March 6–9, 2013
Denver, Colorado, USA

Association for Computing Machinery

Advancing Computing as a Science & Profession

SIGCSE'13

Proceedings of the 44th ACM Technical Symposium on Computer Science Education

Sponsored by:

ACM SIGCSE

Editors:

Renee McCauley, College of Charleston

Tracy Camp, Colorado School of Mines

Paul Tymann, Rochester Institute of Technology

J.D. Dougherty, Haverford College

Kris Nagel, Georgia Gwinnett College

Association for
Computing Machinery

Advancing Computing as a Science & Profession

The Association for Computing Machinery
2 Penn Plaza, Suite 701
New York, New York 10121-0701

Notice to Past Authors of ACM-Published Articles
ACM intends to create a complete electronic archive of all articles and/or other material previously published by ACM. If you have written a work that has been previously published by ACM in any journal or conference proceedings prior to 1978, or any SIG Newsletter at any time, and you do NOT want this work to appear in the ACM Digital Library, please inform permissions@acm.org, stating the title of the work, the author(s), and where and when published.

ISBN: 978-1-4503-1868-6 (Digital)

ISBN: 978-1-4503-2030-6 (Print)

ACM Order Number: 457130

Additional copies may be ordered prepaid from:

ACM Order Department
PO Box 30777
New York, NY 10087-0777, USA

Phone: 1-800-342-6626 (USA and Canada)
+1-212-626-0500 (Global)
Fax: +1-212-944-1318
E-mail: acmhelp@acm.org
Hours of Operation: 8:30 am – 4:30 pm ET

Printed in the USA

Welcome from the SIGCSE Chair

Welcome to the *44th SIGCSE Technical Symposium on Computer Science Education* (*SIGCSE 2013*) - the premiere technical conference for computer science educators. *SIGCSE 2013* is sponsored by the ACM Special Interest Group on Computer Science Education (the SIGCSE organization).

The SIGCSE organization consists of approximately 2600 members, whose interests include a desire to improve computer science education. Many of these members are also volunteers who carry out the various activities associated with the organization. Chief among the volunteers responsible for this 2013 conference are Tracy Camp and Paul Tymann, symposium co-chairs, who have spent more than two years planning this conference. Tracy and Paul steered a committee of more than 40 colleagues in organizing all aspects of this event. On behalf of the SIGCSE organization I thank Tracy and Paul for their countless contributions in managing this huge event and coordinating all of the members of their committee.

During this conference you will hear influential keynote addresses and learn about new resources and pedagogies. I hope that you will also make new connections, renew friendships, meet future collaborators, learn a lot, and have fun!

2013 is an election year – look for participants wearing special "candidate" ribbons. These are candidates for positions on the new SIGCSE Executive Board that takes office in July 2013. Feel free to approach these candidates to ask questions and offer input. In a couple of months, ACM will send you a note letting you know it is time to vote - please do so.

Finally, I encourage you to become more involved in the SIGCSE community and the workings of the SIGCSE organization. I encourage you to attend the annual SIGCSE Business meeting on Friday, from 5:10 to 5:55p.m., in Plaza Ballroom E. This is an opportunity to meet the members of the current SIGCSE board: Daniel Joyce (vice chair), Doug Baldwin (treasurer), Susan Rodger (secretary) and at-large members Tiffany Barnes, Mark Guzdial and Amber Settle. Most importantly, it is an opportunity to learn how the organization works – a first step in becoming more involved.

Enjoy the conference!

Renée McCauley
SIGCSE Chair, 2010-2013

Message from the Symposium & Program Chairs

Welcome to the proceedings of the 44th ACM Technical Symposium on Computer Science Education, or SIGCSE 2013, where you will find over one hundred papers as well as multiple other session formats that document the latest in computer science education: research, tool building, teaching, curriculum and philosophy. The theme of this year's symposium is "The Changing Face of Computing", and features a number of talks and sessions focused on how changes in computing technology and changes in student demographics requires a change in the way computing is taught.

SIGCSE 2013's opening keynote session on Thursday will be different from anything seen at SIGCSE previously. It consists of "flash talks" (where several "all stars" in computing will be given five minutes to share 20 slides, each of which automatically advance) that answer the question: "What can WE do to change the face of computing?" Jane Margolis of UCLA will provide SIGCE 2013's closing keynote session on Saturday, where she'll examine how underrepresentation in computing relates to a larger educational crisis and issues we face as world citizens. In addition, during a special keynote session on Friday, Stanford's Provost (John Etchemendy) will discuss whether massively open online courses will change our universities as we know them or be a "flash in the pan".

We are pleased to announce the winners of the two annual SIGCSE awards. Professor Michael Kölling of University of Kent will receive the SIGCSE award for Outstanding Contribution to Computer Science Education, and will provide Friday's keynote address. Henry Walker of Grinnell College will accept the SIGCSE Award for Lifetime Service to the Computer Science Education Community and speak at our First Timer's Lunch. (SIGCSE First Timers will receive the lunch for free; SIGCSE Old Timers can purchase a ticket and (a) enjoy a delicious meal, (b) mentor a First Timer, and (c) listen to Professor Walker's talk.)

Symposium statistics are presented in the following table. We thank the authors, reviewers, and Program Committee members whose enormous and vital service generated this program. This year's program includes the usual wide selection of events, including the Evening Reception on Thursday and the ACM SIGCSE Student Research Competition, as well as some unusual offerings, such as the Codebreaker drama-documentary on Alan Turing's remarkable and tragic life story, a puzzle extravaganza with a raffle for those who complete it, and a CSTA K-13 Computing Teachers Workshop. Our exhibit hall features a number of exhibitors showcasing the latest in hardware, software tools, textbooks and educational programs and research. We also continue to offer accessibility at SIGCSE 2013 for the deaf and hard of hearing.

Proposal type	*Accepted*	*Received*	*Acceptance Rate*
Paper	111	293	37.9%
Panel	11	23	47.8%
Special Session	16	23	69.5%
Workshop	35	84	41.7 %
Poster	52	103	50.5 %
Birds of a Feather	36	49	73.5 %

We are excited about the variety of pre-symposium events that will exist at SIGCSE 2013. As of the press deadline for this overview, meetings on the following topics will occur on Wednesday: Managing the Academic Career for Women, Open Source Software, Computational Thinking Through Computing and Music, CSAB Computing Accreditation Workshop, Git & GitHub Foundations for Educators, SIGCAS Share and Learn, Using the GENI Networking Testbed, Exploring the Next Generation of Scratch, and Integrating Computing Ethics into the Curriculum.

Our sincere thanks go out to the people who made this Symposium extraordinary. First, our symposium committee: Joel Adams, Dan Bogaard, Marilyn Cadenhead, Adrienne Decker, Lynn Degler, John Dooley,

James Early, Sue Fitzgerald, Susan Fox, Ria Galanos, Scott Grissom, Susan Haller, Sarah Heckman, Steven Huss-Lederman, Catherine Lang, Cary Lazer, James Maher, Lester I. McCann, Larry Merkle, Jody Paul, Susan Rodger, Ann Sobel, Jodi Tims, Kimberly Voll, Henry Walker, Steven Wolfman, Jian Zhang, and Steve Zilora. Additional thanks go to our Associate Program Chairs who provided meta-reviews for papers: Allison Elliott Tew, Brad Richards, Stephen Cooper, Mary Anne Egan, Eric Aaron, Charles Leska, Pam Cutter, Ruth E. Anderson, Sara Miner More, and Suzanne Fox Buchele. We'd also like to thank all of our student volunteers who help us with all of the small details and our International Liaison Committee (Reyyan Ayfer, Mordechai Ben-Ari, Janet Carter, Alison Clear, Mohamed Hamada, Sridhar Iyer, Maria Knobelsdorf, Chi-Un Lei, Claudia Bauzer Madeiros, Cecille Marsh, Guido Rößling, Yasuto Shirai, Su White, and Gary K.W. Wong) for helping ensure SIGCSE 2013 is welcoming to attendees from around the world.

In difficult economic times, we extend a *very* grateful thank you to our supporters, vendors, exhibitors and in-kind donors whose participation literally make the symposium possible. We especially thank Microsoft as the Platinum Plus Supporter, ABET, Google and Intel as Platinum Supporters, and Oracle as a Silver Supporter. Special thanks go to Dorothea Heck and her team at D. Lawrence Planners for coordinating an outstanding exhibition and to Susan Rodger, our amazing supporter/exhibitor liaison.

We thank SIGCSE President Renée McCauley and the entire SIGCSE Board for their support and guidance, and acknowledge the contributions of SIGCSE Symposium Site Coordinators Bob Beck and Scott Grissom, as well as Ashley Cozzi of ACM. Lisa Tolles of Sheridan Communications brought all materials together. Also, the City of Denver provided valuable information through their excellent Visit Denver site, and SIGCSE 2013 attendees owe Soulaiman Bahalla (our main contact at Sheraton) a 'high five' for all his efforts.

Special thanks to our home institutions for providing needed resources: Colorado School of Mines, Georgia Gwinnett College, Haverford College, and Rochester Institute of Technology. We genuinely hope you enjoy the Symposium and find the SIGCSE 2013 Proceedings of use for your work now and your future projects and activities.

Symposium Chairs

Tracy Camp
Colorado School of Mines

Paul Tymann
Rochester Institute of Technology

Program Chairs

John Dougherty
Haverford College

Kris Nagel
Georgia Gwinnett College

Table of Contents

Session 6: Paper - Peer Instruction

Session Chair: Adrian German *(Indiana University)*

Session 7: Paper – Student Dynamics

Session Chair: Suzanne Buchele *(Southwestern University)*

Session 8: Paper - Non-Majors

Session Chair: Debra Goldberg *(University of Colorado at Boulder)*

Session 9: Paper - Approaches for Outreach

Session Chair: Adam Anthony *(Baldwin-Wallace University)*

Session 10: Panel Session

Session 11: Panel Session

Session 12: Panel Session

Session 13: Paper - Alternatives to Lectures

Session Chair: Sherri Goings *(Carleton College)*

Session 14: Paper – Instructional Technologies

Session Chair: Ashish Amresh *(Arizona State University)*

Session 15: Paper - Tough Curricular Challenges

Session Chair: Andrea Danyluk *(Williams College)*

Session 16: Paper - Retention

Session Chair: Carl Alphonce *(University at Buffalo, SUNY)*

Session 17: Paper - CS Education Research

Session Chair: Kristy Boyer *(North Carolina State University)*

Session 30: Paper - Underserved Populations

Session Chair: Eric Aaron *(Wesleyan University)*

Session 31: Paper - Architecture and Hardware

Session Chair: Timothy Stanley *(Utah Valley University)*

Session 32: Paper - Teaching CS1

Session Chair: Jian Zhang *(Texas Woman's University)*

Session 33: Paper - Assessment

Session Chair: Eric Snow *(SRI International)*

Session 34: Panel Session

Session 35: Panel Session

Session 36: Special Session

Session 37: Special Session

Session 38: Paper - Tools for Teaching the Core

Session Chair: Marie Bienkowski *(SRI International)*

Session 39: Paper - Parallel Distributed Computing

Session Chair: Michael Helmick *(Google)*

Session 40: Paper - Teacher Preparation

Session Chair: Shaileen Pokress *(Massachusetts Institute of Technology)*

Session 47: Paper - Active Learning

Session Chair: Richard A. Brown *(St. Olaf College)*

Session 48: Paper - Tools to Support Novice Programmer

Session Chair: Brad Richards *(University of Puget)*

Session 49: Paper - SE and Professional Practice

Session Chair: Colleen Lewis *(Harvey Mudd College)*

Session 50: Special Session

Session 51: Special Session

Session 52: Special Session

Session 53: Paper - Curricular Innovations

Session Chair: Kurt Eiselt *(University of British Columbia)*

Session 54: Paper - Improving Student Learning in Courses

Session Chair: Pamela Cutter *(Kalamazoo College)*

Session 55: Paper – Working the Web

Session Chair: Timothy Fossum *(SUNY College at Potsdam)*

Session 56: Paper - Computational Thinking

Session Chair: Catherine Lang *(Swinburne University of Technology)*

Session 57: Paper - Camps and Mobile Computing

Session Chair: Jakita Thomas *(Spelman College)*

Session 64: Paper - Capstones

Session Chair: Haklin Kimm *(East Stroudsburg University)*

Session 65: Paper – Educational Research

Session Chair: James Maher *(Colorado School of Mines)*

Session 66: Poster Session 1

Session 67: Poster Session 2

Session 68: Birds of a Feather - Flock I

Session 69: Birds of a Feather - Flock II

Session 70: Wednesday Workshops

Session 71: Friday Workshops

Session 72: Saturday Workshops

Session 73: Back Matter

SIGCSE 2013 Symposium Committee

Symposium Chairs
Tracy Camp, *Colorado School of Mines*
Paul Tymann, *Rochester Institute of Technology*

Program Chairs
J.D. Dougherty, *Haverford College*
Kris Nagel, *Georgia Gwinnett College*

Panels and Special Sessions
Sue Fitzgerald, *Metropolitan State University*

Workshops
Susan Haller, *SUNY Potsdam*
Lester McCann, *University of Arizona*

Publications
Joel Adams, *Calvin College*

Database Administrators
John Dooley, *Knox College*
Henry Walker, *Grinnell College*

Registration
Lynn Degler, *Rose-Hulman Institute of Technology*
Cary Laxer, *Rose-Hulman Institute of Technology*
Larry Merkle, *Computational Optimization Services*

Posters
Jodi Tims, *Baldwin Wallace University*

Birds of a Feather
Jian Zhang, *Texas Women's University*

Student Volunteers and Activities
Steven Huss-Lederman, *Beloit College*
Steven Wolfman, *University of British Columbia*

Webmasters
Dan Bogaard, *Rochester Institute of Technology*
Steve Zilora, *Rochester Institute of Technology*

Treasurer
Scott Grissom, *Grand Valley State University*

Evaluations
James Early, *SUNY Oswego*

Kids Camp
Susan Fox, *Macalester College*
James Maher, *Colorado School of Mines*

Publicity / Social Media
Kimberly Voll, *University of British Columbia*

Support / Exhibitor Liaison
Susan Rodger, *Duke University*

Pre-Conference Events Liaison
Adrienne Decker, *Rochester Institute of Technology*

Affiliated Events Liaison
Sarah Heckman, *North Carolina State University*

K-12 Liaison
Marilyn Cadenhead, *School of Science and Engr. Magnet*
Ria Galanos, *Thomas Jefferson HS for Science and Tech.*

Local Arrangements
Jody Paul, *Metropolitan State University of Denver*

Student Research Competition
Ann Sobel, *Miami University (Ohio)*

International Liaison
Catherine Lang, *Swinburne University of Technology*

International Liaison Committee
Rayyan Ayfer, *Bilkent University, Turkey*
Mordechai Ben-Ari, *Weizmann Inst. of Science, Israel*
Janet Carter, *University of Kent, UK*
Alison Clear, *Christchurch Polytechnic Inst. of Technology, New Zealand*
Maria Knobelsdorf, *University of Potsdam, Germany*
Claudia Bauzer Madeiros, *UNICAMP, Brazil*
Cecille Marsh, *Walter Sisulu University, South Africa*
Guido Rößling, *Technische Universität Darmstadt, Germany*
Su White, *University of Southampton, UK*
Mohamed Hamada, *University of Aizu, Japan*
Yasuto Shirai, *Shizuoka University, Japan*
Sridhar Iyer, *Indian Institute of Tech., India*
Chi-Un Lei, *EEE University of Hong Kong*
Gary K. W. Wong, *The Hong Kong Institute of Education*

Associate Program Chairs
Eric Aaron, *Wesleyan University*
Ruth E. Anderson, *University of Washington*
Suzanne Fox Buchele, *Southwestern University*
Stephen C. Cooper, *Stanford University*
Pam Cutter, *Kalamazoo College*
Mary Anne Egan, *Siena College*
Charles Leska, *Randolph-Macon College*
Sara Miner More, *McDaniel College*
Brad Richards, *University of Puget Sound*
Allison Elliott Tew, *University of British Columbia*

SIGCSE 2013 Reviewers

Eric Aaron, *Wesleyan University*
Safurah Abdul Jalil, *University of Auckland*
Adel Abunawass, *University of West Georgia*
Donald Acton, *University of British Columbia*
Raman Adaikkalavan, *Indiana University South Bend*
Elizabeth Adams, *James Madison University*
Robert Adams, *Grand Valley State University*
Paul Addison, *Ivy Tech Community College*
Ravi Agarwal, *St. Norbert College*
Rajeev Agrawal, *North Carolina A&T State University*
Shakil Akhtar, *Clayton State University*
Farha Ali, *Lander University*
Vicki Almstrum, *University of Texas at Austin*
Hana Alnuaim, *King Abdulaziz University*
Carl Alphonce, *University at Buffalo, The State University of New York*
Peter Alston, *Edge Hill University*
Christine Alvarado, *Harvey Mudd College*
Peter Anderson, *Rochester Institute of Technology*
Ruth Anderson, *University of Washington*
Peter Andreae, *Victoria University of Wellington*
Stefan Andrei, *Lamar University*
Peter Andrews, *Eastern Illinois University*
Steven Andrianoff, *St. Bonaventure University*
Marvin Andujar, *Clemson University*
Karen Anewalt, *University of Mary Washington*
Adam Anthony, *Baldwin Wallace University*
Barbara Anthony, *Southwestern University*
Florence Appel, *Saint Xavier University*
Antonio Araujo, *Faculdade de Engenharia da Universidade do Porto*
Michal Armoni, *Weizmann Institute of Science*
Tom Armstrong, *Wheaton College*
David Arnow, *Brooklyn College*
Charles Ashbacher, *Charles Ashbacher Technologies*
John Avitabile, *College of Saint Rose*
John Aycock, *University of Calgary*
Pavel Azalov, *Penn State*
Isabel Azevedo, *ISEP*
Serhat Azgur, *Bilkent University*
Abdel Hameed Badawy, *University of Maryland*
Dinabandhu Bag, *National Institute of Technology*
Mark Bailey, *Hamilton College*
Laura Baker, *St. Edward's University*
Doug Baldwin, *SUNY Geneseo*
Catherine Bareiss, *Olivet Nazarene University*
Ian Barland, *Radford University*
David Barnes, *University of Kent*
Tiffany Barnes, *University of North Carolina at Charlotte*
Lewis Barnett, *University of Richmond*
N. Barnette, *Virginia Tech*
John Barr, *Ithaca College*
Valerie Barr, *Union College*
Martin Barrett, *East Tennessee State University*
Joao Barros, *Instituto Politecnico de Beja - ESTIG*
Phillip Barry, *University of Minnesota*
Carlos Barto, *Universidad Nacional de Cordoba*
Rebecca Bates, *Minnesota State University, Mankato*
Michael Bauer, *University of Hawaii & Leeward Community College*
Robert Beck, *Villanova University*
Byron Becker, *University of Waterloo*
Andrew Begel, *Microsoft Research*
Tim Bell, *University of Canterbury*
Mordechai Ben-Ari, *Weizmann Institute of Science*
Jens Bennedsen, *Aarhus School of Engineering*
Audrey Bennett, *Rensselaer Polytechnic Institute*
Mikael Berndtsson, *School of Humanities and Informatics, University of Skovde*
Lasse Berntzen, *Vestfold University College*
Gian Besana, *CTI DePaul University*
Anne Beug, *California Polytechnic State University*
Ivona Bezakova, *Rochester Institute of Technology*
Marie Bienkowski, *SRI International*
William Birmingham, *Grove City College*
Judith Bishop, *Microsoft Research*
Stephen Bloch, *Adelphi University*
Michael Blumenstein, *Griffith University*
Cory Boatright, *University of Pennsylvania*
Steven Bogaerts, *Wittenberg University*
Esmail Bonakdarian, *Dominican University*
William Booth, *Baylor University*
Kristy Boyer, *North Carolina State University*
Evelyn Brannock, *Georgia Gwinnett College*
Robert Bryant, *Gonzaga University*
Renee Bryce, *Utah State University*
Dennis Brylow, *Marquette University*

Joel Brynielsson, *Royal Institute of Technology*
Suzanne Buchele, *Southwestern University*
Duane Buck, *Otterbein University*
Kevin Buell, *Arizona State University*
Everett Bull, *Pomona College*
David Bunde, *Knox College*
Barry Burd, *Drew University*
Darci Burdge, *Nassau Community College*
Richard Burns, *West Chester University*
Vicky Bush, *University of Gloucestershire*
Mary Califf, *Illinois State University*
Andre Calitz, *Nelson Mandela Metropolitan University*
Johan Calu, *KHBO*
Vivian Campbell, *Edith Cowan University*
Daniel Canas, *Wake Forest University*
Roxanne Canosa, *Rochester Institute of Technology*
James Caristi, *Valparaiso University*
Andrew Carle, *UC Berkeley*
Martin Carlisle, *US Air Force Academy*
Janet Carter, *University of Kent at Canterbury*
Lori Carter, *Point Loma Nazarene University*
Jeffrey Carver, *University of Alabama*
Lori Case, *University of Waterloo*
Steven Case, *University of West Florida*
Sheila Castaneda, *Clarke University*
Tim Chamillard, *University of Colorado at Colorado Springs*
Albert Chan, *Fayetteville State University*
Maiga Chang, *Athabasca University*
Mahesh Chaudhari, *Arizona State University*
Ranjan Chaudhuri, *Eastern Michigan University*
Tom Cheatham, *Middle Tennessee State University*
Jimmy Chen, *Salt Lake Community College*
Peng-Wen Chen, *Oriental Institute of Technology*
Ping Chen, *University of Houston-Downtown*
Tzu-Yi Chen, *Pomona College*
Wei Chen, *Champlain College*
Li-hsiang Cheo, *William Paterson University of New Jersey*
Ho Yin Cheung, *The Community College at Lingnan University*
Chia-Chu Chiang, *University of Arkansas at Little Rock*
Donald Chinn, *University of Washington, Tacoma*
Jayan Chirayath, *Royal Melbourne Institute of Technology*
David Chiu, *Washington State University, Vancouver*
Radhouane Chouchane, *Columbus State University*
Vincent Cicirello, *Richard Stockton College*
John Cigas, *Park University*
Liezel Cilliers, *University of Fort Hare*
Dawn Cizmar, *St. Edward's University*
Michael Clancy, *University of California, Berkeley*
Peter Clarke, *Florida International University*
Tony Clear, *Auckland University of Technology*
Daniel Cliburn, *University of the Pacific*
Joe Clifton, *University of Wisconsin, Platteville*
Osvaldo Clua, *Universidad de Buenos Aires*
Marge Coahran, *University of Toronto*
Cara Cocking, *Portland Community College*
Ben Coleman, *Moravian College*
John Colville, *University of Technology, Sydney*
Tim Comber, *Southern Cross University*
Randy Connolly, *Mount Royal University*
Phillip Conrad, *UC Santa Barbara*
Kevin Coogan, *Pomona College*
Robert Cook, *Georgia Southern University*
Stephen Cooper, *Stanford University*
Jean Coppola, *Pace University*
David Cordes, *University of Alabama*
Jose Cordova, *University of Louisiana at Monroe*
Thomas Cortina, *Carnegie Mellon University*
Monica Costa, *IPCB*
Mary Courtney, *Pace University*
Annemieke Craig, *Deakin University*
Michelle Craig, *University of Toronto*
James Cross, *Auburn University*
Mark Crouch, *Angelo State University*
Joyce Crowell, *Belmont University*
Diana Cukierman, *Simon Fraser University*
Jose Cunha, *New University of Lisbon*
Steve Cunningham, *Brown Cunningham Associates*
Edwin Curran, *University of Ulster*
Judith Cushing, *The Evergreen State College*
Pamela Cutter, *Kalamazoo College*
Quintin Cutts, *University of Glasgow*
Lawrence D'Antonio, *Ramapo College of New Jersey*
Mohammad Dadfar, *Bowling Green State University*
Lucia Dale, *Sewanee*
Andrew Dalton, *Western Carolina University*
Douglas Dankel, *University of Florida*
Andrew Danner, *Swarthmore College*
Brahma Dathan, *Metropolitan State University*

Janet Davis, *Grinnell College*
Renzo Davoli, *Dept. of Computer Science - University of Bologna*
Susan Dean, *UMUC - Europe*
Adrienne Decker, *Rochester Institute of Technology*
Hannah Dee, *Grenoble Institute of Technology*
Katherine Deibel, *University of Washington-Seattle*
Stavros Demetriadis, *Aristotle University of Thessaloniki*
Marie-Anne Demuynck, *Texas Woman's University*
Peter DePasquale, *The College of New Jersey*
Molisa Derk, *Dickinson State University*
Yogesh Deshpande, *University of Western Sydney*
Lucia Dettori, *DePaul University – College of Computing & Digital Media*
Kamyar Dezhgosha, *University of Illinois at Springfield*
Martin Dick, *RMIT University*
Suzanne Dietrich, *Arizona State University*
Wei Ding, *University of Massachusetts-Boston*
Adair Dingle, *Seattle University*
Betsy DiSalvo, *Georgia Institute of Technology*
William Doane, *College of Saint Rose*
Zachary Dodds, *Harvey Mudd College*
Michael Doherty, *University of the Pacific*
Toby Donaldson, *Simon Fraser University*
Aijuan Dong, *Hood College*
John Dooley, *Knox College*
Brian Dorn, *University of Hartford*
Maureen Doyle, *Northern Kentucky University*
Peter Drexel, *Plymouth State University*
John Duncan, *Indiana University*
James Early, *SUNY Oswego*
J. East, *University of Northern Iowa*
Jeffrey Edgington, *University of Denver*
Stephen Edwards, *Virginia Tech*
Mary Anne Egan, *Siena College*
Roger Eggen, *University of North Florida*
Kurt Eiselt, *University of British Columbia*
Joseph Ekstrom, *Brigham Young University*
Ahmed El-Deeb, *Nile University*
Richard Enbody, *Michigan State University*
Alec Engebretson, *Doane College*
Gerald Engel, *University of Connecticut, Stamford*
Ed Epp, *Intel Corporation*
Barbara Ericson, *Georgia Institute of Technology*
Daniel Ernst, *Cray, Inc.*
John Estell, *Ohio Northern University*
Yadran Eterovic, *Pontificia Universidad Catolica de Chile*
Barry Fagin, *US Air Force Academy*
Daisy Fan, *Cornell University*
Homma Farian, *SUNY Geneseo*
David Farrell, *Glasgow Caledonian University*
Mili Fatma, *Purdue University*
Alan Fekete, *University of Sydney*
Maria Feldgen, *Universidad de Buenos Aires*
Roger Ferguson, *Grand Valley State University*
Francesc Ferri, *Universitat de Valencia*
Georgios Fesakis, *University of the Aegean*
Ronald Finkbine, *Indiana University Southeast*
Robin Flatland, *Siena College*
Samantha Foley, *University of Wisconsin-La Crosse*
Timothy Fossum, *SUNY College at Potsdam*
Kent Foster, *Winthrop University*
Susan Fox, *Macalester College*
Charles Frank, *Northern Kentucky University*
Robert Franks, *Central College*
Karen Fraser, *University of Ulster*
Andre Freire, *University of York*
Bill Freitas, *The Lawrenceville School*
Frank Friedman, *Temple University*
S. Fritz, *St. Joseph's College*
Daniel Frost, *University of California, Irvine*
Mohammad Fuad, *Winston-Salem State University*
Kenneth Funk, *Kirkwood Community College*
Jacob Furst, *DePaul University*
Galal Galal-Edeen, *Cairo University*
Angel Garcia-Beltran, *Universidad Politecnica de Madrid*
David Gardner, *Texas Woman's University*
Charlie Garrod, *Carnegie Mellon University*
Alessio Gaspar, *University of South Florida Polytechnic*
Dick Gayler, *Kennesaw State University*
Rick Gee, *Okanagan College*
Edward Gehringer, *North Carolina State University*
Joe Geigel, *Rochester Institute of Technology*
Jill Gerhardt, *Richard Stockton College of New Jersey*
Adrian German, *Indiana University*
Judith Gersting, *Indiana University-Purdue University at Indianapolis*
Paul Gestwicki, *Ball State University*
Lila Ghemri, *Texas Southern University*
J Gibson, *T&M Sud Paris*
Mark Goadrich, *Centenary College of Louisiana*
Don Goelman, *Villanova University*
Sherri Goings, *Carleton College*
Michael Goldweber, *Xavier University*
Evan Golub, *University of Maryland*

Mercedes Gomez-Albarran, *Dept. Ingenieria del Software e Inteligencia Artificial*
Marco Gomez-Martin, *Universidad Complutense de Madrid*
Pedro Gomez-Martin, *Universidad Complutense de Madrid*
Aaron Gordon, *Metropolitan State College of Denver*
Jean Goulet, *Universite de Sherbrooke*
Michael Gousie, *Wheaton College (MA)*
Mary Granger, *George Washington University*
Jonathan Gratch, *University of North Texas*
Scott Grissom, *Grand Valley State University*
Joshua Gross, *University of North Carolina at Charlotte*
Paul Gross, *Washington University in St. Louis*
Andrew Grover, *Thiel College*
Joshua Guerin, *University of Tennessee at Martin*
Carlos Guerrero, *University of the Balearic Islands*
Mario Guimaraes, *Zayed University*
Mark Guzdial, *Georgia Institute of Technology*
Max Hailperin, *Gustavus Adolphus College*
Ranette Halverson, *Midwestern State University*
John Hamer, *University of Auckland*
Nadeem Hamid, *Berry College*
Brian Hanks, *BFH Educational Consulting*
Arthur Hanna, *St. Mary's University*
Stuart Hansen, *University of Wisconsin - Parkside*
Mindy Hart, *Purdue University*
Jessen Havill, *Denison University*
Scott Hawker, *Rochester Institute of Technology*
Orit Hazzan, *Technion -- Israel Institute of Technology*
Sarah Heckman, *North Carolina State University*
Phillip Heeler, *Northwest Missouri State University*
Cecily Heiner, *Southern Utah University*
James Heliotis, *Rochester Institute of Technology*
Keith Hellman, *Colorado School of Mines*
Michael Helmick, *Google*
David Hemmendinger, *Union College*
Dean Hendrix, *Auburn University*
Tyson Henry, *California State University, Chico*
Katherine Herbert, *Montclair State University*
Matthew Hertz, *Canisius College*
Michael Hewner, *Duke University*
Jose Hilera, *University of Alcala*
Rachelle Hippler, *Bowling Green State University*
Gregory Hislop, *Drexel University*
William Hochstettler, *Franklin*
Mark Holliday, *Western Carolina University*
Joe Hollingsworth, *Indiana University*
Christopher Homan, *Rochester Institute of Technology*
William Hooper, *Belmont University*
Charles Hoot, *Oklahoma City University*
Cay Horstmann, *San Jose State University*
Hoda Hosny, *The American University in Cairo*
Mahmood Hossain, *Fairmont State University*
Dwight House, *Fayetteville State University*
David Hovemeyer, *York College of Pennsylvania*
Brian Howard, *DePauw University*
Trudy Howles, *Rochester Institute of Technology*
Michelle Hribar, *OHSU*
Wen-Jung Hsin, *Park University*
Chenglie Hu, *Carroll University*
Helen Hu, *Westminster College*
Meriel Huggard, *Trinity College, Dublin*
James Huggins, *Kettering University*
Janet Hughes, *University of Dundee*
Richard Hull, *Lenoir-Rhyne University*
Dalton Hunkins, *St. Bonaventure University*
Frances Hunt, *Educational Testing Service*
Kenny Hunt, *University of Wisconsin - La Crosse*
Michelle Hutton, *Stanford University*
Deborah Hwang, *University of Evansville*
Jorge Ibarra-Esquer, *Universidad Autonoma de Baja California*
Lubomir Ivanov, *Iona College*
Sridhar Iyer, *Indian Institute of Technology, Bombay*
Clemente Izurieta, *Montana State University*
Jana Jackova, *Slovak University of Technology in Bratislava*
Mark Jaeger, *Baker College*
Giti Javidi, *Virginia State University*
Mike Jipping, *Hope College*
David John, *Wake Forest University*
Chris Johnson, *University of Wisconsin, Eau Claire*
Colin Johnson, *University of Kent at Canterbury*
Julie Johnson, *Vanderbilt University*
Mark Johnson, *Central College*
Edward Jones, *Florida A&M University*
Anthony Joseph, *Pace University*
Mike Joy, *University of Warwick*
Daniel Joyce, *Villanova University*
Maria Jump, *King's College*
Ilker Kalender, *Bilkent University*
Alan Kaminsky, *Rochester Institute of Technology*
Pankaj Kamthan, *Concordia University*
Debbie Kaneko, *Old Dominion University*
Ville Karavirta, *Aalto University*

Elizabeth Katz, *Millersville University*
David Kauchak, *Middlebury College*
David Kay, *University of California, Irvine*
Jennifer Kay, *Rowan University*
Judy Kay, *University of Sydney*
Fereydoun Kazemian, *Rochester Institute of Technology*
Petros Kefalas, *University of Sheffield*
Charles Kelemen, *Swarthmore College*
Thomas Kelliher, *Goucher College*
Andreas Kerren, *Linnaeus University*
Mark Kerstetter, *Western Michigan University*
Arshia Khan, *The College of St. Scholastica*
Sami Khuri, *San Jose State University*
Laurie King, *College of the Holy Cross*
Jeff Kinne, *Indiana State University*
Nancy Kinnersley, *University of Kansas*
David Klappholz, *Stevens Institute of Technology*
Myungsook Klassen, *California Lutheran University*
Frank Klassner, *Villanova University*
Carsten Kleiner, *University of Applied Sciences & Arts Hannover*
Jane Kochanov, *Pennsylvania State University - Capital College*
James Kolasa, *Bluegrass Community and Technical College*
Michael Kolling, *University of Kent*
April Kontostathis, *Ursinus College*
Yana Kortsarts, *Widener University, Chester*
David Kosbie, *Carnegie Mellon University*
Janet Kourik, *Webster University*
Douglas Kranch, *North Central State College*
Joan Krone, *Denison University*
Jan Kruger, *Unisa School for Business Leadership*
Marja Kuittinen, *University of Joensuu*
Amruth Kumar, *Ramapo College of New Jersey*
Deepak Kumar, *Bryn Mawr College*
Benjamin Kuperman, *Oberlin College*
Zachary Kurmas, *Grand Valley State University*
Clif Kussmaul, *Muhlenberg College*
Lynn Lambert, *Christopher Newport University*
H. Lane, *University of Southern California*
Catherine Lang, *Swinburne University of Technology*
Matthew Lang, *Moravian College*
Joan Langdon, *Bowie State University*
Yedidyah Langsam, *CIS Department Brooklyn College of CUNY*
Mick Lantis, *Purdue University North Central*
David Largent, *Ball State University*
Brian Larkins, *Coastal Carolina University*
Edurne Larraza-Mendiluze, *University of the Basque Country*
Eric Larson, *Seattle University*
Mary Last, *self-employed*
Daisy Lau, *Lingnan University*
Robert Law, *Glasgow Caledonian University*
Barry Lawson, *University of Richmond*
Lucas Layman, *Fraunhofer USA*
Alina Lazar, *Youngstown State University*
Cathie LeBlanc, *Plymouth State College*
Mark LeBlanc, *Wheaton College*
Arthur Lee, *Claremont McKenna College*
Byong Lee, *Bennett College*
Cornell Lee, *Minnesota State University*
Cynthia Lee, *UC San Diego*
Gilliean Lee, *Lander University*
Chi Un Lei, *The University of Hong Kong*
Charles Leska, *Randolph-Macon College*
David Levine, *St. Bonaventure University*
Dalit Levy, *Zefat Academic College*
Gary Lewandowski, *Xavier University*
Colleen Lewis, *University of California, Berkeley*
John Lewis, *Virginia Tech*
Hai-Ning Liang, *Xi'an Jiaotong-Liverpool University*
Weidong Liao, *Shepherd University*
Billy Lim, *Illinois State University*
Panagiotis Linos, *Butler University*
Jiang-Jiang Liu, *Lamar University*
Jigang Liu, *Metropolitan State University*
Peter Liu, *Seneca College*
Yue Liu, *National University of Defense Technology*
William Lloyd, *University of West Georgia*
Kate Lockwood, *California State University, Monterey Bay*
Sergio Lopes, *University of Minho*
Jake Luo, *Case Western Reserve University*
Andrew Luxton-Reilly, *The University of Auckland*
William Lyle, *Murray State University*
Bonnie MacKellar, *St John's University*
Peter Macpherson, *Rogers State University*
Joaquim Madeira, *University of Aveiro*
Francesco Maiorana, *University of Catania*

Mercedes Marques, *University Jaume I*
Fred Martin, *University of Massachusetts Lowell*
Hélène Martin, *University of Washington*
Kenneth Martin, *University of North Florida*
Manuel Martins Barata, *ISEL - Instituto Superior de Engenharia de Lisboa*
Dave Mason, *Ryerson University*
Bruce Maxim, *University of Michigan-Dearborn*
Bruce Maxwell, *Colby College*
Christopher Mayfield, *James Madison University*
Robert McCloskey, *University of Scranton*
O. McClung, *Nebraska Wesleyan University*
Jeffrey McConnell, *Canisius College*
Frank McCown, *Harding University*
W. McCracken, *Georgia Institute of Technology*
Sean McCulloch, *Ohio Wesleyan University*
Charlie McDowell, *UC Santa Cruz*
Scott McElfresh, *Wake Forest University*
James McGuffee, *St. Edward's University*
Hugh McGuire, *Grand Valley State University*
Tim McGuire, *Sam Houston State University*
Bonita McVey, *St. Norbert College*
Pedro Medeiros, *Universidade Nova de Lisboa*
Lisa Meeden, *Swarthmore College*
Gloria Melara, *California State University, Northridge*
Antonio Mendes, *University of Coimbra*
Susan Mengel, *Texas Tech University*
Suzanne Menzel, *Indiana University*
Laurence Merkle, *Wright State University*
Joseph Mertz, *Carnegie Mellon University*
Jose Metrolho, *Polytechnic Institute of Castelo Branco*
Timothy Meyer, *Edinboro University of Pennsylvania*
Mark Meysenburg, *Doane College*
Lisa Michaud, *Merrimack College*
Gail Miles, *Lenoir-Rhyne College*
James Miller, *Bradley University*
James Miller, *University of Alberta*
Keith Miller, *University of Illinois at Springfield*
Afsaneh Minaie, *Utah Valley University*
Joe Miro, *Universitat de les Illes Balears*
Susan Mitchell, *University of Maryland, Baltimore County*
Roland Mittermeir, *Universität Klagenfurt*
Sriram Mohan, *Rose-Hulman Institute of Technology*
William Mongan, *Drexel University*
Michael Moorman, *Saint Leo University*
Sara More, *McDaniel College*
Nelma Moreira, *University of Porto*
Patricia Morreale, *Kean University*
Briana Morrison, *Southern Polytechnic State University*
Srikanth Mudigonda, *Saint Louis University*
Christian Murphy, *University of Pennsylvania*
Laurie Murphy, *Pacific Lutheran University*
Michael Murphy, *Concordia University Texas*
David Musicant, *Carleton College*
Bill Myers, *Belmont Abbey Collge*
Mario Nakazawa, *Berea College*
Nannette Napier, *Georgia Gwinnett College*
Krish Narayanan, *Eastern Michigan University*
Pavol Navrat, *Slovak University of Technology*
Rance Necaise, *College of William and Mary*
Tia Newhall, *Swarthmore College*
Lijun Ni, *Georgia Institute of Technology*
Robert Noonan, *College of William and Mary*
Victor Norman, *Calvin College*
Cindy Norris, *Appalachian State University*
Linda Null, *Penn State University*
Keith O'Hara, *Bard College*
William Oblitey, *Indiana University of Pennsylvania*
Rainer Oechsle, *University of Applied Sciences, Trier*
Chris Okasaki, *United States Military Academy*
Amos Olagunju, *St. Cloud State University*
Joseph Oldham, *Centre College*
Nina Onesti, *Indiana University*
Lawrence Osborne, *Lamar University*
Youwen Ouyang, *California State University at San Marcos*
Barbara Owens, *Southwestern University*
Jill Pala, *Girls Preparatory School*
Greta Pangborn, *Saint Michael's College*
Iraklis Paraskakis, *City College, Intern. Faculty of the University of Sheffield*
Abelardo Pardo, *Carlos III University of Madrid*
Crist'obal Pareja-Flores, *Universidad Complutense de Madrid*
Young Park, *Bradley University*
Brenda Parker, *Middle Tennessee State University*
David Parker, *Salisbury University*
Jeff Parker, *Harvard Extension*
Rembert Parker, *Anderson University*
James Paterson, *Glasgow Caledonian University*
Elizabeth Patitsas, *University of Toronto*
Brian Patterson, *Oglethorpe University*
Laurie Patterson, *University of North Carolina Wilmington*

Richard Pattis, *University of California, Irvine*
Thaddeus Pawlicki, *University of Rochester Computer Science*
Arnold Pears, *Uppsala University*
Ramanee Peiris, *University of Dundee*
Eileen Peluso, *Lycoming College*
Bin Peng, *Southwestern College*
Manuel Perez-Quinones, *Virginia Tech*
Teresa Peterman, *Grand Valley State University*
Andrew Petersen, *University of Toronto Mississauga*
Chrisila Pettey, *Middle Tennessee State University*
Charles Pheatt, *Emporia State University*
Vreda Pieterse, *University of Pretoria*
Nelishia Pillay, *University of KwaZulu-Natal*
Francois Pitt, *University of Toronto*
Tony Pittarese, *East Tennessee State University*
Paul Piwowarski, *University of Kentucky*
Shannon Pollard, *Elon University*
Lori Pollock, *University of Delaware*
Wayne Pollock, *Hillsborough Community College*
Irene Polycarpou, *UCLan Cyprus*
Elvira Popescu, *University of Craiova*
Jeffrey Popyack, *Drexel University*
Lori Postner, *Nassau Community College*
George Pothering, *College of Charleston*
Wendy Powley, *Queen's University*
Jon Preston, *Southern Polytechnic State University*
Roger Priebe, *Texas State University - San Marcos*
Philip Prins, *Seattle Pacific University*
Viera Proulx, *Northeastern University*
William Pugh, *University of Maryland*
Sarah Pulimood, *The College of New Jersey*
Semmy Purewal, *University of North Carolina at Asheville*
John Rabung, *Randolph-Macon College*
Cyndi Rader, *Colorado School of Mines*
John Rager, *Amherst College*
Rajendra Raj, *Rochester Institute of Technology*
Muthu Ramachandran, *Leeds Metropolitan University*
Bina Ramamurthy, *University at Buffalo, SUNY*
Saquib Razak, *Carnegie Mellon University*
Eliseo Reategui, *Universidade Federal do Rio Grande do Sul*
Samuel Rebelsky, *Grinnell College*
Michael Redmond, *La Salle University*
David Reed, *Creighton University*
Donna Reese, *Mississippi State University*
Susan Reiser, *UNC Asheville*
Dan Resler, *Virginia Commonwealth University*
Eugene Ressler, *United States Military Academy*
Loren Rhodes, *Juniata College*
Catherine Ricardo, *Iona College*
Brad Richards, *University of Puget Sound*
Detlef Rick, *Universität Hamburg*
Charles Riedesel, *University of Nebraska - Lincoln*
Kelly Rivers, *Carnegie Mellon University*
Suzanne Rivoire, *Sonoma State University*
Steven Robbins, *University of Texas at San Antonio*
Christian Roberson, *Plymouth State University*
Eric Roberts, *Stanford University*
Stefan Robila, *Montclair State University*
Susan Rodger, *Duke University*
Guido Roessling, *Technische Universitaet Darmstadt*
Joel Ross, *University of Puget Sound*
John Ross, *Indiana University Kokomo*
Rockford Ross, *Montana State University*
Jerry Roth, *Vanderbilt University*
Krishnendu Roy, *Valdosta State University*
Martin Ruckert, *Munich University of Applied Sciences*
Anthony Ruocco, *Roger Williams University*
Ingrid Russell, *University of Hartford*
Adrian Rusu, *Rowan University*
Amalia Rusu, *Fairfield University*
Rebecca Rutherfoord, *Southern Polytechnic State University*
Roberta Sabin, *Loyola College*
Shazia Sadiq, *The University of Queensland*
Mehran Sahami, *Stanford University*
Samuel Sambasivam, *Azusa Pacific University*
Ian Sanders, *University of South Africa*
William Sanders, *University of Hartford*
Pete Sanderson, *Otterbein University*
André Santos, *Lisbon University Institute*
Vijayalakshmi Saravanan, *Ryerson University & VIT University*
Amit Sawant, *NetApp*
Suzanne Schaefer, *N/A (retired)*
Christelle Scharff, *Pace University*
Walter Schilling, *Milwaukee School of Engineering*
Karl Schmitt, *University of Maryland, College Park*
Diane Schwartz, *California State University Northridge*
Stephanie Schwartz, *Millersville University*
Leslie Schwartzman, *UIS*
Dino Schweitzer, *United States Air Force Academy*
Otto Seppälä, *Aalto University*
Amber Settle, *DePaul University*

Behrooz Seyed-Abbassi, *University of North Florida*
Cliff Shaffer, *Virginia Tech*
Samir Shah, *Penn State University, York*
Bonita Sharif, *Youngstown State University*
Fangyang Shen, *New York City College of Technology (CUNY)*
Ching-Kuang Shene, *Michigan Technological University*
Mark Sherriff, *University of Virginia*
Yasuto Shirai, *Shizuoka University*
Keith Shomper, *Cedarville University*
Charles Shub, *University of Colorado at Colorado Springs*
Scott Sigman, *Drury University*
Gavin Sim, *University of Central Lancashire*
Maria Simi, *Universita di Pisa*
Beth Simon, *University of California, San Diego*
William Slough, *Eastern Illinois University*
Joslyn Smith, *Florida International University*
Peter Smith, *California State University - Channel Islands*
Robert Snapp, *University of Vermont*
Takako Soma, *Illinois College*
Joel Sommers, *Colgate University*
Raja Sooriamurthi, *Carnegie Mellon University*
Jonathan Sorenson, *Butler University*
Barry Soroka, *Cal Poly Pomona*
Jaime Spacco, *Knox College*
Greg Speegle, *Baylor University*
David Spooner, *Rensselaer Polytechnic Institute*
Carol Spradling, *Northwest Missouri State University*
Nathan Sprague, *James Madison University*
Denbigh Starkey, *Montana State University*
Mark Stehlik, *Carnegie Mellon University*
Michael Stein, *Metropolitan State University*
Josh Steinhurst, *Bucknell University*
Ben Stephenson, *University of Calgary*
Daniel Stevenson, *University of Wisconsin - Eau Claire*
Khadija Stewart, *DePauw University*
Evelyn Stiller, *Plymouth State University*
Vojislav Stojkovic, *Morgan State University*
Christopher Stone, *Harvey Mudd College*
Jeffrey Stone, *Pennsylvania State University*
Forrest Stonedahl, *Centre College*
Fred Strickland, *South University*
Kristina Striegnitz, *Union College*
Catherine Stringfellow, *Midwestern State University*
Deborah Sturm, *College of Staten Island CUNY*
Dario Suarez Gracia, *Universidad de Zaragoza*
Jose Such, *Lancaster University*
Leigh Sudol, *Carnegie Mellon University*
John Sullins, *Youngstown State University*
Fred Sullivan, *Wilkes University*
Wayne Summers, *Columbus State University*
Valerie Summet, *Emory University*
Weiqing Sun, *University of Toledo*
Ken Surendran, *Southeast Missouri State University*
Joo Tan, *Kutztown University*
Stewart Tansley, *Microsoft Research*
Rahman Tashakkori, *Appalachian State University*
Michael Tashbook, *Stony Brook University*
Blair Taylor, *Towson University*
James Teresco, *The College of Saint Rose*
Allison Tew, *Georgia Institute of Technology*
William Thacker, *Winthrop University*
Lynda Thomas, *Aberystwyth University*
Megan Thomas, *California State University Stanislaus*
Rebecca Thomas, *Bard College*
Stan Thomas, *Wake Forest University*
Jodi Tims, *Baldwin-Wallace College*
Fergus Toolan, *University College Dublin*
Gloria Townsend, *DePauw University*
Christian Trefftz, *Grand Valley State University*
Deborah Trytten, *University of Oklahoma*
Shengru Tu, *University of New Orleans*
David Tucker, *Midwestern State University*
William Turner, *Wabash College*
Sharon Tuttle, *Humboldt State University*
Hakan Tuzun, *Hacettepe University*
Suleyman Uludag, *The University of Michigan - Flint*
Susan Urban, *Texas Tech University*
Timothy Urness, *Drake University*
Ian Utting, *University of Kent at Canterbury*
Jan Vahrenhold, *Technische Universität Dortmund*
Ignatios Vakalis, *California Polytechnic and State University*
David Valentine, *Slippery Rock University*
James Vallino, *Rochester Institute of Technology*
Robert Van Camp, *Marietta College*
Tammy VanDeGrift, *University of Portland*
Brad Vander Zanden, *University of Tennessee*
James Vanderhyde, *Benedictine College*
Yaakov Varol, *University of Nevada Reno*

Jorge Vasconcelos, *Johns Hopkins University*
Troy Vasiga, *University of Waterloo*
Kam Vat, *University of Macau*
Steven Vegdahl, *University of Portland*
Nanette Veilleux, *Simmons College*
J. Velazquez-Iturbide, *Universidad Rey Juan Carlos*
Tamar Vilner, *The Open University of Israel*
Giovanni Vincenti, *Towson University*
Ken Vollmar, *Missouri State University*
David Voorhees, *Le Moyne College*
Rosita Wachenchauzer, *Facultad de Ingeniería. Universidad de Buenos Aires*
Paul Wagner, *University of Wisconsin - Eau Claire*
Sally Wahba, *Clemson University*
Gursimran Walia, *North Dakota State University*
Ellen Walker, *Hiram College*
Henry Walker, *Grinnell College*
Xinli Wang, *Michigan Technological University*
Xueyi Wang, *Northwest Nazarene University*
Xusheng Wang, *Winthrop University*
Karen Ward, *University of Portland*
Stan Warford, *Pepperdine University*
Richard Wasniowski, *California State University Dominguez Hills*
Thomas Way, *Villanova University*
Stephen Weiss, *University of North Carolina at Chapel Hill*
Emily Wenk, *Penn State York*
Linda Werner, *University of California, Santa Cruz*
Roger West, *University of Illinois at Springfield*
Curt White, *DePaul University*
Elizabeth White, *George Mason University*
Laurie White, *Mercer University*
Howard Whitston, *University of South Alabama*
Richard Wicentowski, *Swarthmore College*
Sheila Wiggins, *retired*
Linda Wilkens, *Providence College*
Judith Williams, *William Penn University*
Ken Williams, *NC A&T State University*
Craig Wills, *Worcester Polytechnic Institute*
Michael Wirth, *University of Guelph*
Marty Wolf, *Bemidji State University*
Christine Wolfe, *Ohio University*
Rosalee Wolfe, *DePaul University*
David Wolff, *Pacific Lutheran University*
Greg Wolffe, *Grand Valley State University*
Steven Wolfman, *University of British Columbia*
Ka Wai Wong, *The Hong Kong Institute of Education*
Wilson Wong, *Bentley University*
Stelios Xinogalos, *Technology Management Department, University of Macedonia*
T. Yang, *University of Houston – Clear Lake*
Arthur Yanushka, *Christian Brothers University*
Dowming Yeh, *National Kaohsiung Normal University*
Juang Yih-Ruey, *Jinwen University of Science & Technology*
Duane Yoder, *University of West Georgia*
Kwok-Bun Yue, *University of Houston-Clear Lake*
Timothy Yuen, *UTSA*
Marsha Zaidman, *University of Mary Washington*
Carol Zander, *University of Washington, Bothell*
Julie Zelenski, *Stanford University*
Jian Zhang, *Texas Womans' University*
Jinghua Zhang, *Winston-Salem State University*
Lynn Ziegler, *College of St. Benedict/St. John's University*
Stephen Zilora, *Rochester Institute of Technology*
Jill Zimmerman, *Goucher College*
Daniel Zingaro, *University of Toronto*
Fani Zlatarova, *Elizabethtown College*

Recipients of the SIGCSE Award for Outstanding Contributions to Computer Science Education

1981 **William F. Atchison**, *University of Maryland*

1982 **Alan Perlis**, *Yale University*

1983 **Karl V. Karlstrom**, *Prentice-Hall*

1985 **Elliot I. Organick**, *University of Utah*

1986 **Donald Knuth**, *Stanford University*

1987 **Niklaus Wirth**, *ETH, Zurich*

1988 **Grace Murray Hopper**, *Rear Admiral, USN, Digital Equipment Corp.*

1989 **Edsger W. Dijkstra**, *The University of Texas at Austin*

1990 **Curriculum '68 Committee**:
William F. Atchison, Samuel D. Conte, John Hamblen, Thomas E. Hull, Thomas A. Keenan, William B. Kehl, Edward J. McClusey, Silvio O. Navarro, Werner Rheinboldt, Earl J. Schweppe, William Viavant, David M. Young, Jr.

1991 **David Gries**, *Cornell University*

1992 **Daniel D. McCraken**, *City College, City University of New York*

1993 **Alan C. Kay**, *Apple Computer*

1994 **Norman E. Gibbs**, *Software Engineering Institute*

1995 **Robert M. Aiken**, *Temple University*

1996 **Nell B. Dale**, *The University of Texas at Austin*

1997 **Andrew Tannenbaum**, *Vrije University*

1998 **William A. Wulf**, *University of Virginia and National Academy of Engineering*

1999 **Peter J. Denning**, *George Mason University*

2000 **Andries Van Dam**, *Brown University*

2001 **Allen B. Tucker**, *Bowdoin College*

2002 **Elliot Soloway**, *University of Michigan*

2003 **Eric Roberts**, *Stanford University*

2004 **Mordechai Ben-Ari**, *Weizmann Institute of Science*

2005 **Kim Bruce**, *Williams College*

2006 **Richard Pattis**, *Carnegie Mellon University*

2007 **Judith Gal-Ezer**, *Open University of Israel* and **John Hughes**, *University of Technology, Sydney*

2008 **Randy Pausch**, *Carnegie Mellon University*

2009 **Elliot B. Koffman**, *Temple University*

2010 **Sally Fincher**, *University of Kent, Canterbury*

2011 **Matthias Felleisen**, *Northeastern University*

2012 **Harold (Hal) Abelson**, *Massachusetts Institute of Technology*

2013 **Michael Kölling**, *University of Kent, Canterbury*

Recipients of the SIGCSE Lifetime Service Award

1997 **Richard Austing**, *University of Maryland*

1998 **Della Bonnette**, *University of Southwestern Louisiana*

1999 **Robert Aiken**, *Temple University*

2000 **James E. Miller**, *University of Southern Mississippi*

2001 **Lillian N. (Boots) Cassel**, *Villanova University*

2002 **Joe Turner**, *Clemson University and Zayed University*

2003 **Harriet Taylor**, *National Science Foundation and Louisiana State University*

2004 **Bruce Klein**, *Grand Valley State University*

2005 **Andrew McGettrick**, *University of Strathclyde*

2006 **Joyce Currie Little**, *Towson State University*

2007 **John Impagliazzo**, *Hofstra University*

2008 **Dennis Frailey**, *Raytheon Corporation*

2009 **Michael J. Clancy**, *University of California, Berkeley*

2010 **Peter Denning**, *Naval Postgraduate School*

2011 **Gordon Davies**, *Open University*

2012 **Jane Prey**, *Microsoft Research*

2013 **Henry Walker**, *Grinnell College*

CALL FOR PARTICIPATION

SIGCSE 2014

Leveraging Computing to Change Education

The 45th ACM Technical Symposium on Computer Science Education

March 5 – 8, 2014, Atlanta, Georgia, USA

http://www.sigcse.org/sigcse2014

SIGCSE 2014 continues our long tradition of bringing together colleagues from around the world to present papers, panels, posters, special sessions, and workshops, and to discuss computer science education in birds-of-a-feather sessions and informal settings. The SIGCSE Technical Symposium addresses problems common among educators working to develop, implement and/or evaluate computing programs, curricula, and courses. The symposium provides a forum for sharing new ideas for syllabi, laboratories, and other elements of teaching and pedagogy, at all levels of instruction.

Submissions in line with the conference theme, "**Leveraging Computing to Change Education**," are encouraged. The theme focuses our attention on how computing influences the way we educate at all levels. This influence includes applications designed to support student learning, the curricular impact of computing, learning research, and the impact of technology in all forms of education. We want to look beyond the conventional computer science education boundaries for connections as well.

PAPERS

Papers describe an educational research project, classroom experience, teaching technique, curricular initiative, or pedagogical tool. Two versions of a submission are required: a full version having author names and affiliations and an anonymous version for use in reviewing. Papers will undergo a blind reviewing process and must not exceed six pages. Authors will have approximately 25 minutes for their presentations, including questions and answers.

PANELS

Panels present multiple perspectives on a specific topic. To allow each panelist sufficient time to present his or her perspective and still enable audience participation, a panel will normally have at most four panelists, including one moderator. Panel submissions should include a list of the panelists, their affiliations, and a description of the topic, with brief position statements from panelists. Proposals with more than four panelists must provide a statement connecting the extra panelist to the effectiveness of the panel and must convincingly show that each panelist will be able to speak, and the audience able to respond, within the session time. Panel abstracts must not exceed two pages. A panel session is approximately 75 minutes.

SPECIAL SESSIONS

Special sessions are your opportunity to customize and experiment with the SIGCSE conference format. Possible special sessions include a seminar on a new topic, a committee report, or a forum on curriculum issues. More generally, they must be 75 minutes in length, held in standard conference spaces, and justifiably distinct from the panel, paper, and poster tracks. Within those constraints, the form is yours to design. Special session abstracts must not exceed two pages.

WORKSHOPS

Workshops offer participants opportunities to learn new techniques and technologies designed to foster education, scholarship, and collaborations. A workshop proposal (including abstract) must not exceed two pages. Proposals must specify equipment needs (e.g., participant-supplied laptops, room configurations, and A/V equipment) and any limitation on the number of participants. Workshops are scheduled for a three-hour session and do not conflict with the technical sessions.

BIRDS OF A FEATHER SESSIONS

Birds of a Feather (BOF) sessions provide an environment for colleagues with similar interests to meet for informal discussions. A maximum one-page description (including abstract) is requested to describe the informal discussion topic. A/V equipment will not be provided for these sessions. Approximately 45 minutes are allocated to each BOF topic.

POSTERS

Posters describe computer science education materials or research, particularly works in progress. Proposals (including abstract) are limited to two pages. Poster demonstrations are scheduled to permit one-on-one discussion with conference attendees, typically during session breaks. Prepared handouts are encouraged in order to share your work.

STUDENT RESEARCH COMPETITION

Research from all areas of computer science is considered for awards in two categories of competition: graduate and undergraduate. All submissions must represent a student's individual research contribution and a student must be an ACM student member to qualify for awards and travel grants. Entry due date is September 29, 2013.

IMPORTANT DUE DATES

Friday, September 6, 2013: *Paper, Panel, Special Session, and Workshop submissions*
Monday, October 28, 2013: *Birds of a Feather and Poster submissions*

PROGRAM COMMITTEE

Symposium Chairs

J.D. Dougherty
Haverford College
jd@cs.haverford.edu

Kris Nagel
Georgia Gwinnett College
knagel@ggc.edu

Program Chairs

Adrienne Decker
Rochester Institute of Technology
amdigm@rit.edu

Kurt Eiselt
University of British Columbia
eiselt@cs.ubc.ca

Panels and Special Sessions

Stephen Cooper
Stanford University
coopers@stanford.edu

Workshops

Susan Haller
SUNY Potsdam
hallersm@potsdam.edu

Sue Fitzgerald
Metropolitan State University
sue.fitzgerald@metrostate.edu

Publications

Dennis J. Bouvier
Southern Illinois University
djb@acm.org

Database Administrators

John Dooley
Knox College
jdooley@knox.edu

Henry Walker
Grinnell College
walker@cs.grinnell.edu

Registration

Lynn Degler
Rose-Hulman Institute of Technology

Cary Laxer
Rose-Hulman Institute of Technology

Larry Merkle
Computational Optimization Services

Posters

Michael T. Helmick
University of Cincinnati
mike.helmick@gmail.com

Birds Of A Feather

Marc Rubin
Colorado School of Mines
mrubin@mymail.mines.edu

Student Volunteers and Student Activities

Steven Wolfman
University of British Columbia
wolf@cs.ubc.ca

Pam Cutter
Kalamazoo College
Pam.Cutter@kzoo.edu

Webmaster

Jaime Spacco
Knox College
jspacco@knox.edu

Treasurer

Scott McElfresh
Wake Forest University
scottmcelfresh@acm.org

Evaluations

Carl Alphonce
University at Buffalo
alphonce@buffalo.edu

Kids' Camp

James Maher
Colorado School of Mines
jmaher@mymail.mines.edu

Cheryl Seals
Auburn University
sealscd@auburn.edu

Support/Exhibitor Liaison

Susan Rodger
Duke University
rodger@cs.duke.edu

Pre-Conference Events Liaison

Mary Anne Egan
Siena College
maegan@siena.edu

K-12 Liaison

Crystal Furman
Brookwood High School
crystal.furman@gmail.com

International Liaison

Annemieke Craig
Deakin University
annemieke.craig@deakin.edu.au

Local Arrangements

Deepa Muralidhar
North Gwinnett High School
deepa.muralidhar@gmail.com

Student Research Competition

Ann Sobel
Miami University (Ohio)
sobelae@muohio.edu

Association for Computing Machinery
Advancing Computing as a Science & Profession

SIGCSE
ACM Special Interest Group on Computer Science Education

Changing the Face of Computing

Tracy Camp, Moderator
Colorado School of Mines
tcamp@mines.edu

ABSTRACT

The demand for computing professionals continues to grow, while women and minorities remain severely underrepresented at all levels. This opening SIGCSE 2013 keynote asks the crucial question "What can WE do to change the face of computing?" Several answers to this question will be provided in an unusual format with the following all-star cast. Each speaker will take five minutes to share 20 slides (which automatically advance every 15 seconds) to provide a stimulating presentation that ends with "What can YOU do to change the face of computing?"

Categories and Subject Descriptors

K.3.2 [**Computers and Education**]: Computer and Information Science Education – *Computer science education*

General Terms

Human Factors

Keywords

Broadening Participation

BIOGRAPHIES

Ed Lazowska holds the Bill & Melinda Gates Chair in Computer Science & Engineering at the University of Washington, where he has served on the faculty for 35 years. Lazowska received his A.B. from Brown University and his Ph.D. from the University of Toronto. His research and teaching concern the design, implementation, and analysis of high performance computing and communication systems, and, more recently, the techniques and technologies of data-driven discovery. He has also been active in public policy issues, ranging from STEM education to Federal strategies for research and innovation.

Lazowska is a Member of the National Academy of Engineering and a Fellow of the American Academy of Arts & Sciences. He co-chairs (with Susan Graham) the Computing Community Consortium, whose goal is to better align computing research with pressing national and global challenges. He has served on the Technical Advisory Board for Microsoft Research since its inception, and serves as a technical advisor to a number of high-tech companies and venture firms. Lazowska has advised 22 Ph.D. students and 23 Masters students, and has received the University of Washington Computer Science & Engineering Undergraduate Teaching Award.

Bobby Schnabel is Dean of the School of Informatics and Computing at Indiana University. In this position he leads a multi-campus school of approximately 100 faculty and 2400 students at the Bloomington and Indianapolis campuses, including undergraduate and graduate programs in computer science and informatics. From 2009-2010 he also served as interim IU vice president for research. Prior to joining IU in July 2007, Schnabel was on the computer science faculty of the University of Colorado at Boulder from 1977-2007. He served as Vice Provost for Academic and Campus Technology and Chief Information Officer at the University of Colorado at Boulder from 1998-2007, and as founding director of the Alliance for Technology, Learning and Society (ATLAS), a campus-wide information technology institute, from 1997-2007.

Schnabel is a co-founder and executive team member of the National Center for Women & Information Technology, and is chair of the ACM Education Policy Committee. He currently serves on the advisory committee for the NSF Directorate for Computer and Information Science and Engineering. He is a fellow of ACM and of SIAM.

Mary Lou Soffa is the Owen R. Cheatham Professor in the Computer Science Department at the University of Virginia and served as Department Chair from 2004 to 2012. From 1977 to 2004, she was a Professor of Computer Science at the University of Pittsburgh and also served as the Dean of Graduate Studies in the College of Arts and Sciences from 1991 to 1996. Her research

SIGCSE'13, March 6–9, 2013, Denver, Colorado, USA.
ACM 978-1-4503-1868-6/13/03.

interests include optimizing compilers, virtual execution environments, software testing, program analysis, software security, and performance for multi-core architectures.

Soffa received the ACM/IEEE Ken Kennedy Award in 2012 and the Anita Borg Technical Leadership Award in 2011. She was elected an ACM Fellow in 1999 and received the Presidential Award for Excellence in Science, Mathematics and Engineering Mentoring the same year. She was selected as a Girl Scout Woman of Distinction in 2003 and received the Computing Research Association (CRA) Nico Habermann Award in 2006. She has served on the Executive Committees of both ACM SIGSOFT and SIGPLAN, as well as conference chair, program chair or program committee member for numerous conferences. She had directed 30 Ph.D. students to completion, half of whom are women, and over 60 M.S. students. She currently serves ACM Council.

Lucy Sanders is CEO and Co-founder of the National Center for Women & Information Technology (NCWIT) and also serves as Executive-in-Residence for the ATLAS Institute at the University of Colorado at Boulder (CU). Lucy has an extensive industry background, having worked in R&D and executive (VP) positions at AT&T Bell Labs, Lucent Bell Labs, and Avaya Labs for over 20 years. Lucy is a Bell Labs Fellow and has six patents in the communications technology area. Lucy serves on several boards, including the Mathematical Sciences Research Institute (MSRI) Board of Trustees at the University of California at Berkeley, the Information Technology Research and Development Ecosystem Commission for the National Academies, and the U.S. Commerce Department's Innovation Advisory Board.

Lucy is a recipient - along with NCWIT co-founders Robert Schnabel and Telle Whitney - of the Computing Research Association's 2012 A. Nico Habermann Award. In 2011 Lucy was recognized with CU's George Norlin Distinguished Service Award. She has been inducted into the Women in Technology International (WITI) Hall of Fame. Lucy received her BS and MS in computer science from Louisiana State University and the University of Colorado at Boulder, respectively.

Since 2004, **Jan Cuny** has been a Program Officer at the National Science Foundation. Before coming to NSF, she was a faculty member in Computer Science at Purdue University, the University of Massachusetts, and the University of Oregon. At NSF, Jan leads the Education Workforce Cluster and its two programs: Computing Education for the 21st Century (CE21) and the Broadening Participation in Computing Alliance (BPC-A) program. Together these programs aim to increase the number and diversity of students majoring in computing. Jan has had a particular focus on the inclusion of students from those groups that have been traditionally underrepresented in computing: women, African Americans, Hispanics, Native Americans, and persons with disabilities. For her efforts with underserved populations, she is the recipient of one of the 2006 ACM President's Awards, the 2007 CRA A. Nico Haberman Award, and the 2009 Anita Borg Institute's Woman of Vision Award for Social Impact.

Patty Lopez is a Platform Applications Engineer at Intel Corporation. Prior to joining Intel in 2008, she spent 19 years as an Imaging Scientist for Hewlett Packard, creating and transferring technology in imaging into scanner, camera, and all-in-one products. She has released over fifty products and holds seven imaging patents. She earned her BS, MS, and PhD in Computer Science from New Mexico State University (NMSU).

Dr. Lopez serves on the advisory boards of CRA-W, CAHSI, the Anita Borg Institute, and the NMSU Foundation. She is a Distinguished Alumna for the NMSU College of Arts and Sciences received the HENAAC/Great Minds in STEM Community Service Award in 2010. A founding member of Latinas in Computing, a MentorNet mentor, a member of the NCWIT Workforce Alliance, and active for the past several years on the Grace Hopper Celebration of Women in Computing Conference organizing committee, she is currently serving as the 2013 GHC General Co-Chair (Industry). Her current passion is building the STEM pipeline for K-16 and beyond, and creating an inclusive organizational culture in the workplace.

Juan E. Gilbert is the Presidential Endowed Chair in Computing, an IDEaS Professor and Chair of the Human-Centered Computing Division in the School of Computing at Clemson University where he leads the HCC Lab. He is also a Professor in the Automotive Engineering Department at Clemson University. Dr. Gilbert is a Fellow of the American Association for the Advancement Science (AAAS), an ACM Distinguished Scientist, National Associate of the National Research Council of the National Academies, an ACM Distinguished Speaker and a Senior Member of the IEEE Computer Society. In 2011, Dr. Gilbert was given a Presidential Award for Excellence in Science, Engineering and Mathematics Mentoring by President Barack Obama.

Principles, Priorities, and Pressures: Personal and Organizational

Henry Walker
Samuel R. and Marie-Louise Rosenthal Professor of Natural Science and Mathematics
Chair and Professor of Computer Science
Department of Computer Science
Grinnell College
Grinnell, Iowa 50112-1690
(641) 269-4208
walker@cs.grinnell.edu

ABSTRACT

Early discussion regarding a talk at the First-Timers Luncheon highlighted the opportunity for an oldtimer to welcome first timers, encourage participation, and provide perspectives.

Throughout my career, I have been privileged to be able to connect my personal career with activities for the broad, educational-computing community. This talk reflects on factors that have impacted both my own career and the evolution of broader groups --- particularly SIGCSE.

Some general principles (e.g., inclusion, respect, service and social responsibility) seem clear, but even then circumstances present challenges and contradictions. Other principles (e.g., encouraging creative brainstorming, utilizing serendipity, listening to people) may be less obvious, but equally vital.

Many have described the SIGCSE community as a professional family, and this talk seeks to celebrate that community as promotes a vision for fulfilling personal careers and continued organizational development.

Categories and Subject Descriptors

K.3.2 [**Computers and Education**]: Computer and Information Science Education – *Computer science education*

General Terms

Human Factors

Keywords

Career Perspectives

BIOGRAPHY

Throughout his career, Professor Walker has thrived on activities related to students, teaching, and computing education: curricula, pedagogy, environments, teaching, learning, mentoring, and the broad community of educators. He has collaborated with many individuals and groups on a wide range of articles and reports. He works with the Liberal Arts Computer Science Consortium on curricular recommendations; he founded and periodically organizes meetings of the Iowa Undergraduate Computer Science Consortium; he works with the Advanced Placement Computer Science A program; he recently served as Chair of the Program Study Group on Computing and Computation for the Mathematical Association of America (MAA); and he has participated in over 30 external reviews of mathematics and/or computer science programs.

Professor Walker has worked within SIGCSE in many roles, including SIGCSE Chair, Secretary/Treasurer, and SIGCSE 2001 Symposium Chair. The paper submission and review system he began for SIGCSE 2000 is now used by a half-dozen conferences (including SIGCSE 2013). He is author of nine textbooks (most recently, "The Tao of Computing, Second Edition"), an Associate Editor and Columnist for ACM Inroads, a lifetime member of ACM (membership designated as Distinguished Educator), and a lifetime member of MAA.

SIGCSE'13, March 6–9, 2013, Denver, Colorado, USA.
ACM 978-1-4503-1868-6/13/03.

This Much I Know – Thoughts on the Past, Present and Future of Educational Programming Tools

Michael Kölling
Professor of Computer Science
School of Computing
University of Kent
Canterbury, Kent, CT2 7NF
+44 (0) 1227 823821
m.kolling@kent.ac.uk

ABSTRACT
Tools to support and improve the learning and teaching of programming have been developed, used and researched for many years. Yet, sometimes it seems we are still faced with exactly the same problems we were trying to tackle a decade ago, or two decades ago.

In this talk I will look back on educational software tools, through very subjective blinkers, and present a highly personal slice of the history of some of these efforts. This is followed by an attempt to speculate about the future. Where my crystal balls fail me, I will simply stipulate wishes, requirements and challenges – always much easier than presenting facts. Overall, I hope that some current trends in educational software tools emerge.

Categories and Subject Descriptors
K.3.2 [**Computers and Education**]: Computer and Information Science Education – *Computer science education*

General Terms
Human Factors

Keywords
Educational Tools

BIOGRAPHY

Michael Kölling is a Professor at the School of Computing, University of Kent, in Canterbury, UK. He holds a PhD in computer science from Sydney University, and has worked in Australia, Denmark and the UK. Michael's research interests are in the areas of object-oriented systems, programming languages, software tools, computing education and HCI. He has published numerous papers on object-orientation and computing education topics and is the author and co-author of two Java textbooks. Michael is the lead developer of BlueJ and Greenfoot, two educational programming environments. He is a UK National Teaching Fellow, Fellow of the UK Higher Education Academy and a Distinguished Educator of the ACM.

SIGCSE'13, March 6–9, 2013, Denver, Colorado, USA.
ACM 978-1-4503-1868-6/13/03.

Online Education

John Etchemendy
Provost & the Patrick Suppes Family Professor of Humanities and Sciences
Office of the Provost
Stanford University
Building 10
Stanford, CA 94305
(650) 724-4075
etch@stanford.edu

ABSTRACT

There has been an explosion of interest in Online Education since Stanford made three computer science courses freely available in September 2011 and attracted 300,000 "students." Yet Online Education has been around in various forms for thirty plus years. What accounts for the sudden inflection point sparked by these courses? Will the rush to put courses online prove to be (a) a flash in the pan, (b) the savior of higher education, (c) the death knell of universities as we know them, (d) all of the above?

Categories and Subject Descriptors

K.3.2 [**Computers and Education**]: Computer and Information Science Education – *Computer science education*

General Terms

Human Factors

Keywords

Online Education

BIOGRAPHY

John Etchemendy is the Provost at Stanford University and the Patrick Suppes Family Professor of Humanities and Sciences. He received his BA and MA in Philosophy from the University of Nevada, Reno, and his PhD from Stanford University in 1982, where he specialized in logic. He is the author or co-author of seven books and numerous articles in logic, including the popular text/software package Language, Proof and Logic, and has been the co-editor of the Journal of Symbolic Logic and on the editorial boards of several other journals. He was awarded the Educom Medal in 1997 for leadership in the application of technology to the teaching of logic.

Etchemendy has been on the faculty at Princeton University and Stanford University. At Stanford, he served as Director of the Center for the Study of Language and Information from 1990 to 1993, and Associate Dean for the Humanities from 1993 to 1997. He has been Provost of the university since 2000, and is the longest serving provost in Stanford's history.

SIGCSE'13, March 6–9, 2013, Denver, Colorado, USA.
ACM 978-1-4503-1868-6/13/03.

Keynote Talk

Unlocking the Clubhouse: A Decade Later and Now What?

Jane Margolis
Senior Research
University of California at Los Angeles
Graduate School of Education and Information Studies
405 Hilgard Avenue
Los Angeles, CA 90095
(310) 794-4481
margolis@gseis.ucla.edu

ABSTRACT

In the decade since *Unlocking the Clubhouse: Women in Computing* (MIT Press, 2002) was published, educational institutions have coalesced around the mission of increasing women's participation in computing. Yet, despite the uptick of interest in computer science majors and the surge of technology shaping all aspects of our lives, the numbers of women majoring in computer science are still abysmally small. In this talk, I will further reflect on why this is the case, and make connections to the issues raised in *Stuck in the Shallow End: Education, Race, and Computing*---the underrepresentation in computer science of students of color. I will examine how underrepresentation in computing relates to the larger educational crisis in this country and issues we face as world citizens. This talk is part of an overarching mission to understand how inequality is produced in this country and the types of social action required to equalize opportunities and broaden participation in computing.

Categories and Subject Descriptors

K.3.2 [**Computers and Education**]: Computer and Information Science Education – *Computer science education*

General Terms

Human Factors

Author Keywords

broadening participation

SIGCSE'13, March 6–9, 2013, Denver, Colorado, USA.
ACM 978-1-4503-1868-6/13/03.

BIOGRAPHY

Jane Margolis is a Senior Researcher at UCLA's Graduate School of Education and Information Studies. She is a social scientist and the author of two books on the inequities in computer science education. Her book *Unlocking the Clubhouse: Women in Computing* (MIT Press, 2002) examines the gender gap in computer science at the college level, and her book, *Stuck in the Shallow End: Education Race, and Computing* (MIT Press, 2008) examines the daily experiences of students and teachers in three Los Angeles public high schools, all with high numbers of African-American and Latino/a students. Margolis studies the interaction of structural inequalities and belief systems that perpetuate denied access of equal opportunities and segregation. *Stuck in the Shallow End* received the 2008 Prose Award in the Education category from the Association of American Publishers.

Margolis is the PI of the NSF BPC *Into the Loop Alliance.* She is also co-PI on the NSF Math-Science Partnership grant *Mobilize: Mobilizing for Innovation of Computer Science Teaching and Learning.* These grants are all focused on democratizing computer science education and addressing the underrepresentation in the field. Margolis is a member of the National Center for Women in Technology Social Sciences Advisory Board.

Shifting the Paradigm of African-American Students from Consumers of Computer Science to Producers of Computer Science

Yolanda Rankin (Moderator)
Jakita O. Thomas
Spelman College
350 Spelman Lane, Box 1257
Atlanta, GA 30314
{yrankin, jthoma41}@spelman.edu

Quincy Brown
Bowie State University
14000 Jericho Park Road, CS Dept
Bowie, MD 20715
qbrown@bowiestate.edu

Leshell Hatley
Uplift, Inc.
1500 D Street, S.E.
Washington, D.C. 20003
leshell@upliftdc.org

Categories and Subject Descriptors

K.3.2 [**Computers and Education**]: Computer and Information Science Education - *Computer science education*

Keywords

Game Design; Mobile Apps; Entrepreneurship; African American; Middle School; High School

SUMMARY

Recent statistics indicate that 4.6% of Bachelor of Science degrees in Computer Science, Computer Engineering and Information in 2011 were awarded to African American college students compared to 64.8% of Bachelor of Science degrees which were awarded to Caucasian students or 15.3% to Asian students enrolled in U.S. institutions [6]. Because of the low numbers of underrepresented minorities, specifically African Americans in Computer Science, the U.S. federal government, private industries and concerned American educators seek effective measures to increase the number of African Americans in Computer Science programs across the nation. One strategic approach is to leverage African American college students' interest in technology (e.g. testing video games) that enables them to construct computing identities in the context of serving as a technical resource to their peers [2]. As a result, many voices representing different perspectives have begun to engage in a discussion of different approaches that stimulate African American students' interest in Computer Science and how to best propel that interest into educational and career choices that increase the number of African Americans in Computer Science [1 – 5].

However, within the African American community, the discussion is very different from mainstream's perception that African American students are not interested in doing Computer Science [1, 3]. In fact, the discussion among African Americans in Computer Science is one that reveals that we have a wealth of experience educating and utilizing pedagogical strategies that mobilize African American students' interest in Computer Science as well as other STEM related disciplines [1, 3]. We know what works and have been doing CS outreach within our communities for years. However, many African Americans in Computer Science who do outreach within their communities often fail to publish their work for political reasons (e.g. outreach is not valued as part of the tenure-track dossier). Unsurprisingly, our strategic approaches have not been recognized within the larger CS education community.

The purpose of this panel is to make salient pedagogical strategies that positively influence African American middle school and high school students' interests in CS. As African Americans in Computer Science, we provide a framework that is based upon a crucial paradigm shift from African Americans as consumers of technology to African Americans as producers of technology. Our approach goes beyond the premise that "computer science is for everyone, including African Americans" or that "by simply exposing African Americans to computing, you will increase the percentage of African Americans in the CS pipeline." This paradigm shift from one of consumer to one of producer emphasizes students' ideas over prior knowledge of CS concepts and values those ideas over what others consider to be "proper foundation" required for entry into CS courses, challenging the myth that African American students aren't interested in Computer Science [1,3,5]. Thus, learning and applying CS concepts becomes a means to an end as African American students transform their ideas into reality.

Our framework embodies four key principles: 1) African American students interact with African American Computer Scientists who serve as role models. This first principle affirms that African Americans do Computer Science and do it well, and that they too can be Computer Scientists. 2) African American students get hands-on experience learning how to use computing tools and equipment, helping them to develop computing skills. 3) African American students engage in tasks that leverage their creativity to solve problems relevant to them. This principle belies the importance of creating a level playing field that does not rely on prior knowledge of CS concepts. 4) As a result of the three principles in action, educators create a learning environment that embraces African American students' culture, thereby

SIGCSE'13, March 6–9, 2013, Denver, Colorado, USA.
ACM 978-1-4503-1868-6/13/03.

empowering African American students to utilize computing skills to produce artifacts that are culturally relevant. We emphasize that this is a significant outcome given that African American students are not instructed to create culturally relevant artifacts, and yet they naturally do so. These four principles enable African American students to rise to the challenge of both understanding CS concepts as well as applying them in the context of creating technology for a purpose.

Panelists

Each panelist will discuss her approach to engaging African American students in understanding computer science concepts and how the students demonstrate their enthusiasm while completing activities in a week's time that are normally taught on a college level over an entire semester. The expected outcome is a framework that leverages the experiences and cultural background of African American students in the learning activities encountered in the different approaches.

Though this framework has been developed in the context of working with African American students, the lessons learned from these experiences can provide insight into best practices for engaging additional underrepresented groups in learning CS concepts in an effective manner. The panel format will consist of three phases. In the first phase, panel presentations, panelists will introduce themselves and briefly describe their efforts in K-12 CS outreach. In the second phase, discussion, participants and panelists will discuss the presentations and identify emerging themes. In the final phase, identifying next steps, participants and panelists will discuss concrete actions that they can implement in their K-12 CS outreach efforts.

Yolanda Rankin

Yolanda Rankin will serve as moderator for this proposed panel. She is an instructor at Spelman College in Atlanta, GA where she teaches Computer Science courses for both CS and non-CS majors. Yolanda has facilitated several game design workshops for middle school, high school, and college students over the past 5 years and has conducted technology seminars that expose African Americans to career opportunities in computing. Prior to beginning her academic career, Yolanda has accumulated more than twelve years experience in industry as a researcher at IBM, software engineer at Lucent Technologies-Bell Labs and as a senior program manager at Luxcore Networks.

Jakita O. Thomas

Jakita O. Thomas is an Assistant Professor of Computer & Information Science at Spelman College and Founder and Director of the Imagine Computer & Information Science (ICIS) Camps held at Spelman College. The ICIS Camps provide year-round opportunities for students from 3rd grade through 12th grade to learn about game design, mobile app development, and robotics. Her goal is to arm participants with the skills and capabilities they need to engage in technology production as entrepreneurship, producing the tools, products, and services that can address the needs of underserved groups and change the world.

Quincy Brown

Quincy Brown has taught STEM Concepts to African American middle and high school students since she was a NSF GK-12 Fellow in graduate school. She is an Assistant Professor at Bowie State University and the Director of Girls Who Will..., a summer CS Education program for middle and high school girls in the Prince Georges County, Maryland area. Her approach to introducing students to computing includes female-only students being instructed by female African American undergraduate and graduate students. The goal of her program is to introduce the breadth of computing to African American girls with a focus on innovation and technology creation.

Leshell Hatley

Leshell Hatley has over 15,000 hours teaching CS concepts to African-American elementary, middle, and high school students in formal and informal environments in NY, NJ, and Washington, DC. She is the Executive Director of Uplift, Inc., a nonprofit in Washington, DC, which offers year-around courses in science, technology, engineering, and mathematics (STEM) and introduces the concept of creating solutions to relevant problems to students between the ages of 4-19. This past summer, she led a team of African-American teenagers to become the first team of youth to develop an app for the One Laptop Per Child's XO laptop.

REFERENCES

[1] Clark, K. (2012). E-Learning and underserved students. In J.A. Banks (Ed.), Encyclopedia of Diversity in Education. Newbury Park, CA: Sage Publications.

[2] DiSalvo, B., Yardi, S., Guzdial, M., McKlin, T., Meadows, C., Perry, K. and Bruckman, A. "African American Males Constructing Computing Identity." In the Conference Proceedings for ACM CHI 2011 May 7 - 12, 2011, pp. 2967 - 2970.

[3] Eugene, W. and Clark, K. (2012). E-Learning, Engineering and Learners of African Descent: A Needs Analysis. Journal of STEM Education: Innovations and Research, 13(2), 45-57.

[4] Kafai, Y. B., Peppler, K. A., & Chapman, R. N. (Eds.): *The Computer Clubhouse: Constructionism and Creativity in Youth Communities*. New York: Teachers College Press 2009.

[5] Margolis, J., Estrella, R., Goode, J., Holme, J.J., and Nao, K. Stuck in the Shallow End. The MIT Press, Cambridge, MA 2008.

[6] Sweben, S. Computing Degree and Enrollment Trends From the 2010-2011 CRA Taulbee Survey. Computing Research Association, Washington, D.C., 2011.

ACM/IEEE-CS Computer Science Curriculum 2013: Reviewing the Ironman Report

Mehran Sahami (moderator)
Stanford University
Computer Science Department
sahami@cs.stanford.edu

Steve Roach
University of Texas at El Paso
Computer Science Department
sroach@utep.edu

Ernesto Cuadros-Vargas
San Pablo Catholic University
School of Computer Science
ecuadros@ucsp.edu.pe

Richard LeBlanc
Seattle University
Department of Computer Science & Software Engineering
leblanc@seattleu.edu

Categories and Subject Descriptors
K.3.2 [**Computers and Education**]: Computer Science Education; Curriculum

General Terms
Documentation, Design, Standardization.

Keywords
Computing Curricula 2013: Computer Science, CS2013.

1. SUMMARY
For over 40 years, the major professional societies in computing—ACM and IEEE-Computer Society—have sponsored the creation of international curricular guidelines for undergraduate program in computing. These efforts began with the publication of Curriculum 68 [1], and as the field has grown and diversified, so too have the recommendations for curricula. The rapid evolution and expansion of the computing field and the growing number of topics in computer science has made regular revision of curricular recommendations necessary. Thus, the Computing Curricula volumes are updated on an approximately 10-year cycle, with the aim of keeping curricula modern and relevant. The most recent complete Computer Science curricular volume was released in 2001 (CC2001) [3] and was followed by a review effort that concluded in 2008 (CS2008) [2].

The next volume in the series, Computer Science 2013 (CS2013), is currently in progress, and a first draft of the CS2013 report (known as the Strawman report) was previously released in February 2012. A significant revision of this draft (called the Ironman report) is due for release in February 2013. This panel seeks to update and engage the SIGCSE community in providing feedback on the Ironman report, which will be available shortly prior to the SIGCSE conference. Indeed, prior SIGCSE panels on the CS2013 effort [4, 5] have resulted in useful feedback that has helped shape the evolving report. Since the Ironman report is the penultimate draft of the CS2013 report, this panel is an especially important venue for starting the last round of feedback that will impact the final CS2013 curricular guidelines.

SIGCSE'13, March 6–9, 2013, Denver, Colorado, USA.
ACM 978-1-4503-1868-6/13/03.

CS2013 aims to provide advice and guidance to the computing education community throughout the coming decade by redefining the knowledge areas in CS, rethinking the essentials necessary for a CS curriculum, and identifying working exemplars of courses and curricula along these lines. The integration of computing with other disciplines creates additional opportunities for defining innovative computing curricula. Balancing this topical growth with the need to keep recommendations realistic and implementable in the context of undergraduate education is particularly challenging. As a result, it is important to engage the broader computer science education community in a dialog to better understand new opportunities, local needs, and novel successful models of computing curriculum.

The high-level themes on which the CS2013 effort is based include:

- *The "Big Tent" view of CS* – As CS expands to include more multi-disciplinary work and new programs of the form "Computational X" are developed, it is important to embrace an outward looking view in computing that sees CS as a discipline actively seeking to work with and integrate into other disciplines.
- *Managing the size of the curriculum* – Although the field of Computer Science has expanded significantly in the past decade, it is simply not feasible to proportionately expand the size of the curriculum. As a result, CS2013 seeks to re-evaluate what are considered essential topics in computing so as to make room for new topics without requiring more total instructional hours than the prior CC2001 guidelines. The circumscription of curriculum size is necessary to promote more flexible models for curricula without losing the essence of a rigorous CS education.
- *Actual course exemplars as opposed to stylized course guidance* – CS2001 took on the significant challenge of providing descriptions of stylized courses incorporating the knowledge units defined in that report. While this was a valiant effort, it was felt in retrospect that such course guidance did not have much impact on actual course design. As a result, CS2013 plans to take a different approach: identifying existing

successful courses and curricula as fielded exemplars of how relevant knowledge units can be addressed in actual programs.

- *Institutional needs* Curricula exist in the context of specific institutional needs, goals, and resource constraints. As a result, CS2013 allows for explicit flexibility in curricular structure through a *tiered* set of core topics, where a small set of Tier 1 topics are considered essential for all CS programs, but individual programs have flexibility with regard to their coverage of Tier 2 topics.

The CS2013 Ironman draft includes a complete update to the Body of Knowledge in computer science, organized around 18 Knowledge Areas, outlined below:

- Algorithms and Complexity (AL)
- Architecture and Organization (AR)
- Computational Science (CN)
- Discrete Structures (DS)
- Graphics and Visual Computing (GV)
- Human-Computer Interaction (HC)
- Information Assurance and Security (IAS)
- Information Management (IM)
- Intelligent Systems (IS)
- Networking and Communications (NC)
- Operating Systems (OS)
- Platform-Based Development (PBD)
- Parallel and Distributed Computing (PD)
- Programming Languages (PL)
- Software Development Fundamentals (SDF)
- Software Engineering (SE)
- System Fundamentals (SF)
- Social and Professional Issues (SP)

Two substantial reorganizations in the Body of Knowledge include introductory programming and systems. In the area now called Software Development Fundamentals (previously called Programming Fundamentals), we have extracted fundamental software development concepts, including topics in algorithms, design, programming, and software development processes. A new area called Systems Fundamentals indentifies common themes among operating systems, networking, and computer architecture. Additionally, recent developments in the field (such as the ubiquity of parallel computing and the need for better understanding computer security) have given rise to the development of knowledge areas in Parallel and Distributed Computing, Information Assurance and Security, and Platform-Based Development.

While the CS2013 Strawman draft focused primarily on the Body of Knowledge described above, the Ironman draft provides a complete draft of the CS2013 guidelines, notably including a set of exemplar courses and curricula reflecting diverse implementations of the Body of Knowledge as well as discussion of institutional challenges in updating curricula. This panel will engage participants via:

- providing the opportunity to comment further on Body of Knowledge (which includes several changes since the release of the Strawman draft),
- discussion of course/curricular exemplars and ways for members of the community to provide additional exemplars,
- discussion of broad issues related to curricular reinvigoration, including new models for distributing topics across courses while dealing with institutional resource constraints.

To reiterate, this panel not only provides an update on the current state of CS2013, but seeks to actively engage the community in the discussions and work that will eventually manifest into the final published volume. Holding this panel at SIGCSE is an important step in the on-going engagement of the computing education community with the CS2013 effort. Indeed, SIGCSE-13 will be the most relevant venue to start the discussions on the last CS2013 *draft*, prior to the publication of the final report later in 2013.

2. MEHRAN SAHAMI

Mehran Sahami is co-chair of the Steering Committee for the Computing Curricula: Computer Science 2013 volume. He is an Associate Professor and Associate Chair for Education in the Computer Science Department at Stanford University, where he led a redesign of the undergraduate Computer Science curriculum.

3. STEVE ROACH

Steve Roach is co-chair of the Steering Committee for the Computing Curricula: Computer Science 2013 volume. He is an Associate Professor in the Department of Computer Science at the University of Texas at El Paso. He was involved in Computing Curricula Software Engineering 2004 and the Graduate Software Engineering 2009 efforts.

4. ERNESTO CUADROS-VARGAS

Ernesto Cuadros-Vargas is a member of the Steering Committee for the Computing Curricula: Computer Science 2013 volume. He is a Professor of Computer Science and Dean of the School of Engineering and Computing at San Pablo Catholic University in Arequipa, Peru. He is Executive Secretary of the Latin American Center on Computer Science and former President of the Peruvian Computing Society.

5. RICHARD LEBLANC

Richard LeBlanc is a member of the Steering Committee for the Computing Curricula: Computer Science 2013 volume. He is a Professor in and Chair of the Department of Computer Science and Software Engineering at Seattle University. He was co-chair of the Computing Curricula Software Engineering 2004 effort.

6. REFERENCES

[1] ACM Curriculum Committee on Computer Science. 1968. Curriculum 68: Recommendations for Academic Programs in Computer Science. *Comm. ACM* 11, 3 (Mar. 1968), 151-197.

[2] ACM/IEEE-CS Joint Interim Review Task Force. 2008. Computer Science Curriculum 2008: An Interim Revision of CS 2001, Report from the Interim Review Task Force. http://www.acm.org/education/curricula/ComputerScience2008.pdf

[3] ACM/IEEE-CS Joint Task Force on Computing Curricula. 2001. ACM/IEEE Computing Curricula 2001 Final Report. http://www.acm.org/sigcse/cc2001.

[4] Sahami, M., Guzdial, M., McGettrick, A., and Roach, S. 2011. Setting the Stage for Computing Curricula 2013: Computer Science – Report from the ACM/IEEE-CS Joint Task Force. In *Proc. SIGCSE '11*, 161-162.

[5] Sahami, M., Roach, S., Cuadros-Vargas, E., and Reed, D. 2012. Computing Curricula 2013: Computer Science – Update on the Strawman Report from the ACM/IEEE-CS Task Force. In *Proc. SIGCSE '12*, 3-4.

Computer Science Education for Social Good

Michael Goldweber
Xavier University
Cincinnati, Ohio, USA
mikeyg@cs.xu.edu

John Barr
Ithaca College
Ithaca, New York, USA
barr@ithaca.edu

Elizabeth Patitsas
University of Toronto
Toronto, Canada
patitsas@cs.toronto.edu

Categories and Subject Descriptors

K.3.2 [**Computer and Information Science Education**]: [Computer Science Education]

General Terms

Design, Experimentation

Keywords

Introductory Programming Projects, Computing for the Social Good

1. SUMMARY

Computation and algorithmic thinking have become essential components for solving problems in many different fields. As such, computer scientists are intimately involved in finding solutions to some of the most pressing social, economic, and scientific problems of our day. Yet students' perception of computing reflects the longstanding myths and stereotypes perpetuated in popular media. One often cited study of STEM oriented high school students describes students' perception of the computing discipline(s) as boring, tedious and irrelevant[6, 12].

Though CS educators cannot change popular media, they do have an ideal opportunity to change student misconceptions in the introductory computing curriculum. An introductory curriculum can reinforce student held myths or work to dismantle them. Which does the typical curriculum do? Buckley, in a 2009 CACM Viewpoint column[1], complained that introductory computing students, based on the unscientific examination of the textbooks in his office, are seemingly obsessed with animals (e.g. counting ducks, separating cows from horses), games (e.g. Tetris, Checkers), and food (e.g. donut counting, lemonade stands). He concludes with empathy for the student exposed to such motivating examples who quits CS and goes on to study something important.

This special session will present the work of the ITiCSE 2012 working group "A Framework for Enhancing the Social Good in Computing Education: A Values Approach." The working group's report[4] makes a case for the merits of Computer Science Education for Social Good (CSG-Ed) projects from an early stage in the computing curriculum. The working group considered the background of computing for the social good, motivated the work, proposed a categorisation, and provided an illustrative set of exemplar case study projects intended for CS educators to adopt in their own institutions.

In particular this special session will:

- Provide definition of a CSG-Ed activity or programming project.
- Motivate the inclusion of CSG-Ed projects in the computing curriculum in general and in the introductory courses in particular.
- Present subjective evidence as to why this approach is not more widespread in the introductory curriculum and present strategies to overcome the perceived barriers for adoption.
- Describe in appropriate detail 6 exemplar examples of introductory CSG-Ed programming projects.

A tenet of CSG-Ed proponents is that for any non-theoretical computer science domain, topic, or even task, one should be able to articulate a useful CSG-Ed assignment. The balance of the special session will be a challenge to this position. The panelists will open the discussion to the audience, fielding introductory computing concepts and proposing a CSG-Ed assignment for each.[1]

2. SOCIAL GOOD

"Social good" is a vague and potentially misleading term. Good for who? Good in what way? The goal of CSG-Ed, a refinement of the acronym CSG[5], is not to define "good" for CS students, however, but to demonstrate that computation is a powerful tool to use in the search for robust solutions to deep problems. CSG-Ed is an umbrella term meant to incorporate any educational activity, from small to large, that endeavors to convey and reinforce computing's social relevance and potential for positive societal impact.

As described in the introduction, Computer Science has long had a problem attracting a diverse body of students. Perceptions persist of computer science as an arcane and dull discipline that ranks with rebuilding hot-rod engines as an interesting career (and which tends to appeal to a similar demographic). With the decline in computer science courses in secondary school, the one place where CS educators can

[1]It is hoped that by this point in the session, some audience members will have gotten into a CSG-Ed mindset and also assist the panelists at proposing satisfactory CSG-Ed assignments.

SIGCSE'13, March 6–9, 2013, Denver, Colorado, USA.
ACM 978-1-4503-1775-7/13/03.

correct this misperception is in the introductory computing curriculum.

The crucial question for CS educators thus becomes how we can best showcase the broad creative problem-solving that programming enables while at the same time teaching the crucial concepts and skills of computer science. The traditional solution has been to interject projects into the introductory computer science curriculum that appeal to current students; e.g. games. Yet recent studies such as Buckley's[2] find that it is students' desire to have a positive societal impact that is one of the strong determinants in their selection of a major. This suggests that a path to a more diverse and inclusive student body in computer science would be to demonstrate computer science's vital role in addressing social problems through CSG-Ed projects.

The idea of using CSG-Ed projects in CS education is not new. Schneiderman, for example, argued in a 1971 paper that students should be equally stimulated to study sociological modeling as to study faster algorithms for eigenvalue calculations[10]. Along with an increasing recognition of the socially valuable contributions of computing [7, 11], there is a consequent call for inclusion of CSG-Ed activities in the computing curricula [3, 5, 8, 9].

Beyond the usefulness of CSG-Ed for introductory CS curricula, these types of projects provide obvious good to society, enable the linking of CS with the liberal arts and social sciences, and provide a more realistic view of the field of computer science. They even help address some of the common complaints about CS majors, that written and oral communication skills are often lacking.

Given these strong arguments for CSG-Ed projects, the obvious question is why so few such projects exist for the introductory level. There is, of course, no simple answer, but rather many interrelated factors that have delayed CSG-Ed development. Some of these, such as instructors' lack of domain knowledge, provided textbook examples, extraneous (cognitive) load, overloaded instructors, and scoping issues for CS 1, were addressed in the ITiCSE 2012 working group report referenced previously and will be addressed by this panel. In particular, this panel will present six example projects that are illustrative of the CSG-Ed approach and that can be easily integrated by CS educators into existing CS introductory courses. The goal is not to present an exhaustive selection of projects, but to reduce the friction to using CSG-Ed projects by providing a convenient starting point.

Presented projects cover traditional CS concepts such as graph algorithms (Red Cross disaster relief, STI modeling), list manipulation (Radioactive Mice), 2-d arrays (Water Pollution), introductory selection and 1-d arrays (Nuclear Power), and dictionaries (Voting). The projects are all centered around social issues that have been shown to resonate with students, yet require instructors to have little domaine knowledge outside computer science. Some of the problems ((Red Cross disaster relief and Radioactive Mice) recast familiar introductory CS problems. Several projects such as the Voting project and the Nuclear Power project, provide scaffolding in the form of code given to students. And some of the projects (nuclear power and water pollution) provide a simple interface into appealing technologies such as geographic information systems.

3. REFERENCES

[1] M. Buckley. Viewpoint: Computing as social science. *Commun. ACM*, 52(4):29–30, Apr. 2009.

[2] M. Buckley, J. Nordlinger, and D. Subramanian. Socially relevant computing. In *Proceedings of the 39th SIGCSE Technical Symposium on Computer Science Education*, SIGCSE '08, pages 347–351, New York, NY, USA, 2008. ACM.

[3] R. W. Connolly. Beyond good and evil impacts: rethinking the social issues components in our computing curricula. In *Proceedings of the 16th annual joint conference on Innovation and Technology in Computer Science Education*, ITiCSE '11, pages 228–232, New York, NY, USA, 2011. ACM.

[4] M. Goldweber, J. Barr, T. Clear, R. Davoli, S. Mann, E. Patitsas, and S. Portnoff. A framework for enhancing the social good in computing education: A values approach. In *Proceedings of the 17th Annual Conference reports on Innovation and Technology in Computer Science Education - working group reports*, ITiCSE-WGR '12, 2012.

[5] M. Goldweber, R. Davoli, J. C. Little, C. Riedesel, H. Walker, G. Cross, and B. R. Von Konsky. Enhancing the social issues components in our computing curriculum: computing for the social good. *ACM Inroads*, 2:64–82, February 2011.

[6] M. Guzdial. Teaching computing to everyone. *Commun. ACM*, 52(5), 2009.

[7] L. C. Kaczmarczyk. *Computers and Society: Computing for Good.* Chapman and Hall, 2011.

[8] L. Layman, L. Williams, and K. Slaten. Note to self: make assignments meaningful. In *Proceedings of the 38th SIGCSE Technical Symposium on Computer Science Education*, SIGCSE '07, pages 459–463, New York, NY, USA, 2007. ACM.

[9] S. Mann, L. Smith, and L. Muller. Computing education for sustainability. *SIGCSE Bull.*, 40(4):183–193, Nov. 2008.

[10] B. Shneiderman. Computer science education and social relevance. *SIGCSE Bull.*, 3(1):21–24, Mar. 1971.

[11] B. Tomlinson. *Greening through IT: Information Technology for Environmental Sustainability.* The MIT Press, 2010.

[12] S. Yardi and A. Bruckman. What is computing?: Bridging the gap between teenagers' perceptions and graduate students' experiences. In *ICER '07: Proceedings of the 3rd International Workshop on Computing Education Research.*

Board Game Strategies in Introductory Computer Science

Ivona Bezáková
Rochester Institute of Technology
102 Lomb Memorial Drive
Rochester, NY 14623, U.S.A.
ib@cs.rit.edu.edu

James E. Heliotis
Rochester Institute of Technology
102 Lomb Memorial Drive
Rochester, NY 14623, U.S.A.
jeh@cs.rit.edu.edu

Sean P. Strout
Rochester Institute of Technology
102 Lomb Memorial Drive
Rochester, NY 14623, U.S.A.
sps@cs.rit.edu.edu

ABSTRACT

We present three open-ended freshman projects where students design and implement their own player strategies for well-established board games: Quoridor by Mirko Marchesi (Gigamic), San Francisco Cable Cars by Dirk Henn (Queen Games), and The aMAZEing Labyrinth by Max J. Kobbert (Ravensburger). Unlike modern computer-based games, most board games are inherently discrete. For example, the board tends to have a fixed number of allowed positions for the game pieces and every player performs a search through a finite number of possible moves to decide which move to take next. As such, designing a player strategy for a board game provides a very natural context for basic data structures, searching algorithms, and other concepts typically covered in a freshman-level computer science sequence. Furthermore, the project allows for continual improvements to one's strategy, targeting both beginners as well as more advanced programmers.

Categories and Subject Descriptors

K.3.2 [**Computers and Education**]: Computer and Information Science Education

General Terms

Algorithms, Experimentation, Performance

Keywords

Introductory computer science, Learning in context, Basic data structures and algorithms, Open-ended project

1. INTRODUCTION

Motivating a full class of students in a freshman computer science course is challenging, especially if the students come from a variety of backgrounds and previous programming experiences. We address this situation by developing CS2-level projects where students design and implement player strategies for well-established (yet not necessarily widely known) board games. Board games provide a natural context for introductory data structures and algorithms, as both the layout of the game and the playing style (i. e., turn-taking) are typically discrete. Depending on the game, it might require the students to implement a graph search, or continually update and search through a 2D data structure. Previous research has demonstrated that learning to program in context increases student motivation [23, 24].

The students implement player modules that compute their players' moves and keep track of the current game state. We provide the "engine," a program that makes round-robin calls on the student modules to make their moves, enforces the rules of the game, and graphically displays the current state of the game. It also informs the student modules of the other players' moves so that the modules can update their data structures to reflect the current state of the game.

To achieve full credit we simply ask our students to consistently beat an unsophisticated or random playing strategy – we feel that this difficulty is compatible with a CS2-level project. In other words, we do not base the actual grading on competitiveness. However, the motivated student has the opportunity to keep improving their strategy and have it tested against their classmates' strategies in the end-of-term tournament that we dubbed the "Battle Royale." Our preliminary findings indicate that board games not only provide a suitable context but that programming player strategies further increases student motivation by being open-ended and providing opportunities for experimentation.

1.1 Related work

Games have been used as a motivation tool [2, 5, 6, 16] in computer science curriculum for several decades and have flourished into an active area in computer science educational research. The majority of approaches using games for educational purposes fall into these categories: game design and development (for a sample of recent publications, see, e. g., [3, 25, 13, 17, 28]), and playing games to learn (e. g., [8]). "Game design and development" typically means to implement a human-controlled game, not a player strategy, with student excitement often stemming from the accompanying multimedia experience [26, 19].

Our projects do not follow either approach – we use a well-established board game to provide the context for the concepts from introductory computer science courses and ask the students to design and implement a player strategy. As far as we know, the closest works related to our projects are Davies' Uno [22], the last part of Bayliss' Unreal Tournament [3], and Kurkovsky's games for mobile de-

SIGCSE'13, March 6–9, 2013, Denver, Colorado, USA.

vices [14]. Davies' Uno is a CS1 project where students use variables, conditionals, and simple loops to experiment with possible player strategies for the card game Uno. This project provides an excellent context for introductory programming concepts but, naturally since it addresses CS1 audience, not introductory data structures and algorithms. Bayliss' students spent the majority of the time implementing the Unreal Tournament (i. e., doing game development), with the last three weeks devoted to programming their own bot behaviors. Unlike in our case, the nature of the game is continuous where bots turn, move and face opponents in shooting matches. In the end, the bot-behavior part received much less attention than the traditional game development.

Similarly, Kurkovsky's students focused on game development, with a short amount of time devoted to programming game elements reacting to the actions of a human player. In this case the setup was also continuous and, moreover, the students did not implement a strategy of a human player but presumably a simpler behavior of various game creatures.

Summet, et al. [27] proposed an interesting context for CS1 centered around programming robot strategies: their students implemented various robot behaviors, using physical robot devices. However, the robots do not competitively interact.

Another interesting group of recent publications centers around using board games in CS1/2. Drake and Sung [7], and Kurmas and Vanderhyde [15, 22] discuss an interesting variety of board (and dice and card) games and their relevance to CS1/2 topics; however, none of these works take advantage of implementing player strategies. On the other hand, player strategies for games like Tic-Tac-Toe are a favorite topic in introductory artificial intelligence courses [9].

2. THE BOARD GAMES

We briefly sketch the rules for all three board games; see Figure 1 for snapshots of the games.

2.1 The aMAZEing Labyrinth

Designed by Max J. Kobbert and published by Ravensburger [12], the game consists of a 7x7 tiled area, where every tile is an I-shaped, T-shaped, or L-shaped corridor. Every other row and column can be shifted. There is an extra tile that is used to do so, thereby changing the paths in the labyrinth. Each player has a wizard with a distinct home position on the board, plus a randomly generated list of treasures to collect before returning home. Treasures are depicted on some of the tiles and the treasure is collected whenever a player's wizard lands on the corresponding tile. In every turn, a player first changes the board by inserting the extra tile and then moves his or her wizard any distance along an existing path. The game works for 2-4 players.

2.2 Quoridor

Designed by Mirko Marchesi and published by Gigamic [20], this game consists of a 9x9 board and works for 2 or 4 players. Each player places a single piece in the middle of one edge of the board. Its goal is to arrive somewhere along the edge at the opposite side of the board. Additionally to their piece, each player has ten walls of length 2. In each move, a player either moves their piece to an adjacent location, or places a wall. A wall must be aligned with the grid lines and it cannot cross an already placed wall or extend out of the board. Walls are used to obstruct and therefore detour opponents' movement. However, the wall placement cannot completely block the opponent from reaching their destination.

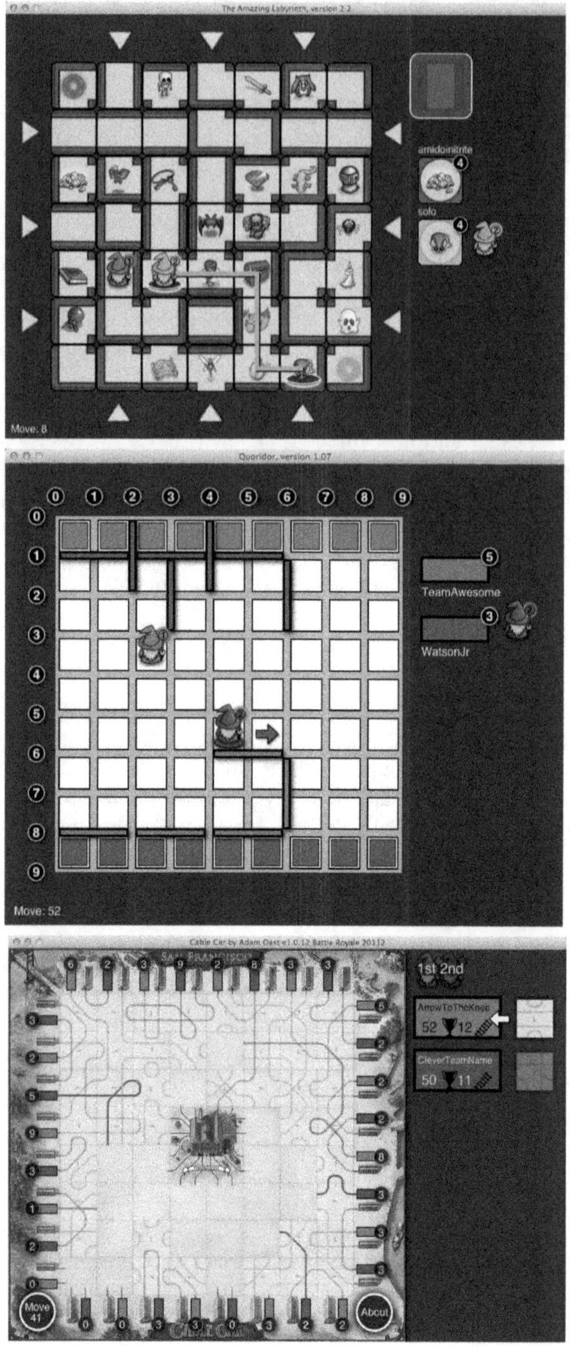

Figure 1: Labyrinth, Quoridor, and San Francisco Cable Cars depicted by our engines. The figures show games in progress, in each case a battle between the top two student players of the respective academic year.

2.3 San Francisco Cable Cars

Designed by Dirk Henn (art by Michael Menzel) and published by Queen Games [11], this game for 2-6 players is played on an 8x8 initially empty board, with 32 cable car stations distributed along the sides of the board. The rules specify which stations belong to each player. Each player gets a randomly drawn tile that specifies four connections, each between two of the eight end-points on the tile's sides. In every move, a player rotates their tile and places it on the board adjacently to an already placed tile or to a side of the board. By doing so, the players build cable car routes (theirs or their opponents' – or both). The game finishes after all tiles have been placed and the player with the overall longest cable car routes wins.

3. HOW THE PROJECT WORKS

3.1 The student module

The students implement three functions:

An initialization function. This function is called by the engine at the beginning of the game. The parameters of the function specify the initial state of the game, including the number of players, the student's player ID (to determine order of play), the initial game layout (e. g., in Labyrinth, the initial tile layout), etc. Students initialize their data structures accordingly – from this moment on the engine does not communicate the current game state; it is the student's responsibility to keep track of it.

A move function. This function is called whenever it is the student's turn to move. The student returns a move object specifying the move of their player.

An update function. This function informs the student of other player's moves, so that the student can update their data structures accordingly.

As a side note, to help the students with their strategies in Labyrinth, we opted to reveal the sequence of treasures to be collected for each player. Similarly in Cable Cars, we opted to reveal the tiles currently held by every player.

3.2 The engine

The engine starts by initializing all student modules. Then, it calls the first player's move function, followed by a call to each player's update function[1], informing them of the first player's move. Then, the engine calls the second player's move function, followed by the update function of the other players. This scenario continues until the game is over.

3.3 The project assignments

To guide the students during this project, we split it into four assignments. Roughly speaking, the first assignment is a "get started" part that asks the students to implement some useful function, for example graph search in Labyrinth. The second assignment is a "single player mode," where the students implement their move function but they do not need to worry about other players yet. In the third assignment, a "multi player mode," the students update their data structures based on other player's moves – they need to be able to play the full game. In the fourth "strategy" assignment we ask the students to design and implement a strategy that beats an unsophisticated player that we provide.

[1]Our design is evolving to inform the player module of its own move as well. This allows us to sometimes provide additional useful information, and it makes the student code's handling of game state updates more consistent.

We opted to have the students do the first assignment individually to fully understand how the engine works. For the subsequent assignments they work in teams of two. We devote three problem-solving (active learning) and laboratory sessions to the first three assignments, typically in the second, fourth, and seventh week of the (10 week) quarter.

3.4 Battle Royale

On the Saturday between the end of classes and the start of final exams, a friendly competition called Battle Royale takes place. An auditorium is outfitted with computer screens for the currently playing game and for a chart showing the winners of each round. Pizza is provided in the area just outside the auditorium for the students, instructors, and their guests. This voluntary competition is completely outside of the grade scheme for the course itself. Instead, prizes are awarded to the top teams (gift certificates at the college book store).

3.5 Grading

We de-emphasized the competitive aspect of the project for grading purposes – a correctly implemented strategy that used basic data structures and searching algorithms easily earned a top score. (For a full score in functionality we only require the player strategy to consistently beat the weaker of the modules that we provide with the engine, i. e., a randomly playing strategy.) We based our decision to suppress competitiveness on research suggesting that underrepresented groups tend to dislike, and not perform well, in a competitive environment [10]. We had very favorable experience with our proposed grading scheme: a vast majority of the teams eventually beat the provided module, reporting to have learned the underlying concepts and stating that the project "was fun."

4. WHY BOARD GAME STRATEGIES

We based the project on programming board game strategies for a number of reasons:

Discrete context to demonstrate basic CS concepts. Board games tend to be discrete. We argue that a discrete model fits better with the introductory courses and basic concepts such as searching algorithms and data structures ranging through arrays, lists, queues, and graphs.

In the Labyrinth project students stored the data in a 2D array (some even contemplated a 1D array) or as a graph representing the labyrinth, using either the adjacency matrix or adjacency lists. The variety led to a nice problem solving discussion of advantages and drawbacks of each data structure. Additionally, independently of the strategy, the students needed to search for their current treasure, search the tile layout for possible paths, and enumerate through several possible moves (for example different insertion locations for the extra tile) to choose what they consider to be the most appropriate move. Different strategies, ranging from heuristics to searching through the configuration space while anticipating the opponents' moves, may be incorporated.

Similar algorithms and data structure concerns relate to the Quoridor project. Even though the maze does not continually shift, the students needed to account for wall placement. This added an interesting dimension as the students needed to keep track of objects (game pieces) on the board as well as on the grid lines (walls). Unlike in Labyrinth, in Quoridor it is desirable to move along a shortest path, requiring the students to implement this functionality.

Cable Cars brought a set of different programming concerns. Since a cable route never splits, this project did not require graph search – a simple linear traversal was enough. The main hurdle to deal with was the representation of the game state, namely the connections of the route segments in the tiles placed on the board.

Established games. Board games are well-tested. If they were not interesting, they would not achieve popularity. We have found this preferable to the difficult task of inventing games that are both well-designed and interesting [4].

Room for experimentation. There is a wide variety of strategies. (If there were only one dominant strategy, the game would loose its appeal.) Typically there are some obvious strategies that are good enough to beat a random player, but the teams have the option to go beyond the required part of the project and experiment further. This means that the project has a clearly defined objective, yet it is open-ended.

Variety. There is a wide variety of board games [1] to choose from, allowing us to rotate through games and reduce the risk of plagiarism from previous students.

Visual feedback. The students get immediate visual feedback on the performance of their modules.

Why have we decided to have our students implement player strategies instead of doing traditional game development? While game development provides an interesting and relevant context for basic computer science concepts (and often for advanced concepts as well), the design of a player strategy is much more open-ended, providing motivation to complete the work, and to keep working on the project beyond the typical call of duty. Also, game development assignments often motivate students to put a lot of effort into the multimedia experience [18]. This tendency is natural, since the stimulation of the senses sparks student excitement. However, in our experience multimedia development can detract from data structures and algorithmic concepts. By providing the engine which includes the graphics, we give the students the satisfaction of a visual feedback, yet they concentrate on the implementation of the concepts in the underlying data structures and algorithms.

Another advantage of using a real-life established board game is that we are able to show the students the physical game and leave it in the student center for them to play (and study its properties!) during their leisure time.

5. GAME SELECTION CRITERIA AND EXPERIENCES

We started with the following list of selection criteria for the board games.

- Reasonably simple rules.
- Underlying data structures and algorithms that fit within the scope of CS2-level courses.
- Well-ranked at an on-line game review website [1]. (This implies the existence of a variety of strategies and an overall appeal of the game.)
- Non-violent and ethnicity- and gender-neutral.

Over the years we started adding other criteria, that, while not deal-breaking, influenced our game selection decisions.

- Playable by 2 and 4 players. Two player mode is important for our grading scheme (described below). The four player mode is not as crucial but it became a Battle Royale tradition and it gives the students a chance to play against multiple opponents at once and see what that does to their strategies.
- Few ties. Some games (e. g., Tsuro [21]) often end up in a tie, especially in the two player mode. This does not make for an interesting strategy development or match-watching.
- Not much randomness. If there is a lot of randomness, the game might be fun for real people but the strategy may not determine the winner.
- Some randomness. Quoridor does not include any randomness and many students opted to not use a randomized strategy. Thus, if there was a tie, we could switch the starting order for a second match but the third rematch was identical to one of the two earlier matches. We are addressing this by including different starting positions for the game.
- Game progress. With Labyrinth some students implemented overly defensive strategies where a match consisted of blocking the opponent from reaching their destination. This led to never-ending games. We started enforcing a maximum number of moves to solve this issue, as well as limiting the amount of time allotted for each player's computation.
- Reasonable visual display. Thus far we avoided 3D games, as well as games that do not use a bounded play area (such as Carcassonne [29]).

6. COURSE SETUP AND STUDENT DEMOGRAPHICS

We used The aMAZEing Labyrinth project in 2009/10, the Quoridor project in 2010/11, and the San Francisco Cable Cars project in 2011/12. We used the projects in the CS2 course in the winter quarter (December through February). The course covers introductory data structures and algorithms such as graphs, breadth and depth first search, backtracking, and hashing. The course was taken by 202 students in the first year, followed by about 350-400 students in both subsequent years. The course is offered in multiple sections of 50-60 students each, taught by a variety of instructors (overall, 10 instructors have taught the course so far). The majority of the students declared themselves as computer science majors, followed by software engineering majors, then computer engineering majors, as well as applied math and bioinformatics majors. Additionally, one or two sections of the course were offered to up to 90 students in the spring quarters. Thus far over a thousand students have taken part in this project.

7. PRELIMINARY FINDINGS

The project motivated the students to understand basic computer science concepts and see beyond the "computer science is just programming" view that we frequently encounter with freshman students. Many students enjoyed the experimenting part and were eager to learn more about upper-level topics such as artificial intelligence. These sentiments are captured by the following sample of student comments:

- *I am proud of every part of this project. When introduced to the idea at the beginning of the quarter I was flabbergasted and did not believe I could accomplish such a task but now that I have I am very confident that computer science is where I belong.*
- *Being very interested in AI, I'll probably return to this program down the road as I learn more about artificial intelligence.*
- *It was a fun project, and I might try to improve my player to win more often, or at least not get closed in so easily. I should probably stop making it rotate to the left every time.*
- *Overall, it was a pretty good project.*
- *The project overall is very interesting and fun. I really enjoy it.*
- *I think the competition was a good idea, since it gave a lot of people motivation to work harder on the project.*
- *The project wasn't necessarily hard. Meeting the minimum requirements was definitely not that much of a challenge. It was the competitive aspect that provoked me to do a bit more than what is required.*
- *The project was fun. (several times)*
- *Nice project idea, can't wait until CS3.*
- *The project was helpful and enjoyable. I liked the way the class was set up.*
- *The project is what made this course interesting. Rather than 4 more individual, disjointed, labs, the project gave us a chance to put several things we had learned together into one thing.*
- *I really like cable car. It's a creative game, and it was challenging to design an AI for but yet it was doable.*
- *I think competition is a great way to foster creativity and pride in one's accomplishments.*
- *This was such a cool project. Not only did we learn a lot, it was a fun experience. I really enjoyed the fact that we could write the code the way we wanted. Overall it was an awesome experience!*
- *Overall, however, the project was interesting and useful in demonstrating practical application of programming skills taught in class.*
- *I really liked the project and how it related to the course materials.*
- *Overall, I believe this project was a very good opportunity for me to improve my programming abilities. Along with the algorithms that we covered in class, the project allowed me to try some new techniques to improve the strategy for the many different parts. Without this experience, I don't think I would be as confident about my programming abilities as I am following its completion.*
- *I guess what I'd like to communicate is that while I don't think I learned much in terms of coding or algorithms over the course of this project, I learned an incredibly important design lesson, which was not to over-complicate things. I'd say this project provides a good testing grounds for students with some self-taught programming knowledge, or students with knowledge from prior courses, to realize what parts of their current programming strategies are stupid.*
- *It was tough. I barely pulled through. Probably worth it.*

We encountered several negative comments as well. Mainly they were about team collaboration and not specific to this project, thus we do not cite them here.

We also report preliminary evaluation results stemming from a post-quarter survey from winter 2011/12. The students responded to a list of statements with their sentiments ranging from "not true at all" to "very true". Out of 217 student responses, 152 students (70%) agreed with "Having to develop the algorithms helped me to see that the project was more than just programming."; 139 students (64%) agreed with "I enjoyed the competition aspect of the project.", 134 students (62%) agreed with "The project helped me to better understand computer science."; 132 students (61%) agreed with "I enjoyed the experimentation with different problem solving strategies." The majority of the other responses were neutral: the disagreeing percentages are 14%, 18%, 19%, and 18%, respectively. The main project evaluation will take place in 2012/13; see Section 8.1.

8. FUTURE PLANS

8.1 Formal evaluation

In 2012/13 we will compare strategy design to game development. We will split the students randomly into a control group and study group. The control group will implement parts of the engine, namely rule enforcement, keeping track of players in the game, score computation, but not graphics. The study group will design and implement player strategies as before. Both groups will need to keep track of the current game state and implement very similar search algorithms to generate/verify moves. Both groups will end the quarter with a voluntary mini competition: Battle Royale for the study group and a "best engine" for the control group (this will be judged by a panel of instructors). We will compare the groups through normal grade keeping but also with before and after surveys that measure how much they learned during the quarter, their interest in the project, their motivation to keep improving their code, and their enthusiasm for computer science in general.

8.2 Programming language support

All the game engines from the previous years ran under Python 2.6 due to the graphical environment Pyglet that is, unfortunately, not supported in later versions of Python. Through a very different approach developed in the summer of 2012, we have now successfully migrated to Python 3. The new architecture has also allowed us to add a Java version of the engine. The reason is that the graphical component has moved to a web browser, thus minimizing the amount of code that has to be rewritten when a new language is adopted. Once stable, these engines, along with the supporting documentation, will be available for use by other instructors and institutions.

8.3 Web interface

In the future, we envision a web site hosting a variety of tournaments, some devoted to a single course, as well as those where students can try their strategies against those written by teams from different universities.

9. ACKNOWLEDGMENTS

We gratefully acknowledge NSF funding, award ID 1044721. The Labyrinth and Quoridor engines were developed by Sean Strout and Paul Solt. The Cable Cars engine development and overhaul of the Quoridor engine in 2012 was done by Adam Oest.

Additionally, we are thankful for the feedback of our evaluation team led by Trudy Howles, with consultants Doug Baldwin, and Sage Miller.

10. REFERENCES

[1] BoardGameGeek / Gaming Unplugged Since 2000, a database of player reviews, session reports, images, and news. `http://www.boardgamegeek.com/`.

[2] T. Barnes, H. Richter, E. Powell, A. Chaffin, and A. Godwin. Game2Learn: building CS1 learning games for retention. In *Proceedings of the 12th Annual SIGCSE Conference on Innovation and Technology in Computer Science Education (ITiCSE '07)*, pages 121–125, 2007.

[3] J. D. Bayliss. Using games in introductory courses: tips from the trenches. In *Proceedings of the ACM SIGCSE '09*, pages 337–341, 2009.

[4] B. Burd, J. Goulden, B. Ladd, M. Rogers, and K. Stewart. Computer games in the classroom, or, how to get perfect attendance, even at 8 am. In *Proceedings of the ACM SIGCSE '07*, page 496, 2007.

[5] D. C. Cliburn. The effectiveness of games as assignments in an introductory programming course. In *Proceedings of the Thirty-Sixth ASEE/IEEE Frontiers in Education Conference (FIE '06)*, 2006.

[6] D. C. Cliburn and S. Miller. Games, stories, or something more traditional: the types of assignments college students prefer. In *Proceedings of the ACM SIGCSE '08*, pages 138–142, 2008.

[7] P. Drake and K. Sung. Teaching introductory programming with popular board games. In *Proceedings of the ACM SIGCSE '11*, pages 619–624, 2011.

[8] M. Eagle and T. Barnes. Experimental evaluation of an educational game for improved learning in introductory computing. In *Proceedings of the ACM SIGCSE '09*, pages 321–325, 2009.

[9] E. El-Sheikh and L. Prayaga. Development and use of AI and game applications in undergraduate computer science courses. *Journal of Computing Sciences in Colleges*, 27(2):114–122, 2011.

[10] S. M. Haller, B. Ladd, S. T. Leutenegger, J. Nordlinger, J. Paul, H. M. Walker, and C. Zander. Games: good/evil. In *Proceedings of the ACM SIGCSE '08*, pages 219–220, 2008.

[11] D. Henn. *San Francisco Cable Cars*. Queen Games, 2009. `http://www.queen-games.de`.

[12] M. J. Kobbert. *The aMAZEing Labyrinth Board Game*. Ravensburger, 1986. `http://www.ravensburger.com`.

[13] M. Kölling and P. Henriksen. Game programming in introductory courses with direct state manipulation. In *Proceedings of the 10th Annual SIGCSE Conference on Innovation and Technology in Computer Science Education (ITiCSE '05)*, pages 59–63, 2005.

[14] S. Kurkovsky. Engaging students through mobile game development. In *Proceedings of the ACM SIGCSE '09*, pages 44–48, 2009.

[15] Z. Kurmas and J. Vanderhyde. Board game project ideas for CS 1 and CS 2 (abstract only). In *Proceedings of the ACM SIGCSE '12*, page 658, 2012.

[16] S. T. Leutenegger and J. Edgington. A games first approach to teaching introductory programming. In *Proceedings of the ACM SIGCSE '07*, pages 115–118, 2007.

[17] M. C. Lewis and B. L. Massingill. Graphical game development in CS2: a flexible infrastructure for a semester long project. In *Proceedings of the ACM SIGCSE '06*, pages 505–509, 2006.

[18] S. Ludi. The benefits and challenges of using educational game projects in an undergraduate software engineering course. In *Games and Software Engineering Workshop, as part of the International Conference on Software Engineering (ICSE 2011)*, 2011.

[19] A. Luxton-Reilly and P. Denny. A simple framework for interactive games in CS1. In *Proceedings of the ACM SIGCSE '09*, pages 216–220, 2009.

[20] M. Marchesi. *Quoridor*. Gigamic, 1997. `http://www.gigamic.com`.

[21] T. McMurchie. *Tsuro*. Calliope Games, 2004. `http://www.tsuro.com/`.

[22] N. Parlante, J. Zelenski, D. Zingaro, K. Wayne, D. O'Hallaron, J. T. Guerin, S. Davies, Z. Kurmas, and K. Debby. Nifty assignments. In *Proceedings of the ACM SIGCSE '12*, pages 475–476, 2012.

[23] M. Savin-Baden. *Facilitating Problem-Based Learning*. McGraw-Hill, 2003. Berkshire, UK.

[24] M. Savin-Baden and C. H. Major. *Foundations of Problem-Based Learning*. McGraw-Hill, 2004. Berkshire, UK.

[25] D. L. Schuster. CS1, arcade games and the free java book. In *Proceedings of the ACM SIGCSE '10*, pages 549–553, 2010.

[26] B. Stephenson and C. Taube-Schock. QuickDraw: bringing graphics into first year. In *Proceedings of the ACM SIGCSE '09*, pages 211–215, 2009.

[27] J. Summet, D. Kumar, K. J. O'Hara, D. Walker, L. Ni, D. S. Blank, and T. R. Balch. Personalizing CS1 with robots. In *Proceedings of the ACM SIGCSE '09*, pages 433–437, 2009.

[28] K. Sung, M. Panitz, S. A. Wallace, R. Anderson, and J. Nordlinger. Game-themed programming assignments: the faculty perspective. In *Proceedings of the ACM SIGCSE '08*, pages 300–304, 2008.

[29] K.-J. Wrede. *Carcassonne*. Rio Grande Games, 2000. `http://www.riograndegames.com/`.

Integrating Theoretical and Empirical Computer Science in a Data Structures Course

John W. Coffey
Department of Computer Science
The University of West Florida
Pensacola, FL 32514
001-850-474-3183
jcoffey@uwf.edu

ABSTRACT

A significant rethinking of the computer science curriculum at a regional comprehensive university has led to a much tighter integration of discrete mathematics, data structures and algorithm analysis in a two-course Data Structures and Algorithms sequence. The courses are 4 semester hours each with two hour weekly labs. The new approach provides good support for a substantially increased emphasis on the reinforcement of theoretical constructs with empirical studies. The nature of the programming assignments has been particularly impacted by these efforts to reinforce the theoretical with the empirical. This article has a focus on the second course content and conduct, and how these modifications support a different approach to the course projects. This article also contains a report of favorable trends in completion percentages of the course under the new regime.

Categories and Subject Descriptors

K.3.2 Computer and Information Science Education

General Terms

Algorithms, Experimentation, Theory

Keywords

computer science education, data structures, algorithms, theoretical computer science, empirical computer science,

1. INTRODUCTION

Courses in data structures and algorithms provide the foundation for all that follows and are truly central to the computer science curriculum. A solid understanding of mathematical techniques as they relate to data structures and algorithm analysis might be reinforced with empirical studies and their comparisons to predicted behaviors. Typically, computer science curricula present these topics in one course on data structures, a second in discrete mathematics, and a third in the analysis of the complexity of algorithms. The data structures class presents a standard collection of structures such as lists, stacks, queues, heaps, trees, graphs, and hash tables. The discrete math course provides (among other topics) counting techniques involving permutations and combinations that are useful in understanding why some algorithms are intractable, and proof techniques such as math induction that are used to prove performance characteristics of algorithms. The analysis of algorithms course is typically the culminating experience in these three courses, offering advanced techniques such as probabilistic algorithms and dynamic programming.

SIGCSE'13, March 6-9, 2013, Denver, Colorado, USA.

In an effort to gain greater integration among relevant mathematics, data structures and the analysis of algorithms, the curriculum within the computer science, computer science (traditional) option at the University of West Florida was radically revised. The result is a unique course organization featuring a greater integration of these topics combined with a co-requisite 2 hour/week lab that provides substantial flexibility in how the course may be conducted. As experience was gained with the delivery of the revised course, it became evident that good potential existed to work from a theoretical, mathematical view of algorithms to a highly confirmatory, empirical study in the programming assignments, and that the empirical studies powerfully reinforced the theory.

The rest of the paper contains an effort to describe this course, including its virtues and drawbacks. After a review of relevant literature, the rationale and organization of the new course are described. The course projects, which have proven to be integral in helping students to appreciate empirical aspects of computer science, are described in some detail. The paper provides a comparison of the results of several offerings of the course with the previous, more traditional data structures course it replaced. A comparison of completion rates between the current version of the course and the previous version of the course is presented. The paper concludes with an assessment of the benefits and problematic aspects of the new course.

2. LITERATURE

The ACM 2008 model curriculum for computer science [1] contains a specification for topics in discrete mathematics, data structures and algorithms. Mention is made of the "traditional, topic-based" approach which includes separate courses for elements such as math, data structures, and algorithm analysis. Also mentioned are a "compressed approach," a "systems-based approach," and a "Web-based approach." The traditional approach is the one to which the current work presents an alternative; the other approaches are orthogonal classifications to the traditional approach and to the one described here.

Much of the literature in the ACM digital library pertaining specifically to data structures courses espouse alternative or higher-level pedagogical approaches, tools such as graphical programs that afford manipulation of a data structure, or approaches emphasizing why data structures are important. For example, Yue-sheng & Ji-yi [15] describe a standard "knowledge structure" for the data structures course drawing boundaries around standard topics: lists, trees, graphs, storage as sequential or in chained lists, algorithms for searching, sorting, etc. Their goal is to afford students a better understanding of why these topics are deemed so important to their educations.

Lister et al. [9] identified five major categories of goals for data structures courses: developing transferable thinking, improving students' programming skills, knowing "what's under the hood", knowledge of software libraries and component thinking. They discuss the conflicting nature of some of these goals, particularly between those who advocate for high-level use of libraries and those who insist on students understanding implementation details. It is a fundamental part of understanding implementation details to be able to analyze and determine the computational complexities of alternative implementations.

Tenenberg [12] advocates using application frameworks such as the C++ standard template library to teach data structures, foregoing details of how to implement data structures to focus on higher-level design and extension of the basic structures. Fekete [6] goes so far as to claim that the ability to read documentation on a collection class library is a critical outcome of a data structures course.

Graphical tools are often described as pedagogical aids for data structures, related mathematics, and algorithm analysis. Wu [14] describes a visual tool that helps students understand graph algorithms. Cigas and Hsin [4] advocate teaching proof techniques with non-algebraic, visual logic puzzles. They are able to tie their novel approach to teaching proof techniques to algorithm development, a critical goal of the current work. Becker and Beachum [3] describe a B-Tree program that can be used to help students understand the workings of those data structures. Kerren et al. [8] bemoan failures of graphical tools because of inflexibility in how they can be tailored to specific examples, and inability to support programming the data structure under consideration in a variety of languages. Their focus is very narrow with emphasis placed on algorithm understanding.

Forisek and Steinova [7] present an interesting take on the use of metaphor and analogy to help students form mental models of how algorithms work. For instance, they explain and elaborate the "balls and strings" analogy to understand Dijkstra's shortest path algorithm. Moore [10] provides insights regarding how to teach students to solve optimization problems using genetic algorithms. Her example is of an approximation algorithm to solve an intractable problem. Moore describes the introduction of an important concept for the current work – the use of approximation algorithms.

Impetus for the organization of the current course came from "Foundations of Computer Science, C Edition" [2]. That book, which is no longer in print, presented a remarkably integrated (and atypical) view of foundational computer science concepts interspersed with traditional data structures. The book included (long) chapters on iteration, induction and recursion, Big O analysis, combinatorics and probability, trees, lists, sets, graphs, the relational model, and propositional and predicate calculus. Implementation of the current course drew upon the organization of concepts in that book, extending them with a strongly experimental, empirical perspective on work students performed. The course is described in the next section.

3. THE NEW COURSE STRUCTURE

The current course was designed to allow a greater integration of the various concepts pertaining to data structures, algorithms, and associated mathematics. Prerequisites are a beginning course entitled "Algorithms and Program Design," and "Data Structures and Algorithms I." The first course is an introduction to procedural programming, and the second covers basic data structures. All three courses (including the current one) are conducted in the C programming language, which remains an extremely popular production language [13]. All of these courses have a very clear emphasis on algorithms first as opposed to an objects-first approach.

The "Algorithms and Program Design" course has no prerequisites. It contains a fairly standard introduction to programming including variables, iterators and selectors, file processing and arrays. The Data Structures and Algorithms I course precedes the current course and includes multi-dimensional arrays, lists, stacks, queues, trees and hashing. Big O analysis is introduced in this course.

The current course addresses height-balanced trees, recurrences and their solutions including recurrence trees, substitution method, and Master Theorem, counting methods (pigeonhole principle, counting trees), permutations and combinations, greedy algorithms, heaps, graphs, and dynamic programming. Students complete five programming projects, two semester exams, and a final exam in this course. Both this course and the first data structures course have two-hour weekly labs that accompany the three hour lecture.

The labs are used in a variety of ways. First, certain labs address topics that require reinforcement such as counting problems and recurrence creation and proofs. The first lab following a programming assignment is used by students to create functional decomposition designs for the project. Additionally, students demonstrate their projects for the instructor in labs as part of the evaluation process. This practice has proven extremely useful in helping the instructor to understand the programming strengths and weaknesses of students generally, and specific aspects of the assignments that give particular trouble.

Students take a separate math course entitled "Set Theory and Mathematical Logic" which introduces various proof techniques (direct proof, proof by contradiction, proof by contrapositive, proof by math induction). The current course utilizes some concepts from Set Theory, but it strongly emphasizes how these techniques can be applied to computer science problems. To this list of proof techniques is added "existence proofs" in which students learn to prove assertions regarding algorithms by showing the existence of datasets or other conditions that lead to some behavior that is meant to be proven (eg: show a data set that requires 3/2 * optimal number of bins for all online bin packing heuristic algorithms).

All programs are carefully chosen to illustrate mathematical concepts and to tie them to basic algorithm analysis techniques. As the course unfolds, students are sometimes surprised by jumps from math to data structures to algorithm analysis, until they see how closely the various concepts being presented are related to one another. The benefit of having the topics treated in a single course is that the math appears just at the correct time for its application to the data structures and algorithms. Such close coordination is more difficult to achieve with separate discrete math courses that include other topics, and that lack the immediate relevance to the current algorithms and data structures. The projects are the glue that ties together the various pieces of the course. They are the subject of the next section.

4. PROJECTS

Five projects are required in the course. The first one is designed to help students make the transition from Data Structures and Algorithms I to the current course. It is also used to assess programming strengths of the students, useful input that informs conduct of the labs. The second introduces event-driven programming with modeling and simulation and a comparison of results obtained in a simulation to an a-priori analytical model of a multi-channel queuing system. Students compare predicted results side-by-side with the empirical results provided by the simulation. The third and fourth projects likewise require empirical study of runtime performance compared to the theoretical result that is anticipated. The final project is one of several dynamic programming projects that illustrate differences in runtime among different classes of computational complexity. Additional details regarding these projects are provided next.

4.1 Analytical Model and Simulation

The modeling and simulation project addresses multi-channel queuing systems. Input is Lambda (λ), the average number of arrivals per unit time, Mu (μ) the average number served per unit time, M, the number of service channels and, for the simulation, the number of arrivals to simulate. Students must code formulas for the analytical model from Render and Stair [11] that provide predicted values for system idle time, average number of items in the system and queue, average time spent in the system, etc. The simulation requires implementation of both FIFO and priority queues. The priority queue is used to process arrival and departure events. Well-written programs obtain results that are very similar to the analytical model predictions, given sufficiently large n. This project is useful for the data structures it requires, as a demonstration of how empirical study can be done with computer science, as a way of demonstrating that accurate modeling and simulation can yield predicted results, and as an introduction to queuing theory as groundwork for the Networks course.

4.2 Intractable Problem with Genetic Algorithm Approximation

The third project is drawn from graph theory – the traveling salesman problem. Students implement a brute force permutation program to test all possible ways to visit n cities, given a designated first/last city, a `O((n-1)!)` algorithm. Students also implement a permutation-based genetic algorithm with elites, mutations and new permutations. The genetic algorithm takes input for the number of tours per generation, number of generations to run, number of elites/generation, number of mutations, and a mutation policy. Students start with 10 cities running both the brute force program and the genetic algorithm. They report the runtime of each program and the percentage of optimal tour cost that the best genetic algorithm tour yields (eg: 115% of optimal).

The assignment requires that the students increase the number of cities by 1 until the brute force algorithm runs for more than 5 minutes (typically at approximately 15 cities). They are asked to experiment with the input parameters to the genetic algorithm to find out what provides the best performance relative to optimum. This project makes the idea of the explosion of computational complexity and the idea of heuristic approximation algorithms that provide nearly optimal results very real to the students. The empirical nature of the experiments: varying generations, mutation policy, number of elites, etc. in the genetic algorithm, coupled with the fact that the genetic algorithm (running in milli-seconds) obtains results that are almost as good as the brute force method that runs in minutes, makes a very strong impression on the students.

This project illustrates how math theory is tied to empirical computer science. A thread runs through the sequence of learning about:

1. permutations, in which order of the permuted items matters
2. a recursive algorithm to produce permutations
3. the graph theoretic introduction to the Traveling Salesman Problem
4. the fact that the optimal solution to TSP is one or more permutations of the order in which cities are visited
5. the search space for solutions is therefore `O(n!)` (and the computational complexity is as well, using a brute force approach)
6. a good, if not optimal solution might be obtained by being clever about how one examines a subset of the `O(n!)` potential solutions
7. an implementation of the clever approach and a comparison of the results to the brute force by determining the runtime of both algorithms over some range in the number of cities.

4.3. Intractable Problem with Heuristic Algorithm Approximations

The fourth project also has an empirical element. It is concerned with greedy algorithms, particularly the bin packing problem. In one version of the assignment, constraints are removed from the canonical bin-packing problem: bins can be of different sizes, objects might be too large to fit in any bin, and various relationships among object sizes and container sizes are examined. Students must provide online (must place the current object without knowledge of any of the remaining ones) first-fit, best-fit and next-fit algorithms and offline (all items known in advance) first-fit and best-fit algorithms. Output requires a summary table for runs over all the storage policies for: small items/big bins, variable-sized items/big bins, and variable-sized items/variable-sized bins. Students summarize how empirical results reflect proofs regarding efficiency of bin utilization in the canonical problem.

4.4 Intractable Brute Force Algorithm with Efficient (DP-based) Optimal Solution

The final problem utilizes dynamic programming, typically either dealing with longest common subsequence or matrix chain multiplication [5]. The LCS problem typically employs 2 `MxN` matrices where `m` is the length of the first sequence and `n` is the length of the comparison sequence. The brute force LCS algorithm has computational complexity of $O(m*2^n)$ and the dynamic programming solution $O(m*n)$. In the first part of the project, students must compute the actual LCS (rather than just its length) from the sequences themselves and from the matrix with the numeric result indicating length. In the second part of the problem, students compare many sequences and build a table indicating "similarity" in the sequences based upon contrived measures of similarity of overall and LCS length. They do this with a single `2*n` (rather than `m*n`) matrix by computing a row at a time. This enables an asymptotic improvement in space consumption at the expense of not being able to recount actual LCSs. The important ideas in this project are that there exist efficient algorithms that provide exact (rather than approximate) answers to problems for which the obvious approach is intractable, and that, within such efficient problems, asymptotic improvement in time or space efficiency can be made.

5. AN ASSESSMENT OF THE COURSE

This section contains a comparison of outcomes (completion percentages and aggregate gpa) for this course and the course it replaced. It also addresses some identified shortcomings in the current course structure.

5.1 Course Outcomes

An attempt was made to assess student success in the new version of the course compared to the older version. Two factors were compared: percentage of students completing the courses and the average gpas of the completers. The new version of Data Structures and Algorithms II has been offered a total of 6 times since fall, 2008. In that time frame, 177 students have attempted the course and 144 have completed it, a completion rate of 81%. The course average and standard deviation in gpa for students in that period were 73.2% and 17.9 points.

Between spring 2006 and spring 2008, an approximately equivalent number of students (n = 165) took the old Data Structures course. Of the 165 in this cohort, 118 completed, a completion rate of 72%. The average gpa and standard deviation in gpa for students in that period were 74.2% and 14.45 points. An F test revealed unequal variances between these groups ($p < 0.01$), so a two tailed T-test for equality of means with unequal variances was performed. Results, which indicated no difference in the mean values of the gpas, are summarized in Table 1.

Table 1. A comparison of the average gpas of completers in the two cohorts in the study.

	2008-present	2006-08
Mean gpa score	73.18	74.16
Variance	320.06	208.94
Observations	143	118
HypothesizedDifferenc e	0	
df	259	
P(T<=t) two-tail	0.625	
T(critical) two-tail	1.96	

A Two-Sample Proportion Z Test was performed on the completion data. The null and alternate hypotheses used in the analysis were no difference in the completion proportion or a difference in the completion proportion between groups. The null and alternate hypotheses lead to a two-tailed Z test of the proportions. Results of the test were $Z = 2.79$, $p < 0.05$, leading to rejection of the null hypothesis and the conclusion that a difference exists in the completion rates of the two groups. The data used in this non-parametric test are summarized in Table 2.

Table 2. The number of students in each cohort and the percentage of completers.

Course	Completed	N	Proportion
Prior	118	165	0.72
Current	144	177	0.81

It must be acknowledged that, while this analysis is interesting and points to a favorable completion trend, it has at least two confounding (but in some sense, offsetting) variables – separation of CIS option students from CS option students in the new course and substantially larger section sizes in the new course. Additionally, factors such as complexity of the new programming assignments (which are probably more difficult) and requiring students to solve math problems on exams are hard to quantify, but likely mediate in favor of worsening, rather than improving, completion rates.

It is important to note that before the new version of Data Structures and Algorithms was implemented, both CS, CS option and CS, CIS option (a business-oriented technical degree with less emphasis on math and theory than the CS option) students were combined in the same sections. Unfortunately, differential completion rates for CS option and CIS option students in this period are not available, but it is possible that the CIS option students had lower completion rates, accounting for at least some of the difference.

Further complicating the comparison is the fact that the 2006-2008 time period was near the bottom of the precipitous decrease in CS student enrollment nationwide that started in 2000-2001. Average students per section from that time was 20.6. Average students per section for the fall 2008 – present (the time frame of the revised course) was 29.5, assuring that the students under the old curriculum had much less competition for the instructor's time and resources. One would expect that these averages would have mediated in favor of higher completion percentages for the earlier version of the course. Just the opposite outcome actually occurred.

Accordingly, it can be concluded that offsetting confounding variables – one mediating in favor of improved completion percentages in the current course, and one mediating against improvement – were in evidence. An extremely conservative analysis would lead one to conclude that, despite the greater demands placed upon students in the new curriculum, completion outcomes were at least as good (and likely better) than those under the old curriculum.

5.2 Problems with this Course Organization

The current curriculum is not without problems. One problem with the current course layout is that the content for courses listed on students' transcripts is more difficult to determine than it is with more traditional structuring. No mention is made of courses in Discrete Mathematics or Analysis of Algorithms, even though the content of these courses is in the curriculum. The department has no clear evidence that the idiosyncratic organization of these courses has caused students trouble getting into graduate schools.

Another problem with the current course arrangement from the faculty's viewpoint is that classes do not fall into convenient 3 hour groups. A consequence of this fact is that tenure-earning faculty who are required to conduct 9 hours of courses (with 3 hours for research) typically have 10 or 11 academic hours and 12 to 14 actual contact hours with student per week. A third minor difficulty that has been identified pertains to the scheduling of the labs. The computer science department has a great many classes over several sub-disciplines, and some difficulty has been created scheduling two-hour blocks in several courses that students take concurrently. These difficulties are perceived as relatively minor, and not viewed as impediments to a curriculum modification that is broadly viewed as very positive.

6. ACKNOWLEDGMENTS

The author would like to acknowledge the efforts of Dennis Edwards, Jackie Huband, Jim Lewis, Bernd Owsnicki-Klewe, and Sharon Simmons, who were responsible for the high-level curriculum decisions that created the framework for the course described here.

7. CONCLUSIONS AND DISCUSSION

This article contains a description of attempts to create a more tight integration between theoretical and empirical approaches to computer science instruction in an advanced data structures course. The approach starts by a reorganization of topics typically addressed in three courses, discrete mathematics, data structures, and analysis of algorithms, into an extended, four hour Data Structures and Algorithms II course with lab. The more tight integration of mathematical topics with data structures supports greater understanding of the a-priori mathematical basis of algorithm analysis and proof. The programming assignments are carefully designed to emphasize determination of both the theoretical, a-priori, expected answer and the validation of the theory with empirical results. Such comparison of results takes both the form of comparing simulation results with those obtained through an analytical model and comparison of the analysis of computational complexity with actual timed empirical runtime results.

The new course evidences both very good and a few bad aspects. Over several years of offering the course, completion percentages have been better for the new course than for the old version. Students respond very favorably to very direct measures that confirm predictions through observed results. The immediacy of actually seeing and timing intractable algorithms (such as brute-force TSP) compared to good approximations or more efficient optimal algorithms strongly reinforces learning.

Several drawbacks, mostly relatively minor, have been identified. The first is that the two-hour blocks that must be reserved for the labs complicate scheduling to some degree. The fact that other disciplines have routinely dealt with such difficulties suggests that this is a minor problem. Another difficulty pertains to the fact that, while this curriculum addresses all the topics in the ACM model curriculum, students' transcripts do not evidence expected courses such as discrete math and analysis of algorithms. To date no evidence exists that this anomaly has caused difficulties for students applying to graduate schools.

8. REFERENCES

[1] ACM, Computer Science Curriculum 2008: An Interim Revision of CS 2001. Retrieved September 4, 2012 from http://www.acm.org/education/curricula/ComputerScience2008.pdf

[2] Aho, A.V., and Ullman, J.D. Foundations of Computer Science, C Edition. Computer Science Press. (1995).

[3] Becker, K., and Beachum, M. A Tool for Teaching Advanced Data Structures to Computer Science Students: An Overview of the BDP System. Journal of Computing in Schools and Colleges, 16(2) pp 66 – 72.

[4] Cigas, J., and Hsin, W-J. Teaching Proofs and Algorithms in Discrete Mathematics with Online Visual Logic Puzzles. ACM Journal of Educational Resources in Computing 5(2) 2005.

[5] Cormen, T. H., Leiserson, C. E., Rivest, R. L., Stein, C.: Introduction to Algorithms (3rd ed.). The MIT Press (2009).

[6] Fekete, A. Teaching Data Structures with Multiple Collection Class Libraries. SIGCSE 2002, Covington, Kentucky pp 396-400.

[7] Forisek, M., and Steinova, M. Metaphors and Analogies for Teaching Algorithms. Proceedings of SIGCSE 2012, pp 15 – 20, ACM (2012) .

[8] Kerren, A., Muldner, T., and Shakuhuki, E. Novel Algorithm Explanation Techniques for Improving Algorithm Teaching. SOFTVIS 2006, Brighton, United Kingdom, September 04–05, 2006.

[9] Lister, R., Box, I., Morrison, B, Tenenberg, J., and Westbrook, S. The Dimensions of Variation in the Teaching of Data Structures. *ITiCSE '04*, June 28-30, 2004, Leeds, United Kingdom.

[10] Moore, M.: Teaching Students to use Genetic Algorithms to Solve Optimization Problems. Journal of Computing in Schools and Colleges, 16(3) pp 19 – 25.

[11] Render, B., and Stair, R.M., and Hanna, M.E. Quantitative Analysis for Management (11th ed.). Prentice Hall. (2012).

[12] Tenenberg, J.: A Framework Approach to Teaching Data Structures. Proceedings of SIGCSE 2003, pp 210 – 214, ACM (2003) .

[13] Tiobe, TIOBE Programming Community Index for August 2012. Retrieved September 4, 2012 from http://www.tiobe.com/index.php/content/paperinfo/tpci/index.html. Retrieved on 8/13/2012.

[14] Wu, M. Teaching Graph Algorithms Using Online Java Package IAPPGA. SIGCSE Bulletin 37(4). pp 64 – 68. (2005)

[15] Yue-sheng, G., & Ji-yi, Z. Teaching Research and Practice of Data Structure Based on Knowledge Structure In Proceedings of ACM SCE'08, Beijing, China. ACM ISBN: 978-1-60558-441-6 (2008)

Hunting High and Low: Instruments to Detect Misconceptions Related to Algorithms and Data Structures

Wolfgang Paul
Technische Universität Dortmund
Faculty of Computer Science
44227 Dortmund, Germany
wolfgang.paul@cs.tu-dortmund.de

Jan Vahrenhold
Westfälische Wilhelms-Universität Münster
Department of Computer Science
48149 Münster, Germany
jan.vahrenhold@uni-muenster.de

ABSTRACT

We present the result of assessing first-year students' misconceptions related to algorithms and data structures. Our study confirms findings from previous small-scale studies but additionally broadens the scope of the topics and methods investigated. The evaluation of our experiments sheds light on dependencies between active and passive knowledge as well as on the instruments used; in particular, we conclude that there is no "one size fits all" instrument but that instruments should be selected depending on the topic at hand.

Categories and Subject Descriptors: K.3.2 [Computers and Education]: Computer and Information Science Education

Keywords: Misconceptions, Instruments, CS1/2.

1. INTRODUCTION

In recent years, computer science researchers have repeatedly issued a call for the development and adoption of cross-institutional tools for assessing and comparing student's understanding of topics in computer science [1, 8, 11, 17]. Developing such tools, however, is difficult, as they have to be applicable to different curricula at different institutions while at the same time having to provide reliable measures.

Motivated by the success of the *Force Concept Inventory* [9] used in physics education, first steps towards building concept inventories for selected areas in computer science have been undertaken [1, 4, 7, 8, 17]. Concept inventories are standardized assessment tools to assess students' understanding or misconceptions regarding a collection of accepted conceptual frameworks. Most studies on misconceptions in computer science focus on object-orientation, e.g., [4, 5, 13, 14]; only little attention has been paid so far to algorithms and data structures, e.g., [4, 6, 15].

In contrast to the broad adoption and repeated validation of the above mentioned *Force Concept Inventory*, only few reports on validating instruments designed to detect misconceptions in computer science are available, e.g., [8, 12].

SIGCSE'13, March 6–9, 2013, Denver, Colorado, USA.

In this paper, we add to these reports by presenting a comparative, large-scale evaluation of instruments to detect students' misconceptions related to algorithms and data structures. The central questions underlying our research were how the sensitivity of easy-to-evaluate instruments compares to the instruments used in previous studies, i.e., audio and video recordings, concept maps, or the analysis of artifacts, and to which extent the instruments used and developed could be shown to be valid and internally consistent.

2. METHODS AND PROCEDURE

Our study was conducted accompanying the cohort of approximately 400 students taking the first-year computer science classes at Technische Universität Dortmund during the academic year 2011/2012. The instruments were administered to all students attending the recital sessions of collaborating instructors; the students' participation was optional and not compensated for. Due to fluctuations in attendance, the average number of responses was around 80.

2.1 Experimental Design

The experiments were conducted as part of the recital sessions. For each topic investigated, we administered the instrument after the homework assignments pertaining to the respective topic were due, thus making sure that students had had incentive and time to recapitulate the topic, but before the solutions were discussed. The instruments used were designed such that their administration never took more than ten minutes of class time; we used multiple-choice, fill-the-blanks, and free-form test items (see Section 3). To reduce the influence of guessing and to gain insights into the quality of the distractors used, all multiple-choice tests allowed for backup answers: students could indicate a backup answer if they were not confident about their choice.

2.2 Baseline Validation

As detailed in section 3, the topics investigated spanned a rather broad range from object-orientation to algorithm design. To calibrate our evaluation with respect to the material taught in class, we conducted semi-structured think-aloud interviews aimed at assessing students' conceptual and procedural knowledge concerning *loop invariants*, *divide-and-conquer*, and *dynamic programming*. Seven students were invited on the basis of their exceptionally good performance in the homework assignments. They participated in the interviews voluntarily and were not compensated for this.

Following our previous study [4], the students were given an iterative program which computes the series $\sum_{i=1}^{n} i$ and asked to formally define the associated loop invariant; all students gave correct answers. All students correctly explained the concepts behind divide-and-conquer and dynamic programming and could successfully be probed for active knowledge. Finally, the students were given a template for the "coin changing" problem and asked the to fill two missing lines of code. All students could either fill in the lines or identify the correct answer among four alternatives.

3. EXPERIMENTS AND EVALUATION

In our study, we tried not only to cover a broad range of topics and methods but also to internally and externally cross-validate instruments. Thus, investigating most topics took more than a week each and only the following, limited number of validated experiments can be reported upon.

Topic	Instrument(s)
Object/Class	free-form text
Identity/State	multiple-choice
Call-by-Value/Reference	multiple-choice
Invariants	multiple-choice & free-form text
Heaps	multiple-choice
Divide-and-Conquer	multiple-choice & fill-the-blanks
Dynamic Programming	multiple-choice

3.1 Object-Orientation

Based on previous studies [3, 10, 13], we investigated alternative approaches for two frequent misconceptions: "object"/"class" conflation and "identity"/"state" conflation.

3.1.1 Objects and Classes

Just as we would ask in an interview, we asked students to first write down definitions of "object" and "class".

The results were disappointing with respect to our objective: 65 of the 73 students asked for a definition of "class" would write down a verbatim reproduction of a popular analogy used in class ("classes are blueprints for objects"). Only few students would give either different descriptions ($4*$"classes generate objects"; $4*$"classes are containers for objects"), or add to an otherwise verbatim reproduction of the above analogy ($6*$"classes operate on local variables only"). Similarly, 45 students would give a verbatim reproduction of the description used in class for relating objects to classes ("objects are instances of classes"). Only few students gave an answer that implied one of the misconceptions known from the literature ($4*$"objects are abstract data types"; $3*$"objects are complex data types"; $3*$"objects are data structures"; $2*$"objects are components of classes").

The verbatim reproductions certainly showed that the students had paid attention to the class material; in a think-aloud interview, however, the interviewer would have chosen to probe deeper. Since such a probing was not possible in our experiment, we conclude that the instrument is at most suited to detect the presence of misconceptions consolidated well enough to override the analogy presented in class but not suited to reliably show the absence of misconceptions.

3.1.2 Identity and State

The second experiment was directed towards detecting a conflation of an object's identity and state. Based upon two misconceptions identified by Ragonis and Ben-Ari [13], we designed a multiple-choice test item in which students were asked to select an answer to the following question: "*What happens if two objects of the same class are about to be initialized with identical values for all of their attributes?*"

The first distractor ($D_{\text{Identity},1}$) suggested a run-time error because the objects were indistinguishable to the run-time environment (Misconception 1.4.1 in [13]) while the second distractor ($D_{\text{Identity},2}$) stated that the answer depended on whether or not the objects had a private `name` attribute (Misconception 1.4.4 in [13]). To have two options for the case that no problem occurred, we then added a third distractor ($D_{\text{Identity},3}$) that stated that an object was identified by the name of the variable referencing it and that different objects were always required to be referenced by different variables.

The result of administering this instrument to 43 students did not confirm the presence of Misconceptions 1.4.1 and 1.4.4 noted by Ben-Ari and Ragonis [13]: No student chose distractor $D_{\text{Identity},1}$, not even as a backup answer (cf. Section 2.1), and only three students chose distractor $D_{\text{Identity},2}$. Most students opted for the answers not suggesting a run-time error: 31 students chose the new distractor $D_{\text{Identity},3}$ and the remaining nine students chose the correct answer. The evaluation showed that students were remarkably sure about their answers: only 13 students provided backup answers. All these students had selected distractor $D_{\text{Identity},3}$ as their final answer; nine of them said that they had been thinking about the option that indeed was the correct answer and four had considered distractor $D_{\text{Identity},2}$.

The interpretation of the striking preference to answers that did not suggest a run-time error may be explained on the basis of cognitivism, i.e., students related the test item to previously acquired knowledge: The course was accompanied by mandatory lab sessions in which they had to pass a short programming test each week. In addition, we conjecture that the contextualization of the test item, i.e., stating the distractors related to a program's run-time behavior made the students reflect on their knowledge before choosing an answer. These two factors seemed to help students to exclude the first two distractors as they had never seen such a behavior before. Yet, a large part of the students was shown to have developed a consolidated misconception: they were under the impression that no object was allowed to be referenced by more than one variable ($D_{\text{Identity},3}$).

In addition to this newly detected misconception, we thus conclude from this experiment that contextualization can implicitly suggest to reflect on previous experience and knowledge in a way that can help avoiding the formation of misconceptions. Supporting evidence comes from the *Force Concept Inventory* [9] where all test items are contextualized and more than two thirds are augmented by sketches or drawings. Which contexts are used exactly, however, seems to be of little statistical significance [16].

3.2 Call-by-Value vs. Call-by-Reference

The Java programming language uses call-by-value for parameter passing [2, Sec. 2.6.5]. In particular, "when the parameter is an object reference, it is the object *reference*—not the object itself—that is passed "by value."" [2, p. 63]. Anecdotal evidence, however, suggests the misconception that call-by-value applies to built-in data types only.

Since (parameter) scoping had been identified by Goldman *et al.* [7] as both an important and difficult topic, we constructed a test item to detect whether the above misconception could be confirmed reliably: students were given the code shown below and asked whether or not the values of the variables a and i when examined in main-method after the call to modify were different from their initial values.

```
public static void modify(MyClass a, int i) {
  a = null; i = i + 1;
}

public static void main(String[] args) {
  MyClass a = new MyClass();
  int     i = 0;
  modify(a, i);  // Call above method.
}
```

A total number of 92 students participated in this experiment and 83 of them were confident enough to not provide a backup answer. Only 21 students gave the correct answer; none of them provided a backup answer. Only one of the students not giving a correct answer considered the answer that turned out to be correct. Thus, the instrument appears to clearly separate correct from incorrect understanding.

With respect to our initial objective, we could indeed detect the misconception we originally set out to find (different methods of passing parameters depending on the type) for another 21 students. The much more surprising finding, however, was that more than 50% of the students were under the impression that Java used call-by-reference. Thus, the instrument not only confirmed the existence of a misconception but also detected a misconception previously unknown.

3.3 Invariants

In their small-scale, qualitative investigation of students' understanding of invariants, Danielsiek *et al.* [4] noticed the influence of a drill-and-practice effect: the interviews conducted showed that students' would be able to correctly name loop invariants as the method of choice to prove the correctness of a given iterative program but at the same time revealed that most students interviewed lacked procedural and conceptual knowledge to actively use this method.

To follow up on this, we evaluated two test items related to invariants. The first test item, directed towards probing passive knowledge, was the test item presented by Danielsiek *et al.* [4, Fig. 3]. The second, newly constructed test item probed active knowledge. It presented a pseudocode description of a loop iterating from 1 to n while in each iteration adding 5 to a variable initially set to zero; students then were asked to give a closed-form description of the result of this program and to provide a matching loop invariant.

The results for the 92 students participating in both experiments are presented below. The imbalance of "Correct (*passive*)/Incorrect (*active*)" (three students) versus "Correct (*active*)/Incorrect (*passive*)" (eleven students) can be explained by the observation that the first test item (*passive*) consisted of three distractors each of which varied the correct answer in only one detail. In fact, the eleven wrong answers were distributed evenly over these distractors.

"Invariants" Test Items	Correct (*active*)	Incorrect (*active*)
Correct (*passive*)	28	3
Incorrect (*passive*)	11	50

For the analysis of these results, we used a χ^2-test and assumed for the the null hypothesis that the characteristics were statistically independent across both dimensions, i.e., that the active knowledge was independent of the passive knowledge. This hypothesis could be strongly rejected ($\chi^2 =$ 43.98, $\alpha = 0.001$, power $= 0.99$). Thus, our experiments not only confirm that active knowledge of invariants indeed is a major issue (more than half of the students did not give a correct answer) but also show that an easy-to-evaluate multiple-choice test for passive knowledge may be used as an indicator for problems pertaining to active knowledge.

3.4 Heaps

Seppälä *et al.* [15] used simulations to investigate misconceptions of the build-heap algorithm on an abstraction level higher than that of the actual implementation. In contrast, our study focuses on the influence of the heap's representation on procedural knowledge and on structural properties.

3.4.1 Influence of the Representation

The study of Seppälä *et al.* used a graphical, tree-based representation. The course examined by us used both representations of heaps, i.e., binary trees and arrays. We thus were interested in finding out whether the representation of the heap affected the result of a multiple-choice instrument. To this end, we administered a test item where students first were presented with a heap in array representation and then with another heap in tree representation. Both heaps were of equal size and complexity. Each of the representations had four corresponding answers and the distractors in both items (omitted due to space constraints) were equivalent.

The evaluation of the 155 answers obtained during the first semester and summarized below yields two conclusions: firstly, a χ^2-test rejects the null hypothesis that the answers are statistically independent across both items ($\chi^2 = 15.92$, $\alpha = 0.001$, power $= 0.98$). Secondly, a relatively high number of students appears to have developed a mental model restricted to one representation. Thus, it is highly recommendable to explicitly address both models when teaching.

"Build-Heap" Test Items	Correct (*array*)	Incorrect (*array*)
Correct (*tree*)	52	31
Incorrect (*tree*)	22	50

3.4.2 Conflation with Binary Search Trees

Based on our previous study [4], we conjectured a conflation of heaps and binary search trees to contribute to difficulties running heapsort. To cross-validate these findings, we repeated one of our experiments in the second semester after heaps had been revisited in the context of priority queues; 90 students were given four binary trees [4, Fig. 2(top)] (see below) and asked to determine for each tree whether it was a heap, a binary search tree, both, or none.

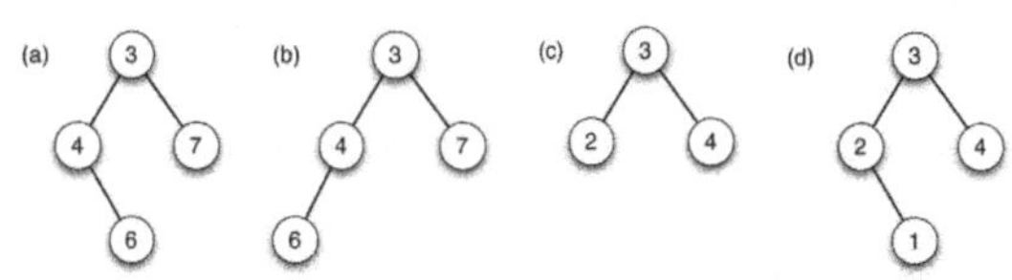

The top part of the table given below (correct answers set in bold face) shows that a conflation of heaps and binary search trees could indeed be re-confirmed to the extent that 14 students who gave otherwise correct answers considered a binary search tree to also be a heap. Another misconception previously observed [4] was that more than half of the students were not aware of the left-completeness of heaps since they considered tree (a) to be a heap. These numbers have to be relativized as left-completeness had not been mentioned explicitly in the lecture notes and could only be inferred from the first semester's material and array representation.

Answers	(a)	(b)	(c)	(d)
19	**neither**	**heap**	**BST**	**neither**
14	**neither**	**heap**	both	**neither**
0	*	*	heap	*
35	heap	**heap**	**BST**	**neither**
10	heap	**heap**	**BST**	BST
3	heap	**heap**	both	heap
9	other			

3.5 Divide-and-Conquer

In our previous study [4], we analyzed several think-aloud interviews which implied a conflation of *divide-and-conquer* and *dynamic programming*. Here, we were interested in investigating whether less resource-demanding instruments were also suited to confirm these findings. Thus, after the divide-and-conquer paradigm had been covered in class, we investigated whether misconceptions about this paradigm might induce a conflation with *dynamic programming*, which, at this point, had not been mentioned in class.

3.5.1 Passive Knowledge

To probe passive knowledge, we administered a multiple-choice test. To refresh the students' memory, the test first presented a divide-and-conquer implementation of binary search and then asked to select the correct of four prosecode descriptions of the general divide-and-conquer template.

Two of the distractors were aimed explicitly at preconditions that would facilitate a conflation with dynamic programming: distractor $D_{\text{D\&C},1}$ suggested to subdivide the problem into several dependent subproblems which then were solved iteratively and distractor $D_{\text{D\&C},2}$ suggested to recursively solve a linear number of subproblems. To detect terminology problems, distractor $D_{\text{D\&C},3}$ suggested to subdivide into two subproblems and to solve them iteratively.

Of the 91 students participating in this assessment, only 13 gave a backup answer. The distributions for both the 78 confident answers the all 91 answers are listed below.

Answers	N	Correct	$D_{\text{D\&C},1}$	$D_{\text{D\&C},2}$	$D_{\text{D\&C},3}$
Confident	78	14	23	20	21
All	91	15	27	26	23

A single student correctly answered this question *and* gave a backup answer; here, the distractor $D_{\text{D\&C},3}$ was considered, i.e., he or she was distracted by the limitation to exactly two subproblems (the examples in class included up to four subproblems) or conflated "iterative" and "recursive".

The interpretation of this first experiment is that students appear to be self-confident about their knowledge, and this seems to imply that established misconceptions can be detected *when probing is directed at passive knowledge.*

3.5.2 Active Knowledge

By design, the instrument in the above experiment was limited to probe passive knowledge. To follow up on this experiment while probing active knowledge, we designed a test item where students were asked to reflect on their knowledge. We presented students with a prosecode template for divide-and-conquer algorithms (see below) with two blanks to be filled in; in these places, we had previously modified the template to obtain distractors for the first assignment.

```
function DivideAndConquerForProblemP(set A)
    if input size in O(1) then
        Solve P directly for A; return result.
    else
        // DIVIDE
        Subdivide A into ________________ subsets.
        // CONQUER
        Solve P for the resulting sets ______________.
        Combine these results to a solution of P for A.
        Return result.
```

To make students reflect on their knowledge, we asked them to fill the blanks such that the resulting template would *not* be correct and to write down a justification for why it would not be correct. The classifications of 83 student's answers to the first item, i.e., the description of how to subdivide the input set A, are summarized below.

N	"Wrong" Answer	Justification
20	"*no* subset"	"*multiple* subsets"
3	"*one* subset"	
8	"*no* subset"	N/A
6	"*n* subsets"	
18	"*n* subsets"	"*two* subsets"
4	"*multiple* subsets"	
5	"*multiple* subsets"	N/A
7	(parity)	(parity)
3	(other)	(other)
3	"*multiple* subsets"	"*multiple equal-sized* subs."
2	"*multiple* subsets"	"*as few equal-sized* subsets as possible"
1	"*no* subset"	"*equal-sized* subsets"
1	"*one* subset"	"*two equal-sized* subsets"
1	"*multiple* subsets"	
1	"*two unequal-sized* subs."	

The "wrong" answers of 74 students were based on the number of subsets. Of these answers, 23 were perfectly right and correctly justified and 14 were correct but not justified. Another 27 answers indicated that students restricted the divide-and-conquer paradigm to the case of exactly two subsets as compared to the more general case discussed in class. Seven students argued that one should always have an even number of subsets or that a subdivision into two subsets would be impossible for an input of odd size. The remaining nine students based their answer on the size of the subsets. While all of them correctly insisted on subsets of equal size, two students restricted the paradigm to the binary case.

The analysis of the second item (given below) showed that 60 out of 83 answers were perfectly right and correctly justified; an additional 11 answers were correct but not justified. An incorrect use of the term "recursively" could be observed in only nine cases; in all of these cases, the "wrong" answer was said to be "solve ... recursively" but no justification indicating that "solve ... iteratively" was given. Only three students did not provide any answer.

N	"Wrong Answer"	Justification
55	"solve ... iteratively"	"solve ... recursively"
3	"solve ... not at all"	
2	"solve ... directly"	
9	"solve ... iteratively"	N/A
1	"solve ... directly"	
1	"solve ... not at all"	
9	"solve ... recursively"	N/A
1		"solve ... recursively"
3	N/A	N/A

When evaluating these items for internal consistency, we distinguished three variants of rating the answers. In the first, "strict" version, an answer was rated as correct if and only if a correct "wrong answer" was justified correctly; in this version, a correct "wrong answer" was rated as incorrect if no justification was given. The second, "relaxed" version of the rating adjusted for this by giving a correct rating in such cases as well. As mentioned above, the instructor presented several examples with multiple subsets resulting from the "divide" step; additionally, the homework due on the day before this instrument was administered included an exercise specifically geared towards multi-way recursion. Nonetheless, the third, "unrestricted" rating relaxed the second rating by also accepting all justifications that referred to "two subsets" resulting from the "divide" step.

D&C Active Knowledge (strict/relaxed/unrestricted)	Correct (*divide*)	Incorrect (*divide*)
Correct (*conquer*)	36/45/67	3/ 2/ 3
Incorrect (*conquer*)	24/24/ 2	20/12/12

While the above results of using these three rating variants obviously differ by the absolute numbers, the internal consistency is not affected. For all variants, a χ^2-test rejected the null hypothesis that the answers to the "divide" item and "conquer" item were statistically independent ($\chi^2 = 14.72/12.29/56.93$, $\alpha = 0.001$, power $= 0.95/0.92/0.99$).

The interpretation of this second experiment shows that a large percentage of students is able to correctly characterize both the "divide" and "conquer" step of the general template; depending on the rating variant between 43% and 80% of the students appear not to have developed misconceptions about divide-and-conquer.

At first, this result seems to be strangely at odds with the first experiment which showed a rather diverse and almost uniformly distributed set of misconceptions. A closer look, however, reveals that the assignment used in this second experiment was not just an instrument. Instead, since the items required the students to actively reflect their knowledge and to check their reasoning, this instrument *by design* was also an intervention.

In conclusion, both instruments serve different purposes: the first, easy-to-evaluate instrument exclusively is geared towards detecting susceptibilities to the type of conflations of divide-and-conquer and dynamic programming as reported previously [4]. The second instrument integrates an intervention by requesting the students to reflect their conceptions on cross-validated items and thus is well suited to follow up on the results of administering the first instrument.

3.6 Dynamic Programming

In addition to the possible influence of divide-and-conquer misconception on the understanding of dynamic programming, one of the hypotheses put forward in our previous study [4] was that the modeling complexity of the problem used for the test item might interfere with detecting possible misconceptions about dynamic programming. To detect such possible influences, we re-ran the experiment using the *coin-changing* test items as presented by Danielsiek *et al.* [4, Fig. 4] and additionally performed a second experiment for the *knapsack* test items also mentioned in this context.

Comparing these two experiments, we point out that the *knapsack problem* is conceptually simpler since it has less parameters; furthermore, the corresponding *test item* is also simpler since the correct answers can be inferred from the code presented. In particular, and in contrast to the *coin-changing* item, the `if`-clause contains the relevant parts of correct answers—see Figure 1. Thus, even if the precise model of the problem can not be derived by a student, the correct answer could, at least in principle, be deduced on the basis of a general understanding of dynamic programming. We added to the difference in complexity by first presenting the more complex problem, i.e., the *coin-changing* problem, and then presenting the second, easier problem one week later, i.e., we allowed for learning effects to take place.

In the evaluation of these experiments, our focus was on whether—and if so, how—the distribution of correct answers depended (1) on the particular problem and (2) on whether the test item related to updating or copying a previously computed value. To answer the first question, we compared the answers given for the "update" and "copy" item across both experiments. The two tables given below present the frequencies for all combinations of answers for all 77 participating students.

"Copy" Test Item	Correct (*knapsack*)	Incorrect (*knapsack*)
Correct (*coin changing*)	8	9
Incorrect (*coin changing*)	23	37

"Update" Test Item	Correct (*knapsack*)	Incorrect (*knapsack*)
Correct (*coin changing*)	8	3
Incorrect (*coin changing*)	23	43

The obvious, unsurprising interpretation of these results is that the "knapsack" problem indeed is less difficult than the "coin-changing" problem: 23 students correctly solved the "knapsack" problem but failed the "coin-changing" problem while only three students correctly solved the "coin-changing" problem but failed the "knapsack" problem.

When further analyzing these results, we assumed for the null hypothesis of a χ^2-test that the characteristics in one dimension were statistically independent of the characteristics in the other dimension, i.e., that giving correct answers in the "knapsack" experiment occurred statistically independent of giving correct answers in the "coin-changing" experiment. This hypothesis could not be rejected for the "copy" test item ($\chi^2 = 0.42$). For the "update" test item, the hypothesis could be rejected ($\chi^2 = 5.63$, $\alpha = 0.025$), the result of the power analysis, however, was rather weak (power $= 0.50$). In particular, giving correct answers in the "coin-changing" experiment appeared to be a good indicator for also giving correct answers in the "knapsack" experiment while the converse is not the case. This again confirms the relative difficulty of the two problems.

To evaluate the internal consistency of the items in each experiment, we analyzed the answers as given below:

"Knapsack" Problem	Correct (*copy*)	Incorrect (*copy*)
Correct (*update*)	31	10
Incorrect (*update*)	12	40

"Coin-Changing" Problem	Correct (*copy*)	Incorrect (*copy*)
Correct (*update*)	10	5
Incorrect (*update*)	11	63

The analysis of the above results again used a χ^2-test where the null hypothesis assumed no statistical dependency

Input: Knapsack of size k; n items with weights $g_1, \ldots, g_n$ and weights $w_1, \ldots, w_n$.
Output: Optimal solution with respect to k and n.

1: $F \leftarrow$ new int$[0, \ldots, n][0, \ldots, k]$ $\quad\triangleright$ Result F with $n+1$ rows and k columns
2: **for** $j \leftarrow 0$ **to** $k+1$ **do** $F[0][j] \leftarrow 0$ $\quad\triangleright$ First row: no items to chose from
3: **for** $j \leftarrow 0$ **to** $g_i - 1$ **do**
4: $\quad F[i][j] \leftarrow \underline{F[i-1][j]}$ $\quad\triangleright$ Row i: For $j \leq g_1 - 1$ copy values from row $i-1$
5: **for** $j \leftarrow g_i$ **to** k **do**
6: $\quad$ **if** $\underline{F[i-1][j-g_i] + w_i} > \underline{F[i-1][j]}$ **then**
7: $\quad\quad$ FILL IN ASSIGNMENT FOR $F[i][j]$
8: $\quad$ **else**
9: $\quad\quad$ FILL IN ALTERNATIVE ASSIGNMENT FOR $F[i][j]$
10: **return** C

Options for Line 7:

1. $F[i][j] \leftarrow F[i-1][j] + w_i$
2. $F[i][j] \leftarrow \underline{F[i-1][j-g_i] + w_i}$
3. $F[i][j] \leftarrow F[i-1][j-g_i]$
4. $F[i][j] \leftarrow F[i][j-w_i]$

Options for Line 9:

1. $F[i][j] \leftarrow F[i][j-1]$
2. $F[i][j] \leftarrow F[i][j]$
3. $F[i][j] \leftarrow \underline{F[i-1][j]}$
4. $F[i][j] \leftarrow F[j][i]$

Figure 1: Dynamic-programming algorithm (knapsack). Underlined expressions are part of correct answers.

between correctly answering the "copy" test item and the "update" test item. For both the "knapsack" experiment ($N = 93$, $\chi^2 = 25.45$, $\alpha = 0.001$) and the "coin-changing" experiment ($N = 89$, $\chi^2 = 18.56$, $\alpha = 0.001$, power ≥ 0.99), this hypothesis could be strongly rejected. This implies that both items are highly correlated within one experiment, i.e., they can be used to cross-validate each other. Thus, the instrument is relatively robust against guessing.

4. CONCLUSIONS

In our study, we have assessed and validated a variety of instruments that can be used to detect misconceptions related to algorithms and data structures. The main findings besides the items' reliability and validity are that, for several topics, low-cost instruments can be used to detect misconceptions known from the literature and that easy-to-evaluate passive knowledge seems to be a good indicator for active knowledge related to invariants and divide-and-conquer. On the other hand, there are topics, e.g., objects and classes, where the low evaluation cost of an instrument comes at a price; previous studies' resources for evaluating recordings or artifacts appear to have been well allocated.

Implication for teaching can be derived from the analysis of the test items related to identity and state, heaps, and divide-and-conquer: the results of our study suggest that integrating incentives to reflect on knowledge before answering a test is strongly beneficial to avoiding the formation or consolidation of misconceptions.

Acknowledgement We thank all instructors for allowing us to administer the instruments in the recital sessions.

5. REFERENCES

[1] V. L. Almstrum, P. B. Henderson, V. J. Harvey, C. Heeren, W. A. Marion, C. Riedesel, L.-K. Soh, and A. E. Tew. Concept inventories in computer science for the topic discrete mathematics. *SIGCSE Bull.*, 38(4):132–145, 2006.

[2] K. Arnold, J. Gosling, and D. Holmes. *The Java^{TM} Programming Language.* Addison-Wesley, 2005.

[3] F. Culwin. Object imperatives! In *Proc. 30th SIGCSE Symp. Comp. Sci. Ed.*, pp. 31–36. 1999.

[4] H. Danielsiek, W. Paul, and J. Vahrenhold. Detecting and understanding students' misconceptions related to algorithms and data structures. In *Proc. 43rd SIGCSE Comp. Sci. Ed.*, pp. 21–26. 2012.

[5] A. Eckerdal and M. Thuné. Novice Java programmers' conceptions of "object" and "class", and variation theory. In *Proc. 10th Conf. Innovation and Technology in Comp. Sci. Ed.*, pp. 89–93. 2005.

[6] J. Gal-Ezer and E. Zur. The efficiency of algorithms – misconceptions. *Comp. & Ed.*, 42:215–226, 2004.

[7] K. Goldman, P. Gross, C. Heeren, G. L. Herman, L. C. Kaczmarczyk, M. C. Loui, and C. Zilles. Identifying important and difficult concepts in introductory computing courses using a Delphi process. In *Proc. 39th SIGCSE Symp. Comp. Sci. Ed.*, pp. 256–260. 2008.

[8] G. L. Herman, M. C. Loui, and C. Zilles. Creating the digital logic concept inventory. In *Proc. 41st SIGCSE Symp. Comp. Sci. Ed.*, pp. 102–106. 2010.

[9] D. Hestenes, M. Wells, and G. Swackhamer. Force Concept Inventory. *The Physics Teacher*, 30:141–158, 1992.

[10] S. Holland, R. Griffiths, and M. Woodmann. Avoiding object misconceptions. In *Proc. 28th SIGCSE Symp. Comp. Sci. Ed.*, pp. 131–134. 1997.

[11] M. McCracken, V. Almstrum, D. Diaz, M. Guzdial, D. Hagan, Y. B.-D. Kolikant, C. Laxer, L. Thomas, I. Utting, and T. Wilusz. A multi-national, multi-institutional study of assessment of programming skills of first-year CS students. *SIGCSE Bull.*, 33:125–180, 2001.

[12] N. Özdener. A comparison of the misconceptions about the time-efficiency of algorithms by various profiles of computer-programming students. *Comp. & Ed.*, 51:1094–1102, 2008.

[13] N. Ragonis and M. Ben-Ari. A long-term investigation of the comprehension of OOP concepts by novices. *Comp. Sci. Ed.*, 15(3):203–221, 2005.

[14] K. Sanders, J. Boustedt, A. Eckerdal, R. McCartney, J. E. Moström, L. Thomas, and C. Zander. Student understanding of object-oriented programming as expressed in concept maps. In *Proc. 39th SIGCSE Symp. Comp. Sci. Ed.*, pp. 332—336. 2008.

[15] O. Seppälä, L. Malmi, and A. Korhonen. Observations on student misconceptions – a case study of the build-heap algorithm. *Comp. Sci. Ed.*, 16(3):241–255, 2006.

[16] J. Stewart, H. Griffin, and G. Stewart. Context sensitivity in the force concept inventory. *Physical Review Special Topics – Physics Education Research*, 3(1):010102–1–010102–6, 2007.

[17] A. E. Tew and M. Guzdial. Developing a validated assess- ment of fundamental CS1 concepts. In *Proc. 41st SIGCSE Symp. Comp. Sci. Ed.*, pp. 97–101. 2010.

Experience Report: CS1 in MATLAB for Non-Majors, with Media Computation and Peer Instruction

Cynthia Bailey Lee
Department of Computer Science and Engineering
University of California, San Diego
La Jolla, CA, USA
clbailey@ucsd.edu

ABSTRACT

As computer programming is increasingly considered an essential literacy skill for all students, MATLAB courses in particular can play a role in introducing non-major students to a tool commonly used in many of their fields. This paper reports on our department's experience introducing a CS1 in MATLAB for non-majors course. The course assumed no prior programming experience and no training in linear algebra. Without linear algebra and without the ability to do domain-specific tailoring, we turned to Media Computation to contextualize the skills and motivate students. Media Computation is an approach to programming instruction that focuses on manipulation of visual, audio, and video media. The course design also featured the Peer Instruction lecture format, in which lectures are punctuated by frequent questions that students answer individually and in small groups. To our knowledge, this represents the first time that Media Computation and Peer Instruction pedagogies have been comprehensively adapted to a MATLAB course. This work shares selected materials designed for this course, and reports outcomes of the two terms the course has been offered.

Categories and Subject Descriptors

K.3.2 [**Computer Science Education**].

General Terms

Design, Human Factors

Keywords

Media Computation, Peer Instruction, Clickers, Classroom response, Active learning, MATLAB, CS1.

1. INTRODUCTION

Our work on an introductory MATLAB course began in close collaboration with the Cognitive Science department, who wanted a required lower-division preparation for their upper-division coursework that uses MATLAB to perform domain-specific tasks, such as statistical analysis of experimental data and simulations of cognitive processes (e.g. neural nets). This course was to redress concerns about poor student preparation in their upper-division courses, and low student satisfaction with existing options for attaining introductory programming skills. The course is also part of our department's movement towards centralizing introductory programming instruction within the department—rather than having such courses scattered across departments—and assuming a larger service role on campus. This shift sets the stage for computer programming to be considered a fundamental literacy skill for all majors and a component of any liberal education, a vision articulated as early as 1961 by Alan Perlis. [9,10]

SIGCSE'13, March 6–9, 2013, Denver, Colorado, USA.

The design constraints and goals for the course were as follows:

- Assume no prior programming experience.
- Assume no training in linear algebra.
- Proactively address differences in demographics, self-efficacy, and long-term goals that distinguish a non-majors audience from a majors audience.
- Build a solid foundation of basic programming skills (variables, conditionals, loops, functions, etc.), with special emphasis on unique MATLAB features for matrix handling.
- Do *not* include topics specific to cognitive science.

Without the ability to assume students have a foundation in linear algebra, an interesting question for a MATLAB course, what should they *do* with MATLAB, then? And with the request that the focus be on foundational programming constructs, and not cognitive science-specific content, another interesting question was, how can we contextualize and motivate the material being presented in this course? Media Computation (MediaComp) provided an attractive answer to both these questions. However, no textbook or other materials introducing MATLAB from a MediaComp perspective were available. This paper presents our efforts in creating our own.

To help foster an atmosphere of community learning and supportive collaboration, keep non-major students focused and engaged with the course material, and emphasize "big picture" conceptual understanding that can form a foundation for lifelong computer literacy, we adopted the Peer Instruction (PI) lecture format.

In this paper, we first define MediaComp and PI and review the existing literature on their benefits—benefits we hoped to obtain for our students. Then selected course materials are introduced, demonstrating how even very early beginning MATLAB concepts can be accessibly introduced using MediaComp and PI. Next follows a summary of evidence of the success of the course design, including student survey results. Finally, we discuss lessons learned and concluding advice for instructors interested in MATALB courses targeted to non-majors that are effective and well received by students.

2. RELATED WORK

Programming courses for non-majors present a particularly fraught pedagogical design challenge. Previous work notes issues with *self-efficacy* in introductory programming courses for non-majors [19]. Self-efficacy is the belief in one's own competence and ability to attain a goal. Many students entering this course have expressed low self-efficacy in relation to anything having to do with computers.

MediaComp is an approach to introductory programming designed with outreach and appeal to non-major students in mind [9,10]. Developed by Georgia Tech faculty Mark Guzdial and Barbara Ericson, MediaComp frames computer programming as a skill that enables students' expressive manipulation of digital media. This coupling of creativity and computing provides students with the context to see the utility of course topics. MediaComp textbooks and other materials are available for Java [7], Python [8], and Alice (Java) [4] programming languages. Comprehensive MediaComp materials were not yet available for MATLAB. We did take inspiration from *Introduction to Scientific Computation and Programming* [12], which also served as the students' textbook for the course. The text introduces MATLAB in a conventional (non-MediaComp) format, but includes extensive image, sound, and other media manipulation content in later chapters.

The MATLAB MediaComp materials described in this paper consist of both programming exercises (labs and homework) and lecture materials. All lectures in this course were conducted using the Peer Instruction (PI) pedagogy [13]. The PI methodology is as follows: (1) Before class, students prepare by reading the textbook. (2) In class, the instructor presents students with several multiple-choice problems. There may or may not be periods of traditional lecture between the questions. (3) For each question, students begin by individually answering and "voting" their response. (4) Then students discuss the question in small groups, ideally coming to a consensus, and vote again. (5) The instructor leads a discussion with the whole class.

PI was created by physics professor Eric Mazur to address concerns he had about the failure of introductory physics courses to change the way students thought about the physical world in their daily lives. Non-majors students in particular could pass their exams by rote regurgitation of formulas, but failed to correctly reason about high-level conceptual questions [2, 13]. Mazur wanted to effect a lifelong change in his students' understanding of the physical world, just as effecting a lifelong change in the way students think about computing is an important goal of this non-majors course.

The crux of productive PI is well-designed questions, often called ConcepTests [13]. ConcepTests are unlike most multiple-choice exam questions in that the purpose is to teach and spark discussion rather than evaluate, and to focus on core concept understanding rather than performance of formulaic procedures. After enjoying years of study and success in physics, studies of PI in computing are now being reported [1,3,14,15,16,17,20]. To our knowledge, there are no reports of PI use in a MATLAB course.

3. SETTING

This section outlines the conditions of the classes reported on in this paper.

3.1 Classes and Instructor

The instructor who designed the course has now taught it twice at a large research intensive public university in the United States. The instructor had previously designed and taught other courses using PI, but had not previously taught a MATLAB course nor a MediaComp course.

The winter class had an enrollment of 100, and the spring class had an enrollment of 131. The course is targeted to cognitive science majors exclusively; however the registrar did not bar other interested students from enrolling. Cognitive science majors were 86% of the class in winter, but this dropped to 66% in spring when more students became aware of the course (CS/CE rose from 2% to 8%, bioengineering rose from 0% to 6%). The influx of non-cognitive science majors also contributed to the drop from 70% female in winter to 57% female in spring. Both figures stand in contrast to our majors-targeted CS1 classes, which were 71% and 84% male for the regular and accelerated versions, respectively, in fall of that year.

An i>Clicker brand clicker device was required for all students. Like a textbook, students may purchase clickers at the bookstore for $20-40. A majority had already obtained one for previous courses in other departments. Clickers offer the instructor detailed record-keeping of student votes, and offer students vote anonymity to their peers; both are advantages over lower-cost alternatives such as colored index cards.

The class format was three 50-minute lectures and one 2-hour lab per week. Additional drop-in assistance from department tutors was available throughout the week in the computer lab.

3.2 Assessments

Summative assessment for the course consisted of three in-class written exams: two midterms and a final. In a beginning, non-majors course, adequate formative assessment and feedback is especially important for supporting student learning and calibrating student expectations. Four categories of formative assessment were used in this course: reading quizzes, PI questions in lecture, lab assignments, and homework assignments.

3.2.1 Reading Quizzes

Advance preparation for lecture is essential for students in PI classes, because they will be responsible to their groupmates for productive participation. Reading quizzes were 5% of the course grade and simply provided some enforcement of advance reading.

3.2.2 PI Questions in Lecture

Clicker participation comprised 5% of the course grade, and points were awarded for participation, not correctness. PI questions were the most timely source of formative feedback—students were able to measure their understanding of concepts just moments after they were taught. Students could also situate their performance relative to their peers, because the software instantly tabulates and displays graphs of all students' responses.

3.2.3 Lab Assignments

Weekly lab assignments were guided explorations of new topics necessary for that week's homework. Pair programming was used for all lab assignments—sometimes randomly assigned and sometimes student self-selected.

3.2.4 Homework Assignments

Weekly homework assignments challenged students to complete a more independent and complex programming task, applying skills

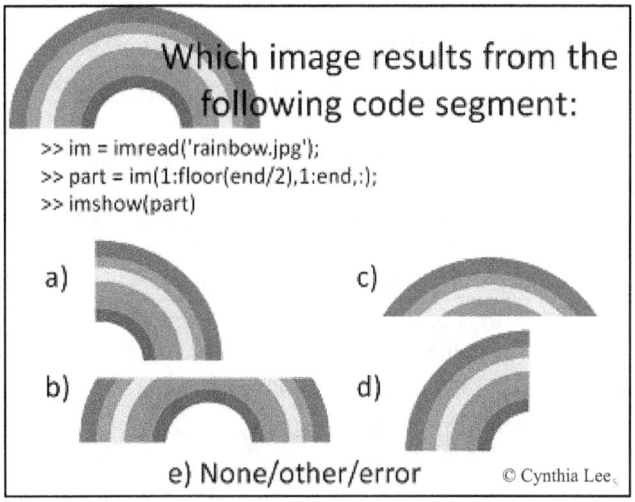

Figure 1. PI question on matrix row/column indexing.

introduced in the lectures and lab. Pair programming was used for all homework assignments, using the same pairing as that week's lab. Homework culminated in a two-week art or animation project of each pair of students' own design.

4. COURSE MATERIALS

In this section, we share the syllabus design process, as well as MediaComp and PI content artifacts created for this course. Examples were selected to highlight materials about programming constructs that are characteristic to MATLAB (e.g. matrix indexing), as opposed to those in common with other languages already taught using PI and/or MediaComp (e.g. while loops). Source code solutions are provided one of the programming assignments to allow the reader to gauge the difficulty for students.

Additional PI materials for the course are available to instructors for non-commercial use at http://PeerInstruction4CS.org, under a Creative Commons license.

4.1 Syllabus Design Process

To apply MediaComp to a new language, MATLAB, the first task was to find a textbook that teaches the desired MATLAB content, and a MediaComp textbook for a different language (Java) to provide project ideas, and try to reconcile the two. Starting with the Kaplan MATLAB text [12], we looked at the chapter (near to the end) where digital media is introduced. Taking the most basic exercises found there, we listed every skill necessary to minimally completing each of the exercises (e.g. call a function with an argument—the image file name, create a variable to save the output of a function, etc). Then we mapped out dependencies between all the skills on those lists and the skills leading up to those skills, and determined the shortest possible path to them. In other words, a single-minded emphasis on reaching key MediaComp-relevant skills as soon as possible dictated the ordering of topics at the beginning of the course. The result is to teach as much of the course as possible using MediaComp.

We determined that simple imperative programming turtle graphics commands could be introduced in the first lab (midweek in the first week of class), including allowing students to specify RGB hues to change the color of the turtle's line. Full RGB images (matrices) could be introduced as soon as the first lecture

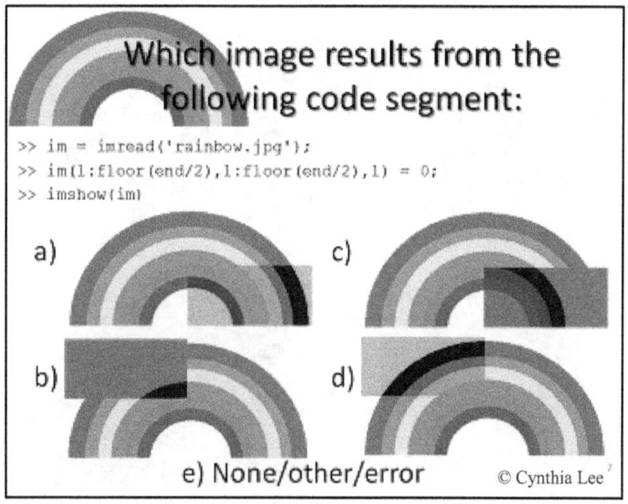

Figure 2. PI question on scalar assignment to a matrix region. ***(This figure best viewed in color)***

of the second week. Once RGB images were introduced, nearly all topics thereafter could be taught using MediaComp methods with RGB images. Green screen effects were introduced in the fourth week, and animation with green screen effects in the eighth week.

4.2 MediaComp Matrix Indexing

Although it has grown to encompass many things, MATLAB, as the name implies, specializes in handling of matrices of numeric data. Fluency with these features was a key learning goal for the course, enabling students to rapidly analyze data throughout their science careers.

4.2.1 PI lectures with MediaComp

MATLAB has a rich syntactic toolkit for matrix indexing by row and column, but it can take time for beginners to acclimate to mentally parsing everything that is going on in a line of code that does multidimensional indexing. Figure 1 shows a lecture slide that demonstrates how the synergy between PI and MediaComp creates a simple and effective way for students to work on this skill.

Throughout the course, we worked with RGB images, which, in MATLAB, are represented as three-dimensional matrices of type unsigned 8-bit integer ("uint8"). The first dimension is the rows, the second is the columns, and the third is the layers (always of size three—one layer for each of the red, green, and blue values in the RGB color scheme). MATLAB automatically decompresses JPEG and other image formats into full matrices of this format using the *imread* function, as shown in the code in Figure 1.

Matrix indexing syntax consists of comma-separated row, column, and layer subscripts. (In MATLAB, these are encased in parentheses, not square brackets, as array indices are in languages such as C/C++.) The colon operator is used to specify a range of values, and the *end* keyword means the last cell in that dimension. So the code snippet in Figure 1 selects the top half of the rows, all the columns, and all three color layers (colon operator by itself is equivalent to `1:end`), giving an answer of (c).

Figure 2 shows a similar question, this time with the matrix indexing occurring on the left hand side of the assignment operator. Students needed to puzzle out both which row/column region of the matrix was being selected, and what should happen to the color in the image when that region is set to zero. The

Figure 3. MakeWarhol homework assignment output. ***(This figure best viewed in color)***

selected region is the first (red) layer of the top left quadrant of the image. Students should recall that in the RGB color scheme, saturated green and blue together, with no red, gives teal. So the correct answer is (d).

These questions show how MediaComp supports implementation of the PI ConcepTest philosophy by enabling instructors to write questions that are stripped of distracting details, and engage students directly with important "big picture" concepts in the course. With a firm grasp of the big picture in hand, students can go forward to master the details—still a critical aspect of computer programming—in lab and homework settings.

4.2.2 Assignments with MediaComp

The matrix handling theme was carried over from lecture to the lab and homework assignments, where students wrote their own code. Figure 3 shows a sample output for the lab project from the 3rd week of the term. The image was created using what we call the `MakeWarhol` function: it takes as input an RGB image matrix, extracts the individual RGB layers, and tiles them (plus the original) onto the four quadrants of a new RGB image. The result is something loosely inspired by Andy Warhol's colorful repeating tiled images. Even more Warholesque results can be achieved by selecting pairs of layers (e.g. red-green) and applying a negative effect to some or all of the quadrants, things some students experimented with.

After writing the required code for assignments like this, students ran the code on images of their choosing, and posted the results on the course discussion board. This provided a chance for students to express their identity to other students, and to build a sense of accomplishment and community.

The solution code for MakeWarhol is as follows:

```
function res = MakeWarhol(im)
  red = im(:,:,1);
  green = im(:,:,2);
  blue = im(:,:,3);
  res = zeros(2*size(im,1),2*size(im,2),3);
  res(1:end/2,1:end/2,2) = red;
  res(1:end/2,end/2+1:end,1) = green;
  res(end/2+1:end,1:end/2,3) = im;
  res(end/2+1:end,end/2+1:end,:) = blue;
end
```

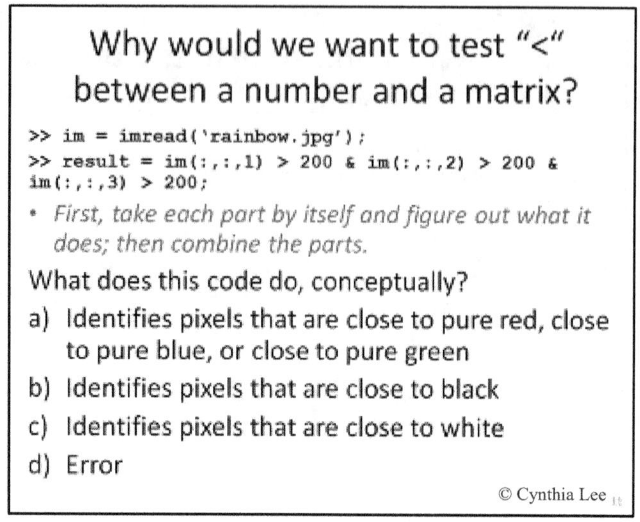

Figure 4. Selecting image regions by hue using logical matrix indexing.

Other matrix-indexing homework and lab exercises included using the increment specification option for the colon operator to select every other row (or column), or every third row (or column), to achieve proportional or out-of-proportion image resizing effects. In the 2nd week assignment, students wrote code that performed static-ratio resizing of an image. In the 3rd week assignment, students generalized their code by packaging it as a function, and parameterizing the horizontal and vertical resize factors.

4.3 MediaComp Logical Indexing

One of the most powerful features of matrix handling in MATLAB—and one of the most challenging for students to understand—is *logical indexing.* This feature allows users to index a vector or matrix of data using a matrix of type logical (i.e. true/false), rather than the row/column ranges shown in the examples above. A cell of the matrix is selected iff the corresponding cell in the logical matrix is true/1, and is not selected if the corresponding cell in the logical matrix is false/0. This feature allows users to easily create filter views of data—for example, from a matrix of health data, select the systolic blood pressure for only those individuals whose age is between 50 and 65.

It also happens that the feature is well suited to doing *green screen* special effects. Green screen effects (also called *chroma key* effects) are used widely in digital video production, from TV news to advertising to Hollywood films. A scene is filmed or photographed with elements (often a background) that is a very specific hue (often bright green). Later, during digital post-production work, that region of the scene will be selected by hue and replaced with some other image.

4.3.1 Creating matrices of type logical in PI

In lecture on the day prior to the lab on green screen effects, the use of logical operators (and/&, or/|) and relational operators (<,>,<=,>=,==) on matrices is introduced. MATLAB allows relational operators to be used between a matrix variable and a scalar variable. The output is a matrix where each entry is the result of the pairwise comparison between the scalar and the corresponding cell in the input matrix. This is illustrated in the PI question shown in Figure 4. (The answer is (c)—the closer the three component colors are to 255, the closer to white the color is.)

The purpose of this question was to introduce the syntax and its functioning, but also to start a dialog about why a user would want to do such a thing. The green screen concept was introduced with examples from popular media. Students were then prepared to create their own hue-selecting filters in lab.

4.3.2 Logical indexing lab assignment

In lab, students were provided with three images of equal size: a man with a red and black shirt on a white background, a telescope photograph of a starry sky, and a multicolor "tie-dye" pattern. Students were to select the man—but not his white background—and overwrite it with the space photo, creating a new background. For this task, they could use the selection code from class (Figure 4), with slight adaptations. The code from class used a very forgiving definition of "close to white." Using this included not only the pure white background, but also other white objects such as the man's teeth. Students can adjust the threshold to include a very small margin, or even only include pure white.

Next, they were to change the man's red shirt fabric to tie-dye by selecting the red part of the shirt and overwriting it with pixels from the tie-dye image. This required more careful hue thresholding calibration. The shirt has wrinkles and shadows, and even the best solutions include some false positives and false negatives in identifying all the red shirt pixels.

That students were largely content spending lengthy amounts of time writing and re-writing compound logical expressions and conditional statements illustrates the power of MediaComp as a motivating context for student exploration of computing. In course evaluations, many students mentioned the green screen lab as a compelling one, and in MATLAB the code was straightforward enough to use as soon as week 4.

For most assignments, students were encouraged to provide their own images as input to their code. This allowed students to spend time with images that are meaningful to them. For this assignment, we provided the three specific input images because the code only works for images that have exactly the same dimensions. Adjusting for different sizes adds several steps, something students were able to master soon after mastering this lab assignment. Students made pervasive use of the different-size image green screen effects on their final projects in the course.

5. RESULTS

University evaluations show the average student approval of the course that existed before this one was 73% (14 classes offered since 2007). For the new course, student approval was 81% the first time it was offered, rising to 88% the second time. The rate of students dropping the class is low: 2% of students dropped in winter and 11% in spring, compared to 17% average in the old course (ranging from 10% to 27%). Comments from students on the evaluations were overwhelmingly positive, many validating achievement of key design goals for the course (these comments summarized below). By all anecdotal accounts, stakeholders in both the computer science and cognitive science departments have been pleased with these outcomes.

There are three sources of information for evaluating the students' perspective of whether the course design was successful in the two times the course has been offered thus far (Winter 2012 and Spring 2012 terms): first, the usual university-conducted end of term course and professor evaluations quoted above (64% and 38% response rates, respectively[1]), second, attitudinal surveys of the students on use of PI (94% and 83% response rates), and third, an attitudinal survey about lab and homework design (winter only, 75% response rate). Student quotes from these three sources are combined and presented below by topic. At the time of this writing, the first alumni of this course are currently enrolled in the post-requisite cognitive science course. Therefore, evaluation in terms of their success there is not yet possible.

5.1 Lab and Homework Assignments

In the homework survey, students reported an average of 5.6 hours per week of outside study for the course (stdev=2.7, max=12.5 hours), which is within the department's guidelines for appropriate student workload. When asked to name the "most rewarding" assignment, "whether it was easy or hard," the most commonly listed assignments were a tile puzzle game[2], MakeWarhol, and the green screen assignment (collectively accounting for about 70% of responses).

For the MakeWarhol assignment, even a few students who mentioned struggling with it said it was still the most rewarding in the end. One student said, "I use the picture we made with the MakeWarhol code as a background on my computer." Another student said, "MakeWarhol because we did something with an image that we might actually want to do sometime for a project or just for fun."

5.1.1 Final projects

The students' digital art and animation final projects were especially successful. The assignment requirements and rubric were set in terms of which programming constructs needed to be employed (at least 4 functions, 3 for loops, 2 while loops, 2 if/else, 2 row/column matrix indexing and 2 logical indexing), leaving the artistic design entirely in the hands of the students. The requirements could be filled by creating a static image using custom filters and green screen effects; however, nearly all of the students elected to do animation. Even considering they worked in groups of two, the scale of effort was considerable. In the spring class, projects included an average of 451 lines of code in 11 source code files (this could include reuse of code from earlier assignments), 23 input image files, and 0.4 sound files. Samples of the students' work may be found in the "MATLAB (CSE 7)" area of this web page: http://www.cse.ucsd.edu/~clbailey.

5.2 MediaComp Pedagogy

Though not everyone agreed ("I think this...course should teach more about how to apply it to math and data rather than images"), most students reported extremely positive reactions to the MediaComp approach used throughout the course. "I have never taken a [computer science] class before and I was really worried because I had heard about how difficult [computer science] was but you have not only made it easy to understand but fun as well."

Students valued the way the MediaComp approach provided immediate visual feedback during debugging. One student noted, "I think the ones that involve images are most rewarding because the results are very apparent when they are done correctly."

[1] The median response rate at the university is 28%.

[2] The tile puzzle game took as input any RGB image, divided the image into a 4x4 grid of tiles, mixed up the order of the tiles (removing one to create an empty space), and let the user play an interactive game of "sliding" the tiles back into the correct order.

Another student said, "It was nice to be able to implement code to [do] something more interesting, [it] helped make it easier to understand how the code worked."

Some did see a connection between skills developed using MediaComp and more traditional applications of those skills. A student commented, "The course was interesting. Although most of the programming was done with media the processes that we learned are very applicable to data analysis."

Students also enjoyed how working with digital media gave them a new, insider's view of computing in their daily lives. One student said, "Interesting course, I enjoyed that it dealt a lot with manipulating images with code—showing us the inner workings of functions we use at the click of a button with programs like photoshop, etc." Another student declared, "I have new found respect for computer programers [*sic*]."

5.3 PI Pedagogy

On the PI survey, 87% and 83% of students (winter and spring, respectively) said they would recommend that other instructors adopt the PI method. One student expressed his or her perception of its impact on learning, "Looking back, it felt that I learned the material automatically by coming to class since it was an engaging class, instead of having to spend time after class and before exams reviewing the material as in normal lectures. Compared to other lectures, I felt like an active participant instead of a passive listener, and I much preferred this role as a student instead of the normal role since in the normal role I usually feel the need to fall asleep."

93% and 91% of students on the same survey agreed with the statement, "The immediate feedback from clickers helped me focus on weaknesses in my understanding of the course material."

6. CONCLUSIONS

MediaComp is an effective pedagogical means to contextualize computing concepts and motivate non-major students in a MATLAB CS1 course. In this way, MediaComp has mitigated the problem created by our course design constraint that we not include cognitive science domain-specific applications of MATLAB in this course.

Using MediaComp contexts for Peer Instruction (PI) ConcepTest questions often creates a synergy between the two pedagogies. This is because ideal ConcepTests confront students with scenarios they can reason about and discuss at a high level, without unnecessary detail and process interfering. When the inputs to and outputs from a piece of code are concrete images, students have a powerful language of programmatic cause and effect to use in their peer discussions.

The success of these pedagogies in a MATLAB course is especially significant because of the role the MATLAB language plays as a commonly used tool for students, professionals, and academics in disciplines outside of computer science. If computer programming is to become a critical component of a liberal education, regardless of major field of study, languages such as MATLAB may become an important vehicle for that education.

7. ACKNOWLEDGEMENTS

The author wishes to recognize Qiushi Wang, who served as Teaching Assistant for this course. His creative work, such as the tile puzzle game assignment, contributed greatly to the success of the course.

8. REFERENCES

[1] Carter, P. An experiment with online instruction and active learning in an introductory computing course for engineers: JiTT meets CS. 14th Western Canadian Conference on Computing Education, 2009.

[2] Crouch, C. H., and Mazur, E. Peer instruction: Ten years of experience and results. Am. Journal of Physics 69, 2001.

[3] Cutts, Q., Carbone, A., and van Haaster, K. Using an Electronic Voting System to Promote Active Reflection on Coursework Feedback. In Proceedings of International Conference on Computers in Education, 2004.

[4] Dann, W. P., Cooper, S. P. and Ericson, B. Exploring Wonderland: Java Programming Using Alice and Media Computation. Prentice Hall. 2009.

[5] Greenberger, M. Computers and the World of the Future. Transcribed recordings of lectures held at the Sloan School of Business Administration, April, 1961. MIT Press, Cambridge, MA, 1962.

[6] Guzdial, M. A media computation course for non-majors. In Proceedings of the 8th Conference on Innovation and Technology in Computer Science Education (ITiCSE), 2003.

[7] Guzdial, M. and Ericson, B. Introduction to Computing and Programming in Java: A Multimedia Approach. Prentice Hall. 2006.

[8] Guzdial, M. and Ericson, B. Introduction to Computing and Programming in Python: A Multimedia Approach. Prentice Hall. 2009.

[9] Guzdial, M. and Forte, A. Design process for a non-majors computing course. SIGCSE Bulletin 37, 1. 2005.

[10] Guzdial, M. and Soloway, E. Computer science is more important than calculus: the challenge of living up to our potential. SIGCSE Bulletin 35, 2. June 2003.

[11] Hake, R. R. Interactive-engagement vs. traditional methods: A six-thousand-student survey of mechanics test data for introductory physics courses. Am. J. of Physics 66, 1998.

[12] Kaplan, D. T. Introduction to Scientific Computation and Programming. Cengage Learning. 2003.

[13] Mazur, E. Peer Instruction: A User's Manual. Benjamin Cummings. 1996.

[14] Pargas, R. P., and Shah, D. M. Things are clicking in computer science courses. In Proceedings of the 37th SIGCSE, 2006.

[15] Porter, L., Lee, C. B., Simon, B., Cutts, Q., and Zingaro, D. Experience Report: A Multi-classroom Report on the Value of Peer Instruction. In proceedings of the 16th ITICSE, 2011.

[16] Porter, L., Lee, C. B., Simon, B., and Zingaro, D. Peer Instruction: Do Students Really Learn from Peer Discussion in Computing? In proceedings of 7th ICER, 2011.

[17] Simon, B., Kohanfars, M., Lee, J, Tamayo, K., and Cutts, Q. Experience report: Peer instruction in introductory computing. In Proceedings of the 41st SIGCSE, 2010.

[18] Smith, M., Wood, W., Adams, W., Wieman, C., Knight, J., Guild, N., and Su, T. Why Peer Discussion Improves Student Performance on In-Class Concept Questions. Science, 2009.

[19] Wiedenbeck, S. Factors affecting the success of non-majors in learning to program. In Proceedings of the 1st ICER, 2005.

[20] Zingaro, D. Experience report: Peer instruction in remedial computer science. In Proceedings of the 22nd World Conference on Educational Multimedia, Hypermedia & Telecommunications, 2010.

How We Teach Impacts Student Learning: Peer Instruction vs. Lecture in CS0

Jaime Spacco
Dept. of Computer Science
Knox College
Galesburg, IL 61401 USA
jspacco@knox.edu

Julian Parris, Beth Simon
Dept. of Psychology, Computer Science and Engr.
University of California, San Diego
La Jolla, CA 92093 USA
{jlparris, bsimon}@ucsd.edu

ABSTRACT
In this paper we look at the impact on student learning of *how* a class is taught. We compare 2 sections of a non-majors CS0 course offered in the same term, by the same instructor, covering the same content and utilizing the same book, labs and exams. One section was taught using standard lecture practices including lecture from slides, live coding and weekly quizzes. The other section was taught using the Peer Instruction (PI) method that actively engages students in constructing their own learning, instead of absorbing understanding from the instructor's explanations. Using a factorial analysis of variance, we find a main effect of instructional method on final exam grade ($F(1,200) = 5.87$, $p = 0.016$) with students in the Peer Instruction section scoring an average 5.7% higher than in the standard lecture practices section. We find no significant interactions among gender and grade or class status (lower or upper division) and grade. In a separate analysis, we also find the interaction of instructional method and high school background to be significant ($F(1,147) = 7.48$, $p = 0.007$). In discussion we consider the meaning of these results for educators and describe questions for future work.

Categories and Subject Descriptors
K.3.2 [**Computer Science Education**]

General Terms
Human Factors.

Keywords
Peer Instruction, Active Learning, Student-Centric Learning.

1. INTRODUCTION
What a course "is" and "does" can be viewed through the lens of instructional design. Any course should be based around the learning goals we have for students taking the course – what it is we want them to know and be able to do when they finish the course[1]. Describing how we go about supporting students in achieving those goals can be broken into two parts: a) the content (e.g. for loops, methods) and materials (e.g. Java or Scratch) we choose and b) the methods or pedagogical approaches (e.g. lecture, lab-centric [18]) we employ. In this work we explore the impacts of changing only the methods used in a course – just changing *how* we teach without changing what we teach (in terms of learning goals, content covered, and materials used). Specifically, we ask the following question:

> *Can a CS0 course designed around Peer Instruction (a student-centric instructional method) produce greater learning gains than a "traditional" lecture approach covering the same content?*

We are interested in the potential of Peer Instruction as an instructional method because it is one of a set of recommended evidence-based, active learning (or student-centric) teaching approaches which have been shown to increase student learning [15]. Peer Instruction (PI) is a formalized technique developed by Eric Mazur whereby students engage in answering and discussing challenging questions in class – often responding with a clicker [6,12]. The motivation for PI comes from research showing that learning is not passively transferred (e.g. from expert to learner), but rather actively constructed by the learner. Learning requires physical change in the learner's brain [16]. PI is one approach which makes the learner more central to what is happening in the classroom, engaging them individually and in peer groups to foster individuals' construction of their understanding.

We report the results of an in-situ study of changing how we teach. We are interested in in-situ results (rather than more controllable lab-based experiments, for example) because of the myriad of factors that come into play to impact a student's learning experience in a course – including their motivation, their accustomed "techniques" for learning in traditional lecture classes, and their time constraints and time management choices. We want to know if adopting PI in the "real world" of university computing classes will better support student learning. However, an in-situ study comes with a variety of complications that pose threats to the validity our results. We report identified threats, the steps taken to manage these threats and possible implications in our threats to validity section.

We find that students in a PI-designed offering of a non-majors CS0 course perform statistically significantly better than students in a concurrently offered course designed to replicate a "standard" course offering at our institution. This result is reported based on performance on the final exam. We choose to report only results of the final exam as the most directly indicative measure of performance. Other measures, such as course grade, may be affected by confounding factors (e.g., other components of the grading scheme). There is no interaction of exam score and gender or exam score and academic level. We measure academic

[1] Attitudinal goals can also be important for a course – e.g. increasing students' interest and/or confidence in using computers to solve problems.

SIGCSE'13, March 6–9, 2013, Denver, Colorado, USA.

level as either upper division or lower division based on number of units a student has completed towards a degree. A subset of students self-reported a metric of their high school background (whether a majority of students in their high school went on to attend college). We find a statistically significant interaction between instructional method and high school background, $F(1,147)=7.48$, $p = 0.007$, providing evidence that the effect of instructional method may be different for students of different high school backgrounds.

2. BACKGROUND AND RELATED WORK

2.1 Measuring Learning Impact

The computing education community has a strong history of exploring materials and tools to support improved learning – from contextualized approaches (e.g., media computation, games, robots) to supportive languages and development environments (e.g., Scratch, Alice, Greenfoot) to various visualization supports (e.g. AlgoViz and many simulators). Indeed, work in this area is too extensive to cite; the reader is referred to SIGCSE Symposia Proceedings. Additionally, one can find numerous reports on teaching methods – for many years SIGCSE has had sessions with titles such as Active Learning or Cooperative Learning. Much of this work takes the form of experience reports – describing what was done in a course in a manner that would allow another instructor to be able to adopt the described approach. In many of these reports evidence of the success of the tool, material, or approach comes in the form of student-self reported attitudinal impact. Certainly attitude or affect can be critical to issues of recruitment and retention of computing studiers. Additionally, student enjoyment of or interest in a course may impact the time spent "on task" studying, working, or learning in that course. Certainly, motivation is one of the key components underlying human activity.

However, even marginally controlled measures of increases in learning outcomes have been relatively rare in our community. Why? One contributor is that, compared to disciplines such as physics, biology, and chemistry, we lack broadly deployable instruments such as concept inventories [10], or measures of student understanding of the "nature of the discipline" [1].

Additionally, computing education has a brief history and, even within that time, our discipline has undergone major transformation. Both the *learning goals* we target and the *materials* (computing languages, tools, environments) to support this learning are changing more rapidly than in other disciplines. And to some extent, we must keep up with these tools – we seek to train both computer scientists and computing professionals – graduates capable of engaging in society to create new things and to solve society's problems. But this constantly changing set of goals and materials has often left us with a challenge in assessing the impact of our instructional *methods*. It seems that many times we have the opportunity to "redesign" a course, even if we want to adopt new methods, the goals and/or materials need to change as well. This study contributes to the field in that it *specifically and consciously focuses only on the instructional method.*

2.2 Peer Instruction

Peer Instruction (PI) is considered a student-centric learning method because the focus of the classroom is moved from the instructor to the student. The basics of a PI course design include having students prepare for lecture (covering basic knowledge before lecture) and designing a lecture-time focused on engaging students in answering challenging questions to confront misunderstandings and deepen existing understandings (often through a process of answering multiple-choice questions with a clicker). Critically, a PI classroom structures this engagement such that students spend time discussing problems in small groups, with the expectation of developing their own ability to verbally analyze the question and to explain why distractor options are incorrect. This aspect of PI is sometimes not clearly understood. In PI, clickers are not as important for measuring *if students understand* as they are for engaging students in discussion to *develop their understanding.* We chose to compare this method to a standard instructional approach for a number of reasons:

- It has 20+ years of documented success in improving student learning in the college physics environment – with seminal work in both intra-instructor [6] and inter-instructor studies [10]. Its impacts have been studied in various environments including community colleges [11]. Results show increase in learning gain as well as improvements in other measures such as pass rate. Nonetheless, PI has not, to our knowledge, become a commonly used approach in computing courses.
- Its tenets address some of the core issues raised by, for example Tobias [19] which may negatively impact student interest and retention in the sciences (and likely computing): e.g., lack of belonging or being right for the discipline, one-way dispensing of information by the instructor, and competitiveness among students.
- The emphasis on student verbal analysis and discussion practice in teams – core "soft" skills regularly identified as missing skills among our graduates [5]. Though in this case we report on a CS Principles CS0 class – many of these same issues appear in the computational thinking practices that are learning goals for that course [2].

In computing, PI has been mostly described in experience reports often showing positive attitudinal impacts on students [9,13,17]. But often these are results presented in conjunction with other instructional change, or by instructors who have not had the opportunity to teach a course using multiple methods (graduate students or junior instructors who cannot risk such). One attempt to measure the impact of PI on learning in computing is that of [14] where they test whether students are really learning from peer discussion using an in-class approach with isomorphic questions.

3. METHODOLOGY

The course. Author Simon had revamped and taught this CS0-type course in 2010-2011 to >1000 students in two terms. The course serves a large variety of non-majors at UCSD and was one of the original 5 university pilots for the CS Principles course -- part of the CS10K project in the US [3]. The course was originally taught using PI -- and a focus of the course was on getting students to think like computing people -- not just to be able to "do" like computing people (e.g., code) [7]. However, PI is not to our knowledge a commonly adopted instructional method in computing courses. This study was designed to provide some evidence on whether the method of instruction would have a significant impact on student learning. Student attitudes about computing and their confidence levels are also of interest, and will be analyzed in future work.

The design. In the Winter 2012 quarter (10 weeks), author Simon served as instructor of record for 2 sections of the course. With appropriate administrative approval, she taught one of the sections using a Peer Instruction instructional approach ($PI\_N = 90$); the other was taught using a "standard" lecture-based instructional approach (SI_N = 124). The standard instructional model was based in the following: her previous experiences lecturing, the book author's (Steve Cooper) materials and personal discussion of how he teaches to complement the textbook, and author Simon's cultural understanding of how other instructors teach introductory programming courses – especially at this institution. Students enrolled in one of the two sections with no prior knowledge of the intended instructional design, though they were informed on the first day of class and given a chance to switch sections (none did). More detail is provided Section 3.1.

Course similarity and variation. The same textbooks were required for both courses -- though the PI section also had to purchase a clicker if they didn't already have one ($20-40 at the bookstore, used or new). The class used the following identical assessments (% of grade): closed labs (20%), written technology and society assignments (5%), project (10%), midterm exam (15%) and final exam (35%). This grade breakdown falls within common practices at our institution. The remaining breakdown of the course grade was as similar as feasible, as indicated in Table 1. To receive full credit for discussion questions, students had to be present at 80% of lectures and get at least 50% of questions correct in each lecture – reflecting that the discussion questions support learning, not summative assessment. Both courses allowed students to drop their 2 lowest quizzes.

The PI class was assigned guided reading (called *exploratory homework* [8]) and given a short quiz on the reading at the beginning of each class. In class much of "lecture" was replaced with clicker questions which they answered individually, discussed in assigned groups, answered again, and then participated in or listened to whole-class discussion. 83 clicker questions and 43 quiz questions were used in the term. In the SI class a quiz was given each Friday lasting 10-15 minutes. It was made of 2-3 multiple-choice questions (all taken from PI clicker questions, with slight modification as needed). Each quiz had one question that asked students to answer, and write an explanation of their answer, in order to provide a summative version of the discussion experiences found in PI and to support SI students in developing written explanation skills which would be tested on the exams. (Note: PI students did not have such written explanation practice – just the oral peer discussions from class.) To support studying for the midterm and final, both groups were provided with a "sample exam" which was comprised of all of the quiz and clicker questions used in the PI class. Answers to the sample exams were provided for students. In addition, for the final, several sample code writing questions were provided.

Comparative metrics. We explore differences in the performance of students in these two sections. We report descriptive statistics and provide statistical analyses on the final exam score. As we are not including students who withdrew from the course before the end of the term (which students can do through the end of week 8 out of 10), it is important to report that the withdraw rates in the two sections were not statistically significantly different (PI Ws: 3, SI Ws: 3). Finally, we also report on performance differences broken down by a number of demographics including: gender, class status (upper or lower division as measured by number of credits completed), and student self-reported high school background. Self-reported data was incomplete, so some results include only the 151 students submitting this data.

Fairness to students. While a course's instructional approach (especially method within the classroom) is generally left to the choice of the instructor, in this case extra precautions were taken to promote fairness to the students. With the consent of both the department and the Provost of the college for which this class serves as a requirement, at the end of the course, final scores in the class were examined for statistically significant differences. As agreed upon, since significant differences existed, students in the lower performing class each had their formally reported grade increased by the average difference between the classes. However, the grades reported in this paper are the original, unmodified scores. Additionally, this work was carried out under exempt IRB status.

	PI	**SI**
# Students	90	124
% Upper Division	22%	63%
Quiz Questions	43 (before class)	16 (end of week)
Written Explanation Questions	0	7 (end of week)
Discussion Questions	83 (in class)	N/A
%grade for Quizzes	5%	15%
%grade for Discussion	10%	N/A

Table 1. Varying aspects for the Peer Instruction (PI) and Standard Instruction (SI) sections.

3.1 Threats to Validity

As an in-situ study of real courses, there are a number of threats to the validity of this study. We report on those here, including the steps that were taken to manage these threats. It is recommended that the reader consider these issues when considering whether the results reported would be valid in another place and time.

- Student background was dissimilar. There are a number of ways in which students' backgrounds could impact their likelihood of succeeding in the course. As this is a non-majors course with no pre-requisites, there is no obvious metric to use in predicting success from past performance. To complicate the issue, many students are freshman, with only one term's worth of GPA – making incoming GPA comparisons suspect. Nonetheless, as a rough check of the equivalence in terms of GPA, average GPA in the PI and SI sections was compared, but no evidence was found for a difference in average GPA ($t(212)=0.15$, $p = 0.870$). The SI course had more upper division students than the PI course (63% to 22%) -- which we expected might have an impact. However, an analysis of the previous year course data (using PI, same instructor) revealed no statistically significant difference in student performance by academic level.

- Student interest level was dissimilar. As a non-majors course that is required by both a university college as a GE requirement and by the psychology department it is likely that students come to the class with varying interests and intentions. On a pre-survey, 14.2% of SI students were dreading or not interested in the course, with 21% saying they were interested. These numbers were similar in the PI course with 12.9% and 21%, respectively.

- Instructor effect. The instructor was already invested in the PI approach and would, perhaps unconsciously, "do better" in the PI classroom. The nuances of instructor behavior and their impact on student learning would be very challenging to measure. As the instructor, author Simon made extra effort to make the lecture course exciting, interesting, and engaging. Additionally, an external observer attended 3 class sessions across the term and found the instructor to be similarly enthusiastic in both courses. Finally, in the end-of-term survey required of all students in the course, students in both sections overwhelmingly indicated that they would "recommend the instructor" (98.8% SI, 98.4% PI).

- Students attended the other course. Students were informed of the two different approaches being used and invited to switch sections if concerned. None switched, though scheduling could have been an issue for some. Students were asked not to attend the other lecture (and the PI class had assigned seats which would have made drop-ins more noticeable). Finally, podcasts for both courses were restricted to each class rather than publicly available.

- Experience with multiple-choice questions (MCQs). PI students had more "experience" with MCQs of the style that would be on the exam. This is a natural consequence of the PI pedagogy. The use MCQs in the course is reasonable given the large course sizes (200-600 per term). To manage this threat, SI students were given weekly quizzes made of 2-3 PI clicker questions (sometimes slightly modified for clarity). In addition, both groups received a "sample midterm" and "sample final" comprised of a compilation of all the quiz and clicker questions asked in the PI class (with solutions). In addition, SI students were asked on weekly summative quizzes to provide written explanations in the style asked on the midterm and final. PI students did not practice writing explanations -- they engaged in explanatory oral discussions through the PI process. PI students were told that they would be asked to write explanations on exams, provided the exact same advice given to SI students, and exhorted to practice writing explanations. However, there was no check as to whether students heeded this advice.

- SI students didn't have access to "exploratory homeworks" which the PI students did to prepare for class. Exploratory homeworks (which are not actually homeworks, but guided reading, nothing turned in [8]) are integral to the PI design. SI students were informed ahead of time what chapters would be covered in a given lecture. They were asked to read the chapters before coming to class, so they would be better prepared to ask questions and to understand the in-class live coding sessions. However, we chose not to implement "reading quizzes" in the SI lectures as that would not be representative of common instructional practice in this course.

- Attendance was not required in SI lectures and was probably lower. Several times during the term the TA sitting in the SI class took a head count during the middle of the class. Attendance was in the 70-90% range. While an experimental option would have been to require attendance in the SI class, this not representative of common instructional practice at our institution and for a non-majors course, specifically. As such, we felt it would not be reasonable to require student attendance in the SI section. However, we recognize one of the intrinsic benefits of the PI approach is the increase in attendance.

4. RESULTS

To assess the overall effect of instructional method on student performance we performed a factorial analysis of variance assessing the factors of instructional approach, gender, and academic level (upper or lower division status). Additionally, a subset of students (N=151) self-reported information on their high school background – indicating whether or not a majority of students in their high school went on to attend college. To assess the effect of high-school background we performed a separate 2-way ANOVA with the factors of instructional method and high school background.

4.1 Comparing Learning Outcomes: Instructional Method, Gender, and Academic Level

In the analysis comparing learning outcomes on the basis of instructional approach, gender, and academic level, we find only a main effect of instructional method on final exam grade ($F(1,200) = 5.87$, $p = 0.0163$), with students in the Peer Instruction section scoring an average 5.7% higher than in the standard instructional practices section (PI M=87.8%, SD: 13.1%; SI: M=82.1%, SD=13.0%). There were no statistically significant main effects of any other factors, nor were there any statistically significant interactions between factors. Overall, this indicates that Peer Instruction provided a benefit in terms of final exam score, and that there is no evidence this benefit is different for males and females, or for upper-division and lower-division students.

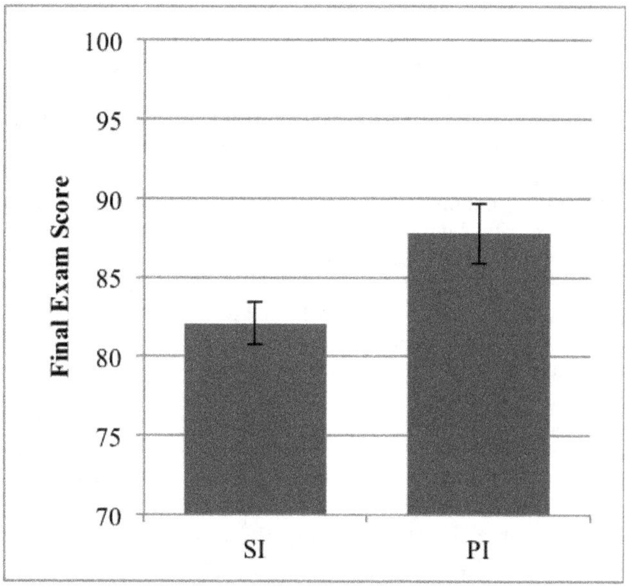

Figure 1. Final exam performance average and standard error in the Standard Instruction section and the Peer Instruction section.

4.2 Comparing Learning Outcomes: Instructional Method and High School Background

A subset of students (n=151) self-reported their high school background – indicating whether a majority of students at their high school went on to attend college. Overall, final exam scores did not differ on the basis of high school background, $t(149)=0.952$, $p = 0.339$.

To assess the effect of peer instruction for both of these groups of students, a two-way analysis of variance was conducted with class section and high school background as factors. There was a statistically significant interaction between instructional method and high school background, $F(1,147)=7.48$, $p = 0.007$, providing

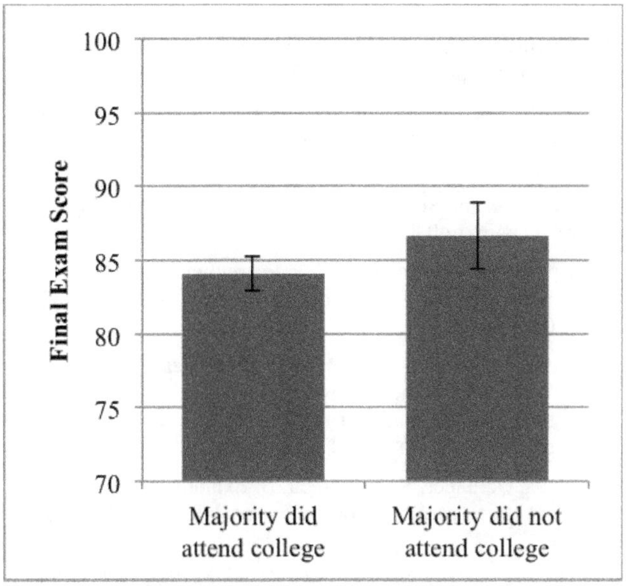

Figure 2. Final exam performance average and standard error of students based on their self-reported high school background.

evidence that the effect of instructional method may be different for students of different high school backgrounds. Follow-up Bonferroni-corrected t-tests provide evidence that among students where the majority of their high school went to college, there was a positive and statistically significant effect of peer instruction when compared to standard lecture, $t(147)=4.22$, $p < 0.001$. Among students for which the majority of their high school did not attend college, there was a slight negative effect of peer instruction vs. standard lecture; but, this effect was not statistically significant, $t(147)=1.04$, $p = 0.3012$, and should not be regarded as evidence for a detrimental effect of peer instruction for these students. However, given the statistically significant interaction, these results do suggest a potential difference in the efficacy of peer instruction for these two populations, but at best these results should be taken as preliminary until future work can investigate these subgroups with a larger sample of each.

5. DISCUSSION

Can differences in *how* a computing course is taught impact student performance? Any experimental design enacted in the "real world" of university instruction must be subject to a number of complicating factors that serve to threaten the validity of its findings. The contribution of this study is to have isolated the teaching method and to describe in detail extant complications. We report the following: ***Students in a standard lecture-based CS0 scored ~½ letter grade worse on the final than their fellows in a PI-based version.*** As educators, we see interesting potential. Could we improve all our students' learning by ½ letter grade if we switched from "lecturing" through our materials to this approach?

Aside from student performance gains, we would be remiss not to mention how much more fun it is to teach with PI. We get to spend more time answering important, deep questions and students are animatedly trying to figure out how things work (rather than texting, facebooking, etc). Finally, in a world excited by massive-open online courses (MOOCs), PI does seem to bring out the value and importance of the expert-student interaction.

Moreover, there are additional factors that, taken together, make the improvement of ½ letter grade seem quite substantial:

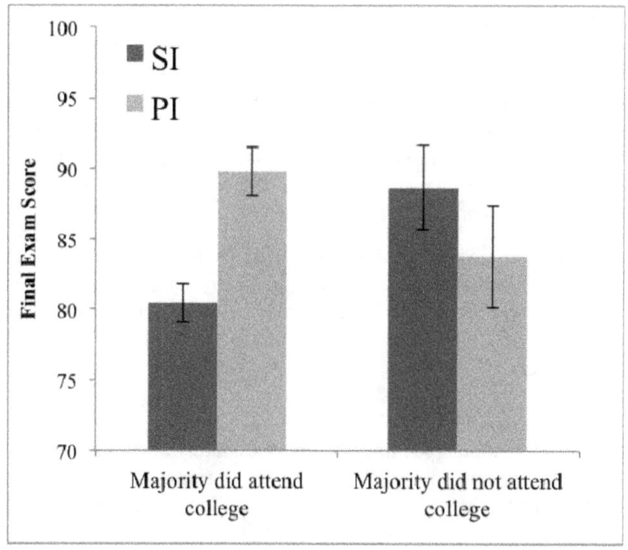

Figure 3. Final exam performance average and standard error in SI and PI sections for students of varying high school background. The difference for students from high schools where a majority did not attend college is not statistically significant and should not be regarded as evidence for a detrimental effect for these students.

1. **Not all learning occurs in the classroom.** There are so many uncontrollable and even unknown factors that play into student performance in a class. Especially when taking a required course, students can be expected to do what it takes to pass. Students have, in general, learned to survive in our educational system. Given this, that only changing the teaching method used (primarily) in the classroom made a ~1/2 letter grade difference on the final exam is fairly surprising.

2. **Students are "used" to standard instruction models (and how to succeed in them).** One might expect that it would take more than one term to "train students" to be effective learners in such a radically different classroom model. Resources supporting PI instructors emphasize that students shouldn't be expected to "love" this new teaching approach. In fact, one can expect resistance to most any new instructional approach, and significant effort needs to be taken to explain to students why the approach is being used and why it will be beneficial for them [4]. Additionally, it may be that students would perform even better if they had more experience learning in PI environments.

3. **The exam tested "real computing understanding".** Though beyond the scope of this paper, performance in this course, and specifically on the exam, measured computational thinking and understanding of core programming concepts like methods, parameters, if statements, loops, and arrays. There were no questions that tested definitions or that could, to our knowledge, be answered by memorization. In [7] we further describe the exam.

5.1 Effects in Sub-Populations

This study found no significant difference on the impact of instructional method when considering subpopulations defined by gender or academic level. We were interested in whether the more student-centric learning environment PI supports would address some of the negative classroom issues raised in Sheila

Tobias' study of university science courses. If it did, this did not manifest itself differently for women versus men. On the other hand, this study was carried out in a non-majors course (no computing majors would be in the course) and women were a majority in both sections. It would be interesting to further explore this hypothesis through a qualitative study of student experience in a more traditionally "unwelcoming" computing course where women are in the minority.

We were interested in the possible impact of academic level because of personal experience with faculty claiming that PI is "clearly appropriate for lower division courses, but not upper division." And vice versa. Whether this is speculated to be due to course content or student maturity, we don't know. Peer Instruction has been used successfully at both lower and upper division in many STEM fields, including computing. However, in those courses, the students themselves are likely all lower division or all upper division – because of the background required in the course. Our course allows us to explore whether student experience or maturity as measured by time spent in the university environment impacts learning gains measured in Peer Instruction. Here we are able to document no significant difference on the impact of instructional method by academic level.

Finally, we did identify a positive effect for students from high schools where a majority of students go on to attend college. Whereas we did not find this effect among students reporting that a majority did not attend college. This should not be interpreted to mean that PI has a detrimental impact for this subgroup. However, it may be worthwhile to consider a more detailed study of the experiences of students from different kinds of educational backgrounds and possible instructional supports or interventions that may help them to benefit as thoroughly as possible from PI methods.

6. CONCLUSION

In this paper, we report on an in-situ study of two sections of the same CS0 course that differed only in *how* they were taught. The two sections used the same textbooks, labs, and exams, and differed *only* in their instructional method: one section used Peer-Instruction while the other section employed a standard lecture-based approach. We observed statistically significant improvements for the PI section of 5.7% on the final exam. There was no interaction effect for gender or academic level (upper or lower division). Students in the PI section who attended high schools where a majority of graduates attend college saw statistically significant improvements; though this effect was not found among students from high schools where a majority of graduates don't attend college.

7. ACKNOWLEDGEMENTS

This material is based upon work supported by NSF 1140731.

REFERENCES

[1] Colorado Learning Attitudes about Science Survey. 2012, September 4. DOI=http://www.colorado.edu/sei/class

[2] Astrachan, O., Briggs, A. and Diaz, L. CS Principles. Retrieved September 2 2012 from http://www.csprinciples.org.

[3] Astrachan, O., Cuny, J., Stephenson, C. and Wilson, C. The CS10K project: mobilizing the community to transform high school computing. In SIGCSE 2011, 85-86.

[4] Bailey Lee, C. and Simon, B. Peer Instruction For Computer Science. 2012, September 4 (). DOI=http://www.peerinstruction4cs.org.

[5] Begel, A. and Simon, B. Novice software developers, all over again. In ICER 2008, 3-14.

[6] Crouch, C. and Mazur, E. Peer Instruction: Ten years of experience and results. American. Journal of. Physics, 69, 9 (2001), 970-977.

[7] Cutts, Q., Esper, S., Fecho, M., Foster, S. and Simon, B. The Abstraction Transition Taxonomy: Developing Desired Learning Outcomes through the Lens of Situated Cognition. In ICER 2012.

[8] Cutts, Q., Esper, S. and Simon, B. Exploratory Homeworks: An Active Learning Tool for Textbook Reading. In ICER 2012.

[9] Cutts, Q., Esper, S. and Simon, B. Computing as the 4th R: a general education approach to computing education. In ICER 2011, 133-138.

[10] Hake, R. R. Interactive-engagement versus traditional methods. A six-thousand-student survey of mechanics test data for introductory physics courses. American Journal of Physics, 66(1998), 64-74.

[11] Lasry, N., Mazur, E. and Watkins, J. Peer instruction: From Harvard to the two-year college. American Journal of Physics, 76, 11 (2008), 1066.

[12] Mazur, E. Farewell, Lecture? Science, 323, 5910 (2009), 50-51.

[13] Porter, L., Bailey Lee, C., Simon, B., Cutts, Q. and Zingaro, D. Experience report: a multi-classroom report on the value of peer instruction. In ITiCSE 2011, 138-142.

[14] Porter, L., Bailey Lee, C., Simon, B. and Zingaro, D. Peer instruction: do students really learn from peer discussion in computing? In ICER, 2011, 45-52.

[15] Prince, M. Does active learning work? A review of the research. J.Engr.Education, (), 223-231.

[16] Shors, T. Saving New Brain Cells. Scientific American, Mar. (2009), 47.

[17] Simon, B., Kohanfars, M., Lee, J., Tamayo, K. and Cutts, Q. Experience report: peer instruction in introductory computing. In SIGCSE 2010, 341-345.

[18] Titterton, N., Lewis, C. M. and Clancy, M. J. Experiences with lab-centric instruction. Computer Science Education, 20, 2 (06/01; 2012/09 2010), 79-102.

[19] Tobias, S. They're Not Dumb, They're Different: Stalking the Second Tier. Science News Books, Washington, DC, 1990.

[20] VanDeGrift, T., Caruso, T., Hill, N. and Simon, B. Experience report: getting novice programmers to THINK about improving their software development process. (2011), 493-498

Peer Instruction in Computing: the Role of Reading Quizzes

Daniel Zingaro
Department of Computer Science
University of Toronto
Toronto, ON, Canada
daniel.zingaro@utoronto.ca

Cynthia Bailey Lee
Computer Science and Engineering Department
University of California, San Diego
La Jolla, CA, USA
clbailey@cs.ucsd.edu

Leo Porter
Department of Mathematics and Computer Science
Skidmore College
Saratoga Springs, NY, USA
leo.porter@skidmore.edu

ABSTRACT

Peer Instruction has recently gained interest in computing as an effective active learning pedagogy. The general focus of PI research has been on the in-class portion of PI: multiple choice questions and group discussion. Here, our focus is the reading quizzes completed by students for purposes of class preparation. These quizzes contain content questions but also ask for difficulties or confusion with course material. Consistent with expectations, we demonstrate that providing correct responses to quiz questions positively correlates with other course assessments. Somewhat counter-intuitively, we find that identifying confusions, noting problematic sections, or asking questions about the reading are also correlated with lab grades.

Categories and Subject Descriptors

K.3.2 [**Computer Science Education**]: Computer and Information Science Education

Keywords

CS1; peer instruction; clickers; classroom response; active learning

1. INTRODUCTION

Peer Instruction (PI) is a pedagogical technique developed in physics that has since been used with considerable success in computing. Physics educators realized that standard lectures are ineffective for teaching core concepts and addressing misconceptions [4], and PI has been shown to remedy such concerns as measured through course-based assessments and standardized concept inventories. The core of PI is the multiple-choice question (MCQ) posed by instructors and answered by students. Lecture meetings hence become sequences of posing questions, answering questions, and discussing the questions in small groups. As detailed below, such activity driven by MCQs has received significant attention from those CS educators interested in PI. However, PI consists of much more than this "MCQ core". In particular, in order to engage in productive in-class discussions, students are expected to complete reading and a corresponding assessment prior to each class. Typically, such quizzes, like the MCQs they portend, are graded based on participation and not correctness. To what extent do students complete such reading quizzes? Do students tend to provide complete (correct or incorrect) responses or provide only minimal information? Do students acknowledge confusion or difficulty, and how does this relate to in-class or course-based performance? We seek to broaden understanding of PI in CS through such analyses of reading quizzes. In particular, we demonstrate that quiz completion and quiz correctness positively correlate with other areas of course performance. In addition, we demonstrate that the ability or willingness to identify confusions about the reading also positively correlates with other measures of course performance.

2. WHAT IS PI?

Each PI meeting consists of the following steps. The instructor begins with a mini-lecture that quickly overviews what the students read for the pre-lecture quiz. Then, the instructor poses a ConcepTest [4]—a multiple-choice question designed both to focus attention on and raise awareness of the key course concept from the mini-lecture [1]. After individually thinking about and voting on the correct answer (the solo vote), students discuss the question in small groups, reach a consensus, and vote again (the group vote). Students are encouraged to discuss each answer, verbalizing why it is correct or incorrect [16].

While student voting patterns can be estimated using flashcards [10], instructors can more easily obtain and communicate clicker data. Clickers also afford immediate, accurate vote counts to the instructor, as well as compelling graphical displays for the students. Ideally, each response option for a ConcepTest will correspond to a common student misconception, so that the instructor can identify the range of understandings present among the students [6]. Seeing the histogram of results, students come to realize that they are not alone in their confusion [9].

Following the group vote and displaying of response graphs, the instructor leads a class-wide discussion. Students are asked to support various response options as the class moves toward consensus. Once the discussion is complete, a new PI cycle begins.

3. WHY PI IN COMPUTING?

Since 2010, many investigations of PI in CS have been published. The first wave of papers focused exclusively on the gains exhibited between the solo and group votes of an MCQ [16, 18]. To measure such improvements, the normalized gain metric (NG) is frequently used. NG captures the proportion of students who answer incorrectly in the solo vote but correctly in the group vote. For example, if 60% of students answer correctly in the solo vote and 80% answer correctly in the group vote, the NG for the question is 50% (i.e. 50% of "potential learners" demonstrated new understanding). Representative findings include NGs of 41% in CS1 [16] and 29% in a CS1 where all students were taking the course for the second time [18]. These NG increases are particularly promising in light of the fact that peer discussions generally last only a couple of minutes, suggesting that learning occurs in a relatively brief timeframe.

Unfortunately, NG does not discriminate active learning from passive copying. Perhaps NG increases are due partly or mostly to students copying from peers whom they perceive as more knowledgeable. To help determine the extent to which the cited NG measures reflect one or the other of these scenarios, more recent papers have measured learning through the use of *isomorphic questions*. The methodology was first used in 2009 in the context of a biology course [17]. A pair of isomorphic questions tests the same concept, but the questions have different cover stories. In CS, this might reflect two questions both testing understanding of variables, but with different values being assigned or variable assignments occurring in different orders. Answered individually, the second question of a pair can give an idea of what students can now do on their own, outside of their PI groups. In both biology and CS [17, 14], isomorphic questions have been used to demonstrate that significant learning takes place during peer discussion.

The present wave of CS-PI research moves beyond per-question gains to an understanding of how PI as a whole confers conceptual understanding to students. One recent argument suggests that PI enables a form of cognitive apprenticeship, where the MCQs set by the instructor can help inculcate students into the professional discipline of CS [5]. When instructors use MCQs to lead students toward the types of thinking engaged in by experts, PI can provide opportunities for the deliberate practice and scaffolding that have been lauded by decades of educational research [7]. Yet, all of this research presupposes, at least implicitly, the requirement for students to be well-prepared to deliberately engage with PI materials. There is little time to "lecture" in a PI class, so preliminary material cannot be taught in the traditional way.

In the physics PI literature, student preparation typically comes in the form of reading quizzes [4], and it is likely that student experiences on reading quizzes are important in order for the core of PI to be effective. Authors of seminal physics PI research [3] note that it can be effective to administer short, three-question web-based quizzes prior to each lecture. The first two questions relate directly to the content covered in the required pre-class reading, and the third question asks, "what did you find difficult or confusing about the reading? If nothing was difficult or confusing, tell us what you found most interesting. Please be as specific as possible." Instructors can use the responses to these quizzes to support a form of just-in-time teaching whose focus is problematic areas reflected in students' quiz responses.

Though the use of reading quizzes is a PI best-practice, CS-PI courses sometimes do not use such quizzes [15]. When CS instructors do administer reading quizzes, research publications tend to jump straight to an analysis of in-class MCQs without reference to the preliminary reading quizzes. For example, [18] note that reading quizzes were used in the style of [3] and offer a sampling of the types of questions included in the quizzes, but say little in regard to correctness, completion, effort, acknowledgment of confusion, and so on. That said, we do know that students find reading quizzes valuable. For example, in work using clickers, occasionally in the PI format, it was found that 76% of Data Structures students agreed that reading quizzes helped them recognize and focus on difficult course concepts [13].

One recent paper suggests that the form of reading quizzes in CS should leverage the activity-based nature of our subject [8]. Rather than decoupling reading from experimentation, these authors support students in experiment-based learning where book and programming environment are used concurrently. Interspersed with reading, students are guided to emulate expert-like behavior: identifying learning goals, exploring small code segments, making predictions, and so on. Then, at the start of each lecture, students are quizzed on the homework material before the instructor launches into the first PI cycle. Student usage and valuation of the *exploratory homeworks* were promising: 50% of students "almost always" or "always" completed the homeworks; 58% of students "always" felt that homework helped them understand lecture; and those who read the text and wrote code before, during or after that reading outperformed the students who did not write the code. At the same time, only 30% of students completed the homeworks as intended: flexibly moving between reading, experimenting, and exploring (rather than, for example, serially reading and then coding).

The work of [8] is similar to the present work, but with two important differences. First, those authors used exploratory homeworks rather than standard PI reading quizzes, and it is the latter that is currently in more common use. In particular, these authors did not seek input from students on what they find difficult or confusing, which is a key role of PI reading quizzes. Second, they did not report on actual student performance on the quizzes, instead relying on student perceptions of the utility of doing the homework. Here, we seek to explore traditional PI reading quizzes by examining completion, correctness, confusion, and the ways in which these variables relate to course-based performance.

4. SETTING

We implemented PI in a small (40 students) remedial CS1 course for Computer Engineers taught by the primary author at a research-intensive Canadian university. All students in the class were unsuccessful in completing a traditional (non-interactive) 12-week version of the same course the previous semester, and require this course to continue in the engineering program. We used C to teach the major topics of the course: selection, iteration, functions, arrays, recursion, sorting, pointers and memory allocation (linked lists were taught in the prior offering but not in this remedial offering). We met for three fifty-minute lectures each

1 Is the expression `'a' < 'C'` true (1) or false (0). Please carefully explain your answer.
2 The following program does not run.

```
#include <stdio.h>

int main (void) {
  int q = 4;
  if (q == 4)
    printf ("The if-statement is running.\n");
    printf ("Another printf.\n");
  else
    printf ("This is the else.\n");
  return 0;
}
```

Try to compile the program. Explain each error that your compiler gives, and suggest a solution.
3 What did you find particularly difficult or confusing about the material you read? If nothing was difficult or confusing, tell us what you found most interesting. Please be as specific as possible: this is meant to help you focus on problematic areas, as well as help me make more meaningful lectures.

Figure 1: The fifth reading quiz.

week for 10 weeks, and were supported by weekly practical lab sessions and weekly tutorials.

Our motivation for using PI in this remedial setting was based on a reported interaction between pedagogy (PI or traditional) and experience [11]. This study found that students with low background knowledge gain as much from PI as students with high background knowledge gain from traditional instruction. It is likely that students in our remedial CS course lack significant background knowledge; therefore, we believed that PI would be particularly effective for achieving learning gains commensurate with those of the successful students from the semester prior.

Before each class, students were required to read one or two sections of our textbook [2], and complete an online reading quiz, typically with three questions. We used the format suggested in [3] and described above (i.e. two or three content questions followed by the "confusion question"). 6% of students' grades were allocated to completion of the quizzes: marks were awarded for effort, not correctness. In general, reading quiz questions were designed to skim the surface of what the students had read, while deeper application of that material was designated for in-class ConcepTests. Figure 1 contains one example reading quiz from week 2; the remainder are available on a PI resource page [19]. An additional 6% of students' grades were allocated to participation in ConcepTests and, again, marks were awarded for effort, rather than correct answers. Further details of the class offering can be found in [18].

5. DATA ANALYSIS AND RESULTS

5.1 Completion and Correctness

In total, there were 27 reading quizzes. On average, students submitted 21.2 reading quizzes, for an average submission rate of 78.5 percent. As will be shown, some of these "submissions" contained empty (or essentially empty) responses.

The reading quizzes contained a total of 52 content-based questions (i.e. not including the "confusion question"). To investigate the quality of the responses submitted, the primary author (also the course instructor) graded each response to a content-based question on a four-point scale:

- G0-Empty: Essentially no response (e.g. submitting "no" or "not sure", or leaving the response completely blank).
- G1-Incomplete: something submitted, but very incomplete (e.g. answering half of a question or tracing only partway through a program).
- G2-Incorrect: complete response, but incorrect.
- G3-Correct: complete and correct response.

Table 1: Average per-student responses on content-based questions, broken down by response category.

Category	Percentage
G0-Empty	1.8
G1-Incomplete	10.5
G2-Incorrect	37.6
G3-Correct	50

Table 1 contains the average per-student percentage of responses that fell in each of these four categories.

G2-Incorrect and G3-Correct reflect complete responses to the question. In the case of G2-Incorrect, students worked through a problem with misconceptions that led them toward incorrect conclusions, but the execution was nevertheless complete. For this reason, we argue that 87.6 percent of responses may be educationally useful as they represent students engaging with questions prior to lecture. 12.3 percent of responses, plus the questions not submitted at all (22.5 percent), may suggest inadequate preparation for lecture. Lastly, we see the rate of G3-Correct responses as surprisingly high: students knew that they were being graded only on submission (not correctness), so there was no immediate mark-based benefit for students to answer questions correctly. In addition, these are students that struggled in the past, and it is encouraging that half of the responses submitted by such "weak" students are correct with no further instructor intervention.

5.2 Confusion Question

On all but two of the reading quizzes, we provided the "confusion question" as the final question for students to answer. As indicated in Figure 1, we suggested to students that their responses might help the instructor create more accurately-targeted lectures. There is also recent evidence that students who are able to acknowledge confusion or difficulty can be well-positioned to excel in post-secondary courses [12].

To determine the extent to which students use this question for such purposes, we read through the responses searching for themes. Themes were initially based on the wording of the question itself, and were refined until all data could be captured and no themes failed to represent data. The following themes emerged:

C0-Interesting: identifies something interesting.

C1-Not Interesting: states that nothing in the reading was interesting.

C2-Confusing: identifies something confusing or unclear.

C3-Not Confusing: states that nothing in the reading was confusing.

C4-Difficult: identifies something that is difficult or "hard".

C5-Not Difficult: states that nothing in the reading was difficult.

C6-Forward: identifies something difficult that has not yet been reached in the course. (This is an artifact of the students having taken the course unsuccessfully once before.)

C7-Problematic: identifies something that cannot be understood or that something is proving problematic or troublesome. (This likely overlaps with student conceptions of difficulty, though with different word choice. For example, students often used phrases such as "I did not understand" or "I had trouble with this concept". When they did not explicitly use the word "difficult" or "hard", we coded the response as problematic rather than difficult.)

C8-Not Problematic: explicitly states that something is understood.

C9-Questioning: poses a question without explicitly indicating confusion or difficulty.

C10-Ambiguous: identifies a topic, but does not indicate whether that topic is interesting, confusing, difficult, etc. For example, a student might indicate simply "recursion".

C11-Other: comments relating to midterms or exams, or comments too short to otherwise classify (e.g. "so far so good").

C12-Empty: completely blank submission or a submission containing no information (e.g. "N/A", "nothing", "no").

Figure 2 provides the average per-student percentages of these codes in the 25 reading quizzes where the "confusion question" was asked. A total of 786 student responses were coded. The sum of the averages is more than 100% because responses could be coded by multiple codes (e.g. a response that asks a question but also acknowledges confusion).

Striking in this data is the number of questions posed to the instructor by students, an indication that areas of difficulty were not only uncovered but explicitly framed in the form of questions to which the instructor could respond. As a case in point, the responses to the quiz in Figure 1 contained eight instances of students asking questions. Two of these asked about the C `switch` statement that was topical but not tested in this quiz. A further two questions asked about the code that had been supplied, and why the code works at all without a `scanf` statement. The remainder of the questions asked how to chain `else if` branches. In our experience, students simply do not ask about course material to this degree when reading quizzes are not used; in such cases we find the vast majority of questions specifically focused on the students' current assignment rather than course material per se. We hypothesize that reading quizzes have the desirable effect of encouraging students to ask questions continuously, rather than clustering questions around assignment deadlines.

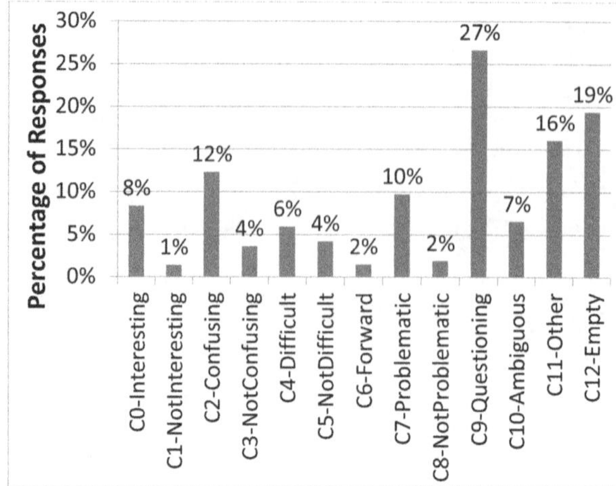

Figure 2: Average per-student response percentages, broken down by codes on the 786 submitted responses to the "confusion question".

Unfortunately, the mingling of confusing, difficult, and interesting in the question text also led to 51 ambiguous responses. For example, again in the responses to the quiz in Figure 1, one student provided simply "the flowcharts". This referred to the approach used in our text that depicted control statements in the form of flowcharts, though whether this was problematic or interesting is unclear.

The codes representing students who are not confused or who found nothing difficult mostly reflect a rephrasing of the question text. That is, we received many responses of the form "nothing was confusing or difficult". Given no further elaboration, it is not clear whether this was an attempt to submit content for the question (rather than leaving it blank), or whether they genuinely believed that nothing was confusing or difficult.

The 111 C11-Other responses were made mostly of high-level comments on the course, students' favourite C constructs, reflections on the prior course offering, and suggestions for how lectures could be improved (though of course without providing explicit questions).

5.3 Correlations with Course Performance

Table 2 gives the significant Spearman correlations ($p < .05$) between reading quiz codes and final exam grade. The final exam was worth 45% of students' grade. Perhaps unsurprisingly, students submitting many G1-incomplete responses do poorly on the final exam, and those submitting many G3-Correct responses do well. G2-Incorrect was negatively but insignificantly correlated ($r = -.23$) with final exam grade. None of the codes from the "confusion question" were significantly correlated with exam performance, though C7-Problematic approached significance ($p = .08; r = .28$).

Students' unsupervised term work (worth 18% of the final grade) involved the completion of five labs on which stu-

Table 2: Significant Spearman correlations between reading quiz codes and final exam grade.

Code	Correlation
Questions submitted	0.32
G1-Incomplete	−0.37
G3-Correct	0.51

Table 3: Significant Spearman correlations between reading quiz codes and unsupervised grade.

Questions submitted	.8
G0-Empty	−.35
G3-Correct	0.72
C2-Confusing	.4
C7-Problematic	.31
C9-Questioning	.57

dents worked alone. Table 3 provides the significant Spearman correlations ($p < .05$) between codes on the reading quizzes and students' unsupervised term work grade. Number of questions submitted, a clear effort measure, had the strongest correlation with unsupervised term work. Unlike with final exam score, students willingness to ask questions and acknowledge difficulty and confusion were significantly correlated with unsupervised work. In addition, G2-Incorrect was positively but insignificantly correlated with unsupervised term work ($r = .29$).

5.4 Correlations with Clicker Scores

Clicker responses, like reading quizzes, were assessed by contribution rather than correctness. Still, we wondered to what extent scores on reading quizzes correlated with clicker correctness. Our hypothesis was that students who did well on reading quizzes would be well-prepared for lecture and hence correctly answer more clicker questions. We focus here only on solo votes (i.e. those votes occurring prior to group discussion). Our rationale for excluding the group vote is that such scores comingle students' incoming knowledge and knowledge obtained through group discussions. We found significant positive correlations between number of clicker questions answered correctly and both the number of reading quiz questions submitted ($r = .65$) and number of G3-Correct submissions ($r = .48$). There was also a significant correlation between clicker correctness and C9-Questioning ($r = .33$). Interestingly, though nonsignificant, there was a moderate negative correlation (−.16) between clicker correctness and C3-Not Confusing. There were two other insignificant but positive correlations between clicker correctness and C7-Problematic and C2-Confusing (both $r = .25$).

6. DISCUSSION

The fact that students submitted almost 80 percent of reading quizzes and that 87.6 percent of question submissions were of acceptable quality suggests that students took reading quizzes seriously. There was no obligation for students to answer questions completely; the instructor explicitly told students that any submission counts. It is heartening that students took it upon themselves to put forth effort rather than simply answering for the sake of answering. This corroborates an end-of-term survey finding reported in [18] where 92 percent of these same students agreed with the claim that reading quizzes helped identify difficult concepts in the reading. The current paper strengthens the belief that students find reading quizzes valuable.

The "confusion question" provided useful data in terms of student questions and confusions, though the wording of the question sometimes led to responses that could not be unambiguously categorized. We argue that receiving this quantity of questions and feedback is further evidence that students cared about the quizzes and used the opportunity to communicate with the instructor. The course instructor was careful to address this feedback personally or at the beginning of the next lecture, which we suspect contributed to the quantity of feedback received. Though feasible in small classes, the workload involved in responding personally to quiz submissions in large classes is likely prohibitive. That said, we believe it is important for students to understand that we take quizzes seriously and treat them as a core component of PI practice.

There were no relationships between codes on the "confusion question" and final exam performance. Yet, codes related to confusion and questioning were highly correlated with unsupervised term work, affirming the relationships discussed by [12]. The reason for this difference is unclear and deserves future consideration. We do note that confusions were largely local ("pointers") rather than global ("what is the relationship between the heap, pointers, and the memory model"), and so perhaps related more strongly to small-scale assignments rather than the integrative exam. Also, assignments provide students some time in which to acknowledge confusions, obtain answers or clarifications, and then apply that knowledge in the context of their deliverable. Such feedback-driven progress is not possible in an exam setting.

Correlations between reading quiz correctness and clicker questions suggest that the quizzes might prepare students for and increase learning in the course. Importantly, we cannot rule out alternate hypotheses: it is equally plausible, for example, that stronger students do well on both quizzes and clicker questions, or that those putting forth more effort on the quizzes also put forth more effort toward answering clicker questions correctly. The relationship does give us confidence that students are finding reading quiz questions and clicker questions to be similar in terms of content and/or difficulty.

7. FUTURE WORK

There are several areas requiring future work. First, we suggest that the "confusion" question be disaggregated to make interpretation of responses more straightforward. For example, the question could be divided into prompts that ask for confusing, difficult, and interesting aspects of the course reading; students could be required to respond to at least one of these prompts. Students could also be provided a space explicitly for asking questions. An analysis of responses to these new questions would be interesting as a comparison to what we have offered here. Second, it will be interesting to compare traditional PI reading quizzes as discussed here and other preparatory assignments such as exploratory homeworks, effectively bridging the span between our work and that presented in [8]. Third, student perceptions of reading quizzes would be useful in the context of our correlation-based causation hypotheses. Do students feel that reading quizzes prepare them for lectures, labs, exams, or the course in general? Do they see relationships between quiz questions and clicker questions? Further student perceptions of reading quizzes are required to determine the accuracy of our correlation-based causation claims.

8. CONCLUSION

Analysis of reading quizzes is underaddressed in the current PI literature in computing. We provide one such analysis here, focusing on completion, correctness, confusion, and relationships to course-based assessments and PI questions. We find that students complete a large portion of reading quiz questions and that their responses suggest a reasonable level of effort and correctness. Students' responses to the "confusion question" demonstrate similar levels of attention: students ask many questions, acknowledge significant confusion, and note particular difficulties. We demonstrate that reading quiz performance correlates with performance in other areas of the course, suggesting that reading quizzes target important course material and may confer advantages to students who expend (or are willing to expend) the effort required to answer the reading quizzes correctly. We also find correlations between identifying confusions and questions on the one hand and performance on unsupervised term work and clicker questions on the other. We encourage further investigations into the utility of reading quizzes, their relationship to learning and the rest of the course, and their applicability to other CS courses in which PI is implemented.

9. REFERENCES

[1] I. D. Beatty, W. J. Gerace, W. J. Leonard, and R. J. Dufresne. Designing effective questions for classroom response system teaching. *American Journal of Physics*, 74:31–39, 2006.

[2] J. Carter. *Introduction to Computer Science Using C.* McGraw-Hill Ryerson, 2008.

[3] C. H. Crouch and E. Mazur. Peer instruction: Ten years of experience and results. *American Journal of Physics*, 69:970–977, 2001.

[4] C. H. Crouch, J. Watkins, A. P. Fagen, and E. Mazur. Peer instruction: Engaging students one-on-one, all at once. In E. F. Redish and P. J. Cooney, editors, *Research-Based Reform of University Physics.* American Association of Physics Teachers, 2007.

[5] Q. Cutts, S. Esper, M. Fecho, S. R. Foster, and B. Simon. The abstraction transition taxonomy: Developing desired learning outcomes through the lens of situated cognition. In *ICER '12: Proceedings of the Eighth international Workshop on Computing Education Research*, New York, NY, USA, 2012. ACM.

[6] Q. Cutts, G. Kennedy, C. Mitchell, and S. Draper. Maximising dialogue in lectures using group response systems. 7th IASTED international conference on computers and advanced technology in education. `www.dcs.gla.ac.uk/~quintin/papers/cate2004.pdf` (accessed August 19, 2011)., 2004.

[7] K. A. Ericsson, R. T. Krampe, and C. Tesch-Roemer. The role of deliberate practice in the acquisition of expert performance. *Psychological Review*, 100(3):363–406, 1993.

[8] S. Esper, B. Simon, and Q. Cutts. Exploratory homeworks: An active learning tool for textbook reading. In *ICER '12: Proceedings of the Eighth international Workshop on Computing Education Research*, New York, NY, USA, 2012. ACM.

[9] J. K. Knight and W. B. Wood. Teaching more by lecturing less. *Cell Biology Education*, 4:298–310, 2005.

[10] N. Lasry. Clickers or flashcards: Is there really a difference? *The Physics Teacher*, 46:242–244, 2008.

[11] N. Lasry, E. Mazur, and J. Watkins. Peer instruction: From Harvard to the two-year college. *American Journal of Physics*, 76:1066–1069, 2008.

[12] E. Mazur. ICER 2011 keynote address, 2011.

[13] R. P. Pargas and D. M. Shah. Things are clicking in computer science courses. In *SIGCSE '06: Proceedings of the 37th SIGCSE technical symposium on Computer science education*, pages 474–478, New York, NY, USA, 2006. ACM.

[14] L. Porter, C. Bailey-Lee, B. Simon, and D. Zingaro. Peer instruction: Do students really learn from peer discussion in computing? In *ICER '11: Proceedings of the Seventh international Workshop on Computing Education Research*, New York, NY, USA, 2011. ACM.

[15] B. Simon and Q. Cutts. CS principles pilot at University of California, San Diego. *ACM Inroads*, 3(2):61–63, June 2012.

[16] B. Simon, M. Kohanfars, J. Lee, K. Tamayo, and Q. Cutts. Experience report: Peer instruction in introductory computing. In *SIGCSE '10: Proceedings of the 41st SIGCSE technical symposium on Computer science education*, pages 341–345, New York, NY, USA, 2010. ACM.

[17] M. K. Smith, W. B. Wood, W. K. Adams, C. Wieman, J. K. Knight, N. Guild, and T. T. Su. Why peer discussion improves student performance on in-class concept questions. *Science*, 323:122–124, 2009.

[18] D. Zingaro. Experience report: Peer instruction in remedial computer science. In *Ed-Media 2010: Proceedings of the 22nd World Conference on Educational Multimedia, Hypermedia & Telecommunications*, pages 5030–5035. AACE, 2010.

[19] D. Zingaro. Pi-cs resource page. `www.danielzingaro.com/pics.php`, 2012.

Incorporating Metacognition into Learning

Murali Mani, Quamrul Mazumder
University of Michigan, Flint
303 E. Kearsley St, Flint, MI, 48502
{mmani, qmazumde}@umflint.edu

ABSTRACT

Metacognition refers to one's knowledge about one's cognitive processes, and is often associated with intelligence. Students who have good metacognition skills typically perform better in their cognitive tasks. For the Fall and Winter semesters in 2011-12, we incorporated metacognition into our computer science courses (both undergraduate and graduate level courses), so that the student becomes more aware of his/her own understanding of the various topics of the course. In this paper, we describe how we incorporated metacognition into our courses, and present results from our analysis of the data that we have gathered over the various courses.

Categories and Subject Descriptors

K.3.2 [**Computer and Information Science Education**]: Self-assessment.

General Terms

Measurement, Experimentation, Human Factors.

Keywords

Metacognition; regression; active learning.

1. INTRODUCTION

Metacognition, or thinking about thinking, was defined by Flavell [5, 6], and refers to one's knowledge about one's cognitive processes or anything related to them. It consists of metacognitive knowledge and metacognitive experiences or regulation. Metacognition enables students to be successful learners and has been associated with intelligence [1, 3]. Individuals who have more metacognitive abilities tend to be more successful in their cognitive endeavors. Other terms used synonymously with metacognition include self-regulation and executive control [10].

Metacognitive knowledge can be considered to include knowledge of person variables (e.g., a student knowing that he/she is more productive in a quiet environment), task variables (for example, a student knowing that he/she will need more time to comprehend a science text than a novel), and strategy variables (for example, a student knowing when to find extra resources from the library) [6, 7, 10]. Metacognitive regulation refers to the use of strategies in order to meet a cognitive goal (for example, a student using self-questioning in order to comprehend a chapter).

SIGCSE'13, March 6–9, 2013, Denver, Colorado, USA.

If the student finds that the cognitive goal is not met, then the student can use cognitive techniques as guided by the metacognitive knowledge till the goal is met. Though cognitive and metacognitive strategies might appear similar, there are significant differences: we can consider cognitive strategies as helping a student achieve his/her goal and metacognitive strategies as helping a student assess whether the goals have been met [10]. How instructors and students can incorporate metacognitive strategies is outlined in [13].

At UM Flint, we have incorporated metacognition in our under-graduate and graduate instruction for the last several semesters. Our goal is to make students aware of their own level of understanding of the topics. This forms a type of metacognitive knowledge, specifically a person variable (using the terminology from [6, 10]). A student can use this knowledge, along with other metacognitive knowledge of task variables, strategy variables and other person variables, and metacognitive regulation to ensure that cognitive goals are met.

Providing such metacognitive knowledge to the student has been done in the past. In [9, 4], the authors observe that weaker students typically have a poor metacognition, and are typically overconfident about their level of understanding. Further, Peirce [13] observes that understanding metacognition is important, as it affects motivation. Students who achieve good results tend to attribute the result to their abilities and effort, which in turn develops confidence in their abilities and promotes future success. On the other hand, students who achieve poor results may attribute their failure to their ability; this in turn results in reduced self-confidence for future tasks. Such students may also be unwilling to seek help from tutors and other support services, as they believe it will not be worth their effort. Such students may put little effort into future tasks so that they can attribute their failure to lack of effort and not lack of ability. Several strategies that can be initiated by the instructor to provide the student with the metacognitive knowledge about the understanding of the topic are discussed in [13], including the 1-minute paper [11].

Contributions: Our contributions in this paper include:

(a) We outline how to effectively incorporate metacognition in our courses, so that students are aware of their own level of understanding of the various topics in the course.

(b) We present large amounts of data obtained from exams for six different courses (both undergraduate and graduate level).

(c) We outline the benefits from incorporating metacognition to both the student, and to the instructor.

Outline: The rest of the paper is organized as follows. In Section 2, we describe our approach for incorporating metacognition into student learning, so that students and instructor are aware of the metacognitive knowledge of the students with regards to the understanding of various topics. In Section 3, we describe how we implemented our data gathering process, and some characteristics of the data. In Section 4, we present the results from our analysis of the data gathered from various courses, and Section 5 concludes this work.

2. APPROACH

As mentioned in the SIGCSE 2012 plenary session [2], the scarcest resource in a course is student time. We need to help the student gauge his/her level of understanding effectively; the student can then take the necessary steps to achieve the necessary cognitive goals. When a student receives a graded test back, the student may only examine the questions that he/she got incorrect. However, the premise that a correct answer indicates good understanding of the topic may not always be right; especially, for questions where the answer is known to be one of a set of choices, the student has a non-insignificant chance of getting the answer correct (could be as high as 50% if there are only two choices). It is worth noting that aggregating over several students gives the instructor a fairly accurate picture as to the level of understanding of the class as a whole for the various topics, even when the questions are multiple-choice questions.

To help the student gauge his/her level of understanding, we have incorporated metacognition as follows. For each question, we ask the student to specify their confidence level in their solution on a scale from [0, 10]. When a student gets a test back, he/she can look at the confidence level and the scores and look more closely at questions for which he/she had low confidence (irrespective of the score), because it indicates that the student does not have a satisfactory understanding of the topics for those questions; similarly a student can look at questions where he/she had low score and high confidence (indicating a gap in understanding). Now the students can use appropriate cognitive and metacognitive strategies to ensure that the cognitive goals are met.

However, a question we need to answer is whether the confidence values are an accurate measure of the metacognitive knowledge of the student. This will be the case if there is a significant positive correlation between the students' confidence levels and scores. We first did a basic analysis, where we used the students' reported confidence levels to come up with an overall expected score for each student, and compared it against the actual score obtained. We did this for the midterm exam in CS1 (that is based on the C++ programming language) in Fall 2011; 25 students reported their confidence levels. The graph is shown in Figure 1.

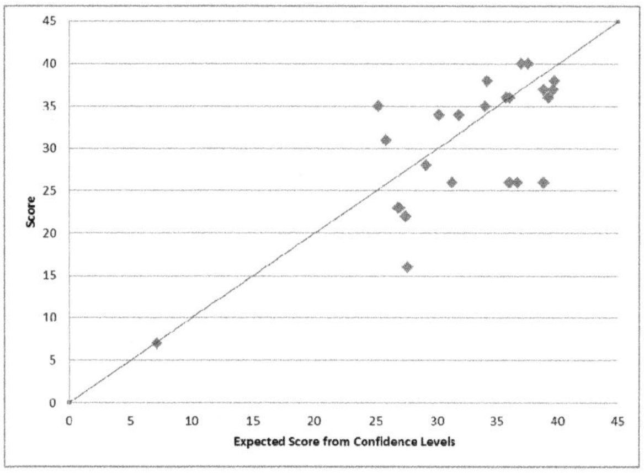

Figure 1. Score .vs. Expected Score from Confidence Levels for CS1, Midterm, Fall 2011

This figure shows an aggregate over all the questions for each student, and is largely as expected. First, we see that students with higher expected score (higher confidence levels) tend to have higher scores. Further, we see that students who have high scores tend to have their expected scores almost equal to their actual scores, whereas students who have low scores tend to have a bigger difference between their actual and expected scores. This is also reported by [4], where Dr. Chew argues that students who score higher tend to have a better metacognitive knowledge of their understanding of the topics. However, this need not be the rule and we may see students who score lower accurately predict their score with great accuracy. In Figure 1, the student with the lowest score (about 7) appears to have accurately predicted the score. Our detailed analysis (discussed below) show that this student's metacognitive knowledge is actually very low.

Incorporating this additional confidence level gives more feedback to the instructor as well. For instance, consider two questions for which the class did equally poorly; for one the students in the class had low confidence level and the other the students had high confidence level. The instructor may want to use different strategies to increase the students' learning for these two types of problems. For instance, self-learning by students most likely will not be effective for the second set of problems, whereas it could be considered for the first set of problems.

Let us consider two problems from the same midterm exam in CS1, Fall 2011.

Q1: `If integer variables a, b, c have the following values: a = 7, b = 4, c = 10, the expression a + b % c has the value 11. (Note: % has higher precedence than +) (Answer True/False)`

Q2: `What value of flag will be printed when the loop exits (in the cout statement)?`

```
bool flag = false;
while (!flag) {
    … // do something, update flag as needed
}
cout << flag << endl;
```

For both the above questions, the class had the same number of correct answers (31.03%). However, for the first question, the students had high confidence (reported expected score was 76.80%), and the second question, the students had low confidence (reported expected score was 52%). When we prepared the test, we expected that Q2 was much harder than Q1. If we look at Q1 more closely, we see that the problem is testing whether students understand the modulus (%) operator, as well as the meaning of precedence rules. But the fact that students have a high confidence in their understanding, but most got it incorrect, implies students believe they understand, but do not really understand at least one of % operator and precedence rules.

Confidence levels also provide other types of feedback to the instructor: for instance, "unexpected" low confidence levels reported by students might mean that the question is ambiguous or possibly even incorrect, or that the learning objectives necessary for answering the question have not been met.

However Figure 1 does not show the complete picture. For instance, consider a student who predicts a score of 0 for a question and gets 100% and predicts a score of 100% for a question and gets 0. This will be shown as an accurate prediction of the aggregate score. Similarly aggregating by questions also does not provide the complete picture. Instead, we need to do a detailed analysis on a problem-by-problem basis for each student. See Figure 2. When we do such a detailed analysis, we find that the student who had the lowest score (shown in Figure 1) did have lower metacognitive knowledge (this student had reported a confidence of 2 on the [0, 10] scale for almost all the questions).

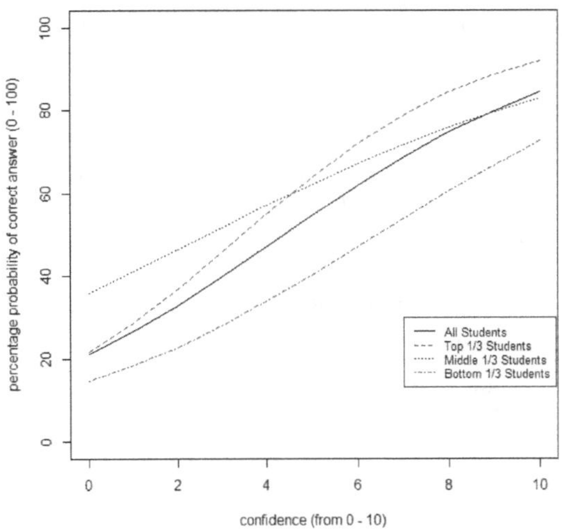

Figure 2. Predicted Scores for Various Student Groups for different Confidence Levels for CS1, Midterm, Fall 2011

We used logistic regression [8] to perform this analysis, which is used when there are only 2 possible scores (in our course the possible scores are 1 or 0, depending on whether the student answered the question correctly or not). We used repeated measurements model, where we had several measurements for each student (for different questions). We used glmer model available in the R statistical software, where we assume different baselines for different students, and we incorporate random effects due to different students using the default normal distribution. We expect the following: students who have an excellent metacognitive knowledge of their understanding will report a confidence of 0 for questions that they do not answer correctly, and will report a confidence of 10 for questions that they answer correctly. We divided the number of students into 3 groups. The top 1/3 students are those who got the top 1/3 scores when we consider the entire course (note this is based on the performance over the entire course and not based on only on the midterm performance). Similarly we had the middle 1/3 students and the bottom 1/3 students. We can see that in Figure 2, the top 1/3 students have greater accuracy than the middle 1/3 students when they answer incorrectly, and also when they answer correctly (because the predicted score for the top students is closer to 0 when they indicate a confidence level of 0, and their predicted score is closer to 100% when they indicate a confidence level of 10). More information about this data and also the results from other courses are described in Sections 3 and 4.

3. Implementation

We incorporated metacognition in a total of six different offerings of our courses over two semesters in the academic year 2011-2012. The courses and their descriptions are shown in table below. Note that two of the offerings were for the same course (Junior-Level Databases). For convenience, we will refer to the six course offerings as C-1 to C-6 from now on.

Semester	List of Courses	Level
Semester 1	CS1 (C++) (C-1)	Freshman
	Databases-I (C-3)	Junior
	Information Retrieval (C-5)	Graduate
Semester 2	Web Application Development (C-2)	Junior
	Databases-I (C-4)	Junior
	Databases-II (C-6)	Graduate

For each of these courses, the students reported their confidence levels on their solution to each exam question and each homework problem on a [0, 10] scale. Due to space constraints, we will consider only exams in this paper. There were two exams for each course, a midterm and a final. All the exams were conducted in class, and were open book, open notes. For CS1 and Web Application Development courses, there were only two outcomes for each question in the exam: 1 or 0 (depending on whether the student got the question right or not). For all the other courses, there were multiple possible outcomes for several questions, as a student can get partial credits and thus get a score anywhere from 0 to 100% (for these courses, we used linear regression with repeated measurements).

Reporting of the confidence levels was optional for the student, and not considered part of the grade. However most of the students reported their confidence levels for all the courses as shown below (a student who reported at least one confidence score is counted in rows 2 and 3). Also, note that the total number of measurements for each exam for a course is quite large; these numbers for C-1 and C-2 are larger because the questions are multiple-choice questions or deal with coming up with one answer (see example problems Q1 and Q2 discussed in Section 2). There were typically 40 questions on the midterm and 60 questions on the final, and all questions have equal weight. For the courses C3 – C6, there were larger problems in the exams, in addition to several short answer and multiple choice questions.

	C-1	C-2	C-3	C-4	C-5	C-6
Total # of students	28	22	29	25	27	26
# students reporting confidence level (midterm)	24	21	26	24	24	26
# students reporting confidence level (final)	24	20	26	23	24	25
Total # of student-questions with confidence (midterm)	1032	804	482	547	366	679
Total # of student-questions with confidence (final)	1318	1263	770	703	538	674

The data was entered and maintained on an excel spreadsheet. We record for each student, the score for the problem and the confidence level reported by the student (whenever it was reported). The instructor used the confidence levels to discuss the exams when they were returned. Once all the data was entered for the entire course, we analyzed the data using R statistical computing package (http://cran.r-project.org/); for this analysis we utilized the assistance of statisticians available at our university.

4. Results from our Analysis

Let us now examine the results of analyzing the data we have gathered from the various courses. For space considerations, we show only the results from analyzing data for three courses (C-1, C-2 and C-3). C-4 is another offering of C-3 and the analysis results looks similar to that of C-3, and hence we will skip the discussion completely. For the two graduate courses, C-5 and C-

6, again the analysis looks similar to that of C3, and hence we skip their discussion; instead we show only the aggregated data.

4.1 C-1: CS1 using C++

Let us examine the CS1 midterm data first. As mentioned earlier, we divided the set of students into three groups: Top 1/3, Middle 1/3 and Bottom 1/3, based on their performance for the whole class. This was done so that we can compare the same set of students over different tests for a course. For each question, a student either gets a 1 or 0 (depending on whether the student answered the question correctly or not). If we look at the table below, we can see that for the Top 1/3 students, for each confidence level > 3, they have correct answers for at least 50% of the questions (in aggregate). Middle 1/3 students have at least 50% of the questions correct for each confidence level > 4, and Bottom 1/3 students have at least 50% of the questions correct for each confidence level > 8.

	Top 1/3		Middle 1/3		Bottom 1/3		Total	
Confidence \ Score	0	1	0	1	0	1	0	1
0	0	0	1	0	16	2	17	2
1	1	0	1	1	10	3	12	4
2	0	2	0	4	33	7	33	13
3	2	1	1	4	2	7	5	12
4	5	5	4	3	0	1	9	9
5	3	3	11	10	27	10	41	23
6	4	10	3	7	4	3	11	20
7	6	23	10	24	6	12	22	59
8	7	30	5	22	18	16	30	68
9	3	61	13	33	19	34	35	128
10	17	161	32	155	26	88	75	404

We have already discussed the analysis results of the midterm data (Figure 2); let us now examine how the different sets of students performed in the final. We aggregate the different confidence levels for space considerations, and this is shown below.

	Top 1/3		Middle 1/3		Bottom 1/3		Total	
Confidence \ Score	0	1	0	1	0	1	0	1
0 – 3	10	9	35	20	70	15	115	44
4 – 7	60	64	104	63	89	75	253	202
8 - 10	72	231	81	138	80	102	233	471

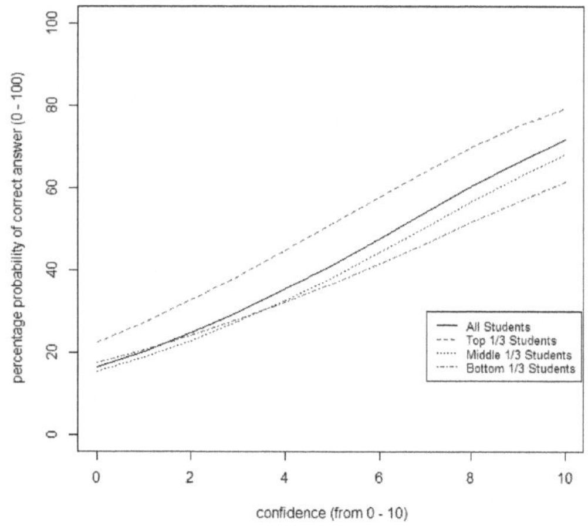

Figure 3. Predicted Scores for CS1, Final, Semester 1

The topics for this final exam included arrays, functions, pass by value and reference and pointers. Further, we believe that the exam turned out to be a hard exam, and students overall had lower scores. The models for the three groups of students are shown in Figure 3. For the top students, the model predicts their score as 22.40% when they report a confidence of 0, and a score of 79.47% when they report a confidence of 10. On the other hand, for the middle 1/3 students, the scores predicted by the model for confidence levels of 0 and 10 are 15.26% and 68.24%, for the bottom 1/3 students, these scores are 17.58% and 61.42% respectively. Again, we can see that the weaker students tend to expect a higher score than what they actually get.

4.2 C-2: Web Application Development

The midterm data is shown below, and we can see that the top 1/3 students had overall very few incorrect answers.

	Top 1/3		Middle 1/3		Bottom 1/3		Total	
Confidence \ Score	0	1	0	1	0	1	0	1
0 – 3	0	0	4	11	1	2	5	13
4 – 7	7	43	35	78	42	69	84	190
8 - 10	7	216	16	110	22	137	45	463

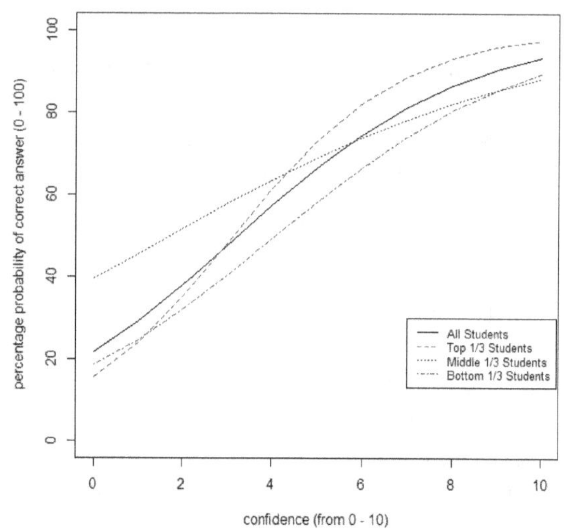

Figure 4. Predicted Scores for C-2, Midterm, Semester 2

When we look at the model in Figure 4, we see that the Top 1/3 students have better metacognitive knowledge about what they know and also about what they do not know: they get closer to 0 when they expect a 0, and get closer to 100% when they expect a 100%, when compared with the rest of the students.

The final exam for C-2 also shows a similar story (Figure 5).

	Top 1/3		Middle 1/3		Bottom 1/3		Total	
Confidence \ Score	0	1	0	1	0	1	0	1
0 – 3	3	0	21	35	17	5	41	40
4 – 7	19	60	57	72	80	75	156	207
8 - 10	32	330	50	201	43	160	125	691

4.3 C-3: Databases-I

Let us now examine a course, undergraduate level databases, where each question had multiple possible outcomes for the score (student can obtain partial credit for some questions). Here, we see that students might have low confidence because some part of

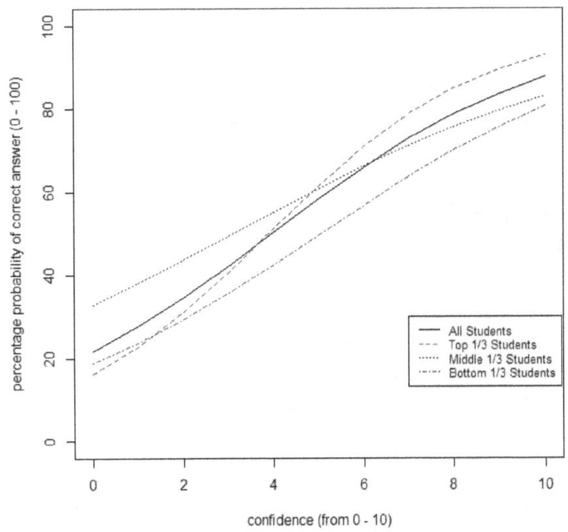

Figure 5. Predicted Scores for C-2, Final, Semester 2

the answer is incorrect; however, their actual score will be higher than their expected score.

Confidence \ Score	Top 1/3			Middle 1/3			Bottom 1/3			Total		
	[0,30]	(30,70]	(70,100]	[0,30]	(30,70]	(70,100]	[0,30]	(30,70]	(70,100]	[0,30]	(30,70]	(70,100]
0-3	0	0	0	0	0	0	2	0	2	2	0	2
4-7	9	0	32	25	1	46	23	10	33	57	11	111
8-10	7	0	104	16	2	83	14	4	69	37	6	256

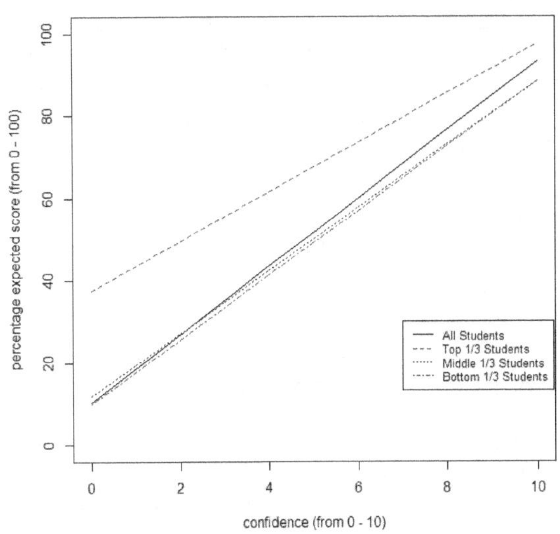

Figure 6. Predicted Scores for C-3, Midterm, Semester 1

For this analysis, we used linear regression model (as the number of outcomes is more than two) with repeated measurements for each student, as shown in Figure 6. Here, top students are expected to score 97.45% which is more than other students (the bottom students and the middle students are expected to score about 88%) when they all report a confidence level of 100%. When the top students, middle students and bottom students report a confidence of 0, their expected scores are 37.51%, 11.84% and 9.80% respectively. We believe this relatively high expected score when top students report 0 confidence is because of partial points that are given, and because the instructor was lenient and gave high partial points. This seems to indicate that top students who have low confidence get closer to the solution (and hence they get more partial points) than other students.

Similar to midterm, the models for the final exam also seem to indicate partial points even when the confidence level is 0. Again, the top students are expected to get higher score than the rest of the students for all confidence levels. The data is shown below and the models are shown in Figure 7.

Confidence \ Score	Top 1/3			Middle 1/3			Bottom 1/3			Total		
	[0,30]	(30,70]	(70,100]	[0,30]	(30,70]	(70,100]	[0,30]	(30,70]	(70,100]	[0,30]	(30,70]	(70,100]
0-3	1	2	4	2	9	20	5	4	7	8	15	31
4-7	8	6	33	29	18	64	37	50	65	74	74	162
8-10	12	8	155	23	18	86	24	18	56	59	44	297

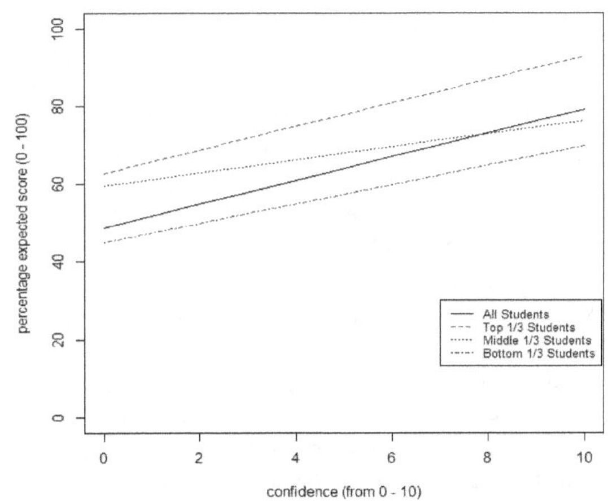

Figure 7. Predicted Scores for C-3, Final, Semester 1

Even though we have analyzed the data from the other three courses, we omit showing the results due to lack of space. For C-4 (which is another offering of C-3), and for C-5 and C-6 (which are graduate level courses), the possible scores for a question are not just 1 or 0, but can be one of several outcomes similar to that of the C-3 course. However, it is worth noting that the results of data analysis for these courses are very similar to what we observed for course C-3. Below, we show the summary data for midterm and final exams for the two graduate level courses in the order: C-5 midterm, C-5 final, C-6 midterm and C-6 final.

Confidence \ Score	Top 1/3			Middle 1/3			Bottom 1/3			Total		
	[0,30]	(30,70]	(70,100]	[0,30]	(30,70]	(70,100]	[0,30]	(30,70]	(70,100]	[0,30]	(30,70]	(70,100]
0-3	0	0	0	0	1	2	3	0	0	3	1	2
4-7	3	3	18	3	3	21	2	4	22	8	10	61
8-10	2	3	98	5	14	68	11	7	73	18	24	239

Confidence \ Score	Top 1/3			Middle 1/3			Bottom 1/3			Total		
	[0,30]	(30,70]	(70,100]	[0,30]	(30,70]	(70,100]	[0,30]	(30,70]	(70,100]	[0,30]	(30,70]	(70,100]
0-3	0	0	0	0	1	0	1	0	0	1	1	0
4-7	2	4	18	1	6	27	7	11	15	10	21	60
8-10	4	16	141	8	27	119	9	21	100	21	64	360

	Top 1/3			Middle 1/3			Bottom 1/3			Total		
Score / Confidence	[0,30]	(30,70]	(70,100]	[0,30]	(30,70]	(70,100]	[0,30]	(30,70]	(70,100]	[0,30]	(30,70]	(70,100]
0 – 3	0	1	2	0	0	2	0	0	0	0	1	4
4 – 7	9	5	37	22	8	55	19	12	27	50	25	119
8 - 10	22	7	130	31	10	95	39	20	126	92	37	351

	Top 1/3			Middle 1/3			Bottom 1/3			Total		
Score / Confidence	[0,30]	(30,70]	(70,100]	[0,30]	(30,70]	(70,100]	[0,30]	(30,70]	(70,100]	[0,30]	(30,70]	(70,100]
0 – 3	0	0	8	3	6	6	2	6	1	5	12	15
4 – 7	5	4	37	14	18	68	18	25	28	37	47	133
8 - 10	4	10	170	6	17	104	21	29	64	31	56	338

5. CONCLUSIONS AND FUTURE WORK

In this paper, we discussed incorporating metacognitive skills, especially metacognitive knowledge about the understanding of the topics of the course. Such metacognitive knowledge can be incorporated effectively in a course by asking the student to report their confidence levels for different assignments and tests, and by analyzing these reported confidence levels. As we have gathered this information from six different course offerings that we have taught, we are able to perform analysis of the data and come to several meaningful conclusions. Both students and instructors benefit from such metacognitive knowledge: a student can effectively manage his/her time to meet the cognitive goals; an instructor can choose appropriate strategies when the necessary learning outcomes are not being met. Further, unexpected low confidence reported by students for an individual problem may indicate issues with the problem, such as ambiguity, that the instructor may have overlooked.

We also discussed how the data about confidence levels may be analyzed. For tests where every problem has only two outcomes (correct or incorrect), the confidence levels can be analyzed by using logistic regression with repeated measurements for each student. For tests where partial credits are given (more than two outcomes), linear regression with repeated measurements can be used. However, partial credits appear to impact the correlation between confidence levels and score in more ways than desired. A student who does not understand the last step of a problem, and a student who does not understand the first step of a problem may both report low confidence levels; however, the first student will get higher partial score. As part of future work, we plan to take tests where some problems have two outcomes and some problems have more than two outcomes (like tests for courses C3 – C6), and perform separate analyses on the two sets of problems.

There are several avenues for future work. As mentioned, we already have data about the confidence levels in the homework questions. In this paper, we looked only at the confidence levels of exam questions; incorporating homework questions might give a good indication of how students are progressing over the course with regards to their metacognitive skills. An extension of this is to monitor the student's metacognitive skills over formative assessments in the course, which can again indicate how the student's metacognitive skills are improving over the duration of the course. A major extension of this is to consider how the student is progressing over his entire degree program by monitoring his metacognitive skills over different classes. Other factors to consider are whether we can obtain the student's metacognitive knowledge in non-exam environments, as an exam setting could be threatening to a student; also whether we can obtain more qualitative data about how a student feels about the whole process. From an ease-of-use point of view, we can consider providing easily usable data entry interfaces and data analysis tools; for instance reporting and analyzing such data can be integrated into blackboard.

6. ACKNOWLEDGMENTS

Our thanks to the statistics consultants at UM Flint and at CSCAR for their tremendous help.

7. REFERENCES

[1] Borkowski, J., Carr, M., and Pressley, M. *Spontaneous Strategy Use: Perspectives from Metacognitive Theory*, Intelligence, 11, 61-75, 1987.

[2] Brooks Jr, F. P., *The Teacher's Job is to Design Learning Experiences; Not Primarily to Impart Information*, Plenary Session, ACM SIGCSE, 2012.

[3] Brown, A. L., *Metacognition, Executive Control, Self-Regulation and other Mysterious Mechanisms*, F. E. Weinart and R. H. Kluwe (Eds.) Metacognition, motivation and understanding, 65-116, 1987.

[4] Chew, S., *How to Get the Most Out of Studying: A Video Series*, Retrieved December 11, 2012 from http://www.samford.edu/how-to-study/

[5] Flavell, J. H., *Metacognitive Aspects of Problem Solving*, The Nature of Intelligence, 231-236, 1976.

[6] Flavell, J. H., *Metacognition and Cognitive Monitoring: A New Area of Cognitive-Developmental Enquiry*, American Psychologist, 34, 1979.

[7] Hartman, H. J., *Metacognition in Learning and Instruction: Theory, Research and Practice*, Dodrecht: Kluwer Academic Publishers, 2001.

[8] Kleinbaum, D. G., Kupper, L. L., Nizam, A., and Muller, K. E. *Applied Regression Analysis and Other Multivariable Methods*, Duxbury Press, 2007.

[9] Lang, J. M., *Metacognition and Student Learning*, The Chronicle of Higher Education, 2012.

[10] Livingston, J., *Metacognition: An Overview*, 1997, Retrieved December 11, 2012 from http://gse.buffalo.edu/fas/shuell/cep564/metacog.htm

[11] Lucas, G., *Initiating Student-Teacher Contact via Personalized Responses to One-Minute Papers*, College Teaching, 58 (2), 39-42, 2010.

[12] Mazumder, Q. H., and Ainsworth, A., *Metacognition Strategies to Improve Confidence and Academic Performance of First Year Engineering Students*, American Society for Engineering Education, North Central Section Conference, April 1-2, 2011, Midland, Michigan, USA.

[13] Peirce, W., *Metacognition: Study Strategies, Monitoring and Motivation*, Workshop presented at Price George's Community College, 2004. Retrieved Dec 11, 2012 from http://academic.pg.cc.md.us/~wpeirce/MCCCTR/metacognition.htm

Teaching Computer Science Soft Skills as Soft Concepts

Orit Hazzan
Department of Education in Technology and Science
Technion – Israel Institute of Technology
Haifa, 32000
Israel
oritha@technion.ac.il

Gadi Har-Shai
Department of Education in Technology and Science
Technion – Israel Institute of Technology
Haifa, 32000
Israel
gadi.harshai@gmail.com

ABSTRACT

In this paper, we describe a course on computer science and software engineering soft skills offered by the Department of Computer Science (CS) at the Technion – Israel Institute of Technology. The course was developed in response to a call by the Israeli hi-tech industry to equip the Technion's CS graduates with such skills. This request actually reflects the industry's recognition of the importance of soft skills in software development processes, not only on the managerial level, but also among software team members. The paper describes the course and aims to deliver the message that like soft *concepts* of computer science (e.g., abstraction and readability), which cannot be imparted rigidly using formal definitions, soft *skills* too cannot be studied and taught formally and, rather, should be learned and grasped gradually over a certain period of time, based on students' engagement, active learning, and reflection. Furthermore, students must accept such soft skills as concepts that can neither be defined formally nor evaluated adequately.

Categories and Subject Descriptors

K.3.0 [**Computing Milieux**]: Computers and Education – *General.*

Keywords

Soft skills, teamwork, reflection, diversity, communication, time management, ethics.

1. INTRODUCTION

This paper describes a course offered by the Technion's Department of Computer Science (CS) to undergraduate CS students. According to a report by an international review committee, which reviewed the department in May 2008, "The Technion's Computer Science Faculty is an excellent department of computer science, comparable to the top ten in the United States"[1]. In 2011, it was ranked 15th in the Academic Ranking of World Universities in CS (Shanghai ranking)[2].

The Department is the second largest academic unit in the Technion, with about 1,300 undergraduate students (about one-eighth of the total number of Technion students) and over 200 graduate students. Its 50 or so faculty members are of international repute and have expertise in a wide variety of fields. The faculty's main areas of research are CS theory, systems, artificial intelligence, intelligent systems, and scientific computation.

The Technion's Department of CS is also the largest CS department in Israel, supplying the Israeli hi-tech industry with its most talented graduates. Thus, it can be argued that the department played a central role in Israel's becoming *The Startup Nation* (Senor and Singer, 2009). The department's unique standing with the Israeli hi-tech industry enables structured interaction between the department and the Israeli and international hi-tech industries. As part of this interaction, calls have been received from several high-tech companies for the department to equip its graduates not only with excellent scientific and engineering skills, but also with soft skills, such as teamwork, interpersonal communication skills, and presentation skills.

The course described in this paper was designed especially for CS students as a response to this call[3]. The course, which is given by the Technion's Department of Education in Technology and Science, was designed so as, first, to expose the students to a variety of soft skills, and second, to enable them to acquire these skills gradually by experiencing them and reflecting upon them. In addition, the close acquaintance of the course instructor and TA with the software industry enabled them to teach the course within various practical contexts and share real-life situations with the students.

In this paper we first present the nature of soft CS skills. Then, we describe the course schedule (taught in the 2012 Spring semester) as well as the teaching principles applied in the course. Finally, we show how, during the course, the students gradually constructed a mental perception of soft CS skills.

2. BACKGROUND

We first describe the concept of soft CS *concepts* in general and soft CS *skills* in particular. Then, we elaborate on existing courses

[1] See: https://www.cs.technion.ac.il/about/

[2] See: http://www.shanghairanking.com/SubjectCS2011.html

[3] The Department of CS approached the first author of the paper, a researcher of human aspects of software engineering with a long and deep acquaintance with the Israeli hi-tech industry, to teach the course. The second author of the paper, who was the course TA, has over 20 years of managerial experience in international hi-tech companies, in product development, business development, and global customer support.

SIGCSE'13, March 6–9, 2013, Denver, Colorado, USA.

on soft CS skills and explain the uniqueness of the course described in this paper.

2.1 Soft CS Concepts

According to Hazzan (2008), a soft idea is a concept that can be neither rigidly nor formally defined, nor is it possible to guide students as to its precise application. Indeed, how can stepwise refinement be presented formally? How can one outline a list of "How to" actions to find a good algorithm? And how can the transition between different levels of abstraction be taught formally? To grasp the essence of soft ideas and the way in which they differ from rigid concepts, it is sufficient to compare the answers to the above questions with answers to questions such as: Is it possible to formulate the syntax of a programming language? What is the formal definition of a heap?

That said, it should be noted that CS concepts are in fact neither soft nor rigid; each CS concept has some soft aspects and some rigid aspects. Nevertheless, some CS concepts, such as the ones mentioned above, lend themselves to be softer than other.

2.2 Soft CS Skills

According to Sukhoo *et al.* (2005) "Soft skills [...] is concerned with managing and working with people, ensuring customer satisfaction with the intention of retaining them and creating a conducive environment for the project team to deliver high quality products within budget and on time and exceeding stakeholders expectations." (p. 693-694)

Like soft CS *concepts*, soft CS *skills* cannot be formally defined or instructed. This stems from the fact that the expression of soft skills depends, among other factors, on the individual's personality and on the specific human interaction in which that individual is involved.

A fast Google search suffices to reveal that almost all problems associated with software development processes are connected to people (mainly customers and team members) and that their origin is rooted not in technological aspects but in cognitive and social aspects – i.e., the expression of soft skills.

It is suggested that since software is an intangible product, the importance attributed to soft skills in CS is indeed crucial. This, combined with the fact that software is often produced by distributed teams, opens room for a great deal of interpretation and misunderstanding. Enhanced communication is, therefore, vital for the success of software projects. As it turns out, the intangibility of software influences almost all activities conducted during software development processes. For example, the fact that software is an intangible entity limits our ability to use our senses to communicate software-related issues, increasing the importance of *verbal* communication between teammates and between teammates and customers. In addition, when a software team develops a software project, i.e. an intangible product, it is harder to build trust among teammates since the actual status of the project is not always transparent. This lack of trust in turn influences communications between teammates and consequently impacts and hampers the development process.

2.3 Courses on Soft CS skills

The contents of the course described in this paper comply with the recommendations of the ACM/IEEE-CS Computer Science Curricula 2013 - Strawman draft[4].

> The education that undergraduates in Computer Science receive must adequately prepare them for the workforce in a more holistic way than simply conveying technical facts. Indeed, "soft skills" (such as teamwork and communication) and personal attributes (such as identification of opportunity and risk) play a critical role in the workplace. Successfully applying technical knowledge in practice often requires an ability to tolerate ambiguity and work well with others from different backgrounds and disciplines. These overarching considerations are important for promoting successful professional practice in a variety of career paths. (p. 11)

In practice, however, not many courses on soft skills are offered. Following are several examples of courses which are offered by other institutions and universities.

- Carnegie-Mellon, School of Computer Science: Courses *17-656/7 Communications for Software Engineers I*[5] *and II*[6]. These seminars are designed for graduate students in software engineering. Technical communication experts introduce principles and approaches for writing and speaking effectively, and students practice writing, speaking, and listening skills.
- MIT, Electrical Engineering and Computer Science: Course *6.982J Teaching College-Level Science and Engineering*[7]. This seminar focuses on the knowledge and skills needed to teach science and engineering in institution of higher education. Topics include theories of adult learning; course development; promoting active learning, problem solving, and critical thinking in students; communicating with a diverse student body; using educational technology to further learning; lecturing; creating effective tests and assignments; and assessment and evaluation.
- Berkeley, Electrical Engineering and Computer Sciences: Course *301 Teaching Techniques for Computer Science*[8]. This course discusses and practices techniques for effective teaching, focusing on issues most relevant to teaching assistants in computer science courses.
- A course on Fred Brooks' seminal book *"The Mythical Man-Month"* (1975). Port and Klappholz (2006) describe a course they taught to both graduate and undergraduate students of software engineering at multiple universities. The course is based on Brooks' established classic on software engineering – *The Mythical Man-Month.* The course was designed to educate students to appreciate and practice the fundamentals of the field. Specific objectives include the concept of project risk, the reasons people and months are not interchangeable, and the impact of non-technical issues, such as communications, overhead, training, integration of parts, and staffing profiles on the effort required to complete a project.

As is explained and exemplified in the next section, the uniqueness of the course described in this paper is in (a) the special attention devoted to the concept of soft skills and to its characteristics; (b) the wide range of soft CS skills addressed both theoretically and practically in the context of the hi-tech industry.

[4] See: http://cs2013.org/strawman-draft/cs2013-strawman.pdf

[5] See: http://msc.isri.cmu.edu/software-engineering/Courses/17-656-communication-for-software-engineers-i.html

[6] See: http://msc.isri.cmu.edu/software-engineering/Courses/17-657-communication-for-software-engineers-ii.html

[7] See: http://student.mit.edu/catalog/m6c.html

[8] See: http://general-catalog.berkeley.edu/catalog/gcc_list_crse_req?p_dept_name=Electrical+Engineering+and+Computer+Sciences&p_dept_cd=EECS&p_path=*

3. COURSE DESCRIPTION

3.1 Course Structure

The course was taught during the 2012 Spring semester and lasted 14 weeks. Each weekly session consisted of 3 academic hours (150 minutes). The course was held at the Department of Education in Technology and Science, which is approximately a 10-minute in-campus walk from the Department of CS[9]. Twenty-four students were enrolled in the course.

Since this was the first time this course was being offered at the Technion, the course was continuously developed in parallel with its teaching so as to adapt its contents to the specific teaching situation. Table 1 outlines the final course schedule.

As can be seen, each session highlighted one soft skill, but other soft skills were addressed as well. For example, although reflective processes were fostered in most sessions, either individually or in teams, reflection was the "official" topic of two sessions (Nos. 5 and 7), in which other soft skills were naturally applied as well (such as diversity and time management).

Table 1. Course Schedule

Session	Topic
1	Introduction – soft *concepts* in CS
2	Feedback skills
3	Diversity
4	Simulation of an international software company
5	Reflection in teams
6	Change management and time management.
7	Time management (cont.) The reflective practitioner's perspective: Reflection on the individual level
8	Business writing – email and more
9	Business writing – email and more (cont.) Midterm summary – Part I: Elicitation of students' questions
10	Midterm summary – Part II: Answering students' questions Conflicts in teamwork Characteristics of soft skills Collaboration and reward in teamwork
11	Collaboration and reward in teamwork (cont.) Guest lecturer Basic principles of effective presentations
12	Knowledge transfer in global companies Ethics of software engineering
13	Guest lecturer Ethics of software engineering (cont.)
14	Summary: Students' suggestions for topics to be included in a second, consecutive course on soft skills

3.2 Evaluation

Homework assignments were given on alternating two weeks during the semester (Weeks Nos. 1, 3, 5, 7, 9, 11, 13) and had to be submitted within two weeks each. In addition, a final assignment was submitted one month after the end of the semester.

To enable the students to construct the concept of soft skills gradually, each homework assignment included at least one task that related explicitly to soft skills; such tasks were given even before the term *soft skill* was defined *by the students* towards the end of the course[10]. For example, in the 4th homework assignment, students were asked to specify which soft skills they wished to learn during the remainder of the semester.

Attendance in the course was compulsory and the final grade was composed as follows:

- 75% - average grade of top 5 homework assignments (out of 7)
- 25% - final assignment[11]

3.3 Teaching principles

We elaborate on two types of teaching principles employed in the course. The first includes general teaching principles, which are highly relevant for this course, and the second type are soft skills themselves.

3.3.1 General teaching principles

3.3.1.1 Active learning

Active learning is widely accepted nowadays as a quality form of education. According to Silberman (1996), in active learning "students need to 'do it' – figure things out by themselves, come up with examples, try out skills, and do assignments that depend on the knowledge they already have or must acquire".

Active learning is especially suitable for the soft skills course for several reasons, among which we mention three. First, according to constructivist educators (Davis et al. 1990; Smith et al., 1993, Ben Ari 2001), learning is an active rather than passive process of acquiring ideas and constructing knowledge. In other words, learning requires the individual to be active and to engage in his or her own construction of mental models (in our case, the CS students' mental construction of soft skills). We suggest that experience is highly important in this process, since soft skills require sensitivity in order to apply them effectively, depending on the given situation. Second, active learning enables the CS students to work on tasks that enhance high-order thinking skills, such as case study analysis and synthesis, which are highly relevant for the successful implementation of soft skills in software projects. Finally, active learning provides students with a great opportunity to interact with one another, which in itself requires the application of important soft skills.

3.3.1.2 Semi-situated learning

Since the CS students who attended the course were either already working part time in the hi-tech industry or planned to work in this industry after completing their bachelor's degree, we made it a point to constantly relate the course topics to real-world situations. To that end, we tried, as much as possible, to apply situated

[9] In the second session of the course, students admitted that the fact that the course was held at a different location (than the Department of CS) contributed to the legitimization they needed to experience and express skills which are not always required in other CS courses.

[10] In the spirit of active learning and constructivist (see below), we did not define the concept of soft skills at any time during the semester. Rather, when the students asked for a definition of the concept, we put the question in context and let them explore the question themselves.

[11] Towards the end of the semester, the students were asked to suggest their preferred topics for the final assignment. Based on the 10 options offered by the students, we presented 6 options and each student had to work on one of them.

learning, which means that knowledge is presented in an authentic context and learning is based on social interaction and collaboration (Lave and Wenger, 1991).

Specifically, situated learning was applied by holding open discussions, giving examples of real cases, encouraging students to reflect on their own experiences, facilitating activities with real software teams, and role-playing and simulating real life situations. For example, in the fourth session of the course the students simulated an international software company, *GO*, which was established in 2012 in order to develop the best electronic wallet in the world within 18 months. The class was divided into three groups – customers, a development team and a marketing team. The students' task was to understand the potential customers' needs, translate them into a work plan, and manage the process. Students were required to observe several rules, such as the requirement that each group must speak two languages and that communications between groups must be electronic only, unless team members "fly" and meet face to face. Each 5 minutes in class was equivalent to one real-life month and since the given time for the project was 18 month, this exercise lasted 90 minutes. While almost completely avoiding the use of email and "flights", the students' engagement in this session was reflected by their use of a variety of electronic communication channels: Facebook, video cameras, Skype, smart phones, and presentations.

3.3.2 *Soft skills teaching principles*

The second group of teaching principles we employed in the course reflects the actual soft skills that were taught. Due to space limitations, we illustrate only three such teaching principles. Additional teaching principles, such as metaphor and feedback, were also applied.

3.3.2.1 *Teamwork*

Since work processes in hi-tech organizations, in which students often are employed, are performed mostly in teams, teamwork should be practiced in the course. Teamwork is also an accepted pedagogical method for the implementation of the general teaching principles mentioned above, namely active learning and situated learning. Thus, the importance attributed to soft skills in teamwork is highlighted, practiced, and reflected upon during the course.

3.3.2.2 *Reflection*

Reflective practitioners are professionals who continuously improve their professional skills based on their on-going reflection with respect to their professional performance, either while or after accomplishing a specific task (Schön 1983, 1987). Reflection was encouraged in the course in two main ways: (a) most homework assignments required students to reflect on what they had learned in the previous lessons; and (b) one stage of most class activities was dedicated to a reflective examination of the activity performance on the team level. For example, following the simulation of GO company in the 4th session, the 5th session began with a reflection on that simulation. Furthermore, the students were asked in their homework to reflect *on the reflection* conducted in class, that is, to practice the skill of meta-reflection. Two additional sessions in the course were dedicated to reflective processes in software development processes: Session No. 5 – reflection on the team level and Session No. 7 – reflection on the individual level.

3.3.2.3 *Diversity*

Recent years have seen an increase in the attention given to diversity by the hi-tech industry. This attention can be partially explained by the fact that diversity enhances and promotes the use of soft skills, such as teamwork, time management, negotiation, and presentation skills, both on the individual level and on the team level.

Specifically, since soft skills are implemented differently by different people (according to the individual's personality and skills) and should be implemented differently according to the specific circumstances, no one person can successfully implement them all in the myriad of possible situations encountered in the changing world. Thus, diversity not only sharpens each team member's sensitivity to different kinds of people, but also compensates for the individual's limitations in successfully expressing all soft skills in all possible situations.

Based on the acknowledgment that diversity fosters the implementation of soft skills, its importance was recognized in different sessions throughout the course, in a variety of learning situations. We also dedicated the third session of the course specifically to diversity. As it turns out, students' awareness to diversity from the early stages of the course developed their performance of a variety of soft skills and enhanced their understanding of the concept of soft skills. This awareness was reflected, for example, in the presentations the students prepared when asked to consider different kinds of audiences.

4. STUDENTS GRADUAL CONSTRUCTION OF SOFT CS SKILLS

In this section we illustrate students' gradual mental construction of the concept of soft CS skills. We base our description on class observations, homework assignments, and occasional talks with the students. Table 2 presents four main stages of the gradual understanding we aim to illustrate. In our talk we present a more complete description of the learning process.

Table 2. Stages in Students' Mental Construction of Soft Skills

Stage	Students' conception of soft skills
1	Students distinguish between soft skills and the skills acquired during their studies at the Department of CS
2	students *characterize* soft skills
3	Students *rank* soft skills
4	Students *define* the concept of a soft skill

Stage 1: Students distinguish between soft skills and the skills acquired during their studies at the Department of CS

We illustrate the students' perceptions of soft skills at the earlier stages of the course using their answers to the following two homework assignments (out of 5), submitted during the third week of the course:

a. Specify 3-5 reasons that caused you to enroll in the course.
b. Specify 3-5 ways in which, in your opinion, the course will contribute to you in the future.

As can be seen, the questions did not explicitly ask the students to address soft skills. Nevertheless, most of the students did address soft skills in their answers, mainly quoting those listed in the notice sent to them by the CS department in which they were encouraged to enroll in the course (e.g., presentations, teamwork, and ethics).

Students' perceptions of soft skills at this stage of the course reflect differences they observed between what they usually learn in the Department of CS and the topics they expect to study in the course. In other words, at this stage the students perceived soft skills as skills that *differ* in some sense from the skills they acquired elsewhere in the Department of CS. Here are several examples of students' answers to the above questions, which reflect this observation:

- A desire to deal with things other than writing code all the day.
- My studies at the department [of CS] prepared me for the technological challenges I am expected to deal with, and this course will prepare me for the many soft challenges I will face.
- [I enrolled in the course] to experience learning of a different kind, to get out of the equations and code segments [and] into a different content world, to a collective learning experience with active discussions, presentations, etc.
- From a professional perspective, the course can enhance my attention and awareness to soft topics in the field [of CS] as they were presented to us in the first [two] sessions. Sometimes, we don't even think about specific topics because we assume they have nothing to do with us [...], only out of a lack of awareness. The fact that the course develops [our] attention to these subjects and says "Guys! There are other things beside the compiler!" indeed awakes us and opens the mind.
- Despite the fact that the course is taught in a different format than that used in other courses [...], it is still connected to the field [of CS], but from a different perspective.

Stage 2: Students characterize soft skills

As mentioned earlier, students were not presented with a definition of the concept of soft skills; rather they were requested, in the homework assignment submitted in the fifth week, to list 5 soft skills that they learned in the course so far and, for each soft skill, to explain why it is a soft skill.

Among the soft skills the students mentioned were: give and get feedback, time management, teamwork, listening, sensitivity to the environment, negotiation, and presentation skills.

To illustrate this stage of the students' mental construction of the concept of soft skills, we focus on the characteristics of soft skills specified by the students when asked to explain why a specific skill is soft. According to students' answers, *a soft skill*

- cannot be measured (or defined by a formula)
- depends on the individual's personality
- can be implemented in different ways
- should be implemented differently in different situations according to the specific circumstances
- is developed gradually.

Table 3 illustrates these characteristics using different soft skills to which the students referred in their answers.

Stage 3: Students rank soft skills

This stage of the students' conception of soft skills was identified by students' answers to the following questions:

a. List 5 soft skills that, in your opinion, are important in teamwork. For each soft skill, explain why it is a soft skill and why it is important for teamwork.

b. Rate the 5 skills you mentioned above according to their contribution to teamwork. Explain your rating.

These homework assignments were given before teamwork was addressed as the main topic of a session (Sessions Nos. 10 and 11; see Table 1); at this stage of the course, however, the students had already worked in teams many times and had a sense of what teamwork is about.

Table 3. Students' Characterizations of Soft Skills

Cannot be measured
- *Time and pressure management* is a soft skill since it cannot be measured precisely with absolute numbers. - *Sensitivity to the environment* is not a measurable characteristic. It is a characteristic that when present can be recognized clearly. - *Creativity* is a soft skill since it is a personal capability that is difficult to measure and evaluate objectively.
Depends on the individual's personality
- *Problem-solving skills* are soft skills because their development requires certain personal characteristics: one must know when to suggest the solution, how to promote it, and how to manage it. - *Communication* between one person and another is very different from the communication between that same person and another, third person, since it depends on the personalities of each of the persons involved.
Can be implemented in different ways
- There is no one way to present a presentation/specific content/ lecture. Each person is different and so will choose a different way of presentation. This is what makes *abstraction and creativity capability* a soft skill. - A *soft skill* (in my opinion) is something that characterizes the "inside" of each individual person. And because people are different, there is no unique way to perform these said skills, unlike rigid skills that, in my opinion, define clear limits.
Should be implemented differently in different situations according to the specific circumstances
- *Teamwork* is a soft skill because a person's behavior in one team differs from that same person's behavior in another team and depends, in each case, on the other team members and on the task, and it [...] cannot be known a-priori. - *Teamwork* is not something that can be explained [...]. The range of possibilities is infinite. We can join different teams, [which work on] different projects, in different situations and periods in our lives. *Adaptation to teamwork* is, therefore, a soft skill to which it is very important to be open, to know it exists, and to try to learn from each experience of working in a new team.
Is developed gradually
- *Feedback* is not something that can be learned using equations and the like. It is a capability that can be developed and in order to be successful, it should be practiced. - *The ability to examine known subjects from different perspectives* is a soft skill since it contributes to the person's professional development without teaching the person a new programming language or mathematical equation.

Table 4 presents soft skills that were mentioned by at least 25% of the students as being important for teamwork. It also specifies the number of students who mentioned each of these soft skills and the total rating of each skill[12].

We note that listening skills, flexibility, and patience are included in this list. Since these skills were not addressed explicitly in the course, it is only natural that the students realized their importance based on their class experiences. For example, with respect to flexibility, one student wrote: *Flexibility and the ability to adjust*

[12] Each soft skill was ranked between 1 and 5 according to its position in a student's rating: 1 – lowest; 5 – highest.

to changes: A team that does not have these skills is stable only for a short period of time, [but] we are interested in long-time production and practical results.

Table 4. Students' Ranking of Soft Skills (n=24)

Skill	Times mentioned	Total rating
Listening skills	17	58
Different aspects of teamwork	13	46
Interpersonal communication	11	47
Giving feedback	10	24
Flexibility	9	22
Time and pressure management	9	25
Knowledge transfer	8	14
Patience	6	17

To express the wide range of considerations that the students expressed in this task, we present one student's explanation of his rating: *While I was trying to rate the contribution of the soft skills to teamwork, I tried to do it by* [addressing] *the question: Which soft skill could I forfeit if I had to, and which must I have in my team? After different considerations, I realized that even though tolerance is important, it is the least important, since a team can survive also without it. [...] the same goes for flexibility, since the team has a management and any disagreement or case of stubbornness can be solved by the manager [...]. At the same time, cooperation, communication and patience are almost synonymous with teamwork. If a team does not have them, then there is no team.*

Stage 4: Students define the concept of a soft skill

Up until the course's 11th session, the concept of soft skill had not yet been defined. Yet, as illustrated above, the students had already gained some sense of the meaning of the concept.

One of the homework assignments the students were given at this time required them to define the concept of a soft skill. In preparation for this assignment, we facilitated the following 2-stage class activity. First, we asked the students to suggest characteristics of soft skills and listed them on the board; then, each student was asked to suggest one soft skill that has one of the characteristics listed. The students suggested ten characteristics two of which are presented below along with the corresponding soft skills that the students suggested:

- *is characterized by interaction with the environment*: listening ability, team management skills, interpersonal communication, giving feedback, teamwork, tolerance.
- *is developed based on experience in different life situations*: presentation skills, conflict-solving skills, ability to cope with stress, flexibility, expression of diversity, abstraction skills.

Next, as homework, the students were asked to define the concept of a soft skill. We present the definitions of two students, which highlight another aspect of soft skills not mentioned in the class discussion, specifically, that soft skills help achieve targets and improve the performance of both the team and the individual:

- A soft skill is a skill that accompanies work processes and is acquired by interaction with the environment and its feedback, and aims for better performance and continuous improvement for better fulfillment of the target.
- Soft skills are *tools* that determine behaviors which reflect efficiency in either individual or cooperative achievements [emphasis added by authors].

5. SUMMARY AND FUTURE WORK

The course described in this paper focuses on social and cognitive soft skills. It also communicates the importance of learning processes within software development processes as well as the need to allocate time for learning, practice, and improvement. In the future, we plan to design a second course on soft skills, based partially on the soft skill topics suggested by the students at the end of the first course, which, in their opinion, should be included in a second, consecutive course on soft skills. Such topics included knowledge management, simulations of start-up companies, reflection processes, and different kinds of presentations for presenting their experiences.

6. REFERENCES

[1] Ben Ari, M. (2001) Constructivism in computer science education' *Journal of Computers in Mathematics and Science Teaching* **20**(1), pp. 45–73.

[2] Brooks, F. P. (1975). *The Mythical Man-Month: Essays on Software Engineering*, (Paperback), Addison-Wesley Professional.

[3] Davis, R. B., Maher, C. A., Noddings, N. (1990, eds.) Constructivist views on the teaching and learning of mathematics. *Journal of Research in Mathematics Education*, Monograph 4, The National Council of Teachers of Mathematics, Inc.

[4] Hazzan, O. (2008) Reflections on teaching abstraction and other soft ideas, *Inroads – the SIGCSE Bulletin* **40**(2), pp. 40-43.

[5] Lave, J. and Wenger, E. (1991). *Situated Learning: Legitimate Peripheral Participation* (Learning in Doing: Social, Cognitive and Computational Perspectives), Cambridge University Press.

[6] Port, D. and Klappholz, D. (2006). So you want brooks in your classroom? *Proceeding of ICSE '06 - the 28th International Conference on Software Engineering*, pp. 655-660.

[7] Schön, D. A. (1983) *The Reflective Practitioner.* BasicBooks, New York, NY.

[8] Schön, D. A. (1987) *Educating the Reflective Practitioner: Towards a New Design for Teaching and Learning in the Profession.* Jossey-Bass, San Francisco.

[9] Silberman, M. (1996) *Active Learning: 101 Strategies to Teach Any Subject.* Pearson Higher Education.

[10] Senor, D. and Singer, S. (2008). *Start-up Nation: The Story of Israel's Economic Miracle*, Twelve.

[11] Smith, J. P., diSessa, A. A. and Roschelle, J. (1993) Misconceptions reconceived: A constructivist analysis of knowledge in transition. *Journal of the Learning Sciences* **3**, pp. 115-163.

[12] Sukhoo, A., Barnard, A., Eloff, M. M and Van der Poll J. A. (2005). Accommodating soft skills in software project management, *Issues in Informing Science and Information Technology*, Vol. 2, pp. 691-704.

The Relationship between Belonging and Ability in Computer Science

Nanette Veilleux
Simmons College
300 The Fenway
Boston, MA 02115
+1-617-521-2705
veilleux@simmons.edu

Rebecca Bates
Minnesota State University Mankato
Mankato, MN 56001
+1-617-389-5587
bates@mnsu.edu

Diane Jones
Joy Crawford
Cheryl Allendoerfer
University of Washington
Seatttle, WA 98195
{jonesd,callendo}@u.washington.edu

Tamara Floyd Smith
Tuskegee University
Tuskegee, AL 36088
tfloyd@mytu.tuskegee.edu

ABSTRACT

Retaining students in computer science majors has been a persistent topic among computer science educators for almost two decades. Researchers have examined the relationship between belonging and engagement, self-efficacy, retention and persistence. Our quantitative research suggests that a student's sense of belonging is related to a student's perception of his ability, possibly more so than to actual performance. Our qualitative analysis further suggests that feelings of belonging can influence students' attitudes toward the mutability of ability, based on conversation and support from their academic and non-academic communities. Supporting a student's sense of belonging both to the discipline and their supportive communities can improve the academic resilience of computer science students, thus improving retention.

Categories and Subject Descriptors

K.3.2 [**Computer and Information Science Education**]: Computer science education

General Terms

Human Factors.

Keywords

Computer science education research, belonging, mixed-methods research

1. INTRODUCTION

Even though there are indications that undergraduate computer science (CS) enrollment in the U.S. is emerging from its decline, increases are unlikely to fill the current and projected needs of industry. There are several key points that can influence the number of new practicing computer scientists. Initially students must be recruited into the major, either from high school or within the university population. Once recruited, students must remain in the major and finally, they must persist into the professional field.

SIGCSE'13, March 6–9, 2013, Denver, Colorado, USA.

Recruitment aside, this pattern highlights the need for comprehensive approaches to promoting retention and persistence. Multiple education studies in computer science [4,14] and other STEM domains [5,22] have called attention to the problem of lack of belonging and its impact on interest, achievement, and retention, particularly for underrepresented groups.

Belonging has proven to be especially relevant to engagement, persistence, and drop-out at the K–12 level (e.g., [8,9,20]). Various studies have investigated the role of belonging in undergraduate programs and its relationship to various factors that influence persistence and success [1,21]. Tinto's seminal work on social and academic integration with respect to retention focuses on the life of the student in the context of belonging in academic communities [21]. On the other hand, Allendoerfer et al. [1] show that students' belonging needs were frequently met through participation in non-academic, often family-related, communities, and that students strategically identify needs, linking their community participation with increased ability to engage in their academic endeavors. As a whole, STEM educators have been particularly interested in the relationship between a student's perception of belonging to a STEM major and attracting and retaining students to the discipline.

One factor in the retention/persistence puzzle is the specific connection between belonging and the student's perception of his academic ability. Wilson et al. [23] found that an increased sense of belonging is connected to perceptions of technical competence. Floyd-Smith et al. posit conceptual connections between belonging and academic outcomes for undergraduate engineers. Belonging is also linked to self-efficacy, that is, the belief in one's ability to succeed, in academic environments [24]. Lewis et al. have identified ability as one of several factors that students use in selecting a major along with fit, enjoyment, utility and opportunity cost [12]. In that study, the authors chose specifically to focus on ability using grounded theory to probe how a student's attitude towards the fixed versus mutable nature of ability impacts a student's choice to major in computer science. Students who view ability as fixed are less likely to choose to major in CS if they perceive that they cannot perform assignments as quickly or as easily as their peers or if they receive poor grades. That is, if students perceive that they are performing badly and their ability is indeed innate, then they conclude that they simply are not "cut out" for computer science.

The work presented here is part of a broader five year, multi-campus study focusing on the key concept of belonging [7,19] and academic engagement. In the larger study, we seek to explain the mechanisms by which a sense of belonging can lead to enhanced and authentic classroom engagement and, in turn, a greater likelihood that the student will remain in a computer science or other STEM major. In the work presented here, we focus on a more narrow aspect of this larger question: what is the relationship between a sense of belonging and a student's assessment of their own ability to perform in a given field?

The motivation for examining this specific question has its genesis in the possible interaction between (at least) two interpretations of the use of term "belonging." For example, studies on students' sense of belonging, including this one, pose some variation of the broad question, "Do you feel you belong to this environment, classroom, major, institution, etc.?" [2] in order to measure a student's subjective feeling of belonging. In answering, students may be conflating interpretations of belonging. In the first interpretation, the student might be responding to feelings of belonging as in to belong to communities determined by social context ("Do I feel socially appropriate and welcomed in this environment?"). For example, a student's race, gender and social class have been found to be related to not having a sense of belonging [10,11,14,16]. However, there is a subtly different, and less studied, interpretation that could lead to a different response. A student might be conceptualizing belonging as belonging to a group granted access by ability ("Do I have the ability to perform/succeed in this discipline?"). These two interpretations may be related in a student's mind and serve, unarticulated and undifferentiated, to inform each other in a fluid way throughout the student's time in the STEM pipeline. Muddying the waters even further is the student's perception of whether either social integration or ability is fixed or can be adjusted positively.

Our research suggests that a student's sense of belonging is related to a student's perception of his ability, possibly more so than actual performance. Our qualitative analysis, however, suggests that feelings of belonging can influence students' attitudes toward the mutability of ability, based on conversation and support from their communities, both academic and non-academic. Having the belief that ability, or at least performance, is not fixed, allows the student to respond with greater resiliency and is perhaps responsible for the results found in Lewis' work [12].

In this paper, the methods used in our mixed qualitative/ quantitative approach are described, followed by results showing relationships between a sense of belonging and perceived ability as measured by self-efficacy and self-reported GPA (both reported current and expected). The paper closes with a discussion of the impact of our results, including possible interventions that could address issues of community and thus belonging in computer science education.

2. METHODS

This research study is a multi-year, multi-university, mixed methods project. The five institutions range from small private colleges to large research institutions and were selected to achieve over-sampling of students from underrepresented populations. The STEM-major population of our study is institution-dependent and includes multiple engineering majors, chemistry, mathematics, and computer science. These majors were selected because of similar retention and persistence concerns and in order to pool data from diverse institutions.

The data for the current research were derived from survey responses and focus groups. Paper surveys were administered in the middle of fall term for sophomores and in the middle of spring term for juniors. Informed consent was obtained and various incentives were offered in order to encourage participation, including small gift cards and free food. Students who completed the survey were invited to participate in focus groups (or individual interviews when more feasible) to gather more detailed information about their experience with communities. A total of 944 students from the five institutions participated in the survey data collection and 169 in the focus groups.

2.1 Survey Scales

The surveys included several scales that assessed the students' self-reported self-efficacy, academic performance, and sense of belonging. The first two scales will be used as evidence of students' perceptions of their ability in their STEM classes, and relationships between these self-reported performance measures and the students' sense of belonging will be examined.

2.1.1 Self-efficacy

Self-efficacy was defined as the self-appraisal of one's ability to master a task, and included judgments about one's ability to accomplish a task as well as one's confidence in one's skills to perform that task. Positive self-efficacy is related to stronger academic outcomes, including achievement and learning, as well as higher levels of effort seen in persistence on difficult tasks [3, 17]. Self-efficacy was measured using five items (Table 1) from the Motivated Strategies for Learning Questionnaire (MSLQ) [17, 18]. Students responded to each item using a 5-point Likert scale (strongly disagree to strongly agree). Responses were summed for a total score with higher values representing a greater sense of self-efficacy. The internal consistency of the scale was strong (Cronbach's alpha = .88).

Table 1. Self-efficacy Survey Items. All responses are given on a 5-point Likert scale.

Statements
I believe I will receive excellent grades in the classes in my major.
I'm confident I can understand the most complex material presented by the instructors in the classes in my major.
I expect to do well in the classes in my major.
I'm certain I can understand the most difficult material taught in the classes in my major.
I'm confident I can do an excellent job on the assignments and tests given in the classes in my major.

2.1.2 Belonging

The survey included questions that directly asked about a student's perception of belonging at several different levels of the educational organization: a specific class, the major, the university (Table 2). Class and Major Belonging were adapted from [13] and were designed to assess students' feelings of support, acceptance, comfort and membership in class and in their specified major. For each scale, students responded to four items using a 5-point Likert scale (strongly disagree to strongly agree). University Belonging and University Community Belonging measured students' sense of belonging and community. The seven university level items were drawn from the Collegiate Psychological Sense of Community scale [5]. Students responded to all belonging statements using a 5-point Likert scale (strongly disagree to strongly agree). Item responses were summed to create four separate measures (scales). Higher scores for each of the belonging scales indicated a greater sense of belonging. Cronbach's alpha for the scales ranged from .80-.88.

Table 2. Belonging to Class, Major, School and Community Survey Items. All responses are given on a 5-point Likert scale.

I feel that I am supported in this class. I feel that I am a part of this class. I feel that I am accepted in this class. I feel comfortable in this class.
I feel that I am a part of this major. I feel that I am supported in this major. I feel comfortable in this major. I feel that I am accepted in this major.
I really enjoy going to school here. I feel like I really belong at this school. I wish I had gone to another school instead of this one. I wish I were at a different school.

2.1.3 Academic performance

Academic performance was assessed through two items. Students indicated the GPA they expected to achieve in their major and their current GPA. Self-reports of grades are used here as proxies for a student's perceived ability. The two measures, however, can be seen to capture two different perspectives on performance. As sophomores and juniors, the students' expected GPA in their major reflects an estimation of their own overall (eventual) performance. The current GPA, on the other hand, would reflect a more objective, institutional assessment of their current academic performance (sophomore or junior).

2.2 Focus Groups

Survey respondents were invited to participate in follow-up focus groups. Those who agreed took part in either a focus group or an individual interview, depending on scheduling logistics. In these focus groups and interviews, students were probed for connections between communities to which they felt they belonged (or not) and the effect of these connections on their academic performance. The format was semi-structured in that interviewers followed a set of guiding questions and were encouraged to follow up with probing questions in order to more deeply gather student perceptions. Sample questions included:

1. Of all the academic communities you participate in (laboratory groups, informal study groups, the classroom, student groups, activities sponsored by the department and so on), which help you the most to engage in your education? How do they help you?
2. Of all the non-academic communities you participate in (athletics, church groups, work communities, international student groups, fraternities and sororities, church groups, and so on), which help you the most to engage in your education? How do they help you?
3. How much does it change how well you do in a class/lab when you feel that you belong in the class/lab? How does it change your performance or participation/engagement in the class/lab?

Focus groups and interviews were audio recorded and transcribed for coding and analysis.

3. RESULTS

This section presents the results of our quantitative research (surveys) and our qualitative research (focus groups and interviews). As a reminder, our goal is to examine how a sense of belonging relates to students' perceptions of their ability.

3.1 Survey Results

In order to examine relationships between a student's sense of belonging and her perception of her ability, we examined the correlation between responses to several key variables.

As shown in the Table 3, belonging at all institutional levels correlated significantly with both self-efficacy and expected GPA. In fact, self-efficacy correlated more strongly with belonging than expected GPA, indicating that students are not merely basing their sense of belonging on grading, but on the larger set of attributes that contribute to a positive self-efficacy. To rephrase, a sense of competence and confidence is more strongly related to all indices of belonging and support than grades.

Perhaps as interesting is the finding that students' actual (reported) GPAs are not correlated with any sense of belonging. This may indicate that actual grades, per se, do not dissuade students from feeling they belong in the major, nor do majors retain students through granting good grades. If belonging is indeed correlated with perceived ability, this suggests that a "weeding out" of poor students from STEM fields with putative grading systems may not be effective. In any case, actual grades do not seem to strongly impact students' sense of belonging to their major community.

Table 3. Mean and standard deviation for the key study scales and variables. Self-efficacy and the belonging variables are comprised of multiple items.

Study Scales (Survey Questions Used)	Mean	Standard Deviation
Self Efficacy (5)	18.70	3.47
Expected GPA in Major (1)	3.43	.53
Current GPA (1)	3.32	.44
Belonging in "this" class (4)	15.24	2.74
Belonging in Major (4)	15.92	2.85
Belonging-University (4)	15.93	3.22

Table 4. Pearson Correlations for Belonging as correlated with self-efficacy, expected and current (reported) GPA. Correlations above 0.15 are significant, p at least < 0.01. Not all students answered every survey question.

Pearson Correlation s	Self-Efficacy	Expected GPA in Major	Current GPA
	N = 944	N= 811	N = 861
Belonging in "this" class	0.37	0.31	0.04
Belonging in Major	0.58	0.22	0.10

Belonging-University	0.33	0.17	0.06

3.2 Focus Group Results

The survey results show that factors that are related to a student's perception of her ability, in particular self-efficacy, are related to a student's sense of belonging at all levels in the institution. Lewis [12] found that students who saw ability as immutable were more likely to leave computer science majors. If belonging is related to a positive perception of ability, how might this relationship be operationalized?

Certainly the different results for self-efficacy and current GPA suggest that actual academic performance may not be the foundational factor, but perhaps confidence in ability and a sense of belonging impact each other, perhaps bi-directionally. Practically speaking, this confidence seems able to transcend even solid data about actual performance, implying that students somehow believe that their demonstrated ability can change.

More detailed insights into the relationship between perceived ability and a sense of belonging can be found in focus group data. We find confirmation that students do indeed weigh "ability" as an important factor in whether or not to remain in STEM fields, and some evidence that many students describe ability as a fixed attribute. For example, one student who transferred from a community college to a university reported,

> *"Definitely coming from community college definitely can give you that impression. I mean, coming here was like, 'Can I make it? Was I sold a bunch of false tickets? Disney Dollars?'"*

This student's perception of his ability to perform adequately in the university is a source of concern, reminiscent of descriptions of the impostor phenomenon. He seems to imply that he came to the university with a set ability level, which he is concerned will not be sufficient. Another student was more explicit in her assessment that performance is related to immutable, fixed abilities.

> *"I feel really uncomfortable being in those classes. ... - it's not my learning style, and yet I still had to take the class because it was a mode [general education] and required."*

From responses like these where students describe ability as possibly faked or "not my learning style" we see confirming evidence of held beliefs that certain abilities are binary and fixed: one either has it or one doesn't. The lack of student control is key, creating a view that no amount of effort can offset negative feedback on performance. This is precisely the perception that would push a student to leave the field once faced with evidence that impacts negatively on the student's perception of her ability.

However, when probing students about their communities, we find that there is some inconsistency, or perhaps volatility in these beliefs. Students do not steadfastly express the uniform opinion that ability is binary and fixed. In fact, many described failure or lack of confidence with a more nuanced perspective. In these instances, respondents described how support communities help them to see that ability might be gradient, reassuringly variable at different points in a student's history and, importantly, within the student's control. For example, during focus groups, students reported that student-student peer communities influence their belief that ability, as determined by graded performance, can be put into a more positive perspective by peers. In one student's words, *"It's ridiculously comforting to know that you're not the only person who did really badly on the tests."*

Another student discussed his choice to remain in the major:

> *"Let's say that you do bad on a midterm and you're thinking, 'Oh, maybe I shouldn't have taken this class. Maybe I should have studied better.' But when you're supported by your peers when you're down about it, that actually helps bring you back and helps you be able to come back and take the second midterm and then 'destroy' [do well on] it pretty much. It's more or less a confidence builder and support."*

Of course, one would expect peer study groups to create a context in which ability, or at least performance, is malleable; study groups are created with the expressed purpose of strengthening performance. However, it is interesting to note that students also credited non-academic communities with providing support to strengthen ability. As different students described:

> *"I did horrible on my first physics test. After the test I was upset and having a horrible day. I went home that weekend and I was able to enjoy time with my family and not think about physics. Next week I was able to do my homework...and I started understanding better. Then I did better on my next test."*

> *"I'm on the swim team. ... In the off-season...my grades would go down – my effort in school would go down because I'd be like, 'Oh, I have a couple of hours.' Next thing you know, it's 9:00 at night. If I have practice at 4:30, I know I have 2 hours where I need to get my work done. It really helps me organize my time. I procrastinate, but swimming counteracts that."*

> *"My sister is on the track team [at this university] and they are highly recommended to go to their study tables, and she gets her stuff done and learning from the other girls in the class. ... You are representing the school."*

> *"If you just have a fun day with your roommate or something. You did something and you feel motivated and you want to get your homework done, finish everything, and you want to do more."*

These students attributed their academic performance, at least in part, to belonging to various non-academic, and in some cases, non-collegial communities (family, team, sister, roommate).

We see evidence, therefore, that suggests that a student's communities, both academic and non-academic, can serve to support a student's academic performance, in some part by counteracting the notion that negative performance indicates a predetermined lack of ability. Instead, peers, family and friends can present perspective on performance. This perspective allows students a greater resilience as they view their performance in an alternate light as an activity that is within their control.

4. DISCUSSION AND IMPLICATIONS

Students decide to enter and remain in majors based on a set of interacting factors. In this work, the concept of ability, as demonstrated in performance, is found to be inconsistently viewed by students. Although they may entertain ideas about a fixed ability, a sense of belonging is related more to an abstract sense of ability, not necessarily reflected in actual performance.

One of the ways that students may maintain the possibility of demonstrating more positive ability is through support derived from belonging to various communities, some academic, others not.

Using anecdotal evidence about the effect of grading on retention, and feeling pressure to either weed students out in some institutions or to hold on to every student in others, faculty often use grades to encourage or discourage students. What is the impact of students' seeming indifference to this very granular evidence of performance and their responsiveness to a broader perception of ability? If the grades themselves are not the most influential factor, might the environment created by arbitrary competition perhaps be amplifying a social barrier that jeopardizes a feeling of belonging?

Students in collaborative relationships (e.g., in study groups or social clubs) are in a position to provide feedback to each other and offset negative implications conveyed by a poor grade. On the other hand, some families and friends might not provide the same level of positive support (e.g., for first generation college students, women, or underrepresented minorities) leaving these students vulnerable compared to classmates with stronger social support. For example, several studies [5,6], find that women may leave STEM fields with equivalent or higher grades to men. In fact, Correll [6] finds that women, discounting specific grades in the opposite way, tend to believe that they must be exceptional to stay in mathematical fields. Using competitive grading schemes as a pruning tool might thereby have the unintended consequence of discouraging students by social factors rather than academic ones. Taken with the results presented here, grades themselves do not seem to be having the intended consequence of weeding out weak students.

This work suggests that, not only are students discounting actual grades in their calculations about whether they have the requisite ability, but that other structures might be more effective in attracting and retaining good students. Within computer science departments, the question becomes how to not only give students appropriate feedback about their work through grades, but also help create a sense of belonging that can reinforce student self-efficacy and connections to community that support student perceptions of their ability within in the field. One straightforward way is to incorporate social instruction strategies, like active and cooperative learning, in the classroom to help students connect with their peers who may provide feedback about a student's ability. Faculty themselves can include comments with graded (or ungraded) work to provide a realistic and holistic perspective on student ability. Finally, faculty can recognize non-academic communities, such as families and social groups, as allies rather than distractions. Faculty mentoring in student liaison groups and social clubs, attendance at college events, and interactions with students' family members provide opportunities to bolster the alliance and provide students with informal feedback that conveys, broadly speaking, whether a student belongs, socially and academically, in the major.

5. ACKNOWLEDGMENTS

The authors would like to gratefully acknowledge the National Science Foundation for their support of this work under the REESE program (grant numbers DRL-0909817, 0910143, 0909659, 0909900, and 0909850). Any opinions, findings, and conclusions or recommendations expressed in this material are those of the author(s) and do not necessarily reflect the views of the National Science Foundation.

6. REFERENCES

[1] Allendoerfer, C., Wilson, D., Bates, R., Crawford, J., Jones, D., Floyd-Smith, T., Plett, M., Scott, E. and Veilleux, N., (2012) Influences of Outside Community on Academic Engagement, Journal of Engineering Education, 101 (3) July.

[2] Baker, R., & Siryk, B. (1999). SACQ: Student Adaptation to College Questionnaire Manual. Los Angeles: Western Psychological Services.

[3] Bandura, A. (1997) *Self-efficacy: The Exercise of Control.* W.H. Freeman and Company.

[4] Biggers, M., Brauer, A., & Yilmaz, T. (2008). Student perceptions of computer science. In *Proceedings of the 39th SIGCSE Technical Symposium on Computer Science Education.* Association for Computing Machinery.

[5] Brainard, S. G., & Carlin, L. (1998). A six-year longitudinal study of undergraduate women in engineering and science. *Journal of Engineering Education, 87*(4).

[6] Correll, S. J. (2004). Constraints into preferences: Gender, status, and emerging career aspirations. *American Sociological Review* 69:93-113.

[7] Floyd-Smith, T., Wilson, D., Campbell, R., Jones, D., Bates, R., Peter, D., Plett, M., Scott, E., Veilleux, N. (2010). A multi-institutional study of connection, community and engagement in STEM education: Tool development, *Proc. 2010 American Society for Engineering Education Annual Conference & Exposition.*

[8] Goodenow, C. (1993). Classroom belonging among early adolescent students: Relationships to motivation and achievement. *Journal of Early Adolescence*, 13, 21-43

[9] Goodenow, C. (1993). The psychological sense of school membership among adolescents: Scale development and educational correlates. *Psychology in Schools*, 30, 79-90.

[10] Hausmann, L. R. M., Schofield, J. W., & Woods, R. L. (2006). Sense of belonging as a predictor of intentions to persist among African American and White first year college students. Paper presented at the Biannual Meeting of the Society for the Psychological Study of Social Issues, Long Beach, CA.

[11] Langhout, R. D., Rosselli, F., & Feinstein, J. (2006). What's class got to do with it? Assessing classism in academic settings. The Review of Higher Education, 30(2), 145–184.

[12] Lewis, C. M., Yasuhara, K. & Anderson, R. E. (2011). Deciding to major in computer science: A grounded theory of students' self-assessment of ability, In *Proceedings of the International Workshop on Computer Science Education Research (ICER)*, Providence, RI, USA, Association for Computing Machinery.

[13] Lounsbury, J.W. and De Neui, D. (1996) Collegiate pyshlogical sense of community in relation to size of college/university and extroversion, Journal of Community Pyschology, 24 (4), 381-394.

[14] Margolis, J., & Fisher, A. (2002). *Unlocking the Clubhouse.* MIT Press.

[15] Mendoza-Denton, R., Downey, G., Purdie, V. J., Davis, A., Pietrzak, J. (2002). Sensitivity to status-based rejection: Implications for African American students'college experience. *Journal of Personality and Social Psychology*, 83, 896–98.

[16] Ostrove, *The Review of Higher Education,* Summer 2007, Volume 30, No. 4, pp. 363–389.

[17] Pintrich, P.R. and DeGroot, E. V., (1990) Motivational and self-regulated learning components of classroom academic performance, *Journal of Educational Psychology* 82(1), 33-40.

[18] Pintrich, P.R., and Schunk, D (1996), *Motivation in education: Theory, research and application, Ch.3,* Englewood Cliffs, NJ, Prentice-Hall.

[19] Plett, M., Floyd-Smith, T., Wilson, D., Jones, D., Veilleux, N., Bates, R. (2011). STEM seniors: Strong connections to community are associated with identity and positive affect in the classroom, *Proc. 2011 American Society for Engineering Education Annual Conference & Exposition.*

[20] Ryan, A.M. & Patrick, H. (2001). The classroom social environment and changes in adolescents' motivation and engagement during middle school. *American Educational Research Journal*, 38 (2), 437- 460.

[21] Tinto, V., (1987). Leaving College: Rethinking the Causes and Cures of Student Attrition. Chicago: The University of Chicago Press.

[22] Treisman, U. (1992). Studying students studying calculus. *College Mathematics Journal, 23.*

[23] Wilson, D., Bell, P., Jones, D., Spring, D. and Hansen, L., (2010). Cross sectional study of belonging in engineering education, International Journal of Engineering Education, 26(3), 1-12.

[24] Wilson, D., Schaffer, J., and Freed, L. (2011) Differences in self-effacacy: is it women or is it engineering? Presented at WEPAN (Women in Engineering Program Advocates Network), Seattle, WA.

A Data-Centric Introduction to Computer Science for Non-Majors

David G. Sullivan
Computer Science Department
College of Arts and Sciences
Boston University
dgs@cs.bu.edu

ABSTRACT

Relational databases and other collections of data are increasingly prevalent across a wide range of professions and disciplines. However, most courses on databases and data mining are designed for computer science majors, and students who wish to familiarize themselves with these topics must first take several prerequisite courses. This paper presents the design and implementation of a course for non-majors that provides a data-centric introduction to computer science. The course covers the basics of databases and data mining, and it also offers an introduction to programming and data visualization. By teaching a variety of computational methods for processing collections of data, the course provides students with tools they can use in their fields of study and future professions, while also exposing them to key concepts from computer science. The course has been well received by students from a variety of majors, and survey results suggest that it has had a positive impact on their perceptions of computer science.

Categories and Subject Descriptors

K.3.2 [**Computers and Education**]: Computer and Information Science Education – *computer science education, curriculum*

General Terms

Design, Experimentation, Human Factors

Keywords

Computer science education; non-majors; curriculum; relational databases; data mining; programming; data visualization

1. INTRODUCTION

Increasingly, professionals from a wide range of disciplines need to manage and analyze collections of data. Researchers from the physical and biological sciences process large datasets in their quest to understand the natural world. Policymakers analyze socioeconomic data to gain insights that guide their decisions. Online music and video services perform data mining to deliver customized recommendations to their users. Retailers develop strategies based on data about customers and their purchases.

SIGCSE'13, March 6-9, 2013, Denver, Colorado, USA.

Given the growing importance of databases and data mining in so many different domains, many if not all undergraduates would benefit from an understanding of the computational methods that are used to organize, store, and process collections of data. However, most undergraduate courses on databases and data mining are aimed at upper-level computer science majors, rather than at a general audience [4].

At Boston University, we have developed a one-semester course that introduces non-majors to computer science through the prism of data processing. The course has four main components: (1) an introduction to databases, including the relational model and SQL; (2) an introduction to programming using Python, with the goal of allowing students to process collections of data that are stored in text files; (3) a one-week unit on data visualization; and (4) an introduction to the basics of data mining, including examples of the types of algorithms that can be used to discover patterns in data. At the end of the course, students complete a final project in which they choose a dataset that interests them and analyze it using techniques they have learned during the course. The course has no prerequisites and it counts towards our institution's general studies requirements. We have offered it two semesters a year for the past six years, and student feedback has been extremely positive.

The remainder of this paper will describe the design and organization of the course in greater detail, including a summary of the topics covered and the resources used in each of the four units. It will also provide information about the labs, assignments, and final project, and discuss and evaluate our experience thus far in offering the course.

2. COURSE DESIGN

2.1 Goals

Our approach to designing and teaching the course has been guided by several goals. First, we want to introduce students to a variety of computational methods for processing collections of data, giving them practical tools that they can use in their other courses and their future professions. This emphasis on practicality has the added benefit of recruiting and motivating students, who are more likely to wrestle with challenging material if they are able to see its potential benefit in the future.

However, we also want the course to be much more than a series of lessons in how to use a particular application or programming language. Rather, we seek to provide students with insights into the concepts that underlie these practical techniques, and thus into computer science as a discipline. These concepts include the use of abstraction to manage complexity, and the use of models to capture the essential aspects of real-world entities or concepts. Throughout the course, we attempt to show students how computer scientists think about and solve problems, and to give them an appreciation for how they can apply these same ways of thinking in their own lives.

This dual focus on practicality and underlying concepts is well-suited to our target audience of non-majors who are fulfilling a general education requirement. Because this course is the only computer science course that many of them will take, we want them to leave the course with both useful skills and an understanding of essential themes and ways of thinking in computer science.

Our final goal in designing and teaching the course is accessibility. Much of the material, if not presented carefully and well, could easily overwhelm a non-technical audience. In order for a wide range of students to benefit from the course, it is essential that it be structured in a way that allows students from non-technical backgrounds to succeed. On the other hand, we also need the course to be sufficiently challenging and comprehensive to accomplish our other goals.

2.2 Topics Covered

The course is taught during a traditional, 14-week semester. The units on databases, programming, and data mining each take up roughly one-third of the course, while the section on data visualization is a shorter, one-week unit. Below we discuss each of the four units in greater detail.

2.2.1 Relational Databases and SQL

Our coverage of databases begins with an examination of database fundamentals. We discuss how data is stored in memory and on secondary storage devices, and the distinction between a database and the database management system (DBMS) that is used to manage it. In addition, we touch briefly on four key functions of a DBMS: providing efficient storage, offering a logical view of data, query processing, and transaction management. Each of these functions would receive in-depth coverage in a database systems course, but we seek only to give students a basic understanding of each of them. Doing so motivates students to learn how to use a DBMS, and it introduces them to key computer science concepts, such as the use of abstraction in the logical view of data that a DBMS provides.

Next, we examine data modeling, with a focus on the key concepts of the relational model. We study primary and foreign keys and the constraints that accompany them. We also briefly discuss the need for normalization, but rather than covering a formal method for removing anomalies from a relation, we recommend rules of thumb for ensuring that relations are normalized in the first place. And we give students practice in developing a well-formed relational schema in the context of an e-commerce domain.

After laying the foundations of the relational model, we spend over two weeks covering the use of SQL to create, manage, and query a database. We take a gradual approach, beginning with single-table queries on an existing database, and moving on to commands for creating a table and adding data to it, multi-table queries (i.e., joins), and commands for updating and removing data. Students get extensive practice in the lectures and labs, and in two separate homework assignments. By taking this gradual approach, and by providing hints in the assignments when more complicated constructs are needed, we are able to introduce students to most of the aspects of SQL that would be covered in a database course for majors, including simple subqueries, aggregate functions, and outer joins.

Despite the relative depth that we achieve in our coverage of the relational model and SQL, we attempt to strike a balance when it comes to the explicit discussion of the underlying theoretical concepts. For example, we do not explicitly discuss most of the relational-algebra operations (projection, selection, etc.) on which SQL is based, but we introduce the concept of a Cartesian product so that students can understand how multi-table queries work. This unit of the course also provides a natural way to introduce a number of key concepts such data types and operators. And the students' use of SQL in this unit facilitates the introduction of more general programming concepts in the next section.

2.2.2 Programming in Python

The second unit introduces students to the writing of simple programs using the Python programming language. We take advantage of Python's simplified syntax and its powerful built-in facilities for list and file processing, which make it easy for beginners to quickly begin writing useful programs. We focus on those features that are most useful to the data-centric tasks that we want students to be able to perform—in particular, the processing of datasets that are stored in a text file. For example, we do not cover `while` loops at all, but we cover `for` loops extensively, because Python makes it easy to use `for` loops to read one line at a time from a text file, or one tuple at a time from the results of a database query. In learning the skills needed for these types of tasks, students are also exposed to foundational programming concepts, and to the problem-solving process that programmers employ.

The following is a summary of the topics covered in this unit:

- *programming basics:* algorithms; expressions, statements, and variables; assignments; built-in functions; simple I/O; simple `for` loops.
- *working with numbers:* data types (building on the students' earlier exposure to types in SQL); representing integers; numeric operators; floating-point and integer division; Python's `math` module; type conversions.
- *making decisions:* flow of control; conditional execution; boolean values and expressions; relational and logical operators (again building on earlier exposure in SQL).
- *working with strings and lists:* strings and lists as sequences; using an index to access an individual value; using slicing to obtain a substring or sublist; other operators for sequences; converting between a line of text and a list of words using the `split` and `join` functions.
- *accessing a database:* writing a program that serves as a simple front-end to a database; database handles and cursors; using a `for` loop to process query results; using parameterized queries to prevent SQL injection faults.
- *working with text files:* file handles; opening and closing a file; writing to a text file; using a `for` loop to read one line at a time from a text file.

All of these topics are covered in just over four weeks. This may seem ambitious, but we have found it to be doable as a result of several factors, including Python's relative simplicity and the students' exposure to some of these concepts in the context of SQL. In addition, we have found it helpful to structure the assignments for this unit in a way that is similar to the applied apprenticeship approach advocated by Astrachan and Reed [2]. In the first Python assignment, students are given an existing program and asked to modify it in order to obtain different results. In subsequent assignments, students are asked to write programs that are close variations of programs that we have covered in lecture, and we provide a fair amount of "scaffolding" in the form of step-by-step guidelines that help students who would otherwise find it challenging to write a program from scratch.

2.2.3 Data Visualization

The unit on programming is followed by a one-week unit on data visualization that has been developed and taught by Wayne Snyder, a colleague with a keen interest in the topic. Snyder bases his lectures on the work of Edward Tufte [18], who presents guiding principles for the creation of data graphics that combine simplicity of design with complexity of data. Students see how well-designed data graphics can enable one to discover insights about the underlying data, and they learn how to construct visualizations that communicate relationships among variables, comparisons between entities, and potential instances of causality.

We also show students a video of an engaging talk given by Hans Rosling at the 2006 TED conference [17]. Rosling demonstrates how well-designed data graphics can challenge one's assumptions about the world and provide surprising new insights. And because Rosling displays his data using software that illustrates changes in the variables over time, students are able to see the value that computational tools can add to the process of understanding data.

2.2.4 Data Mining

The final unit of the course introduces students to the use of data mining to discover patterns in data. We begin with an overview of the topic, in which we contrast the types of questions that can be answered using database queries with those that data mining attempts to answer. As part of this overview, we also briefly introduce three types of machine learning that are employed as part of the data-mining process—classification learning, numeric estimation, and association learning—as well as related concepts like training and test data, input and output variables, classifiers and other types of models learned from data, and ways of assessing the goodness of a given model.

After laying this groundwork, we then look at each type of machine learning in greater detail. We spend the most time on classification learning, because it allows us to teach students two simple algorithms that can be used to perform this type of learning. The first is Holte's 1R algorithm [10], which learns a rule-based model that is based on a single input variable. For example, if 1R were applied to a medical dataset containing the symptoms and diagnoses of a collection of patients, it might learn rules that make a diagnosis based solely on whether or not the patient has a fever. This algorithm is a relatively straightforward one to teach, and students can easily apply it "by hand" to a small collection of training examples.

The second classification-learning algorithm that we cover is one for learning a decision tree. The algorithm is essentially a variation of Quinlan's classic ID3 algorithm [15], but one that uses a more straightforward metric when determining the next variable to include in the decision tree. This algorithm also allows us to introduce students to the notion of recursion, because we repeatedly apply the same procedure to smaller and smaller subsets of the training data.

In our coverage of numeric estimation—a variant of classification learning in which the output variable is numeric rather than nominal—we discuss the essential features of linear regression. We remind students of the notion of a best-fit line that most of them have seen in high-school science classes, but we omit the mathematical details. For association learning—which looks for relationships among variables without singling out one of the variables as the output variable—we discuss the classic *a priori* algorithm [1], which is a relatively straightforward one for students to understand. It also allows us to discuss the importance of taking measures to improve the efficiency of algorithms that operate on large collections of data.

Finally, we discuss the process of preparing data for mining—including the possible need to discretize one or more of the continuous variables—and we look at several case studies.

Here again, the material covered in this section may seem ambitious in the context of a course for non-majors. However, we have found it possible to present the essential concepts in an accessible way. One key is to provide examples of applying the algorithms to "toy" datasets that are small enough to be processed manually. Seeing an application of one of these algorithms allows students to understand its key features better than they could from simply reading a description of the algorithm—either in text or in pseudocode. These toy examples also allow us to provide concrete illustrations the associated data-mining concepts.

2.2.5 Possible Modifications to the Syllabus

While the combination of topics described above has worked well at our institution, it would be relatively easy to modify the course to suit the needs and interests of students and faculty members elsewhere, or to fit a different academic calendar. For example, the unit on data visualization could be omitted, perhaps to allow additional coverage of data modeling (e.g., material on semi-structured and unstructured data). The units on programming and data mining could also be abbreviated or simplified.

2.3 Textbooks and Software

To the best of our knowledge, there is no one textbook that covers all of the topics of this course. Moreover, textbooks for the individual topics tend to cover a large amount of additional material, and most are not well suited to non-majors. As a result, we ask students to buy a coursepack containing detailed lecture notes for the course. This coursepack also includes questions and problems that we work through together during lecture.

For students who are interested in a supplement to the coursepack, we currently recommend Kroenke and Auer's database concepts text [12] and Zelle's Python text [20]. The closest thing we have found to a data-mining text for non-majors is one by Roiger and Geatz [16]. Our coverage of data mining draws inspiration from their presentation, as well as from Witten and Frank's excellent, more comprehensive book [19].

We use freely available software for all of the sections of the course. For the unit on databases, we use SQLite and a related visual tool called SQLite Database Browser. While SQLite does have limitations, it also has two key advantages: it does not require a separate server program and the associated system-administration headaches; and it stores a database in a single file using a cross-platform format, which makes it easy for us to give students databases to work with for the labs and assignments.

For the unit on Python, we currently use version 2.7 of the language and the accompanying IDLE integrated development environment. For data visualizations, we give students flexibility in the tools that they use, but we introduce them to a number of online tools, including those at IBM's Many Eyes website. Finally, for the data-mining unit, we employ a powerful yet easy-to-use program called WEKA that includes tools for preparing a dataset and learning models from it [9]. Students subsequently use WEKA to explore and analyze a dataset in their final project.

2.4 Labs

The concepts of the course are reinforced through weekly small-group lab sessions led by a teaching fellow. The TF may briefly review aspects of the material during these one-hour sessions, but the bulk of each lab is devoted to students solving problems, either individually or in pairs. The lab sessions also allow students to prepare for the problem sets and final project, and to become familiar with the software that they will use on the assignments.

2.5 Student Assessment

Students complete a series of nine problem sets and a final project. The course also includes three hour-long "quizzes" and a two-hour, comprehensive final exam. The problem sets and final exam each count for 30% of the final grade, the quizzes count for 20%, the final project 10%, and attendance and participation 10%.

2.5.1 Problem Sets

There are more or less weekly assignments for the first two-thirds of the course, and then two additional problem sets during the final third:

- *PS 1:* Short-answer questions on database fundamentals and the relational model, including the development of a relational schema for a simple domain.
- *PS 2:* Writing SQL queries on a database of movie data. Each query only accesses one of the tables in the database.
- *PS 3:* More practice writing SQL queries on the movie database, including joins of two or more tables.
- *PS 4:* Getting started with Python. Experimenting with operators, built-in functions, and simple `for` loops. Understanding an existing program, and modifying it to obtain different behavior.
- *PS 5:* Numbers and decisions in Python. Short-answer questions on expressions, assignments, and conditional code. Writing a program with conditional execution.
- *PS 6:* Experimenting with string and list operations in Python, and building expressions using these operations. Writing a short program that manipulates strings and lists.
- *PS 7:* Working with databases and files in Python. Writing programs for querying a database and writing to a text file. Short-answer questions reviewing earlier Python material.
- *PS 8:* Writing a program that reads from a text file. Creating a simple visualization for a dataset. Short-answer questions on basic data-mining concepts.
- *PS 9:* "Hands-on" data-mining problems in which students reinforce their understanding of the algorithms discussed in lecture by applying them to small datasets.

2.5.2 Final Project

The final project allows students to bring together concepts and techniques from all of the units of the course. After they have been exposed to the material in the first few lectures on data mining, students complete a proposal in which they choose a dataset that is amenable to data mining—in particular, to either classification learning or numeric estimation—and provide a preliminary plan for analyzing it. Once the proposal has been approved, they spend the rest of the course completing the project. Students can work as individuals or in pairs, in which case they complete a small amount of extra work.

As part of their project, students are required to use WEKA to apply one or more data-mining algorithms to their dataset, and to discuss the features and accuracy of the resulting models. The other mandatory component of the project is a data visualization that illustrates interesting features or relationships found in the dataset. In addition, students choose two tasks from the following list: writing a program that either prepares the dataset (e.g., by discretizing one of the continuous variables) or that provides a programmatic implementation of one the models learned from data mining; creating a relational database from the dataset and using SQL queries in some way (e.g., to compute summary statistics); and including one or more additional visualizations.

We encourage students to select a dataset that interests them—possibly one that is related to their major. Possible online sources of data include: the datasets associated with Google's Public Data Explorer website; FedStats, which includes a large number of datasets compiled by federal agencies; NASA's National Space Science Data Center; datasets available from the U.S. Census Bureau; and UNdata, a collection of socioeconomic and demographic databases compiled by the United Nations.

Most students are able to create projects that successfully integrate what they have learned. We have developed a Hall of Fame that highlights the best projects from each semester, both as an honor for the students who created them and as an inspiration for future students [21].

3. EXPERIENCE AND EVALUATION

The course has now been offered 12 times: from the spring of 2007 to the fall of 2012, and it is being offered again this spring. This section of the paper evaluates these initial offerings.

3.1 Context of the Course

The course is one of several that our department provides for non-majors who need to satisfy the math and computer science portion of the general education requirements for the College of Arts and Sciences at Boston University. All students who are not majoring in math or CS must take two courses from these departments that count towards the requirement. The course can also be taken as one of the six courses needed for a CS minor. It does *not* count towards the CS major, although some of our majors do take it as an elective.

3.2 Enrollment

This year's entering class at BU has an average combined SAT score of 2005. Several hundred students enroll each semester in one of our department's courses for non-majors. Roughly half of them have typically enrolled in the traditional, breadth-based CS 0 course that we offer. Of the remaining students, between 25 and 45 of them take the course described in this paper each semester; the total enrollments per year are shown in Table 1.

Table 1. Number of students enrolled per calendar year

Semesters	Enrollment
Spring/Fall 2007	22
Spring/Fall 2008	61
Spring/Fall 2009	65
Spring/Fall 2010	55
Spring/Fall 2011	62
Spring/Fall 2012	89

The students come from a wide variety of majors, including a relatively large number of students from the social sciences and business (Table 2). We believe that the course would also be well-suited to biological and physical science majors, but we have not succeeded in attracting many of them thus far. We suspect that students from these majors often take two mathematics courses to satisfy their math/CS requirement or, if they do take a CS course, they choose our Java-based CS 1 course instead.

Table 2. The 10 most common majors of students enrolled in the course, fall 2007 - spring 2011

Major	Number of Students
Economics	32
Business Admin / Management	30
Computer Science	21
International Relations	19
Archeology	16
Mathematics	16
Anthropology	14
Undeclared	13
Political Science	13
English	11

3.3 Reasons Students Take the Course

To obtain a better understanding of students who enroll in the course, we asked students to complete a short survey at the start of the spring 2011 semester. When asked why they had chosen to take the course, a majority of the students (24 of the 39) indicated that they wanted to learn information and skills that could be used in the future—either in their field of study or their career. Other reasons included: the course seemed interesting (10 students); they wanted to fulfill the math/CS distribution requirement (5 students); and they wanted to learn more about computer science (2 students).

Given the relatively small number of students who mentioned a desire to learn about computer science in general, it is possible that at least some of the students who enroll in this course might not take a CS course if the only options were a breadth-based CS 0 course and a CS 1 course that focuses primarily on programming. By combining programming with other topics that are seen to be more widely applicable (databases and data mining), this type of course has the potential to attract and expose additional students to computer science.

3.4 End-of-Semester Evaluations

The course has consistently received positive end-of-semester evaluations. The scores summarized in Table 3 suggest that the course does a reasonable job of making potentially difficult material accessible, while still providing an experience that is seen as useful and valuable. The students' written comments on the evaluations support that view.

Table 3. Summary of average student-evaluation scores

Semester	Difficulty (1 = easy, 5 = difficult)	Usefulness of assignments (1-5)	Overall rating (1-5)
Spring 2007	3.39	4.46	4.54
Fall 2007	3.38	4.50	4.50
Spring 2008	3.16	4.48	4.16
Fall 2008	3.35	4.38	4.41
Spring 2009	3.13	4.47	4.39
Fall 2009	3.56	4.67	4.37
Spring 2010	3.27	4.65	4.54
Fall 2010	3.56	4.67	4.50
Spring 2011	3.23	4.50	4.38
Fall 2011	3.24	4.56	4.36
Spring 2012	3.13	4.65	4.50

3.5 Follow-Up Survey

To further assess the course's impact, we recently asked students who took the course from 2007 to 2011 to complete an anonymous online survey. We sent invitations to 276 former students, and we received responses from 96 of them (35%). Respondents were asked to assess their degree of agreement with a number of statements. Two-thirds of respondents agreed that the course material has been useful in subsequent classes (24% strongly agree, 43.8% agree, 22.9% uncertain/neutral, 8.3% disagree, 1.0% strongly disagree). A similar number indicated that it has been useful in non-academic pursuits like internships and jobs (37.5% strongly agree, 34.4% agree, 20.8% uncertain/neutral, 7.3% disagree, 0% strongly disagree).

The course also had a positive impact on the respondents' perceptions of computer science. Roughly 57% of them recalled thinking that computer science was relevant to their own interests and pursuits before they took the course (16.7% strongly agree, 40.6% agree, 24.0% uncertain/neutral, 17.7% disagree, 1.0% strongly disagree), whereas a full 90% of them now acknowledge its relevance (46.9% strongly agree, 43.8% agree, 5.2% uncertain/neutral, 4.2% disagree, 0% strongly disagree). In addition, three quarters of respondents indicated that the course had increased their interest in learning more about computer science (41.7% strongly agree, 34.4% agree, 18.8% uncertain/neutral, 5.2% disagree, 0% strongly disagree).

4. RELATED WORK

While courses designed for non-majors have typically provided a broad survey of computer science topics, recent efforts have been made to develop courses that focus on particular themes like web programming, multimedia, or principles of computation [5, 7, 8]. The course presented in this paper also sacrifices some breadth to focus on the theme of processing collections of data. Goelman presents a course on databases for non-majors [6], but that course spends more time on database design rather than on other computational methods for processing and analyzing data. Banerjee and Kawash present a course that focuses on different methods for problem solving, including databases and programming [3], but it appears to offer more breadth and less depth than our course.

Some CS 1 courses have also included material on databases. Phillips, Stevenson, and Wick present one such course [14]. Kaplan teaches a CS 1 course for scientists that touches on databases, and he makes a persuasive case for the value of having scientists learn this material [11]. We concur with his argument, and we believe that a similar case can be made for students from other disciplines, and for the value of exposing them to other data-processing methods as well. Approaches have been developed for teaching data mining to CS majors [13, 19] and to MIS/IT majors [16], but we are not aware of other CS courses that introduce it to non-majors.

5. CONCLUSIONS

Our experience indicates that it is possible to offer non-majors a data-centric introduction to computer science that is both challenging and accessible. By exposing students to several computational methods for processing collections of data, such a course offers students practical and marketable skills, while also introducing them to key concepts from computer science. Although this type of course may not be a perfect fit for all non-majors, we believe that it can be a useful option for students from a wide range of disciplines.

6. REFERENCES

[1] Rakesh Agrawal and Ramakrishnan Srikant. 1994. Fast algorithms for mining association rules in large databases. In *Proceedings of the 20th International Conference on Very Large Databases* (VLDB '94), pages 487-499.

[2] Owen Astrachan and David Reed. 1995. AAA and CS 1: the applied apprenticeship approach to CS 1. In *Proceedings of the Twenty-Sixth SIGCSE Technical Symposium on Computer Science Education* (SIGCSE '95), pages 1-5.

[3] Satindranath Banerjee and Jalal Kawash. 2009. Re-thinking computer literacy in post-secondary education. In *Proceedings of the 14th Western Canadian Conference on Computing Education* (WCCCE '09), pages 17-21.

[4] 2001. Computing curricula 2001. *J. Educ. Resour. Comput.* 1, 3es, Article 1 (September 2001).

[5] Thomas J. Cortina. 2007. An introduction to computer science for non-majors using principles of computation. In *Proceedings of the 38th SIGCSE Technical Symposium on Computer Science Education* (SIGCSE '07), pages 218-222.

[6] Don Goelman. 2008. Databases, non-majors and collaborative learning: a ternary relationship. In *Proceedings of the 13th Annual Conference on Innovation and Technology in Computer Science Education* (ITiCSE '08), pages 27-31.

[7] Michael B. Gousie. 2006. A robust web programming and graphics course for non-majors. In *Proceedings of the 37th SIGCSE Technical Symposium on Computer Science Education* (SIGCSE '06), pages 72-76.

[8] Mark Guzdial. 2003. A media computation course for non-majors. In *Proceedings of the 8th Annual Conference on Innovation and Technology in Computer Science Education* (ITiCSE '03), pages 104-108.

[9] Mark Hall et al. 2009. The WEKA data mining software: an update. *SIGKDD Explorations* 11(1): 10-18.

[10] R.C. Holte. 1993. Very simple classification rules perform well on most commonly used datasets. *Machine Learning* 11(2003): 63-91.

[11] Daniel T. Kaplan. 2004. Teaching computation to undergraduate scientists. In *Proceedings of the 35th SIGCSE Technical Symposium on Computer Science Education* (SIGCSE '04), pages 358-362.

[12] David M. Kroenke and David Auer. 2011. *Database Concepts, 5th ed.* Prentice Hall, Upper Saddle River, NJ.

[13] David R. Musicant. 2006. A data mining course for computer science: primary sources and implementations. In *Proceedings of the 37th SIGCSE Technical Symposium on Computer Science Education* (SIGCSE '06), pages 538-542.

[14] Andrew T. Phillips, Daniel E. Stevenson, and Michael R. Wick. 2003. Implementing CC2001: a breadth-first introductory course for a just-in-time curriculum design. In *Proceedings of the 34th SIGCSE Technical Symposium on Computer Science Education* (SIGCSE '03), pages 238-242.

[15] J.R. Quinlan. 1986. Induction of decision trees. *Machine Learning* 1(1986): 81-106.

[16] Richard Roiger and Michael Geatz. 2003. *Data Mining: A Tutorial-Based Primer.* Addison Wesley, Boston, MA.

[17] Hans Rosling. 2006. http://www.ted.com/talks/hans_rosling_shows_the_best_stats_you_ve_ever_seen.html

[18] Edward R. Tufte. 2001. *The Visual Display of Quantitative Information, 2nd ed.* Graphics Press, Cheshire, CT.

[19] Ian H. Witten and Eibe Frank. 2005. *Data Mining:Practical Machine Learning Tools and Techniques, 2nd ed.* Morgan Kaufmann, Waltham, MA.

[20] John Zelle. 2003. *Python Programming: An Introduction to Computer Science, 1st ed.* Franklin Beedle & Assoc., Sherwood, OR.

[21] The CS 105 Hall of Fame: http://cs-people.bu.edu/dgs/courses/cs105/hall_of_fame

Demystifying Networking: Teaching Non-Majors via Analogical Problem-Solving

Sridhar Iyer
Department of Computer Science and Engineering
Indian Institute of Technology Bombay
Powai, Mumbai, India
+91-22-25767905
sri@iitb.ac.in

Sahana Murthy
Educational Technology Inter-Disciplinary Programme
Indian Institute of Technology Bombay
Powai, Mumbai, India
+91-22-25764860
sahanamurthy@iitb.ac.in

ABSTRACT
The goals of a typical Networking course for Computer Science majors include getting students to learn the relevant concepts, delving into details of various protocols, and using Networking utilities. Such focus on low-level details is unlikely to be interesting to non-majors. Also, there is a larger danger of students not understanding the basic concepts due to the perceived complexity in the details and technical jargon. We address both these issues by teaching Networking concepts through solving problems in analogical real-life scenarios. The main idea of our approach is: The instructor poses an analogy problem, students work in groups to devise solutions, followed by a class discussion to map the analogy problem as well as its solution to their corresponding technical details in Networking domain. Thus we emphasize the core concepts of Networking and demystify the specialized technical details. Across three offerings of this course, we have found that: (i) our students' performance on typical Networking questions is comparable or higher than traditionally taught students, (ii) students can solve unseen technical problems, (iii) students' confidence in tackling technical questions is high.

Categories and Subject Descriptors
K.3.2 [Computer Science Education]

General Terms
Design, Human factors

Keywords
Networking, non-majors, analogies, active learning

1. INTRODUCTION
Networking is a course commonly taught to all Computer Science (CS) majors. Often, undergraduate students who choose CS as a minor, or students from other engineering disciplines such as Electrical Engineering, need to take this course. The typical goals of an introductory Networking course for non-majors are to get students to learn the technical aspects of: (i) Concepts such as layering, multiple-access, routing, transport and (ii) Protocols such as Ethernet, OSPF, TCP, SMTP. Sometimes an additional goal is to build familiarity with configuring and using such protocols, either through in-class demonstrations or in laboratory settings.

However, the focus on such low-level details such as protocols or configuration of networks is unlikely to be relevant or interesting to non-CS majors [8]. There is a larger danger of students not understanding the basic concepts due to the perceived complexity. Students might get mired in the details, thereby losing the view of the underlying conceptual framework. The abundant use of technical jargon may be a deterrent to students being able to apply the concepts. A Networking course need not emphasize minute details or use lots of specialized vocabulary to achieve the primary goals of understanding and applying concepts. At its core, the subject contains a straightforward application of common concepts, such as modularity, abstraction, resource-sharing, addressing, correctness and efficiency. An important objective of a course for non-majors is to get students to apply these concepts in a stepwise manner, in the appropriate situations.

In this paper, we describe a course in Networking, based on solving problems in analogical real-life scenarios. Analogies have been known to promote learning of the properties of unfamiliar concepts as well as develop new abstractions [4]. Students work in groups in the classroom to devise solutions to real-life open design problems. The real-life problem as well as its solution are then mapped to their corresponding technical details in the Networking domain. This process of mapping between the real-life analogy and the technical problem emphasizes the core concepts of Networking and demystifies the specialized technical details, which are the two key goals of our course. We found that the analogical problem-solving method is comparable or better in terms of students' performance on typical Networking questions, when compared with traditional students. Students are able to apply concepts from the analogy domain to solve Networking problems in previously unseen topics. After undergoing the analogical problem-solving course, students' confidence in attempting complex Networking design problems is high.

We begin this paper with the goals of the course and describe how the instructional method addresses the goals (Section 2). We illustrate the process of developing instructional material for the analogies and problems with a detailed example, report how a typical class is structured, and describe the implementation steps of problem-solving with analogies (Section 3). To examine the effectiveness of the instructional method, we analyze students' reasoning via analogies in questions, and investigate student perceptions of the non-traditional learning environment (Section 4). We discuss the benefits and challenges for an instructor in teaching the course, and conclude with guidelines for instructors who potentially want to adopt our technique.

2. COURSE GOALS AND INSTRUCTIONAL METHOD

A course on Networking is a staple in all Computer Science departments, both for majors and non-majors. Typical goals of such courses include exposure to concepts such as ARQ mechanisms, graph algorithms and familiarity with protocol details such as RTS-CTS in WiFi, LSPs in OSPF, TCP variants, and use of Networking utilities such as ifconfig, traceroute, tcpdump. There is wide a range of innovative pedagogies and software tools that have been used in Networking courses to address these goals, for example in [7, 9]. Some courses specifically address 'non-specialists' by the use of hands-on experiences of networking concepts such as packet-tracing and network simulations [10].

Our course goals include the typical goals as mentioned above. An additional explicit goal is to get students to engage deeply with the content by (i) drawing connections between Networking topics and real-life analogies, and (ii) retracing the evolutionary steps in the invention of any technology. Specifically, the main learning objectives of our course are:

1. Get students to demonstrate conceptual understanding of Networking protocols.
2. Demystify Networking technologies so that:
   a. Students recognize that design choices for various technologies often stem from commonly known concepts in other real-world applications.
   b. Students recognize that inventing technology is mostly a matter of systematically applying logical thinking towards a goal.

To address the above goals, we emphasize conceptual understanding of the basic ideas underlying various technologies before delving into details of specific technologies. For example, we emphasize understanding of multiple access mechanisms and get students to recognize that GSM is a combination of FDMA and TDMA, before delving into the intricate details of GSM channel structure.

The overview of our instructional method is to use analogical problem-solving through real-life scenarios to develop fundamental concepts. The instructor poses design problems in real-life scenarios which the students solve by working in groups. The instructor then facilitates a class discussion of the solutions to the analogy problem, followed by mapping the analogy problem and solution(s) to the technical domain. Figure 1 shows the overview of the method. The analogy problems have been carefully designed so that the abstract structure of the problem and its solutions, map to corresponding core Networking concepts (see section 3.1 for how these problems were developed). Care is taken to ensure that the mapping does not lead to any ambiguity or misconceptions at the conceptual understanding level [1].

Analogies have been long promoted as a cognitive tool to understand the properties of an unfamiliar idea using a familiar idea and are central to the development of scientific ideas [6]. Analogies are being used in teaching computer science subjects such as programming [3] and algorithms [11]. One role played by analogies in our course is to demonstrate that the subject is a straightforward application of familiar concepts. Further, the power of analogies lies not only in comparing the properties of two domains, but also in the development of new abstraction and mental models [4]. Experts frequently reason through analogies while developing new theories [2]. Analogies have been reported

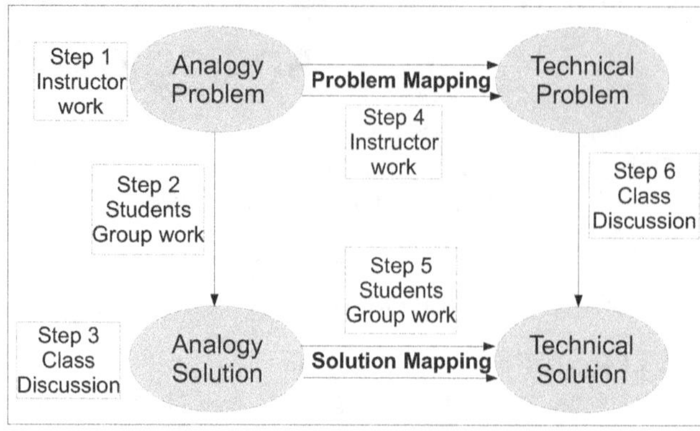

Figure 1. Overview of instructional method

to be an important tool in solving complex problems [5]. It is this power of analogies that we harness in the problem-solving process in our course: students solve complex problems in familiar real-life scenarios, and develop the necessary abstractions, which are then mapped to the Networking domain.

The choice of a familiar real-life scenario especially addresses our second objective of demystifying technology. Studies have shown that success of using analogies for teaching and learning depends on students' understanding of the base domain [4]. In our course, the base domain consists of real-life situations, which have been chosen to maximize students' familiarity. In terms of learning problem-solving skills, students first encounter the problem and attempt its solution in the real-life scenario. Since students learn these new skills in a familiar domain, the initial barrier to begin solving a complex problem is overcome. Finally, real life scenarios increase personalization through connections and relevance, thereby enhancing students' motivation to learn abstract topics. Use of collaborative problem solving further eases the initial barrier and facilitates tackling of complex design problems [12].

3. IMPLEMENTATION DETAILS

3.1 Development of instructional material

Since the basis of the instructional method involves analogies, we first describe how we identified and developed analogies to the relevant Networking concepts. Given the syllabus, we developed instructional material for each topic as follows:

1. Identify the important concepts in that topic. Examine if the basic ideas associated with the concept occur repeatedly, either in Networking or elsewhere.
2. Decide whether an analogy would be useful. We use analogy to (i) emphasize the broad applicability of the concept, or (ii) to overcome the initial barrier of learning the details of a new technology. An example for (i) is: Analogy is useful for teaching multiple access mechanisms since they are similar to resource sharing mechanisms in other areas. An example for (ii) is: Analogy is useful for teaching about the layering, interfaces and protocols. An example where an analogy is not required (by our definition) is: TCP window size.
3. Develop the analogy problem. Consider real-world scenarios or fictitious situations using real-world elements that have an abstract structure similar to the Networking concept. Identify constraints to be imposed on the real-world scenario that can mimic the properties of the network. For example, the CEO

scenario described below (section 3.2, step 1) captures many important concepts in Networking, such as layering, packetization and retransmission.

Throughout the course, students repeatedly get exposed to real-life problems in which they have to design protocols for the given requirements and constraints. These analogy problems build from simple scenarios to complex ones, mimicking the evolution of the corresponding technologies. The explicit use of analogies and asking students to apply skills required to design systems, addresses our instructional goals 2(a) and 2(b) respectively.

3.2 Classroom learning environment

The treatment of a typical topic involves: introduction and motivation of the problem in the analogy domain, group-problem solving of a question in an analogy domain, analysis of various solutions and then mapping of the analogy problem and solution(s) to the technical domain. This process takes about 90 minutes. An overview of the treatment is given in Figure 1. The details of each step in the treatment are as below.

Process of problem solving using analogies:

STEP 1 (5 minutes): Instructor poses question in analogy domain.

The instructor briefly describes what the question entails and what students are expected to do. One example, which we call the CEO scenario, used as an analogy for Networking layers and TCP/IP actions, is given below:

There are two companies A and B, located in cities about 200 km apart. The CEO of company A wants to send a document, of 100 pages, to the CEO of company B. How can this be done, given the following constraints:

- *There is no email, no fax, no phone, no post office - no form of modern communication whatsoever.*
- *The only means of communication are messenger boys.*
- *The messenger boys are weak. Each can carry only 10 pages at a time!*
- *The messenger boys are fickle. They may decide to quit without notice at any, even while carrying pages!*

STEP 2 (20 minutes): Group problem-solving.

Students work in groups of 4-6 to solve the problem in the analogy domain. The instructor helps students structure their problem-solving process.

STEP 3 (20 minutes): Entire-class discussion.

The instructor facilitates a discussion in which various solutions are analyzed. Each group presents their solution and students critique each others' solution. The class evaluates trade-offs and benefits between different solutions. The instructor guides the discussion by bringing out any missing pieces required for correctness of the various solutions and converges on a 'suitable' solution. For the CEO scenario, the instructor first brings out the need for Secretaries and Dispatch sections at each end, and also the need to specify actions of each entity clearly. Then the instructor discusses the details of the chosen 'suitable' solution. An overview of the solution to the CEO scenario is given in Fig. 2. The problem solving steps are listed below.

- *CEO-A gives data - document (D) and name (CEO-B) to Secretary-A, along with control – send this by tomorrow.*

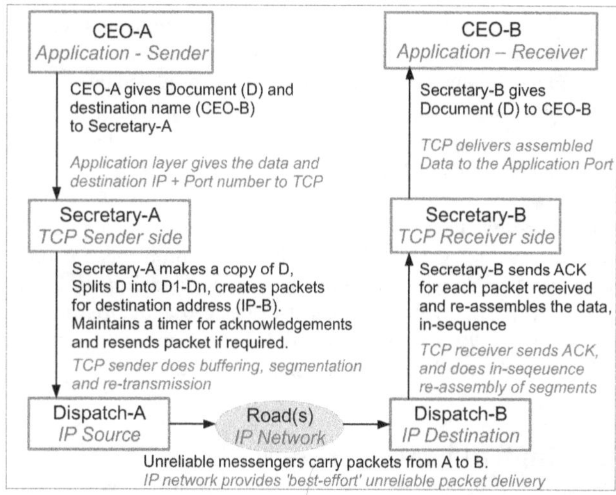

Figure 2: Overview of solution to CEO scenario

- *Secretary-A finds the address for CEO-B, makes a copy of D, creates 10 packets of 10 pages each, and numbers each packet sequentially.*
- *Secretary-A and Secretary-B have an agreed upon protocol for handling packets and sending acknowledgements.*
- *Secretary-A gives each packet to Dispatch-A and waits for acknowledgement from Secretary-B. If the acknowledgement for a packet is not received within a pre-decided time (say due to missing messenger), Secretary-A creates another identical packet (using the copy of D) and re-sends it.*
- *When a messenger arrives at Dispatch-B, Dispatch-B verifies the address and sends the packet to Secretary-B.*
- *Secretary-B sends the acknowledgement for the packet, extracts the 10 pages from the packet and re-assembles the document appropriately. Upon completion, Secretary-B hands over the document to CEO-B.*

STEP 4 (5 minutes): Instructor maps the analogy problem to the technical problem.

For the CEO scenario, the corresponding technical problem is "How does reliable communication happen in a client-server application, despite an unreliable IP network?" The instructor highlights the correspondence between the layers of the company 'stack' (CEO-Secretary-Dispatch) and a networking stack (Application-TCP-IP) (Fig.2). The instructor illustrates the technical problem using examples.

STEP 5 (10 minutes): Students map their solution.

Students work in the same groups as before to map their analogy solution to the technical solution.

STEP 6 (30 minutes): Entire-class discussion.

The class discusses the finer details of the technical solution. The instructor emphasizes which common concepts carry over from the analogy to the technical domain, and where, if any, breakdown occurs.

For the CEO scenario, the instructor brings out:

- The notion of layers, protocols and interfaces. The concerns and functions at each layer are different. The interfaces need to be clearly specified for the abstraction to work.

- The similarity between the Secretary's actions and reliable service provided by TCP. The similarity between the messenger boys and best-effort service provided by IP.
- Other topics that have a mapping from the analogy to technical domain. For example: Secretary-A looking up address of CEO-B corresponds to DNS lookup.

In this paper we have presented only one analogy problem, due to want of space. We have developed analogy problems for other concepts such as Multiple Access, Routing, and Roaming. For each concept, the overall treatment (Steps 1-6 above) is done in one class of 90 minutes, followed by delving into detailed technical aspects of relevant technologies in the subsequent 2-3 classes.

3.3 Student characteristics

The students were from Master's level programs across various domains, such as electronics, reliability, mechanical and chemical engineering. Most of them did not have any prior undergraduate course in Networking. Their objective in registering for this course was to get an exposure to communication networks and a working knowledge of various technologies such as TCP/IP, CDMA.

4. EVALUATING EFFECTIVENESS

Our Networking course taught via analogical problem-solving method was offered as a semester-long course three times, once each in 2009 (30 students), 2010 (62 students) and 2011 (28 students). We evaluated if the primary course goals- demonstrate conceptual understanding and demystify technology - have been met by the instructional method. In this section, we report some of these effectiveness studies.

To test conceptual understanding, we show results from exam questions of two kinds: traditional questions testing conceptual understanding in the Networking domain, and analogy-based problems in which students apply concepts from a real-life situation to solve a Networking problem (section 4.1). We analyze data from focus group interviews and classroom observations to determine student perceptions (section 4.2). We report the benefits and challenges to the course instructor from class logs and classroom observations (section 4.3).

4.1 Is analogical problem solving productive to develop conceptual understanding?

We first analyzed how our students perform on typical textbook questions, in which they have to apply Networking concepts to solve a problem. We then studied to what extent our students are able to apply the analogical problem-solving method in attempting problems in a new topic in the Networking domain.

A) Students' performance on traditional Networking questions is comparable to traditionally taught students

Table 1 shows the comparative data of four final exam questions of students from a traditional course without analogical problem solving and our students (analogical problem-solving group). Such questions are common to most standard Networking courses. An example of such a question is: "It has been observed that as the RTS_Threshold in IEEE 802.11 (WiFi). increases from zero, the network throughput initially increases. The network throughput reaches a peak for a certain value of RTS_Threshold and then starts to drop. Explain."

The traditional group consisted of 63 students at the Masters level in the Information Technology department. The analogical problem-solving group consisted of 30 students who took our course in the first course offering in 2009. Students from both groups enter the program via a similar entrance test. Both courses ran in the 1st year of the Masters program and were taught by the same instructor. Hence we consider the groups as equivalent for purposes of comparison.

Table 1. Comparative performance on Networking problems

Final exam question	**Traditional group Mean (SD)** (N=63)	**Analogical problem-solving group Mean (SD)** (N=30)	**Difference significant?**
Problem 1	6.3 (3.6)	5.9 (4.4)	Not significant, $p>0.05$
Problem 2	3.5 (2.8)	5.0 (3.9)	Significant, $p=0.04$
Problem 3	4.7 (2.1)	5.0 (3.9)	Not significant, $p>0.05$
Problem 4	4.9 (3.8)	6.0 (4.4)	Not significant, $p>0.05$

We find that on three out of four questions, there is no significant difference between the mean performance of the two groups of students. In Problem 2, students who learnt via analogical problem-solving had a higher mean score than traditional students, and this difference was found to be significant. This shows that the analogical problem-solving method is comparable or better than traditional methods in terms of students' performance on typical Networking questions, despite the instructor not spending as much class time on typical questions.

In addition, we have analyzed students' performance on more than 20 test questions over the three years our course was offered. We find that students' are indeed successful in solving such questions. Even though students spend significant class time discussing real life scenarios, they are able to abstract the underlying technical principles and successfully apply them to the relevant Networking topics.

B) Students are able to apply concepts from real life domain to new unseen topic in Networking domain

In each course offering, there were 2-3 problems in various exams in which students had to first solve a problem in the analogy domain (from a real-life scenario or a fictitious scenario in a day-to-day context), then had to map its solution to a problem in a *previously unseen* Networking topic. An example is shown below:

> *Analogy problem:* Consider 3 mountains in a straight line, A-B-C. There is a watch-tower on top of each mountain, each having a security guard. The only mode of communication between the guards is by shouting! The distances between A-B-C are such that A-B are within shouting and hearing range of each other. Similarly, B-C are within range. However, A-C are not within range of each other. Now, the guards want to talk to each other, every once in a while. For example, A and C may want to talk to B, while B wants to talk to C, and so on. Design a protocol to be

used in the above scenario, such that A-B-C may communicate meaningfully with each other.

Technical problem: Consider computers connected using wireless links instead of Ethernet cables. WiFi is a popular Ethernet-like protocol for such wireless LANs. WiFi also uses CSMA (Carrier Sense Multiple Access) in a manner similar to Ethernet. but instead of Collision Detection (CD), it uses Collision Avoidance (CA). Suppose you are asked to design such a CSMA/CA protocol. What would be the main steps of your protocol?

Our goal was to investigate if students can productively use analogy based reasoning to solve new problems. We show results on the above pair of problems, which were given to students in a mid-term exam during the first offering. Table 2 shows students' performance (N=29) on the analogical problem, and its corresponding technical Networking problem. It is important to note that students were not explicitly taught the Networking topic when they encountered this problem. We coded the solutions to both problems into three categories: A) Broad solution and details correct, B) Broad solution and a few details missing and C) Solution reported does not solve the problem.

Table 2. Students' performance on analogy and Networking problems

	Analogy problem (number of students)	Networking problem (number of students)	Mapping done? (number of students)
A: Broad solution and details correct	13	11	11
B: Broad solution correct but a few details missing	13	12	7
C: Solution does not answer the question	3	6	0

We found that 79% students (23 out of 29 from categories A and B in Table 2) were able to solve the Networking problem either with all details correct or at least to the level where the broad solution and some details were correct. Out of students who got the broad solution and details of the Networking problem correct (A), 100% students were found to have explicitly used mapping between the analogy problem and the technical problem to arrive at their solution. Out of students who got only the broad solution of the Networking problem correct but missed some details (B), 7 out of 12 (58%) and students had explicitly used mapping between the analogy problem and the technical problem. However, the students who did not solve the Networking problem correctly did not use mapping at all.

These results show that i) students are able to productively abstract the relevant concepts from the analogy to solve a previously unseen technical problem and ii) students who are successful in solving technical problem use mapping from the analogy. Secondly, from the instructor's point of view, this result shows that using analogies instead of directly teaching in the technical domain is a feasible technique. Thirdly, the fact that students are able to solve a problem in a hitherto unknown technical topic by first solving the analogical real-life problem shows that our goal of using analogies - to demystify technology has been achieved.

4.2 How do students perceive the course environment?

We explore how students react to the non-traditional learning environment in this course, and their perceptions about their learning in this course. To study student perceptions, we conducted focus group interview of 16 students at the end of the course in the first offering. The interview lasted for 45 minutes and was conducted by an external observer (2nd author of this paper). Data were audio-recorded and transcribed. We also show course evaluation data from each of the three offerings

From the focus group interview, we found that students' confidence in tackling technical problems is high, by having been exposed to the analogical problem solving method. Several comments in the focus group interview related to the usefulness of analogies in problem-solving.

> *"When I was solving a technical problem [in an exam], I only had to worry about a few minute technical details. The rest – the broad solution – was very clear because of the analogy."*
>
> *"We keep going back to the analogy while solving the technical problem."*
>
> *"Learning with analogies was a completely new way of thinking, this is thinking out of the box. ... We are made to think about the actual problem underlying the scenario. Concept becomes easier to learn."*

The overall percentages of the end of semester course evaluation were 89.6, 84.2 and 87.8, for the three offerings respectively. These are comparable to the top course scores in our institution.

4.3 What are the instructor's perceptions of teaching with analogies and problem solving?

In this section, we discuss the benefits and challenges to an instructor in teaching Networking using analogical problem-solving. We have three data sources: i) The instructor (1st author of this paper) maintained detailed logs of each class. ii) In addition, the other author of this paper attended all classes as an external observer in the first offering and maintained notes and audio-recordings of classroom observations. About 20% of the classes were also video-recorded. (iii) Interview of the course instructor to determine why his motivation to use analogical problem-solving to teach Networking, and his experiences.

Benefits:

1) The instructor found that not only was the course goal of conceptual understanding met but also that students reasoned at greater depth. The instructor observed that (i) a higher number of students were able to keep up with the technical discussion (in all topics) and (ii) some students were able to come up with scenarios and explanations that indicate depth. For example, on the topic of placement of buffers in routers, some students came up with the idea of parallel iterated matching, which was beyond the syllabus.

2) The instructor found that students could systematically 'invent' current technologies by starting with simple ideas and following the logical steps in the evolution of the technology. The instructor led students through the historical discovery process of many technologies and posed the same question that researchers posed

decades ago. Students were able to replicate the evolution process: they asked questions at the points where problems existed in the historical process and arrived at similar answers. For example, on the topic of packet scheduling, students came up with weighted round-robin for variable packet size, by progressing systematically from first-in-first-out scheduling for fixed packet size.

3) The instructor found that the analogical problem-solving method led to increased efficiency. For example, class logs showed that the instructor had prepared for a 90 minute class on two topics (buffers and scheduling), but due to students leading the discussion, the topics were covered in 60 minutes, whereas a traditional treatment would need 120 minutes. While this was not an explicit course goal, we report this finding as an important side-effect of the instructional method.

Challenges:

1) Almost every student is able to come up with a solution in the analogy domain. When the similarities with the technical domain are pointed out, some of them feel that they understand the technical topic and gloss over the details. In reality, they have only got a start to understanding the technical topic and the details are as important to understand why/how a solution actually works.

2) Caution is needed to ensure that the analogy is not extended to its breakdown point, which could lead to student misconceptions.

3) Some students get overwhelmed with the multiple possibilities while solving the analogy problem, and do not proceed. They find it hard to eliminate possibilities required to converge on one fully working and correct solution, even if it is not optimal.

4) Students who are already somewhat familiar with the technical topic may attempt to reverse map their incomplete understanding.

5. CONCLUSION

Analogies are routinely used by experts to understand new ideas by a process of productive abstraction [2]. In our course, the analogical problem-solving technique helps students focus on the core concepts necessary to solve the problem without getting distracted by the details. It is important to note that in our technique, it is the students who collaboratively devise the solutions to the analogy problems, and thereby construct their own knowledge of new concepts. This technique is more powerful than merely telling students the similarity between two domains, since it is rooted in the principles of active engagement and collaborative learning.

The primary intention of the instructor to use analogical problem solving as a teaching technique was to demystify the technical details that are ubiquitous in Networking courses. For this goal, analogies play the role of engaging students, and helping them see real life connections. Our studies showed that even novice students (to CS topics) are not daunted by the technical details. In fact, they are more likely to begin solving the problem if it is presented in the analogy domain. This technique gets students to overcome the initial barrier of attempting a new problem and thus erases the perceived difficulty. Their confidence in attempting further complex technical problems is increased. Students get over the perception that only a specialist can design network protocols.

For an instructor interested in using the analogical problem-solving technique to teach Networking, we have the following recommendations:

- Choose the problems in the analogy domain carefully. Use analogy problems that map well to the technical problem. Make sure that the analogy problem is in a scenario culturally familiar to the students. (The authors would be happy to provide interested readers with their problems).
- During the problem-solving step, use the analogy to draw students' attention to the core concepts. Help students differentiate between the essential points and the non-essential details.
- Do not be discouraged if no immediate productive discussion seems to happen during group discussion or if some students do not seem to participate. We found that it often took 10-12 minutes of 'floundering' (or silence) before students began to solve the problem. Since the problem is in a familiar domain, students will eventually come up with *a* solution.
- Let each student-group describe their solution during the class-wide discussion. This builds ownership to the problem. They get more involved with topic, as they want to see their analogy solution ideas appear in the technical domain. They also question - why is my analogy solution not exactly suitable – which helps all students become familiar with the nature of technological problem-solving.

6. REFERENCES

[1] Dijkstra, E. W. 1989. On the cruelty of really teaching Computer Science. Comm. of the ACM 32.

[2] Dunbar, K. 1995. In Mechanisms of Insight, edited by R. J. Sternberg and J. E. Davidson MIT Press, Cambridge, MA. pp. 365 - 395.

[3] Forišek, M. and Steinová, M. 2012. Metaphors and analogies for teaching algorithms.Proceedings of the 43rd ACM technical symposium on Computer Science Education. pp 15-20.

[4] Gentner, D. and Gentner, D. R. 1983. In Mental Models, edited by D. Gentner and A. L. Stevens (Lawrence Erlbaum Associates, Hillsdale, New Jersey, 1983, pp. 99 –130.

[5] Gick, M. L. and Holyoak, K. J. 1980. Cognitive Psychology.

[6] Hesse, M. B. Models and analogies in science. University of Notre Dame Press, Notre Dame, Indiana, 1966.

[7] Holliday, M. 2003. Animation of computer networking concepts. Journal on Educational Resources in Computing. Volume 3 Issue 2, Article No. 2.

[8] Margolis, J., and Fisher, A. 2002. Unlocking the Clubhouse: Women in Computing. MIT Press, Cambridge, MA.

[9] Read, Simon. 2005. Teaching networking with TIM. Journal of Computing Sciences in Colleges, Volume 20 Issue 3.

[10] Stratton, D. "Network protocols and services": a non-specialist approach to teaching networking. 2000. Proceedings of the 5th annual conference on Innovation and Technology in Computer Science Education, pp. 194.

[11] Waguespack, L. J. 1989. Visual Metaphors for Teaching Programming Concepts. Proceedings of SIGCSE 1989, pp. 141.

[12] Webb, N. M., & Palincsar, A. S. (1996). Group processes in the classroom. In D. C. Berliner & R. C. Cafree (Eds.), Handbook of Educational Psychology (pp. 841-873). New York: Simon & Shuster Macmillan.

Computation, Complexity, and Emergence: An Interdisciplinary Honors Seminar

Marie desJardins
Department of Computer Science and Electrical Engineering
University of Maryland, Baltimore County
Baltimore MD 21250
mariedj@umbc.edu

ABSTRACT

The *Computation, Complexity, and Emergence* honors seminar at UMBC is designed to introduce an interdisciplinary undergraduate audience to the principles of complex systems that permeate our world. The course goals are for students to understand how simple individual behaviors can lead to complex global behaviors and to be able to identify the sources and effects of complexity in natural and artificial systems. The course is designed to increase students' comfort and skill level in scientific writing, participating actively in written and oral discussions, and learning collaboratively in an interdisciplinary community. The paper describes the course and the innovative elements that lead to student engagement, then presents data from pre- and post-assessments about student attitudes and perceptions.

Categories and Subject Descriptors

K.3.2 [**Computers and Education**]: Computer and Information Science Education—*Curriculum*

Keywords

Complexity; Computing; Curriculum; Interdisciplinary

1. INTRODUCTION

Complex systems consist of large numbers of individual "agents" (such as ants, molecules, cells, or people) who interact with each other (through pheromones, intermolecular forces, chemical transmitters, or social interactions) and their environment (an anthill, a crystal, the human brain, or a university). In a complex system, relatively simple individual behaviors, decisions, and interactions can lead to complex and unforeseen or "emergent" global properties.

Honors seminars at UMBC emphasize critical thinking, writing, oral communication, and collaborative learning among students from different majors in a small-class setting. My intention in creating the *Computation, Complexity, and Emergence* seminar was to introduce the ideas of complex systems to an interdisciplinary student audience. I hoped to change the way that they think about the world, and to show them how computation and complexity can be used as tools to understand a wide range of phenomena in natural and social systems.

Many researchers and educators have noted the importance of an interdisciplinary approach to computing for both majors and non-majors. Elarde and Fatt-Fei [3] surveyed faculty and students about the topics and approaches that were most likely to broaden participation in computing in introductory courses; the top three were using relevant problems, emphasizing the social good of computing, and exploring interdisciplinary applications of computing. The new AP CS Principles curriculum similarly emphasizes interdisciplinarity from multiple perspectives [1]. The complexity course extends the idea of broadening participation through an interdisciplinary approach to an upper-level seminar.

My content-level learning objectives were for students to (1) understand how simple individual behaviors can lead to complex global behaviors; (2) be able to identify the sources and effects of complexity in natural and artificial systems; and (3) gain hands-on experience using mathematical and computational tools for analyzing complex systems. Additional course objectives involve cognitive skills: students should (1) increase their comfort and ability to write effectively on scientific topics; (2) improve their ability to participate in written and oral discussions; and (3) learn collaboratively and actively in an interdisciplinary community.

2. COURSE DESCRIPTION

The website for the most recent course offering is:
`http://www.csee.umbc.edu/ mariedj/complexity/2012/`
The seminar touches on a wide range of topics, including fractals and L-systems, measuring effective complexity, chaotic systems, producer-consumer (predator-prey) dynamics, swarm systems, cellular automata, self-organizing systems, multiagent systems, phase transitions in complex systems, and genetic algorithms and evolution.

The seminar is a mix of short lectures, active learning exercises in which students work through conceptual examples as a class, and open discussion of topics covered in the assigned reading. The primary textbook for the class is Gary Flake's *The Computational Beauty of Nature* [5], chosen for its integration of mathematical and computational topics, its breadth of coverage, and its level of detail (the presentation is technical but not overly so). The textbook is supplemented by articles and excerpts from a wide variety of sources (books, popular press, scientific articles, and news

SIGCSE'13, March 6–9, 2013, Denver, Colorado, USA.

media). Each offering of the course also includes several guest lectures on various topics, such as swarm systems and evolutionary biology.

The NetLogo modeling language is taught using several laboratory assignments and provides students with a hands-on way to experiment with models of complex systems. CS majors are also expected to implement a NetLogo model of the system described in their final research paper. Students are required to give two formal in-class presentations.

Written assignments include reading journal entries, written exercises, and a term paper describing a research investigation of a complex system. Many of the written exercises are followup activities to in-class labs using NetLogo. For example, in a laboratory using one of NetLogo's predator-prey models, students extend the existing model to include a refuge area for the prey and answer a series of questions about the resulting model's behavior. In a followup assignment, they explore another chaotic system (the logistic map), answer questions about that system's observed behavior in NetLogo, and implement their own chaotic system. All assignments are linked from the course website.

Section 2.1 discusses the reading journal assigments that were used to encourage and assess student writing; Section 2.2 presents strategies for active learning and encouraging student participation.

2.1 Reading Journal

To encourage students to analyze, process, and discuss the readings, I assigned a "reading journal" entry prior to each class in which the students had assigned reading. The journal entries were posted on the Piazza[1] discussion area, and could be either a commentary, a thoughtful question, or a response to another student's comment or question. The shared reading journal was very effective at getting the students to do the readings in advance of the class and to think deeply about the ideas covered in the readings.

Piazza discussions, and in particular the question/answer dynamic, also engendered high-quality interaction across the majors in both directions: CS majors liked to find different ways to explain mathematical/computational concepts, while the non-majors appreciated the opportunity to clarify concepts from reading assignments in their own areas, such as plant growth and the spread of disease.

In order to encourage students to reflect on the thoughtfulness of their contributions and the quality of their writings, I developed a self-grading rubric for the postings. Falchikov and Boud [4] provide support for the efficacy and accuracy of self-evaluation, particularly with well designed assignments to students in science-based higher-level courses. Rolheiser and Ross [8] argue that self-evaluation leads to increased self-efficacy, intrinsic motivation, and overall performance.

Students were required to submit three "participation portfolios," each covering about six reading assignments and associated postings. Half of the grade was based on participation; the other half was based on quality. Students selected their two best postings to self-grade using the rubric, which included 10 points for "substantive content" and 5 points each for "effective organization and presentation," "relevance and context dependence," and "correct English usage." Students were optionally able to explain why they gave themselves the grade that they did. I reviewed these portfolios and assigned my own grades using the same rubric. Although I did not use the students' grades directly, I did observe that students' self-grades were generally highly correlated with my own grades.

[1]Piazza is a free course management system that provides a discussion board, Q&A postings, and student polling. See `http://piazza.com`.

2.2 Student Interaction

Student interaction is an essential part of the course. Philosophically, the course design is centered around the idea that students can best learn from other students and from interdisciplinary, interactive conversations about the relevance of complex concepts in a variety of real-world contexts.

Students were invited to post a short introduction on the Piazza site before the semester began, and most of the students did so. This invitation led to a comfortable environment: on the first day, the students recognized each other's names and knew who else was in the class. As the instructor, I found that this exercise made the first day of class extremely approachable, because I had a good sense of who the students were and why they were there.

I next describe three areas in which innovative course design was especially successful: methods for having students self-organize into small groups; specific techniques for creating effective and balanced student discussions; and active learning through specialized group activities.

Self-Organizing Small Groups. On the first day of class, I introduced a lively way for students to self-organize into groups, inspired by swarm systems. Each student was given an index card with a word on it that was one of five parts of speech: a number, an adjective, a plural noun, a verb, or an adverb. They were told to find the largest possible group of students who all had different parts of speech.

To ensure diversity in the groups, I gave the numbers, adjectives, and nouns to the CS majors, and the other parts of speech to the non-CS majors, ensuring that each group had a mix of majors. A similar approach could be used to introduce any sort of desired diversity into groups (gender, class standing (freshman, sophomore), first language, etc.).

The groups then had three minutes to create a short story of which the last sentence was the sentence formed by their words. This process was remarkably successful at breaking the ice, creating energy in the room, and getting all students participating in a lively interaction. I deliberately used unexpected and sometimes unfamilar words (some students actually had to look up vocabulary on their smartphones), resulting in sentences like "Forty-seven gregarious aliens leapt mercurially" and "6.2 insipid anemones sniveled unctuously."

These groups worked together again on Day Two to play *20 Questions* (see below), on Day Four in the first lab, and on Day Five for a mini-competition (a "numeracy" exercise in which students were asked to rank the size of different sets such as "the volume water in the oceans of Earth, in gallons," "the number of molecules in the universe," and "the set of all rational numbers"). While the assigned groups did not persist throughout the semester, this series of group activities created connections across groups of students who hadn't previously met each other.

Encouraging Individual Participation. Much of the class time was devoted to active discussion of the assigned readings. As usual, some students were very comfortable with participating (sometimes overly so) and others were more reticent. I have developed a number of active techniques to address this perennial challenge and to help students improve their class participation (whether it is to *contribute* more actively or to *listen* more actively).

The class meets in a "seminar-style" classroom, with a long table that seats about 18 students and extra chairs around the periphery. On the first day, I tell students that they should sit in a different chair every day. This prevents students from "hiding" in the back or being consistent "front-row attention getters," and changes the dynamics of student interactions throughout the semester.

Around the second or third week of class, after I've identified which students fall into each category (dominant, average, or quiet), I arrive early and place colored index cards with student names at each place. Quiet students have green cards and are placed near the front of the class. Average students have yellow cards and are in the middle. Dominant students receive red cards and are near the periphery or in the back. After students arrive and seat themselves as directed, I explain that green means, "You're the discussion leaders today, and can and should speak frequently"; yellow means, "You should listen carefully but can participate once or twice, if you think you have something really important/unique to contribute"; and red means "Today you are a listener and should learn from the other students." The "green students" still require some encouragement, but with the dominant students in "listening mode," they find that they have the space and time to contribute. Some of the "red students" find it very hard to just listen: I once had a student who literally fell out of his seat trying to get my attention and obtain permission to speak. This exercise leads to a greatly increased awareness of each other's styles and roles, an increased sensitivity on the part of the vocal students, and an "ice breaking" opportunity for the quieter students that makes it easier for them to contribute later in the semester.

Group Activities. Interactive, community-building exercises continued on the second day of class: after a short lecture about the general course topics and an open discussion about the first day's readings, we went outside to play *20 Questions: Complex Systems*, in which one group thought of a complex system and the other groups asked yes-no questions to guess what the first group was thinking of. This game-based group activity stimulates thinking and engages the entire class in community-based learning. The diverse backgrounds of the students led to a wide range of systems and some very creative questions and guesses.

Another successful activity for increasing group interaction was *Fractal Show and Tell:* after several lectures and reading-based discussions on fractals, students were asked to bring an example of a fractal to class and share it with the other students. This activity made for a lively and diverse session, with fractals ranging from the physical (broccoli, tree branches, a YouTube video of frost formation) to the mathematical (Koch curves and L-system ferns) to the whimsical (a Vi Hart fractal video, a T-shirt with a Mandelbrot graphic).

The final very interactive class day was "Game Day," when we went outside and played three "complex system" games: distributed map coloring (in which each student was a region of the map and had to "color" themselves a different color from that chosen by any of their "neighbors"), a game theory activity derived from cognitive psychology research (a group version of the *Ultimatum Game* [6]), and a flocking activity (in which students pretended to be "boids" [7] following different interaction rules to create flocks of students on the library lawn). Many students said they liked this event because it was held outside, but the students' written reflection assignments also showed that the experience gave them deep insights into the relationships between individual decisions and group behaviors.

Table 2: Student demographics

	2012			2011		
	CS	Other	Total	CS	Other	Total
Male	15	2	17	9	2	11
Female	6	1	7	5	4	9
URM	2	0	0	1	0	1

3. EVALUATION AND DISCUSSION

Student demographics for both offerings are discussed in Section 3.1. For the second offering (Spring 2012), I kept copies of the first assignment ("Complexity in Everyday Life") to use as a formative assessment (Section 3.2) and distributed a post-assessment survey to measure student perceptions at the end of the course (Section 3.3). Although these pre- and post-assessments are not directly aligned, the areas of overlap provide some insight into how student perceptions changed over the course of the semester. No formal assessment was done in 2011, but the campuswide course survey instrument was used in both 2011 and 2012 (Section 3.4).

3.1 Student Demographics

Slightly more than half (55%) of undergraduates at UMBC are male; 17% are African American; and 4% are Hispanic. By contrast, as is typical for CS departments nationally, only about 12% of CS majors are women and about 8% of CS majors are underrepresented minorities (primarily African-American and Hispanic). All of the non-CS majors and most of the CS majors in the complexity course are in the Honors College program, a selective program that includes about 5% of undergraduates.

In 2011 and 2012, 24 and 20 students, respectively, took the class.[2] Table 2 shows the distribution of students in the course, based on their major: CS[3] or Other. In 2011, almost all of the students (88%) were CS majors. However, many of these students had a second major (including Ancient Studies, Visual Arts, and Mathematics) or a minor (including Music, Art History, and Psychology). Other majors were Physics, Mathematics, and Interdisciplinary Studies. That year, the course was also very male-dominated overall (71% male), although 29% of the CS majors were female (over twice their departmental proportions).

In 2012, I asked the Honors College advisors to more actively promote the class to non-CS majors, and wrote an "advertising blurb" for them to distribute about the class. This advertising, plus some word of mouth from the previous year's students, was successful at recruiting a more diverse group of students: only 70% of the students were CS or CE majors, again with several second majors (Mathematics and Visual Arts) and minors (English Studies). The six

[2]In 2012, 22 students were registered initially, but two students stopped attending for reasons unrelated to the course content or structure, so only 20 students completed the course. All statistics refer to these 20 students only.

[3]The "CS" designation includes Computer Engineering majors.

Table 1: Pre-assessment responses

	Writing (instructor)	Writing (self)		Participation level		Discussion experience	Participation attitude
Excellent	2	0	Very high	3	Very positive	5	9
Good	5	10	Somewhat high	3	Somewhat positive	3	4
Average	3	0	Average	3	Neutral	2	1
Needs work	3	5	Somewhat low	4	Somewhat negative	2	1
Poor	3	0	Very low	2	Very negative	3	0

non-CS majors came from disparate disciplines: Mechanical Engineering, Visual Arts, Chemistry, Physics, Mathematics, and Modern Languages and Linguistics, with a variety of second majors and minors.

The 2012 recruiting effort was particularly successful at attracting female students: that year, 36% of the CS majors were female, and the class overall was 45% female.

Few underrepresented minority students took the class in either year, all of them African-American CS majors, but their numbers were about what would be expected for CS majors. It is not clear why there were no minority students among the non-CS students in the class, but the numbers are not statistically significant.

3.2 Pre-Assessment

The first written assignment of the semester provides a formative assessment: students were asked to reflect on their writing ability and on their comfort level and experiences with in-class discussions. This section presents a quantitative and qualitative analysis of the findings from this assessment for the 2012 offering.

Writing Effectively. Students were provided with a handout summarizing important rules of writing and describing grammatical and stylistic errors that are often seen in student writing. They were asked to write a short commentary about the rules in this guide and what (if anything) they thought they needed to work on. I assessed the overall writing *quality* of this assignment into one of five categories (excellent, good, average, needs work, or poor), and also interpreted the student's self-assessment on this same scale. (They were not asked to use this scale, so the categorization is coarser.) As can be seen in Table 1, both my assessment and the students' self-assessment for about a third of the class was "needs work" or "poor." However, I also assessed only two of the students as having "excellent" writing, so even those students not in the "needs work" category in fact had ample room for improvement.

Classroom Discussions. Students were assigned to read an article called "It's Time to Raise My Hand" [2] and to reflect on their own experiences (positive or negative) with in-class discussion, their normal level of participation, and their attitude towards their own participation (ranging from "looking forward" to "dreading"). I categorized the responses to each of these three topics (experiences, level of participation, and attitude towards participation) into one of five appropriate categories (Table 1). Students' self-described participation level was fairly uniformly distributed across the five categories, from "very low" to "very high." Similarly, students' experiences with previous discussion-based classes were almost uniformly distributed, with only slightly more "very positive" responses than the others. However, the dominant response to the question asking them about their attitude towards the expectations for participation in *this* class was "very positive."

3.3 Post-Assessment

Of the 20 students in the 2012 class, 17 completed an anonymous exit survey, consisting of multiple-choice and short answer questions that were designed to assess their experience with different aspects of the class and their impressions of the class overall.

Writing and Participation. Students were asked to describe their comfort level and confidence in their ability to write research papers, and their comfort level and the perceived quality of their contributions to class discussions. The answers are shown in Table 3, with the majority response for each question in bold.

Student perceptions of their writing comfort and ability clearly showed an increase, with nearly two-thirds of the students describing these as having "increased somewhat." Several students said that their comfort and ability "significantly increased," and the remainder said they "stayed about the same," with no students describing a decrease.

Fewer students described an increase in the comfort level and quality of their contributions to class discussions: one-third said that these "increased somewhat," and just over half said they "stayed about the same." Only one student described their discussion quality as having "significantly increased," and one student actually said that their comfort level and quality "decreased somewhat."

My own perception as the professor was that the quality and diversity of classroom discussions increased markedly over the course of the semester. At the first few classes, the discussion tended to be dominated by a few vocal students with strong opinions. The techniques that I described earlier to increase and broaden participation by all students were extremely successful. While the quieter students never came to dominate the discussion, the conversations were far more balanced in the latter part of the semester, with the naturally vocal students having learned to listen more effectively to the other students, and the quieter students having become more wililng and able to speak up.

Course Elements. The next question asked how useful students found different aspects of the course to be. "Extremely useful" was the dominant answer for two categories: the research paper (47.1%) and the NetLogo project (35.3%). My impression is that students welcomed the opportunity to perform in-depth investigations of the subject over an extended period of time. The students found eight course aspects "very useful" overall: in-class discussions (64.7%), online discussions and in-class presentations (both 52.9%), written exercises and in-class lectures by the professor (both 47.1%), student in-class presentations (41.2%), laboratory exercises (35.3%), and assigned readings (29.4%,

Table 3: **Post-assessment survey responses regarding writing and in-class discussions**

	Writing		Discussions	
	Comfort level	Ability	Comfort level	Quality
Significantly increased	5.9%	11.8%	0.0%	5.9%
Increased somewhat	**64.7%**	**64.7%**	35.3%	35.3%
Stayed about the same	29.4%	23.5%	**58.8%**	**52.9%**
Decreased somewhat	0.0%	0.0%	5.9%	5.9%
Significantly decreased	0.0%	0.0%	0.0%	0.0%

Table 4: **Post-assessment survey responses regarding overall impressions**

	Interesting	Changed thinking	Relevant	Enjoyable	Learned a lot	Glad I took it	Recommend it
Extremely	**52.9%**	**35.3%**	5.9%	**41.2%**	**52.9%**	**47.1%**	**47.1%**
Very	35.3%	**35.3%**	11.8%	29.4%	41.2%	23.5%	17.6%
Moderately	11.8%	23.5%	**64.7%**	29.4%	5.9%	29.4%	23.5%
A little	0.0%	5.9%	17.6%	0.0%	0.0%	0.0%	11.8%
Not at all	0.0%	0.0%	0.0%	0.0%	0.0%	0.0%	0.0%

the same frequency as "moderately useful" for that category). These course aspects were generally the most interactive, and gave the students the most opportunity to interact with each other; the positive attitudes towards these course components support a hypothesis that students were enthusiastic about learning from and with each other.

Several course elements were seen as only "moderately useful," including guest lectures and presentations (70.6%), other assigned readings (35.3%), and the course Game Day (35.3%). Students' written feedback about the assigned readings focused on the textbook being too dry and mathematical; the other assigned readings were generally found to be more useful. While the Game Day was not rated as "extremely useful," students' written comments about the day were universally positive.

None of the course elements had a majority answer of "not at all useful" or "a little useful," although more than one student gave "a little useful" responses for several elements: textbook reading (23.5%), laboratory exercises and Game Day (17.6%), and written exercises (11.8%).

Student Impressions. The remaining questions asked students about their general impressions (Table 4). The dominant responses in all categories but one were "extreme" agreement with the positive sentiment. The majority said they found the class extremely interesting, with a third describing it as "very interesting." All but one of the students said that it was a "very" or "extremely" good learning experience. Similarly, three-quarters of the students were "very" or "extremely" glad that they took the class; two-thirds would "very" or "extremely" recommend it to another student; and 70% thought it was "very" or "extremely" enjoyable.

Interestingly, student responses were slightly less positive when asked whether they would recommend the class to another student than whether they thought it was enjoyable, interesting, or a good learning experience themselves. The overall answer to this question was still yes, but a few students would only recommend it "a little" even though there were no answers in this category to the other questions. This is a small sample size that may not have great significance, but it is also possible that while students felt they got a lot out of a class from which they hadn't been sure what to expect, they weren't as certain whether their fellow students would benefit from the novelty of the experience.

Perceived relevance to students' careers was somewhat lower than the other overall perceptions, but was still generally positive. Two-thirds (64.7%) of the students said that the class was "moderately" relevant, with 17.6% reporting "a little" relevance, 11.8% "very" relevant, and 5.9% "extremely" relevant. This is unsurprising and in part may reflect a tendency to think that only specific skills and concepts that are directly useful to one's job are "relevant" to a career. The fact that two-thirds of the students agreed "very" or "extremely" with the statement, "The class changed the way I think about the world," may say more about what these students will bring into their future careers in terms of a broad ability to understand complex systems and their relevance.

3.4 SCEQ Scores

Table 5 shows student responses to selected questions from the SCEQ course survey in 2011 and 2012. These are the questions that pertain to whether the student gained new insights and skills; how much learning was facilitated by assigned readings, written assignments, lectures, research projects, student presentations, and class discussions; the degree to which students were actively encouraged to participate and the instructor encouraged fair and open discussion; and the instructor's overall teaching effectiveness. The table gives responses for this course in each semester, followed by averages for the Computer Science and Electrical Engineering (CSEE) department, Honors (HONR) courses, and UMBC overall.

In 2011, students in the courses rated it higher in every category than departmental and UMBC averages, but somewhat below HONR course in all categories except two of the questions pertaining to class discussions (did they facilitate student learning, and were students actively encouraged to participate). Interestingly, though, the course was rated *higher* than the HONR average on "overall teaching effectiveness."

In 2012, with the adjustments and improvements to the class, and with a more diverse set of students, scores increased in nearly every category. The class was again rated higher than departmental and UMBC averages in all categories, but it was now also rated similarly (within 0.1) or

[4]The seminar-specific questions are not asked in CSEE classes.

Table 5: Selected SCEQ responses from 2011 ($n = 22$) and 2012 ($n = 20$). Answers are averages in the range 1 (low) to 5 (high).

	2011				2012			
Question	Course	CSEE	HONR	UMBC	Course	CSEE	HONR	UMBC
New insights and skills?	4.36	4.20	4.66	4.33	4.45	4.29	4.27	4.33
Assigned readings	4.18	3.75	4.57	4.13	4.55	3.75	4.53	4.12
Written assignments	4.18	4.08	4.29	4.16	4.20	4.17	4.16	4.15
Lectures	4.40	4.20	4.73	4.36	4.40	4.19	4.47	4.33
Research projects[4]	4.20	4.10	4.23	4.25	4.17	N/A	4.24	4.50
Presentations[2]	4.45	4.10	4.63	4.32	4.50	N/A	4.58	4.54
Class discussions	4.58	3.99	4.55	4.18	4.46	3.88	4.50	4.18
Actively encouraged to participate	5.00	4.13	4.78	4.36	4.62	4.17	4.65	4.37
Encouraged fair and open discussion	4.50	4.20	4.72	4.40	4.77	4.22	4.35	4.41
Overall teaching effectiveness	4.58	4.02	4.45	4.12	4.47	3.98	4.24	4.11

higher than other HONR classes in most categories. The scores were particularly high in "new insights and skills," "fair and open discussion," and "overall teaching effectiveness."

Student comments from the open-ended written part of the SCEQ included:

- "This class definitely expanded my world view and introduced me to concepts I had never thought about. I enjoyed interacting with other students.... Extremely unique and interesting class."
- "The professor made it a goal to hear from everyone. The open format of discussion made difficult topics more accessible."
- "Awesome topic, great variety, a great tie between the details of computation & nature."
- "I really enjoyed this class. I did more outside work because I wanted to than was assigned. I don't think any class has been so captivating and fun. Thanks for a great semester."
- "She encouraged student-led discussion by identifying students who spoke too little or too much."

A final comment perhaps best sums up the challenging nature of the class and its positive student outcomes:

> To be honest, I went thru this semester feeling out-of-my-league and barely catching a true (technical) understanding of the concepts. However, looking back, even though some of the finer aspects may have brushed by me, I think I have a better/wider view on what goes on around me. And I can't look at trees without thinking of fractals. Thanks for a great semester.

With this student, at least, I succeeded in my goal to "change the way that they think about the world."

4. CONCLUSIONS

The course was very successful at its core content goal of enabling students to identify the sources and effects of complexity in the world around them, and to look at the world differently. It also helped students to improve their writing skills, to participate more effectively in class discussions, and to learn collaboratively in an interdisciplinary context.

The core elements of the class—active discussions, NetLogo modeling projects, the research paper, and student presentations—work very well and I would not make any changes to the basic structure. There are, however, a few improvements that I would make. Many students enjoyed the outside readings but did not like the textbook. I would make the textbook optional, and add more outside and varied readings on the course topics, focusing in particular on locating broadly accessible articles on the more difficult mathematical topics such as fractal dimensions and chaotic systems. Finally, the guest lectures were a mixed success because it was difficult to find outside speakers who were able to fit into the tone of the class, so I would be very selective about who to invite.

Acknowledgements

This material is based upon work supported by the National Science Foundation under grant number CAREER-0545726.

5. REFERENCES

[1] Computer science principles: Computational thinking practices: Big ideas, key concepts, and supporting concepts. Technical report, The College Baord, 2012.

[2] S. M. Chang. It's time to raise my hand. *Harvard Gazette*, December 1 2011.

[3] J. Elarde and C. Fatt-Fei. Introductory computing course content: Educator and student perspectives. In *SIGITE'11*, October 2011.

[4] N. Falchikov and D. Boud. Student self-assessment in higher education: A meta-analysis. *Review of Educational Research*, 59(4):395–430, Winter 1989.

[5] G. Flake. *The Computational Beauty of Nature: Computer Explorations of Fractals, Chaos, Complex Systems, and Adaptation.* MIT Press, 1998.

[6] M. A. Nowak, K. M. Page, and K. Sigmund. Fairness versus reason in the ultimatum game. *Science*, 289(5485):1773–1775, 2000.

[7] C. Reynolds. Flocks, herds and schools: A distributed behavioral model. In *SIGGRAPH '87: Proceedings of the 14th Annual Conference on Computer Graphics and Interactive Techniques*, pages 25–34, 1987.

[8] C. Rolheiser and J. A. Ross. Student self-evaluation: What research says and what practice shows. Technical report, Center for Development and Learning, 2012.

Application of the Cognitive Apprenticeship Framework to a Middle School Robotics Camp

D. Brian Larkins*
Computer Science
Coastal Carolina University
P.O. Box 261954
Conway, SC 29528-6054
blarkins@coastal.edu

J. Christopher Moore
Chemistry and Physics
Coastal Carolina University
moorejc@coastal.edu

Laura R. Covington†
Chemistry and Physics
Coastal Carolina University
lrcoving@g.coastal.edu

Louis J. Rubbo
Chemistry and Physics
Coastal Carolina University
lrubbo@coastal.edu

ABSTRACT

This paper details the development and implementation of a summer robotics camp for middle school children. The Cognitive Apprenticeship (CA) model is used as the framework for developing the camp. Specifically, methods such as modeling, coaching, scaffolding, articulation, reflection, and exploration are integrated throughout the camp structure. Activities include the use of an engineering notebook, debugging logs, and various cognitive challenges, all supervised by a team of expert mentors. During the two-week summer camp, participants realized a positive shift in attitudes towards science, developed common engineering design skills, and showed increased proficiency in the reasoning pattern of isolation of variables. The CA framework, in conjunction with robotics are an excellent way to build interest in STEM and develop skills in engineering, science, and computational thinking.

Categories and Subject Descriptors

K.3.2 [**Computers and Education**]: Computer and Information Science Education

General Terms

Design, Human Factors

Keywords

Cognitive Apprenticeship, Education, Robotics, K-12, STEM

---

*Corresponding author.

†Undergraduate student.

SIGCSE'13, March 6–9, 2013, Denver, Colorado, USA.

1. INTRODUCTION

A troubling trend in education is the lack of proficiency with K-12 students in STEM (Science, Technology, Engineering, and Math) subjects. Even more concerning is that the problem is not limited to aptitude, but also a lack of *interest* in STEM fields. Building interest and improving student proficiency can be accomplished by establishing a personal connection with STEM ideas and activities at an early age [7]. Early intervention through out-of-school programs can foster a lifelong interest in science and technology for all students and is crucial to the long-term success of struggling students [4].

Early intervention and full immersion in STEM-based activities is of critical importance. At this stage of development, immersion in a guided-inquiry environment is necessary but not sufficient in developing scientific reasoning. Research has shown that explicit instruction is necessary to successfully develop reasoning skills for all age levels [6, 11].

In this paper, we describe the application of the *cognitive apprenticeship* (CA) model applied to Robocamp, a summer camp program for middle school students. This program provides students a fully immersive experience at an early age with three principal objectives: a) improving their perception of STEM subjects b) developing scientific reasoning skills, and c) to consider the pursuit of a career in a STEM-related field. The Robocamp program is designed as two weeks of half-day sessions in which middle school students are introduced to a robotics curriculum and learn how to construct robotic hardware and software systems to solve "missions". The Robocamp program uses LEGO Mindstorms educational kits in conjunction with the Carnegie Mellon University *Robotics Academy* curriculum to motivate the application of STEM-related tasks and ideas.

Throughout the course of the robotics camp, students construct a variety of different Mindstorms robots and software programs to solve a set of problems related to terraforming distant planets. The robots and terraforming setting provide the backdrop for teaching topics such as design, problem solving and teamwork in addition to traditional STEM topics such as math, science, and technology using the cognitive apprenticeship approach.

Our approach is based on the following insights: First, cognitive apprenticeship, being a recent instructional design model, is well suited to provide early intervention and full immersion for middle school students. Second, that using affordable educational robotics systems provides a natural problem domain in which to apply cognitive apprenticeship.

This work makes the following contributions: First, we describe how CA can be applied to teaching scientific reasoning and computational thinking to middle school students. Second, we provide a set of techniques and activities that can be used in conjunction with this approach. Lastly, we demonstrate that upon completion of the camp, students leave with an improved perception of science, math, and technology, as well as a more positive opinion of pursuing a STEM-related career.

2. BACKGROUND

Situated cognition theory postulates that all knowledge is situated in actions that occur within cultural, social, and physical contexts [2]. The "Zone of Proximal Development" (ZPD) construct introduced by Vygotsky is defined as the difference between what a learner can do on their own as opposed what he or she can do with help (i.e. in a social/cultural context) [10]. It is this area, where situated learning approaches such as *cognitive apprenticeship* can be useful in increasing the abilities of the learner.

Cognitive apprenticeship borrows from traditional apprenticeship as an applied teaching technique for learners constrained to classroom environments. The application of cognitive apprenticeship is focused on improving proficiency and ability in an assisted learning context. Expanding the abilities of the learner in an assisted setting leads to an increase of their abilities in an unaided setting [3]. The application of CA has been studied in the context of undergraduate CS education, but with different objectives than increasing STEM perception and proficiency [8].

The principal teaching methods of cognitive apprenticeship are summarized as follows [1]:

Modeling: This technique involves an expert within the subject domain explicitly demonstrating a task to a student observer with the intention that the learner is able to build a conceptual model for the task at hand. Implicit processes are exposed so that students can observe and understand the rationale for the problem-solving process.

Coaching: The master observes students in the process of trying to perform a task and gives them individual feedback and can offer assistance at critical moments. Students are actively involved in the problem-solving process and are required to integrate subskills and conceptual knowledge.

Scaffolding: The expert assists students in performing a task, some parts involving skills that are beyond the student's abilities. Assistance is slowly withdrawn (*fading*) as the learner is able to manage more of the task on their own. Scaffolding helps students develop self-awareness and self-correction skills allowing them to be less dependent on external help.

Articulation: This method requires learners to think about their own actions and explain them to others, making their knowledge explicit. This allows students to reorganize their knowledge and generalize its application to related problem domains.

Reflection: Students reflect on their own performance in solving a problem through analysis and deconstruction. Students can increase their self-awareness of knowledge and compare their own understanding with that of others. Students can also compare their own performance with that of an expert and adjust their own conceptual model accordingly.

Exploration: In exploration, students investigate new methods, strategies, and test new hypotheses by exploring the problem domain. Students can set their own goals and develop their own testing strategies, all of which fosters independent learning.

The first three methods (modeling, coaching, and scaffolding) are the principal techniques for CA. They are designed to help students construct a conceptual model for the problem domain and develop a set of cognitive skills through observation and practice. Both articulation and reflection serve to internalize their observations and experience, as well as aid in integrating new knowledge and problem-solving skills. Lastly, exploration fosters independence and encourages autonomous problem formulations and solutions.

3. ROBOCAMP

3.1 Overview

The Robocamp program is delivered over a two-week period with 3-4 hours of instruction each day. The camp was developed around a theme of terraforming foreign planets through the use of autonomous robots to accomplish this objective. During the first day of camp, students construct a basic LEGO Mindstorms robot configuration and program it to perform some simple tasks.

The remainder of the camp is broken down into two parts, a set of four *Moon Missions* and the *Pantheon*. The Moon Missions span the first week of camp, where students are tasked with outfitting their robots with sensors and actuators to complete four specified tasks (such as collecting objects on the playfield, etc.). During the second week of camp (Pantheon), students compete to complete as many tasks as possible by the end of the camp. Tasks vary in difficulty, with more difficult challenges being worth more points in the competition.

The challenges involve maneuvering a LEGO Mindstorms robot around a 4 × 8 foot game board containing a number of obstacles and objectives. For example, one challenge might be to have the robot leave the starting position, follow a blue line to a "frozen lunar lake", then to insert a "water extraction pipeline" into it. The game board configuration and challenges were provided as part of the CMU curriculum.

Each day of camp consisted of several activities. Early in the week, mentors would use the beginning of the camp day to demonstrate new sensors, their capabilities and limits, as well as how to use them in the Mindstorms software environment. Later in the camp, this time is replaced with modules on terraforming and space exploration with the aim to increase science literacy, interest in STEM topics, and to connect camp activities with actual scientific challenges.

The camp was comprised of 27 middle school students assigned to groups of 2-3 students each. Participating students were from a diverse range of schools in the Horry County School District. There were a total of seven mentors for

Figure 1: Picture of one of the authors (Louis Rubbo, left) demonstrating a new technique to students.

Figure 2: Picture of an undergraduate student mentor (Laura Covington, left) actively coaching a group through a difficult challenge.

the camp, three faculty mentors and four upper-level undergraduate assistants. Typically six mentors were available to assist the approximately 10 groups every day.

3.2 Engineering Notebooks

Each group of students were given an Engineering Notebook to record their designs and problem-solving processes over the course of the camp. Every task (for both the warm-up Moon Missions and the Pantheon competition) has its own section in the notebook. For a given task, the engineering notebook contains a detailed description of the problem to be solved, a diagram that illustrates the problem visually, and a scoring rubric specifying the points awarded for each component subtask.

Additional pages provide space for students to brainstorm possible solutions, sketch out ideas and strategies, and to record a description of their final design. During the build/test phase, students record the problems that they encounter in a debugging log, along with a short description of how they resolved the issue.

4. ROBOTICS VIA COGNITIVE APPRENTICESHIP

Over the course of the two-week period, students learn problem-solving skills, computational thinking, and scientific reasoning using cognitive apprenticeship techniques. The CA methods described above were integrated into a variety of activities throughout Robocamp.

Modeling Activities: Each day begins with the entire group observing a mentor demonstrating a new technique that can be used with the Mindstorms robots to solve a challenge. Different sessions cover light and touch sensors, dead reckoning and navigation, actuator control, etc. Figure 1 shows an example of one of the authors modeling an approach to a challenge based on dead reckoning and discussing some of the problems commonly associated with this type of solution.

A common task for robots is *line following*, where the robot uses a light sensor to detect the presence of a contrasting line on the floor. The program idiom used to perform this task is to loop between two states: (`no-line` → `turn-left`) and (`see-line` → `turn-right`). This approach is simple to implement, but the insight of having the robot simply oscillate between the two states is difficult for students new to robotics and programming. By demonstrating the basic line following algorithm, students are then able to construct a conceptual model for themselves and adapt the approach for their own purposes.

Additional modeling happens within each group throughout the remainder of the day. When a group becomes overwhelmed by a problem, a mentor works with them directly. Often times, modeling occurs as the mentor simply describes their own thought process aloud, rather than through explicit demonstration. This exposes techniques such as cost-benefit analysis and allows students to understand the reasoning and rationale behind decision making.

Coaching Activities: Students spend the majority of their time in Robocamp working in their group on solving either the Moon Missions or Pantheon challenges. During this time, mentors are in continuous rotation checking in with each group and observing their progress. As shown in Figure 2, mentors help the students work through difficult challenges conceptually and pragmatically by employing inquiry-based learning methods. This approach keeps the students cognitively active in the problem-solving process, providing confidence while simultaneously building problem decomposition and reasoning skills.

After camp participants leave for the day, mentors discuss their observations made throughout the camp session. This allows mentors to understand each individual student and to develop a specific strategy for coaching each group throughout the entire camp.

Aside from the direct coaching during the robot missions, other coaching activities are integrated into the morning sessions involving the entire camp. The students are presented with a goal and a proposed "solution" for solving the problem. The proposed solution contains one or more errors within the program, illustrating a specific logic flaw or nuance which is easy to overlook by inspection.

For example, early in the camp students are shown a program that is intended to have the robot navigate in a square pattern. The turns are intentionally programmed to an angle slightly larger than 90°. When demonstrated, the robot appears to start off behaving correctly, but after a few repetitions is clearly not tracking a square path. Students then analyze the program and are coached by mentors to develop a hypothesis for the incorrect behavior (error propagation) as well as a debugging scheme (unit testing) to test the validity of their hypothesis.

Scaffolding Activities: Since many of the students have never used or programmed robots prior to participating in Robocamp, early activities are heavily scaffolded. Some scaffolding is provided by LEGO directly, through detailed instructions on how to construct a basic robot along with a large number of tutorials and examples contained within the Mindstorms software. Additionally, the CMU Robotics Academy curriculum also provides mission specifications and game board configuration, along with more tutorials and sample programs.

Aside from externally provided materials, the engineering notebook is a mechanism designed to help students structure the problem-solving process. The notebook provides a place for students to work through the process of completing a mission in a methodical manner and encourages the sequencing of sub-steps when constructing a solution.

Some group demonstrations are scaffolded to develop intuition and assist with the construction of a conceptual model. An example of this is with the introduction of sensors. When introducing the ultrasonic sensor (used for range determination), a student is selected to "be a robot" and is tasked with walking a fixed distance using only input from a sensor. Walking too far ends in the destruction of the robot by means of lava, acid, or similar device. The student is then blindfolded and allowed to move while only receiving perceptual input from the "sensor". The sensor input is provided verbally as the distance from the goal. The participating student steps normally at first, but slows down as the range becomes closer to zero, to avoid stepping off the edge. Once students understand the robot as being blindfolded, save for its sensors, they intuitively understand many of the challenges involved in navigation and perception.

Articulation Activities: One of the key activities in having groups work to solve a task is that each individual participant must communicate their own ideas and plans to the other group members. Throughout the camp, much of a groups success or failure can be directly attributed to the ability of its members to communicate effectively. Groups with poor communication dynamics receive additional coaching to help individuals make their knowledge concrete and sharable with others. In some cases, students need to be reassigned to alternate groups with a more compatible communication dynamic.

At the end of Robocamp, there is a graduation ceremony and an opportunity for students to demonstrate their robot to their parents. As with the group work, this forces each participant to explain their understanding and reasoning to others, allowing them to recast and generalize their knowledge for a different audience.

Beyond explicit articulation via communication, the engineering notebook is an invaluable tool. One aspect of the engineering notebook is to provide a structured process to solve problems, another intention is that students consider their actions and provide a document that can be shared with group members or mentors. The documentation provided by the notebook was especially useful if participants missed a day of camp, for example.

Reflection Activities: Students reflect on their understanding and performance as they progress through the mission campaigns. In addition to working in their groups throughout the problem solving process, they also use the engineering notebook to annotate knowledge gained during each task. Each engineering notebook contains a log which tracks their steps in debugging their robot for each mission. By making a written record of this process, students are able to analyze and generalize both problems and solutions for a variety of tasks.

Additionally, groups are also able to observe each other and their relative progress. This permits creative ideas to be shared amongst groups and promotes a self-awareness of a student's abilities relative to others.

Exploration Activities: Throughout the first week of Robocamp, students follow a more prescribed program, designed to provide a foundation for completing tasks with the LEGO robot and Mindstorms software. The second week of Robocamp, however, is far less structured and provides more freedom to experiment and innovate. The Pantheon missions are setup as a large set of tasks of variable difficulty and points. Students compete to maximize the points obtained within the fixed time remaining in the camp. This allows some groups to select difficult challenges that require more time investment, but have a larger point payoff. Alternatively, weaker groups may choose a strategy based on quantity of tasks completed, rather than difficulty.

Students have freedom to work on tasks that utilize skills and concepts previously mastered (specialization) or to try and solve tasks that require new skills and programming techniques (generalization). The Pantheon activities foster both self-confidence and independent learning.

5. EVALUATION

A mixed-methods evaluation plan was designed and implemented for assessment of the camp goals. Specifically, we looked at quantitative gains in student perceptions of and interest in the various STEM areas using the STEM Semantic Survey (SSS) [9]. We also implemented a pre/post research design to investigate student use of "fair testing" via a common isolation of variables Piagetian task [5]. A qualitative evaluation of student engineering notebooks was used to asses the development of design and troubleshooting skills.

The SSS measures student interest in five STEM areas: (1) science, (2) math, (3) engineering, (4) technology, and (5) interest in STEM careers more broadly. Figure 3 shows pre- and post-camp results from the SSS. Responses from a group (n = 43) of STEM professionals, as reported in [9], are also shown for comparison. For all areas, a score greater than 4 indicates a positive attitude, whereas a score less than 4 indicates a negative attitude toward the particular area.

Our goal for this project was for students to approach attitudes consistent with STEM professionals [9]. As indicated in Figure 3, this goal was achieved. Interestingly, before the start of camp students expressed interest in engineering and technology at levels similar to STEM professionals. Furthermore, the average camper arrived with positive at-

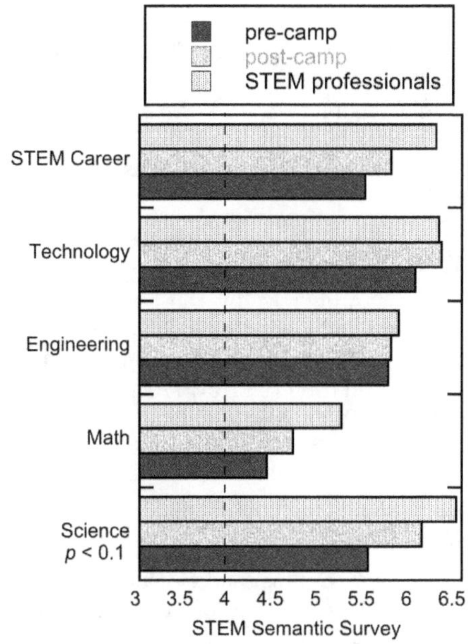

Figure 3: Pre- and post-camp results from the STEM Semantic Survey. Responses from a group of STEM professionals are also shown for comparison. As evaluated, a score greater than 4 indicates a positive attitude, whereas a score less than 4 indicates a negative attitude, as indicated by the vertical dashed line.

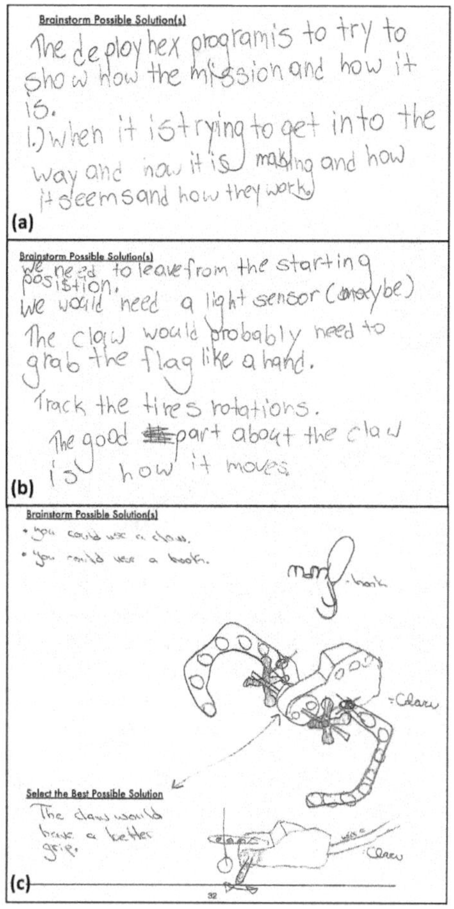

Figure 4: Scanned images from a student group's engineering notebook (a) during an early camp mission, and (b) during a later camp mission. (c) As camp progressed, students began to include more sketches and multiple design options.

titudes about all STEM areas. This is not particularly surprising, since the camp consisted of a self-selecting group and camp promotional materials clearly indicated a focus on engineering. No statistically significant shift (p>0.1) in student attitudes towards math or STEM careers was observed, though students arrived at camp with an already high interest in STEM careers. Student attitudes towards science demonstrated a positive shift significant at the 10% level, which may be attributed to the scientific content incorporated throughout the engineering tasks.

Engineering notebooks were evaluated to determine if the camp was successful at developing common engineering design skills, such as articulation, rapid prototyping, design evaluation, and troubleshooting. Figure 4(a) shows a scanned image from one group's engineering notebook during an early camp mission, whereas Figure 4(b) shows an excerpt from the same group's notebook during a later camp mission. Comparison of the excerpts in Figure 4(a) and (b) demonstrate significant improvement in the student's articulation of their design plan and goals for a particular mission.

As camp progressed, we also noticed an increase in effective pre-design through the use of sketches, multiple design options, and evaluation of options based on certain criteria either expressed or implied. Figure 4(c) shows an excerpt from an engineering notebook during a late-camp mission where the group proposed and sketched three different design options for achieving a task and articulated a decision based on perceived constraints. Furthermore, student debugging logs (not shown) demonstrated increased sophistication with isolating and correcting problems in design and code as camp progressed.

To assess development of "fair testing" use in the form of variable isolation, we implemented a pencil and paper test based on a common Piagetian task [5]. Figure 5(a) shows a drawing of three balls, a ramp, and a small block. Ball 1 and Ball 3 are the same size. Ball 2 is larger, however, both Ball 1 and Ball 2 have a weight of 5 units. Ball 3 has a weight of 10 units. Ball 1 is released from a low position on an inclined block of wood, as shown in the drawing. The ball hits the small block at the bottom of the ramp causing it to move a distance of 1 unit. The students are told that Ball 3 is then released from the top of the ramp and strikes the block. The block moves 2 units. The block is then replaced with another block having twice the density. Ball 1 is released from the top of the ramp and strikes the more dense block. The dense block moves only 1 unit. The students are asked if the result of the experiment shows that Ball 3 can move a target a greater distance than Ball 1.

In order to earn credit for a correct response, the student must answer correctly and provide a coherent and correct explanation. Figure 5(b) shows the percent of the popula-

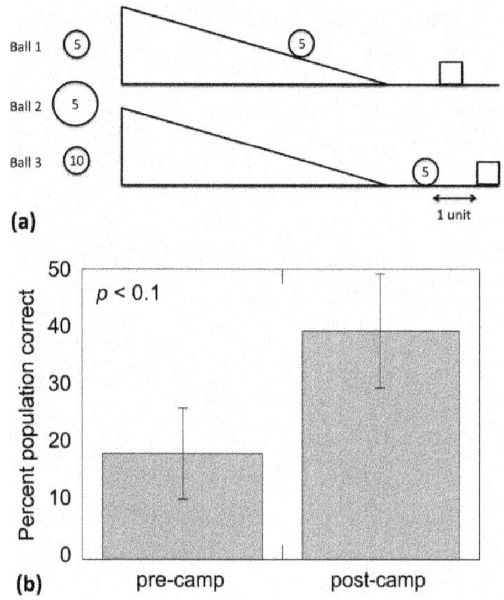

Figure 5: (a) Schematic of the set-up for the Piagetian task used to identify correct use of the isolation of variables reasoning pattern. Three different balls may strike a block after rolling down a ramp. Ball 1 and Ball 2 have the same mass of 5 units, but different diameters. Ball 1 and Ball 3 have the same diameter, but different masses. (b) Percent of the student population that correctly answered and demonstrated correct reasoning for the isolation of variables question.

tion that correctly answered the question and explained their reasoning both before the start of camp and after the completion of the camp. An increase significant at the 10% level was observed, suggesting emphasis on "fair testing" throughout the camp led to improvements in the scientific reasoning pattern of isolation of variables.

6. CONCLUSIONS AND FUTURE WORK

The decline of both aptitude and interest in STEM subjects will have a dramatic impact on the ability of future generations to solve the many significant challenges that lie ahead. Addressing raw skill deficiencies in science and math is a daunting challenge in and of itself. This challenge is only compounded with increasing apathy in STEM professions and subjects. It is understood that addressing these two crucial problems is of critical import, not only at an early age – but also with techniques that work to develop the skills needed for success in STEM. To address these challenges, we have described the application of the cognitive apprenticeship model to change perceptions about STEM subjects and improve student ability for scientific reasoning.

By providing an environment which is fully immersive and targets students at an early age, we have shown the CA approach to be successful in changing STEM perceptions. The approach described is based on the notion that the proximal development of participants can be improved by a combination of modeling, coaching, scaffolding, articulation, reflection, and exploration. This approach has been demonstrated to be successful both quantitatively and also qualitatively.

Moving forward, we are currently in the process of bringing the Robocamp experience to a number of other schools in the Horry County School District. The Robocamp model is affordable, effective, and can be easily transferred to others, such as middle school teachers. We see the cognitive apprenticeship model as being applicable to both traditional education in middle schools, as well as rural schools and home schooling.

7. ACKNOWLEDGMENTS

This work was supported by the South Carolina Space Grant Consortium under the Research and Education Awards Program (REAP). Partial funding was provided by the National Science Foundation (DMR #1104600) and the College of Science at CCU. We would also like to thank our student mentors and the participants of the CCU Robocamp 2012 program.

8. REFERENCES

[1] J. S. Brown, A. Collins, and P. Duguid. Situated Cognition and the Culture of Learning. *Educational Researcher*, 18(1):32–42, Jan. 1989.

[2] A. Collins, J. S. Brown, and A. Holum. Cognitive Apprenticeship: Making Thinking Visible. *American Educator*, 6:38–46, 1991.

[3] A. Ghefaili. Cognitive Apprenticeship, Technology, and the Contextualization of Learning Environments. *Journal of Educational Computing, Design, and Online Learning*, 4, Fall 2003.

[4] P. Lauer, M. Akiba, S. Wilkerson, Apthorp, H.S., D. Snow, and M. Martin-Glenn. Out-of-School-Time Programs: A Meta-Analysis of Effects for At-Risk Students. *Review of Educational Research*, 76:275–313, 2006.

[5] A. Lawson. The development and validation of a classroom test of formal reasoning. *Journal of Research in Science Teaching*, 15(1):11–24, 1978.

[6] W. Overton, editor. *Reasoning, Necessity, and Logic: Developmental Perspectives.* Lawrence Erlbaum Associates, 1990.

[7] President's Council of Advisors on Science and Technology. Prepare and Inspire: K-12 Education in Science, Technology, Engineering, and Math (STEM) For America's Future, September 2010. Executive Office of the President.

[8] A. Shabo, M. Guzdial, and J. Stasko. Computer Science Apprenticeship: Creating Support for Intermediate Computer Science Students. In *Proceedings of the 1996 International Conference on Learning Sciences*, ICLS '96, pages 308–315. International Society of the Learning Sciences, 1996.

[9] T. Tyler-Wood, G. Knezek, and R. Christensen. Instruments for Assessing Interest in STEM Content and Careers. *Journal of Technology and Teacher Education*, 18(2):341–363, 2010.

[10] L. S. Vygotskiĭ. *Mind in Society: Development of Higher Psychological Processes.* Harvard University Press, 1978.

[11] B. White and J. Frederiksen. Inquiry, Modeling, and Metacognition: Making Science Accessible to All Students. *Cognition and Instruction*, 16(1):3–118, 1998.

Using Scaffolded Examples to Teach Computational Thinking Concepts

Heidi C. Webb
The Pennsylvania State University
College of IST
University Park, PA 16802
+1 814-863-2478
hcw120@psu.edu

Mary Beth Rosson
The Pennsylvania State University
College of IST
University Park, PA 16802
+1 814-863-2478
mrosson@psu.edu

ABSTRACT

In this paper we describe a set of computing activities that were used in an outreach enrichment program for middle school girls. The computing activities used a combination of scaffolded examples and minimalist workbooks to introduce and support interaction with computational thinking (CT) concepts, including problem solving, abstraction and basic computational vocabulary. We describe the activities briefly, followed by a discussion of the girls' experiences, drawing primarily from interviews conducted at the end of each activity.

Categories and Subject Descriptors

K.3.0 [**Computers and Education**]: General Education

General Terms

Design, Human Factors

Keywords

Scaffolded example, Scratch, middle school girls

1. INTRODUCTION

Children learn by interacting with people and materials in their environment; they use what they learn to refine their subsequent behavior. Often children learn in social settings, for example by imitating their peers in a group setting, or seeking help from adults to carry out behaviors that are just beyond their current skills or understandings [1]. The pedagogical concept of *scaffolding* refers to forms of assistance in a learning setting –human help or other aids embedded within tools or activities – to help a young learner accomplish activities that would otherwise be difficult or impossible [2].

The application of minimalist design to learning activities often results in scaffolding [3]. For example, a brief manual or "guided exploration card" can be used to both offer learning and reflection goals and to provide just-in-time tips or feedback that can help to coordinate progress on a novel task. In the context of example-based learning, a *scaffolded example* is one that is carefully designed to guide learners to just the pieces of the example that are believed to be most relevant to their current understanding [4]. One of the benefits of scaffolding can be an increase in learning engagement and motivation, because the scaffolding may allow learners to be introduced to unfamiliar concepts and skills while also permitting them to work with artifacts that are complex enough to be meaningful and fun. In the work presented here we are exploring the use of scaffolding techniques for introducing computational concepts to students of middle school age.

In a complex skill-based problem domain like programming, scaffolded examples provide an opportunity for learners to gradually encounter a set of concepts and skills. Novices quickly become overwhelmed when faced with a blank screen when using a computing technology for the first time; in these cases the availability of working examples offers an opportunity to explore and build confidence as new skills are acquired. In prior work, we have shown that high school girls learning about web development can benefit from scaffolded examples in building their skills with databases and webpages [5].

When people develop computational solutions to problems (i.e. when they program) they activate a problem solving process during which they first analyze the problem, then consider and choose among different possible solutions. The abstractions needed for these solutions may range from simple concepts related to stored information to more complex concepts like list processing that relies on searching and sorting. As design ideas are implemented in a computer language the solutions will generally also require testing and debugging. These different aspects of building a computational solution are among those under the umbrella of *computational thinking* (CT) [6]. In the past few years there has been a growing movement to specify and include such concepts in high school curricula (www.exploringcs.org) and teacher education [7].

In the summer of 2009, the Computer Science Teachers Association (CSTA) and the International Society for Technology in Education (ISTE) began a multi-phased project aimed at developing an operational definition of computational thinking for K-12 [8]. Four of the main elements were problem solving, abstraction, testing/debugging, and computational vocabulary. Because this definitional work emerged through thoughtful discussions by stakeholders intimately involved in K-12 teaching standards, we elected to work from these concepts in our own study. We are exploring the role of scaffolded learning activities for middle school girls to learn these basic computational concepts and skills:

How can we use the educational strategy of scaffolded examples to engage middle school girls in computer activities, while also introducing and building an understanding of CT concepts?

In the balance of the paper we first present the design and rationale for the learning activities, and then describe the girls' experiences, drawing primarily from interview data. We conclude with a brief discussion of implications and future directions.

SIGCSE'13, March 6–9, 2013, Denver, Colorado, USA.

2. SCAFFOLDED LEARNING ACTIVITIES

In the context of teaching CT concepts to middle school girls, we have built scaffolded examples that are games, stories or other interactive activities. These examples "work" in the sense that the girls can run the program, but at the same time they exhibit some sort of faulty characteristic or other quirk that requires investigation. Through the investigation process, the learners encounter and learn about computational features of interest. Each activity also includes a workbook that is modeled on the minimalist concept of a "guided exploration card" [3]. That is, it introduces the example and related concepts in a deliberately incomplete way and includes questions designed to provoke reflection or further exploration of the example. We also intended these workbooks to be a source of data, as we provided space next to the embedded questions for the girls to write down their responses.

During Fall 2011 and Spring 2012 a preliminary study was conducted using several different computing technologies – Alice 2.0, Scratch, a custom web development tool, and Lego® Mindstorms [9]. In the initial studies we found that the middle school girls tended to become confused when the activities moved from one platform to another, and that they appeared to be most successful and engaged when working with Scratch. We also observed the workbooks were useful in guiding the activities. Almost all of the girls were able to complete their projects, but we noted that they often did not write down answers to all of the reflective questions embedded in the workbooks. As a result, we decided to simplify the learning to use just one platform (Scratch) and to include interviews after each activity to assess the learning that may or may not have occurred.

In the new set of activities, we followed a similar scheme, with activity designed to exercise particular CT concepts or skills. Each activity revolved around a scaffolded example – working code that exemplified the concepts of interest, to be discovered via exploration and subsequent extension or modification [4]. For instance in the first activity the scaffolded example is a story that requires problem solving to analyze what is wrong with the story line and how to fix it; essential Scratch terminology like "sprite" and "broadcast" are also introduced. In the second we used a simple interactive game to expand the girls' problem solving to include new abstractions such as variables. Table 1 provides a summary of the four activities, key questions from the workbook designed to promote discovery learning, and sample interview questions asked after the activity to probe understanding of the CT concepts being illustrated by the activity. In the activities studied here, a vacation theme was used to provide an overall story line. We turn now to a more detailed description of each activity.

Table 1- Learning Activity and Questions Mapped to CT Concepts

Scaffolded Example	Workbook Questions	Interview Questions	CT Concepts
An animated story that has a character missing from a scene and not reacting in the manner one would expect when they aren't happy with a friend's suggestion	• What characters are/are not being used at this time in the story? • What do you think the problem might be? (A character is not in the scene.) • What sprite receives the getBall message?	• How would you bring Holly (a new character into the scene? • Can you describe what broadcasting is and can you give me an example of using broadcasting with Holly?	Problem solving to include analysis and designing solutions Understanding Computing Concepts
A simple game involving a maze where the barriers are working, the items aren't being counted correctly and the win screen isn't displaying when the player has won.	• Which vacation items are being counted correctly? Write down a plan so all the other sprites increase the itemCount variable by 1 • What instructions within the forever loop make our game stop?	• You also used the variable **itemCount** today; what was it used for? What did you need to do to get it working in the scripts? • An instruction block called forever was used in your scripts. What does it do?	Problem solving to include analysis, designing solutions and implementing Understanding Computing Concepts Testing and debugging
An animation illustrating a simple language translator that needs error handling for user input and can be expanded to include a new language and translated phrases.	• Test your project using a language that isn't on the list, does your fix work? • Create a new list of language phrases with new phrases	• What did you need to fix? • What do you need to do to create and then use a list in Scratch?	Testing and debugging Abstractions
An interactive story where the Lego WeDo tilt sensor, used to control the character only works for up and down movement, and an external structure that uses a Lego WeDo motor to enhance the story.	• How many items does Holly have to pack in her suitcase? • What tilt sensor values are not set up correctly in the if instruction block?	• How did your story know when to close the suitcase? • During this past week you tested a lot of different parts of stories and games. What did you do to test and debug the "Pack the suitcase" activity?	Problem solving to include analysis, designing solutions and implementing Testing and Debugging

2.1 Story Activity

The first activity had two high level goals; one was to provide an introduction to the Scratch language and interface, and a second was to introduce some of the computing concepts and terminology that would be used in all the projects. The scaffolded example was an animated story in which friends planned a vacation.

Exploration of the story revealed that a character (Billy) was missing from a scene, and that Billy had an odd reaction to a friend's vacation idea. The girls were guided through a problem solving process to discover and correct these problems. For example, they were guided to introduce a new scene for Billy's vacation idea. These modifications included replacing or adding instruction blocks to control character movement, what the characters said and controlling when they should be visible or hidden. The concept of broadcasting, which is often used in Scratch for controlling events, was introduced as a way to inject Billy into the scene, and later for adding a new scene to the story.

Before making changes to the story the participants first completed a sub-activity that provided a general overview of the Scratch programming environment, introducing them to sprites, the stage, the instruction blocks they would use for coding and how to run their animations. Once they completed the overview in their workbooks, they began to explore the story, documenting in their workbooks the sprites and backgrounds used by the story. They were also asked to indicate if any sprites had not been included in the story (i.e. Billy). When the participants had ideas on what needed to be changed, they were encouraged to document the instruction blocks they would use and their plan to make the necessary changes. After the story was modified to include Billy, the participants worked with broadcasting to add characters to a new scene. This provided opportunities for the participants to create an alternate ending to the existing story.

2.2 Game Activity

The second activity was an interactive maze game; it was designed for continued practice in computational problem solving, while also introducing decision logic (if statements, loops) and variables. In the game (figure 1) girls pressed the arrow keys to move a character through a timed maze of yellow barriers, looking for vacation items to be packed in the car (finish line).

The game had several embedded problems: 1) the cat was able to move through the yellow barriers; 2) there were items that the cat could not collect (i.e. didn't increase the count and did not disappear when encountered); and 3) the "lose" message did not display when the time was up. The discovery and correction of these "bugs" required the use of decision logic (e.g., executing different instructions when the cat was "touching" something that was yellow); the fixes also required the creation and use of a counting variable that could be tested to see when the game was won. The overall structure of the game introduced the concept of iteration, because the basic action block repeated forever until time ran out or (when fixed) the counter indicated a win. Finally, although the win and lose display messages had been included as sprites in the scaffolded example, the messages were not being broadcast at the appropriate time. The workbook guided participants through the discovery and correction of all of these problems, producing a satisfying and working game.

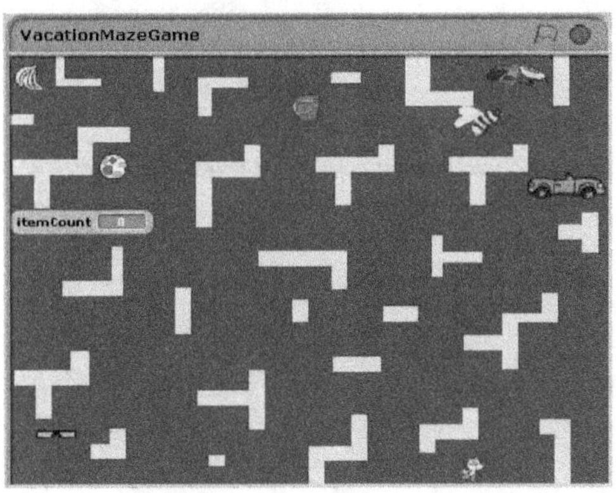

Figure 1-Vacation Maze Game

2.3 Working with Data Activity

For the third activity we built a simple language "translator" that could be used to introduce the concept of related information stored in a set of different lists. The translator activity provided opportunities for the participants to work with user input, create new lists and add to existing lists.

From a story perspective, the example was quite simple, with a single cat character that interacted with the user, asking for a language like to use and a phrase to translate. This was done using the *ask and wait* instruction block and *answer* variable provided in the Scratch programming environment (figure 2). The user's response is stored in a system-provided variable, *answer*. The information held in *answer* must be transferred to some other place in order to save it (i.e., before the next input request). In this way the example focused participants on user input, variables and lists.

The problem embedded in the example was that the user input was not tested appropriately, leading to nonsense responses when non-matching characters were typed. The correction involved modifying the code to use a *repeat until* instruction block, causing the cat repeat the question until a valid numeric value was entered.

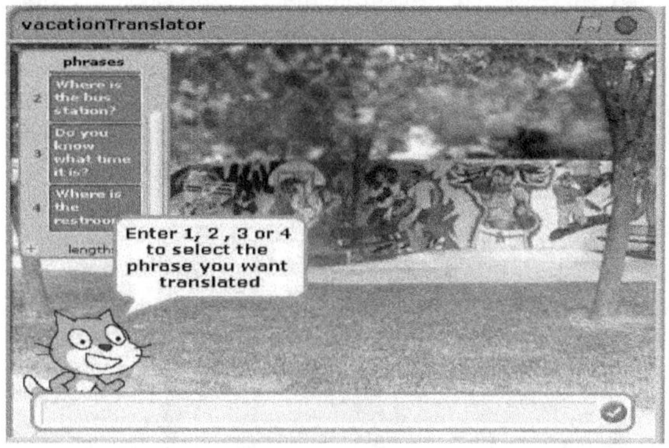

Figure 2-Working with Data Activity - Language Translator

The participants were also able to reinforce the *repeat until* concept when making a similar change to the script for the question "What language do you want me to speak in?". Instead of having the translator abruptly end when the user misspelled a language, the script was modified to keep asking the question until a matching language name was entered.

2.4 Sensors and Motors Activity

The scaffolded example for the fourth activity was an interactive story that worked with the Lego® WeDo tilt sensor and motor. In the story a character (Holly) moved around her room collecting vacation items to pack in her suitcase (figure 3). Users control Holly's movement with a tilt sensor. The problem is that Holly can only move up and down. To correct the problem the *if* statements in the script needed to include values that correspond to right and left tilts.

Figure 3-Vacation Story and Tilt Sensor

Within the animated story the suitcase closed when all the items were packed, however not only did instructions need to be added to the existing scaffolded example, a motorized suitcase structure needed to be built using Lego® bricks. The workbooks provided assistance on how to lower the speed of the motor and how many seconds the motor should run.

3. EVALUATING THE ACTIVITIES

The scaffolded learning activities were evaluated during a summer outreach program for middle school girls. The program took place over four days, with 15 girls in 6th, 7th and 8th grade; informed consent was obtained for 14. Background and post-workshop survey data were collected; however in this preliminary analysis, we focus primarily on the qualitative data collected through the semi-structured interviews conducted after each activity.

3.1 Participants

The participants ranged from 10 to 13 years of age with an average age of 11.4 years. The background survey revealed that 30% of the girls had some experience with Scratch; 50% of the girls indicated they had worked with other computer tools including Alice and Lego Robotics. Classroom observations confirmed that while these girls were not complete novices they had little experience understanding or creating Scratch applications.

3.2 Workshop Process

Each day, the girls worked on a different scaffolded example and workbook that introduced new features of the Scratch application and CT concepts. On the first day the majority of the girls formed into pairs; one girl with prior Scratch experience worked alone.

Each day the girls were guided by the workshop instructor to try out the scaffolded example and were given the corresponding workbook to work through the learning activity. After 90 minutes of work on the scheduled activity they were allowed to work on their own for another 90 minutes, with the option to continue previous projects or to create an original story or game. On the last day parents and family members were invited to an event showcasing the projects they had worked on during the past week.

During each "on your own" period (i.e., the second 90 minutes), two researchers conducted individual semi-structured interviews the girls. These interviews consisted of 3 to 5 open-ended questions probing the girl's understanding of CT concepts explored that day (see, e.g. the third column in Table 2); a complete list of the interview questions can be obtained by request from the first author. Each interview lasted from 3 to 5 minutes. These interviews were transcribed and the discussion in the following sections draws primarily from these interview data.

4. LEARNING OUTCOMES

Although our focus in this paper is on what the girls told us about their understanding of computational concepts, we did gather a small amount of self-report data before and after the program. For instance, we created a set of scales that assessed self-efficacy for computational problem solving, abstraction, debugging, and terminology. We measured these in advance and after the four activities had been completed. On a scale from 1-7 (where 1 is lowest efficacy), average ratings increased from 4.4 at the start to 5.2 after the workshop, $t(11)=3.26$, $p<.01$. We also assessed the extent to which the girls had fun in the program (6.1 out of 7), and whether they felt they had been successful (5.9 out of 7). All of these summary results are positive and consistent with our informal observations that girls were engaged and active throughout the program.

4.1 Story

On the first day, the girls worked with the story, became familiar with the Scratch environment and got used to working with the scaffolded example and workbook. We observed that the girls at times forgot they had a workbook that would guide them through the story and often asked questions for which the answer was "Have you turned the page? You will be doing that in the next part of the exercise." It was encouraging to see the girls excited to work with the Scratch tool and eager to learn more.

The entries in the workbook did indicate that the girls were able to answer the questions related to the programming environment and also document their understanding of what was working or not working with the sprites and scenes in the vacation planning story. However, from the workbook entries we noted difficulties in understanding the computational concept of broadcasting, which is used in Scratch for event handling. In the example broadcasts were sent or received by sprites to cause them to hide, show or carry out other similar behaviors. The workbook offered a diagram to help with this concept (figure 4).

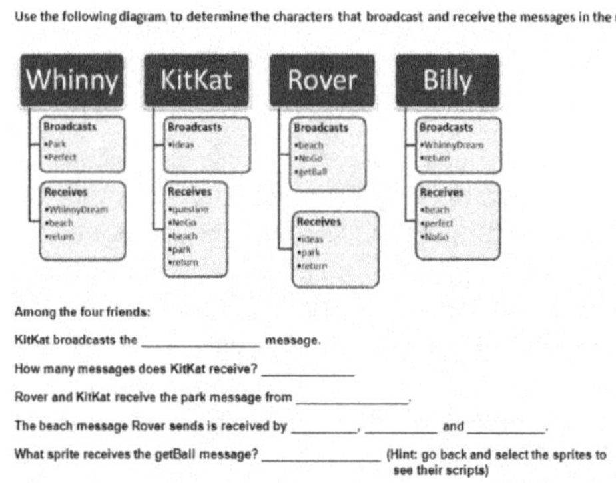

Figure 4-Workbook Broadcasting Exercise

While all 14 participants answered the first four questions related to the diagram in Figure 4, not all could tell us "What sprite receives the *getball* message?" even though we provided a hint (look at the scripts listed for each sprite). Despite the problem we saw in the workbook, the interview responses for day one suggested that they girls had at least a general understanding of broadcasting. When asked "Can you describe broadcasting?" most said it involved sending and receiving messages; some were also able to describe how broadcasting is used to control behaviors:

> *P5: Broadcasting is like talking to all of the sprites.*

> *P14: like sending a message to all the sprites or characters*

> *P2: broadcasting is where the characters say something and then you have to make sure they all hear it so they go on to the next scene.*

> *P10: It's basically when a character, it's a form of conversation, so like one character is like saying like if KitKat were to say to Billy go work that would be a broadcast*

> *P11: Broadcasting is like one of the characters sends a message to all the other characters that triggers them to do some other sequence of things*

As other researchers have noted, learners often understand new concepts by relating it to familiar material [3]:

> *P8: It's sending out a message that, it's a script that broadcast something and there's another script, when I receive and*

so it's like kind of when I say Hi you say Bye thing, like when I receive Hi you say bye

P7: Broadcasting is where someone is like speaking and like a news reporter broadcasts the weather every day and maybe every couple of hours.

After observing the girls during their "on your own" time, it became apparent that a short review of broadcasting would be helpful as the program continued. Some girls were still confusing text displayed in a scene with the messages being broadcast by sprites to control the flow of the story.

In contrast to broadcasting, the concept of Sprite was relatively concrete and grasped by almost all of the girls:

P1: a sprite is basically a character in Scratch ... it's kind of the person you're kind of programming

Interviewer: Can you give me an example?

P1: It's kind of like the cat on it, like the main one that comes with it. And there's a bunch of other ones

Classroom observations revealed considerable enthusiasm among the girls as they worked with Scratch and the Sprites. Some even added their own embellishments to the example story.

4.2 Game

Before starting the game activity the girls reviewed the Scratch environment, again answering questions in the workbooks. They then began to explore the maze, first by testing it to see what was working and not working, and then gradually correcting the bugs that had been inserted.

Afterwards, we probed their understanding of variables with the interview question "You also used the variable **itemCount** today; what was it used for?" The girls' responses suggested that they did understand the concept of a counter variable:

P1: itemCount is whenever you collect a certain amount of things in the maze today, KitKat she went out and collected all those items so whenever she would collect an item what we did she would, oh whenever she would touch it, it would increase her score by one saying that she got it and it would just hide

P2: to count how many items you had so you could go to the car at the end so you could either win or just to show how many items you had and how many more you have to get

P12: to count up all the items you collected

We also asked about iteration: "An instruction block called **forever** was used in your scripts. What does it do?" The girls seemed to have a basic understanding of iteration, though they could not articulate how the loop stopped:

P10: it works so that throughout the game KitKat would repeatedly get stung by the bee, she would repeatedly go back to the start, it'd keep doing it, it wouldn't just be like once.

P12: that it will just keep repeating, it wouldn't really stop so like if one game ended and if you clicked the green flag again it would keep on going

These interview data suggest that many of the girls were grasping the basic constructs of variables and iteration, namely that a count of items was being maintained and that there was a mechanism for doing things over and over. It is less clear that they understood how variables like counts might be used to terminate a loop.

4.3 Data (Lists)

The third activity introduced the girls the concept of a list that stored a set of related data; it also illustrated error handling for user input. Again the girls began by testing what did or did not work in the example, then followed a problem solving process to figure out what changes to make. In this case, they needed to add the some error handling code so that the translator program would refuse user input that would cause nonsensical information to display on the screen.

Once the girls fixed this problem they were guided to extend the translator by adding a new language and phrases. In this, they worked with Google Translator to convert English phrases to the new language of their choosing.

After the activity, we probed their understanding of the list concept: "In Scratch how would you create a list?" We found little evidence that a "data structure" abstraction of a list had been grasped. For example, some girls simply described the physical procedure they would follow to create a list:

P6: I would go to the variables and you can go to the make variable and the variable would be make a list, and you could make a list

P2: you click the list button and typed in the name of the list and it came with some list

Other girls' understanding was tied even more concretely to the specific (language translation) example they had been using:

P7: you create a list, gosh what was that thing called, you create a list by using your languages that you already have then you put your new language in and then there's this little tab thing where you have to put that language in there so you know if you put in another language you know how many languages you have.

Note however, that these answers were undoubtedly influenced by the fact that we asked a "how" question rather than a "what" question. This is further evidenced by comments that mentioned very specific user interface actions needed to manipulate a list:

P7: you touch the, if you want to use a new phrase you're going to have to touch the circle that has a plus sign and type in the phrase and then you're going to have to put it in on every one of them and you're going to have to translate it.

P9: click the plus sign in the list box

P10: I would click the little plus button down in the corner and then type in what I needed

In general, these responses seem to indicate a rather concrete understanding of the list concept we were introducing, tied to the physical procedures that one uses in this environment for manipulating what is otherwise an abstract concept for data storage.

4.4 Sensors and Motors

In the fourth learning activity, the girls integrated input from a tilt sensor with corresponding output in the form of a motor movement, using the Lego® WeDo framework. Answers to questions in the workbooks confirmed that most of the girls could distinguish between input and output when we connected the concepts to input from a computer mouse and output on a printer; however when examples were drawn from their Scratch activities on earlier days (for example, prompts or text displayed on the screen) the answers were much more varied. This suggests that at least at this early phase, their concepts for input and output are somewhat narrow and tied to physical objects.

The interviews suggested that at least some girls understood how their scripts were controlling the activity. In response to "How did your story know when to close the suitcase?" some of them revealed comfort with broadcasting and how it is used:

P10: when the items broadcasted close suitcase

P12: when Holly broadcasts a word and when it received the word it triggered the motor to close the suitcase

However, other girls shared a more literal understanding of the closing function, tying it simply to the story line in place:

P5: when everything was picked up all the toys and things she needed to pick up it automatically closed

P14: when Holly collected all 5 items

These girls seemed to miss the connection of what was happening in their script to what they observed in the physical structures, almost implying that the structures were responding directly to the "plot" of the story acted out by the script.

After this activity, we also asked the girls about their efforts to test and debug the activity they had worked on that day. All of the girls grasped the role of testing and fixing the project, with some detailed answers containing references to program constructs such as if statements and variables:

P1: well first whenever we came in we used the sensor and it wouldn't move left to right because instead of having it controls the value 1, 2 3 and 4 for the ifs it was 1, 20, 3 and 40, so I figured out that it was 1, 2, 3, 4 instead of 1, 20, 3 and 40. We also had some problems where it was with the item count where we figured out it was six, we used 5 and the second to last item would close the suitcase.

P6: we made sure that the tilt sensing control thing went up by one instead of by 19 and 20 and then we had to make sure that the motor was not too fast and not too strong

During classroom observations we heard a lot of laughter when structures did not respond in the manner expected. However many of them needed encouragement to 'play' with the Lego bricks. When we asked one girl "What do you build with Lego's?" she started her response with "My brother likes," which may explain why some girls seemed uncomfortable working with the bricks.

5. SUMMARY AND DISCUSSION

We have described four activities designed to introduce CT concepts and skills to middle school girls. They responded well to the opportunity to learn by testing and debugging example applications that could "run" but had logical or plot-related errors. Though some activities included concepts (broadcasting, list processing) that were too abstract for some of the girls, they were nonetheless able to complete each task, and to carry over their learning to activities on subsequent days.

Subjectively, the girls' reactions to the learning activities were quite positive. They often used the workbooks to document what they had discovered, especially at the start of an activity. However, as the girls became involved in fixing problems and expanding the activity they tended to turn away from the workbook and concentrated instead on fixing or expanding their projects. We also noticed a trend across the program: the girls were more likely to document their plans of action on the first day than the last. However, this may also have been caused by their eagerness to complete the scheduled activity, so that they could finish their "on your own" projects for the parent showcase.

In addition to the daily activity the girls were encouraged to work on extra projects of their choosing. Interestingly, all of them chose to do another story. A story is relatively easy to "program", as a largely linear logical flow; thus it seems that while these girls are able to test and debug complex examples like games, their ability to plan and create applications is much less developed. This of course is one of the assumptions motivating the use of scaffolded examples, providing a mechanism for learners to work on rich projects that are beyond their ability to create on their own.

In summary, our preliminary findings suggest that scaffolded examples in Scratch are an effective way to convey CT concepts and skills in a short amount of time, while serving as a fun and engaging learning activity. Not surprisingly, the girls were more able to describe concepts like Sprites or a simple count variable than more abstract concepts like a list for storing related data. They understood the idea of iteration but less about the logic of controlling iteration. Importantly, they seemed quite able to pick up on the central concept of broadcasting. Finally, we observed considerable success in overall problem solving and the use of testing and debugging for learning how a program works. In the future we will conduct more detailed analysis of the projects built by the girls (including their own creations) and use these findings to guide the design of additional scaffolded learning activities.

6. ACKNOWLEDGMENTS

We would like to thank Neha Sharma for her assistance in the workshops.

7. REFERENCES

[1] Vygotsky, L. S. *Mind in Society: The Development of Higher Psychological Processes*. Harvard University Press, City, 1978.

[2] Reiser, B. J. Scaffolding Complex Learning: The Mechanisms of Structuring and Problematizing Student Work. *The Journal of the Learning Sciences*, 13, 3 2004), 273-304.

[3] Carroll, J. M. The Nurnberg Funnel: Designing Minimalist Instruction for Practical Computer Skill. MIT Press, Cambridge, MA, USA, 1990.

[4] Rosson, M. B. and Carroll, J. M. Scaffolded examples for learning object-oriented design. *Commununications of the ACM*, 39, (4 1996), 46-47.

[5] Rosson, M. B., Ioujanina, A., Paone, T., Sheasley, G., Sinha, H., Ganoe, C., Carroll, J. M. and Mahar, J. A scaffolded introduction to dynamic website development for female high school students. In *Proceedings of the Proceedings of the 40th ACM technical symposium on Computer science education* (Chattanooga, TN, USA, 2009). ACM,.

[6] Wing, J. M. Computational thinking. *Communications of the ACM*, 49, (3 2006), 33.

[7] Repenning, A., Webb, D. and Ioannidou, A. Scalable game design and the development of a checklist for getting computational thinking into public schools. In *Proceedings of the Proceedings of the 41st ACM technical symposium on Computer science education* (Milwaukee, Wisconsin, USA, 2010). ACM,.

[8] Barr, V. and Stephenson, C. Bringing computational thinking to K-12: what is Involved and what is the role of the computer science education community? *ACM Inroads*, 2, 1 2011), 48-54.

[9] Webb, H. and Rosson, M. B. Using Scaffolded Activities to Teach Computational Thinking to Middle School Girls. FECS'12.

A Cascading Mentoring Pedagogy in a CS Service Learning Course to Broaden Participation and Perceptions

Yasmin B. Kafai, Jean Griffin*, Quinn Burke, Michelle Slattery+, Deborah A. Fields, Rita M. Powell*, Michele Grab*, Susan B. Davidson, & Joseph S. Sun*
University of Pennsylvania Graduate School of Education
*Department of Computer and Information Science
+Peak Research
3700 Walnut Street
Philadelphia, PA 19106

kafai@upenn.edu, griffin@seas.upenn.edu, burkeqq@cofc.edu, peakresearch@usa.net, deborah.fields@usu.edu, rpowell@seas.upenn.edu, mgrab@seas.upenn.edu, susan@cis.upenn.edu, sunj@seas.upenn.edu

ABSTRACT

This study reports on the design, implementation, and evaluation of a service-learning course based on a "cascading mentoring" model linking together the faculty, administration, and undergraduates of an urban university's computer science department with local high school students. We present findings from surveys and post-interviews that illustrate undergraduates' and high school students' experiences in the program and how their perceptions of computing and mentoring changed based upon the outreach. In our discussion, we focus on the institutional and conceptual challenges of implementing the community service course within the university's computer science department, while also highlighting the learning opportunities for streamlining such a model for future iterations.

Categories and Subject Descriptors
K.3.0 **[Computers and Education]:** General

General Terms
Human Factors

Keywords
Community service, mentoring programming

1. INTRODUCTION

Despite years of interventions aimed at broadening participation in computer science, research [7, 8] continues to report barriers to participation for entire populations of our citizenry. Mired in the longstanding view that programming is an innate skill meant only for a select few [4], computer science's failure to attract a broad range and number of participants directly correlates with the wider public's equally narrow perception of the field. Yet what has received considerably less attention in this dual focus on participation and perception is the role of effective pedagogy (the third "p") to introduce CS as a tenable course of study and potential career field. Based on prior research [16, 17, 24] citing the unique potential of service-based learning as a pedagogical bridge across the rift between undergraduate and K-12 computing curricula, this paper investigates how college and also high school students can undertake both the role of teacher and learner to create a reciprocal rather than hierarchical mentoring relationship within the surrounding community.

Current discussions of service learning [14, 15] stress the pedagogical importance of reciprocity to generate more authentic and longstanding relationships, and the cascading model we present here emphasizes the interchangeability of the mentor-mentee roles, grounding undergraduates' CS-knowledge in hands-on activity while also introducing underprivileged high school students to the academic and career potential of computing. Developed through a partnership between a university's computer science and education departments, the cascading model emphasizes not only CS-based content but also the modes of delivery for such content. For the past two years we implemented the cascading model with four different cohorts of undergraduates through CS-based service learning courses, each of which was paired with accompanying workshops or a summer camp for local high school students. In our presentation of the cascading model, we report on (1) its implementation on both the undergraduate and high school levels as a means to attract a wider range of youth to CS, (2) its function as a pedagogical tool in shifting perceptions of what it means to mentor, and (3) the resultant changing perceptions of CS as a course of study and career. In the discussion we address the challenges and opportunities of developing and implementing this type of a service learning course and how the cascading model may be additionally streamlined for future iterations.

SIGCSE'13, March 6-9, 2013, Denver, Colorado, USA.

2. BACKGROUND

Despite a recent report from the Computing Research Association (2012) citing a fourth straight year of increased CS undergraduate enrollments, there continues to be significant concern over the development of a viable "pipeline" into CS when it comes to attracting and retaining a diverse range of students [2]. Problems in participation are very much problems in perception as Kelleher and Pausch [18] aptly point out in their taxonomy of introductory programming environments, citing the underlying social and cultural stigmas surrounding programming (and not technical "know-how") as the field's most immediate issue. This conclusion points to a wider issue within the CS community. For while there have been great strides in making the field more accessible technologically, CS severely lacks such innovation in terms of classroom pedagogy, still doggedly relying on "top-down" lecture-style delivery as its default form of instruction on both the undergraduate and high school levels [10, 12].

In this paper, we focus on the role of pedagogy that is inherently connected to these interrelated issues of participation and perception. There are two elements to the pedagogical approach we present with the cascading model. First, there is the overall design of the program, a *service learning* course, in which learners' acquisition of CS concepts and skills is directly tied to the authentic social connections they develop outside of the college classroom. Formally defined by the U.S. National and Community Service Act of 1990 as academically-integrated learning through active participation in community outreach, service learning has demonstrated the potential to enhance students' academic comprehension while also fostering an understanding and caring about other individuals [20]. In terms of CS, service learning coursework has been found to particularly appeal to women and underrepresented minorities, helping dispel the entrenched view among some communities that computer science is asocial and inapplicable [23, 24]. While CS service learning programs have been implemented in some universities [9], research on service learning is not highly visible in either the computer science education community or in the service learning community [24]. One of the goals of our study is to contribute to this growing body of knowledge around CS-based service learning and to promote such outreach as a viable way to broaden participation in and perceptions of computing.

Second, there is the particular instructional design of the service-learning approach, namely *mentoring* through a reciprocal "learning-by-teaching" model. While scholars and practitioners do not agree on a single definition of mentoring, there is consensus aligned with the popular view that mentoring involves acting as a guide, advisor, and/ or counselor to a mentee [22]. Previous discussions of the learning benefits in mentoring have included improved self-esteem, increased opportunities to interact with peers, increased social competence [3] and civic participation [26]. Within the CS department, engaging undergraduates in campus-based mentoring experiences has demonstrated success in raising students' sense of self-efficacy [5] as well as modestly increasing enrollment numbers [11]. Noticeably absent however from such research (and of particular interest to us), is the notion of the mentor as learner. Little research expands the continuum of mentoring roles from learners to teachers and thus would be more inclusive of a view that sees mentoring as a reciprocal rather than a hierarchical relationship. Focusing on mentoring as a process by which one transforms from learner to teacher offers the possibility of a more equitable and reciprocal relationship that opposes the deficit perspective prevalent in many mentoring and service-learning outreach efforts [25, 26], and for this reason may be especially promising in working with underrepresented groups in CS with whom issues of participation and perception are especially prevalent.

3. METHODS

3.1 Mentors and Mentee Participants

Mentors. Our cascading mentoring model was developed through a partnership between the university's computer science and education departments via a service learning course for undergraduates. During the two years, 16 undergraduate students (75% male, 25% female; 38% African American males, 13% Asian females, 50% Caucasian) completed the EAS 285 service learning course and participated in mentoring activities to broaden participation among surrounding local high school students. More than half (56%) reported that they were considering or had declared CS or CE as a major or minor in college; other majors included bioengineering, electrical engineering, and chemical bio-molecular engineering. All undergraduates had taken at least taken one introductory CS course that was a requirement for enrolling in EAS 285.

Mentees. On the high school side, 54 students (33% females, 67% males; 37% Caucasian, 33% African American, 20% Asian, 4% Hispanic, 2% Native American/Alaskan Native, 4% other) participated in the program as mentees. All participants were 14-18 years of age and were high school students in grades 9-12.

3.2. Service Learning Course

The EAS 285 Teaching Computer Science Basics was the community service learning course offered in spring '10, summer '10, spring '11, and summer '11. It was co-taught by a CS faculty member (Griffin) and a school of education doctoral student (Burke). Initially undergraduates undertook the role of mentees, learning about educational theories and practices as well issues surrounding K-12 CS education. Of particular significance was the theory of Constructionsim [21] and grounding CS learning in the design and building of tangible objects that could be then shared with others, be it video games, digital stories, or even programmable plush dolls and clothing accessories. Undergraduates also learned several new educational technologies: the Scratch introductory programming language, and, depending on the course offering, the electronic textile kit Lilypad Arduino, Processing (with Java), or Python. They studied software engineering principles, which then informed the design and development of their educational software projects. In addition to completing reading, writing, and programming assignments, the undergraduates created a variety of lesson plans, which included "unplugged" activities, programming projects and puzzles, demos, tutorials, and Jeopardy-style quiz games. In the spring, workshops were held at two local high schools. During the summer, *Boot Up!* week-long intensive computing camps were held for high school students.

3.3 Data Sources and Analyses

Surveys. All participants, undergraduates and high school students, completed pre- and post- surveys. Depending upon access to computers, some participants completed paper surveys, while others completed surveys online. The survey questions included demographic items, interest ratings, confidence with computing, and satisfaction with participating in the camp, course, or workshop. Both mentors and mentees also completed pre- and post-workshop surveys on their experiences and computing attitudes. The undergraduates took an additional survey, using Retrospective Pre-Test (RPT) methodology [19], in which they rated their level of interest on five items by reflecting back to how they felt before their mentoring experience and then to rate how they felt now. Surveys were analyzed with 2-tailed paired samples t-tests (95% CI) to determine the significance of differences in ratings before and after computing experiences.

Post Interviews. We also conducted post interviews with undergraduates about their mentoring experience in-person or over the telephone, all within one week after the actual workshop experiences. These recorded interviews were then transcribed and analyzed in terms of the three themes identified in an earlier study

[17] that specifically describe the transition from mentee to mentor in terms of the (1) social challenges of mentoring, (2) facilitating others' understanding, and (3) reinforcing one's own learning through the mentoring process (see Figure 1).

Reflections	Sample Interview Statement
Social Issues	[B]e yourself....Don't obsess about the image of how a mentor should be. You know, be malleable and you know, work with the students. Don't, like, assume that you're coming from the university, which is a very nice institution, and you were probably one of the better students in your high school, like realize that not everyone's going to be like you. *(Undergraduate Senior, following the Spring 2011 Course)*
Facilitating	What I've done in the past 3 or 4 months would likely shape sort of what I would do as a mentor going forward. I would really try and help students focus on more of the technical aspects of what they are doing. It's really nice to be able to work with students one-on-one rather than in a big group. I do like the style of teaching where you give them a project, where they have some ultimate goal that they have to work towards on their own. They have to be self-driven and then they come to you for questions rather than you providing just a full lecture. *(Undergraduate Senior, following the Spring 2011 Course)*
Learning	I knew I'd be able to help out because a lot of the stuff we did last year, but also went there as a mentor, but I went there to learn too, so I was like, in the same shoes as the other students because I was learning some stuff too. So we could learn together and I can help them know what I know. *(High School Junior, following the Summer 2011 CS Camp)*

Figure 1: Themes & Sample Interview Responses

In addition, we interviewed five high school students who participated as mentees in workshops at one high school as 9th graders and then became mentors to a new crop of students as 10th graders. They served with us for an entire year. At the end of the year, we conducted hour-long interviews with these students to capture their reflections on their experiences on how they saw their roles as a mentors socially develop, what they learned about mentoring, and what they learned about computing through their mentoring experiences.

4. RESULTS

4.1 Service Learning Course and Mentoring Experiences

Undergraduate Mentors. In the pre-survey, mentors listed a number of areas/ skills that they hoped to learn through the experience. Roughly half of the respondents listed creative design skills, a third listed a greater understanding of how technology works, and 39% expressed the hope to learn whether computer science would be a good fit as a career. In terms of the mentoring experience, the two primary reasons undergraduates chose to become a mentor were to develop leadership skills (89%) and to develop their own computing skills (79%). When the undergraduates were asked to rate their experience in the service-learning course, all agreed that (1) their learning of CS principles was reinforced through teaching; (2) their overall awareness of the field of computer science education increased; and (3) their capacity to serve as role models to aspiring young technologists was very much heightened by the high school students' willingness to turn to them for support. They also reported improvements in their abilities to problem solve, deliver effective presentations, teach hands-on skills, make positive changes in the community through leadership activities, and set clear boundaries with participants. Eight of the eleven skills improved significantly ($p<.05$) as the result of their mentoring experience. Through this service learning experience, student mentors described their experiences as not just helping them develop mentoring skills but also "life skills" such as being able to think on one's feet, adapting as needed, setting clear and realistic boundaries, and using small-talk as a way to get to know others and develop a relationship. These ratings very much support the feasibility of having undergraduate students serve as mentors.

High School Mentees. We also asked high school students mentees what they hoped to learn from the camp or workshop experience. High school students listed creative design skills (71%), how technology works (60%), and if computer science would be a good fit as a career (50%). The camps or workshops overall were rated as "effective" or "very effective" by 91% of high school mentees and 83% of them reported that their level of participation in the camp or workshop was "active" or "very active." While 51% of high school mentees were considering computer science or computer engineering as a major or minor in college before the camp or workshop, this number increased to 65% after the mentoring experiences. The mentees agreed or strongly agreed with the following statements on the post-surveys: "I know more about computing now" (81%); "I increased my knowledge of computing" (89%); "I have a better understanding of concepts like computational thinking" (82%); "I have more confidence about computing" (85%). According to high school students' ratings, both the mentors (41%) and the program (37%) had an impact on their decisions about college major. High school mentors considered their most important role models to be the undergraduate mentors (54%) over the adult teachers (24%).

4.2 Computer Science Career Interests and Computing Attitudes

Undergraduate Mentors. After participation as a mentor, undergraduates' career interests increased across all dimensions: computer science in general, teaching computer science, mentoring younger students, majoring or minoring in computer science in college, and working in computer science. Mean interest rating scores ranged from 3.1 to 4.3 on a 5-point scale, from "extremely low" (1) to "extremely high" (5). Interest in teaching computer science was moderate at the start of the course, but increased significantly ($p<.01$) by the end of the course. Not surprisingly, interest in mentoring younger students was high at the start of the course, but increased significantly ($p<.05$) by the end of the course. While a greater number of undergraduate mentors considered declaring a computer science or computer engineering major or minor in college (from 62% pre-mentoring to 77% post-mentoring), this increase was not significant. In contrast to career aspirations, students' computing attitudes such as "computer jobs are boring" or "women can have jobs in computing" did not change significantly in the positive direction after the mentoring experience. Mentors rated their level of agreement for 15 items on a 4-point scale from "strongly disagree" to "strongly agree." We predicted that computing attitudes would become more positive with more computing experience, yet 8 of 15 attitudes changed in a negative direction, but not significantly so.

High School Mentees. We found that participation in the summer camp or school workshop significantly impacted ($p<.05$) high school students' consideration of computer science or computer engineering as a major or minor in college. In the pre-survey just over half of the high school mentees (51%) were interested as compared to 65% in the post-workshop survey. Much of this appears to be the influence of the undergraduate mentors, all of whom were rated as either "effective" or "very effective" by all mentees who completed the post-workshop survey. Mentees' attitudes towards computing were investigated with 15 items on a 4-point scale from "strongly disagree" to "strongly agree." Like the undergraduate mentors, high school mentee's ratings went down, rather than up on items such as: "computing is fun; women can have jobs in computing; men can have jobs in computing; I like computing; I can become good at computing; I think computing is useful; I want to find out more about computing; and I am interested in a career in computing." Their attitudes did not shift significantly with the exception of one item: "I am good at computing." In contrast to the undergraduates, high school mentees all rated themselves higher after being mentored but again, none of these shifts were significant.

4.3 Reflections on Cascading Mentoring

Undergraduate Mentors. Our analyses of the 16 interview transcripts revealed that all undergraduate and high school mentors reflected upon this transition from mentee to mentor in terms of all three themes with reflections about facilitating (n=27) as the most frequent in occurrence, followed closely by social observations (n=25) and then by direct references to their own technical and pedagogical learning throughout the process (n=19). This is not altogether surprising as all participants spent the majority of the time reflecting upon the mentorship role and the high school students they encountered over their respective workshops and camps. Interestingly though, the undergraduate participants were much more likely to reflect on the social conditions of the students whom they were mentoring—particularly in terms of comparing their mentees' classroom environments to their own previous high school experiences.

High School Mentors. The five returning high school students who spent an entire year mentoring others spoke reflectively about what they had learned both about mentoring and about computing through their experiences. Initially, most thought that mentoring would be easy because they would simply need to tell students what to do and that they would be in positions of authority. Later however, they realized that mentoring was a complex mixture of figuring out students' interests, helping them become interested in computing, and helping them discover the answers to their own problems rather than telling them what the answers were. For instance, Corbin (a pseudonym, as are all names herein) explained that many students who needed help did not recognize that they needed help, while others thought they needed more help than they actually did. Jackson came to the realization that providing expertise with a joke or a "nudge" worked better with mentees than "telling them." Or as Jackson explained, "Instead of trying to point them where I think they should go… I tried to allow them to learn in the same way that I did, which was sort of use whatever appealed to you for whatever reason and just feel your way around. And if you had any questions about what anything did, to the best of my knowledge, I would help you understand."

These high school mentors also described how they had learned things about programming (specifically with Scratch, the software they used) directly from their mentoring experiences. As William put it, some kids would ask him questions about things that they were interested in doing, "so I had to learn it myself to be able to show them how to do it." Or as Chase described, "[S]ometimes people would come to me with more complex things that I've never actually done before and I would figure it out with them." William provided an example of this: "Jenny was one of the people who um, I had to teach about variables… [S]he needed a solution to a problem and I had dabbled a little bit in variables before, so I went onto that part of Scratch and started experimenting with it, and then I got the hang of it and we were able to solve the problem." Finally, in an example of the possibilities of a cascading mentoring model, Corbin described his experiences with undergraduate mentors in the same workshop where he too was a mentor of younger high school students than himself: "I felt like I was a mentor being mentored," he said. The high school mentors expressed gratitude for what they learned from the undergraduate mentors, most of whom knew more about programming or mathematics than they did and who were able to help the high school mentors follow their own interests in programming, as they in turn helped the more novice high school mentees design and implement their programs. This learning from others while teaching at the same time highlights the benefits of the cascading model of mentorship.

5. DISCUSSION

We examined the opportunities and challenges in integrating cascading mentoring into a CS service learning to address the role of pedagogy—the third "p"—that is inherently connected to issues in broadening participation in and perceptions of computing. Our findings suggest that implementing cascading mentoring is a promising but also complex pedagogical effort in addressing the multiple challenges associated with broadening participation and perceptions of computing.

In terms of opportunities, we found that the service learning course was successful, in particular in recruiting a high percentage of underrepresented groups of students, both on the mentor and mentee side. The cascading mentoring model also proved to be successful in broadening participants' interest in computer science and developing a more sophisticated perspective of what it means to mentor, teach and learn. It provided rich opportunities for participants to engage in reciprocal mentoring, a process that created a more equitable relationship between mentors and mentees. While many efforts in broadening participation focus on raising interest in computing and increasing participants' ideas of computing, it is equally important to promote different pedagogies that address learners' needs, interests, and backgrounds. With the increasing need for technology fluency, there is a primacy placed on promoting content. Indeed, there is a great need in building technical skills and conceptual knowledge of computing, particularly among underrepresented groups who often do not have access to courses and activities involving computation. By the same token, by just focusing on content, we leave out instrumental insights from the pedagogical side developed over the last 30 years that content coverage alone is not sufficient, but rather learning needs to start with students' informal knowledge and take advantage of scaffolded instruction [6]. As evident in both the mentor and mentee pre- and post-workshop surveys and mentor interviews, while computing was a significant reason participants chose to be part of the service learning outreach, it certainly was not the only reason for participating nor the only skill set the undergraduates and high school students developed. Participants cited leadership ability, time management skills, and creative design as both the reason for and takeaways from the experience, and it is clear that they very much valued the practical (e.g., "life skills") reasons for service learning coursework as well. The cascading mentoring model illustrated that by "turning the tables"—namely, by having mentees become mentors—we provided undergraduates and returning high school participants with powerful insights about their own learning through their own nascent teaching efforts. Namely, the design of the service learning course turned them into reflective practitioners or learners who became more finely attuned to the needs of others and their own expertise. After all, helping someone to learn in an efficient and respectful manner is of value beyond schooling and is especially crucial to succeeding in the workplace, where much learning about and with technology does not, in fact, happen through top-down content delivery but in far less formal interactions with others that directly relate to knowing how to effectively offer (as well as graciously receive) assistance.

The feasibility of having undergraduates and high school students shift from mentee to mentor and become impactful mentors was demonstrated for both groups of students. The impact of mentors on students at all levels was significant in terms of decision for considering a college major. Mentoring abilities improved significantly, as did confidence, interest in teaching computer science, and interest in mentoring. Minority and underrepresented groups participated in numbers far exceeding their normal representation in computing. The effects of learning by teaching were also significant, increasing student interest in both teaching computer science and mentoring younger students and reinforcing student learning through teaching. Broadly speaking, our findings support the assertion that this sense of having been in the "same shoes" is an imperative in terms of developing future mentors out of the mentee role [14, 15]. The mentor reflections of returning high school students suggests that those who engaged in the actual workshops (rather than just the undergraduate coursework) may very well have a claim to better understand how mentees feel and engage during such outreach. Of course, while some of this may simply be attributed to a similarity in age (high school students reflecting upon other high school students), future iterations of the cascading model need to be mindful that its currents need not be simply "down-pours" but potentially "up-pours" as well. That is, contrasting the mentoring styles and experiences of returning high school participants with those of the college undergraduates offers an ascending insight within a cascading model.

There was, however, one conflicting finding that deserves further discussion. While we were able to confirm some of the expected positive changes in college and career aspirations, we also recorded more stagnant views on computing attitudes among both undergraduate mentors and high school mentees. It may simply be that attitudes change more slowly over time, and in the case of high school students, they had much less understanding of computing before they became mentors so their pre-camp workshop ratings might have been inflated. An alternative explanation is that these post-workshop survey ratings reflected improved understanding of computing, rather than negative attitudes. After all, as the aphorism reads, we tend to only begin to understand a topic when we realize how little we ourselves know. It is difficult to accurately rate one's feelings on a pre-workshop survey when one may not yet fully understand what he or she is actually rating. This suggests that it might be more appropriate to assess attitudes with a retrospective pre-test methodology so that respondents have had the exposure, training, or learning required to accurately rate their pre and post experiences.

We faced several challenges, mostly concerning institutional and administrative issues. One of the biggest challenges was in recruiting undergraduates to the EAS285 class. Although a relatively high percentage of African American males enrolled, the overall enrollment numbers were low, averaging only four undergraduates in four course offerings. The course was an engineering elective course but we were unable to get it rostered as part of the core CS curriculum. This administrative integration would have been critical for many undergraduates who expressed interest in the course but couldn't fit the course in their otherwise booked schedule with required courses and little room for electives. The remarkably busy schedules characteristic of undergraduate curricular life proved to be another challenge—and integrating these schedules into the far more regimented schedules of middle and high school students only compounded this challenge. The undergraduate mentors typically needed two college course periods in order to have enough time to travel and visit their high school mentees.

Perhaps one of the biggest challenges in bringing the cascading model to fruition is the issue of moving from seeding to scaling up the model. We largely underestimated the time it would take to implement and maintain a mentoring cascade over several iterations. While the service learning course was offered both years as a traditional spring semester-long course as well as a more compact summer-based course, the service-learning component of each course varied considerably. Whereas undergraduates in the spring course enacted the cascading model through on-site mentoring at a public middle school and two high schools, undergraduates from the summer course served as mentors at an on-site intensive week-long summer *Boot-Up!* camp. This unique mix of off-site and on-site mentoring certainly offered us a glimpse into the range of service-learning possibilities, but there needed to be more attention directed to weighing and adjusting mentoring styles based on whether undergraduates were on site at public schools or whether the public school students were on the university campus. Going forward we would like to develop curricula that specifically address the tacit yet remarkably significant role of "place" when it comes to mentoring students, especially those in underserved communities. To a degree, the range of locales also affects the generalizability of our results as the context in which the cascading mentoring can occur may be a tacit variable affecting the overall shifts in attitudes toward computing and mentoring.

Moving ahead into the third and last year of implementing the cascading mentoring model, we made adjustments to address some of the challenges. Due to persistently low enrollment, we discontinued EAS 285 and introduced a new service learning course in spring 2012, called CIS 101 *Compute to Create*, an official pilot of the CS Principles project [1]. As an introductory CS course for non-engineering students with no prerequisite, the new course satisfies a formal reasoning requirement (as does introductory calculus). As we had hoped, enrollment in CIS 101 was high; it filled to capacity (15 undergraduate students) with a minimum of advertising. The service component of the new course involved some mentoring of high school students but significantly less so (only three hours per semester) and did not include the depth of CS engagement that high school students experienced in the summer camp and school workshops. Instead, mentoring activities focused on short weekend and school day workshops as well as public computing demonstrations at the outdoor Philadelphia Science Festival. While these reductions in time and engagement allowed us to reach a much larger number of K-12 students than previously, we need to examine in more detail the differences in impacting and broadening participation and perceptions in computing.

There is an urgent need to think about how to create communities of learners, whether it is college classroom, or as in our case, across schools. This of course is no easy feat, particularly because the social and academic divide between high school and college is already so significant for students from underserved communities. However, such a network of communities of learning—formal and informal and across grade levels—represents an essential first step to begin to systematically address these longstanding issues of participation in and perception of CS, as well as a means to both distill and distribute a pedagogy of best practices.

6. ACKNOWLEDGMENTS

This material is based upon work supported by the National Science Foundation (CIS-0940511). Any opinions, findings, and conclusions or recommendations expressed in this chapter are those of the authors and do not necessarily reflect the views of the National Science Foundation or the University of Pennsylvania.

7. REFERENCES

[1] Astrachan, O., Briggs, A. 2012. The CS Principles Project. *ACM Inroads*, 3, 2, 38-42.

[2] Barker, L., McDowell, C., and Kalahar, K. 2009. Exploring factors that influence computer science introductory course students to persist in the major. *ACM SIGCSE Bulletin,* 41, 2, 282-286.

[3] Barton-Arwood, S., Jolivette, K. and Massey, N. G. 2000. Mentoring with elementary-age students. *Intervention in School and Clinic*, 36, 1, 36-44.

[4] Biggers, M. Brauer, A. and Yilmaz, T. 2008. Student perceptions of computer science: A retention study comparing graduating seniors with CS leavers. In *Proceedings of the 39th SIGCSE Technical Symposium on Computer Science Education* (Portland, OR USA March 12-15). ACM, New York, NY, 402-406.

[5] Boyer, K., E. Thomas, A. Rorrer, D. Cooper, and Vouk, M. 2010. Increasing technical excellence, leadership and commitment of computing students through identity-based mentoring. Paper presented at the *Proceedings of the 41st SIGCSE Technical Symposium on Computer Science Education* (Milwaukee, Wisconsin, USA March 10-13). ACM, New York, NY, 167-171.

[6] Bransford, J., Brown, A., and Cocking., R. 2000. *How People Learn.* Washington, DC: National Academy Press.

[7] Bruckman, A., Biggers, M., Ericson, B., McKlin, T., Dimond, J., DiSalvo, B., Hewner, M., Ni, L. and Yardi. S. 2008. "Georgia Computes!": Improving the computing education pipeline. In *Proceedings of the 41st SIGCSE Technical Symposium on Computer Science Education* (Chattanooga, Tennessee, USA March 03-07). ACM, New York, NY, 86-90.

[8] Carter, L. 2006. Why students with an apparent aptitude for computer science don't choose to major in computer science. *ACM SIGCSE Bulletin*, 38, 1, 27-31.

[9] Dodds, Z., and Karp, L. 2006. The evolution of a computational outreach program to secondary school students. In *Proceedings of the 39th SIGCSE Technical Symposium on Computer Science Education* (Houston, Texas, USA March 01-05). ACM, New York, NY, 448-452.

[10] Donaldson, S. 2011. Teaching computer science in a big questions framework. *Journal of Computing Science in College*, 26, 5, 72-79.

[11] Egan, M. and Johnson, M. 2010. Service learning in introductory computer science. Paper presented at the Proceedings of the 15th Annual Conference on Innovation and Technology in Computer Science Education (Bikent, Ankara, Turkey June 26-30).

[12] Goode, J., Chamna, G., and Margolis, J. 2012. Beyond curriculum: The exploring computer science program. *ACM Inroads*, 3, 2, 47-53.

[13] Guzdial, M. 2004. Programming environments for novices. In S. Fincher and M. Petre (Eds.), *Computer Science Education Research* (pp. 127-154). Philadelphia, PA: Taylor & Francis.

[14] Hart, S. 2006. Breaking literacy boundaries through critical service-learning: education for the silenced and marginalized, *Mentoring and Tutoring,* 14, 1, 17-32.

[15] Howard, R. W. 2006. Bending towards justice: service learning and social capital as means to the tipping point, *Mentoring and Tutoring,* 14, 1, 5-15.

[16] Hug, S., Thiry, H., and Tedford, P. 2011. Learning to love computer science: Peer leaders gain teaching skill, communicative ability and content knowledge in the CS classroom. In *Proceedings of the 42nd ACM Technical Symposium on Computer Science Education* (Dallas, TX USA March 09-12). ACM, New York, NY, 201-206.

[17] Kafai, Y. B., Desai, S., Peppler, K., Chiu, G. and Moya, J. 2008. Mentoring partnerships in a community technology center: A Constructionist approach for fostering equitable service learning. *Mentoring & Tutoring*, 16, 2, 194-201.

[18] Kelleher, C., and Pausch, R. 2005. Lowering the barriers to programming: A taxonomy of programming environments and languages for novice programmers. *ACM Computing Surveys*, 37, 2, 83-137.

[19] Lamb, T.A. 2005. An imperfect but useful tool: The retrospective pretest. *The Evaluation Exchange,11*(2). Retrieved July 5th, 2012 at http://www.gse.harvard.edu/hfrp/eval/issue30/ ttp://www.gse.harvard.edu/hfrp/eval/issue30/spotlight.html.

[20] McIver, W., and Rachell, T. 2002. Social informatics and service learning as teaching models. *IEEE Technology and Society Magazine*, 21, 3, 24-31.

[21] Papert, S. 1980. *Mindstorms: Children, Computers, and Powerful Ideas.* New York, NY: Basic Books.

[22] Roberts, A. 2000. Mentoring revisited: A phenomenological reading of the literature. *Mentoring and Tutoring*, 8, 2, 145-170.

[23] Rosmaita, B. 2007. Making service learning accessible to computer scientists. In *Proceedings of the 38th Technical Symposium on Computer Science Education* (Covington, KY, USA March 07-10). ACM, New York, NY, 541-545.

[24] Sanderson, P. 2003. Where's (the) computer science in service-learning? *Junior Computer Science College*, 19, 1 (Oct. 2003), 83-89.

[25] Villalpando, O., and Solorzano, D. G. 2005. The role of culture in college preparation programs: a review of the research literature. In W. Tierney, Z. Corwin and J. Colyar (Eds.), *Preparing for College: Nine Elements of Effective Outreach.* Albany, NY: State University of New York Press.

[26] Walker, G. 1996. Social change one on one: the new mentoring movement, *American Prospect,* 7, 27, 75-81.

Panel: Mobile Application Development in Computing Curricula

Stoney Jackson (Moderator) Western New England U. hjackson@wne.edu

Stan Kurkovsky Central Connecticut State U. kurkovsky@ccsu.edu

Eni Mustafaraj Wellesley College emustafa@wellesley.edu

Lori Postner Nassau Community College Lori.Postner@ncc.edu

Categories and Subject Descriptors

K.3.2 [**Computer and Information Science Education**]: Curriculum

Keywords

Mobile Application Development

1. SUMMARY

Mobile application development is a hot topic that has great appeal to computing students. Harnessing this popularity is important to our programs to help attract new majors, retain those we have and to generally motivate learning. Many institutions are considering offering a course on mobile application development. Some already have.

It is time to begin a discussion about developing mobile applications in our curricula. Where does it belong? Does it belong? What are some of the challenges and risks in creating a mobile application development course and how do we mitigate them? What other potential offerings are there? Can it be used to attract non-majors into the major?

The panelists below present four experiences in teaching a course in mobile application development. They will share their experiences and help start the discussion about mobile application development in our curricula. In the first half of the session, each panelist will present their experience including: an overview of their course; its audience, position in the curriculum, and pre-requisites; the platform, language, and development environment used; positives about the course; and roadblocks and negatives about the course. This explanation will provide the foundation for the second half of the session, which will involve audience discussion of the questions identified above.

2. STONEY JACKSON

Industry Partners: In addition to being attractive to students, mobile applications have the benefit of relatively easy deployment and broad accessibility to a range of users. It is not surprising that many businesses are strongly focusing on mobile apps to reach their customers and to support their business goals. However, mobile application development faces the challenge of developing for a rapidly evolving technology resulting in problems of version control, backwards and forward compatibility, maintenance, and more.

The Mobile Application Development course offered at Western New England University focuses on the development and maintenance of real-world mobile applications. The use of real-world applications allows students to become self-directed learners within a professional environment while understanding development for mobile devices under real world constraints and requirements. Students developed or enhanced two main applications. The WNE Mobile application is aimed at WNE students, and provides students with access to course schedules, library, professor information, and more. In addition, Financial Partners Inc. provided an application for supporting loan initiation for farm credit bureau representatives working with agricultural business folks in the field. This application was developed from requirements defined by FPI and with direct input and oversight from FPI.

Both projects were developed for the Android platform and written in Java using the Eclipse development environment. This course was offered as an elective for upper division Computer Science and Information Technology majors. Students were required to have completed an introductory course in programming in Java.

3. STAN KURKOVSKY

Mobile Games: Computer games gained a wide acceptance as an engaging and motivating tool in the CS curriculum. However, designing and implementing a playable game is a very challenging task and is best implemented in advanced courses where students already have a sufficient experience in software development and exposure to other CS topics. Mobile games offer an advantage of being simpler by nature and thus easier to program. This makes it more feasible to lower-level students to develop playable games as a part of their classroom experience.

Mobile applications are often easy for students to relate to, because mobile technology plays an increasingly important role in the lives of today's students. For many of them, their mobile phone is replacing a desktop computer as their primary computing device. Mobile applications and games offer instant gratification in the sense that students can download them to their mobile phones almost immediately and show them off to their friends. In our approach, we strive to make connections to advanced CS topics as early in the curriculum as possible. By exposing students to a wide range of advanced CS topics early in their academic career, our approach aims to show students that CS can be much more exciting than coding and that there are so many areas in which programming plays a supplementary role.

This approach has been applied in two separate instances, as a standalone course and as a set of curricular modules. An Introduction to Mobile game Development course has been offered at Central Connecticut State University for the three three years. CS I is the only prerequisite for this course, which makes it open to any student with basic knowledge of Java. This course uses Java 2 Mobile Edition (J2ME), which can be installed on any platform. J2ME applications are typically developed in an emulator, but then can be transferred to a mobile device. In parallel with the course, we developed a number of learning

SIGCSE'13, March 6–9, 2013, Denver, Colorado, USA.
ACM 978-1-4503-1868-6/13/03.

modules leveraging the engaging and motivational nature of mobile game development. Each module focuses on a mobile implementation of a single casual game (e.g. Frogger or Battleship) to reinforce a core programming topic (e.g. loops or arrays) and introduce students to an advance are of CS (e.g. computer networking or databases).

4. ENI MUSTAFARAJ

Attracting students to programming: The generation of current students grew up with iPods and Facebook. Mobile devices and access to the Internet are the most natural aspect of their everyday life. With the widespread adoption of smartphones and tablets, which are very powerful generic computing devices, it is only natural to think of how to leverage their appeal into attracting more students (especially minorities) into programming and Computer Science. However, developing mobile applications with the current technologies requires that students have already completed at least two CS courses in programming. Can we make programming mobile apps attractive and easy for non-programmers? It turns out that we can, with the new visual programming environment, App Inventor for Android, that uses the blocks-language technology underlying another popular platform, Scratch. With App Inventor it is simple to create functional apps in a matter of minutes. This is made possible by a built-in library of powerful components that simplify the interface design and behavior programming through event-handlers. In fact, because it is so easy to build interesting apps, very soon students embark in very ambitious projects. App Inventor has been recently open-sourced and this creates new opportunities for educators and hobbyists to develop new libraries that will simplify access to more sophisticated features of the Android SDK. This means that App Inventor can be used both as a platform for non-programmers, and as an open-source project in which advanced CS students can make their contribution, with the goal to make programming more accessible to everyone.

5. LORI POSTNER

Retention: One challenge of teaching in a community college is retaining students through graduation. Many students take Computer Science I and II and then transfer to a four-year institution. In an effort to encourage students to complete their CS degree at Nassau Community College, we created a mobile application development course as a 2nd year elective. From an educational point of view, developing mobile applications provides students with a new perspective on program design and efficiency. It provides a context for discussing topics such as threads, real time applications, databases, and user interface design. From a motivational perspective, students are thoroughly engaged. The ability to put a program they created on their phone or tablet and show it to their friends makes students want to go above and beyond the basics.

The Mobile Application Development course at NCC was offered for the first time Fall 2011 and has run each semester since. Our CS I/CS II sequence is taught in Java using the Eclipse programming environment. To leverage off students' prior knowledge, the course teaches Android application development allowing us to continue with Java and Eclipse. The energy and enthusiasm of the students in the course is unparalleled in any other course I've taught. The students have become part of the learning process. They research ideas and contribute solutions to the class. Not only are they learning an emerging technology, they are able to witness, first hand, the endless possibilities that CS as a discipline provides. Although it is too early to know how the course will affect our retention efforts, it certainly looks promising.

Strategies for Adding the Emerging PDC Curriculum Recommendations into CS Courses

Richard A. Brown (Moderator)
St. Olaf College
rab@stolaf.edu

Joel C. Adams
Calvin College
adams@calvin.edu

David P. Bunde
Knox College
dbunde@knox.edu

Jens Mache
Lewis & Clark College
jmache@lclark.edu

Elizabeth Shoop
Macalester College
shoop@macalester.edu

SUMMARY

The emerging body of knowledge in the ACM-IEEE/CS Computer Science Curricula 2013 recommendations call for a new Parallel and Distributed Computing knowledge area, in response to the explosive growth of multi-core processors, "cloud" distributed computing, and other forms of multiprocessor computing. Those recommendations follow on the NSF-TCPP Curricular Recommendations and other recent efforts to identify the parallel and distributed computing (PDC) education that undergraduate CS majors must now possess as they compete for technology careers requiring ever-increasing parallelism. Given the urgency of this curricular change for our students, the complexity and breadth of this knowledge area, and today's rapid pace of innovation in PDC technology, how can an educator incorporate this new priority into undergraduate CS courses?

This panel offers four distinct examples of curricular responses to this challenge, unified by a common strategy of adding PDC components that address the new curricular recommendations into existing courses:

- exploring GPU architecture and programming in a Computer Organization course;
- incorporating brief units on shared memory parallelism into several core CS courses;
- adding various aspects of the PDC notion of *reduction* to several CS courses; and
- inserting short, course-relevant segments on a broad variety of PDC topics into many courses at multiple levels throughout CS curricula.

In each case, an educator adds conceptual principles of parallel and distributed computing, reinforced by active learning through programming experience with present-day technologies, in curricular units of modest size that are relevant to a course's traditional goals. Thus, the four panelists (who direct NSF-funded projects to develop instructional materials for teaching parallelism and distributed computing) articulate contrasting approaches to augmenting a CS major program with PDC content in response to the new curricular recommendations, within the feasibility constraint of incrementally modifying individual courses.

SIGCSE'13, March 6–9, 2013, Denver, Colorado, USA.
ACM 978-1-4503-1868-6/13/03.

Categories and Subject Descriptors

K.3.2 [**Computers and Education**]: Computer and Information Science Education – *Curriculum.*

General Terms

Algorithms, Design, Performance.

Keywords

Parallel computing, parallelism, distributed computing, education, curricular recommendations, curriculum.

1. RICHARD BROWN (MODERATOR)

Dick Brown co-directs (with panelist Shoop) the CSinParallel project (csinparallel.org), which produces and shares modular materials for incrementally adding parallelism to existing undergraduate computer science courses[1]. He has directed the creation of parallel platform resources, including the MistRider virtual cluster[2] and the WebMapReduce interface to Hadoop map-reduce computing[3]. A longtime director of CS at St. Olaf, he serves as an executive board member of the EAPF (eapf.org). Brown will briefly review the goals of the session (3-4 min), introduce each panelist (10 min each), and moderate discussion.

2. JENS MACHE

Jens Mache is Professor of Computer Science at Lewis & Clark College. He has taught parallelism to undergraduates since 2001. He and panelist Bunde direct an NSF TUES project about teaching parallel computing with activity-based laboratories.

Statement: We introduced a unit on GPU parallelism to our 200-level Intro to Computer Architecture (aka Computer Organization) course. Students nowadays enjoy access to hundreds of cores in graphics cards (GPUs) in desktop or laptop computers. With languages such as CUDA and OpenCL, students can program GPUs for computational tasks and achieve orders of magnitude improvement in performance. This type of programming demands a detailed understanding of GPU architecture. Parallel programming with GPUs also provides opportunity for much programmer control, thus rewarding an understanding of computer architecture. This presentation will show our Game of Life CUDA assignments. It has been popular with students, having interesting visual output that makes it easy to spot erroneous computations.

3. JOEL ADAMS

Joel Adams is Professor and Chair of the Department of Computer Science at Calvin College, and has been teaching his students about concurrency and parallelism for 20 years[4], [5].

Statement: Since 2006, manufacturers have produced processors with multiple cores instead of faster clock speeds. Shared-memory parallelism via multithreading is the industry-standard means of taking advantage of such hardware, so we believe it is essential that all CS students receive significant experience with shared-memory parallelism. Prior to 2008, our students' exposure to these topics was limited to our *Operating Systems and Networking* course. We began increasing our coverage in 2008 by adding a 1-week module on shared-memory parallelism (including a hands-on OpenMP exercise) into our *Data Structures* course (aka CS2), and by increasing our coverage of multithreading in the *Operating Systems and Networking* course. In 2011 and 2012, we have integrated additional coverage of shared-memory parallelism into the following courses: *Algorithms* (aka *CS3*), *Intro to Computer Architecture* (aka *Computer Organization*), and *Programming Language Concepts*. Since these courses are taken by all our CS majors, these changes ensure that all of our majors receive exposure to shared-memory parallelism in nearly every core course, and in a variety of programming languages. Beyond this, our students may choose to study distributed-memory parallelism in our elective *High Performance Computing* course. This presentation will provide an overview of our core curriculum, and will detail how we are integrating parallelism into that curriculum.

4. DAVID BUNDE

David Bunde is Associate Professor of Computer Science at Knox College. He has taught concurrency and parallelism in a variety of courses. He and panelist Mache have written about the need for higher-level approaches in parallel education[6] and now direct an NSF TUES project developing this approach.

Statement: Knox College teaches parallelism in most of our core courses (Computer Organization, OS and networking, Software Development, and Algorithms), in CS2, and in many electives. A particular emphasis in our curricula is on getting students to think in terms of higher-level primitives. Reductions are the most common of these, being directly provided by many parallel languages/libraries and also serving as a useful building block for programs in languages without direct support for them. I will highlight assignments given to Algorithms students that require them to specify algorithms in terms of reductions and also to describe their implementation in a framework that makes the process similar to dynamic programming.

5. ELIZABETH SHOOP

Libby Shoop co-directs (with moderator Brown) the CSinParallel project (csinparallel.org)[1]. She teaches several courses in the CS curriculum, ranging from the introductory level to computer systems organization, software development, and parallel and distributed systems.

Statement: In the CSInParallel project, moderator Brown and I have developed and class-tested over a dozen computer science course modules, each designed to take a short amount of class time to introduce a particular PDC concept and reinforce it through active student exercises. We have deployed these in most courses in our curricula. I will discuss how these modules align with PDC curriculum recommendations, and how those module-knowledge unit relationships have appeared in our CS courses. This approach enables us to instill parallel thinking into our students with incremental, small modifications to our curricula over time.

6. ACKNOWLEDGMENTS

Adams, Brown, and Shoop are supported by NSF DUE-1225739/1225796/1226172. Bunde and Mache are supported by NSF DUE-1044299/1044932.

7. REFERENCES

[1] R. Brown and E. Shoop, "Modules in Community: Injecting More Parallelism Into Computer Science Curricula," in *Proceedings of The 42nd ACM Technical Symposium on Computer Science Education*, 2011, p. to appear.

[2] R. A. Brown, "Hadoop at home: large-scale computing at a small college," in *Proceedings of the 40th ACM technical symposium on Computer science education*, Chattanooga, TN, USA, 2009, pp. 106–110.

[3] P. Garrity, T. Yates, R. Brown, and E. Shoop, "WebMapReduce: An accessible and adaptable tool for teaching map-reduce computing," in *Proceedings of The 42nd ACM Technical Symposium on Computer Science Education*, Dallas, TX, 2011, p. to appear.

[4] J. Adams, C. Nevison, and N. C. Schaller, "Parallel computing to start the millennium," *SIGCSE Bull.*, vol. 32, no. 1, pp. 65–69, Mar. 2000.

[5] J. C. Adams, K. Hoobeboom, and J. Walz, "A cluster for CS education in the manycore era," in *Proceedings of the 42nd ACM technical symposium on Computer science education*, New York, NY, USA, 2011, pp. 27–32.

[6] D. P. Bunde and J. Mache, "Teaching concurrency beyond HPC." 1st Workshop on Curricula in Concurrency and Parallelism, OOPSLA, 2009.

Fulbrights Abroad in Computer Science

Tom Armstrong	Matthew Boutell (moderator)	Linda Ott
Wheaton College	Rose-Hulman Institute of Technology	Michigan Technological University
26 E. Main Street	5500 Wabash Avenue	1400 Townsend Drive
Norton, MA 02766	Terre Haute, IN 47803	Houghton, MI 49931
508.286.5686	812.877.8534	906.487.2315
tarmstro@wheatoncollege.edu	boutell@rose-hulman.edu	linda@mtu.edu

SUMMARY

The Fulbright Scholar Program is the flagship academic exchange program of the U.S. Department of State; approximately 1,100 American scholars travel worldwide annually to lecture and conduct research. The program is open to all U.S. citizens with university teaching experience and a Ph.D. or equivalent professional/terminal degree [1]. Opportunities for Computer Science educators to win Fulbright scholarships are many. The goal of this panel is to inform the community of computer science educators about the Fulbright program, including the application process, and to answer questions about the program. After an introduction to the program at large, the panelists will each give a 10-15 minute overview of their personal experience as a Fulbright scholar in 2011-2012, leaving ample time for questions from educators considering applying for a Fulbright scholarship. The panelists will offer diverse perspectives based on their experiences in India, Zambia, and Siberia.

Categories and Subject Descriptors

K.3.0 [**Computers and Education**]: General

Keywords

Fulbright, international experience, international exchange, teaching abroad

1. TOM ARMSTRONG

Tom is Assistant Professor of Computer Science at Wheaton College in Norton, Massachusetts. He was named a Fulbright-Nehru Scholar to the Republic of India for 2011-2012 to Hemchandracharya North Gujarat University (HNGU) in Patan, Gujarat, India – a location that, while not achieving gender parity in the STEM (science, technology, engineering, and mathematics) disciplines, is notably more successful than institutions in the United States in the attraction to and retention of women in Computer Science. Wheaton holds the honor and distinction of being the nation's first four-year baccalaureate institution of higher education for women. In keeping with that tradition, he is conscious of the need to increase the participation of women and students from underrepresented minority groups in Computer Science.

Tom spent a semester teaching in the Department of Computer Science at HNGU. During his time at the University, his goals were to: 1) develop curricula and expand the scope of their Computer Science department; 2) explore their practices and environments that result in recruitment and retention of women in Computer Science; and 3) actively learn a new language in a multilingual environment to inform course content and build a collaborative research agenda. He taught a course in Artificial Intelligence to 5th and 9th semester MCA and MScIT students, respectively, at the University.

He chose India, in part, because of nascent relationships during his graduate studies to, now, collaborators and friends in the professoriate. He expanded his social network to include computer scientists from many states in India. Among the intangible benefits, the sheer linguistic diversity of the group speaks to the broader multilingualism of India. A multilingual environment is ideal for two of his research and teaching interests: 1) language immersion to study language acquisition; and 2) language change and genesis. Speakers in multilingual environments frequently use multiple languages concurrently (e.g., English, Hindi, and Gujarati). He wanted firsthand experience in that type of environment to inform his research on computational language acquisition Language.

The academic successes and failures were personally and professionally fruitful. The entire experience resulted in establishing new and renewed connections. Tom plans to return to India annually between the fall and spring semesters with students from Wheaton.

2. MATTHEW BOUTELL

Matt is Associate Professor of Computer Science and Software Engineering at Rose-Hulman Institute of Technology. He won a 10-month lecturing/research grant to the Computer Science Department at Copperbelt University in Kitwe, Zambia for the 2011-2012 academic year. His initial contact with the university was very positive, since the Dean at CBU had worked with a Fulbright scholar previously to create a syllabus for Zambia's first MSc program in Computer Science. The plan was for Matt to teach the first intake of students in May. After teaching classes on Android Application Development and preparing for the new MSc courses for several months, he found out less than two weeks before MSc classes were to start that the program would not begin until after he left Zambia, due to circumstances at the University beyond his control. Instead, he taught undergraduate courses on software development, which is his passion. He also developed an Android application which will soon be available on Google Play.

His greatest contributions to the department were mentoring young faculty members, working with lecturers to update the curriculum to include more software development, and teaching the BSc program's first course in Java. In all, he modeled active learning and a greater emphasis on hands-on programming in practice and assessment than had previously been the case.

Matt's wife and five children, ages 13, 11, 9, 7, and 4, accompanied him to Kitwe. They homeschooled their children in both the US and in Zambia, which, along with electronic book readers, made that part of the transition incredibly easy.

SIGCSE'13, March 6–9, 2013, Denver, Colorado, USA.
ACM 978-1-4503-1868-6/13/03.

While in Zambia, they especially appreciated the friendliness of the Zambian people, the fresh locally-grown food, the predictable weather, and the simplicity of life. Back home in Indiana, they now appreciate clean and plentiful tap water, consistent electricity, and smooth roads.

Matt attended a similar panel at SIGCSE two years ago, and was greatly encouraged by the panelists; he hopes that this panel will be as encouraging to fellow educators considering applying for a Fulbright scholarship.

3. LINDA OTT

Linda is Professor of Computer Science at Michigan Technological University. She was awarded a three month Fulbright to visit Siberian State Aerospace University (SibSAU) in Krasnoyarsk, Russia. Krasnoyarsk is a city of over one million people located in Siberia along the Trans-Siberian Railroad.

While at SIBSAU, Linda interacted with three different groups: faculty members and students in the Institute of Computer Science and Telecommunications, teachers and students in the Foreign Languages Department, and staff in the International Cooperation Department. Her primary teaching responsibility was a course on advanced software engineering for Masters students in computer science. In addition to teaching the software engineering course, she was involved in a range of other educationally related activities. She consulted with faculty members on course materials, discussing issues related to both content and their presentation in English. She also consulted with several faculty members and graduate students on their research projects.

She lectured in an English course for scientific and technical Ph.D. students covering such topics as the types of venues for publishing research results and preparing papers for submitting to international technical conferences and journals. She visited a class for students learning to be specialized English interpreters. She also held informal English Clubs with students desiring to practice English with a native speaker and/or to learn more about the United States.

With members of the International Cooperation Department, she drafted a cooperation agreement between SibSAU and Michigan Tech. Through the International Cooperation Department she also had the opportunity to interact with international students and visiting faculty members.

She enjoyed the variety of experiences and the opportunities to interact with the Russian people, particularly the students. She found it rewarding to discover that she could comfortably cope with walking into a class thinking she was going to lecture to an upper level computing class and finding out as she began her lecture on privacy that it was actually a class for students majoring in tourism. Finally, she found that a vegetarian can survive a Siberian winter.

4. ACKNOWLEDGMENTS

We thank the U.S. Department of State for continuing to support the Fulbright Scholars program.

5. REFERENCES

[1] Council for International Exchange of Scholars (CIES) Fulbright, Retrieved September 07, 2012 from http://www.cies.org/about_fulb.htm.

The Inverted Classroom and the CS Curriculum

Kate Lockwood
CSIT, CSU Monterey Bay
100 Campus Center
Seaside, CA 93955
831-402-2424
klockwood@csumb.edu

Rachel Esselstein
Math, CSU Monterey Bay
100 Campus Center
Seaside, CA 93955
831-582-3217
resselstein@csumb.edu

ABSTRACT

The inverted classroom is a pedagogical technique in which passive knowledge acquisitions activities (e.g. lecture, readings) are assigned as homework and hands-on knowledge assimilation tasks (e.g. problem solving, lab, creative work) replace traditional lecture during classroom contact hours. Recent initiatives like the Kahn Academy [1] have raised the visibility of the inverted classroom and it is being adopted in disciplines across the curriculum from Economics [2] to Biology [3]. In this experience report we present successful inverted classroom pilots in linear algebra and introductory programming classes. In particular, this pilot focused on combining the inverted classroom philosophy with other proven pedagogical techniques (e.g. inquiry based learning) there was also a focus on creating free materials that could replace traditional, expensive textbooks when using the inverted classroom. We explain how the inverted classroom pedagogy is well aligned with the hands-on practice required in both math and computer science and discuss our plans to continue our experiment and to expand it beyond the original two classes.

Categories and Subject Descriptors

K.3.2 [**Computer and Information Science Education**]: Computer Science Education.

Keywords

Pedagogy, Inverted Classroom, Linear Algebra, Introductory Programming, Instructional Technology.

1. INTRODUCTION

1.1 The Inverted Classroom

The inverted classroom [2] is a pedagogical technique in which passive knowledge acquisitions activities such as lectures and practice are assigned as homework. In-class contact hours are then used for hands-on, active learning, and knowledge assimilation tasks. This allows instructors to spend the bulk of their in-class time directly interacting with students and mentoring them through advanced problem solving activities. Students are able to do the tasks that most often require expert help while they have direct access to their instructor. Due to popular initiatives such as the Kahn academy [1], there have been a number of recent pilot projects involving implementations of the inverted classroom. These range across disciplines, educational level, and level of inversion.

This experience report describes a pilot project involving two courses available to students in the computer science program at an undergraduate teaching institution: introductory programming and linear algebra. In both cases, inverted classroom methods were combined with other proven pedagogical techniques (pair programming in the programming class, and inquiry-based learning in the math class) in an attempt to maximize the level of learning attained during contact hours without compromising topic coverage.

The paper begins by describing the motivation for this pilot and places it in the context of related work on the inverted classroom. Then it provides a detailed description of the inverted classroom as deployed in each of the pilot courses. Some preliminary data based on student surveys, course evaluations, and informal student feedback is provided. To aid others who may wish to try similar experiments the paper then describes the technology used, most of which was free or relatively inexpensive, and the lessons learned as the courses enter the second year of inverted classroom piloting. The paper closes by discussing plans for continuing this work and for distributing the materials we created during the pilot courses.

1.2 Motivation for CS/Math Pilot

The authors were motivated to experiment with inverted classroom techniques by a number of circumstances. Being based at a teaching focused institution, both authors attempt to stay abreast of pedagogical techniques and research and both had been interested in previous work in the inverted classroom. Both authors teach classes where practice and hands-on experimentation with the material are among the best ways to master the course content, yet felt that students were not getting enough time to spend in guided exploration. In both math and computer science, the ability of students to apply techniques and knowledge to novel problems is paramount. These are often the types of tasks relegated to homework that students complete outside of class and on their own. Yet they are also the tasks that most benefit from instructor support and expert modeling. The authors hoped that by scaffolding advanced problem solving through in-class activities, students would gain more experience with applied skills, would better assimilate the material, and that this would lead to better student success and retention.

In addition to pedagogical issues, financial pressures played into the decision to explore the inverted classroom as well. As instructional budgets are slashed, instructors are faced with taking on more classes with more students, and fewer resources (e.g. TAs, lab assistants). These pressures serve to further limit the amount of contact time that instructors can spend with each student helping them explore and interpret the material. Faced with these kinds of limitations, many instructors feel that the only option is to reduce the time spent on interactive activities and fall back on increased traditional lecture. The authors were determined to find a way to include the interactive activities they (and their students) enjoyed without compromising the amount of material covered in a semester.

Students can also feel frustrated by the lack of contact with their professors and by the increasing cost of course materials. Many textbooks in math and computer science retail for well over $100 and are often used for only one semester. Frequent new editions reduce the sell-back value of books and cause further financial pressure on students. Many online solutions provided by traditional publishers do little to alleviate these problems as they are not substantially cheaper. The pilot courses here made all inverted classroom materials available for free to students, often replacing costly traditional resources. The authors are refining the materials used in order to be able to offer them as free online packages to students in their classes and at other institutions. When inverted classroom materials can be produced and distributed cheaply (or for free), it benefits both students and instructors. These materials can also be offered in multiple formats (e.g. videos and text) to accommodate different learning styles without extensive additional work.

2. PREVIOUS WORK

While the inverted classroom technique has been gaining traction lately due to the prevalence of enabling technologies, it is not a new pedagogy. Many instructors in the humanities and social sciences would say that they have been using the inverted classroom for years by assigning substantial reading assignments (often with accompanying reflection questions) and then devoting class time to expert-facilitated discussion. The authors were inspired by these "analog" inverted classrooms, but found that students often did not do assigned reading (even when they were also required to take a quiz) and that some students who did actually do the reading were unable to extract important concepts from technical textbooks. At the same time, the authors knew that students at home should be able to easily cover some basic, introductory material, freeing class time for high-level problem solving activities. Clearly, some other media, besides textbooks, was needed to provide students with the background material necessary to enable participation in class time activities. The authors turned to the inverted classroom literature.

Many inverted classroom implementations use lecture capture technology to broadcast entire lectures to students either via video or audio with podcasting being a popular medium [e.g. 4]. Many courses that employ video lectures (including many of those available online) show an instructor at a whiteboard and try to digitally recreate the experience of sitting in a lecture hall. The approach in these pilots was to completely do away with a traditional lecture format and to replace it with different types of materials that would engage students and appeal to different types of learners. Inspiration was drawn from inverted classroom experiments that used intelligent tutoring systems [6], student worksheets or other low-stakes assessment of pre-class activities [3], screen capture [7], and shorter, topic-based study materials.

3. PILOT COURSES

The pilot sections described in this paper were both offered during the 2011-2012 academic year. Here we briefly described the courses as traditionally offered and outline the structure of the courses when offered in inverted format.

3.1 Linear Algebra

3.1.1 Traditional Format

Math 330, the introductory Linear Algebra course is a 4-unit course taken by many mathematics and computer science majors. In the past, the course has been taught in traditional lecture format with one section offered each semester. While the course is offered every semester, the instruction duties rotate through the math faculty. Grades are typically assigned based on homework assignments, midterms and a final exam.

3.1.2 Inverted Classroom

The first inverted classroom pilot for Math 330 was offered in Fall semester 2011. The Math 330 implementation of the inverted classroom moved all instructor delivered material to videos that were watched prior to attending class. Student groups then worked through problem sets and proofs during class time and presented results to the class. During the in-class active learning exercises, the instructor used inquiry-based learning techniques, pushing the students to discover solutions on their own and to come to consensus rather than relying on the teacher to tell them whether they were correct. In this pilot course, student work was broken into three main components:

(1) **Preclass videos.** The videos for Math 330 were recorded using screen capture software and a tablet PC. The instructor covered basic, introductory material much like what might be covered in an assigned textbook reading in a similar course. Each video was 15-30 minutes long and was coupled with 1-3 questions for the students to answer. Solutions to the questions were collected at the beginning of each class period and the video and question activities were worth 10% of the student's grade for the semester.

(2) **In-class discussion**. Rather than spend the majority of class time in passive lecture, all of the class time in the inverted linear algebra course was devoted to inquiry-based learning. Active participation in these activities was worth 25% of a student's total grade. The instructor would provide problems for students to work through in small groups. Groups would then present their solution to the class and lead a discussion in which the class arrived at consensus regarding whether the solution was correct. During this discussion the instructor recorded participation for each student, but tried to refrain from commenting on the work as presented, allowing the students to discover mistakes on their own.

(3) **Exams.** Students were further evaluated on whether they had met learning outcomes for the course through midterm and final exams.

3.2 Introduction to Problem Solving and Programming (C++)

3.2.1 Traditional Format

CST 231, the introductory programming class is a 4-unit course that has traditionally been a combination of lecture and lab activities. The course meets in a computer lab that seats 30 students, but is often over-subscribed with at least 35 students enrolled in each section. Each section is taught by a single instructor with no TA support in twice weekly, two hour meetings. Different formats had been tried in the past, although they were typically rearrangements of lecture and lab (e.g. lecture one day, lab the following or mix of lecture and lab on both days).

CST 231 has traditionally had a fail rate between 25 and 30 percent with grades based on a combination of homework, in-class lab assignments and exams. Lectures tended to use a combination of lecture notes (PowerPoint slides) and demonstrations using Visual Studio.

3.2.2 Inverted Classroom

The inverted classroom pilot of CST 231 consisted of five main components.

(1) **Online workbooks** that students were to complete before each class period. Each workbook page included a short summary of the material covered, 3-7 videos demonstrating or explaining the concept, and clearly marked "TO DO" sections directing the student to download code and try different manipulations or experiments with the code. Students were expected to come to class ready to discuss the results of the TO DO activities, but all were exploratory in nature and did not require extensive application of the concepts being covered. Some workbook pages also included links to automatically graded online quizzes allowing students to check their understanding of concepts before attending class.

The workbook is currently in its second revision. Initially all videos were under 5 minutes due to a limitation of the screen capture software used. Videos are still kept short when possible, but new software is being used to allow for a longer explanation of more complex concepts. While many implementations of the inverted classroom use lecture capture technology where an entire lecture is broadcast either via video or audio (e.g. a podcast), the approach in this class was to completely do away with hour long traditional lecture and to segment the material into meaningful, accessible chunks.

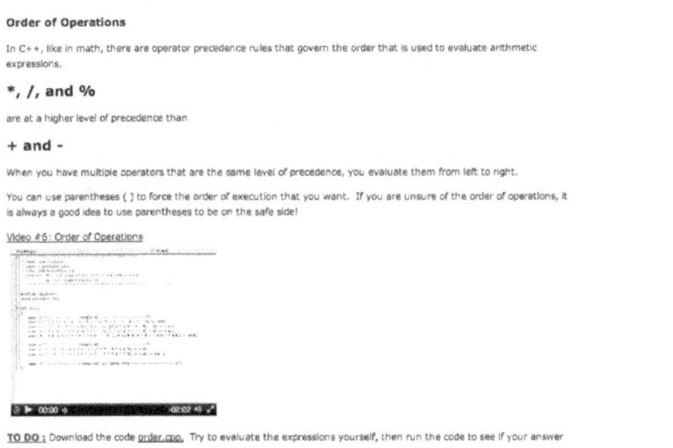

Figure 1. A screen shot of the online workbook for CST 231. Students would read a short summary and watch a video demonstrating a concept. Clearly labeled "TO DO" sections would instruct them to download the code associated with a video and try different manipulations/additions.

(2) **Guided problem-solving activities** done in small groups at the beginning of each class. These activities either asked students to apply knowledge from the day's workbook assignment or introduced a new topic that students were encouraged to extract from the activity. For example, after completing workbook assignments on arithmetic operators and order of operations one of the in class activities involved giving students code using increment, decrement, and abbreviated operators and asking them to run the code and try to determine the rules for how each operator worked. Another activity involved asking them to solve a problem (making change) using the operators they had learned. Each activity would be completed in small groups and then discussed as a class with different groups demonstrating their solution or explaining their result. The presenting groups would answer questions from classmates and multiple groups would present for each activity to allow the class to compare and contrast the solutions found.

(3) **Lab exercises** done primarily in class using pair-programming partners. These exercises were opportunities for the students to practice and apply the concepts they had learned in the workbook and problem solving activities. Students were encouraged to complete the labs in class and credit for labs was only given when the pair could demonstrate the running lab for the instructor and answer a few short questions about how the program worked. During lab work time, the instructor would circulate through the classroom, answering questions and checking off groups who had finished.

(4) **Homework** assigned on a regular basis throughout the semester. Homework was completed individually by students and required the application of the concepts learned in workbooks and labs to more complex problems.

(5) **Exams** including two midterms and a final. Exams included both a written portion and a programming portion where students had access to all their own notes, programs, and their preferred development environment

The labs, homework assignments and exams were actually very similar to those from previous semesters. With the exception that the homework was scaled down slightly to accommodate the additional time required outside of class to watch the videos and do the pre-class activities. With the addition of the group problem solving tasks and the TO DO activities in the workbooks, students are exposed to substantially more code than in traditional implementations of the course when they may see just one or two examples for each concept. The bulk of the work required to implement the inverted classroom pedagogy went towards creating the workbook pages and developing the in-class problem solving activities.

4. PRELIMINARY RESULTS

The authors are involved in additional pilots of the inverted classroom and are creating thorough experimental evaluations of student learning in these courses. While there was no formal evaluation of the initial pilot sections, the authors collected a variety of informal, preliminary results from students to inform further development. These results are extracted from: online student surveys, course evaluations, and student demonstration of course outcomes (both in the pilot courses themselves and in the courses for which the pilot sections are prerequisites.).

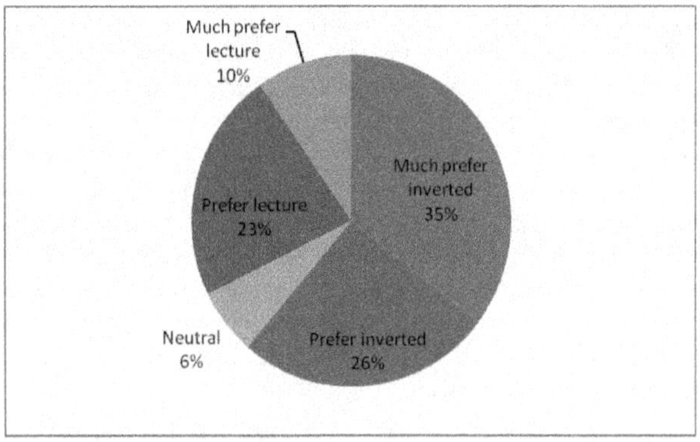

Figure 2. Results from survey of CST 231 students during the inverted classroom pilot. Over 60% of the students preferred the inverted format to a traditional lecture approach.

4.1 Student Engagement

Using the existing course management system, the instructors were able to track which students accessed the pre-class materials, when they were accessed, and how long the students kept them open. The majority of the students in both classes did access the pre-class materials most of the time, particularly once they became familiar with the scope of the in-class activities and learned that they would clearly be unable to participate if they were not adequately prepared. In a survey of the CST 231 students, over 70% of the students reported that they always or almost always watched the videos before the course for which they were assigned. In Math 330, 92% of the students earned perfect scores on the problem sets related to the video assignments. While some students struggled with the additional responsibility of doing the pre-class activities, most eventually found a strategy that worked for setting aside time for the activities. Many students also enjoyed the flexibility offered by the inverted classroom materials with almost 40% of the CST 231 students in the survey responding that they often referred back to videos from past course sessions to review concepts. When asked to account for the time they spent on the course outside of contact hours, the CST 231 students estimated that they spent around 3 hours a week on average watching videos and doing workbook activities and another 6 hours doing homework and finishing labs. The Math 330 students reported less than 1 hour a week watching videos but 5-7 hours a week meeting with groups outside of class to complete packets from in class. The total time spent outside of class then is keeping within the guidelines for a 4-unit class and is similar to numbers reported by students in past semesters when the course was offered in a traditional lecture-based format.

4.2 Student Feedback

4.2.1 Course Evaluations

Both authors have consistently achieved fairly high course evaluations at the end of the semester. The evaluations for the pilot inverted classroom courses were not significantly different from course evaluations in traditional semesters, although in the computer science course it was noted that more students than usual took the time to write comments in the free response portion of the survey. While there was some backlash to the new technique, the majority of the comments tended to be positive. Complaints included students upset about the time management required to examine the materials "on their own time", the requirement to attend class regularly to get the points for the active learning activities, and requests for more traditional lectures. As mentioned in previous work on the inverted classroom [5] a lot of student complaints about the inverted classroom may come from students who are just more comfortable with the familiar, traditional lecture format. These complaints will hopefully fade as students become more comfortable with new course delivery methods.

While there is some dissent, the majority of students prefer the inverted classroom pedagogy. Figure 2 shows results from a survey of the students in the pilot section of CST 231. Over 60% of the students preferred the inverted classroom over traditional lectures. A particularly telling number is that while 35% of students much preferred the inverted classroom, only 10% of students responded that they much preferred a traditional lecture format. The positive feedback found on the survey was also echoed in end of the semester course evaluations.

Sample Comments from CST 231 Students:

"I honestly thought that the videos were great. I would be able to learn at my pace with the videos, repeat anything I didn't understand (or if I needed a break, or couldn't pay attention)"

"I like the way it is because we get introduced the new material before class"

Sample Comments from Math 330 Students:

"The videos let me learn at my own pace. I could pause and rewind. I have ADD so this was good for me."

"I am more focused and engaged during the whole class period. [The course] helped me think on my own and use the tools... to prove my answer rather than looking in the book. I was able to retain more information since I understand the concepts."

4.3 Student Preparation

As both introductory programming and linear algebra are prerequisites for later courses in the curriculum, a prominent concern is that students be prepared to pursue future courses. As most students involved in the pilot are just now taking later courses in the sequence, full data on performance is not available. However, the author who taught the pilot section of CST 231 is now teaching the data structures course. Students from the pilot 231 section have expressed disappointment that the data structures course is not yet inverted and on several occasions they have referred back to videos from the 231 course to review key concepts. Students from the non-pilot section of 231 (taught by a different instructor) have asked for access to the videos as well.

5. TOOLS & TECHNOLOGY

One motivation for the timing of these pilot courses was the prevalence of free or low cost technology to enable the creation of the study materials provided for students. In addition, most students have had extensive experience consuming digital media and are savvy users of media players, e-publications, and productivity software. In an informal survey of students in a 231 section, all but three had personal laptops and all but one had access to a computer in their primary residence. While the digital divide and access to computing resources was a concern for the instructors, the campus has 24-hour computing resources available for free and it was decided that this was sufficient to provide access to all students, much like placing an expensive textbook on course reserve would ensure access to (analog) print materials.

While the mention of educational videos may bring to mind highly edited, professionally produced documentaries, the approach taken for the pilot courses was much smaller scale. Neither author had any previous video production or editing experience so it was essential that all tools be accessible to novice videographers and have a low-enough bar to entry that class prep time would not be prohibitively increased.

5.1 Software

Both authors used commercial screen capture software for the majority of their videos. The Math course used Camtasia Relay and the CST course used Jing (both tools are produced by TechSmith[8]). There are an increasing number of options for screen capture software available on both the Mac and PC as well as for devices such as the iPad and other tablets. This software can range from free to relatively expensive, however, the authors found that many advanced features were not necessary for their first round pilot courses.

The Math 330 screen capture videos were mostly the instructor explaining a concept while inking on a blank screen using a tablet PC. The CST 231 screen captures included live demonstrations using Visual Studio, narrated PowerPoint animations, and ink captures.

5.2 Hardware

Both authors used their personal laptops or tablet PCs for the majority of the media creation they undertook. Recording was done using the built in cameras and microphones. Additional hardware used in some videos included a simple USB tablet to allow on screen inking (both inking on top of existing resources and treating a blank document like a virtual white board). Many Universities, the authors' included, have high-tech recording studies that allow the capture of smart boards, document cameras, and multiple video streams. However, the authors found that relatively low-tech solutions that could be accessed from home lent themselves more easily to the just-in-time media production they found themselves engaging in. Expensive video and audio equipment was not required to create engaging and accessible learning materials.

5.3 Support

The inverted classroom materials developed would not have been possible without institutional IT support. The authors' institution has a faculty instructional technology office that was able to help the authors by suggesting software, providing access to licenses and hardware, and directing them to tutorial materials. Additionally, the authors found that collaboration with other instructors interested in instructional technology was vital to maintaining enthusiasm for the project throughout the semester.

6. LESSONS LEARNED

6.1 Material Creation

The largest investment in moving to the inverted classroom was the creation of all new materials for the students to use to prepare for class. While technology made the process of creating the videos very accessible and low-cost, it was still a time consuming and error prone process. Probably the most important lesson learned in the early days of video creation was: it will never be perfect. Due to the just-in-time nature of developing video materials for a course in progress there was very little to no time available to edit the videos produced. Not to mention, neither instructor had experience editing video so all recording had to be done in a manner that it could be published directly. Both authors briefly outlined the content of videos and carefully chose examples prior to recording, but neither wrote complete scripts making the videos informal and conversational in nature. Many early videos were recorded many times to fix small errors. By the end of the semester, small errors were simply corrected in real-time and interruptions involving pets, children and dishwashers were often left in the published videos as long as the interruption was minimal and did not distract from the material being presented. The instructors found that students actually enjoyed these small interruptions and would often mention them in class.

6.2 Student buy-in

One component crucial to the success of the inverted classroom, is garnering sufficient student buy-in. The pedagogy will be unfamiliar to students who are accustomed to sitting passively in lecture during contact hours. The level of engagement needed for both the at home materials and the classroom activities will require students to be more focused and actively involved than they are used to. The informal student feedback and teaching evaluations collected during our pilot both highlight that some students struggled with this class format as it forced them out of their educational comfort zone.

Both authors found that taking time in the first few class periods to motivate the use of inverted techniques was important to encouraging students to try the new materials. Both now include language (referred to as a manifesto) in course syllabi describing the inverted classroom technique, explaining what is required of students, and motivating our decision to use this pedagogy in terms of learning outcomes for the course and student mastery of the material.

In addition to providing background and motivation at the beginning of the semester, we found that it is important to periodically remind students of the benefits of participating fully in the inverted classroom. By embedding course materials in an existing CMS, both instructors were able to monitor when (and if) students were accessing pre-class materials. When viewing rates dropped, or when student engagement waned, it was important to remind them of class expectations and the benefit to them and their educational goals. Most students were able to understand the benefits and tended to try to push themselves to participate fully in the new pedagogy. For example, one student remarked on his course evaluations: "I feel like I became stronger at analyzing… [the class] challenged my mind… my critical thinking skills have improved." By end of the semester teaching evaluations, one student even said, "I actually enjoyed class time", which might not be a ringing endorsement but does indicate that most students not only adapted to the new technique, but actually enjoyed it as well.

7. FUTURE WORK AND ONGOING PILOTS

Both authors found their initial pilot courses to be informative and successful and both plan to continue to implement the inverted classroom in classes across the computer science and math curriculum. The materials from the CST 231 pilot are being packaged as a free, interactive e-workbook for students that can be easily distributed and shared with other institutions interested in trying this technique. An additional pilot is planned in which an adjunct instructor, unfamiliar with the technique or the materials will use them to teach a separate section of programming under the supervision of one of the authors. This will provide an additional avenue for critiquing and improving the e-workbook.

The success of the Linear Algebra pilot has led to the expansion of the inverted classroom technique to other courses in the math curriculum and to interest in the technique from instructors across the University.

Encouraged by the availability and usability of low cost technical tools, the authors are also working on creating a free, interactive discrete math textbook incorporating many of the principle of the inverted classroom. This book is intended to provide the homework lessons and discovery activities for students participating in an inverted discrete mathematics course while also providing activities that help students learn how to successfully read a more traditional textbook. A pilot chapter is under development and a draft of the book will be available soon

In addition to the successes of the authors, other faculty members at our home institution have begun to adopt the inverted classroom for parts of their courses. While each course is different and commands its own unique set of pedagogical approaches, many of our colleagues have found that their students appreciate the increased hands-on guidance in class and make extensive use of the materials for home study. Formal and informal communities of instructors have been formed to support the development of additional inverted classroom materials and the instructional technology department has expanded both the software and hardware offerings available to support inverted classroom implementations.

As efforts continue to expand inverted classroom techniques across the curriculum, it will be important to address lingering issues related to accessibility both to technology and of the materials created. Given the vast literature on learning styles and the types of materials that support different learners, it will be important to make sure that all learners have access to appropriate materials to prepare for inverted classroom activities. In addition, steps like captioning of videos and creation of accessible PDFs can insure that students with physical and learning disabilities are not excluded from participating fully in inverted classroom activities.

8. REFERENCES

[1] The Kahn Academy. Retrieved September, 1, 2012, from http://www.khanacademy.org/

[2] Lage, M.J., Platt, G.J., and Treglia, M. 2000. Inverting the Classroom: A gateway to creating an inclusive learning environment. *The Journal of Economic Education*, 31, 1 (Winter, 2000), 30-43.

[3] Moravec, M., Williams, A., Aguilar-Roca, N. and O'Dowd DK (2010). Learn before lecture: a strategy that improves learning outcomes in a large introductory biology class. *CBE Life Sciences Education*, 9, 4, (December 21, 2010), 473-481. DOI= 10.1187/cbe.10-04-0063

[4] Gannod, G. C., Burge, J. E., and Helmic, M.T. 2008. Using the inverted classroom to teach software engineering. *In Proceedings of the 30th international conference on Software engineering* (ICSE '08). ACM, New York, NY, USA, 777-786. DOI=10.1145/1368088.1368198 http://doi.acm.org/10.1145/1368088.1368198.

[5] Talbert, R. (2012, February 6). Resistance to the inverted classroom can show up anywhere. [Blog post]. Retrieved from http://chronicle.com/blognetwork/castingoutnines/2012/02/06/resistance-to-the-inverted-classroom-can-show-up-anywhere/

[6] Strayer, J. F. (2012). How learning in an inverted classroom influences cooperation, innovation and task orientation. *Learning Environments Research*, 15, 2, (July 2012), 171-193. DOI=1 0.1007/s10984-012-9108-4

[7] Talbert, Robert (2012) "Inverted Classroom," *Colleagues*: 9, 1, Article 7. Available at: http://scholarworks.gvsu.edu/colleagues/vol9/iss1/7

[8] TechSmith. http://www.techsmith.com/

Integrating Fantasy Role-Play into the Programming Lab: Exploring the 'Projective Identity' Hypothesis

Michael James Scott
Information Systems, Computing & Mathematics
Brunel University
Uxbridge, Middlesex, UB8 3PH
United Kingdom
michael.scott@brunel.ac.uk

Gheorghita Ghinea
Information Systems, Computing & Mathematics
Brunel University
Uxbridge, Middlesex, UB8 3PH
United Kingdom
george.ghinea@brunel.ac.uk

ABSTRACT

It has been claimed that learning can be facilitated by a positive academic self-concept. Therefore, reinforcing this construct may benefit students and the application of 'projective identity' in educational multimedia could be a means of achieving this. To test this hypothesis, two versions of a debugging exercise were developed, with one incorporating elements of fantasy role-play. They were compared through a double-blind parallel-group randomised trial using a sample of 36 undergraduate computing students. Factor scores for academic self-concept in programming were imputed from responses to a 5-point Likert scale, validated through a confirmatory factor analysis of 91 responses. An ANCOVA revealed that students using the fantasy role-play learning activity developed a stronger self-concept than the control group, with respective gains of 2.4% and 1.1%. However, further work is required to determine if such modest gains are practically significant, can be further enhanced and maintained.

Categories and Subject Descriptors

K.3.1 [**Computers and Education**]: Computer Uses in Education – *computer-assisted instruction (CAI).*

General Terms: Design, Experimentation, Human Factors

Keywords

Academic Self-Concept, Programming, Fantasy, Roleplay, Projective Identity, Learning, Education.

1. INTRODUCTION

Positive psychology claims that a reciprocal relationship exists between achievement and academic self-concept (ASC), defined here as "a person's self-perceptions that are formed through experience with and interpretations of one's environment" in relation to a specific academic context [10]. Therefore, reinforcing this construct during the delivery of teaching material could lead to the emergence of more effective learners. However, it is not clear what practices could be applied in learning environments for introductory programming courses to achieve this. Due to the increasing adoption of educational multimedia in such environments, it would seem sensible to identify how such tools can be leveraged to enhance academic self-concept effectively.

SIGCSE'13, March 6–9, 2013, Denver, Colorado, USA.

The use of fantasy role-play [7,8] within a dramatic narrative [5] could be one such practice. It has demonstrated some qualitative success in *Space Mission: Ice Moon*, enabling students to "think and act like scientists" [4]. Among creative learning environments [14], a similar approach can also be seen in *GameStar Mechanic*. There, novice designers are immersed in a series of story-driven scenarios while they learn basic concepts and skills before proceeding onto more practical design activities. While the latter tool addresses games design, rather than programming, a similar approach could effectively prepare students for creative programming activities, as in [13]—but conveying preparatory material in an engaging manner, rather than using just-in-time delivery where the pace can be uncomfortable for some students, which is undesirable [1]. Thus, to what extent could the application of fantasy role-play contribute to the development of academic self-concept?

During an exploration of learning in games, Gee [7] considered the role of identity. A three-way relationship was proposed between: real-world identity; virtual identity; and a mediating projective identity. It was argued that the virtual and projective identities formed when immersed in a fantasy role could reinforce the real-world identity relating to the activity of that role. During a separate investigation of self-representation in virtual reality, Yee and Bailenson [16] empirically demonstrated a somewhat similar phenomenon relating to identity and self-beliefs: the Proteus Effect. Using specialist equipment under experimental conditions, it was shown that manipulating the avatars of participants immersed in a virtual environment had some impact on their attitudes and behavior within the virtual world. Subsequently, some of this difference was maintained when measured a short time after the experiment. However, the extensibility of this effect to other domains, such as educational multimedia, is unclear.

If the phenomenon does extend to educational multimedia, it could have significant implications for the design of learning environments and the delivery of e-learning material. Thus, this paper describes an initial experimental study, in which fantasy role-play is integrated into a prototype virtual lab exercise that aims to enhance debugging skills. It then explores the following research question: assuming an equal baseline, does the incorporation of fantasy role-play in an e-learning activity increase its impact on academic self-concept development for undergraduates enrolled on a programming course?

2. DEBUGGING EXERCISE

The e-learning activity used in this study was inspired by Logo Geometry [11] and Karel the Robot [12]. It aims to increase student confidence by teaching how to identify and correct simple syntax and logic errors in snippets of Java code. Students are first shown an instructional video within the tool, explaining how to trace code to identify errors. A fragment of code containing faulty instructions to navigate a maze is then displayed. Once a student has identified and corrected the mistakes, an animation shows an object moving through the maze, revealing whether all of the errors have been removed. Advice is offered at various intervals, helping students to improve their ability in analyzing faulty code and enabling them to identify common mistakes in their own programs more readily. The interface is shown below in Figure 1:

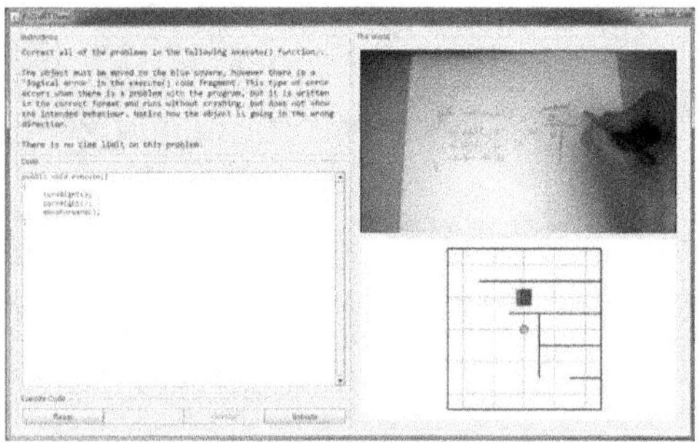

Figure 1. Learning to Trace Code

In order to embed virtual and projective identities within the tool, elements of fantasy role-play were incorporated. In this new version, students would select an avatar, assuming the role of a computer systems specialist on an advanced interstellar spaceship. In this role, students would program repair robots to navigate the ship's maintenance areas in order to fix all of the problems. A video is shown as the tool is launched, setting the scene, and several graphical improvements were added to the user interface, as shown below in Figure 2:

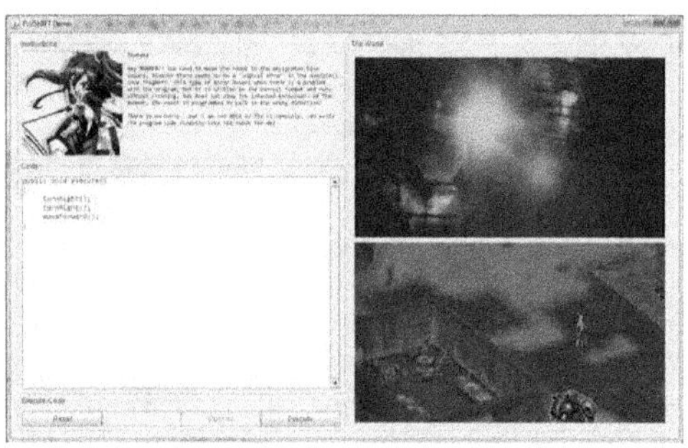

Figure 2. Integrating Fantasy Role-Play

This version of the tool is almost functionally identical to the original. The exercises are the same, requiring about 20 minutes to complete, however each problem is recast into a narrative context. This is conveyed by characters who relate the learning content, instructions and the story through dialogue. The virtual environment is also updated with new graphics, similar to those in a 2D computer game. These changes were necessary to make the exercise more immersive.

3. METHOD

A between-subjects experimental design was adopted due to the potential for preference to bias the self-belief measure. The design consisted of a parallel-group double-blind randomised trial, incorporating balanced allocation between two groups (1:1). Two versions of the virtual lab activity were compared, one incorporating fantasy role-play (experimental condition) and an ablated version, omitting elements of fantasy role-play (control condition). Scores were imputed from a self-completed measurement of academic self-beliefs towards programming, which were measured at pre-test and post-test. The difference between the two groups were compared using an ANCOVA on the post-test scores, using pre-test scores as a covariate.

3.1 Sample

An *a priori* power analysis in G*Power 3.1 showed that for a study of typical significance (α = .05) attempting to detect a "large" effect (f = .5) [2,3], a sample size of 34 would be sufficient to achieve acceptable power (1-β = .80). A sample size of 36 was obtained for this study.

The participants were recruited from a pool of students that had registered interest online (http://www.p-shift.org) in April 2012. To be eligible, participants had to be first or second year undergraduate students enrolled on programming modules at the authors' institution. Furthermore, they had to be aged 18 or over. Although some details were omitted in order to practice blinding, each participant provided informed consent.

3.2 Measurement

A psychometric scale was adapted from an exploration of mathematic self-beliefs by Ferla, Valcke and Cai [6]. This included items relating to academic self-concept (ASC), subject interest (SI), academic self-efficacy (ASE) and learning anxiety (ANX), which were repurposed for use within the programming context. It was not expected that any meaningful change in terms of overall programming could occur within the short timescale of the experiment, so the measure was calibrated to the specific learning domain of the proposed activity: errors and debugging. The items were arranged as a 5-point Likert scale, from strongly disagree to strongly agree, consisting of 22 items.

A pilot study was conducted to validate the scale as a research tool prior to the trial, in which the proposed items were administered to 91 undergraduate students that satisfied the eligibility criteria. A confirmatory factor analysis was performed in AMOS 18.0.0 for Windows. Maximum likelihood estimation was applied to the covariance matrix, but as some multivariate non-normality was discovered (kurtosis = 12.52, c.r = 2.35) a 2000-sample Bollen-Stein bootstrap was applied. During the analysis, several indicators were removed: one due to significant divergence from normality (c.r > 4.0); three due to poor path estimates ($r < .5$); and one due to excess standard residual covariance ($cov > 4.0$). Covariance was allowed between pairs of error terms on the same factor, as recommended by the modification indices. The model demonstrated adequate fit to the data ($\chi^2 = 153.56$, $df = 108$, $p = .003$), as determined by the fit indices presented below in Table 1:

Table 1. Model Fit Indicies and Fit Criteria

Fit Index	Value	Fit Criteria [9]
SRMR	.057	< .08
CFI	.957	> .90
RMSEA	.068	< .08
Bollen-Stein *p*	.149	> .05

A *post-hoc* analysis of sample size and power using Westland's tool [15] indicated the data was sufficient for model testing. Common method bias, measured by common latent factor, was small. Furthermore, adequate reliability, convergent validity and discriminant validity were found in terms of composite reliability (CR), average variance explained (AVE), maximum shared squared variance (MSV), and average shared squared variance (ASV) [9], as shown on the following page in Table 2:

Table 2. Support for Construct Validity in the Factor Model

	Variance and Reliability				Factor Correlations[a]			
	CR	*AVE*	*MSV*	*ASV*	*ASC*	*ASE*	*SI*	*ANX*
ASC	.881	.654	.358	.266	.809			
ASE	.876	.588	.540	.404	.395	.767		
SI	.890	.672	.540	.397	.533	.735	.820	
ANX	.865	.617	.517	.414	-.598	-.719	-.605	.786

(a) values on the diagonal indicate √AVE

Consequently, factor score weights generated by AMOS can be utilized to impute composite scores, by a weighted sum procedure using the Likert-type responses, as shown below in Table 3:

Table 3. Factor Score Weights for Each Subscale[a]

Indicator	*ASC*	*ASE*	*SI*	*ANX*
I am just not good at programming	**-.035**	.001	-.001	.004
I learn programming quickly	**.583**	-.010	.023	-.074
I have always believed that programming is one of my best subjects	**.063**	-.001	.003	-.008
In my programming labs, I can solve even the most challenging problems	**.017**	.000	.001	-.002
I am confident with organising code into a readable format	-.001	**.051**	.004	-.010
I am confident I can understand Java exceptions (e.g. NullPointerException)	-.001	**.040**	.004	-.008
I am confident I can solve simple problems with my programs	-.005	**.335**	.029	-.066
I am confident I can implement a method from a description of a problem or algorithm	-.007	**.416**	.036	-.083
I am confident I can debug a program that calculates prime numbers	-.001	**.042**	.004	-.008
I enjoy reading about programming	.003	.007	**.116**	-.001
I do programming because I enjoy it	.016	.036	**.638**	-.003
I am interested in the things I learn in programming classes	.003	.006	**.104**	-.001
I think programming is interesting	.003	.007	**.123**	-.001
I often worry that it will be difficult for me to complete debugging exercises	-.005	-.008	.000	**.137**
I often get tense when I have to debug a program on my own	-.007	-.011	.000	**.179**
I get nervous when trying to solve programming bugs	-.011	-.019	-.001	**.302**
I feel helpless when trying to solve some bugs in my programs	-.003	-.004	.000	**.070**

(a) significant loadings have been given in bold face, all items used to impute factor scores

3.3 Procedure

As participants registered interest in the experiment, they immediately completed the online pre-test questionnaire. Once an appropriate number had signed up, they were assigned to one of two groups, of equal size, and then emailed a link to download the relevant version of the tool.

The allocation procedure was performed in Microsoft Excel 2007 (12.0 SP3). First, the identity of each participant was obfuscated using an identification number and arbitrarily allocated a row. The rows were then sorted according to a RAND() value in a separate column. Then, the worksheet was divided into two halves, representing each group.

Participants were free to complete the exercise and the online post-test questionnaire within 10 days. Although this resulted in less control over experimental conditions, it is more representative of how a virtual lab exercise may be used by students in practice, thus enhancing ecological validity. It should be noted, however, that no formal teaching (such as lectures, seminars, or labs) occurred during the time period of the trial. Furthermore, while the pre-test and post-test questionnaires contained the same items, the order in which they were presented was randomised.

4. RESULTS

The data was analyzed using PASW 18.0.3 for Windows. All cases were included in the analysis, with any missing ASC values in the raw pre-test data being replaced by the sample mean and any missing ASC values in the raw post-test data being replaced by the allocation mean.

4.1 Data Analysis

After the allocation, one-way ANOVAs demonstrated that no significant differences existed in terms of pre-test ASC score ($F[1,35] = .214$, $p = .646$, $\eta_p^2 = .006$) or academic grade profile ($F[1,35] = .332$, $p = .568$, $\eta_p^2 = .010$) between the two groups. Descriptive statistics are shown below in Table 4:

Table 4. Descriptive Statistics for Each Group

	Variable	Mean	Std Dev	Confidence Intervals	
				Lower	*Upper*
Experimental	Pre-Test ASC	1.7056	.8411	1.2873	2.1239
	Post-Test ASC	1.7443	.8303	1.3313	2.1572
	ASC Gain	.3866	.0352	.0211	.0561
	Grade	3.8900	1.1320	3.3300	4.4500
Control	Pre-Test ASC	1.5804	.7807	1.1922	1.9686
	Post-Test ASC	1.5991	.7739	1.2142	1.9839
	ASC Gain	.0186	.0291	.0041	.0331
	Grade	4.1100	1.1830	3.5200	4.7000

An ANCOVA examined the impact of fantasy role-play on developing academic self-concept. Assumptions of normality, homogeneity of variance and homogeneity of regression were verified. The results are summarized below in Table 5:

Table 5. ANCOVA Results (*dv* = Post-Test ASC)

Source	SS	*df*	MS	F	*p*	η_p^2
Pre-Test ASC	21.872	1	21.872	5.679	.000	.999
Allocation	.004	1	.004	4.181	.049	.112
Error	.032	33	44.326			

Corrected Model R Squared =.999 (Adjusted R Squared =.998)

Hence, after controlling for pre-test scores, there was a significant difference ($p < .05$) in the post-test ASC between the two groups, which constitutes an effect size between "medium" and "large" [2,3]. This difference can be demonstrated by the estimated marginal means, as shown below in Table 6:

Table 6. Estimated Marginal Means (*dv* = Post-Test ASC)

GROUP	Mean[a]	Std Error	Confidence Interval	
			Lower	*Upper*
Experimental	1.682	.007	1.667	1.698
Control	1.661	.007	1.646	1.676

(a) Pre-Test ASC Score = 1.643 (Covariate)

Based on the means and baseline score (1.643) presented above, the gain in academic self-concept for those allocated to the fantasy role-play condition (2.4%) was greater than those in the control condition (1.1%).

5. LESSONS LEARNED

Although a significant difference was detected ($p < .05$), the effect was lower than predicted, resulting in low power ($1\text{-}\beta = .54$). This effect, from the η_p^2 value, being $f = 0.355$, and from the observed difference in gain scores, being $d = 0.619$. These results support the notion that fantasy role-play can enhance the development of self-concept, as shown by the gain scores in Figure 3 below:

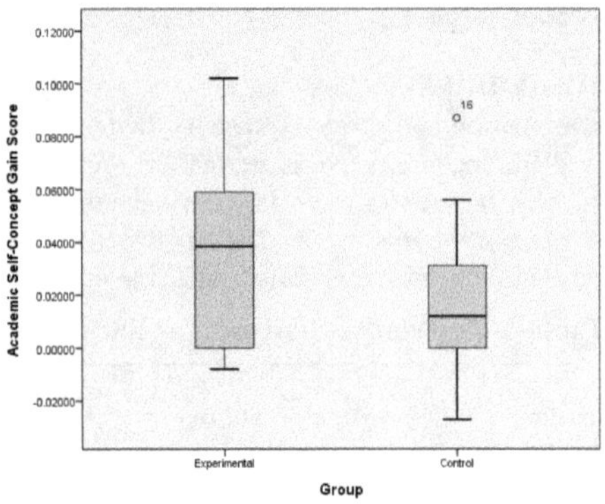

Figure 3. Distribution of ASC Gain Scores

However, there was no significant difference between the two groups at post-test ($F[1,35] = .227, p = .591, \eta_p^2 = .082$). Thus, the isolated exercise was not sufficient to produce a meaningful difference in academic self-concept. Nevertheless, paired t-tests showed that small gains were present ($t[17] = 4.660$, $p < .001$, $d = .327$; and $t[17] = 2.720$, $p = .015$, $d = .240$). If these small effects can be sustained, then it might result in a more practically significant difference over multiple tasks. Thus, a longitudinal trial is appropriate. Assuming that the observed difference remains consistent ($d = .087$), then perhaps eight activities could produce a more meaningful change ($d \approx .69$).

Of note, the item that emerged as the greatest contributor to academic self-concept was "I learn programming quickly" (.583). This may imply that experiences providing a sense of learning something quickly contribute the most to ASC development. Thus, unnecessary narrative may impede this aim. On the other hand, fantasy role-play can increase engagement [7]. Potentially, maintaining interest and supporting persistent attitudes, enabling more learning to occur within the time available. A goal for further study could be to investigate whether this assertion holds and how to convey such an experience.

The item with the largest mean increase at post-test in the experimental group was "I can solve the most challenging problems". Perhaps the fantasy context can encourage senses of pride and fiero in some students. Thus, helping them to feel they can overcome greater challenges. However, further enquiry is required to corroborate this interpretation.

6. CONCLUSION

An early prototype of a debugging exercise that incorporates elements of fantasy role-play has been shown to strengthen academic self-concept to a greater extent than a conventional approach. This supports the hypothesis that projective identities enhance the self-concept development of novice programmers on a computing course. However, the difference was only of medium size and neither condition had a practically significant impact. Due to the limited scope of this initial study, it remains unclear whether such a modest gain could be further enhanced over time and then maintained. Thus, additional longitudinal study is appropriate. Moreover, qualitative enquiry is necessary to reveal how the fantasy role-play could be improved for greater impact. Future research should anticipate "medium" differences and "small" effects for individual tasks [2,3].

7. REFERENCES

[1] Barker, L., McDowell, C. and Kalahar, K. 2009. Exploring Factors that Influence Computer Science Introductory Course Students to Persist in the Major. ACM SIGCSE Bulletin. 41, 1 (Mar. '09), 153-157. DOI = http://dx.doi.org/10.1145/1539024.1508923.

[2] Cohen, J. 1992. A Power Primer. Psychological Bulletin. 112, 1 (Jul. '92), 155-159. DOI = http://dx.doi.org/10.1037/0033-2909.112.1.155.

[3] Cohen, J. 1977. Statistical Power Analysis for the Behavioral Sciences (Revised Edition). New York: Academic Press.

[4] Daanen, H. and Grant, L. 2007. Space Mission: Ice Moon. In Proceedings of the ACM SIGGRAPH Educators Conference (San Diego, USA, 5-9 Aug., '07), GRAPH'07, ACM, NY, 19. DOI = http://dx.doi.org/10.1145/1282040.1282060.

[5] Erion, P. 1996. Drama in the Classroom: Creative Activities for Teachers, Parents & Friends. New York: Lost Cost.

[6] Ferla, J., Valcke, M., and Cai, Y. 2009. Academic Self-Efficacy and Academic Self-Concept: Reconsidering Structural Relationships. Learning and Individual Differences. 19, 4 (Jun. '09), 499-505. DOI = http://dx.doi.org/10.1016/j.lindif.2009.05.004.

[7] Gee, J.P. 2003. What Video Games Have to Teach Us About Learning and Literacy. New York: Palgrave/Macmillan.

[8] Habgood, M.P., Ainsworth, S.E., and Benford, S. 2005. Endogenous Fantasy and Learning in Digital Games. Simulation and Gaming. 36, 4 (Dec. '05), 483-498. DOI = http://dx.doi.org/10.1177/1046878105282276.

[9] Hair, J., Black, W., Babin, B. and Anderson, R. 2010. Multivariate Data Analysis, Seventh Edition. Upper Saddle River, New Jersey: Prentice-Hall.

[10] Marsh, H. and Martin, A. 2011. Academic Self-Concept and Academic Achievement. British Journal of Educational Psychology. 81, 1 (Mar. '11), 59-77. DOI = http://dx.doi.org/10.1348/000709910X503501.

[11] Papert, S. 1980. Mindstorms: Children, Computers, and Powerful Ideas. New York: Basic Books.

[12] Pattis, R., Roberts, J., and Stehlik, M. 1995. Karel the Robot: A Gentle Introduction to the Art of Object-Orientated Programming, Second Edition. New York: John Wiley & Sons.

[13] Repenning, A. 2012. Programming Goes Back to School. Communications of the ACM.55, 5, (May '12), 38-40. DOI = http://dx.doi.org/10.1145/2160718.2160729.

[14] Resnick, M. et al. 2009. Growing Up Programming: Democratizing the Creation of Dynamic, Interactive Media. In Extended Abstracts from the SIGCHI Conference on Human Factors in Computing Systems (Boston, USA, 4-9 Apr. '09), CHI'09, ACM, NY, 3293-3296. DOI = http://dx.doi.org/10.1145/1520340.1520472.

[15] Westland, J.C. 2010. Lower Bounds on Sample Size in Structural Equation Modeling. Electronic Commerce Research and Applications. 9, 6 (Jul. '10), 476-487. DOI = http://dx.doi.org/10.1016/j.elerap.2010.07.003.

[16] Yee, N. and Bailenson, J. 2007. The Proteus Effect: The Effect of Transformed Self-Representation on Behavior. Human Communication Research, 33, 3 (Jul. '07), 270-290. DOI = http://dx.doi.org/10.1111/j.1468-2958.2007.00299.x.

Teaching Creativity in Computer Science

Andrea Salgian
Dept. of Computer Science
The College of New Jersey
Ewing, NJ 08628
+1 609 771 2933
salgian@tcnj.edu

Teresa M. Nakra
Dept. of Music
The College of New Jersey
Ewing, NJ 08628
+1 609 771 2759
nakra@tcnj.edu

Christopher Ault
Interactive Multimedia Program
The College of New Jersey
Ewing, NJ 08628
+1 609 771 2236
ault@tcnj.edu

Yunfeng Wang
Dept. of Mechanical Engineering
The College of New Jersey
Ewing, NJ 08628
+1 609 771 2458
jwang@tcnj.edu

ABSTRACT

In this paper, we describe how a multidisciplinary undergraduate course in Conducting Robots becomes a venue for fostering creativity and teaching strategies for creativity enhancement. We perform a number of creativity measurements and explain our results in the context of creativity research.

Categories and Subject Descriptors

K.3.2. **[Computers and Education]**: Computer and Information Science Education – Computer science education; J.2. **[Computer Applications]**: Physical Sciences and Engineering – Engineering; J.5. **[Computer Applications]:** Arts and Humanities – Music

General Terms

Algorithms, Design, Human Factors.

Keywords

creativity, multidisciplinary, music, orchestral conducting, robotics

1. INTRODUCTION

A problem that we encounter as computer science educators is the perceived lack of creativity of our subject. Although computers are highly valued in our world, when asked to name some creative activities, people will rarely say computer science. There are many possible reasons for this. One is that creativity tends to be seen as mystified, inspired by a muse, and applicable only to performance in one or more of the arts [13]. The other is that computer scientists, more so than other scientists, are perceived as "geeks" who spend their lives in a cubicle in front of the computer, doing things that nobody else understands.

SIGCSE'13, March 6–9, 2013, Denver, Colorado, USA.

Even our majors often have a hard time seeing the creativity of the subject, especially when constrained by the boundaries of traditional courses. Yet computer science is creative in more than one way: not only can one apply creativity to it, it can also be applied to other fields creatively.

Keeping this reality in mind, we designed and taught an undergraduate seminar whose goal was to engage students – majors and non-majors alike – creatively in computer science. We went one step further and attempted to teach students creativity. In the seminar, undergraduate students majoring in computer science, interactive multimedia, mechanical engineering and music, worked in multidisciplinary teams to develop robotic or animated systems that could conduct an orchestra.

Were we successful? Did our students become more creative? Can creativity be taught and learned? The easy approach to answering these questions would be to measure student creativity at the beginning of the semester, and once again at the end of the semester, and look for a significant increase. Unfortunately our analysis cannot be that simple. Creativity has several different definitions, and, accordingly, several different measures. Many of them are difficult to administer twice. Moreover, the results of different measurements seem to be inconsistent at first.

In this paper we argue that creativity in computer science is different from creativity in the arts. Although some researchers argue that creativity is innate, we show that certain traits of certain types of creativities can be learned, resulting in increased creativity. We present a number of quantitative and qualitative creativity measurements that we performed on the students enrolled in our class, and we explain our results using theories from creativity research. Finally we conclude that our approach was successful, and attractive multidisciplinary settings in general are good venues for teaching students to think and problem solve creatively.

2. DEFINING, MEASURING AND ENHANCING CREATIVITY

Theories about the nature of creativity and how to measure it are still actively debated among researchers. Some theories propose that creativity is the generation of imaginative new ideas [10], involving radical innovations. Other definitions claim that creativity can be demonstrated by simply integrating existing knowledge in new ways, or require a creative solution to have value or utility [7]. Yet other definitions attempt to reconcile these approaches, such as the one by Plucker et al: Creativity is "the interaction among *aptitude, process, and environment* by which an individual or group produces a *perceptible product* that is both *novel and useful* as defined within a *social context*" [12]. We find that this definition best reflects the field of computer science.

One of the most popular ways to assess creativity is through the Torrance Test of Creative Thinking, which has been refined over the course of several decades [18]. It is a divergent thinking test, which asks participants to produce several responses to a specific prompt (e.g., alternate uses for a shoe, which may include bug killing device, door stop, container etc.) [19]. However, many researchers agree that while divergent thinking is useful, and maybe even necessary in the creative process, as it provides a variety of starting points, it is not sufficient [19].

An alternative is assessment through an inventory of self-reported creative activities and accomplishments [8]. This approach implies that individuals become more creative by participating in creative endeavors.

Another approach is the consensual assessment technique proposed by Amabile [1], which measures the creativity of a product, not an individual. According to her, "a product or response is creative to the extent that appropriate observers independently agree it is creative. Appropriate observers are those familiar with the domain in which the product was created or the response articulated".

We used all three types of measurement in our class setting.

Once we have a definition for creativity and a way to measure it, we can set out to answer our original question: can creativity be taught? Can individuals be made more creative? We set out with the optimistic assumptions of Nickerson: all people of normal intelligence have the potential to be creative to some degree, but few people realize anything close to their potential in this regard. Therefore creativity can be enhanced, although it is not well understood how to do this [11].

3. THE MULTIDISCIPLINARY SETTING

The vehicle for our investigation was a multidisciplinary undergraduate seminar that we developed, in which student teams built non-human systems that conducted our college orchestra. Called "Conducting Robots", this semester-long course has been offered four times so far. Each time the course was cross-listed in the departments of Computer Science, Interactive Multimedia, Mechanical Engineering, and Music, and was taught by a team of four instructors, one from each department (the authors). We worked with an independent evaluator to develop and administer student surveys and interviews. In addition, students were asked to keep a reflection journal. These tools were used to assess creativity and document the creative process.

Since it is a multidisciplinary seminar, open to students with different backgrounds, the structure of the Conducting Robots course is different from that of a traditional course. Students form interdisciplinary teams from the first week and start brainstorming design ideas right away. The semester starts with one or two lectures specific to each discipline, which serve as a refresher to in-major students while providing out of major students with a basic introduction. Topics include robotics, visual music, abstract animation, algorithms, data processing, procedural animation, music conducting, and project management. Homeworks are assigned in each discipline, and students are expected to rely on their in-major teammates for problem solving. After this introductory period, teams spend their time designing and building their systems. The structure of classes changes from the traditional lecture to an informal conversational setting, where teams share progress reports and discuss specific project related problems with the instructors. Depending on the situation, instructors invite guest speakers who can better address some of the issues encountered by the teams.

The final objective of the course is to have students build graphical and/or robotic non-human conductors that can conduct an orchestra. The minimum requirement for each system is to indicate beat patterns, tempo, dynamics and cueing to a human ensemble in real-time.

Throughout the course, students work together in multidisciplinary teams, contributing and developing knowledge from within their own fields, as well as learning fundamentals from the other fields involved. Each time the course was offered so far, at the end of the semester, all teams were able to demonstrate functional systems that performed in a concert with student musicians. Systems were either animations or robots, depending on whether the team had mechanical engineers. Each system fit one of four categories: humanoid robots (like Honda's ASIMO whose conducting performance [9] inspired some of the students), humanoid animations, non-humanoid robots (including devices tailored for individual musicians), and non-humanoid animations (some of them akin to video game interfaces). Some of the prototypes are pictured in Figure 1.

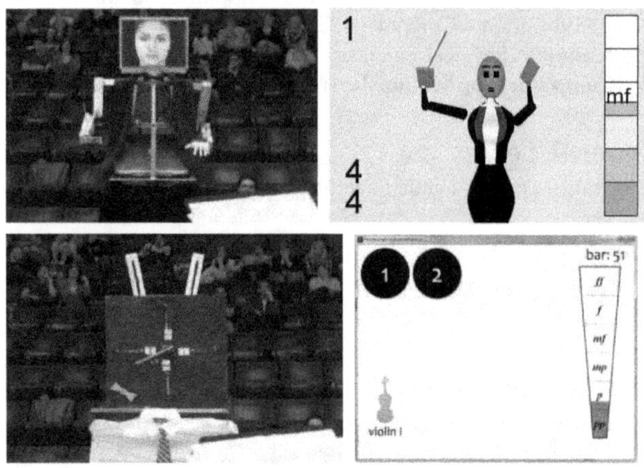

Figure 1. Conducting robot prototypes developed by students. Clockwise from top right: humanoid robot, humanoid animation, non-humanoid animation, and non-humanoid robot

The course presented a number of challenges for students and faculty alike, but all students built working conducting systems at a level that is rare in an undergraduate class setting, and is more characteristic of graduate research. While doing so, they learned to collaborate with other students and apply their knowledge to other fields, as well as communicate cogently about their own disciplines to non-specialists. The collaboration between these fundamentally different fields motivated and inspired our students.

A more detailed description of the course can be found in [14].

4. OUR MEASUREMENTS

4.1 Torrance Test

In an attempt to get a baseline for student creativity, we started each semester by administering the Abbreviated Torrance Test for Adults (ATTA) to the students. This test provides a creativity index, a standardized score that takes into account the raw test score for fluency, originality, elaboration, flexibility and adds extra points for ten different creativity indicators such as sound or movement, resistance to closure, synthesis of two or more figures, abstractness of title, etc. We have found that, in spite of the small number of data points (over the four semesters we taught the class we administered the test to 60 students), the creativity index distribution was very close to the ATTA standardized score distribution. In other words our students scored very similarly to the national sample on which the test was standardized.

In general our students seemed to have average creativity. We found no significant difference between the creativity index of males and females, between classes, or between majors. The only significant difference was between music majors and engineering majors, with the music majors scoring higher, enforcing yet again the popular view of music being a more creative field than engineering.

4.2 Self-reported Creativity

We also asked the students to rate their own creativity on a scale from 1 (least creative) to 10 (most creative). This self-ranking was based on students' creative activities and accomplishments, following the approach in [8]. Interestingly, the only correlation that we found between the self-ranking and the ATTA creativity index was at the two ends of the spectrum, for the most and the least creative students.

As discussed above, the definition of creativity is still a matter of debate among researchers and laypeople alike. When we asked students to rate their own creativity, we also asked them to define it. A vast majority replied that creativity was "thinking outside the box", and the ability to create something new. Only two or three students each semester mentioned using other people's ideas as part of the creative process. By the end of the semester, when students were asked to rate how the diversity of their team influenced the creativity of their solution, it was the exact opposite: only two or three students per semester did not give credit to other people's ideas.

At the end of the semester most students agreed that the multidisciplinary team environment increased the creativity of their project. They also reported that they were able to come up with creative solutions that they would not have found while working alone. This aspect was consistent, regardless of major. On a scale from 1 to 10 where 1 meant "not much at all" and 10 meant "an extraordinary amount", the average rating of the multidisciplinary team's impact was 7.3, 7.4, and 6.4 in the three semesters when we recorded this data.

Here is how some students described the influence of the diverse environment:

"A lot of ideas were thrown around and it was nice to see how everyone tackled the same problem in different ways."

"The knowledge, and also at times lack-there-of, of my group mates helped to force me to explore more creative solutions, musically. "

"If I had done this with just music majors our project would not have been as creative, I believe. We would have only come from one angle (plus we wouldn't have been able to build it!)"

"Whenever I drew a blank, someone else in my team was able to give an alternative approach to the problem. So many different minds collaborated within one group that it was easy to see outside the box."

4.3 Consensual Assessment

At the end of each semester we used the consensual assessment technique [1] to rate the creativity of the student projects. The non-human conductors were ranked by three categories of observers: the student orchestra that performed while being conducted by the non-human prototype (i.e. the users of these systems), the course instructors, and a multidisciplinary advisory board comprised of faculty members from each discipline who were not involved with the course.

All evaluators agreed that all solutions were very creative in their own ways. However, creativity rankings varied from one evaluator to another based on their area of expertise: engineers appreciated the technical details, while musicians favored systems that conveyed all the information required from a conductor. What is more creative? A non-humanoid robot that is unlike anything we have seen before, or a humanoid robot that performs very close to a human? The first requires new definitions for all the information that is being conveyed to the musicians, an original solution that is not usually appreciated by the orchestra used to human gestures. The second may not seem very original to the outsider, but building a humanoid robot requires creative engineering.

Meanwhile, the course instructors ranked the creativity of the entire process, based on details unknown to outsiders. These included the creativity of solutions to various problems students encountered on the way, and the flexibility of students, some of whom made significant contributions in areas that were not related to their major.

Some of the musicians were tempted to give high rankings to the non-humanoid systems – after all, these were the most original – but most of them ended up favoring usefulness, and ranked the most useful systems (the ones that provided a good amount of correct and easy to understand information) as most creative.

5. CREATIVITY ANALYSIS

Even though our measurements are quantitative (creativity indexes, rankings and self-rankings), it is impossible to devise a quantitative measure for the creativity enhancement that we observed by the end of each semester.

5.1 Individual and Group Creativity

One of the reasons is that our baseline measurements targeted each individual, while the final measure, the creativity ranking of the products, pertains to teams of students. Although the creativity literature documents experiments that demonstrate how collaborative emergence results from the interaction of individuals, the phenomenon is difficult to understand by analyzing the members of the group individually [15].

In our setting students were asked to form teams without any specific input from the instructors. The only requirements were the number of teams, the number of students per team (which varied every semester based on the class makeup), and the fact that each major had to be represented on each team (with a couple of exceptions imposed by low numbers of students from a specific discipline who registered for the class in a particular semester). We encouraged students to "advertise themselves" by listing qualities that they thought would be useful for the project, and they self-selected. Invariably, at the end of the selection process there was one team made up of students who were not picked by other teams. Usually these were the students who were not proactive enough and did not advertise themselves as well as others.

Interestingly, the mean creativity index per team was either the same or higher than the class average, with the exception of the last team whose average creativity index was below the class average. Often this team ended up being ranked lowest by the observers participating in the consensual assessment.

It appears that, probably because of the self-promotion that we encouraged, students gravitated towards students who would compensate for their own knowledge gaps and insecurities.

5.2 Types of Creativity

Our individual measurements also seem inconsistent at first: with the exception of the most and least creative students, the ATTA creativity index does not correlate with self-reported creativity ratings. Such inconsistencies have often been observed in creativity research however, and have been explained through domain specificity. Baer has argued that the skills, aptitudes and motivations that lead to creative performance vary from domain to domain [2]. Similarly, Howard Gardner has proposed a theory of multiple intelligences [5], which he then applied to creativity [6]. He suggested that great creative minds often have relied on different intelligences to manifest their creativity. For example, T.S. Eliot made his reputation through linguistic intelligence, Einstein through logical–mathematical intelligence, while Igor Stravinsky became famous through musical intelligence. Sternberg sees creativity as a set of multiple attributes, which are not mutually exclusive [17]. According to him, people might show consistent individual differences in processes, domains, and styles of creative thinking. Dietrich classifies creativity into deliberate and/or spontaneous modes of processing, each of which can direct computations in cognitive and/or emotional structures [4].

Similar to the creativity types described by Gardner [6], we were able to distinguish at least four different types of creativity as follows:

1. Creativity of design – meeting objectives within constraints, adding additional features to the product that are not necessarily required (i.e., visually pleasing details, etc.).
2. Creativity of problem solving – innovative solutions to a variety of problems that need to be solved before the product can be fully built.
3. Creativity of knowledge acquisition – the various ways in which students looked for information that could help build their product
4. Creativity of self-definition – the flexibility in which students perceived their skill sets, regardless of their major.

5.3 Functional Creativity

The goal of our seminar was to foster functional creativity, which focuses on novel, useful, practical products, as opposed to the traditional aesthetic creativity, which characterizes art [3]. When self-reporting, students thought about creative products they might have built in the past. They were all able to relate creativity to their major, regardless of whether that major was art, science or engineering.

On the other hand, the Torrance test, and its ATTA variant that we administered, looks to measure divergent thinking in the aesthetical realm. This explains why the music majors obtained higher scores than the engineering majors. This is also why we chose not to administer them again at the end of the semester, as we were not expecting an improvement in aesthetic creativity.

Our assessment therefore becomes more qualitative, as we look at the way students self-reported at the beginning and at the end of the semester. As mentioned above, most students found that the environment increased the creativity of their project. And since, according to [8], individual creativity can be characterized by the list of creative products that one builds, students' individual creativity was enhanced through this process.

We have stated, based on student reports, that the multidisciplinary environment that included fundamentally different fields motivated and inspired our students. The class provided an environment with lots of learning opportunities that boosted self-confidence. Some interesting comments from student reflection journals are quoted below:

"It makes you take a step back and forces you to explain things in a way that you're not used to with your fellow engineers. That is one of the major things I enjoy about this class, everyone trying to convey their knowledge to people who might not have any idea about what they are talking about. I think it's a great challenge for all the majors"

"I feel it is good to try to understand a new subject which I previously did not even think about, because it has forced me to learn what feels like a new language... really made me see how different it must be for the mechanical engineers in the class to study the musical aspect, because compared to mechanical engineering theory, music theory has an almost mystic quality."

The motivation and self-confidence that students acquired was reflected in the creativity of their products. Without making it explicit, our students were taught a number of ways in which creativity can occur [16]: conceptual replication (the known is transferred to a new setting), redefinition (the known is seen in a new way), forward incrementation (the known is extended in an existing direction), redirection (the known is extended in a new direction), and reinitiation (thinking begins at a radically different point from the current one and takes off in a new direction).

The team setting compensated for the lack of divergent thinking some students may have had: even if each student provided just one idea, the final result had to be a list of divergent and very creative suggestions.

Our students also learned what experienced scientists, engineers, and even artists already know: functionally creative products don't happen overnight. They are the result of hard work and a lot of brainstorming and experimentation [3]. In their reflection journals, students documented their "aha" moments (i.e. a breakthrough moment when new understanding "fell into place"), along with what conversation, interaction or activity lead them to a different way of looking at or solving an issue with respect to a class. Some examples are listed below.

"It was shocking to hear that all the other students from the "smart" majors (mechanical engineering and computer science) were as confused about conducting and music as I had been about their subject areas."

"Trying to wrap my mind around having my right hand do something and my left hand do something entirely different was surprisingly difficult. It was really trying it (conducting) out for myself that made me realize how much cognitive multitasking this feat required."

"I learned that robots are powered by numbers and not just wheels and motors."

While we saw little breakthroughs everywhere throughout the semester that eventually led to functional conducting systems, no one provided us with an account of a big idea that happened in an unexpected place. Students got to see that although myths like Isaac Newton being hit by an apple in the head are highly unlikely, with hard work creative endeavors are accessible to all of us.

6. CONCLUSION

We presented a framework for fostering creativity in and through computer science. The "Conducting Robots" undergraduate multidisciplinary seminar that we designed and offered not only encourages students to be more creative, but it also effectively teaches strategies that increase creativity.

Through working in multidisciplinary teams that include students majoring in computer science, mechanical engineering, interactive multimedia and music, students are able to build products that are more creative. From the different creativity types that were described in the literature, our approach targets functional creativity, which focuses on useful products, as opposed to the more traditional aesthetic creativity that can be seen in art, and is more relevant to computer science.

Our measures are mostly qualitative. We show that although we collected different quantitative measurements according to multiple strategies from creativity research, these measurements could not be used to quantitatively assess improvement in the creativity of participating students. There are two reasons for this: traditional creativity measures are designed for aesthetic, not functional creativity, and the relationship between individual and group creativity is not yet fully understood.

Our experience can easily be adapted to any multidisciplinary environment. All that is needed is an attractive challenge and a team of diverse backgrounds.

7. ACKNOWLEDGMENTS

This work has been supported in part by National Science Foundation grant #0855973.

8. REFERENCES

[1] Amabile, T. 1982. Social Psychology of Creativity: A consensual Assessment Technique, *Journal of Personality and Social Psychology*, vol. 43, no. 5.

[2] Baer, J. 2010. Is creativity domain specific? in *The Cambridge Handbook of Creativity*, eds. J. Kaufman, R. Sternberg, Cambridge University Press, pp. 321-341.

[3] Cropley, D. and Cropley, A. 2010. Functional Creativity. "Products" and the Generation of Effective Novelty, in *The Cambridge Handbook of Creativity*, eds. J. Kaufman, R. Sternberg, Cambridge University Press, pp. 301-317.

[4] Dietrich, A. 2004. The cognitive neuroscience of creativity. *Psychonomic Bulletin & Review*, 11 (6), pp. 1011-1026.

[5] Gardner, H. 1983. *Frames of Mind: The Theory of Multiple Intelligences.* Basic Books, New York.

[6] Gardner, H. 1993. *Creating Minds.* BasicBooks, New York.

[7] Higgins, L.F. 1999. Applying principles of creativity management to marketing research efforts in high-technology markets. *Industrial Marketing Management*, No. 28, pp. 305-317.

[8] Hocevar, D. 1981. Measurement of Creativity: Review and Critique. *Journal of Personality Assessment*, Vol. 45, No. 5, pages 450-464.

[9] Honda. 2008. *Honda Asimo Robot conducting the Detroit Symphony Orchestra.* Retrieved December 4, 2012 from http://world.honda.com/news/2008/c080423ASIMO/ and http://www.youtube.com/watch?v=qRUyVCfFh1U

[10] Newell, A. and Shaw, J.C. 1972. The process of creative thinking. In A. Newell and H.A. Simon (eds), *Human Problem Solving*, Prentice Hall, Englewood Cliffs, NJ, pp. 144-174.

[11] Nickerson, R. S. 1999. Enhancing creativity. In *Handbook of Creativity,* ed. R. J. Sternberg, Cambridge University Press, 392-430.

[12] Plucker, J. A., Beghetto, R. A., Dow, G. 2004. Why isn't creativity more important to educational psychologists? Potential, pitfalls, and future directions in creativity research. *Educational Psychologist*, 39 (2004) 83-96.

[13] Plucker, J. A., and Makel, M. C. 2010. Assessment of creativity. In *The Cambridge Handbook of Creativity*, eds. J. Kaufman, R. Sternberg, Cambridge University Press, pp. 48-73.

[14] Salgian, A., Ault, C., Nakra, T. M., Wang, Y., Stone, M. K. 2011. Multidisciplinary Computer Science through Conducting Robots. In *SIGCSE '11. Proceedings of the 42nd ACM technical symposium on Computer science education.*

[15] Sawyer, R. K. 2010. Individual and Group Creativity. In *The Cambridge Handbook of Creativity*, eds. J. Kaufman, R. Sternberg, Cambridge University Press.

[16] Sternberg, R. J., Kaufman, J. C., Pretz, J. E. 2002. *The creativity conundrum: A propulsion model of kinds of creative contributions.* Psychology Press, New York.

[17] Sternberg, R. J. 2005. Creativity or creativities? *Int. J. Human-Computer Studies* 63 (2005) pp. 370–382.

[18] Torrance, E. P. 1988. The nature of creativity as manifest in its testing. In R. J. Sternberg (Ed.), *The Nature of Creativity*, Cambridge University Press, pp. 43-75.

[19] Ward, T. B., and Kolomyts, Y. 2010. Cognition and creativity. In *The Cambridge Handbook of Creativity*, eds. J. Kaufman, R. Sternberg, Cambridge University Press, pp. 93-112.

Seeking Grace: A New Object-Oriented Language for Novices

Andrew P. Black
Portland State Univ.
black@cs.pdx.edu

Kim B. Bruce
Pomona College
kim@cs.pomona.edu

Michael Homer
Victoria Univ. of Wellington
mwh@ecs.vuw.ac.nz

James Noble
Victoria Univ. of Wellington
kjx@ecs.vuw.ac.nz

Amy Ruskin
Pomona College
asr02010@pomona.edu

Richard Yannow
Pomona College
rmy02010@mymail.pomona.edu

Grace is the absence of everything that indicates pain or difficulty, hesitation or incongruity.
William Hazlitt

ABSTRACT

Grace is a new object-oriented language that supports a variety of approaches to teaching programming. It integrates accepted new ideas in programming languages into a simple language that allows students and teachers to focus on the essential complexities of programming rather than the accidental complexities of the language. We motivate Grace, review its design, and evaluate it against Kölling's criteria.

Categories and Subject Descriptors

K.3.2 [**Computer and Information Science Education**]: Computer Science Education; D.3.2 [**Language Classifications**]: Object-oriented languages

Keywords

Object-oriented language; novice; CS1; CS2

1. INTRODUCTION

At SIGPLAN's SPLASH conference in 2010, Black, Bruce, and Noble presented a "design manifesto" for a new educational programming language [16], arguing that no existing object-oriented programming language was the obvious choice for teaching novices. Now we are ready to describe the (still incomplete) design for the language, which we call Grace, both to honor the late Admiral Grace Hopper and because we hope that it will enable more graceful programs.

1.1 Why a new language?

Object-oriented programming is the dominant paradigm for commercial software development. At many colleges, it is also the paradigm for the introductory programming courses.

SIGCSE'13, March 6–9, 2013, Denver, Colorado, USA.

Other institutions prefer to start by teaching functional or procedural programming, but even at these places, object-oriented techniques must be taught to relative novices.

What language should be used? Instructors and novice programmers need a conceptually simple language with minimal "accidental" complexity, so that class time can be spent on the key ideas of objects. Today's most widely used teaching languages are overly complex, were designed 20 years ago or more, and often fail to provide good support for features like first-class functions, type parameters, and parallelism.

Instructors preferring statically typed languages have tried C++ and Java, but have not always found success. C++ is a large and complicated language, and novices are often overwhelmed by its complexity. While Java began as a simpler language than C++, over the years it has added features, not always gracefully, and too often requires syntax that cannot be easily explained. Instructors preferring dynamically typed languages have gravitated to Python, but Python has some anomalies as an object-oriented language. Methods must be written with an explicit self parameter that disappears when they are used, and there is no support for information hiding, a key concept in object-oriented programming.

There are other interesting object-oriented languages, like Smalltalk and Eiffel, that are candidates for introductory programming courses. However, they are not now in widespread use in courses, despite being available for many years.

Our focus is on object-oriented programming for general-purpose computing. Thus, while we appreciate the advantages of instructional languages like Karel [14] and Alice [3] that introduce simplified or restricted "computational worlds", we do not wish to restrict our students — typically computer science majors — to programming in a narrow domain.

Much has been written about the choice of languages for introductory computer science courses. Pears *et al.* present a good introduction to this literature in their survey [15, §3.3].

1.2 History of Pedagogical Languages

There is a long history of the use of pedagogical languages in Computer Science. BASIC [10] and Pascal [9] were extremely successful from the 1960's through the 80's, but have fallen out of favor with the rise of new programming paradigms. Other pedagogical languages like Turing [7] have been proposed, but never gained widespread acceptance. Blue [13] was a particularly interesting object-oriented pedagogical language, but had the misfortune of being developed at about the same time as Java, which meant that it did not receive the attention it deserved. Its main legacy is the excellent BlueJ programming environment [12].

One criticism of introducing programming using a pedagogical language is students are less well-equipped to take on internships or other projects with industry. Basic and Pascal overcame this problem to a degree by becoming used in industry; the original Macintosh operating system, for example, was written in an object-oriented extension of Pascal.

We believe that the assumption behind this criticism is that the most difficult and time-consuming part of learning to program is learning the syntax and semantics of a programming language. Instructors who believe this, perhaps teaching at institutions where employment as a programmer immediately after the first course or two is an important goal, will not be interested in using a pedagogical language.

We challenge this assumption. We believe that the most difficult and time-consuming part of learning to program is learning how to solve problems and to represent those solutions as program designs. Once these conceptual tasks are mastered, learning a new language syntax and semantics, at least within the same paradigm, is a straightforward task. Moreover, there are significant advantages to learning programming with a simple and consistent language: students can focus on the important learning tasks without a complex and feature-laden language "getting in the way".

2. GOALS OF GRACE

In this section we list the high-level goals for Grace, along with some specific objectives to reach those goals.

- Grace should integrate proven new ideas in programming languages into a simple object-oriented language.
- The language should gracefully represent the key concepts underlying programming, particularly object-oriented programming, in a way that can be easily explained.
- Grace should allow students to focus on the essential, rather than the accidental, difficulties of programming, problem solving and system modeling.

Let's elaborate on the final point. Brooks, remarking on the difficulties of software technology, divides them "into *essence*, the difficulties inherent in the nature of software, and *accidents*, those difficulties that today attend its production but are not inherent." [1]. We make the same division for programming. The essential difficulties that students must master include concepts like variable binding, conditional execution, iteration, parameter passing, recursion, and information hiding. It is essential to understand these notions to be a good programmer in any language. To these, object-oriented programming adds concepts like dynamic binding and incremental programming (as when using inheritance). In contrast, the accidental difficulties encompass those features of the programming process that have no lasting value, but which must be mastered simply to make progress. For example, to pick on Java, there is no good reason to subject novices to **public static void** *main*(*String* [] *args*) early in a first course, or to have them obsess over which lines should end with semicolons. Thus, a goal of Grace is to eliminate as many of these accidental difficulties as possible, not only because students and instructors have quite enough to do mastering the essential difficulties, but also because we do not want to give students the false impression that programming is about the placement of semicolons.

Some of our specific objectives in achieving these goals are as follows.

- Programs to accomplish simple tasks should be simple, with little or no syntactic overhead.
- Novice programmers should have access to a programming environment (IDE) specifically designed to support novices.
- Language concepts should have simple semantic models.
- Grace should support a variety of approaches to teaching, including:
  - introducing objects first, introducing objects late, and (to a limited extent) starting with functions;
  - an emphasis on static types (like Java), a preference for dynamic types (like Python), and gradual typing, which makes types optional; and
  - a series of "language-levels", so that students may learn progressively in a supportive environment.
- Students who have mastered programming in Grace should find it easy to transition to other languages.

3. AN OVERVIEW OF GRACE

In this section we provide a brief and informal description of Grace, and invite the reader to assess how well we have met the above goals and objectives. More details and examples, including a draft specification, can be found on the Grace website at gracelang.org.

3.1 Declarations and Statements

A Grace program consists of a sequence of declarations and statements, which are executed in the order written. Thus,

```
print "hello world"
```

is a complete Grace program. A more complicated program with the same effect is

```
def greet = "hello "
var subject := "world"
print (greet ++ subject)
```

This illustrates two kinds of declaration: **def** introduces a named constant, which must be given a value when it is introduced; **var** introduces a variable, which can optionally be given a value when it is declared, and can subsequently be assigned a new value. We use = for definitional equality, and := for assignment, as in Algol 60, Pascal, and Eiffel.

3.2 Objects and Classes

Grace classes and objects contain field declarations (both **def**s and **var**s), methods, and code.

```
class aCat.named(n) {
    def name = n
    var livesLeft := 9
    method speak { print "Meow" }
    print "A cat named {n} has been created"
}
var theFirstCat := aCat.named "Timothy"
theFirstCat.speak
```

The class aCat has a constructor called named that takes a single parameter n. When the constructor is invoked by the expression aCat.named "Timothy", an object is created containing three attributes: the constant name, which is bound to the string "Timothy", the variable livesLeft, which is assigned the number 9, and the parameterless method speak. This object is returned as the result of the constructor.

As an effect of creating this object, the string *A cat named Timothy has been created* will be printed; in general, a class can contain arbitrary executable code, which will execute every time an object is created. This example also shows that string literals support interpolation, using a syntax like that of Ruby: the expression inside the braces is evaluated and the resulting object asked to convert itself to a string; this string is then inserted into the quoted text.

We refer to an expression like aCat.named "Timothy" as a "method request", to indicate that an object (here aCat) is being asked to execute a method (here named). There is no need to parenthesize an argument like "Timothy" that is delimited by quotes or braces. Parameterless methods like speak are requested without extraneous parentheses, so Grace programmers write theFirstCat.speak and not theFirstCat.speak().

We use empty parentheses () to indicate the location of a parameter list in a method name, so the above method is more properly called named(). Grace allows multi-part method names (sometimes called mixfix operations), but using a syntax more like Algol than Smalltalk. Thus

```
myVector.at(i)put(newValue)
```

represents a request to myVector to execute the at()put() method with arguments i and newValue.

If only one object of a particular shape is needed there is no need to define a class; the object can be created directly by executing an object constructor. Thus

```
def theSecondCat = object {
  def name = "Timothy"
  var livesLeft := 9
  method speak { print "Meow" }
  print "A cat named {name} has been created"
}
```

results in a object operationally equivalent to theFirstCat.

Everything in the language is an object, including classes, numbers and booleans. Grace does not have a built-in nil or null value. Uninitialized variables are given the special value uninitialized, but this cannot be used as a null reference because attempting to access an uninitialized variable is an error. Instead programmers should create sentinel objects like emptyTree, or use matching as discussed in Section 3.6.

3.3 Types & Information hiding

So far, our examples have not mentioned types, but type annotations are part of the language, as are annotations for information hiding. To support a variety of approaches to teaching, types in Grace programs may be completely omitted, completely supplied, or partially supplied. In all cases, enough dynamic checks are inserted to guarantee that Grace is type-safe.

The default visibility of methods is public. This can be changed by annotating a method as confidential, meaning that it can be requested only of **self**[1] or **super**. In contrast, fields are lexically bound, so are visible only in the object constructor in which they are declared. To make a field accessible to other objects, it may be annotated as readable, which creates a public "reader" method, or writable, which creates a public "writer" method, or both.

Types describe the public interface of objects, like Java interfaces; types can be parameterized by other types, as in List<Number>. Grace types are structural; they are completely separate from classes, and say nothing at all about an object's implementation. So the type Number describes both exact rational numbers and inexact numbers approximated to 64-bit precision, since they have the same methods. This separation of type and class is deliberate. Classes specify how to construct an object, and objects contain the code that gives them their behavior. Types support abstraction and the clear specification of intent, by making explicit the methods that may be requested of an object.

To illustrate the use of types, let's define

```
type Mouse = {
  name -> String
  mass -> Number
  speak -> Done
  increaseMassBy (n:Number) -> Done
}
```

This names a type with four methods — name, mass, speak, and increaseMassBy(). The -> symbol after a method name indicates the return type of that method. The built-in type Done is used to indicate that a method has an effect but does not return an interesting object.

Here is a class whose constructor method named() is annotated to say explicitly that it returns a Mouse object:

```
class aMouse.named(n:String) -> Mouse {
  def name is readable = n
  var mass: Number is readable := 50
  method increaseMassBy (m:Number) {
    mass := mass + m }
  method speak -> Done { print "Squeak" }
}
def jeremy:Mouse = aMouse.named "Jeremy"
```

The type annotation :String indicates that the parameter of the method named() must be a String, and the type annotation -> Mouse indicates that the method returns a Mouse object. The compiler will check that the latter annotation is correct. The returned object has public methods increaseMassBy() and speak, and also methods name and mass generated as a consequence of the **is** readable annotations. The type of name can be inferred to be String because that is the type of n. Because Grace types are structural, jeremy would still be a Mouse even if the declarations of jeremy and aMouse.named contained no type information.

The writer method generated by an annotated declaration

```
var age:Number is writable
```

is called age:=() and is requested using a syntax that is deliberately like assignment: age := 3.

3.4 Inheritance

Grace supports inheritance for both objects and classes. For example we can extend our cat example as follows:

```
class aHipCat.named(n) {
  inherits aCat.named(n)
  def vibe = "Cool"
  method speak is override { print "Meow, man!" }
}
```

The **inherits** clause contains an expression generating a fresh

[1] Grace uses **self** to refer to the current object, corresponding to **this** in Java and C++.

object, typically a request of a constructor method on a class. All of the methods of the inherited object are available on the inheriting object; overriding methods must be flagged with the **is override** annotation.

Because fields are local to the object that defines them, inheriting objects cannot access them directly. However, the annotation confidential, readable, writable will generate reader and writer methods that are restricted to heirs. These methods can be overridden, like any other inherited method.

3.5 Blocks

The Grace *block* represents an anonymous function, otherwise known as a lambda-expression; blocks may be assigned to variables and passed as arguments. A block is written between braces, for example {x −> 2∗x}. The −> separates the parameters of the block from the body; if there are no parameters, the −> is omitted. As is normal in Grace, type annotations on the parameters are optional. The body can be an arbitrary sequence of statements and expressions; the value of the block is that of the last expression executed. Thus, the above example doubles its argument. The body of a block can access identifiers from the surrounding scope, so blocks must be implemented as closures. Blocks are objects; they are evaluated by requesting their apply method:

```
def double = {x −> 2∗x}
print (double.apply(5))        // prints 10
```

Blocks play a central role in Grace, because they enable us to define "control structures" using methods that take blocks as arguments. For example, if()then()else() is a method, defined in a standard library, that takes as arguments a boolean-valued expression and two blocks:

```
if (graceLanguage.isGreat) then {
    print "Adopt it now"
} else {
    print "Come up with a better design"
}
```

The statements in braces are parameterless blocks, which are arguments to if()then()else(). As noted in Section 3.2, parentheses are not required around these arguments because they are delimited by braces. Grace also uses blocks to define internal iterators like map and do over its collections:

```
method averageAge(people) {
    // people is a sequence of Person objects.
    // Compute their average age.
    def ages = people.map{each:Person −> each.age}
    var sum := 0
    ages.do{each:Number −> sum := sum + each}
    sum/ages.size
}
```

This code first uses the map method with the argument block {each:Person −> each.age} to create a sequence of ages, and then the do method with the argument block {each:Number −> sum := sum + each} to compute their sum.

A method returns the value of the last expression evaluated, which in the method above is sum/ages.size. An explicit **return** statement can be used to specify an early return; this is useful inside a block, because **return** means return from the enclosing method, *not* from the block itself. For example, the following method might be defined on a collection that has a do() method for iteration.

```
method detect(p:PredicateBlock)ifNone(a:ActionBlock) {
    // find element in this collection that
    // satisfies predicate p. If none, execute a.
    self.do{each −>
        if (p.apply(each)) then {return each}
    }
    a.apply
}
```

As in many other object-oriented languages, the receiver **self** can be omitted.

Grace's use of parentheses and braces is not arbitrary. The expression used as the test in if()then()else() is evaluated once when the method is requested, so it is parenthesized. In contrast, because the code following the then and else parameters must be evaluated conditionally, those expressions must be blocks. While this is different from some other languages, it provides an opportunity for instructors to discuss conditional and repeated execution of code.

A benefit of first-class blocks is that library writers, instructors, and students can write methods that provide high-level operations on their data objects. Being able to write and reuse common abstractions like the detect()ifNone() method, rather than requiring that clients "roll their own" using an iterator and a loop, is something that we consider an important part of object-oriented programming.

3.6 Pattern matching

Grace provides pattern matching similar to that found in languages like ML, Haskell, and Scala. Unlike these languages, Grace's pattern matching facilities are mostly definable using the core features of Grace, and hence can be supported through libraries. A complete description is the subject of another paper [8]; here we confine ourselves to a brief sketch.

The programmer can use pattern matching on both literal values (like the switch statements in the C family of languages) and on types. For example:

```
match (exp)
    case { 0 −> "Zero" }
    case { n:Number −> "Number less than {n+1}" }
    case { s:String −> "String \"{s}\"" }
```

This expression first evaluates exp to yield an object, and then selects a string describing that object.

Pattern matching can also be used to extract information from an object, but only if the object provides a method to make that information available. For example, suppose that we wish to sum the elements of a list of numbers

```
type List<T> = {
    head −> T
    tail −> List<T>
    isEmpty −> Boolean
    extract −> Tuple<T,List<T>>
    ...
}
method sum(aList:List<Number>) −> Number {
    match(aList)
      case {(emptyList) −> 0}
      case {xs:List<Number> −> xs.head + sum(xs.tail)}
}
```

The method sum first matches aList against the constant emptyList. If this fails, aList must have a head and a tail, and the method can perform the obvious recursion. However, because List also provides the method extract, sum can also be written using a so-called destructuring match:

```
method sum(aList:List<Number>) -> Number {
   match(aList)
      case {(emptyList) -> 0}
      case {List<Number>(hd, tl) -> hd + sum(tl)}
}
```

Here, hd and tl are not arguments, but sub-patterns that bind variables. They are bound to the values returned by the extract method on aList. Destructuring matches can be nested arbitrarily deeply.

Patterns are just objects that understand a particular protocol. Consequently, in addition to the built-in patterns described so far, users and library writers can define their own patterns. For example, it is possible to provide a library that supports the matching of strings against regular expressions.

It is useful, particularly for novices, if the compiler can provide a static warning when a pattern match is not exhaustive, and when cases are unreachable. To permit this, Grace includes tagless *variant types* of the form T | U. To have the type T | U, an object must have either type T or type U. The combination of variant types and *singleton types* make it straightforward to program without nil. For example, the object emptyList above, which does not have all of the methods of type List, has the type singleton(emptyList); we call this a singleton type because emptyList is the only object with this type. We could then declare

```
type ListOption<T> = List<T> | singleton(emptyList)
```

Methods operating on a ListOption object can use pattern matching, or explicit emptiness tests, to deal with the two cases. The advantage of pattern matching is that in the body of the case {xs:List -> ...}, xs is statically known to be non-empty.

4. THE STATE OF GRACE

Most of the details of the language design have now been worked out, though we expect refinements to be made as we gather experience with the language. We have written a substantial amount of Grace code, including a self-hosting compiler for Grace itself. The compiler is called *minigrace*; it generates either JavaScript, which can be run in a web browser, or C, which can run on any platform with a C compiler. We have also written parts of a collections library for Grace, and a selection of typical assignments for a data structures course. All code can be reached from the Grace language web site at gracelang.org.

We are convinced that the success of a language for novices depends on having a supportive interactive development environment (IDE). Rather than designing such an environment from scratch, we have examined the feasibility of modifying BlueJ and DrRacket (formerly DrScheme) to support Grace.

We currently have a partial implementation of Grace inside of DrRacket [5], and intend to complete that implementation and to create language levels for Grace in DrRacket. We anticipate having a directed graph of languages rather than a linear progression so that we can support multiple approaches to teaching object-oriented programming.

A BlueJ implementation requires an implementation of Grace on the JVM. While we would eventually like to build such an implementation, it is currently on a back burner.

There is a wide consensus that teaching parallel programming is of growing importance. Unfortunately, there is no consensus on what kind of parallelism to teach: message-passing, shared variables, futures, actors, or whatever. To avoid committing to a model that will be wrong for a large fraction of our intended audience, Grace will provide a variety of libraries for supporting parallelism in a variety of styles. We don't believe that such support need be "second class", because most of the basic features of Grace, including all of the control structures, are also provided by libraries.

We have had good experience with an undergraduate assistant writing libraries for data structures, but must develop tool support and teaching materials to class-test Grace. We plan on using Grace in small classes of novices in late 2013. We expect to make revisions to Grace as we respond to any learning difficulties we find in these early classes.

We intend to develop at least two different approaches to teaching with Grace, one based on the text by Felleisen *et al.* [4], which emphasizes "design recipes", and one based on the text by Bruce *et al.* [2], which takes an objects-first approach. We will make the lecture notes and examples from these courses freely available online.

5. EVALUATING GRACE

While it is difficult to evaluate Grace without direct teaching experience, we can provide a first evaluation based on criteria that others have presented on language choices for novices. For this purpose we adopt the checklist of eleven criteria proposed by Michael Kölling [11].

1. **Clean concepts.** We have provided uncluttered features with a straight-forward semantics. Students can begin by defining objects directly before being introduced to classes, and simple objects can be created fully formed, without need for complex initialization. Types and classes are separate concepts: classes are used to create objects, while types are used to specify the interface of an object, without reference to any particular implementation.
2. **Pure object-orientation.** Everything in Grace is an object, including numbers, booleans and blocks. As a result, there is no need for the complications of value versus reference. While Grace supports functional constructs, they are obtained in an object-oriented way.
3. **Safety.** Grace is strongly typed, with type errors caught at either compile time or run time. Because types are gradual, students may write programs across a spectrum from no type annotations, resulting in dynamic checks, to complete annotations, resulting in static checks. We have designed Grace to make it possible to check for access to uninitialized variables, exhaustiveness of type-case matches, and other common errors.
4. **High level.** Grace is high-level in several ways. Of course, Grace uses automatically managed memory, eliminating the possibility of some of the most frustrating errors for students. More importantly, blocks are first-class in Grace; this provides students (and teachers) with the ability to write methods that accept blocks as parameters, which in turn makes it easy to treat data structures as "whole objects". A good example is a method that traverses a tree, searching for a value that satisfies a predicate represented as a boolean-valued block.
5. **Simple object/execution model.** All objects are on the heap, and all computation takes place by requesting that an object execute a method.
6. **Readable syntax.** All declarations are introduced by

keywords; we chose keywords that directly signify the concept that we wish to teach. So, for example, methods are introduced by the **method** keyword, not **fun** or **mdef**.

Because we expect students to transition to languages that use C-style syntax, we have adopted features that are close to those languages, though normally with a twist. For example, we use braces to delimit blocks, but those blocks must *also* be consistently indented. Semicolons can always be omitted at the end of a line.

In declarations, names come before types, making the names more visible. We distinguish between "=" for definitions and ":=" for assignment to variables because they represent different concepts.

7. **No redundancy.** This is difficult to verify, but we have worked to build Grace from a small number of primitive constructs. Because blocks are first class, we can build any number of looping constructs. That might be considered redundant, but we feel it is important to be able to use the most appropriate loop for a given traversal.

   Pattern-matching may seem to be redundant: most object-oriented languages don't have it, and some programmers feel that pattern-matching is inherently non-object-oriented. Most languages *do* provide a construct to check the type of a run-time value; pattern matching provides similar facilities, and in a way that facilitates static type-checking. Moreover, pattern matching can be excluded from the beginning language levels.

   However, the real argument for including pattern matching in Grace is that it makes Grace *a more effective teaching language*. Students should be able to compare code written with and without pattern matching, and learn from experience which is more readable and easier to maintain. This comparison is most effective if all other variables can be help constant, which means comparing two equivalent programs written in the same language.
8. **Small.** The core of Grace is quite small; we avoided enlarging the language with anything that can be defined in a library. Grace does include a simple module facility for importing features from libraries, but does not provide many facilities for programming-in-the-large, as would be needed in an industrial-strength language. Students should be able to learn all of Grace in one or two semesters.
9. **Easy transition.** The basic concepts supported by Grace are available in other object-oriented languages, though often obscured by complicated syntax. Even blocks, not currently part of Java, will be added in the next revision. They are already included in C# 3.0 [6].
10. **Correctness assurance.** We do not currently have annotations for pre- and post-condition, variants and invariants, but we expect to provide them in libraries.
11. **Environment.** We are well aware of the importance of a good programming environment for Grace. As described in Section 4, development of an environment is underway.

We believe that Grace stacks up very well against languages like Java, C#, Python, and Eiffel with respect to Kölling's criteria. We are well aware that a positive reception by students is crucial to the success of the language. Thus, formative evaluations with real classes of students will be essential to the further development of the language.

6. CONCLUSION

While this project is still in relatively early stages, we feel that it is now far enough along to present to potential adopters. We are eager to have feedback on the language design to this point, and are happy to have others pitch in with library designs, work on programming environments, improvements in the implementation, and in testing the language on novices.

More information on the project, including information on the current prototype compiler, is available at gracelang.org.

7. REFERENCES

[1] F. P. Brooks, Jr. No silver bullet: Essence and accidents of software engineering. *IEEE Computer*, 20(4):10–19, April 1987.

[2] K. Bruce, A. Danyluk, and T. Murtagh. *Java: An Eventful Approach.* Prentice-Hall, 2005.

[3] W. P. Dann, S. Cooper, and R. Pausch. *Learning to Program with Alice.* Pearson Prentice Hall, 2011.

[4] M. Felleisen, R. B. Findler, M. Flatt, and S. Krishnamurthi. *How to design programs: an introduction to programming and computing.* MIT Press, Cambridge, MA, USA, 2001.

[5] R. B. Findler, J. Clements, C. Flanagan, M. Flatt, S. Krishnamurthi, P. Steckler, and M. Felleisen. DrScheme: a programming environment for Scheme. *J. Funct. Program.*, 12(2):159–182, 2002.

[6] A. Hejlsberg, M. Torgersen, S. Wiltamuth, and P. Golde. *C# Programming Language.* Addison-Wesley, 4th edition, 2010.

[7] R. C. Holt and J. R. Cordy. The Turing programming language. *Commun. ACM*, 31(12):1410–1423, 1988.

[8] M. Homer, J. Noble, K. B. Bruce, A. P. Black, and D. J. Pearce. Patterns as objects in Grace. In *Proc. 8th symp. on Dynamic languages*, DLS '12, pages 17–28, New York, NY, USA, 2012. ACM.

[9] K. Jensen and N. Wirth. *Pascal User Manual and Report.* Springer, 1975.

[10] J. G. Kemeny and T. E. Kurtz. *Back to Basic; The History, Corruption, and Future of the Language.* Addison-Wesley, 1985.

[11] M. Kölling. The problem of teaching object-oriented programming, Part I: Languages. *JOOP*, 11(8):8–15, 1999.

[12] M. Kölling, B. Quig, A. Patterson, and J. Rosenberg. The BlueJ system and its pedagogy. *Journal of Computer Science Education*, 13(4), Dec 2003.

[13] M. Kölling and J. Rosenberg. Blue—a language for teaching object-oriented programming. In *Proc. 27th SIGCSE technical symp. on Computer science education*, SIGCSE '96, pages 190–194, 1996.

[14] R. E. Pattis. *Karel The Robot: A Gentle Introduction to the Art of Programming.* Wiley, 1995.

[15] A. Pears, S. Seidman, L. Malmi, L. Mannila, E. Adams, J. Bennedsen, M. Devlin, and J. Paterson. A survey of literature on the teaching of introductory programming. In *Working group reports on ITiCSE on Innovation and technology in computer science education*, ITiCSE-WGR '07, pages 204–223. ACM, 2007.

[16] J. Rosenberger. Grace: A manifesto for a new educational object-oriented programming language. Blog@CACM, October 2010. Retrieved Dec 2012. http://cacm.acm.org/blogs/blog-cacm/100389.

Developing a Highly Interactive eBook for CS Instruction

James B. Fenwick Jr. Barry L. Kurtz Philip Meznar
Reed Phillips Alex Weidner

Appalachian State University
Computer Science Department
Boone, NC 28608
828-262-2370

{jbf,blk}@cs.appstate.edu

ABSTRACT

Electronic books (ebooks) are becoming commonplace and widespread. Highly interactive ebooks actively engage the reader and have great potential to increase student learning. With the recent release of Apple's iBooks Author application, instructors can develop highly interactive ebooks. This paper reports on our experience of creating an interactive Prolog programming ebook using iBooks Author. A particular focus is placed on ebook features pertinent to undergraduate computer science instruction including code listings, coding tutorials, and integration with course management systems and automated grading systems. This work is supported, in part, by two NSF grants.

Categories and Subject Descriptors K.3.2 [Computer and Information Science Education] Computer Science Education

General Terms Human Factors

Keywords eBook, active learning, authoring tools

1. INTRODUCTION

Electronic books, also called e-books, ebooks, or digital books, are finding their way into the daily reading activities of more and more people. While electronic versions of printed books have been available for reading on electronic devices (i.e., computers) for at least 40 years, recent hardware and software offerings have sparked an ebook revolution. In particular, Amazon's 2007 release of the Kindle and Apple's 2010 release of the iPad dramatically propelled the widespread use of ebooks.

We have always had a research interest in understanding how new technologies can be adopted and adapted for computer science education. Podcasts and tablet PCs were an integral aspect of a "flipped classroom" approach for delivering course content [6]. New courses help students learn skills in cutting-edge, web-based technologies [5], and automated grading systems have been built that can be used inside or outside of the classroom [4,7]. Ebooks may offer a new way to integrate many of these capabilities. In particular, they may be able to turn the passive learning that is reading the textbook into a more interactive engagement that may reap the benefits of active learning [1,10].

Like many teachers, we are curious how ebooks can be used to increase our students' learning. With Apple's 2012 release of the iBooks Author application, it became possible to easily create highly interactive ebooks. This paper reports on an "early adopter" experience of creating an iBook version of course content and provides a preliminary evaluation of the effect on student learning.

2. ELECTRONIC BOOKS OVERVIEW

The history of ebooks is debatable, yet many recognize Michael S. Hart's digitizing of the U.S. Declaration of Independence for Project Gutenberg as the origin of the modern ebook [13]. Until recently, ebooks were not interactive. They were just an electronic form of the printed book text and images. Hyperlinks to Internet websites became available from within the ebook text, yet often this deploys a separate application requiring the reader to navigate back to the book. More recently, ebooks have become much more interactive. They allow the reader to highlight text, add notes, and bookmark pages. Newer interactive features include embedded audio, video, slideshows, and image galleries. Questions assessing reader understanding can also be embedded. Interactive images and 3-D objects provide readers a unique, interactive experience. Yet the educational value of these features has not been formally studied.

From a hardware perspective, early ebooks were simply read on standard computer terminals. Web-accessible ebooks could be viewed via a browser interface. The past decade, however, has seen the emergence of hiqh-quality, small screen devices. Some devices, such as Amazon's Kindle and the Barnes and Noble Nook, are intended primarily as reading devices. Other devices, such as Apple's iPad, provide a wider variety of applications of which ebook reading is just one. Display technologies have ranged from "e-ink" (e.g., Amazon's Kindle) to backlit LCD technologies. Entourage Systems combined these into its dual screen eDGe device where one side used an e-ink display and the other side was an LCD. Manufacturers have also explored a variety of device sizes, and the market seems to be converging to a 7"-10" device size.

SIGCSE '13, March 6–9, 2013, Denver, Colorado, USA.

Ebook file formats have varied as well. Non-interactive formats such as HTML and PDF were early ways to publish ebooks. However, the more modern and interactive ebooks use different formats. There is an open-source standard format (EPUB) that is based on XML. The International Digital Publishing Forum released ePub3 in October 2011. Amazon's Kindle uses proprietary formats for their ebooks (AZW and KF8), but will display other formats (e.g., PDF). Apple's iBook format (IAB) is a customized format based on the open-source ePub format. Proprietary formats and the ongoing evolution of the EPUB standard complicates widespread authorship of interactive ebooks.

In 2011, University of Washington researchers reported results of a study using the Amazon Kindle DX of the effectiveness of ebooks on student learning [14]. They report that seven months into the study less than 40% of students were using the Kindle for academic reading. A number of device-related problems were cited including a lack of support for note taking. A conclusion of the study stated that the device was well suited for leisure reading but not academic reading. Newer devices have addressed many of the deficiencies reported in the study.

3. IBOOKS AUTHOR

In January 2012 Apple released the free iBooks Author application. It can be downloaded from Apple's online store. Using a WYSIWYG interface, novices can quickly create highly interactive ebooks that can be read on an iPad mobile device. An ebook can also be exported as a PDF document, but some of the interactive features will not export.

The iBooks Author application supports a wide variety of content types including text, images, shapes, tables, charts, and interactive widgets (see below). Each content type has changeable characteristics, such as text font size, shape color, etc. The content types can be placed anywhere on a page.

A number of interactive widgets are available including

- image galleries,
- audio media (m4a format),
- video media (m4v format),
- slideshow presentations,
- multiple-choice review questions,
- an "interactive image" that supports image zooming and labeling,
- COLLADA format 3-D objects allowing the reader to manipulate the object, and
- embedded Dashcode HTML [9].

Widgets occur within the space of the ebook and do not deploy an external application giving a tightly integrated feel to reading the ebook. Unfortunately, it is not possible for an instructor author to know if their student reader is engaging these interactive elements.

In addition to the content pages themselves, the application also gives control to various book elements such as the cover, a glossary, and a table of contents. The latter two elements are integrated with the content pages such that creating a numbered section of content updates the table of contents as well. There is even an optional "introduction media" that plays when the book is first opened. In addition, a number of document templates are provided that ease the task of authoring.

4. IMPLEMENTING A PROLOG IBOOK

As part of an upper-level, required computer science course, students learn the logic programming language Prolog. We created an iBook version of our own teaching materials [2].

4.1. Goals

This iBook authoring effort had several goals.

- Understand the issues involved in creating an iBook for college level material.
- Make a challenging topic more understandable for students.
- Explore the use of the iBooks Author features in the context of computer science content.
- Explore the use of iBook features in the context of instructional requirements (e.g., integration with course management systems).

4.2. Basic iBook Nuts and Bolts

All of our original material (text and images) was contained in a Microsoft Word file. While iBooks Author allows the direct importing of this bulk of content material, we preferred the results of creating sections and subsections within iBooks Author and cutting/pasting from the Word document. Since the "paper" of an iBook is free, one of the first changes was to add many more figures than in the original document. Figure 1 shows a sample page with a new isolated figure that presents ancillary information about John Alan Robinson, the developer of resolution theorem proving that made Prolog a feasible language to implement. In the printed version this kind of interesting but non-critical information was not included.

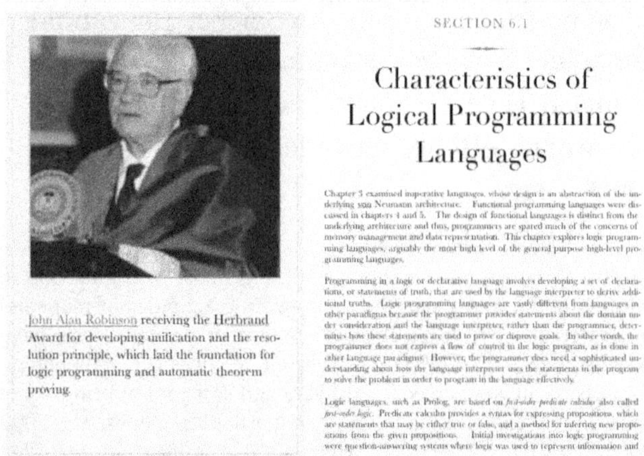
SECTION 6.1

Characteristics of Logical Programming Languages

John Alan Robinson receiving the Herbrand Award for developing unification and the resolution principle, which laid the foundation for logic programming and automatic theorem proving

Figure 1: A Sample Textbook Page

Another change was to add hyperlinks to external sources of information throughout the textual material as appropriate. This allows students to explore topics not covered in detail in the printed textbook. Notice in Figure 1 that Robinson's name in the caption is hyperlinked to a more detailed source of information (e.g., a Wikipedia page). In addition to text and figures, color-filled shapes were positioned behind code fragments to help them stand out from surrounding text as shown in Figure 2. Our materials did not include tables or charts.

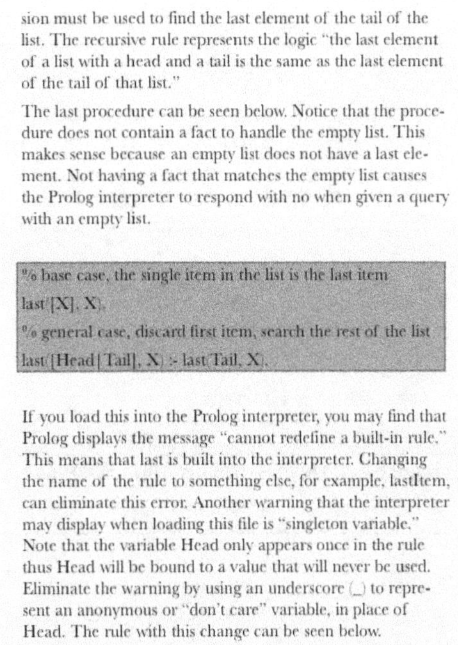

sion must be used to find the last element of the tail of the list. The recursive rule represents the logic "the last element of a list with a head and a tail is the same as the last element of the tail of that list."

The last procedure can be seen below. Notice that the procedure does not contain a fact to handle the empty list. This makes sense because an empty list does not have a last element. Not having a fact that matches the empty list causes the Prolog interpreter to respond with no when given a query with an empty list.

```
% base case, the single item in the list is the last item
last([X], X).
% general case, discard first item, search the rest of the list
last([Head|Tail], X) :- last(Tail, X).
```

If you load this into the Prolog interpreter, you may find that Prolog displays the message "cannot redefine a built-in rule." This means that last is built into the interpreter. Changing the name of the rule to something else, for example, lastItem, can eliminate this error. Another warning that the interpreter may display when loading this file is "singleton variable." Note that the variable Head only appears once in the rule thus Head will be bound to a value that will never be used. Eliminate the warning by using an underscore (_) to represent an anonymous or "don't care" variable, in place of Head. The rule with this change can be seen below.

Figure 2: Shapes Used to Highlight Text

4.3. Interactive Widgets

In a paper textbook all content is visible all the time. By contrast, ebook content can be displayed selectively when the reader clicks on an icon. This is very useful so that:

- High resolution figures are only displayed when requested
- Program code listings are displayed on request
- Interactive activities are only activated on request

Our book content does not have a need for galleries of images, however we did employ this widget successfully to show a multiple page code listing as shown in Figure 3. The arrows and the dots at the bottom are navigation controls to move among the "pages" of code.

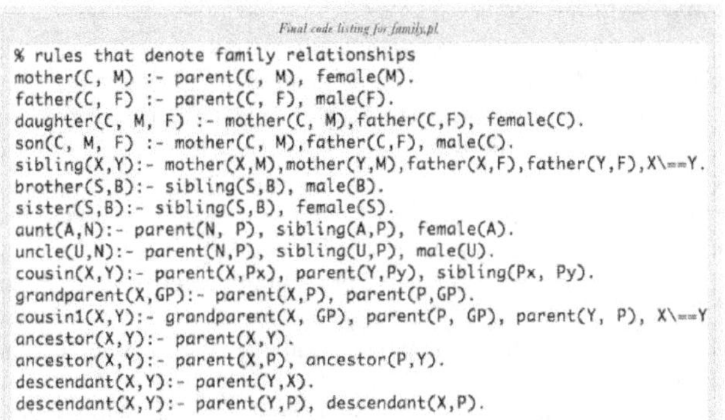

Final code listing for family.pl

```
% rules that denote family relationships
mother(C, M) :- parent(C, M), female(M).
father(C, F) :- parent(C, F), male(F).
daughter(C, M, F) :- mother(C, M),father(C,F), female(C).
son(C, M, F) :- mother(C, M),father(C,F), male(C).
sibling(X,Y):- mother(X,M),mother(Y,M),father(X,F),father(Y,F),X\==Y.
brother(S,B):- sibling(S,B), male(B).
sister(S,B):- sibling(S,B), female(S).
aunt(A,N):- parent(N, P), sibling(A,P), female(A).
uncle(U,N):- parent(N,P), sibling(U,P), male(U).
cousin(X,Y):- parent(X,Px), parent(Y,Py), sibling(Px, Py).
grandparent(X,GP):- parent(X,P), parent(P,GP).
cousin1(X,Y):- grandparent(X, GP), parent(P, GP), parent(Y, P), X\==Y
ancestor(X,Y):- parent(X,Y).
ancestor(X,Y):- parent(X,P), ancestor(P,Y).
descendant(X,Y):- parent(Y,X).
descendant(X,Y):- parent(Y,P), descendant(X,P).
```

Figure 3: An Image Gallery Multi-page Code Listing

Entire slideshows can also be embedded in a page as a widget. Figure 4 shows an embedded slideshow and Figure 5 shows an enlarged view of the last slide in the slideshow. When the student touches this widget, it advances to the next slide with the last slide advancing back around to the beginning. In this example, the code and associated "explanation bubbles" are introduced over the course of 8 slides, one code line or bubble per slide. As with all of these widgets, the student can "stretch" the widget to a full screen size. Slideshows must be created using Apple's Keynote application, but Microsoft Powerpoint files can be imported.

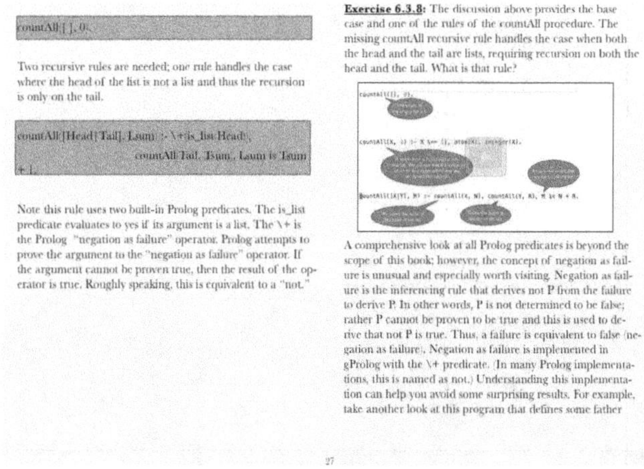

```
countAll([ ], 0).
```

Two recursive rules are needed; one rule handles the case where the head of the list is not a list and thus the recursion is only on the tail.

```
countAll([Head|Tail], Lsum) :- \+(is_list(Head)),
                    countAll(Tail, Tsum), Lsum is Tsum
+ 1.
```

Note this rule uses two built-in Prolog predicates. The is_list predicate evaluates to yes if its argument is a list. The \+ is the Prolog "negation as failure" operator. Prolog attempts to prove the argument to the "negation as failure" operator. If the argument cannot be proven true, then the result of the operator is true. Roughly speaking, this is equivalent to a "not."

Exercise 6.3.8: The discussion above provides the base case and one of the rules of the countAll procedure. The missing countAll recursive rule handles the case when both the head and the tail are lists, requiring recursion on both the head and the tail. What is that rule?

A comprehensive look at all Prolog predicates is beyond the scope of this book; however, the concept of negation as failure is unusual and especially worth visiting. Negation as failure is the inferencing rule that derives not P from the failure to derive P. In other words, P is not determined to be false; rather P cannot be proven to be true and this is used to derive that not P is true. Thus, a failure is equivalent to false (negation as failure). Negation as failure is implemented in gProlog with the \+ predicate. (In many Prolog implementations, this is named as not.) Understanding this implementation can help you avoid some surprising results. For example, take another look at this program that defines some father

27

Figure 4: An Embedded Slideshow

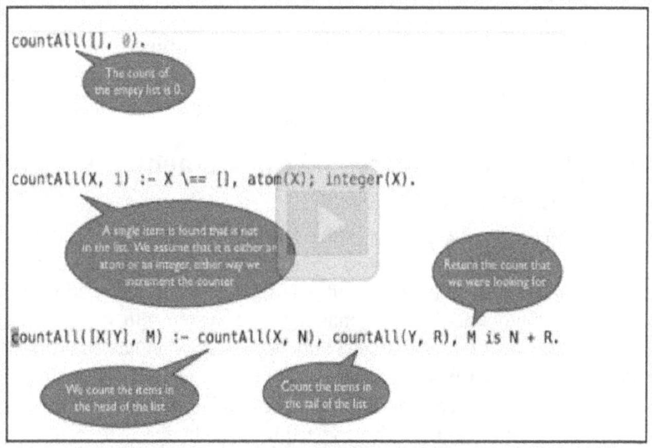

Figure 5: Enlarged View of Slideshow

The iBooks Author application provides a review question widget that is basically a multiple-choice question. Clicking an answer or drag and drop interactive answering is supported. However, there is no way to provide feedback on each separate choice or record student performance. To provide answer feedback, we used a transition-controlled slideshow with answers that were hyperlinks to other slides containing feedback. We also linked to an external course management quizzing system (see section 4.4).

Audio (m4a) and video (m4v) media files can also be embedded on a page. Touching the widget presents a control bar allowing students to play, pause or restart the media. We embedded short screencasts narrating Prolog programming sessions. Figure 6 shows how this looks in the iBook. Again, these can be expanded to full screen if desired. The Quicktime application was used to develop these media clips. Multiple attempts were needed to become comfortable with producing the video in terms of both hardware/software requirements and the targeted focus of the tutorial concept. Prolog is unlike other languages our students have experienced, so these embedded video tutorials were highly valued by our students.

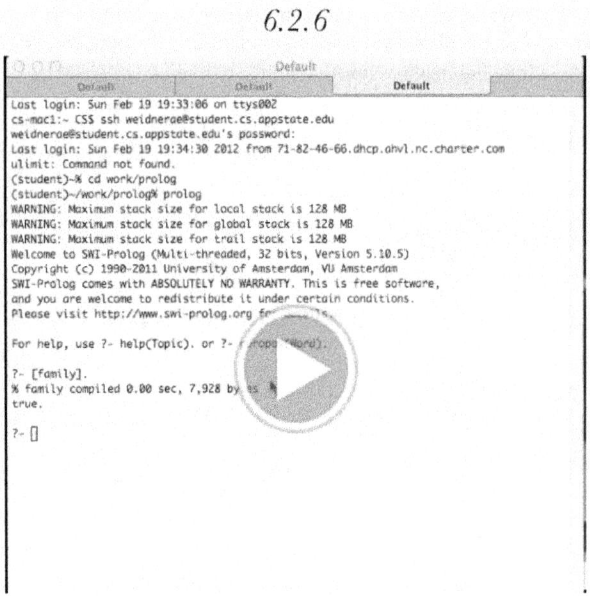

Figure 6: An Embedded Video Tutorial

Our programming language content did not lend itself well to the other widget types: interactive images, 3-D objects, embedded Dashcode HTML.

4.4. Moodle Course Management System Integration

As explained above, the embedded review question widget does not provide feedback or record performance. An iBook used in an instructional setting needs to support these elements. In addition, most instructors use course management systems to consolidate content materials, activities, and assessment. Our university deploys a system based on Moodle [11]. Hyperlinks were added to the text that when clicked cause the device to leave the iBook and open a browser to the hyperlinked webpage which was a Moodle quiz. Figure 7 shows two external hyperlinks, the top box contains a link to a Moodle quiz (see Figure 8) and the bottom box contains a link to a Prolog microlab (see Figure 9).

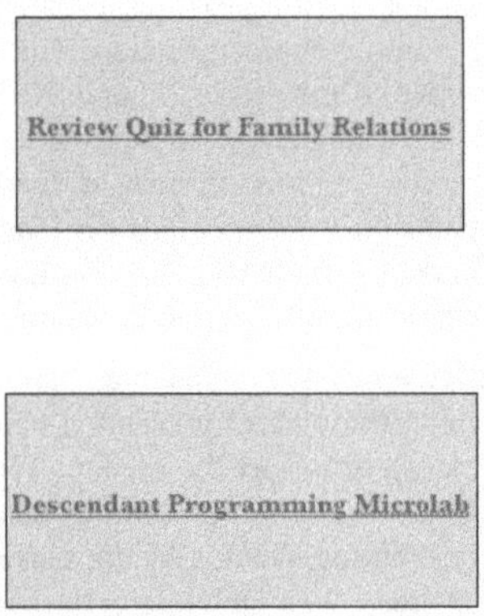

Figure 7: Embedded Hyperlinks to External Web Pages

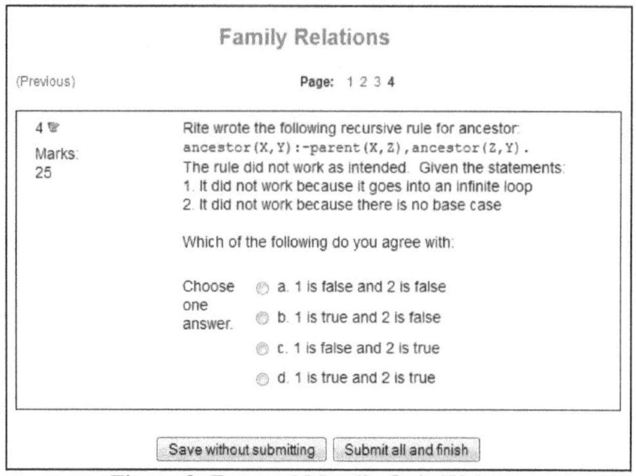

Figure 8: External Moodle Quiz Webpage

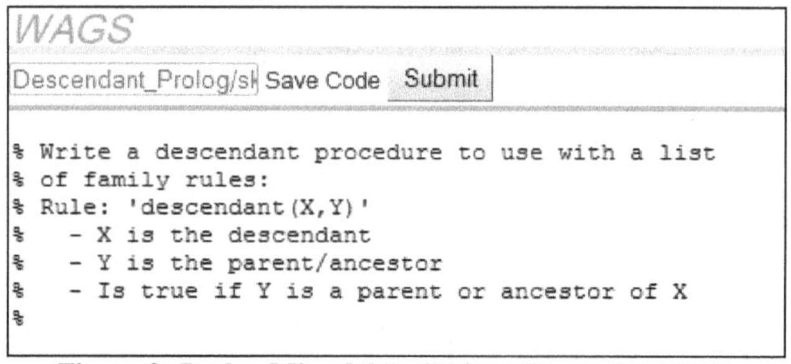

Figure 9: Prolog Microlab to Write a Descendant Rule

If the user had not already logged in to the Moodle system, they would need to authenticate with the course management system. After having authenticated once, the iBook reader is automatically taken directly to the selected quiz. When the user completes the quiz in the browser, they can return to the iBook application on the same page they were previously viewing. This has many significant advantages over the multiple choice question review widget built-into iBooks Author:

- Student performance can be recorded and monitored
- A wider variety of question formats are available
- Detailed feedback can be provided both for correct and incorrect responses

Hyperlinks were also added that connect to the WAGS microlab automated grading system [4]. The bottom box in Figure 7 contains a hyperlink to a WAGS programming activity and Figure 9 shows the resulting browser page for this activity. WAGS also has an authentication component and provides active learning exercises that can be used as monitored formative or summative assessments. The behavior for performing the microlab activities and returning to the iBook is the same as for the Moodle quizzes.

Six Prolog programming microlab activities were incorporated into the course materials. WAGS records the number of attempts each student makes on each microlab activity before succeeding or giving up. The number of attempts varies widely as students tend to exhibit a "try this try that" approach to learning new languages. However, the immediate feedback causes students to nearly always continue to work until succeeding. [3] contains detailed information on the evaluation of the Prolog microlabs.

5. AN EPUB EBOOK

Experiencing the highly interactive features available in the iBook format requires using an iPad mobile device. The open-source EPUB format is readable by a wider variety of hardware platforms, so we are interested in supporting this format as well. The ePub3 standard, adopted in October 2011, is based on HTML5 which provides audio and video tags. While some of the iBook interactive features may not be possible, we felt the most important ones could be achieved with the ePub3 format. However, there was not an easy way to create the ePub3 document.

One of our students developed an application that provides for the authoring of ePub3 documents [12]. We have successfully used this tool to create ePub3 documents that can be read using the Azardi Reader [8]. Unfortunately, at this time most tablet devices do not yet support the ePub3 format. We are awaiting more widespread adoption of the standard.

6. EVALUATION

6.1. Authoring Issues

Using the iBooks Author application is no more difficult than other applications. The WYSIWYG interface allows for quick exploration of various features. If an iPad device is connected during the authoring process, you can preview the iBook on the device directly which allows you to see how the iBook looks and acts to the reader.

There is some learning curve associated with understanding the various content types and widgets available within iBooks Author. However, the steeper learning curve is deciding which content types and widgets to use. No one wants to read an iBook that is simply text and images. Rather there is an expectation of a highly interactive reading and learning experience. So the iBook author must constantly ask himself or herself "new content" types of questions, such as these.

- Would this image become "more alive" by making it an interactive image or a 3-D object?
- Would additional content, such as a narrated screencast, be helpful here?
- What information could be hyperlinked to external sources to enrich the presentation?

While the iBook author asks content enrichment questions such as these that are enabled by the technology, the teacher also wonders if the learning will be improved. Believing that reading an iBook can be an active learning [1,10] exercise, we decided to experiment.

6.2. Student Attitudes

The interactive features of ebooks can increase student engagement and is being reported to increase test scores [15]. We were hoping to be able to determine that the interactive presentation of the content could be correlated to increased student learning. In Spring 2012 semester, 8 out of 18 students received an iPad loaded with the interactive ebook. All students had access to a non-interactive PDF version of the material. The sample is too small to be valid, but there was not a noticeable difference in student performance on standard quiz and exam assessments.

As a part of our funded grant activities, an external evaluator conducted an anonymous survey of students. When asked "What did you like about the eBook materials?" typical responses were:

- I liked having the videos available to be able to get an example of how people created the programs. It helped to see how their programs were organized and gave a "lecture" that I could go back and review whenever I needed it.
- I really liked the video tutorials, and the ease of access to everything.
- It was not very hard to read on the iPad
- The videos that came along with the material.
- Videos that teach
- You can search for key words and it links to many other teaching media
- I could use an iPad for a few weeks

When asked "What did you dislike about the eBook materials?" typical responses were:

- The videos could definitely be fine-tuned, perhaps made a little bit longer with more in-depth explanations.
- Lots of page scrolling
- It was formatted somewhat poorly and is hard to type code on
- Sometimes seemed a little unorganized.
- Nothing

We also wished to measure the degree of exploration performed by students with regards to hyperlinks to external, deeper information. We routed all links to external resources through our own server that recorded this active step of clicking on the link. This was possible because we assigned devices to students and so could correlate MAC address device identification data to a specific student. Preliminary analysis indicates that most students did not take advantage of these deeper information sources.

7. CONCLUSIONS AND FUTURE WORK

The iBooks Author application has created an opportunity for college instructors to engage students with an interactive textbook. An iBook was created for a Prolog programming module of an upper-level computer science course. The authoring application is easy to use, but there are new authoring decisions to make. We were able to successfully connect iBook content to a Moodle-based course management system and an external automated grading system. Several video screencasts were produced and embedded into the iBook that demonstrated actual narrated Prolog programming sessions. Students found these especially valuable.

We were surprised to discover that the process of creating the iBook offered the author a valuable way to engage the content material because of the interactive features. For example, considering turning text into interactive slideshows causes the author to engage the material in new and exciting ways. One way we are considering to involve students in this exciting engagement is to have them publish their own notes in iBook format.

We will expand the Prolog iBook with additional material in the Spring 2013 term, and also plan to expand coverage of the ebook to include content on functional languages and F# in the Spring 2013 term. Screencasts will be reshot to provide a higher quality. Some of the unused interactive widgets, such as embedded Dashcode, will be reconsidered.

We have also developed an authoring tool that creates an ePub3 ebook document [12]. As manufacturers support this newer version of the EPUB standard we can offer a greater variety of devices and book distribution.

8. ACKNOWLEDGMENTS

This work has been supported in part by two NSF grants: Developing Software and Methodologies for eBook/Browsers to Enhance Learning (DUE1044572), and Transforming Computer Science Education with Microlabs (DUE1122752).

9. REFERENCES

[1] Bonwell, C. and Eison, J. Active Learning: Creating Excitement in the Classroom., ASHE ERIC Higher Education Report No. 1, Washington, D, C.: The George Washington University, School of Education & Human Development, 1991.

[2] J. Fenwick, B. Kurtz, C. Norris, Programming Languages and Paradigms, under contract, Jones and Bartlett Learning, to be published 2013.

[3] B. Kurtz, J. Fenwick, R. Tashakkori, A. Peterfreund, E. Costache, A. Germuth, "Evaluation of Microlabs in Computer Science Education", manuscript in preparation.

[4] Barry Kurtz, James B. Fenwick Jr., and Philip Meznar, "Developing Microlabs Using Google Web Toolkit," *Proceedings of the 43rd SIGCSE Technical Symposium on Computer Science Education (SIGCSE '12),* 2012.

[5] Barry Kurtz, James B. Fenwick, Jr., and Joel Hollingsworth "Teaching Mobile Computing and Developing Software to Support Computer Science Education," *Proceedings of the 42nd SIGCSE Technical Symposium on Computer Science Education (SIGCSE '11),* 2011.

[6] Barry L. Kurtz, James B. Fenwick Jr., Christopher C. Ellsworth "Using Podcasts and Tablet PCs in Computer Science," *Proceedings of the 45th Annual ACM Southeast Conference,* Winston-Salem, NC, March 2007.

[7] Barry L. Kurtz, James B. Fenwick Jr., Christopher C. Ellsworth, "The Quiver System," *SIGCSE Technical Symposium on Computer Science Education,* Norfolk, February 2004.

[8] Infogrid Pacific, Azardi Free ePub Reader, 2012, http://azardi.infogridpacific.com/.

[9] Maria Langer, "iBooks Author: Publishing Your First Ebook," Flying M Productions, Inc., 2012, ISBN-10: 1886637075.

[10] Jeffrey J. McConnell, "Active learning and its use in computer science," in Proceedings of the 1st conference on Integrating technology into computer science education (ITiCSE), 1996.

[11] Moodle, website: moodle.org

[12] John Price, "An EPUB3 Authoring Tool," Senior Honors Thesis, Appalachian State University, Boone, NC, 2012.

[13] Project Gutenberg, "About", http://www.gutenberg.org/wiki/Gutenberg:About.

[14] A. Thayer, C.P.Lee, L.H.Hwang, H.Sales, P.Sen, N.Dalal, "The imposition and superimposition of digital reading technology: the academic potential of e-readers," Proceedings 2011 Annual Conference on Human Factors in Computing Systems (CHI'11), ACM, 2011.

[15] Alex Wright, "Tablets Over Textbooks?" Communications of the ACM, Vol. 55, No. 3, March 2012.

CS50 Sandbox

Secure Execution of Untrusted Code

David J. Malan
School of Engineering and Applied Sciences
Harvard University
Cambridge, Massachusetts, USA
malan@harvard.edu

ABSTRACT

We introduce CS50 Sandbox, an environment for secure execution of untrusted code. Implemented as an asynchronous HTTP server, CS50 Sandbox offers clients the ability to execute programs (both interactive and non-interactive) written in any compiled or interpreted language in a tightly controlled, resource-constrained environment. CS50 Sandbox's HTTP-based API takes files, command lines, and standard input as inputs and returns standard output and error plus exit codes as outputs.

Atop CS50 Sandbox, we have built CS50 Run, a web-based code editor that enables students to write code in a browser in any language, whether compiled or interpreted, that's executed server-side within a sandboxed environment. And we have built CS50 Check, an autograding framework that supports black- and white-box testing of students' code, leveraging CS50 Sandbox to run series of checks against students' programs, no matter the language of implementation.

We present in this work the pedagogical motivations for each of these tools, along with the underlying designs thereof. Each is available as open source.

Categories and Subject Descriptors

K.3.1 [COMPUTERS AND EDUCATION]: Computer Uses in Education—*Collaborative learning, Computer-assisted instruction*; K.3.2 [COMPUTERS AND EDUCATION]: Computer and Information Science Education—*Computer science education, Self-assessment*

General Terms

Design, Security, Verification

1. INTRODUCTION

Computer Science 50 (CS50) is Harvard University's "introduction to the intellectual enterprises of computer science and the art of programming" for majors and non-majors alike, a one-semester amalgam of courses generally known as CS1 and CS2. The course is required of majors, but most of the course's students are non-majors. In Fall 2011, enrollment was 607, 76% of whom had no prior CS experience, 18% of whom had taken one prior course, and 6% of whom had taken two or more. The course is taught mostly in C in a command-line environment, with PHP and JavaScript introduced toward term's end in the context of web programming. Weekly problem sets (i.e., programming assignments) demand upwards of 15 hours per week of most students.

In years past, students wrote most of their code on a load-balanced cluster of Linux servers on which they had shells and home directories, primarily using `gcc` and `gdb` to compile and debug. In Fall 2011, students instead used a virtual machine (VM) running on their own Mac or PC. As a result, Internet connectivity was no longer requisite, and students could more easily use graphical editors like `gedit`. Moreover, server load (particularly on nights before deadlines) was no longer an issue, since programs were executed on students' own CPUs. But for the very same reason could technical difficulties no longer be resolved server-side for students by staff. And some netbooks struggled under the weight of a VM.

For Fall 2012, then, we wanted to craft an alternative, not to replace the VM but to supplement it. Our objective was to provide students with a lighter-weight, web-based mechanism for trying out code, particularly in lectures and sections (i.e., recitations), where it's much faster to open a browser than boot a VM. The VM, meanwhile, would still be used by students for larger-scale projects that warrant a full-fledged command-line environment or GUI.

We did not wish to sacrifice C, though, for the sake of browser-based coding. Whereas languages like JavaScript and Python can be interpreted client-side using JavaScript itself [13, 16], compilers for languages like C are not so easily ported. Server-side execution of code would therefore be necessary.

Meanwhile, we faced an orthogonal problem. Over the years, the course has written a variety of scripts (e.g., in Perl and Python) with which the course's teaching fellows (TFs) could test the correctness of students' submissions. But those scripts were generally quite fragile, with unanticipated corner cases sometimes causing all tests to fail. Moreover, because the scripts were custom-written for specific assignments without any unifying framework, both writing and running them was rather laborious. The TFs, too, would generally run students' code under the TFs' own UIDs, and so there was always a risk of buggy or malicious code wreaking havoc in TFs' accounts. We've long wanted some form

SIGCSE'13, March 6–9, 2013, Denver, Colorado, USA.

of sandboxing for students' code, then, simple enough that TFs aren't disinclined to use it.

We thus set out to tackle both problems at once. In the sections that follow, we present our solution. CS50 Sandbox is our environment for secure execution of untrusted code. In Section 2, we present the design goals therefor. In Section 3, we present CS50 Sandbox's implementation details, including its front end (an HTTP-based API) and back end (a Linux-based cluster). In Section 4, meanwhile, we introduce CS50 Run, a web-based code editor built atop CS50 Sandbox that enables students to write code in a browser that's compiled and executed server-side. In Section 5, we introduce CS50 Check, an autograding framework built into CS50 Sandbox that enables students and instructors alike to assess the correctness of code. In Section 6, we present future work and conclude.

2. DESIGN GOALS

Even though CS50 happens to introduce students to C, along with PHP and JavaScript, we wanted our sandboxed environment to be language-agnostic so that courses besides ours could leverage the platform. Moreover, we needed it to withstand execution of buggy (if not adversarial) code, lest infinite loops or fork bombs throttle the system. And we wanted the environment to accommodate the course's style of homework, fairly complex programs that can often be designed in any number of ways, rather than have to alter the course's workload to accommodate technology. And so we set out with these design goals in mind:

- support interactive and non-interactive execution of programs written in any language, particularly those commonly used in introductory courses (e.g., C, C++, Java, JavaScript, OCaml, Perl, PHP, Python, Ruby, Scheme, et al.);
- support build tools like `ant` and `make`;
- support standard error, input, and output;
- limit consumption of CPU cycles, disk space, file descriptors, and RAM;
- restrict network access, both inbound and outbound;
- prevent reading and writing of unsandboxed files; and
- prevent denial-of-service attacks.

Before proceeding to implement, we vetted existing solutions. In the web-based space are ideone [14], codepad [15], CodeEval [2], and compilr [3], all of which support browser-based compilation and interpretation of code. But only the last supports interactive execution of programs, though it lacks an API. Even so, we would want more control over our environment than a third party would likely allow. In particular, we would want it to behave identically to our VM, with the same OS, binaries, and libraries installed on both, so that students' programs behave the same, no matter the context.

In the autograding space, related works abound [7–9], although many are now dated and don't support many languages. Most closely related is Web-CAT [1], perhaps the best known, but Web-CAT doesn't sandbox code to the degree that we sought. Nor does it support interactivity or clustering. Unit-testing frameworks also abound for C (and other languages), but none offer the simplicity that we wanted for the course's earliest projects especially. Autolab [5], meanwhile, is the closest incarnation of our own vision for sandboxing but isn't yet available as open source. It also spawns entire virtual machines for sandboxing tests, overhead that we wished to avoid.

3. IMPLEMENTATION DETAILS

At a high level, CS50 Sandbox is a web-based black box that allows for secure execution of untrusted code. Its inputs include files (e.g., `hello.c`), commands (e.g., `./a.out`), signals (e.g., `SIGINT`), and standard input. And its outputs include exit codes plus standard output and error.

CS50 Sandbox is not meant to be used by humans directly, as via a GUI. Rather, it accepts inputs via HTTP through API calls, and it returns outputs via HTTP as JSON objects [4]. Clients (e.g., CS50 Run, per Section 4) can issue those calls via Ajax (if sandboxing non-interactive programs) or via WebSocket [17] (if sandboxing interactive programs).

CS50 Sandbox is currently packaged for Red Hat-based systems (among them CentOS, Fedora, RHEL, and Scientific Linux) but could be ported to Debian-based systems as well. It is available as open source at
`http://cs.harvard.edu/malan/`.

3.1 Front End

CS50 Sandbox's front end is an HTTP-based API, among whose endpoints are `/upload` and `/run`.

3.1.1 /upload

To upload one or more files to the environment, a client need only POST them to `/upload` (as `multipart/form-data`). CS50 Sandbox's response will be a JSON object with two keys: `files`, whose value is an array of the filenames POSTed, and `id`, whose value is a unique identifier for the collection of files, per the below.

```
{
 "files": [String, ...]
 "id": String
}
```

3.1.2 /run

To execute a non-interactive command (e.g., `clang hello.c`) inside of CS50 Sandbox, a client need only POST to `/run` a JSON object with two keys: `cmd`, whose value is the command line to execute, and `sandbox`, whose value is a JSON object with one key, `homedir`, whose value is the unique identifier for a previously uploaded collection of files, per the below.

```
{
 "cmd": String,
 "sandbox": { homedir: String }
}
```

CS50 Sandbox will then copy those files into a temporary `$HOME`, in which `cmd` will be executed. Upon successful execution, the server will respond with a JSON object of the form

```
{
  "code": Number,
  "sandbox": String,
  "script": String,
  "stderr": String,
  "stdout": String
}
```

where `code` is the command's exit code, `sandbox` is a unique identifier for the temporary `$HOME` so that the client may execute subsequent commands (e.g., `./a.out`) in the same sandboxed environment, `script` is the command's terminal output (with standard error and standard output interwoven), `stderr` is the command's standard error, and `stdout` is the command's standard output

To execute an interactive command that expects standard input (e.g., `./a.out`) inside of CS50 Sandbox, a client can instead establish (or emulate, as with socket.io [12]) a WebSocket with CS50 Sandbox and emit a `run` event, whose payload is also a JSON object whose keys are, as before, `cmd` and `sandbox`. CS50 Sandbox will then execute `cmd`, emitting `stdout` and `stderr` events over the socket as standard output and error, respectively, are generated. CS50 Sandbox will also emit a `stdin` event when it detects that `cmd` is blocking for input so that the client knows to provide. Once `cmd` exits, CS50 Sandbox will emit an `exit` event, whose payload is an exit code plus standard output and error, along with a unique identifier for the `$HOME` used. A client can also interrupt `cmd` prematurely by emitting a `SIGINT` event.

3.2 Back End

Underneath the hood, CS50 Sandbox is an HTTP server written in JavaScript for Node.js [11], an open-source runtime built atop V8 [6] whose event-driven architecture is well-suited for handling asynchronous events (e.g., interactive standard I/O). Moreover, Node.js supports non-blocking I/O, which means that execution of one (slow-running) `cmd` won't block that of another. The architecture supports clustering, whereby CS50 Sandbox can be run on any number of load-balanced servers.

Upon receiving an HTTP request whose endpoint is `/upload`, CS50 Sandbox saves each file POSTed asynchronously to disk in a directory whose name serves as the unique identifier for that collection of files, which is then returned to the client.

Upon receiving an HTTP request whose endpoint is `/run` or a `run` event over a socket, CS50 Sandbox sets up a "sandbox," a temporary `$HOME` in which a `cmd` will be executed. It copies a collection of files (identified by an `id`) into that sandbox, creates a new user (whose username is also `id` and whose password is locked), and then assigns `$HOME` to that user. It then executes `cmd` on behalf of that user, via `sudo`. But it first wraps `cmd` with a call to `nice`, so as to prioritize its execution below the HTTP server itself. It also wraps `cmd` with a call to `seunshare`, which further confines `cmd` to the temporary `$HOME` (and its own `/tmp`) within an alternate "context," a feature of SELinux [10] that restricts processes' behavior, blocking access to `/etc/passwd`, `/proc`, and more. Finally, `cmd` is wrapped further with a call to `strace`, which allows CS50 Sandbox to detect writes on standard output and error (as well as reads on standard input).

So that `cmd` can only consume its fair share of resources, CS50 Sandbox imposes constraints using `pam_limits`, which caps processes' consumption of CPU cycles, disk space, file descriptors, RAM, and more on a per-user basis, ergo the creation of a user per sandbox. Meanwhile, `iptables` restricts network access. CS50 Sandbox's own HTTP server additionally monitors wall time, killing long-running processes (in addition to fork bombs).

Once `cmd` exits, CS50 Sandbox responds to the client and tears down the sandbox after waiting a few minutes for any subsequent `cmd`.

We happen to run CS50 Sandbox on Amazon EC2, using Amazon ELB for load-balancing and Amazon S3 for shared storage, but the environment can just as easily be run locally on one or more servers, using DNS or layer-3 alternatives for load-balancing and NFS or SMB for shared storage as needed. Indeed, the environment can be installed with a single command (`yum`).

4. CS50 Run

CS50 Run is a web-based code editor that lives at `https://run.cs50.net/`. Built atop CS50 Sandbox, CS50 Run enables students to write, within a browser, code in any language, execution of which happens server-side. Implemented in JavaScript, HTML, and CSS, CS50 Run leverages CS50 Sandbox's API to create an illusion that execution is local, even providing students with a terminal window in which they can not only see standard output and error but provide standard input as well. Via a drop-down can students select the language in which they wish to write code, each of which maps to a particular `cmd` (e.g., `clang` for C). Each `cmd` is executed automatically for students, based on that drop-down's selection, but each `cmd` is displayed in the illusory terminal window so that students can see exactly what's happening under the hood. Lines of code, meanwhile, are automatically numbered and syntax-highlighted. And via a button can students save revisions of their code, so that they can roll back in time and recover from crashes. Figure 1 depicts.

Not only does CS50 Run enable students to work on small programs in lectures and sections without booting a VM, it also empowers students to check their code's correctness instantly via integration with CS50 Check.

5. CS50 Check

CS50 Check is an autograding framework built into CS50 Sandbox that enables black- and white-box testing of students' code. Like CS50 Sandbox itself, its front end is an HTTP-based API. Its back end, meanwhile, comprises series of checks (i.e., tests) that are written in JavaScript (but can check the correctness of programs written in any compiled or interpreted language).

5.1 Front End

To run some program (i.e., `cmd`) through a series of checks, a client (e.g., CS50 Run, which itself uses CS50 Check to provide students with browser-based feedback) need only POST the program's file(s) to CS50 Sandbox via `/upload`, at which point it can then contact `/check`, CS50 Check's sole endpoint, to initiate testing.

5.1.1 /check

To run a series of (instructor-defined) checks against a previously uploaded collection files, a client need only POST to `/check` a JSON object of the following form, where `checks`

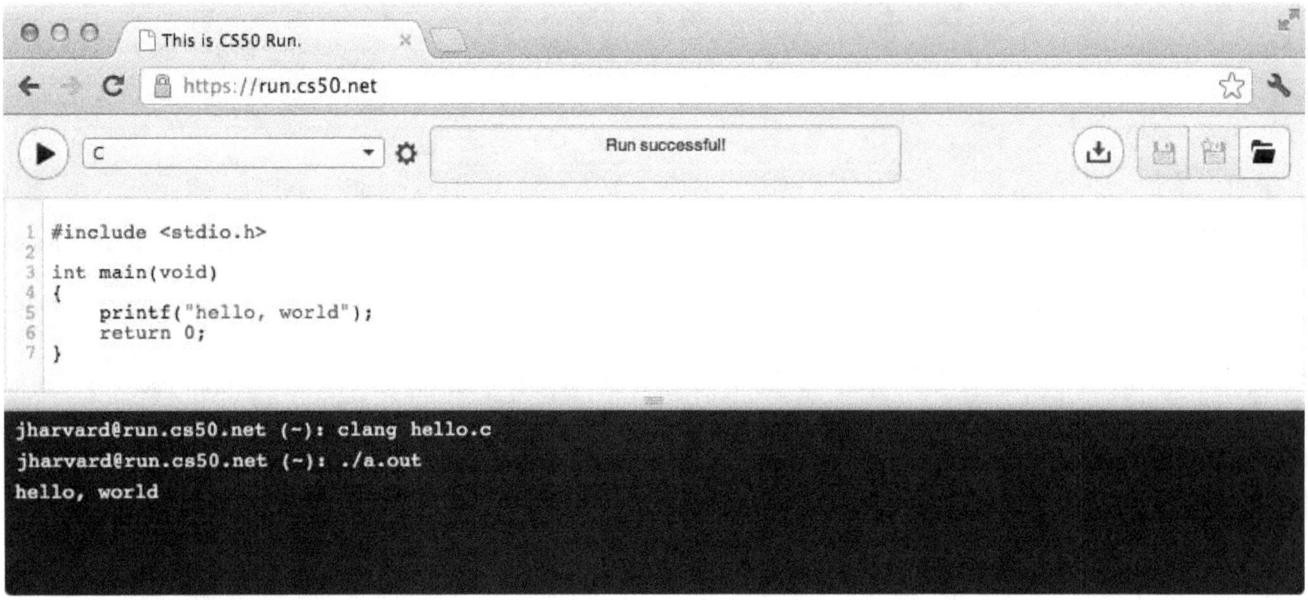

Figure 1: This is CS50 Run, a web-based code editor built atop CS50 Sandbox that enables students to write programs in any language within a browser.

is a unique identifier for the series of checks, and `sandbox` defines (as it also does for `/run`) a sandbox to use for the checks' execution, where `homedir` is the unique identifier for a previously uploaded directory of files, a copy of which will be mounted as `$HOME` for each of the checks in the series.

```
{
 "checks": String,
 "sandbox": { homedir: String }
}
```

Upon execution of checks, the server will return a JSON object of the form

```
{
 "results": Object
}
```

where `results` is an object, each of whose keys is the unique identifier for a check in the series, the value of which is an object of the form

```
{
 "dependencies": [String, ...],
 "description": String,
 "result": Boolean,
 "script": [Object, ...]
}
```

where `dependencies` is an array, each of whose elements is the unique identifier for another check on which the check depends, `description` is a human-friendly description of the check, `result` is either

- `true`, which signifies that the check passed,
- `null`, which signifies that the check was not executed because of a failed or erred dependency, or
- `false`, which signifies that the check failed,

and `script` is an array of objects, each of the form

```
{
 "actual": { type: String, value: String },
 "expected": { type: String, value: String }
}
```

where `expected` describes what was expected, and `actual` describes what actually occurred, if anything, up until the point when the check passed or failed. For instance, this response indicates that two checks (`compiles` and `runs`) passed:

```
{
 "results": {
  "compiles": {
   "dependencies": [],
   "description": "Does hello.c compile?",
   "result": true,
   "script": [Object, ...]
  },
  "runs": {
   "dependencies": [
    "compiles"
   ],
   "description": "Does a.out run?",
   "result": true,
   "script": [Object, ...]
  }
 }
}
```

By contrast, this response indicates that one check passed whereas another check failed (because of an unexpected exit code):

```
{
 "results": {
  "compiles": {
   "dependencies": [],
   "description": "Does hello.c compile?",
   "result": true,
   "script": [Object, ...]
  },
  "runs": {
   "dependencies": [
    "compiles"
   ],
   "description": "Does a.out exit with 0?",
   "result": false,
   "script": [
    ...,
    {
     "actual": {
      "type": "exit",
      "value": 1
     },
     "expected": {
      "type": "exit",
      "value": 0
     }
    }
   ]
  }
 }
}
```


Similarly does this response indicate that one check passed whereas another check failed (because of unexpected standard output):


```
{
 "results": {
  "compiles": {
   "dependencies": [],
   "description": "Does hello.c compile?",
   "result": true
  },
  "runs": {
   "dependencies": [
    "compiles"
   ],
   "description": "Does a.out print \"hello, world\"?",
   "result": false,
   "script": [
    ...,
    {
     "actual": {
      "type": "stdout",
      "value": "goodbye, world"
     },
     "expected": {
      "type": "stdout",
      "value": "hello, world"
     }
    }
   ]
  }
 }
}
```


And this response indicates that two checks failed, one of which wasn't even executed because of its dependency on the other:


```
{
 "results": {
  "compiles": {
   "dependencies": [],
   "description": "Does hello.c compile?",
   "result": false,
   "script": [
    ...,
    {
     "actual": {
      "type": "exit",
      "value": 1
     },
     "expected": {
      "type": "exit",
      "value": 0
     }
    }
   ]
  },
  "runs": {
   "dependencies": [
    "compiles"
   ],
   "description": "Does a.out run?",
   "result": null,
   "script": []
  }
 }
}
```


5.1.2 Back End

On the back end, series of checks are implemented in JavaScript as Node.js "modules," objects whose keys are checks' names, whose values are anonymous functions that return functional tests. Checks themselves are implemented as "chains," sequences of asynchronous methods, each of whose execution is delayed until its preceding sibling invokes a callback. These chains hide from instructors the underlying implementation details of asynchronous code, which is not always easy to write. After all, the objective of CS50 Check is to challenge students to pass checks, not instructors to write them! Below is a representative series of two checks, the first of which checks, by running `clang` (with `.run`, which runs a `cmd` in a sandbox), whether `hello.c` compiles with an exit code of 0, the second of which checks whether the resulting `a.out` says hello, as per the `RegExp` (which could alternatively be a `String` specifying a file on disk against which to compare standard output).

```
module.exports = {
 "compiles": function(check) {
  return check("Does hello.c compile?")
  .run("clang hello.c")
  .exit(0);
 },
 "runs": ["compiles", function(check) {
  return check("Does a.out print \"hello, world\"?")
  .run("./a.out")
  .stdout(/^hello, world$/)
  .exit(0);
 }
};
```

CS50 Check includes support for other "links" in checks' chains as well, including `.diff` (which compares two files for differences), `.exists` (which checks whether a file exists), `.stderr` (which checks students' standard error against a `RegExp` or file), and `stdin` (which checks whether a program is blocking for standard input).

CS50 Check also supports specification of dependencies. Indeed, in the above, the value of `runs` is actually an array, the first of whose values is `"compiles"`, which prescribes that the second check should be executed only if the first of the two passes.

6. FUTURE WORK, CONCLUSION

CS50 Sandbox is an environment for secure execution of untrusted code that we designed underneath both CS50 Run, a web-based code editor that enables students to write code in any compiled or interpreted language, and CS50 Check, an autograding framework that enables students and instructors alike to assess the correctness of code.

In Fall 2012, we will deploy CS50 Sandbox not only to our own undergraduates but to as many as 120,000 edX students as well. Coupled with CS50 Run and CS50 Check, CS50 Sandbox will ultimately enable students to work on problems within browsers during lectures and sections, without the need for client-side VMs. Moreover, it will enable us to embed alongside curricular materials real-time coding exercises on which students will receive instant feedback.

So that the infrastructure scales dynamically with load, we may eventually utilize Amazon Auto Scaling, which will allow us to define thresholds for load, beyond which additional servers will be spawned automatically. We anticipate adversarial attacks on the system, and so we plan to harden the system over time as we detect weaknesses. In particular, we expect to write our own SELinux policy with which to confine each `cmd` all the more. We plan, too, to augment CS50 Check's pool of methods to support measurement of resources consumed during runtime (e.g., CPU cycles and RAM).

Meanwhile, we expect that the thousands of submissions that CS50 Sandbox will collect over time will yield insights into the process by which students write code and respond to continual feedback.

7. ACKNOWLEDGMENTS

Many thanks to Dan Walsh of RedHat and to Glenn Holloway, Joseph Ong, Mike Tucker, Nate Hardison, Rob Bowden, and Tommy MacWilliam of Harvard for their assistance with this work.

8. REFERENCES

[1] Anuj R. Shah. Web-CAT: A Web-based Center for Automated Testing. Master's thesis, Virginia Polytechnic Institute and State University, 2003.

[2] CodeEval Inc. CodeEval. http://www.codeeval.com/.

[3] Compilr Inc. compilr. https://compilr.com/.

[4] D. Crockford. The application/json Media Type for JavaScript Object Notation (JSON). http://www.ietf.org/rfc/rfc4627.txt?number=4627.

[5] Dave O'Hallaron et al. Autolab. http://autolab.cs.cmu.edu/.

[6] Google Inc. V8 JavaScript Engine. http://code.google.com/p/v8/.

[7] J. A. Harris, E. S. Adams, and N. L. Harris. Making program grading easier: but not totally automatic. *J. Comput. Sci. Coll.*, 20(1):248–261, Oct. 2004.

[8] D. Jackson. A semi-automated approach to online assessment. In *Proceedings of the 5th annual SIGCSE/SIGCUE ITiCSE conference on Innovation and technology in computer science education*, ITiCSE '00, pages 164–167, New York, NY, USA, 2000. ACM.

[9] D. Jackson and M. Usher. Grading student programs using assyst. In *Proceedings of the twenty-eighth SIGCSE technical symposium on Computer science education*, SIGCSE '97, pages 335–339, New York, NY, USA, 1997. ACM.

[10] James Morris. SELinux Project Wiki. http://selinuxproject.org/.

[11] Joyent, Inc. Node.js. http://nodejs.org/.

[12] LearnBoost, Inc. Socket.IO. http://socket.io/.

[13] Scott Graham. Skulpt. http://www.skulpt.org/.

[14] Sphere Research Labs. ideone. http://ideone.com/.

[15] Steven Hazel. codepad. http://codepad.org/.

[16] Syntensity. Python on the Web. http://syntensity.com/static/python.html.

[17] World Wide Web Consortium. The WebSocket API. http://dev.w3.org/html5/websockets/.

Cloud Computing in the Curriculum: Fundamental and Enabling Technologies

Charles Border
Department of Information Science and Technologies
Rochester Institute of Technology
Rochester, NY 14623, U.S.A.
cbbics@rit.edu

ABSTRACT

Cloud computing is a new buzzword for a group of old technologies that have been integrated to create a system that is more than the sum of its parts. After teaching a seminar in cloud computing three times over the last year I have gained a better understanding of the fundamental and enabling technologies that should be brought into our curriculum to facilitate our students becoming competent users of cloud computing. Developing and deploying an application on a cloud architecture appears very similar to working with any remotely accessible server architecture but to work with it effectively our students need to understand the following technologies: firewalls, addressing and sub-netting, encryption, scripting, storage architectures, and virtualization. There are several enabling technologies that make the cloud more than just the sum of its parts. Some of the most important enabling technologies include: segregation of services and multi-systems architectures, workload characterization, identity federation, load balancing, and content distribution networks.

Categories and Subject Descriptors

K.3.2 [Computers and Education]: Computer and Information Science Education- Computer science education, curriculum

Keywords

Cloud computing, virtualization, curriculum, load balancing, multi-system, workload characterization

1. INTRODUCTION

Cloud computing is a new buzzword for a group of old technologies that have been integrated to create a system that is more than the sum of its parts. After teaching a seminar on cloud computing three times over the last year I have gained a better understanding of the technologies involved, what is new and deserves to be brought into the curriculum and what is already in the curriculum and does covers what needs to be said. To be clear much about the cloud is very familiar as in many ways it appears to a user just like any other remotely accessible server. So, how does deploying a service in the cloud differ from deploying that same service in a private architecture and by extension what do we need to teach our students to make them competent users of public and private clouds? In many ways we do not have to change what we teach, but we do need to recognize that teaching our students to marshal the incredible resources that are at our fingertips in the cloud requires that we understand the fundamentals of deploying services, and also the retooled set of options that can be used to create global applications.

This paper is not so much about the cloud as about the cloud in our curriculum and will be based on my experiences teaching this seminar using the Amazon Web Services (AWS) Infrastructure As A Service (IAAS) Cloud and my thoughts on the impact of cloud computing on the CS curriculum.

SIGCSE'13, March 6–9, 2013, Denver, Colorado, USA.

2. PERSPECTIVES ON THE CLOUD

There are two distinct perspectives on the cloud, either you are a user of someone else's public/private cloud, or you are the provider of cloud services to others on a public or private basis. While it is tempting to think that we need to teach all our students to be builders of clouds and providers of cloud services and other authors have taken this approach to the cloud [Wang], this in many ways ignores one of the fundamental facts about the cloud. The cloud is built around the idea that a small number of people can develop scripts that can control a huge number of servers and that these servers can be managed and deployed by outsiders to the organization that owns them. The reason this is so important is that it argues against the existence of a large number of independent clouds and the need for large numbers of people to build and maintain them. We are clearly in the early days of cloud computing so it is natural to expect an overbuilding of capacity followed by a severe competition for dominance in the industry and a subsequent shakedown of cloud service providers. After the dust settles, if it ever does, there will remain a small number of very well funded CSPs.

From the users perspective this process will be inconvenient and somewhat tumultuous, but will leave the best CSPs as the last ones standing and providing a very high level of service to the many users of their services. From a curricular perspective this argument is very persuasive in its pointing to concentrating our curriculum on educating students to be competent users of clouds rather than builders and deployers of clouds.

To make our students competent users of the cloud we need to modify our curriculum to include two groups of technologies. Those technologies that are best described as fundamental technologies and services including firewalling technologies, the basics of networking, and network services, encryption, scripting, storage architectures, and virtualization. We also need to include a discussion of a set of enabling technologies that, while not new, are very important in making the cloud a more useful architecture for service deployment including, segregation of services and multi-server systems architectures, workload characterization, identity federation, load balancing, and content distribution networks. Finally, for our students to fully appreciate the power of the cloud they need to understand its application in two very important domains, big data analytics using Hadoop and map reduce, and the use of the cloud as a platform for global application deployment.

3. FUNDAMENTAL TECHNOLOGIES AND SERVICES

Deploying a service in the cloud involves working with some of the fundamental network services that we are used to working with, but in a slightly different way.

3.1 Firewalls

In a physical environment firewalls are usually deployed on the perimeter of the network with the goal of stopping traffic using unauthorized protocols and ports that originates on the Internet from gaining ingress to the network. While this is effective in mitigating malicious attacks that originate from an outsider, it does little to police the activities of malicious insiders. The concept of using ports and protocols to police traffic is also used in the cloud. The complicating factor that we do not face in a physical environment involves the fact that services deployed in a public cloud are located outside the periphery of the organization's network but might be expected to operate as though they were located inside the periphery. To allow servers in the cloud to operate as though they were located inside the network periphery firewalls can be established on each individual server that block all traffic not meeting the firewall rule set. As part of deploying an AWS server you are required to designate the server as a member of a security group. Security groups function much like firewall rule sets and allow you to select the ports, protocols and source and destination IP addresses or ranges of IP addresses that can be used to access the deployed server.

3.2 Addressing and Sub-netting

In a physical network environment it is common practice to use sub-netting to create a single point of ingress and egress to a subnet by deploying a service as part of a subnet. This has the effect of allowing members of the subnet to quickly find the service and establish a connection to the service without going through any intermediary connectivity devices while preventing those who are not in the subnet from accessing the service without passing through a designated connectivity device such as a router. The router thus becomes a convenient point of traffic monitoring, filtering and blocking. In the cloud this concept is also used, but it is harder to "see". The AWS cloud allows you to deploy servers as members of a "Virtual Private Cloud (VPC)". By deploying servers in a VPC the user tells AWS to establish a private address space within the AWS cloud whose points of ingress and egress can be connected to a Virtual Private Network (VPN) and easily controlled.

3.3 Encryption

One of the chief concerns most users have about the cloud relates to the security of their data as it traverses the Internet to and from the cloud, is processed on cloud based servers, and as it is stored in cloud based storage architectures. This is a valid concern that is primarily addressed through the use of encryption. Encrypted tunnels can be set up between the user's network and the cloud to make sure that traffic between the user's network and the cloud cannot be intercepted in a man-in-the-middle attack. Data can also be stored in cloud based storage arrays in a wholly encrypted fashion. At the moment it is very difficult to process encrypted data. If an organization wants to use the cloud to process data it must first be decrypted before it can be processed after which it can be stored once again in an encrypted fashion. Developing a way to process encrypted data is an on-going research project for many people in the mathematics and computing areas.

3.4 Scripting

There are two ways to access and manage the AWS cloud, through a web based front end based at aws.amazon.com, or programmatically through the use of Software Development Kits that are available for the following languages and platforms: Android, IOS, Java, .NET, PHP, and Ruby. There is a wide range of sample code, libraries, documentation, templates, sample applications, and tools available that provide a very real alternative for monitoring and managing multi-system cloud based architectures programmatically rather than using the web based front end.

3.5 Storage Architectures

The storage architecture behind AWS is truly vast, very complex, and the source of much of the angst around the deployment of services on the AWS cloud by organizations both large and small. The problem lies in the idea that the replication technology that makes the architecture useful at the same time makes it very scary. While organizations want to have their cloud based data replicated throughout the AWS cloud to ensure that the data survives the failure of one or more AWS datacenters, they also are accustomed to the comfort that comes from knowing where their data is stored and what needs to be done to destroy the data when it reaches the end of its useful life. It is hard to have both, and the AWS model is based on the idea that data needs to be protected from inadvertent deletion and the failure of one or more datacenters through replication.

3.6 Virtualization

While it is possible to lease an entire physical server from most CSPs, this is not the typical use of the cloud. Typically in a public or private cloud the flexibility and better alignment of cost with load comes from the CSP's ability to distribute the overall workload to particular servers on a mix and match basis implemented at their discretion. The net result of this is that the user has little control over what physical server is used to run their workload and who they share this physical server with and virtualization is the key to making this happen. From a security perspective there have been few if any successful attacks on the industry standard hypervisors that allow multiple virtual servers/users to share one physical server. The discomfort that organizations feel about the situation where they share a physical server with anyone who has a credit card remains and the prospect of this changing in the future is not good. The compliance organizations to which many organizations must report are also uncomfortable with this situation and have been slow to issue guidelines around in-scope data being processed and stored in the cloud.

4. ENABLING TECHNOLOGIES

The cloud is more than just a whole bunch of remotely accessible servers. There are a small number of technologies that make the synergy of the cloud possible that our students need to know about. Below I will introduce these technologies and give a short overview of each as they relate to the cloud.

4.1 Segregation of Services and Multi-Systems Architecture

In a physical environment it is sometimes difficult to create multi-server systems, in the cloud this is the normal course of events. While it is possible to create a single server web hosting environment in the cloud, with a few additions you can create a multi-tier web hosting environment that includes the tools that make that environment elastic so that it can grow and shrink in response to changes in load (as defined by the user). The technologies involved with this capability are not particularly revolutionary; using load balancers to spread the traffic between hosts; a consistent storage environment to house system images that are used as the basis for additional hosts; and virtualization to allow system images to move from host-to-host; what is interesting about this is that they are all integrated into the AWS architecture and configurable both from the command line and a web interface in a fairly easy and logical fashion. There are extensive amounts of reference architecture documentation available on the AWS site (http://aws.amazon.com/architecture/) that both illustrate and describe systems architectures for many popular applications. The key concept that pervades all the reference architectures is segregating services between multiple virtual servers so that a single virtual server does a single task. A reason why this is so attractive is that when this concept is combined with the presence of firewalls (security groups in AWS speak) on each individual server, a clear delineation of the type of traffic that should be entering and exiting a server can be defined and enforced.

4.2 Workload Characterization

From a teaching perspective our students need to understand the way that broad classes of applications work so that they can understand what needs to happen when the load on a application changes over time. This again is not a new technology. Workload characterization has been a topic of computing research for a long time. What is different is that in the past the workload generated by an application changed relatively slowly and the process of matching that workload with appropriate resources could be a fairly leisurely activity by today's standards. In the world of the Internet applications can see their workload spike very quickly as they receive favorable notice from an influential site (the slash-dot effect is a well known example of how workloads can spike on a web site after its content has been recommended on the Slashdot web site http://slashdot.org).

What our students need to know to be effective in managing the incredible resources that the cloud makes available to them is how our application servers respond to an change in workload? What are the options available to them to respond to the Slashdot effect in real time? Once again this is not a new topic in the computing profession. Practitioners and academics have studied workload characterization for a very long time and the predominance of multi-tiered web applications as a baseline architecture for many seemingly divergent applications makes this area easier to understand.

4.3 Identity Federation

Identity federation is not a new technology or area of interest, but it has taken on renewed importance in the cloud as the cloud becomes a place for organizations to work together on common projects. Organizations can share identities in many ways in the cloud. This can run the gamut of anything from encrypted tunnels into cloud based applications using VPNs or SSH to establishing new identities for users of specific cloud applications. For our students it is important that they have a basis to understand the importance of identity and the set of ideas around this issue.

4.4 Load Balancing

One of the key capabilities that the cloud brings to hosting modern applications is the ability to create elastic applications that can change in scope and scale in response to changes in load. The technology that makes much of this possible is load balancing. Once again this is not a new technology, what makes it so powerful in the cloud is its ease of implementation and deep integration into the architecture. In the cloud it is relatively easy to assemble an architecture that relies on a set of load balancing nodes to keep track of changes in load on the system and respond to those changes by either spawning new instances of operating systems located at the datacenter closest to the origin of the traffic (if your web application becomes popular in Japan instances could be spawned at the Tokyo AWS datacenter rather than in Northern Virginia). The method by which this is implemented relies on changing DNS records to pint incoming traffic to the least busy server. The metrics by which you determine which machine is busier than the next are entirely up to the user. Students can implement this technology in their cloud based application with little understanding of the underlying mechanisms by which it works, but this is an important technology in the cloud and would make a very good subject to bring into our curriculum.

4.5 Content Distribution Networks

Closely coupled to the technologies around load balancing are those around content distribution networks (CDNs). CDNs allow users to access content from servers located more closely to them while maintaining a connection to the home content for that information that must be consistent across the entire set of users. The best example of this type of architecture is an e-commerce site that uses large graphics files to let users around the world see pictures of the merchandise that is for sale while relying on a central database to maintain consistent inventory information. Users in Japan would access a version of the site cached on web servers located in Tokyo for images of the merchandise but would rely on a connection back to the main database located in the US for relevant inventory numbers.

The ease with which this is implemented and integrated with other technologies in the cloud makes the cloud a great place to deploy global applications. When content distribution networks are combined with load balancing assembling a multi-system architecture that turns a local web site or other application into an application that can serve customers or users around the world becomes much easier and economical. CDNs become a key technology in the context of the cloud. Understanding the protocols by which they are created and the interconnections that they require is a valid topic for our curriculum and would make our students better users of the cloud.

4.6 Big Data Analytics

Another important technology that fits well into the capabilities of the cloud is big data analytics. One of the things that the internet is very good at is the generation of very large log files and many organizations would like to be able to gain some business intelligence from the analysis of these files. The problem is that while the analysis of these large files is not conceptually very difficult, finding and harnessing the computing infrastructure to analyze these often embarrassing parallel files can be difficult and very costly. The cloud with its flexible usage based pricing model and high speed interconnection of both compute nodes and storage arrays provides a perfect architecture for this application. AWS has developed its own implementation of Google's MapReduce and Google File System technologies that they call Elastic Map Reduce and deployed that as Amazon Machine Images (AMIs) in the AWS environment. Users can either upload their data to the nearest AWS datacenter (or more likely with large files ship it on standard formatted hard disks) and then use some standard technologies and as many servers as necessary to conduct their analysis. This is not just a popular application for large web implementations. It is also very useful for the analysis of some big science questions in areas such as genomics, and high energy physics. The technology used to implement this capability is not very new, as with the other technologies discussed previously it is the deep integration of the technology into the overall cloud architecture that makes this such an important topic for our students to understand and use.

5. RELATED WORK

Although much has been written about how to integrate new technology into the curriculum very little has been written about the integration of cloud computing in the curriculum. Wang takes the perspective of teaching students about the cloud by having them build a cloud based on open source technologies [4]. While this is an interesting assignment for students it is very capital intensive and would be hard to support with larger classes over the long-term. The goal of this paper was to describe the long-term impact of the needs of our students to be skilled users of the existing public and private clouds. Yuan takes another tack on the integration of cloud computing into the curriculum [5]. He discusses a project where he and his co-authors used a local private cloud to host the applications used to run an IP telephony class. Radenski looks at the use of a computing cloud as the basis to teach a data-intensive high performance computing class [3]. Cappos described his work with the "Seattle" community cloud computing platform to create a platform for student's work and research [1]. Seattle, as described by Cappos, allows many educational organizations to loan computing power to others to create a grid that can support many pedagogical uses. Hollingsworth discusses changes that were made at Elon University to the core of their computer science curriculum to better support the need of their students to understand web and mobile computing and their integration with the cloud [2]. The goal of the seminar which was the basis for my thoughts contained in this paper was a more general purpose use of the cloud. While it is important for our students to understand these different sides of the cloud and it is laudable that the above authors used the cloud in the way that they did it is the goal of this paper to look beyond these special use cases to present the underlying technologies of a platform that will have a big impact on our students for a long time to come.

6. CONCLUSION

The strength of the cloud does not come from single server implementations or relying on a single technology to get a standard job done, it comes from the building block fashion in which multiple services can be deployed on multi-server architectures located in datacenters around the world to create global applications for the internet. The technologies involved are not by themselves revolutionary, or even new, in many cases, it is the deep integration of the technologies into the overall structure of the cloud and the speed and dexterity with which they can combined that makes the cloud such an important technology for our students to understand. Do we need to radically revise our curriculum to make our students competent users of the cloud? No, but we do need to revise and rethink the way that we think about applications and their deployment in the world of the cloud.

7. REFERENCES

[1] J. Cappos, I Beschastnikh, A. Krishnamurthy, T. Anderson, "Seattle: A Platform for Educational Cloud Computing," *SIGCSE'09,* 2009.

[2] J. Hollingsworth, D. Powell: "Requiring Web-based Cloud and Mobile Computing in a Computer Science Undergraduate Curriculum," 49th ACM Southeast Conference, 2011.

[3] A. Radenski, "Integrating Data-Intensive Cloud Computing with Multicores and Clusters inan HPC Course," ITiCSE'12, 2012.

[4] X. Wang, G. Hembroff, A. Cerier, B. Perrault, "Introducing Cloud Computing with a Senior Design Project in Undergraduate Education of Computer System and Network Administration," SIGITE'11, 2011.

[5] D. Yuan, C. Lewandowski, J. Zhong, "Developing IP Telephony Laboratory and Curriculum with Private Cloud Computing," SIGITE'11, 2011.

Characterizing the Need for Graduate Ethics Education

Scott Dexter
Dept. of Computer & Information Science
Brooklyn College
2900 Bedford Avenue
Brooklyn, NY 11210
+1-718-951-5657
sdexter@brooklyn.cuny.edu

Elizabeth Buchanan   Kellen Dins
Center for Applied Ethics
University of Wisconsin-Stout
PO Box 790
Menomonie, WI 54751
+1-715-232-5184
buchanane@uwstout.edu
dinsk4020@my.uwstout.edu

Kenneth R. Fleischmann
School of Information
University of Texas at Austin
1616 Guadalupe Suite #5.202
Austin, TX 78701-1213
+1-512-471-8291
kfleisch@ischool.utexas.edu

Keith Miller
Dept. of Computer Science
University of Illinois Springfield
One University Plaza, UHB 3100
Springfield, IL 62703
+1-217-206-7327
miller.keith@uis.edu

ABSTRACT
We report on some initial findings of an investigation into current practices in, and the need for, information/computer ethics curricula at the graduate level. We give some results and analysis from a survey of faculty and graduate students at four diverse U.S. institutions. Faculty and students agree that students will face professional ethical challenges after graduation, but assessment of students' preparedness for these challenges differs widely across the surveyed institutions. A clear majority of faculty and students expressed support for an elective graduate-level ethics course, and roughly half supported a required graduate-level ethics course.

Categories and Subject Descriptors
K.3.2 [**Computers and Education**]: Computer and Information Science Education – *computer science education.* K.7.4 [**The Computing Profession**]: Professional Ethics

Keywords
Computer ethics, professionalization, graduate education, pedagogy

1. INTRODUCTION
Are computing professionals adequately prepared for the ethical challenges they will face in an increasingly global and interdisciplinary workplace? In this paper, we report on research undertaken to characterize the state of, and need for, ethics education at the graduate level. We take the category of computing professionals to include not only those generally understood as computer scientists, software engineers, and so on, but also those trained in library and/or information science.

SIGCSE'13, March 6–9, 2013, Denver, Colorado, USA.

We focus on graduate (specifically, master's-level) education for a number of reasons. First, it is under-studied and under-discussed, particularly within computer science: both the ACM and IEEE have curricular recommendations pertaining to ethics at the undergraduate level, but neither ACM or IEEE-CS have published any such advice at the graduate level. (The American Library Association, however, has recently included ethics in its curricular standards for accredited master's programs.) Second, for some students, the master's level is the first time they encounter any formal computing content whatsoever; it is nearly as fundamental a period as an undergraduate computing major, and thus no less in need of an ethically-inflected foundation. Finally, because master's students generally have specific professional aspirations, the master's level is a particularly good moment for studying an alignment with the needs of the computing professions, and the need for a commitment to professional ethics.

Computing disciplines continue to grow increasingly complex and methodologically diverse. Changes in technology always introduce new possibilities as well as a range of ethical and social challenges. Globalization juxtaposes multiple cultures, legal systems, and work environments even as projects and work groups become larger and geographically scattered. Inherently multidisciplinary problems engage computer scientists outside traditional boundaries of disciplines, departments, and professions. These new challenges raise interesting questions about ethics education for graduate students in computing. Has computer ethics education kept pace with these changes? How can better ethics education in the computing professions promote better science, broadly conceived? How do computer professionals, particularly those working across a range of disciplines and across geographic borders, learn ethics in and for their professions? What effect does the globalization of computing have on ethical theory and practice? How might scientists and engineers work more effectively and more ethically across cultures in increasingly interconnected, global scientific communities? Our research begins to explore these and related questions.

This study unfolds in the context of a surprising dearth of literature on graduate-level information/computing ethics education. Discussion of pedagogical and curricular matters as they pertain to undergraduate CS/IT programs are plentiful, and suggest that social, professional, and ethical issues have achieved a high degree of penetration in undergraduate curricula (for example, see [4]). But even works which discuss the importance of "professional ethics" focus exclusively (as far as we can tell) on the undergraduate context (for example, [5], [7], and [9]); though Stoodley et al [8] proposes a broad framework for "influencing IT professionals to adopt ethically mature practice," (p. 379) which might in principle be adopted at any level of the curriculum, as well as by "industry leaders" and "individual professionals" (p. 380). Davis et al. [1] report on an investigation of the effectiveness of "micro-insertions, that is, small-scale insertions of ethics instruction into technical courses" (p. 25) in graduate level engineering courses, specifically in a "nanotechnology lab because . . . students' engagement with practical projects in an emerging technology should provide illuminatingly new micro-insertion problems, useful questions related to them, and useful insights" (p. 26). A similar approach might be effective in graduate information/computing pedagogy, but we are unaware of published discussions of this nature. Thus, while there has been some study of computing/information ethics education as well as some study of graduate-level engineering ethics education, there is a relative lacuna around the study of graduate-level computing ethics education.

2. PROJECT DESIGN

In the first phase of our study, we carried out web-based surveys and face-to-face focus groups with faculty and master's students at four diverse public institutions. Our intent was to begin to understand the goals for and strategies used in graduate computing ethics education at these sites, as well as something of the ethical issues under discussion and the pedagogical approaches and materials used.

The four institutions differ both in their demographics and in the ways that ethics relate to curricula.

The University of Illinois Springfield (UIS) is an award-winning developer of quality online education; the online "Graduate Research Seminar" offered by the Computer Science Department includes an emphasis on ethics organized around the Software Engineering Code of Ethics and Practice, and the department offers an elective stand-alone computer ethics course. **Undergraduate . . .**

At the University of Maryland (UMD), a high-activity research university, the College of Information Studies (the only Information/Library program in the study) offers three professional degrees: Master of Library Science, Master of Information Management, and Master of Science in Human–Computer Interaction. The College offers an elective ethics course designed by the third author with support from the NSF's Ethics Education in Science and Engineering program (described in [3]). The College has no undergraduate program.

At the University of Wisconsin-Stout (UWS), a rural master's-granting polytechnic university, the Department of Mathematics, Statistics and Computer Science and the Department of Information and Communication Technology are the study sites; neither department has a stand-alone ethics course, but the institution has a strong commitment to ethics education across its polytechnic focus, with a Mission which includes, "preparing lifelong learners and ethical leaders." In particular, the campus has an Ethical Reasoning and Social Responsibility general education requirement, so all undergraduate students have exposure to ethics curricula. In addition, all faculty are encouraged to bring ethics into their specific program or discipline; an Ethics and IT course was introduced recently.

Finally, at Brooklyn College (BC), an urban nonresidential master's-granting liberal arts college in Brooklyn, NY, our study site is the Department of Computer and Information Science, which has a required stand-alone ethics course—cross-listed with the Philosophy department, and fulfilling the College's writing-intensive requirement—for the undergraduate computer science major but no explicit curricular commitment to ethics at the graduate level.

Below, we report on selected results from the surveys; future reports will include more in-depth analysis based on qualitative results from the analysis of focus groups as well as from the next phase of our study, a survey of professionals affiliated with ACM and IEEE which will characterize the need for ethics education from the perspective of the workplace and of professional societies.

3. SELECTED SURVEY RESULTS

The student survey was administered to 924 students at the four institutions; 249 responded for an overall response rate of 27%. Institutional response rates varied from 16% to 32%. The faculty survey was administered to 167 faculty members at computer and information science departments of the four institutions; 55 responded for an overall response rate of 33%. Institutional response rates varied from 22% to 69%. See Table 1.

Table 1: Survey response rates

	Total	UIS	UMD	UWS	BC
Students	249 (29%)	89 (32%)	115 (27%)	20 (30%)	25 (16%)
Faculty	55 (33%)	11 (69%)	15 (44%)	13 (33%)	16 (22%)

The student surveys focused on the students' exposure to ethical concepts in their prior education and during their current studies, as well as their expectations about the significance of ethical issues in their profession/workplace. Additionally, the survey asks for students' perspective on the pedagogies to which they have been exposed in the teaching of ethics. Faculty were asked, similarly, about their experiences and techniques teaching ethics, as well as their expectations for their students' professional experiences.

While faculty response was low in an absolute sense, sometimes limiting the power of statistical analysis, we believe the responses are generally representative and are unlikely to suffer from significant self-selection bias. Faculty responses from relatively high-responding institutions (UIS and UMD) were often notably dissimilar (see, for example, Table 5 and Table 6). Responses from BC, the lowest-responding institution, were not wildly out of line with responses from the other institutions, with the possible exception of faculty assessment of student preparation for ethical challenges post-graduation.

3.1 Student Age

The mean age of all respondents was 32.19 years, ranging from 30.55 for University of Maryland to 36.73 for UW-Stout. The maturity of these students illustrates why the more copious research results for undergraduate students and professional ethics are not always directly applicable to graduate students. The graduate students are at a different stage of life than a traditional undergraduate, and this is likely to affect their approach to ethics.

3.2 Students' Exposure to Ethics

As Table 2 shows, students generally believe themselves to be familiar with ethics (as measured by their agreement with the statement, "I understand what information/computer ethics is"), even though they may not have encountered the subject in formal academic circumstances.

Table 2: Students' familiarity with and academic exposure to computer/information ethics

	All	UIS	UMD	UWS	BC
Understand ethics	223 (90%)	84 (94%)	98 (85%)	17 (85%)	24 (96%)
Undergrad Exposure	78 (31%)	37 (42%)	25 (22%)	7 (35%)	9 (36%)
Graduate Exposure	131 (59%)	44 (51%)	78 (77%)	6 (35%)	3 (17%)

While nearly 60% of students reported that they had been exposed to ethics in their graduate degree studies, only 9% of students overall reported having taken a required ethics course in their current program, and 18% reported having taken an elective course.

About 45% of students indicated they had read a professional code of ethics as part of their graduate studies (Table 3). Those who had were asked to name the code they had read. 21% named the IEEE; 19% named the ACM (the joint ACM/IEEE-CS code was published as [5]); 24% (all at Maryland) named the American Library Association Code of Ethics [1]. Some of the students taking the survey at UIS had not yet encountered a code, but later in the semester did; that was not reflected in these figures but was reported to an investigator in this study.

Table 3: Students' exposure to professional codes of ethics

	All	UIS	UMD	UWS	BC
I have read a code of ethics	102 (45%)	28 (33%)	66 (65%)	6 (33%)	2 (10%)

3.3 Student Notions of Ethics

We also asked students to give a definition of ethics; we then classified their responses into themes. The most frequently cited theme was *Doing Right* (20.08%). *Morality* was the second most frequently cited theme at (9.64%). Other themes included *Decision-Making* (8.84%), *Code of Conduct* (6.43%), *Common Good* (6.02%) and *Religion* (1.61%). The classification of *Other* (8.43%) were comments that seemed unrelated to the other themes, and to each other.

In addition, we gave students the opportunity to provide an example of a *major ethical issue* they see in their profession. Thematically, the most commonly invoked issue was *Collecting and Storage of Personal Data*, with 11.24% of the students naming an example related to that theme. The second most frequent theme overall was concerns with *Copyright Infringement vs. Fair Use* (9%). Other responses were categorized as *Business Concerns* (7.63%), *Access to Information* (6.02%), *Piracy* (4.02%), *Plagiarism* (2.41%), and *Licensing* (2.01%).

In both these free-form questions, individual responses are interesting in themselves. Data and responses are available upon request.

3.4 Students' Professional Preparation

As Table 4 shows, students and faculty strongly agree that our students will face ethical challenges in their professional lives. However, there is a wide disparity in opinion about how well these students are actually prepared for these challenges, with 82% of students believing they are prepared, but only 33% of faculty agreeing (see Table 5). Interestingly, Maryland students are most pessimistic and Maryland faculty are most optimistic.

Table 4: Students will face professional ethical challenges after graduation

	All	UIS	UMD	UWS	BC
Students Agree	195 (97%)	71 (95%)	93 (99%)	17 (95%)	14 (93%)
Faculty Agree	53 (100%)	11 (100%)	14 (100%)	13 (100%)	15 (100%)

Table 5: I/my students are prepared for professional ethical challenges after graduation

	All	UIS	UMD	UWS	BC
Students Agree	166 (82%)	71 (92%)	69 (74%)	14 (82%)	12 (80%)
Faculty Agree	17 (33%)	4 (36%)	8 (57%)	5 (45%)	0 (0%)

3.5 Support for graduate ethics course

Surveyed faculty (Table 6) and students (Table 7) were well-aligned in their support for a graduate ethics course. About half the faculty and students agreed that "all students seeking Master's degrees in information/computer sciences should have a required ethics course;" this ratio rose to three-quarters for an elective ethics course.

Table 6: Faculty support for a graduate ethics course

	All	UIS	UMD	UWS	BC
Required	27 (49%)	8 (72%)	6 (40%)	9 (69%)	4 (25%)
Elective	40 (72%)	7 (63%)	13 (87%)	10 (77%)	10 (63%)

Table 7: Student support for a graduate ethics course

	All	UIS	UMD	UWS	BC
Required	128 (52%)	42 (47%)	63 (55%)	13 (65%)	10 (40%)
Elective	181 (73%)	65 (72%)	87 (77%)	12 (60%)	17 (68%)

3.6 Student Gender

We have not yet studied second order statistics associated with these surveys. However, a few results seem intriguing even at this early stage. For example, female students and male students differed in their responses to several questions, as shown in Table 8: Male and Female Student Agreement with 3 StatementsTable 8.

Table 8: Male and Female Student Agreement with 3 Statements

	Females Agreeing	Males Agreeing
I understand what information/ computer ethics is.	77 (87%)	98 (93%)
I will experience ethical challenges in my profession when I graduate.	85 (98%)	99 (95%)
I am prepared for ethical challenges in my profession when I graduate.	67 (78%)	90 (86%)

Male and female students agree (almost unanimously) that they will experience professional ethical challenges after graduation. But males seem to be more confident that they understand what ethics is in their field, and that they are prepared for those challenges (these differences are not significant, according to Pearson's chi-squared test).

3.7 Faculty Gender

Female students and male faculty members differed in their responses to several questions, as shown in Table 9.

Table 9: Male and Female Faculty Agreement with 3 Statements

	Females Agreeing	Males Agreeing
All students seeking Master's degrees in information/computer sciences should have a REQUIRED ethics course	9 (53%)	14 (44%)
Students seeking Master's degrees in information/computer sciences should have an elective ethics course.	15 (89%)	22 (69%)
[My students] are prepared for ethical challenges in their profession when they graduate.	7 (41%)	8 (28%)

Male faculty are less confident about their students' ethical preparation, but are less favorable toward required or elective courses in ethics. The numbers of responses are much smaller than the student responses, and thus do not rise to the level of statistical significance, but the differences are suggestive of avenues for future research.

3.8 Pedagogy and Learning

We asked faculty two questions about pedagogy: first, we provided a list of pedagogical strategies and asked them to select which they had used in teaching ethics (whether in a standalone course or as part of a course with a different focus); second, we asked an open-ended question, "I believe the best way to teach information/computing ethics is through . . ."

Table 10 summarizes responses to the first question. The two respondents from UMD who selected *Other* elaborated this as "Design games, a paper assignment" and "Discussion of codes of ethics." The overall ranking was consistent across institutions, except that role-playing and guest lectures were more frequently cited at UMD and reading current events was more frequently cited at UIS.

Table 10: Instructional Strategies

	All	UIS	UMD	UWS	BC
Lecture—Instructor	29 (53%)	8 (73%)	9 (60%)	4 (31%)	8 (50%)
Case Studies	24 (44%)	6 (55%)	9 (60%)	3 (23%)	6 (38%)
Reading Current Events	22 (40%)	7 (64%)	7 (47%)	3 (23%)	5 (31%)
Lecture—Guests	11 (20%)	5 (45%)	4 (27%)	1 (0%)	1 (6%)
Role Playing	10 (18%)	2 (18%)	5 (33%)	2 (15%)	1 (6%)
Simulations	2 (4%)	1 (9%)	0 (0%)	1 (0%)	0 (0%)
Other	2 (4%)	0 (0%)	2 (13%)	0 (0%)	0 (0%)

Faculty were also asked an open-ended question, "I believe the best way to teach information/computing ethics is through . . ." We grouped these responses into themes, as shown in Table 11. *Curriculum Integration* captures sentiments that ethics should be infused in the curriculum rather than contained in a particular course. *All* responses refer to the strategies listed in Table 10; *Other* responses included higher-level strategies such as "Teach consequences, not 'ethics,'" "K-12 and family education," and "Look at a familiar issue from a different perspective." *Case Studies* was most commonly mentioned overall, with particular favor at UIS and UMD; the idea of *Curriculum Integration* was volunteered by about 15% of the total respondents.

We also asked students about preferred modes of learning through the open-ended question, "I believe the best way to learn about information/computing ethics is through..." Students reported a clear favorite: 22% overall had a response with the theme of *Case Studies*, with particularly strong responses from UIS (19%), UMD (27%), and UWS (30%). Other themes were endorsed by relatively few students: Eight percent of students each endorsed *Classroom Discussion*, *Simulation/Roleplay*, and *Discussion of Current Events*; seven percent each supported *Lecture* and having a *Stand-alone Course*; six percent each endorsed *Integrating Ethics Across the Curriculum* and *Self-Directed Informal Education.*

Table 11: Best instructional strategies

	All	UIS	UMD	UWS	BC
Case Studies	10 (18%)	3 (27%)	4 (27%)	2 (15%)	1 (6%)
Curriculum Integration	9 (16%)	2 (18%)	2 (13%)	3 (23%)	2 (13%)
Real-World Examples	7 (13%)	3 (27%)	2 (13%)	1 (8%)	1 (6%)
Discussion	5 (9%)	2 (18%)	1 (7%)	0 (0%)	2 (13%)
Mixed Methods	4 (7%)	1 (9%)	1 (7%)	0 (0%	2 (13%)
Lectures	3 (5%)	2 (18%)	1 (7%)	0 (0%	0 (0%)
Hands-on Activities	3 (5%)	0 (0%)	3 (20%)	0 (0%)	0 (0%)
All	4 (7%)	1 (9%)	1 (7%)	0 (0%)	2 (13%)
Other	4 (7%)	2 (18%)	0 (0%)	0 (0%)	2 (13%)

3.9 Institutional Differences

We tested the significance (using Pearson's chi-squared) of the institution in student and faculty responses to several survey questions. Asserting significance in the faculty responses is problematic because of the relatively low expected values; thus we report these results as suggestive. Responses to "all students seeking Master's degrees in information/computer sciences should have a required ethics course" (see the first line of Table 6) differed by institution with significance $p < 0.05$—Illinois Springfield and Wisconsin-Stout faculty were favorable, and Maryland and Brooklyn faculty were unfavorable—but the expected values of the responses from Brooklyn College were only slightly above the minimum of 5. Responses to "[My students] are prepared for ethical challenges in their profession when they graduate" (see the second line of Table 5) were different with significance $p < 0.01$—a majority of Maryland faculty agreed, a majority of Illinois Springfield and Wisconsin-Stout faculty disagreed, and Brooklyn faculty unanimously disagreed—but three of the eight cells in the calculation had expected counts less than 5.

Student responses to two survey questions differed significantly across institution, though again some results can only be judged as suggestive because of low expected values. Exposure to computer/information ethics at the undergraduate level (see line 2 of Table 2) was significant, $p < 0.05$—students at Illinois Springfield are more likely to have had undergraduate exposure; belief that "I am prepared for ethical challenges in my profession when I graduate" (see line 1 of Table 5) was significant, $p < 0.05$—a majority of students at each institution agree, but the level of agreement ranges from 74% at Maryland to 92% at Illinois Springfield. However, two of the eight cells in the crosstabulation had expected values less than five, so this result is only suggestive.

3.10 The Role of Undergraduate Ethics

Some student responses showed significant relationships (again, using Pearson's chi-squared) with each other. In particular, undergraduate exposure to information/computer ethics nakes a significant difference to both the belief that "I understand what information/computer ethics is," and the belief that "I am prepared for ethical challenges in my profession when I graduate."

Table 12: Crosstabulation of undergraduate exposure to ethics

		I had undergraduate exposure to ethics	
		YES	NO
I understand what ethics is	YES	77	145
	NO	1	25
I am prepared for ethical challenges	YES	61	105
	NO	5	31

As Table 12 shows, students who report undergraduate exposure to ethics are much more likely to report understanding what ethics is and to assert preparedness for professional challenges than students who had no such exposure. Both differences are significant with $p < 0.01$. Interestingly, graduate coursework in ethics (either required, elective, or their aggregate) does not show a significant relationship with self-reporting of either understanding of ethics or professional preparedness.

4. CONCLUSIONS

Our survey showed generally strong support for graduate-level coursework in information/computer ethics from both faculty and students. Faculty and students generally agreed that students will face ethical challenges in the workplace, though the assessment of students' preparedness diverged fairly widely. Faculty assessment of student preparedness seems to be related to the degree of curricular/institutional emphasis placed on ethics in the graduate curriculum: faculty at Maryland, the only information science department in the study, were most optimistic; Illinois Springfield and Wisconsin-Stout faculty were slightly pessimistic; these sites have some commitment to graduate ethics but not at the level of a required course; faculty at Brooklyn, where there is no explicit programmatic commitment to ethics at the graduate level, were unanimous in believing their students unprepared.

Incidentally, our study provides some support for the role of undergraduate ethics curricula: exposure to ethics at the undergraduate level interacts much more strongly with students' feelings of preparedness than exposure in their current graduate studies. This may be due to the recentness of any exposure at the graduate level.

Even though our results are preliminary, they suggest fascinating lines for further research, including broadening the number of institutions, and carefully examining relationships between demographic information and responses.

5. ACKNOWLEDGMENTS

This material is based upon work supported by the National Science Foundation under Grant No. EESE-1135163. We thank the anonymous reviewers for their generous and constructive comments.

6. REFERENCES

[1] American Library Association. (2008) *American Library Association Code of Ethics.* http://www.ala.org/advocacy/proethics/codeofethics/codeethics

[2] Davis, M., and Riley, K. 2008. Ethics Across the Graduate Engineering Curriculum: An Experiment in Teaching and Assessment. *Teaching Ethics* 9, 1 (Fall 2008), 25-42.

[3] Fleischmann, K. R., Robbins, R. W., and Wallace, W. A. 2011. Information Ethics for a Multicultural World. *Journal of Information Systems Education* 22, 3 (Fall 2011), 191-201.

[4] Goldweber, M. et al. 2010. Enhancing the Social Issues Components in our Computing Curriculum: Computing for the Social Good. In Proceedings of the 2010 ITiCSE Working Group Reports. (ITiCSE '10). ACM, New Yorky, NY, 117-133. DOI=http://dx.doi.org/10.1145/1971681.1988996.

[5] Gotterbarn, D., Miller, K., and Rogerson, S. 1999. Computer Society Connection: Computer Society and ACM approve software engineering code of ethics. *Computer* 32, 10 (October 1999), 84–88. DOI=doi:10.1109/MC.1999.10112

[6] Preston, D. 1998. What makes professionals so difficult: an investigation into professional ethics teaching. In *Proceedings of the ethics and social impact component on Shaping policy in the information age* (ACM POLICY '98), Tom Jewett and Keith Miller. (Eds.). ACM, New York, NY, USA, 58-67. DOI=http://doi.acm.org/10.1145/276755.276778.

[7] Shichtman, D. C. and Wheeler, P. A. 2011. Social and professional issues: online naturally. In *Proceedings of the 2011 conference on Information technology education* (SIGITE '11). ACM, New York, NY, USA, 317-318. DOI= http://doi.acm.org/10.1145/2047594.2047681.

[8] Stoodley, I., Bruce, C., and Edwards, S. 2010. Expanding ethical vistas of IT professionals. *Information Systems Frontiers* 12, 4 (September 2010), 379-387. DOI= http://dx.doi.org/10.1007/s10796-009-9207-7.

[9] Wang, Z. 2009. Team, Leadership, Ethic, and Profession in Software Engineering Education. In *Proceedings of the 2009 WRI World Congress on Software Engineering - Volume 04* (WCSE '09), Vol. 4. IEEE Computer Society, Washington, DC, USA, 81-83. DOI=10.1109/WCSE.2009.360.

Methodology Education in Computing

Towards a Congruent Design Approach

Matti Tedre
Stockholm University
Department of Computer and Systems Sciences
Kista, Sweden
firstname.lastname@acm.org

ABSTRACT

All major computing curricula recommendations mention methodological skills and knowledge as an important learning objective in undergraduate and graduate education. None of those curricula recommendations, however, include a methodology course for students. One reason for that lack might be the stunning diversity of computing fields and the unique methods each branch of computing uses in their research. A methodology course in computing has to make a choice between three options: a narrow but deep specialization in some techniques and methods, a broad but superficial covering of a large number of methods, and a higher-level view on the principles of methodology and research design. This paper adopts the high-level approach, and presents a course description for a methodology course that aims at providing students understanding of how the elements of a research study link together.

Categories and Subject Descriptors

K.3.2 [**Computers and Education**]: Computer and Information Science Education—*computer science education*

Keywords

Methodology, research design, thesis work, computing education, congruent design, computer science education, methodology education

1. INTRODUCTION

Methodology is an overlooked area of computer science education. It has been argued that students in computing fields typically learn research skills through mentoring (in a master–apprentice relationship with seniors in their educational program) and through patterning activities (examining the writings of successful prior researchers) [11]. Despite some criticism [11], there is nothing fundamentally wrong in that sort of learning—it is indeed characteristic of any scientific paradigm [14, pp.187–191]. It can be argued, though, that such informal transfer of research skills might not provide a balanced view of research methodology.

One of the most influential curriculum recommendations in computing disciplines, the ACM/IEEE report CC2001 [8], did not include a single course on methodology. Courses in that report involve 'techniques' and 'methods'—take, for instance, formal methods, proof techniques, algorithmic strategies, and methods and tools of analysis in social and professional issues. The CC2001 briefly mentions that students ought to have an understanding of the scientific method [8, Sect. 9.2.1]. However, the scientific method is not a method of inquiry but a broad set of abstract principles. The scientific method does not present any tangible directions that could guide a student's work in a research project.

The most influential set of curriculum recommendations is continuously designed and improved by a joint task force of the ACM and IEEE, in collaboration with a number of other influential organizations in computing fields, such as AIS. The most recent guidelines can be found online at www.acm.org/education/curricula.htm.

Of those guidelines, the CS2008 curriculum update for computer science is vague on methodology, although it does mention a stunning list of computing-specific methods and techniques. Similar to CS2008, the 2009 curriculum guidelines for graduate degree programs in software engineering (GSwE2009) are technique-oriented, and do not propose a methodology course. Although the ACM/IEEE curriculum guidelines for information technology (IT2008) are explicit about the need for methodology education, they also focus on techniques without any actual methodology education. The IS2010 information systems curriculum update extends learning outcomes to qualitative research methods, too, but again does not propose how students should learn methodology. The CE2004 curriculum recommendations for computer engineering, are much more explicit about methodological aspects of undergraduate education than the other documents are. Finally, the CC2005 overview report, which covers the fields of CS, CE, IS, IT, and SE, does not mention the magic word "methodology" at all. Although all the five curriculum recommendations mention methodology as a learning outcome on a program level, and although they all do include a number of techniques and methods, none of them includes a course on *methodology*—on the principles and assumptions for selecting and using a set of methods.

Insofar as curriculum recommendations are serious about students' methodological training, there is a clear need for a course on research methodology. The term *methodology* is sometimes understood strictly as the study of methods

SIGCSE'13, March 6–9, 2013, Denver, Colorado, USA.

(akin to biology, psychology, and zoology), but in this paper, methodology refers to another common interpretation of the term as the principles and assumptions for selecting and using a set of methods. Under that interpretation, the main task for a methodology course is not to introduce a bunch of techniques or methods (means and procedures for achieving something), but to train students for making an informed choice between various methods, understanding their limitations and applicability to different tasks, and using them in a coherent and consistent way.

2. METHODOLOGY COURSE DESIGN

The students in our methodology course are M.Sc. students from two relatively large computer science institutions (around 10.000 computing students combined), where research areas span two dozen specializations as different as text mining, theoretical computer science, security, health informatics, HCI, e-learning, media technology, and computational biology. Hence, a narrow specialist education was not a viable choice for our methodology course. Instead, our course was aimed at teaching students the principles of methodology and research design. This section presents the building blocks of our course design.

2.1 Research Problem and Research Aim

Students start our course by finding a research problem and stating the aim of a mini-study that they conduct during the course. Research problem and research aim are tightly interwoven. A research problem states the reason, rationale, or background for research, and research aim (or 'purpose') describes, in general terms, what the research study will do to address that problem. It is, hence, important to emphasize to students the logical link between problem and aims. Although the research problem often develops and focuses throughout the study, it is very hard to think of a study that lacks problem and aims. Scholarly problems are concerned with lack of theoretical knowledge, evaluation problems are concerned with lack of knowledge about how well something works, and development problems are concerned with lack of knowledge about the best designs, architectures, or processes for constructing something [21]. Consider, for instance, the following problem that is of the evaluation type:

P_{ev} *"There is a lack of knowledge about the educational effects of the one-laptop-per-child program."*

Due to the topics taught at our institution, we adopted, as examples, the four 'aims' verbs from Cronjé's four-quadrant model: explore, describe, develop, and evaluate [7]. Cronjé's model arises from the instructional technology tradition, but one could adopt any set of verbs that properly describe research aims; other such characterizations include, for instance, exploratory, explanatory, descriptive, and emancipatory research [15], or observation, description, prediction, and experimentation (e.g., [12, 20]).

Exploratory research is the starting point for investigation of any poorly understood phenomenon, and it refers to developing an initial understanding of that yet uncharted phenomenon [23]. Descriptive research attempts to systematically record and model the phenomenon and its connections to other phenomena [23]. Development—a central part of design research—brings one to computing disciplines' home

Table 1: Example verbs for objectives in relation to four different research aims

Exploration	Description	Development	Evaluation
To observe	To classify	To synthesize	To analyze
To identify	To pinpoint	To design	To test
To characterize	To extrapolate	To implement	To predict
To clarify	To define	To devise	To determine
To interpret	To organize	To construct	To compare
To narrate	To simplify	To introduce	To assess
To estimate	To generalize	To specify	
To depict	To rank	To build	
	To measure		
	To detail		
	To distinguish		

turf, where engineering, design, and evaluation meet (e.g., [9, 13]). Evaluation—or testing of claims and designs—is the cornerstone of the scientific method, where its job is to identify and eliminate claims that cannot be backed up by solid evidence (e.g., [20]). Consider, for instance, the following aim for the research problem above:

A_{ev}: *"This research study aims at evaluating the educational effects of the OLPC program at Highlands School."*

2.2 Research Objectives and Research Questions

The next building blocks in research design are research objectives and research questions. While aims describe the broad goals of the study, objectives are specific statements about how the research aim is going to be met. Each objective contributes to meeting the aim, and success in meeting those objectives can be assessed. Hence, strong active verbs are recommended for objectives. Table 1 presents a number of examples of common verbs for objectives, categorized under the four example aims described in the previous section (the literature has numerous lists similar to Table 1).

For instance, consider the example research aim A_{eval} above. There are an endless number of ways of conducting such evaluation. One could study how laptops affect learning outcomes, or whether laptops unlock some unintended outcomes or triggers, how laptops affect the learning environment and dynamics, if laptops affect learning strategies or approaches, and so forth. It is, however, not possible to study all those aspects in one M.Sc. thesis. The choice of perspective is tightly anchored in the research study's theoretical or conceptual framework. Consider, for instance, an example research objective that addresses the question A_{eval} above:

O_1: *"To compare the learning outcomes between randomly assigned OLPC and non-OLPC groups by using authentic national examination questions."*

Objectives should focus on well defined aspects of the phenomenon. In the OLPC case above, the laptop intervention may change a countless number of things. But a student's thesis should focus on a few aspects and study those well. Once research aims and objectives are set, research questions follow directly from those aims and objectives. The main research question (RQ) can be derived directly from the research aim and subquestions ($SQ_1..SQ_n$) can be derived from research objectives.

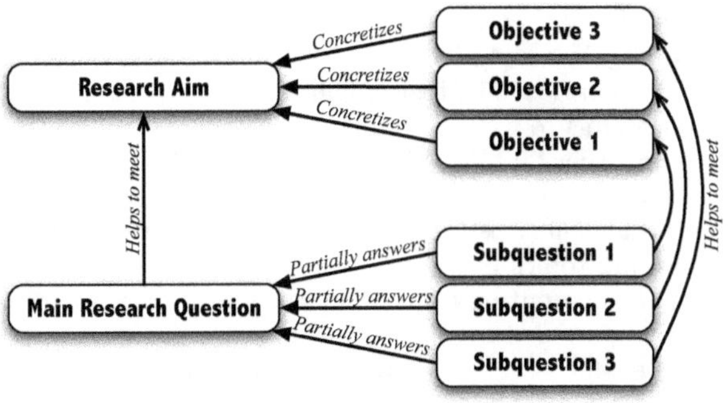

Figure 1: Functional relationship of aims, objectives, and research questions.

RQ *"How do laptops affect learning outcomes at Highlands School?"*

SQ_1 *"Do laptops affect students' learning outcomes as measured by national examination questions?"*

Figure 1 portrays the relationships between the research aim, objectives, main question, and subquestions. In Figure 1, the function of subquestions is two-fold: Each subquestion contributes one perspective that helps to answer the main research question, and each subquestion also helps to meet one or more research objectives. Each objective frames, in concrete terms, one perspective that contributes to the broad research aim. And the research aim is met, at least partially, by answering the main research question. However, in design research studies, questions sometimes become rather artificial, or tacked-on, so in some cases we allow students to have objectives only (see [13]).

2.3 The Role of Theory

In many types of research the theory choice is seamlessly intertwined with the research question and there is no logical order, 'first step,' between them. In various types of descriptive and evaluation research, for example, research literature provides a model or framework that can be tested, or variables that can be measured [6, 58–59]. In various types of exploratory research, literature provides a 'vocabulary', or conceptual framework, for the study by naming and describing, for instance, variables, constructs, phenomena, or categories of interest. In many types of qualitative research, literature offers a theoretical 'lens' for interpreting results [6, Ch.3]. In the mini-research papers that students write in this course, theory choice should not be very complex.

2.4 Research Ethics

It is difficult to think of a practical research study where research ethics would not play a role—in terms of intellectual property issues and ethics of reporting if nothing else. Ethical questions are such a cross-cutting issue that they should be discussed throughout the research study and not only as a separate learning module. Especially if the study deals with human participants—as respondents, interviewees, subjects, collaborators, or any other stakeholders—that study must explicitly plan to protect people from any negative consequences. In the fields of psychology and medicine ethical regulations and procedures are very well developed and worth presenting to students (e.g., [1]).

Table 2: Using the six "W" questions to narrow the research focus

W-word	*Question*	*Example*
What?	What is the theme of your study?	M-banking
Where?	Where do you want to study it?	Iringa Town in Tanzania
When?	When does your study start and finish?	2012/3–2012/5
Who?	Who are your informants or stakeholders?	Small businesses
Why?	Why or for which purpose is technology used?	For business transactions
hoW?	How / which technology will be used?	Using M-Pesa

Computing research often involves human participants, and in those cases *informed consent* is one of the key concepts. Informed consent is established by giving participants enough information about the study so that they can decide whether they want to participate or not. Other concepts emphasized in our M.Sc. level methods course are security (data must be kept secure and preferably anonymous), anonymity (no-one should be directly or indirectly identifiable from the report, unless they explicitly request it), and the various types of research permits. We do not consider the ethics of publishing (e.g., authorship, intellectual property, conflicts of interest, or non-disclosure) to be absolutely necessary for a B.Sc. level or M.Sc. level course, but definitely for a graduate (Ph.D.) student course.

2.5 Focus and Feasibility

The question of feasibility stands between what one would like to achieve and what really can be achieved within the resources of a research study. Research focus is a tool for making a research study feasible. An M.Sc. research study should not try to do everything. Broad aims can, however, be easily narrowed down to feasible studies, for instance, by employing the six "W" questions (or 'five Ws and one H'). Instead of a sweeping statement "*This study explores the use of mobile money in developing countries*" one could apply the six W questions presented in Table 2. Those six W questions narrow the study down to "*This study explores the use of M-Pesa for business transactions among small business holders in Iringa Town, Tanzania, between March 2012 and May 2012.*"

Aside from making the study feasible, there are several positive side-effects of making focus very clear from early on. Firstly, a clear focus helps to narrow down literature review and to make a theory choice. Secondly, a clear focus makes it easier to plan sampling, hone instruments, and arrange time tables for a research study. Third, a well documented focus is easily converted into limitations of research at the end of a research study.

2.6 Data Types

Research studies are not built around the research method. On the contrary, the method selection is based on what kinds of information are needed for answering the research questions. Each research question creates some expectations for what kinds of data will be able to answer that research question, which, in turn, limits the choice of data collection methods. Hence, an explicit discussion of different kinds of

Table 3: Data types and some related research objectives

Data type	*Typical objectives*
Interview data	To characterize, clarify, interpret, narrate, depict, specify
Observational data (qual.)	To observe, identify, characterize, clarify, interpret
Documents	To identify, clarify, interpret, estimate, synthesize, design, specify, analyze, compare
Audiovisual data	To identify, characterize, interpret, estimate, analyze, compare
Performance data	To classify, pinpoint, extrapolate, generalize, measure, detail, distinguish, design, test, predict, compare, assess
Attitude data (quant.)	To identify, estimate, pinpoint, generalize, rank, measure, detail, design, test, predict, compare, assess
Observational data (quant.)	To identify, estimate, pinpoint, rank, measure, distinguish, design, test, predict, determine, compare, assess
Census data	To classify, extrapolate, organize, generalize, distinguish, analyze, test, predict, determine, compare

data is necessary in order to establish congruence between research questions and method choice.

The basic choice regarding data (or information) type is famously that between qualitative and quantitative data. Creswell [6, p.15] divided types of information in qualitative research into four broad categories: interview data, observational data, documents, and audiovisual data. He also divided quantitative data into four categories: performance data, attitude data, observational data, and census data. Although any type of data can be used, in one way or another, in nearly any empirical research study, every data type has characteristics that make it especially suitable for specific types of studies. Table 3 presents data types and typical objectives that are connected with each type of data.

There are many natural matches between objectives and data types in Table 3, while other data types are found with a variety of research studies. For instance, interview data is a natural choice if the research objective is to narrate life stories. There again, if the objective is to identify key variables of a phenomenon, a broad variety of data types can be used. In order to keep the research elements well aligned, it is also important to consider the fit between data type required and focus of research. A research study that is concerned with a small number of things (be they people, web pages, data sets, or events) may not always benefit from quantitative data, while researchers of a large-scale survey may be overwhelmed if each survey produces a large amount of qualitative data.

2.7 Method Choice for Data Collection and Sampling

As the method choice for data collection depends on the type of data needed for answering the research questions, the data collection method can be decided rather late in the research, yet it must be in agreement with the aims and objectives of the study. Understanding the basics of sampling is not only a skill for doing research, but it is also essential for one's ability to critically read research studies. Hence, sampling vocabulary (e.g., population, sample, sampling frame, inference, bias) is as important as understanding why specific types of sampling strategies are needed. Sampling strategies (random, systematic, comprehensive, and others) can be taught by clearly connecting them with aims and focus, what kinds of inferences can one make from various strategies, and which kinds of statistical tools one aims to use at the analysis phase. Therefore, similar to the other building blocks of research studies, sampling is not a choice that one makes in a linear order after the previous topics, but it is tightly tied with both previous as well as following topics in the course.

In many computing fields, data consists of program inputs and outputs. Data can also include, for instance, execution times, file sizes, or accuracy of program outputs. Computer science research uses a stunning variety of quantitative data. Computing studies do not, however, typically employ the blinding principle familiar from fields like medicine and psychology, which is something that a methodology course should try to instill. That is, if a research study claims "our algorithm A is faster than algorithms B and C with data set D, machine m, and parameters p", the researchers should not be able to select B, C, D, m, and p favorably for their own algorithm.

In many types of qualitative research one cannot strictly define the sample size before the data collection, as sample size bears no value as such. Instead, researcher keeps on collecting data—interviewing, for instance—until the data reaches a point of saturation [16]. The point of saturation is based on diminishing returns: for example, in interviews it typically happens that after some point, each additional interview adds less and less to the overall story, model, theory, or framework [22]. Various rules of thumb do, however, exist for the number of informants needed for qualitative research studies [2, 4, 5, 16, 17].

2.8 Data Analysis and Interpretation

Although data analysis comes temporally after data collection, the decisions regarding analysis methods are, however, tightly tied with the rest of the research elements. Analysis methods are tools for answering the research questions: for instance, if the objective is 'to characterize', analysis should yield rich descriptions, and if the objective is 'to measure', analysis should yield numbers. In data analysis, the first step is preparing the data for analysis—transcription, data entry, or formatting for the right software, for instance.

Based on the aims and objectives, one can use any of the four combinations of qualitative–quantitative data and analysis methods [21]. Qualitative analysis of qualitative data produces rich descriptions and looks at the meanings and affects found in the data. Quantitative analysis of qualitative data looks at occurrences, frequencies, and other statistical measures found in data. Quantitative analysis of quantitative data has a research field dedicated to it—statistics—and it is also the most common analysis approach in computing fields. Qualitative analysis of quantitative data looks at interpretations and judgments of otherwise "hard data", such as visual inspection of the results of image compression algorithm, or a judgment-based grouping of scatterplot data. Table 4 presents intermediate questions from each of the four combinations of qualitative data–quantitative data and qualitative analysis–quantitative analysis.

Statistical data analysis is one of the basic skills one should obtain from a methodology course in computing, and students should get considerable understanding and experience in descriptive and inferential statistics. A graduate's vocab-

Table 4: **Example intermediate questions in the four quadrants of data types and analysis types**

	Qualitative data	*Quantitative data*
Qualitative analysis	Why did the learners start collaborating at around half an hour mark?	What does it mean that 48% of respondents agreed with the claim that laptops cause students to lose focus?
Quantitative analysis	How much difference was there in accessibility terms between European and American web pages?	What was the gender ratio in the survey responses?

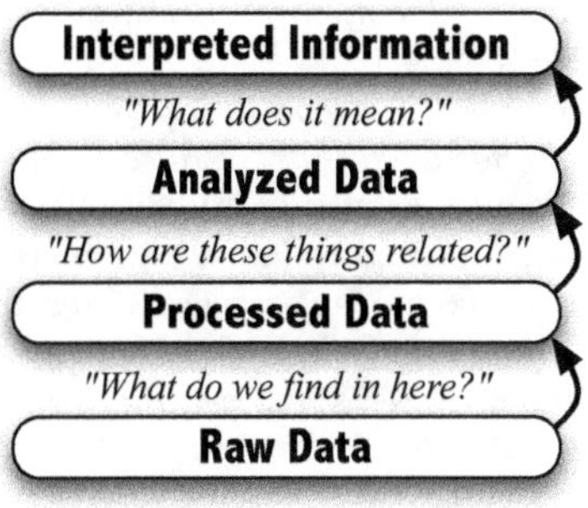

Figure 2: Layers of qualitative data analysis.

ulary should include things like basic types of measurement (nominal, ordinal, interval, ratio), discrete and continuous data, types of midpoints, vocabulary for spread of data, and statistical tests for significance and association. Concerning qualitative analysis, we present students a layered approach to the analysis of qualitative data (Fig. 2). In Figure 2 'raw data' refers to things like unprocessed interview recordings, video footage, documents, web pages, and so forth. On this level tasks are mostly technical, such as managing data into files, units, or databases [5, p.151].

In Figure 2 'processed data' refers to the same data after tasks like reading, indexing, coding, or tagging have been done. After those tasks the data is supplemented with low-level reflections or codes, such as notes, memos, or tags. The next step is the analysis of processed data by, for instance, describing, classifying or interpreting the identified codes and categories in their context. Outcomes on the data analysis level are things like comparisons or categories found in the data [5]. A research study should not end on this level, but it should continue to the level of context-tied, interpreted information. At this level, the understanding that emerged from the data is related to the research aim, context of research, other research studies, and the broader context of the study. Descriptive statistics and 'processed data' are in some senses similar layers, and inferential statistics and 'analyzed data' also share conceptual similarities—although the processes that lead to them are very different.

2.9 Evaluating the Results

Students' research reports also include a higher level of analysis, where students look at the limits of their research study, its strengths and weaknesses, what could have been done differently, and what recommendations there are for future research. The limitations of research study come nearly automatically from the selection of focus, and if that was justified well, limitations can be easily described and justified. Similar, discussions on methods and sampling tie back to argument for their selection. Limitations and discussion on method and sampling also lead naturally to future research: "Given more resources and what we know after the study, what should we do next?"

The strengths and weaknesses of research can be analyzed from a number of perspectives, including the various biases (e.g., sampling bias, design bias, and non-response bias [21]), methodological rigor, and research design. The twin pillars of quality in quantitative research are validity and reliability, with all their variations, while the most common qualitative measures are credibility, confirmability, transferability, and dependability—which assess how believable, neutral, applicable, and consistent the study was. Again, those measures are not a certificate of approval that a study gets after it is done, but those measures should be kept in mind at all phases of research work. There are various techniques for improving each of those measures, and none of them can be applied post hoc.

2.10 Reporting Research Outcomes

Language of research varies greatly between traditions. Interpretive research and statistical research differ in how they, for instance, assert factual statements, construct a disagreeing or agreeing paragraph, present uncertain results, portray competing or conflicting theories, and cite literature. A report on an ethnographic study uses different vocabulary and constructs than a report on a controlled experiment. We advise students to imitate—but not plagiarize—the style of writing in their literature.

We also encourage students to choose their preferred citation system, but emphasize their suitability for different types of research. The IEEE bracket citation system is well suited for factual statements ("*There is a causal link between x and y* [81].") The various systems for parenthetical referencing are well suited for discussing various authors' viewpoints ("*Doe (2008) argued that...*"). If a student's thesis makes texts talk to each other, the APA style could be a good choice, but if its literature review mostly summarizes previous findings, the IEEE style might be preferred.

3. DISCUSSION

Research methods can be taught well in various ways (see, e.g., [19]). Our situation—a large number of students and a broad variety of research fields—led us to teach students the principles of methodology and research design instead of specialized techniques and methods. Surely other institutions with a different research profile and student body would come up with a different course.

From a methodological perspective, one of the central features of a good research study is *congruence* of the elements that the study is made of, such as the research problem, aims, and method choices. A research study is a puzzle-like activity where each element of the study must fit all the others well, and changing one element is usually difficult without changing all the other elements, too. In the above description of elements of research study, there is no linear succession of 'steps' in research; rather, each piece of the research puzzle is connected to every other piece so that changing one affects the others. The driving methodological question in students' thesis work is how to make the elements agree. One must think of the study as a whole, and not as disconnected pieces. We call this view *congruent research design*.

The term 'aligned research design' would be inappropriate, for it suggests a linear succession of steps. The term 'congruence' emphasizes a systemic view, where the building blocks of research are developed together, constantly keeping in mind their consistency within the high-level research design. Various methodology experts have noted that logically prior elements of research typically do not precede the others in research action [5, 18]. Instead, in research activity the researcher moves back and forth between the research components "in an integrated, consistent manner so that all parts interrelate" [5, p.101]. One way of improving the congruence of research elements in a study is to follow a research strategy. Strategies—such as survey strategy, case study strategy, and experiment strategy—offer a tool for organizing the research study into a coherent whole [10, Ch.1–Ch.8]. Especially the strategies for experimental computer science have been stressed in methodology debates in computing. Each strategy offers directions for tackling specific types of issues, yet they also leave a lot to researcher's discretion. Strategies should be a part of methodology education at least on the Ph.D. training level.

Pedagogically speaking, our congruent design approach fits well the SOLO taxonomy of learning outcomes [3]. If that course were taught as a list of techniques and methods, or as a linear list of elements, the learning outcomes might be directed towards a multistructural list of things that students should know. Combined with the backwash effect (students thinking that they will be tested for their knowledge of specific methods) that might lead to undesirable learning outcomes. The systemic view of congruent design is conceptually closely related to the highest levels of SOLO taxonomy: the relational level, where students appreciate the relationships between the parts and the whole; as well as the extended abstract level, where students are able to transfer the course concepts to new contexts [3]. That is what our methodology course aims to teach students.

Acknowledgments

The author expresses his gratitude to the co-designers of the course: associate professor Harko Verhagen and professor Paul Johannesson. This research received funding from the Academy of Finland grant #132572.

4. REFERENCES

[1] *Publication Manual of the American Psychological Association.* American Psychological Association, Washington, D.C., USA, 6th edition, 2009.

[2] H. R. Bernard. *Social Research Methods.* Sage Publications, Thousand Oaks, CA, USA, 2000.

[3] J. Biggs and C. Tang. *Teaching for Quality Learning at University: What the Student Does.* Open University Press, New York, NY, USA, 4th edition, 2011.

[4] K. Charmaz. *Constructing Grounded Theory: A Practical Guide Through Qualitative Analysis.* Sage Publications, Thousand Oaks, CA, USA, 2006.

[5] J. W. Creswell. *Qualitative Inquiry and Research Design: Choosing Among Five Approaches.* Sage Publications, Thousand Oaks, CA, USA, 3rd edition, 2007.

[6] J. W. Creswell. *Research Design: Qualitative, Quantitative, and Mixed Methods Approaches.* Sage Publications, Thousand Oaks, CA, USA, 3rd edition, 2009.

[7] J. C. Cronjé. The ABC (aim, belief, concern) instant research question generator. Unpublished Manuscript, 2012.

[8] P. J. Denning, C. Chang, and CC2001 Joint Task Force. Computing curricula 2001: Computer science volume. pdf, March 2001.

[9] P. J. Denning, D. E. Comer, D. Gries, M. C. Mulder, A. Tucker, A. J. Turner, and P. R. Young. Computing as a discipline. *Communications of the ACM*, 32(1):9–23, 1989.

[10] M. Denscombe. *The Good Research Guide for Small-Scale Social Research Projects.* Open University Press, Berkshire, England, 3rd edition, 2007.

[11] R. L. Glass. A structure-based critique of contemporary computing research. *Journal of Systems and Software*, 28(1):3–7, 1995.

[12] C. G. Hempel. *Aspects of Scientific Explanation And Other Essays in the Philosophy of Science.* The Free Press, New York, NY, USA, 1965.

[13] P. Johannesson and E. Perjons. A design science primer. Unpublished Manuscript, February 25 2012.

[14] T. S. Kuhn. *The Structure of Scientific Revolutions.* The University of Chicago Press, Chicago, USA, 3rd edition, 1996.

[15] C. Marshall and G. B. Rossman. *Designing Qualitative Research.* Sage Publications, Thousand Oaks, CA, USA, 4th edition, 2006.

[16] M. Mason. Sample size and saturation in PhD studies using qualitative interviews. *Forum Qualitative Sozialforschung / Forum: Qualitative Social Research*, 11(3), 2010.

[17] J. M. Morse. Designing funded qualitative research. In N. K. Denzin and Y. S. Lincoln, editors, *Handbook of Qualitative Research*, pages 220–235. Sage Publications, Thousand Oaks, CA, USA, 2nd edition, 1994.

[18] J. M. Morse and L. G. Richards. *README FIRST for a User's Guide to Qualitative Methods.* Sage Publications, Thousand Oaks, CA, USA, 2002.

[19] B. J. Oates. *Researching Information Systems and Computing.* Sage Publications, London / Thousand Oaks / New Delhi, 2006.

[20] K. Popper. *The Logic of Scientific Discovery.* Routledge, London, UK, 1959.

[21] J. J. Randolph. *Multidisciplinary Methods in Educational Technology Research and Development.* HAMK University of Applied Sciences, Hämeenlinna, Finland, 2008.

[22] A. L. Strauss and J. M. Corbin. *Basics of Qualitative Research: Techniques and Procedures for Developing Grounded Theory.* Sage Publications, Thousand Oaks, CA, USA, 2nd edition, 1998.

[23] G. H. von Wright. *Explanation and Understanding.* Routledge & Kegan Paul, London, UK, 1971.

Retaining Nearly One-Third more Majors with a Trio of Instructional Best Practices in CS1

Leo Porter
Skidmore College
Saratoga Springs, NY 12866
Leo.Porter@skidmore.edu

Beth Simon
University of California, San Diego
La Jolla, CA 92093
bsimon@cs.ucsd.edu

ABSTRACT
Beginning in 2008, we introduced a new CS1 incorporating a trio of best practices intended to improve the quality of the course, appeal to a broader student body, and, hopefully, improve retention in the major. This trio included Media Computation, Pair Programming, and Peer Instruction. After 3 and 1/2 years (8 CS1 classes, 3 different instructors, and 1011 students passing the course) we find that 89% of the majors who pass the course are still studying computing one year later. This is an improvement of 18% over our average retention of 71% for the previous version of the course (measured since Fall 2001). If the focus shifts from retention of *passing* CS1 majors to retention of CS1 *initially enrolled* majors, multiple improvements—fewer students drop, more students pass, and more passing students are retained—compound to increase retention by 31% (from 51% to 82%). In this paper we analyze further aspects of these results, detail the three instructional design choices, and consider how they impact issues known to affect retention.

Categories and Subject Descriptors
K.3.2 [**Computer Science Education**]: Introductory Programming

General Terms
Human Factors.

Keywords
Peer Instruction, Active Learning, Student-Centric Learning, Contextualized Computing, Pair Programming.

1. INTRODUCTION
Many of us agree that attracting and retaining majors in computing is an important goal. In addition to preparing more computer scientists, there is an increasing societal need for graduates with computational thinking skills. We believe a broad spectrum of changes are needed to support the necessary sea change of getting more students computationally capable and increasing the number attaining secondary degrees in computing. These changes will almost certainly involve not only K-12 education and university education, but also the way the computing community represents itself in society. As one example, the US CS10K project is seeking to train 10,000 teachers to teach a quality high school computing course in the US [10]. It is critical that university-level computing educators be involved in such efforts across the board. *But we also need to be ready to make the most of whatever successes may drive more computing majors to our door. In our own universities, in our own departments, and in our own classrooms we need to support all, and hopefully more diverse, students in both enjoying and succeeding in computing.*

Here we report on the impact of redesigning our major's "front door" —CS1. In Fall 2008 at our large, research-intensive public university, we implemented a new CS1 course redesigned around three practices with research evidence supporting their benefits for learning:

- Contextualized computing: Media Computation
- Engaging classroom pedagogy: Peer Instruction
- Supportive programming assignments: Pair Programming

After 3.5 years of offering the course, taught by 3 different instructors, and taken by 1011 students, through post-hoc analysis we discover a dramatic improvement in *programmatic retention* (measured based on the enrollment of majors one year after CS1). In the 7 years prior to our changes, the retention rate among students passing the course was 71%. After our changes, the retention rate among students passing the course became 89%.

However, describing retention only by the number of students passing the course is not the complete picture—focusing only on those students who pass omits those students who start the course and drop it or finish it with a non-passing grade. In this work we evaluate retention from a number of different angles: by gender, by students passing, by students enrolled after the drop deadline (week 4), and by students enrolled at the end of week 1. In the most optimistic sense (based on students enrolled in the course at the end of week 1), we see an increase in retention of 31% (from 51% to 82%). Finally, we discuss potential threats to the validity of this post-hoc study and describe key features of our trio of best practices identified by Tobias [12] as issues for retention: context, engagement, competition, and community.

2. RELATED WORK
Providing students with a familiar domain and context for computing in the form of multimedia has been shown to improve pass rates, reduce negative impressions by students, and increase their potential willingness to take more CS courses [3].

Peer Instruction (PI) has been widely successful in improving student learning in physics [1]. In computer science, most of the previously reported PI results have been attitudinal—demonstrating that students value PI in their classroom [2,6,10]. The first, to our knowledge, quasi-controlled experiment to establish learning gains in computer science from PI was based on asking isomorphic questions following group discussion [7].

From that work, the peer discussion portion of the PI process was shown to improve student understanding [7].

Pair Programming is the process of assigning students to work in pairs when programming [5]. Pair Programming has been shown to produce more confident and proficient introductory programmers and has also been shown to improve retention, particularly for women [5].

In 2010, we reported preliminary findings on major retention in this course focusing on the aspect of what we teach—Java through the context of Media Computation [9]. In this work, we bring a more holistic review of the collective changes in the course. While it would be theoretically possible to explore the impact of each of our three instructional design choices, we doubt that any one alone would have the same impact; and as computing educators we would be uncomfortable with the experiment. In this paper we utilize the theoretical backing of each of the instructional design components to produce a post-hoc argument of the value of the trio of changes and how they complement each other.

3. METHODOLOGY

The course. The work reported here occurred at UC San Diego, a large, public US research-intensive university currently enrolling >1200 computing majors (class sizes 40-200). Author Simon designed the CS1 course in summer 2008 with the guidance of the department's undergraduate curriculum committee. Specifically, the committee considered various options in contextualized computing approaches including robots, gaming, and media computation. Media computation was selected primarily for its compelling research-reported results [3]. We used Guzdial and Ericson's Introduction to Computing and Programming with Java – a Multimedia Approach and completed content in Chapters 1-6 and 8-11 (1- and 2-D arrays, loops and nested loops, if statements, object use, and class design) [4]. In [9] we reported a comparison of author Simon's media computation final exam versus her final exam in the previous instance of the course. We found the media computation exam had comparable coverage of content (with less class design and much more coverage of the other topics) and notably more questions requiring application of multiple concepts.

Similarly, the compelling Pair Programming results reported at UC Santa Cruz led to consideration of pair programming [5]. Our institution already had a strong culture of undergraduate use of in-building labs due to a strong undergraduate tutoring program. In many lower-division computer science courses it is common to have course-specific tutors staffed 20-100 hours a week. From formal interviews with under-represented students who had previously left the major, but were completing studies in another major, we found that lack of use of the labs was both ubiquitous and something they felt contributed to their struggles in computing courses. We chose to implement fixed pairs (students kept the same partner the entire 10-week term) for programming assignments. Students were responsible to identify at least six hours a week they could both meet to do their assignments. Students were given quite basic "training" in that we described the roles of the driver and navigator and expressly told them only to work on the code together. This verbal instruction was reinforced in our closed, 1-hour weekly labs where students worked with different (and sometimes rotating) partners and the lab explicitly told them when to switch roles. We cannot document whether or not students faithfully implemented the pair programming model (and we are not so naïve as to think all partnerships went well). However, we attempted to limit complete free-riding by having

Table 1: Dataset Characteristics including Week 1 Enrollment Characteristics.

	CS1-Before Previous Version	CS1-BP New Version
Timeframe	FA01-SP08	FA08-FA11
Course Instances	18	8
Instructors	5	3
Overall Enrollment Week 1	2067	1231
Percentage CS/E Majors	46%	52%
Non-Majors (Male/Female)	66% / 34%	61% / 39%
Majors (Male/Female)	81% / 19%	77% / 23%

10% of each assignment be graded via a short (usually 2 question) interview given by a tutor in the open lab hours for the course. These questions were chosen by the tutors with the guidance that they should ask first for the student to describe what one of the main structures in the program did ("what does this if statement do?") and second for the student to describe how they would make a small change to the program. In general, students should get 100% on these questions. The procedure allowed tutors to identify students who were incapable of answering both questions in order to recommend better working styles. It also served to reinforce simply that students are expected to understand the program produced by their partnership. As necessary, issues could be escalated to the professor in (rare) cases of partner disbanding, etc.

Finally, author Simon's experience in working with physics education researcher Carl Wieman led to the consideration of Peer Instruction (PI) to support an effective in-lecture learning environment [1]. Again, the physics education research community has extensive evidence for the value of PI in various university physics courses. Simon created clicker questions based on assigned reading in the textbook. An experience report on the adoption of PI in the course can be found in [9] and the materials themselves are available on the Peer Instruction for Computer Science (CS) website [8].

The analysis. We obtained official grade reports from a university database for all offerings of CS1 back to and including 2001[1]. We call our original version CS1-Before and our new version CS1-BP (Best Practices). We purposefully elided data from summer session courses as these are very different from regular year offerings (e.g., often very small classes, students take only one course at a time, etc.). Table 1 identifies characteristics of our dataset and Table 2 identifies immediate student outcomes in those courses.

Students not listed as a Computer Science or Computer Engineering (CS/E) major may take CS1 for a variety of reasons—but it is a requirement for these majors: computer science, interdisciplinary computing and the arts, bioinformatics, and math.

True retention in the major would be measured at the time of degree conferral. However, given that this is a first year course, we are still not able to report graduation rates. Furthermore, 1-yr retention is potentially a more meaningful metric for evaluating

[1] Note: For legal reasons ethnicity data is not available from this database.

Table 2: Student course outcomes among CS/E majors and non-majors including (M)ales, (F)emales, and (O)verall.

	CS1-Before Previous Version	CS1-BP New Version
CS/E Majors Drop by Week 4 deadline (M/F/O)	10%/ 15%/ 11%	1%/ 2%/ 2%
CS/E Non-Majors Drop by Week 4 deadline (M/F/O)	17%/ 22%/ 19%	17%/16%/16%
CS/E Majors Passing	677	587
CS/E Non-Majors Passing	663	424
Pass rate Majors (M/F/O)	80%/ 81%/ 80%	93%/96%/94%
Pass rate Non-Majors (M/F/O)	73%/ 72%/ 73%	86%/84%/86%
Gender of Passing Non-majors (M/F)	69%/ 32%	61%/ 39%
Gender of Passing CS/E Majors (M/F)	81%/ 19%	76%/ 24%

the impact of CS1—before other factors (later classes, instructors, etc.) add additional noise. For the purposes of this study, we define the following forms of retention (note all denominators are the same):

- **Programmatic Retention**: (#of CS1 students taking a computing course and majoring in CS/E one year later) / (#of students in CS1 listed as a CS/E major at time of enrollment).

Contributing to Programmatic Retention are the number of original CS/E majors who are retained as well as the number of new majors (students who were not CS/E majors at the time of CS1 who become CS/E majors 1-yr later). We define programmatic retention as the sum of these forms of retention:

- **Original Majors Retention**: (#of students listed as a CS/E major at time of enrollment in CS1 who are majoring in and taking a computer science course one year later) / (#of students in CS1 listed as a CS/E major at time of enrollment)
- **New Majors Retention**: (#of students not listed as a CS/E major at time of enrollment in CS1 who are in a CS/E course and CS/E major 1 year later) / (#of students in CS1 listed as a CS/E major at time of enrollment)

Measuring the addition of new majors to the program is difficult for the following reason: students may make the decision to change major and enroll in CS/E classes but delay in officially changing their major (as recorded). One potential measurement would be to infer that students enrolled in a CS/E class one year later have changed their major to CS/E but this could be problematic as it may capture students minoring in CS/E, taking more classes out of interest, etc. We instead take a conservative approach and only count those students enrolled in a CS/E class one year later who have also changed their major to CS/E. We recognize that this may undercount new majors, but it does so to both classes (CS1-Before and CS1-BP). Future work can more accurately measure major outcomes after graduation.

We are most interested in programmatic retention for the following reason: we enroll a certain number of students in our program—if they start in CS1, how many are still in our "pipeline" after a year? This number will include students we "kept" in the pipeline and students we "added" to the pipeline (e.g., changed into our major).

Statistical significance. We determine statistical significance using a two-tailed two-proportion z-test for two independent groups. These groups were created by summing students across classes to produce a group of students who had taken CS1-Before and another group having taken CS1-BP.

3.1 Threats to Validity

As a retrospective study of real courses, there are a number of threats to the validity of this study.

Instructor Variation — Instructors may vary in their appeal to students and, potentially, their ability to retain students in the major. To isolate this issue, we present a within-instructor analysis, looking at the results of just that instructor who taught both versions of the course four times (for a total of eight). This assumes that the instructor was equally charismatic in all classes (which cannot be measured).

Change in Students — Student abilities, perceptions of computing, and interest in the major may have shifted during the study. Specifically, students enrolled during our standard course (2001-2008) may differ from our new course (2008-2011). In the following section, we examine a different advanced-track CS1 course not part of this study for changes in these two time periods.

Impacted vs. not Impacted — The CS/E major was impacted (had higher standards for admission) for much of the time period of the standard course (2001-2007) and was not impacted during the duration of our new course (2008-2011). Again, we compare to the advanced-track CS1 course for impacts this might have had.

4. RESULTS

We evaluate the retention of students in the CS1-BP course using the metrics defined in Section 3.

4.1 Retention of Students Who Pass CS1

Figure 1 provides overall 1-yr programmatic retention by gender and overall based on the number of CS/E majors who pass CS1. First we focus on the two components of Programmatic Retention: retained original majors and new majors. In terms of retained original majors, CS1-BP increased retention from 68% to 81% ($p<0.01$). Although both genders improved in the retention of original CS/E majors, males improved slightly more than females. Male improvement from 68% to 82% was statistically significant ($p<0.01$) however the improvement for females from 68% to 79% was not ($p=0.058$). A similar story appears for new majors. New majors, as a component measured out of the number of initial majors, went from 3% to 8% overall. Males benefitted slightly more, experiencing a gain from 3% to 8% whereas females went from 5% to 9%.

The New Major Retention metric allows for us to evaluate the contribution to programmatic retention from new majors, but may hide details concerning from where these new majors come. Non-majors enrolled in our CS1 course vary widely by term and consist of a variety of students, many of whom are taking CS1 as a requirement for a related major. As such, reporting the number of new majors as a percentage of passing non-majors can be deceptively low as non-majors are often non-freshman in a required course for their major and are not "potential majors." However, even when evaluating this metric (new majors one year later divided by CS1 non-majors) we find substantial improvements for CS1-BP. For CS1-Before, 3% of passing non-majors become majors 1-yr later for males, females, and overall.

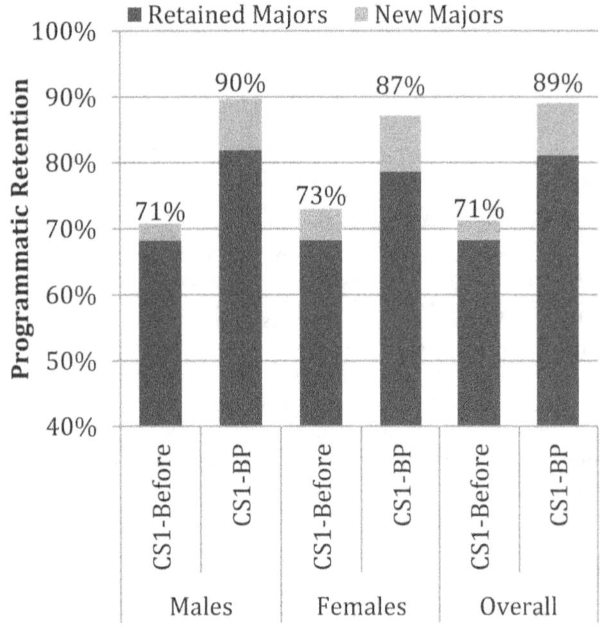

Figure 1. Programmatic Retention by gender for both versions of CS1. Includes retained majors and new majors. Differences in Programmatic Retention are statistically significant (p<0.05).

For CS1-BP, these numbers rise to 14% (p<0.01), 7% (p=0.046), and 11% (p<0.01) respectively. Although these improvements in new majors are large (factor of 3.7 increase overall), the large variance in reasons for students taking the class limits potential conclusions.

The primary result from Figure 1 is that of overall programmatic retention. Although programmatic retention improves for both males and females, the improvement in male retention is slightly higher than that of females. Overall improvement in retention is substantial: 18% (p<0.01). As a measure of improvement, 29% of programmatic majors were lost after one year, whereas only 11% were lost after revising the course. This represents a 62% reduction in lost programmatic majors.

4.2 Instructor Effect

A common criticism of results for new course design is that those most apt to change the course tend to be "good" instructors who, of course, "do well." To address this potential concern, Figure 2 provides the programmatic retention for a single instructor who taught the course four times in each of the two styles. These results are comparable with the overall results, demonstrating a 14% increase in programmatic retention (p<0.01). The benefit is again more substantial for males (15% p<0.01) than females (12%, not statistically significant p=0.08).

4.3 Retention by Students Enrolled in CS1 (Pass, Fail, Withdraw)

The results thus far have focused on the percentage of students retained relative to the number of majors who pass the CS1 course. This could also be a potential threat to validity, as one might substantially reduce the number of students passing the course to artificially affect retention. However, in the case of this new course, the number of students who pass increases as does the number of those students who are retained.

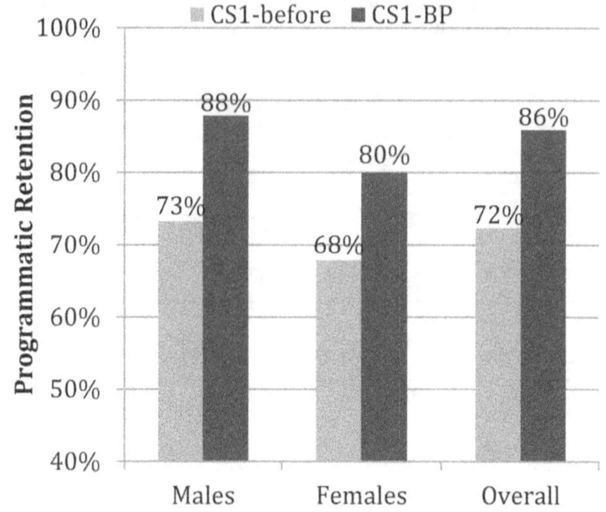

Figure 2. Programmatic Retention by gender for both versions of CS1 for a single instructor. Differences for Males and Overall are statistically significant (p<0.05).

As reported in Section 3, the pass rate for majors increases from 80% in the original course to 94% in the new course. By changing the denominator in the equations from Section 3 to be the number of computer science/engineering majors who are enrolled after the deadline to withdraw from the course (week 4) instead of those who pass, we can further evaluate the impact of these changes. This adds in those students who did not pass the course (earning a D or F grade, or withdrawing from the course). Figure 3 provides these results. The impact of the new course is more pronounced as the two effects—an increased pass rate and an increased retention rate—compound to increase the programmatic retention from 57% to 84% (p<0.01). Improvements in male and female programmatic retention are statistically significant (p<0.01).

It was surprising to us to discover that in our CS-Before course only 57% of the number of declared CS/E majors at the end of week 4 persisted one year later. Although this is a derivative of the change in majors' pass rate in the course (80% increasing to 94%), the view from the programmatic level is a bit more stark.

4.4 Retention by Students Enrolled at Week 1

In Figures 1 and 3, we excluded students who start the course, but drop it before week 4 (an event unrecorded on their transcript). For this work, we make the reasonable assumption that CS/E declared majors enrolled in the course at the end of week 1 intend to give the course (and perhaps computing) a serious try. As another potential threat to validity, if more students drop the CS1-BP class than the traditional CS1 class in the first 4 weeks, one could again argue that CS1-BP artificially inflates the retention and pass rates. We actually found the opposite effect had occurred in that fewer majors dropped before week 4 in CS1-BP (2%) than in CS1-Before (11%).

Figure 4 provides the programmatic retention for each of the CS1 variants for majors enrolled in CS1 at the end of week 1. The denominator for numbers in this graph includes majors who pass, fail, withdraw, or drop after week 1. The impact of the new course is now magnified by three effects: fewer drops, fewer failures (withdraw, D, or F), and increased retention among those

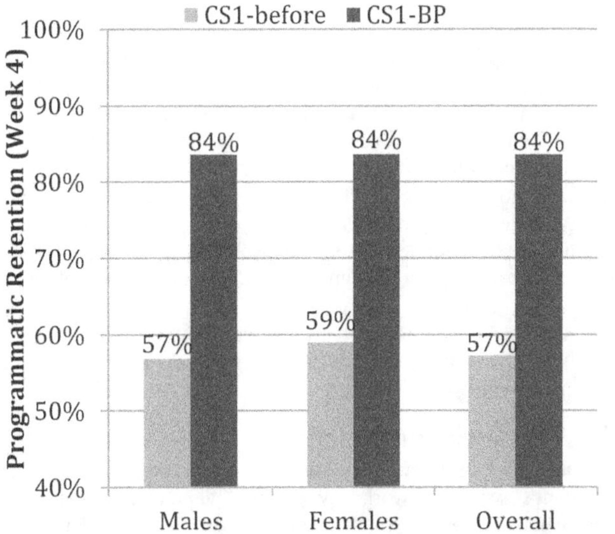

Figure 3. Programmatic Retention by gender for majors original enrolled in CS1 at Week 4. Differences are statistically significant ($p<0.05$).

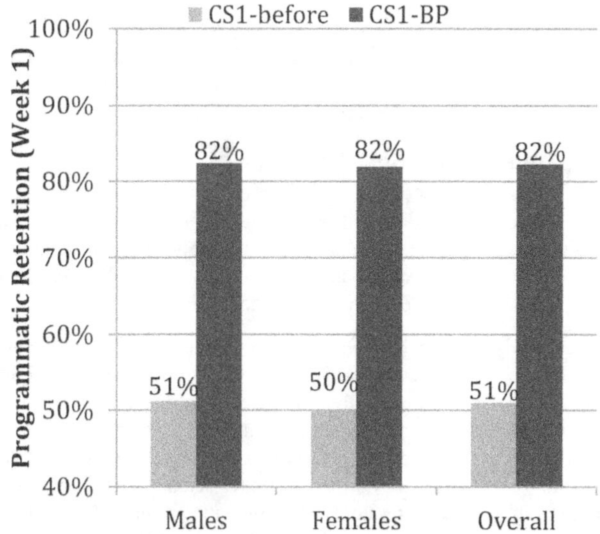

Figure 4. Programmatic Retention by gender for majors original enrolled in CS1 at Week 1. Differences are statistically significant ($p<0.05$).

who remain. These effects compound: increasing programmatic retention from 51% to 82% ($p<0.01$). Differences in both male and female programmatic retention based on week 1 are also statistically significant ($p<0.01$).

4.5 Advanced Track CS1

In Section 3 we discussed the potential threat to validity that our major was impacted (admission to the major was more selective) during the timeframe of CS1-Before (2001-2008) and not-impacted during the timeframe of CS1-BP (2008-2011). Those timeframes were also different in terms of national climate regarding computing as a field. Lastly, students from those different timeframes may have differed in terms of ability, interest in CS, and perceptions of CS.

To inform us as to the effect of timeframe on our results, we evaluated another class at our institution which had not changed. The course studied and modified here was for our standard CS1 track designed for students without (much) programming experience. The alternative advanced CS1 track is designed for students with programming experience. We hypothesized that national change in climate, change in students over time, and the shift of the major from impacted to not-impacted would benefit both sections of CS1. Analyzing programmatic retention for the advanced CS1 course, we found a minor improvement (83% to 87%); however the result was not statistically significant ($p=0.12$). Although the advanced and standard CS1 tracks may have a different composition of students, this result strengthens our belief that the retention improvements for CS1-BP were from the changes to the course, rather than the timeframe.

5. DISCUSSION

Our implementation of Media Computation, Pair Programming, and Peer Instruction appear to provide a proverbial hat-trick of instructional design resulting in significantly increased programmatic retention. This increase comes from both the retention of original majors and the addition of new majors. These results include data from 10 years of instruction including 26 different sections taught by 8 different instructors impacting over 3,000 students. Of those students who pass the course, the new course design increases retention by 18% (71%-89%). But what about the experience students have coming in our "front door"? It is when we evaluate the number of initially enrolled majors that we believe the true story is told. Previously, students, perhaps with little idea of what computing is about and what one does to "study" and "learn" computing, would start in our course, but one year later only 51% of that number would still be studying computing. **By adopting a complementary set of best practices, we seem to have patched up some major leaks in our pipeline—improving retention to 82%.** In this section, we first revisit threats to the validity of this work and specifically consider the impact on the female pipeline. We then discuss potential reasons why the trio of best practices has positively impacted retention.

5.1 Threats to Validity

The threats to validity from Section 3 remain relevant. The student population in our courses could have changed due, perhaps, to perception of the computing field or to our varying admission standards (impacted status). Additionally, this post-hoc study reports data from 10 years of real course data. We have no control over instructors and their very real and possibly varying, effects. That said, we report our best efforts to provide the readers a chance to assess these threats for themselves. We find that an alternate CS1 at our institution did not experience a statistically significant increase in retention over the period of our study. We also show results attempting to control for the instructor effect by providing a within-instructor comparison for the one instructor who has taught the course the most, covering both versions. We find similar gains for courses just taught by that instructor; although we do not analyze these courses at any finer granularity for factors which might impact retention.

5.2 Gender Differences

In Section 4.1 we found that CS-BP had a larger beneficial impact on males than females. However, that section analyzed retention among students who *pass* the course. As previously mentioned, one might artificially increase retention by passing fewer students (or by encouraging students to drop). After excluding these effects in Sections 4.3 and 4.4, males now benefit slightly less from the new course as there is a 31% improvement for males versus a 32% improvement for females. This effect is much less substantial than the difference in 4.1 and occurs because female pass rates improve in CS1-BP over CS1-Before more than males (female 15% and male 13%). Thus, evaluating retention based on week 1 and week 4 enrollments provides a potentially more accurate picture than retention among those students who pass.

5.3 Benefits of Best Practices

As previously mentioned, all three best practices—Media Computation, Pair Programming, and Peer Instruction—were selected because of the body of research supporting their benefits. Here we wish to provide our intuition as to why these best practices, combined, may provide increased retention.

A key study of why students are not retained in the sciences, *They're Not Dumb, They're Different* [12], may provide insight into this course. In that study, non-science graduate students and a non-science Ph.D. enrolled in introductory science classes and reported their experiences. From our analysis of the work, there are four key themes relevant to computer science that stem from Tobias' subjects' impressions of university science classes that make them unappealing: **Context** – science classes lack relevance to the real world; **Engagement** – student comments are not valued and they are uninvolved in lecture; **Competition** – students are in adversarial relationships with each other for grades; and **Community** – students are on their own without support. We believe the trio of best practices addresses each of these concerns:

Context. Media Computation provides the highly relevant and familiar domain of images and sounds for students. Moreover, the homework assignments designed for the course allow for a level of creativity in the solutions (photo collages, etc.) which might be difficult in different domains.

Engagement. Peer Instruction involves students directly into lecture in that they are frequently solving problems and discussing the material with other students and/or the professor. The applicable contextual domain from media computation also helps improve student interest and, hence, engagement.

Competition. Our changes result in student grades no longer being entirely individualistic, as parts of students' grades are now based on cooperative efforts. Homework assignments and Labs are done as pairs using Pair Programming. Class participation is graded on their answering of questions, not correctness. Peer Instruction has them working in cooperative groups during class. As such, the environment is much more collaborative.

Community. The same elements that reduce competitiveness also foster community. Pair Programming in assignments and labs provides students support avenues in the form of classmates. Peer Instruction provides each student with a group of other classmates with whom they work in each lecture, potentially creating an out-of-class support group as well.

In summary, one can see how Media Computation, Peer Instruction, and Pair Programming facilitate an engaging and cooperative classroom where students work with a domain relevant to their experiences.

6. CONCLUSION

In the fall of 2008 we adopted a trio of CS1 best practices including Media Computation, Peer Instruction, and Pair Programming. These were chosen because of supporting evidence from computing education research literature. In an in-situ study, we evaluate retention for students who pass the CS1 course and find an 18% absolute improvement in programmatic retention (students in the major one year later). Although these numbers summarize results from multiple instructors, we also find a 14% improvement for an individual instructor having taught multiple terms both with and without these improvements. Lastly, we find that failure rates and drop rates decreased in the best practices course. The combination of fewer students dropping, more students passing, and more passing students retained resulted in an absolute improvement of 31% (from 51% to 82%) in programmatic retention among students initially enrolling in our CS1 course. In this work we discussed our rationale for adopting these changes, potential threats to the validity of our results, and how these three best practices synergistically combine to improve retention.

7. Acknowledgements

Thank you to Dr. Rachel Roe-Dale and Dr. Jaime Spacco for their assistance with this work. We would also like to thank our anonymous reviewers for their constructive feedback. This work was supported in part by NSF grants 0933635 and 1140731.

8. REFERENCES

[1] Crouch, C. H., and Mazur, E. Peer instruction: Ten years of experience and results. *American Journal of Physics 69*. 2001.

[2] Cutts, Q., Esper, S., and Simon, B. Computing as the 4th "R": a general education approach to computing education. In *Proceedings of the seventh international workshop on Computing education research*. 2011.

[3] Forte, A., Guzdial, M. Motivation and nonmajors in computer science: identifying discrete audiences for introductory courses. *IEEE Trans on Education*, 48(2). 2005.

[4] Guzdial, M. and Ericson, B. Introduction to computing and programming with java: a multimedia approach. Prentice-Hall. 2007.

[5] McDowell, C., Werner, L., Bullock, H. E., Fernald, J. Pair programming improves student retention, confidence, and program quality. *Commun. ACM* 49, 8, 90-95. 2006.

[6] Porter, L., Bailey-Lee, C., Simon, B., Cutts, Q., and Zingaro, D. Experience report: a multi-classroom report on the value of peer instruction. *In proceedings of the 16th Annual Conference on Innovation and Technology in Computer Science Education*. 2011.

[7] Porter, L., Bailey-Lee, C. Simon, B., Zingaro, D. Peer instruction: do students really learn from peer discussion? *In the 7th Annual International Computing Education Research Workshop*. 2011.

[8] Simon, B. http://www.peerinstruction4cs.org/

[9] Simon, B., Kinnunen, P., Porter, L., Zazkis, D. Experience report: CS1 for majors with media computation. *In Proc. of 15th Annual Conference on Innovation and Technology in Computer Science Education*. 2010.

[10] Simon, B., Kohanfars, M., Lee, J, Tamayo, K., and Cutts, Q. Experience report: peer instruction in introductory computing. *In Proceedings of the 41st SIGCSE technical symposium on computer science education*, 2010.

[11] Snyder, L. Barnes, T., Garcia, D., Paul, J., and Simon, B. The first five computer science principles pilots: summary and comparisons. *ACM Inroads* 3, 2, 54-57. 2012.

[12] Tobias, S. They're not dumb, they're different: stalking the second tier. Research Corporation, Tucson. 1990.

Retention of STEM majors using Early Undergraduate Research Experiences

Bethany Bowling*, Heather Bullen†‡, Maureen Doyle§, John Filaseta‖
Northern Kentucky University
Nunn Drive
Highland Heights, KY 41099
bowlingb1@nku.edu, sieveb1@nku.edu, doylem3@nku.edu, filaseta@nku.edu

ABSTRACT
An early undergraduate research program for rising sophomores and juniors at risk of leaving STEM degree programs is described. Students are paid a stipend to work part-time, at a maximum of twenty hours per week, as part of a research team. Faculty researchers are not financially compensated for working with students. The program successfully brings together STEM departments to target students who are at risk of leaving their major. Initial results demonstrate a positive influence of undergraduate research in retaining STEM majors and improvements in Student Assessment of Learning Gains. Future work, including institutionalization of the project, is discussed.

Categories and Subject Descriptors
K.3.2. [**Computing Milieux**]: Computers and Education - *Computer and Information Science Education*

Keywords
Undergraduate research, STEM, Recruitment and Retention

1. INTRODUCTION
In 2010, NKU (Northern Kentucky University, a Midwest regional comprehensive university) received a five-year NSF grant (NSF-DUE-STEP award #0969280) to recruit and retain STEM majors. This award funded a project named FORCE (Focus on Occupation, Recruiting, Community and Engagement) which implemented six activities to achieve the goal of increasing the number of Science, Technology, Engineering and Mathematics (STEM) majors.

This paper reports the initial results of one of these 6 activities: UR STEM, an effort to increase the opportunities for rising sophomore and juniors to participate in paid undergraduate STEM research with an objective to retain undergraduate students in the STEM disciplines.

All five STEM departments are involved in the project. The PI is from Biological Sciences and the co-PI's are from Chemistry, Computer Science (CS), Mathematics and Statistics, and Physics and Geology.

The undergraduate research projects are interdisciplinary or specific to the discipline. Undergraduates can explore a computer science research project independent of their declared major.

Undergraduate research experiences have been shown to influence retention[12]. We were curious whether this could apply to rising sophomores and juniors who are at risk for leaving STEM? This paper discusses the implementation and evaluation of first three years of the UR STEM program.

2. BACKROUND
Tinto's influential theoretical work[14] about persistence in college suggests that the level of academic and social integration that a student feels at an institution has a direct relationship to the likelihood that the student will persist in their undergraduate studies. Empirical studies that produced only partial support for Tinto's theory motivated subsequent theories, many of which focus on the importance of institution culture and students' sense of belonging[1]. Although this body of work is not STEM-specific, we believe that the ideas apply to STEM departments as entities within institutions. For example, the cultural theory proposition, "Students who belong to one or more enclaves in the cultures of immersion are more likely to persist, especially if group members value achievement and persistence" ([6] p. 201), suggests that we should attend to activities that enable students to establish kinship within STEM.

Building on the outstanding work of Seymour and Hewitt[10], a team of researchers at the University of Oklahoma (OU), who conducted an ethnographic study focused on the success of one department, Industrial Engineering (IE), in attracting, retaining, and graduating women as well as men[7]. Among the results in the seminal Seymour and Hewitt work was the *push-pull* issue described by some students, including many high-performing ones, who switched out of STEM majors. In the OU study was a population of such students, termed *relocators* [7], who such experienced a *push* (e.g., "a lack of personal resonance with the perceived profession") or a *pull* from their original majors (e.g., visibility of the major through talks, printed information, word of mouth).

* : Department of Biological Sciences
† : Department of Chemistry
‡ : Deceased July 11, 2012
§ : Department of Computer Science
‖ : Department of Physics and Geology

There is strong research supporting success in student retention as a result of effective undergraduate research programs[3][4][6]. In addition, providing undergraduate research experiences to females is one of the recommendations for increasing women in computer science[2].

Margolis and Fisher had similar results to Oklahoma University in retaining females. They showed that efforts to retain and recruit female computer science undergraduate majors also recruited and retained more students overall[7].

Building on these successes we are investigating whether providing undergraduate research experiences to students early in their post-secondary academic career helps them persist in STEM majors by providing them with direct attention from faculty, involving them in a learner-centered community, and exposure to research and unanswered questions.

3. UR STEM PROGRAM

3.1 How it works

The UR STEM program follows a traditional, yet simplified, summer research application process. Faculty projects are solicited starting in December and closing mid-January. The program is advertised heavily within the university emphasizing students will be paid to work with a faculty member over the summer, 'no experience' is necessary and they can apply for projects outside of their major field of study. Students can apply online between the beginning of February and the first week of March. All student applications are given a rating of 0-4, where a higher rating indicates the student may be more at risk to leave STEM and not their qualifications. Faculty is encouraged to hire students with higher ratings. Faculty is given contact information and ratings for students interested in their project. Faculty independently interview and select the student(s) they want to work with. During the summer, an orientation and a scientific communication seminar are conducted with the students and they present research posters outlining their work during the first weeks of the fall semester. Students are also required to write a short summary and reflection of their research experience.

3.2 Faculty Research Projects

Faculty are recruited from the five STEM departments to submit research projects accessible to rising sophomores and juniors. Faculty understand the purpose of the program and are not financially compensated for participating. The application process is done online. Faculty provide a description of their research project, size of their research team, faculty collaborator(s) (if they exist), and what a student researcher would do. Faculty can submit multiple proposals and work with multiple students. We offer two research experiences: The mini-experience is ten hours per week for four weeks. The part-time experience is twenty hours of work per week for 10 weeks. The mini-experience stipend is 20% of the part-time stipend.

Department chairs and project personnel review proposals and work with faculty researchers to ensure that the proposed research is appropriate for rising sophomores and juniors.

Concern was raised by some department chairs that faculty would not be interested in participating since the target student population typically does not have the expertise required to contribute significantly to their research. The students also require more training and instruction than typical upperclass research students. Concern about participation was also raised because faculty are not paid. This may be an issue for individual faculty; however, faculty applications and interest have exceeded our funding capabilities for the past three years. We suspect that the large number of faculty projects is due to faculty supplementing their research teams with UR STEM students. There are exceptions to this: we have faculty who developed undergraduate research projects specifically for rising sophomores and juniors and approach this project as service. We also have faculty who have designed mini-experiences to allow a larger number of students to participate. Mini-experiences are used sparingly and are specifically defined. Mini-experiences have included data analysis in support of a grant, fossil extraction or a dinosaur remains dig in Utah.

3.3 Student Applications

UR STEM is advertised aggressively through student group web sites, course management web sites, flyers and personal invitations in classrooms and study sessions. Students can find all information online including pay, project descriptions, faculty research advisor, and time commitment.

The bar for student applications is purposefully low to encourage students to apply. Students simply fill out a brief form online. Students are asked to list their demographic information, work experience and a name of a faculty member with whom they have taken a class. We ask a few additional questions to ensure the student is eligible.

3.4 Rating Students Risk Factor

Student applications are reviewed by the PI's and co-PI's to ensure they meet the eligibility requirements for the program. Students' applications are eliminated if: they have done some type of STEM research on campus, either as an independent study or as a paid researcher; they are employed in a job in their field of study (e.g., pharmacy pre-major working in a pharmacy); have earned a baccalaureate degree in a STEM discipline; or are not enrolled at NKU for the current semester.

Eligible students are rated to encourage selection of students at risk of leaving the STEM discipline. Attributes of students at risk of leaving STEM were defined as rising sophomores and juniors, students who were not yet part of the university community[7], did not have experiences in research or the profession and might be susceptible to the push-pull issue[11], and students who struggled in a STEM course[4]. Students can earn a maximum of 4 points. Students who have earned all A's may not be at risk of leaving and get no points for grades. Students who have an F in a STEM class also earn 0 points. Students' whose lowest STEM grade is a B earns one point. Students whose lowest grade is a C or a D in a STEM class are awarded 2 points. Students earn one point for not working in a STEM-related field and one point for being a rising sophomore or junior.

The rating may be construed as punishing students who have earned a high GPA. As a regional comprehensive university, faculty typically include outstanding upper-class undergraduates on their research, teams thus this program is meant to expand the types of students involved in research. We suggest that UR STEM students be added to existing research projects as a supplement to their team. The program is intended to primarily benefit the students and not further faculties' specific research. There are many opportunities for outstanding students including multiple full-time research opportunities on our campus

In 2011, the Chemistry Department used the ratings most effectively and this model was used for all departments in 2012. Faculty receive a list of students interested in the project sorted by ranking. Faculty is instructed to interview students with higher ranks and the ranks of hired students are checked prior to final confirmation of student hires. They are also given the ground rule that students with higher rankings will be funded first. This is not a threat in departments that will not use all of their funds such as Computer Science and Mathematics and Statistics. However, it has challenged faculty in the Biological Sciences and Chemistry to choose at-risk students.

3.4.1 At Risk Identifier Results

In 2011, 78 students applied to participate in UR STEM and thirty students were selected to participate. Of the thirty, twenty-two were juniors or seniors at the time they conducted their research. In 2012, 113 students applied to the UR STEM program and thirty students were again selected. After implementation of the rating system, a smaller proportion, only 16/30, were upper-classmen. Table 1 presents the distribution of UR STEM students group by ratings. Of the three students with a rating of 1, all are female and one student was paired with a student with a rating of 4. The two other students with a rating of one worked with tenure-track assistant professors. The Computer Science department emphasized higher ratings and all UR STEM CS students had a rating greater than 2. This is a substantial improvement from 2010 where all three students had a rank of 1 or 2 from Computer Science.

Table 1. Distribution of UR STEM Students by Rank

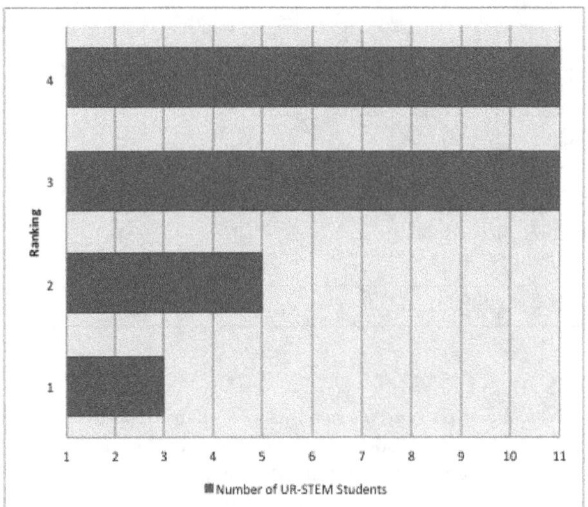

3.5 Summer Work

Most students work twenty hours per week for ten weeks. We initially offered more options for the research experience. In 2011 we offered full time (forty hours) experiences, which is standard for Research Experiences for Undergraduates[10], part-time research experiences and mini-experiences. Only two faculty members out of thirty-eight requested full time UR STEM students. In 2012 full-time was eliminated and only two options were offered to simplify the coordination and management of the project. Faculty preferred the part time option for two primary reasons. First, given a limit of funds we could impact more students. Second, students without a lot of background need more coaching, instruction, and oversight.

The faculty member and student researcher define the student's work schedule and research tasks. The student is required to submit a poster to a Celebration of Summer Research event held at NKU at the beginning of the fall semester. In addition, the student must submit a report on the work they did on the project and they are asked to complete a final survey.

Two lunch meetings are held during the summer with all of the UR STEM students. Their faculty advisors are invited. The initial meeting is a kick-off to inform students about the program and provide them with an overview of what to expect doing research and what is expected from them. Students are encouraged to ask questions, take notes and collaborate. UR STEM students often need a lot of coaching and the kick-off lays the groundwork for that. In particular, weekly meeting attendance and lab notebook protocol must be reviewed regularly. Students are required to take an online course on research ethics.

The second lunch meeting is held in July. Students are taught how to create a research poster and the logistics of getting it printed. This prepares them for creating their end-of-summer poster. It is held a month before classes start to provide adequate time for students and faculty to finish their research posters.

Figure 1 is a thumbnail of a poster done by a computer science research team of five students: three were UR STEM 2012 students and one a UR STEM 2011 student.

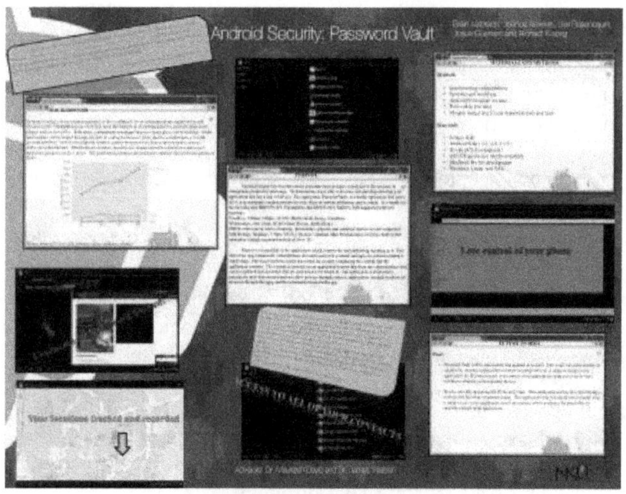

Figure 1. UR STEM Security Research Poster

4. UR STEM EVALUATION

The UR STEM evaluations for 2010 are not included due to the small sample size of three students. The formative evaluation results were used to improve the program for 2011.

4.1 Retention

In 2011, seventy-eight students applied to participate in UR STEM and thirty students were hired. We compared the preliminary retention numbers for the two groups. The first group were UR STEM students and the second group consisted of students who applied to UR STEM but were not selected. This analysis allows us to compare the retention of students in UR STEM to non-UR STEM students who were interested enough in STEM to apply for the program.

As of fall, 2012 84% of the non-UR STEM students either graduated in a STEM discipline or were majoring in a STEM discipline versus 87% of the UR STEM students. Of the 74 students who persisted at NKU, 11% (5) of the non-UR STEM students declared a non-STEM major while only 6% (2) of the UR STEM students declared a non-STEM major. Data continues to be collected on retention.

It should be noted that retention of STEM majors at our institution is lower than 80%. Retention within the STEM disciplines computed for 2009 graduates was only 28%.

4.2 Survey results

In 2011, twenty-two of the twenty-eight research mentors completed a questionnaire regarding their experience with the UR STEM program. The responses were overwhelmingly positive with all respondents saying they were strongly satisfied or satisfied with the UR STEM experience overall. Eighteen said they would consider being a mentor for the program again (four did not respond to the question), and sixteen of them proposed projects in 2012. An additional eight new faculty mentors proposed projects in 2012.

Also in 2011, eleven students (just under 37%) completed the voluntary questionnaire asking about their UR STEM experience. Over 80% of the students were strongly satisfied with the UR STEM experience overall. All of the student respondents reported spending 'a great deal' or 'a fair amount' of time engaged in meaningful research and they all felt the research was appropriately challenging. Since the intent of the UR STEM program is to encourage persistence, it was positive that two-thirds of the students 'strongly agreed' and the other one-third 'agreed,' that the experience confirmed their interest in continuing in a STEM field. While not a major goal of the program, the majority of students 'strongly agreed' or 'agreed' that the experience encouraged them to consider advanced study in their field.

The students were also asked about their gains in particular areas, similar to the Student Assessment of Learning Gains (SALG; Table 1) [13]. The vast majority felt they gained skills in problem solving, keeping data, working with technology, conducting procedures, and managing their time. The respondents also expressed gains in knowledge about specific theories and concepts and increased comfort in talking about research with others. While some of the projects were explicitly interdisciplinary, it does appear that roughly 20% of the students did not see the connections between the STEM disciplines.

In 2012, with the addition of orientation, we administered both a pre- and post-experience questionnaire. Although results are not available at the time of submission of this paper, improved response rates were observed, with over twenty students completing both questionnaires, we suspect due to the added structure of the summer events.

4.3 Threats to Validity

All students attended the same regional comprehensive University in the Midwest during spring, 2011. These results may not extend to different types of universities. In addition, the retention number computations were done using a pool of self-selecting students interested in exploring research. This is not a random sample of undergraduates.

An additional threat to validity is the assumption that students were involved in hands-on research. We did not monitor day-to-day student research activities and assignments. It can be argued that students may have been lab technicians instead of researchers.

Table 2. Percentage of students responding to their perceived gain in various areas related to skills, knowledge, and dispositions.

How much did you gain in the following areas as a result of the UR STEM experience?	**Great gain (%)**	**Good gain (%)**	**Mod gain (%)**	**Little gain (%)**	**No Gain**
Problem solving	36.4	36.4	27.2		
Understanding theory and concepts guiding my research project	72.7	27.3			
Understanding the connections among STEM disciplines	45.4	36.4		9.1	9.1
Confidence in my ability to contribute to science	63.6	27.3		9.1	
Keeping data and/or notes organized	45.4	36.4	9.1	9.1	
Working with technology	63.6	27.3	9.1		
Comfort in discussing scientific concepts with others	63.6	18.2	9.1	9.1	
Comfort in working collaboratively	63.6	27.3	9.1		
Understanding what everyday research work is like	63.6	27.3		9.1	
Taking greater care in conducting procedures in the lab or field	36.4	27.3	18.2	9.1	
Managing my time	36.4	54.5	9.1		

5. CS or STEM

There have been unforeseen benefits of collaborating with other STEM faculty on a student-success-centered project. CS has implemented others' successful efforts, such as a department-wide news web site. The department has also increased the percentage of students involved in undergraduate research. In addition, the CS department is being asked to participate in more outreach events. For example, there is a middle school STEM camp that is held each year at our university. In 2012, CS was asked to participate. We have also been invited to participate in high school outreach events.

Importantly, by collaborating with other STEM faculty who are passionate about recruiting and retaining students, we can examine the issue of retention for at-risk students. We could not have studied this for just our major due to other department commitments and interest.

6. CHALLENGES

The UR STEM program has evolved over the last three summers. Students and faculty have been interviewed and filled out surveys and their input helped us to improve the UR STEM process and program. There were also some challenges that required refinement of the program and process. Initial student and faculty feedback from the summer 2012 program indicate that the UR STEM process and program is stable.

The five departments involved have a large range of enrollment and different undergraduate research expectations. For example, all students majoring in Chemistry are expected to have a research experience prior to graduating. In Computer Science, fewer than 20% graduate having done research. The number of majors is also different in the five departments. Table 3 illustrates the differences in the number of students enrolled in the specified BS degree program. In addition to the degrees listed in table 3, all departments offer other degree programs and Biological Sciences students do not declare their first year, so the numbers below are not the total majors.

Table 3. Fall 2012 Enrollment by declared BS Majors

STEM Degree	Fall 2012 BS Majors
Biological Sciences	168
Chemistry	159
Computer Science	262
Mathematics	83
Physics	37

Their are funds for thirty students to participate in the part-time research experiences. One might argue that each department should be allotted funding to fund the same percentage of majors in each department. One might also argue that departments with low enrollment should be awarded additional funds to help increase their enrollment numbers. Our team decided that each department would be funds for five part-time UR STEM students and the department decides whether to use the funds for 5 part-time researchers or to offer a combination of mini-experiences and part-time experiences. Each department has until May 1st for their research students to sign UR STEM contracts. Remaining funds are 'returned' and are used by departments that have additional research projects. In the past two years, Mathematics and Statistics have not used all of their funds. The funds were used to support Computer Science and Chemistry researchers.

The student selection process has improved significantly since 2010. In 2010, only three UR STEM students were hired and all were in computer science. The max students ratings was a 2. This was not a concern in 2010 because the three students were able to be our alpha UR STEM testers. There feedback helped improve the UR STEM experience for the students.

Our goal is to retain students in the major. We used research to identify students who were at risk for leaving the major based on research of persistence in STEM. We revisit the ratings each year based on feedback from students, faculty and department chairs.

The quality of a number of UR STEM posters at the Summer Celebration of Summer Research in 2010 and 2011 were fair to poor. The UR STEM students needed detailed instructions on how to create a poster, the purpose of research poster and its content. In summer 2012 UR STEM students and their advisors were invited to a 'How to Create a Research Poster' talk and luncheon. The presentation was done by a junior faculty member not directly affiliated with this grant. The quality of the posters improved dramatically and the summer training will continue each summer.

Logistics, as expected, has been a challenge. The first two years, 2010 and 2011, the logistics were primarily handled by the PI and co-PI's with some assistance from departments on campus. In 2012, two campus centers contributed to the project with web development work and advertising.

7. FUTURE WORK

The UR STEM program for at-risk students interested in STEM has completed its third year. Feedback from affiliated students and faculty is reviewed annually to refine the program and steps have been taken to institutionalize the program.

UR STEM has been positively received and each year more of the organization work is being done by two centers on campus. The Kentucky Center of Mathematics (KCM) support has included website support. The Center for Integrative Science And Mathematics (CINSAM) is the logical home for this program once this grant has ended. Each year CINSAM takes on more of the logistics and leadership. In the final two years we will work on transitioning the remaining work to CINSAM.

UR STEM is supported by a NSF DUE-STEP grant and provides student stipends totaling $42K per summer, with $8400 allotted to each department. The university has committed to sustaining this program. Our retention numbers are positive and we hope to be able to demonstrate the effectiveness of this program using graduation rates starting in 2014. We will use these positive results to solicit external funding to supplement university-provided funds.

UR STEM does not consider underrepresented groups in the rating factors because underrepresented groups vary by department. For example, the department Biological Sciences does not have an issue with low gender representation unlike the departments of Computer Science and Physics. In 2010-2012, individual faculty could recruit underrepresented groups with high ranks when interviewing and hiring. In particular, Computer Science and Computer Information Technology faculty have interviewed and hired females, Hispanics and African American students. In 2011, 47% (15/32) UR STEM projects were awarded to females and in 2012 30% (9/30) were awarded to women and 6% (2/32) to Hispanic students. We will develop a process during the fall of 2012 to identify students from underrepresented groups. Departments will decide whether this information should be considered when selecting students or not. The departments of Computer Science and Physics and Geology have both committed to using this information when selecting students.

8. ACKNOWLEDGMENTS

Thank you to Dr. Brooke Buckley who selflessly joined our team and provided excellent ideas and suggestions which greatly improved our work. We received leadership and financial support from Northern Kentucky University's Center for Integrated Natural Sciences and Mathematics (CINSAM), the Kentucky Center for Mathematics (KCM), the Provost and the following departments: Biological Sciences, Chemistry, Computer Science, Mathematics and Statistics, and Physics. The improvements to this project are a direct result of the contributions of Dr. Teri J. Murphy of Northern Kentucky University and Dr. Cindy Foor from Oklahoma University. This material is based upon work supported by the National Science Foundation's STEM Talent Expansion Program (DUE-STEP) program under Grant No. 0969280. Any opinions, findings and conclusions or recommendations expressed in this material are those of the authors and do not necessarily reflect the views of the National Science Foundation.

9. REFERENCES

[1] Braxton, J. M. (Ed.). (2000). *Reworking the Student Departure Puzzle*. Nashville, TN: Vanderbilt University Press.

[2] Cuny, J., Aspray W., (2000). *Recruitment and Retention of Women Graduate Students in Computer Science and Engineering.* Washington, DC, Computing Research Associates.

[3] Gutierrez, C. G., Tunstad, L. M., Fratiello, A., & Nickolaisen, S. L. (2003). Undergraduate Research Participation Increases Minority Retention and Success in Chemistry, Abstracts of Papers, 225th ACS National Meeting, New Orleans, LA.

[4] Gregerman, S. R., Lerner, J. S., Hippel, W. von. , Jonides, J. & Nagda, B. A. (1998) Undergraduate Student-Faculty Research Partnerships Affect Student Retention. *The Review of Higher Education* 22.1, 55-72.

[5] Karukstis, K. & Elgren, T. (Eds.). (2007). *Developing and Sustaining a Research- Supportive Curriculum: A Compendium of Successful Practices*. Council on Undergraduate Research: Washington, DC.

[6] Kuh, G. D. & Love, P. G. (2000). A cultural perspective on student departure. In J. M. Braxton (Ed.), *Reworking the Student Departure Puzzle* (pp. 196-212). Nashville, TN: Vanderbilt University Press.

[7] Lopatto, D. (2004a). Survey of Undergraduate Research Experiences (SURE): First findings. Cell Biology Education, 3, 270 – 277.

[8] Margolis, J., Fisher, A., (2003). *Unlocking the Clubhouse: Women in Computing.* MIT Press.

[9] Murphy, T. J., Shehab, R. L., Reed-Rhoads, T., Foor, C. E., Harris, B. J., Trytten, D. A., et al. (2007). Achieving parity of the sexes at the undergraduate level: A study of success. *Journal of Engineering Education, 96*(3), 241-252.

[10] NSF Computer and Information System REU's http://www.nsf.gov/crssprgm/reu/list_result.cfm?unitid=5049 (referenced September 6, 2012)

[11] Seymour, E., & Hewitt, N. M. (1997). *Talking About Leaving: Why Undergraduates Leave the Sciences*. Oxford: Westview Press.

[12] Seymour, E., Hunter, A., Laursen, S. L., & Deantoni, T. (2004). Establishing the benefits of research experiences for undergraduates in the sciences: First findings from a three-year study. *Science Education, 88*, 493-534.

[13] Seymour, E., Wiese, D., Hunter, A. & Daffinrud, S.M. (Marzo del 2000). Creating a Better Mousetrap: On-line Student Assessment of their Learning Gains. Paper presentation at the National Meeting of the American Chemical Society, San Francisco, CA.

[14] Tinto, V..1993.. *Leaving College: Rethinking the Causes and Cures of Student Attrition, (2nd ed.)*. Chicago: University of Chicago Press.

[15] Walden, S. E., & Foor, C. E. (2008). "What's to keep you from dropping out? Student Immigration into and within Engineering. *Journal of Engineering Education, 97*(2), 191-205.

Halving Fail Rates using Peer Instruction: A Study of Four Computer Science Courses

Leo Porter
Skidmore College
Saratoga Springs, NY 12866
Leo.Porter@skidmore.edu

Cynthia Bailey-Lee and Beth Simon
University of California, San Diego
La Jolla, CA 92093
{clbailey, bsimon}@cs.ucsd.edu

ABSTRACT

Peer Instruction (PI) is a teaching method that supports student-centric classrooms, where students construct their own understanding through a structured approach featuring questions with peer discussions. PI has been shown to increase learning in STEM disciplines such as physics and biology. In this report we look at another indicator of student success — the rate at which students pass the course or, conversely, the rate at which they fail. Evaluating 10 years of instruction of 4 different courses spanning 16 PI course instances, we find that adoption of the PI methodology in the classroom reduces fail rates by a per-course average of 61% (20% reduced to 7%) compared to standard instruction (SI). Moreover, we also find statistically significant improvements within-instructor. For the same instructor teaching the same course, we find PI decreases the fail rate, on average, by 67% (from 23% to 8%) compared to SI. As an in-situ study, we discuss the various threats to the validity of this work and consider implications of wide-spread adoption of PI in computing programs.

Categories and Subject Descriptors

K.3.2 [**Computer Science Education**]

General Terms

Performance, Human Factors.

Keywords

Peer Instruction, Active Learning, Student-Centric Learning, Assessment, Flipped Classroom.

1. INTRODUCTION

Peer Instruction (PI) is a teaching method — an instructional approach applicable to a range of disciplines and content. PI supports a student-centered learning environment by replacing some of lecture time's traditional "sage on the stage" activity with "guide on the side" student-focused activity. That is, instructor explanation is augmented and/or replaced with carefully crafted questions designed to engage students in learning. The "peer" in PI comes from the core of the PI methodology — having students discuss and analyze questions in small groups. While many of us may ask students to "work in groups" at times, PI generally uses clickers to motivate full participation and to enable quick gathering and review of the entire class' views. The combination of personal responsibility (perhaps by assigning points for clicking), peer discussion, and student feedback (including seeing and hearing how their peers are doing) underlie the PI experience. As one of a number of student-centric learning approaches (including collaborative learning, active learning, cooperative learning, guided inquiry learning, and problem-based learning [3]), PI has appeal because it can be implemented in "standard" lecture halls and with relatively fewer course modifications than other techniques.

There is a significant body of research showing the positive impact of PI on learning gains, most notably in physics (where performance on a standardized concept inventory improved two-fold) [1], but also in chemistry and biology [2,5,6]. Numerous calls have been made in the U.S. encouraging university faculty to adopt such evidence-based practices — including in reports from the National Research Council and the President's Council of Advisors on Science and Technology [11]. Such efforts are considered critical to increasing the populace's preparation in STEM areas.

In support of this call, PI has been adopted at our institution in a variety of computing courses by various instructors over the past four years. Here we perform a *post-hoc, in-situ study of the adoption of PI in 4 different courses (CS1, CS1.5, Theory of Computation, and Computer Architecture), spanning 16 course instances, taught by 7 different instructors.* Due to the lack of standardized assessments and the nature of the in-situ study (instructors retain academic freedom, set their own exams, etc.), it is not possible to report strict learning gains. However, in this report we seek to consider the impact of PI from a programmatic point of view. Specifically we seek to answer the question: *Do fewer students in PI classes have to retake the course due to withdrawing or earning a D or F grade (WDF) than in standard instruction courses?*

Obviously, there are many benefits to more students passing a course — reduced time to degree, smaller class sizes (assuming students re-take the course to pass it), possibly increased retention in the major, and even reduced student and instructor angst.

The results from our study are very encouraging:

- Course fail rates are reduced 25-81% — with an average (by course) reduction of 61% ($p<0.01$).
- It is not simply that instructors who adopt PI are "better" than others who teach that course. We measured the change in fail rate for four instructors who had taught the course using standard instruction (lecture) before adopting PI. In this within-instructor study, fail rates are reduced by 40-87% with an average (by instructor) reduction of 67%.
- Finally, in a 10-year retrospective of one specific course, CS1, we find a) the *average* fail rate in non-PI offerings (N=18) is higher than the fail rate in *any* PI offering (N=9)

and b) the average fail rate in PI offerings is lower than all but one instance of non-PI offerings.

Throughout this paper, *fail rate* refers to the number of students earning a W (withdraw), D, or F grade out of the total number of students earning a passing (A,B,C) or failing (W,D,F) grade.

2. BACKGROUND - PI

The PI methodology commonly consists of the following components [1]:

1. **Before class.** Students are assigned to complete preparatory work (often textbook reading, but this could include watching online lectures). The goal is to have students learn some of the more basic items, concepts, or definitions before class, so that these do not have to be presented in class, thus creating time for student engagement. To incentivize students to complete this work, a quiz or other assessment of some sort is given before each "lecture" (either online, or perhaps at the beginning of the lecture [1,6,14]).

2. **During class.** Students engage with questions designed to help them confront and explore challenging concepts. Often these questions are posed as multiple-choice and students gain credit for answering the questions with a clicker (or other electronic polling device). Specifically, the algorithm of a clicker question episode in class should be:
    a. Pose a question, students answer individually (generally, results not displayed for class).
    b. Small group discussion (2-3 students) where students discuss their thinking and share their analyses with each other.
    c. Students all answer a second time, perhaps changing their answer based on group discussion. (The results of student responses can be shown at this point, or after the discussion below.)
    d. Class-wide discussion facilitated by the instructor is preferably led by first asking students to share the explanations and discussions they had in their group. The instructor provides clarification of how the question can be analyzed. The correct answer is clearly indicated.

Traditional explanatory lecture materials are likely reduced or removed (e.g. basic materials to be learned in pre-class work). However, lecture-style explanation or examples may either precede or follow clicker questions to provide further explanation or clarify challenging issues or concepts from pre-class preparation.

Colloquially, instructors implementing the PI methodology are often described as using clickers in their class. This is not always the case. Clickers are a technology that can be used in many ways. In this paper we report specifically on the use of clickers to implement the PI methodology[1].

3. RELATED WORK

Peer Instruction is an active learning pedagogy that utilizes lecture time to engage students in problem solving and group discussion. PI was introduced by physics professor Eric Mazur [1] and has been extensively studied in university physics classrooms. It has subsequently been adopted in other natural sciences [2,5,6]. PI in physics courses has been shown to significantly increase student learning, doubling the normalized learning gains [1].

PI use is associated with lower failure rates in introductory biology classes [5]. In physics classes using PI, a factor of two to three reduction in mid-course withdrawals was reported [7].

In recent years, PI has begun to be adopted in computer science [3,8,9,10,14,15,18]. In computer science, PI has been shown to be valued by students [9, 14], be valued by instructors [9], and result in individual learning [10,15]. We are not aware of any study of the impact of PI on pass/fail rates in computer science courses.

4. METHODS

This work reports fail rates, that is, incidence of students withdrawing from the class or completing the course with a grade of D or F. The study draws data from the previous 10 years for 4 courses, encompassing 120 classes, taught by more than 20 different instructors, and a total enrollment of more than 10,000.

4.1 Institution

All results reported are for courses taught at a large, public, research-oriented institution. The academic year at this institution consists of three 10-week quarters. All summer session classes were excluded from this study, because the student and instructor demographics diverge from the regular school year, and because summer sessions are often run on an intensive five-week schedule.

At this institution, students may drop classes up to four weeks into the term without any record. After the fourth week and until the end of the ninth week, students may drop classes with a W ("withdraw") grade recorded. All others completing the course either earn a passing grade (A, B, C, P (pass)) or a failing grade (D, F, NP (no pass)).

4.2 Courses and Instructors

We collected all enrollment history and grade data for the past 10 years for 4 courses that have been taught using PI at this institution. All course instances not using PI are reported as standard instruction (SI) courses. The numbers of SI instances and PI instances of each course occurring in those years are shown in Table 1. The "Total Enrollment" figure in Table 1 is not the number of distinct students, because many students took more than one of the four classes.

Most results are reported in aggregate by course, combining classes taught by different instructors. We have additionally separated out data for courses that have both SI and PI instances for the same instructor. We will identify the four instructors in this category by number (1-4). Of these, one instructor taught Computer Architecture and the other three taught CS1.

Statistical significance was determined using a two-tailed z-test for two independent groups, comparing the population of students impacted by SI against the population impacted by PI. Statistical significance is denoted as a p-value of less than 0.05.

4.3 Instructor Background

The instructors reflect a range of career stages and history with PI. Of the seven who used PI, two are active in research about PI and mentoring others in the practice, and developed their own PI materials. The five others used materials developed by others. Some had little or no exposure to PI until immediately before the start of the quarter. All of the following career titles and ranks are represented amongst both the SI and PI instructor pools in this

[1] Although the PI pedagogy may be implemented with lower-tech alternatives (e.g. colored cards), research on effectiveness is mixed. A large study in biology showed an advantage for clickers over cards [4], though a smaller physics study showed no benefit [6]. In any case, clickers are bought by students like textbooks and are generally re-sellable.

Table 1. Profile of classes studied. Instructor Totals may not reflect sum as instructors may teach more than one course.

		CS1	CS1.5	Theory	Arch.	Total
Number of Classes	SI	18	23	31	32	104
	PI	9	4	2	1	16
Number of Different Instructors	SI	5	5	9	9	23
	PI	4	1	2	1	7
Total Enrollment	SI	1764	1937	2674	2237	8612
	PI	1296	361	343	68	2068

study: tenure-track faculty, teaching-oriented faculty, adjunct faculty, lecturers, and graduate students.

4.4 Threats to Validity

This study is a post-hoc, in-situ study of independently run university classes and, by that nature, cannot impose experimental controls. We identify various threats to the validity of this work, and in some cases, efforts made to manage these threats. Readers are encouraged to consider these as they evaluate likeliness of replication of the results.

Variation in Difficulty between Instances of the Same Course. As a post-hoc study, no controls were imposed to ensure that instructors did not make their classes easier (which could impact W rate), or their final exams and grades more lenient (which could impact D/F rates). Instructors retain academic freedom over their classes and hence determine assignments, exams, and grades. Even for our Instructors 1-4, for whom we have both SI and PI data, we cannot assume that exam and grading difficulty was constant between classes, as PI might change an instructor's perspective on what is fair. On the other hand, students have continued in our program and there has been no noticeable increase in "drop outs" or poorer performance in follow-on courses, though this has not been formally measured.

High-Quality Instructors Self-Select to Use PI. Perhaps the population of instructors who would adopt a new teaching practice, such as PI, self-selects for instructors who are better overall. For this threat, we present two mitigating factors. First, three of the seven PI instructors (two in CS1 and one in theory) did not adopt PI in a way characteristic of pure self-selection. They were assigned to a class within a week or two of the start of the term and they adopted PI, in part, because PI materials were available for the course and there was no time to prepare anything else. Second, we report intra-instructor results for Instructors 1-4, who taught the same course in both SI and PI modes. These results therefore control for general quality of the person as an instructor (though, as noted earlier, changes in grading difficulty are still possible).

Variation in Other Aspects of Course Design. Due to principles of academic freedom, instances of a given course can vary, sometimes widely, in course design and even in the topics covered. In particular, we note that CS1 was changed in several significant ways at the same time that it was switched to PI — adopting pair programming for assignments and a contextualized media computation approach similar to those reported in [9,13]. These changes apply to all CS1 PI instructors.

Reproducibility of Outcomes Depends on Quality of PI Materials. The materials for two courses were developed by an instructor with a background in computing education research and who had notable experience in best-practices uses in physics. Both of the other courses had materials developed by instructors who TAed for, or were otherwise advised by, the first instructor.

Students may have Changed over Time. The first PI course at our institution occurred in the Fall of 2008. Hence, when comparing PI vs. SI, many of the PI classes were taught later in our 10 year window than the SI classes. The decrease in fail rate may be partially attributable to a potential improvement in our students. We first analyzed fail rates for the past 5 years (rather than 10 years) and found similar results. In Section 5.4, we extend this analysis by evaluating another introductory CS course to determine if a change occurred between the SI and PI time-periods of study and no statistically significant change is found.

5. RESULTS

We look at the impact of PI adoption in three ways: a longitudinal review of fail rates in PI and SI classes in the Fall 2001-Spring 2012 timeframe, a within-instructor comparison of fail rates for those who taught a course at least once using each method (PI and SI), and a detailed, per term, longitudinal look at fail rates in CS1 (PI course N=9, SI course N=18).

5.1 Longitudinal Effects

In Figure 1, we provide the reduction in fail rate for the course. We define reduction in fail rate as:

$$\textbf{\textit{Reduction}} = (\textbf{\textit{Fail\_Rate}}_{SI} - \textbf{\textit{Fail\_Rate}}_{PI})/\textbf{\textit{Fail\_Rate}}_{SI}$$

We can see from Figure 1 that the PI adoption reduces fail rates dramatically (59% or more) in 3 of the 4 courses with statistically significant improvements ($p<0.05$) in all but the CS1.5 course ($p=0.066$). There are a number of issues that might explain why PI had less of an impact in CS1.5 — including that it is a direct follow-on of CS1 — which are further explored in the Discussion.

It is also of value to look at the raw fail rates of students in both SI and PI courses. Figure 2 provides these results. Somewhat surprisingly, Theory edges out CS1 for highest fail rate in the SI setting. PI reduces fail rates in the lower division courses to around 10% and in upper division courses to around 5%. Particularly noteworthy is the reduction in fail rate in the theory course. In general, this course has a reputation at our institution of being challenging and not-well-loved — both because of its math-based nature and because students do not generally feel it relevant to their future careers. Exactly what aspects of PI might be contributing to this increased success and why is a subject for future work.

5.2 Within-Instructor Effects

A potential threat to validity is that those who would choose to adopt PI are "excellent" instructors. To partially address this concern, we compared the fail rates of four instructors who had taught the same course using both SI and PI methods.

Figure 3 shows reduction in fail rates and Figure 4 provides absolute fail rates for these four instructors. All instructors experience a statistically significant ($p<0.05$) reduction in fail rate. Averaged by instructor, switching to PI lowers absolute fail rate by 15% — a reduction of 67%. The instructor who originally adopted PI at our institution and has served as a mentor for many of the other adopters is Instructor 1. Oddly, that instructor experiences one of the smallest benefits. Instructors 2 and 4 were mentored in the PI adoption process by Instructor 1 with Instructor 4 receiving the most support. The improvement by

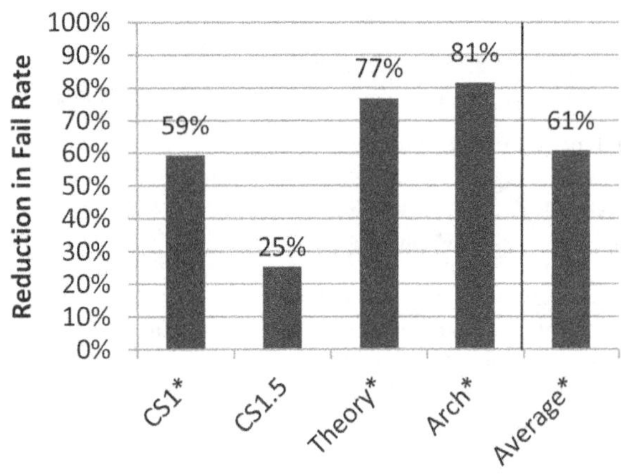

Figure 1. Reduction in Fail rates by course. Changes marked with a * are statistically significant (p<0.05).

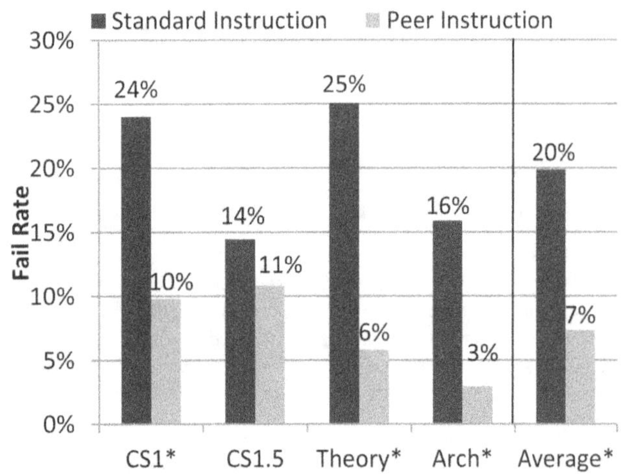

Figure 2. Comparison in Fail Rates in SI and PI course offerings. Changes marked with a * are statistically significant.

Instructor 4 bodes well for other faculty looking to adopt PI and may emphasize the value of mentoring. It bears noting that no instructor who taught with PI in a given course has subsequently returned to SI for that course.

5.3 Further Analysis: CS1

CS1 has the largest number of PI adopters (4) and PI sections (9), which makes looking at variations across SI and PI instances more meaningful. Figure 5 provides the fail rates per section of CS1 arranged with SI on the left and PI on the right, and within method, sorted by fail rate. The overall average for SI and PI sections is on the far right. The number of students is provided as well is the term: those without a + were taught in the Fall, those with a + were taught in the Winter or Spring. Winter and Spring classes commonly have a different student demographic (fewer majors, etc.) than Fall classes.

Of interest is that although the Winter/Spring sections were among the worst instances with SI, this does not appear to be the case for PI instances. Another point of interest is that class size does not appear to contribute to fail rate trend in either instructional mode. PI again stands out as providing a significant

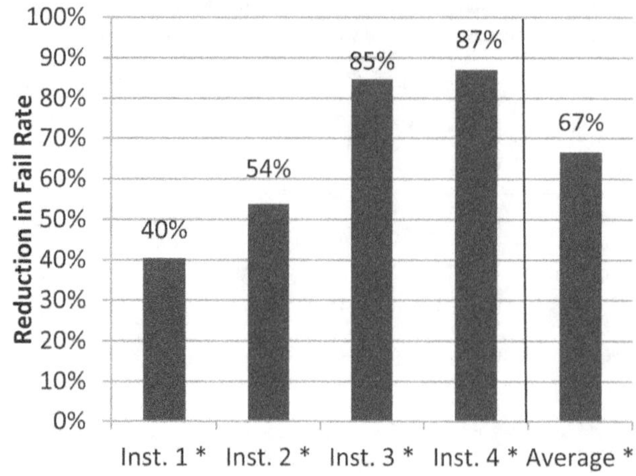

Figure 3. Reduction in Fail rates for instructors who taught both SI and PI instantiations of the same course. Changes marked with a * are statistically significant.

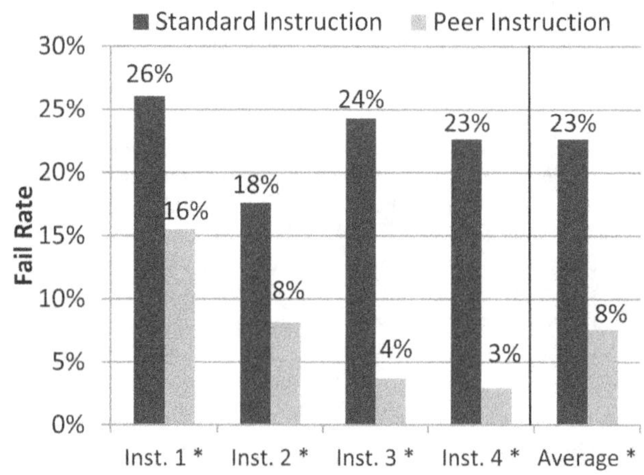

Figure 4. Fail rates for instructors who taught both SI and PI instantiations of the same course. Changes marked with a * are statistically significant.

reduction in fail rates. In fact, the *worst* PI instance has a lower fail rate than the *average* SI instance.

5.4 Student Improvement

One challenge to the validity of the study might be that students at our institution have been getting stronger (as evidenced by their ability to pass courses) over the past few years. To help evaluate this possibility we evaluated the fail rates for a different advanced-track CS1 course (for those with prior programming experience). The fail rates in the advanced track CS1 for more recent instances (Fall 2008-present) were actually slightly higher than older instances (Fall 2001-Spring 2007) (21% vs. 20%) and are not significantly different (p=0.54). Although the course makeup may be different for each track of CS1, this provides some contradictory evidence to the claim of students improving with time. Additional analysis in Theory and Architecture do not evidence notable differences in SI fail rate averages when considered for the last 10 years or just the last 5.

5.5 Statistical Significance

Table 2 provides the statistical significance of the evaluations in pass rates reported above using a two-tailed z-test for two independent groups.

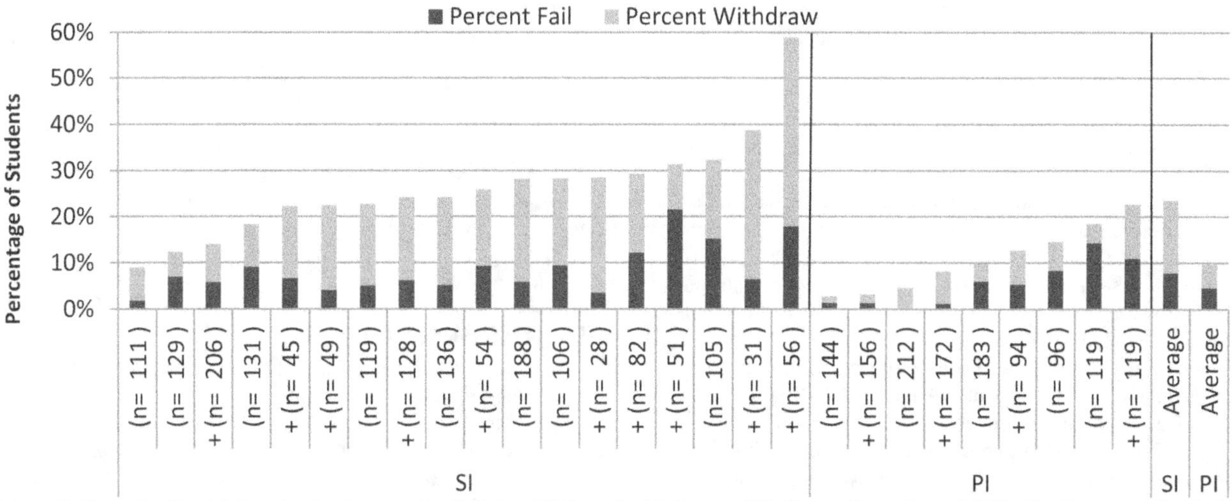

Figure 5. Longitudinal fail rates broken up by failures (DF) and withdraws (W) for each section of CS1. Sections are divided by SI or PI. The number of students (n) is provided. + denotes a class taught in the Winter or Spring.

6. DISCUSSION

6.1 Better Learning or Lowered Standards

In classes where instructors adopted PI, failure rates were, on average, reduced by more than half. Is this a good thing? Are more students learning what they need to pass the class or are the instructors lowering standards? This study does not allow us to answer these questions. We note that ultimate responsibility falls on the instructor to maintain the rigor of a course such that passing students have the requisite knowledge, understanding, and skills for future coursework and careers. The extent to which this is regularly measured may vary by institution depending on, for example, whether courses use common exams, have detailed course learning goals [17], and/or departments analyze exam scores or other student work.

"Making a course easier to pass" can be something to support — not avoid — depending on how it is accomplished. The obvious approach to avoid is to lower standards, effectively reducing the required knowledge, understanding, or skill required to pass. Alternatively, what if a course is "easier" without lowering standards? *By designing a course to better support students in their attainment of learning goals, standards can be preserved while facilitating "easier" learning.* For example, a course may be "easier" if is designed to offer students a better learning environment: one tailored to support learning experiences based on what is known about how the brain learns.

Whether PI facilitated such a learning environment or if standards eroded (or some combination of the two) during the ten years' worth of courses analyzed, we cannot say. We can say that none of our follow-on courses has seen a spike in failure rates, but that has issues in itself and provides only a partial answer. Even a post-hoc study would be of limited use as variation in course evaluation schemes may mean that for Course X an "A" could be earned with a 45% on the final exam whereas in Course Y 90% might be required for the same grade. A concurrently reported study that might inform these questions had a single instructor teach the "same" course with all the same components except for the teaching method [15]. This study reports that students experiencing the PI method score 5.7% better on the final exam than their SI counterparts.

Table 2. Statistical significance of pass rate comparisons.

Comparison	Pass Rate SI	Pass Rate PI	p-value
CS1	76.0%	90.2%	<0.01*
CS1.5	85.5%	89.2%	0.066
Theory	74.9%	94.2%	<0.01*
Architecture	84.1%	94.1%	<0.01*
Inst. 1	74.0%	84.5%	<0.01*
Inst. 2	82.4%	91.9%	<0.01*
Inst. 3	75.7%	96.3%	<0.01*
Inst. 4	77.4%	97.1%	<0.01*

We reiterate that we make an explicit assumption in this study that instructors did not intentionally or otherwise make their courses easier by reducing what students were expected to know. To the extent that this assumption may be violated, the results of the study may not be replicable.

6.2 CS 1.5

CS1.5 experienced a considerably lower change in fail rate. This can be partially explained by the low CS1.5 SI fail rate of 15%, as this provides less room for improvement. However, we suspect the more likely cause is that CS1.5 is the direct follow-on to CS1. In the SI classes, the high CS1 fail rate of 35% may have removed many of the students who might have struggled in CS1.5, contributing to the low SI CS1.5 fail rate. In the PI classes, the greater number of students who pass PI CS1 courses can continue on and pass PI CS1.5. Thus the finding of a large impact on the front-end and a smaller impact on the backend of this two course sequence is unsurprising.

6.3 Programmatic Responsibilities

These results can have a potentially large impact from a departmental or programmatic view in the following ways:

1. **Retention** – Students failing CS1 are at high risk for leaving the major. Having more students succeed in CS1 may result in higher retention of students in the major [13]. There is the

potential that these additional students ultimately struggle in later classes, which we plan to study as our PI CS1 cohorts continue.

2. **Efficiency** – Particularly in upper-division courses needed for the major, students who fail the course are likely to repeat it. The 16-percentage-point reduction in failed students in our theory and architecture courses could potentially result in fewer (or smaller) courses needing to be taught.
3. **Time to Degree** – Student failures can result in additional terms before degree conferral. Although a more comprehensive study is warranted, our average time to degree is 4.3 years which is 0.3 years longer than the standard 4 year plan. Reducing failure rates by 60% should conceivably reduce time to degree.
4. **Student Satisfaction** – Evaluating student failure as mere percentages can lose sight of the fact that failing a course can be devastating for students. Failure not only impacts self-worth but can also impact financial student aid and, in some cases, the ability of a student to stay at the institution. For those who persevere, one wonders at negative feelings they might harbor toward that experience. These feelings may result in lower degree/institution satisfaction and alumni participation.

The impact of these reductions in failure rates is an interesting topic within itself and is the topic of ongoing research. While it is undeniably the student's work (or lack of work) that fails a course, these results do contribute to a consideration of whether students would be right to wonder whether our instructional practices are supporting, or failing, them.

6.4 Recommendations

For readers interested in adopting PI in their courses to achieve similar reductions in fail rate, we provide the following recommendations:

1. **Best Practices** – Best Practices for Peer Instruction can be found online [12,16] and can serve as an excellent starting point for potential adopters.
2. **Materials** – The development of materials for PI requires time and effort and materials improve with use. We encourage potential adopters to review the materials available for a number of computer science classes online [12].
3. **Support** – Each of the instructors in this study, other than the initial adopter, had at least one PI mentor assisting them in the adoption of PI in their course. We highly recommend potential adopters seek out personal mentorship (feel free to contact the authors who can serve as mentors or point you to a potential mentor in your area). We are interested in further study of the factors supporting instructors in adoption of PI.

7. CONCLUSIONS

Classes implementing the Peer Instruction methodology have been shown to improve student learning outcomes in other STEM disciplines. This result is challenging to convincingly replicate in computing, due to our lack of standardized assessment instruments. However, we consider an important programmatic metric of success — student pass rates. Comparing against a 10-year, 10,000+ student, longitudinal set of course data from our own institution, we find that in courses where instructors adopt PI, course fail rates are reduced by an average of 61% (a reduction in absolute fail rates of 13%). Additionally, we identify that this effect is likely not due to student improvement with time or due to PI being implemented by "better" instructors. From a within-instructor comparison of four instructors, we find fail rates to decrease an average of 67% (a reduction in absolute fail rates of 15%). While this in-situ, retrospective study lacks some perhaps desirable controls, we believe its real-world nature lends the results additional credence.

8. ACKNOWLEDGEMENTS

In memoriam of Dr. Allan Snavely. Thank you to Dr. Rachel Roe-Dale, Dr. Jaime Spacco, and the anonymous reviewers for their contributions to this work. This work was supported in part by NSF grant 1140731.

9. REFERENCES

[1] Crouch, C. H., and Mazur, E. Peer instruction: Ten years of experience and results. *American J. of Physics 69*, 2001.

[2] Caldwell, J. E. Clickers in the large classroom: Current research and best-practice tips. *CBE-Life Sciences Education* 6, 2007.

[3] Cutts, Q., Esper, S., and Simon, B. Computing as the 4th "R": a general education approach to computing education. *Proc. 7th ICER*, 2011.

[4] Eberlein T, Kampmeier J, Minderhout V, Moog RS, Platt T, Varma-Nelson P, White HB. Pedagogies of engagement in science. A comparison of PBL, POGIL, and PLTL. Biochem Mol Biol Educ 36, 262–273, 2008.

[5] Freeman S, O'Connor E, Parks JW, Cunningham M, Hurley D, et al. Prescribed active learning increases performance in introductory biology. *CBE-Life Science Education. 6:132–39*. 2007.

[6] Knight, J. K., and Wood, W. B. Teaching more by lecturing less. *Cell Biology Education 4*, 2005.

[7] Lasry, N., Mazur, E., and Watkins, J. Peer instruction: From Harvard to the two-year college, *" Am. J. Phys. 76 (11), 1066-1069*, 2008.

[8] Pargas, R. P., and Shah, D. M. Things are clicking in computer science courses. *Proc. of 37th SIGCSE*, 2006.

[9] Porter, L., Bailey-Lee, C., Simon, B., Cutts, Q., and Zingaro, D. Experience Report: A Multi-classroom Report on the Value of Peer Instruction. *Pro. of 16th ITiCSE*, 2011.

[10] Porter, L., Bailey-Lee, C. Simon, B., Zingaro, D. Peer Instruction: Do Students Really Learn from Peer Discussion*? In Proc. 7th ICER*, 2011.

[11] Prepare and Inspire: K–12 Education in Science, Technology, Engineering, and Math (STEM) for America's Future. Executive Office of the President, Washington, D.C., 2010.

[12] Simon, B. http://www.peerinstruction4cs.org/

[13] Simon, B., Kinnunen, P., Porter, L., Zazkis, D. Experience Report: CS1 for Majors with Media Computation. *Proc. of 15th ITiCSE*, 2010.

[14] Simon, B., Kohanfars, M., Lee, J, Tamayo, K., and Cutts, Q. Experience report: Peer instruction in introductory computing. *Proc. of 41st SIGCSE,* 2010.

[15] Spacco, J., Parris, J., Simon, B. How we teach impacts learning: peer instruction vs. lecture in CS0. *Proc. of 44th SIGCSE*, 2013.

[16] UBC Science Education Initiatives. Clicker Resource Guide, http://cwsei.ubc.ca/resources/clickers.htm.

[17] UBC Science Education Initiatives. Learning Goals, http://cwsei.ubc.ca/resources/learn_goals.htm.

[18] Zingaro, D. Experience report: Peer instruction in remedial computer science. *Proc. of 22nd Ed-Media*, 2010.

Becoming Experts: Measuring Attitude Development in Introductory Computer Science

Brian Dorn
University of Hartford
200 Bloomfield Ave
West Hartford, CT 06117
bdorn@hartford.edu

Allison Elliott Tew
University of Washington Tacoma
1900 Commerce Street
Tacoma, WA 98402
aetew@u.washington.edu

ABSTRACT

We have begun the process of examining how students perceive the field of computer science by employing a novice-to-expert continuum framework. As part of this exploration we have developed and are validating the Computing Attitudes Survey (CAS). In this study, our research focuses on how students develop expert-like attitudes and what effect an introductory course may have on that development. In particular, we find that the CAS instrument can be used to detect pre/post attitude shifts after a single introductory course of instruction and that individual subpopulations show positive attitude gains across gender, area of study and pedagogy. Further, the CAS can also be used to identify significant pre/post attitude shifts among individual component factors, groupings of items on the survey that characterize different aspects of novice thought processes.

Categories and Subject Descriptors

K.3.2 [**Computers and Education**]: Computer and Information Science Education—*computer science education*

Keywords

Assessment, surveys, attitudes

1. INTRODUCTION

With concerns about negative perceptions of computing and declining enrollments [3, 13], many researchers have developed curricular innovations in computer science education to address these issues. Accordingly there is a recognized need to evaluate the impact of these changes on learning outcomes as well as students' beliefs about the field. Our work seeks to respond to this need by developing the Computing Attitudes Survey (CAS)—a validated attitudes instrument designed to measure the growth of expert-like attitudes about computer science for students studying at the university level.

Researchers across various STEM disciplines have found evidence of a relationship between student perceptions and learning outcomes within an academic discipline. Valentine et al. provide an in-depth meta-analysis of the relationship between student self-beliefs and achievement [18]. Studies by House have demonstrated that students' achievement expectations and self-concept were better predictors of success in chemistry and mathematics courses than previous mathematics or science instruction [10, 11]. A recent study by Lewis et al. links students' self-assessment of ability to their decision to major in computer science [12]. Student beliefs affect how they learn new information, and student experiences both inside and outside of the classroom can shape their beliefs [4, 16]. Thus, it is imperative that we understand how our educational practices impact the underlying perceptions students have about computer science.

Our research examines how students perceive the field of computer science by employing Hammer's novice-to-expert continuum framework [9]. The CAS was adapted from the Colorado Learning Attitudes about Science Survey (CLASS). The CLASS is a validated attitudes survey measuring student perceptions of physics according to Hammer's framework [1], and it has been used to demonstrate the link between educational practices in introductory courses and student perceptions. Further, the CLASS has been used as a recruitment tool to identify and retain students who enter university with more expert-like perceptions within a major [14]. The CLASS has been successfully adapted in both chemistry [2] and biology [15] with similar results.

The current version of our CAS instrument is a 53 item Likert scale questionnaire exploring problem solving in CS as well as attitudes about discipline-specific topics such as abstraction and scalability. In an earlier study we identified a set of components characterizing different aspects of novice beliefs through factor analysis of post-term data [7].

In this study, our research focuses on how students *develop* expert-like attitudes and what effect an introductory course may have on that development. In particular, we investigate four questions regarding assessment of computing attitudes among students enrolled in introductory CS courses.

- RQ1 To what extent does the CAS instrument detect pre/-post attitude shifts during an introductory course in computing?
- RQ2 To what extent are there significant differences in pre/-post attitude shifts for demographic subgroups like gender and area of study?
- RQ3 To what extent does the instrument detect pre/post attitude shifts according to varying course pedagogies?
- RQ4 To what extent does the instrument detect pre/post attitude shifts on the previously identified components characterizing different aspects of novices' beliefs?

SIGCSE'13, March 6–9, 2013, Denver, Colorado, USA.

The remainder of this paper proceeds as follows. Section 2 provides an overview of the current version of the CAS instrument and describes the study design. We present the results of our overall pre/post attitude shift analysis in Section 3. An in-depth analysis of the pre/post shift on individual component factors is provided in Section 4, and we then compare our results to those found in other sciences (Section 5). We conclude with a discussion of our progress towards validation of the instrument and future work (Section 6).

2. METHODOLOGY

2.1 The CAS Instrument

Following Hammer's theoretical framework for investigating novice-to-expert differences [9], CAS statements were designed to probe a range of student attitudes and beliefs about computing, focused in the following areas: 1) learning computer science, 2) problem solving in computer science, and 3) the connection of computer science to the real world.

Many items in the CAS were able to be directly replicated from the CLASS, simply changing the word "physics" to "computer science." Others were adapted by using terms more appropriate to the discipline (e.g., substituting the notion of algorithms for equations or formulas). Some remaining statements were not applicable to computing and were replaced by new discipline-specific statements. These additional computer science topics focused on notions of abstraction, data representation and scalability, errors and testing, and problem solving strategies. Sample items include:

- After I study a topic in computer science and feel that I understand it, I have difficulty solving problems on the same topic.
- When working on a complex computer science problem, I have to understand all of the details of the program implementation before I am able to make progress on a solution.
- I am confident my solution to a computer science problem is correct when the output matches the sample output provided in the problem set.
- Spending a lot of time understanding where algorithms come from is a waste of time.

To date, the CAS instrument has undergone revisions following expert reviews, think-aloud interviews, and pilot testing with undergraduate students. The current draft (version 3) contains 53 statements designed to be be used in a wide range of undergraduate computer science courses, for both majors and non-majors alike. Our prior work established the set of items on which there is expert consensus, enabling analysis of shifts towards the expert opinion. We also have identified groups of statements through factor analysis indicating potential subscales on the instrument (discussed in Section 4). Full details about the CAS development process can be found in [7].

2.2 Courses and Recruitment

Students were recruited from a variety of introductory Computer Science courses at the authors' institutions to examine CAS performance in a wide range of courses. Data was collected in five different courses:

UH-NonMjr An introductory programming course for non-CS majors at University of Hartford (UH) taught in Visual Basic.

UH-CS A first course in the CS major and required by some other science/engineering majors at UH. This course provides an introduction to object-oriented problem solving in Java, and one of the two sections surveyed made extensive use of the IPRE Robot Kit [17] and the MyroJava API.

UBC-NonMjr A general education course at University of British Columbia (UBC) designed for non-majors as a broad introduction to the field of computing. In addition to other coursework, students complete programming projects using Scratch and Javascript.

UBC-CS The first course for CS majors and required by some other science majors at UBC taught using Scheme and the *How to Design Programs* curriculum [8].

UBC-Eng An introductory computation course for engineering majors at UBC taught using the C language and primarily an inverted, just-in-time-teaching classroom pedagogy [5].

All students enrolled in these five courses were recruited via email for participation in the study prior to the start of the term (for the pre-term data) and during the final exam period (for the post-term data). Students were offered extra credit for completing the survey. Results presented here include only those students who completed the study and consented for their data to be included in the analysis.

2.3 Data Cleaning and Question Scoring

The data from pre- and post-term surveys were systematically cleaned to filter out meaningless responses. First we filtered out all responses that incorrectly answered Q43 which read: "We use this statement to discard the surveys of people who are not reading the questions. Please select 'Agree' for this question to preserve your answers." We then eliminated any duplicate entries in the data set based on student ID number. In such cases, only the first set of responses was preserved. We then eliminated any instances where a single student ID appeared in the data set for multiple courses. In these situations, all data was eliminated to avoid a confound while examining course-level attitude shifts. Lastly, data from the pre- and post-term surveys were paired using the student ID field, and any student who had not completed both surveys was dropped from this analysis.

Individual question responses were then scored using the standard procedure for this instrument described in [7]. The 5-point Likert scale responses were first collapsed to a simple 3-point range (Disagree, Neutral, Agree), and then the student's response was compared to the established expert consensus opinion. If a student response to a particular question matched that of the experts, it was given a score of +1. Responses opposing the expert opinion were given a score of -1, and neutral responses were scored as 0. These individual question scores were then aggregated to statistically examine the research questions posed earlier.

2.4 Demographics

Following the data cleaning and scoring procedures, we were left with 253 participants who had completed both the pre- and post-term surveys. Given variation in class sizes the raw number of students in the data set from each course differed markedly: UH-NonMjr (12 participants), UH-CS (9), UBC-NonMjr (32), UBC-CS (50), and UBC-Eng (150).

Of the 253 participants, 167 were men (65.2%) and 85 were women (33.2%), though the distribution fluctuated across

Table 1: Pre-Post Attitude Shifts

Group	Avg Pre % Agree	Avg Post % Agree	Avg % Shift (std err)	N	t (paired)	p (2-tail)
Overall	43.5%	59.6%	16.0% (1.4%)	253	11.60	< 0.001*
By Gender						
Women	40.0	59.6	19.5 (2.4)	85	8.09	< 0.001*
Men	45.3	59.6	14.3 (1.7)	167	8.52	< 0.001*
By Area of Study						
Education	21.6	45.5	23.9 (23.9)	2	—	—
Health Professions	46.2	57.6	11.4 (8.6)	3	—	—
Business	56.8	66.5	9.7 (8.2)	8	—	—
Visual/Perf Arts	34.1	56.3	22.2 (6.7)	12	3.29	0.007*
Humanities & Soc Sci	43.3	62.0	18.7 (4.9)	18	3.85	0.001*
Sci, Tech, Math	44.2	61.4	17.2 (3.2)	55	5.34	< 0.001*
Engineering	43.6	58.8	15.1 (1.7)	155	8.78	< 0.001*
By Course						
UH-CS	48.5	57.1	8.6 (8.0)	9	—	—
UH-NonMjr	43.6	54.6	11.0 (3.9)	12	2.81	0.017*
UBC-NonMjr	41.2	62.8	21.6 (4.0)	32	5.42	< 0.001*
UBC-CS	45.0	61.4	16.5 (3.4)	50	4.90	< 0.001*
UBC-Eng	43.3	58.8	15.6 (1.8)	150	8.79	< 0.001*

* denotes significant p values for $\alpha = 0.05$

— indicates that no statistics were computed due to insufficient sample sizes ($n < 10$)

the courses.[1] Participation in all but the UBC-Eng course was nearly evenly split between men and women. UBC-Eng, on the other hand, had a split of 78% men and 22% women.

Participants came from all levels of class standing, but the vast majority of them were first year students. 71% were in their first year at the university, as expected given the courses were all at the introductory level. 17% were second year students, and the remaining 12% were in their third year or more.

Overall, the respondent demographics are similar to those of the underlying class populations, though we note that in some courses women appear to be overrepresented in our sample. Nonetheless, this dataset provides a useful tool for exploring attitude shifts among various subgroups.

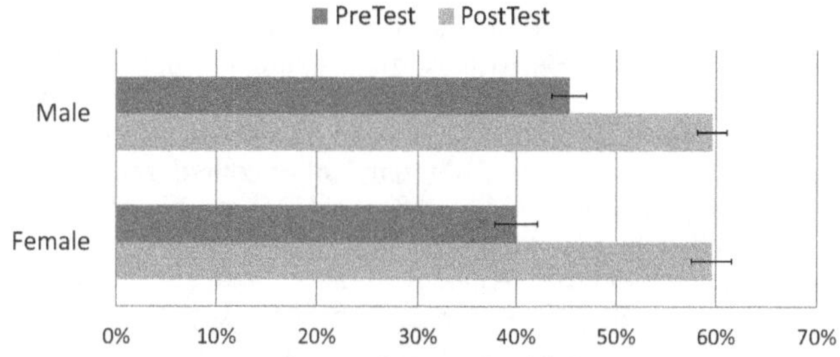

Figure 1: Pre/Post Term Attitude Shift by Gender with ±1 Standard Error

3. OVERALL ATTITUDE SHIFTS

This section focuses on the first three research questions, presenting an analysis of overall shifts in student attitudes from pre-term to post-term. Table 1 presents data for attitude shifts for various cross-sections of the data. In the subsections to follow, we discuss shifts in overall attitudes and attitude change by gender, by students' majors, and by individual course population.

3.1 Overall

At the most basic level, the CAS instrument is intended to identify attitude shifts over time. The simplest question one might ask is to what extent does the instrument indeed detect shifts during an introductory CS course (RQ1). For each student, we computed the percentage of survey items on which he or she agreed with the expert opinion both before and after the course. We also computed the difference between these two values for each student. As seen in "Overall" group from Table 1, the mean pre-term agreement level was 43.5% and increased to 59.6% post-term. The 16.0% average positive shift was statistically significant ($paired\ t(252) = 11.60; p < 0.001$).

Encouraged by this overall result, we then turned the analysis to various sub-populations within the dataset to investigate attitude shifts at a finer granularity.

[1] One participant did not indicate a gender and was excluded from the gender-related analyses.

3.2 By Gender

Breaking the data down by gender confirms statistically significant positive attitude shifts over the academic term for both women and men (+19.5% and +14.3% mean shifts, respectively). The "By Gender" group in Table 1 provides results of the paired t-tests, and these sizable attitude shifts are further illustrated in Figure 1. While it appears that women may have started off with a slightly lower level of expert agreement than their male counterparts, the difference in pre-term values was not statistically significant ($t(250) = 1.816, p = 0.071$). We noted that men and women ended up with the same post-term agreement level. Further, while the average increase in agreement was approximately 5% greater for women, there was not a statistically significant difference in the degree to which participants shifted based on gender ($t(250) = 1.772, p = 0.078$).

3.3 By Area of Study

We then considered the data by the students' areas of study. As part of the survey's demographic questionnaire, we collected data about a participant's major. Participants were also able to select "other" and complete a free-form text field. We grouped majors into seven larger categories: Education; Health Professions (e.g., nursing, pre-medicine); Business; Visual & Performing Arts; Humanities & Social Science; Engineering (all sub-disciplines); and Science, Technology & Mathematics, including CS.

In all areas of study, there was a positive attitude shift during the introductory computing course. These shifts ranged from +9.7% agreement for Business-related majors to over +20% for Arts and Education majors. The "By Area of Study" group in Table 1 provides details for all seven categories; rows are sorted by the total number of students in that category. Small sample sizes for the Education, Health Professions, and Business groups preclude meaningful statistical analysis, but for all other major areas there is a statistically significant positive shift towards expert attitudes following the first semester of instruction. These results verify that the instrument behaves consistently across different areas of study. They also provide encouraging evidence that a single semester of instruction can have a significant impact on "non-major" populations. For example, students in the Arts held some of the least expert-like attitudes at the outset, but gained expert-like attitudes at a dramatic rate by the end of the course.

3.4 By Pedagogy

Given the variety of pedagogies and target audiences in the five courses, we were also interested in how the instrument behaved in these different introductory settings (RQ3). Ultimately, the goal is to have an instrument that can be meaningfully applied in a variety of different course settings across the curriculum. While one might expect some variation in the results based on particular course goals, on the whole, one would hope that the CAS is able to capture growth towards expert-like attitudes regardless of the particular introductory experience.

Participants in all five courses showed a positive shift towards expert attitudes on average. The last group in Table 1 presents data disaggregated by course. Due to insufficient sample size, statistics for UH-CS were not computed. However, in all other cases the shifts were statistically significant, with average shifts ranging from +8.6% to +21.6%.

The distributions of attitudes pre-term and post-term illustrate the pronounced positive shift. Distributions of agreement from the three University of British Columbia courses are provided in Figures 2–4. In each of these courses, the pre-term data appears distributed around a mean of $\approx$ 40%. Post-term, the distributions shift upward, though novice attitudes persist for some. We note that few students exhibit the maximum level of agreement with experts after a single course—as one might expect.

4. CANDIDATE SUB-SCALE SHIFTS

Having identified significant positive shifts on the CAS instrument in both the overall scores and by gender, area of study, and pedagogy, we now turn our investigation to an analysis of possible shifts on individual component factors. Our previous work posited a model of eight separate components that were meaningfully interpretable groupings of the individual items on the CAS [7]. Derived through an exploratory factor analysis, these groupings theoretically represent underlying latent variables that play a role in novice attitudes. Once the CAS is fully validated, these groups will comprise the sub-scales on the survey. The current candidate factors are summarized below, and the number of items in each factor is given in parentheses:

1. *Abstraction*: The items in this component reflected key notions of abstraction related to level of detail and information hiding. (3 questions)

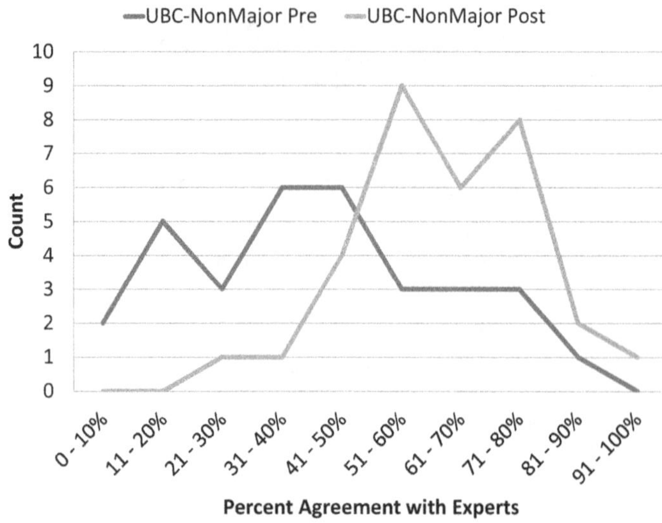

Figure 2: Distribution of Attitude Shift Pre/Post Term in the UBC-NonMjr Course

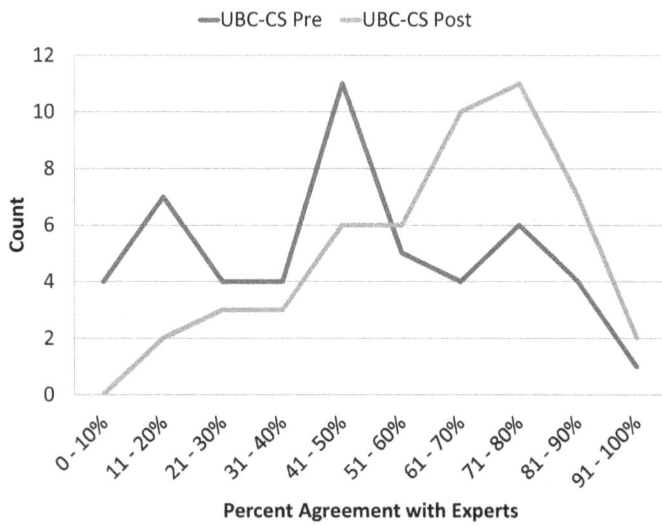

Figure 3: Distribution of Attitude Shift Pre/Post in the UBC-CS Course

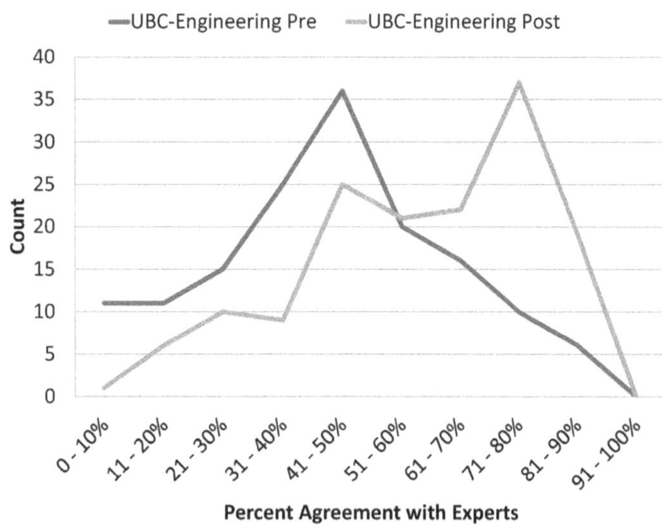

Figure 4: Distribution of Attitude Shift Pre/Post Term in the UBC-Eng Course

Table 2: Pre-Post Attitude on Potential Factors ($n = 253$)

Factor	Avg Pre % Agree	Avg Post % Agree	Avg % Shift (std err)	t (paired)	p (2-tail)
Real World Connections	48.1	58.2	10.1 (1.9)	-5.20	< 0.001*
Prob Solv-Fixed Mindset	43.5	61.1	17.5 (2.0)	-8.86	< 0.001*
Personal Interest	45.8	65.7	19.8 (2.0)	-10.15	< 0.001*
Prob Solv-Transfer	35.2	58.0	22.9 (1.9)	-11.90	< 0.001*
Prob Solv-Strategies	44.5	69.8	25.3 (2.3)	-10.79	< 0.001*

* denotes significant p values for $\alpha = 0.05$

2. *Problem Solving–Confidence*: This component represented students' confidence or ability at being able to succeed in learning to program or solve computer science problems. (3 questions)
3. *Problem Solving–Sense Making*: This factor captured how students make use of resources and employ strategies to help them solve problems. (3 questions)
4. *Real World Connections*: This category dealt with the relationship between the discipline of computer science and everyday life and the connectedness of CS and other disciplines. (6 questions)
5. *Problem Solving–Fixed Mindset*: This factor focused on a student's belief of predetermined fate or learned helpless within the discipline, related to Dweck's notion of fixed or malleable mindset [6]. (10 questions)
6. *Personal Interest & Enjoyment*: This component was comprised of items related to personal interest, motivation, and engagement with computer science. (10 questions)
7. *Problem Solving–Transfer*: The items in this factor concentrated on students' ability to see and apply connections between concepts in order to solve problems. (6 questions)
8. *Problem Solving–Strategies*: Items here are related to classic problem solving techniques in the discipline such as problem decomposition, code commenting, and planning. (4 questions)

For the purposes of this analysis, we focus our investigation on those factors that contain four or more items, as these were the strongest and most stable of the proposed candidate factors in the prior work. The remaining factors will be examined in subsequent analyses once verified through additional confirmatory factor analysis. The research question under investigation here is to what extent does the instrument detect pre/post attitude shifts on these individual components in the proposed factor model: real world connections, problem solving–fixed mindset, personal interest & enjoyment, problem solving–transfer, problem solving–strategies (RQ4)?

Statistics for pre-post results on each of these five components are presented in Table 2, sorted by increasing magnitude of attitude shift. Values for percent agreement here are computed as the average number of participant responses in a factor matching the expert opinion divided by the total number of items in that factor. There were statistically significant positive gains in attitudes in all five factors. Prior to the start of the term, participants showed less than 50% agreement with experts across the board but were well above this threshold by the post-term survey. The largest attitude gains were on the factors for problem solving–transfer and –strategies, which one might hope for following exposure to a term of hands-on problem solving in the discipline.

While still a statistically significant increase, the real world connections factor had the smallest degree of shift on average. However, further analysis showed that shifts on this factor appeared responsive to differences in pedagogy. For example, when we considered University of British Columbia courses we found that the UBC-NonMjr course had a +18.2% shift on this factor, with UBC-CS and UBC-Eng having only +13.0% and +7.1%, respectively. Additionally, analysis of post-term attitudes on this factor showed statistically significant differences between the three courses at University of British Columbia (UBC-NonMjr 72.9%, UBC-CS 63.3%, UBC-Eng 53.2%) (one-way ANOVA, $F(2, 229) = 7.58$, $p = 0.001$). At first glance it is surprising that a non-majors course would result in the most expert-like attitudes about computing's real world connections, however we note that two of the five course-level learning goals for the UBC-NonMjr course were about topics related to this factor.

These results are encouraging in that they demonstrate the instrument's ability to measure attitudes at a finer level of detail through subscales, and they suggest potential avenues for future investigation by disaggregating data by both factor and demographic variables.

5. DISCUSSION

Overall, the results of this pre/post administration of the CAS in introductory courses are positive and enlightening. The instrument performed well and clearly measured attitude growth both overall and when grouped by demographics or candidate sub-scales. Further, the results suggest that course pedagogy can have a measurable impact on the degree of shift in student attitudes for at least one CAS sub-scale (real world connections). Having a validated instrument capable of measuring such fine-grained shifts in student attitudes would be a powerful means to evaluate potential effects of novel curricular interventions and to measure longitudinal development of expertise.

When conducting a replication study, it is worthwhile to consider the performance of the adapted instrument (CAS) to the original (CLASS-Physics) and other adaptations. Interestingly, the results presented here for the CAS stand in stark contrast to typical results for administrations of CLASS-based instruments in other science disciplines. In a study using the CLASS-Physics instrument in 6 different courses, the maximum average attitude shift overall was only 1.5%, and two courses showed declines in expert-like attitudes of approximately 8 and 9% [14]. Results obtained using CLASS-Chemistry also found negative shifts in attitudes of 5% overall following an introductory chemistry course [2]. In a study of six different introductory Biology courses, five showed statistically significant declines in student attitudes on the CLASS-Bio survey [15].

An obvious question arises: why do students demonstrate such marked *gains* in expert attitudes in introductory computer science courses when other sciences show the exact opposite? One hypothesis is that students entering introductory CS courses, even those designated for CS majors, have a much less well developed notion of what computer science is when compared to the other sciences. Most high school students have prior experience with chemistry, biology, or physics, but high school CS exposure is much less common. Perhaps they simply have fewer pre-conceived notions of the discipline before the first course begins. Generally lower pre-term expert agreement scores on the CAS compared to the published results with the CLASS in the other sciences support this theory. Future work is needed to examine this phenomena and test our hypothesis.

6. FUTURE WORK

The results of the study presented here are early indications of the success of the CAS as a validated instrument for measuring the development of expertise in student attitudes about computer science. As an active research project, the iterative process of refining and validating the instrument is ongoing. We are currently gathering additional CAS data Fall term 2012 in order to finalize the construct validity of our factor model, that is confirming or revising the individual sub-scales as needed to accurately reflect novice thought patterns. We will also replicate the study presented here to confirm the ability of the instrument to reliably measure pre/post term shifts in attitudes.

Beyond the immediate ongoing work, a critical piece to the final validation of the instrument is a large scale effort to gather data from students at many different institutions worldwide. This will ensure that the final instrument is broadly applicable in a wide variety of institutional and pedagogical settings.

Upon completion of this final validation effort, we plan to make the CAS publicly available under a Creative Commons license for use by instructors and researchers alike. Once available, the CAS will enable instructors to reliably measure attitude shifts resulting from a course or intervention, and it will enable departments to measure long-term development of expert attitudes among students over an entire degree program. For researchers it will allow for comparison of results between institutions, and it will permit meaningful explorations on the relationship between attitudes and skills-based outcomes. Given the connection between student perceptions and learning outcomes [18], the CAS contributes an important piece to the assessment toolkit for beginning to understand how students learn computer science.

Acknowledgments

We thank University of British Columbia and University of Hartford faculty and students who participated in this study, and all who have participated in earlier CAS development studies. This work was funded in part by the Carl Wieman Science Education Initiative at the University of British Columbia.

References

[1] W. K. Adams, K. K. Perkins, N. S. Podolefsky, M. Dubson, N. D. Finkelstein, and C. E. Wieman. A new instrument for measuring student beliefs about physics and learning physics: The Colorado Learning Attitudes about Science Survey. *Physical Review Special Topics–Physics Education Research*, 2(010101): 1–14, 2006.

[2] J. Barbera, W. K. Adams, C. E. Wieman, and K. K. Perkins. Modifying and validating the Colorado Learning Attitudes about Science Survey for use in chemistry. *Journal of Chemical Education*, 85(10): 1435–1439, 2008.

[3] L. J. Barker, K. Garvin-Doxas, and M. Jackson. Defensive climate in the computer science classroom. In *Proc. of SIGCSE '02*, pages 43–47, 2002.

[4] J. D. Bransford, A. L. Brown, and R. R. Cocking. *How People Learn: Brain, Mind, Experience, and School.* National Academy Press, Washington, D.C., expanded edition, 2000.

[5] P. Carter. An experience report: On the use of multimedia pre-instruction and just-in-time teaching in a CS1 course. In *Proc. of SIGCSE '12:*, pages 361–366, 2012.

[6] C. S. Dweck. Motivational processes affecting learning. *American Psychologist*, 41(10):1040–1048, 1986.

[7] A. Elliott Tew, B. Dorn, and O. Schneider. Toward a validated computing attitudes survey. In *Proc. of ICER'12*, pages 135–142, 2012.

[8] M. Felleisen, R. B. Findler, M. Flatt, and S. Krishnamurthi. *How to Design Programs.* MIT Press, Cambridge, MA, 2nd edition, 2012.

[9] D. Hammer. Epistemological beliefs in introductory physics. *Cognition and Instruction*, 12(2):151–183, 1994.

[10] J. D. House. Student motivation and achievement in college chemistry. *International Journal of Instructional Media*, 21(1):1–11, 1994.

[11] J. D. House. Student motivation, previous instructional experience, and prior achievement as predictors of performance in college mathematics. *International Journal of Instructional Media*, 22(2): 157–167, 1995.

[12] C. M. Lewis, K. Yasuhara, and R. E. Anderson. Deciding to major in computer science: A grounded theory of students' self-assessment of ability. In *Proc. of ICER'11*, pages 3–10, 2011.

[13] J. Margolis and A. Fisher. *Unlocking the Clubhouse: Women in Computing.* MIT Press, Cambridge, MA, 2002.

[14] K. K. Perkins, W. K. Adams, S. J. Pollock, N. D. Finkelstein, and C. E. Wieman. Correlating student beliefs with student learning using the Colorado Learning Attitudes about Science Survey. In *Proc. of the 2004 Physics Education Research Conference*, pages 61–64, 2004.

[15] K. Semsar, J. K. Knight, G. Birol, and M. K. Smith. The Colorado Learning Attitudes about Science Survey (CLASS) for use in biology. *Life Sciences Education*, 10:268–278, 2011.

[16] E. Seymour and N. M. Hewitt. *Talking About Leaving: Why Undergraduates Leave the Sciences.* Westview Press, Boulder, CO, 1997.

[17] J. Summet, D. Kumar, K. O'Hara, D. Walker, L. Ni, D. Blank, and T. Balch. Personalizing CS1 with robots. In *Proc. of SIGCSE '09*, pages 433–437, 2009.

[18] J. C. Valentine, D. L. DuBois, and H. Cooper. The relation between self-beliefs and academic achievement: A meta-analytic review. *Educational Psychologist*, 39(2):111–133, 2004.

What Is It We Are Asking: Interpreting Problem-Solving Questions in Computer Science and Linguistics

Noa Ragonis
School of Education – Computer Science Department
Beit Berl College, Israel
Department of Education in Technology and Science
Technion – IIT
noarag@beitberl.ac.il

Gila Shilo
School of Education – Linguistics Department
Beit Berl College, Israel
gilas@beitberl.ac.il

ABSTRACT

The cognitive abilities of learners have been studied extensively in both psychological and educational contexts. In the field of education, attention is placed on high-order thinking strategies, while in computer science education the focus is on cognitive skills required for solving problems. Since any process of problem solving is based on answering questions, it is worth looking at the questions we ask. In this conceptual framework, the current study aims to investigate the cognitive requirements from learners answering questions that arise from the questions' formulation. The study focuses on a linguistic investigation of keywords that appear in questions aimed at promoting the learners' high-order thinking when solving problems. To sharpen our attention to the uses of particular keywords in questions, we present a comparison between questions used in two different disciplines, computer science and linguistics. The paper outlines and describes nine question keyword categories, demonstrates the question keyword categories, and argues that the cognitive requirements from learners answering those questions are very similar for both disciplines.

Categories and Subject Descriptors

K.3.2 [**Computers and Education**]: Computer and Information Science Education – *Computer science education, Curriculum.*

Keywords

Computer science education, linguistics, questions, answers, cognition, problem solving, high order thinking.

1. INTRODUCTION

Much attention is placed on students thinking strategies in any educational framework. Education policy makers as well as curriculum developers aim to enable students to develop their skills, in addition to acquiring knowledge. The development of high thinking strategies relies on teaching scenarios that include problem solving, which involves questioning and answering processes. Based on that premise, we analyzed the keywords used in questions and examined whether there are differences between questions in different subject matters. Here we present part of our study that relates to computer science and linguistics. The comparison with linguistics is interesting, first, because we obviously use language to formulate questions and second, since linguistics may be considered as a "totally" different discipline when focusing on problem-solving questions. In our study we reviewed previous works that involved thinking strategies, taxonomies relating to learning objectives, and research works that focused on questions (presented in Section 2). The study refers to problem-solving questions and distinguishes between this type of questions and other types of questions (presented in Section 3). Different keywords used in the wording of questions were examined. The list of keywords was restricted to keywords that can be used in problem-solving questions, which were classified into nine categories according to the cognitive requirements of learners while answering questions with the specific keywords (presented in Section 4). In what follows we present four questions for each category, two in computer science and two in linguistics, to demonstrate how the keyword is used in the category (Section 5). To finalize, we discuss and summarize our interpretations and insights from the study (Section 6 and Section 7). It is important to mention that this paper does not relate to any issues that involve answer assessment.

SIGCSE'13, March 6–9, 2013, Denver, Colorado, USA.

2. BACKGROUND

In this section we present some of the main theoretical research references that led us in the construction of our interpretation. First, we address cognitive and high-order thinking skills; then, we relate to asking questions in different disciplines; next, we discuss previous works in computer science (CS) on cognition and asking questions; and finally, we summarize the background and locate the current study with reference to past researches.

2.1 Cognition and high-order cognitive skills

Part of the discussion on the process of thinking, is formulated in different suggested taxonomies. The taxonomy considered to be most foundational is that of Bloom [4] who classified learning objectives in education. Bloom's taxonomy consists of six parts that relate to planning students' learning and evaluating their achievements: 1- knowledge, 2- comprehension, 3- application, 4- analysis, 5- synthesis, and 6- evaluation. Anderson and Krathwohl [1] suggested a revision of Blooms' taxonomy that regarded levels 4, 5 and 6 as being similar with respect to cognitive abilities – metacognitive knowledge. Passig [12], a future studies researcher, adapted Bloom's taxonomy of cognitive skills to reflect future needs. He expanded the interpretation of Bloom's six levels with relation to currently needed skills and added a seventh level, melioration, which deals with cognitive functions in the futuristic society.

Bigges and Collis [3] offered another taxonomy, i.e. the Structure of Observed Learning Outcome taxonomy (SOLO) [2], which describes levels of increasing complexity in students' understanding of subjects. The levels are: 1- pre-structural, 2- uni-structural, 3- multi-structural, 4- relational, 5- extended abstract. The first three levels are categorized as quantitative phases, while the latter two are regarded as qualitative phases. The SOLO taxonomy is used in assessment; it facilitates classifying of learning outcomes in terms of their complexity and enables educators to assess students' work in terms of its quality. The SOLO can also be used to design curricula in terms of the intended learning outcomes.

Verbs are used, in these two main taxonomies. In Bloom's taxonomy, verbs are offered to explain the skills expected from students at each level, while in the SOLO taxonomy, key verbs are used to assess students' outcomes, categorizing them into different levels. Our keyword categories include keywords that appear particularly in problem-solving questions. The categorization we propose can scaffold the planning of teaching processes that: (a) involve the development of questions aimed at enhancing students' cognitive skills – as presented in Bloom's taxonomy, and (b) aimed at elevating the levels of complexity expected from students' outcomes – as presented in the SOLO taxonomy. In the Discussion, we will elaborate further on the connections between our categories of problem-solving questions and these two fundamental taxonomies.

Our focus on questions is also related to the broad research area of higher-order cognitive skills - HOCS. Investigators in this field claim that it is important to pose questions during the process of learning, with different investigators highlighting different aspects. Zohar and Ben David [20], for example claims that high-order cognitive skills are not systematic; they include skills of asking questions, solving problems and critical thinking. Paul and Elder [13] suggest improving HOCS using eight differentiated components, the second of which deals with the subject of questions. Costa [6,7] suggests a way of teaching HOCS based on three levels. One level relates to asking questions whose answers require high-order cognitive skills. Costa [7] also presented a five-part curriculum development process, which is adapted to the new millennium, and includes the topic of asking questions. Attention is given in the literature also to class discussions and awareness is raised to asking "fruitful questions" (e.g. Harpaz [8]).

This indicates that HOCS research regards the issue of asking questions as central and important and our interpretation can be seen as deepening and enhancing that viewpoint.

2.2 Questions in different disciplines

Previous researchers who addressed and/or compared questions used in different disciplines referred to the understanding of texts. Shepherd [16] claimed that questions targeted at various levels of understating require the same types of skills in all disciplines. For example, eliciting the main idea of a text or drawing conclusions from a text require the use of similar skills such as data organization, interpretation, inference, comparison, and confrontation. Shilo [17] compared types of questions and difficulty levels of questions across the language and history disciplines, examining questions that appear in books, on tests and in homework assignments. Unlike Shepherd, Shilo did find differences between the questions used in the two disciplines. Specifically she found that questions in the discipline of language tend to be of a higher level since they may be regarded requiring the solution of problems rather than the understanding of texts.

2.3 Questions, answers and cognition in CS

The issue of questions versus answers, in the context of cognition, has been discussed in CS research from diverse points of view. Thompson et al. [18] reviewed the work done over the past decade on teaching-learning processes so as to apply Bloom's taxonomy to CS course design, evaluation, and assessment, and to provide an interpretation of the taxonomy that can be applied to introductory programming exams. Although they provided examples of questions for each of Bloom's cognitive categories, their focus was on writing and evaluating exams, and not specifically on problem-solving questions. Jones et al. [10] focused explicitly on written examinations. They determined three difficulty levels for questions, in the light of Bloom's taxonomy, and analyzed examination papers based on the criteria of keywords found in the questions. The study included a cross-analysis across student performance, cognitive skill requirements, and module learning outcomes. Here too, the researchers did not focus on problem-solving questions nor was it their intention to present a keyword categorization.

Like the works presented earlier that dealt with class discussions during question-answer sessions, Boyer et al. [5] address recommended questions for instructors to use to promote students' problem-solving skills in CS classes. The main issue is the climate of the debate, in which answers are not provided and questions are posed to encourage thinking. In their study, Boyer et al. categorized the instructional goals of question asking.

Ragonis [15] explored twelve types of questions. Her center of attention was on the diverse use of questions pattern to enable the investigation of concepts from multiple viewpoints, enabling different students to express their knowledge in different ways and to vary the teaching-learning process.

Although these researches do address questions and keywords that appear in questions, they do not focus on keyword categorization, and they did not delve into the issue of problem-solving questions.

Question answering systems (QA) is a research domain that relates to questions and answers and integrates language issues into computerized systems. Extensive research has been done in this area [eg. 9,11,19]. Pomerantz [14], for example, evaluated four taxonomies of question types to determine the expressiveness of each with respect to questions received from digital reference services. He offered a faceted classification scheme that can be used as a basis for automating parts of a reference question-answering process. QA systems are used, among other things, in search engines or in expert systems, and their purpose is to find a high-quality answer to a human question. This kind of research involves the ability of a computerized system to identify question keywords as well as subjects and relations, to "understand" the question better, and to offer answers. Although such research indeed combines linguistics aspects with programming aspects, these attempts actually concern the understanding of texts rather than cognitive aspects of answering questions.

2.4 Background summary

To summarize, the current study does not concern the understanding of questions, nor does it examine questions that involve the understanding of texts. It addresses different cognitive aspect than those presented in the familiar taxonomies, which mainly target learning objectives. Still, we learned a lot from those researches and they affected our investigation.

The objective of the present study was to focus on keywords that appear in problem-solving questions as they reflect the cognitive resources required from learners when answering those questions. We also aimed to characterize and categorize keywords in problem-solving questions and to investigate the application of our interpretation in two disciplines, namely computer science and linguistics.

3. QUESTIONS SCOPE

The study focuses on a linguistic investigation of keywords that appear in questions, based on an extensive review of textbooks, worksheets and exams. We especially targeted questions that were described by their authors as aiming to examine high-order thinking skills. We then classified the keywords into categories and reduced the categories to questions that are attributed to problem-solving processes. We did not include questions that focus on analyzing or understanding texts. Although it is but natural to refer to problem solving in the field of computer science, it is important to emphasize that the questions we investigated did not relate to the understanding of texts or to any other verbal summarizing of concepts. For example, we did not relate to questions such as: "What types of variables exist" or "What are the differences between Stack and Queue" or "Describe the four sort approaches we learned". In the field of linguistics, on the other hand, it is less natural to talk about problem solving, and yet questions in the fields of syntax and morphology actually express problem-solving processes. Hence, the questions we examined from the discipline of linguistics were based on the sub-domains syntax and morphology, and did not relate to sub-domains like understanding expressions or text comprehension. For example, we do not address questions such as: "What is the meaning of the following expression" or "What was the writer's intention " or "What is your opinion on the writer's claim".

In our study, we investigated a variety of question keywords and grouped together those questions that according to our interpretation can be referenced as problem-solving questions. Some question keywords are obviously synonymous, and we checked whether the question keywords in each category reflect similar cognitive requirements from learners in both disciplines. As a result, we eliminated question keywords that, in our opinion, are not naturally suited for use in problem-solving questions. Some examples of such keywords are: speculate, suggest, describe, and express.

Since questions are always located in a particular content knowledge, the issue whether the complexity of the content knowledge influences the high-order thinking strategies, or further influences our categorization, must be explored. Our starting position is the assumption that neither the complexity of the topics nor the fact that a topic is considered to be "advanced", affect the classification of the question keywords. In any subject of study, fundamental or advanced, questions can lead to high-order thinking.

4. QUESTIONS CATEGORIES

In this section we present the nine categories of questions we defined. Table 1 displays the categories, the keywords that express each category and a short interpretation of their meaning and usage. The main issue that led to this categorization is the cognitive resources the learner needs in order to solve a question. In Section 5 we further elaborate on the implementation of the categories using examples of concrete questions in the two disciplines.

Table 1. Problem-solving question categories and keywords

Category	Keywords	Interpretation
1. **Address / define criteria**	Address / apply / note / mention / specify / indicate / sort / mark	Address and apply different kinds of criteria and attribute the criteria to a list of elements; define criteria.
2. **Argue and justify**	argue / state / assert / determine, follow by justification: explain / argue / prove / justify / demonstrate / illustrate / clarify	State opinion and further establish the claim using any kind of justification.
3. **Analyze**	analyze / examine / investigate / explore	Identify and analyze the meaning or significance of components and factors.
4. **Compare**	compare / classify	Compare different objects/issues by applying principles, and observing from different view points; generalize insights.
5. **Complete**	complete / add	Complete or add components to a given structure according to detailed requirements.
6. **Convert**	convert / represent in different forms / modify / adjust / change / transform	Convert a given paragraph/section/clause according to specified, meaningful qualitative - related instructions (not technical translation).
7. **Discover**	discover / identify / find out / say what	Discover a phenomenon / indicate an occurrence / find out the purpose / identify components and the relations between them.
8. **Develop**	develop / compose / write / create new elements	Develop a new component / write a new module.
9. **Integrate**	integrate / order / arrange / merge / combine	Integrate some given components to a new structure.

The question categories we proposed cannot be completely distinguished from one another. In some cases, the categories are indistinct and a question keyword can serve different categories of questions.

Two representative examples of such categories are:

(1) The Category 3 keyword – *Analyze* can be used in questions that belong to Category 2 keywords – *Argue and justify*, since students analyze phenomena as a basis for supporting their justifications.

(2) The Category 7 keyword - *Discover* is actually part of the Category 5 keyword *complete*, since it is necessary to first discover the purpose of a section as the basis for answering a "complete" question. In other words, students must first understand – "discover" – the purpose of a section so as to be able to complete some missing parts of it.

Despite the partial overlap between the categories, our categorization outlines different types of questions. Furthermore, this overlap is expected and reasonable, since different thinking strategies lean on and/or supports each other.

A missing category? – execution tracing

One of the more frequently asked questions in CS is posed when students are required to monitor the execution of a given solution using, for instance, a tracing table or a tree of method calls. Since this kind of question refers to execution, we considered it inapposite to the super-category of "problem solving". This kind of questions indeed requires the application of knowledge, and in some cases even very complicated and advanced knowledge, but requires something different than the creation of "something new".

5. EXAMPLES OF QUESTIONS

In this section we present two representative questions from each discipline – computer science (CS) and linguistics (Lin). The examples aim to demonstrate the various question categories and to illustrate the usage of some of the category keywords.

1. Apply / define criteria

CS-1: A problem is presented and three different, correct solutions are offered. Specify different considerations that could be taken into account when determining which of the solutions is "better".

CS-2: A list of open tasks is presented. Apply criteria and determine which of the abstract data types, Linked-list, Stack, Queue or Tree, is most suitable to be used for solving the task.

Lin-1: Determine the syntactic type of each sentence (simple, compound or complex).

Lin-2: Classify words with a common root into two groups according to the meaning of the root.

2. Argue and justify

CS-1: A solution for a problem using a loop is given. State whether the loop execution is finite for each input and provide an explanation or a contrary example.

CS-2: A solution for a problem is given. For each input, state whether the solution is logically correct, and justify your answer.

Lin-1: Which word, in the presented list of words, is exceptional in its formation? Justify your answer.

Lin-2: What phenomenon is expressed in the following sentences? Explain your answer.

3. Analyze

CS-1: A problem is presented. Divide the problem to several sub-tasks that together will lead to the desired solution.

CS-2: An algorithm is presented. Examine the algorithm's complexity.

Lin-1: Analyze the syntactic structure of the sentence, refer to: subject, predicate, object and adverb.

Lin-2: Analyze the attributes of the following verbs, refer to: root, time, person and verbal stem.

4. Compare

CS-1: A problem is presented. Compare the use of Queue or Stack to solve it, specifying the advantages and disadvantages of each data type.

CS-2: Describe and explain the type of problems that are best solved using a counters array as opposed to those best solved using an indication array (Boolean).

Lin-1: Compare the following two sentences and explain their similarities and dissimilarities.

Lin-2: Compare the words in the following list and explain the differences you find between them.

5. Complete

CS-1: A problem is presented along with a solution with some missing instructions. Complete the missing instructions so that the solution solves the problem correctly.

CS-2: A problem is given along with its solution. Add instructions to the solution so as to fulfill a presented extended task.

Lin-1: For each of the verbs presented in the table, complete the verb root, conjugation, tense and person.

Lin-2: Complete the sentence by using appropriate syntactic word categories: "The _____ ate ______ before ________."

6. Convert

CS-1: A problem and its solution are given. Transform the solution from a procedural approach to a functional approach.

CS-2: Transform a method that uses a specific data type so that it uses the same algorithmic approach with a different data type. (For example: transform a bubble sort algorithm implemented with array so that it is implemented by a linked-list).

Lin-1: Convert the following complex sentence into a coordinated sentence using a suitable logical connective.

Lin-2: Change the following present tense sentence to a past tense sentence and to a future tense sentence.

7. Discover

CS-1: Determine the goal of the presented algorithm.

CS-2: Discover what algorithmic patterns are used in the solution to the following problem.

Lin-1: What linguistics phenomenon do the following words express?

Lin-2: What kind of subject is found in the main part of the sentence? Why is such a subject used?

8. Develop

CS-1: A problem is presented. Write a solution. (The most classic question asked in CS.)

CS-2: A problem is presented along with a solution to a module. Write a solution that uses the given module

Lin-1: Construct a meaningful sentence from the following words.

Lin-2: Create a new complex sentence in past tense using the two given present-tense sentences.

9. Integrate

CS-1: Two algorithmic patterns are given. Compose a problem whose solution requires combining the two patterns.

CS-2: Several methods are given, and a problem is presented. Write an algorithm that solves the problem using a sequence of method calls with appropriate parameters.

Lin-1: Convert the following three simple sentences into one coordinated sentence.

Lin-2: Merge the following three simple sentences, which are each in a different tense, into one complex sentence.

6. DISCUSSION

The study focuses on categories of keywords that appear in problem-solving questions. Our interpretation is that all nine categories presented in Section 3 relate to high-order thinking. Students are required to develop "something" new, based on multiple facets of different kinds of knowledge they previously acquired. The categories reflect the essence of the questions, but are not part of any cognitive taxonomy. Nevertheless, we have associated our categories with the known cognitive taxonomies.

Referring to Bloom's taxonomy [4], we see that none of the keyword categories relate to Bloom's lower levels (1-Knowledge and 2-Comprehension); some of them can be attributed to the 3rd level (Application); and all of them are attributed to the three high levels that Anderson and Krathwohl [1] consider as being at the metacognition level, (4-Analysis, 5-Synthesis and 6-Evaluation). Our interpretation, however, must be further developed to accommodate the new level addressed by Pasig [12] – Melioration, which concerns a personal cognitive link between two areas that seem far apart and is a higher interpretation of our category 9 – Integration. The current research may be regarded as an implementation of the Melioration level.

Referring to SOLO taxonomy [2,3], we found that none of the keyword categories relate to the lower levels of the taxonomy (1-pre-structural and 2-uni-structural), some of the them can be associated with level 3 (multi-structural), and all of them can be attributed to the qualitative phases (4-relational, and 5-extended abstract).

Although the questions are all about solving problems, it is evident that the categories express different levels of difficulty. For example, the Category 5 keyword, "complete", seems easier (as a task) than Category 9 keyword, "integrate". Yet, the list of categories can not be sorted base on their "difficulty" since difficulty is an undefined measure and it depends on a wide range of factors. For example, students' ability to answer questions depends on their previous knowledge and experience. If a type of question has already been presented and solved in the class, students will find it easier to cope with the same type of question when presented in slightly different scenario.

A comparison between the two disciplines reveals the extensive common aspects of the use of keywords that appears in problem-solving questions. Still, we believe there are vague aspects that capture the complexity dimensions of answers (width or depth). Some conspicuous aspects can be seen in the resources students require in order to answer the questions. In most cases, we assume that answering questions in computer science requires more time (particularly in categories 3-Analyze, 5-Complete, 6-Convert, 7-Discover, 8-Develop, and 9-Integrate) or that the answers will be longer and more extensive (particularly in categories 6-Convert, 8-Develop, and 9-Integrate).

7. SUMMARY

The categorization presented defines nine categories of keywords that are used in problem-solving questions. This categorization is new and adopts a different point of view from the well-known taxonomies. This study is unique in its interpretation of the comparison between the two disciplines of computer science and linguistics. Several interesting aspects were observed in the analysis process and are worth mentioning:

(1) The ability to widely interpret questions in linguistics as problem-solving questions;

(2) The ability to define categories that can be presented conveniently and interpreted similarly in both disciplines;

(3) Completeness of the categorization. We did not find any category or keyword within a category that could not be integrated into a problem-solving question in the both disciplines. Our presumption was that we would find a category that would fit only one discipline and not the other – but we found that all of the categories may be interpreted in both disciplines.

The categorization we presented groups together keywords that are used in questions aimed at practicing or testing problem-solving skills. As demonstrated in our research, the categorization was applied successfully in two different disciplines that are considered to be seemingly unrelated. We believe that educators can benefit from this study and use the proposed categorization as a guideline when developing questions. It would be of value to expand the study to other disciplines in which problem-solving questions are similarly rooted.

8. REFERENCES

[1] Anderson, L. and Krathwohl, D.A. (2001). *Taxonomy for Learning, Teaching and Assessing: A Revision of Bloom's Taxonomy of Educational Objectives.* New York: Longman.

[2] Atherton, J.S. (2005). *Learning and Teaching: SOLO taxonomy*. [On-line] http://www.learningandteaching.info/learning/solo. Accessed: 19 August 2012.

[3] Biggs, J. B. and Collis, K. (1982). *Evaluating the Quality of Learning: the SOLO taxonomy.* New York, Academic Press.

[4] Bloom, B.S. (1956) .*Taxonomy of Educational Objectives, Handbook I the Cognitive Domain* .New York: David McKay Co Inc.

[5] Boyer, K.E., Lahti, W., Phillips, R., Wallis, M.D., Vouk, M.A. and Lester, J.C. (2010). Principles of asking effective questions during student problem solving. *Proceedings of the 41st ACM technical symposium on Computer science education* (SIGCSE '10).

[6] Costa, A.L. (2001). Teaching For, Of, and About thinking, A.L. Costa (Ed.), *Developing Minds: A Resource Book for Teaching Thinking*, ASCD Publication, USA, pp. 192-196.

[7] Costa, A.L. (2006). Five Themes in a Thought-full curriculum. *Thinking Skills and Creativity*, 1, 62-66.

[8] Harpaz, Y. (2002). Teaching and Learning in a Community of Thinking. http://www.learningtolearn.sa.edu.au/Colleagues/pages/default/harpaz/ Accessed: 19 August 2012.

[9] Hermjakob, U. (2001). Parsing and question classification for question answering. In *Proceedings of the workshop on Open-domain question answering* (ODQA '01), Vol. 12.

Association for Computational Linguistics, Stroudsburg, PA, USA, 1-6.

[10] Jones, K.O., Harland, J., Reid, J.M., and Bartlett, R. (2009). Relationship between examination questions and Bloom's taxonomy. *Proceedings of the 39th IEEE international Conference on Frontiers in Education Conference*, San Antonio, Texas, USA, October 18 - 21, 2009.

[11] Krishnan, V., Das, S. and Chakrabarti, S. (2005). Enhanced answer type inference from questions using sequential models. In *Proceedings of the conference on Human Language Technology and Empirical Methods in Natural Language Processing* (HLT '05). Association for Computational Linguistics, Stroudsburg, PA, USA, 315-322.

[12] Passig, D. (2007). Melioration as a Higher Thinking Skill to Enhance Future Intelligence. *Teachers College Record.* Columbia University, 109 (1), 24–50.

[13] Paul, R., and Elder L. (2008). The Thinker's guide to the Nature and Functions of Critical and Creative Thinking. http://www.criticalthinking.org/files/CCThink_6.12.08.pdf Accessed: 19 August 2012.

[14] Pomerantz, J. (2005). A linguistic analysis of question taxonomies. *Journal of the American Society for Information Science and Technology*, 56(7), pp. 715–728.

[15] Ragonis, N. (2012). Type of Questions - The Case of Computer Science. *Olympiads in Informatics*, Vol. 6, 115-132.

[16] Shepherd, D.L. (1973). Reading in the Subject Areas. in Karlin, R. (Ed). *Reading for All* .IRA 173- 179

[17] Shilo, G. (2002). Asking Questions by three levels of understanding, *Dapim*, 37, pp.154 – 167.

[18] Thompson, E., Luxton-Reilly, A., Whalley, J., HU, M., and Robbins, P. (2008). Bloom's Taxonomy for CS assessment. In *Proc. Tenth Australasian Computing Education Conference (ACE 2008*), Wollongong, NSW, Australia. CRPIT, 78. Simon and Hamilton, M., Eds. ACS, 155-162.

[19] Yang, A., WU, J., and Wang, L. (2008). Research and design of test question database management system based on the three-tier structure. *WTOS*, 7, 12 (Dec. 2008), 1473-1483.

[20] Zohar, A. and Ben David, A. (2008). Explicit teaching of meta-strategic knowledge in authentic classroom situations, *Metacognition and Learning*, 3(1), pp. 59-82.

Investigating Factors of Student Learning in Introductory Courses

Matthew Hertz
Computer Science Department
Canisius College
Buffalo, NY 14208
hertzm@canisius.edu

Sarah Michele Ford
Department of Sociology
University of Massachusetts, Amherst
Amherst, MA 01003
ford@soc.umass.edu

ABSTRACT

Instructors of the introductory computer science courses, commonly called "CS1" and "CS2", face a large number of choices when designing their classes. Instructors have available to them a multitude of ways to explain each topic as well as course-wide choices such as objects-first or objects-late or using a functional or procedural language. Understanding how these options can affect student learning would help simplify these decisions. Unfortunately, just comparing how well students perform may not be accurate as it ignores the many confounding factors that could also have made a difference. To get beyond that problem, this study investigates underlying factors that affect student learning.

Using a survey of instructors, we find that students' abilities are nearly always correlated with the importance that the instructor placed on a particular topic. Our results also highlight several "hard" topics for which student mastery and topic importance were not correlated in CS1 and only weakly correlated in CS2. While one might expect the time spent covering a topic in class to also be correlated with student mastery, we find little evidence of this. In fact, for some basic programming concepts, we document *negative* correlations between instructional time and learning. We discuss how instructors can use these results when organizing their courses and how the computer science education community can use this finding of "hard" topics to focus their efforts.

Categories and Subject Descriptors

K.3.2 [**Computers and Education**]: Computers and Information Science Education—*Computer science education; Curriculum*

General Terms

Measurement, Standardization

Keywords

CS1, CS2, Survey, Curriculum Design

SIGCSE'13, March 6–9, 2013, Denver, Colorado, USA.

1. INTRODUCTION

When designing a course, CS1 and CS2 instructors must consider the relative importance of and how much class time to devote to each of the topics they cover. These decisions then influence, and are influenced by, a number of other pedagogical options, such as the programming language used or if and when to introduce objects. Following the course, all of these choices may be adjusted or the entire focus of the course changed to try to improve student learning. But knowing which change or changes to make is difficult. Research exists examining each individual option and, generally, shows that switching to or using any option improves student learning, but can they all be "right"? Little has been done to understand why all these choices work and what the underlying factors are that influence student learning.

Finding that the importance an instructor places on a topic, and not the amount of time spent on that topic, is important to student learning and would help instructors make these decisions. Understanding these details will also help identify "difficult" or "hard to teach" topics – topics where learning is not correlated with either time or importance. With this identification, the computer science education community can focus its attention on those areas where it is most needed.

To uncover these relationships, this paper uses a survey that was taken by 58 CS1 instructors and 41 CS2 instructors teaching classes that represent the full range of class sizes, languages, paradigms and teaching pedagogies. The survey asked instructors about their course practices including the class time spent and importance placed on a range of topics. This survey also asked instructors how well their students mastered each topic. Using these data, we examine what relationship, if any, exists between the time spent or importance placed on a topic and the resulting level of student ability. The level of correlation will be tested in two different ways. Spearman's ρ determines if any monotonic correlation exists between the data; Pearson's r determines if there exists a linear correlation. Pearson's r also allows us to compute r^2, the percentage of the variation in students' abilities that can be explained by differences in the level of importance or class time spent on a topic.

For nearly all of the topics we examined, we will show that students' abilities at the completion of the course are closely correlated with the level of importance the instructor placed on that topic. This result suggests that students usually follow their instructor's lead and focus on those topics the instructor believes to be most important. Two commonly taught lessons in CS1, SUBROUTINES/FUNCTIONS and TYPES, do not exhibit this relationship, however, suggesting that they are very difficult to teach. Unlike importance and learning, both CS1 and CS2 had few instances where the time spent teaching a topic and student learning were closely correlated. While usually not statistically significant, we did find a number of topics which

Control constructs	Methods, functions, subroutines
Variables, types, expressions	Arrays, strings
I/O (e.g., files, printing to screen)	Style (e.g., indentation, variable names)
Object-oriented programming (e.g., inheritance, class anatomy)	Abstraction mechnisms (e.g., interfaces, abstract classes)
Testing	Debugging
Error handling (e.g., exceptions)	Recursion
Sorting	Stacks, queues, lists
Trees	Graphs
Other data structures	

Table 1: Listing of topics used in the survey. These topics were derived from CS1 and CS2 topics detailed in the LACS Model Curriculum.

even exhibited negative correlations. These correlations suggest that one could improve student learning by *reducing* the time spent teaching these topics.

These results highlight factors that help explain the results found in computer science education research. While the amount of time spent on a topic may not make of a difference, the importance placed on a topic clearly does. By changing a class to focus on different topics, instructors should find that student learning on those topics improves. This analysis also provides quantitative data documenting topics that are "hard". With this in mind, future researchers could document which factors enable students to master these topics and disseminate these best practices.

We begin by presenting related works in Section 2. The design and methodology of the survey and an analysis of our respondents are in Section 3. The results of our survey appear in Section 4. We analyze these results and discuss future directions for this research in Section 5. Our conclusions are presented in Section 6.

2. RELATED WORK

Several papers have presented the range of approaches that are used to teach introductory programming courses. Model curricula, such as those developed by the ACM-IEEE committee [13] and the Liberal Arts Computer Science Consortium [8], not only guide curricular choices, but also map out how the curricula should be applied to different paradigms (e.g., objects-early, objects-late, functional, scripting-based). Other work has used surveys to investigate the different programming languages used in CS1 and CS2 [4], the time spent covering a list of topics [2], level of emphasis instructors place upon topics [5] and level of student learning on a variety of topics [6]. All of these past works document the current practices of instructors. Unlike this work, however, they do not attempt to examine how these factors affect student learning nor do they use this to determine what topics are most difficult to teach or learn.

Other past work has investigated which of the introductory computer science concepts are the most difficult. The SIGCSE Bulletin contained two articles by Dale [2, 3] in which she investigated which topics instructors felt were the most difficult. Goldman, et al., provided another approach to determine which topics were most difficult [5]. This work used a survey-driven multi-step Delphi process to enable a panel of 20 experts to reach consensus on the level of difficulty for a number of topics. Like our current work, these past studies used surveys to find the difficult topics. Unlike the previous studies, however, our research determines topic difficulty by analyzing respondents' instructional practices to find where student learning cannot be correlated with instructors' efforts.

3. SURVEY DESIGN & RESPONSE

We now discuss how we constructed the survey and present an overview of the courses taught by our respondents. Other details about the design of this survey can be found in our previous work [6].

3.1 Survey Design

We began designing the survey by developing a list of topics that would appear in introductory computer science courses. The ACM-IEEE Model Curriculum [13] provided an obvious starting point, but the curriculum only contains high-level topics and would limit possible analyses. We therefore began with the more detailed topic listing from the LACS Model Curriculum [8]. While the LACS Model Curriculum is focused on programs offering liberal arts degrees, it is based upon the ACM-IEEE Model Curriculum and so we felt its concept listing would apply broadly. Our previous work documents the process we used to determine the final list of topics [6] and these topics can be found in Table 1.

This research analyzes the current practices of CS1 and CS2 instructors. This required gathering as many responses, from as wide a range of instructors and institutions, as possible. For the questions asking instructors for the amount of time they spent covering each topic, respondents selected from "Not a part of this course/No time", "1 hour", "2 hours", "3 hours", ..., "9 hours", "10+ hours", and "Don't Know". For responses to how important the respondent felt the topic was to their course and the level of student mastery at the conclusion of the course we used Likert-type scales [7] and included a "Don't Know" option. For levels of importance, the possible answers were: "Unrelated", "Tangential", "Beneficial", "Important", "Critical", and "Don't Know". For levels of mastery, respondents could choose between "None", "Limited", "Capable", "Knowledgeable", "Mastered", and "Don't Know".[1] When analyzing the data, we pruned responses on a topic when the respondent answered "Don't Know" or did not respond to all questions for that topic. We also pruned responses to topics instructors recorded as being "Unrelated" to their course. Including these data could not help inform us about what affects student learning or identify difficult to teach topics and so could only serve as a potential bias.

3.2 Survey Responses

Requests for instructors to complete the survey were sent periodically to the SIGCSE e-mail discussion list. Using an approach known as targeted snowball sampling [1], each announcement included a link to the survey website and a request that the mail be forwarded to appropriate instructors and related mailing lists. This led to 143 unique survey responses. After removing incomplete and abandoned surveys, we were left with 99 valid responses. 58 of these completed surveys were from CS1 instructors and 41 were from

[1]Purely objective measures of mastery are not feasible. This type of analysis would require language-independent tests of CS1 and CS2 concepts such as that proposed in [11, 12]. Unfortunately, these tests are not publicly available and could not be given to a large enough sample to analyze the range of current teaching practices.

instructors of CS2 courses. (Some respondents filled out surveys for both CS1 and CS2. The data were entered separately and we do not analyze data across courses, so we count these respondents as instructors of both CS1 and CS2.)

Language Used	CS1	CS2
Java	55%	59%
C++ (with objects)/C#	12%	2%
Pascal/C/C++ (without objects)	14%	22%
Lisp	12%	7%
Other	7%	10%

Class Size	CS1	CS2
Min. - Max.	9 - 150	4 - 150
Mean	37	27
Median	23	20
1st - 3rd Quartile	18 - 39	10 - 30
	CS1	CS2

Table 2: The range of teaching approaches used by instructors responding to our survey. Though not directly comparable, the use of languages we find is similar to those found in earlier surveys [4]. Though we know of no census of class sizes, our responses cover a diverse range of courses.

Table 2 shows the diversity of the courses taught by the respondents. Because our survey was not limited to US-based institutions, a direct comparison with a previous survey of educational practices [4] is not possible, but our respondents differ from the results of that earlier survey only in that our respondents are slightly more likely to use either Java or a functional language. The number of students taking respondents' courses also varied from a minimum of 4 to a maximum of 150 students. CS2 courses tended to be much smaller than CS1 courses, but CS2 classes of 75 or more students still made up 10% of our survey.

Our results may be biased by the survey design and participant recruitment. The initial survey solicitations were posted on education-focused discussion lists. While these postings included a request to forward the e-mail, it is likely that most of the instructors who saw this have an active interest in computer science education. It is reasonable to assume the respondents would also place a greater emphasis on teaching than other faculty. While our results may thus skew away from average computer science educators and towards those most focused on student learning, this should only strengthen any conclusions we draw as to which topics are difficult and the effect that classroom time and importance has on student learning.

4. RESULTS

When designing or modifying a course to achieve student learning goals, two factors instructors control are the importance placed on a topic and the amount of class time spent covering each topic. It is reasonable to expect that making a topic more important to a course would increase student learning. Similarly, one would hope and expect that instructional time and levels of student learning are positively correlated. To test for this relationship, we use *Pearson's r* to measure the linear correlation between students' abilities and how important the instructor felt a topic is or how much time was spent on the topic in class. Pearson's r provides two different ways to evaluate what correlation, if any, exists. First, the resulting p value establishes the statistical significance of the correlation. Additionally, the value of r^2 calculates the percentage of variability in one factor that can be explained by the other [14]. Only linear correlations can be detected by Pearson's r, however. Using *Spearman's* ρ we can test for any monotonic relationship [9] and, in combination with the earlier correlation statistic, will highlight cases where supra- or super-linear relationships exist.

4.1 Topic importance & student learning

We first examined the correlation between students' abilities on a topic and the importance the instructor placed on the topic. We found that the correlations were statistically significant for all but a few topics in CS1 courses. Figure 1a illustrates the responses for a typical topic, I/O, which exhibits this correlation. As Figure 1a shows, students did well when the topic was emphasized and had little ability when the topic was considered less important. For the majority of topics in which significant correlations were not found, it was due to the topics being covered by VERY few instructors (84 - 91% of respondents marked these topics as being "unrelated" to their course). Even after including "unrelated" responses, there were 2 topics for which we could not find significant correlations: SUBROUTINES/FUNCTIONS and TYPES. Both topics are commonly taught, all of our respondents covered both of these topics in their courses, but students' abilities were highly variable. As the bubble plot in Figure 1c shows, most instructors think SUBROUTINES/FUNCTIONS are important for their course. This agreement does not translate to equal levels of student learning, however. In fact, only 4% of the variation in students' abilities can be explained by differences in how important instructors felt the topic was. Clearly, teaching SUBROUTINES/FUNCTIONS is *difficult*. But the difficulty of teaching SUBROUTINES/FUNCTIONS pales in comparison to the teaching of TYPES in CS1. As Figure 1d shows, nearly every respondent rated TYPES as either important or very important. Students' abilities are again highly variable, however, with less than 0.5% of the variation in students' abilities being explainable by differences in importance the instructor placed on TYPES.

While the correlation between a topic's importance and student learning is statistically significant for all other topics in CS1, the strength of this correlation varies greatly. For some topics, CS1 students' ability is closely tied to the importance the instructor placed on it. For example, the importance placed on a topic explains nearly 65% of the variation in students' abilities with RECURSION and almost 60% of the variation with ABSTRACTION MECHANISMS. For the plurality of topics in CS1, the correlation is weaker and explains less than half of the variation in student learning.

Unlike in CS1, the responses from CS2 show clear correlations between student learning and topic importance for every topic. But for two of the topics, SUBROUTINES/FUNCTIONS and CONTROL STRUCTURES, this correlation is statistically significant only when using Spearman's ρ, meaning the relationship is monotonic, but not linear. As before, the strength of the correlations varies greatly between topics. A summary of these results for both CS1 and CS2 can be seen in Table 3. More interestingly, the topics with weak correlations found in CS1 carry forward into CS2. In addition, the levels of correlation found in the second course are often lower than those found in first course. That the same topics come up as having the lowest levels of association in both of these courses suggests that these truly are among the most difficult to teach.

4.2 Time spent on a topic & student learning

Students' abilities and the total class time spent on a topic should be closely aligned – one would expect student learning to increase along with the time spent in class working on the topic. Finding low or non-existent levels of correlation would suggest there exist efficient, but not widely used, ways of teaching the topic. This could provide a list of areas ripe for greater scrutiny to find how some instructors do so well or what causes students to struggle with a topic. As the results in Table 4 show, we find that correlations between

		Control Construct.	Procedure/Func.	Types	Arrays	I/O	Style	OO	Abstraction Mech.	Testing	Debugging	Error Handling	Recursion	Sorting	Lists	Trees	Graphs	Other
	n	56	54	56	52	53	55	44	31	53	54	39	27	31	19	9	5	15
CS1	ρ	**0.263**	0.197	0.097	**0.389**	**0.609**	**0.314**	**0.660**	**0.753**	**0.719**	**0.638**	**0.526**	**0.809**	**0.575**	**0.666**	0.467	0.356	0.368
	r	**0.307**	0.207	0.062	**0.491**	**0.615**	**0.350**	**0.649**	**0.773**	**0.698**	**0.610**	**0.516**	**0.806**	**0.556**	**0.671**	0.473	0.327	**0.492**
	n	38	38	38	38	37	38	37	36	38	38	37	36	35	36	32	23	27
CS2	ρ	**0.522**	**0.349**	**0.574**	**0.578**	**0.594**	**0.552**	**0.577**	**0.675**	**0.416**	**0.505**	**0.546**	**0.373**	**0.578**	**0.336**	**0.457**	**0.752**	**0.693**
	r	0.288	0.174	**0.362**	**0.567**	**0.584**	**0.564**	**0.626**	**0.676**	**0.417**	**0.499**	**0.547**	**0.425**	**0.625**	**0.402**	**0.539**	**0.783**	**0.698**

Table 3: Summary of the correlation of an instructors rating of the importance of a topic and students' abilities at the end of CS1 and CS2 by topic. Values listed in bold are statistically significant ($p \leq 0.5$).

		Control Construct.	Subroutines/Func.	Types	Arrays	I/O	Style	OO	Abstraction Mech.	Testing	Debugging	Error Handling	Recursion	Sorting	Lists	Trees	Graphs	Other
	n	55	54	56	52	53	55	44	30	53	54	38	26	31	19	9	5	15
CS1	ρ	-0.143	-0.098	-0.088	0.030	0.239	0.074	**0.385**	**0.779**	**0.433**	**0.266**	**0.619**	**0.659**	0.343	**0.750**	0.506	0.700	**0.790**
	r	-0.146	-0.078	-0.118	0.094	0.151	0.099	**0.367**	**0.699**	**0.330**	0.234	**0.421**	**0.654**	0.340	**0.664**	0.456	0.623	**0.721**
	n	38	38	38	38	37	38	37	36	38	38	37	36	35	36	32	23	27
CS2	ρ	-0.193	-0.099	-0.265	**-0.352**	0.053	0.026	-0.030	0.106	0.184	0.178	0.241	-0.105	0.051	-0.177	0.057	**0.466**	**0.487**
	r	-0.172	-0.183	**-0.355**	**-0.335**	0.076	0.038	-0.021	0.163	0.160	0.110	0.224	-0.511	0.102	-0.144	0.145	0.373	**0.547**

Table 4: Summary of the the correlation of the number of hours spent covering a topic and students' abilities at the end of CS1 and CS2 on that topic. Values listed in bold are statistically significant ($p \leq 0.5$).

instructional time on a topic and student learning are ***much*** weaker than correlations between topic importance and student learning levels. For several topics, in fact, we could not document ANY positive correlation between instructional time and student learning. As we now discuss, this pattern can be seen for both CS1 and CS2 courses.

In CS1, there was not a statistically significant correlation between class time spent on a topic and student learning for a majority of topics. Even when the responses labeling a topic "unrelated" are included, we could not find statistically significant evidence of a relationship between teaching time and student learning. This result holds for both the linear and monotonic correlation metrics. Where the correlation is significant, either the strength of this correlation is weak (e.g., TESTING, DEBUGGING) or the topic was taught by a small subset of instructors (e.g., ABSTRACTION MECHANISMS, RECURSION). For three of the most basic topics, CONTROL STRUCTURES, SUBROUTINES/FUNCTIONS, and TYPES, the correlations are weakly negative. While not statistically significant, these correlations suggest that increasing the time spent on these topics is associated with *decreased* student ability. For other commonly taught topics, ARRAYS being the strongest example, the level of correlation means that differences in time spent on a topic could explain as little as 10% of the variations in student ability. In CS1, just spending more time on a subject would result in very little improvement in student learning.

If the correlations seen by CS1 instructors were weakly significant, it is almost impossible for us to conclude that the time spent on a topic in CS2 has any relationship with student learning. In fact, of the four topics for which we find statistically significant correlations, an equal number have negative correlations (TYPES and ARRAYS) as have a positive correlation (GRAPHS and OTHER). Nor are these relationships very strong; only for RECURSION and OTHER does the time spent teaching explain at least 14% of the variation in student ability. For a majority of topics (10 out of 17), in fact,differences in time spent teaching a topic explain less than 3% of the variation in student ability. The two topics in which we see significant positive correlation (GRAPHS and OTHER) are also the only topics which were identified by some respondents as "unrelated" to their course (33% and 20% of respondents, respectively).

5. ANALYSIS

Survey responses suggest that students' abilities are largely a factor of how important the instructor considered a topic. This result is unsurprising, as the respondents were recruited via a computer science education-related mailing list. This is an important consideration when examining educational studies and assessments. By making a topic more (or less) important, student learning should also be improved (or decreased). While this result is to be expected, it also highlights a fact reflecting the experience of many of our students: some of our most basic concepts are also the ones that are hardest to teach. In CS1, students' abilities on SUBROUTINES/FUNCTIONS and TYPES are unrelated to the importance we place on the subject. That SUBROUTINES/FUNCTIONS is one of the topics in CS2 in which importance and ability are not significantly linearly correlated suggests that something about this topic is truly "hard".

That the results show negative correlations between the time spent on a topic and students' ability ***is*** surprising. That several of the

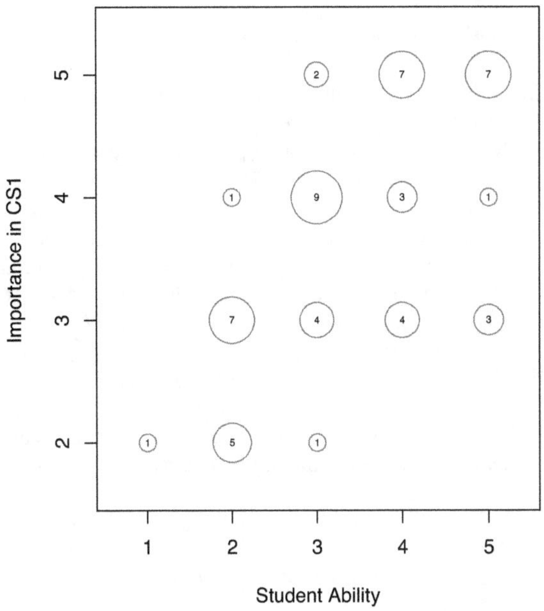

(a) Plot showing the very strong correlation for I/O.

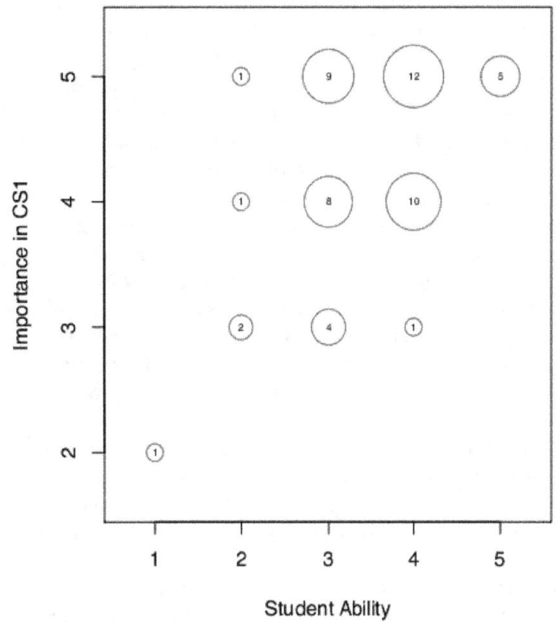

(b) Plot showing a weak, but statically significant, connection for ARRAYS.

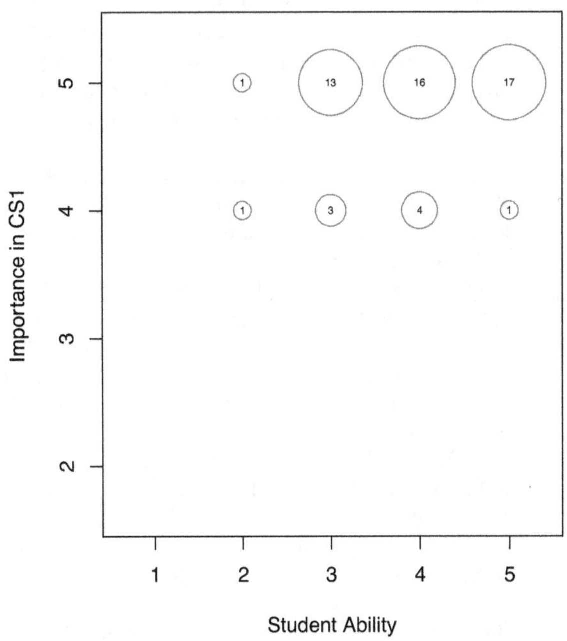

(c) Plot showing the weak connection for SUBROUTINES/FUNCTIONS

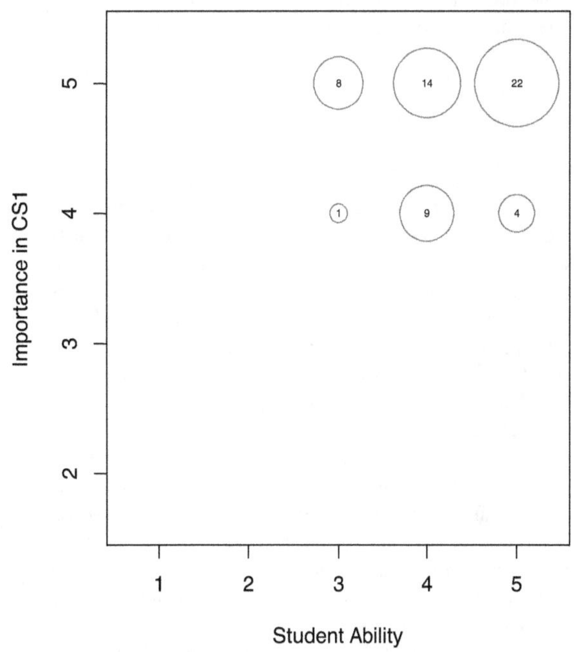

(d) Plot showing that there is almost no connection for TYPES.

Figure 1: Bubble plots showing a range of relationships between topic importance and student learning in CS1 courses. In each of these graphs, the size of each bubble represents the number of people who responded with that combination of importance and ability. This number is also written at the center of the bubble.

most basic topics have weak, negative correlations in CS1 could reflect a number of possible causes. Differences in how prepared students are at the start of the course, the instructors' comfort with teaching, and the energy and eagerness of the instructor could all help explain these odd results. The lack of significant correlations seen in CS2 may further reflect these differences. That the CS2 correlations are so much weaker than CS1 correlations could also be an indication of differences in students' strength: it is natural to assume that schools with "better" students should need less time to achieve the same level of mastery. These explanations still fail to explain the consistent, albeit weak, negative correlations that appear in CS2. Nor do they explain why the correlations with a topic's importance is so much higher than with the time spent on a topic.

All of this highlights the need for more detailed studies into best teaching practices in introductory courses. Are there approaches or techniques that help students master these topics efficiently? Could topic importance's greater effect on student learning levels be due to student's understanding key ideas or concepts earlier in the course? What underlying ideas or concepts must students possess to learn this material?

Finally, this work emphasizes the need for opportunities such as Ensemble [10] that enable the sharing of teaching material. The results strongly suggest that some instructors have ways of increasing student learning in time efficient ways. In addition to creating a space to share and discuss materials, this work suggests it could help answer important research questions. If posted material specified the time required and resulting level of student mastery, best practices could be identified and disseminated. More importantly, researchers could identify what, if any, common themes exist within those teaching approaches that are the most efficient. This could help improve the teaching of our introductory courses further or create entirely new approaches derived from these best practices.

6. CONCLUSION

Our results show that introductory students' abilities on a topic generally correlate with how important an instructor thought the topic was. This result can help explain the diversity of successful approaches towards teaching these introductory courses. Because the importance placed on each topic changes, our results show that different levels of student learning are to be expected. For nearly every topic, instructors *should* see student learning improve when using an approach that makes the topic more important to the course. We further identified several "hard" topics for which there is no correlation or very weak correlation between importance and ability. These topics – CONTROL STRUCTURES, SUBROUTINES/FUNCTIONS, and TYPES – cover many of the basic programming concepts and were rated as important or very important by nearly all of our respondents. This paper suggests that more research is needed to better understand why these topics are so difficult to teach and investigate better ways to teach these ideas.

Our results also show that there is little correlation between the time spent covering a topic and students' abilities on that topic. In CS1, this is often seen as weak or no correlation for most topics. Worse, in CS2, this is frequently seen as negative correlations suggesting that student learning is improved by decreasing the time topics are taught. There are many possible explanations for this result; future research is needed to understand which explanation or explanations are the cause. Even so, this research highlights the need to share those best practices that best help students learn the material efficiently.

Acknowledgements

The authors would like to thank the survey respondents and anonymous reviewers for their help in improving this paper.

7. REFERENCES

[1] *Implementation and Analysis of Respondent Driven Sampling*, New York, NY, Nov. 2006. Springer New York.

[2] N. B. Dale. Content and emphasis in CS1. *SIGCSE Bulletin*, 37(4):69–73, Dec. 2005.

[3] N. B. Dale. Most difficult topics in CS1: results of an online survey of educators. *SIGCSE Bulletin*, 38(2):49–53, June 2006.

[4] S. Davies, J. A. Polack-Wahl, and K. Anewalt. A snapshot of current practices in teaching the introductory programming sequence. In *SIGCSE '11: Proceedings of the 42nd ACM technical symposium on Computer science education*, pages 625–630, 2011.

[5] K. Goldman, P. Gross, C. Heeren, G. L. Herman, L. Kaczmarczyk, M. C. Loui, and C. Zilles. Setting the scope of concept inventories for introductory computing subjects. *Transactions on Computing Education*, 10(2):1–29, June 2010.

[6] M. Hertz. What do 'CS1' and 'CS2' mean? investigating differences in early courses. In *Proceedings of the 41st SIGCSE technical symposium on Computer science education*, pages 199–203, 2010.

[7] K. Kapp. Likert-type scales: Examples, samples, and information. In *Kapp Notes*, Retrieved 14 Sept. 2010. Available at: `http://www.uleduneering.com/kappnotes/index.php/2010/09/likert-type-scales-examples-samples-and`.

[8] Liberal Arts Computer Science Consortium. A 2007 model curriculum for a liberal arts degree in computer science. *Journal on Educational Resources in Computing*, 7(2):2, 2007.

[9] Spearman's rho is a 'quasi-ordinal' correlation coefficient. Retrieved 26 Aug., 2012. Available at: `https://www.msu.edu/~nurse/classes/summer2002/813/week8spearman.htm`.

[10] F. M. Shipman, L. Cassel, E. Fox, R. Furuta, L. Delcambre, P. Brusilovsky, B. S. Carpenter, G. Hislop, S. Edwards, and D. D. Garcia. Ensemble: a distributed portal for the distributed community of computing education. In *Proceedings of the 14th European conference on Research and advanced technology for digital libraries*, pages 506–509, 2010.

[11] A. E. Tew and M. Guzdial. Developing a validated assessment of fundamental CS1 concepts. In *SIGCSE '10: Proceedings of the 41st ACM technical symposium on Computer science education*, pages 97–101, 2010.

[12] A. E. Tew and M. Guzdial. The FCS1: a language independent assessment of CS1 knowledge. In *SIGCSE '11: Proceedings of the 42nd ACM technical symposium on Computer science education*, pages 111–116, 2011.

[13] The Joint Task Force on Computing Curricula. Computing curricula 2001. *Journal on Educational Resources in Computing*, page 1, 2001.

[14] E. W. Weisstein. Correlation coefficient, Retrieved 26 Aug., 2011. From MathWorld–A Wolfram Web Resource. `http://mathworld.wolfram.com/CorrelationCoefficient.html`.

Computer Science Curriculum 2013: Social and Professional Recommendations from the ACM/IEEE-CS Task Force

Elizabeth K. Hawthorne (Moderator)
Union County College
Department of Computer Science
Cranford, NJ 07016
hawthorne@ucc.edu

Florence A. Appel
Saint Xavier University
Department of Computer Science
Chicago, IL 60655
appel@sxu.edu

Carol L. Spradling
Northwest Missouri State University
Department of Mathematics, Computer Science and Information Systems
Maryville, MO 64468
c_sprad@nwmissouri.edu

Lisa C. Kaczmarczyk
Independent Evaluation Consultant
San Diego, CA, USA
lisakacz@gmail.com

ABSTRACT

Social and professional principles were included in ABET computer science accreditation standards in 1987 and first appeared in the *ACM/IEEE-CS Computing Curricula* in 1991. This moderated panel presented the Social Issues and Professional Practice Knowledge Area (SP KA) of the 2013 ACM/IEEE-CS draft curricular guidelines for computer science. Specific knowledge units from the Ironman version were highlighted for discussion along with course and module exemplars.

Categories and Subject Descriptors

K.2 [History of Computing]; K.3.2 [Computers and Education]: Computer Science Education; Curriculum; K.4.0 [Computers and Society]; K.5.0 [Legal Aspects of Computing]; K.7.0 [The Computing Professional].

General Terms

Design, Documentation, Human Factors, Legal Aspects, Security

Keywords

Computing Curricula 2013; Computer Science; Computer Ethics Pedagogy; Social and Legal Aspects of Computing; Access to Computing; Sustainability; Sustainable Computing; Professional Communication; Professional Ethics; Professional Practice

1. INTRODUCTION

Social and professional principles were included in ABET computer science accreditation standards in 1987 [5] and first The Special Interest Group on Computers and Society (SIGCAS) was approached to provide input to the CS2013 Task Force on the social issues and professional practice knowledge area (SP KA), and a special SIGCAS subcommittee was formed to review, revise and update the 2008 curricular guidelines to reflect current social and professional topics, needs and practice. The result has been a significant contribution to the first and second drafts of CS2013, known as Strawman [3] and Ironman [4], respectively. The panel seeks to inform and solicit feedback from the SIGCSE community on the contents of the SP KA of CS2013, Ironman draft. Core Tier-1, Core Tier-2 and Electives will be highlighted for the areas shown in Table 1.

Table 1. Social Issues & Professional Practice Knowledge Area [11 Core Tier-1 hours, 5 Core Tier-2 hours]

SP Knowledge Unit	Core Tier-1 Hours	Core Tier-2 Hours	Includes Electives
Social Context	1	2	N
Analytical Tools	2		N
Professional Ethics	2	2	N
Intellectual Property	2		Y
Privacy and Civil Liberties	2		Y
Professional Communication	1		Y
Sustainability	1	1	Y
History			Y
Economics of Computing			Y
Security Policies, Laws and Computer Crimes			Y

SIGCSE'13, March 6–9, 2013, Denver, Colorado, USA.
ACM 978-1-4503-1868-6/13/03.

In particular, the panel will highlight significant changes such as the inclusion of two new core knowledge units: sustainability in computing and professional communication and other changes to the social and professional knowledge unit. The panel will also highlight course and module exemplars that are being collected for the final report. Audience participants will be encouraged to share exemplars from their colleges.

2. ELIZABETH K. HAWTHORNE

Elizabeth Hawthorne is a member of the Steering Committee for the Computing Curricula 2013: Computer Science volume and serves as the chair of the Social and Professional Knowledge Area (SP KA). She is a Senior Professor in the Department of Computer Science at Union County College and is the chair of the Two-Year College Education Committee of the ACM Education Board. Elizabeth will moderate the panel, describe the process that was utilized to update the SP KA, and discuss how social issues and professional practice relate to community and technical college curricular via course exemplars.

3. FLORENCE A. APPEL

Florence Appel is the former chair of the Special Interest Group: Computers and Society (SIGCAS) where she worked extensively to set the direction of social and professional issues in the SIGCAS community. She currently represents SIGCAS on the ACM Education Council. She is a professor of Computer Science at Saint Xavier University. Florence will discuss the value of SP KA course and module exemplars to the growing number of computer science educators who seek direction in incorporating this content into their curricula. Central to this discussion is addressing the decision to offer a stand-alone course or to integrate the content throughout the curriculum.

4. CAROL L. SPRADLING

Carol Spradling is a former member of the ACM Education Council and has worked on the social and professional knowledge units for the 2008 Computer Science interim curriculum [2], 2008 Informational Technology curriculum, 2010 Information Systems 2010 curriculum as well as the 2013 SP KA. She is an Associate Professor in the Department of Mathematics, Computer Science and Information Systems. Carol will discuss the new professional communication knowledge unit in the SP KA and will present a modular exemplar.

5. LISA C. KACZMARCZYK

Lisa Kaczmarczyk is a member of the ACM Education Council and an Associate Editor for Inroads Magazine. Her book [7] "Computers and Society – Computing For Good" was published in 2011. She was a member of the ITiCSE 2008 working group on sustainability and computing. Lisa is currently an independent evaluation and assessment consultant for computing education research projects. Lisa will discuss the controversial core knowledge unit of the SP KA that infusing sustainability into the undergraduate computer science curriculum. She will provide a sustainability example.

6. ACKNOWLEDGMENTS

We extend our sincere appreciation to the SIGCAS community as well as numerous internal and external reviewers.

7. REFERENCES

[1] ACM/IEEE-CS Joint Curriculum Task Force. (1991, December). *Computing Curricula 1991 Communications of the ACM, 34*(6), 68-84.

[2] ACM/IEEE-CS 2008 Interim Review Task Force. (2008, December). *Computer Science Curriculum 2008: An Interim Revision of CS 2001.* Retireved August 1, 2012 from www.acm.org/education/curricula/ComputerScience2008.pdf

[3] ACM/IEEE-CS 2013 Joint Task Force on Computing Curricula. (2012, February). *Computer Science Curricula 2013 Strawman Draft.* Retrieved August 1, 2012 from www.cs2013.org/strawman-draft/cs2013-strawman.pdf

[4] ACM/IEEE-CS 2013 Joint Task Force on Computing Curricula. (2012, November). *Computer Science Curricula 2013 Ironman Draft Version 0.8.* Retrieved December 1, 2012 from www.cs2013.org/ironman-draft/cs2013-ironman-v0.8.pdf

[5] Huff, C. & Martin, C. D. (1995). Computing consequences: A framework for teaching ethical computing. *Communications of the ACM, 38*(12), 75.84.

[6] IEEE-CS/ACM Joint Task Force on Computing Curricula. (2002). *Computing Curricula 2001 Computer Science. (Final Report IEEE-CS/ACM Joint Task Force on Computing Curricula).* Los Alamitos, CA: IEEE Computer Society.

[7] Kaczmarczyk, L. (2011). *Computers and Society - Computing for Good.* Boca Rotan, FL: CRC Press.

[8] Sahami, M., Roach, S., Cuadros-Vargas, E. & Reed, D. (2012, March). Computer Science Curriculum 2013: Reviewing the Strawman Report from the ACM/IEEE-CS Task Force, *SIGCSE '12 Proceedings of the 43rd ACM technical symposium on Computer Science Education,* 3-4, doi: 10.1145/2157136.2157

Understanding NSF Funding Opportunities

Jeffrey Forbes
National Science Foundation
Directorate of Computer and Information Science and Engineering
jforbes@nsf.gov

Victor Piotrowski, Jane Prey, & D. Suzanne Westbrook
National Science Foundation
Directorate of Education and Human Resources
vpiotrow@nsf.gov, jprey@nsf.gov, swestbro@nsf.gov

SUMMARY

This session highlights programs in the National Science Foundation's (NSF) Education and Human Resources (EHR) and Computer and Information Science and Engineering (CISE) directorates. The focus is on providing descriptions of several programs of interest to college faculty and discussing the requirements and guidelines for programs in these areas. The session includes a description of the proposal and review processes as well as strategies for writing competitive proposals. Participants are encouraged to discuss procedural issues with the presenters.

Categories and Subject Descriptors

K.3.2 Computer and Information Science Education

General Terms

Documentation.

Keywords

Grants, awards, proposals, National Science Foundation, education.

1. OVERALL OBJECTIVE, AUDIENCE, SUITABILITY

NSF supports projects to improve education in science, technology, engineering, and mathematics (STEM) through several programs in its Education and Human Resources (EHR) directorate, as well as in its research directorates, including Computer and Information Science and Engineering (CISE). This forum presents a description of some education-related programs in the EHR and CISE directorates, and enables faculty to interact with the presenters concerning specific project ideas that could be appropriate for the various programs. This type of forum is best suited to a special session to encourage audience interaction and for making connections between faculty and NSF program directors.

2. SESSION OUTLINE

The presenters will describe each of the following programs and encourage questions from the audience. Complete details about the programs can be found on the NSF websites for the Directorate of Education and Human Resources [1] and the Directorate for Computer & Information Science & Engineering (CISE) [2].

SIGCSE'13, March 6–9, 2013, Denver, Colorado, USA.
ACM 978-1-4503-1868-6/13/03.

2.1 Advanced Technological Education (ATE)

ATE is a program specifically geared for community colleges, or for four-year schools working closely with community colleges. This program focuses on improvement in the "education of science and engineering technicians at the undergraduate and the secondary school levels. [2]" Specific technological fields include computer and information technology, cybersecurity, forensics, and telecommunications.

2.2 Transforming Undergraduate Education in STEM (TUES)

The TUES program supports efforts to create, adapt, and disseminate new learning materials and teaching strategies to reflect advances both in STEM disciplines and in what is known about teaching and learning. It funds projects that develop faculty expertise, implement educational innovations, assess learning and evaluate innovations, prepare K-12 teachers, or conduct research on STEM teaching and learning. It also supports projects that further the work of the program itself, for example, synthesis and dissemination of findings across the program. The program supports projects representing different stages of development, ranging from small, exploratory investigations to large, comprehensive projects.

2.3 Widening Implementation and Demonstration of Evidence-based Reforms (WIDER)

The WIDER program supports research on how to achieve widespread sustainable implementation of undergraduate instructional practices leading to improved student outcomes in STEM at academic institutions through demonstration models. The goal is to change practice across the institution, not simply in one or two courses. Proposals should describe how they employ innovative strategies, develop dynamic partnerships, and implement catalytic approaches toward achieving this goal.

2.4 CyberCorps: Scholarships for Service (SFS)

The SFS program seeks to increase the number of qualified students entering information assurance and cybersecurity and to increase the capacity of the US higher education enterprise to produce professionals in these fields. The SFS program has two tracks: (1) the Scholarship Track which provides funding for scholarships to students in information assurance and cybersecurity, and (2) the Capacity Track which provides funding for professional development of information assurance and cybersecurity faculty and for the development of academic programs in these fields.

2.5 Innovative Technology Experiences for Students and Teachers (ITEST)

The ITEST program seeks to encourage K-12 students to develop interest in and to be prepared for careers in STEM and information and communications technology (ICT). ITEST projects must engage K-12 students and may also provide opportunities for teachers. While there are four types of ITEST projects, the two most likely to be of interest are (1) Strategies projects that develop, implement, and evaluate novel interventions for K-12 students, and (2) Research projects that contribute to the knowledge base about which approaches, models, and interventions with K-12 students and teachers are most likely to increase capacity in the STEM and ICT-intensive workforce of the future.

2.6 Research Experiences for Undergraduates Sites (REU Sites)

Research experience is one of the most effective ways of attracting talented undergraduates to, and retaining them in careers in science and engineering, including careers in teaching and research. The REU Sites program aims to provide appropriate and valuable educational experiences for cohorts of 8-10 undergraduate students in the summer through participation in research and professional development activities. REU projects engage students, most of whom are from institutions different than the host institution, in meaningful ways in ongoing research programs or in research projects specifically designed for the REU program. REU projects feature high-quality interaction of students with faculty and/or other research mentors and access to appropriate facilities and professional development opportunities.

2.7 Research Experiences for Teachers in Engineering and Computer Science (RET Sites)

The RET Sites program provides support for the active participation of in-service and pre-service K-12 STEM teachers and community college faculty in ongoing engineering and computer science research. Institutions build bridges with their communities through hosting a cohort of 10-15 teachers for summer research and ongoing community activities during the school year. Encouraging active participation of K-12 educators and community college faculty in research is an excellent way to broaden and increase the capacity of the teacher pool in the U. S. to teach engineering and computer science concepts to their students and to encourage students to pursue engineering and computer science careers.

2.8 Computing Education for the 21st Century (CE21)

The CE21 program goals are to build a robust computing research community, a computationally competent 21st century workforce, and a computationally empowered citizenry. The program addresses three interrelated challenges: the significant underproduction of degrees needed for the computing and computing-related workforce, the longstanding underrepresentation of many segments of our population, and the lack of a presence of computing in K-12. CE21 has three tracks: (1) CS10K projects develop the partnershiops and knowledge base necessary to ensure broad access to engaging, rigorous computer science courses in 10,000 high schools taught by 10,000 well-trained teachers; (2) Computing Education Research projects will contribute to the knowledge base for computing education by conducting basic research on the teaching and learning of computational competencies at any level from elementary school through undergraduate study; and (3) Broadeining Participation projects develop and assess novel interventions that contribute to our knowledge base on the effective teaching and learning of computing for students from groups underrepresented in computing.

2.9 STEM Talent Expansion Program (STEP)

STEP grants fall into two categories of activities. Type 1 activities are aimed at implementing recruitment or retention strategies that will lead to a measurable increase in the number of students obtaining STEM degrees in baccalaureate or associate degree programs or completing credits toward transfer to a baccalaureate degree program in STEM fields at community colleges. Type 2 activities focus on educational research on factors affecting associate or baccalaureate degree attainment in STEM.

3. WRITING COMPETITIVE PROPOSALS

NSF programs are quite competitive but there are simple strategies you should be aware of when writing proposals to improve your chances of success. First and foremost, read the Program Solicitation carefully. Your goal is to help reviewers quickly understand *what* you intend to do and that you have given sufficient thought of *how* you intend to do it. Organize the proposal to address the essential components described in the solicitation. Use headings, boldface and bulleted lists to help the reader quickly understand the organization of the proposals. Address each point thoroughly but succinctly. And finally, start well before the submission deadline. Include sufficient lead time to allow colleagues to provide feedback and for your research office to approve the proposal. Specific directions for completing your proposal can be found online [3].

4. REFERENCES

[1] http://nsf.gov/div/index.jsp?org=EHR

[2] http://nsf.gov/dir/index.jsp?org=CISE

[3] http://nsf.gov/funding/preparing/

An Interactive Exploration of Gender and Computing: Unpacking the Student Experience

Lynn Andrea Stein, Debbie Chachra, Yevgeniya V. Zastavker,
Caitrin Lynch, Alisha Sarang-Sieminski
Franklin W. Olin College of Engineering
1 Olin Way
Needham, MA 02492 USA
+1 781 292 2500
corresponding author: las@olin.edu
all authors: gender@olin.edu

ABSTRACT
Being a computer science and engineering student is experienced differently by male and female students; gendered interactions affect the development of academic and professional role confidence as well as professional identity. In this hands-on special session, participants explore concepts of gender schemas, privilege, and identity using a range of interactive activities. We have found these concepts useful in framing discussion with our students and in understanding and improving student experiences. The session introduces – and obtains feedback on – a Gender and Engineering Exploration Kit, which the participants are encouraged to review, use, and share at their home institutions.

Categories and Subject Descriptors
K.7 [**The Computing Profession**]. K.3.2 [**Computers and Education**]: Computer and Information Science Education. K.4.2 [**Computers and Society**]: Social Issues – *employment.*

General Terms
Human Factors.

Keywords
Gender, diversity, classroom climate, meritocracy.

1. BACKGROUND AND OBJECTIVES
Being a computer science or engineering student is experienced differently by male and female students. Relevant factors include lower numbers of women enrolled in computer science and engineering programs [1,2], lower self-confidence among these women [3,4,5], and lower retention rates [4,6]. These factors in turn influence differential formation of professional identity and affiliation [7]. This is not an exhaustive list; it merely serves to illustrate some of the ways in which gender affects the experience of being in a computer science or engineering program and in the profession at large.

While considerable effort has been centered on studying the student experience, the focus of this special session is not academic. Rather, we use conceptual frameworks drawn from research to provide members of the educational community with concrete tools for understanding in academic computer science environments. The session further builds participant insight into how these interactions affect the student experience and empowers participants to put this understanding to use – facilitating further activities and improving climate – in their home institutions.

SIGCSE'13, March 6–9, 2013, Denver, Colorado, USA.
ACM 978-1-4503-1868-6/13/03.

The special session consists almost entirely of structured interactive activities and facilitated small group discussion, with introductory and concluding presentation bookends used to scaffold participant understanding and effective engagement.

This special session has several goals. The first is to engage participants in a discussion-centered learning experience about gendered experiences in CS/E education. The second is to provide participants with the tools and confidence to lead such a discussion at their home institutions. To this end, we are developing a Gender and Engineering Exploration Kit, which provides the materials and information necessary to facilitate this conversation. As a part of this session, we introduce participants to the kit, help prepare them to use it at their home institutions, and solicit their feedback on its design and content.

2. SESSION OUTLINE
This session engages its participants in interactive exercises and facilitated discussion to explore conceptual frameworks around gender and computer science as well as their implications in educational environments. While these ideas are based in and drawn from extensive research, the purpose of this session is to translate frameworks into actionable models, new understandings, and scaffolding for productive interactions. A minimum of the session is spent presenting information; the majority of time participants are actively engaged in exploring these tools and their own experiences. The session focuses on self-reflection, discussion, and sharing among the participants. The content and format of the discussion are guided by the Gender and Engineering Exploration Kit. The session includes:

- Introduction of frameworks and relation to student experience: gender schemas, implicit awareness; student confidence, self-efficacy, and identity.
- Interactive exploration of privilege and its relationship to experience using Kit materials.
- Interactive exploration of (micro)messaging and its relationship to experience using Kit materials.

- Guided exploration of Kit materials. Participants review and discuss the Kit in small/facilitated groups, recording feedback and envisioning home institution activities.

The Kit and the workshop emphasize structured discussions. A discussion format leverages the participants' own experiences, allowing participants to reflect on their interactions in the context of schemas and privilege, thereby reinterpreting their own discourse and that of others. By sharing these interactions, facilitators and participants demonstrate that a) there are a wide range of gendered interactions, b) these interactions are a part of our daily communications, and c) these types of interactions have affected all of us. Further, sharing experiences in an interactive session helps participants to develop a common understanding and awareness of these issues within our community.

3. EXPCTATIONS AND OUTCOMES

The session is intended for computer science and engineering faculty members and students. We have previously offered variants on this session at engineering education conferences with strongly positive feedback. Participants appreciate acquiring language, conceptual frameworks, and tools with which to engage this issue. They benefit from the opportunity to explore with colleagues both their own observations and experiences and the ways in which they might translate these tools to their home contexts. Finally, the Gender and Engineering Exploration Kit contains concrete support for follow-on activities. This workshop provides experience with the Kit, feedback for its continued development, and an expanding community of concerned educators supporting ongoing discussion.

4. SUITABILITY AS SPECIAL SESSION

This session would not be feasible at SIGCSE within the traditional formats. Similar sessions –not explicitly focused on computer science – have been run using special session formats at the American Society for Engineering Education's annual conference and at the ASEE/IEEE's Frontiers in Education conferences as well as the hands-on session format at the Workshop on Active Learning in Engineering Education (ALE).

While we recognize that the SIGCSE Special Session format differs somewhat from these, it is the closest environment to provide this important topic an appropriately interactive forum. Based on our previous experiences, we anticipate that workshop participants will have many personal experiences related to gender and CS/E education. We feel it is critical to give them an opportunity both to share these experiences and to integrate what they learn in the session with their own professional lives. Finally, we will ask participants to provide feedback regarding the Kit with the goal of further refining the materials.

5. SAMPLE ACTIVITIES

During the session and through the Gender and Engineering Exploration Kit, participants explore their own understandings of and relationship to gender. Kit-facilitated activities include:

> *"Unpacking the Invisible Knapsack":* Participants are introduced to the concept of 'privilege,' based on the essay by Peggy McIntosh [8]. They are asked to "experience privilege" through a set of exercises, to write a list of examples of privilege based on their gender and other dimensions of identity, and to share and discuss these lists.
>
> *Gender Schemas:* Workshop facilitators introduce the concept of gender schemas – our mental models of the behavior of others – and describe how these schemas affect social and other interactions [9]. Participants provide examples of gender schemas in action and discuss them in small groups.
>
> *Implicit Awareness Test:* A series of images is shown; and participants are asked to immediately respond by noting and recording images they associate with women and men. (The Kit includes a pointer to the interactive online version of this activity.) As the goal of implicit awareness tests is to reveal unconscious biases, this activity allows participants to better understand and reflect on their own implicit biases [10].
>
> *Micromessaging:* Curated images selected from current media are the basis for a discussion of how each of us perceives both intended and unintended messages, as well as the effects of these messages on our senses of self [11].

While time permits us to run only some of these as interactive activities during the special session, participants receive previews of each of these and will leave with materials to enable facilitation of these activities at home.

All kit materials are available from http://gender.olin.edu

6. REFERENCES

[1] Vesgo, J. "CRA Taulbee Trends: Female Students and Faculty." http://archive.cra.org/info/taulbee/women.html

[2] Sax, L. 2008. *The Gender Gap in College*. Jossey-Bass, San Francisco, CA, USA.

[3] Chachra D., and Kilgore, D. 2009. Exploring gender and self-confidence in engineering students: a multi-method approach. *Proceedings of the American Society for Engineering Education Annual Conference* (Austin, TX).

[4] Margolis, J., and A. Fisher. *Unlocking the Clubhouse: Women in Computing.* MIT Press, 2002.

[5] Cech, E., Rubineau, B., Silbey, S., and Seron, C. 2011. "Professional role confidence and gendered persistence in engineering," *American Sociological Review*, vol. 76, pp. 641-666, October 2011.

[6] Seymour, E., and Hewitt, N. M. 1997. Talking About Leaving. Westview Press, Boulder, CO, USA.

[7] Smyth, F., and W. Guilford. "First-year engineers are strikingly impoverished in their self-concept as professional engineers." *Proceedings of the American Society for Engineering Education Annual Conference*, 2011

[8] Macintosh, P. 1988. "White privilege and male privilege: a personal account of coming to see correspondences through work in women's studies," in *Reconstructing Gender: A Multicultural Anthology*, E. Disch, Ed. Boston: McGraw-Hill Higher Education, pp. 79-80.

[9] Valian, V. 1999. *Why So Slow? The Advancement of Women.* Cambridge: MIT Press.

[10] Greenwald, A. G., McGhee, D. E., Schwartz, J. L. K. 1998. "Measuring individual differences in implicit cognition: the implicit association test." *Journal of Personality and Social Psychology,* 74, 1464-1480.

[11] Rowe, M. 2008. "Micro-Affirmations and Micro-inequities." *Journal of the International Ombudsman Association,* 1(1).

Demystifying Computing with Magic, continued

Daniel D. Garcia
University of California, Berkeley
777 Soda Hall
Berkeley, CA 94720-1776
+1 510-517-4041
ddgarcia@cs.berkeley.edu

David Ginat
Tel-Aviv University
Sharet Building; Ramat Aviv
Tel-Aviv, Israel
+972 3-640-8151
ginat@post.tau.ac.il

SUMMARY

One man's "magic" is another man's engineering.
– Robert A. Heinlein

Some beginning students have fuzzy mental models of how the computer works, or worse, sincerely believe that the computer works unpredictably, "by magic" [2]. We seek to demystify computing for these students using analogy, by showing them something that even magic itself isn't really mystical, it is just computation. This is a continuation of our standing-room only SIGCSE 2012 special session [4].

Magic is one of the most colorful examples of "unplugged" (i.e., without-computer, active learning) activities. It adds a unique facet in that it holds a *hidden secret* that the audience can be challenged to unfold. Once solved, students are often enthusiastic to perform the magic in front of others. In this session, we will share a variety of new magic tricks whose answer is grounded in computer science: modulo arithmetic, human-computer interfaces, algorithms, binary encoding, invariants, etc. For each trick, we will have an interactive discussion of its underlying computing fundamentals, and tips for successful showmanship. Audience participation will be critical, for helping us perform the magic, discussing the solution, and contributing other magic tricks.

Categories and Subject Descriptors

K.3.2 [**Computer and Information Science Education**]: Computer Science Education

General Terms

Algorithms, Design, Human Factors, Theory

Keywords

Computational thinking, magic, card tricks, unplugged activities

1. OBJECTIVE

Magic is a lot of fun. Yet, it can be more than fun – it can be used to illustrate and teach scientific and mathematical notions, including those of computer science [1, 3, 5, 6]. Our objective in this special session is to show how magic can motivate particular computational ideas, by challenging the students to figure out the idea *behind* the trick, then elaborating on these notions and relating them to the material. Students may also be encouraged to practice the magic, and even perform in front of the class. In our primary experience, students (majors and non-majors) are enthusiastic to take part.

SIGCSE'13, March 6–9, 2013, Denver, Colorado, USA.
ACM 978-1-4503-1868-6/13/03.

2. OUTLINE

The session will be an interactive seminar. It will include motivation, illustrations, audience participation, and conclusion. The general structure will be as follows.

- **Rationale.** The relevance of magic, as a special unplugged activity, will be described and presented. An emphasis will be put on magic's baffling impact on one hand, and the enthusiastic characteristic to discover the secret – on the other.
- **Aspects and illustrations.** We will display several magic tricks. The presentations will sometimes involve volunteers from the audience. The secrets behind the presented magic will be related to various CS principles, e.g., modulo arithmetic, human-computer interfaces, algorithms, binary encoding, invariants, and more. Suggestions will be offered on how one may elaborate on the underlying CS notions following a magic presentation.
- **Audience participation.** The audience will participate in three ways. Volunteers may take part in some presentations. The audience will be challenged to discover the secrets. Audience participants may offer further, enriching, unplugged ideas for magic, including those presented, and will be invited to perform them, if they wish.
- **Suggestions for educators.** Pedagogical lessons of ways to embed magic will be displayed and discussed. We will share our experience with students, who like to perform (sometimes more than once) in front of their friends. This yields active assimilation of studied principles.

Here are but eight of the magic tricks we will perform, and the youngest group that could present the tricks on their own with no hints. We will have more ready to present, if time permits.

2.1 The Real-Time 4x4 Magic Square

The magician asks a spectator for a number, and quickly creates a 4x4 Magic Square, in which all the rows, columns and diagonals add to the original number [7].

Youngest group: Grade School (~10 years old)

Lesson: Algorithms, functions.

2.2 The Six-Sided Piece of Paper

The magician produces a folded piece of paper (a flexagon) that apparently has *six* sides, revealed by continuously unfolding it, but not changing its overall size [8].

Youngest group: Grade School (~7 years old)

Lesson: Algorithms, topology.

2.3 The Tricky Dice

The magician asks a spectator to drop a pair of dice into a cup of water, and peek under to see the two numbers hidden from view (facing down). The magician dips their finger in the water, and tells the person what numbers they saw [7].

Youngest group: Grade School (~7 years old)

Lesson: Algorithms, functions.

2.4 The Guess the Missing Digit Game

The magician thinks of a 4-digit number, and asks a spectator to think of a 3-digit number, multiply the two together, and hide one of the digits. Seeing the product, the magician guesses the digit.

Youngest group: Grade School (~10 years old)

Lesson: Abstraction, modulo arithmetic.

2.5 The Trick that Fooled Einstein

The magician tells a spectator he knows the difference in the amount of change they're both carrying. The magician makes three claims: (a) "I've got as much change as you", (b) "I've then got another 2 quarters", and (c) "I'm left with just enough change left to make your change add to $2.35". The magician proceeds to count out the same change as the spectator, plus 2 quarters, and the remainder plus the spectator's sums to $2.35 [6].

Youngest group: Grade School (~10 years old)

Lesson: Algorithms, model-checking.

2.6 The Birthday Day in the Week

The magician asks a spectator for their birthday and correctly reports the day in the week it was [5].

Youngest group: Grade School (~10 years old)

Lesson: Algorithms, functions, modulo arithmetic, arrays.

2.7 Split-Second Calculations

This magic involves computations that appear difficult to be calculated quickly. It is composed of three parts. In part 1, the magician defines a sequence of positive integers (all those for which no one is an average of any other two in the sequence), the spectator calls the number n and the magician immediately tells the nth integer in the sequence. In part 2, the magician describes a process of emptying a jar with black and white beans, the spectator calls the initial numbers of white beans and black beans, and the magician immediately tells the color of the last remaining bean. Finally, in part 3, the magician describes a system with three buckets and a rule for pouring water from one bucket to another, the spectator says the (integer) water amounts in the buckets, and the magician reveals the number of steps to empty a bucket.

Youngest group: College students

Lesson: Algorithms, invariance, binary representation, encoding.

2.8 The Numbers Game

The magician asks a spectator to call out 10 numbers, which the magician writes on separate pieces of paper, places face down, and shuffles. The magician turns around, asks the spectator to pick turn over a pile, and the magician guesses that number [6].

Youngest group: Grade School (~7 years old)

Lesson: Abstraction, human-computer interfaces.

3. EXPECTATIONS

The intended audience for the special session is the broad community of computing educators, especially those who enjoy magic but have not used it in their classes or during occasions of computing outreach. They will hear (and hopefully, contribute) magic tricks, the computing fundamentals behind them, showmanship tips, and how to direct a follow-up discussion.

4. SUITABILITY

Our presentation is interactive and engaging, with active audience participation. Anyone in attendance who knows magic tricks based on computing fundamentals is encouraged to contribute. A special session affords and encourages this unique format with the most audience involvement.

5. REFERENCES

[1] CS Unplugged. *Error Detection*. Retrieved January 1, 2012 from `http://csunplugged.org/error-detection`

[2] Clancy, M. Misconceptions and attitudes that interfere with learning to program. In *Computer Science Education Research*, s. Fincher and M. Petre, eds. Taylor and Francis Group, London, 2004, 85–100.

[3] Curzon, P. and McOwan, P. W. 2008. Engaging with computer science through magic shows. In *Proceedings of the 13th Annual Conference on innovation and Technology in Computer Science Education* (Madrid, Spain, June 30 - July 02, 2008). ITiCSE '08. ACM, New York, NY, 179-183. `http://doi.acm.org/10.1145/1384271.1384320`

[4] Garcia, D. and Ginat, D. 2012. DeMystifying computing with magic. In *Proceedings of the 43rd ACM technical symposium on Computer Science Education* (SIGCSE '12). ACM, New York, NY, USA, 83-84. `http://doi.acm.org/10.1145/2157136.2157164`

[5] Ginat, D.; Garcia, D.; and Gasarch, W. 2002. Aha! an illuminating perspective. In *Proceedings of the 33rd SIGCSE Technical Symposium on Computer Science Education* (Cincinnati, Kentucky, February 27 - March 03, 2002). SIGCSE '02. ACM, New York, NY, 1-2. `http://doi.acm.org/10.1145/563340.563342`

[6] CS4FN. 2012. *The Magic of Computer Science.* Retrieved September 6, 2012 from `http://www.cs4fn.org/magic/`

[7] Math Magic. 2011. *Kidz Labs Fun Science Products.* `http://m-ind.com/product_view.php?id=233`

[8] singingbanana. 2010. *A Flexagon for Martin Gardner*. Retrieved September 6, 2012 from `http://youtu.be/4DETMhTC0H0`

Reading Mobile Games Throughout the Curriculum[*]

Jennifer Bayzick, Bradley Askins, Sharon Kalafut, and Michael Spear
Computer Science and Engineering Department
Lehigh University
{jlb411, bja206, smk5, spear}@cse.lehigh.edu

ABSTRACT

We introduce ALE, a new framework for writing games for the Android platform. The primary motivation behind ALE is to emphasize reading code before writing it. Beginners read game code to learn how levels can be made, and advanced users read the code of ALE itself to learn how to create useful and extensible libraries. To date, roughly 200 students at our university have used ALE, ranging from first-semester engineering undergraduates through Masters students. ALE has proven useful in teaching non-majors about CS, in making introductory CS programming courses more exciting, and in encouraging creativity, entrepreneurship, and good program design in upper-level electives. Based on these experiences, we encourage educators at all levels to consider using ALE to improve students' ability to learn by reading code.

Categories and Subject Descriptors

K.3.2 [**Computers and Education**]: Computer and Information Science Education – Computer science education

General Terms

Design, Languages

Keywords

Android, CS1, Games, Java, OpenGL

1. INTRODUCTION

While the authors of this paper are generally optimists, we worry that too many of today's CS students are not passionate about programming. They see it as drudgery. They do not enjoy it. They might abandon CS to avoid it. If not, too often they remain in CS but never learn to program well. And while programming is only a part of CS, it is an integral part. Just as calculus cannot be hidden from math majors forever, neither can programming be hidden from CS majors. In this paper, we describe our effort to make learning to program more fun.

We argue that there are four causes of this problem that are understudied, all of which can be addressed in part through a new framework we developed for Android game development, called ALE (the AndEngine Lehigh Extension). To date, we have employed projects based on ALE at three points in the curriculum: an 18-hour first-year experience course for first-year engineers, an introductory programming course for CS majors, and an upper-level mobile programming elective. Though informal, our experiences have been positive enough that we are now releasing ALE to educators worldwide, so others may benefit from our effort.

Projects involving ALE are fun, social, and output-focused. By design, they address the following four concerns:

- Students do not read source code, and indeed do not consider it a valuable resource for learning. Likewise, faculty do not treat source code as a pedagogical tool.
- Students do not write code to test hypotheses, only to produce solutions.
- Early curriculum programming projects fail to make programming a form of entertainment and self expression.
- Many instructors are not willing to redesign an entire course, but will integrate new ideas that are packaged as standalone projects requiring little infrastructure or support.

ALE is a Java-based platform for developing 2D games for the Android platform. It is an intermediate library that sits between the programmer and the complex AndEngine OpenGL ES 2.0 game development framework [8]. Using ALE, beginners can produce a variety of styles of game, with each level requiring as little as a dozen lines of declarative code. In this project configuration, students read the code of a sample game, select those levels that possess the features they desire for their game, and then write code using a simple copy-paste-modify model. Unique and enjoyable games can be created without writing a single loop or defining a single class: only basic uses of variables and methods are required.

Advanced courses can require students to extend ALE, either by modifying and combining existing ALE features, or by providing clean new abstractions built directly atop AndEngine. Again, the emphasis is on reading code first, and writing code second. However, at this level arbitrarily advanced programming topics can be taught, to include events, callbacks, and asynchrony.

ALE encourages social interaction and self expression. Students must find or create their own artwork, music, and sound effects. Students work together to design their games, and then they debug their code by playing games together. When logic bugs manifest, they usually have an amusing visual manifestation (e.g., throwing the puppy to the stick, instead of throwing the stick to the puppy).

*This work was supported in part by the US National Science Foundation under grant CNS-1016828; and by financial and equipment support from Google.

SIGCSE'13, March 6–9, 2013, Denver, Colorado, USA.

Furthermore, ALE is a pure Java project. It uses familiar, industry standard tools that we bundle in a pre-packaged virtual machine. Since it is fun, students learn to use ALE quickly. Consequently, it is possible to use it as a capstone or enrichment experience, without redesigning an entire course around it. This also allows ALE to be integrated at many points in the curriculum without risking overexposure or watering down the curriculum.

In this paper, we discuss our motivation in designing ALE. We then provide some details about the framework, followed by a discussion how ALE can be integrated into curricula. We conclude with lessons learned and suggestions for instructors looking to increase excitement and improve programming proficiency without redesigning entire courses or learning complex software packages.

2. MOTIVATION AND RELATED WORK

Over the last few years, both mobile programming and game design have been embraced by educators seeking to increase excitement about CS and increase its appeal to a diverse audience. Much of this work forms the motivation for ALE, though there are some noteworthy distinctions. Below we discuss the industrial, social, and administrative trends that shaped the design of our project.

2.1 Industrial Trends

Nothing is from Scratch: In industry, a programmer usually starts with existing code, and then bends and changes it to create something new. Yet in many academic game projects, students still write the core game loop and low-level simulation code. desJardins and Littman note that too much programming decreases the appeal of a project to non-majors [4]. Particularly in projects that entice students to study CS, every line of code should directly correlate to an observable output.

Collaboration is the Norm: Not only do modern programmers typically work with other programmers, they also often must work closely with experts in other disciplines [28]. If students are not permitted to use copyrighted material, then there is an incentive to either develop friendships with students majoring in digital design and music, or to explore their own latent artistic abilities, even if only to modify royalty-free media. We believe that the interaction between art and code, born out of the interaction between artist and programmer, is the source of value in many programs, particularly those with which students are most familiar.

Code Writers Must Read Code: In order to extend existing software, a programmer must learn about its behavior. This typically comes from three areas: reading code itself, reading on-line documentation, and reading generated documentation (e.g., JavaDoc) from within an IDE. Professional programmers are expected to generate both code and documentation, and to review their peers' code. Preparing for these roles requires a fluency in reading code that is rarely emphasized.

Programming is not the Only Job Skill: Today's students worry about employment upon completion of their degrees. While CS jobs are plentiful, employers have high expectations. Projects that use industry-standard languages and tools, and that result in marketable software, distinguish job applicants. As a simple example, a student who has independently released software on a mobile application marketplace offers an employer evidence of her ability (measured in the program's ranking and number of downloads), creativity, customer focus, and entrepreneurship.

2.2 Social Factors

In addition, the following social factors play a significant role in student outcomes. To be clear, we believe today's student possesses tremendous ability and skill, and the discussion below is not intended to imply a negative attitude towards them. In raising these issues, we are instead sharing an opinion about student motivation and attitudes that we have formed through interactions with hundreds of students, both CS majors and non-majors. These observations are, at least at our university, an accepted fact. Our project treats them as an opportunity.

Fun Projects Matter: Throughout the curriculum, the use of mobile phones in general, and Android in particular, leads to an increased perception that projects are fun and relevant to future employment prospects. Andrus and Nieh observed this in an upper-division operating systems class [2], and Loveland similarly noted that both mobile programs and the Google brand made HCI projects more "cool" [13]. Independently, mobile programming [6, 7, 18, 27], graphics [9], and computer games [19–21,26] have been shown to improve student experiences in introductory courses. Clearly, mobile games are the sweet spot for maximizing enthusiasm, especially since they are *easier* to write than traditional games [11].

Students Expect Instant Gratification: Wolber discusses how the hour-long effort of getting a first "hello world" program working from scratch is anticlimactic, and might repel prospective students [27]. Today's students are too fluent in media-rich computing for such an introductory experience to succeed. If the effort required to create early programs seems too great, and the resulting software artifacts appear too simple, students may develop a sense of hopelessness and feel that creating production-quality software requires a skill set that is beyond their ability.

Passion Matters: Assignments with a single "right answer" stifle creativity. In such assignments, students are reluctant to push themselves toward abstract goals such as quality, user experience, and robustness. While these goals are difficult to grade, failing to encourage their pursuit is dangerous. Without them, students will not develop the enthusiasm observed by Greenberg et al., whose students would give themselves extra assignments, due to the passion they developed through their projects [9].

Bragging is OK, if not Good: Finally, programming projects should appeal to basic human nature. Students gain a sense of satisfaction, and departments receive free publicity, when projects result in tangible artifacts that students can show to peers. This has certainly been a common trend in engineering courses, yet CS courses rarely result in "boast-worthy" projects or useful take-home artifacts.

2.3 Administrative Constraints

Finally, many administrative constraints come into play. These issues deal with instructors and institutions, and capture the sources of reluctance that prevent even exceptional educators from adopting innovative material.

System Administration is not Free: Course administration has a real cost, particularly in sysadmin time. Projects that require custom software, or a particular operating platform, are difficult to adopt [5, 22]. The problem is worst when changing an existing course, one project at a time.

Service Expectations do not Include Games: Not all deans are as open-minded as ours, and as willing to allow 25% of incoming engineers to participate in a project involving games. Other departments, similarly, may worry that too much emphasis on art, music, and game-play will not satisfy learning objectives related to computational science and engineering, particularly in departments with a substantial "service" enrollment.

Pedagogy Cannot be Sacrificed: New projects must still support core educational objectives. Malan discusses the redesign of CS1 at Harvard, and notes the danger of reducing the pedagogical value of courses in order to broaden participation [14]. A project must not require instructors to devote lecture time to framework details, or encourage them to de-emphasize learning objectives that do not lend themselves to projects within the framework.

Expertise is Limited: Finally, Sung [22] argues that it is difficult for faculty without game or graphic experience to get involved in mobile game projects. This suggests both that gradual adoption is a necessary strategy, and that the underlying framework cannot be too complex. The same social factors that affect our students apply here: faculty want fun projects, instant gratification, and the ability to boast to their peers. If a project is not easy for an instructor to master, it will not be useful in her classroom.

3. ALE DESIGN

3.1 System Administration

ALE's requirements are simple: inspired by Laadan et al. [12], we provide a Linux virtual machine (VM) with Eclipse, the Android SDK, a web browser, and image and audio editors. Each VM also includes a checkout of the ALE repository. The VM infrastructure eliminates the need for phone-specific drivers, or indeed any software on the host apart from virtualization software. Installing ALE consists of (a) copying a single file (the VM image), and (b) running a 10-line non-interactive script to import and configure the VM. Since we use Android, there is no lock-in [5]: the host can use Windows, Linux, or MacOS.

3.2 Core Objects

ALE exposes 11 core objects, with which games can be written in a declarative fashion. These objects are grouped as follows:

First, the `Level`, `Media`, and `Controls` objects are used to define the shape of a level, the forces that occur on objects in that level, the images and sounds used by that level, and the level's on-screen controls (buttons and timers). In all, there are 36 methods for these purposes, though a typical game will use less than 10.

Second, the `Hero`, `Goodie`, `Enemy`, `Obstacle`, `Destination`, and `Projectile` objects are used to place individual entities into a game level. These entities indicate the main character in the game, items that must be collected, characters that must be avoided, barriers that prevent passage across the screen, a goal that the hero must reach, and items that the hero can throw at enemies. The interactions among these objects are complex, but are configured only through declarative code. All aspects of interaction are handled invisibly by AndEngine's physics simulator. 75 methods are available for placing and configuring these entities.

Third, the `HelpScene` and `PopUpScene` objects are used to generate on-screen help and tips. These features are simpler than those for defining levels, and we do not discuss them further in this paper. Their use entails up to 7 methods.

3.3 Game Configuration

Students modify a well-commented XML configuration file to specify game configuration. The file exposes 12 properties, relating to the customization of strings (such as the game name), the number of levels, and the orientation of the game (portrait or landscape).

```
public class MyGame extends ALEGame {
  public void nameResources()    {
    // see Figure 3
  }
  public void configureLevel(int whichLevel) {
    // use Level, Controls, and 6 entity
    // object types to define each level
    if (whichLevel == 1) { // see Figure 2 }
    else if (whichLevel == 2) { ... }
    ...
  }
  public void configureHelp(int whichScene) {
    // use HelpScene object to draw
    // help screens
    if (whichScene == 1) { ... }
    else if (whichScene == 2) { ... }
    ...
  }
}
```

Figure 1: ALE game shell. There are only 3 required methods, which load images, describe levels, and draw help screens.

```
// Set screen size, max/initial gravity, & tilt
Level.reset(460, 320, 10, 10, 0, 0, true);
// Put a border on the screen.  (1, .3f, 1) are
// density, elasticity, and friction
Obstacle.drawBorder(0, 0, 460, 320, "black.png",
    1, .3f, 1);
// Hero starts at (40,70), is 30x30 in size
Hero.addHero(40, 70, 30, 30, "hero.png",
    1, 0, 0.6f);
// Put the destination in the top right
Destination.addDestination(290, 60, 10, 10,
    "bullseye.png", 1, 0);
// Draw a wall that isn't bouncy
Obstacle.addStationarySquareObstacle(50, 0, 10,
    200, "wall.png", 1, 0, 1);
// Win when 1 hero reaches the destination
Level.setVictoryDestination(1);
```

Figure 2: Java code for a level of a simple tilt-based maze game.

3.4 The ALE Game Shell

While ALE exposes callback mechanisms, we exclude it from this discussion. Not counting callbacks, ALE games consist of only three methods, as depicted in Figure 1. Each level is declared within the corresponding `if` block. For example, Figure 2 shows the code for a maze level, with the main character in the top left, the goal in the top right, and a vertical wall between them. Only 6 lines of code are required, with no variables or control flow.

The parameters for this code fall into three categories: (x,y) dimensions specifying the location of an object, (width,height) dimensions indicating the size of an object, and (density, elasticity, friction) values to govern the behavior of an object when it experiences a collision. Since the underlying methods carry JavaDoc comments, the Eclipse IDE generates tooltip-style documentation for these fields to aid the programmer. Extending the behavior of an object is achieved with syntax such as:

```
Destination d = addDestination(...);
d.applyRotation(...);
```

```
// sound when the hero reaches the destination
Media.registerSound("happy.ogg");
// background music: ''true'' means to loop
Media.registerMusic("music.ogg", true);
// load the images that are used in level 1
Media.registerImage("black.png");
Media.registerImage("hero.png");
Media.registerImage("bullseye.png");
Media.registerImage("wall.png");
```

Figure 3: Registration of media files for simple tilt-based maze.

ALE consists of 3700 lines of code and 4400 lines of comments. Its primary purpose is to hide AndEngine behind a clean, simple, and well commented interface. ALE supports a wide array of game types through just 118 methods. Levels can be infinitely long, heroes can throw, jump, and duck, there is a health scoring system, levels can have time limits, and a variety of game types are possible. To date, students have built side-scrollers (like Temple Run), platform games (pinball, mazes), puzzles that involve creating a path for a laser beam to travel (laserlight), and games involving throwing projectiles at falling/moving enemies (asteroid).

4. CURRICULAR INTEGRATION

ALE can be used in CS projects at any level. Below, we discuss recent and ongoing uses of ALE at our university.

4.1 Undeclared First-Year "Projects" Courses

At our university, all engineering students arrive with an undeclared major, and in the course of a common first-year curriculum, participate in a "projects" course. Through this course, they gain exposure to engineering disciplines by participating in two 6-week projects. Each project meets for one 3-hour lab per week. No prior knowledge is assumed.

This project allows us to reach a very diverse audience. We use ALE as the basis for a project titled "Mobile Game Programming for Fun and (non)Profit". Students have 6 weeks to produce a game that *could be* sold to raise money and awareness for the cause of their choosing. By merging gaming with social relevance, we accrue benefits similar to those observed by Pauca and Guy [16], while accommodating the fact that "fun" is more valuable than "important" to students [17]. By letting students choose their theme, we are, to a degree, following the advice of McFall and DeJongh, who use students' personal interests to make CS attractive [15], though we differ in that programming remains the focal activity.

Our goals are to reinforce general problem solving skills and to demystify programming. Recognizing that our class population is primarily non-CS engineers, the course is oriented toward non-majors, employing practices recommended by Adams and Pruim [1].

The only rules we impose are that (a) no copyrighted material can be used, (b) the game must relate to a social cause, and (c) games must be violence-free and gender-neutral [3, 22].

Teams of three work to produce a game. They begin by playing a sample game, for which they have the source code. This game consists of 60+ levels that demonstrate ALE features, each requiring between 6 and 33 lines of code (the average is 12.5). Students decide which levels possess features that they would like to integrate into their game. They then base their game on the source code for those levels. We also provide on-line resources, consisting of traditional documentation and a guided walk-through of the behavior of the sample game.

Our experience matches past observations [10, 25], in that students tend not to need much lecture, but that guided programming coupled with hands-on interaction with the professor and lab assistant results in rapid progress. We encourage all students to program, critique programs, and design levels.

A few of the sample levels include variables, and two include `for` loops in order to simplify the drawing of geometric patterns. A limited number of levels also include frame-based animation, which requires the use of simple arrays. Otherwise, individual levels require only declarative, straight-line code. For the most part, programming only entails placing objects on the screen, and configuring the images and sounds that are used. However, since a game can have an arbitrary number of levels, with each level arbitrarily long and complex, we have no trouble keeping even advanced students occupied for the entire 6-week project.

To summarize, the main goals of the project at this level are:

- Make computing fun
- Foster teamwork and relationship-building
- Demystify programming for engineers
- Encourage students to consider a major or minor in CS
- Ensure that each team completes the project
- Emphasize general problem solving skills
- Reward attention to detail and creativity

These goals are achieved by having students *read* source code, and then modify it. Self-expression and enjoyment are encouraged, especially by debugging (i.e., playing) each others' games.

4.2 Introductory Programming Courses

In introductory programming courses, we use ALE in a similar fashion. A key difference is that ALE is reserved for the end of the semester, when students will be able to enjoy it the most. When two weeks remain in class, we assign the ALE project, with the hope of mimicking the "wax on, wax off" trope [23]: after enduring a semester learning to program using traditional techniques, students discover that they've actually learned enough to write games!

Since students have much more fluency in Java, we expect more of them. We require them to use arrays for animation, and to use `for` loops to draw patterns of obstacles. We offer extra credit for using the callback mechanism, which may, in turn, require students to declare new fields and use references with complex object lifecycles. As before, we do not require modification of ALE itself, and instruction is primarily through on-line materials, not lectures. Students are encouraged to refactor the single `configureLevel` method through additional functions that improve both code reuse and organization. They also see first-hand the value of code documentation, since ALE's comments, which they encounter as tooltips in Eclipse, directly improve their productivity.

Grading involves two parts. First, the instructor grades the code according to the standards of the class. Second, students share their games with the class, which rates games subjectively, based on perceived quality and a "fun factor". Students learn about quality, since the most complex source code does not necessarily produce the highest-rated games.

Using ALE in this manner does not water down the course. All of the rigor of the original course is preserved, but ALE makes the final project more fun. This avoids the pitfall raised by Malan [14]: without sacrificing quality, a final large project can be a form of entertainment and self expression.

4.3 Upper-Level Courses

Whether or not they are familiar with ALE from previous experiences, students in upper-level courses can also benefit. In our mobile programming class ALE provides a gentle introduction to the mobile development environment: the framework hides the Android SDK, but the games themselves expose the nuance required to use touch and small screens effectively. Thus ALE helps get students into the right mindset: they have to think about the relationship between the device and the experience of using the application, but can do so without having to simultaneously learn complex Android APIs. Emphasizing marketability helps show students the importance of an intuitive interface and visual appeal.

ALE also encourages students to think about software development in general, and the design of reusable libraries in particular, making it a convenient project for reinforcing self-reflection about development [24]. In a software engineering course, students could be tasked with expanding ALE with new features. These would entail reading hundreds of lines of code, and then realizing that 10 lines or less suffice to add a powerful new feature. In reading code and navigating the layout of the library, students will gain exposure to the fruit of a good software engineering effort, which then provides a case study for their own work. Their work can also be contributed back to ALE as open-source. A more complex requirement is to extend ALE to provide a clean interface to more of the underlying AndEngine framework. In truth, this assignment is somewhat sadistic, in that ALE is well commented, whereas AndEngine is virtually comment-free, with support coming from a loosely-moderated online forum. The stark difference is likely to leave a lasting impression on students.

Example projects in the former category include:

- Extending a base class so that any `Enemy`, `Goodie`, `Destination` can appear or disappear according to a timer.
- Extending `Goodie` to cause a `Hero` to move in slow motion for a period of time.

A programmer who has experience with ALE could complete either project in less than ten minutes, writing less than 15 lines of code. However, a new user might take an hour to read enough code to know where to begin, and would need to think carefully about the object hierarchy and interaction routines to ensure a clean interface.

Example projects in the latter category include:

- Adding an obstacle that behaves like a pinball flipper
- Adding a "volcano" that spews `Goodies` or `Enemies`.

Neither of these projects would require more than 100 lines of code, but could likely take several hours of grappling with AndEngine.

5. LESSONS LEARNED

Many of our experiences with ALE confirm observations that others have made in the literature. Our informal experience strongly confirms the importance of keeping games violence-free and gender-neutral [3, 22]. This is not just a matter of preventing underrepresented students from losing interest: it also provides a challenge to violence-focused teams. Our requirement that games relate to social causes made it easy to emphasize the point, since students could not deny that they would never reach a large segment of their target market with violence.

The second critical lesson is that a framework like ALE must be bulletproof, and that ease of use trumps efficiency. The first version of ALE required students to manually register images by creating fields within their game class, computing image dimensions, allocating texture memory, and then loading image files into that memory. Though media registration is not critical code, it was the overwhelming source of bugs. Replacing this with less-efficient code that refers to media by filename virtually eliminated crashes in student code.

Third, forbidding the use of copyrighted material is essential. The first time we used ALE, every project had copyrighted material. These students could not market their games. However, as we grew more strict, creativity blossomed. Engineers drew animation sequences, wrote music, and recorded their own sound effects. For our upper-level mobile programming class, we paired teams of students with "consultants" who were actually Graphic Design majors registered for an independent study in their home department. The quality of the artwork was exceptional, and the designers were graded and supervised by an expert in their field, rather than a computer scientist. By coordinating with an independent study, we were able to overcome some of the administrative challenges discussed by Wolz et al. [28]. Furthermore, we made it explicit that the artists were on equal footing: CS students who made last-minute requests for artwork changes, or who did not work with their consultant early to specify their needs, received no sympathy from the artists or instructor.

The main lesson for designers of new projects is that up-front work and a continuing effort to nurture creativity are essential. If ALE did not have significant documentation and thousands of lines of comments, the project would have failed. Furthermore, during our first trial with ALE, we would field requests from students after each lab, and then upgrade the framework for the following week. This produced more than a dozen new features during the course of the semester, but enabled every student to realize their game, even if they had no programming background. It also taught the students about how to specify requirements, and helped us converge toward a robust framework.

Finally, and perhaps most importantly, our experience shows that students can write compelling mobile games in under 18 hours, even without a CS background. They quickly learned how to bend interfaces to overcome seeming deficiencies in a library (the most popular example was the use of an "invisible enemy" as a catch-all for terminating a level). Even when programming skills themselves were not a learning objective, students saw that programming could be fun, while also reinforcing attention to detail, clearly articulating specifications, and entrepreneurship.

6. CONCLUSIONS AND FUTURE WORK

Our experiences developing ALE and using it in CS projects has thus far been extremely positive. By emphasizing code reading as a core skill, we have helped students to enjoy programming while producing visually impressive, fun, and socially relevant games for smartphones.

In addition to the experiences we have shared in this paper, we believe that there are many more opportunities for researchers and educators alike. Among the most exciting are the following:

- ALE can serve as the foundation for campus-wide programming competitions. Since the barrier to entry is low, and since the need for rich media often trumps the quality of the source code, it is possible that non-majors and new majors can "win" despite the greater programming experience of more senior competitors. This project can also encourage campus-wide engagement, since all students, staff, and faculty can participate in judging.
- We also believe that ALE is suitable for middle-school and high-school outreach. While ALE requires students to write Java, many styles of game can be written without anything more than declarative code.
- We are also hopeful that researchers can formally evaluate the effectiveness of ALE in broadening participation and improving student outcomes and retention.

The key point, however, remains that by emphasizing reading code, a complex project like writing Java-based games for Android smartphones becomes tractable and enjoyable even for students without programming experience. As a project with tunable complexity and low administrative overhead, ALE is suitable for use as a capstone project in a non-ALE course, as a means of teaching software introduction, as an introduction to HCI issues related to smartphones, or as a fun interdisciplinary way to increase excitement and broaden participation in CS.

Acknowledgments

We would like to thank our reviewers for their many helpful suggestions. We also thank the students in CSE-15, Eng-98, and CSE-398 for their patience and encouragement. ALE is available for download from `http://code.google.com/p/andengine-lehigh-extension`.

7. REFERENCES

[1] J. Adams and R. Pruim. Computing For STEM Majors: Enhancing Non CS Majors. Computing Skills. In *Proceedings of the 43rd ACM Technical Symposium on Computer Science Education*, Raleigh, NC, Feb. 2012.

[2] J. Andrus and J. Nieh. Teaching Operating Systems Using Android. In *Proceedings of the 43rd ACM Technical Symposium on Computer Science Education*, Raleigh, NC, Feb. 2012.

[3] L. Cassel. Personal Conversation, Dec. 2011.

[4] M. desJardins and M. Littman. Broadening Student Enthusiasm for Computer Science with a Great Insights Course. In *Proceedings of the 41st ACM Technical Symposium on Computer Science Education*, Milwaukee, WI, Mar. 2010.

[5] P. Dickson. Experiences Building A College Video Game Design Course. *Journal of Computing in Small Colleges*, 25(6):104–110, 2010.

[6] P. Dickson. Cabana: A Cross-platform Mobile Development System. In *Proceedings of the 43rd ACM Technical Symposium on Computer Science Education*, Raleigh, NC, Feb. 2012.

[7] M. Goadrich and M. Rogers. Smart Smartphone Development: iOS versus Android. In *Proceedings of the 42nd ACM Technical Symposium on Computer Science Education*, Dallas, TX, Mar. 2011.

[8] N. Gramlich. AndEngine – Free Android 2d OpenGL Game Engine, 2012. http://www.andengine.org/.

[9] I. Greenberg, D. Kumar, and D. Xu. Creative Coding and Visual Portfolios for CS1. In *Proceedings of the 43rd ACM Technical Symposium on Computer Science Education*, Raleigh, NC, Feb. 2012.

[10] P. Hubwieser and M. Berges. Minimally Invasive Programming Courses - Learning OOP With(out) Instruction. In *Proceedings of the 42nd ACM Technical Symposium on Computer Science Education*, Dallas, TX, Mar. 2011.

[11] S. Kurkovsky. Engaging Students through Mobile Game Development. In *Proceedings of the 40th ACM Technical Symposium on Computer Science Education*, Chattanooga, TN, Mar. 2009.

[12] O. Laadan, J. Nieh, and N. Viennot. Teaching Operating Systems Using Virtual Appliances and Distributed Version Control. In *Proceedings of the 41st ACM Technical Symposium on Computer Science Education*, Milwaukee, WI, Mar. 2010.

[13] S. Loveland. Human Computer Interaction That Reaches Beyond Desktop Applications. In *Proceedings of the 42nd ACM Technical Symposium on Computer Science Education*, Dallas, TX, Mar. 2011.

[14] D. Malan. Reinventing CS50. In *Proceedings of the 41st ACM Technical Symposium on Computer Science Education*, Milwaukee, WI, Mar. 2010.

[15] R. McFall and M. DeJongh. Increasing Engagement and Enrollment in Breadth-First Introductory Courses Using Authentic Computing Tasks. In *Proceedings of the 42nd ACM Technical Symposium on Computer Science Education*, Dallas, TX, Mar. 2011.

[16] V. Pauca and R. Guy. Mobile Apps for the Greater Good: A Socially Relevant Approach to Software Engineering. In *Proceedings of the 43rd ACM Technical Symposium on Computer Science Education*, Raleigh, NC, Feb. 2012.

[17] C. Rader, D. Hakkarinen, B. Moskal, and K. Hellman. Exploring the Appeal of Socially Relevant Computing: Are Students Interested in Socially Relevant Problems? In *Proceedings of the 42nd ACM Technical Symposium on Computer Science Education*, Dallas, TX, Mar. 2011.

[18] D. Riley. Using Mobile Phone Programming to Teach Java and Advanced Programming to Computer Scientists. In *Proceedings of the 43rd ACM Technical Symposium on Computer Science Education*, Raleigh, NC, Feb. 2012.

[19] D. Schuster. CS1, Arcade Games and the Free Java Book. In *Proceedings of the 41st ACM Technical Symposium on Computer Science Education*, Milwaukee, WI, Mar. 2010.

[20] G. Smith and A. Sullivan. The Five Year Evolution of a Game Programming Course. In *Proceedings of the 43rd ACM Technical Symposium on Computer Science Education*, Raleigh, NC, Feb. 2012.

[21] K. Stolee and T. Fristoe. Expressing Computer Science Concepts Through Kodu Game Lab. In *Proceedings of the 42nd ACM Technical Symposium on Computer Science Education*, Dallas, TX, Mar. 2011.

[22] K. Sung. Computer Games and Traditional CS Courses. *Communications of the ACM*, 52(12):75–78, 2009.

[23] tvtropes.org. Wax On, Wax Off, 2012. http://tvtropes.org/pmwiki/pmwiki.php/Main/WaxOnWaxOff.

[24] T. VanDeGrift, T. Caruso, N. Hill, and B. Simon. Experience Report: Getting Novice Programmers to THINK about Improving their Software Development Process. In *Proceedings of the 42nd ACM Technical Symposium on Computer Science Education*, Dallas, TX, Mar. 2011.

[25] A. Vihavainen, M. Paksula, and M. Luukkainen. Extreme Apprenticeship Method in Teaching Programming for Beginners. In *Proceedings of the 42nd ACM Technical Symposium on Computer Science Education*, Dallas, TX, Mar. 2011.

[26] D. Webb, A. Repenning, and K. H. Koh. Toward an Emergent Theory of Broadening Participation in Computer Science Education. In *Proceedings of the 43rd ACM Technical Symposium on Computer Science Education*, Raleigh, NC, Feb. 2012.

[27] D. Wolber. App Inventor and Real-World Motivation. In *Proceedings of the 42nd ACM Technical Symposium on Computer Science Education*, Dallas, TX, Mar. 2011.

[28] U. Wolz, L. Cassel, T. Way, and K. Pearson. Cooperative Expertise For Multidisciplinary Computing. In *Proceedings of the 42nd ACM Technical Symposium on Computer Science Education*, Dallas, TX, Mar. 2011.

Hairball: Lint-inspired Static Analysis of Scratch Projects

Bryce Boe
UC Santa Barbara
bboe@cs.ucsb.edu

Charlotte Hill
UC Santa Barbara
charlottehill@cs.ucsb.edu

Michelle Len
UC Santa Barbara
mlen@cs.ucsb.edu

Greg Dreschler
UC Santa Barbara
gdreschler@umail.ucsb.edu

Phillip Conrad
UC Santa Barbara
pconrad@cs.ucsb.edu

Diana Franklin
UC Santa Barbara
franklin@cs.ucsb.edu

ABSTRACT

Scratch programming has risen in prominence, not only as a potential language for K-12 computer science, but also in introductory college courses. Unfortunately, grading Scratch programs is time-consuming, requiring manual execution of each program. Automation of this process is greatly complicated by the very reason Scratch is an attractive introductory language—the projects are multimedia in nature, requiring eyes and ears to fully appreciate.

We propose Hairball, an automated system that can be used both by a student to point out potential errors or unsafe practices, and by a grader to assist in inspecting the implementation of Scratch programs. Because automatic analysis will not be able to determine the sensory effect, Hairball focuses instead on the implementation, including safe/robust programming practices, providing a "lint-like" tool for Scratch.

In this case study, we have created an initial set of Hairball plugins that detect and label instances of initialization of Scratch state, synchronization between say and sound blocks, synchronization between broadcast and receive blocks, and use of timing and loops for complex animation. Our evaluation shows that Hairball is very useful in conjunction with manual analysis. Overall, Hairball was actually slightly more accurate than manual analysis at labeling these instances. Specifically for broadcast/receive, Hairball's analysis correctly classified 99% of the 432 instances, manual analysis only 81%. Overall, if Hairball was only used to identify correctly implemented instances, with manual analysis for the remainder, it would remove 76% of the instances for the manual analysis and assist in the rest, with a false positive rate of less than 0.5%.

Categories and Subject Descriptors

K.3.2 [**Computers and Education**]: General

General Terms

Languages, Measurement

Keywords

Scratch; automated assessment; static analysis

SIGCSE'13, March 6–9, 2013, Denver, Colorado, USA.

1. INTRODUCTION

There is a movement toward less industrial and more engaging projects and languages for introductory and AP computer science courses. This movement includes the push for Python with Multimedia approaches [1, 7, 13], the various approaches to the AP CS Principles course [14], as well as Alice [4] and Scratch [11].

One drawback of visual and auditory projects is that their evaluation can be more difficult than traditional text-based programming assignments. A common and straightforward practice in evaluating text-based assignments is to perform functional testing. That is, to write a script to run all submitted programs and compare their output with solution files [9]. More recently, unit testing frameworks have been employed as part of automated assessment [6, 15]. When students are given creative freedom with a sensory project—which is an integral feature of languages such as Alice and Scratch—there is neither a text-based output file with which to diff, nor a straightforward way to perform unit testing. For Scratch, for example, evaluation typically requires that each project be individually opened and run. Inspection of the code requires many mouse clicks and navigation through the stage, sprites, and all of their associated scripts.

To assist with assessment of Scratch projects, we propose a static analysis tool. Inspired by the Scratch mascot (a cat), and the concept of lint (a static analysis utility for C that looks for potential defects [10]), we call our system Hairball. We propose two roles for Hairball: (1) formative assessment—inspired by lint, we envision students using Hairball to check their Scratch programs for potential problems, and (2) summative assessment—accelerating manual analysis of assignments by verifying the presence and correctness of certain programming constructs as well as directing the manual analysis toward potential problems. We have developed a plugin architecture so that, in Python, Hairball can be extended and adapted for evaluation of specific assignments.

The challenges we explore in this paper relate to where the line should be drawn between what Hairball can do with static analysis, and where manual examination of the Scratch program is necessary. We find that each has its own strengths. Hairball can quickly differentiate between Scratch programs that do, or do not, contain certain targeted constructs, and is particularly helpful for identifying instances of particular constructs and implementations that are not robust but may not immediately cause obvious errors at runtime. Manual analysis, however, is still needed to evaluate the overall aesthetic effect and cohesion of a visual or auditory project.

We begin in Section 2 by giving background on automated analysis in general and Scratch in particular. We then describe our Hairball framework in Section 3. Section 4 describes the Hairball plugins we developed for our analysis. We describe our methodology and results in Sections 5 and 6. Finally, in Section 7 we conclude.

2. BACKGROUND AND RELATED WORK

Providing automation for analyzing programs is not a new concept. ASSYST is an automated assessment system that performs end-to-end, or input/output, type testing of submissions [9]. Both the Marmoset system by Spacco et al., and the Web-CAT system, by Edwards, perform testing of code using student written unit tests [6, 15]. All of the aforementioned tools supplement the feedback the student receives with code coverage analysis and feedback from static analysis tools such as FindBugs by Cole et al. [3]. Douce et al. performed a more detailed analysis of existing automated assessment systems [5]. The problem with existing assessment systems is that they are not applicable to Scratch programs.

Scratch is a block-based programming language from MIT [11]. Programs consist of 2-dimensional interactive animations. Objects, or sprites, move on the screen as a result of user input or scripts in the program. Sound and video can also be integrated into Scratch programs. Scratch was designed to allow students to learn computer science projects while employing great creativity in their work. This creative freedom is one of the reasons that Scratch projects are challenging to analyze.

An additional challenge in Scratch analysis is that Scratch programs are developed and run within a graphical user interface (GUI). Independent segments of code, known as scripts, are associated with Scratch sprites (e.g. the Scratch Cat) and tied to a triggering event. There is no central "main" point of execution. Instead, programs might begin when a parallel set of scripts beginning with a "when green flag clicked" hat block are triggered.

At least two other projects have looked at automated Scratch analysis. Adams and Webster describe using scripts and custom modifications to the Squeak source code of Scratch to perform their quantitative analysis of programs from the Imaginary Worlds summer camp [1]. Additionally, Burke and Kafai developed Scrape [16] as a visualization tool to aid humans in understanding patterns across Scratch files. Scrape was used to assess Scratch projects produced in a middle school writing workshop [2]. Scrape is useful in answering questions such as:

- How many programs use loops?
- How many loops are present in each program?
- What level of nesting does the program use?

Hairball has two purposes. Like Scrape, Hairball can help verify the use of the required constructs of an assignment. The main contribution of Hairball, however, is the framework and set of available plugins that support more sophisticated analysis. We want to answer questions not just about the use of Computer Science (CS) constructs, but about the competence demonstrated for different CS concepts. Hairball can be used to answer questions such as:

- Which programs contain unmatched broadcast and receive blocks?
- Which programs contain broadcast/receive events that result in infinite loops?
- Which programs do not properly initialize the start state?
- Which programs do not properly implement complex animations (requiring the application of timing, costume changes, motion, and loops)?

3. DESIGN CONSIDERATIONS

We have two goals in designing Hairball. Our first goal is to perform analysis on a set of Scratch programs automatically. Without automated analysis, each Scratch program must be opened manually in order to be inspected and executed. This manual process is time-consuming and error-prone. Our second goal is that Hairball is easily extendable so that new Scratch analysis plugins can be created with only a basic amount of Python experience, and anyone can make use of available plugins.

Plugin Architecture

We used the object-oriented features of Python to develop a base class from which Hairball plugins can be derived. Python was chosen due to the authors' experience with Python and its increased adoption in introductory CS classes. However, Python was mainly chosen due to the open source Python package *Kurt* that provides simple access to all the elements contained within a Scratch program, i.e., the images, sounds, stages (backgrounds), sprites and most importantly the scripts [12].[1]

Implementing a Hairball plugin simply requires extending the base class and overloading a single method. The method's sole parameter is a handle to the Scratch program (from *Kurt*) and the method should return a dictionary containing the results of the desired static analysis. In principle, any type of static analysis of a Scratch program that can be described algorithmically can be implemented as a Hairball plugin in a straightforward manner by anyone with basic Python programming skills. The following code provides an example of a simple Hairball plugin that counts the number of times each Scratch block is used in a program.

```
class BlockCounts(HairballPlugin):
  def analyze(self, scratch):
    blocks = Counter()
    for block, _, _ in iter_blocks(scratch):
      blocks.update({block: 1})
    return blocks
```

4. HAIRBALL PLUGINS

In this section we describe four Hairball plugins written to perform Scratch static analysis. The plugins were designed to analyze projects submitted as part of our two-week interdisciplinary Animal Tlatoque summer camp [8]. Notice that some of the traditional topics, i.e., variables and conditionals, are not represented, and that loops are represented in a very specific way (defined as animation). The plugins target the CS concepts used in the camp's cumulative project, an interactive movie about an animal. For this project, students were to demonstrate state initialization, use of broadcast and receive blocks, synchronization between say and sound blocks, and creation of complex animation. While these plugins were developed for our summer camp, each provides valuable feedback that is generally useful both as a lint-like tool for individual developers of Scratch programs and for others who are tasked with analyzing numerous Scratch programs.

Each Hairball plugin for the camp strives to evaluate whether, or to what extent, the program demonstrated competence in an area. These plugins attempt to discover instances of the aforementioned concepts contained within a Scratch program and label each instance as **correct**, **semantically incorrect**, **incorrect**, or **incomplete**. Instances labeled "correct" should indicate that the concept

[1] As part of our work, we made a few contributions that are now a core part of the *Kurt* Python package.

Category	Relative	Absolute
Costume	next costume	switch to costume x
Visibility		show/hide
Orientation	turn clockwise x degrees	point in direction x
Position	move x steps, go to x,y, glide z secs to x,y, etc.	go to x,y go to x,y
Size	change size by x%	set size to x%
Background	next background	switch to background x

Table 1: Five categories of initial state, along with example relative and absolute modification blocks

was implemented correctly. Instances labeled "semantically incorrect" should indicate that the concept was implemented in a way that may not always work when executed. Intuitively, instances labeled "incorrect" should indicate the concept was implemented incorrectly. Finally, instances labeled "incomplete" should indicate that only a subset of the required blocks for a concept were discovered. A single program may contain multiple instances of a concept distributed across any or all of the labels. Ideally instances labeled "correct" should not require manual analysis, whereas instances with any other label should be inspected manually.

Initial State

In any program, correctly setting the initial state is important. In Scratch programs, the significance is different. Scratch programs are comprised of animations, and in the runtime environment, they may run from start to finish and be restarted again. Alternatively, they may be stopped in the middle and restarted again. We want to determine statically whether the code runs the same way in these two events. For reasons described below, the environment is different than in traditional programming.

The first problem is where to start the analysis. In traditional programs, execution starts at "main". Scratch programs have no such globally-defined starting point. We taught our students to start their programs using the green flag button, so the starting point for our evaluation is the "when green flag clicked" block.

The most complex problem, and the problem that introduces the possibility of error into our analysis, is that sprites are placed on the stage during implementation thus giving them an implicit set of attributes, which we will refer to as the base attributes. Explicit initialization for a particular attribute, e.g., position or orientation, is only required when one of the program's scripts modifies the attribute. Thus, the challenge is distinguishing segments of scripts that perform initialization from those that perform general modification. To discover instances of initialization, we first determine the set of blocks that can be considered initialization blocks and then we restrict the location such blocks can appear in a script. We call this location the "initilization zone"

Attribute modifying Scratch blocks can be labeled as "relative" or "absolute". Relative Scratch blocks alter the attribute based upon its current value whereas absolute Scratch blocks directly set the attribute. As such only absolute blocks can be considered initialization blocks. Table 1 shows our categorization for a subset of attribute modifying Scratch blocks.

For an absolute block to be considered an initialization block, it must appear in the initialization zone. We define the initialization zone only for scripts beginning with a "when green flag clicked" block. The initialization zone begins at the start of the script and ends when either a relative block or a broadcast block is encountered. We take a conservative approach when encountering blocks contained within loops or conditionals—absolute blocks are ignored due to the possibility that the block is not executed, and relative blocks continue to signify the end of the initialization zone due to the possibility that the block is executed.

The initialization plugin considers a modified attribute of a sprite as correctly initialized when an absolute block for the same attribute exists in the initialization zone. Instances are labeled as incorrect otherwise. Non-modified attributes are ignored. Finally, despite this plugin's ability to detect unnecessary initialization, we did not include it as part of our analysis.

Say/Sound Synchronization

Synchronization between a speech bubble (say block) and sound file (play sound block) is not straightforward in Scratch. The desired behavior is that, at the same time, a speech bubble appears with the message, and a sound file plays of a voice speaking the message. When the sound is complete, the speech bubble disappears.

Achieving this effect is complicated by the timing semantics of the two forms of the say block, and the two forms of the play sound block in Scratch. One form of the say block places the speech bubble on the screen indefinitely (until replaced by another say block, or "erased" with an empty say block), while the other puts a speech bubble on the screen for n seconds (and, as a side-effect, delays execution of the script for n seconds.) Similarly, there are two forms of the block for playing a sound clip: "play sound until done" plays the sound synchronously, while "play sound" plays the sound asynchronously.

There are two methods to produce the desired effect. The first is to asynchronously play the sound via the "play sound block" followed by a "say for" block with a duration equal to the elapsed time of the sound. Unfortunately, the timing must be manually determined and needs to be updated whenever the sound file changes. The second, is to use a "say" block to display the message, followed by a "play sound until done" block, ending with an empty "say" block to clear the previous speech bubble. The campers were taught the latter method as the correct approach.

This plugin detects instances of this concept by looking for sequential say and sound blocks and verifies the instances are implemented using the appropriate method. A correct instance contains the previously described three blocks in the proper order. Instances following the method requiring manual timing are labeled semantically incorrect. Instances that have both say and sound blocks but do not match either of these methods are labeled incorrect, and isolated uses of say or sound blocks are labeled incomplete.

Broadcast and Receive

One use of Scratch's broadcast blocks is to trigger the execution of other sprites' scripts beginning with the appropriate receive block. We taught our campers the broadcast and receive concept in the context of two animal sprites conversing, where each sprite would signal the other's turn via broadcasting an event. In the camp's cumulative project, campers demonstrated an understanding of the broadcast and receive concept by triggering scene changes in their interactive movie.

The broadcast and receive plugin verifies that for each broadcast or receive event, there is a broadcast block and at least one corresponding receive block. Such instances are labeled correct. All instances with a broadcast block appearing in the same script with another instance's broadcast block are labeled as semantically incorrect. All other instances are labeled incomplete. Note that this plugin does not use the incorrect label.

Complex Animation

We have a very specific definition of the term *complex animation* for purposes of assessment. We use this term to refer to animation involving integration of costumes, motion, timing, and repetition control structures such as loops. This definition of complex animation is to distinguish from, for example, the "glide to" block built into Scratch. One example of complex animation is realistic motion of sprites that represent people and animals. E.g., people walking, birds flying and snakes slithering. Creating such animations requires the correct integration of several Scratch and CS concepts. For example, creating an animation sequence where a sprite spins around requires integration of loops, rotation, and timing.

A necessary component of a complex animation instance is either rotation blocks, or motion blocks paired with costume change blocks. We define a complex animation instance as either a loop containing these necessary components or a sequence of these necessary components, since a sequence can be considered an unrolled loop. In order to be labeled correct, an instance must also make use of a Scratch block that introduces a delay, otherwise the instance is labeled semantically incorrect. The plugin additionally labels instances that use sequences instead of loops as semantically incorrect because the student did not demonstrate competence in the CS concept of loops. Finally, if the program is missing any critical element, e.g., repetition, it is labeled incomplete.

5. METHODOLOGY

In the remainder of this paper, we will use Hairball to refer to both the framework and the set of plugins described in section 4.

We tested Hairball on the projects submitted during our two week summer camp. There were five assignments total, with a distribution of concept requirements. For example, complex animations were taught toward the end of the camp, so they were only present in the last two assignments whereas initialization was present in all [8].

We first perfomed a manual analysis on all 58 of the submitted Scratch projects. Three members of our project staff independently analyzed the first five projects submitted for a given assignment using a common rubric. We discussed any discrepancies in our scores and after coming to agreement, we analyzed the remaining projects. Once again, any score discrepancies were reconciled.

Hairball was then programmed to match the methodology agreed upon by the staff members when classifying the concepts. Hairball was run on all of the projects. When there were discrepancies between Hairball and the manual analysis, there was a second manual analysis to determine which was correct—Hairball or the manual analysis. In the results section, we compare the results between Hairball and the reconciled manual analysis using the second analysis results as a ground truth.

Because the projects are sensory in nature (auditory, visual), we are not attempting to create Hairball to replace manual analysis. Instead, we are automating the identification of the "easy" cases in order to accelerate analysis. The methodology is not perfect because Hairball was informed by the manual analysis - sort of like a fourth entity whose answers needed to be reconciled in the group. As the results show, Hairball did an excellent job of identifying issues that all three of our staff members missed.

6. RESULTS

In this section, we present the results of using Hairball to assist in determining the level of competence demonstrated by students' Scratch projects for several CS concepts. For each concept, we will compare the labels Hairball assigned to instances of the concept with those assigned via manual analysis. We will use the second manual analysis as the ground truth, and look at both false positive and false negative rates for Hairball and the manual analysis. Although our results include the labels "semantically incorrect," "incorrect," and "incomplete" to demonstrate that Hairball can be used for more than binary labeling, our assessment focuses on instances that are either labeled "correct" or not. Thus, we consider a false positive to be an instance that was labeled correct, when in fact it is not, and a false negative to be an instance that is actually correct, but was not labeled as such. For manual analysis both false positives and false negatives represent the inaccuracies of manual assessment. For Hairball, false negatives can be considered warnings, i.e., they are used to indicate the need for additional manual analysis. However, any false positives produced by Hairball are cause for concern.

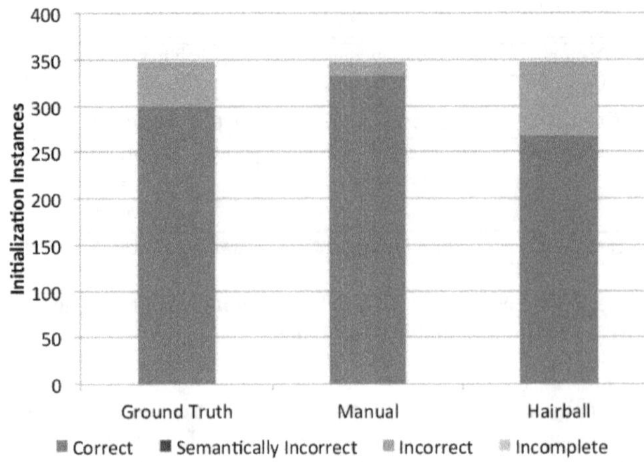

Figure 1: Compares the initialization instance labels. Note that, this analysis used only the "correct" and "incorrect" labels. Manual analysis resulted in 32 false positives, and Hairball resulted in 33 false negatives.

6.1 Initialization

We begin with initialization. Recall from section 4 that Hairball looks for attributes that are modified, and expects to find a corresponding absolute block in the initialization zone in order to consider an instance correct. The manual analysis, on the other hand, only involved running the program twice, and confirming that the two executions matched.

Figure 1 provides the classification of the 348 initialization instances discovered across the 58 projects. Of the 65 instances that Hairball and the manual analysis labeled differently, Hairball was correct for 32 of the instances. Many of the remaining 33 instances were not possible for Hairball to label as correct due to initialization taking place outside of the initialization zone. For example, an initially hidden sprite, can correctly have its position initialized just before the sprite becomes visible. In spite of this discrepancy, these results overall indicate that Hairball is successful at pointing out problems in initialization.

6.2 Sound/Say Synchronization

Figure 2 shows the results of identifying and labeling instances of synchronization between speech bubbles and sound files. Manual analysis identified 237 correct instances, and a total of 31 other instances. Hairball, identified 229 correct instances and 37 others. Manual analysis and Hairball failed to find two and four instances respectively.

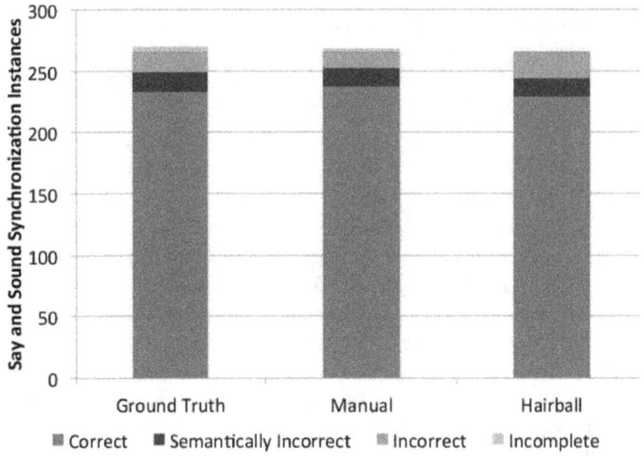

Figure 2: Compares the say and sound synchronization instance labels. Manual analysis and Hairball failed to detect two and four instances respectively and manual analysis resulted in 4 false positives.

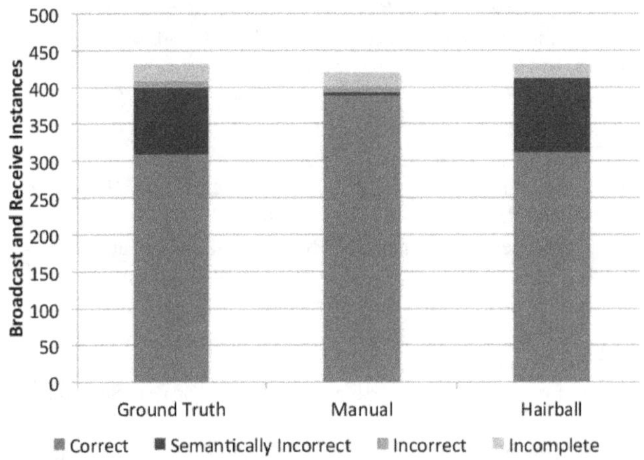

Figure 3: Compares the broadcast and receive instance labels. Manual analysis failed to discover 12 instances, and resulted in 79 false positives. Hairball detected 100% of the instances with three false positives.

Comparison with the ground truth results in four false positives for manual analysis. Hairball labeled its instances with 100% accuracy. Two of the four instances undetected by Hairball were labeled incomplete by manual analysis. Hairball failed to detect these instances due to a separation of the say and sound blocks with a broadcast block. To detect such instances, Hairball would need to additionally inspect all scripts triggered by the broadcast message to ensure none of them interfered with either the speech bubble or the playing of the sound file.

6.3 Broadcast/Receive

Figure 3 shows the results of detecting and labeling broadcast and receive instances. Here, the manual analysis differed from Hairball by additionally verifying that the intended action is performed for correct instances. Hairball is limited to static analysis, thus it is unable to perform this additional step.

Overall, Manual analysis failed to discover 12 instances, and identified 388 correct instances, of which 79 were false positives. Hairball discovered 100% of the instances with zero false negatives. However, three of the 312 instances Hairball labeled as correct were false positives. Although these three instances represent "correct" usage of broadcast and receive blocks, the ground truth analysis determined the evaluation behavior to be incorrect.

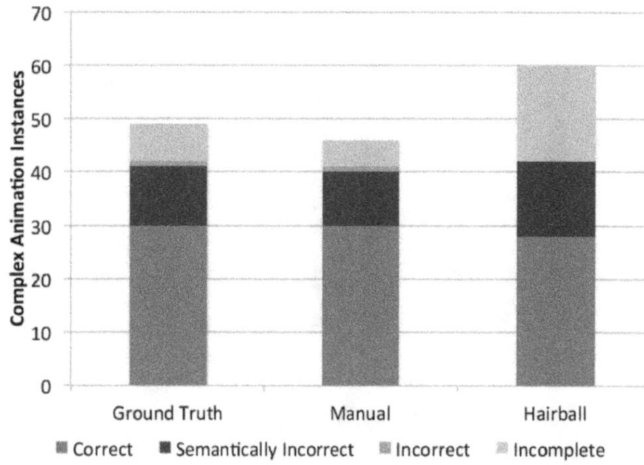

Figure 4: Compares the complex animation instance labels. Manual analysis failed to detect three instances whereas Hairball found 11 items that were determined to not be instances of complex animation. Hairball resulted in two false negatives.

6.4 Complex Animation

Complex animation was especially difficult for Hairball to detect. As Figure 4 shows, the manual analysis was 100% accurate at labeling the 46 instances found, and only failed to detect three instances. Hairball, on the other hand, discovered 11 incomplete instances that the ground truth analysis determined to not be instances at all. Excluding these instances, Hairball identified 28 correct instances, and 21 others with only two false negatives.

Hairball identified too many instances of complex animation due to the subjective nature of what is considered an animation. For example, Hairball detects an animation according to where the loops and repetition are located. Several times, Hairball detected two separate animations, when manual analysis determined that those two actions were working together to create a single larger animation. Additionally, Hairball considered a move, wait, and change in appearance as an incomplete animation instance. In such cases, manual analysis recorded nothing.

6.4.1 *Summary Results*

Figure 5 shows three sets of results across all four CS concepts and the overall average. The first is the mislabel rate of manual analysis and Hairball. Percentages closer to zero indicate higher accuracy. We can see that Hairball is actually slightly more accurate overall than manual analysis, largely in part of its accuracy in labeling broadcast and receive instances.

The second set of results are the rate of false positives. Manual analysis, with an overall false positive rate of 11.7%, indicates that manual analysis is quite error prone. On the other hand, Hairball's false positive rate of 0.4% strongly indicates that instances Hairball labels as "correct" can be trusted.

Finally, the third set of results are the rate of false negatives. The lack of false negatives for manual analysis makes sense, considering Hairball was created according to the first manual analysis. Although Hairball has an overall false negative rate of 13.5%, we believe this rate to be acceptable due to the fact that four out of five instances in our ground truth set were labeled "correct".

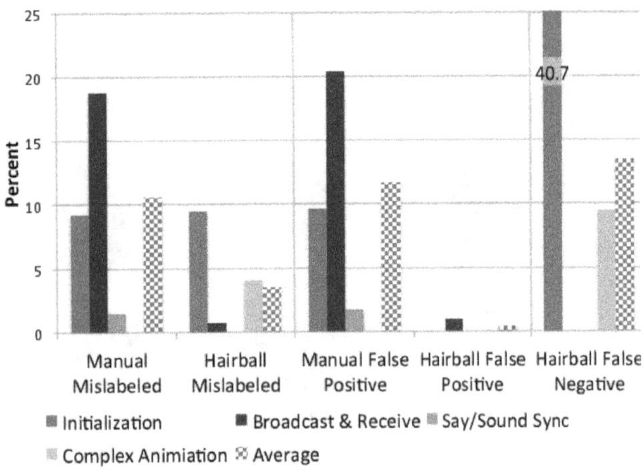

Figure 5: Provides a summary of the percent of mislabeled, false positive, and false negative instances from manual analysis and Hairball for each of the four CS concepts and the average. The "Manual False Negative" category was omitted as manual analysis resulted in zero false negatives. The y-axis is truncated for the smaller values, thus the tallest bar should extend to 40.7%. Missing bars represent 0%.

7. CONCLUSIONS AND FUTURE WORK

We presented a case studying showing a new static analysis tool, Hairball, that provides an extendable framework for automatically analyzing Scratch programs. In addition, we provide an initial set of plugins that analyze the implementation of Scratch programs for competence in four areas: initialization, broadcast and receive, say and sound synchronization, and animation. Our evaluation shows that Hairball is extremely usful in identifying correctly implemented instances, with a false positive rate of less than 0.5%. Overall, the mislabel rate of Hairball is less than half that of manual analysis. Therefore, we propose Hairball as an addition to, not replacement of, manual analysis.

We have made the complete Hairball source code available under the open source simplified BSD license. The source is hosted on github at `github.com/ucsb-cs-education/hairball`.

Our future work entails writing Hairball plugins suitable for widespread summative assessment in both AP CS Principles courses, and other summer camps. Finally we want to launch a web service that provides a convenient way to utilize Hairball for formative assessment of individual Scratch projects.

8. REFERENCES

[1] J. C. Adams and A. R. Webster. What do students learn about programming from game, music video, and storytelling projects? In *SIGCSE '12*, pages 643–648, 2012.

[2] Q. Burke and Y. B. Kafai. The writers' workshop for youth programmers: digital storytelling with scratch in middle school classrooms. In *Proceedings of the 43rd ACM technical symposium on Computer Science Education*, SIGCSE '12, pages 433–438. ACM, 2012.

[3] B. Cole, D. Hakim, D. Hovemeyer, R. Lazarus, W. Pugh, and K. Stephens. Improving your software using static analysis to find bugs. In *Companion to the 21st ACM SIGPLAN symposium on Object-oriented programming systems, languages, and applications*, OOPSLA '06, pages 673–674. ACM, 2006.

[4] S. Cooper, W. Dann, and R. Pausch. Teaching objects-first in introductory computer science. In *Proceedings of the 34th SIGCSE technical symposium on Computer science education*, SIGCSE '03, pages 191–195. ACM, 2003.

[5] C. Douce, D. Livingstone, and J. Orwell. Automatic test-based assessment of programming: A review. *J. Educ. Resour. Comput.*, 5(3), Sept. 2005.

[6] S. H. Edwards. Rethinking computer science education from a test-first perspective. In *Companion of the 18th annual ACM SIGPLAN conference on Object-oriented programming, systems, languages, and applications*, OOPSLA '03, pages 148–155. ACM, 2003.

[7] A. Forte and M. Guzdial. Computers for communication, not calculation: Media as a motivation and context for learning. In *Proceedings of the Proceedings of the 37th Annual Hawaii International Conference on System Sciences (HICSS'04) - Track 4 - Volume 4*, HICSS '04, pages 40096.1–, Washington, DC, USA, 2004. IEEE Computer Society.

[8] D. Franklin, P. Conrad, B. Boe, K. Nilsen, C. Hill, M. Len, G. Dreschler, and G. Aldana. Assessment of computer science learning in a scratch-based outreach program. In *Proceedings of the 44th SIGCSE technical symposium on Computer science education*, SIGCSE '13. ACM, 2013.

[9] D. Jackson and M. Usher. Grading student programs using assyst. In *Proceedings of the twenty-eighth SIGCSE technical symposium on Computer science education*, SIGCSE '97, pages 335–339. ACM, 1997.

[10] S. C. Johnson. Lint, a c program checker. In *COMP. SCI. TECH. REP*, pages 78–1273, 1978.

[11] J. Maloney, M. Resnick, N. Rusk, B. Silverman, and E. Eastmond. The scratch programming language and environment. *Trans. Comput. Educ.*, 10(4):16:1–16:15, Nov. 2010.

[12] T. Radvan. Kurt. `https://github.com/blob8108/kurt`, September 2012.

[13] B. Simon, P. Kinnunen, L. Porter, and D. Zazkis. Experience report: Cs1 for majors with media computation. In *Proceedings of the fifteenth annual conference on Innovation and technology in computer science education*, ITiCSE '10, pages 214–218. ACM, 2010.

[14] L. Snyder, T. Barnes, D. Garcia, J. Paul, and B. Simon. The first five computer science principles pilots: summary and comparisons. *ACM Inroads*, 3(2):54–57, June 2012.

[15] J. Spacco, D. Hovemeyer, W. Pugh, F. Emad, J. K. Hollingsworth, and N. Padua-Perez. Experiences with marmoset: designing and using an advanced submission and testing system for programming courses. In *Proceedings of the 11th annual SIGCSE conference on Innovation and technology in computer science education*, ITICSE '06, pages 13–17. ACM, 2006.

[16] U. Wolz, C. Hallberg, and B. Taylor. Scrape: A tool for visualizing the code of scratch programs. Poster presented at the 42nd ACM Technical Symposium on Computer Science Education, Dallas, TX., March 2011.

GSK: Universally Accessible Graph SKetching

Suzanne Balik, Sean Mealin, Matthias Stallmann, and Robert Rodman
Dept. of Computer Science
North Carolina State University
Raleigh, NC 27695-8206
{spbalik, spmealin, mfms, rodman} @ncsu.edu

ABSTRACT

Combinatorial graphs, often conveyed as node-link diagrams, figure prominently in Computer Science and other Science, Technology, Engineering, and Mathematics (STEM) disciplines. Unfortunately, they are most often inaccessible to blind students and professionals. This paper introduces GSK, a self-contained Graph SKetching tool that allows blind and sighted people to easily create, edit, and share graphs in real-time using interaction mechanisms (mouse, keyboard, monitor, screen reader) that are standard for them. GSK was successfully used by a blind Computer Science student and his sighted instructors to create and access graphs specific to his automata theory and operating systems courses. Our hope is that GSK will enable more blind STEM students and professionals to actively participate in their disciplines by providing them and their sighted colleagues with a cross-collaboration tool that allows them to share graphs just as easily as they share text and word processing documents.

Categories and Subject Descriptors

H.5.2 [**Information Interfaces and Presentation**]: User Interfaces; K.4.2 [**Computers and Society**]: Social Issues – *assistive technologies for persons with disabilities;* K.3.2 [**Computers and Education**]: Computer and Information Science Education; G.2.2 [**Discrete Mathematics**]: Graph Theory.

General Terms

Human Factors.

Keywords

Universal Design, Accessibility, Computational Equivalence.

1. INTRODUCTION

We developed GSK, a self-contained Graph SKetching tool, to provide a universally accessible means of creating, editing, and sharing combinatorial graphs, also known as node-link diagrams. A combinatorial graph consists of nodes joined by edges. While a very simple structure, it figures prominently in Computer Science and other Science, Technology, Engineering, and Mathematics (STEM) disciplines. Entity relationship diagrams, finite-state machines, various Universal Modeling Language (UML) diagrams, resource-allocation graphs, chemical molecules, etc., are all represented using (combinatorial) graphs.[1] Unfortunately, these representations are generally not accessible to blind students and professionals forming a barrier between the blind user and active participation in STEM fields. Our goal is to help remove that barrier by providing blind people with the means to independently create and use graphs in a variety of disciplines for knowledge representation and problem solving, and to easily share them with sighted people.

2. DESIGN CONSIDERATIONS

The principles of *universal design* and *computational equivalence* as well as a desire to *level the playing field* for blind people guided our design of GSK.

2.1 Universal Design

Universal design principles espouse the development of products that are equitable in use without segregating users [3]. A number of applications have been developed *separately* and *specifically* to provide blind users with access to various types of graphs [1, 2, 4, 6, 7, 9]. However, separate is most often not equal and it is important that blind users be included in software applications intended for universal use. Work is now underway to include blind students in the use of JFLAP, a popular automata theory platform [5]. Our prior experience with making our graph-based automata theory application, ProofChecker, accessible to blind students without affecting the sighted interface [11] inspired us to do the same for generalized graph editing.

Text editors and word processing programs are useable by both sighted and blind people via interaction mechanisms that are standard for them (mouse, keyboard, monitor, screen reader). When a blind and a sighted person are working together on a text or word processing document, they have immediate access to changes made by the other. GSK is designed to provide the same type of experience for graph editing for both blind and sighted people in terms of ease of use and document sharing.

2.2 Computational Equivalence

In order to use graphs for problem solving, it is important that blind people have graph representations that are *computationally equivalent* and not simply *informationally equivalent* to those available to sighted people. Larkin and Simon distinguish between informational and computational equivalence as follows:

Two representations are informationally equivalent if all of the information in the one is also inferable from the other, and vice

[1] A recent issue of the Communications of the ACM (June 2011) contained over 20 graphs representing networks, structural equation analysis, page ranking, record assembly, and verification pipelines, among other things, within its 128 pages.

*versa. Each could be constructed from the information in the other. Two representations are computationally equivalent if they are informationally equivalent and, in addition, any inference that can be drawn **easily and quickly** from the information given explicitly in the one can be drawn easily and quickly from the information given explicitly in the other, and vice versa.* [8]

Oftentimes graphs are provided to blind people in the form of tables which are informationally equivalent, but not generally computationally equivalent to the node-link diagrams typically used by sighted people. As one blind student studying finite-state machines (FSMs) succinctly put it, he was "stuck in table mode" while his sighted peers had the advantage of easily moving from state to state of an FSM by following the edges (transitions) of a node-link diagram representation.

To further illustrate this point, consider the following example from automata theory [11]. A deterministic finite automaton (DFA) is a form of directed graph that is used to determine whether or not a string (sequence of characters) is a member of a regular language. A DFA is said to "accept" or "reject" a string in terms of membership in its language. Table 1 and Figure 1 below provide *informationally equivalent* representations of the same DFA, i.e., each could be created from the information provided in the other.

Table 1. Transition table representation of a DFA [11]

δ	a	b
q_0	q_2	q_3
$*q_1$	q_0	q_1
q_2	q_0	q_1
q_3	q_2	q_3

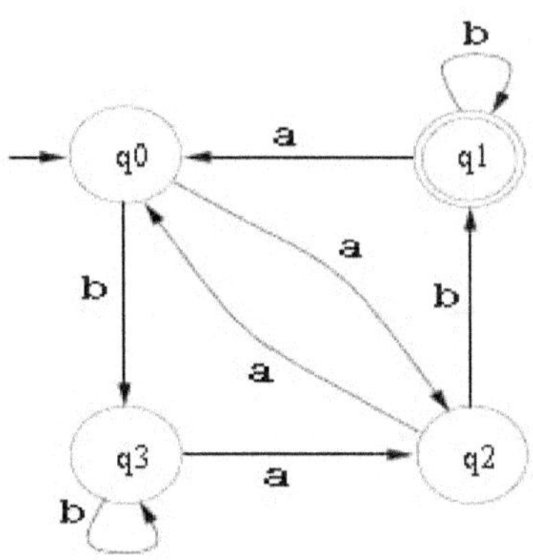

Figure 1. Node-link diagram representation of a DFA [11]

In this example, the alphabet $\Sigma = \{a, b\}$ and the set of states $Q = \{q_0, q_1, q_2, q_3\}$. The first state in the transition table, q_0, is the start state and is designated as such by an incoming arrow in the node-link diagram. The accepting state, q_1 is preceded by an asterisk (*) in the table and denoted by a double circle in the diagram. This DFA may be used to tell whether or not a string consisting of 0 or more a's and b's has an odd number of a's and ends with b.

For example, determining whether the string *abbabab* is accepted by the DFA above involves moving from state to state while reading the current input symbol as illustrated by the following sequence of configurations:

$(q_0, \text{abbabab}) \vdash (q_2, \text{bbabab}) \vdash (q_1, \text{babab}) \vdash (q_1, \text{abab}) \vdash$

$(q_0, \text{bab}) \vdash (q_3, \text{ab}) \vdash (q_2, \text{b}) \vdash (q_1, \varepsilon)$

Because q_1, the last state reached in the computation, is an accepting state, the string is indeed in the language of the DFA.

Imagine a sighted person carrying out the above computation by moving a finger back and forth and up and down the rows of the transition table, which is analogous to the way a blind person would access an electronic form of the table. Using a table, the time to determine the inclusion of a string w in the language of a DFA is proportional to the number of states times the size of its alphabet times the length of the string, ($|Q|\ |\Sigma|\ |w|$). On the other hand a sighted person moving a finger from state to state of a node-link diagram following the transition corresponding to the current input symbol could complete the computation in time proportional to the size of the alphabet times the length of the string, ($|\Sigma|\ |w|$). For a DFA with a large number of states, the time savings would be considerable. Thus, the two representations are *not computationally equivalent*.

Our design of GSK aims to relieve blind students and professionals of the tedium of using tables to solve graph-related problems and instead provides them with the computational advantage of being able to easily traverse the edges of a graph and otherwise efficiently create, edit, and access graphs.

2.3 Leveling the Playing Field

Besides providing blind people with computationally equivalent graph representations, we would like to help enable them to function as independently and efficiently as possible in academic and professional settings. All of the graphs shown in Figures 2, 7, 8, and 10 were drawn independently by a blind student, who is also the second author of this paper. Using GSK, he was able to communicate graphs with his automata theory instructors, create and include graphs in documents for homework assignments, and quickly render the graphs necessary to solve problems on an operating system quiz. Our hope is that GSK will help to level the playing field for more blind students and professionals allowing them to fully participate in their disciplines alongside their sighted peers.

3. OVERVIEW OF GSK

GSK is a Java application built using standard Swing components that leverages the Java Accessibility API. It was developed and tested on a Windows platform using the JAWS screen reader, which requires the installation of the Java Access Bridge. The bridge provides a communication mechanism between the screen reader and the Java Virtual Machine (JVM). Being written in Java, our hope is that GSK would port well to other systems and use by other screen readers.

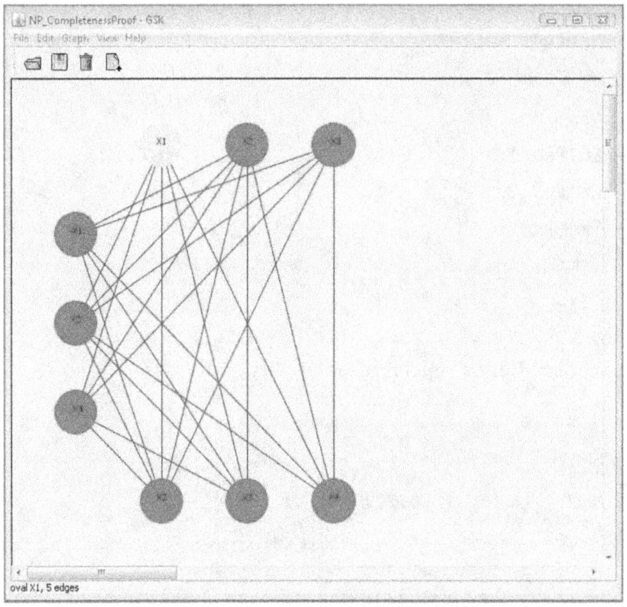

Figure 2. Connection View of an NP-Completeness Graph

GSK was developed as a collaboration between the sighted first author and the aforementioned blind second author, which was itself an exercise in universal accessibility. We found that the Eclipse platform using SVN for version control worked well for both of us. The ability provided by Eclipse to specify the indentation level of our source code and correct the indentation when necessary was particularly helpful. We used Microsoft Word to prepare our initial design documents and a raised print drawing kit whenever we needed to share a drawing of the interface, control flow, etc. Eventually, we were able to use GSK instead of the drawing kit to create and share simple flowcharts that we used in the design of subsequent functionality.

3.1 Universal Accessibility Features

GSK is intended to appeal to both sighted and blind users. In addition to providing a point-and-click interface, GSK is fully *keyboard accessible* which is crucial for blind users and in fact required by Sec. 508 accessibility guidelines [10]. This helps make GSK useable by a wide group of users including those with mobility or other impairments.

Providing *programmatic focus* and an effective *navigation scheme* is also crucial for blind users. While sighted users can easily rest their gaze on any item on the screen, blind users must use the keyboard to navigate from item to item. When using GSK to examine a graph, the node or edge with focus is designated as the current or selected node/edge. Whenever focus is changed to a different node or edge, its name is announced by the screen reader in use by the blind user. The currently selected node or edge is also highlighted thus providing a visual focus indicator, especially important for sighted users navigating via the keyboard.

In order for blind users to create and share graphs with sighted people, they must be able to position the nodes in such a way that they are visually viewable. GSK facilitates this by providing blind users (and other users) with the means to specify the *spatial layout* of a graph.

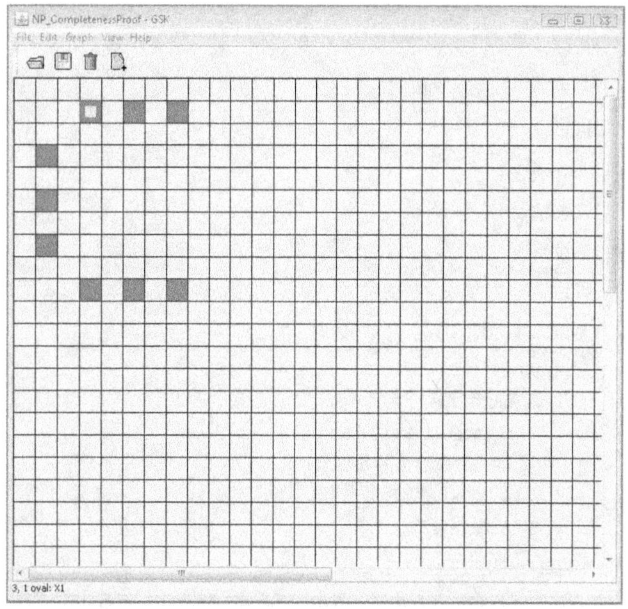

Figure 3. Grid View of Graph in Figure 2

3.2 The GSK Interface

The GSK interface shown in Figures 2 and 3 above provides two different views of the same graph, *Connection View* and *Grid View*. Connection View displays a graph as a conventional node-link diagram. Grid View allows blind (and other) users to spatially lay out the nodes of a graph, but does not display its edges. Using the View Menu, the user may easily switch between them depending on which is more appropriate for the task at hand.

In addition to the large central panel where the graph is displayed, the interface contains a menu bar with File, Edit, Graph, View, and Help menus as well as a tool bar with Open, Save, Remove, and Add Edge buttons. A status bar at the bottom provides information about the currently selected node/edge or, in the absence of a graph, the name of the view. When a screen reader is in use, the status is announced whenever it changes thus allowing a blind user to track focus changes. Appropriate mnemonics and keyboard shortcuts are also provided thus allowing for multiple means of accessing each function of the interface. Graphs may be saved in .gsk format and/or exported as PNG images.

3.2.1 Connection View

Connection View provides the typical point-and-click interface and node-link diagram representation of a graph to which sighted users are accustomed. It is also useful for blind users in that it allows them to navigate a graph via the keyboard. When working together, changes to a graph that are immediately visible to a sighted user are announced to a blind user via the screen reader.

Creating, Editing, and Removing Nodes

In Connection View, a new node is created by double-clicking on an empty space on the graph panel. The Node Properties dialog box shown in Figure 4 is then displayed with default values for the node name, X and Y Locations in Grid View, shape, height, width, and color, any of which may be changed, if desired. Currently available node shapes include general *oval* and *rectangle* shapes as well as shapes pertaining to automata theory – *accepting state*, *accepting/start state*, *start state*, and *state*. We plan to add shapes for other domains such as flow charts, UML

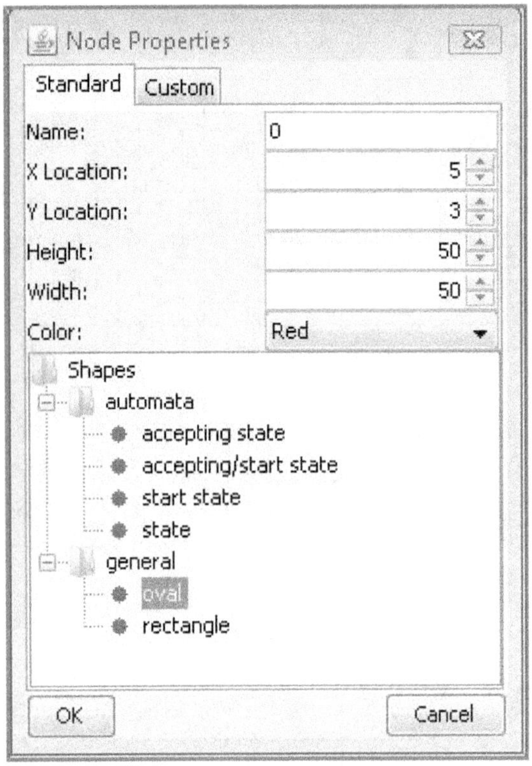

Figure 4. Node Properties Dialog Box

diagrams, etc. and have designed GSK to make this extension relatively straightforward.

The properties of an existing node may be edited by double-clicking on the node or by selecting the node and pressing Enter, both of which bring up the Node Properties dialog box. A node may be moved by changing its X and/or Y position or by dragging it to a different position. A node may be removed by selecting it and pressing the Delete key, selecting Remove from the Graph menu, or pushing the Remove button on the toolbar. Whenever a node is removed, its edges are removed as well.

Adding, Editing, and Removing Edges

An edge may be added to the selected node by pushing the Add Edge button on the toolbar, selecting Add Edge... from the Graph menu, or entering CTRL+E. The Edge Properties dialog box shown in Figure 5 is then displayed with default values for the edge name, endpoints, color, and direction. The direction choices are Undirected, Incoming, Outgoing, and Bidirected.

The properties of an existing edge may be edited by double-clicking on the edge or by selecting the edge and pressing Enter, both of which bring up the Edge Properties dialog box. An edge may be removed by selecting it and pressing the Delete key, selecting Remove from the Graph menu, or pushing the Remove button on the toolbar.

Graph Navigation

A node is selected by clicking on it, selecting Jump to Node... from the Graph menu, or by entering CTRL+J. The latter two options bring up the Jump to Node dialog shown in Figure 6 which allows the user to choose a node from a list. The left/right arrow keys are used to move between and select the edge(s) of the

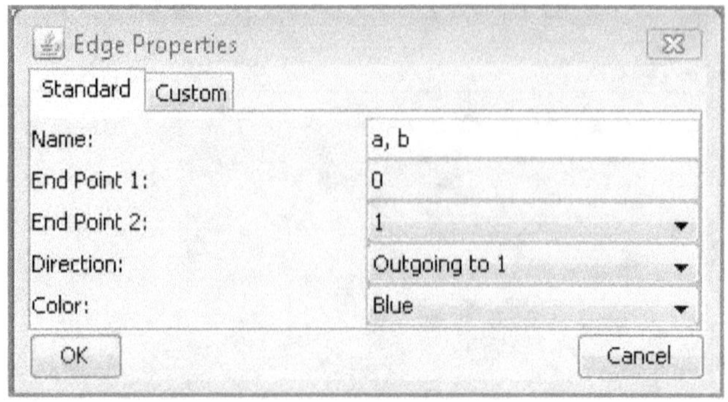

Figure 5. Edge Properties Dialog Box

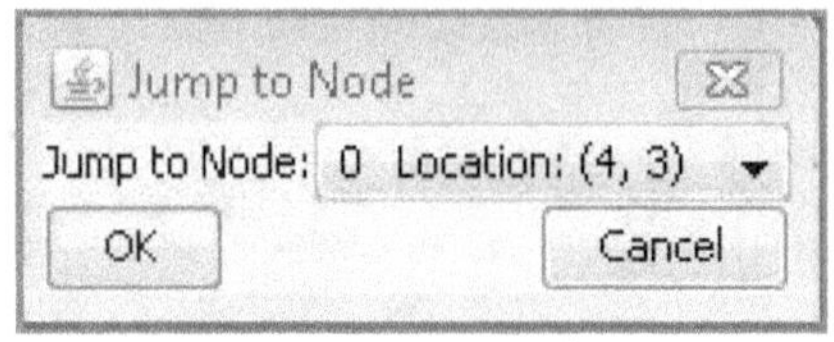

Figure 6. Jump to Node Dialog Box

node. Pressing up arrow when an edge is selected, moves focus to (selects) the opposite endpoint; pressing Escape returns focus back to the original endpoint. Each time focus changes to a node or edge, information about the selected node/edge is displayed in the status bar and announced by the screen reader, if one is in use.

3.2.2 Grid View

Grid View provides blind (and other) users with the ability to spatially lay out a graph. In this view, the graph panel is divided into a grid of squares, each one of which corresponds to a potential or actual node position in Connection View. The squares are referenced by their X, Y Location in the grid with the X values starting at 0 and running horizontally across the grid and the Y values starting at 0 and running vertically down the grid. The grid squares are much smaller than the default size of nodes in Connection View and are intended to show the location of nodes relative to each other. Figures 2 and 3 provide a side by side comparison of the same graph displayed in both views.

A grid square may be selected by clicking on it or navigating to it with the up/down/left/right arrow keys. If the square contains a node, it may also be selected using the Jump to Node action. The X, Y Location for the selected square is displayed in the status bar. If the square contains a node, the node shape and name is displayed as well. For example, in a graph used for automata theory, information about a start state named q0 with 6, 5 as its X, Y Location would be displayed as "6, 5 start state: q0." Whenever focus changes to a new square, its status bar information is announced by the screen reader, if one is in use.

Creating, Editing, and Removing Nodes

In Grid View, a new node is created by double-clicking on an empty square or by pressing Enter when focus is on an empty square. This brings up the Node Properties dialog box as previously described which allows for changing the default values of the node, such as name, X and Y Locations, shape, and color.

The properties of an existing node may be edited by double-clicking on the square containing the node or by pressing Enter when focus is on the node's square, both of which bring up the Node Properties dialog box. A node may be moved by changing

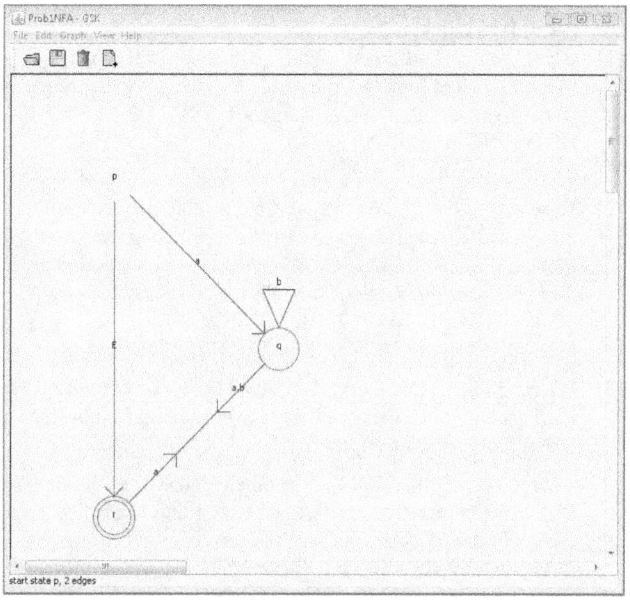

Figure 7. Nondeterministic Finite Automaton (NFA)

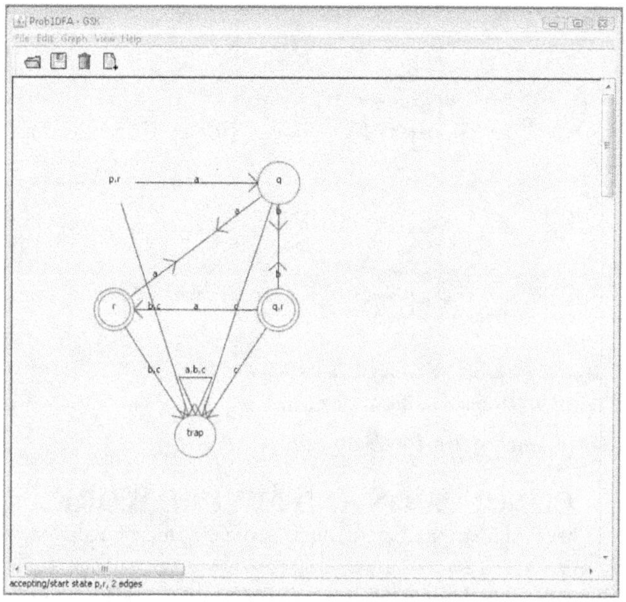

Figure 8. Deterministic Finite Automaton (DFA)

its X and/or Y Location via the Node Properties dialog or by cutting and pasting it in a different square using the standard CTRL+X, CTRL+V sequence. A node may be removed by selecting the square containing the node and pressing the Delete key, selecting Remove from the Graph menu, or pushing the Remove button on the toolbar. Whenever a node is removed, all of its edges are removed as well.

Adding, Editing, and Removing Edges

When in Grid View, an edge may be added to the selected node in the same way as previously described in Section 3.2.1. However, editing and removing existing edges requires the use of Connection View.

4. GSK IN PRACTICE

The second author, who is a blind third year Computer Science undergraduate student, successfully used GSK for assignments, tests, and quizzes in his Fall 2011 Automata Theory and Operating Systems courses. In addition to making it possible for him to create graphs to include in his course work, GSK provided him with an important problem-solving tool. It also functioned as a means for cross communication between him and the teaching staff in terms of sharing graphs. The student's use of GSK in both courses is described below.

4.1 Automata Theory Course

Graphs were used extensively throughout the Automata Theory course during the Graph Theory review, as part of NP-completeness proofs, and to represent automata – Deterministic and Nondeterministic Finite Automata (DFAs / NFAs), Pushdown Automata (PDAs), and Turing Machines. Examples of the use of GSK by the teaching staff and the second author for each of these topics are provided below.

4.1.1 Graph Theory

GSK was used by the teaching staff to render undirected graphs in the lecture notes, quizzes, and homework assignments and communicate them to the student. He found Connection View particularly helpful when examining the graphs to answer quiz and homework questions about Eulerian and Hamiltonian paths, cliques, independent sets, etc. He felt that these tasks would have been much more difficult had he been restricted to examining the graphs in table form.

4.1.2 NP-Completeness Proofs

As part of an NP-Completeness proof, the student was required to create a graph representation of the Boolean expression $(x_1 \vee x_2 \vee \neg x_3) \wedge (\neg x_1 \vee x_2 \vee \neg x_4) \wedge (x_2 \vee x_3 \vee x_4)$. He used GSK to create this graph as shown in Figure 2, which he then exported as a PNG image and included in his LaTeX homework document. Using Grid View as shown in Figure 3 to lay out the graph was very helpful.

4.1.3 Automata

Besides using GSK to render the various types of automata, the student used it to convert an NFA to an equivalent DFA as shown in Figures 7 and 8. To determine whether a DFA was equivalent to a given regular expression, he generated strings using the regular expression and then used Connection View to check if the strings were accepted by the DFA. Again, he felt that using GSK was much more efficient than having to rely on transition table representations of the automata and that it provided him with computationally equivalent graph representations to those available to sighted students.

4.2 Operating Systems Course

The Operating Systems course only made use of one type of graph – a system resource-allocation graph. The student used GSK to create modified resource allocation graphs to help him detect deadlock and other resource contention problems and determine how they might be resolved. For a quiz, he was given a textual description of the resource-allocation graph in Figure 9. He was able to render it using GSK as shown in Figure 10 and solve the related problems using only 5 minutes more than his sighted peers, who were provided with the node-link diagram version of the graph.

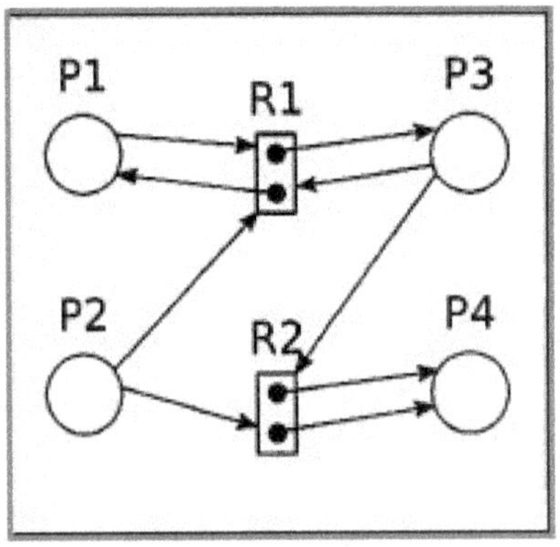

Figure 9. Resource-allocation Graph

Image courtesy Dr. David Sturgill

5. CONCLUSION AND FUTURE WORK

We have demonstrated the usefulness of GSK for a blind student in two CS courses – Automata Theory and Operating Systems; the student regrets not having had such a tool for his prior Discrete Mathematics and Data Structures courses for which it would have been invaluable. His sighted Automata Theory teaching assistant found creating graphs with GSK to be quite simple and straightforward, and expressed interest in using it to create homework solution sets. Thus, GSK appears to have universal appeal.

We plan to carry out controlled user studies with more blind participants to help determine whether the interface and paradigm are intuitive, as well as how close GSK comes to providing blind and sighted people with computationally equivalent access to graphs. We will continue to improve GSK, incorporating feedback from the user studies as well as our own ideas, in hopes of providing blind students and professionals with greater access to graphs in a universally accessible and appealing way. Our ultimate goal is to provide a graph sketching tool that is beneficial for all users regardless of their means of computer interaction.

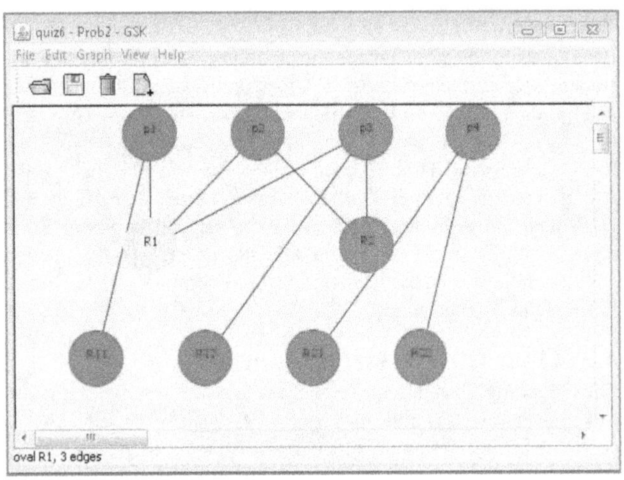

Figure 10. Resource-allocation Graph

6. ACKNOWLEDGMENTS

We would like to thank Dr. Richard Ladner for the AccessComputing mini-grant that supported this work via NSF Award #CNS-0837508.

7. REFERENCES

[1] Blenkhorn, P. and Evans, D. G. 1998. Using speech and touch to enable blind people to access schematic diagrams. *J. Netw. Comput. Appl.* 21, 1 (January 1998), 17-29. DOI=10.1006/jnca.1998.0060 http://dx.doi.org/10.1006/jnca.1998.0060

[2] Brown, A., Pettifer, S. and Stevens, R. 2003. Evaluation of a non-visual molecule browser. In *Proceedings of the 6th international ACM SIGACCESS conference on Computers and accessibility* (Assets '04). ACM, New York, NY, USA, 40-47. DOI=10.1145/1028630.1028639 http://doi.acm.org/10.1145/1028630.1028639

[3] Burgstahler, S., and Cory, R. (2008). *Universal design in higher education: From principles to practice*. Cambridge, Mass: Harvard Education Press.

[4] Calder, M., Cohen, R. F., Lanzoni, J. and Xu, Y. 2006. PLUMB: an interface for users who are blind to display, create, and modify graphs. In *Proceedings of the 8th international ACM SIGACCESS conference on Computers and accessibility* (Assets '06). ACM, New York, NY, USA, 263-264. DOI=10.1145/1168987.1169046 http://doi.acm.org/10.1145/1168987.1169046

[5] Crescenzi, P., Rossi, L. and Apollaro, G. 2012. Making Turing machines accessible to blind students. In *Proceedings of the 43rd ACM technical symposium on Computer Science Education* (SIGCSE '12). ACM, New York, NY, USA, 167-172. DOI=10.1145/2157136.2157190 http://doi.acm.org/10.1145/2157136.2157190

[6] Kennel, A. R. 1996. Audiograf: a diagram-reader for the blind. In *Proceedings of the second annual ACM conference on Assistive technologies* (Assets '96). ACM, New York, NY, USA, 51-56. DOI=10.1145/228347.228357 http://doi.acm.org/10.1145/228347.228357

[7] King, A., Blenkhorn, P., Crombie, D., Dijkstra, S., Evans, D.G., and Wood, J. Presenting UML Software Engineering Diagrams to Blind People. In *Proceedings of ICCHP*. 2004, 522-529.

[8] Larkin, J. H. and Simon, H. A. 1987. Why a diagram is (sometimes) worth ten thousand words. *Cognitive Science* 11, 1 (January - March 1987), 65-100.

[9] Miller, D. 2009. *Can we work together?* Ph.D. Thesis, University of North Carolina at Chapel Hill, Chapel Hill, North Carolina. Retrieved November 9, 2012 from http://search.lib.unc.edu/search?R=UNCb5970444

[10] Sec. 508 Electronic and Information Technology Accessibility Standards. Retrieved November 9, 2012 from http://www.access-board.gov/sec508/standards.htm

[11] Stallmann, M. F., Balik, S. P., Rodman, R. D., Bahram, S., Grace, M. C. and High, S. D. 2007. ProofChecker: an accessible environment for automata theory correctness proofs. *SIGCSE Bull.* 39, 3 (June 2007), 48-52. DOI=10.1145/1269900.1268801 http://doi.acm.org/10.1145/1269900.1268801

Collaborative Learning and Anxiety

A phenomenographic study of collaborative learning activities

Katrina Falkner
katrina.falkner@adelaide.edu.au

Nickolas J.G. Falkner
nicholas.falkner@adelaide.edu.au

Rebecca Vivian
rebecca.vivian@adelaide.edu.au

School of Computer Science
The University of Adelaide
Adelaide, South Australia, Australia, 5005

ABSTRACT

Collaborative learning encourages deeper learning, producing significant benefit in learning outcomes. There has been an increasing trend to adopt collaborative activities, due to the expected learning benefits but also because of the expected social benefits and their impact on transition concerns. However, collaborative activities may also introduce additional stress and anxiety for students as they cope with altered participation expectations, and the need to develop collaboration, communication and management skills concurrently with their discipline skills. In this paper we describe a phenomenographic analysis of student's reflections on collaborative activities, including their perceptions of the purpose of such activities, and corresponding behaviours.

Categories and Subject Descriptors

K.3.2 [**Computing Milieux**]: Computers and Education-Computer and Information Science Education

General Terms

Human Factors

Keywords

Computer Science Education, Collaborative Learning, Phenomenography

1. INTRODUCTION

Constructivist pedagogy encourages students to engage with and develop ownership over their learning processes, encouraging reflective and deep learning. There has been significant research into the application of constructivist learning strategies, in both small and large classes, with significant benefit in learning outcome [4, 11]. Constructivist learning techniques are commonly, although not exclusively, collaborative; these forms of *social* constructivism leverage increased engagement and deeper learning resulting from the benefits of group discussion and group learning. Collaborative learning techniques have received significant practical and research focus within first year tertiary courses in particular, due to the evidence of increased engagement and the impact of social education structures upon progression and retention [10]. However, when collaborative learning activities place undue cognitive or metacognitive load upon students, they may introduce problems with anxiety and indeed decrease learning. The learning objectives buried within collaborative activities are complex - we frequently intertwine objectives related to discipline experience and skill, with professional skill and metacognitive development. Wiggberg [24] identifies that unclear learning objectives may confound the learning outcome; when participants are not clear on their role within the community, learning effectiveness may actually be decreased (p.129).

A self-regulating student will set their goals, marshal their resources and then manage their time effectively [20] - without this fundamental level of metacognition they cannot direct their knowledge in a useful and constructive manner. Unsurprisingly, given that we expect our students to move on and take their place within the community, it is their ability to use their knowledge in accordance with others' expectations and time frames that will be one of the greatest tests of their self-regulation.

Students who are not experienced with collaboration, i.e. they have not as yet been able to extend self-regulation to group self-regulation, frequently break up collaborative activities into parts, assign each part to a participant in the collaboration, continue their work primarily independently, and then undertake a brief integration exercise prior to submission [1]. Wiggberg identifies that stress introduced through unclear learning objectives can lead to a predisposition to this behaviour (p. 114). In these cases, students also have a tendency to adopt those roles within a collaboration that they are most comfortable with, meaning that they may never be exposed to activities that address particular skill development. When contributions are not equally made, or equally respected within the collaboration, knowledge asymmetry can lead to decreases in peer learning and self-confidence [1]. Issues of power inequality and cross-cultural concerns [12] may arise that impact upon the ease of adoption of certain roles; where students represent cultures with greatly varying power distances they may be reluctant to participate fully and equally in the collaboration.

In this paper we describe a phenomenographic study exploring the variation in student experiences of collaborative learning activities. Our analysis shows that students

SIGCSE'13, March 6–9, 2013, Denver, Colorado, USA.

view collaborative learning activities as exhibiting a range of learning objectives, ranging from task-oriented through to metacognitive, and that the choice of learning objective impacts upon their behaviour and experiences within those activities. When students recognise metacognitive learning objectives they are more readily able to disassociate their individual performance and focus on the metacognitive development of the group. In contrast, students who exhibit a task focus, incorporating an assumption of group self-regulation skill along with the need to demonstrate technical expertise, exhibit degrees of anxiety and stress.

2. RELATED WORK

The crucial role of community within learning has been long established, and forms the basis for many collaborative and cooperative learning techniques. Vygotsky [23] elaborates the ideas of social constructivism through his observation that learning awakens a variety of internal development processes that operate only when one is working with others, i.e. the *zone of proximal development*, where learning is achieved within a group and as a direct result of the group activities. In this model, the learning of new concepts and processes is achieved by first establishing mastery as a group, and only then, developing mastery as an individual through continued practice and internalisation of knowledge.

Liu, Joy and Griffiths [15] describe a national survey-based study on student perceptions on group work, encompassing both online and face-to-face collaborations. They incorporate a significant literature review that identifies three key problems in collaborative group work: poor motivation, lack in individual accountability and negative interdependence, where one or more students within the group complete the majority of the work, decreasing the overall group contribution. Drury, Kay and Losberg [9] describe a cross-sectional evaluation on perceptions of group work, combining analysis of focus group interviews and an extensive questionnaire to monitor changes in students' perceptions of collaborative group work throughout their studies. They identified the need to model group work within foundation courses, due to the complexity of learning both discipline concepts and metacognitive aspects of group collaboration. The majority of students reported positive experiences, however a significant minority indicated negative experiences within their collaborations.

Beven, Warner and McDowell [6] explore successful structuring mechanisms for pair programming, a form of collaborative learning where two students work together on the one program, with one acting as driver and one as navigator. In this study, the authors identify that students at a high skill level prefer not to be paired with a student of a lower skill level, while Thomas et al [21] find that students perform at their best when they are paired with a student of equivalent skill and confidence level. Begel and Nagappan [3] explore industry-level pair programming, identifying consistent issues related to differences in skill and confidence level, and communication issues. In these studies, anxiety is linked to the degree of cognitive and metacognitive dissonance.

Plonka *et al* [17] explore the causes and impact of disengagement in pair programming; they identify five reasons why disengagement may occur, primarily focussed on differences in skill level, and the structuring of tasks, including degree of difficulty and time co-ordination. They identify that disengagement may be invisible, in that a collaboration may dissolve without explicit agreement or discussion.

Vartiainen [22] describes a phenomenographic study of the moral conflicts perceived by students within collaborative projects, exploring the conceptions underlying student responses to issues such as differing skill level and communication problems. Vartiainen identifies two dimensions of variation in his analysis, namely whether the student focusses on the impact of issues on the self, or on the other, i.e. the other members of the group.

Wiggberg [24] presents arguably the most comprehensive study in this area, exploring students' experience with collaborative group work and how they correspond to teachers' expectations. Wiggberg presents three different stories of students' experiences with a industry-standard software development project, exploring issues such as work allocation practices, responsibility for learning and degree of ownership of project goals. One key finding from this study is that unclear learning objectives, such as whether the purpose of the collaboration is to achieve deeper discipline learning or collaboration skills, may hinder learning outcomes and introduce additional stresses.

3. RESEARCH METHOD

In this project, we explore student's experiences with collaborative learning activities and their understanding of the purpose of these activities within their curriculum. Phenomenography [16, 7] is a qualitative and empirical research method that aims to explore how groups of people experience and understand certain events. The basis of phenomenography is the establishment of descriptive categories that describe the variation in the experiences of the participants in the study. The participants are selected in order to represent varied interpretations and understandings rather than to form a statistically representative sample.

The research methodology underpinning a phenomenographic study typically consists of qualitative analysis of interview transcriptions, identifying quotes of experiences that reflect categories within one or more dimensions of variation. These dimensions, and corresponding categories, may be pre-determined from related literature and analysis and/or may evolve from the analysis process. Although a perceived weakness of qualitative studies is the inability to generalize from the small sample size, studies such as this capture the complexities of a phenomenon; such detailed observations cannot be captured in surveys or experimental designs [19]. A typical interview cohort consists of 10-15 participants, to support deep analysis of variation of experience and understanding [5].

3.1 Data Collection

In our project, we undertook a pilot stage refining an initial set of interview questions derived from the literature, before conducting a series of in-depth semi-structured interviews with our participant cohort. Participants were sought from those students who were currently studying, or who had recently completed, undergraduate Computer Science courses, with 10 students agreeing to participate in interviews of approximately 45 minutes duration. The participants represented a diverse cross section of our cohort: of our cohort 3 were female, and 7 were male; 4 were international students, while 6 were domestic; and 3 were enrolled in first year studies, 2 in second year, and the remainder in advanced level courses. All students had been exposed to a variety of collaborative learning activities within their courses, ranging from formative, informal pair programming, peer collaboration and group discussions within tutorials and lectures, through to more formal, structured group assignments and industry-related projects.

Each interview commenced with a series of key positioning questions, designing to orient the participants towards the area of interest, following by a series of followup questions. The purpose of the unstructured followup questions, specific to the context of the individual interview, was to explore further each student's experiences and construct a common understanding of the student's experiences and understanding. The key positioning questions used within the interviews were formed from three question areas (QAs):

- QA1: How do students understand the purpose of collaborative learning activities?
- QA2: Do students view collaborative learning activities as positive or negative experiences?
- QA3: How do students perceive their relationship with their group?

Each interview was transcribed verbatim and analysed in an iterative process using NVivo (Version 9) to refine both the dimensions of variation and the internal categories, identifying logical relationships between the qualitatively different categories. Within phenomenographic research, individual interviews are not categorised, rather, individual expressions and experiences are categorised according to the identified dimensions of variations.

4. ANALYSIS

The results of a phenomenographic study consist of a description of the categories of understanding that have been isolated within the interview transcripts, and the relationships between those categories. We have identified five categories relating to how collaborative learning activities are experienced in the outcome space, illustrated in Table 1.

4.1 Category 1: Anxiety

In Category 1, the focus of the student is upon the emotional pressure and anxiety that they experience as a result of the multifaceted skill requirement of collaborative activities. The student does not acknowledge group or self-regulation as a learning objective, but instead assumes it as a required skill, which places additional pressure upon both themselves and the group. They view the purpose of the activity as task-oriented, but their focus is not so much on the achievement itself, but upon any potential compromises to their individual achievement that may occur. Some of the comments focussed on the structuring of groups, identifying differing skill levels and familiarity as the source of anxiety and pressure (identified by participant and quote):

> P3: I hated it, especially if it was randomised groups where we didn't get to pick our groups, that was terrible. I didn't like it because if you got a bad group, it really destroyed your mark for the subject, or you have to do a lot more work. (q1).

Some comments relate the pressure of collaborative activities to a lack of control over group decisions, such as time management and goal setting:

> P10: I still don't enjoy the pressure of having to do the work at someone else's pace; I try to do a good job anyway, but I have to do a certain degree of, like a good job, and I have to have done that good job by a certain time so that I am not disappointing the other person. (q2)

In contrast, some students identified the degree of pressure and anxiety as having a positive impact upon their studies:

> P4: if we are doing the group project, we have a schedule in the group, we have our own schedule, so that can push you so that you don't get behind. You are feeling that someone is pushing you, you have to do it by tomorrow, or something, so it is good. (q3)

In our discussion, we explored potential causes of this anxiety, including group assessment, and alternatives such as individual and peer assessment. Interestingly, students also exhibited variation in response here, with some comments focussing on the impact upon their individual achievement, while others adopted responsibility for the group, defining their individual achievement through that of the group.

> P8: It is still important, as the rest of the assignment obviously has to get completed and a lot of the time, if you are trying to drag the rest of the group through you end up leaving your own section to the very end and that can suffer because you have to put the rest of the group through (q4)

4.2 Category 2: Achievement

In Category 2, students experience collaborative learning activities as a way of producing a substantial achievement. The focus is less on the learning outcomes, either discipline or higher order, that are achieved but on the completion of a task where the outcome is greater than what an individual could achieve on their own.

Some students identified the expected efficiencies to be gained by having multiple people contributing and collaborating. This contrasts with (q4), where responsibility for the group achievement is taken on board by the individual, whereas in this experience, we have a student who appreciates only having to adopt part of the total task load.

> P5: I like it. and it sort of splits the work in half a bit, so it's sort of easier? (q5)

While others recognise the synergy available in such activities:

> P4: We were working in groups, me and my friend, well, my partner, we've actually come up with two totally separate solutions, and we sort of joined them together to make one awesome solution. (q6)

There is a tension here between achievement and cognition: students may have a focus on achieving a substantial goal, but also want to access all of the available skill development. This represents a cognitive disconnect:

Table 1: How Collaborative Learning Activities are experienced.

Category	Collaboration is experienced as...	Focus
Anxiety	a stressful experience that introduces emotional responses and pressure without substantial learning benefit.	potential compromise to individual achievement
Achievement	an opportunity to complete a larger, more complex task.	discipline achievement
Professionalism	an opportunity to develop professional skills and awareness.	professional skill development
Cognition	an opportunity to develop new skills, techniques and discipline knowledge.	individual knowledge development
Metacognition	an opportunity to share and develop cultural awareness and higher order thinking skills.	Higher order development and self-regulation

> P8: If you can break the topic up into small elements, you can just divide it up amongst the group and work on isolated bits and that may mean that you don't actually ever work on particular pieces in a subject ... you get an imbalance between which parts of the group know which parts. (q7)

4.3 Category 3: Professionalism

For some students, the development of professional behaviours is their primary understanding of the purpose of collaborative activities. Students' conceptions of professional behaviour were quite mature, exhibiting a deeper understanding than the simplistic development of generic skills, extending to the importance of those skills to achieving something greater than yourself. One student identifies the scale of output expected of a professional, and the ability to take on larger and more complex projects as a group.

> P5: Definitely teamwork is very important in society and even if you are quite smart you are just a single person, you can not make all of the things by yourself. (q8)

Another student focusses on the mentorship and leadership aspects, identifying the role of an ICT professional in managing others and helping develop skills in less experiences colleagues.

> P9: Most of the time you are going to have a group or a team of people where you are going to have to work with them and even if you are not working with them you'll have meetings with them or that sort of thing, and I think it represents what will happen once you leave university, rather than just, yeah, you might be able to do it, but you might not be able to work with other people to help them do it ... (q9)

4.4 Category 4: Cognition

In this category, the student's understanding of collaborative activity is a means to achieve new knowledge or skills, and a means to share knowledge and techniques with others. Many of the comments expressed the benefit to self, i.e. the ability to gain knowledge or skills from working with others.

> P3: I can do something by myself , but sometimes I need some very, very good idea to enlighten me because i need to enlighten myself to solve the problem. (q10)

Some students identified this as a move from independent study and self reliance to a more community-focussed model, identifying the need to work with others to achieve the zone of proximal development and, hence, deeper learning:

> P8: I like to work on my own, I need to work with others... so I like working by myself but I know I need the help, and it is better for me to work with other people. (q11)

One student describes this as the "a ha!" moment, where the group works in a united fashion to achieve knowledge construction:

> P8: But I think it is that *a ha!* moment, where someone says something and you are like, there you go, and then you just go and do it.... and it falls into place. (q12)

The impact of different learning objectives can be seen here, where competing learning objectives of cognition and achievement introduce group coordination problems and block learning outcomes. The following student identifies the issue at hand, but considers this mismatch just part of the standard practice – the roulette of group construction:

> P10: I never really learnt a lot because I was never really lucky with groups ... The problems were that people in my groups either were just interested in getting the assignment done and not really learning anything from it... (q13)

4.5 Category 5: Metacognition

In Category 5, the student's understanding of collaborative activities is focussed on the ability to develop and share higher order problem solving and analysis skills, and in learning to develop both self-regulation and group self-regulation skills.

This comment makes reference to the ability to develop these skills within a multi-cultural context, incorporating multiple understandings of processes and technical content:

> P6: Yeah, I learn a lot of things, actually, even if I just pass in a group project, I think I learn that what I am thinking about is not always right, because other people come from different hierarchies, different cultural background, they have their own ideas on the course work, even when we are focusing on the same topic they have different experiences of it... we collect all of the

ideas, and use our judgement to improve - it is interesting learning process. (q14)

One student identifies the ability to learn not only technical content from others, but also their learning processes:

> P10: When people work together to share ideas and share the processes that they use to get to solutions, so that other people can learn from what their peers do. (q15)

Some students recognised the tension inherent here between anxiety and metacognition - many students identified group structure and the need to develop relationships and communication networks with new people as a significant source of anxiety, however some students also recognised the embedded benefits of such actions:

> P4: It is easy to stick with the old friends, it is easier, but it is not good in the future... you can get more different opinions, and you can... because everyone has their way to do things, maybe you never thought of the thing that they are doing, the way that they are doing, that can surprise you. (q16)

5. DISCUSSION

Collaborative activity asks a lot of our students; while they are learning technical and professional skills, they are also having to master self-regulation skills, and then move those into the space of group self-regulation, coordinating their own self-regulation with that of other group members and learning how to integrate group self-regulation into their skill set. These so-called *soft skills*, including monitoring of group progress, group decision making, and evaluating and providing feedback on other's contributions, are not given high priority within university pedagogy. In contrast, our experiences with industry, as a community, identify that our students are inadequately prepared, and more consideration needs to be given to these areas [2].

In their analysis of industry-level collaboration, Begel and Nagappan [3] identify that the issues involved in their form of collaborative activity can be traced back to sources of anxiety. However, our analysis identifies that in an educational setting, additional complexities related to learning objective may introduce further issues and problems for collaborative groups. We identify that the conceptualisation of purpose of the activity is closely tied to the way that the student approaches the activity and the development of relationships with their group. Students have a complex understanding of the benefits and costs of collaborative learning, and adopt a range of approaches based upon assumptions of purpose. When learning objectives are unclear, and students must determine them for themselves, this introduces a degree of tension and impacts upon the behavioural choices of the students involved in the collaborative activity [24].

The five categories in our outcome space correspond to the different ways that students experience collaborative learning activities. We do not view these categories in a strict hierarchy or spectrum, instead identifying individual relationships as follows. In our analysis, we view anxiety and achievement as being closely related categories, representing two ends of a spectrum. Both exhibit task-orientation, moving towards anxiety when cognitive or metacognitive overload occurs. We view cognition and metacognition as elements of process-orientation, where metacognition subsumes cognition in terms of higher order development. We see professionalism as representing a separate point within our outcome space.

Where students are able to focus on the development of the group, and the development of group self-regulation skills, they are able to move beyond the focus on self achievement. Correspondingly, where students have unclear metacognitive learning objectives, or where students are overwhelmed by the metacognitive or cognitive load, associated anxieties and pressures modify their behavioural responses.

Interestingly, one category that we had expected to identify, that of social development, was not one that was explicitly identified by our participants. As academics, we frequently utilise collaborative learning activities as a way of promoting social bonds to help address transition concerns, however this conceptualisation was not readily recognised by our participants. Several students identified friendships and relationships that had developed as part of their activities, but hesitated to articulate the connection between the activity itself and their social development. Rather, they viewed these relationships as resulting from their own initiation, coincidentally placed within the structure of the activity.

So what can we say about how we should structure collaborative learning activities? We conclude our discussion by connecting what we have observed through our analysis with support from the literature.

Collaborations are more likely to break up into disjoint, and unequal activities if the learning objectives are not clear. It is therefore imperative to make the learning conditions of the activity clear, enabling students to adapt their assumptions and behaviours from the outset. However, in some cases, the learning objectives of our collaborative activities are primarily task-oriented and are therefore open to metacognitive overload. Ideally, at this point, we will have provided sufficient scaffolding for our students so that they are not overwhelmed by the metacognitive requirements. Unfortunately, with the realistic knowledge that this is unlikely to be the case for all of our students we need to identify strategies for minimising anxiety.

Cohen [8] identifies that open-ended ill-structured collaboration activities may be better positioned to encourage participation by reluctant students, as they tend to avoid potential causes of stress. We concur, in that these kinds of problems promote problem solving discussion and move away from an achievement or task-oriented focus. Rick and Guzdial [18] further identify that this form of structuring is more important for STEM students, due to their tendency to initially adopt a dualist view towards their activities, making them reluctant to contribute collaboratively. Although variably experienced by our participants, incorporation of individual and peer assessment components is also recognised as alleviating stress [13].

Perhaps the most successful measures for alleviating stress are through the explicit development of team management, group decision making and problem solving skills. Kavanagh *et al* [13] describe a detailed process of activity design and team management skill development, which utilises peer and self-assessment, in part, for their assistance in self-reflection and support for metacognitive development. Leeper [14] adopts a progressive project process designed to build student self-confidence in stages as they approach increasingly difficult tasks. Subsequent tasks can be customised in degree of difficulty to support varying skill levels. Wiggberg [24] identifies that students are more likely to value other's contributions when they perceive that the other student is competent, either through the demonstration of skill or the presumption of skill. This supports structured activities where each student is provided with opportunities, relative to their experience, to demonstrate skill within any collaboration.

6. CONCLUSIONS

Collaborative learning presents many opportunities for educators and students, supporting increased engagement, deeper learning and opportunities to develop and reflect upon group communication and self-regulation. However, sources of anxiety may be introduced that impact upon the success of the collaboration where students are unclear on, or have conflicting perceptions of, expected learning outcomes.

In this study, we have explored students' experiences of collaborative learning activities, identifying themes in terms of their understanding of the purpose of said activities and how that impacts upon their behaviour and expectations of other students. We have adopted phenomenography as the research method for this study, identifying five categories of variation associated with task- and process-oriented views. Our analysis extends and improves our understanding of how to structure collaborative activities, supporting moves to explicitly address group management and decision making skills, and viewing the development of these skills not only as a professional requirement but as essential to group success, and discipline learning.

The connection between metacognitive overload and anxiety appears promising, and warrants further investigation. We intend to expand our analysis through the development of a broader survey study to gather statistically representative data reflecting students' experiences with collaborative learning activities and learning outcomes.

7. REFERENCES

[1] L. J. Barker. When do group projects widen the student experience gap? In *In Proceedings of iTiCSE'05*, pages 276–280, June 2006.

[2] A. Begel and S. B. Novice software developers, all over again. In *Proceedings of ICER'08*, pages 3–14, 2008.

[3] A. Begel and N. Nagappan. Pair programming: What's in it for me? In *Proceedings of ESEM'08*, pages 120–128, 2008.

[4] M. Ben-Ari. Constructivism in computer science education. In *Proceedings of SIGCSE'98*, pages 257–261, 1998.

[5] A. Berglund and M. Wiggberg. Students learn cs in different ways: Insights from a empirical study. In *Proceedings of iTiCSE'06*, pages 265–269, 2006.

[6] J. Bevan, L. Werner, and C. McDowell. Guidelines for the user of pair programming in a freshman programming class. In *Proceedings of the 15th Conference Software Engineering Education and Training*, pages 100–107, 2002.

[7] S. Booth. On phenomenography, learning and teaching. *Higher Education Research & Development*, 16(2):135–158, 1997.

[8] E. Cohen. Restructuring the classroom: Conditions for production small groups. *Review of Educational Research*, 64(1):1–35, 1994.

[9] H. Drury, J. Kay, and W. Losberg. Student satisfaction with group work in undergraduate computer science: do things get better? In *Proceedings of ACE'03*, pages 77–85, 2002.

[10] K. Falkner and D. Munro. Easing the transition: A collaborative learning approach. In *Proceedings of ACE'09)*, volume 95, pages 65–74. ACS, 2009.

[11] U. Geer and D. Rudge. A review of research on constructivist-based strategies for large lecture science classes. *Journal of Science Education*, 7(2), December 2002.

[12] G. Hofstede. National cultures in four dimensions: A research-based theory of cultural differences. *International Studies of Management & Organisation*, 13(1/2):46–74, 1983.

[13] L. Kavanagh, D. Neil, and J. Cockley. Developing and disseminating team skills capacities using interactive online tools for team formation, learning, assessment and mentoring. Technical report, The Australian Learning and Teaching Council, 2011.

[14] R. Leeper. Progressive project assignments in computer courses. In *Proceedings of the 20th Technical Symposium on Computer Science Education (SIGCSE'89)*, pages 88–92, 1989.

[15] S. Liu, M. Joy, and N. Griffths. Students' perceptions of the factors leading to unsuccessful group collaboration. In *Proceedings of the 10th IEEE International Conference on Advanced Learning Technologies*, pages 565–569, 2010.

[16] F. Marton and S. Booth. *Learning and awareness*. New Jersey: Lawrence Erlbaum Associates, 1997.

[17] L. Plonka, H. Sharp, and J. van der Linden. Disengagement in pair programming: does it matter? In *Proceedings of the 2012 International Conference on Software Engineering*, pages 496–506, 2012.

[18] J. Rick and M. Guzdial. Situating coweb: a scholarship of application. *Journal of Computer-Supported Collaborative Learning*, 1(1):89–115, 2006.

[19] M. Sandelowski. Sample size in qualitative research. *Research in Nursing & Health*, 18(2):179–183, 1995.

[20] G. Schraw, K. Crippen, and K. Hartley. Promoting self-regulation in science education: Metacognition as part of a broader perspective on learning. *Research in Science Education*, 36(1-2):111–139, 2006.

[21] L. Thomas, M. Ratcliffe, and A. Robertson. Code warriors and code-a-phobes: a study in attitude and pair programming. In *Proceedings of SIGCSE'03*, pages 363–367, 2003.

[22] T. Vartiainen. Moral conflicts perceived by students of a project course. In *Proceedings of the 6th Baltic Sea Conference on Computing Education Research (Koli Calling 2006)*, pages 77–84, 2006.

[23] L. Vygotsky. *Mind in Society: The Development of Higher Psychological Processes*. Harvard University Press, 1978.

[24] M. Wiggberg. *Computer Science Project Courses: Contrasting Students' Experiences with Teachers' Expectations*. Doctor of Philosophy, Acta Universitatis Upsaliensis, 2010.

Life's a Game and the Game of Life: How Making a Game Out of it Can Change Student Behavior

Adrienne Decker, Elizabeth Lane Lawley
School of Interactive Games and Media
Rochester Institute of Technology
Rochester, NY 14623-5608
+1 (585) 475- {4653, 6896}
{adrienne, ell} @mail.rit.edu

ABSTRACT
There is little argument that creating experiences for students that will increase student success and retention is a goal that is shared by anyone teaching courses. In computing courses, we have seen a lot of focused attention on the first year introductory courses as it has been shown that it is failure in these courses that drives students away from the discipline. In this paper we describe success we have had with first year students through the creation of achievement system for the undergraduate experience. Through the Just Press Play project and its associated achievements, we observed a significant shift in student behavior in relation to our first year students which lead to a greater level of student success in their first course.

Categories and Subject Descriptors
K.3.2 [**Computing Milieux**]: Computers and Education – *computer and information science education.*

General Terms
Human Factors

Keywords
Gamification, student mentoring, CS1, retention

1. OUR STORY BEGINS
Our story begins with a simple question that one student asked innocently enough, "Why can't we get achievements for being awesome?" The student was referring to the idea that achievements in online systems and in life come from doing some particularly structured thing. The faculty members who heard the question felt that the student had the right idea. Student success is based on more than simply completing academic goals, prerequisite courses, and the fulfilling of requirements. Successful undergraduate students also engage with the people and activities on their campus, and use the skills gained in classes in their extracurricular activities.

SIGCSE'13, March 6–9, 2013, Denver, Colorado, USA.

From this recognition was born the idea of creating a "gaming layer" for the undergraduate experience. Students could choose to become involved in this game-like experience, which would allow them to receive recognition for activities that as faculty we know are important to their future success. The prototype phase of this gaming layer, which was implemented during the 2011-12 academic year, demonstrated its potential value through the successful of achievement of its key goals. We created an environment that allowed the students to engage with one another and encouraged the student community to come together to enable the academic success of the first year students.

2. RULES OF THE GAME
2.1 Gamification
Gamification is generally considered to be the use of game design elements in non-gaming contexts [10]. While critics have dismissed gamification as a crass attempt to manipulate consumers [3], others have pointed to this use of games as a way to significantly enhance everyday experiences [17]. The difference in perspective arises in large part from the motivation for the use of game design elements in a given experiential context. When that use is intended primarily to encourage participants to engage in activities that they would otherwise find unpleasant for the benefit of the sponsoring organization, the risk of manipulation and exploitation is high. When the implementation is instead intended to improve the experience of the participant, the potential for positive impact is much higher.

A primary concern in developing "gamified" applications is the impact on participant motivation. Research into motivation has shown that using extrinsic rewards can have a damaging effect on individual motivation to participate in activities. These rewards can undermine the intrinsic sense of satisfaction that engaging in creative and productive work can generate. Used well, however, game elements can reinforce intrinsic satisfaction and reward rather than replacing them. Effective gamification allows participants to use the game elements as a reflection of their sense of pride in completing an activity, rather than as a replacement, as noted by Deterding in his "Gamificaton by Design: Response to O'Reilly" essay [8]:

> Indeed, games are full of points, scores, tokens, and so on, and digital games are full of virtual currency and items that players can gain in the course of play. My point is that the "fun", the pleasure of these elements does not come from some extrinsic reward value of those elements, but chiefly from the experience of competence they give rise to.

While the Just Press Play system has frequently been described as an attempt to "gamify" education [4], we saw it instead as a pervasive game [6, 19], one that used not just game elements but also game design principles and an underlying narrative to engage players in a real-world context.

2.2 First Year Computing

Much focus has been paid to the first year computing curriculum in order to ensure a strong foundation experience for students in their study of computing. Two of the main intervention techniques have been innovative curriculum and enhanced student experiences.

Curriculum techniques and innovations have been created, discussed, presented, advocated and/or maligned en masse in the past several years. We have seen the growth in object-oriented curriculums and tools (BlueJ, Alice) [1, 2], media computation [13], robotics [5], Processing and digital art [12], and finally a call for a return to basics [21]. For each of the innovative tools or techniques, various advocates have discussed their successes in the classroom and each has found a place in the pantheon of curriculums for the first year.

However, many believe that it is not just about what you present or how it is presented, or what projects the students work on, but rather that student experience in the classroom plays a large role in creating success for students. Pair programming has been found to be successful in helping students learn to program in the first course/year [16, 20]. Mentoring of students in various ways has also proven to be valuable to first year students [11, 18]. And most recently, the trend of flipping the classroom has made its way into the first year of programming instruction, especially as the advent of massive online education appears to be growing [15].

For each of these ideas, we can find evidence that supports the approach and shows that it helps students to succeed in the course. While this is important to a particular course, the goal of the Just Press Play project was to create an atmosphere for success outside of individual courses and inclusive of them. In a way, we are looking to umbrella the undergraduate experience and support it, not just support one or more particular courses, or particular sets of topics.

3. JUST PRESS PLAY

Begun in 2011, the Just Press Play (JPP) project is a game-based achievement system designed to help students traverse their undergraduate experience. It was designed to address the intellectual, social, and developmental challenges that students face attempting to navigate the waters of earning an undergraduate degree. It also allows for faculty to have a clearer picture of the students' progress on this journey.

In order to facilitate this, JPP provides a web-based networked environment that allows students to identify opportunities, collect recognition for achievements, and build connections with others through both social and creative activities.

In Fall 2011, the prototype version of this system was used in the School of Interactive Games and Media at Rochester Institute of Technology. The primary audience was undergraduate students enrolled in the school's two programs, Game Design & Development and New Media Interactive Design. Graduate students in the department and faculty and staff were also encouraged to participate in the pilot phase, but the main goal of the system was to support the needs of the undergraduate population. No achievements or activities were designed around the graduate student or faculty/staff populations. The pilot study ran until the end of Winter Quarter 2011/2012.

3.1 Project Goals

The JPP prototype had four main goals:

1) Provide students with a clearer sense of their accomplishments in various areas (academic, social, and creative) of their college experience, and provide them with tools to reflect on their range and balance of activities.
2) Increase students' awareness of activities and opportunities outside their academic coursework, from wellness to collaboration to knowledge of the campus and city, and inspire them to sample a range of experiences.
3) Enable students to maintain and share a record of their activities.
4) Provide students with a sense of fantasy, whimsy and playful abstraction in dealing with the stress and growth associated with the transformational nature of undergraduate education

3.2 Core Design Principles

The JPP team has been guided by the following principles in designing the system.

3.2.1 Non-Curricular and Voluntary

The activities within JPP should not be a requirement for any course, and lack of participation in the game should not impose penalties on a student. However, completion of some achievements could require skills typically gained in one or more courses in the curriculum.

3.2.2 Game Activities External to Website

Most of the activities in JPP should take place outside of the context of the website. The website should be used primarily for discovering and validating activities, viewing progress, and communicating and collaborating with other players.

3.2.3 Varied Achievement Types and Contexts

Players should be offered stand-alone, grouped, and/or sequenced achievements within the game. Some of the achievements should be possible to complete independently, while others should require collaboration among students. Some achievements may be repeatable. Achievements can include creative work, social activities, and exploration of physical and online resources.

3.2.4 Accessible to Casual Players

The game is designed to be accessible to both core and casual players. Core gamers are those who are interested in conquering all aspects of the game and who engage fully in the narrative of the play. Casual gamers may elect to do some of the achievements, but will not typically attempt achievements that will require significant effort outside of their existing routine. In order for the project to be truly successful, the game had to appeal to both player types. The barrier to entry could not be too high for casual players, nor for players who chose to join the game well after it had begun in October.

3.3 Achievements and Quests

In the game, achievements were situated on two axes: one representing the balance between creative and cultural activities and technical or skill-focused activities; the other representing the balance between individual and social activities. As players collected achievements, they moved along the axes to show how much they have grown in that quadrant.

Quests, made up of collections of achievements, were also a part of the system. Some quests required completing a sequence of achievements, while others allowed players to choose a subset of achievements from a large collection. Completing a particular quest awarded the player that quest's achievement.

To earn an achievement, the player would complete the required task or tasks and then be awarded the achievement in the game through one of three mechanisms: collectible cards, location checkins, or administrative assignment. Collectible cards were used for achievements associated with specific individuals or events. These cards had the name of the achievement as well as photos, descriptions, or trivia related to the specific person or event. The card also included a unique 25-character alphanumeric code that players needed to enter on the website to register their achievement with the system. For some achievements, going to a particular place was important. Once there, the players would check in with an RFID tag to indicate their attendance and register them for the achievement. For other achievements, administrators of the game awarded the achievement to all eligible users at the appropriate time.

3.4 Pilot Phase

The pilot phase of the JPP project began in October 2011. Registration in the system was only available to the students within the IGM department for the pilot phase. Launch day, October 14, 2011 saw the registration of 155 players in the game. By the end of the first week, 384 students had registered in the system. By the end of the fall quarter (mid-November 2011), there were 423 users. Out of the 423 registered participants, 261 had completed the apprentice level and could really be considered full players of the game. To complete the apprentice level, a player needed to sign up for the game, pick up an RFID key fob and interact with at least one faculty or staff member within the department to earn some achievement.

These numbers were very encouraging for us. Our school had just over 700 undergraduate students, and the registration numbers for the pilot indicate that over 60% of those students registered for the experience and nearly 40% completed the tutorial phase and participated actively in the game. We found that a higher percentage of freshmen and sophomores participated compared to juniors and seniors, but since one of our goals was to engage those populations early in their academic careers, those numbers were indicative of a successful launch.

During the pilot, there were several different types of achievements that the students could earn. Almost all involved interactions with other people in some way, be it faculty/staff or other students.

Students could engage with faculty and staff in a number of ways. Achievements could be earned for students simply attending an instructor's office hours, or meeting with their academic advisor. The department held a number of faculty/student mixers throughout the year and attendance at the events earned you an achievement.

Faculty and staff could also choose to have a collectible card, associated with a unique achievement. If a student completed the relevant requirements, they earned the special faculty/staff achievement and a collectible card for that faculty/staff member. Because those achievements were intended to increase informal and playful interactions with faculty and staff, the achievements were generally not academic in their content. Some of the achievements included:

- Simply using "the magic word" ("please") when asking for the achievement.
- Making the faculty member laugh.
- Doing a little dance for the faculty member.
- Showing a faculty member a picture of the player eating pie.
- Showing a faculty member a picture of the player on a boat.
- Finding the hidden achievement card in a faculty member's office.

Increasing our students' engagement in extra-curricular social activities was also an important part of the project's goal. Students could earn achievements for attending a variety of on-campus events and checking in with the JPP representative at the event. This included sporting events, concerts, and lectures.

Having students create a social experience with their peers was another popular set of achievements. For example, the achievement entitled "The Last Supper" was awarded if a student went out for dinner off campus with at least 12 other people, took a picture, and submitted it online. Students could also organize and participate in a flash mob; one of these was successfully completed around Halloween to Michael Jackson's Thriller, while a second in February involved the creation of a giant human-powered Rube Goldberg machine in the college's atrium. The students help to organize, make costumes for, and practice these events. In each case, someone "leaked" the news to the university press and the event was well attended both for participants and spectators.

Overall, by the end of the winter quarter (in March) and the end of the pilot, the game had 283 active players (those who had completed the tutorial), who had collectively completed 3,504 achievements (an average of 21.6 achievements per player). The highest number of achievements collected was 49.

4. THE GAME CHANGER

4.1 Challenge Issued

Of all of the achievements, the most interesting and encouraging to us from an educational and student experience perspective came was the *Undying* achievement. This achievement was devised because historically, no more than 85% of our freshmen pass their introductory programming course. While that level of success is actually quite high for such a class, the team felt that it provided an interesting target for an achievement. The intent of the achievement was to engage the student community as a whole to help the freshmen pass the class. Thus, the achievement would be granted to *all* players if the freshmen had a passing level of 90% for the first course. By taking this approach, we did not single out students who had done poorly in the class, nor did we limit the impact of their success to simply those who had done well.

4.2 Student Response

Soon after the achievement was announced, discussion ensued in the department's Facebook group about it. When a freshman posted late in the quarter about having difficulty with one of the concepts, an upperclassman responded by exhorting his classmates to help the freshmen, so that everyone would be able to earn the achievement.

Two students in particular, took the lead and decided to organize a study session for the final exams. In doing so, they first approached the department leadership for permission, and asked for help finding space to hold the study session. Also, they approached the faculty teaching the first course via email for help.

> Hi Prof. XXX,
> YYY (cc'd on this email) and I are arranging a study session for people in GSD I the weekend before finals. We were wondering if we could meet with you at some point this week or next to get an idea of what you have covered in your class this quarter, and what you are expecting your students to know for your final. If you could let us know when you are free to meet, that would be great.
>
> Thanks.
> --
> ZZZ
> 3rd Year Game Design & Development Major
> Rochester Institute of Technology

First year faculty were eager to help with this endeavor and the study sessions drew a large number of the students from the introductory course.

The final passing percentage for the first-quarter programming class was a record-breaking 91%. While it is not possible to prove a direct causal relationship between our game and the increase in the number of successful students in the course, we can show a direct relationship between the game and the emergence of peer tutoring sessions, which in turn have been shown to be a highly effective mechanism for increasing student performance [22].

4.3 Seasons Change

While the acquisition of the *Undying* achievement was something that the students valued, the real value of the exercise became clear to us in the following quarter when the upperclassmen once again approached the faculty about organizing study sessions. The upperclass students had found that organizing and running the study sessions was an intrinsically rewarding activity, and they wanted to continue offering this peer support to the new students. They went on to run study sessions for midterms and finals in the winter quarter, with an increasing number of upperclass students attending each session to assist with the tutoring.

Once again, in winter quarter the passing percentage of students in the freshman programming class was well over 90%. Many of the students participating in the tutoring, however, expressed no interest in the achievement, finding that the reward of helping other students was the real value in this activity.

5. LEVEL UP

While the pilot project was successful in many ways, most notably in increasing information interactions between students and faculty, and in encouraging peer tutoring in our programming courses, there were a number of technical problems with our implementation that hindered adoption by students and restricted our ability to implement content. Achievement redemption via lengthy alphanumeric code entry had a very negative impact on participation, and resulted in many students participating in activities but not bothering to actually record that in the achievement system; this, in turn, made our participation statistics far less accurate. We also encountered significant problems in implementing the RFID readers for checkins around campus, which reduced student trust in the reliability of our infrastructure and limited our ability to assign achievements for many activities.

During the summer of 2012, we rebuilt the technical infrastructure of the system, and implemented a significant number of changes to the overall game mechanics and presentation of content. Most notably, this included a shift from code entry and RFID scanners to the use of QR codes associated with individual players that can be scanned by any admin with an Android or iOS mobile device [14]. Version 2 of Just Press Play launched in late August of 2012, and we are already seeing much higher levels of participation and engagement, as well as much more accurate recording of player participation.

We plan to test the new version of the system with other departments at RIT, as well as other educational institutions, during the 2012-13 academic year, with a long-term goal of making the software and a set of best practices for content available in an open-source format to other educators.

6. ACKNOWLEDGMENTS

The Just Press Play project has been made possible through the generous support of Microsoft Research Connections. In addition, the Just Press Play project would not have been possible without the work of the dedicated individuals on the design and development team. We stand on their shoulders (https://play.rit.edu/credits).

7. REFERENCES

[1] Alice website. Retrieved September 5, 2012 from http://www.alice.org

[2] BlueJ website. Retrieved September 5, 2012 from http://www.bluej.org

[3] Bogost, I. 2011. Gamification is Bullshit. Retrieved September 5, 2012 from http://www.bogost.com/blog/gamification_is_bullshit.shtml

[4] Cheston, D. 2012. College as a Video Game? *The John William Pope Center for Higher Education Policy*. Retrieved September 5, 2012 http://www.popecenter.org/commentaries/article.html?id=2726

[5] Cowden, D., et al. 2012. A C-based introductory course using robots. In *Proceedings of the 43rd ACM technical symposium on Computer Science Education* (Raleigh, NC, USA, February 29–March 3, 2012). SIGCSE '12. ACM, New York, NY, USA, 27-32.

[6] Davies, H. 2007. Place as media in pervasive games. Proceedings of the 4th Australasian conference on Interactive entertainment (2007), 1–4.

[7] Deci, E. L. and Ryan, R. 2002. *The handbook of self-determination research.* University of Rochester Press, Rochester, NY.

[8] Deterding, S. 2011. Gamification by Design: Response to O'Reilly. *Gamification Research Network*. Retrieved September 5, 2012 from http://gamification-research.org/2011/09/gamification-by-design-response-to-oreilly/

[9] Deterding, S. 2012. Gamification: designing for motivation. interactions. 19, 4 (Jul. 2012), 14–17.

[10] Deterding, S. et al. 2011. Gamification. using game-design elements in non-gaming contexts. In *Proceedings of the 2011 annual conference extended abstracts on Human factors in computing systems* (2011), 2425–2428.

[11] D'Souza, D. et al. 2008. Transforming learning of programming: a mentoring project. In *Proceedings of Tenth Australasian Computing Education Conference* (Wollongong, Australia, January 2008). ACE2008. 75-84.

[12] Greenberg, I., Kumar, D. and Xu, D. 2012. Creative coding and visual portfolios for CS1. In *Proceedings of the 43rd ACM Technical Symposium on Computer Science Education* (Raleigh, NC, USA, February 29–March 3, 2012). SIGCSE '12. ACM. New York, NY, 247-252.

[13] Guzdial, M. et al. 2010. Variations on a theme: role of media in motivating computing education. *Proceedings of the 41st ACM Technical Symposium on Computer Science Education* (Milwaukee, WI, USA, March 10-13, 2010). SIGCSE '10. ACM. New York, NY, 66-67.

[14] Lawley, E. 2012. Ch-ch-ch-ch-changes: Revising the JPP User Experience. Retrieved September 6, 2012 from http://games.rit.edu/~thinkplay/2012/07/ch-ch-ch-ch-changes-revising-the-jpp-user-experience/

[15] Martin, F. 2012. Will massive open online courses change how we teach?. *Commun. ACM* 55, 8 (August 2012), 26-28.

[16] McDowell, C. et al. 2006. Pair programming improves student retention, confidence, and program quality. *Commun. ACM* 49, 8 (August 2006), 90-95.

[17] McGonigal, J. 2011. *Reality Is Broken: Why Games Make Us Better and How They Can Change the World.* Penguin Press.

[18] Miller, A. and Kay, J. A mentor program in CS1. In *Proceedings of ITiCSE 2002* (Aarhus, Denmark, June 24-26, 2002). ITiCSE '02. ACM. New York, NY, 9-13.

[19] Montola, M. et al. 2009. Pervasive games: Theory and design. Morgan Kaufmann.

[20] Nagappan, N. et al. 2003. Improving the CS1 experience with pair programming. In *Proceedings of the 34th ACM Technical Symposium on Computer Science Education* (Reno, Nevada, USA, February 19-23, 2003). SIGCSE '03. ACM. New York, NY, 359-362.

[21] Reges, S. 2006. Back to basics in CS1 and CS2. In *Proceedings of the 37th ACM Technical Symposium on Computer Science Education* (Houston, Texas, USA, March 1–5, 2006). SIGCSE '06. ACM. New York, NY, 293-297.

[22] Topping, K.J. 1996. The effectiveness of peer tutoring in further and higher education: A typology and review of the literature. Higher education. 32, 3 (1996), 321–345.

A Student Perspective on Prior Experience in CS1

Anya Tafliovich
Department of Computer and Mathematical Sciences
University of Toronto Scarborough
atafliovich@utsc.toronto.edu

Jennifer Campbell
Department of Computer Science
University of Toronto
campbell@cs.toronto.edu

Andrew Petersen
Department of Mathematical and Computational Sciences
University of Toronto Mississauga
andrew.petersen@utoronto.ca

ABSTRACT

This work explores the effects of prior exposure to programming on student experiences in an introductory computer programming course (CS1). We take a student-focused approach: using a combination of surveys and semi-structured interviews, we obtain information on the student experiences in CS1 and their relationship to prior programming experience (PE). The analysis of the results provides insight into the following two questions: a) How does PE affect peer interaction: pair programming sessions, assignment partnerships, and online and in-class interactions? b) What are the students' beliefs on the relationship between PE and success in the course?

Categories and Subject Descriptors

K.3.2 [**Computers and Education**]: Computer and Information Science Education—*Computer Science Education*

General Terms

Human Factors

Keywords

novice programming, previous experience, CS1

1. INTRODUCTION

The wide range of prior programming experience that introductory programming (CS1) students bring to the course can present a significant challenge to instructors. In our experience, many CS1 students have never been introduced to programming before starting the course, while others have taken one or two programming courses in high school or have taught themselves one or more programming languages. Still others have work experience involving programming.

This work explores how students perceive and are affected by the wide range of previous experience (PE) that their peers have. Using a combination of surveys and semi-structured interviews with 24 students (see Section 3), we collected information about the student experience in CS1, focusing on their impressions affected by their own or their peer's prior programming experience. Then, we examined the data for perspectives to the following two questions:

- How does PE (or lack of PE) affect peer interaction including pair programming sessions, assignment partnerships, and online and in-class interactions?
- What are the students' beliefs on the relationship between PE and success in the course?

The remainder of this paper presents student perspectives on these questions. Section 2 introduces related studies and work on beliefs about success and pair programming. Section 3 describes the course and the research methodology. Section 4 reports on the results of the study. Section 5 draws conclusions, makes suggestions on improving student experiences in CS1, and suggests directions of future research.

2. RELATED WORK

2.1 Prior Programming Experience

Over the past decade, computer science education researchers have examined whether having PE helps students succeed in CS1. Several recent studies investigate whether PE is a predictor of success in the first programming course, and results vary based on the type of course offered.

In a study by Hagan and Markham [5], students with PE performed significantly better than those with no experience in a Java-based introductory CS course, and the difference in performance was systematically related to the number of programming languages previously used. Wilson and Shrock [28] investigate twelve factors as possible predictors of success in CS1. Marks at the midterm are used as a measure of success. When PE includes both a previous programming course and self-initiated programming, PE is not a significant predictor of success. However, having taken a previous programming course by itself is a significant predictor.

In contrast, Ventura and Ramamurthy [25, 24] describe a design-centred, graphical, object-first CS1 taught in Java, in which elements of program design and object orientation supersede more traditional for CS1 concepts such as iteration or recursion. They find that in this course PE is not a predictor of success. Bennedsen and Caspersen [2] follow up with similar research focused on their model-driven CS1.

To ensure that students obtain consistent programming skills from the intro sequence, Holden and Weeden [8, 9] propose a sequence designed to stream students based on the level of their PE. They find that in the first course of

SIGCSE'13, March 6–9, 2013, Denver, Colorado, USA.

the sequence, PE is a strong predictor of success. However, in the last course, it is no longer the case. They conclude that the difficulty in learning to program is in mastering the basic concepts such as sequence, iteration, and decision. Once these are learnt, the students with no PE perform at the same level as the experienced students.

Rauchas et al. [18] used Scheme as the language of CS1 to level the playing field with respect to the varying levels of students PE. They report success in their Fundamental Algorithmic Concepts module. However, in the Basic Computer Organization module, the students with PE still outperform their less experienced peers.

2.2 Predictors of Success in CS1

A number of studies attempt to identify student characteristics that (fail to) predict success in CS1. Most studies take a quantitative approach, but several recent studies solicited perspectives from students [7] or faculty [11].

Several large studies considered multiple factors. Bergin and Reilly [3] looked at 15 factors as possible predictors of success in CS1. They found that students' perception of their understanding, comfort level, pre-university maths score, and gender were the best predictors of success. Byrne and Lyons [4] investigate a number of factors including PE, gender, and learning styles. Barker et al. [1] conclude that student-student interaction is the best predictor of intention to persist in CS major. Other factors include pace, workload, PE, and gender.

Several researchers considered prior exposure to mathematical ideas or computers. Ramalingam et al. [17] show that self-efficacy for programming is influenced by PE, and that both self-efficacy and the student's mental model of programming affect course performance. Pillay and Jugoo [15] focus on identifying those student characteristics that affect procedural programming performance. They find that problem solving ability (measured by success in math-related courses) positively correlates with programming performance, while gender and prior exposure to computers do not.

Other researchers focused on attitude. Rountree et al. [19, 20] find that the best predictor of success is the student's expectation to receive an A in the course. Simon et al. [22] report on a multi-institutional, multi-national study that investigates correlations between a number of cognitive, behavioural, and attitudinal factors and success in introductory programming.

2.3 Pair Programming

We include a review of related work on PP since a number of our findings relate to student experiences with PP. More of the relevant literature on PP can be found in Preston [16] and Salleh at al. [21].

A number of studies report on the effectiveness of PP as a pedagogical tool in CS1. Williams et al. [26, 27] summarize their experiences with PP and suggest guidelines for successfully implementing the PP model. Nagappan et al. [14] report that students who worked in the PP model performed better and were more likely to complete the class with a grade of C or better. McDowell at al. [13] found that in addition to better performance, pair programmers are more likely to pursue computer science related majors. Moreover, students who learned through PP in CS1 do better in subsequent courses, even if they are required to work solo in those courses.

Other studies report on student experiences with PP. Hanks et al. [6, 23] reports on student attitudes towards PP and links to confidence. Katira et al. [10] studied the compatibilities of students in the PP model at different levels of their university careers.

3. BACKGROUND

3.1 Environment

The study was performed in a first year programming sequence at a North American, research-intensive public university. The sequence is composed of two courses: an introduction to programming and a broader introduction to computer science that introduces design and abstract data types. The course sequence is taught on several campuses by separate teams of instructors, and the study was run on two of the campuses.

The study focused on experience in the first-term programming course which uses Python as the language in an objects-late structure. The course met three times per week for a 1-hour lecture as well as one additional time for a 2-hour lab. Lectures normally featured live coding, and the labs featured exercises to be completed using a pair-programming model. In the first lab, students were introduced to the pair-programming model and its objectives; they were reminded of the driver and navigator roles at the beginning of all subsequent labs.

Students spend most of the term on variable assignment, conditionals, counted and conditional loops, functions, and the built-in Python datatypes. They are also introduced to the concepts of testing (and test-driven design), modular design, algorithms (searching and sorting), complexity, and classes. Students were expected to complete weekly programming exercises, three programming assignments, two midterms, and a final exam.

The investigators visited the course lectures in the second week of the term to obtain informed consent from the students in the course. An email follow-up was sent to students who did not attend lecture, but uptake was minimal from the email. The enrolment in the larger campus at that time was 659 students, of whom 212 provided consent (32% uptake). The enrolment in the smaller campus was 265, of whom 99 provided consent (37% uptake).

Of the 311 students across both campuses who provided consent, 162 were definitely planning on completing a program in CS (52%), and an additional 70 were considering that path (23%). Since many programs (statistics, cognitive science, etc.) require CS1, many of the remaining students were likely fulfilling a program requirement.

3.2 Methodology

The study contained three data components:

- A demographic survey provided at the same time that informed consent was obtained augmented by end-of-term marks for the first-term course.
- A 30-minute interview at the end of the first term in which students were asked to describe their experience in the course and, in particular, their impressions about previous programming experience.
- A 30-minute interview at the end of the second term in which students who completed a first-term interview were asked similar questions to determine if their responses changed after a second term of CS.

All students who consented to participate in the study, including those who chose not to complete the course, were sent an email at the end of the term that invited them to participate in an interview. Interviews were scheduled after the end of the term to avoid any appearance that responses were linked to marks. A total of 311 interview requests were sent with 24 students actually attending a first interview (7.8% uptake). 9 of the interviews were from the smaller campus. Across the two campuses, no students who chose not to complete the course participated in an interview.

The interviewers followed a script that consisted of a series of icebreaker questions, a grand-tour question designed to get the student's overall impression of the course, and then a series of questions about interactions with other members of the course community. The interviews were recorded by the interviewer and then notes were transcribed from the audio recording. Identifying information was removed from the transcript before it was shared with the other investigators.

After the second term, all students who completed a first round interview were invited to complete a second interview. Some students declined because they had not enrolled in the second term, and a total of 5 interviews were completed (20% uptake). As before, the instructors followed an interview guide, and an anonymized transcript was produced based on an audio recording of the interview.

After all interviews were completed, the investigators coded the interviews using a grounded theory approach [12]. All three investigators independently coded the same subset of interviews and then met to discuss their codes and identify overlaps. After two rounds of discussions on different sets of interviews, the codes were deemed to have converged, and each interview was coded by two separate investigators. The third investigator was reserved in case it became necessary for a third party to review text that had been analyzed differently by the two coders. Once all of the text was coded, all text linked to a specific code was gathered and analyzed.

4. RESULTS

4.1 Quantitative Results

We surveyed the students about their PE at the time they provided consent. We also collected final marks for consenting students, in order to determine if there is a quantitative difference in performance between the groups of students who self-identified as having and not having experience.

Of the 311 students who consented to participate, only 26 claimed previous Python experience (8.4%) but 155 claimed PE of some sort (49.8%). About half of the students who identified PE (46%, or 23% of the total class) claimed experience with more than one language. Java was the most prevalent, with 92 students claiming PE. Students also claimed Visual Basic (39), C/C++ (20), Turing (19), HTML (13), Pascal (9), Flash (5), and various other languages.

At the end of the term, 265 students completed the final exam (85%), and 239 passed the course (77% of the original consenting students). However, only 23 students with PE failed or did not complete the course (15% of students with PE), while 49 students without PE failed or did not complete (31% of students without PE). The marks of students with PE were also higher by half a letter grade (76.8 vs. 70.8). The two sample populations have similar negatively-skewed distributions, and using a Wilcoxon rank-sum test indicates that the median for students with no experience is less than the median for students with experience ($W = 9169.5$, p-value $= 0.0006$).

Unfortunately, these results also indicate that our student sample is skewed toward more successful students. The completion rate of the students who consented is higher than the general course population. Identifying and recruiting students who choose not to complete the course is ongoing work, and this work profiles the experience of those students who successfully complete the course.

4.2 Student Partners

Comments on pair programming and assignment partners were among the most ubiquitous. Students commented on the process of choosing a partner or deciding to work independently, interaction with the partner, the outcomes, and the level of satisfaction with the partnership.

The majority of the students interviewed thought that, overall, having a partner was helpful. For example:

1161 We worked well together because we understood each other. He knew what I had trouble with, and I knew what I could do better than him. We could help each other. We brought each other up.

Students commonly mentioned the usefulness of getting another opinion, having someone to bounce ideas off, and simply having someone to talk to.

1161 When you are working with a partner, you can see things that he ... may or may not see. ... It is almost as though you are putting together pieces of a puzzle.

184 It's just more fun and more productive to work with someone.

In analyzing the students' comments, we have categorized them as they address the following three questions. What are the ingredients of a successful partnership? When is a partnership unsatisfying? Why do some students choose to work solo? We have found that prior experience of the partners is an important factor in each of these categories.

4.2.1 A Successful Partnership — Similar PE

Virtually universally students reported that in a successful partnership the two partners have similar levels of PE, show comparable aptitude, and are able to make equal contributions to the shared task. Students commonly referred to being "at the same level" as a recipe for a fruitful partnership.

1200 There were two people I tried to work with...We had the same level of understanding, so we could work through the exercises together. No rushing ahead or feeling slowed down.

246 On the third assignment, I just picked a partner who had relatively the same skills that I do. We kind of shared the work and had lots of debates and stuff, like you know people have, and, well, it turned out good.

One student commented that although she and her partner had differing levels of PE, the outcome was positive, since they contributed different but equally valuable skills to the project.

262 We kind of complemented each other, because I could get the steps and then she would know how to put it onto the computer.

Only two students reported taking advantage of the fact that the partner had more PE. Note that in the latter case, the gap in PE is minimal and the student comments on the value of both partners learning.

1195 But he had prior experience doing GUIs in Java, so this helped a lot for the enhancements. Otherwise, wouldn't know where to start with the GUIs.

23 He knew a little bit more than me and he helped me out, but throughout the process it was a new assignment for both of us, so we were both learning.

4.2.2 A Failed Partnership — Gap in PE

The single most common cause of a failed partnership was the gap in the partners' levels of PE. The students with less PE felt they were not contributing to the partnership, which left them feeling unsatisfied with their work. They also reported they were not learning as much in these situations.

184 In ... the first few labs, my partners knew a lot more than I did, and I didn't want to slow them down ... so I didn't learn anything.
146 sometimes, it went really badly. ... Sometimes your partner understands the lab better and they just take over. They won't let you do anything... My TA didn't spend much time with us because my partner could do the work.

Interestingly, the belief that a student with less PE is disadvantaged in the partnership was shared by the more experienced students. A common sentiment is that the less experienced student does not adequately learn the material when working with a more experienced partner.

244 I felt that it is not good for the partner. Because we have some tests on the assignment, and if they don't do it then they won't be able to get good marks.
279 But when I was the one who knew more, I felt like I was hurting my partner. They needed to do it to get it, but I already knew how to do it.

In 3 cases the less experienced partner ended up learning nothing or very little as a result of an unequal partnership, with grave consequences for the student.

1200 [Having taken CS1 before] doesn't mean anything. It didn't help. I had a partner in the labs and for the assignments, and I wasn't getting it, but they could do it. ... Yeah, some stuff I remember seeing ... setting a value equal or, like, lists, but I didn't remember anything about them.
1221 I cruised with this one guy...about half of the labs... He had done some Java before, so he knew what to do. He did most of the labs, and I watched... I [hurt] myself for the tests...I didn't know what I didn't know until I started the test.

The dissatisfaction with an unequal partnership is mutual. Several students with PE felt they were not benefiting from a partnership with a less experienced student. They felt the partner was holding them back.

1195 For the first lab ... my partner didn't know what he was doing... I didn't get anywhere because I was always having to explain basic stuff.
1200 Once, my partner had no clue. He had no idea what I was doing, and I had to stop a lot. ... he slowed me down.

Finally, having a partner who does not contribute her fair share was another reported cause of a failed partnership. Interestingly, in each of these four cases, the complaining partner had PE.

16 Partners never helped. ... No, I never worked in a real 'driver-navigator' pair. I'd drive and my partner could catch typos. Partners couldn't help develop a solution or a plan.
296 I tried to work with a partner, but more or less they either didn't do anything or they just watched me. Or they just looked at the screen.

4.2.3 Choosing to Program Solo

Why do some students choose to program solo? It seems the answer depends largely on their level of PE. Several less experienced students reported having less confidence in their abilities after working with a more experienced partner. The students with little or no PE choose to program solo since they believe that independent work ensures better learning of the material.

23 The last assignment was on your own, which was good because you are not really depending on anyone else, so you know that you can do the stuff yourself.
239 I just want to do the things by myself so that I will have the confidence and then I will feel more comfortable.

Experienced students, on the other hand, choose to work independently since they are very comfortable with the material and feel no need for having a partner.

1195 The few people who did have experience ... didn't have partners often because really we could just work on things and if there was a problem we would just talk to each other.
16 many students are still having trouble. They had trouble in [CS1] and don't know what they're doing yet. I don't want to do most of the work if I am going to work with a partner.

4.2.4 Other Forms of Peer Interaction

Even when students did not work in groups, they did not work in isolation. Students often use interactions with others to measure progress. **1161** used conversation with people in lectures and from his first-year learning community (FLC) group. **183** also used his FLC as a peer group. **146** found peers at the help centre:

I didn't pay attention to other people in labs or class, but the help centre was useful. I saw people there who were at my level ... or who were doing worse than me.

and **279** used lecture:

You sort of ... get where everyone is by what they ask about in lecture. ... you never really see them anywhere else.

23 used the discussion board to get multiple perspectives and to find people in similar situations:

At first it was primarily [the professor] answering; I guess people were shy. But towards the end everyone started to contribute and help out each other. Just getting different opinions on different things was very helpful, especially since they were getting lost and confused on some of the same things you are.

One experienced student used answering questions online as a form of studying for tests and exams:

244 It's actually a good source to study, because then I get the hardest questions. ... that's how I studied.

Some students became quite dedicated to the community and appeared to get involved for reasons other than self-evaluation or support:

1195 Sometimes I answered questions. ... I enjoy helping others online.

4.3 Prior Experience and Success in CS1

Many students form beliefs about what helps them or others succeed in CS1. PE is one of the most reported factors of success; not only as it relates to programming, but also to awareness and application of various other factors of success.

4.3.1 Experience Helps

Most of the students with PE and a minority of those without felt that PE was a factor of success (it made things easier for those who had PE or more challenging for those who did not).

296 I think that it was a very powerful advantage.
182 He was really excited about programming, but he just didn't know what he needed to do. [This student without experience] was at a major disadvantage.
239 Those who didn't learn it before would find it much harder. Compared with them I would feel confident.

4.3.2 *Effort and Time — Experience Shows*

Several students mentioned that putting in effort or time contributes to success. We assume the main advantage of PE to be programming skills, but students reported that another advantage is knowing how much effort and time is required.

> **239** Before CSC programming, you will never know how much time it will take you. So what you can do is just work and work and work until the time when you get through it.
> **296** They were more disabled, because computer science is a very time-consuming process and also very trial and error based learning. Most people don't know those two secrets until, like, the assignments, which I feel that without proper time management at the start coming into university, most people would definitely fail computer science in first year, almost guaranteed.

Underestimating the amount of time or effort that an assignment will take to complete can lead to negative outcomes. Looking back at the course, students reported turning points that prompted them to increase the amount of effort or time spent on the course.

> **146** Getting a bad mark on T1 actually helped. It woke me up. I knew I had to focus, and I spent more time on [CS1].
> **23** [A1] was a wake-up call. When we were first assigned it, we were assigned it with a good enough amount of time, but I didn't assume it would be as difficult as it actually was. We ended up pulling a lot of late nights to work on it towards the due date.

4.3.3 *Experience and Confidence*

Students also suggest that having confidence in one's abilities is a key to success. Students reported that PE contributes to confidence.

> **239** If you have learned some computer language before and then you have that thinking way and then you learn that other language, then you will find it more comfortable and [will be] more confident.
> **246** They just knew the stuff. They have more confidence in what they are doing and it is based on their experience.
> **259** It helped me, in terms of at the beginning it gave me the confidence.

4.3.4 *Succeeding with No Prior Experience*

Several students mentioned that putting in effort or time contributes to success. There seemed to be common sentiment that putting in effort could help those with or without PE succeed and that with effort it was possible to overcome the disadvantage of having no PE.

> **118** I don't ... no, you can succeed without experience. The course already has what you need ... if you do your work. That's a big if.

Independent work was identified by some students as a key to learning the material and some students correlate successful independent work with gaining confidence.

> **246** You have to just work on it and you have to just try to do the stuff on your own.
> **246** Closer to the end of the course, they [people without PE] might be able to write something a little bit on their own and they might feel a little bit more confident in themselves.

4.3.5 *Others with Experience*

In Section 4.2.4, we discussed how students often use the community around them to self-evaluate while other students become involved in helpful ways. In some cases, they are well appreciated by their peers.

> **1161** there's one guy who always posts on it. He's on point with everything, and it is very helpful. Really want to meet him! There's a small group of people who are always on point. With every year there's going to be that group of people, and they really know what they are doing, and it is really good.
> **1195** There's this one guy on Piazza who always answers questions in like 10 minutes, he's like a prof in this way.

But that means that the discussion board can be a significant source of stress, as students often identified others on the board who they asserted must have had PE.

> **1195** A lot of people have past programming experience, and you can see it on Piazza posts.
> **1200** You could tell that some people were ahead. ... from the discussion board. They would talk about finishing the assignment, and it would be a day after it was posted. ... I didn't see those people in lecture.

1161 notes that seeing students with PE on the forums lead to self-doubt.

> Coming into [university], I checked the forums, and there were people there who had like websites and applications and had tons of experience. And I felt smaller than I should have had. Whenever I was stressed out, I would think about that, and I set a bunch of limitations for myself.

1161 believes that some behaviour on the discussion board is posturing.

> A lot of people, when they are behind the screen, they have the same fear. So they try to make themselves look bigger. And this makes the rest of us feel intimidating.

Some students are intimidated by these experts even before the course starts.

> **115** I'd been told that everyone else would know how to program from high school, so I found some tutorials online and tried to figure some of it out ... before school started.

5. CONCLUSIONS

Computer science educators agree that pair programming and, more generally, programming with a partner are beneficial for CS1 students. Many of the students interviewed report having a positive experience with PP, but partnerships have a significant risk of failure. In particular, when partners are at different skill levels, students feel that the less skilled partner is unable to adequately contribute to the common task. Students who experienced the role of "less skilled partner" felt unsatisfied with their role and reported that they learned less in the process. Meanwhile, the more skilled partners may experience frustration at being held back. Students also report feeling more confident about their abilities when programming solo.

While students may have different skill levels for various reasons, at the beginning of the course the largest contributing factor is PE. We suggest that CS1 students are advised to form partnerships in which the parties have comparable levels of PE. If PP is used in a lab setting, we suggest that lab TAs receive additional training in identifying potential sources of failed partnerships that stem from gaps in students' PE. We also reiterate that the students be actively educated about the value of PP and the risks associated with misusing the PP model.

In addition, PE affects students' perceptions of self and of their peers. We observe that students, both with and without PE, tend to attribute their successes to time and effort and attribute the success of more skilled classmates to PE. In particular, the students interviewed identified a small group of "experts" among their classmates. The "experts" are students who became very visible early in the course through comments in lecture, success in the lab, or posts on the discussion board. Students identified these "experts" as having PE, and they also identified this group as a source of help (especially online help). We are unable to determine if the "experts" did have PE, but the instructor of one of the courses notes that several of the most active and helpful posters on the discussion board did *not* have PE.

While some students found the "experts" helpful, they also indicated that the existence of this group contributed to stress, low self-confidence, and feelings of intimidation. However, the students seem to be unwilling to admit to being intimidated by the "experts" until after the end of CS2 (the second round of our interviews). This may be related to the population, as we were unable to interview students who chose not to complete the course. We speculate that these students may also have been intimidated; investigating the effects of PE on a student's decision to withdraw from CS1 is the subject of ongoing work.

Finally, many students spoke about a "gap" between students with and without PE. Many students indicated that the gap narrowed over the course of CS1, but other students commented that the gap remained significant. Students who had PE indicated that they continued to learn independently, thus maintaining the gap. We also identified students whose PE is extensive enough to contribute to a large gap even in CS2. This situation is an argument for more careful "streaming" of students into appropriate courses.

6. SUMMARY

This work presents a student perspective on the impact of previous programming experience in CS1 courses. We interviewed 24 students who completed CS1 and found that prior exposure to programming affects many aspects of student experience in CS1. We normally think of the ability to code as the main benefit of having PE, but student interviews suggest that the impact of PE is more complex: it affects students' expectations, work habits, attitude and confidence, and perceptions of self and peers. Of particular note, a gap in the level of students' PE can negatively impact peer interactions including pair programming sessions, assignment partnerships, and online and in-class interactions.

7. REFERENCES

[1] L. J. Barker, C. McDowell, and K. Kalahar. Exploring factors that influence computer science introductory course students to persist in the major. *SIGCSE Bull.*, 41(1):153–157, 2009.

[2] J. Bennedsen and M. E. Caspersen. An investigation of potential success factors for an introductory model-driven programming course. In *Proceedings of the 1st international workshop on computing education research*, pages 155–163, New York, NY, USA, 2005. ACM.

[3] S. Bergin and R. Reilly. Programming: factors that influence success. *SIGCSE Bull.*, 37:411–415, 2005.

[4] P. Byrne and G. Lyons. The effect of student attributes on success in programming. *SIGCSE Bull.*, 33(3):49–52, 2001.

[5] D. Hagan and S. Markham. Does it help to have some programming experience before beginning a computing degree program? *SIGCSE Bull.*, 32:25–28, 2000.

[6] B. Hanks. Student attitudes toward pair programming. *SIGCSE Bull.*, 38(3):113–117, 2006.

[7] B. Hanks, L. Murphy, B. Simon, R. McCauley, and C. Zander. CS1 students speak: advice for students by students. *SIGCSE Bull.*, 41(1):19–23, 2009.

[8] E. Holden and E. Weeden. The impact of prior experience in an information technology programming course sequence. In *Proceedings of the 4th conference on Information technology curriculum*, pages 41–46, New York, NY, USA, 2003. ACM.

[9] E. Holden and E. Weeden. The experience factor in early programming education. In *Proceedings of the 5th conference on Information technology education*, pages 211–218, New York, NY, USA, 2004. ACM.

[10] N. Katira, L. Williams, E. Wiebe, C. Miller, S. Balik, and E. Gehringer. On understanding compatibility of student pair programmers. *SIGCSE Bull.*, 36(1):7–11, 2004.

[11] P. Kinnunen, R. McCartney, L. Murphy, and L. Thomas. Through the eyes of instructors: a phenomenographic investigation of student success. In *Proceedings of the third international workshop on Computing education research*, pages 61–72, New York, NY, USA, 2007. ACM.

[12] P. Y. Martin and B. A. Turner. Grounded theory and organizational research. *The Journal of Applied Behavioral Science*, 22(2):141–157, 1986.

[13] C. McDowell, L. Werner, H. E. Bullock, and J. Fernald. Pair programming improves student retention, confidence, and program quality. *Commun. ACM*, 49(8):90–95, 2006.

[14] N. Nagappan, L. Williams, M. Ferzli, E. Wiebe, K. Yang, C. Miller, and S. Balik. Improving the CS1 experience with pair programming. *SIGCSE Bull.*, 35(1):359–362, 2003.

[15] N. Pillay and V. R. Jugoo. An investigation into student characteristics affecting novice programming performance. *SIGCSE Bull.*, 37(4):107–110, 2005.

[16] D. Preston. Pair programming as a model of collaborative learning: a review of the research. *J. Comput. Sci. Coll.*, 20(4):39–45, 2005.

[17] V. Ramalingam, D. LaBelle, and S. Wiedenbeck. Self-efficacy and mental models in learning to program. *SIGCSE Bull.*, 36(3):171–175, 2004.

[18] S. Rauchas, I. Sanders, and B. Kumwenda. The effect of prior programming experience in a Scheme-based breadth-first curriculum at wits. *SIGCSE Bull.*, 38:326–326, 2006.

[19] N. Rountree, J. Rountree, and A. Robins. Predictors of success and failure in a CS1 course. *SIGCSE Bull.*, 34(4):121–124, 2002.

[20] N. Rountree, J. Rountree, A. Robins, and R. Hannah. Interacting factors that predict success and failure in a CS1 course. *SIGCSE Bull.*, 36(4):101–104, 2004.

[21] N. Salleh, E. Mendes, and J. C. Grundy. Empirical studies of pair programming for CS/SE teaching in higher education: A systematic literature review. *IEEE Transactions on Software Engineering*, 37:509–525, 2011.

[22] Simon, S. Fincher, A. Robins, B. Baker, I. Box, Q. Cutts, M. de Raadt, P. Haden, J. Hamer, M. Hamilton, R. Lister, M. Petre, K. Sutton, D. Tolhurst, and J. Tutty. Predictors of success in a first programming course. In *Proceedings of the 8th Australasian Conference on Computing Education*, pages 189–196, Darlinghurst, Australia, 2006.

[23] B. Simon and B. Hanks. First-year students' impressions of pair programming in CS1. *J. Educ. Resour. Comput.*, 7(4):5:1–5:28, 2008.

[24] P. Ventura. *On the origins of programmers: identifying predictors of success for an objects first CS1.* PhD thesis, State University of New York at Buffalo, NY, USA, 2004.

[25] P. Ventura and B. Ramamurthy. Wanted: CS1 students. No experience required. *SIGCSE Bull.*, 36(1):240–244, 2004.

[26] L. Williams. Lessons learned from seven years of pair programming at North Carolina State University. *SIGCSE Bull.*, 39(4):79–83, 2007.

[27] L. Williams, D. S. McCrickard, L. Layman, and K. Hussein. Eleven guidelines for implementing pair programming in the classroom. In *Proceedings of the Agile 2008*, pages 445–452, Washington, DC, USA, 2008. IEEE Computer Society.

[28] B. C. Wilson and S. Shrock. Contributing to success in an introductory computer science course: a study of twelve factors. *SIGCSE Bull.*, 33:184–188, 2001.

The Role of Teachers in Implementing Curriculum Changes

David Thompson
Department of Computer Science and Software Engineering
University of Canterbury
Christchurch, New Zealand
dr.curiosity@gmail.com

Tim Bell
Department of Computer Science and Software Engineering
University of Canterbury
Christchurch, New Zealand
tim.bell@canterbury.ac.nz

Peter Andreae
School of Engineering and Computer Science
Victoria University of Wellington
Wellington, New Zealand
peter.andreae@ecs.vuw.ac.nz

Anthony Robins
Computer Science Department
University of Otago
Dunedin, New Zealand
anthony@cs.otago.ac.nz

ABSTRACT

In 2011 New Zealand introduced computer science into high schools after a long period when computing was mainly focussed on training students to be users. The transition was rapid, and teachers had little time to upskill to prepare for the new topics, and yet there was widespread voluntary adoption of the new standards. The role of teachers and the national teachers' organisation in making the change has been pivotal, and this paper reviews the changes from the teachers' perspective. This story is intended to inform those planning similar changes in other countries, and provide a context for the next steps in NZ. The discussion centres around a survey of 91 teachers, which reveals strong intrinsic motivation from teachers to make the changes, a mixture of prior knowledge and skills that teachers shared with each other through peer support and online communication, a low level of confidence as teachers of computer science, and a need for further professional development.

Categories and Subject Descriptors

K.3.2 [**Computer and Information Science Education**]: Computer Science education

Keywords

teacher professional development, curriculum implementation

SIGCSE'13, March 6–9, 2013, Denver, Colorado, USA.

1. INTRODUCTION

Considerable work has been done around the world to introduce Computer Science (CS) and Computational Thinking (CT) concepts into formal school curricula, and some countries and states have initiated significant changes. For example, in early 2012 the Royal Society in the UK released a report that advocated sweeping changes to the ICT curriculum [11] that received support from the government; in New Zealand (NZ) new computer science standards were introduced in the final three years of high school in 2011 [3, 4]; in Germany new compulsory standards have been introduced in some regions since 2008 [7]; and in the US, the "CS10K" project aims to have 10,000 CS teachers in 10,000 high schools by 2015 [1].

Implementing such changes to school systems has required major structural changes to curricula and standards, but the key element in the success of the changes is having well-trained and confident teachers to deliver the new curriculum, and growing the numbers of such teachers has been of widespread interest [1, 8, 11, 12]. New teachers need to have subject knowledge *and* pedagogical knowledge to deliver the topics effectively. The history of computing in schools has often seen the subject evolve from areas such as commerce or using applications, where teachers have less technical knowledge and therefore need considerable upskilling to be able to teach CS topics as diverse as programming, algorithms, data representation, security, HCI and so on.

The ability to teach also depends on the teacher's self-perception. Ni and Guzdial [15] observe that teachers' perception of their professional identity can be a significant issue, and that in addition to appropriate training they need to be part of a community of CS teachers who can support each other and build a strong sense of identity.

To understand this better, we investigate the role that teachers have played in implementing the significant changes in the New Zealand computer science curriculum that was phased in from 2011. In this case almost no formal training was available, and furthermore, the changes were made quickly so teachers have had to upskill at short notice in a resource-constrained environment, which could lead to issues of teachers feeling out of their depth or unsupported. This ad-hoc and under-resourced approach raises doubts about whether the introduction can succeed, as the importance of dedicated computer science teacher training is well established [16].

Despite these issues, a strong teacher community emerged in NZ, and with some support from universities, industry and government, ad-hoc professional development became available which enabled teachers to essentially bootstrap the teaching of the new topics. Consequently a new CS curriculum was delivered in NZ in 2011 with positive student engagement and some good learning outcomes [5]. It is important to investigate such changes from a teacher's point of view, since they have borne the brunt of the changes, and are still developing confidence teaching the new material.

In this paper we begin by looking at the role of teachers in implementing the introduction of computer science to high schools, and then report on a survey of teachers conducted in early 2012 in which teachers were able to reflect on the introduction of computer science in 2011.

2. IMPLEMENTING A NEW CURRICULUM

Computer science as a school subject was introduced to NZ high schools to be taught at the start of the school year in February 2011 as part of a range of new standards covering five strands within the "Digital Technologies" area. The standards are specifications of assessment requirements and effectively define curriculum content. The process of introducing the curriculum has been documented elsewhere [3, 4], but some key points to note are that computing in schools had a low status prior to the 2011 changes [9], the introduction was extremely fast (two years from conception to implementation), there was very little formal training for teachers, and yet there was remarkably widespread adoption of the new topics [4].

During the period that the new standards were introduced, the formal training offered to teachers mainly comprised a 3-day national symposium in November 2010 on the range of computing topics in schools (not all teachers could attend), regional workshops, and training on technology teaching in general. The recently formed NZ Association of Computing Digital and Information Technology Teachers (NZACDITT) organised local workshops and set up a national mailing list which was very active (over a thousand *topics* were discussed on the list in the year leading up to the standards going live). The association also developed a website for sharing resources (nzacditt.org.nz). A collaboration between the Ministry of Education and all Computer Science departments in NZ created a project to develop resources for this site, and to date some 7,000 links have been created that identify relevant (mainly free) resources for teaching the standards [14]. At the end of 2011 two duplicate two-day "CS4HS" (computer science for high schools) workshops were run, sponsored by Google Inc., and these were attended by about 90 teachers. Although the workshops are based on the model originated in the US [6], they were primarily focussed on upskilling teachers for the new standards.

The survey reported here was conducted after the first year of teaching the Level 1 standards (Level 1 corresponds to the third to last year of high school), and also after the CS4HS workshops, where teachers had been able to reflect on the year and prepare for the new Level 2 standards that were to be introduced in 2012.

Given the rapid introduction of the subject in NZ, the main source of qualified teachers has had to be existing teachers, most of whom had to upskill. There are other approaches to "growing" CS teachers, including retraining unemployed IT workers [13], coaching teachers as they introduce CS in their classes [8, 12], having academics partner with teachers to teach the topic initially [2, 10], and providing specific CS teaching training programs [16] including summer programs [8]. While there has been some progress in NZ on these approaches, the first year was primarily a grassroots approach to training, and the following survey reflects on how this worked from the teachers' point of view.

3. METHODOLOGY

New Zealand digital technology teachers were surveyed between 24 January and 7 February 2012. Respondents were recruited through emails sent to the NZACDITT mailing list, which currently has 404 members. Because the group was formed to support teachers through the changes, this will have covered most teachers with an interest in the new standards (the description of the group is that it was "formed to strengthen, encourage and improve the teaching of a broad range of Computing, Digital and Information Technologies in NZ secondary schools"). As an incentive, the first 25 respondents were offered a $20 voucher, with a draw for one of 10 vouchers for the remaining respondents.

91 teachers from 71 schools responded to the survey (to put this in perspective, this is about 23% of the NZACDITT mailing list, and there are about 490 high schools in NZ). Of the respondents, 75 had used or intended to use the new Programming and/or CS standards. The remaining 16 would be involved in the other areas of digital technologies: information systems, infrastructure, digital media and electronics.

A range of schools was represented, with 82% of the respondents from public (state) schools, 12% from "integrated" schools (combined private and public funding), 4% from private schools, and one from a school support organisation.

51% of the survey respondents were female, and 46% of the respondents intending to use the Programming and CS standards were female. This is a reasonably balanced number considering that role models are an important influence in this discipline, and this balance is not normally found in university computer science departments where female students and staff are typically a significant minority. Despite this balance, a larger proportion of male teachers (91%) than female teachers (73%) intended to use the new programming and CS standards.

A majority (60%) of the respondents were aged 50 or older, with 45% in the range of 50 to 59 years old, and none under 30 years old. The low numbers of younger high school teachers in NZ is a general concern, but the near-absence of new recruits in the survey is particularly concerning for the future of the topic and is a matter that would benefit from further research. It will be interesting to see if the new standards attract more teachers; there is anecdotal evidence that this is the case, but it will take a few years for them to flow through the system. While the age of the teacher population is a concern for the long-term future of the subject, it does indicate that teachers with considerable experience are involved in the new subject, and with that they bring skills and influence that will be of value getting the subject established. 68% of the teachers had 10 or more years experience teaching, and only 4% had less than 4 years experience.

For those who did not intend to use the new Programming and CS standards, the most common reason was "Not confident to teach them" (51%), followed by the related issue of "Insufficient information / support available to know how to teach them" (39%). Note that respondents could give multiple reasons, so these categories can be overlapping. Only 22% indicated that they couldn't fit the subject into their school program, indicating that if suitable support was available most could have adopted the new standards.

4. TEACHERS' BACKGROUND

The background that teachers bring to the new subjects can include both subject knowledge and pedagogical knowledge. In computer science, the ability to program is a fundamental skill, but we also need to consider other areas of CS, as well as mathematical skills to underpin them, and pedagogical skills for fostering learning.

In terms of programming knowledge, 41% of all respondents were confident and/or experienced in programming in one or more languages, with 47% reporting only rudimentary programming skills and 12% unable to program. Looking at specifically at the respondents who are teaching the Programming and Computer Science standards, those figures are in relatively similar proportion: 45%, 48% and 7% respectively. With under half of the respondents reporting confidence or experience in programming, professional development materials or programmes cannot assume that teachers will have strong programming skills. Developing programming skills takes time, although fortunately there are now a number of on-line and in-person courses available to teach programming to beginners.

Only 56% of all survey respondents indicated any specific qualification in the computing field. Specialist computer science qualifications were uncommon, with only 11% reporting a full computer science degree and a further 11% having full degrees in other computing or ICT areas (such as information systems). 10% had taken only some first- or second-year university papers, and another 10% had some other related qualification, such as a degree or certificate with a computing component. The most common qualification was having a sub-degree computing qualification such as a certificate or diploma (14%). 44% reported that they had no related qualification.

Looking at mathematical qualifications, 16% of all respondents had a degree in mathematics. 41% had some university papers or College of Education study, with a further 8% having some other kind of mathematics-related education or certification. 27% of respondents had only high school mathematics, and 7% reported no mathematical qualification at all.

5. COURSE IMPLEMENTATION

Respondents teaching the standards reported a range of motivations, both intrinsic and extrinsic, for adopting them during 2011. Of the 51 who reported their motivation, 90% wanted to provide better opportunities for students. Most (62%) had a personal interest in the topics. Some believed that adopting the new standards was good for the country (45%) or simply the right thing to do (47%). 2% felt it would give credibility to computing as a subject, and 8% were motivated by school management's requirements. These responses reflect the grass-roots nature of the support for the new curriculum, rather than change being driven by a top-down mandate.

Table 1: Adoption of the new standards in 2011, and plans for 2012

Standard	2011 ($N = 44$)	2012 ($N = 61$)
1.44 (Computer science)	40%	56%
1.45 (Program design)	77%	77%
1.46 (Program implementation)	97%	93%
2.44 (Computer science)	n/a	54%
2.45 (Program design)	n/a	59%
2.46 (Program implementation)	n/a	66%

The new standards offer a lot of flexibility with course design. Teachers can combine a variety of standards to put together a course; typically programming and computer science would be combined to fill about half a course, and the remainder could be chosen from, say, media standards (such as web design) to make a course on web programming, or with electronics to make a course on embedded systems.

Table 1 shows the proportion of respondents able to adopt the new Level 1 standards (1.xx) in 2011, and their plans for 2012. Note that the Level 2 standards (2.xx) only became available in 2012. (Levels 1, 2 and 3 correspond to the last three years of high school respectively; Level 3 will be phased in during 2013). There are two programming standards (separating program design and implementation) and one CS standard available at each level[1]. The Level 1 CS standard covers algorithms, programming languages and HCI, and the Level 2 CS standard covers number representation, coding (cryptography, error detection and compression), and usability. Although 75 respondents had reported an intention to use the new standards earlier in the survey, only 44 had reported adopting them in 2011, and only 61 indicated plans to use them in 2012. It is possible that the remainder chose not to answer this question, or that they intend to introduce them after 2012.

The program implementation standard (1.46) was the most popular, which reflects it being the topic that teachers had the highest confidence in. This isn't surprising since this is the area where more had qualifications and experience. The low adoption of the CS standard reflects the much lower levels of prior knowledge, experience, and confidence in this area. Considerable PD on this topic was provided at the end of 2011 through a CS4HS event, and more peer support would be available in 2012, which may have contributed to the significant increase in planned adoption, as well as a higher interest in Level 2 CS (54%) compared with the Level 1 CS (40%) in their first years of being offered. This increase is in contrast to the programming standards, which show a substantially lower rate of adoption planned at Level 2.

The choice of programming languages for the standards is flexible; at Level 1 the language only needs to support simple structures, whereas at Level 2 it must include functions or methods with parameters, and at Level 3 is requires some OO features. Of course, the same language could be

[1]The codes (1.44 etc.) used here are the draft numbers for the standards, and were in common use at the time of the survey. The standards now have formal codes: AS91074, AS91075, AS91076, AS91371, AS91372 and AS91373 respectively.

used throughout, but introductory languages like Scratch are popular (73%) at Level 1, and the wealth of material available to support teaching such specialist languages can make them an appealing choice for teachers. Visual Basic was the next most popular Level 1 language (15%) followed by Alice (13%) and Python (6%).

A broad range of programming languages have been chosen for use in programming at Level 2 or above, with some respondents considering multiple languages. Python is the most popular (78%) followed by Java (25%) and Visual Basic (18%). Other languages include Alice (10%), C# (10%) and ActionScript (3%). A number of other languages were in use at either Level 1 or Level 2 by one respondent each.

Student reactions to courses using the standards were mixed. Teachers reported that (in their view) courses attracted either a significant number of the highly capable (40%) or those who lacked the academic ability to perform well (46%), though typically not both at once (12%). This reflects the change of the subject from being a non-academic option to one that is academically demanding; some schools would have managed to communicate this to students and get the message across, but others may have found that they had cohorts who were expecting a course on using computers rather than challenging concepts and programming.

48% of teachers believed they had significant numbers of students who were pleased that they took the course, and 18% thought they had students who wish they *hadn't* (with 10% of teachers in both categories). 42% felt they had classes with significant student numbers who had difficulty completing the work in the time available.

32% of teachers thought that a significant number of students found the content different to what they expected, suggesting a need to more clearly explain the courses to students and prime their learning expectations. From a positive point of view, it is apparent that many students were learning what CS is for the first time.

6. TEACHER CONFIDENCE

The confidence of teachers and their sense of identity relative to the subject area is an important consideration [15]. The responses show relatively low confidence among teachers in their ability to teach the new topics. Only 64% of those who taught the programming standard reported that they felt a positive level of confidence about teaching it; and only 44% of those who taught the computer science (algorithms, programming languages and HCI) standard expressed confidence. The latter topics are new to most teachers, but there was also a lack of cohesive material such as textbooks or websites that set out how to teach the topics at high school level. Many disconnected resources have been identified that teach a part of the topics [14], but teachers need material specifically written for the standard so that they don't have to weed through a large variety of options.

Table 2 shows the details of the responses about confidence. It is notable that confidence in the programming standards was more highly polarised between confident and unconfident — this observation is also made of students learning programming [17]!

No distinctive patterns of confidence levels were found based on age categories or years of experience teaching, but in almost all cases, greater experience and confidence in programming is an indicator of greater confidence in both understanding and teaching the achievement standards, especially for the areas that require more implementation (1.46) compared with conceptual (1.44) or design work (1.45). The broad range in teacher experience levels can be a concern in peer support; for example, one respondent observed: "...I know that I am capable of learning this but feel totally useless and alone trying to sort it out myself. Everyone else seems to know exactly what programming is about."

Table 2: Teacher self-rated confidence to teach new standards (number of teachers)

	Standard		
	1.44	1.45	1.46
Confident	6	14	19
Quite confident	5	7	9
Quite unconfident	3	4	2
Unconfident	11	15	14

Table 3: Mathematical problems posed to teachers

Topic	Question
Logarithm	What is $log_2 1024$? (log to base 2 of 1024)
Hexadecimal	Convert the following hexadecimal number to decimal: 1A
Checksum	A checksum that is calculated by multiplying all the odd numbered digits by 2, and the even numbered ones by 1; sum the total and take the remainder when divided by 10.
Algebra	If $n = 10$, what is $n(n-1)/2$?
Exponent	What is 2^{10}? (2 to the power of 10)
Binary	Convert the following binary number to decimal: 11001
Pixels	How many pixels are there on a 780 by 1024 screen?

Teachers generally reported a lower level of confidence in teaching a topic than their level of understanding of it. It is rare for a respondent to be more confident about teaching the standard than they are about understanding it — a possible consequence of this being the first year of using the standards, and the limited availability of targeted support for CS pedagogy. One respondent commented: "I don't need to know any more programming and CS, I need to know how to *teach* programming and CS better."

Computer science topics inevitably involve some mathematics, and the teachers were asked to indicate if they would be comfortable explaining some specific CS-related math problems to a class. The problems are shown in Table 3, and Figure 1 shows the number of teachers who said they would be confident explaining them, grouped according to those who used the 1.44 (CS) standard, those who showed interest in using the new standards, and those who don't intend to use them.

Note that the question was posed in terms of pedagogical knowledge; the teachers were asked about *explaining* the problems, not whether they understand them themselves. More confidence was expressed by the respondents who will be teaching the new standards, and (except for algebra) those who taught the new 1.44 CS standard were more confident, with a particularly dramatic difference between confidence with binary representation for the groups. From this, it isn't surprising that we have observed in other contexts that adults find it very empowering to find out how binary numbers work. The results do show a relatively low level of

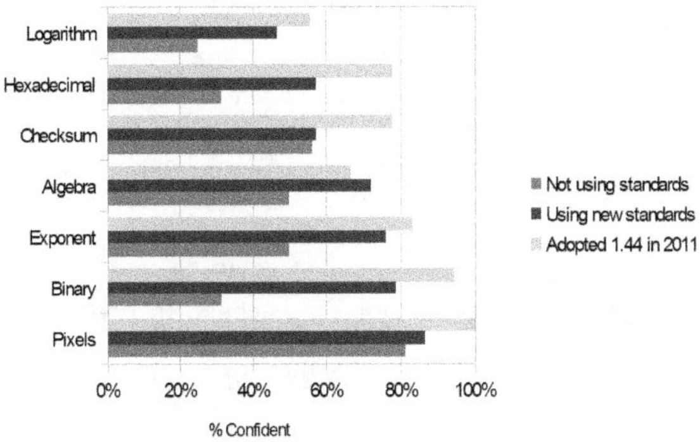

Figure 1: Proportion of teachers confident to explain mathematical problems

confidence explaining fairly fundamental mathematical topics (such as dealing with the expression $n(n-1)/2$, which is common in the analysis of simple sorting algorithms, or calculating a checksum, which uses a relatively simple formula to achieve a powerful result), and they also indicate a relationship between confidence teaching mathematical topics and willingness to use the new standards.

All of these math topics are relevant to the new NZ standards, although some can be avoided with alternative approaches. For example, while logarithms are heavily used in CS (e.g. binary search, binary numbers, divide and conquer) and are associated with highly scalable algorithms, at high school level the notation needn't be used. Students can simply address questions like "how many times can we repeatedly halve 1024 until we have just one item" or "how many bits do you need to represent 1023 in binary?"

Clearly there is a need for professional development (PD), and the survey also explored how it would be best delivered in a way that teachers could access it. Figure 2 shows the kind of PD that teachers were interested in. The graphs are separated into two groups: those who were less than a one-hour drive from a University / College of Education (66%), and those more than an hour away (34%). Access to PD is an issue for teachers out of town — 9 of the teachers surveyed had to drive over 3 hours to get to a main centre, and so could feel quite isolated. From Figure 2 we can see that for both groups most found having lesson plans provided to be a top priority, with self-paced study and short workshops also being attractive[2]. Regular courses (full-time or part-time) and evening workshops were less useful to those from out of town, and travel would be impractical for many in this situation, although there was still a group of these teachers who expressed interest in such courses. A total of 13 of the teachers said that a full-time course would be very useful, indicating that they would be prepared to take time away from teaching to upskill.

Regarding *assessing* students' work in the new standards, 7% of respondents were quite confident in their ability. The number who felt confident or unconfident was similar (41% each) and 12% were quite unconfident. In assessing the fairness of external grading of their students' results, 74%

[2]The length of the bars varies because the survey allowed teachers to give no response to each question.

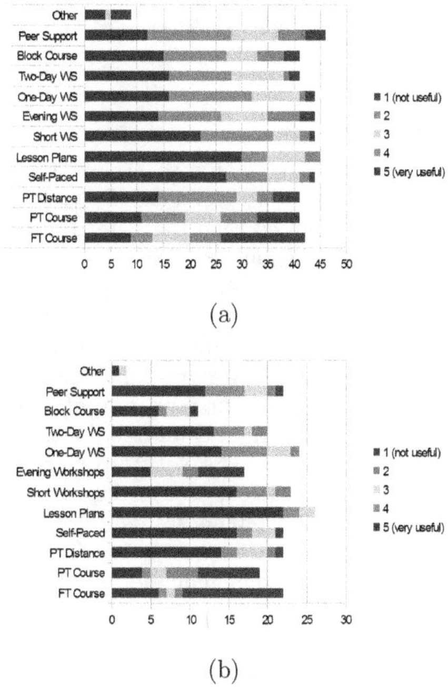

Figure 2: Teacher preferences for professional development delivery (a) teachers less than one hour from a university (b) teachers more than one hour from a university

agreed or strongly agreed that they seemed fair, with 26% disagreeing or strongly disagreeing. Grading is an important issue, because in the first year of a course being offered there is a lack of experience for advising students on what examiners might be looking for. This is examined in more detail for these students in [5].

We have looked for information about teacher attitudes from their comments in their surveys. While generally well-motivated, several respondents reported a number of roadblocks to implementation, including:

- a lack of available support resources such as lesson plans, assessment exemplars and workbooks,
- difficulty finding quality material appropriate for familiarizing themselves with the topic,
- a lack of confidence or experience with programming, and the need for more beginner-level explanation, support and practice, and
- insufficient time or available PD opportunities to adequately prepare for the new standards.

When available, PD opportunities such as the CS4HS workshops and support from university-based experts have been well-received, and appear to boost confidence and self-efficacy. Support through the NZACDITT online community and local groups is also highly valued. However, calls for more regional PD and peer support outside of major centres underline the frustration and isolation of some of the smaller and more remote regional schools. There were also a few concerns raised about how to accommodate students opting to take the Level 2 standards without having first completed the Level 1 standard, and students who may be more focused on the design aspects of computing than the underlying mathematical concepts.

7. CONCLUSION

Although the new NZ computer science standards weren't compulsory in schools, it has had a significant level of adoption. Based on the survey reported here, the impetus for rapid change has largely come from teachers' intrinsic motivation rather than government or school leadership directives. The top reason given for adopting new standards was to "provide better opportunities for students". Teachers have used familiar values from computing culture to achieve this: there has been open source sharing of resources and ideas; agile development of teaching methods; a bootstrap approach where a few teachers with advanced knowledge were able to help others get up to speed; peer-to-peer communication where local communities developed practices in the safe environment of relationships between individuals; and heavy use of online communication to share ideas and debate issues.

The introduction of the new material has largely relied on "grassroots" development of teacher expertise, and many teachers and their support networks have put in countless voluntary hours to take hold of this window of opportunity. This is feasible in the short term, but in the long term well-supported formal teacher professional development is needed [16]. Several teachers have indicated that they would be prepared to take time out from their career to upskill.

The survey has shown that teacher confidence is an issue. Lack of confidence was the main reason given by teachers who didn't adopt the standards, and about half the teachers who delivered the standards were not confident about teaching them. There is a clear call for professional development delivered in a way that is accessible for teachers in a variety of situations, as well as providing resources that will make it easier for them to deliver courses.

8. REFERENCES

[1] O. Astrachan, J. Cuny, C. Stephenson, and C. Wilson. The CS10K project: mobilizing the community to transform high school computing. *Proceedings of the 42nd ACM Technical Symposium on Computer Science Education, SIGCSE 2011*, pages 85–86, 2011.

[2] O. Astrachan, R. Morelli, D. Barnette, and J. Gray. CS principles: piloting a national course. *Proceedings of the 43rd ACM technical symposium on Computer Science Education, Raleigh, NC, USA*, pages 319–320, 2012.

[3] T. Bell, P. Andreae, and L. Lambert. Computer Science in New Zealand High Schools. In T. Clear and J. Hamer, editors, *ACE '10: Proceedings of the 12th conference on Australasian Computing Education*, volume 32 of *Australian Computer Science Communications*, pages 15–22, Brisbane, Australia, Jan. 2010. Australian Computer Society, Inc.

[4] T. Bell, P. Andreae, and A. Robins. Computer Science in NZ High Schools: The First Year of the New Standards. In L. A. S. King, D. R. Musicant, T. Camp, and P. Tymann, editors, *Proceedings of the 43rd ACM technical symposium on Computer Science Education, Raleigh, NC, USA*, pages 343–348, New York, 2012. ACM.

[5] T. Bell, H. Newton, P. Andreae, and A. Robins. The introduction of Computer Science to NZ High Schools — an analysis of student work. In M. Knobelsdorf and R. Romeike, editors, *The 7th Workshop in Primary and Secondary Computing Education (WiPSCE 2012)*, page to appear, Hamburg, Germany, 2012.

[6] L. Blum and T. J. Cortina. CS4HS: an outreach program for high school CS teachers. In I. Russell, S. M. Haller, J. D. Dougherty, and S. H. Rodger, editors, *Proceedings of the 38th SIGCSE Technical Symposium on Computer Science Education, SIGCSE 2007, Covington, Kentucky, USA*, pages 19–23. ACM, 2007.

[7] T. Brinda, H. Puhlmann, and C. Schulte. Bridging ICT and CS: Educational standards for computer science in lower secondary education. *ACM SIGCSE Bulletin*, 41(3):288–292, 2009.

[8] A. Bruckman, M. Biggers, B. Ericson, T. McKlin, J. Dimond, B. DiSalvo, M. Hewner, L. Ni, and S. Yardi. "Georgia computes!": Improving the Computing Education Pipeline. *ACM SIGCSE Bulletin*, 41(1):86–90, Mar. 2009.

[9] T. Carrell, V. Gough-Jones, and K. Fahy. The future of Computer Science and Digital Technologies in New Zealand secondary schools: Issues of 21st teaching and learning, senior courses and suitable assessments. Technical report, 2008.

[10] Q. Cutts, M. Brown, and L. Kemp. Enthusing and informing potential computer science students and their teachers. *ACM SIGCSE Bulletin*, 2007.

[11] S. Furber, editor. *Shut down or restart? The way forward for computing in UK schools.* The Royal Society, London, 2012.

[12] J. Goode and J. Margolis. Exploring Computer Science. *ACM Transactions on Computing Education*, 11(2):1–16, July 2011.

[13] M. Guzdial. Learning How to Prepare Computer Science High School Teachers. *Computer*, 44(10):95–97, Oct. 2011.

[14] S. Murugesh, T. Bell, and A. McGrath. A Review of Computer Science Resources to Support NCEA. In S. Mann and M. Veerhaart, editors, *First annual conference of Computing and Information Technology Research and Education NZ (CITRENZ2010)*, pages 173–181, July 2010.

[15] L. Ni and M. Guzdial. Who AM I? Understanding High School Computer Science Teachers' Professional Identity. In *Proceedings of the 43rd ACM technical symposium on Computer Science Education, Raleigh, NC, USA*, pages 499–504, 2012.

[16] N. Ragonis, O. Hazzan, and J. Gal-Ezer. A survey of computer science teacher preparation programs in Israel tells us: computer science deserves a designated high school teacher preparation! In *Proceedings of the 41st ACM technical symposium on Computer science education*, SIGCSE '10, pages 401–405, New York, NY, USA, 2010. ACM.

[17] A. Robins. Learning edge momentum: A new account of outcomes. *Computer Science Education*, 20:37 – 71, 2010.

Computer Science Principles: Analysis of a Proposed Advanced Placement Course

Andrea Arpaci-Dusseau
University of Wisconsin, Madison
dusseau@cs.wisc.edu

Owen Astrachan
Duke University
ola@cs.duke.edu

Dwight Barnett
Virginia Tech
barnette@vt.edu

Matthew Bauer
Illinois Institute of Technology
bauerm@iit.edu

Marilyn Carrell
Springdale High School
mcarrell@sdale.org

Rebecca Dovi
Patrick Henry High School
rdovi@hcps.us

Baker Franke
Chicago Lab High School
bfranke@ucls.uchicago.edu

Christina Gardner
Georgia Tech
cmgardner@cc.gatech.edu

Jeff Gray
University of Alabama
gray@cs.ua.edu

Jean Griffin
University of Pennsylvania
griffin@seas.upenn.edu

Richard Kick
Newbury Park High School
kickrg@gmail.com

Andy Kuemmel
West High School
andykuemmel@yahoo.com

Ralph Morelli
Trinity College
ralph.morelli@trincoll.edu

Deepa Muralidhar
North Gwinnett High School
deepa.muralidhar@gmail.com

R Brook Osborne
Duke University
rbo@cs.duke.edu

Chinma Uche
GHAMAS
cuche@crec.org

ABSTRACT

In this paper we analyze the CS Principles project, a proposed Advanced Placement course, by focusing on the second pilot that took place in 2011-2012. In a previous publication the first pilot of the course was explained, but not in a context related to relevant educational research and philosophy. In this paper we analyze the content and the pedagogical approaches used in the second pilot of the project. We include information about the third pilot being conducted in 2012-2013 and the portfolio exam that is part of that pilot. Both the second and third pilots provide evidence that the CS Principles course is succeeding in changing how computer science is taught and to whom it is taught.

Categories and Subject Descriptors

K.3.2 [**Computers & Education**]: Computer & Information Science Education --- *Computer Science Education.*

Keywords

Advanced Placement, Portfolio Assessment, National Pilot.

1. Introduction

We report on and analyze the Computer Science Principles project, a project sponsored by both the National Science Foundation (NSF) and the College Board. CS Principles is intended and designed to be a rigorous, engaging, and broadly appealing Advanced Placement (AP) course taught in high schools for which students can earn placement and/or credit for a college course. In this paper we provide an historical context that helps explain the development of CS Principles in the AP program, we describe the process by which the CS Principles exam is being designed and planned, we analyze the second and third pilots of the course, and we describe the next phase of the project leading to a national, AP exam.

SIGCSE'13, March 6–9, 2013, Denver, Colorado, USA.

2. Historical Perspectives of APCS

The development of the current AP Computer Science exam provides both insight and foundation for the development of the CS Principles project. The College Board developed and delivered the first Advanced Placement Computer Science exam in the early 1980s --- the first exam was given to students in May of 1984 [1]. That exam covered what are conventionally called CS1 and CS2 using the language Pascal. Over thirty years that exam changed in many ways: first to report a CS1 (called the A exam) sub score, then to create two exams and courses: CS1 (APCS A) and CS2 (APCS AB), and then to discontinue the AB exam. The course and exam went through several changes including changing the language from Pascal to C++ and then to Java [2, 3]. Perhaps more important were changes made more for pedagogical reasons rather than to track the conventions used in college courses. The pedagogical changes included the adoption of case studies that were fundamental to both the curriculum and the exam [4]. These case studies permitted students to write small functions that fit into a much larger code-base that had been (presumably) the object of study throughout the AP course leading up to the exam. The case studies engendered both robust and reliable questions on the AP exam, but they also allowed teachers to structure a course around a software artifact that was accompanied by a written design document. Very few colleges use a similar approach --- so case studies were used for purposes of pedagogy and assessment rather than to track the conventions used in most colleges. The College Board has plans to replace the case study by a set of labs that students would use during the year and that would be the basis of questions on the exam. The growth-rate in the number of students taking the AP Computer Science exam has lagged far behind the growth rate of the AP program in general, and the demographics [see Sections 2.1 and 3.2] of students taking the AP Computer Science exams have not included sufficient representation by women and under represented minorities (URMs). These characteristics of the student population were a principle impetus in the development of the CS Principles course and exam.

2.1 Underproduction, Underrepresentation

The issues of underproduction and underrepresentation are clear in the demographics of students currently taking AP CS as well as in historical trends of this population. In 2011, AP CS A accounted for 21,139 of the 3,365,617 total AP Exams taken by students in the US --- that is .62% of all AP Exams scored in the US. Of these 21,139 students, 19% were from underrepresented racial and ethnic groups. Women accounted for 19% of APCS test takers while women account for 54% of all AP test takers [5]. The data for 2012 have the same percentages for both URMs and women [6]. Between 2002 and 2012 the number of AP test takers across all exams increased by 57%. In the STEM fields of Statistics, Calculus, Physics, Biology, and Computer Science the corresponding increases were 68%, 45%, 52%, 49%, and 11% [7].

According to a longitudinal study of nearly 40,000 college and university students released by the College Board in 2011, 17.9% of students who took the AP CS A Exam went on to major in Computer and Information Sciences, compared to 2.3% of the total sample. The findings of this report are in line with prior research indicating students who take an AP Exam in a particular content area are more likely to major in a related discipline in college [8]. The low enrollment in AP CS means this positive relationship does not translate into a large cohort of CS majors. Under enrollment and underproduction of degrees in computer science is a particularly salient problem given the high demand for qualified employees in the field. For years there has been a gap between the number of available jobs requiring a background in computer science and the number of qualified job hunters --- in 2010 there were a total of 1.3 million job-openings (from both job creation and replacement) that fit into the Bureau of Labor Statistics "Computer Occupations" category, with expected job growth of 22% between 2012 and 2020 [9]. These data sit in stark contrast to the number of students majoring in Computer Science; according to the Taulbee survey from the same year, there were only 12,501 bachelor's degrees awarded in Computer Science. Of those degrees 13.8% were awarded to women, 3.4% to Blacks or African Americans, and 5.3% to resident Hispanics [10].

From these data two things are clear: the CS community must motivate and educate a substantially larger number of students to fulfill the demands of the market while reaching a broader, more diverse segment of the population. The Mattern et al. study demonstrates a strong relationship between AP CS A Exam participation and pursuing a major in a related field. The creation of CS Principles, an AP course that increases opportunities for engagement with CS and develops new ways to interest potential students that have not fit into prior paradigms of learning CS, has the potential to increase the number and diversity of students majoring in the field. By attracting more students into AP CS, we will see more students completing courses of study that will prepare them to enter the computer science workforce. Beyond addressing the issues of overall access to learning opportunities, both the content and structure of the CS Principles course and exam described below aim to attract students who do not traditionally enroll in CS courses.

2.2 Development of CS Principles

The approach recently adopted across the AP program for the revision or creation of an exam is based on evidence-centered design [11]. This design methodology has led to revisions in AP Calculus, Biology, Physics, and was used in drafting the curriculum framework for CS Principles. Detailed learning objectives (LOs) with evidence statements are used to determine whether the objectives have been met. These objectives are constructed by matching the so-called seven *Big Ideas* of CS Principles with six *Computational Thinking Practices*. Details can be found on the CS Principles website [12]. Here we use one example to illustrate how the 35 learning objectives were developed. One of the Big Ideas is Abstraction: *Abstraction reduces information and detail to facilitate focus on relevant concepts*. This Big Idea is divided into three key concepts, each of which is divided into three-to-four supporting concepts. Using the Big Idea and the Computational Thinking Practice of *Developing Computational Artifacts*, leads to the following learning objective: The student can develop an abstraction. The following points are the evidence statements used to determine if a student has met the learning objective described above.

- Creation of an abstraction for a hardware, software, or conceptual purpose
- Use of appropriate abstractions in the creation of the artifact
- Selection of appropriate algorithmic and information-management abstractions

More details on learning objectives and evidence statements can be found by examining all 35 learning objectives and their associated evidence statements.

The seven big ideas are:

1. Creativity: Computing is a creative activity
2. Abstraction: Abstraction reduces information and detail to focus on relevant concepts
3. Data: Data and information facilitate the creation of knowledge
4. Algorithms: Algorithms are used to develop and express solutions to computational problems
5. Programming: Programming enables problem solving, human expression, and creation of knowledge
6. Internet: The Internet pervades modern computing
7. Impact: Computing has global impacts.

The six Computational Thinking Practices are:

1. Connecting Computing
2. Developing Computational Artifacts
3. Abstracting
4. Analyzing problems and artifacts
5. Communicating
6. Collaborating

The entire curriculum framework was developed by a group of ten educators and professionals whose work was overseen by an advisory board of thirty drawn from colleges, secondary schools, and professional organizations.

2.3 Future of CS Principles

The CS Principles project is building toward a national AP exam by the 2016-2017 academic year. The next phase of the project is the expansion of the pilot program described in the next section and the development of portfolio questions and rubrics that will form the foundation of the CS Principles exam. This phase is underway in academic year 2012-2013 and is an integral part of the third pilot described in the next section. A new advisory board is overseeing the development of the course, the portfolio, and the professional development that the College Board supplies to all AP courses. This board is working to ensure that the approach taken appeals to a broad audience while maintaining the rigor that is an essential part of all AP courses.

3. Summary of Pilots

Three years of piloting the framework were planned in the first phase of the CS Principles project between 2010-2013. Phase II of the project begins in 2013 and includes a larger pilot program designed to lead to the launch of an AP course. In this section we describe the three pilots that are part of the first phase of CS Principles, these are Pilots I, II, and III.

3.1 Pilot I

The first phase, in 2010-2011, consisted of five institutions and courses with instructors drawn from the advisory board since they would be familiar with the framework and the rationale by which it was developed. These included: Beth Simon, UCSD; Dan Garcia, UC Berkeley; Jody Paul, Metropolitan University of Denver; Tiffany Barnes, UNC Charlotte; Larry Snyder, U. Washington. This first pilot was designed to determine how the curriculum framework could support many different approaches. For example, as reported in [13], the type of software and the programming languages used was different across the five pilots. The size of the classes and the pedagogical approaches used varied drastically. The number of contact hours per week with students varied, as did the kind of artifacts that students produced. As the first pilot took place, the CS Principles team coordinated a national survey of colleges and universities designed to assess the curriculum framework and to determine if it could lead to widespread adoption in terms of college placement and/or credit. This ultimately led to revisions to the framework, e.g., the Internet replaced a more generic and abstract Big Idea on networking and topics based on algorithmic and complexity concepts such as intractability, P, and NP, were replaced by topics that are less theory-centric.

3.2 Pilot II

A second pilot was conducted in 2011-2012 using the revised curriculum framework that resulted from the first pilot. This pilot consisted of ten high schools partnered with eight colleges.[1] The schools in this pilot were North Gwinnet HS/Georgia Institute of Technology; Northside College Prep with Chicago Lab School/Illinois Institute of Technology; Greater Hartford Academy of Math and Science/Trinity College; Booker T Washington Magnet High School/University of Alabama; Springdale High School/University of Arkansas, Little Rock; South Philadelphia HS/University of Pennsylvania; West High School/University of Wisconsin, Madison; Patrick Henry HS/Virginia Tech; Newbury Park HS (California). The student demographics from the second pilot are shown in Table 1, and provide evidence that CS Principles is addressing the issue of enrollment of underrepresented minorities in computer science (see Section 2.2).

Table 1. Aggregated Demographic Data for Pilot II

Race/ Ethnicity	American Indian	Asian/ Asian American	Black
	.23%	18.0%	23.4%
	Hispanic/ Latino	White	Other
	15.0%	41.3%	1.8%
Gender	Male	Female	
	60.5%	39.5%	

Instructors in the first pilot often differentiated their courses by emphasizing the programming languages used in their courses [13]. In the first pilot each of the five instructors used a language that was not used by another instructor though more than one of the five pilots used Snap! (formerly BYOB).[2] In contrast, more than half of the 18 schools in the second pilot used App Inventor [14]. The attraction of creating an app that can be used on a phone or tablet is a real draw for many students. However, it is not clear that using App Inventor will scale across hundreds of schools. Given the limitations of the simulator used in App Inventor (as opposed to deploying apps on a real device), testing and demonstrating code on an actual device is often necessary, and funds for cell phones, tablets, or other Android devices will almost certainly not be available for all schools. In the second pilot, two courses used the code-in-the-browser website [15]. This is a zero footprint, browser-only programming environment that has been met with reasonable success.[3] In the third pilot, instructors have indicated that they will make use of the new Khan Academy Computer Science program. This environment is based on work done by Resig and Bibeault [16] and provides a real-time, read-eval-print loop in the browser for experimenting and playing with code. The learning environment is unique in that each keystroke is immediately evaluated so that changes to a program are visualized as they are made rather than as part of an edit, compile, run, debug cycle. The quick adoption of this tool by the third pilot group indicates the potential of this approach, though its longevity and success in the context of CS Principles will arguably be a function of the degree of adoption by the much larger Phase II pilot program in 2013-2014.

3.3 Pilot III

A third pilot is being conducted in 2012-2013. The schools and teachers participating in this pilot were all drawn from the second pilot group. The third pilot group includes North Gwinnet HS, Greater Hartford Academy of Math and Science, Patrick Henry HS, Newbury Park HS, University of Alabama, and University of

[1] Two high schools in Chicago were partnered with the same college. One of the colleges originally in the pilot had to drop out before the pilot course was finished, but the partnership with the high school continued.

[2] In 2010-2011 Snap! was called BYOB (Build Your Own Blocks) and was used in two of the five pilots, though one of these two also used App Inventor.

[3] This environment was used in the Coursera offering of Compsci 101 (see coursera.org).

Wisconsin, Madison. This group of pilots will use an open-ended portfolio assessment during the course. The portfolio questions are available on the csprinciples.org website for use by the entire educational community.

Portfolio-based assessment often centers on a collection of student work that demonstrates achievement or improvement [17]. While the particular structure of a portfolio assessment can vary, two approaches are the most prevalent within the education research literature. The first approach treats the use of a portfolio as a capstone experience where the best student work is selected and placed into the portfolio, representing the student's current level of mastery of knowledge and skills in a domain. The second portfolio structure represents a student's learning process that demonstrates growth or relative change rather than the final level of achievement. Student work for this type of portfolio is selected along a continuum of student progress toward mastery throughout the duration of a course. Two national exams include a portfolio component: AP Studio Art [18] and the National Board Certification for teachers [19].

Portfolio assessments are ideal for capturing non-traditional, project, or performance-based student work. They have also been lauded for their ability to better capture the authentic application of a student's acquired knowledge [20, 21]. Portfolio assessments have been found to produce positive effects on students, teachers, and instruction [22]. Portfolios can also provide the opportunity for students to actively engage in and understand a rubric that can provide pre-determined criteria for success. Thus, portfolio-based assessments provide greater levels of student awareness of the process of gaining and applying knowledge and skill.

3.4 Future Pilots

Phase II of CS Principles includes three more years of pilots at roughly 40-50 high schools and colleges in each year. More schools than these 40-50 will certainly be involved in delivering a CS Principles course, but not as part of the formal research project carried out by The College Board. Thus, they will not be part of annual meetings, nor will these early adopters receive the same level of community support provided to the formal pilots in the CS Principles project. However, ongoing efforts supported by the NSF and industry to support CS Principles will extend beyond these 50 schools. Each of the Phase II pilot schools will use the portfolio assessment and participate in the research-based approach to grading the portfolios that is part of the ongoing development of the CS Principles project.

4. Prototype Assessment in Pilot II

As discussed in Section 3.2, seventeen high schools, colleges, and universities took part in Pilot II. While the first pilot was focused on determining if instructors would be able to create engaging and rigorous courses in diverse settings based on the curriculum framework, the second pilot was centered on investigating the feasibility of assessing student understanding of the Big Ideas and Computational Thinking Practices. To this end, each pilot course culminated in a prototype assessment with both objectively and subjectively scored questions. In this section we discuss and analyze the assessments used in Pilot II. In the next section we discuss and analyze the courses that were part of Pilot II.

Students in the Pilot II courses participated in an end-of-course exam intended to assess the feasibility of an online testing platform as well as both objectively scored questions (e.g., matching or multiple choice) and subjectively scored questions (e.g., open-ended, free-response questions (FRQs)). In a separate report, information about these results is available[4], we provide a quick summary of the results here as they affect the development of the portfolio used in current (Pilot III) and future pilots. Objectively scored questions will be a component of the planned AP exam for CS Principles. The chief lesson learned from the use of such questions in the online, computer-based exam that was part of Pilot II is that students will need practice with new kinds of questions --- those that go beyond simple multiple choice to include multiple-correct responses, drag-and-drop completion questions, and animated questions that require students to manipulate sliders to change values. The free-response questions illustrated what an analysis of the time-in-class on each big idea had already provided in a preliminary analysis of the second pilot courses: instructors did not have sufficient guidance in the depth-of-coverage anticipated in all areas of the curriculum framework. As an example, student performance on the question below was very poor:

> *The Internet Protocol IPv4 was in widespread use from 1980-2012. There is a more recent protocol named IPv6 now used more frequently than in the past. With IPv6 128 bits specify an IP address whereas 32 bits specify an address using IPv4. IPv6 also includes support for Internet security that is not present in IPv4. Describe an example for why the change in the number of bits per address is necessary and an example for why security is necessary in the new, more recent IPv6 protocol compared to the IPv4 protocol.*

The open-ended nature of the portfolio questions used in Pilot III is due in part to the desire to stay away from fact-based questions such as the one above since the release of such questions will likely have an immediate effect on what teachers discuss and cover in subsequent years.

5. Exploration and Analysis of Pilot II

This section will explore and analyze how courses in Pilot II were structured in terms of both content and pedagogy. This analysis is holistic rather than quantitative, aimed at providing an understanding of how courses were implemented and conducted.

5.1 The Curriculum Framework

The planning and development of the 18 courses in Pilot II differed in substantial ways from Pilot I. The instructors in Pilot II were not part of the development of the curriculum framework as were the instructors in Pilot I; Pilot II included high schools whereas Pilot I only included colleges; and high schools were partnered with universities. Perhaps as a result of these differences Pilot II instructors engaged directly with the curriculum framework while building and maintaining their CS Principles courses. For example, one instructor notes that when he was developing materials and activities during the year, he would turn to the CS Principles framework, find a learning objective that had not been covered thoroughly in the course, develop a sequence of activities leading to a project that both illuminated the objective and developed new skills as well. Many instructors report that they covered several Learning Objectives in each class project and revisited those LOs frequently in different contexts. By contextualizing topics across several domains students had more opportunities to experiment with those concepts. This is an

[4] This report will be published after all the FRQs have been completely graded.

important feature of Constructivism [24]; a learning theory adopted by many of the Pilot II instructors.

5.2 Constructivist Classroom

In his 1916 book, *Democracy and Education*, John Dewey says of education: "It is that reconstruction or reorganization of experience which adds to the meaning of experience, and which increases ability to direct the course of subsequent experience. The increment of meaning corresponds to the increased perception of the connections of the activities in which we are engaged." [23] This is the backbone of constructivist learning theory, or the high-level process in which the learner builds understanding of a concept through first-hand experience [24]. In his 2002 book *The Art of Changing the Brain*, James Zull highlights how the experiential learning model of David Kolb is tied to the biology of the brain. Kolb's model, which supports a constructivist approach, is broken down into four parts: (1) concrete experience with a topic, (2) reflection about the experience with the topic, (3) extending the topic to form generalizations and make connections to broader concepts, and (4) testing these concepts and generalizations in new situations [25]. Zull makes a case that this model is supported by neuroscience, that each of Kolb's parts is supported by the brain: (1) sensory cortex, (2) temporal integrative cortex, (3) frontal integrative cortex, (4) premotor and motor brain [26].

Many Pilot II instructors delivered courses built on the educational tenets of experiential learning and constructivism, a paradigm facilitated by the CS Principles framework. Perhaps the synergy engendered by including high school teachers in the second pilot facilitated this approach. Rather than conducting lecture-based courses, the overwhelming majority of Pilot II instructors produced curricula based on a constructivist theory.

5.2.1 Experiential Learning

Many of the instructors focused on student comprehension through the model of experiential learning. In one case, an instructor designed projects that were specifically open-ended and co-curricular. Students started by learning about and exploring tools and concepts, and then leveraged this new knowledge to complete projects that featured content from other courses. Another instructor structured projects similarly, giving students the option to explore topics and create artifacts that related to their personal areas of interest. This resulted in a variety of projects, from recreations of childhood games to tools for use in other courses. One of the instructors who used a drag-and-drop language early in the semester, but later switched to a text-based, procedural language, noted that students benefitted from working out logic in the visual programming language and using that as a blueprint for coding in the text-based language. In this case, students were abstracting a solution from an established context into a newer, less familiar situation. Another strategy employed was the creation of student-maintained concept dictionaries. In one case, the definitions were revisited daily and refined as the course progressed, providing students with a record of the growth of their understanding of the topics. In another case, students created and maintained a 'computing concept dictionary' where they translated their understanding of topics into jargon-free definitions.

One instructor integrated Service Learning into her course, with each student performing at least 3 hours of course-relevant community service for K-12 youth using drag-and-drop languages. Another pilot instructor noted the increase in student inspiration when topics were put into context and made relevant after completing a project. In another course, students would first examine magnified details of a topic and then explore the topic in the context of the "big picture" with the direction of exploration guided by student suggestions and preferences. In that same class, quizzes and tests were formatted in such a way that students were required to do much more than just answer questions; rather, they would speculate about possible solutions to problems, compare their speculations with sample solutions that were made available to them after their initial speculations, and then resolve any differences that were identified. Each of these examples highlight experiential learning and are rooted in the natural learning cycle, demonstrating instances of students extending the topic of instruction and making connections to broader concepts, and then testing these concepts in new situations.

5.2.2 Reflection

As a tenet of experiential learning, reflection gives students the opportunity to abstract their understanding of a topic, thereby creating versatile content knowledge that can be applied to new and different tasks. As such, reflection is a hugely important component of the teaching and learning process and was embraced by the Pilot II instructors. In many courses, the reflection process was formalized. Students would share their written reflections with other students or the instructor in a number of different ways --- from writing papers, to journaling in a shared Googledoc, to blogging. In several cases, students were encouraged to reflect on what they were learning about computing in the context of its impact on their lives and future careers. This exercise prompts the learner to consider the broader implications and applications of the content knowledge she is amassing; an important part of the learning cycle. As noted, students often reflected publically and online; these online spaces often went beyond repositories for self-reflection. Many students posted both their work products and their reflections in these spaces throughout the year. They would discuss their work with their peers and reflect on prior work after these discussions. This feedback and shared reflection process presents the learner with an opportunity to refine her understanding of the content, and in some cases, refine the actual work product.

Many instructors noted the need for providing guidance during the reflection process. When done correctly, reflection gives the teacher an opportunity to see the depth of a student's understanding; however many students have no experience with deep reflection. In one case where an instructor invested time in building an understanding of the mechanics of reflection, she saw the students' ability to write and reflect improve dramatically throughout the year, giving her a snapshot of how well they understood the material covered in class. All of these examples point to the usefulness of reflection as a tool for gaining and demonstrating comprehension. Reflection is a cornerstone of the portfolio tasks being used in Pilot III, especially for those tasks that are collaborative.

6. Future Directions

The next steps in the Phase II CS Principles project are grounded in ensuring that the portfolio exam can be successfully administered on a much larger scale. This includes the possibility of a distributed grading of the portfolios --- a distinct contrast to existing grading of AP free response questions which requires travel and housing for more than a week to support the grading of each subjectively scored question in AP exams. As an example, nearly one thousand educators convene centrally to grade the AP English and Composition exam. Since the digital components of the CS Principles portfolio can be duplicated, a distributed grading is more than feasible. The development of such a process is an important component of the CS Principles project.

Professional development (PD) supported by the College Board is another important component. All AP courses have short, focused PD opportunities for educators, however, successful professional development requires an emphasis on pedagogical content knowledge, not simply on content [27]. As such, it is important that educators have access to PD that facilitates deep understanding and retention of pedagogical content knowledge.

7. ACKNOWLEDGMENTS

We thank the CS Principles commission, the advisory board and all the pilot instructors across all three pilots. We also thank the staff at College Board and our external evaluator.

8. REFERENCES

[1] D. Rine, J. R. J. W. Wadkins, and G. Steven, "Advanced Placement Program in Computer Science," *Proceedings of the SIGCSE Symposium,* vol. 15, p. 204, 1983.

[2] M. Stehlik, S. Rodger, K. Larson, A. Brady, and C. Nevison, "Current and Future Directions of the Advanced Placement Exam," in *Proceedings of the SIGCSE Symposium*, New Orleans, LA, 1999, p. 358.

[3] O. Astrachan, G. Chapman, S. Rodger, and M. Weiss, "The reasoning for the advanced placement C++ subset," *ACM SIGCSE Bulletin,* vol. 29, pp. 62-65, 1997.

[4] M. Linn and M. Clancy, "The case for case studies of programming problems," *Commun. ACM,* vol. 35, pp. 121-132, 1992.

[5] (2011, November 29, 2012). *AP Summary Reports: 2011.* Available http://bit.ly/apscores2011

[6] (2012, November 29, 2012). *AP Summary Reports: 2012.* Available http://bit.ly/apscores2012

[7] (2012, November 29, 2012). *AP Program Participation and Performance Data 2012.*

[8] K. Mattern, E. Shaw, and M. Ewing, "Advanced Placement Exam Participation: Is AP Exam Participation and Performance Related to Choice of College Major?," 2011.

[9] B.L. Statistics. (2010). *Employment by occupation* Available: http://www.bls.gov/emp/ep_table_102.htm

[10] C.R. Association, "Computing Research Association: Taulbee Survey Report 2009-2010," 2011.

[11] R. J. Mislevy and G. D. Haertel, "Implications of Evidence-Centered Design for Educational Testing," *Educational Measurement: Issues and Practice,* vol. 25, pp. 6-20, 2006.

[12] C. P. Commission. (2012, Computer Science Principles Big Ideas and Key Concepts Learning Objectives and Evidence Statements. Available:

[13] T. B. Larry Snyder, Dan Garcia , Jody Paul, Beth Simon. (2013, June, 2012) The First Five Computer Science Principles Project. *ACM Inroads*.

[14] D. Wolber, H. Abelson, E. Spertus, and L. Looney, *App Inventor*: O'Reilly, 2011.

[15] N. Parlante. (2012). *Code in the Browser.* Available: http://codeinthebrowser.org/

[16] J. Resig and B. Bibeault, *Secrets of the JavaScript Ninja*: Manning, 2012.

[17] G. Wiggins, "A true test: toward more authentic and equitable assessment," *Phi Delta Kappan,* vol. 70, pp. 703-713, 1989.

[18] N. Chudowsky and J. Pelligrino, "Large Scale Assessments that Support Learning: Will it Take?," *Theory into Practice,* vol. 42, pp. 75-83, 2003 2003.

[19] D. Goldhaber and E. Anthony, "Can Teacher Quality Be Effectively Assessed? National Board Certfication as a Signal of Effective Teaching," *The Review of Economics and Statistics,* vol. 89, pp. 134-150, 2007.

[20] D. P. Wolf, "Assessment as an episode of learning," in *Construction Versus Choice in Cognitive Measurement*, R.E. Bennett and W.C. Ward, Ed., Hilllsdale, NJ: Lawrenece Erlbaum Associates, 1993, pp. 213-240.

[21] F. L. Paulson, P.R. Paulson and C.A. Meyer, "What makes a portfolio a portfolio?," *Educational Leadership,* vol. 48, pp. 60-61, 1991.

[22] M. Gearhart and E. Osmundsun, "Assessment portfolios as opportunities for teacher learning.," *Educational Assessment,* vol. 14, pp. 1-24, 2009.

[23] J. Dewey, *Democracy and Education.* New York: MacMillan, 1916.

[24] C. T. Fosnot, Ed., *Constructivism: Theory, Perspectives, and Practice.* New York: Teachers College Press, 1996.

[25] D. Kolb, *Experiential Learning: Experience as the Source of Learning and Development.* New Jersey: Prentice Hall, 1984.

[26] J. Zull, *The art of changing the brain: Enriching the practice of teaching by exploring the biology of learning.* Virginia: Stylus, 2002.

[27] L. Darling-Hammond and N. Richardson, "Teacher Learning: What Matters," *Educational Leadership,* vol. 6, pp. 46-53, 2009.

A More Formal Approach to "Computer Science: Principles"

Rex Page
University of Oklahoma
Norman, OK, USA
page@ou.edu

Ruben Gamboa
University of Wyoming
Laramie, WY, USA
ruben@uwyo.edu

ABSTRACT

We report on a course, entitled "How Computers Work: Logic in Action", which we have offered the past few years at the University of Oklahoma, and which will be offered soon at the University of Wyoming. Intended for non-CS majors, this course is our answer to the question, *What would you teach if you had only one course to help students grasp the essence of computation and perhaps inspire a few of them to make computing a subject of further study?* Assuming no prior knowledge of computers or mathematics beyond high school algebra, the course is compatible with the *Computer Science: Principles* approach proposed by the College Board, although it is a significant departure from the pilot courses that are currently following this approach.

Categories and Subject Descriptors

K.3.2 [**Computers and Education**]: Computer and Information Science Education; F.4.1 [**Mathematical Logic and Formal Languages**]: Mathematical Logic—*Mechanical theorem proving*; D.1.1 [**Programming Techniques**]: Applicative (Functional) Programming

Keywords

First year, service course, formal computation.

1. BACKGROUND

For the past few years, we have had the opportunity to teach a broad computer science course to honors students at the University of Oklahoma. The corps of honors students is a self-selected group, with above average abilities, motivation, or both. To qualify for the honors program, students must hold a grade point average (GPA) of at least 3.4 out of 4.0 when they join the honors program, and they must maintain this GPA at the time of graduation to receive an honors designation in their diploma. Because of their high academic engagement, these students can succeed in almost any course, so they make our job as professors easy. However, their diverse backgrounds also make them particularly challenging: 44% of the students who have taken our course are science majors, ranging from physics and chemistry to meteorology; 31% are engineering majors, including computer science and computer engineering, as well as many traditional engineering disciplines; and 22% are humanities, social sciences, or business majors. Another measure of the students' disparate backgrounds is provided by their computing experience: 60% had some prior exposure to programming, primarily in high school, but the others knew very little of computing. One place where the students were similar to each other was in academic classification: nearly all of them were in their first two years of college.

So our challenge was clear: How to design a course that presents an overview of the essential principles of computation to a group of talented students with varying degrees of computing experience and mathematical preparation. This immediately presented us with two seemingly conflicting challenges. Since the students were majoring in many different disciplines, the only guarantee we had with regards to mathematical background was the minimum required by the university, namely high school algebra. So it was imperative that the course be accessible to a student with only this minimum background. Of course, this also means that the course is accessible to many, if not most, high school students. And this leads into the second challenge. While the course must remain accessible to students with little mathematical preparation and no prior exposure to computer science, it must also be engaging and challenging to those students who have had some programming experience.

But this only masks the deeper issue. What exactly are these "essential principles of computation" that we wish students to learn? Our answer to this question is influenced by the First Year curriculum proposed by Felleisen and the PLT group[7, 8], but adapted and pared down so that it can be fruitfully presented in a single semester to students who may not take another computer science course. In particular, the First Year blends program design, discrete math, and the beginnings of software verification using the automated theorem prover ACL2, and all these are also features of our course [12, 6].

Here are the principles we wanted to impart to students. To start with, students should build a mental model of computation, so they can see how it's possible for mechanical devices to perform computations. So one essential principle is as follows:

1. Algebraic formulas can specify computations.

SIGCSE'13, March 6–9, 2013, Denver, Colorado, USA.

Once students understand that computations can be specified using ordinary algebra, it is possible to discuss how software systems can be constructed. This leads to the next essential principles:

2. Abstractions allow solutions to small problems to be arranged into the solution to big ones.

3. Important, complex algorithms derive from simple, definitional properties.

The relevance of these ideas is made clear by considering some applications of software. Our goal is to make sure that students see the connection between software systems—specified as sets of algebraic equations—and the real world. We also stress the importance of getting the software right, precisely because the software is solving real-world problems.

4. There is a strong correspondence between logic formulas and digital circuits.

5. Models expressed in software capture the behavior of processes and devices.

6. Testing and reasoning critically about software are important tools in ensuring that the software works as intended.

The relevance of the material is supported even more by considering applications familiar to students, e.g,. the internet. What we want the students to understand is that computers work on the concept of *scale*. The big applications they are familiar with operate on the exact same concepts they learn in class. The only difference is that the problems are bigger, so abstraction plays a major role, and the final solution is composed of many, many steps. In other words, the main difference between computing as they see it in class and computing as practiced in, say, Google, is one of scale. Solving the scale problem is an engineering problem, the main problem studied in a computer science degree.

7. Different definitional properties can specify the same functions, but at vastly different computational expense.

8. Computational expense makes some useful devices feasible and others infeasible.

9. All of the ideas in the course bear on the ability of computers to deal with information on the massive scale needed to provide services like search engines, internet storefronts, and social networks.

This is not the typical introductory computer science course! The material does not overlap directly with the mainstream material from a computer science or computer engineering program, so those students with prior exposure to computers find it new and challenging.

A feature of this course is that it includes topics from logic and software verification, which are usually not included in the computer science curriculum. We believe that the course has been successful because of the algebraic description of computation that we use. In this view, programs are really ordinary equations, very similar to the equations students have seen in high school algebra. So the students learn about computation in a comfortable framework. Moreover, this framework lends itself to automatic verification, and students learn how to use the theorem prover ACL2 to automate many of the reasoning tasks. ACL2 is not completely automatic, usually requiring much assistance from its users. However, the necessary assistance can be minimized by carefully choosing the programs to study and the properties under consideration, so that the proofs of these properties can be readily found using ACL2's heuristics. Others who have also incorporated ACL2 into lower division computer science courses have also found that students can benefit from using ACL2 for the purposes of the course, without having to become ACL2 experts [6, 2]. The end result is that students learn how to think formally about computation, without being overwhelmed by the logical machinery that would normally be required.

In its approach and objectives, this course has much in common with the *Computer Science: Principles* course proposed by the college board [15]. For instance, our course is not designed to teach students how to program. Students do learn some programming, but not enough to take on any serious development project. Instead, the course tries to provide insight into the nature and relevance of computation.

Our course differs significantly from other courses in the *Computer Science: Principles* vein. Currently, a number of pilot courses are running nationwide [16]. The majority of these use scripting languages to facilitate programming. Python is popular for this purpose, as are visual scripting languages like BYOB (aka SNAP!) and App Inventor [10, 9]. Doing so has a major advantage, in that it allows to create software that is very similar to what they use daily, e.g., App Inventor allows them to build mobile applications with only minimum effort. It also allows more time to be spent on the social aspects of computing, so many of these courses feature topics from privacy and security, as covered in the textbook from Abelson et al [1]. There are many things we like about this approach, but we chose to go in a different direction because we wanted students to really understand the layers of abstraction that allow simple ideas from logic, which are readily implemented as circuits, to implement complex applications, e.g., mobile apps or popular websites. And we also wanted to emphasize how mistakes in software can be avoided and the importance of doing so, since software is increasingly relevant in our lives in many different contexts.

We will address the connections between our course and the principles approach in Sect. 3. But first, we will describe the course in more detail in Sect. 2, and we share the results from the previous offerings of this course in Sect. 4.

2. COURSE CONTENTS

We use equations extensively, both to describe functions and to present properties that these functions should have. Equations are a good fit for a computational approach based on algebra, but they are not the usual way in which software is described. For example, the imperative model of programming introduces variables to hold state, assignment statements to mutate state, and other programming constructs to control the execution of the program. Consequently, we chose to use a purely functional approach to programming, and in particular we use the language ACL2, which is a variant of Common Lisp. To our knowledge, undergraduate students are only exposed to ACL2 in a few courses nationwide. But what makes it ideal for our purpose is that it is not just a programming language. It is also a logic of computation and an automated theorem prover for this logic. So students learn the basics of programming *and* of reasoning about such programs.

We introduce the equational style of programming with a handful of examples. For example, the classic Lisp list operations can be introduced with the following equations:

$$
\begin{array}{lcll}
(\texttt{cons}\ x\ [x_1\ x_2\ ...\ x_n]) & = & [x\ x_1\ x_2\ ...\ x_n] & \{cons\} \\
(\texttt{first}\ [x_1\ x_2\ ...\ x_{n+1}]) & = & x_1 & \{fst\} \\
(\texttt{rest}\ [x_1\ x_2\ ...\ x_{n+1}]) & = & [x_2\ ...\ x_{n+1}] & \{rst\}
\end{array}
$$

Note that the equations are labeled, so that we can refer to them later.

Students have no problems understanding these equations, and they quickly gain an understanding of what these functions are. In fact, they readily accept (without any sense of proof) that the following two equations must also hold:

$$
\begin{array}{lcll}
(\texttt{first}\ (\texttt{cons}\ x\ [x_1\ x_2\ ...\ x_n])\ ) & = & x & \{fst\text{-}id\} \\
(\texttt{rest}\ (\texttt{cons}\ x\ [x_1\ x_2\ ...\ x_n])\ ) & = & [x_1\ x_2\ ...\ x_n] & \\
 & & & \{rst\text{-}id\}
\end{array}
$$

Even at this early stage, we can introduce one of the main ideas of the course, namely that testing and critical reasoning are necessary to ensure that the functions work as expected. Students certainly believe the last two equations—but are they actually true? To verify this, we make use of the `DoubleCheck` testing framework of Dracula [6, 5]. In the style of Racket (formerly known as DrScheme), Dracula is a front-end that makes it easier for many students to interact with ACL2. One of its most useful features is `DoubleCheck`, which was inspired by the `QuickCheck` testing framework for Haskell. It allows students to specify properties that should be true of either built-in functions or new functions they write. For example, a student could submit the property *fst-id* to `DoubleCheck`, which would then generate random tests to see if the property is likely. If the tests pass—and in this case, they surely will—the library moves on to the second ("double") check. I.e., it submits the property to the ACL2 theorem prover, which tries to prove it automatically. In the case of *fst-id*, the theorem prover is able to verify the property automatically, so the student can be assured that the property in fact holds for all inputs.

The equations *fst* and *rst* capture the essence of `first` and `rest`, but neither equation fully captures the corresponding function. For example, what is `first` of the empty list? The actual answer to this question is not important, and different programmers (and even programming languages) will provide different answers. But what *is* important is that there be some answer. E.g., we may choose to use the following equation to resolve the matter:

$$(\texttt{first}\ [])\ =\ []\quad \{fst\text{-}empty\}$$

Thus students are introduced to the concept of function definitions. In this model, functions are defined by a set of equations. We stress that the equations must satisfy two key properties. First, they must be *consistent*. That is, no two equations can provide different results for the same input. Second, they must be *comprehensive*. All forms of input must match the left-hand side of at least one equation.

Things become more complicated when inductive (also called recursive) definitions are necessary. Opinions certainly vary as to whether recursion is a topic suitable for beginning programmers [13, 17, 3, 11]. However, we find that inductive definitions arise naturally in the context of properties. To see this point, consider the square root function, which is very familiar to all students. They would certainly believe that $\sqrt{x \cdot y} = \sqrt{x}\sqrt{y}$ is true, and nobody would remark that this is an inductive property. Of course, this one equation is not a definition of square root, but that is precisely the point. Properties that use the same function symbol in the left and right-hand sides pose no immediate problem, and *some* inductive properties can be used to define functions.

In fact, students readily accept the following properties for the `append` function:

$$
\begin{array}{lcll}
(\texttt{append}\ (\texttt{cons}\ x\ xs)\ ys) & = & (\texttt{cons}\ x\ (\texttt{append}\ xs\ ys)) & \\
 & & & \{app1\} \\
(\texttt{append}\ [\ ]\ ys) & = & ys & \{app0\}
\end{array}
$$

In the beginning, we encourage students to think of these equations simply as properties that any reasonable definition of `append` must satisfy. Once the students are comfortable with these equations, we extend the notion of function definition—that is, definitions by way of equations—to include inductive definitions. As before, such equations should be *consistent* and *comprehensive*, but now we add a third criteria for a valid definition. The equations must be *constructive*, i.e., any inductive reference to an operator must be on a reduced computation. In the case above, the inductive reference to `append` is on the value of xs which is smaller than `(cons` x xs`)` in the left-hand side.

What students learn is that all properties of any function derive from a set of equations, as long as these are *consistent*, *comprehensive*, and *constructive*. These three characteristics of definitional equations, which we refer to as "The Three Cs," form a recurring theme throughout the course.

Students analyze functions defined inductively in the same way as they do other functions. For instance, students (or the instructors) can state properties that they believe the functions should hold, such as the associativity of `append`. These properties can be expressed using the `DoubleCheck` testing framework, and Dracula will test the properties on random values. If the tests pass, the property is then submitted to the ACL2 theorem prover for formal verification. The difference is that in this case the proof requires induction.

At this point, students mostly believe that all properties of the function `append` must follow algebraically from its defining equations. We reinforce this concept now by demonstrating how the associativity of `append` can be proved formally. A pencil-and-paper proof of this property is based on induction on the length of the list xs. The base case uses the defining equation $\{app0\}$, while the inductive case relies on $\{app1\}$ and, of course, the inductive hypothesis. While students do not necessarily learn how to carry out these proofs by themselves, they come to appreciate that the same algebra they learned in high school, albeit with less familiar functions, such as `cons`, can be used effectively to think about software and to guarantee that a particular function works as expected.

It should be noted that proofs of basic facts, such as the associativity of `append`, can be quite challenging. Students do learn how to write down some of these proofs, and they certainly learn how to read them. Mostly, however, they use ACL2 to find proofs of the more substantial theorems. Here, too, the students can run into trouble, because even though ACL2 is fully automated, it does not always find proofs of even basic theorems. This means that students must also discover (with some help) key lemmas that can be used to guide ACL2 to the desired results. To minimize the students' frustration, we have designed specific problems that work exceptionally well with ACL2's heuristics, so that many proofs are found fully automatically.

In the remainder of the course, students gain more experience with programming using equations to define functions. Our approach is to introduce programs in a variety of small application domains, and to ask students to write (or complete) some of the functions that are useful in that domain.

Of course, discovering equations satisfying "The Three Cs" that can define a particular function is no easy task! This requires more than an understanding of algebraic rules. We tell students, and they soon agree, that it requires insight and creativity, even though defining functions entails "nothing more than" working with ordinary, algebraic equations and classical logic. In fact, this is another recurring theme in the class. Simple mechanisms can combine to produce extremely complex results, sometimes by accident, and sometimes not—and doing it intentionally is profoundly creative.

The first application domain that we use as a programming playground is the world of propositional logic and combinational digital circuits. This domain is advantageous, because the equations of Boolean algebra are very similar to the familiar equations from high school algebra. We show students how all properties of Boolean algebra, including the traditional truth tables, can be derived from a handful of equations that suffice to capture the meaning of the propositional connectives. This gives students practice in the type of algebraic reasoning that they will later employ when reasoning about more complicated functions.

After introducing propositional logic, we move on to digital circuits. This serves two distinct purposes. First, it allows us to directly connect what the students have been doing in the course so far to working, physical computing devices. Second, and more important, it begins an explicit discussion on the nature of abstraction: propositional formulas and combinational circuits are quite obviously related, and students can analyze one of them by studying the other.

Next, we provide a brief introduction to computer arithmetic, culminating in a ripple-carry adder circuit. Again, this provides us with an excellent opportunity to discuss abstraction. At the top level is ordinary arithmetic, which the students take for granted. Below that are the rules of numerals, i.e., lists of digits and arithmetic operators on those lists. Numerals are a representation for numbers, and different strings of numerals can represent the same number. This point is driven home by considering the binary representation of numbers. The process of abstraction continues, because binary digits themselves represent different voltages in wires of digital circuits. The result of all this is that students see how it is that physical devices can perform meaningful computations. I.e., they can see how a particular circuit consisting of logical gates can seem to compute the sum of two numbers. More than that, the different layers of abstraction are precisely defined, and the transitions between these layers can be formalized by a set of equations which be checked with `DoubleCheck` and verified informally with hand proofs and formally with ACL2. This culminates in the following ACL2 theorem, which is presented in class:

```
(implies (and (bitp c0) (bit-listp x) (bit-listp y)
              (= (len x) (len y)))
         (let* ((a (adder c0 x y))
                (s (first a))
                (c (second a)))
           (= (num (append s (list c)))
              (+ c0 (num x) (num y)))))
```

This theorem uses the "type-checking" functions `bitp` and `bit-listp` which recognize bits and lists of bits, respectively. It also uses the function `num` which converts a list of bits into a number, and `adder` which adds two lists of bits encoding numbers in two's complement notation. All of these functions were previously defined in our equational style.

This process continues with the introduction of some typical data structures, such as trees and hashes, and different combinational circuits, such as multiplexers. As the problems get bigger, we provide the students with more and more guidance and supporting artifacts, so that they can continue learning without having to write (and reason about) an inordinate amount of code. Eventually, we reach the top of the abstraction pyramid in a very high-level discussion of computing systems that students use in their daily lives. Here the discussion is at the conceptual level, and not at all at the nuts-and-bolts level of a ripple-carry adder.

The first major application comes from Facebook. Throughout the course, we have been convincing students that simple mechanisms can combine to produce extremely complex results, and that the same basic mechanism they learn about in class have been put together in creative ways to produce all the computing artifacts they have already seen. The only mystery is how to deal with scale, both the scale of the program itself and the scale of the data it works on—and Facebook is a perfect case study on scale.

We tell the students that Facebook must combine data from two large datasets in order to produce a single page. It must consult its dataset of "friends" so that it knows which status updates to post, and it must also ccons-first-rest-defonsult its dataset of "statuses" so that it knows what your friends have been saying. Without providing any evidence, we tell them that combining these two datasets is conceptually simple but computationally infeasible with traditional technology because of the sheer number of facts. As a consequence, Facebook developed its own database solution, the NoSQL database Cassandra [14]. We do not expect students to learn much about databases, whether relational or NoSQL in this course. However, students can grasp the essence of Cassandra replication, and they can readily see how this affords the massive scalability required by Facebook. Students also see how Cassandra uses many of the algorithms and data structures they have already seen, such as hash functions and lists.

Next, students learn a little about scaling at Google. Again, the need for scale is easily motivated because of the sheer size of the web. We ask students to consider the difficulty of doing something as simple as finding how many other web pages link to each page in the web, a key metric in the PageRank algorithm that Google uses for ranking search results. The answer, we show them, is Google's distributed platform MapReduce [4]. With its roots in functional programming, MapReduce is actually easy to introduce to students who are already familiar with Lisp in the form of ACL2, so we can present relevant examples with actual code.

For example, WordCount is one of Google's simple MapReduce examples. In this case, the input to the map function is a word appearing in some document and a partial count, which can simply be 1. Our initial sample consists of each word from the Gettysburg Address and an initial count of 1. In general, a main program would process a document and produce such calls to map. The output of map is a list of partial word counts. Only one word (the input word) appears in this list, but the MapReduce framework requires that the function return a more general list of values. The inputs to the reduce function are a word and a list of all the counts that were seen for this word. The output is a list of words and their combined sums, computed using the auxiliary function **sumlist**—again, there is only one word in the list, although the extra container is required by the MapReduce framework.

$$
\begin{array}{lcll}
(\texttt{wc-map}\ w\ c) & = & [\ [w\ c]\ ] & \{\textit{wc-map}\} \\
(\texttt{wc-reduce}\ w\ cs) & = & [\ [w\ (\texttt{sumlist}\ cs)]\ ] & \\
 & & & \{\textit{wc-reduce}\} \\
(\texttt{sumlist}\ [\,]) & = & 0 & \{\textit{sumlist-0}\} \\
(\texttt{sumlist}\ [x_1\ x_2\ ...\ x_n]) & = & x_1 + (\texttt{sumlist}\ [x_2\ ...\ x_n]) & \\
 & & & \{\textit{sumlist-0}\}
\end{array}
$$

3. CONCORDANCE

Although our course is very different than the official pilot courses for the *Computer Science: Principles* initiative, we believe that it can be used in that setting [16]. In this section, we explore how our course satisfies the theme and topics covered in *Computer Science: Principles* (henceforth, CSP).

For instance, the CSP contains seven "big ideas," further divided into specific learning objectives and evidence that supporting them. The first big idea is that computing is a creative activity, and the associated learning objectives include understanding that tools and techniques from computer science are used to *create* and analyze computing artifacts, but it goes beyond that. It also involves using computing as a means for creative expression and as a tool to build artifacts that have some practical applications (even if only for personal reasons.) This idea is central to our course (as to many other introductory and advanced courses in computer science.) Students have the opportunity to create several programs *and* to analyze many of their properties, mostly of the correctness flavor, e.g., "the circuit for a ripple-carry adder correctly performs addition of n-bit binary integers." Students readily agree that writing programs that can perform specific tasks is an intensely creative process. Moreover, students are exposed to a number of different application domains and they see how very practical problems, such as solving arithmetic problems or indexing the world-wide web, can be solved using computation.

The second big idea is abstraction, which comes in a variety of flavors. In our course, abstraction is one of the main ideas. This is the reason why we present boolean expressions and combinational digital circuits, and why we go on to build machine representations of arithmetic. The students quickly appreciate the benefit of abstraction in information hiding. In addition, students explore properties of the various abstractions and mappings between them, and they learn that some properties of a complex model can be more easily explored by analyzing a simpler one.

The third big idea involves data. Students are expected to use computers to explore data sets and understand how the different ways in which the data can be represented affect the exploration. Our course does expose students to this idea, although we have not had the time to explore it as deeply as other CSP courses. We do stress that the big difference between toy applications and real-world applications is a matter of scaling, both in data and program size. And we show students examples of how large data sets are used and processed, e.g., by Google and Facebook.

The next two big ideas encompass algorithms and programming, and both of these are very much at the center of our course. We describe algorithms using algebraic equalities, and this is something that students start doing from the first few classes. Students learn to develop their own algorithms in different applications, and they learn to express these algorithms in ACL2, which as a programming language is almost identical to the pure functional subset of Common Lisp. Students also evaluate these algorithms, mostly in terms of correctness, but also in terms of performance, and they learn that some algorithms yield efficient computations while other algorithms to the same problem result in infeasible computations. This last point is especially central to the discussion of data structures, e.g, when describing binary trees, balanced trees, and hashtables.

The sixth idea is concerned with the internet, and it includes knowing basic networking concepts, characteristics of the internet, and basic concepts from cybersecurity. Our course does address the internet, but not as much as other CSP courses. In particular, we discuss the structure of the web and the notion of indexing and ranking as it relates to search engines. We also discuss different types of web applications, including traditional Web 1.0 storefronts and the more social Web 2.0 applications. In addition, we describe how web applications are implemented and discuss specific components of the solution, such as web servers and databases, but without going into any depth.

The seventh and final big idea concerns the global impact of computers. This actually fits in very well with our approach, because the course is currently directed at honors students, who bring a diverse background to the course, including prior exposure to courses in the humanities. The impact of computers, both good and bad, is a topic for discussion in class. More important, it is a topic that students explore more fully in a research paper and class presentation.

4. OUTCOMES AND CONCLUSION

We have offered this course twice at the University of Oklahoma, and it is scheduled for the current academic year. As of this writing, we are also in the process of migrating the course to the honors program at the University of Wyoming, where it will be offered for the first time this year.

This is not an easy course. Although the material is couched in the familiar framework of algebraic equations, it includes topics in logic, digital circuits, programming, testing, verification, and selected topics from data structures, algorithms, and other areas of computer science. Nevertheless, the course is accessible to students who have had only the standard college preparatory work, in particular high school algebra.

What we found is that all students do well in the course,

despite their different backgrounds. The engineering students outperformed the students in the arts and sciences, but not by much. And the difference between students in the arts and those in the sciences was negligible.

Students have been satisfied with the course. They found the course challenging but rewarding. Their anonymous comments suggest that they gained a fundamental understanding of what computers can actually do and how they can do such things. This is, in our opinion, the basis for computational thinking.

Because the course has been offered under the framework of the honors program, we have another way to judge student satisfaction. Every year, different honors courses are proposed, and the students have an important voice in determining which of these courses are actually offered. Our course has been selected three times now, and placed prominently as one of a handful of options that can satisfy one of the major requirements for the honors program.

When we started this effort, we believed that it was possible to offer a course that could introduce students from many different backgrounds, not just computer science majors, to formal ways of thinking about programs. We also believed that such a course could demystify computers and place them in a larger historical context. However, we were concerned that students would find the mathematical rigor to be too challenging. We can now report that the more optimistic viewpoint was the correct one, and we are convinced this is due in large part to the presentation of computation as a form of equational reasoning and the use of tools to aid in proof discovery. Specifically, writing programs as simple equations means that reasoning about those programs follows the exact same patterns and tools that students learned in high school algebra (and that we reinforce in the early parts of the course.) And by carefully choosing the programs that we ask students to write and the properties that we ask them to verify, we can ensure that the proofs can be found by the theorem prover ACL2 with only a minimum of assistance from the students.

In the end, students learn much about software, how to build it and how to think about it. The majority of students will not take any further courses in computer science, but they will take with them a new way of thinking about computation to their diverse disciplines. And those students who do end up pursuing advanced courses in computer science will have a bird's eye view of the field that we hope will stay with them and give them a unique perspective as they study the engineering details that are needed to construct large-scale computing systems.

5. ACKNOWLEDGMENTS

The authors would like to thank the National Science Foundation for supporting the work described in this paper under Grant No. 1016532.

6. REFERENCES

[1] Hal Abelson, Ken Ledeen, and Harry Lewis. *Blown to Bits: Your Life, Liberty, and Happiness After the Digital Explosion.* Addison-Wesley Professional, 2008.

[2] Harsh Chamarthi, Peter Dillinger, Matt Kaufmann, and Panagiotis Manolios. Interactive testing and interactive theorem proving. In *Proceedings of the Tenth International Workshop of the ACL2 Theorem Prover and its Applications (ACL2-2011)*, 2011.

[3] Stephen Cooper, Wanda Dann, and Randy Pausch. Teaching objects-first in introductory computer science. *SIGCSE Bull.*, 35(1):191–195, Jan. 2003.

[4] Jeffrey Dean and Sanjay Ghemawat. Mapreduce: simplified data processing on large clusters. *Commun. ACM*, 51(1):107–113, Jan. 2008.

[5] Carl Eastlund. DoubleCheck your theorems. In *Proceedings of the Eighth International Workshop on the ACL2 Theorem Prover and its Applications (ACL2-09)*, 2009.

[6] Carl Eastlund, Dale Vaillancourt, and Matthias Felleisen. ACL2 for freshmen: First experiences. In *Proceedings of the Seventh International Workshop of the ACL2 Theorem Prover and its Applications (ACL2-2007)*, 2007.

[7] Matthias Felleisen. The first year. `http://www.ccs.neu.edu/home/matthias/Presentations/FirstYear/first%20year.pdf`.

[8] Matthias Felleisen, Robert Bruce Findler, Matthew Flatt, and Shriram Krishnamurthi. *How to Design Programs: An Introduction to Programming and Computing.* MIT Press, Boston, 2001.

[9] Brian Harvey and Jens Mönig. Bringing "no ceiling" to scratch: Can one language serve kids and computer scientists? In *Constructionism 2010 (Paris)*, 2010.

[10] Yu-Chang Hsu, Kerry Rice, and Lisa Dawley. Empowering educators with google's android app inventor: An online workshop in mobile app design. *British Journal of Educational Technology*, 43(1):E1–E5, Jan. 2012.

[11] Joint Task Force on Computing Curricula. Computing curricula 2001 computer science. *Journal of Educational Resources in Computing (JERIC)*, 1(3es), Sept. 2001.

[12] Matt Kaufmann, Panagiotis Manolios, and J Strother Moore. *Computer-Aided Reasoning: An Approach.* Kluwer Academic Press, 2000.

[13] Takayuki Kimura. Recursive programming in english for freshmen. *SIGCSE Bull.*, 9(1):129–132, Feb. 1977.

[14] Avinash Lakshman and Prashant Malik. Cassandra: a decentralized structured storage system. *SIGOPS Oper. Syst. Rev.*, 44(2):35–40, Apr. 2010.

[15] The College Board. Computer science: Principles. `http://www.collegeboard.com/prod\_downloads/computerscience/ComputationalThinkingCS_Principles.pdf`, 2011.

[16] The College Board. CS principles pilot sites. http://www.csprinciples.org/home/pilot-sites, 2012.

[17] Franklyn Turbak, Constance Royden, Jennifer Stephan, and Jean Herbst. Teaching recursion before loops in CS1. *The Journal of Computing in Small Colleges*, 14(4):86–101, 1999.

Building Equitable Computer Science Classrooms: Elements of a Teaching Approach

Niral Shah
University of California, Berkeley
niral@berkeley.edu

Colleen M. Lewis
Harvey Mudd College
lewis@cs.hmc.edu

Roxane Caires
University of California, Berkeley
roxane.caires@berkeley.edu

Nasar Khan
University of California, Berkeley
nasarmkhan@gmail.com

Amirah Qureshi
University of California, Berkeley
amirahqureshi@gmail.com

Danielle Ehsanipour
University of California, Berkeley
d.ehsanipour@berkeley.edu

Noopur Gupta
University of California, Berkeley
noopurgupta@berkeley.edu

ABSTRACT

This paper offers a framework for equitable instruction that emerged while designing a computer science course for students entering the sixth grade. Leveraging research from a range of fields, including sociology, mathematics education, and the learning sciences, we argue that in addition to material resources, such as rich course content and quality instruction, equity also depends on students' access to non-material resources, such as productive domain identities and peer relationships. We illustrate each dimension of the framework by describing in detail a core set of pedagogical practices implemented during a summer course.

Categories and Subject Descriptors

K.3.2 **[Computers and Education]:** Computer and Information Science Education—*computer science education*

General Terms

Human Factors

Keywords

Scratch, equity, identity

1. INTRODUCTION

A primary goal of the National Science Foundation's *Computing Education for the 21st Century* (CE21) program is to identify pedagogical practices that may broaden participation among students from groups who are underrepresented in computer science, such as women and racial minorities. In fact, the CE21 initiative reflects an increasingly field-wide concern for equity, which is the idea that opportunities to learn computational thinking should be equally accessible to all segments of the population [1]. In this paper we elaborate a multidimensional framework for equitable computer science instruction that aims to disrupt inequities that occur at the level of classroom interaction.

SIGCSE '13, March 6–9, 2013, Denver, CO, USA.

Equity can be conceptualized in terms of students' access to material resources (e.g., computer labs, substantive coursework beyond basic computer literacy) [12]. We argue that equitable classrooms also require pedagogical practices that account for the social and emotional aspects of learning [1][4]. To that end, we propose a framework for equitable teaching that consists of four distinct but interrelated dimensions: (1) access to rich course content; (2) access to quality instruction; (3) access to identities as computer scientists; and (4) access to productive peer relationships. To illustrate each dimension, we report on our experience designing and implementing a suite of equity-oriented teaching practices in a computer science course for students entering the sixth grade.

This article makes two primary contributions that can support the computer science education community in researching and implementing equitable pedagogy. First, it provides a theoretical framework consisting of four dimensions of equity that we believe are important for designing and evaluating teaching practices that support equity in computer science classrooms. And second, it presents our experiences developing and implementing concrete practices that may support educators in building equitable learning environments.

2. THEORIZING "EQUITY"

Educational equity is predicated on the idea that all students should have equal access to the particular resources they need to succeed in school [9]. Some of these resources, such as rich course content and quality instruction, are material in nature. In their longitudinal study of computing programs at three, racially diverse Los Angeles high schools, Margolis, Estrella, Goode, Jellison Holme, and Nao [12] illuminated some of the ways in which differences in students' access to material resources can lead to systemic inequities in computer science education. For example, while two of the schools in the study had ample technological resources (e.g., computer labs), the only coursework available to students focused on basic computer literacy—these schools were "technology rich but curriculum poor" ([12], p. 14).

And yet, Margolis and her colleagues found that disparities in material resources were but one driver of inequity. Unlike the first two schools, the third school in their study did offer advanced computing courses (i.e., rich course content). However, few African American and Latina/o students enrolled in the school's Advanced Placement (AP) Computer Science class, which was instead disproportionately dominated by White male students. In part, the researchers attributed this participation gap to a learning environment that positioned less experienced and less confident students—all of whom in this particular study happened to be either female or from historically underrepresented racial groups—as less capable of learning the subject. In their words, such an environment "constrains the choices [students] make about whether or not to engage in AP computer science specifically, and the AP pipeline in general" ([12], p. 87).

Other researchers have also investigated the ways in which the quality and configuration of computer science learning environments mediate student engagement. Garvin-Doxas and Jackson [8] analyzed undergraduate computer science classrooms that engendered an impersonal, "defensive climate," which they attributed to particular classroom norms. For instance, instructors rarely used students' names, and students rarely interacted with instructors or even spoke in class. Further, similar to the AP Computer Science classroom in the previous study, status hierarchies formed between students with prior experience and students who were relatively newer to the discipline. These hierarchies were reproduced in everyday classroom interactions, including moments when certain "high-status" students asked public questions that—from the researchers' perspectives—seemed to be more about showing off expert-level knowledge than genuine requests for clarification.

Together, these studies speak to the role of *non-material* resources in student learning. Specifically, classroom environments that engender status hierarchies between students are problematic because they can cause those students who are positioned as "low-status" to disengage from the learning process [4]. Disengagement can occur because hierarchies prevent students from forming relationships with their peers and seeing them as resources [4], but also because, as learning theorists have argued, learning and identity are closely intertwined [13][16]. That is, when students do not perceive themselves as capable of academic success, they are less likely to persist in learning: If a computer science learner does not believe that she or he can be successful in learning computer science, then why make the effort? [7] In this sense, students' access to identities as computer scientists and access to peer relationships are both components of equity, and carry at least as much weight as students' access to physical resources, rich course content, or highly qualified teachers [9].

To summarize, then, equitable teaching approaches must simultaneously account for students' access to both the material *and* non-material resources necessary for learning. The multi-dimensional framework for equitable instruction we present here is grounded in this conceptualization of equity (see Figure 1). In subsequent sections we describe the specific pedagogical practices we implemented, as well as the research base that informed their design.

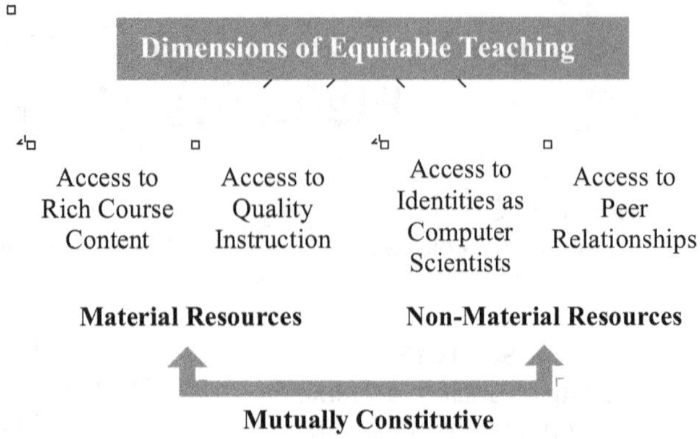

Figure 1. Framework for Equitable Teaching

3. DESCRIPTION OF CLASSROOM SETTING

Our team of seven researchers collaborated to design and implement plans for equitable instruction in a course titled, "Creating Music, Movies, and Games with Computers." The course took place over three weeks in the summer of 2012, and was part of a university-sponsored summer enrichment program. The enrichment program is designed for academically high-achieving students, and students without need-based financial aid paid 650 dollars to participate in the course.

There were two offerings of the course: a morning class and an afternoon class. Overall, there were 36 hours of instruction per course. Each course offering met four days a week for three weeks, and each class session lasted 3 hours, consisting of two 90-minute sessions separated by a 30-minute break. During the course students used the following programming languages: Scratch (24 hours), BYOB (3 hours), and Logo (1.5 hours) [14], and completed a final project in their choice of these languages (7.5 hours).

The seven researchers met daily throughout the three weeks to discuss the experiences and perceived needs of the students. During the class sessions, three of the researchers served as ethnographers, and took detailed field notes about the learning environment and students' experiences within it. The remaining four researchers worked as instructors for the course. Two of the instructors, one female and one male, facilitated the majority of whole-class discussion. One of these instructors originally designed the course and had taught three previous offerings, while the other instructor had taught the course the previous summer. The two remaining instructors were female and had never taught this course but had experience with computer science.

Forty-five students were enrolled across both classes: 22 students in the morning class, and 23 students in the afternoon class. With the exception of two students who were entering the fifth grade in the fall, all of the students were entering the sixth grade. Based on gender data collected by the enrichment program, 23 students were parent-identified as female and 22 students as male (51% female, 49% male). Although the female-male ratio was lower in the morning class (43:57 in the morning class, and 59:41 in the afternoon class), we note that these demographics do not mirror the underrepresentation of women at the college or career level for computer science [5]. And for the purpose of this paper, we will refer to our course as "gender balanced."

A typical class session involved work within an online curriculum, a 15-minute paper-based assessment, lecture with whole class discussion, and a 30-minute paper-based assignment to be completed at home. For each of the 12 class sessions, the online curriculum contained a set of formative assessments and programming tasks. All students began with the same activity each day and were allowed to move at their own pace. Topics covered included: conditionals, looping, iteration, problem decomposition, and event-based programming. Previous research provides additional details regarding the course content [10][11].

Each day the students alternated between working in the online curriculum individually and working with a partner. On "solo programming" days, although students worked on their own computers, they were still assigned a partner who they were encouraged to turn to for help. On days that students worked with other students, we employed a practice referred to as *pair programming*, in which students are paired in groups of two (and, in our class, occasionally groups of three) while working together on one computer [3]. The student who was in control of the mouse and keyboard is called the "driver," while the student responsible for guiding the driver and giving instructions or advice is called the "navigator."

Further details on the curriculum and pedagogy of the course are discussed below in relation to our specific equity-based goals.

4. IMPLEMENTING EQUITY IN PRACTICE

In this section we introduce the four dimensions of our equity framework, and exemplify each with practices implemented in our course. Our primary pedagogical goal was to build a learning environment that gave all of our students equal access to both the material resources (i.e., rich course content, quality instruction) *and* non-material-resources (i.e., identities as computer scientists, peer relationships) needed for learning. The practices described here and listed in Table 1 constitute a representative sample of our teaching approach.

Table 1. Pedagogical practices listed by dimension.

Dimension	Pedagogical Practices
Access to Rich Course Content	• Emphasizing Multiple Solutions • Using Metaphors to Introduce Concepts • Debugging by "Acting Out"
Access to Quality Instruction	• Tracking Student Progress • Customizing Teaching Plans for Individual Students • Using iClickers for Formative Assessment
Access to Identities as Computer Scientists	• Exposing Students to a Diverse Set of Computer Scientists • Managing Public Displays of Status • Encouraging Connections to "Out-of-School" Identities
Access to Peer Relationships	• Strategically Partnering Students • Encouraging and Structuring Peer Interaction • Modeling Ideal Peer Collaboration

4.1 Access to Rich Course Content

The first dimension of our framework for equitable teaching concerns students' *access to rich course content.* As was noted earlier, curriculum mediates students' opportunities to learn. That is, taking a course in basic computer literacy (e.g., word processing) does not afford the same level of learning opportunities as a course in computer programming [12]. Our course content covered the same material as the first four weeks of an introductory computer science course at a local university. Moreover, the curriculum required students to learn above-grade level mathematics content. For these reasons, we consider the course content presented to our rising sixth grade students to be rich and, for our students, challenging.

In addition to the actual content of the curriculum materials, *access to rich course content* includes teaching practices that make the curriculum accessible. We implemented three practices to help students develop robust problem solving strategies, and to help students access this rich computer science content, which is often seen as abstract and inaccessible. These practices were: 1) emphasizing multiple solutions; 2) using metaphors to introduce concepts; and 3) debugging by "acting out."

4.1.1 Emphasizing Multiple Solutions

Traditional approaches to STEM education tend to convey the message that problems have only "one right answer." This is problematic because it can discourage students from building robust problem solving repertoires and perpetuate narrow, procedural views of rich disciplines like computer science [1]. Instead, we structured our curriculum to emphasize the idea that problems have multiple solution paths. For example, the online curriculum included a task that required students to draw a rainbow in Scratch. The curriculum described two different methods for creating the rainbow, and students were afforded the opportunity to select one of these methods or invent a method of their own.

The theme of "multiple solutions" was also promoted on homework assignments. For instance, a typical homework task involved students being given both a problem and its solution script, and then asked to provide an alternate script that would solve that same problem in a different way. In general, open-ended problems were a staple of the course, and during whole-class discussions the instructors would not let students settle on an initial solution unless alternate solutions had been considered.

4.1.2 Using Metaphors to Introduce Concepts

Students with little or no prior experience in computer science can find the subject abstract and thus difficult to learn. To address this issue, instructors employed specific metaphors to introduce students to the concepts of programming. For example, on the first day of class students were told that they would be learning a language with which to communicate with the computer [6]. We did an activity in which one of the instructors acted as a "computer" and the other instructor acted as a computer scientist. The "computer" left the classroom, and the class agreed on an image (e.g., a house) for the "computer" to draw on the chalkboard, knowing that the "computer" could only understand basic commands about shape, size, and direction. When the "computer" returned, the "computer scientist" gave instructions on how to draw the image without looking at what the "computer" was drawing. The result was a nonsensical picture, as no instruction was clear enough to produce a coherent version of the desired image. This metaphorical activity, which students then repeated with their partners, was intended to teach students about the relationship between computer and computer scientist.

4.1.3 Debugging by "Acting Out"

In keeping with our effort to make computer science more concrete for our students, we sought to support our students in using physical intuition to solve problems [14]. One practice we encouraged students to use in debugging was to physically "act out" the code they had written. As a foundation for incorporating this strategy, students participated in an interactive, outdoor geometry exercise where students acted as "sprites," while their partners gave them instructions to trace squares, triangles, and circles that had previously been drawn in chalk on the ground. Teachers continued to engage the strategy of "acting out" when helping students, and would often have the student instruct them as they acted out the motions for the students to observe. In fact, we noticed a number of occasions when students independently used this strategy with a partner to successfully debug a program. Thus, by having students physically act out code, we aimed to provide a more concrete understanding of programming concepts that are traditionally difficult to grasp.

4.2 Access to Quality Instruction

The second dimension of our framework pertains to students' *access to quality instruction.* While the previous dimension referred to students' opportunities to engage with appropriate and rich computer science curriculum, this dimension focuses on equity-oriented pedagogical practices that are not necessarily specific to computer science. Below we note structural factors that contributed to students' *access to quality instruction* and highlight three practices in the service of this goal: 1) tracking student progress; 2) customizing teaching plans for individual students; and 3) using iClickers for formative assessment.

4.2.1 Structural Factors

A common problem in education is that large class sizes make it difficult for teachers to provide students the individualized support they need. Several structural factors in our particular learning setting mitigated this issue for our students. First, course enrollment in the summer enrichment program was capped at 24 students. Second, many courses in the program were co-taught by two instructors. In our case, not only did the two primary instructors have extensive experience teaching computer science to upper elementary students, but there were two additional instructors who further reduced the student-teacher ratio. These additional teacher resources allowed us to provide prolonged, individual attention to students who were experiencing difficulty, as well as to students who had been absent from a previous class session. In some cases an instructor worked with an individual student for more than an hour, scaffolding where appropriate. While many of these structural affordances are not generalizable, the following practices can be extended to classrooms with fewer resources.

4.2.2 Tracking Student Progress

Although some students will ask for help when they get stuck, others will struggle without calling for an instructor. This can present an inequity in access to instruction, because students who are less comfortable asking for help do not have access to the same resources.

The majority of class time was spent with students working individually or in pairs on the activities from the online curriculum. In order to identify students who were progressing more slowly, or who may need additional support to complete the activities for the day, we maintained a document tracking students' progress through the online curriculum. This document was a matrix consisting of our student roster along one axis and selected steps in the online curriculum along the other. Instructors would mark timestamps when a student was observed completing a particular activity. This tracking document allowed us to approach students that we believed to be in need of additional support, which is a practice that has been referred to as "targeted tutoring" [15]. Having four instructors in the room provided an uncommon level of resources to support students in this way, but the tracker document is a replicable practice that focuses an instructor on the needs of students that may not otherwise seek assistance.

4.2.3 Customizing Teaching Plans for Individual Students

Assuming that all students learn at the same pace and through the same methods can make instruction inaccessible to students progressing both slower and faster than average. Using the idea that "equity" does not necessarily mean that all students have the same needs, we attempted to address each student's unique needs instead of employing a "one size fits all" approach [9]. A primary support for this customized instruction was team conversations before and after class sessions. During these conversations, instructors and ethnographers shared concerns about particular students and developed plans to support these students. For example, one of our students had prior experience with Scratch and tended to go through the curriculum very quickly and with minor difficulties. The teachers were conscious to give the student extra challenges when appropriate. On the other hand, with a student who experienced difficulty, we attempted to identify strengths in this student's understanding and build upon that when working with this student one-on-one.

4.2.4 Using iClickers for Formative Assessment

To assess students' current understanding of a topic, we integrated into our daily routine a set of formative assessment questions in the form of multiple-choice questions. We used iClickers, which are wireless devices used to anonymously vote on multiple-choice questions projected to a classroom of students.

In the case of conceptually rich questions, we had students discuss their solutions with a partner. One concern we had about this arrangement was its potential to reify status hierarchies between students. That is, a student who does not know the correct answer may be embarrassed by attempting to explain what they later find out is an incorrect answer, or one student may dominate the discussion and not provide opportunities for other students to explain their reasoning. To avoid unnecessary embarrassment for students, we made a habit of publicly announcing the correct answer before students discussed their responses with each other. This provided the opportunity for students to work together to explain in their own words the answer or solution without concern that their explanation justifies the wrong answer choice. To avoid one student dominating the discussion, we directed students to alternate which partner should be the first to explain. This was intended to provide both partners equal opportunity to explain their answer even if they were not the more confident or dominant student in the partnership.

4.3 Access to Identities as Computer Scientists

The third dimension in our framework concerns students' *access to identities as computer scientists.* Our commitment to this dimension of equity stems from research demonstrating that students' self-perceptions of their disciplinary capabilities are closely related to the ways in which they take up or reject opportunities to learn [13]. Put simply, we wanted our students to identify as someone capable of doing computer science, and to accept the idea that with enough time and effort, anyone could become a computer scientist. In this section we describe three practices intended to facilitate students' access to productive domain identities: 1) exposing students to a diverse set of computer scientists; 2) managing public displays of status; and 3) encouraging connections to "out-of-school" identities.

4.3.1 Exposing Students to a Diverse Set of Computer Scientists

Part of supporting students' identities as computer scientists was to provide them an expansive sense of who could be a computer scientist, and we did this by creating a classroom that showcased diversity. The team chose 12 computer scientists—six males and six females from historically underrepresented racial and ethnic groups—and displayed prominently on a classroom wall their names, pictures, and brief quotes about why they love computer science. Each day we introduced one of these individuals, who in addition to their ethnic and gender diversity, also worked in a variety of fields including healthcare, film, and business. Beyond these computer scientists, the gender balance of both the instructional team and the students themselves may have implicitly sent the message that both genders are equally capable of being computer scientists.

4.3.2 Managing Public Displays of Status

Students' access to identities as computer scientists is also mediated by public displays of status, which can result in a defensive classroom climate [8]. Based on our previous years of collective teaching experience, we anticipated several ways in which student behavior might create status hierarchies. One way students position themselves (and others) is in whole-class discussion. Students who frequently raise their hand and answer questions correctly can gain higher status because they appear more confident or somehow innately more capable than students who may be just as proficient but do not raise their hand.

To address this issue, we used a system to randomly call on students. All students were told from the first day that when they were called on, they could "pass," and it was emphasized that "passing" should not be viewed negatively. The randomization of student contributions helped avoid discussion being dominated by a limited number of students. This method allowed us to facilitate student participation in a more equitable fashion.

Another potential problem we sought to preempt was the perception that "faster" students are "smarter" students. In the past, we had observed that when students finish an activity before the rest of the class, they tend to display this publicly, which may unintentionally be perceived by their classmates as signifying domain competence. We implemented several practices to mitigate this issue. First, instead of collecting students' paper-based assessments as students finished them, we collected them all at the same time when the instructors saw that most or all of the students were finished. If a student finished early, she or he would begin working in an "extra time" packet provided at the beginning of the course. Second, if on a given day students finished the core lessons of the online curriculum, the last activity for that day was open-ended, thereby engaging students who had moved more quickly through the curriculum. Of course, because students could look around the room and see what their peers were working on, we acknowledge that these practices by themselves could not completely prevent public displays of status. However, these practices helped us to work toward that goal.

4.3.3 Encouraging Connections to "Out-of-School" Identities

Educational researchers have argued that, in part, learning depends on the synchronization between students' personal, out-of-school identities and their in-class domain identities [2]. That is, the more students are able to bring in "who they are" into the classroom, the more likely they are to engage and persist academically. One practice we used to foster this connection was to give students autonomy to design their own final projects, which were shown on the last day of class at an open house attended by friends and family. For instance, one student was extremely fond of horseback riding, and chose to build a computer game around it. The opportunity for students to design their own final projects encouraged students to make a connection between their "personal identity" and "computer scientist identity," thereby fostering the notion that students are capable of being computer scientists.

4.4 Access to Peer Relationships

The final dimension of our framework for equitable teaching pertains to students' *access to peer relationships*. Social relationships are a central component of classroom learning because when students know and treat their peers with respect, they are more likely to view them as resources to learn from [1]. We implemented the following practices to promote all students' access in this area: 1) strategically partnering students; 2) encouraging and structuring peer interaction; and 3) modeling ideal peer collaboration.

4.4.1 Strategically Partnering Students

Students entering a new class will naturally gravitate toward classmates they previously know, and these peer relationships can be a positive influence on learning. However, this can be problematic for students who do not know anyone in the class, and therefore do not have access to an established social group. To address this potential inequity, we strategically assigned students' to new seats each day so as to maximize their opportunity to meet and work with new classmates. Taking into account students' temperament and interaction patterns over time, we also attempted to pair students who we thought would be more likely to engage in productive collaboration (i.e., without one student dominating the conversation or physical resources, without discouraging a weaker student, and without becoming distracted with off-task behavior). As a rule we avoided partnering the most advanced students with students who we perceived to be lacking confidence or to be experiencing extreme difficulty with the material.

4.4.2 Encouraging and Structuring Peer Interaction

A critical component of students' access to peer relationships was for students to come to respect their partners as mutually integral to their respective learning experiences. To facilitate familiarity between partners, we allotted several minutes each day for partners to get to know each other on a social level by discussing a light-hearted prompt, such as "would you rather be 15 feet tall or 2 inches tall?" As previously mentioned, instructors also emphasized that there were multiple ways of determining an answer, and that there was value in understanding how their partners thought through a problem. Finally, when students were doing independent work the teachers encouraged them to consult with their partners when they had a question about a particular task prior to requesting assistance from a teacher.

On pair programming days, it was necessary to provide more explicit interaction structures. For example, every five minutes a

Scratch program played music to signal the switching of roles between "driver" and "navigator." Occasionally some students would show reluctance to give up the "driver" role. To ensure students shared duties in an equitable way, we had them enact an explicit routine that involved both partners standing up, exchanging a "high five," and switching seats.

4.4.3 Modeling Ideal Peer Collaboration

A final practice we implemented to foster productive peer relationships was to have the instructors "role play" exaggerated versions of positive and negative partner interactions as a way of modeling desired student behavior. Themes discussed in the role plays included: encouraging students to ask their partners for help, respecting the switching of roles from "driver" to "navigator" during pair programming, not boasting when they got a question correct, not putting classmates down for going at a different pace, checking in with partners about coding choices, and staying focused. While students often found the teacher-led role-plays amusing, on multiple occasions we also observed students using language and specific problem solving strategies presented during the role-plays in their interactions with each other. By providing a model for students to emulate, we sought to scaffold access to positive peer relationships within the framework of the course content.

5. DISCUSSION

In this paper we outlined a multi-dimensional framework for equitable teaching in computer science. Further, we demonstrated how each dimension was generative of specific pedagogical practices aimed at equalizing students' access to the resources necessary for learning. Equity can be defined as students' access to material resources, such as curriculum and qualified teachers. Leveraging research from a wide range of fields, including psychology, sociology, and mathematics education, we argued that *non-material* resources (e.g., identities as computer scientists, peer relationships) also play a significant role in the learning process, and therefore also hold implications for equity.

For the sake of clarity, we presented each of the four dimensions in our framework as distinct. In reality, however, these dimensions are necessarily interrelated. For example, rich course content is about more than exposing students to certain skills and concepts. It is also about identity, in that it sends a message to students about their capabilities: what kinds of learners they are and what kinds of learners they can become. Conversely, if classroom status hierarchies push students to become increasingly disidentified from a content domain like computer science, they will also become less willing to engage with a rich, challenging task. In general, then, the four access points we highlight are mutually constitutive of each other, and equitable outcomes are more likely when all of the dimensions are considered in parallel.

We should also note that although prior research gives us reason to hypothesize that the practices we implemented were effective in promoting equity, our empirical study of our teaching is ongoing, and at present we do not purport to make such a claim. Still, we are hopeful that educational researchers and practitioners will find ways to adapt elements of our approach to the particular circumstances of their local teaching and learning contexts.

6. ACKNOWLEDGMENTS

We would like to thank the students and staff of the summer enrichment program. The research reported here was supported in part by a grant from the National Science Foundation (Award #1044106), the Institute of Education Sciences pre-doctoral training grant R305B090026 to the University of California, Berkeley, and a NAEd/Spencer Dissertation Fellowship. The opinions expressed are those of the authors and do not represent views of the National Science Foundation, the Institute of Education Sciences, the U.S. Department of Education, or the National Academy of Education/Spencer Foundation.

7. REFERENCES

[1] Boaler, J. (2008). Promoting 'relational equity' and high mathematics achievement through an innovative mixed-ability approach. *British Educational Research Journal, 34(2)*, 167-194.

[2] Cobb, P., & Hodge, L. L. (2002). A relational perspective on issues of cultural diversity and equity as they play out in the mathematics classroom. *Mathematical Thinking and Learning*, 4(2 & 3), 249-284.

[3] Cockburn, A. & Williams, L. (2001). The costs and benefits of pair programming. In G. Succi & M. Marchesi (Eds.), *Extreme Programming Examined* (pp. 223-243). Boston, MA: Addison-Wesley Longman Publishing Co., Inc.

[4] Cohen, E. G., & Lotan, R. A. (1995). Producing equal-status interaction in the heterogeneous classroom. *American Educational Research Journal, 32(1)*, 99-120.

[5] Computing Research Association. Taulbee Survey, 2010-2011. http://www.cra.org/resources/taulbee/.

[6] http://csunplugged.org "Marching Orders: Programming Languages."

[7] Dweck, C. S. (2007). Mindset: The new psychology of success. New York, NY: Random House, Inc.

[8] Garvin-Doxas, K. & Barker, L. J. (2004). Communication in computer science classrooms: Understanding defensive climates as a means of creating supportive behaviors. *Journal of Educational Research in Computing, 4(1)*, 1-18.

[9] Gutierrez, R. (2007). Context matters: Equity, success, and the future of mathematics education. Paper presented at the Proceedings of the 29th annual meeting of the North American Chapter of the International Group for the Psychology of Mathematics Education.

[10] Lewis, C. M. (2011). Is pair programming more effective than other forms of collaboration for young students? *Computer Science Education. 21(2).* 105-134.

[11] Lewis, C. M. & Shah, N. (2012). Building upon and enriching grade four mathematics standards with programming curriculum. *ACM SIGCSE Bulletin. 43(1).* 57-62.

[12] Margolis, M., Estrella, R., Goode, J., Jellison Holme, J., & Nao, K. (2008). Stuck in the shallow end: Education, race, and computing. Cambridge, MA: MIT Press.

[13] Nasir, N. S., & Cooks, J. (2009). Becoming a hurdler: How learning settings afford identities. *Anthropology & Education Quarterly, 40(1)*, 41-61.

[14] Papert, S. (1980). Mindstorms: Children, computers, and powerful ideas. New York, NY: Basic Books, Inc.

[15] Titterton, N., Lewis, C. M., & Clancy, M. (2010). Experiences with lab-centric instruction. *Computer Science Education (Ed. Y. Ben-David Kolikant) 20(2)*, 79-102.

[16] Wortham, S. (2006). Learning identity: The joint emergence of social identification and academic learning. New York, NY: Cambridge University Press.

Bringing Computer Science Back into Schools: Lessons from the UK

Neil C. C. Brown
School of Computing
University of Kent
Canterbury, UK
nccb@kent.ac.uk

Michael Kölling
School of Computing
University of Kent
Canterbury, UK
mik@kent.ac.uk

Tom Crick
Department of Computing
Cardiff Metropolitan University
Cardiff, UK
tcrick@cardiffmet.ac.uk

Simon Peyton Jones
Microsoft Research
7 J J Thomson Ave
Cambridge, UK
simonpj@microsoft.com

Simon Humphreys
BCS
Cambridge, UK
simon.humphreys@computingatschool.org.uk

Sue Sentance
Department of Education
Anglia Ruskin University
Essex, UK
sue.sentance@anglia.ac.uk

ABSTRACT

Computer science in UK schools is a subject in decline: the ratio of Computing to Maths A-Level students (i.e. ages 16–18) has fallen from 1:2 in 2003 to 1:20 in 2011 and in 2012. In 2011 and again in 2012, the ratio for female students was 1:100, with less than 300 female students taking Computing A-Level in the whole of the UK each year. Similar problems have been observed in the USA and other countries, despite the increased need for computer science skills caused by IT growth in industry and society. In the UK, the Computing At School (CAS) group was formed to try to improve the state of computer science in schools. Using a combination of grassroots teacher activities and policy lobbying at a national level, CAS has been able to rapidly gain traction in the fight for computer science in schools. We examine the reasons for this success, the challenges and dangers that lie ahead, and suggest how the experience of CAS in the UK can benefit other similar organisations, such as the CSTA in the USA.

Categories and Subject Descriptors

K.3.2 [**Computers and Education**]: Computer and Information Science Education—*Computer science education*; K.4.1 [**Computers And Society**]: Public Policy Issues

General Terms

Human Factors

Keywords

Computer Science Education; High School; Teachers

SIGCSE'13, March 6–9, 2013, Denver, Colorado, USA.

1. INTRODUCTION

The computing industry is prospering and evolving: the smartphone 'app' market has become worth billions of dollars within a few years of its inception [6], the video game industry is now worth more than the film industry [14] – which itself uses increasing amounts of technology [9] – not to mention the growth of companies such as Google and Facebook. Computing is also increasingly being used in a wide range of disciplines – such as bioinformatics, which is forecast to soon be worth billions of dollars [7].

UK industry reports a shortage of quality computer science graduates to support this growth [4]. However, the computer science education pipeline is stalling. The number of UK computer science degree entrants remains relatively static: a decline until 2007/2008 has been followed by a recent slight uptick (see Figure 1), with a similar pattern in the USA [15]. The situation in schools is worse, where the numbers taking the pre-university A-Level qualification have roughly halved since 2005 [8] (see Figure 1).

Increasing the computing workforce requires more computer science graduates. However, computer science take-up in higher education cannot realistically be increased simply by improving advertising of the course to 18 year-old degree applicants; typically, UK students choose their degree subject much earlier, as they must choose their subject specialisms at ages 16–18 (and even at ages 14–16) to support their degree choice. Thus, the drive to increase interest in computer science must focus on schools, not universities.

It is against this backdrop that Computing At School (CAS) was formed in the UK in 2008, to promote the cause of computer science in schools. This paper examines the challenges that were/are faced in promoting computer science in schools, and highlights successes and failures of CAS in the UK, which can inform efforts in other countries, such as the USA.

2. A BRIEF GUIDE TO UK EDUCATION

This paper will discuss computer science education in the UK, specifically. As a brief guide to education in the UK: typically, students will be given little choice in their subjects (and take no qualifications) before age 14. At age 14–16 they will usually study for around ten GCSE qualifications.

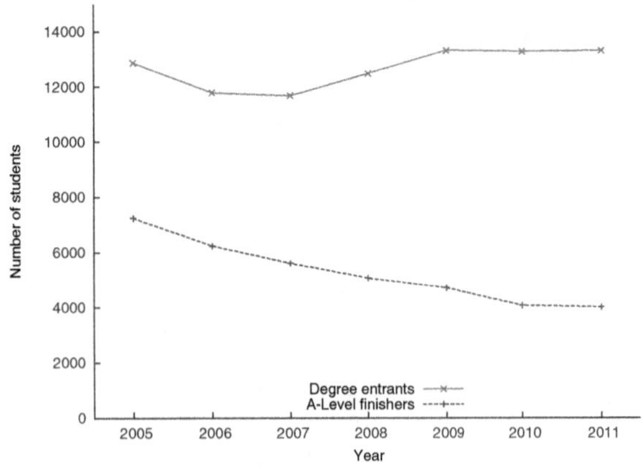

Figure 1: Numbers of A-Level completions and degree entrants for computer science in the UK. Source: UCAS and JCQ.

Sufficient grades will allow students to take 16–18 qualifications: normally, three or four A-Levels. Grades from A-Levels (commonly, dependent on subject) will allow entry to universities for a degree taken from age 18–21.

GCSE and A-Level exams are designed and examined by a small set of government-approved awarding bodies. Other qualifications do exist for these age groups, and due to devolution the system differs in some regions (especially in Scotland), but that will not be discussed in this paper.

3. THE DECLINE OF COMPUTER SCIENCE IN UK SCHOOLS

The state of computer science A-Level qualifications has become such that it is not considered suitable support for any degree [3] – including computer science itself [1] [11, p67]! Many teachers have told the authors of advising students not to take computing A-Level despite an intention to take a computer science degree.

This is partly a chicken-and-egg problem: not enough schools offer computer science to allow universities to require it for entry, so many universities are indifferent to prior qualifications in computer science. This can be seen numerically in Figure 1 – the number of students entering computer science degrees is not related to the number taking computing A-Level. Maths and physics do not suffer the same problem.

One noticeable effect on the numbers taking computer science in UK schools was an overshadowing by the subject of ICT (Information and Communication Technology). Although some teachers delivered excellent ICT or bent the curriculum to teach computer science, too often ICT featured basic IT skills, which were considered dull and pedestrian, and which are also of little relevance to computer science [10, 12]. To give an idea of the impact of ICT on computing: in 2003, computing A-Level split into ICT and computing [12, p59][1]. Before the split, 28,000 students took computing. Immediately afterwards, 16,000 took ICT and 8,000 took computing, dropping to 11,000 and 4,000 respectively by 2012 [8]. By contrast, maths went from 56,000 in 2003 to 85,000 in 2012.

In the late 2000s there was no organisation that was advancing the cause of computer science. ICT had its own subject association, Naace, but computer science did not. BCS, The (UK) Chartered Institute for IT[2], was focused on professional development, not schools. Universities were aware of the problem, but did not have enough contact with schools and awarding bodies to make a difference. Computer science in schools had no visible champion.

4. COMPUTING AT SCHOOL GROUP

The *Computing At School* (CAS) group was founded in 2008 to investigate ways to improve the teaching of computer science in UK schools. CAS started as a truly grassroots initiative, with no organisation or funding, but was unified both by a shared recognition that the representation of computer science in UK schools was dismal and by a collective desire to improve the situation.

A wide variety of institutions was represented at the first meeting, with people from a range of backgrounds: school teachers and academics, as well as representatives from industry and awarding bodies. The lack of hierarchy and composition of the group turned out to have a significant impact on the operation of CAS, which lasts to this day. While some formal structures were slowly added over time, its flat-structured grassroots origins remain, and are hugely influential in the way CAS operates.

Over the last four years, CAS has transformed from a small action and lobbying group into a membership organisation for UK school teachers with over 2,000 members. Its activities have diversified, and include the development of model curriculums, political lobbying, organisation of training for teachers and the staging of an annual national conference for teachers.

At its foundation in 2008, CAS seemed to fight a lonely battle against the odds. While many individuals agreed that the state of computer science teaching in UK schools was problematic, few organisations or institutions of influence seemed inclined to act to improve it.

In 2011, however, the tide started to change. Several organisations became actively involved in promoting improvements in UK computer science teaching, including e-skills UK [5], UCU [13], and the *Next Gen.* Report [9], culminating in a highly-noted report by the Royal Society, the UK's Academy of Sciences [12]. These reports were supported by various statements from industry, one of the most publicised being a speech by Google's executive chairman Eric Schmidt in Edinburgh in 2011[3]. As a result, in early 2012 the UK Department for Education declared the re-introduction of computer science teaching into UK schools an official goal. The CAS agenda had become mainstream.

With this rising tide of various organisations and individuals pushing in the same direction came, however, problems of success: thousands of teachers now have to be trained, curriculums need to be developed, infrastructure put into place. CAS is one of the organisations working on supporting these changes.

[1]We have received private correspondence contesting this interpretation of the JCQ figures by the Royal Society report, suggesting that the 2003 figures already included some ICT qualifications, but there are no published figures to corroborate this.

[2]`http://www.bcs.org.uk/`

[3]`http://www.guardian.co.uk/media/interactive/2011/aug/26/eric-schmidt-mactaggart-lecture-full-text`

5. ACTIVITIES AND CHALLENGES

The CAS activities fall broadly into two major categories: initiatives for teachers, and activities opposite established organisations of influence, such as awarding bodies and government. For teachers, CAS aims at providing support for the delivery of computer science content in the classroom. For decision makers, CAS aims at influencing overall policy and strategy to improve the environment that computer science teachers work in.

Initially, one of the main problems for teachers was a lack of infrastructure for communication and exchange of ideas. Teachers worked in isolation from each other, with no overarching organisation or support. This isolation of individual teachers contributed greatly to stifling progress. Even for dedicated, motivated and capable teachers it was essentially impossible to engender change beyond the boundaries of their own school. Accordingly, many of the teacher-related initiatives of CAS aim at improving exchange of experiences between teachers and provide platforms to communicate. This includes communication online, local face-to-face "hub" meetings, and a national conference.

5.1 Peer communication

One of the first actions of CAS was to create a static website[4] and set up a national mailing list for anyone interested in furthering computer science teaching at school. Members subscribed to this list included many school computer science teachers, but also academics, representatives from industry, members of awarding bodies and other regulatory bodies [2]. As membership grew and the number of activities diversified, these tools were insufficient to maintain good group communication. Members started complaining about the amount of traffic on the mailing list and many unsubscribed from the list, losing some contact with CAS.

In August 2012, the mailing list was replaced by a custom-designed community website[5], which provides richer functionality for communication. In addition to providing discussion forums, the community site offers functionality to share resources and collaborate on their development, disseminate news items and display geographical locations of other members and CAS Hubs (see Figure 2). Early indications of the effect of the new site are very promising: the number of members participating has tripled. There is also an active CAS community of UK computer science education blogs, written by teachers and academics[6].

A further strong communication mechanism has been the CAS newsletter. The newsletter is published three times a year, and is produced to a high standard. It is professionally printed and distributed to schools throughout the UK. This has served both as useful offline publicity for CAS (reaching further than just the CAS membership), and allowed sharing of news and information about CAS members' activities at a more measured pace than the online community.

5.2 The CAS Hubs

In addition to these distributed communication mechanisms, CAS aimed very early on to facilitate face-to-face contact between teachers. This is most feasible where teachers are geographically close, and is supported by CAS Hubs.

[4]http://www.computingatschool.org.uk/

[5]http://community.computingatschool.org.uk/

[6]http://planetcas.org.uk/

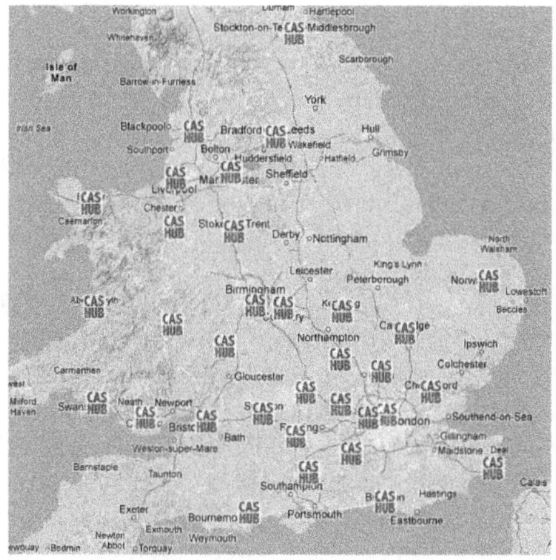

Figure 2: The CAS Hubs in England and Wales.

CAS Hubs are run by volunteers from the CAS membership and serve a geographical region. Their activities vary in nature and frequency, depending on the situation of the local hub leader and members. A typical pattern would be monthly or quarterly meetings in the evening, often at the school of one of the hub members. At these meetings, members share knowledge, often via demonstrations of particular teaching tools and general discussions.

Establishing a local hub is supported by CAS through the provision of a hub handbook to get started, and technology infrastructure (mainly on the community website) to promote the hub and its activities. CAS also provides advice, suggestions and contacts for external speakers (typically volunteers from industry or academia), and can provide funding for those speakers' travel expenses.

At the time of writing, around 40 CAS Hubs exist in the UK – most of which are shown in Figure 2. This provides a density where most teachers have a CAS Hub within an hour's travel of their home location.

5.3 The CAS conference

Since 2009, CAS has organised an annual national conference. Attendance at the conference has been free for all participants. Teachers have to pay only for their own travel and accommodation, and speakers donate their time free of charge. The conference programme usually spans one full day (with a social reception the evening before) and consists of a number of plenary talks and a set of workshops.

The conference has been very successful from the start, with over 200 participants attending in its first year. The capacity was increased to 250 in following years, with the event booked out every year since then. Feedback for the conference has been very good, and afterwards teachers usually report an increased level of excitement and enthusiasm; the conference serves to seed new ideas and to encourage teachers to start new initiatives. However, the nature of the conference has given rise to several challenges, which can be seen as representing larger challenges to CAS as a whole.

One challenge is the size limit of the venue, compared to growing interest in the conference. The conference has been held each year in space made available to CAS free of charge by the University of Birmingham. CAS has greatly benefited from this arrangement, but it imposes a hard limit on the size of the conference. It is unrealistic to be able to continue to increase participation without switching to paying for the conference venue. More generally, it is increasingly becoming a problem that where CAS used to be able to rely on freely donated time or resources, scaling up will require a switch to having a more traditional funding scheme.

One possible method of funding is registration fees for attendees, but an alternative is sponsorship from industry. In the past, the conference was essentially non-commercial and vendor free: it contained no commercial booths or sales talks. This purely collegial and academic nature has created a positive atmosphere that has contributed much to the success of the conference, and sponsorship may jeopardise this. More generally, as CAS scales, it must continue to monitor and adjust its position with respect to vendors and commercial interests, treading a line between useful cooperation and vendor-independence.

In summary, the conference is one of the clearly successful activities with high impact. For any teacher organisation, this is an activity well worth considering. As CAS – and with it, the conference – evolves and grows, a number of challenges arise in managing the increased interest and scale. This model has been successfully replicated at CAS regional conferences in Wales (2011 and 2012) and Scotland (2012).

5.4 Teacher Professional Development

One obvious activity for CAS from the start was the organisation and provision of training for existing teachers. Initially, this consisted of occasional courses, scheduled irregularly and on demand, varying in duration from a few hours to several days. Topics and technologies covered in these workshops included Greenfoot, Python and Scratch/BYOB. Some courses also offered more theoretical background of specific areas of computer science, such as algorithms, but workshops on specific technologies – especially programming technology – were the most frequent and most popular.

More recently, demand for teacher CPD (Continuous Professional Development) has increased sharply. With the goal of increasing computer science teaching in schools now widely supported by a broad alliance of organisations, including the Department for Education, many schools aim to improve their offerings. Very often, this necessitates further training for teachers, who frequently have no formal training in computer science or programming [1].

One reason for the lack of expertise in computer science teaching is the background of the teachers. When ICT grew in the 2000s, many teachers were conscripted from other subjects without any additional training [12, p72]. CAS now faces the challenge that many ICT teachers may be expected to now transfer to computer science, again without training.

This increase in demand for teacher CPD opens up a number of new questions and challenges. Teacher CPD is currently not well funded, nor centrally organised. Teachers often have a low or non-existent budget for training, and some teachers end up paying for training using their own personal money. Not only is paying for the training an issue, but teachers must either attend in their own time (evenings, weekends, holidays) or a substitute teacher must be found to cover their classes – which is either logistically difficult/impossible, or too costly for the school to allow it (often overshadowing the cost of the training itself).

CAS is preparing to play a role in the planning and provision of teacher CPD. It cannot provide the content itself, but can have a role in organising and advertising courses provided by partners, such as universities or other organisations. Due to the aforementioned problems, to be currently accessible to teachers, these courses must be both short and cheap to attend. Many initial courses are being run at cost or at a loss by enthusiastic universities or other teachers, but this is not sustainable in the long term.

A long list of problems thus remain to be solved as CPD is scaled up in future. These include questions of funding, setting content, unified certification, and quality control of course delivery. It is envisaged that CAS-certified CPD will be delivered by a number of independent institutions, with CAS providing administrative support, announcement and advertising, coordination and certification. The exact nature of the relationship of CAS and the content providers, including the formalisation of certification and quality control, remains to be decided.

5.5 Organisation

A further challenge caused by the growth of CAS is that of organisation. The initial CAS membership was a group of concerned individuals who fitted in one meeting room. Small working groups were often formed at regular group meetings or via the mailing list, e.g. to produce a model curriculum. Members were always encouraged to volunteer and take the lead on issues that concerned them, with the motto *"there is no them, there is only us"*.

While the organisation has had much success, it is hard to measure the opportunity cost, where issues may not have been followed up due to the lack of a volunteer with an interest. There is also the issue of scale: having no organisational structure may not scale well enough to accommodate the increasing membership. Currently, CAS has only two paid, part-time members of staff (funded by the BCS), supporting over 30 hubs and 2,000 members. It is anticipated that more staff will be needed to support future growth.

6. POLICY

While CAS has been successful at getting teachers to support each other, the struggles of computer science as a subject could not have been solved solely at this low level. In addition, CAS has engaged successfully with government and awarding bodies (examination boards) at a policy level.

6.1 Government

Government were initially unconcerned with the problem of computer science in schools. The subject of ICT was widely taught in schools, and as far as most government officials were concerned, ICT addressed all computing-related needs. This belief was only unseated by the publication of several reports, combined with interventions by industry[7]. An early leader was the *Next Gen.* report [9], headed by two respected industry members, followed by Eric Schmidt's aforementioned speech and then a comprehensive report from the Royal Society [12] in January 2012.

These interventions made the government aware that there was a problem to be solved, and that it was not just computer science teachers who felt this way. This contact was followed first by a campaign by CAS to educate government ministers on the difference between computer science

[7]For example, see `http://academy.bcs.org/content/promoting-computing-schools`

(academically rigorous, long-lasting core principles, full of programming and software creation) and ICT (too often changing to fit the latest technology, dependent on specific applications such as Microsoft Office, focused more on using existing software than creating new software).

Once this difference had been made clear, the government became more understanding of the issues, and more willing to act on them, ultimately culminating in the Education Secretary declaring in a January 2012 speech[8] that the ICT curriculum would be rewritten and that the government supported the development of "new, high-quality Computer Science GCSEs". The speech made explicit mention of the *Next Gen.* report and of Eric Schmidt's comment and, not coincidentally, preceded the publication of the Royal Society report by only a few days.

CAS has had a remarkable impact at the policy level. Its weight when talking to government was boosted by several factors. One factor was the support of industry and other bodies to whose needs government was attentive. Another factor was the core aspect of CAS: the teachers who are members. Being an organisation that represents hundreds of school-teachers gave more weight than being purely a lobbying organisation. The final factor was that CAS gained the support of the BCS, an established industry-associated organisation, which helped to legitimise them.

6.2 Awarding Body Engagement

In England and Wales, qualifications (syllabuses and assessment) are the responsibility of a small number of awarding bodies (a.k.a. examination boards, primarily: OCR, AQA, Edexcel, WJEC), audited by the government agency Ofqual. In order to have computer science as a subject in schools, it was necessary to ensure that exam boards were offering computer science qualifications with a suitable syllabus that focused on computer science, rather than ICT.

The OCR exam board decided to design a computer science GCSE (ages 14–16), which was piloted in 2010/2011, and launched a year later. Following this and various other policy developments, the other three largest exam boards announced the development of their own computer science GCSEs, targeted for launch in 2012/2013.

The focus on GCSE is an interesting development. An initially more obvious route would have been to work "backwards" from universities (where computer science was still reasonably popular) and develop a new A-Level. However, students only take three or four A-Levels, so taking computing A-Level (which is not well respected by universities, including by "neighbouring" subjects such as maths or physics) would be a significant commitment, and of little benefit – even if the students want to take computer science at university. The GCSE (of which students typically take ten) is more likely to see uptake from those who are not already dedicated to the subject.

6.3 Schools

Although CAS has a large number of computer science teachers as members, many of whom are heads of department[9], their influence within their own school was typically quite limited. Headteachers were generally unreceptive to the idea of increasing computer science teaching: like government, they believed that ICT covered all the computing-related educational needs of the students. Furthermore, without a computer science GCSE, there was no possibility of offering computer science at ages 14–16 (when almost all teaching is towards a GCSE) nor before age 14 (without an ensuing GCSE to follow, it would be seen as a dead-end).

With the GCSE issue being resolved, CAS have worked to try to inform and support headteachers with regards to computer science in schools. One significant step was a mass mailout to every headteacher of a state school in England and Wales[10], explaining how and why computer science could be delivered in their school, and offering an invitation to join the CAS/BCS Network of Computer Science Teaching Excellence. This network will get underway in the 2012/2013 academic year, headed by a seconded teacher and university academic, who will look to support schools in the new push to teach computer science.

6.4 Devolution

The UK is comprised of four major geographical regions: England, Wales, Scotland and Northern Ireland. England is the biggest region geographically and in terms of population (over 80%), and thus tends to dominate politically. Since 2000, devolution has seen power shifted to local assemblies in Wales, Scotland and Northern Ireland (but not in England, which has no separate government than the overall UK government). Education (and in particular, school qualifications) has historically differed between the four regions, and devolution means that some aspects of education policy are devolved to the three regions, while some power remains with the overall UK government.

Devolution brings advantages and disadvantages when trying to effect change. The smaller governments in the devolved regions can be more accessible and more agile when it comes to making change, allowing easier and more effective access to policymakers. On the other hand, it can also mean fighting the same battle four times over to convince different regional governments. (Thankfully, this problem is not as large as, say, in the USA, where each of the fifty states may have power over their own education systems.)

Nevertheless, there has been significant success in driving the computer science education agenda in the devolved nations, especially by leveraging commitments made in the others. At the 2012 CAS Wales conference[11], the Welsh Government's Minister for Education and Skills announced a £3m investment in computer science and digital literacy, along with clear commitments to promote and support computer science education. As this issue grows in prominence, can Scotland et al. be seen to fall behind?

7. CONCLUSIONS

The Computing At School (CAS) group was formed in 2008 against the backdrop of a decline in computer science in UK schools: declining numbers, declining visibility and declining respect. In just four years the organisation has grown to over 2,000 members, has successfully lobbied the national government to support computer science in schools, has con-

[8] `http://www.education.gov.uk/inthenews/speeches/a00201868/michael-gove-speech-at-the-bett-show-2012`

[9] A computer science department in a UK school typically has 1–3 members, including the head of department.

[10] Strategic Information Pack: `http://academy.bcs.org/content/strategic-information-schools`

[11] In partnership with the Technocamps project based at Swansea University.

tacted all state headteachers regarding re-introducing computer science, has begun to set up a national network of excellence for computer science in schools with over 250 member schools, has been instrumental in the reintroduction of rigorous computer science qualifications in schools and has set up over 30 hubs nationwide to support teacher communication, as well as organising an annual national conference and many teacher training sessions.

One key aspect to the success of CAS has been the composition of its membership – a mix of teachers (albeit rarely headteachers), industry professionals, university academics and members of various other stakeholder bodies. The teachers formed a large grassroots membership that could perform peer support (nationally through the Internet, and locally through face-to-face meetings), which in turn gave weight to the policy-level lobbying performed by some of the industry-based and academic members.

One of the first, vital steps was re-education about the nature of computer science. In the UK, too many people – both in society at large, but also specifically in government – conflate computer science (which involves programming and rigorous analytical thinking, with a consistent set of core principles) with ICT (which typically involves learning to use – rather than create – current computer software). The success in lobbying the government only followed after this distinction was made clear.

The process of promoting computer science required addressing several fronts at once. Some teachers were keen to re-introduce computer science, but needed a suitable qualification (determined in the UK by awarding bodies) to be allowed to teach it at ages 14–18. Many schools felt that ICT was sufficient and saw no need for computer science – taking their lead from government, who in turn became more receptive after reports from distinguished academic bodies [12] and industry [9]. (In the UK, recent governments' education policies have, sadly, been more receptive to industry views than the views of schools or universities.)

Although CAS has managed to grow quickly, not all teachers have been receptive. Some ICT teachers feel threatened by the push of computer science: some because they are worried that they will be called on to teach the subject they are unfamiliar with, some because they feel computer science is a niche subject, some because they worry that the computer science bandwagon may now overshadow (or denigrate) their own subject of ICT. And indeed, computer science runs the risk of falling into the same trap that damaged ICT's reputation: demand for running computer science in schools may outstrip the supply of trained teachers, which could lead to computer science being taught by a cohort of undertrained teachers. Without funding from government for teacher training, this is a major concern.

The CAS grassroots activities, coordinated locally, have been very successful, and have scaled well, with new regional coordinators volunteering to serve each area until the point has been reached where most of the country is served by a nearby hub (see Figure 2). The forthcoming challenge will be to scale the national coordination of CAS activities (particularly teacher training) effectively as more teachers continue to join the organisation. Pleasingly, there has been much industry support for CAS, but a further challenge is how to make effective use of industry goodwill, by encouraging liaisons between developers and their local teachers, or coming up with some other partnership of the two.

7.1 Lessons

Each country will have its own unique set of challenges when looking to promote the cause of computer science in schools, but here is a summary of the lessons from the UK:

- A varied composition (featuring many or all of: teachers, headteachers, industry, academia and other organisations) will provide strength – for example, teachers can provide weight to lobbying carried out by non-teachers.
- Part of the challenge will be making clear what computer science is (rigorous, academic, centred on programming), and how it differs from digital literacy, computer maintenance and other areas of IT.
- It is key to understand the pressures and motivations of different interdependent stakeholders – teachers, headteachers, government – and solve the problems of each.

8. REFERENCES

[1] R. D. Boyle and M. A. C. Clark. A-Level Computing: its content and value. Technical Report 2002.15, University of Leeds, 2002.

[2] P. Bradshaw and J. Woollard. Computing at school: an emergent community of practice for a re-emergent subject. In *Proceedings of the International Conference on ICT in Education (ICICTE 2012)*, 2012.

[3] T. Crick and S. Sentance. Computing at School: Stimulating Computing Education in the UK. In *Proceedings of the 11th Koli Calling International Conference on Computing Education Research*, 2012.

[4] Department for Innovation, Universities & Skills (UK). *The Demand for Science, Technology, Engineering and Mathematics (STEM) Skills.* 2009.

[5] e-skills UK. *Technology Insights 2012.* 2012.

[6] Gartner. *Gartner Says Worldwide Mobile Application Store Revenue Forecast to Surpass $15 Billion in 2011.* `http://www.gartner.com/it/page.jsp?id=1529214`.

[7] Global Industry Analysts. *Bioinformatics – A Global Strategic Business Report.* 2012. `http://www.strategyr.com/Bioinformatics_Market_Report.asp`.

[8] Joint Council for Qualifications. *A-Level Results.* 2011.

[9] I. Livingstone and A. Hope. Next Gen. Nesta, 2011.

[10] R. Pau, W. Hall, and M. Grace. 'It's boring': female students' experience of studying ICT and computing. *School Science Review*, 92(341):89–94, 2011.

[11] S. Peyton Jones. *Computing at School: the state of the nation.* UK Computing Research Committee, 2010.

[12] The Royal Society. Shutdown or restart? *The way forward for computing in UK schools.* 2012.

[13] Universities and Colleges Union. Choice cuts*: How choice has declined in higher education.* 2012.

[14] H. Wallop. Video games bigger than film. *The Telegraph*, 2009. `http://www.telegraph.co.uk/technology/video-games/6852383/Video-games-bigger-than-film.html`.

[15] S. Zweben. *Computing Degree and Enrollment Trends.* Computing Research Association, 2011.

Cultivating a K12 Computer Science Community: A Case Study

Sarah Hug
ATLAS Institute
320 UCB
University of Colorado, Boulder
Boulder, CO 80309
(303) 735-0993
hug@colorado.edu

Richard Guenther
St. Vrain Valley School District
395 South Pratt Parkway
Longmont, CO 80501
(303) 776-6200
guenther_richard@svvd.edu

Michael Wenk
School of Education
240 UCB
University of Colorado, Boulder
Boulder, CO 80309
(303) 492-6237
Michael.wenk@colorado.edu

ABSTRACT

In this paper, we use a sociocultural lens to provide an in-depth case study of a computer science program at a high school serving traditionally underserved youth. The study illuminates the contextual factors that supported dramatic programmatic growth, including the policy, curriculum, pedagogy, community, and school factors leading to student recruitment and retention in computer science. By focusing on computer science classroom practices and beyond, the study sheds light on the role multiple stakeholders can take in supporting computer science education in a K12 setting, and suggests strategies for program development in other K12 computer science settings.

Categories and Subject Descriptors

K.3.2 [**Computers and Education**]: Computers and Information Science Education – *computer science education.* J.4 [**Social and Behavioral Science**]: *psychology.*

Keywords

K-12 education, case study, recruitment, diverse student populations

1. Introduction

In the fall of 2008, Mountain View High School (school name has been changed) held one computer science course that served 15 students. Utilizing a set of laptops the course took place in a classroom trailer behind the school, and the teacher spent the rest of his academic assignment teaching mathematics to English language learners. By the fall of 2012, the computer science department had grown to 1.25 full time teachers, with five distinct course offerings (Alice programming language through AP computer science) and 335 student enrollments, in a school of 1300 total students. This growth rate is an astonishing 2233% over four years.

SIGCSE'13, March 6–9, 2013, Denver, Colorado, USA.

Our study takes a sociocultural approach to understanding phenomena [1], and as such assumes that school and community cultures shape student experiences of content, including the courses they take. In this work, we investigate the contextual factors that influenced the growth of computer science as a field of study at Mountain View High School.

The research questions we address are:

1. What supportive factors led to the increase in computer science course enrollment and in discrete course offerings?

2. In what ways has the program redefined/reconceptualized computer science to meet the needs of students?

2. Background and Related Work

The study described here is an in-depth portrait of a unique case. It provides an opportunity to develop strategies for growth in other K12 settings. The rate of programmatic growth experienced at Mountain View is exceptional, particularly given the current decline of computer science in K12 education. According to the Computer Science Teachers Association, the low level adoption of computer science standards at the state and local levels is discouraging, and the policies that determine teacher qualification in computer science are varied and, evidence suggests, not well understood locally [2]. Computer science teachers from across the country report that lack of student interest (80%) and lack of support for their programs (74%) are challenges they face in their positions [3]. In the majority of US states, course credits are not valued as mathematics or science courses would be, and student achievement and success is increasingly measured with standardized tests of reading, writing, and physical and natural science [2].

Little information regarding K12 computer science program development is available in the scholarly literature. The most notable study of formal, schooled computer science education at the K12 level is that conducted by Goode, Margolis, and colleagues from the Exploring Computer Science collaborative (www.exploringcs.org) [4,5,6] Their in-depth study of computer science and computing-related education as a socially constructed set of educational practices, both formalized in policy and informal as implemented locally, shows how school communities can shape who learns high-status computer science concepts, and who is relegated to learning how to "use" technology as consumers. Data from case studies in three diverse Los Angeles high schools illustrate that even when schools have supportive technological infrastructure and course accessibility, underrepresented populations are not learning the high status computer science content that their Caucasian and Asian male peers receive. The "Into the Loop" project has shown how teacher agency and targeted recruiting of students can begin to change the computer science landscape of high schools—these schools have seen dramatic increases in the number of students who take the AP computer science test, particularly those from underrepresented students.

Like the schools referenced above, Mountain View High School is a diverse school: forty five percent of the student population identifies as Hispanic, and nearly half (48%) receive free and/or reduced price lunch, a proxy for low income status. In essence, the school is a site with a large portion of underserved and underrepresented students, yet the enrollment in computer science is growing. This case study serves as a modest counterpoint to the work described above—it tells the story of an economically underserved, diverse high school that has made progress in attracting and retaining students in computer science.

3. Research Methods

This work is a case study in line with the following definition [7]:

"*A case study is an empirical inquiry that is explanatory, investigates a continuous phenomenon within its real-life context, when the boundaries between phenomenon and context are not clearly evident, and in which multiple sources of evidence are used.*"

The computing department analyzed in this paper is an example of an extreme or unique case, one worthy of explanatory analysis as a method for uncovering the contextual factors that led to the computer department's success in recruiting high school students to the study of computer science.

Data collection took place as part of a National Science Foundation-funded program over three academic school years, and included the following:

- 2-4 classroom observations per year;
- 3-6 informal interviews with the classroom teacher per year;
- 1 formal interview with the classroom teacher per year;
- 2-4 informal interviews with each of three classroom fellows per year;
- 2 formal interviews with classroom fellows per year (individual and group);
- 1 formal interview with administrators, counselors, related personnel (year 3); and
- Document analysis (brochures, student handbook, website for Mountain View, website for computer science department, syllabi for courses).

As the computer science teacher of record, the second author served as a facilitator and observer of the research; he did not participate in the data collection or analysis except in his role as stakeholder, though his expertise and "insider" knowledge of the department were valuable assets in the collection, analysis, and interpretation of data. As the first and third authors collected data and interpreted findings, the second author provided "member checking," or validation (or, in some cases, lack of validation) of analyses [8].

Data were analyzed iteratively, and codes were developed to capture themes in the data. Codes or themes were triangulated across subjects, referred to as data triangulation (teachers, administrators, graduate student fellows) and across data types, called methodological triangulation [9] (e.g., interview, observation, documentation).

4. Results

The results section is organized in two parts. The first is a brief presentation of code analysis to highlight how the data were gathered, interpreted, and validated for this case study. The second section is a narrative description of factors that supported CS department development from 2008-2012 at Mountain View, based on the themes uncovered in our data analysis.

4.1 Coded themes in the case study

A subset of developed codes is presented in the table below. The table lists the overarching theme for each code, the name of the code, the number of occurrences of the theme in the corpus of the data, and the data sources that support the theme. Each overarching theme had from 5 to 13 sub themes, or specific codes, that related to the theme. There were a total of 58 codes. Those reported in this document were validated either through confirmation via multiple interviewees, or through confirmation from multiple data types.

Table 1: Selected codes in the Mountain View CS dataset

Overarching theme	Specific code	#	Data sources
Policy factors that support CS	Students have few to no prerequisites for CS courses across levels	4	Interview (multiple stakeholders) and documentation
Community factors that support CS	Students experience connections to CS careers through industry involvement	7	Interview (multiple stakeholders) and observation
Pedagogical factors that support CS	CS teacher fosters sense of belonging/ community in courses	4	Interview (multiple stakeholders) and observation
School culture factors that support CS	School stakeholders view CS as a way to empower underrepresented students	8	Interview (multiple stakeholders) and documentation

4.2 Social and cultural factors that support CS at Mountain View

Our data indicate that multiple factors supported the development of computer science at Mountain View High School: school culture and community factors, policy factors (both formal and informal), and pedagogical and curricular factors. This "perfect storm" of circumstances seems to be responsible for 2233% growth in the CS program over four years. The following sections describe, from multiple perspectives, how these factors may influence student engagement in computer science.

4.2.1 School culture and community connections

Data from administrators, fellows, and the computer science teacher indicate multiple community factors have supported computer science program development, in particular, school partnerships with industry and higher education institutions. One of the most significant partnerships has evolved over the past three years, and is based on the supposition that high school students are capable of high level technical work. A local technical entrepreneur has invested his time and expertise in the after school application development team (App Dev team) at Mountain View High School. Observations during work sessions verify how the business leader offered assignments, provided technical support for students, and described how the project might best be implemented. In collaboration with the business leader, graduate fellows, and the computer science teacher, students worked in groups on real-world projects with actual clients. To date, students have developed a website for a local business, a school district classroom observation application for the iPad, and a multimedia platform for the STEM program at the high school.

Through US Department of Education funds, high school students receive pay for their work after school, allowing for stronger home-to-school connections and continuity between academic experience and career opportunities. The practice of having high school students build apps for actual clients led to the newest course offering at Mountain View, software engineering. Data indicate the administration values strong community partnerships, as evidenced in the quote from the principal: *"We have gone to the community with computer science just because we feel like it is a shining star for us. When we are talking with the community, we talk about the computer science department and what it is doing for students, especially when we are saying we are creating a 21st-century learning environment."* At the same time, offering students opportunities to build real world projects for specific clients mirrors strong undergraduate curricular design [10].

Two National Science Foundation-funded university programs are engaged with Mountain View students—both serve K12 students through the development of graduate fellows who engage regularly with K12 science and engineering teachers and classrooms, creating new lessons and offering new perspectives on STEM. One such program has worked with the computer science program at Mountain View for the past 3 academic years. Graduate student fellows from the university collaborate with the computer science teacher to develop and enhance curriculum to incorporate rich computational thinking concepts.

According to administrators, fellows, and teachers, participation with the GK12 program serves the computer science department well, and may have had some influence regarding its growth. Fellows bring added technical expertise into the computer science classroom, and serve as mentors for students. They support instruction by providing additional perspectives from their own computing backgrounds and serving as additional resources for students. For example, the fellow who participated in the classroom during the 2011-2012 school year led web development in the afterschool club, given his expertise in that realm of computing.

All program stakeholders note the importance of Mountain View students learning scientific, technical content, no matter their post-secondary career path. In many cases, they highlight the need for STEM education *because of* rather *than in spite of* their status as underserved, underrepresented youth. Computer science (along with other STEM content) is viewed as an opportunity out of poverty for students from low income families. The theme that computer science knowledge can empower underrepresented youth is echoed in each of the interviews held with Mountain View personnel. A representative quote appears below.

"For us, (computer science) is an opportunity for students to see and make career choices that are going to be beneficial for them. With our student population being 52% minority and 48% free and reduced lunch, they are looking for ways to get out of poverty and I think that a lot of students are really engaged with technology. This is one way for them to see a career path that is very relevant to them."

4.2.2 Policy factors

Multiple school policies, both formal and informal, have influenced the successful growth of computer science at Mountain View High School.

4.2.2.1 Curricular requirements and related coursework

In 2008, Mountain View developed academic focus academies that operate in a "school within a school" model. A bond effort in the school district provided funds to support technological upgrades, among other school renovations. Students enrolling at Mountain View can choose to join the STEM Academy, join the Visual and Performing Arts Academy, or choose to enroll as a traditional high school student. The computer science program has natural ties to both STEM and the arts—in fact as of 2012 STEM academy students are *required* to take one computer science course. These connections were visible to multiple stakeholders in this school, including the school counselor, principal, and academy director. Administrators highlight the purposeful development of flexibility within academies, such that students who choose an academy have multiple ways to fulfill their focus requirements, and non-academy students have access to all curricular choices.

This curricular flexibility allows for student exploration, and prevents "de facto tracking," in which students with particular strengths and weaknesses take courses together because of scheduling constraints. The five computer science courses have few to no prerequisite courses within or outside of the department (e.g., no requirement to take computer science level 1, no mathematics requirements). This allows students to take the courses early in their high school careers, and continue their computer science studies throughout their high school careers. In addition, computer science courses fulfill multiple graduation requirements at Mountain View High School, including STEM electives for STEM Academy students and a practical art course for traditional and VPA Academy students. The role of computer science at Mountain View was communicated online via the high school website, on academy documents available online, on the computer science program website, and verbally by administration, counselor, and computer science teacher.

Computer science's clear connections to both technical and artistic pursuits were leveraged at Mountain View, leading to program growth. "Computer science pathways" students took were varied, as is often the case; however at Mountain View multiple stakeholders were cognizant of those multiple paths. This perspective runs counter to social science research, which indicates outsiders are often unaware of the breadth of computer science [11]. The quotes below illustrate the ways administration at Mountain View High view computer science as a multifaceted discipline.

"(Computer science at Mountain View) is student centered and engaging ...we are very much able to capitalize on their current interests and put in that computer science component or that programming piece, whether it is software or app design. There is a lot of choice for students depending on their interests and through that they're able to learn the technical aspects of computing."

"I think computing is definitely a career choice that is very exciting to students especially once they start learning where it can take them. I think that it lends itself to really be adaptable for kids—if I'm really an arts kid I could be in developing websites or be an animator or be a game maker and have that artistic value of putting together the animation. At the same time, some hard-core science and tech kid who really gets the math and physics—computer science allows them to use programming in a lot of different venues...so I think it complements both arts and sciences."

4.2.2.2 Informal school policies that support CS growth

Formal policy, at the federal, state, or school level, can influence student enrollment in courses, as, for example, stated requirements must be met for graduation in any high school. Our analysis uncovered another way that policy can influence student course taking—the informal policies developed by social actors in a community. These unofficial policies are developed as the "way things are done" within an organization or institution, are malleable, and often leave room for discretion. [12.13] An example of informal policy that K12 computer science researchers cite as influencing enrollments is the tendency for teachers and counselors to steer academically elite and high status students towards computer science [4,5,6]. Our study shows how informal policy, when supportive of underrepresented students, can in fact support computer science enrollment.

The ninth grade counselor at Mountain View High School is in a unique position to schedule students for their first high school courses. Over the last 4 years, one of the ninth grade counselors developed informal policies that have helped build the computer science program to its current state. The informal policy practices of this counselor are in line with school and academy goals, which include preparing underserved youth for careers of the future.

The counselor reports casting a wide net for computer science students—she based her advisement for elective courses on multiple variables, including teacher recommendation, test scores, and students expressed interests. Rather than advising students into computer science when all of the factors align, (e.g., when test scores show high achievement in science, teachers recommend the course, and students describe interest) the ninth grade counselor described a low threshold for recommending computer science. For example, students who may not appear to be prepared for high level math or science are not discouraged from enrolling in CS.

"If students put computer science on their course request form, it is worth a conversation with them. ... They seem to be doing a good job at the middle school focusing on the girls—I am seeing a lot of girls that I wouldn't have guessed would be interested listing computer science on their forms, and (their test scores show) they may be only partially proficient in math or unsatisfactory in science."

The counselor acknowledges her lack of knowledge about computer science as a discipline. To supplement her description of the course, the counselor made it a common practice to invite students who were highly engaged in computer science to describe the courses to new students: *"I have students from (CS teacher's class) come down and describe what they are doing in the class currently... I say, 'Hey, would you feel more comfortable having someone talk to you about what they do in computer science?'"* Lastly, the counselor describes her personal and professional ambition to increase the number of girls, particularly Latinas, engaging in technical fields. She notes the influence students' interests in computing have for her as a Latina academic counselor:

"It is awesome to see too, being Latina and a girl, it is so awesome to see these girls coming in from the middle school with the course requests with a last name like Quintana ... and she wants Intro to Programming. Done! I tell them we are going to build your courses around this interest. They are starting to think about careers as freshmen. When I see kids who show interest in computer science or something out of the ordinary, as freshmen I encourage them to try things out—computers and science—(knowledge of those subjects is) what is going to set them above the rest."

4.2.3 Pedagogical and curricular factors

4.2.3.1 The changing face of computing: defining CS as a broad field

It is apparent in the data that stakeholders have a broad view of computer science as it pertains to Mountain View High School opportunities. In an effort to capture the breadth of perceptions regarding computer science, data was coded using the newly developed Advanced Placement CS Principles core practices document
http://apcsprinciples.org/docs/BigIdeasPracticesJune2011.pdf
This document details what an introduction to computer science might look like, and focuses on the "changing face of computing" supported in this conference. Data were viewed through this lens, to understand how stakeholders at Mountain View describe computer science and how the artifacts of CS (e.g., website, syllabi) reflect opportunities to try out these practices. Asterisks indicate that data come from sources beyond classroom insiders (e.g., classroom teacher, fellow) and the course documentation.

Table 2: CS Practices Evidence from Mountain View

CS Practice	#	Data sources
Practice with abstraction (e.g., modeling)	7	Interviews (multiple) and documentation
Practice analyzing problems	14*	Interviews (multiple), documentation, and observation
Practice communicating	3*	Interviews (multiple)
Practice connecting computing	5*	Interviews (multiple), documentation, and observation
Practice developing computational artifacts	10*	Interviews (multiple), documentation, and observation
Practice working in teams	5*	Interviews (multiple) and observation

These data indicate that multiple school stakeholders understand the diversity of computing, and can speak to multiple facets of CS learning.

4.2.3.2 Classroom Practice

Mr. Guenther has been described by school administrators as a "facilitator of learning," a teacher with vast expertise willing to let students uncover concepts through inquiry learning and problem solving. He offers demonstrations on programming, but much of his time is spent circulating among students, watching them do the work of learning, coaching on skills and concepts, posing problems, and offering resources. His approach mimics how adults learn in the workplace, through "apprenticeship and sustained internships," which school administrators at Mountain View note are also very effective in promoting learning among students in computer science classes [14]. Graduate fellows serve as additional in-school and out-of-school resources for students, sharing their expertise in aspects of computing and serving as role models for students as they consider a post-secondary pathway.

Course observations, teacher and administrator accounts confirm the computer science classroom is busy, with students consulting with other students about projects, participating in dialogue about coding issues, or interjecting ideas at team meetings. All sorts of leaders emerge organically or are fostered by the teacher through individualized instruction and support, so that teaching and learning becomes a community enterprise.

While each course focuses on learning a programming language (currently Alice, Processing, Python, and Java) and performing "programming challenge" assignments, tasks are rooted in what the student cares about, and allow for multiple entry points into the curriculum. For example, students may learn key programming concepts as they use Alice to animate a character, or they may apply their computer science studies to master a programming sequence as they develop a mobile app. Mountain View administrators note that Mr. Guenther encourages students to *"find out what part of computer science interests them,"* whether it's human-centered design, visual art, programming or developing network systems. Student interests are leveraged for learning.

According to interviews and observational data, the pursuit of skills in computer science courses is a means to an end. Student motivation for learning this concept or this skill is clear: it makes an animated character move, it solves a coding conundrum, it makes an app functional. Because of partnerships with local businesses, nonprofits, and government agencies, students begin to see that there is a connection between what they learn in the classroom and what they may aspire to do as a career.

The CS teacher has been given great latitude from administration to develop new courses, and to innovate in his practice. Because of the pedagogical approach and the engaging curriculum, many students want to enroll in Mountain View's computer science courses—the counselor reports a unique problem of not having room for all of the students who want to take computer science at Mountain View. Mr. Guenther is not content just to fill his classes; instead, he envisions classes with young women and students of color, he says, in part, because of his background focusing on the education of English Language Learners. He actively and purposefully recruits underrepresented students and encourages them to not only enroll in the courses but also to participate in afterschool and summer programs. In addition, Mr. Guenther culls leaders from nontraditional CS students, and positions them as resources in the classroom and experts in the school. As these students experience success in computer science courses, they begin to view themselves as capable students.

The principal of Mountain View tells a story that highlights the way the computer science teacher positions students for success in the classroom. As the principal was briefed on a high level genetic algorithm project that students were working on after school, the teacher told her, *"Well, let me introduce you to Emelda. She is a newcomer with ELL[1] and she has the best logical mind and is my best thinker when it comes to algorithms."* The principal notes how singling out a struggling student for specific praise about her work made an impact. The principal continues: *"Richard sees (her) potential and... she is on top of the world."* In this school setting, Mr. Guenther realizes that his underrepresented students not only compose the majority of actual and potential CS students, but also have intelligence, creativity, and unique perspectives to offer his CS classes.

This academic year, the computer science teacher and his part-time colleague have redesigned the curriculum to not only map to CSTA standards, as they have done in previous years, but also to develop a standard template for each unit with a specific number and type of activities and assessments. These units are context independent, and allow for use in multiple contexts, with a mapping of standards to course levels. Major concepts will be revisited in new applications across the 5 courses. In response to low standardized test scores earned at this school, the team included a "computational thinking problem of the week" that addresses mathematics standards as well; in this way, computer science can show how it addresses school-wide improvement goals in high stakes subjects.

The instructional practices in Mr. Guenther's classes reflect the tenets of high school reform efforts across the United States: he brings *rigor* to coursework, situates learning activities in ways that students find *relevant*, and develops *relationships* with his students as well as among his students [14]. These practices have led to strong student interest in computer science at Mountain View High School.

5. DISCUSSION & IMPLICATIONS

Mountain View High School has developed a computer science program that serves a large portion of the school's students, with curriculum that focuses on computational concepts beyond mere technology use. Multiple social and cultural factors influence the growth of the department over time, including the pedagogical strengths of the classroom teacher, the support for STEM for all students that permeates the school, the benefits of community partnerships and financial support via the school bond initiative, and a broad view of computer science taken by multiple school stakeholders. Informal and formal policies that shape student course enrollment can have an impact: cultivating counselors who champion computer science can influence who chooses to take courses offered.

The case study suggests the following recommendations for K12 computer science stakeholders in other settings:

[1] "ELL newcomer" is a term that refers to students in the school who had recently emigrated from Mexico. Emelda had been in the United States school system for 2 months when she met the principal in Mr. Guenther's classroom.

- Consider the need for prerequisites, particularly in entry level courses. Small modifications to curriculum might make courses accessible to a larger, more diverse audience.
- Communicate about CS courses to administration and academic counselors, in multiple ways. Offer to display student work in multiple venues, and have a description of courses that highlights an inclusive CS.
- Cultivate community partnerships that show students clear paths towards the world of work.

6. Future directions

This initial case study analysis demonstrates that Mountain View High School is a unique setting for studying computer science learning. In future work, we aim to focus on student experiences in computer science at Mountain View, and on the assessment of student knowledge of computing concepts.

7. Acknowledgements

Our thanks to the fellows, teachers, administrators, and students involved with ECSITE. This material is based upon work supported by the National Science Foundation under Grant No. DGE 0841423.

8. REFERENCES

[1] Vygotsky, L. 1978. Mind in society: Development of higher psychological processes. Harvard University Press, Cambridge, MA.

[2] Wilson, C., Sudol, L., Stephenson, C., and Stehlik, M. 2010. *Running on empty: The failure to teach k–12 computer science in the digital age*. ACM. Available as: http://www.acm.org/runningonempty/fullreport.pdf

[3] http://csta.acm.org/Research/sub/Projects/ResearchFiles/CSTASurvey11CSResults.pdf

[4] Goode, J., Chapman, G. and Margolis, J. 2012. Beyond curriculum: the exploring computer science program. *ACM Inroads* 3, 2 (June 2012), 47-53.

[5] Margolis, J., Estrella, R., Goode, J., Holme, J. J. and Nao, K. 2008. *Stuck in the shallow end: Education, race, and computing*. MIT Press, Cambridge, MA.

[6] Goode, J. and Margolis, J. 2011. Exploring Computer Science: A Case Study of School Reform. *Trans. Comput. Educ.* 11, 2, Article 12 (July 2011), 16 pages.

[7] Yin, R. K. 2003. Applications of case study research . Sage, Thousand Oaks, CA.

[8] Lincoln, Y. S. and Guba, E.G. 1985. *Naturalistic inquiry*. Sage, Newbury Park, CA.

[9] Patton, M. Q. 2002. *Qualitative Research and Evaluation Methods. (3rd Ed.)*Sage Publications: Newbury Park, CA.

[10] ABET (Accreditation Board for Engineering and Technology). 2009. Criteria for accrediting computing programs: Effective for evaluations during the 2010–2011 accreditation cycle. Retrieved August 17, 2012. http://www.abet.org/Linked%20DocumentsUPDATE/Criteria%20and%20PP/C001%201011%20CAC%20Criteria%2011-16-09.pdf .

[11] Clarke, V. and Teague, J. 1996. Characteristics of computing career: Students and professionals disagree. *Computers and Education,* 24,4, 241-246.

[12] Levinson, B. a. U. et al. 2009. Education Policy as a Practice of Power: Theoretical Tools, Ethnographic Methods, Democratic Options. *Educational Policy*. 23, 6 (Oct. 2009), 767–795.

[13] Ogawa, R.T. 2012. The Institutional Sources of Educational Reform□: The Case of School-Based Management. *American Educational Research Journal*. 31, 3 (2012), 519–548.

[14] Harvard Graduate School of Education. (2011, February). *Pathways to prosperity: Meeting the challenge of preparing young Americans for the 21st century.* Retrieved from http://www.gse.harvard.edu/news_events/features/2011/Pathways_to_Prosperity_Feb2011.pdf

Teaching Secure Coding- The Myths and the Realities

Matt Bishop
University of California at Davis
Davis, CA
bishop@cs.ucdavis.edu

Elizabeth Hawthorne
Union County College
Cranfield, NJ
ehawthorne@acm.org

Kara Nance
University of Alaska Fairbanks
Fairbanks, AL
klnance@alaska.edu

Blair Taylor (moderator)
Towson University
Towson, MD
btaylor@towson.edu

1. SUMMARY

Teaching secure coding has never been more important. As attacks on financial, medical, government, and critical infrastructure systems increase in number and severity, there is a need for curriculum that prepares all computer science graduates to design and implement secure software. Accordingly, the CS2013 Ironman draft has added Information Assurance and Security as a new Knowledge Area in undergraduate computer science education and recommended that security content be cross-cutting across all curricula. In 2010, the Summit on Education in Secure Software provided a series of recommendations to facilitate secure coding education, including: 1) increasing the number of faculty who understand the importance of secure programming principles, and will require students to practice them; 2) integrating computer security content into existing technical and non-technical courses to reach students across disciplines; and 3) using innovative teaching methods to strengthen the foundation of computer security knowledge across a variety of student constituencies.

In this panel, we will speak to these recommendations and the new curricular guidelines outlined in CS2013 and discuss the importance and challenges of teaching secure coding. The panelists have been active participants in security education and will share their experiences teaching secure coding.

Categories and Subject Descriptors

D.2.4 [**Software**]: Software/Program Verification - *reliability*

K.3.2 [**Computers and Education**]: Computer and Information Science Education – *computer science education*

General Terms

Reliability, Security

Keywords

Secure Coding

SIGCSE'13, March 6–9, 2013, Denver, Colorado, USA.
ACM 978-1-4503-1868-6/13/03.

2. MATT BISHOP

Teaching robust programming, or how to write programs that are reliable, in the sense that they perform the tasks they are supposed to, and handle any unexpected inputs or events in a reasonable manner, has several myths.

Myth #1. There is no room in the curriculum for a course on secure programming. This statement assumes that a separate course is required. But introductory and second programming classes teach the basics of secure programming: how to check for bad inputs, to do bounds checking, check return values, catch and handle exceptions, and so forth. When students program for more advanced classes, the focus is on the class material and not on the mechanics of programming. That students will write secure programs is assumed, and rarely checked.

Myth #2. If students learn to write secure programs, the state of software and system security will dramatically improve. Programs rely on operating system, library, and other services. Further, system security relies on systems being set up and configured as required *for the particular environment in which the system is used*; the size of the gap between this and practice is unknown, but probably large. Companies must also provide support for the use of these skills. Whether organizations that develop software and systems will be willing to pay this price *in practice* is unclear, as is whether customers will be willing to pay higher prices, and endure longer development times.

Myth #3. Academic institutions are hierarchical educationally. Few academic institutions allow a university president, chancellor, or dean to require faculty to teach a specific topic, and how to teach it. The best ideas and methods of learning and teaching are developed through trying different ways, and seeing which works best. There may be no "best way" to do something; often, several different ways work equally well.

Myth #4: We know what to do and how to do it. We don't know how to teach secure programming. We have ideas, but we *do not know what will work, and when.*

3. ELIZABETH HAWTHORNE

Software is an intrinsic part of our personal lives. Nearly every facet of modern society depends on complex software systems:

business, energy, transportation, education, communication, government, and defense communities. The Strawman release of Computer Science Curricula 2013 (CS2013) recognizes the urgent need to teach secure coding in the undergraduate computer science curriculum [2]. CS2013 includes a new, dedicated Knowledge Area (KA) on *Information Assurance and Security* (IAS). The IAS KA is comprised of several knowledge units with one specifically on secure software design and engineering. Other knowledge units distributed throughout the proposed CS2013 Body of Knowledge (Bok) - especially in the *Software Development Fundamentals* and *Software Engineering* KAs - also address secure coding practices, defensive programming techniques, and software assurance methodologies. The next iteration of CS2013, called Ironman, is scheduled for public release and comment in February 2013. This panel will highlight the places secure coding topics and learning outcomes appear in Ironman and provide the opportunity for community feedback and input.

According to CERT, software assurance is an important discipline to ensure that software systems and services function reliably and securely. In September 2011, the Software Engineering Institute at Carnegie Mellon University published a technical report entitled, "Software Assurance Curriculum Project Volume IV: Community College Education" [3] sponsored by the U.S. Department of Homeland Security (DHS) National Cyber Security Division (NCSD). This report focuses on community college courses for software assurance and includes a review of related curricula, outcomes and body of knowledge, and outlines for six courses.

4. KARA NANCE

Many faculty members are overwhelmed with the thought of preparing original materials that demonstrate and emphasize the importance of secure coding. Further, creating a lab environment to allow students to gain hands-on experience with the potential effects of insecure coding can be challenging and may require resources and isolated environments that are not available at many institutions. The RAVE Project, funded by NSF, provides a remotely accessible virtualized environment that can be leveraged by instructors to demonstrate these effects in a safe and easy-to-use environment. The shareable instructional materials available through the RAVE Project have been developed through an ever-growing cadre of CS educators and facilitate easy inclusion of these important foundational concepts in a wide range of CS courses. Instructors can utilize these resources in a number of ways -- from setting up their students with accounts in the RAVE (if local resources are limited) -- to adapting the materials for use in a local environment. The emphasis of the RAVE Project is on sharing resources to minimize duplication of effort as instructors with common educational objectives work together.

5. BLAIR TAYLOR (moderator)

To adequately prepare computer science graduates for current and future cybersecurity challenges, security and secure coding can no longer be elective or relegated to a track for select students. All computing students should learn secure coding, starting with their first programming course, and security principles should be reiterated throughout the computer science curriculum. The challenges to security integration are significant and include: faculty lacking security skills; programming textbooks that include insecure coding examples; and courses that leave little room for additional topics.

To help address these issues, the Security Injections @ Towson project (www.towson.edu/securityinjections) includes over 30 security injection modules, available to all instructors. (This work is supported by NSF – 0817267) *Security injections* are security-related modules which address top security concerns, including integer error, input validation, and buffer overflow, that are particularly relevant for introductory programming courses. Modules are available at varying levels for CS0, CS1, and CS2, and in a variety of languages, including Java, C++, pseudocode and Python. Each module is self-contained and can be easily inserted into a course with no additional instruction required by the faculty. Modules have been tested across a variety of two and four-year institutions. Additional modules are also available for the Computer Literacy (for non-majors), Database, Networking, and Web Development courses.

Security injections allow faculty to easily incorporate important security topics that are often not well-addressed in textbooks. Teaching undergraduates to validate input and avoid integer errors and buffer overflow goes a long way towards producing more secure code, as these errors lead to a large number of the top vulnerabilities. Another important goal of the security injections is to "create a security mindset" amongst faculty and students, which many security experts consider to be one of the most important strategies towards improving security. Each security injection module includes a "Code Responsibly" section which includes guidelines for writing code that is robust and secure. Through this project, we have integrated secure coding concepts in CS0, CS1, and CS2 to over 1000 students; coached faculty at two and four year institutions to implement the security injections; and piloted a "build-a-lab" workshop to grow the modules library and foster engagement. The next step, recently funded by NSF - 1241738, is to expand the build-a-labs and create a community of "security ambassadors" to extend security integration to more institutions. **Blair will serve as moderator of the session.**

6. REFERENCES

[1] Burley, D and Bishop, M. 2011. Summit on Education in Secure Software Final Report. http://nob.cs.ucdavis.edu/bishop/notes/2010-sess/2010-sess.pdf

[2] ACM/IEEE-CS 2013 Joint Task Force on Computing Curricula. (2012, February). *Computer Science Curricula 2013 Strawman Draft.* Retrieved from www.cs2013.org/strawman-draft/cs2013-strawman.pdf

[3] Mead, N., Hawthorne, E. and Ardis, M. *Software Assurance Curriculum Project Volume IV: Community College Education.* Retrieved from http://www.sei.cmu.edu/library/abstracts/reports/11tr017.cfm

Alternatives to Lecture: Revealing the Power of Peer Instruction and Cooperative Learning

Scott Grissom
Grand Valley State University
grissom@gvsu.edu

Beth Simon
University of California, San Diego
bsimon@cs.ucsd.edu

Leland Beck
San Diego State University
beck@cs.sdsu.edu

Alexander Chizhik
San Diego State University
achizhik@mail.sdsu.edu

SUMMARY

This session will demonstrate best practices for integrating a variety of student engagement pedagogies into the classroom. Presenters play the role of instructors on the first day of class. Audience members play the role of students as they collaborate on a variety of sample activities. By providing models of active learning in computing contexts, we seek to motivate instructors to adopt these pedagogies in their classrooms. Attendees will be invited to join a growing community of faculty who share resources and best practices. Sufficient time will be reserved for questions and discussion.

Categories and Subject Descriptors

K.3.1 [**Computing Milieux**]: Computers and Education – *Collaborative learning*

General Terms

Design, Human Factors

Keywords

Active learning, student engagement pedagogies, student-centered learning, collaborative learning, peer instruction, cooperative learning

1. ENGAGEMENT PEDAGOGIES

There is significant evidence that student engagement pedagogies are more effective than traditional lecture and have benefits including improved student performance, increased attendance, and better retention in the major [10]. These approaches are also referred to as student-centered, active learning or cooperative learning. Calls for faculty to adopt these approaches have been widespread for many years but their impact remains limited.

For example, a majority of Physics faculty report awareness of these strategies but their students spend no more than a third of class time interacting with each other [8]. A survey of over 12,000 university professors suggests that well over half of class time in STEM fields is devoted to lecture [14]. A recent survey revealed that just over a third of 116 computer science faculty use cooperative learning on a consistent basis [1].

SIGCSE'13, March 6–9, 2013, Denver, Colorado, USA.
ACM 978-1-4503-1868-6/13/03.

Each of the following pedagogies share three key features that make them well-suited to the varying needs of CS educators: scalabilty, adaptability and technology independence. The approaches **scale** well to different computing courses and class sizes. Large lecture classes can have students break into small groups. Best practices can be **adapted** to meet the local needs of specific institutions and instructors. For instance, peer instruction can collect student responses with clickers, colored paper or a show of hands. There are a variety of computing platforms, programming languages and development environments used in computer science education. However, each of these pedagogies is designed to be **technology independent**.

2. SESSION FORMAT

The session begins with a brief introduction to student engagement pedagogies. Thirty-minute demonstrations are then devoted to each of two pedagogies: cooperative learning and peer instruction. Attendees play the role of students and complete carefully selected exercises that demonstrate each approach. Session leaders play the role of instructors on the first day of class and present evidence why the approach is being used with respect to increased student learning, performance and motivation. The final fifteen minutes are reserved for questions and comments from the audience. Attendees will be invited to join a growing community of faculty who share resources and best practices.

3. COOPERATIVE LEARNING

Cooperative learning involves students working together in the classroom to understand material or complete a task. Accumulated evidence suggests that cooperative learning results in higher student achievement, more positive attitudes toward the subject, improved student retention, and a variety of other benefits [9, 13]. Positive results have been reported in computer science courses [2, 6, 15].

Cooperative learning activities are most effective when they are designed to promote high-level verbal interactions. Groups can include members with a variety of backgrounds and tasks can be structured to involve all members. Students are motivated to complete, and understand, the problem-solving process they began in their groups. Thus they are primed to connect material presented during the instructor's debriefing to their own problem-solving experience [4].

4. PEER INSTRUCTION

Peer Instruction (PI) is a multi-part pedagogy, often referred to by the physical object used during lecture – clickers [3]. Students initially engage with the material, perhaps through assigned readings or watching videos of lectures, prior to class. Students are held accountable by completing an online quiz before class or at the start of class using clickers.

During class, students are posed a challenging multiple-choice question, and vote on an answer using a clicker. Students then discuss in small groups and are encouraged to explain their thinking to each other. After the discussion, everyone votes a second time. The instructor uses the responses to facilitate a class-wide discussion.

PI is based in constructivist learning theory, which tells us that information can't be dumped into the brain, but in fact that every person individually constructs their own understanding of new material. PI has been documented most thoroughly in physics but results can be found in biology, chemistry, and math [5, 7]. Positive experiences have been described in computing [11, 12].

5. ACKNOWLEDGMENTS

Our thanks to the National Science Foundation for funding a workshop in San Diego, CA (June13-14, 2011). The meeting included fifteen faculty to develop a plan to increase the adoption of student engagement pedagogies in the CS classroom.

6. REFERENCES

[1] Beck, Leland. 2011. personal communication.

[2] Beck, L. L. and Chizhik, A. W. 2008. "An Experimental Study of Cooperative Learning in CS1", *Proceedings of SIGCSE 2008*, pp. 205-209.

[3] Carl Wieman Science Education Initiative, Clicker Resource Website. http://cwsei.ubc.ca/resources/clickers.htm

[4] Chizhik, A. W., Shelly, R. K., and Troyer, L. 2009. "Intragroup Conflict and Cooperation: An Introduction," *Journal of Social Issues 65*(2), pp. 251-259.

[5] Crouch, C. H., & Mazur, E. 2001. Peer instruction: Ten years of experience and results. *American Journal of Physics,* 69.

[6] Falkner, K., and Palmer, E. 2009. "Developing Authentic Problem Solving Skills in Introductory Computing Classes", *Proceedings of SIGCSE 2009*, pp. 4-8.

[7] Hake, R. R. 1998. Interactive-engagement vs. traditional methods: A six-thousand-student survey of mechanics test data for introductory physics courses. *American Journal of Physics*. 66 (1).

[8] Henderson, C., & Dancy, M.H. 2009. "The Impact of Physics Education Research on the Teaching of Introductory Quantitative Physics," Proceedings of the Physics Education Research Conference.

[9] Johnson, D. W., Johnson, R. T., and Smith, K. A. 1991. *Active Learning: Cooperation in the College Classroom,* Interaction Book Company, Edina, MN.

[10] Michael, J. 2006. "Where's the Evidence that Active Learning Works?" *Advances in Physiology Education*, 30, pp. 159-167.

[11] Porter, L., Bailey-Lee, C., Simon, B, Zingaro, D. 2011. Peer Instruction: Do Students Really Learn from Peer Discussion in Computing? ICER 2011.

[12] Simon, B. Kohanfars, M., Lee, J., Tamayo, K. and Cutts, Q. 2010. "Experience report: peer instruction in introductory computing". *Proceedings of SIGCSE 2009.*

[13] Slavin, R. E. 1995. *Cooperative Learning: Theory, Research, and Practice* (2nd edition), Allyn & Bacon, Boston, MA.

[14] Trustees of Indiana University. 2011. Faculty Survey of Student Engagement.

[15] Walker, H. M. 2011. "A Lab-Based Approach for Introductory Computing that Emphasizes Collaboration", Computer Science Education Research Conference (www.cs.grinnell.edu/~walker/talks/lab-based-heerlen/)

ACM/IEEE Computer Science 2013 Exemplar-Fest

Andrea Danyluk
Williams College
47 Lab Campus Drive
Williamstown, MA 01267
andrea@cs.williams.edu

Steve Roach
ITT Exelis
1650 Tysons Blvd Suite 1700
McLean, VA 22102
sroach55@hotmail.com

Elizabeth K. Hawthorne
Union County College
1033 Springfield Avenue
Cranford, NJ 07016
hawthorne@ucc.edu

Henry M. Walker
Grinnell College
Noyce Science Center
Grinnell, IA 50112
walker@cs.grinnell.edu

Ruth E. Anderson
University of Washington
Paul G. Allen Center
Seattle, WA 98195
rea@cs.washington.edu

Christa M. Chewar
U.S. Military Academy
600 Thayer Road
West Point, NY 10996
Christa.Chewar@usma.edu

ABSTRACT

Beginning with the publication of Curriculum 68, ACM and IEEE-Computer Society have sponsored various efforts to establish international curricular guidelines for undergraduate programs in computing. Work on the next volume, Computer Science 2013 is well underway, with the Ironman draft out shortly before SIGCSE 2013. The Ironman draft includes course and curricular exemplars, which should serve as a rich resource for those trying to meet the curriculum standards. This special session highlights the exemplar section of the Ironman report through a description of its purpose, presentation of several exemplars, and an invitation to the SIGCSE community to participate by submitting exemplars and providing feedback on what they would find useful in this section of the CS 2013 final report.

Categories and Subject Descriptors

K.3.2 [**Computers and Education**]: Computer and Information Science Education

General Terms

Design

Keywords

Computing Curricula 2013; CS 2013; Curriculum Exemplars

1. INTRODUCTION

Beginning over 40 years ago with the publication of Curriculum 68[1], the major professional societies in computing – ACM and IEEE-Computer Society – have sponsored various efforts to establish international curricular guidelines for undergraduate programs in computing. As the field has grown and diversified, so too have the recommendations for curricula. There are now guidelines for Computer Engineering, Information Systems, Information Technology, and Software Engineering in addition to Computer Science. These volumes are updated regularly with the aim of keeping computing curricula modern and relevant.

SIGCSE'13, March 6–9, 2013, Denver, Colorado, USA.
ACM 978-1-4503-1868-6/13/03.

Work on the next volume, Computer Science 2013 (CS 2013), is well underway. The first draft, known as the Strawman report [2], was made available in February 2012; the next draft, known as the Ironman report, will be available shortly before SIGCSE 2013. New to the Ironman draft will be course and curricular exemplars. These will be descriptions of existing, fielded courses and curricula from a wide variety of institutions. The exemplar section of the Ironman draft will explicitly identify how the exemplars intersect the CS 2013 Body of Knowledge in diverse ways. The CS 2013 Steering Committee recognizes that there are many successful ways to teach computer science. Including exemplars will provide a rich resource for those trying to meet the curriculum standards.

This special session will focus on course exemplars. The goals of the session are to

- Highlight the exemplar section of the CS 2013 Ironman report.
- Illustrate a range of ways in which the Body of Knowledge can be translated into successful courses. Demonstrate that the organizational units in the Body of Knowledge (i.e., Knowledge Areas) need not be in one-to-one correspondence with courses.
- Provide the audience with an opportunity to give feedback on the range and types of exemplars in the Ironman draft, as well as the opportunity to suggest additional types of exemplars for the final CS 2013 document.

Four faculty will present exemplar courses from their institutions. Two were invited to participate before this special session was proposed for SIGCSE 2013; an additional two were selected after a call for exemplars was sent out to the SIGCSE community. The CS 2013 Ironman report will include many more exemplars, and authors of several of those will be available to talk to SIGCSE attendees informally at the end of the session. We will distribute a list of those authors, along with brief descriptions of their courses, before the session.

2. OUTLINE AND PRESENTERS

Andrea Danyluk, a member of the CS 2013 Steering Committee, will begin by giving a very brief overview of the "Course Exemplar" chapter of the CS 2013 Ironman report. This will be followed by presentations of the exemplars.

2.1 Henry Walker: A Three-Course Introductory Sequence

Henry Walker will present Grinnell College's three-course introductory sequence. The CS program at Grinnell follows a multi-paradigm approach in its introductory curriculum. Since each course emphasizes problem solving following a specified paradigm, students gain practice by tackling a range of problems. Toward that end, the first two courses utilize application themes to generate interest in interdisciplinary connections of computer science. The following outlines the main elements of this approach:

- Functional Problem Solving (CS1)
  - Primary Paradigm: Functional problem solving
  - Supporting language: Scheme
  - Application area: image processing, media scripting
- Imperative Problem Solving and Data Structures (CS2)
  - Primary Paradigm: Imperative problem solving
  - Supporting language: C (no objects as in C++)
  - Application area: robotics
- Algorithms and Object-Oriented Design (CS3)
  - Primary Paradigm: Object-oriented problem solving
  - Supporting language: Java
  - Application areas: large-scale problems

These three courses cover topics and learning outcomes selected from 12 of the 18 Knowledge Areas in the CS 2013 Strawman Body of Knowledge.

Henry Walker is a Professor of Computer Science at Grinnell College. He has served as Chair of SIGCSE, is a regular columnist on "Classroom Issues" for the *SIGCSE Bulletin*, and was designated an ACM "Distinguished Educator" in 2009. He will receive the SIGCSE Award for Lifetime Service to the Computer Science Education Community at this conference.

2.2 Ruth Anderson: Multithreading and Data Structures

Ruth Anderson will describe a required data structures course that comes after CS2 and discrete structures and that integrates a 3-week introduction to multithreading[3]. This University of Washington course emphasizes a distinction between utilizing parallelism to speed up computations and managing concurrency to ensure correct access to shared resources. It approaches multithreading with the same mix of algorithms, programming, and asymptotic analysis that makes the data structures course such a keystone in the curriculum. This course covers topics and learning outcomes from 4 of the 18 Knowledge Areas in the Strawman Body of Knowledge.

Ruth Anderson is a Lecturer in the Department of Computer Science and Engineering at the University of Washington. She is a regular SIGCSE conference contributor, including former workshops co-chair.

2.3 Elizabeth Hawthorne: Discrete Math at a Community College

Union County College is a comprehensive community college in Cranford, NJ offering associate degree programs in computer science/engineering and in mathematics. Both programs were designed to transfer into respective baccalaureate degree programs throughout the New York metropolitan region and require a sophomore level course in discrete mathematics, MAT 267. The presentation of this course exemplar will highlight not only the topics and student learning outcomes, which adhere closely to the CS 2013 guidelines, but also the assessment of student learning.

The course is the work of Cynthia Roemer and Jean Lane. Dr. Cynthia Roemer chairs the Mathematics department and Professor Jean Lane coordinates the Mathematics program at Union County College. As department chair, Cynthia directs the assessment of all mathematics courses for institutional accreditation. As program coordinator, Jean developed the discrete mathematics course based on the 1991 ACM/IEEE-CS computer science guidelines and has kept it current in accordance with ACM/IEEE-CS curricular revisions (CS2001, CS2013). Elizabeth Hawthorne, a member of the CS 2013 Steering Committee, will present the exemplar.

2.4 Christa Chewar: Information Assurance

Christa Chewar will discuss how Information Assurance topics are infused throughout the computer science curriculum at the United States Military Academy (West Point). Coverage of information-assurance fundamentals begins in the CS0 and CS1 courses, where students are exposed to topics such as personal and global cyber threats, while developing problem solving and programming skills with exercises in steganography, ciphering, and "Facebook scraping." Students have several choices of more advanced coursework to fulfill their networking and information assurance and security requirements, including courses in Digital Forensics and Exploitation. However, the most popular option is the Cyber Security course. Serving both the IT and CS programs, this course focuses on offensive and defensive information operations, with a culminating week-long "Cyber Defense Exercise" that challenges students to protect a production network from external intrusions.

Christa Chewar has served as an Assistant Professor at West Point for five years, and is currently the curriculum coordinator for the CS and IT programs.

2.5 Audience Participation

Three members of the CS 2013 Steering Committee – Andrea Danyluk, Steve Roach (CS 2013 Co-Chair), and Elizabeth Hawthorne – will invite the audience to provide feedback on the range of exemplars in the Ironman draft, with an eye to fleshing out the set of exemplars for the final report.

As described above, authors of exemplars in the Ironman will be invited to the front of the room so that session attendees may speak with them as well as with session presenters.

3. REFERENCES

[1] ACM Curriculum Committee on Computer Science. Curriculum 68: Recommendations for academic programs in computer science. *Comm. ACM*, 11(3):151–197, Mar 1968.

[2] ACM/IEEE-CS Joint Task Force on Computer Science Curricula. Computer science curricula 2013 strawman draft, February 2012.

[3] D. Grossman and R. E. Anderson. Introducing parallelism and concurrency in the data structures course. In *SIGCSE'12*, pages 505–510, 2012.

Studio-Based Learning and App Inventor for Android in an Introductory CS Course for non-Majors

Khuloud Ahmad and Paul Gestwicki
Computer Science Department
Ball State University
Muncie, IN 47306
knahmad@bsugmail.net pvgestwicki@bsu.edu

ABSTRACT

In this study, an experimental introductory CS course was implemented focusing on two pedagogic factors: the use of App Inventor for Android (AIA), a visual blocks programming environment for creating smart phone applications; and the adoption of studio-based learning (SBL) as the main teaching methodology. Participants included 18 non-CS major undergraduates. The Motivated Strategies for Learning Questionnaire (MSLQ) was implemented at several stages. With the exception of the Peer Learning scale in the mid-MSLQ, all participants scored in the high range in the three MSLQs. Results indicated that participants were comfortable collaborating with peers and asking questions. Additional data were collected from entry and exit interviews as well as student-created mind maps. The study revealed positive student response to the pedagogic factors and positive attitudes towards CS, and the subjects also demonstrated significant academic achievement. The experimental approach was found to have a positive effect on students' motivation, creativity, achievement, and attitude towards CS.

Categories and Subject Descriptors

K.3.2 [**Computers and Education**] Computer and Information Science Education- *Computer science education*

Keywords

AIA, Studio-Based Learning, Introductory Computer Science, MSLQ, Mind Map, Computer Science Education

1. INTRODUCTION

A reexamination of the traditional instruction in introductory computer science (CS) courses is becoming a necessity. In many universities, the CS department has suffered from low enrollment for several years [27]. There were slight increases in enrollment over the past few years [29]. However, Cooper and Cunningham [8] argue that there are "some promising results here and there, but an overall pattern of change and improvement is not yet evident" (p. 5).

SIGCSE'13, March 6–9, 2013, Denver, Colorado, USA.

In addition to low enrolment, introductory CS courses tend to have low success rates [7,10,27]. Multiple studies have linked these phenomena with low student motivation, specifically with respect to attitudes towards overtly mathematics-oriented assignments and lecture-oriented pedagogy [10,26]. Students' criticisms are directed at the major for its lack of creativity, relevance, and interest [14,26]. The industry, as well, noted "a lack of creativity in school graduates" (p. 149) [26]. Research on creativity in CS education, however, is very rare [20]. One study found the traditional computer science education approach focused on problem solving and lacked creative activities [26]. Gottel and Schild [13] found that students are "not well-trained in creative thinking" (p. 98). They observed "discomfort amongst students when asking them to realize their own ideas." However, according to the Bureau of Labor Statistics (BLS) there is still an increasing demand for workers with technical computer skills and computer related services [4,15]. To provide CS graduates with better job prospects, they need to be creative and versatile programmers.

Studies showed that the introductory CS course failed to reach the wide range of students taking the course [14]. Forte and Guzdial [10] found that "traditional introductions to computer science are more likely to frustrate students than attract them to the field" (p. 2). Students conceded the intro course to be "overly-technical," not applicable in the real world, and lacking opportunities for creativity. Forte and Guzdial [10] stated that the reason behind students failing and dropping out of CS was not perceiving it as interesting or useful. According to Freudenthal et al. [11], "programming techniques in early [introductory] courses should be chosen to minimize cognitive load while maximizing pedagogical value" (p. 37).

1.1. Purpose of This Study

The purpose of this study was to implement an experimental introductory CS course for non-CS majors focusing on two pedagogic factors and to evaluate their effects on students' motivation, achievement, and attitude towards CS; evaluating them as a comprehensive learning environment. These factors were: 1) The use of App Inventor for Android (AIA); and 2) the adoption of Studio-Based Learning (SBL) as the main teaching methodology and using lectures only to reinforce the SBL sessions when needed. This study attempts to address some of the problems in introductory CS courses, such as lack of interest, lack of creativity, and suitability of the learning environment.

1.1.1. Why AIA?

The practice of using a professional-grade development language in introductory CS courses started when languages were easy for beginners [9]. Today, Java and C++, two professional-grade development languages that are the standard languages used in introductory CS courses. However, these languages were created for developing large-scale software and not intended for instructional settings [25]. In using those, students struggle, get distracted, and frustrated. According to Denning [9], "students are being overwhelmed by the complexities of languages that many experts find challenging. . . . Many students have turned to cheating and plagiarism as ways to pass these courses, and 35%-50% drop out prematurely" (p. 20). Meyer and Masterson [23] found that "students in 'CS 0' courses and even early programming courses find algorithm design difficult and seldom much fun" (p. 184).

Many studies have used languages that depend on a visual or graphical environment in introductory CS courses, for example Alice and Scratch, rather than textual syntax languages. These languages are known as visual blocks programming languages; since a program is built through snapping together building blocks. Surprisingly, novice programmers often find difficulty in understanding the simple concept of consistent indentation [23]. Where in visual blocks programming languages, blocks fit together a certain way using drag and drop actions, much like a puzzle, eliminating the need for indentations all together; thus eliminating the struggle students have with language syntax and the trivial syntactical errors. Overall, Meyers and Masterson [23] found that the "visual metaphor of containment and subordination of control" (p. 184) in visual blocks programming languages aid in understanding algorithmic design principles.

Unlike its counterparts, that is Alice and Scratch, AIA was developed for college level education purposes and has the capability of developing all types of applications not just animation. Furthermore, AIA was chosen due to its mobile application development capability. It allows instructors to leverage students' interest in mobile applications and the ubiquity of mobile devices in order to increase students' motivation.

1.1.2. Why SBL?

One of the reasons posited for the low interest in CS and the low retention rates is the anti-social image the discipline has [16], the image of a computer scientist as a socially-challenged person sitting in front of the computer all day. Lewis et al. [21] argue that "integration of cooperative and collaborative learning might challenge cultural stereotypes and set more accurate expectations of CS professions" (p. 10). Hundhausen et al. [16] claim that this image is due to the association of computing with programming, since many early CS courses tend to focus mainly on programming and learning the syntax of a language. The industry does demand proficient programmers which makes this focus understandable and even necessary. However, even after taking many CS courses that focus on programming, students still have poor programming skills [28]. Woodley and Kamin argue that learning skillful programming requires constant feedback. Here Studio-Based Learning, with its social setting and its periodical discussion sessions (aka *design crits)*, may offer a solution.

SBL has been studied on its own in many research papers and have been proven to be beneficial as well as motivational. It is worth mentioning, however, that most studies that implemented SBL so far used "SBL to reinforce lecture material" (p. 110) [6]. The reverse is worth investigating; where the main teaching methodology used in the course would be SBL and lectures are used to reinforce the SBL sessions. There is a need for "additional comparative studies" (p. 110), as Carter and Hundhausen [6] believed, where SBL is compared to other methodologies. They believe, moreover, "the interplay between lecture and SBL" (p. 110) should be further studied. This study further investigates this interplay focusing on SBL as the main teaching methodology and using, very few, lectures only as reinforcement to the SBL sessions. Furthermore, the SBL approach is a natural fit with the AIA tool and provides the educational setting and environment needed for such a language: this synergistic combination brings the advantages of active learning, peer learning, and motivational contexts to introductory CS.

2. IMPLEMENTATION

The experimental course was implemented in an introductory CS course for non-CS majors offered in fall 2009 at Ball State University known as CS116-Visual Programming. A total of 18 undergraduates attended this course. The course was restricted to non-CS majors in order to find students that had little to no programming experience; students that may exhibit a negative attitude towards CS as a discipline or at least did not have one.

2.1. Course Structure

The format of the course involved learning basic algorithmic and programming concepts through completing project-based programming assignments. The course was taught in a lab that included work stations equipped and ready for use. Each student had his/her own workstation and G1 phone to use during class meetings. Whenever the instructors felt students were unable to complete a given assignment on their own, or that they needed to comprehend a concept in order to reach a solution, mini-lectures were given with hands-on tutorials. These mini-lectures were to simply reinforce concepts covered during SBL class sessions. In other words, the need for and the topics covered in the lectures were driven by the studio experiences. A total of five mini-lectures were given throughout the semester.

2.1.1. Programming Projects

The first week of the semester was spent on introducing the students to the structure of the course (see Table 1). For the next few weeks, students were given the assignment of completing the tutorials provided on the official AIA site[1]. This was to provide the students with the chance to familiarize themselves with the AIA IDE and the G1 phone. Throughout the rest of the semester, students completed a total of eight projects; six one week programming assignments, one midterm project, and one final project. Furthermore, of these six programming assignments two were completed individually and four in groups. In group programming assignments, groups were formed by the instructors using several methods: by major, by gender, by GPA, or simply by random selection.

Following the SBL model, each project was discussed in the *design crits* on three progressive stages: *The Pitch*, *The Studio*, and *The Presentation* [12]. *The Pitch* starts before any programming is actually done, during which students were to formulate their ideas and design and "pitch" their project to the rest of the class and get feedback. During *The Studio*, students would spend time in class working on their projects. This allowed the implementation of active learning. When obstacles were faced, students were encouraged to open a discussion session with the

[1] For more information go to http://www.appinventor.mit.edu/

entire class. For large-scaled projects, one or more status reports were presented where each student discussed his/her progress and received feedback during class session. *The Presentation* is the last stage of the projects where students would "present" their finished, in rare cases close to finished, projects to the entire class and get feedback. This feedback was intended to help students in their upcoming projects.

Table 1. Course structure

Content	Week
Introduction to the course structure	1
Complete AIA tutorials	2-4
Complete five programming assignments	5-8
Complete the midterm project	9-10
Complete a programming assignment	11
Complete the final project	12-15
Presentations of final projects	16

2.1.2. Reflection Papers

After each programming assignment, students were asked to write a reflection paper; in which they were to write a paragraph of self-evaluation. This evaluation would include a reflection on their contributions on the assignment, the difficulties and issues they faced and what they found to be effective approaches to solving them. There were two purposes to this assignment. One was to get a deeper insight into what the students faced during class and in working on their assignments. The other was to foster metacognition and reflective practice.

2.1.3. Group Page

To facilitate communication and collaboration between students and with instructors outside of the class, a group page was created using Google Groups. This site was restricted to CS116 students only. It allowed students to post their assignments and comments and ask any questions they may have. The students used the group page to upload their assignments and comment on their classmates' work as well. This helped in promoting active learning and student communications, two integral parts of SBL. The instructors, also, used the group page to post assignments, reminders, reading materials, and comment on the students' work.

2.1.4. Formative Assessment

Essential to the SBL model is the process of formative assessment, both formal and informal. It is the basis for the active learning process that is intrinsic to the structure of SBL [6]. Therefore, the structure of the course was developed to incorporate formative assessment. This is most evident in the structure of the programming assignment and their division into the three stages: *The Studio, The Pitch, and The Presentation.* At each stage, the instructors gave students immediate feedback on their efforts.

2.1.5. Summative Assessment

One of the challenges faced in structuring this experimental introductory CS course was summative assessment. Students often worked in groups and, if not, solicited the help of others in their work. Therefore it was not fair to use submitted programming assignments alone for the purposes of summative assessment. Therefore, an individual midterm assessment process was devised in an interview setting in lieu of a written exam [12]. Students would schedule an individual meeting with the instructors outside of the class for this assessment-by-interview process. This process included two parts. The first part was the sample application test. The second was the submitted midterm project. In the sample application test, a medium-size example application was created and students were asked to read and explain its functionality during the individual meeting. The aim was to test their ability to distinguish and understand specific programming concepts that were taught in class up to that point. At the end of the semester, a final programming project was assessed as part of the students' final grade. The students were expected to deliver a more complex application that showcased their understanding of the more complex concepts in CS covered during the course. The final grade students received at the end of the course included their cumulative work throughout the course.

2.2. Evaluation Tools

Evaluation of this experience was based on three different forms of data. The Motivated Strategies for Learning Questionnaire (MSLQ) [24] was administered at several stages to evaluate the effect on student motivation and interest. Interviews were conducted to elicit specific factors that were influential in this experience. Mind map analysis was implemented to study the effect on student attitudes towards the course in particular and CS in general.

2.2.1. Motivated Strategies for Learning Questionnaire

Variations on the MSLQ were administered in this study. The original MSLQ was modified slightly and three variants were developed, an entry-MSLQ, a mid-MSLQ, and an exit-MSLQ. The modifications included the elimination of scales in all three modified MSLQs that were not relevant to the purpose of the study; they were Test Anxiety, Rehearsal, and Organization. The modified MSLQs were paper-based questionnaires administered during class time. In CS116 the entry-MSLQ was administered at the beginning of the semester, the mid-MSLQ was at a mid point during the semester, and the exit-MSLQ was at the end. This was done in order to evaluate any changes in motivation and learning as the course progressed.

2.2.2. Interviews

Two interviews were conducted in CS116, an entry interview at the beginning of the semester, and an exit interview at the end. Participation was voluntary and anonymous. Both interviews included questions that elicited responses about the participant's attitude towards this CS course in particular, towards CS as a major, as well as towards active learning and SBL. The exit interview, however, included in addition a few questions about AIA eliciting their attitudes toward it as a learning language.

2.2.3. Mind Maps

One critical assignment that was included to analyze students' understanding of CS was the creation of mind maps with reference to computer science. A mind map is "a diagram that shows topics and how they are connected" (p. 171) [17]. It is a technique developed by Tony Buzan with Barry Buzan in *The Mind Map Book* [5]. According to Buzan et. al, "the Mind Map is your external mirror of your own Radiant Thinking and allows you access into this vast thinking powerhouse" (p. 31). They suggest that mind maps offer away to represent the internal mental image on an external piece of paper which would allow the chance for analysis and interpretation.

In this study, CS116 students were asked to submit two mind maps, one at the beginning of the semester and one near the end. Each mind map was to start with Computer Science as the root and students were to add as many nodes and subnodes as they see fit (see Figure 1 for an example). Analyzing the change from the first mind map to the second would show any change in the students' understanding of CS. This would help investigate whether the course had an effect on the students' view of CS and their understanding of it.

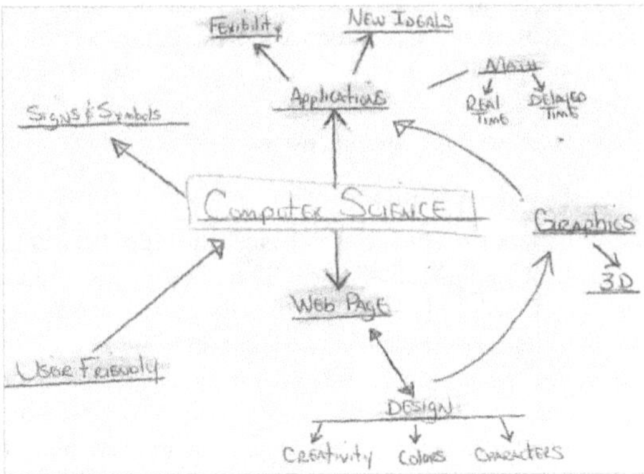

Figure 1. A Student-created Mind Map.

Since in this study we were examining CS as a discipline, the examination of the mind maps was based on a well devised and formal description of the discipline found in the *Computing Curricula 2001* [1] and its revision report titled the *Computer Science Curriculum 2008* [2]. In those reports, CS as a "body of Knowledge" (CS BoK) is described and organized into a hierarchy that provides a good basis for examining the mind maps. Thus an elimination process was implemented where the nodes and subnodes that do not correspond to the areas and units in the CS BoK were removed from consideration.

Many studies have shown the importance of going beyond the individual words within the nodes in evaluating mind maps [e.g. 18,19,22]; they suggest the use of propositions. There were subtle differences in their definition of propositions. They all agree, however, that a proposition is the meaning of a node relative to its connecting node(s). McClure et al. [22] found the use of propositions in assessing mind maps the highest in terms of reliability. Such propositions were found to be important in this CS BoK examination process.

3. ANALYSIS

Analysis was based on triangulation of the three forms of data described above, namely, the MSLQ, interviews, and mind maps. In addition, students' submitted course work and instructors' observations were included in this process. The results were studied and analyzed to identify this experimental course's effect on the students' motivation, achievement, and attitude towards CS.

3.1. MSLQ

Students in CS116 (N=18) answered three modified MSLQs. All students scored in the 4-7 range, which is defined as high, on all scales in all three MSLQs, with the exception of the Peer Learning scale in the mid-MSLQ. As part of the MSLQ, background information was also elicited. These showed that the students in CS116 did not find the course to be difficult, did not find the course intimidating, and were comfortable in collaborative situations. By the end of the semester, students were more comfortable collaborating with and asking questions of their peers than their instructors.

3.2. Interviews

Two interviews were implemented in CS116. Only one student participated in the entry-interview while seven students responded to the exit-interview. The entry-interview showed the common attitudes and misconceptions exhibited in non-CS students. The exit-interview showed that the respondents had a positive reaction to the experimental course. Almost all respondents expressed that they would not change anything about the design of the course. Most respondents had positive responses about using AIA; even though most respondents had no programming experience before taking this course. For most respondents working on the projects and collaborating with others were enjoyable as well as beneficial. One student commented on that in the exit-interview, "this class helped me to become more open to working with others[*sic*] classmates to solve the problems that would arise." Most respondents had positive attitudes towards CS and found it relevant to their major and their lives, "coming into college, I wasn't exactly sure what['s] the difference between a CS major and a IT major. This made me appreciate the CS major more and I definitely hope to take more classes on this material," as one student commented. However, most respondents still showed some misconceptions regarding CS as a discipline. One student acquainted it with programming and only programming. Another stated that he only used CS "for entertainment," probably thinking of the computer as a device. A few others shared a similar viewpoint, "if you can know as much as possible with[*sic*] computers than[*sic*] computer science will come easy," as one stated.

3.3. Mind Maps

In order to examine whether the change in view was related to the students' understanding of CS and the way they viewed CS, the student-created mind maps were examined using the CS BoK with considerations for propositions. Fourteen students' mind maps were analyzed for any significant differences. A dependent t-test was administered and the difference between the number of nodes in first mind map and in the second was found to be statistically significant: $t(13)$=-2.709, p<.02. These results indicated that there was a significantly positive change in the image and understanding of CS and an ability to find more connections and topics relating to CS in the second mind map than in the first (M=10.07 and M=5.93 respectively).

In a qualitative analysis of the mind maps, specific observations were noted on each mind map and on the differences between the two. This analysis confirmed the results found above. Moreover, even though programming was mentioned equally in both mind maps, students were able to make many new connections and expand their image of CS to go beyond programming. This was a desirable outcome for programming is an integral element of CS but not the only element, and the students were able to see that. Students, furthermore, found that CS connects to other disciplines, such as biology, chemistry, engineering, and art. Some students established connections to CS as a place for innovative ideas and "helping needs," others saw the need for people skills in CS, such as communication and collaboration. Such connections did not exist in their first mind maps.

3.4. Students' Submitted Course Work

CS116 students' were able to complete all given assignments and showed creativity in their work. They were able to understand the basic programming concepts taught in the course and to utilize AIA and create applications for their G1 phones. In the reflection papers, most students found collaboration to be a helpful part of the course, "working in groups not only brings everyone's ideas together to come up with some very interesting app work, but it also gives a chance for members to work on their strengths and weaknesses," as one student commented. They, moreover, found the experimental course to provide an interactive environment that cultivated collaboration and motivation to learn.

3.5. Assessment

Students, for the most part, were doing very well throughout the semester (see Figure 2). It was evident in their submitted work that they were making use of the feedback given, both formal and informal. Students were able to actively learn with very few interjections from the instructors. It is important to note, however, that at first students did not relate to the idea of formative assessment and were always seeking ways were they could get a tangible grade. For the most part, however, students did appreciate the process of formative assessment and did find it very helpful to their learning.

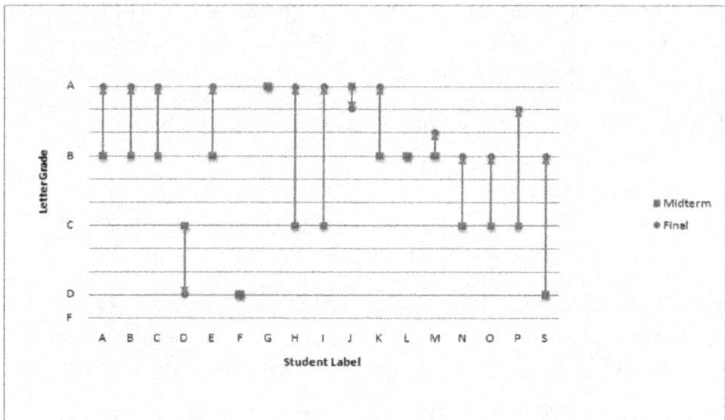

Figure 2. Individual Grade Progress Linechart.

Students did well in the midterm assessment-by-interview process. Over half of the students were above the C letter grade with approximately 12% getting an A, 41% getting a B, 35% getting a C, and 12% getting a D. No student failed this assessment process. The concepts that some of the students struggled with in this assessment-by-interview included string operations–nesting of the 'join' command specifically–and the difference in the logic of 'if' vs. 'ifelse'. A few students seemed to have difficulty understanding the difference between defining a variable and setting a value to a variable. Generally, there were some concerns about the ability of those struggling students to turn their grades around and do better at this stage.

The final grade was assigned taking into consideration the cumulative work the progress each student has shown throughout the course. Overall students did very well where 47% of the students got an A, about 12% got an A-, 6% got a B+, approximately 23% got a B, and about 12% got a D. No students failed the course. More importantly, they had shown an understanding of the basic concepts covered in the course, some of them were concepts they had struggled with in their midterm assessment. One student, however, withdrew from the course. These results indicated that the experimental course had a high success rate with 83% of the participants not withdrawing, failing, or getting a D.

4. CONCLUSIONS

The use of SBL as the main teaching methodology is rarely reported in the literature; when examined, SBL is often used as reinforcement for lectures that were the main method for delivering the knowledge. In this study, however, only five mini-lectures were given throughout the semester and were guided by the *design crits*. The instructors saw little need to interject or interfere in the learning process. Students were able to learn on their own and, at the same time, have a positive attitude about the course. Students scored in the high range on all the scales of the MSLQ. This indicated that they were doing well in terms of motivation and learning skills.

The experimental course as a whole was found to be a positive experience. Creating mobile applications through AIA was found to be one of the factors that contributed to increasing motivation. Basing the pedagogy on SBL was a factor in increasing collaboration and comfort levels. Both pedagogic factors resulted in positive outcomes in terms of students' motivation, performance, and attitude. Students were able to pick up basic concepts and actively learn through this course. This study indicated that this experimental course resulted in positive attitudes towards the discipline. Most students, at the end of the semester, no longer acquainted it with programming alone. Students were able to appreciate other factors related to the discipline, such as design and HCI issues. The anti-social image of the discipline was also affected. They found CS inviting, challenging, and interesting. In both mind maps and interview results, students associated collaboration with CS. This result appears to confirm previous research by Hundhausen et al. [16]: the anti-social image the discipline has is due to associating computing with programming and tending to focus mainly on learning syntax of a language in early CS course. In Fact, this approach had a deeper effect on a couple of students which resulted in their desire to change their minor to CS.

In conclusion, this study suggests that a course merging a visual blocks language, with the use of a medium that is of interest to students at the time of study–in this case mobile technology, along with the use of an active learning pedagogy, creates a learning environment that cultures creativity and trains student in creative thinking. It, furthermore, shows that SBL can stand on its own as the main teaching methodology used in an introductory CS course. Even though the sample size is relatively small, this study provides validation and new perspectives on the literature on the use of SBL, as the main teaching methodology, and visual blocks programming languages in Computer Science. Furthermore, the analysis of data collected in this study may help to improve recruitment and retention of CS majors in addition to improving the understanding of how to make CS accessible and interesting to non-majors.

5. ACKNOWLEDGMENTS

Our thanks to Google and the AIA development team for their contributions and support throughout the implementation of this study; special thanks to Google for providing the G1phones used in this study. Our gratitude is extended to Hal Abelson for his effort and continuous support.

6. REFERENCES

[1] ACM/IEEE-CS Joint Task Force. 2001. Computing Curricula 2001: Computer Science. *Journal on Educational Resources in Computing (JERIC)*, *1*(3).

[2] ACM/IEEE-CS Joint Task Force. 2008. *Computer Science Curriculum 2008: An Interim Revision of CS 2001*, Retrieved May 20, 2012 from, http://www.acm.org/education/curricula/ComputerScience2008.pdf

[3] Ahmad, K. 2012. Measuring the impact of app inventor for android and studio-based learning in an introductory computer science course for non-majors. *Dissertation Abstract International, 73*(12), 227A. (Publication No. AAT 3521731).

[4] Bureau of Labor Statistics. 2009. Tomorrow's Jobs. *Occupational Outlook Handbook, 2008-2009 Edition.*

[5] Buzan, T., & Buzan, B. 1994. T*he Mind Map Book: How to Use Radiant Thinking to Maximize Your Brain's Untapped Potential.* Penguin Books, NY.

[6] Carter, A., & Hundhausen, C. 2011. A Review of Studio-Based Learning in Computer Science. *Journal of Computing Sciences in Colleges, 27*(1).

[7] Cohoon, J., & Chen, L. 2003. Migrating Out of Computer Science. *Computing Research News, 15*(2): 2-3.

[8] Cooper, S., & Cunningham, S. 2010. Teaching Computer Science in Context. *ACM Inroads*, *1*(1): 5-8.

[9] Denning, P. 2003. Great Principles of Computing. *Communications of the ACM, 46*(11): 15-20.

[10] Forte, A., & Guzdial, M. 2004. Computers for Communication, Not Calculation: Media as a Motivation and Context for Learning. *Proceedings of the 37th Annual Hawaii International Conference on System Sciences*, 1- 10.

[11] Freudenthal, E., Roy, M., Ogrey, A., Magoc, T., & Siegel, A. 2010. MPCT - Media Propelled Computational Thinking. *Proceedings of the 41st ACM technical symposium on Computer science education*, 37-41.

[12] Gestwicki, P., & Ahmad, K. 2011. App Inventor for Android with Studio-based Learning. *Journal of Computing Sciences in Colleges, 27*(1): 55-63.

[13] Gottel, T., & Schild, J. 2011. Creativity Room 5555: Evoking Creativity in Game Design Amongst CS Students. *Proceedings of the 16th annual joint conference on Innovation and technology in computer science education*, 98-102.

[14] Guzdial, M. 2003. A Media Computation Course for Non-Majors. *Proceedings of the 8th annual conference on Innovation and technology in computer science education*, *35*(3): 104-108.

[15] Henderson, R. 2012. Industry employment and output projections to 2020. *Monthly Labor Review, 135*(1): 65-83.

[16] Hundhausen, C., Narayanan, N., & Crosby, M. 2008. Exploring studio-based instructional models for computing education. *Proceedings of the 39th SIGCSE technical symposium on Computer science education*, 392–396.

[17] Hunt, A. 2008. *Pragmatic Thinking and Learning: Refactor Your "Wetware"*. The Pragmatic Bookshelf, Dallas, TX.

[18] Kintsch, W. 1998. *Comprehension: A paradigm for cognition*. Cambridge University Press, Cambridge, UK.

[19] Kintsch, W., & Dijk, T. 1978. Toward a Model of Text Comprehension and Production. *Psychological Review, 85* (5): 363-394.

[20] Knobelsdorf, M., & Romeike, R. 2008. Creativity as a Pathway to Computer Science. *Proceedings of the 13th annual conference on Innovation and technology in computer science education,* 286-290.

[21] Lewis, C., Yasuhara, K., & Anderson, R. 2011. Deciding to Major in Computer Science: A Grounded Theory of Students' Self-Assessment of Ability. *Proceedings of the Seventh International Workshop on Computing Education Research*, 3-10.

[22] McClure, J., Sonak, B., & Suen, H. 1999. Concept Map Assessment of Classroom Learning: Reliability, Validity, and Logistical Practicality. *Journal of Research in Science Teaching, 36*(4): 475–492.

[23] Meyer, R., & Masterson, T. 2000. Towards a better visual programming language: critiquing Prograph's control structures. *Proceedings of the fifth annual CCSC northeastern conference on The journal of computing in small colleges*, 181–193.

[24] Pintrich, P., Smith, F., Garcia, T., & McKeachie, W. 1991. *A Manual for the Use of the Motivated Strategies for Learning Questionnaire (MSLQ).*The University of Michigan.

[25] Radenski, A. 2006. "Python First": A Lab-Based Digital Introduction to Computer Science. *Proceedings of the 11th annual SIGCSE conference on Innovation and technology in computer science education,*197-201.

[26] Romeike, R. 2006. Creative Student – What can we Learn from Them for Teaching Computer Science?. *Proceedings of the 6th Baltic Sea conference on Computing education research*, 149-150.

[27] Sloan, R., & Troy, P. 2008. CS 0.5: A Better Approach to Introductory Computer Science Majors. *Proceedings of the 39th SIGCSE technical symposium on Computer science education*, 271 – 275.

[28] Woodly, M., & Kamin, S. 2007. Programming studio: a course for improving programming skills in undergraduates. *Proceedings of the 38th SIGCSE technical symposium on Computer science education,* 531 - 535.

[29] Zweben, S. 2010. 2009-2010 Taulbee Survey: Undergraduate CS Degree Production Rises; Doctoral Production Steady. *Computing Research Association,* Retrieved June, 20, 2012 from, http://www.cra.org/uploads/documents/resources/taulbee/CRA_ Taulbee_2009-2010_Results.pdf

Impacts of Adaptive Feedback on Teaching Test-Driven Development

Kevin Buffardi
Virginia Tech
114 McBryde Hall (0106)
Blacksburg, Virginia
+1 540-231-5723
kbuffardi@vt.edu

Stephen H. Edwards
Virginia Tech
114 McBryde Hall (0106)
Blacksburg, Virginia
+1 540-231-5723
edwards@cs.vt.edu

ABSTRACT
Studies have found that following Test-Driven Development (TDD) can improve code and testing quality. However, a preliminary investigation was consistent with concerns raised by other educators about programmers resisting TDD. In this paper, we describe an adaptive, pedagogical system for tracking and encouraging students' adherence to TDD. Along with an empirical evaluation of the system, we discuss challenges and opportunities for persuading student behavior through adaptive technology.

Categories and Subject Descriptors
K.3.2 [**Computers and Education**]: Computer and Information Science Education; D.1.5 [**Programming Techniques**]: Object oriented Programming; D.2.5 [**Software Engineering**]: Testing and Debugging.

General Terms
Measurement, Human Factors, Verification.

Keywords
Test-Driven Development (TDD), Automated Testing, Test-first, Unit testing, Adherence, Instructional Technology, Web-CAT.

1. INTRODUCTION
Test-Driven Development (TDD) is a software development process used in industry [10] that is emerging in computing education. At our university, we teach TDD in introductory CS1 and CS2 courses. However, to weigh the possible benefits and shortcomings of TDD in an academic setting, we focused on investigating how well students follow TDD and assessing how it affected their code quality.

In several instances, we observed anecdotal evidence of students resisting TDD. For example, while working on a programming project, one student explained, "*I will worry about my testing [...] later; I just want to get it working first.*" Another student worried about failing software tests and lamented, "*[The program] is my baby and I don't want to be told that my baby is bad!*" Both cases demonstrate attitudes that discourage TDD adoption.

Other studies have also identified challenges to motivating TDD adherence. Researchers identified students' reluctance to accept TDD especially from less experienced programmers [11][12][15]. Our preliminary investigation confirmed claims that following TDD contributes to code and test quality. We also supplemented our anecdotal observations with evidence of some students' reluctance to follow TDD. Students' project code identified some behaviors that violate TDD principles. Furthermore, our survey linked poor attitudes toward some aspects of TDD as a reason for non-adherence [3].

Consequentially, while we recognize educational value in continuing to teach TDD, we also acknowledge a need to improve TDD adherence. We sought pedagogical interventions to foster better attitudes toward TDD and encourage its use. As a result, we developed an adaptive feedback system to track students' programming behaviors and to reinforce TDD. This paper describes the system's design and a preliminary evaluation of its effects.

2. BACKGROUND
Test-Driven Development (TDD) is a process involving incremental development of solution code and test validation. In TDD, programmers write unit tests—meant to test a small segment of code, such as a single function—throughout development of the solution. In particular, Beck advocates a "test a little, code a little" test-first approach [1] where programmers write a unit test preceding its corresponding solution code. He also promotes TDD for helping developers gain confidence in their solutions and localize bugs with greater ease.

TDD is popular in the software industry, often as part of Extreme Programming (XP) and Agile Methods [1]. Canfora performed empirical studies comparing professionals' use of TDD and test-after-coding approaches and found TDD improves testing quality [4]. Likewise, Microsoft reported substantial benefits to TDD's impact on code quality, documentation, and maintenance [2]. Nevertheless, professionals hedge TDD endorsements with caveats of initial increased workload [2] and a particular need to promote its adoption [10].

Meanwhile, schools have begun to adopt TDD in their computer science curricula. A survey of TDD education reaffirmed findings from industry that TDD may increase workload but also improves both code and testing quality [5]. One study found students produced 45% fewer defects per line of code when using TDD [9].

In an academic setting, it is important to consider how TDD affects learning in addition to implications on improving code quality. Through exposure to TDD, students gain practical experience with a technique they may use during their professional careers. Furthermore, by practicing TDD, students may replace inferior "trial-and-error" problem-solving techniques with higher order thinking skills involved in deliberate reflection [8].

Despite its advantages, independent academic reports echo difficulties in motivating students to adopt TDD. Specifically, less mature and inexperienced programmers demonstrate reluctance to adopt TDD [11][12][15]. In a previous study, we found students held generally positive perceptions of TDD and unit testing but had particular reservations about following a test-first approach [3]. Correspondingly, Spacco and Pugh suggest that special incentives are necessary to motivate students to adopt a "test-first mentality" instead of resorting to test-after-coding [15].

Persuading students to change their behavior and adhere to TDD principles is a formidable challenge. Schwarz reasons that persuasion relies on emotional valence and appraisal of anticipated effects [14]. A student's positive mood can foster easier coaxing. In addition, students' expectations for the outcomes of changing their behavior play a significant role. Without perceived benefit, a student is unlikely to change methods. Accordingly, students will appraise the effects of adhering to TDD and their appraisal will influence the prospect of continuing that behavior. Therefore, demonstrating valuable results from following TDD will positively reinforce that behavior.

Another challenge in influencing student behavior is intervening while they program. Ideally, when a student does not exhibit TDD techniques, a pedagogical intervention persuades a change in behavior. Likewise, exhibiting proper TDD would earn positive reinforcement. However, it is impractical to expect a teacher to provide supervision and prompt feedback to each student in class as they work on programming assignments.

To the contrary, automated grading systems can provide students with feedback at their convenience without placing an extra burden on instructors. Web-CAT [7] is an automated grading tool that provides students with unlimited opportunities to receive prompt feedback on their solution and test code. It assesses students' solutions based on instructor-provided reference tests. It also runs students' tests against their own solutions, validates that the tests pass, and measures the percentage of solution code covered by the tests. In addition, Web-CAT can deliver hints to students that correspond to failed reference tests.

Since Web-CAT evaluates students' work, its feedback may be positive or negative. The feedback reflects the quality of the student's work so poor or incomplete work will show failed tests and other negative results. Web-CAT is a promising medium for delivering interventions to persuade student behavior. However, because of the possible impact of negative feedback on students' mood, it is important to design feedback strategically to cultivate persuasion.

3. AN ADAPTIVE FEEDBACK SYSTEM

We designed and evaluated a pedagogical intervention for improving student adherence to Test-Driven Development (TDD). The intervention intends to monitor students' development habits and persuade them to follow TDD's incremental process. We implemented this intervention by developing a plugin for Web-CAT that provides adaptive feedback based on how well the student is adhering to incremental unit testing. Since Web-CAT allows students to resubmit multiple times to improve their scores, the plugin monitors how a student's code changes from one submission to the next. The plugin particularly takes note of changes in: the amount of solution code, the amount of test code, the correctness of the solution (as determined by the instructor's reference tests), and the test coverage achieved (as determined by the student's tests run against her own code).

As mentioned previously, Web-CAT displays hints to the student when a submitted solution fails any instructor reference tests to help guide the student in the right direction. These hints have obvious value to the students because they provide some guidance on where to look for problems in their programs. By default, Web-CAT shows three hints to the student (the exact number can be configured by the instructor) and obscures the rest until one or more of the displayed hints are resolved. However, since hints help students, we decided to use the hints as incentives to follow TDD.

The plugin monitors progress on correctness and coverage as indicators of whether a student is testing incrementally while developing a solution. When students satisfy a threshold in making progress on testing, they earn a credit for a hint. With the plugin, students no longer receive three "free" hints automatically. Instead, with each credit they earn, they receive a hint. If a problem that triggers a hint is resolved, the credit remains and a new (previously obscured) hint displays instead. As students continue to make progress on their solution and testing, they can accumulate multiple hint credits. *Figure 1* shows an example of adaptive feedback where the student has earned two hints by following TDD practices.

However, if a student's submission pattern does not indicate sufficient adherence to TDD, he will not earn any hint credits. Instead of displaying hints, the plugin displays an image and message that encourages the student to improve their testing in order to earn hints.

In addition to earning and showing hints, the plugin also displays affirming messages to acknowledge good habits, even when they are insufficient to warrant earning another hint. For example, if the plugin detects that the student has increased the amount of test

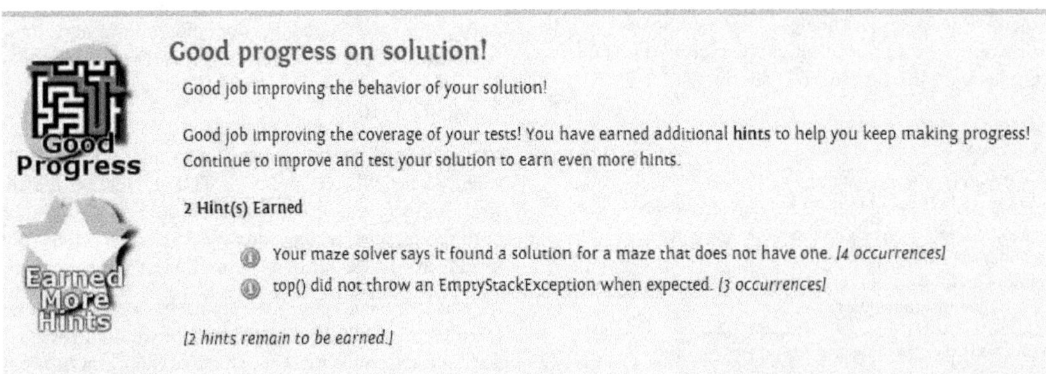

Figure 1. The Web-CAT plugin displays adaptive feedback with hints earned.

code but has not improved coverage, the message praises the work done and suggests continuing to improve test coverage. All adaptive messages and accompanying images purposely use only *positive reinforcement* to encourage and gently persuade students to follow TDD. The choice of wording was influenced by the need to promote and maintain a more positive mood regarding the feedback received.

We also engineered the adaptive feedback system to account for students who may try to manipulate or cheat in hopes to gain more (unearned) hints. First, students may only earn hints by making improvements to their solution and testing. While the feedback messages acknowledge added solution and test code, simply adding lines of code without improving test coverage or solution correctness does not earn hint credit.

Second, a student might remove code in between submissions with the hope of earning more hints on the following submission by adding the code back and "faking" an impression of improving coverage and/or correctness. However, the plugin compares the latest submission to whichever previous submission had the highest coverage and correctness, rather than simply comparing to the preceding submission. Therefore, attempts to manipulate indicators of progress in this way will not earn hints.

4. EVALUATING IMPACT

4.1 Metrics for Test-Driven Development

Actual student grades included manual evaluation by instructors or teaching assistants. However, for consistency, our data analysis only considered Web-CAT's automated assessment. Web-CAT calculated correctness as the percentage of instructor-provided reference tests passed. Coverage is the percent of methods, branches, and statements present in the student solution that were executed by student-written tests. Correctness and coverage scores were normalized for the maximum possible score on the automatic assessment alone.

Reviewing a completed assignment allows us to evaluate the quality of code and testing. However, Test-Driven Development (TDD) should be followed throughout the development process so only a single representation of students' work is insufficient for describing how well they conformed to TDD principles. By allowing students unlimited submissions to Web-CAT, we can observe their development habits as their code evolves from first to last submission.

Therefore, to judge adherence to incremental unit testing, we considered two metrics for evaluating testing quality and quantity over time: *average coverage* and *average test-methods-per-solution-method (TMSM)*. The average coverage across all submissions a student makes to Web-CAT for an assignment provides insight into how consistently she covered her solution with corresponding tests. Furthermore, average TMSM indicates how consistently students incrementally wrote test methods to correspond with each solution method.

To examine these metrics, we analyzed their effects using a comprehensive data set of project submissions to Web-CAT from five years (ten semesters of two courses) of introductory computer science classes. Spearman's rank coefficient (ρ) indicated statistically significant relationships between both average coverage and average TMSM and final outcome correctness and coverage. Average TMSM (M=1.08, sd=0.58) had small, positive correlations (ρ=0.29, p<0.0001) with final correctness (M=0.79, sd=0.30) and with final coverage (M=0.87, sd=0.21, ρ=0.27, p<0.0001). Meanwhile, average coverage (M=0.77, sd=0.24) had moderate, positive correlations with final correctness (ρ=0.44, p<0.0001) and final coverage (ρ=0.63, p<0.0001). The correlation with final coverage is expected since its measurement is not independent of the average coverage metric.

We considered the possibility these correlations demonstrated an effect of student motivation instead of TDD adherence. For example, a highly motivated student may produce high-quality code regardless of her adherence to TDD; this student may choose to follow TDD because they heed the instructor's advice. Meanwhile, a poorly motivated student may produce poor-quality code not only because she did not follow TDD. Both potential student profiles would reinforce a positive correlation but would not indicate whether TDD adherence helped produce good outcomes.

Consequently, we grouped students into three groups: the High Achieving group earned at least 80% correctness on every one of their projects; the Low Achieving group earned less than 80% correctness on each project; and the Mixed Achieving group earned 80% correctness or better on at least one project, and less than 80% correctness on at least one project. We found that the average TMSM and average coverage maintained a positive correlation with final correctness and coverage for each group, as summarized in *Table 1*.

Since the Mixed Achieving group showed capabilities of producing both high- and poor-quality work, we performed a Mann–Whitney–Wilcoxon test for repeated measures comparing the average TMSM and average coverage between assignments with high-($\geq$80%) and low- (<80%) scoring correctness. Average TMSM was significantly greater (p<0.0001) on high-scoring assignments (M=1.18, sd=0.62) than low-scoring assignments (M=0.93, sd=0.50). Likewise, average coverage was significantly greater (p<0.0001) for high-scoring assignments (M=0.83, sd=0.17) than for low-scoring assignments (M=0.63, sd=0.29). Given the relationships between indicators of unit testing (average

Table 1. Correlations grouped by high-, mixed-, and low-achieving students.

			Correctness (M=0.79, sd=0.30)		Coverage (M=0.87, sd=0.21)	
Metric	**M**	**sd**	**ρ**	**p**	**ρ**	**p**
Average TMSM						
High Achieving	1.16	0.59	0.2110	< 0.0001	0.1361	< 0.0001
Mixed Achieving	1.08	0.58	0.2680	< 0.0001	0.2796	< 0.0001
Low Achieving	0.79	0.39	0.2135	< 0.0001	0.3712	< 0.0001
Average Coverage						
High Achieving	0.83	0.18	0.2116	< 0.0001	*0.4741*†	*< 0.0001*
Mixed Achieving	0.75	0.25	0.4624	< 0.0001	*0.6623*†	*< 0.0001*
Low Achieving	0.59	0.29	0.4243	< 0.0001	*0.8305*†	*< 0.0001*

† - Final Coverage data are subsets of Average Coverage calculations, so strong positive correlations are expected

TMSM and average coverage) and positive outcomes (final correctness and final coverage), the metrics provide evidence for adherence to incremental unit testing improving quality of code and testing.

4.2 Method

To evaluate the impact of this adaptive feedback intervention, we collected data from student submissions to Web-CAT for two semesters of our CS2 course, *Software Design and Data Structures*. The programming projects for the first semester did not use our intervention, so Web-CAT feedback always showed (up to a maximum of) three hints to each student, whenever hints were available. The second semester used the adaptive feedback system to provide encouragement for following TDD, but required students to earn hints as incentives for doing so. Both semesters used the same four project assignments.

Students signed consent forms to allow their submission data to be included in the analysis at the conclusion of each semester. Participation was voluntary and participants did not receive any form of compensation. 87 of 130 (66%) students enrolled in the first (control) semester and 78 of 129 (60%) students enrolled in the second (experimental) semester opted to participate. Code analysis excluded faulty Web-CAT submissions (typically, submissions that were cancelled before they were processed, or where a student accidentally submitted the wrong files). Students who did not submit at least once for each of the four programming projects were omitted from analysis. Students averaged roughly 22 submissions per project.

If the pedagogical intervention succeeds in persuading students to adhere to TDD, we may observe multiple effects. Primarily, increased average TMSM and increased average coverage both indicate closer adherence to unit testing. Since we previously found positive correlations for both metrics with final correctness and coverage, we may also observe improved outcomes because of TDD adherence. Persuading TDD adherence may produce longer-term results as well. As students follow TDD, we may see increasing average TMSM and increasing average coverage over the span of the semester for the experimental group as they adopt TDD habits and mature in their practice. Statistical analysis of the data will evaluate the following hypotheses:

H1) The experimental group will have significantly greater average TMSM and average coverage than the control group.

H2) The experimental group will have significantly greater project correctness and coverage scores than the control group.

H3) The experimental group's average TMSM and average coverage will increase over time relative to the control group's average TMSM and average coverage trends.

4.3 Survey

We also collected surveys at the conclusion of each semester to investigate student attitudes and perceptions of TDD. With the survey, we gathered information about attitudes and perceptions of TDD, self-reported adherence to TDD principles, and anxieties. The following survey items addressed these issues:

Rate each item individually on a 5-point scale from 1 (Very Harmful) to 5 (Very Helpful) on the impact the following behaviors have on developing programs:

- *Developing thorough test code*
- *Developing code and corresponding tests in small units at a time*
- *Developing code and corresponding tests in large portions at a time*
- *Developing tests before writing solution code*
- *Developing tests after writing solution code*

The survey also asked students to indicate how frequently they practiced each of the behaviors listed above using the following scale: *Rate each item individually on a 5-point scale from 1 (Very Rarely) to 5 (Very Often) on how often you practice the behavior.* Students also reflected on the effect of TDD:

Rate each item individually on a 5-point scale from 1 (Strongly Disagree) to 5 (Strongly Agree) based on your experience with Test-Driven Development (TDD) by incrementally developing tests and then solution code one unit at a time:

- *I consistently followed TDD in my programming projects during this course*
- *TDD helped me write better test code*
- *TDD helped me write better solution code*
- *TDD helped me better design my programs*
- *In the future, I will choose to follow TDD when developing programs outside of this course*

Since we are concerned about how negative feedback may affect student attitudes and behaviors, we also used two questionnaires to measure anxiety: the Brief Fear of Negative Evaluation Scale (BFNES) [13] and the Westside Test Anxiety Scale (WTAS) [6]. Both are brief, validated questionnaires. We adapted WTAS specifically for programming projects with the following items:

- *The closer I am to a programming project deadline, the harder it is for me to concentrate on it*
- *When I prepare for programming projects, I worry I will not understand the necessary material*
- *While working on programming projects, I think that I am doing awful or that I may fail*
- *I lose focus on programming projects, and I cannot understand material that I knew before the project*
- *I finally understand solutions to programming projects after the deadline passes*
- *I worry so much before a programming project deadline that I am too worn out to do my best on the project*
- *I feel out of sorts or not really myself when I work on programming projects*
- *I find that my mind sometimes wanders when I am working on important programming projects*
- *After the project deadline, I worry about whether I did well enough*
- *I struggle with developing programming projects, or avoid them as long as I can. I feel that what I do will not be good enough.*

Students completed the survey at the end of each semester. Participation was voluntary and participants did not receive compensation. 61 students from the control and 54 students from the experimental group completed the survey. Using the results from the surveys, we evaluate the following hypotheses:

H4) Students' perceptions of the helpfulness of test-first and unit testing will have a positive correlation with their self-reported adherence to the same behaviors.

H5) The experimental group will value the helpfulness of test-first and unit testing behaviors significantly higher than the control group.

H6) The experimental group will score significantly lower on WTAS (project anxiety) scale relative to their BFNES (fear of negative evaluation) scale when compared to the control group.

H7) The experimental group will respond more positively to following TDD in the future than the control group.

5. RESULTS

Before testing hypotheses H1-H3 on code analysis, we used the Shapiro-Wilk test to check for normal distributions. None of the following code metrics fit normal distributions, where low p-values reject the null hypothesis that the data is normally distributed: correctness (M=0.84, sd=0.27, p<0.0001), coverage (M=0.93, sd=0.17, p<0.0001), average TMSM (M=0.68, sd=0.27, p<0.0001), and average coverage (M=0.79, sd=0.20, p<0.0001). Consequentially, we used the Mann-Whitney-Wilcoxon test to check for significant differences between independent, non-parametric samples.

H1 hypothesizes that the experimental group will have greater average coverage and average TMSM than the control group. However, the experimental group did not have significantly different (p=0.80) average coverage (M=0.79, sd=0.20) than the control (M=0.79, sd=0.19). Likewise, there was no significant difference (p=0.81) between the average TMSM for the experimental group (M=0.69, sd=0.28) and the control (M=0.68, sd=0.26). Results do not provide any support for H1.

H2 hypothesizes that the experimental group's correctness will be greater than that of the control. However, no significant difference (p=0.41) was found between the experimental (M=0.83, sd=0.27) and the control (M=0.84, sd=0.26) groups. Furthermore, the coverage for the control (M=0.94, sd=0.17) was significantly greater (p<0.001) than the experimental group (M=0.92, sd=0.17), contradicting H2.

The third hypothesis compares the trends of average TMSM and average coverage over the entire semester. First, we calculated the difference in average TMSM and average coverage between the first and last projects for each subject. The Mann-Whitney-Wilcoxon test showed no significant differences (p=0.73) in the change in average TMSM between the control (M=-0.12, sd=0.48) and experimental group (M=-0.11, sd=0.48).

The average TMSM decreased over the course of the semester for both groups, but this decrease may be attributed to assignment difficulty. The first project only involved developing a business logic model, while latter projects additionally required developing user interfaces and event handling, which are typically less straight-forward to test. Both groups showed a similar decrease in average TMSM from the first project to the last. No significant difference between the two groups indicates that there is insufficient evidence to support H3 that the experimental group would mature over the semester to increase TMSM when compared to the control.

On the other hand, the experimental group's change in average coverage (M=0.10, sd=0.19) is greater than that of the control group (M=0.05, sd=0.20) and is approaching significance (p=0.10). Since this result suggests there might be an effect between groups, we performed a multivariate analysis of variance testing effects for PROJECT (representing the repeated measure for four projects) and PROJECT*TREATMENT interaction. We found an effect for PROJECT (p<0.0001), but no significant interaction for PROJECT*TREATMENT (p=0.22), so there was no observed treatment effect. *Table 2* shows the average coverage for each project.

Table 2. The average coverage on each project, separated by treatment

	Project 1	Project 2	Project 3	Project 4
Control	M=0.82	M=0.68	M=0.79	M=0.87
	sd=0.16	sd=0.23	sd=0.18	sd=0.17
Experimental	M=0.79	M=0.69	M=0.78	M=0.90
	sd=0.18	sd=0.22	sd=0.18	sd=0.11

The final four hypotheses address attitudes observed from survey results. We used the Shapiro-Wilk test to find that unit testing helpfulness (M=4.09, sd=0.83, p<0.0001) and adherence (M=3.07, sd=1.14, p<0.0001) responses are not normally distributed. Likewise neither test-first helpfulness (M=3.04, sd=0.99, p<0.0001) nor adherence (M=2.04, sd=1.05, p<0.0001) are normally distributed. We used Spearman's ρ to investigate relationships between non-parametric samples. There is a moderately strong positive correlation (ρ=0.57, p<0.0001) between unit testing helpfulness and adherence ratings. Similarly, there is a moderately positive correlation (ρ=0.50, p<0.0001) between test-first helpfulness and adherence. These correlations verify the relationship between perceived helpfulness and adherence found in our previous study and supports H4.

As described in H5, we expected the experimental group to rate the helpfulness of test-first and unit testing behaviors higher than the control group. To the contrary, a Mann-Whitney-Wilcoxon test found the control group (M=4.20, sd=0.82) rated unit testing helpfulness greater than the experimental group (M=3.96, sd=0.82) at a difference approaching significance (p=0.09). On the other hand, the experimental group (M=3.20, sd=1.05) rated test-first helpfulness greater than the control group (M=2.90, sd=0.93) at a difference approaching significance (p=0.06). Neither difference appears to translate into a meaningful distinction at the level of the response scale used, however.

H6 addresses comparing scores from the WTAS and BFNES scales. Cronbach's coefficient for WTAS (α=0.90) and BFNES (α=0.95) confirmed each scale's internal reliability. Students in the experimental group scored slightly lower for project anxiety (M=2.10, sd=0.91) than the control group (M=2.2, sd=0.81) but this difference was not significant (p=0.48). When WTAS scores were adjusted relative to each subject's BFNES score, there was still no significant difference (p=0.68) between the experimental (M=1.12, sd=0.58) and control groups (M=1.07, sd=0.41).

Finally, we compared each group's reported likelihood of using TDD in the future. The experimental group (M=3.59, sd=1.09) provided higher ratings than the control group (M=3.38, sd=1.21) but the difference is not statistically significant (p=0.38).

6. DISCUSSION

We based each of the seven hypotheses on the expectation that the adaptive feedback system would persuade adherence to Test-Driven Development (TDD). However, none of the statistical analyses provided sufficient evidence to claim it did so. Nevertheless, the results provide insight into the plugin's strengths and weaknesses and can serve as a formative assessment of its use as an educational and persuasive tool.

Although the differences were not quite significant, the experimental group's higher rating of test-first's helpfulness is worth noting since our previous study identified attitudes toward the test-first approach as the primary factor hindering acceptance of TDD. This insight into opinions of test-first approach is particularly useful in this research since the programming metrics concentrate on incremental unit testing, but cannot explicitly observe test-first adherence. Continuing to improve upon that impression of a test-first approach has potential for persuading changes in student behavior.

Improving attitudes toward test-first development may be a matter of better demonstrating its immediate value. Benefits of early testing—such as improved confidence—are difficult to portray concretely. Consequently, it would be valuable to investigate students' expectations and appraisals to build a mental model and make the effects of test-first development more salient.

Likewise, the trends in changing adherence to TDD over the course of a semester show promise for potential long-term persuasion. Several factors may contribute to the apparent lack of immediate changes in student behavior. Primarily, by the time a student receives adaptive feedback, it may be too late to persuade considerable change. Our studies have found that students' first submission for any given assignment often has over half the number of lines of code of their final submission [3][9]. Instead, students may be more inclined to change their behavior if persuasive interventions begin *before* they have established a pattern of behavior. For this reason, it would be worthwhile to explore ways to increase how soon and how often students receive adaptive feedback.

7. CONCLUSIONS

After previous studies identified problems motivating students to adhere to Test-Driven Development (TDD), we implemented a novel adaptive feedback system to persuade changes in student behavior. Our system takes advantage of Web-CAT's automated analysis to provide students with encouraging messages and feedback catered to their needs multiple times throughout development. The system also leverages automated hints as incentives that students can earn through demonstrating desired development techniques. Further, it focuses on positive reinforcement, using wording intended to promote a more positive mood.

We evaluated the system after its use in a semester of CS2 and compared effects with a control group from a previous semester. In addition, we gathered attitudinal data regarding students' opinions and behaviors. The evaluation did not identify any significant improvement in TDD adherence, however. We noted the adaptive feedback system's strengths and explained opportunities for improving its persuasiveness in future work.

8. REFERENCES

[1] Beck, K. (1999). "Embracing change with extreme programming." Computer 32(10): 70-77.

[2] Bhat, T. and N. Nagappan (2006). Evaluating the efficacy of test-driven development: industrial case studies. Proceedings of the 2006 ACM/IEEE international symposium on Empirical software engineering. Rio de Janeiro, Brazil, ACM: 356-363.

[3] Buffardi, K. and S. H. Edwards (2012). Exploring influences on student adherence to test-driven development. Proceedings of the 17th ACM annual conference on Innovation and technology in computer science education. Haifa, Israel, ACM: 105-110.

[4] Canfora, G., A. Cimitile, et al. (2006). Evaluating advantages of test driven development: a controlled experiment with professionals. Proceedings of the 2006 ACM/IEEE international symposium on Empirical software engineering. Rio de Janeiro, Brazil, ACM: 364-371.

[5] Desai, C., D. S. Janzen, et al. (2009). "Implications of integrating test-driven development into CS1/CS2 curricula." SIGCSE Bull. 41(1): 148-152.

[6] Driscoll, R. (2007). "Westside Test Anxiety Scale Validation." Education Resources Information Center: 6.

[7] Edwards, S. H. "Web-CAT." 2012, from https://web-cat.cs.vt.edu.

[8] Edwards, S. H. (2004). "Using software testing to move students from trial-and-error to reflection-in-action." SIGCSE Bull. 36(1): 26-30.

[9] Edwards, S. H., J. Snyder, et al. (2009). Comparing effective and ineffective behaviors of student programmers. Proceedings of the fifth international workshop on Computing education research workshop. Berkeley, CA, USA, ACM: 3-14.

[10] Fraser, S., D. Astels, et al. (2003). Discipline and practices of TDD: (test driven development). Companion of the 18th annual ACM SIGPLAN conference on Object-oriented programming, systems, languages, and applications. Anaheim, CA, USA, ACM: 268-270.

[11] Janzen, D. S. and H. Saiedian (2007). A Leveled Examination of Test-Driven Development Acceptance. Proceedings of the 29th international conference on Software Engineering, IEEE Computer Society: 719-722.

[12] Melnik, G. and F. Maurer (2005). A cross-program investigation of students' perceptions of agile methods. Proceedings of the 27th international conference on Software engineering. St. Louis, MO, USA, ACM: 481-488.

[13] Rodebaugh, T. L., C. M. Woods, et al. (2004). "More Information From Fewer Questions: The Factor Structure and Item Properties of the Original and Brief Fear of Negative Evaluation Scale." Psychological Assessment 16(2): 169-181.

[14] Schwarz, N. (2000). "Emotion, cognition, and decision making." Cognition & Emotion 14(4): 433-440.

[15] Spacco, J. and W. Pugh (2006). Helping students appreciate test-driven development (TDD). Companion to the 21st ACM SIGPLAN symposium on Object-oriented programming systems, languages, and applications. Portland, Oregon, USA: 907-913

Adding a Contributing Student Pedagogy Component to an Introductory Database Course

Henry A. Etlinger
Rochester Institute of Technology
Department of Computer Science
Rochester, NY 14623 USA
(585) 475-2097
hae@cs.rit.edu

ABSTRACT

An introductory database course is well established within computer science curricula. Instructors in this course are challenged to select a subset of possible topics to cover and emphasize and also to design appropriate assignments to help students master those topics. As theories regarding effective educational practice continue to emerge and become known, we also seek to invigorate our courses by including some of these newer techniques.

Contributing Student Pedagogy is an umbrella term that refers to a family of techniques that involves finding ways for students to become directly involved in the production of course content utilized by other students. Students not only make use of content provided by other students, but they come to view that content as valuable. This paper reports on initial efforts to incorporate an assignment based on contributing student pedagogy into a standard database course. Several iterations took place, with improvements made between the first and second iterations. Plans for future iterations are included and implications, not only for the database course, but other Computer Science courses, are discussed.

Categories and Subject Descriptors

K.3.2 [**Computer and Information Science Education**]: Computer science education

General Terms

None

Keywords

Contributing Student Pedagogy, database course design and tradeoffs, active learning

SIGCSE '13, March 6–9, 2013, Denver, Colorado, USA.

1. INTRODUCTION

Numerous Computer Science programs have an introductory database course, either required or offered as an elective. While the scope and contents of such a course is fairly well standardized, instructors still face important choice points. Commonly used textbooks, such as [1,9], run well over 1150 pages long and consist of approximately 30 chapters. Recommendations made by the authors of such textbooks suggest that perhaps one could cover the topics contained in 15 chapters, or half of these textbooks, in a one-semester course. To teach such a course in one-quarter, as is the case at this author's home institution, makes the selection of course content even more severe.

Experienced instructors also recognize that once course content is chosen, issues still remain. What degree of depth will students be held accountable for in each course topic? What activities will students engage in to learn material? How will they be assessed? When we successfully answer all of these questions and map out an entire course, we're relieved if nothing else. However, when we reach this stage, this accomplishment sometimes works against us!

While all instructors refine their courses over time, many changes represent incremental adjustments. In contrast to such changes, introducing a contributing student pedagogy (CSP) component represents a more significant change. When we introduce something we're unfamiliar with, this task quickly becomes formidable as we inevitably struggle with numerous course design choices that have to be balanced in order to incorporate our new ideas. Still, the nature of what we do demands that we continually reassess what we teach and also how we teach. This paper reports on some early efforts to bring an entirely new dimension to our database course and some of the decision making that took place in order to do so. We review some of the compromises made, present some promising early results and suggest some possible future enhancements.

2. SETTING THE CONTEXT

2.1 Course Background

We attempt to offer students a broad introduction to the database field, recognizing that in one quarter, we cannot possible cover even half of the topics found in one of the standard database textbooks. Fortunately for us, we have for many years also offered a course directed at database system implementation and more recently, we have begun to offer a course in data mining. Having these courses available permits us to give our introductory database course primarily a high-level focus. After introducing and motivating database systems, we cover: E-R diagrams and data modeling; assorted query languages, including relational algebra, relational calculus, and SQL; the relational model and relational design, with a focus on normalization; selected integrity and quality goals (aka constraints); transactions; DBMS programming; and the emergence of and growing interest in non-relational data and systems that support such. As time permits, different instructors try to introduce additional topics.

Historically our course has been taught primarily through lectures, with student performance measured through some number of exams. The course is an elective in our curriculum, most often taken by upper-level students. While we have never viewed our database course as essentially equivalent to an "SQL course", we nonetheless recognized early on that our students would benefit from some type of activity that allowed them to gain some first-hand experience using SQL, both interactively and through a programming interface, as well as to carry out some form of non-trivial data modeling exercise. With this in mind, we have students complete a loosely structured, team-oriented project that involves modeling some data domain, converting their model to a well normalized relational database, implementing that database using Oracle (more recently, Postgres), demonstrating a variety of SQL features through both an interactive interface as well as through a Java program, giving a short presentation in class, and documenting both the process and the products developed.

The database project offers students a more realistic and larger-scale opportunity to enhance their understanding of data modeling, relational design, and SQL, but the course also demands that students master a number of distinct concepts. To help students prepare for exams, we offer students a fair number of homeworks on specific topics such as relational algebra, relational calculus, SQL, basic E-R modeling, normalization, indexing, and so on. Students submit their solutions, which count a "small amount" toward their course grade, but the primary use of the homework is to guide classroom discussions and reveal possible misconceptions regarding specific topics.

While the course is "crowded" and already "packed", it was felt that students could also benefit from an assignment that allowed them to expand the course by going more deeply into or extending a database topic not covered by the instructor, since most students do not take additional database courses. This assignment provides students with a modest opportunity to search the scholarly literature. It also provides students with an opportunity to improve their written communications and analytical skills, something that we attempt to make pervasive throughout the curriculum. This led to an assignment that required students to identify a scholarly paper on a database topic not covered in class that they would summarize and also critique. Papers must be instructor-approved; if proposed papers are rejected, then students must find another potential paper to review. Students appear to enjoy this activity, but in some ways, the instructor seemed to benefit more than the students since the instructor saw all the papers and read all of the reviews. A few years ago, one additional element was added to this assignment. Students were asked to prepare one PowerPoint slide based on their paper, which they submitted to the instructor. The instructor assembled all of the slides into a single slide show and on the last day of classes, students were given two-to-three minutes to briefly summarize key points from their paper as well as to offer their reactions to the paper. This allowed all students to gain from the work done by the other students and it provided a low-stress, enjoyable way to end the course.

2.2 Contributing Student Pedagogy

The version of the database course just described accomplishes many goals. Due to our aggressive schedule, we cover considerable content for those students who elect to take only one database course while also preparing those students who move on to take additional database coursework. We offer students a chance to engage in practical and useful activities and point the way toward resources so that once they leave the course, they will have some experience in finding additional information, should they need to. Students are given opportunities to improve communications skills, both written and verbal. In addition, students work in a group on the project and can work with other students on homeworks.

Even though the database course has evolved and incorporates a number of desirable elements, we can still look for ways to increase student motivation and engagement. Numerous authors over the last several decades have championed active learning strategies and promoted a variety of techniques designed to reach today's students more effectively. One interesting family of approaches is termed Contributing Student Pedagogy (CSP) [2,3,4,5,7]. Several of the references cited do an excellent job of connecting CSP to deeper models of learning theory and we will not repeat those discussions here. Rather, we present the definition of CSP given in [5] as well as identify some of the common characteristics that seem to go hand in hand with CSP, and then move on to how we attempted to instantiate CSP in our database course.

The authors in [5] "define a Contributing Student Pedagogy (CSP)" as:

> "A pedagogy that encourages students to contribute to the learning of others and to value the contributions of others."

This definition evolved from several other earlier works and highlights two critical aspects of CSP: (1) students become actively engaged in the production of learning materials, the delivery of instruction, and quite often participation in helping others evaluate the degree to which they understood the material and (2) students come to recognize that their own learning has benefitted directly from the work of their fellow students and that this should be considered a positive outcome.

Roles of students (and the instructor) change dramatically when CSP is involved. Students are active participants and instructors relinquish some control over course decisions. Changes to roles and expectations, for both students and the instructor, are likely to produce some anxiety, which needs to be acknowledged upfront. CSP extends typical group activities by taking into account the fact that other students (in fact, all other students in a class) will be affected by the effort and results produced by each group. Measures have to be put in place that allow for assessment of group work and products produced. And, in the ideal setting, students utilize a variety of technologies to facilitate communication and collaboration and to allow instructors opportunities to monitor student efforts.

3. THE DILEMMA OF HOW TO START

Sometimes when we contemplate making a major change to a course, especially one that we're already satisfied with, we may get "hung up" with trying to make too many changes all at once or trying to "get it right" the first time. Do we just "jump in the deep end of the pool right away" or do we first "put our toe in"? In this case, after considering the nature of the course and the environment in which it's taught and identifying several aspects of the course that perhaps could be improved, we opted to "put our toe in first".

3.1 Course Background Revisited

Having already set the context, we need to "drill down" a bit further into some of the operational details of the course prior to the introduction of a CSP component. The course typically meets twice per week for ten weeks, with each class lasting two hours. One more class session follows in week eleven, most often used for a final exam.

Some topics (e.g., advanced data modeling issues or normalization) in a database course typically prove to be more difficult for students than others. In order to give students sufficient time to master some of the more difficult topics, the course structure includes three exams. Each exam covers roughly a third of the course material, although the third exam also includes a few more comprehensive questions that span the entire term. Exams account for 60% of a student's grade, but are weighed unequally so that the best exam counts for 25% while the worst exam counts for only 15%. The database project counts for 20% of a student's overall grade, with all students within a group receiving the same project grade. The scholarly paper assignment accounts for 15% of a student's overall grade. The final 5% of a student's grade stems primarily from attendance and homeworks as well as the instructor's subjective assessment of each student. It should be noted that several homeworks allow students to reflect on exams and exam grades. One homework assignment gives students a chance to review the database project, making note of their own contributions as well as those of other group members. If there is compelling and uniform evidence that one or more group members contributed very little (or a great deal) to the project, that can be accounted for through the instructor's subjective assessment component.

It typically takes a while to cover enough topics in the course to provide students with sufficient background to tackle the database project. If they start too soon, they are likely to produce ill-conceived designs or poor implementations. Thus, the database project tends to start about midway through the course, with final materials due toward the end of the term. Likewise, the scholarly paper review also starts later in the term because students need to gain an appreciation for the topics that will be covered in class so that they can then identify papers from other topics that they might like to review. Student reviews are due at the end of the term and as stated previously, students also present their paper during the last class session. The end of the term becomes quite busy as students are simultaneously working on multiple assignments and so typically any topics covered in lecture toward the end of the term have been covered relatively lightly.

Exams primarily cover lecture material and assigned readings in the textbook. It's reasonable to expect that students increase their knowledge about design and SQL through their participation in the database project, but exams do not contain questions directly related to the project. Likewise, students learn additional course material through their own individual efforts on the scholarly paper review as well as the collective efforts made by the class during the presentations, but questions on this material is not included on an exam. The third and final exam, in particular, tends to measure lower-level thinking skills (e.g., remembering and simple understanding) since material has been covered quickly, students are busy completing multiple assignments, and the exam must be graded quickly.

3.2 First Iteration

It did not seem reasonable to add another assignment to an already crowded course. Rather, the decision was made to replace one assignment with another and then to see what further adjustments needed to be made to other aspects of the course. Given that the database project was deemed an essential aspect of the course, the decision was made to replace the scholarly paper review with a new assignment centered on contributing student pedagogy.

The most recent versions of the course made use of [9]. Chapters covered during the term included: 1 (introduction); 2 (relational model); 3-5 (SQL); 6 (relational algebra/calculus); 7-8 (data modeling and database design); 10-11 (brief; primarily for indexing); and 14 (transactions). Lectures on topics related to these chapters made use of slides (which were extensive) provided to textbook adopters, although the instructor frequently annotated the slides to highlight material or to make additional points. For some topics, separate materials prepared or selected by the instructor were provided. As previously mentioned, toward the end of the term, students were quite busy working on assignments. Time for group work in class was provided during some of the later classes and "short" introductory lectures were given on a few additional topics. These topics varied, but often were chosen from concurrency control (found in chapter 15), data warehousing and data mining (found in chapter 20), or XML (found in chapter 23).

3.2.1 The Basic CSP Assignment

Students were presented with the basic motivation and benefits for including an assignment based on contributing student pedagogy in the course. At the time the assignment was given out, there were approximately 20 students in the class and there were five groups of four students each. Since students had already been grouped for the purpose of the project, the same groups worked on this assignment. Groups were given a list containing five possible topics (with the corresponding textbook chapters): concurrency control (chapter 15); distributed databases (chapter 19); object-based databases (chapter 22); XML (chapter 23); spatial and temporal data and mobility (chapter 25). Students were told that each group would be responsible for one of the five topics. They would prepare and deliver a presentation in class and also prepare and deliver a study guide.

An initial deliverable for each group was the submission of a preference memo in which each group rank ordered the five topics and gave a rationale behind each ranking. The instructor made the final decision as to which topic was assigned to each group based on the rankings, the rationales provided, and the order in which memos were received. Once this assignment was made, the instructor met with a representative from each group and established the presentation schedule. Each group would speak for approximately 50 minutes or half of a class session. One of the advantages of the set of topics chosen was that they were independent of one another and so the order in which topics were presented did not really matter. As an incentive for those groups that gave their presentations earlier, they were given more time to develop and deliver their study guides.

Groups were expected to prepare slides for use in their presentation and then to submit those slides to the instructor. While it was expected that slides would be submitted in Adobe PDF format, some groups neglected to do that and so the instructor made the conversion for them. Once slides were in Adobe PDF format, they were posted "as is". Students were free to structure their presentations in any way that they wanted to, but were reminded that they had seen several models during the term. There were some lectures in which the slides provided with the textbook were used almost verbatim. At other times, the base slides were heavily annotated and in other cases, separate materials had been displayed. In fact, students were allowed to base their presentations on the slides that came with the textbook, provided that they were annotated and augmented by additional examples developed by the group. Groups were also told that they should view the textbook coverage of a topic as a "starting point". One strength of [9] is that it contains extensive references for each chapter and it was hoped that groups would make use of these to bring additional material to the attention of the class.

Study guides were intended to serve as "high level" introductions to topics. Important terms and concepts would be defined and highlighted. Connections between the topic under discussion and the set of topics already covered by the instructor would be made. Groups could also provide advice on how to go about mastering the topic (e.g., what to read first, what examples to try, etc.). Each study guide was also expected to include a set of potential exam questions along with suggested answers. Questions could take multiple forms and students were pointed to Bloom's taxonomy [6,8] for ways to connect types of questions with levels of expected learning. Some number of the questions provided by a group had to be original, although groups were also free to use some suggested questions provided with the textbook. Once again, study guides were to be delivered in Adobe PDF format. Once all study guides were in such format, they were posted for the entire class to view.

As a means of motivating groups to treat study guides seriously, they were told that the third and final exam would include questions, subject to editorial changes only, from each of the study guides. Thus, students could know ahead of time, a significant percentage of the last exam (i.e., both the questions and the correct answers)!

3.2.2 Positives and Negatives

In many respects, especially for a first pass, the assignment worked! By and large, groups produced the expected products. Most groups directly utilized and annotated the slides that came with the textbook, while several created their own slides, but based the order in which topics were addressed along the same lines as used by the textbook authors. All students in a group participated in that group's presentation. It should be noted that as a term winds down, some students withdraw from a course. That occurred in this course and that left a few groups short a person (the instructor tried to take this into account in grading the assignment).

While students were directed to think about many issues, especially in terms of organizing material in support of desired learning outcomes and also framing possible exam questions to support those outcomes, it was not immediately apparent that this took place. For the most part, study guides were fairly straightforward, no frills documents that included lists or primarily objective type questions (e.g., multiple choice, true-false, fill-in-the-blank, etc.). Questions were also generally straightforward and reflected material that had been covered in presentations or covered in study guides. There was some, but not much evidence that outside sources had been consulted and reviewed.

As might be expected, assignment grades were high, ranging from 80 (or B-) to 92 (A). If students delivered the required materials on time and met assignment specifications, it was unlikely that much credit was deducted based on actual content or (lack of) creativity. Most deductions came from not following specifications, some oversights during presentations, or turning in items late.

In this course, exam grades typically range from 60 to 75% while project, outside assignment, and attendance/homework/subjective grades are typically much higher. The net effect is that the distribution of final course grades typically works out reasonably well. It turned out that for this instance of the course, the exam average for exams 1 and 2 was around 64% while the exam average for the third exam was around 67%. So, even by including known questions on the third exam, there did not seem to be a significant grade spike for the third exam. In addition, the contribution from the database project was slightly reduced in this version of the course and the contribution of the CSP assignment was slightly greater than that from the scholarly paper review in the original version of the course. In the end, the distribution of final course grades was as expected.

The take-away message from the first iteration was that students were willing to participate in this assignment and did a credible job with it. Presentations covered topics at a level comparable to how the instructor typically dealt with similar topics toward the end of the course. In order to accommodate the presentation schedule, the instructor carved out additional time from the course schedule (typically devoted to topics of particular interest to the instructor) and gave students a greater chance to "own" more of the course content. This resulted in a somewhat broader course, with minimal sacrifice in time devoted to foundational topics.

3.3 Second Iteration

There were enough encouraging signs from the first iteration of the CSP assignment that it could be used again. In the second iteration, we would strive to make incremental improvements as well as a more concerted effort to gather some direct data related to the assignment and how well it fit within the course structure.

3.3.1 *The Revised CSP Assignment*

In order to try and improve what groups delivered (and, hence, how useful materials would be to the other students in the class), the instructor became a bit more intrusive. Two additional deliverables were added to the assignment. Groups were required to prepare a two-to-four page outline. In this outline, groups went through their assigned chapter and identified sections they might cover or skip and which sections or topics they planned to focus on. Groups gave an initial idea as to whether they would annotate the slides that came with the textbook or whether they planned to develop their own materials. Groups had to provide a preliminary list of outside references that they planned to consult and what ideas, examples, and concepts from these outside sources they might use. Finally, groups were asked to provide a list of the main learning objectives they had in mind for their topic.

Groups handed in their outlines and then met individually with the instructor a few days later. The outline was not binding and the purpose of the discussion was to allow the instructor to comment on planned topic overage, make suggestions with regards to learning objectives and to offer advice on various aspects of the assignment. Some groups modified their plans based on these discussions, others did not.

There were more students in this version of the class, although more students also withdrew from the course throughout the term. In order to accommodate the number of students, we started with six groups and six topics listed as possible group choices. Added to the previous list of possible topics was coverage of recovery systems (which corresponded to chapter 16 in the textbook). Groups once again delivered presentations and study guides, with Adobe PDF format versions of slides and study guides posted for the entire class to use. Questions from each of the six topics were included on the third exam in such a way that the points for any one topic accounted for 10% of the exam points. In other words, 60% of the points for the third exam came from the study guides produced by the students.

3.3.2 *Positives and Negatives*

It became slightly more difficult for groups to earn As on the assignment compared to the first iteration, with more grades of B or B+. This most likely was due to the simple fact that there were increased expectations and additional deliverables. The overall quality of both the presentation slides as well as the study guides increased. More groups made concerted efforts to include material from outside sources and to point students in the class to those sources. More groups opted to build their own slides and structure presentations around those topics they identified as priority topics. Study guides showed more evidence of structure and a willingness to create sample exam questions that tied in with the group's main learning objectives.

All three exam grades were slightly higher in this iteration of the course. Exam averages for the first two exams were 70% and 69%. The third exam average was 70.5%, so once again, there did not seem to be an undue influence on exam or course grades due to the inclusion of student generated questions on one of the exams. Copies of the third exam were made before the exams were returned to students so that individual student performance on the exam could be examined.

Given the nature of the activity and the expectations for coverage of the six topics chosen, it seemed reasonable to choose primarily objective questions for inclusion on the third exam, although in some cases, some simple problems or short answer questions were also included. Five points in total stemmed from the questions chosen from each topic. Mean grades for the class on each of the six topics ranged from 3.5 to 4.4 out of 5 and the overall mean for the class across all six topics was 4 out of 5 (when rounded). The range of points students earned on various topics proved to be interesting. On two topics, the range of points was 3 to 5; on two topics, the range of points was 2 to 5; on two topics, the range of points was 1 to 5! Experienced instructors will recognize that students often surprise us on exams, scoring well in places we wouldn't expect and doing poorly on topics we felt they probably would do well on.

When we examine how students did on the third exam on the questions chosen from their own topic, we see their mean score is only 4.1 out of 5. While a majority of students had means for the questions taken from their group's topic greater than the overall class mean for that topic, only half of the students in the class earned all 5 points on the questions chosen from their own topic! It would seem that the approach of including student generated questions (with correct answers known ahead of time) on an exam did not unfairly bias overall course grades.

4. SUMMARY

We've described initial efforts to infuse a standard database course with an activity that makes students responsible for content delivery and presentation. Students research an assigned topic, prepare a one-hour class presentation on their topic, and make available to all students in the class their presentation slides as well as a study guide that can be used by all students to help them prepare for the last exam given in the class.

Students were given the option to complete a homework that allowed them to evaluate the CSP assignment from a number of different perspectives. Unfortunately (and perhaps, predictably), only approximately half the class took advantage of this opportunity, so we must temper our interpretation of the results taken from this homework. Still, it may be instructive to review some of the findings. Students strongly agreed or agreed 81% of the time that their own contributions to the CSP assignment were 'outstanding'. When evaluating others on their groups, most of the time, students strongly agreed or agreed 63% of the time that their colleagues' contributions to the CSP assignment were 'outstanding'. Usually there was one individual per group who was perceived as underperforming and for that one student, ratings were much lower.

How did students feel about presentations made by other groups? On average, presentations were rated outstanding (or excellent) to good 87.5% of the time, with a range of 80% to 100%!. On average, study guides were rated outstanding (or excellent) to good 87.3% of the time, with a range of 80% to 91%. Given the timing of when activities had to be completed, students probably had less time to carefully review study guides before submitting their homework, so it's possible they did not fully appreciate whether a study guide was or was not useful in preparing for the exam. In a series of telling questions, students speculated on whether they learned more (or believed they learned more) on a topic from the student-led presentations and study guides versus whether they had listened to a lecture, read the corresponding chapter in the textbook, and had a chance to try a homework on the topic. For three of the six topics, students strongly agreed or agreed that they learned more from other students over 50% of the time, although there were wide variations in responses. Finally, nearly 75% of those students responding indicating 'yes' when asked if they "had fun with this assignment".

4.1 Next Steps and Broader Implications

We plan to maintain the structure of the basic assignment and continue to build in more support for students as they carry out the assigned tasks. More can be done with guiding students to understand the implications of Bloom's taxonomy and how to translate that taxonomy to match up with their learning goals for selected topics. Study guides can more clearly identify individual learning goals and include questions that address those learning goals. Students also need more guidance in how to construct reasonable questions that match various levels of expected learning. Study guides can also be more direct in establishing minimum thresholds for students to reach when preparing for the exam (for example, on this topic, "you should be able to correctly answer four of the five following questions").

Deadlines for some deliverables and assignment grading guidelines can be adjusted slightly so that virtually all students complete an evaluation (i.e., homework) related to the assignment. Having data for all (or virtually all students) in the class will allow for more meaningful assessment of the assignment and its impact on the course, especially moving forward.

Will this assignment work as well for larger class sizes or a greater number of groups in the database course? Could the assignment be extended to include an even greater percentage of the course content? For example, could groups work on two topics over the term, with feedback from their first effort folded into their second topic? A new version of the course will be rolled out next year and is likely to be taken by students who are second-year and higher. Will students with less background than students in the version of the course reported upon here still be able to handle such an assignment? As pointed out at the beginning of section 3, we eased our way into using this approach. [4,5] make the point that central to CSP is the use of technology and various tools to help students collaborate, produce artifacts, and communicate with other students. We can certainly extend our assignment in this direction.

Finally, it seemed as if the database course provided a suitable vehicle for testing out this type of assignment. What was it about a database course that provided a positive level of support and can we characterize or define this more precisely to see what other Computer Science courses might also be appropriate? Informally, the database course is so broad as well as deep that it is virtually impossible to cover all possible topics in one term. There are key concepts and topics that must be covered (perhaps by the instructor), but there are a range of additional topics that allow for choice and can be covered more than adequately by students.

Individuals interested in looking at the assignment or discussing student presentations and study guides in more detail may contact the author via email.

5. ACKNOWLEDGMENTS

Thank you to students from several sections of our introductory database course who embraced the concept and willingly participated in the learning module activity. While these students learned a considerable amount and helped other students do the same, the instructor learned right along with them. In addition, thanks go to the anonymous reviewers for raising questions regarding assessment and calling for creating better measures of student learning from this assignment.

6. REFERENCES

[1] Elmasri, Ramez and Navathe, Shamkant B.2011. *Fundamentals of Database Systems*. Addison-Wesley. Sixth edition.

[2] Hamer, J. 2006. Some Experiences with the "Contributing Student Approach". In *Proceedings of the 11th Annual SIGCSE Conference on Innovation and Technology in Computer Science Education* (Bologna, Italy, June 26-28, 2006). ITiCSE '06. ACM, New York, NY, 68-72. DOI=http://dx.doi.org/10.1145/1140123.1140145.

[3] Hamer, J. 2006. Contribution-based Pedagogies in Engineering Education. In *Proceedings of the 17th Annual Conference of the Australasian Association for Engineering Education*. (December 10-13, 2006). AAEE'06. Auckland, New Zealand, 1-8.

[4] Hamer, J., Cutts, Q., Jackova, J., Luxton-Reilly, A., McCartney, R., Purchase, H., et. al. 2008. Contributing Student Pedagogy. *SIGCSE Bulletin*. 40(4), November, 2008. ACM, New York, NY 194-212. DOI=http://dx.doi.org/10.1145/1473195.1473242.

[5] Hamer, J., Luxton-Reilly, A., Purchase, H., and Sheard, J. 2011. Tools for "Contributing Student Learning". *Inroads*. 2(2), June, 2011. ACM, New York, NY 78-91.

[6] Heer, R. 2012. A Model of Learning Objectives. Retrieved August 7, 2012 from http://www.celt.iastate.edu/teaching/RevisedBlooms1.html

[7] Luxton-Reilly, A., Plimmer, B., Sheehan, R. 2012. Activities, Affordances and Attitude – How Student-generated Questions Assist Learning. In *Proceedings of the 17th ACM Annual Conference on Innovation and Technology in Computer Science Education* (Haifa, Israel, July 3-5, 2012). ITiCSE '12. ACM, New York, NY, 4-9. DOI=http://dx.doi.org/10.1145/2325296.2325302.

[8] Overbaugh, R. and Schultz, L. Bloom's Taxonomy. Retrieved August 7, 2012 from http://www.odu.edu/educ/roverbau/Bloom/blooms_taxonomy.htm

[9] Silberschatz, Abraham, Korth, Henry F., and Sudarshan, S. 2011. *Database System Concepts*. McGraw-Hill. Sixth edition.

On the Nature of Fires and How to Spark Them When You're Not There

Sarah Esper
University of California, San Diego
La Jolla, CA
sesper@eng.ucsd.edu

Stephen R. Foster
University of California, San Diego
La Jolla, CA
srfoster@eng.ucsd.edu

William G. Griswold
University of California, San Diego
La Jolla, CA
wgg@cs.ucsd.edu

ABSTRACT
Traditionally, computer science education research contributes new tools, techniques, and theories to improve *institutionalized* learning spaces – e.g. classrooms. However, we take the position that the study and improvement of computer science learning spaces *outside* the classroom are just as important.

We take a step toward illuminating the critical qualities of non-institutional computer science learning spaces by engaging in a grounded-theoretical examination of first-hand accounts of non-institutional learning. To further study the topic, we attempted to recreate (in the lab) a learning environment with many qualities that characterize non-institutional learning. To make this possible, we employed a modified version of *CodeSpells* – a video game designed to teach Java programming in a way that engenders the sense of sustained, playful, creative exploration driven entirely by the learner. This study introduced 40 girls, ages 10 to 12, to programming for the first time. We use the results of both studies to develop a theoretical framework which we use to examine existing tools such as Scratch, Alice, and educational games in a new light.

Categories and Subject Descriptors
K.3.2 [**Computer Science Education**]: Introductory Programming

General Terms
Human Factors

Keywords
Grounded Theory, Authentic Practice, Origin Stories, CS0, CS1, Gamification, Active Learning, Informal Learning Spaces

1. INTRODUCTION
That minds are "fires to be kindled rather than vessels to be filled" was first expressed by Plutarch and has become one of the most oft employed quotations within pedagogical discourse. Still, there would appear to be some magic and mystery to the sparking of flames: it is much easier to develop curricula and textbooks that seek to fill up minds with material rather than to spark a love of learning. Not surprisingly, it is a rare student indeed that catches fire in a classroom. Furthermore, our "factory" model of education has come under such heavy criticism in recent years, [1, 2, 3] that one might begin to suspect that some forms of institutional instruction may have a dampening effect on the sparking of flames. This suspicion (further supported anecdotally by several decades of the authors' personal experiences in academia), prompted us to study the nature of flame-sparking by investigating how such flames manifest themselves "in the wild" – i.e. outside of classrooms.

Indeed, the field of computer science is rife with stories of children (many strikingly young) who discovered computers and taught themselves to program without the benefit of formal instruction. We collected various such accounts from a variety of sources. The following section gives a grounded-theoretical analysis of these accounts and begins to set forth a list of five qualities that appear to correlate with the eventual sparking of a lifelong love of programming.

We then sought to recreate these five qualities in a laboratory study with 40 girls, ages 10 to 12, exposing them to programming for the first time using a video game called *CodeSpells*, which supports many of the aforementioned qualities by default. Our goal was to study these qualities "up close", in order to refine our understanding of them. We present the results of this second study in Section 4.

Ultimately, using the insights gained from our grounded-theoretical analysis and our laboratory study, we are able to further illuminate how a passion for programming spark "in the wild". Although our studies are both of non-institutional learning environments, we believe (as in [4]) that the study of these environments can help shed new light on the process of learning in general. Thus, in Section 5, we discuss various contemporary software tools for teaching programming – looking at them in the new light offered by our analysis of non-institutional learning.

2. *FORMAL* VS. *INFORMAL* LEARNING
In related literature, a distinction is generally made between "formal" and "informal" learning. However, we prefer the terms "institutional" and "non-institutional" because, as pointed out by Sefton-Green [4], the terms "formal" and "informal" are somewhat overloaded. "Formal" can refer either to "organized" (as opposed to "disorganized") knowledge acquisition or to "institutional" (as opposed to "non-institutional") settings. This can lead to confusions: for example, one could imagine a disorganized (or student-driven) acquisition of material within the confines of an academic classroom – which is difficult to classify as a "formal" or "informal" experience. Thus, we use "institutional" (and "non-institutional") to make clear that we are discussing settings that fall within (or out side of) traditional academic institutions.

There has been wide research on informal learning spaces, but relatively little that pertains directly to non-institutional *computer science education*. The only two studies that we know of both involve ethnographic research on how Scratch (a novice programming environment) has been employed voluntarily by minority teenagers in a Los Angeles-based Computer Clubhouse [5, 6]. Although, the clubhouse environment is technically an institution, we classify the setting as non-institutional because it is not a traditional academic classroom environment. Students have free rein over their activities and can even play video games if they wish.

Thus, this paper adds to the small amount of prior knowledge on non-institutionalized computer science education by performing two new studies, using two new methodologies, and offering novel analysis of non-institutional learning to better illuminate the nature of learning in general.

3. ORIGIN STORIES STUDY

Since our research interest lies in the notion of sparking flames that lead to *lifelong* passions, we elected not to begin by studying existing non-institutional learning spaces – e.g. the clubhouse-like settings mentioned above, or after-school programs. After all, the children partaking in these spaces are (at best) only just *beginning* a lifelong computer science career. Instead, we collected first-hand accounts from contemporary computer science professionals, whose lifelong passions began in non-institutional settings. In this way, we hoped to be better equipped to draw conclusions about the non-institutional learning qualities that correlate with long-term excitement toward programming.

Ultimately, we accumulated 30 of these "autobiographical origin stories" (as we call them) from 3 different sources. We first drew 12 such stories from: 1) the Computing Educators Oral History Project [7], and 2) a qualitative study performed by Hewner and Guzdial [8]. To obtain more data, we also obtained 18 origin stories from 3) a survey we conducted ourselves, wherein we instructed participants to respond to the simple prompt: "Describe your first experiences with programming." We sent out this survey to the faculty and graduate student population at our university as well as to industry professionals via email and LinkedIn. In all cases, we selected only first-hand accounts where it was clear that the participants were describing their first experience as a programmer within a non-institutional setting.

The demographics of the autobiographers were intentionally quite diverse: ranging in age from graduating college seniors to industry professionals to retired. There were 11 males and 14 females. The genders of the 5 authors acquired from the study performed by Hewner and Guzdial is not directly reported. Some accounts involved programming on ancient Teletype machines, whereas others used modern hardware and environments like Alice. Since our intention was to begin constructing a very general theory of effective non-institutional learning environments, we felt that diversity was key.

3.1 Methodology for Origin Stories Study

Following the well-accepted procedures of grounded theory as set forth by Strauss and Corbin [9], we first engaged in open coding [9, ch5], where we coded each sentence and often time partial sentences. In the open coding, we found 13 subcategories: self-drive, enjoyable/emotional connection, "flow state" while programming, confidence/belief that you can succeed, investment in the results of the code, empowerment, creation of "meaningful" artifacts, lots of hours/re-visitation, access to immediate feedback, wrongness is on a spectrum and is therefore not binary, access to support, feeling addicted, losing track of time.

We followed open coding with axial coding [9, ch7], which allowed us to derive 5 distinct categories based on the open coding. Table 1 shows how the open coding results were connected to the 5 categories found in the axial coding and in the next section we define and give examples to our 5 categories.

Table 1. Results of Grounded Theory coding of Origin Stories

Axial Coding Results	Open Coding Results
Learner-Structured Activities	Self-driven, Access to immediate feedback, Access to support
Exploration/ Creativity/ Play	Creation of "meaningful" artifacts, Investment in the results of the code
Programming as Empowerment	Enjoyable/emotional connection, confidence/belief that you can succeed, wrongness is on a spectrum; not binary
Difficulty Stopping	"Flow-state" while programming, Feeling addicted
"Countless" Hours	Lots of hours/re-visitation, Losing track of time

3.2 Results of Origin Stories Study

All 30 origin stories exhibited at least 1 of the 5 qualities. 20 of the origin stories exhibited 3 or more.

Learner-Structured Activities: An activity is learner-structured when the learner engages in activities that are not at all (or not entirely) structured by some outside force:

- "...when the Commodore PET came along and **I took it home one summer and taught myself** BASIC",
- "I was **by myself** with no assignments - **just me and the computer** to play with."
- "I... **bought books and wrote programs instead of taking courses** in high school."

Exploration / Creativity / Play: The act of creation through experimentation and play was common – a mentality of "What would happen if...?"

- "I'd also **try to add things**, so if it was print a 'hello world' string, I would make it ask for your name, and print 'hello <name>', and if your name was a friend's name, **I'd add an inside joke or something**."
- "I would **purposely try changing some of the parameters to see what would happen**"
- "And we had gotten a Radio Shack computer and I had **played around** with that."

Programming as Empowerment: Programming was commonly viewed as a means of increasing one's personal efficacy, self-esteem, sense of purpose, or social standing.

- "…so I was able to do it, and that **gave me confidence** that '**I knew computers**'"
- "To me, **computers are freedom**, they are entertainment and above all they are a **symbol of power and adulthood**."
- "Soon enough the computer was asking me what my name was and then asking me how I was and addressing me by name. **I'd made a new friend**! I think my most impressive program was when I got the computer to make different sounds."

Difficulty Stopping: We expected to discover that the autobiographers found programming enjoyable, but the origin stories included many accounts of how frustrating the process was. The common thread, however, is that the act of programming was perceived as an engaging and often addictive one – with descriptions liked being "hooked".

- "That was a moment where **I got hooked** because just the sense that you could program a loop that could do an array of any number of any size, any number of numbers, just seemed to be such a fantastic thing."
- "When that actually worked, I thought it was the coolest thing ever, and after that **I was hooked** =P"
- "[I was] becoming **so closely involved** with technology... [that] I was a little afraid of **being sucked into** the CS major stereotype..."
- "I went for Mechanical Engineering. But **my liking for computers never died...** and I took some private computer courses on the side"

"Countless" Hours: This is closely related, but distinct from, difficulty stopping. (Some autobiographers did not exhibit signs of addiction but still invested large amounts of time for other reasons.) Many origin stories describe spending so much time that the autobiographers could not readily quantify the amount, tending to use abstract generalizations like "countless" or "dozens" or metaphors like "journey" (which imply a large time-investment).

- "I wrote **countless Pascal programs** on my old PC. (I still have some of the old code, printed out, somewhere!)"
- "**My journey** has been full of excitements. **Since the beginning** I have enjoyed computers."
- "So back then it was really **very labor intensive**, was **not instantaneous by any stretch of the imagination**.."
- "I read the guide to my TI-89 calculator a **dozen times**, learning to make simple games or programs in it."

We stress that this study was intended to be a preliminary theory-building endeavor, not a means by which a definitive, overarching theory was to be achieved. Indeed, the main intent was to inform and structure the laboratory study that followed it.

4. LAB STUDY

Our laboratory study was intended to "enhance theoretical sensitivity" [9, ch6] through the use of questioning – moving a step beyond the brief, straightforward nature of the origin stories.

We wanted to be able to determine if 1) the above five qualities could be recreated under laboratory conditions, and if so 2) to study them "up close" in order to enrich our theoretical understanding of them. Furthermore, we contend that performing laboratory studies on non-institutional learning is extremely important if one's ultimate goal is to learn from non-institutional learning in order to help inform institutional learning environments. After all, a laboratory lies somewhere between a fully institutional setting and a fully non-institutional setting. This means that lessons learned in a laboratory may be more easily transferable to a classroom than lessons learned in the wild.

4.1 Methodology for Lab Study

4.1.1 Software and Experimental Setup

CodeSpells is an educational video game – more specifically, an immersive fantasy role playing game designed to teach Java programming by immersing the player inside a 3D virtual world and a first-person storyline wherein she plays the part of an apprentice wizard [10]. *CodeSpells* teaches Java by giving players access to a novice-friendly API for crafting novel magic spells. We chose to use *CodeSpells* because its magic metaphor has been shown to be compelling and exciting to novice learners [ibid]. We felt that the game would be an engaging environment for girls in the 10- to 12-year-old age group.

Normally, learning in *CodeSpells* is encouraged by way of a series of quests that must be completed with the use of Java-based spell crafting. However, we particularly wished to study **learner-structured activities** and **creative exploration**. So we employed a version of *CodeSpells* that did not have explicit quests to complete. (The *CodeSpells* platform is quite extensible). Rather, players could walk up to in-game gnome-like characters who would give various spells to the player, along with simple explanations. Our hope was that these spells would serve as starting points for code exploration.

We recruited forty girls (ages 10 to 12) who had no prior programming experience in any language or programming environment. We gave them a short overview of the *CodeSpells* game mechanics – including how to write and edit code with the in-game IDE. We divided them into 12 groups of three and 2 groups of two, and encouraged them to explore the 3D world and to see if they could "do interesting things". We were purposefully vague, as we hoped to encourage a largely unstructured learning environment.

We then allowed the subjects to play *CodeSpells* for one hour while we observed. Data collection techniques during this time involved video and audio recordings of 6 groups; video was of the computer monitor so that we could record actual gameplay. We also assigned one undergraduate computer science major to each group; each undergraduate took notes on what the girls struggled with. Our main research team also took observational notes as they walked around the lab.

After one hour, we split the girls into groups of 12 to 15 members and engaged each group in a semi-structured group interview. The interview involved questions such as: "Describe what you have been doing for the past hour.", "Can anyone share something interesting they did in *CodeSpells*?", "Can anyone share something they were trying to do, what did you do to try to make it happen?", "Did anyone get stuck while playing, what did you do when you got stuck?", "If you had more time, what would you want to do next?", and "Can anyone describe to me what spells are and how you use them?". Data collection during the group interview was videotaped and the interviewer took brief notes.

4.2 Results of Lab Study

Our subjects played *CodeSpells* for the entire hour before we had to ask them to stop. Students expressed disappointment that it was "over so soon". 25 of the subjects showed interest in playing *CodeSpells* at home and wanted to know when it would be available for them to play. We consider this to be evidence that students experienced some **difficulty stopping**. And the lingering excitement is a rough indicator that novices might indeed play such a game for **"countless" hours** – though we would need to allow our users to play *CodeSpells* at home to measure this further.

Of the 6 groups of girls we recorded, roughly 90% of their time was spent exploring the 3D world and/or editing code (as opposed to, say, chatting amongst themselves). Also interesting is that the quest-less version of *CodeSpells* provides considerably less structure than most video games. In spite of this, subjects did not ask "What am I supposed to be doing?", nor did they seem at a loss for activities to engage in. The simple directive to "do interesting things" was sufficient for inspiring subjects to give structure and shape to their own activities. This strongly suggests that a **learner-structured mentality** arose within the lab study.

Some subjects tried changing method calls like `thing.levitate(3)` to `thing.hop()` or to `thing.blowup()` (which are not available in the API but are surprisingly correct syntactically). Even though these attempts failed to evoke the desired effect, students did not appear to become discouraged. Subjects also discovered quite valid changes in this way too – e.g. `thing.levitate(300000)`. This suggests a drive to **explore, play, and create.** And furthermore, this drive appeared to be *fueled* (rather than dampened) by syntax errors. Of the 6 groups video taped, 4 of them encountered some syntax error that they resolved either by undoing the error they introduced (55% of the time) or asking the undergraduate student that was near them (45% of the time). In all cases, acts of **self-structured activities** followed these interludes.

A particularly interesting phenomenon occurred with regard to what one might call "logic errors". One group of girls made the mistake of levitating an object so high into the air that it could not be reached. They were able to retrieve the object, however, by jumping onto *another* object and levitating it (and thus themselves) sufficiently high enough to reach the original object. This emergent use of code to surmount challenges of one's own making is an act that fits our definition of **exploratory play**. Logic errors were seen in all 6 groups recorded, but we note again that the exploration seemed to be *fueled* (rather than dampened) by things going awry.

During the lab study and more so in the group interviews we were encouraged to hear that the girls felt **empowered**. When changes to the code didn't accomplish what they wanted, they kept working towards their goal, trying different spells or different code changes until they eventually reached it. When asked about how they reached their goals, they conveyed that they "knew it could be done" and that they "just needed to figure out how". They described code as a "way to accomplish anything" within the 3D environment. At no point did they describe programming as a barrier to the **self-structured activities** and **creative exploration** in which they chose to engage.

5. DISCUSSION

5.1 Refining the Theory

With the benefit of the laboratory study, we were able to study 4 of the aforementioned qualities (with the exception of **"countless" hours**) up close. Our observations allow us to add a quality that seems to go hand in hand with **exploratory play**. Namely,

A positive attitude toward "failure": An institutional setting often provides an objective and authoritarian definition of what "success" and "failure" are. It was striking to observe that, when left to their own devices in a *non*-institutional setting, subjects approached what would traditionally be labeled as "failures" (syntax and logic errors) without the slightest apparent awareness that they had done something "wrong". No one had ever told them that syntax errors were bad or that code ought to do what one expects it to.

Thus far, we have presented two studies, 1) a study of origin stories in computer science and 2) a laboratory study of 40 novice 10- to 12-year-old pre-programmers. In the first study, we were able to tentatively identify 5 qualities that correlate with non-institutional learning in such a way that leads to the sparking of a lifelong passion for computer science. In the second study, we showed that at least 4 of these qualities (all but **"countless" hours**) could be recreated in a laboratory setting. We further observed a striking relationship between a **positive attitude toward "failure"** and the tendency to engage in **exploratory play** – allowing us to further enrich our theoretical framework.

We believe that further study of non-institutional learning is critical if we, as educators, wish to better understand how the sparking of young minds happens in the wild. We feel that a clearer understanding of the conditions under which such a seemingly mysterious phenomenon naturally occurs can serve to shed light on how to recreate this phenomenon more readily within institutional settings.

Moreover, though, the theory we have developed so far can help enrich modern pedagogical discourses – for example, the ongoing discourse about tools for teaching novice programmers.

5.2 Applying the Theory

Even though a comprehensive theory of non-institutional learning is perhaps a long way off, the aforementioned theoretical framework is already sufficient to allow for existing tools to be discussed with a new vocabulary, leading to new insights. Consider, for example, some common tools for teaching introductory programming.

5.2.1 Novice IDEs

Scratch is a visual programming environment designed to allow novice programmers, particularly young programmers, to create media-rich results by dragging programming blocks into place to create programs [11]. The 3D *Alice* environment is a friendly IDE serving as a "stepping stone to computer science careers" [12]. *Alice* provides an experience that allows users to make their own movies or video games.

Such environments allow the production of visually stimulating effects – which certainly gives young pre-programmers more avenues for **exploration, play, and creativity**.

On the other hand, it is not clear whether such environments encourage the other four qualities. For example, these environments do not *overtly* seek to motivate **learner-structured activities**. Likewise, there is no overt effort to induce **"countless" hours** of practice. On the other hand, nothing in Alice or Scratch overtly *prevents* learners from spending **"countless" hours** on **learner-structured activities**. Then again, nothing overtly *prevents* a student from opening up Eclipse and playing around with Java for hours on end. It is no doubt a rare occurrence though.

When the above are embedded within a classroom environment, **"countless" hours** can easily be required of students – but at the risk of sacrificing **learner-structured activities** and **exploratory play**. A natural place to look for solutions to this problem is in educational video games.

5.2.2 Educational Video Games

There exists a long history of educational video games, some of which are intended to teach programming [13, 14, 15, 16]. Although programming-related educational games to date have not gained widespread popularity, one can still examine video games (in general) in light of the framework.

Learner-Structured Activities: Video gaming tends to be a self-driven and self-structured activity – even for individuals who are too young to apply the same kind of self-motivation to academic subjects.

Exploration / Play / Creativity: Games can be used to create rich 3D worlds that facilitate exploration. In *CodeSpells*, for example, the interplay between objects, physical laws, and magic makes for emergent properties that drive play and exploration.

Programming as Empowerment: In *CodeSpells*, for example, the code a player can write directly correlates with the efficacy of that player within the 3D world. What one can *code* and what one is empowered to *do* go hand-in-hand.

Positive attitude toward "failure": Games are not always enjoyable. Players can lose. Characters can die. Tetris blocks don't always fit. Frustration is as common as euphoria. Yet it doesn't seem to phase gamers and is indeed an integral part of the experience.

Difficulty Stopping: Indeed, while not always strictly an enjoyable experience, video games inspire an unprecedented level of active engagement that (for some) borders on addiction.

"Countless" Hours: The gaming industry is a multi-billion dollar industry. At least one study shows that children spend 10,000 hours playing video games throughout childhood [17]. Clearly non-educational video games *do* spark lifelong passions… for playing video games.

One might then ask, if video games have all the requisite qualities, why aren't educational video games routinely sparking lifelong passions for all sorts of academic disciplines? Our response would be to point out that many explicitly *educational* video games actually lack some of the above qualities.

It is difficult for many educational games to support **creative exploration.** Consider, for example, the classic *Math Blaster*. In order to provide positive and negative feedback to the player, the game must be able check the player's answers to mathematical problems. This means that the game can only serve-up a series of checkable problems, each with an objective right or wrong answer. There is no room for creativity. The game cannot say to the player: "Do something mathematically creative. You'll get more points the more creative it is."

Similarly, many educational games have been criticized and called "chocolate-covered broccoli" [18] because the educational material interrupts what would otherwise be smooth gameplay. In other words, the education interrupts the fun stuff. Or, to put it the other way around, the fun stuff (chocolate) is intended to thinly disguise the education (broccoli). No doubt this has a detrimental effect on the **difficulty stopping** and the tendency to engage in **"countless" hours.**

In conclusion, it would appear that both novice-friendly IDEs and educational games alike leave something to be desired from the standpoint of sparking lifelong passions for programming. The gamification of programing environments like Alice or Scratch might be one solution. *CodeSpells*, for example, seeks to combine the best aspects of educational games with the best aspects of novice-friendly IDEs.

6. FUTURE WORK

Our main goal is to use lessons learned from highly successful non-institutional learning to shape and inform institutional learning. To this end, we are currently conducting a 6-week-long class in which unstructured play time in *CodeSpells* is supplemented with in-class instruction. Also, we have developed a multi-player, competitive version of *CodeSpells*, which we are utilizing to examine the non-institutional learning environment that has sprung up around a competitive *CodeSpells* team that practices three times a week while we observe.

Our grounded theory study on origin stories was somewhat limited because we reviewed static, written text and were not engaging in interviews. We would like to further define our 6 categories that classify non-institutionalized learning spaces through a series of interviews where we could employ the grounded theory technique more rigorously. This study has introduced us to the theory, but we would like to define this theory more detailed so that other education researchers may apply it when examining and creating tools and environments for novice programmers.

7. CONCLUSION

We take the position that it is highly relevant to study non-institutional learning in which young people teach themselves to program. We analyzed the origin stories of 30 individuals who eventually became successful in computer science. We identified five qualities that tended to occur across multiple origin stories and that can be tentatively posited to correlate with the sparking of lifelong passions for computer science.

To more deeply study these qualities, we performed a laboratory study with 40 girls (ages 10 to 12) and analyzed their experiences according to the aforementioned five qualities. This allowed us to refine our understanding of these qualities and even to observe a sixth quality – further deepening the theoretical framework.

Our contributions are three-fold:

- We give the first theoretical framework for understanding the conditions under which the sparks of lifelong learning are sparked in non-institutional computer science learning environments.
- We demonstrate two novel methodologies for further examining non-institutional computer science learning. (The small amount of prior work that exists uses only *in situ* ethnographic methodologies.)
- We contribute a new vocabulary for discussing and designing tools for novices, using our theoretical framework to point out opportunities for improvement in both novice-friendly IDEs and educational games.

Ultimately, we take the position put forth in [11] – namely, that studying non-institutional learning is a means by which to understand learning in general. After all, non-institutional learning has a unique character. It is unstructured. It is creative. It is play. Also, as we saw in our laboratory study, the absence of values implicitly instilled in institutional settings (e.g. that syntax errors are bad) can lead to differences in behavior. As such, the study of non-institutional spaces may serve as an untapped resource for computer science educators – a resource that can help inform how we structure our institutional spaces. We believe the study of these space can yield surprising new insights about what we're doing right as well as what we may be doing wrong. Ultimately, it is a line of research that can give us new ways to light fires and to keep them lit.

8. ACKNOWLEDGMENTS

This research is funded, in part, by two NSF Graduate Fellowships. Any opinions, findings, and conclusions or recommendations expressed in this material are those of the author(s) and do not necessarily reflect the views of the NSF. Our thanks to ACM SIGCHI for allowing us to modify templates they had developed.

9. REFERENCES

[1] Eric Mazur. 2009. Farewell, Lecture? Science, 323, 50-51 (2009).

[2] Christopher D. Hundhausen, N Hari Narayanan, and Martha E. Crosby. 2008. Exploring studio-based instructional models for computing education. In *Proceedings of the 39th SIGCSE technical symposium on Computer science education* (SIGCSE '08). ACM, New York, NY, USA, 392-396. DOI=10.1145/1352135.1352271

[3] Andrew Luxton-Reilly and Paul Denny. 2009. A simple framework for interactive games in CS1. *SIGCSE Bull.* 41, 1 (March 2009), 216-220. DOI=10.1145/1539024.1508947

[4] Julian Sefton-Green. 2004. Literature Review in Informal Learning with Technology Outside School, 2004. A NESTA Futurelab Series -report 7.

[5] Kylie A. Peppler and Yasmin B. Kafai. 2007. From supergoo to scratch: exploring creative digital media production in informal learning. Learning, Media and Technology 32, 2 (2007), 149–166.

[6] John H. Maloney, Kylie Peppler, Yasmin Kafai, Mitchel Resnick, and Natalie Rusk. 2008. Programming by choice: urban youth learning programming with scratch. In *Proceedings of the 39th SIGCSE technical symposium on Computer science education* (SIGCSE '08). ACM, New York, NY, USA, 367-371. DOI=10.1145/1352135.1352260.

[7] CEOHP. 2008. Computing Educators Oral History Project. (April 2012). www.ceohp.org/.

[8] Michael Hewner and Mark Guzdial. 2008. Attitudes about computing in postsecondary graduates. In *Proceedings of the Fourth international Workshop on Computing Education Research* (ICER '08). ACM, New York, NY, USA, 71-78. DOI=10.1145/1404520.1404528.

[9] Anselm Strauss and Juliet Corbin. 1990. Basics of qualitative research: grounded theory procedures and techniques. Sage Publications, Newbury Park, Calif.

[10] http://sarahesper.ucsd.edu/CodeSpells, August 2012.

[11] John Maloney, Mitchel Resnick, Natalie Rusk, Brian Silverman, and Evelyn Eastmond. 2010. The Scratch Programming Language and Environment. *Trans. Comput. Educ.* 10, 4, Article 16 (November 2010), 15 pages. DOI=10.1145/1868358.1868363.

[12] Stephen Cooper, Wanda Dann, and Randy Pausch. 2000. Alice: a 3-D tool for introductory programming concepts. *J. Comput. Small Coll.* 15, 5 (April 2000), 107-116.

[13] Matthew Dickerson. 2011. Multi-agent simulation and netlogo in the introductory computer science curriculum. J. Comput. Sci. Coll. 27, 1 (October 2011), 102–104.

[14] Michael K¨olling. The greenfoot programming environment. 2010, Trans. Comput. Educ. 10, 4 (November 2010), 14:1–14:21.

[15] William H. Bares, Luke S. Zettlemoyer, and James C. Lester. 1998. Habitable 3d learning environments for situated learning. In Proceedings of the 4th International Conference on Intelligent Tutoring Systems, ITS '98, Springer-Verlag (London, UK, UK, 1998), 76–85.

[16] http://robocode.sourceforge.net/, August 2012.

[17] Clare Richards. 2003. Teach the world to twitch: An interview with Marc Prensky, CEO and founder Games2train.com. Futurelab. www.futurelab.org.uk/resources/publications_reports_articles/web_articles/Web_Article578.

[18] Amy Bruckman. 1999. "Can Educational Be Fun?" Game Developer's Conference, San Jose, California. (March 17th, 1999).

Cupcake Cushions, Scooby Doo Shirts, and Soft Boomboxes: E-Textiles in High School to Promote Computational Concepts, Practices, and Perceptions

Yasmin Kafai, Kristin Searle, Eliot Kaplan*, Deborah Fields**, Eunkyoung Lee, & Debora Lui

University of Pennsylvania *The Westminster Schools **Utah State University

3700 Walnut Street

Philadelphia, PA 19104

kafai@gse.upenn.edu, searle@dolphin.upenn.edu, eliotkaplan@westminster.net, deborah.fields@usu.edu, eunklee@upenn.edu, dlui@asc.upenn.edu

ABSTRACT

In this paper, we present and discuss the use of electronic textiles (e-textiles) for introducing key computational concepts and practices and broadening participation and perceptions about computing. The starting point of our work was the design and implementation of a curriculum module using the Lilypad Arduino in a pre-AP high school class. To understand students' learning of concepts, practices, and perceptions of computing, we focused on the structure and functionality of circuits and program code and their design approaches to making and debugging their e-textile creations, and on their views on computing by examining pre-post interviews. Our discussion addresses the challenges and potential of using e-textiles materials and activities for designing introductory courses that can reach a broader student population.

Categories and Subject Descriptors

K.3.0 **[Computers and Education]:** General

Keywords

Electronic textiles, education, K-12

1. INTRODUCTION

In the past decade, many efforts have focused on broadening access to and participation in computer science education to address the generally low number of students interested in CS and the underrepresentation of women and minorities in the US [21]. Some have developed programming tools to simplify the mechanics of learning to program thus helping young, novice programmers to become more fluent and expressive with new technologies [17]. Others have examined the social and cultural barriers that impede participation [18] or focused on the use of new activities like game and story design to recruit more girls and women into computing [8; 10; 13]. Efforts are also underway to create networks of opportunities through statewide alliances between schools, afterschool programs and college outreach [3].

SIGCSE'13, March 6-9, 2013, Denver, Colorado, USA.

New developments of tangible construction kits such as the Lilypad Arduino [4] include sewable microcontrollers, sensors and actuators, to teach programming and engineering concepts. While e-textile construction kits are similar in many functional aspects to robotics construction kits that connect to engineering and computing, they use soft materials rather than motors and gears, and bring in crafting techniques such as sewing that historically have a more feminine orientation. In previous work [14], we described youth's learning with e-textiles in an after school environment as taking place at the intersections of crafting, coding, and circuitry, which allowed us to capture the interdisciplinary nature of e-textile designs. Here, we extend these descriptions to current developments in computational thinking [21] using a framework developed by Brennan & Resnick [2] to make it relevant for in-school application.

In this paper, we report on the design and implementation of a 10-week e-textile module we conducted with 15 high school students (16 - 18 years) as part of a pre-AP CS class. We analyzed students' completed artifacts, design approaches (and how they evolved over time), and reflective interviews guided by the following research questions: (1) How were computational concepts and practices reflected in the design of students' e-textiles? (2) What changed in students' perceptions of computing? In the discussion, we highlight what we can learn from our experiences about developing new introductory courses in K-12 computing.

2. BACKGROUND

There are many compelling examples of how computing curricula can not only provide a rich introduction into computational concepts and practices but also generate personally relevant contexts, provide bridges to real-world applications, and connect to larger groups of students. Successful approaches on the college level have used programming multimedia applications [12], testing game designs [10], or designing mobile apps [22]. On the K-12 level, robotics [1], interface designs [23], game design [13] and storytelling classes [16] have been also successful in broadening students' participation in and perceptions of programming.

However, curricular extensions that build on arts and crafts oriented activities and materials have received far less attention. The recent development of commercially available e-textile construction kits such as the LilyPad Arduino and others provides the missing connection between craft-based activities and computing [6]. But so far, most activities have focused on afterschool programs, leaving the 'more serious' programming to traditional activities. In order to expand the portfolio of available computing curricula, we developed and implemented an e-textile unit as one component of a pre-AP CS class in high school.

Bringing e-textiles into the classroom requires us to articulate what exactly that is that students are engaged in and how their learning relates to what is valued in computing. In previous work [14], we conceptualized youth's learning with e-textiles as taking place at the intersections of crafting, coding, and circuitry, which allowed us to capture the interdisciplinary nature of e-textile designs. Equally important is to establish a connection to computational thinking that Wing [21] described as the "ability to engage in problem solving, designing systems, and understand human behavior" (p. 6). Brennan & Resnick [2] distinguished between computational concepts, practices and perspectives to highlight the multiple dimensions of computational thinking. Computational concepts refer to elements such as sequences, loops, parallelism, events, conditionals, operators, and data structures that are present in many programming languages. Computational practices refer to activities such as being incremental, reusing and remixing, testing and debugging, and modularizing and abstracting that designers use to create programs. While some aspects of concepts and practices appear to be easily applicable to what is being accomplished in making with e-textiles, it is not clear how the interdisciplinary elements such as the circuitry and crafting will be being accounted for in students' learning.

Computational perspectives such as expressing, connecting, and questioning refer to worldviews that designers develop as they engage with digital media. Computational perspectives connect to a core concern in broadening participation that focuses on learners' perceptions of computing, how students define computing, where they see applications for computing, and how they see themselves within the field and future careers. Studies that have examined students' perceptions of computing [8; 27] often hear descriptions such as "being boring or tedious", "only for smart students", "antisocial", and "lacking creativity." The classroom implementation we conducted affords us the opportunity to re-examine these perceptions because of the particular positioning of e-textiles within a larger computing culture. By design, e-textiles are a hybrid, combining traditionally masculine activities such as engineering and computing with traditionally feminine activities such as crafting and sewing. We were interested in whether learning with e-textile materials could indeed broaden not only participation but also perceptions of computing. Taken together, the focus on computational concepts, practices, and perspectives allows us to examine students' understanding of core CS concepts, the generative thinking practices students developed through the process of bringing their e-textile designs to fruition, and students changing perceptions of computer science.

3. METHODS

3.1 Participants

A class of 15 students (7 girls and 8 boys) ages 16-18 years from a public high school participated in a 10-week (19 meetings) e-textiles module as part of their elective computer science class. The students reflected the demographic makeup of the school: 49% African American, 8% Latino, 7% Asian/Pacific Islander, 34% White, and 2% Other. Because the school is a public science and technology magnet school, each student is issued a laptop. Students in the class had spent September to March working with programming in Alice and many had also taken a physics course where they programmed robots, but students had no prior experience with e-textiles. The course met twice a week for 65 minutes per session. While the course was implemented twice, with 15 different students each, in this paper we report only on the second implementation from March to May 2012. The designer and teacher of the course was one of the co-authors (Kaplan), a fourth-year undergraduate majoring in digital media design with an interest in becoming a computer science teacher. He created curricular materials and had two years of experience teaching after-school e-textile workshops but had little classroom teaching experience. He developed the e-textiles curriculum (described in more detail in 4.1) and taught it as part of his senior capstone project for his education minor. Additionally, a graduate student (Searle) with prior experience in both e-textiles and teaching collected observational data. She aided students with e-textile design, construction, and coding as needed and documented research in field notes and interviews.

3.2 Analysis of E-Textile Projects

We documented students' design processes through collection of hand drawn "blueprints" of designs, hourly photographs of their e-textile designs, and copies of their Arduino code. We then created portfolios for each student where we combined the elements described above to provide a more complete portrait of the learning of computational concepts and practices as students moved through the process of creating their e-textile artifacts. To understand students' learning of computational *concepts*, we examined circuit designs, code and final artifacts to evaluate how students used input/output, digital and analog connections, control flow, and structures such as sequences, conditionals, loops, operators, and variables in Arduino. Then, to get a grasp on students' learning of computational *practices*, we inductively identified different approaches to computing evident in our observation notes about students' design processes and within students' designs themselves. We classified these approaches as incremental practices (developing a little bit, trying out), reusing and remixing practices, and testing and debugging practices.

3.3 Analysis of Interviews

In order to understand students' computational *perceptions*, we analyzed pre/post interviews in which students reflected on their e-textile designs as indicators for how they saw computation as a medium for expression. We conducted substantive (30+ minutes each), semi-structured pre- and post-interviews with 11 of the 15 students in which we asked students how their project had changed from their early ideas to completion, what they were most proud of and what was most challenging, what they felt they had learned about computer science in the process, whether their ideas about computer science had changed, and whether the project had influenced their future goals. All interviews were logged and then analyzed [7] focusing on the three aspects: personal relevancy of computing, potential study and career path in computing, and expanded understanding of computing at large.

4. FINDINGS

4.1 Design of e-Textile High School Class

The design of the e-textile class initially followed an outline proposed by Buechley and colleagues [5] that structured the course into six units focusing on circuit designs, code, and materials. While we used some of these units in our course (such as learning about circuits and code), we decided to design activities around students' completion of individual e-textiles projects that included four or more LEDs (light-emitting diodes) and two or more electrically conductive patches. Table 1 provides an overview of the focal daily class activities and materials (e.g., sample designs, starter projects, debugging activities, design consultations, flexible lessons and assessments) that proved to be instrumental in communicating key ideas and helping students complete their projects.

Table 1: Overview of e-Textile Class Activities

Days	Activity	Description
1 -3	Simple Electric Circuits & Conductive Sewing with Starter Projects	Brief review of electricity (how it works, using a flashlight, introducing basic notations); Students make simple circuits using alligator clips, a battery, a switch, and 1 LED followed by learning how to sew with conductive thread to create their first soft circuits. Finally, in pairs or small groups, students work through a series of simple circuit debugging activities.
4 - 5	Programming with Arduino & LilyPad ProtoSnap Boards	Instructor demonstrates on screen how to program LEDs on the ProtoSnap board. Students then program in pairs, turning on multiple LEDs and exploring various blinking patterns and other actuators (e.g., vibe board and sound buzzer). Variables introduced at the end of day 4.
6-8	Basic E-Textile Design Schemes & Individual Design Consultations	Introduction of computational circuit diagrams showing two conductive patches and four LEDs connected to the LilyPad. Students generate their own designs, focusing first on their chosen aesthetic and later on the logistics of circuitry and coding. "Design Consultations" were required before construction could begin; a course instructor or expert research team member met individually with students to finalize their design diagrams.
9 - 18	Culminating E-Textile Design: Crafting, Coding, & Debugging	Students implement their designs, first cutting pieces of conductive and non-conductive fabric and ironing these on their project. Then students sew electrical components together to the LilyPad, testing each line with alligator clips and/or a multimeter. Short lessons on code concepts are interspersed amidst longer periods where students work on their individual projects. More complex coding concepts are introduced on an individual basis as they are relevant to students' projects. Students iteratively test and debug their designs, developing solutions to address them. Some students add new components on toward the end.
19	Final Presentations	Students demonstrate and explain their e-textile project.

In completing their e-textile projects, students demonstrated the ability to customize designs in ways that were both functional but also aesthetic, with a personal touch. Projects had to follow certain guidelines, namely to include a LilyPad microcontroller, 4 LEDs, and at least 2 conductive patches that, when pressed at the same time, acted as a sensor of electrical resistance. It was the freedom within these design requirements that afforded creativity for students' designs in terms of what they made and how they made this, which in turn led to deeper learning [11]. In addition, we provided a *template* for students showing how these components could be connected together and required one-on-one *design consultations* to help them finalize their circuit designs. Yet, the diversity of students' projects surprised us; these included a stuffed octopus, a soft boombox, a cupcake pillow, a Scooby Doo shirt, and a Jamaica-themed shirt. Students' adapted the template to the requirements of their own projects. For instance, in making his soft boombox, Lloyd created two sets of 5 LEDs in parallel circuits that interacted with two conductive patches and a sound buzzer. In his Scooby Doo t-shirt, Will used 4 positive patches that each acted as separate sensors when connected to a central negative patch. These and other innovations required intricate circuit topology both for efficiency (e.g. using a common negative thread to connect multiple LEDs) and insulation (i.e., keeping positive and negative lines from touching). Variations of circuitry further led to innovative coding in order to determine the conditions and effects of the size of the conductive patches, which provided different ranges of resistance (from 800-1000, from 450-1000, etc.), the number of patches that allowed for multiple inputs, and the numbers and placement of LEDs and other actuators. Thus, the design constraints allowed for creative variance that provided unique technical challenges for each students. Additionally, this creative freedom helped students feel a great deal of ownership in designing their projects, something we discuss further in section 4.3.

4.2 Computational Concepts and Practices

Another way to understand the complexity and learning in making e-textile artifacts, is to examine more closely *how* students approached making them, their computational practices, and *what* they included in terms of computational concepts. Before any e-textile can be programmed, it needs to have functional circuits that connect sensors and actuators to the LilyPad Arduino. All students accomplished this in their e-textile designs. However, the actual circuit diagrams varied significantly. Students differed in how many pieces they connected, what kind of circuits they used to accomplish their desired efforts, and most importantly, how they coordinated functionality with their aesthetic requirements. How much functionality drove aesthetics and vice versa, is difficult to gauge, but it was a constant tension in students' design processes, complicated further when coding demands were integrated that required particular circuit designs [14].

Many of the initial circuit blueprints had some mistakes and demonstrated a lack of efficiency. For example, students did not make connections between negative pins and devices, crossed negative and positive lines, made redundant circuit lines, or lacked efficiency in connecting positive or negative lines (i.e., making many independent lines instead of strategically utilizing continuous ones). However, we observed that all students developed final designs that were refined and efficient, customized to their aesthetic requirements and the functionalities they implemented through coding. For instance, in making her cupcake pillow, Trinity changed her initial circuit design to minimize redundancy. Instead of having negative lines from five LEDs criss-crossing her design, she directed them all to one large negatively charged patch which acted as a common ground. She also re-ordered the positives lines from the 5 LEDs such that they made more sense spatially. Her final design was more symmetric, made better use of space, and was more efficient to sew (see Figure 1). Similarly with his octopus, Marty came up with a clever design solution, replacing 8 independent lines from the LilyPad to 8 LEDs by making the back of his stuffed octopus one large conductive patch that acted as a continuous negative line to the LilyPad and the 8 LEDs. Other students utilized parallel circuits in order to connect multiple LEDs that they wanted to behave similarly or expanded their projects to include additional components like speakers or extra LEDs. Of course, these changes affected each student's development of code for his or her project.

Lloyd	Trinity	Giuliana

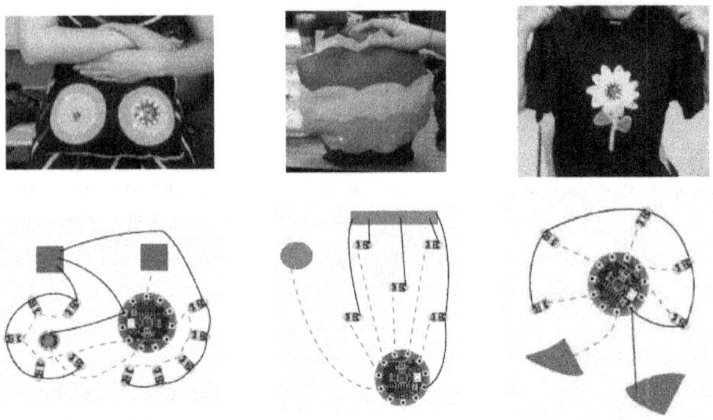

Lloyd	Trinity	Giuliana
If 2 patches touched, - each LED ring blinks on and off in turn while sound buzzer plays "Super Mario's theme" song. *Else if two patches squeezed, each LED ring blinks on and off in turn without music.* *Else, all LEDs off.*	*If two patches touched, - all LEDs fade in and out.* *Else, all LEDs turned off.*	*If two conductive patches touched, - each LED blink on and off in a counter-clockwise direction* *Else, all LEDs e turned off.*

Figure 1: Selection of student e-textile designs: Lloyd's boombox, Trinity's Cupcake Cushion, Giuliana's Sunflower shirt

While each project had different layouts and programmed behaviors, the Arduino program code for these final projects all incorporated key computational concepts such as sequences, loops, conditionals, operators, and variables. First, to set up the digital or analog pins on the LilyPad Arduino that connected input or output devices, students had to understand the relationship between the layout of their electronic circuit and the program code. Second, students had to define output of four or more LEDs. Some students added a speaker to their circuits and remixed the starter code (which we provided) to make sound. To accomplish these tasks, students learned how to include delay functions to adjust how long an LED stayed on or to synchronize LED lights with the beep sounds. Third, students had to code output behaviors for the sensors that connected to the two or more conductive patches. This required the use of conditional statements and loops with variables for storing input values. Some programs featured more complex functionality using multiple conditional statements.

Students engaged in various computational practices to design circuits and code, but mostly in an iterative cycle of imagining and designing and constructing a little bit, then trying it out, and then developing it further when they designed circuits and code. While we provided two basic starter code examples, all students had to customize the code to work with their particular physical designs. We found that all students were able to use and remix starter code examples to create specific behaviors for their circuit designs. In this process, students needed to test and debug the code to make sure that their projects worked as expected. Debugging e-textiles is a complicated process, more so than debugging regular program code, because not only the code but also the circuit design or crafting can cause bugs that need to be fixed. It is these interdependencies [14] that engage students in complex problem solving.

4.3 Perceptions of Computing

Relevancy of Computing. Previous studies have found that students often see computing as irrelevant to their own lives [9; 24]. In pre-interviews, most students revealed that coding remained a mystery removed from their everyday interactions with computers. Carlton expressed a common theme when he said, "I'm sure computers are lovely, but it's not something I'd like to delve into." This sentiment was shared by other students who stressed a disconnect between their everyday lives, future career aspirations, and computer programming. Megan described wanting to go into a career in international relations and said, "I think that I'd use computers, but it's not like I'll be doing coding or anything." We highlight this gap between the perceived need for computing in current and future lives, in particular because it is still prevalent even in science and technology magnet high schools.

In post-interviews conducted after the e-textiles module, students demonstrated a shift towards viewing computing as more relevant to their identities, their daily lives, and their career choices. Students stressed that e-textiles provided the opportunity to use computing as an outlet for personal creativity, or customizability. Many students (7 out of 11) focused on the *aesthetic customizability* of a project. Lloyd, for instance, said that he had been tuning out in the course prior to the e-textiles module but contrasted this with his positive engagement in making a soft boombox. Describing his project he said, "This is music, it's a boombox. A boombox expresses how I feel....Music is my identity." Fewer students (4 of 11) focused on *behavioral customizability* noting that they could shape not only how a project looked but also how it technically functioned.

In addition, more than half of the students (6 of 11) articulated how their e-textiles projects could fit in with or be used in their everyday lives and, by extension, recognized other devices they used in their daily lives that were programmed (cell phones, for instance) or could be programmed (a doorbell). For instance, Megans's project allowed her to transform an "ugly" shirt from her uncle into a useful object, which she can both use to scare her younger siblings and as a Halloween costume. Abeni and Trinity initially conceived of their projects as gifts for others. Keenan and Lloyd both described how they wanted to include their e-textile projects within their personal trophy collections as proof of their accomplishments.

Ability to See Oneself as a Computer Scientist. While all the students saw themselves as fairly competent in using technology on a daily basis—this self-assessment should not come as a surprise since all of them elected to be part of a science and technology magnet school—there were still substantial differences in how their perceptions of themselves as programmers shifted. A large group (7 out of 11) was initially intimidated or even completely disinterested in programming but felt greater competency after the class, expressing a sense of accomplishment, or even surprise about the fact that 'I did this.' Giuliana initially described herself as someone who was not good at programming but after the class she talked about her project (and specifically learning to write in Arduino) as a huge accomplishment, "I think it's just this moment like, "I did it! Finally... Yup. I'm that cool. I programmed a shirt to light up.... I think it's just that moment of accomplishment."

The remainder of the interviewed students (4 out of 11) felt more expertise in programming at the beginning, but after class felt more validated in this expertise after having demonstrated their increased ability to identify and solve programming problems with e-textiles. Reflecting on the class Raven described how exciting it was to speak the same language, "Like we're talking in terms that I've never thought I would never speak… And I'm like, 'I'm understanding everything that you're saying', which is really nice." She connected her ability to understand problem solving and computing with being part of a larger community, with which she now shares a common vocabulary and understanding. Some students like Will, who self-identified as someone who knew about programming before class, proclaimed that they now more clearly understood the connection between programming an e-textiles project in class to programming in other situations, like video games at Activision.

Perceptions of Computing as a Field. Most students also gained a better idea of the field at large, initially conceptualizing computing as something contained only "within the screen" but expanding it after class to see included tangible, real world objects. This perception was most clearly connected to the unique e-textiles projects themselves; almost all students noted that the class was more "hands-on" and that you could really "touch" the products you were working on (as opposed to computer programs in Alice). Trinity liked the e-textiles took programming "outside of [the] computer", while Megan pointed out, "we can touch it, we can feel it, we know what's going on". Several students also described the tangibility of the project with respect to how they could more easily 'show off' their projects to their friends and family once it was done. When asked what she would do with her project, Abeni replied, "Hang it in my room. So when my friends come in, they can touch it. My parents don't know about this, so... it's really cool." Some students even went further by relating projects to professional applications in the real world. In some cases, this meant seeing their individual projects as being on a trajectory toward professional e-textile projects, such as LED sneakers for children or costumes worn by celebrity musicians.

5. DISCUSSION

We see the introduction of e-textiles into high school curriculum as part of a larger effort to broaden the portfolio of available materials, activities, and pedagogies in CS education in K-12. Our findings indicate that the class was successful in promoting a rich array of computing concepts and practices while at the same time broadening perceptions of computing. Designing e-textiles addressed many of the reservations that youth often have expressed about computing: it integrated multiple disciplines of computing, engineering and crafting, had real-world relevance since it involved repurposing and augmenting everyday items, and allowed for creative expression through the creation of personal e-textile artifacts within given design constraints [24]. It was the unique combination of all these aspects, not a single one alone, that accounted for the success. Through our analysis of the students' perceptions of computing before and after the e-textiles class, we demonstrated how creating e-textiles artifacts shifted their perspectives on computing. Students expanded in their thinking about relevancy of computing to their personal lives, understanding of themselves as computer scientists, and their understanding of computing as a field. Admittedly, we have downplayed the role of crafts and the physical techniques of creating soft computational circuits in order to emphasize more traditionally valued academic learning in circuitry and coding. Yet these aspects are intricately related to the particular development of circuits and code in e-textiles [14].

While we didn't have the room to describe in much detail the various curricular activities beyond the final culmination e-textile project, we believe these played an equally important role in helping students to learn computational concepts and to engage in computational practices. Like robotics workshops, we did structure the e-textile class around the activity of designing a final artifact as its ultimate outcome. But we also made generous use of a series of smaller stepping stone starter and debugging projects along the way that provided additional experiences for students to understand the complexities of particular design aspects. For instance, *starter projects* with a simple circuit that includes an LED, battery, and switch provided introductions to conductive sewing. Students learned sewing techniques as well as key rules of thumb: (1) connect positive to positive and negative to negative, (2) do not sew through both the positive and negative ends of a component, and (3) do not cross positive and negative threads/lines. Alternatively, *debugging projects* [15], presented students with problems in circuit or code design of finished e-textile projects. For instance, one debugging project tested students' knowledge of short circuits while in another they had to correctly connect a series of positive and negative lines to create a functional circuit, and in yet a third they had to alter the connections to obtain the desired behavior when a button switch was pressed. As students worked through the debugging projects they were asked to complete a series of questions about each circuitry problem.

All high school students were equally engaged in the various aspects of crafting, circuitry and coding and this should perhaps be counted as the biggest success. Many of the other curricular innovations such as game design and robotics workshops are often heavily geared towards male students because of how the professional communities are structured. In designing e-textiles, we found present what Resnick and Silverman [19] called the "wide walls" of construction kits that allow for diverse set of interests to expressed in programmable activities. But rather than to work in the "existing clubhouse" we opened a new one, or new doors, to stay with the metaphors of low floors, high ceilings, and wide walls that are often used in thinking about creating computational construction kits for beginners. Making personal and portable computational projects with materials that connect to everyday experiences and mundane activities such as crafting and sewing provided a new window to see the general and personal relevance of computing.

6. ACKNOWLEDGMENTS

This work was supported by a collaborative grant (0855868) from the National Science Foundation to Yasmin Kafai, Leah Buechley and Kylie Peppler. Any opinions, findings, and conclusions or recommendations expressed in this paper are those of the authors and do not necessarily reflect the views of the National Science Foundation, the University of Pennsylvania, Utah State University, or The Westminster Schools.

7. REFERENCES

[1] Baretto, F. & Benitti, V. (2012). Exploring the educational potential of robotics in schools: A systematic review. *Computers & Education, 58*, 978–988.

[2] Brennan, K. & Resnick, M. (2012, April). New frameworks for studying and assessing the development of computational thinking. Paper presented at the annual meeting of the American Educational Research Association, Vancouver, BC, Canada.

[3] Bruckman, A., Biggers, M., Ericson, E., McKlin, T., Dimond, J., DiSalvo, B., Hewner, M., Ni, L., & Yardi, S. "Georgia Computes!": Improving the Computing Education Pipeline. Proceedings of SIGCSE '09 (pp. 86-90). Chattanooga, TN.

[4] Buechley, L. (2006). A construction kit for electronic textiles. In Proceedings of *IEEE International Symposium on Wearable Computers* (ISWC) (pp. 83-92). Montreux, Switzerland.

[5] Buechley, L., Eisenberg, M., & Elumeze, N. (2007). Towards a curriculum for electronic textiles in the high school classroom. In *Proceedings of the Conference on Innovation and Technology in Computer science Education* (ITiCS). Dundee, Scotland.

[6] Buechley, L., Peppler, K., Eisenberg, M. & Kafai, Y. (Eds.). (in press). *Textile messages: Dispatches from the world of e-textiles and education.* New York: Peter Lang.

[7] Charmaz, K. (2000). Grounded theory: Objectivist and constructivist methods. In N.K. Denzin & Y.S. Lincoln (Eds.), *Handbook of qualitative research* (pp. 509–535). Thousand Oaks, CA: Sage Publications.

[8] Denner, J., Werner, L. & Ortiz, E. (2012). Computer games created by middle school girls: Can they be used to measure understanding of computer science concepts? *Computers & Education,* 58(1), 240-249.

[9] Dimond, J. & Guzdial, M. (2008). More than paradoxes to Offer: Exploring motivations to attract women to computing. Georgia Institute of Technology Technical Report. Retrieved on August 27, 2012 from: http://gacomputes.cc.gatech.edu/ Members/jpdimond/dimondParadoxes.pdf

[10] Disalvo, B.& Bruckman, A. (2011). From Interests To Values: Computer science is not that difficult but wanting to learn it is. *Communications of the ACM*, 27-29.

[11] Fields, D. A. Kafai, Y. B. & Searle, K.A. (2012). Functional aesthetics for learning: Creative tensions in youth e-textiles designs. In *Proceedings of the 10th International Conference of the Learning Sciences (ICLS 2012) (*196-203). ICLS: Sydney, NSW, Australia.

[12] Forte, A. & Guzdial, M. (2004). Motivation and nonmajors in computer ccience: Identifying discrete audiences from introductory courses. *IEEE Transactions on Education,* 48 (2), 248-253.

[13] Kafai, Y. B. (1995). *Minds in Play.* Hillsdale, NJ: Lawrence Erlbaum Associates.

[14] Kafai, Y. B., Fields, D. A., & Searle, K.A. (2012). Making learning visible: Connecting crafts, circuitry & coding in e-textile designs. In *Proceedings of the 10th International Conference of the Learning Sciences (ICLS 2012)* (pp. 188-195). ICLS: Sydney, NSW, Australia.

[15] Kaplan, E., Griffin, J., Kafai, Y. B., & Burke, W. Q. (2011, March). A deconstruction kit for the LilyPad Arduino: Designing debugging sets for learning about circuitry & programming for high school students. Poster presented at The 42nd ACM Technical Symposium on Computer Science Education (SIGCSE 2011), Dallas, TX.

[16] Kelleher, C. (2008). Using storytelling to introduce girls to computer programming. . In Y.B. Kafai, C. Heeter, J. Denner, & J.Y. Sun (Eds.), *Beyond Barbie & Mortal Kombat: New perspectives on gender and gaming* (pp. 247-264). Cambridge, MA: The MIT Press.

[17] Kelleher,C. & Pausch, R. (2005). Lowering the barriers to programming: A taxonomy of programming environments and languages for novice programmers. *ACM Computing Surveys*, 37, 2, 83-137.

[18] Margolis, J., Estrella, R., Goode, J., Holme, J. J., & Nao, K. (2008). *Stuck in the shallow end.* Cambridge, MA: The MIT Press.

[19] Resnick, M., & Silverman, B. (2005, June). Some reflections on designing construction kits for kids. *Proceedings of Interaction Design and Children* conference (pp. 117-122), Boulder, CO.

[20] Wilson, C., Sudol, L., Stephenson, C., & Stehlik, M. (2010). *Running on empty: The failure to teach K–12 computer science in the digital age.* ACM. DOI = http://www.acm.org/runningonempty/fullreport.pdf.

[21] Wing, J. (2006). Computational thinking. *Communications of the ACM, 49,* 33-35.

[22] Wolber, D., Abelson, H., Spertus, E. & Looney, L. (2011). *App Inventor: Create your own Android apps.* Sebastopol, CA: O'Reilly Media, Inc.

[23] Yardi, S., Krolikowski, P, Marshall, T., & Bruckman, A.. (2008). An HCI approach to computing in the real world. *ACM Journal on Educational Resources in Computing* 8(3), 1-20.

[24] Yardi, S. & Bruckman, A. (2007). What is computing? Bridging the gap between teenagers' perceptions and graduate students' experiences. *Proceedings of the 3rd International Workshop on Computing Education Research* (pp. 39-50), Atlanta, GA.

Workifying Games: Successfully Engaging African American Gamers with Computer Science

Betsy DiSalvo[1], Mark Guzdial[1], Charles Meadows[2], Tom McKlin[3], Ken Perry[2], Amy Bruckman[1]

[1]Georgia Institute of Technology
Atlanta, GA
[bdisalvo | guzdial | asb]
@cc.gatech.edu

[2]Morehouse College
Atlanta, GA
[kperry | cmeadows]
@morehouse.edu

[3]The Findings Group
Decatur, GA
tom.mcklin@gmail.com

ABSTRACT
We report on the implementation and evaluation of a three-year program to increase interest in studying computer science (CS) among African American male high school students. Over the course of 3 years, the Glitch Game Tester (Glitch) program employed 25 African American male high school students. These students tested pre-release digital games, full-time in the summer and part-time in the school year, with an hour of each day dedicated to learning introductory CS. Initially, only 20% of our participants expressed interest in pursing computing as a career. After Glitch, 65% have pursued some form of post-secondary computing studies. These outcomes, and the participants' enthusiasm for engaging in computing, are in sharp contrast to the crisis in African American male education and learning motivation. The research presented in this report discusses lessons learned through implementation of the Glitch program and higher education outcomes after graduation from the program.

Categories and Subject Descriptors:
K.3.2 Computer and Information Science Education.

General Terms
Design, Human Factors

Keywords
Games, Learning, Design, Intent to persist

1. INTRODUCTION
There is a concern in the United States (US) that we are not training enough citizens to fill the need for computer scientists. The pool of individuals who historically have filled these positions, white males, is a shrinking part of our population [9, 12]. African American males have historically underperformed in academic settings, and have high rates of unemployment and underemployed [10]. We propose that increasing the number of African American males who enter higher education to study CS is one strategy to improve the number of trained computer scientists in the US, improve educational outcomes for African American males, and increase their participation in computing, a field that holds the promise of high-paying and secure employment [1].

To address these objectives, researchers from a public technical university and a Historically Black College or University (HBCU) developed a targeted program to leverage young African American males interest in digital games into an interest in computing. Our formative work showed that many current computer scientists (mostly white males) were drawn to computing through hacking and modding video games [4]. However, we found that while African American males played games more frequently, they valued sportsmanship in their play practices, and felt that hacking or modding was cheating. [5]. We sought to build on practices with games that seeded interest in computing (i.e. breaking open the game through hacking or modding), while still respecting the play practices of African American males (i.e. a value on sportsmanship). We pursued the idea of game testing as a learning practice because it engages breaking open the games, while still respecting the culture of sportsmanship.

2. DESIGN & IMPLEMENTATION
From 2009 – 2011, twenty-five high school students participated in the Glitch Game Testers program. These participants worked full-time in the summer and part-time in the school year as game testers. They did quality assurance work on pre-release digital games for industry clients. The testers also participated in CS workshops and classes. There were other factors that made Glitch successful with the students, like holding it on a university campus, and offering a competitive point system (e.g. giving points for documenting a bug in a game) with significant rewards.

2.1 Schedule and Pay
During the summer, the testers worked full-time from 10:00 AM – 5:00 PM, Monday – Friday for 8 weeks. Testers were paid an hourly rate of $8.00. During the school year, testers worked part-time on Saturdays from 9:00 AM – 10:00 PM. While we began our summer days a little later to match adolescent sleep patterns, when we established the schedule for the school year, participants asked to start a little earlier so they could "get more hours in."

A typical day consisted of testing from 10:00 AM to noon, lunch, a CS workshop after lunch, and then more testing until 5:00 PM. We began the day with testing to make sure we established that this was a work environment rather than an educational environment. The weekly activities varied, but the majority of the time was spent on testing or tasks related to testing.

SIGCSE'13, March 6–9, 2013, Denver, Colorado, USA.

On Monday mornings there would frequently be quality assurance training and review, which included exploring new concepts or reviewing bug reports. This was another strategy to focus the participants on the work for the week. On Fridays there were pizza lunches with computer scientist speakers, and we held a game tournament late Friday afternoon. These more social aspects of the program helped to facilitate a number of friendships that extended beyond the program – and likely provided social support for their interest in CS. There were other activities, such as tours of colleges or game development companies. We also had visits from our clients, who would conduct training or help with technical issues.

The schedule and activities were based around participant input, what would work with their schedule, and what was of value to them. For example, we held resume writing, college application and HTML workshops based upon the participants' request.

2.2 Recruitment and Consent

Participants were recruited to become part of the Glitch program through an email flyer with a one-page application sent to local youth leaders, teachers and community members in predominantly African American communities and schools. The recruitment language was focused on recruiting individuals who loved playing games, not individuals with an interest in technology or computing. Of the approximately 200 applications we received in the first two weeks after these emails were sent each spring, we selected 15 - 18 students to interview for the summer session. Selections were made based upon the date the application was received, meaning that participation was primarily based on a first-in, first-hired basis. The only other qualifying criteria for an interview were age; participants needed to be between 16 and 18 years of age, and currently enrolled in high school.

In all cases, the first 20 applicants that met these criteria were African American males. We generally interviewed more applicants than the 7 – 12 openings. Final selection gave priority to those who, were passionate about playing video games, qualified for free or reduced lunch, and were rising juniors. All data was collected between May 2009 and July 2012 with 25 participants. All participants and their parents were informed of the human subjects protocol. We obtained assent from minor participants and consent from adult participants and adult guardians. Protection of participants was annually reviewed and renewed through our Institutional Review Board (IRB).

2.3 Participants

From the beginning of the Glitch program in June of 2009 to the end of the summer program in July of 2011, we had 33 participants. Only the 25 participants who have graduated from high school are considered in this evaluation. All other participants are still in high school and on track to graduate on time. All participants self-identified as African American males. Two participants also self-identified as Latino. The participants ranged in age from 16 – 18 years of age, with an average age of 17. Of the 25 participants, 19 qualified for free or reduced lunch.

2.4 Location and Transportation

Prototype workshops demonstrated that transportation was an important issue in maintaining participation. We originally intended to hold the program on the HBCU campus; however, it rapidly became apparent that this would not work because of limited public transportation [3]. Instead, the program was held on the public university campus, where public transportation is more accessible. This set an expectation, similar to any job, that testers were responsible for their own transportation and would not be paid if they did not show up. Testing occurred in a dedicated space in an academic building that primarily houses computing classrooms, chemistry class labs, and robotics project labs.

The location became an important issue for the participants. The responsibility of getting to and from work each day using public transportation was something that made Glitch feasible. In addition, it emerged that participants were quite proud of being independent and responsible for their own transportation. The campus location was also important to participants because they began to see themselves as members of a prestigious university community where classes and research happened [3].

2.5 Game Testing

Game testing is a form of software quality assurance (QA) work. In Glitch, testers would receive early versions of games from our clients, and then look for instances where the code did not perform as expected. There are different types of testing that engaged participants in the software development community of practice. Some were very directed, such as *planned testing* where participants systematically tested specific lists of functionalities that developers requested. On the other end of the spectrum, *play testing* engaged participants in open ended and subjective critique on the balance and playability of the game. The participants also saw the iterative process of software development through *regression testing*, in which a tester checks previously-reported bugs to see if they have been fixed correctly. When participants found an error, they would write up a bug report using online bug tracking software. This report includes a detailed step-by-step description of how to reproduce the bug. Developers then look at these reports and respond to them by fixing the bug or engaging the testers with questions about the bug report.

2.5 Computer Science Learning

We anticipated that testing was one method for encouraging these young men to see video games as computation. In addition, we held computing workshops and classes to increase the opportunities for learning. Our goal was to seed an interest in computing. The workshops helped to make sure that students learned CS. Without the CS workshops, the game "seed" would never sprout.

The introductory CS workshops were built upon existing curriculum that had previously been successfully in teaching non-CS majors basic computing concepts [7]. In their first year in Glitch, participants took part in CS workshops based on the media computation approach (Guzdial, 2003) using *Alice*, a drag and drop programming language (Cooper, Dann, & Pausch, 2000), and Jython.

Initially we had no plan for different CS workshops for the participants' second year in the program – we thought they would just do more in-depth projects with Alice and Jython. However, the participants' requested an opportunity to learn a more realistic programming language (they felt Jython was not a real language). In response, we offered them a chance to take an Advanced Placement Computer Science (APCS) course to prepare them for the Advanced Placement exam. All of the participants voluntarily chose to take this class rather than taking the first workshop again.

Finally, both first- and second-year students built computers that were used in our testing (it was cheaper to build them than to buy them) and used as prizes in the *Glitch Competition* (see section 2.6). The participants seemed to appreciate authentic work, such a building computers we really needed, and working towards taking a test that would mean something for their future in computing. We continued to design elements of what they were doing with game testing into the development of our curriculum including the development of a Java class using *Greenfoot* [8] to create their own games in 2011.

Another way we contextualized the CS learning was through our teachers. Most CS workshops and classes were taught or assisted by African American CS majors from the partnering institutions. These young people (most of whom were male) were paid to help manage and teach in the Glitch program, and they were motivated to make a difference in the education of young African American males. The contribution these young people provided the program was immeasurable. Of particular note is how they became role models for success in CS and college, and they were able to inform the older, White and African American researchers about the interest of the high school participants. For example, the young men who taught the first APCS course used an elaborate description of basketball positions, teams, and individual players to introduce object oriented programming.

2.6 Competition

Formative work indicated that competition was important to young African American males when gaming and in their everyday lives [5]. Because of this, we designed competitive elements into the Glitch program. During workshops and classes, mentors and teachers used competition and rewards to motivate the participants. The types of rewards and prizes varied. Sometimes participants were awarded candy as a prize, or rewarded intangibles, such as being voted as having the "best" presentation, or with points in the overall *Glitch Competition.*

The *Glitch Competition* was an ongoing tally of the points posted on a white board in the room. Keeping track of points became an important part of each day for the participants. When updates were made on the board, everyone stopped what they were doing, turned to look at the manager writing the new scores down, and started bragging, making excuses or trash talking (using insulting or boastful speech) with each other based upon the outcome. The points were added up each week to determine a winner. In the summer, the weekly winner received a video game or a gift certificate. At the end of the summer and the school year, the winner won one of the computers the group had built.

2.7 Notes on Implementation

The point system, weekly Friday speakers, CS workshops and QA training were iterated upon over the 3-year implementation. This ongoing effort was based upon participants' opinions and insured they had a voice in designing the learning environment. Perhaps due to this flexible implementation, participants frequently asked for additional help, training and mentorship.

2.8 Funding

The project was primarily funded through a National Science Foundation grant which covered the most of the cost of undergraduate staff, about half of the technology and materials, and all of the hourly wages of the participants for the first two summers. Wages for the third summer were paid with funds from foundations Arthur Blank Foundation and Yahoo! Games.

So while we were testing pre-release games companies were not willing to pay us directly for our services. There seem to be three main issues that contributed to this. First, we did not have trained and dedicated sales staff member. Second, the payment structure proved to be difficult to coordinate with an academic institution and for profit companies. Third, we did not attain consistent quality in our game testing services. To address these issues we are now working with a for profit company that has a sales staff for technology serves, a business model for more traditional client structures, and better trained managers for quality assurance. The academic institutions were good at the CS educational components, and will continue those aspects of the program.

3. DATA COLLECTION AND METHODS

Quantitative and qualitative methods were used to evaluate Glitch. This report will focus on quantitative measures including two online tools developed and administered with the assistance of The Findings Group, LCC,[1] and follow-up communications with participants one year after their high school graduation. The surveys were administered in 2010 when 22 of the 25 graduates of Glitch participated.

3.5 Confidence & Interest in Computing

We used a survey instrument to measure participants' *interest in and confidence with computing* [15] based upon two validated instruments that measure self-efficacy, outcome expectancy, and computer attitudes,. The first validated surveys used was the Microcomputer Beliefs Inventory (MBI), which assessed the participants' self-efficacy and outcome expectancy beliefs toward computers [6]. Item analysis, scale reliability assessment, and factor analysis of scale integrity were previously conducted and both scales performed with "good" reliability (Cronbach's Alpha r = 0.80, 0.85, respectively) [6].

The second validated instrument we used was the Computer Attitude Questionnaire (CAQ), which was designed to measure attitudes and disposition towards computers and was shown to have "very good" internal consistency [2]. This version of the CAQ used three of the eight possible subscales: Computer Importance, Computer Enjoyment, and Creative Tendencies (Cronbach's Alpha r = 0.80, 0.80, 0.87, respectively).

Both surveys used a 5-point scale where 1=Strongly Disagree, 3 = Not Sure, and 5 = Strongly Agree. In the first year, 2009, we administered this survey as a pre (N = 12) and post (N = 12) measure at the beginning and end of the 8-week summer program. For some questions, participants' post surveys reported lower self-efficacy. We suspected that students were overconfident about their computing abilities pre-Glitch, and after participating in the 8-week program discovered the breadth and depth of computing knowledge that was available, and gave more conservative

[1] The Findings Group, LCC. is the independent firm hired to evaluate the Glitch project with funding from NSF.

estimates of their confidence and knowledge. In response to this, we modified the survey in 2010 and delivered it as a retrospective survey to participants (N = 21), which allowed us to ask the participants to evaluate how they changed in their attitudes, self-efficacy and outcome expectancy. The reported findings are from these retrospective surveys from 2010.

3.2 Intent to Persist Scale

Toker and Ackerman [13] developed a validated measure on *Intent to Persist* to assess vocational interest in STEM fields. We used a modified version of this survey that included focused questions on computing. Participants were asked to rate the truth of statements regarding intention to persist with education, STEM interest, and interest in computing on a 6 point scale, with 1 being Very Untrue of Me and 6 being Very True of Me (N = 22). Wyer's [14] short-term, mid-level, and long-term commitments were used to frame the 12 items in this survey. Six additional computing questions were added and these followed the same framework, but which were specific to intent to persist in computer science. In 2009, the survey was given as a pre and post measure. In 2010 and 2011, we gave the survey only at the end of the 8-week summer program and added retrospective questions to gauge more exact reflections on changes in participants' intent to persist in education, technology and computing. The reported findings are from the retrospective surveys.

3.3 Post High School Graduation Follow-up

The lead author maintained a relationship with most of the participants through occasional emails and participation on social network sites. Through these correspondences and direct email appeals, we have data on the post high school activities of 23 of the 25 participants who have graduated from high school. In this paper we report actual persistence: whether the participants have attended a higher education or training program, the type of education program they are involved in and the subject they study, within one year of leaving the Glitch program.

4. RESULTS

In this section we will report on the results from surveys on confidence with computing and interest in computing, scores on *intent to persist* with computing, and details on the post-secondary education outcomes. Throughout these findings, we can see demonstrations of Glitch's success in motivating this group of young African American males to study computer science.

4.1 Confidence with Computing Results

The retrospective surveys measuring confidence in computing from the summer of 2010, showed statistically significant gains and small to medium effect sizes. Participants' responses to indicated that they gained computing confidence. Particularly participants demonstrated increased confidence in computing on two questions; "I know how to use the computer" (p=0.005) and on the negatively worded "I get a sinking feeling when I think of trying to use a computer" (p=0.046) (Table 1).

4.2 Interest in Computing Results

Glitch participants self-reported interest in computing and other factors involving technology before and after the summer 2010 (Table 2). We see statistically significant gains in their interest in computer programming (p=0.008), in their interest in information technology (p=0.013), and in their interest in computer engineering (p=0.013). Comparatively, we did not find significant gains in other items of interest such as music programming, web programming and game design. Further, Vargha and Delaney's A is used to measure effect size, and we see small to medium effect sizes for computer programming, information technology, computer engineering, graphic design, web programming, and game design. Table 2 indicates that the program has increased student interest in our primary target, computer programming.

Table 1: Participants' Confidence in Computing (n=21)

Statement	Time	Mean†	A	Wilcoxon
1. I know how to use the computer.	Before	4.43	0.690[c]	0.005**
	After	4.81		
2. I am not very good at using a computer.	Before	2.19	0.532[a]	0.610
	After	2.29		
3. Even when I try hard, I do not use the computer as well as others do.	Before	1.90	0.502[a]	1.000
	After	1.95		
4. I think I generally use the computer poorly.	Before	1.86	0.517[a]	0.157
	After	1.67		
5. I understand what a computer can do well enough to use it correctly.	Before	4.10	0.590[b]	0.102
	After	4.29		
6. I get a sinking feeling when I think of trying to use a computer.	Before	1.71	0.544[a]	0.046*
	After	1.57		

Note. Vargha & Delaney's *A* is a non-parametric measure of effect size. An *A* value of 0.50 indicates no difference between group means; an *A* of 0.56 equates to a small effect size (d=0.20), an *A* of 0.64 equates to a medium effect size (d=0.50), and an *A* of 0.71 is equivalent to a large effect size (d = 0.80). Effect size ranges are denoted with the letters a-d to indicate the range within which the effect size statistic falls.

[a] none to a small effect; [b] small to medium effect; [c] medium to large effect; [d] large effect †Scale ranges from 1 (Strongly Disagree) to 5 (Strongly Agree) with "I'm not sure" as the midpoint.

*Statistically significant (p<0.05)

**Statistically significant (p<0.01)

4.3 Intent to Persist Results

The *Intent to Persist* scale indicates that participants intended to pursue CS in their future careers. Table 3 indicates that participants' plans to attend and graduate from college began and remained high. While, there was no significant increase in these numbers, their stability gives us more trust in the measure. The participants' plans to pursue computing while in college did change positively and significantly from pre to post. These findings indicate that the Glitch program had an impact on the participants' intent to study computing in both college and graduate school (Mcklin et al., 2010).

Table 2: Participants' Interest in Computing (n=21)

		Mean	A	Wilcoxon
I was interested in computer programming.	Before	4.48	0.600^b	0.008**
I am interested in computer programming.	After	5.05		
I was interested in information technology.	Before	4.40	0.592^b	0.013*
I am interested in information technology.	After	4.79		
I was interested in computer engineering.	Before	4.36	0.582^b	0.013*
I am interested in computer engineering.	After	4.81		
I was interested in graphic design.	Before	4.15	0.576^b	0.347
I am interested in graphic design.	After	4.45		
I was interested in music programming.	Before	4.23	0.476	0.861
I am interested in music programming.	After	4.05		
I was interested in web programming.	Before	4.29	0.595^b	0.062
I am interested in web programming.	After	4.70		
I was interested in game design.	Before	4.62	0.564^b	0.054
I am interested in game design.	After	5.00		
See notes from Table 1				

Table 3: Glitch Participants' Intention to Persist in CS (n=22)

Statement	Time	Mean†	A	Wilcoxon
1. I plan to apply to college.	Before	5.86	0.478	0.317
	After	5.82		
2. I plan on graduating from college.	Before	5.86	0.457	0.157
	After	5.77		
3. I plan on graduating from college with a computing-related degree.	Before	4.05	0.648^c	0.026*
	After	4.55		
4. I would like to go to graduate school after college.	Before	4.41	0.571^b	0.096
	After	4.68		
5. I would like to go to graduate school after college for a computing-related degree.	Before	3.59	0.653^c	0.028*
	After	4.14		
See notes from Table 1				

Participants were also asked about their career aspirations (see Table 4). Again, there are significant changes from pre to post in their "plans to work in a technology-related field" (p=0.02), "plans to find a job as a computer scientist or computer programmer" (p=0.01), "plans to earn a living as a computer scientist or programmer" (p=0.004), and "plans to devote my career to an area related to computer science" (p=0.026). As with their intentions to continue their education in computing, the participants expressed a growing interest in pursuing computing as a career.

Table 4: Participants' Interest in Pursuing a Computing Career (n=22)

Statement	Time	Mean†	A	Wilcoxon
1. I am planning on working in a technology-related field.	Before	4.86	0.589^b	0.02*
	After	5.18		
2. I can see myself working as a computer scientist or programmer in the future.	Before	4.23	0.582^b	0.07
	After	4.68		
3. I am planning to find a job as a computer scientist or computer programmer.	Before	3.77	0.624^b	0.01*
	After	4.36		
4. I am planning on earning a living as a computer scientist or programmer.	Before	3.55	0.640^c	0.004**
	After	4.27		
5. I am planning to devote my career to an area related to computer science.	Before	3.77	0.582^b	0.026*
	After	4.27		
See notes from Table 1				

4.4 Post High School Graduation Outcomes.

As of May 2012, twenty-five participants had graduated, and the remaining participants were still enrolled in high schools. Of the twenty-three graduates that responded, twenty-one have pursued post-secondary education and as of one year after their graduation all but one were still enrolled in school.

The five students pursuing non-CS related education generally came from families with a stronger history of educational attainment. These students are attending in-state pubic schools and majoring in education, marine biology, business and film.

The sixteen students who are pursuing additional computing education are taking several different paths to pursue careers as computer scientist, game developers, web developers and software engineers. Only four of these students had indicated that computing was a possible major before the Glitch program started. As of one year after graduation, 11 were continuing on in four-year schools majoring in computer science. Most of these students are attending in-state public schools, but one is attending a private HBCU and one transferred to a military academy after his first year. Three students started in 2-year institutes studying computer information technology, but one dropped out at the end of the year and enlisted in the military with hopes of pursing technology training as a soldier. Finally, Two students were pursing arts degrees with digital media as their focus, one in a 4-year college and one in a 2-year institute.

5. DISCUSSION & CONCLUSION

The design of the Glitch program was based in extensive formative work that informed the initial concepts, but Glitch was also continually refined. We approached Glitch as a prototype and worked daily with the young African American participants in shaping this environment to their values. These ongoing iterations to the program helped us polish the implementation. Through these iterations the program began to focus on three things that may be key for creating CS learning environments for young African American males. First, we found that real work and authentic contributions to valued artifacts were significant motivators for enthusiasm in all aspects of the program. Second, we found that competition was often used as a tactic for making it socially acceptable to make a concerted effort to learn. Third, we found that integration of the program on a college campus, with undergraduates teaching, gave the participants a sense of belonging in a higher education environment.

The qualitative data presented suggest that the focus areas were on target and most participants increased their confidence with computing, interest in computing, intend to persist in computing and are seeking CS educational options post graduation. However, there are still real barriers to success outside of the Glitch environment that these young men may not be equipped to handle. After entering college, some of the participants have not made good grades as easily as they thought they would with their prior CS experience. One participant did not attend school at first because of finances, then went to a technical school, then dropped out to enter the military. Another participant completed his first year but dropped out in his second year. While the findings are compelling that, over time, these young men have the intent to persist in computing, long-term effects may be tempered with the reality of the barriers that young lower-income African American males face.

While we began the Glitch program leveraging the fun of video games to learn CS, through the iterative process with our participants, we discovered that a real world work environment about a product (video games) that young African American men care about was more motivating than making something "fun." For future work we hope to take a different approach than the gamification advocates [11]. We seek to focus on the work of game making, rather than the gaming of work.

6. ACKNOWLEDGMENT

The Glitch Game Testers was made possible by the National Science Foundation through support of grant # 0837733. Additional funding was provided by the Arthur Blank Family Foundation and Yahoo!.

7. REFERENCES

[1] Bureau of Labor Statistics U. S. Department of Labor *The 30 Fastest-growing Occupations, 2006 - 2016*. City, 2007.

[2] Christensen, R. and Knezek, G. Instruments for assessing the impact of technology in education. *Computers in the Schools*, 18, 2-3 (2001/06/24 2001), 5-25.

[3] DiSalvo, B. *The Glitch Game Testers: The Design and Study of a Learning Environment for Computational Production with Young African American Males*. Georgia Institute of Technology, Atlanta, GA, 2012.

[4] DiSalvo, B. and Bruckman, A. *Questioning video games' influence on CS interest*. ACM, City, 2009.

[5] DiSalvo, B. and Bruckman, A. *Race and gender in play practices: Young African American males*. ACM, City, 2010.

[6] Enochs, L. G., Riggs, I. M. and Ellis, J. D. The development and partial validation of microcomputer utilization in teaching efficacy beliefs instrument in a science setting. *School Science and Mathematics*, 93, 5 1993), 257-263.

[7] Forte, A. and Guzdial, M. Computers for communication, not calculation: media as a motivation and context for learning. *System Sciences, 2004. Proceedings of the 37th Annual Hawaii International Conference on*2004), 96-105.

[8] Kölling, M., Utting, I., McCall, D., Brown, N., Stevens, P. and Berry, M. *Greenfoot* Programming Education Tools Group, Computing Education Research Group at the School of Computing, University of Kent, City, 2011.

[9] Lee, J. M. J. and Ransom, T. *The Educational Experience of Young Men of Color: A review of Research, Pathways and Progress*. The College Board Advocacy & Policy Center, New York, 2011.

[10] Lewis, S., Simon, C., Uzzell, R., Horwitz, A. and Casserly, M. *A Call for Change: The social and educational factors contributing to the outcomes of black males in urban schools*. The Council of the Great City Schools, Washington, DC, 2010.

[11] McGonigal, J. *Reality is Broken: Why Games Make Us Better and How They Can Change the World*. Penguin Group (USA) Inc., New York, NY, 2011.

[12] NSF *Broadening Participation in Computing (BPC) Program Solicitation* The National Science Foundation, Directorate for Computer & Information Science & Engineering, City, 2008.

[13] Toker, Y. and Ackerman, P. L. Utilizing occupational complexity levels in vocational interest assessments: Assessing interests for STEM areas. *Journal of Vocational Behavior*, 80, 2 2011), 524-544.

[14] Wyer, M. Intending to stay: Images of scientist, attitutes toward women, and gender as influences on persistence amoung sscience and engineering majors. *Journal of Women and Minorities in Science and Engineering*, 9, 1 2003), 1-16.

[15] Yardi, S., Krolikowski, P., Marshall, T. and Bruckman, A. An HCI approach to computing in the real world. *Journal on Educational Resources in Computing (JERIC)*, 8, 3 2008), 9.

Emumaker86: A Hardware Simulator for Teaching CPU Design

Michael Black
Dept of Computer Science, American University
Washington, DC, USA
mblack@american.edu

Nathaniel Waggoner
Dept of Computer Science, American University
Washington, DC, USA
waggoner@gxmconsulting.com

ABSTRACT

This paper describes a new GUI-based tool to teach undergraduate students to design their own CPUs. The tool was purpose-built to teach a wide range of computer organization topics, including digital logic, instruction set encoding, datapath and control units, and pipelining. A datapath builder allows microarchitecture building blocks, such as registers, ALUs, and multiplexors, to be laid out, wired together, and simulated. A control builder allows students to develop control states and microinstructions for the datapath. Both units are integrated with a full PC emulator, allowing student-designed processors to use emulated devices, such as drives, video, and I/O ports. A tutorial teaches students to use the simulator to build a pipelined RISC processor.

Categories and Subject Descriptors

C.0 [**Computer Systems Organization**]: General

Keywords

Processor, Simulator, Digital Logic, Datapath, x86

1. INTRODUCTION

CPU simulators are frequently employed in computer organization and computer architecture courses, as well as in academic research, allowing students to experiment with the course materials and produce designs without having to physically construct the device [19]. This paper describes a new hardware simulator that allows students to develop their own processors. The simulator is entirely graphics-based and does not require the user to write code. It nevertheless is powerful enough that more advanced architectural techniques, such as pipelining, speculation, and real instruction sets can be modeled. We built this tool from the ground-up to integrate with a Computer Organization class and teach a wide range of material, from digital logic to instruction sets to processor architecture.

SIGCSE'13, March 6–9, 2013, Denver, Colorado, USA.

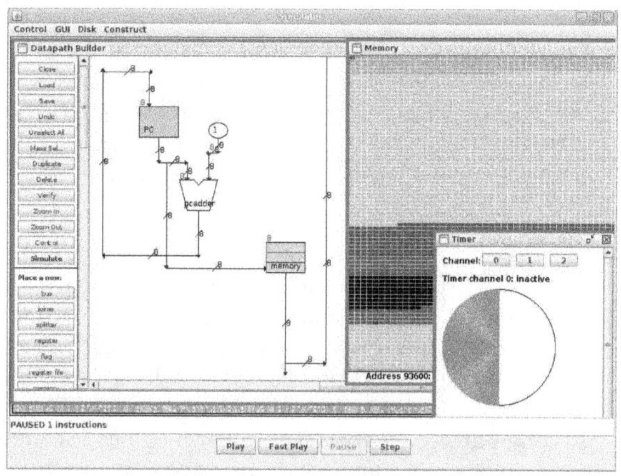

Figure 1: PC Simulator with Datapath Builder, Memory Viewer, Interval Timer

Several factors make our hardware simulator unique. It is integrated into a Java-based x86 full personal computer emulator that was previously developed for teaching computer organization and operating systems [4]. This integration allows student processor designs to access a simulated physical memory, video, interrupt controller, and CD drive; students can even design PC-compatible peripherals. It encourages users to design at a higher abstraction level than typical digital circuit simulators: registers replace flip-flops, ALUs replace gates, and all storage units are clocked synchronously. The simulator includes a Control Unit Builder that allows users the option of making microprograms for their datapath. Also included is a "wizard" that takes an instruction set from the user, suggests an encoding, and creates a simple template processor. This simulator may be run as browser applet or freely downloaded as a stand-alone Java utility from our website: *http://blackware.org.*

Accompanying the simulator is an extensive tutorial intended for undergraduate students taking a computer architecture course. The tutorial teaches students to use the simulator to construct simple logic circuits, and builds up to a pipelined RISC processor with hazard detection. The authors conducted the tutorial with computer science students at their own university and computer engineering students at a different university, and most students successfully designed and simulated the pipelined processor.

We mentioned an initial prototype of our hardware simulator in our earlier paper [4], as a component in our full

PC emulator. This paper describes the hardware simulator, which we have greatly expanded, in far more depth. We provide examples of sample designs and labs using the simulator, and discuss the tutorial and the student experiences completing it.

2. RELATED WORK

Many excellent hardware simulators and tools have been developed for teaching digital logic and computer hardware, and a number of them are freely available and widely used. Our simulator borrows ideas from several of them, and is targeted specifically for an undergraduate computer organization audience with only basic knowledge of programming. The following open-source tools greatly influenced our work:

- Logisim [6]: A GUI-based digital design tool intended for teaching digital logic. Like Logicworks and PSpice, it allows the user to lay out digital blocks on a grid and wire them together. Based on student feedback, we have given our datapath builder a similar look and feel.
- Simplescalar [7]: One of the more widely used tools for academic research. Simplescalar models a complete out-of-order pipeline and gives realistic performance estimates. However, as it is not GUI-based and requires the user to understand and modify source code, it is not appropriate for most undergraduate classes. Among our design goals is to allow advanced students to make processor models of similar complexity to Simplescalar, but within an entirely GUI environment.
- Procsim [10]: Provides a GUI specifically for beginners to design and simulate CPUs. Though somewhat underpowered, it has an attractive user interface, and is the closest example to the system we are designing and the target student userbase.
- Any number of Verilog and VHDL compilers, such as Icarus [18]: The user writes a hardware model in a C-like descriptor language, which can then be simulated or compiled to run on actual hardware. Our simulator saves user work in an XML format that is similar to (and potentially compilable into) HDL.
- Java PC [13]: A full-system PC emulator that runs as an applet and inspired our PC emulator. It is not a teaching tool per-se (its target seems to be DOS game emulation) nor an architecture design tool, but it provides accurate implementations of common PC devices, and its source code tends to be easy to read and modify.

3. SIMULATOR DETAILS

Traditionally, CPUs are designed as two discrete units: a datapath of buses and microarchitecture blocks, and a state-machine-based control unit that issues microcodes to move values through the datapath. While the physical implementations of processors have varied over time, this model is presented in most popular computer organization textbooks [12, 16], and in the experience of the authors, relatively easily grasped by students. Our simulator consequently has two GUIs within the PC emulator, a Datapath Builder and a Control Builder, each with its own frame, data structure,

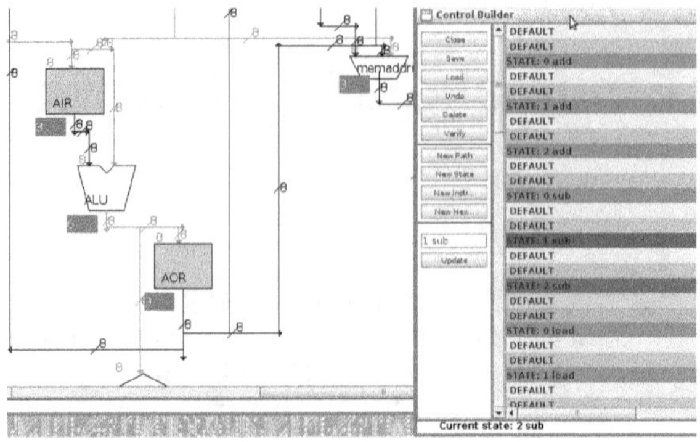

Figure 2: Datapath and Control, Executing a Subtract Instruction

and save file. The Datapath contains the digital circuit blocks and buses. The Control models the control state machine and issues signals to manage data flow and clock registers. This separation of datapath and control differentiates our work from other tools we have encountered; circuit design tools like Logisim model only a datapath, while C or HDL microarchitecture simulators like Simplescalar model only microinstructions. Among the reasons for our approach: With a Control Builder, students may create or modify the instruction set at a high level by adding control states, rather than by rewiring the circuit. Students can be provided with a template datapath by the instructor and develop their own instruction set with the Control Builder. Figure 2 shows a partial screenshot of these two units together. The Control Builder shows at runtime which assembly instruction is running, and how many cycles each instruction takes. At the same time students can see (and modify) the data values moving through the datapath.

Running a hardware simulation normally takes four steps: 1) opening the PC emulator, 2) creating or loading a datapath with the Datapath Builder, 3) creating or loading a control with the Control Builder, 4) pressing "Simulate", which simulates the design and allows the user to see it run. The Control Builder step, however, is optional; if the user skips it a control unit is automatically generated. This allows students to learn digital logic design with the Datapath Builder before they learn about control states. Once simulation starts it runs within the PC emulator as a "custom processor", sharing the same devices as the x86 processor. Port number FF, unused in PCs, mediates between the processors: a 0 written to that port enables the x86 processor and disables the custom processor, a 1 enables the custom and disables the x86, and a 2 enables them both to run simultaneously. In this way, the simulated design can function within the computer as a peripheral or a co-processor: an x86 program can voluntarily pass control to the simulated processor, which can in turn return to the x86. Figure 1 shows how the hardware simulator is integrated – at the same time the user can see the datapath, the contents of physical memory, and peripherals such as the system timer.

3.1 Datapath Builder

Figure 3 shows a screenshot of the Datapath Builder window. The Datapath Builder's look and feel is patterned after other GUI logic circuit building tools, such as Logisim, but is intended specifically for microarchitecture design. Like sim-

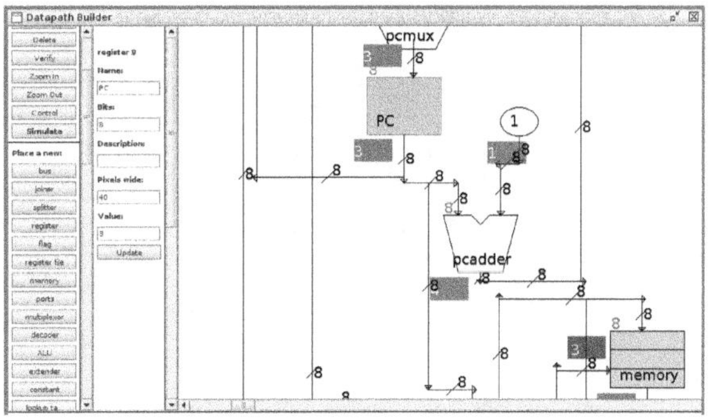

Figure 3: Datapath Builder

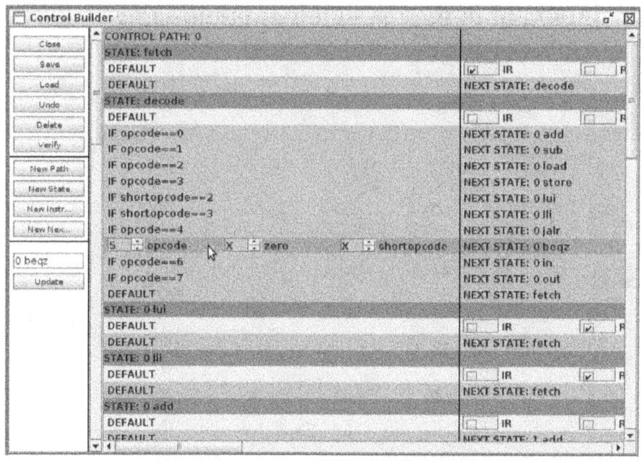

Figure 4: Control Builder

ilar tools, the user places component blocks and draws buses between them. The 33 components that are modeled include standard combinational blocks, like NAND and XOR gates, adders, shifters, and comparators. Electrical components, such as pull-up resistors or transistors, are not included so as to keep the interface entirely digital. Buses, by design, take the same number of bits as the block sourcing them, and must be sourced by only one component.

Several components are handled in a unique way to take advantage of the control unit. Registers, with a single multi-bit input and output, and register files are the only sequential blocks. Registers are synchronized with the system clock; they do not have a clock input but rather an enable/disable input that determines whether a value is stored on the next processor cycle. A register's enable input can be connected to a 1-bit bus within the datapath, but by default it is sourced by the control unit, and is enabled only if the current microinstruction tells the register to receive data. Likewise multiplexors have an optional selector input in the datapath, and are controlled from the control unit by default. An ALU block combines the functions of all of the logic and arithmetic blocks, and its operation is also specified by the control microinstruction. Control-input blocks pass data values to the control unit to allow for conditional control statements. These are the main components: our template processors are almost entirely designed from registers, multiplexors, ALUs, and control-inputs.

A few additional components interface with the computer simulator. A memory block and a port block act and appear as register files, but connect to physical memory and the I/O ports, respectively. Interrupt pins allow the datapath to respond to hardware interrupts and pass exceptions to the interrupt controller.

Users can also create datapath modules. A module component can be created from a datapath and control and is packaged as a single block, to allow custom components and abstraction. When simulation is started, each module instance is loaded as a separate device within the simulator and runs in parallel.

The Datapath Builder, in addition to the standard block placing and manipulation operations, can validate, save, and load designs. The validation tool is run before the datapath is simulated. It searches for misconnected blocks, unsourced buses, and other errors, selects the erroneous blocks so they can be easily deleted, and prints error messages next to the blocks. A datapath can be saved and reloaded as an XML file. An advanced user can edit the XML to expand the datapath.

3.2 Control Builder

Figure 4 shows the Control Builder and its unique interface. The Control Builder lets users design one or more control unit state machines for a datapath. The Control Builder depicts the state machine as a table of color-coded rows. At the top level are Control Path rows (purple), each path a separate state machine running in parallel. These allow for pipelining and parallel execution. Within each Control Path are one or more State rows (blue), corresponding to a processor cycle. State transitions are synchronized with the system clock, with register clocking occurring only on state transitions. Within the state are one or more Microcode rows (yellow) and Next State rows (green). A Microcode row allows the user to set multiplexors and ALUs during the cycle, and specify which registers will be clocked at the cycle's end. Mux and register controls appear as check boxes and selection boxes, and are automatically generated based from the corresponding datapath. A Next State row chooses the state, within the control path, that will run on the next cycle.

Both Microcode rows and Next State rows can be absolute or conditional. Each control input block in the datapath appears as a selection box on the left side of the row, and allows the user to make the row conditional, by selecting a value that must be present at that control input for that row to run. A row will be active only if all the control inputs selections are satisfied, or are set to X (don't care). A state may have more than one Microcode or Next State row with a different set of conditions, much like a series of "if/else-if" statements, and when the row is not selected by the user the corresponding if-statement is shown instead of the control input boxes.

On the right side of a Microcode row is a selection box for each multiplexor and ALU, and a checkbox for each register. These boxes allow the user to choose, for that state, which mux input line is routed to the output, and which registers will store values. The user can manually enter this information. Alternatively, the user can press a "Trace" button, and draw a path from a source register to a destination. If the path is valid, a microinstruction is generated, and the boxes are filled automatically. Afterwards, if the row is selected at runtime, the path will be highlighted on the datapath.

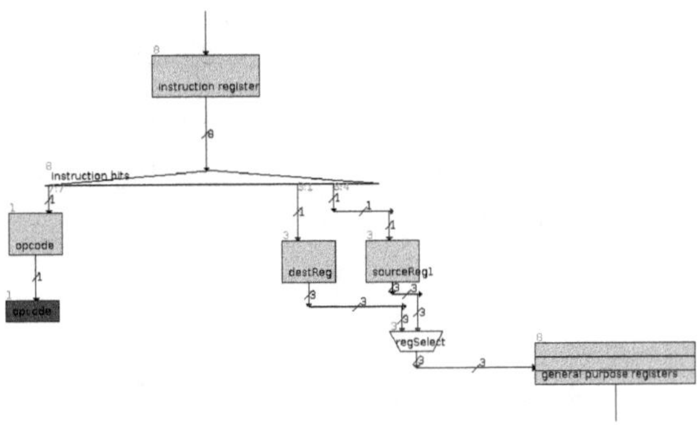

Figure 5: Autogenerated Decode Stage with 2 instructions, 2 operands

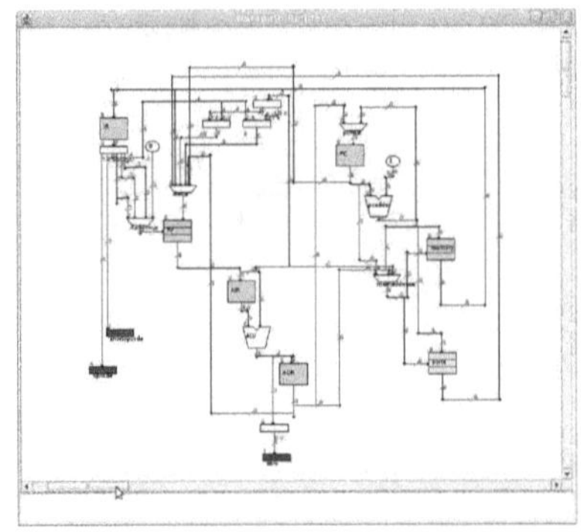

Figure 6: RISC Processor Datapath

Part of the purpose to this layout is to show the user how the control unit transforms easily to a truth table. Each table entry contains bits specifying the next state number, mux, ALU, and register clocking codes. The table is in turn indexed by the current state and control input blocks.

Like the Datapath Builder, the Control Builder can save the design and reload it from an XML file. The XML file can be easily modified.

It is not strictly necessary that the user create a control unit. If a simulation is started without a control, a simple control unit is automatically generated. This unit consists of one path, one state, and a microcode line that enables every register. This allows students to learn logic design with the Datapath Builder and build purely combinational circuits without needing to understand control units.

3.3 Processor Wizard

The Processor Wizard is a unit intended to help students get started on a processor. It asks the user a series of questions and generates a datapath and control from a template. For a simple instruction set, the processor wizard can create an instruction encoding, a complete datapath, and all of the necessary control paths and states. To complete the processor, the user must only trace the microinstructions for each state.

The unit starts by prompting the user to enter the number of address bits and the number of instruction bits, whereupon it constructs an instruction fetch stage with a program counter, instruction register, and link to physical memory. It then prompts the user to enter a set of assembly instructions, each instruction containing an opcode and up to three operand fields. The user may choose up to five addressing modes (register direct, indirect, immediate, indirect with displacement, PC with displacement) and three different registers (two sources and a destination). The unit will attempt to create an instruction encoding that handles each instruction within the bit constraints. If successful, it generates the datapath for a decode stage and, optionally, an execute stage. If the user selects, it will generate a control template consisting of a fetch state, an decode state, and one execute state for each opcode. Empty microcode lines are given, leaving the user responsible for implementing the instructions.

4. TUTORIAL EXAMPLES

We developed a tutorial intended for undergraduate students in a computer architecture class. The tutorial assumes that the students have had exposure to digital design and assembly programming, and are familiar with the basic concepts of an instruction set, datapath, control, and in-order pipelining. The tutorial has four parts. An introductory lab teaches how to use the simulator, and guides the student through making a simple counter and a programmable adder. In subsequent labs, students build the control for a datapath given to them, make a 4-stage pipeline for that processor, and detect and remove pipeline hazards to improve performance.

4.1 RISC Processor

Figure 6 shows the complete datapath for a 10-instruction Turing complete RISC processor. Students are given the datapath and the instruction encodings, and must write the control unit. A short machine code program that adds a series of numbers is given as verification, which the students load into the bottom of the PC emulator's physical memory. Figure 4 shows part of the finished control unit. Because each instruction has a fetch, decode, and one or more execute states, students can measure the processor's cycles-per-instruction performance.

4.2 RISC with pipelining

In the next step, students devise a four stage in-order pipeline consisting of fetch, decode, execute, and writeback stages, as partially shown in Figure 4.2 . Students must create both the datapath and the control. By following the tutorial, the control for this pipeline will have four Control Paths with one State per path, allowing for a theoretical average performance of one instruction per cycle. Because of pipeline hazards, the sample program will not achieve this performance. To verify this step in the presence of hazards, students are instructed to put two NOP instructions after every read-after-write hazard, and three after every branch. If completed correctly, students will see approximately the same instruction-per-cycle performance when running the sample program as they did with the first processor, despite the pipeline.

4.3 RISC with pipelining and hazard detection

In the final tutorial step, students build additional units to detect read-after-write hazards and implement data forwarding, and squash pipeline stages when a branch instruction occurs. This involves upgrading the datapath to add

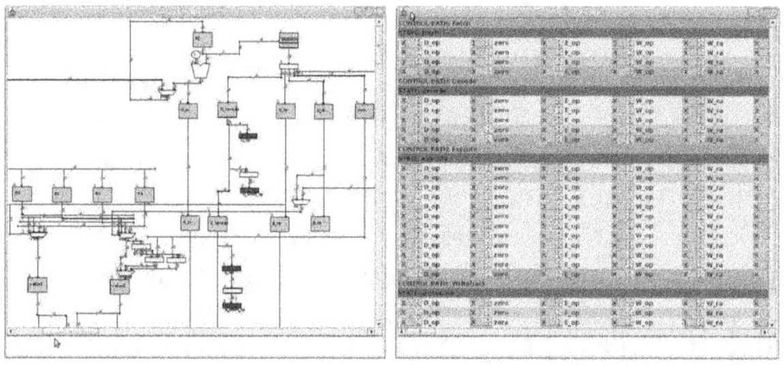

Figure 7: Pipelined RISC Processor, Fetch and Decode Stages

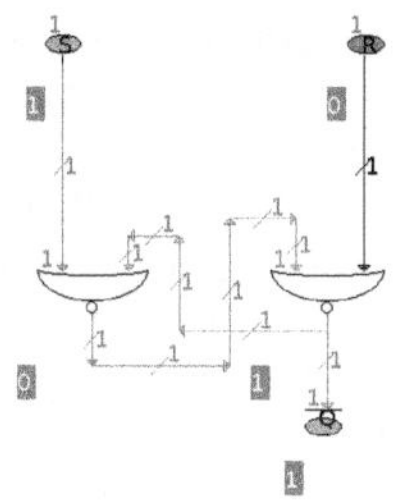

Figure 8: RS Flip Flop

a hazard detection unit. On completion, students can run the original program without any NOPs added, and see a significant performance improvement.

5. OTHER DESIGNS

The following designs demonstrate additional ways the simulator can be used in the classroom.

- Digital logic design

  Although the focus of the hardware simulator is processor architecture, it can nevertheless teach the fundamentals of digital logic design. Figure 8 shows a basic RS flip flop with input and output pins. When the user clicks on the appropriate input pin, the flip flop changes state.

- Z-80

  Figure 9 shows the datapath of a Z-80 processor, and demonstrates that a real-world instruction set can be implemented in the simulator. Despite performing very slowly – at about 2 seconds per cycle – it was able to correctly execute part of the Nintendo Gameboy BIOS [15].

- Custom Peripherals

  Because the tool is embedded within a PC emulator, connects to physical memory and I/O ports, and can be run from the x86 processor, it can be used to design peripheral device controllers. As a proof of concept, Figure 10 shows the datapath and control for a simple "Print-to-Screen" DMA. When activated, it copies an ASCII text string from memory address 0 to video memory so that it displays at the top left of the screen.

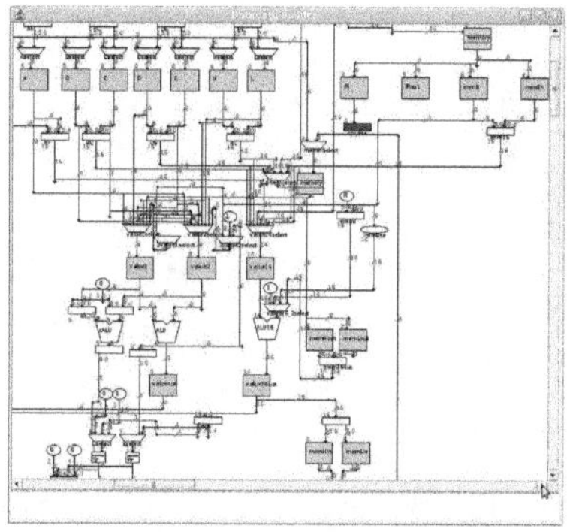

Figure 9: Z-80 Processor

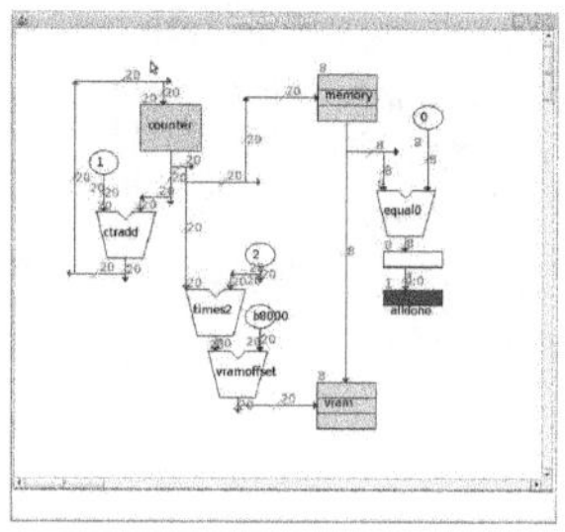

Figure 10: Print-to-Screen Device

6. STUDENT EXPERIENCES

Undergraduate students have been continuously involved in the design process from the conception of the project to the present. Students have been given a variety of design projects using the simulator, in some cases redoing projects as the tool has been revised, and have been asked to keep journals on their experience. The user interface has been dramatically improved in response to this feedback. The following are examples of how student experiences have shaped the tool.

The RISC tutorial was tested as part of a Computer Architecture course for electrical and computer engineering majors at the University of Maryland, College Park. The tutorial was given to a class of 60 students at about 10 weeks into the 15 week semester, after the lectures on pipelining were completed. Students were given homework credit for completing labs 1 and 2 of the tutorial. Part 3, as well as the introductory part, were optional. All students completed the tutorial in groups of 2, for 30 teams total. Of these, all 30 teams successfully completed the introductory lab and lab 1 (the RISC control). 22 teams successfully completed lab 2 (the pipelined processor). Because lab 3 (hazard detection) was optional, only 3 teams attempted it; of these, 2 teams completed it successfully.

Students reported that their biggest difficulty was learning the Datapath Builder's then-cumbersome user interface. Relatively fewer students had trouble with the Control Builder. Most students reported their greatest struggle was in the introductory lab with the mechanics of placing and manipulating components. Zooming, verification, bus placing, an undo command, and shortcut keys were the most requested additions, and have now been added.

Two computer science students at American University, neither of whom had taken computer organization, attempted

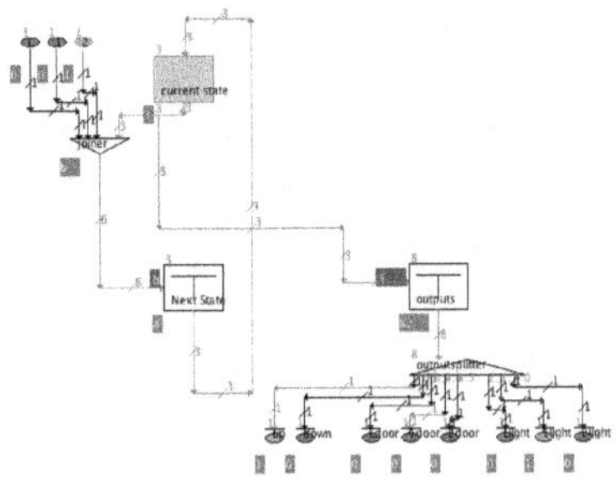

Figure 11: Student elevator controller

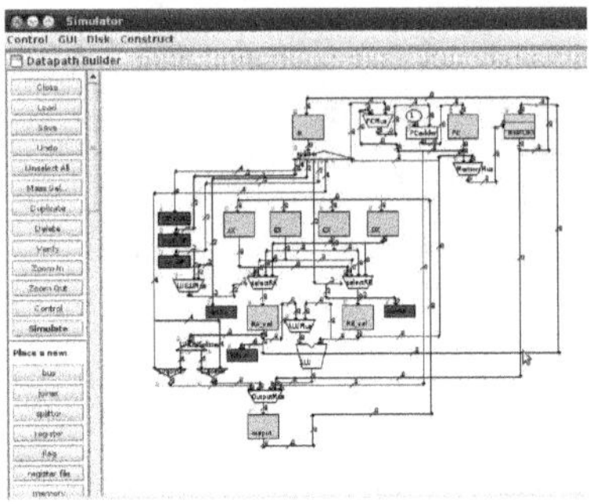

Figure 12: Student processor submission

the RISC tutorial. Unlike the computer engineering students, neither had prior exposure to digital logic, and this proved to be the main stumbling block. In response to their suggestions, elements from circuit simulators were added so that the students could learn digital logic, including gates, lookup tables, and input/output pins.

A computer science student at American University was assigned the task of building an ARM processor emulator. The student initially developed an ARM7-TDMI instruction set emulator in Python, and then designed the microarchitecture for it on the simulator. With the student's assistance, modules and interrupt support were added, bus manipulation was simplified, and the Processor Wizard was developed. The student found the Control Builder to be the most intuitive part because it most resembled a higher-level language.

Most recently, the simulator was used throughout a computer organization course at American University to teach digital design, instruction set encoding, and processor architecture to sophomore-level computer science students. Students used it to learn finite state machine circuits by designing an elevator controller and a traffic light controller, and then simulated their own RISC processor. Figures 11, 12 show examples of student submissions (used with permission). Of 28 students, all of them successfully completed the digital controller projects and 21 simulated a working processor. Students kept journals during the semester and listed their frustrations when using the simulator and recommendations for improvement.

7. ACKNOWLEDGMENTS

This work was made possible by NSF CCLI/TUES grant 0941057. The author would additionally like to thank Dr. Manoj Franklin for trying the tutorial in his class.

8. REFERENCES

[1] M. Becvar. Teaching Basics of Instruction Pipelining with HDLDLX. Proc. 2004 workshop on Comp. arch. ed., held in conjunction with the 31st International Symposium on Computer Architecture, 2004.

[2] A. Beg, W. Ibrahim. PerfPred: A Web-Based Tool for Exploring Computer Architecture Design Space. Computer Applications in Engineering Education, Wiley Periodicals, Inc. 2009.

[3] Bem, E., Petelczyc, L. MiniMIPS:Âăa simulation project for the computer architecture laboratory. Proceedings of the 34th Technical Symposium on Computer Science Education, 2003.

[4] Black, M., Komala, P. A Full System x86 Simulator for Teaching Computer Organization. Proceedings of the 34th Technical Symposium on Computer Science Education, 2011.

[5] Branovic, R. Giorgi, E Martinelli WebMIPS: a new web-based MIPS simulation environment for computer architecture education. Proceedings of the 2004 workshop on Computer architecture, 2004.

[6] C.Burch. A graphical system for logic circuit design and simulation. Journal on Educational Resources in Computing 2:1, 2002, pages 5-16.

[7] D. Burger, T.M. Austin The SimpleScalar Tool Set, Version 2.0. University of Wisconsin-Madison Computer Sciences Department, Technical Report 1342, June, 1997

[8] A Visual Tool to Enhance Comprehension and Design in Micro-processing Systems Department of Electrical and Computer Engineering, University of Manitoba, 2007.

[9] Garcia, Rodriguez, Perez, Garcia. p88110: A Graphical Simulator for Computer Architecture and Organization Courses. IEEE Transactions on Education, May, 2009

[10] Garton, J. 2005. ProcessorSim - a visual MIPS R2000 Processor Simulator. http://jamesgart.com/procsim/

[11] Grunbacher, Khosravipour. WinDLX and MIPSim pipeline simulators for teaching computer architecture, IEEE Symposium on Engineering of Computer-Based Systems, March 1996.

[12] Hennessy and Patterson. Computer Architecture, A Quantitative Analysis, 2nd Edition Morgan Kaufman, 1996.

[13] Java PC http://jpc.sourceforge.net/

[14] J.C. Moure, D.I. Rexachs, E. Luque The KScalar simulator. Journal on Educational Resources in Computing Volume 2, Issue 1 Pages: 73-116 2002.

[15] I.Nazar http://imrannazar.com/GameBoy-Emulation-in-JavaScript

[16] Patterson and Hennessy. Computer Organization and Design, 3rd Edition. Morgan Kaufman, 2005.

[17] C.W. Smullen, T.M. Taha. PSATSim: An Interactive Graphical Superscalar Architecture Simulator for Power and Performance Analysis. 2006 workshop on Computer architecture education

[18] S.Williams. http://iverilog.icarus.com/

[19] G.Wolffe,W.Yurcik,H.Osborne,M.Holliday. Teaching Computer Organization/Architecture with Limited Resources using Simulators. ACM SIGCSE Bulletin Volume 34, Issue 1, Pages 176-180.

Helping Students Understand the Datapath with Simulators and Crazy Models

Michael B. Gousie
Department of Math & Computer Science
Wheaton College
26 E. Main Street
Norton, MA 02766
mgousie@wheatoncollege.edu

James D. Teresco
Department of Computer Science
The College of Saint Rose
432 Western Ave.
Albany, NY 12203
terescoj@strose.edu

ABSTRACT

Undergraduate computer science programs at many small colleges often include only one course focused on hardware. Many important concepts are covered in such a course, including the basics of computer architecture. By the end of such a course, students should have a good understanding of how a binary machine instruction is executed in hardware. Unfortunately, even a simplified diagram of a datapath is often difficult for students to master. We present two approaches that use lab exercises to help to address this problem. In one, students build a working model of the datapath out of ordinary materials; in the other, a software simulator is designed and implemented. These approaches are described and their merits discussed.

Categories and Subject Descriptors

K.3.2 [**Computer and Information Science Education**]: Computer science education; C.0 [**Computer Systems Organization**]: General

Keywords

Computer organization pedagogy, laboratory assignments, modeling computer architecture, simulating computer architecture

1. INTRODUCTION

Many small colleges require and/or offer only one course focused on hardware/computer organization. As such, this course could be the only place students will be exposed to a variety of important topics from circuits and binary representations to assembly language programming. Ultimately, we would like students in such a course to understand how a circuit can be constructed that is capable of executing a machine language program for a (relatively) simple instruction set architecture. This means being able to look at a complex diagram of the datapath and control of an architecture implementation and understand how it can possibly execute machine language programs.

How can we best maximize student understanding of this fundamental but challenging concept, working within the constraints of a semester course? We can present diagrams in class, examine individual components, and show how instructions work their way through the architecture. Students often grasp the concepts abstractly from this approach. However, they are not gaining concrete understanding that would allow them, for example, to be able to complete an exam question that asks what bits are found on each line given a particular binary instruction, or to be able to augment an architecture to implement a new instruction.

Staring at a diagram and/or watching a simulation run can aid in understanding, but not to the level that "getting your hands dirty" and examining the underlying details would permit. Constructing a circuit (*e.g.*, as in [10]) on breadboards, using a logic simulator or even with a hardware definition language, would certainly qualify as getting your hands dirty, but any of these is likely to be too large a project for our context. In the era where many of the instruction set architectures were heavily microcoded, a microcode design project (*e.g.*, [6]) could serve this purpose well. However, many architectures studied in classes today (we use MIPS) do not lend themselves well to a microcoding approach.

We present two approaches to improving the teaching and the student understanding of the single-cycle MIPS datapath, a summary of which is found in Section 2, and described in detail in Patterson & Hennessy [8]. In each case, one or more closed lab sessions are used to provide additional student hands-on experience compared to lecture-only classes. In Gousie's course, developed at Wheaton College, students are given a project to create a simulation of the single-cycle MIPS datapath. The simulation must show the movement of data through the various parts of the hardware for (ideally) an R-format instruction. The novel idea is that the simulation consists of a working model made out of any material *except* the usual datapath diagram(s). Electronic simulations are acceptable if they are sufficiently unique; that is, different from commonly available software.

In Teresco's course, which has been taught at Mount Holyoke College, Rensselaer Polytechnic Institute, and Siena College, students develop their own software simulator for the single-cycle MIPS datapath. Previous class and lab work in this course focuses on both digital logic and MIPS assem-

SIGCSE'13, March 6–9, 2013, Denver, Colorado, USA.

bly language programming leading up to a unit on datapath and control that brings these two extremes together. The goal is to ensure that students understand how the components used in the example datapath can be constructed using the building blocks and techniques they have used to construct similar components using breadboards and/or a logic simulator (such as Logisim [3]). They should also be able to see that while the datapath and control we study only implements a subset of the MIPS instruction set, they understand how they would implement remaining instructions. By developing their own simulator, not just to simulate the effect of MIPS instructions (as done in tools such as [5, 11]), but to simulate them by modeling the underlying datapath and control, they can gain a much deeper insight into how the datapath and control components work together to achieve the desired effect for each instruction.

2. THE SINGLE-CYCLE MIPS DATAPATH

Patterson & Hennessy [8] present the single-cycle datapath (Figure 1) for a subset of 9 MIPS instructions as their introduction to an implementation scheme for a MIPS processor[1]. This representative set of instructions includes load (`lw`) and store (`sw`), 5 arithmetic and logical instructions (`add`, `sub`, `and`, `or`, and `slt`), and a conditional (`beq`) and an unconditional (`j`) branch. This includes 5 R-format instructions, which take the form

op	rs	rt	rd	shmat	funct
6 bits	5 bits	5 bits	5 bits	5 bits	6 bits

3 I-format instructions, which take the form

op	rs	rt	address
6 bits	5 bits	5 bits	16 bits

and one J-format instruction, which takes the form

op	address
6 bits	26 bits

Instructions outside the subset require similar implementation techniques and are omitted for simplicity. Some of these, such as immediate mode arithmetic operators and bit shifts, are later considered on homework or exam questions that ask students to show how they would augment the architecture to implement these instructions.

3. TWO WAYS TO AID UNDERSTANDING OF THE DATAPATH

Of course, there are many approaches to presenting the datapath. While students have seen and should be able to understand every component in the diagram in Figure 1 by the time they encounter it, its complexity is intimidating if not overwhelming for many students. In our experience, students have tremendous difficulty understanding the way data flows from an instruction through the various hardware devices to finally achieve a (partial) result. We have found that building up the datapath in parts, as is done in [8] is not effective, nor is tracing the datapath in lecture. Nevertheless, a Google search will show that this is the approach that is taken by many instructors. Other authors of similar textbooks include datapath simulators, such as [7]. In Gousie's

[1]This figure was published in [8] on Page 329, Copyright Elsevier (2009). Used with permission.

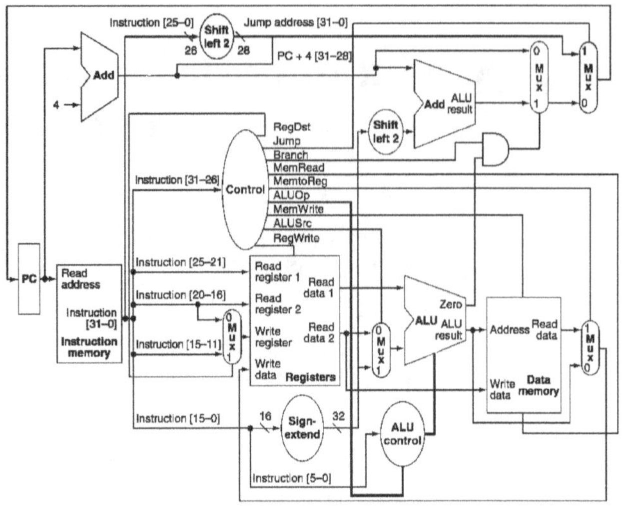

Figure 1: The single-cycle MIPS datapath of [8].

course, the Knob & Switch computer [2] has been used for many years; students seem to understand the broader workings of the hardware but then still can not show the value of individual bits on a given line in a comprehensive datapath diagram. What follows is not meant to supplant current best practices, but rather to add a hands-on layer to augment what is currently being taught.

3.1 Computer Organization Model Expo

Gousie's course includes a lab that attempts to teach the datapath using a new method called the Comp Org *Crazy* Model Expo. The intent of this lab is to have student groups present a working model showing how data flows through the CPU for a given R-format instruction.

3.1.1 Model Expo Rules

Students are given an assignment with the following parameters:

1. Students can form groups of up to three.
2. Given an R-format instruction, the group must build a model simulating the flow of data through the CPU, using whatever material that is convenient. Normally, this means that the model will be made of physical materials. Crazy ideas are encouraged, as long as the resulting model adequately shows the datapath.
3. A formal poster must be created that explains the workings of the model in the context of one of the diagrams from Patterson & Hennessy.
4. The group must present the model in no more than ten minutes at the Comp Org *Crazy* Model Expo. The event takes place during one of the regularly scheduled lab sessions.

Before embarking on the project, students must gain approval of the topic from the instructor; that is, which R-format instruction they are going to simulate so that multiple groups do not simulate the same instruction. Students can also amend the rules somewhat through negotiation; for

Figure 2: The Rube Goldberg contraption that simulates the jump instruction.

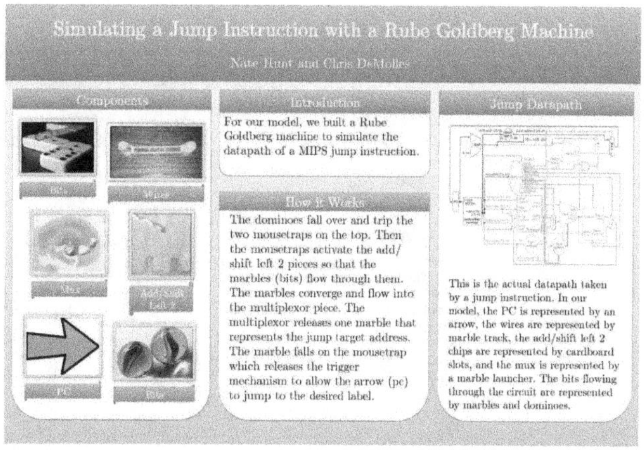

Figure 3: Poster that explains the workings of the Rube Goldberg contraption.

example, one group used Alice for the simulation, which obviously is not a physical model, and another group used a J-format instruction.

The idea behind this project is that students must think carefully about how the datapath actually works so that they can translate their understanding to some sort of physical device that models how the electrons (bits) are moving through the hardware. By leaving the type of materials completely open (indeed, crazy is encouraged), and stressing that this should be a fun and not arduous exercise (as well as promising pizza during the actual lab), most students seem to take on the challenge with aplomb.

The class during the spring of 2012 had 23 students, divided into 10 groups. Many groups simulated the datapath in somewhat predictable ways. For example, several groups used water (similar to [1]) or marbles and tubing to simulate data flowing through components. One group built a small cardboard town with roads; the flow of data was simulated by cars driving through the town. Three of the more successful and original models/presentations are described in the following sections.

3.1.2 Model One: Rube Goldberg Device

In this model, a working machine made of dowels, string, pulleys, and other assorted parts (see Figure 2), showed how the MIPS jump instruction (`j`) works. The user triggers the Instruction Decode phase by touching the first of a series of dominoes; these fall until the shift left component is hit. Marbles represent a subsequent portion of the datapath; these flow until an arrow representing the instruction address is moved from its initial position signifying the original instruction to its new position. This, then, completes the instruction. Figure 3 shows the poster that accompanied the project.

3.1.3 Model Two: R-Format Carnage

Alice [9] was used as a way to quickly build a model of the datapath. The various hardware parts were modeled as buildings in a city. A suite of avatars represent the portions of instructions or data moving about the city between various buildings. In this case, the R-format instructions were modeled. Running the simulation for the MIPS instruction `add $t0, $t1, $t2` results in the actions shown below. Only the data portions are covered here; see Figure 4 for information on all parts of the datapath.

1. An airplane is sent to City Hall (instruction memory) to fetch the instruction.

2. The 32-bit instruction is split into its constituent parts. Two Eskimos represent the address of the two read registers (`$t1` and `$t2`), Prince Charming represents the address of the write register (`$t0`), a toy soldier represents the funct code, and a teacher represents the opcode. Parts that are not used in the instruction (for example, the shamt code) die off.

3. The two Eskimos (`$t1` and `$t2`) move to the register file (a townhouse) and transform into a shark and penguin (two data values).

4. The shark and penguin (two data values) move to the ALU (a farmhouse), where the sum is computed and stored in a knight.

5. The knight moves to the register file (townhouse) and its data is written into the write register addressed by Prince Charming (`$t0`; see Step 1) completing the instruction.

Note that the above describes only the movement of data; the control lines are also modeled, and work similarly. When the program runs, many avatars, representing the data and the control signals, are moving simultaneously, giving the impression that there is chaos. However, the instructions work themselves out as expected.

Although this implementation may seem somewhat silly, the students working on the project had fun, as did those watching the demo. More importantly, the students must have a good understanding of the underlying mechanism of the datapath in order to implement the program.

3.1.4 Model Three: Sonification of the Datapath

In this project, the flow of binary instructions through the datapath is represented as short duration "musical" structures by means of a simple parameter mapping scheme. The datapath is divided into segments that roughly correspond to the stages of a pipeline. Each segment is divided into n

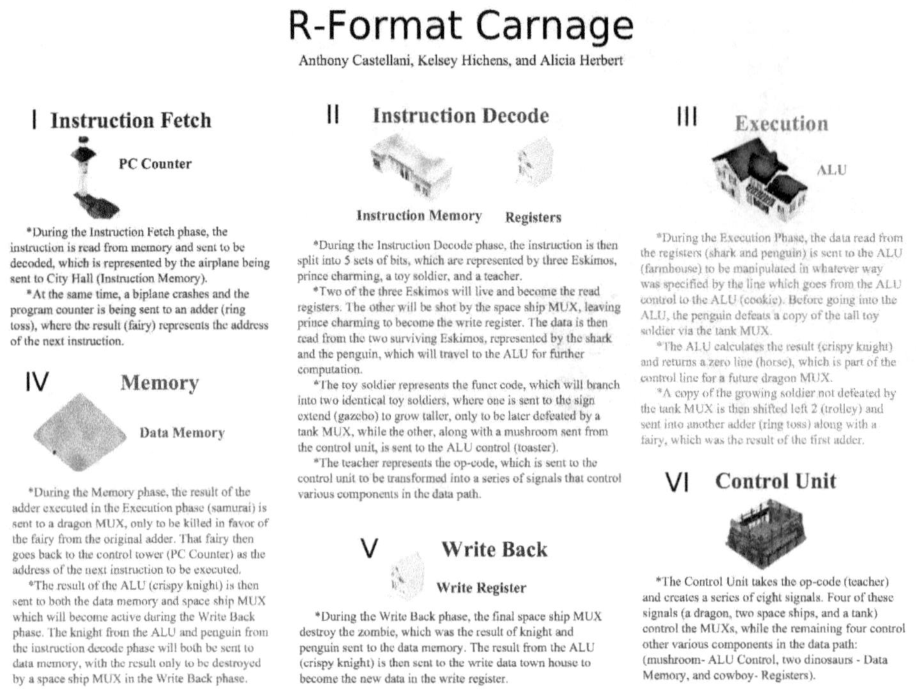

Figure 4: Poster showing the datapath components simulated in Alice.

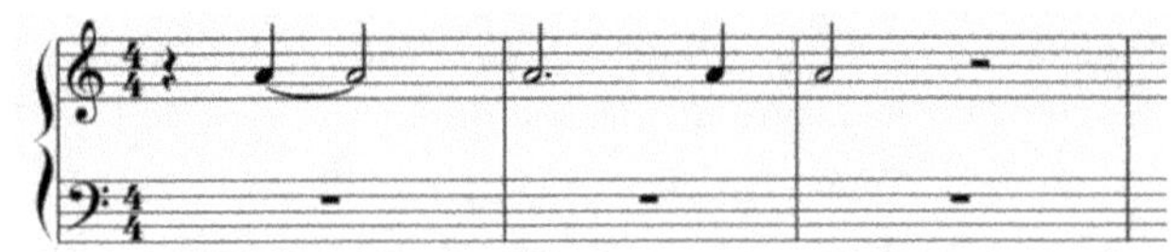

Figure 5: Mapping the binary string 0100100110 to a rhythm.

quarter notes, where n is the maximum number of bits in a binary string passing through that segment. The binary string is mapped to a rhythm in which a one represents the beginning of a note and a zero represents a rest if it is not preceded by any ones in its segment; otherwise, a zero sustains the last note that was played. Figure 5 shows an example of rhythmic mapping.

With a rhythm established, a pitch must be mapped from the data lines. The pitch value of a note is a function of the data line its corresponding binary string is passing through. The individual bits within a binary string together form a chord for that segment.

The program is given a MIPS instruction which is then decoded into its constituent binary strings. These strings are mapped to rhythm and pitch, and the corresponding chords are played. If a pipeline is being simulated, multiple chords will be played for each segment. Thus, choosing the notes for each data line was done so as to produce a pleasing combination of chords when played simultaneously.

3.1.5 *Results*

Every group presented an acceptable model of a datapath (or approved component). As shown in the previous section, several of the projects were quite novel and showed particular ingenuity. Each group prepared a poster of varying quality; this warrants better specifications the next time the project is assigned. Anecdotally, on the final exam that included a major question regarding the datapath, the scores were better than similar final exams (same instructor) in the previous two iterations of the course. Specifically, the mean was 75 with a median of 73 this year, compared to 67/67 and 69/70 in the previous iterations. Furthermore, the average score was a very good 12.3/14 (88%) on the datapath question that typically is problematic for many students. Perhaps of more significance was that the students really took to the project and were interested in not only their own models but their classmates' as well.

3.2 Software Simulation of the Datapath

The implementation of a software simulation of the MIPS datapath and control in Figure 1 serves as a final lab exercise and project for Teresco's course. It is one thing to use an existing simulator, but quite another to have to understand it to the level of detail required to write your own simulator.

3.2.1 *Software Simulation Assignment*

The single-cycle simulator the students are required to implement consists of a number of components.

- A command-line parameter specifies a memory file,

```
0x8c010024 ! 0: lw %1 36(%0) a
0x8c020028 ! 4: lw %2 40(%0) b
0x8c03002c ! 8: lw %3 44(%0) 1
0x00002020 ! 12: add %4 %0 %0 prod = 0
0x00822020 ! 16: add %4 %4 %2 prod += b
0x00230822 ! 20: sub %1 %1 %3 a--
0x10200001 ! 24: beq 1 %1 %0
0x08000004 ! 28: j 16
0xffffffff ! 32: halt
0x00000003 ! 36: a
0x00000004 ! 40: b
0x00000001 ! 44: 1
```

Figure 6: A sample memory file specifying a program to perform multiplication by repeated addition. Only the hexadecimal numbers are relevant – the remainder of each line is treated as a comment by the simulator.

which is simply a list of 32-bit hexadecimal values that are placed into the simulation's memory component. These values may be treated as instructions or as data.

For example, the memory file in Figure 6 loads a program that multiplies two numbers `a` (3, from memory location 36), and `b` (4, from 40), using repeated addition, accumulating the result in register %4.

- A simple command line interface is used to control the simulation. This includes commands to execute one or more instructions from memory, print the contents of the registers or a range of memory locations, print the control line values for the current instruction, turn on a debug mode, and quit the simulation. The command-line parser is usually provided in starter code to keep the project more manageable.
- The simulator needs to be able to break down a MIPS instruction into the fields that will be used to drive the simulation of the instruction. In a previous lab assignment, students were required to read in a sequence of MIPS machine instructions, print out the opcode, instruction format, and value of each relevant field for that instruction format.
- The values of each control line in the datapath are computed by a function which shares that control line's name, *e.g.*, the *MemRead* control line's value is obtained as needed (by the data memory unit) by calling the `MemRead()` function in the control unit module. The only permitted use of the opcode field of the instruction is to pass it as a parameter to the control unit module.

The heart of the simulator is the simulation of a single instruction. The simulator models physical components as high-level language constructs. Memory and register components become variables or arrays, multiplexers become conditional statements, and data and control lines become variables.

Each component is then simulated, using only the information that would be available to that component in the circuit, to produce its output or change its state. For example, the instruction memory uses the value presented to it from the program counter, and produces the 32-bit instruction at that location on its output (which becomes a variable, usually named `ir` for the instruction register). Meanwhile, the program counter value is also passed to the adder that is always adding 4 to its input, producing the address of the next instruction that will eventually make its way back into the program counter should that value not be replaced by a branch target later in the instruction simulation. Concurrency is not simulated directly, but part of the exercise is to think carefully about what order things happen in the datapath as an instruction is executed. Students also are forced to realize that these two components are combinational, and will continue to produce their current output values so long as the program counter's value does not change. And they know that will not happen until the final phase of the instruction. This also forces students to realize that the circuit is always computing useless information concurrently with useful information. For example, an arithmetic instruction will never make use of the branch target or jump target ALU results, but those values are computed nonetheless.

The next step is the essential one to implementing a simulation that is true to the datapath. Parts of the instruction (the bit fields determined by the instruction formats) are delivered to several components directly. The opcode is sent only to the control unit, from which all of the control line values can be computed. This simulator does print out the name of the instruction based on the opcode, but this is not used to drive the simulation in any way other than to compute control line values in the control unit. That is, nowhere in the simulation outside of the control unit should there be a place where decisions are made based on opcode. All other decisions are made based on the control line values as computed by the main control or the ALU control.

To ensure that the simulation accurately models the circuit, a debug mode is required. In debug mode, each component reports on its function as the instruction works its way through the circuit. For example, Figure 7 shows what the debug output for the first instruction from the example in Figure 6 above (a memory read, `lw`) might look like. Each component's action is shown, even those whose actions end up not being used by the instruction. Even the ALU, where students may be tempted to implement a subtract instruction using subtraction, the action is modeled as an addition with the subtrahend negated, as this is how the ALU would be implemented in hardware.

Students are encouraged to develop their simulators in C, as one of the goals of the course is to introduce them to that language, but some choose to use Java or another language they know well. We use a standard high-level language without a library like SystemC [4], as the architecture we simulate is simple enough that the additional cost of learning the library is likely more significant than any potential savings in implementation time.

In addition to the simulator, students are required to provide a new MIPS machine code program along the lines of the one shown in Figure 6 to perform some simple but hopefully interesting computation. This helps to reinforce their understanding of the relationships among the MIPS assembly instructions they wish to use, the MIPS machine instructions that represent them, and the actions of the circuit to execute the instructions.

Finally, students are required to describe in detail how the architecture and their simulator would need to be modified

```
Executing instruction: 0x8c010024
op=0x23/35, format=I, rs=0x00/0,
   rt=0x01/1, imm=0x0024/36
PC+4: 0x00000004
Sign Extend: 0x00000024
ReadReg 1: R[0]=0x00000000
ReadReg 2: R[1]=0x00000000
Jump address: 0x00040090
ALU input MUX (from sign extend): 0x00000024
Branch offset: 0x00000090
ALU input A not inverted: 0x00000000
ALU input B not negated: 0x00000024
ALU result (ADD): 0x00000024, Zero=0
Read from memory at 0x00000024, value 0x00000003
Branch target: 0x00000094
Branch selection MUX not taking branch: 0x00000004
Write reg number: 0x01
Write reg data from memory: 0x00000003
New PC no jump: 0x00000004
Write reg: 0x00000003 to R[1]
```

Figure 7: Debug mode output for the execution of the first `lw` instruction in the program in Figure 6.

to implement some of the instructions which are not part of the required MIPS subset. For bonus points, they can augment their simulator to implement those instructions and provide example programs to demonstrate them.

3.2.2 Results

The project has successfully forced students to think carefully about how each component in the datapath works, what information it has available as input, and what it produces as output. Considering each in isolation (as a small segment of code) and planning the simulation order to ensure proper interaction of components is an intense and fairly painful process for the students, not to mention the instructor who has a class full of students inside and outside his office for the duration of the project.

While there is no meaningful way to compare students who have completed the project with those who have not (the course is typically taught to one section of students once per year), we can examine some grading information. In the most recent course which used this project (Fall 2011), 20 of the 23 students who were still actively engaged in the course submitted a substantially complete simulator. The others were in group of 3 that made an honest effort but continued to have fundamental misunderstandings and did not ask for help until it was too late. The final exam question that was directly related to the project was very successful. The overall score on the question was 84%, and over 90% if we remove the scores of those students who did not complete the project.

The most encouraging results from the project are also those which are harder to quantify. Students coming for help regularly ask the right questions. With many of them, there is that moment when it clicks – they not only understand how they need to implement the simulator, but the datapath diagram and the whole concept of a circuit running a program suddenly makes sense. Also, when class discussion turned to the more complex pipelined datapath, it was clear that their extensive experience with the single-cycle datapath helped them to understand pipelining.

4. CONCLUSION AND FUTURE WORK

We have presented two approaches to laboratory projects that help students grasp the workings of the datapath. In one approach, students build a physical device that simulates the flow of information from one component to another until a particular instruction is completed. Students applauded the lab and anecdotal evidence showed that exam scores improved. The second approach requires students to understand how the datapath circuit executes an instruction by simulating the low-level hardware components in software.

It is extremely difficult to test the efficacy of such labs, making it dangerous to draw any firm conclusions. However, we believe that such hands-on projects help students learn, as has been shown in other areas in general. At the very least, the material is presented in a fresh way that students enjoy much more than a traditional lecture. We will continue our work on these labs and attempt to add more hands-on experiences in the computer organization courses.

5. REFERENCES

[1] D. Berque, I. Serlin, and A. Vlahov. A brief water excursion: introducing computer organization students to a water driven 1-bit half-adder. *SIGCSE Bull.*, 36(2):52–56, June 2004.

[2] G. Braught. Computer organization in the breadth-first course. *J. Comput. Sci. Coll.*, 16(4):182–195, 2001.

[3] C. Burch. Logisim: A graphical system for logic circuit design and simulation. *J. Educ. Resour. Comput.*, 2(1):5–16, 2002.

[4] E. Harcourt. Teaching computer organization and architecture using SystemC. *J. Comput. Sci. Coll.*, 21(2):27–39, Dec. 2005.

[5] J. Larus. 2012. SPIM: A MIPS32 simulator. Retrieved September 6, 2012 from `http://sourceforge.net/projects/spimsimulator/`.

[6] D. Magagnosc. Simulation in computer organization: a goals based study. *SIGCSE Bull.*, 26(1):178–182, Mar. 1994.

[7] L. Null and J. Lobur. MarieSim: The MARIE computer simulator. *J. Educ. Resour. Comput.*, 3(2):1–29, June 2003.

[8] D. A. Patterson and J. L. Hennessy. *Computer Organization and Design: The Hardware/Software Interface.* Morgan Kaufmann, 2009.

[9] R. Pausch, T. Burnette, A. Capehart, M. Conway, D. Cosgrove, R. DeLine, J. Durbin, R. Gossweiler, S. Koga, and J. White. Alice: Rapid prototyping system for virtual reality. *IEEE Computer Graphics and Applications*, 15(3):8–11, 1995.

[10] J. Phillips. Simulation of a simple CPU design and its use as an instructional tool in a computer organization course. *J. Comput. Sci. Coll.*, 22(6):140–146, June 2007.

[11] K. Vollmar and P. Sanderson. MARS: an education-oriented MIPS assembly language simulator. *SIGCSE Bull.*, 38(1):239–243, Mar. 2006.

Step-by-Step Design and Simulation of a Simple CPU Architecture

Derek C. Schuurman
Redeemer University College
777 Garner Road East
Ancaster, Ontario, CANADA
dschuurman@cs.redeemer.ca

ABSTRACT

This paper describes a sequence of assignments, each building upon the next, leading students to a working simulation of a simple 8-bit CPU (Central Processing Unit). The design features a classic Von Neumann architecture comprising a simple data path with a few registers, a simple ALU (Arithmetic Logic Unit), and a microprogram to direct all the control signals. The first step involves the design of the ALU which is capable of eight basic operations. The second step guides students to construct a datapath complete with several 8-bit registers. The third step involves the design and implementation of a control unit which uses a microprogram to implement machine code instructions. The microprogram implements nine basic machine language instructions which are sufficient for writing many simple programs. The final step involves adding program memory and an input and output device to form a simple working simulation of a computer. At this point, students may hand-assemble code for their CPU and simulate its execution.

All simulations are performed using a free and open source simulator called Logisim which performs digital logic simulations with the ability to build larger circuits from smaller subcircuits. Students can set an adjustable clock rate and observe the internal CPU state and registers as it retrieves instructions and steps through the microcode. The basic CPU architecture provides many opportunities for more advanced exercises, such as adding an instruction fetch unit, adding pipelining, or adding more machine language instructions. The assignments were introduced in a second year course on computer organization, providing an effective hands-on approach to understanding how a CPU actually operates.

Categories and Subject Descriptors

C.0 [**General**]: Modeling of computer architecture

General Terms

Design, Theory

Keywords

computer organization; CPU simulation; education

1. INTRODUCTION

Computer organization and architecture form important parts of the computer science "body of knowledge" as identified by the ACM and IEEE computing curriculum task force. The 2008 computer science curriculum guidelines continue to identify computer organization and architecture as important topics in the computer science curriculum. According to this report "A professional in any field of computing should not regard the computer as just a black box that executes programs by magic ... Students need to understand computer architecture in order to make best use of the software tools and computer languages they use to create programs" [2].

One way to learn about this topic is to study existing CPU architectures. Many different CPU architectures abound, and different textbooks have selected different processor architectures as examples. Several commercial processors have been used as exemplars to describe computer organization and architecture concepts, including the 8051 [7], the MIPS processor [6], and the popular x86 and ARM architectures [9].

Other authors have developed their own architectures designed with pedagogical principles in mind to help students understand the fundamentals of computer organization. Some simple processors used for pedagogical purposes include the picocontroller described in [5] and the Mic-1 described in [11]. Other simple computer architectures can be found in popular textbooks such as [3] and [8].

Another strategy is to guide students in a step-by-step manner to construct their own basic processor. This approach seeks to help students go beyond simply understanding computer architecture and guide them to apply the concepts to the design of a simple computer architecture.

There are many different approaches to having students build a CPU. Using real digital hardware is fraught with many engineering pitfalls: chip fan-outs, ground bounce, clock ringing, stray inductance and capacitance, open and short circuits, and propagation delays to name just a few. These low-level issues are important for electrical and computer engineers to master, but can be a source of frustration and distraction when the objectives are to teach basic computer architecture principles. Using programmable logic de-

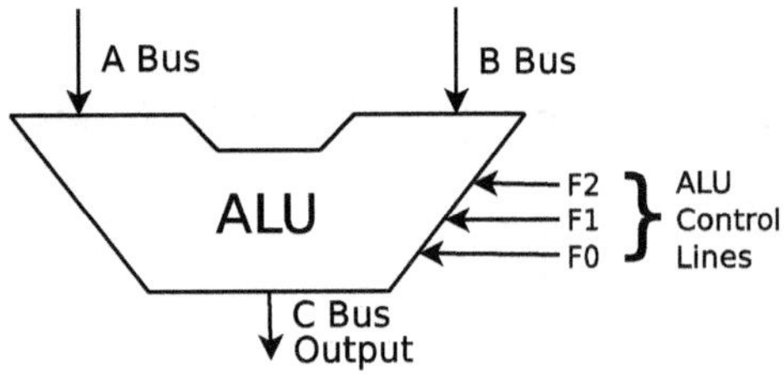

Figure 1: Block diagram of a simple ALU.

vices such as FPGAs (Field Programmable Gate Arrays) can reduce the issues associated with assembling digital circuits, but the development environments associated with FPGAs are complex and can take considerable time to master.

A better approach is to use a basic logic simulator, which provides a simpler environment free of FPGA architecture constraints and low-level electrical issues. These environments provide digital logic elements at a level of abstraction that allows students to experiment with basic digital design issues. In particular, Logisim provides a friendly educational tool for performing basic digital simulations [4]. Logisim enables designing and simulating digital circuits ranging from small logic circuits up to entire CPUs. A recent comparison of logic simulators for computer design courses found Logisim to be a good option for educational use [10]. Furthermore, Logisim is an open source tool that can be freely downloaded by students from the web [1].

2. THE SIMPLE CPU DESIGN

This paper will describe a series of assignments using Logisim to provide a step-by-step design and simulation of a simple CPU. The design of the processor is inspired and derived from the Mic-1 architecture as described by Andrew Tanenbaum and Todd Austin in their text *Structured Computer Organization* [11]. The steps are broken down into several assignments, each building upon the next. These steps are described in the following subsections.

2.1 Step 1: A Simple ALU

The students are first provided with a hands-on lab tutorial to teach them the fundamentals of using Logisim. The first assignment includes some initial logic design exercises such as designing a 2-bit demultiplexer and testing it using Logisim.

After the students gain a working knowledge of Logisim, they are given the first assignment. This assignment requires the students to design and simulate an 8-bit ALU using logic gates. The ALU must have two 8-bit bus inputs (labelled A and B) and one 8-bit output as illustrated in Figure 1. The function of the ALU is selected using three ALU control lines ($F0$, $F1$ and $F2$) which select one of eight operations in the ALU as indicated in Table 1. The ALU can be constructed in a straightforward manner by building the digital circuit for each operation and using a 1-of-8 multiplexer to select which appears at the output. Once the ALU is constructed and tested, the ALU can be turned into a subcircuit and used as a building block in subsequent assignments.

2.2 Step 2: The CPU Datapath

The next step in the process is to take the ALU subcircuit built in the previous step and place it inside a datapath using

Table 1: Summary of simple ALU operations.

F2	F1	F0	Output
0	0	0	A
0	0	1	B
0	1	0	A+1
0	1	1	B+1
1	0	0	A+B
1	0	1	A-B
1	1	0	A AND B
1	1	1	A OR B

Table 2: List of CPU Registers.

Register	Description
A	General purpose A register
B	General purpose B register
OUT	Output register
MBR	Memory Byte Register
PC	Program Counter
MIR	Microprogram Instruction Register
MPC	Microprogram Program Counter

Logisim. The datapath is a simplified version of the Mic-1 datapath and represents a basic Von Neumann architecture. Using 8-bit buses and registers, the students are guided to create a datapath that forms the basis of a simple CPU as illustrated in Figure 2. (Note that the 7-segment display and input switch are not part of the CPU, but are included as helpful diagnostic devices). The CPU will eventually include two general-purpose registers, one output register, and four special-purpose registers as summarized in Table 2. The destination register for the output of the ALU (C bus) is determined by selecting the write control line on the appropriate register. The A Bus input to the ALU is tied directly to the A register, hence the A register figures prominently in nearly all ALU operations. The B Bus input to the ALU uses a multiplexer to select which register output will appear on the bus. The control of the multiplexer is summarized in Table 3.

Operation of the CPU datapath can be simulated by preloading the A register with a preset value (a helpful feature in Logisim allows pre-loading registers with a click of the mouse). Next, students must discern how to toggle the appropriate ALU control lines and write lines to move the value in the A register through the ALU and into the OUT register. If the operation is done correctly, the current value in the A register will appear in the OUT register. At this point, the students have just simulated a "Move" operation in a simple CPU datapath!

After completing this step, students can either demonstrate their working CPU datapath, or submit a screenshot of Logisim showing the 7-segment display output along with a description of the sequence of control lines that were asserted to perform the move operation. At this point, the students are manually performing operations that will later be automated by the control unit.

2.3 Step 3: The Control Unit

The manual control of the datapath simulated in the previous step highlights the need to manage the control signals in the CPU. In previous assignments, the students built an

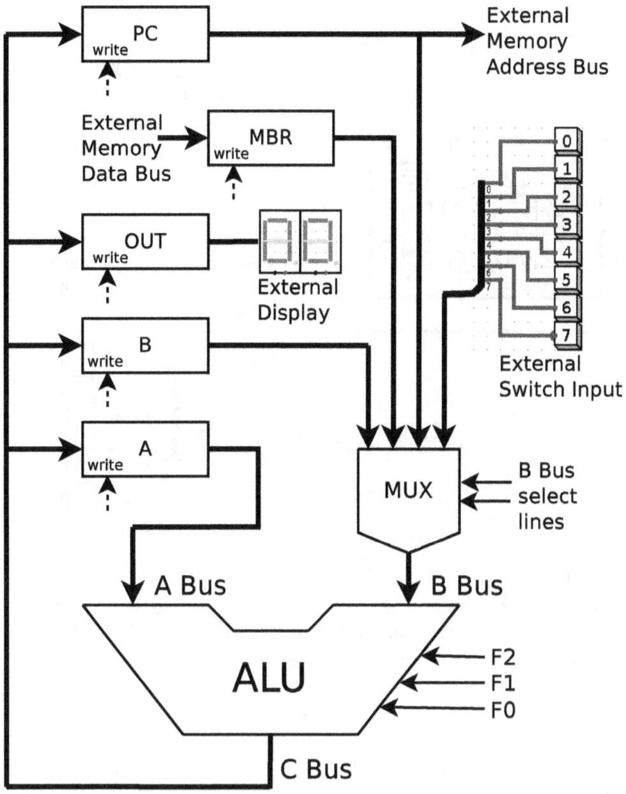

Figure 2: The block diagram of the CPU datapath.

Table 3: B Bus Multiplexer Select Lines.

Select Lines	ALU B Bus Input
00	B Register
01	MBR (Memory Byte Register)
10	PC (Program Counter)
11	External input

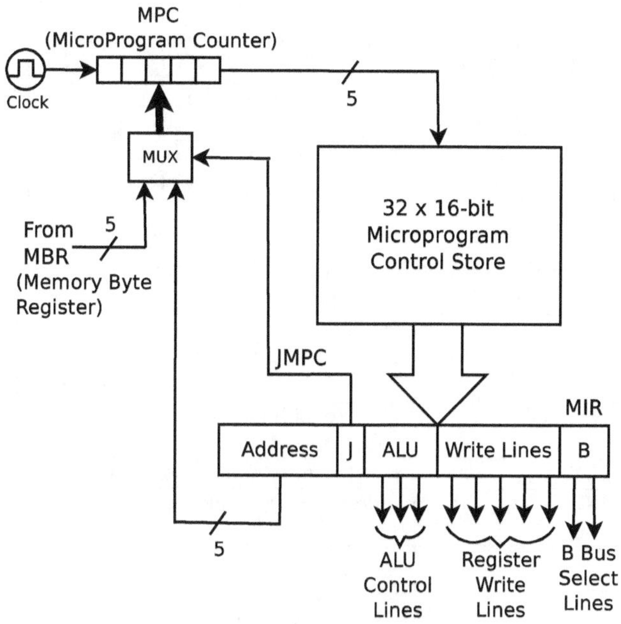

Figure 3: Block diagram of the control unit.

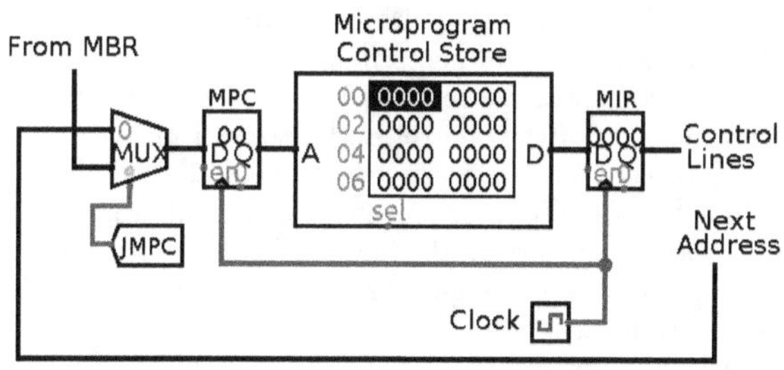

Figure 4: Logisim blocks for the control unit.

ALU and added registers to simulate a simple CPU datapath using Logisim. In this next step, students complete the final piece in the CPU puzzle by adding the control unit.

The CPU requires a sequencer to step through the operations necessary to execute each machine language instruction. A microprogram can be used to orchestrate and coordinate the various registers and control lines within the CPU. To accomplish this, a ROM (Read Only Memory) is used as the control store for the microprogram. The microprogram and control unit used in the assignment are derived from the Mic-1 architecture as described in sections 4.1 and 4.3 of *Structured Computer Organization* [11]. For this assignment, students are required to use a 32x16-bit ROM for the control store as arranged in Figure 3. The 5-bit address bus for the control store is connected to a special purpose register called the Microprogram Program Counter (MPC). The 32-bit data bus from the control store is latched into another special purpose register called the Microprogram Instruction Register (MIR).

Students are given the following specifications for the control store and surrounding logic:

- the control store ROM address is provided by a 5-bit MPC register. It is synchronized by the rising edge of the clock
- the next address loaded into the MPC register should be selected by a multiplexer controlled by a JMPC line as defined in Table 4
- a 16-bit data bus from the control store ROM connects to the MIR register and is synchronized by the falling edge of the clock
- The MIR bits are arranged as follows (from most-significant to least-significant bits):
  - Next address (5-bits)
  - JMPC (Jump control) bit
  - ALU control lines (3-bits)
  - Register write control lines (5 bits)
  - ALU B Bus input select lines (2 bits to select one of four registers)

Students are then coached to connect the output bits from the MIR to the various control lines within the CPU. Logisim provides a convenient "tunnel" connector to connect

Table 4: **JMPC Operation.**

JMPC	Description
0	Next address loaded from the top 5-bits of MIR
1	Next address is loaded from MBR (bottom 5-bits of the Memory Byte Register)

Table 5: List of simple CPU instructions.

Instruction	Description
`NOP`	No operation
`INPUT`	Load Input into A register
`OUTPUT`	Move A register to Output register
`JMP <addr>`	JMP to address <addr> in program memory
`LOAD A,#<value>`	Load <value> into the A register
`INC A`	Increment the value in register A by 1
`MOV B,A`	Move register A into register B
`ADD A,B`	Add register A to register B and store result in register A
`HALT`	Halt execution

lines using labels rather than drawing individual wires. This avoids having a diagram containing a "rat's nest" of wires and connections which are hard to follow and debug. A Logisim diagram of the control unit is shown in Figure 4.

Once the control unit wiring is complete, students will need to enter a microprogram into the control store ROM. The microprogram directs the flow of the datapath for each of the various machine language instructions. For simplicity, the instruction set is limited to the nine simple instructions summarized in Table 5.

The microcode begins at location 00h in the control store with the main loop which continually fetches and executes instructions from program memory. The main loop fetches the machine language instructions (opcodes) from program memory at the address stored in the Program Counter (PC) register and loads them into the MBR (Memory Byte Register). After the instruction is loaded, the PC register is incremented to the next location. The main loop then branches to execute the microcode for the current instruction (for convenience in this design, the opcode corresponds to the actual address in the control store). Once the microcode for the current instruction is completed (which may require several microinstructions and clock cycles) control is transferred back to the main loop (at location 00h in the control store) and the process repeats.

The microcode for each of the assembly language instructions can be given to the students, or added as a further assignment. The use of a spreadsheet can be helpful in coding the microprogram by assigning a column to each control signal and a row to each memory location in the control store (a sample of a few spreadsheet rows is shown in Figure 5). The bit patterns in the resulting table can be converted into 16-bit hexadecimal words which are then placed in the corresponding locations in the control store. Logisim provides an intuitive interface for entering data into a ROM device.

Once the microprogram has been entered into the control store ROM, the CPU is complete. The CPU, including the registers, ALU and control unit can all be placed inside a single Logisim subcircuit and represented using a single block. The CPU block can now be connected to an external program memory and input/output components to simulate a simple computer. The address and data bus of the program memory should connect to the CPU block. The address bus should internally connect to the output of the PC register, and the data bus should internally connect to the input of the MBR register. The CPU block can also be connected to external input switches and the 7-segment output display as illustrated in Figure 6.

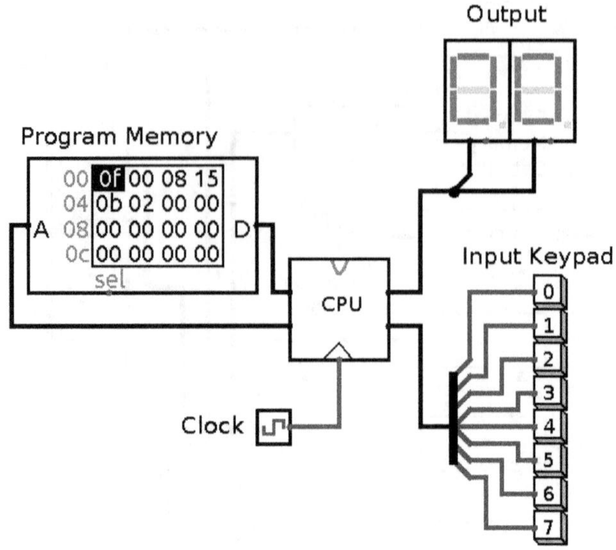

Figure 6: Final schematic diagram of computer with CPU represented as a Logisim subcircuit and connected to input and output devices and program memory.

2.4 Step 4: Putting It All Together

Students are given the following simple assembly language program to test their design. The students must first hand-assemble the program into machine language and then enter it into program memory starting at address 00h. The opcodes for each assembly language instruction can be deduced from their starting addresses in the microprogram ROM. Students can then run this program on their CPUs and observe what it does.

```
00h  LOAD A,#0
02h  OUTPUT
03h  INC A
04h  JMP 2
```

If everything is working properly, students should observe the CPU counting in the 7-segment display output. If something is not working correctly, students can debug their design in Logisim by single-stepping the clock and tracking the state of the program or even the microprogram. Logisim also supports adjustment of the clock speed, so students can observe how the CPU clock rate effects the counting speed on the 7-segment display.

Even with the limited set of assembly language instructions, a variety of additional programs can be assigned. For example, students can code a program that continuously

Opcode	Hex Address	Decimal Address	Next Addr	JMPC	ALU2	ALU1	ALU0	R1	R0	OUTwr	PCwr	MBRwr	Bwr	Awr	Comment
(main)	00	0	1	0	0	0	0	0	0	0	0	1	0	0	Fetch MBR
	01	1	2	0	0	1	1	1	0	0	0	0	0	0	PC = PC + 1
	02	2	3	0	0	1	1	1	0	0	1	0	0	0	Store PC
	03	3	0	1	0	0	0	0	0	0	0	0	0	0	Goto MBR
NOP	04	4	0	0	0	0	0	0	0	0	0	0	0	0	goto main
	⋮														

Figure 5: Sample of a spreadsheet showing a portion of the microprogram listing.

reads the input switches and displays their values (in hexadecimal) on the 7-segment display output. For homework submissions, students can be asked to hand in their assembly code and machine language translation along with a print out of the completed CPU with the input/output devices and program memory.

3. FUTURE WORK

This simple CPU design provides a foundation for many possible future enhancements. One obvious enhancement is to add support for additional instructions in the microprogram. Some instructions that are conspicuously absent in the instruction set include compare operations and conditional jump instructions. The ALU could be further enhanced by adding a more elaborate status register to support more useful compare operations. Furthermore, the ALU could be modified to provide an 8-bit integer multiply or divide instruction. Moreover, students could be asked to enhance the architecture by adding an instruction fetch unit to independently update the PC register and fetch the next instructions. Additional enhancements can be explored such as adding various stages of pipelining.

To give students a glimpse of all the levels of computer organization from the digital logic layer up to the assembly language layer, the students can be guided to make a simple two-pass assembler for the CPU they have designed. Logisim has support for a binary text file format that can be loaded into a ROM block rather than typing in the hex codes manually. The assembler could be programmed to output an assembled program directly to a binary text file that can be read directly into Logisim. The students will then be able to write assembly language programs in a text editor, assemble them them with their assembler, load the resulting binary code into the program memory block, and then run it on their CPU.

4. CONCLUSIONS

Logisim is a friendly and simple tool for performing digital logic simulations, yet it is powerful enough to simulate a basic CPU. Using a simulator avoids many of the pitfalls that accompany working with real hardware and allows students to focus on understanding basic computer organization concepts. Having students build their own simple CPU has pedagogical value which augments the description of existing industrial CPU architectures. This paper describes a sequence of step-by-step assignments that gradually guide students to create their own simple CPU simulation. As each assignment builds on the next, students gain an insight into the layers of computer organization from the digital logic level up to the assembly language level. Designing a simple CPU from the ground up provides an opportunity to grasp basic computer architecture concepts while students experience the satisfaction of making their own CPU. The simulation provides many opportunities for further exercises such as adding additional instructions, features and performance enhancements to the basic CPU architecture.

5. ACKNOWLEDGEMENTS

The author would like to thank all the contributors to the Logisim project for making it available to educators and students.

6. REFERENCES

[1] http://ozark.hendrix.edu/~burch/logisim/.

[2] Computer science curriculum 2008. http://www.acm.org/education/curricula-recommendations, 2008. Report from the ACM/IEEE Interim Review Task Force.

[3] S. Brown and Z. Vranesic. *Fundamentals of Digital Logic with VHDL Design.* McGraw Hill, second edition, 2005.

[4] C. Burch. Logisim: a graphical system for logic circuit design and simulation. *Journal on Educational Resources in Computing*, 2(1):5–16, Mar. 2002.

[5] F. Cady. *Microcontrollers and Microcomputers: Principles of Software and Hardware Engineering.* Oxford University Press, second edition, 2010.

[6] J. L. Hennessy and D. A. Patterson. *Computer Architecture: A Quantitative Approach.* Morgan Kaufmann, third edition, 2003.

[7] I. S. MacKenzie. *The 8051 Microcontroller.* Prentice Hall, 1999.

[8] M. M. Mano and C. R. Kime. *Logic and Computer Design Fundamentals.* Prentice Hall, second edition, 2004.

[9] W. Stallings. *Computer Organization and Architecture: Designing for Performance.* Prentice Hall, eighth edition, 2010.

[10] T. Stanley, V. Chetty, M. Styles, S.-Y. Jung, F. Duarte, T.-W. J. Lee, M. Gunter, and L. Fife. Teaching computer architecture through simulation: (a brief evaluation of cpu simulators). *Journal of Computing Sciences in Colleges*, 27(4):37–44, Apr. 2012.

[11] A. S. Tanenbaum and T. Austin. *Structured Computer Organization.* Prentice Hall, sixth edition, 2013.

Introducing Computer Science in an Integrated Science Course

Barry Lawson
blawson@richmond.edu

Doug Szajda
dszajda@richmond.edu

Lewis Barnett
lbarnett@richmond.edu

Department of Mathematics and Computer Science
University of Richmond
Richmond, VA 23173-0001 USA

ABSTRACT

This paper describes our implementation and experience of incorporating computer science concepts into a team-taught, first-year interdisciplinary course for prospective science majors at the University of Richmond. The course integrates essential concepts from each of five STEM disciplines: biology, chemistry, computer science, mathematics, and physics. Including computer science in this course faces three primary challenges: few of the students have any CS background; the time devoted to CS instruction is reduced compared to a traditional introductory CS course; and the spirit of the course requires the CS material to be highly integrated with the other disciplines. Here we discuss our experience from three-plus years of offering the course and its impact on the major/minor pool of students in our own discipline.

Categories and Subject Descriptors

K.3.2 [**Computer and Information Science Education**]: *computer science education, curriculum*

Keywords

CS1; Integrated Science

1. INTRODUCTION

At the University of Richmond, faculty from the disciplines of biology, chemistry, computer science, mathematics, and physics have designed an innovative year-long course with the intent of more fully integrating essential concepts from each of these science, technology, engineering, and mathematics (STEM) disciplines. The course, named Integrated Quantitative Science (IQS), spans two academic semesters, and each semester the course is team-taught by five faculty, one from each of the disciplines above.

The overall goals of this course include: (a) increasing understanding by students of essential disciplinary and interdisciplinary concepts; (b) increasing understanding by faculty of interdisciplinary concepts and connections; (c) increasing the ability of faculty to develop future courses that draw on and integrate material from multiple scientific disciplines; (d) increasing the number of undergraduates who participate in cross-disciplinary academic and research opportunities at the university and beyond; and (e) allowing faculty to bring new material, from a variety of disciplines, into existing courses within their own disciplines.

The course is open to first-year students only. Students apply for admission to the course, and preference is given to those students who meaningfully express a strong yet broad interest in the sciences and in scientific exploration. Student load for the course is equivalent to two courses per semester for each of the first two semesters. At the end of the two semesters, students will have received sufficient background to allow them to move into a major of their choice in any of the STEM disciplines listed above, and they receive general-education credit for the natural science and symbolic reasoning fields of study at our university.

To facilitate the necessary integration, we selected a unifying theme for each semester that allowed all five disciplines to be involved and that leveraged the expertise of the participating faculty. For the first semester, the current theme is antibiotic resistance; for the second semester, the current theme is cell signaling. As much as possible, each semester is structured so that no single discipline receives a large contiguous block of lecture time — the challenge is to balance a sense of integration with a sense of topic continuity.

In this paper, we focus on implementation details and our experience with this course from the computer science perspective, referring the interested reader to [6] for a more broad treatment of the course, constraints, and outcomes. When initially designing the IQS course, all parties involved felt strongly that computer science should be included. In addition to recognizing CS as an important field of study in its own right, there is clear recognition of the impact CS has in research areas of each of the other disciplines. Although none of the science majors at our university currently requires CS, many of our science colleagues understand the importance of strong CS skills for their own research and for their students. We see this course as an opportunity to present early the discipline of computer science to many science students who might not otherwise take a CS course (or might only take one very late in their course of study).

However, including CS does present challenges:

- Computer science is but one of five disciplines to receive coverage in this course. Our experience indicates

SIGCSE'13, March 6–9, 2013, Denver, Colorado, USA.

that it is more difficult to present computer science effectively when, in the same course, the students' responsibilities and time are divided. Indeed, the total amount of time and the frequency at which the students focus on CS topics is significantly reduced compared to a traditional CS1 course.

- Few of the students who have taken the course have had any background in computer science. The same is not true for the other four disciplines. Therefore, while our science and mathematics colleagues can try to move quickly into more advanced material, we in CS must start at square zero[1].
- In the integrated spirit of the course, we feel it is very important to include applications and projects which are meaningful within the theme of each semester and, as much as possible, are highly integrated with other of the disciplines. The primary challenge in this regard is to choose topics that are sufficiently meaningful yet accessible by students new to CS.

2. IQS: CS INTEGRATION

Our IQS course is split across two motivating topics in consecutive semesters, and, especially from the CS viewpoint, there is an unfortunate gap that occurs with the winter break. Because most of our students are new to computer science—in terms of learning a programming language and thinking algorithmically—we believe the students benefit from frequent, smaller assignments, especially initially. The winter break presents a period of four weeks during which the students are unlikely to be actively working.

Accordingly, our approach is to introduce most of the traditional CS1 concepts within the framework of the first semester of IQS: basic computer organization, variables, assignment and expressions, control structures, loops, methods and parameter passing, fundamental object-oriented programming, arrays, and file I/O. These concepts are presented using projects and assignments that fit within the antibiotic-resistance theme of the first semester. Our language of choice is Java, to maintain consistency with our standard CS1 and CS2 courses.

We then use the second semester of IQS to reinforce those fundamental concepts through applications and assignments that relate to the second-semester theme of cell signaling. Students understand from the beginning that, because we are including five disciplines into the time equivalent of four courses, at the conclusion of the course they may need to pick up some small amount of additional material on their own before moving into subsequent courses within a particular discipline. So in the second semester, we also try to include any remaining CS1 concepts (more advanced OOP, recursion, searching, and sorting), but a full coverage of these remaining topics has not always appeared in the three offerings of this course.

2.1 First Semester Topics and Projects

The first semester of IQS currently focuses on the theme of antibiotic resistance. We use projects on agent-based simulation, Monte Carlo methods, and DNA sequence comparison to motivate the presentation of particular CS1 topics.

[1]As computer scientists, we feel compelled to start here rather than at square one.

Agent-based Simulation.

The first full CS project is an agent-based simulation model of antibiotic resistance. In this model, students implement methods which use strings of binary characters to model the binding sites of antigens, antibodies, and antibiotics [15]. Students also write a simple class to represent an agent in the model, its corresponding characteristics (e.g., spatial location, strings for binding sites), and its necessary behaviors (e.g., immune response, antigen mutation).

The CS1 concepts necessary for implementation of this project include variables, strings, conditional execution, for-loops, writing and using methods, and elementary OOP (using objects and writing a new class). We use roughly the first half of the first semester to introduce these topics in small, manageable chunks. For example, in the CS lessons during the first two weeks of class, we introduce variable declarations and assignments followed by strings and string methods through simple written homework and programming exercises. In the next two weeks of class, we introduce conditional execution and for-loops, again through manageable assignments similar to those in a typical CS1 course but with IQS-specific contexts. We then progress to writing a simple agent class, which the students later extend for use in the simulation model. Implementation of this first project is not due until slightly over halfway through the semester.

Admittedly, the entire agent-based model is not one that first-year students can reasonably complete on their own. We provide most of the framework for the interactive model, including code for a front-end GUI and the simulation engine. The students must implement an agent class which can then plug into the provided simulation framework.

Beyond writing the code for the agent class, we require the students to use their model once implementation is complete. We believe this is very important as the students see early the idea of CS as an area of study unto itself, not simply as a field of potential tools for the other sciences. Using the GUI, students are able to perform experiments by changing various parameter values (e.g., probability of infection, antibiotic string length) and evaluating the result on the number of infected, uninfected, and living agents over time. A screen shot of the GUI is provided in Figure 1.

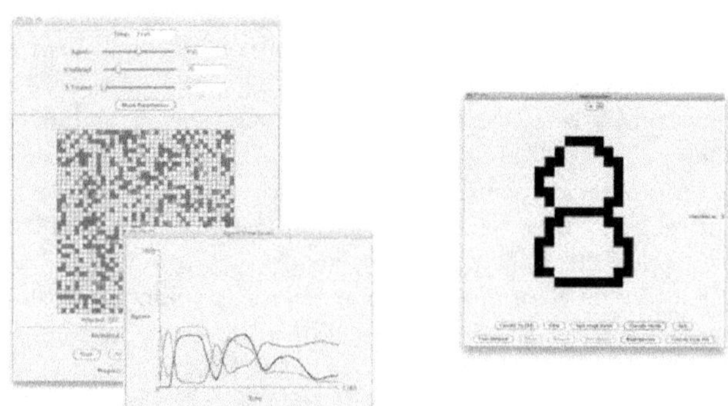

Figure 1: Agent-based simulation model GUI (L) and neural network character classifier GUI (R)

Monte Carlo Methods.

The next CS project involves a Monte Carlo approach for determining low energy structures of antibiotic molecules, integrating CS with chemistry and mathematics. Motivation for this project lies in determining stable (low energy) conformations of molecules, since they are more likely to occur in nature than higher energy conformations. Steric crowding (when atoms are closer to one another) generally leads to a higher energy state due to repulsion among the atoms. Hence, the energy of a molecular conformation is most affected by modifying dihedral angles within the molecule.

One approach for searching the energy state space is to generate an *ensemble* of different conformations of a given molecule by varying random dihedral angles, and then minimizing that ensemble to identify only the low energy conformations. Generating the ensemble is a natural application of the Monte Carlo technique. Given a molecular conformation, select at random a number of dihedral angles to vary, select at random the actual angles to vary, and then select at random the values for the angles. Repeat this process many times, adding each new conformation to the ensemble.

Again, we provide some framework for the students: classes for representing a conformation and an ensemble, and tools for reading and writing appropriate file formats. Students should be capable of writing the classes for a conformation and an ensemble, but we provide them because of time constraints. We use a straightforward file format (Z-matrix) for representing a conformation, providing an additional context for the chemistry professor to cover bond lengths, bond angles, and dihedral angles, and allowing the CS professor to introduce the algorithmic process of file I/O.

Integration with mathematics occurs via discussion of minimization techniques (e.g., gradient descent) during lecture. Students understand the mathematics behind minimization of the ensemble, but do not implement the minimization step within the CS project, again because of time constraints. Rather, we have the students use research-grade molecular modeling software to visualize the conformations generated by their own code, and then to conduct a full Monte-Carlo minimization process (generate and minimize an ensemble, and visualize the results).

There are no new CS1 concepts required for this project (requiring primarily looping, random number generation, and use of objects), providing a means of reinforcing ideas in a different context. In our allotted lesson times during this period, we cover data representation, low-level program execution, and the overall concept of Monte Carlo methods.

DNA Sequence Comparison.

The final project in the first semester integrates biology and computer science. Throughout the semester, students conduct a sequence of wet-lab experiments to sequence the 16S ribosomal DNA gene of bacterial symbionts isolated from marine sponges, specifically looking to identify novel antibiotic-resistant species of bacteria in the sponge cultures. Given the resulting DNA sequences, students use NCBI's BLAST utility [9] to identify good matches with DNA in other organisms. Working in groups of five, students write code that allows repeated searching of the BLAST results, which then permits the students to analyze those results for hypothesizing about antibiotic resistant bacteria in nature and potential therapeutic uses.

This project requires students to understand and implement basic file I/O, arrays, and searching. The students download BLAST results in XML format and then use a simple approach for reading necessary information (sequence accession number and species description) from the files. Students store all data using a multi-dimensional array of strings, and searches are performed using sequential search.

Additionally, in class we provide an introduction to algorithm analysis, including big-O notation and scalability. We present the concept of binary search (with the notion that data must be sorted) as an alternative to sequential search, but because there is not time to meaningfully cover sorting algorithms, students are not required to implement binary search. We also cover the Needleman-Wunsch algorithm [10] for performing global alignment of two DNA sequences, which provides an introduction to the dynamic programming technique. Students do not implement Needleman-Wunsch in code, but working with the algorithm by hand provides them an understanding of a technique similar to those used in the BLAST utility.

Final Poster Presentation.

A final requirement in the first semester is for each group to present a poster about their work. The poster, primarily driven by the marine sponge experiments and data analyses, must incorporate and integrate all five disciplines. Students are graded (a) as a group on poster content and integration, and (b) individually during a one-on-one oral presentation of the poster to a faculty member from the course. We also open the presentations to the university at large.

2.2 Second Semester Topics and Projects

The first semester of IQS includes at least some front-loading of required topics from all disciplines. The front-loading is particularly pronounced for CS, for reasons described earlier. This results in greater flexibility regarding selection of topics for the second semester of the course. For the computer science components, we try to choose topics that a computer science researcher might address, to counterbalance the focus on skills acquisition in the first semester, and to dispel any notion that computer science is "just programming".

We have offered a variety of second-semester topics and projects over the first three years of IQS, some of which are mentioned in Section 4. For the remainder of this section we discuss the topic, and its organization, that will be covered in the second semester of the current academic year.

Artificial Neural Networks.

During the coming spring semester, the CS component of IQS will focus on the theory and implementation of artificial neural networks, the first time that only a single research area will be covered in the second semester of IQS. In each of the previous three years, three or four different topics were covered. However, our experience is that even gifted first-year students respond better to advanced topics when those topics are introduced in small chunks. Moreover, discussing a single topic allows for a more detailed exploration, and one that potentially covers more advanced CS concepts. The use of a single overarching topic for the CS material also has the advantage of avoiding the startup costs of introducing several different topics. And because the performance of a neural network is well quantified, students see and understand the need for additional mechanisms that improve observed results. Note that, although we used this project as one of three during the previous offering of IQS, a full-semester version of the project will allow for more theoretical detail, more time for experimentation, and increased student understanding.

The students implement a neural network intended to classify the ten base-10 digits. A digit is represented as an image, which is then cropped, centered, scaled, and vectorized. The network contains perceptrons that use a logistic activation function, and the cost function is regularized. Optimal weight values for the network are computed using gradient descent and the back propagation algorithm. Correctness of back propagation implementations is verified using gradient checking, which is subsequently disabled.

Students are provided with a base GUI (see Figure 1), and are required to write methods to handle the corresponding events (e.g., outputting drawn digits into appropriate file format). Students are also supplied with default values for required parameters (such as number of hidden layers, regularization parameter, gradient descent step size, delta value for gradient checking, and stopping threshold), but are required (and encouraged) to experiment with the values of these parameters. A single training set with roughly 1000 training vectors is created by pooling a small number of drawn digits (in file format as generated by the GUI) from each student.

Few outside packages are used for the project. In particular, students code the perceptron class, the back propagation and gradient checking algorithms, the gradient descent algorithm, methods for reading matrices from and writing to files, and methods for vectorizing and preprocessing images. Basic matrix arithmetic operations are performed using the Jama Matrix package [3].

Not all of the neural network processing and checking is performed or discussed from the start. Rather, students experiment with methods for improving the performance of the initial version of the network. For example, they do very little preprocessing of the data at the outset, using raw pixel data, and attempt to implement the neural network and back propagation without performing any checking, other than final network output. When the neural network performs poorly (as it will at this stage), we discuss gradient checking, which the students then implement. This has the bonus of demonstrating that numerical approximation of partial derivatives for performing gradient descent is, in this context, generally infeasible. When back propagation implementations are verified, and network performance is still poor, we discuss image preprocessing steps, which students then implement. The final product is a neural network that classifies with a success rate of approximately 75-80%.

The theory of neural networks includes fundamental CS issues and integrates well with topics from mathematics and biology. We discuss machine learning, and in particular that machine learning methods often require the minimization of functions of several variables. This prompts a review of functions of several variables, partial derivatives, and gradient descent (covered in the first semester), as well as brief coverage of some improved minimization algorithms. The neural network concept is motivated by brief discussion of biological neurons, a topic which is subsequently covered in greater detail by the biologist teaching IQS. We also discuss the choice of a logistic activation function, as well as why, and how, this function classifies behavior that cannot be modeled in the absence of a non-linear transformation. Bias and variance are covered when discussing the concept of regularization. Finally, because the implementation is vectorized, the basics of matrix arithmetic are also discussed.

Among the desirable properties of this particular project is that the concepts can be handled by first-year students, and that when the project is completed, students have a tool that allows for further exploration, including testing additional preprocessing algorithms and comparing neural network configurations and parameters. Most important, however, is that students have been exposed to some of the types of "non-programming" questions considered by research computer scientists.

3. OUTCOMES

From the CS perspective, benefits to offering a course like IQS include the following:

- Early exposure to CS is beneficial for students. Our university has no CS requirement, and generally natural science students either do not take a CS course or wait until late in their course of study. IQS is one way to present CS early to alleviate these issues. Anecdotally, a few of our science colleagues have indicated IQS students in their research labs demonstrating coding skills and algorithmic thinking not present in their more traditional research students.

- A significant number of IQS students have gone on to take a subsequent course in CS, boosting our enrollments. Moreover, we have garnered additional CS majors and minors from among those students.

- Faculty development is an important component of IQS. Working in a highly interdisciplinary setting provides CS faculty with more applications from a variety of disciplines which we can bring into our own courses. For example, one of us has incorporated the topic of Monte Carlo conformational search into an upper-level Simulation elective.

- Because the course development process promotes conversation among STEM faculty, new research opportunities for faculty can be discovered. Anecdotally, one of us is currently working on an interdisciplinary research project that resulted from the initial IQS development.

To quantify the second bullet above, we have collected data about students from the first four years of IQS. Of the 78 students who have taken IQS, 19 have gone on to take at least one course at the CS2 level or above — nearly 25%. This is a larger percentage than we had initially expected, but certainly is welcomed. In the same time period, we have had 230 students in our traditional CS1 courses. Of those students, 86 have gone on to take at least one course at the CS2 level or above — roughly 37%. We are thrilled with a 25% retention from IQS for a group of students that, in general, we would not see (or see early) in our courses.

We polled those 19 students about their perceived influence of CS within IQS: 12 of them indicated that early exposure to CS in IQS was the primary reason they took additional CS courses; only 3 of that 12 indicated they may have taken a CS course anyway but later in their course of study. Of the 7 who, prior to IQS, already felt they wanted to pursue CS, all but one indicated that the CS experience in IQS firmly established that desire (the remaining student decided to pursue a non-STEM major). The absence of IQS would not have precluded these students from taking a traditional CS1 course, but these data support the notion that early exposure to CS is important.

Moreover, of the 19 IQS students who have taken at least one course at CS2 or above, 16 are eligible to be declared majors or minors. Of those 16 students, currently 6 are declared as CS majors and 1 as a CS minor. Based on discussions with last year's IQS students (now eligible to declare), we expect those to increase to 9 majors and 2 minors — a 14% yield of all IQS students. Finally, 6 of the 14 have conducted summer research in CS at the university. Admittedly, we cannot claim that IQS is the *sole* reason these students have taken an additional CS course or declared CS as a major, but we can claim IQS had a strong influence in that regard.

From our most recent report to the primary funding agency for development of the course, the Howard Hughes Medical Institute, we also have data from the students who applied to IQS during the inaugural year but were not accepted (54 students). From that control group, only 13% (7 of 54) took a CS1 course and only 2% (1 of 54) took a CS2 course. In contrast, 26% of IQS students (5 of 19) from the same year as the control group took a CS2 course; 24% of all IQS students (19 of 78) have taken a CS2 course (plus several from the current year expressing an interest to do so in a future semester). Again, these data support the need for early exposure to CS.

Development and delivery of this course is not without issues, however. The impact of IQS-required faculty resources on staffing within CS is a primary issue. In the absence of IQS, we in CS would likely have never seen most of these students in our traditional CS1 courses. However, we are essentially staffing two additional sections of a CS course per year, roughly 10% of our total course offerings, to serve 20 IQS students — a significant impact. The initial development year, in which two faculty obtained reassigned time specifically for planning and development, exacerbated this issue. In the absence of IQS, we could have offered additional upper-level electives or general-audience service courses. (While enrollment in our traditional CS1 courses grew during this period, the demand was not sufficient to require additional sections.) These faculty resource impacts, especially on small disciplines such as CS and physics, are a major issue that must be addressed, both for the sustainability of IQS at our university and for its ability to be adopted by other institutions. Our university has received a grant renewal from HHMI to address ways to make IQS sustainable and exportable, specifically in terms of the faculty resources required.

A significant issue with the current state of the course is the requirement that certain topics from each discipline be presented. Because this is a first-year course that counts for the first course in each of the five disciplines, buy-in from the five departments depended on including minimum content from each discipline (typically a subset of the standard-course minimum content). As a result, course development was constrained by the opposing goals of trying to present challenging interdisciplinary problems and the need to cover a specific set of disciplinary topics.

Another primary challenge of this course is to identify meaningful programming projects that are well integrated with the course yet pitched at the appropriate level for the students. It is not reasonable, for example, to expect students to be able to code their own worms and viruses, despite the many interesting ways in which the topic integrates with biology and mathematics. In the first semester, in which we cover the fundamental CS concepts, it is appropriate to have several different, smaller projects. In the second semester, in which we have more flexibility, a semester-long theme for projects seems more appropriate. For example, neural networks and genetic algorithms share the important aspects of integrating well with several disciplines, covering sufficient material for a full-semester theme, and allowing for interesting experimentation, while still being feasible for first-year students to implement. In either semester, providing to the students some initial code framework for particular projects mitigates the latter issue of feasible implementation.

4. OBSERVATIONS

The course content and its delivery have evolved each year we have offered IQS, and there are several lessons we have learned in the process.

- An objects-first approach to CS, which we tried in the first year, is difficult to execute successfully. This is due in no small part to the divided attention of the students and to the somewhat abbreviated nature of overall topic coverage. Moving to a procedural approach early, with plenty of simple exercises, works better in our experience with this course.
- Our expectations of the students in the course were too high initially. Because the students are accepted into IQS through an application process, we expected them to be able to handle an initial introduction to CS through carefully-crafted offline tutorials. This was not the case, and we had to request more lecture time. In hindsight, the mixture of student abilities we encounter in our CS1 courses is very similar to those in the IQS course. Moreover, we need to keep in mind that, based on the structure of this two-semester course, students in the second semester are "equivalent" to students in the second half of a one-semester CS1 course.
- It is critical in this setting for students to encounter CS on a frequent basis, particularly with regular, accessible coding exercises. Large blocks of time between CS assignments/lectures is not conducive to success.
- In the second semester of IQS, there are several integrated topics we used initially that in hindsight are not especially well-suited to the current version of this course. For example, topics in image processing related to the automation of two-dimensional gel electrophoresis present an interesting interdisciplinary research problem. However, the general problem itself is too advanced, and, as currently structured, involves too many individual stages to be feasible in a single semester first-year level course (e.g., requiring coverage of frequency domain processes and complex number theory). Other topics, such as implementing the Needleman-Wunsch sequence alignment algorithm or a Brownian motion simulator, suffer from the opposite problem: insufficient material to comprise a full-semester theme or to retain student interest over the course of a semester.

5. CONTEXT AND RELATED WORK

Similar efforts fall roughly into three categories. The first comprises courses intended to introduce science majors to computing skills required by their majors [1, 5, 8, 11, 14]. The second has been characterized as *contextualized CS*. Related courses in this category draw on the sciences or mathematics for organizing themes in introductory courses [2, 7]. The third category includes science courses that attempt to combine two or more disciplines in an integrated fashion.

The University of Richmond's IQS course falls squarely into the third category. There are several relevant examples from other institutions. The Accelerated Integrated Science Sequence at the Claremont Colleges [13] integrates biology, chemistry, and physics. Students are introduced to computer modeling with Matlab, but no computer science credit is awarded. The closest match for the Richmond course is Princeton's *Integrated Science* course [12], which served as a motivating example for the design of IQS. The course has been described in several articles in the *Daily Princetonian*, e.g., [16]. Both courses have a strong problem-solving orientation and present material from biology, chemistry, computer science, mathematics and physics. They differ primarily on distribution of emphasis among the disciplines, with the Princeton IS course providing "a mathematically and computationally sophisticated introduction to physics and chemistry, drawing on examples from biological systems" [12] (Freshman Year course description), while Richmond's IQS course provides students with preparation equivalent to the initial course in all five disciplines. The Richmond and Princeton courses are the only ones in this category that prepare students to move directly into CS2. The first year curriculum of Princeton's Integrated Science course takes as its organizing framework the set of quantitative skills and techniques needed for tackling big problems, particularly in the area of quantitative biology. Each of the techniques is developed through applications in the participating disciplines [4]. Richmond's course, on the other hand, is organized about a research theme for each semester, with the quantitative tools introduced as needed to develop the theme. The strategies are different, though the ultimate goals are similar.

6. CONCLUSIONS

Along with faculty from four other STEM disciplines, we have developed for prospective science students a first-year interdisciplinary course which has CS as a significant component. Challenges include students with generally no CS background, reduced presentation time compared to a traditional CS1 course, and the need to balance complex integrated problems with accessibility for students. Benefits include non-traditional students who proceed to additional courses and/or major in CS, the opportunity to present some advanced topics early, and faculty development. We are currently working to reduce staffing impacts and to make the course exportable. We will gladly provide materials and additional details to interested parties.

7. ACKNOWLEDGMENTS

The authors and their faculty colleagues gratefully acknowledge the support of the Howard Hughes Medical Institute, PKAL/KECK FIDL, the National Science Foundation, and the University of Richmond.

8. REFERENCES

[1] J. C. Adams and R. J. Pruim. Computing for STEM majors: enhancing non CS majors' computing skills. In *Proc. SIGCSE 2012*, pages 457–462, Raleigh, NC, March 2012.

[2] V. Barr. Create two, three, many courses: an experiment in contextualized introductory computer science. *J. Comput. Sci. Coll.*, 27(6):19–25, June 2012.

[3] R. F. Boisvert, J. Hicklin, B. Miller, C. Moler, R. Pozo, K. Remington, and P. Webb. JAMA: A Java Matrix Package. Retrieved Sep 5, 2012 from `http://math.nist.gov/javanumerics/jama/`.

[4] D. Botstein. An Integrated Science Curriculum at Princeton. *iBioMagazine*, June 2011. Retrieved Sep 3, 2012 from `http://ibiomagazine.org/issues/june-2011-issue/david-botstein.html`.

[5] Z. Dodds, R. Libeskind-Hadas, C. Alvarado, and G. Kuenning. Evaluating a breadth-first CS 1 for scientists. In *Proc. SIGCSE 2008*, pages 266 – 270, Portland, OR, March 12 – 15 2008.

[6] L. N. Gentile, L. Caudill, M. Fetea, A. Hill, K. Hoke, B. Lawson, O. Lipan, M. Kerckhove, C. Parish, K. Stenger, and D. Szajda. Challenging disciplinary boundaries in the first year: A new introductory integrated science course for STEM majors. *J. College Sci. Teaching*, 41(5):24 – 30, May 2012.

[7] M. Guzdial. A media computation course for non-majors. In *Proc. of ITiCSE '03*, pages 104–108, Thessaloniki, Greece, 2003.

[8] S. Hambrusch, C. Hoffmann, J. T. Korb, M. Haugan, and A. L. Hosking. A multidisciplinary approach toward computational thinking for science majors. In *Proc. SIGCSE 2009*, pages 183 – 187, Chattanooga, TN, March 2009.

[9] National Center for Biotechnology Information. BLAST: Basic Local Alignment Search Tool. Retrieved Sep 5, 2012 from `http://blast.ncbi.nlm.nih.gov/`.

[10] S. Needleman and C. Wunsch. A general method applicable to the search for similarities in the amino acid sequence of two proteins. *J. Mol. Bio.*, 48:443–453, 1970.

[11] Princeton University Computer Science. Computer Science 126, April 1 2012. Retrieved Aug 17, 2012 from `http://www.cs.princeton.edu/~cos126`.

[12] Princeton University Lewis-Sigler Institute for Integrative Genomics. Integrated Science, March 1 2012. Retrieved Aug 17, 2012 from `http://www.princeton.edu/integratedscience/`.

[13] K. L. Purvis-Roberts, G. Edwalds-Gilbert, A. S. Landsberg, N. Copp, L. Ulsh, and D. E. Drew. Accelerated Integrated Science Sequence. *J. Chem. Ed.*, 86(11):1295 – 1299, Nov. 2009.

[14] R. Sedgwick and K. Wayne. *Introduction to Programming in Java: An Interdisciplinary Approach.* Addison-Wesley, 2008.

[15] P. Seiden and F. Celada. A model for simulating cognate recognition and response in the immune system. *J. Theor. Biol.*, 158:329–340, 1992.

[16] T. Thein. Integrated science pays off for graduates. *Daily Princetonian*, October 12 2009.

Teaching the Security Mindset to CS 1 Students

Vahab Pournaghshband
Computer Science Department
University of California, Los Angeles
Los Angeles, CA 90024
vahab@cs.ucla.edu

ABSTRACT

In this 21st century technological world, the inherent problems of computer security are becoming increasingly important, and it is critical that our students gain the necessary skills and knowledge, early in their academic programs, to handle these problems. Specifically, the lack of security mindset is responsible for many overlooked and exploitable security bugs in the computer programs that these students design. While learning the security concepts generally requires a more advanced knowledge of computer science, learning the security mindset can be, and should be, addressed as early as CS 1.

Although the primary focus of any traditional CS 1 course is that of basic programming concepts, we believe that teaching the security mindset in this course is valuable and effective. In this paper we discuss the course that we have taught for four terms—an introductory course that teaches the security mindset to beginner programmers.

We start out by using the term-long incremental development of a security-sensitive program—the login program. Students develop the security mindset by thinking as both hackers and defenders, in order to catch and fix the logical and run-time errors that may lead to security breaches in the program.

Categories and Subject Descriptors

K.3.2 [**Computer and Information Science Education**]: Computer Science Education; D.4.6 [**Operating Systems**]: Security and Protection

General Terms

Design, Security

Keywords

CS 1, computer security, C++, security mindset

SIGCSE'13, March 6–9, 2013, Denver, Colorado, USA.

1. INTRODUCTION

Over the past several decades, software has become a crucial element in our lives, allowing us to manage and control systems that provide critical infrastructures in areas such as communications, energy, and transportation. Unfortunately, hackers are capable of interrupting these connections by exploiting software vulnerabilities and breaching software security. For instance, in 2011 programming flaws allowed hackers to steal millions of dollars through stolen credit cards in a single cyber attack incident [3]. Very recently, a flaw in Java put millions of Windows and Mac users worldwide at risk, and the damage cost is still rising [6]. New threats are further emerging as computers become more embedded and more intimately into our environment and daily lives, e.g., recent security vulnerabilities found in mobile medical devices [14]. Flaws in programs have also been exploited (e.g., by Stuxnet worm [11]) to sabotage critical infrastructures as an act of cyberwarfare.

Software security vulnerabilities are the most common cause of software security breaches. Most security problems can be traced back to underlying errors in a program's source code. For example, 64% of the nearly 2,500 vulnerabilities in the National Vulnerability Database in 2004 were caused by programming errors [7]. Fixing these bugs through constant security patches has its own problems, since security patch management and distribution are known to be fairly ineffective [2]. This suggests that catching security bugs in the pre-release version of programs is what is most effective.

These errors exist in programs mostly because programmers often fail to notice how the programs might fail and how those failures might be exploited. Among the numerous factors that explain this problem, the lack of a security mindset plays an important role in being unable to spot the exploitable bugs in programs in the early stages of development. The following is an excerpt from Bruce Schneier's blog on the security mindset [15]:

> "Security requires a particular mindset. Security professionals – at least the good ones – see the world differently...This kind of thinking is not natural for most people. It's not natural for engineers. Good engineering involves thinking about how things can be made to work; the security mindset involves thinking about how things can be made to fail. It involves thinking like an attacker, an adversary or a criminal. You don't have to exploit the vulnerabilities you find, but if you don't see the world that way, you'll never notice most security problems."

Therefore, if we teach programmers the security mindset, it will go a long way toward making a world with fewer cyber attacks and will substantially improve the security of future technological systems.

We believe that this security mindset should be taught to beginning programmers in classes as basic as CS 1, and that it should be emphasized throughout a student's computer science undergraduate program. In this paper we illustrate how to develop and teach this mindset in a CS introductory course. Through an example, we will show how to effectively teach the basic programming concepts, which is the primary goal of any CS introductory course, while developing the necessary security mindset for the students. The rationale for teaching the security mindset in an introductory course is elaborated on in Section 2.

This paper is organized as follows: Section 2 presents the advantages offered by this course. Section 3 presents related work. Methodology is presented in Section 4. Section 5 presents an informal evaluation of our work, and Section 6 concludes this paper.

2. ADVANTAGES

In this section we discuss why it is important to teach the security mindset in the first CS introductory course, while still keeping the primary focus on teaching basic programming concepts.

1) An early exposure to security issues is essential to a student's foundational appreciation and understanding of computer security. If the security mindset is developed at an early stage, students are more prone to naturally have security in mind while programming. From a practical point of view, this is a more effective approach than the one that only emphasizes program correctness and then, later in a student's programming career, attempts to change the undesirable habit of overlooking security bugs.

2) Students will also learn the significance of security bugs by understanding how these minor inaccuracies in detail, if overlooked, can lead to security breaches even though their code might be free of syntax, logical, and run-time errors. Moreover, it forces students to realize the importance of programming mistakes that can result in minor logical or run-time errors. Students will realize that these errors not only cause simple mistakes in program correctness, but they create an opportunity for hackers to attack the systems that run their programs.

3) Our proposed curriculum changes in the introductory course still emphasize learning the basic concepts of programming. By incorporating simple attack/defense scenarios to teach and verify program correctness interactively, we make learning those concepts more attractive to our students. As Fanelli et al. [5] state, "Security can make the *other stuff* more interesting. Studying security can lead students to a deeper understanding of computer science and information technology concepts. In many cases a thorough understanding of how a program works is needed to effectively attack or defend it."

4) Many students outside of the CS major are required to take only CS 1 (and/or CS 2), and quite possibly will never take any other CS course beyond the introductory courses. Therefore, it might be their last chance (within the curriculum) to learn about computer security. Even if a student never pursues a programming career, or programs only infrequently, this is still an opportunity for him to learn about the technical aspects of computer security. Students will understand the root cause of known security problems, why they behave maliciously, and how to protect themselves from them effectively. For instance, once students learn about how powerful brute force attacks are, they will understand the importance of choosing a strong password. In any and all cases, "The security mindset is a valuable skill that everyone can benefit from, regardless of career path." [15]

5) Secure programming takes extensive practice in order for it to evolve into a skill. While gaining this knowledge is valuable, a single course in computer security in the undergraduate curriculum often fails to actually build this skill for students. This suggests that exposing students to security issues, as early as an introductory course, establishes the security mindset and provides more practice in secure programming; hence, skill will be built faster and better.

3. RELATED WORK

An extensive body of literature has been created that focuses on computer security education. Some methods use active learning and visualization tools to teach security effectively. As an example, IPsecLite [8] was developed as a tool to demonstrate the inner-networking of IP security standards. Other methods emphasize the importance of teaching the physical and social aspects of computer security, along with technical aspects [4, 9]. A different class of work in this area, such as Peterson et al. [13], has developed hands-on laboratory exercises for a term-long security course.

There have also been proposals that emphasize introducing security concepts in the CS 1 course [10]. Validating user input, array range checking, numeric overflow and underflow, operator precedence, and rounding errors are a number of concepts that are suggested for course material in CS 1. The list is, however, not very long due to the limited knowledge of students in a CS introductory class.

Finally, there have been several papers on how security education fits into the CS undergraduate curriculum. Some introduced various ways to teach a single course [12]. Some presented effective track approaches, where a sequence of specialized courses on security is offered [1]. And some support the thread approach that is used as a unifying theme across the standard core CS curriculum [12].

4. METHODOLOGY

In this section we present the methods used to teach this introductory course at UCLA. C++ is used in the introductory CS course sequence. The material we present here, however, can be applied to other programming languages with some modifications, except for some topics such as pointers and C strings that are unique to a specific set of languages.

In our approach we used a widely known practical program as our example—the login program. Our login program asks for username and password from the user and will reveal a secret word if the credentials are provided correctly. It generates an error message if the username or the password entered is invalid. This program evolved throughout the school term, as the students learned new concepts. Note that traditional examples were still used to teach the materials, in addition to examples relevant to our login program case study.

We used the login program for teaching purposes for various reasons: (1) the basic concept of the program is familiar to students since it is a program that students use multiple times in an average day, ranging from logging into the department laboratory systems, to Facebook, and e-mail accounts. This would also make interacting with the program interesting, whether one was hacking into it or preventing hackers from breaching it. (2) This program has the unique feature of being able to vary from being a very simple program to a complex one. (3) As more programming concepts are introduced in the course, the program can be incrementally built up from a simple program to a coherent complex program. (4) The program is security-sensitive by its nature, making defensive programming even more essential.

In many cases, a thorough understanding of how a program works is needed to effectively attack or defend it. Moreover, to be a good defender you must be a good attacker; hence, we constantly guide the students to wear a hacker's hat to spot the vulnerability, and then switch to a defender's hat to fix the problem. Note that we use the term "hacking" in the most non-pejorative sense possible. Hacking, for our purposes, is a process for pointing out programming bugs rather than any negative use of such skills. For instance, we present a faulty program containing a particular logical error. We then ask the students to spot the error and exploit that vulnerability as if they were hacking into the system. We then further ask them to fix the error in the program to protect it against that particular attack.

Below, we outline, in order, some of the concepts and approaches that we use to simultaneously introduce core programming ideas and to develop the security mindset.

4.1 Introduction and Variables

Early in the course, variables are introduced. For the login program, we discuss how to define and use variables to hold the username and the password. Integer overflow is also introduced, and is illustrated through an example involving simple arithmetic operations. However, an example of how integer overflow is exactly exploited will be presented later in the course when introducing dynamic memory allocation.

4.2 Conditional (if-else) Statements

A very simple login program is implemented. This program will only support a single user and only accepts an all-numeric (`int`) password. If the password matches a hard-coded password, the secret word will be revealed (Figure 1).

```
if ( password==12345 )
  cout << "The secret word is Kosar.";
else
  cout << "Invalid password!";
```

Figure 1: Our first login program.

Even in such a simple implementation, common beginner mistakes, like using the assignment operator "=" in the condition instead of the equality operator "==," can be illustrated to students as an error that can lead to revealing the secret, even in the case of an incorrect entered password.

4.3 String Class

A major problem that variables of type `int` used to store passwords have is that they are vulnerable to brute force attacks due to relatively short range of values they can hold. To alleviate this security problem, we change our program to use the C++ string class to store the password instead.

4.4 Nested if-else and switch Statements

The program evolves into a two-user login program. We start our presentation with a faulty version of a two-user program (Figure 2). We then lead the students into a discussion of how this code is problematic, and examine the set of information that hackers would need in order to get into the system without entering the correct credentials. Finally, through a class discussion, we explain how to fix this problem by replacing the inner ||'s by `&&`'s.

```
if ((username=="vahab" || password=="Ta#3rEh") ||
    (username=="peter" || password=="hOo$H@Ng"))
  cout << "The secret word is Kosar.";
else
  cout << "Invalid username and/or password!"
```

Figure 2: An erroneous two-user login program.

Afterwards, this program is converted to a nested `if-else` statement, where outer `if` statements now check the usernames and inner `if` statements check the validity of the corresponding password. In this case, a more specific error message will be produced that indicates whether the username or the password entered is invalid. As this is being implemented, the emphasis will be on not only the possibility of errors in the code, but also the magnitude of problems caused by those errors. Ultimately, this program will be converted to use a `switch` statement in the same way.

4.5 Loops

The program shall be enhanced to allow multiple login attempts in such a way that it will quit after a predefined number of successive failed attempts. This illustrates a simple way to prevent brute force attacks, introduced earlier in the course. We also emphasize the magnitude of logical errors in the loop condition. For instance, an infinite loop will give the hacker a virtually unbounded number of attempts.

4.6 Nested Loops

When choosing a new password, the program should determine if it is a legitimately strong password. In our example, with the help of nested loops, we will write code to validate the password strength. The restrictions that define the level of strength of passwords is arbitrary. In this example, we make a strength requirement that the password must be at least eight characters long, and must include at least one uppercase and one lowercase letter, one digit, and one visible non-alphanumeric character. In addition, it must contain at least one string of at least four letters long. Again, failing to write this piece of code in the program correctly may result in accepting weak and vulnerable passwords.

4.7 Functions

After familiarizing students with the concept of functions, we implement the following two functions as examples of how to modularize our login program using functions:

```
bool isStrongPassword(std::string);
int authenticate();
```

The first function reuses the code implemented in the nested loops section to validate the strength of passwords. The latter function abstracts away the entire authentication process by moving all the details of how it is done into the function `authenticate()`. This way, only a simple `if` statement is needed to decide on revealing the secret word:

```
if ( authenticate()==0 )
  cout << "The secret word is Kosar.";
```

The function has no argument. It returns a non-zero value only when authentication fails (1=excessive failed attempts, and 2=user gave up trying prematurely).

And last, as we introduce some popular functions from the standard library, we mention the importance of knowing the difference between safe and unsafe functions.

4.8 Arrays and C Strings

In addition to learning and interacting with arrays, the students learn about C strings and some popular library functions associated to it. C strings can now replace the string class that was used as the type for the username and the password earlier in the course (`char username[SIZE]; char password[SIZE];`). At this point we present the students with the code presented in Figure 3 and ask them to examine it for potential problems.

```
char password[SIZE];
bool logged_in = false;

cin >> password;

if ( strcmp(password,correct_password)==0 )
  logged_in = true;

if ( logged_in==true )
  cout << "The secret word is Kosar.";
else
  cout << "Invalid password!";
```

Figure 3: A login program that is prone to buffer overflow.

There is no logical error here but at run-time, entering a password larger than the length of the array is problematic. Technically, among numerous undesirable consequences that could happen in this case, crashing at run-time is most desirable, from the security point of view. We explain why by showing how this could be an opportunity for the attacker to successfully overwrite `logged_in` to `true`, bypassing the entire authentication process. Even worse, the attacker can exploit the buffer overflow vulnerability in this piece of code and gain full control of the system. The latter, however, would be only explained in a very high level discussion since the students are not expected to have any knowledge of the operating systems concepts required to fully understand this details of this effect.

4.9 Multidimensional Arrays

The program should now support multiple users. One way to store the required information could be as follows:

```
char credentials[2][MAX_NUM_USERS][SIZE];
```

In this case, the corresponding password for username `credentials[0][i]` is `credentials[1][i]`.

4.10 Parallel Arrays

Our multiple user login program will contain meta information about users in addition to their corresponding passwords: first name, last name, age, date of birth ("MMDDYY"), the security question and its corresponding answer, and whether the user has administrative privileges or not (Figure 4). This is also a good way to teach array traversal and basic sorting to the students.

```
char username[MAX_NUM_USERS][SIZE];
char password[MAX_NUM_USERS][SIZE];
char first_name[MAX_NUM_USERS][SIZE];
char last_name[MAX_NUM_USERS][SIZE];
int age[MAX_NUM_USERS];
bool admin[MAX_NUM_USERS];
long dob[MAX_NUM_USERS];
char security_question[MAX_NUM_USERS][SIZE];
char answer_security_question[MAX_NUM_USERS][SIZE];
```

Figure 4: List of parallel arrays used in the login program.

4.11 File I/O

Hardcoding passwords into an executable file is considered a bad security practice for numerous reasons. Reverse-code engineering the executable file may leak the passwords. Also, if the passwords are exposed by other means, changing them would require changing the source code—making it a virtually impractical task.

Instead, the credentials should be stored in a separate file. At this point, students learn how to read the already stored usernames and passwords from a file designated for this purpose—the *credentials file*. Furthermore, they learn how to modify this file to add new users, remove users, and update users' passwords. We also use this opportunity to touch upon using cryptographically secure one-way hash functions (e.g., `crypt`) for storing credentials in files, and to point out the disadvantages of storing passwords in plaintext.

4.12 Pointers and Dynamic Memory Allocation

Previously, we have used the constant `MAX_NUM_USERS` as the size of the parallel arrays. By taking this approach, we are bound to either wasting memory resources by allocating more than necessary, or that our array runs out of space if there are more users than the predefined size of the arrays. To alleviate this problem we need to allocate arrays dynamically.

We first need to know how many users are there before being able to allocate enough memory to hold that information. Hence, we first call a function that is assumed to read a file and returns the number of rows in it, representing the total number of users.

```
int n = getNumberOfRows("credentials_file");
```

We then dynamically allocate the parallel arrays. Here we create a two dimensional array to hold the usernames:

```
char** username = new char*[n];

for(int i=0; i<n; i++)
  username[i] = new char[SIZE];
```

Finally, we call a function that would iterate through the file and copy the information for each user in the corresponding arrays including `username`, one user at a time.

The students are then asked to examine the code for problems. Basically, the problem with this code is that if the number of lines are too large (beyond the range of `int`), it would result in integer overflow. This means that `username` is not large enough to hold the information about all users stored in the file. Technically, this would lead to accessing and writing into elements out of range, and hence, leading this cascading effects to heap overflow. A subtle attacker could corrupt the credentials file maliciously to cause integer overflows.

Note that in teaching the basics of how to dynamically allocate memory, we ensure that the students understand both the security and performance implications of not checking for `NULL` immediately after the `new` statement as well as deallocating that chunk of memory improperly. We further mention the importance of clearing (by setting the value to zero) the allocated memory right before deallocating, for security purposes. We explain that if the allocated memory holds sensitive information, as it does in our case, deallocation without clearing could potentially expose the sensitive information.

4.13 Classes and Structs

By now we are ready to wrap our implementation of the login program into an API, for other programs to use. We have defined two classes, as illustrated in Figure 5: `Credentials` and `UserInfo`. `Credentials` is designed to perform user management tasks such as adding and removing users, and `UserInfo` is designed to hold and update the information about a particular user.

Here, we omit the details of implementation of the functions and limit ourselves to the discussion of the constructor for `Credentials` that takes the credentials filename as an argument. The constructor parses through the file, sets the total number of users, dynamically allocates memory for `users_list`, and at last, copies all the information from the file into the array.

While teaching the basics of C++ classes, it is important to address clearly that the access specifiers (private and public keywords) are not designed to be used for security, and rather they are designed for abstraction in object oriented programming. In fact, declaring methods or data as private, enables the compiler to find programming mistakes before they become bugs. In other words, this C++ access control mechanism provides protection against accidents and not against fraud. Therefore, an effective design would protect careless programmers, who will be using our API, from unwillingly committing to such bugs.

For instance, in `UserInfo` class, by design, you can never change the `username`, after it is set by the constructor. This design would protect against accidental attempts to change

```
class Credentials {
public:
  Credentials(char* filename);
  bool addNewUser(char*,char*,char*,char*,int,
                  long,char*,char*,char);
  int deleteUser(UserInfo*);
  UserInfo* getUserInfo(char* username);

private:
  int num_of_users;
  UserInfo* users_list;
};

class UserInfo {
public:
  UserInfo(char*,char*,char*,char*,int,
           long,char*,char*,char);
  char* getUsername();
  char* getPassword();
  bool resetPassword(char* password);
  bool isStrongPassword(char* password);

  char first_name[SIZE];
  char last_name[SIZE];
  int  age;
  long dob;
  char security_question[SIZE];
  char answer_security_question[SIZE];
  char privileges;

private:
   char username[SIZE];
   char password[SIZE];
};
```

Figure 5: The login program API.

the username after its creation which should never happen. Another design choice we are making here is forcing indirect access to `password`. One advantage of this approach is to ensure calling `isStrongPassword()` to check for its validity before changing it (as it is called inside `resetPassword()`). Finally, by not allowing direct access to `users_list`, we leave all memory management tasks associated to it to the `Credential` class and out of the the burden of the API user. This is desirable to avoid the possibility of potential programming mistakes in doing so that could lead to memory leaks by the API users.

5. AN INFORMAL EVALUATION

While we have not conducted a formal evaluation of the course materials, we do have several indicators that suggest that our approach was successful. Remember that we used two sets of examples to teach each concept: a set of traditional examples and the examples related to our login program case study.

At the end of the Spring 2010 term, we asked the CS 1 students to rank these two sets of examples that we used to cover the materials in various categories. These categories were (1) helpfulness in learning the programming concepts, (2) level of difficulty understanding the materials, and (3) was it or was it not a "fun" experience? We used a scale of 1 (low) to 5 (high) in this survey, and provided 32 students with questionnaires to be completed. The results from this survey are shown in Table 1.

Table 1: Student evaluation of materials we used in CS 1. (H: Helpfulness, D: Difficulty, F: Fun)

	Login Program			Other Examples		
Topics	H	D	F	H	D	F
Intro/Variables	3.2	1.4	3.1	3.0	1.4	2.1
if-else Statements	3.8	2.0	3.9	4.0	2.1	3.1
Nested if-else	4.3	2.4	4.6	3.3	2.6	3.0
String Class	3.3	2.1	3.8	3.5	1.7	3.3
Loops	4.1	2.7	4.2	3.8	2.7	3.4
Nested Loops	3.4	3.5	3.7	3.9	3.2	3.8
Functions	3.2	3.1	3.9	3.9	3.4	3.7
Arrays/C strings	3.7	3.2	4.0	3.7	2.9	3.8
Multi-dim Arrays	3.2	3.6	4.1	3.5	3.4	2.9
Parallel Arrays	3.8	3.0	4.4	3.7	3.1	3.2
File I/O	3.6	4.0	4.5	3.4	3.4	3.1
Pointers/DMA	3.6	4.0	4.5	3.5	3.9	2.8
Structs/Classes	4.2	4.3	4.2	3.7	4.2	3.5

Interestingly, the ratings for "fun" averaged around 4 for the login program example through all the topics, which was higher than ratings for traditional examples. Average ratings on whether the examples were helpful for learning programming concepts were almost the same for both sets of examples. We also observed that as the concepts got harder, the average rating for difficulty rose almost equally.

In the questionnaire that we gave to students, we also asked if they thought that the login program example we used in the course helped them to be more aware of security bugs, and in general, if it had any educational value. 93% of respondents answered "Yes" to this question.

However, in our evaluation, we did not test the students for security mindset and awareness to see if we had achieved our goal. Hence, in future work we plan to construct the following experiment to evaluate that mindset and awareness. We plan to choose two CS 1 classes in the same term, and run them with two different teaching styles: one with our traditional style, and the other with the same teaching style presented in this paper. At the end of the term, we will then evaluate students' security mindset and awareness in programming through an informal exam (one with no effect on the final grade in the course). We will also compare students' average final grades for two classes to see if the methods we used have any effect (positive or negative) on learning the basic concepts of programming. These grades, while not a perfect measure for student learning, should indicate whether students were able to learn the basic concepts, along with the security concepts, without experiencing problems.

6. CONCLUSIONS

In this paper we described the process of teaching the security mindset for beginning programming students in the CS 1 course that this author taught for four terms. Students, by and large, reacted very positively to this course. They enjoyed the material and found it educationally valuable and helpful for understanding the basic programming concepts. What we have described in this paper is only the first step toward achieving our goals, but we believe it to be an important step that can be built on later in more advanced undergraduate courses.

7. ACKNOWLEDGMENTS

The author is very much obliged to Peter Reiher for his valuable input on technical aspects of the paper.

8. REFERENCES

[1] S. Azadegan, M. Lavine, M. O'Leary, A. Wijesinha, and M. Zimand. An undergraduate track in computer security. In *Proc of the 8th ITiCSE*, 2003.

[2] H. Cavusoglu, H. Cavusoglu, and J. Zhang. Security patch management: Share the burden or share the damage? *Management Science*, 54(4):657–670, 2008.

[3] CNNMoney. *Citi: millions stolen in May hack attack.* http://money.cnn.com/2011/06/27/technology/citi_credit_card/index.htm, 2011.

[4] T. Dimkov, W. Pieters, and P. Hartel. Training students to steal: a practical assignment in computer security education. In *Proc. of the 42nd SIGCSE*, '11.

[5] R. Fanelli and T. O'connor. Experiences with practice-focused undergraduate security education. In *Proc. of the 3rd USENEX CSET*, 2010.

[6] Forbes.com. Java flaw puts millions of Windows and Mac users at risk, 2012. http://www.forbes.com/sites/adriankingsleyhughes/2012/08/29/java-flaw-puts-millions-of-windows-and-mac-users-at-risk/.

[7] J. Heffley and P. Meunier. Can source code auditing software identify common vulnerabilities and be used to evaluate software security? In *Proc. of the 37th HICSS*, 2004.

[8] N. Kazemi and S. Azadegan. IPsecLite: a tool for teaching security concepts. In *Proc. of the 41st ACM SIGCSE*, pages 138–142. ACM, 2010.

[9] T. Kohno and B. D. Johnson. Science fiction prototyping and security education: cultivating contextual and societal thinking in computer security education and beyond. In *Proc. of SIGCSE*, 2011.

[10] K. Nance. Teach them when they aren't looking: Introducing security in CS1. *IEEE Security and Privacy*, 7(5):53–55, Sept. 2009.

[11] NYtimes.com. Cyberattacks on Iran - Stuxnet and Flame, 2012. http://topics.nytimes.com/top/reference/timestopics/subjects/c/computer_malware/stuxnet/index.html.

[12] L. Perrone, M. Aburdene, and X. Meng. Approaches to undergraduate instruction in computer security. In *Proc. of ASEE*, 2005.

[13] P. Peterson and P. Reiher. Security exercises for the online classroom with DETER. In *Proc. of the 3rd USENIX CSET*, 2010.

[14] V. Pournaghshband, M. Sarrafzadeh, and P. Reiher. Securing legacy mobile medical devices. In *Proc. of the 3rd International Conference on Wireless Mobile Communication and Healthcare (MobiHealth)*, 2012.

[15] B. Schneier. Schneier on Security: The Security Mindset, 2008. http://www.schneier.com/blog/archives/2008/03/the_security_mi_1.html.

Constructive Use of Errors in Teaching CS1

David Ginat*
CS Group, Science Education Department
Tel-Aviv University
ginat@post.tau.ac.il

Ronit Shmallo
Science Education Department, Tel-Aviv University
and SCE - Shamoon College of Engineering
ronits1@sce.ac.il

ABSTRACT

We developed an approach of learning from errors in CS1, taught in OOP. The approach is based on a set of principles, which include: cognitive conflict, constructivist characteristics, error attribution, self explanation, reflection, and *refinement of concept images* of fundamental OOP terms and mechanisms. The approach is presented, and some of its activities are illustrated. The developed activities aim at erroneous OOP conceptions that we have observed in a previous study. We applied the approach with CS1 college students, and conducted a comparative study, with an experiment group and a control group. We display a summary of the study's results, together with the students' opinions about the applied approach.

Categories and Subject Descriptors

K.3.2 **[Computers and Education]:** Computer and Information Science Education – Computer science education.

Keywords

OOP, Constructivism, Learning from errors.

1. INTRODUCTION

Errors involve wrong doing. Yet, everyone errs, and one may learn from wrong no less, and perhaps even more than from right. Learning from wrong may be beneficial when conducted constructively. In this paper, we display a study of constructive learning from wrong in CS1.

In Computer Science (CS), the common practice of learning from wrong appears mostly implicitly, in the form of debugging a program. Debugging is typically considered a process of "cleaning" a program from rather local programming "bugs", in order to have it run successfully. Programming textbooks and tutors usually mention the important phase of debugging, without *explicitly* focusing on learning from errors.

Yet, errors may not necessarily be programming bugs. They may derive from limited conceptual understanding, lack of fundamental notions, or improper problem solving. Two studies of capitalizing on errors, for enhancing algorithmic problem solving skills were conducted by us during the last decade [4,5]. But such studies are rather the exception. In this paper, we extend the perspective of capitalizing on errors, by using errors for developing coherent knowledge in CS1.

In the last two decades, mathematics and science educators attempted various ways of using errors as a means for learning. Ohlsson [9] proposed a theory of how people detect and correct errors during skill practice, and conjectured that errors are primarily caused by overly general knowledge structures. He advocated the development of domain-specific declarative knowledge. One of his primary themes is "re-conceptualization" of declarative knowledge as prescriptive rather than descriptive.

Borasi [1] recognized the stimulating potential of errors, and developed a framework of capitalizing on errors as a springboard for inquiry about the nature of mathematics. She offered a teaching approach based on problem exploration, errors, conflict, doubt and reflection, for elaborating on mathematical concepts and problem solving. Melis et al. [7,8] examined the pedagogical value of erroneous examples. They posed to students erroneous examples of others, both directly, and using ActiveMath – a web-based, user-adaptive learning environment, and observed both a cognitive (mathematical) contribution and a meta-cognitive (analysis) contribution of such an activity.

Physics educators guided students to learn from mistakes by analyzing their own and others' mistakes. Pinkeron [10] conducted a "second round" for a test, in which he asked the students to identify, explain, and correct their conceptual mistakes in their original test solutions. Yerushalmi & Polingher [17] handed students a sheet of incorrect answers, with erroneous statements, and asked the students' analysis and diagnosis of the statements, in a homework assignment and a class discussion.

Siegler [15] and Grobe & Renkl [6] examined whether students benefit from explaining to themselves "worked-out examples", and observed that students who self-explained both correct and incorrect solutions benefited more than those who only self-explained correct solutions. The benefit was particularly noticeable when the learners maintained "favourable prior knowledge" of the studied material.

The above studies of learning from errors involve an aspect of constructivism, as the utilization of errors was based on students' prior knowledge, which was imprecise, or vague to some extent. The goal was to refine their knowledge and skills by raising conflict, or cognitive dissonance, in using errors. Constructivist psychologies support the idea of conflict as a catalyst for learning. Conflict causes review of one's knowledge and procedures [2].

The review of one's knowledge and procedures involves a meta-cognitive aspect, as one becomes better aware of both her solution process and her conceptual notions. The enhancement of one's

*This study was supported by ISF grant #937/08

SIGCSE'13, March 6–9, 2013, Denver, Colorado, USA.

meta-cognitive practice is advocated by mathematics and science educators [13] as an additional constructive means for learning.

In this paper, we display a constructive approach of using errors in developing basic programming concepts. Our approach is based on the embedment of elements of the studies described above in the teaching of CS1. The approach addresses novice difficulties with OOP conceptions, which were revealed in previous studies.

We applied our approach in a class of 52 undergraduates in their CS1 course in Java. In order to obtain assessment information, we conducted a comparative study, in which the performance of these students was compared to that of another group of 47 undergraduates, who studies the same CS1 material in the more common, non error-oriented way.

In the next section – Section 2 – we display and exemplify our learning-from-errors approach. In Sections 3, we display the methodology of our comparative study and present the study's results, including students' affective views. In Section 4, we discuss the presented results and their implication for teaching.

2. LEARNING FROM ERRORS IN OOP

Programming involves several primary elements, among them: comprehension of programming language features, understanding of the computer model, I/O analysis, modeling of the "world", algorithmic design, and problem solving.

Novices demonstrate difficulties, of different kinds, with all these elements. We focus on the first element above – comprehension of the programming language features. We do not aim at problem-solving. The programming language is Java. Our focus is also related, to some extent, to comprehension of the computer model.

Previous studies of novice difficulties revealed limited understanding of the most elementary terms of the OOP paradigm, including the terms: *class*, *object*, and *constructor* (e.g., [11]). A recent study of ours revealed novices' vague perceptions of term characteristics [14], particularly in the sense of novices' tendencies to *expand* or *reduce* term features.

For example, some novices perceive a particular static variable as an entity that may have many occurrences, thus expanding its number of occurrences. Other novices are unaware of the necessity of invoking a constructor in creating an object, thus reducing, or oversimplifying the mechanism of object creation. Some novices are aware of the essential role of constructors, but believe that only one constructor may be defined in a class, thus reducing the number of ways possible for constructor definition.

The Learning-From-Errors Approach

The findings in our previous study imply a few themes:

- For quite a few elementary terms, the *concept image* [16] of a term, or mechanism, is not equivalent to the actual definition of the term features, and divert from these features by either expansion or reduction of their actual characteristics.
- Some of the inaccurate conceptions develop from particular examples shown to novices, which they use with *improper analogy* or *improper generalization*.
- Some of the terms', or mechanisms' features are perceived as collections of actions, rather than well-defined features. This encapsulates an *operative*, rather than *declarative* view of features.

Following the above themes, and the elements of learning from wrong described in the Introduction, we devised guidelines for an approach of learning from errors in elementary OOP. We introduce them below.

- **Declarative conceptions.** The objective is to develop declarative conceptions of elementary OOP terms, so that novices' *concept images* of these terms will suite their accurate definitions.
- **Constructivist approach.** Activities will "build upon" (possibly inaccurate) *prior knowledge*. This may assist in the reduction of cognitive load (during the activities).
- **Tasks that refine conceptions.** The constructivist approach tasks may be aimed at erroneously expanded or reduced conceptions of term features and notions. In the case of expanded conceptions, the tasks will be aimed at *narrowing the conceptions*; and in the case of reduced conceptions, the tasks will be aimed at *expanding the conceptions*.
- **Task format.** The tasks will be of three forms: 1. Description of the execution result of a given code; 2. Evaluation of an assertion about a term feature, or about a given programming statement; 3. A code development task (either "from scratch", or from a given partial code).
- **Cognitive conflict.** The tasks should raise cognitive conflicts. Students who follow a task should reach a point in which they realize that the task cannot be properly solved if an erroneous conception is applied.
- **Error attribution.** The point at which the cognitive conflict will arise should evoke a process of "blame assignment", which will yield error attribution [9]; i.e., the recognition of the source of the error. The recognition of the error's source will, in turn, yield *knowledge revision*, in the sense of refinement of one's concept image.
- **Class activity.** A task solution process, which will eventually yield knowledge revision, may be conducted in one of several ways: 1. Each student will solve the task alone; 2. A pair of students will solve the task; 3. A class discussion will be conducted.
- **Explanation.** During the activity of single students and pairs of students, *self-explanation* may be conducted. The explanation should involve an emphasis of both the wrong conception and the suitable "refinement".
- **Reflection.** A class discussion will conclude with reflection on the solution process. Wrong conceptions will be discussed, and students may be encouraged to suggest their possible origins, including previous examples that were over-generalized or analogically misused. The reflection will also illuminate the type of activity that was conducted, raising awareness of possible meta-cognitive elements.

The above guidelines were utilized to develop a set of tasks and activities that were applied in class as means for learning from errors. We describe some of them below.

Learning-From-Errors Examples

In our previous study [14], we noticed particular difficulties with several OOP aspects, among them the aspects of *addressing*, *creation*, *scope*, and *method invocation*.

We illustrate the application of the above learning-from-errors guidelines with three examples. Each example was part of an activity on one aspect or a few related aspects. Each example is displayed with accordance to the guidelines presented above.

Difficulty with *addressing*

Example 1. Address vs content

Prior knowledge: Objects are accessed through their name.

Erroneous, reduced conception (which should be expanded): An object name yields the object attributes. But, conception of the object name as a variable that keeps the object's address (in memory) is vague or missing.

Task: Determine the following code's output.

```
public class Point
{   private int x_coord; private int y_coord;
    public Point(int x,int y) {
      x_coord = x; y_coord = y;
}}
public class ComparePoints
{   public static void main() {
      Point p1=new Point(1,2);
      Point p2=new Point(1,2);
      if (p1==p2)
        System.out.println("equal");
      else
        System.out.println("not equal");
}}
```

Cognitive conflict: The correct output is "not equal", yet some students said "equal", as the objects' attributes are equal.

Error attribution: The incorrect conception was the following: the statement `p1==p2` yields comparison of the contents pointed-at by p1 and p2. But, the comparison is between the values of p1 and p2.

Class activity: Each student was given the task in a handout, and was requested to self-explain her answer (and train-of-thought) to herself. Then, a class discussion followed, and both the erroneous answer ("equal") and the correct answer ("unequal") were discussed and explained.

Reflection: Students acknowledged that the reason for the above erroneous conception seemed to be *vague conception* of the computer model and the mechanism of object addressing. The declarative definition of object addressing was displayed, emphasizing that the reference "p1" keeps the object address, and not the attributes of the object.

Refined conception: Object accessing involves two elements: the object's *address* and the object's *attributes*. The address is kept in a variable, which is the object's name, and the attributes are kept in some location in the computer memory, which is pointed-at by the object name.

We developed an additional task, with a similar objective. In this task, we set two pointers, with different names – p1 and p2 – on the same object, and asked whether the attributes pointed-at by p1 are equal to the attributes pointed-at by p2. This task underlined, again, the notions of address and content.

Difficulty with *creation*

Example 2. The role of the constructor

Prior knowledge: An object name is the pointer for reaching an object in memory.

Erroneous, reduced conception (which should be expanded): The creation of an object occurs by declaring a name of the object. But, the conception of the essential role of the constructor during object creation is missing.

Task: Identify the error(s) in the following code:

```
public class Time
{   private int hour; private int minute;
    public Time(int hr,int mnt) {
      hour = hr; minute = mnt;
    }
    public boolean equal(Time other) {
      if (hour==other.hour &&
          minute==other.minute)
          return true;
      else return false;
}}
public class CompareTime
{   public static void main() {
      Time t1,t2;
      if (t1.equal(t2))
        System.out.println("equal");
}}
```

Cognitive conflict: Students who held the erroneous conception did not recognize an error, although they were told in the task that there is an error in the code.

Error attribution: The incorrect conception was the following: declaration of names of objects also yields creation of the objects themselves.

Class activity: The students were divided into pairs, and each pair was directed to discuss the task and offer its solution. Then, a class discussion followed, and different (suitable and unsuitable) errors were suggested.

Reflection: Students conjectured that they employed *improper analogy* and *over-generalized* the utilization of simple variables. The constructor's role was elaborated, and the specification of the process of object creation was displayed and explained in detail.

Refined conception: The creation of an object requires both the declaration of its name, and the allocation of the memory cells that keep the values of the object's attributes. In addition, the initial object values are set by the constructor.

The role and specification of constructors are unclear to novices in various respects. We developed several activities of learning-from-errors for addressing erroneous conceptions of constructors.

Difficulty with *scope*

Example 3. Access of private attributes

Prior knowledge: Class attributes may be accessed from other classes.

Erroneous, expanded conception (which should be reduced): A class attribute may be accessed from another class, regardless of the way the attribute is specified.

Task: Given the following code:

```
public class Time
{   private int hour;
    private int minute;
    public Time(int hr,int mnt) {
      hour = hr; minute = mnt;
 }}
public class SetTime
{   public static void main() {
      Time t = new Time(12,30);
      t.hour = 11;
      System.out.println(t.hour);
}}
```

Is the following assertion correct? "The program will compile and run successfully, and the output will be 11."

Cognitive conflict: Some students did not recognize any error in the above code, yet the answer "Correct" is wrong.

Error attribution: The incorrect conception was that of overlooking the attribute's specification as *private*.

Class activity: A class discussion was conducted. Those who answered that the program will compile and run successfully realized the compilation difficulty, due to the attempt to improperly assign a value to the private variable `t.hour`.

Reflection: In earlier learning stages students used only one class. The expansion into programming with more than one class was *oversimplified*; overlooking the term *private*. The declarative specification of class attributes was displayed, emphasizing the roles of the terms *private* and *public*.

3. ASSESSMENT

We embedded the learning-from-errors approach in the teaching of college CS1 students, and compared their OOP conceptions to those of CS1 college students who learned in the traditional way. We display below the methodology of our comparative study and then present its results. In addition, we display the student opinions about the learning-from-errors approach.

Methodology

Population

The comparative study involved two populations – an experiment group of 52 students, and a control group of 47 students. The students in both groups were college students, of the Information Systems program in the Industrial Engineering department, in the SCE College of Engineering in our country. Their program included CS1 studies, in two courses – CS1a and CS1b. Both courses involved the Java programming language, yet the CS1a course focused on fundamental procedural features (e.g., *if, for, while, arrays*), using a single class; and the CS1b course expanded the perspective to fundamental OOP notions, including multiple classes, different constructors, inheritance, and more.

Both groups started the CS1b course in Winter 2011. The groups were of similar competence in CS1a - the average CS1a grade of the control group was 70.2, and the average CS1a grade of the experiment group was 67.9.

The course lasted 15 weeks (for both groups). Each week involved 3-hour class meetings and 2-hour lab meetings. The control group studied the CS1b material in the traditional way, without particular focus on learning from errors. The experiment group studied the same material, at the same pace, yet during 6 of the weeks in the first half of the course, the OOP notions were displayed with an extra focus on learning from errors.

Before the middle of the course we posed a 1.5-hour questionnaire to both groups, with which we examined and compared their OOP conceptions. We also posed an attitudes questionnaire to the experiment group students.

Tools

Three tools were used: the learning-from-errors activities, a comparative questionnaire about OOP concepts, and an attitudes questionnaire about the learning-from-errors approach.

The Learning-from-errors Activities: We developed a total of 6 activities, each composed of a few parts. Each activity lasted between one and two hours. In the previous section we displayed the guidelines for the activities, and illustrated them with three examples – each displaying a part of a complete activity. The complete activity involved a few additional parts about the same terms, or related terms. The activities particularly focused on basic aspects of OOP terms, including: addressing, creation, scope, default conceptions, the difference between a class and an object, assignment characteristics, and method invocations. The activities particularly underlined accurate definitions and mechanism comprehension.

The Comparative Questionnaire: The questionnaire was posed to the students of both groups, before the middle of the course, and included three questions, each of a different kind. Question 1 involved code comprehension; Question 2 required code design; and Question 3 required code completion (combining code comprehension and code design).

In Question 1, we displayed a code, and asked the students various questions about the code.

In Question 2, we posed several tasks, among them the formulation of a class `Date`, which involved: three attributes (`day`, `month`, `year`), two constructors, one of which is a copy constructor, and several methods (including `get` and `set` methods and some comparison methods).

In Question 3, we specified two classes, one which created an object and two pointers (references) to that object. We asked the students to answer questions about the given code and add a component to the code.

The Attitudes Questionnaire: The questionnaire was posed to the experiment group students, and asked about their opinions on different aspects of the embedment of the learning-from-errors approach in their studies.

Process

The two groups of students studied the first half of the CS1b course as described (in the Population part) above. It is important to note that the embedment of the learning-from-errors approach did not slow down the teaching progress of the experiment group. Only the teaching means were different. After posing the comparative questionnaire we interviewed about 10% of the students from both groups about their answers. We display a summary of our findings below.

Results

We analyzed the student's written and oral (interview) answers. Our focus was on the erroneous, reduced and expanded conceptions that we recognized in our earlier study [14]. The erroneous conceptions could be seen in the pieces of code that the student designed, as well as in the answers to the code-comprehension and code completion questions. They involved vague or erroneous conceptions of: OOP term definitions, the mechanisms of the OOP paradigm, and the underlying computer model.

The students of the experiment group demonstrated fewer erroneous conceptions than those of the control group. We display below a statistical summary of erroneous conceptions of the students in both groups.

Statistics of the two groups' erroneous conceptions:

Address as content. The comparison of names of objects is the comparison of all their attributes.

Control: 34%	Experiment: 22%

And, assignment of an additional name to the same object creates a new object.

Control: 24%	Experiment: 18%

Oversimplified creation. The creation of an object is equivalent to the declaration of a variable – its name.

Control: 30%	Experiment: 18%

(Some students even perceived that there is no need at all to create an object in order to use it, as "it is just there".)

Method invocation as an assignment. A method invocation is an assignment statement (e.g., *obj.set = 5*, instead of *obj.set(5)*) .

Control: 16%	Experiment: 6%

Method reference without an object. It is suitable to invoke a method without indicating an (its) object.

Control: 16%	Experiment: 0%

Erroneous scope. It is possible to access from an outer class an attribute that is defined as private.

Control: 12%	Experiment: 4%

The default constructor is always there. The default constructor always exists, even if not defined when another constructor is defined.

Control: 18%	Experiment: 8%

In the answer to Question 2, one student from the control group, did not invoke a constructor, and only wrote the following statement: `Date d1={3,5,2011}`. In a following interview he explained: "I initialized the object d1 in a similar way to array initialization". This expresses erroneous conception of object creation, and improper analogy to the notion of assignment in procedural programming.

Another students, from the experiment group, designed a correct code in her answer to the Question, and said: "It is insufficient just to declare, you have to create the object ... I realized from our learning-from-errors activities that we have to declare the object, create it and initialize it using the constructor ...".

Unfortunately, due to lack of space, we do not display more student quotations.

We display below a summary of answers of the experiment group students to some of the questions in the attitudes questionnaire. In the table below, "1" represents "strongly disagree, "2" – disagree, "3" – agree, and "4" – strongly agree.

Summary of answers to the Attitudes Questionnaire:

	1	2	3	4
Working with self-explanation sheets contributed to my understanding.		2	26	24
The activity of telling whether an assertion is correct was helpful.	1	11	23	17
The activity of telling whether a code is erroneous was helpful for me.	2	10	14	26
Class discussions of erroneous solutions were contributing.		9	11	32
Learning from errors offered critical thinking and intellectual challenge.		4	15	33
I would like to learn other topics with learning-from-errors.	3	8	12	29

Some quotations from the students' answer sheets are:

"Sometimes I realized that I don't know things I thought I knew."

"The explanation (to myself) was very helpful, as I had to tell myself what is wrong ... between similar things ..."

"The activity helped me remember not to repeat the same error."

"It was fun ... clever to divert from the routine way of learning."

4. DISCUSSION

Errors may trigger cognitive conflicts, which, in turn, yield a process of reflection and critical thinking [1]. Such a process may be used for developing coherent knowledge. We developed, and presented in the previous sections an approach, which involves activities that yield such a process.

Our approach capitalizes on previous knowledge that is vague or partly erroneous. It is aimed at correcting erroneous conceptions and decreasing declarative vagueness. We view our approach as reducing OOP knowledge gaps. The approach involves constructivist characteristics.

Constructivism is apparent in the approach activities, in the sense that each activity assumes prior knowledge and focuses on only one or two, possibly vague conceptions.

The activities involve self-explanation, pair discussions, reasoning and reflection. Such elements deepen understanding (e.g., [6]). So do class discussions in which the incorrect is compared to the correct. In such discussions, one may better comprehend the correct, as well as remember and become more aware of the incorrect. Furthermore, discussions and reasoning about the possible origins of errors (as indicated in the "reflection" parts of the examples of section 2) enhance meta-cognitive competence.

Some students indicated that they realized their previous erroneous conceptions, of which they were unaware. They conjectured about the origins of their faulty perspectives. These origins seem similar to previous observations of the characteristics of novice difficulties, among them those of Du Boulay [3] and Rath & Brown [12].

Du Boulay revealed novice's *improper use of analogies, metaphors, and projection* (from one entity to another), as well as *overgeneralization*. These were present also here. Students acknowledged their tendencies to apply procedural programming notion in OOP. One such example is students' perceptions of method invocation without indication of the method's object.

Rath & Brown [12] illuminated novice tendencies to relate capacities of "*independent thinking*" to the computer. Here too, some students demonstrated an oversimplified conception of the process of object creation, believing that the computer "takes care" of the necessary operations involved in object creation, without them telling it explicitly to do so (and invoking the constructor).

Quiet a few students of the experiment group indicated that they deepened their understanding with the learning-from-errors activities. They were able to specify terms and mechanisms clearer and more accurately.

The results displayed in the previous section show the relevance and potential of the embedment of our approach in teaching. The experiment group students demonstrated fewer erroneous conceptions than the control group students. And, they liked the learning-from-errors activities. Thus, one of the benefits of our developed activities is that of raising student motivation.

It seems that the experiment group students refined through the activities their concept images of terms and notions. In [16], Vinner revealed student tendencies to turn to *concept images* rather than concept definitions, in mathematical problem solving. He noticed that some students "adopt" various associations from examples, of which some are suitable but others are not. Our learning-from-errors emphasis on declarative definitions helped students modify and correct undesired associations, and refine their concept images.

In conclusion, we offer some suggestions for tutors, based on our experience: **1.** Identify erroneous conceptions of your students; **2.** Address these conceptions with a constructivist approach, while trying to reduce knowledge gaps; **3.** Develop activities such as those illustrated here; **4.** Embed the activities in selected places in your CS1 teaching; **5.** The activities may involve self-explanation, working in pairs, and class discussion; **6.** The class discussions will involve a process of error attribution and reflection on both erroneous and correct solutions; **7.** The discussion will conclude with accurate declarative specifications of the studied terms and notions; and **8.** Throughout the activities and the discussion, try to raise the students' enthusiasm so they will feel they are both learning and having fun.

5. REFERENCES

[1] Borasi, R. (1996). *Reconceiving Mathematics Instruction: A Focus on Errors*, Ablex Pub.

[2] Confrey, J. (1990). What constructivism implies for teaching. *Journal for Research in Mathematics Education. Monograph Vol 4*, NCTM Inc, 107–122.

[3] Du Boulay, B. (1986). Some Difficulties of Learning to Program, *Journal of Educational Computing Research*, 2(1), 57-73.

[4] Ginat, D. (2003). The greedy trap and learning from mistakes, *Proc of SIGCSE 34*, ACM Press, 11-15.

[5] Ginat, D. (2008). Learning from wrong and creative algorithm design, *Proc of SIGCSE 39*, ACM Press, 26-30.

[6] Grobe, C. S. & Renkl, A. (2007). Finding and fixing errors in worked examples: can this foster learning outcomes?, *Learning and Instruction*, 17, 612-634.

[7] Melis, E. (2004). Erroneous examples as a source of learning mathematics, *Proc of CELDA 2004*, 311-318.

[8] Melis, E., Sander, A., & Tsovaltzi, D. (2010). How to support meta-cognitive skills for finding and correcting errors, *Proc of the AAAI Fall 2010 Symposium*, 64-68.

[9] Ohlsson, S. (1996). Learning from performance errors, *Psychological Review* 103:241–262.

[10] Pinkerton, K. D. (2005). Learning from errors, *The Physics Teacher, 43* (8), 510-513.

[11] Ragonis, N. & Ben-Ari, M. (2005). A long-term investigation of the comprehension of OOP concepts by novices, *Computer Science Education*, 15(3), 203-221.

[12] Rath, A. & Brown, D.E. (1995). Conceptions of human-computer interaction: A model for understanding student errors, *Journal of. Educational Computing Research*, Vol. 12(4), 395-409.

[13] Schoenfeld, A. E. (1992). Learning to think mathematically: problem solving, metacognition, and sense making in mathematics, in Grouws D. A. (ed.), *Handbook of Research on Mathematics Teaching and Learning,* 334-370.

[14] Shmalo, R., Ragonis, N. & Ginat, D. (2012). Fuzzy OOP: expanded and reduced term interpretations, *Proc of ITiCSE 12*, ACM Press, 309-314.

[15] Siegler, R. (2002). Microgenetic studies of self-explanation, in Granott, N. & Parziale, J. (eds.), *Microdevelopment, Transition Processes in Development and Learning*, Cambridge University Press, 31–58.

[16] Vinner, S. (1983). Concept definition, concept image and the notion of function, *Intl Journal of Mathematics Education in Science and Technology*, 14, 293-305.

[17] Yerushalmi, E. & Polingher, C. (2006). Guiding students to learn from mistakes, *Physics Education, 41,* 532-538.

Computing Creativity: Divergence in Computational Thinking

Vicki Bennett
Department of Communication
University of Colorado at Boulder
Boulder, CO 80309
+1 (303) 995-2802
Vicki.Bennett@colorado.edu

Kyu Han Koh
Department of Computer Science
University of Colorado at Boulder
Boulder, CO 80309
+1 (303) 495-0357
kohkh@colorado.edu

Alexander Repenning
University of Colorado at Boulder
430 UCB
Boulder, CO 80309
+1 (303) 492-1349
ralex@cs.colorado.edu

ABSTRACT

Conventionally creativity is often conceived as an aptitude to be discovered in an individual that cannot be mathematically measured. But the concept of creative thinking as a divergence from a standard "norm" is used in creativity research for the purpose of assessing creativity and is also linked to non-traditional or creative processes that lead to unique and divergent artifacts [1,2]. Using Computational Thinking Pattern Analysis (CTPA)[3], the divergence between implemented computational thinking patterns in a student-created game, and that game's tutorial "norm" is calculated as an indicator of creativity. Through a case study of one teacher using three unique learning conditions, CTPA's computed divergence is explored as a valid measurement of creativity in these student games.

Categories and Subject Descriptors

K.3.2 [**Computers and Education**]: Computers and Information Science Education

Keywords

ACM proceedings, Computational Thinking, Computational Thinking Pattern Analysis, Creativity Measurement, Game Design

1. INTRODUCTION

In our previous research, we reported that a game design class could foster student creativity in public schools [4]. The aspects of game design documented were character/agent design and level/worksheet design. A visual inspection of authored agents and worksheets, plus classroom observations yielded the data for our conclusions. This type of data assessment was necessary due to the lack of a computational tool capable of measuring creativity in game design programming solutions.

Measuring the creative aspects of programming decisions that students employ can reveal teaching protocols for successful increases in the quality and quantity of those creative solutions. Measuring creativity in programming presents a unique obstacle. Since manually analyzing game programming patterns for creative divergence is labor intensive, a computational tool for creative assessment was sought. CTPA was developed as a tool for teachers and researchers to gauge game design accuracy. We surmised that a further expansion of CTPA could possibly assess indications of creativity as "divergence from the norm," where the "norm" is defined as the standard tutorial for each specific game.

SIGCSE'13, March 6–9, 2013, Denver, Colorado USA.

1.1 Creativity Defined as Divergence

Defining a multi-faceted concept such as creativity presents measurement difficulties. Research investigations into creative processes usually describe them as the identifying or discovery of a problem and/or its solution. The solution or outcome must be significantly unique or divergent from other possible solutions [5], especially from the predetermined solution of the test. Herring et al [6], report that creativity can be produced regularly through the exposure to multiple visual examples of a similar nature, and multiple examples usually support a more divergent perspective of the problem, which in turn fosters more creative or divergent solutions. Currently, the most common measure of creativity for creativity research purposes is based on tests of divergence [1, 5, 7]. Tasks designed to distinguish divergence are currently the most recognized creative assessments [2, 8]. Although the quality and quantity of the solutions to the task must be considered, divergence from the accepted "norm" is commonly considered to be a significant indicator of creativity. The solution does not need to be totally unique or of high quality to be assessed as creative.

For example, the figure below (Fig. 1) illustrates several different Frogger design examples from different Frogger games created by 6th graders. All of them are divergent from the standard solution, provided by their teachers (Fig. 2). Similar to other skills, creativity can be learned and practiced. Consequently, creative efforts are not always of high quality, especially in the beginning. But, can creativity be measured computationally?

Inspired by the notion of divergent thinking tasks, we devised a method or tool (CTPA), divergence calculation [9], to more accurately assess creativity in programming solutions. Using comparative divergent thinking tasks as a measurement criteria for creativity in programming solutions should yield valid results, since computer programming lends itself to computational solutions and assessing divergent elements in programming solutions should be possible through a mathematical calculation.

Throughout the 2010/2011 school year, some early stages of mathematical measurement were investigated to calculate divergence in game programming in the Scalable Game Design project [10, 11]. One teacher presented lessons in three different conditions during 2010/2011 school-year. Since these three conditions lent themselves to a traditional experimental set-up, already accounting for the teacher influence as a variable, the game divergence from the tutorial norm was calculated with the addition of the implications of the creativity measurement.

Figure 1. Frogger Design by Students

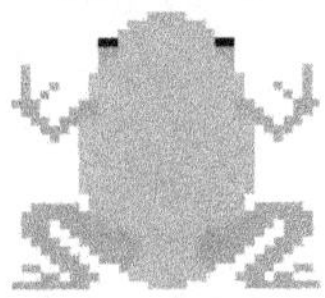

Figure 2. Standard Frogger Design

1.2 Scalable Game Design Project

Although game design is often believed to be a creative endeavor, for the programming novice, this is not usually the case. A student's first experience can often be boring or disappointing at best and debilitatingly frustrating at worst. The Scalable Game Design (SGD) Project investigates the use of game design as a means to encourage interest in programming and computer science in middle school students. As members of SGD project research team, the authors often have opportunities to visit and observe middle school teachers during project implementation classes. During these classes the authors often observed an outpouring of creativity. Even though participating classes follow specific curriculum content and upload their self-created games to the Scalable Game Design Arcade (SGDA) at the completion of each course module, individual teachers add their own style to the curriculum parameters. This is observed in person and from the submitted games' programming analyses with the CTPA. A visual inspection for agent and worksheet creativity is also conducted.

1.3 Scalable Game Design Arcade

In support of the Scalable Game Design project, we designed and operated a cyberlearning infrastructure, Scalable Game Design Arcade (SGDA). SGDA works as an online repository for collecting games/simulations that are created by middle school students from participating schools. SGDA consists of three parts: a main page, an assignment gallery, and an individual page. The main page displays recently submitted games, the most downloaded games, and the most played games, while the assignments gallery shows multiple submitted games/simulations that are submitted by participant school students in one unit class (not shown). The individual page displays a screenshot of a submitted game/simulation, the Computational Thinking Pattern Analysis (CTPA) graph [[9], links for playing and downloading games/simulations, and a similarity score between a given game/simulation and four tutorial games (Fig 3). Any user who accesses SGDA can play, download, and/or rate a game without a time lag after the submission is made.

1.4 Using Examples for Creativity

Examples are one of the most commonly employed methods of facilitating creativity. The use of multiple examples of other people's creative activities, often give rise to ideas and solutions we would not otherwise consider. Most project teachers choose to have their students play the games on SGDA before formal instruction, as a motivational tool to engender interest and encourage familiarity with a specific game. Promoting creativity in their students' games was an unexpected effect. The teachers saw a creative increase in their students' abilities in comparison to other project lessons [4]. The use of multiple examples on SGDA is consistent with stimulating creativity, while providing motivation, as intended.

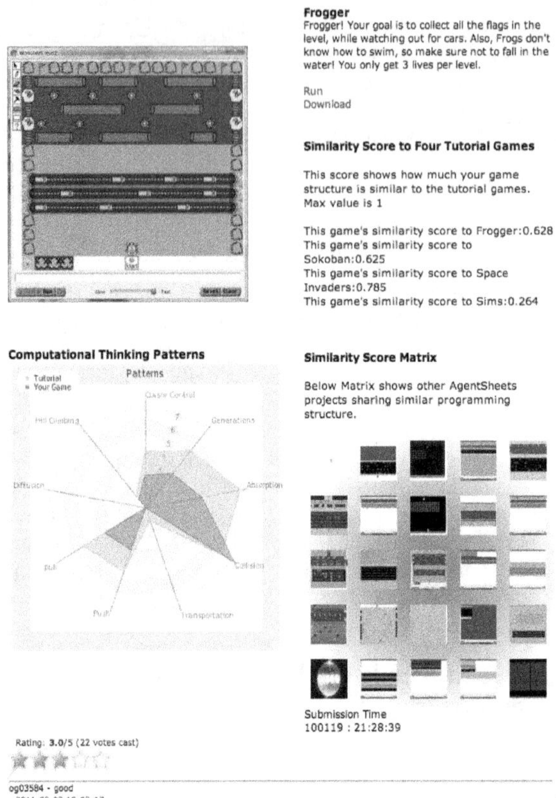

Galler

y Page of SGDA

Figure 3. The Individual Page of SGDA. Individual page illustrates the screenshot of the game (upper left), Run and Download button (upper right), the game's similarity score compared to four tutorial games (middle right), a similarity score matrix showing similarly programmed games to the submitted game, and the CTPA graph (bottom right & left).

2. METHODS

Methodology for this case study incorporated multiple classroom observations, the CTPA of submitted student games, and the divergence calculation to assess creativity. Inspired by Latent Semantic Analysis [12], we developed the concept of Semantic Subject Analysis (SSA) that uses multiple high dimensional cosine calculations to analyze semantic meanings of a given context with several pre-defined subjects.

Latent Semantic Analysis (LSA) was devised to compute the similarity between two given essays: a student-written essay and a sample essay [12]. LSA can be used as a grading-aid tool for text assignments by calculating the high dimensional cosine value between the student-created text and sample/standard text. However in LSA, the high dimensional cosine value calculations between the text and the target-text can express the similarity between these two texts as a single value, only. On the other hand, SSA can show the semantic meaning of a given text by calculating multiple high dimensional cosine calculations. These value calculations compare the similarity of the given context to the pre-defined subjects semantically within that context.

2.1 Computational Thinking Patterns

Computational thinking is a high level concept, and still has not been clearly defined in one sentence [13]. So we conceptualized Computational Thinking Patterns within the game design context to help students and teachers understand how CT can be practically utilized [10]. A Computational Thinking Pattern (CTP) is an abstract form of programming, which can be easily found in game and simulation programming. For example, the CTP, Generation, represents one agent creating another agent (i.e. a gun shoots a bullet or one cell splits in two). While CTP, Absorption represents that same bullet 'disappearing' as it enters the target. In this way, each CTP represents only one complete phenomenon or behavioral concept in a game or science simulation design.

2.2 Computational Thinking Pattern Analysis

The Computational Thinking Pattern Analysis (CTPA) is a specified version of SSA, within which nine canonical computational thinking patterns work as pre-defined subjects within a given game's context. The SSA structure appeared to be a good fit for comparing computational thinking patterns within student-submitted games to the tutorial standard used to teach those specific games. Consequently, SSA was revised to analyze the semantic meaning of the computational thinking pattern concept. To reflect the tool's analysis capabilities, we named the tool, the Computational Thinking Pattern Analysis [3].

CTPA tool consists of two parts: a computational thinking pattern analysis (CTPA) and a computational thinking pattern analysis graph (CTPAG). CTPA compares the similarity between a given programmed artifact and the nine pre-defined subjects (nine canonical CT patterns). For each programmed artifact nine high dimensional cosine calculations are computed which results in nine values between 0 and 1. The result of this CTPA is visualized as a form of spider graph with nine values displayed graphically in comparison to the same nine values calculated for the standard tutorial. The CT patterns for the standard tutorial of a given game overlap the CT patterns of the submitted game in different colors. The graphic display is called the CTPA graph or CTPAG. The CTPAG (Fig 4) visualizes the semantic similarity between a given game/simulation through each computational thinking pattern available. The equation below illustrates a high dimensional cosine calculation for the CTPA [3].

In this equation (below), u and v mean a given game/simulation and one canonical computational thinking pattern respectively. Also, n means he vector size of a game/simulation or CT pattern, and m means the number of computational thinking patterns that are applied to CTPA, currently 9. The calculated result of CTPA through CTPA (1) to CTPA (*m*) could be represented as an *m* length vector.

$$\textbf{CTPA}\ (m) = \left[\frac{\sum_{i=1}^{n} u_i v_i}{\sqrt{\sum_{i=1}^{n} u_i^2}\sqrt{\sum_{i=1}^{n} v_i^2}} \right]_1^m$$

Specifically for the above equation, the Computational Thinking Pattern Analysis (CTPA) is computed by calculating the value of cosine □ between two n-dimensional vectors that represent a given game and one computational thinking pattern. Thus, the CTPA graph in Fig 4 requires nine high dimensional cosine calculations between the Frogger game and the nine computational thinking patterns: Cursor Control, Generation, Absorption, Collision, Transportation, Push, Pull, Diffusion, and Hill Climbing. The CTPA graph visually depicts the difference or divergence between the norm (tutorial standard-green) and each individual student's submitted artifact (brown) by overlapping the two images in different colors in one graph.

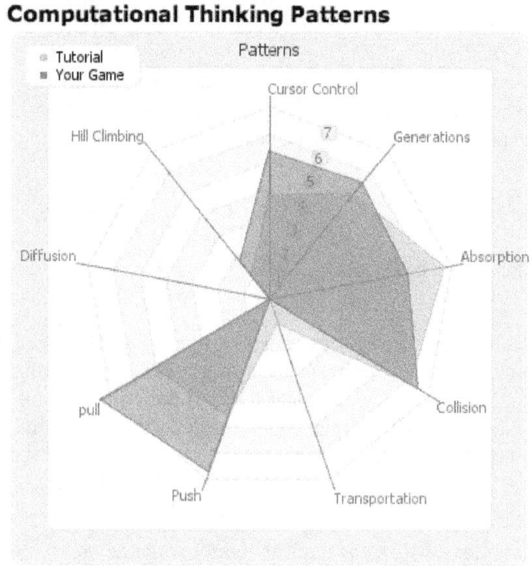

Figure 4. CTPA Graph Example 1. This graph is an actual student's example of a game of Frogger.

2.3 Divergence Calculation

The data previously collected from our class observations and interviews illustrate that the students' game artifacts showed increased creativity within the Scalable Game Design project. Previously some of these students referred to the making of the game (agent & worksheet design) as "all their own" [4]. This type of ownership appears to be consistent throughout the design of the agent depictions and worksheets. Our classroom observations confirmed that this "ownership" was related to divergence from the norm and/or creativity. We wanted to find evidence of creative ownership in the programming element of the student game artifacts, as well. With a mathematical method of calculating the divergence in the game programming, it seemed possible. Divergence in programming could be assessed through the evaluation of the differing approaches each student employed within the specified design parameters. In other words, when faced with a difficult challenge for agent behavior design, each student defined that programming challenge in a way that specified an accurate programming solution [7]. Consequently, creativity in game programming could be described as the divergence of a specific programming solution utilized by one student and not another in comparison to the SGD online tutorial standard. From this we devised the divergence calculation to demonstrate student-programming creativity as a divergence calculation from the "norm" or SGD online tutorial standard.

We recognized that computing creativity as divergence from the "norm" within the framework of CTPA could be possible. CTPA was already used to validate the students' game artifact solution divergence in comparison to the tutorial. So, it seemed logical to investigate its use for computing creativity. Figure 4 depicts a student-submitted game in comparison to the standard SGD online tutorial [3]. In figure 4, the difference or space between the tutorial (green) and the submitted artifact (brown) visually displays the divergence of a student's Frogger game from the tutorial "norm." Since each axis on the CTPA graph represents one element in a vector, the CTPA graph represents a nine-element vector, where each element represents a CT programming pattern that could be chosen by the student as part of his/her programming solution. Thus, the divergence of a student-created artifact from the tutorial "norm" can be calculated as the difference between two nine-element vectors; one is from the tutorial and the other is from the submitted artifact. The Divergence Score is calculated from the length of vector difference of the nine-element vector. The equation of the Divergence Calculation is depicted below.

$$Divergence(x) = \frac{\sqrt{\sum_{i=1}^{n}(u_i - v_i)^2}}{\sqrt{n}}$$

In this equation, u and v represent a tutorial and a given game respectively, and n represents the number of computational thinking patterns, which is equal to 9. At the current point in our research, 9 computational thinking patterns are used to accommodate the Agentsheets software, as well as the nine patterns taught within the Scalable Game Design project curriculum.

For example in Fig 4, the student-submitted game and the tutorial can be represented as nine dimensional vectors respectively (0.525, 0.557, 0.432, 0.641, 0, 0.687, 0.721, 0, 0.197) and (0.373, 0.499, 0.679, 0.623, 0.096, 0.455, 0.51, 0, 0.106). The difference of those two vectors is (0.152, 0.058, -0.247, 0.018, -0.096, 0.232, 0.211, 0, 0.091). The normalized (divided by the value of rooted n) length value of that vector is 0.15, and this is the value of divergence score of the given game.

Equally, when a student-submitted game is exactly the same as the tutorial, there is no difference between those graphs. So the submitted game and the tutorial can be represented as following vectors, (0.373, 0.499, 0.679, 0.623, 0.096, 0.455, 0.51, 0, 0.106) and (0.373, 0.499, 0.679, 0.623, 0.096, 0.455, 0.51, 0, 0.106). The difference of those two vectors, of course, is (0, 0, 0, 0, 0, 0, 0, 0, 0). The value of 0 represents no difference between a given game and the tutorial, so the game's programming is identical.

2.4 Three Class Conditions

Sheryle (pseudonym), the teacher selected for this study, taught three unique class conditions. Initially she taught the project class based on the SGD online tutorial. Subsequently, she designed her own tutorial for her regular in-class students and then transferred her tutorial adaptation to an online version of the project class. This offered a rare opportunity to compare three unique class conditions without having to consider teacher influence as a random variable. In all three class conditions the uploaded student games were noticeably divergent from the SGD tutorial "norm."

Common factors identified from all three class conditions taught by Sheryle are as follows:

- Sheryle is the teacher of record for all classes
- She alone helps the students complete their games
- She followed the project curriculum content parameters
- Frogger is the first project game taught to all classes
- Frogger is the game uploaded by all students
- Frogger is the only uploaded game analyzed

3. CREATIVITY IN GAME DESIGN

Runco and Okuda [5] describe creativity as divergence from the norm. Through observations of the project classes and the sets of games produced by these classes, we conceptualized that the differences between the individual student-created games and the tutorial could logically indicate creativity as computed divergence from the "norm." So, the CTPA processed data comparisons were utilized for measuring/computing creativity from the games uploaded to the Scalable Game Design Arcade (SGDA).

3.1 Game Dimensions and Creativity

The game design process allows for variations and/or individual divergence along three main dimensions: character, level and behavior (descriptions below). Creativity can be expressed within all three of these described game dimensions. Assessing the creativity or divergence from the "norm" in agent and level design can be detected by a simple visual inspection of the artifacts. In our previous research [4], we demonstrated that divergence in character design and level design can indicate creativity.

Characters: The characters or agents in AgentSheets [14], make up the entire game worksheet. If an agent doesn't exist for a specific object, that object does not exist in that particular game. In Frogger, agent depictions include frogs, trucks, streets, turtles and a river.

Levels: Levels may vary enormously. The only constant is that each succeeding level should be more difficult than the proceeding one. In AgentSheets, each game level is represented by a worksheet, similar to a blank painter's canvas. The student lays out his/her created agents into a configuration that is most pleasing to them. The game level sequence, as well as the difficulty of the levels can show a students' creativity or divergence from the tutorial "norm."

Behavior: The programming that students create, determines the behavior of characters, and is the most complex aspect of the game-design process.

Our current study anticipates the clarification and/or development of assessment possibilities for the behavioral dimension as well.

3.2 Creativity: Programming (Behavior)

Programming an agent as the student envisions can be problematic due to multiple available programming solutions. The specific approach an individual student uses to program his/her game differently than the tutorial is a divergence from that standard "norm" and an indication of creative programming. Although a game's programming (behavior) can also be examined through a visual inspection, the process is labor intensive and time-consuming. Consequently, when evaluating programming, originality and/or "divergence from the norm" the process is not as simple as the assessment of the agents and levels. Manually inspecting each game for creativity in the same manner would be an extremely time-consuming process. So in order to find a method for calculating divergence in game programming that was less time consuming the divergence calculation was developed.

Figure 5. Scattered Divergence Calculation Graph: X-axis represents time by order of submission. Y-axis represents Divergence Score. Each dot means individual submission. 296 Frogger games are displayed in this graph.

4. FINDINGS

For this investigation we chose three unique class conditions that were taught by a single teacher. This allowed us to keep the experimental focus on the divergence calculation as an indication of creativity, as opposed to teacher influence. Findings show a marked difference between the three class conditions in regards to programming divergence, as well as class difference, as represented in Figure 5.

4.1 Divergence Calculation Graph

In Figure 5 (above), the graph depicts the collected data of all Frogger games during 2010-2011 academic year from Sheryle's three-class conditions, using the divergence calculation above. Each individual student-submitted game is placed on the graph according to the calculated divergence represented by his/her game. The different colors represent the three class conditions. The three distinguishable clusters accurately represent the three distinct class conditions. The left cluster (blue) displays a sparser more scattered pattern than the middle (purple) and right (red) clusters. In this analysis, 296 Frogger games are represented by this graph. Until the 171st game submission, the students' Frogger games were highly divergent from each other. From the 172nd submission the games started to converge into each other. Coincidentally, the 172nd game submission was the exact time frame when Sheryle started using her own tutorial in place of the official SGD online tutorial. It appears that although her teaching style was unchanged, her presentation of the material had evolved in some fashion.

Table 1. Standard Deviation Calculation

$$f(x;\mu,\sigma^2) = \frac{1}{\sigma\sqrt{2\pi}} e^{-\frac{1}{2}\left(\frac{x-\mu}{\sigma}\right)^2}$$

Using the standard deviation equation above we also calculated the class standard deviation, as well as the class divergence average. Those are displayed in Table 2 (below). It appears that while the "2010 In-class" condition (blue) with the widest pattern spread in Figure 5, also shows the largest standard deviation within the class, while the "2011 Online class" (red) with the narrowest spread, has the smallest standard deviation within the class. This means that the games in the "2010 In-class" condition are more divergent to each other than the games in "2011 Online" class condition.

Table 2. Divergence Calculation Score in Each Class

Divergence Score	Standard Deviation	Average
In Class 2010	0.074	0.135
In Class 2011	0.057	0.186
Online 2011	0.011	0.314

We conjecture that not only is the revised tutorial a significant factor in the represented divergence between class conditions, but that the in-class/online condition comparison also appears to be a significant factor affecting the divergence calculation for at least two class conditions, effecting calculated creativity.

5. DISCUSSION

Previously, we have documented indications of creativity in two game design aspects, agent design and level/worksheet design [4]. Showing creativity in the programming aspect of game design through the divergence calculation is the goal of this study. Currently, the most common indication of creativity is based on divergence assessments [1,5,7]. Using this standard, we have developed a mathematical measure of divergence for game programming, that calculates the difference of each programming sequence of a submitted game from the game tutorial "norm." The main difference in our measurement of creativity, is the use of a mathematical calculation in place of the subjective appraisal by a trained rater. The "norm" for standard creativity tests is usually a predetermined standard solution, similar to the SGD online tutorial. Since, the SGD tutorial is commonly used by most project teachers, it is the "norm" for the SGD curriculum or standard by which the teachers judge or grade their students' work. So, based on traditional measures of creativity, individual game divergence from the SGD tutorial should indicate the presence of individual and/or group creativity.

Although the same teacher conducted the three, class-conditions discussed in this paper, operationally eliminating teacher influence as a mitigating variable in the divergence calculation, we recognize a teacher rarely teaches multiple classes exactly the same. However, for the present purpose of beginning a validation process for the divergence calculation as a measurement method of creativity, we believe we have documented compelling support. So, when looking at the Scattered Divergence Calculation graph (Fig. 5) the three separate clusters, representing these three class conditions, are obvious. Even without the designating colors, the three class conditions stand apart from each other, as distinct clusters. So, although the implications and meanings of the different cluster spreads is not clear at present, the most significant feature of the Scattered Divergence Calculation graph in Figure 5 is that each of the three separate class-learning conditions generates a unique divergence pattern. Since each of the separate conditions is unique, then the first validity test should be to show that the divergence calculation can demonstrate that uniqueness in the game programming analyses and it does. The amount of creativity from divergence that each cluster pattern represents is not as important as the fact that it displays programming distinctiveness within the divergence calculation model, in general, in three separate learning conditions.

The divergence calculations are supported by other data sources, such as the teacher's unsolicited comments about her students' creativity and our observations of student enthusiasm and creativity in the physical classroom settings. Space limitations prevent us from more disbursing more details of these sources. Previous research on the use of examples for promoting creativity would also tend to support the divergence calculation since SGDA examples are a common teaching tool for student motivation. We additionally conducted a manual inspection of the programming code to support the actual divergence calculation within a random sample of the chosen uploaded games as a fail-safe.

Current creativity research for showing indications of creativity is founded on common comparisons for divergence. Similarly, our divergence calculation was utilized for three separate class conditions and resulted in three separate divergence patterns. Indications show that these divergence calculations could demonstrate, not only creativity indications within programming solutions, but that these calculations are subtle enough to differentiate between different class learning conditions of the same teacher.

So grounded on the basis that creativity can be shown through divergence in thinking [1,5,7], it is logical to conclude that creativity in game programming solutions can be exposed through a similar divergence in programming pattern solutions from a consistent format, in this case the SGD tutorial "norm." Consequently, we believe that the divergence calculation model can significantly inform the measurement of creativity within programming and possibly other scientific areas. We look forward to further investigating the more specific indications and meanings of the divergence calculations, cluster spreads and how these might relate to the quality of the creative solutions employed, especially to gain an understanding of how individual students determine the solutions they use to program their games and how that relates to the tutorial "norm" within the curriculum.

6. ACKNOWLEDGMENTS

This work is supported by the National Science Foundation under Grant Numbers DLR-0833612 and IIP-0848962. Any opinions, findings, and conclusions or recommendations expressed in this material are those of the authors and do not necessarily reflect the views of the National Science Foundation.

7. REFERENCES

[1] Torrance, E.P. "Creative teaching makes a difference." In J.C. Gowan, J. Khatena, & E.P. Torrance (Eds.), Creativity: Its Educational Implications (2nd ed., pp. 99-108). Dubuque, IA: Kendall-Hunt, 1981.

[2] Kaufman, J. C., Plucker, J. A., & Baer, J. "Essentials of creativity assessment." Hoboken, NJ: Wiley, 2008.

[3] Koh, K. H., Basawapatna, A., Bennett, V., Repenning, A., "Towards the Automatic Recognition of Computational Thinking for Adaptive Visual Language Learning." IEEE International Symposium on Visual Languages and Human-Centric Computing 2010, Leganés-Madrid, Spain, September 21-25, 2010

[4] Bennett, V., Koh, K. H., Repenning, A., "CS Education Re-Kindles Creativity in Public Schools." ITiCSE '11: Annual Conference on Innovation and Technology in Computer Science Education, Darmstadt, Germany, June 27-29, 2011.

[5] Runco, M.A. & Okuda, S.M. "Problem discovery, divergent thinking, and the creative process." Journal of Youth and Adolescence, 17:3, 211-220, 1988.

[6] Herring, S.R., Chang, C.C., Krantzler, J. & Bailey, B.P. "Getting inspired! Understanding how & why examples are used in creative design practice." CHI2009, 87-96, 2009.

[7] Csikszentmihalyi, M., and Getzels, J. W. "Discovery-oriented behavior and the originality of creative products: A study with artists." J. Personal. & Social. Psychol. 19: 47-52, 1971.

[8] Williams, F.E. "Creativity assessment packet examiner's manual." Austin TX: PRO-ED, 1993.

[9] Koh, K. H., Bennett, V., Repenning, A., "Computing Indicators of Creativity." ACM Creativity & Cognition 2011, The High Museum of Art · Atlanta, Georgia, USA, November 3-6, 2011

[10] Basawapatna, A., Koh, K. H., Repenning, A., Webb, D., Marshall, K., "Recognizing Computational Thinking Patterns." SIGCSE 2011: Reaching Out The 42nd ACM Technical Symposium on Computer Science Education, Dallas, Texas, USA, March 9-12, 201

[11] Koh, K. H., Bennett, V., Repenning, A., "Inspiring Collaborative Benefits: An Interaction between a Virtual and a Physical Group Learning Infrastructure." Western Canadian Conference on Computing Education (WCCCE 2010), Okanagan, B.C., Canada May 7-8, 2010.

[12] Landauer, T.K., Foltz, P.W. & Laham, D., "Introduction to Latent Semantic Analysis. Discourse Processes." 25, 1998, 259-284.

[13] Wing, J.M. "Computational Thinking." Communications of the ACM, 49:3, 33-35, 2006.

[14] Repenning, A. "AgentSheets®: an Interactive Simulation Environment with End-User Programmable Agents." In Proc. Interaction 2000, Tokyo, Japan, 2000.

On Plugging "Unplugged" into CS Classes

Renate Thies
Cusanus-Gymnasium Erkelenz and
Technische Universität Dortmund
44227 Dortmund, Germany
renate.thies@cs.tu-dortmund.de

Jan Vahrenhold
Westfälische Wilhelms-Universität Münster
Department of Computer Science
48149 Münster, Germany
jan.vahrenhold@uni-muenster.de

ABSTRACT

A variety of experience reports and studies has shown *Computer Science Unplugged* to be an effective resource for outreach, and it has been suggested to build upon these benefits to augment teaching in a regular classroom as well. Based upon an analysis of the learning objectives, "Unplugged" activities seem to be particularly well suited to serve as an introduction to Computer Science concepts and algorithms; whether or not the effectiveness of using these activities compares to that of traditional teaching methods, however, has remained an open question so far.

We present the first experimental study of using *Computer Science Unplugged* material as part of a regular Computer Science class in lower secondary education. The evaluation of our study affirmatively answers the above question, i.e., teaching using "Unplugged" activities can be at least as effective as when following more conventional approaches.

Categories and Subject Descriptors: K.3.2 [Computers and Education]: Computer and Information Science Education

Keywords: Computer Science Unplugged, Assessment.

1. INTRODUCTION

In response to the discrepancy between the demand for highly-skilled professionals in Science, Technology, Engineering, and Mathematics (STEM) and students' relatively low interest in studying Computer Science [26], recent years have seen a broad variety of outreach programs aimed at attracting Computer Science majors; see, e.g., [4, 6, 8, 10, 13, 17]. These programs repeatedly have been shown to have strong beneficial effects on motivation and attitude towards Computer Science [3, 8, 12, 16, 19, 22].

Among these programs, *Computer Science Unplugged* [4] is probably the most widely known outreach program, in part because example activities are included in the *Model Curriculum for K-12 Computer Science* of the ACM K-12 task force [24]. Also, several studies document the beneficial effects of *Computer Science Unplugged* towards recruitment and motivation [3, 12, 16, 22]. However, in contrast to the explicit connection to a curriculum and despite that *Computer Science Unplugged* is said to be a useful teaching resource [7], there are surprisingly few studies related to the actual use of this material in a regular classroom setting.

Manabe *et al.* [15] discuss using (a digitally augmented form of) *Computer Science Unplugged* materials in classes for physically handicapped students; the focus of their study, however, is the motivating aspect of the material for students recovering from a severe injury or illness and the question of how to adapt kinesthetic activities for physically handicapped students.

Feaster *et al.* [9] report on using *Computer Science Unplugged* material to teach Computer Science concepts in highschool. Based upon a pre/post survey using Likert-type test items, they measured attitude to Computer Science and content understanding over the course of one semester per test group. The conclusion the authors drew from their evaluation was that *Computer Science Unplugged* was not well suited to improve content understanding but that some (non-significant) detrimental effects of this teaching method could be observed; some of these effects were attributed to the students' self-perception as experienced programmers and the resulting diminished interest to learn about concepts. With respect to the validity of their study, the authors point out that "a number of experimental factors" including "adjusting for preexisting differences in student attitudes and content understanding, adjusting for instructor-induced impacts" were outside their control [9, p. 252].

In our previous work [23], we evaluated the *Computer Science Unplugged* activities with respect to the type of learning objectives that can be inferred from the *Computer Science Unplugged* teachers' book [4]. We observed that teaching using *Computer Science Unplugged* activities only, at least when used in an unmodified form, seems to exclude learning objectives on higher levels of Bloom's revised taxonomy [1]. This observation can be seen as a partial explanation of the "limited success" of the experiment of Feaster *et al.* [9], since the higher-level learning objectives are essential in higher secondary education.

One hypothesis that can be derived from the above results is that using *Computer Science Unplugged* materials can be adequate and effective when carefully integrated into Computer Science classes in lower secondary education. In this work, we present the results of a first experimental study directed towards evaluating this hypothesis.

SIGCSE'13, March 6–9, 2013, Denver, Colorado, USA.

2. (LEARNING) OBJECTIVES

From the large body of literature on using *Computer Science Unplugged* (and related programs) for outreach purposes, it can be concluded that these activities are a very successful resource when it comes to motivation and attitude towards Computer Science. In addition to this, the *Computer Science Unplugged* activities can be interpreted as a set of kinesthetic learning activities as thus have been advocated also as a resource for teaching [7].

Referring to the use of kinesthetic learning activities in the classroom, Begel *et al.* [2, p. 183] point out that they "can be challenging to use in the classroom" and that it "is easy to create [...] [a kinesthetic learning activity] that misfires because it is socially inappropriate, physically challenging, difficult to manage, *or simply incomprehensible*" [emphasis added]. Hence, despite encouraging reports on using *Computer Science Unplugged* for outreach, it remains an open question to which extent *Computer Science Unplugged* can be used to *teach* in a *regular classroom* setting.

When selecting *Computer Science Unplugged* activities for our experimental study directed towards answering this question and thus conducted embedded into a regular Computer Science course (see Section 3.1), the set of activities from which we could chose was determined by the school's Computer Science curriculum. Nonetheless, we aimed at selecting activities whose combined learning objectives covered the range of learning objectives of all *Computer Science Unplugged* activities (see [23, Fig. 4]) as much as possible. Combining these two constraints, we chose the following three activities as the basis for our experiments:

Activity 1: Binary Numbers Activity 1 addresses only cognitive processes on a relatively high level (*apply/analyze*) but spans *Computer Science Unplugged*'s full knowledge range (*factual/conceptual/procedural*).

Activity 6: Binary Search Among all activities, Activity 6 spans the largest range across both dimensions, see [23, Fig. 4]. In addition, it is one of two activities pertinent to highest cognitive process (*evaluate*) aimed at by *Computer Science Unplugged.*

Activity 8: Sorting Networks Among all *Computer Science Unplugged* activities, this is arguably the most kinesthetic activity.

3. METHOD

The focus of our study was to investigate the effectiveness of using *Computer Science Unplugged* compared to more conventional methods of introducing Computer Science concepts in lower secondary education. The design of the experiments was directed at resembling a controlled experiment as closely as possible. In the remainder of this section, we describe the resulting choices regarding the subjects, materials, procedures, and the experimental design.

3.1 Subjects

All experiments were conducted at Cusanus-Gymnasium Erkelenz, a German middle school where approximately 200 students enroll in the lowest grade each year. Parents registering their children can opt to choose classes with a special focus on either languages, music, or STEM. In the case of the STEM class, two extra class sessions per week are devoted to STEM subjects; the first semester is devoted to Computer Science. Since usually there are more registrations for the STEM class than slots available, students are selected by the results of a proficiency test.

The subjects were 25 students from the STEM class in the lowest grade, i.e., students of age 11–12, at Cusanus-Gymnasium Erkelenz during the 2011/2012 school year. This class was taught by the first author who is also the Mathematics teacher of this class.

Since we aimed at a controlled experimental setting, the teacher was asked to group the students into two groups of roughly the same intellectual characteristics. An analysis of the results of a *Culture Fair Intelligence Test*[1] using the Mann-Whitney test showed no statistically significant difference ($p \geq 0.05$, two-tailed test) between the groups. Even though the focus of this study is not on gender issues we note that both groups had four female students each.

3.2 Materials and Procedure

The experiment took place as part of the Computer Science section of the above-mentioned STEM course. To provide a closed experimental setting, all sessions were taught by the first author, i.e., the regular instructor for this course.

The alternative, i.e., non-*Unplugged*, material was selected such that each topic was taught using one of three almost orthogonal methods: textbook-based teaching, collaborative teaching, and media-supported teaching. In the selection of alternative material and design of the worksheets, we made sure that the material addressed the same learning objectives and contextual information as in the *Unplugged* case.

In the following subsections, we discuss the material, learning objectives, and methods for each experiment in turn.

3.2.1 Binary Numbers

The *Unplugged* material was taken from Activity 1 ("Count the Dots") of the *Computer Science Unplugged* teachers' book [4, pp. 3–13]; while teaching the teacher followed the instructions given in the book.

Following the approach of our previous work [23], we used the anchors provided by Anderson *et al.* [1] to evaluate the activity's description and extracted the following learning objectives (presented along with their classifications):

(i) Students are able to transform a number from decimal into binary representation (*apply/factual*).

(ii) Students are able to transform a number from binary into decimal representation (*apply/factual*).

(iii) Students analyze the binary system by working on the worksheet activity "More on Binary Numbers" [4, p. 11] (*analyze/conceptual*).

(iv) Students gain an understanding of the connections to Computer Science by working on the worksheet activities "E-mail and modems" [4, p. 9] and "More on Binary Numbers" [4, p. 11] (*analyze/procedural*).

In the case of teaching the binary number system, the alternative material consisted of a self-contained section from a Mathematics textbook approved for this grade but not used at Cusanus-Gymnasium Erkelenz.[2] This textbook was selected since the exposition and the exercises clearly were

[1]Written consent for participation in this study was obtained from all parents/guardians.

[2]The Mathematics curriculum at Cusanus-Gymnasium Erkelenz does not include binary numbers for this grade.

aligned with the above learning objectives and also because the introductory text of this section extensively referred to the use of binary numbers as a mean of representation in computers (learning objective (iv)).

The teacher organized the session following the textbook, i.e., in a rather traditional way: after an introduction to the topic, the concept of the decimal system was presented, and based upon this, the binary system was introduced. The students then were asked to work on the exercises given in the book; "cheat sheets" were accessible upon request (learning objectives (i)–(ii)). At the end of the session, the exercises and their solutions were discussed and presented on the chalkboard (learning objectives (iii)).

3.2.2 Binary Search

The *Unplugged* material was taken from Activity 6 ("Battleships") of the *Computer Science Unplugged* teachers' book [4, pp. 45–63]; while teaching the teacher followed the instructions given in the book. To allow the topic to be taught within a 45-minutes slot (see Section 3.3), the material was limited to sequential and binary search; this did not change the set of classifications of learning objectives.

The learning objectives for this activity as extracted previously [23, p. 490] are given below:

(i) Students discover linear search [...] (*understand/procedural*).

(ii) Students discover the disadvantages of linear search (*understand/factual*).

(iii) Students discover binary search [...] (*apply/procedural*).

(iv) Students discover the advantages of binary search as compared to linear search (*evaluate/factual*).

(v) Students gain an understanding about when to use which searching algorithm (*analyze/procedural*).

The alternative material was taken from *Algorithms Unplugged*, a textbook written by computer scientists aiming to explain algorithms to the general public [20]. This chapter was selected since it presents the problem by discussing how a young boy tries to locate a CD in his older sister's CD collection—a context readily accessible to the students. Since this material did not contain any exercises, we augmented the material by a *Think-Pair-Share* [14] activity which closely matched the process suggested in the *Computer Science Unplugged* teachers' book. This augmented material made sure that students in both groups were given the opportunity to discover linear and binary search themselves (learning objectives (i)–(iii)).

After an introduction to the methodology, the teacher presented the context which was also given to the students in writing and handed out worksheets describing the activity. In the first part of this activity, students were asked to *think* on their own about how many CDs the boy would need to look at if the CDs were unsorted and how long this would take assuming a rate of two CDs per second. The students were also asked to redo this exercise for the case of CDs sorted by name. In the second part of the activity, students were asked to *pair* with their neighbor and to discuss whether any strategy better than linear search could be developed if the CDs were sorted. The final phase of the activity consisted of all students getting together and to *share* the results of the previous phase (learning objective (iv)). At the end of the session, the binary search algorithm was summarized on the chalkboard (learning objective (v)).

3.2.3 Sorting Networks

The *Unplugged* material was taken from Activity 8 ("Beat the Clock") of the *Computer Science Unplugged* teachers' book [4, pp. 71–75]; while teaching the teacher followed the instructions given in the book. To allow the topic to be taught within a 45-minutes slot (see Section 3.3), the material did not include the extension activities.

The learning objective extracted from this activity used Anderson *et al.*'s [1] anchors are listed below:

(i) Students are able to run a sorting algorithm using a sorting network (*apply/procedural*).

(ii) Students gain an understanding of the concept of sorting networks (*understand/conceptual*).

Since the "Sorting Networks" activity seems to be original to the *Computer Science Unplugged* approach, we decided to use a short movie as the alternative teaching material. This movie was a reproduction of the original *Unplugged* video where we made sure to leave out all scenes showing the setup of the kinesthetic activity and children actually performing this activity. After the presentation of the video, the teacher summarized the central concepts on the chalkboard. The students then were given a paper copy of the sorting network shown in the video (which in turn was the same sorting network on which the *Unplugged* activity was performed) and asked to individually use this network to sort a set of numbers (learning objective (i)). At the end of the session, the exercises and their solutions were discussed and presented on the chalkboard (learning objective (ii)).

3.3 Experimental Design

Both groups were taught during the same class session. Group A was taught the topic during the first half of the class (45 mins.) while Group B, assigned to a different room, was given exercises related to the topic of the previous class session unrelated to the current topic; for the second half of the session, the roles were reversed.

Following the experimental design used by Ward and Sweller in the context of worked examples [25], we performed a counterbalancing to ensure that differences between instructional methods were not contaminated by differences between topics or groups. In particular, Group A was taught "Binary Search" and "Sorting Networks" using the *Unplugged* material and "Binary Numbers" using the alternate material while Group B was taught "Binary Numbers" using the *Unplugged* material and "Binary Search" and "Sorting Networks" using the alternate material.

The first assessment was conducted on the day following this instruction. After a period of three weeks, a short recapitulation of the topic was presented by the teacher making sure not to reference either teaching material. After another three weeks, the first assessment was repeated.

4. EVALUATION

In our experiments, we used both *Computer Science Unplugged* activities and alternative material to teach in the context of a regular Computer Science class. The focus of our evaluation thus was on the effectiveness of the *Computer Science Unplugged* approach compared to alternative methods. In particular, we prepared an assessment worksheet for each topic; the items (assignments and free-form questions) were designed to obtain answers the following questions:

(1) To which extent can students successfully solve exercises related to each subject matter? (*factual and procedural knowledge*)
(2) On which level of abstraction can students describe each subject matter? (*conceptual knowledge*)
(3) To which extent can students relate each subject matter to Computer Science? (*conceptual knowledge*)

Since *Computer Science Unplugged* has repeatedly shown to be very successful both with respect to motivation and attitude towards Computer Science (see Section 1) and in order not to dilute the experimental results related to contextualization, we decided not to include yet another verification of the above observation by running a pre/post survey related to motivation and attitude.

As mentioned in Section 3.3, we performed one assessment immediately following the instruction ("Round 1") and, to also capture long-term effects, repeated the assessment after a period of six weeks ("Round 2"). Due to various reasons, the number of students participating in either round varied but never by more than one person.

4.1 Factual and Procedural Knowledge

To assess the factual and procedural knowledge, students were given short exercises related to the topic taught. These exercises were designed to match the type of test items used in closed-book written exams.

4.1.1 Binary Numbers

Students were asked to transform two numbers (10101_2 and 11_2) from binary into decimal representation and two numbers (16_{10} and 112_{10}) from decimal into binary representation. The number of correct answers are given below.

Round 1	N	10101_2	11_2	16_{10}	112_{10}
Unplugged	13	13	11	13	7
Alternative	12	10	12	11	6

Round 2	N	10101_2	11_2	16_{10}	112_{10}
Unplugged	12	9	10	9	4
Alternative	11	8	9	10	4

For the statistical evaluation, we ran a χ^2-test for each test item in turn where we assumed for the null hypothesis that the correctness of the answer and the teaching method experienced were statistically independent. For none of the eight tests comparing the groups for each test item in Round 1 and Round 2, a higher χ^2-value than 2.31 was computed, only two values were above 1.2. Thus, we were unable to reject the null hypothesis, i.e., we could not detect a statistically significant difference between the groups.

Comparing the answers within either group but over the two rounds, we could neither reject the null hypothesis that the correctness of the answer and the time of assessing it were statistically independent ($\chi^2 \leq 1.69$).

4.1.2 Binary Search

Students were given a sorted array containing fifteen numbers and were asked to execute and describe the steps of the binary search algorithm when run on this array and a given number. This element was located in the fifth slot of the array, so the search algorithm would recurse on the left, right, and left subarray in turn. Since the array contained fifteen numbers, all ambiguities due to round-off errors when determining the median element were eliminated.

In the first round, six out of 13 students in the group taught using the *Unplugged* material and seven out of ten students in the groups taught using the alternative material gave correct answers. A χ^2-test for the null hypothesis that the correctness of the answer and the material used for teaching were statistically independent gave only statistically insignificant grounds for rejection of this hypothesis ($\chi^2 = 1.31$, power: 10%). If we consider the two answers given by "Unplugged" students that correctly described the concept but introduced round-off errors as correct answers as well, the null hypothesis cannot be rejected ($\chi^2 = 0.18$).

In the second round, all 13 students taught using the *Unplugged* material and all ten students taught using the alternative material gave correct answers, so obviously no difference between the groups could be detected.

4.1.3 Sorting Networks

Students were given a sorting network from the *Computer Science Unplugged* Extension Activity 8.3 [4, p. 74] (not covered in class) and asked to sort four numbers into ascending order. In the first round, the "linear" sample network was used, in the second round, the "parallel" network was used.

In both rounds, *all* students from both groups correctly solved the exercises, so no difference related to the groups or the time of the assessment could be detected. In both groups, however, several students were observed to first write down the numbers in sorted order in the last "column" and to then work their way backwards through the network. Since this effect could be observed across both groups, the threat to the validity of our assessment seems to be minor.

4.2 Conceptual Knowledge

To assess the conceptual knowledge, we asked students to first give a written explanation of what they had learned in the respective lesson. The second item then asked to write down how the topic taught related to Computer Science.

4.2.1 Data Analysis Method

While analyzing the data collected, we realized that a large percentage of students intermixed their answers: a common answer to the first question was "We learned about binary numbers/binary search/sorting", while most answers to the second question contained detailed descriptions that implied correct answers to the first question. We thus decided to analyze the combined answers.

For the analysis of the written answers, we used the *Structure of the Observed Learning Outcomes* (SOLO) taxonomy [5], that can be used "to identify in broad terms the stage at which the student is currently operating" [11, p. 103]. This taxonomy, which has been applied previously to subjects in Computer Science education (see [18] and the references therein), is a classification scheme with five stages (explanations adapted from Hattie *et al.* [11, p. 104]):

(1) Prestructural: Only a preliminary comprehension of the topic is apparent.
(2) Unistructural: One aspect of the topic is mentioned.
(3) Multistructural: Several aspects of the topic are mentioned but not interrelated.
(4) Relational: Several aspects of the topic are integrated.
(5) Extended Abstract: A generalization to a higher level of abstraction is apparent.

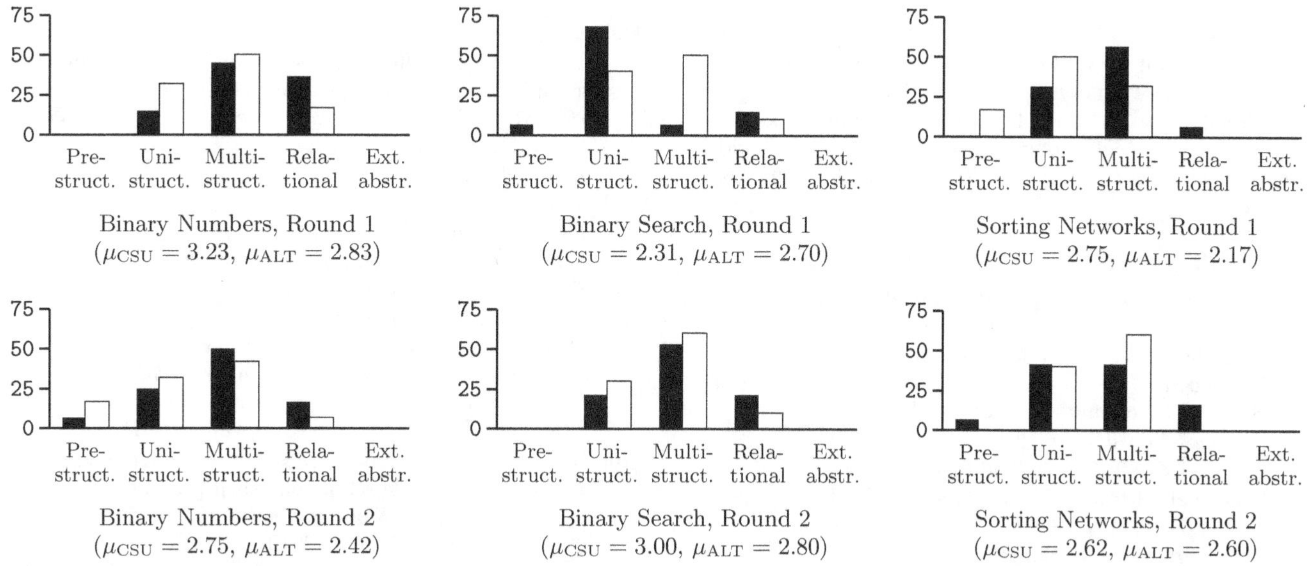

Figure 1: Classification according to SOLO (in percent). Black: Unplugged (CSU), white: Alternative (ALT).

4.2.2 *Interpretation of the Results*

The results of our classification are summarized in Figure 1. The mean values for all groups and experiments are between 2.17 and 3.23, i.e., on average, students showed more than unistructural understanding. Given that the duration of the teaching unit was only 45 mins. and that no more than 15 mins. were devoted to the recapitulation unit three weeks later, it comes as no surprise that no student worked on the highest operational stage (*extended abstract*). Instead, we can conclude that all conceptual learning objectives were reached reasonably well.

While the mean values given in this figure seem to imply that, on average, students taught using "Unplugged" material almost always reach higher operational states, an analysis using Student's t-test did not show any statistically significant difference except in the first round of the "Sorting Networks" topic ($p = 0.045$). This difference, which most likely can be attributed to the fact that the "Unplugged" activity and the alternative method (media-based teaching) differed most with respect to the kinesthetic factors, completely disappeared in the second round ($p = 0.96$). We conjecture that this is related to the fact that the mental barriers impeding an understanding of a comparator or a sorting network are much lower than for the other two topics; this conjecture is also based on the fact that all students exhibited factual and procedural knowledge in both rounds of assessing this topic.

Comparing the distribution of operational stages within each groups but across time, a statistically significant change could only be detected for the "Unplugged" group and "Binary Search", where Student's t-test showed a significant increase ($p = 0.034$). More precisely, the mean in the first round was below the mean of the group taught using alternative material while it was the other way around in the second round. Combining the observations by Feaster *et al.* [9] and our previous observations [23], one possible explanation we can offer is that the "Binary Search" activity simply leads to more learning objectives (including one objective on the *evaluate* level) than can be accommodated in a single teaching unit. The additional recapitulation unit three weeks after the first round, however, was effective enough to compensate for this deficit. This observation supports our earlier hypothesis that *Computer Science Unplugged* material should not be used "in lieu of fully-fledged teaching material or as stand-alone teaching units" [23, p. 491] but instead needs to be augmented and embedded into the curriculum.

The final comment related to the classification of the students' answers pertains to within-class ability grouping—see, e.g., Slavin [21] and the references therein. Figure 1 shows that in all experiments more students taught using the "Unplugged" material than students taught using the alternative material reached the *relational* operational stage. Since, in the design of the teaching material and worksheets, we had taken care to provide the same content to each group, and since the intellectual characteristics were the same across the groups (see Section 3.1), we conclude that this difference is likely to be related to the *Computer Science Unplugged* concept as such. The immediate implication of this conclusion would be that the "Unplugged" material facilitates students whose intellectual abilities allow for reaching the *relational* stage to actually reach this stage and thus can be used, e.g., in mastery learning.

5. CONCLUSIONS

In our study, we have investigated the effectiveness of using *Computer Science Unplugged* material as part of a lower secondary Computer Science class. The results of our controlled experiments indicate that for none of the introductory topics taught and alternative methods used, a statistically significant difference could be observed in either short- or mid-term assessments. We thus conclude that it is indeed possible to weave *Computer Science Unplugged* activities into lower secondary Computer Science classes without a negative effect on factual, procedural, or conceptual knowledge. Building upon previous studies documenting the motivating effects of using *Computer Science Unplugged* [3, 12, 16, 22], our study thus demonstrates that *Computer Science Unplugged* materials can be adequate and effective when used in lower secondary education. In addition, our analysis of the students' answers using the SOLO taxonomy indicates that the *Computer Science Unplugged* materials can prove helpful for ability grouping within a class, since, on average, more students are enabled to reach a higher operational stage. To reach higher-level learning objectives and, on average, higher operational stages, however, additional teaching units and thus additional teaching material is necessary.

6. REFERENCES

[1] L. W. Anderson, D. R. Krathwohl, P. W. Airasian, K. A. Cruikshank, R. E. Mayer, P. R. Pintrich, J. Raths, and M. C. Wittrock, editors. *A Taxonomy for Learning, Teaching, and Assessing: A Revision of* Bloom's Taxonomy of Educational Objectives. *Abridged Edition.* Longman, New York, 2001.

[2] A. Begel, D. D. Garcia, and S. A. Wolfman. Kinesthetic learning in the classroom. In *Proc. 35th SIGCSE Technical Symp. on Computer Science Education*, pp. 183–184. 2004.

[3] T. Bell, P. Curzon, Q. I. Cutts, V. Dagiene, and B. Haberman. Overcoming obstacles to CS education by using non-programming outreach programmes. In *Proc. 5th International Conf. on Informatics in Schools (ISSEP 2011), LNCS* 7013, pp. 71–81. Springer, 2011.

[4] T. Bell, I. H. Witten, M. Fellows, and R. Adams. *Computer science unplugged. an enrichment and extension programme for primary-aged children.* Unplugged, Canterbury, 2002.

[5] J. Biggs and K. Collis. *Evaluating the quality of learning: the SOLO taxonomy.* Academic Press, New York, 1982.

[6] P. Curzon, J. Black, L. R. Meagher, and P. W. McOwan. cs4fn.org: Enthusing students about computer science. In *Proceedings of Informatics Education Europe IV*, pp. 73–80, 2009.

[7] P. Curzon, P. W. McOwan, Q. I. Cutts, and T. Bell. Enthusing & inspiring with reusable kinaesthetic activities. In *Proc. 14th SIGCSE Conf. on Innovation and Technology in Computer Science Education, ITiCSE 2009*, pp. 94–98, 2009.

[8] Q. I. Cutts, M. I. Brown, L. Kemp, and C. Matheson. Enthusing and informing potential computer science students and their teachers. In *Proc. 12th SIGCSE Conf. on Innovation and Technology in Computer Science Education, ITiCSE 2007*, pp. 196–200, 2007.

[9] Y. Feaster, L. Segars, S. K. Wahba, and J. O. Hallstrom. Teaching CS unplugged in the high school (with limited success). In *Proc. 16th Conf. on Innovation and Technology in Computer Science Education, ITiCSE 2011*, pp. 248–252, 2011.

[10] S. Graham and C. Latulipe. CS girls rock: Sparking interest in computer science and debunking the stereotypes. In *Proc. 34th SIGCSE Technical Symp. on Computer Science Education*, pp. 322–326, 2003.

[11] J. Hattie, J. Biggs, and N. Purdie. Effects of learning skills interventions on student learning: A meta-analysis. *Review of Educational Research*, 66(2):99–136, 1996.

[12] L. Lambert and H. Guiffre. Computer science outreach in an elementary school. *Journal of Computing Sciences in Colleges*, 24(3):118–124, Jan. 2009.

[13] C. Lang, A. Craig, J. Fisher, and H. Forgasz. Creating digital divas: Scaffolding perception change through secondary school and university alliances. In *Proc. 15th SIGCSE Conf. on Innovation and Technology in Computer Science Education, ITiCSE 2010*, pp. 38–42, 2010.

[14] F. T. Lyman. The responsive classroom discussion: The inclusion of all students. In A. Anderson, editor, *Mainstreaming Digest*, pp. 109–113. University of Maryland Press, College Park, 1981.

[15] H. Manabe, S. Kanemune, M. Namiki, and Y. Nakano. CS Unplugged assisted by digital materials for handicapped people at schools. In *Proc. 5th International Conf. on Informatics in Schools (ISSEP 2011), LNCS* 7013, pp. 82–93. Springer, 2011.

[16] C. Mano, V. Allan, and D. Cooley. Effective in-class activities for middle school outreach programs. In *Proc. 40th Annual Frontiers in Education Conf. (FIE 2010)*, pp. F2E–1–F2E–6. 2010.

[17] R. Mittermeir, E. Bischof, and K. Hodnigg. Showing core-concepts of informatics to kids and their teachers. In *Teaching Fundamentals Concepts of Informatics, 4th International Conf. on Informatics in Secondary Schools - Evolution and Perspectives, ISSEP 2010, LNCS 5090*, pp. 143–154, Springer 2010.

[18] L. Murphy, R. McCauley, and S. Fitzgerald. 'Explain in Plain English' questions: Implications for teaching. In *Proc. 43rd SIGCSE Technical Symp. on Computer Science Education (SICGSE 2012)*, pp. 385–390. 2012.

[19] C. Myketiak, P. Curzon, J. Black, P. W. McOwan, and L. R. Meagher. cs4fn: A flexible model for computer science outreach. In *Proc. 17th Annual SIGCSE Conf. on Innovation and Technology in Computer Science Education, ITiCSE 2012*, pp. 297–302, 2012.

[20] T. Seid and J. Enderle. Binary search. In B. Vöcking, H. Alt, M. Dietzfelbinger, R. Reischuk, C. Scheideler, H. Vollmer, and D. Wagner, editors, *Algorithms Unplugged*, chapter 1, pp. 5–11. Springer, 2011.

[21] R. E. Slavin. Ability grouping in the middle grades: Achievement effects and alternatives. *The Elementary School Journal*, 93(5):99–136, 1993.

[22] R. Taub, M. Ben-Ari, and M. Armoni. The effect of CS unplugged on middle-school students' views of CS. In *Proc. 14th Annual SIGCSE Conf. on Innovation and Technology in Computer Science Education, ITiCSE 2009*, pp. 99–103, 2009.

[23] R. Thies and J. Vahrenhold. Reflections on outreach programs in CS classes: learning objectives for "Unplugged" activities. In *Proc. 43rd SIGCSE Technical Symp. on Computer Science Education (SICGSE 2012)*, pp. 487–492. 2012.

[24] A. Tucker, F. Deek, J. Jones, D. McCowan, C. Stephenson, and A. Verno. A model curriculum for K-12 computer science: Final report of the ACM K-12 task force curriculum committee, 2004.

[25] M. Ward and J. Sweller. Structuring effective worked examples. *Cognition and Instruction*, 7(1):1–39, 1990.

[26] C. Wilson, L. A. Sudol, C. Stephenson, and M. Stehlik. Running on empty: The failure to teach K-12 computer science in the digital age. ACM / CSTA, 2010. Also available via `http://www.acm.org/Runningonempty`.

Assessment of Computer Science Learning in a Scratch-Based Outreach Program

Diana Franklin[†], Phillip Conrad[†], Bryce Boe[†], Katy Nilsen[‡], Charlotte Hill[†], Michelle Len[†], Greg Dreschler[†], Gerardo Aldana[§], Paulo Almeida-Tanaka[†], Brynn Kiefer[†], Chelsea Laird[♯], Felicia Lopez[§], Christine Pham[†], Jessica Suarez[§], Robert Waite[†]

† Department of Computer Science
‡ Gevirtz School of Education
§Chicana/o Studies Department
♯Biology Department
UC Santa Barbara

ABSTRACT

Many institutions have created and deployed outreach programs for middle school students with the goal of increasing the number and diversity of students who later pursue careers in computer science. While these programs have been shown to *increase interest* in computer science, there has been less work on showing whether participants *learn computer science content*.

We address two questions, one specific, and the other more general: (1) "What computer science did our middle school students learn in our interdisciplinary two-week summer camp?" (2) "How can computer science concepts be assessed in the context of Scratch-based outreach programs"? We address both questions by presenting the design of our summer camp, an overview of our curriculum, our assessment methodology, and our assessment results.

Though the sample size is not statistically significant, the results show that a two-week, interdisciplinary, non-academic summer camp can be effective not only for engaging students, but also for imparting CS content. In just two weeks, with a curriculum not entirely focused on computer science, students displayed competence with event-driven programming, initialization of state, message passing, and say/sound synchronization[1]. We have employed assessment methodologies that avoid written exams, an approach both outreach and classroom-based programs may find useful.

Categories and Subject Descriptors

K.3.2 [**Computers and Education**]: Computer and Information Science Education; K.4.m [**Computers and Society**]: Miscellaneous—*Diversity and Outreach*

General Terms

Design, Human Factors

[1]A timing issue between say bubbles and sound in Scratch

Keywords

diversity, K-12 education, outreach, assessment, Scratch

1. INTRODUCTION

The desire to expose more students to computer science has led to the development of many educational activities[15, 9, 12, 5] and outreach programs to broaden participation in computer science [4, 3, 10] . Unfortunately, these outreach programs can reach only a small segment of the population. To truly broaden participation in computing, we must help computer science find a place at the table in K-12 schools—and that requires the development of standards, curricula, and assessments.

Previous work shows that Scratch-based outreach can be effective at increasing students' *interest* in computing [19, 10] . With this paper, we contribute to a small but growing body of work assessing the effectiveness of Scratch for teaching CS *content*—in our case, in the context of a two-week interdisciplinary summer camp for middle school students, based on Scratch programming [15] presented along with culturally-relevant non-CS themes aimed at broadening participation among underrepresented groups.

We present this work both to (1) address the question of whether outreach activities can really teach computer science ("Sure, they had fun, but did they learn anything?") and (2) provide a starting point for further development of assessment for Scratch programming; techniques that can be adapted not only to assessing outreach activities, but also in any computing curriculum based on Scratch programming.

We found that in just two weeks of our interdisciplinary camp, students displayed competence in several areas, including event-driven programming, initializing state, synchronization between audio and visual elements as well as between objects, and some proficiency in creating complex animations requiring the integration of several concepts including loops. Our assessment techniques resulted in fairly low-overhead note-taking and program analysis, with very little reliance on written exams.

The rest of the paper is organized as follows. We provide a brief summary of related work in Section 2. Section 3 describes our camp and curriculum. Sections 4 and 5 describe our assessment methodology, and the results of our assessment. Finally, Section 6 describes future work.

2. RELATED WORK

We are adding to a small but growing body of work assessing student learning with Scratch programming—work that spans a variety of approaches, settings, and contexts. A general framework for such assessments is described by Brennan and Resnick [7].

Adams and Webster[1] conducted a thorough analysis of programs from nine years of CS-centric summer camps for middle and high school students. By inspecting which and how many blocks of each type were used, they answered interesting questions about how the project types, gender, etc. influenced the CS constructs used.

A series of papers [16, 17, 11] assessed learning of CS concepts through Scratch in the school setting, examining, among other things, whether the programming approaches learned through Scratch were beneficial or detrimental to later success in CS. Their methodology used traditional classroom tests.

Burke and Kafai [8] found that students following a similar curriculum to ours (digital story-telling) in a school setting (vs. our summer-camp setting) over seven weeks demonstrate competence in several key CS concepts (event-driven programming, synchronization/coordination of multiple threads, and loops). Like us, they had a small sample size (10).

Lewis and Shah [14] describe an assessment of Scratch programming quizzes in a summer enrichment course focused primarily on math and computer science and containing high-achieving students. They administered paper-based quizzes on the 2nd through 10th day of instruction in a 12 day course.

Building on this prior work, our work has two major differences. First, we adapt the assessment methodology to a non-academic camp setting with a broad spectrum of students (academically and culturally). We cross-reference help received with the programs to more accurately reflect the competence, and we analyze the implementation of the Scratch programs deeply to rate the competence displayed. Second, we show that with just a two-week, interdisciplinary, non-academic camp program, students demonstrate competence in many CS areas.

3. CAMP AND CURRICULUM

Animal Tlatoque, our two-week summer camp, was initially designed with two specific goals: (1) to attract a target audience of middle school students from underrepresented groups with non-CS themes[2, 13, 18] that appeal to both parents and children (at which we have succeeded [10]), and (2) to engage participants in interdisciplinary activities that allow them to learn about computer science and develop skills for computational thinking in the context of those non-CS themes. This past year, we took on a third goal: (3) to assess the learning of CS content that took place during the camp.

The Summer 2012 instance of our camp had 35 campers. Ten of these were enrolling in the camp for a second or third year; these campers progressed through the Scratch curriculum on an accelerated track. Our assessment efforts are focused on students participating in the camp for the first time; of these we had IRB permission and informed consent to report data for 22 campers.

3.1 Curriculum Design Constraints

The curriculum design was heavily influenced by two constraints:

(1) The interdisciplinary themes influenced the computer science *content* of the lessons because of the culminating project—a digital story-telling project.

Week 1 lessons consisted entirely—and only—of lessons that taught skills and concepts needed to complete that final project. Concepts not strictly needed for that project—such as user-defined variables and conditional control flow—were deferred to Week 2, and students had less opportunity to practice them.

(2) Assessment influenced the *structure* of the lessons. Each

Lesson	event-driven prog.	Initial State: size	orientation	background	visibility	costume	position	synchronization	broadcast/receive	complex animation
1) Scratch Basics	X	X								
2) Conversations	X	X	X					X	X	
3) Scene Changes	X	X	X	X	X			X	X	
4) Complex Anim.	X	X	X			X	X			X
Final project	X	X	X	X	X	X	X	X	X	X

X: item required by the project's checklist.

Table 1: Computer science concepts assessed through Scratch projects.

lesson has two parts: a warm-up exercise (not assessed) in which students learn one or more new CS concepts with substantial scaffolding and support, and a small project (assessed) in which students apply their new knowledge to a similar, but new, problem.

Our core Scratch curriculum is summarized in Table 1. The columns to the right of the table show the major CS concepts that formed the learning objectives, and the targets of assessment, namely: Event-Driven Programming, Initial State, Synchronization, Broadcast/Receive, and Complex Animation. In addition, we offered an additional lesson covering interactive input, user-defined variables and conditional control flow (if/then/else) and an optional project involving a side-scroller game. The remainder of this section describes each of these lessons in more detail.

3.2 Lesson Descriptions

Students work in pairs at a single computer. Each pair is assigned an endangered animal from Mesoamerica that is used in several projects.For reasons of space we omit detailed descriptions of the warm-up exercises.

Lesson 1: Scratch Basics familiarizes students with the basic elements of Scratch programming, including concepts such as the stage, sprites, the way blocks are combined into scripts and two core CS concepts.

Event-driven programming is used in interactive programs, using blocks such as "When Green Flag clicked" and "When Sprite clicked" to determine when actions should occur.

Initial state, in particular its initialization, was previously observed (anecdotally) to be a common source of bugs. Sprites have certain attributes (e.g.position, orientation) that, if changed during the program, need to be initialized if the "green flag" is clicked again to restart after completion or the "red flag" is clicked.

Lesson 1 Project: Name Poem [20] is based on the camper pair's assigned animal—the name of their animal is spelled out, and when each letter is clicked, a descriptive word appears starting with that letter appears. For example, the character "fish" might become Friendly, Intelligent, Shy, Hairless.

Lesson 2: Conversations teaches multi-sprite synchronization through "conversations" between two characters, where the dialog is simultaneously in say bubbles and sound, requiring a tricky Scratch solution. This introduces two new CS concepts.

Broadcast/Receive is used to control timing between sprits. In Scratch programming, a collection of scripts can be associated with each sprite, and each script runs as a separate parallel thread. To create order between threads, students use broadcast/receive blocks. This can be considered an example of the more general CS concepts of "message-passing" and "event driven programming".

Say/Sound Synchronization is used when displaying a "say" bubble – the kind used to show dialog in comics – at the same time as an audio file narrating the text. It turns out not be nearly as straightforward to implement as one might hope. We found the most robust and pedagogically straightforward solution to be placing an indefinite say bubble on the screen, playing the sound until finished, and then removing the say bubble using a blank say bubble. This approach emphasizes an important CS concept—one so basic, that we sometimes forget that novice programmers have to *learn* it—the importance of putting blocks in the correct *sequence* to achieve the desired effect.

Lesson 2 Project: Animal Conversation allows students to teach others about their animals. Students split up and pair with others, implementing a conversation between their two animals in which they are trying to learn about each other. This reinforces their new knowledge in synchronization.

Lesson 3: Scene Changes expands on message passing and sequential instructions by introducing visibility(hide/show) and backgrounds in order to make scene changes.

Lesson 3 Project: Mayan Conversation reinforces message passing, sequential instructions, and visibility (hide/show) to make a conversation in the Mayan language. Students are given the first two glyphs and recordings. They sequence them like scenes.

Lesson 4: Complex Animation teaches students how to create realistic motion (e.g. people walk, birds fly, snakes slither, fish swim), and requires several CS concepts to complete.

Complex Animation goes beyond the simple "glide to" block provided by Scratch. To make the motion realistic requires costume changes, motion, timing, and repetition control structures (loops).

Lesson 4 Project: Name Poem w/ Motion has students add several complex animations to their name poem from lesson 1, including one of their animal.

Culminating Project: Animating a Mesoamerican Animal Myth involving their animal, containing at least three scenes and two characters. A checklist contained require elements to ensure that the resulting Scratch program would allow us to assess CS concepts taught.

Lesson 5: Interactive Conversation was taught after the students had already started the culminating project, and consisted of a series of warm-ups introducing input, variables, and conditionals (if/then/else).

Optional Project: Side-Scrolling Game contains a main character (Scratch the cat) who must battle foes such as the banana-throwing monkey, a field of thorns, bees, and a giant bat, with nothing more than foul-smelling fish as weapons. Although too complex for students to code on their own, students explored parts of implementation. Due to the lack of a project, we used a written quiz-like assessment (Table 4) for the concepts taught in this lesson.

4. ASSESSMENT METHODOLOGY

We faced several challenges in designing an assessment plan for our curriculum. The major hurdles were (1) the short timescale (this is a 2-week camp that combines several subjects, so time is very tight) (2) the student perspective that camps are supposed to be fun, so anything that reminds them of "school" (e.g. anything that smells like a "test") is to be avoided, and (3) our use of pair programming for all projects (preventing data-gathering by individual student).

In particular, we did not control for prior knowledge using pre-tests, nor did staff members take extensive notes because of negative camper feedback last year. We did ask about prior programming experience on a survey, but found this to be inaccurate because campers differ in their interpretation of what "programming" is. Instead, we relied on informal discussions with campers, and only two reported specific programming knowledge (one in Scratch). For this reason, we are not stating definitively that students *learned* these concepts within the two-week camp, but that they *demonstrated competence* by the end of the two-week camp.

#	Explanation
0	**Validation:** Students want confirmation, not information
1	**Where:** Only needed help navigating the Scratch gui
2	**What:** Only needed a reminder of the name of the concept
3	**How:** Given name of concept, still needed help to complete task
4	**Reteach:** Had to reteach the entire lesson (concept and execution)

Table 2: Help levels recorded in field notes.

Our major artifacts are the completed projects, but it is not sufficient to analyze these in isolation, since completion of the project does not necessarily imply competence in the material. Throughout the camp, we had at least one staff member available for every six students, so students were able to receive ample help, including being stepped through the solution, if necessary.

Therefore, we use a combination of analysis of the artifacts and information from the staff members about what help they gave the students on the projects associated with each lesson, as well as the culminating project. Note that we do not assess competence based on completion of the warm-up lessons—we assess only the final projects in each lesson.

While working, students have access to a set of Scratch Reference Cards, including a relevant subset of the original MIT Scratch Cards as well as cards we designed for each lesson. These are tied directly to the project in the lesson, and they are used as reference for the smaller projects and culminating projects. If a student completes the project using only Scratch cards, we consider that the student learned/understood the material.

4.1 Staff Notes

Campers have staff members available for help. Each time a student asks a question related to a concept that has been taught, staff members explore the level of understanding of the student. The levels of help are listed in Table 2. The goal of the staff member is to first attempt to give help as if the student required only level 0 help, then proceed to level 1, etc., until the student is able to figure out the solution. As long as at least level 1 help was given, the staff member records the level of help given and the concept covered. Some also recorded level 0 help.

4.2 Project Analysis

Each assessed project has a list of concepts required to complete it, as shown in Table 1. For the competence, we looked at the projects in two ways—the execution and the implementation. For each category, we have four levels. The top level is "perfect"—looking at the project playing and the implementation. The next level is that the project itself looks fine when played, but the implementation is not robust or did not apply the computer science concept correctly (i.e. synchronization has a potential timing issue or the student used repetitive code where a loop would have been more appropriate). The next level is that there is a noticeable defect when running the project (i.e. two sounds play at the same time, or the animation was too fast to see). The lowest level is used when the implementation is absent or incomplete—i.e. a critical piece is missing.

Our assessment involved several phases. First, for each project, three students independently scored the first five programs manu-

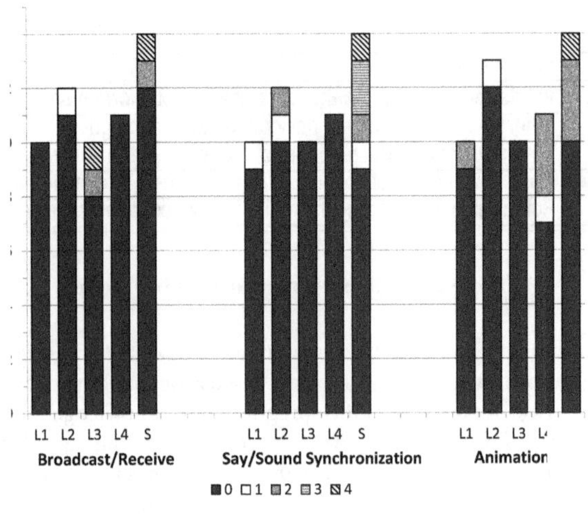

Figure 1: Field notes taken by staff members.

ally, discussed and reconciled their scores, independently scored the rest of the programs, and reconciled the rest of their scores. Our Scratch static analysis tool, Hairball, was developed to determine the scores as a fourth entity [6]. Whenever Hairball's results disagreed with what the manual assessors concluded, a final, more detailed manual assessment occurred to determine which was correct.

Lesson and Event Descrption	Results	
(1) click green flag⇒character says something	8/10	80%
(1) click letter⇒letter says word	9/10	90%
(2) click green flag ⇒conversation starts	10/10	100%
(4) click letter⇒turn into animal	6/11	55%
Final Project: click green flag⇒ story begins	10/10	100%

Table 3: Assessments of event-driven programming.

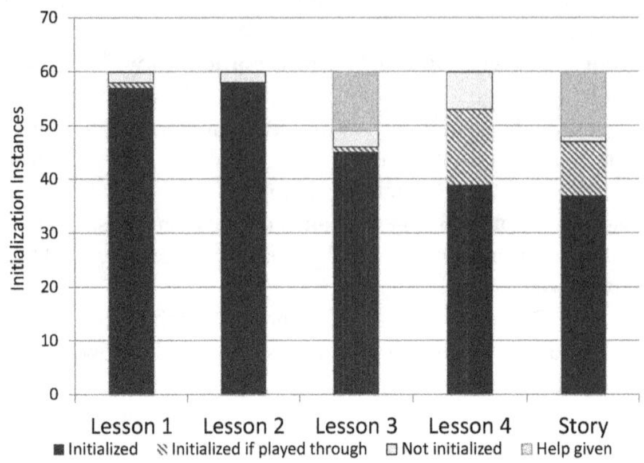

Figure 2: Initialization results broken down by project.

5. ASSESSMENT RESULTS

In this section, we present the results of our assessment. We preface these results with a frank recognition of the fact that the population under study is very small—results are reported for only 10 campers pairs. Our purpose in presenting these results, therefore, is not to claim anything "statistically significant". Rather it is to provide a model for integrating assessment of learning into the design of a Scratch-based curriculum—one that can be followed both by future designers of outreach programs, and in-school curricula alike. This allows us to not only gain insights into student competence in certain subjects, it can tell us if students were rushed through particular assignments.

In our camp, because of the complex integration of different subjects and the scheduling involved, students were a little bit rushed with the projects for Lessons 3 and 4 (Mayan Conversation and Name Poem with Motion).

5.1 Field Notes

Each staff member recorded a note for each interaction that required them to help the students. Figure 1 shows the level of help given to each pair for each concept. For the most part, students asked validation question such as: "Should I do this?" and the staff member merely confirmed the students' own knowledge. Only a few pairs needed what we consider substantive help—help levels 3 and 4. We believe this is for one of three reasons. First, by placing the warm-up exercise immediately before the transfer project, students are able to ask questions and practice once a short time before being expected to complete it by themselves.

Second, because students were working in pairs, only one of the two needs to understand the material. Pairs were assigned randomly by age and school, so we had no opportunity to match them by learning speed / skill level. Anecdotally, we did find that some pairs contained one strong partner and one weak partner. Finally, students could be completing the projects incorrectly or avoiding challenging implementations. We will see that this is true for several pairs when implementing animations in the culminating project.

5.2 Event-Driven Programming

Table 3 shows part of our results of assessing understanding of event-driven programming, i.e. implementing scripts that are triggered by specific events (the other part being the results for Broadcast/Receive, discussed later in this section.)

In the project for Lesson 1, students were required to implement event-handling for both green flag and sprite clicked events—80% and 90% were successful. By Lesson 2, students has mastered "green flag" events; 100% correctly started the required actions this way as instructed.

We are not showing results for Lesson 3, because very few students completed that Lesson successfully. We believe that this, and the fact that only 55% of the students correctly implemented the assessed click event in Lesson 4 have more to do with extraneous factors; at this point in the camp, students may have felt more rushed. In addition, in Lesson 4, they may have been concentrating more on realistic motion (presented later) rather than this checklist item.

5.3 Initialization

We performed two tests for initialization. The first is to manually open the program and run it twice from beginning to end to see if the second execution matches the first. The second is to use our Hairball tool to assist in detecting if something is not initialized before it is used, leading to incorrect execution if it is stopped in the middle and restarted. Hairball is not perfect—it flags possible changes that do not have an initialization in the beginning of the program, but it misses some valid later initializations, so a manual check is still necessary.

We first show initialization broken down by project in Figure 2. The X axis shows the project, and the Y axis shows initialization errors or successes. Initialization attempts are broken down by category, not sprite, so each project has 6 initialization checks.

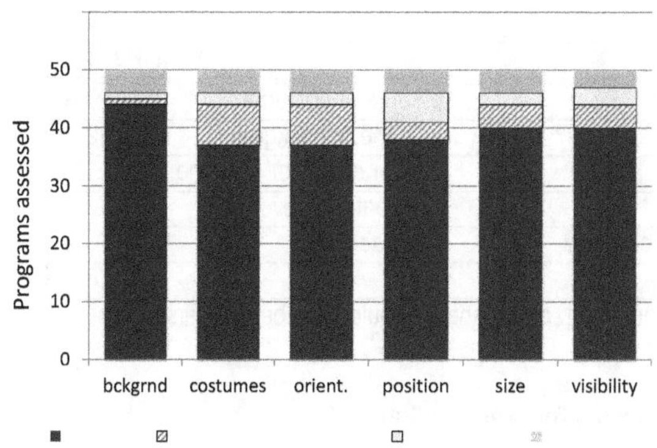

Figure 3: Initialization results broken down by category.

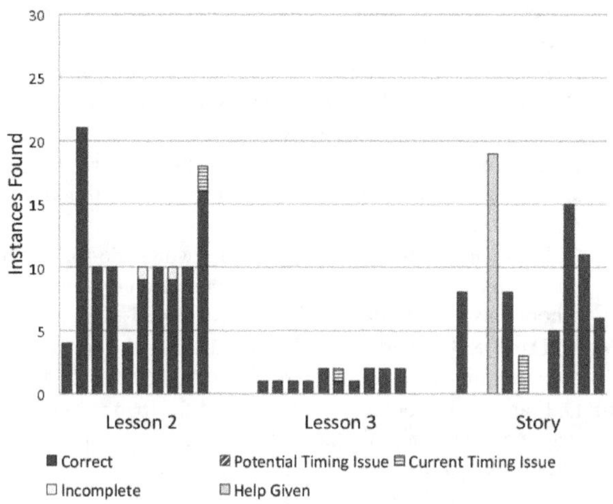

Figure 4: Results for Sound/Say Synchronization.

For the most part, students remembered to initialize items that needed to be reset when the project was played to completion and restarted. As the projects became more complex, there were more opportunities to forget initialization, especially if the program ran correctly twice in a row. For each of Lesson 3 and the story, two groups were retaught initialization (one of which was the same group both times). We do not have a record of which type of initialization was retaught, so we deducted all initialization opportunities.

We now present the initialization errors by category in Figure 3. There was not one particular category that dominated the errors. Instead, the errors were fairly evenly distributed across all the categories except for backgrounds, where there were virtually no errors.

5.4 Sound/Say Synchronization

Figure 4 shows that few of our students had any trouble with the concept of say/sound synchronization. The issues that did arise were evident on playback, so given additional time to work on the project, the pair may have been able to detect and fix the bug. There were a few students who did not choose to implement synchronized say/sound blocks in the culminating project; they chose other ways of incorporating sound.

5.5 Broadcast/Receive

Results for Broadcast/Receive are shown in Figure 5. These results show that it is often the case that a project has one incomplete Broadcast/Receive, either because they did not clean up their dead code or they did not quite complete the project. In Lesson 3, especially, many students were rushed in their implementations. We see that for the Story, almost all students used Broadcast/Receive properly, except for one group that required level 4 help and another that had timing issues due to two sequential broadcasts.

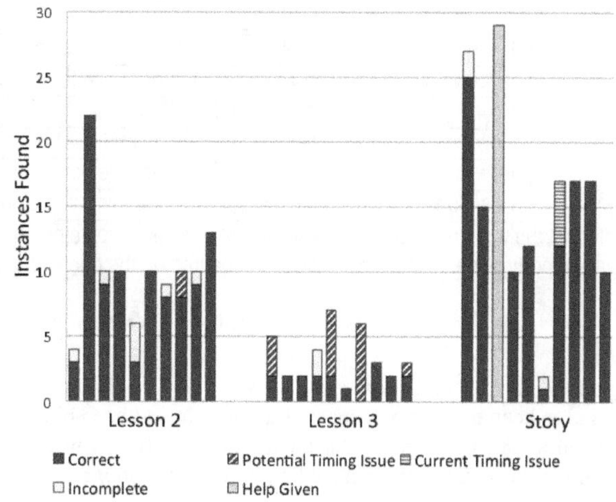

Figure 5: Results for Broadcast/Receive.

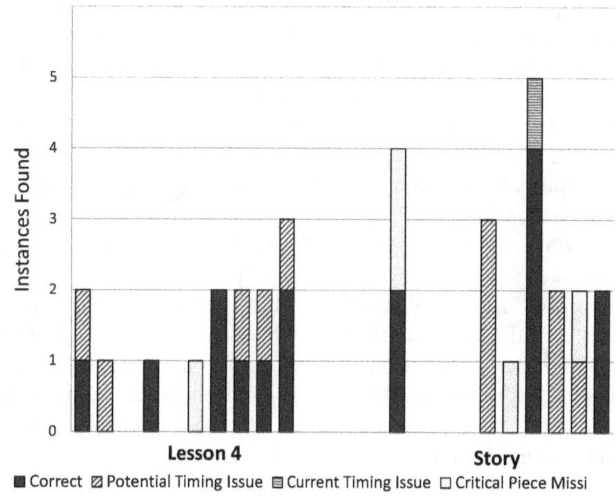

Figure 6: Results for Animation.

5.6 Complex Animation

The checklist for the name poem with motion and the culminating project specifically indicated that campers should include Complex Animation in the form of realistic motion of their animal in their projects. Most pairs added realistic motion to their name poem, but four had current timing issues, and two were missing something critical in the code. For the culminating project, we found that many students chose not to implement realistic motion, instead using the "glide" block to slide their sprite across the screen. In the end, only three pairs out of ten successfully implemented complex animation in their culminating project.

5.7 Side-Scroller Warmup Assessment

Table 4 shows the questions and results from the side-scroller quiz. Most of the students assessed knew when to employ costumes and background changes (91% and 82%). 73% of the students knew to use a repeat or forever block to make the bees keep go-

Question	Answer	Results
If you want the cat rather than a panda, what would you change?†	sprite or costume	100%
If you want the cat to go into a cave rather than a temple, what do you change?	scene or background	82%
How do you make the monkey turn red?	color effects or costume	91%
How do you make the bees keep going up and down?	repeat or forever	73%
How can you keep track of how many times the bat has been hit by a banana?	variable	73%
How do you make the bat disappear on the third hit, not the first hit?	if	28%

†Note that the first question on the assessment worksheet contained a typo—the words "cat" and "panda" should have been reversed. We are reporting the question as it actually appeared on the questionaire.

Table 4: Written assessment of concepts for side-scroller.

ing up and down and the same number knew that a variable should be used to keep track of how many times the bat had been hit. Only three pairs (28%) recognized that the difference between disappearing on the third hit rather than the first hit required an *if* block.

6. CONCLUSIONS AND FUTURE WORK

Despite the constraints of our camp—a two-week, non-academic, interdisplinary, "fun oriented" camp—we were able to perform assessments demostrating that students attained competence with several computer science concepts. In just two weeks, with a curriculum not entirely focused on computer science, students displayed—and we were able to assess—competence with event-driven programming, initialization of state, message passing, and say/sound synchronization.

Further, we have adapted and piloted a technique for asssessing computer science competence that relies very little on written assessments in the context of Scratch programming. Our technique uses a scaffolded curriculum, with warm-up lessons, projects to assess mastery, measurment of help given, and both automated and manual examination of the Scratch programs produced by students. Our approach can be adapted for other Scratch-based curricula, and/or other Computer Science concepts.

As with similar research, we have only a small sample size—thus, future work may include applying this assessment technique with a larger sample size. This could take place across multiple instances of an outreach program or in the context of a K-12 CS curriculum implemented within the regular school day.

We also note that, outreach programs, while valuable for the students that participate, reach only a small segment of the population. It is likely that integration of computer science into K-12 standards and curricula will have a broader impact. By pairing our curriculum with a curriculum teaching variables, loops, and conditionals, students can be exposed to a broad set of topics that can be applied to many different subjects required in schools today.

7. ACKNOWLEDGMENTS

This work is supported by the National Science Foundation BPC Award CNS-0940491 to Franklin, Aldana, and Conrad.

8. REFERENCES

[1] J. C. Adams and A. R. Webster. What do students learn about programming from game, music video, and storytelling projects? In *SIGCSE '12*, pages 643–648, 2012.

[2] G. Aikenhead. Students' ease in crossing cultural borders into school science. *Science Education*, 85(2):180–188, March 2001.

[3] S. Alliance. The stars alliance: A southeastern partnership for diverse participation in computing. NSF STARS Alliance Proposal. http://www.itstars.org/.

[4] I. Arroyo et al. Effects of web-based tutoring software on students' math achievement. In *AERA*, 2004.

[5] T. Bell, I. H. Witten, and M. Fellows. *Computer Science Unplugged*. 2006.

[6] B. Boe, C. Hill, M. Len, G. Dreschler, P. Conrad, and D. Franklin. Hairball: Lint-inspired static analysis of scratch projects. In *SIGCSE '13*, March 2013.

[7] K. Brennan and M. Resnick. New frameworks for studying and assessing the development of computational thinking. In *AERA 2012*, 2012.

[8] Q. Burke and Y. B. Kafai. The writers' workshop for youth programmers: digital storytelling with scratch in middle school classrooms. In *SIGCSE '12*, pages 433–438, 2012.

[9] W. Dann, S. Cooper, and R. Pausch. Making the connection: programming with animated small world. *ITiCSE*, 2000.

[10] D. Franklin, P. Conrad, G. Aldana, and S. Hough. Animal tlatoque: attracting middle school students to computing through culturally-relevant themes. In *SIGCSE '11*.

[11] M. Gordon et al. Spaghetti for the main course?: observations on the naturalness of scenario-based programming. In *ITiCSE '12*, 2012.

[12] C. S. Hood and D. J. Hood. Teaching programming and language concepts using legos. In *ITiCSE*, June 2005.

[13] C. Lee. Why we need to re-think race and ethnicity in educational research. *Educational Researcher*, 32(5):3–5, June 2003.

[14] C. M. Lewis and N. Shah. Building upon and enriching grade four mathematics standards with programming curriculum. In *SIGCSE '12*, pages 57–62, 2012.

[15] J. Maloney et al. The scratch programming language and environment. *Trans. Comput. Educ.*, 10(4):16:1–16:15, Nov. 2010.

[16] O. Meerbaum-Salant et al. Learning computer science concepts with scratch. In *ICER '10*, pages 69–76, 2010.

[17] O. Meerbaum-Salant et al. Habits of programming in scratch. In *ITiCSE '11*, pages 168–172, 2011.

[18] J. Moschkovich. A situated and sociocultural perspective on bilingual mathematics learners. *Mathematical Thinking and Learning*, 4(2/3), 2002.

[19] P. A. G. Sivilotti and S. A. Laugel. Scratching the surface of advanced topics in software engineering: a workshop module for middle school students. In *SIGCSE '08*, 2008.

[20] U. Wolz et al. Computational thinking via interactive journalism in middle school. In *SIGCSE*, 2010.

Growing Female Undergraduate Enrollments in Computer Science: What's the Secret?

Wendy DuBow
(Moderator)
National Center for Women & IT
University of Colorado
303.492.5462
wendy@ncwit.org

Ignatios Vakalis
Computer Science
Cal Poly, San Luis Obispo
(805) 756-2824
ivakalis@calpoly.edu

Manuel A. Perez-Quinones
Computer Science
Virginia Tech
540-231-2646
perez@cs.vt.edu

Jason T. Black
Computer & Information Sciences
Florida A&M University
850-412-7354
jblack@cis.famu.edu

SUMMARY

For the past decade, computer science and other computing-focused departments in universities and colleges around the nation have seen dramatic decreases, or at best, stagnation in their enrollments in the major, particularly among females and other populations under-represented in computing. Recently, some institutions have begun to see a shift in student interest in their major. What are these departments doing to reverse this 12-year, or in some cases, 35-year trend?

This panel will share interventions undertaken by three U.S. universities that have shown increased undergraduate enrollments overall, with particular increases in female enrollment; increased faculty engagement with outreach, recruitment and retention for diversity; and increased commitment from minority women to pursue graduate degrees in CS/IT. These departments have not only implemented evidence-based practices to make these dramatic changes, but have tried new ideas as well.

National Center for Women & Information Technology (NCWIT) will share equivalent enrollment increases from other institutions that have implemented evidence-based practices. She also will make available hardcopy materials and website links that describe practical interventions faculty can implement.

Categories and Subject Descriptors

K.3.2 Computer and Information Science Education

Keywords

Broadening Participation; Gender; Diversity; Evidence-based Practices; Women

1. WENDY DUBOW

Evaluation evidence from 65 academic departments indicates that use of evidence-based practices is positively correlated with an increased number of females enrolled in computing at those institutions [1]. The moderator will describe these results and point attendees to the vast repository of free, evidence-based practices that NCWIT provides to the public (www.ncwit.org/resources).

SIGCSE'13, March 6–9, 2013, Denver, Colorado, USA.
ACM 978-1-4503-1868-6/13/03.

2. IGNATIOS VAKALIS

The Department of Computer Science at Cal Poly (San Luis Obispo) has implemented a cadre of approaches in order to attract and retain more women in Computer Science and Software Engineering. These approaches include evidence-based practices [2], as well as new tactics, as follows:

- Instituting a unique first year (first quarter) course, featuring different "tracks" and reflecting student interests (e.g., robotics, games, visual art, music, mobile apps) [3]. All "tracks" employ project-based learning [4] with common learning outcomes. Each section provides a "big picture" view of computing. External clients supply projects that are implemented using group-based pedagogies.
- Enriching mentoring [5]. Female students are paired with upper-division female students for mentoring during first-year courses to build academic self-confidence, social support, and motivation to achieve.
- Providing support for female students (cohorts of first year and upper division) to attend the Annual Grace Hopper Celebration.
- Deploying the female students to recruit additional female students from their respective high schools to create a distributed and scalable approach. Roadshow materials [6], supplemented by personal experiences of our female majors, make captivating presentations.

During the last three years, Cal Poly's enrollments in computer science and software engineering are monotonically increasing. Female students constitute 33% of first-year students in Software Engineering. In addition, the retention rate of students, including the female majors, has increased by 70%.

3. MANUEL A. PEREZ-QUINONES

The Computer Science Department at Virginia Tech has included in their service activities a set of diversity events as opportunities for faculty to be engaged in increasing the number of females in our student ranks [7,8]. As a result, we have seen an increase in participation in outreach from both faculty and current students.

We have been tracking our enrollments to enable us to monitor our progress [9]. In fall 2010, we had 337 CS majors, with only 26 females (7.7%). In fall 2011, there were 427 majors with 38 females (8.9%). As of this writing (fall 2012), we have 434 majors with 60 female students (13.82%!).

We have been actively engaged in the following activities:

- Summer high-school teacher workshops using funding from NCWIT, Microsoft, Google and our industrial partners. The workshop helps create an atmosphere of collaboration and partnership between high-school teachers and our faculty.
- Regional high school visits. We have presented at traditional engineering fairs and female-dominant engineering classes, spoken in girl-only classes in magnet schools. Having a female department head also conveys a strong message to prospective female students of a favorable climate.
- Undergraduate support. The College of Engineering (CoE) has two special dorms for its students, Hypatia for females and Galileo for males. We have discussed CS careers with these students and encouraged them to consider a CS major. We also offer CS modules to about 75 first-year students through a program organized by the CoE and offered the summer before students arrive on campus.
- Diversity-oriented conferences. We send students to both the Grace Hopper Celebration and the Richard Tapia Celebration of Diversity in Computing annually, and have been among the top academic sponsors of Tapia.
- We co-coordinate the regional affiliate of the NCWIT Award for Aspirations in Computing, along with George Mason University and the University of Virginia, to honor high-school teachers and students for their efforts in computing.

4. JASON T. BLACK

The Computer and Information Sciences Department at Florida Agricultural and Mechanical University (FAMU), a Historically-Black College or University (HBCU), has seen a decline in female enrollment of close to 70% from 2001 through 2007. While HBCUs like FAMU have had significantly higher success than the national average at producing BS degrees in computer science compared to majority-serving institutions, the number of female students majoring in CS has declined. Consistent with national trends among HBCUs, the number of women graduates in CIS at FAMU dropped from 31 in 2001 to just 9 in 2006, a 71% decline. It is with this backdrop that the African-American Women in Computer Science (AAWCS) scholarship program was formed in 2008, with funding from NSF. Its goal is to increase the number of women pursuing degrees in CS-related fields.

The objectives of the AAWCS program are five-fold:

- Financial Support. Stipends to reduce strain and to help them focus on their studies rather than second (or third) jobs.
- Academic Advancement. Services to increase the academic progress of students, including tutoring, academic advisement, and mentoring.
- Progression. Close monitoring of class schedules during registration; peer-teams, and other coordinated efforts.
- Graduation. Exposure to research opportunities through REUs and other opportunities; tours of graduate schools and other research labs.
- Employment. Professional development and corporate career activities; internship and research opportunities.

AAWCS students are involved in leadership skill-building activities as well, including middle- and high-school career days and roadshows; academic workshops for middle- and high-school girls; and mentoring for community and school-based programs, such as K-12 computer clubs and Boys and Girls Clubs.

As a result of these efforts, we have seen a significant jump in our enrollment of women in computing disciplines at FAMU of almost 20%; additionally, we have seen increased commitment from AAWCS participants to pursuing graduate degrees in CS/IT (80% of the women that graduated from the AAWCS program have either enrolled in a graduate program in CS/IT or state that they plan to in the near future).

5. ACKNOWLEDGEMENTS

The authors thank the National Science Foundation for support under award CNS-0813956, NCWIT's Strategic Partners National Science Foundation, Microsoft and Bank of America, and Investment Partners Avaya, Pfizer, Merck and Turner. Data collection for the NCWIT external evaluation was only possible with the cooperation of Academic Alliance institutions. All opinions reflected in this paper are those of the authors and not necessarily those of the National Science Foundation.

6. REFERENCES

[1] Litzler, E. 2010. NCWIT External Evaluation Report. Center for Workforce Development, Seattle, WA. Unpublished.

[2] Barker, L.J. & Cohoon, J.M. How Can You Re-Engineer Your Undergraduate Program to Increase Women's Representation in Computing? Small Steps Toward Systemic Change. NCWIT, Boulder, CO. http://www.ncwit.org/reengineerundergrad

[3] Haungs, M., Clark, M., Clements, J. & Janzen, D. Improving First-year Success and Retention through Interest-Based CS0 Courses. In Proceedings of the 43rd ACM Technical Symposium on Computer Science Education (Raleigh, NC, USA, February 29- March 3, 2012). SIGCSE 2012. ACM, New York, NY.

[4] Barg, M., Fekete, A., Greening, T., Hollands, O., Kay, J. & Kingston, J. Problem-based Learning for Foundation Computer Science Courses. Computer Science Education, 10(2): 109- 128, 2000.

[5] Lotkowski, V. Robbins, S. & Noeth, R. The Role of Academic and Non-academic Factors in Improving College Retention. ACT Policy Report, 2004.

[6] Roadshow-in-a-Box: Capitalizing on Models for Outreach. NCWIT, Boulder, CO. http://www.ncwit.org/ roadshow

[7] Barker, L.J. & Cohoon, J.M. How Can You Re-Engineer Your Undergraduate Program to Increase Women's Representation in Computing? Small Steps Toward Systemic Change. NCWIT, Boulder, CO. http://www.ncwit.org/reengineerundergrad

[8] Communicating for Change: Persuade Colleagues to Get on Board. NCWIT, Boulder, CO. http://www.ncwit.org/commchange

[9] Barker, L. and Cohoon, J. Key Practices for Retaining Undergraduates in Computing. NCWIT, Boulder, CO. http://www.ncwit.org/retainundergrads

Rediscovering the Passion, Beauty, Joy, and Awe: Making Computing Fun Again, part 6

Daniel D. Garcia (moderator)
University of California, Berkeley
777 Soda Hall
Berkeley, CA 94720
+1 (510) 517-4041
ddgarcia@cs.berkeley.edu

Valerie Barr
Union College
Computer Science Dept
Schenectady, NY, 12308
+1 (518) 388-8361
barrv@union.edu

Mark Guzdial
College of Computing/GVU
Georgia Institute of Technology
Atlanta, GA 30332-0280
+1 (404) 894-5618
guzdial@cc.gatech.edu

David J. Malan
Harvard University
33 Oxford Street
Cambridge, MA 02138
+1 (617) 329-1205
malan@harvard.edu

Categories and Subject Descriptors
K.3.2 [**Computer and Information Science Education**]: Computer science education

General Terms
Experimentation

Keywords
Computer science education, alternative entries into the major

1. SUMMARY

In his keynote at SIGCSE 2007, Grady Booch exhorted us to share the "passion, beauty, joy and awe" (PBJA) of computing [2]. This led to a series of room-packed sessions at the following five SIGCSE symposia to explore that idea from different angles [5, 6, 7, 8, 10]. They have provided a forum for sharing:

- **What we've done**: Highlighting successful PBJA initiatives the presenters have undertaken or seen and wish to trumpet.
- **What we should do (curriculum)**: Pointing out where our curriculum is lacking in PBJA, and how to fix it.
- **How we should do it (pedagogy)**: Sharing how a change in attitude / focus / etc. can make strides to improving PBJA.

While the initial PBJA sessions evolved from a need to understand and combat the enrollment crisis of seven years ago, we are now seeing a resurgence in interest in our field, partially because "coders are hip and computer science is hot" [13]. Some point to "the Facebook Factor" as the source of inspiration for many young students, claiming this is a "Sputnik moment" [11]. Many dispute this, however, citing statistics that indicate under-represented students have not returned, and continuing negative connotations about the field [1]. Free computer science online courses are drawing hundreds of thousands of students [14], and there are colleges where the numbers have so exceeded historic highs, that some rightfully claim the crisis is over [12, 15]. This PBJA "movement" was born out of this enrollment crisis, but is not tied to it. There is always value in sharing novel best practices and advocating techniques that make computing fun.

In the past, we either tried to gather educators who either brought a wide variety of perspectives, or who would focus on a particular issue (e.g., K-12 education or broadening participation). This year we've gathered educators whose introductory class numbers are exploding or who have instituted very creative and successful paths into the major. The hope with this panel is to explore best practices in these crucial early years, in terms of extolling the PBJA of computing.

2. VALERIE BARR

In 2004, the Union College CS department was offering two sections per year of a typical CS1 course. Only 9% of annual enrollment was in the introductory class; 14% of those students were women. At that time, 31% of annual enrollment was in non-major courses. Beginning in 2005, inspired by the Georgia Tech media computation course, we embarked on an experiment in the use of contextualized computing. Today we offer *six* theme-based introductory CS courses, each of which covers the same concepts and skills. The course themes are big data, robotics, game development, artificial intelligence, media computation, and programming for engineers. In 2011-2012, 50% of the enrollments were in introductory CS, and 29% of the students were women (33% if we do not consider the *Programming for Engineers* course). In raw numbers we now enroll 3 to 5 times as many students in the introductory course per year as we did in 2004. While CS is not required college-wide, several majors (notably neuroscience and managerial economics) have joined the engineers in requiring the introductory CS course. It is a key component of the digital media minor and the computational methods minor. Finally, we have seen an increasing number of departments add CS to their lists of allowable electives to satisfy math and science requirements.

SIGCSE'13, March 6–9, 2013, Denver, Colorado, USA.
ACM 978-1-4503-1868-6/13/03.

3. MARK GUZDIAL

In 1999, Georgia Tech implemented a new general education requirement: everyone on campus had to take computer science, and it was the same introductory course for everyone. Students in Liberal Arts, Architecture, and Business programs withdrew-or-failed over 50% per term. In 2003, we decided to create three courses: One for CS and Science majors, one for Engineering majors (in MATLAB), and one for the rest. Media Computation was developed as an introduction to computing that answered the question for the other majors, "Why learn about computing?"

The idea of Media Computation is to learn the same introductory computing as a traditional CS1, while playing with the pixels in a picture (to implement Photoshop™ effects), the samples in a sound (to reverse or splice sounds), the characters in a Web page, or the frames in a video. Changing the data changes the context, which creates a purpose. Assignments in a Media Computation course involve creativity, as students build collages, music, animations, and comic strips. The average pass rate today in Media Computation is around 85%. We do get new CS majors or minors through Media Computation, but our greater goal is computational literacy across campus.

4. DAVID J. MALAN

CS50 is Harvard College's introductory course for majors and non-majors alike, enrollment in which both rose and fell along with the dot-coms. Although enrollment peaked in 1996 at 386 students, it had settled by 2002 in the neighborhood of 100.

We set out in 2007 to combat that trend by tackling two problems. We hypothesized that CS50 suffered from two problems, one of perception and one of design. Although, according to end-of-term surveys, the course had never lacked for good teachers or good content, the consensus on campus for years had been to beware this particular course. And the course's own syllabus may very well have been dated in the eyes of students who had begun to carry regularly modern hardware and software in their backpacks and pockets. Not only did we proceed to revamp every one of CS50's problem sets, we brought its syllabus more in line with technological trends already familiar to students.

We also altered the tone of the course to appeal to those "less comfortable" with computing on campus. But we took care to preserve the course's rigor and underlying fundamentals, lest we do our own students a disservice. Our new approach appears to be working [9]. Between 2006 and 2007, enrollment in CS50 more than doubled from 132 to 282 (+114%). Between 2007 and 2008, enrollment increased another 17% to 330, though even more striking was that year's 48% increase in female enrollment. By 2010, enrollment had risen to 494 students. In 2011, CS50 became the second-largest course at Harvard College, with 607 students (+360% since 2006) [3]. In 2014, the department itself will graduate 74 majors, up from 25 in 2006 (+204%) [4].

5. REFERENCES

[1] ACM, WGBH. Interim report. *New Image for Computing*. April, 2009. **www.acm.org/membership/NIC.pdf**

[2] Booch, G. 2007. Readn', writ'n, 'rithmetic... and code'n. *SIGCSE Bull.* 39, 1 (Mar. 2007), 197-197. **doi.acm.org/10.1145/1227504.1227380**

[3] CS50 Manual. **manual.cs50.net/Enrollment**

[4] CS50 Manual. **manual.cs50.net/Concentrators**

[5] Garcia, D. D., Cutler, R., Dodds, Z., Roberts, E., and Young, A. 2009. Rediscovering the passion, beauty, joy, and awe: making computing fun again, continued. In *Proceedings of the 40th ACM Technical Symposium on CS Education* (Chattanooga, TN, USA, March 04-07, 2009). SIGCSE '09. ACM, New York, NY, 65-66. **doi.acm.org/10.1145/1508865.1508889**

[6] Garcia, D. D., Chapman, G., Hazzan, O., Johnson, M., and Sudol, L. A. 2010. Rediscovering the passion, beauty, joy, and awe: making computing fun again, part 3. In *Proceedings of the 41st ACM Technical Symposium on CS Education* (Milwaukee, WI, USA, March 10 - 13, 2010). SIGCSE '10. ACM, New York, NY, 394-395. **doi.acm.org/10.1145/1734263.1734399**

[7] Garcia, D. D., Hutton, M. F., Lemon, E., and Paley, J. 2011. Rediscovering the passion, beauty, joy, and awe: making computing fun again, part 4. In *Proceedings of the 42nd ACM technical symposium on Computer science education* (SIGCSE '11). ACM, New York, NY, USA, 613-614. **doi.acm.org/10.1145/1953163.1953332**

[8] Garcia, D. D., Ericson, B., Goode, J. and Lewis, C. 2012. Rediscovering the passion, beauty, joy, and awe: making computing fun again, part 5. In *Proceedings of the 43rd ACM technical symposium on Computer Science Education* (SIGCSE '12). ACM, New York, NY, USA, 577-578. **doi.acm.org/10.1145/2157136.2157300**

[9] Malan, D. 2009. Reinventing CS50. In *Proceedings of the 41st ACM Technical Symposium on CS Education* (Milwaukee, WI, USA, March 10 - 13, 2010). SIGCSE '10. ACM, New York, NY.

[10] McGettrick, A., Roberts, E., Garcia, D. D., and Stevenson, C. 2008. Rediscovering the passion, beauty, joy and awe: making computing fun again. In *Proceedings of the 39th SIGCSE Technical Symposium on Computer Science Education* (Portland, OR, USA, March 12 - 15, 2008). SIGCSE '08. ACM, New York, NY, 217-218. **doi.acm.org/10.1145/1352135.1352213**

[11] NY Times. *Computer Studies Made Cool, on Film and Now on Campus*. **www.nytimes.com/2011/06/11/technology/11computing.html**

[12] NY Times. *CS Programs Make a Comeback in Enrollment*. **www.nytimes.com/2009/03/17/science/17comp.html**

[13] NY Times. *Giving Women the Access Code*. **www.nytimes.com/2012/04/03/science/giving-women-the-access-code.html**

[14] NY Times. *Instruction for Masses Knocks Down Campus Walls*. **www.nytimes.com/2012/03/05/education/moocs-large-courses-open-to-all-topple-campus-walls.html**

[15] Reges, S. Email to SIGCSE-members mailing list. *enrollment crisis over?* 2009-05-21.

AP CS A Exploration of a Change from GridWorld to Labs

Renee L. Ciezki
Estrella Mountain Community College
Glendale, AZ
+1 623-878-4958 country code
renee.ciezki@estrellamountain.edu

Lien Diaz
College Board
Atlanta, GA
+1 678-787-9445
ldiaz@collegeboard.org

Robert Glen Martin
School for the Talented and Gifted
Dallas, TX
+1 972-925-6311
gmart039@dallasisd.org

Henry M. Walker
Grinnell College
Noyce Science Center
1116 8th Avenue, Grinnell, IA 50112
+1 641-269-4208
walker@cs.grinnell.edu

ABSTRACT

The AP CS A program is exploring the possibility of moving from the utilization of the GridWorld case study to the inclusion of several in-class laboratory exercises, beginning in 2014-2015 or later. The Development Committee believes labs may achieve many benefits of the past case studies, but a lab format will allow teachers more flexibility in teaching and a more agile development cycle for new materials.

This Special Session will review the motivations, experiences, limitations, and constraints of case studies, motivations for the use of in-class laboratory exercises, and some components of three laboratory exercises that currently are under development by the AP CS A program.

Categories and Subject Descriptors

K.3.2 [**Computer and Information Science Education**]: computer science education, curriculum Language

General Terms

Algorithms, Design, Experimentation

Keywords

Laboratory exercises, case studies, active learning. computing applications.

1. SUMMARY

The AP CS A program is exploring the possibility of moving from the utilization of the GridWorld case study to the inclusion of several in-class laboratory exercises, beginning in 2014-2015 or later. The Development Committee believes labs may achieve many benefits of the past case studies, but a lab format will allow teachers more flexibility in teaching and a more agile development cycle for new materials.

This Special Session will review

- the motivations and experiences of the use of case studies, which were first used on the 1995 AP CS exams,
- limitations and constraints with the case-study model,
- motivations for the use of in-class laboratory exercises, and
- the main components of three laboratory exercises that currently are under development by the AP CS A program.

SIGCSE '13, March 6–9, 2013, Denver, Colorado, USA.
ACM 978-1-4503-1868-6/13/03.

2. INTRODUCTION AND BACKGROUND

Beginning with the 1995 AP CS exams, the Advanced Placement Computer Science program has utilized case studies. Three goals articulated in the original AP CS Directory Manager Case Study included:

a. "They emphasize process over end product ...providing a sort of apprenticeship in the craft of programing.

b. They make large programs accessible. ...

c. They provide a good vehicle for assessment." [7]

In recent years, case studies also have been a vehicle to highlight principles of object-oriented problem solving. [3]

Although case studies have important benefits, their size and complexity have constrained the AP CS program in adapting to new course content and pedagogy. As a result, the AP CS A Development Committee is exploring a shift from the case study (GridWorld [5, 6]) to in-class laboratory exercises [2], perhaps in 2014-2015. The AP CS A Development Committee believes that a lab format may promote student learning, just as the case studies did. In addition, several lab experiences could provide a venue to suggest some real world applications. (A lab may not provide extensive details regarding an application, but a lab can suggest directions and encourage further investigation.) Altogether, the lab format allows flexibility for teachers, encourages creativity, allows courses to address local needs of students, encourages consideration of application areas, and allows an agile development cycle for new materials.

Should the AP CS A course move to lab-based experiences, The AP CS A program will identify important characteristics of lab-based experiences, and teachers will be able to choose labs that fit their courses [4].

Since the development of labs is time intensive, the AP CS A Development Committee, working with the College Board, is developing three new labs that may meet identified goals and objectives for an introductory computer science course [2]. These labs may be used at various times throughout a course, and may be of interest to both high school and college teachers.

3. SESSION OBJECTIVES

This session is designed to provide information to high school and college faculty alike on a possible transition of the AP CS A course from the GridWorld case study [5, 6] to in-class laboratory exercises. More specifically, the session has these objectives:

- Clarify the motivation and experiences with past AP CS case studies, especially the use of case studies as a pedagogical device for student learning of key concepts. [1]
- Review limitations of the case study approach for AP CS.
- Explain the approach of active student engagement through in-class labs, as described in many papers, such as [8-13].
- Outline the possible role of labs for AP CS A for 2014-1015 or later, including a review of important lab characteristics for a AP CS A course. [4].
- Present an overview of three draft AP CS A Labs, being developed by the AP CS A Development Committee to provide hands-on experiences with many topics of the course. [2]

4. OUTLINE OF THE SESSION

The following outline provides time to review the main topics (described above), followed by audience questions and feedback.

- Introduction and welcome --5 minutes, Walker
- Historical use of case studies (e.g., in AP CS) -- 5 minutes, Martin
- Limitations of the case study approach -- 5 minutes, Ciezki
- Use of labs within introductory computer science -- 5 minutes, Walker
- Role of labs for the AP CS course and exam, 5 minutes, Diaz
- Characteristics of in-class labs for AP CS A -- 5 minutes, Diaz
- Three draft lab resources under development for AP CS A
    - Overview, use in classes -- 5 minutes, Ciezki
    - Magpie Lab, 5 minutes, Walker
    - Picture Lab, 5 minutes, Ciezki
    - Elevens Lab, 5 minutes, Martin
- Questions, audience feedback, discussion, 25 minutes

5. EXPECTATIONS

This proposal has at least two primary audiences:

- Secondary school teachers (particularly AP CS A teachers) who organize introductory CS courses and who want to utilize current pedagogy and resources. These teachers want their students to be well prepared for the AP CS A course, so possible changes in content, exam coverage, and pedagogy can make a difference as courses are planned and taught.
- Teachers of introductory computer science at all levels, who wish to engage students and utilize laboratory exercises effectively. The new AP CS A Labs provide a new resource for teachers that could be useful in many settings.

Both of these audiences are likely to have questions regarding the possible dropping of the GridWorld case study and the inclusion of in-class labs, so the session will conclude with a 25-minute question-answer session with attendees.

6. ACKNOWLEDGMENTS

The Advanced Placement Computer Science Development Committee thanks the College Board for its support of the Lab concept and the development of these draft labs. The Committee also thanks authors Michael Clancy, Judy Hromcik, Barbara Ericson, and Laurie White for their efforts in this project.

7. REFERENCES

[1] Clancy, Michael J, and M. C. Linn. 1992. "Case Studies in the Classroom," *Proceedings of the 23rd SIGCSE Technical Symposium on Computer Science*, Kansas City, MO, March 1992.

[2] College Board. 2013 (forthcoming). *Advanced Placement Computer Science A Labs.*

[3] College Board. 2010. *The Computer Science A Course Description.* http://apcentral.collegeboard.com/apc/public/repository/ap-computer-science-course-description.pdf

[4] College Board, 2014 (forthcoming). *The Computer Science A Course Description.*

[5] College Board. 2010. *GridWorld: A Curriculum Module for AP Computer Science.* http://apcentral.collegeboard.com/apc/public/repository/GridWorld_AP_CompScience.pdf

[6] College Board. 2007. *GridWorld Case Study,.* http://apcentral.collegeboard.com/apc/public/repository/ap-sf-computer-science-gridworld.pdf

[7] College Board, 1994. *A Teacher's Manual for the "Directory Manager" Case Study.*

[8] McConnell, Jeffrey J. 2005. "Active and Cooperative Learning: Final Tips and Tricks (Part I)," *SIGCSE Bulletin inroads*, Vol. 37, No. 2, June 2005, pp. 27-30.

[9] McConnell, Jeffrey J. 2005. "Active and Cooperative Learning: Final Tips and Tricks (Part II)," *SIGCSE Bulletin inroads*, Vol. 37, No. 4, December 2005, pp. 34-38.

[10] McConnell, Jeffrey J. 2006. "Active and Cooperative Learning: Final Tips and Tricks (Part III)," *SIGCSE Bulletin inroads*, Vol. 38, No. 2. June 2006, pp. 24-28.

[11] McConnell, Jeffrey J. 2006. "Active and Cooperative Learning: Final Tips and Tricks (Part IV)," *SIGCSE Bulletin inroads*, Vol. 38, No. 2, December 2006, pp. 25-28.

[12] Parker, J, R. Cupper, C. Kelemen, D. Molnar, and G. Scragg,. 1990. "Laboratories in the computer science curriculum," *Computer Science Education*, 1990, pp. 205-221.

[13] Walker, Henry M. 2011. "A Lab-based Approach for Introductory Computing that Emphasizes Collaboration," *CSERC '11 Proceedings, 'The Computer Science Education Research Conference, Heerlen, the Netherlands, April 7-8, 2011, pp. 9-20.*

Revision of the SE 2004 Curriculum Model

Gregory W. Hislop
Drexel University
Philadelphia, PA
011-216-895-2179
hislop@drexel.edu

Mark Ardis
Stevens Institute of Technology
Hoboken, NJ
011-201-216-5143
mark.ardis@stevens.edu

David Budgen
Durham University
Durham, UK
44 (0) 191 33 41724
david.budgen@durham.ac.uk

Mark J. Sebern
Milwaukee School of Engineering
Milwaukee, WI
011-414-277-7213
sebern@msoe.edu

Jeff Offut
George Mason University
Fairfax, VA
011-703-993-1654
offutt@gmu.edu

Willem Visser
University of Stellenbosch
Stellenbosch, South Africa
27-21-808-4235
visserw@sun.ac.za

SUMMARY

Software Engineering 2004: Curriculum Guidelines for Undergraduate Degree Programs in Software Engineering (*SE 2004*) [1] is one volume in a set of computing curricula adopted and supported by the ACM and the IEEE Computer Society. In order to keep the software engineering guidelines up to date the two professional societies began a review and revision project in early 2011. This special session will present the results of the review, present a first draft of the revision, and provide time for discussion and input from the computing education community.

Categories and Subject Descriptors

K.3.2 [**Computers and Education**]: Computer and Information Science Education – *Computer Science Education.*

General Terms

Management, Human Factors

Keywords

Software Engineering education; Curriculum guideline; SE 2004

1. OVERVIEW

This section provides key information points for the session:

Objective of the session: This session will present the first draft of a revision to the SE 2004 curriculum guideline. The session will provide an update to the computing education community and an important opportunity for community discussion and input on the revision.

Session outline: The session will begin with a summary of the curriculum guideline review results. This will be followed by a summary of the first revision draft. These presentations should take about 30 minutes in total. The other 45 minutes will be used for questions, discussion, and audience input.

SIGCSE'13, March 6–9, 2013, Denver, Colorado, USA.
ACM 978-1-4503-1868-6/13/03.

Expectations: The audience for this presentation is the set of computing educators who teach software engineering topics. While the SE curriculum guideline addresses entire BSSE degrees, it is highly relevant for computing programs that have an SE minor, and all computing degrees that incorporate SE topics in other Computer Science courses or other computing courses.

The remainder of this paper provides a brief summary of the review and revision phases of this project.

2. REVIEW

The first phase of the project was a review of SE 2004. The charge for the SE2004 Review Team was as follows:

1. Conduct a "consultation process" to collect information and opinion from the principal curriculum stakeholders (industry and academia) about the need for modification of the curriculum model (body of knowledge, curriculum architecture, pedagogy, infrastructure, etc.).
2. Analyze and assess the results of the consultation process to determine the type and extent of change needed.
3. Prepare a report for the IEEE-CS Educational Activities Board and the ACM Education Board including recommendations concerning a) the type and extent of revision needed to SE2004, b) an estimate of the amount of effort needed, and c) a proposed schedule for the recommended revision.

The team first constructed a comprehensive list of stakeholder groups from academia, industry and government. Groups included accredited academic programs, special interest groups, and software engineering programs in several countries. We were especially interested in identifying people from industry or government who had an interest in software engineering education. We established a community portal page on the Ensemble Computing Portal website [2]. This provided a convenient place to advertise our survey, and it placed us near other curriculum efforts that have portals there.

We created a survey on SurveyMonkey to collect feedback about the current state and use of *SE 2004*. The first part of the survey asked about the respondent's background and familiarity with *SE 2004*, while later sections asked about specific sections of the guidelines. We allowed respondents to skip some of the more detailed questions about the Software Engineering Education

Knowledge (SEEK) section if they felt unprepared to answer those. Respondent background data was important to us, as we were concerned about reaching stakeholders across a wide spectrum of occupations and localities.

We received about 480 usable responses from 42 different countries. The majority of survey participants were from North America, even though we worked hard to recruit responses from other parts of the world. We sent email to hundreds of potential participants in Central and South America, Europe and Asia as part of our publicity campaign.

Most of the respondents had graduate degrees. This is not surprising, since our main stakeholder group consists of faculty at colleges and universities. We asked respondents about their role in software engineering education, and the set of responses indicated good representation of both educators and practitioners.. Table 1 lists the breakdown of roles.

Teacher	134
Researcher	88
Software Developer	156
Administrator	26
Retired	13
Other	60
Not Answered	1

Table 1. Role of respondents

A key element of SE 2004 is the structure of the SEEK. We asked survey participants about the overall structure and about specific sections. Most participants agreed that the Knowledge Areas were still relevant.

We received useful feedback from some respondents about the relative percentage of time that should be spent on individual topics within knowledge areas. For example, respondents felt that more time should be spent on requirements fundamentals within the Software Modeling and Analysis area.

We also asked about elements that were missing from the SE2004 Curriculum Guidelines or from the SEEK. There were a few trends, especially the incorporation of more modern software development methods, and a need for more emphasis on security.

Additional details of the survey result will be presented in the special session.

3. REVISION

Based on the results of the survey of constituents, we found that the overall structure of *SE 2004* is sound and does not need to be changed. The SEEK was found to need only minor revisions. The areas of revision identified include:

- agile methods: these have become more popular and successful
- security: increasingly important as more software systems are exposed to attack
- service-oriented computing: techniques in this area have become more popular and important

A revision plan was created by the review group and accepted by the two professional societies. The revision group began work in August 2012, with a target of creating an internal draft by December, 2012. The goal is to revise that draft primarily within the group and have a first draft for public review by the time of SIGCSE 2013. That draft will be presented at this special session and be the focus of discussion and request for input.

Other curriculum revision efforts are being conducted concurrently with SE 2013. Two of particular interest are CS 2013, a revised set of guidelines for computer science curricula, and the Guide to the Software Engineering Body of Knowledge (SWEBOK) [3], which is undergoing review of recent updates. We expect to work closely with members of both of those projects.

4. REFERENCES

[1] ACM/IEEE-CS Joint Task Force on Computing Curricula, Software Engineering 2004: Curriculum Guidelines for Undergraduate Degree Programs in Software Engineering, August 2004. http://www.acm.org/education/curricula.html

[2] Ensemble Computing Portal, http://www.computingportal.org/se2004rtf

[3] Abran, Alain. et al. (editors) Guide to the Software Engineering Body of Knowledge (SWEBOK), IEEE CS Press. www.computer.org/portal/web/swebok/htmlformat

Teaching Garbage Collection without Implementing Compilers or Interpreters

Gregory H. Cooper
Google, Inc.
ghc@google.com

Arjun Guha
Cornell University
arjun@cs.cornell.edu

Shriram Krishnamurthi
Brown University
sk@cs.brown.edu

Jay McCarthy
Brigham Young University
jay@cs.byu.edu

Robert Bruce Findler
Northwestern University
robby@northwestern.edu

ABSTRACT

Given the widespread use of memory-safe languages, students must understand garbage collection well. Following a constructivist philosophy, an effective approach would be to have them implement garbage collectors. Unfortunately, a full implementation depends on substantial knowledge of compilers and runtime systems, which many courses do not cover or cannot assume.

This paper presents an instructive approach to teaching GC, where students implement it atop a simplified stack and heap. Our approach eliminates enormous curricular dependencies while preserving the essence of GC algorithms. We take pains to enable testability, comprehensibility, and facilitates debugging. Our approach has been successfully classroom-tested for several years at several institutions.

Categories and Subject Descriptors K.3.2 [**Computers and Education**]: Computer and Information Science Education

General Terms Languages

Keywords Garbage collection

1. INTRODUCTION

Many students appear to have a poor grasp of garbage collection (GC) [8], because it is an automated process that runs without their control. This makes some students intimidated and untrusting of it (which can result in their using unsafe programming languages), while others use it without understanding its impact on performance.

Our antidote is to lay bare the underlying mechanisms by having students *implement* them, in keeping with constructivist educational principles. This approach is consistent with what many programming languages courses already do, following the venerable tradition of studying languages through *definitional interpreters* [11]. A definitional interpreter defines a language by a lightweight implementation, in lieu of abstract mathematics. These interpreters allow students to actually run programs in their languages and explore the consequences of alternate definitions.

There are several programming language texts and courses based on definitional interpreters [1, 6, 9], but most of them do not cover GC within the implementation-oriented tradition. Implementing a GC is taxing because it requires a grasp of low-level concepts such as walking the stack, pointer arithmetic, manipulating raw memory, and so on, and most real-world runtime systems—which focus on performance—are not designed to enable easy modification. The alternative is to provide students with a toy language's implementation, but such a language will necessarily be small and hence hard to write interesting programs in, thereby discouraging testing and experimentation.

Furthermore, even to work with a toy language, students must first learn about interpreters or compilers, which is a significant curricular prerequisite. In contrast, many other university-level courses could and do teach GC, including runtime systems, operating systems, and even middleware. Thus, finding a way to implement GC without a heavy language implementation prerequisite could have broad use.

In this paper, we present a framework for building, debugging, and exploring garbage collectors. It meets several important criteria:

- It *minimizes curricular dependencies*: we enable students to learn and write garbage collection algorithms in a full-fledged language with an IDE. Students do not have to master other complex topics, such as compilers and continuation-passing style, to implement their GC. This makes the approach fit better as a module in a variety of different courses that might want to teach this material.

- It is *flexible*: students can investigate several strategies, including copying collectors, generational collectors, and conservative collectors. We design our framework so that students can trivially change the type of collector their program uses (Figure 1).

- It *encourages exploration*: our framework lets student-written collectors manage memory for a regular programming language. Thus, they are not limited to the (much smaller) set of examples and tests they could write in a toy language. This is especially valuable

SIGCSE'13, March 6–9, 2013, Denver, Colorado, USA.

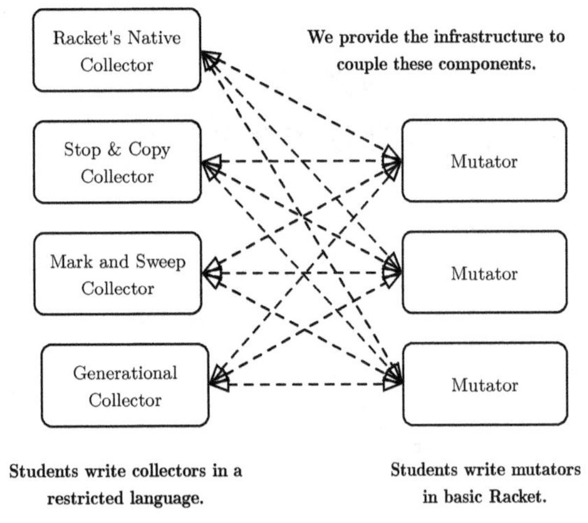

Figure 1: High-Level Assignment Architecture

when students believe they have a working collector and now want to stress-test it on non-trivial inputs.

- It *facilitates testing and debugging*: our framework can use a native garbage collector instead of a student-written collector. This allows the student to validate behavior and to isolate errors. In addition, students have powerful debugging tools as their disposal. We include a *heap visualizer*, and engineer our system so that the IDE's debugger allows students to *single-step between collector and program.*

In end-of-semester surveys, students indicate that whereas they had been apprehensive before, they are now much more likely to trust and rely on garbage collection as a result of their implementation experience. Beyond the pure pedagogic value, this could have a salutary impact on the software students write in their careers.

The solution described in this paper has already been implemented in actual courses at several institutions. Before adopting this solution, some of them used a more conventional approach that depended on compiling to continuation-passing style. Since switching to the new framework, all have noticed a marked improvement in the quality of students' solutions and the extent of their testing and exploration.

Background and Terminology.

We use standard terminology from the garbage collection literature. A language runtime's memory subsystem, or *collector*, has two principal duties. (1) It allocates and de-allocates values on the heap on behalf of programs, or *mutators.* (2) It provides facilities for reading and writing values and inspecting their types at runtime.

When *allocating* a new value, the collector first searches for a free slot of appropriate size on the heap. If found, it stores the value along with metadata, e.g., a *type-tag* for runtime type-inspection. *Garbage collection* usually starts if there are no free slots. GC de-allocates values that are not reachable by following references from local variables on the stack and in registers; these variables are called the *root set.* To follow references through arbitrary values, the GC inspects their type-tags. Accessing and mutating values is straightforward provided type-tags are respected; languages use a combination of static and runtime checks to do so.

The outline above encompasses several kinds of collectors, including mark-and-sweep, stop-and-copy, and generational collectors. Advanced techniques such as concurrent collectors are beyond the scope of our GC assignment.

Linguistic Dependence.

The work in this paper is done for Racket [3], a descendant of Scheme. We use Racket for two reasons. Historically, Scheme and Racket are widely used in definitional interpreter courses (thanks to several influential textbooks [1, 6, 9]). Much more importantly, Racket (but not Scheme) provides us with the linguistic mechanisms needed to implement this solution seamlessly from the student's perspective, through its cutting-edge ability to treat languages as libraries [5, 13]; other languages lack the module systems needed to enable such a solution. Readers who would prefer our solution in a different linguistic context can regard this paper as a technical challenge for the module mechanisms of their preferred language.

2. PROBLEM CONTEXT

Our garbage collection assignment, along with classroom discussions contrasting garbage collection with the cost of manual memory management and the impact of garbage collection on programming style, constitutes about one fifth of a roughly 13-week programming languages course for upper-level undergraduates and beginning graduate (master's and PhD) students. We ask students to implement memory allocation and garbage collection algorithms for a small number of Racket primitives. We assign multiple algorithms to avoid the risk of presenting too narrow a perspective: traditionally, *mark-and-sweep* (which later also provides a starting point for discussing conservative collection) and *semispace swapping* (because it confronts the challenge of moving objects in memory). Students are given about two weeks to complete these implementations.

We often grade the assignment by *code inspection*, in which students present their collectors to the course staff and answer questions about their design decisions. We discuss code inspection for GC in more detail in Section 6.

3. WRITING COLLECTORS

We provide a general framework that allows students to implement several kinds of collectors. The framework exposes essential concepts such as memory layout and roots on the stack. However, we hide lower-level machine details, including registers and the binary representation of data.

A student-written collector is a module that implements the interface in Figure 2a. These functions allocate values, query type-tags, and read values. The depicted functions only manipulate lists and flat values (i.e., numbers and booleans), though it is trivial to add support for other datatypes. For example, we also require students to allocate closures for higher-order functions.

These student-written functions determine the location, layout, and size of values on the heap. Therefore, students can experiment with collectors that add metadata (e.g., lifetimes for generational collectors) or don't (e.g., conservative collectors). Students can also explore simple optimizations, such as reusing allocated constants.

$$
\begin{array}{rcl}
\textbf{addr} & \in & 0 \le n < (\textit{heap-size}) \\
\textbf{flat} & \equiv & \textbf{num} \mid \textbf{bool} \mid \textbf{empty}
\end{array}
$$

$$
\begin{array}{r}
\textit{gc:cons} :: \textbf{addr} \times \textbf{addr} \rightarrow \textbf{addr} \\
\textit{gc:cons?} :: \textbf{addr} \rightarrow \textbf{bool} \\
\textit{gc:first} :: \textbf{addr} \rightarrow \textbf{addr} \\
\textit{gc:rest} :: \textbf{addr} \rightarrow \textbf{addr} \\
\textit{gc:set-first!} :: \textbf{addr} \times \textbf{addr} \rightarrow \textbf{void} \\
\textit{gc:set-rest!} :: \textbf{addr} \times \textbf{addr} \rightarrow \textbf{void} \\
\hline
\textit{gc:flat} :: \textbf{flat} \rightarrow \textbf{addr} \\
\textit{gc:flat?} :: \textbf{addr} \rightarrow \textbf{bool} \\
\textit{gc:deref} :: \textbf{addr} \rightarrow \textbf{flat}
\end{array}
$$

(a) Garbage Collector Interface (student-implemented)

$$
\begin{array}{r}
\textit{heap-size} :: \rightarrow \textbf{int} \\
\textit{heap-set!} :: \textbf{addr} \times \textbf{flat} \rightarrow \textbf{void} \\
\textit{heap-ref} :: \textbf{addr} \rightarrow \textbf{flat}
\end{array}
$$

(b) Heap manipulation (provided)

$$
\begin{array}{r}
\textit{get-root-set} :: \rightarrow \textbf{listof root} \\
\textit{read-root} :: \textbf{root} \rightarrow \textbf{addr} \\
\textit{set-root!} :: \textbf{root} \times \textbf{addr} \rightarrow \textbf{void}
\end{array}
$$

(c) Root manipulation (provided)

Figure 2: Generic Allocator Interface

```
(define (incr-list lst)
  (if (empty? lst)
    empty
    (cons (+ 1 (first lst)) (incr-list (rest lst)))))
```

↓ **Use students' GC primitives**

```
(define (incr-list lst)
  (if (and (gc:flat? lst) (empty? (gc:deref lst)))
    (gc:flat empty)
    (gc:cons (gc:alloc-flat (+ (gc:deref (gc:flat 1))
                               (gc:deref (gc:first lst))))
             (incr-list (gc:rest lst)))))
```

↓ **Name intermediate results (A-normal form)**

```
(define (incr-list lst)
  (if (and (gc:flat? lst) (empty? (gc:deref lst)))
    (gc:flat empty)
    (let* ([t0 (gc:flat 1)]
           [t1 (gc:first lst)]
           [t2 (gc:flat (+ (gc:deref t0) (gc:deref t1)))]
           [t3 (incr-list (gc:rest lst))])
      (gc:cons t2 t3))))
```

Figure 3: Sketch of Program Transformations

Our framework provides functions to manipulate the heap as an array of cells (Figure 2b). The collector can store (*heap-set!*) and retrieve (*heap-ref*) **flat** values in heap cells—storing structured-data in a single cell would violate the intent of the assignment. The *heap-size* function returns the size of the heap, which is set by each mutator (Section 4).

Our framework provides functions to manipulate the roots on the stack (Figure 2c). A **root** is an updatable reference to the heap: updates are needed by moving collectors, such as stop-and-copy or compacting mark-and-sweep. We do not require students to walk the mutator's stack to find roots themselves; the **get-root-set** function provides this functionality. The next section explains why having students implement root-finding is neither essential nor desirable.

4. TESTING AND CALCULATING ROOTS

To truly exercise a collector we must use it to allocate memory for a program. In traditional courses, students test collectors by writing mutators in small, toy, classroom-only languages. It is difficult to write substantial tests in these toy languages. However, in our framework *students write mutators in Racket itself.* This enables students to write much more rigorous tests: student submissions have included non-trivial programs such as entire interpreters for other languages, and complex graph algorithms. In addition, by automating stack-walking, our approach *eliminates a curricular dependency* on program transformations.

The Traditional Approach.

In a traditional setting, such as a compilers course, writing a collector requires mastery of semantics-preserving program transformations. We sketch these transformations for a simple mutator that increments the numbers in a list (top of Figure 3).

Given a mutator, such as *incr-list*, students have to first instrument it to call their collector at memory-manipulation points. Although this first transformation is conceptually simple, it is orthogonal to GC algorithms and quickly becomes complex for non-toy languages. In addition, the collector must save the state of the mutator, collect garbage if necessary, perform the memory operation, and then restore the state of the mutator. Implementing these steps in a low-level language requires considerable effort and knowledge.

Students must then transform the mutator to an intermediate form that names all sub-expressions. Such representations (e.g., continuation-passing style, static single assignment, or A-normal form) are advanced topics, tricky to implement, and tedious for even modestly-sized languages.

As a result, a traditional approach incurs several curricular dependencies and is only realistic for a toy, classroom-only mutator language.

Our Approach.

Our framework automates the transformations in Figure 3 for a large subset of the Racket language, eliminating the curricular dependencies described above, and allowing students to test and explore their collectors by writing mutators in ordinary Racket. Our students are familiar with Racket, since it is the language they use to write the collector itself! Mutators do have one non-standard line, which specifies the collector to use and the size of the heap:

(**collector-setup** ⟨*collector-filename*⟩ ⟨*heap-size*⟩)

By varying the GC algorithm and heap size, students can test for more corner-case behaviors.

Finally, our framework allows students to easily run sequences of collector functions on hand-crafted heaps. This allows them to unit-test with complex heaps without crafting complex mutators. To help students further, we provide a program that generates mutators that allocate and traverse random graphs.

5. DEBUGGING

Despite the efforts described above, building a collector remains subtle and error-prone. Bugs often corrupt the heap, and heap corruption may only cause errors and incorrect answers several steps later. Students thus need good debugging support. Building a debugger in this context is a challenge, because bugs manifest in the interaction between collectors and mutators. We thus need to *co-debug the mutator and collector*, set breakpoints in either piece, and single-step between them.

The Traditional Approach.

In a traditional setting, the mutator is first compiled to a low-level, intermediate representation, and then coupled with the collector, which is also written in a low-level language, such as C. A debugger for this low-level language (GDB) can debug both components. However, without extensive tooling, the debugger can only show the mutator's intermediate form, so students have to fully absorb the very program transformations we were trying to hide.

Our Approach.

Figure 4 shows our framework co-debugging a mutator and collector. The collector has a breakpoint at the start of GC. We are paused a few steps beyond this breakpoint, which we reached because the heap filled up after a few recursive calls in the mutator. Note that the stack shows both mutator and collector stack frames. Most significantly, we can debug both in their original source language.

Our approach reuses Racket's native debugger [10] by carefully transforming the mutator using Racket's macros. The debugger works at the original source level, and does not step into intermediate expressions introduced by macros. This is possible because macros can attach original source locations and variable names to generated code. Simple macros can track names and locations automatically, but our more complex, whole-program transformations require more careful engineering. In particular, we are careful to leave the shape of the control stack unmolested by our macros.

Heap Visualization.

Debugging is not enough. Not surprisingly, we noticed that in practice, students have as much difficulty interpreting their data as they do debugging the flow of control. Specifically, we found that they repeatedly printed the entire heap, often as frequently as before and after every allocation (to answer questions like, *What exactly is at location 14?*). They then had to pore over the output to reconstruct its meaning as a heap of values.

While such activity builds character, it may not fit the constraints of some teaching schedules. Fortunately, we can provide a much better interface for this domain. Keeping the heap data structure under the control of our code—a decision made to guard the size of and kinds of values stored in the heap—has a (perhaps unexpected) advantage: we can find the heap without difficulty (whereas otherwise it would be just another datum in the collector code) and employ the student's heap-inspection routines to display it.

Figure 5 shows the heap at the point shown in Figure 4. From this, it is relatively easy to reconstruct what datum is at location 27.

Naturally, the visualizer and debugger are especially useful in conjunction. For instance, it is often convenient to avoid stepping through code that sets up initial data structures in the mutator. The student can thus set a breakpoint in the mutator past this stage. Upon control arriving there, the student can then enable breakpoints in the collector, or use single-stepping, to proceed methodically through the program's execution—using the visualizer to avoid having to manually inspect the heap at each point along the way.

6. PEDAGOGY

Implementing collectors forces students to confront intricacies of the problem that would be difficult to convey through an abstract verbal treatment alone. To evaluate student understanding we often augment the implementation assignment with a *code inspection*, in which students explain their programs to the course staff, then answer questions about their design decisions and how they might handle potential extensions. Our questions include:

basic concepts How did they represent data on the heap, and why? Did they inline the free list in mark-and-sweep? What are forwarding pointers in stop-and-copy, and what purpose do they serve? Is their collector realistic, or have they over-simplified the problem by exploiting high-level features, or even cheated (e.g., ignoring the provided heap interface and relying instead on Racket's collector)?

representations What representations did they choose for flat values? Did every mention of a flat value result in fresh allocation? Did they reuse existing allocated values (and if so, what are the time-space tradeoffs)? Did they pre-allocate any values? Did they make intelligent use of addresses to encode some values in the address itself and, if so, how did this affect their ability to address all of the heap?

cycles How does the collector handle cyclic data? How does it avoid getting stuck in an infinite loop if it traverses data with cycles? Do we need to check for sharing even in programs that do not create cyclic data, and what impact does this have on a copying collector?

subtleties What happens if the collector needs to run in the middle of a recursive procedure? Could the collector run out of memory in the middle of allocating an object? Is the collector idempotent?

testing Did they have test cases to exercise salient features of the language? Did they try nested data structures, such as lists of lists? The assignment does not provide a canonical mutator, so students are forced to exercise their imagination.

extensions What would it take to add support for coalescing adjacent free blocks in the mark-and-sweep collector? How difficult would it be to support other kinds of objects?

invariants What invariants hold for the mark-and-sweep collector? What about semispace swapping?

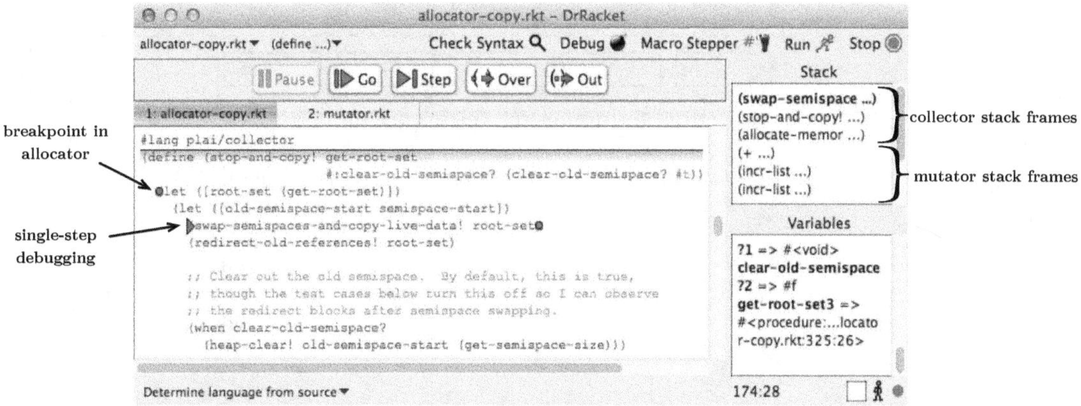

Figure 4: Co-debugging a collector and a mutator

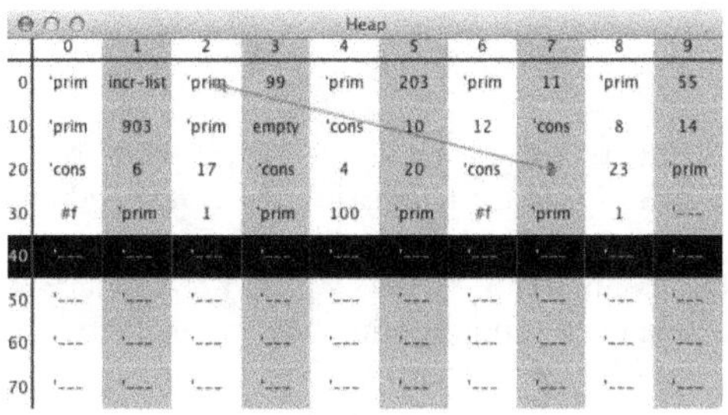

Figure 5: Heap visualization: a filled semi-space

By having a concrete implementation in front of us (that the student has hopefully thought long and hard about), we can ask specific, detailed questions that would otherwise be difficult to frame. Code inspection thus gives us a very strong sense of the student's understanding of the concepts.

Student Feedback.

Many faculty have reported success using this framework. For example, one author, Jay McCarthy, surveyed 258 students over 4 years. Before doing the assignment, 40 students agreed with the statement, "Manual memory management is usually preferable to GC," but only 10 agreed after the assignment. Before the assignment, 80% believed that manual memory management is always faster than GC, but only 40% agree after; the others answer that GC is as fast or faster, given enough memory. The students were also asked what part of the class they learned from and enjoyed the most. Of the 258, only 15 mentioned anything other than GC.

7. IMPLEMENTATION

Our GC framework could be built for any programming language, but Racket provides a combination of several technologies that ease its implementation [13]. Whereas syntactic extensions are part of the Scheme tradition, a Racket language can have entirely different syntax and semantics. Our GC framework is an extreme example of the latter: the semantics of the mutator language changes as students fix bugs in their collectors. The implementation is a separate research contribution beyond the scope of this paper. But, we note some key techniques below.

Collector The collector language provides a heap abstraction to students. The language itself ensures that students do not store structured data directly on the heap using contracts [4]. In addition, the collector language itself starts the graphical heap visualizer.

Mutator The mutator language implements the transformations that students have to learn in traditional GC courses (Section 4). Throughout these transformations, we ensure that generated code is carefully tagged with the source-location of original code. This ensures that runtime errors have correct locations and that the transformations are transparent to the debugger [10].

The mutator language uses students' collectors instead of Racket to manipulate memory (e.g., it rewrites *cons* to *gc:cons*). If done naively, e.g., with macros, we would have to instrument all syntactic forms (that we remember). Instead, we use Racket's ability to precisely control macro expansion: we first transform mutators to primitive syntax and then instrument code. This ensures that students can write mutators with convenient syntax.

Mutators must expose their root set to collectors, which we do with an internal *roots* variable at each program point. To calculate *roots*, we first name all intermediate expressions and then calculate free variables at each program point. By doing so, as Figure 6 illustrates, the set of free variables and the root set coincide *for a single stack frame*. We also augment all functions with an additional *caller-roots* parameter. Thus at each point, the root set is the union of *caller-roots* and the local *roots*.[1]

8. RELATED WORK

We surveyed faculty who teach implementation-based languages courses, as well as experts in the field of garbage collection, and none of them appear to use an infrastructure similar to ours. The only assignments we found involving implementation of garbage collection were in courses on compilers and run-time systems.

At the University of Victoria, Nigel Horspool's course on virtual machines treats GC in depth [7]. Students study the

[1]N.B., we use *continuation marks* to obviate parts of this transformation and preserve tail-calls [2].

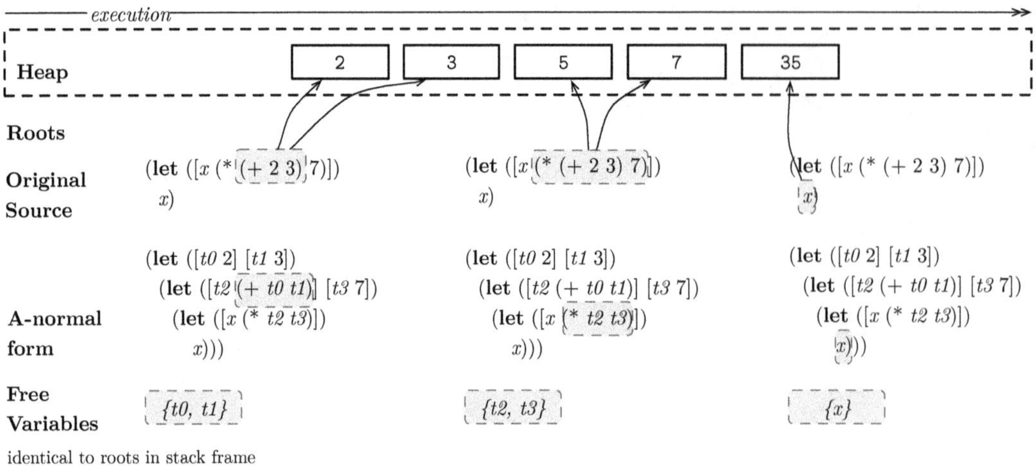

Figure 6: Naming intermediate results allows us to track roots

implementation of a conservative mark-and-sweep collector inside a JVM, then answer questions pertaining to design decisions. Students do not implement collection algorithms, but they instrument the collector to obtain statistics.

At Cornell, Greg Morrisett's course on data structures and functional programming [12] included an assignment to implement parts of a compiler and runtime system for a subset of ML, including generational GC. Programs are first compiled to lambda terms, which are evaluated by an abstract machine. The course framework specifies the heap layout and handles allocation; students only implement collection. At Princeton, David Walker assigned a similar project that had students write a semispace collector for a simple, functional language interpreter [14]. All the interfaces between the elements of the system (memory layout, stack, heap, collector) are spelled out explicitly in the module system. Abelson and Sussman detail the implementation of another semispace collector for a register-based Scheme evaluator [1].

The main difference between all these assignments and ours is their use of explicit compilers, interpreters, and abstract machines, which expose a lower-level model of the runtime system, encouraging a more systems-oriented view of garbage collection. Our approach involves fewer curricular dependencies and allows the students to focus on the collection algorithms. Our unobtrusive transformation strategy allows students to write mutators in a full-fledged language and exploit graphical debugging and testing features in the DrRacket IDE. These variations reflect a difference in course content and philosophy; our approach seems advantageous for instructors interested in covering garbage collection without assuming much low-level background or context.

Acknowledgments

We thank our students for enduring GC, Matthew Flatt for making Racket awesome, and the NSF for partially supporting this work.

9. REFERENCES

[1] H. Abelson and G. J. Sussman. *Structure and Interpretation of Computer Programs.* MIT Press, Cambridge, MA, 1985.

[2] J. Clements and M. Felleisen. A tail-recursive semantics for stack inspection. In *ESOP*, 2003.

[3] R. B. Findler, J. Clements, C. Flanagan, M. Flatt, S. Krishnamurthi, P. Steckler, and M. Felleisen. DrScheme: A programming environment for Scheme. *JFP*, 12(2):159–182, 2002.

[4] R. B. Findler and M. Felleisen. Contracts for higher-order functions. In *ICFP*, 2002.

[5] M. Flatt. Composable and compilable macros. In *ICFP*, 2002.

[6] D. P. Friedman, M. Wand, and C. T. Haynes. *Essentials of Programming Languages.* MIT Press, second edition, 2001.

[7] N. Horspool. Topics in virtual machine implementation. `http://www.cs.uvic.ca/~nigelh/Courses/csc586a-2008/`.

[8] R. Jones and R. Lins. *Garbage Collection: Algorithms for Automatic Dynamic Memory Management.* John Wiley & Sons, 1996.

[9] S. Krishnamurthi. *Programming Languages: Application and Interpretation.* 2006. `http://www.cs.brown.edu/~sk/Publications/Books/ProgLangs/`.

[10] G. Marceau, G. H. Cooper, J. P. Spiro, S. Krishnamurthi, and S. P. Reiss. The design and implementation of a dataflow language for scriptable debugging. *ASE Journal*, 14(1):59–86, 2007.

[11] J. McCarthy. Recursive functions of symbolic expressions and their computation by machine. *CACM*, 3(3):184–185, 1960.

[12] J. G. Morrisett. Mini-ML Compiler. `http://www.cs.cornell.edu/Courses/cs312/2002fa/hw/ps5/ps5.html`.

[13] S. Tobin-Hochstadt, V. St-Amour, R. Culpepper, M. Flatt, and M. Felleisen. Languages as libraries. In *PLDI*, 2011.

[14] D. Walker. Garbage collection programming assignment. `http://www.cs.princeton.edu/courses/archive/spr05/cos320`.

.NET Gadgeteer: A New Platform for K-12 Computer Science Education

Steve Hodges[a], James Scott[a], Sue Sentance[b], Colin Miller[c], Nicolas Villar[a], Scarlet Schwiderski-Grosche[a], Kerry Hammil[c], Steven Johnston[a]

a: Microsoft Research Cambridge
7 JJ Thomson Avenue
Cambridge, CB3 0FB
+44 1223 479700

b: Anglia Ruskin University
Bishop Hall Lane, Chelmsford
Essex, CM1 1SQ
+44 845 196 3519

c: Microsoft Corporation
Microsoft Way
Redmond, WA 98052
+1 425 703 4530

{shodges,jws,colinmil,nvillar,scarlets,khammil,v-stejo}@microsoft.com

sue.sentance@anglia.ac.uk

ABSTRACT
In this paper we present the features of a new physical device prototyping platform called Microsoft .NET Gadgeteer along with our initial experiences using it to teach computer science in high schools. Gadgeteer makes it easy for newcomers to electronics and computing to plug together modules with varied functionality and to program the resulting system's behavior. We believe the platform is particularly suited to teaching modern programming concepts such as object-oriented, event-based programming and it could be a timely addition to established teaching tools given the current interest in improving high school computer science education in some regions. We have run a number of pilot studies in the US and in the UK with students of varying age and ability. Our results indicate that the tangible and expressive nature of Gadgeteer helps to engage and motivate a diverse set of students. We were also pleasantly surprised by the level of polish and sophistication of the devices which were built. We hope to further explore the potential of Gadgeteer for teaching in future work and we encourage others to build on our experiences.

Categories and Subject Descriptors
K.3.2 [**Computers and Education**]: Computer and Information Science Education–*computer science education, curriculum, information systems education, literacy*. D.2.6 [**Software Engineering**]: Programming Environments–*graphical, integrated & interactive environments*. D2.m [**Software Engineering**]: Miscellaneous–*rapid prototyping, reusable software*.

General Terms
Algorithms, Design, Experimentation, Languages, Theory.

Keywords
K-12 computer science education, prototyping platform, modular hardware, tactile learning, Microsoft .NET Gadgeteer.

1. INTRODUCTION
There is a growing acknowledgement that computer science teaching in high schools has not kept pace with the remarkable growth of computing and related technologies in society. For several years, bodies such as the Computing At School (CAS) group in the UK and the Computer Science Teachers Association (CSTA) in the US have actively promoted the need for a stronger emphasis on computer science in the curriculum and associated facilities and expertise in schools [3], [13]. A recent report by the UK Royal Society highlights an unsatisfactory level of computing education in many UK schools and states that computer science is sufficiently foundational that it should be recognized with equal importance as subjects like mathematics, physics and history [8].

As a result of this awareness, we are starting to see changes in the curriculum coupled with additional qualification options for students aged 14-18 along with increased adoption of computing-related content in schools for younger students [4]. Consequently, more than ever there is a need for engaging resources and vehicles for teaching computer science. Given the dramatic change in the way in which computer-related technologies are used in homes and workplaces – from smartphones and tablets to social networking – it is also timely to re-examine exactly what should be taught within the curriculum to "bridge the gap" between computer literacy and computer science [2].

A number of different programming environments and tools are well-established in a secondary computing education context. In particular systems such as Scratch[1] Alice[2], Greenfoot[3] and Kodu[4] have been shown to motivate and engage young people. The constructivist learning theory claims that knowledge is actively constructed by the student [1]. This suggests that active participation in problem-solving is very valuable, and critical thinking regarding a learning activity which the students find relevant and engaging is encouraged. Papert built on this concept by introducing the term 'constructionism' to indicate a combination of constructivism and hands-on construction [6].

We have recently been exploring how a new platform which we have developed – Microsoft .NET Gadgeteer[5] [11], [12] – might be used as a tool to support hands-on constuctionist computer

[1] http://scratch.mit.edu/

[2] http://www.alice.org/

[3] http://www.greenfoot.org/

[4] http://www.kodugamelab.com/

[5] http://netmf.com/gadgeteer/

science learning in high schools. Gadgeteer enables rapid creation of small electronic gadgets and digital devices. A key property of Gadgeteer is the use of physical hardware rather than the virtual environment approach taken by systems like Greenfoot, Logo and Kodu. This provides the excitement of a hands-on experience and the reward of physically building something, while also making it easy to introduce modern programming concepts like object-orientation and event-based programming.

The use of physical hardware in the context of K-12 computer science education has been explored previously through systems such as Logo-based turtles, Lego MindStorms and a variety of robot-based education products. These constructionist tools have engaged many students but are not yet established in support of the complete K-12 CS curriculum. The ScratchBoard/PicoBoard provides a tangible, hardware-based extension to Scratch which can be useful for younger students but is still quite limited both in terms of hardware flexibility and the programming experience. Modkit [5] extends the Scratch environment with a 'code view' and supports a wider variety of Arduino-based hardware but does not have the flexibility of Gadgeteer or the ability to create stand-alone electronic devices. The Sense system [7] similarly builds on Scratch and provides a modular tangible hardware experience through the SenseBoard, but is primarily aimed at adult learners.

In this paper we describe the Gadgeteer system and explain the features which we feel make it suitable for teaching. We present two initial pilots where Gadgeteer was used to teach aspects of computer science to students aged 11-18 in schools in the UK and US. We give an overview of our methodology and report on classroom experiences. We end by presenting avenues for future work which our pilots have uncovered. Our aim is to inform others who are active in the field of high-school computer science education of the potential of Gadgeteer as part of a portfolio of tools which teachers can use to engage a diverse set of students.

2. MICROSOFT .NET GADGETEER

The Microsoft .NET Gadgeteer system is an open and modular platform we created to facilitate the design, programing and construction of digital devices [12]. The ease of building new hardware coupled with powerful software development results in a very low hurdle for creating simple projects, but also supports more sophisticated applications. The open source nature of the platform[6] enables multiple manufacturers to create a diverse set of interoperable hardware. We now discuss the particular features we feel make Gadgeteer an interesting platform for CS education.

2.1 Hardware

At the heart of each Gadgeteer project there is a central 'mainboard' which includes a processor and a number of electrical sockets. The sockets may be used to attach a variety of 'modules' – different sensors, actuators, displays, communication and storage elements. Gadgeteer supports well-established protocols and formats such as USB, TCP/IP, FAT file systems, JPG/BMP/GIF images and WAV/MP3 audio files. Consequently modules can support quite sophisticated functionality including audio playback, color image display, Ethernet, WiFi, SD cards, USB keyboards, mice and cameras etc. Of course, Gadgeteer also supports simpler modules such as LED lights, buttons, joysticks, buzzers, light sensors etc. A growing number of modules are commercially available, around 100 at the time of writing.

[6] http://gadgeteer.codeplex.com/

The use of modules creates a very flexible platform with which many different devices can be built and programmed, promoting creativity. The solder-less composability of the elements means that students can construct sophisticated devices in minutes, and these can subsequently be re-configured and extended just as quickly. By using modules rather than the underlying hardware components such as individual LEDs or ICs, Gadgeteer is easier and faster to use and is more robust. It also encourages students to approach the corresponding software in a modular way.

2.2 Software development

From a programming point of view, code may be written in either C# or Visual Basic (VB). These high-level languages enable relatively sophisticated yet robust programs to be created quickly and as a result are very popular with professional programmers. The Gadgeteer system is tightly integrated with the Visual Studio (VS) integrated development environment (IDE) which is freely available as the "Express Edition" in addition to its commercial variants. While Visual Studio has a steeper learning curve than bespoke educational programming environments, it familiarizes students with the kind of professional tools used in modern software development. In particular, students can take advantage of features like automatic inline API documentation, dynamic syntax checking, real-time debugging and auto-completion of variable names, method calls, code snippets etc., see Figure 1. Also, there are no artificial ceilings in terms of the complexity of the projects and the development experience since any of Visual Studio's features can be used. For example, a shared library can be created for use by many students and projects, source control systems can be used for group project work, and so on.

2.3 Visual designer experience

Gadgeteer support is integrated into the VS IDE via Visual Studio's "plug-in" architecture. We have created a new visual representation for Gadgeteer projects which we call the "designer view", see Figure 2. This acts as the bridge between hardware and software and is the first screen that a user sees on creating a new Gadgeteer project. It specifies to the software which hardware modules are included, provides editable names for each of these, and assists the user with connecting the cables from modules to compatible mainboard sockets. The user can then go on to write C# or VB code to specify what this device actually does. Figure 2 shows the designer view during the creation of a digital camera.

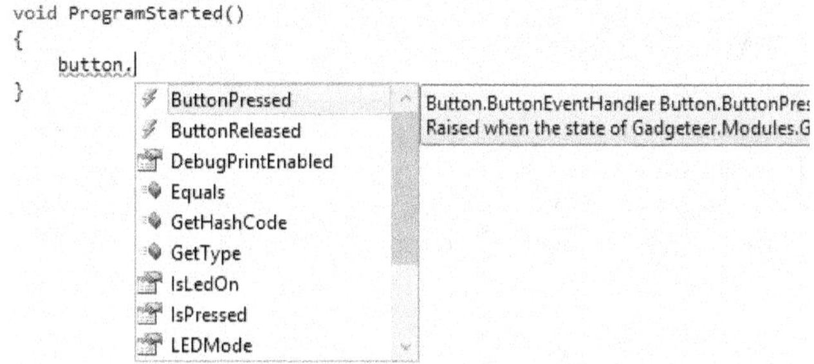

Figure 1. Real-time auto-completion in Visual Studio lists object methods, properties and so on in real-time as you type.

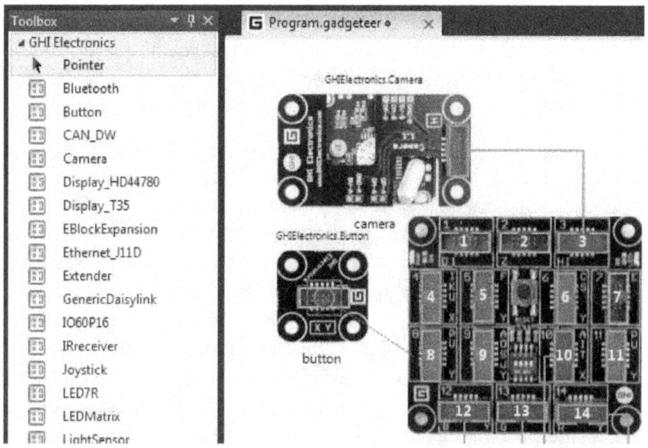

Figure 2. A 'designer view' in Visual Studio lets students create a graphical representation of the modules in a project and how they are connected to each other.

```
void camera_PictureCaptured(Camera sender, GT.Picture picture)
{
    display.SimpleGraphics.DisplayImage(picture, 0, 0);
}
                                    display.BBackLightOn 1
                                    display.Height       240
                                    display.Width        320
                                    display              {Display_T35}

                                    picture.Encoding     BMP
                                    picture.PictureData  {byte[230454]}
```

Figure 3. Real-time debugging allows students to pause program execution and examine and edit variables.

2.4 Real-time remote debugging

Through Visual Studio and the underlying .NET Micro Framework, Gadgeteer supports real-time debugging of whatever code is running on a mainboard. This debugging channel is established via USB and it enables a number of features. "Breakpoints" can be set up to cause execution to pause at specific places in a program. The state of variables can then be examined (see Figure 3) and even modified during execution; the program can be "stepped through"; and "immediate" commands can be executed as if the device was interpreting code rather than running compiled code. These features, commonly found in desktop environments, are much less common on embedded platforms but are immensely useful in a teaching context. For example, it is possible to "step through" algorithms to see how the variables interact and how control structures operate. It also gives students a realistic professional software development experience.

2.5 Programming model

Gadgeteer uses an event-driven programming model. This is in line with many modern programming environments such as Javascript, and lends itself to programming parallel behaviors like blinking two LEDs at different rates in a thread-safe manner.

The functionality of each Gadgeteer module is wrapped up in a software class which acts as an object-oriented "device driver" for the relevant hardware. This hides the underlying complexity of initializing, communicating with, and controlling that module. For example, an accelerometer driver can provide a high-level API that might include a "GetReading()" method which returns an "Acceleration" class with floating-point fields "X", "Y" and "Z" and a "Magnitude" property. The driver might also provide a "HighAcceleration" event. In this way drivers expose module functionality in a very accessible manner. Of course, it is possible for more capable students to develop their own drivers if appropriate. Note that objects can be instantiated multiple times if several identical hardware modules are used in a single project.

2.6 Bringing it all together

One short example which simultaneously illustrates the simplicity and the sophistication of Gadgeteer is the construction of a self-contained digital camera. Until very recently this would have required considerable hardware and software development skills. With Gadgeteer the first step is to use the VS Designer to specify the hardware components and how they are connected. In the case of a digital camera, an image sensor, an SD storage card, a touchscreen and a push button are needed along with the mainboard and power supply modules. Having "wired these up" graphically on-screen, it takes just a couple of minutes to construct the corresponding physical hardware, Figure 4. The basic operation of taking a photo, displaying it and saving it to a memory card can be specified in essentially just five lines of code. Auto-completion and dynamic syntax highlighting make coding incredibly easy. Figure 5 shows the resulting application in its entirety. When this application starts up, two methods which serve as event handlers are registered. The first executes when the "shutter" button is pressed, and this requests the camera to take a picture. Once the picture is captured, the second method is triggered and the picture is displayed and saved to the SD card.

Figure 4. An example digital camera built with Gadgeteer.

```
void ProgramStarted()
{
    button.ButtonPressed +=
        new Button.ButtonEventHandler     (button_ButtonPressed);
    camera.PictureCaptured +=
        new Camera.PictureCapturedEventHandler(camera_PictureCaptured);
}

void camera_PictureCaptured(Camera sender, GT.Picture picture)

{
    //Show the picture on the display
    display_T35.SimpleGraphics.DisplayImage(picture,0,0);

    //Save the picture to the SD card
    sdCard.GetStorageDevice().WriteFile("picture.bmp",
                                        picture.PictureData);
}

void button_ButtonPressed(Button sender, Button.ButtonState state)
{
    camera.TakePicture();
}
```

Figure 5. The entire camera application is just 5 lines of code.

3. CLASSROOM EXPERIENCES

In the 2011/2012 school year we trialed Gadgeteer in the classroom to gain experience of its suitability for high school computer science education. We ran a total of five pilot studies: two in the UK with 11-17 year-olds and three in the US with 14-18 year-olds. These pilots were implemented differently in the two regions, and are described in more detail below.

3.1 UK Pilots

The two UK pilots involved 16 secondary schools, mostly state-funded and mixed gender. Teachers willing to trial Gadgeteer in the classroom were recruited and given initial training either in groups or 1:1. They were also provided with session plans and example projects; C# was used throughout. Gadgeteer was then taught for around 12 weeks, mostly in extra-curricular 'lunchtime' or 'after-school' clubs attended by students ranging from 11 to 17 years old. The students typically worked in groups of 3-4 with one Gadgeteer Fez Spider[7] starter kit from GHI electronics per group.

The session plans consisted of 8 separate modules with approximately one hour's teaching material in each. They contained all the instructions for carrying out the tasks including code samples. Following the first UK pilot all the materials were refined based on feedback and observations and they are available online[8]. Towards the end of the 12 week duration of each pilot, students were invited to invent and program a device of their own design, and enter this into a competition. The students enjoyed being creative and implementing their own ideas. Prizes were given for originality and technical merit.

Approximately 150 students were involved in the UK pilot, attending an average of 8 sessions each, although this varied significantly from school to school. More details of the first pilot are presented in [10]. Feedback gathered from students and staff is presented in Section 3.3.

3.2 US Pilots

In the US Gadgeteer was used in direct support of computer science curriculum teaching in three suburban public high schools around Seattle, WA. Two courses were offered, 'Introduction to Computer Science' and 'High School Computer Programming'. The latter class provided an option for college credits. Both courses were one semester long, about 75 class hours of instruction, and as a result covered much more depth than the UK pilots. One course was taught by an accredited teacher and one was taught under supervision of an accredited teacher. Both classes were open to students from freshman through senior (14-18 years old).

The courses were intended to raise the students' proficiency in computer science concepts and computer programming to allow them to progress to more advanced high school classes like Advanced Placement (AP) and International Baccalaureate (IB) or to pursue engineering at college level. In addition to material on computer organization, data structures, algorithms and programming constructs (looping, conditional logic, variables) the courses focused on 'computational thinking' [14]. This provided students with exposure to generally applicable problem decomposition and analysis techniques.

In the 'Introduction to Computer Science' course, the students spent several weeks becoming familiar with programming constructs by using Scratch to create several games, one of which they controlled using an Xbox Kinect gaming controller.

Following the introductory period, for the remainder of the semester the students worked in Visual Studio C# Express Edition and used Gadgeteer. They completed several small projects and one larger one. The large project involved creating a fully functional digital camera. The students programmed the camera so that it could take multiple pictures, store them to an SD card, scroll through them, etc. User interaction with the camera was supported via a large Gadgeteer touch screen, requiring the students to create an on-screen menu system and interpret user input. The hardware modules were encased in a laser-cut wooden enclosure provided to the students which allowed them to take the camera out of the classroom to take part in a photo contest.

3.3 Feedback and outcomes

Students were generally very positive about the way that Gadgeteer gave them the freedom to develop their own devices:

> *"You're allowed to be sort of creative and sort of like make anything – so you weren't really limited to what you can make. You're in control; you can take an idea anywhere and use the hardware that's available..."* (Student, 1st UK pilot)

> *"It's nice when you finish a product ...and you're always looking to improve in certain areas, like can I make this camera function better, could I make it hook to an SD card, could I enable it so that it has internet connectivity. It's asking those sort of questions .. that's really enabled me to enjoy such projects."* (Student, 1st UK pilot)

> *"I thought overall this semester was a success. It got really confusing sometimes but once you got it, it was awesome."* (Student, 1st Semester US Pilot)

> *"Overall it was a great learning experience for me and has helped me to want to get into the computer field more."* (Student, 1st Semester US Pilot)

> *"Now I have an idea of how most of the electronics I own works. It gave me higher expectations for the future."* (Student, 1st Semester US Pilot)

Feedback from the teachers confirmed the students' views, they felt that the Gadgeteer kits were engaging to use and in particular developed determination and resilience in students because they were motivated to get their devices to work and to extend them:

> *"The technology of gadgets inspired them to work a little harder & play with ideas more."* (Teacher, second UK pilot)

> *"... they actually wanted to solve it and they would keep trying to solve it ... that kind of resilience you need to have to be able to keep going"* (Teacher, first UK pilot)

Interestingly, several students indicated that they would like to gain a deeper understanding of and experience with Gadgeteer:

> *"I would much rather this class be a year long instead of a semester."* (Student, 1st Semester US Pilot)

> *"Now that I know how to use it, I want to learn more with it. I think that it is amazing how you can make something work with simple computer code."* (Student, 1st Semester US Pilot)

Devices built by our high school participants included iSpyder and Gadgesketch. The iSpyder (Figure 6) is a double-sided device

---

[7] http://www.ghielectronics.com/catalog/product/297

[8] http://netmf.com/gadgeteer/forum/

in a wooden case built by the students. One side has a touch screen which displays the temperature when a button is pressed. The other side acts as a coaster for a hot drink. The iSpyder tests the temperature of the drink; when it reaches a temperature cool enough to drink an internal buzzer will sound to alert the user.

Gadgesketch (Figure 6) is a remake of a classic children's sketching toy, by a pair of 17 year-olds. The students programmed the device by reading potentiometer values and translating them to on-screen graphics. The housing was designed in the Pro/Desktop CAD package and then vacuum formed from acrylic. The modules were mounted inside using engineering materials. The students are now planning to revise the housing and add a tilt switch via the extender module allowing the iconic "shake to erase" feature.

Other devices built by students demonstrated their ability to design graphics for the 3.5" touch screen and build engaging and interactive games, for example the "How wide is your goal" game, "FaceBooth" and "Rainbow Press", all shown in Figure 6.

3.4 Discussion

The pilots were successful in their primary objective of assessing whether Gadgeteer has potential for computer science education in the classroom. In our work with high-school students of a range of ages from both the US and the UK its tangible nature seemed to engender curiosity and motivate the students to push themselves. They enjoyed the creativity the platform supports and gained a great deal of satisfaction from building real, tangible devices. We also saw how Gadgeteer lends itself to collaborative working, whereby students with a range of skills and abilities can support and learn from each other. In this way we believe that Gadgeteer engenders valuable inter-personal skills in addition to the specific technical skills which are actively being taught.

We were pleased how quickly the students mastered the VS professional development environment. One 13 year-old student commented that he was using a *"proper programming language"* and appreciated that he was using real tools rather than an educational environment. Initial feedback from the first UK pilot suggested that the younger students (aged 11-13) found the programming difficult unless they had had some prior experience. More engagement was experienced with students in the 14-18 age range. We also saw more engagement from those pupils who were able to use Gadgeteer within the curriculum rather than solely as an extra-curricular activity.

As with the UK experience, in the US the age of the students played a role in the level of difficulty that they encountered mastering programming. Students who had at least been taught geometry seemed to be better equipped for the challenge. However, all students were able to complete the projects with support from the instructors, in part because of the larger time commitment in these courses.

In summary, the qualitative feedback to date indicates that Gadgeteer is a motivating environment for teaching programming to 14-18 year-olds. Recent changes in the computer science curriculum [9] mean that this will now be possible in the UK, as it was during our US pilot. With Gadgeteer we hope to engage students of all abilities, many ages and both genders. In addition to teaching computing, we hope to give students a better understanding of modern devices and technology in general.

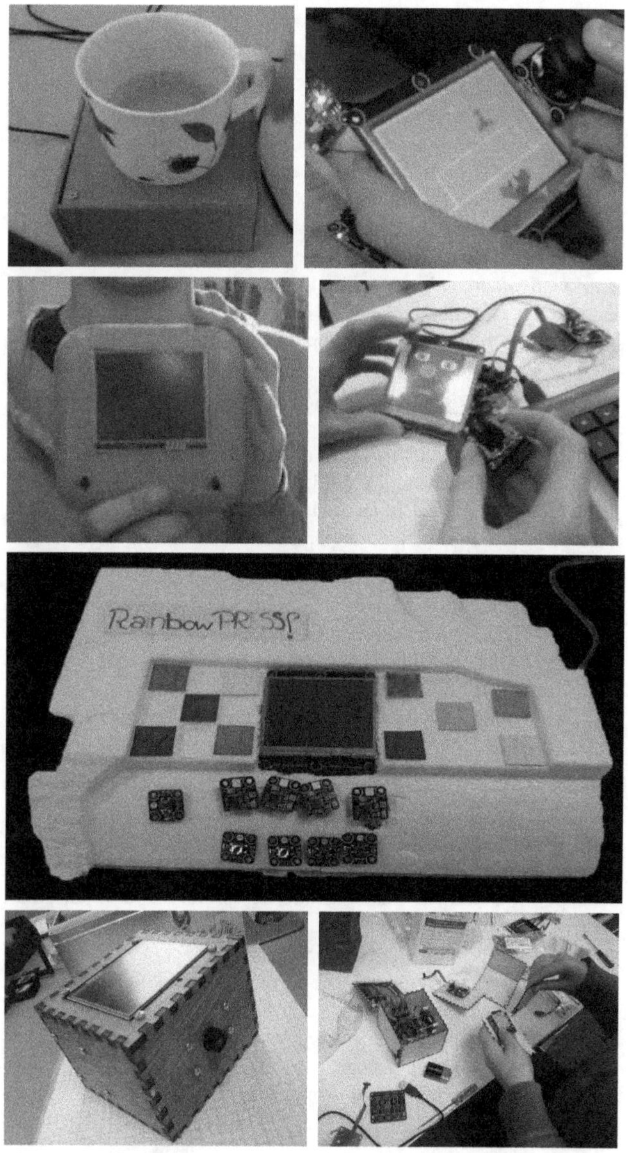

Figure 6. Example devices built during our high-school pilots. The "i-Spyder" (top left) alerts you when your drink is cool; "How wide is your goal" is a football game (top right); the GadgeSketch drawing device with its vacuum-formed case (middle left); "FaceBooth" (middle right) lets you take a photo and then annotate it with cartoon eyes, nose and mouth; "Rainbow Press" is a reaction game. The bottom row shows digital camera construction in the US trials.

4. FUTURE PLANS

As an initial pilot study with a new platform, our work with Gadgeteer has inevitably highlighted a large number of interesting avenues for future research. We discuss some of these here.

Initial feedback from teachers in indicates that Visual Basic would have a much wider appeal than C# because it is relatively well-established for high-school teaching. Following recent technical improvements to the Gadgeteer software framework, the platform now supports VB and we are currently developing new teaching materials which cover key programming concepts in the K-12 CS curriculum such as variables, functions, conditionals, file handling, looping and arrays. We would like to get experience with VB in the classroom and compare this with C#.

We hope to leverage the appeal of building real, tangible devices to engage a more diverse set of students than has traditionally been the case in computer science. We would also like to gain experience of a more holistic approach to education which cuts across the wider curriculum by including Gadgeteer in the teaching of subjects beyond computer science. Perhaps the most obvious example is the creation of enclosures for devices built with Gadgeteer, which could be integrated with design and technology teaching. Each Gadgeteer module includes standardized mounting holes which facilitate the use of a number of physical construction tools ranging from hot melt glue and self-adhesive tape right up to 3D CAD tools and rapid prototyping equipment such as laser cutters and 3D printers. Other examples of potential cross-curriculum integration include building an environmental sensor and recorder which could be deployed and subsequently analyzed in an environmental studies session, or the creation of experimental equipment such as a light-beam-triggered digital timer as part of a physics experiment.

We want to create a wider range of example projects that will inspire students and teach deeper computer science principles in a way which is particularly relevant to today's sophisticated consumer electronics devices. Examples would include a portable games console, an MP3 player and even a smartphone – the elements of which are all available as Gadgeteer modules.

At the same time as extending the depth and breadth of our Gadgeteer teaching materials, we think it is also very important to investigate the ways in which Gadgeteer can facilitate the students' understanding and acquisition of programming concepts. We want to maintain the exploratory and experiential approach which seemed to work so well in our pilots to date, and enhance it with more staged support which leverages the sense of challenge and creativity we saw in our participants. We hope to explore whether Gadgeteer can assist and motivate students who typically find it harder to engage with computer science and in particular address the gender imbalance which has traditionally been seen in the uptake of computing. Ultimately we hope to facilitate a secure and robust understanding of computer science.

Finally, we would like to trial Gadgeteer at university level for teaching undergraduate computer science courses. There is a lot of headroom in Gadgeteer for supporting sophisticated programming concepts such as threading, inter-process communication, device drivers, algorithms, data structures, and advanced networking.

5. CONCLUSIONS

This paper presented the Microsoft .NET Gadgeteer platform, highlighting in particular the various features which lend themselves to teaching computer science at high school level. In particular, Gadgeteer exposes students to many of the concepts which are an intrinsic part of modern software development. It facilitates a pedagogy based around teaching events first and object orientation naturally follows the modular hardware. The platform is growing rapidly and the increasing range of modules means it can be incorporated in cross-curricular contexts.

Our experience of using Gadgeteer and the initial feedback from teachers and students alike has been favorable. In addition to technical skills, Gadgeteer also appears to support the development of personal and inter-personal skills such as creativity, problem-solving, independent learning and collaborative working.

The Gadgeteer platform is still in its infancy and there are clearly a great many unanswered research questions relating to its use as a tool for teaching. Nonetheless, we hope that others will find our initial experiences valuable and build on them in future work.

6. ACKNOWLEDGMENTS

We would like to thank to the many teachers and students who supported our pilots so enthusiastically and the large number of people who have contributed to the Gadgeteer platform.

7. REFERENCES

[1] Ben-Ari, M. Constructivism in Computer Science Education. In proceedings of the 29th SIGCSE Technical Symposium, ACM. 1998.

[2] T. Brinda, H. Puhlmann and C. Schulte. Bridging ICT & CS - Educational Standards for Computer Science in Lower Secondary Education. In Proceedings of ITICSE, July 2009.

[3] T. Crick and S. Sentance. Computing At School: Stimulating Computing Education in the UK. In Proceedings of the 11th Koli Calling International Conference on Computing Education Research, pages 122-123, ACM, 2011.

[4] O. Hazzan, J. Gal-Ezer and L. Blum. A Model for High School Computer Science Education: The Four Key Elements That Make It! In Proceedings of the 39th SIGCSE Technical Symposium, pages 281–285. ACM, 2008.

[5] A. Millner and E. Baafi. Modkit: Blending and Extending Approachable Platforms for Creating Computer Programs and Interactive Objects, In Proceedings of the 2011 ACM Interaction Design and Children Conference.

[6] S. Papert. Mindstorms: Children, Computers and Powerful Ideas. Basic Books, 1993. 92053249.

[7] M. Richards, M. Petre and A. K. Bandara. Starting with UbiComp: Using the Senseboard to Introduce Computing. In Proceedings of the 43rd SIGCSE Technical Symposium, pages 583-588, ACM, 2012.

[8] The Royal Society. Shut Down or Restart? The Way Forward for Computing in UK Schools. Technical Report, January 2012 DES2448, The Royal Society, 2012.

[9] S. Sentance. Changes Afoot in the UK. CSTA Voice, Volume 8 Issue 3. July 2012. Available at: http://csta.acm.org/Communications/sub/CSTAVoice.html

[10] S. Sentence and S. Schwiderski-Grosche, Challenge and Creativity: Using .NET Gadgeteer in Schools, In Proceedings of the 7th Workshop on Primary and Secondary Computing Education, WIPCSE 2012.

[11] N. Villar, J. Scott and S. Hodges. Prototyping with Microsoft .NET Gadgeteer. In Proceedings of the 5th International Conference on Tangible, Embedded, and Embodied Interaction, TEI '11, pages 377-380. ACM.

[12] N. Villar, et al., .NET Gadgeteer: A Platform for Custom Devices. In Proceedings of Pervasive 2012, Lecture Notes in Computer Science.

[13] C. Wilson, L. A. Sudol, C. Stephenson and M. Stehlik. Running on Empty: The Failure to Teach K-12 Computer Science in the Digital Age. Technical Report CSTA. 2010.

[14] J. Wing "Computational Thinking", Communications of the ACM, March 2006.

Using FPGAs as a Reconfigurable Teaching Tool Throughout CS Systems Curriculum

D. Brian Larkins*, William M. Jones, H. Erin Rickard
Department of Computer Science
Coastal Carolina University
P.O. Box 261954
Conway, SC 29528-6054
{blarkins, wjones, hrickard}@coastal.edu

ABSTRACT

This paper describes the adaptation of several common computer science courses to include the use of FPGA-based systems for project and assignment work. One of the principal challenges in modern curriculum design is balancing between breadth and depth of course topics while simultaneously reinforcing the interconnections among topics in the field. To address these challenges, faculty are often forced to approximate real-world systems, sometimes at the expense of any hands-on experience. At Coastal Carolina, we have integrated FPGA systems first used in our hardware-based courses into several higher-level systems and applications courses. This allows us to leverage student familiarity with a hands-on, flexible hardware platform and also strengthens the relationships between different subfields within computer science. We discuss both the changes made to our curriculum and the effectiveness of our approach.

Categories and Subject Descriptors

K.3.2 [**Computers and Education**]: Computer and Information Science Education

General Terms

Design, Human Factors, Standardization

Keywords

FPGA, Education, Curriculum, Hardware Platforms

1. INTRODUCTION

The field of computer science is ever expanding, continuously challenging curriculum designers to make tradeoffs between depth and breadth at every advance. The wide range of topics that are encompassed by computer science necessitate a pedagogy which utilizes a variety of different tools, programming environments, languages, etc. One of the primary challenges in designing a modern CS curriculum is achieving balance with the overwhelming amount of information to convey within a limited time frame. For the most part, increasing program length to accommodate new material is intractable. This constraint forces faculty to look for new ways to communicate more concepts in a fixed number of contact hours as well as to look for techniques which reinforce interrelated concepts across multiple courses.

Not only are there a large variety of topics to fit into the curriculum, but each topic requires its own level of abstraction, tools, programming languages, and other infrastructure. The greater diversity in the set of environments that are used for teaching adds additional burdens to our students and further constrains what can be reasonably expected of them. Any opportunity to minimize the effort which must be spent by students learning new tools or environments at the expense of learning new concepts is welcomed.

Several recent trends highlight the importance of students being able to reason about the end-to-end operation of an entire system. For example, being able to comprehend the relationships between a number of hardware and software components that provide either a system-level service or support an application is critical to understanding issues of performance or security [2]. Ensuring that students construct a coherent model which encompasses all aspects of a system is vital to reasoning about and solving such problems.

In this paper, we describe the use of field-programmable gate array (FPGA) systems as a flexible hardware platform that can be modified to suit the needs of a variety of classes. FPGA devices are a natural vehicle for teaching hardware concepts in organization and architecture classes, however a key benefit is that these systems can also be used as simple general-purpose computers in a multitude of roles throughout the CS curriculum. Our approach is based on the following insights: First, since FPGAs are reconfigurable hardware systems, they allow adaptation to a variety of courses. Second, by using these systems in multiple courses, students gain greater familiarity with them and can use this knowledge throughout their coursework. Lastly, these systems offer a hands-on, big picture learning experience, allowing students to focus on how the entire system works together, rather than as a disjoint set of topics and ideas.

This work makes the following contributions: First, we describe the integration of FPGA-based computer systems into several curriculum modules as a means of reusing earlier

*Corresponding author.

SIGCSE'13, March 6–9, 2013, Denver, Colorado, USA.

student experience, connecting loosely related topics, and providing a hands-on learning experience. Second, we briefly describe how several typical CS courses can be adapted to include FPGA-based hardware to accomplish traditional learning objectives. Lastly, we discuss the effectiveness of the approach to date.

2. BACKGROUND

At Coastal Carolina, we elected to replace our aging breadboards and simulator software with FPGA units to teach our organization and architecture classes. We have found that while FPGA systems are commonly used throughout electrical engineering programs, their use in computer science programs has been limited. The focus of this paper is to advocate for increasing their role in the curriculum beyond simply a "better breadboard" and also to demonstrate how their flexibility allows for them to be an ideal platform for conventional CS topics throughout the curriculum.

The use of an FPGA-based system as a model hardware platform provides many benefits. First, our students are exposed to the platform in hardware-focused organization and architecture classes. In later classes, they can re-use their knowledge of the system architecture and related software without needing to learn new hardware or simulation software. Second, the FPGA kit that we use, the Altera DE2, is a stand-alone unit designed specifically for educational use. Other models are available both from Altera or other vendors, such as Xilinx, with a wide range of features and prices (typically between $50 and $275 per unit).

As shown in Figure 1, the DE2 is outfitted with binary input switches, LEDs, an LCD display, and seven-segment displays for output. Since these input and output devices are integrated into the hardware unit, using them to control the device provides a kinesthetic learning experience. In addition to the LCD/LED/switch interface, these systems support modern peripherals such as VGA output, USB, Ethernet, and other interfaces used on ordinary PC's.

Figure 1: The Altera DE2 FPGA system used in several CS courses throughout the curriculum

The DE2 hardware connects to a Windows or Linux host (or virtual host) via USB. The board is programmed with free Altera design software that is used to define the actual system design and the connectivity to other chips provided on the board. A stand-alone monitoring program allows students to view register contents, memory contents, and step through program execution one instruction at a time.

With increasing transistor counts and shrinking process scales, it has become difficult to use modern, general-purpose hardware platforms in a classroom setting due to their inherent complexity. The strength of using an FPGA-based platform is that such systems can be constructed with "enough" sophistication to teach the task at hand, without the unneeded complexity of commodity hardware platforms. Even default, vendor-provided CPU configurations are powerful and flexible enough to apply to a wide range of courses, without the need to resort to simulation or scaffolding which can obscure the realism of the underlying system.

At the simplest level, the FPGA can be used as a programmable circuit board, capable of implementing combinational and sequential circuits. In addition to custom circuit design, vendors also provide pre-built circuit modules (IP cores) which allow for the development of a hardware platform that contains components too sophisticated for students (or faculty, for that matter) to develop in a timely manner. In particular, the use of a modern soft-processor, such as Altera's MIPS-like NIOS II, allows the FPGA to operate as a fully-functional computer, but with a simple architecture that is conducive to teaching.

Since the system permits many different configurations, it can be tailored to the needs of a particular class. As an example, for our compiler course, the use of the NIOS RISC soft-processor makes the FPGA a more attractive target platform than either a complex x86 architecture or a software-only simulator setup. For other courses, peripherals can be connected via a parallel port, such as a camera for image processing or a motor controller for robotics. Students can interact with the FPGA system using logic development tools for hardware topics, a MIPS-like assembly language for low-level systems topics, or using Eclipse and the C programming language for higher-level concepts.

Often, it is difficult to find a single common platform which can gain broad buy-in from faculty members. We have found the FPGA platform to be a popular choice in our department because it provides a common system that students can become proficient with and is flexible enough to be adapted by faculty to meet the needs of a specific course.

3. COMPUTER ORGANIZATION AND ARCHITECTURE

By their very nature, FPGAs provide an ideal platform for the implementation of structures addressed during the study of CPU organization and the accompanying subsystems discussed in a typical computer organization and architecture course sequence. FPGAs are an excellent vehicle to explore digital logic design ranging from the most basic introductory concepts such as combinational and sequential logic design to the more sophisticated design of an entire CPU. FPGAs were initially integrated into our computer organization and architecture courses during the Fall 2009 semester and our experiences are detailed in [8]. In this section, we discuss an introductory design project that has evolved over the past few semesters and that is particularly well suited for implementation on an FPGA platform.

3.1 Motivation

The computer science curriculum at Coastal Carolina integrates digital logic design pedagogy across its two-course sequence of computer organization and architecture. In these two courses, as well as in many others that we offer, we stress the importance of evaluating the impact that design choices have across a range of characteristics including performance, flexibility and cost.

As such, we firmly believe that being able to devise multiple solutions to a problem and subsequently analyzing the tradeoffs among them is central to computer science education. One such design choice that inevitably surfaces is whether a software- or hardware-based solution to a given problem is "better."

In order to allow us to explore this question at an early point in the curriculum, we have devised a project that allows our students to design two competing solutions to the problem of driving two seven segment displays (SSDs) as the primary output device of an embedded computing system.

3.2 Example Design Project

Students are tasked with the responsibility of taking the contents of a data register and displaying it in hexadecimal format on the two SSDs. As such, the system should be able to correctly display all 256 possible numbers ranging from 0x00 to 0xFF.

In the case of both the hardware and software approaches, the students make use of the NIOS embedded soft processor that is also instantiated alongside their designs in the FPGA fabric. By using a set of development tools provided by the FPGA manufacturer, the students are able to write the necessary assembly code to output the contents of the data register to a parallel I/O port, whether it is connected directly to the SSDs or via their display driver logic.

3.2.1 *The Hardware Approach*

In the hardware approach, the students are expected to explore the fundamental issue: deriving the expressions that will correctly drive all seven independent LEDs that make up the SSD. Although such chip models as the 7447 are already available in the IDE library that will perform binary to BCD or binary to hex display decoding, students are not permitted to use them. Furthermore, they must come to the realization that the same hardware they derive for one display will also work for the second display (Figure 2), which helps reinforce the concept of design reuse.

Solving this problem amounts to utilizing elementary digital logic design techniques such as truth tables and Karnaugh maps to derive Boolean expressions for each LED within the seven segment display.

3.2.2 *The Software Approach*

After having finished the purely hardware-based implementation of the SSD drivers, the students have now seen a functioning project and are familiar with the challenges associated with building these structures from the ground up. Additionally, students are familiar with the relatively simple assembly code that loads the contents of the given data register onto the SSD displays. At this point, students are tasked to implement the *same behavior* without the use of their hardware SSD drivers by connecting the NIOS I/O ports directly to the individual LEDs.

A common software technique used to map numbers to symbol data is through the use of a lookup table (or LUT). In this case, the index into the table is the value to be displayed and the contents at that index is a bit vector which corresponds to the correct LEDs on the seven-segment display. In this case, the contents of a register must be properly displayed in hexadecimal format using two adjacent and independent SSDs.

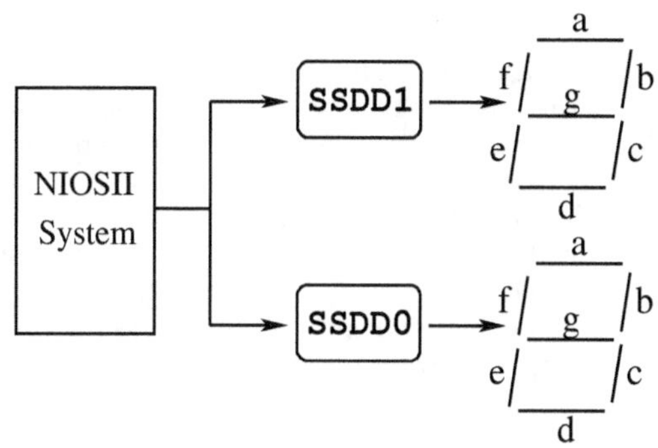

Figure 2: Using combinational logic to implement the binary-to-hex seven-segment display drivers (SSDDs). Here a parallel I/O port is instantiated on the NIOS system and is split to feed both drivers. In this case, the contents of a register can be written directly to the I/O port using an assembly primitive.

Although this project presents a number of concurrent challenges that cover both basic hardware design as well as assembly programming which requires judicious use of bitwise and shifting operators, many students have expressed that this project allowed them to tie together concepts that had previously seemed disjoint. In addition, our intention is to allow students to make comparisons between the two solutions and to critically analyze the tradeoffs involved.

3.2.3 *Tradeoff Analysis*

After completing both parts of this project, the students are asked to comment on the benefits and drawbacks of each approach. This typically evokes responses related to how difficult each part was relative to the other in terms of their own effort. In most cases, students feel that the hardware solution is "easier" to implement because it avoids the intricacies of dealing with the lookup table and bit-wise operations. However after we move past the initial response, when pressed further to evaluate each design, students begin to critically analyze the issues involved. Chief among the ideas discussed are:

Flexibility: The LUT approach is more flexible in that the characters displayed on the SSDs can easily be changed by simply altering the contents of the array. This is in stark contrast to the challenge of re-deriving Boolean expressions for a similarly altered truth table.

Speed: The hardware approach allows the display to be driven with far fewer instructions as there are fewer operations to perform on the contents of the displayed register and there are no memory accesses to a LUT. Furthermore, there is no on-chip memory overhead associated with a LUT, which leaves more logic elements on the FPGA to be used for other hardware, if desired.

Time versus Space: Using a larger LUT allows for half as many assembly operations; however, in doing so, 16 times as much memory is required to store the array.

This sort of tradeoff analysis reinforces the concept of matching a design with a specific set of requirements. For example, in this case the requirements given did not include the need to provide for a changing set of characters to be displayed on the SSDs; therefore, the hardware solution might seem to be the "better solution" since it is both faster and requires less on-chip memory. However, the software solution provides a modicum of flexibility that more easily accommodates incomplete or changing specifications, an unfortunately common occurrence in the field.

3.2.4 Survey Results

During the Fall 2010 semester, a short, anonymous, and voluntary survey was given to students in two different courses, CSCI 210 and 310. CSCI 210 is a course that covers digital logic design, computer organization, and introduces assembly programming while CSCI 310 further covers assembly programming and advanced logic design with a significant focus on computer architecture.

The general trend across both courses is that, of the students that had a preference, 100% preferred the use of the Altera DE2 board and and its associated development environment over the use of a simulator for executing their assembly programs. To a lesser extent, 90% of those that responded preferred the use of the Altera DE2 over the use of breadboards and discrete logic gates for implementing their digital logic designs. Additionally, 78% of CSCI 210 students indicated that using the NIOS processor played a significant role in helping them to better understand assembly programming over lecture alone. Moreover, a full 100% of CSCI 310 respondents indicated that the new FPGA platform played a significant role in helping them understand how software and hardware interact.

4. COMPILER DESIGN AND IMPLEMENTATION

Compiler design and program translation has long been an important part of the computer science curriculum. With recent architectures trending towards multicore systems, compiler design is still an valuable component of a modern computer science curriculum [5]. Given the wide range of topics that can be covered in a course on compiler design, tradeoffs must be made in order to limit the scope of knowledge and maintain a reasonable student workload [14].

In this course, students use a Java-based framework to implement a compiler for the Tiger programming language, an ML-variant source language described in [1]. As shown in Fig. 3, students only interact with platform-specific details in two of the six assignments that they complete throughout the class: stack frame construction and instruction selection.

Compiler implementation projects traditionally target one of three classes of platforms [7, 13]:

x86 ISA: Given the ubiquity of the x86 architecture, using this platform allows the project compiler output to be executed directly on the hardware. While the convenience and availability of x86 hardware is advantageous, the complex instruction set and conventions governing register usage is, at best, cumbersome in a classroom project.

Simulated Hardware: One of the most popular architectures to target is MIPS, due to its straightforward instruction set. Unfortunately, finding MIPS-based hardware systems for this purpose can be problematic, often necessitating the use of simulators, such as SPIM to execute the compiled code[12].

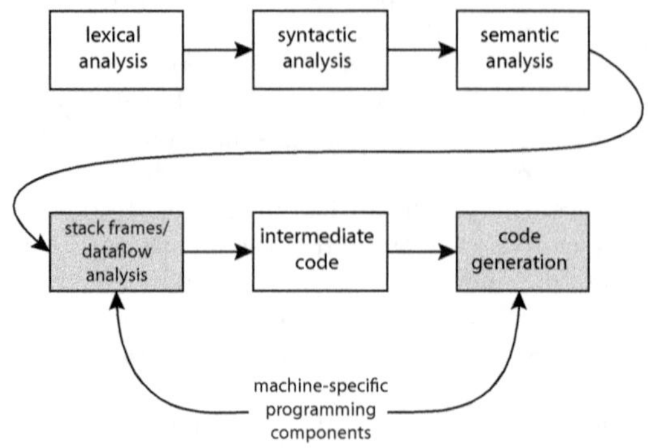

Figure 3: Programming assignments in the compiler construction course.

Bytecode / Virtual Hardware: Some projects instead target virtual hardware, such as Java bytecode, or use lower-level virtual hardware instructions, such as LLVM. While this avoids both instruction set complexity and the reliance on simulation, using virtual hardware still entails at least one more level of translation software in between the student-compiled code and hardware execution.

Using an FPGA-based system target for our project compiler provides several advantages. First, the FPGA system is configured with a NIOS CPU which allows our students to leverage experience gained in their earlier organization course. As a result, little time is spent on hardware specifics and students are able to implement a fully functional compiler during a semester, as opposed to a set of separate components. Also, since the system is physical, executing the output of their compiler is a hands-on, tangible experience, rather than just handing it over to another set of programs.

Student generated code is executed directly on the hardware and only requires a small runtime library to provide rudimentary memory management and I/O device support. Adapting the course to the FPGA target involved re-writing the compiler runtime library which consists of approximately 1000 lines of assembly language. The compiler framework was originally targeted to MIPS and needed very minor changes to adapt it to the FPGA soft-processor.

We initially adapted this class to use the FPGA target in the Fall 2010 semester, our experience is detailed in [9]. The class was taught to 21 junior and senior rank undergraduate students. These students were surveyed anonymously at the end of the class, which 17 students responded to. Of the 17 students, 15 had prior experience with the FPGA systems. Out of these, 12 out of 15 (80%) students felt that their prior experience was very helpful to them in the compiler implementation course. Of those that expressed a preference (8/17), 100% of the students preferred using a physical system over a simulator. We are currently in the third iteration of the compiler implementation class using FPGAs.

5. SECURITY

Issues of computer security are woven throughout the curriculum at Coastal Carolina. In addition to this broad integration, we also offer a course dedicated to software security. A popular topic often discussed in this course is the concept of buffer overflow exploits and stack smashing. These topics are generally covered during lecture; however they were not being reinforced through actual programming assignments.

We have developed a laboratory activity that makes use of a pre-configured FPGA-based computer system and provides students the opportunity to explore buffer overflows in a detailed and hands-on fashion. The students are provided with a section of undocumented NIOS II assembly code that represents a function which copies array data from the heap into a fixed-size automatic array present on the callee's stack. The arguments to the function are source and destination addresses, as well as the number of items to copy. The function copies data from the source on the heap to the destination on the stack, and uses the item count passed to the function to terminate the loop. The function does not first check that the number of items is less than or equal to the fixed-size of the array on the stack, thus leading to potential buffer overflow.

The students are instructed to identify and exploit the buffer overflow flaw to corrupt the return address in the callee's stack frame. The grading rubric used for this assignment incentivizes more sophisticated exploits. In particular, simply overwriting the return address such that the program returns to an undefined location is the easiest to accomplish, and therefore earns the student a base grade of a B. More clever solutions that cause the program to return to a known location that contains executable and presumably malicious code, will earn them higher marks. Finally, the students are required to modify the provided code to prevent the given exploit.

A trial run of this assignment was conducted in a Spring 2011 course, and is presently being integrated and expanded as part of our security course that runs each Fall. We have received positive qualitative feedback from students indicating that this assignment was especially illuminating. Specifically, several students admitted that although they were familiar with the idea of a buffer overflow, that being forced to exploit the flaw via a programming assignment made them realize that their earlier understanding of the mechanics underlying these types of exploits was incomplete.

Moreover, students indicated that they were intrigued with the puzzle-like characteristics of this particular assignment and that they were fond of the idea of figuring out how to "break" the code provided by the professor and alter the intended flow of control of the target program. While this type of assignment can be accomplished on a traditional computer using an appropriate set of tools, an FPGA-based computer system provides the type of platform that makes it easy to see exactly what the hardware is doing, without all of the levels of abstraction, including the operating system and memory manager of a typical modern-day computer. This simplicity makes it an excellent starting point to explore these types of security issues in isolation, with the possibility of moving to more sophisticated computer systems later in the course.

6. ROBOTICS

The robotics course at Coastal Carolina takes an AI-based approach that emphasizes software control systems [11]. Since robotics systems have a heavy dependence on hardware control systems, the software/hardware interface must be addressed. Many R/C-based robotics systems rely on actuator controls that use a pulse-width-modulated (PWM) system with a variable 1-2ms pulse sent every 20ms to control motor velocity [6]. We have created a course module which uses the FPGA processor to generate the PWM signal that is used to control brushless motors. These motors are also used in the quadrotor UAV robots throughout the course and are similar to motors used in a range of robotic systems.

To implement the programmable speed control system, students use a C programming environment with an instantiated NIOS CPU on the FPGA. The NIOS C API provides access to an interval timer which is capable of sub-millisecond resolution. Students write C code to read a 4-bit integer value from the input switches signifying the desired motor speed (0=off, 15=max speed). This value is then used to set the duration of the interval timer, which determines the PWM duty cycle.

An interrupt handler is invoked whenever the interval timer expires. The handler simply writes a bit value to the output pin which changes the pulse state, then recomputes the next interval needed by the timer. When implemented correctly, the FPGA switch input causes the brushless motor to spin up and change speeds depending on switch values.

To implement this lab, students do not deal directly with the FPGA configuration, this is provided to them as a scaffolded component of the assignment. In fact, the same hardware configuration used for the compiler and security assignments will also work with this setup. While students are writing C code targeting an FPGA soft-processor, what they are focused on is learning how to program in an asynchronous, interrupt-driven style and not burdened with the specific hardware details of the system. What makes the FPGA an ideal platform for this activity is the availability of a C API with an interval timer, direct tactile input using switches, and a parallel I/O output port that is directly mapped into the CPUs memory, which can be wired directly (with a single wire) to the brushless motor controller.

This assignment was given to 12 students in the Spring 2012 offering of the robotics course at CCU. Of these students, 10 students were able to submit fully functional interrupt driven motor controller solutions. The PWM project was used to bridge the gap between the more theoretical-driven AI approach to robotics and the practical side of constructing and operating a functional UAV robotic system in the open world.

7. ADDITIONAL COURSES

There are several additional courses which we feel that using FPGA systems are a good fit and have developed some course materials for. We are in the process of retrofitting these courses and will present the adapted versions when they are next offered.

7.1 Image Processing

Extensive experimentation is required to solve many image processing problems. Implementation of the theoretical concepts often necessitates parameter estimation, algorithm revision, and the evaluation of a set of solutions on a large collection of test images. The critical importance of algorithm development and analysis is highlighted by using tools such as MATLAB and Simulink. These tools force students to focus on algorithms rather than low-level system details.

As such, students are more aware of how algorithmic design choices affect results.

While much of the course focuses on the algorithms and theory of image processing, it is also beneficial for students to understand how such techniques are realized in practice. We have specialized FPGA systems with both camera and monitor peripherals which we are using to emphasize the connection between theory and implementation.

At the most basic level, FPGAs may be used as a simplistic processing system which provides a 2-D matrix of intensity values to the student, who is assigned to manipulate the image using a basic image processing technique such as Gaussian blurring or edge detection. Alternatively, MATLAB programs can be used in conjunction with Simulink to generate entire hardware systems that can be programmed directly onto FPGA hardware for spatial filtering and morphological operations such as edge detection, image perception, and object detection [15, 3].

We have configured the DE2 FPGA system to act as a closed system which provides image data generated from an attached camera device as a 2-D matrix to the student programmer, who implements the image processing algorithm and is able to display it through the video output. The raw image is scaled and resampled by hardware modules.

7.2 Operating Systems

Operating systems classes are a natural place for utilizing FPGAs in order to reduce the complexity of the hardware environment. The FPGA platform can provide a system with enough functionality to merit the need for an operating system, yet be simple enough for didactic purposes. The same FPGA system in use at Coastal Carolina has been shown to be an effective tool for teaching operating systems design and demonstrating implementation issues [4].

We have had success using the *uClinux* operating system [10] on the Altera FPGA boards, as well. As with the use of the FPGA in the compiler course, students are already familiar with the particulars of the hardware platform and can focus on the details specific to operating systems. We will integrate FPGAs into our operating systems course beginning Fall 2013.

8. CONCLUSIONS

In an ideal setting, students completing an undergraduate education in computer science should be exposed to a broad range of topics within the field. Not only should they have sufficient depth in each of these areas, but students should be able to reason about all aspects of both system and application design. To facilitate this objective, we have described the integration of FPGA devices throughout several systems classes in the computer science curriculum.

The use of these systems throughout the curriculum enables students to gain familiarity with a single flexible tool that can be used in a variety of different contexts. This familiarity in turn allows students to re-use their knowledge of this system throughout the curriculum and builds confidence in understanding issues of end-to-end system construction. Where we have measured the effectiveness of our approach, it has been shown to be a useful tool in increasing student understanding and engagement.

The course materials used for these courses (assignments, FPGA hardware configurations, supporting software, etc.) are available upon request.

9. REFERENCES

[1] A. W. Appel. *Modern Compiler Implementation in Java.* Cambridge University Press, 1998.

[2] Association for Computing Machinery and IEEE Computer Society. Computer Science Curriculum 2008: An Interim Revision of CS 2001. http://www.acm.org/education/curricula/ComputerScience2008.pdf.

[3] A. Bochem, K. B. Kent, and R. Herpers. FPGA Based Real-Time Object Detection with Validation of Precision and Performance. In *Proceedings of the 22nd Annual IEEE Int. Symposium on Rapid System Prototyping (RSP '11)*, May. 24–27 2011.

[4] M. L. Corliss and M. Melara. VIREOS: An Integrated, Bottom-up, Educational Operating Systems Project with FPGA Support. In *Proceedings of the 42nd ACM technical symposium on Computer science education*, SIGCSE '11, pages 39–44, New York, NY, USA, 2011.

[5] M. Hall, D. Padua, and K. Pingali. Compiler Research: The Next 50 Years. *Commun. ACM*, 52:60–67, Feb. 2009.

[6] J. O. Hamblen and T. S. Hall. Engaging Undergraduate Students with Robotic Design Projects. In *in Proc. of the 2nd IEEE Int'l Workshop of Electronic Design, Test and Applications*, 2004.

[7] J. Hickey and A. Nogin. Formal Compiler Construction in a Logical Framework. *Higher-Order and Symbolic Computation*, 19:197–230, 2006.

[8] W. M. Jones and D. B. Larkins. Integrating Digital Logic Design and Assembly Programming Using FPGAs in the Classroom. In *Proceedings of the 49th Annual Southeast Regional Conference*, ACM-SE '11, pages 13–18, New York, NY, USA, 2011. ACM.

[9] D. B. Larkins and W. M. Jones. Targeting FPGA-based Processors for an Implementation-driven Compiler Construction Course. In *Proceedings of the 49th Annual Southeast Regional Conference*, ACM-SE '11, pages 31–35, New York, NY, USA, 2011. ACM.

[10] D. McCullough. *uCLinux* for Linux Programmers. *Linux Journal*, 2004:7–, July 2004.

[11] R. R. Murphy. *Introduction to AI Robotics.* MIT Press, Cambridge, MA, USA, 1st edition, 2000.

[12] D. A. Patterson and J. L. Hennessy. *Computer Organization and Design: The Hardware/Software Interface.* Morgan Kaufmann, August 1997.

[13] W. M. Waite. The Compiler Course in Today's Curriculum: Three Strategies. In *Proceedings of the 37th SIGCSE technical symposium on Computer science education*, SIGCSE '06, pages 87–91, New York, NY, USA, 2006. ACM.

[14] W. M. Waite, A. Jarrahian, M. H. Jackson, and A. Diwan. Design and Implementation of a Modern Compiler Course. In *Proceedings of the 11th annual SIGCSE conference on Innovation and technology in computer science education*, ITICSE '06, pages 18–22, New York, NY, USA, 2006. ACM.

[15] Q. Xu, C. Chakrabarti, and L. Karam. A Distributed Canny Edge Detector and its Implementation on FPGA. In *Digital Signal Processing Workshop and IEEE Signal Processing Education Workshop*, Jan. 4–7 2011.

MDAT: A Multithreading Debugging and Testing Tool

Eric Larson
Seattle University
901 12th Avenue
Seattle, WA 98122
(206) 296-5513
elarson@seattleu.edu

Rochelle Palting
Seattle University
901 12th Avenue
Seattle, WA 98122
rcpalting@gmail.com

ABSTRACT
MDAT is a multithreaded testing and debugging tool designed for students learning to program with multiple threads. MDAT automatically generates random schedules to allow students to more thoroughly test their programs. The design of MDAT takes full control over the scheduling allowing a failing run to be reproduced. To assist debugging, MDAT includes an output trace that shows the status of all threads, locks, and semaphores in the program and has an interactive mode that allows students to try out their own schedules. MDAT was effective at detecting deadlock and mutual exclusion violations in student submissions of the unisex restroom problem.

Categories and Subject Descriptors
D.1.3 [**Programming Techniques**]: Concurrent programming.
D.2.5 [**Software Engineering**]: Testing and Debugging – *debugging aids, testing tools.*
K.3.2 [**Computers and Education**]: Computer and Information Science Education – *computer science education.*

General Terms
Reliability, Verification.

Keywords
concurrency, synchronization, multithreading, testing, debugging

1. INTRODUCTION
One of the primary challenges of developing multithreaded applications is testing and debugging, especially for students who are first learning how to program with multiple threads. Testing and debugging are particularly important when designing programs that use synchronization primitives, such as locks and semaphores, as their programs may suffer from race conditions or deadlock. The paper presents MDAT – a multithreaded testing and debugging tool designed for students learning to program with multiple threads.

Students are often given problems such as the unisex restroom problem: *There is a single restroom that can be used by both men and women but not at the same time. There is no limit to how many people can be in the restroom at once but they all have to be the same gender.* This problem serves as a running example throughout the paper. There are two versions of this problem: the initial version as described above and the restricted version which is the same as the initial version with the added restriction of having at most four people in the restroom at once.

It is difficult to test for race conditions and deadlock as they are often dependent on how the operating system schedules the individual threads. As a result, it is necessary to execute the same test with the same inputs multiple times to test different operating system schedules. This is a confusing concept to comprehend for students who are used to deterministic results each time a test is run. A further complication is that the schedules exercised by the operating system are very unlikely to be very aggressive in terms of finding race conditions. Since the first programs written by students are often small, the program rarely gets interrupted due to the expiration of a time slice. Instead the program runs until it encounters a system call (such as acquiring a lock or printing something to the screen). This means that it is highly unlikely for a program to get interrupted in the middle of a series of statements such as this:

```
countFemale++;
if (countFemale == 1)
  sem_wait(&male);
```

A common mistake for beginners is to not protect shared variables such as `countFemale` with a lock. However, a race condition may only surface if the operating system interrupts the thread after the if statement but before the wait statement (such that another thread can alter `countFemale` making the condition false). As noted earlier, the small size of these programs makes it highly unlikely that the thread will get interrupted in between those statements even for long-running programs.

Our MDAT tool alleviates these testing challenges in two ways. First, MDAT instruments the program by placing calls to invoke the scheduler after each statement allowing for more varied and aggressive schedules. Second, MDAT can be run to automatically test the program using a user-controlled number of random schedules. This permits students to easily test their programs several times without manual intervention.

If an error does occur in a multithreaded program, it can be difficult to debug. First, the bug may be dependent on a particular schedule and it may be difficult to reproduce that schedule. In addition, using a debugger to examine the state of different threads, locks, and semaphores can be intimidating to students who are new to multithreading programming.

MDAT addresses these concerns by having full control of scheduling. The tool is designed such that only one thread executes at a time so the underlying operating system has no decisions to make on what threads to execute. This permits the schedules produced by MDAT to be fully reproducible. When schedules are randomly generated, a random seed is displayed. The user can generate the exact same schedule using that random seed. In addition, MDAT creates a trace that displays the status of each thread, lock, and semaphore after each scheduler invocation.

SIGCSE'13, March 6–9, 2013, Denver, Colorado, USA.

Using this trace, a programmer can follow the steps that led to a particular problem.

For further testing and debugging, MDAT features an interactive mode that allows students to select which threads to run while displaying the program status on the screen. This mode encourages students to try different scenarios within their programs. More importantly, students can simply play around with their program increasing their comprehension on how multithreaded programs and synchronization primitives behave.

MDAT also has several benefits for the instructor. Using the interactive mode, MDAT can be used as an instructional aid in classroom presentations to demonstrate how locks and semaphores work. The interactive mode could also be used in a lab setting where students are given a buggy program and must devise a schedule that exposes the bug. MDAT can also help with evaluating student work. The instructor can run MDAT on student submissions to see if MDAT can find any errors. However, manual inspection of the submissions is still necessary since not every schedule is run. Exhaustively running all possible schedules is not computationally feasible.

2. MDAT OVERVIEW

The architecture of MDAT is shown in Figure 1. MDAT is designed for UNIX-based systems and programs written in the C programming language using the pthreads threading library.

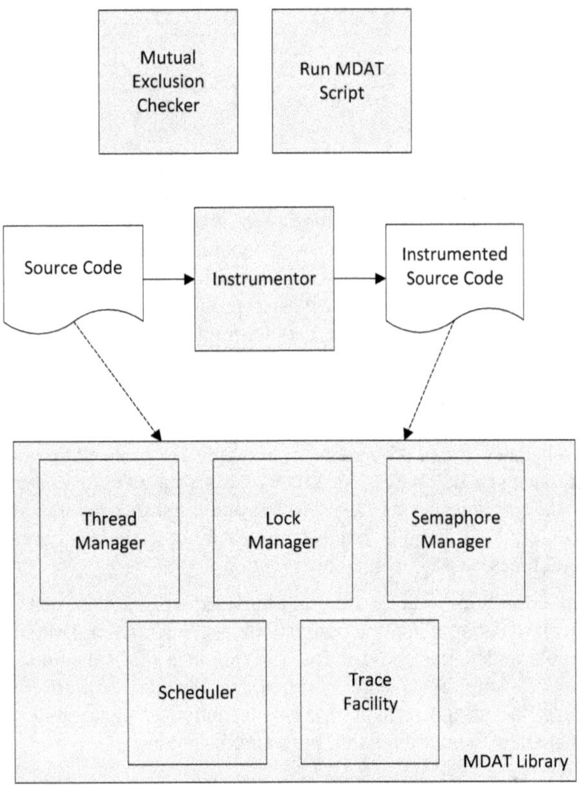

Figure 1. MDAT Architecture

The primary component of MDAT is the MDAT library which contains replacements for each of the lock and semaphore functions. The separation of the MDAT library permits it to be used with existing multithread applications with minimal effort. When writing a multithreaded program using MDAT, a student would use the corresponding MDAT functions instead of the normal pthreads functions commonly used in UNIX as shown in Table 1. To maximize realism, the argument lists for the MDAT functions are identical to those of the pthreads except for `mdat_mutex_init` and `mdat_sem_init`. These functions have an additional string argument that serves as the name of that entity that is subsequently used in the trace.

Table 1. MDAT Lock and Semaphore Functions

Pthreads function name	***MDAT function name***
`pthread_mutex_init`	`mdat_mutex_init`
`pthread_mutex_lock`	`mdat_mutex_lock`
`pthread_mutex_unlock`	`mdat_mutex_unlock`
`sem_init`	`mdat_sem_init`
`sem_wait`	`mdat_sem_wait`
`sem_post`	`mdat_sem_post`

MDAT only supports locks and semaphores as synchronization primitives. Furthermore, it only supports the basic operations shown in Table 1. Other operations such as `pthread_mutex_trylock` are not supported. This decision reflects what we covered in the class. In particular, only the basic lock and semaphore operations are taught. This choice is consistent with operating system textbooks which often only use these basic operations when introducing synchronization using locks and semaphores.

The MDAT library interface contains four additional functions:

- `mdat_init`: Initializes the MDAT library.
- `mdat_thread_start`: Registers a thread. Must be called by each thread at the beginning.
- `mdat_thread_finish`: Notifies MDAT that the thread has finished and not to schedule the thread any longer. Must be called by each thread once it completes.
- `mdat_invoke_scheduler`: Forces MDAT to invoke the scheduler and select a thread to run out of the threads that are ready (including the currently executing thread). In random mode, it will select a thread at random. In interactive mode, a prompt will be given to the user.

The calls to `mdat_invoke_scheduler` are automatically added by the *Instrumentor*, not by the programmer. The instrumentor adds a call to `mdat_invoke_scheduler` after each statement in the program. Furthermore, the instrumentor splits complex statements into two or more basic statements adding a call to `mdat_invoke_scheduler` after each one. This allows the tool to catch some, but not all, concurrency issues that arise if students incorrectly assume each statement is atomic. Splitting the statements further is left as future work.

The instrumentor only needs to be run on files that contain code that can be run concurrently. Optionally, a list of functions can be supplied to the instrumentor such that it will only instrument the functions specified on the list. To improve the debugging capabilities, `mdat_invoke_scheduler` has a location argument, a unique integer that is assigned by the instrumentor to each call it adds. As shown in Section 3, the location appears in the trace allowing the user to see where each thread is currently executing in the program. In addition to `mdat_invoke_scheduler` calls, the scheduler is invoked at the end of lock, unlock, wait, and post operations.

Internally, the MDAT library contains the following:

- *Scheduler*: The scheduler permits only one thread to be executed at a time. It also detects deadlock if no threads are able to run.
- *Thread Manager*: Manages all of the threads. Keeps tracks of which threads are ready to run and which threads are waiting due to a lock or semaphore.
- *Lock Manager*: Manages the locks. Keeps track of which thread holds each lock and which threads, if any, are waiting for each of the locks.
- *Semaphore Manager*: Manages the semaphores. Stores the current values of each semaphore and which threads, if any, are waiting for a post operation.
- *Trace Facility*: Responsible for displaying important events and the current state in the trace file.

The scheduler is implemented using signals. When a thread is not executing, it calls `sigwait` which causes the thread to wait until it receives the Linux user-defined signal SIGUSR1. When a thread switch occurs, the thread that is currently active sends the next thread to execute the SIGUSR1 signal using `pthread_kill`. To avoid issues at start up, all threads must call `mdat_thread_start` to register with MDAT. All threads must register before execution can start. Once all the threads have registered, the thread selected to start (chosen randomly or by the user in interactive mode) will begin execution. All other threads will wait for their turns using `sigwait`. A thread must call `mdat_thread_finish` when it completes. This lets the scheduler know not to schedule that particular thread anymore.

The thread manager, lock manager, and semaphore manager are essentially tables that keep track of the threads, locks, and semaphores respectively. The various operations update these tables accordingly. An important field in the thread manager is the current state of each thread: running, ready, waiting for a lock, waiting for a semaphore, or completed. The scheduler will only select from threads that are running or ready. If no thread is running or ready, the scheduler will report deadlock and abort the program. The state of each lock (locked or unlocked) is tracked by the lock manager. If a thread needs to wait due to a lock that is already acquired by a different thread, the state of the thread is updated and the scheduler is invoked to choose a different thread. The semaphore manager works in a similar fashion.

While the MDAT library can check for deadlock, it cannot check for mutual exclusion violations as these are specific to the programming task. The *Mutual Exclusion Checker* checks for these types of violations relying on output statements that are produced by the program. The mutual exclusion checker will need to be modified based on the mutual exclusion requirements of the program. For example, a checker for the reader / writer problem would ensure that a writer has exclusive access in the critical section. The checker implementation for the unisex restroom problem is described in Section 4.

Finally, the *Run MDAT Script* is a Python script that will run the program a user-specified number of times. This allows students to test their programs on as many random schedules as they desire. Once an error is detected, either due to deadlock or a mutual exclusion violation, the script will stop. The random seed for each run is displayed, and the trace files of the failing run are saved so students are able to reproduce the failing run.

3. USER INTERFACE

To use MDAT, simply compile the instrumented source code produced by the instrumentor and link with the MDAT library. We altered our source code such that the MDAT configuration could be controlled using command line arguments. For instance, one command line switch directs MDAT to run in interactive mode. The command line arguments are parsed and passed into MDAT using `mdat_init`.

An excerpt of a trace is shown in Figure 2. For consistency, the trace and interactive outputs are identical except when interactive mode prompts the user for a thread. The first three lines are informational messages. Messages are displayed any time a thread is switched or a synchronization function is executed. The status table that follows is divided into three sections: threads, locks, and semaphores. For each thread, the current location is given – the unique identifier of the last `mdat_invoke_scheduler` call executed by that thread. Looking at the first line of Figure 2, thread 6 executed `mdat_invoke_scheduler` with unique identifier 7 and this is reflected in the status table that follows. Programmers, using the instrumented source code, can follow along using this location field.

Within the thread section of the status table, the status column shows the current state of the thread. It can be one of the following states: ready, running, waiting-lock, waiting-sem, or completed. If the thread is waiting, the name of the lock or semaphore it is waiting on is displayed in the last column.

The lock section displays the name of each lock, the status of the lock (which includes the thread currently holding the lock if it is held), and a list of threads waiting for that lock. The semaphore section is similar. It displays the name of the semaphore, its current value, and a list of threads waiting for that semaphore. We chose to use a semaphore implementation that decrements for every wait operation allowing the value to be negative. For example, `genderBlock` in Figure 2 has a value of -1.

When running in interactive mode, a prompt appears anytime there is a choice regarding threads. At the start, the user is prompted on which thread should start running first. Each time the scheduler is invoked, the user is prompted on which thread to run next. Only the threads that are ready are acceptable; the user is asked to select a different thread if their selected thread is waiting or has already completed. If threads are waiting, the user is also prompted on which thread to wake up when a lock is released or a semaphore is incremented. Referring back to Figure 2, thread 2 releases lock `maleMutex`. MDAT randomly chose to wake up thread 4 but it could have selected threads 0, 8 or 10. In interactive mode, the user would have been given the choice to wake up either thread 0, 4, 8, or 10. Note that selecting a thread to wake up is independent of the choice of which thread to schedule next. Even though the lock was transferred to thread 4, thread 6 was selected to run next.

```
[Call 7] Switching from thread 6 to thread 2
Thread 2 is releasing lock maleMutex
Transferring lock maleMutex from thread 2 to thread 4
*****************************************************************************
|THREAD ID    |LOCATION       |STATUS         |WAITING ON                    |
|0            |7              |waiting-lock   |maleMutex                     |
|1            |3              |waiting-lock   |femaleMutex                   |
|2            |9              |running        |                              |
|3            |21             |completed      |                              |
|4            |17             |ready          |                              |
|5            |6              |waiting-sem    |genderBlock                   |
|6            |7              |ready          |                              |
|7            |21             |completed      |                              |
|8            |7              |waiting-lock   |maleMutex                     |
|9            |21             |completed      |                              |
|10           |17             |waiting-lock   |maleMutex                     |
-----------------------------------------------------------------------------
|LOCK NAME                    |STATUS         |WAITING THREADS               |
|femaleMutex                  |held by 5      |1                             |
|maleMutex                    |held by 4      |0 8 10                        |
-----------------------------------------------------------------------------
|SEMAPHORE NAME               |VALUE          |WAITING THREADS               |
|occupancy                    |2              |                              |
|genderBlock                  |-1             |5                             |
*****************************************************************************
[mdat-mutex-unlock] Switching from thread 2 to thread 6
Thread 6 tried to acquired held lock maleMutex - thread 6 must wait
*****************************************************************************
|THREAD ID    |LOCATION       |STATUS         |WAITING ON                    |
|0            |7              |waiting-lock   |maleMutex                     |
|1            |3              |waiting-lock   |femaleMutex                   |
|2            |9              |ready          |                              |
|3            |21             |completed      |                              |
|4            |17             |ready          |                              |
|5            |6              |waiting-sem    |genderBlock                   |
|6            |7              |waiting-lock   |maleMutex                     |
|7            |21             |completed      |                              |
|8            |7              |waiting-lock   |maleMutex                     |
|9            |21             |completed      |                              |
|10           |17             |waiting-lock   |maleMutex                     |
-----------------------------------------------------------------------------
|LOCK NAME                    |STATUS         |WAITING THREADS               |
|femaleMutex                  |held by 5      |1                             |
|maleMutex                    |held by 4      |0 6 8 10                      |
-----------------------------------------------------------------------------
|SEMAPHORE NAME               |VALUE          |WAITING THREADS               |
|occupancy                    |2              |                              |
|genderBlock                  |-1             |5                             |
*****************************************************************************
```

Figure 2. Example of MDAT trace file

4. UNISEX RESTROOM IMPLEMENTATION

The unisex restroom problem can be structured like many classic synchronization problems and divided into four sections:

- Entry section (person is entering the restroom)
- Critical section (person is using the restroom)
- Exit section (person is leaving the restroom)
- Remainder section (person is outside drinking more water)

The critical and remainder sections are actually uninteresting in enforcing mutual exclusion – all of the work is done in the entry and exit sections. The students were given these four functions. Each of the functions started with an output statement that logged the start of the function. The resulting log was then used by the checker. Students could only add code to the entry and exit sections after the output statement. Students also had to add code to a fifth function that initialized shared variables, locks, and semaphores. These five functions are resided in a standalone file.

Students were also given a driver file that is responsible for setting up the threads. Each thread executes the four sections in order for a user-specified number of times. The driver file can be reused for other programs and the classical synchronization problems that are set up using these four sections.

The mutual exclusion checker is invoked after a run has concluded and uses the log to determine if a mutual exclusion violation has occurred. The log consists of entries that describe which section each thread has entered along with the gender of that thread. To enforce the mutual exclusion rule, the checker uses two counters: one for the number of males in the restroom and one for the number of females. The checker scans the log entries in order. When someone enters the critical section, the appropriate counter is incremented. When someone leaves the critical section, the appropriate counter is decremented. Mutual exclusion occurs if both counters are non-zero at the same time.

Students were also asked to write a second implementation to the restricted version of the unisex restroom problem such that at most four people could be in the restroom at once. To support this restriction, the checker was modified to flag an error if either gender's counter is greater than four. A command line switch was also added to the checker so this check could be turned off or on depending on which version of the problem was being worked on.

5. RESULTS

To assess the potential impact of MDAT, we used the student submissions of the unisex restroom problem that were assigned in the Fall 2011 and Fall 2012 offerings of the first author's Operating Systems and Networks class. Students had to provide solutions for both the initial problem and the more restrictive version. Solutions did not need to ensure fairness or lack starvation but they could not be overly restrictive (such as allowing only one person in the restroom at once).

In the Fall 2011 offering, students did ***not*** have access to the MDAT library at the time; they had to test and debug their programs themselves manually. However, as part of their assignment, students had to create a mutual exclusion checker that they could use to help test their programs. The assignments were graded manually looking for mutual exclusion violations and possible cases of deadlock. Once MDAT was completed (which occurred well after the completion of the course), 21 submissions were converted so they could run with MDAT.

In the Fall 2012 offering, students did have access to MDAT. There were 28 submissions for the assignment. To reduce copying from the previous offering, the problem was changed to an identical problem with a different situation: prohibiting old children and young children from simultaneously being on a play structure at once. For clarity, the remainder of this section is written in the context of the unisex bathroom problem. Students were also given a survey at the end of the assignment to provide feedback on their experience using MDAT.

We ran the submissions from both quarters using MDAT for 200 different randomly-generated schedules with 12 threads and 10 rounds per run. The results are shown in Table 2.

Table 2. Results of using MDAT on Student Submissions

MDAT reported...	Fall 2011 (w/o MDAT)	Fall 2012 (MDAT)
No errors (correct solution)	6	23
No errors (incorrect solution)	0	1
Deadlock (all 200 runs)	10	0
Deadlock (some runs)	1	0
Mutual exclusion violation (all 200 runs)	1	1
Mutual exclusion violation (some runs)	0	2
Both deadlock & mutual exclusion	2	1
Hung due to incorrect spin loop	1	0

The fact that 15 of the 21 submissions are incorrect in the Fall 2011 offering clearly demonstrate the need for such a tool. While using MDAT, only 5 of the 28 submissions were incorrect in the Fall 2012 offering. MDAT was able to detect four of the five faulty submissions. In the incorrect submission that was not detected by MDAT, the synchronization was too restrictive in that it only allowed one person to use the restroom at once. MDAT does not catch this particular problem but the mutual exclusion checker could be modified to warn the user of this situation.

In addition, in virtually all of the cases, very few runs are needed to catch the error. This implies the aggressive scheduling with more opportunities to switch threads has a significant impact on finding multithreaded problems. The only exception to this are the two solutions from Fall 2012 that encountered mutual exclusion violations on only some of the runs. In both cases, mutual exclusion violations were only detected in 4 of the 200 runs.

For the Fall 2011 offering, we compared the results returned from MDAT with our manual grading of the assignments. Quite embarrassingly, the manual grading of these assignments only caught 6 of the 14 deadlock cases. Manual grading did properly detect the three mutual exclusion violations and deemed the six solutions with no errors to be correct.

Now consider the restricted version of the problem where the restroom has a maximum capacity of four people. Solutions that got the initial part wrong were not considered further since the corresponding solution to the restricted version of the problem was incorrect for the same initial reason. Of the 29 solutions that remained, MDAT did not find any errors. Of these 29 solutions, 27 solutions correctly implemented the restriction. Two solutions (both from the Fall 2012 offering) were incorrect in that it was possible to have more than four people use the restroom but MDAT did not generate a random schedule for this scenario.

To address the lack of data, we used a solution of the initial unrestricted version of the problem with the more restrictive mutual exclusion checker. Since the solution lacks a mechanism for restricting capacity, it is capable of allowing more than four people in the restroom. The solution was run 10,000 times. Only 1 of the 10,000 runs reported a case where four people were in the restroom at once. In this particular situation, using a randomized scheduler was not effective.

The students in the Fall 2012 offering were asked a variety of questions regarding their experience using MDAT. Here is the set of YES / NO questions and their responses:

- Q1. Did MDAT detect deadlock? *24 YES, 2 NO*
- Q2. Did MDAT detect a case where men and women used the restroom at the same time? *16 YES, 9 NO*
- Q3. Did MDAT detect a case where more than four people used the restroom at once? *8 YES, 16 NO*
- Q4. Did you look at the output trace? *22 YES, 4 NO*
- Q5. Did you use interactive mode? *17 YES, 9 NO*

Considering the number of correct solutions that were ultimately received, MDAT was successful in detecting errors. We found it surprising that eight students encountered an error with more than four people using the restroom at once given how rare it was encountered when evaluating the final submissions.

Students who answered yes to Q4 were asked to gauge the usefulness of the output trace on a five point scale from 1 (very useless) to 5 (very useful). They were also asked to provide comments on the trace. The same two questions were posed to those who answered yes to Q5 asking them to assess the usefulness of the interactive mode. The results of the two multiple choice questions are listed in Table 3.

Table 3. Usefulness of MDAT Features

Usefulness of...	*(Very Useless)* 1	*2*	*3*	*(Very Useful)* 4	*5*
output trace	1	3	7	4	7
interative mode	0	2	0	7	7

The usefulness of the output trace was mixed. While some students found the trace to be useful, several felt that the trace was hard to follow, very dense, and a lot of data to scroll through. One comment that really stood out was "Once I understood what I was looking at it was useful, but that took a long time to do."

Based on Table 3, the students who used interactive mode found it to be useful. Looking at the comments, some students used interactive mode to get a better understanding of how context switching, locks, and semaphores worked. Other students found interactive mode to be very helpful in debugging and testing their implementations. One student noted that using output statements he/she added to the code was more helpful.

Lastly, students were asked what improvements should be made to MDAT. Several students suggested on reducing the level of detail on the trace output. Another common suggestion was to better correlate the position on the trace to the source code and to the errors reported by the mutual exclusion checker. In particular, it was difficult to find an error detected by the mutual exclusion checker in the trace.

6. RELATED WORK

The design of MDAT was inspired from CHESS [1]. CHESS is a multithreaded testing tool that systematically generates different schedules for testing, an improvement over simply randomly generating schedules. CHESS works on Win32 and .NET platforms. Inspect [8] is a similar tool but works on C programs with pthreads. ConTest [4] and CalFuzzer [6] generate multithreaded tests for Java. ConTest biases the scheduler towards obtaining multithreaded coverage. CalFuzzer focuses on potential concurrency bugs that were flagged by different tools. All four of these tools are designed for real-world programs where MDAT is focused on assisting students with multithreaded programming.

From an education perspective, Bi and Biedler [2] developed a Java thread visualization tool that helps students see graphically the states of the different threads over time. Ricken and Cartwright [7] propose using a test-first approach to writing concurrent programs in Java. They use a specially designed unit testing framework that overcomes problems with using traditional unit testing frameworks. Currently, their testing is dependent on the schedule produced by the JVM but they plan to incorporate a technique that systematically generates schedules based on heuristics in the future. Bruce et al. [3] propose introducing concurrency as a topic in the first computer science course. They initially select examples that avoid or minimize race conditions but eventually introduce the topic later in the course. A more thorough treatment of testing and debugging is left for future courses. Gopalakrishnan et al. [5] give an extensive list of resources for teaching concurrency and describe how they use Inspect [8] and CHESS [1] in their course.

7. CONCLUSION AND FUTURE WORK

MDAT is a multithreaded testing and debugging tool designed for students learning to program with multiple threads. For the unisex restroom problem, it was effective in helping students find deadlock and mutual exclusion violations where men and women used the restroom at the same time. It was not effective at finding violations of the added restriction that only four people could use the restroom at once. While many students found MDAT to be useful for testing and debugging, some students felt that the output trace was too long and difficult to parse.

For future work, the first obvious step is to improve the tracing facility so it is easier to understand. One enhancement is to have the mutual exclusion checker be integrated into MDAT instead of a separate entity. This will allow state associated with mutual exclusion state to be part of the trace making it easier to debug. Another enhancement is to create a GUI with the ability to collapse and expand the trace. Initially the trace would contain a description of the different events that occurred and the user could click on an event to see the various tables at that point. This would allow the user to find where the error is taking place and then only investigate the state near where the error occurred.

Another direction of future work is to improve the ability to catch concurrency bugs such as the restriction of having four people in the restroom at once. Are there improvements to the scheduler to catch this particular type of bug? Another source of bugs is forgetting that individual statements cannot be assumed to be atomic. By breaking individual statements into smaller pieces, the instrumentor will be able to insert more scheduler invocations in the middle of individual statements. The downside of more scheduler invocations is that the resulting trace is longer.

Lastly, the MDAT interface can be adjusted to use the actual locking and semaphore functions. This would allow the student to write their program that would compile and execute normally with or without MDAT. This would make the exercise seem more real and demonstrate the benefit of creating testing and debugging tools. It would also permit students to use MDAT on other concurrent programs.

ACKNOWLEDGMENTS

The authors would like to thank the anonymous reviewers for their valuable comments. We also thank the students in the Fall 2012 offering of Operating Systems and Networks at Seattle University for providing feedback on MDAT.

REFERENCES

[1] Ball, T., Burckhardt, S., de Halleux, P., Musuvathi, M., and Qadeer, S. 2011. Predictable and Progressive Testing of Multithreaded Code. *IEEE Software* (May/June 2011), 77-83.

[2] Bi, Y., and Beidler, J. 2007. A Visual Tool for Teaching Multithreading in Java. *Journal of Computing Sciences in Colleges* 22, 6 (Jun. 2007), 156-163.

[3] Bruce, K., Danyluk, A., and Murtagh, T. 2010. Introducing Concurrency in CS 1. In *Proceedings of the 41st ACM Technical Symposium on Computer Science Education* (Mar. 2010), 224-228.

[4] Edelstein, O., Farchi, E., Goldin, E., Nir, Y., Ratsaby G., and Ur, S. 2003. Framework for testing multi-threaded Java programs. *Concurrency and Computation: Practice and Experience* 15 (2003), 485-499.

[5] Gopalakrishnan, G., Yang, Y., Vakkalanka, S., Vo, A., Aananthakrishnan, S., Szubzda, G., Sawaya, G., Williams, J., Sharma, S., DeLisi, M., and Atzeni, S. 2009. Some resources for testing concurrency. In *Proceedings of the 7th Workshop on Parallel and Distributed Systems: Testing, Analysis, and Debugging* (Jul. 2009).

[6] Joshi, P., Naik, M., Park, C., and Sen, K. 2009. CalFuzzer: An Extensible Active Testing Framework for Concurrent Programs. In *Proceedings of the 21st International Conference on Computer Aided Verification* (Jun. 2009), 675-681.

[7] Ricken, M., and Cartwright, R. 2010. Test-First Java Concurrency for the Classroom. In *Proceedings of the 41st ACM Technical Symposium on Computer Science Education* (Mar. 2010), 219-223.

[8] Yang, Y., Chen, X., and Gopalakrishnan, G. 2008. *Inspect: A Runtime Model Checker for Multithread C Programs.* Technical Report UUCS-08-004. University of Utah.

Pattern Programming Approach for Teaching Parallel and Distributed Computing

Barry Wilkinson
University of North Carolina Charlotte
9201 University City Blvd.
Charlotte, NC 28223 USA
abw@uncc.edu

Jeremy Villalobos
Formerly of
University of North Carolina Charlotte
9201 University City Blvd.
Charlotte, NC 28223 USA
jeremyvillalobos@gmail.com

Clayton Ferner
University of North Carolina Wilmington
601 S. College Rd.
Wilmington, NC 28409 USA
cferner@uncw.edu

ABSTRACT
In this paper, we describe an approach for teaching parallel and distributed computing at the undergraduate level using computational patterns. The goal is to promote higher-level structured design for parallel programming and make parallel programming easier and more scalable. A pattern programming framework has been developed to create a distributed application that avoids the need to write code in low level message–passing APIs such as MPI. Several patterns have been implemented including workpool, pipeline, synchronous and iterative all-to-all, and stencil. We have redesigned a regular senior undergraduate parallel programming course to begin with a pattern strategy using our framework and provide a detailed syllabus around patterns.

Categories and Subject Descriptors
D.1.3 [**Programming Techniques**]: Concurrent Programming – *distributed programming, parallel programming.*

General Terms
Design, Languages.

Keywords
Pattern Programming; Undergraduate Education.

1. INTRODUCTION
With the widespread introduction of processors with multiple cores, multicore processors have mostly replaced single core designs. Present processors typically have four execution cores. We can expect an increasing number of cores in the future. Intel's first commercial product in its recent Many Integrated Core (MIC) architecture has 32 Intel cores in one package [7]. Systems with a small number of cores such as present 4-core designs have a so-called shared-memory architecture where the cores share common main memory. As the number of cores increases, it becomes necessary to use distributed-memory and hierarchical-memory models. Programming shared-memory and distributed-memory systems is taught in senior undergraduate and first year graduate courses typically called parallel programming. Parallel programming has a very long history as a specialty area for those interested in high performance computing. However, with advent of multicore systems, all computer science students should now be trained in dealing with these systems. A typical parallel programming course focuses on using low-level libraries – MPI for message passing distributed memory systems, OpenMP and other thread tools for shared memory systems, and CUDA/OpenCL for high performance GPU computing. A course typically uses these tools to solve simple problems such as matrix multiplication and sorting. Unfortunately, this approach does not give the student programmer the skills to tackle larger problems nor skills in computational thinking for parallel applications. In addition, programmers have to deal with issues such as deadlock and mutual exclusion. A programming approach is needed that raises the level of abstraction to make parallel programming easier and also more scalable.

To address the above problems, we have developed a new software environment that creates a higher level of abstraction for parallel and distributed programming based upon a pattern programming approach. In this approach, the programmer first identifies an appropriate parallel computational pattern or patterns to solve the problem rather than immediately starting with a low-level API such as MPI or OpenMP. We focus on higher level computational patterns such as workpool, pipeline, stencil, divide and conquer, and synchronous all-to-all rather than lower level constructs such as fork-join and loop. Our pattern programming framework was developed as part of a PhD project exploring distributed computing by Jeremy Villalobos [13]. The framework will automatically distribute tasks across distributed computers and processors, once the programmer has selected the pattern, specified the data to be sent to and from the processors/processes, and specified the computation to be performed by the processors/processes. The framework has built-in patterns including workpool, pipeline, stencil, and synchronous all-to-all. Other patterns can be implemented by the programmer using more advanced knowledge of the framework. The framework will self-deploy on distributed computers, clusters, and multicore processors, or a combination of distributed- and shared-memory computers. More details of the framework will be given later, but the key aspects are the programmer does not program using low level message passing APIs such as MPI or OpenMP. Instead, the patterns are implemented automatically, relieving the programmer of concerns for message-passing deadlock. The programmer has a very simple programing interface avoiding the complexities of putting message-passing statements in the actual code.

The rest of this paper is organized as follows. Existing work is briefly reviewed in Section 2. Various patterns and the programmer interface for our framework are described in Section 3. In Section 4, we describe how our parallel programming course has been re-structured to start with patterns and Section 5 provides conclusions.

2. EXISTING WORK ON PATTERN PROGRAMMING

Design patterns, that is, "reusable solutions to commonly occurring problems" [12], have been part of software engineering for many years and are well-established [1], [5]. Design patterns provide a guide to "best practices" but not a final implementation. They provide scalable design structures allowing one to focus, understand, and reason more easily about the parallel algorithms. With the widespread introduction of multicore and many core systems, there has been some effort to make parallel and distributed programming easier and useable by using design patterns. Mattson, Sanders, and Massingill wrote an influential book promoting patterns for parallel programs in 2004 [8]. A pattern programming language called OPL (Our Pattern Language) was co-developed at the Universal Parallel Computing Research Centers (UPCRC) at University of Illinois at Urbana-Champaign and University of California, Berkeley with significant funding support from Microsoft and Intel. OPL is described by Keutzer and Mattson [6]. Twelve computational patterns are used: Finite State Machines, Circuits, Graph Algorithms, Structured Grid, Dense Matrix, Sparse Matrix, Spectral (FFT), Dynamic Programming, Particle Methods, Backtrack, Graphical Models, and Unstructured Grid, in seven general application areas. UPCRC promotes patterns in workshops on parallel programming patterns, ParaPLoP 2009, 2010, and 2011, and the Pattern Languages for Programs conference PloP'2009.

Intel has developed somewhat competing tools that use patterns; Thread Building blocks (TBB), Cilk Plus, and Array Building Blocks (ArBB). They embody low-level patterns such as fork-join. McCool, Reinders, and Robison wrote a recent book on using patterns in parallel programming, focusing on the Intel tools [9]. Microsoft describes using patterns in the .NET/C# environment [10] but again with low level patterns such as parallel for loops.

The closest to our work is Fastflow [4] from the University of Torino, Italy/Università di Pisa but uses C++ and focuses on shared-memory platforms.

Much of the quoted work tends to concentrate upon lower-level constructs such as fork-join and parallel loops – we concentrate upon a few higher-level and widely applicable computational patterns such as workpool and synchronous all-to-all. We also provide an automatic and seamless conversion into executable code for parallel and distributed platforms. All the related work mentioned in this section concentrates upon professional or research environments. We are interested in training students in a better way and introducing the pattern programming strategy in an undergraduate parallel programming course with automated pattern programming tools.

Note on terminology. Sometimes term "skeleton" is used to describe a "pattern", especially a directed acyclic graph with a source, a computation, and a sink. We do not make that distinction and use the term "pattern" whether a directed or undirected graph and whether acyclic or cyclic.

3. PATTERN PROGRAMMING FRAMEWORK

3.1 Patterns

Figure 1 shows perhaps the most useful pattern, the workpool pattern. In this pattern, the master process sends tasks to worker or slave processes for them to perform. Our framework implements this pattern with a task queue within the master that hands out tasks to waiting worker processes. When a worker process completes a task and returns results to the master, the master gives it a new task to do, which provides automatic load balancing for the programmer. A tutorial has been written to use this pattern in our framework, complete with sample code [15].

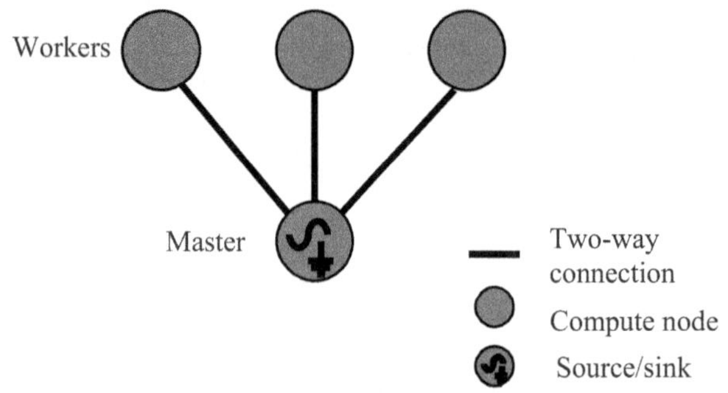

Figure 1 Workpool pattern.

Figure 2 shows another pattern implemented in our framework, the pipeline pattern. The master process sends a task to the first worker, which does some computation and passes the result onto the next worker and so on. In some ways, a pipeline models a normal sequential program, which has statements executed one after the other and could be introduced to students that way, but the pattern would particularly suit a situation in which data is fed from one process to the next. Bubble sort can map onto a pipeline as well as digital filtering. A tutorial has been written to use this pattern in our framework, complete with sample code [16].

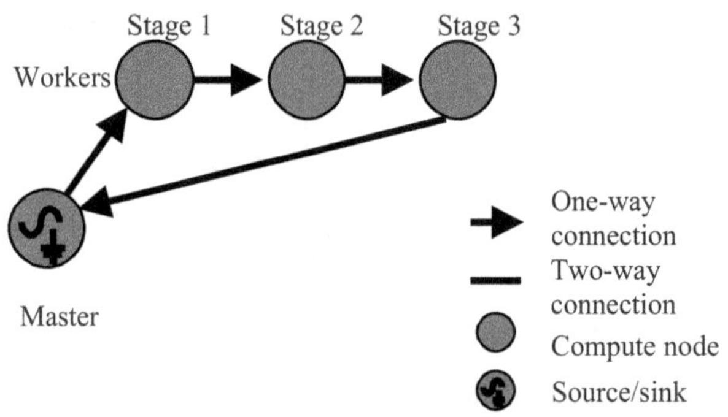

Figure 2 Pipeline pattern.

Figure 3 show the divide and conquer pattern, which has not yet been fully implemented in the framework, but the programmer can create it using more advanced tools in the framework. In the (binary) divide and conquer pattern, a problem is divided into two parts and then these parts are divided into two parts and so on until the problems has been divided into sufficiently small sub-problems. These are then computed and a reverse process is used to create the final result. Several well-known algorithms use divide and conquer such as Quicksort and Mergesort.

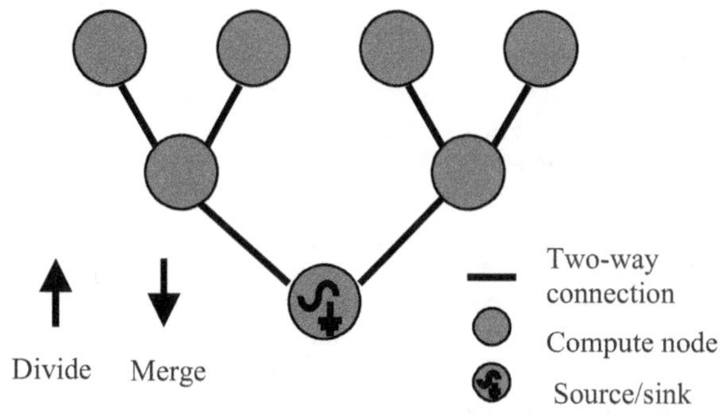

Figure 3 Divide and conquer pattern.

Figure 4 shows the synchronous stencil pattern, which is implemented in our framework. This pattern performs a number of iterations to converge on a solution, for example for solving Laplace's/heat equation by iteration. A tutorial has been written to use this pattern in our framework, complete with sample code [17].

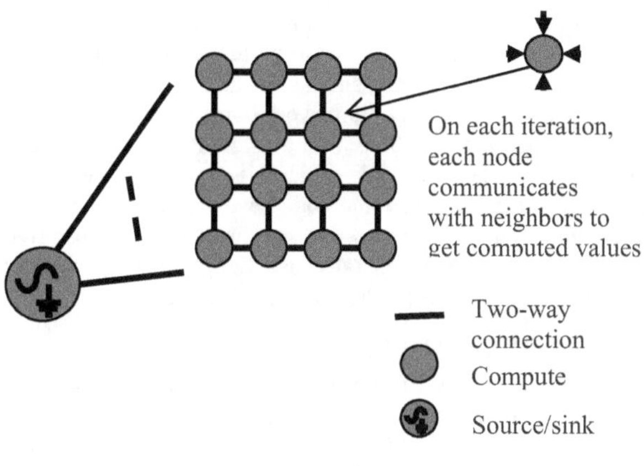

Figure 4 Stencil pattern.

Figure 5 shows the all-to-all pattern. In this pattern, each slave process can communicate with any of the other slave processes, which provides the most general of communication pattern. This is also the worst case scenario for message passing but certain problems may require it. An example of this pattern is the gravitational N-body problem using the brute force $O(N^2)$ algorithm that computes the force on each body due to all the other bodies. Solving a dense system of linear equations with n equations and n unknowns may also use an all-to-all pattern.

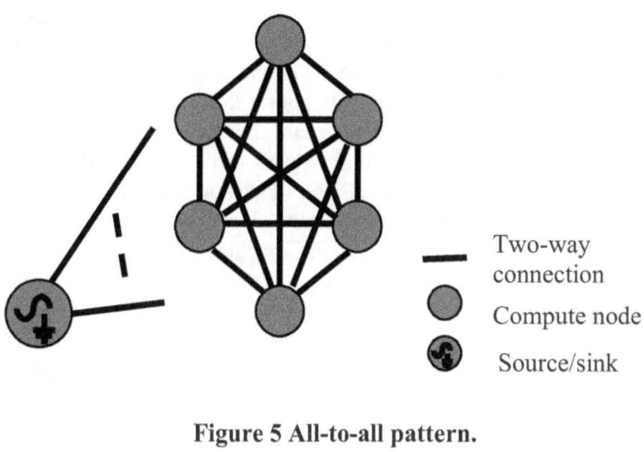

Figure 5 All-to-all pattern.

Both the N-body problem and iterative problems that converge on a solution such as solving linear equations by iteration require the all-to-all pattern to be repeated a number of times with the results of one iteration passed to all the nodes before the next iteration. Our framework implements the all-to-all pattern that includes this synchronous iteration feature. We call the pattern the CompleteSyncGraph pattern. At the end of each iteration, workers synchronize and update their data and proceed to new computations. The master node and framework will not gain control of the data flow until all the iterations have finished. A tutorial has been written to use this pattern in our framework, complete with sample code [20].

Our CompleteSyncGraph pattern is really two patterns, an all-to-all pattern and a loop iteration. We do have a pattern operator that can combine patterns. An example is shown in Figure 6. Here, the synchronous all-to-all pattern is added to a stencil pattern.

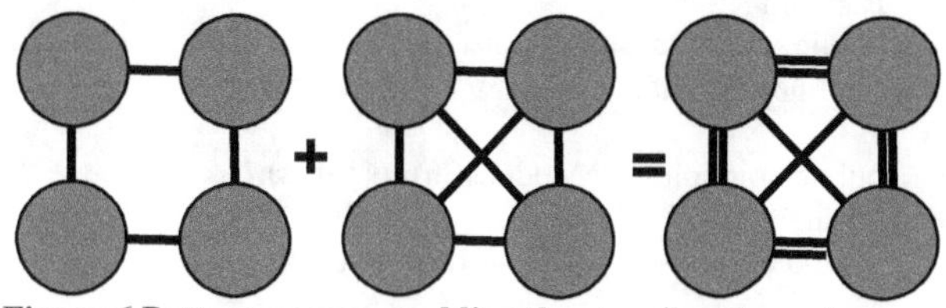

Figure 6 Pattern operator adding the stencil and synchronous all-to-all pattern.

An example use of the pattern in Figure 6 would be solving the Heat equation (which calculates static heat distribution). The stencil pattern is repeated until global termination conditions are met. Since the programmer does not have direct control over the repeating pattern, it is difficult to check for termination based upon computed values without stopping the computation completely. The added all-to-all pattern enables termination to be checked at each node. More information on using our pattern operator in this fashion can be found at [18].

3.2 User Interface

The framework is constructed in three layers, the "basic" layer, the "advanced" layer, and the "expert" layer. The basic layer provides standard well-established patterns, and the programmer need only implement a few simple Java interface methods. The advanced layer exposes some of the internal routines to enable new patterns to be created or existing patterns to be optimized. The expert layer exposes the deployment and security services for the programmer who wants to increase the performance. We use the basic layer in our undergraduate parallel programming class.

To create and execute parallel programs, the basic layer programmer selects an existing pattern and implements three principal Java methods:

- Diffuse method – to distribute pieces of data.
- Compute method – the actual computation
- Gather method – to gather the results

The programmer also completes a "bootstrap" class to deploy and start the framework with the selected pattern. The framework self-deploys on a single multicore computer, a local cluster, or a geographically distributed platform and executes the pattern with the programmer's computation.

As an illustration, consider deploying a workpool pattern to compute π using the well-known Monte Carlo method [15]. The basis of Monte Carlo calculations is the use of random selections. To compute π, a circle is formed within and touching a 2 x 2 square so that the radius of the circle is 1. Points are chosen randomly within the square. The fraction of points that fall within the circle will converge on $\pi/4$ as the number of points increases because (area of circle)/(area of the square) = $\pi r^2/(2 \times 2)$. The code implementing the required framework interface is shown below. Points are chosen in one quadrant in the code.

```
package edu.uncc.grid.example.workpool;
... // import statements
public class MonteCarloPiModule extends Workpool {
    private static final long serialVersionUID = 1L;
    private static final int DoubleDataSize = 1000;
    double total;
    int random_samples;
    Random R;
    public MonteCarloPiModule() {
      R = new Random();
    }
    public void initializeModule(String[] args) {
      total = 0;
      random_samples = 3000; // random samples
    }
    public Data Compute (Data data) {
      DataMap<String,Object>
        input= (DataMap<String,Object>)data;
      DataMap<String, Object>
        output = new DataMap<String, Object>();
      Long seed = (Long) input.get("seed");
      Random r = new Random();
      r.setSeed(seed);
      Long inside = 0L;
    for (int i = 0; i < DoubleDataSize ; i++) {
      double x = r.nextDouble();
      double y = r.nextDouble();
      double dist = x * x + y * y;
      if (dist <= 1.0) ++inside;
    }
    output.put("inside", inside);
    return output;
  }
  public Data DiffuseData (int segment) {
    DataMap<String, Object>
      d =new DataMap<String, Object>();
    d.put("seed", R.nextLong());
    return d; // returns a random seed for each job unit
  }
  public void GatherData (int segment, Data dat) {
    DataMap<String,Object>
      out = (DataMap<String,Object>) dat;
    Long inside = (Long) out.get("inside");
    total += inside; // aggregate answer from all the worker nodes.
    }
    public double getPi() {
      double pi = (total /(random_samples*DoubleDataSize)) * 4;
      return pi;
    }
    public int getDataCount() {
      return random_samples;
    }
  }
```

The bootstrap class to start the framework and deploy the code is given below.

```
package edu.uncc.grid.example.workpool;
... //import statements
public class RunMonteCarloPiModule {
  public static void main(String[] args) {
  try {
    MonteCarloPiModule pi = new MonteCarloPiModule();
    Seeds.start( "/path-to-seeds-folder" , false);
    PipeID id = Seeds.startPattern(new Operand( (String[])null,
      new Anchor( "hostname" ,
      Types.DataFlowRoll.SINK_SOURCE), pi ) );
    System.out.println(id.toString() );
    Seeds.waitOnPattern(id);
    System.out.println( "The result is: " + pi.getPi() ) ;
    Seeds.stop();
    } catch
      ... // exceptions
    }
}
```

The code is given to show the simplicity of the approach. Note that the programmer does not have to write any message passing code. Other patterns are very similar in their requirements, and template code is given on the framework home page [14] together with sample code that can be run on a single PC or a distributed platform. In our class, we ask students to use their own PCs. Tutorials are provided describing code development, compilation and execution using a command line and through the Eclipse IDE [19], [21]. Our students generally use Eclipse because syntax errors and missing classes/methods are quickly highlighted.

4. TEACHING WITH PATTERNS

We propose a new way of teaching parallel programming using the framework described above and have tried this approach at the two universities: UNC-Charlotte and UNC-Wilmington. Classroom teaching at UNC-Charlotte and UNC-Wilmington is based upon a 15-week semester. The regular parallel programming course at UNC-Charlotte is the senior undergraduate course/first year graduate course ITCS 4145/5145, which has been taught for many years. Previously, the course followed the traditional approach of teaching low-level parallel programming tools - MPI message passing programming, OpenMP and thread-based shared memory programming, and since 2010, high performance computing GPU programming using CUDA. Parallel algorithms (numerical algorithms, sorting, searching, and other applications) are covered after the programming tools but over the years fewer algorithms as the focus has been on learning the tools. Similarly, theoretical aspects have been given less prominence. Some of this is driven by the desire to provide students with programming skills using MPI, OpenMP, and CUDA. The applications that students tackle are quite limited – such as matrix multiplication, sorting, and the gravitational N-body problem. Students use a cluster of servers dedicated to teaching parallel and distributed computing. The course is very popular and typically closes very quickly at its maximum of 50 students. A similar class has been taught at UNC-Wilmington for many years.

For the Fall 2012 class, we substantially revised the course to start with the pattern approach. In addition, the course was co-taught between UNC-Charlotte and UNC-Wilmington on the North Carolina Research and Education Network (NCREN), a televideo network that connects most North Carolina universities and colleges. The course now focuses on higher-level computational strategies and not only uses the pattern programming approach described here but also introduces a C/C++ based compiler directive approach described elsewhere [2], [3]. We still cover MPI, OpenMP, and CUDA but after computation strategies and using patterns with our framework. Students will still need to understand how to program at a lower level but now with a design philosophy that is applicable to larger applications. Table 1 shows the outline of the re-designed course.

Table 1. Course topics

Parallel Computing	Demand for computational speed, grand challenge problems, potential speed-up using multiple processors, speed-up factor, max speed-up, Amdahl's law, Gustafson's law.
Parallel Computers	Types of parallel computers, shared memory systems, multicore, distributed memory systems, networked computers clusters, GPU systems.
Pattern Programming	Parallel patterns for structured parallel programming, workpool, pipeline, divide and conquer, stencil, all-to-all patterns, advantages of patterns, Seeds framework, user interface, programming examples
Assignment 1	Using the Seeds Pattern Programming Framework: 1 - Workpool
Lower-level message-passing computing - MPI	Message-passing programming, MPI, point-to-point message passing, message tags, MPI communicator, blocking send/recv, compiling and executing MPI programs, instrumenting code for execution time, Eclipse IDE Parallel Tools Platform. MPI collective routines, broadcast, scatter, gather, reduce, barrier, synchronous message passing, asynchronous (non-blocking) message passing, changing to synchronous message passing.
Assignment 2	Compiling and executing MPI programs. Comparison with pattern framework
Synchronous All-To-All pattern	Synchronous All-To-All pattern, gravitational *N*-body problem, Barnes-Hut algorithm, Seeds CompleteSynchGraph pattern, pattern framework code for *N*-body problem.
Divide and conquer pattern	Recursive divide and conquer pattern, example: numerical integration with adaptive quadrature.
Pipeline pattern	Pipeline pattern, examples unfolding loops, insertion sort, prime numbers, upper triangular linear equations. Seeds pipeline pattern, sorting code.
Iterative synchronous All-To-All pattern	Iterative synchronous All-To-All pattern, solving system of linear equations by iteration, Seeds CompleteSynchGraph pattern, Jacobi iteration, convergence rate.
Stencil pattern	Stencil pattern, applications, heat distribution problem, Seeds code, cellular automata, game of life, partially synchronous method.
Compiler directive approach	Introduction to Paraguin compiler, parallel region, forall, broadcast, gather, examples
Assignment 3	Using Paraguin to create MPI programs using the workpool pattern.
Programming with Shared Memory	Processes, threads, issues, interleaved statements, thread safe routines, re-ordering code, compiler/processor optimizations, accessing shared data, critical sections, locks, condition variables, deadlock, semaphores, monitors, Pthreads program example, dependency analysis (Bernstein's conditions), serializing code, cache false sharing, sequential consistency.
OpenMP	OpenMP directives/constructs, parallel, shared and local variables, work-sharing, sections, for, loop scheduling, for reduction, single master, critical, barrier, atomic, flush.
Assignment 4	Using Paraguin to create MPI programs, Sobel edge detection, and hybrid MPI/OpenMP
Data parallel pattern	Data parallel pattern, examples, data parallel prefix sum algorithm, matrix multiplication, introduction to HPC GPU systems and CUDA
Assignment 5	CUDA programs using GPU server, vector addition and heat distribution problem, with graphics.
Parallel algorithms (in various places throughout course)	Parallelizing matrix multiplication, block multiplication, recursive algorithm, mesh algorithms, Cannon's algorithm, systolic array, solving system of linear equations, direct and iterative methods, red-black, multigrid, potential speedup of sorting in parallel, compare and exchange, bubble sort, odd-even transposition sort, mergesort, quicksort, odd-even mergesort, bitonic mergesort, shearsort, rank sort, counting sort, radix sort.

As with the pre-pattern programming version of the parallel programming course, we have programming assignments (one every 2-3 weeks) to support the concepts presented in the lectures. The first programming assignment asks students to use our framework with the workpool pattern on their own PC (or a lab computer). From our previous experiences in large distributed computing courses [11], we find it much better to have students use their own computers rather than log onto centralized servers to do assignments, especially for code development, when possible to avoid servers being overloaded with a large number of concurrent processes. For Assignment 1, students have to install our framework (and Java and Eclipse if they do not have these). The basic Monte Carlo π code is given but students also have to develop code to perform matrix multiplication. The next assignment asks students to implement the same problems with the workpool pattern but using MPI. Students compare using the pattern framework with lower-level MPI coding approach. Subsequent assignments explore more patterns and also OpenMP with MPI. Compiler directives are also explored as a higher-level approach. Finally, we cover GPUs and CUDA as in previous course offerings but only after introducing the data parallel pattern that is the basis of GPUs and CUDA.

5. CONCLUSIONS

This paper describes an approach for teaching parallel programming by first starting with higher-level computational patterns. We have developed a new software framework that enables parallel and distributed programs to be implemented and executed on a parallel or distributed platform without needing to write low-level message passing code. Advantages of patterns include:

- Reduces programmer errors
- Abstracts/hides underlying computing environment
- Reduces source code size (lines of code)
- Leads to an automated conversion into parallel programs without using low level message-passing routines.
- Hierarchical designs can be created with patterns embedded into patterns, and pattern operators to combine patterns.

Disadvantages of patterns include:

- New approach to learn
- Takes away some of the freedom from programmer
- Performance is reduced slightly

We strongly believe that our approach builds a foundation for students to tackle larger professional applications by thinking about established higher-level patterns first.

6. ACKNOWLEDGMENTS

This material is based upon work supported by the National Science Foundation under the collaborative grant #1141005/1141006. Any opinions, findings, and conclusions or recommendations expressed in this material are those of the authors and do not necessarily reflect the views of the National Science Foundation.

7. REFERENCES

[1] Astrachan, O. 1998. Design Patterns: An Essential Component of CS Curricula, *SIGCSE Bulletin and Proceedings*. 30, 1, 153-160.

[2] Ferner, C.S. 2006. Revisiting communication code generation algorithms for message-passing systems, *International Journal of Parallel, Emergent and Distributed Systems (JPEDS) 21(5)*, 323-344.

[3] Ferner, C. F. 2002. The Paraguin compiler---Message-passing code generation using SUIF, in *Proceedings of the IEEE SoutheastCon 2002*, Columbia, SC, 1-6.

[4] Fastflow. University of Torino, Italy /Università di Pisa. Retrieved December 5, 2012 from http://calvados.di.unipi.it/dokuwiki/doku.php?id=ffnamespace:about

[5] Gamma, E., Helm., R., Johnson, R., and Vlissides, V. 1995. *Design Patterns*. Addison-Wesley, New York.

[6] Keutzer, K., and Mattson, T. n.d. Our Pattern Language (OPL): A Design Pattern Language for Engineering (Parallel) Software. Retrieved December 5, 2012 from http://parlab.eecs.berkeley.edu/wiki/_media/patterns/paraplop_g1_1.pdf.

[7] Intel. n.d. Introducing Intel Many Integrated Core Architecture. Retrieved December 5, 2012 from http://www.intel.com/technology/architecture-silicon/mic/index.htm.

[8] Mattson, T. G., Sanders, B. A., and Massingill, B. L. 2004. *Patterns for Parallel Programming*. Addison Wesley.

[9] McCool, M., Reinders, J., and Robison, A. 2012. *Structured Parallel Programming: Patterns for Efficient Computation*. Morgan Kaufmann.

[10] Microsoft. n.d. Patterns of Parallel Programming Understanding and Applying Parallel Patterns with the .Net Framework 4. Retrieved December 5, 2012 from http://www.microsoft.com/download/en/details.aspx?displaylang=en&id=19222

[11] Wilkinson, B., and Ferner, C. 2008. Towards a Top-Down Approach to Teaching an Undergraduate Grid Computing Course. *SIGCSE 2008 Technical Symposium on Computer Science Education*. Portland, Oregon.

[12] Wikipedia. n.d. Software Design Patterns. Retrieved December 5, 2012 from http://en.wikipedia.org/wiki/Design_pattern_(computer_science)

[13] Villalobos, J. 2011. *Running Parallel Applications on a Heterogeneous Environment with Accessible Development Practices and Automatic Scalability*. PhD diss. University of North Carolina Charlotte.

[14] Villalobos, J. n.d. Parallel Grid Application Framework. Retrieved December 5, 2012 from http://coit-grid01.uncc.edu/seeds/

[15] Villalobos, J. and Adibolo, Y. K. 2012. Seeds Framework Workpool Template Tutorial. Retrieved December 5, 2012 from http://coitweb.uncc.edu/~abw/seeds/docs/WorkpoolTutorial.pdf

[16] Villalobos, J. n.d. Seeds Framework Pipeline Template Tutorial. Retrieved December 5, 2012 from http://coit-grid01.uncc.edu/seeds/docs/pipeline_tutorial.pdf

[17] Villalobos, J. n.d. Seeds Framework Stencil Template Tutorial. Retrieved December 5, 2012 from http://coit-grid01.uncc.edu/seeds/docs/stencil.pdf

[18] Villalobos, J. n.d. Seeds Framework Pattern Operator Template Tutorial. Retrieved December 5, 2012 from http://coit-grid01.uncc.edu/seeds/docs/PatternOperator.pdf

[19] Villalobos, J. n.d. Seeds Development with Eclipse. Retrieved December 5, 2012 from http://coit-grid01.uncc.edu/seeds/docs/seeds_eclipse_tutorial.pdf

[20] Villalobos, J., and Adibolo, Y. K. 2012. Seeds Framework. The CompleteSynchGraph Template Tutorial. Retrieved December 5, 2012 from http://coitweb.uncc.edu/~abw/seeds/docs/CompleteSynchGraphTutorial.pdf

[21] Villalobos, J., and Adibolo, Y. K. 2012. Getting Started With the Seeds Framework: An Introduction to the Seeds Framework in a Shared Memory Environment. Retrieved December 5, 2012 from http://coitweb.uncc.edu/~abw/seeds/docs/GettingStartedSeeds.pdf

Parallel from the Beginning: The Case for Multicore Programming in the Computer Science Undergraduate Curriculum

Yousun Ko
Yonsei University
Seoul, Korea
yousun.ko@cs.yonsei.ac.kr

Bernd Burgstaller
Yonsei University
Seoul, Korea
bburg@cs.yonsei.ac.kr

Bernhard Scholz
The University of Sydney
Syndney, Australia
scholz@it.usyd.edu.au

ABSTRACT

The computing landscape has shifted towards multicore architectures. To learn about software development, it is increasingly important for students to gain hands-on parallel programming experience in multicore environments. This experience will be significantly different from programming for uniprocessors, because it involves a profound understanding of how to write software that is (1) free of concurrency bugs and (2) able to effectively utilize the underlying parallel hardware architecture. We present our work at Yonsei University and The University of Sydney to teach parallel programming to first and second-year undergraduate students. Our objective is to introduce parallelism early on in the curriculum, to instill it as a first principle of computation. We introduce a series of five parallel programming course modules suitable for a one semester introductory programming course. Each module teaches one fundamental concept of parallel programming: parallelism and execution indeterminism, thread-and-lock based programming, performance of parallel programs, hardware acceleration using OpenCL, and stream-parallel programming with StreamIt. We report our experience from four course offerings (2008–2011) at Yonsei University, and two course offerings at The University of Sydney. Over 73% of students surveyed enjoyed this multicore programming experience and preferred exposure to parallelism at this early stage of their CS education. Our course has been awarded an Intel microgrant for "Parallelism in the Classroom", and it is available online at Intel's Multicore Curriculum Initiative Website.

Categories and Subject Descriptors

K.3.2 [**Computers and Education**]: Computer and Information Science Education—*Computer Science Education*

General Terms

Human Factors, Languages, Theory, Experimentation

SIGCSE'13, March 6–9, 2013, Denver, Colorado, USA.

Keywords

Introductory programming; multicore computing development/education; computer science education; course design

1. INTRODUCTION

The recent shift to multicore processors has made concurrency a core concept of Computer Science. Because of the rapid proliferation of multicore processors in all areas of computing, there is now demand for a large number of computer science graduates who can exploit the power of these architectures through efficient and reliable concurrent programming. This growing importance for concurrency in the classroom is recognized in the ACM CS2008 Curriculum Update [2], which recommends a course on "Parallel Computation" to support "*effective parallel programming*".

The increased emphasis on concurrency contrasts with current practice, which frequently considers parallelism as an afterthought to writing single-threaded applications. In particular, introductory programming courses are commonly taught using sequential programming. Parallel programming concepts are often introduced at a later stage in the curriculum, as a senior-level undergraduate or graduate elective. When students finally encounter parallel programming, many perceive the transition from sequential to parallel thinking as difficult.

To overcome the above difficulties, we argue that students should be introduced to the fundamentals of multicore programming already early on in the CS curriculum. Learning about the ubiquity of multicore architectures raises students' awareness and interest, and existing parallel programming hurdles are then accepted by necessity. The popularity of multicore architectures can be used to create engaging course materials and programming projects.

We present our work on an introductory one-semester parallel programming course that we have developed and taught over a four-year period at Yonsei University and The University of Sydney. Target students were in their second or third semester, and they had no prior knowledge of computer architectures, operating systems or algorithms. All students had experience with C programming.

Because our target students had no prior knowledge on parallelism and were at a very early stage of their computer science education, we put thorough emphasis on the foundations of parallel programming. Programming for performance was particularly highlighted, because it is the main reason for utilizing multicore architectures. We included thread-and-lock based programming in C, to acquaint students with the current state-of-the-art, and we chose the stream-parallel programming language StreamIt [17] as a representative for the yet-to-come multicore productivity languages. (With StreamIt, a programmer writes programs in the form of actors that communicate through first-in/first-out data channels. All synchronization and parallelization is left to the compiler and run-time system.) We decided to include hardware accelerators, because heterogeneous architectures consisting of a multicore CPU and a general-purpose graphics processing unit (GPGPU) nowadays constitute the major computing platform with desktops, servers and embedded systems. For GPGPU-programming we selected OpenCL [11] over CUDA-C [1], because OpenCL is a platform-independent standard supported by all major GPGPU manufacturers. For historical reasons and a lack of stable, available OpenCL platforms, the initial three course offerings used the Sony PS3 as the underlying hardware platform [3]. On several occasions in the course, we applied parallel programming design patterns from [13].

We structured the course as five course modules suitable for a one semester parallel programming course. Each module teaches one fundamental concept of parallel programming, i.e., (1) parallelism and execution indeterminism, (2) thread-and-lock based programming, (3) performance of parallel programs, (4) hardware acceleration using OpenCL, and (5) stream-parallelism with StreamIt. Each module is accompanied by individual programming assignments. A team term project gave students free choice of programming language and programming problem.

All parallel programming concepts were introduced with the help of very small, worked-out programming examples. Considerable time was spent on stripping off all possible clutter, to put the concept under investigation figuratively under a magnifying glass. Compileable versions of the example programs were made available for student experimentation. Example programs turned out as valuable code-templates for assignments and term projects, too.

Over 73% of students surveyed enjoyed this multicore programming experience and preferred exposure to parallelism at this early stage of their CS education. Our course has been awarded an Intel microgrant for "Parallelism in the Classroom", and it is available online at Intel's Multicore Curriculum Initiative Website.

2. COURSE MODULES

2.1 Parallelism and Execution Indeterminism

This module starts with a brief outline of the history of computing, to motivate the recent shift to multicore architectures. We chose an analogy from cooking to introduce task, data and pipeline parallelism: A cooking recipe asks to (1) wash salad, (2) chop tomatoes, and (3) apply dressing to prepare a salad. A single chef can only manage these tasks sequentially. To speed up the process, a second chef is introduced. The availability of the second chef allows us to task-parallelize tasks (1) and (2). We observe the dependency of task (3) on tasks (1) and (2). The dependence relation on task dependence graphs is formally introduced. By introducing additional chefs we are able to data-parallelize tasks (1) and (2) among several chefs. Students observe that at some stage (e.g., with 100 chefs) the amount of work per chef and hence the achievable speedup becomes too small to justify further parallelization. The example concludes with the analogy of pipeline-parallelism and factory assembly lines.

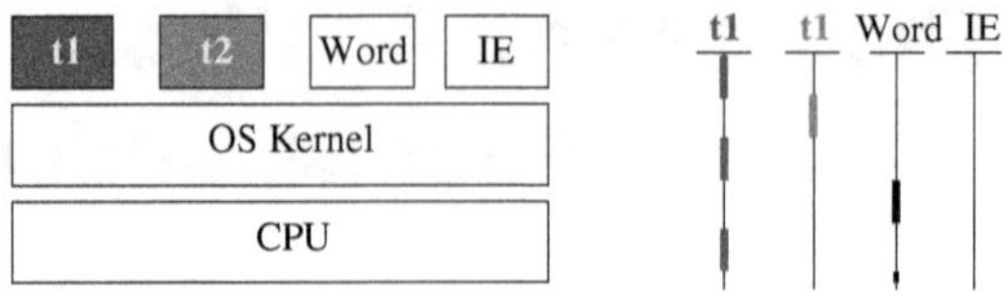

Figure 1: OS scheduling, concurrency and execution indeterminism between threads on a uniprocessor. Word processor ("Word") and web browser ("IE") are examples of applications first-year students are already familiar with.

To relate task-parallelism to a concrete example from computer science, a task-parallel loop to sum up an array of integers is shown. Data-parallelism is illustrated with CPU vector registers.

With the initial three course offerings we used the vector registers of the Cell BE synergistic processing units (SPE), which provide an accessible programming model through intrinsics [7]. With the 2011 offering, we employed the newly-introduced x86 AVX vector extensions [8]. AVX2 vector extensions will first be introduced with Intel's Haswell processor in 2013, but we had students execute AVX2-based programs on Intel's SDE emulator [9] that we provided with our lab environment. For stream-parallelism, we mention rendering pipelines of graphic cards, and our treatment of StreamIt in Module 5.

Fig. 1 depicts the basic view of OSs and thread scheduling to explain execution indeterminism and concurrency on a uniprocessor (it should be noted that for students without prior training on OSs, the provided explanations have turned out to be the minimum amount of prerequisites necessary for this course). Students understand that a single CPU is multiplexed by the OS between several threads (time-sharing). No assumption must be made about the execution order of threads. A similar figure is used to introduce physical parallelism of threads on a multicore CPU. We then discuss how to create POSIX threads (pthreads). Students are asked to create four threads with each thread executing a distinct a `printf()` statement in a loop. Reflection on the order of the print statements (execution indeterminism) and on the thread-safety of `printf()` conclude the module.

2.2 Thread-and-Lock Based Programming

We introduce race-conditions through another real-world example: a procedure to withdraw money from a bank-account is used concurrently from two ATMs. The total amount of money is a shared data-item, and the simultaneous withdrawal exhibits a race condition where one ATM overwrites the new total written back by the other ATM. We then illustrate the fact that even a variable update, e.g., `i++`, bears a potential race-condition due to its read-modify-write semantics. We provide the example program illustrated in Fig. 2 to allow students to observe race-conditions. The thread function in lines 4–8 of Fig. 2 is executed by multiple threads in parallel. Access to the shared `ctr` variable is heavily affected by race conditions. A `printf()` statement before program termination (lines 12–14) compares the expected (race-free) counter value with the observed counter value,

```
1  #define ITER 10000000
2  long ctr = 0;
3
4  void * thread_function(void * arg) {
5      long l;
6      for (l=0; l < ITER; l++)
7          ctr = ctr + 1; //critical section
8  }
9
10 ...
11
12 printf("Expected value: %lld , "
13        "observed value: %lld\n",
14        ITER * nr_threads, ctr);
```

Figure 2: Code to enforce race conditions between threads accessing the shared `ctr` variable.

to determine the number of occurred data-races. (Note that the `void *` argument of the thread function (line 4) is required with POSIX threads, even if the argument is not used.) This example serves as the motivation for synchronization to establish mutual exclusion for access to shared data. By enclosing the critical section in line 7 with a POSIX mutex, the program becomes race-free. Students observe the dramatic speed-down compared to a sequential solution, which is due to *serialization* of threads. We observe the potentially adverse effect of synchronization on performance and scalability. An example where a long-running, non-race computation is moved out of the critical section, illustrates the necessity to keep the time spent inside critical sections to a minimum.

Deadlocks are introduced through Dijkstra's Dining Philosophers problem. Demonstrating this problem with students in class turned out to be a valuable change to the classroom routine. Each student embodies one philosopher, and philosophers are asked to eat and think, while synchronizing on their left-hand and right-hand side pens (chopsticks). Students are then asked to proceed at the same time, to experience the resulting deadlock.

Locking-hierarchies are introduced to overcome deadlocks. A thread-based implementation of dinning philosophers is provided to students to (1) observe the deadlock and (2) fix the concurrency bug by introducing a locking hierarchy. Students are asked to implement a linked list where each node is protected by a lock. Operations on multiple nodes (e.g., adding and deleting nodes) requires students to decide on a locking hierarchy. We introduce semaphores as an extension of mutexes, to allow acquisition (`P()`) and relinquishing (`V()`) operations from different threads. With this mechanism students are asked to enforce particular execution orders among threads. Coarse-grained and fine-grained locks are introduced using an example of a data-structure consisting of several linked lists. The module concludes with the discussion of barriers and a parallel implementation of Conway's game of life based on a barrier.

2.3 Performance of Parallel Programs

At this stage of the course we usually observed students asking the inevitable question on the course discussion forum: "Why is my parallel program slower than the sequential version?". This course module on performance thus discusses profiling, quantification of performance, and common performance bottlenecks.

We start with the definition of *speedup*, scalability and efficiency, and then present Amdahl's Law, to make students aware of the sequential portion of an application that is going to limit the possible speedup. We then discuss profiling of program code, to enable students to compute the achieved speedup. In the simplest case, students employ the Linux time utility to derive the overall program execution time. To measure particular portions of code, glibc's `gettimeofday()` function is used. For the 2011 offering of the course we gratefully received a classroom license for Intel's VTune performance profiler, which turned out an effective and easy-to-use tool (we provided students with a guideline on how to run VTune on our lab environment).

The major portion of this module is about performance bottlenecks and how to avoid them. We based our slides on Lin and Snyder's excellent description of sources of performance loss [12]. Our case-study focuses on false sharing of cachelines, a performance bug where two threads share a single cache-line to store thread-private data. Because the memory hierarchy is managed in units of cache-lines, the shared cache-line needs to be copied back and forth between the L1-caches of the associated threads, resulting in a huge performance degradation. Because our target students do not have prior training with computer architecture, we again extracted those concepts related to caches which are necessary to understand false sharing (see e.g., Fig. 3). A similar case-study for false sharing has already been described elsewhere [12], so we omit ours here for space considerations.

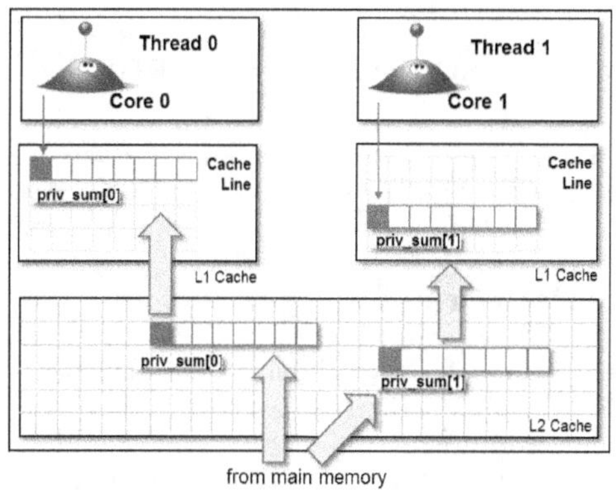


```
struct padded_int {
    unsigned long long value;
    char padding[56]; //64-byte cache lines
} private_sum[nr_threads];
```

Figure 3: Caches and padded thread-local counters to avoid false sharing.

2.4 Programming of Hardware Accelerators Using OpenCL

We introduce heterogeneous multicore architectures, i.e., multicore computers that contain processing cores of diverse hardware architectures. For the initial three offerings of this course we used the Cell BE processor, which consists of a PowerPC core and 8 synergistic processing units. For the 2011 offering, we switched to the OpenCL platform model, which consists of a general-purpose host CPU (e.g., an x86 multicore CPU), and one or more OpenCL GPGPU devices. Each GPGPU device contains several compute units (CUs), with each CU providing a number of processing elements

(PEs). The OpenCL platform model is supported by all major CPU and GPGPU vendors, which makes it attractive as a hardware platform for a parallel programming course.

To be able to program GPGPUs, students need to understand the data-parallel, kernel-based OpenCL execution model and the software-exposed local memories provided by GPGPUs. (For a comprehensive treatment, we refer to the courses' reference textbooks [14, 4].)

```
float in[MAX];
float result[MAX];

void scalar_sqr(int n,
                const float *in,
                float *result) {
   int i;
   for (i=0; i<n; i++)
      result[i] = in[i] * in[i];
}
```

(a) Scalar execution model of CPUs

```
__kernel void sqr_kernel(__global const float *in,
                         __global float *result)
{
    int id = get_global_id(0);

    result[id] = in[id] * in[id];

} // execute in parallel over n work-items
```

(b) Kernel-based OpenCL execution model

Figure 4: Comparison of the execution models of CPUs and OpenCL-programmed GPGPUs.

In Fig. 4 we show how the well-known scalar execution model of CPUs relates to GPGPUs. The example routine squares an array of integers. The key point to understand for students is that the n iterations of the `for`-loop of the scalar execution model are replaced by n data-parallel invocations of the OpenCL kernel of Fig. 4(b). Each kernel invocation processes one so-called work-item. Work-items receive their thread-id through function `get_global_id()`. Based on this thread-id, a work item locates its assigned work-item.

To make the transition from pthreads to OpenCL kernels easier for students, we provide a programming assignment where students are asked to emulate the OpenCL kernel of Fig. 4(b) using pthreads. Students need to create a thread for each work item; the kernel function becomes the thread's work function, and the work-item is accessed through the pthread id. At this stage of the course students are already very familiar with pthreads, which facilitates the transition to OpenCL kernels.

OpenCL work-items need to be partitioned into workgroups, because workgroups are assigned to the CUs of a GPGPU device. We introduce this partitioning mechanism to students, but we also encourage students to experiment with the auto-partitioning mechanism that recent versions of the OpenCL standard provide.

We found that students understand quickly how to work with software-exposed local memories. From a schematic diagram of a heterogeneous multicore architecture, separated memories are easily explained. However, to point out the consequences for software, we employ the code-snippet depicted in Fig. 5. The purpose of this code-snippet is to illustrate that the CPU (host) cannot directly access GPGPU

```
int i; // Variable in host memory

int main(int argc, char **argv) {
   i++; // ok
   j++; // Forbidden, the host
        // cannot access GPGPU memory!
}

__kernel void f(__global float *in) {

    int j; // variable in GPGPU memory

    j++; // ok
    i++; // Forbidden, GPGPU kernel
         // cannot access host memory!
}
```

Figure 5: Illustration of the separate memory spaces of CPU (host) and GPGPU (device).

memory and vice versa. We conclude this example with the data transfer mechanisms to copy data between host and GPGPU. Before a kernel can execute, data buffers need to be allocated on the GPGPU, and the kernel's input data needs to be transferred from CPU main memory to a data buffer on the GPGPU. After kernel execution, the kernel's output data needs to be transferred back to main memory. Data-transfers constitute mostly boiler-plate code, that we provide to students in source-code as well. The same holds for the code to load, compile and run OpenCL kernels on a GPGPU [14, 4].

In the final part of our module on hardware accelerators we discuss matrix multiplication on the GPGPU. Matrix multiplication is a computation that contains plenty of data-parallelism, and hence maps well onto GPGPUs. Starting with the sequential version, we develop a series of OpenCL kernels to improve kernel performance. In particular, we (1) let each work-item compute one row of the result matrix, and (2) we utilize the local and private memories of the GPGPU. We continue with an exposition of the memory consistency on GPGPUs. Because GPGPU memory consistency is extremely weak, and the rules are simple, students did not experience difficulties with this issue. We conclude this module with a discussion of kernel profiling. We deliberately excluded memory-coalescing and branch divergence optimizations, as those are very involved, and increasingly ineffective with newer GPGPU generations.

2.5 StreamIt

As the final module of the course, after a large amount of at times laborious work to acquire the state-of-the-art in parallel programming, we wanted to provide students with an outlook on the possible future of multicore programming. We chose StreamIt [17] as our representative for the yet-to-come multicore productivity languages. StreamIt was designed for applications that process regular streams of data. With StreamIt, a programmer writes code for so-called actors, which are connected through first-in/first-out data channels. All synchronization and parallelization is left to the compiler and run-time system. The StreamIt actor model abstracts away the underlying hardware, and the semantics of the language is compact so that it can be explained in a short amount of time. To compare the thread-and-lock based programming with StreamIt, students were

	2010 (Cell BE)	2011 (GPGPU)
Average	44%	73%
Stddev.	30%	32%

Table 1: Average and standard deviation of exam scores for programming questions related to hardware accelerators, i.e., the Cell BE and GPGPUs.

asked to implement a gray-scale conversion algorithm for RGB images both with threads and for StreamIt.

3. STUDENT WORK AND RESULTS

Students worked on individual programming assignments during the course of the semester. For space limitations, we only enumerate these assignments here: Monte-Carlo Pi computation, gray-scale conversion of PPM images, concurrent linked-list data structure, semaphores-based ordering of threads, Conway's Game of Life, performance profiling and elimination of false sharing, maze solving, OpenCL kernel simulation with pthreads, computing the power of a matrix with OpenCL.

Term projects were conducted in teams of 1–6 students. Students were free to choose a particular programming problem and implementation language. For the initial three course offerings, term project development was conducted on 8 Sony PS3s; In 2011, two PCs with NVIDIA GTX 275 GPGPUs were introduced. For all course offerings, a 2-CPU (8 cores) server was provided, too. This server was used by students who did not employ hardware accelerators. All computers were running Linux.

Categories	2010 (Cell)		2011 (GPGPU)	
Game alg.	12	(13.3%)	7	(10.4%)
AI	—	—	7	(10.4%)
Math	6	(6.6%)	17	(25.3%)
Ray tracing	7	(7.7%)	4	(5.9%)
Particle simulation	1	(1.1%)	4	(5.9%)
Security	27	(30.0%)	8	(11.9%)
Audio/Image/Video	32	(35.5%)	11	(16.4%)
Others	—	—	2	(2.9%)
Withdrawal	5	(5.5%)	9	(13.4%)
Total	90		67	

Table 2: Preference of students on term project topics

Table 2 depicts the number of students grouped according to term-project application areas, for the 2010 and 2011 course offerings. "Withdrawal" denotes students who did not submit a term project, and "Total" denotes the overall number of students who finished the course. Students seemed slightly more comfortable on GPGPUs than on the Cell BE. On the Cell BE, students showed a tendency to pick Audio/Image/Video analysis & transformations, as well as Security, which they could have experienced from programming assignments. With GPGPUs, the selected topics show a broader spectrum.

Because this course has a particular emphasis on performance, we surveyed term-projects with respect to utilization of hardware accelerators and achieved performance. In Table 3, row "Pthread" denotes the number of students who managed to parallelize their project using pthreads.

	2010 (Cell)	2011 (GPGPU)
Pthreads	82 (96.4%)	52 (89.6%)
Pthreads & accelerator	35 (41.1%)	32 (55.1%)
Speedup	36 (42.3%)	27 (46.5%)
Total	85	58

Table 3: Term project parallelization approach

Row "Pthread with accelerator" denotes the number of students who utilized the provided hardware accelerators (CELL SPEs for the year 2010, and GPGPUs in 2011). With the Cell BE, some teams performed vectorization to utilize the vector-registers of the SPEs. Slightly more students (55.1%) were able to extend their programs to the GPGPU, as opposed to 41.1% on the Cell BE. Row "Speedup" denotes the percentage of term projects where the achieved speedup was according to the expectation for the programming problem at hand (achieved with pthreads and/or accelerators). Again, students achieved better performance on GPGPUs event though their topics had a broader scope and were more challenging. This is backed by the data from Table 1, which indicates that during exams (paper and pencil programming), students achieved a substantially higher score on GPGPU-related topics than on the Cell.

More than half of the class (57.6% for the Cell and 53.5% for GPGPUs) could not achieve reasonable speedups even from POSIX threads alone. This seems like a high number; however, parallel programming of heterogeneous multicore architectures is by no means a trivial task, and less so for early undergraduate students. Some students had the tendency to start late or they underestimated the complexity of their term project topic, which might also have had impact on speedups. In general we believe that having almost half of an undergraduate class achieving competitive speedups on a heterogeneous multicore architecture is a reasonable achievement.

We conducted a survey among the students of the 2011 course offering at Yonsei University, where students are expected to take this course during their second year. The majority of students (72%) prefers to learn about parallel programming in Year 2, twenty percent would prefer Year 3, the remaining eight percent are evenly divided between Year 1 and Year 4. Students provided feedback on the course:

- *"I think this class could not be better."*
- *"Without this course, learning OS will be impossible."*
- *"It was the most interesting class I'd ever take."*
- *"Good for job."*
- *"I found something like forward-seeing feelings."*
- *"This lecture was first of a kind, I like that."*

When asked, on what topic students want to develop further, 35% of the 2011 students named OpenCL.

4. RELATED WORK

Several researchers have already investigated teaching parallel programming at the undergraduate level. Parallel programming with data-structures has been considered in [10, 6]. The application of parallel computing to all areas of the undergraduate curriculum is discussed in [15]. A parallel language and an interactive programming environment for teaching elementary school students are introduced in [5]. A parallelism analysis tool for Java is introduced in [16]. The primary intention is to allow students to find parallelism within Java source code. In contrast, our approach focuses more on programming foundations on heterogeneous multicore architectures, and on performance. Our implementation languages are C, OpenCL and StreamIt. We report the results from four years of teaching experience, and we compare student ability to program GPGPUs vs. the Cell BE processor. There is noticeable agreement that students are motivated to study parallel programming, and that concrete parallel programming examples are beneficial to the students' learning experience.

5. CONCLUSIONS

We have introduced a series of five parallel programming course modules suitable for a one semester introductory multicore programming course for 1st and 2nd-year students. Modules are sufficiently self-contained to be added on a per-module basis to existing introductory sequential programming courses. Our target-students had no prior knowledge of hardware architectures and OSs, which required us to select and convey the minimum prerequisite knowledge that allowed students to comprehend concurrency and execution indeterminism, cache coherence and false sharing, and communication-exposed hardware accelerators. During a one-semester multicore programming course, students became capable of determining the parallelism in a programming problem, apply synchronization where necessary, and we observed a general awareness of performance bugs (esp., false sharing). Programming hardware accelerators was achievable, with a success-rate of 46% for obtaining speed-ups. Our experience from four course offerings at Yonsei University, and two course offerings at The University of Sydney show that undergraduate students are both eager and capable to master multicore programming. Over 73% of students surveyed prefer to learn about parallel programming in the 2nd year of their undergraduate education. Early undergraduate students who had acquired thread-and-lock based programming skills were more open to novel and "unusual" multicore programming languages such as StreamIt than a control-group of graduate students with no prior training on parallel programming. At the time of writing, four capstone projects have applied multicore programming as a direct result of this course [18]. Our course has been awarded an Intel microgrant for "Parallelism in the Classroom", and it is available online at Intel's Multicore Curriculum Initiative Website.

6. ACKNOWLEDGMENTS

Research partially supported by the National Research Foundation of Korea through the Global Ph.D. Fellowship Program 2011 and through grant 2010-0005234; by the Australian Research Council through ARC DP grant DP1096445; by Intel through a microgrant awarded for "Parallelism in the Classroom".

7. REFERENCES

[1] *NVIDIA CUDA Compute Unified Device Architecture—Programming Guide*, 2012. version 4.2.

[2] ACM and IEEE Computer Society. *Computer Science Curriculum 2008: An Interim Revision of CS 2001.* http://www.acm.org/education/curricula/ComputerScience2008.pdf Accessed August 7, 2012.

[3] T. Chen, R. Raghavan, J. N. Dale, and E. Iwata. Cell broadband engine architecture and its first implementation: a performance view. *IBM J. Res. Dev.*, 51(5):559–572, Sept. 2007.

[4] B. R. Gaster, L. Howes, D. R. Kaeli, P. Mistry, and D. Schaa. *Heterogeneous Computing with OpenCL.* Morgan Kaufmann, 2011.

[5] C. Gregg, L. Tychonievich, J. Cohoon, and K. Hazelwood. Ecosim: a language and experience teaching parallel programming in elementary school. In *Proceedings of the 43rd ACM technical symposium on Computer Science Education*, SIGCSE '12, pages 51–56. ACM, 2012.

[6] D. Grossman and R. E. Anderson. Introducing parallelism and concurrency in the data structures course. In *Proceedings of the 43rd ACM technical symposium on Computer Science Education*, SIGCSE '12, pages 505–510, New York, NY, USA, 2012. ACM.

[7] IBM Redbooks. *Programming the Cell BE Architecture: Examples and Best Practices.* 2008.

[8] Intel Advanced Vector Extensions Programming Reference. `http://software.intel.com/en-us/avx`, retrieved Aug. 2012. JUNE 2011 version.

[9] Intel Software Development Emulator (SDE) Web Site. `http://software.intel.com/en-us/articles/intel-software-development-emulator`, retrieved Aug. 2012. SDE version 4.46.0.

[10] D. Johnson, D. Kotz, and F. Makedon. Teaching parallel computing to freshmen. In C. Nevison, editor, *Conference on Parallel Computing for Undergraduates.* Colgate University, June 1994.

[11] Khronos Group. *The OpenCL Specification*, Ver. 1.1, Sep 2010.

[12] C. Lin and L. Snyder. *Principles of Parallel Programming.* Addison-Wesley, 2009.

[13] T. Mattson, B. Sanders, and B. Massingill. *Patterns for parallel programming.* Addison-Wesley, 2004.

[14] A. Munshi, B. Gaster, and T. Mattson. *OpenCL Programming Guide.* Addison-Wesley, 2011.

[15] C. H. Nevison. Parallel computing in the undergraduate curriculum. *Computer*, 28(12):51–56, Dec. 1995.

[16] B. W. Rague. Exploring concurrency using the parallel analysis tool. In *Proceedings of the 43rd ACM technical symposium on Computer Science Education*, SIGCSE '12, pages 511–516, New York, NY, USA, 2012. ACM.

[17] W. Thies, M. Karczmarek, and S. P. Amarasinghe. StreamIt: A language for streaming applications. In *Proceedings of the 11th International Conference on Compiler Construction*, CC '02, pages 179–196, London, UK, UK, 2002. Springer-Verlag.

[18] Yousun Ko et al. Parallel from the beginning: the case for multicore programming in the computer science undergraduate curriculum. Technical Report TR-0004, Dept. Computer Science, Yonsei University, Seoul 120-749, Korea, `http://elc.yonsei.ac.kr`, 2012.

Pair Programming for Middle School Students: Does Friendship Influence Academic Outcomes?

Linda Werner
University of California
Santa Cruz, CA
831-459-1017
linda@soe.ucsc.edu

Jill Denner, Shannon Campe, Eloy Ortiz
ETR Associates
4 Carbonero Way
Scotts Valley, CA
831-438-4060
{jilld, shannonc,eloyo}@etr.org

Dawn DeLay, Amy C. Hartl, Brett Laursen
Florida Atlantic University
Boca Raton, FL

ABSTRACT

Research shows the benefits of pair programming for retention and performance in computing, but little is known about how relationship dynamics influence outcomes. We describe results from our study of middle school students programming games using Alice and pair programming. From our analysis using statistical procedures that take into account the interdependence of pair data, we found evidence for partner influence moderated by the role of confidence over improvements in Alice programming knowledge in friend partnerships but not non-friend partnerships. We discuss implications for researchers and educators.

Categories and Subject Descriptors

K.3.2 [Computers and Education]: Computer and Information Science Education – *Computer science education.*

Keywords

Pair Programming, Game Programming, Middle School, Alice, Friendship, Computational Thinking.

1. INTRODUCTION

Educators and researchers are trying to change the 'face of computing'. Those at the K-12 level are hopeful that initial programming environments such as Alice and Scratch [22] and techniques such as collaboration via pair programming and game programming will make computing accessible to all students at an early age. Since computer science (CS) is not yet widely accepted as one of the K-12 core topics [3], we need to provide evidence-based results that show using these programming environments and techniques holds promise for introducing CS concepts and bringing real gains in computational thinking (CT) to K-12 students. We recently presented results supporting the introduction of CS concepts using Alice and game programming for middle school youth [24]. In this paper, we describe results pertaining to the use of friendship in the partnerships, referred to as dyads, with respect to pair programming and gains in aspects of CT.

As a review, "CT is a problem-solving process that includes (but is not limited to) the following characteristics:

- Formulating problems in a way that enables us to use a computer and other tools to help solve them.
- Logically organizing and analyzing data,
- Representing data through abstractions such as models and simulations,
- Automating solutions through algorithmic thinking (a series of ordered steps)
- Identifying, analyzing, and implementing possible solutions with the goal of achieving the most efficient and effective combination of steps and resources,
- Generalizing and transferring this problem solving process to a wide variety of problems." [11]

We ran semester-long game-programming courses called iGame that involved 189 middle school students using Alice and pair programming across four semesters (in and after school). iGame is a study where we address many research questions including the following: Under what conditions does pair programming benefit the learning outcomes of middle school students programming games using Alice? Are the dyadic data interdependent?

We looked closely at pair programming to determine if there were moderating effects of this form of dyadic learning processes. To address this research question, we conducted surveys containing questions about student confidence in computing and Alice programming knowledge. Additionally students rated the degree to which their partner was a friend.

In this paper, we first discuss prior work with pair programming, followed by a description of the iGame course including participant demographics, procedures of the study, measures, and the analysis process. Next, we list the results of the analyses using statistical procedures that take into account the interdependence of dyadic data and discuss these results. The paper concludes with a discussion of future work.

2. PRIOR WORK

A long history of research describes the benefits of collaborative learning [4] and specifically pair programming for individual performance and persistence rates at the college level [6][18][26] but there are very few studies of pair programming in K-12 [15][25]. Building on the research of Vygotsky [23], socio constructivists have studied how discussion and reflection on a specific task can help children construct an understanding that goes beyond what they can achieve on their own. For example, working with a partner encourages students to summarize and explain what they know, respond to immediate feedback, take time to work through what they do not understand, and ask questions--all high level thinking skills that improve performance [20].

In pair programming, two students share one computer and there are suggested roles: one is the driver (working the keyboard and mouse) while the other navigates. Pair programming is a particularly promising means to promote computational thinking because it encourages peer scaffolding, clear roles, and frequent feedback. But simply working with any partner is not enough to promote learning. Students must be involved in the selection of their partner [9], and are more likely to articulate and internalize what they are learning when their partner is on an equal social level and is a friend [2]. This is particularly important for collaboration on an open ended, creative task (unlike tasks in which there is a single 'right' answer) because friends know how to develop a shared space and generate ideas together [19]. In addition, other characteristics of the students, such as previous knowledge or self confidence, may promote or interfere with the development of computational thinking in each of the partners. Few studies examine the association between interdependence of dyads and change in learning outcomes, and none have done this in the context of pair programming.

Studies of friendship dyads are flawed, however, when they do not correct for statistical biases inherent in interdependent dyadic data. Previous studies have either involved separate analyses of individuals in dyads, which often produces conflicting results, or treated partners as if their data were independent, violating key assumptions of statistical tests and typically inflating Type II errors [10]. In our study, we distinguished partners based on computer confidence, reasoning that confident partners would be better collaborators, such that they would be both persuasive in, and open to suggestions for, obtaining task mastery [16]. Thus we expected confident partners to be both influential and open to influence.

3. METHOD

3.1 Participants

The data described in this paper were collected over two years as part of a study of how game creation and pair programming can promote CT. A total of 189 students with parental consent participated in pair programming classes at seven public schools along the central California coast. Participation in all parts of the study was voluntary. We measured students' experience programming, closeness with partner, Alice programming knowledge, and student confidence with computing.

Of these 189 students, all but 18 were members of same-gender dyads. Because most adolescent friendships are same-gender, our analyses focuses on these students. Paired students were either initially paired with a partner or were a replacement for a partner who left the course sometime before the final survey. The current sample was reduced by nine students who dropped out of the study and their partners had to be repaired and two students (one dyad) who were excluded because they were twins (since the focus of the current investigation was not on sibling relationships). Individuals with partners who dropped out were immediately paired with other students in the class who did not have a partner. New partners were assigned after 2 to 12 hours of instruction (M=7.38). New partners completed the measure of friendship at the start of their first session of joint instruction. Participants in dyads with reassigned partners did not differ on any study variable from the remainder of the sample. Neither were there differences between students who participated in the after-school program (n=58) and those who participated in a computer class during school hours (n=102).

Of the remaining 160 pair programming students, (60 girls, 100 boys), there were 61 students in grade 6, 49 students in grade 7, and 50 students in grade 8. Students ranged from 10 to 14 (M =12.05, SD=1.01) years old. The parental consent form indicated that a total of 64.38% (n=103 students) lived with both biological parents, 18.13% (n=29 students) lived with one biological parent, 3.13% (n=5 students) lived in other types of households, and 14.38% (n=23 students) had not reported living arrangements. The final sample included 73 (45.6%) who described themselves as White Caucasian, 22 (13.8%) as Hispanic Latino, 8 (5.0%) as Asian Pacific Islander, 5 (3.1%) as Native American, 3 (1.9%) as African American, 44 (27.5%) as mixed ethnic background, and 5 (3.1%) who did not report their ethnicity.

3.2 Procedure

In-school participants were recruited from eight classrooms and from four extended learning programs in seven schools in four cities (or school districts). The schools represented lower and middle socioeconomic status communities. Schools were selected for participation if a technology teacher indicated interest in the project. In some schools (n=3), students participated in the project as part of their technology elective class (n= 62 boys and 40 girls). All students in the technology elective classrooms were invited to participate in the study through in-class announcements and a letter sent home to parents. One student declined to participate. In other schools (n=4), students participated as part of an after-school enrichment program (n= 38 boys and 20 girls). Recruitment for the after-school program involved announcements made by the extended learning site coordinator and by teachers. Two students in the after-school technology program declined to participate. Written parent consent and student assent were required for participation. Students participated for 20 hours (usually 10 weeks).

Students worked in dyads assigned by their teachers with input from the students themselves. Students worked with various other (typically) same gender classmates during the first two or three class sessions at which time students submitted a short list of classmates' names with whom they would like to partner. Students spent the remainder of the sessions working in the assigned dyads.

Students used one of two programming environments in the Alice [1] series developed at Carnegie Mellon. In year 1, students used Storytelling Alice (SA), and in year 2 they used Alice 2.2 because SA was only available on PCs, which were limited at our partner schools. In the rest of this paper, we will refer to both SA and Alice 2.2 as Alice unless it is necessary to distinguish between the two. Alice allows users to control characters in 3D environments using drag-and-drop programming, a language that is closely related to Java and many other modern imperative programming languages. Most code is written in the methods of objects that have properties that store state and functions that return values. Each property, method, and function is attached to an object, with

World being the global object. The event system in Alice is primarily used to handle user interactions, such as mouse clicks, although it can also handle in-World events, such as when the value of a variable changes.

Students engaged with CT in a three-stage progression called Use-Modify-Create[14] over approximately 20 hours during a semester. In the first half of the semester, students played games, completed tutorials, and worked through a series of self-paced instructional exercises built to provide scaffolding, which we call "challenges." During the last half of the course, the students freely designed and developed their own games [8]. Most students completed eight to 10 of 11 required challenges, though some completed up to six additional optional challenges. The student dyad shared one computer, with one driving (controlling the mouse and keyboard) and the other navigating (checking for bugs, consulting resources, and providing input). We asked students to reverse roles approximately every 20 minutes.

Alice programming knowledge assessments were administered as online surveys at the beginning of the first and the end of the last (or second to last) class meeting. Friendship assessments were completed in paper-pencil format at the beginning of the third or fourth class meeting after partners were assigned (or at the start of the first class for students who were re-partnered) and online at the end of the last or second to last class meeting. Students were not permitted to collaborate or share answers. Surveys were administered by research staff.

3.3 Measures and Analysis Process

Participants separately completed the same assessments: a) pre-test at the beginning of the project, at the start of the introductory class meeting; and b) post-test at the conclusion of the project, after the last class meeting approximately 10 weeks later.

Alice programming knowledge was assessed with an 8-item measure of sample programming code. Students were presented with screenshots of the programming interface (e.g., *What would happen if you were to play the above 3 lines of code?*). Students selected one of five possible response options. Each student received a score that indicated the number of correct responses (range=0 to 8).

Computer confidence was assessed with a 3-item scale that measured perceived computing abilities [5]. Items were rated on a scale from 1 (*Strongly disagree)* to 5 (*Strongly agree) (*e.g., *I feel confident about my ability to use computers).* Item scores were averaged; internal reliability was good (Cronbach's α=.84). Each partner in each dyad was classified as either relatively more confident using computers (M=4.27, SD=0.76) or relatively less confident using computers (pretest M=2.99, SD=0.89). These classifications did not change from pretest to posttest. In most dyads (n = 50), the computer confidence scores of partners differed by at least 0.50 standard deviations (pretest M =1.03, SD=.61).

The Friendship score used the Friendship Quality Scale [7]. This scale measures perceptions of closeness and intimacy with the partner. Items were rated on a 1 (*Not true*) to 5 (*Really true*) scale. Dyads were classified as friends or non-friends using responses to a single item (i.e., *My partner is my friend*). To qualify as friends (n=48), both partners had to respond to this item with a rating of 3 (*Usually true*) or higher at the pretest. All other dyads were classified as non-friends (n=32), meaning that at least one partner responded with a score of 2 (*Might be true*) or lower at the pretest. In six cases, both partners rated the other as 2 or lower on the friendship item.

Our analysis using the Actor-Partner Interdependence Model (APIM), which is designed for correlated data in distinguishable dyads, permits the analysis of non-independent data across multiple time points [13]. It partitions variance shared across partners on the same variable from variance that uniquely describes associations within and between partners. This 4-step analyses process estimates the influence that partners have on changes in each other's computer programming skills as measured by pre and posttest Alice programming knowledge assessment. We distinguished partners on the basis of computer confidence, reasoning that confident partners would be better collaborators, such that they would be both persuasive in, and open to suggestions for, obtaining task mastery [16]. Thus we expected confident partners to be both influential and open to influence [12].

In step one of the APIM analyses, 30 dyads were omitted from our analyses because partners in these dyads differed in computer confidence by less than 0.50 standard deviations from the mean. In step two, the remaining 50 dyads with partners distinguishable on the basis of computer confidence are analyzed looking at the influence high confidence partners have over changes in Alice programming knowledge of low confidence partners and vice versa. In the third step, we conducted a multiple group APIM to examine whether there were differences between friend and non-friend dyads on the magnitude and direction of influence in Alice programming knowledge. In the fourth step, we conducted a repeated measure ANOVA to determine whether the rate of change in Alice programming knowledge differed for more confident students paired with partners who had greater Alice programming knowledge, as compared to those paired with partners who had less Alice programming knowledge.

4. RESULTS

As expected, the data were not independent. There were significant (p<.001) concurrent pretest and posttest correlations between Alice programming knowledge and computer confidence (range: r=.24 to .35). Autocorrelations indicated that pretest scores were positively (p<.001) associated with posttest scores, for both Alice programming knowledge (r=.47) and computer confidence (r=.66). There was a significant (p<.001) over time correlation (r=.26) between pretest Alice programming knowledge and posttest computer confidence, but not between pretest computer confidence and posttest Alice programming knowledge (r = .09).

Alice programming knowledge increased over time, $t(153)$= 12.38, p<.001 (Pretest: M=2.22 SD=1.69; Posttest: M=4.01 SD=1.76), but computer confidence did not (Pretest: M=3.69 SD=.93; Posttest: M=3.71 SD=.87). There were no gender differences on either computer programming knowledge or computer confidence.

Figures 1 and 2 show the partner influence on Alice programming knowledge as a function of relative computer confidence in friend (n=30) dyads and non-friend (n=20) dyads. APIM analysis results for friends revealed statistically significant actor paths for the less confident partner (a2), but not the more confident partner (a1). For less confident partners, pretest Alice programming knowledge scores were positively associated with posttest scores (β=.57). For more confident partners, there was no statistically significant association between pretest Alice programming knowledge scores and posttest scores (β=.15). The lack of stability among more confident partners is an indication of change in Alice programming knowledge. Partner paths revealed influence of the less confident partner on the more confident partner (p2), but not the reverse (p1). The less confident partner's initial Alice programming knowledge was associated with positive changes in the more confident partner's Alice programming knowledge (β=.47), but the more confident partner's initial Alice programming knowledge did not predict change in the less confident partner's Alice programming knowledge (β=-.23).

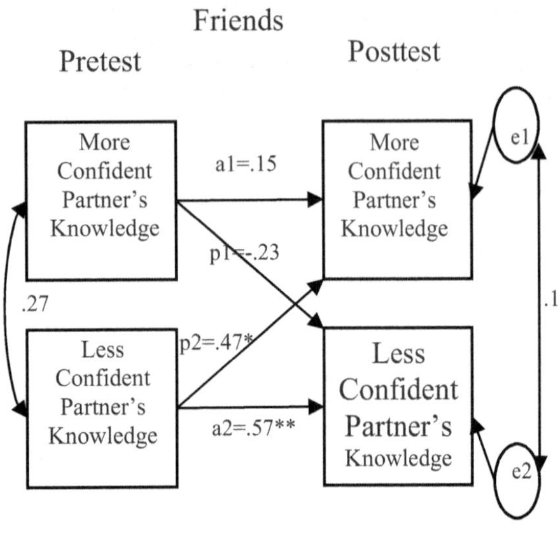

Figure 1. Friend influence; *p<.05, **p<.01, two-tailed.

Among non-friends, actor paths revealed stability for both partners (a1 and a2). Pretest Alice programming knowledge scores were positively associated with posttest scores (more confident: β=.58; less confident: β=.47). There were no statistically significant partner paths (p1 and p2), indicating that neither partner influenced the other (more confident: β=.12; less confident: β=.20).

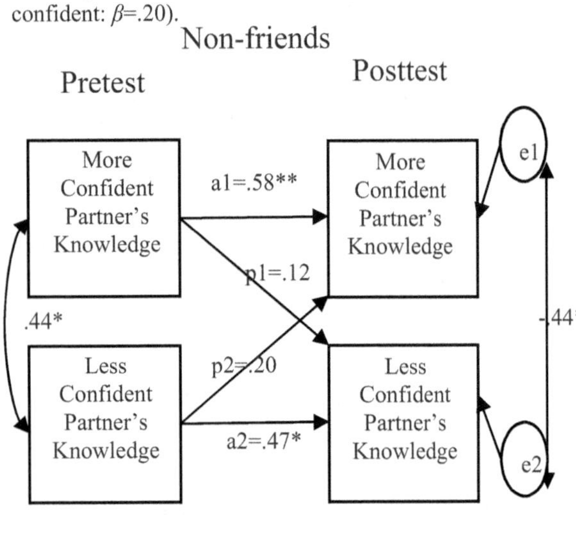

Figure 2. Non-friend influence; *p<.05, **p<.01, two-tailed.

Multiple group contrasts compared friends and non-friends on each actor and partner path. There were no statistically significant differences on partner influence paths (Range: $\chi^2(1, N=50) = 1.51$-1.67, $p>.05$). There were statistically significant differences between friends and non-friends on the stability of the more confident partner's Alice knowledge score, $\chi^2(1, N=50) = 4.01$, $p<.05$, but not on the stability of the less confident partner's Alice knowledge score, $\chi^2(1, N=50) = 0.90$, $p<.001$.

Within group contrasts compared the partner influence and actor stability paths of the more confident and the less confident partners, separately within friend dyads and within non-friend dyads. For friends, there were statistically significant differences between the more and less confident partner on partner influence paths, $\chi^2(1, N=30) = 8.86$, $p<.05$, such that the less confident partner had more influence than the more confident partner. Additionally, there were statistically significant differences between the more and less confident partner on actor stability paths, $\chi^2(1, N=30) = 4.23$, $p<.05$, such that the more confident partners' Alice programming knowledge scores were less stable than the less confident partners' scores. For non-friends, there were no statistically significant differences between more and less confident partners on partner influence or actor stability paths (Range: $\chi^2(1, N=20) = 0.19$-1.13, $p>.05$).

Step 3 revealed a statistically significant partner influence path in friend dyads, wherein the less confident partner's Alice programming knowledge pretest score predicted change in the more confident partner's Alice programming knowledge posttest score. To better understand the nature of this influence, we divided friend dyads into two groups: (1) Those where the less confident partner had more pretest Alice programming knowledge than the more confident partner did (n=10), and (2) those where the less confident partner had less pretest Alice programming knowledge than the more confident partner (n=15). Partners who had equivalent levels of pretest Alice programming knowledge were removed (n = 5).

A 2 (Time) X 2 (Alice programming knowledge of partner at pretest) repeated measures ANOVA was conducted. The Alice programming knowledge score of the more confident partner was the dependent variable. There was a statistically significant time by partner Alice programming knowledge interaction, $F(1,23)=24.309$, $p<.001$. The more confident partner experienced the greatest increases in Alice programming knowledge when paired with a friend who had more Alice programming knowledge at the outset. Follow-up paired t-tests revealed a significant increase in Alice programming knowledge for the more confident partner when paired with a more knowledgeable partner, $t(9) = 8.72$, p<.001, but not when paired with a less knowledgeable partner, $t(14) = 1.10$, p>.05.

A similar pattern of results emerged when dyads whose computer confidence differed by less than .50 *SD* (n=30) were included. Additional multiple group APIM analyses were conducted using gender and instructional setting (during or after-school) as moderators. There were no statistically significant χ^2 differences, suggesting that the influence of more confident partners and less confident partners did not vary as a function of these variables. Age, grade, length of training (numbers of hours), ethnicity, and household structure were separately entered into the model as control variables. In each case, model fit significantly worsened and the pattern of statistically significant paths did not change.

5. DISCUSSION

The investigation of friend influence over learning processes presents an analytic challenge because of the interdependent nature of dyadic data. Taking advantage of recent advances in non-independent statistical analyses, we used a longitudinal APIM for distinguishable dyads to determine the degree and magnitude of friend influence over change in Alice programming knowledge. We found that computing confidence determines who influences whom. We also found that friendship status moderated the findings such that the less confident partner influenced the more confident partner only if partners were also friends. Follow-up analyses illustrated these influence processes. The greatest increases in Alice programming knowledge occurred among confident partners who were paired with a friend who had relatively more initial Alice programming knowledge.

What are the implications of these results for teachers? Since the benefit of working with more knowledgeable peers is greater when students are confident, it is important for teachers to focus on increasing confidence, as well as knowledge.

This study had several limitations. "Friendship" was assessed by a single question at a single point in time, and we know that middle school friendships tend to fluctuate. This may have introduced some error in the categorization of dyads as friends and non-friends, which suggests that these findings may underestimate the magnitude of results. We had limited statistical power to detect differences between friends and non-friends, suggesting that some non-significant group contrasts may have been a result of a small sample size. Small sample sizes prevented us from definitively determining whether age moderated the pattern of results.

6. CONCLUSIONS AND FUTURE WORK

The next set of questions involves looking at intervention efforts to guide positive forms of influence. Also additional analyses will contribute to an understanding of what makes pair programming effective, and how that varies across gender and culture. Longitudinal dyadic data analysis is beginning to show the conditions under which partners learn more, such as when they are paired with friends. The findings have implications for teachers, who often resist pairing children with friends for fear that students will be disruptive and spend time off task. The APIM methodological approach is being used in studies of pathology, but this is the first application of its use in Computer Science education research.

The role of pair versus solo programming is also being investigated by looking at the nature of pair programming. There was great variation in the effectiveness with which partners worked together, and we expect that will impact how much they learn. To this end, we have begun to describe what pair programming looks like, and the conditions under which it is advantageous. This includes a "pair effectiveness" score, based on video recordings of 71 pairs working together for approximately 20 minutes with each partner in both of the two pair programming roles. Our scale includes collaboration categories for inclusiveness, responsiveness, and negative behaviors.

In addition, we are drawing on socio-cultural theory, to focus on the collaborative aspects of the learning process, specifically how students of different cultural backgrounds collaborate during pair programming. We are in the process of clarification of collaboration categories from an earlier study [21] after which we will catagorize all interactions in the recordings. Understanding how partners interact by supporting or undermining each other's goals during pair programming will provide useful information for strengthening classroom practices. Although pair programming has shown benefits for students' learning in general, more research is needed on which collaborative qualities can support girls and Latino-heritage students, who are underrepresented in the computer science and related fields.

7. ACKNOWLEDGMENTS

Our thanks go to the teachers and administrators at our seven schools, specifically Anne Guerrero, Shelly Laschkewitsch, Don Jacobs, Sue Seibolt, Karen Snedeker, Susan Rivas, and Katie Ziparo. Thanks also to teaching assistants, Will Park, Chizu Kawamoto, and Joanne Sanchez; and to Pat Rex, for her support with instructional matierials design. Thanks to all of the students who participated. This research is funded by a grant from NSF 0909733 "The Development of Computational Thinking among Middle School Students Creating Computer Games." Any opinions, findings, conclusions or recommendations expressed in this material are those of the authors and do not necessarily reflect the views of the National Science Foundation.

8. REFERENCES

[1] Alice website, September 1, 2011. www.alice.org.

[2] Azmitia, M. and Montgomery, R. 1993. Friendship, transactive dialogues, and the development of scientific reasoning. *Social Development*, 2: 202–221. doi: 10.1111/j.1467-9507.1993.tb00014.x

[3] Barr, V. and Stephenson, C., 2011. Bringing computational thinking to K-12: what is Involved and what is the role of the computer science education community? *ACM Inroads* 2, 1, 48-54.

[4] Barron, B. 2000. Achieving coordination in collaborative problem-solving groups. *Journal of the Learning Sciences*, 9(4), 403-436.

[5] Barron, B., Walter, S.E., Martin, C.K., and Schatz, C. 2010. Predictors of creative computing participation and profiles of experience in two Silicon Valley middle schools. *Computers & Education*, 54, 178-189.

[6] Braught, G., Eby, M., and Wahls. T., 2008. The effects of pair-programming on individual programming skill. In *Proceedings of the 39th SIGCSE technical symposium on Computer science education* (SIGCSE '08). ACM, New York, NY, USA, 200-204.

[7] Bukowski, W. M., Hoza, B., and Boivin, M. 1994. Measuring friendship quality during pre and early adolescence: The development and psychometric properties of the Friendship Qualities Scale. *Journal of Social and Personal Relationships*, 11, 471–484.

[8] Campe, S., Werner, L., and Denner, J. 2012. Game programming with Alice. In P. Phillips, S. Cooper, and C. Stephenson, *CSTA Voice Special Issue Computer Science K-8: Building a Strong Foundation*, 13-14.

[9] Ciani, K., Summers, J., Easter, M., and Sheldon, K. 2008. Collaborative learning and positive experiences: Does letting students choose their own groups matter? *Educational Psychology*, 28(6).

[10] Cook, W. L., and Kenny, D. A. 2005. The actor-partner interdependence model: A model of bidirectional effects in developmental studies. *International Journal of Behavioral Development, 29,* 101-109.

[11] CSTA, 2011. Operational Definition of Computational Thinking for K-12 Education. Accessed on August 10, 2012 at http://csta.acm.org/Curriculum/sub/CompThinking.html.

[12] Delay, D., Hartl, A., Laursen, B., Denner, J., Werner, L., Campe, S., and Ortiz, E. Submitted for review. Learning from friends: Measuring influence in a dyadic computer instructional setting. Submitted to special issue Methodological Issues with the Measurement of Change in Education: The Use of Longitudinal Studies in *International Journal of Research and Method in Education.*

[13] Kenny, D. A., Kashy, D. A., and Cook, W. L. 2006. *The Analysis of Dyadic Data.* New York: Guilford Press.

[14] Lee, L., Martin, F., Denner, J., Coulter, B., Allan, W., Erickson, J., Malyn-Smith, J., and Werner, L., 2011. Computational thinking for youth in practice. *ACM Inroads* 2(1), 32-37.

[15] Lewis, C., 2011. Is pair programming more effective than other forms of collaboration for young students? *Computer Science Education,* 21(2), 105-134.

[16] Liem, A. D., Lau, S., and Nie, Y. 2008. The role of self-efficacy, task value, and achievement goals in predicting learning strategies, task disengagement, peer relationship, and achievement outcome. *Contemporary Educational Psychology,* 33, 486-512.

[17] Linn, M. C., 1985. The Cognitive Consequences of Programming Instruction in Classrooms. *Educational Researcher*, 14(5), pp. 14-16+25-29 at http://www.jstor.org/stable/1174202.

[18] McDowell, C, Werner, L., Bullock, H., and Fernald, J. 2006. Pair programming improves student retention, confidence, and program quality. *Communications of the ACM,* 48(8), 90-95.

[19] Miell, D. and MacDonald, R. 2000. Children's creative collaborations: The importance of friendship when working together on a musical composition. *Social Development,* 9: 348–369. doi: 10.1111/1467-9507.00130

[20] Palincsar, A.S., and Brown, A.L. 1984. Reciprocal teaching of comprehension-fostering and comprehension-monitoring activities. *Cognition and Instruction*, 1(2), 117-175.

[21] Ruvalcaba, O., Werner, L., and Campe, S. 2012. Computer-based collaboration in middle school: A sociocultural perspective on pair programming with Mexican-heritage and European-heritage students. *Proceedings of the 2012 Conference of American Educational Research Association,* Vancouver, British Columbia, Canada.

[22] Utting, I., Cooper, S., Kölling, M., Maloney, J., and Resnick, M. 2010. Alice, Greenfoot, and Scratch -- A Discussion. *ACM Transactions on Computing Education* 10(4), Article 17 (November 2010), 11 pages. DOI=10.1145/1868358.1868364 http://doi.acm.org/10.1145/1868358.1868364

[23] Vygotsky, L.S. 1978. *Mind in Society.* Cambridge, MA: Harvard University Press.

[24] Werner, L., Campe, S., Denner, J. 2012. Children learning computer science concepts via Alice game-programming, *Proceedings of the 43rd ACM Technical Symposium on Computer Science Education,* SIGCSE, Raleigh, N. Carolina, USA.

[25] Werner, L., Denner, J. 2009. Pair programming in middle school: What does it look like? *Journal of Research on Technology in Education*, 42(1), 29-49.

[26] Werner, L., Hanks, B., & McDowell, C. 2004. Pair programming helps female computer science students. *ACM Journal of Educational Resources in Computing*, 4(1).

CS4Impact: Measuring Computational Thinking Concepts Present in CS4HS Participant Lesson Plans

Heather Bort and Dennis Brylow
Marquette University
MSCS Department – Cudahy Hall
1313 W. Wisconsin Ave.
Milwaukee, WI 53233
{heather.bort, dennis.brylow}@mu.edu

ABSTRACT

In this paper, we aim to directly measure a CS4HS workshop's participating teachers' ability to synthesize CSTA computational thinking core concepts into actionable lesson plans for courses in their current teaching repertoire. Participants were expected to present a lesson plan on the final day of the workshop, highlighting the integration of their classroom curriculum with computing and computational thinking skills. We present our evaluation rubric, used to rate the teachers effective use of the computational thinking core concepts in their lesson plans, and describe how our method of evaluation may more accurately gauge the overall impact that CS4HS workshops have on their participants.

Categories and Subject Descriptors

K.3.2 [**Computer and Info Science Education**]: Computer Science Education

General Terms

Measurement, Human Factors

Keywords

CS4HS, Computational Thinking, K-12 Outreach, Lesson Planning

1. INTRODUCTION

Many current K-12 outreach efforts attempt to increase the number of students interested in majoring in computer science and related fields, with goals such as creating awareness of computer science, developing an interest in CS as a discipline, and communicating CS concepts in a way that is accessible to an audience broad in both interests and experience. These initiatives include workshops for K-12 teachers such as the Tapestry Workshop at Tennessee Technological University [20], the Computer Science for High School (CS4HS) workshops started at Carnegie Mellon and subsequently funded by Google [18, 7], and a variety of workshops sponsored either by single universities or through national funding agencies such as the National Science Foundation [3, 13, 15, 12]. Other efforts work to incorporate computer science and computational thinking into existing curricula [24, 19], develop new curricula to ensure student exposure to computer science and computational thinking principals [11], and use various media to inform teachers and students of the value of computer science [16, 6].

Most of these professional development efforts use pre- and post-test methodology to assess the transfer of factual knowledge about computer science and/or computational thinking to their target audience. While teaching the teacher is a laudable goal in itself, there has been little effort in prior and related work to directly assess the impact of these professional development designs on actual teacher practice.

One recent study [14] attempted to measure how much of an impact programs like these actually have on teachers. This study concluded that the teachers had an improved understanding of computational thinking after the workshop they attended based off of an increased percentage of correct answers to a multiple choice survey asking for a definition of the term and why they thought it might be important. Another measure that they used to determine the significance of the workshop was to ask the teachers if and how much of the material presented they thought could immediately be incorporated into their classrooms [14].

While this analysis directly measures some factual knowledge about computational thinking, it only indirectly addresses teachers' ability to incorporate this knowledge into teaching practice. Our anecdotal experience from many such previous workshops has been that teachers are typically very enthusiastic about the material immediately after a well-designed session; however, follow-up surveys taken months later usually show that only a small number of teachers are able to transform the content of a 2- to 4-day CS4HS-style workshop into viable classroom practice.

In this paper, we aim to directly measure a CS4HS workshop's participating teachers' ability to synthesize the CSTA computational thinking core concepts [4] into actionable lesson plans for courses in their current teaching repertoire.

2. THE WORKSHOP

Over this past summer we received a grant from Google's Education Group to develop a CS4HS workshop for high school and middle school teachers to promote Computer

Science and Computational Thinking in their classrooms. We undertook several goals in presenting this workshop, initially building on goals set at previous summer workshops [3, 12] to help high school and middle school teachers incorporate computer science and computational thinking into their classrooms. One of the goals was to show the direct correlation between the subjects taught by the teachers and computational thinking, and to show the teachers how to use computational examples to teach current standards [3, 12]. Behind this aim is the prospect of cultivating a new crop of computer science teachers to renew the depleted resources available in our state. A second goal for this workshop was to take advantage of having assembled a number of our states computer science teachers in one space for network building, discussion of computer science education standards, and to launch a chapter of the CSTA (Computer Science Teachers' Association) for our state. Finally, we specifically targeted an audience of teachers with a background in teaching computer science in order to identify schools and lend support to those schools interested in piloting the Exploring Computer Science [2] and AP Computer Science Principles [1] courses for the 2013 school year [8].

The participants were split into two tracks, a "basic" track A for teachers with little or no computer science background, and an "advanced" track B for those with experience teaching computer science. Both tracks had time allotted to learn and practice hands-on programming skills with either Scratch or Alice. The summary schedule is shown in Figure 1.

The basic track concentrated on computational thinking, some aspects of the Exploring Computer Science [2] curriculum, and ideas for working more computing-centric modules and motivations into existing high school STEM courses while still addressing relevant state standards.

The advanced track included sessions on the new AP Computer Science Principles exam being developed, with particular focus on topics that the AP CSP pilot sites have shown to be more troublesome in translating between the university context and the high school context. Some sessions met with everyone, and teachers were permitted to cross tracks if they were more interested in the opposing session.

Workshop structure included a variety of lecture-style presentations, hands-on lab sessions, mixed sessions, and panel discussions. We had two 2-hour sessions for lesson plan preparation late in the day on Monday and Tuesday, and then participants shared highlights of their lessons plans with the full group on the final day.

Because we drew participants almost exclusively from our state, we included sessions on state-specific curriculum and licensure issues, and worked hard on getting critical mass together for a pending CSTA chapter application.

Participants were given the opportunity to fill out an evaluation at the end of each day to inform us of which parts of the workshop they found most valuable, and in what areas we could improve.

2.1 Focus on Computational Thinking

A major focus common to both tracks in this workshop was to impart a working definition of computational thinking, how it is an entity separate from computer science, and how to integrate the computational thinking skill set and vocabulary in a classroom setting.

CSTA's K-12 Computer Science Standards manual makes the distinction between computer science and computational thinking, defining *computer science* as:

> "...the study of computer and algorithmic processes, including their principles, their hardware and software designs, their application, and their impact on society"

Whereas *computational thinking* is defined as:

> "...a problem-solving methodology that can interweave computer science with all disciplines, providing a distinctive means of analyzing and developing solutions to problems that can be solved computationally" [4]

In an article explaining her thoughts on computational thinking, Jeannette Wing states that:

> "...it represents a universally applicable attitude and skill set everyone, not just computer scientists, would be eager to learn and use" [21].

Day 1	
7:30	Breakfast/Registration
9:00	Welcome and Introductions
9:45	Session 1: [A] Exploring CS and Computational Thinking [B] AP CS Principles
11:00	Session 2: Algorithms
12:15	Lunch
1:00	Session 3: Scratch
3:15	Session 4: [A] Boolean Building Blocks [B] Creativity
5:00	Dinner
6:00	TechSpots: Augmented Reality, POV Copter, Embedded Xinu
6:00	Lesson Planning / Open Laboratory
8:00	Daily Evaluation
Day 2	
7:30	Breakfast
8:30	Session 6: [A] HPC and Sciences [B] Big Data
9:45	Session 7: State and Curriculum Issues
11:00	Session 8: [A] CT and the Sciences [B] Impact and the Internet
12:15	Lunch
1:00	Session 9: [A] Alice [B] Scratch
3:15	Session 10: Problem/Project-Based Learning and Computational Thinking
5:00	Dinner
6:00	TechSpots: Mobile Computing, Finch, Lego MindStorms
6:00	Lesson Planning / Open Laboratory
8:00	Daily Evaluation
Day 3	
7:30	Breakfast
8:30	Presenting Lesson Plans
11:00	Google Keynote Speaker: *Go* Language
12:15	Lunch
1:00	Session 15: Careers Panel
2:00	Closing and Final Evaluations

Figure 1: Workshop Schedule

Computational thinking is a method of problem solving, using abstraction and analytical thinking to arrive at a *best* answer. It is not about using a computer to solve a problem, it is more about thinking in an algorithmic way [22].

While applications of computational thinking in computer science may seem rather obvious and even redundant to those of us steeped in the field, when we try to define computational thinking outside of computer science it tends to be a somewhat esoteric concept; this can lead to some common misconceptions regarding the subject.

Firstly, computational thinking does not imply computer programming; a computer programmer can use computational thinking but so can any other person. Computational thinking is a way of conceptualizing a problem that

> "requires thinking at multiple levels of abstraction" [21].

Next, Computational thinking should not be defined as thinking like a computer. It is a fundamentally human way of thinking, drawing on concepts from mathematical and engineering thinking. Also, computational thinking does not promote cookie cutter approaches to problems; it provides a method for thought organization and process optimization for solving complex problems. The computer is a tool, and it can be used to help us visualize abstract concepts [21, 22]. As there is not a concrete, finite definition of computational thinking, the CSTA and the International Society for Technology in Education (ISTE) have entered into a project to develop one. They have compiled a list of core computational thinking concepts and capabilities and given examples of how to incorporate them in a variety of disciplines. The concepts are data collection, data analysis, data representation, problem decomposition, abstraction, algorithms and procedures, automation, parallelization, and simulation [5].

All of our workshop participants were given this information on computational thinking and spent time during sessions engaged in group and individual projects designed to give them experience using the CSTA and ISTE developed capabilities to highlight the core concepts in problem solving activities. The participants were also provided with information regarding the decline in computer science graduates, particularly the sharp drop in the participation of women in computer science, and the increased demand for qualified individuals in this field.

2.2 Under-representation

In an economy where people are struggling to find jobs, the field of computer science is expected to have an increase in employment of 22 percent over the next decade and yield an average income 74.07 percent higher than the national average yearly income over all occupations [10]. There has been a concerning trend of decreased enrollment in computer science programs, particularly in the case of women. 2.61 percent of all bachelor's degrees awarded in 1990 were computer science degrees and in 2009 that percentage dropped to 2.38. In 1990, 30.24 percent of the bachelor's degrees awarded in computer sciences went to women; in 2009, it was only 17.91 percent. In fact, while the percentage of bachelor's degrees in all majors earned by women has increased from 53.31 percent in 1990 to 57.29 percent in 2009, the percentage of those women who majored in computer sciences has decreased from 0.79 percent in 1990 to 0.43 percent in 2009 [17].

2.3 Feedback

Overall, the participants gave favorable feedback. They were asked to complete an anonymous survey; some of the questions gave an opportunity to leave essay style feedback and others used a 5-point Likert scale (1=not at all, 5=extremely). The mean values of the Likert type questions are as follows:

1. Overall, I found this workshop to be worthwhile. 4.94
2. I felt a sense of community among participants of this workshop. 4.71
3. If you are a teacher, how likely is it that you will incorporate knowledge you've learned into your curriculum? 4.93

When asked if they would recommend this workshop to other colleagues, all respondents answered in the affirmative.

From this we conclude that our goal for helping teachers develop lesson plans incorporating the material from the workshop into their current teaching field was successful. As noted in an earlier section, it appears that most workshops of this type that ask teachers to rate the likelihood of incorporating workshop material into their classroom get reasonably positive responses. However, a separate follow-up survey will be necessary to determine if the teachers' self-assessment on this point was correct – that they did, indeed, incorporate material from the workshop into their teaching practice during the following school year.

Our secondary goal of network building and establishing support for a new CSTA chapter was accomplished as evidenced by the response to the question 2 and that all participants that were not currently on the CSTA mailing list did sign up to begin receiving materials and information from the CSTA.

3. EVALUATION OF LESSON PLANS

Most prior work on examining the impact of professional development interventions for K-12 CS teachers stops with the indirect measures detailed in the previous section. Teachers are surveyed to see if they have learned anything, asked how much they liked the workshop, and asked to guess how much of it they'll use in the future.

Proper longitudinal follow-up studies of teacher participants are much rarer, and again only involve indirect measures. Follow-up with their students is even more unusual; the authors of this paper are not familiar with any such work in the literature specific to K-12 computer science. This is not a surprising state of affairs; longer-term studies are expensive and require a dedicated cadre of participating teachers – typically in a funding category beyond most K-12 outreach grants. Studies involving K-12 students directly present significantly higher barriers in terms of proper institutional review board approvals, and again require more resources than are available from the majority of funding agencies focused on K-12 CS outreach.

While we were not able to directly measure the impact of our workshop on participants' students in the subsequent school year, or to directly observe changes in teacher practice in their home classrooms, the structure of our workshop allows us to directly measure the next best thing – lesson plans crafted by participants during the course of the workshop, ready to incorporate computational thinking concepts into courses they already teach.

Core Concept	0	1	2
Data Collection	Not incorporated	Provides the data that student will use	Students are required to collect their own data
Data Analysis	Not incorporated	An interpretation of the data is given to the student	Students will analyze the data
Data Representation	Not incorporated	The student is given a specific method to use	Students are able to choose their own method
Problem Decomposition	Not incorporated	An outline or similar structure is provided to the student	Students are required to break the problem down on their own
Abstraction	Not incorporated	Provides an expected outcome	Student arrives at an outcome
Algorithms and Procedures	Not incorporated	The basic steps for an algorithmic solution are provided	Students develop an algorithm or procedure
Automation	Not incorporated	Students are provided with a program or some other technology that automates their process	Students are able to automate their process
Parallelization	Not incorporated	Students are instructed to work in parallel	Students will decide how to distribute their workload
Simulation	Not incorporated	Students are shown a simulation	Students will produce their own simulation
Connection to Other Fields	Not incorporated	The connection is given to the student	Students are required to make a connection to another field

Figure 2: Lesson Plan Evaluation Rubric

We have developed an evaluation rubric (Figure 2) to rate the teachers' effective use of the computational thinking core concepts based on a structure similar to the inquiry level rubric [9]. The lesson plans could receive a possible rating from zero to eighteen, each of the nine core concepts were assigned a level based off of the teachers use of that concept in their lesson plan. Points were awarded for each of the core concepts; zero points for not incorporating the concept, one point for incorporating the concept, and two points for incorporating the concept in a way that encourages high-level inquiry in their students. The teachers could then earn up to two additional points for connecting their lesson to another field, for a total possible score of twenty points.

Core Concept	0	1	2
Data Collection	7	6	3
Data Analysis	9	4	3
Data Representation	8	6	2
Problem Decomposition	5	10	1
Abstraction	5	9	2
Algorithms and Procedures	4	9	3
Automation	3	12	1
Parallelization	12	2	2
Simulation	0	13	3
Connection to Other Fields	10	6	0

Figure 3: Lesson Plan Evaluation Results

3.1 Results

Videotaped recordings of 28 participant lesson plan presentations and the written deliverables shared with the group were categorized and coded according the the rubric described in the previous section.

The average score was 7.31, with no lesson plan scoring higher than 14. One of the most successful presented lessons required the students to learn about DNA molecules and then create a model of the molecule through a process using the computational thinking concepts. Other well-planned lessons involved creating truth tables to determine the care for patients in an emergency room and a project requiring students to present a report on an historical figure in computer science by programming an animated interview. The lesson plans that scored the least number of points did not involve any activity for the students; the teachers did not plan an activity, instead they gave an example of a program that they had written or found online. Figure 3 tabulates the number of lesson plans scored in each category.

Our evaluation of the lesson plans shows that the participants were largely unable to effectively integrate the computational thinking core concepts into lessons that would hold any meaningful significance with the students in their classrooms.

The large number of lesson plans scoring 0 levels on the rubric are to be expected. Our workshop specifically targeted a cohort of non-CS STEM teachers, most of whom were attending their first professional development experience in computing. Demonstrating proficiency in developing computational thinking core concepts in domain-specific lesson plans cannot be expected of everyone after only two days of instruction. Among the experienced CS teachers, some are firmly entrenched in a pedagogical style that still emphasizes conveying facts and programming language syntax, not in focusing on skill building. Nevertheless, after only two days of instruction, a large number of participants were able to produce lesson plans with level 1 or level 2 components, sometimes in multiple core areas.

In the absence of other similar data for comparison, it is not yet possible to objectively quantify how good these results are. However, that was not the point of this iteration of data collection. With a baseline and a rubric, we can now design more specific interventions to increase the number of high-scoring lesson plans at next summer's workshop – to measure if we can improve teachers' abilities to construct lesson plans that should challenge students to a deeper level of inquiry in computational thinking tasks.

3.2 Other Analyses

Based upon a careful analysis of free-response survey results, it is not clear that most workshop participants were able to make the distinction between computational thinking and computer science. Of the 231 comments made through the daily evaluations and workshop survey, only 6 mentioned computational thinking; and while all of the lesson plans presented used some element of computer science, only 4 of them mentioned computational thinking explicitly or used the associated vocabulary.

There were 2 comments concerning the gender issues that were discussed in one of the sessions:

- "Gender divide: It was the males that were able to talk the tech talk about network configurations and hardware and electronic specs."
- "Lets talk about specific ways to improve middle school cs and females in CS – not just that we need to do it."

The first comment highlights our failure to present women as having an equal role in the field of computer science. While our sessions decry the stereotypes that inhibit women from entering into computer science, the only female presence we were able to recruit for our careers panel had the epitome of a typecast soft science non-technical job. Like many smaller computer science programs, we have graduated only a handful of female majors in the recent past, and our network of female alumnae working in the field and in our metropolitan area is nearly an empty set.

The second comment is concerning, as it implies that the concept of integrating computational thinking and computing concepts into existing non-computer science course content to increase awareness and interest in computer science was not realized. We feel that this may be due to an under-generalization of the computational thinking concepts and a failure to present this problem solving method in a way that fully expounds upon its multi-disciplinary reach.

It seems that the normal operating mode is that these workshops specifically target CS and STEM field teachers and therefore the goal of raising awareness and interest in computer science can only permeate about 30 percent of the student population [17].

In response to this trend, Towson University has recently added a series of general education courses focusing on computational thinking; they have developed outcome objectives for these courses. For their Computational Thinking in the Humanities course, students learn to design and use mapping and modeling tools, to put representational dynamics in perspective by applying the basic principals of graphs, networks, and systems, and also they will learn about the challenges associated with applying technology to the arts and humanities. Students develop algorithms and build models to define steps toward weight management in the Computational Thinking: Developing Life Skills for Weight Management course. They can use graph theory to explore social networks as well as learn to identify opportunities to use concurrency or parallel processing in everyday problem solving in the course for Everyday Computational Thinking. These along with the several other courses in this series exposes students to computational thinking as it relates to processes that they are already engaged in [11].

While the effort at Towson University is sure to have a substantial impact on the undergraduate students in their program and is a commendable endeavor that we hope to see spread to other universities, we hold that the first line for recruitment of future computer scientists and computational thinkers alike is the K-12 classroom. We feel that engaging students throughout their elementary and secondary education will promote an increased interest in computer science.

In an effort to correct the deficiency present in our workshop, we are working in collaboration with the Humanities department at a local women's college to develop lesson plans that adhere to the Department of Public Instruction common core standards [23] with the computational thinking core concepts as a problem-solving framework. Our goal is to pilot this initiative in select humanities courses offered to education majors in the Spring 2013 semester and then open our summer workshop to high school teachers in the humanities in an effort to reach a broader, more diverse audience of educators and consequently a greater percentage of the student population that might not have had the opportunity for exposure previously.

4. SUMMARY AND CONCLUSIONS

Enrollment trends in university CS programs – while showing recent improvements – continue to lag disturbingly behind projected needs for graduates, and to show disheartening, persistent under-representation issues. These trends are driving a growing number of K-12 outreach efforts in the form of CS4HS-style summer workshops and other professional development interventions for K-12 teachers. The vast majority of these efforts, while well-intentioned and arguably effective in many dimensions, (teacher morale, more effective university and industrial contacts, updated tool and concept knowledge,) have done little to directly measure their results on participants' classroom teaching practice.

This paper leverages the structure of our workshop – which includes significant time dedicated to preparing and sharing discipline-specific lesson plans to incorporate core CSTA standards – to directly measure our participants' ability to construct lesson plans that encourage higher-level student inquiry with computational thinking concepts.

Our mixed results show that teacher enthusiasm about the workshop remains predictably high. (They're getting free professional development from experts, and STEM teachers of all sorts generally love to play with new instructional technology.) However, the quality of lesson plans developed leaves ample room for improvement in next year's workshop.

4.1 Future Work

While it is beneficial to us as researchers to be able to evaluate the impact that our workshop has on participants, we suspect that participants themselves may also benefit directly. It is one thing to check a box indicating that you have learned something about a topic and quite another to be able to show how you will use what you have learned in your classroom; this is the reasoning behind our asking the participants to present a lesson plan in which they show how they have incorporated the ideas that they learned about computer science and computational thinking into their curriculum. We will go a step further at our next workshop by asking participants to complete an evaluation rubric for each of their peers, as well as a self-assessment of their work. We will provide them with our feedback and the anonymous feedback of their peers, as well as resources and support necessary to improve the assimilation of these concepts into their classrooms.

A brief, non-intrusive follow-up survey next spring will allow us to correlate our initial rating of lesson plans with subsequent teacher reporting of classroom usage.

4.2 Acknowledgments

The authors are grateful to Google for funding our CS4HS workshop, and remain indebted to the many high school and university colleagues who contributed to planning and execution over the summer.

5. REFERENCES

[1] Computer Science: Principles. Retrieved August 31, 2012 from `http://www.csprinciples.org/`.

[2] Exploring Computer Science. Retrieved August 31, 2012 from `http://www.exploringcs.org/`.

[3] S. I. Ahamed, D. Brylow, R. Ge, P. Madiraju, S. J. Merrill, C. A. Struble, and J. P. Early. Computational thinking for the sciences: a three day workshop for high school science teachers. In *SIGCSE '10: Proceedings of the 41st ACM technical symposium on Computer science education*, pages 42–46. ACM, March 2010.

[4] Association for Computing Machinery. Curricula Recommendations, CSTA K-12 Computer Science Standards, Revised 2011. Retrieved August 31, 2012 from `http://www.acm.org/education/curricula-recommendations`.

[5] V. Barr and C. Stephenson. Bringing computational thinking to K-12: what is involved and what is the role of the computer science education community? *Inroads*, 2(1):48–54, February 2011.

[6] T. Bell, I. Witten, and M. Fellows. CS Unplugged. Retrieved August 31, 2012 from `http://csunplugged.org/`.

[7] L. Blum and T. J. Cortina. CS4HS: an outreach program for high school CS teachers. In *SIGCSE'07: Proceedings of the 38th SIGCSE technical symposium on Computer science education*, pages 19–23. ACM, March 2007.

[8] D. Brylow, et al. CS4HS @ MU. Retrieved August 31, 2012 from `http://www.mscs.mu.edu/~brylow/cs4hs/`.

[9] L. B. Buck, S. L. Bretz, and M. H. Towns. Characterizing the level of inquiry in the undergraduate laboratory. *Journal of College Science Teaching*, 38(1):52–58, September 2008. NSTA.

[10] Bureau of Labor Statistics, U.S. Department of Labor. Occupational Outlook Handbook, 2012-13 edition. Retrieved August 31, 2012 from `http://www.bls.gov/ooh/`.

[11] C. Dierbach, H. Hochheiser, S. Collins, G. Jerome, C. Ariza, T. Kelleher, W. Kleinsasser, J. Dehlinger, and S. Kaza. A model for piloting pathways for computational thinking in a general education curriculum. In *SIGCSE'11: Proceedings of the 42nd ACM technical symposium on Computer science education*, pages 257–262. ACM, March 2011.

[12] M. Hart, J. P. Early, and D. Brylow. A novel approach to K-12 CS education: linking mathematics and computer science. In *SIGCSE'08: Proceedings of the 39th SIGCSE technical symposium on Computer science education*, pages 286–290. ACM, February 2008.

[13] J. Liu, C.-H. Lin, E. P. Hasson, and Z. D. Barnett. Introducing computer science to K-12 through a summer computing workshop for teachers. In *SIGCSE '11: Proceedings of the 42nd ACM technical symposium on Computer science education*, pages 389–394. ACM, March 2011.

[14] P. Morreale, C. Goski, L. Jimenez, and C. Stewart-Gardiner. Measuring the impact of computational thinking workshops on high school teachers. *Journal of Computing Sciences in Colleges*, 27(6):151–157, June 2012.

[15] P. Morreale, D. Joiner, and G. Chang. Connecting undergraduate programs to high school students: teacher workshops on computational thinking and computer science. *Journal of Computing Sciences in Colleges*, 25(6):191–197, June 2010.

[16] C. Myketiak, P. Curzon, J. Black, P. W. McOwan, and L. R. Meagher. cs4fn: a flexible model for computer science outreach. In *ITiCSE'12: Proceedings of the 17th ACM annual conference on Innovation and technology in computer science education*, pages 297–302. ACM, July 2012.

[17] National Science Foundation, Division of Science Resources Statistics. Women, Minorities, and Persons with Disabilities in Science and Engineering: 2011. Special Report NSF 11-309. Retrieved August 31, 2012 from `http://www.nsf.gov/statistics/wmpd/`.

[18] K. L. Pokorny and N. White. Computational thinking outreach: reaching across the K-12 curriculum. *Journal of Computing Sciences in Colleges*, 27(5):234–242, May 2012.

[19] J. A. Qualls and L. B. Sherrell. Why computational thinking should be integrated into the curriculum. *Journal of Computing Sciences in Colleges*, 25(5):66–71, May 2012.

[20] A. Siraj, M. J. Kosa, and S.-M. Olmstead. Weaving a tapestry: creating a satellite workshop to support HS CS teachers in attracting and engaging students. In *SIGCSE'12: Proceedings of the 43rd ACM technical symposium on Computer Science Education*, pages 493–498. ACM, February 2012.

[21] J. M. Wing. Computational thinking. *Communications of the ACM*, 49(3):33–35, March 2006.

[22] J. M. Wing. Computational thinking and thinking about computing. *Philosophical Transactions of the Royal Society A: Mathematical, Physical and Engineering Sciences*, 366(1881):3717–3725, October 2008.

[23] Wisconsin Department of Public Instruction. Academic Standards. Retrieved August 31, 2012 from `http://dpi.wi.gov/standards/`.

[24] A. Yadav, N. Zhou, C. Mayfield, S. Hambrusch, and J. T. Korb. Introducing computational thinking in education courses. In *SIGCSE'11: Proceedings of the 42nd ACM technical symposium on Computer science education*, pages 465–470. ACM, March 2011.

Going Mobile with App Inventor for Android: A One-Week Computing Workshop for K-12 Teachers

Jiangjiang Liu
Dept. of Computer Science
Lamar University,
Beaumont, TX 77706
001 (409) 880-7741
Jane.liu@lamar.edu

Cheng-Hsien Lin
Dept. of Sociology, Social Work, and Criminal Justice
Lamar University
Beaumont, TX 77706
001 (409) 880-8339
cheng-hsien.lin@lamar.edu

Phillip Potter, Ethan Philip Hasson, Zebulun David Barnett, and Michael Singleton
Dept. of Computer Science
Lamar University
Beaumont, TX 77706
001 (409) 880-7741
{ppotter, ephasson, zdbarnett, msingleton} @lamar.edu

ABSTRACT
More and more students are interested in developing their own mobile applications. Incorporating mobile technology into classrooms can greatly capture student attention, better student engagement, and improve student achievement. In this paper, we present our experience, findings, and lessons learned from conducting a one-week App Inventor for Android summer computing workshop for K-12 teachers. Our workshop focuses on using App Inventor, a drag-and-drop Android development environment, introduce computing concepts to K-12 teachers in all subjects. During the workshop the teachers developed curriculum applications for the subjects they will teach in the following semesters with the help of our workshop tutors. Workshop assessment results show a 29.5% increase in confidence level in teaching computer science and a 109% computing knowledge level increase.

Categories and Subject Descriptors
K.3.2 [Computers and Education]: Computer and Information Science Education – *computer science education, information systems education, curriculum.*

General Terms
Experimentations, Design, Human factors.

Keywords
Computer science education, computing education K-12 outreach, K-12 teacher training, computing workshop, summer workshop, summer outreach program.

1. INTRODUCTION
Between the years 2001 and 2007, the number of degrees earned in computer science (CS) has been decreasing. According to the Higher Education Research Institute (HERI) at the University of California, Los Angeles (UCLA), between 2000 and 2005 there was a 50% decline in the number of newly declared CS majors and a 70% decline in the number of incoming freshmen who expressed an interest in CS majors [8]. A similar decline had been reported in the Computing Research Association (CRA) Taulbee Survey during the 2000's. Even though the 2010-2011 CRA Taulbee Survey reported an increase of 9.6% in the number of undergraduate C.S. majors, the College Board discontinued the Advanced Placement (AP) Computer Science "AB" course following the May 2009 exam administration due to the low participation in that course [5]. However, the Bureau of Labor Statistics predicts that the demand for software developers will grow more than twice as fast as the average for all occupations in the U. S. over the next decade [4]. Therefore, the computing workforce might face a shortfall in the next decade. The education crisis in computer science has been drawing critical attention and compelling educators to produce more computer scientists.

Computer science educators have tried different ways to attract more students to computing fields: computing camps for K-12 students, outreach programs for K-12 teachers, new teaching tools, changes of policy, professional networks, etc. Mobile devices, such as Android phones/tablets, iPhones, iPads, are becoming increasingly popular among K-12 teachers and students. More and more students are interested in developing their own mobile applications (apps). Most of these apps would be in the form of a game which would require functionality such as basic graphics, sound, touch-screen inputs, and other sensors. Creating a game requires an understanding of all aspects of programming, so we are convinced that encouraging game development is a very effective way to inspire students to pursue a career in computer science. Incorporating mobile technology into classrooms can greatly capture student attention, better student engagement, and improve student achievement. App Inventor narrows the gap between a student's current ability and the ability required to create the types of games he/she would like to create.

App Inventor was released in 2010 by Google as an easy way of creating applications for their mobile platform. In 2011, development of the project was transferred to the Center for Mobile Learning at MIT where they continue to support and improve App Inventor. Over the past two years of development, many Android features have been implemented in App Inventor; most important of which include the ability to: place or accept

SIGCSE'13, March 6–9, 2013, Denver, Colorado, USA.

phone calls, send or receive text messages, interface the various built-in sensors, use the text-to-speech and speech-recognition modules, play audio, and manipulate graphics. However, App Inventor does have limitations, some of which include: inability to create fully object-oriented programs, no access to internet resources without a pre-existing API (e.g. Facebook, YouTube, Amazon) and inability to upload apps to the Google Play Store.

In this paper, we present our experience, findings, and lessons learned from conducting a one-week App Inventor summer computing workshop for K-12 teachers. Our workshop focused on introducing fundamental computing concepts to K-12 teachers using App Inventor for Android, a drag-and-drop Android development environment. The workshop was designed for K-12 teachers of all subjects at all levels. K-12 teachers play an important role in preparing students for college and helping them thrive in the 21st-century global workforce. During the workshop, the participants developed their own App Inventor curriculum materials that they could take back and use in their classrooms to introducing fundamental computing concepts to students. The workshop was assessed by an outside program evaluator for future improvements.

The organization of the rest of this paper is as follows. We review related work in Sec. 2. Next, in Sec. 3, we describe workshop organization including learning objectives, schedules, and lesson plans. Then, in Sec. 4, we discuss various App Inventor curriculum projects designed and developed by the participants using the computing concepts learned at the workshop. In Sec. 5, we present assessment results. Finally, we conclude in Sec. 6.

2. RELATED WORK

K-12 teacher outreach programs have been shown to be an effective means of making computer science accessible to those teachers. A survey was conducted by Lamar University on computer science K-12 teacher training programs in 2011 [12].

Carnegie Mellon University offered the CS4HS and CSbots programs which targeted high school computer science teachers [2][10]. In 2010, Marquette University led the "Computational Thinking for the Sciences" workshop, a three-day summer workshop for high school science and mathematics teachers [1]. Lamar University offered summer workshops for K-12 teachers in 2010 [11]. During the summer of 2008, Duke University conducted a three-week Alice training course for middle school teachers [13]. Saint Joseph's University became the site at which the Teacher Enrichment in Computer Science course was based [7]. The Georgia Institute of Technology also put in an effort to improve the aging computer science education pipeline currently employed in the state by offering a series of teacher workshops, starting in 2006, to influence CS teaching styles in a positive manner [3].

However, to the best of our knowledge, App Inventor has not been used in any K-12 teacher outreach programs before 2012. In 2009, Google launched a pilot program with ten universities where App Inventor was taught as a core college curriculum course [13]. In summer 2011, Valdosta State University offered an App Inventor summer camp for high school students [9].

3. WORKSHOP OVERVIEW

The five-day workshop was divided into morning and afternoon periods. The participants were given pre- and post-session quizzes at the beginning and the end of each day relevant to the computing topics covered. These pre- and post-session quizzes were designed to assess if the concepts presented were actually absorbed upon the participants. Table 1 shows the workshop schedule and the computing concepts covered at the workshop.

The morning period was usually broken into two sessions, each introducing fundamental computing concepts along with sample exercises and class assignments used to specifically demonstrate the session's programming topic. The step-by-step sample programs taught during the class often introduced additional capabilities available for Android devices through the App Inventor program.

The afternoons were used by the participants to develop their own curriculum projects that could be taken back and used in their own classrooms. During the afternoon curriculum development period, our tutors would assist the participants as needed. The participants presented their App Inventor curriculum apps on the last day of the workshop.

Table 1: Workshop Schedule & Computing Concepts Covered

	Day				
	Mon.	Tue.	Wed.	Thur.	Fri.
9:00am-9:30am	Opening Session	S-2 Conditional Branching	S-4 Methods	S-6 Advanced Topics 1	CD Demo
9:30am-10:30am	Session-0 (S-0) App Inventor Overview				
10:30am - 11:00am	S-1a Variables	S-3 Loops	S-5 Lists (Arrays)	S-7 Advanced Topics 2	
11:20am - 12:00pm	S-1b User input				Closing Session
1:00pm-3:00pm	Curriculum Development (CD)	CD	CD	CD	

3.1 Session-0: App Inventor Overview

After the opening registration, an overview of the App Inventor was presented introducing the software development environment to be used in the workshop. The App Inventor Overview was sectioned into three parts, one for each component of the program: the Component Designer, the Blocks Editor, and the Android Emulator. The participants were also shown how to launch the Android Emulator to simulate execution of the newly designed program.

Each of the following sessions consisted of a presentation explaining fundamental computing concepts. The presentation also included a sample program, which was developed together by the workshop instructor and participants to demonstrate the concept presented. The participants were then given an assignment to develop individually with the help of the tutors.

3.2 Session-1a Variables

The first concept presented was the creation and use of variables. Variables for the three App Inventor data types: text (or string), number, and Boolean were explained. Several variables were created, renamed, and given initial values. **Sample:** The sample program showed the use of a global variable to store the number of times a button is clicked. The counter variable named "total is incremented every time a button is clicked. **Assignment:** The participants were then assigned the task to create an app that changed the contents of two different kinds of variables using a button click event to trigger the change.

3.3 Session-1b: User Input

This concept of the textbox component was presented to the participants as the primary method of collecting numeric or textual information from the user. Adding a textbox component, located in the Palette Basic Panel, was shown to the participants. The textbox's two events, *GotFocus* and *LostFocus*, were explained as well as the *hint*, *text*, *numeric only restriction*, and *multiline* properties. **Sample:** The textbox functionality was demonstrated in a sample program that asks the users to input their name and the grade they taught. The program would then concatenate that information into a single sentence that stated their name and the grade they taught using two labels to display the information. **Assignment:** The project assigned to the class asked the participants to design a program that asks the user to input a string and then, upon a button click, manipulate the string using three labels to display the resulting output. The first label was to show the input in uppercase, the second label was to show only a portion of the string, and the third label was to show the result of appending another string to the original string.

3.4 Session-2: Conditional Branching, Boolean Expressions

Session-2 introduced two types of *if* blocks provided by the App Inventor as well as the use of Boolean values and expressions used in the decision making processes of a program. The structure of both the *if/then-do* and the *if/then-do/else-do* blocks were explained. Also, briefly introduced were the Boolean operators and their functions on Boolean variables and values. **Sample:** The sample program graphically demonstrated a coin flip by changing the picture of an *image* component between a picture of the head of a quarter and a picture of the tail of a quarter. The picture to display was determined by the Math function block, *random integer*. The generator function was set to return a value of 1 or 2, and conditional branching was used to determine which image would be displayed. The App Inventor block code is shown in Figure 1. **Assignment:** The assignment for the conditional branching concept required the participants to create a program that asked the user a question, had the user provide the answer in a textbox, and then told the user if the answer was correct or not.

3.5 Session-3: Loops

Three type of looping control blocks were explained using the Built-In Control Blocks in the Block Editor. The structure and the parameters used with the *for range* loop, *while* loop, and "infinite while loop" were presented and explained. The *for range* loop block's *start*, *end*, and *step* parameters were explained. **Sample:** The sample allowed the user to enter the number of seconds a ball would be allowed to move across the canvas bouncing from side to side. **Assignment:** The project assigned to the participants called for the creation of a program that displays a list of random numbers between 1 and 9 that initially prompts the user for the

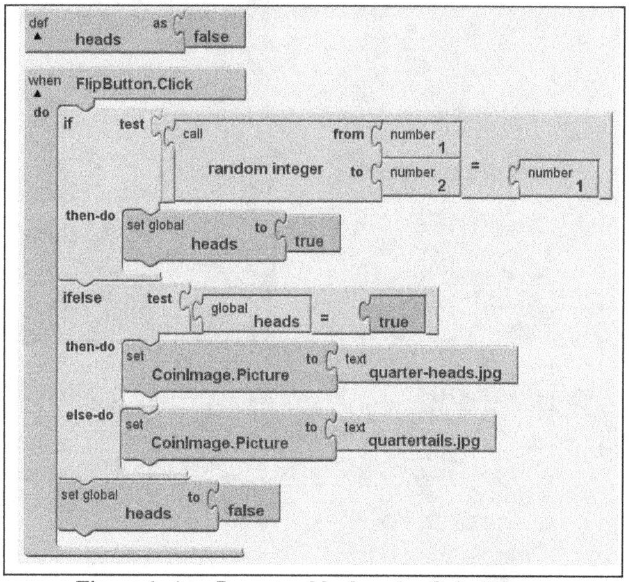

Figure 1. App Inventor block code: Coin Flip.

number of random numbers to be displayed. The solution would involve the use of the *for range loop* block with the upper bound set to the value entered by the user.

3.6 Session-4: Procedures (Methods and Functions)

Session-4 discussed the implementation of procedures and their functionality. It was explained that the App Inventor provides two types of procedure blocks, one that returned a value and one that did not. It was shown that a procedure may or may not include arguments. The participants were shown how to create a procedure from the Blocks Editor Built-In definitions. It was also explained that newly created procedures must be renamed to a meaningful description of the functions they performed. **Sample:** The sample program created a procedure, App Inventor's equivalent to a function or method, that calculated the length of the hypotenuse of a right triangle using textboxes to input the length of the opposite and adjacent sides of the triangle. The resulting length of the hypotenuse was calculated in a procedure that accepted the two sides' lengths as arguments and returned the hypotenuse length that was displayed using a label. **Assignment:** The assignment required the participants to ask the user for three inputs and create any kind of output using the inputs through use of procedures.

3.7 Session-5: Advanced Boolean and Lists

A more detailed explanation of Boolean operators was presented including Boolean values, variables and. The comparison operator blocks for both textual and numerical data were demonstrated. The Block Editor's Built-In Lists functions such as *make a list*, *select list item*, and *length of list* were presented to the participants. The Built-In List functions to manipulate the list, such as *add items to list*, *append to list*, *insert list item*, *replace list item*, and *remove list item*, were also discussed. **Sample:** This sample program was designed based on the tutorial given on the App Inventor web site. The sample program created a rudimentary "Quiz" program where the questions and answers were "hard coded" into the app. This was done by using a list for

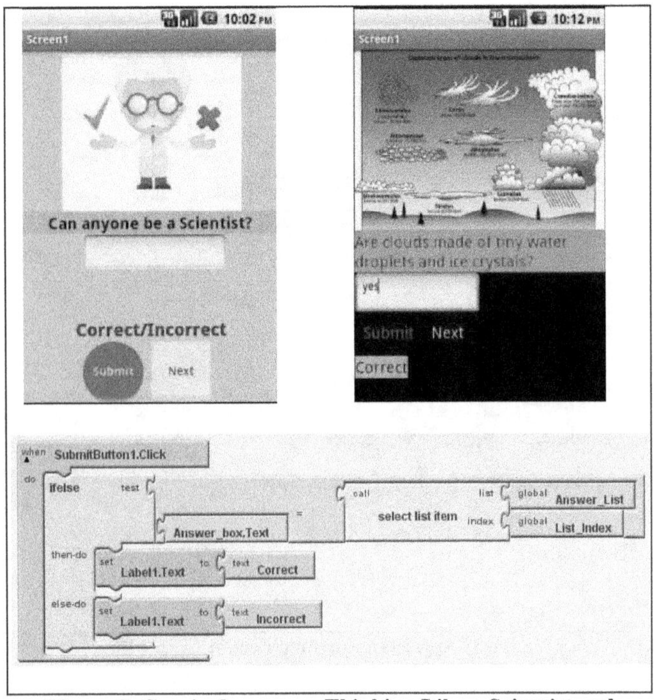

Figure 2. Curriculum apps: Thinking Like a Scientist and Weather Review.

the questions and another list for the answers. The program would cycle through questions while continuing to increment an index variable to check the answer. **Assignments:** The project asked the participants to modify the sample "Quiz" program by adding an image for each of the questions asked and by having one question have multiple answers.

3.8 Session-6 and Session-7: Advanced Topics

Session-6 introduced data storage implemented with the App Inventor and Android devices. Two components were discussed, *tinyDB* and *tinyWebDB*, that are available for storing data locally to the Android device or online using a shared database. **Sample:** The sample program expanded on the Quiz example from the previous session. This sample was modeled based on the App Inventor Tutorial MakeQuiz on the App Inventor website. The tutorial was modified to allow for two additional incorrect answers for each of the questions, which allows for multiple-choice answers in the TakeQuiz sample. Once all the information was inputted, the lists were saved to the online testing database using the *tinyWebDB* component.

Session-7 discussed more of the components available with an Android device. The use of the media components, sensor components, and other device dependent functions were reviewed. **Sample:** The sample program for Session-7 built the corresponding TakeQuiz app used in association with the MakeQuiz app presented in Session-6.

4. CURRICULUM MATERIALS DEVELOPED BY WORKSHOP PARTICIPANTS

During the workshop, the participants also designed interesting curriculum materials using App Inventor for various subjects in science, math, etc. Table 2 shows the detailed information of all curriculum apps designed by the participants. The curriculum materials were developed for grades ranging from kindergarten to 12th grade. Most materials require 30-45 minute lecture times. The participants were able to use App Inventor to implement the apps and incorporate computing concepts, such as variables, inputs, conditional branches, lists, and methods in their apps.

As shown in Figure 2, the Thinking Like A Scientist app was to test users' knowledge about the requirements of a Scientists career. The question is presented, followed by an answer box for the user to type the correct answer into. The answer the user supplies is compared to the correct answer in the answer list using the current index. In the Weather Review app, all questions were related to weather, so the grade range focus was fairly limited. Two lists were used: one containing the correct answers, one containing the question. An index was used to step through and compare the answer, which was supplied by the application user and was the same as the one found in the answer list.

Figure 3 shows the Reading for Kindergarteners app and its App Inventor block code. It starts with the name of an animal that the students will be learning about. The app consists of a button that displays the picture of the animal, another button that pronounces the word when the user clicks it, a third button that makes a sound that is associated to the specific animal shown, and a fourth button that cycles through a list of animals.

Figure 3. Curriculum app: Reading for Kindergarteners.

5. ASSESSMENT AND FEEDBACK

5.1 ASSESSMENT RESULTS

Our outside program evaluator collected multiple pre- and post workshop assessment materials for the evaluation of the workshop's effectiveness. There were two types of assessment: workshop participant self-assessment and assessment by the workshop instructors to avoid self-interest issues in the workshop effectiveness outcomes. In addition, participants completed a workshop evaluation questionnaire and accepted a face-to-face interview to provide some in-depth feedback to the workshop administration. The summary of the assessment results are given below.

Among the fourteen participants, there was only one male teacher. The majority of the group were 50 years old or older (mean = 46.1 years old). Results from the pre-workshop survey showed that five participants completed a bachelor's degree and nine participants earned a master's degree. The workshop had a good mix of elementary school, middle school, and high school teachers. The elementary school teachers accounted for 57% of the participants

Table 2. App Inventor Curriculum Materials Developed by Workshop Participants

Project Name	Grade	Target Subject	Time Required	Computing Concepts Used in Project
Science				
Thinking Like a Scientist	2nd grade	Science	Two class periods	Lists, conditionals, variables
Weather Review	2nd grade	Science	Two 10-20 minutes	Lists, variables, conditionals
The Sun	5th	Science	15 minutes	Variables, lists, conditionals
Formula Practice	8th grade	Science	30 minutes	User input
Auto Hetero	9th grade	Biology	6-7 minutes	Conditionals, variables
Math				
Counting by Tens	2nd grade	Math	35 minutes	Conditionals, variables
Balancing Check Book	3rd Grade	Math	30 minutes	Variables, loops, conditionals
Estimation	5th	Math	45 minutes	Variables, conditionals
Average Temperatures	9-12	Tech., Math, Sci.	1-2 weeks	Lists, variables, user input, loops
Other				
Reading with Kindergarteners!	Kindergarten	Reading	20 minutes	Variables, lists, conditionals,
Vocabulary Building	3rd to 5th	Reading/Writing	10 min. daily	Lists
Understanding Colors	3rd - 9th	Art	1 hour	*Unavailable*
GPA Calculator	6,7,8	Cross-Curriculum	Two 45 minutes	Variables, user input
Info-Final	9th - 12th grade	Introduction	45 minutes	Lists, variables, user input, methods

(eight out of fourteen). Three participants teach middle school, and the other three teach high school. Their areas of teaching range from Social Science, Science (Biology/Chemistry), Math, English, Reading, to computer related subjects; however, two teach almost all subjects in elementary schools. Our participants, on average, have taught for more than 11 years.

Pre- and post- self-assessment surveys were given at the beginning and ending of the workshop, allowing participants to rank themselves in their conceptual knowledge of the items taught. All self-assessment questions are ranked on a scale from 1 to 5; 1 indicating they felt very uncertain and 5 indicating they felt very comfortable with the concept. The post-workshop self-assessment per-person average was 3.60, which was an appreciable improvement from the pre-workshop average score of 2.78. Compared to the last year, participants' post self-assessment seemed to be rather moderate. Some further analyses may be needed to examine the difference.

From our in-depth face-to-face interviews, participants mentioned that there are a few areas of the Computing Workshop that could be changed to create a better experience for the participants: Most participants feel like the timeframe is not enough to comprehend the more advanced concepts showcased, and they suggest either two weeks or slightly extended hours each day being used instead. Also, a few participants expressed wanting prior knowledge of the workshop's software and lesson scheduling.

Although there is room for improvement in the workshop, there are plenty of aspects that participants find positive. The most prominent compliments given to the workshop is the high ratio of tutors-to-participants (2:1) and the frequent assistance in general. There seemed to be a consensus that having help at arm's reach was vital to keep the participants on track with the fast pace of the course. It also established a more comfortable atmosphere for them to work in and succeed. The participants very much appreciated the App Inventor with Android as the development software and platform of choice. They consider it very relevant to both their work environments and students' interests at school. All participants found that the App Inventor was an excellent program as a part of their teaching tools; especially because it is a new technology that may intrigue their students and colleagues. From the participants' perspective, the strong points of the workshop are the easily accessible help and the relevant nature of what is being developed and developed on.

We also developed a number of questions for instructors to measure the amount of material the participants would take away from the workshop. We did this by creating pre- and post-questions to test their knowledge of the subject discussed during each session. Each student was evaluated by both of our instructors to improve the measurement reliability. Table 3 shows average percentage increases ranging from 56.2% to 150.3%. The rubric used for grading these tests is given in Table 3.

6. CONCLUSIONS

Our workshop focuses on using App Inventor, an easy-to-use, drag-and-drop Android development environment, to introduce computing concepts to K-12 teachers at all K-12 levels to expose students to computing at an early age and to reach more students. During the workshop, the teachers develop App Inventor curriculum apps for the subjects they will teach in the following semesters. Based on the pre- and post-workshop assessment results, the participants were able to indicate their confidence in the concepts presented in the workshop. In the pre-workshop assessment, the results indicate a confidence level average of 2.78 out of 5. However, the average post-workshop assessment score was 3.60 out of 5, a 29.5% increase in confidence level. A similar change was observed upon analysis of the pre- and post-tests (graded by workshop instructors) for each session. Participants scored an average 1.55 out of 5 on the pre-session tests, but that score rose to 3.24 on the post-session tests, a 109% knowledge level increase.

Table 3. Pre-Test and Post-Test Assessment Results

Session	Pre-Test Average score/ per participant in each session	Post-Test Average Score/per participant in each section	Score changed (percentage increased)
Day-1	1.42	3.10	+1.68(118.3%)
Day-2	1.53	3.83	+2.30(150.3%)
Day-3	1.94	3.03	+1.09(56.2%)
Day-4	1.31	3.01	+1.70(129.8%)
Rubrics: 1. No understanding of the concept 2. Very little understanding of the concept 3. Little understanding of the concept 4. Moderate understanding of the concept 5. Complete understanding of the concept			

7. ACKNOWLEDGMENTS

This project was supported by US National Science Foundation grant #0846053. All opinions reflected in this paper are those of the authors and not necessarily those of NSF.

8. REFERENCES

[1] Ahamed, S. I., Brylow, D., Ge, R., Madiraju, P., Merrill, S. J., Struble, C. A., and Early, J. P. 2010. Computational thinking for the sciences: a three day workshop for high school science teachers. In Proceedings of the 41st ACM Technical Symposium on Computer Science Education (Milwaukee, Wisconsin, USA, March 10 - 13, 2010). SIGCSE '10. ACM, New York, NY, 42-46. DOI= http://doi.acm.org/10.1145/1734263.1734277

[2] Blum, L. and Cortina, T. J. 2007. CS4HS: an outreach program for high school CS teachers. In Proceedings of the 38th SIGCSE Technical Symposium on Computer Science Education (Covington, Kentucky, USA, March 07 - 11, 2007). SIGCSE '07. ACM, New York, NY, 19-23. DOI= http://doi.acm.org/10.1145/1227310.1227320

[3] Bruckman, A., Biggers, M., Ericson, B., McKlin, T., Dimond, J., DiSalvo, B., Hewner, M., Ni, L., and Yardi, S. 2009. "Georgia computes!": improving the computing education pipeline. In Proceedings of the 40th ACM Technical Symposium on Computer Science Education (Chattanooga, TN, USA, March 04 - 07, 2009). SIGCSE '09. ACM, New York, NY, 86-90. DOI= http://doi.acm.org/10.1145/1508865.1508899

[4] Bureau of Labor Statistics, 2010. Occupational Outlook Handbook, 2010-2011 Edition. DOI=http://www.bls.gov/oco/oco2003.htm.

[5] College Board, 2008. Important Announcement about AP Computer Science AB, April 2008. DOI= http://apcentral.collegeboard.com/apc/public/courses/teachers_corner/195948.html.

[6] Computing Research Association Taulbee Survey, 2010. Computing degree and enrollment trends. DOI= http://www.cra.org/govaffairs/blog/wp-content/uploads/2010/03/CRATaulbee-2010-ComputingDegreeandEnrollmentTrends.pdf.

[7] Cooper, S., Dann, W., and Harrison, J. 2010. A k-12 college partnership. In Proceedings of the 41st ACM Technical Symposium on Computer Science Education (Milwaukee, Wisconsin, USA, March 10 - 13, 2010). SIGCSE '10. ACM, New York, NY, 320-324. DOI= http://doi.acm.org/10.1145/1734263.1734371

[8] Higher Education Research Institute (HERI), 2006. CIRP freshman survey. University of California at Los Angeles. DOI= http://www.gseis.ucla.edu/heri/freshman.html.

[9] Krishnendu Roy. 2012. App inventor for android: report from a summer camp. In Proceedings of the 43rd ACM technical symposium on Computer Science Education (SIGCSE '12). ACM, New York, NY, USA, 283-288. DOI=10.1145/2157136.2157222 http://doi.acm.org/10.1145/2157136.2157222

[10] Lauwers, T., Hamner, E., and Nourbakhsh, I.. 2010. A Strategy for Collaborative Outreach: Lessons from the CSbots Project. In Proceedings of the 41st ACM technical symposium on Computer Science Education (Milwaukee, WI, USA, March 10-13, 2010).SIGCSE '10. ACM, New York, NY, USA, 315-319. DOI= http://doi.acm.org/10.1145/1734263.1734370.

[11] Liu, J., Lin, C., Hasson, E., and Barnett, Z. 2011. Introducing computer science to K-12 through a summer computing workshop for teachers. In Proceedings of the 42nd ACM technical symposium on Computer science education (SIGCSE '11). ACM, New York, NY, USA, 389-394. DOI=10.1145/1953163.1953277 http://doi.acm.org/10.1145/1953163.1953277

[12] Liu, J., Lin, C., Hasson, E., and Barnett, Z., and Zhang, P. "A Survey on Computer Science K-12 Outreach: Teacher Training Programs," In Proceedings of the 41st Annual IEEE Frontiers in Education Conference (FIE 2011), pp. T4F-1 – T4F-6, Rapid City, SD, Oct. 12-15, 2011

[13] Rodger, S. H., Hayes, J., Lezin, G., Qin, H., Nelson, D., Tucker, R., Lopez, M., Cooper, S., Dann, W., and Slater, D. 2009. Engaging middle school teachers and students with Alice in a diverse set of subjects. In Proceedings of the 40th ACM technical symposium on Computer science education (SIGCSE '09). ACM, New York, NY, USA, 271-275. DOI=10.1145/1508865.1508967 http://doi.acm.org/10.1145/1508865.1508967

[14] Wolber, D. 2011. App inventor and real-world motivation. In *Proceedings of the 42nd ACM technical symposium on Computer science education* (SIGCSE '11). ACM, New York, NY, USA, 601-606. DOI=10.1145/1953163.1953329 http://doi.acm.org/10.1145/1953163.1953329

A Large-Scale Quantitative Study of Women in Computer Science at Stanford University

Katie Redmond
Computer Science Department
Stanford University
Stanford, CA 94305, USA
kredmond@cs.stanford.edu

Sarah Evans
Computer Science Department
Stanford University
Stanford, CA 94305, USA
sevans1@stanford.edu

Mehran Sahami
Computer Science Department
Stanford University
Stanford, CA 94305, USA
sahami@cs.stanford.edu

ABSTRACT

In this paper, we analyze gender dynamics in the undergraduate Computer Science program at Stanford University through a quantitative analysis of 7209 academic transcripts and 536 survey responses. We examine previously studied effects as well as present new findings. We also introduce Fisher's Noncentral Hypergeometric Distribution as a model for estimating the impact of program changes on underrepresented populations and explain why it is a more robust measure than changes in the *percentage* of minority participants.

Categories and Subject Descriptors

K.3.2 [**Computers and Education**]: Computer and Information Science Education – *Computer science education*

Keywords

Gender diversity, women in computing science.

1. INTRODUCTION

Despite the awareness of the need to increase participation by women in computing, the National Center for Women and Information Technology reports that only 18% of 2010 Computer and Information Sciences undergraduate degree recipients were female [16]. The Computer Research Association reports that less than 12% of Bachelor's degrees in Computer Science were awarded to women at North American research universities in 2011 [22]. While there has been much qualitative analysis about what drives women's relationship with computing, there are few large-scale quantitative studies that offer actionable results.

In this paper, we examine a number of factors related to women's participation in Computer Science through a quantitative analysis of 7209 academic transcripts and 536 survey responses from students at Stanford University. We examine previously studied effects as well as present new findings.

As part of our study, we also examine the impact of a recent CS curriculum change at Stanford on gender dynamics in the major. We also present Fisher's Noncentral Hypergeometric Distribution [6] as an effective model for gauging the impact of a curriculum change on female participation and show that simply measuring growth in the percentage of women in a program can be a flawed indicator when program changes lead to a total increase in the number of participants.

SIGCSE'13, March 6–9, 2013, Denver, Colorado, USA.

Our study examines students at Stanford University, where the Computer Science department is housed within the School of Engineering. Students have until the end of their sophomore year to declare a major. Stanford has a set of introductory programming/systems courses numbered CS106A, CS106B and CS107. CS106A and CS106B correspond to CS1 and CS2, respectively, with the former being taught in Java and the latter in C++. Additionally, an accelerated course, CS106X, is offered as an alternative to the CS106A/B sequence for students with previous computing background. CS107 is the first systems course that CS majors are required to take. It is taught in C, and the main emphasis of the course is on understanding low-level topics (such as memory management and compilation) as opposed to the mechanics of programming.

While CS106A (and to some extent CS106B) are required for a variety of majors and are taken by a large percentage of the entire undergraduate population, CS107 is only required for students majoring in Computer Science or a few other highly-related majors. CS107 is commonly regarded by students as a "weeder" class, a critical juncture for students to decide whether they wish to continue on with a major in CS. As mentioned previously, there was a significant curriculum change made in the CS program during the 2008/09 school year that created a track (i.e., concentration area) structure in the major, including adding multi-disciplinary course options [18]. While the curricula for CS106A/B/X remained unchanged, there was a revision of the contents of CS107, with the class transitioning from significant coverage of C language mechanics to include more of an emphasis on understanding systems concepts such as code compilation, basic computer organization, and memory management. Thus, we give CS107 special consideration in our study to both understand its impact on CS declarations as well as see if the curriculum revision had any impact on participation by women. Additional details of the curriculum revision are available in [18].

2. RELATED WORK

The level of gender diversity in computing has far reaching consequences. On a purely economic level, the projected significant shortfall in computing graduates [5] could be better addressed by broadening participation by women in the field. More socially, the lack of women in computing enables sexism and perpetuates stereotype threat [3, 13, 19] by corroborating the misconception that the small number of women in computing is indicative of a lack of belonging or ability. It has also been suggested that lack of gender diversity may potentially inhibit the diversity of ideas generated in the field [7]. As a result, understanding the factors that contribute to a woman's choice whether or not to pursue computing has been studied from different perspectives for more than two decades [2, 8, 14, 20].

Two similar studies have been conducted at Stanford in the past decade. The first [11] analyzed women's attitudes and participation in Stanford's introductory curriculum in 2003. This study concluded that while CS107 did not seem to filter more women than men out of the CS pipeline, the women studied reported lower self-confidence and comfort with computers than their male counterparts. The study focused primarily on a qualitative analysis of women's confidence in CS classes in the context of gendered communication and self-presentation. Although this study was performed before the curriculum change we analyze here, it provides a crucial context for our understanding of CS107 and the way such "gatekeeper" classes are experienced by each gender.

The second Stanford study [9] provided an ethnographic analysis of the importance of family influence and interactions with instructors as a means for encouraging women in CS, reinforcing the importance of mentoring previously posited as a crucial factor in helping retain women in computing majors [4]. The study also raised broader social issues, such as the degree to which women self-identified as "engineers" and the perceived relevance of one's major toward future career paths—themes also studied qualitatively by Margolis, Fisher, and Miller [15] that we revisit more quantitatively in this study.

The finding that women self-report lower skills with computing technology upon entering college has been documented in other settings as well [1, 10, 17], and is related to fact that men generally have more experience than women in computing prior to entering college [1, 15, 17]. This observed difference between men and women in prior computing experience sets an important foundation for the study we conduct here. Indeed, we not only provide further quantitative validation of this phenomenon in our setting, but delve further into its implications with respect to gender differences in course performance, finding significant downstream impacts. Moreover, prior familiarity with computing also influences the point in a student's academic career when CS courses are taken, and we find clear gender differences along these lines. This point ultimately becomes a crucial feature in the dynamic of whether students choose to pursue a major in CS.

3. DATA GATHERING

To analyze gender differences related to academic performance as well as issues related to confidence, prior computing experience and views of computing, our study gathered two types of information: academic transcripts and survey data.

3.1 Academic Transcripts

We obtained partial academic transcripts for all students at Stanford from 1995 to 2012 who had taken either CS106B or CS106X. We chose to include all students who had taken CS106B/X (equivalent to CS2) as this population includes those students who had shown a level of interest in computing beyond CS106A (CS1). The anonymous partial transcripts include students' grades for the courses CS106A/B/X and CS107 (if taken) as well as the students' major and major declaration date. This data was used to analyze gender differences in the choice of major and CS course performance. This data set includes transcripts for 7209 students, 4281 of whom also took CS107.

3.2 Surveys

To gather information related to confidence, prior computing experience, and views of computing, we distributed an online survey to all students who had taken CS106A/B/X or CS105 (Stanford's CS0 course) during the 2011-12 year, as well as to all current Computer Science and Symbolic Systems majors. By surveying students in CS105 as well as Symbolic Systems (a non-CS, but computing-related major in the School of Humanities and Sciences) we could get a broader sampling of students across majors and programs. Survey questions included both free response questions (which were independently coded by the first two authors until consistency was achieved) and Likert-scale rating questions on a range of issues addressing self-perception and views of one's major. Students were incentivized to complete the anonymous survey by being entered into a drawing for one of eight $50 Amazon.com gift cards. The survey was distributed to approximately 2500 students and we received 536 responses.

4. A NEW STATISTICAL MODEL

As we report below, for many comparisons of gender differences with respect to some variable or attribute, classical statistical models (e.g., t-tests, Pearson correlation, Cramer's V measure of association, etc.) are useful and appropriate, given the quantity of data available. However, when reporting increases in participation by women in computing, the traditionally used measure of the *percentage* of women in a particular population (e.g., in a specific class, majoring in CS, etc.) can be (surprisingly) problematic when the overall size of that population is also in flux. For example, consider a college that has (as many do) a total population that is roughly 50% women, but a population of CS majors which is only 18% women. As the number of CS majors as a whole grows (hypothetically approaching the population of the whole college), the *percentage* of women majoring in CS must also grow to approach the total college percentage of women (50%). Thus, it would appear that CS was becoming more attractive to women (relative to men), even if the true dynamic was simply that CS had become more attractive to *both* genders. The increase in the percentage of women is simply a statistical artifact of growth in the CS major population, not an indication that the major has actually become more attractive to women (relative to men) than it was before.

To provide a more robust statistical model that better measures the likelihood of women choosing to pursue a major in CS relative to men, we suggest the use of Fisher's Noncentral Hypergeometric (FNCH) distribution [6]. FNCH is a generalization of the Hypergeometric distribution where sampling probabilities (of black and white balls in an urn) are *unequally* weighted. The probability mass function of the FNCH distribution is given by:

$$P(X=i)=\frac{\binom{m_1}{i}\binom{m_2}{n-i}w^i}{\sum_{j=x_{\min}}^{x_{\max}}\binom{m_1}{j}\binom{m_2}{n-j}w^j},$$

where m_1 = number of white balls in the urn, m_2 = number of black balls in the urn, n = number of balls drawn (simultaneously) from the urn, $x_{\min} = \max(0, n - m_2)$, $x_{\max} = \min(n, m_1)$, and w = relative weight of drawing a white ball as opposed to a black ball. The variable X denotes the number of white balls drawn from the urn (after n draws).

To explain the analogy with gender composition in CS, consider an urn (college) which contains a particular number of black balls (men) and white balls (women). We then choose as many balls (simultaneously) from the urn as the number of CS majors, where the color of the chosen balls reflects the gender composition in CS. If the numbers of black and white balls in the urn were the same to begin with and either color was *equally* likely to be drawn ($w = 1$), then our sample representing CS majors would have a maximum likelihood outcome of containing the same number of black and white balls (men and women). However, if the white balls were to be *weighted* so as to be less likely to be drawn than black balls, then our sample would likely contain a higher proportion of black balls (men), as we see in real-world CS enrollments. Note that if there are the same number of black and white balls in the urn, and all the balls are drawn, we would still produce the a 50/50 outcome regardless of the weighting used.

To reiterate, the weight of the white balls in the FNCH model reflects the likelihood of a woman choosing to major in CS relative to a man. Given the other parameters (m_1, m_2, n, i) we can obtain a maximum likelihood estimate for w using numerical optimization, allowing us to measure the weighting factor in different populations. By focusing on this weighting factor (instead of percentages) we are able to more accurately measure the impact of changes aimed at making CS more attractive to women even in the face of changes in overall enrollment levels in CS. The underlying FNCH model dynamics are not distorted by the size of the sample of balls taken from the urn in the same way that a simple percentage measurement would be (as it would be forced to approach the population mean). This is especially important in accurately comparing women's participation in computing over time as overall enrollment levels fluctuate, which has certainly been the case in recent years.

5. RESULTS

5.1 Role Models and Social Factors

One of the main goals of the study was to provide quantitative evidence to support or refute issues that are often mentioned in relation to gender and computer science. In this vein, a frequent hypothesis is that women's decision to pursue computing is affected by the lack of female professors and role models [4, 9]. While we did not investigate the effect of industry role models, we found there was no significant impact of a professors' gender on women's propensity to take a class with him/her (t-test based on 2885 classes taught by men and 347 classes taught be women, $p = 0.2$). While this result is impacted by the fact that some courses are required rather than elective (and may only be taught by faculty of one gender), it still provides evidence that female students did not seem to seek out courses with female instructors.

On the other hand, we found that having parental support, especially maternal support, was a greater influence for women in computing than their male counterparts. The Cramer's V association between maternal/paternal support and sureness of one's career aspirations was measured stratifying by gender (male/female) and major (CS/non-CS). The results are below.

Association with sureness of career	Female CS	Male CS	Female non-CS	Male non-CS
Maternal support	0.26	0.18	0.18	0.15
Paternal support	0.24	0.15	0.18	0.16

Similarly, we found parental support (either maternal or paternal) to be highly associated with women calling themselves "hardcore" about CS. And while we found a similar high associate among men, the correlation is more pronounced for women:

Association with being "hardcore"	Female CS	Male CS
Maternal support	0.33	0.30
Paternal support	0.25	0.21

These results show that that parental support has a significant impact on female students' attitudes toward their academic and career paths, especially with regard to computing.

Another social factor that has been posited for why women may not pursue CS is the solitary nature of computing and lack of interaction with others. We found conflicting evidence regarding this claim. On a free-response survey question asking students for potential "cons" of majoring in CS, 14.7% of female CS majors (N=34) and 15.5% of female non-computing related majors (N=71) listed the solitariness of CS as a "con." However, only 11.9% of male CS majors (N=84) and 13% of male non-computing related majors (N=83) did so. Interestingly, women, regardless of whether they major in CS or not, seem to find CS a more solitary discipline (in a negative sense) than their male counterparts.

Paradoxically, based on transcript data we did not find evidence that women were more likely to take courses involving group work as a potential means to avoid a solitary working environment. Fitting weight parameters in the FNCH model across classes involving group projects (N=444) and those involving individual work (N=5680), we did not find that women were statistically any more likely to take CS classes involving group projects than CS classes involving only individual work ($p = 0.3$). From this finding we posit that simply developing a CS curriculum including more group projects may not necessarily help address women's view of solitary working conditions in the field unless there is a commensurate compelling reason for women to take such courses.

Another common belief regarding women in computing is that feeling like a "minority" in the field may deter women from considering or continuing on in CS. In our survey data, 84% of female CS majors (N=50) self-reported feeling like a gender minority in a free-response question asking if they identified as any form of minority in their major. This number was 52% for women survey respondents overall (N=229). However, feeling like a minority did not appear to be correlated with students' self-reported grades in CS106A or self-reported confidence asking questions of a CS professor. Since the survey and transcript data are both anonymous, we unfortunately cannot cross-correlate answers across them to validate actual grades in CS106A or grades in other CS courses. Nevertheless, we note that the high proportion of women who feel like a minority in CS creates greater potential for stereotype threat, which has been observed in other settings [13].

5.2 Confidence and Enjoyment

Next, we analyzed women's confidence with and enjoyment of factors related to computing (on 5 point scale). First, we examined women's self-reported confidence in their mathematical abilities. Female CS majors' (N=51, μ=3.3) rating of confidence in their math abilities was statistically indistinguishable from that of their female non-CS (N=180, μ=3.3) counterparts ($p = 0.7$). Thus, confidence in one's math abilities did not appear to be an important factor in women's choice to pursue CS. Nevertheless, in the overall population, men's self-reported confidence in their math abilities (N=299, μ=3.8) was higher than women's (N=231, μ=3.3) at a statistically significant level ($p < 0.001$).

Perhaps more importantly, we also observed a statistically significant ($p < 0.001$) gender discrepancy with respect to confidence asking questions in CS classes, as males (N=294, μ=3.7) rated themselves more confident asking questions than females (N=226, μ=3.2) did. Such gender differences are important for instructors to be aware of in classroom dynamics.

Moving from confidence to enjoyment, we wanted to better understand how factors related to the enjoyment of CS might reveal gender differences. Looking specifically at the introductory programming course CS106A, men (N=204, μ=4.5) self-reported enjoying this course more than women (N=164, μ=4.3) at a statistically significant level ($p = 0.02$). Restricting the data to only CS majors, this gender difference is no longer statistically significant ($p = 0.2$). This provides quantitative evidence for the unsurprising conclusion that the enjoyment of CS106A is an important factor in choosing to continue on in computing, but that the level of enjoyment is not gender balanced. It is important to consider how such a gender discrepancy can be decreased when designing introductory CS courses as it indeed has significant downstream impact (i.e., choice of major).

One possible cause for the discrepancy in enjoyment of CS106A is that we also found a gender difference in the enjoyment of problem solving, a more general factor we hypothesized would be strongly related to computing. Indeed, male survey respondents (N=299, μ=4.4) reported enjoying problem solving more than females (N=230, μ=4.1) by a significant margin ($p < 0.001$). And enjoyment of problem solving was indeed correlated with enjoying CS106A (Cramer's V value = 0.291). We also found that the enjoyment of problem solving is linked to the likelihood of majoring in CS, and we found significantly ($p = 0.01$) higher enjoyment of problem solving among women who major in CS (N=51, μ=4.3) versus those who do not (N=179, μ=4.0).

5.3 Prior Experience and Grades

Corroborating previous findings [1, 15, 17], we found higher rates of self-reported CS experience prior to college for males (N=298) than females (N=232):

Prior CS experience	All students	CS majors	Non-CS majors
Female	42.4%	45.1%	41.7%
Male	66.3%	75.0%	59.0%

Indeed, the difference in prior CS experience between all men and women was highly statistically significant ($p < 0.001$). So was the difference between prior CS experience for CS major men and women ($p < 0.001$) and for non-CS major men and women ($p < 0.002$). Of note, while some difference in the level of prior CS experience does exist between female CS majors and non-CS majors, this difference is much less pronounced than among men. This would seem to indicate that women's prior experiences with CS before coming to college were not as compelling a driver of their collegiate major choices as they were for men.

We hypothesized that having prior CS experience would improve students' performance in the introductory programming class (CS106A) and may also be one of the contributing factors to the gender-based confidence gap in the course, discussed in the previous section. Indeed, we found a relatively high (Cramer's V value = 0.293) correlation between having prior CS experience and students' grades in CS106A. Indeed, comparing the grades for students in the class with and without prior CS experience revealed a clear statistically significant difference ($p < 0.001$).

This finding led to a larger-scale comparison of course performance between men and women using transcript data. We examined the mean course grades (GPA) for men and women in our introductory series of programming/systems courses (CS106A, CS106B, CS106X, and CS107) from 1995 to 2012. We found statistically significant differences in grades by gender in every course examined (N is total number of students in all offerings of the course over the period examined):

Course grades	CS106A		CS106B		CS106X		CS107	
	N	GPA	N	GPA	N	GPA	N	GPA
Female	1367	3.63	1330	3.30	269	3.22	870	3.22
Male	3467	3.68	3590	3.41	1538	3.51	3408	3.33
p-value	0.005		< 0.001		< 0.001		< 0.001	

Interestingly, our results agree with smaller-scale studies conducted at other institutions [21], but contradict the conclusions of a previous study conducted by Irani a decade prior at our own institution [12]. We believe the difference stems from the fact that the previous study was based on only one year's worth of data. While it found that men did receive slightly higher grades than women in CS107, it did not include a large enough sample to detect statistical significance in this difference.

It is also important to point out that while we detect a clear difference in grades for men and women in these courses, we do not have a clear explanation as to *why*. Indeed, many factors shown to have gender differences, such as experience with CS before college, enjoyment of problem solving, or confidence asking questions may all be contributing factors to the difference in grades. We believe that this is a rich area for further study.

We did want to assess the potential impact of grades on whether women choose to continue on in CS beyond the introductory courses. Since CS107 is informally considered a "weeder" class by students, we examined women's grade differences between CS106B and CS107 (using transcript data) to see if students who chose not to major in CS after taking CS107 experienced a more significant drop in grade from CS106B than students who did major in CS. Interestingly, we found no significant difference in grade drop between women who became CS majors and those who did not ($p = 0.6$). We also found no significant difference in grade drop between women and men ($p = 0.6$). These results suggest that performance differences from the introductory classes do not affect women's choice of major after CS107 any more than men's choice, in alignment with the previous work of Irani that came to a similar conclusion using a different analysis.

5.4 Dynamics of Choosing a Major

Examining the theme of choice of major, our survey asked students how sure they were of their major upon entering college. We found that among CS majors, men (N=143, μ=2.8) were more sure of what their major would be upon entering college than were women (N=51, μ=1.9) at a highly statistically significant level ($p < 0.001$). This difference is likely related to the differing rates of experience with CS prior to college between

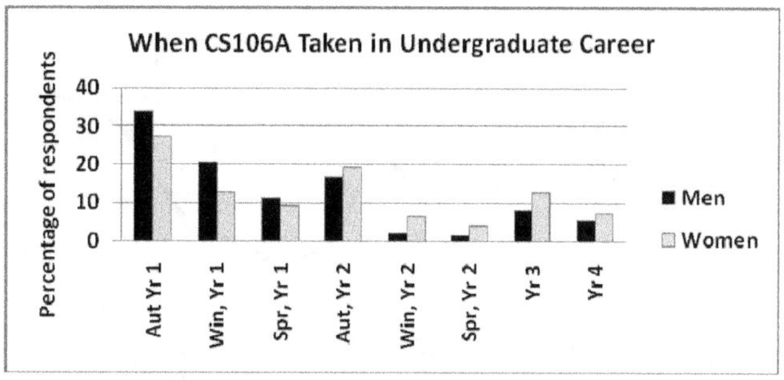

Figure 1. Percentage of survey respondents who took CS106A during various quarters/years of their undergraduate career. Aut, Win, and Spr refer to Autumn, Winter and Spring quarters of the year (1 = Freshman, 4 = Senior).

men and women, further punctuating the importance of early CS exposure.

Unfortunately, we found women (perhaps exacerbated by less CS familiarity prior to college) typically take their first college CS class later than men—a pattern seen in both survey responses and transcript data. Figure 1 shows the quarter/year in which men and women took CS106A (in the survey data, N_{men}=185, N_{women}=149).

The idea of encouraging women to take a CS class early in their college years takes on even greater importance in light of the fact that 25.4% of female non-CS majors taking the survey (N=71) reported that they had started taking CS courses too late in their academic career, a factor that was cited by only 8.8% of female respondents who did major in CS (N=34). Even more strikingly, 61% of female survey respondents said they would have considered a CS major more strongly if they had taken CS106A earlier. Indeed, we believe that encouraging women to take a CS course as early as possible as undergraduates is one of the most critical factors in promoting the number of women CS majors.

We also asked students to rate how relevant they believed their choice of major was to their future careers. Overall, men (N=299, μ=4.3) viewed their major as significantly more relevant to their career ($p < 0.001$) than women (N=231, μ=3.9). Restricting to just CS majors data (men: N=144, μ=4.6; women: N=51, μ=4.4), this pattern was still present, though not as significant ($p = 0.1$). This finding aligns with previous qualitative work [14] indicating that women look more at the broader social impacts of computing rather than focusing primarily on the technology itself, reflecting that the technology they learn as a result of their major is just a facet of what they will do in their careers after graduation.

5.5 Curriculum Changes

Finally, we want to understand the gender impact of the recent curriculum revision made in our CS program. While locally, we are interested in whether the curriculum change resulted in more gender diversity, the broader research question is one of how to robustly evaluate the impact of curricular changes on gender diversity, especially in light of overall fluctuating enrollments. Hence, we identified the FNCH model, and used it extensively in evaluating our curriculum revision.

We began by focusing on CS107, since—as part of the curriculum revision—the content of CS107 was also significantly revised. We examined the relative propensity for women (vs. men) from the entire campus population to take CS107 based on weight estimation in the FNCH model. We looked at a symmetric (7 year total) period before and after the curriculum revision. The results are given in Figure 2.

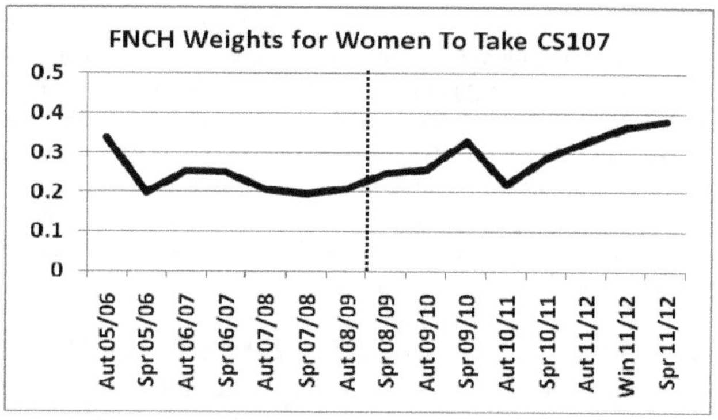

Figure 2. FNCH weights for women to take CS107. The dashed line delineates when the course content was revised.

We find that the average weight after the curriculum revision (w = 0.30) is notably higher than the average weight before (w = 0.23). Using a (non-parametric) Mann-Whitney test, we find this difference in weights to be statistically significant ($p = 0.02$), indicating a higher propensity for women to take CS107 after the curriculum revision.

To be precise, we noted one possible confounding factor of this analysis, which is that all offerings of CS107 examined before the curriculum revision were taught by the same (male) instructor (Prof. A) and all but one offering of the CS107 after the curriculum revision were taught by the same (female) instructor (Prof. B). Thus, we wanted to see if the difference observed above was potentially due to the instructor as opposed to the course content. Luckily, we found that these two instructors had both taught several offerings of CS106B and CS106X in the past (during which time the content for those courses remained stable), so we examined those classes to see if they exhibited a similar difference in mean FNCH weights across instructors:

FNCH weights	CS106B	CS106X
Prof. A	0.322	0.209
Prof. B	0.341	0.202

Here we found no statistically significant difference between Prof. A and Prof. B in the FNCH weights for either of the other courses they teach, leading us to believe that the difference observed with respect to CS107 is not due to the instructor, but rather due to the revision in the course content.

Moving from CS107 to majoring in CS, we considered the same 7 year population of CS107 students and calculated the weights in the FNCH model based of the number of men and women who eventually became CS majors. We found that prior to the curriculum revision, the mean relative weight for women vs. men who had taken CS107 to major in CS was w = 0.66, and after the curriculum revision it was 0.80, showing that women are more likely to major in CS after completing the revised CS107 course.

Our final analysis involved looking at the revised curriculum as a whole to determine if it has positive impact on female enrollment. Again, the FNCH model was employed using CS enrollment data over the past 14 years. We grouped the data by students' year of graduation. Thus most students who were juniors (and had likely declared their major previously) when the curriculum revision went into effect would be in the graduating class of 2009/10. Students in later graduating classes would likely have declared their major after the new curriculum was in effect, so we consider the class of 2009/10 an approximate delineating point between the old and new curriculum. (Note that students who have declared their major, but not yet graduated are projected to be on a 4-year program, common at Stanford. So, students who were freshman in 2010/11 would be reported in the (projected) graduating class of 2013/14.) The weights estimated using the FNCH model are reported in Figure 3. A Mann-Whitney test finds the difference in weights between the old and new curriculum to be statistically significant ($p < 0.05$), indicating a higher propensity for women to major in CS after the curriculum revision.

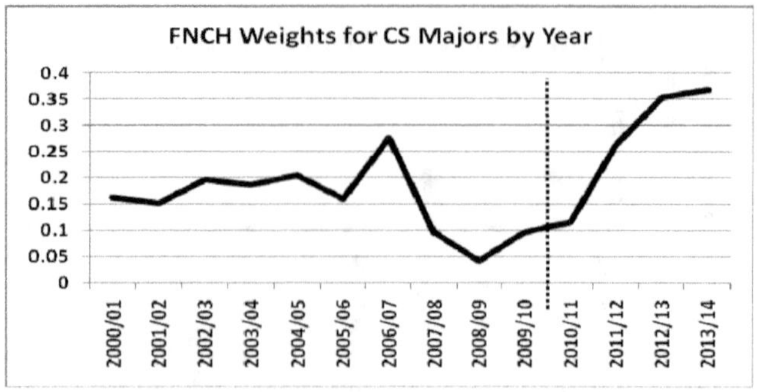

Figure 3. FNCH weights for CS majors, grouped by year of graduation. Graduating classes beyond 2011/12 are projected based on a 4-year program. The dashed line indicates the approximate change point from the old to the new curriculum.

6. CONCLUSIONS AND FUTURE WORK

The results reported here provide large-scale quantitative evidence for several gender-related issues in computing, both in relation to previously observed phenomena as well as newly discovered ones. We highlight three of our more significant conclusions.

- At the college level, we found that one of the biggest obstacles between women and a CS major was starting CS classes too late in their undergraduate education. We believe that providing strong encouragement for women to take a CS course early in their academic career is a key factor to promoting greater gender diversity in the field.
- Corroborating previous studies, we believe CS educators should be aware of the differences in confidence and previous background in computing that men and women bring with them into courses. These differences can impact interactions with instructors (such as asking questions or seeking help) and potentially overall performance in courses. Providing strong encouragement and mentorship, including parental support, can potentially help to address some of these issues.
- Curricular revision has the potential to have a real impact on gender diversity, as we have witnessed with our own curriculum change. Trying to identify the aspects of our new curriculum that appear most responsible for greater female participation is part of our future work. We conjecture that the program's track structure provides more options and a broader context for impactful work in computing.

Of course, much work still remains to be done, including building better structures for mentorship and community to help increase women's confidence and comfort in CS classes. Our study also highlights the importance of gender dynamics in computing before students even start college, especially the need to expose more women to computing early and engender parental support for their pursuits. It may also be instructive to examine in more detail the factors that inhibit women from taking CS classes earlier in the academic careers. We are hopeful that with continued study we may make further progress toward reaching equitable gender representation in computing.

7. ACKNOWLEDGMENTS

We thank Paddy McGowan and Claire Stager for providing data that was essential to our study. This work was supported by a gift from the Holtzschue/Schloss family.

8. REFERENCES

[1] Beyer, S., Rynes, K., Perrault, J., Hay, K., and Haller, S. Gender differences in computer science students. In *Proc. of SIGCSE '03.*

[2] Camp, T. The Incredible Shrinking Pipeline, Communications of the ACM (CACM), Volume 40 Issue 10, Oct. 1997.

[3] Beyer, S., Rynes, K., Perrault, J., Hay, K., and Haller, S. Gender differences in computer science students. In *Proc. of SIGCSE '03.*

[4] Camp, T. The Incredible Shrinking Pipeline, Communications of the ACM (CACM), Volume 40 Issue 10, Oct. 1997.

[5] Cheryan, S., Plaut, V. C., Davies, P., and Steele, C. M. Ambient belonging: How stereotypical environments impact gender participation in computer science. *Journal of Personality and Social Psychology*, 97, 1045-1060.

[6] Cohoon, J.M. Recruiting and retaining women in undergraduate computing majors. *SIGCSE Bull.*, v.34 n.2, June 2002.

[7] Computer Science Teachers' Association, United States' Annual STEM Job Openings vs College Graduates through 2018, *Voice Newsletter*, v.6, n.5, 2010.

[8] Fisher's Noncentral Hypergeometric Distribution. *Wikipedia.* Wikimedia Foundation, 20 July 2012. http://en.wikipedia.org/wiki/Fisher's_noncentral_hypergeometric_distribution.

[9] Gendered Innovations in Science, Health & Medicine, and Engineering. http://genderedinnovations.stanford.edu/

[10] Gürer, D., and Camp, T. An ACM-W Literature Review on Women in Computing, *SIGCSE Bull.*, v.34 n.2, June 2002.

[11] Heddleston, K. Women in Computer Science: An Ethnographic Study of Women in Computer Science at Stanford University. Undergraduate Honors Thesis. Stanford University, 2010.

[12] Hoffman, M.E. and Vance, D.R. Gender difference trends in computer literacy of first-year students, *SIGCSE Bull.*, v39, n1. 2007

[13] Irani, L. A Different Voice: Women Exploring Stanford Computer Science. Undergraduate Honors Thesis. Stanford University, 2003.

[14] Irani, L. Understanding gender and confidence in CS course culture. In *Proceedings of SIGCSE '04*, 195-199.

[15] Kumar, A.N. A Study of Stereotype Threat in Computer Science. In *Proceedings of ITiCSE '12*, 273-278.

[16] Margolis, J. and Fisher, A. *Unlocking the Clubhouse: Women in Computing.* MIT Press, Cambridge, MA. 2002.

[17] Margolis, J., Fisher, A., and Miller, F. The Anatomy of Interest: Women in Undergraduate Computer Science. *Women's Studies Quarterly*, 28(1/2).

[18] National Center for Women & IT, By the Numbers, 2012. www.ncwit.org/sites/default/files/legacy/pdf/BytheNumbers09.pdf

[19] Ogan, C., Robinson, J.C., Ahuja, M., and Herring, S.C. Gender differences among students in computer science and applied information technology. In W. Aspray & J. McGrath Cohoon (Eds.), Women and Information Technology: Research on the Reasons for Under-Representation, MIT Press, 2006.

[20] Sahami, M., Aiken, A., and Zelenski, J. Expanding the frontiers of computer science: designing a curriculum to reflect a diverse field. *Proc. of SIGCSE '10.*

[21] Spencer, S.J., Steele, C.M., and Quinn, D.M. Stereotype threat and women's math performance, *Journal of Experimental Social Psychology*, 35, 1999, 4-28.

[22] Spertus, E., *Why Are There So Few Female Computer Scientists?*, MIT Artificial Intelligence Laboratory Technical Report 1315, 1991.

[23] Vilner, T., and Zur, E. Once she makes it, she is there: gender differences in computer science study. In *Proc. of ITiCSE'06.*

[24] Zweben, S., and Bizot, B. 2010-2011 Taulbee Survey. Computing Research News, May 2012.

From Difference to Diversity: Including Women in *The Changing Face of Computing*

Carol Frieze
School of Computer Science
Carnegie Mellon University
5000 Forbes Avenue
Pittsburgh, PA 15213
412-268-9071
cfrieze@cs.cmu.edu

Jeria L. Quesenberry
Information Systems
Carnegie Mellon University
5000 Forbes Avenue
Pittsburgh, PA 15213
412-268-4573
jeriaq@andrew.cmu.edu

ABSTRACT

In this paper we argue that gender difference thinking, with regards to attitudes towards computing, can work against diversity in the field of computing. Indeed, gender difference approaches to the participation of women in computing have not provided adequate explanations for women's declining interest in computer science (CS) and related technical fields. As yet "The Changing Face of Computing" has not led to significant changes in the levels of women's participation. Indeed, the number of computer science degrees awarded to women has steadily declined since 1984. Our objective in this paper is to present a critique on why gender difference approaches may be problematic and propose that a cultural approach offers a more effective framework for investigating and increasing women's participation in CS. We support our findings and recommendations from the most recent research in a series of studies carried out at Carnegie Mellon University (CMU) over the past 10 years. In brief, we found the Women-CS fit at CMU continues to present a positive and encouraging story. Our findings demonstrate that under certain conditions women, alongside their male peers, can fit successfully into a CS environment and help shape that environment and computing culture, for the benefit of everyone, *without accommodating presumed gender differences* or any compromises to academic integrity.

Categories and Subject Descriptors

K.3.2 Computers and Information Science Education

General Terms

Management, Human Factors

Keywords

Computer science education, women, culture, gender similarities, gender differences, diversity, retention, Women-CS fit

SIGCSE'13, March 6-9, 2013, Denver, Colorado, USA.

1. INTRODUCTION

In this paper we argue that gender difference thinking, with regards to attitudes towards computing, can work against diversity. Indeed, gender difference approaches to the participation of women in computing have not provided adequate explanations for women's declining interest in computer science and related technical fields [1, 6, 14, 15]. We raise the question: is a focus on gender differences within the culture of the USA reaffirming essentialist thinking (i.e. the belief that innate differences between men and women suit them to different fields) thus contributing to the low participation of women in CS?

The 2012 Taulbee survey[1] reports that enrollments in undergraduate computer science programs rose for the fourth straight year. The number of bachelor's degrees in computer science awarded also increased. While this is welcome news and certainly contributes to *the changing face of computing*, the situation for women has not improved. The 2012 Taulbee survey also shows discouraging data on the national graduation rates for women in CS, rates which now stand at 11.7% down from last year's 13.8%. Indeed, the number of computer science degrees awarded to women has steadily declined since 1984 [28]; "a stark reminder that women's progress cannot be taken for granted" [17].

At the same time we face a critical situation in the history of computing in the USA when jobs in computing outnumber graduates with the necessary skills to fill them [7]. Clearly, it is in the interest of women, of the nation, and the field of computing to attract and train talent from a diverse pool of potential participants. The question that begs is why are we failing to do this?

In CMU's School of Computer Science (SCS) a shift towards a more balanced environment, and ensuing changes in the micro-culture, have contributed to a successful undergraduate experience for most students–women and men–but the changes have been particularly dramatic and positive for women. While cultural attitudes within the USA may often work against women's inclusion in male dominated fields, our studies have shown that localized cultural changes can influence student experiences and attitudes and help buck any trend towards a gender divide.

---

[1] The 2012 Taulbee Survey provides data from Ph.D. granting schools for the 2010-2011 school year.

This paper has two primary goals: a) to present our thoughts on why gender difference approaches may be problematic and why a cultural approach is necessary; and b) to support our ideas with findings and recommendations from studies at CMU.

2. BACKGROUND

CMU has not been immune to national trends. However, even in the face of a nationwide decline in the number of new female CS majors, SCS has sustained a critical mass of female students within the entire CS undergraduate student body (currently around 25% female). For the past few years, the percentage of women enrolling in the CS major at CMU has held steady or increased at well above national averages. Indeed, since 2002 the percentage of bachelor's degrees granted to women in the CS major at CMU has exceeded and stayed well above the national average. We believe this success is due in large part to the school's commitment to building and sustaining a culture and environment which works for *both men and women.*

A full account of actions leading to changes in the CS culture at CMU has been well documented [5, 6, 13, 19]. In brief, prior to 1999 CMU maintained a very traditional male dominated CS culture, a culture that tended to support the personalities of stereotypical computer science students. By the time our research began in 2002, CMU had a more diverse student body in CS including increased numbers of women but also more men with wide ranging characteristics. All of whom were selected and admitted for their "community" and leadership potential along with high SATs. We began to observe what we believed to be the evolution of a new culture of computing as the environment shifted from an *unbalanced* to a more *balanced environment.* By balance we refer to three specific areas: balance in terms of gender, in terms of breadth of student personalities, and in terms of the development of a professional and social organization, *Women@SCS*[2]. Women@SCS provides crucial educational and professional experiences often taken for granted by the majority in the community (e.g. the networking and mentoring) that often goes on quite naturally among the majority male population [13]. In this more balanced environment women began to participate, contribute, and be successful, in the CS major, *without accommodating presumed gender differences* or any compromises to academic integrity.

For the past ten years, we have been paying close attention to the culture of computing and monitoring the Women-CS fit. Our research findings (2002, 2004, 2009-2010, 2011-2012) show that in this new culture of computing, women and men relate to CS through a spectrum of attitudes, including many gender similarities, rather than the gender divide observed prior to 1999. It is also important to note that while the SCS at CMU clearly allows for diversity and a more balanced environment, *the academic curriculum was not adapted to become "female-friendly".* In fact it has continued to be an extremely rigorous and highly competitive program receiving, for example, over 4000 applications in 2012 for the 130 places offered the same year.

3. CULTURE

It seems reasonable to assume that a multitude of factors are involved in women's participation in CS–biological, educational, psychological, cognitive, social, etc.–factors which this paper cannot hope to untangle. This concept was nicely illustrated by Barnett and Rivers [2] when they explained, "We are all a product of many interacting forces, including our genes, our personalities, our environment, and chance". Their book promotes the view, and provides evidence to show, that factors relating to culture and environment which encompass so many of these "interacting forces", play critical roles in determining women's participation in CS [2, 15].

So what do we mean by culture and employing a cultural approach? Williams [27] suggests that culture belongs to everyone being part of our everyday experiences and being *"made and remade"* by us on both the personal and the societal levels. This definition allows us to see culture as a *synergistic* process for change. We are shaped by the cultures we occupy while also being active contributors to those cultures. Hence, we use the term culture as previously defined [6, 14, 15] to refer to the complex and broad set of relationships, values, attitudes and behaviors that bind a specific community *consciously and unconsciously.* This community can be localized as in the micro-culture of a department or extensive as in the culture of a nation. In all cases this definition posits that culture is bound by context and history and that we are born into specific cultures with prevailing values and structures of opportunity.

A cultural perspective can both *broaden* and *focus* our thinking. It can broaden our thinking as we think outside of our own cultures and it can focus our thinking as we recognize specific factors affecting specific situations. Taking a cultural perspective on women's participation in CS is an approach which allows us to look at *factors outside of gender* as leading contributors to different levels of participation. As gender is often constructed differently in different cultures taking a cultural approach allows us to see quite clearly and *convincingly* that many characteristics ascribed as natural to men and to women are actually produced in specific cultures. Indeed, several researchers have brought this fact to our attention describing examples of countries and cultures where women are well represented in computing [1, 9, 21, 25].

4. IS THE RHETORIC OF ESSENTIALISM CONTRIBUTING TO THE GENDER GAP IN COMPUTING?

Essentialism is the belief that people have properties that are essential to their composition. In this sense, all members of a particular demographic group (e.g. gender, race, sexual orientation) share common and finite characteristics. Gender essentialism is epitomized and popularized in such best sellers as John Gray's *Men are from Mars, Women are from Venus* (1992), which has sold more than 7 million copies and was the "highest ranked work of nonfiction" of the 1990s. "The book and its central metaphor have become a part of popular culture".[3] According to research examined in the 2010 AAUW report gender difference thinking is still prevalent in attitudes towards STEM fields in the USA: "Most people associate science and math fields with "male" and humanities and arts fields with "female" [17].

---

[2] For details of *Women@SCS* please see http://women.cs.cmu.edu/

[3] See Wikipedia: http://en.wikipedia.org/wiki/Men_Are_from_Mars,_Women_Are_from_Venus

At the core of essentialism is the belief that men and women are inherently different in their physical bodies, and hence they are also different in the ways in which they act, behave and think. Marini [20] adds that this frequently leads to the assumption that biological features can be used to explain other observed differences between men and women. Further, DeCecco and Elia [8] explain that biological characteristics constitute the primary influencing factor influencing human behavior, thereby minimizing the effects of culture or social shaping.

Researchers argue that essentialism uses biological differences between the sexes to explain differences in male and female decisions to study CS [23, 25, 26]. Consequently, essentialism studies generally conclude that men relate to technology in differing and opposing ways from those of women. For instance, Pinker [22] suggests that the lack of women in technical careers could be due to biological differences in average temperaments and talents. Furthermore, Baron-Cohen [3] argues, "the female brain is predominantly hard-wired for empathy. The male brain is predominantly hard-wired for understanding and building systems".

Essentialist rhetoric has become more noticeable in relation to CS and technology, and more broadly to some areas of science in general, as we have struggled to address the low participation of women. Signs of essentialist thinking are not only evidenced in the remarks of Larry Summers, when he was president of Harvard and should have known better, but also in the way we are constantly searching for ways to make science *appeal to girls and women*, as if tapping into something inherent in girls and women, or re-shaping science to suit women's interests, will provide the answers. Such approaches, though well intentioned, may ultimately play into essentialist thinking and serve to reinforce a gender divide. By identifying gender differences and *subsequently accommodating those differences* we can be our own worst enemies playing a harmful role in *perpetuating stereotypes and differences.*

These differences, which are often only *perceived* differences that can change according to situation, can serve to *deny diversity* and the cross-gender spectrum of characteristics, interests and identities that can emerge. Gender difference approaches can result in setting up men and women as separate categories when research has shown that there are more differences within each gender than between them [15, 18, 25]. This is not an easy message to broadcast to children and parents when difference approaches seem to be the mainstay of marketing in our culture. Recent discussions on LEGO, for example, showed that sales went from only 9% purchased specifically for girls at the end of 2011 to 27% after the introduction of the LEGO Friends playsets designed especially for girls.[4] LEGO is famous for its creative, building and construction challenges. "Lego play develops spatial, mathematical, and fine motor skills, and lets kids build almost anything they can imagine".[5] These skills are valuable to all children but critics of the new LEGO Friends, suggest that such skill building has been downplayed and replaced by "shapely female figures and playsets like the Butterfly Beauty Shop (which) reinforced the idea that women should focus on their looks". While this may seem a far cry from computer science it is an example of how accommodating perceived gender differences and perpetuating a gender divide within our culture can mean that sections of the population easily miss out on valuable experiences, experiences which could serve them well later in life.

Without an awareness of cultural contexts gender difference approaches can serve: a) to reinforce the belief that men and women are two distinct and fundamentally different categories, which in turn can support an essentialist position; and b) to exclude significant cultural factors that are impacting participation in CS. We propose that taking a cultural approach can offer more prudent insights and open up new possibilities for thinking about participation in computing without contributing to a gender divide.

5. NEW RESEARCH AND INGREDIENTS FOR SUCCESS

There is a growing body of research that challenges the historical notions of essentialism. Epstein [11] argues that men and women are overwhelmingly similar and that any differences between them are socially constructed. For instance, Fine [12] argues that sloppy science is frequently used to justify gender stereotypes, which she labels "neurosexism". She critiques the use of fMRIs and high-tech scanners to explain how sex hormones shape the brain, which then shapes behavior and intellectual ability, from mathematics to nurturance. It is not that she is opposed to neuroscience or brain imaging; quite the opposite, she strongly argues against making authoritative interpretations of ambiguous data. Supporting her argument is research emerging from the fields of psychology and neuroscience, which suggests that men and women may not be so different after all. For example, Halpern [16] recognizes that the female brain is slightly smaller than the male brain, but studies show this to have no significant effect on a woman's intellectual performance. Further, through empirical analysis, Barnett and Rivers [2] show that the idea of a "math gene" or the hardwiring of a male or female brain is a fallacy.

Scientists are showing that more and more behaviors once thought to be hard wired can be seen to change when behavior is changed. For example, Eliot [10] uses the notion of the brain's plasticity to explain how human brains are works in progress. She argues that brains change based on experience, especially in early childhood. Consequently, a child's environment can dramatically influence how he or she develops in terms of skills and interests. Eliot also argues that the brain-based differences that seem so immovable in childhood can lessen with age.

For our purposes we are reminded that at one time different math abilities in men and women, with women having poorer ability, were attributed to "different brains" [4]. Such "scientific" explanations have been used to explain women's weaker performance in math and to uphold and justify a culture entrenched in beliefs that men and women are fundamentally very different in their intellectual abilities. By paying attention to girls and math, by increasing their levels of encouragement, of experience and practice, girls have caught up with their male peers and indeed women now earn almost half of bachelors in the field of mathematics [17].

We believe there are several important ingredients outside of gender which contribute to any student's participation and success in the STEM fields at all levels of academic and personal growth.

[4] See http://abcnews.go.com/blogs/business/2012/09/lego-friends-triples-sales-to-girls-despite-feminist-critique/

[5] http://www.businessweek.com/magazine/lego-is-for-girls-12142011.html

Factors such as opportunities, experience, and exposure to computing are outside of gender and not intrinsic to one gender or the other. Thus, we can be very pragmatic in recommending that we pay close attention to a small but effective set of best practices such as hands-on experience to gain important skills and exposure to role models to inspire and allow students to see themselves as next generation scientists. Students should be encouraged to see ability in computer science (or any STEM field) as an educational process of learning concepts and practicing skills, not as "gifts" more prevalent among one gender or another [17]. We particularly welcome the efforts of the Association for Computing Machinery (ACM), the National Science Foundation (NSF), the College Board, the CS Teachers Association (CSTA), the National Center for Women in Information Technology and others working to include a solid program of CS studies in the US national K-12 curriculum. We see K-12 curricular changes in CS as *essential ingredients in ensuring that ALL students are exposed to computer science.*

6. THE 2011-2012 CASE STUDY AT CMU

As with our initial study in 2002, our latest study, 2011-2012, was prompted by a newly revised curriculum in 2010, providing greater emphasis on computational thinking. We monitored how these changes impacted the academic and social fit of the CS students at CMU.

6.1 Methodology

In this study, as with previous studies, we sought to understand how a cohort of CMU CS students perceived their relationship to CS. The primary data collection tools included interviews (for depth) and surveys (for breadth). Interview and survey questionnaires covered a wide range of topics ranging from background in computing, reasons for choosing the CS major, favorite classes, attitudes to programming, and many more.

CS sophomores (first to experience the new curriculum as freshmen) were invited by email to participate in interviews. We identified and interviewed a cohort of 20 men and 20 women. We also interviewed 4 students who had switched out of CS. Interviews, which lasted approximately 30-60 minutes, were audio taped, transcribed and analyzed. Surveys targeting the entire undergraduate student body were conducted in spring 2012. We collected 200 survey responses (52 women and 148 men) from freshmen through seniors. We used traditional qualitative (selective and open coding) and quantitative processes (descriptive statistics) for the analyses and evaluation of the data.

6.2 Findings

Our survey findings showed little to no difference to findings from surveys carried out 2009-2010 and reported in detail [15]. Both our 2011-2012 interview and survey findings were in agreement with previous findings that men and women relate to CS through a spectrum of attitudes including many gender similarities. *In brief, we found no evidence of a strong gender divide.* For the purposes of this paper we focus on findings relating to culture and environment, atmosphere of gender inclusion and perceptions of fit.

6.2.1 Culture and Environment

The students were asked to describe the atmosphere or the environment in the computer science department. This interview question provoked a range of responses with several gender similarities. Both men and women commented on the hard working atmosphere (7/20 women, 9/20 men). Several students felt the atmosphere was friendly and comfortable (9/20 women, 7/20 men). Only 4 men and 4 women felt the atmosphere was stressful or too competitive. Otherwise one of the most interesting findings was the collaborative nature of the environment as noted by the women. Even when they commented on competition they suggested it was a healthy kind of competition *"It's not cut-throat tech like other schools ... Here, we're all just in it for the love of it"*. One woman noted *"It's competitive in that you want to do well, but, it's a collaborative environment"*. Men also noted the collaborative nature of the environment *"collaborative and helpful"*. Four women and five men used very positive descriptions in response to this question using words like *love, enjoy, fun, great, cool,* and *amazing*.

Students were also asked if they found their computer science advisors and professors to be approachable. We saw this as another indication of whether or not we were sustaining a good environment. The interview responses were overwhelmingly positive with 14/20 women and 15/20 men saying yes. One man said *"Everybody is approachable... You can send the professor an email or go talk to him after class, and it's awesome"*. One woman compared CS faculty to non-CS faculty *"I actually think the computer science professors are a lot more approachable than other professors"*.

Responses to this question on the survey were similar to interview responses and amazingly gender balanced with just over 50% men and women *dis*agreeing with the statement "Professors at CMU are not approachable". In the interviews, six women and five men gave mixed or unsure responses. One woman felt *"some of the professors are a little scary but (my advisor) is very approachable"*. Some students pointed to their own reluctance or need to approach faculty who they knew are busy. Likewise, approximately 35% of the men and 35% of the women who completed the survey were unsure.

No students gave completely negative replies in the interviews. And only 15% of the women and 17% of the survey respondents felt their professors were not approachable.

Overall the responses were more positive than negative about the approachability of professors. We also found very strong gender similarities in the responses to this question. We were very pleased to see how well faculty were contributing to an atmosphere in which both men and women could find help when needed and work towards success.

6.2.2 Atmosphere of Gender Inclusion

We asked several questions relating specifically to gender giving them the opportunity to raise any gender related issues. We asked the female interviewees "what has it been like being a woman in CS overall?" Responses to this question were very positive from the women with 12/20 women noting they did not feel or experience anything they thought was different to the men. One woman said *"Most people don't really seem to care about my gender. They care about whether or not I can solve problems"*. Some commented on how great it was to have female friends, for others there were still too few women. Several women noted advantages e.g. more attention from recruiters, feeling admired by non-CS majors, special events for women only provided by Women@SCS.

We asked the men to speculate on what they thought it was like for women in the program. Responses proved particularly interesting with men often pointing to the difficulties women must face because of being outnumbered. One student said that some of the CS clusters look *like "someone's idea of a frat house. I think that it's gotta be tough"*. At the same time when asked if they had any advantages being men none of the men thought they did although 2/20 men (including one minority) did allude to the gender imbalance and the possibility of women having fewer friends. This was phrased as a negative for women rather than an advantage for the men.

6.2.3 Attitudes to Programming

During the interviews, students were asked if they liked or disliked programming and why. We asked this in part because earlier research at CMU had found a strong gender divide in student attitudes towards programming [19]. In contrast, we have asked the question throughout our studies and always found that women like programming as much if not more than the men and they held similar reasons for doing so.

From among our interview cohort 16/20 women and 13/20 men expressed they either love or like programming. Responses ranged from expressing the sense of accomplishment that programming can provide to the creative side of programming. A male student noted *"It's amazing how much you can do with just writing code"* while a female student said *"You can create so many things with it"*. Twice as many men as women had mixed attitudes (6/20 men, 3/20 women). Mixed attitudes usually referred to students who like programming at times but did not see themselves as programming for long periods of time, an attitude exemplified by one man who said although he liked programming *"When I think about doing it 40 hours a week, I feel I would get bored. I don't want to do that the rest of my life"*. Only one man and one woman indicated they did not like programming at all. Clearly, our cohort does not suggest a gender divide in terms of attitudes to programming.

6.2.4 Perceptions of Fit

Two important interview and survey questions were intended to give us an overall sense of how students perceived themselves as fitting into CS academically and socially.

We asked students in the interviews and surveys if, overall, they felt they fit into CS academically. The interview responses produced striking gender similarities and were highly positive. 17/20 women and 17/20 men answered with very direct and simple comments like "yes", "I think I fit okay", "Yeah, I think so", "I think now more so yes". While the surveys were less gender balanced, most women, 52%, felt they had a positive academic fit (strongly agreed or agreed) and 78% of men felt they had a positive academic fit (strongly agreed or agreed). We saw gender similarities in the way students expressed their sense of academic fit. For instance, one male said he was *"...wondering if I'm up to par with everybody else. But I think that's something that most everyone here also has"*. A female explained, *"You're always feeling that you're trying to fit in struggling with all the academic concepts and things. Overall I think everyone is doing the same thing"*.

In the surveys 33% women and 14% men were unsure about their sense of academic fit and expressed ambiguity in their responses. In the interviews 2/20 women expressed sentiments of uncertainty; one said *"I think to some extent, I do. .... I'm honestly not sure"*. One male interviewee also expressed uncertainty saying it was a hard question for him to answer and he couldn't say yes or no.

In the surveys only 15% of the women and 7% of the men disagreed that they fit in academically. In the interviews, only one woman was definite about not feeling she fit saying *"Not really, just because I'm not doing so well academically here"*. Two men felt they did not fit academically one saying "not really" and another saying *"academically, no. I am not going to do well as a computer science student"*. We were pleased to see so many women express a sense of positive academic fit.

We asked students in the interviews and surveys if, overall, they felt they fit into CS socially. Once again the responses were highly positive and produced striking gender similarities even to the point of the language they used: e.g. one woman said, *"Yeah, I'm definitely a CS major at heart"*, while one man responded *"Yes. I am a CS major at heart"*. With regard to the survey, most women, 71%, felt they had a positive social fit (strongly agreed or agreed) and 69% of men felt they had a positive social fit (strongly agreed or agreed). The comments of one woman in her interview clearly challenged the stereotype that computer scientists are not social: *"You make friends easily with people here. They're actually really social people"*. Another woman also said "Yeah, yeah. We nerd out and have fun."

A number of the surveyed students, 17% women and 14% men, were unsure about their sense of social fit and expressed ambiguity in their responses. Only 12% of the surveyed women and 18% of the men disagreed that they fit in socially. One female interviewee said, *"I think sometimes I feel like I'm not nerdy or geeky enough"*. The 3/20 men who responded negatively in the interviews did so saying most of their friends were "outside of CS".

7. CONCLUSION

The *changing face of computing* has brought many exciting and promising advancements to the field. Unfortunately, a key concern remains–the persistent under representation of women in post-secondary computing educational programs. We know it is in the interest of women, of the nation, and the field of computing to attract and train talent from a diverse pool of potential participants. *Yet, sadly, years of attention and funding applied to women in computing issues have not paid off.*

We believe reframing the problem lens is a critical step to attracting and retaining more women in the discipline. By moving beyond old frameworks and essentialism rhetoric that situate the problem as a male-female dichotomy, we are able to employ more sophisticated and robust tools for analysis and interventions. Findings from our most recent study suggest many gender similarities and a spectrum of attitudes towards CS exist rather than a divide between the genders. We suggest that researchers and practitioners be hesitant to assume the factors that attract and retain men to the field are opposite and at times in conflict to those of women.

Further, our research demonstrates that in order to promote the participation of women in computing, attention should be focused on cultural change and conditions in the environment, not on gender and gender differences. Indeed, we suggest caution in searching for ways to make science *appeal to girls and women*, since we know the Women-CS fit is already evident in certain cultures and micro-cultures. Findings in this paper demonstrate that student attitudes to factors of faculty approachability, environment, social fit, academic fit, are more similar than different between the genders. Our findings also demonstrate that these factors are important indicators in building and maintaining an inclusive atmosphere. These factors are built on attention to diversity—not gender differences—and are positively related to a Women-CS fit. Conditions that foster diversity, not gender divides, are essential for changing the face of computing to include and reflect the face of the population it serves.

8. ACKNOWLEDGMENTS

We would like to thank the Microsoft Research-Carnegie Mellon Center for Computational Thinking, and Carnegie Mellon's School of Computer Science for their support of the 2011-2012 research.

9. REFERENCES

[1] Adams, J. C., Vimala Bauer and Shakuntala Baichoo. 2003. An Expanding Pipeline: Gender in Mauritius, *SIGCSE 2003*, 59-63.

[2] Barnett, R. and Rivers, C. 2004. *Same Difference: How Gender Myths Are Hurting Our Relationships, Our Children, and Our Jobs.* Basic Books: New York, New York.

[3] Baron-Cohen, S. 2003. *The Essential Difference: The Truth about the Male and Female Brain.* Basic Books: New York, New York.

[4] Benbow, C.P. and J. Stanley, J. 1983. Sex Differences in Mathematical Reasoning Ability: More Facts. *Science,* 222, 1029-1031.

[5] Blum, L. 2001. Women in Computer Science: The Carnegie Mellon Experience. In Resnick D.P. and Scott , D. (Eds.) *The University of the Future: The Future of the University.*

[6] Blum, L., Frieze, C., Hazzan, O., and Dias, D. 2007. A Cultural Perspective on Gender Diversity in Computing. In Burger, C.J., Creamer, E.G., and Meszaros, P.S. (Eds.) *Reconfiguring the Firewall: Recruiting Women to Information Technology across Cultures and Continents.* AK Peters, Ltd.

[7] Computing Consortium Blog RA. 2012. Taulbee Report (downloaded August, 2012). http://www.cccblog.org/2010/01/04/where-the-jobs-are/.

[8] DeCecco, J.P., and Elia, J.P. 1993. A Critique and Synthesis of Biological Essentialism and Social Constructionist Views of Sexuality and Gender. *Journal of Homosexuality,* 24(3/4), 1-26.

[9] Eidelman, L. and Hazzan, O. 2005. Factors Influencing the Shrinking Pipeline in High Schools: A Sector-based Analysis of the Israeli High School System. *SIGCSE,* 406-410.

[10] Eliot, L. 2010. *Pink Brain, Blue Brain: How Small Differences Grow Into Troublesome Gaps – And What We Can Do About It?* Mariner Books.

[11] Epstein, C. F. 1990. *Deceptive Distinctions: Sex, Gender and the Social Order.* Yale University Press, New Haven, CT.

[12] Fine, C. 2010. *Delusions of Gender: How Our Minds, Society, and Neurosexism Create Difference.* W. W. Norton & Company.

[13] Frieze, C. and Blum, L. 2002. Building an Effective Computer Science Student Organization: The Carnegie Mellon Women@SCS Action Plan. *Inroads SIGCSE Bulletin Women in Computing* 34(2), 74-78.

[14] Frieze, C., Hazzan, O., Blum, L., and Dias, D. 2006. Culture and Environment as Determinants of Women's Participation in Computing: Revealing the 'Women-CS Fit.' *SIGCSE,* 22-26.

[15] Frieze, C., Quesenberry, J., Kemp, E., and Velaszquez, A. 2011. Diversity or Difference? New Research Supports the Case for a Cultural Perspective on Women in Computing, *Journal of Science Education and Technology.*

[16] Halpern, D.F. 2000. *Sex Differences in Cognitive Abilities* (3rd ed.). L. Erlbaum Associates, Mahwah, New Jersey.

[17] Hill, C., Corbett, and Rose, A. 2010. "Why So Few: Women in Science, Technology, Engineering, and Mathematics", AAUW 2010.

[18] Kvasny, L., Trauth, E. and Morgan, A. 2009. Power Relations in IT Education and Work: The Intersectionality of Gender, Race and Class. *Journal of Information, Communication and Ethics in Society*, 7(2/3), 96-118.

[19] Margolis, J. and Fisher, A. 2002. *Unlocking the Clubhouse: Women in Computing*, MIT Press.

[20] Marini, M.M. 1990. Sex and Gender: What Do We Know? *Sociological Forum,* 5(1), 95-120.

[21] Othman, M. and Latih, R. 2006. Women in Computer Science: NO SHORTAGE HERE! *Communications of the ACM,* 49(3).

[22] Pinker, S. 2002. *The Blank Slate: The Modern Denial of Human Nature.* Penguin Putnam, New York, New York.

[23] Ratliff, C. 2005. Essentialism. In Heywood, L.L. (Ed.), *The Women's Movement Today: An Encyclopedia of Third Wave Feminism.* Greenwood Press, Westport, Connecticut, 122-123.

[24] Trauth, E.M. 2006. Theorizing Gender and Information Technology Research Using the Individual Differences Theory of Gender and IT. In E.M. Trauth (Ed.), *The Encyclopedia of Gender and Information Technology,* Idea Group Publishing, Hershey, Pennsylvania, 1154-1159.

[25] Trauth, E.M., Quesenberry, J.L., and Huang, H. 2008. A Multicultural Analysis of Factors Influencing Career Choice for Women in the Information Technology Workforce. *Journal of Global Information Management,* 16(4), 1-23.

[26] Wajcman, J. 1991. *Feminism Confronts Technology.* The Pennsylvania University Press, University Park, Pennsylvania.

[27] Williams, R. 1958. Culture is Ordinary. Originally published in N. McKenzie (Ed.), *Convictions.*

[28] Zweben, S. 2012. Computing Degree and Enrollment Trends from the 2010-2011 CRA Taulbee Survey: Computing Research Association. Retrieved from: http://cra.org/govaffairs/blog/2012/04/undergrad-computer-science-enrollments-rise-for-fourth-straight-year-cra-taulbee-report/.

Are IT Interventions for Girls a Special Case?

Annemieke Craig
School of Information Systems
Deakin University
Geelong, Australia
+61 3 5227 2152
acraig@deakin.edu.au

Jo Coldwell-Neilson
School of Information Technology
Deakin University
Geelong, Australia
+61 3 5227 1417
jojo@deakin.edu.au

Jenine Beekhuyzen
School of IS and School of IT
Deakin University
Geelong, Australia
+61 3 5227 2152
jeninebeek@gmail.com

ABSTRACT
Over the past two decades, numerous interventions have been conducted to inform and inspire schoolgirls into studies and a career in computing and technology. Two successful intervention of this kind have been held over a number of years, and this paper presents the initial stages of a longitudinal study which evaluates the qualitative data from the survey from six Australian events in total. The paper explores the motivational aspects of the presentations in the context of the responses from students and teachers, and it highlights the importance of ensuring that presentation sessions at these events are fun, funny and interesting, and the importance of considering the age of the target audience. It concludes by raising a concern.

Categories and Subject Descriptors
K.3.2 [**Computers and Education**]: Computer and Information Science Education - *Computer science education, Curriculum, Information systems education.*

General Terms
Human Factors.

Keywords
Outreach programs; Intervention; Gender and diversity; K-12 education; Girls and IT

1. INTRODUCTION
The issue of the gender imbalance in Information Technology (IT) is well documented in the literature [1, 4, 11, 12]. Over the last two decades numerous intervention programs have been conducted to try to redress this imbalance [3, 5, 7, 8, 13, 20].

The *Go Girl, Go for IT* (Go Girl) initiative, in the state of Victoria, is a two day intervention event that aims to increase secondary school girls' awareness of IT careers as well as debunking the myth that a career in IT will be boring. In the state of Queensland *Technology Takes You Anywhere* (TTYA) is another such intervention, with a focus on younger girls of primary school age, and it is conducted on one day only. Its aim is to increase the girls' interest in technology and their confidence with using it. Post event evaluation is conducted at both events with participants (students and teachers) being asked to complete a two-page questionnaire at the conclusion of the day. The general feedback received from participants is usually very positive. But, in the context of IT, what do schoolgirls in the target age ranges find engaging or motivational?

The aim of this study is to present the initial findings which will contribute to developing a framework that can be used to maximize the impact of future presentations. The goal is to better understand how to ensure presentations meet at least some of the positively identified characteristics from the evaluation data. This information can then be used when planning similar interventions to maximize their impact on the audience.

The data set to be evaluated for this purpose will primarily be the open ended responses from the survey deployed at Go Girl events conducted in 2006, 2008, and 2010, and from TTYA events conducted in 2008, 2009 and 2010. Similar questions were purposely asked in the evaluation of all events enabling the comparison of responses. The entire study consists of four phases:

Phase 1: Initial exploration of the entire data set to identify positive characteristics of presentations followed by detailed analysis of Go Girl 2006 data to develop a framework of what contributes to a good, well-received presentation.

Phase 2: Analysis of Go Girl 2008, and 2010 data to test the developed framework (from phase 1).

Phase 3: Analysis of TTYA data from 2008, 2009 and 2010 to test the developed framework (from phase 1) against a different age group.

Phase 4: Comparison of all TTYA data to all Go Girl data to further refine the framework.

This paper reports on Phase one of the research, which identified characteristics of presentations that participants have identified positively. An initial framework is then developed, based on the 2006 Go Girl data set to explain the characteristics of what makes a good session through the eyes of the participants.

2. LITERATURE
An intervention programme is an activity designed to change a state of affairs and over the last two decades numerous intervention programs have been conducted to try to redress the gender imbalance by recruiting, retaining or advancing women in IT [2, 5, 7, 14, 17].

While the date of the first intervention programme focusing on women in IT is difficult to identify the first IFIP WG 9.1 working conference on Women, Work and Computerization was held in Italy in 1984 [18]. At this conference reports of intervention strategies were presented. Since then many different intervention programmes and strategies have been reported in the literature. Most recently Klawe et al. [14] briefly described a range of North American based intervention approaches which they suggest show success however, there were no examples provided of how success was defined or determined. These programmes [14] are typical of the many programmes reported in the literature.

Previous literature on intervention programmes for women and IT has often lacked discussion on the impact of the intervention or its evaluation [6, 15, 16 19]. Clewell and Campbell [6] note that some interventions may have helped narrow the IT gender gap but there may be other influences such as changes in society and technology which have had an impact. A major conclusion of the *Under the Microscope* report which examined a decade of gender equity projects in the Science Technology Engineering and Mathematics (STEM) fields was that across all STEM fields 'a lack of project evaluation make[s] it difficult to determine who is being served and if and how project outcomes are measured'[10]. The literature focuses predominantly on 'access' to computing and courses, and the 'process' of intervention programmes, with little written about what change has occurred as a result of a specific intervention programme. It has therefore been difficult to determine which interventions have had an impact and to be able to learn from the work of others. Successful programmes create positive change and are built on a foundation of what works.

3. METHOD

The analysis was aided by Nvivo9 software, which enabled easy access to the open-ended responses as well for coding, searching and comparing responses. This paper focuses on the following question which was included on the post-event evaluation questionnaires at each of the events: "Of the sessions you attended today, which was the best and why?"

At the conclusion of each event the participants were asked to complete an evaluation form. In exchange for submitting a completed form the girls received a show bag containing a range of goodies provided by participating organizations. Table 1 summarizes the number of responses received in this study (4932 responses in total).

Event	Day 1	Day 2	Total
Go Girl 2006	948	720	1668
Go Girl 2008	691	385	1076
Go Girl 2010	335	457	792
TTYA 2008	502	N/A	502
TTYA 2009	522	N/A	522
TTYA 2010	378	N/A	378
Total			4932

Table 1: Study Sample

Nvivo9 was particularly useful for managing the large amount of data collected through the qualitative responses. Once imported from a spreadsheet, the column containing the response to the above question was auto-coded into a more usable format for the qualitative analysis. Then the responses from Day 1 and Day 2 were merged together (see Figure 1) for each event to provide a starting point for analysis.

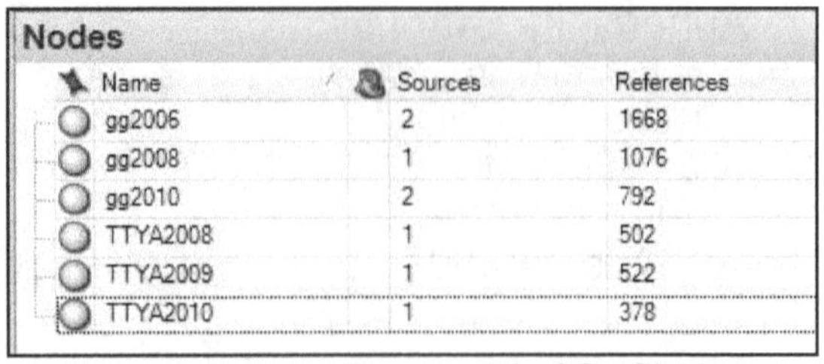

Figure 1: Merging Day 1 and 2 of Go Girl Data

4. CHARACTERISTICS OF A GOOD SESSION

4.1 Interesting, Fun and Funny

In order to identify the characteristics of a good session, the entire data set was used for the initial content analysis. A word frequency query was undertaken on the favourite session responses for all 6 events. The most frequently occurring word returned was *because* (2445 times) but this was determined not to be useful for the analysis and hence added to the stop words (exclusion) list. The amended query provided the 50 most frequently used words in students' open-ended responses with the top three concepts of *interesting, fun* and *funny* being identified as useful characteristics of the sessions. Figure 2 shows a tag cloud representation of these results.

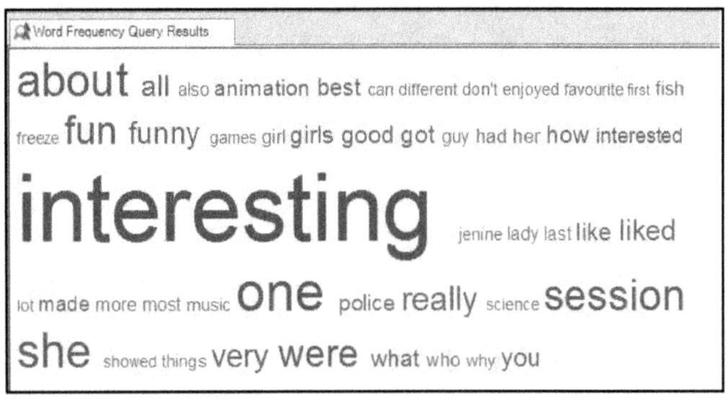

Figure 2: Tag Cloud of Favourite Session Reason

This tag cloud shows the relative significance of the concept *interesting*; however a count of how many times these terms appear is better represented in Table 2. This shows that *interesting* was mentioned by 1459 participants at events, *fun* by 576 participants and *funny* 408 times by participants. Note: words with less than three letters were not included in the search, and the software includes some default stop words of its own (e.g. these, with) which do not appear in the result. To explore this further, we conducted a word frequency query on the Go Girl dataset (3 events) and on the TTYA dataset (3 events) separately, and this provided the results shown in Table 3.

Consistent with the previously run word frequency of terms, the Go Girl result identified *interesting* as the term used most often to describe the participant's favourite session by far, followed by *funny* and *fun*. However the word frequency for Technology Takes You Anywhere reveals that the term *fun* is more commonly used to describe the girls' favourite session. This is a useful distinction when considering that Go Girl is targeted at secondary school girls and TTYA at primary school girls. It can then be argued that developing strategies for sessions to be *interesting* is more important for interventions targeting secondary school students, and *fun* needs to be incorporated into interventions targeting a younger cohort such as primary school girls. However the results so far suggest that regardless of the age group, strategies for making a session *interesting*, *fun* and *funny* are important for interventions targeted at any age group.

Word Frequency Query Result		
Word	**Length**	**Count**
interesting	11	1459
one	3	796
she	3	698
about	5	675
session	7	621
fun	3	576
were	4	548
really	6	452
very	4	424
funny	5	408
all	3	382
liked	5	375
you	3	324

Table 2:Characteristics of a Good Session

Event	Interesting	Fun	Funny
Go Girl 2006/ 2008 / 2010	1325	257	311
TTYA 2008 / 2009 / 2010	134	319	97

Table 3: Reporting of Interesting, Fun and Funny

Having identified these three characteristics from the entire data set, the next task was to develop a theory of what makes a session *interesting*, *fun* and *funny* by focusing on the Go Girl 2006 data.

A text search query to pull out every instance of the word *interesting* from Go Girl 2006 was undertaken and the result displayed the entire response that contained the word. From here, the responses were manually coded based on why the session was reported as a favourite. Each response was coded by identifying the concept(s) that the response best related to. Some responses used the actual word that had been defined for the concept e.g. *engaging* or *passionate* and some were interpreted e.g. "I learnt a lot" was coded at *informative* and "it was interesting to see what a scientist does" was coded at *role model*. Responses relating to a specific presenter(s) were coded to a node for that presenter(s).

Responses such as "I loved them all" were eliminated from the coding. If a response indicated which session as well as why the girl liked the session, the response was coded more than once accordingly. This was also the case if a response referred to a session as *fun*, *funny* and *entertaining*; it was coded three times. Some responses indicated "the first one" as being their favourite; unless further information was provided such responses were not included in the thematic coding.

After completing the thematic coding, attention was returned to the text search query to ensure that every instance of useful words were captured in the coding scheme e.g. animation, inspiring (inspir* - to include inspiring, inspiration etc.), engaging.

4.2 Characteristics of Presenters and Presentations

Having completed the initial round of coding it was noted that the concepts could be logically classified into three broad categories:

1. Presenters
2. Characteristics of presenters, and
3. Characteristics of presentations.

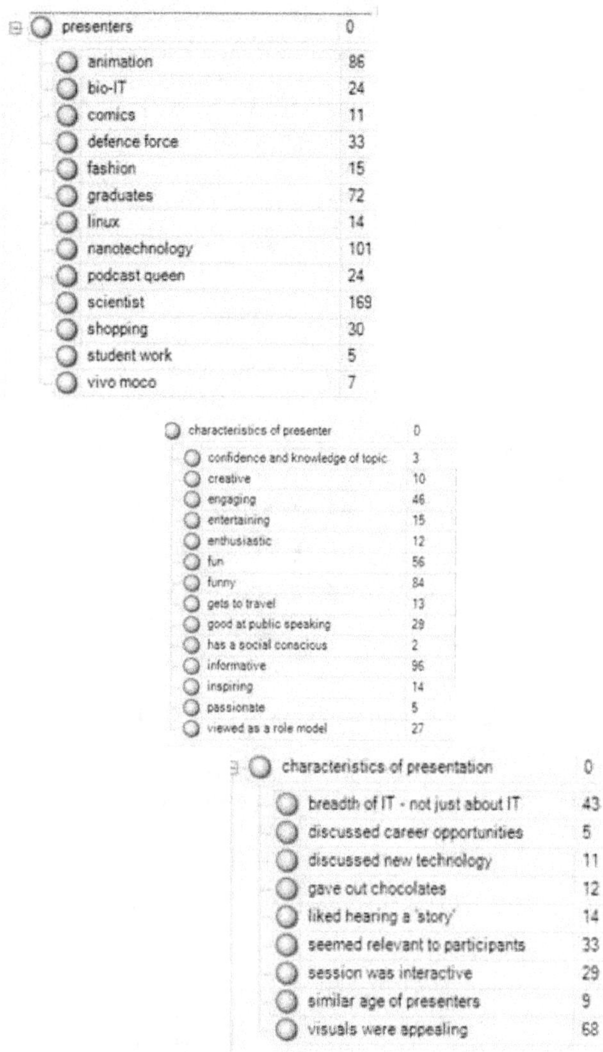

Figure 3: Categories of Concepts

Figure 3 shows all of the concepts used to code the qualitative responses to the "best session and why" question in the survey. The numbers next to each concept indicates the coding references (how many times reference to that concept appeared). Note that in Figure 3 the nodes are shown in alphabetical order rather than frequency of mention. It is however more useful if we consider the top four responses in each category to guide our discussion.

In the following, we start by looking at characteristics of presentations, then characteristics of presenters and finally the presenters themselves. The rationale here is that all presentations were related in some way to IT. All presenters were just that, presenters, but the organisations they came from represented the huge range of industries IT has an impact on.

4.2.1 Characteristics of Presentations

Figure 4 highlights the characteristics of presentations valued most highly by the participants. The top four reported characteristics highlighted in red are *visuals are appealing, breadth of IT, seemed relevant to participants,* and *session was interactive.*

Because of the large number of participants the sessions were conducted in lecture theatres with seating capacities in the hundreds. This is a very different environment from the secondary school classroom the girls would have been familiar with. The large screens at the front of the theatres are the focus of attention, rather than the speakers themselves. Hence imagery that excites and appeals to the audience will have a considerable impact on their engagement with the content of the presentation.

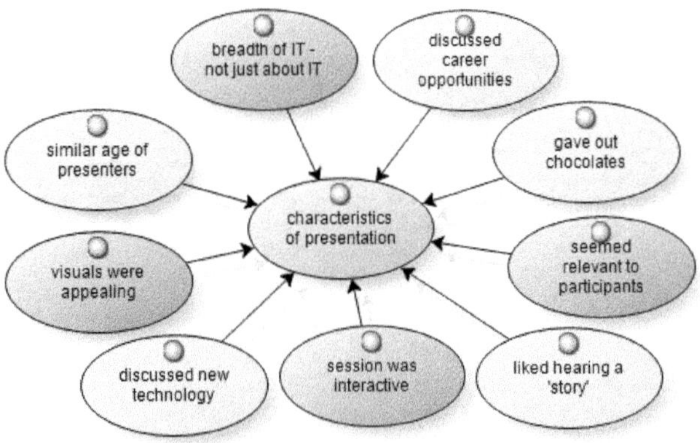

Figure 4: Characteristics of Presentations

The overall aim of Go Girl as an intervention strategy is to demonstrate to participants that IT provides many and varied opportunities. Therefore it is satisfying to note that this aim is reflected in the girls' perception of a good presentation. Similarly making IT seem relevant and hence feature in their choices made about future studies and careers is a key goal of these interventions.

A major challenge in a lecture theatre setting is to incorporate elements of interactivity with the audience. However the school classroom is quite the opposite and so including interactive elements in presentations will increase the appeal of the presentations generally but also contribute to the perceived accessibility of the content.

4.2.2 Characteristics of Presenters

Now armed with an understanding of which aspects of Go Girl sessions were the most favorable and some of the reasons why those sessions were successful, Figure 5 highlights the characteristics of presenters valued most highly by the participants. The top four reported characteristics of presenters are highlighted in green in Figure 5 and these are *informative, funny, fun,* and *engaging.*

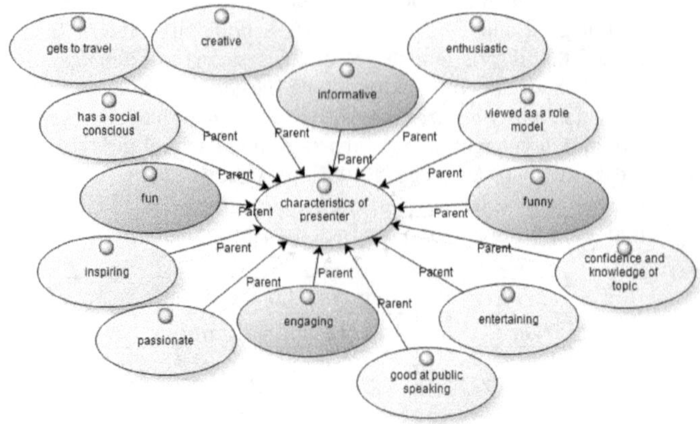

Figure 5: Characteristics of Presenters

Table 4 presents the evidence for this model, presenting the coding references to each of the concepts. The top four characteristics for a presentation are informative (96), funny (84), fun (56) and engaging (46).

Characteristic	Count
Informative	96
Funny	84
Fun	56
Engaging	46
Good at public speaking	29
Viewed as a role model	27
Entertaining	15
Inspiring	14
Gets to travel	13
Enthusiastic	12
Creative	10
Passionate	5
Confidence and knowledge of topic	3
Has a social conscious	2

Table 4: Characteristics of a Good Presenter

THE PRESENTERS

The most frequently mentioned presenters/sessions are identified in Figure 6. The male scientist was highly popular, as was the animation session also run by a male. A senior female IT consultant ran the nanotechology session, and many indicated the four graduates from a multinational consulting firm as their favourite.

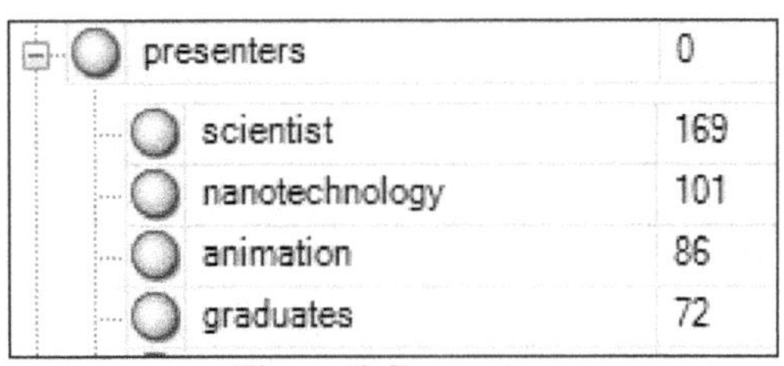

Figure 6: Presenters

The following section explores these four presenters/sessions and why they were considered to be a favourite in detail. This was achieved by running a matrix coding query on each of the top 4 presenters and the characteristics of presenters.

1. The Scientist

Participants reported that they found the scientist *interesting* mostly because his visuals were appealing and because his presentation highlighted the breadth of the application of information technology (Table 5). The title of his presentation "Why fish don't freeze" proved not only significant but indicated a level of entertainment as well.

Characteristic	Count
Visuals were appealing	26
Breadth of IT – not just about IT	18
Liked hearing a 'story'	8
Session was interactive	7
Seemed relevant to participants	4
Discussed career opportunities	1

Table 5: Scientist Session

The scientist's presentation seemed to appeal to the girls at a number of levels. Although he focused on the biological factors that contribute to fishes' anti-freezing capabilities, he weaved into his story where and how IT supports his research into these properties of fish. However, this could be perceived as a double-edged sword. Would the audience's recollections of the presentation be about freezing fish or the application of IT in the research area?

2. The Consultant - Nanotechnology

Participants reported that they found the consultant who discussed nanotechnology was *interesting* mostly because she gave out chocolates, and because her session was interactive. The visuals were reported to be appealing, and some reported being somewhat surprised that nanotechnology was relevant to them (Table 6).

Characteristic	Count
Gave out chocolates	12
Session was interactive	10
Visuals were appealing	7
Seemed relevant to participants	5
Breadth of IT – not just about IT	1
Discussed career opportunities	1

Table 6: Nanotechnology Session

The presenter discussed the application of nanotechnology in everyday products including sunscreens and makeup, both significant items of interest to the young adults making up the audience! Imagery at the nano-level would, if nothing else hold some curiosity value for the audience. However, the lever into their curiosity is primarily the fact that every-day products that they use on a regular basis have developed as a result of research in IT.

3. The Animator

Participants reported that they found the animation session *interesting* mostly because of the visuals used in the session were appealing (Table 7). Some participants reported being somewhat surprised that animation was relevant to them.

The focus of this presentation was very much about visual imagery. The speaker demonstrated how he uses IT in the production of animated sequences, for games etc. and how these can be built using a number of basic elements. The visual imagery had been set to music, both of which were targeting the predominant age group in the audience.

Characteristic	Count
Visuals were appealing	26
Seemed relevant to participants	8
Breadth of IT – not just about IT	1
Discussed career opportunities	1
Liked hearing a 'story'	1
Session was interactive	1

Table 7: Animation Session

4. The Graduates

Participants reported that they found the four graduates in their session *interesting* mostly because the presenters were of a similar age to the participants, and also the session was interactive (Table 8). The graduates talked about how the Google search engine worked, using lots of small scale hardware in a distributed system with lots of redundancy built in, "copying" and storing the internet overnight, and how a Google search is not actually of the Internet but rather of Google's copy of the Internet. Google searching was still a novelty in 2006 and the fact that such searches were not "live" searches certainly piqued the audiences' interest. More importantly the young presenters made all the IT concepts embodied in their presentation very real, not complex and very accessible to the audience.

Characteristic	Count
Session was interactive	9
Similar age to presenters	8
Breadth of IT – not just about IT	4
Seemed relevant to participants	2
Visuals were appealing	1

Table 8: Graduates Session

The graduates also talked about why they chose IT as their area of study, what interested them about working in the area and what their typical work day looked like in a large organization such as Google.

5. CONCLUSIONS

Based on this analysis of the 2006 Go Girl data there appears to be a number of characteristics that contribute to a successful presentation of the type that occurred in this intervention event. These characteristics include:

- Appealing visuals
- Building in some interactive elements
- Making the talk relevant to the audience context
- Ensuring presentations are varied and include the breadth of IT

Each of the presentations analyzed here had at least one of these key characteristics. Stronger presentations had more than one. Further, there are a number of characteristics of the presenter(s) that appear to influence audience engagement with the presentation. These included being:

- Informative
- Funny
- Fun, and
- Engaging

Having a "story" to tell, rather than an information-based presentation, appears to be the glue that holds the various elements of this framework together, contributing to the overall characteristic identified initially as *interesting*. Further, younger presenters seem to be able to communicate more readily with the younger audience although this does not seem to be an essential characteristic – the nanotechnology presenter being the counter example to youth.

The outcomes of this study raise a concern however. Any text on communication skills articulates exactly the points raised here as those of a good presentation (see Dwyer, 2002 for example). This analysis shows that the target audience is not a special case; they do not need to have the subject matter presented in a specially tailored way. They are seeking good, soundly constructed presentations delivered in accordance with the accepted norms for such presentations. Assuming that the girls are willing to receive such information (attending the event would imply, at least in part, that this is the case) the reason they have not taken it on board previously must be that it was not given to them. This begs the question why are the usual communication channels of school, family, friends and entertainment media failing to transmit a positive message about the IT industry?

6. FUTURE WORK

Data from the 2008 and 2010 events will be analyzed to determine whether the characteristics identified so far are sufficient (Phase 2). Undertaking a similar analysis with the TTYA data from 2008, 2009 and 2010 (phase 3) will provide a wider perspective relating to the age range of the audience. With the longitudinal nature of the events themselves it will be interesting to note whether elapsed time between events has an impact on the outcomes.

The ongoing developments in modern technologies, the accessibility of many of the mobile technologies and acceptance of social media, particularly amongst the generation being targeted by the Go Girl intervention strategy could have a significant impact on perceptions of ICT. A further Go Girl event was held recently, in June 2012. Data from this event will be used as a comparison with that from 2006 to investigate if the level of awareness of technology has been influenced by the increasing level of adoption of social media and mobile technologies amongst the participants.

7. REFERENCES

[1] Adam, A., D. Howcroft and H. Richardson (2004). A decade of neglect: reflecting on gender and IS. *New Technology, Work and Employment* **19**(3): 222-240.

[2] Beekhuyzen, J., A. Puikkonen, J. Hakkila and L. Venta (2008). Playing, Performing, Reporting: A Case Study of Mobile Minimovies Composed by Teenage Girls. *Australasian Computer-Human Interaction Conference (OZCHI)*. Cairns, Australia.

[3] Beekhuyzen, J., L. von Hellens and K. Clayton (2006). Mentoring Australian girls in IT. *Gender Research Encyclopaedia*. E. Trauth. Pennsylvania, USA, Idea Group Publishing.

[4] Clarke, V. (1990). Sex Differences in Computing Participation: Concerns, Extent, Reasons and Strategies. *Australian Journal of Education* **34**(1): 52 - 66.

[5] Clayton, D. and T. Lynch (2002). "Ten years of strategies to increase participation of women in computing programs - The Central Queensland University experience: 1999-2001." *Inroads SIGCSE Bulletin* **34**(2): 89 - 93.

[6] Clewell, B. and P. Campbell (2002). Taking stock: where we've been, where we are, where we're going. *Journal of Women and Minorities in Science and Engineering* **8**: 255-284.

[7] Craig, A. and J. Coldwell (2010). An initiative to address the gender imbalance in tertiary IT studies. *Interdisciplinary Journal of Information, Knowledge, and Management* **5**: 177 - 190.

[8] Craig, A., J. Fisher, A. Scollary and M. Singh (1998). Closing the gap: Women education and information technology courses in Australia. *Journal of Systems Software* **40**(1): 7 - 15.

[9] Dwyer, J (2002) *Communication in Business: Strategies and Skills*. 2nd edition Prentice Hall. Pp500-503

[10] Dyer, S. (2004). *Under the microscope: A decade of gender equity projects in the Sciences report*, American Association of University Women Education Foundation.

[11] Edwards, J. and J. Kay (2001). A Sorry Tale-A Study of Women's Participation in IT Higher Education in Australia. *Journal of Research and Practice in Information Technology* **33**(4): 329 - 335.

[12] Galpin, V. (2002). Women in computing around the world. *Inroads SIGCSE Bulletin* **34**(2): 94-100.

[13] Goral, C. (2006). *How to Increase Women's Impact on Technology - Changing Culture, Curriculum and Technology*, Anita Borg Institute.

[14] Klawe, M., T. Whitney and C. Simard (2009). Women in computing -Take 2. *Communications of the ACM* **52**: 68-76.

[15] Lang, C. (2007). Twenty-first century Australian women and IT: Exercising the power of choice. *Computer Science Education* **17**: 215-226.

[16] Lyon, A. (2003). *Broadening Pathways for Young Women through VET*. Collingwood, Victoria, Equity Research Centre.

[17] Nielsen, S. and J. Beekhuyzen (2009). Narratives of identity formation: Tech Girls are Chic (not just Geek). *Australasian Women in Information Technology (OZWIT)*. Melbourne, Australia, Monash University.

[18] Olerup, A., L. Schneider and E. Monod (1985). *Women, work and computerization: Opportunities and disadvantages*. Proceedings of the IFIP WG9.1 Working Conference, Amsterdam, Netherlands, Riva del Sole, Italy.

[19] Parker, L. (2004). *Gender and technology in the information society: Networking to influence ICT in education*. Bremen, Germany, GIST - Gender Perspectives Opening Diversity for Information Society Technology.

[20] Tsagala, E. and M. Kordaki (2007). Critical factors influencing secondary school pupil's decisions to study computing in tertiary education: Gender differences. *Educational Information Technologies* **12**: 281-295

The Revolution Will Be Televised: Perspectives on Massive Open Online Education

Mehran Sahami (moderator)
Stanford University
Computer Science Department
sahami@cs.stanford.edu

Mark Guzdial
Georgia Institute of Technology
College of Computing
guzdial@cc.gatech.edu

Fred G. Martin
University of Massachusetts Lowell
Computer Science Department
fredm@cs.uml.edu

Nick Parlante
Stanford University
Computer Science Department
nick.parlante@cs.stanford.edu

Categories and Subject Descriptors
K.3.1 [**Computers and Education**]: Computer Uses in Education, K.3.2 [**Computers and Education**]: Computer and Information Science Education

General Terms
Human Factors, Design, Economics.

Keywords
Online education; Massive open online courses; MOOC.

1. SUMMARY
While online educational resources have existed for decades, the past year has seen a tremendous acceleration in the adoption and potential disruption afforded by recent online education initiatives. In the Fall of 2011 the concept of Massive Open Online Courses (MOOCs) more broadly entered the public consciousness with a group of three Stanford CS courses collectively enrolling over 200,000 students, and gaining national press coverage from the New York Times [2] and other outlets. Since that time, a number of new platforms have emerged for online course delivery, including Udacity and Coursera (two for-profit companies started by Stanford faculty, the latter of which partners with over 30 elite universities), EdX (a not-for-profit consortium, composed of MIT, Harvard, UC Berkeley, and the University of Texas system), and the Minerva Project (a for-profit online university with $25 million in funding).

The level of recent activity in online education has lead Stanford University president John Hennessy to proclaim "There's a tsunami coming" [1], implying that educational institutions can either ride the coming wave or be washed away by the resultant sea change. While this analogy is prone to hyperbole, we do believe that online education poses real opportunities and challenges going forward. The economic dynamics of massive open online education may be a disruptive force to many traditional educational institutions.

SIGCSE'13, March 6–9, 2013, Denver, Colorado, USA.
ACM 978-1-4503-1868-6/13/03.

In this panel we seek to provide a variety of diverse perspectives on online education, including opportunities and challenges that many in the computing education community are likely to face. The panelists, who all have experience with online education in different contexts, will discuss the following topics (among others):

- Issues and lessons learned from preparing and teaching a MOOC to over 50,000 students, including the challenges in delivering such a course and guidance for those who might be considering doing the same,
- Using online education resources/MOOCs as a way to enhance live, on-campus learning, including models for making online instruction more effective,
- Experiences garnered over several years of making educational materials available online (outside the context of the more recent MOOCs), and novel ways that these resources can and have been used in a variety of contexts,
- Perspectives on online education from the standpoint of learning research to better understand and analyze how the online model can foster learning.

The panelists aim to provide a data-driven context for more in-depth community discussion of issues related to online education. We believe (to differing degrees) that online education has the potential to be transformative at all levels of the CS educational pipeline (from "K to gray"), and that it is imperative to more broadly engage the CS education community in this discussion. If a tsunami is coming then we will do better to learn from each other's experiences and surf it together than to each try to stay afloat alone.

2. MEHRAN SAHAMI
In 2008, Stanford University launched the Stanford Engineering Everywhere (SEE) initiative (see.stanford.edu), freely releasing online several CS courses, including full videos of class lectures and all course materials (including handouts, assignments, and software). The course videos were released through YouTube, Apple's iTunes University, and on Stanford's own website. Among the classes released was an offering of CS106A (Stanford's Java-based CS1 course) which I taught in the Fall of 2007.

While, the SEE initiative was not novel (bearing similarity to MIT's OpenCourseWare), the response to the open online materials was tremendous. Specifically for CS106A, the course's (hour-long) lecture videos were viewed more than *2 million* times on YouTube alone, and were ranked in the top 20 videos at iTunes University. Viewer response to the videos includes over 1,000 emails from individuals around the world, including unsolicited offers of gifts.

Beyond the publicity, however, the availability of such online materials has resulted in universities in the US, China, India, and South America using these videos as part of teaching their own introductory programming courses. And since the CS106A course covers much of the same material as the AP Computer Science curriculum, students without traditional CS courses at their high schools have reported being able to study for and pass the AP CS exam as a result of watching the course videos (either alone or through a teacher-guided independent study at their school).

Of note is the fact that these online materials generated such a strong response without any of the affordances of the most recent generation of MOOCs (enrollment, quizzes and assessments, statements of accomplishment, etc.). Based on these experiences, we believe that online education has the potential to be transformative in CS education, regardless of whether appropriate business models or methods for verifiable assessment or certification are developed for the most recent wave of MOOCs.

3. MARK GUZDIAL

Learning in an online collaborative setting dates back at least three decades. Researchers back in the 1980s learned some of the lessons still being learned today. Indeed, many of the early lessons from computer-supported collaborative learning environments are not yet influencing the design of MOOCs, but that's okay.

MOOCs are an exciting new form of educational technology that have advantages of scale that previous systems have not had. Like all new technologies, there is a certain amount of thrashing, as the most critical features are defined and developed. As in all new educational technologies, there is a certain amount of re-inventing the wheel as the developers and pioneers focus on innovation, not on what's been done before. MOOCs currently don't build upon what we know about constructing multimedia learning environments that support a broad range of learners [3].

The greatest danger of MOOCs is seeing them as panaceas, as a technological form that will work across the spectrum of learners ("from K to gray") for all subjects. No educational technology has yet been successful across such a broad spectrum. The scale of MOOCs can lead us to believe that it is working broadly, but most MOOC offerings have had an 80-90% non-completion rate. Most MOOC teachers have spoken of the impassioned missives they've received, but even at several hundred, it means that we have feedback from only a fraction of a percent of the enrollees. We have little evidence that MOOCs are successful for "K" or "gray."

4. FRED G. MARTIN

In Fall 2011, I participated in the first large-scale content-based MOOC—Thrun and Norvig's `ai-class.com`. I was both a student, viewing the lectures and working through the assigned problems, and a teacher, facilitating the learning of the 16 students who had enrolled in my university's Artificial Intelligence course.

With an inspiring teacher, learning from recorded lectures definitely brings material alive, in a way that's more interactive than reading from a textbook. Having the MOOC's backend server give you immediate feedback during lecture's mini-problems is fun and practical, keeping you engaged in the content.

I ran my class "flipped classroom"-style—after students had worked through the lectures and problems each week, we held a discussion meeting. Also, separately from the MOOC content, my students each completed a research-and-implementation term project. This structure and support that I added was instrumental to my students' learning. In the weekly class meetings, we discussed things we didn't understand, and more interestingly, *things we didn't realize we didn't understand.* In the term projects, students put into practice a subset of the AI ideas they had been taught in the class—transforming their relationship with AI from knowing *about* AI to knowing *how to do* AI.

I do see great potential for MOOCs. They can address the task of straight-up "explaining stuff," providing material to students in a more engaging way than a before-class reading. And they're definitely better than the usual lecture. But delivering content is the easy part. Without our role in probing students' understandings, encouraging them to discuss and share, and mentoring them in applying their nascent knowing new situations, a MOOC will only produce "knowing about"—not "knowing how to do."

5. NICK PARLANTE

This past year I taught an online course (CS101) with an initial enrollment of over 50,000 students. I am very optimistic about MOOCs. They will greatly extend the availability of high quality education to the world. In 10 years it will be difficult to explain to a high school student how you couldn't always just pull up a selection of high quality courses at will. A MOOC is not as good as the ideal live classroom experience, but it has its own profound advantages.

The obvious techniques for teaching a great live course apply to a MOOC as well: choose good topics, build great assignments, fit the lectures and examples to support the assignments. That said, here are three things I found to be different about MOOCs:

- *Drop rate.* A big challenge for MOOCs is that it's not only easy (and cheap) for students to sign up, but it's easy for them to drop out as well. The initial decision is easy to make compared to the follow through; with live courses, the students are more invested. Online students may not persevere through bad instructions or exercise breakage the way a live student does.
- *Fast cycle between seeing it and trying it.* Instead of lecturing for an hour, and then students try it later on the homework. Lecture and demo for 15 minutes, and then they immediately have students try it. Actually I run the live CS101 at Stanford this way now too, with everyone in the class bringing a laptop.
- *Big range of students.* The range between the worst and best students is enormous. One technique I'd like to try is having additional optional problems for students who want more practice. I had many CS101 students asking for more work, reflecting the bizarrely wide range of the students.

6. REFERENCES

[1] Auletta, K., April 30, 2012. *Get Rich U.*, The New Yorker.

[2] Markoff, J., August 16, 2011. *Free Course in Artificial Intelligence Is Offered Online, and 58,000 Sign Up.* New York Times, p. A11.

[3] Mayer, R. 2009. Multimedia Learning, Second Edition. New York, NY, Cambridge University Press.

Special Session: Engaging Mathematical Reasoning Exercises

Joseph Hollingsworth
Indiana University Southeast
Computer Science
New Albany, IN 47150
1-812-941-2425
jholly@ius.edu

Joan Krone
Denison University
Mathematics and Computer Science
Granville, OH
1-740-587-6484
krone@denison.edu

Bruce Weide
The Ohio State University
Computer Science and Engineering
Columbus, OH 43210
1-614-292-1517
weide@cse.ohio-state.edu

Jason O. Hallstrom
Murali Sitaraman
Clemson University
School of Computing
Clemson, SC 29634
1-864-656-3444
jasonoh@cs.clemson.edu
murali@clemson.edu

SUMMARY

SIGCSE has for a long time nourished an audience excited about teaching mathematical reasoning principles across the curriculum. A math thinking-related *Birds-of-a-Feather* (BoF) session is perhaps the longest running such session at SIGCSE, and every year it has attracted 30 or so participants. Every two or three years, there has been a panel devoted to related topics; recent examples include [1,3,4] with the 2012 SIGCSE panel attracting well over 100 attendees. The "Math Thinking" group started in 1999 by Doug Baldwin and Peter Henderson still remains a source for ongoing discussion among regular SIGCSE participants through a mailing list [5] several years after its founding. While these other forums are useful for discussing reasoning topics, they do not provide a consistent venue for sharing math reasoning activities. Therefore, SIGCSE attendees interested in math thinking have routinely wished for a place where engaging math reasoning examples and assignments that help connect mathematics and software development can be shared and discussed. Providing such a forum is the purpose of this session. The exercises and assignments will help faculty find ways to incorporate mathematical reasoning in CS1, CS2, data structures and algorithms, discrete math, and software engineering courses.

Categories and Subject Descriptors

D.2.4 [**Software Engineering**]: Software/Program Verification – *class invariants, correctness proofs, formal methods, programming by contract.*

F.3.1 [**Logics and Meanings of Programs**]: Specifying and Verifying and Reasoning about Programs – *assertions, invariants, pre- and post-conditions, specification techniques.*

F.4.1 [**Mathematical Logic and Formal Languages**]: Mathematical Logic – *proof theory, set theory.*

General Terms

Algorithms, Design, Reliability, Theory, Verification.

SIGCSE'13, March 6–9, 2013, Denver, Colorado, USA.
ACM 978-1-4503-1868-6/13/03.

Keywords

Correctness proofs, discrete structures, induction, invariants, programming by contract, specification, and verification.

1. OVERALL OBJECTIVE

There is near universal agreement in the community that computing students should learn analytical reasoning principles and understand the connections between mathematics and software construction. In the process they realize the importance of the mathematics they learn for software development. Educators need compelling examples and assignments to make such connections, and often they are difficult to come up with, because the environments and background of students at different institutions vary widely. This session aims to provide a forum at SIGCSE where educators can share joys of teaching mathematical reasoning principles throughout the computing curriculum.

2. OUTLINE

The proposed special session will borrow much from the organization of the highly successful, annual "Nifty Assignments" session at SIGCSE. Unlike that session which focuses on programming assignments, the focus of the present session will be on exercises that are engaging essentially because of the mathematical reasoning involved. Also, unlike that session, this session will feature innovative classroom exercises and activities that help highlight the connections between mathematics and software development, not necessarily just major, take-home projects. Ideally, the exercises can be done within one class period and will have corresponding reasoning projects that can be assigned offline to reinforce the concepts considered.

The session will be organized as follows. The proposers will take about 5 minutes to motivate and introduce the special session. Following the introduction, we expect to feature about four engaging exercises over a period of 55 minutes. Each presenter will have 10 minutes to share their reasoning exercises and assignments that help connect mathematics to computing and the engineering of high quality software. The next 15 minutes will be devoted to seeking feedback from session participants on the format of the session, the choice of exercises and assignments presented, the selection process, and any other ways the session could be improved if it were to be considered for a future offering. At this time, feedback from the audience will be gathered using a short anonymous survey asking about quality of the special session as well as their thoughts on future such sessions.

To give the reviewers an idea of the kinds of exercises that may be proposed, we provide an example using specific headings to capture tangible aspects of the activity/assignment. This example is based on loop invariants; others might involve induction proofs on recursive operations; yet others might involve objects and invariants, and various discrete structures.

Example: Computing x^p: Reasoning with a Loop Invariant Leads to Discovery of an Efficient Implementation

Objectives – The nominal objectives of this two-part exercise are for students to be exposed to using loop invariants to trace over a loop (without simulating its execution through even one iteration), and to be exposed to using loop invariants to reason about the correctness of a loop body (by tracing only one iteration).

Why It Is Engaging – Students like to optimize code. The obvious algorithm for this problem takes linear time. In the absence of reasoning with a loop invariant, a log-time algorithm (which is different from the usual recursive one) is far from apparent. The instructor can illustrate the value of loop invariants and formal methods in general by interactively, with the class, deriving the efficient algorithm while using a modern software verification tool, e.g., Dafny or Resolve, to prove that it is correct.

The Exercise – The example is a function that computes a non-negative integral power of a real number. Tracing over the loop using the invariant, without simulating execution of its body even once, is rather straightforward. However, it is interesting that the loop invariant (shown below) is appropriate for two entirely different loop bodies: one that computes the power in linear time and the other in logarithmic time. The process of reasoning about how to write the loop body that is correct for this invariant reveals how the more efficient implementation might be discovered, making it less mysterious than otherwise is the case.

Below is a skeleton for computing x to the integer power $p \geq 0$, with the loop invariant appearing in the maintains clause.

```
double result = 1.0;
double factor = x;
int pLeft = p;
/*
    updates
        result, factor, pLeft
    maintains
        result * factor ^ (pLeft) = x ^ (p)
    decreases
        pLeft
*/
while (pLeft != 0) {
    ...
}
return result;
```

Topics – Correctness, alternative implementations, performance.

Audience – Data structures/algorithms, programming language, or software engineering students.

Difficulty – Medium.

Strengths – The strength of this in-class activity (or related assignments) is that it connects motivation for loop invariants and improved software performance in a novel way.

Weaknesses – Instructors need to teach loop invariants.

Dependencies – None.

Variants – Minor mutations of the loops and their loop invariants.

3. EXPECTATIONS

The intended audience is the group of SIGCSE educators that have been regularly attending the "Math Thinking" BoFs at recent SIGCSEs as well as the over 100 participants at last year's panel [1]. The session will include approximately four engaging mathematical reasoning exercises and assignments with details, slides, and other related material made available at a website for later download. The repository of examples can be hosted at the Math Thinking website [6], for example. The audience will learn how others are injecting excitement in teaching mathematical reasoning in their courses, as well as acquire some specific exercises to expand their repertoire.

4. SUITABILITY FOR SPECIAL SESSION

The strong interest in mathematical reasoning by many SIGCSE attendees is our main justification for this special session. The rationale for the session is indeed similar to that of the present "Nifty Assignments" session. The participants in the session will be chosen by reviewers based on a selection process from several possible submissions. For the session, the proposers of this session will serve as the reviewers. If the session is accepted, the proposers will publicize the session widely and immediately through dedicated mailing lists, internet, and other suitable forums to seek submissions. If the session is continued into the future, past presenters will serve as reviewers.

One possible question is whether the exercises and assignments presented in this session could be presented in the "Nifty Assignments" session itself. A close inspection of the "Nifty Assignments" website information page [2] does not explicitly indicate that "Nifty Assignments" is only for programming assignments; it does however make clear that the emphasis is on nifty programming assignments. The types of mathematical reasoning exercises and assignments we envision would not nominally fit there. Furthermore, this session is at least as concerned with classroom activities in mathematical thinking, as it is with offline assignments.

5. ACKNOWLEDGMENTS

We would like to acknowledge Doug Baldwin and Peter Henderson for their contributions in developing this proposal. We would also like to acknowledge NSF grants CCF-0811748, CCF-1161916, CCF-1162331, CNS-0745846, DUE-0942542, and DUE-1022191.

6. REFERENCES

[1] Krone, J., Baldwin, D., Carver, J. C., Hollingsworth, J. E., Kumar, A., and Sitaraman, M., Panel: Teaching Mathematical Reasoning across the Curriculum, *Procs. 43rd ACM SIGCSE Conference*, March 2012.

[2] Parlante, N., "Nifty Assignments Info", Web, 31 August 2012, http://nifty.stanford.edu/info.html.

[3] Baldwin, D., Marion, W., Sitaraman, M., and Heeren, C., Panel: Some Developments in Mathematical Thinking for Computer Science Education Since Computing Curricula 2001, *Procs. 41st ACM SIGCSE Conference*, March 2010.

[4] Marion, W., Bloss, A., Powers, K., Baldwin, D., Panel: How Departments are Responding to the Mathematics Recommendations in CC2001, *Procs. 34th ACM SIGCSE Conference*, February 2003.

[5] Baldwin, D., "Math-thinking-l – Mathematical reasoning in CS curricula", Web, 4 September 2012, http://mail.geneseo.edu/mailman/listinfo/math-thinking-l/.

How AP CS A Matches College Courses

Renee L. Ciezki
Estrella Mountain Community College
Glendale, AZ
+1 623-878-4958
renee.ciezki@estrellamountain.edu

Lien Diaz
College Board
Atlanta, GA
+1 678-787-9445
ldiaz@collegeboard.org

Frances E. Hunt
Educational Testing Service
Princeton, NJ 08541
+1 609-243-6602
fhunt@ets.org

Henry M. Walker
Grinnell College
Noyce Science Center
1116 8th Avenue, Grinnell, IA 50112
+1 641-269-4208
walker@cs.grinnell.edu

ABSTRACT

The Advanced Placement (AP) Program provides a framework for high school students to obtain college credit and/or placement for work done in high school. Toward this end, the College Board outlines course descriptions and organizes examinations in several dozen disciplines, including computer science. To meet its goals, each AP course must align with college courses, so students taking an AP course will master needed content Several approaches are used to monitor this connection between AP courses and college-level courses. This session will review these approaches, considering how the AP CS A course matches introductory college computer science courses.

Categories and Subject Descriptors

K.3.2 [**Computer and Information Science Education**]: computer science education, curriculum

General Terms

Algorithms, Design, Experimentation

Keywords

Laboratory exercises, case studies, active learning. computing applications.

1. SUMMARY

The Advanced Placement (AP) Program provides a framework for high school students to obtain college credit and/or placement for work done in high school. Toward this end, the College Board outlines course descriptions and organizes examinations in several dozen disciplines, including computer science. To meet its goals, each AP course must align with college courses, so students taking an AP course will master needed content Several approaches are used to monitor this connection between AP courses and college-level courses, including

- Representation on the course Development Committee
- Curriculum surveys
- Pretesting
- Comparability studies

SIGCSE '13, March 6–9, 2013, Denver, Colorado, USA.
ACM 978-1-4503-1868-6/13/03.

This session will review these elements, considering how the AP CS A course matches introductory college computer science courses.

2. INTRODUCTION

The content of the Advanced Placement (AP) Computer Science (CS) A course is driven by introductory computer science courses at colleges and universities. A major goal of the AP CS A program is to identify and assess appropriate content, so that students performing well on the AP CS A examination will be able to obtain college credit for their CS work in high school and then be well prepared for the next CS course in college.

With the range of introductory CS courses offered at the college level, achievement of this goal is a significant challenge. Over the years, many sessions at SIGCSE symposia and at other conferences have discussed a wide range of visions for introductory CS at the college level,

Rather than expect complete consensus, the AP CS A course seeks to identify common themes and content --- material that resonates well with a large number of colleges and universities. With such diversity of introductory CS options around the country, it is unreasonable to expect that a single course will fit perfectly with college practices. However, the AP CS A course does strive to reflect widespread practice at the college level.

The AP CS A program uses many tools to identify and articulate common themes and content in introductory CS courses at the college level, This special session will review many of these approaches.

3. SESSION OBJECTIVES

In recent years, the AP CS A course and examination has been the subject of substantial discussion and debate. How should computer science be introduced? What topics should be included? What pedagogy is appropriate? To what extent should programing be involved? Much of this discussion has seemed to miss the underlying motivation for Advanced Placement (AP) courses as a mechanism for students to receive college credit for work they have done in high school. This session seeks to clarify the role of the AP CS A course and examine how the current AP CS A course matches the college courses for which students might receive credit and/or placement. This motivation leads to the following session objectives.

- Clarify the role of the AP Program in general and the purpose of the AP CS A course in particular
- Review the main elements of the current AP CS A course, as a basis for discussion
- Examine some mechanisms used to ensure that the AP CS A course and examination align with introductory CS courses at the college level.
- Outline how feedback from multiple sources leads to refinements in the AP CS A course
- Consider how recent feedback fits within long-term plans to review the alignment of AP CS A with college courses.

4. OUTLINE OF THE SESSION

The following outline envisions questions and discussion during the last 25 minutes of the session. Realistically, some questions may arise during the initial presentations, so the question-answer time may be revised as the session progresses.

- The AP CS A course and examination --- 5 minutes, Diaz
  - Purpose: college credit and/or placement
  - Content overview [2]
- Approaches and tools to help match AP CS A with introductory college courses -- 5 minutes, Hunt
  - Overview, Need for comparability
  - Make-up of the Development Committee (with inclusion of college faculty)
  - Curriculum surveys --- 5 minutes, Ciezki
  - Pretesting --- 5 minutes, Walker
    - Approach
    - Need for involvement from college teachers
  - 2008 Faculty Colloquium [5] --- 7 minutes, Walker
  - 2011 College Curriculum Survey [1] --- 6 minutes, Diaz
  - 2012 Comparability Study [4] --- 7 minutes, Hunt
    - Motivation
    - Some characteristics of college courses
    - Relationship between AP CS A and typical college courses
- Use of feedback results --- 5 minutes, Walker
  - Adjustments in AP CS A coverage [3]
  - On-going elements for both colleges and AP CS A
- Long-term evolution of AP CS A (e.g., review commission, new course description) --- 5 minutes, Ciezki
- Questions, audience feedback, discussion --- 25 minutes

5. EXPECTATIONS

This proposed session will serve several audiences:

- Teachers of introductory computer science who are interested in nation-wide trends and practices regarding their courses.
- Educators and administrators who want to better understand the role and goals of AP CS A.
- Guidance counselors and student advisors who want to guide students in the transition from high school CS courses to college courses.
- Department chairs and deans who are monitoring placement and credit policies regarding AP courses.
- AP CS A teachers who are interested in having their students receive college credit

With the diversity of practices regarding introductory CS at the college level, the results reported in this session will likely generate considerable discussion and debate. Thus, the session will conclude with a 25-minute question-answer-feedback session involving attendees.

6. ACKNOWLEDGMENTS

The Advanced Placement Computer Science A Development Committee thanks the College Board for its efforts in obtaining feedback from community college, college, and university faculty throughout the United States regarding introductory courses at the college level. The Committee also thanks these faculty for their time, interest, insights, and suggestions. Finally, the Committee thanks the many high school teachers who teach the students who are taking AP CS A and who provide extensive feedback and insight regarding course materials, professional development, and assessment activities.

7. REFERENCES

[1] College Board. 2011. *Advanced Placement Computer Science College Curriculum Study,* June 2011.

[2] College Board. 2010. *The Computer Science A Course Description,* http://apcentral.collegeboard.com/apc/public/repository/ap-computer-science-course-description.pdf

[3] College Board. 2014 (forthcoming). *The Computer Science A Course Description.*

[4] College Board. 2012. *Computer Science College Comparability Study.*

[5] College Board. 2010. *AP Computer Science Faculty Colloquium Results*, December 10, 2008.

Stories from the Scratch Community: Connecting with Ideas, Interests, and People

Karen Brennan
Harvard University
324 Longfellow Hall
Cambridge, MA 02138
+1-617-495-4341
karen_brennan@gse.harvard.edu

Mitchel Resnick
MIT Media Lab
75 Amherst Street, E14-445A
Cambridge, MA 02142
+1-617-253-9783
mres@media.mit.edu

SUMMARY

This special session aims to provoke discussion about new strategies for engaging young people in computer programming, drawing on experiences of educators and young people using the Scratch programming environment and online communities. The session will combine several different formats, including research presentations and analysis by two members of the team that develops and supports Scratch, short presentations and demonstrations by five educators and young people working with Scratch, and discussions among audience participants.

Categories and Subject Descriptors

K.3.1 [**Computers and Education**]: Computer Uses in Education – *collaborative learning.*

Keywords

Learning, Education, Programming, Community, Computational Thinking, Creativity, Scratch.

1. OBJECTIVES

Young people (ages 8 and up) are using the Scratch programming environment [5] to create interactive stories, games, animations, and simulations, and then share their creations with one another online (scratch.mit.edu). Since the launch of Scratch in 2007, young people around the world have shared more than 2.7 million projects on the Scratch website, adding more than 2000 new projects every day. At the same time, thousands of teachers have shared ideas, exchanged resources, and connected with one another through the ScratchEd website (scratched.media.mit.edu).

This special session will provide examples and analysis of how educators and young people are using Scratch in a variety of different contexts – and what they are learning in the process. More broadly, the session aims to provoke discussion about new strategies for engaging young people in computer programming and helping them develop as computational thinkers and computational creators.

SIGCSE'13, March 6–9, 2013, Denver, Colorado, USA.
ACM 978-1-4503-1868-6/13/03.

The session will use specific examples from the Scratch community to explore how Scratch supports and encourages three types of connections: with ideas, interests, and people.

- *Connecting with ideas.* The session will examine how Scratch activities can help educators and young people make connections with computational concepts, practices, and perspectives – the three dimensions in our framework for computational thinking [1].
- *Connecting with interests.* The session will discuss how Scratch provides beginning programmers with opportunities to work on projects based on their own interests, such as simulations of environmental issues affecting their communities, games featuring characters from their favorite books, and animated stories with original soundtracks.
- *Connecting with people.* The session will describe how young people use the Scratch online community to work together on collaborative programming teams and to remix one another's projects (sharing programming scripts and media assets), while educators use the ScratchEd online community to share classroom experiences, lesson plans, and assessment rubrics.

In addition to exploring how these three types of connections support learning with Scratch, the session will also describe how this framework has guided the design of the next generation of Scratch, called Scratch 2.0.

2. OUTLINE

The session will combine several different formats, including research presentations and analyses by members of the Scratch Team, stories and demonstrations by Scratch-using educators and young people, small-group discussions among audience participants, and question-and-answer opportunities among the full group.

Here is our proposed schedule for the session:

- *Motivations and framework (15 minutes).* Karen Brennan and Mitchel Resnick will describe the ideas and motivations underlying the design of Scratch and ScratchEd, their research framework for studying learning in the Scratch and ScratchEd communities, and an overview of experiences and results from the first five years of Scratch.
- *Presentations by community members (25 minutes).* Several educators and young people from the Scratch community will each make presentations about their work with Scratch, including demonstrations of projects and classroom activities.

The presenters will situate their experiences within the framework of connecting with ideas, interests, and people.

- *Small-group discussions (15 minutes).* Audience participants will divide into small groups to discuss how the three-connections framework (connections with ideas, interests, people) relates to their own personal experiences teaching and learning computer programming.
- *Question-answer session (20 minutes).* The full group comes back together for questions from the audience and reactions from the presenters.

3. EXPECTATIONS

Although Scratch is used in many different contexts (in informal as well as formal education, in elementary schools through universities), this session is intended primarily for K-12 educators. The presentations by educators and students will focus especially on the use of Scratch in K-12 settings.

We are designing the session so that people with all different levels of Scratch experience will find the session useful and interesting. The presentations will not assume any previous Scratch experience, so they will be appropriate for those who are new to Scratch. At the same time, educators who are already familiar with Scratch will have the opportunity to learn new strategies for using Scratch and will be able to share their Scratch experiences in the breakout groups.

4. SUITABILITY

In this session, we want to share experiences from multiple perspectives: from researchers as well as from educators and young learners. We know from the situated-learning literature and the teacher-education literature that stories and testimonials (i.e., teachers hearing from other teachers and/or from young learners) are an important part of learning and effectuating changes in teaching practice [2][3][4].

In addition, we also want to provide audience participants the opportunity to discuss how the ideas in the session relate to their own experiences.

None of the traditional formats (papers, panels, birds-of-a-feather) would allow all of these elements. We had considered a panel format, but the constraint of a four-person panel was too limiting. So we feel that a special session is needed.

5. ACKNOWLEDGMENTS

Many members of the Lifelong Kindergarten research group at the MIT Media Lab contributed to the ideas and technologies described in this proposal. We are deeply grateful to all of the educators and young people who have participated in the Scratch community and shared their ideas with one another (and with us). Our work has received generous financial support from the National Science Foundation (grants 1019396, 1002713, and 1027848), the MacArthur Foundation, and Google.

6. REFERENCES

[1] Brennan, K., & Resnick, M. 2012. New Frameworks for Studying and Assessing the Development of Computational Thinking. Proceedings of the 2012 annual meeting of the American Educational Research Association, Vancouver, Canada.

[2] Dexter, S., Seashore, K., & Anderson, R. 2002. Contributions of professional community to exemplary use of ICT. *Journal of Computer Assisted Learning, 18*(4), 489–497.

[3] Kirschner, P. & Lai, K. 2007. Online communities of practice in education. *Technology, Pedagogy and Education, 16*(2), 127-131.

[4] Lave, J., & Wenger, E. 1991. *Situated learning: Legitimate peripheral participation.* New York, NY: Cambridge University Press.

[5] Resnick, M., Maloney, J., Monroy-Hernandez, A., Rusk, N., Eastmond, E., Brennan, K., Millner, A., Rosenbaum, E., Silver, J., Silverman, B., & Kafai, Y. 2009. Scratch: Programming for All. *Communications of the ACM*, vol. 52, no. 11, pp. 60-67 (Nov. 2009).

Measuring Increased Engagement Using Tablet PCs in a Code Review Class

Wade Fagen
Computer Science Dept.
University of Illinois
wfagen2@illinois.edu

Samuel Kamin
Computer Science Dept.
University of Illinois
kamin@illinois.edu

ABSTRACT

The Programming Studio in the University of Illinois Computer Science department is a required course in which small groups of students participate in weekly code reviews of each other's programs. To increase student engagement in the discussions, Tablet PCs were introduced for several weeks in the middle of the semester. By recording the discussions before, during, and after the use of tablets, we measure the effectiveness of this intervention. In doing so, we develop a simple metric to measure the "active engagement" of the participants. We found each section was significantly more engaging when using Tablet PCs ($p<0.0001$) and the large majority of individual participants were more engaged. This paper contributes both an objective measurement of "active engagement" and a successful intervention in a programming studio-type course.

Categories and Subject Descriptors

K3.2 [**Computer and Information Science Education**]: Computer Science Education

General Terms

Education, software engineering, tablet computers, audio analysis

Keywords

Code reviews, Tablet PC

1. INTRODUCTION

Students in the Computer Science department at the University of Illinois are required to take CS 242, Programming Studio. Normally taken in the first semester of the junior year — after the core programming courses — the Studio is intended to build individual programming skills. The overall approach is drawn from studio courses in architecture and fine arts: students present their work "in public," and get feedback. Specifically, students meet every week in discussion sections of 3 to 6 students, plus a moderator, where each student has twenty minutes to present their program. With some exceptions, the discussions focus on the code itself, rather than the functionality of the program. Assignments are not as structured as in traditional classes, but the students generally have an idea of what the other students' programs do. (The main exception is in the last four weeks of the semester, where student-selected term projects are presented; during that time, program demos are mixed with code discussions.)

The Studio course was described in 2007 [10]. Although the Studio seemed to be useful to most students, there were some difficulties. We noted, "We need to continually work on maintaining the quality of the discussion in the discussion sections." Programs are complicated, and it is hard to have a stimulating discussion on something that only one of the interlocutors understands. The fear was that the discussions would be closer to monologues, the critiques offered would be superficial, and the discussion would be unengaging. [10] describes various mechanisms to help stimulate discussion. Using Tablet PCs is another such a mechanism. This paper discusses how they were used in the programming studio, and how we attempted to verify that they were having the desired effect.

Tablet PCs are ordinary PC laptops with the added feature of a screen that can be written upon, using Microsoft's digital ink API. These machines have an "active digitizer" screen which can only be written upon with a special stylus. In this paper, we refer to these devices as "tablets," but we caution the reader that these are not iPads or Android tablets, which mostly lack the active digitizer and are not as easy to write on. Writing on Tablet PCs is very natural, and students adjust to them easily. In the Studio, each student has a tablet, and all comments written by any student are instantly shared with all other students. The system we used provides in effect a shared whiteboard, with a student's code forming the background image.

Traditionally, the Studio operates by having each student explain his or her program as it is displayed on a large screen. Adding the tablets provides two benefits: First, writing, which makes it easier to ask and answer questions about code. Second, private copies of the presenter's code, allowing each student to explore it independently, rather than following the presenter. In introducing the tablets, we hoped these benefits would help make the discussions more engaging and efficient.

The study reported here was peformed in the Spring, 2011,

SIGCSE'13, March 6–9, 2013, Denver, Colorado, USA.

semester. Its goal was to test whether the tablets had a positive effect on the discussions. We set up a simple experiment: In six sections, we had students alternate between tablet use and the traditional Studio. We gathered data by using personal audio recorders to record the interactions during each meeting of each of the six sections. In this paper, we report on the results of the analysis of this data.

This paper makes three contributions to the study of Computer Science education:

- We describe a Tablet PC system supporting code reviews in the Programming Studio, and explain why it is helpful.
- We give a method for mechanically measuring "active engagement" of the Studio discussions, based on analyzing audio recordings of the participants.
- We describe an experiment to test the hypothesis that the introduction of Tablet PCs lead to livelier discussions. We present data from voice recording analyses that confirm the hypothesis.

The next two sections of the paper describe the Programming Studio and the use of Tablet PCs. Section 4 describes the experimental set-up, and then sections 5 gives the results obtained from the recordings. These are followed by a discussion of related work, and our conclusions.

2. PROGRAMMING STUDIO

CS 242, Programming Studio [10], is a required class for CS majors at the University of Illinois, providing individualized instruction on programming by having students critique each other's programs in a code review setting. The class grew out of a concern that, despite many hours spent programming in CS courses, not all of our students were becoming proficient at it. A student could get through our program — we are undoubtedly not unique in this regard — without ever having a detailed, one-on-one, discussion about a program he or she had written.

The Studio is taken in the junior year, after all the core courses have been completed. Students get fairly open-ended assignments each week, and are expected to show up at the weekly discussion with a working program. In a group of three to six students, plus a moderator — a graduate student or upper-level undergraduate — each student presents his or her program for 20–25 minutes. The presentation may include a demo, but usually it is simply a discussion of the code. (This changes in the last few weeks of the semester, when students do self-chosen projects; then, more of the discussion is devoted to demos.) In the presentation, the presenter stands in front of the group and explains his or her program, while showing it on a large display. The arrangement is shown in Figure 1.

Most students find the studio beneficial, and many report that it played a key role in their development as a Computer Scientist. However, others complain that the discussions tend to focus on superficial aspects of their programs. This points to a fundamental issue that we identified in [10]: how can a discussion of programs be kept lively and engaging? Some mechanisms for addressing this issue are described in [10]. The tablets are our latest effort in this direction.

Terminology: We refer to the presenting student as the *presenter*; non-presenting students as *reviewers*; everyone in

Figure 1: Non-Tablet PC Studio structure: students follow presenter

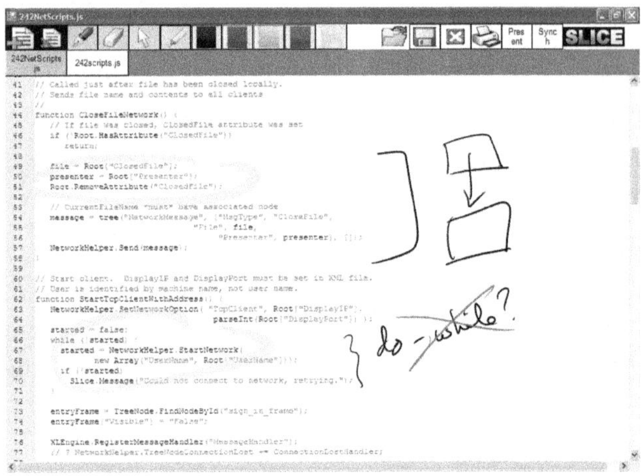

Figure 2: SLICE screenshot

the studio except the moderator as *students*; and everyone in the studio, including the moderator, as *participants*. A *section* is a regular meeting of a particular group of students; the experiment involved six sections (Thursdays at 5PM and 7PM, Fridays at 9AM, 11AM, 1PM, and 3PM). A *meeting* is a single meeting of a section, lasting from one to two hours depending upon the number of participants.

3. TABLET PCS IN THE STUDIO

The system used in the Studio is a straightforward "shared whiteboard" application. It was developed using the SLICE framework [5,8], and is customized for our course. As each student takes a turn as presenter, he or she loads the program files into the system, where each is represented by a tab. Within each tab, the text of the file forms the background of the whiteboard; the text cannot be directly edited, but simply annotated upon. Figure 2 shows the SLICE screen during a studio discussion.

Each student in the discussion, as well as the moderator, has a tablet, and all share the same data. That is, any program loaded into the presenter's tablet, and any stroke made by anyone, is immediately sent to all others. The arrangement is otherwise identcal to that shown in Figure 1.

The tablets provide two capabilities: (1) The ability to write, draw, and point. Drawing is useful to explain the deep structure of a program, data structure, or algorithm; writing makes it easier for reviewers to ask "what if you did it this way?" questions; pointing makes it easier to draw attention to a particular spot in the program. In general, writing helps make the discussion more efficient. (2) The ability to explore the presented program independent of the presenter. Each student can switch tabs and scroll through the files in the presented programs. This allows a reviewer to spend time understanding a section of code after the presenter has moved on, or simply to explore it in a different order than the presenter uses. (A button on the interface allows a student to synch up with the presenter.) This can allow a reviewer to gain a better understanding of the presented program — or at least of some part of it — and thus make more substantive comments about it.[1]

4. EXPERIMENT

The Studio discussion can switch easily from the traditional structure to the tablet structure. The design of our experiment was to have the discussions operate first in the traditional setting, introduce tablets for several weeks in the middle, and then move back the traditional setting towards the end of the semester. During this entire time, we took audio recordings of each meeting.

We ran the experiment in the Spring, 2011 semester for ten weeks, with six sections participating, with a total of 17 students and 4 moderators. We began recording students and moderators, using small personal recorders with lapel microphones on each participant, in week 5 and continued through the end of the semester (week 14). In weeks 5–6 and 11–14, the Studio ran in its traditional structure; in weeks 7–10, the tablets were used.

When we first introduced tablets into the course, in a pilot project in Fall, 2010, we assumed the digital communication channel provided by the tablets would *displace* the traditional oral channel. However, we began to observe that the tablets might have the *opposite* effect, actually enhancing oral communication in the meetings. That observation gave rise to the current study.

In particular, we postulated that the tablets would help make each student more individually engaged in the discussion. That is, each student would contribute to the conversation more often when the class used tablets than when it did not.

5. AUDIO RECORDINGS

To measure this form of engagement, which we call "active egnagement", we wanted to capture how long has passed since a given participant spoke. This metric would need to rate a conversation poorly if only a single speaker spoke for minutes on end without any participation by others and rate a conversation as productive if the entire class was engaged in the dialog.

[1]We made little attempt to distinguish the impact of these two features. It would be worthwhile to do so, in particular, because this second capability could be provided with ordinary computers, which may be more readily available than tablets.

Week	All	5–6	7–10	11–14
Tablet usage?		No	Yes	No
Recorded meetings	49	11	20	18
Total recordings	222	47	97	78
Hours	195.1	53.81	72.3	69.0
Size (GB)	10.46	2.89	3.88	3.70

Table 1: Basic information on audio recordings

In this section, we present our analysis. Following an explanation of the data collection process, we present a mathematical measure of "active engagement" of a meeting, which we call ϵ, and show strong, statistically-significant results of a substantial increase in ϵ for tablet vs. non-tablet sections. We then define a related measure of "active engagement" of individuals, called γ, and give evidence that almost all participants showed increased γ in the tablet sections.

5.1 Data collection

To gather audio data, each participant was asked to wear a small, personal voice recorder with a lapel microphone. We used the VR5220 RCA Digital Voice Recorder, a consumer-level voice recorder that captures audio in a single-channel format at 8000 Hz.

To have minimal impact on the meetings, we attended only the first few minutes of the first meeting where recorders were used, to show the participants how to use them. We instructed the students not to stop the class if the recorders malfunctioned. After each week, we collected the audio from the devices for storage. The stored recordings were tagged with the participant's name, and the time and date of the meeting.

The large majority of participants from each section had successful recordings. However, for both mechanical reasons and human error, we did not always obtain a complete recording for every participant in every section. Table 1 presents the basic statistics about the recordings.

5.2 Data processing

After the semester concluded, we had collected over nine days of audio recordings. Although each recording was made by a single student with an individual microphone, the recordings were corrupted by "cross talk" that sometimes made it difficult to isolate the actual speaker. We needed to determine who was actually speaking when.

The "cross talk" turned out to be useful for this, as we could use it to precisely synchronize the audio recordings in each meeting. Effectively, this process gave us a multi-channel audio file where each channel was the microphone of one of the participants. The next phase of our analysis relied on the observation that the channel with the loudest volume (over a threshold of background static) was almost certainly the speaker at that time. To validate this assumption, we had three different humans tag a recording with the times that a participant spoke. We found that the small differences between the human interpretations of the audio was within the same margin as the differences between any human's interpretation and the algorithm's result.

Finally, with individual "volume events" identified and attributed to a speaker, the final analysis was to combine adjoining "volume events" by the same person into a *turn*. This

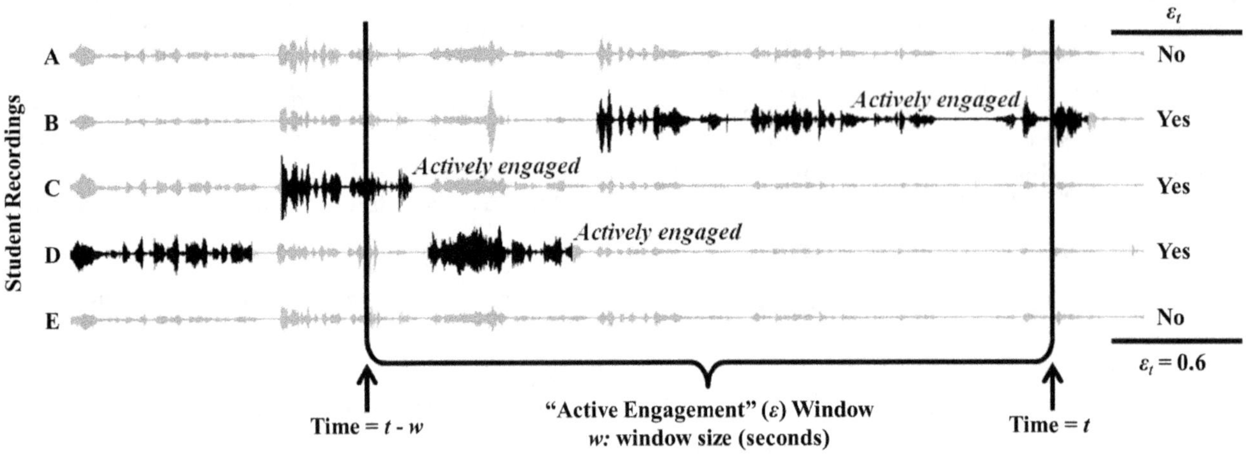

Figure 3: A visual overview of the "active engagement" metric, ϵ. Five participants in a studio meeting, labeled A–E, have their raw waveform displayed. The darkened areas of the waveforms were identified as turns in the discussion. Speakers B, C, and D had a speaking turn within the "active engagement window," resulting in $\epsilon_t = 0.6$. The value of ϵ is found by taking the average of all ϵ_t values across an entire section.

combines individual words, eg: "How did your algorithm sort this list?", into a single speaking *turn*.

As a whole, our treatment of the raw data transformed groups of 8000 Hz input waveforms into a series of turns of each speaker. For all the analysis from this point forward, we work only with the turns that we identified through this process.

5.3 Active engagement

Our hypothesis was that the tablets would have a positive effect on the oral channel. Specifically, we were interested in how often an individual in a meeting of the studio section would contribute to the conversation. To measure this, we developed an "active engagement" metric, which we call ϵ.

This metric asks a simple question: "At a given moment in time, how many of a meeting's participants had a speaking turn within the last *(*time window)?". ϵ is the ratio between the number of participants who had a speaking turn within the time window and the number who were present at that time. If our window was one minute, and all the participants spoke within the past minute, ϵ would be 1.0. If only two of the six participants spoke, ϵ would be 0.33. Figure 3 shows a visual overview of the ϵ metric.

We analyzed the average ϵ across the full meeting, for several window sizes. For each hundredth of a second (0.01s) in each meeting, ϵ is calculated. For an hour long section, this would result in 360,000 individual values. Effectively, we have performed a detailed approximation of an integration across the entire meeting.

Consider an average ϵ of 0.7 for a given meeting. This value would indicate that, across the entire meeting, an average of 70% of the participants contributed to the conversation within the last *(time window)* of time.

We have not yet said what a correct window size would be. Using a small window, on the order of only a few seconds, would be uninteresting as one wouldn't consider someone unengaged in a conversation if they went just ten seconds without speaking. On the other hand, a large window would be equally uninteresting as *everyone* is likely to get a turn

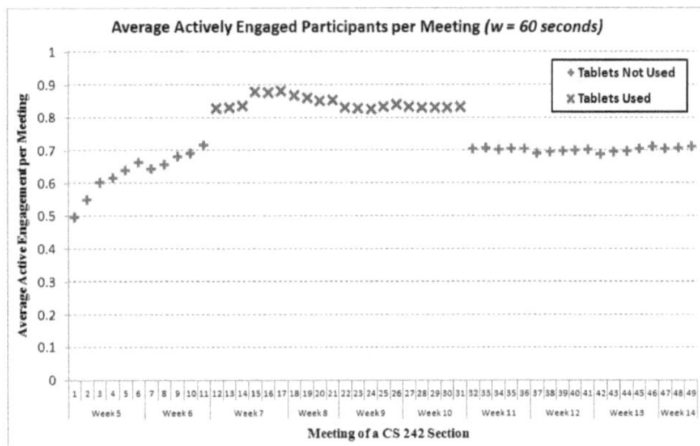

Figure 4: Average "active engagement" (ϵ) per meeting

in each window. We present data for windows ranging from 30 seconds to 300 seconds, but often focus on a window of one minute.

Figure 4 shows the average ϵ of all 49 meetings that were recorded, using a one-minute window. On average, the introduction of tablets significantly boosted the average ϵ from less than 70% to nearly 85%. Table 2 shows the average ϵ for various windows, showing the result remains statistically significant with windows from 30 seconds up to five minutes.[2]

Looking deeper into the data, we compared the meetings on a section by section basis. As the CS 242 studio course was a graded course and students signed up for a single,

[2]The numbers presented are from the analysis of all participants, including both students and moderators. We also performed analysis using only the students. Both forms of analysis resulted in the same trends when graphed, nearly identical raw values, and the same level of statistical significance.

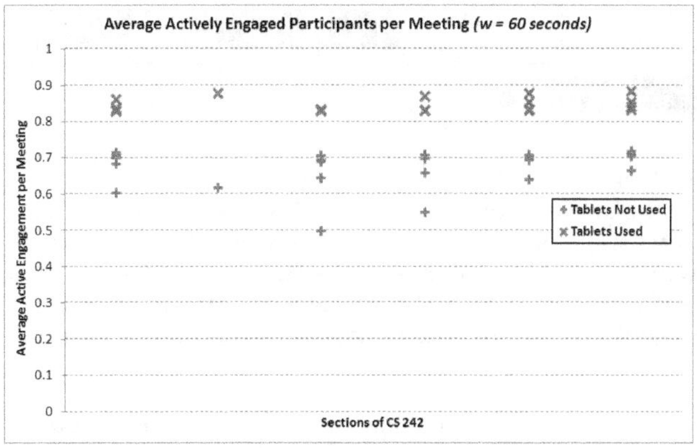

Figure 5: Average ϵ per meeting, grouped by the six sections that were recorded as part of this study

Window	No Tablets		Tablets		p
	Mean	StDev	Mean	StDev	
30s	0.5682	0.0508	0.7401	0.0230	<0.001
60s	0.6765	0.0519	0.8446	0.0189	<0.001
120s	0.7902	0.0438	0.9292	0.0135	<0.001
180s	0.8526	0.0343	0.9607	0.0095	<0.001
300s	0.9190	0.0209	0.9818	0.0056	<0.001

Table 2: Average ϵ across all meetings for various windows

specific section, there was little variance week-to-week in the students who attended each section.[3]

Figure 5 shows the same ϵ values grouped by section. We find that the sections are very similar, and all showed improvement when using tablets.

We next asked if there were significantly more *turns* in the conversation. An increase in the number of turns might signify that a different type of conversation occurred, where each person spoke for shorter segments of speech. However, an analysis on the average number of turns per minute, displayed in the table below, shows no meaningful difference:

	No Tablets	Tablets	p
All	10.5934	10.4143	0.9278

Further analysis of the data allows us to look at individual participants. For individuals, we use a metric related to ϵ, which we call γ: the percentage of time in the meeting that the individual is "engaged" in the sense of having had a turn within the the previous time window. For example, a γ of 0.8 indicates that, at any given time in that meeting, there was an 80% chance that this participant had spoken within the previous window. In the following, we again use a 60-second window.

Figure 6 graphs each participant's average γ over all meetings they attended, grouped into tablet and non-tablet meetings. Starred participants are moderators. We make several observations on this figure:

[3]When students were unable to attend their assigned section due to a conflict, they were allowed to attend other sections. Our analysis used all students present at the section, even when a student only appeared once.

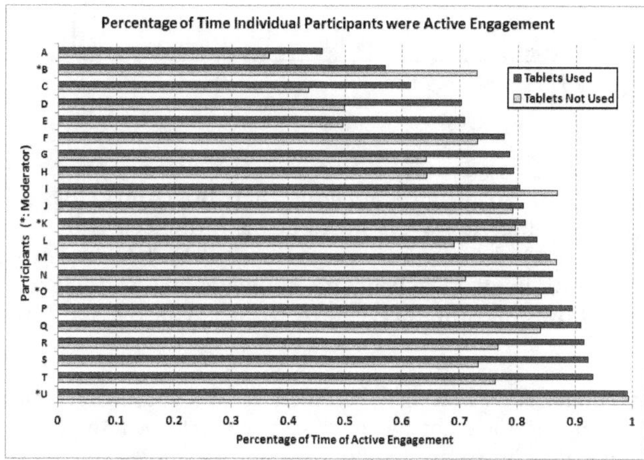

Figure 6: Average "individual active engagement" (γ) per participant (w = 60 seconds)

1. The vast majority of students (15 of 17) were more "actively engaged" using tablets. The average student saw a boost to their γ by 0.0834 (an increase of 11.64%) with tablets.

2. Of the students who were least engaged without the use of tablets (participants A, C, D, and E all had $\gamma < 0.50$), all saw a significant boost from the tablets (an average increase in γ of 0.1726, or 38%).

3. For three of the moderators, γ increased when using tablets, but the increases were small. For the fourth moderator (B), γ decreased, and by a much greater amount (0.73 to 0.57) than either of the two students whose γ decreased. It is not surprising that moderators should show up differently from students — after all, if the students are *un*engaged, we might expect the moderators to talk more — but we do not have enough data to draw definite conclusions in this regard.

4. Performing a paired, two-tailed t-test on the participants' data graph in Figure 6, we find these results are statistically significant (p=0.000914). If we choose to exclude the moderators, the p-value decreases to 0.0000416.

To make these measures more concrete, we show more detail on the speech of a single student. Figure 6 shows that student "D" was a shy student who increased his γ by more than 40% when tablets were used. Figure 7 shows this student's turns in two meetings, one with and one without tablets. ("Turns" are explained in section 5.2; in Figure 3 these are the parts of the signal shown in black.) Observe that in both meetings, there is a period of high speech activity; this is to be expected: it is when student D is presenting. More interesting are the other parts of the graphs, when student D was not presenting but was one of six reviewers. The graphs show pretty clearly that student D was a more engaged reviewer when using the tablets.

6. RELATED WORK

The use of the studio concept in programming classes seems to be increasing [7]. There is a considerable literature on the use of Tablet PCs in classrooms, some with

Figure 7: Student D's turns in the discussion from two differnet meetings, each approximately 75 minutes in length. At full resolution, each horizontal pixel represents one second of the meeting. A black line at a specific pixel for a given meeting indicates that a speaker was speaking during that second of the meeting. Graph (A) shows a meeting where Tablet PCs were used while Graph (B) shows a meeting where Tablet PCs were not used. Each graph shows a large, dark area where Student D was the presenter. However, Graph (A) shows significantly more total turns by Student D throughout the meeting outside of his presentation.

an emphasis on how they can increase student engagement [1,3,4,6]. We are not aware of any research on integrating Tablet PCs into a studio, nor of analyzing audio recordings to assess engagement. We drew the idea of using individual lapel microphones from "Conversation Clock" [2]; in that research, participants in a small meeting employed a system that visually displayed each individual's contribution to the conversation in real time; the researchers studied the subtle effects that this had on the conversation.

7. CONCLUSIONS AND FUTURE WORK

We have described how, in a course in which Computer Science students gather for mutual code reviews, Tablet PCs were introduced to help facilitate and enliven the discussions. Through the recording of ten weeks of weekly meetings across six different sections, we presented detailed analysis of the engagment of the various participants in each section.

To perform this analysis, we established an "active engagement" metric that evaluated how lively or engaging the discussions were in each meeting. This metric is defined simply as how many participants had a "turn" in the discussion within a window of time before the current time. Using this metric, we found the use of tablets, for every reasonable window of time (from 30 seconds to 5 minutes), significantly increased the "active engagement" in all of the discussion sections ($p < 0.001$).

Further, we examined the percentage of time each individual student was "actively engaged" in each of the meetings they attended. We found that, with the introduction of tablets, the large majority of students were more engaged (15 of 17), and, interestingly, the students who were least engaged gained the most in our metric (an average of +17.26%). We found strong significance in the increase in "active engagement" of the participants as a result of the use of tablets ($p=0.000914$).

In this paper, we did not perform any analysis that made use of the various roles of the participants, such as distinguishing which student was presenting at any time. It would be interesting future work to see how the interactions between the presenter, reviewers, and moderator differ with and without the tablets.

Further, the analysis performed on this audio was done without reference to the topic of conversation. While the meetings are lead by a moderator (a member of the course staff) that kept the discussions largely on-topic, it would be of value to understand if the introduction of tablets aided to keep the discussion on-topic more often.

The quest for increased student engagement is a long one; a Google search for "strategies for increasing student engagement" gets over two million hits. In those circumstances where "active engagement" is a good proxy for increasing student engagement, we believe our work can contribute to studying engagement using more objective measurements.

Acknowledgements

We thank Chris Cortez for his help in running the experiments, and Studio instructors Mike Woodley and Charlie Meyer, and the CS 242 moderators, for their cooperation.

References

[1] R. Anderson, R. Anderson, L. McDowell and B. Simon. Use of Classroom Presenter in Engineering Courses. Frontiers in Education, 2005.

[2] T. Bergstrom, K. Karahalios. Conversation Clock: Visualizing audio patterns in co-located groups. In Proc. 40th Annual Hawaii Intl. Conf. on System Sciences (HICSS '07), 2007.

[3] T. L. Derting, J. R. Cox, Using a Tablet PC To Enhance Student Engagement and Learning in an Introductory Organic Chemistry Course J. Chem. Educ., 2008, 85 (12), p 1638

[4] A. Hurford and E. Hamilton, Effects of Tablet Computers and Collaborative Classroom Software on Student Engagement and Learning, 38th ASEE/IEEE Frontiers in Education Conference, Saratoga Springs, NY, 2008.

[5] S. N. Kamin, M. Hines, C. Peiper, B. Capitanu, A System for Developing Tablet PC Applications for Education. SIGCSE, Portland, OR, March, 2008.

[6] P. Lafontant. Using Tablet PCs and DyKnow Vision to Enhance Student Engagement In A Human Anatomy Class. Workshop on the Impact of Pen-Based Technology on Education (WIPTE) West Lafayette, IN. 2008.

[7] N. H. Narayanan, C. Hundhausen, D. Hendrix, M. Crosby, Transforming the CS Classroom with Studio-Based Learning, SIGCSE 2012, Raleigh, North Carolina, USA, 165–166.

[8] SLICE website: slice.cs.illinois.edu

[9] K. Wiegers, Peer Reviews in Software, Addison-Wesley Professional, 2001.

[10] M. Woodley, S.N. Kamin, Programming Studio: A Course for Improving Programming Skills in Undergraduates. SIGCSE, Covington, KY, March, 2007.

What Are We Thinking When We Grade Programs?

Sue Fitzgerald
Metropolitan State University
sue.fitzgeral@metrostate.edu

Brian Hanks
BFH Educational Consulting
brianhanks@acm.org

Raymond Lister
University of Technology, Sydney
Raymond.Lister@uts.edu.au

Renée McCauley
College of Charleston
mccauleyr@cofc.edu

Laurie Murphy
Pacific Lutheran University
lmurphy@plu.edu

ABSTRACT
This paper reports on a mixed methods study which examines how four experienced instructors approached the grading of a programming problem. Two instructors used a detailed, analytic approach and two instructors employed a holistic approach. One instructor exhibited elements of a primary trait approach. Even though the four instructors used different grading scales and philosophies, their raw scores were highly correlated (Spearman's *rho* of .81) supporting the conclusion that experienced instructors usually agree on whether a program is 'very good' or 'very bad'. Clearly there is no single right way to grade programs. Further discourse should be encouraged for the benefit of both educators and students.

Categories and Subject Descriptors
K.3 [**Computers & Education**]: Computer & Information Science Education - *Computer Science Education.*

General Terms
Management, Measurement, Documentation.

Keywords
Grading, scoring, programming, rubrics.

1. INTRODUCTION
Grading is the Cinderella activity of teaching – often overlooked yet critically essential. Educators talk more about many other topics – attracting and retaining students, first languages, IDEs, nifty assignments and the latest technology – than we do about grading. But grades are crucial. Within the academic term, formative assessment provides the critical feedback that guides both students and teachers. At the end of the term, summative assessment – the final grade – has a profound influence on a student's subsequent choice of major and eventual career. Class grade distributions also have an effect on driving pedagogic change by teachers.

Both students and teachers benefit from a methodical and consistent approach to scoring assignments and exam questions. "Learning increases, even in its serendipitous aspects, when learners have a sense of what they are setting out to learn, a statement of explicit standards they must meet, and a way of seeing what they have learned...Assessment requires [faculty] to articulate...explicit and public statements of criteria of performance. By doing so, faculty refine their own understanding of expected abilities, clarify for their colleagues the basis of their judgment, and enable students to understand what performance is required" [7 as quoted in 2].

This paper reports on a mixed qualitative and quantitative study which closely examines how four experienced instructors approached the grading of a programming problem. The differences in how the instructors approached the grading process and the rubrics they developed are revealing and may serve as a set of good alternatives for novice programming instructors.

Our thoughts may also serve as useful input for those who develop automatic graders. In the coming age of Massive Open Online Courses (MOOCs), automatic grading will be crucial. It is not clear to us that existing automatic graders accommodate the variety of approaches illustrated by the set of expert instructors as outlined in this paper. This is particularly true for those instructors who use the holistic approach.

This paper is organized as follows: Section 2 describes some of the theoretical background on developing rubrics and summarizes previous reports on using rubrics for grading programs. Section 3 describes how the student solutions were collected and Section 4 describes how four different instructors graded a programming problem. In Section 5 we analyze our approaches statistically. In Section 6 we discuss the implications of our work and we conclude in Section 7.

2. BACKGROUND
2.1 Manual Marking
Surprisingly little has been published on the grading of programming assignments.

Howatt wrote a practical paper which provides an example of a rubric, including a detailed explanation of how the authors arrived at it and how they used it [6]. The paper reflects on teaching (grading) practice and provides some insights for the novice teacher. However, it has no theoretical basis.

Miller and Peterson devised a problem-independent rubric for grading programs written by undergraduates [8]. One hundred points were available in their rubric, with 80 points for "minimum requirements" and the remaining points for "refinements above minimum". There were 13 items in the rubric, with 10 items for minimum requirements. The smallest item was worth 2 points (for "author at the beginning") and the largest was worth 20 points ("correct output"). Only one item was worth 20%, with the next

SIGCSE'13, March 6-9, 2013, Denver, Colorado, USA.

highest weighting being 10 points, for 5 items. Miller and Peterson evaluated their rubric by having three professors grade ten programs. Using a statistical test, they rejected the null hypothesis that their rubric was not reliable. However, the average scores across the ten programs for each of the three professors were 72%, 75% and 81%. In some institutions this would result in different letter grades for many students, depending upon which professor graded their program.

Hamm et al. presented a scale for use in grading computer programs [5]. Their goal was to facilitate consistent grading among graders and across courses, and to speed up the grading process. The scale, called the Jacksonville University Scale, lists seven factors (execution of the program, correctness of the output, design of the output, design of the logic, design of test data, internal documentation and external documentation), along with a point system for distinguishing "poor", "average" and "good" performance on programs. Their development of the scale was informed by similar work on grading English composition papers. They built a tool to generate grading forms based on the scale. The programs were graded manually, but the forms were used to guide the grading. They reported anecdotal support for the effectiveness of the grading scale within their own institution.

Olson [10] compared two approaches, analytic and holistic, for grading programs. "In analytic scoring, sub-scores on a series of specific criteria are totaled to give the program an overall score. In holistic scoring, raters read an entire program to obtain a general impression of its overall quality and assign the program a single score". Each approach was used by two evaluators on a set of thirty end-of-term programming exams. Surprisingly, Olson found that "The inter-rater reliability for the student's scores on holistically scored hands-on programming ability test was significant (r=.73) and higher than the inter-rater reliability for the analytically scored tests" (r=.56). The "low correlation between the scoring methods indicates that only 45% of the variance in students' scores on the hands-on final from one scoring method could be explained by use of the other scoring method."

Smith and Cordova [11] discussed a theoretical foundation for developing grading rubrics based on primary trait analysis (PTA), often used when evaluating writing and other topics in the liberal arts [11]. "PTA uses specific criteria for evaluating performance and defines the factors or 'traits' that are to be evaluated as part of the assignment evaluation. For each trait, a grading scale is used to determine the level to which a particular criterion is satisfied. The scale is defined by providing specific descriptions of the levels of achievement that correspond to each point in the scale." Smith and Cordova provide a detailed rubric for grading programs based on PTA. They offer a six-part description of how to evaluate fourteen separate criteria. The criteria can be weighted. The identification of traits/criteria is analogous to the analytic approach but the level to which a criterion is satisfied more closely resembles the holistic approach as described by Olson [10]. Smith and Cordova developed a spreadsheet version of the tool and reported anecdotally that students liked the feedback it provides and that the tool increased consistency in grading.

2.2 Automatic Marking

A striking feature of the literature on manual grading is its age. In recent years, the bulk of the literature on grading has been in the context of automatic grading. Automatic grading tools have been used to grade student programs for decades, with many of those tools being developed and used within a single institution. According to a survey performed by Carter et al. approximately 70% of first-year programming courses use computer-aided assessment to some extent although not all of these computer-aided assessment techniques were tools for grading programs [3].

More automatic program grading tools have been developed than can be reviewed in this paper. We refer readers to reviews by Ala-Mutka [1] and Douce et al. [4]. Ala-Mutka identified several ways in which automatic graders assess programs, including: (1) functionality, which usually involves running programs against test data sets, (2) efficiency, which can be measured as run time or by number of statements executed, (3) coding style, which can measure one or more aspects of code, such as module length, number of comment lines and use of indentation, and (4) software metrics, such as cyclomatic complexity.

2.3 Types of Rubrics

Rubrics in general (i.e., not just rubrics for grading programs) are often classified into one of three types [12]:

- **Holistic:** Grading is done against a small number of criteria. For each criterion, a small point range is used, often 4 – 6 points (e.g., from 0 for "not attempted" to 4 for "exemplary"). There may also be some trade off between scores for each criterion. Thus the grader forms an overall impression of the piece of work. Speed is one advantage of this approach.
- **Analytic:** Grading is done against a larger and more detailed set of criteria than for holistic grading. Points are assigned to each criterion independently of other criteria and those points are summed to give the total score.
- **Primary trait:** Grading is focused on a very small number of aspects (perhaps one aspect) considered crucial. Like the holistic approach, primary trait grading is often quick, but the difference is that aspects considered secondary are ignored.

3. EXAM DATA

The data examined for this study were collected from a final exam given to 20 introductory students who learnt Java at a small liberal arts university in the United States. Students were given a two-part exam during a one hour and 45 minute period. The first part was taken on paper and comprised matching, expression evaluation, short essay, error detection, and code reading problems. The code reading questions included tracing and Explain in Plain English questions [9].

After turning in the first part, students logged onto classroom machines and completed a set of short Java programs by adding basic constructs and simple object oriented code to a series of templates. Students were given three reference sheets to use during the programming exam. They used temporary accounts to prevent access to previous homework solutions and examples. Classroom management software was used to monitor students as they worked. The programming exam counted for 45 of 100 exam points with an opportunity to earn 5 extra credit points.

We used one of the programming questions from the exam in this study. In that question, students wrote a program to prompt the user to enter a series of integers (using -99 to signal the end of input) and then display the largest and smallest numbers entered.

4. FOUR GRADERS IN ACTION

Four of the authors, all of them experienced university faculty members, graded the 20 student programs. Each instructor approached the problem independently without prior consultation although all the graders were aware that the original intention of the programming exam was to separate those students who should continue to the next course from those for whom this was not advisable. The instructors did not discuss grading criteria or rubrics before grading. Analysis of the grading techniques showed that the graders approached the problem with very different goals.

4.1 Author Murphy

Author Murphy designed the test problem and was the instructor of the class that completed the test. She teaches at a small, undergraduate liberal arts institution in the northwestern part of the United States. Her class sizes are small and her students are primarily residential and traditionally aged. She has over 20 years of teaching experience. Murphy's intended purpose for the machine-based portion of the final exam was to provide a "litmus test" to determine if students with borderline (C/C-) overall grades should advance to the next course. Her approach was simple and direct. Students' source files were compiled and executed using a script containing typical input values. Programs were not tested for incorrect or illegal input values. If the program passed the test cases, the source code was manually scanned for general correctness. If everything appeared in order, the program was awarded full points. If any errors or oddities were noticed, they were examined more closely to determine how they should impact the score. Programs that did not compile or contained serious errors were given closer scrutiny. Because the source files contained multiple problems, students were sometimes given full or partial credit for one or more problems that appeared to be implemented correctly, even if the code overall did not compile or contained a runtime error.

Murphy deducted points if the program:

- did not have a priming read
- did not display the smallest or largest value
- read data, but did not check for the smallest or largest
- initialized the smallest or largest to an arbitrary number

Murphy gave no credit if the student did not attempt to solve the problem, and she gave full credit even if the code potentially returned the loop sentinel (-99) as the highest or lowest value. As Murphy noted, "I clearly wasn't that picky and in some cases I gave pity points." Her intention, again, was simply to separate those students who programmed well enough to continue to the next course, from those who did not.

4.2 Author Fitzgerald

Author Fitzgerald teaches at a comprehensive university in the US Midwest with approximately 10,000 undergraduate and master's level students. Her students are non-residential adult learners and her class sizes are usually 25-35 students. She has over 25 years of teaching experience at the graduate and undergraduate level.

Fitzgerald graded the programs by reading the solutions and mentally tracing them, as if they were answers to a problem given on a written exam. She did not run the solutions. She began by developing a rubric based on her understanding of the problem. The rubric identified key program elements and assigned points values for each element. The first version of the rubric was created after looking at the skeleton code but before looking at any student answers.

Correct functionality was considered the most important part of solving the problem and the rubric assigned points accordingly, identifying two large pieces of functionality (find the smallest and find the largest) and assigning them approximately one-third of the points each. Correctly reading the data and stopping at the sentinel value was also considered important, but to a lesser degree.

Fitzgerald's first rubric was quite simple, checking to see if the program displayed the largest and smallest values, prompted for and read the input values and ended with the sentinel value (-99). However, the rubric was quickly revised after she made a first attempt to use it. She added more details to the generic descriptions, 'Displays largest' and 'Displays smallest', having failed to anticipate that students might choose arbitrary initial values for 'Largest' and 'Smallest' which could exclude ranges of numbers. Fitzgerald also discerned that other key elements of the solution included: considering all of the elements entered, avoiding any possibility of choosing the sentinel as the highest or lowest value, and actually displaying the correct results.

After grading the first student's program using the second version of the rubric, Fitzgerald asked herself if the total score reflected her gut feeling about the student's understanding. The answer was, "probably not". The first student's program did not find the correct answer since it used incorrect initial values and included the sentinel value when comparing for largest and smallest, yet it earned 71% of the possible points (a C). The rubric was revised again by placing more weight on finding the largest/smallest number and by distinguishing between finding and displaying the correct result. The first student's program was re-graded, and the resulting score of 53% of the possible points (an F) was a more accurate representation of this student's understanding of the problem. One final adjustment was made to the rubric after grading the second student's answer. Neither of the first two participants accounted for the case where the user entered no numbers to compare but instead entered the sentinel as the first input value. The fourth and final version of the rubric included one point for catching this error condition. Sadly, none of the students wrote code which caught this error. Fitzgerald concluded that rubrics cannot be finalized before they are tested against actual student work and may require adjustment even toward the middle or end of the grading process.

She noted, "I commonly create the rubric at the same time I design the test problem. I usually solve programming problems using a computer before administering the test to discover unanticipated quirks in the solution and to focus my attention on what it took to solve the problem. But I'm really not very good at anticipating the sorts of mistakes the students will make."

4.3 Author McCauley

Author McCauley is an experienced educator with more than 25 years experience teaching at the undergraduate level, including introductory programming. Her institution is a state-supported liberal arts and sciences institution with a focus on undergraduate education. Class sizes in the introductory courses are about 25 students. McCauley graded by inspecting hardcopies of the code and graded them as though they were part of a written, rather than computer-based, programming test. She started by reading the problem and listing what she considered the characteristics of a correct solution were:

1. Should work for any set of integers, including the empty set.
    a. If the data set is empty (-99 is the first value entered), an error message indicating that there is no largest or smallest value should be displayed.
    b. If the data set is non-empty, a message displaying the correct values is printed.
2. Should include a proper sentinel-controlled loop, with a priming read before the loop, a next read at the end of loop, and no checks for the sentinel value within the body of the loop.

3. Should not contain any superfluous assignments, control structures or other statements even if the program generated correct results (see point 1 above).
4. Should be logically correct, even if not syntactically correct or beautiful.
    a. The programs were not executed, since they were received in PDF format.
    b. The grader ignored issues related to indentation, documentation and meaningful identifier names.

After listing the characteristics of a correct solution, McCauley glanced at several participant submissions, to inform herself of the types of solutions to expect. This convinced her that seeing a correct solution, before proceeding further, would be helpful. She produced a solution that satisfied 1-4 above; this reminded her of how difficult the problem actually was.

With a correct solution in hand, McCauley read through all 20 solutions, building a spreadsheet of notes, with column headings such as "bad initialization", "good loop form", and "produces correct results for non-empty data". She noted these characteristics for each program while reading through it. Since new column headings were generated as the McCauley read through all of the programs on the first pass, she made a second pass through the programs and updated the notes for each. A 10-point grading scale was established:

- Any program that satisfied 1-4 above received a grade of 10.
- Any program that satisfied 1-4 above, but only for non-empty data sets received a grade of 8.
- If a program returned a correct result for non-empty data, but had one imperfection (such as an extra if statement, bad initial values or worked only for the given sample data), it received a score of 7.
- For other programs close to returning a correct result for non-empty data except for one or two minor mistakes, a grade of 6 was assigned.

Submissions that did not receive 6 points or more as described above were placed into buckets and awarded scores based on the buckets into which they fell:

- No work (no loop for input or any logic to find the largest or smallest value): score of 0
- Contained a loop and possibly some logic, but the purpose of the logic was not clear: score of 2
- Serious attempt but not close to a correct solution: score of 3.5. A serious attempt had at least one of the following elements:
    a. Correct sentinel controlled loop
    b. Correct initialization of variables holding min and max
    c. Correct logical structure for updating min and max variables

McCauley made a third pass through the programs, noting the score earned in the spreadsheet and looking at all programs that earned the same score to verify that they were equivalent. A few scoring adjustments were made during this pass. Since no solution satisfied point 1 above, the highest score given was an 8.

4.4 Author Lister

Author Lister teaches at a large research institution in Australia. He has large class sizes, typically 200-400 students. He has 20 years of teaching experience. Lister reasoned that the students completed this task on a computer, which provided them with the opportunity to iteratively write-test-debug. Furthermore, the exam question provided an example set of inputs: 9, 11, 4, 6 and -99, along with the expected output, Largest: 11 Smallest: 4. Therefore, Lister decided that a solution would receive zero points if it did not output either the correct largest value or the correct smallest value for the sample input. His thinking was that the most important factor is the student's capacity to reason about their own code – so, if a student cannot reason well enough to get at least one of the minimum or maximum correct, then that student is not ready to proceed to the next programming course. Moreover, to let them move on the next course would almost certainly condemn them to failure. Lister notes, "Had this been a pen-and-paper test I would have awarded non-zero points to solutions that scored zero in this test, since a pen-and-paper test does not provide the opportunity to iteratively write-test-debug."

Lister started with a test of functionality. Most students declared two variables which they used to remember the smallest and largest input values inputted thus far. However, many initialized those two variables to a constant value, often zero. Thus, if the input data consisted entirely of positive numbers (as the sample test data does) then an incorrect smallest value would be output, and if the test data consisted entirely of negative numbers then an incorrect largest value would be output. One point was awarded for solutions that exhibited this problem, and two points to solutions that did not exhibit this problem (even when the chosen initial values only worked for the single given test case). Lister had originally intended to subtract functionality points for solutions that did not handle the case where -99 is the first number input. However, none of the students' solutions handled that case, so he decided to ignore that problem, as did Murphy.

Lister considered the quality of the code if and only if a student scored the two full points for functionality. The only measure of code quality that was considered was indentation. Lister commented, "I don't expect end-of-first-semester students to understand good design beyond choice of variable names, writing some comments, and indentation. In the context of this machine-based exam, with a tiny amount of code to write (including only two new variables), plus a little bit of time pressure, I didn't want to be harsh about variable names and comments, but I did feel that even under these circumstances a programmer should still use indenting to keep their own thoughts clear, and to some degree just out of habit. But I only wanted to reward indentation if the code met my minimum criteria for functionality." After inspecting the first few student solutions, Lister decided to award one point if a student had indented the code within the body of the loop, and another point if the student had indented "if" statements appropriately. These two indenting points were awarded independently of each other.

Thus, in Lister's grading scheme, the highest possible score was 4. At Lister's institution, letter grades are awarded on the basis of a total set of points out of 100, and 50 points is considered the minimum passing score that allows a student to proceed to the next programming course. Therefore, after completing the initial grading, Lister then chose to change the total number of points to 2 for students who scored only one functionality point (i.e., a passing score). However, those students who had their score lifted remained ineligible for points from indentation.

4.5 Comparing the Four Instructors

Table 1 offers a summary of the grading approaches of these four instructors. Fitzgerald and McCauley both used a detailed, analytic approach. Murphy and Lister used simpler approaches, because of their focus on the test as a "gate keeping" exercise, to stop weaker students from progressing to the next course. Murphy tended toward a holistic approach while Lister tended toward a primary trait approach, given his emphasis on minimum functionality.

Table 1. What instructors were thinking

Instructor	Objectives	Characteristics
Murphy	Is the student sufficiently competent at programming to move to the next class?	Holistic (simplified) Focus on pass/fail
Fitzgerald	How did the student perform on this problem, based on a set of criteria?	Analytic
McCauley	How did the student perform on this problem, based on a set of criteria?	Analytic
Lister	Is the student sufficiently competent at programming to move to the next class?	Primary Trait. Focus on pass/fail

5. ANALYSIS

5.1 Statistical Analysis

As discussed above, the four instructors used different approaches and rubrics to grade the programs. As a result, the largest score possible under each rubric differed for each instructor, ranging from 4 to 18. The differences in scale granularity allowed instructors with larger scales to be more discriminating in their grading. Fitzgerald and McCauley, who had the most granular scales, did not give full credit to any students, while Murphy and Lister gave full credit to 12 and 10 students respectively.

Even though the four instructors used different grading scales and philosophies, the raw scores they gave to the programs were highly correlated, with an average Spearman's *rho* of .81. The individual correlations, as shown by the values of Spearman's *rho* are shown in Table 2. All correlations were significant at the p=.05 level (adjusted using Bonferroni's correction technique for multiple comparisons).

Table 2: Correlation of assigned scores

	Fitzgerald	McCauley	Lister
Murphy	0.89	0.79	0.84
Fitzgerald		0.92	0.81
McCauley			0.60

Although this study considered only one exam question, we were curious to see how the different scoring rubrics would have determined the number of students who passed or failed assuming that this single question was the sole basis for a pass/fail decision. For Murphy, Fitzgerald and McCauley, passing was considered to be 70% of the possible points in their grading scale, while Lister considered passing to be a score of 50%. Although the number of scores that were deemed passing by the instructors varied from 10 to 16 (see Table 3), this difference was not statistically significant based on a χ^2 test ($\chi^2(3)=4.396$, p=0.222). According to the χ^2 test, the expected pass/fail counts were 13 passes and 7 fails.

Table 3: Extrapolated pass and fail Counts

	Instructor			
	Murphy	**Fitzgerald**	**McCauley**	**Lister**
Pass	16	12	10	14
Fail	4	8	10	6

5.2 Dealing with Exceptions to the Norm

Overall scoring was highly correlated despite the different approaches chosen by the instructors. However, there were notable exceptions. One student wrote the following rather unusual solution:

```
int tempNum = 0, lowNum, highNum;
print("Enter a number (-99 to stop): ");
tempNum = Integer.parseInt(kbd.nextLine());
lowNum = tempNum; highNum = tempNum;
while (0 == 0) {
 print("Enter a number (-99 to stop): ");
 tempNum=Integer.parseInt(kbd.nextLine());
 if (tempNum == -99)
        break;
 else if (tempNum < lowNum)
        lowNum = tempNum;
 else if (tempNum > highNum)
        highNum = tempNum;
}
```

Murphy gave this student full marks, although it clearly it does not work correctly if the sentinel is the only input value. She attributed the rather odd use of Integer.parseInt for reading, the expression (0 == 0) for the loop condition, and the break statement to terminate the loop to the student's previous programming experience in C and generally eccentric nature, which led him to enjoy writing unusual code. Fitzgerald and McCauley both deducted some points, assigning the solution 14/18 and 7/10 points, respectively, but gave it an overall passing grade. Because the code threw a runtime exception when tested, Lister gave the solution 0 points, reasoning that since students had the opportunity to compile, run, and test the code on a machine, there was no excuse for compilation or runtime errors.

The variation in scores for this solution highlights potential differences in grading manually vs. machine or automatic grading. It is also an example of the role that personal knowledge of a given student may play in the grading process, which is unlikely to be a factor with automatic grading or in a larger class setting.

6. DISCUSSION

While the graders were consistent in a statistical sense, the combination of the sample size and the traditional 1–in–20 criteria of statistics might provide a false sense of security. Consider McCauley and Lister, who had the poorest correlation in the scores among the four instructors, but still achieved a surprisingly high correlation of 0.60. Table 4 shows how the scores of those two instructors compared on each student with McCauley's scoring range of 0 to 8 shown on the x axis and Lister's scores of 0 to 4 shown on the y axis.

The top right cell of the table indicates that four students received the highest possible score from both instructors. A total of eight students are clustered at or near the top score for both instructors. Also, two students scored zero from both instructors. Despite the large differences in how these two instructors graded, very good solutions and very poor solutions tended to receive similar scores from both instructors – perhaps indicating why the graders were consistent in a statistical sense. The heavy lines in Table 4 indicate the pass/fail threshold for these two instructors. The eight students represented by the shaded cells (i.e., 40% of the sample) were passed by one instructor, but failed by the other. Furthermore, other students may have received different letter grades from these two instructors. There is more to a fair and transparent grading scheme then statistical tests may indicate.

Table 4: Comparison of scores by McCauley and Lister.

	0	1	2	3.5	4	5	6	7	8
4				1			2	3	4
3									1
2				2		1			
1									
0	2		1	1				2	

All four of the instructors have many years experience teaching introductory programming. Despite that experience, it is interesting that all four instructors revised their initial approach to grading. One reason for a revision was a mismatch between the score from an analytic rubric and the rubric creator's "gut feel". Another reason for revision was the initial expectation that students would successfully treat the case where the sentinel was the first input element, which proved unrealistic as none of the students successfully treated that case.

7. CONCLUSION

In this paper we described how four experienced instructors approach the grading of programs, placing those approaches in the context of the literature on holistic grading, analytic grading and primary trait analysis. The four instructors usually agreed on whether a program is 'very good' or 'very bad'. However, there is no single right way to grade, and the very different motivations of the graders sometimes led to very different grading of programs that lay between the two extremes.

As a learning and teaching community, computer science educators rarely discuss how and what they grade; instead educators just assume that they hold similar values and grade in similar ways. We advocate further reflection and discussion of approaches to grading programs. As a community we should be able to articulate the reasons for our choices for the benefit of our students and to clarify our own thinking. Furthermore, we should discuss those reasons with our colleagues, not competitively, but to learn from each other.

A striking feature of the literature on grading programs is the age of the papers describing manual grading. Most of the recent literature occurs in the context of automatic grading. Even if more and more grading is done automatically in the future, we need to continue discussing how we think grading should be done. Otherwise, automatic grading systems will implement solutions which may not cover the full range of useful approaches to grading. This is especially apparent when holistic and revisionary approaches are considered.

Perhaps even more important than talking to our colleagues, we need to communicate with our students about how we intend to grade their programs. Given the variation in approaches to grading (and resulting scores) presented in this paper, while every educator may think their own approach to grading is obvious, it clearly is not obvious – not even to their colleagues, let alone their students.

8. REFERENCES

[1] Ala-Mutka, K. 2005. A survey of automated assessment approaches for programming assignments. *Computer Science Education* 15, 2 (June 2005), 83–102.

[2] Becker, K. 2003. Grading programming assignments using rubrics. In *Proceedings of the 8th Annual Conference on Innovation and Technology in Computer Science Education* (ITiCSE '03), David Finkel (Ed.). ACM, New York, NY, USA, 253-253. DOI=10.1145/961511.961613 http://doi.acm.org/10.1145/961511.961613.

[3] Carter, J., Ala-Mutka, K., Fuller, U., Dick, M., English, J., Fone, W. and Sheard, J. 2003. How shall we assess this?. SIGCSE Bull. 35, 4 (June 2003), 107-123. DOI=10.1145/960492.960539 http://doi.acm.org/10.1145/960492.960539.

[4] Douce, C., Livingstone, D., and Orwell, J. 2006. Automatic test-based assessment of programming: A review. *ACM Journal of Educational* Resources *in Computing* 5, 3 (September 2005).

[5] Hamm, R. W., Henderson, K. D., Repsher, M. L. and Timmer, K. L. 1983. A tool for program grading: The Jacksonville University scale. In *Proceedings of the 14th SIGCSE Technical Symposium on Computer Science Education* (SIGCSE '83). ACM, New York, NY, USA, 248-252. DOI=10.1145/800038.801059 http://doi.acm.org/10.1145/800038.801059.

[6] Howatt, J. 1994. On criteria for grading student programs. *SIGCSE Bull.* 26, 3 (September 1994), 3-7. DOI=10.1145/187387.187389 http://doi.acm.org/10.1145/187387.187389.

[7] Loacker, G., Cromwell, C. and O'Brien, K. 1986. Assessment in higher education: To serve the learner. In Adelman, C. (ed.), *Assessment in American Higher Education.* U.S. Department of Education, Office of Educational Research and Improvement, Washington, DC, 47-62.

[8] Miller, N. E. and Peterson, C. G. 1980. A method for evaluating student written computer programs in an undergraduate computer science programming language course. *SIGCSE Bull.* 12, 4 (December 1980), 9-17. DOI=10.1145/989274.989276 http://doi.acm.org/10.1145/989274.989276.

[9] Murphy, L. McCauley, R. and Fitzgerald, S. 2012. 'Explain in plain English' questions: Implications for teaching. In *Proceedings of the 43rd ACM Technical Symposium on Computer Science Education* (SIGCSE '12). ACM, New York, NY, USA, 385-390.

[10] Olson, D. 1988. The reliability of analytic and holistic methods in rating students' computer programs. *SIGCSE Bull.* 20, 1 (February 1988), 293-298. DOI=10.1145/52965.53037 http://doi.acm.org/10.1145/52965.53037.

[11] Smith, L. and Cordova, J. 2005. Weighted primary trait analysis for computer program evaluation. *J. Comput. Small Coll.* 20, 6 (June 2005), 14-19. http://dl.acm.org/citation.cfm?id=1060405.1060409&coll=DL&dl=ACM&CFID=106820723&CFTOKEN=10091255.

[12] Taggart, G., Phifer, S. and Nixon, J. 2001. In Wood, M. (ed.), *Rubrics: A Handbook for Construction and Use.* Scarecrow Press, Latham, MD, USA.

Automated Online Grading for Virtual Machine-based Systems Administration Courses

Lewis Baumstark
Dept. of Computer Science
University of West Georgia
Carrollton, GA 30118
1 (678) 839-6663
lewisb@westga.edu

Edwin Rudolph
Dept. of Computer Science
University of West Georgia
Carrollton, GA 30118
1 (678) 839-6650
erudolph@westga.edu

ABSTRACT
We present a system for automatically and iteratively grading student work in a Systems Administration course. This system can grade – and give feedback regarding – live (running) virtual machines the students have configured. It is appropriate for both face-to-face and online course offerings.

Categories and Subject Descriptors
K.3.1 [**Computers and Education**]: Computer Uses in Education – *Computer-managed instruction, Distance learning.*

K.3.2 [**Computers and Education**]: Computer and Information Science Education – *Computer science education.*

General Terms
Design, Human Factors

Keywords
Online Grading; Automated Grading; Virtual Machines; Systems Administration; Networking

1. INTRODUCTION
The Department of Computer Science at the University of West Georgia offers two system and network administration courses, one each at the undergraduate and graduate level. Both are intended as a blend of theory (e.g., TCP/IP protocol stacks) with hands-on lab work (e.g., configuring DNS and DHCP servers). As others, e.g., [10][8][2] have done, we have transitioned from hardware-based labs full of racks of physical routers and servers to assignments that use virtual machines (VMs) running Linux. One benefit of this approach is our students are no longer required to be physically present in a laboratory to work on their network and server-configuration assignments; instead, they can work on them at home or wherever they have an available Internet connection.

This approach presented logistical problems of its own, however, particularly with respect to grading. Most of our CS courses use the Moodle courseware, which allows assignment and project work to be uploaded for the instructor to grade later. While a virtual machine is nothing more than a collection of files and could theoretically be uploaded, its size (typically in the 5-10 gigabyte range for each assignment) makes that impractical in terms of both network bandwidth and server disk storage. An alternate approach is to require students to demonstrate their work in-person, but this is time-consuming. (Further, our graduate systems administration course is now 100% on-line, making in-person demonstrations impossible.) We have even had students upload screen shot pictures of their configured systems.

One offering of the graduate course was taught using VMware Server. This product allows multiple virtual machines to be stored and run from a single physical server. Each VMs desktop can be accessed remotely using a web-based tool. This arrangement facilitated grading: the instructor could simply log into a student's VM directly and evaluate the quality of their running system. Unfortunately, with eleven students there were serious performance issues (note the undergraduate version of the course usually has 30-40 students, so VMware Server would be even less appropriate). For both the graduate and undergraduate courses we now use VMware Workstation, which allows students to run VMs on their own computers.

With this in mind (students running VMs on their own computers), we desired a grading system with the following qualities:

- *Is modular* in that new assignments can be "plugged-in" to the system.
- *Can evaluate running systems.* For example, test whether a student's DNS server can, in fact, properly resolve host names.
- *Is initiated by the student* when the student is working on the assignment.
- *Can be graded remotely* (e.g., from the student's residence). This means the system must work from behind the typical residential NAT-based router as well as tunnel through our campus firewall.
- *Is asynchronous.* The instructor should not have to be on-line when the work is submitted.
- *Should provide automatic feedback.* The student should receive an immediate score along with some indication of what is incorrect.
- *Allows for an iterative learning process.* Similar to iterative design-implement-test software development cycles, we want these assignments to be completed incrementally, with students working on one part, testing it, and re-working until that part is completed. After completing a step, they can move on to next part of the assignment.

SIGCSE'13, March 6–9, 2013, Denver, Colorado, USA.

- *Secure*. To avoid cheating, each student should be authenticated and the details of their grading sessions should only be visible to the student and the instructor.

2. Related Work

As an alternative to live demonstrations, [10] suggest grading virtual machine assignments by having the students submit a CD-RW disk that has a file diff between the as-assigned VM state and its as-completed state. This means less data transfer than submitting an entire VM file for grading, but it does introduce the overhead in patching a test VM on the grader side, plus the turn-in logistics. It also requires all students start with the same VM for each assignment; our approach allows students who want to experiment with different Linux distributions to do so.

There are several existing approaches for automated and semi-automated grading for programming projects. APOGEE [3] is targeted at web-design projects and uses a specially-designed web client to run testing scripts against student work. Infandango [5] and Web-CAT [1] are examples of systems that accept submitted program code, compile it, and compare the output against expected results.

We were initially inspired by the judging systems such as those used in ACM student programming competitions. The PCSS3 [7] and PC^2 [9] systems use a submit/receive feedback/revise cycle similar to our system; both can be configured to automatically judge submissions.

3. ONLINE GRADING SYSTEM

3.1 System Use Cases

There are three main interactions with the system:

1. **Student solicits feedback**: The student, having completed a part (or the entirety) of an assignment, submits the work to the autograder for review. The system returns a human-readable report with a current grade for the assignment and text giving feedback on correct/incorrect items. (*Note that the grade is not recorded in the course grade book at this time.*) This process takes approximately one minute.
2. **Instructor records grades**: After an assignment is due, the instructor sifts through the records of all grading attempts, by all students, for the assignment, recording each student's highest grade over all their attempts for the assignment.
3. **Student-Instructor conference**: If a student needs instructor help (via email, instant messaging, face-to-face, etc.) beyond the automated feedback for an assignment, the instructor can look at records of that student's previous attempts as a guide to the student's current issues with the assignment. (We have also used this information to aid other tasks such as debugging assignment scripts and network-connection issues.)

3.2 Running Example: DNS Server

In the remainder of this paper we will use as an example an assignment where students configure the BIND domain name system (DNS) server. [6] The requirements are that they:

- Install the BIND package (along with some useful command-line tools).
- Make the DNS server authoritative for the assigned domain.
- Configure the DNS server to resolve host names in that domain.
- Configure the DNS server to forward lookups for hosts not in its own domain to another DNS server.
- Configure the VM's network settings so that it uses itself to resolve host names.

The source code for this and other assignment scripts can be viewed at http://lewisb.wiki.westga.edu/autograder.

3.3 Shell Script Solution

Our system is implemented as a set of Linux shell scripts, written in the bash [4] scripting language. The main script, `grade.sh`, operates as follows: a student (working on their own computer) contacts the grading server requesting it grade, in our example, the `dnsserver` assignment. The assignment is a separate bash shell script, which is transferred to the student's computer and executed locally. After execution of the assignment script, the results are both presented to the student and uploaded to the grading server where they are available for the instructor to view at her convenience. (The assignment script is also deleted from the student's computer once grading is complete.) We strove to make invocation of the grading script as simple as possible; for the example, a student would execute:

```
bash grade.sh dnsserver
```

i.e., just `grade.sh` followed by a parameter indicating the name of the assignment script. This arrangement provides us with modularity; all an instructor need do to create a new assignment is to write a separate, custom assignment script and save it on the server. There is no need to modify `grade.sh`.

By executing a grading script directly on the student's VM, we are able to evaluate the entire state of the running system as a user of that system. Any program that can be run from the command line and whose output can be parsed can be used for evaluation. For example, in `dnsserver`, we want to find out if the student's DNS server has a name server (NS) record defined for their domain, so we execute the command:

```
NS=$(dig ns sysadmin.cs3280 +short)
```

This uses the `dig` command to query the DNS server for a name server that is authoritative for our `sysadmin.cs3280` domain. If the command succeeds (Linux return status 0, available from special bash variable `$?`) we go on to use the value it stored in the `$NS` variable to perform host name resolutions using that server. If it does not succeed, the student receives an informational message describing the error.

Note that there is only a small amount of network data transfer during the grading attempt: the student receives the script file (to date, the largest is 4 kilobytes) and sends back a log of the grading attempt (a few kilobytes or less, depending on the assignment). Compare this to a solution where a student would upload a 5 gigabyte VM file and then wait until an instructor can run and evaluate the system manually.

3.4 The Role of Secure Shell

The `grade.sh` script creates a Secure Shell (`ssh`) tunnel between the student's PC and our grading server. This authenticates the student to the grading server. (Previously, in a one-time setup operation, the student has provided the server with a public key for authentication). It also sets up port-forwarding from the server back to the student's PC, which allows the server to transfer the assignment script (e.g., `dnsserver`) to the student's PC. This step may seem like overkill, but consider that,

Table 1. Results of Previous Course Offerings

Assignment	Description	Average Grade	Average Number of Attempts
`vminstall`	Get a virtual machine installed; also insures the student understands and can perform the auto-grading process.	100	3.1
`static_ip`	Configure a static IP address, including DNS and gateway information, for a server machine	96.4	5.2
`dchp`	Configure a dynamic host configuration protocol (DHCP) server to dynamically assign IP addresses and other configuration information to a DHCP client.	88.3	7.0
`dnsserver`	Configure a domain name system (DNS) server to resolve IP addresses for a domain.	92.5	15.7
`fileserver`	Configure an server message block (SMB) file server to share files across a network	90.8	6.1
`webserver`	Install and configure a webserver hosting static and dynamic content.	92.1	4.2
`firewall`	Configure and write filtering rules for a firewall.	75.0	8.4
`users-and-groups`	Create user accounts and privilege groups.	99.5	2.2
`ldap-server`	Install and configure a lightweight directory access protocol (LDAP) server; populate with directory information.	90.7	4.1
`nat`	Configure a gateway to perform network address translation (NAT) between two private networks.	94.0	3.0
`mrtg`	Configure the MRTG software package, which uses the simple network messaging protocol (SNMP) to display system information as a web page.	86.7	4.0
Unique students: 61			
Total attempts: 2642			
Number of course offerings: 4 (*not all course offerings used every assignment.*)			

typically, the system being graded is a virtual machine behind two layers of Network Address Translation (NAT): one provided by the VM software itself to define a virtual network on the host machine, the other a student's broadband router defining a private network (e.g., 192.168.1.0/24) behind the single non-private IP address given them by their Internet Service Provider (ISP). The port-forwarding hides this complexity from the grading server, which needs to treat the VM as an `ssh` "server" for purposes of running the assignment script.

3.5 Sample Results File

In Figure 1 (on the last page due to its size), an anonymous student has initiated grading of `dnsserver` and received their results. The results are condensed for brevity and line numbers have been added. These results are copied to the grading server so the instructors can review them.

- Lines 00-01: For troubleshooting purposes, the IP address and the Ethernet adaptor in-use by the VM are reported.
- Lines 03-18: It is useful, again for debugging purposes, to include any relevant configuration files in the results. Shown are the contents of a BIND "zone" file, which contains host and name server records for a DNS zone. The instructor can review these files and advise a student on mistakes they have made. In this example, the student has erred in configuring the NS record for the domain.
- Lines 20-21: These show successful completion of two parts of the assignment (installing the dnsutils and bind9 packages).
- Lines 22-46: These show errors on most of the remaining items of the assignment (setting up an authoritative name server and successfully resolving host names using proper "A" records). Note that the student is told what parts of the assignment that did not succeed.
- Line 47: Part of the assignment is to have the VM look to itself (instead of an external DNS server) to perform its own DNS lookups. The student has configured this part correctly.
- Line 48: The overall score for this attempt.

4. Iterative Completion of Assignments and Instructor Feedback

Students are allowed to attempt these assignments as many times as they wish before the due date. On each attempt, the student sees their current score and results similar to those described in the previous section. Only the grade for the highest-scoring attempt is recorded.

This gives students a feedback cycle for learning as they are not required to "get it right the first time" and can learn from their mistakes and correct them. As each set of results is copied to the instructor, the instructor can use them to guide students through the difficult parts.

Table 1 shows the various assignments made over the (to date) four course offerings where our online grading system has been used. The last column shows that students do make use of the iterative nature of the assignments, bringing them to grades that in most cases are in the A or B range (second-to-last column).

5. Summary and Future Work

Our online grading system allows students in our systems administration courses to engage with hands-on assignments using virtual machines at home but with the benefit of immediate grading and feedback. Further, the nature of the assignments allows for iterative refinement of their assignments, providing feedback along the way.

As this system is capable of remotely grading running virtual machines, it could be adapted to grade a range of student projects that require a system of running software components such as a web design project with a web server, database, and runtime platform such as Java or .NET.

In the future, there are several features we would like to add:

- Scripts to link final grades for an assignment to the student's grade book on Moodle
- Ability to run root-level (administrator) commands on the student's VM. Not having this ability limits some of the analysis we can perform.
- Perform analyses of Internet-based services as a remote client. In other words, we would not just run local commands on a student's machine, but have the ability to make TCP/IP connections to it (for example, acting as an external HTTP client to test a student's webserver configuration).

6. REFERENCES

[1] Allowatt, A. and Edwards, S. 2005. IDE Support for Test-driven Development and Automated Grading in Both Java and C++. *Proceedings of the 2005 OOPSLA workshop on Eclipse technology* (San Diego, CA. Oct. 2005). eclipse'05. 100 – 104. DOI= http://dx.doi.org/10.1145/1117696.1117717

[2] Bullerw, Jr., W.I., Burd, S., and Seazzu, A.F. 2006. Virtual Machines – An Idea Whose Time Has Returned: Application to Network, Security, and Database Courses. *Proceedings of the 37th SIGCSE Technical Symposium on Computer Science Education* (Houston, TX, USA. March 2006). SIGCSE'06. 102 – 106. DOI= http://dx.doi.org/10.1145/1124706.1121375

[3] Fu, X., Peltsverger, B., Qian, K., Tao, L., and Liu, J. 2008. APOGEE – Automated Project Grading and Instant Feedback System for Web Based Computing. *Proceedings of the 39th SIGCSE Technical Symposium on Computer Science Education* (Portland, OR, USA. March 2008). SIGCSE'08. 77 – 81. DOI= http://dx.doi.org/10.1145/1352135.1352163

[4] GNU.org. 2010. GNU bash Manual. Retrieved November 13, 2012 from http://www.gnu.org/software/bash/manual/

[5] Hull, M., Powell, D., and Klein, E. 2011. Infandango: Automated Grading for Student Programming. *Proceedings of the 16th Annual Conference on Innovation and Technology in Computer Science Education* (Darmstadt, Germany. June 2011). ITiCSE'11. 330. DOI=http://dx.doi.org/10.1145/1999747.1999841

[6] Internet Systems Consortium. 2012. BIND 9 Administrator Reference Manual. Retreived November 13, 2012 from http://ftp.isc.org/isc/bind9/cur/9.9/doc/arm/Bv9ARM.pdf

[7] Kăcer, M. and Mannová, B., 2008. PCSS3: Programming Contest Scoring System. *Proceedings of Competitive Learning Institute Symposium* (Banff, Alberta Canada. April 2008).

[8] Laadan, O., Nieh, J., and Viennot, N. 2010. Teaching Operating Systems Using Virtual Appliances and Distributed Version Control. *Proceedings of the 41st SIGCSE Technical Symposium on Computer Science Education* (Milwaukee, WI, USA. March 2010). SIGCSE'10. 480 – 484. DOI= http://dx.doi.org/10.1145/1734263.1734427

[9] PC^2 Project. 2011. Programming Contest Control System. Retreived November 13, 2012 from http://www.ecs.csus.edu/pc2/

[10] Volrath, A. and Jenkins, S. 2004. Using Virtual Machines for Teaching System Administration. *Journal of Computing Sciences in Colleges*. 20, 2 (Dec. 2004), 287 – 292.

```
You are using ethernet adapter eth0
Your IP address is 192.168.244.3
================================================
.db/.zone files

$TTL 3D
@ IN SOA   ns.sysadmin.cs3280. admin.sysadmin.cs3280. (

                  2006071801
                  28800
                  3600
                  604800
                  38400
          );
sysadmin.cs3280. IN       NS      ns.sysadmin.cs3280.
www.sysadmin.cs3280. IN  NS  ns1.sysadmin.cs3280.

www IN     A      192.168.244.3
ns1 IN     A      192.168.244.3
================================================
dnsutils installed
bind9 installed
Found k.root-servers.net.
e.root-servers.net.
d.root-servers.net.
i.root-servers.net.
l.root-servers.net.
c.root-servers.net.
b.root-servers.net.
m.root-servers.net.
j.root-servers.net.
f.root-servers.net.
g.root-servers.net.
h.root-servers.net.
a.root-servers.net. (variable QUERYIP) via nameserver
Your VM is not authoritative for sysadmin.cs3280
Partial score: 50
Did not find www.sysadmin.cs3280
Partial score: 50
Did not find ftp.sysadmin.cs3280
Partial score: 50
Did not find pop3.sysadmin.cs3280
Partial score: 50
Did not find ns1.sysadmin.cs3280
Partial score: 50
Did not find smtp.sysadmin.cs3280
Partial score: 50
Your VM is set to use itself to resolve host names.
Final score: 65
```

Figure 1. Sample Grading Session Results

Building Knowledge and Confidence with Mediascripting: A Successful Interdisciplinary Approach to CS1

Samuel A. Rebelsky, Janet Davis, and Jerod Weinman
Grinnell College
1116 8th Avenue
Grinnell, IA 50112
641-269-4410
{rebelsky,davisjan,weinmanj}@cs.grinnell.edu

ABSTRACT
As the Media Computing approach [5] has shown, writing programs that make images excites a wide variety of students. In this paper, we report on five years of experience with a new approach to media computation, which we call "media scripting". In our introductory class, students build images by interactively scripting an application, so they can experiment easily and mix work "by hand" and "by code"; we collaborate with studio art faculty, so students build works meeting design criteria; and we emphasize multiple paradigms, so students make images using functional, declarative, imperative, and object-oriented techniques. Our approach has proven quite successful—enrollments are up (at least 33% in CS1, 50% in CS2) and we attract more women (currently 40% of the students in the first course, 25% of those in the second course). Other outcomes are equally positive. For example, comparative data show that our students gain significantly more confidence in their abilities than students in other introductory science courses.

Categories and Subject Descriptors
K.3.2 [**Computers and Education**]: Computer and Information Science Education-*computer science education.*

General Terms
Design, Languages.

Keywords
Computer science education. CS1. Media computation. Multi-paradigm programing. Scheme. Functional programming. Scripting. Interdisciplinary approaches.

1. NEW APPROACHES TO THE INTRODUCTORY COURSE
For much of the past decade, computer science educators have worried about significant drops in enrollment, particularly in the enrollment of women and domestic students of color. A range of techniques have been developed to attract students to and retain students in the discipline, including appraoches as diverse as bottom up [12] "Passion, Beauty, Joy, and Awe" [4,10].

Perhaps for these reasons, perhaps for others, we as a discipline are fortunate that enrollments are again on an upswing. But rising enrollments do not mean that we should stop revisiting the introductory course and the overall curriculum; we still need to focus on attracting and retaining a diverse group of students.

SIGCSE'13, March 6–9, 2013, Denver, Colorado, USA.

Many of the successful introductory approaches, such as Alice-first [9,11] or Media Computation [5], have shown that images can motivate students. By writing programs that make and modify images, students see concrete results from their work, have projects that they can share with friends and family who might not otherwise understand what they are doing in the intro course, and explore open-ended projects [5]. Media computation, in particular, has proven successful at attracting students in contexts from community colleges to R1 universities. Students are clearly excited by writing programs that make images.

Starting in Fall 2007, we have been using media computation in an introductory course that serves all students, not only prospective majors (for whom it is the first CS course), but also students who just want to see what CS is like. We vary the media computation model in many important ways. We teach the course using a *workshop-style approach*: In the typical class session, students have read a short piece (3-5 pages) before class, and spend most of class time working in pairs on a set of problems. Rather than focusing on stand-alone programs, we have students build images by *interactively scripting* an application, which means that they can more easily experiment and mix work that they create "by hand" with work that they create "by programming". Because we want students to think beyond the discipline, we *collaborate with studio art faculty*, so students build works that must meet underlying design criteria. As Clayson [1] has shown, mixing CS with formal discussions of art practice can transform how students think about computing. Finally, we use a *multi-paradigm approach* – students make images using functional, declarative, imperative, and object-oriented techniques. We revisit course design in two sections. In Section 2, we discuss general course issues, particularly institutional context. In section 3, we elaborate on the design of the new mediascripting course.

Two of the most successful aspects of the course are the use of multiple paradigms early in the course and an interdisciplinary group final project. We discuss the group project in Section 5.

In section 4, we discuss an approach that we use to address changes in professional practice. The past few decades have seen a remarkable transformation in the way professionals think about programming. Structured programming gave way to object-oriented programming. Now, modern languages are increasingly including functional components – witness the growth of languages like Scala and Erlang. At the same time, software developers increasingly work closely in pairs and small teams, while software applications have always relied on domain-specific knowledge, often building on other disciplines. We address these changes by giving students multi-paradigm training, which we expect will allow them to adapt to new approaches and paradigms.

Because we have now taught the course for five years, we have substantial data we can use to assess our successes and failures. We have assessed the course in multiple ways, from gathering data about enrollments to using national survey instruments. In section 6, we discuss these results, which are remarkably positive,

2. INSTITUTIONAL AND COURSE CONTEXT

Grinnell College is a small, highly selective, liberal arts college with approximately 1600 undergraduate students. As is the case at many liberal arts colleges, students enter Grinnell without a declared major. Most do not declare a major until midway through their second year of college.

CSC151 is our primary introductory course, intended to serve all students. The course is the first in the introductory sequence for prospective majors. But it also serves as a course for students who just want to learn some programming or explore an unfamiliar discipline. CSC151 does not meet any general education requirements and Grinnell does not have minors, so students are either prospective majors (perhaps 1/3 to 1/2 of the students) or students who are taking the course out of general interest (the remainder). We only get students if we (or their peers) convince them it's an interesting course to take. Of course, one of our goals is to recruit prospective majors whose general interest leads them to the introductory course.

Even though CSC151 serves a wide audience, it is not a scaled-down course. Students engage with some fairly sophisticated issues, such as recursion (including a bit of tail recursion), higher-order procedures, refactoring, a few sorting algorithms (typically insertion sort and Quicksort), and some fundamental data structures, such as linked lists and trees.

For nearly three decades, the department has taught CSC151 as a "flipped classroom".[1] Students are expected to read a short introduction to the topic of the day (usually three to five pages) before most class sessions and then spend in-class time working in pairs on a set of problems, while the faculty member and student mentor move through the classroom asking questions, making suggestions, and helping with student difficulties.

Figure 1. A Typical Class Session.

The class was originally taught in Fortran, then in Pascal. About fifteen years ago, the department made the transition to Scheme.

[1] When our colleagues started teaching that way, no one called it "flipped", it was just a "collaborative, hands-on course" or a "workshop-style course" or "constructivist education".

While there are clearly many opinions on the use of Scheme in the introductory course, we have found that it plays several valuable roles. First, Scheme provides a syntax and an approach that few, if any students have seen. Students who come in with previous programming experience are challenged to deal with an approach in which assignment and iterative loops are typically eschewed. This change in approach helps level the playing field, making students with no background feel much less intimidated by those with prior experience.[2] Second, Scheme is small enough and the syntax is straightforward enough that students can master most of the language in a semester.[3] Third, Scheme lets us teach students multiple ways of thinking about problem solving. Finally, because Scheme is not often used in commercial software development, we do not inflict upon the world people who think that they can program professionally after one course.

Although Scheme is not the typical introductory course, the simplicity of the language design allows us to cover a wide range of material typical to CS1 and CS2. An analysis of our introductory curriculum suggests that students leaving our introductory sequence (which adds C and Java in subsequent courses) have not only studied the material expected in traditional introductory sequences, and also encountered new material, such as the multiparadigm approach.

3. A NEW INTRODUCTORY COURSE

For the first decade, our Scheme-based, workshop-style introductory course showed many strengths. We attracted students and the workshop-style classroom clearly helped us support a variety of learners and make the class more welcoming to women. Our students also learned deep concepts.

However, in the mid 2000's, we noted that there were two issues that needed to be addressed. First, like CS departments at many other institutions, we found that our enrollments were starting to slip. (Our enrollments did not slip as dramatically as elsewhere, but they still slipped.) Second, we were seeing too many cases of students, particularly women, who took CSC151 in their junior year, excelled at it, and said things like, "If only I had taken this my first year, I would have majored in CS."

Our challenge was therefore to retain what we saw as strengths of the course (workshop-style teaching, the use of Scheme, deep coverage) while looking for ways to attract a wider variety of students to the course earlier. Media Computation seemed like the natural approach.

Because we planned to continue to use Scheme, we decided to look at having students "script" the GNU Image Manipulation Program (GIMP), an open-source alternative to Photoshop that includes Scheme as a scripting language.[4] Scripting a graphics

[2] We have been fortunate that most students with prior experience are not overly frustrated by having to learn a different approach. While we recommend that all prospective majors start in CSC151, our first course, we are sometimes able to let students with significant experience skip the second course.

[3] One of our colleagues jokes that there are fewer words in the Fifth Revised Scheme specification than there are methods in the standard Java library

[4] Unfortunately, the Scheme now shipped with the GIMP is not particularly amenable to novice programmers. After one semester using the default Scheme, we found a way to incorporate the robust MzScheme implementation of Scheme into the GIMP and developed a student-friendly UI.

application provides good motivation; most students are used to drawing with such applications. Once we teach them to script, they learn they can do things more quickly and more precisely with a script than by hand. And, as importantly, they can use scripts to explore design spaces; it's much easier to write a program to generate 100 alternative designs than it is to make them by hand. Using the GIMP also helps students make more powerful images – because they can script the powerful brushes and textures that come with the GIMP, they can produce much more expressive works than they could do just using the tools usually available with Java or Python.

But such power also brings responsibility. Rather than just having students create images that "look cool" (and that meet the learning requirements for the assignment), we thought it important to involve our studio art faculty in thinking about how to talk to students about image making. For the first few years of the course, a studio art faculty member would visit the class three times: once early in the semester to present some inspirational works (often from students in a studio course) and to discuss color theory, once midway through the semester to discuss some general principles of visual design, and once toward the end of the semester to discuss works that our students created. By now, our colleague tells us that we've now heard about these issues enough that we're prepared to teach them.

4. MULTIPLE PARADIGMS EARLY

Our students need to be prepared to work in a world in which they must regularly adopt and understand a diversity of new perspectives. We find that we best prepare students for this complexity if we introduce multiple paradigms early and return to them regularly throughout the curriculum. In this course, we do the same thing on a smaller scale. That is, we ask them to think about image making in multiple ways on day one and then delve more deeply into those approaches throughout the semester.

On the first day of class, we assign students to small groups (three to five students) and challenge them to write instructions for making the prototypical "smiley face". Each group is limited in what kinds of instructions they can give. For example, one group is only allowed to tell people to draw circles. Another is only allowed to write a function that, given an (x,y) coordinate, tells you what color to draw at that coordinate. A third is told that they will be instructing a Logo-style turtle (although we don't call it that). A fourth can only instruct a person about how to move their body. The exercise helps students not only learn that there are multiple ways to solve a problem, but also discover the interplay between languages, algorithms, and qualities of the resulting solutions.

Throughout the semester, we return to these models in code. Students first construct images by sending direct instructions to the GIMP: e.g., select this ellipse, deselect this portion of the selection, and fill what remains. That approach gives them experience with imperative programming. It is also closely tied to what they do "by hand" on the GIMP. They also get to deal with "state", but a limited state that they can only change, not query.

Next, we challenge students to think about a "pure" functional approach. They start with a few basic pictures (a circle and a square) and need to make more complex images by scaling, shifting, recoloring, and composing pictures. Here, students get one of their first "aha" moments (or moments of significant frustration): It takes a while for some to understand that when they scale a picture, this doesn't affect the original picture, but rather produces a new, scaled, version of the picture. This model also gives students an early experience in recursive data definition.

We then turn to another functional model in which students represent images as functions. The `image-compute` procedure, given an image size and a function from position to color, builds an image by applying that function at each pixel in the image. For example, to draw a circle using one color scheme on a background that uses a second color scheme, they might write something like the code in Figure 2. Clearly, this approach is not particularly amenable to representational works. However, it makes it very easy for them to build interesting color patterns and textures, such as the one in Figure 3, which is generated by the code in Figure 2, with simple color functions for `colorfun1` and `colorfun2`.

```
(image-compute
  (lambda (x y)
    (if (< (+ (square (- x xcenter))
              (square (- y ycenter)))
           radius-squared)
        (colorfun1 x y)
        (colorfun2 x y)
    256 256)
```

Figure 2. A Functional Circle.

Figure 3. Textures Generated in the Functional Circle.

We return to Logo-style turtles as an exercise in a combined object-oriented (no inheritance) and imperative system.

Finally, depending on student or instructor interest, we may cover other models.

Figure 4. Student Project Work.

5. AN INTERDISCIPLINARY PROJECT

About two-thirds of the way through the semester, we assign a project we call *A Procedure is Worth A Thousand Pictures*. This assignment challenges students to tie together what they have learned in computing with some of the visual design principles they've learned. Their goal is simple: Write a program that, given an integer *N* and a width and a height, generates an image of the given width and height. However, different values of *N* must give different images, and different widths and heights must appropriately scale the image. That is, a 50x50 and a 500x500 image should look essentially the same, perhaps with more detail in the 500x500 image. A 500x500 image and a 500x1000 image will also look similar, although the latter image will appear more "stretched out".

They must begin with a proposal that incorporates sketches with text and addresses questions such as the following: What will the images generally look like? How do they apply visual design principles? What will they vary with *N*? What invariants will they maintain as images scale? Students know that an art design critic (either a member of the Art faculty or a student with experience jurying art) will assess their design and their success in achieving the design, while a computer science design critic (typically the faculty member anc class mentor) will assess the quality and design of their code. The week of discussions and presentations are exciting. Figure 4 presents a selection of student work.

6. ASSESSING THE COURSE

In planning the course, one of our goals was to assess what differences the new approach made. We hypothesized that the approach would (a) bring more students in to the course and the computer science major, (b) attract a greater percentage of students from underrepresented groups; and (c) help students develop a deeper understanding of important concepts, such as higher-order procedures and refactoring.

We had hoped to look at general learning outcomes. Unfortunately, when we began in 2007, our discipline lacked a common assessment instrument for CS1 concepts. And still, the best instrument available [14] emphasizes imperative concepts, and is therefore inappropriate for a Scheme-based course. For example, questions ask things like "what is the value of the variable after this loop", focusing on two issues (assignment and iterative loops) that many Scheme courses downplay.

Because of the lack of a common instrument, we have relied on a variety of other mechanisms for assessing the success and failure of the course. Some of our data are quite informal. For example, we hear from many students that "seeing what the program does visually helps me better understand the program and track down errors." We seem to be seeing a larger variety of student interests, and in particular, more students who have interests outside the sciences. Of course, students are not uniformly positive; for example, some note that the course doesn't feel like "real" CS, even though we address many "real" and complex issues.

Beyond these informal data, we have assessed the course in three ways: We track enrollment data across changes in the course, we developed our own instrument for looking at how students deal with complex problems, and we rely on a national instrument for exploring student experiences in introductory science courses.

6.1 Enrollment Data

Our enrollments are up, and they are up a lot. We now fill all offerings of our introductory course each fall. Table 1 compares enrollments in the two years of the prior course, and the first year of the course (before students had heard about the new approach) to the next three years of the course.[5]

We cannot attribute the increases to our courses alone; factors could have led to the change in the enrollments. Certainly, many institutions have seen upswings in recent years. However, our more telling change is in the shape of the enrollments. In particular, we are seeing significantly more women enroll in the first course and the second course. In Fall 2011, 33% of the students in CSC151 were women. In Fall 2012, nearly 50% of the students were women. Clearly, something is going right.

Average yearly enrollment	Years -2,-1,1	Years 2 to 4
First course	74	93
Second course	25	37

Table 1. Enrollment Changes.

Unfortunately, we do not seem to have significantly changed our number of majors. In the past few years, the number of women majors has been small, but we seem to have made progress. Of the twelve CS graduates in the class of 2013, five are women. We are not doing as well in the class of 2014, with only three women of sixteen majors. However, we have two other women who are effectively doing minors in CS.

6.2 A Custom Assessment Instrument

In planning the course, we wanted to explore how well students learned some of the deeper aspects of the course, such as higher-order procedures and factoring out common control. We hypothesized that functions like `image-compute` would encourage them to think more deeply about such issues. We decided on a simple, two-problem instrument. For each problem, the students have ten minutes to develop an answer. We hoped that the time pressure would reveal natural student inclinations.

Problem 1: Use of Higher-Order Techniques

For the first problem, they are to write a function that, given a list of numbers, generates a new list consisting of the successor to the square of the corresponding number. So, the list (1 2 3 4) would become (2 5 10 17). The straightforward solution (in Scheme) is recursive, and shown in Figure 5. We hypothesized that because students have significant experience using higher-order functions, such as `map`, `compose`, and `left-section` (all of which they use for color transforms), they would use higher-order procedures in their solutions, as in Figures 6 and 7.

```
(define probl
  (lambda (lst)
    (if (null? lst)
        null
        (cons (+ 1 (square (car lst)))
              (probl (cdr lst))))))
```

Figure 5. A Recursive Solution.

```
(define probl
  (lambda (lst)
    (map (compose increment square) lst)))
```

Figure 6. A Typical Higher-Order Solution.

```
(define probl
  (left-section map (compose increment square)))
```

Figure 7. A More Concise Higher-Order Solution.

In our most recent uses of this instrument, 76% of the students used a higher-order solution (`map`, `compose`, `section`, or some combination) and another 12% developed recursive solutions. The remaining 12% did not develop correct solutions in the time provided. Still, we consider that large use of `map` and similar functions a great success.[6]

[5] Varying course offerings make it difficult to compare enrollment on a semester-by-semester basis.

[6] We do not offer non-mediascripting versions of the course, so we cannot provide comparative data. Anecdotally, the students seem to be doing better at these topics.

Problem 2: Refactoring Under Pressure

For the second problem, we ask students to write three functions that each take an integer *n* and compute a list of *n* numbers. The first function computes the squares of the numbers from 1 to *n*: (1 4 9 16 ...). The second computes the cubes of the numbers from 1 to *n*: (1 8 27 64 ...). The third computes 2^k for each *k* from 1 to *n*: (2 4 8 16 ...). Because students had experience writing their own higher-order procedures, we had hoped that students would note the common pattern: Build a list of "some function" applied to the numbers from 1 to n. Since there's a common pattern, they should write a helper that encapsulates that pattern, as in Figure 8.

```
(define helper
  (lambda (func n)
    (map (compose func increment) (iota n))))
(define prob2-a
  (lambda (n) (helper square n)))
  ; Alt:
  ;  (define prob2-a (left-section helper square))
(define prob2-b
  (lambda (n) (helper (right-section expt 3))))
(define prob2-c
  (lambda (n) (helper (left-section expt 2))))
```

Figure 8. Factoring Out Common Control.

However, students rarely make that leap. Perhaps one in twenty writes the general solution. A few more (about one in five) note that the first two are similar, and write a common helper. Nonetheless, the solutions show other successes. Many (roughly one-third to one-half) use left- and right-section in their solutions.

We have talked with students about why they don't identify the common part of the three functions. A common answer is "I had to write three functions in ten minutes. I didn't take the time to think about generalizing." So, we've had less success in this than we might like. We accept that it's likely to continue to challenge students, and that we need to consider ways to encourage them to think through problems, even in time-limited situations.

6.3 Research on the Integrated Science Curriculum

To look beyond the particular details of this course, we turned to a national instrument intended to assess student development in introductory science courses. The RISC (Research on the Integrative Science Curriculum) instrument is an outgrowth of the SURE (Survey of Undergraduate Research Experiences) and CURE (Survey of Classroom Undergraduate Research Experiences) instruments, which are intended to assess student attitudinal gains in significant research experiences, such as summer research (SURE) or the new research-based introductory science classroom (CURE) [8]. The RISC instrument is used in introductory science classes at a wide variety of institutions. After asking students about particular experiences in the class (e.g., working with others, making a poster), RISC asks students about 21 types of learning gains.

We conducted RISC in two separate sections of CSC151. 48 students in the two sections responded and were compared to a sample of 598 RISC respondents.

Our students reported higher learning gains than their peers in other courses at a highly significant level ($p < 0.01$) for three categories: "tolerance for obstacles faced in the research process"; "self confidence"; and "learning to work independently". Not surprisingly, these are also the categories for which they reported the highest learning gains. We are particularly encouraged by the high report of gains in self-confidence, which may explain the increased enrollments in the second course.

While we appreciate that students have learned to tolerate obstacles, we note that the high response here may suggest that they perhaps encountered too many obstacles. Of course, many students experience unexpected obstacles in CS: Computers and programs often just don't work they way students expect. We consider it positive that students clearly overcame obstacles (since they persevered in the course) and that they learned to tolerate such obstacles. We note that it may be that their ability to tolerate obstacles relates to their newfound confidence. ("Yes, it's a problem, but I can deal with it.")

Our students also reported higher learning gains than their peers in other courses at a significant level ($0.01 < p < 0.05$) for two categories: "understanding how knowledge is constructed" and "ability to integrate theory and practice". Both seem to be good and important gains for students in introductory computer science.

Our students reported lower learning gains than their peers in other courses at a significant level ($0.01 < p < 0.05$) for only one category: "skill in how to give an effective presentation". Since we do not have students give presentations in this class, that outcome is not surprising.

For the remaining fifteen categories, there was no significant difference between our students and the overall sample RISC population.

7. SUMMARY

Six years ago, we made significant changes to our introductory course to bring in not only more students, but also a wider variety of students. These changes included a focus on image making with an interdisciplinary perspective and an increased emphasis on a multi-paradigm approach to problem solving. Evidence suggests that these changes have been successful. We see success through enrollments: We have more students, we have more women students, we seem to have students with a more diverse group of interests. We see success in learning outcomes: Our students are clearly mastering difficult concepts, such as higher-order procedures. We see success in other important factors: Our students show important learning gains, particularly gains in self-confidence and in integrating theory and practice.

8. LOOKING TOWARD THE FUTURE

While we find the course successful, we know there is always room for improvement.

First, we are looking for new ways to collaborate with our Art department, particularly as new faculty members join that department. We have begun to look at how we can have students in CSC151 work with students in the Introduction to Studio Art class. That class includes a project in which students build a simple pattern and then look at different ways to tile that pattern in a grid, rotating the tile in different ways to create new, more complex patterns. This exercise seems like an excellent opportunity to have CS students work with the art students to develop simple programs that let the art students explore their design space, just as students in [7] found benefit in designing musical interfaces for music students. The project is likely to give the CS students more experience in thinking about working with people who think differently and in designing procedures. (What are the options that I should provide to the user in making tiles? How should they describe potential patterns?)

Second, it is time to rethink the development environment we provide to students. When we began the project, we found that we could not easily make DrScheme (now DrRacket) work directly with the GIMP, and ended up building our own development environment. However, our students would be better served by the richer environment that DrRacket provides. New inter-process communication tools, such as D-Bus [13] have made it easier for us to prototype a new approach that allows students to use DrRacket as the development environment. We expect to have a link between DrRacket and GIMP ready for the next school year.

Third, we are investigating ideas of "self-disclosing code", wherein the application (in this case, the GIMP) displays underlying code when the user does something by hand [3]. When the student selects a brush, she sees `(image-select-brush! ....)`. When the student draws a line or curve, she sees `(image-draw-line! ....)`. Past experience [3,6] suggests that self-disclosing applications provide a good initial learning environment. We think it would smooth the first week or two of the class. The self-disclosing code may also provide an alternate form of reference for the students.

Finally, we are considering adding vector graphics to the course. Certainly, there is an appeal to working with a format like SVG, in which students can read the underlying code for the image after they construct it. This declarative representation of images provides yet another way to think about image making. There are also some interesting opportunities for different kinds of images (say, by recursively drawing a shape at each of its control points).

ACKNOWLEDGEMENTS

Matthew Kluber, of Grinnell's Art department, was instrumental in helping us bridge perspectives on image making. Jeremy Chen, also of Grinnell's Art department, is working with us on making new links with the introductory studio art course. Andrew Kaufman is helping create links with the Digital Art course.

A wide variety of students, particularly Soren Berg '08, helped with the implementation of this software.

We appreciate our students who have graciously allowed us to use their work as examples in this paper.

We thank David Lopatto for his RISC instrument. We thank both David and Leslie Jaworski and for their analysis of our RISC data.

This project was partially supported, by the National Science Foundation under Grant Number CCLI-0633090 and by Grinnell. Any opinions, findings, and conclusions or recommendations expressed in this article are those of the authors and do not necessarily reflect the views of the Foundation or the College.

Henry Walker and John David Stone designed and wrote our original introductory Scheme course nearly two decades ago. Many of their materials still live on in the current course.

REFERENCES

[1] James Edward Clayson. 2008. Radical bricolage: building coherence in the liberal arts using art, modeling, and language. *International Journal of Education Through Art* 4(2), pp. 141-161.

[2] Andrea Danyluk, Steven Roach, Elizabeth Hawthorne, Henry Walker, and Ruth Anderson. 2013. ACM/IEEE Computer Science 2013 Exemplar-Fest. In *Proceedings of the 44th ACM technical symposium on Computer science education* (SIGCSE '13). ACM, New York, NY, USA. Forthcoming.

[3] Chris DiGiano and Mike Eisenberg. 1995. Self-disclosing design tools: a gentle introduction to end-user programming. In *Proceedings of the 1st conference on Designing interactive systems: processes, practices, methods, \& techniques* (DIS '95), Gary M. Olson and Sue Schuon (Eds.). ACM, New York, NY, USA, 189-197. DOI=10.1145/225434.225455

[4] Daniel D. Garcia, Barbara Ericson, Joanna Goode, and Colleen Lewis. 2012. Rediscovering the passion, beauty, joy, and awe: making computing fun again, part 5. In *Proceedings of the 43rd ACM technical symposium on Computer Science Education* (SIGCSE '12). ACM, New York, NY, USA, 577-578. DOI=10.1145/2157136.2157300

[5] Mark Guzdial. 2003. A media computation course for non-majors. In *Proceedings of the 8th annual conference on Innovation and technology in computer science education* (ITiCSE '03), David Finkel (Ed.). ACM, New York, NY, USA, 104-108. DOI=10.1145/961511.961542 http://doi.acm.org/10.1145/961511.961542

[6] Pelle Hall, Andrew Hirakawa, Jennelle Nystrom, and Samuel A. Rebelsky. 2012. From drawing to programming: attracting middle-school students to programming through self-disclosing code (abstract only). In *Proceedings of the 43rd ACM technical symposium on Computer Science Education* (SIGCSE '12). ACM, New York, NY, USA, 673-673. DOI=10.1145/2157136.2157401

[7] Jesse M. Heines, Gena R. Greher, S. Alex Ruthmann, Brendan L. Reilly, "Two Approaches to Interdisciplinary Computing+Music Courses," *Computer*, vol. 44, no. 12, pp. 25-32, Dec. 2011, doi:10.1109/MC.2011.355

[8] David Lopatto, 2010. *Science in Solution: The Impact of Undergraduate Research on Student Learning*. The Research Corporation.

[9] Torben Lorenzen and Abdul Sattar. 2008. Objects first using Alice to introduce object constructs in CS1. *SIGCSE Bull.* 40, 2 (June 2008), 62-64. DOI=10.1145/1383602.1383636

[10] Andrew McGettrick, Eric Roberts, Daniel D. Garcia, and Chris Stevenson. 2008. Rediscovering the passion, beauty, joy and awe: making computing fun again. In *Proceedings of the 39th SIGCSE technical symposium on Computer science education* (SIGCSE '08). ACM, New York, NY, USA, 217-218. DOI=10.1145/1352135.1352213

[11] Paul Mullins, Deborah Whitfield, and Michael Conlon. 2009. Using Alice 2.0 as a first language. *J. Comput. Small Coll.* 24, 3 (January 2009), 136-143.

[12] Noam Nisan and Shimon Schocken. 2008. *The Elements of Computing Systems: Building a Modern Computer from First Principles* (History of Computing S.). The MIT Press.

[13] Havoc Pennington, Anders Carlson, Alexander Larsson, Sven Herzberg, Simon McVIttie, and David Zeuthen. 2012. *D-Bus Specification*, Version 0.19. Online document at http://dbus.freedesktop.org/doc/dbus-specification.html (Dated 20 February 2012; Accessed 7 September 2012).

[14] Allison Elliott Tew and Mark Guzdial. 2010. Developing a validated assessment of fundamental CS1 concepts. In *Proceedings of the 41st ACM technical symposium on Computer science education* (SIGCSE '10). ACM, New York, NY, USA, 97-101. DOI=10.1145/1734263.1734297

The Inverted-Lecture Model: A Case Study in Computer Architecture

Edward F. Gehringer
Department of Computer Science
North Carolina State University
Raleigh, NC 27606-8206
efg@ncsu.edu

Barry W. Peddycord III
Department of Computer Science
North Carolina State University
Raleigh, NC 27606-8206
bwpeddyc@ncsu.edu

ABSTRACT

This paper reports on an experience in using the inverted-lecture model (a.k.a. "flipping the classroom") in computer architecture. The first author concurrently taught two courses in computer architecture. One of these courses was CSC/ECE 506: Architecture of Parallel Computers, an introductory Graduate-level course. It was taught in a traditional format which was mostly lecture with interspersed active-learning exercises. Lecture videos were recorded to be used by distance-education students; however, on-campus students also had access to the recordings. The other was the inverted CSC 456: Computer Architecture and Multiprocessing, a senior-level undergraduate course. Students in this class watched the recorded CSC/ECE 506 lectures at home, with class time devoted to working problems, writing programs, and writing papers related to the course material. All "homework" was done in pairs, with a requirement that each student pair with each other student at least once during the semester.

Students in the inverted-lecture class exhibited high levels of engagement. Their performance on exams was not quite up to the level of the students in the graduate class, but the difference was not wide, and could be related to the fact that the students in the inverted classroom were undergraduates. From this experience, we offer observations and suggestions about inverted classes in general.

Categories and Subject Descriptors

K.3.2 [**Computers in Education**]: Computer and Information Science Education—*Computer Science Education*

General Terms

Human Factors; Management

Keywords

Inverted-lecture model; inverted classroom; flipped classroom; case study

SIGCSE'13, March 6–9, 2013, Denver, Colorado, USA.

1. INTRODUCTION

Technology is changing the classroom. Wifi is ubiquitous. Students come to class with a variety of electronic devices, including laptop computers. While these devices have many pedagogical applications, they frequently end up becoming a distraction as whole areas of the classroom can be "tuned out." [3, 12]. In response, some instructors have banned these devices during lecture [3], but this approach is suboptimal, especially in Computer Science, as it means depriving students of the ability to immediately practice what they are being taught.

Active learning is an effective way to mitigate distraction, as students are kept engaged by answering questions, sharing their thoughts, and working problems. Active learning takes time from lecturing, but the benefits are worth it [14]. The inverted-lecture model suggests that we maximize this benefit by using class time *exclusively* for active learning.

2. INVERTING LECTURES AND "HOMEWORK"

The inverted-lecture model, also known as an "inverted classroom" or "flipped classroom" [1], is an instructional approach that reverses the traditional position of lecture and homework. In an inverted classroom, students watch or listen to a presentation on the day's material at any convenient time prior to class. During class, they work what would usually be "homework" activities, such as solving problems, performing experiments, or discussing concepts with their classmates. What was once a lecture becomes more of a hands-on laboratory environment where students learn the material both from doing the assignments and collaborating with their peers.

In the classes of yesteryear, the only time an instructor had available to deliver content was during the scheduled class period. Mastery activities, therefore, had to be undertaken at home. It is through these activities that students have a chance to practice concepts from lecture, reflect on their knowledge, and identify misconceptions they may have. At home, when they come across a misconception, they have to turn to class notes or the textbook to resolve them.

In today's technology-rich environment, multimedia can explain a concept more effectively than a talking head. Unlike a live lecture, the presentation can be scripted and rehearsed until it is just right, used across multiple semesters, and students can replay it until they understand. This frees up class time for collaborative learning – which works best when students work out their ideas together in front of the instructor and any teaching assistants. In this environment, misconceptions can be quickly clarified and misstatements can be immediately corrected. Class time is convenient in this case as it ensures that the instructor and students will not have to schedule around time commitments to meet.

3. PREVIOUS WORK

The earliest systematic attempt at inverted lectures was in an economics course [9]. Students were asked to read a topic from the textbook and either watch or listen to a lecture before coming to class. Students were then given an opportunity to ask the professor to explain points that they had trouble understanding, leading to student-focused "mini-lectures," after which students were asked to work problems or perform experiments.

While these were small courses with no more than 40 students, the inverted approach has also been tried in courses with substantially higher enrollment, e.g., a business course that typically lectures to 300 students per section was broken down where students worked in groups of 24 students each [17].

Gannod,et al. [5] identified a number of issues raised by flipped classes. First, they found it necessary to mandate attendance, as the experiments and group work done during class time could not be replicated outside of class. They required students to view the lectures before class in order to ensure they were prepared for the in-class exercises. This can be enforced by interspersing machine-scored questions in the videos, or having door-quizzes when students arrive in class.

One barrier to implementing inverted lectures in practice is the need for developing lectures and other courseware for students. As some institutions are already recording lectures for the purposes of distance education, enterprising instructors have experimented in leveraging these already available resources to implement inverted lectures in their own classes [18].

However, many students dislike the videotaped lectures, some reporting that recorded lectures are not appropriate for more difficult course material [5], with others saying they are too long [18]. This has led some instructors to believe there is a need for courseware that is is specifically designed with inverted teaching in mind [8]. However, many reports find that students find the inverted-lecture model to be a more enjoyable learning experience, and typically express more confidence in their performance [9, 18, 17].

4. THE COURSES

In Spring 2012, the first author taught two courses covering very similar material, the first being a senior-level elective, CSC 456: Computer Architecture and Multiprocessing. It had not been taught for several years, due to the retirement of the previous instructor. The subject matter is becoming more important because of the need to educate students in parallelism and concurrency. Moreover, parallel architecture is the most relevant aspect of computer architecture for CS students, because it affects the programming model. However, only ten students registered for the course, and only eight completed it.

The other course was CSC/ECE 506: Architecture of Parallel Computers. It is a masters-level course also open to advanced undergraduates. It is a required course for Electrical and Computer Engineering graduate students and fulfills a "core" course requirement in "systems" (as opposed to "theory") for Computer Science graduate students. This course has been taught every semester for the last several years, serving about 100 students annually. In Spring 2012, forty-four students completed the course, of whom 17 were distance-education students.

CSC 456 and CSC/ECE 506 both enroll students with similar backgrounds. The main difference is the presence of ECE students in CSC/ECE 506; they have considerably more experience in logic and hardware design. Of course, the masters students are more experienced; mainly because most of them have worked in industry for a year or two. All of CSC 456 students were American, but about 2/3 of the CSC/ECE 506 students were foreign nationals. About 85% of the course material overlapped between the two classes with the following differences: The CSC 456 students studied pipelining and cache design in the place of the CSC/ECE 506 lessons on data dependencies and thread-level speculation.

As with most distance-education courses in the College of Engineering, the on-campus lectures of CSC/ECE 506 were recorded so they could be watched later by off-campus students. Similar to work by Toto [18], students in the inverted CSC 456 class were asked to watch these recorded lectures. Before coming to class, students in both classes were required to take and pass a 5-question pre-quiz over the reading for the day. If they got at least 4 of the 5 questions right, they received credit for the quiz. Each quiz could be retaken up to 7 times to obtain credit. Every student was allowed to miss at least one quiz without penalty, but for each additional quiz not completed with a passing grade, they lost 0.5% from their semester average. The purpose of the pre-quizzes was to make sure the students came to class prepared. In the case of CSC/ECE 506, they needed to be prepared to do active-learning exercises at several points during the class, usually 3 or 4 during a 75-minute class session. The CSC 456 students, on the other hand, needed to be prepared to work on "homework" during class.

Homework was similar in the two classes, including many identical problems. The CSC 456 students completed six problem sets, two more than the CSC/ECE 506 students, though the 456 problem sets were shorter so that they could be mostly finished within a single class session. There were also writing assignments, in which the students wrote articles for a textbook supplement on the class wiki. The topics included "The limits to speedup", "On-chip interconnects," and "TLB coherence," among many others. Again, the CSC 456 students did more of these (3 vs. 2), but each individual article was shorter than in CSC/ECE 506. Each article was written over three or four class periods. The articles were peer-reviewed, with the last period being used to revise their articles based on other students' comments. The last type of homework involved programming assignments, one on parallelizing a simple algorithm and the other two simulating cache-coherence protocols. The two classes were given identical programming assignments; the CSC 456 students had two class periods to work on each.

Table 1: Comparison between CSC 456 (inverted) and CSC/ECE 506 (traditional)

	CSC 456	CSC/ECE 506
Predominant student population	Senior undergraduate	Beginning masters
Class size	8	44 (27 on-campus, 17 distance)
Class preparation	Read text, pass quiz, watch video	Read text, pass quiz
Class time	Ask questions, do "homework"	In-class active-learning exercises
Partnering requirement	All assignments	At least three assignments
Attendance requirement	None	At least 20 of the 27 classes
Actual on-campus attendance	95%	50% + virtual participants
Number of problem sets	6	4
Length of each problem set	Shorter	Longer
Number of programming assignments	3	3
Number of writing assignments	3	2
Length of writing assignments	Shorter	Longer
Number of exams	2 midterms + final	2 midterms + final

One collaborative feature of CSC 456 work was that all assignments were done in pairs, with each student required to pair with all 7 other students at least once during the semester. The rationale was that each student comes into the class with a unique set of skills and experience, and that by pairing with all other students, students could diffuse their skills as widely as possible. Although CSC/ECE 506 students were only required to work together on projects with three other students, they were encouraged to pair on other assignments as well.

Each CSC 456 class day began with the instructor introducing the work for the class and answering questions on it. The students then broke into pairs, with the instructor visiting each pair several times during class to see how they were doing and answer questions or offer suggestions.

The exams in both courses consisted of two midterms and a final. Two-thirds of the questions were common across the two classes, allowing us to compare the two classes' mastery of the material. We had several hypotheses about how the two classes would compare.

- CSC 456 students will learn better from video lectures, because they can replay parts.
- CSC 456 students will be more engaged, as manifested by better attendance and more effort.
- CSC 456 students will score better on exams.

We kept track of each student's score on each exam question. The last class of the semester was structured as a focus group. Students were asked several questions and answered them anonymously on a Google form. The answers were then displayed to the class and discussed for a few minutes. Based on the discussion, another set of questions was generated and posed to the students on a Google form. This process was repeated three times during the class period.

5. RESULTS

Students in the inverted class did appear to be better motivated. Attendance was approximately 95%, despite the lack of an attendance requirement. At least 2/3 of the time, all eight students were present. They skipped class only for important events, like interviews and illness, sometimes notifying the instructor in advance when they were going to be absent. Students identified several factors contributing to high attendance.

1. Class time was already reserved, so it was the most convenient time for students to meet with their partners.
2. Doing homework in class made it convenient to ask questions of the instructor and get answers quickly.
3. Students would disadvantage their partner if they skipped a class.
4. The class was small, so students and the instructor all knew each other and would easily notice when someone was missing.
5. Since the class was an elective, students only enrolled if they were interested in the material.

Note that two of these factors (1 and 3) are dependent on working collaboratively, one (4) is related to the class being small, and one (5) is related to it being an elective. Factor 2 is the only reason that would be applicable to all inverted classes.

By and large, students came to class prepared to work on the "homework." Few of the questions they asked reflected a lack of background knowledge. They might have prepared so as not to disadvantage their partner, but it seems more likely that the pre-quizzes forced them to keep up with the material.

The fact that all students started on the homework at the same time with the instructor present meant that any confusion about the requirements was noticed quickly and resolved before students wasted time acting on their misunderstandings. This helped the students make better use of class time, but perhaps more importantly, it may serve as a model for assigning homework in an environment where the use of textbook problems is increasingly risky because of student access to solution manuals [20, 16, 13]. If instructors create their own questions to use in place of "canned" questions, they need a way to fix mis-specifications quickly. Having a class available to do an on-the-spot requirements inspection makes this possible.

Table 2: Exam performance between CSC 456 and CSC/ECE 506

	CSC 456 $n = 8$ students	CSC/ECE 506 $n = 44$ students
Test 1, Q1	18.2 (3.4)	17.6 (3.4)
Test 1, Q2*	6.7 (4.2)	12.3 (6.3)
Test 1, Q6 (4)**	5.10 (4.4)	10.4 (5.7)
Test 2, Q1	18.7 (0.7)	19.4 (0.8)
Test 2, Q2	18.4 (2.3)	18.6 (2.4)
Test 2, Q3	12.7 (5.9)	13.9 (4.2)
Test 2, Q5 (4)**	16.1 (3.6)	17.0 (3.9)
Test 2, Q6	8.3 (6.1)	15.5 (5.3)
Final exam, Q1	16.0 (4.73)	14.4 (5.8)
Final exam, Q3	12.1 (3.40)	13.7 (3.6)
Final exam, Q4	11.9 (4.6)	13.4 (5.2)
Final exam, Q6	13.0 (2.4)	14.8 (4.6)
Test 1, total	**64.9 (16.4)**	**65.4 (12.6)**
Test 2, total	**72.1 (13.4)**	**89.6 (7.1)**
Final exam, total	**75.1 (12.5)**	**79.1 (12.3)**

* *Students were free to skip one problem without penalty. Only three 456 students answered question 2 on the first midterm.*
** *The question numbers in parentheses are the corresponding question numbers for the tests in CSC/ECE 506.*

That said, an inverted classroom also makes it harder to cheat in the first place. Procrastination is a major reason that students cheat [7]; they put off starting an assignment until it is too late, and then panic and copy from another student or the Web. In an inverted classroom, procrastination is virtually impossible, since everyone starts at the same time. Moreover, working collaboratively with another person tends to diminish cheating, as has been observed in pair-programming studies [19]. Cheating would literally require a conspiracy of several students under the nose of the instructor.

Despite the engagement successes of the inverted model, our hypothesis that students taught in this way would do better on exams was not borne out. Of the twelve exam questions common to the two classes, CSC 456 students outscored CSC/ECE 506 students on only two (Table 2). The average score on common questions was 13.6 for the CSC 456 students and 15.6 for the CSC/ECE 506 students (each question was worth 20 points). Most of the difference, though, was on the last question of each of the three exams; if one excludes these questions from the computation, the CSC 456 students averaged 15.2 and the CSC/ECE 506 students averaged 15.7. This might suggest that the CSC 456 students knew the material nearly as well, but were slower at test-taking. We must note, though, that there was no requirement to attempt the questions in order.

Table 3: Exposure to course material in CSC 456 and CSC/ECE 506

	Avg	How measured
CSC 456		
# of times book was read	18.7	(self-reported)
# of lectures watched	11.6	(self-reported)
Total Exposure	**30.3**	
CSC/ECE 506		
# of times book was read	25.1	(pre-quizzes passed)
# of lectures watched	19.7	(in-class exercises)
Total Exposure	**44.8**	

Of course, we are comparing undergraduate students with graduate students. Any differences may reflect the greater maturity of the grad students (most of whom had work experience after their bachelor's degree), or the fact that our graduate program is more selective than our undergraduate program. It might also bespeak the fact that graduate students can afford to spend more time on each course, since they are typically taking 3 courses per semester, while undergraduates are taking 5 or 6.

An alternative explanation is that the CSC/ECE 506 students had more of an opportunity to reinforce the material in their minds, because they needed both to read the book and watch the lectures, while the CSC 456 students could get by by doing one or the other but not both. Not only were the 506 students required to pass a pre-quiz; they were also obligated to do in-class exercises during the class sessions and submit their answers on Google forms. If they failed to do this in at least 20 of the 27 class sessions, they were penalized 0.5% for each additional class missed on their final average. On the other hand, the CSC 456 students could probably pass the pre-quiz by either reading the textbook or watching the lecture.

The CSC 456 students self-reported that they read the book before an average of 18.7 classes in the semester, and watched an average of 11.6 lecture videos. There were 27 classes (75 minutes each), but there was no reading assigned for the first class, and the inverted-lecture model was not used during the first week of class, so the students could have done the reading a maximum of 26 times and watched the lecture a maximum of 25 times. The CSC/ECE 506 students passed an average of 25.1 quizzes based on the readings, and received attendance credit for an average of 19.7 lectures, based on responses to in-class exercises. Computing the totals reveals that the CSC 456 students were exposed to class material 30.3 times, whereas the CSC/ECE 506 students were exposed an average of 44.8 times. By this calculation, the 506 students spent 48% more time on the material, which should have translated to higher scores. And this may underestimate the difference, since the 456 data is based on self-reporting, whereas the 506 data comes from tallying submitted work.

This has two implications. First, it supports the notion that the CSC/ECE 506 students scored higher because they had more time to spend on the course. If the comparison had been between a traditional and inverted-lecture class where the students were taking the same number of other courses, our findings might have been much different. Second, it raises the question of how best to combine textbook readings with lecture videos in an inverted class. Should students be asked

- to read the textbook first, then watch the videos,
- to watch the videos first, then read the book, or
- to cover some material by reading, and other material by watching?

Of the five students who offered an opinion one way or another, four said that they would rather read the book first. The one student who said watch the lecture first said that (s)he could understand much of the material from the video, and only go back to the book to study what was unclear. Which is better for a particular student may depend on that student's learning style [4]. But it bears mention that at conferences, when attendees have a choice of whether to watch the presentation or read the paper first, virtually all of them choose to watch the presentation.

In our experiment, reading the book necessarily came first for the CSC/ECE 506 students, and that influenced the way the material was presented in the video. Videos could instead be designed to give an overview of what is written in the textbook, and in that case, more students might be inclined to watch first, read later. Whether the video or the book should come first is an open question for future research.

The inverted classroom can be a "gentler" way to learn a subject, because students can get help from other members of their group or the instructor (or TA) at any time during the class. All students thought it was helpful to some degree to have someone to talk to; two of them said it was very useful. One student, though said (s)he learned more from having to "grow around challenges," even if it took more time.

One innovation in this class was that every student was required to pair with every other student in the class at least once during the semester. This was fairly easy to achieve since the class was small and there were many different assignments. Opinions were mixed about whether this was helpful. Three students said yes, but the others cited two problems: First, it was not possible to finish the homework in class, so they had to look for times when they could meet outside of class, and such times were not easy to find. Second, some students were stronger than others; it was sometimes a burden to work with slower students, but at least the burden was shared roughly equally. Students were asked how many of the other 7 students they learned from while doing homework. The average student reported learning from 4.9 of their 7 classmates.

Our philosophy of shuffling pairs is derived from agile development practices, which stress the importance of everyone learning from everyone else so that knowledge diffuses across the group [10]. It is in contrast to team-based learning [6], which keeps the same team together for an extended period (often the whole semester) so that members learn to take advantage of each other's strengths. We observe greater student buy-in with the agile approach, primarily because no one feels shortchanged for very long by having a partner who puts forth inadequate effort.

6. OBSERVATIONS AND FUTURE WORK

Our inverted-lecture class used 75-minute videos recorded from traditional classes for the purposes of distance education. This is similar to work by Toto [18], as we chose to leverage existing resources rather than creating new material specifically for this course. Five of our eight students said the videos should be shorter, which is reasonable, as research shows that adult learners have a 10-15 minute attention span at the beginning of a class [11]. While the attention span does drop later in the class, students watching short videos do not need to watch them in a single sitting; they can fit them around other activities. Shorter videos are also more likely to be watched repeatedly to reinforce knowledge, since it is easier to find the relevant material in shorter videos.

We asked about creating shorter videos from the recorded lectures, but were told by the production staff that it would require too much time. However, over the longer term, it does make sense to record shorter videos. Students can be asked to write the script for such videos (or even record them) as a homework assignment. In a current class, we are having students peer-review each other's online lesson videos. Beare [2] reports that students preferred videos that were edited and touched up to mere classroom recordings.

Other researchers, e.g., Lage [9], have reported that inverted classes take more time for students than traditional classes. All but one of our students thought it took more time than most other classes. Two of the eight said it took a lot more time. Two reasons were cited: the quizzes, and the need to meet with partners outside of class to finish assignments. The quizzes were short (only 5 multiple-choice or checkbox questions), so the extra time was probably mostly for reviewing the material to be able to pass the quiz.

At this point, we know little about how best to structure class time. Should students be given short tasks, should they be given tasks that they can just complete in class, or should they be given longer assignments that can only be started during class? In any class, students will work at different paces, so that some finish before others. When this happens, there are at least three choices.

1. Interrupt those who are not done; tell them the answer, and go on to the next question.
2. Allow the faster students to work additional problems at their own pace.
3. Structure activities so that those who got the answer first work with others who are slower [15].

In this class, we chose the second approach, but were left with the impression that the class was less interactive than it might have been.

7. CONCLUSIONS

The inverted classroom is a relatively new approach, which is driven by at least three contemporary phenomena: the proven efficacy of active learning, the availability of online technology to present and illustrate course material, and the tendency of portable electronic devices to serve as distractions when students are not actively engaged in learning activities. Class time is uniquely valuable because it permits all students to co-locate in the same room, where they can work with their classmates and immediately receive help from the course staff. Several of our students said that this made it a high priority for them to attend class. Unusually high attendance and serious collaborative effort was the most favorable experience with our class.

The students in our inverted classroom did not do as well on exams as the students in our traditional classroom, scoring about 10% lower (2 points less on 20-point problems). However, it's unlikely that this difference was due to the mode of instruction. More likely, it was due to the fact that the students in the inverted class were undergraduates being compared to graduate students in the traditional class, and that the graduate students had more time to spend on the course due to having a lighter course load (2-4 classes) than undergraduates (4-6 classes). Based upon our experience, we have several recommendations for improving the inverted classroom: Divide online lectures into learning modules of 10 to 15 minutes duration, emphasize shorter in-class assignments that can be completed in class, and have students pair with many other students on different collaborative assignments in order to learn most effectively from the lectures, the exercises, and their peers, respectively.

In the years to come, we can expect more research on how best to use class time in an inverted classroom. We also anticipate more study on how to divide learning time optimally between solo preparation (reading the textbook, watching videos, doing exercises alone) and collaborative practice (discussions, experiments, and other group work).

8. REFERENCES

[1] J. Baker. The "classroom flip". using web course management tools to become the guide on the side. In *11th International Conference on College Teaching and Learning, Jacksonville, FL*, Jacksonville, FL, 2000.

[2] P. L. Beare. Media: The comparative effectiveness of videotape, audiotape, and telelecture in delivering continuing teacher education. *American Journal of Distance Education*, 3(2):57–66, 1989.

[3] B. Fang. From distraction to engagement: Wireless devices in the classroom. *EDUCAUSE Quarterly*, 32(4):4–9, 2009.

[4] R. Felder and J. Spurlin. Applications, reliability and validity of the index of learning styles. *International Journal of Engineering Education*, 21(1):103–112, 2005.

[5] G. C. Gannod, J. E. Burge, and M. T. Helmick. Using the inverted classroom to teach software engineering. In *Proceedings of the 30th international conference on Software engineering*, ICSE '08, pages 777–786, New York, NY, USA, 2008. ACM.

[6] E. Gomez, D. Wu, and K. Passerini. Traditional, hybrid and online teamwork: Lessons from the field. *Communications of the Association for Information Systems*, 25(1):33, 2009.

[7] D. L. R. Jones. Academic dishonesty: Are more students cheating? *Business Communication Quarterly*, 74(2):141, 2011.

[8] S. Kellogg. Developing online materials to facilitate an inverted classroom approach. In *Frontiers in Education Conference, 2009. FIE '09. 39th IEEE*, pages 1 –6, San Antonio, TX, Oct. 2009.

[9] M. J. Lage, G. J. Platt, and M. Treglia. Inverting the classroom: A gateway to creating an inclusive learning environment. *The Journal of Economic Education*, 31(1):pp. 30–43, 2000.

[10] L. Lindstrom and R. Jeffries. Extreme programming and agile software development methodologies. *Information Systems Management*, 21(3):41–52, 2004.

[11] J. Middendorf and A. Kalish. The "change-up" in lectures. In *Natl. Teach. Learn. Forum*, volume 5, pages 1–5, 1996.

[12] S. Miller and J. Connor. Student use of technology in a large lecture. In *2010 ASEE Annual Conference & Exposition*, 2010.

[13] A. Minichiello, L. McNeill, and C. Hailey. Comparing engineering student use of solution manuals and Student/Faculty perceptions of academic dishonesty. In *2012 ASEE Annual Conference & Exposition*, 2012.

[14] M. Prince. Does active learning work? a review of the research. *JOURNAL OF ENGINEERING EDUCATION-WASHINGTON-*, 93:223–232, 2004.

[15] S. Robbins. Beyond clickers: using ClassQue for multidimensional electronic classroom interaction. In *Proceedings of the 42nd ACM technical symposium on Computer science education*, pages 661–666, 2011.

[16] S. T. Santillan. Correlation between homework solution website use and course performance. Vancouver, BC, 2011.

[17] N. Schullery, R. Reck, and S. Schullery. Toward solving the high enrollment, low engagement dilemma: A case study in introductory business. *International Journal of Business, Humanities and Technology*, 1(2):1–9, 2011.

[18] R. Toto and H. Nguyen. Flipping the work design in an industrial engineering course. In *Frontiers in Education Conference, 2009. FIE '09. 39th IEEE*, pages 1 –4, San Antonio, TX, Oct. 2009.

[19] T. Urness. Assessment using peer evaluations, random pair assignment, and collaborative programing in CS1. *Journal of Computing Sciences in Colleges*, 25(1):87–93, 2009.

[20] J. Widmann, J. Kennedy, and K. Shollenberger. Student use of author's textbook solution manuals: Effect on student learning of mechanics fundamentals. In *2007 ASEE Annual Conference & Exposition*, 2007.

Learning Computer Science in the "Comfort Zone of Proximal Development"

Nicole Anderson Tim Gegg-Harrison
Department of Computer Science
Winona State University
Winona, Minnesota 55987
{nanderson,tgeggharrison}@winona.edu

ABSTRACT

As computer science faculty, we are always looking for better ways to recruit and retain new majors. One way to achieve this goal is to incorporate material into the introductory courses that lies within the intersection of the student's "zone of proximal development" (which contains concepts that the student is capable of understanding) and "comfort zone" (which contains concepts that motivate the student and are presented in a way in which the student is familiar and comfortable). We refer to this region as the "comfort zone of proximal development." In this paper, we present a "comfort zone of proximal development" that we have created for computer science students which consists of a collaborative learning environment where programming concepts are introduced with gaming applications.

Categories and Subject Descriptors

[**Computing education**]: Computing education programs—*Computer science education*

General Terms

Algorithms, Design

Keywords

Active Learning, Scaffolding, Pair Programming/Teaching, Mobile Game Development

1. INTRODUCTION

Students enter the world of computer science expecting to harness new and exciting technology. When the introductory courses fail to realize their expectations, many students leave the major. Teachers want to make introductory courses enjoyable for their students, and are looking to recruit and retain new majors. However, they understand that strong fundamental knowledge must be conveyed in these courses in order for students to be successful in the field. The core concepts cannot be sacrificed. We have found a solution that provides the best of both worlds. In our approach, the introductory programming sequence is not disturbed. Instead, we developed companion courses which reinforce fundamental concepts using mobile game development and a collaborative approach, giving both students and faculty what they want.

We believe that optimal learning takes place for students when the material is within their cognitive capabilities, it is presented in a way that is familiar to them, and uses an application that is relevant or interesting to them. This is a region that lies within the intersection of the *zone of proximal development* [28] and their *comfort zone* (which contains concepts and topics that the students are interested in and comfortable with, and that are presented in a way in which they are familiar and comfortable) as depicted in Figure 1. To be effective, we need to both stay within the students' developmental zone of proximal development as well as within their comfort zone. In other words, we need to be talking about something of interest in an environment that motivates them and it needs to be concepts that the students are capable of understanding. Our notion of a *comfort zone of proximal development* is related to situated cognition (or authentic learning) [6]. Situated cognition relies on the idea that conceptual knowledge can be more easily internalized when context is provided, especially when that context is integrated with everyday life activities. According to Brown, Collins, and Duguid, "Activity, concept, and culture are interdependent. No one can be totally understood without the other two. Learning must involve all three" [6]. By relating problems to the students' lives, authentic learning occurs.

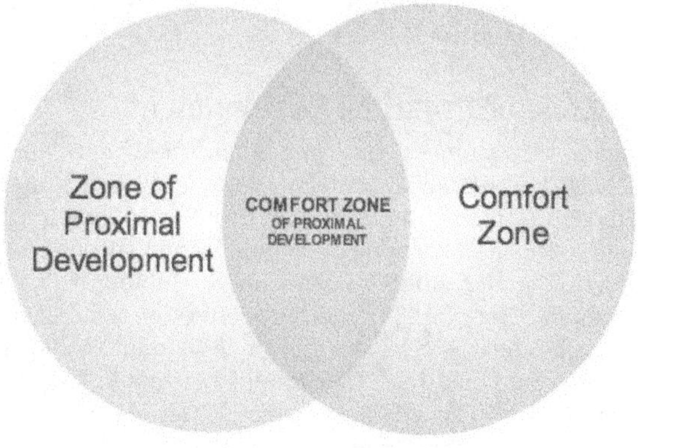

Figure 1: Comfort Zone of Proximal Development

SIGCSE'13, March 6–9, 2013, Denver, Colorado, USA.

Children's playgrounds are significantly different today than they were 50 years ago. They are safer, void of "dangerous" equipment, made from various composites that provide an environment for children to play without the risk of getting hurt. That's a good thing, right? The simple answer is *yes*. Upon closer analysis, however, it is possible that the benefits in safety come at a price. Sandseter and Kennair argue that playgrounds have become too safe [27]. They see playgrounds as environments where children "test possibilities and boundaries for action," arguing that "the rehearsal of handling real-life risky situations through risky play is thus an important issue." In essence, the playground and the other children are part of the child's comfort zone. A playground with proper equipment (i.e., equipment that is safe enough but also capable of providing physical and mental challenges for children of all ages) becomes the child's zone of proximal development. Together, with an attentive parent who places restrictions when necessary, these aspects of the playground become a comfort zone of proximal development for the child. Our pair^2 learning environment that introduces computer programming through gaming applications provides an appropriate playground for individuals wanting to learn computer science. They have an opportunity to collaborate with their peers, construct useful artifacts like computer games, and challenge themselves with the security of a partner and an attentive teacher to help keep them from becoming overwhelmed. As a side-effect of "playing" in this comfortable environment, they learn computer science.

2. COMFORT ZONE OF PROXIMAL DEVELOPMENT FOR CS

Over the past several years, we have been developing a comfort zone of proximal development for our computer science students. We began by updating the discrete mathematics course to make the material more relevant to computer science students [12], and more recently changed the introductory programming sequence. The comfort zone of proximal development contains both concept-dependent and concept-independent components. The zone of proximal development is concept-dependent, requiring the selection of a concept (or topic) that is within the student's intellectual capability and one that the student is interested in so as to help motivate her to learn the new concept (or topic area). The comfort zone, on the other hand, is concept-independent, requiring the creation of a learning environment that is more conducive to student learning.

2.1 Zone of Proximal Development

Vygotsky introduced the *zone of proximal development* (ZPD) as "the distance between the actual developmental level as determined by independent problem solving and the level of potential development as determined through problem solving under adult guidance or in collaboration with more capable peers" [28]. In other words, the zone of proximal development is what a child or individual can achieve with some guidance that they would be unable to achieve independently. The goal is to stretch the learner beyond her innate capabilities, challenging her while providing support to meet her challenges. The ZPD is unique to each individual, and varies according to her capabilities and the environment and context in which the development is occurring.

Apprenticeship and scaffolding are some common approaches to reaching the ZPD [10]. Scaffolding involves the construction of appropriate supportive conditions for a learner [11, 13]. Consider the scaffolding that is constructed for maintenance or repair of a building. It allows a worker to do jobs that they would not be capable of doing without climbing on the scaffolding. For example, scaffolding allows a worker to wash higher windows, provides a work surface for holding necessary construction tools, and often provides a level of safety and stability that gives comfort to the worker and thus the confidence to perform the job at hand. The term scaffolding may be used more abstractly in our context, but with familiar goals. Scaffolding for a learner may consist of providing the appropriate tools, support, and confidence building to allow the learner to succeed. When these types of models are employed, after spending time working with an expert to grasp a new concept an individual is able to internalize what she has learned, and eventually the scaffolding/assistance can be removed. This is reflected by Vygotsky, as he believed that "what the child is able to do in collaboration today he will be able to do independently tomorrow" [29].

In the ZPD the expert engages in a "dialogue with the novice (learner) to focus on emerging skills and abilities" [24]. Another method in which knowledge can be passed from an expert to a novice is when the novice utilizes imitation to mirror what the expert has already mastered. However, this is only effective when the action being imitated is at the appropriate developmental level. "It is well established that the child can imitate only what lies within the zone of his intellectual potential... [T]he child can enter into imitation through intellectual actions more or less far beyond what he is capable of in independent mental and purposeful actions or intellectual operations" [30]. One of the authors is the parent of a young child, and witnesses this phenomenon frequently. As an example, describing how to blow up a balloon to a child is a futile task. But while blowing up a balloon for the child, the author noted how the child began to purse his lips, puff out his cheeks, and blow out air through his mouth. Without an intended lesson, the child was imitating the actions of the "balloon blowing expert." Later, the author witnessed the child blowing up the balloon independently. The child could not inflate the balloon as large as the adult, nor could he tie the balloon to keep it inflated, but incremental development was indeed occurring to move him toward mastering these skills.

What we see is that these types of collaborations occur intentionally and unintentionally, they occur with teacher-student pairs, when mentoring and apprenticeship roles have been established, and also seemingly randomly through imitation or observation when the necessary context and environment are present. It has been noted that "the term 'collaboration' should not be understood as a joint, coordinated effort to move forward, where the more expert partner is always providing support at the moments where maturing functions are inadequate. Rather it appears that this term is being used to refer to any situation in which a child is being offered some interaction with another person in relation to a problem to be solved" [7].

As teachers, we wish to utilize these ideas to make our interaction with students as effective as possible. According to Vygotsky, teaching "is effective only when it awakens and rouses to life those functions which are in a stage of maturing, which lie in the zone of proximal development" [30]. The expert is able to empower the learner through dialogue and guided participation [26]. While some prior research encourages the teacher to attempt to find each student's ZPD, Meira and Lerman argue that the "ZPD emerges, or not, in the moment, as part of the microculture of the classroom" [17]. We believe this emergence is really the discovery of the student's *comfort zone of proximal development* (CZPD), where each individual's ZPD intersects with their comfort zone.

2.2 Comfort Zone

One of the most important factors that impacts college students' persistence is the degree of social connectedness that they experience [14, 19]. Bean argues that "few would deny that the social lives of students in college and their exchanges with others inside and outside the institution are important in retention decisions" [4]. The teacher's role in establishing the sense of connectedness is vital. Roberts and Styron argue that "effective faculty-student interaction will help establish an environment where students feel that faculty members truly care about them as individuals, which will facilitate the attainment of academic success" [25].

According to Oblinger, today's *millennial* students gravitate towards groupwork, preferring "teamwork, experiential learning, structure, and the use of technology" [21]. Ironically, however, social networking technologies appear to have a negative impact on students' social connectedness at universities. Because of the ease with which to stay "connected" with their friends from high school via FaceBook and text messaging, even those attending colleges that are geographically disconnected, today's college students do not feel the need to establish new friendships. We are finding that over half of our students will choose to have the teachers define groups rather than self-selecting partners for group work claiming that they "really don't know anyone in the class." The computer science discipline tends to attract individuals who have more introverted personality types. As such, the need to establish connectedness is both more difficult and more important for the retention of computer science students.

When properly administered, pair teaching increases both the amount and quality of teacher-student interaction. Pair programming [32] appears to be a mechanism that forces computer science students to establish a social connectedness with fellow students, something they would likely not do on their own. In addition to their social uneasiness, many of today's students have *helicopter parents* [9] with whom they have become very dependent. When pair teaching is employed, students have more opportunity to establish relationships and build stronger bonds with their teachers, which provides them with a "safety net" away from home and enables them to establish some independence and thereby feel a higher degree of connectedness to the university community. In an effort to harness the positive benefits to student learning from both pair programming and pair teaching, we recently employed *pair*^{2} *learning*, which combines pair programming with pair teaching, in the first course of our introductory Computer Science programming sequence [1]. We believe that the combination of pair programming and pair teaching produces a learning environment that is better than when one or both of these techniques is not used, creating an appropriate comfort zone of learning for beginning CS students.

Having two teachers enables the distribution of course preparation work, placing a second set of eyes on the course material to help make it more effective. Responsibility for preparing the course materials can be divided up between topics. For each topic, one of the teachers takes on the role of the *driver*, the teacher responsible for both preparing the lecture notes and corresponding evaluations (in-class laboratory assignments, out-of-class programming assignments, and examinations), and the other teacher assumes the role of *navigator*, the teacher responsible for reviewing the course materials for defects (typos, ambiguities, and potential points of confusion). The *driver* then delivers the lecture with the *navigator* advancing the slides and demonstrating the in-class programming examples. There is constant feedback and communication between the *driver* and *navigator* during the preparation phase, delivery phase, and reflection phase. Williams argues that one of the benefits of pair programming results from the fact that "because the navigator is not as deeply involved with the design, algorithm, code or test, he or she can have a more objective point of view and can better think strategically about the direction of the work" [32]. The same applies to pair teaching. When pair teaching is employed in developing a course, the teacher's time is shifted somewhat from preparing course materials to time spent in the classroom. Of course, even though the primary responsibility for material development for a given section of the course is given to one teacher, additional time is spent by the other teacher to review the materials produced. We believe the end result is higher quality materials, which will be beneficial to the students.

2.3 CZPD for CS Students

Although it is hard to imagine anything more awe-inspiring than the closed form of the Fibonacci sequence, most of today's potential computer science students are not that impressed. As a general rule, computer science faculty members expect that every student who arrives at her university with an intention to major in computer science is excited by computation and formal reasoning. It is a reasonable assumption given that many computer science faculty members pursued advanced degrees in computer science precisely because they were awed with the beauty and elegance of computation and formal reasoning. The new generation of computer scientists, on the other hand, does not share that intrinsic love of formalism. There are other things that excite them. Towards the top of this list is their iPhone and the various gaming apps that it contains. Studies have found that students prefer gaming assignments to non-gaming assignments. Cliburn and Miller found that 78.9% of their students preferred projects that were game related, and 84% of their students claimed that games provided extra motivation to both complete their projects and improve the quality of their projects [8].

Mobile game development provides a new and exciting avenue to recruit and retain the new generation of computer scientists. There have been various approaches to incorporate game and/or mobile device programming into the computer science curriculum as a way of making the curriculum more inviting to today's college student. Several programs have restructured their introductory programming sequence courses to incorporate game development [3, 5, 16, 22, 33]. Other programs introduce students to mobile game development after they have already gained some programming experience [15], some provide game development in upper-level courses [2, 31], while still others have threaded gaming throughout their curriculum [18]. All of these approaches required significant revisions to their curriculum. Although we share their enthusiasm of using mobile game development to better engage today's students, we believe that we can achieve the same goal without completely restructuring the curriculum. We have developed an approach that captures the enthusiasm that students have with mobile devices and gaming without sacrificing the integrity of the computer science curriculum.

Rather than changing the introductory programming sequence courses to teach mobile game programming, we introduced an optional one credit companion course that augments the fundamental concepts of object-oriented programming and problem solving that are taught in the first programming course. The introductory programming course continues to introduce computer science students to object-oriented programming in Java using an objects-first approach [20], while the companion course introduces students to iPhone app development using Objective C. By using Objective C to create apps on an iPhone, the companion courses serves two primary purposes: (1) it provides students with a fun environment that increases their motivation to continue studying computer science, and (2) it strengthens their understanding of the underlying object-oriented programming concepts by reinforcing the concepts using a different programming environment.

One of the potential concerns with our approach is that we are forcing the students to switch programming languages from Java to Objective C. Although it does pose some difficulties for some of the students, we believe that the use of multiple programming languages is actually good from a pedagogical point of view. It forces students to transition from a "what do I type in" mode of thinking to the "what do I need to do" mode. Because the syntax of Objective C and Java are sufficiently different from one another, the students shift their focus from what they need to type to what they are trying to accomplish. Thus, they become more concerned with the semantics than the syntax of the programming language. This belief is supported by the results of a survey given at the end of class.

We created a set of seven iPhone labs for the companion course. The companion course meets every other week, so the students were exposed to two weeks of material in the introductory Java programming course between each lab assignment in the companion course. In the first lab, students install XCode, Apple's IDE for developing iPhone apps. The students are given a sliding puzzle iPhone app that they are able to compile and run on the iPhone simulator provided by XCode. We chose this particular app because sliding puzzles are familiar to students, it is a fairly straightforward app to implement, it has different levels (starting with a 3×3 board and going up to a 12×12 board), and it has a slight twist on standard sliding puzzle apps in that the solution to this puzzle is to find a configuration in which no two tiles of the same color are adjacent to one another.

The second lab takes the app from the first lab and has students add a `Counter` class that supports the timer and move counts that are displayed at the top of the screen. This

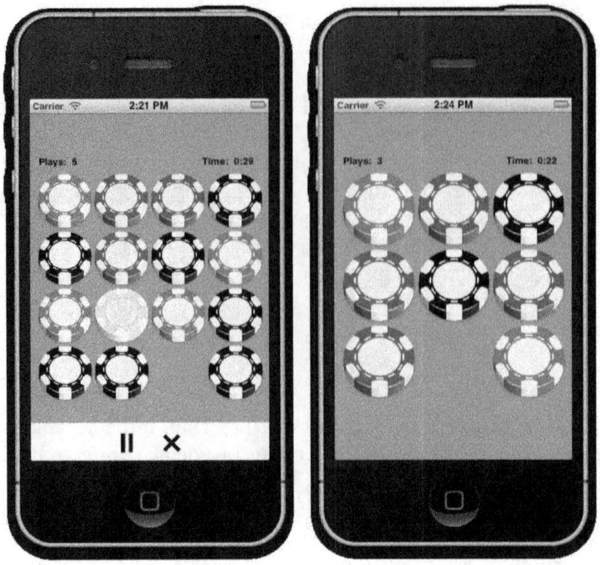

(a) ColorClash app (b) SlidingTile app

Figure 2: iPhone Apps

is an example of scaffolding the app so that the students are able to produce an app without having to code the entire app from scratch. The `Counter` class is the first class that is presented in Niño and Hosch's text, so the students have already studied and produced this class in Java. The key concepts for this lab include classes, variables, and methods. None of the methods and the constructor for this class have parameters. We use this class to introduce the differences between Java and Objective C. We also talk about specification and implementation (.h vs. .m files) and the difference in compilation between Objective C and Java as well as import issues. Note that in the first lab, the students merely load XCode on their machines and run the ColorClash app. In this second lab, they *create* the ColorClash app by adding the `Counter` class. Rather than merely constructing a `Counter` class that they can create, increment, and test with various values, they are able to construct a `Counter` class that has an actual purpose. They can test the class by playing a game and checking the timer and move counts to ensure that their implementation is correct. Rather than relying on their imaginations (or suggestions provided by the instructor) that their `Counter` class is useful, they see first hand the role that it plays with the implementation of the sliding puzzle as shown in Figure 2(a).

In the third lab, the students create the *HelloWorld* app. Traditionally, the *HelloWorld* app is the first app that students write. Although it is nice tradition to write *HelloWorld* as the first program when learning a new programming language, it is not particularly useful for a student learning to program for the first time. It is, however, useful for a student who has already constructed a component of larger, more sophisticated app. The key concepts for this lab include an introduction to XCode projects (including the creation of an iPhone app from scratch), the declaration and allocation of objects (specifically a `UILabel`), and the invocation of methods with parameters. Students are also introduced to the Cocoa Touch API. It is important to note that we do not use *Interface Builder* in our app development, so students create and place labels (and all other *views*) programmatically. Thus, they learn about the geometry of the views along with the use of Cocoa Touch objects.

The fourth lab is another scaffolded lab. In the introductory Java programming course, students are introduced to class interaction with a maze game example. The key concept introduced with this lab is the construction of methods and constructors with parameters. Students have the concept of parameter passing reinforced by seeing the difference between the way in which parameters are expressed in Objective C vs. Java. In Objective C, parameters are labeled as compared to having unlabeled parameters defined by position in Java. Students see, however, that parameters are still defined by position in Objective C, they are just labeled as well for better readability. Parameters provide an ideal example for discussing syntactic differences and the pros and cons of these decisions. Students are reminded that the concept and underlying use of parameters is the same in both Objective C and Java. It is merely two different syntactic approaches to the same problem. Such discussion helps differentiate the key conceptual similarities from the superficial syntactic differences in the two programming languages.

The remaining labs have the students creating their own sliding puzzle. In the end, they create a 3×3 standard sliding puzzle as shown in Figure 2(b). In the first of the *SlidingPuzzle* app labs, the students start by creating an app from scratch that contains one tile which is stored as a `UIImageView`. They complete the lab by adding several more tiles at various places on the screen. The second of the *SlidingPuzzle* app labs introduces the students to event handling through the `touchesBegan`, `touchesMoved`, and `touchesEnded` methods. Students practice with conditionals to identify when the user is touching one of the tiles. Students begin by tracking the finger movement precisely by updating the x and y coordinates of the tile to match the x and y coordinates of the touch. They then modify their code to restrict moving the tiles to strict vertical and horizontal movement. This lab activity is useful at this stage in the student programmer's development because it eliminates any lingering belief in the *magic* of computing, since they see firsthand that what is displayed on the screen is dictated by their code, not the actual finger movement. In the final *SlidingPuzzle* app lab, students complete the sliding puzzle by creating an array of tiles.

Scaffolding in the initial labs is at the code implementation level, where students are given a partial program solution and are asked to complete the app by writing the missing code. This implementation-level scaffolding is important for beginning programmers because they lack sufficient programming experience and knowledge to construct a complete solution on their own. Scaffolding in the final labs is at the design level, where students are guided through the design steps for the program solution and are asked to complete all of the coding. This design-level scaffolding is important for beginning programmers as they transition into more independent programmers.

3. RESULTS AND CONCLUSION

We recently offered two sections of the first course in the Computer Science introductory sequence along with the companion courses, where both sections were pair taught. We invited students to complete a survey that asked them to give some feedback on how pair teaching was influencing them in terms of learning, attitudes, and likelihood to continue on in the Computer Science course sequence. The survey included some questions they answered using a modified Likert scale with four options. The neutral option was removed so that students were forced to choose either a positive or negative response. It also included some open-ended questions on the benefits and problems students experienced from having a course that was pair taught. Finally, the survey asked students whether or not they planned to continue with the next course in the CS introductory sequence, and if their experiences in the current course influenced this decision.

The results of the survey indicated that students liked the the use of scaffolding with gaming applications in a pair^2 learning environment, with 92% indicating that they "looked forward to coming to class each day" and 29% indicating that they "greatly looked forward to coming to class each day." They also felt like they benefitted from the pair teaching with 82% of students indicating that they received "more individual attention" due to the pair model and 29% indicating that they received "a lot more individual attention" than they would have received with a single teacher. The students' positive experience in the classroom lead to higher retention, with 49% of them continuing to the next course in the sequence. This represented a significant improvement in our retention rates. The average retention rate (which is calculated based on the number of students who continue into the second programming course in the following semester) was 39% for the previous four semesters when the pair^2 learning environment was not used. We have enjoyed a high success rate in the second course in the CS introductory sequence, with 82% of our students receiving a passing grade over the past four semesters. We continued that success, with 91% of the students that participated in the pair^2 learning environment receiving a passing grade in the follow-on course (that was not taught by either of the instructors who taught the first course). These results support the claim that our approach improved retention without sacrificing student learning outcomes.

Reynolds recently noted that "bringing a spirit of play to work - and the feeling of exploration and discovery that it instills in the moment - improves learning and stimulates creative thinking" [23]. We believe that play for a child or an adult, as well as specifically for a computer science student includes two key factors. The first is exploring something that is relevant and interesting to the individual, and the second is doing this in a social environment. We have found a formula that incorporates both of these factors into our introductory CS course by using game development as our application area and utilizing pair^2 learning to create a truly collaborative learning environment. This formula has produced successful results, both in terms of student feedback and in terms of student retention in the CS program.

4. REFERENCES

[1] N. Anderson and T. Gegg-Harrison. Pair^2 learning = pair programming $\times$ pair teaching. In *WCCCE 2012*, pages 2–6, Vancouver, Canada, May 2012.

[2] T. Barnes, E. Powell, A. Chaffin, A. Godwin, and H. Richter. Game2Learn: Building CS1 learning games for retention. In *ITiCSE 2007*, pages 121–125, Dundee, Scotland, June 2007.

[3] J. D. Bayliss and S. Strout. Games as a "Flavor" of CS1. In *SIGCSE 2006*, pages 500–504, Houston, Texas, March 2006.

[4] J. P. Bean. Nine themes of college student retention. In A. Seidman, editor, *College Student Retention*. Praeger, 2005.

[5] H. Boudreaux, J. Etheridge, and T. Roden. Adding handheld game programming to a computer science curriculum. In *GDCSE 2008*, pages 16–20, Miami, Florida, March 2008.

[6] J. S. Brown, A. Collins, and P. Duguid. Situated cognition and the culture of learning. *Educational Researcher*, 18(1):32–41, 1989.

[7] S. Chaiklin. The zone of proximal development in Vygotsky's analysis of learning and instruction. In *Vygotsky's educational theory in cultural context*. Cambridge University Press, 2003.

[8] D. C. Cliburn and S. M. Miller. Games, stories, or something more traditional: The types of assignments college students prefer. In *SIGCSE 2008*, pages 138–142, Portland, Oregon, March 2008.

[9] F. W. Cline and J. Fay. *Parenting with Love and Logic: Teaching Children Responsibility*. Pinon, 1990.

[10] A. Collins, J. S. Brown, and S. E. Newman. Cognitive apprenticeship: Teaching the craft of reading, reading, and mathematics. In L. B. Resnick, editor, *Knowing, Learning, and Instruction: Essays in Honor of Robert Glaser*, pages 453–494. Lawrence Erlbaum, 1989.

[11] R. Donato. Collective scaffolding in second language learning. In *Vygotskian approaches to second language research*. Ablex, 1994.

[12] T. S. Gegg-Harrison. Constructing contracts: Making discrete mathematics relevant to beginning programmers. *ACM Journal of Educational Resources in Computing*, 5(2):3:1–3:28, 2005.

[13] P. M. Greenfield, B. Rogoff, and J. Lave. A theory of the teacher in the learning activities of everyday life. In *Everyday cofnition: Its development in social context*, pages 117–138. Harvard University Press, Cambridge, Massachusetts, 1984.

[14] G. D. Kuh, J. Schuh, E. Whitt, R. Andreas, J. Lyons, and C. Strange. *Involving Colleges: Successful Approaches to Fostering Student Learning and Personal Development Outside the Classroom*. Jossey-Bass, 2000.

[15] S. Kurkovsky. Engaging students through mobile game development. In *SIGCSE 2009*, pages 44–48, Chattanooga, Tennessee, March 2009.

[16] S. Leutenegger and J. Edgington. A games first approach to teaching introductory programming. In *SIGCSE 2007*, pages 115–118, Covington, Kentucky, March 2007.

[17] L. Meira and S. Lerman. The zone of proximal development as a symbolic space. *Social Science Research Papers*, 1991.

[18] B. B. Morrison and J. A. Preston. Engagement: Gaming throughout the curriculum. In *SIGCSE 2009*, pages 342–346, Chattanooga, Tennessee, March 2009.

[19] D. Moxley, A. Najor-Durack, and C. Dumbrigue. *Keeping Students in Higher Education: Successful Practices and Strategies for Retention*. Kogan Page Limited, 2001.

[20] J. Nino and F. A. Hosch. *Introduction to Programming and Object Oriented Design Using Java*. John Wiley and Sons, 3rd edition, 2008.

[21] D. Oblinger. Boomers, gen-xers, and milliennials: Understanding the new students. *Educause Review*, 38(4):37–47, 2003.

[22] R. Rajarvivarma. A games-based approach for teaching the introductory programming course. *SIGCSE Bulletin*, 37(4):98–102, 2005.

[23] G. Reynolds. The secret to great work is great play. *http://www.presentationzen.com/presentationzen/2010/03/we-were-born-to-play-play-is-how-we-learn-and-develop-our-minds-and-our-bodies-and-its-also-how-we-express-ourselves-play.html*, 3/26/2010.

[24] P. Richard-Amato. *Making it happen: Interaction in the second language classroom*. Longman, 1988.

[25] J. Roberts and R. Styron. Student satisfaction and persistence: Factors vital to student retention. *Research in Higher Education Journal*, 6(3):1–18, 2010.

[26] B. Rogoff. *Apprenticeship in thinking*. Oxford University Press, 1990.

[27] E. B. H. Sandseter and L. E. O. Kennair. Children's risky play from an evolutionary perspective: The anti-phobic effects of thrilling experiences. *Evolutionary Psychology*, 9(2):257–284, 2011.

[28] L. S. Vygotsky. *Mind in Society: The Development of Higher Psychological Processes*. Harvard University Press, Cambridge, Massachusetts, 1978.

[29] L. S. Vygotsky. Thinking and speech. In *The collected works of L. S. Vygotsky*, volume 1, pages 249–250. Plenum, 1987.

[30] L. S. Vygotsky. The problem of age. In *The collected works of L. S. Vygotsky*, volume 5, pages 187–205. Springer, 1998.

[31] S. A. Wallace, I. Russell, and A. Markov. Integrating games and machine learning in the undergraduate computer science classroom. In *GDCSE 2008*, pages 56–60, Miami, Florida, March 2008.

[32] L. Williams. Pair programming. In P. A. Laplante, editor, *Encyclopedia of Software Engineering*, volume II. Taylor and Francis Group, 2011.

[33] D. Xu, D. Blank, and D. Kumar. Games, robots, and robot games: Complementary contexts for introductory computing education. In *GDCSE 2008*, pages 66–70, Miami, Florida, March 2008.

The Simulation Creation Toolkit: An Initial Exploration Into Making Programming Accessible While Preserving Computational Thinking

Ashok Basawapatna
University of Colorado Boulder
Department of Computer Science
Boulder, CO 80303
(720) 838-5838, 001
basawapa@colorado.edu

Alexander Repenning
University of Colorado Boulder
Department of Computer Science
Boulder, CO 80303
(303) 492-1349, 001
ralex@cs.colorado.edu

Clayton Lewis
University of Colorado Boulder
Department of Computer Science
Boulder, CO 80303
(303) 492-6657, 001
clayton.lewis@colorado.edu

ABSTRACT

Computational thinking aims to outline fundamental skills from computer science that everyone should learn. These skills include problem formulation, logically organizing data, automating solutions through algorithmic thinking, and representing data through abstraction. One aim of the NSF is to integrate these and other computational thinking concepts into the classroom. This paper introduces a tool called the *Simulation Creation Toolkit* wherein users apply high-level agent interactions called *Computational Thinking Patterns* (CTPs) to create simulations. Programming at the Computational Thinking Pattern level allows users to directly create agent interactions in a simulation by employing generic icons acting out a scientific phenomenon they are trying to represent. The Simulation Creation Toolkit aims to preserve the computational thinking benefits of simulation creation while enabling higher-level implementation of agent behaviors. Initial study data collected from sixth grade students with no prior programming experience indicates that students can work the mechanics necessary to create simulations in the classroom environment using the Simulation Creation Toolkit.

Categories and Subject Descriptors

K.3.2 Computer and Information Science Education

General Terms

Algorithms, Design, Experimentation, Human Factors.

Keywords

University Programming Education, Middle School Computer Education, Scalable Game Design, Computational Thinking, Computational Thinking Patterns, Student Observation.

1. INTRODUCTION

Currently, a major emphasis of many educational end-user programming tools is to empower students with the ability to easily and very quickly program games [1,2,3]. There are multiple advantages to introducing students to programming through game design rather than more conventional techniques such as C++ and/or Java. For one thing, students tend to like and are engaged by games [4,5]. Often, these game programming tools are able to eliminate confusing and tedious syntax rules of conventional programming languages by having students program visually instead, for example, with drag and drop rules. This quickly introduces students to the underlying problem-solving logic of programming [6]. Finally, these tools allow students to create 2-D and even 3-D games rather quickly as opposed to having to learn sophisticated graphics packages that accompany traditional programming languages such as C++ and/or Java [6,7].

Two such end-user game programming tools that we currently employ is AgentSheets and its subsequent 3-D version AgentCubes. AgentSheets/AgentCubes is a rapid agent-based visual game and simulation prototyping environment [8]. In AgentSheets, middle school students can go from having no prior programming experience to programming their first graphical 2-D game within 5 hours [7]. As students gain expertise, the games they program can become more complex integrating higher-level concepts from both math and science [3].

End-user game programming tools, such as AgentSheets/AgentCubes, have been shown to increase student motivation in I.T. and computer science [4,5]. Though increased motivation is arguably a valuable result of any end-user programming tool, the question arises as to what exactly students are learning from this practice of game design? Many end-user programming tools claim that students learn "computational thinking" [9,10,12]. At present computational thinking defined (by the 2011 CSTA, ISTE, NSF standard on computational thinking) includes the following six items: problem formulation, logically organizing and analyzing data, representing data through abstractions such as models, automating solutions through algorithmic thinking, implementing effective solutions optimally, and transferring the solution to solve a wide variety of problems [11].

Given this definition, it is helpful to look at an example of what thinking computationally might look like in the domain of end-user programming. Len Scrogan, former Director of Technology for the Boulder Valley School District (BVSD) in Boulder, Colorado, asked a student an enlightening question as to the actual educational content of a given AgentSheets project. Mr. Scrogan admitted that he was confused as to the definition of

SIGCSE '13, March 6–9, 2013, Denver, Colorado, USA.

computational thinking, but he went up to a student designing 'Space Invaders' and asked:

> *"Now that you've made 'Space Invaders' can you create a science simulation?"* [10]

For our purposes in game design, the actual game creation gives students the skills necessary to program. Students are thinking computationally when they *transfer* these skills learned in game design to using the computer to help solve a real world problem. The above Len Scrogan quote uses the idea of creating a "science simulation" as an example of how the student's skills garnered through programming "Space Invaders" can be applied in a way that would be classified as computational thinking. This idea is underlined by the computational thinking definition above, which emphasizes problem solving, abstraction and transfer. Ideally, students would take a problem from the real world, represent this problem in the computer domain (in our case AgentSheets/AgentCubes), and do things like running simulation trials and varying parameters and in general, experiment on this created simulation to hopefully gain a better understanding of the real world concept being represented.

Even with this connection between creating simulations and computational thinking, and access to the aforementioned end-user programming tools, in-class units that involve modeling have not readily been adopted into classrooms nation wide. For example, a study by the U.S. Department of Education entitled "Teachers Use Of Educational Technology In U.S. Public Schools" combined statistics for computer, math and science classes. In this combined category, the study found that only a quarter of all computer science/math/science classes ever tried to expose their students to modeling exercises once, half of these classes never tried a modeling exercise at all, and a quarter of these classes tried it more than once [14]. An interview conducted with Marco Cornacine, a Life Science teacher at Millenial Middle School, Boulder, Colorado, shed some light on why this might be the case. When asked what he thought might be the biggest obstacle to integrating simulations into the classroom, Mr. Cornacine stated the following:

> *"Time to put together the resources, finding activities that are appropriate."*

In our experiences with AgentSheets, for example, often simulation creation exercises are taught after first teaching an introductory game creation exercise for a week. This enables students to transfer the skills they have learned from game design to creating simulations; however, given classroom time constraints, this adds a week of additional exercises. Furthermore, these exercises require that the teacher lesson plan by figuring out how to create a given simulation using an end-user programming tool that can sometimes be complex and time consuming to a teacher who has never programmed before. One wonders if there is a way to decouple the conceptualization and creation of the simulation, preserving the computational thinking benefits while programming at a higher level to save on classroom time.

One method we have found of abstracting the concepts learned in simulation creation and end-user game design is through what we call Computational Thinking Patterns (CTPs). A Computational Thinking Pattern describes interactions between objects that are common to a large set of applications including game design and computational science. CTPs are design patterns that students initially learn in game design and implementation, but then transfer to the creation of science simulations [7,10]. They are groups of behaviors (conditions/actions) given to one or more agents in games that are very similar to groups of behaviors one would use to create corresponding agent interactions in science simulations. In this way, CTPs can be thought of as the units of transfer between game design and science simulations.

Examples of Computational Thinking Patterns include things like the Generation Pattern, wherein one agent generates another agent; the Absorption Pattern, wherein one agent makes another agent disappear; and the Tracking Pattern, wherein one agent chases another agent. From this list, one can begin to see how Computational Thinking Patterns link interactions in games with interactions in simulations. For example, when programming Frogger, a student might use the Generate Pattern to have the tunnel create trucks; when creating a Predator/Prey simulation a student might use the Generate Pattern to simulate reproduction. Similarly, when programming Pacman a student might implement the Tracking Pattern to enable the Ghost Agents to chase Pacman; in the Predator/Prey simulation a student might use the Tracking Pattern to have a hungry Fox Agent chase after a Rabbit Agent.

An in depth list of Computational Thinking Patterns can be found in [7]; Computational Thinking Patterns are a work in progress with new patterns being discovered as a growing number of teachers expose students to increasingly diverse projects.

2. SIMULATION CREATION TOOLKIT

We have described Computational Thinking Patterns as the units of transfer between game programming and science simulations. Given the aforementioned shortcomings of end-user programming tools in integrating simulations into the classroom, one might wonder whether it would be useful to program at this Computational Thinking Pattern level itself.

For example, let us say that a student studied a given interaction in science class. At this point we give the student a palette consisting of animated icons acting out various Computational Thinking Patterns, and by combining these patterns, students could quickly create a simulation of the interaction they just learned and experiment on it. Students would program at the interaction level wherein conditions and actions would automatically be added subject to the pattern chosen by the student. This stands in contrast to the typical way someone programs behaviors using a tool like AgentSheets/AgentCubes wherein students add individual conditions and actions to multiple agents to realize these interactions. The following big picture question emerges: can we use the idea of Computational Thinking Patterns as an abstraction that lowers the programming barrier enabling students to quickly create science simulations. In other words, instead of students implementing these patterns, can students utilize these high-level patterns directly, as the elemental units of programming, in order to create simulations quickly and to better understand the concepts they are learning in the classroom? If this could indeed occur, such a tool wherein students programmed by exclusively using agent interactions as defined by Computational Thinking Patterns could be a major first step towards classroom integration of computer science and modeling concepts as well as increasing student understanding on a particular topic.

The Simulation Creation Toolkit is an initial attempt at the idea of using high-level Computational Thinking Patterns directly. Integrated into AgentCubes, the Simulation Creation Toolkit employs a palette of "interacticons", which are generic agents acting out various Computational Thinking Patterns that users can choose from. These interacticons are in part inspired by agent interactions described in "The Perception of Causality" by Albert Michotte and the study of phenomenological perception [13]. The following figure is three sequential interacticon frames of the Absorb Pattern.

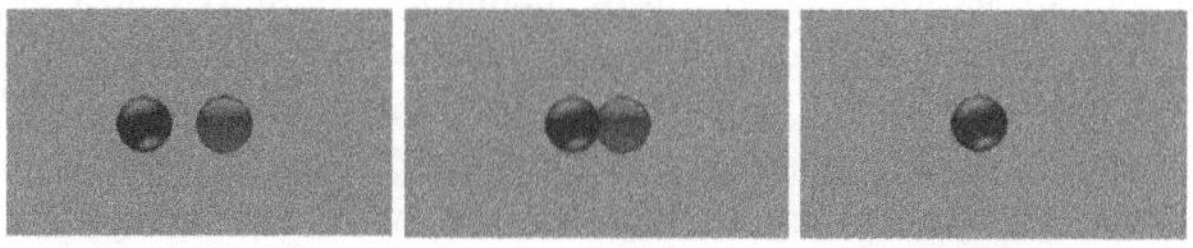

Figure 1: Three sequential frames of the absorb pattern. Left disk and right disk meet and right disk disappears

Figure 1 shows how interacticons describe Computational Thinking Patterns; namely by having the disk on the right disappear as the two disks come together, the user perceives that the disk on the left caused the disk on the right to disappear.

The Simulation Creation Toolkit relies on the ability of students to make analogies between generic interacticons and the real world scientific phenomenon attempting to be recreated. The student must be able to see that the left disk in Figure 1 is absorbing the right disk and realize that this is similar to the Predator/Prey simulation, for example, wherein the predator makes the prey disappear. Students must be able to abstract out the agents present in the interaction while preserving the interaction itself.

The following figure depicts the main screen of the Simulation Creation Toolkit called the Pattern Picker window.

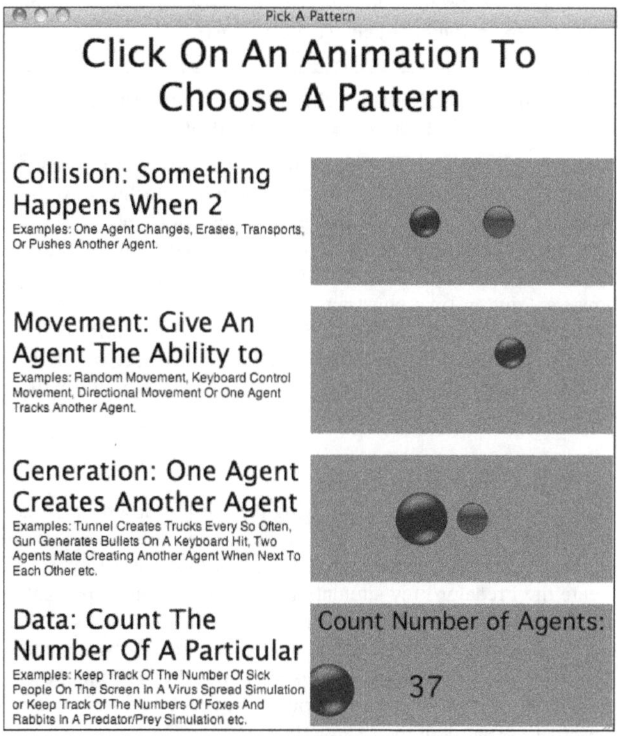

Figure 2:The Simulation Creation Toolkit Pattern Picker Window

Students can use the Pattern Picker window to select from 10 patterns provided by the Simulation Creation Toolkit to add to their simulation. The top selection includes "collision" patterns wherein a pattern happens when two agents meet. Under that is the "movement" patterns wherein an agent is given movement. Directly below "movement" is the Generate Pattern wherein one agent creates another agent. Finally, the bottom of the Pattern Picker window depicts the Data pattern which allows a user to keep track of the population data of a given agent. Table 1 outlines the 10 patterns with a brief description of each; the first four patterns are in the collision category of Figure 2, the second four patterns are in the movement category of Figure 2.

- **Change:** One agent changes another agent into a third agent.
- **Absorb:** One agent makes another agent disappear.
- **Transport:** One agent transports another agent.
- **Push:** One agent pushes another agent.
- **Random Movement:** An agent moves randomly
- **Tracking:** One agent tracks another agent.
- **Keyboard Movement:** An agent's movement is controlled by keyboard button presses.
- **Directional Movement:** An agent moves in a single direction at a certain speed.
- **Generate:** One agent creates another agent
- **Data:** Counts the number of agents in existence at a particular instance of a simulation run.

Table 1: Description of the 10 Patterns Users Can Implement Using The Simulation Creation Toolkit

After the pattern is selected, users are given numerous specification choices for the pattern. Let us say the user selects the Absorb Pattern in Figure 2 to have a Fox Agent make a Rabbit Agent disappear in a Predator/Prey simulation. At this point, there is still the question of when does the execution of this pattern occur. To help define the conditions associated with a pattern, the Simulation Creation Toolkit allows users to add specifications to their patterns. "Pattern specification" allows a user to define things such as the time frequency at which a pattern occurs at and the probability associated with the pattern, among many other possible choices. The choices of pattern specification are unique for each pattern; the following picture shows an example pattern specification for an Absorb Pattern in a Predator/Prey simulation.

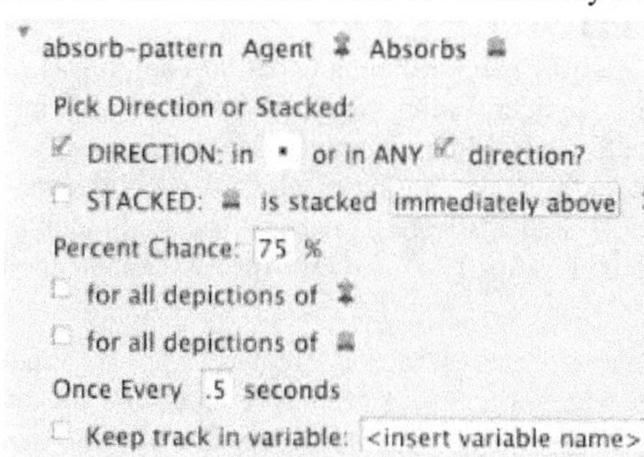

Figure 3: The pattern specification choices for the Absorb Pattern in the Simulation Creation Toolkit

In Figure 3, starting at the top, we see that the Fox Agent absorbs the Rabbit Agent. Next, we see that this absorption happens in any direction (as denoted by the direction checkbox and the "any direction" checkbox being checked). Under that we see that this absorption could also happen if one agent happens to be stacked on top of another agent; in the above example this choice is not selected. Next we see that there is a 75% chance that this pattern occurs. Under that, there are choices wherein the user can specify if just one or any depiction of an agent acts out this pattern (depictions are how an agent looks; one agent can have many depictions). Next the user can specify how often this pattern occurs using the Once Every textbox. If the user wants to keep track of every time a Fox Agent absorbs a Rabbit Agent the user can insert a variable name into the "Keep track in variable" textbox.

As the user makes their selections of patterns, agents to be in the patterns, and specifications for each pattern, the Simulation Creation Toolkit automatically adds the necessary low-level AgentCubes rules to each agent, thus implementing the pattern in real time. Furthermore, if a user makes a change to any part of the specification or deletes a pattern entirely, the Simulation Creation Toolkit will update the agent rules appropriately, again, in real time.

Combining these patterns with their specifications allows users to create simulations by breaking down a given science phenomenon they are trying to represent into constituent units corresponding to Computational Thinking Patterns. Some of the specifications of the patterns can be thought of as simulation parameters, that can easily be varied to run different experiments. For example, if a user implements the Generate Pattern to have one Fox Agent mate with another Fox Agent, the percent chance associated with that pattern can loosely be thought of as a reproduction rate for that particular simulation. By changing these specifications for specific patterns, the user can run multiple experiments with varying parameter values extremely quickly.

The patterns outlined in Table 1 can be used to create a variety of simulations across a wide range of topics found in many school's Guaranteed Viable Curriculums. For example, these patterns can be combined to make simulations pertaining to epidemiology, natural selection, military simulations, and photosynthesis among many others. The Simulation Creation Toolkit has the potential to enable users to create simulations in part by analogy and quickly run experiments. It remains to be seen whether this potential can be realized in a classroom setting; the following study is an initial exploration in testing whether students can create a simulation using the Simulation Creation Toolkit in the classroom.

3. METHODS

An initial study of the Simulation Creation Toolkit was carried out through the Boulder Valley School District at Millenial Middle School located in Boulder Colorado. Data for this study was taken from two sixth grade computer classes: 18 students from 5th period and 21 students from 6th period. The study took place over 3 days: Thursday April 26th, Friday April 27th, and Monday April 28th 2012.

The simulation the students created was a Predator/Prey simulation wherein a Fox Agent represented the predator and a Rabbit Agent represented the prey. Very few of these students had ever created a simulation, programmed a game or simulation of any kind, or knew what a Predator/Prey simulation was. This simulation was split up into 4 days based on teachers' suggestions; because of curriculum and time constraints, students only had 3 days to work on it.

The first day of each class started with an introduction to the Computational Thinking Patterns along with a role-playing exercise wherein students would be given the roles of either a Fox Agent, a Rabbit Agent, or a Grass Agent, and would act out the patterns in the simulation they were about to build. Then students would be handed a worksheet that would help guide them through the simulation building exercise using the Simulation Creation Toolkit. The unit was heavily scaffolded with the worksheets laying out step by step instructions on how to complete the simulation. The merits of such a strategy will be further developed in the discussion section. Subsequent days started with a 5-10 minute review and question and answer period followed by students resuming their simulation building activities. The simulation itself consists of 16 patterns. The following table outlines the simulation at a high level with corresponding pattern numbers that will enable pattern identification later in this paper.

- The Fox Agent and Rabbit Agent start out moving randomly (Pattern 1 and Pattern 2).
- The Fox and Rabbit Agent gets hungry with a given percent chance as they move (Pattern 3 and Pattern 4). A hungry Fox or Rabbit dies with a given percent chance every second it does not find food (Pattern 5 and Pattern 6) and decomposes into a Grass Agent (Pattern 7 and Pattern 8).
- A hungry Fox Agent tracks the Rabbit Agent (Pattern 9). A Hungry Rabbit Agent tracks the Grass Agent (Pattern 10). If a hungry Fox encounters a Rabbit, it eats it and is no longer hungry (Patterns 11,13). If a hungry Rabbit Agent encounters a grass Agent, it eats it and is no longer hungry (Patterns 12,14).
- If a Fox or Rabbit is next to another Fox or Rabbit Agent respectively, it will mate with a given percent chance creating a new Fox or Rabbit Agent. (Patterns 15,16)

Table 2: Description Of Patterns Included In The Predator/Prey Simulation

It should be noted that students were directed to implement the patterns in numerical order though, technically, the implementation order of patterns does not matter in the Simulation Creation Toolkit. As mentioned above, the full simulation outlined in Table 2 is meant to be completed in 4 days; however, due to time constraints students only had 3 days to get as far as they could. Day 3 of the worksheet ends with the implementation of Pattern 10. Though the worksheet was split up into individual days, students were allowed to and routinely worked ahead of schedule.

4. RESULTS

Figure 4 depicts two graphs showing the initial study results. Each graph in Figure 4 contains 16 axes; these axes each represent one of the 16 different patterns students had to program to correctly create the Predator/Prey simulation using the Simulation Creation Toolkit. The graph represents the percentage of students in each class that implemented a particular pattern correctly by the end of Monday's class (i.e. the last day of this unit). For example, by the end of Monday, 95.2% of students in Period 6 had implemented Pattern 1 correctly in their simulation. If every student in the class implemented every pattern correctly, the graph would be a circle.

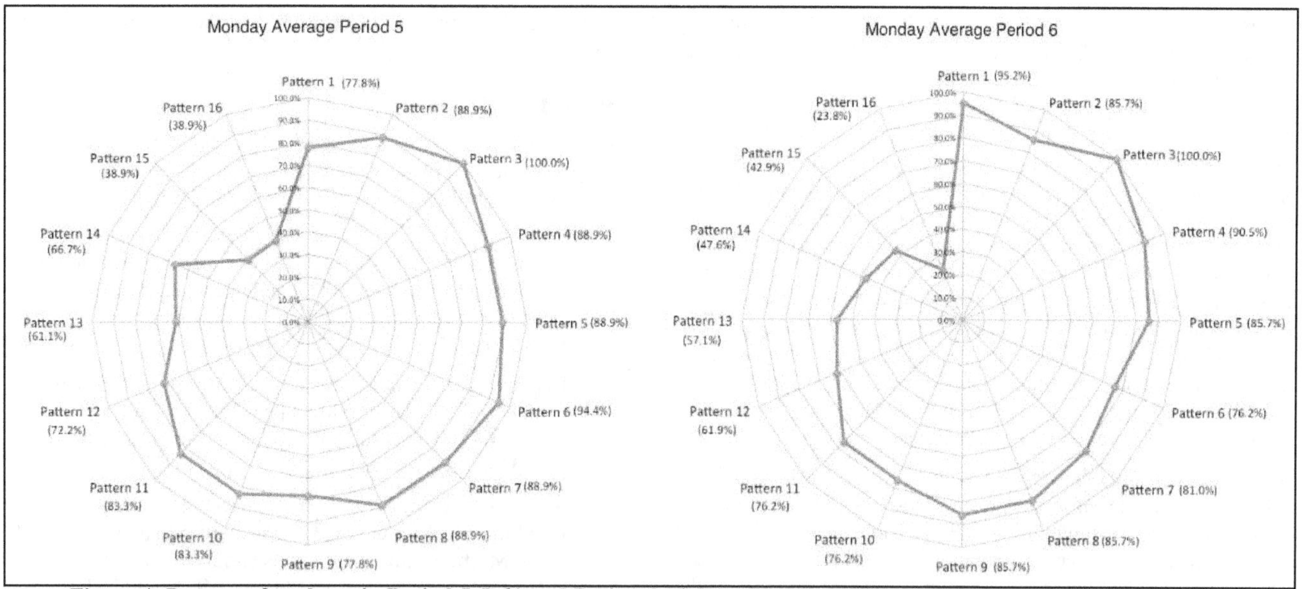

Figure 4: Percent of students in Period 5 (left) and Period 6 (right) who correctly implemented a given pattern in the Predator/Prey simulation by the end of day 3.

There are a few things to note about the results. Both graphs start out loosely resembling a circle, but drop off at the later patterns. This is to be expected as all 16 patterns represent 4 days of work, and as fewer students implement the later patterns, as they were only given 3 days, the graph should decline. However, from Pattern 1 to Pattern 10 (the last pattern of Day 3) the lowest percent correct for any pattern during period 5 was 77.8% and the lowest pattern for Period 6 was 76.2%. This shows that, for the most part, students were able to correctly create the patterns necessary for the first 3 days of the Predator/Prey simulation. The raw data shows that 94% of students in Period 5 and 90.4% of students in Period 6 attempted Pattern 10 by Day 3. The raw data further shows that 55.5% of the students in Period 5 and 42.8% of students in Period 6 had Patterns 1-10 programmed perfectly, meaning no mistakes on any of the Patterns including their corresponding specifications. Many students were able to get beyond Pattern 10 in 3 days as shown in Figure 4 by 66.7% of students implementing Pattern 14 correctly in Period 5 and 47.6% implementing Pattern 14 correctly in Period 6. In fact, the raw data shows that 38.8% in Period 5 got to the last simulation step, with 27.7% of the students completing all 16 patterns perfectly; in Period 6, 23.8% got to the last simulation step with 9.5% of the kids completing the whole simulation correct.

5. DISCUSSION

These results indicate that programming at the Computational Thinking Pattern level is an important avenue for investigation into simulation creation in the classroom. Most of these 6th grade students had never programmed before, let alone program a game or create a simulation. Furthermore, most had never been exposed to a Predator/Prey model. In past experiences using AgentSheets to teach the Predator/Prey simulation in a high school class, students started out by taking a week to create the game Frogger. After that, students took a week (5 class periods or 5 hours) to create a less complex Predator/Prey simulation than the one outlined in Table 2. It should be noted that these students were provided with a worksheet similar to the one given out in this exercise. In comparison, these 6th grade kids had a about a 20 minute introduction that included the idea of simulations, the Predator/Prey model, Computational Thinking Patterns, and finally the Simulation Creation Toolkit. Nevertheless, around 77% of students, in both periods, were on pace to finish the simulation in 4 days with almost 30% of the students in Period 5 and 10% of the students in Period 6 actually completing all 4 days of simulation correctly.

This speaks to the power of using patterns for simulation creation. Namely, students can concentrate on making high-level analogies with the real world phenomenon they want to represent without having to worry about lower-level AgentSheets/AgentCubes rules. For example, getting an agent to track another agent in AgentCubes involves having the agent being chased diffuse a scent across the level using a background agent, and the agent that is tracking follow that scent [3]. To accomplish this, a user has to specify 3 methods over 3 agents with one of the method containing 4 rules including 3 conditions for each rule. Furthermore, a user has to employ some fairly sophisticated math in order to get the scent value of the agent being chased to diffuse correctly across the level.

In contrast, using the Simulation Creation Toolkit, a user can have one agent track another agent with a few mouse clicks; namely the user just has to specify which agent does the tracking, which agent gets tracked and what agent(s) diffuse the scent. At this point, all the AgentCubes code is automatically added to the simulation, and the user never has to see or alter this code. Furthermore, if a user wants to make a change to a pattern, the user can simply alter the specifications box for the pattern depicted in Figure 3 and the code will be automatically updated without the user having to alter any of the individual AgentCubes rules. This makes simulation creation much quicker.

The compromise that is made in using the Simulation Creation Toolkit, is that students do not have to think through the if/then conditionality logic present in conventional AgentSheets/AgentCubes game and simulation creation activities. A valid argument can be made that this is a valuable experience for students, as being able to realize an agent interaction as a series of rules is, in itself, an important example of thinking computationally. The Simulation Creation Toolkit is not meant as a replacement for lower level if/then conditionality statement based programming. It could, however, provide classrooms that are short on time the ability to have students create simulations through abstraction of a real-world phenomenon without having to spend vast amounts of overhead time reviewing how students might create a given interaction. One could argue that often the problem solving steps that students go through are sometimes unrelated to the learning goals of the exercise. For example, in a Life Science class, if the aim was to allow students to better understand Predator/Prey interactions by creating and experimenting on a simulation, spending time implementing diffusion equations, though an interesting mathematical concept, does not help meet the curriculum standards relating to the Predator/Prey simulation in that Life Science class.

In this study, a worksheet was used to guide students through the act of creating the simulation using this tool. Ideally, students would use the Simulation Creation Toolkit throughout the semester in their science or computer class. Students could then use the first simulation creation activity to better understand the Simulation Creation Toolkit system, and then in later exercises, figure out how they might create a given simulation with little scaffolding. However, if in this study it was found that students were not able to successfully work the mechanics of this system with scaffolding present, there would be no need to try these later exercises. More research on a larger scale (i.e. over multiple units) must be done to see if this tool really is a sound strategy for integrating computational thinking concepts into the classroom. The above results provide initial hope that this could be the case. Based on this future research, more patterns and specifications should be added as well as improvements to the user interface.

6. CONCLUSION

The Simulation Creation Toolkit is a Computational Thinking Pattern based strategy towards simulation creation. The need for programming at the if/then conditionality statement level is obviated by the use of interacticons. Specifically, this tool allows users to create simulations by making an analogy between the real world interaction they want to represent and the specific Computational Thinking Pattern that would accomplish this. After pattern creation, users have the ability to further specify a pattern and these specifications often act as the simulation parameters.

By enabling students to create simulations, the Simulation Creation Toolkit can potentially facilitate computational thinking, as defined by [11]. The initial data for this tool is extremely promising. More studies have to be done to see to what extent this tool can be used to integrate computational thinking concepts into the classroom. So far, however, we see that students with minimal prior experience in programming and simulation creation can effectively use this tool to model real-world interactions.

7. ACKNOWLEDGMENTS

This material is covered by the University of Colorado IRB number 12-0141. This work is supported by the National Science Foundation under Grant Numbers 0833612, 0848962, 1138526. Any opinions, findings, and conclusions or recommendations expressed in this material are those of the authors and do not necessarily reflect the views of the National Science Foundation. A special thanks to teachers Marco Cornacchione and Mark Savignano for all their help. Thanks to Fred Gluck for invaluable feedback. Alexander Repenning is the founder of AgentSheets Inc.

8. REFERENCES

[1] Cooper, S., Dann, W., Pausch, R., Cooper, S., Dann, W., and Pausch, R., Teaching Objects-first In Introductory Computer Science, In Proc. SIGCSE 2003, Reno, Nevada, USA, 2003

[2] Peppler, K. & Kafai, Y. B., Collaboration, Computation, and Creativity: Media Arts Practices in Urban Youth Culture. In C. Hmelo- Silver & A. O'Donnell (Eds.), In Proc. Computer Supported Collaborative Learning, New Brunswick, NJ, USA, 2007

[3] Repenning, A., Excuse me, I need better AI! Employing Collaborative Diffusion to make Game AI Child's Play. In Proc. ACM SIGGRAPH Video Game Symposium, Boston, MA, USA, ACM Press, 2006.

[4] Sturtevant, N. R., Hoover, H. J., Schaeffer, J., Gouglas, S., Bowling, M. H., Southey, F., Bouchard, M., and Zabaneh, G. 2008. Multidisciplinary students and instructors: a second-year games course. In proc 39th SIGCSE Technical Symposium on Computer Science Education, Portland, OR, USA, 2008.

[5] Squire, K., Video games in education. International Journal of Intelligent Simulations and Gaming, (2) 1. 2003.

[6] Repenning, A. and A. Ioannidou 2005. What makes End-User Development Tick? 13 design guidelines. End-User Development. F. Patern&Mac247; and V. Wolf. Dordrecht, Kluwer

[7] Basawapatna A., Koh, K.H., Repenning, A. 2010. Using Scalable Game Design to Teach Computer Science From Middle School to Graduate School. In Proceedings of ITICSE '10 (Bilkent, Ankara, Turkey, June 26-30, 2010).

[8] Repenning, A., "AgentSheets®: an Interactive Simulation Environment with End-User Programmable Agents," Interaction 2000, Tokyo, Japan, 2000.

[9] Ruthmann, A., Heines, J. M., Greher, G. R., Laidler, P., and Saulters, C. 2010. Teaching computational thinking through musical live coding in scratch. In Proceedings of the 41st ACM Technical Symposium on Computer Science Education Milwaukee, Wisconsin, USA, March 10 - 13, 2010. SIGCSE '10.

[10] Repenning, A., Webb, D., and Ioannidou, A., "Scalable Game Design and the Development of a Checklist for Getting Computational Thinking into Public Schools", Proc. SIGCSE' 10, ACM Press, WI, USA, 2010.

[11] Barr, D., Harrison, J., and Conery, L. (2011) Computational Thinking: A Digital Age Skill For Everyone. ISTE Learning and Leading, 38(6), pp. 20-23. March/April 2011.

[12] Learning Computer Science From Scratch (2009). Retrieved March 27, 2011, NSF Press Release 09-235: http://www.nsf.gov/news/news_summ.jsp?cntn_id=116070.

[13] Michotte, A. The Perception of Causality. Metheun & CO LTD, London, England, 1963.

[14] Gray L., Thomas, N., Lewis, L., Tice, P. Teachers' Use of Educational Technology in U.S. Public Schools: 2009, First Look. US Department of Education Report, National Center for Education Statistics.

Middle School Students Using Alice: What Can We Learn from Logging Data?

Linda Werner
University of California
Santa Cruz, CA
linda@cs.ucsc.edu

Charlie McDowell
University of California
Santa Cruz, CA
charlie@cs.ucsc.edu

Jill Denner
Education, Training, Research Assoc.
Scotts Valley, CA
jilld@etr.org

ABSTRACT

There is growing interest in how we can use computer logging data to improve computational tools and pedagogies to engage children in complex thinking and self-expression, but our techniques lag far behind our theories. Only recently have learning scientists begun to measure, collect, analyze, and report how data informs the science of children's learning. In this paper, we describe our initial efforts towards developing tools to mine computer logging data for information on how to enhance learning opportunities. The data were collected as part of an NSF-funded project, and include logs from 320 middle school students using Alice to program computer games in semester-long courses. We describe some lessons learned and decisions made in the process of reconstructing high-level user actions in Alice from low-level Alice logs.

Categories and Subject Descriptors

K.3.1 [Computers and Education]: Computer Uses in Education – *Computer-managed instruction.* K.3.2 [Computers and Education]: Computer and Information Science Education – *Computer science education.*

Keywords

Educational data mining, Education, Middle school, Alice.

1. INTRODUCTION

Computer logging data has great potential for informing research and tool development in education due to the low-cost ability to track every action with today's computer systems. For many years, computer scientists have been using data analytics techniques with web usage, computer interaction, and game play logs in order to inform tool development and to predict student performance [4]. However, few studies have looked at what can be learned from this data in the middle school context. This paper describes the first steps in the process of using low-level logging data of middle school students using Alice, a 3D environment using drag-and-drop programming [8]. We describe the steps that were required and problems encountered in order to prepare the logging data to be used to describe how students approach two different tasks: programming games (an open-ended task) and a performance assessment (a closed-ended task).

SIGCSE'13, March 6–9, 2013, Denver, Colorado, USA.

Ultimately, we plan to use the logging data to answer a number of questions such as: Can logging data reveal the conditions under which students notice and use key features of an initial programming environment? Do students recognize problem patterns and try creative solutions or do they keep repeating the same ineffective strategies? Do students' strategies vary, depending on whether they are working on a closed-ended or open-ended task? Are student actions related to the sophistication of the games they produce? We hope to distinguish the development of routine expertise, where learners develop a core set of skills that they use with increasing efficiency, from adaptive expertise, which involves a balance between innovation and efficiency where learners develop meaningful knowledge so they can adapt their skills in response to new situations [1].

Before we can get very far into the process of using Alice logging data to understand students' computer programming and problem solving strategies, we need to understand the internal structure of the logs and how that maps to high-level actions of students using Alice. We also need to make a series of decisions that determine how the data will be parsed. This paper describes the problems we have encountered and discoveries we have made, starting with creating and using an Alice log parser, and then applying it to logs created during both open-ended and closed-ended tasks.

We created the parser to combine low-level individual log entries into high-level Alice actions (HLAAs). The description of this process is important for researchers and educators that want to use Alice or similar tools that generate logging data to understand how students learn to program and if and how students develop adaptive expertise. Additionally, this work is important for researchers and tool builders involved with the design of activity logging systems for other programming environments and software tools.

2. PREVIOUS WORK

There is a long-standing interest in novice programming, which forms the basis for our analysis of Alice logs. Publications in the 1980s described how children develop programming skills and ways of thinking [19][20]. Studies of higher education have used phenomenology to analyze interviews with students in an introductory Java programming course to reveal how they experience the act of learning to program [4]. In addition, researchers have studied the strategies used by expert programmers hoping to use this information to teach novices more effective programming strategies [17].

Educational data mining techniques have been used to build models of student behavior when using traditional intelligent tutoring systems. Baker [3] has successfully developed models transferable to different tasks for structured problem solving activities where there are designated correct responses. Using time-consuming (manual) identification of activity by domain experts, progress has been made with understanding and modeling students' exploratory use of interactive simulation systems where there is no clear identification of correct use [15]. More recent work [2] describes a data mining approach used to identify behavioral patterns that then require human labeling in order to model students' use of these unstructured learning environments. For example, researchers create a data point for each student consisting of the frequency of use of every tool action and the mean and standard deviation of the latency between actions representing reflection time. Additionally, researchers collect student pre- and post-test domain knowledge.

Logging data has incredible untapped potential for adding to our understanding of how children learn with technology, especially the class of unstructured learning environments called initial programming environments. The developers of these environments intend for the learners to "be interested to explore, and to represent their explorations" [9]. In one groundbreaking study [16]; researchers used machine-learning techniques to analyze approximately 200,000 logs of code snapshots from beginning university-level programming students using Karel the Robot, an initial programming environment. Their results are that the patterns discovered using machine-learning techniques were more predictive for students' performance on midterm exams than the grades they received on the submitted program solutions. One implication of this is that the process of programming was more predictive than the program produced. In addition, the researchers were able to show applicability of their methodology for use with Java code snapshot logs of beginning university-level programming students.

Our study focuses on Alice, a widely used initial programming environment [21], and one of few for which logs can be captured [12]. Kelleher built an Alice logging system and distinguished a log entry as representing one of three different categories of Alice activities: programming, scene layout, or program play. She found time-based usage patterns when doing open-ended tasks to be different for 12-year old girls using two different variants of Alice: Storytelling Alice or Generic Alice (without storytelling support) over a 4-hour period. Identification of these high-level actions is an informative first step in mining the Alice logs. However, despite the use of Alice in many K-12 and college classrooms around the world (there are over 23,500 members in the Alice online community forum), there is no existing system for capitalizing on these logs to understand novices and how they learn to program [7].

Our log data come from 320 middle school students who were enrolled in voluntary after-school or elective during-school technology courses called iGame. These students ranged in age from 10-14 years (mean=12) and they had, on average, 2.7 computers at home. Students were primarily white (46%) or Latino/a (37%). Sixty-three percent of the students were male. Out of the 134 students who said they spoke another language at home at least some of the time, 108 (81%) of these students named Spanish or Spanish and another language.

The research we describe here will contribute to the growing number of efforts to use educational data mining techniques, and especially learning analytics to describe how students interact with computers and the implications for learning. Eventually, this knowledge can be used to inform strategies for teaching and assessing the learning of novice programmers, as well as for improving programming environments. Specifically, it will help us understand how novice programmers develop adaptive expertise.

3. ANA2, AN ALICE PARSER

Based on Kelleher's description of her research [13], with a few exceptions, she places each individual log entry into one of four categories (programming, layout, play, or ignore) according to the value of the event field of the log entries. It is our desire to understand more about what the user is doing than to determine the amount of time spent doing programming, layout, or play, We want to be able to identify individual high-level user actions. It became clear that looking only at individual low-level log entries was insufficient for identifying high-level actions because most user actions result in sequences of log entries. We have found that combining sequences of one or more low-level log entries into High-Level Alice Actions (HLAAs) is necessary to create the 'primitive pieces' that mirror the user actions. These primitive pieces can then be organized into sequences that are instances of specific problem solving strategies. To this end, we built a parser, Ana2, based on an earlier attempt [18], to combine the log entries into HLAAs. In this section we discuss our approaches to answering a number of questions that arose during the process of building Ana2 and reasons for the choices we made.

3.1 How to combine log entries into HLAAs.

Our efforts to combine log entries into HLAAs were challenged by the lack of formal documentation for the Alice logging system. The source code is public, but it contains essentially no comments. We learned the format of the log entries from various methods [6]7,13,[18]] including the use of reverse-engineering techniques.

We learned that every log file is composed of records called entries; one or more entries are written for each HLAA. For example, inserting a mouse click event handler, generates ten low-level log entries. Each log entry has two required fields and a variable number of optional fields, each with field values. The required fields are time (in milliseconds) and event (with 12 possible values). The number and type of other fields in each log entry are dependent on the value of the event field. Most log entries have many fields and many of the values of the fields are dependent on objects, operations, and other pieces of the story narrative the student chooses to model with their Alice program.

The first version of the Alice log parser, Ana, relied entirely on the time gaps between log entries in order to combine the log entries into HLAAs. Ana used a total accumulated time threshold of 800 milliseconds (ms). This meant that an HLAA was composed of a log entry and all subsequent log entries, provided the total elapsed time was less than 800ms [18].

The threshold of 800ms was somewhat arbitrary and we found that sometimes multiple HLAAs could be found in a sequence of log entries with an elapsed time less than 800ms (e.g. multiple quick mouse clicks to adjust the position of an object would each be a single layout HLAA). Furthermore, we also discovered examples of single HLAAs that spanned more than 800ms (e.g. using Storytelling Alice and switching to a different scene with many objects). In our first attempt to refine this, we switched to using the time gap between two consecutive log entries, rather than the total elapsed time accumulated for the HLAA to decide when to start a new HLAA. If the time gap between two consecutive log entries exceeded a certain value, which we will call the 'maximum log entry gap' (MLEG), then a new HLAA was assumed to start with the log entry following that gap. This seemed to do a better job of separating low-level log entries into HLAAs corresponding to single user actions, but we were still unable to find an appropriate value for the MLEG (on the order of 200-500ms) that satisfactorily separated the sequences of entries into HLAAs.

Some HLAAs can be identified regardless of the time gaps between log entries. Unfortunately, it is not possible to unambiguously reconstruct all of the individual HLAAs from the logs. Our current version of the Alice log parser, Ana2, uses a combination MLEG with a grammar for the types of HLAAs we expect to see in the logs. For example, the sequence of log entries shown in Figure 1 has a 281ms gap between the timestamps for the 2nd and 3rd entries. This could be interpreted as two HLAAs, the recording of a sound (the first two entries) followed by the addition of a play sound method call (the last two entries), or as a single insertion of a play sound method call, selecting the "record new sound" option. The only way to decide between these two choices is based on the time gap between the entries having event field values of objectArrayInsert and insertResponse, which has been observed to be anything from 0 milliseconds to many seconds in the log files we've analyzed. If the time gap is many seconds, then this sequence is clearly two HLAAs; if the time gap is zero or just a few milliseconds, then clearly it is one HLAA. This means we are left making a judgment call about the size of the time gap, if it alone is used to separate two or more HLAAs. Fortunately, for some analyses, the choice between one or two HLAAs is irrelevant provided we categorize both HLAAs the same way (as programming HLAAs in this case). However, we can envision situations where it might matter. For example, we might decide that recording of sounds is more like scene layout and should be included in the layout category rather than the programming category. If it were seen as one HLAA, it would be a programming HLAA. If it were seen as two HLAAs, it would be a layout HLAA followed by a programming HLAA.

Time=1...277921,Event=insertChild,childtype=<...Sound>
Time=1...277**937**,Event=objectArrayInsert,...,<sounds>
Time=1...278**218**,Event=insertResponse,...<SoundResponse>
Time=1...278234,Event=objectArrayInsert

Figure 1: Example of an event sequence yielding one or two HLAAs depending upon the inter-log-entry gap which is 281ms between the 2nd and 3rd events in this sequence.

3.2 How sensitive are our initial key metrics to possible errors in our combining of log entries into HLAAs?

Any choice of MLEG is likely to result in either some high-level user actions being split into two HLAAs because of a large time gap, or two high-level user actions being combined into one HLAA because of a small time gap between the end of the first high-level user action and the start of the next. In this section we examine how sensitive our initial metrics are to our choice of MLEG and discuss our search for an MLEG that would affect the fewest number of HLAAs.

Using an MLEG of zero, there is roughly a uniform distribution of gap times preceding a layout HLAA in the range 300ms to 999ms. For programming HLAAs, the distribution of gap times in this same range is small enough to be of little or no consequence with less than 0.3% of the log entries separated by gaps in the range 200-1000ms. Therefore, the identification of programming HLAAs is relatively insensitive to the choice of an MLEG anywhere in this range.

Based on our manual inspection of the logs, using an MLEG greater than 300ms will result in combining HLAAs that were quite likely from two separate, but closely spaced, high-level user actions. Choosing an MLEG less than 300ms results in splitting many potential HLAAs with small inter-event gap times into two separate HLAAs. In all of the logs we processed moving from a 300ms MLEG to a 200ms MLEG resulted in an 1.4% increase in the number of HLAAs, however, we have not seen clear evidence of log entry sequences that should be split using these small gap times (below 300ms). The identification, via manual inspection, of HLAAs that are separated by approximately 300ms combined with the small increase in total HLAA count when moving below 300ms has led us to use a value of 300ms for the MLEG. Thus, we programmed the parser to split HLAAs when the inter-log-entry gap exceeded an MLEG of 300ms, unless it was overruled by a grammar rule that unambiguously separates or combines the two adjacent log entries (e.g. a stop event immediately followed by a save event which would always be separated).

A key metric reported by Kelleher [12] is the ratio of programming time to layout time. Kelleher used this metric to determine whether students spent most of their time doing layout, programming, or a balance of the two. Table 1 shows this metric, total programming time (computed as the sum of the total gap times prior to all programming HLAAs and the total elapsed times of those programming HLAAs) divided by total layout time (computed as the sum of the total gap times prior to all layout HLAAs and the total elapsed times of those layout HLAAs) and two additional key metrics: average gap time prior to a programming HLAA, and average gap time prior to a layout HLAA. As shown in Table 1, the results are relatively insensitive to an MLEG choice anywhere in the 100-400ms range. The ratio of total programming time to total time doing layout is unchanged when rounded to four significant digits. In addition, in the 200-400ms range, the average gap time prior to a programming HLAA varies by less than one-tenth of a second and the average gap time prior to a layout HLAA varies by less than one-half of a second. The larger change for the average gap time prior to a layout HLAA is expected because this is where we see many individual high-level user actions in close succession (minor adjustments to the position of a character) that are indistinguishable, based on our manual analysis, from compound layout actions triggered by a single high-level user action. When identification is ambiguous using our knowledge of Alice and its logging system, our use of an MLEG of approximately one-third second (i.e., 300ms) allows us to identify quick mouse clicks while doing scene layout as individual layout HLAAs (provided the user pauses for at least 300ms). Yet it correctly identifies as a single layout HLAA, many long sequences of log entries generated when students use the right mouse button to execute a scene layout action.

gap time->	100ms	200ms	300ms	400ms
programming time / layout time	1.627	1.627	1.627	1.627
average programming gap time (secs)	28.30	28.54	28.58	28.60
average layout gap time (secs)	10.43	10.56	10.84	10.96

Table 1: Key **metrics to test gap sensitivity.**

In a few specific situations, primarily related to the initial loading of a scene done for a program play HLAA or related to a scene layout HLAA when done using the right mouse button, we allow even larger inter-log-entry times, up to 5 seconds for log entries within a single HLAA. These gaps always precede a log entry with 'propertyChange' as the value of the event field. In the log files that we analyzed, consisting of over 800,000 log entries combined into over 200,000 HLAAs, we found only 96 instances where this long gap exception occurred.

3.3 How should the time between HLAAs be treated?

During the time interval between HLAAs, the student may think about or reflect on what was just done, what to do next, or some combination of both of these. We call this time "reflection time." When the two bordering HLAAs are both in the same category of either programming or scene layout, then it is reasonable to conclude that the time was spent reflecting about programming or scene layout, respectively. However, when the two bordering HLAAs are from different categories, was the student reflecting on what they just did, or was the student reflecting about what to do next? Of course, it is also possible in either situation that the time between HLAAs could be due to other actions, such as taking a break, or waiting for help from a teacher. When the HLAAs are from different categories, we associate the reflection time with the second HLAA; that is, viewing the time primarily as reflecting about what to do next. For example, the time between a programming HLAA until the start of the following scene layout HLAA is associated with the scene layout HLAA.

An exception to this reflection time allocation involves the 'save' HLAA. Typically students using Alice save their work for three different reasons: because they have completed a series of changes they don't want to lose, because a 'save' prompt appears, or because they are ready to quit their work with Alice. If a student does a save and then quits, we allocate the time leading up to the save as reflection time for the save. If a student does a save and then continues to do more work with Alice, then the time leading up to the one or more saves and the time following the save until the next non-save HLAA is allocated as reflection time for this following HLAA. The reasoning for this becomes clear when one considers the scenario of saving because a 'save' prompt appears. During this scenario, the student is thinking about the next action; is interrupted by the 'save' prompt; saves; then continues with thoughts about the next action. Clearly, all of this reflection should be allocated to thinking about the action following the save HLAA.

3.4 Does the identification of HLAAs distinguish between programming behavior in closed versus open-ended tasks?

As a first-check to see if our identification of HLAAs and the categories adopted from Kelleher are going to be useful for understanding behavior in initial programming environments, we compared our key metrics for two different activities. The first was an open-ended task where students programmed a computer game, either alone or with a partner. The second was a close-ended task of an assessment of computational thinking that we call the Fairy Assessment (FA) done by each student individually. The FA was built in the style of a computer game and students were asked by the dialog of the characters within the FA to solve three subtasks [22].

As shown in Table 2, the metrics are very different for students using Alice when doing the FA versus open-ended game programming. Since we expected students to do little, if any, layout when doing the FA, we are not surprised at the ratio of programming time to layout time for the FA and this finding serves as a validation of our process.

	FA	Games
Ratio of programming time/layout time	8.512	1.435
average programming think time (secs)	25.83	29.31
average layout time (secs)	12.86	11.13

Table 2: Comparing key metrics for FA vs. game programming.

Table 3 shows a summary of our findings for percentages of time spent in layout, programming, and program play, and compares them to the findings of Kelleher [12]. Kelleher's data are from a study of 88 middle school girls using either Generic Alice (GA in the table) or Storytelling Alice (SA). Because Kelleher's time calculation is based on timestamps between log entries; in order to make a comparison of Kelleher's results to ours, we combine the action times with the reflection times for these same HLAA categories. The fact that our values are similar to Kelleher's is an additional validation of our analysis process.

	Ana2	Kelleher GA	Kelleher SA
Programming	36.8%	34.0%	48.3%
Layout	22.7%	40.8%	22.3%
Program play	34.9%	25.1%	29.3%
Other	5.6%	0.1%	0.1%

Table 3: Distribution of time by category from our analysis and that of Kelleher [12].

4. DISCUSSION

This work has implications for tool developers implementing logging systems for programming environments and other software tools. Here we make recommendations for logging systems. They are:

1) Integrate the logging into the design of the software. Researchers looking at introductory programming trace logs from university students have found that the process of program creation is a better predictor of student test scores than the finished program [16]. Logs can give us information about the process of program creation but it is not always easy to identify HLAAs from sequences of low-level log entries. If the programming environment software is designed and built with high-level action logging, then an entry could be logged for each high-level action and each high-level action could have a corresponding log entry, or easily identifiable sequence of log entries (e.g. beginAction … endAction).

2) Include a 'start' log entry when the software opens. We don't know how much reflection time is present before the current first log entry in each file. Currently, the first HLAA in each file has a zero reflection time.

3) Similarly, include a special log entry when a new file/project is opened, or when a new project is created. These are critical boundaries that are obscured in the current Alice logging system.

4) It appears important to capture time-off-task. Certainly eye-tracking hardware can be used to determine if a student is physically present. Alternatively, if privacy and cost are concerns, another strategy that can be used to determine a student's presence is to fade out the display after a time of keyboard or mouse inactivity. Provide a mechanism to set the inactivity time prior to fade out and to disallow student modification of it. When the student makes a keystroke, a log entry can be made to record the

time from the fade out until the keystroke. This will not capture reflection time during which a student goes to another student or the teacher for help, however, it does correctly identify other time-off-task.

5) Assist in the design and development of an open data repository for logs from novice programming environments. Alice has a logging system that needs modification to make it more easily usable for the educational data mining community using the recommendations we give here. BlueJ has a logging system that has been used to study novice compilation behavior [10][11]. Other programming environments designed for novices such as Scratch, Agentsheets, Stagecast Creator, and Greenfoot would benefit from logging features. Alternatively, design the logging data to be consistent with the standards being developed by the PSLC DataShop group [14]. DataShop is an open data repository of logs from intelligent tutoring systems designed for the educational data mining community.

6) The interface to the Alice programming environment has an undo/redo function. This provides an undo mechanism to the Alice user so that any HLAA back to the start of an Alice session can be undone. Similarly, HLAAs can be redone if they have been undone. Unfortunately, the Alice logging system does not capture any redo/undo actions; we have no record of any redo or undo actions a student has done. Future logging systems should ensure that these important high-level user actions are captured in the log.

7) Consider the important questions to be asked from analysis of the logs before the design of the logging system is complete. The answers to these questions should give us a starting place. For us, we want to determine how novices use the Alice software. We want to determine what constitutes a 'problem solving strategy' and if novices use different problem solving strategies. Researchers have used terms like tinkering and flailing. To see flailing in logs, the use of undo and redo needs to be captured.

5. CONCLUSIONS

The study described in this paper adds to the body of literature in learning analytics in two ways:

1) We started the important work of analyzing the logs of young students using initial programming environments, specifically Alice, for the purposes of learning how they use these programming environments when working on open and closed-ended tasks. Eventually, this knowledge can be used to inform strategies for teaching and assessing the learning of novice programmers as well as for improving programming environments.

2) We identified problems and decision-making steps for the analysis of Alice logs so that researchers and tool developers can improve the logging features of other initial programming environments and software tools to facilitate learning analytics.

We have built a parser, Ana2, and used it to identify HLAAs from the logs. The report of our mean time values reaffirms the times reported by Kelleher [12] and prepares us to go further with our plans to use unsupervised and supervised classification techniques similar to those described by Amershi and Conti [2], to address questions such as the following:

1) Can Alice logs be used to distinguish between programming strategies (e.g. linear development based on a plan vs. central algorithm followed by initializations) used by novices when programming games?

2) Can Alice logs be used to distinguish between problem solving strategies (e.g. flailing vs. tinkering) used by novices when working on the FA assessment?

3) Can Alice logs be used to distinguish between programming strategies used by students pair programming compared to strategies used by students working solo when programming games?

4) Can Alice logs be used to determine if there are differences in the findings for the closed versus open-ended tasks? If so, what do these differences mean?

We now have the data we need (logging information) in the form we need (High-Level Alice Actions) to begin to look for patterns and programming strategies that will help us answer the questions we posed in the Introduction, such as "Do students recognize problem patterns and try creative solutions or do they keep repeating the same ineffective strategies?"

6. ACKNOWLEDGMENTS

Thanks go to Shannon Campe and Eloy Ortiz, whose vital support was necessary to run the classes and collect logging data. This research is partially funded by a grant from NSF 0909733 "The Development of Computational Thinking among Middle School Students Creating Computer Games." Any opinions, findings, conclusions or recommendations expressed in this material are those of the authors and do not necessarily reflect the views of the National Science Foundation.

7. REFERENCES

[1] Alexander, P. 2003. The development of expertise: The journey from acclimation to proficiency. *Educational Researcher*, 32, 10-14.

[2] Amershi, S., and Conati, C. 2009. Combining unsupervised and supervised classification to build user models for exploratory learning environments. *The Journal of Educational Data Mining*, 1(1), 18-71.

[3] Baker, R.S.J.d. 2007. Modeling and understanding students' off-task behavior in intelligent tutoring systems, *Proceedings of ACM CHI 2007: Computer-Human Interaction*, 1059-1068.

[4] Baker, R., & Yacef, K. (2009). The state of educational data mining in 2009: A review and future visions. *Journal of Educational Data Mining, 1*(1), 3-17.

[5] Bruce, C., Buckingham, L., Hynd, J., McMahon, C., Roggenkamp, M., and Stoodley, I. 2004. Ways of experiencing the act of learning to program: A phenomenographic study of introductory programming students at university. *Journal of Information Technology Education*, 3, 143-160.

[6] Conway, M.J. 1997. Alice: Easy-to-learn 3D scripting for novices. University of Virginia, Ph.D. Dissertation.

[7] Cooper, S. 2010. Personal conversation. January 24, 2010.

[8] Dann, W., Cooper, S., and Ericson, B. 2009. *Exploring Wonderland: Java Programming Using Alice and Media Computation.* Prentice Hall.

[9] Fincher, S., and Utting, I. 2010. Machines for thinking. *ACM Transactions on Computing Education*, 10(4).

[10] Jadud, M.C. 2005. A 1st look at novice compilation behavior. *Computer Science Education*, 15(1), 25-40.

[11] Jadud, M.C., and Henriksen, P. 2009. Flexible, reusable tools for studying novice programmers. *ICER'09*, August 10-11, 2009, Berkeley, CA. USA.

[12] Kelleher, C. 2006. Motivating programming: Using storytelling to make computer programming attractive to more middle school girls. Carnegie Mellon University Ph.D. Dissertation, September 2006.

[13] Kelleher, C. 2008. Emails July 14, 2008.

[14] Koedinger, K.R., Baker, R.S.J.d., Cunningham, K., Skogsholm, A., Leber, B., Stamper, J. 2010. A data repository for the EDM community: The PSLC DataShop.

[15] Merten, C., and Conati, C. 2006. Eye-tracking to model and adapt to user meta-cognition in intelligent learning environments. In *Proceedings of the 11th International Conference on Intelligent User Interfaces (IUI '06)* ACM, New York, NY, USA, 39-46.

[16] Piech, C., Cooper, S., Sahami, M., Koller, D., and Blikstein, P. 2012. Modeling how students learn to program. In *Proceedings of the 43rd ACM Technical Symposium on Computer Science Education (SIGCSE).* ACM, New York, NY, USA.

[17] Robins, A., Rountree, J., and Rountree, N. 2003. Learning and teaching programming: A review and discussion *Computer Science Education*, 13(2), 137-172.

[18] Smith, B. 2010. Effect of pair programming on middle schoolers using Storytelling Alice. *13th Annual UCSC Undergraduate Research Symposium.*

[19] Soloway, E., Ehrlich, K., Bonar, J., and Greenspan, J. 1983. What do novices know about programming? In B. Shneiderman & A. Badre (Eds.) *Directions in Human-Computer Interactions,* 27-54. Norwood NJ: Ablex.

[20] Soloway, E., and Spohrer, J.C. (Eds.) 1989. *Studying the Novice Programmer.* Hillsdale N.J.: Lawrence Erlbaum.

[21] Utting, I., Cooper, S., Kolling, M., Maloney, J., and Resnick, M. 2010. Alice, Greenfoot, and Scratch – A discussion. *ACM Transactions on Computing Education*, 10(4), 1-11.

[22] Werner, L., Denner, J., Campe, S., Kawamoto, D.C. 2012. The Fairy Performance Assessment: Measuring computational thinking in middle school. In *Proceedings of the 43rd ACM Technical Symposium on Computer Science Education (SIGCSE)*, ACM, New York, NY, USA.

Bug Catcher: A System for Software Testing Competitions

Renée Bryce
Computer Science and Engineering
University of North Texas
Denton, TX 76208
Renee.Bryce@unt.edu

Quentin Mayo, Aaron Andrews,
Daniel Bokser, Michael Burton,
Chelynn Day, Jessica Gonzalez,
Tara Noble
Computer Science
Utah State University (REU Site Program)
Logan, UT 84341
USU.CS.REU@gmail.com

ABSTRACT

Bug Catcher is a web-based system for running software testing competitions. While programming competitions are a way to engage students, they require students to have coding experience. On the other hand, software testing competitions may reach high school students that do not have access to a programming course. In this paper, we present the Bug Catcher system and the results from four sessions of a competition that include a total of 94 high school students. Bug Catcher provides students with requirements, buggy code, and input fields to enter test cases. We observed that most students began entering test cases based on requirements, but then many took an interest in the code as time went on. Our results show that 90% of students would recommend this activity in the future and 72% of students report that the activity increased their interest in Computer Science. Students also provided feedback on the system from the perspective of students without background in Computer Science, allowing us to create and modify features for future use.

Categories and Subject Descriptors

K.3 [COMPUTERS AND EDUCATION]: Computer and Information Science Education—*Computer science education*

Keywords

Computer Science outreach, software testing, software testing competition

1. INTRODUCTION

Competitions are a way to engage students. Many different types of competitions exist. Example competitions include the ACM International Collegiate Programming Contest [1], ACM Student Research Competition [2], National Collegiate Cyber Defense Competition [4] , Facebook Hacker Cup [6] , First Robotics competitions [7], Google Code Jam [8], Google Summer of Code [9], Annual Berkeley Programming Competition [10], SCORE [3], International Olympiad in Informatics [11], and the Microsoft Imagine Cup [12].

To our knowledge, our Bug Catcher system is the first specifically for Software Testing Competitions. We anticipate that this system can be used for students without programming experience, but also tailored to experienced students and programmers by modifying the problem sets. In this paper, we focus on the use of Bug Catcher for high school students that may not have programming experience. We attempt to engage them through the competition so that their interest in Computer Science increases.

2. BACKGROUND

Prior to the creation of Bug Catcher, we conducted a mock software testing competition by modifying the intended use of the "Bug Hunt" software developed by Elbaum et al. [5]. Bug Hunt is an educational tool that was not developed for software testing competitions, but rather as a tool to teach students about software testing topics, including black box testing, white box testing, code coverage, and automated unit testing. In addition to the educational material, Bug Hunt allows students to apply their new knowledge in a fun environment. Bug Hunt displays problems and allows students to create test cases by entering input and expected output. As students submit test cases, the system records the number of bugs found. For the mock competition, Bug Hunt was used with the following modifications: (1) there is a required quiz at the beginning of Bug Hunt - we provided the answers so that students could skip the quiz (particularly for those without programming or software testing experience who were unable to answer the questions), (2) students skipped the tutorials, (3) students did not use the module on JUnit, (4) each team was only allowed to log onto one machine using their team leader's account, and (5) since the system was created to track the total bugs found, not the speed at which bugs are found, a team of volunteers did their best to record the approximate times at which students found the bugs.

For the mock competition, we invited high school, undergraduate, and graduate students to participate. It was

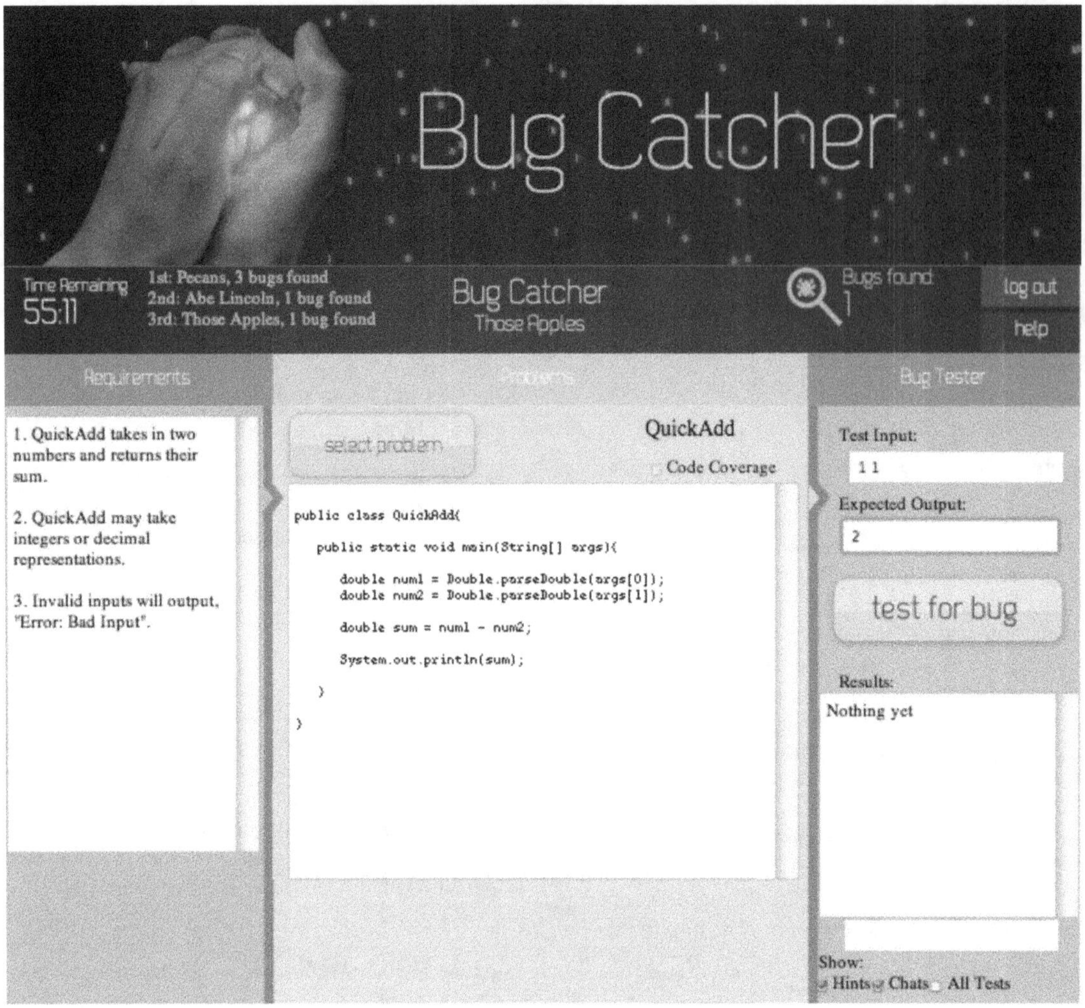

Figure 1: Bug Catcher: Main screen of the student competition

held on a Saturday and a total of 59 students competed. The event gave us firsthand experience running a software testing competition and provided feedback to consider when creating Bug Catcher. The follow-up survey was optionally completed by 55 of the participants. In this survey, the most common comments were on the limitations of Bug Hunt for competitions. Students indicated that they wanted the quiz, tutorials, and unused modules to be removed. They also wanted easy navigation between problem sets and real time views of their scores in comparison to the other teams. On the administrative side, volunteers requested easier methods for enrollment, including account creation for both students and teams. They also want the system to automatically compute the rates at which bugs are found and to sort the teams by rankings.

Though students provided constructive criticism, which we address in Bug Catcher, all 55 students reported that they would recommend the event to future students, 43 students communicated an increased interest in Computer Science, and 44 students said the event had increased their interest in Software Testing. In the comments section, many students wrote that they enjoyed the competition and wanted us to hold another event.

Many of the high school students, as well as their supervising high school teacher, commented that this software testing competition was more accessible for students who are new to programming than programming competitions. They felt that students need a lot of programming experience in order to compete in a programming competition, but students without any programming experience could still compete in a software testing competition.

3. BUG CATCHER

Bug Catcher is available at (*http://renee.cse.unt.edu*). Figure 1 shows a student competing. The header displays the timer, the top three teams, the current team's name, and the total number of bugs that the team has found. The leftmost side shows a requirements, which we also refer to as the problem description. The middle shows the code with options to change the problem and enable code coverage highlighting. The right side has input boxes for the input and expected output. On the right side, where students

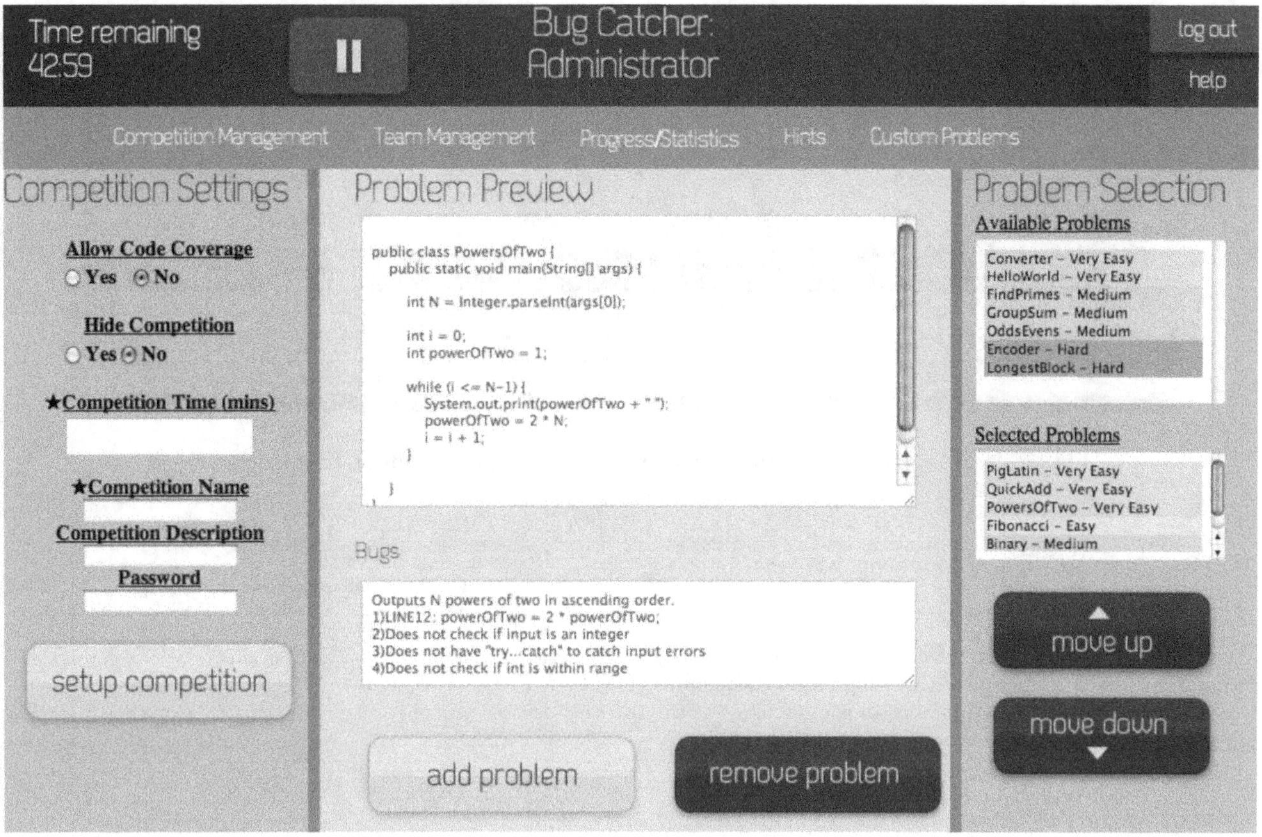

Figure 2: Bug Catcher: Administrator screen to set up a competition

enter test cases, they can hover over the test input and expected output boxes to see an example input and output for the problem. The lower right hand corner has a results box that displays important information such as administrator hints and feedback from test cases that they already entered. We observed that many students relied only on the problem statement (requirements), but some took an interest in the code as time went on. Only a few teams used the code coverage option to highlight executed lines of code.

Figure 2 shows the administrator view for setting up a competition. They select from a list of problems and add the desired problems to the competition. Each problem is ranked by difficulty so that they can plan accordingly for their participant group. The administrator may view the code and list of associated bugs before including them. The administrator also sets a time limit, competition name, competition description, whether the competition is visible to participants yet, and whether to allow code coverage. The password for a competition is optional and facilitates running multiple simultaneous competitions.

Figure 2 shows the administrator view during a competition. The administrator is able to view the scores and rankings for each team in real time. At the top, a timer counts down with the option to pause and resume the competition.

Figure 4 shows the screen for the administrator to push hints to the student screens. We have prewritten hints for the problem sets in the system, but the administrator may also create their own custom hint.

While not shown here, the system also allows the administrator to upload new problem sets, including the code, bugs, and optional hints. We have a similar implementation to that of BugHunt [5]. For each test case, we then run the oracle and each of the buggy versions of code, compare the output, and identify bugs based on mismatches between the expected outputs. We require the administrator to upload a correct version of the code (i.e., the oracle) and then a file for each bug that contains compilable code with the respective bug. We require the use of one file per bug in order to minimize the threat of one bug possibly masking another bug. While our current version of Bug Catcher supports Java code, we believe that it will be easy to extend the system to allow other languages in the future.

4. EXPERIMENT

4.1 Research Questions

We examine four research questions:

- **RQ1:** How many bugs does each team find?
- **RQ2:** Do the students recommend this event for future students?
- **RQ3:** Do the students report an increased interest in Computer Science?

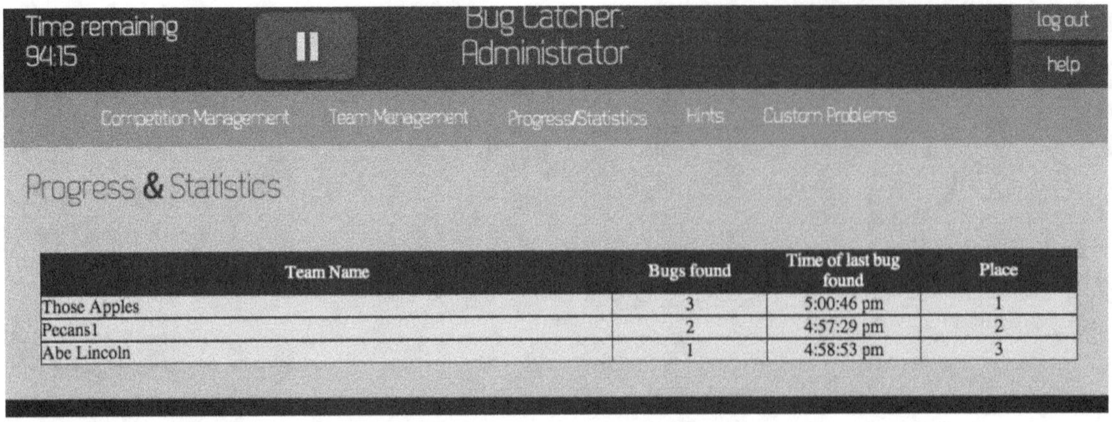

Figure 3: Bug Catcher: Administrator screen to view student team progress

- **RQ4:** What are suggestions for improving the system?

4.2 Experimental Set Up

We conducted four sessions of a Software Testing Competition over a two day period with 94 high school students that visited campus. The students formed teams of 2 to 3 students. Each competition was 80 minutes long. The following is an example schedule:

- **8:00 - 8:20**: Pre-surveys,instructions for the competition, and team registrations
- **8:20 - 9:05**: Competition
- **9:05 - 9:20**: Post-surveys and prize distribution

The competitions each had 6 to 8 problems that contained a total of 12 to 16 bugs. Each problem was written in Java. Problems range in difficulty and covered a variety of bugs. We used our judgement when classifying the level of difficulty of bugs and peer reviewed them with each other as we created them. Example bugs include simple mutations, for-loops that are off-by-one, division by zero, and not accounting for inputs of different types or sizes. For instance, Figure 5 shows our simplest program that adds two numbers, but with a mutation to subtract instead of add. This bug was found by every student team. This was a good problem because students that relied on the problem statement to develop ideas for tests were able to use their problem solving skills to figure out that the code was subtracting instead of adding and then they could point to the minus sign in the code and start to figure out how the code worked.

To simulate real world testing, the students were not told how many bugs were in each problem. This is a feature of Bug Hunt [5] that we adopt. Therefore, part of the competition is to strategically move between problems.

4.3 Results

RQ1: How many bugs does each team find?
Table 1 shows the number of teams, problems, bugs, and percentage of possible bugs that each team found in the four different sections. All of the teams found some of the easy bugs while the most advanced team found as many as

```
public class QuickAdd{
  public static void main(String[]args){
    double num1 = Double.parseDouble(args[0]);
    double num2 = Double.parseDouble(args[1]);
    double sum = num1 - num2;
    System.out.println(sum);
  }
}
```

Figure 5: Bug Catcher: Sample "easy" problem

94% of the bugs in their competition. The lowest ranked team in each of the four competitions found between 2 to 5 bugs. That is 17% to 38% of the possible bugs in the different sections. The highest ranked team in each of the four competitions found between 8 to 16 bugs. That is 67% to 94% of the possible bugs in the different sections. On average, teams in the four sections found 53% to 68% of the possible bugs. The median was close to the average and fell between 53% to 77% for the different sections. We interpret these results positively that most students were able to find over half of the bugs and none of the teams were under-challenged as no team found all of the possible bugs. On the other hand, we'll discuss an observation shortly that the teams that found as few as 2 to 5 bugs during the 40 minutes may have felt frustration and it may be beneficial to insert a larger number of "easy" bugs into the programs to increase their interest and to motivate them to keep trying. Indeed, we observed student excitement when they accomplished finding new bugs.

RQ2. Do the students recommend this event for future students?
In our post-survey, 90% of students said that they would recommend this event for future students. While this is encouraging, we'll discuss points for improvement shortly.

RQ3. Do the students report an increased interest in Computer Science?
Our post-survey results show that the activity increased interest in Computer Science for 73% of the students. This is lower than the number of students that said that they would recommend the event to future students, so we see room for improvement in exciting students about Computer Science.

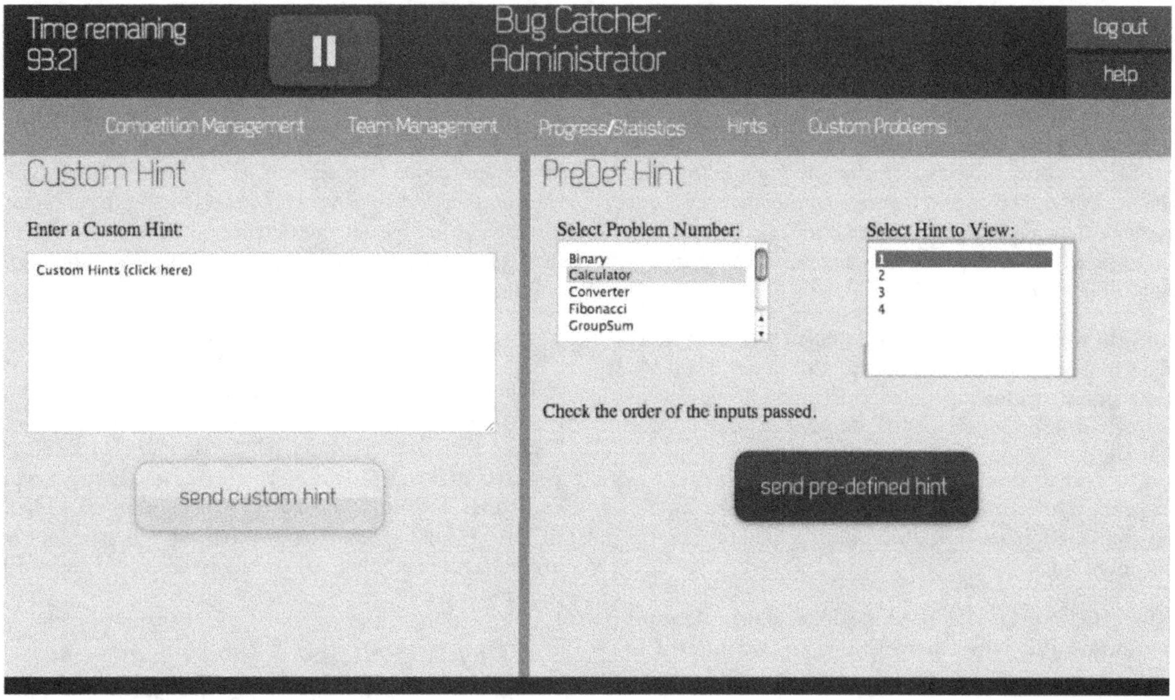

Figure 4: Bug Catcher: Administrator screen to push hints

	Competition 1	Competition 2	Competition 3	Competition 4	Overall
No. of teams	9	12	7	8	36
Total no. of problems in this session	6	6	8	6	n/a
Total no. of bugs in the problems	16	13	17	12	n/a
Average % of bugs found per team	56	68	54	53	58
Median % of bugs found per team	56	77	53	58	61
Low % of bugs found per team	46	38	18	17	17
High % of bugs found per team	92	92	94	67	94

Table 1: Number of teams and the average, median, low, and high percentage of bugs found

We address some ideas for this shortly in our discussion of suggestions to improve the system.

RQ4. What are suggestions for improving the system?
Our post-survey collected comments on how to improve the event in the future. Some of these comments are encouraging as we see ways to possibly better engage students.

- **Practice problems:** We did not provide a practice round before the competition. Students would like to try the system on their own before the competition begins.
- **Provide information on the number of bugs in each problem:** Some students do not like our design choice that we do not tell them how many bugs are in each problem.
- **Talk more about Computer Science careers:** We spent approximately 5 minutes telling students about career paths in Computer Science, but some students would like us to spend more time on this and provide more time to ask questions before the competition.
- **Teach coding:** Some students wanted us to give a lesson on programming.

We will address two of these suggestions in our ongoing work. First, we created a new system called, "Bug Catcher Lite" which is available at (*http://maman.cs.usu.edu/Lite*). This program allows students to log on at any time and practice. They do not compete against other teams, but they have the opportunity to practice with sample problems so that they can familiarize themselves with the system and competitions.

We also plan to dedicate a longer amount of time to talk more about Computer Science and careers. We will add this discussion at the end of the competitions instead of at the beginning because we felt that students had more interest in Computer Science *after* they finished the competition.

We do not plan to provide information on the number of bugs in each problem because we feel that this is an important design decision for our competition and better mimics the real world.

Finally, we found it exciting that students wanted to know more about coding *after* the competition. We observed that many students initially ignored the code on their screens and entered test cases based on the requirements. However, as time went on, some students showed more interest in the code because they were motivated to do what they could to find more bugs. After the competition, some students complained that we should have taught them to code before the competition. We view this as a positive comment because it indicates that they want to learn more about programming!

We also asked our volunteers for suggestions to improve the system. These include:

- **Include more bugs:** Include problem sets with more bugs, including many that are at the "easy" level because many students became frustrated if they went more than approximately 10 minutes without finding new bugs.
- **Increase the time:** Increase the amount of time for the competition so that students have more time to find more bugs
- **Offer the competition to college students and professionals:** Offer competitions to undergraduate students, graduate students, and professionals by using more complex problem sets and bugs

We are currently addressing the comments from volunteers. First, it is straightforward to increase the number of "easy" bugs and the amount of time available during the competition. However, we are looking into more complex problem sets for more advanced students and professionals. Our future work explores competitions for these groups.

5. CONCLUSIONS AND FUTURE WORK

To our knowledge, Bug Catcher is the first system designed specifically for Software Testing Competitions. It is a web-based system that can be administered to anyone through a web browser. Surveys conducted during a prototype competition, prior to the development of Bug Catcher, revealed that students had a strong interest in Software Testing competitions and provided us with feedback to create a web application to administer competitions. We then created the Bug Catcher system with this feedback in mind. Using Bug Catcher, we administered four competitions to 94 high school students. The results showed that 67 high school students, or 73%, report an increased interest in Computer Science. Further, 90% recommend this competition for a future event.

Constructive comments include suggestions that we provide a training mode. We have created "Bug Catcher Lite" to address this concern. Students also reported that they wanted to learn more about programming after the event and that they wish that we would have spent more time telling them about career paths in Computer Science. We view these comments as positive indicators that their interest in Computer Science increased and we plan to look into opportunities to address these comments in our future work. Our volunteers suggested that we include more bugs, particularly "easy" bugs since students feel excitement when they find bugs and it may increase the engagement of the lower ranked teams. They also suggested increasing the amount of time for the competition. Our ongoing work seeks to not only address all of these issues, but also to better understand how to fine tune future competitions. We plan to examine the parameters of the problem sets, types and frequencies of bugs that we use, the amount of time that we allocate for competitions, the sizes of the teams, and how to tailor the competition to high school students with different backgrounds. Finally, our ongoing and future work will develop more complex problem sets and bugs that are geared toward college students and professionals.

6. ACKNOWLEDGEMENTS

Thank you to Sebastian Elbaum for providing us with access to Bug Hunt. Thank you to support from National Science Foundation grants #1139840 and #1156487. Thank you to Google for providing the prizes for these competitions and to Utah State University for their support. Thank you to Dr. Daniel Bryce for co-advising the students on this project and providing valuable feedback that helped to improve this paper.

7. REFERENCES

[1] ACM. ACM International Collegiate Programming Contest. `http://icpc.baylor.edu`, accessed on August 1, 2012.

[2] ACM. ACM Student Research Competition. `http://src.acm.org`, accessed on August 1, 2012.

[3] ACM ICSE. SCORE Student Competition. `http://2013.icse-conferences.org/content/scoreCFP`, accessed on August 1, 2012.

[4] CCDC. National Collegiate Cyber Defense Competition. `http://www.nationalccdc.org`, accessed on August 1, 2012.

[5] S. G. Elbaum, S. Person, J. Dokulil, and M. Jorde. Bug hunt: Making early software testing lessons engaging and affordable. In *Intl. Conf. on Software Engineering (ICSE)*, pages 688–697. ACM, May 2007.

[6] Facebook. Facebook Hacker Cup. `http://www.facebook.com/hackercup`, accessed on August 1, 2012.

[7] FIRST. First Robotics Competitions. `http://www.usfirst.org/`, accessed on August 1, 2012.

[8] Google. Google Code Jam. `http://code.google.com/codejam`, accessed on August 1, 2012.

[9] Google. Google Summer of Code. `http://code.google.com/soc`, accessed on August 1, 2012.

[10] Hilfinger. Annual Berkeley Programming Contest. `http://www.cs.berkeley.edu/~hilfingr/programming-contest/`, accessed on August 1, 2012.

[11] IOI. International Olympiad in Informatics. `http://ioinformatics.org/index.shtml`, accessed on August 1, 2012.

[12] Microsoft. Imagine Cup. `http://www.imaginecup.com`, accessed on August 1, 2012.

Analyzing PHP Frameworks for Use in a Project-Based Software Engineering Course

Lisa Lancor & Samyukta Katha
Southern Connecticut State University
501 Crescent Street
New Haven, CT 06515 USA
203.392.5890
lancorl1@southernct.edu, kathas1@southernct.edu

ABSTRACT

Given the popularity of PHP frameworks used in developing web-based applications, a comparative study is conducted to determine which framework is best suited for incorporation into the curriculum of an undergraduate software engineering course that uses project-based learning. The top six PHP frameworks (Zend, Yii, CakePHP, CodeIgniter, PRADO, and Symphony) were initially considered and then narrowed down to two (CakePHP and CodeIgniter) based on their alignment with common functionality in previous class projects, framework complexity for those new to frameworks (learning curve), and developer friendliness (availability of documentation and online resources). An in-depth comparative study is conducted by developing a functionally-equivalent web application using each of the two frameworks as well as plain PHP (no framework). This work was motivated by the difficulties that were encountered in an evolving, content-rich software engineering course and discusses the educational changes that were made to align student learning with sound software engineering principles and current software development practices used in the computing industry.

Categories and Subject Descriptors

D.2.3 [**Software Engineering**]: Coding Tools and Techniques – *object-oriented programming*

General Terms

Design, Experimentation, Languages.

Keywords

Software design and development; project-based learning; PHP frameworks; software engineering.

1. INTRODUCTION

In the last 10+ years, there has been a pedagogical shift in undergraduate software engineering classes away from learning by lecture on concepts related to the software development life cycle (SDLC) towards requiring students to *experience* the SDLC as they develop an actual application for a real client [1] [2]. It has been argued that this project-based learning pedagogy can better prepare students for software development positions beyond graduation as they are put in a position to learn how to gather and document client requirements, design and implement a solution (often collaboratively for those courses that require teamwork), and finally deliver an application that meets the client's needs. All of this is done within a limited, semester-based timeframe thereby emphasizing additional software engineering concepts such as planning, project management, and software estimation.

Adopting industry-based software tools and development technologies can further align student experiences in the classroom with workplace practices. PHP-based web frameworks are examples of a reusable software platform that has become prevalent for developing robust web applications. Incorporating PHP frameworks into the curriculum can help to emphasize key software engineering principles such as software architecture, reusability and unit testing. But, which PHP framework can be best incorporated into the curriculum of a project-based undergraduate software engineering course? This work performs a comparative study of the development of a small-scale web application (similar to previous student projects) using two popular PHP frameworks (CodeIgniter and CakePHP) as well as an implementation of the same application using plain PHP (without a framework). Both quantitative and qualitative analyses were conducted on the three development approaches. The quantitative analysis compares the web application frameworks in terms of performance, security and development effort (measured by lines of code). The qualitative analysis compares the web application frameworks in terms of ease of installation, developer friendliness, and web application extensibility.

2. BACKGROUND

2.1 The Course

CSC330: Software Design and Development is a course that is required by all computer science students and is typically taken in the last two years of the major. CSC330 follows a typical one-semester software engineering curriculum that focuses on the entire software engineering process. Students are broken into teams of 4-5 students and remain on the same team throughout the semester to develop a real project for an on-campus client. Prior to the start of the semester, a "Request for Projects" is sent out to the entire campus community and after careful analysis, the professor chooses suitable projects for the class to develop. A sampling of completed projects which have benefitted the SCSU community include an on-campus employment website for the Career Services Department, a grant tracking application for the Department of Sponsored Programs and Research, an online competency exam for the Psychology Department and an alumni phone-a-thon application for the Office of Institutional Advancement.

Almost all projects have been developed as a web application using PHP with MySQL. While not a formal prerequisite course, most students have taken our database course prior to taking this course. There are however, no prerequisite courses that teach PHP; students are expected to learn the language on their own.

From a curricular perspective, CSC330 is normally taken one year prior to our capstone experience course (CSC400). Students are expected to incorporate the concepts from this software engineering course into their final individual capstone project in CSC400.

2.2 The Problem

This course has been taught as a project-based course for more than 10 years. During this period, alumni and our Technical Advisory Committee, composed of local IT leaders, have provided significant feedback that has led to a number of curricular components that have been incorporated into the course. At this point however, the course has clearly reached its saturation point. As more material has been added to the course, students are becoming overwhelmed and as a result the final projects are suffering leaving some clients with unusable products.

A detailed review of student experiences in the course reveals that learning a new language in a short period of time, working collaboratively in a team for an entire semester, completing the numerous written assignments associated with the different software phases, in addition to building a software solution for a real client from scratch, is daunting for most, if not all, students. Most troubling however, is that students were experiencing a severe disconnect between the software engineering concepts covered in the course and the development of the client's project. Students admitted that they chose to "take the grade hit on software design, software architecture and security" because they were under pressure to deliver some level of working code to their client. When asked, "if your team had more time to develop the project or had a smaller project to work on, would you have focused more on design, architecture and security?" The overwhelming responses were either "maybe" or "probably not." This obviously was contradictory to the learning goals of the course. Clearly something had to be done.

2.3 Revamping the Course

Attempting to remedy the problems identified in the course has led to a 4-phased approach. The first phase required a systemic look at the overall CS curriculum and the identification of areas in which content from the course could be either completely removed or at least introduced in other courses required in the major. Ideally, we would have liked to extend the course to a two-semester sequence separating the software engineering principles from the client project however, the major had already reached its maximum credit load. By removing project management concepts from the course and requiring students to take a project management course offered in the School of Business, we were able to make room in the course. This project management course requirement did not add additional credits to the major since it was formerly listed as an option in a group of other business course electives. Additionally, testing concepts are now emphasized in all CS prerequisite courses starting as early as our CS1 course thereby freeing up several course sessions that were dedicated to covering general testing concepts.

The second phase of our approach occurred at the course level. Within this phase, we wanted to focus on, not only those areas that overwhelmed students (learning a new language independently, team collaboration, and the documentation requirements), but also on the areas that are critical to the course (software design and development is, in fact, the name of the course).

Three new tools have been added to the course to address the student concerns related to teamwork and the time spent on documentation. For documentation, both Visual Paradigm for UML, Standard Edition along with Visual Paradigm's Agilian, Standard Edition (both free for academic institutions) is currently used in the course. Students can now do detailed UML diagrams (Use-Cases, Class Diagrams and Sequence Diagrams) and then use the Report Generation tool (available in the Standard Edition) to generate formalized reports of their software in HTML, PDF or Word with the touch of a button. This saves a considerable amount of time previously spent on documentation and allows for more time and effort to be spent on software design and development. With respect to team collaboration, BaseCamp [3] has been successfully used in the course to enhance overall collaboration. In addition, a GitHub [4] educational account (free) was recently acquired so that teams now have their own private development repository. The inclusion of GitHub into the course attempts to streamline the development bottleneck that was previously caused by the lack of a revision control system while at the same time, introduces students to a common tool used in industry. The use of all of these tools helps to alleviate the difficulties that students have had with respect to working collaboratively.

Requiring students to independently learn a new language has created some serious issues in the course. Despite the fact that particular resources are recommended for learning PHP, students end up using a variety of other learning resources – some good and some bad. For example, many web-based tutorials and PHP books do not emphasize object-oriented design or an MVC architecture - two critical components that are emphasized throughout the course. As a result, the implementations of the final projects do not follow an object-oriented design and have an ad-hoc architecture at best. Additionally, while software reuse is talked about frequently in the course, few students embrace the concept in their final projects. Students typically attempt to manually develop their own PHP code for common web application features such as form validation, database connectivity, authentication, and session control. It is here that significant security weaknesses are often detected. With the increasing number of security breaches discovered in web applications based on poor programming techniques today, it is critical that our students develop sound programming practices that lead to robust software applications and not just working deliverables.

In an attempt to remedy this problem, the newly revised course will now spend time covering PHP with an emphasis on OO design and web development using a framework and its built-in libraries to handle common web-based features (e.g. authentication, session management). The first offering of the newly modified course, which will include an emphasis on PHP and frameworks, is expected in the Spring of 2013. We are hopeful that the incorporation of frameworks into the course will help to emphasize sound software design architecture (MVC) and code reusability while at the same time yield more robust applications that will better meet the needs of our on-campus clients.

The fact that many PHP frameworks exist leads us to the third phase of our project which tries to determine which PHP-based framework would be most appropriate for our project-based software design and development course. In this phase, the top 6

PHP-based frameworks were reviewed and the two frameworks that seemed most appropriate for the course were chosen for comparison. These two frameworks were then compared and contrasted during the development process of a web application that contains typical features found in student projects. The following sections of this paper describe this phase in detail. The fourth and final phase, yet to be completed, is an assessment of the revamped course that uses the "winning" PHP framework along with the other software development tools previously described in an attempt to determine if the course goals are being met.

3. PHP FRAMEWORKS

3.1 Background

Web application frameworks are collections of libraries aimed at promoting high code reusability that can lead to faster development of web applications. Web application frameworks contain code for common functionalities like database access, session management and security. They help to reduce the development and testing overhead of web applications. They also support folder organization and structure, thereby promoting easier code maintainability.

The Model–View–Controller (MVC) architectural pattern forms the basis for many of the existing web application frameworks. The MVC pattern allows for a well-defined separation of user interface, business logic and data model components of a web application. In addition, the MVC based design also defines the interactions between these components. Since the responsibilities of each component are well defined, it leads to better code modularization.

The features of web application frameworks and the MVC architectural pattern are in perfect alignment with the goals of the course. We are hopeful that the time spent teaching these topics will not only result in the development of more robust applications for our on-campus clients but will also provide students with very marketable skills after graduation.

3.2 Choosing a PHP Framework

Web application frameworks are available for most web programming languages including PHP, ASP.NET, C++, Perl, Python, Java and Ruby. PHP is a widely used, general-purpose scripting language that is especially suited for Web development [5]. It offers several advantages for quick development of dynamic web applications and promotes easy integration with various popular frameworks across multiple platforms. It is open source and also freely available. Because of PHP's popularity, there are many PHP based frameworks that are currently available. Each framework has its specific advantages and disadvantages. Based on the Framework Usage Statistics [6], PHP frameworks are clearly the most popular web application frameworks in use today. In fact, the PHP framework distribution currently captures almost 40% of the top million sites on the Internet as shown in Figure 1.

After reviewing three years of the final projects submitted by students, we identified a common list of web application functions/features that would need to be supported by the PHP-based framework chosen for the course. These include: form handling, form validation, session management, authentication and authorization, database interactivity (supporting CRUD: create, read, update and delete), CAPTCHA, and easy interaction with third party API's (e.g. Google Maps). These functional requirements are in line with the list of common functions that should exist in the domain of web frameworks [8].

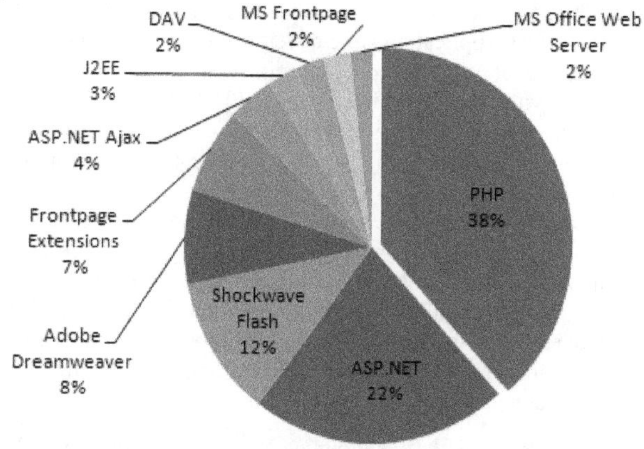

Figure 1.Framework Distribution in Top Million Sites [6].

In selecting the candidate frameworks, we also considered support for the MVC architecture, popularity among the web development community, job marketability for those with particular framework skills, clearly written support documentation, as well as the steepness of the learning curve. At the time of this writing, the top six PHP-based frameworks [7] (listed in order of popularity) were the Zend Framework, the Yii Framework, CodeIgniter, CakePHP, Symfony, and PHP Rapid Application Development Object-oriented (PRADO) and are shown in Figure 2. All of these frameworks support the MVC architecture.

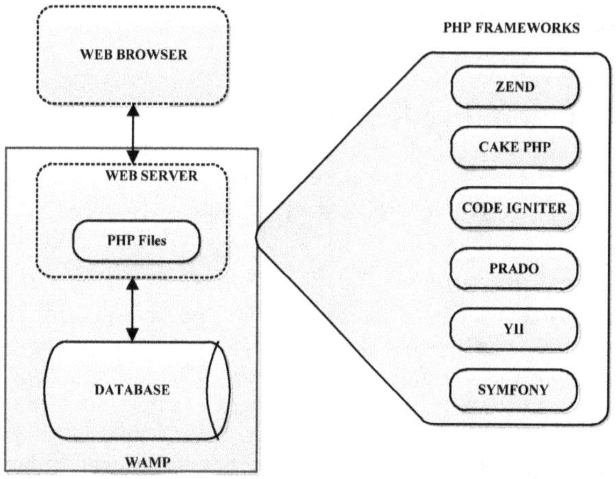

Figure 2. PHP-based frameworks [7]

We then narrowed down the top six frameworks to only two so we could perform a full comparative analysis. While Zend [9] and Yii [10] showed high promise, especially with their increasing support in the web development community and job marketability, the complexity of these frameworks and their high learning curve, led us to exclude them in this comparative study. Because we wanted students to obtain marketable framework development skills for outside employment, we looked at the top IT Job Search sites (dice.com and monster.com) and ranked the number of job postings for each of the remaining four frameworks. At the time of this writing, Symfony and PRADO fell to the bottom of the ranked job listings. Thus, the selected frameworks that were compared in this study are CodeIgniter 2.1.0 by Ellis Lab [11], Inc. and CakePHP 2.1 by Cake Software Foundation, Inc. [12].

3.3 The Comparative Study

To conduct the study, three versions of the same (functionally-equivalent) web application were developed by a graduate student who was adept at PHP programming but had no previous experience with web-based frameworks (PHP or otherwise). The applications were all developed using Eclipse PDT (version 3.0.2) with Eclipse Indigo [13] as the integrated development environment (IDE). This IDE provides intelligent code completion by listing all the possible related methods that allows developers to code faster and helps students to learn more about the language's options. Additionally, this IDE provides features like modifying, compiling, deploying and debugging in the PHP perspective. It also highlights and colors the basic PHP, JavaScript and HTML syntax variables which can lead to faster application development.

The first version of the web application was developed in PHP 5.3.10 from scratch without a framework and did not use any reusable code. There was also no MVC architecture involved in this version. The second and third versions of the application were developed using CakePHP 2.1 and CodeIgniter 2.1.0 both of which incorporate the MVC architecture and support reusable code. All three versions of the code were developed and run on a local WAMP server.

After development of all three implementations, a quantitative and a qualitative analysis was conducted. The quantitative analysis looked at measurements of development/coding effort, performance and security. The qualitative analysis was performed based on the ease of the installation, developer friendliness (availability of documentation and online resources), and the extensibility for adding new features within the frameworks.

4. RESULTS

4.1 Quantitative Results

The quantitative analysis that was conducted across the three implementations in this comparative study focused on coding effort (based on the number of lines of code), performance and security.

4.1.1 Coding effort

The comparative study of coding effort involved a static analysis conducted on the number of lines of code (LOC) written to develop each version of the web application. The number of lines of code is often used to predict the amount of effort required to develop an application. Additionally, it helps estimate programming productivity and maintainability for the application. The number of lines of code for each of the three versions was analyzed using the program Count Lines of Code (CLOC) [14]. CLOC is a program that counts the comment lines, blank lines and the physical lines of source code. The LOC comparison considers only the actual code that was written by the developer of the web application. For comparison purposes, the lines of code for the framework libraries are also reported to show the amount of code included in the framework.

PHP frameworks aim at achieving high code reusability and this is clearly indicated in the results. In the plain PHP implementation, the entire functionality is implemented by manually writing all the application code. PHP frameworks reuse some of the functionality that is built into the framework. The results in Table 1 show that CakePHP and CodeIgniter included libraries and helper classes that were reused in this application. Additionally, because accessing the underlying databases is done automatically through model mapping in CakePHP, CakePHP developers write considerable less code than CodeIgniter developers. This can be seen in the PHP lines of code for CakePHP (1408 LOCs with 16 files) versus CodeIgniter (2321 LOCs with 36 files).

Table 1. Comparative analysis of Lines Of Code for all 3 implementations

	PHP	CSS	# of PHP files	# of CSS files
Plain PHP	3002	650	42	13
CodeIgniter	2321	621	36	13
CakePHP	1408	680	16	13
CI with framework	26714	990	183	14
Cake with framework	139595	1373	655	19

The results clearly indicate that when using CakePHP, the required functionality for student projects requires comparatively fewer lines of code. Fewer lines of code can lead to faster development, easier maintainability (less code to maintain) and comparatively fewer chances of software faults.

4.1.2 Performance

Performance of the three implementations was measured using a PHP extension called XDebug [15]. XDebug provides debugging information such as stack traces, function traces and memory allocation, as well as profiling capabilities that can report on the time consumed for performing tasks in a PHP script. Because XDebug profiler output files are not humanly readable, they had to be passed through WinCacheGrind [16]. WinCacheGrind is an open source Windows tool used to parse XDebug profiler output files and display them in a human readable format.

The performance results are shown in Table 2. As can be seen, there is a significant amount of performance overhead when using frameworks. For each functional component of the web application, the CodeIgniter and CakePHP implementations take significantly longer to complete. For example, the login and logout functions take 96ms in plain PHP whereas it takes more than 23 times that (2291ms) in CodeIgniter and 16 times that (1159ms) in CakePHP. This overhead is related to the fact that PHP frameworks need to load their built-in libraries prior to executing the required functionality of the application. Hence, for student projects, plain PHP provides better performance than PHP frameworks.

Table 2. Comparative analysis of performance by time (ms) and Lines of Code (LOC) for all 3 implementations

Functionality	Plain PHP		CodeIgniter		Cake PHP	
	Time	LOC	Time	LOC	Time	LOC
Login/Logout	96	121	2291	192	1559	83
Session Mgmt	91	132	739	118	1309	102
Database	143	83	762	89	1492	52
Form Handling	487	209	1338	385	2262	191
From Validation	321	292	966	406	2411	310

4.1.3 Security

With respect to our security analysis, we used an all-purpose security tool as well as a specific SQL injection tool since all of the student projects have an SQL database on the backend. Thus, the security of the web applications across all of the implementations was tested using Nessus [17], one of the top vulnerability scanners used in penetration testing, and sqlmap [18], an open source penetration testing tool that automates the process of detecting and exploiting SQL injection flaws and taking over of back-end database servers.

On our initial security analysis, Nessus was able to fingerprint the underlying database server for all three implementations by analyzing the error messages that were returned from various Nessus probes. Additionally, as shown in Figure 3, Nessus was able to identify several vulnerabilities in the version of PHP that was installed. After upgrading to PHP 5.4.1 these vulnerabilities were cleared in all three implementations.

Figure 3. Nessus report showing vulnerabilities

4.1.3.1 SQL Injection

When Nessus was pointed at the plain PHP (no framework) implementation, an error from the underlying database was reported suggesting that the web application might be vulnerable to a SQL injection attack. This error was identified only with the plain PHP implementation. The same was not observed when using CakePHP or CodeIgniter as they provide built-in filtering as a security feature. We then pointed our sqlmap tool at all three applications using URL parameters as well as form parameters. Below are the results for each implementation:

Plain PHP: The SQL injection attack was successful. Sqlmap was able to extract the information about the databases, tables and columns in the underlying database server. In order to fix this critical vulnerability, query binding was used.

CodeIgniter: Although Nessus did not flag the CodeIgniter implementation as being potentially vulnerable to a SQL injection attack, a SQL injection attack by sqlmap was successful. Sqlmap was able to extract the information about the databases, tables and columns in the underlying database server. As was the case in the plain PHP implementation, query binding was used to fix this critical vulnerability.

CakePHP: All SQL injection attacks attempted on the CakePHP implementation were unsuccessful. Further analysis discovered that CakePHP provides a built-in security component (`SecurityComponent`) to thwart SQL injection attacks. Additionally, this component automatically provides restriction on which HTTP methods the application accepts, cross site request forgery (CSRF) protection, form tampering protection and limits on cross controller communication. CakePHP has an additional component (`AuthComponent`) to handle identifying, authenticating and authorizing users which is also appears to be resilient to SQL injection attacks.

4.1.3.2 Cross site scripting

Nessus also has the capability to check if a web application is vulnerable to potential cross-site scripting (XSS) attacks. On the plain PHP version, Nessus was able to inject innocuous strings into passed parameters and read them back in the HTTP response. The ability to do this means that a site is potentially vulnerable to XSS attacks. This can be remedied by neutralizing invalid characters in the input URL parameters. When the same Nessus attack was used against the CakePHP and CodeIgniter versions, it failed. This is because CakePHP and CodeIgniter provide built-in security features like the Security component in CakePHP and the filtering capability for cross site scripting which can be enabled in CodeIgniter's `config.php` file.

4.1.3.3 Security summary

Based on our security findings, it appears that CakePHP is more secure than the implementations in plain PHP and CodeIgniter. CakePHP provides built-in security components that can prevent many common security attacks. While CodeIgniter provides similar security features (CSRF protection and cross site scripting filtering), our results show that CodeIgniter, with its default configuration, failed to handle common SQL injection attacks. If a framework other than CakePHP is chosen for the course, query binding needs to be discussed to alleviate the possibility of SQL injection attacks.

4.2 Qualitative Results

While CakePHP appeared to be the framework of choice with respect to development effort, security and performance, it loses favor in the qualitative analysis that was performed on the ease of installation, developer friendliness (based on the availability of documentation and online resources) and ease of extensibility for adding new features. These results were carefully reviewed to determine the best framework for a course that is typically enrolled with framework newbies.

In an attempt to remove subjectivity from our analysis, we used the document analysis qualitative research method [19] [20]. Our data collection was focused on http://php.net for plain PHP, http://codeigniter.com/forums/ for CodeIgniter and http://www.cakephpforum.net for CakePHP. Posts in the online forums regarding each of the qualitative measures were collected, analyzed and categorized into High, Medium and Low. Our assumption with respect to categorization was that the more posts that were found related to a particular qualitative measure, then the higher the ranking. For example, with respect to extensibility, there were 83 posts related to extensibility in the plain PHP forums, 35 posts in the CodeIgniter forums and 42 posts in the CakePHP forums. In this example, plain PHP would be given a High ranking indicating a high level of extensibility relative to CodeIgniter (Medium) and CakePHP (Low). Table 3 shows a summary of all of the qualitative measures and their results across all three implementations.

Table 3. Summary of qualitative analysis results

Quality Measure	Plain PHP	CodeIgniter	Cake PHP
Ease of installation	High	Medium	Medium
Built-in CAPTCHA support	None	Yes	None
Built-in support for security	None	Medium	High
Extensibility	High	Medium	Low
Documentation/Community Support	High	High	Medium
Learning Curve	Low	Medium	High
Developer friendliness	Medium	High	Low
Development Flexibility	High	High	Medium

5. CONCLUSION

Although plain PHP has certain advantages in areas of performance and flexibility, the development cycle in plain PHP is lengthy as all of the features of the application need to be coded from scratch. Manually coding common web application functions such as session management and authentication can lead to significant security vulnerabilities if not done correctly. Code reuse is essential for these types of critical functions to ensure the development of robust applications. Additionally, development without a framework does not enforce an MVC architecture that is critical in web design.

While CakePHP showed initial promise in the quantitative analysis of our study, when qualitative measures were considered, it lost favor. Indeed, the built-in features available in CakePHP libraries are extensive, but the usage of all those features for student projects may not be applicable. Additionally, CakePHP is comparatively inflexible in terms of naming conventions and folder organization and has a much higher learning curve particularly due to its lack of strong development community at the time of this writing. And finally, the job marketability for those with skills in CakePHP is not near as high as the number of positions that are advertised for skills in CodeIgniter.

Based on our qualitative and quantitative results, we believe that CodeIgniter is best suited for student projects. Although CodeIgniter and CakePHP support many of the same functionalities, the simplicity of CodeIgniter makes it preferable. Additionally, CodeIgniter has advantages in areas of ease of use, quick development, support for components like CAPTCHA, community support, very low learning curve and built in support for security.

As previously stated, this work represents the third phase of a four-phased process to revamp our undergraduate software engineering course. Now that an appropriate PHP framework has been selected, it will be incorporated into the next offering of CSC330 (Spring 2013) and assessment of the course will continue.

6. REFERENCES

[1] N. &. S. G. Piccinini, “Cooperative Project-based Learning in a Web-based Software Engineering Course,” *Educational Technology & Society,* vol. 9, no. 4, pp. 54-62, 2006.

[2] E. &. L. C. Stiller, Project-Based Software Engineering: An Object-Oriented Approach, Addison Wesley, 2005.

[3] “Project management software, online collaboration: Basecamp,” [Online]. Available: http://basecamp.com/. [Accessed 5 September 2012].

[4] “GitHub - Social Coding,” GitHub, Inc., [Online]. Available: https://github.com/. [Accessed 5 September 2012].

[5] “PHP:Hypertext Preprocessor,” [Online]. Available: http://www.php.net/. [Accessed 5 September 2012].

[6] “Framework Technology Web Usage Statistics,” [Online]. Available: http://trends.builtwith.com/framework. [Accessed 4 September 2012].

[7] I. a. K. D. Vosloo, “Server-centric Web frameworks: An overview,” *ACM Computing Surveys (CSUR),* vol. 40, no. 2, 2008.

[8] “Top 5 PHP Frameworks 2012,” [Online]. Available: http://www.phpzag.com/top-5-php-frameworks-2012/. [Accessed 4 September 2012].

[9] “Zend Framework,” [Online]. Available: http://framework.zend.com/. [Accessed 5 September 2012].

[10] “Yii Framework: Best for Web 2.0 Development,” [Online]. Available: http://www.yiiframework.com/. [Accessed 5 September 2012].

[11] “CodeIgniter - Open source PHP web application framework,” [Online]. Available: http://codeigniter.com/. [Accessed 5 September 2012].

[12] “CakePHP: the rapid development php framework. Pages,” [Online]. Available: http://cakephp.org/. [Accessed 5 September 2012].

[13] “Eclipse.org - Indigo Simultaneous Release,” [Online]. Available: http://www.eclipse.org/indigo/. [Accessed 4 September 2012].

[14] “CLOC -- Count Lines of Code,” [Online]. Available: http://cloc.sourceforge.net/. [Accessed 4 September 2012].

[15] “Xdebug - Debugger and Profiler Tool for PHP,” [Online]. Available: http://xdebug.org/. [Accessed 4 September 2012].

[16] “WinCacheGrind | Free Development software downloads at SourceForge.net,” [Online]. Available: http://sourceforge.net/projects/wincachegrind/. [Accessed 4 September 2012].

[17] “Nessus 5 | Tenable Network Security,” Tenable Network Security, [Online]. Available: http://www.tenable.com/products/nessus. [Accessed 3 September 2012].

[18] “sqlmap | Free Development software downloads at SourceForge.net,” [Online]. Available: http://sourceforge.net/projects/sqlmap/. [Accessed 30 August 2012].

[19] M. Grady, Qualitative and Action Research: A Practitioner Handbook, Bloomington: Phi Delta Kappa Edcuational Foundation, 1998.

[20] G. A. Bowen, "Document Analysis as a Qualitative Research Method," *Qualitative Research Journal,* vol. 9, no. 2, pp. 27-40, 2009.

[21] “Xdebug - Debugger and Profiler Tool for PHP,” [Online]. Available: http://xdebug.org/. [Accessed 4 September 2012].

Gaps Between Industry Expectations and the Abilities of Graduates

Alex Radermacher
North Dakota State University
IACC Bldg., Room 258
Fargo, ND, 58102
alex.radermacher@ndsu.edu

Gursimran Walia
North Dakota State University
IACC Bldg., Room 258 B3
Fargo, ND, 58102
gursimran.walia@ndsu.edu

ABSTRACT

Although computer science, information systems, and information technology educators often do an exemplary job of preparing their students for jobs in industry or for further education, there are still many areas where these students do not possess the necessary skills or knowledge based on the expectations of employers or academia. These gaps between the abilities of graduating students and those expectations can prevent them from succeeding in their careers. This paper presents the results of a systematic literature review conducted to determine which areas graduating students most frequently fall short of the expectations of industry or academia. The results of this review indicate that graduating students are lacking in many different areas, including technical abilities (design, testing, configuration management tools, etc.) personal skills (oral and written communication, teamwork, etc.) and professional qualities (e.g. ethics). By raising awareness of these areas, it is possible for educators to become aware of areas where students most frequently fail to meet expectations and to make curriculum changes or other adjustments to address these problems.

Categories and Subject Descriptors

K.3.2 [**Computers and Education**]: Computers and Information Science Education—*curriculum*

General Terms

Human Factors

Keywords

Software developer, Required skills, Computer science pedagogy, Computer science education, Knowledge deficiency

1. INTRODUCTION

One of the main focuses of educators in computer science, software engineering, and related fields is to prepare undergraduate students for their future careers in industry or advanced studies. In order to determine the quality of the education students are receiving, it is necessary to evaluate the abilities and knowledge of graduating students based on the expectations of both academia and industry. Furthermore, it is important to determine the areas in which students are lacking in order to both raise awareness of these shortcomings and understand where improvement is most needed. Many researchers, educators, and industry professionals have indicated that graduating computer science students are deficient in their skills and understanding of concepts that will be important in their future careers [5, 15, 3].

Because graduating students can lack skills or abilities in a variety of different categories, it is necessary to develop a term to collectively describe these different areas. The term "knowledge deficiency" is used for that purpose and is more formally defined as:

> *Any skill, ability, or knowledge of concept which a recently graduated student lacks based on the expectations of industry or academia.*

Less formally stated, knowledge deficiencies can be considered as any knowledge or skills which graduating computer science students lack when first beginning a job in industry or pursuing further education, but are expected to have by their employers or university instructors. Knowledge deficiencies can range from a lack of understanding of computer science concepts (e.g. object orientation, UI design principles, etc.) to poor personal skills (e.g. written or oral communication) to the inability to use software development tools.

As an initial step to gain a better understanding of knowledge deficiencies, a systematic literature review was conducted to identify and classify the knowledge deficiencies previously identified and empirically identified by other researchers. A *systematic literature review* is a formalized, repeatable process in which researchers systematically search a body of literature in order to document the state of knowledge on a particular subject. A primary benefit of performing a systematic review, rather than using an ad hoc approach, is that it provides researchers with more confidence that they have located as much relevant information as possible. Systematic reviews are commonly used in fields such as medicine to document high-level conclusions that can be drawn from a series of detailed studies [12]. To be effective, a systematic review must be driven by an overall goal. The goal of this research is to:

SIGCSE'13, March 6–9, 2013, Denver, Colorado, USA.

> Identify and classify knowledge deficiencies found in graduating computer science students for the purpose of better preparing students for their future careers in academia or industry.

The remainder of this paper is structured as follows: section 2 provides a background information on knowledge deficiencies and related work in the area. Next, a brief description of the process used in this systematic literature review is provided in section 3. Section 4 then provides the results of the systematic literature review, followed by a discussion of those results in section sec:discussion. Finally, section 6 concludes this paper.

2. BACKGROUND

The idea of examining knowledge deficiencies in graduating students in computer science and related fields is not a new idea. During an ad hoc literature review used to determine the feasibility of conducting a systematic reiveiw, several different papers from the 70's and 80's were found [24, 25, 38]. Even then, researchers were interested in ensuring that computer science education was relevant to industry needs [24] and identifying areas where newly hired graduates required further training to become productive at their new jobs [25].

Additional research from the 90's onward was also uncovered [3, 4, 15, 30, 40]. Byrne, et al. researched the similarities and differences between Computing Curriculum 91 [28] and actual software industry managers [4]. A Microsoft employee provided a personal account of multiple instances where he felt unprepared for his career [3]. Ruff, et al. examined and created recommendations for the lack of communication abilities in engineers [30]. Winbladh reported on some of the misconceptions that newly hired requirements engineers possess [40]. A large survey of software developers was conducted by Lethbridge, et al. to examine areas in which they needed to increase their competency past their college education [15].

There is a large amount of research related to knowledge deficiencies in graduating students, but many publications have major shortcomings. For example, some publications contain are based on personal accounts or contain anecdotal evidence, making the identified deficiencies suspect or non-generalizable [3, 40]. Other publications are so old that the information that they contain may no longer be relevant [24]. There are also publications aimed at solving knowledge deficiencies, rather than identifying the extend to which they exist [30]. Another issue is that some research focuses on other domains (e.g. business skills) that is less relevant to computer science students [38].

However, there were still several publications which either explicitly examine knowledge deficiencies or can be used to derive areas where graduating computer science students are not meeting the expectations of academia or industry [1, 4, 15, 21]. McGill reported on the gap between the curriculum for game development at several universities and actual industry needs [21]. The surveys of industry managers and professionals conducted respectively by Byrne, et al. and Lethbridge, et al. also provided a good deal of insight into knowledge deficiencies [4, 15]. Begel and Simon conducted a case study of recently hired developers at Microsoft and reported on the struggles and other issues that these developers frequently experienced [1].

It was these publications based on empirical research that provided the best and most detailed information on knowledge deficiencies. Not only was there clear evidence for the existence of these deficiencies, but in many cases the results could be quantified and compared with the results from other research to determine to which extent a particular knowledge deficiency was prevalent. In order to find additional publications based on empirical evidence, the authors of this research decided to conduct a systematic literature review.

3. REVIEW PROCESS

This section describes the process used for performing the systematic literature review of knowledge deficiencies. This includes a description of the review protocol, which describes the high-level research questions, the sources to be included in the literature review, various criteria used for conducting the study, and the data that was extracted from each research paper included in the review. Due to space limitations, only a brief description of the review process is provided in this paper. A full description of the process can be found in [29].

The systematic review is based on guidelines established by Kitchenham in *Procedures for Undertaking Systematic Reviews* [10, 11]. The purpose of performing a systematic literature review is similar to that of performing any scientific experiment: procedures are established, followed, and reported on so that other researchers are capable of replicating the work. Following a systematic review process also provides a high degree of control over the type and quality of reference works that will be included in the review and helps to provide support for the conclusions of the literature review.

In accordance with the guidelines for a systematic literature review established by Kitchenham, [11] the following steps were implemented: First a review protocol was established. Research questions were created (which can be found in table 1), search strings for searching databases were developed, and criteria were established to determine to quality of potential studies found during the review process. Next, the review was executed, applying search strings to the ACM Digital Library and IEEE publication databases and manually searching through targeted journals and conference proceedings. 14,968 publications were initially screen for inclusion based on their title. After this, the remaining 449 papers were further screened based on their abstract. After this, 143 papers remained and were read in their entirety to evaluate their quality and applicability. After reading all of these papers, 30 remained.

The papers chosen for inclusion in the literature review are all based on empirical research in order to provide greater confidence that the knowledge deficiencies identified are not

Table 1: Research Questions

#	Research Question
1	Is there empirical evidence of knowledge deficiencies in graduating computer science students?
1.1	What are the most common knowledge deficiencies in students?
1.2	Are there trends or changes in knowledge deficiencies in students over time?

anecdotal. All of the selected papers were also published no earlier than 1995, as it was felt that information prior to that time, even if based on empirical evidence, was less likely to be relevant to current academic practices and industry needs. Included papers were also required to be relevant computer science students. However, to provide a larger pool of results and strengthen the conclusions of the review, papers from information technology and information systems conferences and journals were included if they were deemed relevant (i.e. focusing on programming and technical skills rather than business aspects, or identifying knowledge deficiencies among new hires for job positions that could be filed by computer science graduates).

Papers were also required to contain empirical evidence so that the researchers of this study could be confident about the results. Additionally, the papers should either explicitly indicate a gap between the abilities or knowledge of graduating students and the expectations of industry or academia, or otherwise indicate that the identified problems were areas where recent graduates were considered to be weak or under-performing. This was done in order to distinguish between areas where recent graduates were truly not meeting expectations and the skills and abilities that perspective employers felt that recent graduates required.

4. RESULTS

The results include a wide variety of papers, with different types of focus and methodologies. A majority of the papers focus on the expectations of industry managers and hiring personnel [4, 21, 42], but there were also a large number of results based the experiences of software developers, both experienced [15, 33, 35] and new [1, 7, 32], as well as some results that focused on senior level students [5, 6, 26]. Most of the included studies focus on computer science or software engineer, but there were also some relevant results from the information technology and information systems fields [23, 13].

After extracting information from the selected publications, over 50 different knowledge deficiency categories were identified. Several of these categories were similar or shared some overlap, so categories were combined or eliminated until there were 31 categories remaining, each of which contained at least two sources. Table 2 contains a list of the most frequently identified deficiencies. A more detailed description of these knowledge deficiencies is provided in the next section. It should be noted that although 30 papers were included, several have a narrow focus, possibly on a single knowledge deficiency [5, 26]. For this reason, some knowledge deficiencies (e.g. testing) are not proportional to other deficiencies.

The results also cover a variety of different categories, ranging from technical abilities (e.g. programming), to soft skills (e.g. oral and written communication), to software engineering concepts (e.g. design and testing), and the use of software tools (e.g. configuration management).

Research into knowledge deficiencies may also be becoming more frequent. Table 3 shows the distribution of papers included in this literature review over time.

5. DISCUSSION

This section provides a more in-depth description of the different knowledge deficiencies described in table 2 as well

Table 2: Most Identified Knowledge Deficiencies

Knowledge Deficiency	Occurances
Written Communication	10
Oral Communication	10
Project Management	9
Software Tools	9
Testing	9
Teamwork	7
Problem Solving & Critical Thinking	7
Programming	7
Requirements	7
Personal Skills	6
Ethics	5
Leadership	5
Design	5
Databases	5
Development & Improvement Processes	5

as a brief discussion of some trends in knowledge deficiencies over time.

Oral communication was one of the most commonly identified knowledge deficiencies. The ability to communicate with customers and possessing good listening skills were cited as specific examples of how recent graduates did not meet expectations in this area [8]. Tesch, et al. conducted a study where they found that the biggest discrepancy between employer expectations and student ability was their ability to listen [37]. Research conducted by Begel, et al. also identified that recently hired software developers often struggle to adequately communicate when they were in need of assistance or struggling with a problem [1].

Written Communication was another area where recent graduates were found to struggle. One study specifically mentioned technical writing ability as a specific aspect of knowledge deficiencies in written communication [15]. Another commonly cited specific example was that newly hired recent graduates lacked the ability to write and produce documentation [4, 33]. Begel, et al. reported that new developers often did not include an appropriate amount of detail in written communication (e.g. emails) [2].

Project Management was identified in a large number of publications spanning computer science [15, 16], information technology [8], and information systems [23]. An study by Hagan, et al. found that employers were not satisfied with the project management skills of recent graduates. A study conducted by Lethbridge also found that software developers rated their current level of project management much higher than their level of project management when they had graduated college [15]. Another paper indicated that project management was one of the most important topics for curriculum change as there was a large gap between what developers knew when they had graduated and what they needed to know for their current job [9].

Table 3: Knowledge Deficiencies Studies Over Time

Years	Number of Publications
1995 – 2000	9
2001 – 2006	8
2007 – 2012	13

Software Tools is a broad category of knowledge deficiency in which a large number of specific examples exist. The most commonly reported example was configuration management software. A case study conducted by Begel, et al. found that recently hired developers lacked experience using configuration management tools [1]. A study of the skills used by software professionals found a large gap between their current ability levels and what they had been provided with from their education [9]. A similar, earlier study by Lethbridge also reported similar findings [15]. Other research indicated that project management tools (e.g. Microsoft Project), database tools, testing, and debugging tools were other tools with which students lacked proficiency [1, 5, 36].

Testing was a knowledge deficiency which was identified by both industry [4] and academia [5, 39]. Carver, et al. conducted a study of senior-level students that found that they lacked the ability to use test-coverage tools effectively and created spurious test cases [5]. Another study which looked newly hired software developers found that many lacked the ability to conduct thorough code testing [7]. A similar study indicated the new developers often experienced problems when debugging code [2]. Many of the included publications did not provide specific information about any particular type of testing where recent graduates were knowledge deficient.

Teamwork was tied with oral communication as the most identified knowledge deficiency. Begel, et al. reported that new software developers often lacked the kind of teamwork experience that is common in industry, having only worked with small teams of 2 or 3 individuals rather than with dozens of other developers, testers, and others [1]. Scott, et al. indicated that the ability to be work as part of a cross-disciplinary team (something that does not generally occry in a university setting) was often necessary in industry [32]. Another study which surveyed previous graduates who had recently gained employment found that a large number of respondents indicated that their education should give them a more thorough training in teamwork [8].

Problem Solving & Critical Thinking was another commonly identified knowledge deficiency. One paper indicated that new hires often lacked the ability to generate alternate solutions to problems [7]. Another study indicated that the generation and synthesis of new ideas was another area where recent graduates fell short of educators' expectations [36]. Another study conducted by Martz, et al. found that students undervalued analytical and conceptual skills compared to industry hiring personnel and recruiters [20]. Another publication which looked at the importance that educators and practitioners placed on different skills found that while practitioners placed the greatest amount of importance in skill building activities that required critically analyzing problems, whereas educators placed those activities as the least frequently practiced [23].

Programming was one of the most frequently identified technical knowledge deficiency. Lu, et al. reported that recent graduates did meet employer expectations in terms of their programming abilities [19]. Although most publications did not specify particular areas of programming where recent graduates were weak, one paper identified procedural programming [35], and another specifically indicated that students were not learning enough multi-threaded programming and did not have enough exposure to C++ [21]. Miller, et al. also indicated that language independence was another important aspect of programming. Tang, et al. indicated that students did not meet instructor expectations for their proficiency in 4th generation languages [36].

Requirements were another area of software engineering that was identified as a common knowledge deficiency. Several publications identified different sub-areas where students were viewed as knowledge deficient. Wang, et al. identified requirements specification as a knowledge deficiency [39]. Another study reported that requirements elicitation was an issue [33]. A study by Misic, et al. found that educators did not place as much value on teaching students how to prepare for and conduct interviews with users as did industry practitioners [23].

Personal Skills is another broad category that contains multiple different examples. Lee, et al. reported that recruiters placed a significantly larger amount of importance on personal skills such as motivation than did students [14]. Another study found that industry placed a much larger emphasis on attitude and disposition than academia [21]. One study reported that one of the largest gaps in personal skills was the ability to face and learn from errors and openly accept feedback [32]. Tesch, et al. indicated that the ability to listen was where recent graduates fell shortest of expectations [37].

Ethics was the most commonly identified professional skill where students were found to be deficient. A survey of hiring personnel by Tesch, et al. found that recent graduates did not the ethics expectations, but did not provide further information. A study by Woodward, et al. look specifically at the computer ethics of information technology students and found that students were less able than faculty members to distinguish ethical and unethical behavior [41]. Perhaps even more troubling, the same study also indicated that students indicated a greater tendency to act in an unethical manner, irrespective of their ability to identify behaviors an unethical.

Leadership was another commonly reported soft skill. One study which interviewed managers at software development companies indicated that graduates lacked the skills that made them good candidates for group leader roles [4]. Lethbridge's study of software professionals found that their on-the-job learning of leadership was one of the top categories among the 75 that were examined [16]. Another study found that the leadership abilities of newly hired IS professionals was below expectations [37].

Design was a knowledge deficiency that was widely regarded by academia as an area where students did not meet expectations. A study by Wang, et al. indicated that graduating students lacked the ability to describe their designs using formal or semi-formal modeling techniques [39]. Studies conducted by Eckerdal, et al. and Loftus, et al. examined the types of designs that students produced and found that these designs tended to be minimalist with important details left out or portions of the design incomplete [6, 18]. One publication which reported on employers' perceptions of the skills of recent graduates indicated that those graduates did not meet expectations in the area of system design [19].

Databases were another frequently reported knowledge deficiency. Lee, et al. found a wide gap between the importance placed on database query languages between recruiters and students [14]. An earlier study conducted in South Africa found similar results [31]. Misic, et al. found that IS practitioners placed more importance on developing and designing databases than did IS educators [23]. A different study that examined how much software professionals increased their knowledge of topics after graduating college, found that databases was in the top quartile of all topics [17].

Development & Improvement Processes were also widely reported. Lethbridge reported that software developers did not receive an adequate amount of exposure to process standards such as the CMM in their education [16]. Another study indicated that students needed to be familiar with process improvement frameworks (e.g. 6 Sigma and CMMI) [33]. A study of IS professionals found that their current capabilities in several areas related to process improvement were significantly less than their perceived importance of those areas [22]. Woratscheck, et al. reported that IS graduates skills in change management do meet the expectations of their employers.

Knowledge deficiencies have also undergone some changes over time. Teamwork has become more frequently identified within the past 5 years, perhaps indicating that collaboration is becoming more important than ever before. Alternatively, there are some knowledge deficiencies such as software maintenance, object-oriented concepts and presentation skills that have decreased over time. However, without studying these particular deficiencies in more detail, it is difficult to determine precisely what has caused the change. In the case of object-oriented concepts, it is likely that the ACM/IEEE curriculum recommendations have had an impact as they place a much higher emphasis on teaching object oriented languages and concepts to CS majors [27]. Similarly, educators may be incorporating more activities into their courses that allow students to acquire and hone presentation skills. A decrease in reports of knowledge deficiencies related to software maintenance could also indicate that educators have done a better job of incorporating maintenance topics into their course material; however, it could just as easily represent a shift in the work that employers are assigning to their new hires. As such, concrete evidence to suggest why these trends in knowledge deficiencies exist is not available.

6. CONCLUSION

Graduating students experience a wide variety of knowledge deficiencies ranging from personal skills to technical abilities. This paper presents the results of a systematic literature review in order to identify the most common deficiencies from the perspective of educators and industry professionals. A description of the most prevalent knowledge deficiencies is also provided in order to provide specific details about how or why students might be struggling to meet expectations in these areas.

One of the major purposes of disseminating this information is so that it can be used by educators to evaluate their own students for the presence of these knowledge deficiencies and to influence curriculum changes in order to address these deficiencies. This information can also serve as a starting point for future research into knowledge deficiencies by providing researchers with a list of common, existing knowledge deficiencies.

7. REFERENCES

[1] A. Begel and B. Simon. Novice software developers, all over again. In *Proceedings of the Fourth international Workshop on Computing Education Research*, ICER '08, pages 3–14, New York, NY, USA, 2008. ACM.

[2] A. Begel and B. Simon. Struggles of new college graduates in their first software development job. In *Proceedings of the 39th SIGCSE technical symposium on Computer science education*, SIGCSE '08, pages 226–230, New York, NY, USA, 2008. ACM.

[3] E. Brechner. Things they would not teach me of in college: what microsoft developers learn later. In *Companion of the 18th annual ACM SIGPLAN conference on Object-oriented programming, systems, languages, and applications*, OOPSLA '03, pages 134–136, New York, NY, USA, 2003. ACM.

[4] D. J. Byrne and J. L. Moore. A comparison between the recommendations of computing curriculum 1991 and the views of software development managers in ireland. *Comput. Educ.*, 28(3):145–154, Apr. 1997.

[5] J. Carver and N. Kraft. Evaluating the testing ability of senior-level computer science students. In *Software Engineering Education and Training (CSEE T), 2011 24th IEEE-CS Conference on*, pages 169–178, may 2011.

[6] A. Eckerdal, R. McCartney, J. E. Moström, M. Ratcliffe, and C. Zander. Can graduating students design software systems? In *Proceedings of the 37th SIGCSE technical symposium on Computer science education*, SIGCSE '06, pages 403–407, New York, NY, USA, 2006. ACM.

[7] H. Haddad. Post-graduate assessment of cs students: experience and position paper. *J. Comput. Sci. Coll.*, 18(2):189–197, Dec. 2002.

[8] D. Hagan. Employer satisfaction with ict graduates. In *Proceedings of the Sixth Australasian Conference on Computing Education - Volume 30*, ACE '04, pages 119–123, Darlinghurst, Australia, Australia, 2004. Australian Computer Society, Inc.

[9] B. Kitchenham, D. Budgen, P. Brereton, and P. Woodall. An investigation of software engineering curricula. *Journal of Systems and Software*, 74(3):325 – 335, 2005.

[10] B. A. Kitchenham. Procedures for undertaking systematic reviews. Technical report, Computer Science Department, Keele University, 2004.

[11] B. A. Kitchenham and S. Charters. Guidelines for performing Systematic Literature Reviews in Software Engineering. Technical Report EBSE 2007-001, Keele University and Durham University Joint Report, 2007.

[12] B. A. Kitchenham, E. Mendes, and G. Travassos. Cross versus within-company cost estimation studies: A systematic review. *Software Engineering, IEEE Transactions on*, 33(5):316–329, may 2007.

[13] T. Koppi, S. L. Edwards, J. Sheard, F. Naghdy, and W. Brookes. The case for ict work-integrated learning from graduates in the workplace. In *Proceedings of the Twelfth Australasian Conference on Computing Education - Volume 103*, ACE '10, pages 107–116, Darlinghurst, Australia, Australia, 2010. Australian Computer Society, Inc.

[14] S. Lee and X. Fang. Perception gaps about skills

requirements for entry-level is professionals between recruiters and students. *Information Resources Management Journal*, 21(3):39–63, 2008.
[15] T. C. Lethbridge. A survey of the relevance of computer science and software engineering education. In *Proceedings of the 11th Conference on Software Engineering Education and Training*, CSEET '98, pages 56–66, Washington, DC, USA, 1998. IEEE Computer Society.
[16] T. C. Lethbridge. Priorities for the education and training of software engineers. *J. Syst. Softw.*, 53(1):53–71, July 2000.
[17] T. C. Lethbridge. What knowledge is important to a software professional? *Computer*, 33(5):44 –50, may 2000.
[18] C. Loftus, L. Thomas, and C. Zander. Can graduating students design: revisited. In *Proceedings of the 42nd ACM technical symposium on Computer science education*, SIGCSE '11, pages 105–110, New York, NY, USA, 2011. ACM.
[19] M.-T. Lu, C.-W. Chung, and P. Wang. Knowledge and skills of is graduates: A hong kong perspective. *Journal of Computer Information Systems*, 39(2):40–47, 1999.
[20] W. M. B. J. Martz and G. Landof. Information systems careers: A comparison of expectations. *Journal of Computer Information Systems*, 40(2):41–45, 2000.
[21] M. M. McGill. Defining the expectation gap: a comparison of industry needs and existing game development curriculum. In *Proceedings of the 4th International Conference on Foundations of Digital Games*, FDG '09, pages 129–136, New York, NY, USA, 2009. ACM.
[22] E. G. McGuire and K. A. Randall. Process improvement competencies for is professionals: a survey of perceived needs. In *Proceedings of the 1998 ACM SIGCPR conference on Computer personnel research*, SIGCPR '98, pages 1–8, New York, NY, USA, 1998. ACM.
[23] M. M. Misic and N. L. Russo. An assessment of systems analysis and design courses. *Journal of Systems and Software*, 45(3):197 – 202, 1999.
[24] J. L. Mize. Making an academic curriculum relevant to business requirements. *SIGCSE Bull.*, 8(2):24–27, June 1976.
[25] F. L. Moore and J. T. Streib. Identifying the gaps between education and training. In *Proceedings of the twentieth SIGCSE technical symposium on Computer science education*, SIGCSE '89, pages 52–55, New York, NY, USA, 1989. ACM.
[26] L. Murphy and J. Tenenberg. Do computer science students know what they know?: a calibration study of data structure knowledge. In *Proceedings of the 10th annual SIGCSE conference on Innovation and technology in computer science education*, ITiCSE '05, pages 148–152, New York, NY, USA, 2005. ACM.
[27] T. J. T. F. on Computer Curricula. Computing curricula 2001. *J. Educ. Resour. Comput.*, 1(3), Sept. 2001.
[28] T. J. T. F. on Computing Curricula. Computing curricula 1991. *Commun. ACM*, 34(6):68–84, June 1991.
[29] A. Radermacher. Evaluating the gap between the skills and abilities of graduating computer science students and the expectation of industry. Master's thesis, North Dakota State University, 2012.
[30] S. Ruff and M. Carter. Communication learning outcomes from software engineering professionals: A basis for teaching communication in the engineering curriculum. In *Frontiers in Education Conference, 2009. FIE '09. 39th IEEE*, pages 1–6, oct. 2009.
[31] E. Scott, R. Alger, S. Pequeno, and N. Sessions. The skills gap as observed between is graduates and the systems development industry - a south african experience. *Informing Science*, June 2002.
[32] G. Scott and D. N. Wilson. Tracking and profiling successful it graduates: An exploratory study. In *Proceedings of the 13th Australasian Conference on Information Systems*, ACIS '02, pages 1185–1195, 2002.
[33] C. B. Simmons and L. L. Simmons. Gaps in the computer science curriculum: an exploratory study of industry professionals. *J. Comput. Sci. Coll.*, 25(5):60–65, May 2010.
[34] L. A. Sudol and C. Jaspan. Analyzing the strength of undergraduate misconceptions about software engineering. In *Proceedings of the Sixth international workshop on Computing education research*, ICER '10, pages 31–40, New York, NY, USA, 2010. ACM.
[35] S. Surakka. What subjects and skills are important for software developers? *Commun. ACM*, 50(1):73–78, Jan. 2007.
[36] H.-L. Tang, S. Lee, and S. Koh. Educational gaps as perceived by is educators: A survey of knowledge and skill requirements. *Journal of Computer Information Systems*, 41(2):76–84, 2001.
[37] D. B. Tesch, G. F. Braun, and E. A. Crable. An examination of employersâĂŹ perceptions and expectations of is entry-level personal and interpersonal skills. *Information Systems Education Journal*, 6(1):3–16, 2008.
[38] R. H. Trent. Perspectives on the academic preparation of mis professionals. In *Proceedings of the ACM SIGCPR conference on Management of information systems personnel*, SIGCPR '88, pages 119–119, New York, NY, USA, 1988. ACM.
[39] T. G. Wang, D. Schwartz, and R. Lingard. Assessing student learning in software engineering. *J. Comput. Sci. Coll.*, 23(6):239–248, June 2008.
[40] K. Winbladh. Requirements engineering: closing the gap between academic supply and industry demand. *Crossroads*, 10(4):4–4, Aug. 2004.
[41] B. S. Woodward, W. Ceccucci, and M. Whitney. It students and computer ethics: Making the case for further training and ethical development. *Information Systems Education Journal*, 7(77):3–12, 2009.
[42] C. R. Woratschek and T. L. Lenox. Information systems entry-level job skills - a survey of employers. *Journal of Computer Information Systems*, 2(2):119–143, 2002.

A Mid-Career Review of Teaching *Computer Science I*

Amruth N. Kumar
Ramapo College of New Jersey
505 Ramapo Valley Road
Mahwah, NJ 07430, USA
1 201 684 7712
amruth@ramapo.edu

ABSTRACT

A mid-career review is presented, of how the teaching of *Computer Science I* has changed for this instructor over the last two decades. The content of the course has evolved to include algorithm development and program design. Assessment in the course has gone online and moved away from testing how clever the student is, to how much the student has learned in the course. Professional practices are now covered that help students understand and incorporate preferred practices of the discipline. Changes incorporated into the pedagogy include going from using anthropomorphic and ad-hoc to discipline-specific and consistent vocabulary, and from writing code in the class like an experienced programmer to writing it to suit a beginning learner. It is hoped that this review will help new *Computer Science I* instructors avoid some misconceptions with which this instructor started out.

Categories and Subject Descriptors

K.3.2 [**Computer and Information Science Education**]: Computer Science Education

General Terms

Documentation, Experimentation

Keywords

Computer Science I, Problem-Solving, Program Design, Assessment, Professional Practices, Pedagogy.

1. INTRODUCTION

I have been teaching *Computer Science I* for two decades now. This seemed like a good time to stop and reflect on my journey as the instructor of this introductory bread-and-butter Computer Science course. It is a journey many instructors have taken before, and many will take in the years to come. What is striking is how much my teaching of the course has changed over these years – its content, assessment, presentation and pedagogy. It is my hope that this documentation of the changes might help freshly minted Computer Science educators skip a step or two in their own inevitable journeys. Over the years, a lot of good educators and researchers have wrung their hands about dismal retention rates in *Computer Science I.* I have a hunch that some of the reasons for attrition in my own offerings of the course are hiding in plain sight in this article reflecting my journey. It is hoped that cataloging the practices that I have since abandoned might contribute to the discussion on what works and what does not in the teaching of *Computer Science I.*

This account of the evolution of my *Computer Science I* course is not meant to be a qualitative or quantitative study of how novices learn - there is abundant literature on how novice programmers learn (e.g., [5]) as well as the differences in the program comprehension of novices versus experts (or instructors) (e.g., [4]). This article presents what makes for effective student learning in *Computer Science I* from the perspective of one instructor who has taught the course for two decades, and therefore, is in the tradition of phenomenographic studies (e.g., [12]). By necessity, and with apologies to the reader, this account will contain a lot of sentences starting with the first person singular pronoun.

In the following sections, I will present four aspects of teaching *Computer Science I*: content, assessment, presentation and pedagogy. I will present each aspect in terms of prior practice, a retrospective analysis and current practice.

2. CONTENT

Prior Practice: When I first started teaching *Computer Science I,* it was all about teaching the syntax and semantics of a programming language in class. The *piece de resistance* was the sample code written on the board illustrating the programming construct. To be fair, back then, *Computer Science I* was a purely lecture course, and this seemed like the most logical content to teach – this is what the students did not know coming into the course, and this is what could be taught in a lecture format without recourse to computers. In addition, students were assigned half a dozen programming projects to practice programming constructs. This is where students actually got the opportunity to write a program on a computer and try out the concepts "learned" in class. On the tests, students were expected to write code for a given problem, debug given code, and identify the output of given code, all on paper, without the benefit of a computer or compiler.

In Retrospect: It is now common knowledge that writing a program for a given problem involves at least the following steps:

SIGCSE'13, March 6–9, 2013, Denver, Colorado, USA.

1. **Problem-Solving**, the process of designing an algorithm for the given problem;
2. **Program Design**, the process of identifying the variables and designing the control constructs needed to implement each stage of the algorithm;
3. **Coding**, the process of writing code to incorporate the variables and control constructs identified during program design;
4. **Debugging and testing**.

In retrospect, in class, I was teaching to step 3, viz., coding, and some amount of step 4, potential pitfalls of programming constructs. The written tests also assessed only these two steps. However, on the projects, the students were expected to execute all four steps. Clearly, there was a mismatch between what was being taught and what was being assessed. Since projects are the most immediate and on-going form of self-assessment for students, i.e., students decided whether they were keeping up in the course or not based on their project performance, the mismatch may have led to a lot of frustration and eventually, attrition among my students.

Is it really necessary to explicitly teach steps 1 and 2 – problem-solving and program design? *Computer Science I* textbooks generally do not cover these topics at all or in any great detail. Personally, I do not recall ever being taught how to solve problems in class, and it is very likely, neither can most *Computer Science I* educators today - It has always been assumed that students could do problem-solving and program design on their own, without explicit instruction.

Going back to my own experience as a student decades ago, I recall being perplexed, not quite sure how to come up with an algorithm for a given problem. So, when in doubt (or lost), my practice was to just start coding, hoping the solution would transpire as I went along – so much for top-down decomposition! In my experience, average students continue to have trouble designing the algorithm for a given problem. This stands to reason – when confronted with a problem in everyday life, human beings go into an iterative plan-act sequence (e.g., want to get gas? Drive to the nearest gas station. Station is closed? Drive onwards to the next station). In contrast, writing an algorithm involves sketching out all the steps, not just the next one, and taking into account all the possibilities, not just the one immediately confronting us (e.g., what if the gas station has run out of the type of gas I want?). This is further complicated by the push in educational circles to use real-life problems to make computing more interesting and relevant to students (e.g., [13]) - coming up with the algorithm for a real-life problem can be even more daunting to students, who must now also resolve the ambiguities inherent in the problem statement of a real-life problem (e.g., does Ace count as 1 or 10 in Blackjack?).

Students not only have problems coming up with the algorithm, but also struggle with program design, as is clear from reading the code they write – programs with superfluous variables, unnecessary nesting of if-else statements, conjunctive conditions where simple conditions would have sufficed; read-only parameters passed by reference to functions, an entire array passed as parameter to a function that only references one element in it, variables referenced in a single member function declared as class variables, etc.

Current Practice: My conclusion was, yes, it is necessary to explicitly teach problem-solving and program design techniques in *Computer Science I.* I now cover these topics in every class, in the context of every programming construct. In each class, after assigning a new problem, I tease out the algorithm for the problem in collaboration with the students, and write down the algorithm on the board. This is followed by program design in consultation with students:

- Data analysis, i.e., analysis of the variables needed for the program and their desired data types and forms
- Control analysis, i.e., determination of the control structures needed for each step in the algorithm. Control analysis includes showing the students how to translate information in the problem statement into tables and fork diagrams [11] that help them properly nest `if-else` statements; how to design loops [10] and introduce accumulator variables into a loop after it is designed; and how to pick the signature of a function based on its desired input/output characteristic.
- In later classes, control flow analysis, i.e., the desirable order in which functions should be called, and data flow analysis, i.e., the movement of data as parameters among functions and classes.

All of these help students write a program for a given problem from scratch. Explicitly covering them and consistently repeating them for each problem help students develop, practice and internalize algorithm development and program design – the first two steps in programming that I was not covering earlier. Similar program design techniques have been advocated by the very successful Program By Design project [16].

Finally, we now use closed labs [7] in *Computer Science I,* as do many other schools. Closed labs offer the opportunity for students to practice all four steps of programming listed earlier, under the supervision of the instructor. We go through the first two steps – problem-solving and program design – during the lecture, with me taking the lead on the board and students assisting me. Students complete the last two steps – coding, and debugging and testing – in the closed lab – they take the lead (individually) and I assist them when necessary. In other words, the class is now "flipped" [3].

3. ASSESSMENT

Prior Practice: When I started out, the tests in my course were written, not online. Students were expected to write code for a given problem, debug given code, and identify the output of given code, all on paper, without the benefit of a computer or compiler.

In Retrospect: In retrospect, both the form and content of the tests were off the mark. I thought a good test question was one whose answer was not obvious. Now, I understand that a good test question is not about finding out how clever a student is, but how much the student has learned in the class. For example, consider the following C++ problem that I would have assigned to assess knowledge of parameter passing – the student is asked to identify the output of the code.

```
void insert (int value, int data[], int & size )
```

```
{
    for ( int index = size; index > 0; index-- )
      data[index] = data[index-1];

    data[0] = value;
    size++;
}

int main()
{
     int data[5] = {5, 4, 3, 2, 1};
     int location = 0;
     insert( 3, data, location );
     insert( 2, data, location );
     insert( 1, data, location );
     for (int index = 0; index < 5; index++ )
     {
          cout << data[index] << endl;
     }
}
```

Solving the problem correctly requires knowledge of not just parameter passing, but also arrays and loops. If the student solves the problem incorrectly, it does not necessarily mean the student does not understand parameter passing – it could also be that the student does not understand arrays or loops. So, the problem lacks focus and does not really assess what it was meant to assess. Consider another C++ problem to assess knowledge of parameter passing:

```
int var1;
int someFunction( int var5, int & var6 )
{
    int var3 = 11, var4 = 13;
    var5 = 17; var6 = 19; var1 =23;
    cout << var1 << var3 << var5 << endl;
    cout << ::var1 << var4 << var6 << endl;
    return var4;
}

int main ()
{
    int var2, var3, var4;
    var1 = 2; var2 = 4; var3 = 6; var4 = 8;
    cout << var4 << var3 << var2 << var1 << endl;
    var2 = someFunction(var2, var3);
    cout << var1 << var2 << var3 << var4 << endl;
}
```

This program does not have any meaningful purpose. Worse, it uses unhelpful variable names, making it hard to solve correctly even when a student knows the underlying concepts. This problem screams "catch me if you can"! It sets a bad example by presenting inscrutable code and sends the wrong message that programming is hacking,

Current Practice: Pen and paper questions can be properly designed to test whether the student understands programming concepts. But they do not test whether the student can turn around and write a program involving those concepts. Since the objective of introductory Computer Science is problem-solving and programming, I now use online tests in the course [9]. In the online tests, students design, write, and test a program for a given problem. By offering hints during the test, and awarding partial credit for incomplete programs, I try to reduce the stress associated with writing a program under deadline. Online tests reward students who complete the most number of projects and therefore, have independently practiced problem-solving and program design techniques [8].

4. PRESENTING PROFESSIONAL PRACTICES

Prior Practice: Even after I began to cover problem-solving and program-design techniques in class, and started using closed labs in the course, it did not occur to me that it was important to discuss preferred programming practices and that in the absence of such discussion, students would bring to bear, models learned in other disciplines that were inadequate or wrong for programming.

In Retrospect: That, they did. For example, when writing an English essay, one might plough through a draft of the entire essay before stopping to check the cohesion of its narrative. Students often assume that the process of writing a program is similar – write the entire program, call it "mostly done", and then try to compile it. When writing an English essay, one would write the paragraphs and sentences within each paragraph in a linear order. Students assume that a program is written the same way – in a linear order top to bottom, an order that reflects neither the problem-solving process nor the program design process. I found that it was necessary to explicitly clarify the process of programming and proactively disabuse students of misconceptions borrowed from other disciplines.

Current Practice: When students write a program in each class, I insist that they edit, compile, run and test their program after *each* step in the algorithm. For good measure, in addition to writing the steps in the algorithm on the board, I number those steps in the order in which the student must attempt them, and insist that students attempt the steps in this order. The advantages of enumeration and incremental compilation are numerous:

- Any new bugs can be localized to the most recently developed step in the algorithm. This is similar to the concept of Programmer Test (itself a modification of Unit Test) in Extreme Programming [1].
- Students get positive reinforcement from seeing their partial program work, which builds their self-confidence in a virtuous cycle.
- Students do not realize that the order in which they attempt steps in the algorithm is important. In my experience, if students feel they know the code for a step, they will attempt it first, regardless of whether it is the first or the last step in the algorithm. For example, they might attempt to print the value of a variable before assigning to it or in some cases, even declaring it! When they do, and inevitably get stuck, guiding them through the process of climbing out of the mess on their own without just giving away the desired code is very frustrating and time-consuming. (Yet, in a closed lab, when the rest of the class is bored and rearing to go to the next task, it is too tempting to throw in the towel and simply give the student the desired code). Thanks to the ordering of the steps, I now simply ask them to roll back their program

to the earliest step they skipped, either deleting or commenting out the code for all the subsequent steps. This "rollback recovery" (applied here to novice programming) borrows from similar techniques used in computing literature to recover from hardware and software faults (e.g., [6]).

So, in my current practice, I emphasize that *the process is just as important as the product of programming*, a sentiment echoed by other educators (e.g., [2]). I insist that they practice the process just as much as everything else.

When writing control statements such as `if-else` or `while` loop, my students are required to write the shell (language-mandated syntax) first, before filling in details such as the condition expression, if-clause and else-clause. This practice minimizes bugs resulting from mismatched or misplaced closing statements (braces, `end` statements). While this practice is obvious to experienced programmers, it is not obvious to novices who have only seen programs in their finished form, and not as they are being written. So, in addition to explicitly mentioning the practice during the lecture, I compulsively reinforce its use during the laboratory session, reminding students that writing code *hierarchically rather than linearly* will avoid a lot of gratuitous bugs and save them a lot of frustration and time.

When debugging, professional programmers draw upon the wealth of their experience to quickly identify the problem and fix it in the code. For novices though, debugging, i.e., localizing, identifying and fixing bugs is a very time-consuming process. Localizing the bug is aided by the practice of testing code after each step in the algorithm. Identifying and fixing the bug on the other hand, are skills learned through practice. We all know how unhelpful compiler errors can be – if a student fails to enclose a character literal constant (say x) within single quotes, the compiler complains that x has not been declared! This is when a beginner dutifully proceeds to declare x as a variable, which leads the programmer and the program further astray. When students are working on their own after class on a programming project, they could easily spend hours agonizing over such bugs without being the better for it. In order to help students learn from their past mistakes and save time in the process, I now instruct students to maintain a "bug library" – the symptom of each bug and its cause. During the lecture, I point out typical bugs that students should add to the library, e.g., how a semi-colon after the `else` keyword results in a semantic error in most popular languages. Students are allowed to bring the bug library to their online tests.

Students rarely test their code for anything other than the expected values of program input. This can be attributed to two problems: 1) Students do not know how to come up with the correct test cases; 2) Students lack or do not appreciate the discipline of comprehensively testing their code after each stage of development. The first problem is addressed by introducing the concept of boundary values, and using the number line to illustrate conjunctive and disjunctive conditions of `if-else` statements and loops as follows – an arrow is drawn on the number line originating at each boundary value and pointing in the direction prompted by the relational operator, e.g., `hour >= 1` is drawn as an arrow originating at 1 and pointing right; `hour <= 12` is drawn as an arrow originating at 12 and pointing left. Conjunctive conditions are true for the values on the number line that fall under *both* the arrows, and disjunctive conditions are true for the values that fall under *either* arrow. So, test cases must include, in addition to boundary values, at least one value on the number line under either, and both / neither arrow. This technique also helps illustrate why a condition such as `hour >= 1 || hour <= 12` is always true and `hour < 1 && hour > 12` is always false.

The second problem, i.e., instilling the discipline of comprehensive testing is much harder since *Computer Science I* students are usually less interested in taking ownership of their code than they are of meeting the benchmarks established for correct completion of the course project. One option is to record an observation journal - consisting of the test cases used and the code behavior observed – as an integral part of the comments preceding each section of code.

Iterative development of code, writing constructs hierarchically rather than linearly, maintaining a bug library, developing the discipline of testing code – these are some of the professional practices that are not self-evident, but are very helpful to *Computer Science I* students. While many of these ideas are traditionally covered in depth in Software Engineering course, introducing them in some rudimentary form in *Computer Science I* is not just a good idea, it is necessary.

5. PEDAGOGY

Prior Practice: As a beginning programmer and later, as a beginning instructor, I remember anthropomorphizing programming: "this function *grabs* the input, *shoots* its result to this other function, which then *decides* whether to keep it or *toss it*. Huh? I see my students do it now when describing their project, and wonder if they really know what they are talking about. More importantly, I doubt very much that my *Computer Science I* students understood what I was talking about as a beginning instructor.

In Retrospect: Anthropomorphic verbs hide insecurities. Insecurity about whether a program works (my students describing their project), how the program works (someone with a shallow knowledge of a new technology talking about it), or may be how to explain how the program works (I as a beginning instructor). Beginning students cannot replicate *grabbing, shooting, deciding* and *tossing* unless they see the code behind each of these verbs. If so, why not simply call these actions what they stand for in the code - *reading input, returning value,* and using *selection statement*? Each of these terms corresponds to specific syntax in the code and is unambiguous.

Current Practice: At the risk of sounding staid and boring to my students, I no longer use anthropomorphic verbs. Instead, I started using more appropriate computing terms. But, over the years, I found that this was not sufficient; it was also necessary to be consistent.

A case in point is the phrase "returning a value by reference", as applied to functions. Technically, *returning* has a specific meaning in functions, so, it should be *passing* a value by reference, or more generically and evocatively, *sending* a value back by reference. I have found that using words and phrases to consistently mean the same concept every time in class is challenging, but worth it in terms of the clarity of the presentation. It also helps students develop their own professional vocabulary.

Prior Practice: When writing code in class on the board, I would write it as an experienced programmer, not as an experienced teacher. The distinction is important: an experienced programmer expediently combines multiple steps in an algorithm into the same line of code. This conflation often confuses and sometimes misdirects a beginning programmer. An experienced teacher might choose to present code step-by-step, in a manner understandable and replicable by the beginning student.

In Retrospect: When we help a baby learn to walk or a child learn to ride a bike, we stoop to the learner's level. The same should be true of helping novices learn to write programs. Students develop a mental model of programming based on the examples presented to them. They are just as likely to develop incorrect models as correct models. So, the examples presented to them and their sequence are both very important. For example, one of the first programs presented one semester was about calculating simple interest. In the program, unfortunately, I combined two algorithm steps, viz., calculating interest and printing it, into a single statement. Sure enough, several students inferred that all calculations had to be done in print statements! It took me weeks to disabuse them of this notion.

Current Practice: Now, my practice is to let the algorithm dictate the code. I no longer conflate steps in the algorithm, even when it seems very natural to do so. As an example, consider a program to calculate the total cost of a purchase. An experienced programmer might write a statement such as:

totalCost = quantity * costPerItem * (1 + TAX_RATE);

In the algorithm, though, this corresponds to three steps:

// Calculate the cost of all the items

// Calculate the taxes

// Calculate the total cost as the sum of the cost of all the items and taxes

When developing code in class, I write a separate statement for each of these three steps. Moreover, I declare two additional variables to hold the cost of all the items and the taxes. The advantages of such deliberative coding in class are many:

- Since we do not take shortcuts, we tend to repeat the same process of program design over and over again. Repetitive practice makes perfect.
- Math-phobic students find it easier to understand when each calculation involves only one operator.
- It reduces the likelihood of students developing incorrect mental models of programming, such as the one described earlier.

Of course, the faster learners quickly progress to conflating code for multiple steps in the algorithm and eliminating the need for variables to hold intermediate values in expressions. As an added bonus, they feel more empowered because they figured this out on their own rather than being instructed or shown how to do it! At the same time, the slower learners do not feel confused, overwhelmed or lost in class. So, deliberative coding is a win-win for everyone.

Prior Practice: As a beginning *Computer Science I* instructor, I thought it was very important to present in class, every subtlety and nuance of each programming construct. I felt it was important to be comprehensive in my coverage. It made logical sense to present everything related to a programming concept or construct at the same time.

In Retrospect: Presenting everything about a programming construct all at once quickly discharged my responsibility as a teacher, but not my obligation to help my students learn. Cognitive Load Theory recommends that information should be properly segmented and sequenced to avoid overload in learners [14]. Presenting all the nuances, exceptions and subtleties at once meant that information was being neither segmented nor sequenced.

Current Practice: I introduce the most general case of any programming concept or construct first, and allow students time to practice with it for a week before introducing special cases, exceptions, etc. Often, I present alternatives as either exceptions or special cases, e.g., functions returning `void` as a special case of non-`void` functions; simple statement as a special case for the body of a loop, compound statement being the general/default case; and empty statement as the exception to what can be the if-clause in an `if-else` statement. Pedagogically, this makes sense, since students tend to think that what is introduced first is the most typical case, and build out every other case with respect to it, as predicted by anchoring bias [15]. They are better prepared because the general version they learn first is the version applicable to the majority of the programs they will write.

Incidentally, "curse of knowledge" is the term recently coined by Harvard psychologist Steven Pinker for the last two prior practices – when an instructor assumes a certain level of knowledge on the part of the student, and forgets that the student is trying to learn the material for the first time!

Current Practice: Whether it is arrays, parameter passing by reference, or pointers, once a programming construct is introduced, students feel compelled to use it in *all* subsequent programs, often ending up with greatly convoluted and unreadable programs. So, I now find it necessary to remind my students of the "law of the instrument", or a variation of it: *just because they bought a hammer does not mean everything is a nail.* In other words, it is not sufficient to tell students when to use a given programming construct, it is also necessary to tell them when not to. This was so counter-intuitive to me that I do not have a prior practice or retrospection to offer for this current practice.

6. DISCUSSION

In retrospect, the content, assessment, presentation and pedagogy of my *Computer Science I* course have changed significantly over the years. What did all this mean to the learning of students in my course?

In my experience, the benefits of most educational interventions do not accrue to the A-grade students who would have done well even without them. This probably explains why there are always some educators who dismiss most interventions as something their students do not need and would not benefit from – because their student population is skewed towards A-grade. Educational innovations do not often benefit F-grade students either, most of whom would fail regardless of the course pedagogy. This probably explains why numerous solutions have been offered for improving retention in *Computer Science I*, but most have failed to deliver on the promise. It has been my experience that educational interventions primarily benefit the students in the middle – their grade improves by up to a letter grade, thanks to the intervention. I believe, the same has been true for all the changes that have occurred in my *Computer Science I* course as it evolved over the years.

Looking back at myself two decades ago, I would be hard pressed to give myself a passing grade as the instructor of *Computer Science I.* I am curious whether I will feel the same way in two decades about my current practices. Only time will tell.

7. REFERENCES

[1] Beck, K. and Andres, C. *Extreme Programming Explained: Embrace Change.*2nd Edition. Addison-Wesley Professional, 2004.

[2] Bennedsen, J. and Caspersen, M.E. Assessing Process and Product – A Practical lab Exam for an Introductory Programming Course. *Proc. FIE 2006.* San Diego,_ Oct 2006.

[3] Bergmann, J., Overmyer, J. and Willie, B. The Flipped Class: Myths Vs Reality. *The Daily Riff.* June 21, 2011.

[4] Burkhardt, J., Detienne, F., and Wiedenbeck, S. Object-Oriented Program Comprehension: Effect of Expertise, Task and Phase. *Empirical Softw. Engg.* 7, 2 (June 2002), 115-156.

[5] Clear, T., Edwards, J., Lister, R., Simon, B., Thompson, E., and Whalley, J. The teaching of novice computer programmers: bringing the scholarly-research approach to Australia. In *Proceedings of the tenth conference on Australasian computing education - Volume 78* (ACE '08), Simon Hamilton and Margaret Hamilton (Eds.), Vol. 78. Australian Computer Society, Inc., Darlinghurst, Australia, Australia, 2008, 63-68.

[6] Elnozahy, E.N., Alvisi, L., Wang, Y., and Johnson, D.B. A survey of roll-back recovery protocols in message-passing systems. *ACM Computing Surveys.* 34(3). September 2002. 375-408.

[7] Kumar, A.N. The Effect of Closed Labs in Computer Science I: An Assessment. *The Journal of Computing Sciences in Colleges.* 18(5). May 2003. 40-48.

[8] Kumar, A.N. An assessment of On-line Testing in Computer Science I. *Proc. ITiCSE 99*, Krakow, Poland, June 1999, 25-28.

[9] Kumar, A.N. The Design of On-line Tests for Computer Science I and their Effectiveness. *Proc. FIE 99,* Nov 99.

[10] Kumar, A.N. An Algorithm to Design Loops. *The Journal of Computing in Small Colleges.* 12(5). May 97. 89-98.

[11] Kumar, A.N. Fork Diagrams for Teaching Selection in CS I. *Proc. SIGCSE 96.*Philadelphia, PA, Feb 96. 348-352.

[12] Lister, R., Berglund, A., Box, I., Cope, C., Pears, A., Avram, C., Bower, M., Carbone, A., Davey, B., de Raadt, M., Doyle, B., Fitzgerald, S., Mannila, L., Kutay, C., Peltomäki, M., Sheard, J., Simon, Sutton, K., Traynor, D., Tutty, J., and Venables, A. Differing ways that computing academics understand teaching. Proceedings of the ninth Australasian conference on Computing education (ACE '07), Vol 66, January 2007, 97-106.

[13] Roth, W.M. Bridging the Gap Between School and real Life: Toward an Integration of Science, Mathematics, and Technology in the Context of Authentic Practice. *School Science and Mathematics.*92(6) Oct 1992. 307-317.

[14] Sweller, J., Ayres, P. amd Kalyuga, S. *Cognitive Load Theory (Explorations in the Learning Sciences, Instructional Systems and Performance Technologies).* Springer, 2011.

[15] Tversky, A. and Kahneman, D., Judgment under Uncertainty: Heuristics and Biases. *Science.* 185(4157). Sep 27, 1974. 1124-1131.

[16] www.programbydesign.org

Designing and Supporting Collaborative Learning Activities

Katrina Falkner
School of Computer Science
The University of Adelaide
Adelaide, South Australia, Australia, 5005
katrina.falkner@adelaide.edu.au

Nickolas J.G. Falkner
School of Computer Science
The University of Adelaide
Adelaide, South Australia, Australia, 5005
nickolas.falkner@adelaide.edu.au

SUMMARY

This session will help participants understand the importance of, and challenges in, introducing collaborative learning within introductory Computer Science curricula. At the University of Adelaide, we have designed our first year curriculum, a sequence of three courses, around collaborative learning - in this session we explore our experiences in developing collaborative activities, collaborative assessment and appropriate training for staff, academic and sessional, involved in collaborative sessions. Based on a seven year programme of designing and undertaking collaborative activities, we will discuss our successes, and our failures, in the use of collaborative learning techniques.

Categories and Subject Descriptors

K.3.2 [**Computers and Education**]: Computer Science Education, Curriculum

General Terms

Human Factors

Keywords

Computer Science Education, Teaching CS1, Active Learning, Collaborative Learning, Assessment

1. OVERALL OBJECTIVE

The overall objectives of this special session are to: (1) disseminate our experiences in the use of collaborative learning as a way of teaching and structuring CS1, (2) explore the different ways that collaborative learning can be employed in CS1, and (3) share our experiences in the management of a collaborative CS1 curriculum, including faculty development, guidelines for the design and delivery of collaborative activities, and evaluations of the experiences of both students and faculty. This special session blends short presentations with group discussion and interactive activities, designed to illustrate our experiences.

Collaborative Learning [6] encompasses a range of constructivist learning techniques where students work in groups, sharing and constructing their knowledge to achieve a common aim. Collaborative learning is effective in academic development, as students are more engaged with the subject matter, but also supports community and social development. It is seen as a particularly relevant technique in first year education, in that it addresses transition concerns by increasing deeper learning and a sense of belonging [5]. The session provides coverage of our seven year experience with collaborative learning, starting from the inclusion of collaborative activities in lectures through to the complete restructure of our first year curriculum. We describe our experiences in adopting contributing student pedagogy to provide effective and engaging collaborative experiences [1].

Collaborative inquiry supports learning for all parties involved, not simply through the sharing of knowledge, but in the elaboration and discussion that ensues. Successful collaborative learning structures do not impose structures based on ability or previous experience, instead supporting individuality and diversity. Faculty work with students on setting goals and tasks, with the outcomes of individual groups used in the coordination of topics and discussion. An essential aspect of a collaboration is the *authenticity* of the task that they are attempting to solve, and the process by which they solve it. Mutual engagement requires that each member has a genuine motivation for being part of the collaboration, and that learning is associated with a task or problem that the group has to solve. Our collaborations are constructed around problem solving.

What does it mean to teach an authentic problem solving process? The development of software is a creative process, requiring design, innovation and communication skills. Software developers commonly start with a partially defined problem, and must communicate with clients and colleagues in determining the full problem specification. This is just the beginning, however, as what follows is an extensive process of creation, partial solutions and experimentation to determine the final solution. Introductory classes in Computer Science tend to take the opposite approach, focussing on learning syntax and semantics, and the problem solving process as one of immediate success. Introductory Computer Science texts rarely present examples illustrating that problem solving has to deal with failure. This is detrimental for our students, as studies indicate that students tend not to vary their approach to problem solving, instead persisting in applying the same techniques regardless of their success [4].

As software developers we do not always solve problems on our own, or only attempt to solve problems that have already been solved. However, we frequently expect our students to learn how to develop software by doing just that. If we hide the problem solving process away as something

SIGCSE'13, March 6–9, 2013, Denver, Colorado, USA.
ACM 978-1-4503-1775-7/13/03.

done between lectures, then students stand little chance of learning by example. Our approach consists of exposing, and forming learning communities, around the problem solving process. We expose the sound approaches, the blind alleys and the fatal flaws in a supportive, but honest, collaborative environment.

2. SESSION OUTLINE

2.1 Course Structure

Presenter: Dr Katrina Falkner
Duration: 15 minutes

This part of the session reviews the structure of our CS1 curriculum, demonstrating how collaborative activities are used in place of traditional, didactic lecture sessions, and how they are integrated - and changed - as the curriculum progresses. Over our seven year experimentation with collaborative learning, we have introduced a variety of collaborative activities, culminating with a complete restructure of our first year curriculum around collaborative learning. This restructure places collaborative activities at the heart of the curriculum, forming over 70% of scheduled contact time with faculty, through the use of facilitated collaborative workshops, small group tutorial classes and in-lecture collaboration. We also discuss collaborative support structures introduced outside formal contact time, including peer instruction and our use of contributing student pedagogy [1].

Analysis of student and faculty evaluations will be presented as well as the results of in depth interviews with students and faculty on the suitability of, and engagement afforded by, collaborative learning activities. Quantitative and qualitative data will be presented based on the introduction of collaborative learning structures, and resulting increases in student engagement and performance. Analysis of these results has been published in [1, 2, 3].

2.2 Collaborative Assessment Tasks

Presenter: Dr Nickolas Falkner
Duration: 20 minutes

We will discuss the design of collaborative assessment tasks, including the results of qualitative analysis and in-depth interviews regarding what students find *approachable* as a collaborative task. We answer the question 'what kind of tasks do students naturally and comfortably approach in a collaborative way?'

This part of the session will include a hands-on activity to clarify the processes used to design collaborative assessment tasks - what works and what does not. Participants are encouraged to bring along examples of successful (and unsuccessful!) collaborative activities to contribute to the discussion.

2.3 Teaching Impact

Presenter: Dr Katrina Falkner
Duration: 20 minutes

This part of the session focusses on the management and coordination of a course structure built around collaborative learning, including the management of large teaching teams that are typically involved in such courses, and specialised skill development for sessional and faculty staff. We will report on the specific teaching skills required, particularly by those staff leading collaborative sessions, and how collaboration is extended to the development of training resources by the faculty and sessional staff involved in the courses.

We will discuss a common set of teaching templates, designed to provide a degree of consistency across large teaching teams, including common approaches to modelling the software development process, problem solving algorithms, and techniques for describing designs and test cases.

2.4 Group Discussion

Leader: Dr Katrina Falkner
Duration: 20 minutes

We would like to hear from participants regarding their own experiences using collaborative learning - both small scale and large scale. This discussion will focus on the challenges of collaborative learning, and on the interests of the community in identifying future research areas.

3. EXPECTATIONS

The intended audience is CS1 educators who are interested in exploring collaborative learning activities at both a small and a large scale. It is expected that the broader discussion of our, and others, experiences in collaborative learning will provide significant benefit to the participants in terms of understanding underlying principles of collaborative learning, and how to design course, or year-level collaborative learning structures. Feedback will be elicited via a brief voluntary survey after the completion of the session.

4. SUITABILITY FOR SPECIAL SESSION

The format of this proposal makes it an ideal candidate for a SIGCSE Special Session. Unlike a regular paper or panel, this session will incorporate a mixture of short presentations, discussions and hands on experiments designed to explore and aid familiarisation with the collaborative learning style.

5. REFERENCES

[1] K. Falkner and N. Falkner. Supporting and structuring ̀contributing student pedagogỳin computer science curricula. *Computer Science Education*, 22(4):413–443, December 2012.

[2] K. Falkner, N. Falkner, and R. Vivian. Collaborative learning and anxiety: A phenomenographic study of collaborative learning activities. In *Proceedings of the 44th ACM Technical Symposium on Computer Science Education (SIGCSE 2013)*, March 2013.

[3] K. E. Falkner and E. Palmer. Developing authentic problem solving skills in introductory computing classes. In *Proceedings of SIGCSE'09*, pages 4–8, 2009.

[4] D. Ginat. Misleading intuition in algorithmic problem solving. In *Proceedings of the 32nd SIGCSE Symposium*, pages 21–25, 2001.

[5] D. McKinney and L. Denton. Developing collaborative skills early in the CS curriculum in a laboratory environment. In *Proceedings of SIGCSE 2006, Symposium on Computer Science Education*, 2006.

[6] B. Smith and J. MacGregor. *What is Collaborative Learning?* National Centre on Postsecondary Teaching, Learning and Assessment, Pennsylvania State University, 1992.

Nifty Assignments

Nick Parlante, Julie Zelenski
(moderators)
Stanford University
nick.parlante; zelenski
@cs.stanford.edu

John DeNero
Google
denero@google.com

Aditi Muralidharan
UC Berkeley
aditi.shrikumar@gmail.com

Michelle Craig
University of Toronto
mcraig@cs.toronto.edu

Mark Guzdial
Georgia Institute of Technology
guzdial@cc.gatech.edu

Eric Roberts
Stanford University
eroberts@cs.stanford.edu

David J. Malan
Harvard University
malan@harvard.edu

Kevin Wayne
Princeton University
wayne@princeton.edu

Abstract

Every time I re-use a handout, I look it over and make a few little "improvements". I play around with code demos and entertain myself with different slide transitions. However, inevitably, I return to the conclusion that most of what my students learn in my course comes from the assignments. Great assignments are hard to dream up and time-consuming to develop. With that in mind, the Nifty Assignments session is all about promoting and sharing the ideas and ready-to-use materials of successful assignments.

Each presenter will introduce their assignment, give a quick demo, and describe its niche in the curriculum and its strengths and weaknesses. The presentations (and the descriptions below) merely introduce each assignment. A key part of Nifty Assignments is the mundane but vital role of distributing the materials – handouts, data files, starter code – that make each assignment ready to adopt. The Nifty Assignments home page, **http://nifty.stanford.edu**, gathers all the assignments and makes them and their support materials freely available.

If you have an assignment that works well and would be of interest to the CSE community, please consider applying to present at Nifty Assignments. See the nifty.stanford.edu home page for more information.

Nick's standing ACM editorial: a large part of the value of Nifty Assignments is that all the materials are on the internet for anyone to see or use at any time. People (or search engines!) are not screened by requiring some affiliation or login. In keeping with the ACM's mission to promote Computer Science, the ACM should raise funds in some other way, such as by charging authors. I look forward to the day that the ACM makes materials simply and freely available on the internet.

Categories and Subject Descriptors

K.3.0 [**Computers and Education**]: General.

Keywords

Education; assignments; homeworks; examples; repository; library; nifty; pedagogy

SIGCSE'13, March 6–9, 2013, Denver, Colorado, USA.
ACM 978-1-4503-1868-6/13/03.

Sentiment Analysis and Visualization with Twitter (CS0-CS1) - John DeNero and Aditi Muralidharan

In this project, students will develop a geographic visualization of twitter data across the USA. They will need to use dictionaries, tuples, and data abstraction techniques to keep track of intermediate steps and create a modular program. We developed it to show our introductory programming students that their skills could already tackle interesting real-world problems.

They create their visualizations by:

- Filtering public tweets for those that contain the query word

- Assigning a sentiment (positive or negative) to each tweet, based on all of the words it contains

- Aggregating tweets by the state with the closest geographic center

- Coloring each state according to the aggregate sentiment of its tweets. Red means positive sentiment; blue means negative.

By the end of the project, they will be able to map the sentiment of any word or phrase. The nifty result of the completed project is a visualization that combines multiple large data sets and reveals hidden patterns. Students engage with real-world data — filtering by any keywords they choose — to discover geographic and temporal trends in the Twitter stream.

Image Collage (CS0) - Mark Guzdial

Once you've used some of the Nifty image (pixel manipulation) or sound (sample manipulation) processing assignments, you might be wondering what next. Make a collage! A collage assignment involves using some smaller media transformations to create a larger artifact. Students will have to plan and design more (of both code and media). A collage assignment can be graded (by rubric) in terms of the computation, so that the students can choose whatever media elements they want for a creative final product.

Authorship Detection (CS1) - Michelle Craig

Automated authorship detection is the process of using a computer program to analyze a large collection of texts, one of which has an unknown author, and making guesses about the author of that unattributed text. The basic idea is to use different statistics from the text — called "features" in the machine learning community — to form a linguistic "signature" for each text. One example of a simple feature is the number of words per sentence. Some authors may prefer short sentences while others tend to write sentences that go on and on with lots and lots of words and not very concisely, just like this one.

Students write a set of independent functions that each calculate a linguistic feature chosen to require no more complicated data-structures than 1-dimensional arrays. By applying their functions to a mystery text, combining these results into a signature and comparing the signature to a set of known signatures for famous authors, the program predicts the identity of the mystery text's author.

The assignment is a starting point for discussing other CS ideas like weighted averages, natural language understanding, machine learning and the challenges of working with messy real-world data. Automated authorship detection has uses in plagiarism detection, email-filtering, social-science research and as forensic evidence in court cases. Also called authorship attribution, this is a current research field. The state-of-the-art linguistic features are considerably more complicated than the ones used here.

Recursive Turtle Graphics (CS1) - Eric Roberts

With a small extension of the basic Turtle Graphics idea, this assignment enables CS1 students to experiment with nifty recursive drawings.

For the first part of the assignment, students build part of simple interpreter that supports drawing pictures by moving a "turtle" around the graphics window. Unlike a traditional Turtle Graphics assignment, this assignment focusses less on graphics and more on string manipulation. In particular, the students implement a general find-and-replace mechanism, and this enables the nifty recursive feature of the assignment.

The find-and-replace mechanism gives the Turtle Graphics system the power of a Lindenmayer System (or "L System"), which supports the creation of complex patterns through repeated string substitution.

Lindenmayer systems allow students to draw fascinating recursive diagrams without having to use recursion in their implementation. As an example, the following screenshot shows the application drawing a Koch snowflake of order 3:

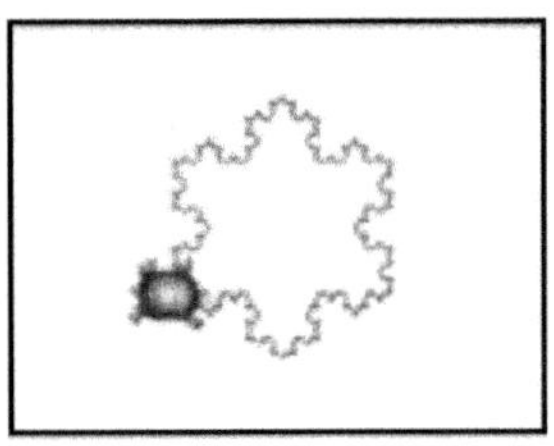

Students can generate amazing fractals diagrams including Koch snowflakes, Sierpinski triangles, and fractal approximations of plant growth without having to understand recursion in depth. The assignment provides students with significant practice using strings and forces them to implement a specialized tokenizer class. The assignment also offers extensive opportunities for extensions and serves as the basis for a contest that encourages highly motivated students to exercise their creativity.

Campus Shuttle (CS1) - David J. Malan

This assignment challenges students to implement a web-based driving game using JavaScript that mashes together the Google Earth and Google Maps APIs. Once implemented, students can drive around their school's campus virtually. The game's objective is to pick up classmates who appear as 2D avatars within Google Earth and drop them off at their respective dormitories.

The assignment assumes familiarity with arrays and objects (in any language) as well as exposure to HTML and CSS. It also assumes exposure to (but not necessarily experience with) JavaScript.

Not only does this assignment reveal to students the applicability of arrays and objects to actual problems, it also introduces students to third-party APIs as well as event handling. Plus, it's incredibly fun to drive around one's own campus virtually.

The assignment can be customized for any school's campus (that's been photographed and mapped by Google). The assignment's difficulty can be tailored to students with different backgrounds by adjusting the amount of distribution code provided.

Estimating Avogadro's Number (CS1-CS2) - Kevin Wayne

Repeat a famous physics experiment to track the motion of particles immersed in a liquid undergoing Brownian motion, fit the data to Einstein's statistical model of molecular motion, and estimate Avogadro's number. This assignment involves a fundamental programming technique (recursion), uses a core computer science concept (depth-first search), and shows an important role of computation in the natural sciences (to analyze experimental data).

The project has two elements: performing the physical experiment and analyzing the resulting data. We supply students with the raw data as sequences of 200 JPEG images. To analyze the data, students must implement the following components:

- Read in an image and use thresholding to separate the image into foreground and background pixels.
- Identify the particles by finding maximal blobs of connected foreground pixels using depth-first search.
- Determine how far each particle moves between observations via a simple nearest neighbor calculation.
- Estimate Avogadro's number by averaging the displacements and plugging the results into Einstein's equations.

This assignment is designed as a two-week capstone assignment in a CS 1 course. No prior physics knowledge is required. This assignment is nifty because, with the aid of modern video microscopes and about 200 lines of code, students can replicate a Nobel-Prize winning scientific experiment and reaffirm the atomic nature of matter.

Expanding Access to K-12 Computer Science Education: Research on the Landscape of Computer Science Professional Development

Baker Franke (Moderator)
University of Chicago Lab Schools
bfranke@ucls.uchicago.edu

Jeanne Century
UEI/CEMSE, University of Chicago
jcentury@uchicago.edu

Michael Lach
UEI/CEMSE,University of Chicago
mlach@uchicago.edu

Cameron Wilson
ACM
wilson_c@hq.acm.org

Mark Guzdial
Georgia Tech
guzdial@cc.gatech.edu

Gail Chapman
UCLA
chapgail@gmail.com

Owen Astrachan
Duke University
ola@cs.duke.edu

SUMMARY

This session will present the research findings to date from an 18-month study commissioned by the ACM in partnership with the National Science Foundation, Google, Computer Science Teachers Association, Microsoft, and the National Center for Woman and Information Technology that started in July, 2012, and invite an open discussion about them. The study seeks to understand the national landscape of K-12 computer science (CS) professional development (PD) and the capacity to provide high quality CS PD on a large scale. The study is being conducted by The University of Chicago's Center for Elementary Mathematics and Science Education (CEMSE) who will present findings from the landscape study conducted in the Summer and Fall of 2012, as well as preliminary findings about the CS community's capacity for increasing the ranks of K-12 CS teachers in light NSF's stated goal of preparing 10,000 secondary education teachers to teach high-quality computer science[1].

A goal for this work is to produce actionable findings that will be of use to the broad CS education community. In the spirit of togetherness and engendering some collective action toward a coherent national strategy for expanding computer science education, it's vital that the SIGCSE community be both aware of this study's findings and be given an opportunity to reflect on its implications. Therefore, over half the time of this session will be devoted to open discussion during which several key questions stemming from the findings will be raised as well as questions raised by audience members. This session is an important opportunity for the SIGCSE community to offer feedback and help to guide the future direction of this study to ensure that the findings and plans for the remainder of the study are useful and actionable.

Categories and Subject Descriptors

K.3.2 Computer and Information Science Education

Keywords

Professional Development, K-12, Scaling, CS10K, Access, Landscape

SIGCSE'13, March 6–9, 2013, Denver, Colorado, USA.
ACM 978-1-4503-1868-6/13/03.

1. BACKGROUND

Numerous sources [2, 3, 4, 5, 6] have identified the critical need to expand the teaching and learning of computer science in K-12 schools in the United States. However, major concerns still exist about our nation's capacity to increase (1) the number of people teaching K-12 computer science, (2) the number of schools in which computer science is taught, and (3) the quality and effectiveness of the computer science instruction. This study will provide a picture of the current CS PD landscape, putting facts and figures behind questions about PD that will help us understand how existing opportunities might fit together in a strategic framework for systematically growing the number of teachers and learners of computer science.

In order to increase the number of K-12 CS teachers it is critical to have a clear understanding of existing PD opportunities so that we may address the needs of not only current K-12 CS teachers but those new teachers we hope to find and recruit to the field. This study will move us toward having the answers to these questions, and provide a foundation for understanding of where we, as a field, have room to grow and of our capacity to increase the number of people teaching high quality computer science in K-12.

2. OUTLINE OF THE SESSION

The presenters will take 40 minutes to explain the motivation for the study, methods of research, the most recent findings, and give some perspective on the findings to provide context for discussion. A 35-minute moderated open forum will follow in which the community at large may comment on the study and ask questions.

2.1 Introduction and Background – 10 min

Cameron Wilson, Director of the Office of Public Policy, ACM, will describe why ACM is interested in understanding the community's capacity to scale K-12 computer science education and the partnership it built to support the study.

Michael Lach, Project Director, UEI/CEMSE, will explain UEI/CEMSE's interest in doing this work, as well as explain the organization of the project and its goals. The project has four main strands: (1) documenting the landscape of K-12 computer science professional development (2) identifying the community's capacity for growing the number of K-12 computer science teachers (3) identifying the professional development and institutional supports needed to both attract new and retain computer science teachers and (4) working with PD providers to help develop models and best practices that will help expand the ranks of K-12 CS teachers.

2.2 Presentation of Research – 20 min

Jeanne Century, Director of Research and Evaluation, CEMSE, with **Michael Lach** and **Baker Franke** will present the research findings to date, as well as the methods and instruments used to collect data. By March, 2013 major findings from the landscape study will be presentable. We also hope to have preliminary findings from the capacity study. Plans for the remainder of the work will also be presented.

2.3 Perspective & Open Forum – 45 min

Three members of the CS education community involved in existing large-scale professional development opportunities, **Owen Astrachan** (CS Principles), **Gail Chapman** (Exploring Computer Science), **and Mark Guzdial** (Georgia Computes!), will kick off the open forum session by providing some perspective on these findings, and suggest what the findings might mean for scaling PD and CS courses in general.

Perspective also includes comparing computer science to other disciplines that conduct PDs at a large scale. This perspective and the research findings will suggest many questions that require input and involvement from the community if a coherent strategy for expanding computer science education is to be developed. Professional development for teachers will need to be a large part of that strategy. Since PD directly impacts what and how CS is taught in classrooms, the voices of the SGICSE community should play a vital role in its future directions, and this open forum is an opportunity to have this discussion.

The open forum will build on questions suggested from the presenters as well as those suggested by the audience. The discussion will be moderated only to the degree necessary to ensure that adequate time be allotted for 1) Q&A about the project, methods and findings and 2) discussion and feedback about the direction of the project and plans for future work that would be most helpful to the CS education community.

Since one of the goals of this project is acceptance of its findings by the computer science education community this feedback and discussion is crucial to its success.

3. EXPECTATIONS AND AUDIENCE

Hundreds of members of the CS community who are providers of PD opportunities, such as workshops, conferences, summer institutes, and PD associated with CE21/CS10K grants, will be aware of this research project since they will have been surveyed as part of the landscape study during the Fall of 2012. Presumably they, along with all of the other stakeholders of those PDs, are interested in the findings. Many who wish to have some tractable information about the national landscape of PD will be interested in how they might use the study's results to inform their own efforts and perhaps contribute to a larger strategy for reaching the CS10K goal.

Furthermore, broad questions about both the need to expand the teaching and learning of CS at the K-12 level, and United States' capacity to do so, are of wide-ranging interest to the CS education community.

4. SUITABILITY

It is vital that the CS community understand and support the goals of this project. This status report is an opportunity for members of the CS community to offer critique of the findings thus far, and contribute suggestions for improving the work and the direction of the study so that it most effectively addresses their questions and needs, as well as those of the broader CS community.

5. REFERENCES

[1] Astrachan, O., Cuny, J., Stephenson, C., Wilson, C. (2011). *The CS10K Project: Mobilizing the Community to Transform High School Computing.* Proceedings of the SIGCSE 2011 Symposium.

[2] CSTA Curriculum Improvement Task Force, Chris Stephenson, Chair. (2005). *The New Educational Imperative: Improving High School Computer Science Education. CSTA.* Retrieved September 1, 2012 from: http://www.csta.acm.org/Communications/sub/DocsPresentationFiles/White_Paper07_06.pdf

[3] CSTA Teacher Certification Task Force, Barbara Ericson, Chair. (2008). *Ensuring Exemplary Teaching in an Essential Discipline: Address the Crisis of Computer Science Teacher Certification.* CSTA, ACM. Retrieved September 1, 2012 from: http://www.csta.acm.org/Communications/sub/DocsPresentationFiles/CertificationFinal.pdf

[4] Margolis, J. (2008). *Stuck in the Shallow End: Education, Race and Computing.* The MIT Press, Cambridge, MA.

[5] United States. President's Council of Advisors on Science and Technology. *Report to the President. Prepare and Inspire: K-12 Education in Science, Technology, Engineering and Math for America's Future.* (2010). Washington, Executive Office of the President. Retrieved Sept. 1, 2012 from: http://www.whitehouse.gov/sites/default/files/microsites/ostp/pcast-stem-ed-final.pdf

[6] Wilson, C., Sudol, L.A., Stephenson, C., Stehlik, M. (2012). *Running on Empty: The Failure to Teach K-12 Computer Science in the Digital Age.* ACM, CSTA. Available: http://www.acm.org/Runningonempt

Two Models of a Cryptography and Computer Security Class in a Liberal Arts Context

Suzanne Fox Buchele
Southwestern University
1001 East University Avenue
Georgetown, TX 78626
bucheles@southwestern.edu

ABSTRACT

The critical need for computer security concepts to be taught in the undergraduate computer science curriculum is evident from current news stories, curricular guidelines, and government initiatives. Beginning to teach a standalone computer security course can be daunting, especially for instructors with little or no background or formal education in computer security. An elective course in cryptography and computer security was developed that matched the talents of the professor and the resources and context of the two Universities and departments in which it was taught. Two models of the course evolved: an elective semester-long computer science and mathematics cross-listed course, and an elective summer computer science course with significant hands-on laboratory exercises. Either course may be used as a model for an accessible course offering involving computer security.

Categories and Subject Descriptors

K.3.2 [**Computer and Information Science Education**]: Computer Science Education.

General Terms

Experimentation, Security.

Keywords

Computer Security Education; Computer Security; Cryptography; Cryptology.

1. INTRODUCTION

There is no doubt that computer security is a requisite component of the education of modern computer scientists. Every day news stories are populated with reports of computer hacking, security breaches, malware, espionage, and/or legislative proposals related to computer, network, or information security. Several U.S. government initiatives are aimed at strengthening the security education of students [9, 17], and several NSF-funded projects have developed resources for teaching security for instructors [2, 5, 18]. In addition, the most recent computer science curriculum guideline proposal features Information Assurance and Security as a Knowledge Area that all students should cover [6]. In the introduction to the CS2013: Ironman Draft (the most recent draft of the computer science curricula available), the authors state, "When questioned about new topical areas that should be added to the Body of Knowledge, survey respondents indicated a strong need to add the topics of *Security* as well as *Parallel and Distributed Computing*" [6]. However, faculty in departments that have not to date offered a computer, network, or information security course may be concerned about the time and resources that implementing such a course would involve, especially in light of time and budget constraints, and lab configurations.

Two models of an elective course in Cryptography and Computer Security that were developed and offered at two different Universities on two different continents are presented here: one, an upper level course cross-listed as a computer science and mathematics elective at a small liberal arts college in the U.S., and the second, an upper-level computer science elective course with a combined lecture and laboratory approach at a new University with a liberal arts focus in West Africa. History, content, and outcomes of the courses follow, as well as a mapping of course topics to CS2013 Ironman Draft Knowledge Areas.

2. HISTORY OF THE COURSE DEVELOPMENT

2.1 Motivation and First Steps

The importance of computer security in modern society and the computer science industry has become more and more evident. For example, computer, network, or information security is a frequently occurring subject in the tri-weekly ACM TechNews digest [1]. However, having no formal experience with computer or information security, no support for new course development, a full curriculum, a set of "standard" electives, and a full teaching schedule meant little incentive for the author to develop a security course.

Student interest in the area led the author to oversee two independent studies involving computer security. Because studying and teaching mathematical concepts can be more straightforward than dealing with differing software and hardware configurations, topics tended toward cryptography and the knowledge-based computer security topics. However, students were also interested in doing hands-on activities that were relevant to the knowledge they were acquiring. The author was reminded of a 2006 paper presentation by Ed Crowley, and Crowley was generous enough to share many of his other resources including several full laboratory exercises using Live DVDs with a Linux distribution and several network utility tools

SIGCSE'13, March 6–9, 2013, Denver, Colorado, USA.

[3]. In addition, course content and objectives were developed and assignments were created during the independent studies, paving the way for a future course offering.

During the first independent study, the author offered to teach a summer course in Cryptography and Computer Security at Ashesi University College, a new University in Ghana, West Africa with a liberal arts focus. The department at Ashesi has a more technical and engineering focus than is typical of a liberal arts computer science department in the U.S., with an expectation of scheduled lab time in CS classes. In addition, a summer course necessitates longer contiguous contact times than a semester-long course, so a lecture-mostly format would not be suitable. Therefore, for the first formal course, a summer course offered in May-June 2010 at Ashesi University College in Ghana, the number of labs was significantly expanded. The course was offered to rising sophomores through seniors as a computer science elective, although several recent alumni working in industry also audited the course.

2.2 Two Models Emerged

In spring of 2012 a version of the course was taught at Southwestern University as an upper-level, cross-listed computer science and mathematics special topics elective. Course topics more appropriate to the mathematics majors were expanded. In addition, course topics necessitating significant computer science expertise were minimized, and explanatory material for the needed concepts was added. For several topics and assignments, differentiated learning and assignments were adopted: for mathematics majors, deep understanding of the proof and mathematical concepts behind certain algorithms was expected, and for computer science majors, the ability to implement certain algorithms was expected. An individual research, applied research, or implementation project was also added, which allowed students to select topics suited to their interest and abilities.

In the summer of 2012, an expanded version of the course was re-taught at Ashesi University College in Ghana. The course was a pilot study abroad program, with one student from Southwestern University accompanying the author to study abroad with 15 West African students for the 5 ½ week summer course. Although similar in content and structure to the initial offering in summer 2010, new material pulled from the Spring 2012 course (e.g. elliptic curve cryptography) was added, although adapted for the more applied computer science context. More labs were also added, so that most content presented now had an associated lab activity.

3. CONTENT AND STRUCTURE OF THE TWO MODELS

3.1 Prerequisites

The mathematics cross-listed course at Southwestern University required sophomore standing, CS1 (which is required of all mathematics majors), and either two mathematics courses or Computer Organization and one mathematics course. This ensured that mathematics majors had already had at least CS1, and the computer science majors had already had topics in data representation and digital logic, and some mathematical maturity; typical sophomore computer science majors had already taken either or both of Statistics or Calculus 1, although junior and senior computer science majors often had Linear Algebra and/or Discrete Mathematics as well. The only computer science course several of the mathematics majors had already taken was CS1.

The computer science summer course with a laboratory focus at Ashesi University College required at least Programming 2 (a course more like a traditional CS1 course), Statistics, a quantitative reasoning course, Calculus 1, and either Discrete Mathematics or Data Structures (CS2). Several students also had courses in Computer Organization and Architecture, Programming 3, Database Management, and Web Technologies.

3.2 Textbooks and Other Resources

Both courses began with students reading Simon Singh's *The Code Book: The Evolution of Secrecy from Mary, Queen of Scots, to Quantum Cryptography* [12]. Singh's book is an excellent and easy-to-read non-fiction book including stories of intrigue, espionage, mathematics, research, discovery and hard work that have characterized the development of cryptography and the algorithms and systems that employ it. Students wrote a summary of the book within the first three weeks, and in the semester-long course engaged in in-class peer review and were encouraged to re-write their papers for increased credit.

Both courses used Brett Tjaden's *Fundamentals of Secure Computing Systems*, and William Stallings, *Cryptography and Network Security* as texts [19, 16]. Tjaden's book was recommended by Crowley; the author was familiar with Stallings from using his books in other courses. Although they cover similar material, Tjaden's book is less technical and more readable by mid-level undergraduates. Stallings' book is more comprehensive and detailed, but also more terse and advanced. Mel and Baker's *Cryptography Decrypted* provides an elemental basis of the mathematical and algorithmic concepts behind many cryptographic processes, and was used as a teaching resource [8]. Their appendix, "Public Key Mathematics (and Some Words on Random Numbers)", is written at a level that is especially accessible to students with a weaker mathematics background, and was used as a roadmap for the mathematical background needed to present the RSA public key algorithm.

Other books and resources were also previewed and may be of interest to those developing a new security course or those interested in enhancing an existing one. The author attended a SWEET (Secure WEb dEvelopment Teaching) workshop at SIGCSE 2011, which proffered laboratory exercises and other resources specifically for teaching secure web development [15]. The SEED project is another NSF-funded initiative with numerous resources including 29 labs as of this writing [11]. Towson University's Security Injections provide security modules that can be injected into several courses throughout the computer science curriculum, from CS0 to a Computer Networks course [10]. Smith's *Elementary Information Security* [13] is a comprehensive text geared more toward information security than the dual cryptographic and computer/network security focus of the course presented. However, those wishing a single resource that covers the new CS2013 Information Assurance and Security Knowledge Area only may consider Smith's book. Lastly, Goodrich and Tamassia's *Introduction to Computer Security* [7] is also a comprehensive self-contained text requiring only a CS2-level background and has a broad focus on security concepts and one chapter on Cryptography. The book integrates some of the labs from the SEED project and may be considered as a lower-level substitute to the Stallings text for a course that is not so heavily focused on Cryptography.

Both courses used Cryptool, a free and open source program originally developed as an employee education tool at a bank in Germany [4]. The Cryptool project has since evolved into a fully-functional tool that allows users to explore, practice, learn about, and/or view demos of all major historic and modern cryptographic algorithms. Originally developed as a Windows-only application, later versions included a limited web-based version called Cryptool-Online, and in 2012, a platform-independent version based on Java, called JCryptool, was released [4]. Cryptool is available in English, German, Polish, and Spanish versions.

The independent studies and the summer courses with a laboratory focus also used either Live DVDs or Virtual Machines (i.e. VMWare or Virtual Box) with Linux distributions. These were used to allow the students to experiment with OpenSSL and network utility tools to send encrypted files and view packet traffic in the local network. The semester-long mathematics cross-listed course did not utilize Linux labs, partly because of the weaker computer science skills and background of some of the students. In addition, the physical lab setup was problematic: the University-wide network does not allow any local network traffic not destined for the host to be observed or intercepted, and the departmental lab did not have enough computers to accommodate the students, even if some students brought their own laptops.

3.3 Course Structure

Both courses began with the students writing summary papers of *The Code Book.* In the semester-long mathematics cross-listed course, students engaged in in-class peer review and had the opportunity to revise their papers based on peer feedback. In the summer courses there was not enough time to accommodate a paper revision, although it would have been a valuable experience, especially since many of the students were non-native English speakers and would have benefitted from reading their peers' papers and having the opportunity for revision.

Both courses had a midterm and comprehensive final exam. In the semester-long mathematics cross-listed course, either a homework or a lab was assigned approximately every-other week. In the summer course with a laboratory focus, there were only 3 homework assignments, but labs were performed most class days (13 labs were assigned over the 5 ½ weeks of the course). In the mathematics cross-listed course, labs involved Cryptool only, while in the summer course with a laboratory focus, labs included both Cryptool and Linux-based labs. Table 1 gives a listing of the topics for both the Cryptool and Linux-based labs. Labs were typically worked on in pairs and consisted of students working through a prescribed set of applied exercises. Most labs also included an individual analysis component that was completed outside of class, which consisted of "big picture" analysis as well as questions that required more detailed work directly related to the lab exercises. Some of the labs were originally obtained from Crowley, although the majority were developed by the author as the course evolved.

Another major component of both courses was the presentation of current news articles by students at the beginning of every class. Students were instructed to choose a news article from a reputable news source from within three months of the date of their presentation that was related to cryptography or computer, network, or information security. A link to the article was posted

Table 2. Lab Topics

Cryptool Labs	Linux Labs
Monoalphabetic ciphers	Symmetric cryptography using OpenSSL
Vigenère and Enigma	
DES, AES, and CBC	Message Digests using OpenSSL
HMACs	Networked key exchange
Pseudo-random number generation	Different key exchange protocols
RSA	Dictionary attack on passwords
Digital Signatures	Traffic/packet analysis

or sent to students ahead of time; at the beginning of class the student gave a brief summary of the news article including its relevance to cryptography or security, and then led a brief discussion over the content of the article. Credit for news article presentations were included as part of the class participation grade.

The semester-long mathematics cross-listed class also included a research, applied research, or implementation project of the student's choosing (with the topic approved by the professor). The project included a paper or implementation and write-up, and class presentation of their work.

In addition, both courses had exposure to professionals currently working in the security industry. In the semester-long mathematics cross-listed course, an alumni working at a security division of Hewlett Packard in Austin, Texas came to guest lecture for a class. The lecture demonstrated the need for mastery of many mathematics and computer science topics and the need for continual learning, to keep up and work in the field of security. In the summer course with a laboratory focus, the class was invited by three recent alumni to a company in Accra, Ghana that develops ATM hardware, software, and services. During the field trip students were able to see the server room and learn about some of their network security issues and safeguards; see their control room and learn about the real-time tracking of ATM transactions and how they use algorithms and protocols discussed in class; and see the insides of an ATM machine and learn about many of the physical and software security mechanisms built into ATMs.

3.4 Course Content

Both courses covered similar material, although for some topics the two courses covered certain material in more or less depth. Both courses began with studying historic cryptosystems using material from the textbooks, which also overlapped material in *The Code Book.* Coverage of the more mathematical Hill cipher was included in mathematics cross-listed course but was skipped for the laboratory focused course. The modern block ciphers DES and AES, and the concept of cipher block chaining (CBC) were also discussed in both courses, with more emphasis placed on the theories of Feistel ciphers and the properties of AES in the mathematics cross-listed course. In both courses the number theory background needed to fully understand RSA public key cryptography was introduced, with more emphasis on the mathematical theory in the mathematics cross-listed course. Cryptographic hash functions, message authentication codes (MACs) and keyed-hashed MACS (HMACs) were also covered in both courses in similar depth. The Diffie-Hellman-Merkle key exchange protocol, other key exchange protocols, and different techniques for producing digital signatures were also covered in both courses. Computer security threats (e.g. classifications of Malware) and network security threats (e.g. DDOS Attacks) were covered in similar depth, and risk analysis was discussed in both courses as well. Finally, secret key management, public key certificates and PKI infrastructure, user authentication protocols, and Kerberos were also covered in both courses.

Three topics were also covered that are not necessarily considered fundamental knowledge but that the author views as significantly important in the fields of cryptography and computer and network security: true and pseudo-random number generation, issues of passwords, and elliptic curve cryptography. True and pseudo-random number generators were discussed in somewhat more detail in the laboratory focused course, which may seem counter-intuitive; the reason is that all students in the laboratory focused course had taken an elementary statistics course and there was no guarantee that even the mathematics majors in the mathematics cross-listed course has taken any probability or statistics course. Passwords were discussed in both courses, including: hashing and storage, their use in authentication protocols, the purpose of salting passwords, and recent studies examining password qualities; in the laboratory course, a detailed Linux-based lab in which students implemented a brute-force attack on both salted and unsalted passwords was also performed. Lastly, elliptic curve cryptography, the most recent major multi-purpose cryptographic method, was also studied; not surprisingly, the mathematics cross-listed course studied this topic in more detail than the applied course.

3.5 Topics Covered and CS2013 Ironman Draft Guidelines

The Ironman Draft of the upcoming CS2013 curricular guidelines separate Information Assurance and Security (IAS) into a separate Knowledge Area, with 2 hours listed as Core-Tier1, 6 hours listed Core-Tier2, and numerous Elective topics [6]. In addition, IAS topics are distributed among other Knowledge Areas, with 23 Core-Tier1 hours and 46 Core-Tier-2 hours distributed among 8 other Knowledge Areas. There is already significant overlap between security concepts presented as the 2 Core-Tier1 and 6 Core-Tier2 IAS topics in the CS2013 Ironman Draft, and courses already taught in a typical computer science curriculum. The versions of the course presented here serve to strengthen and deepen the students' understanding of many of these core topics by providing an in-depth study of the cryptographic principles underlying the concepts and algorithms. In addition, the course expands the students' security breadth by adding other IAS Core-Tier1 and Core-Tier2 topics that are distributed in other Knowledge Areas, or that are listed as IAS Elective topics in the CS2013 Ironman Draft.

The course encompasses all of the Elective IAS/Cryptography category, all of the IAS/Network Security Core-Tier1 and most of the Core-Tier2 hours, most of the IAS/Fundamental Concepts Core-Tier1 and Core-Tier2 hours, and includes a modicum of other topics throughout the CS2013 Ironman Draft IAS Knowledge Area: topics from IAS/Risk Management, IAS/Security Architecture and Systems Administration, IAS/Security Policy and Governance, NC/Introduction, NC/Networked Applications, OS/Security and Protection, SE/Software Project Management, SF/Virtualization and Isolation, and SP/Security Policies, Laws, and Computer Crimes. In addition, discussion of current news articles gave students exposure to additional topics in: IAS/Network Security, OS/Overview of Operating Systems, OS/Operating Systems Principles, SP/Intellectual Property, SP/Professional Ethics, and SP/Security Policies, Laws, and Computer Crimes

Table 2. Course Topics and location in CS2013 Ironman.

Topic(s)	Location in CS2013 Ironman	Tier1, Tier2, or Elective
Introductory security concepts	IAS/Fundamental Concepts	Tier1 and Tier2
	IAS/Security Policy and Governance	Elective
Risk analysis	IAS/Risk Management	Elective
	SE/Software Project Management	Tier2
Classic and historic ciphers	IAS/Cryptography	Elective
Block Ciphers: DES and AES; CBC mode	IAS/Cryptography	Elective
Cryptographic hash functions, message digests, MACS, HMACs	IAS/Cryptography	Elective
True and Pseudo-random number generators	None	N/A
Number theory for RSA	IAS/Cryptography	Elective
RSA Public Key Cryptography	IAS/Cryptography	Elective
Diffie-Hellman-Merkle and other secret-key exchange protocols	IAS/Cryptography	Elective
Digital Signatures	IAS/Cryptography	Elective
Elliptic Curve Cryptography	None	N/A
Secret Key Management and Hybrid Systems	IAS/Cryptography	Elective
Public Key Infrastructure	IAS/Cryptography	Elective
User Authentication Protocols, Access Control, and Kerberos	IAS/Cryptography	Elective
	IAS/Security Arch and Systems Admin	Elective
	OS/Security and Protection	Tier2
Issues of passwords	IAS/Security Arch and Systems Admin	Elective
	SP/Security Policies, Laws, and Computer Crimes	Elective
Computer Security and Threats; Malicious Code	IAS/Fundamental Concepts	Tier2
	SF/Virtualization and Isolation	Tier2

	SP/Security Policies, Laws, and Computer Crimes	Elective
Network Security and Threats; Network Attacks	IAS/Fundamental Concepts	Tier2
	IAS/Network Security	Tier1
	NC/Introduction	Tier1
	NC/Networked Applications	Tier2
Current News Articles	IAS/Network Security	Tier1 and Tier2
	OS/Overview of OS	Tier1
	OS/OS Principles	Tier1
	SP/Intellectual Property	Tier1
	SP/Professional Ethics	Tier1 and Tier2
	SP/Security Policies, Laws, and Computer Crimes	Elective

4. OUTCOMES OF THE TWO COURSES

The course evaluations in both courses were excellent, with overall comments such as, "It inspired me!", "The course was interesting and captivating.", and "I want more." Students were clearly engaged in and excited about the course.

Students consistently reported, both via course evaluations and verbally, that they enjoyed the *The Code Book* assignment, even though it entailed reading a non-fiction book and writing a paper over it in a relatively short amount of time. *The Code Book* is engaging and easy to read, much more like a novel than a textbook, and the students agreed that it was a great way to learn the history. Although published in 1999, the material is not "dated" – it presents a comprehensive history of cryptography from the 5th century B.C. to the late 1990s, with a final chapter on quantum cryptography. Through the paper the students exercised their writing skills, and through the peer review and optional re-write for increased credit (in the semester-long mathematics cross-listed course only) students improved their writing skills as well.

The students also appreciated the daily news articles as a connection between the theory and what is happening in "real life". Sprenkle & Duvall call this the "broader issues" component of a computer science course [14]. The discussion surrounding the articles varied from forced to lively, and often connected to previous articles or previous course material. Due to the plethora of news articles related to security, students had plenty of topics to choose from, and the range of news topics presented throughout each course was largely comprehensive. Interestingly, the American students appeared to put less effort into choosing the news article they presented and preparing for the presentation than the West African students, who spent a lot of effort finding an article that was different from past articles and also relevant to the coinciding or recent course topics; the West African students also spent significant time and effort reading the background information the article referenced. Including student presentations of news articles is an aspect of the course that is highly recommended to anyone teaching a security course, because it serves to consistently highlight the relevance of security in just about every facet of our lives. For the mathematics cross-listed course, which was about ¼ mathematics majors, it also served to demonstrate the importance of security and the applicability of mathematics, and not just computer science, to the field of security. Several course evaluations commented positively on this aspect of the course, including, "The news presentation helped make a clear relationship to what happened in the real world." and "I knew nothing was secure, but Wow! All these articles about attacks is crazy!"

An added benefit of a computer security elective course that is cross-listed with mathematics is the possibility of enticing mathematics majors to take more computer science courses, and encouraging mathematics majors to take CS1 earlier rather than later in their academic careers. Most of the mathematics majors in the Southwestern University mathematics cross-listed course were either graduating seniors or rising seniors with little or no opportunity to fit "extra" CS courses in their degree plan before graduation. However, at the end of the computer security elective course, one rising senior mathematics major switched to a Computational Mathematics major, a major that incorporates much of the mathematics and computer science coursework but that is less than a full double-major. In addition, a Biology major who had taken the course in conjunction with CS 2 registered to take more CS classes the following semester. Although only two students, this points to the interest of non-CS majors desiring to take more computer science courses.

The laboratory exercises were a favorite component of each course. In both courses students commented on this in freeform responses on the course evaluations: in the semester-long mathematics cross-listed course, 7 of the 23 students said that more hands-on labs would have improved the course. A recommended future iteration of the semester-long mathematics cross-listed course would include more contact time so that more labs could be accommodated. In the summer course with a laboratory focus, almost ½ of the students commented on the labs as a strength of the course, including comments such as, "The intensive lab sessions were exciting and demystify the course", and "Labs were very helpful and questions stressed critical understanding and applied logic." Logistically, the labs in the summer course were essential since the course met 2-3 hours per day, 5 days per week; without the more applied laboratory work, students would have been too overwhelmed and/or bored in a 2-3 hour class every day. The students in the summer, laboratory focused course also greatly valued the field trip, and commented both verbally and in the course evaluations about how the trip showed the practicality and relevance of course topics and work being done in the real world.

The semester-long mathematics cross-listed course had an independent project in which students either researched theory, investigated an algorithm or application area of an algorithm not covered in class, implemented an algorithm, or performed a hands-on computer or network security investigation. Overall this was a valuable assignment, since students chose topics particularly interesting to them and further exercised their research and/or independent learning, writing and class presentation skills. However, due to the relatively large class size for the liberal arts setting (23 students), project presentations consumed the last 2 ½ weeks of the semester, which allowed less time for other class topics or labs. In the future, if enrollment in the course remains high, student in-class presentations of projects may be eliminated so that even more time could be devoted to labs or additional topics.

Both courses are expected to continue; the semester-long mathematics cross-listed course may become one of the "standard" electives at Southwestern University. The summer course with a laboratory focus at Ashesi University College in Ghana is expected to continue and expand into a summer study abroad opportunity for American computer science students. In addition to providing an opportunity for both American and West African students to learn about cryptography and computer security, students would also learn from each other about the similar and differing issues surrounding computer and network security in two very different areas of the world.

5. CONCLUSIONS

Two models of an elective Cryptography and Computer Security course in a liberal arts context are presented, one a semester-long course taught at a traditional liberal arts college in the United States, another a summer course taught at a new University with a liberal arts focus in Ghana, West Africa. The semester-long course was cross-listed as a mathematics course and included an independent project and student presentations of their work; the summer course included about the same amount of contact time, but more time was spent in the lab and there was no individual project. Both courses were very successful and covered much of the same material. The courses provided students depth in the cryptographic principles underlying modern security algorithms, as well as background in the history of cryptography and an opportunity to discuss current news articles. In both courses, the laboratory components were considered essential and served to provide the students with opportunities for hands-on engagement with the course material. Future iterations of the semester-long mathematics cross-listed course will endeavor to include more labs. The summer course with a laboratory focus is expected to continue and expand into a summer study abroad opportunity in order for American computer science students to study in Ghana.

6. REFERENCES

[1] ACM TechNews Archive. http://technews.acm.org/archives.cfm.

[2] Chen, L., Tao, L., Li, X. and Lin, C. 2010. A Tool for Teaching Web Application Security. In *Proceedings of the 14th Colloquium for Information Systems Security Education*. CISSE, Severn, MD, 17-24.

[3] Crowley, E. 2006. Developing 'Hands-on' Security Activities with Open Source Software and Live CDs, *Journal for Computing Sciences in Colleges* 21, 4 (Apr. 2006), 139-145.

[4] Cryptool Portal, Cryptography for Everybody. http://www.cryptool.org/en/.

[5] Du, W. SEED: a suite of instructional laboratories for computer SEcurity EDucation. 2007. In *Proceedings of the 38th ACM Technical Symposium on Computer Science Education*, ACM, New York, NY, 486-490, DOI=http://doi.acm.org/10.1145/1227310.1227474.

[6] Joint Task Force on Computing Curricula (Nov. 2012). Computer Science Curricula 2013: Ironman Draft (Version 0.8). http://ai.stanford.edu/users/sahami/CS2013/ironman-draft/cs2013-ironman-v0.8.pdf.

[7] Goodrich, M.T. and Tamassia, R. 2011. *Introduction to Computer Security*. Addison-Wesley, New York.

[8] Mel, H.X. and Baker, D. 2001. *Cryptography Decrypted*. Addison-Wesley, New York.

[9] National Security Agency, Central Security Service. Information Assurance Scholarship Program (IASP). http://www.nsa.gov/careers/opportunities_4_u/students/undergraduate/iasp1.shtml.

[10] Security Injections @ Towson University. http://triton.towson.edu/~cssecinj/secinj/.

[11] SEED Project. http://www.cis.syr.edu/~wedu/seed/.

[12] Singh, S. 1999. *The Code Book: The Science of Secrecy from Ancient Egypt to Quantum Cryptography*. Doubleday, New York.

[13] Smith, R. 2011. *Elementary Information Security*. Jones and Bartlett, Burlington, MA.

[14] Sprenkle, S. and Duvall, S. 2012. Reshaping the Image of Computer Science in Only Fifteen Minutes (of Class) a Week. In *Proceedings of the 43rd ACM Technical Symposium on Computer Science Education*, ACM, New York, NY, 595-600, DOI=http://doi.acm.org/10.1145/2157136.2157308.

[15] SWEET Project. http://csis.pace.edu/~lchen/sweet/.

[16] Stallings, W. 2011. Cryptography and Network Security. Pearson- Prentice Hall, New York.

[17] U.S. Office of Personnel Management. Federal Cyber Service: Scholarship for Service. https://www.sfs.opm.gov/.

[18] Taylor, B. and Kaza, S. 2011. Security Injections: Modules to Help Students Remember, Understand, and Apply Secure Coding Techniques. In *Proceedings of the 16th Annual Joint Conference on Innovation and Technology in Computer Science Education*, ACM, New York, NY, 3-7, DOI=http://doi.acm.org/10.1145/1999747.1999752.

[19] Tjaden B.C. 2004. *Fundamentals of Secure Computer Systems*. Franklin, Beedle & Assoc., Inc. Wilsonville, OR.

The Entrepreneur's Bootcamp: A New Model For Teaching Web/Mobile Development and Software Entrepreneurship

Timothy Hickey
CS Department, MS018
Brandeis University
Waltham, MA 02454
tjhickey@brandeis.edu

Pito Salas
CS Department, MS018
Brandeis University
Waltham, MA 02454
pitosalas@brandeis.edu

ABSTRACT

This paper describes three years of experience with an intensive three course summer semester on web and mobile entrepreneurship for second year CS students and beyond. The program is similar in structure to a high school summer camp or to a summer accelerator/incubator program except that it has a much higher level of academic content and provides the credit equivalent to three Computer Science electives and a full semester of residency. The program has been effective at teaching students production programming and entrepreneurship and has stimulated entrepreneurial activity during the academic year. It is taken by about half of the CS majors in the department which is surprising since it requires them to spend their summer months in a very intense academic and entrepreneurial experience which is quite different from the usual summer experience of their peers.

Categories and Subject Descriptors

D.2 [**Software Engineering**]: [Software Engineering]; K.3.2 [**Computer Science Education**]: [Computer Science Education]

General Terms

Human Factors, Experimentation, Design

Keywords

Entrepreneurship, Mobile Applications, Web Applications

1. INTRODUCTION

In 2010, our university authorized a new summer program that would consist of three co-requisite classes and would provide a semester of residency equivalent to Fall or Spring. The courses were to be experiential and intensive. We created a Computer Science version of this program which debuted in 2010 and was focused on teaching web and mobile application development in the context of entrepreneurship and software engineering to students who had completed a two semester Java programming course.

The program, which we called the COSI JBS program, bears many similarities to the Computer Science summer camps taught on University campuses for high school and middle school students [2], but taught at a much more advanced and intense level. Nevertheless the sense of community bonding and shared purpose is high. It is also very similar to the experience of partipating in an accelerator or incubator (e.g. TechStars or BetaSpring), except that there is a strong academic component with reading and programming assignments, blogging, and both formative and summative assessment (as well as credit for three college level computer science electives). Moreover, we have taught the course with two college faculty (not always present at the same time) and a graduate student TA. This results in an extreme apprenticeship model of learning [9].

The program also emphasizes Lean Startup methodologies [7] which employ an evidenced-based method for product development requiring early and continuous interaction with potential clients, formulation and testing of hypothesis about the potential users, and agile development methodology. We used a variation of Scrum. Social media based marketing was also explored [3] as part of the curriculum.

1.1 Primary features

Here are the main features of the COSI JBS program.

Three co-requisite classes. Students completing the program earned credit for three courses. In the 2012 session, the courses were CS152aj: Web Applications, CS152bj: Social Networks, and CS154aj: The JBS Incubator.

Minimal prerequisites. The program was designed for students who had a solid understanding of Java programming. The program attracted a mix of students, about half had not taken the Data Structures and Algorithms course. The students were required to learn the fundamentals of Ruby on their own and to complete a programming assignment in Ruby before the summer program began.

Intensive pedagogy. The program consists of 10 weeks of classes, with class time from 10-12 and 1-4 every day. The mornings were typically devoted to the two lecture classes CS152aj and C152bj. The afternoons were a combination of invited lectures, workshops, and supervised lab time where students worked in teams to design, build, and launch a web application with a mobile component. Since all students were taking the same courses, the initial part of the summer

SIGCSE'13, March 6–9, 2013, Denver, Colorado, USA.

could focus more on the lecture style courses while the later weeks consists mostly of incubator work where students were completing their projects.

Faculty Workload. The workload for the faculty was much greater than for a summer school course. The COSI JBS program was co-taught with two faculty, one TA and 10-15 students. This is an expensive program in terms of faculty time.

Integration of CS, SE, and Business. The COSI JBS program offered a successful combination of Computer Science concepts, Software Engineering techniques, and Software Entrepreneurship practices.

Playing the Whole Game. The students who completed this course, gained an introduction to the kind of software development that many of them will participate in as graduates if they enter the software industry. The fact that they were spending 10 weeks designing, developing, and launching a product for their CS154aj Incubator course provided strong motivation for the other more academic components of the course.

This program follows the philosophy espoused in Perkin's recent book, "Making Learning Whole." [6] which argues convincingly of the benefits of having students learn skills and concepts in the context of creating a real world artifact using the tools and best practices from the professional world while simultaneously learning the academic components required for this level of software engineering.

2. PEDAGOGICAL STRUCTURE OF THE SUMMER PROGRAM

One of the most distinctive features of the COSI JBS is that it allows great flexibility in structuring the learning environment, providing an experience which is more like a summer camp or a bootcamp or startup than typical summer school. We took advantage of this flexibility in a number of ways. Class time was divided into several different types of pedagogical interaction:

- **Traditional Lectures.** The academic content was covered in traditional lectures where students had assigned reading, the instructor reviewed the material, interspersing the lecture with questions and guiding class discussions. In the beginning of the summer we had lectures every morning, toward the end of the summer several days each week were devoted entirely to experiential learning. The students earned credit for two full semester courses through these traditional lectures. The particular content varied each of the three summers but always included some aspect of web and/or mobile application design and development.

- **Incubator Labs and Summer Projects.** Students also earned a full course credit for an Incubator class which was run as an afternoon lab. In the first week, students were led through a process in which they brainstormed ideas for summer projects and then divided into teams of 2-4 around products that were approved by the faculty. Over the course of the summer the students were introduced to the best practices of collaborative software design using Agile methodology, we discuss this more in detail in the next section. Each team was assigned a client who worked closely with the team to keep it on track.

- **CEO Speaker Series.** Once or twice a week we brought in a distinguished practitioner, typically a CEO or CTO of a local software company, who discussed some aspect of Entrepreneurship using their company to illustrate the points. For example, we had speakers on Agile Development, on Startup Financing, on Social Marketing, on Customer Development, on Hiring and Interviewing, etc. This series was viewed by the students as one of the best parts of the class and it also served to help them build their professional networks. These were typically scheduled in the afternoons after a lunch where 2-3 students would be invited to dine with the speaker and instructors before the talk.

- **Daily Homework.** At the end of each day, the homework assignment for the next morning was discussed. Students typically were required to complete some reading, apply the concepts covered by completing short coding assignments (if appropriate), reflect on the homework through a post in the course blog, and screen record a quick review of their code including a demo of it running. The blogging assignments also required some reflection which greatly helped in fine tuning the amount and type of homework in this intense course. Such reflective blogging has been shown to be useful in other intro level courses as well [8]. Each morning we began with homework cold calls where selected students presented their homework solutions. Students maintained a google doc containing links to all of their homework components (blog, videos, code in github) and a graduate student reviewed these links and assigned grades every day.

- **Weekly Programming Projects.** Each Monday a larger programming project was assigned which required students to solve an interesting problem using the concepts and techniques being taught in the course. For example, in the most recent summer we had a sequence of programming assignments where students created a recommender system for movies using an online open-source movie database with 10 million reviews. The insights and skills they developed working on these problems were directly applicable to their own incubator projects.

- **Weekly Project Presentations.** At the end of every week, each group was required to give a presentation on their project following guidelines provided by the faculty. The goal of this activity was to give them practice in presenting their work to a public audience and giving them the opportunity to reflect on their progress. This activity builds on the Studio Based Learning model [4] but applied in a team context. Each of the 2-4 person teams gave a 10-15 minute presentation of their project, including design documents, results of user studies, architecture of the project, code review when appropriate, live demos, and assessment of project progress based on milestones they created. The audience consisted of the faculty, teaching assistant, all the other students, and a few new reviewers seeing the material for the first time. The audience members critiqued the project (and presentation) and the team responded. This process was repeated each week building up to the Product Showcase in the 10th and last week.

- **Community Building Social Events.** An important component of such an intense program is the inclusion of purely social events such as pot lucks, river cruises, trips to the beach, ice cream socials.

- **Final Product Showcase.** The COSI JBS program concluded with a Product Showcase in which the teams presented their products to a panel of 5-10 professionals and an audience of 50-100 students, staff, and faculty. The professional panel gave comments about the products after each presentation.

3. TEACHING SOFTWARE PRACTICES

One of the goals of the COSI JBS program is to have students learn what it is like to work in a startup creating a product. Most of our graduates do go on to work in software companies and many of those are startups and some of them gain this kind of experience through summer internships. The difference between a COSI JBS and a summer internship at a startup is that the JBS is designed both as an academic experience with lectures, homework, course credit, quizzes, oral presentations, etc. and it gives primary responsibility for the selection, design, development, marketing and launch of the product to the students themselves.

In "Making Learning Whole," David Perkins makes an argument that the most effective teaching engages the students in the process that professionals follow [6]. So when learning Mathematics students should gain a strong sense of what it is that Mathematicians do. Sometimes the instructor needs to create a simplified version of the experience which still captures most of the key features. The COSI JBS is precisely that kind of an experience.

One particularly valuable part of the course is that students are given the opportunity to learn how to rapidly pick up new technologies and teach themselves how to become proficient. In the course we give workshops on the underlying concepts of these technologies but require students to master the details themselves. In the world of professional software development, learning how to seek out and master the latest technologies is a key skill. In the Summer 2012 session, the students were exposed to and mastered the following technologies, none of which had been seen by them prior to taking this summer JBS:

- **Source Control Management.** All programming assignments and code for the team project was managed with git, a collaborative SCM, and hosted on github.com, a web-based code repository. Students learned how to branch, merge, resolve conflicts, tag, review, and fork git repositories.

- **Web Application Frameworks.** The web applications were developed using Ruby on Rails. The students were required to learn Ruby and Ruby on Rails by completing a series of programming projects and using online and print materials to help them master Ruby and the Rails framework.

- **Platform as a Service.** The students learned how to deploy their projects to the web using Heroku, which is a site that allows users to deploy Ruby on Rails apps from a Git repository and to analyze, debug and tune the deployment remotely using a command-line API.

- **Object-Relational Mapping.** We introduced SQL over the summer and students became adept at using the Ruby on Rails ActiveRecord API which models database tables as Ruby objects and provides an API for selecting and modifying records that is independent of the underlying database. Indeed, they develop locally using MySQL or SQLite and using Postgres when porting to Heroku.

- **Test-driven Development.** We introduced unit testing with Rspec and integration testing using Capybara that allowed detailed full-system testing by modelling and validating patterns of interaction with their web applications.

- **Hypertext Markup and Style Sheet Languages.** Students learned to specify the layout and styling of webpages using HTML 5 and CSS 2.3 and in particular they learned the Twitter Bootstrap API as well as the SCSS extension of CSS.

- **Client-side Functionality and REST.** Interaction with the webserver was implemented using the REST approach which required an understanding of the HTTP protocol and the HTTP verbs in particular. jQuery and Ajax were used to facilitate more interactivity in the webpages.

- **Multi-platform Mobile Development.** Mobile application development was presented using the Apache Cordova (previously PhoneGap) framework. This approach provides, for each of the standard platforms (Android, iOS, Blackberry, etc.) a base application in which every mobile screen is defined by HTML, CSS, and Javascript. All interaction between the user interface and the underlying features of the phone (GPS, camera, speakers, microphone, compass, orientation, accelerometer, local storage, etc.) is handled using a Javascript API. Communication with servers is implemented using Ajax. The advantage of this approach is that students can, and do, build a full mobile application that interacts with their website using REST protocols in as little as 1-2 weeks.

- **Cloud-based Multi-media Collaboration Tools.** A less technical, but still quite useful component of the course is learning how to use the google applications (especially google sites and google docs) to create portfolios of their work. They also learn various screen recording tools so they can create videos of code walk throughs to post on their google sites. Finally they blog (and comment on blog posts) almost every day, which develops written communication skills.

- **Agile Project Management and Collaboration Tools.** Students were required to use the Scrum version of Agile methodology in which they specify project goals in the forms of stories which are assigned, weighted, tracked, and classified on a continual basis. There are several different online tools to help support this process and most students used PivotalTracker.

- **Crowd-sourced Technical Support.** One of the key skills students learned over the summer was how to leverage the online presence of fellow coders to solve problems. One of the most effective tools was StackOverflow a Question/Answer site with subdomains devoted to particular technologies (e.g. Ruby on Rails). We have found that many students are reticent to use these online tools, but that after a few required assignments they learned to become both good net citizens (answering questions when appropriate) and good clients (asking appropriate questions only after investing an adequate amount of research into the problem).

4. CURRICULUM

The particular curriculum has varied somewhat over the three summer programs. Each summer we've covered some combination of Web and Mobile development. Usually one of the three courses focused on one technology (e.g. Web Design using RoR, or Mobile App Design using Android) and another on a higher level application domain (e.g. Game Design, or Social Networking). The third course is always the JBS Incubator, which is an experiential course covering Entrepreneurship and Collaborative Software Engineering. The particular content taught in the two academic courses in the COSI JBS can vary considerably and will likely change every year as the students and faculty interests in current technology changes.

What makes the program distinctive is the way in which the content of the two Academic courses is explored more deeply in the Incubator course by applying it to the design, development, and launch of a real product.

5. SUMMER 2012 PROJECTS

As in [1, 5], the COSI JBS was designed to eschew the use of toy programs as a teaching aid and to let students sink their teeth into a real project that would be a fully functioning web and mobile application designed for real users. The role of the faculty is mainly to serve as mentors and guides in a real startup process where the goal is to produce a product that could serve as the initial offering of a company. We believe we have been largely successful as the examples of this year's projects below demonstrate. It is unclear whether the students will continue to work on these projects or will open source them or both. In past years about a third of the students either continued their project (possibly pivoting a time or two) or started a new product effort using the skills they had learned.

The 8-10 week intense experience provides just the amount of time needed for the students to go through the entire process of designing, developing, launching, and marketing a product while at the same time learning all of the web and mobile concepts, skills, and technology as well as agile development methodology.

The Summer 2012 class of 11 students consisted of 1 rising sophomore, 2 postbac/MA students, 1 graduating senior, and 7 rising juniors. All students had completed the first year programming courses but only 3 had completed the data structures course. The students formed into four groups during the first week and all completed working projects with both web and mobile components by the 10th week. Since all students are either taking full-time schedules or are working in the Fall and Spring, any continued work on the projects will be at a reduced rate. Several groups are considering making their projects open source and looking for collaborators with more time.

Where's My Lane. This project was developed with the Office of New Urban Mechanics in the City of Boston in response to concerns of bicycle commuters about double parking in bike lanes. The project consists of a database-backed website showing locations and times of double parkers (selected by time of day and date) as well as feedback from the city. There is also a mobile component consisting of a mobile app (on iOS and Android) that reports the location and time of a double parked car when pressed. The 3 person group ran surveys, held focus group meetings with bicycle commuters, and met regularly with representatives from the Mayor's office.

Volunteer Hours. This website allows community service providers and volunteers to register and login. The providers can create events. The volunteers can register to attend those events. The providers can verify that the volunteers attended (using either a mobile app or a web interface). The volunteers have all of their volunteering hours displayed on a profile page along with verification information from the provider. This can be used for proof of community service. The providers have detailed information online about their volunteers! The two members of this team met with the community service staff at the University and also created several surveys to test their hypotheses.

The Spy Game. This is an ambitious mobile/web project to create a version of hide and seek where the location of the "spy" becomes visible on the mobile device map every 60 seconds. The locations of the police are always available. The goal is for the police to "catch" the spy in 10 minutes.

Wiki Witness. This project provides a wikipedia-like interface for first person accounts of historical events. Users can register, view the narratives for an event, and add their own narrative. Administrators can create events, and remove users (and their posts).

6. RESULTS OF THE COSI JBS PROGRAM

The program has been well-received by the students. Our university graduates about 20-25 CS majors each year and the COSI JBS has attracted about 10-15 students each summer, so if this trend continues about half of all CS majors will be taking this program.

Many students express reservations about enrolling in the JBS program for a variety of reasons:

- The JBS leaves no time for summer recreation. Students are in class all day and completing homework every evening. Even students in internships will typically have their evenings and weekends off. This has pedagogical benefits as the students are able to become totally focused on their product and the related academic content, but it can deter some students from participating.

- Computer Science students typically use the summer for internships which is not possible with the JBS. A partial answer to this is the extended JBS semester in which students take a full-time internship in the Fall as part of a single long semester (June-Dec) and earn credit for five courses: the three JBS courses, an internship course, and an online readings course in the Fall. This option only attracts 1-3 students each year, indicating that the loss of a traditional summer is a concern for many students.

Over the three years that the COSI JBS has been offered as a summer program, we've noticed a considerable increase in entrepreneurial activity among our undergraduates. About a third of the JBS students continue to build products during the year and two or three have been starting companies each year and seeking funding from accelerators and other startup funding sources. Its possible that the students who are attracted to the JBS are the ones who would be starting companies anyway, so we don't have proof of causation, but there has been a noticeable change in the entrepreneurial culture among our majors in the past few years.

One challenge with the COSI JBS is that it requires a tremendous amount of faculty time and the need to compensate the faculty makes this an expensive program for the university, as it brings in less revenue than summer school or regular courses.

7. CONCLUSIONS

This novel approach to CS education has been successful on our campus. About half of our majors are projected to participate in the program at some point in their career. Several students each year describe the program as "transformative" and feel that it was a turning point in their academic and professional lives.

The program has been correlated with a perceived uptick in undergraduate entrepreneurial activity, but requires a major investment in faculty time to implement the apprenticeship-style model of teaching. The degree of faculty investment in teaching such a program is comparable to the time required to engage in and manage a large funded research project. This time requirement can be an impediment to getting research active faculty to participate.

In the future, we may offer a version of the COSI JBS designed as a capstone experience for masters students who are interested in starting their own companies or working in a startup.

8. REFERENCES

[1] Eric Allen, Robert Cartwright, and Charles Reis. Production programming in the classroom. *SIGCSE Bull.*, 35(1):89-93, Jan. 2003.

[2] Barbara Ericson and Tom McKlin. Effective and sustainable computing summer camps. In *Proceedings of the 43rd ACM technical symposium on Computer Science Education*, SIGCSE '12, page 289-294, New York, NY, USA, 2012. ACM.

[3] Francois Gossieaux and Ed Moran. *The Hyper-Social Organization: Eclipse Your Competition by Leveraging Social Media.* McGraw-Hill, 1 edition, June 2010.

[4] N. Hari Narayanan, Christopher Hundhausen, Dean Hendrix, and Martha Crosby. Transforming the CS classroom with studio-based learning. In *Proceedings of the 43rd ACM technical symposium on Computer Science Education*, SIGCSE '12, page 165-166, New York, NY, USA, 2012. ACM.

[5] Tom Nurkkala and Stefan Brandle. Software studio: teaching professional software engineering. In *Proceedings of the 42nd ACM technical symposium on Computer science education*, SIGCSE '11, page 153-158, New York, NY, USA, 2011. ACM.

[6] David N. Perkins. *Making Learning Whole: How Seven Principles of Teaching Can Transform Education.* Jossey-Bass, 1 edition, Dec. 2008.

[7] Eric Ries. *The Lean Startup: How Today's Entrepreneurs Use Continuous Innovation to Create Radically Successful Businesses.* Crown Business, Sept. 2011.

[8] Jeffrey A. Stone. Using reflective blogs for pedagogical feedback in CS1. In *Proceedings of the 43rd ACM technical symposium on Computer Science Education*, SIGCSE '12, page 259-264, New York, NY, USA, 2012. ACM.

[9] Arto Vihavainen, Matti Paksula, and Matti Luukkainen. Extreme apprenticeship method in teaching programming for beginners. In *Proceedings of the 42nd ACM technical symposium on Computer science education*, SIGCSE '11, page 93-98, New York, NY, USA, 2011. ACM.

Growing a Computer Science Program with a Focus on Game Development

Timothy E. Roden
Department of Computer Science
Lamar University
Beaumont, TX, USA
troden@lamar.edu

Rob LeGrand
Department of Mathematics & Computer Science
Angelo State University
San Angelo, TX, USA
rlegrand@angelo.edu

ABSTRACT
A comprehensive undergraduate curriculum in computer game development is described. The program was created as a set of elective courses in the context of a traditional computer science (CS) degree. Primary goals of the program were to increase enrollment in CS and prepare students for careers in the entertainment software industry. In addition, the CS department sought to compete for students with larger state institutions. To do so effectively the department needed to offer a unique program. Results show the new program helped the CS department to nearly triple enrollment over four years and achieve both statewide prominence and national recognition.

Categories and Subject Descriptors
K.3.2 [**Computing Milieux**]: Computers and Information Science Education [**Computer Science Education**]

General Terms
Design, Experimentation.

Keywords
Computer science education, game programming, game development.

1. INTRODUCTION
In 2007, the Computer Science (CS) Department at Angelo State University (ASU) sought to implement a new program in computer game development. The motivation was to increase the number of CS majors and turn around what had been a steady decline in majors over the preceding ten years, a trend not unique to ASU. Computer game development was identified as the single most significant enhancement to the existing CS program that had the potential to increase the number of majors, based on faculty interest and positive reports from other universities [1, 3, 13]. It was decided to add the new curriculum as a set of elective CS courses. The new curriculum was modeled not unlike other similar programs already ongoing in academia in which game development courses are typically targeted at upper-level students (juniors and seniors), and game development is kept within a traditional CS degree as opposed to creating a separate game development degree [3, 13, 14].

Three specific game development courses were added, all of which required students to complete the first three semesters of introductory CS programming courses as a prerequisite. Two of the courses focus on PC game development while one course features development for a handheld platform. An introductory course, open to all majors, was added. To add synergy to the program, the instructor teaching the Artificial Intelligence (AI) course adapted the course to include a focus on games. A dedicated laboratory was also established.

The new program had three goals:

1. Increase the number of students majoring in CS.
2. Prepare student for careers in game development.
3. Align with industry trends and government priorities.

1.1 Goal 1: Increase enrollment
At the beginning of the fall 2007 semester, enrollment in CS at ASU was dangerously low. There were not enough students for the faculty. Small class requests were common. Increasing enrollment was seen as mandatory to maintain the CS department. In addition, the department wanted to hire more faculty to diversify the capabilities of the department with an eventual goal of adding a graduate program within a few years. To increase enrollment significantly the department had to be competitive with larger state schools. With far fewer faculty and resources than other schools ASU needed a unique program. A survey of curricula at other state universities indicated only a few schools had any undergraduate programs in computer game development. The most notable program was at University of North Texas where a faculty member had been teaching game development since 1993 [13].

1.2 Goal 2: Prepare Students
Computer game development was an easy choice to add to the CS program at ASU. A faculty member in the department had experience developing games. Student interest was very high, as has been reported elsewhere [1, 7, 13] . Jobs in the industry pay well with average starting salaries for new graduates near $60,000. Due to the highly competitive nature of securing a job

SIGCSE'13, March 6–9, 2013, Denver, Colorado, USA.

in the industry after graduation the department knew any curriculum would need to prepare students adequately to be successful.

The new program was a good fit since the existing CS degree prepared students well for game development. For the first three semesters, CS majors take programming courses in C++. We believe a foundation in C++ prepares students for careers in game development better than another language such as Java. Other similar programs have taken the same approach in response to perceived industry demands. Also, like similar programs, we want students to graduate from the program with one or two significant game projects to showcase to potential employers [13, 16]. We also want students to leave with a basic understanding of how to develop games for a popular handheld platform since we believe handheld gaming will continue to grow in popularity and market share. In addition, a goal of the new program was to teach students not only how to program games but also how to create game art assets. Since the university art department did not offer classes in content creation for computer games, the department would take on this responsibility as part of the new program. Educating students about the industry was also a priority. Understanding the industry gives students a sense of perspective when working on particular platforms and helps them better identify a segment of the industry they want to target in their job search after graduation. The textbook chosen for the introductory course [12] does a good job surveying the industry.

Some universities have reported success with creating specialized game development degrees [8, 10, 16]. At ASU, we chose to keep the new program in the context of the traditional CS undergraduate degree for several reasons: First, implementing the new program as a set of classes simplified the approval process since only university-level approval was needed. Second, faculty believed a traditional CS degree was more beneficial to a graduate over the course of their career in case they wanted to work in a field of computing other than game development. Despite this, our experience has shown there is a significant population of prospective students who would rather earn a specialized degree.

1.3 Goal 3: Program Alignment

To make sure the new program was successful consideration was given to how the new program aligned with other priorities, including university, local, state, and national.

At the university level, a new president had been hired in summer 2007. One of the president's top priorities was growth. The CS department was able to leverage this to obtain university funding for a new lab and equipment and also to move the new program quickly through the university curriculum approval process. The department also worked with the university communication department to publicize and promote the new program as much as possible including web, newspaper and radio advertising. CS faculty also met regularly with university recruiters to discuss strategies for marketing the new program to prospective students.

At the local level, representatives from the Small Business Development Center, located on campus, were eager to establish new relationships with businesses potentially seeking to relocate to San Angelo. This proved to be very beneficial a few years later when publicity surrounding the program's mobile development course attracted several companies to give the university grants to development mobile software.

At the state level, attracting the game development industry to the state was a priority of the state's Governor. The Governor had recently attended the annual Electronic Entertainment Expo to recruit businesses to the state. It was anticipated the program would apply for state funds to enhance department facilities and equipment. Also, the state has more game development companies than any other state besides California. This was another fact that helped in recruiting.

At the national level, computer science had been identified for several years as one of the best growth areas for jobs by the U.S. Bureau of Labor Statistics. Starting salaries for computer science graduates are typically highly competitive as compared to other disciplines. Both of these facts were highlighted in communication to prospective students. The program also expected to apply for grants at the national level.

2. PROGRAM OVERVIEW

The new program in game development consisted of four elective courses. This presented a problem since the existing CS degree contained only two electives. To manage this, the existing degree was restructured. The existing degree's large kernel of required courses was trimmed to a smaller kernel to incorporate five electives. This allowed students to take the four game development courses and the artificial intelligence course. Courses moved out of the required kernel were programming languages, architecture and software engineering, all of which were retained in the curriculum as electives.

At ASU the academic year is divided into two semesters. Students can optionally complete a third semester in the summer. Beginning students in the CS program take three semesters of C++ programming. Subsequently, many other required and electives courses become available. The core of the game development program is the two-course sequence in PC game development. Since students must take the first three semesters of C++ and the first course in the PC development sequence begins in the fall, students are typically juniors when they enroll in the PC courses. A course in handheld game development is offered in the spring so students can begin developing games in the second half of their sophomore year. An introductory course can be taken at any time in the program. Freshmen interested in game development are especially encouraged to enroll. Having an early course in game development keeps student's enthusiasm high in addition to other benefits as reported elsewhere [3, 8, 10, 17]. Students are also encouraged to take the artificial intelligence course given the topic's importance to game development; they typically take it in their junior or senior year. In addition, students are given the opportunity to enroll in independent research if they express an interest in pursuing a specific topic in game development not covered during the regular courses. These sections require faculty sponsorship and are only approved for outstanding students.

The department allows students to minor in any discipline. Game development students are encouraged to minor in a discipline related to their particular interest in game development such as art, mathematics or English (story-telling).

Figure 1. The game development laboratory.

3. LABORATORY

Before the first course was offered the department received internal funding for a dedicated game development laboratory, shown in Figure 1. The lab has keycard access for only those students enrolled in the game development sequence and new freshmen who indicate they intend to take the game development courses. A projector was installed for both teaching and presenting student projects. Equipment includes twelve high performance dual-monitor PC workstations loaded with appropriate game development software including compilers, image editing software, video editing software, 3D painting software and content libraries. Table 1 lists important installed software. All of the game development courses are taught in the lab if space permits. For larger sections of more than 15 students a lecture room is used. The lab is similar in scope to those found at other universities with dedicated game development labs [13, 14, 17].

Table 1. Software Installed in Game Laboratory

Software	Purpose
Microsoft Windows 7	Operating system
Microsoft Office	Word processing, etc.
Microsoft Visual Studio	PC development tool
Eclipse	Android development tool
Adobe Photoshop	2D image editor
Adobe Audition	Audio editor
Adobe Premiere	Video editor
Lightwave	3D modeling/animation
BodyPaint 3D	3D painting
FaceGen	3D face generator
SnagIt	Video capture program

The importance of the lab and its benefit to the new program cannot be overstated. Small classes can be taught in the lab using hands-on methods of instruction. The lab also serves as an open lab for student use during non-class times. Students use the lab for both working on assignments and meeting with other students. Playing games in the lab is encouraged and promotes student interest and enthusiasm in the subject matter. Even if a general access lab could be equipped with the necessary hardware and software, we agree with others that hosting these activities in a general access lab would be too distracting to other students [13, 14].

In addition to the benefits described, the dedicated lab afforded a unique recruiting opportunity. When shown the lab, visiting prospective students often commented how surprised they were that a university would have the level of equipment contained in the lab and how pleased they were the university appeared to have a high level of commitment to the program. The lab was often featured in marketing materials and on television.

4. COURSES

The following sections describe each of the courses in the game development program in addition to the artificial intelligence course which is complimentary to the program.

4.1 Introductory Course

As the first course in the game development sequence, the introductory course was important to provide a foundation for the program. The course originally had three goals:

1. Retain majors, especially from freshmen to sophomore years.
2. Train students on content creation tools used in the upper-level game development courses.
3. Recruit new CS majors.

Since students needed to complete three courses in C++ programming prior to taking a game development course it was expected that attrition would factor heavily in reducing the number of majors. To keep students enthusiastic and interested in the program the introductory course was created. The content of the course includes lectures covering aspects of the industry starting with the history of computer games. There are no programming assignments. Instead, assignments are heavily oriented toward enabling students to express their creativity through game design and other multimedia-related projects. For the final semester project students create a machinima: a video created using computer game technology. Students record video of a 3D computer game and insert voice, sound effects and still images using a video editing program. The resulting movies are presented in a group setting.

Equally important to retaining majors, the course is designed to teach students how to use content creation tools used in later semesters. Through hands-on demonstrations in the lab, students learn basic 3D modeling, audio editing, video editing and a tool that creates 3D human faces that can be exported to the modeling program for further customization. Since the course was created as an elective and not required for the game programming courses some students did not take the course. As a result, not all students entering the game programming courses were familiar with the content creation tools. A remedy for this would be to require the introductory course as a prerequisite for the other courses. One reason this was not done is the course was open to all majors and due to the popularity of the course CS majors often had a hard time enrolling in the course due to the limited number of sections offered each semester.

Despite the popularity of the course among non-CS majors, the course did not serve to attract a large number of students to the CS program. However, an unexpected benefit of the course was realized. The course fostered a strong sense of community among CS majors and helped new freshman get to know their peers early in the program.

Figure 2. Student project from the PC development course demonstrating lip sync morph animation.

4.2 PC Development Courses

Due to the complexity of PC development and the breadth of topics that can be covered, a one-year, two-semester sequence was created. A similar approach has been taken at other universities teaching game development [3, 13] and recommended as appropriate [11].

The choice of programming tools is an important one. A application programming interface (API) for graphics must be chosen that students can digest and become proficient using in a short amount of time. There is currently no standard in academia for which API to use. Many have used a high-level tool such as Microsoft XNA with mixed success [2, 5, 6, 8, 10] while others have used a custom API [5, 14]. In our experience the best tool to use is what the instructor is most familiar with. We used a custom API based on the Microsoft DirectX 9 fixed-function pipeline. Since a custom API will likely not have extensive documentation the instructor bears the responsibility for carefully instructing students in its use whereas with an industry-standard API students can be left somewhat on their own. During semesters with small groups of students the custom API worked well and students used it with good success. During semesters with larger classes of more than 15 students the instructor was not able to spend as much time with students individually. As a result, the quality of work was lower and student satisfaction was not as high.

Topics covered during the first semester include:

1. 3D computer graphics – 3D concepts, mathematics, hardware and software, APIs, object representation, file formats, camera control.
2. Windows programming – OS architecture, SDKs, event-driven programming, multi-threading.
3. Game architecture – major software components of a 3D game engine.
4. Texturing – texture coordinates, texture filtering, texture animation, mipmapping.

Assignments guide the student from loading and displaying a simple model they create in a modeling program to creating a walkthrough of an outdoor environment. The final semester project requires students to use their knowledge to craft a game. Since the focus of the semester is on outdoor environments most students typically create a game set in a forest or other outdoor space.

During the second semester two primary topics are covered: indoor rendering and character animation. Portal rendering is presented as a method for creating and managing large indoor environments. The instructor provides source code for a project that procedurally generates indoor environment from a set of student-created prefabricated 3D models of sections of the environment such as rooms and corridors. Students can also manually create their own indoor environments although few students have chosen to implement their own portal rendering code due to complexity and time constraints. Since students in the PC development courses are required to author their own artwork they also have to balance the time spent coding and creating art assets.

A second emphasis during the second semester is character animation. Multiple techniques for character animations are explained including morphing and skinned bones. Significant project assignments highlight both methods. To demonstrate their skills with morphing, an assignment requires students to create a 3D head animated using morphing and lip synced with audio. An example of a student project demonstrating morph animation is shown in Figure 2. An example of a student project demonstrating skinned bone animation is shown in Figure 3.

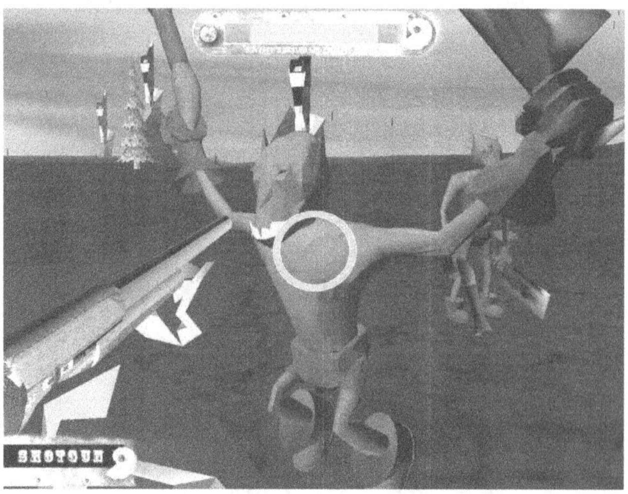

Figure 3. Student project from the PC development course demonstrating bones animation.

4.3 Handheld Development Course

The handheld game development course was designed both to provide students the opportunity to develop games for a mobile platform and to afford students an opportunity to take a game development course during their sophomore year. Another premise for inclusion of the course was to accentuate the uniqueness of the ASU game development program since, at the time it was first offered, no other university in the state offered a similar course.

For the first two years the course was offered the development platform used was Nintendo Gameboy. This was quite popular with students, many of whom had owned a Gameboy at some point in their lives. An example of a student program created for the platform is shown in Figure 4. An advantage of the platform is simplicity—programs are written to run directly on the hardware without an operating system. The course was redesigned in 2011 to use Android. The best supported development language for Android is Java. In the first iteration of the course, in spring 2011, the instructor used Java exclusively. Reactions to the new format were mixed. Students who had not taken the department's only elective Java course expressed some dissatisfaction with the course since they were required to both learn Android and learn to program using Java. A different textbook was chosen for the second iteration of the Android course with good results [15]. Students were still required to learn Java as needed but the textbook helped abstract away many of the operating system specific details, enabling students to concentrate on creating games.

Overall interest in the handheld course among students has been very positive. Many students not interested in game development wanted to take the course in order to learn more about Android programming.

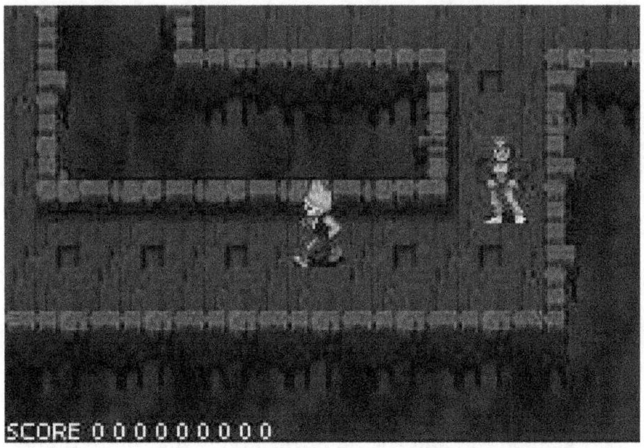

Figure 4. Student project from the Handheld/AI courses.

4.4 Artificial Intelligence Course

The artificial intelligence (AI) course fits into a traditional CS curriculum and covers important AI topics. However, we take every opportunity to relate traditional AI approaches to game development. Almost every topic covered is put into a game-development context, at least briefly. Some techniques, such as A* search, depth-limited alpha-beta pruning and game-theoretical analysis, are widely used in commercial games of different types. Other techniques are pointed out as less useful in game development. For example, most machine learning approaches are too time-intensive to use in games, which usually must react to the human player in real time. Simpler, even hard-coded, approaches often work just as well and can run much faster. Even though a traditional AI approach can be overkill and a simple, approximate solution is often better in game development, students in the AI course benefit from a big-picture understanding of how computers can be made to think.

The programming assignments in the course are organized as a series of "agent challenges." A C++ framework is presented that sets up an environment in which agents can compete and/or cooperate. Each student writes an agent function that takes as input a situation and returns an action. The agent functions are run inside the framework to determine the outcome and the agents' performances are scored and compared. Agent challenges range from simple game-theoretic games (rock-paper-scissors, prisoner's dilemma) to games that require search (Connect Four, Chomp) to explorable environments like a Wumpus world. Agent functions are given time limitations, so realistic efficiency/ accuracy tradeoffs must be considered. The students enjoy the competition and chances for cooperation. The agent challenges add excitement and a real-world-application flavor to balance the theoretical feel of some of the course material.

The course culminates in a final project. Students propose their own projects. Subject to instructor approval, game-related ideas are explicitly encouraged. In fact, many students have overlapped the AI project with the final project in a game-development course. For example, a student concurrently enrolled in both the handheld game development and AI courses produced the program shown in Figure 4 to navigate a maze using help from a custom AI search algorithm.

5. RELATED ACTIVITIES

After the establishment of the new program there were inquiries from prospective students who already had an undergraduate degree in computer science and wanted to attend ASU specifically to enroll in the game development courses. A certificate program was created as a result. A "Certificate of Computer Game Development" is awarded to any student completing the two PC development, handheld development and artificial intelligence courses. The certificate proved to be attractive to both post-graduate students and new undergraduates. It also provided another selling point for marketing purposes.

It was understood that marketing would be vital to the success of the new program and growth of the CS department. The department website was redesigned early to emphasize the game development program. Large posters advertising the program were printed and displayed on campus bulletin boards. Flyers were posted to advertise specific courses. One benefit of this was summer enrollment went up.

A three-day summer workshop was established to attract new students to the program. The workshop was advertised to prospective high school students. While the benefits of the summer workshop were smaller than expected in terms of the number of new students enrolling, the workshop generated an unexpected amount of publicity via newspaper and television.

6. RESULTS

The computer game development curriculum has been offered since the fall 2008 semester. The program has been instrumental in growing the CS program at ASU. The program grew from 71 to 213 majors over a four-year period since the introduction of the game development courses. A fall 2011 survey of 155 freshman and sophomore CS majors indicated 63 chose to attend ASU specifically to study computer game development and 73 planned to enter the game development industry after graduation. Freshman-to-sophomore retention of CS majors increased by 10% from academic year 2008-2009 to 2010-2011. Anecdotal evidence suggests a greater retention among CS students choosing the game development option. Almost all students in the latest upper-level PC programming course, taught in fall 2011, had taken the introductory class, compared to approximately half in fall 2010 and only a few in fall 2009. Two years after the courses were adopted ASU was named one of the Top 50 Game Design Programs in North America by Princeton Review in their 2010 survey of similar programs. By fall 2011 ASU CS enrollment had grown to 3% of total enrolled students, making it the CS program with the highest per capita enrollment of any Texas public university, according to a fall 2011 survey conducted by ASU. The growth of the program mirrors experiences elsewhere where game development courses have increased enrollment [7, 9, 13, 17].

7. CONCLUSION

A new program in computer game development as part of a traditional degree in CS has been described. At the present time nearly half of CS majors at ASU have indicated they chose to attend ASU specifically to study computer game development. It remains a significant challenge to keep the game development curriculum up to date and produce graduates who are competitive in securing industry jobs.

8. REFERENCES

[1] Becker, K. Teaching with Games: The Minesweeper and Asteroids Experience. *The Journal of Computing in Small Colleges*, 17, 2 (Dec. 2001), 23-33.

[2] Bidarra, R., et. al. Bringing a Pioneer Games Project to the Next Level. In *Proceedings of the 3rd International Conference on Game Development in Computer Science Education (GDCSE -08)* (Miami, Florida, February 28-March 3, 2008). ACM Press, 2008, 11-15.

[3] Coleman, R., et. al. Game Design & Programming Concentration within the Computer Science Curriculum. In *Proceedings of the 36th SIGCSE Technical Symposium on Computer Science Education (SIGCSE '05)* (St. Louis, Missouri, February 23-27, 2005) ACM Press, 2005, 545-550.

[4] Distasio, J. and Way, T. Inclusive Computer Science Education Using a Ready-Made Computer Game Framework. In *Proceedings of the 12th SIGCSE Conference on Innovation and Technology in Computer Science Education (ITiCSE '07)* (Dundee, Scotland, June 25-27. ACM Press, 2007, 116-120.

[5] Duvall, S. Creating a Games Class: A Walkthrough. In *Proceedings of the 4th International Conference on Foundations of Digital Games (FDG -09)* (Orlando, Florida, April 26-30). ACM Press, 2009, 279-284.

[6] Harris, J. Teaching Game Programming Using XNA: What Works and What Doesn't. *Journal of Computing Sciences in Colleges.* 27, 2 (Dec. 2011), 174-181.

[7] Haungs, M. et. al. Improving First-Year Success and Retention Through Interest-Based CS0 Courses. In *Proceedings of the 43rd SIGCSE Technical Symposium on Computer Science Education (SIGCSE '12)* (Raleigh, North Carolina, February 29–March 3, 2012). ACM Press, 2012, 589-594.

[8] Kessler, R., van Langeveld, M., and Altizer, R. Entertainment Arts and Engineering (Or How to Fast Track a New Interdisciplinary Program). In *Proceedings of the 40th ACM Technical Symposium on Computer Science Education (SIGCSE '09)* (Chattanooga, Tennessee, March 4-7, 2009). ACM Press, 2009, 539-543.

[9] Leutenegger, S. and Edgington, J. A Games First Approach to Teaching Introductory Programming. In *Proceedings of the 38th SIGCSE Technical Symposium on Computer Science Education (SIGCSE '07)* (Covington, Kentucky, March 7-10, 2007). ACM Press, 2007, 115-118.

[10] Linhoff, J. and Settle, A. Teaching Game Programming Using XNA. In *Proceedings of the 13th Annual Conference on Innovation and Technology in Computer Science Education (ITiCSE '08)* (Madrid, Spain, June 30-July 2, 2008). ACM Press, 2008, 250-254.

[11] McGill, M. Defining the Expectation Gap: A Comparison of Industry Needs and Existing Game Development Curriculum. In *Proceedings of the 4th International Conference on Foundations of Digital Games (FDG -09)* (Orlando, Florida, April 26-30). ACM Press, 2009, 129-136.

[12] Novak, J. *Game Development Essentials: An Introduction.* Third Edition. Delmar Cengage Learning. 2011.

[13] Parberry, I., Kaxemzadeh, M., and Roden, T. The Art and Science of Game Programming. In *Proceedings of the 2006 ACM Technical Symposium on Computer Science Education (SIGCSE '06)* (Houston, Texas, March 1-5, 2006). ACM Press, 2006, 510-514.

[14] Roden, T., and Etheredge, J. Educating Game Programmers, In *Proceedings of the 2nd International Conference on Game Development in Computer Science Education (GDCSE '07)* (Orlando, Florida, February 22-25, 2007). Microsoft Press, 2007, 82-86.

[15] Zechner, M., and Green, R. *Beginning Android 4 Games Development.* Apress, 2011.

[16] Zyda, M. Computer Science in the Conceptual Age. *Communications of the ACM.* 52, 12 (Dec. 2009), 66-72.

[17] Zyda, M., Lacour, V., and Swain, C. Operating a Computer Science Game Degree Program. In *Proceedings of the 3rd International Conference on Game Development in Computer Science Education (GDCSE -08)* (Miami, Florida, February 28-March 3, 2008). ACM Press, 2008, 71-75.

Trace-Based Teaching in Early Programming Courses

Matthew Hertz
Computer Science Department
Canisius College
Buffalo, NY 14208
hertzm@canisius.edu

Maria Jump
Department of Math and Computer Science
King's College
Wilkes-Barre, PA 18711
mariajump@kings.edu

ABSTRACT

Students in introductory programming courses struggle with building the mental models that correctly describe concepts such as variables, subroutine calls, and dynamic memory usage. This struggle leads to lowered student learning outcomes and, it has been argued, the high failure and dropout rates commonly seen in these courses. We will show that accurately modeling what is occurring in memory and requiring students to trace code using this model improves student performance and increases retention.

This paper presents the results of an experiment in which introductory programming courses were organized around code tracing. We present *program memory traces*, a new approach for tracing code that models what occurs in memory as a program executes. We use these traces to drive our lectures and to act as key pieces of our active learning activities. We report the results of student surveys showing that instructor tracing was rated as the most valuable piece of the course and students' overwhelming agreement on the importance of the tracing activities for their learning. Finally, we demonstrate that trace-based teaching led to statistically significant improvements student grades, decreased drop and failure rates, and an improvement in students' programming abilities.

Categories and Subject Descriptors

K.3.2 [**Computers and Education**]: Computers and Information Science Education—*Computer science education; Curriculum*

General Terms

Tracing; Pedagogical Choices

Keywords

CS1, CS2, Pedagogy, Tracing

1. INTRODUCTION

Past research found that many introductory programming students hold impossible mental models of how programs execute. These inviable mental models include ones related to understanding how variables behave [7], how references work [14], and how subroutines get executed [3,5]. It has also been suggested that the difficulty of developing viable models is among the leading reasons these early courses have such high dropout rates [11].

As a result, visual models were investigated as a way of helping introductory students. Nearly a decade ago, Holliday and Luginbuhl documented that a student's ability to draw visual representations of objects in a program's heap and their comprehension of the material were correlated [6]. This led Sorva and Sirkiä to determine that using a program which presents a program's objects visually helps students construct viable models of execution [15]. Given this potential to help students, many programs have been developed that perform this visualization (e.g., [1,4,15]).

This paper presents *program memory traces*, a new trace format that includes abstract representations of both a program's stack and its heap. By abstracting what happens in memory, our program memory trace can be used with many languages and for multiple programming paradigms.

We build on previous research by presenting our experiences organizing instruction in introductory computer science courses around tracing code using this new format. For this study, lectures typically begin with 20–30 minutes of instruction which followed brief introductions to the concepts with the instructor leading the class through tracing prewritten code samples that illustrate the concept. Students spend the remainder of the 50- or 75-minute lecture period working in small groups on activities focused on their tracing sample programs. By actively providing a visual model of the concepts and reinforcing this model with in-class activities in which students trace prewritten code, we help students develop viable models of the concepts and thereby improve student learning and increase the rate at which students successfully complete the course.

To demonstrate the effectiveness of our teaching approach, we examined both quantitative and qualitative measures of student learning and teaching effectiveness. We show that switching to this new approach increased the rate at which students successfully complete a Java-based data structures course from 75% to 91%. This was also met with students' unsolicited comments expressing their belief in the value of these traces. We also show that this increase was accompanied by a considerable improvement in students' lecture grade and a statistically significant increase in students' laboratory grade. Anonymous surveys from both a Java-based data structures course and a C-based introduction to programming course show that a majority of students in each course rated both watching the instructor trace code and tracing code on their own to be "very helpful" to their learning. Furthermore each form of tracing was rated either "helpful" or "very helpful" by at least 90% of each course's students.

The rest of the paper is organized as follows. Section 2 presents

SIGCSE'13, March 6–9, 2013, Denver, Colorado, USA.

an overview of the program memory trace format we used. The organization of courses to focus on the use of these traces is described in Section 3. We analyze the effects of our trace-driven teaching approach in Section 4. Section 5 describes the related work and Section 6 offers suggestions for future work and concludes.

2. PROGRAM MEMORY TRACES

Motivated by a desire to help novice programmers develop valid mental models of many challenging programming concepts, we developed *program memory traces*. A *program memory trace* provides an accurate representation of the program's memory usage in such a way that it balances the abstractness required by introductory students with the accuracy needed for advanced students. We wanted to develop a model that would remain useful to students throughout their education and beyond. As such, a *program memory trace* depicts all of the program's accessible memory by dividing the trace area into different regions representing different types of memory: *stack*, *heap*, and *static*.

The first and most important region represents the program stack; we simply call it the *stack*. In the *stack*, we use blocks to represent the stackframes created whenever a subroutine is called. For each parameter and each local variable, the block contains a space for that variable including its name and its current value. Value variables represent their value in the space within the stackframe, while a reference variable's value is shown as an arrow pointing to the memory block to which they refer. Whenever a method returns (or quits executing), the corresponding block in the stack is disposed of by drawing an "X" through it. By accurately representing each method call with its stackframe, students are able to better understand method calling and variable scoping.

Next is the *heap* where blocks depict dynamically allocated memory. In C this includes any memory allocated using `malloc`, while in Java this includes memory allocated using `new`. In a program memory trace, the return values of `malloc` and `new` are depicted as an arrow from the reference variable to which the return type is assigned to the memory block representing the dynamically allocated memory. Blocks in the heap are disposed of by drawing an "X" through it. This would occur whenever they are freed (in C) or, optionally, are no longer reachable (in Java).

Finally, the *static* region contains any statically allocated memory. For static memory, blocks represent each statically allocated variable labeled according to who allocated it and thus who has the ability to modify it. Since static memory is allocated at the start of a program and "lives" until the end of the program, blocks in the static region are created when they are needed by the trace and are never disposed of.

To illustrate both how these program memory traces work and how they can be used with different languages and programming paradigms, we show two sample programs shown in Figure 1. This figure shows the same program written in both C (Figure 1a) and Java (Figure 1c) and the program memory traces generated for them (Figures 1b and 1d, respectively). These sample programs are intended to illustrate the trace format and so were designed to be small and highlight multiple features of the trace; they are not programs we have used in our classes.

In a *program memory trace*, program execution starts at a method call. In many cases, this is `main` but it does not have to be. At the start of any method, a new stackframe is created and, thus in our trace, we draw a block on the stack to represent that method. The method's parameters are evaluated and given space in the method's block. A common mistake when evaluating the method's parameters in an object-oriented language like Java is to forget the `this` reference. `this` is treated like a method parameter. Once the parameters are evaluated and their initial values recorded, the method can be stepped through one line at a time. With each line, we update the memory trace to reflect its effects. As an example, an assignment statement requires evaluating the right-hand-side. The right-hand-side could simply be a value, an arithmetic expression, or even another method call. The result of the evaluation is used to update the value of the variable named on the left-hand-side of the assignment. These updates are shown by crossing out the old value of the variable and showing the new value. When a method call is encountered, the execution of the current method is interrupted and a new stackframe created at the top of the stack. For most languages, only the method of the most current stackframe can be traced.

3. TRACE-DRIVEN TEACHING

Like many institutions [11], our introductory classes suffered from low retention rates and poor student performance. These problems occurred despite our making a number of pedagogical changes including adding active learning exercises and demonstrating how code features worked using live coding and canned examples. Students seemed to have an especially difficult time with issues such as variable scoping and pointer assignments/aliasing. These problems led to further difficulties. Despite devoting a week or more of class time to the basics of recursion, the majority of students struggled to write recursive methods. These classes slogged on with little of the fun and none of the "passion, awe, and joy" that encourage students to become or continue as computer science majors. Something needed to be done.

While many others had previously documented these *struggles* (e.g., [3,5,7,14]), very few solutions were suggested. The classes already included in-class code tracing and coding activities, labs, small programming homework exercises, larger programming projects, and other opportunities for students to develop valid mental models. We observed that some of these activities seemed to hurt as much as they helped. Even working in groups, activities in which students coded on paper seemed to reinforce inaccurate models and made it more difficult for students to change. Code tracing activities exposed students' inviable models [6] and, more importantly, provided a much clearer starting point with which to discuss correct models. While this should have encouraged students to trace code, students would avoid these questions and instead just guess at program's end state. As others have found, students were *extremely* hesitant to perform any tracing on their own [9, 16].

To improve upon our courses, we decided to surround students with viable models of memory by using traces as the focus of our teaching. We introduce students to tracing and the ideas of a *program memory trace* from the onset of our classes. While concepts such as the heap and stackframes are not needed immediately, we use them in our traces from the beginning to accurately model what is happening in memory. In our lectures, we follow each topic introduction with tracing through sample code to illustrate what the concept does or how it works. Because we continue to use active learning pedagogy, at least half each lecture period has students working on activities in small groups. These activities **always** include problems requiring they trace code and, if they ask students to write code, require students to trace the code they wrote [1].

Our hope was that by organizing instruction around *program memory traces*, students would be more likely to develop viable mental models of how programs execute. Beyond just surrounding them with visual representations, trace-based teaching should help

[1]Examples of these activities can be found at `http://cs.canisius.edu/~hertzm/tracing` and `http://staff.kings.edu/mariajump/tracing`

```
typedef struct Ex {
  int min, max;
} Ex;
void comp(int *arr, Ex *r) {
  for (int i=0; i < 3; i++) {
    r->max = (arr[i]>r->max)?arr[i]:r->max;
    r->min = (arr[i]<r->min)?arr[i]:r->min;
  }
}
int main() {
  Ex *result = malloc(sizeof(Ex));
  int arr[] = {7, 3, 14};
  result.min = 100;
  result.max = -1;
  comp(arr, result);
  return 0;
}
```

(a) Sample program written in C.

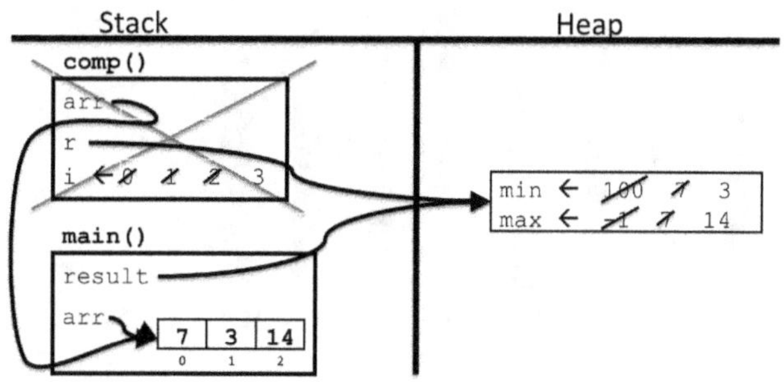

(b) Program memory trace generated for the C program.

```
public class Ex {
  private int min, max;
  void comp(int[] arr) {
    for (int i=0; i < 3; i++) {
      max = (arr[i]>max)?arr[i]:max;
      min = (arr[i]<min)?arr[i]:min;
    }
  }
  public static int main(String[] args) {
    Ex result = new Ex();
    int arr[] = {7, 3, 14};
    result.min = 100;
    result.max = -1;
    result.comp(arr);
    return 0;
  }
}
```

(c) Sample program written in Java.

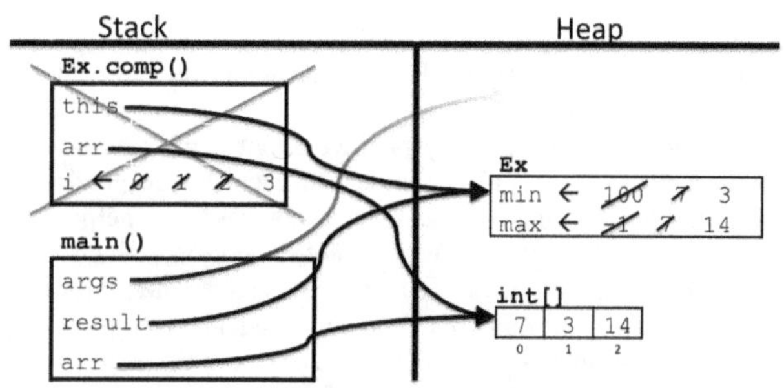

(d) Program memory trace generated for the Java program.

Figure 1: Sample program, written in both C and Java, with which we illustrate how program memory traces are created. Both program use static and dynamic allocation, arrays and scalar variables, and subroutines. These will be used to illustrate how these traces work.

students by "priming" them for many of the concepts with which past research had found students struggle. One example of this is that of stackframes. By including stackframes from the very start, students are comfortable with the mechanics of variable scoping before the course gets to subroutine execution. Similarly, by having our traces represent what occurs in memory, students literally see the parallels between related concepts (e.g., arrays and pointers in C are both represented as arrows). These illustrations highlight these relationships and make reusing knowledge easier.

4. RESULTS AND ANALYSIS

We use this trace-driven teaching approach in two introductory courses at a medium-sized regional college. The first, a CS1 ("Introduction to Programming") course taught in C, is required for, and largely populated by, first-year physics and pre-engineering majors. For nearly all of the students, this CS1 course is their first computer science course and they begin the term with little interest in computer science. Enrollments in this course vary greatly between 12 – 31 students. The second course, a CS2 course taught in Java, is required for computer science majors and minors and is usually taken by second-year students. Course registrations vary from year to year from a low enrollment of 9 to a high of 21 (mean enrollment was 14). A small minority of students come from the CS1 course described above, but would have had to have taken a Java-based CS1 course in the interim. Both the CS1 and CS2 classes in this study have a similar structure including 3 hours per week of instructional time, a 1 hour per week laboratory session, small weekly programming sets, and 3 larger programming projects. Classes are taught using active learning with 15 - 30 minutes of active lecture followed by activities performed in 3 - 5 person groups.

As a quantitative measure of the effectiveness of our teaching approach, we compare students' grades from the 3 years preceding the change to trace-driven teaching with the 4 subsequent years. This comparison can only be performed for the CS2 course because the content and coverage of the CS1 course changed significantly during this time frame.[2] As a qualitative measure, we performed end-of-course assessments during the last week of the course and, during the past 3 years, included questions asking students to rate how helpful each aspect of the course was for their learning the material. Responses to this question were on a 5-point Likert scale ("very unhelpful", "unhelpful", "neither helpful nor unhelpful", "helpful", and "very helpful"). Student participation in the end-of-course assessment was both voluntary and anonymous. Aggregated within each course, we had 53 responses in our CS1 course (a 88.33% response rate) and 36 responses in our CS2 course (a 97.30% response rate). As with most qualitative measures, students often confuse what was most helpful with what they liked the most. Regardless,

[2]In particular, the CS1 course now covers 25% more material and goes deeper into other topics relative to the course before switching trace-driven teaching

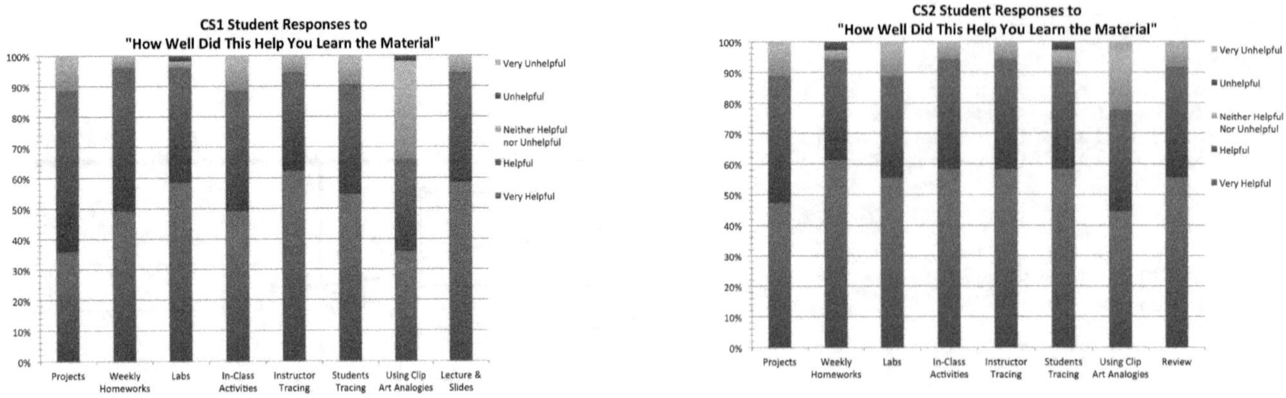

(a) Percentage of students answering how useful each of the aspects of the CS1 course was to their learning (n=53). Almost two-thirds of the students found the instructors tracing code in lectures to be "very helpful," a rate higher than any other aspect of the course.

(b) Percentage of students answering how useful each of the aspects of the CS2 course was to their learning (n=36). The instructor's use of traces continued to be more popular than even the lectures themselves and, along with weekly homework assignments, the aspect of the course that students found to be most helpful.

Figure 2: Results of anonymous surveys of the students in the CS1 (a) and CS2 (b) courses. Students in both classes found traces to really help them learn the material. In particular, students rated the instructor tracing code in the lecture as among the most helpful aspects of the course.

qualitative results often help explain any changes we see in the grades students received.

Students were overwhelmingly positive about using traces to explain the concepts. A majority of students in each class responded that the instructor's tracing code while lecturing was "very helpful" to their learning of the material. Over 94% of students in each class, in fact, stated that the instructor tracing code was either "helpful" or "very helpful" to their learning (the remaining students rated this as "neither helpful nor unhelpful"). As can be seen from the results in Figure 2a, students were more positive about the instructor's tracing of code than they were about the slides which included the traces. In fact, the instructor's tracing of code was found to be more helpful than the lectures as whole. Additionally, the data in Figure 2b shows that students rate the instructor tracing code among the most helpful aspects of both the CS1 and CS2 courses.

While students reported that the instructor tracing code helped them learn, our course design also places an emphasis on having the students trace code. While students had tried to "guess" what code does rather than actually complete a trace previously, students in trace-driven teaching courses willing trace code when a problem requires it .Even with this emphasis, students in trace-driven teaching class were no more likely to use traces on their own than students in our classes before the change. A majority of students in each class responded that they found having to trace code to be "very helpful". While the percentages are lower than for the instructor tracing code, over 90% of students in each class rated students tracing code positively (in fact, only a single CS2 student rated this "unhelpful"). In both courses student tracing code was rated more positively than the multi-week programming projects and in CS1 students tracing code was rated more positively than the daily activities as a whole.

While students clearly feel that trace-driven teaching helps them learn, those results cannot show whether it improves student learning. For this we turn to quantitative data and compared students grades from the 3 years preceding the change to trace-driven teaching with the 4 subsequent years. All of these classes were taught by the same instructor using the same structure, content, and grading scheme. Any changes, therefore, reflect the effect of using trace-driven teaching.[3]

First we examine student's CS2 lecture grade which includes all aspects of the course except weekly labs. The CS2 lab (like the CS1 lab) require students work individually at a computer to complete the programming problems. These labs last 1 to 2 hours and assignments are due at the end of that time. The lab grade reflects students' performance writing the required code (the lab assignments do not require tracing, though students can use this to find bugs). As shown in Figure 3a, the median CS2 lecture grade remains unchanged but the distribution of grades has skewed much higher. Similarly, the CS2 lab grade distribution (see Figure 3b) show grades improved considerably since switching to trace-driven teaching.

To understand the significance of the grade data, we used an analysis of variance (ANOVA) test. ANOVA examines the variance in the data of two groups to determine the confidence with which one can state that two populations' means are different [12]. We evaluated the student grade data using ANOVA to establish if the grade improvements seen with trace-driven teaching are significant. We found that while the differences in the lecture grades are strong, they are not quite statistically significant ($p = 0.0805$). The same cannot be said for students' lab grades, however. The improvement in these grades is very, very strong and well beyond what is necessary for statistical significance ($p = 0.000131$). Initially, this result may seem odd: the improvements from trace-driven teaching are far stronger for the lab portion of the course rather than the portion that uses traces. We argue this makes sense: the improvement reflects students' improved understanding of the material and holding viable mental models. This improvement has the biggest impact on students' programming skills, the skills most directly assessed, and so most visible, within the laboratory portion of the class.

Finally, since one of our motivations for using trace-driven teaching was the high rates that students had been dropping out or failing our introductory courses, we examine student success rate. Fully one-quarter (25.49%) of students did not successfully complete the CS2 course in the three years prior to this change. In the four years

[3]To validate this assumption, we examined grades in the instructor's other courses. They were unchanged during this time.

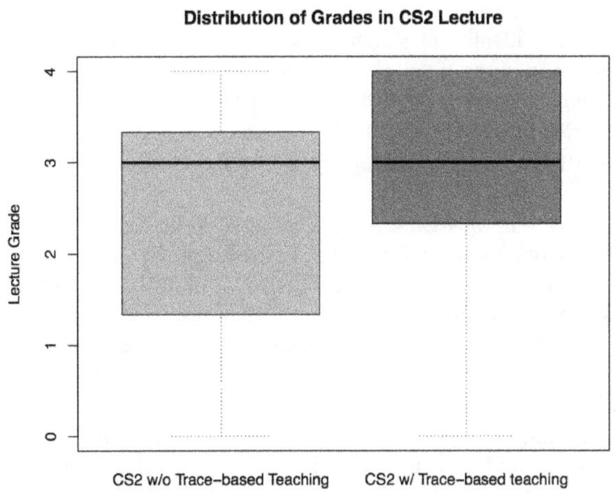

(a) While the median lecture grade in CS2 has not changed, the increase in student learning can be seen in the higher skew of the grade distributions. Using ANOVA, the differences are significant with p=0.08.

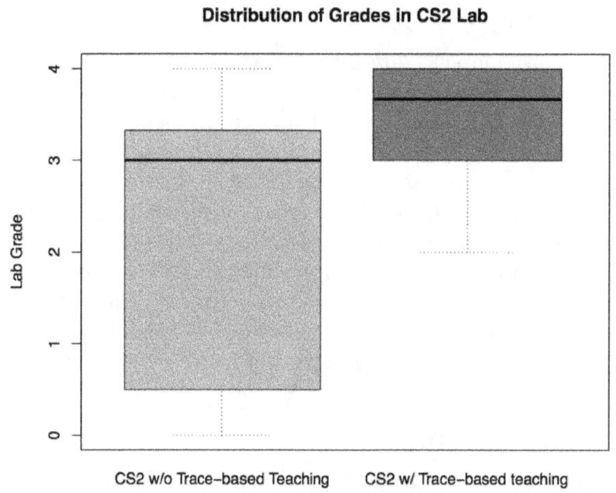

(b) Even while reducing the time students spend writing code in-class, trace-driven teaching improves students coding ability by increasing their understanding of the material. This change is statistically significant with a p=0.000131.

Figure 3: Graphs showing grade distributions in a CS2 class before and after changing to trace-driven teaching. The boxes show the range of grades in the 1 - 3 quartiles, the dashed lines show the range of grades within 1.5 times of the interquartile range beyond these quartiles, and the solid line is the median grade. As shown by these grades, trace-driven teaching has improved student understanding of the material and their ability to program.

following this change, only 4 out of 57 students (8.51%) have failed this course (no students in this time dropped out). As much as the students' reports of our approach's helpfulness and the increase in student grades, this reduction in the rate in which students did not successfully complete our course shows the value of trace-driven teaching.

5. RELATED WORK

While this is the first paper of which we know that studied the effectiveness of organizing classes around traces, there are other works in related topics such as visualizing a program's state or using traces to assess or improve student learning. We discuss these related works now.

Many papers have been published in which ways of visualizing a program's heap state is discussed. These systems include more general means of visualizing such as Heapviz [1], UUWhistle [15], and visualization tools built into IDEs such as BlueJ [8] and jGRASP [4]. Other systems have been designed to visualize more specific data structures. Examples of these latter systems include iSketchmate [13] and CSTutor [2]. While these papers share our goal of creating means to educate students, they cannot be used with only pencil and paper and do not examine the effectiveness of organizing a class around these topics.

Other research has investigated using traces to assess or improve student learning. An early important work in this area found that introductory students were especially weak at tracing [9]. Unlike our research, this earlier work only looked at students' tracing ability and did not examine the benefits of using traces to educate students. While further research examined the correlation between students ability to trace code with their ability to write code [10], the tracing in that research does not model what occurs in memory and so is an assessment tool and not a way to help students develop viable mental models. Further research by Holliday and Luginbuhl [6] used a trace format created by the authors to document a correlation between students' ability to draw traces and their comprehension of the material. Unlike our research, Holliday and Luginbuhl's trace format did not visualize all of a program's memory and their research did not examine the effectiveness of using traces to teach introductory topics. Thomas, et al., examined the effect of providing students with incomplete traces when asked to answer multiple-choice questions [16]. While some of their findings, that students who draw traces are better able to answer questions, match ours, they did not consider the effect of organizing their course around traces and so could not overcome student resistance. Finally, Ma, et al., used visualizations and cognitive conflict to improve student understanding of value assignments [11]. Like us, they found that visualizations can provide statistically significant improvements in student learning, but only considered the gains from a single exposure to visualizations and did not consider the gains possible when visualization is used throughout a course.

6. CONCLUSION

This paper introduces trace-based teaching which centers teaching introductory programming courses around *program memory traces*. *Program memory traces* present an accurate memory model upon which programming concepts can be explained to students. We show that students feel that tracing code help them learn and hold tracing as more important to their learning and understanding the material than writing code. We also document that trace-based teaching led to improvements in student learning by finding a statistically significant improvement in student programming grades. Thus, this paper shows that program memory traces help students develop viable models of programming concepts and increases the rate students successfully complete the course.

Acknowledgements

The authors wish to thank the anonymous reviewers whose comments helped strengthen this work. They also wish to thank Marge Foster for her help in developing this manuscript.

7. REFERENCES

[1] E. E. Aftandilian, S. Kelley, C. Gramazio, N. Ricci, S. L. Su, and S. Z. Guyer. Heapviz: interactive heap visualization for program understanding and debugging. In *Proceedings of the 5th international symposium on Software visualization*, pages 53–62, 2010.

[2] S. Buchanan, B. Ochs, and J. J. LaViola Jr. CSTutor: a pen-based tutor for data structure visualization. In *Proceedings of the 43rd ACM technical symposium on Computer Science Education*, pages 565–570, 2012.

[3] M. Craig, S. Petersen, and A. Petersen. Following a thread: knitting patterns and program tracing. In *Proceedings of the 43rd ACM technical symposium on Computer Science Education*, pages 233–238, 2012.

[4] J. H. Cross, II and T. D. Hendrix. jGRASP: an integrated development environment with visualizations for teaching Java in CS1, CS2, and beyond. *Journal of Computing Sciences in Colleges*, 23(1):5–7, Oct. 2007.

[5] T. Götschi, I. Sanders, and V. Galpin. Mental models of recursion. In *Proceedings of the 34th SIGCSE technical symposium on Computer science education*, pages 346–350, 2003.

[6] M. A. Holliday and D. Luginbuhl. CS1 assessment using memory diagrams. In *Proceedings of the 35th SIGCSE technical symposium on Computer science education*, pages 200–204, 2004.

[7] L. C. Kaczmarczyk, E. R. Petrick, J. P. East, and G. L. Herman. Identifying student misconceptions of programming. In *Proceedings of the 41st ACM technical symposium on Computer science education*, pages 107–111, 2010.

[8] M. Kölling, B. Quig, A. Patterson, and J. Rosenberg. The BlueJ system and its pedagogy. *Journal of Computer Science Education*, 13(4), Dec. 2003.

[9] R. Lister, E. S. Adams, S. Fitzgerald, W. Fone, J. Hamer, M. Lindholm, R. McCartney, J. E. Moström, K. Sanders, O. Seppälä, B. Simon, and L. Thomas. A multi-national study of reading and tracing skills in novice programmers. In *Working group reports from ITiCSE on Innovation and technology in computer science education*, pages 119–150, 2004.

[10] R. Lister, C. Fidge, and D. Teague. Further evidence of a relationship between explaining, tracing and writing skills in introductory programming. In *Proceedings of the 14th annual ACM SIGCSE conference on Innovation and technology in computer science education*, pages 161–165, 2009.

[11] L. Ma, J. D. Ferguson, M. Roper, I. Ross, and M. Wood. Using cognitive conflict and visualisation to improve mental models held by novice programmers. In *Proceedings of the 39th SIGCSE technical symposium on Computer science education*, pages 342–346, 2008.

[12] 7.4.3. Are the means equal? NIST/SEMATECH e-Handbook of Statistical Methods, Retrieved 16 Aug. 2012. Available at: `http://www.itl.nist.gov/div898/handbook/prc/section4/prc43.htm`.

[13] M. C. Orsega, B. T. Vander Zanden, and C. H. Skinner. Experiments with algorithm visualization tool development. In *Proceedings of the 43rd ACM technical symposium on Computer Science Education*, pages 559–564, 2012.

[14] J. Sorva. The same but different. In *Proceedings of the 8th International Conference on Computing Education Research*, pages 5–15, 2008.

[15] J. Sorva and T. Sirkiä. UUhistle: a software tool for visual program simulation. In *Proceedings of the 10th Koli Calling International Conference on Computing Education Research*, pages 49–54, 2010.

[16] L. Thomas, M. Ratcliffe, and B. Thomasson. Scaffolding with object diagrams in first year programming classes: some unexpected results. In *Proceedings of the 35th SIGCSE technical symposium on Computer science education*, SIGCSE '04, pages 250–254, New York, NY, USA, 2004. ACM.

Teaching Cyber-Physical Systems to Computer Scientists via Modeling and Verification

Kostadin Damevski, Badreldin Altayeb, Hui Chen, David Walter
Virginia State University
1 Hayden Dr.
Petersburg, VA 23806
{kdamevski,baltayeb,hchen,dwalter}@vsu.edu

ABSTRACT

The greater versatility and increasingly smaller sizes of computing, sensing, and networking devices have resulted in a new computing paradigm called Cyber-Physical Systems (CPSs), which integrates computation and sensing into physical processes producing a wealth of exciting applications in many domains of life, such as transportation, medicine, and agriculture. In order to equip students with the essential knowledge and skills to be successful in the future, this paradigm requires an expansion in the scope of computer science curricula to enable students to understand and overcome the complexity inherent in CPSs. In this paper, we describe our experience with teaching CPS via a set of course modules that rely heavily on modeling and verification. By using the popular Android platform, we aim to engage students to successfully build CPS applications while enhancing their understanding of intellectually challenging concepts.

Categories and Subject Descriptors

K.3.2 [**Computer and Information Science Education**]: Computer science education

General Terms

Design, Human Factors

Keywords

cyber-physical systems, computer science education

1. INTRODUCTION

Cyber-Physical Systems (CPSs) [4, 5] are a novel class of computing systems intended to enable a new set of applications that have the potential to surpass the 21st century's IT revolution [6]. This new class of applications (e.g., smart home, intelligent transportation, smart electric grid [10, 13]) require rigorous theory and mature engineering principles that combine communication, physical, and computing systems to achieve satisfactory timing, predictability, reliability, and robustness.

Successful CPS design requires an interdisciplinary skill set, including understanding of the discrete characteristics of computer systems, stochastic nature of network protocols, and the continuousness of physical processes. The flourishing development of computer science and physical science in recent years has created barriers between these two disciplines from which CPS is emerging. The barrier "has kept the research communities apart, splitting education into isolated disciplines and resulting in compartmentalized design flows that ultimately lead to major difficulties and failures as complexity has increased" [4].

Traditional computer science education that focuses on teaching programming for ordinary multi-purpose desktop computers does not suffice in preparing students to contribute to this emerging field. For instance, the time delay to perform a computation is a performance issue in a general purpose computer, while it may lead to incorrect control behavior in CPSs [5, 7]. In this paper, we propose a method to infuse CPS concepts into the computer science curriculum via a set of CPS course modules that emphasize modeling and verification.

Our educational approach follows a CPS design methodology, first proposed by Lee and Seshia [7] and depicted in Figure 1, that emphasizes modeling and verification. It is through the process of modeling that engineers gain a deeper understanding of what needs to be built, while performing verification builds confidence that the system adheres to specified properties. In our course modules, students create high-level discrete models of the system that interact with continuous models of physical processes (e.g., movement, sound). Creating these models builds student understanding of the system's overall structure and behavior, instead of becoming too focused on the implementation details. After creating a model, students are able to explore verifications principles and concepts using this model, and, in doing so, consider what properties are necessary to determine correctness and flush out potential errors in the process. During the design and implementation phase, students map the system's model into particular implementation technologies.

Our CPS course modules are designed to be easily applicable to a variety of institutional settings. They rely on the open-source Ptolemy II [3] environment for modeling and verification, and on Android mobile phones and the associated development environment for implementation. Each module follows at least one driving application, which uti-

SIGCSE'13, March 6–9, 2013, Denver, Colorado, USA.

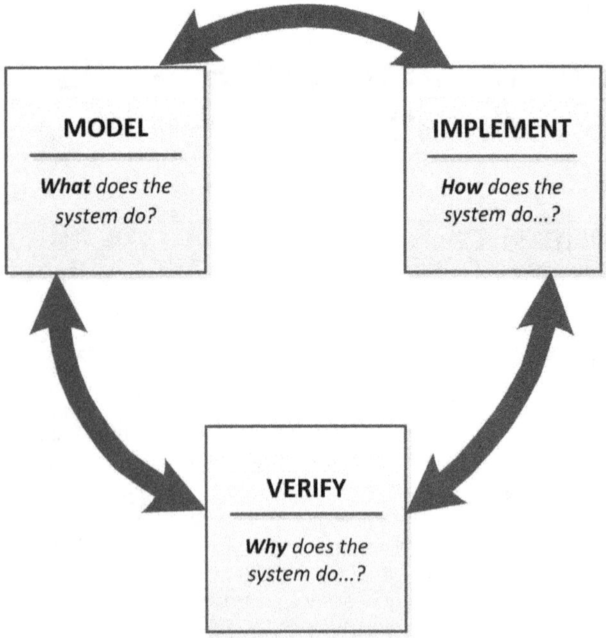

Figure 1: The cyber-physical systems design process.

lizes the smart phone's sensing capabilities and focuses on teaching a specific CPS concept. The Android implementation environment was chosen for these modules due to its attractiveness to students, which has also been previously noted by others [12]. The attractiveness of the mobile platform, in our experience, makes students more willing to engage in discovery of more challenging CPS concepts.

To ease integration with existing CS curricula and effectively teach a number of CPS concepts, we propose to continuously expose students to CPSs and their interesting applications, from freshman to senior year. This type of a longevity-oriented approach has been shown to yield positive benefits in the retention of knowledge [1]. Courses that are utilizing early versions of these modules are currently being offered at Virginia State University. Materials are available on the web at `http://www.sysnetgrp.net/cpsedu`.

2. CORE CPS CONCEPTS

CPS design requires knowledge of a number of topics that present a challenge to existing computer science education. In this section, we list a number of them that we have identified as target areas for our course modules.

- **Resource management:** Resources that require management in CPSs go beyond the usual computing resources, such as CPU cycles, memory, and disk space. They include power consumption and availability, I/O interfacing, and networking.
- **Timing constraints.** Operating system scheduling leads to jitter in system response time, as it takes time to run a program or deliver a packet over a network. Predictable timing and the enforcement of timing constraints are crucial to the robustness of CPSs.
- **Distributed sensing, computation and control.** Many CPS applications require the collection of precise data via sensors that is used to perform control over distributed actuating devices. A number of important issues have to be considered in order to design a CPS that makes correct control decisions within a given deadline, including: when the sensing is performed, how many sensing samples are needed, how to cope with missing, imprecise, and sometimes misleading data, and where computation is to be performed. Furthermore, distributed sensing in CPSs yields continuous streams of data that are managed differently from traditional databases.
- **Modeling and analysis.** A CPS must be dependable and robust in managing a number of complex issues, such as timing, location, power, computational resources, and uncertainties in sensed data. Modeling is an important means to understand system behavior, including both its functional and non-functional aspects.
- **Verification and testing.** CPSs are often used in mission critical tasks, requiring that their behavior is proven or certified to be correct. CPS designers must know how to formally ensure that the system satisfies certain properties.

3. DESIGN OF COURSE MODULES

Each CPS course module centers around a specific CPS concept (e.g., sensor data processing, network reliability, concurrency), which it accomplishes via modeling, verification, and implementation subtasks and is designed to be integrated into a particular CS core or elective course. A list of the current set of course modules mapped to the 2008 ACM/IEEE CS body of knowledge is given in Table 1. In this section, we describe the common aspects of the course modules, their hardware and software requirements, and how they can be integrated in the CS curriculum.

Course modules, such as the ones we have developed, have frequently been used in education as a means to integrate a new concept into existing curricula. For instance, the course module approach was successfully used to embed parallel programming into the CS curriculum at St. Olaf's college by Brown et al. [1]. We argue that there is an additional benefit to this type of approach, stemming from the repeted exposure to CPS concepts and to modeling and verification.

3.1 Structure

The modules are intended to be self-contained in that they provide both lecture and activity instructions, though activity description and hints consume much of the content similar to a tutorial. However, we do not envision the CPS course modules to be used for independent learning by students, as an instructor is necessary to provide greater depth of content and guidance during the activities. Each module's learning outcomes are divided into a number of modeling, implementation or, verification subgoals, an educational approach effective in decreasing cognitive load [9]. These subgoals contribute to building a small to medium size driving application that is intended to be interesting to students while using CPS concepts for its correct function. Each of the current set of modules requires only one prerequisite module, which introduces students to the modeling and implementation environments.

CPS Concept	Driving Application	Target Course	Knowledge Area
Introductory Module	Security Device Baby Rattle	CS1 or CS2	PF/EventDrivenProgramming SE/SoftwareDesign
Concurrency	Parking Helper	Operating Systems	OS/Concurrency NC/Introduction
Digital and Analog Signals	Human Activity Classification	Operating Systems Embedded Systems	AR/InterfacingAndI/OStrategies OS/DeviceManagement
Low-level Communication	Sound Beacon	Networking	NC/Network Communication

Table 1: List of the current set of CPS course modules

The hardware requirements of the course modules are intentionally low in order to facilitate their dissemination to the educational community. Most of the modules require only the use of an Android mobile phone, as those are nowadays widely available to students and CS programs. Recent generation mobile phones contain a set of sensors (e.g., accelerometer, gyroscope, microphone, camera, GPS receiver) as well as advanced networking (e.g., WiFi, bluetooth), which make them appropriate for teaching CPS concepts. Most mobile phones lack on-board actuation capabilities, and therefore we engineered our course modules to be functional without performing actuation, although actuation does contribute to richer CPS application development. This limitation can be overcome by using the Android Accessory Development Kit (ADK)[1].

On the software side, our modules are linked to the Ptolemy II [3] design environment, which is used for modeling (and potentially verification), while implementing the CPS applications requires the Android application development environment. Ptolemy II provides the capability for modeling of discrete computational processes in combination with continuous physical processes, and presents a natural fit for designing and modeling CPSs. Ptolemy II also supports the use of third-party model checkers (e.g., NuSMV, REDLIB, Real Time Maude) which can be utilized for the verification aspects of our modules [2]. All of the required software for the course modules is open source and available for download to a wide set of classroom or laboratory platforms.

3.2 Content

Each module contains at least one modeling activity, usually at the forefront, intended to be completed by students using the Ptolemy II heterogeneous modeling environment. Ptolemy II models are executable as simulations, which is advantageous for building intuition of the modeled system's behavior. A starter Ptolemy II model is provided to students as scaffolding [8] to guide them towards completing the most relevant parts of the model. Commonly, students are asked to design a Finite State Machine (FSM) model of the application to be implemented. This model is often extended with discrete time (timed FSM), or to describe concurrency (concurrent FSM). Based on our experience using the modules, the starter models include completed continuous time sub-models to produce simulated sensor data. However, in upper level courses, those sub-models can be the responsibility of the students.

The purpose of verification activities within the modules is to develop student analytical thinking, to underscore the importance of correctness in CPS design, and expose students to relevant verification concepts such as languages for specifying temporal properties, reachability analysis, and model checking. Students explore verification by being asked to formally specify certain properties of the model (e.g., that a particular FSM state will never be reached) and to perform a state space exploration manually to allow them to check their property. If the property is violated, this indicates a potential problem with the model that the student is asked to re-examine. We are also exploring tool support to execute a model checker directly from Ptolemy II and formally determine the correctness of the property. Currently, we only discuss the specification and verification of discrete parts of the model; while continuous verification is desirable, it is also much more challenging to perform.

The implementation aspect of the course modules uses the Android mobile phone development environment, based on the Java programming language. While the Android APIs require some time for the students to master, we make every effort to provide the necessary documentation within each course module about the relevant APIs. The implementational task usually involves the translation of the FSM model into working Java code. In general, our experience indicates that an accurate and detailed model is not very difficult for the students to translate into a working Android implementation.

4. EXAMPLE MODULE: HUMAN ACTIVITY CLASSIFICATION

In this section, we describe one representative CPS course module in order to illustrate the modules' contents, as well as how modeling and verification are used in the instruction.

The Human Activity Classification module focuses on rudimentary signal processing concepts, such as analog-to-digital conversion, digital-to-analog conversion, noise, and sampling rate. These concepts are illustrated by using input from the the accelerometer sensor, available in a broad set of Android mobile devices. The most common purpose of the accelerometer in mobile devices is to detect the rotation of the device in the user's hands, which is used by the OS to change the screen orientation between portrait and landscape. Our Human Activity Classification application repurposes the accelerometer to measure the amount of shaking the phone is experiencing, translating this information to determine whether the person holding the device is standing (none or almost no shaking), walking (some shaking) or running (a lot of shaking). This application follows the previous research results in human activity classification of Estrin et al. [11]. A functional and robust Human Activity Classification Android application is the students' final goal in this module,

[1]More information on the Android ADK can be found at `http://developer.android.com/tools/adk/index.html`

which is accomplished via a set of modeling, verification, and implementation increments.

This course module begins with the students receiving background information on basic signal processing concepts, usually accomplished with the help of the course instructor, followed by students constructing Ptolemy II models of the aforementioned application.

4.1 Modeling

A Ptolemy II model consists of a set of executable interconnected *actors* whose communication is governed by a *director*. An actor defines one specific activity, such as a mathematical function, a UI element, or a finite state machine. Actors can be *composite*, meaning that they can contain one or more actors and a director within them. Directors allow Ptolemy II to support multiple modes of execution including simple dataflow execution, continuous time, discrete events, and several others, which allows the expression of a wide set of actor interaction patterns.

The Ptolemy II model of the Human Activity Classification application is shown in Figure 2. The `SignalGenerator` composite actor generates accelerometer data that is purposefully noisy to make the simulation more realistic. This acceleration data is processed by a `MagnitudeCalculator` actor, which is also composite, that calculates the magnitude of the acceleration by combining the acceleration in the X, Y and Z axes. The statistical variance of this magnitude is calculated by the `Variance` actor, which contributes this value to the `Classification FSM` actor that, in turn, classifies the data as one of the three states: standing, walking, or running. The result of the the FSM is displayed by the `Android Screen` actor.

When modeling the application, students are provided with a starting Ptolemy II model that defines the application at the highest level of the hierarchy (top box in Figure 2). Certain actors in the the provided starting model are already fully functional, such as the `SignalGenerator` actor that produces the simulated accelerometer data. Students are asked to augment the starting model by completing all of the incomplete composite actors: `Classification FSM` and `MagnitudeCalculator`. In this particular application, student modeling consists of creating models of two of the core parts of the application: (1) the computation of the shaking metric from the data, and (2) the FSM that performs the final classification. While working on these two composite actors, using the already functional actors in the starter model, students are able to debug certain aspects of their models and associated application logic, as well as experiment with several of the important parameters that will govern the effectiveness of the final application, such as the window size for the calculations, and the accelerometer's sampling frequency.

4.2 Verification

Verifying the model of the Human Activity Classification application, based on a set of specified properties, builds confidence about the model's correctness and is an important aspect of CPS design. Through our course modules, we train the students about verification concepts as well as the value of verication to ensure correcteness of the final implementation of the application. The instructor works with the students to identify system invariants which are then written more formally using a temporal logic such as linear temporal logic (LTL) [7]. In this example, an important property may be that the application will be in the standing state when the value of the magnitude of the shaking is at a particular constant or range of values.

After properties have been identified, students are presented with the challenge of algorithmically ensuring that the properties are adhered to. In particular, they are asked to manually do a state space exploration for a part of the problem. In doing so, students will encounter on a first-hand basis the challenge of state explosion, providing an excellent opportunity to discuss additional verification topics such as abstraction and refinement. Ultimately, the goal is for students to use Ptolemy II to convert their model into a format which can be used with a model checker to either show that the property is provably true or provides a counterexample[2]. If a counterexample is provided, the students will be directed to change the application's Ptolemy II model in order to remedy the problem, and then repeat the verification. These activities are taught with ample supervision of the students' effort, in order to develop skill in both expressing verifiable properties and interpreting and acting on the model checker's output.

4.3 Implementation

After the modeling and verification phases are complete, the students are confident that the resulting model is correct and can be implemented and tested on the target hardware, the Android mobile device. Several of the actors in the Ptolemy II models were concerned with simulating the physical process (acceleration), and should not be explicitly implemented. Instead, the students implement the `MagnitudeClassification` and `Classification FSM` actors. Implementing the FSM is usually considered not to be difficult, as students are previously taught how to efficiently convert FSMs into programs. One challenge remains, which is to properly use the Android APIs to sample the accelerometer and interface with the Android UI. As this particular module is usually given to junior students, the students are able to read the Android documentation directly and, with minor guidance, to implement the application. However, with greater instructor involvement in selecting the correct Android API invocations, this module could easily be retargeted to less experienced students.

5. ASSESSMENT PLAN

An initial set of course modules have been recently developed and their assessment is currently underway at Virginia State University. In this section, we present our assessment goals and plan. The results of the assessment will impact the creation of new CPS course modules and guide modification to the existing modules.

Since CPSs require a more comprehensive design process than conventional computer systems, due to their high complexity and reliability goals, our course modules emphasize modeling and verification. The main hypothesis that represents this philosophy for teaching CPS is the following:

Modeling and verification improves the reliability of the design and implementation of CPS applications.

This hypothesis should be evaluated in two dimensions:

[2]This functionallity is a work in progress.

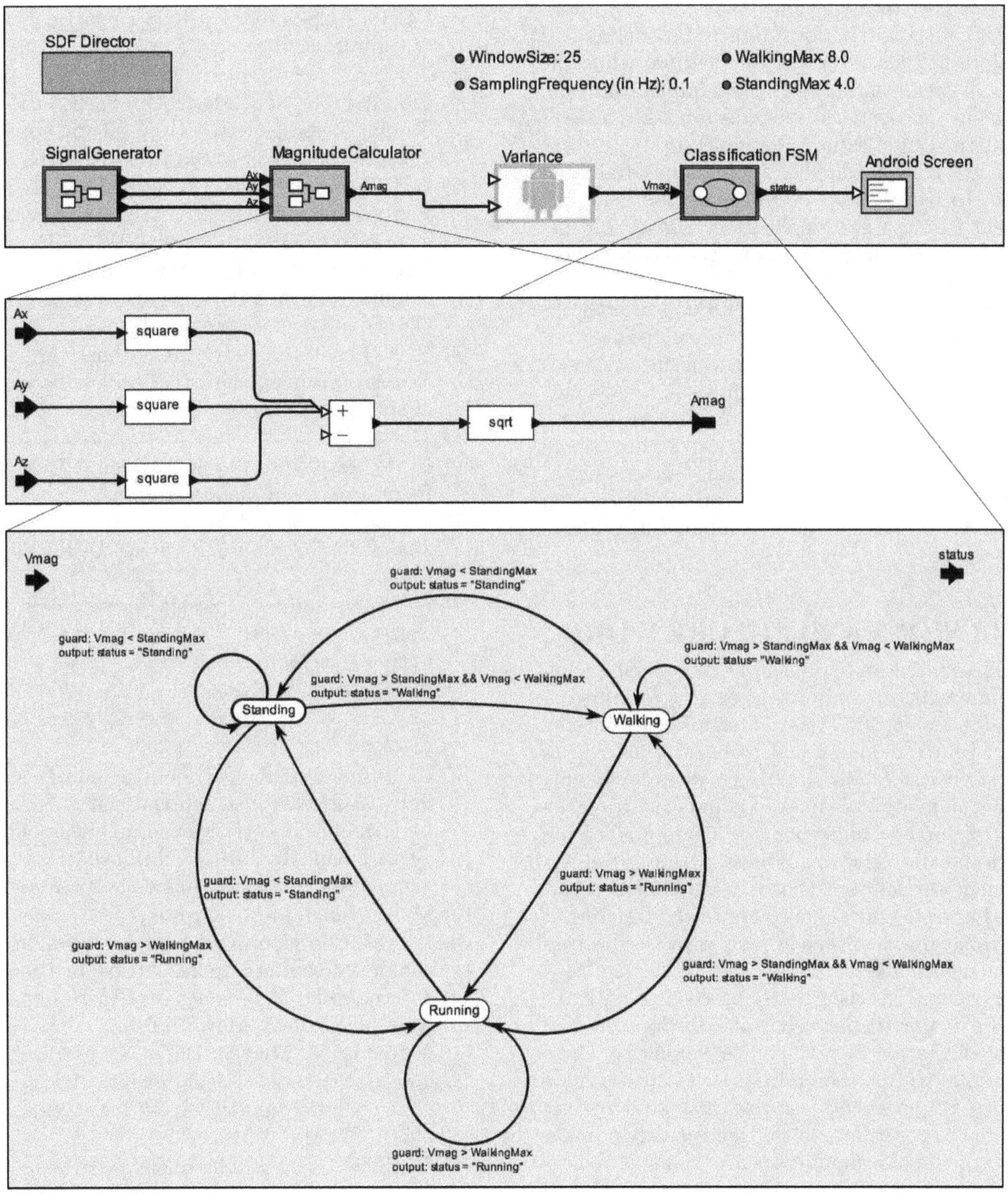

Figure 2: Model of the Human Activity Classification Application in Ptolemy II, including the top level model and inner models of two of the composite actors.

completeness and correctness. First, students should be able to consider all possible scenarios that the application may encounter. Second, students should be able to correctly implement the design and ensure the implementation meets the requirements. Our expectation is that modeling and verification play a key role to enable students to design a complete solution and implement the solution correctly.

Our study plan is to divide the students into two cohorts and assign each cohort to implement a specific CPS application. The first cohort will perform directed modeling and verification before implementing the application, while the second cohort will spend the entire time on implementation. After an equivalent timespan, the students are asked a set of questions about their application's design to evaluate completeness, while the resulting application's code is evaluated for correctness. To reduce bias, we intending to repeat the same experiment (using a new application) while requiring the first cohort to directly implement, and the second cohort to use modeling and verification.

In addition to the assesment of our CPS educational approach, we intend to assess the impact of our course modules on student outcomes over the long term. Specifically, since the course modules are part of several courses in the CS curriculum, we want to evaluate their overall effect on cohorts that have used the modules through their entire educational experience at our university. To perform this assessment, we will survey CPS understanding and perception of groups of students that have used these modules compared to students that were not exposed to the modules.

6. CONCLUSIONS AND FUTURE WORK

This paper introduced an approach for introducing computer science students to concepts necessary for the implementation and design of CPSs. Our approach centered around a set of course modules, consisting of a number of modeling and verification activities, designed to be flexibly integrated into a number of courses in standard CS curricula. Each course module implements a single application that is chosen to be attractive to students, and uses the Android development environment that is capable of also garnering student interest. Our modules are freely available at `http://www.sysnetgrp.net/cpsedu`, and we welcome contributions and suggestions.

Future work consists of concurrently proceeding with the outlined assessment activities as well as the development and classroom implementation of new course modules. These new course modules will be chosen in order to span a more complete set of CPS concepts, ensuring that students are properly prepared to contribute to this increasingly popular and important domain of computer science. Some of the existing modules, as well as newly developed modules, should be enhanced to include actuation using the Android Accessory Development Kit. In addition, we intend to develop one or two complex modules that can be used as a project in a capstone course, and that use multiple CPS concepts and expose the potential complexity of larger CPS applications.

Acknowledgement

The authors gratefully acknowledge support for this work from the U.S. National Science Foundation through award number 1044841.

7. REFERENCES

[1] R. Brown and E. Shoop. Modules in community: injecting more parallelism into computer science curricula. In *Proceedings of the 42nd ACM technical symposium on Computer science education*, SIGCSE '11, pages 447–452, New York, NY, USA, 2011. ACM.

[2] C. P. Cheng, T. Fristoe, and E. A. Lee. Applied verification: The ptolemy approach. Technical Report UCB/EECS-2008-41, EECS Department, University of California, Berkeley, Apr 2008.

[3] J. Eker, J. W. Janneck, E. A. Lee, J. Liu, X. Liu, J. Ludvig, S. Neuendorffer, S. Sachs, and Y. Xiong. Taming heterogeneity - the Ptolemy approach. *Proceedings of the IEEE*, 91(1):127–144, Jan. 2003.

[4] B. H. Krogh, E. Lee, I. Lee, A. Mok, G. Pappas, R. Rajkumar, L. R. Sha, A. S. Vincentelli, K. Shin, J. Stankovic, J. Sztipanovits, W. Wolf, and W. Zhao. The cyber-physical systems summit executive summary, 2006. `http://varma.ece.cmu.edu/Summit/CPS-Executive-Summary.pdf`.

[5] E. A. Lee. Cyber-physical systems - are computing foundations adequate? In *Position Paper for NSF Workshop On Cyber-Physical Systems: Research Motivation, Techniques and Roadmap*, 2006.

[6] E. A. Lee. Cyber physical systems: Design challenges. In *International Symposium on Object/Component/Service-Oriented Real-Time Distributed Computing (ISORC)*, May 2008. Invited Paper.

[7] E. A. Lee and S. A. Seshia. *Introduction to Embedded Systems - A Cyber-Physical Systems Approach.* `http://LeeSeshia.org`, 2011.

[8] L. Lipscomb, J. Swanson, and A. West. Scaffolding. In M. Orey, editor, *Emerging perspectives on learning, teaching, and technology.* 2007.

[9] L. Margulieux, R. Catrambone, and M. Guzdial. Subgoal-labeled instructional material improves performance and transfer in mobile application development. In *Proceedings of the Eight International Computing Education Research Workshop*, 2012.

[10] M. McNaughton, C. Urmson, J. M. Dolan, and J.-W. Lee. Motion planning for autonomous driving with a conformal spatiotemporal lattice. In *Proceedings of the International Conference on Robotics and Automation*, pages 4889–4895, May 2011.

[11] S. Reddy, M. Mun, J. Burke, D. Estrin, M. Hansen, and M. Srivastava. Using mobile phones to determine transportation modes. *ACM Trans. Sen. Netw.*, 6(2):1–27, Mar. 2010.

[12] D. Riley. Using mobile phone programming to teach Java and advanced programming to computer scientists. In *Proceedings of the 43rd ACM technical symposium on Computer Science Education*, SIGCSE '12, pages 541–546, New York, NY, USA, 2012. ACM.

[13] M. U. Tariq, S. Grijalva, and M. Wolf. Towards a Distributed, Service-Oriented Control Infrastructure for Smart Grid. In *Proceedings of the 2011 IEEE/ACM International Conference on Cyber-Physical Systems*, pages 35–44. IEEE, Apr. 2011.

A Derivation-First Approach to Teaching Algorithms

Ran Libeskind-Hadas
Department of Computer Science
Harvey Mudd College
ran@cs.hmc.edu

ABSTRACT

A common approach to teaching algorithms involves describing algorithms first and then proving their correctness afterwards. In this article we advocate a "derivation-first" approach in which algorithms are "derived," either from basic concepts or from simpler algorithms, before they are proved correct. We demonstrate how a number of "classical" algorithms can be derived, providing students with a more intellectually satisfying experience, a deeper intuition into how algorithm design works, and connections between algorithms that can be useful in developing algorithms for other problems.

Categories and Subject Descriptors

K.3.2 [**Computer and Information Science Education**]

Keywords

Computer science education, algorithms, derivations

1. INTRODUCTION

Many undergraduate algorithms curricula have moved from an applications-based approach where material is organized by problem type (e.g., sorting, graph algorithms) to a paradigm-based approach organized by major conceptual and design ideas (e.g., greed, divide-and-conquer, dynamic programming) illustrated by representative problems and algorithms. While the latter approach has been advocated as particularly well-suited for teaching design and problem-solving skills [1, 7], even this mode of organization can miss opportunities to demonstrate important connections between algorithmic ideas and show students how "non-obvious" algorithms can be plausibly "derived."

It is our belief that seeing or participating in the "derivation" of an algorithm – that is, the development of an algorithm from either a simpler algorithm or from a basic principle – is more intellectually satisfying and more effective for student learning than simply being shown the algorithm. In any case, a proof of correctness is ultimately required, but it is likely to be conceptually easier to construct a proof for an algorithm that students have helped derive than for one that has been presented without motivation. Deriving *multiple* algorithms from a single unifying idea can be particularly useful because these connections may offer students cognitive schemata that are useful in solving problems in new situations [8] and leads students to subsequently generalize their results [10]. In our experience, the derivation-based approach substantially mitigates the a commonly heard comment from students: "I understand now how it works, but I would never have come up with that myself!"

In this paper, we describe how some of the most commonly-taught classical algorithms can be derived from conceptually simpler algorithms or fundamental ideas. Specifically, we show how selection sort and merge sort are related and how this relationship allows us to naturally develop heap sort, we demonstrate how the simple breadth-first search algorithm for finding shortest paths in unweighted graphs leads to Dijkstra's algorithm for finding shortest paths in weighted graphs, we show how both the Bellman-Ford and Floyd-Warshall algorithms originate from the same simple recursive idea, and we develop minimum spanning tree algorithms from a single simple observation.

Many of the connections that we discuss here and use in our course are known: Some appear in textbooks, some appear in the academic literature, and some are evidently computer science "folklore." Our emphasis here is not in advancing the field of algorithms but rather on the pedagogical use of these connections to enhance the student learning experience.

We have recently begun using this "derivation-first" approach in the the junior-level algorithms course at Harvey Mudd College. Initial evidence suggests that students enjoy and benefit from this approach. A systematic study on the impact of this approach on student learning is the topic of future work.

2. DERIVING HEAP SORT

Sorting algorithms are foundational in computer science curricula. They are taught both because of their widespread utility and because they illustrate fundamental algorithm design and analysis techniques. The various sorting algorithms that are typically presented can seem entirely unrelated to one another. Moreover, some of the less intuitively "obvious" algorithms, such as heap sort, are often presented with little motivation. The algorithm is clever and makes sense in hindsight, but how would one come up with it? In

SIGCSE'13, March 6–9, 2013, Denver, Colorado, USA.

this section we describe a way of relating three classical sorting algorithms – selection sort, merge sort, and heap sort – and ultimately deriving heap sort from the other two algorithms.

The connections between sorting algorithms are not new, they are just generally not presented to students! When they are presented, they are typically shown after-the-fact rather than as a pedagogical mechanism for developing "non-obvious" algorithms from simpler or more intuitive ones. Some of the connections between sorting algorithms were shown by Knuth [6]. Merritt established a systematic taxonomy of sorting algorithms [9]. More recently, Bell and Aspvall described a way of revisiting sorting algorithms after they have been explained to students in order to show their commonalities and relationships [2]. They use a generalization of a binary heap, called a d-heap, to establish these connections. Our approach uses related ideas but inverts the presentation by deriving heap sort from selection sort and merge sort rather than presenting the algorithms first and then establishing their relationships afterwards.

2.1 Background and Assumptions

In our experience, when students (even those with no prior computing background) are asked to describe a "recipe" for sorting numbers from smallest to largest, the overwhelming majority describe selection sort (or some modest variant). Merge sort is less obvious, but once students are familiar with recursion and the divide-and-conquer idea, this algorithm too is quite natural and can be derived by students with modest encouragement from the instructor (e.g., "If you were going to divide a list into two halves and delegated some of the sorting task to two subordinates – what would you want those subordinates to do with each of the two halves? And once they were done, what would you still need to do?"). Heap sort, on the other hand, is not as naturally "derived," even if students are already familiar with the priority queue abstract data type and the heap data structure.

In fact, these three algorithms can be viewed as special cases of a more general algorithm. Demonstrating this connection to students potentially provides a deeper understanding of sorting but also allows us to motivate heap sort – the least obvious of the three algorithms – in a way that students can later re-derive on their own.

We assume that students have been exposed to both selection sort and merge sort and their asymptotic worst-case running times have been established: selection sort has $\Theta(n^2)$ worst-case running time and merge sort has $\Theta(n \log n)$ worst-case running time. Perhaps students have seen the proof that the lower-bound on comparison-based sorting is $\Omega(n \log n)$ or perhaps they have just been told that this is true. (We prefer the proof, of course, but sometimes students see this later.) The connection between these two algorithms will become evident later. We assume, in this discussion, that students have been previously exposed to the priority queue abstract data type (ADT) and the binary heap data structure.

2.2 From Selection Sort to Heap Sort

One approach for motivating heap sort is based on the observation that selection sort repeatedly seeks to find the minimum remaining element. Initially, it finds the minimum element in the entire array. That element is placed in the first position of the sorted array and then is removed from future consideration. Next, we find the minimum element among those remaining, place it in the growing sorted array, and remove it. This process is repeated until all elements have been placed and there are no more elements to consider. Now we observe that there might be a faster way of finding the minimum at each iteration. "Our goal is to repeatedly find the minimum and delete it. What mechanisms do we have to do this quickly?" Students notice that the priority queue is an ADT that supports the needed operations and recall that the heap is an efficient implementation of that ADT.

This approach is simple and provides insight into how an algorithm like heap sort could have been plausibly derived. However, in our course we use a somewhat different approach that connects selection sort, merge sort, and heap sort through an exploratory activity described next.

2.3 Generalizing Merge Sort

Once merge sort is presented, it's very natural to ask "What would happen if we divided the array into more-or-less equal thirds rather than halves? Would this make the algorithm any faster?" Let's find out. We set up the recurrence relation for this variant of merge sort, observing that the base case when the array has length 1 will still take constant time (c) and the general case involves three recursive calls on arrays of length $n/3$. The merging still takes $\Theta(n)$ time since each merge step compares 3 elements – one in each of the recursively sorted arrays – and writes the smallest of those to the sorted output array. Comparing three elements to find their minimum takes two comparisons, which is constant time, and then we remove the "winner" (the smallest element) from future consideration. Thus, at most n such constant time comparisons are required to merge, for a total of $\Theta(n)$ time. Even if we end up not needing to do all of these comparisons, we still spend $\Theta(n)$ time writing down the merged list. So, our recurrence relation is now:

$$T(1) = c \quad (1)$$
$$T(n) = 3T(n/3) + cn \quad (2)$$

(For simplicity, we use a single constant c here.) Solving this recurrence (e.g., using either work trees, as we do in our course, or the Master Theorem), we get a running time of $cn(1 + \log_3 n) \in \Theta(n \log n)$.

So, no improvement over merge sort. But we should not have expected an asymptotically faster algorithm since $\Omega(n \log n)$ is the theoretical lower bound on comparison-based sorting. But, at least it's not asymptotically *worse* than merge sort! What if we had divided the array into four quarters, or five fifths, or more generally, ℓ pieces of size n/ℓ? Our first attempt at generating the new recurrence relation, generalizing directly from the one above, might be:

$$T(1) = c \quad (3)$$
$$T(n) = \ell \times T(n/\ell) + cn \quad (4)$$

Solving this recurrence, we get a running time of $cn(1 + \log_\ell n)$ which is $\Theta(n \log n)$ for any constant value of ℓ. Nice!

2.4 Heap Sort

Out of curiosity, what happens if we use our generalized merge sort algorithm with a value of ℓ that is not constant – that is, splitting up the array into some number of parts that varies with n? It's a reasonable thing to try and the simplest thing to try is just $\ell = n$. If we substitute n for ℓ in $cn(1+\log_\ell n)$ we get $cn(1+1) \in \Theta(n)$. Something is clearly wrong, because now we're sorting faster than the $\Omega(n \log n)$ theoretical lower bound on comparison-based sorting. It is this discovery of *something wrong* that we find to be particularly useful in this interactive development of heap sort.

Let's take a closer look at what our generalized merge sort algorithm is doing when $\ell = n$. It's making n recursive calls on size 1. Each of those is a base case that takes constant time c. In other words, we spend a total of cn time just touching of those elements and effectively doing nothing! Then, we merge those n elements in (supposedly) cn time. What does the merging do in this case? It looks at the smallest element in each of our n sorted arrays of length 1, finds the minimum of these, and writes that down in the sorted output array. That element is placed in the sorted output array, and we now do the same thing on the remaining $n-1$ elements. This is precisely what selection sort does. In the implementation of selection sort that we may have seen earlier, that smallest element was swapped with the element in the first location of the array, while here we are writing that smallest element in a new output array. But it's otherwise the same algorithm: We compare the current set of elements to find the smallest one, put that in its rightful location, and then repeat with the remaining elements. We know that this takes $n-1$ comparisons to find the minimum element the first time, $n-2$ the second time, for a total of $(n-1)+(n-2)+\cdots+1 = \frac{n(n-1)}{2} \in \Theta(n^2)$.

So, when $\ell = n$, generalized merge sort effectively becomes selection sort and the running time should be $\Theta(n^2)$ not $\Theta(n)$ as we derived from our recurrence relation. Looking back at our recurrence relation, what went wrong? The base case (3) is fine as are the ℓ recursive calls on problems of size $T(n/\ell)$ in (4). The problem must be then with the cn term in (4). Indeed, this term assumes that we always get the next smallest element in constant time, but we saw in selection sort that this is not the case – it takes $n-1$ comparisons the first time, $n-2$ the second and so forth. We correct this term by observing that when we merge ℓ sorted arrays of length ℓ/n, each step of the merge requires $\ell-1$ comparisons since each comparison removes one of the ℓ elements from consideration as the minimum and thus $\ell-1$ comparisons are required to remove $\ell-1$ elements from consideration and leave just one. So, our new recurrence becomes:

$$T(1) = c \quad (5)$$

$$T(n) = \ell \times T(n/\ell) + c(\ell-1)n \quad (6)$$

Solving this recurrence gives us $c(\ell-1)n(1+\log_\ell n)$. For any constant value of ℓ, this is still $\Theta(n \log n)$. For $\ell = n$, it becomes $\Theta(n^2)$ as expected.

Note that this running time is a bit pessimistic because, when $\ell = n$, it assumes that that we'll spend $\ell - 1 = n - 1$ time to find each minimum, when in fact we know that only the first step will take this much time while the second step will take $n-2$ steps, then $n-3$, and so forth. But the sum is asymptotically the same. This observation leads us to another observation – the way that we're finding the minimum at each merge step seems wasteful. For example, imagine that $\ell = 42$. We've divided the array into 42 more-or-less equal sized subarrays and sorted them recursively. Now, we merge those 42 sorted subarrays by comparing the smallest (leftmost) element in each of the arrays using 41 comparisons. Afterwards, we've found the smallest element and have written it to our sorted output array. We advance a metaphorical finger on the subarray where the winner came from but all of our other 41 fingers are where we left them. We now again perform 41 comparisons to find the minimum of these elements. But many of the comparisons that we're doing this time were probably done last time since only one of the 42 elements has changed.

Here's our problem: We have 42 (or in general, ℓ) elements. We'd like to find the minimum element in that set, remove it, and add a new element. We need some efficient mechanism for deleting the minimum and inserting a new element. Under the assumption that students have seen heaps previously (either in this course or in an earlier one), most students enthusiastically volunteer the use of a heap at this point.

Building a heap of ℓ elements takes $O(\ell)$ time. (If students have not seen this analysis, we can also build the heap naively using $O(\ell \log \ell)$ time without any consequences to the final result.) Subsequent deletions of the minimum and insertions of new elements each take $O(\log \ell)$ time. Thus, using a heap to perform the merging operations takes time $\ell + n \log \ell$ (omitting multiplicative constants) resulting in the following new recurrence relation for generalized merge sort:

$$T(1) = c \quad (7)$$

$$T(n) = \ell \times T(n/\ell) + \ell + n \log \ell \quad (8)$$

For any constant value of ℓ, $\ell + n \log \ell$ is $\Theta(n)$, so the running time remains $O(n \log n)$. However, when $\ell = n$, what happens now? In this case, the recurrence relation immediately solves to $T(n) = n \times T(1) + n + n \log n \in \Theta(n \log n)$. So we now get $n \log n$ running time even when $\ell = n$. This version of generalized merge sort, using a heap to do the merging, is called heap sort. We revisit the high level connections between the three algorithms and then probe deeper into heap sort, revisiting what heap sort is actually doing, note that it doesn't actually require any recursion because we began by dividing the array into n subarrays of length 1, and develop the pseudo-code.

3. DERIVING DIJKSTRA'S ALGORITHM

Breadth-first search is a simple and intuitive algorithm for finding shortest paths in unweighted graphs that effectively sends a wave from the start vertex outwards, recording the time when that wave first reaches each vertex. That first "reach time" is rather clearly the length of the shortest path. Dijkstra's algorithm is a considerably more complicated and less intuitive algorithm for finding shortest paths in weighted graphs. The connection between these two algorithms is not often taught, but Dijkstra's algorithm makes perfect sense by first explaining it in the context of breadth-first search. This is presented in [4].

In a nutshell, consider a graph with positive integer edge weights. Then, an edge (u, v) with weight w can be replaced by a sequence of $w+1$ unit-weighted edges $u_0, u_1, \ldots, u_w$ where $u_0 = u$ and $u_w = v$. By performing this transformation on each edge of the original graph, we construct a new unweighted graph. Let those vertices present in the original weighted graph be called *original vertices* and the new vertices used to model weighted edges be called *new vertices*.

We can now find the shortest paths from the designated

start vertex to the original vertices using breadth-first search in our new graph. But this could be potentially very slow. Why? Large edge weights in the original graph result in a large unweighted new graph which in turn results in a large running time.

It would be nice if we could simulate the breadth-first search in the new graph efficiently by skipping many steps of the BFS wave propagation and fast-forwarding to the point when the wave will reach the next original vertex. To that end, we can now revert to the original weighted graph and associate an "arrival time" with each vertex in the original graph that indicates when the breadth-first search wave will reach that vertex (and thus the distance to that vertex). The start vertex s has a time of 0 since the wave begins there. All other vertices currently have undetermined arrival times. Since arrival times are supposed to be numbers, it is reasonable to initialize these times to be comparable to numbers and infinity is therefore a natural choice. The BFS wave now starts moving towards all of the neighbors of the start vertex, s. Thus, for each neighbor v of s, where $w(s,v)$ denotes the weight on that edge, we must update the arrival time for v to be $w(s,v)$. We now find the unvisited vertex v with the least arrival time. This is where the BFS wave would reach next. We now know the distance to that vertex v so we remove v from further consideration and let it inform each of its neighbors when the wave will reach them from v. Each neighbor receiving that information accepts the new arrival time if it is less than its current arrival time.

Thus, we need the ability to insert all of the initial arrival time values, delete the vertex with minimum arrival time, and update the arrival times of vertices. These operations are precisely the ones supported by a priority queue. Students have seen the notion of a priority queue and the heap data structure by this time and now have a complete description of Dijkstra's algorithm using heaps. (We've found that students suggest using a priority queue on their own if we originally motivate priority queues with applications to discrete-event simulation.) Moreover, they can compute the running time of this implementation of Dijkstra's algorithm based on their knowledge of the cost of heap operations.

Of course, we've derived this algorithm under the assumption that the edge weights are integers. A different and more complex proof of correctness is required for the case of arbitrary non-negative edge weights and this development is not intended to replace that course content. However, this intuitive development of Dijkstra's Algorithm provides initial insight that is much more satisfying and useful than simply being told how the algorithm works.

4. DERIVING THE BELLMAN-FORD AND FLOYD-WARSHALL ALGORITHMS

In addition to Dijkstra's shortest path algorithm, many algorithms courses show students the Bellman-Ford and Floyd-Warshall algorithms. Unlike Dijkstra, these algorithms permit negative cost edges. Floyd-Warshall, unlike Dijkstra or Bellman-Ford, finds shortest paths between all-pairs of vertices.

There are a number of nice ways of motivating or deriving these algorithms. For example, Dasgupta *et al.* [4] motivate Bellman-Ford as an extension to Dijkstra's algorithm while Kleinberg and Tardos [5] develop it as a dynamic programming algorithm.

Our approach is to motivate both of these algorithms simultaneously as slightly different variants of the same underlying recursive – and ultimately dynamic programming – approach. In particular, we develop these algorithms without mention of negative edge weights or all-pairs shortest paths; at this point we're just seeking a simple algorithm for finding the shortest path between two vertices under the intuitively reasonable assumption that all edge weights are positive. We revisit and relax some of the assumptions afterwards.

4.1 Bellman-Ford

Recursion is one of our most powerful tools so we begin there. Imagine that we wish to write a function that finds the length of a shortest path from vertex i to vertex j where there are n vertices and i and j are indices $1 \leq i,j \leq n$. Let's call the function $\mathrm{SP}(i,j)$. In the spirit of a recursive solution, we seek the base case first. If $i=j$, the shortest path length is 0 and we're done. Otherwise, what shall we do? Again in the spirit of recursion, we'd like to solve a "smaller" similar problem and use this to answer our question. One possibility is to recursively find the lengths of the shortest paths from i to each vertex k and then add to that the weight of the additional "hop" on the edge from k to j (which is implicitly ∞ if there is no edge (k,j)). Then, the shortest path from i to j is $\mathrm{SP}(i,j) = \min_k \mathrm{SP}(i,k) + w(k,j)$ where $w(k,j)$ is the weight of the edge (k,j).

This all looks good, but there's a subtle problem here. A few moments of reflection by the students leads them to observe that $\mathrm{SP}(i,j)$ will make a recursive call to $\mathrm{SP}(i,k)$ which will, in turn, make a recursive call to $\mathrm{SP}(i,j)$, leading to infinite recursion. We need some way of making the recursion eventually stop. In other words, we need something that gets "smaller" at each recursive step in order to eventually terminate the recursion at a base case. Students generally volunteer that the length of the subpath from i to k being invoked in the recursion should be shorter than the length of the path from i to j. So, path length is getting "smaller" and we can reformulate our recursive function to take in a third argument that is a path length "budget". Our function now becomes $\mathrm{SP}(i,j,\ell)$ where ℓ is the maximum number of edges that are permitted on that shortest path. Clearly, the smallest value of ℓ is 0 and we can easily add a corresponding base case to our recursion. What is the maximum possible value? Again, a few moments of thinking leads students to volunteer that a shortest path between two vertices can have length at most $n-1$; by the pigeonhole principle any longer path would revisit vertices and would not be a shortest path. Now the construction of the recursive function falls out easily. After observing that this algorithm is potentially slow, we apply dynamic programming, resulting in the Bellman-Ford algorithm. Finally, we can now easily show that process of computing one row of the dynamic programming table from the previous row is exactly the same thing as having each vertex make relaxation offers to each of its neighbors. This observation mitigates the frequently asked question "Why does Bellman-Ford have every vertex make relaxation offers to every one of its neighbors at every iteration? It seems wasteful!" Showing that Bellman-Ford is simply implementing the DP for our recursive strategy makes it very clear.

4.2 Floyd-Warshall

Next, we derive the Floyd-Warshall algorithm by observing instead of using the recursive $\mathrm{SP}(i,j) = \min_k \mathrm{SP}(i,k) + w(k,j)$ we could have just as naturally used $\mathrm{SP}(i,j) = \min_k \mathrm{SP}(i,k) + \mathrm{SP}(k,j)$. Again, we run into the problem of infinite recursion because there is no mechanism that ensures that each recursive call gets closer to a base case. The idea of adding a third argument to control the recursion is now quite natural after seeing its utility in the Bellman-Ford algorithm.

We could use the same third argument – a path length budget – but now we have two recursive calls $\mathrm{SP}(i,k)$ and $\mathrm{SP}(k,j)$ rather than one and they don't *both* need a path length budget of $n-1$. So, we might explore other mechanisms for controlling the recursion. Notice that in our expression $\mathrm{SP}(i,j) = \min_k \mathrm{SP}(i,k) + w(k,j)$ we are minimizing over all k, $1 \leq k \leq n$. Our goal is to minimize over the entire range $1 \leq k \leq n$, but perhaps we could do this by recursing on a smaller range. That is, the range on k would be the thing that is getting "smaller" in the recursion. So now we try to make the maximum value of k the third argument rather than the path length ℓ that we used in Bellman-Ford. In other words, we'll let $\mathrm{SP}(i,j,k)$ denote the length of the shortest path from i to j using any intermediate vertex numbered between 1 and k. After exploring the base case, we note that in the general case to compute $\mathrm{SP}(i,j,k)$ we either use vertex k or not. The shortest path using k is $\mathrm{SP}(i,k,k-1) + \mathrm{SP}(k,j,k-1)$ because each of those recursive paths will only use an intermediate vertex of k or less, but neither will actually use k since is one of their endpoints. The other option is not to use vertex k and thus we use $\mathrm{SP}(i,j,k-1)$. Now, $\mathrm{SP}(i,j,k) = \min\{SP(i,k,k-1) + SP(k,j,k-1), SP(i,j,k-1)\}$ and we wish to compute $\mathrm{SP}(i,j,n)$.

After applying dynamic programming to this recursive solution, we compute the running time, and finally observe that this characterization actually computes the shortest paths between all pairs of vertices as a by-product of finding the shortest path between our given pair of vertices. Afterwards, we explore questions such as "do these algorithms assume that edge weights are positive?" among others. By addressing these issues after the algorithms have been derived rather than beforehand, we are able to concentrate on a single simpler problem and a general solution technique for that problem.

5. DERIVING MINIMUM SPANNING TREE ALGORITHMS

The topic of Minimum spanning trees (MST) is taught in most introductory algorithms courses. One approach to teaching this material presents a generic MST algorithm and the notion of "safe" edges and then demonstrates that Kruskal, Prim, and other algorithms are special cases of the generic algorithm [3]. While this an elegant formulation, it is difficult for students to develop the generic algorithm because it is an abstraction – a meta-algorithm for instantiating actual algorithms. Another approach is to present an actual algorithm, such as Prim or Kruskal, and then prove its correctness using the same "safe" edge idea underlying the generic MST algorithm [4, 5]. This too is clean and easily understood, but misses an opportunity for students to develop these algorithms themselves. In contrast, our presentation has students participate in the development of Kruskal's algorithm, then Prim's, then observes a general framework that results in the generic algorithm, and then uses that generic algorithm to generate additional MST algorithms.

Our presentation begins with a review of relevant graph theoretic concepts from discrete mathematics including unrooted trees and their properties, connected components, cuts, spanning trees, and ultimately motivates and formulates the minimum spanning tree problem. Inititally, we make the simplifying assumption that all edge weights in the graph are distinct and prove the simple "safe" edge lemma that states that in such a weighted graph, the unique edge of least weight crossing any cut must be in any MST for that graph. In other words, it's always safe to include such an edge in a MST because that edge must be in the MST. Students are now ready to develop Prim's and Kruskal's algorithms interactively.

5.1 Kruskal's Algorithm

We use a carefully selected small example graph, such as the one shown in Figure 1, on which to develop our algorithms. We ask, "Starting with an empty set of edges and based on the 'safe' edge lemma, which edge of this graph would you be inclined to choose first?" Greed is a natural idea for students (perhaps too natural in some cases, since greedy algorithms seem to be suggested for nearly every problem!), and they volunteer choosing the edge of least weight. "Can you convince me that it's in the MST? You'll need to show me that it's the least weight edge crossing some cut." That's easy because it's the cheapest edge in the entire graph, so it will be the cheapest edge crossing any cut that severs its endpoints. "What edge do you want next?" Clearly, the next cheapest edge! Students easily identify a cut which shows that this edge is safe. This process works for awhile, but eventually our small example graph forces them to choose the next edge to be one between two vertices in the same connected component in the graph of the edges chosen so far (e.g., in the graph in Figure 1, the students have already chosen and justified the selection of the edges with weights 1, 2, and 3, but the edge of weight 4 creates a cycle and thus does not belong in a MST.) Students don't want to choose this edge, but now they seem to be breaking their own rule of choosing edges from lower weight to higher weight. But now they see that this edge is not actually permitted by the lemma because it's not the cheapest edge crossing any cut and they are challenged to explain why. They now reformulate their algorithm to choose edges in increasing order of weight but to exclude edges whose endpoints are in the same connected component. They've now derived Kruskal's algorithm and have developed the idea for how the forthcoming proof of correctness will work.

5.2 Prim's Algorithm

A similar approach is used for Prim's algorithm. "What if we want to grow the tree as a single connected component, starting from an arbitrary vertex v?" This question suffices for the students to now develop Prim's algorithm. Clearly, we want to choose the cheapest edge incident on v and it's easy to demonstrate that this is the cheapest edge crossing a cut (namely the one separating v from all the other vertices). We want the next edge selected to be in this component. Again, it's quite easy for students to see that we

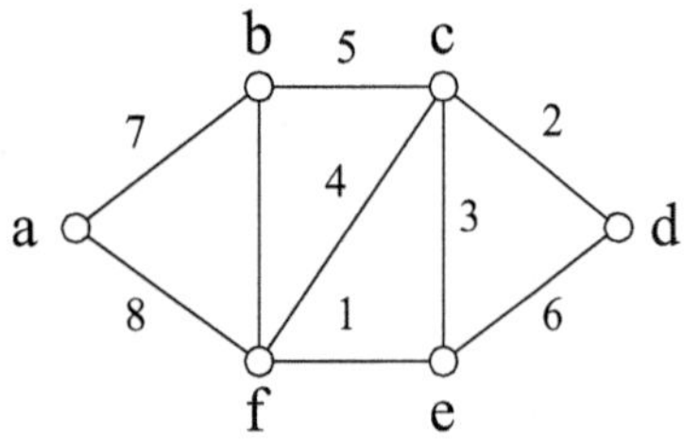

Figure 1: An example graph for developing Kruskal's algorithm.

need to choose the least cost edge incident on one of the two vertices of the current component and they quickly see that in each case the selected edge is the cheapest one separating the current component from the remaining vertices. This is Prim's algorithm.

5.3 Beyond Kruskal and Prim

Once Kruskal and Prim have been derived, we can generalize these to the generic MST algorithm and prove it's correctness. We revisit and relax the unique edge weight assumption and the students prove the more general "safe" edge lemma. Afterwards, students write the proofs of correctness of Kruskal and Prim for the general case and the data structures and running time analyses are developed. Finally, they use the generic algorithm – which they helped derive – to explore and prove the correctness of other MST algorithms such as Bo̊ruvka's algorithm among others.

6. IMPACT AND OUTCOMES

In Spring 2012 we first experimented with presenting some of the major algorithms in the course using this "derivation-first" approach. Approximately five of the 30 lectures in the course emphasized these derivations. Otherwise, this "new" version of the course was virtually identical to the "old" version (taught in Spring 2010 by the same instructor) in organization, content, homework problems, and time of day that the course was taught. The instructor had previously taught this course over 15 times at the college.

Measuring the impact of these curricular changes on student learning is difficult at best. At present, the best measure available are the end-of-semester student evaluations. On a Likert scale (1-7 where 1 is low and 7 is high), the course evaluations between the "old" and "new" offerings were nearly identical (the corresponding means between offerings were within 1% of one another) on all questions related to the performance of the instructor. However, on all three questions related to course content, the differences were notably higher in the new version of the course. For the question "The course was effectively organized to promote the learning objectives," the old version scored 6.52 versus 6.80 for the new version (two-tailed p value for unpaired t test: 0.0552), for the question "The course stimulated my interest in the subject matter," the old version scored 6.41 versus 6.75 for the new version (two-talked p value for unpaired t test: 0.0812), and for the question "I learned a great deal in this course," the old version scored 6.59 versus 6.82 for the new version (two-tailed p value for unpaired t test: 0.1246).

While these analyses fall short of the 0.05 level for statistical significance, they are sufficiently encouraging to merit further experimentation. We plan to post lecture notes on these and future derivations of algorithms on the website `www.cs.hmc.edu/~hadas/AlgorithmDerivations`. A template will be offered for others to use in submitting their contributions to the website as well.

7. CONCLUSION

In this paper we have described a "derivation-first" approach to exposing students to a number of classical algorithms. In our experience, this mode of presentation enhances students' intellectual satisfaction, provides students with more confidence in attacking new algorithmic problems, and largely mitigates a common perception that the development of algorithms is magical. A systematic study of the impact on students is the topic of future work.

8. ACKNOWLEDGEMENTS

The author thanks Professors Zachary Dodds and Darryl Yong for valuable conversations in the preparation of this paper.

9. REFERENCES

[1] R. A. Baeza-Yates. Teaching algorithms. *SIGACT News*, 26(4):51–59, Dec. 1995.

[2] T. Bell and B. Aspvall. Sorting algorithms as special cases of a priority queue sort. In *Proceedings of the 42nd ACM technical symposium on Computer science education*, SIGCSE '11, pages 123–128, New York, NY, USA, 2011. ACM.

[3] T. Cormen, C. Leiserson, and R. Rivest. *Introduction to Algorithms*. The MIT Press, Cambridge, MA, 1990.

[4] S. Dasgupta, C. Papadimitriou, and U. Vazirani. *Algorithms*. McGraw-Hill, New York, NY, USA, 2008.

[5] J. Kleinberg and E. Tardos. *Algorithm Design*. Addison-Wesley Longman Publishing Co., Inc., Boston, MA, USA, 2005.

[6] D. E. Knuth. *The art of computer programming, volume 3: (2nd ed.) sorting and searching*. Addison Wesley Longman Publishing Co., Inc., Redwood City, CA, USA, 1998.

[7] A. Levitin. Design and analysis of algorithms reconsidered. In *Proceedings of the thirty-first SIGCSE technical symposium on Computer science education*, SIGCSE '00, pages 16–20, New York, NY, USA, 2000. ACM.

[8] J. Mason and M. Spence. Beyond mere knowledge of mathematics: The importance of knowing-to act in the moment. *Educational Studies in Mathematics*, 38:135–161, 1999. 10.1023/A:1003622804002.

[9] S. M. Merritt. An inverted taxonomy of sorting algorithms. *Commun. ACM*, 28(1):96–99, 1985.

[10] G. Pólya. *How to solve it: a new aspect of mathematical method*. Science study series. Doubleday, 1957.

Online Python Tutor: Embeddable Web-Based Program Visualization for CS Education

Philip J. Guo
Google, Inc.
Mountain View, CA, USA

ABSTRACT

This paper presents Online Python Tutor, a web-based program visualization tool for Python, which is becoming a popular language for teaching introductory CS courses. Using this tool, teachers and students can write Python programs directly in the web browser (without installing any plugins), step forwards and backwards through execution to view the run-time state of data structures, and share their program visualizations on the web.

In the past three years, over 200,000 people have used Online Python Tutor to visualize their programs. In addition, instructors in a dozen universities such as UC Berkeley, MIT, the University of Washington, and the University of Waterloo have used it in their CS1 courses. Finally, Online Python Tutor visualizations have been embedded within three web-based digital Python textbook projects, which collectively attract around 16,000 viewers per month and are being used in at least 25 universities. Online Python Tutor is free and open source software, available at `pythontutor.com`.

Categories and Subject Descriptors

K.3.1 [**Computers and Education**]: Computer Uses in Education—*Computer-assisted instruction*
; K.3.2 [**Computers and Education**]: Computer and Information Science Education—*Computer science education*

General Terms

Languages, Human Factors, Experimentation

Keywords

CS1, Python, Program Visualization

1. INTRODUCTION

A core challenge in introductory computer science ("CS1") courses is getting students to understand how a static textual representation (source code) maps to a highly dynamic process (program execution). Instructors typically illustrate program execution using graphical PowerPoint lecture slides, which require a great deal of preparation effort, or by drawing diagrams on a whiteboard, which is tedious and error-prone [11]. In the past few decades, many *program visualization* tools have been created to assist instructors in this task. Chapter 11 of Sorva's dissertation [15] provides a comprehensive overview of 40 such tools, which all look similar at first glance: One GUI pane shows source code with the currently-executing line highlighted, another pane shows a visual representation of run-time state (e.g., stack frame contents, heap objects), and control widgets allow the user to step forwards and backwards through execution points.

This paper presents a free and open-source project called Online Python Tutor, which follows in the long tradition of program visualization tools for CS education. In spite of the rich history of related work in this field, three characteristics make Online Python Tutor modern, unique, and effective:

Python: In recent years, Python has been gaining traction as a preferred language for CS1 courses across many universities. For example, two of the largest CS departments—MIT and UC Berkeley—both ported their CS1 curricula from Scheme to Python. Michigan State University switched from C++ to Python and presented empirical evidence that new students were just as prepared for advanced CS courses taught in other languages [7]. Python is also used in free online CS1 courses offered by Udacity, Coursera, and edX, which each enroll tens of thousands of students per term.

Despite the prevalence of Python in teaching, there are almost no program visualization tools for Python. Aside from Online Python Tutor, UUhistle [16] and Jype [9] are the only other Python visualizers[1]. (However, the Jype project seems to be inactive [15], and we cannot find its code online.)

Web-Based: Online Python Tutor is the only Python program visualization tool that runs within a web browser without any required software or plugin installation[1]. UUhistle and Jype are written in Java, so they can be launched from the web on a computer with the proper Java version installed; however, the entire application must first download before launching, which can take a few minutes. In contrast, opening any visualization in Online Python Tutor is as simple and fast as visiting a URL from a web browser.

We believe that this ease of access is a major contributor to adoption: Online Python Tutor has been used in CS1 courses in a dozen universities including UC Berkeley, MIT, the University of Washington, and the University of Water-

[1]to the best of our knowledge

SIGCSE'13, March 6–9, 2013, Denver, Colorado, USA.

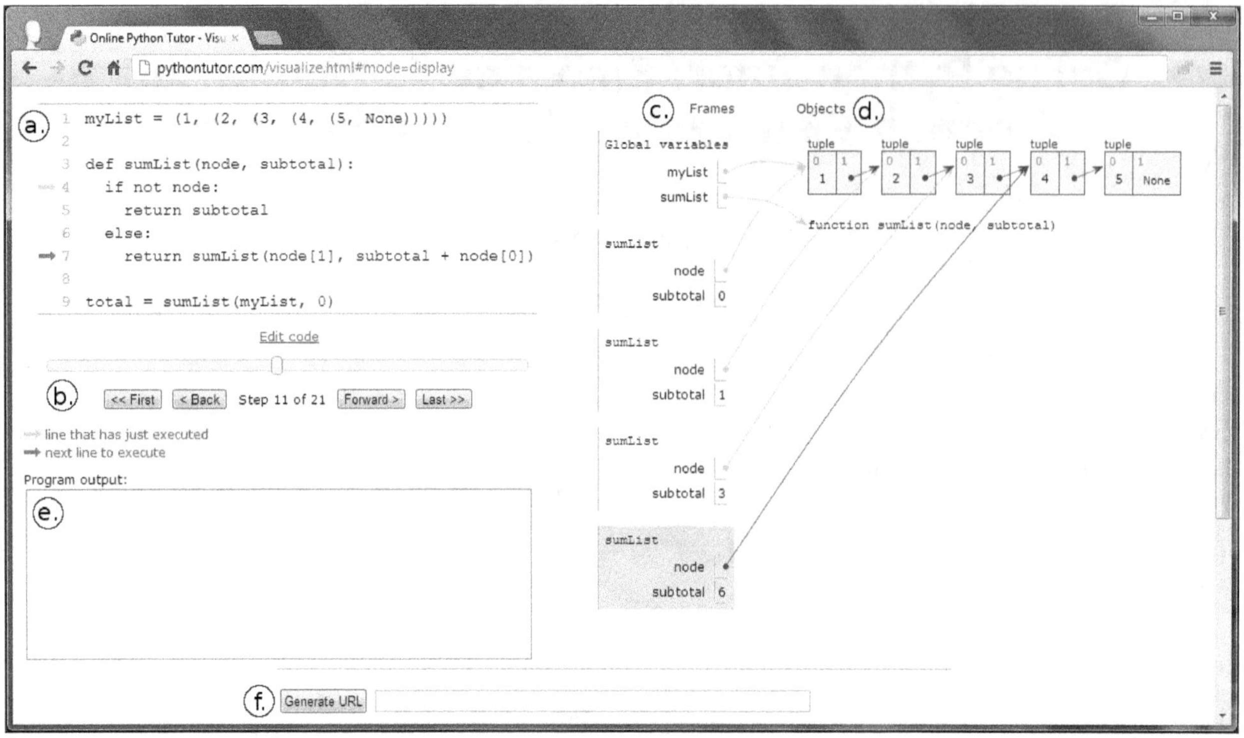

Figure 1: Online Python Tutor is a web-based program visualizer where the user can: a.) view the currently-executing line of code, b.) step forwards and backwards through execution using a slider bar and buttons, c.) view stack frames and variables, d.) view heap object contents and pointers, e.) view the program's text console output, and f.) generate a sharable URL of the current visualization at an exact execution point.

loo. Over 30,000 people (unique IP addresses) per month use Online Python Tutor by visiting `pythontutor.com`.

Embeddable: Finally, Online Python Tutor is the only program visualizer that can be seamlessly embedded within webpages[1]. So far, three web-based interactive digital CS textbooks [6, 10, 14] have embedded Online Python Tutor into their lessons (by inserting one line of JavaScript code per visualization). Students can read lessons and interact with code visualizations within the same webpage (Figure 7).

These three digital textbooks attract around 16,000 unique viewers per month and are being used in at least 25 universities around the world. Alvarado et al. analyzed usage log data from a CS1 course that used one such textbook [10] and found that students who interacted more with the embedded visualizations tended to score higher on midterm exams [2].

2. OVERVIEW

Figure 1 shows the Online Python Tutor webpage loaded in Google Chrome. In this screenshot, the user has previously typed in a 9-line Python program for computing the sum of a linked list and is now visualizing execution step 11 of 21, in the midst of the fourth recursive call to `sumList`.

We now describe the GUI components corresponding to each label in Figure 1:

a.) The source code display shows the program that is being visualized. A red arrow in the left margin points to the next line to be executed (line 7 in this example). A light green arrow points to the line that has just executed, which helps users track non-contiguous control flow (e.g., function calls).

b.) A slider bar and text indicate the current execution point being visualized (in this example, step 11 of 21). Each point represents a single executed line. The user can click on or drag the mouse over the slider bar to jump to a particular point or use the VCR-style navigation buttons to step forwards and backwards over executed lines.

c.) The frames pane shows global variables and stack frames at the current execution point, with the stack growing downward. Each frame shows the function name and a list of local variables. Each variable's value is an arrow that points to a heap object. The currently-active (bottommost) frame is highlighted in blue, as are all arrows emanating from it. To reduce visual clutter, arrows emanating from all other frames are rendered in light gray. In this example, the `node` variable in each recursive call to `sumList` each point to successive elements in the linked list. Finally, even though every object in Python is technically on the heap, we chose to render immutable primitive objects (e.g., numbers, strings, bools) inline within each frame for visual simplicity.

d.) The objects pane shows visual representations of Python objects and their pointer references to one another. Online Python Tutor renders all compound data types necessary for teaching CS1, including list, tuple, set, dict, class, object instance, and closures (see Figure 2). This example shows a linked list of integers built from a chain of five tuples.

e.) The program output text box shows the cumulative output of `print` statements issued by the program at the current execution point.

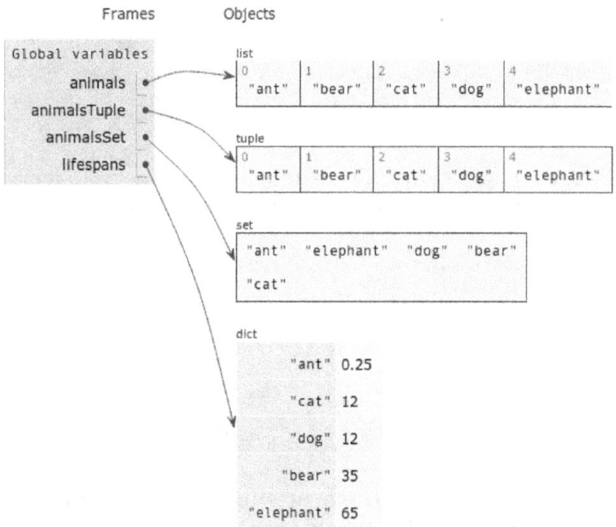

Figure 2: Visualizations of Python's four main compound data types: list, tuple, set, and dict (class, instance, and closure not shown due to space limits)

f.) Clicking the "Generate URL" button creates a URL that uniquely identifies the current program being visualized and also the current execution point. In this example, the URL encodes the complete contents of the 9-line Python program and also includes "step 11 of 21." The user can send that URL in an email or post it to a discussion forum along with a note. When someone clicks on that URL, they are brought to the exact execution point that the sender has specified.

3. DESIGN METHODOLOGY

Online Python Tutor started as a graduate student side project in January 2010, motivated by the creator's experiences with teaching Python by drawing messy stack and heap diagrams on the whiteboard. Around that time, web browsers and technologies were getting sophisticated enough that it became possible to build an educational program visualization tool that could run within the browser.

Our design goal is to make a tool that Python instructors and students prefer to use instead of (or in addition to) traditional whiteboard and PowerPoint diagrams.

We started by taking common features from existing program visualization tools (surveyed in this dissertation [15]) and selectively adapting them to a web browser environment. Over the past three years, the Online Python Tutor user base has grown organically via word-of-mouth publicity. We refined our initial design and implemented new features (e.g., nested function and lambda support) by consulting with our users, which includes a diverse group of CS instructors—teaching assistants, professors at both small and large universities, and an instructor of several free online CS classes with over 200,000 total enrolled students[2].

4. IMPLEMENTATION

Online Python Tutor is a web application with a backend written in Python and a frontend written using standard web technologies: HTML, CSS, and JavaScript.

[2]courses online at `www.ai-class.com` and `www.udacity.com`

4.1 Backend (Python)

The Online Python Tutor backend takes the source code of a Python program as input and produces an *execution trace* as output. The backend executes the input program under supervision of the standard Python debugger module (`bdb`), which stops execution after every executed line and records the program's run-time state. The trace is an ordered list of execution points, where each point contains the state right before a line of code is about to execute, including:

- The line number of the line that is about to execute,
- the instruction type (ordinary single step, exception, function call, or function return),
- a map of global variable names to their current values at this execution point,
- an ordered list of stack frames, where each frame contains a map of local variable names to current values,
- the current state of the heap,
- and the program's output up to this execution point.

After execution terminates, the backend encodes the trace in JSON format [5], serializing Python data types into native JSON types with extra metadata tags. To guard against infinite loops and excessively long traces, the backend halts execution after 300 executed lines. Although this limit is tiny for real programs, it is sufficient for the pedagogical code examples that our users want to visualize. Note that the trace contains a great deal of redundancy, since it stores a complete snapshot of the stack and heap at every execution point. Traces from pedagogical code examples range from 10KB to 200KB in size. We have not found backend running times or trace sizes to be performance bottlenecks in practice and thus have not yet attempted to optimize.

The backend works with both Python 2 and 3, which is important because courses are taught using both of these major language variants.

The backend can be hosted on any webserver capable of running CGI scripts (using Python 2 or 3) or on the Google App Engine platform (Python 2.7). When the user's web browser makes an HTTP GET request to the backend and passes in the Python program to visualize, the backend generates a trace and returns it to the browser in JSON format.

Since the backend is running untrusted Python code from the web, it implements sandboxing to prevent the execution of dangerous constructs such as `eval`, `exec`, file I/O, and most module imports (except for a customizable whitelist of modules such as `math`). In addition, many webservers implement "defense in depth" for additional protections. However, we have not yet conducted a formal security audit.

4.2 Frontend (HTML/CSS/JavaScript)

The frontend is a website located at `pythontutor.com`, which renders in all modern web browsers without requiring the user to install any extensions or plugins. We have tested the website on a wide range of computer monitor sizes and even on tablet devices (see Figure 3).

The user first sees a text box and can type (or paste) a Python program into there. When the user clicks the "Visualize execution" button, the frontend sends that program to the backend; the backend then sends back a JSON execution trace, which the frontend renders in a GUI like Figure 1.

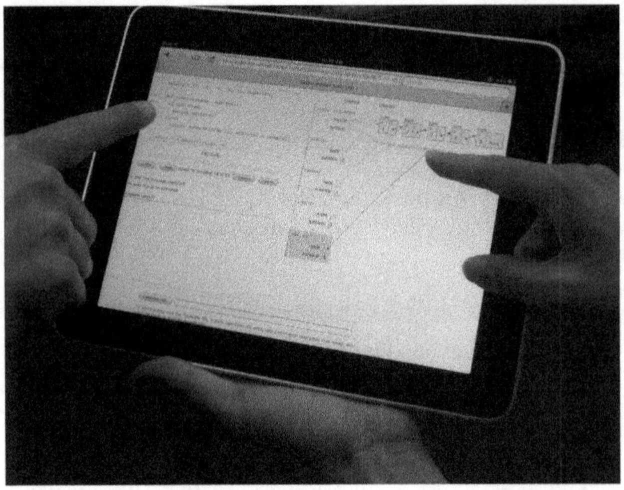

Figure 3: A teacher and student interacting with the Online Python Tutor visualization shown in Figure 1 using the default Safari web browser on an iPad.

From informal testing, the webpage visualizing the code in Figure 1 (and similar code examples) loads in ~ 0.4 seconds on a home broadband Internet connection and in ~ 3 seconds from a shuttle bus with relatively slow Wi-Fi.

After the initial webpage load, all interactions occur in the browser with no additional server calls; thus, stepping forwards and backwards refresh the display instantaneously.

Object layout: The main technical challenge in the frontend is rendering objects in a clear and aesthetically-pleasing way. Since the heap can be an arbitrary graph of objects, a naive rendering scheme could lead to a tangled mess of boxes and pointers. We implemented the following layout heuristics, inspired by looking at diagrams from textbooks and PowerPoint lecture slides from CS1 instructors:

- Each frame variable and heap object is stacked *vertically* in the order in which they were created during the program's execution (see Figure 2). Thus, when the user steps forward through execution, new variables and objects are always appended to the bottom of the display rather than being inserted in the middle.
- Once an object has been rendered, it stays in the same location (relative to other objects) until there are no more pointers to it. This heuristic makes objects not "jiggle" around when the user steps through execution.
- If a new compound object contains pointers to other *new* compound objects, then nest the inner objects inside of the outer one. For example, Figure 4 shows a list of four new Person object instances. Nesting both reduces clutter (instead of rendering more pointers) and also conveys a natural "containment" relationship.
- Since linked lists are common in CS pedagogy, the frontend visualizes them specially by laying out node objects *horizontally* (see Figure 5). The frontend determines that an object is likely a linked list if it contains pointers to identically-structured objects (e.g., a list/tuple of the same size or a dict/instance with the same attribute names). Note that this heuristic fares poorly for tree and graph structures: It simply "flattens" them to one horizontal dimension.

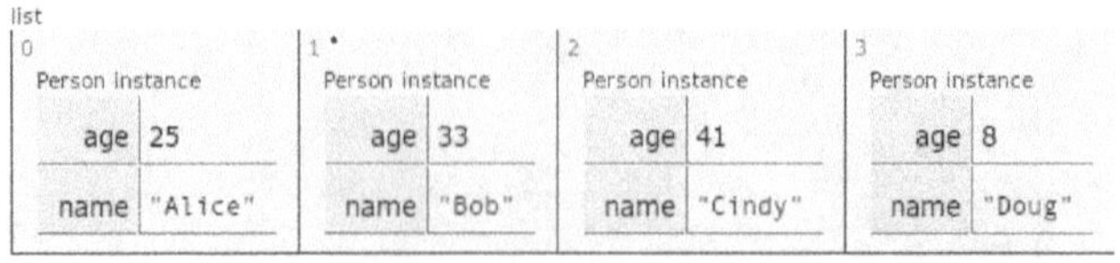

Figure 4: An example visualization of nested data: a list containing four instances of the Person class.

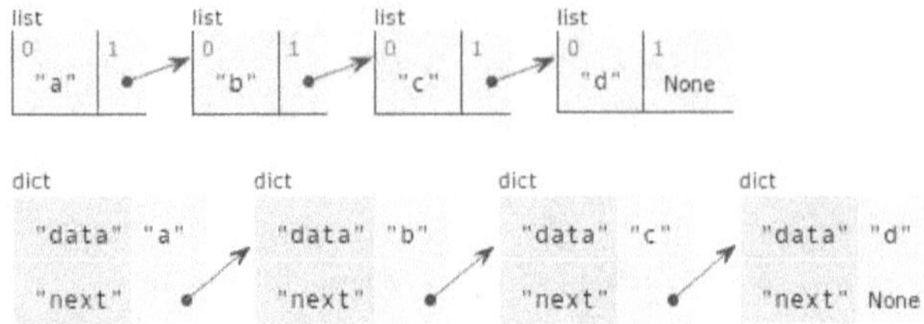

Figure 5: Visualizations of singly-linked lists constructed using Python lists (top) and dicts (bottom).

The frontend uses two main JavaScript libraries: D3 [3] to map execution trace objects to corresponding HTML elements and jsPlumb [13] to draw pointers as arrows.

Embedding: The entire visualizer GUI is encapsulated in a JavaScript `ExecutionVisualizer` class, so embedding it within a webpage takes only one line of code. For example:

```
var v = new ExecutionVisualizer(parentNode, trace);
```

`parentNode` is the HTML DOM element where the visualizer instance should be embedded. The execution `trace` can either be precomputed offline or generated by the web application backend. Multiple visualizer instances with different traces can be simultaneously embedded within one webpage.

5. USE CASES

We conservatively estimate that over 200,000 people have used Online Python Tutor in the past three years since its inception. There are three main categories of use cases:

- Instructors using it as a classroom teaching aid,
- digital textbooks with embedded Python visualizations, which collectively have been deployed in at least 25 universities and have around 16,000 viewers per month,
- students using it either while taking free online CS courses or during self-study for, say, programming interviews (`pythontutor.com` gets around 30,000 visitors per month, estimated by unique IP address hits).

Instructor use cases: Professors, lecturers, and teaching assistants in a dozen universities have used Online Python Tutor in their teaching. Class sizes ranged from 7 students in a summer Python course for non-CS majors at the University of Washington to over 900 students in the Fall 2012 offering of CS1 at UC Berkeley.

Several instructors told us via email that Online Python Tutor helped clarify concepts such as tracing parameters and return values through function calls, control flow, exceptions, scope, recursion, local variable lifetimes, and understanding aliasing when there are multiple identifiers referencing the same object. A professor at UC Davis wrote,

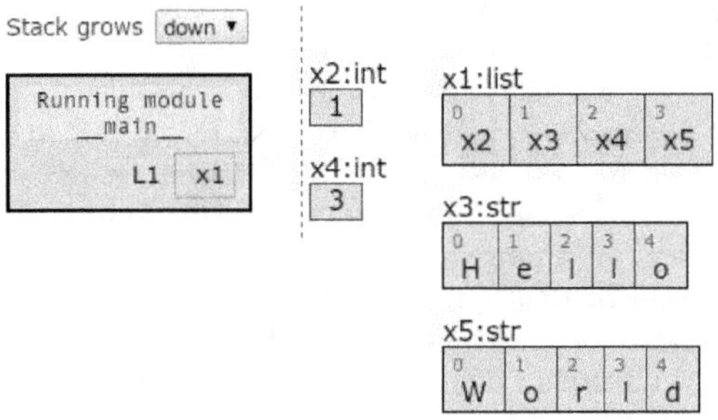

Figure 6: The University of Toronto's customized version of Online Python Tutor, which represents references as labels and strings as character arrays.

"I have students who are currently retaking the class in the summer session, since they dropped out in spring, when they were struggling. I can see from their reaction in class that this tool has literally been an eye-opener for them – it's making a huge difference!"[3] Another wrote, "The diagrams [Online Python Tutor] show[s] are just like the diagrams I'm constantly drawing on the whiteboard. So it matches the model that I try to get the students to see exactly."[3]

Although most instructors simply visited `pythontutor.com` during lectures and lab sessions to step through code examples, several went further:

- A CS1 teaching assistant at MIT augmented Online Python Tutor with beginner-friendly error messages, which his students found more helpful than Python's default error messages [8]. His error message templates were inspired by common mistakes that students in his class made.
- A team from the University of Toronto used Online Python Tutor as the basis for a CS *peer instruction* system, inspired by those used in science classes [12].
- Another team at the University of Toronto spent the summer of 2012 customizing Online Python Tutor to suit their own pedagogical preferences (see Figure 6). They deployed this customized version in their Fall 2012 CS1 offering, which is being concurrently taught at their university and online through the Coursera platform (with ~34,000 enrolled students) [4].

Digital textbook use cases: In preparation for teaching the CS1 course at UC Berkeley, John DeNero ported the classic *Structure and Interpretation of Computer Programs* textbook from Scheme to Python and put it online in HTML format [6]. He embedded Online Python Tutor visualizations directly into the HTML so that students can read the lessons and interact with code examples on the same webpage (see Figure 7), as opposed to simply viewing static, manually-drawn diagrams of code examples.

Miller and Ranum embedded Online Python Tutor into their digital textbook, *How to Think Like a Computer Scientist: Interactive Edition* [10], as a component called CodeLens. This web-based e-textbook attracts around 6,000 viewers per month and has been adopted by 25 universities around the world. Alvarado et al. logged student interactions with this resource in a 61-person CS1 course and found that

[3]via personal email communication, August 2012

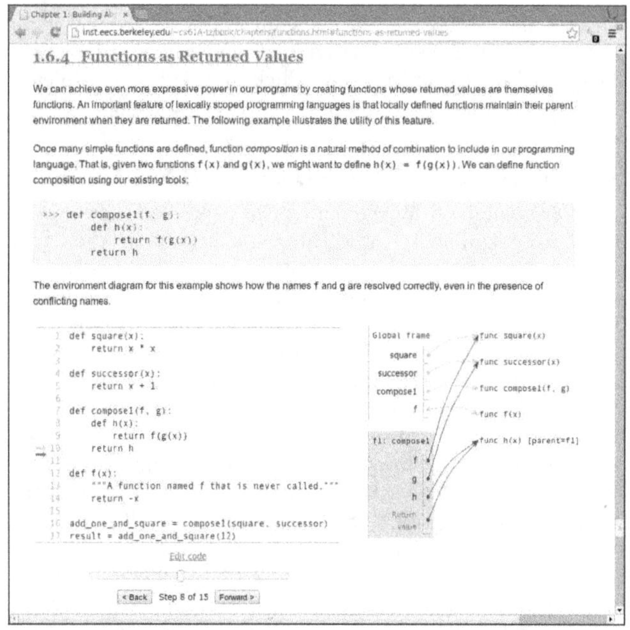

Figure 7: Online Python Tutor visualization of a code example embedded within DeNero's digital textbook (used for UC Berkeley's CS1 course) [6].

students who interacted more with CodeLens visualizations outside of class hours scored higher on midterm exams [2].

Lastly, the Computer Science Circles project [14], a free online introductory programming course and textbook serving 10,000 visitors per month, has integrated Online Python Tutor as its main visualization and debugging tool. According to its creators, an average of 600 code snippets per day are visualized by their embedded Online Python Tutor[3].

Digital textbook authors often ran our Python backend offline to generate traces for individual code examples, which they then embedded directly as JSON objects in JavaScript code. Thus, the textbooks can work offline without needing to make server calls, which Miller found useful for deploying in regions with slow and unreliable Internet connections[3].

Student use cases: Over 30,000 unique IP addresses visit `pythontutor.com` each month, but to our knowledge, instructors in only a dozen universities are using it in their courses. Thus, we suspect that the majority of users are self-directed learners using it without instructor supervision.

Although we do not have detailed demographic information on users, we know at least one major source of users: students taking free online CS courses offered by Udacity [1], such as CS101: *Introduction to Computer Science* (186,000 total students over two offerings) and CS212: *Design of Computer Programs* (almost 40,000 students).

Online Python Tutor was not an official component of these courses, but some students found the tool and shared their use cases in discussion forums. One student posted, "This tool is particularly helpful when debugging recursive functions. I used it for the recursive unit at cs101 and it was a lifesaver." Other students wrote that it was "exactly what I need to solve knotty python questions without cheating" and "exactly what I need to untangle lists and arrays." [1]

Udacity's CS101 students, many of whom are computer novices, liked the web-based nature of Online Python Tutor because they did not need to install or configure software. They also posted custom URLs to accompany questions that they asked in the forums like, "Click on this link and please explain why this program does X at execution point Y."

6. LIMITATIONS AND ONGOING WORK

We are delighted by the number of people who have benefited from Online Python Tutor so far, but at the same time, we acknowledge that numbers and anecdotes are no substitutes for a rigorous evaluation of efficacy. We would like to run some formal studies with academic partners to understand students' attitudes toward and usage of Online Python Tutor, how it correlates with their performance in tracing, explaining, and writing programs, and impacts on their attitudes toward programming in general.

Study results might determine whether we should add new features to encourage active engagement with program visualizations, which prior work has shown to be effective [15], rather than passive viewing. This effort could involve embedding question prompts, mini-quizzes, textual annotations, and discussion threads directly within visualization elements.

Another Online Python Tutor limitation is that it steps through execution one line at a time like a debugger and does not show the details of expression and subexpression evaluation. In contrast, UUhistle [16] visualizes expression evaluation for a subset of Python constructs. Some users have requested such finer-grained stepping functionality.

A limitation we might not immediately address is scalability: Online Python Tutor can visualize only several hundred execution steps of programs with relatively small data structures. It is not meant to be used for debugging production-sized software systems. However, we may investigate how to cache and visually summarize large data structures to scale up to larger pedagogical code examples.

Currently the visualization works well for linked lists, but not for more sophisticated data types. Thus, we are planning to add custom visualizations for trees, graphs, numerical matrices, and other data structures so that Online Python Tutor can be useful in more advanced CS courses.

Another area of ongoing work is determining whether to add animations and smooth transitions between visualization states. The D3 library [3] we already use makes it easy to add animations, but the main design challenge will be determining which animations are pedagogically effective without becoming distractions.

Finally, since the Online Python Tutor frontend can technically visualize programs written in any mainstream language, we are now working with students to write backends for Ruby, JavaScript, and Racket (a Scheme dialect). Also, since the backend generates an execution trace that is not tied to any particular visualization, some users have suggested parsing the trace to render an audio "reading" of execution states to help teach visually-impaired students.

In closing, we have presented Online Python Tutor: a free, open-source, web-based tool following in the long tradition of program visualizations for CS education. Although the high-level ideas embodied by Online Python Tutor are decades-old, our main contribution is adapting and redesigning this sort of tool for a modern web-based environment, where it has been able to reach over 200,000 users thus far.

Acknowledgments: Thanks to Peter Norvig, Andrew Petersen, and David Pritchard for reading drafts of this paper.

7. REFERENCES

[1] Udacity - 21st Century University. `http://www.udacity.com/`.

[2] C. Alvarado, B. Morrison, B. Ericson, M. Guzdial, B. Miller, and D. A. Ranum. Performance and use evaluation of an electronic book for introductory Python programming. Technical Report GT-IC-12-02, Georgia Institute of Technology, 2012.

[3] M. Bostock, V. Ogievetsky, and J. Heer. D3: Data-Driven Documents. *IEEE Trans. Visualization & Comp. Graphics (Proc. InfoVis)*, 2011.

[4] J. Campbell and P. Gries. Learning to Program: The Fundamentals. `https://www.coursera.org/course/programming1`.

[5] D. Crockford. JSON (JavaScript Object Notation). `http://json.org/`.

[6] J. DeNero. CS61A: Structure and Interpretation of Computer Programs. `http://www-inst.eecs.berkeley.edu/~cs61a/`.

[7] R. J. Enbody, W. F. Punch, and M. McCullen. Python CS1 as preparation for C++ CS2. In *Proceedings of the 40th ACM technical symposium on Computer Science Education*, SIGCSE '09, pages 116–120, New York, NY, USA, 2009. ACM.

[8] A. J. Hartz. CAT-SOOP: A tool for automatic collection and assessment of homework exercises. Master's thesis, MIT Department of Electrical Engineering and Computer Science, Cambridge, MA, June 2012.

[9] J. Helminen and L. Malmi. Jype - a program visualization and programming exercise tool for Python. In *Proceedings of the 5th International Symposium on Software Visualization*, SOFTVIS '10, pages 153–162, New York, NY, USA, 2010. ACM.

[10] B. Miller and D. Ranum. Beyond PDF and ePub: toward an interactive textbook. In *Proceedings of the 17th ACM annual conference on Innovation and technology in computer science education*, ITiCSE '12, pages 150–155, New York, NY, USA, 2012. ACM.

[11] M. C. Orsega, B. T. Vander Zanden, and C. H. Skinner. Experiments with algorithm visualization tool development. In *Proceedings of the 43rd ACM technical symposium on Computer Science Education*, SIGCSE '12, pages 559–564, 2012.

[12] A. Petersen, D. Zingaro, Y. Cherenkova, and O. Karpova. Facilitating Code-Writing in PI Classes. In *Proceedings of the ACM technical symposium on Computer Science Education*, SIGCSE '13, 2013.

[13] S. Porritt. The jsPlumb JavaScript library. `http://www.jsplumb.org/`.

[14] D. Pritchard and T. Vasiga. CS Circles: An In-Browser Python Course for Beginners. In *Proceedings of the ACM technical symposium on Computer Science Education*, SIGCSE '13, 2013.

[15] J. Sorva. *Visual Program Simulation in Introductory Programming Education*. Ph.D. dissertation, Aalto University, 2012.

[16] J. Sorva and T. Sirkiä. UUhistle: a software tool for visual program simulation. In *Proceedings of the 10th Koli Calling International Conference on Computing Education Research*, Koli Calling '10, pages 49–54, New York, NY, USA, 2010. ACM.

Facilitating Code-Writing in PI Classes

Daniel Zingaro
Ontario Institute for Studies in Education
University of Toronto
daniel.zingaro@utoronto.ca

Yuliya Cherenkova, Olessia Karpova,
and Andrew Petersen
University of Toronto Mississauga
{yuliya.cherenkova, olessia.karpova,
andrew.petersen}@utoronto.ca

ABSTRACT

We present the Python Classroom Response System, a web-based tool that enables instructors to use code-writing and multiple choice questions in a classroom setting. The system is designed to extend the principles of peer instruction, an active learning technique built around discussion of multiple-choice questions, into the domain of introductory programming education. Code submissions are evaluated by a suite of tests designed to highlight common misconceptions, so the instructor receives real-time feedback as students submit code. The system also allows an instructor to pull specific submissions into an editor and visualizer for use as in-class examples. We motivate the use of this system, describe its support for and extension of peer instruction, and offer use cases and scenarios for classroom implementation.

Categories and Subject Descriptors

K.3.2 [**Computer Science Education**]: Computer and Information Science Education

Keywords

CS1, pair programming, peer investigation, active learning

1. INTRODUCTION

Peer Instruction (PI) is a pedagogical technique developed by the physics education community that has recently been applied to the teaching of computing courses. Physics educators realized that standard lectures are ineffective for teaching core concepts and addressing misconceptions [2], so PI was developed to introduce active, peer-based interaction to the classroom and to focus student attention on key misconceptions. Multiple research projects described in physics education journals demonstrate that PI-students outperform lecture-students on various grade-based and affective measures. For example, PI advantages have been demonstrated on final exams and standard concept inventories [2]. PI also tends to reduce student attrition and improve problem-solving ability [9].

Recent research in computing education suggests that PI may also be valuable as a pedagogical approach to teaching computing. Its focus on conceptual knowledge is appealing to computing educators who seek to confront misconceptions and help students understand core CS material [15]. However, PI focuses on in-class discussions of multiple-choice questions, and such a focus suggests a mismatch between PI and the skill-based practice required of CS1 students. Many of the skills typically expected of CS1 students relate to code-investigation and code-writing [5], and code-writing is disproportionately used to gauge student skill on final exams [12].

In this paper, we introduce a new tool, the Python Classroom Response System (PCRS), that can be used by computing teachers in classroom settings to administer both PI (multiple choice) and code-writing questions. Our goal is to enable PI educators to additionally ask code-writing questions and hence further adapt PI to our disciplinary context.

2. BACKGROUND

A PI course can be described by the pre-class, in-class, and post-class features that differentiate it from a lecture offering. Prior to each lecture, students are expected to read a section of the textbook and complete an associated reading quiz. We then replace the lecture with several iterations of the following four-step loop body:

Presage. Each PI iteration begins with a mini-lecture: a couple of slides that act as a refresher for what students read before class. The mini-lecture lasts at most a few minutes.

Engage. We next pose a ConcepTest [2] — a multiple choice question designed both to focus attention on and raise awareness of the key course concept from the mini-lecture [1]. After individually thinking about and voting on the correct answer (the solo vote), students discuss the question in small groups, reach a consensus, and vote again (the group vote). Students are encouraged to discuss each answer, verbalizing why it is correct or incorrect [15].

Gauge. While student voting data can be estimated using flashcards [8], the effectiveness of the "gauge" step is substantially enhanced by using electronic response systems. Clickers are a popular choice, as they provide immediate, accurate vote counts to the instructor and

SIGCSE'13, March 6–9, 2013, Denver, Colorado, USA.

compelling graphical displays for the students. Ideally, each response option for a ConcepTest will correspond to a common student misconception, so that the instructor can identify the range of understandings present among the students [4]. Seeing the histogram of results, students come to realize that they are not alone in their confusion [7], which may make them more comfortable voicing their concerns in subsequent, class-wide discussion.

Age. Having engaged students in collaborative debate and gauged their progress and understanding, the instructor leads a class discussion meant to solidify a mature conception of the lessons learned. The results of this discussion can be used by the instructor to adapt the lecture in real-time, filling gaps in student knowledge before progressing to the next topic and ConcepTest.

Using PI in combination with clickers provides an important pedagogical benefit to instructors in terms of response data. Following the lecture, the teacher can use this data to shape upcoming class meetings, as analyzing the responses to PI questions may expose points of confusion or difficulty that would benefit from extra class time.

Simon et al.'s paper at SIGCSE 2010 [15] began the investigation into the applicability and effectiveness of PI in CS. This original paper was primarily interested in the following question: do more students answer correctly after a group discussion compared to before the group discussion? To quantify such gains, the authors computed normalized gain (NG) on each question. NG captures the proportion of students who answer incorrectly in the solo vote but correctly in the group vote. For example, if 60% of students answer correctly in the solo vote and 80% answer correctly in the group vote, the NG for the question is 50% (i.e. 50% of "potential learners" demonstrated new understanding). The authors found an NG of 41% in a CS1 course and 35% in a CS1.5 course. Similarly, [17] used PI in a remedial CS1 course and found an NG of 29%.

End-of-course surveys consistently find that students and instructors value PI. A survey reported in [17] found, for example, that 100% of students believed that individually thinking about and responding to a PI question helped them learn the course material. In addition, 100% agreed that group discussion was helpful, and 94% strongly agreed that PI should be used in other courses. Other surveys corroborate these findings [11, 15]. A unique reflection of four instructors' use of PI [13] suggests other observed benefits, including a focus on teamwork and communication; flexible, demand-driven lectures; and opportunities for improving proof-reasoning abilities.

What kinds of questions can be asked using PI? Some of the papers cited above [15, 17] contain examples of questions where students must read and understand code. It is also possible to approach code-writing through the use of Parsons puzzles [17] that involve the rearrangement of existing code. In an analysis of a semester's worth of PI questions [3], three levels of abstraction were prominent: English, CS-speak, and code. Most prominently, questions often transitioned from one category to another; for example, a student might be asked for the code-equivalent of an English statement. Other questions were restricted to only one level of abstraction. Within coding, for example, many questions asked students to trace code to determine the code's output or purpose. However, despite this focus on code, multiple-choice questions inherently cannot require students to generate new code from scratch.

We acknowledge PI's utility in targeting various sought-after skills, such as code-reading, explaining code in English, and translating between levels of abstraction. However, we seek to extend the reach of PI into the domain of code-writing. We believe that having students write code, even small portions of code, is crucially important for success in CS1. Literature shows that code-writing is not equivalent to other code-related tasks such as code-reading or explaining code in plain English. Code-writing is argued to be at the top of a hierarchy with other code-related tasks below [16]. Furthermore, Zingaro et al. examined integrative code-writing questions and a corresponding set of "concept" questions on a final exam. Concept questions are small code-writing questions developed to target single concepts rather than multiple concepts, as is typical of code-writing questions. They found that concept questions were highly predictive of performance on the exam as a whole, suggesting that the ability to write small pieces of code from scratch is a valued outcome in CS1 [18]. This further suggests that code-based ConcepTests, which also focus on a small number of expected misconceptions, may also be effective performance evaluators. Validating this claim is the subject of ongoing work.

3. USE CASES

The design of the Python Classroom Response System (PCRS) emerges directly from our experience with PI pedagogy. Our goal was to extend PI to deal with discipline-specific needs while remaining faithful to the PI philosophy and 4-step cycle. As such, it was important not to lose the PI-support functionality that was previously available through the use of clickers. Therefore, assuming the availability of a wireless network and student handheld devices (e.g., laptop, phone, or tablet), the PCRS's multiple choice question support replaces the functionality of clicker software. Of course, clickers are low-cost devices much more affordable than the devices supported by the PCRS, but we anticipate that many students will already own a phone or other mobile device that will suffice.

Beyond traditional PI support, the PCRS can be used to support lecture-based code reading and code writing exercises. For example, we can use the PCRS to support code-writing exercises. In the past, we would insert programming exercises into lecture by asking students to discuss design issues in small groups and then to write pseudocode on paper. Later, we would implement one possible solution to a problem. However, during these exercises, students lacked many typical debugging resources, and in large classes, the instructor lacked feedback, as it is not feasible to review many students' code. Therefore, we were often unaware of the number of students answering correctly or exactly where students became stuck. The PCRS makes these exercises more effective by providing students and instructors with the support they require: students work interactively with a dynamic visualization tool that supports debugging and program understanding [14, 10], and instructors receive real-time feedback on their students progress.

The PCRS can also support a range of other code-writing exercises. For example, it supports partial-code exercises where students are provided with starter code that they must read and then extend. In this case, the debugging tools aid the students in the code understanding task. In terms of debugging, the PCRS can also support defect triage exercises that are otherwise difficult to conduct in lecture. In this activity, we present students with incorrect or incomplete code that may pass some (but not all) test cases. We then ask students to determine why the specific tests fail and to correct the code using test-driven debugging techniques.

4. TOOL DESCRIPTION

The PCRS is a freely available, open-source system designed to support PI-style multiple choice questions as well as submission and analysis of live coding exercises in a classroom system (*link omitted*). It consists of administrator and student modules backed by a shared database. The administrator module contains functionality for creating questions and analyzing submissions in real-time or outside of class. The student module allows students to view questions, submit answers written in Python, and debug submissions to programming problems. The student module is built around the Online Python Tutor (OPT) developed by Philip Guo [6]. As shown in Figure 3, the OPT supports tracing and debugging activities by providing a visualization of the Python memory model and allowing students to step both forward and backward through the code.

The PCRS is entirely web-based, so it can be accessed through a browser on a laptop or tablet. Submitted code is executed on a server which returns an execution log to be visualized on the client machine. For security reasons, the code that can be executed and visualized is restricted: several built-in Python functions are disabled, and external modules cannot be imported. With the exception of file operations, which cannot be executed, the subset of Python that is supported is sufficient for exercises in a CS1 or CS2 course.

"L1 = [1, 2, 3]
L2 = L1
L2.append(4)
L2 = [0, 1, 2, 3]

After the preceding code has executed, what is the value associated with the variable L1?"

A. [0, 1, 2, 3]
B. [1, 2, 3]
C. [0, 1, 2, 3, 4]
D. [1, 2, 3, 4]

Figure 1: An example ConcepTest-style multiple choice question.

4.1 Multiple Choice Questions

To directly support PI, the PCRS allows instructors to define ConcepTest-style multiple choice questions like the one in Figure 1. Before class, the instructor enters the question and defines the possible answers. During class, the instructor logs into the administrator module of the PCRS and "enables" the problem when she wants students to respond to the question. At that point, it becomes visible to students who are logged into the PRS website, and they can submit responses. The instructor can display a response histogram

"Given a number n and a Python list L, return the index (position) of the first occurrence of n in the list or -1 if n is not in the list."
1. n = 0, L = []
2. n = 0, L = [1, 2, 3]
3. n = 0, L = [1, 2, 0, 3]
4. n = 0, L = [1, 2, 3, 0]
5. n = 0, L = [1, 2, 0, 0, 3]

Figure 2: An example coding problem with the test cases defined by the instructor.

in real-time and can "disable" the problem to stop submissions. The histogram displayed is very similar to the one displayed for programming questions illustrated by Figure 4.

In most cases, PI questions are carefully crafted to uncover specific issues that the instructor anticipates will be misunderstood by students. For example, the question in Figure 1 evaluates whether students understand how assignment of mutable objects works in Python. Option (A) aligns with a common misunderstanding related to assigning variables (rather than the referenced object) and option (B) uncovers a misunderstanding about aliasing.

However, PI instructors often feel the need to quickly poll the students on unanticipated topics or questions raised during the flow of the class. The PCRS also provides instructors with the opportunity to ask a "snap question". From the administrator interface, a single click creates a new, enabled multiple choice question with 5 possible responses. The instructor has the choice of filling in text for the question or any of the responses, but none are required.

4.2 Programming Problems

The PCRS also allows programming instructors to ask PI-inspired programming questions. Like PCRS support for multiple choice questions, the instructor will usually define the problem before class and use real-time analysis functionality to identify misconceptions that are present. To create a coding question, the instructor must formulate the problem and, as in PI, specify a set of expected misconceptions. However, instead of encoding the misconceptions as multiple choice answers, the instructor implements them as a set of test cases. Each student submission is run through the test suite, and as illustrated in Figure 3, the instructor can identify the specific test cases that are proving troublesome for the class. Since each test case represents a typical misconception, the instructor can immediately identify the concepts on which to focus for the next part of the lecture.

Consider the code problem and corresponding test cases in Figure 2. In our experience, students often have difficulty solving it using a conditional ("while") loop. When we build the problem, we consider what problems students might encounter, and we build a test case for each one. We anticipate that students will attempt to access elements before checking the list's length (test case 1), continue iteration beyond the end of the list (case 2), terminate one comparison too early (case 4), or return the later index in cases with duplicate entries (case 5).

Before class, we quickly review the problem: test cases 1, 2, and 4 are related to understanding of list indices, and cases 3 and 5 check for correctness related to the problem

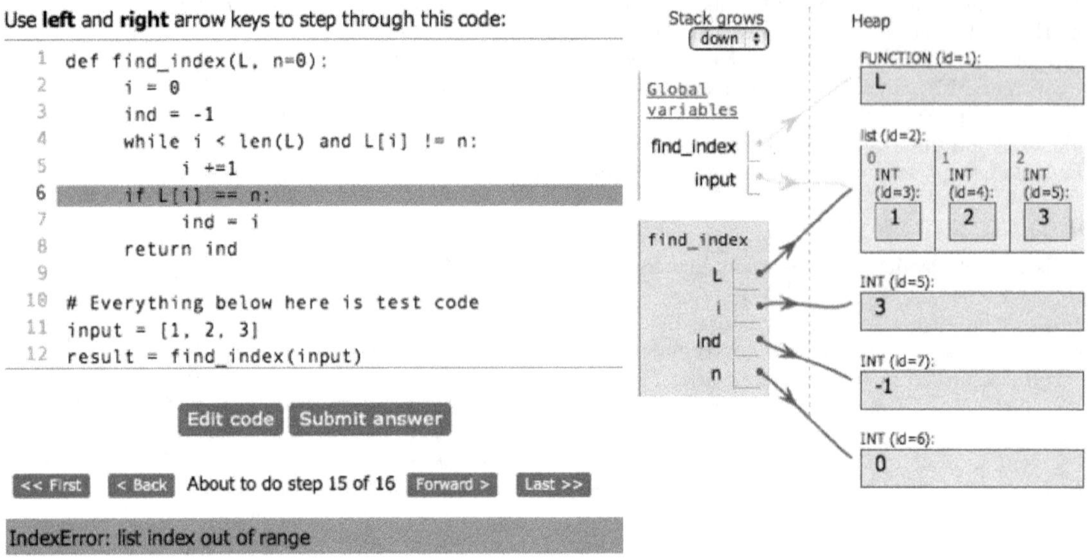

Figure 3: Encountering an error in Python code that iterates over a list.

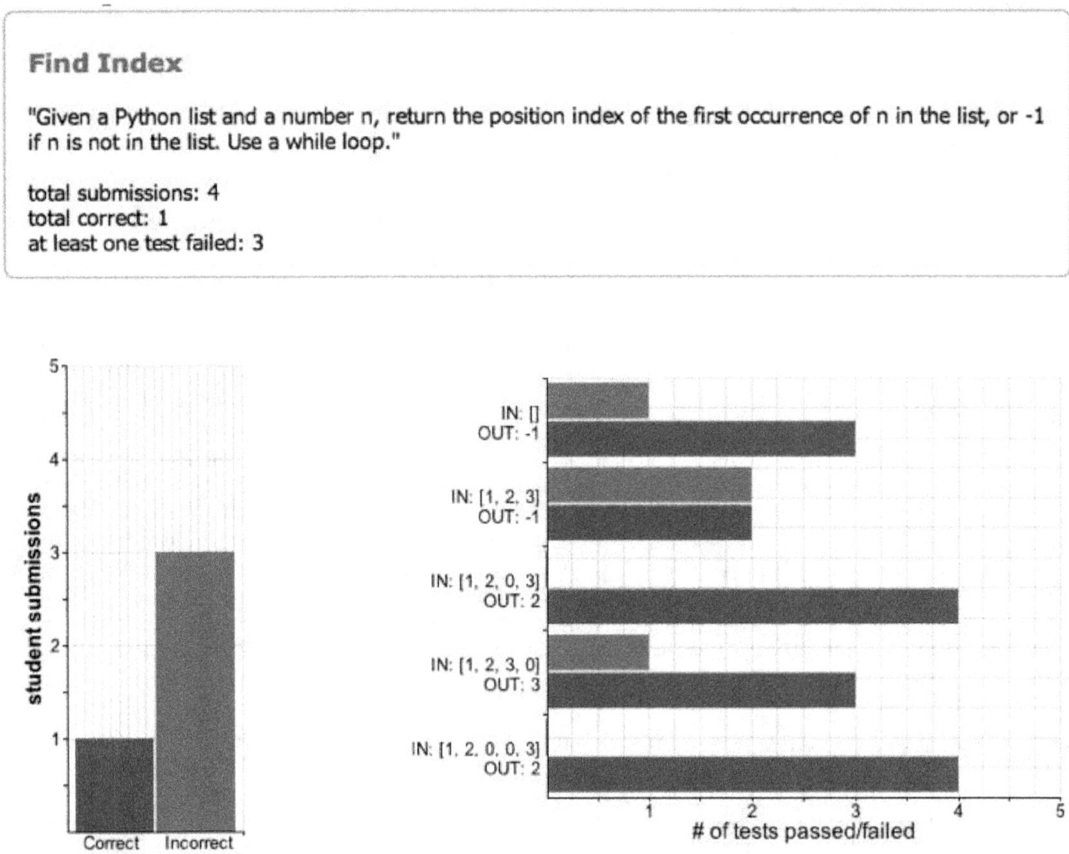

Figure 4: The instructor's view: monitoring submissions to a programming exercise. The graph on the left illustrates the number of submissions that passed all tests, while the graph on the right identifies the success and failure rate on particular tests.

specification. Then, after the problem is introduced, we can use real-time histograms produced by the PCRS to quickly identify the issues that are causing the students the most trouble. In response, we can issue verbal hints or pause the class and use a student submission to demonstrate why a particular test case is failing.

In the meantime, students are receiving feedback on their submissions directly from the system. Each submission is evaluated against the test cases, and the students are told which test cases pass (and fail). If they wish, they can use the visualizer to trace through a failing (or passing) test case, as demonstrated in Figure 3. In that example, the bottom two lines of code (11 and 12) tell the student exactly what test case was run; the top 8 lines are the student's submission. If the instructor desires, she can turn off this feedback feature. In that case, the students are told the number of test cases that fail but are not provided information about the contents of the test case. This might be desirable if an instructor uses the PCRS for marked work.

4.3 Analyzing Submissions

The PCRS provides several real-time and offline tools for analyzing student submissions. The real-time tools keep submissions anonymous, to protect student privacy, but the offline tools generally allow the instructor to identify the student in order to enable marking or credit for participation.

In real-time, the instructor can display a histogram of submissions. By default, each student's most recent submission is counted in the histogram, but all submissions are stored. To follow-up on a misconception, the instructor has access to a rich set of tools. The PCRS allows the instructor to browse submissions that pass (or fail) specific test cases and to display, modify, and trace through selected submissions in the same visualizer environment that the students use. This allows the instructor to find relevant examples submitted by students in the class and to use them in demonstrations. The PCRS also allows the instructor to filter submissions using a regular expression; this allows the instructor to identify submissions that use a specific syntactic structure.

Offline, the instructor can view student-specific information. On request, the PCRS can generate a comma-separated-value file that provides data for each student in the system. The instructor may specify which problems are included in the report; for the problems that are included, the correct (and incorrect) submission counts and pass/fail information for each test is provided.

The students are also provided facilities for analyzing their submissions. Each submission is stored in the database, and students can browse their history and send specific submissions to the visualizer for further investigation. Each submission is annotated with information on the tests that were passed and failed.

5. DISCUSSION

We believe that the PCRS is an effective means of implementing active, PI-inspired activities in a programming classroom. The tool is designed to give the students the opportunity to practice key code writing skills — problem solving, code production, and debugging — in class. At the same time, the instructor is obtaining rapid and rich feedback from the students and has the tools necessary to identify and use relevant student submissions in examples.

However, deploying this system requires planning. While most students have phones that can load the PCRS website, mobile phones do not have sufficient screen real estate to make visualization effective, and beyond that, coding on a phone keyboard is not feasible. While phones can easily be used for multiple-choice questions, we recommend that programming activities be performed on devices, like tablets or laptops, with larger screens and better text input functionality. In our own classes, only about 1 of 3 students normally bring a laptop to class, but we believe that when this tool is integrated into a class and students see its benefit, more will bring appropriate devices to lecture. Furthermore, since we prefer to structure the activities using a pair-programming or small-group model to get students involved in discussions, only 1/3 to 1/2 of the students need to be equipped with mobile devices.

Network resources are another issue that requires forethought. The local wireless point can become overwhelmed by connections if everyone in the classroom is using a device, so the network administrators need to be involved in the deployment of the PCRS in a large course.

Work on the PCRS is progressing in three directions. First, the interface and the analysis features of the tool are being improved based on instructor and student feedback. Support is also envisioned for languages other than Python. Second, we are performing a qualitative study investigating how the availability of tools like the PCRS change how students interact with the material, their peers, and their instructor. Third, we are preparing a set of pre-packaged programming exercises and multiple-choice questions to accompany the PCRS, so that new adopters can quickly deploy the tool.

6. CONCLUSION

While PI has been adopted in computing education contexts, such adoptions have tended to ignore the differences between computing and physics. In particular, recognition of the importance of code-writing exercises in CS1 as a key activity, assessment technique, and outcome measure has been lacking. We suggest that an active learning pedagogy used in a programming context should naturally support code-writing in addition to problem-solving, code-reading, and other valued CS1 skills. Our PCRS efforts seek to adapt PI to this unique disciplinary context to increase the breadth of questions and feedback that move between teacher and student during lectures. We make this tool freely available to the community, will continue development, and will report on its use by teachers that have previously used and not used PI.

7. REFERENCES

[1] I. D. Beatty, W. J. Gerace, W. J. Leonard, and R. J. Dufresne. Designing effective questions for classroom response system teaching. *American Journal of Physics*, 74:31–39, 2006.

[2] C. H. Crouch, J. Watkins, A. P. Fagen, and E. Mazur. Peer instruction: Engaging students one-on-one, all at once. In E. F. Redish and P. J. Cooney, editors, *Research-Based Reform of University Physics.* American Association of Physics Teachers, 2007.

[3] Q. Cutts, S. Esper, M. Fecho, S. R. Foster, and B. Simon. The abstraction transition taxonomy: Developing desired learning outcomes through the lens

of situated cognition. In *Proceedings of the Eighth International Workshop on Computing Education Research*, New York, NY, 2012.

[4] Q. Cutts, G. Kennedy, C. Mitchell, and S. Draper. Maximising dialogue in lectures using group response systems. 7th IASTED International Conference on Computers and Advanced Technology in Education. `www.dcs.gla.ac.uk/~quintin/papers/cate2004.pdf` (accessed August 19, 2011), 2004.

[5] U. Fuller, C. G. Johnson, T. Ahoniemi, D. Cukierman, I. Hernán-Losada, J. Jackova, E. Lahtinen, T. L. Lewis, D. M. Thompson, C. Riedesel, and E. Thompson. Developing a computer science-specific learning taxonomy. *SIGCSE Bulletin*, 39(4):152–170, Dec. 2007.

[6] P. J. Guo. Online Python Tutor: Embeddable web-based program visualization for CS education. In *Proceedings of the 44th SIGCSE Technical Symposium on Computer Science Education*, 2013.

[7] J. K. Knight and W. B. Wood. Teaching more by lecturing less. *Cell Biology Education*, 4:298–310, 2005.

[8] N. Lasry. Clickers or flashcards: Is there really a difference? *The Physics Teacher*, 46:242–244, 2008.

[9] N. Lasry, E. Mazur, and J. Watkins. Peer instruction: From harvard to the two-year college. *American Journal of Physics*, 76:1066–1069, 2008.

[10] T. L. Naps, G. Rössling, V. Almstrum, W. Dann, R. Fleischer, C. Hundhausen, A. Korhonen, L. Malmi, M. McNally, S. Rodger, and J. A. Velázquez-Iturbide. Exploring the role of visualization and engagement in computer science education. *SIGCSE Bulletin*, 35(2):131–152, June 2002.

[11] R. P. Pargas and D. M. Shah. Things are clicking in computer science courses. In *Proceedings of the 37th SIGCSE Technical Symposium on Computer Science Education*, pages 474–478, New York, NY, 2006.

[12] A. Petersen, M. Craig, and D. Zingaro. Reviewing CS1 exam question content. In *Proceedings of the 42nd ACM Technical Symposium on Computer Science Education*, pages 631–636, New York, NY, 2011.

[13] L. Porter, C. Bailey Lee, B. Simon, Q. Cutts, and D. Zingaro. Experience report: a multi-classroom report on the value of peer instruction. In *Proceedings of the 16th Annual Joint Conference on Innovation and Technology in Computer Science Education*, pages 138–142, New York, NY, 2011.

[14] N. Ragonis and M. Ben-Ari. On understanding the statics and dynamics of object-oriented programs. In *Proceedings of the 36th SIGCSE Technical Symposium on Computer Science Education*, pages 226–230, New York, NY, 2005.

[15] B. Simon, M. Kohanfars, J. Lee, K. Tamayo, and Q. Cutts. Experience report: Peer instruction in introductory computing. In *Proceedings of the 41st SIGCSE Technical Symposium on Computer Science Education*, pages 341–345, New York, NY, 2010.

[16] J. L. Whalley, R. Lister, E. Thompson, T. Clear, P. Robbins, P. K. A. Kumar, and C. Prasad. An australasian study of reading and comprehension skills in novice programmers, using the bloom and solo taxonomies. In *Proceedings of the 8th Australasian Conference on Computing Education*, pages 243–252, Darlinghurst, Australia, 2006.

[17] D. Zingaro. Experience report: Peer instruction in remedial computer science. In *Proceedings of the 22nd World Conference on Educational Multimedia, Hypermedia & Telecommunications*, pages 5030–5035. AACE, 2010.

[18] D. Zingaro, A. Petersen, and M. Craig. Stepping up to integrative questions on CS1 exams. In *Proceedings of the 43rd ACM Technical Symposium on Computer Science Education*, pages 253–258, New York, NY, 2012.

CS Circles: An In-Browser Python Course for Beginners

David Pritchard
Department of Computer Science*
Princeton University
Princeton, NJ, USA
dp6@cs.princeton.edu

Troy Vasiga
David R. Cheriton School of Computer Science;
Centre for Education in Mathematics and Computing*
University of Waterloo
Waterloo, ON, Canada
tmjvasiga@cs.uwaterloo.ca

ABSTRACT

Computer Science Circles is a free programming website for beginners that is designed to be fun, easy to use, and accessible to the broadest possible audience. We teach Python since it is simple yet powerful, and the course content is well-structured but written in plain language. The website has over one hundred exercises in thirty lesson pages, plus special features to help teachers support their students. It is available in both English and French. We discuss the philosophy behind the course and its design, we describe how it was implemented, and we give statistics on its use.

Categories and Subject Descriptors

K.3.1 [**Computers and Education**]: Computer Uses in Education; K.3.2 [**Computers and Education**]: Computer and Information Science Education

General Terms

Design, Human Factors, Languages

Keywords

Python, Teacher Tools, MOOCs, CS0/1, WordPress

1. INTRODUCTION

The last decade has seen an explosion of web-based software that runs "in the cloud," jointly with a tremendous improvement in the ability of web browsers to interact with users and servers. Near the end of 2009, we and our colleagues decided to create an interactive introductory programming course using these technologies. The main motivation was that many wonderful online programming judges existed for veteran programmers[1], but at the same time beginners had little to work with. It is unreasonable to expect all novices to download a compiler, or to re-load a webpage and re-upload a file just to debug their very first program. Computer Science Circles (CS Circles) is our way of filling this gap. It is publicly available at

`http://cscircles.cemc.uwaterloo.ca`

Since opening in the fall of 2011, over 150,000 exercises have been completed on the site, by nearly 7000 registered users. On an average day, the website handles 900 visits and 7000 code submissions. Approximately half of the traffic is from users that are not logged in.[2]

We eschew the traditional separation into lessons and sets of exercises. Our position is that such a framework puts students at risk of losing interest mid-lesson, and also splits their attention between exercise comprehension, lesson review, and problem solving when they finally start working hands-on. We think it is pedagogically superior for the exercises to be embedded throughout the lessons: this reduces monotony and keeps the student on a focused progression. Removing page reloads and handling the student/auto-grader communication with asynchronous JavaScript (Ajax) helps keep the experience smooth.

Programming is the ideal topic for computer-based learning: beginners can get immediate detailed feedback on the entirety of their creations from the compiler and auto-grader. But, automatic grading is not a replacement for a real teacher looking over the student's shoulder. To compensate for these issues we have added a human touch by letting students easily send a "Help" message when they are stuck. Any message sent in this way will also automatically include the code currently in the student's code editor for that problem. We and our colleagues have answered over 1000 such student questions. Additionally, teachers wishing to use CS Circles can easily become the "guru" of their students, redirecting all questions to the teacher instead. Teachers also can easily track the progress of their students, which mitigates that CS Circles does not check for plagiarism or style.

The rest of the paper is organized as follows. Section 1.1 discusses related work. Section 2 provides an overview of the CS Circles experience and the philosophy behind it. Section 3 discusses the features of the site, grouped according to the three types of people interacting with the site: students, lesson authors, and teachers. Section 4 describes details of the site's implementation. Finally, Section 5 has some suggestions for future work.

*CS Circles is a project of the Centre for Education in Mathematics and Computing, University of Waterloo.

[1]e.g. TopCoder.com, Sphere Online Judge (`spoj.pj`), the ACM judge (`acm.uva.es`), USA Computing Olympiad training (`train.usaco.org`), the PEG judge (`wcipeg.com`), etc.

[2]Summary statistics cover from when CS Circles opened to the time of writing (mid-December 2012). Daily statistics represent averages for the preceding six months.

SIGCSE'13, March 6–9, 2013, Denver, Colorado, USA.

1.1 Related Work

The year 2012 saw a proliferation of MOOCs (massive open online courses) and in particular, the first courses of the companies Coursera (`coursera.org`) and Udacity (`udacity.com`). Two main distinctions between these platforms are that Coursera offers each course on a specific schedule, while Udacity allows open enrollment at any time; and that Coursera deals with the full range of university subjects, while Udacity is focused on the sciences, especially computer science. Udacity has an auto-grader, and so do a few Coursera courses. Two other educational websites focus on interactive online programming enrichment in a more independent way, without university partnerships or certification processes. The first, Codecademy (`www.codecademy.com`), was launched in October 2011. Initially they only offered JavaScript, but they now offer Python and other languages. The second, Khan Academy (`www.khanacademy.org/cs`), has offered online interactive programming lessons in a dialect of JavaScript since August 2012; previously (since 2011) they offered videos on Python.

The programming environments of both Khan Academy and Codecademy are tailored for learning. Codecademy shows exercises on one side of the browser and a coding window on the other site. Student code is retained in the coding window between steps of a multi-part exercise, which gives the student helpful continuity while progressing through the work. The design of the Khan Academy CS user interface is drastically different from traditional coding environments. Immediately after typing or deleting each character in the program editor, it is re-parsed and re-executed dynamically (with injection to ensure that the current state persists as much as possible). See John Resig's talk [16] for details, as well as Bret Victor's recent re-popularization of "responsive programming" [17]. For example, numeric constants in the code can be changed by dragging a slider, which creates the effect of an animation when there is graphic output. The ubiquitous Khan Academy video takes the form of a narrated replay of the lecturer's code window, which can be interrupted at any time and edited. As an additional feature, syntax/run-time errors come with automatically-generated suggestions on how it can be fixed. These are fantastic tools but beyond the scope of our own project.

Both of these sites have strengths and weaknesses in their pedagogy and interface. For example, Codecademy has some "hints" containing mandatory directions, and occasionally does not give a reason why a user failed a test; while Khan Academy's "semicolon monster" occasionally obfuscates an error rather than clarifying it. Nonetheless these sites both represent the state of the art and their UI and curriculum are improving continuously.

In CS Circles we give some of the benefits of both the university-style sites and the more open-ended ones. We have numbered lessons, giving an easy-to-follow linearly structured curriculum, any page of which can be accessed at any time. Since the whole site is entirely focused on Python, every page uses a consistent, well-polished programming interface. One advantage of CS Circles over the others is that it can easily facilitate teachers helping their students when they have specific questions, by using the guru feature. Lesson layout is sequential like the traditional concept of a web "page." Each lesson, together with its embedded exercises, is laid out in a vertical sequence on a scrollable web page. Despite its old-fashionedness, this has advantages over video/audio tracks: it is simpler for authors and translators, it is easier to review, and it helps students follow at their own speed, including students not fluent in English.

Two other online interactive Python courses date back to 2011. The site `pyschools.com` offers 210 exercises arranged in 14 topics, but without overall narrative. The groundbreaking "How to Think Like a Computer Scientist: Interactive Edition" [12] combines an in-browser Python interpreter (implemented in JavaScript) with Creative Commons-licensed material from Downey's "Think Python" book [2]. The user experience with their site is comparable to ours. On the one hand not all of their exercises are auto-gradeable, but on the other hand their auto-grader is able to run without contacting a central server. See also an interactive sequel on algorithms and data structures [13] and a paper on methodology [14] by the same authors.

2. BIRD'S-EYE VIEW

The CS Circles website is "end-to-end" in the sense that everything is handled through the browser interface: submitting code, seeing the grader's reply, editing (with syntax highlighting), visualization with forward/backward stepping, saving and loading solutions, and asking for help. There is a curriculum to serve as a backbone, but we also make judicious use of flexibility: some lessons are optional, helping each user learn at their own choice of depth, and some lesson groups can be completed in any order, making the course less monotonous.

Content. The content begins with a lesson on "Hello, World!", including a working click-to-run sample program and a crashing one. We continue through variables, function calls, comments, quotes, and all of the fundamentals needed in order to write or understand an elementary program. Most lessons have a narrative where a new feature is motivated and explained, with examples, caveats, and exercises for the user. A few special lessons don't discuss language features but rather practical matters like errors, design, and debugging; and several lessons have only exercises based on material from prior lessons, helping to re-consolidate what the user learned previously. The final lessons discuss basic auto-decryption of Caesar ciphers, recursion, object vs. value identity, and efficiency. We forced ourselves not to make the lessons too long; 1000 words was a soft upper limit on what was reasonable to convey in a single sitting. The end goal for the course as a whole is to give the user enough knowledge and confidence to understand further information available online.

The top half of Figure 1 displays the first exercise on the site, which is to write a program that prints out a particular message, in analogy with the `Hello, World!` example. When the user submits their code, it is compiled, executed, and graded server-side. Then, without a page reload, the grading box is updated according to the result of grading. The bottom half of Figure 1 shows the result of a successful submission for this exercise.

Many of the sites we have mentioned use "gamification" features like points and badges (see also `www.checkio.org`). CS Circles has little of this since we believe that it can be intimidating for beginners, especially when not all users have access to the same content and features. The full extent of gamification in CS Circles is that when an exercise is completed, its box turns green and a checkmark appears. The "My Progress" page keeps a hyperlinked visual list of

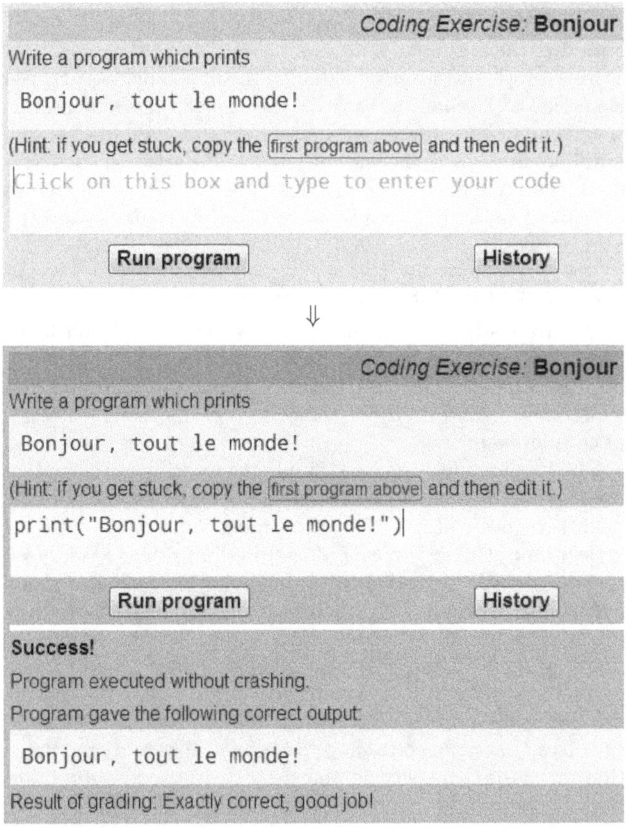

Figure 1: Top: the first exercise in CS Circles. Bottom: when the user submits a correct submission, the grader reply is shown (without a page reload). The box color has changed from blue to green. A checkmark (not shown) also appears in the top right corner.

which exercises are completed, so students can easily pick up where they left off or go back over previously-skipped exercises. We receive a lot of positive user feedback; here are portions of unsolicited quotes from two students about their enjoyment of learning Python and solving the exercises.

Jun 11 2012: *"I'm addicted to how the frustration of getting the function or program wrong at first transitions into excitement as I finally figure it out, and it all makes perfect sense laid out in front of me."*

Aug 14 2012: *"Sites like Codecademy tend to corral you through a safe introduction of 'type this after me' but Computer Science Circles has really helped me apply the things I'm learning in a fun, more thought-intensive way."*

Our position is that games are addictive because they are fun and engaging, and that copying the fun and engagement is more effective than copying more superficial aspects. Likewise, because we assume that anyone completing our exercises is doing so just for the pursuit of learning and/or problem-solving, we don't take any precautions against plagiarism. This means that in an institutional setting, while CS Circles can be used to deliver content, its exercises should not be used as a way of assigning marks.

2.1 Usage Statistics

In Figure 2 we show three different charts describing usage data for CS Circles. The top chart shows the number of users that have completed each of the 105 problems currently on the site, sorted from most completed to least completed. The "outlier" with the least number of completions is the final exercise on the site, which asks the user to look up information from Wikipedia and efficiently compute a list of primes by implementing the Sieve of Eratosthenes.

The middle chart in Figure 2 shows the total number of code fragments submitted by each user. Note that some users have submitted several thousand code fragments.

The bottom chart in Figure 2 shows the typical time elapsed (in octiles) before each problem is completed. The completion time for each problem is approximately normally-distributed over users. Interestingly, for *every* exercise, at least half of all students who ever complete it do so within two weeks.

We have no formal biometric data, but in unsolicited feedback and the help system, a few users have self-identified as a PhD student, a lawyer, a parent and child, a miner working in a remote location, and individuals over age 60. CS Circles can help a school reach out to non-traditional student populations, including "math circles"-style settings [8] where one might assign online exercises between weekly meetings.

3. FEATURES

3.1 Student Tools

While a typical IDE has dozens of buttons, our coding windows start with just 3: submit, help, and history. The remaining features are explicitly introduced and explained one at a time in later sections, so that the student learns the purpose of all the available tools. This technique helps avoid novices from getting overwhelmed.

The "Help" button is for the student to use when they are stuck and want targeted assistance. Clicking on this button opens up a new text field where the student is directed to type a few sentences about what they've tried and where they are stuck. This is sent along with the current contents of the code editor for that problem.

For each user, every coding exercise automatically stores a history of all prior submissions. The history can be accessed on demand, both by the student and their guru. When a user re-visits a page, the most recently submitted version is automatically loaded in the text editor.

In lesson 4, we introduce the two debugging tools for the course. One is simply a "console" that allows the student to run arbitrary code without any grader interference. Every example has a button which allows it to be copied to the console, in a new browser tab, with a single click. The other debugging tool is an open-source Python visualizer [5] that can take an arbitrary program, store the steps of its execution, and replay those steps both forwards and backwards in time along with a visual representation of all the variables and the call stack. This replicates most of the functionality of a client-side debugger but the backwards execution is even more useful than what most IDEs currently offer. Students run the visualizer on 650 pieces of code per day on average.

The ability to specify a test input is introduced in lesson 5, when the command to read from standard input is introduced. In later lessons, when users are tested based on their

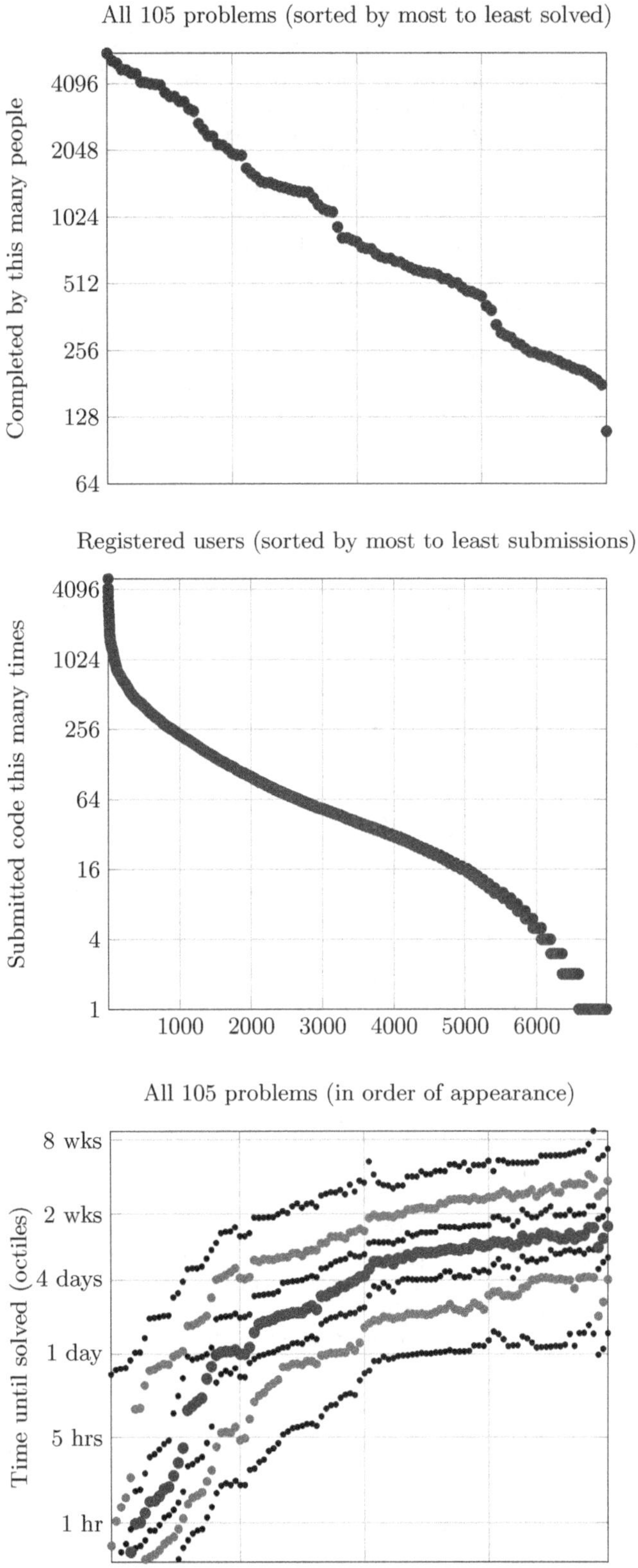

Figure 2: Top: The number of people who have completed each problem. Middle: The number of times each user of the site has submitted code. Bottom: For each problem, conditional on solving it, octiles of time elapsed between registration and completing it.

function definitions, this input box is replaced with a text area for test arguments.

In lesson 7, just after introducing the first block-structured elements of Python, we switch the user to a "rich" editor, specifically the CodeMirror editor [6]. It highlights syntax, numbers lines, matches parentheses, and performs smart indentation. We have customized it to resize automatically up to a fixed limit, but to also be manually sizeable when the user desires.

3.2 Lesson Designer Tools

CS Circles is exercise-centric: since we believe you learn best by active participation, exercises are embedded throughout the lessons. We use traditional exercise formats like short answer and multiple choice as well as many varieties of coding exercises.

The Python auto-grader is similar to existing auto-graders used by olympiads and public problem websites. Aiming for beginners necessitates that the grader offer more grading styles than just the typical stdin/stdout approach. While we teach the `print` function in lesson 0, input reading doesn't occur until lesson 5. For this reason the early exercises specify input through variables that the grader pre-populates with values. In lesson 1, the *swap* exercise — write code to put the value of `x` in `y` and vice-versa — has the grader pre-define variables, and test their values after the user code executes. Later, once we have described how to define functions with `def`, inspecting the values returned by function calls becomes the main testing approach. We believe that each of these three methods (variable-based, stdin/stdout, function-based) has its place in a beginner course.

Our grader uses a number of other techniques in order to maximize the variety and fun of the exercises:

- randomizing test cases, with a model solution to generate answers, to prevent hard-coded solutions;
- pre-defining non-working initial code — additionally, sometimes we limit the (Levenshtein) edit distance to a valid solution;
- pre-defining a function for the student;
- forbidding the student from using some built-in functions;
- requiring that a specific error be produced;
- and plugging in custom graders for problems where more than one answer is correct.

Code Scramble. We present a small fraction of our coding exercises as *code scramble* exercises: a solution is already given in the coding window, but with its lines appearing in the wrong order; users are only permitted to drag-and-drop entire lines of code until they find a correct solution. A nice side effect of writing a problem in this way is that we don't rely on the student to have memorized any past syntax, and they can focus purely on the logical aspect of the problem. See also the studies [10, 3] on "syntax-free programming." The problem type we call "code scramble" has been previously called *Parsons problems* [15]; see Denny et al. [1] for a thoughtful quantitative study of how complex these problems should be for optimal effect. One interesting feature suggested previously that we have not implemented is to have extra lines that must be left out of the solution. Generally, our code scrambles are of medium difficulty, and syntactic considerations alone will partially, but not completely, solve them. See [7] for information on *C-doku*, near-complete programs with specific short answer blanks that the student must fill in, with additional features such as code coverage requirements.

Hints are essential to writing an exercise that can meet the needs of the widest variety of students. As a rule, our problems are always solvable using only the tools that have been previously introduced to the student, even without hints. However, we also want to avoid students getting stuck on a particular problem just because they have overlooked an old idea or they are unable to come up with an innovation on their own. For this reason we offer clickable hints. The most basic version is one whose content appears like a pop-up window when clicked, which can be moved around the page to a convenient place and closed when no longer needed. Occasionally we find that a very conceptually challenging exercise (such as the swap exercise) requires many hints, and in this case we present them in an "accordion" style, where at most one of the hints can be slid open on the page in the midst of the existing content, which avoids overloading the user interface with too many boxes.

Two other features are the result of user feedback: a "cheatsheet" in html and pdf formats, which contains a quick review of all the functions and syntax used by our curriculum; and "previous/next lesson" buttons on the bottom of each page, precluding the need to scroll all the way up to the main navigation menu when a lesson has been completed.

3.3 Teacher Tools

A student can ask any teacher, mentor or friend who has signed up for CS Circles to be their "guru." E.g., in any class using CS Circles the teacher would normally get the students to enter him/her as their guru. Currently, there are 25 gurus that have five or more students registered under them; in total these gurus have almost 400 registered students.

A student with a guru can send their "Help" messages to their guru instead of to the CS Circles staff. When a teacher clicks on the reply link sent in the e-mail that they receive, they are brought to the "mail" webpage. The mail page offers the teacher several tools we found invaluable in providing fast personalized responses:

- the complete submission history for that student on that problem, to see what they've tried that worked or did not, and how close they got;
- a view of the "My Progress" page for that student, to see where they are overall;
- and a list of the teacher's other messages about the same problem, which allows them to cut-and-paste relevant information when several different students have similar questions.

We have found that this system is an extremely efficient way to provide targeted, personalized feedback to hundreds of students without much work, filling in the inherent gaps in what an auto-judge can provide.

There is another surprising benefit of this "Help" button: as lesson authors, we are able to get a tremendous amount of quick feedback when any newly-introduced content is too difficult or badly worded. Many of the hints in the current curriculum are the result of boiling down commonly-asked questions received in this way.

4. IMPLEMENTATION

CS Circles is built on top of the WordPress content management system (CMS). It is estimated[3] to be the most popular CMS, hosting a significant portion of all web traffic. We chose it because it has an easy web-based interface for management and content editing (including instant previews), it has a built-in secure login system we could extend for our own purposes, it is built on a well-maintained and easy-to-modify code base, and it has a plugin system which lets us easily add third-party features. We use plugins for site search, analytics, contact forms, translation, LaTeX, jQuery UI, and translator/admin role management.

As mentioned earlier, CodeMirror [6] and the Python visualizer [5] are two prominent non-WordPress tools that we integrated into CS Circles. Flexigrid[4] is another external library that we use, which allows for smooth and secure user access to database slices — for example this lets you browse through your past code submissions without pulling them all from our server at once.

Lesson pages are stored, like in most CMSes, as html-formatted text in a database. The auto-grader and exercises are specified using WordPress "shortcodes." For example, the code at the top of Figure 3 defines an exercise where students must correctly define variables counting the heads, shoulders, knees, and toes at a party, given a pre-defined count of the number of `people`. The specification, when embedded in the lesson text and rendered, produces the exercise. At the bottom of Figure 3 we show an example of the grader's reply to a partially correct solution. This quick text-based specification system has been instrumental in quick prototyping and lesson editing.

The auto-grader and surrounding code is written in a mix of several languages. There is html/js/css to handle browser interaction, PHP to interface with WordPress and generate dynamic html, Python to do introspective grading, and C++ to call the core "safeexec" sandbox routines. The latter was developed starting from the `safeexec` module of the Mooshak contest system [9] — our fork is available at `http://github.com/cemc/safeexec`. For a survey of the techniques involved in executing arbitrary user code securely, see the excellent survey of Forišek [4] or the recent implementation of Mareš and Blackham [11].

The grader has a run-time limit of 1 second by default. With the sole exception of the Sieve of Eratosthenes exercise, we don't intend that any of the coding problems need to be solved in an optimized way. So far the design has been successful: we've not seen any correct student code that times out on any other problem.

5. FUTURE WORK

Our experiences with WordPress and its great plugin community drive us to ask, would it be useful to distribute the technologies behind CS Circles as a set of plugins? It would be excellent to let individual educators develop and host their own interactive programming lessons.

We would like to extend the technology behind the site to other languages such as JavaScript, R, and Sage. Addi-

[3] `http://trends.builtwith.com/cms`

[4] `http://flexigrid.info/`

```
[pyBox repeats=3 precode="people = _rint(10, 100)"
autotests="heads\nshoulders\nknees\ntoes"
solver="heads, shoulders, knees, toes =
people, 2*people, 2*people, 10*people"]
```

⇓

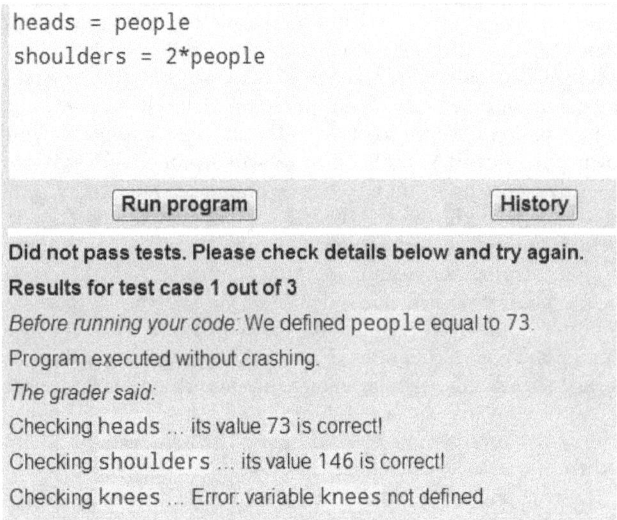

Figure 3: Top: a WordPress-style shortcode that defines an exercise in CS Circles. Bottom: the result of a submission sent to this exercise.

tionally, it would be beneficial to integrate interactive sandboxes (and exercises) into programming languages' online documentation.

Interactive input and output is not currently possible in CS Circles, but it would be an important feature to add in a future version. The Skulpt environment used by [12, 13] would be one way to accomplish this.

While programming generally requires enough English competency to make sense of the syntax and the errors, we have translated everything else (including the UI and grader feedback) to French. Translations into a few other languages are under way, and reaching more students and teachers in this way is an exciting prospect.

Can a useful programming course be taught on a touchscreen/tablet/iPad? Our intuition is that a comfortable keyboard is an important ingredient in making any significant amount of coding enjoyable. However, "code scrambles" might work even better on a touchscreen.

6. ACKNOWLEDGMENTS

We thank our colleagues Graeme Kemkes, Sandy Graham, and Andy Kong for helping with lesson/backend development, answering student questions, and server administration, and Brice Canvel for leading the French translation. We thank the authors of the plug-ins and libraries we use, especially Philip Guo and Peter Wentworth for building the visualizer, and the authors of the Polylang plugin. We are inspired by StarCraft's excellent integrated tutorials and choosable level ordering, and by *Good Eats* for explanations that are at once clear, amusing, scientific, and polished.

7. REFERENCES

[1] P. Denny, A. Luxton-Reilly, and B. Simon. Evaluating a new exam question: Parsons problems. In *Proc. 4th ICER (Int. Workshop Comp. Ed. Research)*, pages 113–124, 2008.

[2] A. B. Downey. *Think Python.* O'Reilly Media, 2012. Earlier version: *How to Think Like a Computer Scientist: Learning with Python*, Green Tea Press, 2008.

[3] C. Fidge and D. Teague. Losing their marbles: syntax-free programming for assessing problem-solving skills. In *Proc. 11th ACE (Australasian Conf. Comp. Ed.)*, pages 75–82, 2009.

[4] M. Forišek. Security of Programming Contest Systems. In V. Dagiene and R. Mittermeir, editors, *Information Technologies at School*, pages 553–563, 2006.

[5] P. Guo. Online Python Tutor: Embeddable web-based program visualization for CS education. In these proceedings, 2012. http://pythontutor.com/.

[6] M. Haverbeke. CodeMirror (Version 2.x), 2011–. http://codemirror.net/.

[7] D. M. Hoffman, M. Lu, and T. Pelton. A web-based generation and delivery system for active code reading. In *Proc. 42nd SIGCSE*, pages 483–488, 2011.

[8] R. Kaplan and E. Kaplan. *Out of the Labyrinth: Setting Mathematics Free.* Oxford University Press, 2007.

[9] J. P. Leal and F. Silva. Mooshak: a web-based multi-site programming contest system. *Software: Practice and Experience*, 33(6):567–581, 2003.

[10] M. Lopez, J. Whalley, P. Robbins, and R. Lister. Relationships between reading, tracing and writing skills in introductory programming. In *Proc. 4th ICER (Int. Workshop Comp. Ed. Research)*, pages 101–112, 2008.

[11] M. Mareš and B. Blackham. A new contest sandbox. *Olympiads in Informatics*, 6:100–109, 2012.

[12] B. Miller and D. Ranum. *How to Think Like a Computer Scientist/Learning with Python: Interactive Edition (Using Python 3.x).* Runestone Interactive, 2011. http://interactivepython.org/courselib/static/thinkcspy/index.html.

[13] B. Miller and D. Ranum. *Problem Solving with Algorithms and Data Structures.* Runestone Interactive, 2012. http://interactivepython.org/courselib/static/pythonds/index.html.

[14] B. N. Miller and D. L. Ranum. Beyond PDF and ePub: toward an interactive textbook. In *Proc. 17th ITiCSE (ACM Conf. Innovation & Tech. in Comp. Sci. Ed.)*, pages 150–155, 2012.

[15] D. Parsons and P. Haden. Parsons' programming puzzles: a fun and effective learning tool for first programming courses. In *Proc. 8th ACE (Australasian Conf. Comp. Ed.)*, ACE '06, pages 157–163, 2006.

[16] J. Resig. Khan Academy computer science (talk). In *EmpireJS*, 2012. http://vimeo.com/36579366.

[17] B. Victor. Inventing on principle (talk). In *4th CUSEC (Canadian University Software Eng. Conf.)*, 2012. http://www.youtube.com/watch?v=2sEvlJKAuos.

Will it Stick? Exploring the Sustainability of Computational Thinking Education Through Game Design

Kyu Han Koh
Department of Computer Science
University of Colorado at Boulder
Boulder, CO 80309
+1 303 492 1349
kohkh@colorado.edu

Alexander Repenning
Department of Computer Science
University of Colorado at Boulder
Boulder, CO 80309
+1 303 492 1349
ralex@cs.colorado.edu

Hilarie Nickerson
Department of Computer Science
University of Colorado at Boulder
Boulder, CO 80309
+1 303 492 1349
hnickerson@colorado.edu

Yasko Endo
Department of Computer Science
University of Colorado at Boulder
Boulder, CO 80309
+1 303 492 1349
yasko.endo@colorado.edu

Pate Motter
Department of Computer Science
University of Colorado at Boulder
Boulder, CO 80309
+1 303 492 1349
Pate.Motter@colorado.edu

ABSTRACT

Exposing middle school students to computer science through game design appears to be a promising means to mitigate the computer science pipeline challenge. Particularly when game design is integrated into already-existing middle school courses, either with an academic or a technology skills focus, there is a high potential for exposure, often reaching hundreds of students per school per year. In contrast to after-school programs, students taking these classes are usually not self selected, creating an important opportunity to vastly broaden participation in computing activities and to include more female and underrepresented students. Research suggests that exposure to short game design activities is effective in motivating large percentages of students in a wide variety of demographic groups. The Scalable Game Design project has trained middle school teachers around the US to teach students how to make one simple arcade-style game in a 1-2 week session. A study with over 10,000 students is exploring the sustainability of this approach and finding positive responses to inquiries such as these: Do teachers continue to use game design? Do they have the desire and capacity to move forward without extrinsic rewards such as research stipends? After building one game, do students advance to building more games or even STEM simulations?

Categories and Subject Descriptors

K.3.2 [**Computers and Education**]: Computers and Information Science Education

Keywords

Sustainability, Game Design, Simulation Design, Computational Thinking, Zone of Proximal Flow.

1. INTRODUCTION

The need to start early with computational thinking (CT) activities in middle school has been widely recognized [4]. Recently, the number of students selecting computer science as a field at the college level has gradually been going up, but the same cannot be said of the participation of women and underrepresented students. Activities such as game design [11, 12], robotics [8], story telling [15] and animation [11] have mostly focused on the motivational angles that are important to address given the rather negative perception of computer science. Many students find that "programming is hard and boring." For some time, the Scalable Game Design (SGD) project has been a proponent of the idea that it is not only important but also quite feasible to integrate CT into public school education [1]. SGD introduces middle school students to CT through game design. Particularly when game design is integrated into already-existing middle school courses, either with an academic or a technology skills focus (e.g., keyboarding, use of office applications), there is a high potential for exposure, often reaching hundreds of students per school per year. Moreover, in contrast to after-school programs, students taking these classes are usually not self-selected. Consequently, this strategy affords an important opportunity to vastly broaden participation by including more female and underrepresented students. For example, research suggests that exposure to short game design activities is effective in motivating large numbers as well as large percentages of women and underrepresented students with respect to interest in computer science [16]. In past surveys, the percentages of students who desired to participate in more game design were as follows: 64% female / 74% male; 69% underrepresented / 71% white [16].

To assess the efficacy of a CT education strategy, it is important to look beyond just tools, activities and curricula. High levels of motivation [16] are most likely essential in achieving efficacy but certainly not sufficient alone. Aside from motivational angles, can game design activities contribute to the core education challenges connected to STEM education? Can teachers with little, if any, programming background be trained to teach students how to design and implement games? Middle schools in particular usually have very little time and even fewer resources for professional development, especially given that CT/computer science/programming is simply "not on the test" and consequently does not factor into strategically important school assessments such as the No Child Left Behind act.

The sustainability of an instructional strategy is a more robust indicator for efficacy but at the same time also harder to evaluate than motivational and educational goals. Implementers must overcome potentially strong novelty effects [2] and address a number of other concerns that typically require longitudinal research to discover. It is often easy to find a number of highly motivated teachers and students to initially participate in some kind of experiment, but what will happen if support structures including the presence of assistants in the classroom or perhaps even financial support and training fade and the research ends? Will the teachers want to continue? Do they have the means to continue? Can students move beyond basic activities? Does school management appreciate these efforts?

This paper compares the theory and practice of the Scalable Game Design project with respect to sustainability. To better interpret the outcomes, it will help to provide a brief introduction to the Scalable Game Design *theory of change*. Designed with sustainability in mind, its essence is that programming challenges and skills should be balanced, providing different paths along which students can increase their skills in order to tackle more advanced challenges. The four core principles of this theory of change [13] address not only motivation, but also scaffolding for schools that is intended to stimulate ongoing interest by administrators, teachers, and students in continuing these CT skill-building activities. These four principles are captures in <approach> *so that* <outcome> format:

1. ***Exposure:*** Develop a highly adoptable middle school CT curriculum integrated into existing computer education and STEM courses *so that* potentially large and diverse groups of children are exposed to CT concepts.
2. ***Motivation:*** Create a scalable set of game design activities ranging from low-threshold to high-ceiling activities *so that* students with no programming background can produce complete and exciting games in a short amount of time, enticing them to move on a gradual trajectory to the creation of highly sophisticated games and STEM simulations.
3. ***Education:*** Build computational instruments that analyze student-produced projects for CT skills *so that* learning outcomes can be objectively measured.
4. ***Pedagogy:*** Systematically investigate the interaction of pedagogical approaches and motivational levels *so that* teachers can broaden participation more strategically.

The resulting Scalable Game Design framework (Figure 1) [3, 6] includes a curriculum of increasingly advanced game design activities that range from basic classic 1980s arcade games such as Frogger (bottom-left in the figure) to more contemporary games such as The Sims. As students progress, they encounter sophisticated concepts such as artificial intelligence (top left in the figure). The right-hand side shows the Zones of Proximal Flow diagram—a combination of Csíkszentmihályi's Flow diagram with Vygotsky's Zone of Proximal Development conceptualization [16]. Project-First learning, a just-in-time approach of introducing skills in context as needed, sustains high student motivation levels throughout the learning process.

To measure the efficacy of this approach, student learning is evaluated by employing a tool called Computational Thinking Pattern Analysis (CTPA) [5]. Every game and simulation produced by students—more than 10,000 over the last 4 years—is not only collected in the Scalable Game Design Arcade [6], but is also analyzed with respect to CT thinking skills expressed by students. CTPA is not looking for constructs such as IF and LOOP statements at the programming level but, instead, is looking for more general object interactions such as collisions and diffusion at a phenomenalistic [9] level through the use of Latent Semantic Analysis [7] inspired methods to find code patterns. These phenomenalistic patterns, Computational Thinking Patterns [3], can be understood as a subset of universal CT skills that are relevant to game design as well as to other applications including the creation of science simulations.

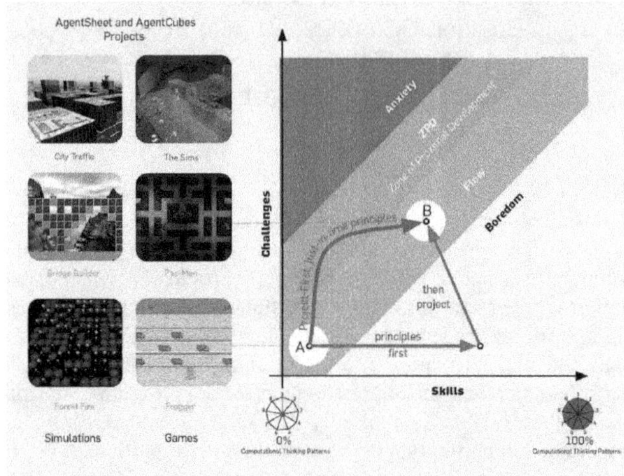

Figure 1. Zones of Proximal Flow: The Scalable Game Design framework includes a CT curriculum that balances CT challenges with CT skills. A Project-First learning path maintains motivation while students advance from basic skills to more advanced ones.

The combination of exposure, motivation, education, and pedagogy afforded by the Zones of Proximal Flow framework provides a favorable environment for sustainability, as it offers an incremental approach for CT skills development that could transform school systems gradually. In other words, it should be possible for schools to get started quickly and then to move along somewhat predicable trajectories toward more advanced game design or STEM simulation building challenges.

So far this has been the theory. The rest of this paper explores the question of sustainability by analyzing data from schools around the USA that are engaging in Scalable Game Design. Specifically, it investigates whether students mentored by teachers with basic training in SCG principles will move beyond the basics, advancing to more sophisticated game design or even applying their skills to non-game design applications such as STEM simulation building. This outcome would be particularly exciting, as it could be interpreted as providing evidence for the transferability of CT skills that are relevant to game design as well as to simulation-building applications.

2. METHOD

The project discussed in this paper was designed to increase students' interests in computer science and STEM by integrating learning about computational thinking with game design at the middle school level. To serve a wide spectrum of communities, this project has worked with more than 80 teachers and 10,000 students from urban, rural, suburban and remote/tribal regions in 9 different states.

Common factors for the project schools are as follows:

- Most students were 6th/7th graders.
- Teachers taught Scalable Game Design to students using the AgentSheets game/simulation programming software, employing the Project-First approach (see Figure 1). They attended a week-long training before their SGD implementation.
- The project offered an official game design curriculum for participating schools, and this curriculum started with a basic design for the game of Frogger.
- At the end of each 1–2 week module, during which students completed either a game or a simulation, the students' creations were uploaded to the Scalable Game Design Arcade (SGDA) [6].
- A fixed stipend was given to teachers who finished one module of any project (game or simulation) per semester. There was no extra incentive for implementing additional modules. This meant that teachers could stay with the basic Frogger implementation to receive their stipend, with no obligation for further levels of implementation.

2.1 Class Implementation

The participating middle school classes are exposed to the Scalable Game Design project curriculum in separate class modules. Each module's curriculum includes one game or simulation. Before each class of students begins its first module, a survey is administered to collect demographic and experience level data. A similar post survey is administered after the games have been uploaded. The middle school course trajectory is structured along a difficulty-oriented pipeline. In other words, from a computational thinking perspective, the second game in the curriculum is more difficult than the first, incorporating new CT patterns, and the third learned game increases in difficulty from the second. The course difficulty continuum also deliberately builds on the acquired knowledge and skills from previously learned game tutorials. Within these parameters, the project teachers are free to present the curriculum in any manner that is comfortable for them, as long as the curriculum integrity is adhered to.

2.2 Game Implementation Trajectory

There are several official tutorials for game design on the Scalable Game Design Wiki [14]. Generally, students are guided to learn general programming patterns through implementing a game of Frogger. After Frogger, students are encouraged to learn more sophisticated programming patterns with more complex games such as Pacman, Space Invaders, or Sims.

The project provides several possible learning paths with game implementations. Each learning path is designed to balance CT challenges in a given game implementation and a student's CT skills. For example, students could learn different computational thinking patterns through a "Frogger–Sokoban–Sims" path. Project implementation complexity is designed to increase over time. The paragraphs below show an example of Frogger-Sokoban-Sims learning path followed by one of the project schools, with actual student-created game screenshots.

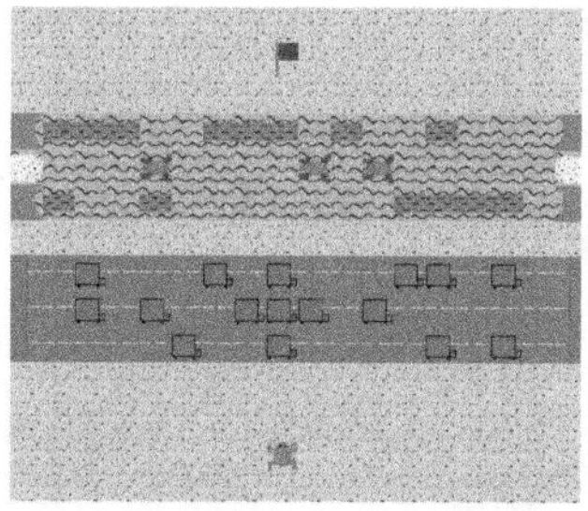

1st game: Frogger

Frogger is typically the first game implemented in the project curriculum. In this simple 80s arcade game, the interactions between agents are relatively simple. Examples include move, hit, and kill.

2nd game: Sokoban

After implementing Frogger, students are asked to implement a game of Sokoban, a classic puzzle game that requires slightly more complicated agent interactions than Frogger.

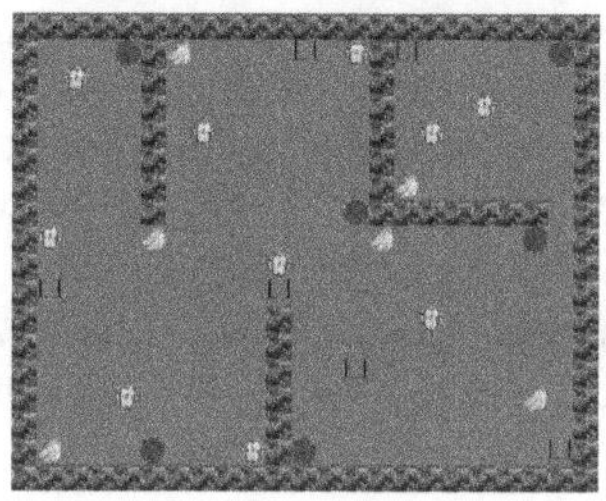

3rd game: Sims

A game of Sims is considered a good stepping-stone between game design and simulation design. Sims adopts some artificial intelligence techniques such that agents in the game interact with other agents without user control.

2.3 Simulation Implementation Trajectory

There are several popular STEM simulation models such as the Virus Contagion model, which shows how a virus could be spread; the Forest Fire model, which simulates forest fire; and the Eco System model, which describes food pyramids in ecosystems.

The STEM simulation examples below were created by students from one of the project schools.

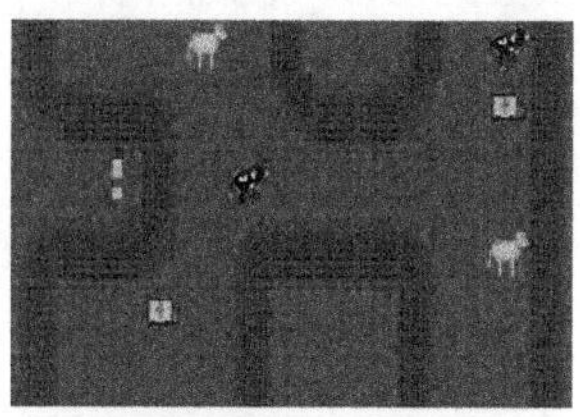

Virus Contagion:

This simulation is often used as an introductory simulation since it requires fewer CT patterns compared to other simulation designs.

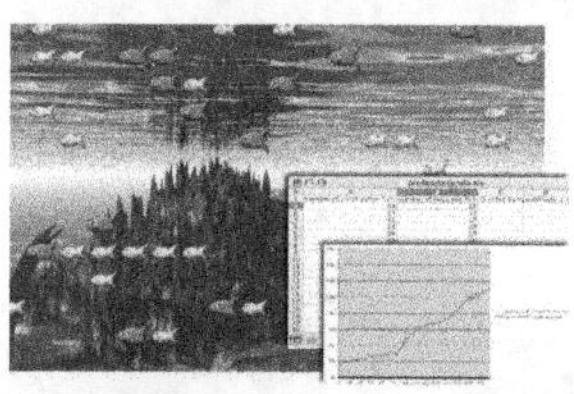

Eco System:

There are several different types of Eco System designs, all based on the Predator-Prey model.

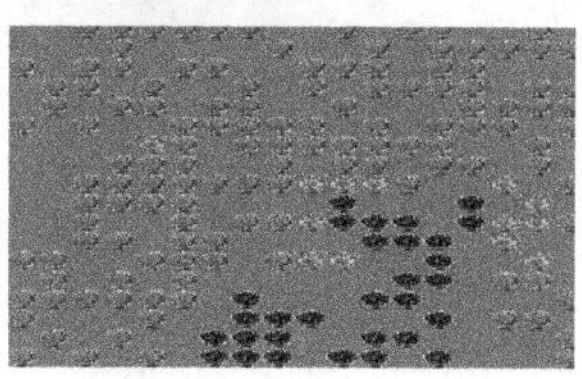

Forest Fire:

This simulation includes mathematical techniques such as calculating probability to estimate the direction of fire spreading.

The implementation complexity could be increased by the teacher, for example by adding multiple levels of reproduction rate, animal life spans, and predator-prey relationships.

The project offers basic implementation tutorials for these popular simulation designs. However, the project does not recommend a specific learning path for simulation design. Teachers can design their own STEM simulation or teach any predesigned simulation offered by the project based on their goals and abilities. Designing and teaching original STEM simulations would require extra effort by the teachers.

3. Results: Exploring the Sustainability

Fostering computational thinking through video game camp, student summer camp, computer workshops, and/or after-school programs has been successful [1]. However, there are few reports showing whether those programs are sustainable over a long time period. To validate a program's CT education benefit, the program should show a sustainability of learning over a period of time; otherwise the program's education benefit would end after one experience with the program. The core benefit of computational thinking education lies in bridging problem solving skills between two or more different problem domains [17]. Through our project, we have witnessed many project schools that were able to extend and transfer their students' learning abilities and problem solving skills to the next level of problem domains.

In the following section, we illustrate three kinds of evidence of sustainability: probability to advance, number of different projects, and advancing from game design to simulation design.

3.1 Sustainability: Probability to Advance

Over the last 3 years, 72 different types of games and simulations have been collected from 46 participating schools. All 46 schools submitted at least one project (game or simulation) to the SGDA, and 37 schools submitted two projects or more. Also, 30 schools and 23 schools submitted 3 and 4 projects or more, respectively (Figure 2). Interestingly, these numbers show that 0.8 appears to be a threshold to move forward: 81% of the schools that submitted at least one project, submitted two projects or more, and 80% of this second group submitted three projects or more.

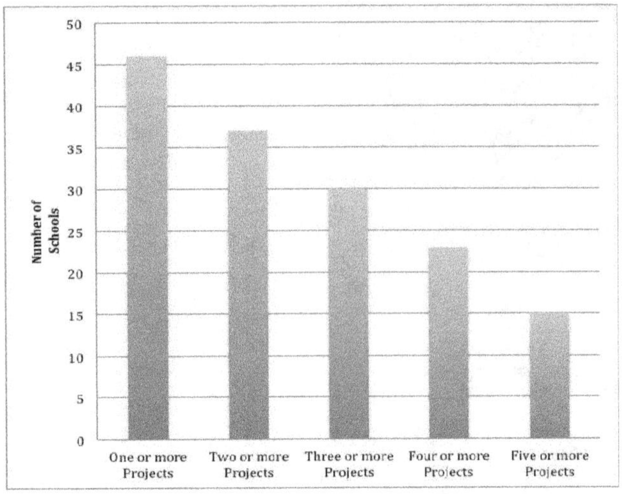

Figure 2. Probability to Advance: A high degree of sustainability is suggested by a large rate of advancement. Over 80% of schools advance to create a second project, of these 80% advance to a third project, of these 80% advance to a fourth project.

Considering teachers' short training timeframe and the lack of financial support after the first module implementation, the 80% success rate can be considered quite high, implying the existence of sustainability. Also, this result possibly indicates that many project schools have successfully helped students follow the Zone of Proximal Flow, spanning students' problem solving skills over multiple problem domains.

3.2 Sustainability: Number of Different Projects

The 46 schools that actively participated in this project submitted students' projects to the Scalable Game Design Arcade. Those schools can be grouped by school locale types. For this project, 9 Tech Hub schools, 22 Urban-City schools, 12 Rural schools, and 3 Tribal schools participated. For school locale definition, we referenced the National Center for Education Statistics (NCES) homepage [10].

Following NCES, the school locale types are defined as below:

- ***Tech Hub:*** Schools within a city with a university and high density of tech support
- ***Urban-City:*** Schools in or very near a city, suburb.
- ***Town:*** Schools less than or equal to 10 miles from urbanized area.
- ***Rural:*** Schools that are less than or equal to 25 miles from an urbanized area.
- ***Tribal/Remote:*** Schools from Ignacio, CO and Oglala, SD, and Native American Indian reservations of Southern Ute and Oglala Sioux.

When project submission data is categorized by region type, schools in tech hubs submitted 46% more projects per school than those in the other three types of regions (Figure 3). However, schools in these region types show similar outcomes to each other. Unique project submission per school in a tech hub is 5.3 while there are 3.6 unique project submissions per school in an urban-city, 3.3 unique project submissions per school in a rural and 3.6 unique project submissions per school in a tribal/remote area.

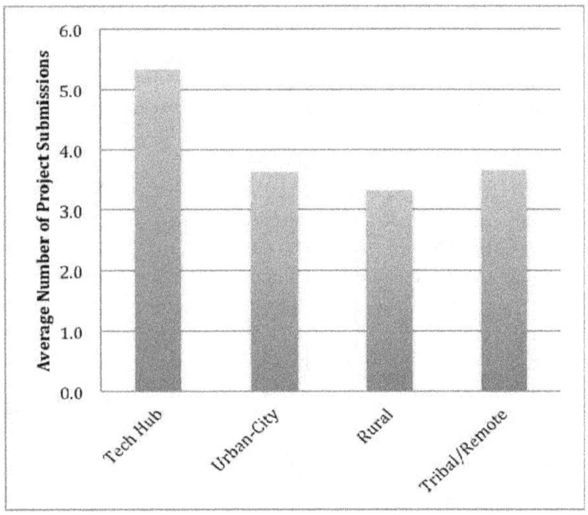

Figure 3. Average Number of Different Project Submissions by School Locale Type

There is one special case that has very large after-school programs and/or summer camp programs in a tech hub area. This organization, called *Girl Start*, submitted 12 different games and simulations. When this organization is excluded from the data, the number of unique project submissions per school in a tech hub goes down to a value of 4.8. Additionally, there is a second tech hub area school that has been working with the project for over 10 years, with a highly skilled teacher using a specialized curriculum for game design and simulation design. This school produced 17 different types of games and simulations. If those games and simulations were not counted, then the number of project submission per school in a tech hub area would be 3.14, which is similar to other three school areas. However, for clear data interpretation, those two organizations are not excluded in any graph or chart.

3.3 Sustainability: Advancing from Game Design to Simulation Design

There are several good strategies to bring computational thinking into student learning activities [17]. Computational thinking could be taught through an activity of transferring problem solving processes from one problem domain to a wide variety of other problem domains. Thus, when a student transfers acquired problem-solving skills from game implementation to simulation implementation, we could say that evidence of a student's ability to use computational thinking emerges. This seems to be related to the sustainability of computational thinking education since the learning continues toward a higher level of problem domain instead of stopping at the same level of problem domain.

For example, one student created a science simulation based on chaos theory with computational thinking patterns that he learned from implementing Frogger and Sokoban [5].

The project's official game design curriculum includes simulation implementation continued from the basic game implementation. The project strongly encourages teachers to move toward simulation implementation for bridging basic programming education and STEM education, but it is not required for teachers. There is no incentive for simulation implementation.

Regardless of the lack of further financial incentive and a more advanced level of implementation, 43% of project schools successfully moved toward simulation implementation (Figure 4).

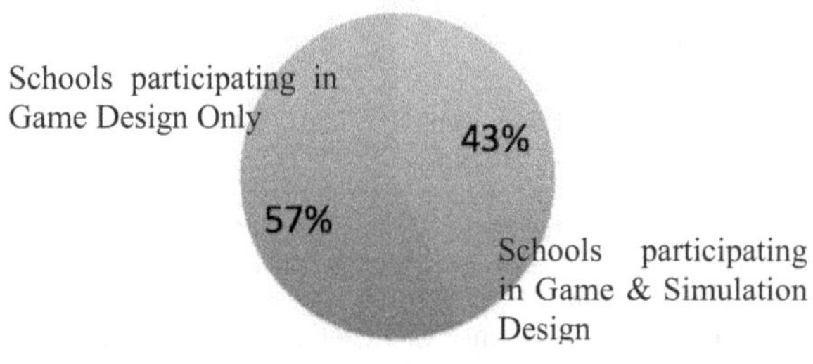

Figure 4. Game Design vs. Game & Simulation Design

In this result, schools in a tech hub area also showed better performance than those in the other three areas. Of the schools in a tech hub area, 66.7% have progressed into simulation implementation. Fewer than half of the project schools not in a tech hub area progressed in this way (Figure 5).

Every project teacher was aware that there was no project incentive for the second module implementation, more advanced levels of implementation, or simulation implementation. Nevertheless, project teachers were willing to move beyond the basic game design as the graphs show.

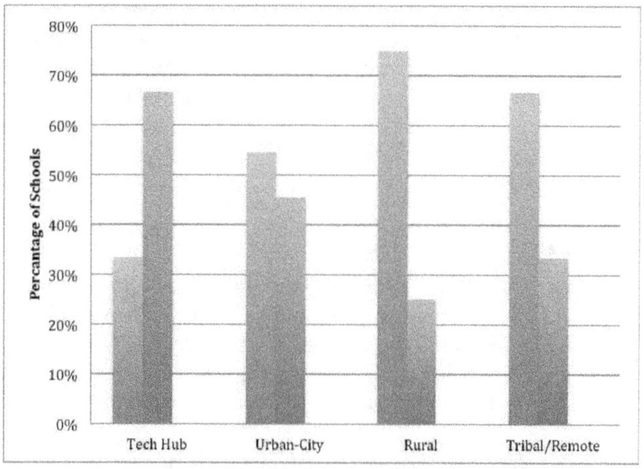

Figure 5. Game Design vs. Game & Simulation Design by School Locale Type

4. DISCUSSION

The large percentage of schools that showed evidence of curricular sustainability by expanding their Scalable Game Design offerings beyond the introductory lessons (80%) is somewhat remarkable given both the typical fate of trial STEM curricula and the many pressures faced by educators. We believe that a combination of student-, teacher- and school-related factors is partially responsible for this outcome. Motivation surveys completed by students in the first two years of the project, which were administered following the completion of SGD activities in their classes, showed that approximately two thirds of the participants would be interested in taking another game or simulation design course and that only 6% offered negative comments regarding their initial experiences [16]. In addition, the number of previously trained teachers who have returned to our Summer Institute for advanced instruction suggests that educators also find value in what the students are learning. In 2012, this professional development opportunity emphasized STEM applications and the design of three-dimensional games. With positive feedback from both students and teachers, schools that have the resources to do so may choose to increase the scope of their Scalable Game Design activities by adding more advanced games and/or promoting the transition to simulation design. It is likely that the higher simulation-to-game ratio of Arcade submissions observed in certain Tech Hub schools versus other types of schools reflects a greater ability to integrate SGD longitudinally into their curricula. Given more time, schools that do not currently have the resources to expand their activities as quickly may show similar patterns of adoption.

Ongoing improvements in how we train and support teachers may also play a role in encouraging schools to proceed beyond basic game design activities. Previous research suggested that guided discovery would be more effective than teacher-directed instruction at increasing interest by girls in pursuing future game design activities, narrowing or eliminating the gender gap even in classrooms where boys significantly outnumber girls [16]. Therefore, for the past two years, our training for teachers new to the SGD curriculum has included demonstrations of alternative teaching styles and a discussion of the efficacy of the guided discovery approach. Classroom observation has shown that growing comfort with the AgentSheets software also affects teacher behavior, with teachers who desire to employ the guiding strategy becoming less prescriptive over time. Greater student interest resulting from these adjustments, coupled with increasing ease in curriculum delivery, could certainly lead to schoolwide sustainability and the expansion of SGD activities. The availability of more and better tutorials may also be a contributing factor for schools that submit several different kinds of games and/or simulations to the arcade.

5. CONCLUSIONS

The use of game design as an instrument to introduce computational thinking early on in K–12 education is gradually emerging as a promising practice, particularly when trying to broaden the participation of female and underrepresented students. Sustainability trends are an important indicator of whether game design activities in schools will remain one-shot activities kept alive largely through research support or will be able to be adopted in the practice of public schools. The Scalable Game Design strategy, outlined in this paper, has been designed with sustainability in mind. The data collected over a period of four years and with more than 10,000 games and simulations produced by students suggests that more than 80% of schools have advanced beyond the basic requirement. That is, teachers and students have created more, and in most cases more advanced, games and simulations than they were trained to do. This is particularly impressive given that these teachers did not receive any financial support to do so. Moreover, we believe that the large percentage of schools that moved on from game design to science simulations (43%) is a positive indicator that there is more going on than just game programming. Instead, the skills acquired through game design could be considered at least an important subset of computational thinking.

6. ACKNOWLEDGMENTS

This work is supported by the National Science Foundation under Grant Numbers DLR-0833612 and IIP-0848962. Any opinions, findings, and conclusions or recommendations expressed in this material are those of the authors and do not necessarily reflect the views of the National Science Foundation. Alexander Repenning is a founder of AgentSheets Inc.

7. REFERENCES

[1] Bennett, V., Koh, K. H., Repenning, A. 2011. CS Education Re-Kindles Creativity in Public Schools. *In Proceedings of ITiCSE '11: Annual Conference on Innovation and Technology in Computer Science Education,* Darmstadt, Germany, June 27-29, 2011

[2] Fraenkel J. R., and N. E. 2005. *How to design and evaluate research in education.* McGraw-Hill, Columbus, OH

[3] Ioannidou, A., Bennett, V., Repenning, A., Koh, K., Basawapatna, A. 2011. Computational Thinking Patterns. *In Proceedings of 2011 Annual Meeting of the American Educational Research Association (AERA) in the symposium "Merging Human Creativity and the Power of Technology: Computational Thinking in the K-12 Classroom".* New Orleans, April 8-12, 2011

[4] James J. Lu and George H.L. Fletcher. 2009. Thinking about computational thinking. *In Proceedings of the 40th ACM technical symposium on Computer science education (SIGCSE '09).* ACM, New York, NY, USA, 260-264

[5] Koh, K. H., Basawapatna, A.,Bennett, V., Repenning, A. 2010. Towards the Automatic Recognition of Computational Thinking. *In Proceedings of IEEE International Symposium on Visual Languages and Human-Centric Computing 2010,* Leganés-Madrid, Spain, September 21-25, 2010

[6] Koh, K. H., Bennett, V., Repenning, A. 2010. Inspiring Collaborative Benefits: An Interaction between a Virtual and a Physical Group Learning Infrastructure, *In Proceedings of Western Canadian Conference on Computing Education (WCCCE 2010),* Okanagan, B.C., Canada May 7-8, 2010

[7] Landauer, T. K., Foltz, P. W., Laham, D. Introduction to Latent Semantic Analysis. Discourse Processes, 25, 1998, 259-284

[8] Lawhead, P. B., Duncan, M. E., Bland, C. G., Goldweber, M., Schep, M., Barnes, D. J., and Hollingsworth, R. G. 2002. A road map for teaching introductory programming using LEGO© mindstorms robots. SIGCSE Bull. 35, 2 (June 2002), 191-201.

[9] Michotte, A. 1963. *The Perception of Causality* (T. R. Miles, Trans.). London: Methuen & Co. Ltd.

[10] National Center for Education Statistics (NCES), 2012. NCES's urban-centric locale categories. http://nces.ed.gov/surveys/urbaned/page2.asp

[11] Resnick, M., Maloney, J., Monroy-Hernández, A., Rusk, N., Eastmond, E., Brennan, K., Millner, A, Rosenbaum, E., Silver, J., Silverman, B., and Kafai, Y. 2009. Scratch: programming for all. Commun. ACM 52, 11 (November 2009), 60-67.

[12] Repenning, A. 2000. AgentSheets®: an Interactive Simulation Environment with End-User Programmable Agents. *In Proceedings of Interaction 2000,* Tokyo, Japan, 2000.

[13] Repenning, A. 2012. Programming goes back to school. Communication of the ACM 55, 5 (May 2012), 38-40.

[14] Scalable Game Design Wiki, 2012. Scalable Game Design Tutorial. http://scalablegamedesign.cs.colorado.edu/wiki/Category:Tutorial

[15] Werner, L., Denner, J., Bliesner, M., and Rex, P. 2009. Can middle-schoolers use Storytelling Alice to make games?: results of a pilot study. In Proceedings of the 4th International Conference on Foundations of Digital Games (FDG '09). ACM, New York, NY, USA, 207-214.

[16] Webb, D. C., Repenning, A., and Koh, K. 2012. Toward an Emergent Theory of Broadening Participation in Computer Science Education, *In Proceedings of ACM Special Interest Group on Computer Science Education Conference, (SIGCSE 2012),* February 29 - March 3, 2012, Raleigh, North Carolina, USA.

[17] Wing, J. M. 2006. Computational Thinking. Communications of the ACM, 49(3), pp. 33-35, March 2006.

The Social Turn in K-12 Programming: Moving from Computational Thinking to Computational Participation

Yasmin B. Kafai
University of Pennsylvania
Graduate School of Education
Philadelphia, PA
215-746-3468
kafai@upenn.edu

Quinn Burke
College of Charleston
School of Education, Health, & Human Performance
Charleston, SC
843-953-7433
burkeqq@cofc.edu

ABSTRACT

In this conceptual paper, we argue that recent developments in K-12 programming education are suggestive of what can be called a "social turn", a shift in the field in which learning to code has shifted from being a predominantly individualistic and tool-oriented approach to now one that is decidedly sociologically and culturally grounded in the creation and sharing of digital media. We discuss in detail three dimensions of this social turn—(1) from writing code to creating applications, (2) from composing "from scratch" to remixing the work of others, and (3) from designing tools to facilitating communities. These three shifts illustrate how the development of artifacts, tools, and communities of programming lead us to move from computational thinking to computational participation. We draw from examples of past and current research, both inside and outside of school, and situate these developments in the context of current discussions around computational thinking, which has become a driving force in revitalizing programming in K-12 curricula and altogether broadening participation in computing.

Categories and Subject Descriptors

K.3.0 [**Computers & Education**]: Computer and Information Science Education

Keywords

Novice programming, tools, networked commons

1. INTRODUCTION

More than 30 years ago, Seymour Papert [28] wrote about computers, children, and powerful ideas promoting the use of Logo programming for learning about mathematics, complex ideas, learning communities, and creative expression. However while Logo grew quite prominent in K-12 schools throughout the 1980s, it literally had disappeared from the curriculum by the 1990s [14]. Schools largely turned away from programming as the availability of pre-assembled multi-media packages arrived via glossy CD-Roms. These, along with the Internet, seemingly negated the need for learning programming. With such a plethora of new content just a mouse-click away, who was still interested in toiling over creating these applications oneself?

SIGCSE'13, March 6–9, 2013, Denver, Colorado, USA.

Logo's departure was only further aided by the difficulty of finding qualified K-12 educators, knowledgeable about computers and programming, who could highlight the long-term merits of such "toil" and even make it palpable.

In the last few years, however, we have witnessed a renewed interest in learning programming in K-12 levels, propelled by several developments, including the educational initiative to promote computational thinking [41], a need to broaden participation in the technology culture at large [25], and perhaps most significantly, the wider "do-it-yourself" (DIY) ethos characteristic of digitally-based youth cultures [15]. Computers indeed now seem to be accessible everywhere, particularly outside of school. But with few students digitally fluent and persistent disparities in participation, it is crucial that computer science education recognizes its role in leveraging significant shifts in (a) what students are interested in programming, (b) the contexts in which they do it, and (c) how they do it. Broadly speaking, we view these shifts as a *social turn*, moving from a predominantly individualistic view of technology to one that includes a greater focus on the underlying sociological and cultural dimensions in learning to code, re-conceptualizing computational thinking as computational participation.

We see three shifts as the key levers of this social turn. The first shift, from code to applications, focuses on the emergence of programming artifacts as the focal point of learning. Learning programming was once a practice that largely prized coding accuracy and efficiency as the signifiers of success. Today however, rather than programming for the sake of programming, students can create authentic applications such as games and stories as part of a larger learning community. It is the quality of these shareable artifacts—a highly playable game, a sophisticated animation, or a particularly nuanced digital story—that offers entry to such coding communities and fosters camaraderie. This is characteristic of the second major social turn in programming, from tools to communities, in which coding is no longer performed as an isolated endeavor but within a shared social context, utilizing open software environments and mutual enthusiasm to spur participation. The third shift, from scratch to remixes, marks the hallmark activity of these new networked communities. Whereas programs once had to be created "from scratch" to demonstrate competency, today, seamless integration via remixing is the new social norm for writing programs. While this certainly presents particularly ethical challenges, remixing also offers newfound networks for participation.

The goal of this paper is to review what we know about these shifts and outcomes from the research literature of educational programming to inform rationales for the design of programming tools, applications and environments for learners and to help us design more appropriate and effective research, interventions, and assessments. We also hope to demonstrate how these shifts build on pedagogical ideas of Constructionist learning theory that were articulated early on in *Mindstorms* [28], but were subsequently neglected because of what Papert himself called a "technocentric" focus, valuing the technology over people and social actions. We argue that understanding this newly emerging social turn in programming can help us to generate better ways of how to think differently about K-12 computing and support the pivotal roles of context and community in learning [8]. Equally important, these shifts provide compelling illustrations of computational thinking [41] in K-12 educational programming. While much attention has focused on different concepts, practices and perspectives [4] and dimensions of programming [5], our goal is to connect to a broader conceptualization of computational thinking that encompasses its functional, political, and personal purposes [36]. Functional purposes usually describe the basic skills and concepts that someone needs to learn in order participate in society; political purposes captures why understanding these skills and concepts are relevant in society; personal purposes describe the role that these skills and concepts plays in personal expression for building and maintaining relationships. These various purposes describe the fundamental aspects of any literacy, whether its reading and writing printed texts or using and programming digital media, but they also make clear that when we talk about computational thinking, we need to understand that basic concepts and skills are situated within a larger cultural and personal context of learning and schooling. For that reason, we begin this review with outlining central ideas of Constructionist theory that situate these shifts in educational programming.

2. CONSTRUCTIONISM: PERSONAL, SOCIAL, & CULTURAL DIMENSIONS OF LEARNING

When Papert wrote *Mindstorms* in 1980, the term "Constructionism" had yet to be coined. He [29] later defined it as, "[C]onstructionism – the *N* Word as opposed to the *V* word – shares Constructivism's connotation to learning as building knowledge structures irrespective of the circumstances of learning. It then adds the idea that this happens especially felicitously in a context where the learner is consciously engaged in constructing a public entity whether it's a sand castle on the beach or a theory of the universe that can be shared with others". The idea that knowledge is represented in a *public entity* foreshadows the social as well as the cultural dimensions of Constructionist learning and their application to learning programming.

2.1 Personal dimensions

Most of Papert's writings have focused on learning programming from a *personal* perspective, very much in the Piagetian tradition. He saw the engagement with Logo programming as a way to facilitate the construction of knowledge structures and what he termed "appropriation" so that learners could make knowledge their own and begin to personally identify with it. Programming the Logo turtle very much makes the construct an "object-to-think-with" [28] linking together artifacts in the physical world (in this case, a turtle) with those of the digital world (e.g., programs, robots, and games). Papert argued that objects-to-think-with such as the Logo turtle are particularly effective at supporting appropriation, because they facilitate the child's personal identification with the object and help to construct, examine, and revise connections between old and new knowledge. By designing a program or game (or, on a more granular level, its procedures, algorithms and data structures) the personal knowledge becomes public and can then be shared with others. Of course, thinking about programs as personal objects that can be shared widely as public entities articulates a phenomenon entirely akin to the growth of Internet culture, which too is built upon the amassment of intimately personal items (e.g., photos, stories, and designs) introduced on an equally massive wider public sphere, taking on entirely new meanings upon this wider scale.

2.2 Social dimensions

The *social* dimensions of Constructionist learning have focused on learning communities, girded by the understanding that personal construction of programs does not happen in a vacuum but very much in a social context. Papert's [28] first-hand experience researching Brazilian samba schools encapsulated his sense of social norms and interactions as pivotal to any form of learning: "[t]hese are not schools as we know them; they are social clubs with memberships that may range from a few hundred to many thousands. Each club owns a building, a place for dancing and getting together. ... During the year each samba school chooses its theme for the next carnival, the stars are selected, the lyrics are written and rewritten, and the dance is choreographed and practiced. Members of the school range in age from children to grandparents and in ability from novice to professional. But they dance together and as they dance everyone is learning and teaching as well as dancing. Even the stars are there to learn their difficult parts" (p. 178). In many ways the proposal of samba schools as an example of learning culture predates the move away from traditional schools to apprenticeship learning that was ushered in years later by Lave and Wenger's seminal work [23] and then again in the form of affinity cultures by Gee [11] in the context of gaming communities.

2.3 Cultural dimensions

Finally, a *cultural* dimension of Constructionist learning has focused on the politics that determine how one way of knowing is valued over others. By studying and interviewing programmers, Turkle and Papert [39] revealed that the officially promoted "top-down" planning approach is not always superior to a more improvised, bricoleur-like approach. The bricoleur style is not a stepping stone towards more advanced forms of knowledge construction, but rather is a qualitatively different way of organizing one's planning and problem solving. Turkle and Papert argued that the bricoleur style favoring concrete thought could be just as advanced as abstract thought and observed that among the sciences, computer science prized abstract thinking. It's not just the approach but also the programming artifacts that we design that reflect these values and provide a context for learners to connect and engage with the practices in the field. The re-evaluation of the concrete finds today perhaps its most popular expression in the interest that youth display for learning programming apps [42] or other digital artifacts illustrating the complex issues can also be learned in the process of making a sharable and usable artifact that can situate learning of algorithms, data structures and other features.

These three dimensions, the personal, social, and cultural, of Constructionist theory highlight that learning to program, and learning anything for that matter, is not solely a technical matter of skills to be mastered. Rather, like Kelleher and Pausch [21] aptly recognized, the social and cultural barriers to learning programming are often "harder to address than mechanical ones because they are harder to identify and some cannot be addressed through programming systems" (p. 132) alone.

3. THE SOCIAL TURN IN K-12 PROGRAMMING

The following three dimensions highlight the social turn of how learning programming has shifted with the wider cultural perceptions and practices of what it is to socialize and produce in the 21st century and how this relates to computational thinking, resulting as we argue in better learning opportunities and, by extension, better teaching opportunities.

3.1 From code to applications

Learning to program is about writing code, developing algorithms, data and control structures that result in functional, if not, efficient programs. We have numerous studies of what students learn about syntax, control structures, conditionals, and recursion as well as data structures and variables while writing code, just as we have documentation on the connected challenges of learning to do so [38]. While much planning and problem solving went into these programs, there was also prompt criticism [30] that the empirical evidence was slim in demonstrating exactly what students were learning and how such learning transferred to other subjects. Others also noticed a lack of integration with the rest of the school curriculum [27]. In its initial foray into K-12 schools, programming largely existed as a stand-alone activity in which students would participate in once or twice a week for an hour at a time. And typically, these isolated moments of coding existed apart from classrooms within the computer lab after which the students were return to their "normal" classes back down the hallway.

On the tail end of this development, a new pedagogical approach to programming emerged, called instructional software design [12]. Rather than simply composing code, students designed full-fledged software applications. This approach was inspired by writings that saw design practices as contexts that could promote open-ended forms of problem solving and situate learners in the application of academic content in the design of meaningful, authentic applications [35]. Harel's seminal study not only illustrated that treating students as designers of instructional mathematics software could make them manifestly more invested in their learning, but also helped the students learn programming and mathematics significantly better than students in control classes. The instructional software design approach has since then successfully applied to other contexts such as game design [17] and integrated with other school subjects such as language arts [6], science [7], as well as music and art [10]. By leading with a particular project within a particular subject matter, be it digital stories in an English class or fraction games in a math course, programming pedagogy engages children with the potential to create "real-world" applications. It also builds on successful instructional practices in which educators can leverage content-based subject matter to informally design software that is meaningful and authentic beyond the classroom [3].

Today, the surge of "app" design courses [42] is a testament to the recruiting pull of such applied programs and ought to be leveraged more intently for broadening participation. It widens the walls [33] in suggesting applicability of programming to a range of activities rather than just narrow technical ones. More broadly speaking, designing applications can also be considered a direct and, more importantly, an accessible application of Wing's computational thinking [41]. It captures key aspects of designing systems, solving problems and understanding human behaviors because designing an application like a game or simulation involves the creation of a system, albeit on a smaller scale, that requires the designers to think carefully about how users will interface with the applications they design as well as solve problems of how to implement features according to their intentions. On a personal level, the idea of designing applications has most likely generated the broadest interest and success rate in getting youth actually interested in computer programming. Perhaps this is why making games for learning has received such widespread attention with so many programs, for-profit and non-profit alike, vying for children's attention. Nowhere is this more evident than in the proliferation of video game-making competitions such as Globaloria's "Globey Awards", Advanced Micro Devices (AMD) "Changing the Game" contest, the Games for Change Awards, as well as the National STEM Video Game Design Challenge sponsored by the White House itself. All of these competitions instill a sense of empowerment, both personal and political, that one can make what one uses and is characteristic of the self-reliance and drive of the wider DIY movement that has grown since the advent of Web. 2.0.

3.2 From programming tools to communities

Many efforts have focused on helping novice programmers to become more fluent and expressive with new technologies by developing programming tools [21]. In particular, addressing issues such as syntax problems have been simplified by using visual programming languages that reduce the amount of typing, or arranging control structures by providing linkages between different levels [38]. Particularly popular have been construction tool kits such as Scratch [34] or Kodu have focused on facilitating the programming of different multimedia applications to create games, animations and music videos, whereas others such as Alice [22] have focused on applications that engage in storytelling by providing characters from the popular program The Sims or have designed tools such as Agentsheets [32] to facilitate the creation of simulations. Both inside and outside of schools tools like these have been successful in lowering the floors of entering into programming. The design of computational construction kits has generated rich insights into how to make programming accessible for beginners and support many styles and interests [33].

One of the primary attractions for youth in creating applications rather than simply generating code is the capacity to share such applications with others and gain status by these shared creations. For instance, early use of the Scratch tool in a Computer Clubhouse illustrated how a vibrant game design community emerged over the course of two years with hundreds of different games developed [20]. The recent creation of Internet-based sharing sites has expanded the tool users into communities of designers. The most prominent example is the Scratch site, one of the largest youth programming communities that was inspired in part by Seymour Papert's samba schools. It is an online community for youth to create and share stories, games, and animation with over one million registered users, primarily between the ages of 8 and 16. Scratch collaborative activities typically revolve around the production of particular types of projects in which dozens of members can participate bringing different skills such as music, graphics or editing to the group [1]. More importantly, it builds on essential insights from educational research that fruitful learning is not done in isolation but in conjunction with others. While some early work by Webb [40] examined some of the challenges as well as opportunities in having students program in small teams, programming in K-12 contexts is still mostly an individual activity. One of the perhaps most successful collaborative designs has been the introduction of pair programming that is now widely practiced on grade levels K-16 because it has shown to be effective in helping and motivating beginning programmers [9].

Today programming and design tools such as Alice, Gamestar Mechanic, and Kodu all include communities, creating open source sites in the style of communities like Linux for youth to share, comment on, and contribute to their coded creations. While such communities have always existed—the pre-Internet Logo community is testament to that—with access to sharing programs online and finding like-minded peers and others, even novice programmers now have an audience that values their artifacts and thus provides a community or affinity group. Designing tools that facilitate particular mechanics of programming is not enough. Rather, providing a social context in which these programming tools are used and where programming artifacts are shared is equally important. It suggests that how we engage beginners in programming can be a collaborative activity. Learning how to program collaboratively brings other elements of computational thinking into the foreground such as decomposing a complex task and coordinating control flow between different components. In addition, we can also use computational thinking as a way for participants to parse the networked commons itself. Many data mining tools rely on algorithms to search for and extract patterns from interactions and behaviors in massive communities. Likewise, tools like crowd-sourcing not only leverage feedback from others but also need to be understood in how those can be used more effectively to not only gauge wider opinion but also promote greater efficiency and reliability in applied programming activities.

3.3 From scratch to remix

In the past, not only did most programs have to be created "from scratch" (no pun intended!) to illustrate programming competencies, but the expectation was that code was very much a proprietary commodity, to be built and ever-refined but certainly not freely shared. This mindset very much set the tone for early computing coursework as children were introduced to the potential of programming in terms of text-based functionality, akin to learning about fiction in a language arts course by being taught the meaning of nouns, verbs, and modifiers. The idea however to design programs on existing building blocks is by no means a new concept. Traditionally, as part of instruction, beginning programmers are given pieces of code to modify for their own programs and this allows novices to build far more complex designs than they could do their own. But the concept of repurposing code has taken on a new life through the Internet, mirroring prominent remix practices in digital media culture.

Today, the repurposing and remixing of code has become standard practice. It has been argued that remixing is a key practice in today's networked culture in support of our knowledge production [16]. Crediting ownership consists of referencing the intellectual origins of "text" used in media productions, be it graphics, animations or music. Remixing is also a particular form of participation within the Scratch community, taking existing Scratch projects and changing them before uploading them back to the website. With nearly 25% of the 3 million project posted at the Scratch site as remixes, members use the practice as means to familiarize oneself with the software as well as to socialize and collaborate with others via their creations [26] and this number has been steadily increasing since its launch. In some instances, authors design programs and explicitly invite others to remix their code, thus using programs as design-starters whereas in other cases remixes can range from direct copying to small tweaks of code or simply serve as inspiration for new, very different programs. Indeed, the culture of remixing in Scratch itself is not without fraught as positive and negative comments are prevalent as evident in previous attempts to introduce the practice within school-based environments. In an after-school club, Scratch programmers ages 10-12 years were adamant that their fellow programmers credited the origins of programs that they had remixed and posted online. Scratch programmers initially were concerned about others taking their programs, but they soon came to understand the remixes as a form of recognition that represented attention they received from others [19]. The issue of intellectual ownership looms large in discussion even among youth scratch members, from feeling complimented for the attention to distraught of the seeming lack of acknowledging the sources of work.

It's perhaps the aspect of computational thinking that raises the most interesting intersection of technical and social issues because what's prevalent in amateur creators cultures such as Scratch might not be considered appropriate in school contexts that value individual authorship and explicitly would consider remixing a violation of their policies. A growing number of media theorists and educators posit remix as very much a new literacy that schools need to address [31]. In fact, school's traditional conception of "copying" sits directly at odds with the wider culture of remix that prevails in children's interactions outside of school. While remixing on the most basic level requires just a few mouse-clicks to copy programs and thus would be a hard-sell for any consideration of computational thinking, we do know that selective remixing can actually require a far greater degree of sophistication. Considering what to modify in selected code segments versus what to keep and where to add or delete procedures or variables within a program are examples of remixing activity that very much requires a deeper, functional understanding of the code, and in some instances remixing here may very well be more complex than starting with a blank slate. On a political level, the issues of copyright in the digital domain (and this extends to code as well as interfaces) present a highly complicated matter that is only in the process of being defined in light of new cultural practices [24]. Personally, for many youth, this is a complex issue to deal with. The remixing dilemma—the difficulty to promote both originality and generativity in projects—suggests that remixing can serve as an opportune case for critically understanding copyright issues and thus address the wider social implications of computational thinking, which too often get neglected in the overt focus on technical prowess.

4. DISCUSSION

We painted in broad strokes a social turn in K-12 educational programming community to emphasize that engaging with computational thinking at large, and with programming in particular, should be thought of as a social practice. Programming applications are increasingly being developed in order to design artifacts of genuine significance for others. Programming in a community suggests that such significance ultimately lies in the fact that we design to share with others. Programming as remixing code makes clear that we build on the work of others and need to better understand the ramifications of this approach. Most importantly, in the context of computational thinking, this means that we need to move beyond seeing programming as an individualistic act but rather begin to understand it as a communal practice steeply grounded in how we think about what students today should learn in order to become full participants in their respective communities. Computational thinking should really be thought of computational participation to emphasize that "objects-to-think-with"—to use one of Papert's core ideas—are indeed "objects-to-share-with" others. To expand on Wing's [41] definition of computational thinking, computational participation is the ability to solve problems with others, design systems for and with others, and understand the cultural and social nature of human behavior, by drawing on concepts, practices, and perspectives fundamental to computer science. Of course, just by having kids program applications, placing them in groups, and encouraging them to remix code hardly addresses all of the problems associated with broadening participation in computing. In fact, a renewed focus on computational participation likely will present whole new set of challenges when it comes to bringing programming activities back into schools. This paper represents a modest start in beginning to address some of the challenges around facilitating such participation in the very design of the programming activities.

If computational thinking is indeed a social practice, then access to participation and collaboration in communities of programming becomes a focal issue. We know from preliminary research in the Scratch community, that this move toward membership in a large-scale community is a complex interplay between how young software designers develop personal agency through programming and how they gain status as "experts" amongst their peers [19]. Despite the myth of children as "digital natives" who naturally migrate online, observations indicated that some children initially resisted going online and uploading their program to the Scratch website, uncomfortable sharing their own work with more experienced members online. Thus suggests that establishing membership in a larger programming community is not as easily achieved as one may think. Rather, navigating online communities requires an array of participation strategies that directly address this sense of vulnerability associated with sharing one's work for others to comment on and even remix for their own purposes.

Likewise, seeing programming as a collaborative, distributed effort requires new types of collaborative agency than are usually found in assigned collaborative group work in many classrooms. For instance, in the Scratch online community collaborative activities typically revolve around the production of particular types of Scratch projects by a small group of individuals that have commonly met one another in the online environment [1]. In our recent research to engineer such forms of collaborative efforts with online and offline groups we found that many students had difficulties in participating in this type of self-organized collaboratives. Educators and researchers that design and study K-12 programming communities need to focus not just on programming but also on how novice participants get to participate. This issue of equity in participation is of course not a new one. On a basic level the classrooms that build around design activities always formed communities where students engaged in forms of peer pedagogy [7] often observed in large online networks [2]. But what's different now, are the large-scale communities that connect hundreds, if not thousands, of young programmers and provide different contexts and opportunities for exchange. How we design communities around tools such as Scratch, Alice or Kodu can and needs to be done both online and offline, in the local classrooms and clubs in which youth participate as well as the online spaces that youth populate to share their designs and comment on others.

Furthermore, we need to broaden our array of computing activities. While the shift towards designing authentic applications is an important step into the right direction, we also need to realize that designing games is not the only acceptable application to achieve this goal. While game design definitely leverages the interest and informal experience of many children and youth, it also happens to cater to a community that is still predominantly male. There are many other types of software applications that can be designed and fulfill the premise of an authentic context. For this reason, we have argued that joining the "existing" clubhouse like you would find in the Scratch community, still leaves many outside. Indeed, in terms of membership in the Scratch online community, only 37 % of its members are girls. Rather than just to focus on games and animations, we also need to further encourage stories and perhaps even introduce different materials and contexts. For instance, design of tangibles like the electronic textile construction kits LilyPad Arduino suggest that new clubhouses can be build that serve other members rather than simply joining existing ones.

From our vantage point, the social turn provides new directions for the design of activities, tools, and communities in K-12 educational computing efforts that are aimed at broadening participation in and perceptions of computing on a considerably larger scale than previous attempts of integration. We are not arguing that all the standard staples of traditional computing courses should be dismissed. The merits of writing code to learn about the nature of algorithms, and developing data structures, compilers and general architecture remain crucially important. But we want to make the case that K-12 educational computing can take the road that K-12 mathematics and science education [3] have taken long ago and leverage with success the insights gained from youth digital media and networked culture in conjunction with learning theory that initially promoted the idea of children programmers against all conventional wisdom.

5. ACKNOWLEDGEMENT

The writing of this paper was supported by a collaborative grant from the National Science Foundation (NSF-CDI-1027736) to Mitchel Resnick, Yasmin Kafai, and Yochai Benkler. The views expressed are those of the authors and do not necessarily represent the views of the Foundation, University of Pennsylvania, or College of Charleston. We wish to think Deborah Fields for comments on earlier draft of the paper.

6. REFERENCES

[1] Aragon, C., Poon, S, and Monroy-Hernandez, A. 2009. A tale of two communities: Fostering collaboration and creativity in scientists and children. In *Proceedings of the 7th ACM Conference on Creativity and Cognition*, (Berkeley, CA, October 27-30). ACM, New York, NY, 9-18.

[2] Benkler, Y. 2006. *The Wealth of Networks: How Social Production Transforms Markets and Freedom.* New Haven, CT: Yale University Press.

[3] Bransford, J., Brown, A., and Cocking., R. 2000. *How People Learn.* Washington, DC: National Academy Press.

[4] Brennan, K., & Resnick, M. (2012). New frameworks for studying and assessing the development of computational thinking. Paper presented at the *2012 Annual Meeting of the American Educational Research Association* (Vancouver, Canada, April 13-17).

[5] Brown, A., Allan, W., Coulter, B., Denner, J., Erickson, J., Lee, I., Malyn-Smith, J., and Martin, F. (2010). Computational thinking for youth. *White Paper for the ITEST Small Working Group on Computational Thinking (CT).*

[6] Burke, Q. and Kafai, Y.B. 2012. *The writers' workshop for youth programmers.* In *Proceedings of the 43rd SIGCSE Technical Symposium on Computer Science Education,* (Raleigh, NC February 29-March 03), ACM, New York, NY, 433-438.

[7] Ching, C., & Kafai, Y. 2008. Peer Pedagogy: Student collaboration and reflection in learning through design. *Teachers College Record*, 110, 12, 2601-2632.

[8] Cole, M. (2005). Cross-cultural and historical perspectives on the developmental consequences of education. *Human Development*, 48, 4, 195-216.

[9] Denner, J. and Werner, L. 2007. Computer programming in middle school: How pairs respond to challenges. *Journal of Education Computing Research*, 37, 2, 131-150.

[10] Gargarian, G. 1996. The art of design. In Y.B. Kafai, & M. Resnick (Eds.), *Constructionism in Practice: Designing Thinking, and Learning in a Digital World* (pp. 125-160). Mahwah, NJ: Lawrence Erlbaum.

[11] Gee, J. 2003. *What Video Games Teach Us about Learning and Literacy*. New York, NY: Palgrave.

[12] Harel, I. 1991. *Children Designers: Interdisciplinary Constructions for Learning and Knowing Mathematics in a Computer-rich School*. Norwood NJ, Ablex Publishing.

[13] Harel, I., and Papert, S. 1990. Software design as a learning environment. *Interactive Learning Environments,* 1, 1–32

[14] Noss, R. & Hoyles, C. 1996. *Windows on Mathematical Meanings: Learning Cultures and Computers*. Norwell, MA: Kluwer Academic Publishers.

[15] Ito, M., Baumer, S., Bittanti, M., boyd, d., Cody, R., Herr, B., Horst, H. A., Lange, P. G., Mahendran, D., Martinez, K., Pascoe, C. J., Perkel, D., Robinson, L., Sims, C., and Tripp, L. 2009. *Hanging Out, Messing Around, Geeking Out: Living and Learning with New Media.* Cambridge, MA: MIT Press.

[16] Jenkins, H. Clinton, K., Purushotma, R., Robison, A., & Weigel, M. (2006). Confronting the challenges of participation culture: Media education for the 21st century. White Paper. Chicago, IL: The John D. & Catherine T. MacArthur Foundation.

[17] Kafai, Y. B. 1995. *Minds in Play: Computer Game Design as a Context for Children's Learning*. Mahwah, NJ: Lawrence Erlbaum.

[18] Kafai, Y. B. 2005. The classroom as living laboratory: Design-based research for understanding, comparing, and evaluating learning science through design. *Educational Technology,* 45, 28–33.

[19] Kafai, Y., Fields, D., and Burke, W. 2010. Entering the clubhouse: Case studies of young programmers joining the online Scratch communities. *Journal of Organizational and End User Computing*. 22, 1, 21-35.

[20] Kafai, Y., Peppler, K.A., & Chapman, R. (Eds.). (2009). *The Computer Clubhouse. Creativity and Constructionism in Youth Communities*. New York, NY: Teachers College Press.

[21] Kelleher,C. and Pausch, R. 2005. Lowering the barriers to programming: A taxonomy of programming environments and languages for novice programmers. *ACM Computing Surveys*, 37, 2, 83-137.

[22] Kelleher, C. and Pausch, R. 2007. Using storytelling to motivate programming. *Communications of the ACM*, 50, 7, 58-64.

[23] Lave, J., and Wenger, E. 1991. *Situated Learning: Legitimate Peripheral Participation*. Cambridge, England: Cambridge University Press.

[24] Lessig, L. 2008. *Remix: Making Art and Commerce Thrive in a Hybrid Economy*. New York: Penguin Press.

[25] McGrath-Cohoon, J. and Asprey, W. (Eds.). 2006. *Women and Information Technology: Research on Under-representation*. Cambridge, MA: MIT Press.

[26] Monroy- Hernández, A. and Resnick, M. 2008. Empowering kids to create and share programmable media. *Interactions*, 15, 2, 50-53.

[27] Palumbo, D.B. 1990. Programming language/problem-solving research: A review of relevant issues. *Review of Educational Research*, 60, 1, 65–89.

[28] Papert, S. 1980. *Mindstorms: Children, Computers, and Powerful Ideas*. New York, NY: Basic Books.

[29] Papert, S. and Harel, I. 1991. *Situating Constructionsim.* Norwood, NJ: Ablex Publishing.

[30] Pea, R.D. and Kurland, D.M. 1983. Logo programming and the development of planning skills. Center for Children & Technology. New York, NY: Bank Street College.

[31] Perkel, D. 2008. "No I don't feel complimented".. *Digital Youth Research*, (February 6). Available at http://digitalyouth.ischool.berekley.edu/node/105.

[32] Repenning, A. and Ioannidou, A. 2008. Broadening participation through scalable game design. In *SIGCSE '08 Proceedings of the 39th SIGCSE Technical Symposium on Computer Science Education* (Portland, OR, March 12-15), ACM, New York, NY, 305-309.

[33] Resnick, M. and Silverman, B. 2005. Some reflections□on designing construction kits for kids. In *Proceedings of the 2005 Conference on Interaction Design and Children,* (Boulder, CO, June 05-08), ACM, New York, NY, 117-122.

[34] Resnick, M., Maloney, J., Hernández, A. M., Rusk, N., Eastmond, E., Brennan, K., Millner, A. D., Rosenbaum, E., Silver, J., Silverman, B., and Kafai, Y.B. 2009. Scratch: Programming for everyone. *Communications of the ACM,* 52, 11, 60-67.

[35] Schön, D. A. (1983). *The Reflective Practitioner*. New York, NY, Basic Books.

[36] Scribner, S. (1984). Literacy in three metaphors. *American Journal of Education*, 93, 1, 6-21.

[37] Shaffer, D. W. and Resnick, M. 1999. Thick authenticity: New media and authentic learning. *Journal of Interactive Learning Research,* 10, 2, 195-215.

[38] Soloway, E., Guzdial, M., and Hay, K. 1994. Learner-centered design: The challenge for HCI in the 21st century. *Interactions*, 1, 22, 36-48.

[39] Turkle, S. & Papert, S. 1990. Epistemological pluralism: Styles and voices within the computer culture. *Signs*, 16,1, 128-157.

[40] Webb, N. 1980. A process-outcome analysis of learning in group and individual settings. *Educational Psychologist*, 15, 69-83.

[41] Wing, J.M. 2006. Computational thinking. *Communications of the ACM*, 49, 3, 33-35.

[42] Wolber, D., Abelson, H., Spertus, E. and Looney, L. 2011. *App Inventor: Create Your Own Android Apps.* Sebastopol, CA: O'Reilly Media.

Accelerating K-12 Computational Thinking Using Scaffolding, Staging, and Abstraction

David S. Touretzky
Computer Science Department
Carnegie Mellon University
Pittsburgh, PA 15213
dst@cs.cmu.edu

Daniela Marghitu
Computer Science and Software Engineering
Auburn University
Auburn, AL 36849
marghda@auburn.edu

Stephanie Ludi
Dept. of Software Engineering
Rochester Institute of Technology
Rochester, NY 14623
salvse@rit.edu

Debra Bernstein
TERC
Cambridge, MA 02140
debra_bernstein@terc.edu

Lijun Ni
Georgia Inst. of Technology
Atlanta, GA 30332-0760
lijun@cc.gatech.edu

ABSTRACT

We describe a three-stage model of computing instruction beginning with a simple, highly scaffolded programming environment (Kodu) and progressing to more challenging frameworks (Alice and Lego NXT-G). In moving between frameworks, students explore the similarities and differences in how concepts such as variables, conditionals, and looping are realized. This can potentially lead to a deeper understanding of programming, bringing students closer to true computational thinking. Some novel strategies for teaching with Kodu are outlined. Finally, we briefly report on our methodology and select preliminary results from a pilot study using this curriculum with students ages 10–17, including several with disabilities.

Categories and Subject Descriptors

K.3.2 [**Computer and Information Science Eduation**]: Curriculum

General Terms

Design, Experimentation

Keywords

Kodu, Alice, robotics, computational thinking

1. INTRODUCTION

Highly scaffolded programming environments offer novices a smoother path to early success in computing [7], but their limited expressiveness must inevitably lead to their abandonment in favor of more powerful conventional languages.

SIGCSE'13, March 6–9, 2013, Denver, Colorado, USA.

We have developed a three-stage model of programming instruction for K-12 students that embraces these transitions between frameworks as part of the learning process. The model was built upon a three-step ladder model developed by Daniela Marghitu since 2005, in which students with varying abilities and experience levels could learn any of three software frameworks and progress at their own pace from one to another [12]. Our new curriculum specifies the ordering and guides students to make explicit analogies between frameworks to develop a deeper, more abstract understanding of fundamental computing concepts.

We conducted a pilot study using Microsoft Kodu [15], Alice [4], and Lego Mindstorms NXT-G [8] as the three stages of a five-day computer camp for 31 children ages 10-17. In this paper we describe our strategy for teaching programming using Kodu, including several innovative ideas that were developed in the course of the project. We also discuss some CS Unplugged-type enrichment activities [2] employed in the camp. We then describe how students transitioned from Kodu to Alice and NXT-G, and how we mapped concepts from one framework to another.

A key design goal for the curriculum was that it be accessible to a wide range of students, including those with disabilities. Our initial offering was not completely universal (e.g., Alice and Kodu cannot be used by students who are blind), but we were able to include students who were partially sighted or had other disabilities, as described in Section 6. We provided assistive technology and adjusted activities to ensure that students with disabilities had equal access to the tools, activities, and interactions that made up the curriculum [13]. Examples included large-print handouts and assessments, legible, high contrast Kodu and Alice worlds, and extra participant support for students who required more assistance. With these aids, the curriculum described here was used by all of the students in the camp.

2. DEEP & ABSTRACT UNDERSTANDING

If the goal of K-12 computing education is to teach students "computational thinking" [20, 21], how should that be facilitated? We believe mastery of computational thinking implies a deep and abstract understanding of the fundamental concepts of computing:

- **Deep:** the ability to recognize fundamental concepts instantiated in progamming contexts. For example, recogzning that a certain task inherently involves conditional execution, or looping, or parallelism, or persistent state.
- **Abstract:** separating the essence of a mechanism from mere syntactic details. For example, appreciating that WHEN/DO in Kodu, If/Then in Alice, and SWITCH blocks in NXT-G all function as *conditional expressions*, even though they look different.

We can promote this style of thinking by guiding students to draw analogies between different formalisms [3, 5]. We transition them betwen these formalisms in a carefully structured way. The increased complexity of instruction is mitigated by this scaffolding.

3. KODU INSTRUCTION STRATEGIES

Microsoft Kodu [15] is an icon-based programming framework designed to allow young children to construct their own computer games. Kodu employs many clever scaffolding mechanisms to keep novice programmers on track [10]. For example, students compose their programs, organized as sequences of WHEN/DO rules, by selecting icons from a context-sensitive menu, making syntax errors impossible. Rather than using named variables, Kodu uses *scores*, such as the "red score" and the "blue score," which children intuitively understand from playing computer games. (Students can actually program in Kodu using an Xbox game controller instead of a keyboard.) Assigning a value to a score automatically causes it to be displayed on the screen, eliminating the need for explicit output statements.

In the course of developing our curriculum, we had some insights into how to use Kodu more effectively to teach programming. We summarize these ideas here.

1. Start with programs in a pre-made world. Some Kodu tutorials begin by teaching the terrain editor and having students construct their own virtual world. But this activity takes significant time and can divert students from the central task of learning programming. We found it preferable to supply students with small worlds with prepositioned characters and objects. They did, however, work with the terrain editor during free exploration periods, and this contributed to their overall enjoyment of Kodu and provided an additional opportunity to practice new programming skills.

2. Show programs in textual form. Kodu programs are sequences of WHEN/DO rules. A rule is a string of tiles, each bearing a word and an icon, as in Figure 1.

Figure 1: A Kodu rule.

The first example code we show to students uses this iconic notation, but we immediately introduce equivalent textual notation, and quickly abandon the iconic version. The textual version is more compact, allowing more to fit on a page. But more importantly, it introduces students to the notion that the same idea can be expressed in multiple forms: a first step toward abstraction. They see sample code on the page in textual form, but when they enter it into the computer they see it in its iconic form.

3. Use parenthesized keywords to guide menu navigation. While Kodu's context-sensitive menus are helpful, the menu structure is deep enough that students may not know where to find a tile. For example, "move" is a top-level menu item, but "glow" is found in the "actions" submenu, while "vanish" is found in the "combat" submenu. The iconic representation of a tile does not indicate how to find it in the menu tree. We addressed this by including the submenus as parenthesized keywords in the textual notation, so the rule in Figure 1 would be written as:

`WHEN see apple close DO` *(actions)* `glow` *(colors)* `red`

4. Use arrows to help students interpret indentation. A Kodu rule can be linked to a preceding rule by indenting it. The linked rule will be considered for execution only if the parent rule's WHEN clause is satisfied. If the linked rule has a non-empty WHEN clause, this mechanism creates a conjunctive test. If the parent rule has a non-empty DO clause, this mechanism creates a compound action. But as Jill Denner of ETR Associates has observed (personal communication), indentation has no inherent significance to young readers and does not imply any sort of attachment relation. Indentation has also been found to be problematic for beginning Python programmers [9]. This is an instance where Kodu's graphical notation fails to scaffold student understanding.

This deficiency could easily be remedied by tweaking Kodu's graphical user interface. In our textual version, we solved the problem by introducing an arrow icon that links an indented rule to its parent, as shown in Figure 2.

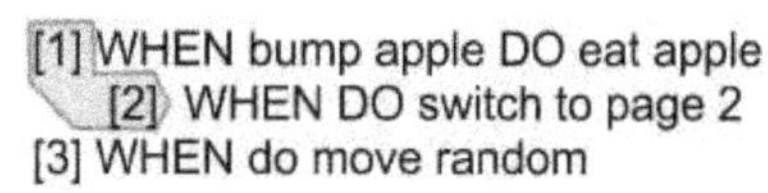

Figure 2: Graphic aid for illustrating how indentation links a rule to its parent rule above.

5. Teach state machines; explicitly identify states with pages. Kodu programs are organized as pages of rules, with all the rules on a page applying simultaneously. Thus, the most general way for a character to change its behavior is to switch to another page. We introduce students to the concept of state machines as a way of reasoning about program behavior, with each page corresponding to a state node [17]. We support this with a CS Unplugged-type activity described in Section 4. State machines are particularly helpful for teaching students about loops.

The Kodu editor displays the page number in a unique color: blue for page 1, green for page 2. etc. We use these same colors for nodes in our state machine diagrams, reinforcing the correspondence between nodes and pages. Instructions to switch pages form the links between nodes.

6. Have the kodu change color to indicate what page it's on. When creating complex behaviors that loop between pages (states), it's helpful to know a character's current page in order to understand its behavior. We established a convention that the first rule on every page would set the kodu's color to the page's color. We used this convention to frame questions about program state such as "Why did the kodu turn red when it bumped the tree?"

7. Distinguish implicit from explicit looping. The Kodu interpreter repeatedly executes all applicable rules on the current page. This can result in *implicit looping* behavior with no use of control structure primitives. For example, the following program loops forever:

```
[1] WHEN DO score red 1 point
```

Kodu's movement actions, such as *move toward,* are incremental; the programmer relies on implicit looping to repeat the actions until a goal is met. For example, to move the kodu toward a tree and then go do something else when the tree is reached, one would write an implicit loop with a termination test that exits the page:

```
[1] WHEN see tree DO move toward
[2] WHEN bump tree DO switch to page 2
```

Implicit looping cannot be used when the loop body contains actions requiring complex sequencing or nested iteration. In this case one must use what we call *explicit looping,* where the program explicitly switches back and forth between the loop's control page and its body pages, which may contain their own implicit or explicit loops.

We introduced the concept of implicit looping to make *explicit* to students the way that Kodu interprets their programs. Students also learn to override implicit looping using the *once* tile, e.g., the following program does not loop:

```
[1] WHEN DO score red 1 point once
```

Drawing a distinction between implicit and explicit looping helps students develop a more abstract understanding of the loop construct by seeing it implemented in two different forms.

8. Provide graphical notation to highlight implicit and explicit looping. Explicit looping is easy to identify in a state machine diagram because the relevant state nodes form a loop in the graph [17]. We go further and label state nodes with their function in the loop: initialization, loop logic (including termination test), loop body, and wrap-up. The latter refers to actions taken after exiting the loop. Not every loop has separate pages for all four of these functions. But students are taught that explicit loops by definition involve page switching, and hence, loops in the state machine diagram.

Because implicit loops confine the body and loop logic to a single page, we introduced an extension to the standard state machine notation to distinguish those pages: a semicircular arrow appearing inside a state node, as in Figure 3.

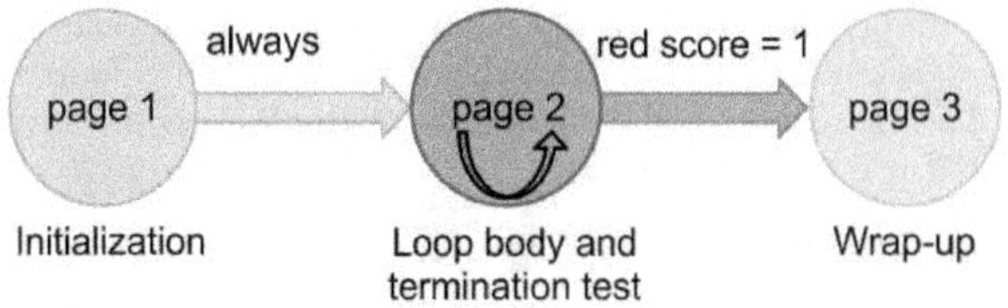

Figure 3: State machine diagram with added arrow indicating implicit looping within a page (state).

There are several conditions under which a page does not implicitly loop. For example, if every rule contains a *once* tile, or if execution of the page always includes a *switch to page* action. In one exercise, students were asked to go through a complex Kodu program and mark on their state machine diagram the pages that do contain implicit loops.

9. Teach bugs explicitly by giving them names and showing sample code. A *program structure* bug could result from incorrect indentation, which changes the dependency relationship between rules. An *order of operations* bug could result from swapping two rules, because in the event of conflicting actions, Kodu gives priority to the lower numbered rule. *Loop initialization* and *loop termination* bugs are straightforward. In the Alice component we introduced the *fencepost error* bug and the *divide by zero* bug.

A series of pins with cartoon bugs illustrated these six bug types. Students earned bug pins by successfully completing bug-related exercises, such as deliberately introducing a bug of the specified type, demonstrating its effects to the instructor, then fixing it.

4. CS UNPLUGGED-TYPE ACTIVITIES

Computer Science Unplugged is a series of activities developed by Bell et al. in which students use their bodies or simple props to simulate algorithms illustrating important computer science concepts [2]. Hence, no computers are involved. This type of kinesthetic learning is fun for students across a broad age range, and has proven effective for reaching students with disabilities [14]. We used three such activities in our summer camp. Two were of our own design; the third came directly from the CS Unplugged book [2].

In the first activity, students hand-simulated the execution of a Kodu program containing two characters: a kodu and an exploding mine. We created a large poster of the state machine for the program that was placed on the floor, and used chess pieces (a white pawn and a black pawn) to track the states of the two characters. We also laid out a map of the Kodu world on the floor, and placed hand-made kodu and mine characters on the map, moving them as the simulation progressed. The kodu character included a rotating mechanism that could be used to change its color. The mine could glow various colors, and we used little flags on stick-pins to simulate that. Students shared the tasks of deciding which rules were able to execute on the current cycle, moving the kodu's pawn when a state change occurred, and moving the kodu and the mine characters around on the map. The exercise reinforced students' understanding of the Kodu rule execution mechanism, including such fairly advanced topics as implicit looping and priority arbitration.

In the second activity, students simulated a bubble sort as an introduction to nested loops and a hint at arrays. (There are no arrays in Kodu, and we did not cover Alice arrays due to time limitations.) Ten students formed a line and each held a card containing a number. Another group acted as sorters. With square dance music playing and the audience encouraged to clap along, the instructor acted as "caller". On each pass, a sorter would start at the left edge of the line, examine the first pair of numbers, and give one of two instructions: "bow to your partner" if the numbers were in the correct order, or "switch with your partner" if the two should switch places. The sorter then advanced to the next pair. As students became proficient at sorting, we sped up the pace, which increased the entertainment value.

The final activity, which came during the Alice portion of the camp, was the network sorting activity from the CS Unplugged book. We laid out a six-element sorting network on the floor, and students moved synchronously through the stages of the network, arriving at the output stage in sorted order. This allowed us to make some interesting comparisons between the two sorting algorithms, e.g., the sorting network requires fewer comparisons than a bubble sort would use.

5. CONCEPTUAL MAPPING

The first two days of the camp were devoted to Kodu, the next two days to Alice (occasionally looking back at Kodu for comparison), and the final day to NXT-G. In this section we discuss the conceptual mapping between Kodu, Alice, and NXT-G that we guided students to develop through direct instruction, group discussion, and exercises.

5.1 Objects

Both Kodu and Alice have named objects ("characters" in Kodu), but Alice objects can have nested components, such as body parts. Also, Alice objects are organized in a tree for convenient inspection, while Kodu objects must be accessed at their location in the world. Alice objects have named user-defined methods that take optional parameters, while Kodu only provides numbered pages. Kodu's simplicity is a deliberate attempt to protect beginners from being overwhelmed by too many details. As students become more comfortable with programming they can learn new constructs such as parameterized methods.

5.2 Variables

Kodu uses predefined *scores* as variables, while Alice has conventional named and type variables. This is one of the areas where trading simplicity for power is evident. Using variables in Kodu is effortless. In Alice it takes some work, since one must first explicitly create the variable and assign it a name and initial value, and take additional steps to display its value. But the benefit of descriptive names soon becomes evident as programs with multiple variables are introduced. VARIABLE blocks in NXT-G are similar to Alice's named and typed variables.

5.3 Conditionals

Since the only Kodu statement is the WHEN/DO rule, every line of a Kodu program is a conditional. Alice also has WHEN/DO rules, mainly used to respond to events such as mouse clicks on objects or single-character keyboard input. We start students out using these events very early, and the analogy with Kodu is immediately apparent. Alice WHEN/DO rules can also include arbitrary expressions as conditions, but since they run asynchronously and in a global context (no access to local variables), they cannot replace the conventional If/Then, which Alice also provides.

We introduce If/Then statements later in the curriculum, after methods, functions, predicates, and parallelism have all been covered. We also introduce If/Then/Else, and explore with the students how this logic can be implemented in Kodu using a pair of WHEN/DO rules with opposite conditions. In NXT-G, the SWITCH block implements If/Then/Else.

5.4 Parallelism

Kodu uses a unique form of parallel execution. All the rules on a page evaluate their conditions simultaneously. Then actions take effect sequentially, and in the event of conflicting actions, the lower numbered rule has priority. So, for example, if one applicable rule moves the kodu north but a later rule that also has a true condition moves it south, the kodu will move north. This can be useful for creating default behaviors whose action will be taken only if no earlier rule is eligible to fire, e.g.:

```
[1] WHEN see apple DO move towards
[2] WHEN DO move random
```

Because all rule evaluations are completed first in Kodu instead of being interleaved with the actions, a rule's action cannot affect the ability of later rules to fire on the same cycle. This can lead to unexpected behavior if the programmer has an incorrect model of the execution cycle. (One of the authors actually experienced this bug.) For example, given that scores are initialized to zero, the following code fragment sets the red score to 5 but also switches to page 2 even though the second rule appears to guard against that:

```
[1] WHEN DO score red 5 points
[2] WHEN scored red 0 points DO switch to page 2
```

In Alice, sequential execution is the norm; parallelism must be explicitly requested via a Do Together block, and there is no conflict resolution mechanism. We examine this difference with the students, comparing Kodu code with Alice code for the same task. NXT-G also provides for explicit parallelism via a "sequence beam", but we did not cover this due to lack of time.

5.5 Looping

Looping in Kodu is both simpler and more difficult than in Alice. Implicit loops occur automatically in Kodu unless blocked by *once* tiles or a page switch. But explicit looping requires at least two page switches, which are the Kodu equivalent of the dreaded "go to". There is also no notion of an associated index variable, so variable updating and testing must be done explicitly. In contrast, Alice's "Loop n times" statement handles all those details invisibly, but also allows the index variable to be exposed if desired. Alice also provides a conventional While loop.

When teaching explicit looping in Kodu we identify four loop components: initialization, loop logic (including termination test), body, and wrap-up. Each of these goes on a separate page, although it is sometimes possible to fit two components on the same page if the required actions are simple enough. When teaching Alice's Loop construct, we expose the loop details and point out how the first three loop components, which make up the loop proper, are realized by this single Loop statement. We also show students Kodu code to implement a specific Alice loop they've studied, to reinforce the mapping between the two formalisms.

NXT-G offers a LOOP block with a variety of options that can cause it to function like either a For or a While loop. As in Alice (but not Kodu), the body of the loop is physically nested inside the block.

5.6 States

We've identified states with pages in Kodu, glossing over the parallelism and implicit looping within. The sequential execution model in Alice suggests that each statement could be regarded as a state, but since Alice statements can nest, the mapping is not quite that straightforward. Due to lack of time, we did not introduce a new graphical notation in the Alice segment, but were we to do so, we would use flowchart notation. The major difference with state machines is that in a flowchart, the boolean expression component of a conditional or loop is depicted as a separate node.

NXT-G has semantics similar to Alice (sequential execution by default, and nesting components), but its graphical layout more closely resembles a state machine. However, NXT-G uses "wires" between "ports" to transmit parameter values between blocks. These extra links distinguish the graph from a pure state machine graph.

6. THE PILOT STUDY

We conducted a five day CS4All summer camp at Auburn University in July 2012. Students were recruited from schools in Alabama and Georgia, and ranged in age from 10 to 17, with a mean age of 13.1. A total of 31 students participated; 13 were female. Seven of the students self-identified as having one or more of the following disabilities: visual impairment (VI), Asperger's syndrome (Asp), cerebral palsy (CP), or dyslexia. The distribution of ages and genders was: 10 (M, Asp), 12 (F, VI), 13 (M, VI), 14 (M, dyslexia), 15 (M, Asp), 16 (F, CP with VI), 17 (F, VI).

Students each had their own computer, but were organized in groups of 3-5 overseen by one or two instructors. Instructors were mainly CS graduate students, plus two CS/ECE undergraduates, several of the authors, and two undergraduate instructional aides from the Auburn University Special Education and Rehabilitation Department. Students worked for seven hours each day, including time for unplugged activities and free exploration.

7. EVALUATION

We conducted an evaluation of the pilot summer camp, focusing on participant outcomes in two primary areas: knowledge development and attitudes. Knowledge development was measured using two short surveys and one programming task. The first Kodu assessment focused on participants' understanding of state machines and the relationship between program state and program output. In the second Kodu assessment, we asked students to program loops. Our analysis of their programs focuses on inclusion of critical loop components (e.g., loop initialization, loop body, and termination test). The Alice assessment focused primarily on students' understanding of relationships within Alice, understanding of core concepts, and ability to draw comparisons between Kodu and Alice. Participant attitudes were assessed using an attitude survey developed by Heersink and Moskal [6]. The attitude survey was administered on days 1 (pre) and 5 (post) of the camp. Participants' overall reactions to the pilot curriculum were collected via written survey at the end of the camp.

This paper presents preliminary findings from the post-camp survey. Analysis of the knowledge surveys, programming task, and attitude assessments are underway.

Participant reactions to camp activities were collected via an 18-question written survey administered on the last day of the camp. This survey included closed- and open-ended questions about participants' enjoyment of camp activities, their intentions to continue using the programming environments introduced during the camp, and whether they had taken steps to make those environments available at home.

Participants' reactions to the summer camp were generally positive, with the majority reporting that they enjoyed the camp, learned a lot, and would recommend it to their friends. See Table 1. (Participants responded to a 5-point scale. However, the end points have been collapsed for ease of presentation.)

Table 1: Participants' reactions.

	n	Disagree; Strongly Disagree	Neut.	Agree; Strongly Agree
I enjoyed participating in this camp.	28	14%	7%	79%
I would recomend this camp to my friends.	29	10%	34%	55%
I learned a lot about computer programming at this camp.	29	17%	10%	72%

When asked whether they would continue to use the programming environments introduced during the camp, nearly half of the participants said they would "probably" or "absolutely" use Kodu, with an additional 25% saying they "might" do so. Fewer reported that they would use Alice after the camp ended. The majority of participants (71%) said they would "probably" or "absolutely" want to continue programming robots if they had access to a robotics kit like Lego Mindstorms (see Table 2).

Table 2: Participants' intent to continue.

Response	Kodu	Alice	Robotics
I absolutely will not	11%	25%	0%
I probably will not	18%	14%	11%
I might	25%	29%	18%
I probably will	21%	25%	25%
I absolutely will	25%	7%	46%

More than half of the participants planned to install Kodu (61%) or Alice (50%) on computers at home. 36% reported that they currently had access to a Lego NXT kit either at home or at school, and an additional 29% reported that they planned to get one.

8. LESSONS LEARNED

The 2012 summer camp was an experiment to test the idea that explicitly transitioning students from more scaffolded to less scaffolded frameworks was feasible and beneficial. An extensive amount of data was collected and is presently being analyzed to determine what students actually learned. However, we can make a few preliminary observations here.

Beginning students sometimes find the Alice interface intimidating due to the multiple panes and tabs. There is a fair amount of typing (e.g., method names, variable names, and numeric values), vs. no typing at all in Kodu except to make a character "speak". And Alice's drag-and-drop editing interface is not entirely intuitive. Based on our experience in previous camps, we expected students to take to

Kodu quickly because of its simpler interface. As predicted, once students mastered the ideas of programming characters in a simulated world and switching between editing and execution modes, the transition to Alice went smoothly.

NXT-G has semantics sufficiently so close to Alice, and its graphical interface so closely resembles a state machine diagram, that students took to it immediately. Working with physical robots is exciting for students [1, 16], and their enthusiasm was reflected in the survey responses.

But NXT-G is not the ideal choice for the third stage of the framework precisely because it adds little beyond what students have encountered in Alice. Introducing students to robot programming is still a good idea, but at least with older students, it could be better done using more sophisticated robots and a more powerful programming formalism. During the camp we gave students a chance to teleoperate a Calliope5KP robot developed at Carnegie Mellon [19] that features a five degree-of-freedom arm with gripper and a Kinect camera on a pan/tilt mount. Students were fascinated by the robot and eager to learn more about it.

9. FUTURE WORK

Our pilot curriculum was compressed and covered a limited set of topics due to time constraints. To apply our ideas in a year-long or multi-year computer science course, and ensure that students fully master the concepts, will require considerable additional work. As we move forward we will be assessing the frameworks used in the pilot study. Scratch [11] might be an attractive alternative to Alice.

We would also like to develop an alternative robotics curriculum for high school students using the Tekkotsu software framework [18] and robots similar to the Calliope series. Tekkotsu is based on C++ and includes modules for computer vision, landmark-based navigation, and manipulation. This would make the third stage of our model a significant advance toward college-level programming. For younger students, NXT-G's limitations aside, it at least allows them to see familiar programming constructs in a novel form, facilitating a more abstract understanding.

10. ACKNOWLEDGMENTS

This work was funded by National Science Foundation awards CNS-1151542, CNS-1151713, CNS-1151980, and CNS-1152003. We thank our camp instructors T. Ben Brahim, J., Weaver, Y. Rawajfih, E. Banu, S. Kulkarni, C. Stephens, Y. Tiang, C. Cira, A. Jain, A. Marshall, and G. Leung.

11. REFERENCES

[1] Barker, B. S., and Ansorge, J. (2007) Robotics as a means to increase achievement scores in an informal learning environment. Journal of Research on Technology in Education, 39(3):229–243.

[2] Bell, T., Witten, I. H., and Fellows, M. (2010) Computer Sciene Unplugged. Available at <http://csunplugged.org/books>.

[3] Bransford, J.D., Brown, A. L., and Cocking, R.R. eds. (2000) How People Learn: Brain, Mind, Experience, and School. Washington, D.C.: National Academy Press

[4] Dann, W. P., Cooper, S., and Pausch, R. (2008) Learning to Program with Alice (2nd Edition). Prentice-Hall.

[5] Gentner, D., Loewenstein, J., and Thompson, L. (2003) Learning and transfer: A general role for analogical encoding. Journal of Educational Psychology, 95(2):393–408.

[6] Heersink, D., and Moskal, B. M. (2010) Measuring high school students' attitudes toward computing. *Proc. SIGCSE'10*, 446–450.

[7] Kelleher, C., & Pausch, R. (2005). Lowering the barriers to programming: A taxonomy of programming environments and languages for novice programmers. ACM Computing Surveys, 37(2), 83–137.

[8] Kelly, J. (2010) LEGO Mindstorms NXT-G Programming Guide. New York, NY: APress.

[9] Konidari, E. and Louridas, P. (2010) When students are not programmers. ACM Inroads 1(1):55–60.

[10] McLaurin, M. (2011) The design of Kodu: A tiny visual programming language for children on the Xbox 360. Proceedings of POPL-11.

[11] Maloney, J., Resnick, M., Rusk, N., Silverman, B., Eastmond, E. (2010) The Scratch programming language and environment. ACM Transactions on Computing Education, November 2010.

[12] Marghitu, D., Ben Brahim, T., Rawajfih, Y., Weaver, J., and Shanahan, J. (2010) Auburn University K-12 inclusive STEM outreach programs. SDPS 2010 Conference, June 6–9, 2010, Dallas, TX USA.

[13] Marghitu, D. (2012) Auburn University K-12 Inclusive STEM Outreach Programs. SIGCSE 2012 workshop slides available at <https://fp.auburn.edu/comp2000/SIGCSE2012_AccessComputingWorkshop.htm>.

[14] Marghitu, D., Bell, T., et al. (2009) Using virtual worlds to engage typical and special needs students in kinesthetic computer science activities: A Computer Science Unplugged case study. AACE EdMedia 2009 Conference, June 22–26, 2009, Honolulu, HI, USA.

[15] Microsoft Kodu Game Lab. Available at <http://www.kodugamelab.com/About>.

[16] Nugent, G., Barker, B., Grandgenett, N., and Adamchuk, V. I. (2010) Impact of robotics and geospatial technology interventions on youth STEM learning and attitudes. Journal of Research on Technology in Education, 42(4), 391–408.

[17] Stolee, K. T., and Fristoe, T. (2011) Expressing computer science concepts through Kodu Game Lab. *Proc. SIGCSE'11*, pp. 99–104.

[18] Touretzky, D. S. (2010) Preparing computer science students for the robotics revolution. Communications of the ACM, 53(8):27–29.

[19] Touretzky, D. S., Watson, O., Allen, C. S., and Russell, R. J. (2010) Calliope: Mobile manipulation from commodity components. In A. Thomaz and M. D. Anderson (Eds.), Papers from the 2010 AAAI Robot Workshop. Technical report WS-10-09. Menlo Park, CA: AAAI Press.

[20] Wilson, et al. (2010). Running On Empty: The Failure to Teach K–12 Computer Science in the Digital Age. Association for Computing Machinery, 2010. Available at <http://www.acm.org/runningonempty/>.

[21] Wing, J. M. (2006) Computational thinking. Communications of the ACM 49(3):33–35.

Girls on the Go: A CS Summer Camp to Attract and Inspire Female High School Students

Janet E. Burge, Gerald C. Gannod
Miami University
205 Benton Hall
Oxford Ohio, 45056
+1 513-529-0347
burgeje@muohio.edu;
gannodg@muohio.edu

Maureen Doyle
Department of Computer Science
Northern Kentucky University
Highland Heights, KY 41099
(859) 572-5468
doylem3@nku.edu

Karen C. Davis
School of Electronic and Computing Systems
University of Cincinnati
Cincinnati, OH 45221-0030
+1 513-556-2214
karen.davis@uc.edu

ABSTRACT
In this paper, we describe our experience running "Girls on the Go: The Mobile Computing College Experience." We decided to do a residential summer camp for HS-age girls to achieve two goals: to encourage our campers to attend college and to interest them in computer science as a possible career option. We centered the camp around the design of a zoo-themed research tool where campers designed a mobile application to be used by researchers to document and study animal behavior. Post-camp surveys gave statistically significant results indicating that the camp increased the girls' confidence in performing computer science and understanding what computer scientists did.

Categories and Subject Descriptors
K3.2 [**Computers and Education**]: Computers and Information Science Education – *computer science education, information systems education, self-assessment.*

Keywords
Summer Camps, Recruiting Women, Mobile Application Development

1. INTRODUCTION
The low number of women studying computer science (CS) has been a concern for many years. One approach that many institutions have taken towards increasing interest in computer science is to offer summer camps. In this paper, we describe our experience running "Girls on the Go: The Mobile Computing College Experience." This camp took place in the summer of 2012, offered free of charge, and was attended by 25 high school girls. The camp was held at Miami University but was a collaboration between three institutions: Miami University (MU), Northern Kentucky University (NKU), and University of Cincinnati (UC).

We decided to do a residential summer camp for HS-age girls to achieve two goals: to encourage our campers to attend college and to interest them in computer science as a possible career option. Our camp was aimed at encouraging interest in CS in several ways. First, we wanted to make it clear to the campers that CS had many interesting applications, involved creativity and inquiry, and that computer scientists are not solitary programmers coding away in cubicles in isolation. We did this by centering the camp around the design of a zoo-themed research tool where campers designed a mobile application to be used by researchers to document and study animal behavior. Part of the design process included a visit to the Cincinnati Zoo where the girls performed studies (called ethograms) using pencil and paper to help design requirements for the application. We also highlighted the importance of computing to everyday life by focusing on mobile application development. Finally, we provided the opportunity for the girls to interact with female computer scientists working in a variety of application areas ranging from education to patent law.

In addition to encouraging interest in CS, we also wanted to give our campers a taste of college life and help them prepare to apply to college. The campers and their parents were provided information about all three universities and all three contributed both personnel and funds to run the camp to supplement NSF-provided funding for camp expenses and equipment.

The following sections describe the camp and its outcomes in more detail. Section 2 outlines related work, Section 3 describes the design of the camp, Section 4 presents an evaluation of camp outcomes, strengths, and lessons learned. Section 5 suggests some future work and Section 6 provides a summary and conclusions.

2. RELATED WORK
Many institutions are conducting summer camps to promote STEM fields. An examination of the most recent ASEE Annual Conference alone contains 37 papers that describe or mention summer camps. In our literature search we were not able to find papers describing other camps that taught mobile application development exclusively to HS girls. Here we describe camps that were similar to ours in either addressing the same population (early HS, girls only) or the same application area (mobile application development).

University of Waterloo conducted residential CS camps for girls that targeted students in the same age range as our camp with similar goals, including introducing students to university life and providing role models [1]. Their camps were structured to allow students to switch between programming (in Tcl/Tk) and digital hardware. The Girls' POWER (Programming Of the WEb

Rocks!) Summer Program, held at the University of Delaware [2] was an eight-week, half-day program that focused on web programming. The students were paid a stipend of $1000 for completing the program. Stipends were also used by the University of New Mexico to attract students to their Young Women in Computing Program [3]. This program lasted five weeks in the summer and then continued into the school year with monthly Friday afternoon meetings with social activities and speakers. The University of Denver held a two week residential Summer Women's Game Camp [4] that used their P4Games curriculum and the Greenfoot programming environment. Survey results showed an increase in both interest in computer science and confidence in programming ability.

Mobile application development is newer and less common than other technologies used in camps. App Inventor, initially developed by Google and now supported by MIT (http://appinventor.mit.edu) has been used in several camps. Georgia Tech taught App Inventor in one of their on-going summer one-week day-camps [5]. These are mixed gender camps (20.8% women in 2011) taught by local teachers who attended teacher workshops. Valdosta University conducted two summer camps [6] that used Android App Inventor and Lego NXT. They surveyed the students to see if there was an increased interest in computing with mixed results--one camp showed a slight increase, the other a slight decrease. Interest in computing was already high when the students started. Their paper did not describe the gender composition of their camp. Sewell and Ringenberg [7] implemented camps and workshops on mobile application development at the University of Michigan for HS students at different levels. All of their participants were underrepresented minorities or females.

3. GIRLS ON THE GO: THE MOBILE COMPUTING COLLEGE EXPERIENCE

Our summer camp was run by four tenured faculty instructors, two from Miami, one from NKU, and one from UC and three undergraduate, assisted by one additional adult (a woman who also holds a Ph.D. in CS) and four undergraduate student counselors, two from Miami and two from NKU. Our campers were recruited through a combination of personal contacts at local schools and e-mail addresses of students who had already expressed interest in Miami. Local schools where we had contacts were strongly represented but we also had several campers who travelled more than five hours to attend the camp. Our original goal was to have twenty campers. We ended up with 27 applications and 25 attendees. The camp was one week long and was preceded by two days of training for instructors and counselors. The following sections describe key features of our camp.

3.1 Design

Early in the planning process we decided on four features that drove our camp design:

1. Mobile application development. One of the reasons stated for a lack of interest in computer science is a perception that it does not have "real-world context" [8]. Many computer camps focus on game development or robotics but we chose to focus on building mobile applications. We felt that the pervasiveness of mobile technology would help underscore the impact of computing on real-life. Each camper was issued an iPod Touch to use for the duration of the camp and was encouraged to experiment with them by downloading apps to use outside of scheduled camp activities.

2. Zoo-themed application development. We wanted to highlight the variety of application domains where computer scientists might work by having the campers apply computing to an area that we thought would be appealing to our campers--studying animals. We leveraged an on-going partnership with the Cincinnati Zoo and Botanical Gardens to bring our campers to the zoo during the camp. The goal was to show the girls that they could use a computer science degree to work in many different domains and that one of the advantages of being a computer scientist was having that career flexibility. We suspect the zoo theme also helped in recruiting campers who might not otherwise be interested in a computing camp.

3. Residential college experience. While many camps are day-camps, which can keep the cost down, we wanted the camp to feel like a camp, not a class. We also wanted to make it available to campers from a variety of backgrounds and locations. Transportation to and from a day camp was likely to be problematic for many campers. We found that the college experience was a big part of the draw for many of the camp applicants.

4. Early HS. We decided to aim our camp at the early HS level by recruiting campers who had just finished their freshman and sophomore years (14-16 years in age). Our hope was that they were early enough in the decision-making process so that they would be open to computer science as an alternative yet also at the point where they could use the information about admissions provided as part of the camp. Many of them already had strong opinions on what they wanted to study in college but we also know from our own personal experience that goals change, even after starting college courses so we viewed that as an opportunity, not an obstacle.

3.2 Camp Activities

The camp was a mixture of technical, informational and social activities meant to mirror an ideal balance of the college experience. Our sessions throughout the week were as follows:

Sessions on CS careers. On the first day of camp we had an introductory session where we asked the girls to form teams and list their impressions of computer science and to provide a list of questions for us. Two of the three female instructors had significant industry experience prior to starting their academic careers and were able to give brief descriptions of their experience. On the last evening of the camp we invited six women working at local companies to conduct a "speed mentoring" session where we rotated groups of campers for eight minute discussions with each mentor. This allowed the girls to ask questions in a small-group session and to learn about a variety of computing careers. We had the speed mentoring sessions prior to dinner with the mentors to encourage continued interaction.

Sessions on Design. Rather than just focusing on programming, we chose to employ a "design-first" approach for app development. In particular, our approach was to provide a big picture view of app development that included problem analysis and interaction design. To facilitate this, our first technical session of the week involved having the students learn how to create app mockups using online tools. For this activity, the students created mockups for a fictitious "Shoe App" suggested by a character from the popular television show *The Big Bang Theory*. In this activity, students first brainstormed features using the KJ Method [9], with the primary features of the app being taken from the affinity groups. Next, students used an iPhone Mockup tool [10] to design the screens to be used for the app. Finally, all the groups presented their results back to the larger group for discussion and evaluation.

Education on the Domain. Part of our goal was to provide campers with an experience that closely models the college experience. In particular, we were interested in having the students work on a significant problem throughout the week (rather than just a simple toy problem). We arrived at the idea of developing an app for supporting ethology (e.g., the study of animal behaviors). In the second half of the first day of the camp, students received instruction from staff at Project Dragonfly (http://www.projectdragonfly.org) on how to observe animal behaviors and design ethograms. On Day 2 of the camp, students, instructors, and counselors visited the Cincinnati Zoo and Botanical Gardens to gain first-hand experience on the difficulties related to performing ethograms. Ultimately, the goal was to have the campers immersed in the problem and thus base their app design activity on experience rather than just classroom work. As we did with the "Shoe App," we had the campers brainstorm and mockup the design of an "Ethogram App."

iBooks Author. To document their experiences during the camp, we had the campers use iBooks Author to create Apple iBooks. We had students use iBooks Author for two activities: to capture their trip to the Cincinnati Zoo, and to document the wireframe of the Ethogram App.

Mobile App Development with Titanium. Many of the campers had little or no previous exposure to programming. Rather than using native development with Objective-C or Java, we chose to use the Appcelerator Titanium cross-platform development environment (www.appcelerator.com). For our audience, the advantages of this platform were two-fold. First, by using a cross-platform environment we were ensured that all of the campers would be able to leave the camp and be able to develop apps using resources available to them. As such, regardless of whether campers had access to Mac or PC platforms they would be able to develop apps when they returned home. Second, the Titanium platform uses a mixture of Javascript, CSS, and HTML for programming, thus providing a gentler path to programming. For teaching programming, we used a hybrid teaching style that included the use of online videos made available on YouTube, and laboratory exercises that brought the students from "zero-to-app" with little effort. Many campers were able to use the instructional videos to create apps that incorporated animation, navigation, color, and other advanced app features. While the campers did not create the Ethogram app in whole, many did use the lab time to develop various screens for the app.

Sessions about College. One of our goals was to design a camp that went beyond just teaching programming but also helped prepare the campers for applying to college. It was clear that even though these students were just starting high school they were already interested in learning about application and entrance requirements, as well as opportunities for scholarships and financial aid. The admissions session was very lively and filled with questions. The campers also attended a session on first year programs and went on a campus tour of the host institution.

Social Activities. In order to provide balance to the experience, we organized a number of social activities for the campers.. The first evening had them baking cookies in the dorm kitchen as campers arrived. The second evening was a game night. This activity was also attended by the children of two of the instructors. The third evening, after the day at the zoo, was a movie night. One instructor brought his five children, making it another family affair. The fourth evening was intended to be social but the campers all wanted more lab time to work on their iBooks and apps. The last night of camp was the speed mentoring, followed by a catered dinner and a chance to explore a bit of the downtown of the host institution. The campers also self-organized their own "end-of-camp" celebration, which demonstrated, in our opinion, that they had the makings of a community.

4. EVALUATION

4.1 Survey Results

In order to study the impact of the summer camp, we administered pre-camp and post-camp surveys. In the pre-camp survey, a number of questions were used to identify campers' usage of technology and measure basic mathematics and algorithmic skills. In addition, we asked students to rate their about **attitudes** towards computing such as "Generally, I feel ***secure*** about attempting X," "X is very ***useful*** to me," and "I am sure I can do ***advanced work*** in X," where X is either *science, mathematics, engineering,* or *computer science.* In addition, we asked the students to rate the following:

- I have a good understanding of what computer scientists do.
- Computer science is relevant to real world issues.

Students were asked to rate each on a Likert scale (1 - strongly disagree, 3 - neutral, 5 - strongly agree). Finally, we asked students to indicate if they would consider a particular **discipline** as a major when they enter college. We measured this series of questions using a three-valued Likert scale (1 - no, 2 - maybe, 3 - yes). In the post-camp survey, in addition to having the campers rate their experience, we repeated the attitude and disciplines sections of the pre-camp survey.

4.1.1 Responses

Campers were female and primarily Caucasian/White (18/25). The remaining participants were African American (3), Asian (3), or self-classified as Other (1). The surveys were administered on the first and last days of the camp. Each response was coded so that the pre- and post-responses could be paired for a *t-test*.

Table 1. Survey Results - Aggregate Summary

SD – Strongly Disagree, N – Neutral, SA – Strongly Agree

	Pre-Camp					Post-Camp					
	SD	D	N	A	SA	SD	D	N	A	SA	p
Computer Science											
Secure	2	3	7	10	3	0	3	5	11	6	0.046*
Useful	0	0	5	13	7	0	1	5	10	9	1.000
Advanced Work	1	0	14	8	2	2	1	7	8	7	0.129
Understand CS	0	3	8	14	0	0	0	0	18	7	0.00005****
Real-world Utility	0	1	4	12	8	0	2	2	8	13	0.233
Mathematics											
Secure	0	1	1	17	6	0	1	2	11	11	0.356
Useful	0	0	2	11	12	0	0	1	9	15	0.043*
Advanced Work	0	1	4	11	9	0	0	7	10	8	0.647
Science											
Secure	0	3	6	6	10	0	0	5	7	13	0.002***
Useful	0	0	1	10	14	0	0	1	8	16	0.491
Advanced Work	0	1	6	9	9	0	0	5	9	11	0.096

Table 2(a) – I feel secure about attempting CS

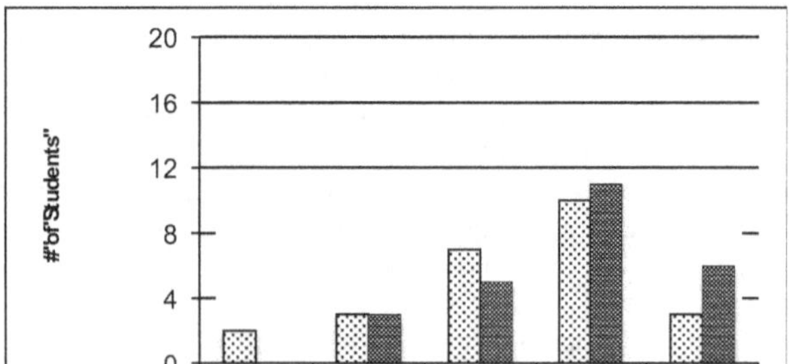

	SD	D	N	A	SA
Pre-Camp	2	3	7	10	3
Post-camp	0	3	5	11	6

Table 2(b) – I have a good understanding of what Computer Scientists do

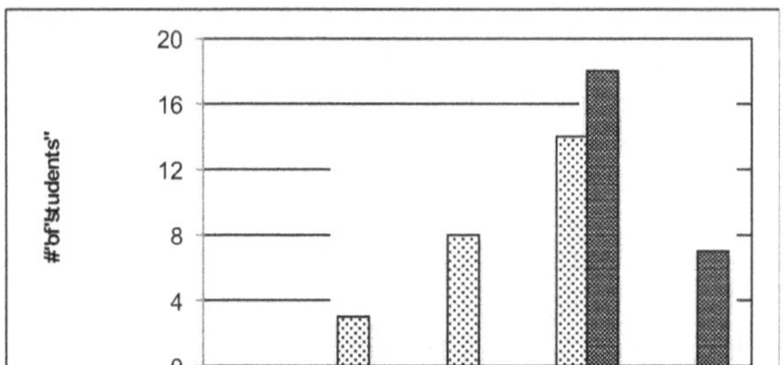

	SD	D	N	A	SA
Pre-Camp	0	3	8	14	0
Post-Camp	0	0	0	18	7

Table 2(c) – I study math because I know how useful it is

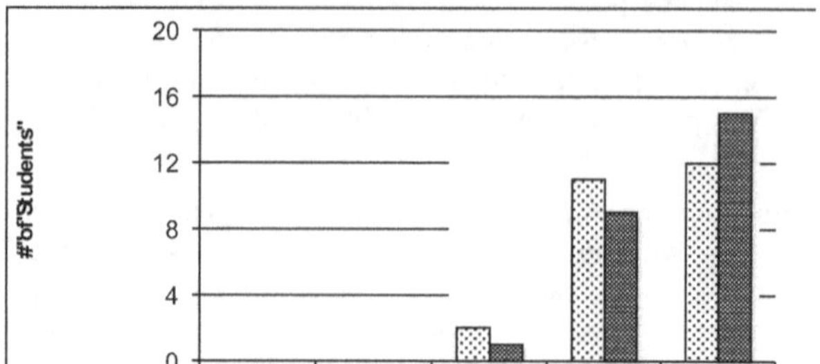

	SD	D	N	A	SA
Pre-Camp	0	0	2	11	12
Post-Camp	0	0	1	9	15

Table 2(d) – I feel secure about attempting science

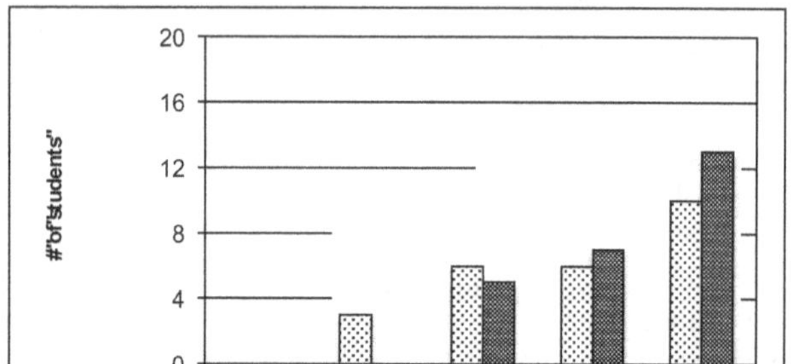

	SD	D	N	A	SA
Pre-Camp	0	3	6	6	10
Post-Camp	0	0	5	7	13

4.1.2 Attitudes

Table 1 shows the aggregate responses for the pre and post camp responses to the attitudinal questions regarding *security, usefulness,* and *advanced work.* We performed a *paired t-test* (n = 25) on individual responses for each of the categories of responses and found a statistically significant positive effect on attitudes on four different questions (highlighted in the table and summarized in Tables 2(a)-(d)). In particular:

1. Generally, I feel secure about attempting computer science.
2. I have a good understanding of what computer scientists do.
3. I study mathematics because I know how useful it is.
4. Generally, I feel secure about attempting science.

Tables 2(a) and (b) are particularly interesting, given the goals of the camp. Each points toward a positive impact on the attitudes towards computer science, with the first 2(a) indicating an increase in confidence, and the second 2(b) indicating an increased awareness of computer science. We believe that these are direct results of the activities of the camp. Specifically, the technical aspects of the camp and the career counseling sessions.

Table 2(c) points towards a general understanding of the importance of mathematics as a foundation, while Table 2(d) seems to point towards a reinforcement of an already existing positive attitude towards science.

4.1.3 Majors

Table 3 shows a table of the aggregate responses on the choice of major. Looking at the raw data, most of the participants began the camp with a leaning towards STEM fields. In particular, for CS, Science, Mathematics, and Engineering, students chose either *maybe,* or *yes* at rates of 24/25, 25/25, 20/25, and 20/25, respectively, on the pre-survey. Comparatively, for English, History, Foreign Languages, Education, and Business, students chose *maybe* or *yes* at rates of 8/25, 5/25, 7/25, 10/25, and 9/25 on the pre-survey.

Table 3 – Intended Choice of Major

STEM	NO	MAYBE	YES	Non-STEM	NO	MAYBE	YES
Computer Science				English/Language Arts			
Pre	1	20	4	Pre	16	7	1
Post	3	14	8	Post	15	6	2
Delta	2	-6	4	Delta	-1	-1	1
Science				History/Social Studies			
Pre	0	14	11	Pre	18	4	1
Post	3	10	12	Post	20	2	1
Delta	3	-4	1	Delta	2	-2	0
Math				Foreign Language			
Pre	5	14	5	Pre	17	7	0
Post	6	13	6	Post	17	8	0
Delta	1	-1	1	Delta	0	1	0
Engineering				Education			
Pre	5	12	8	Pre	14	9	1
Post	3	14	8	Post	15	8	1
Delta	-2	2	0	Delta	1	-1	0
				Business			
				Pre	14	8	1
				Post	11	10	3
				Delta	-3	2	2

Table 4 - Summary of Change in Major Choice for STEM fields

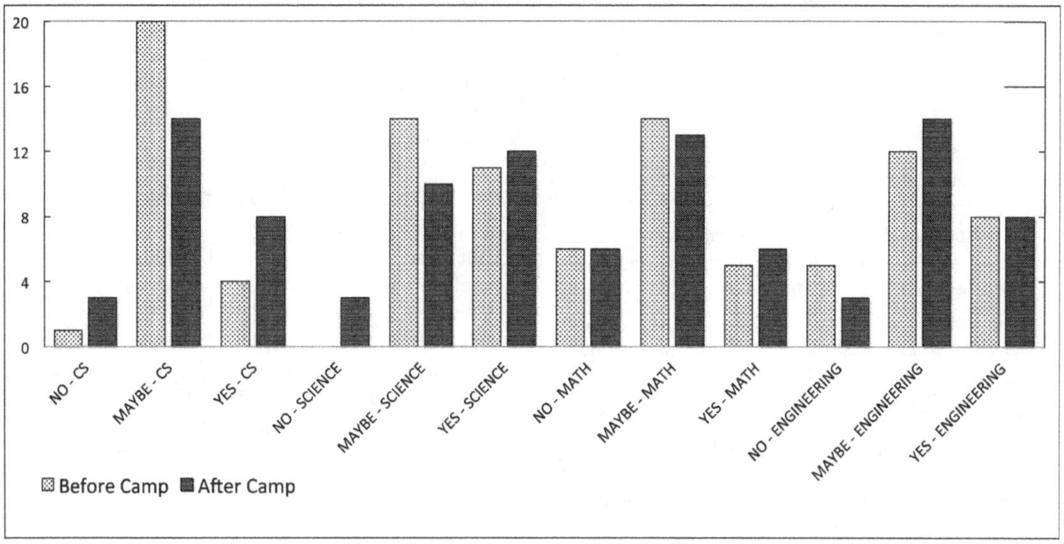

Again, we performed a *paired t-test* on the responses (n = 25) to determine whether a statistically significant change in attitudes towards choice of major had occurred, but none was observed.

Table 4 shows a chart that summarizes the pre- and post-survey responses and highlights the changes (e.g., deltas) in attitudes towards each particular major. The left columns are pre-camp, and right columns are post camp. CS exhibited the largest positive change in movement from *maybe* to *yes* (+4). All other disciplines changed by at most +2.

4.1.4 Discussion and Threats to Validity

The participants in the camp were self-selecting in that they had to apply for the camp in order to be admitted. In particular, as shown by the data in Table 3, they had a propensity towards STEM fields. As such, the data cannot be extended across the general population but given our long-term goal of increasing enrollments in CS, this is acceptable. It is exactly these students that have a leaning towards STEM but do not choose CS that we are ultimately interested in recruiting into CS programs.

4.2 Strengths

There are a number of strengths to this camp that contributed to its success, where success is defined not only by students' improved attitudes about CS but also by the satisfaction of all involved.

Outreach to Parents. Parents have a significant influence on their children's choice of major [11][12] and two different mechanisms were used to engage the parents throughout the week. A "Girls on the Go Mobile Computing" Facebook group was created so parents could follow camp activities from home. Campers presented their work at a closing ceremony, showing their parents and family the work they had accomplished throughout the week.

Counselor Role Models. Another strength of our camp were the four female counselors, all majoring in computing. They shared their experiences as college students and what it is like to study CS. The counselors were chosen based on recommendations of the camp faculty and advisors. Research has shown that social connectedness directly impacts college retention [13] and as we got to know the four counselors we were able to advise and mentor them. As one counselor said "I've never done mobile apps before and I love it." Two of the counselors at the hosting institute are now doing research with one of the camp faculty.

Interdisciplinary Focus. Our collaboration with the Cincinnati Zoo was a strength of the camp. It has been shown [14] that one of the reasons for low female enrollment in CS is because women do not see that computer science is more than writing games. We introduced campers to computer science, but in a larger context of solving a problem for the zoo and zoologists. Campers were able to examine current software tools available at the zoo and see the benefit that an Ethogram App. As one camper stated *"... we can create stuff that Doctors can use! I always wanted to help people ... I love the programming. "*

The College Experience. Another strength was that the program was a mini-college experience in a small college-town. Campers ranged in age from 13-16 and experienced dorm life, dorm food and life away from home. The campers loved this and commented on adjusting to the new experience of roommates and shared bathrooms. There were no complaints from the campers. Campers also got to know the counselors very well and ask them detailed questions about what it was like going to college.

Collaboration. The final strength of the camp was the collaboration between faculty, counselors and institutions. A summer camp is a large time commitment and overwhelming to many faculty. We believe that having four vested faculty coordinate this led to its success. We also learned a lot from our counselors. They offered suggestions on team-building (e.g., let the campers pick their own team for the zoo.) and leisure time (e.g., bring dinner back to the dorms so they could relax before the evening activities). There was a lot of brainstorming and idea generation throughout the camp. Our focus was the best experience for the campers and this made decision making easy. The surprise was how much fun we all had during the camp and our eagerness to do it again next year.

4.3 Lessons Learned

Overall, we feel that the camp was very successful. There were a number of things learned during the process. Some lessons were learned in time to make adjustments, others retained for future reference.

Leverage other camps. All but one of our instructors were new to campus-based summer camp planning. Fortunately the organizers of another camp were kind enough to share application forms with us so that we had the appropriate medical, photo, and transportation releases for the parents. We also received invaluable advice on getting deposits to avoid no-shows and writing ground rules for camper conduct.

Start recruiting campers early. We sent out camp application materials in early April for a camp starting in mid-July. In mid-May, after our application deadline, we heard from several computing instructors that they had just received the materials from the school guidance counselors. In the future we plan to distribute materials earlier and to highlight the application deadline to make sure it gets disseminated in a more timely manner.

Avoid "day campers." We had one camper who was pulled out of camp frequently by her parents to attend class and do homework. She did not have the same quality of camp experience as the other campers, plus some of the other campers resented her lack of contribution to their group projects. For future camps, we will require that all parents sign a form stating that they realize the camp is an immersive experience and that any campers who leave camp for non-emergency reasons will not be allowed to return.

Have contingency plans. Our original plan for the camp was to have all the students working on developing applications using Appcelerator Titanium and the Android simulator. This was for logistical reasons—the only computer lab with a machine for each camper was one of the PC labs. We had technical issues with the Android simulator and had to switch to using Macs to deploy to the iPod touches issued to each student. We put the girls into teams of 2 and had them using two different computer labs to do this.

5. CONCLUSIONS AND FUTURE WORK

The 2012 Girls on the Go Mobile Computing Experience was enjoyed by all involved. Some of the highlights include:

- The campers were enthusiastic about programming and wanted to go back to the lab to work in the evening instead of socializing.
- When asked what was their favorite part of the camp, two of our female campers responded "Coding!"
- Another camper told an interviewer "I thought I knew what programming was, but I learned things I had heard of and am now thinking about doing this. "
- Ten of the 25 campers have volunteered to continue working on the ethogram app.

In addition, the organizing and running of the camp strengthened the working relationship between three universities and their computer science departments, which has strengthened the regional women in computing network.

We have a number of quotations, enthusiastic reviews and heartwarming stories, but most importantly, the campers were provided with a positive mini-college experience and showed significant improvement in attitudes about mathematics, computer science and computing.

In the future, we would like to investigate ways to provide some of the opportunities provided by our camp to larger numbers of students. One option would be to extract or adapt material from our week-long camp curriculum to create shorter workshops for students in higher grades, similar to the approach taken by Sewell and Ringenberg [7]. Another thing we are considering is to follow the example of some of the other camps and include teachers in both the pre-camp technology training sessions and the camp administration so that they can bring the acquired skills back to their classrooms [14].

6. ACKNOWLEDGMENTS

We could not have held the camp without our counselors, the Cincinnati Zoo, and Project Dragonfly. We would also like to thank Jeff Gray for providing us with the basis of our evaluation instruments. Victoria McIe and Julie Rogers (two of our counselors) assisted with data entry and analysis. Financial assistance was provided by all three institutions involved. This work was supported by NSF CAREER Award CCF-0844638 (Burge). Any opinions, findings, and conclusions or recommendations expressed in this material are those of the author(s) and do not necessarily reflect the views of the National Science Foundation (NSF).

7. REFERENCES

[1] Graham, S., Latulipe, C.. 2003. CS girls rock: sparking interest in computer science and debunking the stereotypes. SIGCSE Bull. 35, 1 (January 2003), 322-326

[2] Pollock, L. , McCoy, K., Carberry, S., Hundigopal, N. and You, X. 2004. Increasing high school girls' self confidence and awareness of CS through a positive summer experience. *SIGCSE Bull.* 36, 1 (March 2004), 185-189

[3] Pivkina, I., Pontelli, E., Jensen, R., Haebe, J. 2009. *Young women in computing*: learned from an educational & outreach program. In *Proc SIGCSE 2009,*. 509-513

[4] Al-Bow, M., Austin, D., Edgington, J., Fajardo, R., Fishburn, J., Lara, C., Leutenegger, S., Meyer, S.. 2009. Using game creation for teaching computer programming to high school students and teachers. In *Proc. of* ITiCSE '09, 104-108.

[5] Ericson, B. McKlin, T.. 2012. Effective and sustainable computing summer camps. In *Proc of* SIGCSE '12. 289-294

[6] Roy, K.. 2012. App inventor for android: report from a summer camp. In *Proc of* SIGCSE '12. 283-288

[7] Sewell, K L., Ringenberg, J. 2012, "Accelerating K-12 Interest in Computer Science Using Mobile Application-Based Curriculums," *Proc of ASEE,* San Antonio, TX, USA, June 9-14,.

[8] Yardi, S. Bruckman, A.. 2007. What is computing?: bridging the gap between teenagers' perceptions and graduate students' experiences. In Proc of ICER '07. 39-50.

[9] Kawakita. J. 1975. KJ Method: a Scientific Approach to Problem Solving. Kawakita ResearchInstitute,

[10] Mathis, L. iPhone Mockup Tool, http://bit.ly/OLMFVC [accessed September 4, 2012].

[11] Maple, S.A., Stage, J. K., 1991."Influences on the Choice of Math/Science Major by Gender and Ethnicity," Am Educ Res J March 20, vol. 28 no. 1 37-60

[12] Frome, P., Eccles, J. 1998. "Parents' influence on children's achievement-related perceptions," J of Personality and Social Psychology, vol 74(2), Feb 1998, 435-452.

[13] Allen, J., Robbins, S, Casillas, A., Oh, I.. 2008 "Third-year College Retention and Transfer: Effects of Academic Performance, Motivation, and Social Connectedness," Research in Higher Education, Volume 49, Number 7, 647-664.

[14] Margolis, J., Fisher, A., 2003, Unlocking the clubhouse: Women in Computing. Cambridge, MA: MIT Press..Tims, H., Turner, G. E., Deemer, E., . Corbett, K. 2012 "Using Cyber Discovery to Assess Change in Student Stem-Related Attitudes," *Proc of ASEE,* San Antonio, TX, USA, June 9-14.

Using App Inventor in a K-12 Summer Camp

Amber Wagner, Jeff Gray, Jonathan Corley
Department of Computer Science
University of Alabama
{ankrug, jggray, corle001}@bama.ua.edu

David Wolber
Department of Computer Science
University of San Francisco
wolber@usfca.edu

ABSTRACT
Educators are often seeking new ways to motivate or inspire students to learn. Our past efforts in K-12 outreach included robotics and media computation as the contexts for teaching Computer Science (CS). With the deep interest in mobile technologies among teenagers, our recent outreach has focused on using smartphones as a new context. This paper is an experience report describing our approach and observations from teaching a summer camp for high school students using App Inventor (AI). The paper describes two separate methods (one using a visual block language, and another using Java) that were taught to high school students as a way to create Android applications. We observed that initiating the instruction with the block language, and then showing the direct mapping to an equivalent Java version, assisted students in understanding app development in Java. Our evaluation of the camp includes observations of student work and artifact assessment of student projects. Although the assessment suggests the camp was successful in several areas, we present numerous lessons learned based on our own reflection on the camp content and instruction.

Categories and Subject Descriptors
D.2.6. [**Software Engineering**]: Programming Environments

General Terms
Human Factors

Keywords
App Inventor, Java Bridge, Summer Camp

1. INTRODUCTION
Students learn best when the learning objective is contextualized with topics related to their daily activities [14]. Most teenagers are frequent users of smartphones and texting, which provides a unique context for engagement. The adoption rate of mobile computing among teenage students in the US continues to grow and has been estimated at 58% for smartphone adoption [13]. Based on current US census results [17], this suggests that there are 12.1M teenage students with smartphones. Educators can take advantage of these devices as a springboard for motivating topics involving CS [1], which has always been driven by a love of creative exploration using computational themes and artifacts.

SIGCSE'13, March 6–9, 2013, Denver, Colorado, USA.

Since 2004, we have offered multiple one-week summer camps to K-12 students. As a context for motivation and learning, we have used Lego Mindstorms robots [10], Alice [2], and Media Computation [9] in our past camps. In Summer 2011 and 2012, we offered three one-week camps focusing on Java [1] across multiple themes. The topics and attendance at these camps is summarized in Table 1. Students had the opportunity to attend all three weeks or one week. A dormitory option allowed us to offer the camps to students across the United States (the 2012 camps were attended by high school students from 12 states) in addition to students from Hong Kong and Beijing.

The third week was focused on App Inventor (AI) [3], which enabled us to take advantage of the interest that high school students have in smartphones. AI is a visual programming language that allows users to write apps using a block-oriented drag-and-drop interface to create both the user interface of an app, as well as to specify the app's behavior and functionality. An emulator is available for AI so that apps can be executed on a local desktop. AI also integrates with Android smartphones and tablets, which enables the user-made applications to be tested on a physical device. There is also an alternative to using the block language of AI: the Java Bridge, which allows for the creation of Java programs that use the same components available in the AI block language. From our experience in teaching Android programming to college seniors using the traditional Android SDK with Java, we found the Java Bridge to be a much simpler way to program Android apps and an excellent transition tool for students learning Java.

Table 1. Summary of three camps taught in Summer 2011/2012

Camp	Pre-requisites	Content	Attendance
Week 1: Intro to Java	No experience needed; Grades 9-12	Taught intro to Java using Greenfoot and Media Comp	2011: 28 2012: 33
Week 2: Robotics	Existing knowledge of Java or attendance of the first camp	Taught Java using Lego NXT and Lejos	2011: 12 2012: 25
Week 3: Android App Inventor	Existing knowledge of Java or attendance of the first camp	App Inventor Block Language and App Inventor Java Bridge	2011: 16 2012: 24

There are other mobile platforms that support educational outreach [8]. However, because our camps were for students new to programming, the visual language of AI was found to be a positive way to introduce students to problem solving and

[1] http://outreach.cs.ua.edu/camps/

computational issues. We observed that after students became familiar with the components and events of the block language of AI, they were then more prepared to learn and use the Java Bridge to rewrite the same programs in Java. In Section 3.2, we present our approach for easing the students into the Java Bridge to improve their practice in using Java. The first two days of the camp were taught using the block language of AI, the next two days were focused on using Java, and the final day was focused on student projects (this gave students the ability to be creative and write a program that they wanted to use in their daily lives). In Section 4, we summarize our thoughts on why we believe that teaching the AI block language helped students to be more successful in programming apps using the Java Bridge.

This paper presents related instruction at other institutions (Section 2), the layout and content of the camp (Section 3), observations of student reactions, strengths and weaknesses of the camp (Section 4), and how the summer camp will evolve in future offerings (Section 5).

2. RELATED WORK

The popularity of mobile devices has inspired much interest as a context for teaching computation [12]. In fact, a new learning model has emerged, LOCAL (Location and Context Aware Learning) [4], which combines mobile devices and wireless networks to create a new learning context. In this section, we summarize a portion of the work that has emerged in using smartphones as a context for teaching CS.

At the University of San Francisco (USF), co-author Wolber has integrated AI into a general education course over the past three years and reported that AI was "his most satisfying teaching experience in seventeen years" [19]. Before teaching AI, this course used Lego Robots [10] and Media Computation [9]. The course focuses both on programming and the real-world impact of mobile applications [19]. Because students were able to start building applications immediately with AI, they were motivated as the semester progressed to learn how to solve hard logic problems. Although the students attending the course were not CS majors, they successfully learned how to solve problems and, more importantly, felt empowered at the conclusion of the course (they even presented along with Senior and Master's project students at USF's annual CS Night). There were 11 students, out of 41 total, who went on to take the next course in the CS sequence. In the past, this CS0->CS1 bridge has been very rare, because the students that enroll in CS0 often take it because they have little confidence in mathematics. A video describing student feedback on this course is available[2].

As described in [7], Fenwick and Kurtz (from Appalachian State University) and Hollingsworth (from Elon University), taught their senior classes using the Android SDK [6] and AI. The Elon University course started as a lecture-based course with hands-on activities followed by a project-based approach. The Appalachian State University course was project-based from the start. Both universities found that "students enjoyed the course" and students were once again exhibiting an "entrepreneurial and independent spirit" [7].

To assist in teaching the importance of human-computer interaction, Loveland used AI to motivate students [11]. At the conclusion of the course, one student commented: "It is cool that the course applied the latest technologies in software development to mobile and web design." This statement summarizes other reports [4, 7, 8, 12, and 19] about why mobile computing is being used as a teaching context. Students are able to learn about programming using tools that are very personal and applicable to their daily lives.

A few college courses on mobile computing have been described above; however, these courses focused on college-level students in beginning or non-major programming courses. Roy [15], from Valdosta State University, organized summer camps for high school students using AI in 2011 and found AI to be an effective tool for novice programmers due to the visual environment being similar to Scratch. Moreover, Roy noted that transitioning from AI to Java would be easy due to the Java Bridge functionality, but does not provide an assessed study.

The primary difference between these examples and our summer camp is our approach of presenting a visual language followed by a strategic transition to Java. The gap among first learners using graphical languages and textual languages was also noticed by Cheung et al. [5], who describe an approach for easing into textual languages from a graphical language. The new version of Alice 3 also enables such a transition. However, the benefits of using a common set of examples to support the transition from a graphical to textual programming language is not described deeply in the literature.

3. FROM BLOCK LANGUAGE TO JAVA

AI was the focus of our third and final week of camp, meeting for a total of 35 hours over a 5-day period. Among the 40 students across both summers that attended the AI week of camp, 14 had Java experience from their high school and 26 were introduced to Java in our first week of camp. This section introduces our approach for providing a transition path from a visual language to Java for writing apps.

Given the varied Java experiences of the students, the camp started with two days of using the AI block language, which allows novice programmers to build Android apps quickly (using a blocks metaphor, such as in Scratch [16]). After the students gained confidence with events, components, and the general AI environment, students were then introduced to the Java Bridge. The learning objectives for the camp were to teach the students the following concepts:

> 1. Writing Android apps; 2. Objects; 3. Programming environments; 4. Events; 5. Decision statements; 6. Loops; 7. Method calls; 8. Method creation; 9. Being able to interpret documentation; 10. Creating a GUI and coding the components of the GUI; 11. Using phone sensor components and services (camera, text messaging)

3.1 Starting with the Visual Block Language

The AI environment, components and visual language were covered in days one and two by using examples from co-author Wolber's textbook [18]. Although the students already had some previous experience with Java (either from our week 1, or from an offering at their home school), it was important to introduce the students to AI via the block language due to the complexity of the various components, events, GUI, and general metaphors associated with programming Android apps. The block language helped familiarize the students with these components before jumping into the Java Bridge. The apps we selected from the textbook represent a progressively complex combination of applications that offer benefits to society (e.g., "No texting while driving") as well as entertaining apps such as games (e.g., "MoleMash"). Rather than a traditional lecture, the camp was

[2] http://www.appinventor.org/

approached with an inquiry-based hands-on approach, where a problem was presented and the instructor walked the students through the problem while answering questions as the instructor and students completed the app together. Next, a similar problem was presented that covered one or more new concepts. The students were presented with each exercise and were given approximately thirty minutes to implement each app. For those who implemented an app quickly, an additional challenge was assigned. After the allotted time, students were asked to volunteer to present their solution to the class. To emphasize that more than one solution/approach exists, multiple students were asked to present their solutions, and the instructor aided the students in explaining options for various possibilities.

On Day One, students were introduced to the AI interface and began creating applications immediately. The apps the students focused on throughout the day are from [18]:

1. "HelloPurr" (see Figure 1; notice that only three lines of "code" were required to create this app) – this application is a simple button with an image of a cat. When the button is clicked, a "meow" sound is played, and the phone vibrates for 500ms simulating a purr.
2. "PaintPot" – a paintbrush app that has options for changing pen color, wiping the canvas, drawing circles/lines, and changing the background image through a call to the camera component (see Figure 3 for an emulator image).
3. "MoleMash" – this application simulates the "Mole Mash" game at arcades where a "mole" appears in a random hole, and the player must hit the "mole" before it disappears.

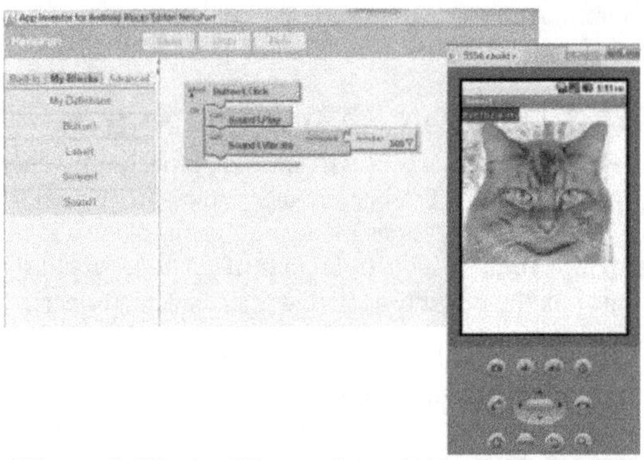

Figure 1. Block editor and emulator (left to right)

Day Two began by asking the students to explore on their own several projects from the textbook to continue their familiarity and confidence in using the visual block language. We then introduced the week-long project and asked the students to design and create their own application to present to the class on Day Five. Students were told they could use either the visual block language or the Java Bridge (described in Section 3.2) that would be introduced on day three. Each student gave a 5-minute presentation to the class of their project idea. Please refer to Figure 2 for an example of the timeline for the 2012 camp.

3.2 Mapping to the Java Bridge

As noted in Section 2, many universities are beginning to offer a mobile computing course focusing on app development. The University of Alabama offers a college senior-level design course focused on Android development that is taught using Java and the Android SDK. Although this is a feasible option at

ID	Task Name	Start	Finish	Aug 2012				
				30	31	1	2	3
1	Introduction to AI: Hello Purr, Paint Pot, and Mole Mash	7/30/2012	7/30/2012					
2	More work on projects from the text [14]	7/31/2012	7/31/2012					
3	Begin final project ideas and proposals	7/31/2012	7/31/2012					
4	Introduction to Java via the Java Bridge: repeat Paint Pot	8/1/2012	8/2/2012					
5	Time to work on final projects	8/2/2012	8/3/2012					
6	Final project presentations	8/3/2012	8/3/2012					

Figure 2. Timing of topics presented in 2012 camps.

the college level, we felt it would be overwhelming for high school students (with limited Java experience) to learn the core Android SDK. Thus, our approach transitioned the students from the visual language of AI into the Java Bridge, which assists in writing a Java-based app that targets the same AI components (the Java Bridge is a .jar file containing all of the AI components that is included in the build path of a Java app in Eclipse). The Java Bridge was first introduced on Day Three of the camp. Our approach was to take the same apps that were developed in days one and two, and show the equivalent implementation in Java. Our reasoning for this strategy is that the students would be able to form a mental mapping to the equivalent Java representation. In fact, the code completion of the Java Bridge components in the Eclipse editor reveals that the component interfaces provided in Java are the exact same as those components in the visual language of AI. We believe that the familiarity with the same components from the first two days of the camp is an asset to students learning to use the Java Bridge.

3.2.1 PaintPot with the Java Bridge

The first exercise the students completed using the Java Bridge was the HelloPurr app. This provided the details on the structure of a Java Bridge application. From that experience, the students were then asked to implement the PaintPot app in Java. We demonstrated how to create the initial setup with the background image and the creation of the first button to select the pen color, including both the GUI and the event method code for the button. Students were asked to create the two remaining pen buttons and a "Clear" button. Those who completed the problem quickly were challenged to add a button, which would take a picture and replace the background image with the newly taken picture. Six students completed the app within nine minutes, and all students completed the initial problem within thirty minutes. Three students successfully implemented the camera challenge without help from the instructors within that same time period. We found this to be a remarkable accomplishment – we estimate that for ourselves to create a similar app using the traditional Android SDK would take approximately six hours. The fact that students with little Java experience were able to do this within 30 minutes attests to the power that the AI Java Bridge offers as a teaching environment, which abstracts many of the accidental complexities found in the Android SDK.

Figure 3 illustrates a portion of a completed implementation of the PaintPot app in Java. As can be seen, in the Java Bridge the "main" method is replaced with `$define`. The code that is shown in Figure 4 is focused on the creation of the GUI. Java components are created and added to the default `Form` object (i.e., the `this` object). Other parts not shown in this figure include the import section, the registration of events for dispatching, and the implementation of event handlers.

The complete implementation of the PaintPot, as well as the other apps given to students, is available at our Google code sites at both the University of San Francisco[3] and the University of Alabama[4].

3.2.2 Skeleton of a Java Bridge App

The skeleton of a Java Bridge app is shown in Figure 4. The required packages from the Java Bridge .jar file include classes for handling the event dispatching, as well as the importation of all the GUI components used in the app. The class representing the app must extend the `Form` class within the Android SDK and implement the interface specified by the event dispatcher. The main class also declares all of the GUI components that will be used, which are then constructed at the beginning of the `$define` method and inserted into the form. At the end of the `$define` method, the events that the app is interested in are registered (sample events include things like Click, Dragged, Touched). A separate dispatching method is then called whenever an event occurs in the app. Those events that are filtered by the dispatcher have their appropriate handlers called, which represent the remaining methods in the class.

We have observed that students very quickly pick up on the mechanism for registering events in a manner that is much more intuitive to them than the listener approach required in the core Android SDK. An important aspect of AI is its event-based nature; i.e., an app is a set of event-handlers. The only challenge that students faced was uncovering the specific names of the handlers, which are available in documentation.

At USF, co-author Wolber explored a different way for Java Bridge programmers to specify event handlers that is a bit higher level than registering them. In this approach, a slightly modified Java Bridge is used, one where the components are not final classes. The programmer subclasses the components (e.g., Canvas), then can override the event methods (e.g., Dragged) to build the event-handler. This simplifies things for beginners because they do not have to worry about the low-level event names and event registration. The event-handler method headings are already in the superclass and the programmer need only override them to program the handler (Eclipse even generates the override method header). For example, consider the following code:

```
class GameCanvas extends Canvas {

  @Override
  public void Touched(float x, float y, boolean touchedSprite) {
```

The downside with this approach is that inheritance is used, but in limited testing novice students have grasped the approach readily and with less problems than the event registration scheme of the traditional Java Bridge.

As an extension of the Java Bridge idea, students at USF have created an application to generate the Java code automatically for an app created within AI[5]. This assists students transitioning from AI to Java from a different perspective. The students can create their own app and then see the Java code required to build the app.

[3] https://sites.google.com/site/mobileprogrammingusf/paintpot-java-bridge

[4] http://code.google.com/p/appinventor-java-translation/downloads/list

[5] http://usfaicg.appspot.com

3.3 Final Project

In addition to the exercises that we used from [18], the students were asked to work on their final project that was initially introduced on Day Two. The primary time for project design and implementation occurred on Days Four and Five. The student projects were often collaborative (done in teams) and very creative. The projects varied from applications that would benefit the community to games and entertainment apps. The final projects serve as the artifacts that are assessed in Section 4.2. These apps are publicly available on our camp website.

One beneficial app created using the Java Bridge assists environmental scientists in collecting information about samples from photos taken of the environment. This app allows a citizen scientist to help collect information by taking a photo of some reactive test and then report details about the image by touching various parts of the image. This project actually turned into a regional science fair project for the student, with continued mentoring by one of the co-authors. The app will return various properties about the pixel that is touched. Another final project, created using Java, acts as a study aid for science. The application asks the user for initial and final data for one or more of the following fields: pressure, temp, moles, molecular mass, and/or density. Based on the information the user enters, the app fills in the remaining information according to laws of gases: Boyle's Law, Charles's Law, Gay-Lussac's Law, Combined Gas Law, and Ideal Gas Law (true and false). This application required the use of data structures, loops, decisions, custom methods, events, objects, and components. Although this student had previous Java experience, this was her first time using Java to program Android phones. Based on the complexity of the project, she mastered the material thoroughly and quickly.

4. EVALUATION AND DISCUSSION

This section introduces two assessment approaches to determine the impact of using AI in our summer camps. In Section 4.1, we summarize our observations made throughout the week; Section 4.2 provides some insight from an artifacts assessment that we performed on the publicly available final student projects.

4.1 Observations from the AI camp

Of the three different camps, students were noticeably most excited for the start of the AI camp. During the PaintPot exercise, students were not initially impressed with the difficulty-level of the application; however, as soon as they completed the app and ran it on their phones, smiles began appearing throughout the classroom. The students enjoyed working with AI and learned how to use the programming environment within a day of its introduction.

When transitioning to the Java Bridge, the students were challenged, but because we repeated the same applications (HelloPurr and PaintPot), they were able to create a mental map between the Java syntax and what they previously created with the blocks language. The majority of the students appeared to understand how to use Java in creating an app. Some of the students preferred using the blocks language to using the Java Bridge, due to the ease of creating GUIs in the blocks language (as compared to programmatic creation of the GUI in Java).

Overall, the students were more engaged this week than in previous weeks. Because students were so enthusiastic about creating their own apps, which they could install on their phone, they wanted to arrive early to the camp and stay later. We did not see this level of engagement in previous weeks.

```
private int count = 0;
private int dotSize = 30;

void $define()
{
    img = new BufferedImage(this);
    img.Visible(false);

    cam = new Camera(this);

    cnv = new Canvas(this);
    cnv.BackgroundImage("resize.jpg");

    Label space = new Label(this);

    btnTakePic = new Button(this);
    btnTakePic.Text("Take Picture");

    Label space1 = new Label(this);

    HorizontalArrangement hrz1 = new HorizontalArrangement(this);
    HorizontalArrangement hrz2 = new HorizontalArrangement(this);
    HorizontalArrangement hrz3 = new HorizontalArrangement(this);
    HorizontalArrangement hrz4 = new HorizontalArrangement(this);
    Label space2 = new Label(this);
    HorizontalArrangement hrz5 = new HorizontalArrangement(this);

    lblX = new Label(hrz1);
    lblX.Text("X: ");
    lblXPosition = new Label(hrz1);
    lblXPosition.Text("");
```

Figure 3. PaintPot application written in Java

```
import com.google.devtools.simple.runtime.components.HandlesEventDispatching;
import com.google.devtools.simple.runtime.events.EventDispatcher;
import com.google.devtools.simple.runtime.components.android.*;

public class MyApp extends Form implements HandlesEventDispatching
{
        /* Declaration of GUI components goes here */

        void $define()
        {
            /* GUI components constructed and added to Form, similar to code in Figure 3 */

            EventDispatcher.registerEventForDelegation( this, "MyApp", "SomeEvent" );
        }

        public void dispatchEvent(Object component, String id, String eventName, Object[] args )
        {
                if( eventName.equals( "SomeEvent" ) )
                        if( component.equals( someComponent ))
                                someComponent_DoAction();

                /* Other event dispatching goes here */
        }

        private void someComponent_DoAction()
        {
            /* Some specific event handler code here */
        }
}
```

Figure 4. Skeleton of a Java Bridge app

4.2 Student Project Assessment

To evaluate what the students learned throughout the week, we reviewed the 23 (9 from 2011 and 14 from 2012) complete and submitted final projects (students gave permission to post online) based on the eleven learning objectives presented in Section 3.1 (several of the projects were team-based). Some students did not submit a project because they were unable to complete it, which indicates either the project was too ambitious or we should start the project time earlier in the week. Table 2 lists the given learning objectives and the number of projects where each learning objective was met (the learning objective had to be used correctly to be counted). The projects used in this assessment were student selected projects; therefore, the difficulty level is indicative of the student's understanding. The results are positive considering only 35% of the students had exposure to Java prior to this summer (i.e., 65% of the students learned Java just from our first week of camp).

It is clear from Table 2 that iteration was not a common need in the final projects (only 3 projects used a looping construct), but many students had no need for loops in their applications because the event processing did not require iteration. 15 projects included decision statements, which is also a critical construct used for problem solving; therefore, most students felt confident using decision statements in their applications. The majority of students also felt comfortable with the use of objects, learning a new environment, working in teams collaboratively, using and programming events, calling methods, reading documentation, creating GUIs, and using components based on project assessment and observations.

Table 2. Number of projects meeting the learning objectives

Learning Objective	Number of projects
How Android apps can be written	23
Objects	23
Programming environments (Block Language and Java)	23
Events	23
Decision statements	15
Loops	3
Method calls	23
Method creation	7
Understanding how to read documentation	14
Creating a GUI	23
Using components	23

5. CONCLUSION

In order to inspire students to study CS and understand its relevancy to their lives, educators should identify meaningful learning contexts. From our experience, we found that mobile computing provides a powerful new context for motivating computational thinking. The 40 students attending our AI week of camp across two years were exposed to both the AI block language and the Java Bridge to familiarize them with multiple environments and solutions, GUI development, and Java.

It was clear that students needed solidification of Java concepts at the beginning of the week. Based on information in Table 2, we feel the approach of teaching a visual language followed by Java (using common examples in each) allowed students to gain the confidence necessary to build applications, while reinforcing core concepts such as objects, decision statements, and methods. In a separate week, we also used AI in a teacher-focused workshop (supported by a Google CS4HS grant) where science teachers were taught how to create apps focused on their classroom needs. Several of these teachers are introducing AI into new CS Principles classes to highlight the way in which computing affects many disciplines[6]. At the University of Alabama, we are also Piloting a CS Principles course with the College Board that uses AI as a core focus.

Moving forward, this camp will be offered in Summer 2013 with improvements made based on student feedback. Our observations after reflecting on the past two years has led us to several activities that we plan to try, including: 1) introduce the Java Bridge earlier (afternoon of Day Two); 2) homework challenges with notes for those who need more help or more challenges; and 3) for those students staying in our dormitory, offer evening sessions for those interested, providing additional help to those who are behind or deeper challenges for advanced students. As a contribution to the AI community, we also developed a prototype tool that will convert AI programs in the block language into a complete Eclipse project representing the same app as translated to Java[7]. This allows an integrated mapping mechanism where students can compare their block language programs to the Java equivalent.

[6] http://outreach.cs.ua.edu/camps/

[7] http://code.google.com/p/appinventor-java-translation/

ACKNOWLEDGMENTS

We acknowledge the support of a Google CS4HS award. Thanks to Josh Swank for assisting in the conversion of several of the AI programs to the Java Bridge.

REFERENCES

[1] Abelson, H., Mobile Ramblings. *EDUCAUSE Quarterly*, vol. 34, no. 1, 2011.

[2] Alice. Carnegie Melon University. http://www.alice.org.

[3] Android App Inventor from MIT Center for Mobile Learning, http://appinventor.mit.edu.

[4] Barbosa, J., Hahn, R., Rabello, S., and Barbosa, D., LOCAL: A model geared towards ubiquitous learning. *SIGCSE Symposium on Computer Science Education*, Portland, OR, March 2008, pp. 432-436.

[5] Cheung, J., Ngai, G., Chan, S., and Lau, W., Filling the gap in programming instruction: A text-enhanced graphical programming environment for junior high students, *SIGCSE Symposium on Computer Science Education*, Chattanooga, TN, March 2009, pp. 276-280.

[6] Eclipse. ADT plugin for eclipse. http://developer.android.com/sdk/eclipse-adt.html.

[7] Fenwick Jr., J., Kurtz, B., and Hollingsworth, J., Teaching mobile computing and developing software to support Computer Science education. *SIGCSE Symposium on Computer Science Education*, Dallas, TX, March 2011, pp. 589-594.

[8] Goadrich, M. and Rogers, M., Smart smartphone development: iOS versus Android. *SIGCSE Symposium on Computer Science Education*, Dallas, TX, March 2011, pp. 607-612.

[9] Guzdial, M. and Ericson, B., *Introduction to Computing and Programming in Python, A Multimedia Approach*. Pearson Education, 2009.

[10] Lego Mindstorms. http://mindstorms.lego.com.

[11] Loveland, S., Human computer interaction that reaches beyond desktop applications. *SIGCSE Symposium on Computer Science Education*, Dallas, TX, March 2011, pp. 595-600.

[12] Mahmoud, Q., Best practices in teaching mobile application development. *ITiCSE Joint Conference on Innovation and Technology in Computer Science Education*, Darmstadt, Germany, June 2011, pg. 333.

[13] Nielsen Wire, Young Adults and Teens Lead Growth Among Smartphone Owners. Written September 10, 2012, retrieved December 7, 2012 from http://blog.nielsen.com/nielsenwire/online_mobile/young-adults-and-teens-lead-growth-among-smartphone-owners/

[14] Perrone, V. Teaching for understanding: How to engage students in learning. *Educational Leadership*, Vol. 51(5), February 1994.

[15] Roy, K. App inventor for Android: report from a summer camp. *SIGCSE Technical Symposium on Computer Science Education*, Raleigh, NC, March 2012, pp. 283-288.

[16] Scratch. Massachusetts Institute of Technology. http://scratch.mit.edu.

[17] U.S. Census Bureau. Age and Sex Composition: 2010. 2010 Census Briefs, May 2011. Retrieved July 9, 2012. http://www.census.gov/prod/cen2010/briefs/c2010br-03.pdf.

[18] Wolber, D., Abelson, H., Spertus, E, and Looney, L., *App Inventor: Create Your Own Android Apps*. O'Reilly, 2011.

[19] Wolber, D., App Inventor and real-world motivation. In *Proceedings of the 42nd ACM SIGCSE Technical Symposium on Computer Science Education*, Dallas, TX, 2011.

No Sensor Left Behind: Enriching Computing Education with Mobile Devices

Matthew H. Dabney, Brian C. Dean
School of Computing, Clemson University
Clemson, SC, USA
{mdabney,bcdean}@clemson.edu

Tom Rogers
Southside High School
Greenvile, SC, USA
tkrogers@greenville.k12.sc.us

ABSTRACT

The use of mobile app development in pre-college computing education is rapidly gaining momentum due to the increasingly widespread use of mobile devices. To fully realize the learning potential of this technology in the classroom, however, one may need to re-examine traditional curricular approaches originating from desktop computing environments. In this work, we describe our experience with a new high-school computing camp designed from the ground up to engage students by taking full advantage of the specific benefits of mobile devices, such as built-in cameras, GPS, networking, and sensors measuring touch, sound, acceleration, and orientation. We describe the design of our camp including materials and examples used. We assess the effectiveness of this instructional approach by demonstrating a statistically significant increase in interest in future computing endeavors. We also comment on the use of MIT App Inventor to ease the transition, particularly for novice programmers, to more sophisticated Java-based apps.

Categories and Subject Descriptors

K.3.2 [**Computer and Information Science Education**]: Computer Science Education

General Terms

Theory, Design, Languages

Keywords

Android, App Inventor, Mobile Computing

1. INTRODUCTION

The computing landscape has recently shifted from desktop and laptop computers to smartphones and tablets. Implications of this trend on computing education are substantial and quite exciting, particularly at the pre-college level, since mobile computing has now moved well beyond just a "gimmick" to enhance new student engagement (cf., video games, robotics) to a mainstream technology that reaches every corner of industry and society.

Mobile computing opens up a number of opportunities as well as challenges for the design of computing curricula. On the opportunity side, many mobile devices are equipped with a vast array of sensors and versatile components (e.g., camera, microphone, speaker, Bluetooth, Wi-Fi), that open the door to curricular modules that make clever use of this technology to showcase computing concepts in new ways that are more effective and more engaging. On the other hand, it can be a non-trivial exercise to design such modules. In this paper, we highlight our experience with a new high-school computing camp designed with student engagement in mind by taking full advantage of the broad range of features on most mobile devices. Students participating in this camp demonstrated a statistically significant increase in self-reported understanding of fundamental computing concepts as well as interest in pursuit of future computing endeavors.

Inspired by the annual "nifty assignments" SIGCSE session, we hope this work will help to build momentum towards a larger-scale effort devoted to the conception and dissemination of curricular ideas in computing education designed to achieve higher effectiveness by leveraging the specific features of mobile devices.

2. BACKGROUND AND MOTIVATION

Computer science education has shown lackluster progress to date in making inroads into high-school curricula across the United States [1]. Several factors are to blame for this state of affairs, including a lack of computing requirements for graduation at the statewide level (in fact, no state requires a computer science course for graduation and only 9 states take computer science credits in place of math or science graduation requirements), and an inadequate supply of qualified computer science educators to teach at the high school level [3, 12]. Faced with a lack of government support and qualified teachers, innovative educational approaches are necessary to attract high school students to the field of computing. Moreover, diversity in the field of computing is nowhere near where it should be; for example, recent figures show low percentages of undergraduate degrees awarded to African-Americans (10-11%), Hispanics (5-8%), and females (11.7%) [8, 13]. Any efforts to increase engagement at the high-school level should ideally also consider strategies for improving participation levels among underrepresented groups.

Mobile devices such as smartphones and tablets have seen

SIGCSE'13, March 6–9, 2013, Denver, Colorado, USA.

explosive growth in the past half-decade, with more than 114 million people in the United States (out of a population of around 314 million) owning smartphones between May and July of 2012 [2]. Smartphones now represent more than half of the mobile phones in the USA. Of particular interest is the fact that a higher fraction of females own smartphones than males, and substantially higher fractions of Hispanic and African-American mobile device owners own smartphones than White mobile device owners [9]. Smartphone adoption also transcends economic barriers: among 18-24-year-olds, a majority of mobile phone owners owned smartphones irrespective of household income level [11]. The growing adoption of smartphones, particularly among females, minorities, and all economic groups, presents a powerful opportunity for drawing high school students to computer science. The ability to develop apps for devices so ubiquitous in students' lives is a powerful motivator, especially considering the possibility to make money by marketing the apps to hundreds of millions of users across the various app markets [4].

App development carries with it a set of unique programming challenges, especially for novices. These include the need to understand event-driven programming, as well as the need to use complicated programming and debugging environments (e.g., an external device or emulator). In order to make programming easier for novice students, block-based programming languages have recently been gaining in popularity [5, 7]. These languages abstract away syntax and object-oriented complexities into blocks that can be pieced together like puzzles to create programs. MIT App Inventor (formerly Google's App Inventor for Android) is one such language that is used to program apps for Android devices. It is particularly helpful because, in addition to the syntax and object-oriented abstraction, it also provides built-in components that handle complex interactions with the Android OS. It also automatically updates the app running on the emulator or physical device, so students do not have to wait for compilation and deployment between code changes.

3. CAMP SETUP

We developed and ran a week-long summer camp for high school students in collaboration between Clemson University, a public university in Clemson, South Carolina, and Southside High School in nearby Greenville, South Carolina. Funding was provided by a Google RISE (Roots in Science and Engineering) grant.

Our camp served twenty-two students from four local high schools and one home-schooled student all between rising ninth and twelfth grades. Six were female, one was African-American, and one was of Hispanic descent. Campers varied in terms of prior computing experience: some had already had AP Computer Science, some had taught themselves Java, and some had had no prior programming experience. The camp staff also included four undergraduate and graduate student assistants.

3.1 Devices

We chose to use the Android operating system as our smartphone platform for several reasons, including its open source approach to software, free standard development kit and development environment, the relative cost of Android phones compared to iOS devices, the ease of availability of App Inventor, and its prominence in the smartphone market [10]. Our funding allowed us to purchase one phone per group of two students. We chose the Samsung Nexus S as our development phone. The Nexus series of devices are produced directly by Google in association with a hardware vendor and come generally free of additional software bloat added by wireless communications providers, so it provides a stock Android OS environment. The phones we purchased did not come from a wireless provider and, therefore, lacked calling, texting, and mobile data functionality (these features are challenging to obtain for a large phone deployment like ours due to the added costs and administrative requirements of purchasing voice and data plans for the phones). The only setup that was required on the devices themselves was the installation of a free barcode scanning app[1] that is required by the App Inventor barcode scanner that we used in one of our example projects.

3.2 Software

The camp consisted of three days of App Inventor development followed by two days of Android Java programming in the Eclipse IDE. While Java has successfully been used in more advanced mobile computing classes [6], we felt it important, despite the short length of our camp, to try at least some Java programming, as this is the only way to fully exploit the rich capabilities of Android smartphones. This also offered us some useful insight into the effectiveness of App Inventor as a transitional step towards the more complicated Java programming environment.

Necessary software installation for our lab Windows machines included Java 6, the App Inventor software (which includes a phone emulator in case you do not have physical devices), and Windows drivers for our phones. Since App Inventor is web-based, we made sure to check that our systems had access through the high-school firewall to the App Inventor website. Setup for using the Android SDK with Eclipse consisted of installing Eclipse, installing the Android SDK manager, setting up firewall exceptions to allow the download of Android SDK components, and installing the Android Development Tools (ADT) Eclipse plugin. Just as the App Inventor software included an emulator, the Android SDK manager also allowed for the installation of device emulators. Because each smartphone in our lab was shared between a pair of students, we relied on emulators for much of our development. However, since our curricular approach involves crucial use of many of the hardware components on the smartphone, the emulator was in some cases of limited use, and students needed to exchange phones periodically to test their apps on a physical device.

4. APPS

Our educational goal was to develop curricular modules that utilized all the "bells and whistles" of our mobile devices, in order to provide a more effective and engaging means of conveying introductory computing topics. The approach is reminiscent of problem-based learning, where relevant computing techniques are learned en route in support of a primary goal ostensibly related to exploiting functionality of our smartphones. By carefully designing our activities, we were able to incorporate a large number of fundamental computing concepts into our curriculum, and we were able to pace these so that students were exposed to concepts at

[1] http://code.google.com/p/zxing/

App (Environment)	Phone Features Demonstrated	Computing Concepts Used
"Hello world" (A)	Phone emulation	Event-driven control, if/else
Mole game (A)	Touch input (click), clock	Variables, timing, animation, boundary checking, random number generation, string manipulation
Drawing canvas (A)	Touch input (drag), camera	Lists and iteration, generic component functions (advanced tab in App Inventor)
Number game (A,W)	Wi-Fi	Menus, networking and web technologies
GPS treasure hunt (A)	Bar/QR codes, GPS, "Google Maps"	UI design, sensor state verification, complex math
3D camera (A,W)	Camera, portability	Image processing
Java "Hello World" (J)	n/a	Scope, functions, classes, loops, arrays, variables
Sensor example (J,S)	Accelerometer, gyroscope, magnetometer, light sensor	Using API for built-in class functions for sensor access
Spiral graphics (J,S)	High-resolution graphics display	Nested for loops
Sound manipulator (J,S)	Microphone and speakers	Arrays, iterators

Figure 1: List of apps developed during camp. A = App Inventor, J = Java and Eclipse, W = Web server used, S = Android SDK.

a comfortable rate, with each new application designed to introduce only a small handful of key concepts.

In this section, we describe the instructional examples we provided over the course of our camp, as well as examples of apps conceived entirely by students during open-ended design exercises in which they were able to build on their recently-acquired knowledge in a more creative, unstructured manner. Figure 1 provides a summary of the example apps used throughout our camp, and Figure 2 shows photos of several of our camp activities.

4.1 App Inventor Examples

Our first two App Inventor examples were adapted from the App Inventor website; the first was the obligatory "Hello, World" app that we used to introduce the App Inventor interface. It simply displayed a label with the text "Hello, World!", an image of the world, and a button that we made make the image vanish and reappear when clicked. With this and all of the following examples, we formulated additional challenges for those students with more experience.

The second example we used was adapted from the "Mole Mash" tutorial from the App Inventor website. Here, a player attempts to tap the image of a mole as it moves across the screen. This example illustrated the concepts of event-driven programming, timing, animation, boundary checking, random number generation, and, once we added in a score counter, manipulation of variables and string concatenation. After programming the basic Mole Mash app, we challenged the campers to introduce some added difficulty, for example, to decrement the score if you touch outside the mole image, to make the mole slide in a random direction in addition to jumping, to have a bad mole and a good mole with opposite score values, etc. The introduction of sliding allowed us to hold one of a series of mini-lectures, in this case covering movement in animation.

Next, we programmed a drawing app similar to the "PaintPot" example from the App Inventor website. We started with the ability to choose one of three colors using buttons and used the chosen color to draw on a canvas. We then added the ability to take a picture to use as the canvas background and the ability to save the image produced after drawing on it to the phone's internal memory. This example allowed us to highlight the phone's drag events, the camera, and saving files to memory. We took the app a step further and introduced lists to allow the user to choose from each of the thirteen built-in colors in App Inventor by iterating through a list. Then, we introduced random element selection from lists by adding a random color button. Finally, we programmed our own red, green, and blue (RGB) sliders (for some reason this incredibly useful design element is not included in App Inventor's built-in components list) that we could use to pick specific colors. In programming these sliders, we were able to make use of the generic component functions provided under the advanced tab of the blocks editor to program generic functions to which we could later pass a specific component to modify, a fairly advanced programming technique with which many of the campers had little trouble.

Our fourth example illustrated networking and web development, where the students implemented one side of a simple multi-player networked game. Their apps communicated with a web server on a laptop hooked up to a portable Wi-Fi hot spot and connected to a projection screen. The game implemented by these apps was relatively simple, yet remarkably entertaining for the students. In each round, every team would use their app to select a number from one to seven that was transmitted over the phone's wireless network interface using an http "get" request to the web server. The team that submitted the highest *unique* number was declared the winner of that round, visualized on the large projection screen. In addition to encouraging the students to think about game theory and to develop an algorithm to maximize their point value, this app example demonstrated the phone's wireless capability, introduced drop-down menus, and provided an opportunity for a mini-lecture on web technologies.

Our most popular App Inventor example app was a GPS "treasure hunt" game. To play the game, students wrote an app that would scan a QR code that encoded a set of coordinates, parse the text string of coordinates into a longitude and latitude value, and calculate and display the distance to that position from the phone's current position. In order to plot this information on a map on the phone's screen (recalling that our phones lacked mobile data plans), we took a screenshot of the grounds surrounding the school in Google Maps and calculated the coordinates of the left, top, right,

Figure 2: Clockwise from upper-left: using a pair of phones to build a 3D camera, students viewing 3D photos taken with this device, superposition of successive screenshots from our GPS "treasure hunt" app showing how students converged to the target by triangulating its location via multiple GPS readings, and students participating in the GPS treasure hunt.

and bottom edges of the screen. Then, each time students found their current position, their app would plot their position on the map and automatically draw a circle at approximately the distance to the current goal. After walking a bit, they were able to calculate their distance again and use triangulation to determine where the goal location was. After the students programmed the app that did all of the above, they scanned a QR code we printed out and laminated at the back door of the school and followed their triangulations through a sequence of five QR code goal markers. The GPS app allowed us to teach several other mini-lectures, including the theory behind QR codes, and the recovery of one's position based on GPS data.

Another favorite application of our students was a 3D camera we built using a pair of phones seated side-by-side, with cameras eye-width apart, in a custom-built Lego mount. We had initially planned this exercise to demonstrate Bluetooth communication between phones, by having one phone initiate simultaneous photographs on both phones. However, this turned out to be impossible using App Inventor (and exceedingly difficult even in Java) since there is no easy way to direct the phones to take a photograph immediately – the standard method for using the camera instead pulls up the camera screen and then waits for the user to press a button to snap a photo. We showed the students how to overlay their images to produce red-blue anaglyph 3D images, which they enjoyed viewing with 3D glasses we supplied.

4.2 Java Examples

To transition the students from App Inventor to using the Android SDK in Java, we spent about 3 hours going through a brief Java introduction using the standard Java Eclipse environment without the Android framework. In this introduction, we introduced data types, variables, scope, functions, classes, loops, and arrays, making sure to refer every new coding concept to something we had learned in App Inventor. For example, we related Java's String class to App Inventor's text type, and we introduced arrays by showing the similarities and differences between them and App Inventor's lists.

After an obligatory "Hello World" Android app written in Java, we prepared three main examples using the Android SDK. The first app we created was a simple app to display sensor data from the device's accelerometer, gyroscope, magnetometer, and light sensors to three labels on the screen. This let us introduce the Eclipse IDE interface, which was made easier by its similarity to the App Inventor interface, using a simple app that showed how easy it is to obtain detailed sensor data. We later challenged the students to make use of this data in interesting ways. For example, we recommended that students use sensor data to control the next example we prepared, an interactive graphics app that drew artistic spiral-shaped forms on the phone's screen, with radius and number of loops decided by the distance from the center of the user's last touch. This allowed us to show off the processor speed of smartphones today as

Question	Pre-Camp Avg	Post-Camp Avg	P-Value
How would you rate your level of...			
Programming experience overall	3.350	5.200	<0.0001
Experience programming mobile devices	1.850	4.575	<0.0001
Please rate your knowledge of the following computer science concepts:			
Conditional blocks	4.650	6.600	0.0009
Loop blocks	4.750	6.150	0.0034
Math comparisons	5.150	6.800	0.0043
Variables and assignments	5.200	6.450	0.0027
Functions/procedures	4.700	6.500	0.0003
Please rate your interest in the following areas			
Studying computer science in college	5.000	5.400	0.0421
Programming apps for mobile devices	5.300	5.800	0.0662
Programming desktop applications	5.050	5.050	1.000
Developing web sites	5.050	4.700	0.1845
Developing video games	5.250	5.350	0.6295
Developing educational apps/applications/games	3.950	4.650	0.0031
Making existing computers and programs faster/more efficient	5.050	5.300	0.2617

Figure 3: Pre-camp and post-camp survey results and corresponding p-value from a paired t-test. Questions were measured using a scale from one to seven.

the devices were able to calculate and display thousands of circles each second without impacting the screen's refresh rate. We challenged the students to update the app so that it took parameters from one of the device's sensors rather than the distance from the center of a touch event.

Our final example, another favorite, was a sound manipulation app. We were able to use the phones' microphones to record several seconds of sound into an array, then use the phones' speakers to play the audio signal slowed down, sped up, in reverse, and with an echo. In doing so, we were able to teach the use of arrays, checking for boundary conditions of arrays, and the different ways to use for loops to iterate over them. We also showed how you could separate the manipulation of the array into a function in order to easily apply the same transformation repeatedly, creating the effect of a repeating echo.

4.3 Student Apps

Due to the breadth of topics and technologies covered in such a short time frame, much of the example app coding was guided programming. However, students were given plenty of time to make their own creations using the concepts they learned through the examples with minimal guidance. The students were very creative and produced several impressive creations. For example, one team enhanced the color picker in their drawing app by using the accelerometer sensor to display a ball that would roll around the screen on top of a gradient with the chosen color being the color underneath the ball. Other students also combined two or more examples into one exciting app idea. Several students combined the 3D anaglyph technique we described with the drawing app so that when you drew on the canvas it would draw a red and a blue line offset from each other at a distance chosen by a depth slider. Another group made the spiral graphics app produce 3D output. Many students implemented entirely new apps. These included a drum set app that included a picture of a drum set and played appropriate sounds when each drum was touched, a virtual piano keyboard, a two-player "Pong" game, and a two-player shooter game with Bluetooth support and on-screen video game controller buttons drawn on a canvas. These extracurricular apps demonstrated mastery of the concepts taught as well as self-directed learning of additional topics required by the student experiments.

5. ASSESSMENT

We measured the self-reported change in student interest in a variety of computing applications, student knowledge of programming techniques, and the students' level of programming experience through a pre- and post-camp survey, the results of which appear in Figure 3. Twenty students completed both the pre- and post-camp surveys, and their responses indicated marked improvement in a positive direction on nearly every survey question. We saw very statistically significant improvement in both overall programming experience and mobile programming experience over the course of the camp with p-values of less than 0.0001. There were also very statistically significant gains in self-reported knowledge of each of the five programming techniques: conditionals, loops, math comparisons, variables and assignments, and functions – with p-values ranging from 0.0003 to 0.0043. These results confirm that students felt more comfortable with programming concepts and with programming in general after participating in the camp.

Notably, the average of student responses about their interest in developing web sites went down during the course of the camp and the average response regarding student interest in developing desktop applications did not change. These results most likely come from the lack of coverage of these two topics during the camp. Aside from these two examples, responses to each of the other interest areas demonstrated some improvement during the camp. Only those subjects focused on during the camp saw significant gains, though, as student interest in developing educational apps/applications/games had a very statistically significant increase with a p-value of 0.0031, interest in studying computer science in college showed a statistically significant increase with p-value 0.0421, and interest in programming apps for mobile devices was not quite statistically significant with p-value 0.0662. Based on this feedback, the camp succeeded in its goal of increasing student interest in pursuing computer science as a focus of their education.

When restricted to responses from students from underrepresented groups, the results were similar to those of the entire group. Each question indicating improvement also did so in the overall survey results. Average responses to the interest in programming desktop applications question saw a slight decrease, whereas it stayed the same in the overall group. Of course, these results are slightly less statistically significant due to the smaller sample size of seven underrepresented students.

Our survey also included short response questions in order to gather additional feedback concerning the effectiveness of camp activities on student interest in computing. We asked students to comment on concepts that Android development made easier and more difficult to learn, to describe problems and positive experiences with the camp, and to comment on their most and least favorite exercises from the camp. The GPS scavenger hunt activity was by far the most preferred with nine out of twenty participants mentioning it as their favorite exercise. Students responded that they enjoyed both coding the app and the physical activity that they were able to do with the completed app. The sound manipulation example was the second favorite. Due to varying levels of prior programming experience, many of the comments noted that the pace was too slow at times while others said the opposite. Those with prior programming experience typically preferred the Java portion of the camp and vice versa.

Many students noted that they became more interested in mobile app programming because it was easy to create fun, personalized apps. One student wrote, "simply working with the phone reminded me how much fun programming can be." One student who adapted the drawing application to include 3D drawing and several other features described their favorite exercise as "programming the drawing app, because there were so many different features you could add to it on your own to make it different." Another described their favorite activity by saying that "all of them were exciting and unique for different reasons. I enjoyed them all."

6. CONCLUSIONS

With this being our first implementation of the camp, we saw several opportunities for improvement. Dividing the camp into novice and advanced groups would help with pacing, especially for a student group (like ours) with widely varying backgrounds. Benefits of this would include smaller camp sizes, higher ratio of teachers to students, and the ability to provide phones for every student, although sharing devices did help facilitate communication between partners, often leading to collaboration. We believe that App Inventor does present a useful transition to Java/Eclipse even for advanced users, but time spent with it could possibly be shortened for advanced students.

Overall, we believe that App Inventor provided an excellent introduction to programming concepts and transitioned well into coding mobile apps in Java using the Android SDK. We found that example app activities that made use of mobile device capabilities provided engaging learning opportunities and sparked interest in camp attendees in computer science and programming. We plan to expand upon this camp's success by establishing a self-sustaining yearly summer camp, and we hope to continue sharing our curricular ideas with the computing education community.

7. ACKNOWLEDGMENTS

The authors would like to acknowledge the Google RISE program for supporting this work. Author Dean is also partially supported by NSF award CCF-0845593.

8. REFERENCES

[1] Computer Science Teachers Association. High school computer science surveys, 2011. `http://csta.acm.org/Research/sub/HighSchoolSurveys.html`.

[2] comScore, Inc. comScore reports July 2012 U.S. mobile subscriber market share. Press Release, Sept. 2012. `http://www.comscore.com/Press_Events/Press_Releases/2012/9/comScore_Rep%orts_July_2012_U.S._Mobile_Subscriber_Market_Share`.

[3] J. Cuny. Transforming high school computing: a call to action. *ACM Inroads*, 3(2):32–36, June 2012.

[4] Mobile Statistics. Quarterly device sales, June 2012. `http://www.mobilestatistics.com/mobile-statistics/`.

[5] S. Mohamad, A. Patel, R. Latih, Q. Qassim, L. Na, and Y. Tew. Block-based programming approach: challenges and benefits. In *Electrical Engineering and Informatics (ICEEI), 2011 International Conference on*, pages 1 –5, July 2011.

[6] D. Riley. Using mobile phone programming to teach Java and advanced programming to computer scientists. In *Proceedings of the 43rd ACM technical symposium on Computer Science Education*, SIGCSE '12, pages 541–546, New York, NY, USA, 2012. ACM.

[7] K. Roy. App inventor for android: report from a summer camp. In *Proceedings of the 43rd ACM technical symposium on Computer Science Education*, SIGCSE '12, pages 283–288, New York, NY, USA, 2012. ACM.

[8] V. Taylor and R. Ladner. Data trends on minorities and people with disabilities in computing. *Commun. ACM*, 54(12):34–37, Dec. 2011.

[9] The Nielsen Company. America's new mobile majority: a look at smartphone owners in the U.S., Mar. 2012. `http://blog.nielsen.com/nielsenwire/?p=31688`.

[10] The Nielsen Company. Mobile and smartphone trends, June 2012. `http://www.nielsen.com/us/en/insights/top10s/mobile.html`.

[11] The Nielsen Company. Survey: New U.S. smartphone growth by age and income, Feb. 2012. `http://blog.nielsen.com/nielsenwire/online_mobile/survey-new-u-s-smartp%hone-growth-by-age-and-income`.

[12] C. Wilson, L. A. Sudol, C. Stephenson, and M. Stehlik. Running on empty: The failure to teach K-12 computer science in the digital age CSTA report. Technical report, 2010. `http://www.acm.org/runningonempty/`.

[13] S. Zweben and B. Bizot. Continued increase in undergraduate CS degree production; slight rise in doctoral production. *Computing Research News*, pages 7–24, May 2012.

Panel: Textbook Pricing, Present and Future

Edward F. Gehringer (moderator)
Dept. of Computer Science
North Carolina State University
Raleigh, NC 27695-8206
+1 919-515-2066
efg@ncsu.edu

Beth Lang Golub
Executive Editor, IS & CS
John Wiley & Sons
111 River Street, 6-01
Hoboken, NJ 07030-5774
+1 802-862-4684
bgolub@wiley.com

Randi Cohen
Computer Science Acquisitions Editor
Taylor & Francis
3108 Rockwater Way
Virginia Beach, VA 23456
+1 757-240-7501
randi.cohen@taylorandfrancis.com

David M. Arnow
Dept. of Computer & Information Science
Brooklyn College
2900 Bedford Avenue
Brooklyn, NY 11210
+1 718-951-5000x2040
arnow@acm.org

Clifford A. Shaffer
Department of Computer Science
Virginia Tech
Blacksburg, VA 24061
+1 540-231-4354
shaffer@cs.vt.edu

SUMMARY

Textbook pricing has become a hot-button issue in academe. Allegations are rife that textbook prices are increasing faster than tuition, and that some students spend even more on textbooks than on tuition. The matter is complicated by rapidly changing technology and the expectations that print textbooks may soon be obsolete. This panel brings together two textbook editors from major publishers and two authors with extensive experience in new media to discuss why textbooks are so expensive and how the market is likely to change in the foreseeable future.

Categories and Subject Descriptors

K.3.2 [**Computers and Education**]: Computer and Information Science Education – *Computer science education.* I.7.2 [**Document and Text Processing**]: Electronic Publishing

General Terms

Economics

Keywords

Textbooks, e-books, pricing

1. BETH LANG GOLUB

Students and professors are moving to online content solutions at an increasing rate. E-book platforms and the variety of devices are proliferating quickly. Publishers are under intense pressure from local, state and the federal government to lower the price of course materials. These and related issues are providing complexity, challenges, and opportunity to the higher education publishing industry.

SIGCSE '13, March 6–9, 2013, Denver, Colorado, USA
ACM 978-1-4503-1868-6/13/03.

Wiley is working on many fronts to keep costs and prices down. Initiatives include sending out complimentary review copies in digital format (via CourseSmart) and offering a broad range of options to students including printed loose-leaf and custom books and a variety of digital formats including CourseSmart, VitalSource, and WileyPLUS.

Wiley is exploring new online models for delivering content and services that meet the needs of professors and students. Wiley is developing new distribution models and building relationships with new technology partners. I will discuss some of the new models and provide an overview of the issues in the quickly changing publishing environment.

2. RANDI COHEN

Publishers consider a host of factors, when determining the price of textbooks. Developmental costs, production and manufacturing costs, sales and marketing costs, and author payments are just some of the many variables that influence the price of a textbook. Publishers make significant financial investments in their textbook publishing programs, with the ultimate goal to develop, produce, and promote high quality textbooks that meet the needs of professors and students worldwide. A number of adverse influences, such as piracy and copyright infringement, can also have an impact on textbook pricing and availability.

The publishing world is quickly evolving to meet the needs of customers today, by offering alternatives to traditional print textbooks, including e-textbooks. While e-publishing is still a dynamic and fast moving area, it has already had a positive impact on the world of publishing, by allowing publishers to broaden the scope of their offerings, and making lower cost alternatives available to students. Textbook rentals, custom publishing, and the ability to purchase individual book chapters are just some of the new options that publishers have been able to offer to customers through e-publishing, and more possibilities are surely on the horizon.

3. DAVID ARNOW

The blame heaped on publishers for CS textbook prices is excessive and unfair. It stems from general academic anti-corporate sentiment combined with a failure of faculty to take partial responsibility for and action against the sharp increases in university fees. The publishers are convenient whipping boys after years of increased tuition and decreased government financial aid packages.

The textbook price controversy is actually a mere coda to an era that is about to vanish. Just as technology forced an upheaval in the music industry, so will the the internet and its associated phenomena force a sea change in the textbook publishing industry. The publishers' old bête noire, The Used Book, pales as a revenue threat in comparison to the ease with which pirated PDFs are obtained, or to the $14 Apple book model, or to the proliferation of MOOCs.

The only way to preserve some portion of textbook publishing is for publishers to change the model: to recognize that passive, fixed texts, no matter how comprehensive, will soon no longer support a viable business model. They will need to be replaced by something else, either employing future technologies that I have no ability to predict or contemporary ones, such as online, interactive, customizable, multi-media, service-offering "etexts". We already see the beginnings of this.

These changes will result in significantly lower prices, but the Used Book will vanish, piracy will be less compelling and the publishers should end up with a sustainable model. The market itself will be very competitive, and in a reversal of increased concentration in the hands of a shrinking field of providers, we will witness a proliferation of providers ranging from individual professors, to depts and colleges, to small startups to The Big Companies.

4. CLIFF SHAFFER

For about a decade I had a data-structures textbook published by Prentice Hall. It was priced at well over $100, and the publisher refused to consider producing it in a lower-cost paperback version due to their marketing model, even though I was sure that it would be more popular in a low-cost format. Eventually, the book went out of print and I recovered the publication rights. While the original book publication was a good thing for me financially, "losing" the support of an in-print publisher was beneficial to me in terms of my research and pedagogical goals. Once I had publication rights back, I completed the third edition of the text and posted it online for free. Since then, Dover Publications has picked up the print rights and offers a low-cost print edition [1], [2] while I retain all on-line publication rights. The online version (a PDF file) is now downloaded thousands of times per month, and I am in contact with a number of instructors who are using the book for their class. Despite survey data that seems to indicate roughly equal preference for print and online text (when price is not a complicating factor), my own experience is that students overwhelmingly prefer the free online version over the print version, even though the print cost is minimal (< $20).

My interst in e-textbooks is an important reason for not wanting to limit my publication rights. Posting the PDF version of the book is intended only as a short-term solution as we transition to a larger online project called OpenDSA (see http://algoviz.org/OpenDSA for more information). The idea is to build an online textbook deeply integrated with algorithm visualizations and automatically assessed exercises. That project benefits from having available complete textbook-quality content. Since I have complete rights to use my own text, I do not need to worry about whether I am violating my publisher's rights as we develop our online project.

A whole new wave of online education projects like OpenDSA, the Khan Academy, and large online classes (MOOCs) have been in the news lately. Whether done independently or in collaboration with a textbook publisher, these represent a new model for textbooks. Under this model, textbooks become sophisticated online systems that integrate multimedia content with assessment. Rather than merely static content, this model transforms the textbook into a flexible learning environment, which can be provided as a service rather than as a commodity. I cannot predict how this will affect "textbook" pricing. On the one hand, the internet allows authors or groups to self-publish content. On the other hand, these learning environments are far more complex and expensive to build than traditional textbooks, which might make self-publication financially impractical. Today these efforts are often supported as research projects. In the future, publishers might play an important role in financing and marketing sophisticated development efforts.

5. FORMAT NOTE

There will be four speakers on this panel. The moderator will not make a presentation, but may address questions to the panelists, or ask different panel members to comment on questions from the audience.

6. REFERENCE

[1] Shaffer, Clifford A., *Data Structures and Algorithm Analysis in C++, 3rd edition*, Dover Books, 2011

CS Principles: Development and Evolution of a Course and a Community

Owen Astrachan
Duke University
ola@cs.duke.edu

Amy Briggs
Middlebury College
briggs@middlebury.edu

Lien Diaz
College Board
ldiaz@collegeboard.org

R. Brook Osborne
Duke University
rbo@cs.duke.edu

Categories and Subject Descriptors

K.3.2 [**Computers and Education**]: Computer and Information Science Education – *computer science education*

General Terms

Measurement, Experimentation, Standardization .

Keywords

Computer Science Education, K-12 Curriculum, CS Principles, Computational Thinking, Outreach.

1. SUMMARY

The Computer Science Principles project is in the fourth year of a roughly eight year project to develop a new Advanced Placement course that broadens participation in computer science while providing a rigorous yet engaging academic experience that will earn college credit and/or placement. In this special session we discuss new developments in the project and share student work and instructor perspectives from those pilot programs that have been part of the project for the past two years. In previous SIGCSE special sessions we have reported on the development of the project and its relationship to a national initiative (CS10K) to broaden participation in high school computing while expanding the number of teachers educating students in high school computing and computer science. [1-3] In this session we report on the conclusion of a second year of pilots that included nine high schools partnered with eight colleges (2011-2012) and a third pilot using a new portfolio exam (2012-2013) being conducted at six schools. The second pilot included new pedagogies and a prototype exam delivered to all students in the pilot. In this session we report on results this second round of piloting; on how the pilots succeeded in reaching goals of broadening participation and delivering a course that maintained fidelity to the curricular framework of the CS Principles project.

We also report on the third pilot --- the first to use a portfolio exam that will be refined over the course of ensuing pilots, and used when the course becomes an AP course with a national exam by 2016-2017. This third pilot will expand to 40-50 schools in 2013-2014. We report on how a community of educators is being developed around these pilots to help ensure their success.

The pilot instructors will talk about their experiences with the portfolio-based exam that students will have submitted at the time of this conference.

SIGCSE'13, March 6–9, 2013, Denver, Colorado, USA.
ACM 978-1-4503-1868-6/13/03.

2. CS Principles (Owen Astrachan)

The CS Principles (CSP) course is one of two national projects partially funded by the NSF that are designed to provide a foundation for change in how computer science is taught and to whom it is taught. Together with the Exploring Computer Science (ECS)[4, 5] project, CSP is part of the foundation that builds on the success of other projects to expand the number and reach of schools and teachers involved in teaching computer science at the high school level.

We provide a brief overview of the project, its development, and its relationship to similar projects and courses of instruction. We introduce the format of this session: including results from both students and teachers delivering the course and the plans for the future including the development of a portfolio assessment at a national scale, e.g., as is included in AP Studio Art [6] and the National Board Certification for teachers [7]. We report on the use of objective and free-response questions in the pilot delivered to 17 schools in 2011-2012 and how exams built on these questions led to the portfolio component of the exam being piloted now and next year. We discuss the future of this project including its relationship to large-scale professional development for teachers.

As the PI of the CS Principles project, Owen Astrachan helps coordinate the group of educators and researchers who oversee the development of the curricular framework, the exam, and the pilots.

3. Broadening Participation (Amy Briggs)

Since its inception the CS Principles course has been designed to broaden participation --- to expand the population of students taking high school computer science courses [8]. In this part of the session we show by example both the rigor and engagement of the assessments and pedagogical approaches that are being developed and encouraged as part of this project. This includes results from the free-response/open-ended questions used in the second pilot and the preliminary results of the portfolio exam questions being used in the current, third pilot.

As co-PI of the CS Principles project Amy Briggs helps oversee development of curricular materials and works with the project team to assess and ensure that the project is following established research and best practices in broadening participation

4. Expansion to a National Exam (Lien Diaz)

This project is funded both by the NSF and the College Board. As part of Advanced Placement program the CS Principles project can leverage resources that are part of every AP program, including professional development for instructors and access to educational and psychometric resources for developing exams. The process of developing new AP exams using evidence-centered design [9] has led to new and richer assessments in several AP exams, including Biology and Physics. This same process was used in the CSP project, connecting assessment design to support: student learning objectives in the AP CSP Curriculum Framework; pilot implementation; and scoring of the computer-based exam. The development of the course and exam continues to foster participation and success in computer science education, especially among students traditionally underrepresented in computer science. We report on this and other aspects of the AP program that impact the stakeholders in this national project: students, teachers, researchers, and others.

As co-PI for the CS Principles project Lien Diaz oversees all aspects of the project related to the development and establishment of the course as an Advanced Placement course including the development of the portfolio exam.

5. Building a Community (Brook Osborne)

Building a community of educators[10] has been an important component of this project. In this part of the session we demonstrate and describe the practices by which we both supported pilot instructors and helped assess and track the project as part of the development of the portfolio-based exam. We discuss future directions for the much larger pilot planned for 2013-2014 and how all educators that are interested in CSP will be able to participate in the community we are building and facilitating.

Brook Osborne is the Outreach and Pilot Coordinator for the CS Principles project. She works to ensure the success of the supported pilot instructors and those who are teaching CS Principles courses but are not officially involved in the pilot courses.

6. Report on Portfolio Exam (Piloters)

The four high school instructors and two college instructors who are delivering a course that uses the three portfolio questions that are the prototype of those to be used on the national, Advanced Placement exam will report on their experiences delivering the course. Each of these instructors participated in the second pilot, delivered in 2011-2012, and will be able to compare the current course with the portfolio assessment with the course they previously delivered that did not include such an assessment. We will share results and student work that were part of each of the pilots.

7. Intended Audience

This special session is designed for all educators interested in the development of a future Advanced Placement course that includes a novel, portfolio exam to be administered by 2016-2017. Best practices in educational research, in using established pedagogical approaches designed to change how students learn, and in providing professional development opportunities for teachers will be discussion topics that transcend their particulars in the case of Computer Science Principles.

8. REFERENCE

[1] O. Astrachan, H. Walker, C. Stephenson, and L. Diaz, "Advanced Placement computer science: the future of tracking the first year of instruction," *Proceedings of the SIGCSE Symposium,* vol. 51, pp. 397-398, 2009.

[2] O. Astrachan, K. Haynie, C. Stephenson, L. Diaz, and A. Briggs, "Re-imagining the first year of computing," presented at the Proceedings of the 41st ACM technical symposium on Computer science education, Milwaukee, Wisconsin, USA, 2010.

[3] O. Astrachan, T. Barnes, D. D. Garcia, J. Paul, B. Simon, and L. Snyder, "CS principles: piloting a new course at national scale," presented at the Proceedings of the 42nd ACM technical symposium on Computer science education, Dallas, TX, USA, 2011.

[4] J. Goode and G. Chapman. (2013, January 2012). *Exploring Computer Science 4.0* http://www.exploringcs.org/

[5] J. Goode and J. Margolis, "Exploring Computer Science: A Case Study of School Reform," *ACM Transactions on Computing Education,* vol. 11, 2011.

[6] N. Chudowsky and J. Pelligrino, "Large Scale Assessments that Support Learning: Will it Take?," *Theory into Practice,* vol. 42, pp. 75-83, 2003 2003.

[7] D. Goldhaber and E. Anthony, "Can Teacher Quality Be Effectively Assessed? National Board Certfication as a Signal of Effective Teaching," *The Review of Economics and Statistics,* vol. 89, pp. 134-150, 2007.

[8] O. Astrachan, G. Chapman, and R. B. Osborne, "Broadening Participation: ECS and CS Principles," presented at the CS&IT, Irvine, CA, 2012.

[9] R. J. Mislevy and G. D. Haertel, "Implications of Evidence-Centered Design for Educational Testing," *Educational Measurement: Issues and Practice,* vol. 25, pp. 6-20, 2006.

[10] R. Dufour, "What is a "Professional Learning Community"," *Educational Leadership,* vol. 61, pp. 6-11, 2004.

Addressing 21st Century Skills by Embedding Computer Science in K-12 Classes

Debra S Goldberg[1] Dirk Grunwald[1] Clayton Lewis[1]
Jessica Feld[1] Kristin Donley[2] Odette Edbrooke[2]

[1]Department of Computer Science, University of Colorado Boulder, 430 UCB, Boulder, CO 80309, USA
[2] Boulder Valley School District, 6500 Arapahoe, Boulder, CO 80303, USA
{debra.goldberg, dirk.grunwald, clayton.lewis, jessica.feld}@colorado.edu
{Kristin.donley, Odette.edbrooke}@bvsd.org

SUMMARY

School districts across the country are embracing 21st century skills, and grappling with how to teach these to their K-12 students. At the same time, computer science educators are grappling with how to broaden participation. These two dilemmas are related, in that computer science can be used to teach many of the 21st century skills, and bringing computer science to all K-12 students can help broaden participation.

For computer scientists, key 21st century skills [4] include creativity & innovation, critical thinking and problem solving, communication & collaboration, information literacy, media literacy and information, communications and technology (ICT) literacy – these skills go beyond traditional "computational thinking" skills because they include reflections on how computation affects social processes (such as the role of computational media in society).

Since 2009, K-12 educators and computer science graduate students in the Engaging Computer Science in Traditional Education (ECSITE, pronounced "excite") project have developed curricular units that are embedded into non-computing K-12 classes [3]. These units collectively address many 21st century skills, and have been introduced into arts, geography, government, health, music, and science classes

Categories and Subject Descriptors

K.3.2 [**Computers and Education**]: Computer and Information Science Education – *curriculum*.

Keywords

K-12, computational thinking, interdisciplinary curriculum

1. OBJECTIVE OF THE SESSION

The Engaging Computer Science in Traditional Education (ECSITE) Program is a 5-year program that began in 2009 to bring computer science into traditional K-12 classrooms. It is one of the first of the 400 programs funded by the U.S. National Science Foundation (NSF) GK-12 program to focus on computer science. We are working with middle schools and high schools in four local school districts. We have partnered with other organizations to bring computer science to a diverse audience, and have provided mentors for high school students to engage in computer science research.

The ECSITE program "embeds" computing into traditional classes by carefully studying the existing curriculum of a particular subject area (*e.g.* biology) and determining how to augment those parts to emphasize 21st century skills such as computational thinking, computing tools and structured problem solving. Other classes with which we engage, such as art, sociology and geography, have little history of using math or computation in their curriculum. In those classes, we have emphasized broader curricular modules that use computational tools (such as maps and developing algorithmic specifications of geographic elements) or descriptive tools that better help students understand how technology impacts a particular topic (such as the role of cryptography, security and voting algorithms in government).

Once teachers have co-taught an ECSITE unit, most are willing to continuing including the unit in future years. However, this involves having an ECSITE fellow (a computer science graduate student) spend time with the teacher developing new curriculum for a school year. One of the biggest challenges we've encountered is disseminating material to other schools and finding a teacher-engagement model that yields sustainable results from our interactions. without requiring an intense commitment from a member of our department. We will discuss one successful method (insertion into district educational guidelines) and one that is on-going (sustainable collaboration between an art and computer science class). Both of these approaches are difficult to achieve in practice, and both depend on successful engagement with K-12 computer science educators. We have also had success having an ECSITE fellow work with a teacher for just a few days, bringing previously developed curriculum to a new school. This approach depends on successful engagement of college computer science departments.

This session will include hands-on activities, so participants can experience for themselves these lessons that incorporate computational thinking and 21st century skills into non-computing high school classes. One key objective of this session is to offer these activities to other computer science educators as effective tools that they may want to offer to high schools near them. Another key objective of this session is to synthesize our experience and that of participants to determine whether the methods we found effective would be applicable to other school districts, and whether methods effective elsewhere would be applicable to our region.

SIGCSE'13, March 6–9, 2013, Denver, Colorado, USA.
ACM 978-1-4503-1868-6/13/03.

2. OUTLINE OF THE SESSION

Through our experience, we have had successfully worked with four school districts, numerous teachers and after school organizations. In this session, we will describe the structure of our curriculum development in two classes (biology and sociology) and briefly provide an overview of our experience in other classes, including math, art and geography.

Table 1. Overview of the session schedule

10 minutes	Overview of ECSITE program and session goals
20 minutes	CS in AP Biology
20 minutes	CS in Civics and Government
25 minutes	Discussion

The sample curricula we will discuss are described below. We have identified 21st century skills listed in the P21 framework definitions with italics.

2.1 Biology (HS)

This unit, which was taught in Advanced Placement (AP) Biology classes and other upper-level high school biology classes, addressed the biology standards of genetics and evolution [2]. Participants will receive handouts for three lessons, and will also work through the third lesson.

After students are introduced to the vocabulary of algorithms by formulating algorithms for every-day tasks, they participate in a "living computer" algorithm: each student is given a numbered instruction that represents one step in the algorithm, perform their step, and hand the "output" to the next participant in line until the final step is reached. In this lesson, students learn to *analyze how parts of a whole interact with each other to produce overall outcomes in complex systems*.

In the second lesson, DNA sequence comparison is explained in terms of word search puzzles containing progressively more error types that model different types of DNA mutations. Students are asked to think about how they solved the puzzles, and other possible ways a person or computer might approach the problem. Then students use online software for comparing DNA sequences. In this lesson, students practice *creativity and innovation* by *brainstorming* and *evaluating their ideas*, then learn to *apply technology effectively*.

The third lesson, which will be worked through during this session, has participants split into groups and use DNA similarity scores to build phylogenetic (evolutionary) trees. Groups are given slightly different algorithms, which produce very different results, showing why software users, and not only developers, need an understanding of the underlying algorithms and parameters. Here students learn *collaboration* skills and enhance their *information literacy* and *critical thinking* skills.

2.2 Civics and Government

As described in [1], ECSITE fellows frequently contribute to classroom discussions with content related to computer science and citizenship, political information, and anonymous speech. The United States' "Founding Fathers" unit, which is a common lecture across our local K-12 educational setting, now asks students to use computational thinking and *critical thinking* skills to determine which decisions should utilize the wisdom of the crowds and which should be left to representatives. After learning Condorcet's Jury Theorem (which argues about the relative probability of a given group reaching a correct decision) the class is divided into two teams to play chess; one team votes on each move and the other team elects a representative to play. This supports their ability to *reason effectively* and to *make judgments and decisions*. Another traditional US Government lesson about the Federalist Papers now involves a discussion of the importance of anonymous speech and an exercise explaining Tor and WikiLeaks. This teaches the ability to *apply a fundamental understanding of the ethical/legal issues surrounding the access and use of information technologies*. In this session, participants will discuss how modern technology has caused changes in the interpretation of the right of privacy, which is not explicitly in the Bill of Rights. We conclude with an encryption exercise that helps to explain the Copyright Act's limitations on the First Amendment to the US constitution, further enhancing students' understanding of *legal issues related to information technologies*. These additions to the curriculum bring a better understanding of computer science into the K-12 system. At the same time, the lessons gain relevance as they are revised to reflect 18th century ideas in a 21st century world.

3. EXPECTATIONS & SUITABILITY

This special session is intended for K-12 educators, as well as education researchers and computer science professionals interested in transforming K-12 and computing education. We hope that all participants are able to both learn and contribute to methods to disseminate existing curriculum and sustain efforts once that curriculum is used in a school.

This session is better suited to be a special session than a panel or paper because of its interactive nature, and the final discussion will have all attendees participate as equals, whereas the format of a panel or paper session is more conducive to treating the presenter(s) as the experts.

4. ORGANIZERS

Debra Goldberg, Dirk Grunwald and Clayton Lewis are faculty in the Computer Science Department at the University of Colorado, Boulder and co-direct the NSF ECSITE program. Jessica Feld is the Program Coordinator for ECSITE, and former elementary educator. Kristin Donley teaches science in the Boulder Valley School District (BVSD), won the 2011 Best Should Teach Award, and was the 2012 Colorado Teacher of the Year. Odette Edbrooke is a civics teacher in BVSD and the Teacher Leader for high school Social Studies in the district. Kristin and Odette are also former ECSITE participants who helped develop the units presented in this special session.

5. REFERENCES

[1] Ambrose, M and Edbrooke, O. 2012. Social Education. to appear.

[2] Gallagher, S.R., et al. 2011. A First Attempt to Bring Computational Biology into Advanced High School Biology Classrooms. *PLoS Computational Biology* 7(10): e1002244, doi/10.1371/journal.pcbi.1002244

[3] Goldberg, D. et al. 2012. Engaging Computer Science in Traditional Education: the ECSITE project. In ITiCSE 2012: The 17th Annual Conference on Innovation and Technology in Computer Science Education, Haifa, Israel.

[4] Trilling, B., Fadel, C. 21st century skills: learning for life in our times. (2009). San Francisco, CA: Jossey-Bass

Git on the Cloud in the Classroom

Joseph Lawrance
Wentworth Institute of Technology
550 Huntington Ave
Boston, MA 02115
lawrancej@wit.edu

Seikyung Jung
Bridgewater State University
131 Summer St
Bridgewater, MA 02324
sjung@bridgew.edu

Charles Wiseman
Wentworth Institute of Technology
550 Huntington Ave
Boston, MA 02115
wisemanc@wit.edu

ABSTRACT

Numerous CS faculty have demonstrated the benefits of using version control in courses other than software engineering. However, they maintained their own servers, and to the best of our knowledge, none published experiences with version control in CS1 courses for non-CS engineering majors. As a result, even faculty experienced with version control may hesitate to adopt it in some classes, fearing that it is too difficult, time consuming or distracting. In this paper, we describe how we adopted version control in a CS1 course for non-CS engineering majors, and how project hosting services facilitated its use. Our experience indicates that undergraduate engineering majors in CS courses can gain competence in version control, and project hosting services simplify course management.

Categories and Subject Descriptors

K.3.1 [**Computer Uses in Education**]: Computer managed instruction; K.3.2 [**Computer and Information Science Education**]: Computer science education

General Terms

Education, Management

Keywords

Version control; course management; software engineering

1. INTRODUCTION

Version control is essential to software development [11, 15, 21] and beneficial in the classroom [6, 10, 12, 18], yet few students gain sufficient experience through undergraduate courses alone [18, 24]. One industry source stated: "I've worked with some twenty-odd interns [...] all of them graduate students at top electrical engineering and computer science departments from around the world. I've also interviewed many more job candidates. One fact that has continually amazed me is what a tiny fraction of them have had any previous experience using version control systems. Not only will using version control help you write better software, but it will help you get a job if you ever want to go into industry." [24]. One student replied: "As an undergraduate I can tell you from experience that there are virtually no classes that expect you to use [version control]" [24]. In an internal survey of Wentworth computer science students in 2012, one said that we need to emphasize in our curriculum: "More mobile development. More micro-controller development. **VERSION CONTROL**" (emphasis theirs).

Students should gain experience in version control, but often do not for lack of faculty experience, time, or early emphasis in the curriculum. Faculty may avoid version control for lack of experience: Clifton et al. noted that only one faculty (and none of the teaching assistants) in their department had prior experience [6]. Experienced faculty may avoid version control in the classroom for lack of time: some authors noted the administrative overhead necessary to set up and manage servers [6], [18]. Faculty may also avoid version control outside of software engineering courses because the ACM Computer Science Curriculum [1, 2, 3] places coverage of the topic in a three hour section called "Software Engineering Tools and Environments." Indeed, Reid and Wilson noted that "undergraduates in CS at the University of Toronto were not introduced to version control until their final-year software engineering course. As a result, most students completed their degree with only a hazy understanding of version control's importance and how best to use it" [18].

In this paper, we do not focus on the benefits of version control in the classroom (as others have already done); instead, we examine how to overcome the obstacles that prevent faculty from using it more frequently. For the inexperienced, this paper briefly reviews relevant background knowledge, surveys related work, cites tutorials, and describes how to set up and use version control in the classroom, step-by-step. For the time-strapped, this paper explains how cloud project hosting services reduce administrative overhead. For faculty who avoid version control outside of software engineering courses, this paper describes how non-CS engineering freshmen successfully used it for work submission in CS1. This paper also describes our experience with version control in object oriented programming, compiler design, and software engineering courses. Finally, this paper calls for the ACM Computer Science curriculum to properly reflect the importance of version control by emphasizing early and repeated exposure to it.

SIGCSE'13, March 6–9, 2013, Denver, Colorado, USA.

2. BACKGROUND AND RELATED WORK

2.1 Version control

Version control systems enable multiple contributors to record changes (make *commits*) to a project over time. Obsolete version control systems locked files to ensure that only one contributor could edit at a time. Modern version control systems (e.g., CVS, Subversion, Git, Mercurial) handle concurrent contributions by *merging* changes together. Merging not only facilitates concurrent contributions, but also enables organizing commits by topic (*branch*) or contributor (*fork*). If changes overlap (*conflict*), then the contributor must *resolve* the conflict manually. Free training resources are available for all of these systems.[1,2]

Version control systems are either *centralized* or *distributed*. Centralized version control systems (such as CVS and Subversion) store the project history (*repository*) on a remote server, not locally. In centralized systems, making a commit records changes to the server; consequently, contributors *must* merge any recent changes from the remote server (and resolve any conflicts) *before* making a commit. Distributed version control systems (such as Git and Mercurial) include all of the operations of centralized systems, but decouple recording changes from publishing them by storing project history locally and on remote servers. In these systems, making a commit records changes locally; contributors must then *push* to publish commits to a server and *fetch* or *pull* to acquire commits from others. Users of distributed version control systems can always make commits off-line without conflicts and decide when (and if) to merge later.

Distributed version control systems are more robust and secure than centralized systems. While centralized systems number commits sequentially, distributed systems use secure hashing algorithms to identify commits and detect tampering with history, such as students rewriting logs to "give the impression that they had completed work earlier than they actually did", as is possible with CVS [18]. Distributed systems store data in a hidden folder in the project root, while centralized systems store data in every subdirectory of the project (e.g., `CVS/` or `.svn/`), making it easy for students to confuse these folders with the working directory and damage both [18]. In the event of a server failure, users of centralized systems lose project history and the ability to make commits; users of distributed systems lose nothing.

2.2 Version control in the classroom

Faculty have noted the benefits of version control for assigning, collecting, and returning student work [6, 12, 18]. Posting assignments using version control enables students to start with skeleton code and test cases, and submit work repeatedly to faculty at any time before or after the deadline, since submissions have timestamps. Version control makes it easy to post grades, give feedback on work in progress [6, 12], review changes (*diffs*), work remotely across multiple machines [16, 18] or assist during office hours [18].

Using version control offers other pedagogical benefits. Version control makes it easy to identify problems in student work habits [6, 12, 18], collaborate in group projects [10, 12, 18], assess individual contributions in group settings [6], coordinate among faculty and teaching assistants [6], and back up work off-site [12]. Students exposed to version control early on improve work habits in time for working on team projects [18] and also build skills for their careers.

The alternatives to version control for course management are worse. Assigning or collecting work via email clutters inboxes, and students may forget (or claim spam filters ate) attachments, requiring follow-up. Collecting work on a server requires system administration. Course management systems such as Blackboard or Moodle solve these problems, but students will not use these systems outside of school.

2.3 Project hosting services

Previously, faculty who published their experiences with version control (ourselves included) administered their own servers [6, 12, 18]. Faculty administering a server can retain full control, but bear the burden of acquiring access to a server, maintaining student rosters, initializing repositories for each student, ensuring sensible permissions, giving each student secure access, and configuring a web interface so students can confirm that they pushed commits properly. Thanks to project hosting services, we no longer maintain our own servers for version control.

Cloud-based *project hosting services* host version control repositories on-line so that contributors on a team can share changes with each other *without* administering their own servers. Examples include: Assembla, Bitbucket, Github, Google Code, ProjectLocker, Sourceforge, and Unfuddle. Many services host open source projects free of charge. In addition, these services may also include an issue tracker and a wiki, similar to systems such as IBM Rational Team Concert [16] or DrProject [19], and include code review features that facilitate rapid feedback to students.

Faculty should adopt project hosting services carefully because the U.S. Family Educational Rights and Privacy Act (FERPA) requires maintaining the privacy of student educational records. Thus, it is necessary to "prevent students from seeing one another's repositories" [18]. However, according the U.S. Department of Education, "*FERPA does not prohibit the use of cloud computing solutions for the purpose of hosting education records*; rather, FERPA requires States to use reasonable methods to ensure the security of their information technology solutions" [23]. Fortunately, Assembla,[3] Bitbucket,[4] and Github[5] offer *private repositories* for educational use free of charge, so that students and faculty can share only with each other, and nobody else.

3. WHY GIT ON THE CLOUD?

We chose Git due to the technical merits of distributed systems and because more project hosting services support Git directly or indirectly than any other version control system. Assembla, Bitbucket and Github all support Git; if any service fails, the class can switch to a competitor. Ensuring such continuity with Subversion would require local backups; fortunately, Git makes local backups by design and works well with Subversion repositories. Git is also the fastest version control system, and has gained market share at the expense of CVS, Mercurial, and Subversion (see Figure 1). Apple, Google, Microsoft, IBM, Facebook, Linux, Perl, Eclipse, Android, and Ruby on Rails all use Git.

[1] `http://www.ericsink.com/vcbe/html/`

[2] `http://software-carpentry.org/4_0/vc/`

[3] `https://assembla.com/`

[4] `https://bitbucket.org/`

[5] `https://github.com/`

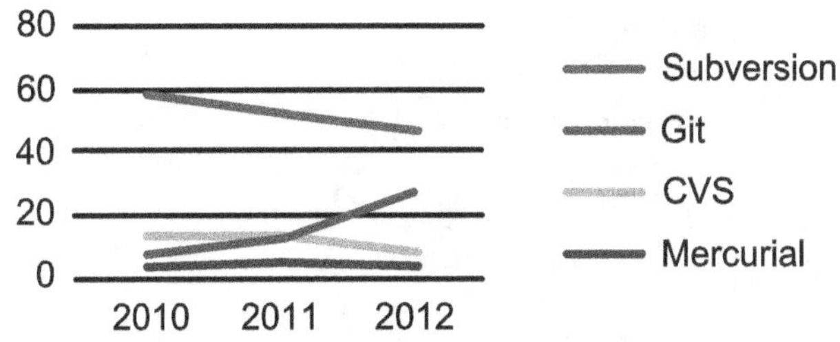

Figure 1: Market share by year. [4, 7, 8, 9]

4. SETTING UP GIT ON THE CLOUD

This section shows how to set up Git on the cloud so that faculty can modify any repository in the classroom, but students cannot see or modify each others' repositories. Section 5 shows an example of using Git for course management. We do not assume familiarity with Git, but cannot cover everything; read these books [5, 13, 22] or tutorials[6,7,8,9] for more information. Graphical interfaces to Git use the same names for commands as Git itself; either way, do not type in $ (the shell prompt) or instruction examples literally.

Faculty must first decide on a project hosting service. Assembla offers free private repositories regardless of purpose, but excludes code review or issue tracking. Bitbucket offers unlimited free private repositories automatically for `.edu` domains. Github offers free private repositories by request.[10]

4.1 Preliminaries for faculty and students

1. Download and install Git[11] and merge tools (e.g., Meld, TortoiseGit, or KDiff3) to handle conflicts easily.
2. Set up the user name and email for Git. For example,

```
$ git config --global user.name    "Jane Smith"
$ git config --global user.email   jane@wit.edu
```

3. (*Optional*) Set up the commit editor. For example, to set up Notepad++ (if it is on the PATH),

```
$ git config --global core.editor \
"'notepad++' -multiInst -notabbar -nosession"
```

4. Create an account on the project hosting service with the school-issued email address. Reuse the school-issued user name if possible; otherwise, collect user names from students (e.g., through Google Forms).
5. (*Recommended*) Create an SSH authentication key to avoid password re-entry for push and pull operations.

```
$ ssh-keygen -t rsa
```

Share the public key (`~/.ssh/id_rsa.pub`) with the project hosting service and use SSH remote repository URLs; otherwise, use HTTPS URLs.

[6] `http://git-scm.com/book`
[7] `http://gitref.org/`
[8] `http://gitimmersion.com/`
[9] `http://try.github.com/`
[10] `https://github.com/edu`
[11] `http://git-scm.com/download/`

4.2 Course repository setup for faculty

1. Create the course repository. For example,

```
$ git init CS1
$ cd CS1
```

2. Put course materials into the new folder (e.g., in `CS1`).
3. (*Recommended*) List paths or file globs for Git to ignore in a file called `.gitignore`. For example,

```
*.class
*.exe
*.o
bin
```

4. Add the current folder to Git, and then commit.

```
$ git add .
$ git commit -m "Added course materials."
```

5. On the project hosting service, create a new *public* course repository for students to clone (e.g., `CS1`).
6. Add the remote repository URL to Git. For example,

```
$ git remote add origin \
git@bitbucket.org:lawrancej/cs1.git
```

7. Publish commits to the project hosting service:

```
$ git push -u origin master
```

8. Instruct students to follow steps in the next subsection.
9. Add each student's private fork to Git. For example,

```
$ git remote add alice \
git@bitbucket.org:alice/cs1.git
$ git remote add bob \
git@bitbucket.org:bob/cs1.git
```

10. (*Recommended*) Verify the class set up Git properly.

```
$ git remote -v    # Is the roster complete?
$ git fetch --all # Did students push?
```

4.3 Setup for students

1. On the hosting service, create a new *private* repository (e.g., `CS1`). Do not fork the course repository.
2. Then, add faculty as the sole collaborator so faculty can view work, offer feedback and post grades.[12]
3. Download (*clone*) the public course repository, and enter the folder. For example,

```
$ git clone \
https://bitbucket.org/lawrancej/cs1.git
$ cd cs1
```

4. Add your remote URL and push to it. For example,

```
$ git remote add my \
https://alice@bitbucket.org/alice/cs1.git
$ git push -u my master
```

[12] If available, give administrator privileges to faculty.

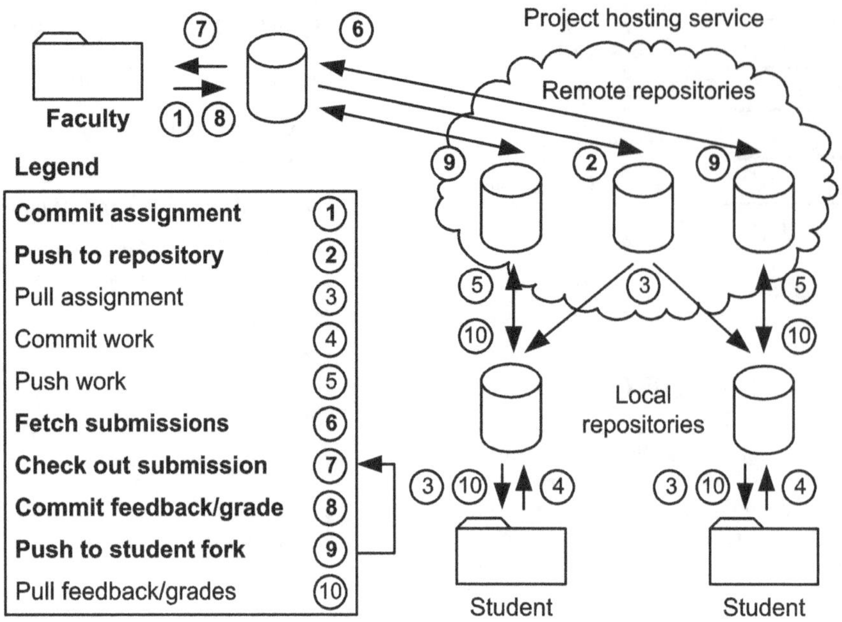

Figure 2: Course management with Git on the cloud (faculty steps in bold).

5. USING GIT: AN EXAMPLE

Figure 2 depicts the steps; Table 1 lists useful commands.

1. (**Faculty**) Commit to a new branch (e.g., `assignment1`), to organize submissions and prevent merge conflicts.

```
$ git checkout -b assignment1 master
$ echo "By Monday, write a C program to print:
Hello, world." > assignment1.txt
$ git add assignment1.txt
$ git commit -m "Assignment 1"
```

2. (**Faculty**) Push to the course repository (`origin`)

```
$ git push origin assignment1
```

3. (Students) Fetch and check out `assignment1` from `origin`.

```
$ git fetch origin
$ git checkout -b assignment1 origin/assignment1
```

4. (Students) Complete and commit the assignment.

```
$ echo "#include <stdio.h>
int main (int argc, char ** argv) {
   printf("Hello, world.\n");
}" > assignment1.c
$ git add assignment1.c
$ git commit -m "Assignment 1 solution"
```

5. (Students) Push work to your private repository.

```
$ git push my assignment1
```

6. (**Faculty**) Collect (fetch) submissions at the deadline.

```
$ git fetch --all
```

7. (**Faculty**) Checkout a student's submission (e.g., `alice`).

```
$ git branch -D assignment1
$ git checkout -b assignment1 alice/assignment1
$ less *.c
```

8. (**Faculty**) Commit feedback or grades.

```
$ echo "Good job. Grade: A" >> assignment1.txt
$ git commit -a -m "Feedback for Alice."
```

9. (**Faculty**) Push `assignment1` feedback to the student. Repeat steps 7-9 for each student.

```
$ git push alice assignment1
```

10. (Students) Pull feedback from faculty.

```
$ git checkout assignment1 # Switch to branch
$ git pull my assignment1  # Fetch and merge
$ less assignment1.txt     # Review feedback
```

Table 1: Useful Git commands

Show status	`git status`
Show unstaged changes	`git diff`
Show commit logs	`gitk --all &`
Git graphical interface	`git gui &`
Merge in `branch`	`git merge branch`
Handle conflicts	`git mergetool`
(Merging) Use their `file`	`git checkout --theirs file`
Set aside (stash) changes	`git stash`
Discard since last commit	`git reset --hard HEAD`
Count commits by author	`git shortlog -s`
Force a push to `remote`	`git push -f remote`

6. CLASSROOM EXPERIENCES

We learned best practices for using version control systems with project hosting services from experience with software engineering, compiler design, and object-oriented programming courses before using it in CS1 for engineering majors.

6.1 For computer science majors

Although faculty can use version control on the cloud for course management (and that is a good way to get started), version control lends itself to complex project-based pedagogy, since it tracks work for real-world projects. In short, students learned well by collaborating with each other.

In our software engineering course, we asked student teams to select and improve an existing open source project. Because Git can interface well with almost every other version control system, students were able to choose any project. Version control was essential to run this course: students needed it to collaborate, and we needed it to distinguish student work from upstream project contributions.

In our compiler design course, we asked student teams to write a toy compiler and also contribute features to a class-wide project. From this experience, everyone (ourselves included) learned how good habits such as topic branching and small, incremental commits reduced the risk of merge conflicts. Many students even contributed fixes to the course materials themselves and asked us to pull in their changes. We discovered that with distributed version control, because we did not *need* to merge in changes, it facilitated conversations about whether code was good enough to be merged in. One student in this course told us: "learning Git was probably the most useful thing for me, personally." Another student told us that they learned more about version control in this course than in their software engineering course.

In our sophomore object-oriented programming course, we asked students to review each others' code and also collaborate in teams on projects of their choosing. Students reviewed each other's code anonymously, learning through practice how to assess quality. Just as peer instruction is more effective than traditional lecture [14], we found that code review engaged peers to learn from each other. In an unsolicited email, one student in this course said:

> I've been meaning to thank you again for being such a progressive teacher as when I was in your class having us use Git, and talking to us about unit testing. My understanding of Git was very important in me getting an awesome summer dev job. Thank you! I even use Git to host my own code so I can code on multiple computers without an issue. I just want to say keep up with the way you're teaching, I wish other teachers were as progressive about using technology like Git. I'm sure other teachers would benefit from using Git as a submission system, or even have the students post onto a personal or school Github.

Another student in this course told us:

> I just got back from an interview, and the guy interviewing me asked me if I knew Git. I said yes, in fact, we used it in the Java course. The interviewer said: "Thank your professor."

6.2 For engineering majors in CS1

In our search through the SIGCSE literature, we found no published experiences with using version control in CS1 courses for non-CS engineering majors.

In our CS1 course, we asked electrical and mechanical engineering freshmen to complete individual assignments and in-class activities in C, using version control for course management as described in Section 5. As in our courses for computer science majors, we adopted the Gutenberg method of teaching by answering questions about the reading in class [17] and the Thayer method of teaching by moving work into the classroom [20]. We programmed in front of the class, and students often typed what we typed. When students asked for our code, we committed to a separate branch to avoid conflicts with their work, and asked them to commit or stash their work first before pulling from us.

In our experience, almost all students were able to learn enough Git commands to receive starter code and submit the first lab on time; however, students often needed reminders about how to use version control. Prior to every deadline, we reminded students to commit first before pushing. When students submitted work before and after the deadline, we asked them to tag the work to be graded; that way, they could decide whether to suffer any late penalty.

7. LESSONS LEARNED AND DISCUSSION

Although distributed version control often confused students, they had little difficulty in adopting its workflows and never asked "when am I ever going to use this?" Students often made multiple commits off-line between pushes, and students on teams who pushed to a single remote repository (adopting a centralized workflow) encountered more difficulty than those who pushed to their private forks and merged later (adopting a distributed workflow). Students appreciated using Git, and did not feel learning it was wasted time. In fact, several of our students continued to use Git outside of our courses.

Despite the benefits of version control systems and project hosting services, they are unsuitable for some uses. Version control systems work well for human-readable text files, but are cumbersome for file formats such as Word, Excel or Powerpoint; cloud services such as Google Drive support collaboration better for those formats. Version control systems do not notify collaborators of changes in real-time (except for Jazz [16]), and cannot replace conversations about revisions. Project hosting services cannot fully replace systems such as Blackboard or Moodle, since they lack features such as online quizzes or mailing lists for announcements; however, cloud services such as Google Forms and Google Groups can serve these purposes, respectively.

We believe that the ACM Computer Science Curriculum should move version control from software engineering into programming fundamentals, to reflect the changing face of computing. Currently, faculty may hesitate to teach students version control outside of software engineering, thinking that it is either too difficult, time consuming, or would distract attention away from relevant course topics. When we tutored sophomores who struggled to collaborate on a project because they were unaware of version control, we decided to emphasize it in all of our programming courses. Immersing students in practice with version control in the programming fundamentals sequence benefits everyone.

8. CONCLUSION

Faculty should use version control in many science and engineering courses for students to gain experience with it. Unlike prior work that focused on computer science majors, we have demonstrated that freshmen in engineering majors can become skilled in version control as part of work submission. This success leads us to believe that science or engineering students can learn how to use version control. Furthermore, unlike prior work in which faculty maintained their own servers, students used private repositories on a cloud project hosting service to coordinate and submit work. We found that using a project hosting service was no more difficult than using existing course management systems. Therefore, we believe that faculty have no reason to avoid using Git on the cloud in the classroom.

9. ACKNOWLEDGMENTS

We thank our anonymous reviewers for their useful feedback. In particular, reviewer B's numerous suggestions and criticisms helped us improve this paper.

10. REFERENCES

[1] ACM and IEEE-CS Joint Task Force on Computing Curricula. Computer Science Curricula 2001. Retrieved August 1, 2012 from `http://bit.ly/csc2001`.

[2] ACM and IEEE-CS Joint Task Force on Computing Curricula. Computer Science Curricula 2008: An Interim Revision of CS 2001. Retrieved August 1, 2012 from `http://bit.ly/csc2008`.

[3] ACM and IEEE-CS Joint Task Force on Computing Curricula. Computer Science Curricula 2013 Ironman Draft. Retrieved December 1, 2012 from `http://ai.stanford.edu/users/sahami/CS2013/`.

[4] Black Duck Software. Compare repositories. Retrieved August 1, 2012 from `https://www.ohloh.net/repositories/compare`.

[5] S. Chacon. *Pro Git*. APress, 2009.

[6] C. Clifton, L. Kaczmarczyk, and M. Mrozek. Subverting the Fundamentals Sequence: Using Version Control to Enhance Course Management. In *Proceedings of SIGCSE 2007*, pages 86–90. ACM, 2007.

[7] Eclipse Foundation. Eclipse open source developer report: 2010. Retrieved August 1, 2012 from `http://bit.ly/eclipse-osr2010`.

[8] Eclipse Foundation. Eclipse open source developer report: 2011. Retrieved August 1, 2012 from `http://bit.ly/eclipse-osr2011`.

[9] Eclipse Foundation. Eclipse open source developer report: 2012. Retrieved August 1, 2012 from `http://bit.ly/eclipse-osr2012`.

[10] K. T. N. Hartness. Eclipse and CVS for Group Projects. *Journal of Computer Sciences in Colleges*, 21(4):217–222, 2006.

[11] A. Hunt and D. Thomas. *The Pragmatic Programmer*. Addison Wesley Longman, Inc., 1999.

[12] O. Laadan, J. Nieh, and N. Viennot. Teaching Operating Systems Using Virtual Appliances and Distributed Version Control. In *Proceedings of SIGCSE 2010*, pages 480–484. ACM, 2010.

[13] J. Loeliger and M. McCullough. *Version Control with Git*. O'Reilly Media, 2nd edition, 2012.

[14] E. Mazur. Farewell, lecture? *Science*, 323(5910):50–51, January 2009.

[15] S. C. McConnell. *Code Complete*. Microsoft Press, 2004.

[16] A. Meneely and L. Williams. On Preparing Students for Distrubted Software Development with a Synchronous, Collaborative Development Platform. In *Proceedings of SIGCSE 2009*, pages 529–533. ACM, 2009.

[17] R. T. Morrison. The lecture system in teaching science. In M. R. Rice, editor, *Proceedings of the Chicago Conferences on Liberal Education*, number 1 in Undergraduate Education in Chemistry and Physics. The College Center for Curricular Thought: The University of Chicago, October 1986.

[18] K. L. Reid and G. V. Wilson. Learning by Doing: Introducing Version Control as a Way to Manage Student Assignments. In *Proceedings of SIGCSE 2005*, pages 272–276. ACM, 2005.

[19] K. L. Reid and G. V. Wilson. DrProject: A Software Project Management Portal to Meet Educational Needs. In *Proceedings of SIGCSE 2007*, pages 317–321. ACM, 2007.

[20] A. E. Shell. The Thayer method of instruction at the United States Military Academy: A modest history and a modern personal account. *Primus: Problems, Resources, and Issues in Mathematics Undergraduate Studies.*, 2002.

[21] J. Spolsky. *Joel on Software*. Springer-Verlag, New York, NY, 2004.

[22] T. Swicegood. *Pragmatic Version Control Using Git*. The Pragmatic Programmers, 2008.

[23] United States Department of Education. Frequently Asked Questions—Cloud Computing. Retrieved August 1, 2012 from `http://1.usa.gov/SNjjsy`.

[24] J. Yedidia. Version Control Using Subversion. Retrieved August 1, 2012 from `http://bit.ly/T3q9d4`.

Creating Effective Student Groups: An Introduction to groupformation.org

Tyson R. Henry
Department of Computer Science
California State University, Chico
trhenry@csuchico.edu

ABSTRACT

Success in the computing industry often depends on an individual's ability to be a productive member of an effective study group or project team. In order to prepare students for successful careers, computer science curriculum often includes group projects. This paper discusses the challenges of forming effective student groups, discusses existing software for forming groups, and introduces groupformation.org [16], a new free and open source group formation service.

Categories and Subject Descriptors

K.3.2 [Computers and Information Science Education]: *Computer Science Education.*

General Terms

Management, Algorithms

Keywords

Student Groups, Student Teams, Group Formation, Team Formation, Grouping, Groupware

1. INTRODUCTION

Success in the computer science and computer engineering industries often depends on an individual's ability to be a productive member of an effective project group (while *team* and *group* are often used interchangeably, the literature often describe teams as being self forming, thus the term group is used in this paper). In order to become successful in industry, students must learn the many skills required to work in groups. When students work in an effective group they are provided three opportunities: to learn how to be a productive group member, to learn about the problem domain from other group members, and to have a positive group experience. These result in tangible skills they can use in their continued education and to present to prospective employers. Thus, the goal is to group students into the most effective groups possible.

There are three traditional approaches to forming student groups: random composition, self selection, and manual creation by the instructor. Each has significant shortcomings: random assignment can result in very unbalanced groups and is not likely to produce effective groups, self selection discriminates against less connected students, and the large number of possible groupings makes manually grouping difficult and unlikely to produce effective groups.

In order to form better groups and to improve the educational outcomes of students' group experiences, a growing body of research on algorithmic group formation has emerged (see Section 2). While most research has focused on specific grouping algorithms, a few research projects have focused on developing web-based systems that encompass the entire group formation process.

Existing algorithmic approaches have three shortcomings. First, the algorithms used for forming groups consider a very small portion of the solution space (see Section 3 for a discussion of the complexity of the grouping problem). Second, the instructor has limited control over the grouping algorithm. Finally, the grouping criteria used to calculate the weight of a group is limited.

These shortcomings have motivated the development of groupformation.org [15], a new group formation system. This system builds on previous work and expands the ability to control the group formation process. It provides an interactive environment which allows the instructor to experiment with different grouping parameters and grouping algorithms, a survey library that allows instructors to share grouping criteria, a mechanism for gathering and considering students' group mate preferences, and a platform for researching, developing, and evaluating new grouping algorithms. Section 4 presents an overview of groupformation.org.

2. RELATED WORK

Many group formation systems are described in the literature [5,7,12,19,20,22,24,27,30,31]. The most documented and the only system available on the Internet is Team-Maker [7]. A large effort is currently underway to provide a thorough assessment of Team-Maker (the Comprehensive Assessment of Team-Member Effectiveness (CATME) system [20]). It provides a web-based system any instructor can use to create groups and is using the data from actual courses to validate the grouping process [26].

The CATME research project is well formed and produces good groups. However, it does not directly analyze the grouping algorithm. It assumes the groupings produced by its algorithm are near optimal. Analysis of running the CATME grouping algorithm on data collected from software engineering courses, indicates that the algorithm is unlikely to find a near optimal solution [16]. This does not invalidate the overall grouping process, it just diminishes the likely strength of the calculated groupings.

SIGCSE'13, March 6–9, 2013, Denver, Colorado, USA.

Instead of focusing on the grouping algorithm, the CATME research project is working to validate the grouping process by collecting feedback from students throughout the life of the group. By comparing student feedback to the group weights calculated by the system, the validity of the entire process can be calculated. Once the process has been validated, the results can be used to validate other approaches (such as the one presented below) and when better grouping algorithms have been found, they can be incorporated into the CATME process.

Three other group formation systems are well defined in the literature: DIANA [31], OptAssign [24], and PEGASUS [19]. None of them appear to be available on the Internet.

The DIANA group formation system uses genetic algorithms to form groups. It was tested with 66 undergraduate computer science students assigned to groups of three either randomly (10 groups) or using their algorithm. The test results indicate their algorithm produces better groups than random group formation. The authors conclude that the small sample size limits the extent their results can be generalized. There is no discussion of using DIANA in the classroom.

OptAssign allows the instructor to specify domain specific questions, but it is not currently available for use. It formulates the grouping problem as a series of constraints. The paper did not report the method used to solve the series of constraints. The groups were evaluated by surveying students for their satisfaction of the groups vs. satisfaction of students in groups formed manually. The results were positive, but the improvement was not large. The paper concludes, "There seems to be a clear need for more analytical tools to investigate the quality of the solution obtained in an interactive and visual way."

The PEGASUS system has two objectives: providing a tool to facilitate reflection on learning and teaching preferences, and providing a group formation tool based on students' learning styles. During the trial study several students rejected the proposed groupings and convinced the instructor to allow them to form their own groups. The remaining students were grouped using the system. The authors suggest that a grouping system should accommodate students' grouping preferences. Accounting for student preferences is an option in groupformation.org (see Section 4).

The literature contains descriptions of many different approaches to formulating groups: genetic algorithms [1, 8, 10, 20, 32], a hybrid grouping genetic algorithm approach [1,2] , fuzzy-genetic decision support system [29] , agent-organized networks [14], fuzzy optimization approach [4] , student performance [13], analytical hierarchy process [33], clustering [9], and integer programming [11]. This long list shows the breadth of research on algorithm based group formation. However, there has been only minimal analysis of the results. Many of the listed researchers compare the groups composed by their algorithms to randomly composed groups or groups created manually by an instructor. Other researchers evaluate their algorithms by comparing the results to results generated by the same algorithm without some portion of the logic. There is clearly a need for a better understanding of the grouping data and a means of evaluating algorithms.

Several authors support the importance of group composition in general and in computer science and software engineering groups. Many factors include personality [18, 17, 28], learning styles [25], shared mental models [6], problem solving style [21], and friendships [23]. No work addressing the specifics of grouping students for computers science and software engineering has been published.

3. GROUPING PROBLEM COMPLEXITY

The number of possible groups of size **g** that can be constructed from a class of **n** students is *n choose g* or $\binom{n}{g}$. This is equivalent to $\left(\frac{n!}{g!\cdot(n-g)!}\right)$. For a typical class, this set is small enough that it can be constructed quickly. For example, there are 1,947,792 distinct groups for a class of 36 students with a group size of six. A modern desktop computer can calculate these groups and their weights in a matter of seconds. The computational road block arises from the task of selecting the best set of groups (or best grouping). The number of possible ways to group all the groups into groupings is

$$\frac{\left(\frac{n!}{g!\cdot(n-g)!}\right)!}{\left(\frac{n}{g}\right)!\cdot\left(\frac{n!}{g!\cdot(n-g)!}-\frac{n}{g}\right)!}$$

For a class of 36 students partitioned into groups of 6 students there are $2.67\text{x}10^{24}$ possible groupings. This problem is intractable; it is not feasible to consider all the possible groupings. In order to find good groupings, a heuristic algorithm that considers only a fraction of possible groupings must be used.

An analysis of sample data [15] has found that good solutions are few and far between. Thus it is very unlikely that the heuristic approaches presented in the previous section are likely to find optimal or even near-optimal solutions.

The next section introduces groupformation.org, a web-based system for forming student groups. In addition to providing a free group formation service, it serves as a platform for researching, developing, and evaluating new grouping algorithms.

4. groupformation.org

The first step in the group forming process is for the instructor to visit groupformation.org and create an account and a course. Both are a matter of filling in forms. The second step is to create a *preliminary survey* for students in the course. The purpose of this survey is to gather relevant information about the student. The instructor can create a survey from scratch, adopt an existing survey from the survey library (the survey library is available to all instructors), or modify a survey from the library. The survey can contain a variety of question types including: multiple-choice, Likert Scale, pick many, schedule availability, text entry/essay, and group member preferences. The survey questions are fully customizable. Figure 1 shows the multiple-choice question editor. The instructor is allows to add and remove choices and specify the minimum and maximum number of answers the student is allowed. All question types are customizable and have similar interfaces. Once created, the instructor can chose to publish the survey in the survey library so other instructors can use it.

Each question in the preliminary survey is classified as public or private (see Figure 1). Answers to public questions (not answers to private questions) are used to automatically generate a public profile for each student. For example, grade point averages would be classified by the instructor as private (i.e., not shown to other students; only to be used by the grouping algorithm). On the other hand, questions such as programming language preferences (i.e., *Which of the following programming languages do you know well?*) could be classified as public. In addition to being used to create the student's profile, public questions are used by the grouping algorithm.

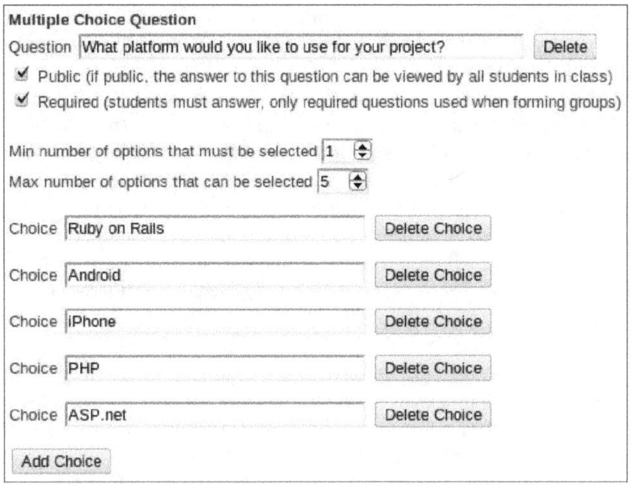

Figure 1. Partial Survey Creation Interface

Sample public questions for groups working on a semester long software engineering project are:

- What language would you like to use?
- What platform (iPhone, Android, web) would you like to use?
- Would you rather focus on programming or documentation?

Sample private questions are:

- What is your major GPA?
- What is your overall GPA?
- What grade did you receive in CS100?
- Complete the personality tests at this link and report the result.

On the student's view of the preliminary survey, public questions are clearly labeled as such so students know their classmates will be able to view their answers.

In addition to the preliminary survey, the instructor can create a *group member preference survey*. The preference survey allows students to specify who they want to work with and who they do not want to work with. The preference survey is configurable by the instructor. The instructor can chose the wording of the question and the wording of each element on the Likert scale. Figure 2 shows the interface for creating and editing the preference survey.

Figure 3 shows the student's view of the preference survey. Notice that the values correspond to those the instructor entered (shown in Figure 2). Each student name is a link to that student's profile. When the link is selected, the public information (including name and picture) are displayed for the selected student.

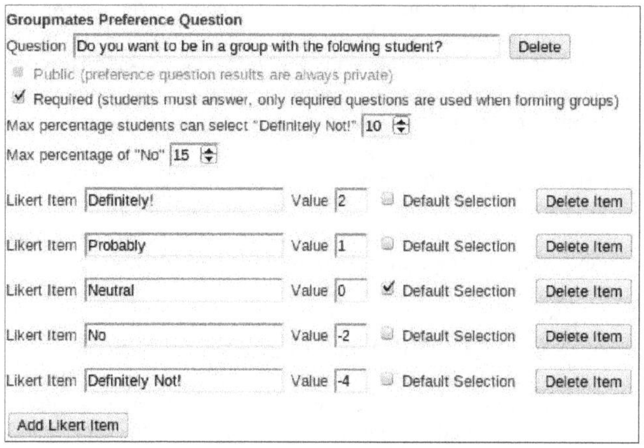

Figure 2. Instructor Group Member Preference Survey Editing Interface

In addition to the basic preference question, the instructor can allow students to construct and recommend one or more groups containing themselves.

After creating the surveys, the instructor creates a group forming event. The event consists of a title, a preliminary survey start time, a preliminary survey stop time, a preference survey stop time (if used), and the associated course. The system assures that students can only access the surveys during the allowed times.

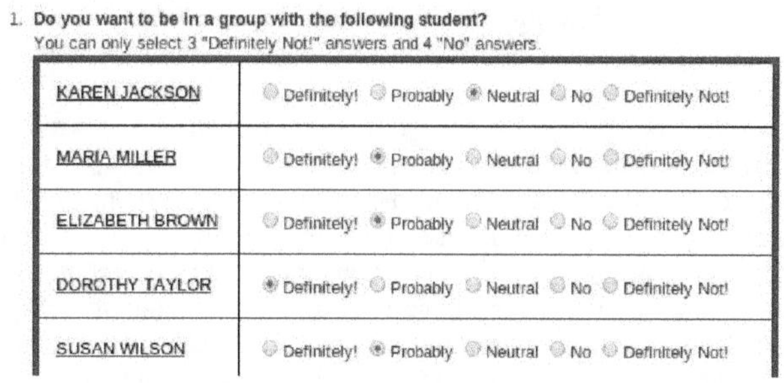

Figure 3. Student Group Member Preference Survey (partial)

The instructor must instruct her students to create an account and enroll in her class. Once enrolled, the student will be shown the tasks he needs to complete (i.e. which surveys must be completed) and the survey deadlines. It is crucial for the instructor to explain the importance of completing the survey before the deadline and to remind them as the deadline approaches. The author's experience is that the consequence of being placed in a group with all the students who did not complete the survey (which students immediately assume is a group of *slackers*) is enough to ensure that virtually all students (99%) complete the survey by the deadline.

If a preference survey is required by the instructor, students must return to the website after the preliminary survey deadline and specify their desire to work with each student in the course. Figure 3 shows the student view of a preference survey. For each student, a link to his or her profile (created from survey answers to questions classified as public) is provided. When deciding preferences, students can view their classmates' profiles by clicking on their names and use the profile to help with their decision. This mechanism allows for students who know few other students in the class to make reasoned decisions. After the students have completed the preliminary survey and entered group preferences (if required), the instructor returns to the website and performs the grouping process.

The first step in the grouping process is to select basic parameters (such as, size of groups). The second step is to assign an importance weight to each survey question and to the preference survey. Weights range from zero (do not consider answers to this question) to ten (answers to this question are very important). Then the instructor must designate if the algorithm should form groups of homogeneous answers or heterogeneous answers. For example, if the instructor wants students with similar grades to be grouped together, the homogeneous grouping approach would be selected for the grade category or categories. On the other hand, if the instructor wanted groups of students with a range of grades, heterogeneous groups should be selected.

In addition to specifying the homogeneity and weight of each question, the instructor can exclude specific students. This allows for the removal of students who have dropped the course and for the manual creation of one or more groups (if the instructor wants to manually create a group, he excludes all the students in the group and the group forming algorithm will not consider them).

The next step is to select the grouping algorithm. Currently the system provides only two effective algorithms, best-first and partial brute force. The system allows for algorithms to be added. Developing new grouping algorithms is the primary focus of this project; several new algorithms are under development.

The best-first algorithm starts by calculating the weights of all possible groups (see [10] for a discussion of calculating weights of groups). The number of groups is relatively small (40M for a class of 35 in groups of 5) so the weights of all groups can be calculated in a fraction of a second. The groups are sorted from the largest weight to the smallest weight. The algorithm then selects the group with the largest weight. All remaining groups that contain one or more students from the selected group are eliminated from consideration. After this elimination, the remaining group with the largest weight is selected and groups that contain its members are eliminated. This process continues until all students are in a group. If at any point a solution cannot be found, the algorithm back-tracks and selects the group with the second largest weight.

If the selected group size is not an integral factor of the class size, the algorithm stops when the maximum number of complete groups has been created. In this situation the number of unmatched students is smaller than the number of groups. That means that at most one student will need to be added to some of the groups. A second phase of the algorithm enumerates all the possible distributions of the leftover students and distributes these students to maximize the grouping weight. Since there are only a small number of ways to distribute left over students, all possible solutions are considered.

The partial brute force algorithm also starts with calculating the weights of all possible groups and then sorting the groups by weight. Analysis of the sample data indicates that the best groupings are very likely to only contain groups with large weights [15]. Thus the partial brute force algorithm is seeded with the group with the largest weight.

The algorithm is implemented using several thousand threads running on two nvidia multi-core CUDA processors (TESLA C2050). Each card contains 498 1Gh processing cores. Each thread is seeded with a highly weighted group. Specifically, if 4,000 threads are executed (the number of threads is a parameter to the algorithm) then the 4,000 highest weighted groups are used for seeds.

In a brute force fashion, each thread considers all groups that follow its seed group (i.e. all groups that have lower weight). The thread terminates when it has considered all possible groupings that include the seed group and all subsequent groups. The search is pruned when it is not possible to improve on the best current solution. For example, consider building groups of five students. Assume the current best solution has a weight of 1000 (the weight of a grouping is the sum of the weights of all the groups in the grouping), and the current solution contains three students and has a weight of 700. In order for the current solution to be better than the current best solution, the remaining two students must add 301 to the weight. If the group currently being considered has a weight of 150, all subsequent groups have a weight equal or less than 150. Since groups are considered in decreasing weight (recall that groups are ordered from highest weight to lowest weight), it is not possible for the current solution to lead to a solution better than the current best solution (the best it could find is two more members each with a weight of 150 which would result in a grouping of weight 1000). When a path is found to be a dead end, it is abandoned. The net result is that each thread finds the largest grouping that contains its seeding group. When a thread finds a grouping with a weight larger than the current best grouping, that grouping becomes the new best grouping.

A subtle advantage of this approach is that threads do not have to consider groups with weights greater than its seeding group. This is because all the groups with weights greater than a thread's seeding group are in turn the seeding group for another thread. Since that thread will find the largest grouping that contains it, there is no need for any other thread that is seeded with a lower weight group to consider it.

The result of this algorithm is that each of the n threads will have calculated the best grouping for the n groups with the highest weight. It is computationally easy to compare these groupings.

Even with this massive computing power, the brute force algorithm is intractable. As described, this algorithm does not reduce the complexity as described in Section 3. In order to reduce the complexity, the number of groups that are considered is limited. This limit is a parameter selected by the instructor in the group forming process.

The larger the set of seed groups the better the results. Running the brute force algorithm with tens of thousands of seed groups results in finding near optimal groupings but takes several days. Very good groups can be found in a matter of hours. Good groups can be found in several minutes. Research is underway to discover how to further prune the number of groups by eliminating groups that are unlikely to belong to a good grouping and thus reduce the time required to find near optimal solutions.

When the instructor selects the grouping algorithm and presses the *Create a Grouping* button, the selected grouping algorithm is executed. The calculated grouping is displayed to the instructor. The display includes the weight of each group, the students in each group, the parameters to the grouping algorithm, and the influence each question has on the group (that is, the weight each question contributes to the weight of the group).

A primary design goal of groupformation.org is to provide the instructor with interactive tools that facilitate an iterative approach to group formation. The idea is for the instructor to analyze each generated grouping and consider the influence of each question, intuition she may have about particular students, and the answers student gave. The current implementation allows the instructor to fine tune the grouping parameters (including which algorithm is used) and create additional groupings. The instructor can compare the different groupings to see how changes in the parameters affect the outcome. Additionally, the instructor can remove specific students (for example, a student who listed limited or unusual availability times) or an entire group (for example, if the group is particularly strong and the instructor wants to assure these students are grouped together) and re-run the process.

5. EXPERIENCE

groupformation.org has been used in four undergraduate software engineering courses for forming semester-long groups. The best-first grouping algorithm has also been used for eight years in an additional ten graduate and undergraduate software engineering courses to form semester-long groups (email was used to communicate preferences and a command line interface was used to run the grouping algorithm). The first ten times it was used, only student preferences were considered. The last four times, other factors (such as grades and project interests) were used, however, student preferences were highly weighted.

Informal surveys and discussions with students have been used to evaluate the success of this approach. Most groups (21 out of 29) worked well together, successfully completed a semester project, and reported high satisfaction with their group. Most group failures resulted from students failing to contribute the necessary time to the project.

Most students speak favorably of the grouping process and the resulting groups. Using an algorithm removes the instructor's culpability in forming *bad* groups. In other words, most students don't blame the instructor for forming a poor group because the group was formed by an algorithm using their own grouping preferences.

One group of students that wanted to ensure they would work together colluded to influence the grouping algorithm. Everyone gave similar and limited answers. For example, the question that asked which platforms they were interested in using, each student selected the same single answer (the answer they assumed would be the least popular among their classmates). However, they reported that they did not lie on questions with distinct answers (e.g. their grades in the prerequisite courses). The result was a group weight that was in the middle of the class. This effort has led to the inclusion of allowing students to specify not just who they want to work with but also an entire group. Ironically, this group did not work well together and did not produce a very good project.

6. FUTURE WORK

There are three primary directions of future work. The first is to develop additional grouping algorithms and a means to validate their effectiveness in finding groupings with near optimal weights (this work will assume the algorithm for calculating the weight of a given group is valid and focus only on validating the grouping algorithm). Validation will be performed by comparing results to those from brute force search algorithms that have been run for extended periods. Second is to develop better visualization of the grouping (e.g. how the impact of each question affects each group). The goal is to provide more information to the instructor allowing intuition to be used in the iterative group formation process. Finally, new ways of interacting with the grouping algorithms are being investigated. The ultimate goal is to give the instructor more control over the grouping algorithms using intuition to fill in where the algorithm falls short.

7. CONCLUSION

The composition of a student group often makes the difference between an excellent group experience and a negative group experience. When asked about past group experiences, most students describe several terrible groups. Often the stories include the instructor forcing students into groups or describe drifting into groups of students they don't know (probably because they sat next to each other on the day the group was formed). Sometimes students talk about being pressured to work with a group of students (often friends) with whom they do not want to work. The unfortunate end result is too often students believing that working with groups is painful, non-productive, and not fun.

Forming groups is too difficult of a task to do by hand. Given the massive number of possible groupings and the limited number of good groupings, leaving group formation to chance is unlikely to produce a good outcome. The best solution is to use an algorithmic approach.

groupformation.org provides an easy to use and highly extensible algorithmic means for creating student groups. Several features make it the most sophisticated group forming system available: choice of algorithms, iterative group formation process, and support for gathering student preferences. Given the high stakes, it is important for faculty to take matters into their own hands and guide the group formation process to ensure students are partitioned into effective groups that promote student success.

8. REFERENCES

[1] Agustín-Blas, L. E. , Salcedo-Sanz , S., Ortiz-García , E. G., Portilla-Figueras , A., Pérez-Bellido , Á. M., Jiménez-Fernández, S. 2011. Team formation based on group technology: A hybrid grouping genetic algorithm approach, Computers and Operations Research, v.38 n.2, p.484-495.

[2] Agustín-Blas, L. E. , Salcedo-Sanz , S., Ortiz-García , E. G., Portilla-Figueras , A. 2008. Assignment of Students to Preferred Laboratory Groups Using a Hybrid Grouping Genetic Algorithm. In Proceedings of the 8th IEEE International Conference on Hybrid Intelligent Systems (HIS '08). DOI=10.1109/HIS.2008.37

[3] Ani, Z., Yasin, A. Husin, M., Hamid, Z., 2010. A Method for Group Formation Using Genetic Algorithm, (IJCSE) International Journal on Computer Science and Engineering Vol. 02, No. 09, 3060-3064

[4] Baykasoglu, A., Dereli, T., Das, S. 2007. Project Team Selection Using Fuzzy Optimization Approach. Cybern. Syst. 38, 2 (February 2007), 155-185. DOI=10.1080/01969720601139041

[5] Beheshtian-Adekani, M., and Mahmood, M. 1986. Development and validation of a tool for assigning students to groups for class projects. Decision Sciences. v17. 92-113.

[6] Carpenter, S., Fortune, J., Delugach, H., Etzkorn, L., Utley, D., Farrington, P., and Virani, S. 2008. Studying team shared mental models. In Proceedings of the 3rd International Conference on the Pragmatic Web: Innovating the Interactive Society (ICPW '08), ACM, New York, NY, USA, 41-48. DOI=10.1145/1479190.1479197

[7] Cavanaugh, R., Ellis, M., Layton, R., and Ardis, M. 2004. Automating the process of assigning students to cooperative-learning teams. In Proceedings of the 2004 ASEE Annual Conference. American Society for Engineering Education.

[8] Chan, T., Chen, C., Wu, Y., Jong, B., Hsia, Y., and Lin, T. 2010. Applying the genetic encoded conceptual graph to grouping learning. Expert Syst. Appl. 37, 6 (June 2010), 4103-4118. DOI=10.1016/j.eswa.2009.11.014

[9] Christodoulopoulos, C.E., Papanikolaou, K. 2007. Investigation of group formation using low complexity algorithms. In: Proc. of PING Workshop, pp. 57-60.

[10] Craig , M., Horton, D., Pitt, F. 2010. Forming reasonably optimal groups: (FROG), Proceedings of the 16th ACM international conference on Supporting group work, November 07-10, 2010, Sanibel Island, Florida, USA.

[11] Cutshall, R., Gavirneni, S., and Schultz, K. 2007. Indiana University's Kelley School of Business Uses Integer Programming to Form Equitable, Cohesive Student Teams. Interfaces 37, 3, 265-276. DOI=10.1287/inte.1060.0248

[12] Doyle, K., Kroha, S., Palchowdhury, A., and Xu, W. 2002. Project Group Assignment System, Proceedings of MASPLAS'02 The Mid-Atlantic Student Workshop on Programming Languages and Systems, Pace University.

[13] Feng, B., Jiang, Z., Fan, Z., Fu, N. 2010. A method for member selection of cross-functional teams using the individual and collaborative performances, European Journal of Operational Research, Volume 203, Issue 3, 16, ISSN 0377-2217, DOI: 10.1016/j.ejor.2009.08.017.

[14] Gaston, M. E., des Jardins, M. 2005. Agent-organized networks for dynamic team formation. In Proceedings of the fourth international joint conference on Autonomous agents and multiagent systems (AAMAS '05), 230-237. DOI=10.1145/1082473.1082508

[15] Henry, T.R. 2013. http://groupformation.org

[16] Henry, T.R. 2013. Algorithmic Issues of Forming Productive Student Groups, TR No. CS-2013-01. http://www.ecst.csuchico.edu/~tyson/tr/TR13-01.pdf

[17] Hishina, M., Okada, R., Suzuki, K. 2005. Group Formation for Web-Based Collaborative Learning with Personality Information, International Journal on E-Learning, v4 n3.

[18] Karn, J., Cowling, T. 2006. A follow up study of the effect of personality on the performance of software engineering teams. In Proceedings of the 2006 ACM/IEEE international symposium on Empirical software engineering (ISESE '06). DOI=10.1145/1159733.1159769

[19] Kyprianidou, M., Demetriadis, S., Pombortsis, A., Karatasios, G. 2009. PEGASUS: designing a system for supporting group activity, Multicultural Education & Technology Journal, Vol. 3 Iss: 1, pp.47 – 60

[20] Layton, R. A., Loughry, M. L., Ohland, M. W., G. D. Rico, G. D. 2010. Design and validation of a web-based system for assigning members to teams using instructor-specified criteria. Advances in Engineering Education, Vol. 2, No. 1.

[21] Lewis, T. L., Smith, W. J., 2008. Creating high performing software engineering teams: the impact of problem solving style dominance on group conflict and performance. J. Comput. Small Colleges. 24, 2, 121-129.

[22] Lin, Y., Huang, Y., Cheng, S. 2010. An automatic group composition system for composing collaborative learning groups using enhanced particle swarm optimization. Comput. Educ. 55, 4. DOI=10.1016/j.compedu.2010.06.014

[23] Mahenthiran, S., and Rouse, P. 2000. The impact of group selection on student performance and satisfaction. The International Journal of Educational Management. v14 i6.

[24] Meyer, D. 2009. OptAssign-A web-based tool for assigning students to groups. Computer Education. 53, 4. DOI=10.1016/j.compedu.2009.05.022

[25] Nielsen, T., Hvas, A. E., Kjaergaard, A. 2009. Student team formation based on learning styles at university start: does it make a difference to the student? Reflection Education. v5 i2. 85-103.

[26] Ohland, M. W. 2012. http://catme.org https://engineering.purdue.edu/CATME

[27] Redmond, M. A. 2001. A computer program to aid assignment of student project groups. In Proceedings of the thirty-second SIGCSE technical symposium on Computer Science Education.

[28] Rutherfoord, R. H. 2006. Using personality inventories to form teams for class projects: a case study. In Proceedings of the 7th conference on Information technology education (ACM SIGITE). DOI=10.1145/1168812.1168817

[29] Strnad, D., Guid, N. 2010. A fuzzy-genetic decision support system for project team formation. Appl. Soft Comput.10, 4, 1178-1187. DOI=10.1016/j.asoc.2009.08.032

[30] Tobar, C. M., de Freita, R. L. 2007.A support tool for student group definition. In proceedings of the 37th ASEE/IEEE Frontiers in Education.

[31] Wang, D., Lin S. S. J., Sun, C. 2010 DIANA: A computer-supported heterogeneous grouping system for teachers to conduct successful small learning groups, Computers in Human Behavior, v.23 n.4 DOI=10.1016/j.chb.2006.02.008

[32] Yeoh, H. K., Nor, M. I. M. 2009. An Algorithm to Form Balanced and Diverse Groups of Students. Computer Applicatons in Engineering Education, v19, i3. DOI=10.1002/cae.20338

[33] Zakarian, A., Kusiak, A. 1999. Forming teams: an analytical approach. IIE Transactions. v31. 85-97.

The Effectiveness of Live-Coding to Teach Introductory Programming

Marc J. Rubin
Dept. of Electrical Engineering and Computer Science
Colorado School of Mines
1610 Illinois St.
Golden, Colorado
mrubin@mines.edu

ABSTRACT

Live-coding is defined as "the process of designing and implementing a [coding] project in front of class during lecture period" [5]. In this article we present our research design and results regarding the effectiveness of live-coding to teach introductory programming.

The research design includes two experimental groups spread across four sections of an introductory C++ course at Colorado School of Mines. In the control group, students were taught using static code, meaning that instructors never typed, but instead viewed, compiled, and executed code examples. In the experimental or "live-coding" group, instructors started each lecture with a blank screen, and taught code examples by systematically typing, compiling, and testing code to solve example problems.

To assess the effectiveness of live-coding, we administered four surveys and analyzed final grades. Two of the surveys were given at the beginning of the course, and were used to measure baseline programming knowledge and student learning preferences (i.e., VARK [2]). The other two surveys, given at the end of the course, were designed to measure the amount of programming knowledge obtained as well as preferences towards live coding. Lastly, final grades were analyzed in terms of its subcomponents: the assignments, exams, final project, and overall grade. Based on our results, we conclude that teaching via live-coding is as good as if not better than using static code examples.

Categories and Subject Descriptors

K.3 [**Computers and Education**]: Computer and Information Science Education

Keywords

Live-coding; Introductory; Programming; Pedagogy

SIGCSE'13, March 6–9, 2013, Denver, Colorado, USA.

1. INTRODUCTION

In mathematics education, instructors often teach concepts by solving example problems, from start to finish, in front of students. By going through each step "live" during lecture, instructors show students the mechanics and techniques required to solve each problem. Now, instead of showing the steps to solve, for example, an algebraic simplification, what if instructors only presented the final solution in its entirety? Would this static version be as effective as the "live" version for teaching mathematical problem solving skills?

In introductory programming courses it is all too common for instructors to present only static versions of code examples. More specifically, instructors teach programming by presenting only the correctly coded final solutions to students (in addition to other lecture materials such as Powerpoint slides and verbal explanations). Since programming is essentially problem solving, how effective is teaching with static code examples? Better yet, is it more effective to teach programming by solving programming problems from start to finish during lecture? This method, known as live-coding, is defined as "the process of designing and implementing a [coding] project in front of class during lecture period" [5]. In this article we present our findings from a semester long research study where we investigated the effects of teaching via live-coding versus static code examples.

This article is organized as follows. First we summarize the previous literature regarding introductory programming pedagogy with a focus on live-coding. Second, we discuss our experimental design including the metrics used. Third, we describe and discuss the quantitative and qualitative results from our metrics. Lastly, we conclude with a summary of our work and hopes for the future.

2. PREVIOUS LITERATURE

Though there is much research regarding introductory programming pedagogy, there is very little research investigating the effectiveness of live-coding as a teaching method [3]. Following is a summary of the existing literature pertaining first to programming pedagogy in general and then specifically live-coding.

2.1 Introductory Programming Pedagogy

The authors of [7] provide a high level and abstract literature review of how novice programmers learn programming. At the end of the article, the authors create a programming framework (page 164 in [7]) that nicely summarizes the relationships between the cognitive theories and practical issues covered in the literature. The framework can be summarized as follows. To learn how to program, novices need to learn 1) knowledge, 2) strategies, and 3) models of programming. Knowledge, though a vague term, is characterized by the concrete concepts required to master programming, and include formal programming language structures (e.g., for loops, if statements, etc.), environments, debugging tools, compilers, etc. The second aspect, known as strategies, involves schemas or concrete design patterns that students use to apply their programming knowledge to different types of problems. Third, over time students develop mental models that are more abstract and generalizable than the schemas, and allow students to design solutions to new and unforeseen problems. The authors of [7] conclude that instructors teaching programming to introductory programmers should be cognizant of these three levels, and should focus their pedagogy on all three, instead of just, for example, the concrete knowledge such as syntax. Teaching novices to program *should* include aspects that develop their abilities to develop these schemas and mental models.

To accomplish this, the authors of [7] further break down the framework by three aspects more directly related to programming pedagogy: i.e., teaching the 1) design, 2) generation, and 3) evaluation of programs. Based on the authors' assessment, most of the introductory programming pedagogy research has focused on these three elements. For example, researchers have studied the effects of teaching using an object-oriented (OO) language (e.g., C++) vs. a procedural language (e.g., Pascal). The thoughts behind using OO vs. procedural languages to teach are many, but include the notion that OO languages may be easier for students to use to design and generate programs, since real life problems can often be broken down into objects. Results from these studies are mixed: in some cases (e.g., code snippet interpretation) the students in the OO language based courses performed better than procedural, while in other cases (e.g., control flow comprehension) the OO students performed worse. The author's in [7] cite several successful results from other areas of introductory programming pedagogy, including the use of pair-programming, visualization and animation based tools, graphical programming languages, the use of reflective writing, and problem-solving based curricula. In sum, the authors of [7] suggest that there is not a "one-size fits all" method for teaching introductory programming effectively, but instead instructors must focus their efforts on teaching the *process* of programming, not just the knowledge (e.g., syntax) required to do so.

In another literature review of introductory programming pedagogy, the authors of [6] offer a nice summary of the literature that is relevant to computer science educators. The aim of [6] was to summarize the existing body of research in order for introductory computer science educators to make informed decisions about how to best teach introductory programming. The authors of [6] do not explicitly state results from specific studies, but instead list methodologies that have proven successful. The article is organized into four main sections regarding teaching introductory programming: 1) curricula, 2) pedagogy, 3) language choice, and 4) teaching tools. While the sections covering introductory programming curricula (e.g., object oriented vs. procedural languages), language choice (e.g., C++ vs. Java), and teaching tools (e.g., auto-graders) summarize many interesting theories and bodies of work, they are outside the scope of this article, which focuses on live-coding as a pedagogical method. In terms of 2) pedagogy, the authors divide the reviewed research into two domains: student learning experiences and instructor didactics. The research focused on student learning includes student approaches (e.g., pair-programming) and different programming environments (e.g., visual debuggers). Didacticism is broken down into three sub-categories (that are not necessarily mutually exclusive): 1) problem solving, 2) syntax specificity, and 3) systemic code production. In the problem solving based approach, the focus of the course is to teach programming as a means to solve problems (i.e., code is taught on a "need to know" basis). Syntax specific teaching, which focuses on the constructs of a programming language, is how introductory programming textbooks are written, and is the most traditional way to teach programming (e.g., here's the code, now let's use it). The final teaching paradigm is systemic code production, where programming is taught in the context of developing a larger software system (e.g., programming a robotic system). The authors conclude by stating that there is no canonical answer regarding how to best teach programming. Instead, each instructor, department, and institution must make decisions that best suit the institutional goals and instructor teaching styles.

In [8], the author summarizes three teaching and three learning based strategies for teaching computer science. For starters, the article surmises that traditional lecture methods (i.e., "chalk and talk" or "teaching by telling") are largely ineffective for teaching introductory computer science. Instead, instructors should focus on using non-traditional teaching strategies: e.g., 1) scaffolding, 2) concept mapping, and 3) constructivism. Scaffolding is the teaching method where an expert facilitator provides necessary support to students as they solve problems, gradually removing support as students become more knowledgable and independent. The second teaching technique, concept mapping, makes use of graphical diagrams as a means to present and organize course material. Concept maps provide an alternative to natural language as a means to convey information. The third teaching method, constructivism, is when students actively "construct" knowledge on their own, as opposed to passively mirroring information presented by the instructor. Instructors following the constructivist model spend considerable time asking explorative and participatory questions to students who are increasingly responsible for learning new material.

The article also describes three learning strategies that may be adopted to help teach introductory programming: 1) problem-based learning, 2) collaborative learning, and 3) active learning. Problem-based learning occurs when students attempt to solve problems using their current knowledge base. This process develops critical thinking skills and helps students identify areas of insufficiency. In collaborative learning, students participate in group activities such as group discussions, projects, games, and competitions. Lastly, active learning occurs when instructors encourage student participation during lecture, including answering questions, posting solutions on the board, or discussing the topic of the day. As with the previous articles presented, [8] does not conclude with a single "best" strategy for teaching programming. Instead the author presents techniques that have proven effective and leaves it up to the reader to decide which method(s) to employ.

2.2 Live Coding

In the previous section, the literature reviews make it abundantly clear that there is no single "best" way to teach introductory programming. In this section we focus on live-coding in particular, starting with research from Finland.

During the Spring of 2010, an instructor at the University of Helsinki taught introductory and advanced computer science courses following a cognitive apprenticeship model [9]. This model has three phases: modeling, scaffolding, and fading. During the modeling phase, the instructor incorporated live-coding into his pedagogy, effectively "modeling" how to solve programming problems. Although student pass-rates increased (when compared to previous semesters), it is not clear whether live-coding was a suitable explanation. The authors indicated that weekly lectures were reduced from five to two hours, and the extra time was spent in the "scaffolding" phase: i.e., helping students with their code and providing immediate feedback.

In another study from Montana State University, an instructor taught a semester of introductory Java programming via live-coding and surveyed 30 of the students [5]. The results indicated that 80% of students surveyed preferred the live-coding teaching method rather than traditional "static" lectures. In a similar study at the University of South Florida [3], 100% of students surveyed (N = 5) from an introductory course and 70% (N = 10) of students surveyed from a programming II course either Agreed or Strongly Agreed to the statement "Seeing the instructor code 'live' solutions was more useful than seeing the final solutions directly." Although most students responded favorably to live-coding, there was no analysis of student grades or knowledge retention. Furthermore, the small sample sizes and lack of control populations limit the generalizability of the results.

In a study from Europe, researchers provided introductory programming students with "process recordings" to supplement lecture material for an online course [1]. These process recordings were 30 to 45 minute how-to videos where the instructor coded an example from start to finish and narrated his thought process. Fifty-five total students were surveyed with regard to the expected learning outcome of the process recordings. The results indicated that 58% of the students expected a "high" or "very high" learning outcome from these process recordings. Although there was no control group or comparison of grades, these findings are encouraging.

From the presented literature it is clear that live-coding may be a favorable teaching method amongst introductory programming students. In addition, the previous literature highlights the lack of quantitative and generalizable results regarding live-coding research. In the following sections, we discuss our experimental design as well as results from our first semester of live-coding research.

3. EXPERIMENTAL DESIGN

At the Colorado School of Mines, CSCI 261 "Programming Concepts in C++" (`http://mines.humanoriented.com/261/`) is a popular introductory programming course that is a requirement for all undergraduates majoring in computer science or any engineering discipline (e.g., electrical, mechanical, petroleum, etc.). During the Fall semester of 2011, this course was taught by three different instructors over six different sections. Two of the instructors (MR and TD), volunteered to help conduct this study. Instructors MR and TD both taught two sections: an experimental (i.e., live-coding) and a control (e.g., Table 1). For each section, the course consisted of two 50-minute lectures and one 50-minute lab per week. Students were not told about the nature of the study (i.e., live-coding vs. control), and were given the option to fill out surveys to "help the computer science department improve CSCI 261." Student participation was voluntary and in no way effected their grades.

Section	Instructor	Group	N
A	MR	Live Coding	41
B	MR	Control	40
D	TD	Live Coding	37
F	TD	Control	28

Table 1: Four sections of CSCI 261 were used in this study. Each instructor (MR and TD) had a live coding as well as control section.

The overall design of our study is as follows. At the beginning of the semester we administered two surveys: a pre-course survey and a VARK (Visual, Auditory, Reading/Writing, Kinesthetic) learning style questionnaire. Likewise, at the end of the semester we administered two surveys: a post-course survey and a live-coding survey. During the semester each instructor taught one experimental and one control section. All sections used the exact same Powerpoint lecture slides, homework assignments, and tests. In addition to identical content and materials, the order of each lecture and proportion of time spent on each component (e.g., slides, code examples) was the same across all sections. The only difference was how the code examples were presented and taught. In the experimental sections, the code examples were taught via live-coding, always starting with a blank screen. In the control sections, the code examples were presented as full and complete solutions. The following sections describe the surveys and pedagogical techniques in much more detail.

3.1 Pre-Course Surveys

During the first two weeks of the course, the instructors administered two surveys. The first survey, which we will refer to as the pre-course survey, asks students to rate their familiarity and experience with programming in any language. In particular, this survey asks students to circle all programming languages they have used, including C++, Java, Python, etc. Students were also asked to circle their experience with C++ programming concepts, such as file input, user output, classes, etc. In addition to language familiarity, students were given two snippets of C++ code and asked to draw conclusions about the code. The first code snippet contained a common bug for introductory programming students: i.e., assignment (=) instead of logical equality (==). The second snippet of code combined an array of strings with modular arithmetic to print an array element to the screen. Both questions were multiple choice and provided an "I don't know" answer.

The second survey was a VARK learning style questionnaire, which is a proven tool used to assess each student's learning preferences [2]. Visual learners prefer visual aids such as pictures and diagrams. Auditory learners like to hear verbal explanations of the topic at hand. Read / write learners prefer reading the details from textbook or other word based references. Kinesthetic learners learn by doing, preferring to use their hands to physically complete a task. It is crucial to note that these four groups are not mutually exclusive, and many learners tend to prefer more than one learning style. The free VARK survey asks 16 multiple choice questions where students select one or more answers per question. The answers are then scored to yield a numerical rating for each of the VARK learning preferences.

Unfortunately we did not collect demographical information from participants. Such information regarding intended major, ethnicity, gender, primary language, and socio-economic status would have been interesting metrics to analyze.

3.2 Pedagogy

As mentioned previously, each 50-minute lecture made use of the exact same material across all four sections. The Powerpoint slides, homework assignments, tests, and lecture handouts were always exactly the same. Although the code examples may have differed slightly between instructors, the examples did not differ between the experimental vs.control sections. In other words, the code instructor MR used was the same between the two sections. Likewise, the code examples instructor TD used across her two sections were identical. The only difference was in how the instructors presented the code, using live-coding in the experimental section.

3.2.1 Lecture Structure

The structure of each 50 minute lecture was basically the same across all four sections. Each lecture started with no more than five minutes for questions about the previous lecture or homework assignments. Next, the instructor went through all the Powerpoint slides, which took between 20 and 25 minutes, depending on the topic. Each lecture ended with 20 to 25 minutes dedicated to going over example code. The instructors did their best to keep the lectures consistent between their two sections.

3.2.2 Code Examples

As previously alluded to, the only difference between each instructor's two sections was the way the code examples were presented. In the experimental or live-coding section, the instructor always started with a blank screen and ended with a working solution. That is, the instructors would posit an example problem to the students and write code to solve the problem, one step at a time. Throughout the coding process, the instructors would narrate their thoughts and actions as well as ask for student input with questions such "what am I missing?" or "what comes next?".

In addition to writing correct code from scratch, both instructors purposefully demonstrated common logic and syntax errors, such as integer division, assignment (=) instead of equality (==), forgetting a semi-colon, poor curly-brace bracketing, etc. In addition to writing buggy code on purpose, occasionally the instructors would create errors on accident. Although unforeseen bugs during live-coding lecture can be time-consuming and embarrassing for the instructor, it provides excellent learning opportunities for the students. Watching an expert track down an unforeseen bug shows students the process of debugging, which is a very useful skill that is rarely taught. Also, seeing an expert instructor make a mistake shows the often imperfect nature of writing software and the importance of incremental development and testing.

In the control sections, the code examples were presented statically and never modified "live" during lecture. Instead, several iterations of code were presented, analyzed line by line, compiled, and executed. Some iterations had purposeful syntax and logic errors as previously mentioned. Other iterations showed different ways to solve the same problem. It is important to note that the code examples did not change between the experimental and control sections, only the manner in which it was presented. Specifically, the control sections saw the same code examples but never saw the instructor typing code.

3.3 Post-Course Surveys

During the last week of lectures, two surveys were administered. The first survey, referred to as the post-course survey, asked students to rate their familiarity with C++ concepts such as user input/output, file input/output, classes, functions, etc. Also, to see how students progressed, the post-course survey asked the same two code snippet questions that were on the pre-course survey.

The second survey, known as the live-coding survey, focused on student's perceptions about how the course was taught. Students rated seven statements on a 4-point Likert scale ranging from Strongly Disagree to Strongly Agree (with no Neutral). Next, the students were asked to rank which aspects of the lecture and course that they learned the most from. In addition to the Likert scales and rankings, students were given the opportunity to comment about live-coding in general, and whether they would prefer such pedagogy in future computer science courses.

3.4 Grades

To help assess the effectiveness of live-coding, we examined student grades on assignments, exams, the final project, and the overall average. Throughout the semester, students in all sections were given the same weekly homework assignments, which were used to help assess and solidify the student's coding abilities. These assignments were graded by graduate teaching assistants based on common grading rubrics. During the semester the students took three exams, which were written by the head instructor and common between all sections. The exams were graded in a fair and balanced way by all three instructors: i.e., each instructor graded specific pages on all exams. Thus there was no bias from instructor grading on the exam results between sections. The final project was a two week, pair programming assignment where students had to implement a GUI version of Conway's "Game of Life" using C++ and OpenFrameworks [4]. The final project was graded by course instructors and was based on a standardized rubric that analyzed game performance and code clarity. Finally, we examined the overall grade of each student, which was based on a weighted combination of the previous elements (i.e., 25% assignments, 15% exam I, 15% exam II, 30% final exam, and 15% final project).

4. RESULTS

In this section we present results that have led us to conclude that live-coding is an effective way to teach an introductory programming course. Due to limited space, we only present results from our key findings. Furthermore, there were no statistical differences between the VARK preferences both between and within experimental groups (T-test, $p < 0.05$). In other words, the relative number of visual, auditory, read/write, and kinesthetic learners were statistically similar across all sections of experimental groups and instructors.

4.1 Grades

For starters, the assignments, exams, and overall grades from both groups were virtually identical, with the live-coding group actually performing better on the final project (e.g., see Figure 1). More specifically, the live-coding group performed statistically better than the control group on the final project (T-test, $p < 0.05$). All other grades were not statistically different between groups.

When tested using the same official performance metrics, live-codings students performed equal if not better than their control counterparts. Thus, it is safe to say that live-coding is as good as, if not better than, teaching with static code. Moreover, our results suggest that live-coding may actually help students prepare and complete the final project.

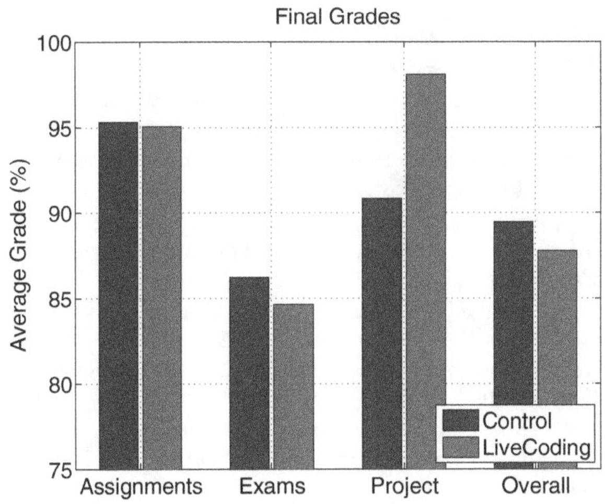

Figure 1: Final grades computed for both groups. The live-coding group performed statistically better than the control on the final project (T-test, $p < 0.05$).

4.2 Live-Coding to Teach Common Bugs

As indicated in Figure 2, live-coding appears to be an effective way to teach and correct common introductory programming mistakes such as assignment (=) versus equivalence (==). This is because live-coding offers instructors the flexibility to purposefully write buggy code and make corrections live in front of students. Watching an instructor debug code is very helpful to students because it: 1) shows the process of debugging code and 2) shows common pitfalls when developing software.

For example, when instructors write code that is conceptually new to students (e.g., pass by reference vs. value) the instructor may purposefully incorporate a bug in the code (e.g., trying to permanently modify a variable that was passed by value) without telling students. When the instructor tests the code and the bug becomes apparent (e.g.,

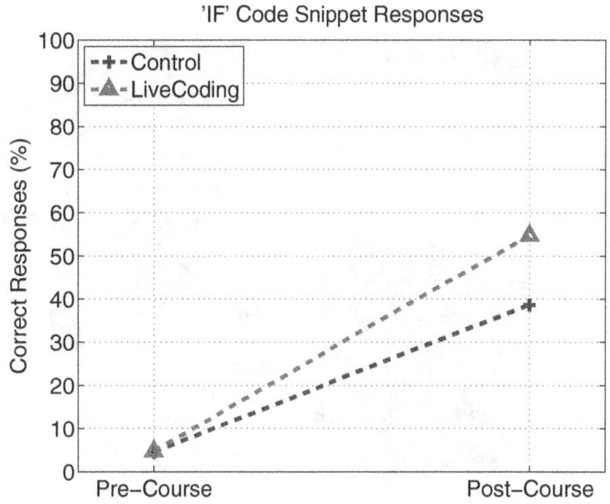

Figure 2: The percentage of students (based on experimental group) who correctly answered the assignment vs. equivalence code snippet questions on the pre and post-course surveys.

the value doesn't persist), the instructor will go back to the code and ask for student help to track down the bug (e.g., using *cout* to output variable values). Then, when the bug is found, the instructor will make the necessary corrections (e.g., pass by reference) and recompile / rerun the code. As the semester progresses, students become more and more adept at locating these on purpose bugs as the instructor types. This attentiveness helps students with their own code, since they most likely develop a keen awareness of locating bugs as they type.

In the control (static code) version, the instructor presents three totally different files: one with a bug, one with debugging statements, and finally the correct solution. Although the instructor would take ample time asking for student input, testing for the bug, and explaining the mistake, students do not seem to grasp the information as well. This is evident in the results from Figure 2, where the control group did not perform as well on the assignment vs. logical equivalence question. One can speculate that live-coding is simply a better way to hold student attention while showing code examples.

4.3 Live-Coding and Lecture Preferences

As indicated in Figures 3 and 4, students in the live-coding group preferred the code examples more than the control group. In particular, 90% of the live-coding group agreed that code examples were more educational than the Powerpoint slides (as opposed to 67% in the control group). This is most likely because the code examples in the live-coding group were more dynamic and interesting for students to pay attention to. Despite the instructors' best efforts, presenting static code examples simply does not draw the same level of attention from students. This is evident from the types of comments we received on the live-coding survey.

5. CONCLUSION

In this article we shared our research design and results to assess the effectiveness of live-coding as a teaching method.

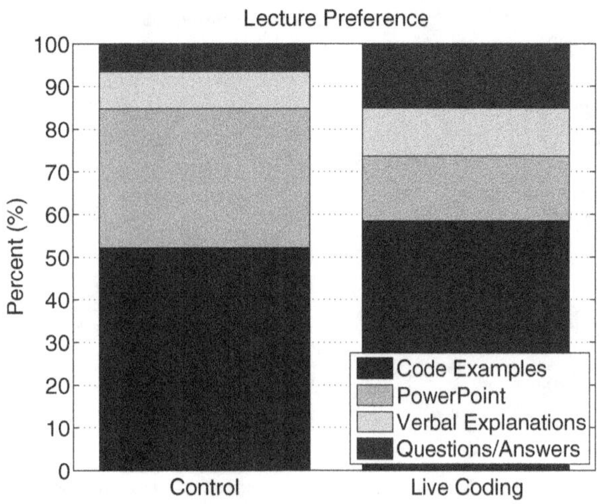

Figure 3: Top lecture preference of the control and live coding sections.

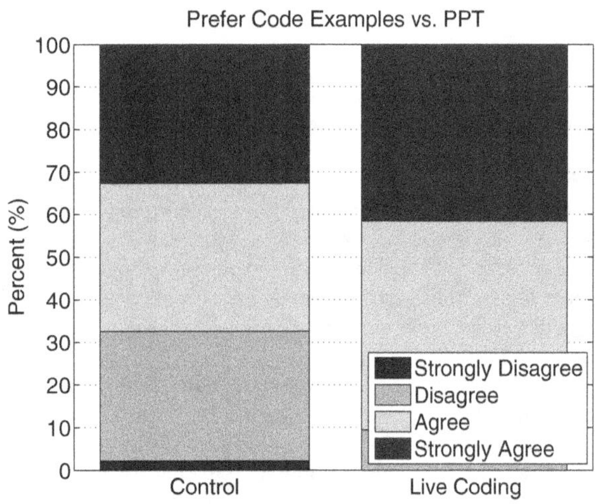

Figure 4: Likert scale responses to the comment: "Watching the instructor code 'live' solutions was more educational than viewing the Powerpoint slides"

Our carefully constructed research design helps insure that our results are admissible, given that all of the course materials, i.e., the Powerpoint slides, lecture handouts, assignments, exams, and final project, were identical between sections. The only aspect that differed between experimental groups was how code examples were presented: either via live-coding or with static examples. Also, we reduced the effects of instructor bias by pooling the four sections of CSCI 261 into only two experimental groups. Thus, the results better reflect the impact of live-coding and not the effectiveness of a particular instructor.

The results of this study show that live-coding is as good as if not better than teaching code via static examples. With the exception of the final project, student grades between experimental groups were not significantly (statistically) different, offering support that live-coding does not detract student learning in any way. For the final project, the statistically significant higher grades reflect the notion that live-coding may better prepare students to tackle large coding assignments by demonstrating good programming habits such as iterative testing. The impact of live-coding is further reflected in the performance on the code-snippet questions, were students in the live-coding group showed more improvement on the assignment vs. equivalence survey question. Additionally, students in the live-coding group showed more preference towards using code examples over Powerpoint slides than the control group. Also, students in the live-coding group preferred code examples more than the control group. Lastly, student comments regarding the use of code examples were much more favorable in the live-coding group.

From the results presented it is clear that live-coding is a viable and effective method to teach code examples to introductory programming students. We hypothesize that the dynamic nature of live-coding helps keep student attention on the task at hand, which can only help students learn the new skill of programming. It is our hope that these results will provide other instructors with ample evidence to consider using live-coding to teach programming at their institutions.

6. REFERENCES

[1] J. Bennedsen and M. Caspersen. Revealing the programming process. *SIGCSE*, pages 186–190, 2005.

[2] N. Fleming. Vark – a guide to learning styles. `http://www.vark-learn.com/english/index.asp`, 2010. Retrieved Sept. 6, 2012.

[3] A. Gaspar and S. Langevin. Restoring "coding with intention" in introductory programming courses. *SIGITE*, pages 91–98, 2007.

[4] Z. Lieberman, T. Watson, and A. Castro. Openframeworks: an open-source c++ toolkit. `http://www.openframeworks.cc/`, 2012. Retrieved Sept. 6, 2012.

[5] J. Paxton. Live programming as a lecture technique. *Journal of Computer Sciences in Colleges*, 18(2):51–56, 2002.

[6] A. Pears, S. Seidman, L. Malmi, L. Mannila, E. Adams, J. Bennedsen, M. Devlin, and J. Paterson. A survey of literature on the teaching of introductory programming. *SIGCSE Bulletin*, pages 204–223, 2007.

[7] A. Robins, J. Rountree, and N. Rountree. Learning and teaching programming: A literature review. *Computer Science Education*, 13(2):137–172, 2003.

[8] A. Sanwar. Effective teaching pedagogies for undergraduate computer science. *Mathematics and Computer Education*, 39(3):243–257, 2005.

[9] A. Vihavainen, M. Pakula, and M. Luukkainen. Extreme apprenticeship method in teaching programmers for beginners. *SIGCSE*, pages 93–98, 2011.

Tackling Engagement in Computing with Computational Music Remixing

Brian Magerko[1], Jason Freeman[2], Tom McKlin[3], Scott McCoid[2], Tom Jenkins[1], Elise Livingston[1]

[1] Digital Media Program
Georgia Institute of Technology
Atlanta, GA 30332
001-404-894-2739
{magerko, tj399, elivingston3}
@gatech.edu

[2]School of Music
Georgia Institute of Technology
Atlanta, GA 30332
001-404-894-8949
{jason.freeman, smccoid3}
@gatech.edu

[3]The Findings Group
1201 Clairmont Road, Suite 305
Decatur, GA 30030
001-404-633-9091
tom@theFindingsGroup.com

ABSTRACT

In this paper, we describe *EarSketch*, an integrated curriculum, software toolset, and social media website, grounded in constructionist principles, that targets introductory high school computing education. We hypothesize that the use of *collaborative computational music composition and remixing* may avoid some of the engagement and culture-specific issues that other approaches, both in music and other media, have had. We discuss the design of *EarSketch*, its use in a pilot summer camp, and the evaluation results from that pilot.

Categories and Subject Descriptors

K.3.2 [**Computers and Education**]: Computer and Information Science Education – *computer science education.*

Keywords

Music, education, computing principles, remixing, collaboration.

1. INTRODUCTION

Computing education in the United States currently struggles to engage students and motivate their further studies in the discipline [6]. This challenge is more pronounced with under-represented groups and particularly with African-Americans [4,29]. Previous research has attempted to increase minority participation in computing education by making it more relevant and engaging through culturally specific technology [3,7,29]. Other approaches to engagement have turned to more general contextual motivators, such as the computational creation and control of movies, music, textiles, animations, robots, and especially computer games as an "in" for motivating students to study computing [5,8,11,12,16,22].

EarSketch, our approach to engaging students in computing principles through *collaborative computational music composition and remixing*, consists of an integrated curriculum, software toolset, and social media website. The *EarSketch* curriculum targets introductory high school computing education. The software toolset enables students to create music by manipulating loops, composing beats, and applying effects with Python code. The social media website invites students to upload their music and source code, view other students' work, and create derivative musical remixes from other students' code. *EarSketch* is built on top of *Reaper*, an intuitive digital audio workstation (DAW) program comparable to those used in professional recording studios. It is extremely practical for educational settings due to its low cost, cross-platform compatibility, and low processor and memory utilization.

EarSketch is designed to enable student creativity, to enhance collaboration, and to leverage cultural relevance. This focus has created unique advantages for our approach to computing education. First, *EarSketch* leverages musical remixing as it relates to popular musical forms, such as hip hop[1], in an attempt to connect to students in a culturally relevant fashion that spans gender, ethnicity, and socioeconomic status. It does so by explicitly connecting the learning environment to popular music production software, by drawing from industry practice in the features it supports, and by visualizing computational output within standard studio paradigms. It also focuses on the level of beats, loops, and effects more than individual notes, enabling students with no background in music theory or composition to begin creating personally relevant music immediately, with a focus on higher-level musical concepts such as formal organization, texture, and mixing. Second, student use of the social media site allows a tight coupling between code sharing / reuse and the musical practice of remixing. Students can grab code snippets from other projects and directly inject them into their own work, modifying them to fit their idiosyncratic musical ideas. Third, unlike more graphically oriented environments such as *Scratch*, *EarSketch* builds on professional development techniques using an industry-relevant, text-based programming language (Python), giving them concrete skills directly applicable to further study.

2. EARSKETCH

2.1 Technical Design

EarSketch integrates three components into the *Reaper* software: an application programming interface (API) for controlling *Reaper*; a sound library of pre-composed audio loops; and utility scripts to seamlessly integrate with other *EarSketch* components.

[1] Hip hop music has widely embraced the remixing of other artists' musical works as a post-modern music composition practice since the 1970's [25].

SIGCSE'13, March 6–9, 2013, Denver, Colorado, USA.

The *EarSketch* API leverages ReaScript, *Reaper*'s own Python API that provides low-level programmatic access to *Reaper*. We have developed our own higher-level Python API for pedagogical use that wraps the ReaScript API. It focuses on typical composition and remixing tasks, such as placing audio files on the timeline, applying effects, and sequencing rhythmic beats.

We have also used ReaScript to customize the functionality of *Reaper*'s user interface, hiding extraneous GUI items and adding menu commands to run and edit Python scripts, upload projects to the social media site, and access *EarSketch* curricular materials.

Since *EarSketch* relies heavily on the manipulation of pre-composed audio loops, it requires an extensive audio loop library. For this workshop, we licensed a commercial loop library that includes a variety of genres, so that students can create pieces that reflect their own interests and tastes: hip hop, soul, R&B, techno, house, drum n bass, and Latin/world.

2.2 Curriculum Design

The curriculum incorporates basic computing concepts grounded in "thick authenticity", which focuses on the interrelated authentic learning practices of: having personally meaningful learning experiences; learning that relates to the world outside of the learning context; learning that encourages thinking within a particular discipline, like music composition; and allowing for assessment that reflects the learning process. The curriculum has been based on the CS Principles topics [31] within the context of loop-based composition (see Section 2.2.1). Students learn how to create music with digital audio workstation (DAW) software, to write code to programmatically generate music in the DAW, and to create both music and code collaboratively.

2.2.1 Overall Design

The *EarSketch* curriculum is currently designed for use in a summer workshop setting (see Section 3) and will soon be adapted for use in an academic high school classroom. The curriculum does not expect students to play a musical instrument or read music notation. It also assumes that students have no prior experience in using DAW software or in programming. Its design emphasizes hands-on, collaborative experiences.

The curriculum also emphasizes some of the unique benefits of approaching music from a computational perspective. In particular, it demonstrates to students how to rapidly experiment with many possible variations on a musical idea by iteratively modifying algorithmic parameters, executing each version of code, and using their musical ears to decide which option(s) are best [8]. (For example, they may explore how many times a loop should be repeated before a new one is introduced.) The curriculum also focuses on the idea of a composer as a "pilot" who uses computation to negotiate low-level details so as to focus more on higher-level musical structures and on the ways in which a computational interface transforms musical thinking [30].

We formulated learning objectives based on the current CS: Principles learning objectives [31], adopting the relevant objectives to our specific domain. For example (italics indicate *EarSketch*-specific language): Learning Objective 5: (CSP-14) The student can analyze the considerations involved in the computational manipulation of *musical sounds and ideas*. These learning objectives were directly used in designing our assessment instruments (see Section 4.1).

2.2.2 Digital Audio Workstation (DAW)

The first topic covered in the curriculum is the *Reaper* DAW. The DAW is the timeline-based software that lets users place sound clips on tracks, as well as add and manipulate effects. Before coding, students first learn how to create music using *Reaper*'s standard graphical interface. This familiarizes them with music industry software paradigms, helps them build a mental model of the DAW as a foundation for further programming abstractions, provides clear connections between API functions and standard DAW functionality, and demonstrates the unique advantages and time savings programming can offer in executing complex tasks.

2.2.3 Programming

Programming concepts in the *EarSketch* curriculum are introduced in hand with DAW capabilities and musical constructs. The current workshop curriculum covers basic Python syntax (e.g. comments, imports); the use and declaration of variables, functions, and parameters; iteration with for loops, index variables, and skip counting; strings; simple math and random functions; and list data structures.

Figure 1. Example of *Reaper*'s graphical interface

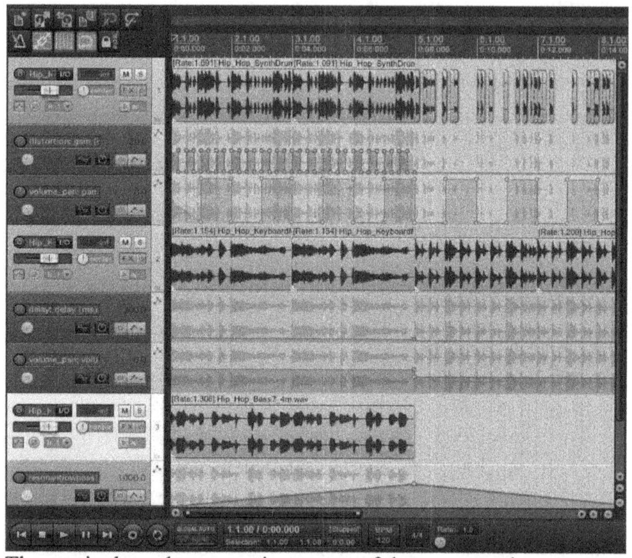

The curriculum always motivates use of these computing concepts by linking them to new methods of musical composition in the DAW. For example, students declare functions to generate A and B sections of music and then use the flexibility that such abstractions enable to quickly modify, move, and repeat these musical passages. They use loops with skip-counting indices to create musical fills that vary a repeating loop at structurally significant time intervals in the music. They create strings to define their own step-sequenced rhythmic patterns within the music (e.g. "111-1-1-" will play an audio file on the first, second, third, fifth, and seventh sixteenth notes of a pattern). They use random functions to select among different audio files or rhythmic patterns stored in a list to create unexpected musical results that change each time a program is executed.

The curriculum also emphasizes the ways in which programming can simplify the execution of complex tasks that would be tedious to do in *Reaper*'s graphical interface, thus permitting rapid, iterative musical experimentation. For example, students first learn how to apply effects — audio techniques such as delay, pitch-shifting, volume, panning, and distortion — by using *Reaper*'s graphical interface to draw connected line segments that change effects parameters over time. They then use the *setEffect()* function to more easily create and control effects and parameter changes programmatically.

Collaboration and sharing are incorporated into the curriculum at all levels. After each lesson, students have time to work on their own projects, frequently collaboratively. We use "round robin" and "pair" style coding, where students work for five minutes on a project, then continually shift one seat over in the classroom to a new project or alternate back and forth with a single collaborator on the same project. All of this work is placed onto the social media web site, allowing students to view and download other students' projects. By appropriating musical ideas and programming techniques from uploaded work, collaborative practices emerge even without direct pairing or contact.

2.3 Social Media Site

Our social media web site facilitates informal sharing and borrowing of code among students. Following the paradigm established by online music remixing communities such as ccMixter [1] and computing education communities such as Scratch [18], the site enables students to browse projects created by their peers, listen to the audio and view the code inside the browser, download the project, add comments and tags, and see how code has been reused and transformed by others. To facilitate seamless integration, we created a menu command within *Reaper* that automatically uploads a user's relevant source code and audio files for a project to his or her social media site account.

3. SUMMER WORKSHOP

During summer of 2012, we conducted the first *EarSketch* workshop to pilot the curriculum, software, and social media site. The workshop consisted of 5 days (5 hours each) of instruction, with each day being divided into 60-minute segments. These segments were designed to provide a comfortable amount of time for instruction and demonstration with longer periods of time for individual student practice and application, followed by sharing and reflection. Students had specific assigned exercises, more open-ended work time, and round robin, pair programming, and kinesthetic activities. Besides the instructor lessons, they also had access to an *EarSketch* curriculum manual and reference documentation. Ultimately, the students worked to create a final project to present and share with family members during an "open house" which took place on the final afternoon of the workshop.

Many of the students enrolled in the workshop due to an interest in music. These students' intrinsic motivation for creating music was used as a foundation for an interest in programming. Students were encouraged to bring an instrument or to utilize the in-room keyboard and a recording system to test musical ideas. Several students were able to record their own music and incorporate it into their projects. In-class jam sessions where the students would improvise and play music occurred a number of times throughout the course. Students also frequently brought in musical ideas from commercial recordings that became seeds for their projects.

4. EVALUATION

The students that participated in the *EarSketch* workshop (n = 17) were from a variety of Metro Atlanta and Atlanta schools. Rising 9th and 10th grade students made up 70% of the group while the remaining 30% was made up of 11th and 12th grade students. The ethnic demographic of the group was relatively diverse with 18% of the students being Asian-American, 24% being African-American, 53% European-American, and 6% of two or more ethnicities. The class was comprised of 75% male and 25% female students. These workshop participants were recruited through the Georgia Tech Institute for Computing Education (ICE). 82% of the students had never been previously involved in a computer science related workshop.

4.1 Methods

Program participants were measured at three time points over their 5-day *EarSketch* experience: a 10-item pre content knowledge assessment on day one, an engagement survey at the end of day four, and the same content knowledge assessment on day five that the students saw on day one. The content knowledge assessment is designed to measure basic knowledge related to programming a digital audio workstation environment and adheres to a set of standards developed by the *EarSketch* curriculum team. We focused on novice-level concepts in teaching materials and assessment, using Bloom's Taxonomy [15] as a guide for focusing on 1st (knowledge) and 2nd level (comprehension) learning. Before administering the assessment, the team rated the difficulty of each item in relation to this taxonomy as: easy, moderate, and difficult. Figure 2 shows an example of a moderate difficulty question.

Figure 2. Example of a moderate content knowledge assessment question

Which code example puts the beat "0+++0+++0+0+0+++" on measures 5, 6, 7, 8?

A.

```
music = HIP_HOP_DRUMS4_2M
for measure in range(5, 9):
   makeBeat(music,1, measure, "0+++0+++0+0+0+++")
```

B.

```
music = HIP_HOP_DRUMS4_2M
for measure in range(1, 5):
   measure = measure * 2
   makeBeat(music,1, measure, "0+++0+++0+0+0+++")
```

C.

```
music = HIP_HOP_DRUMS4_2M
for measure in range(5, 8):
   makeBeat(music,1, measure, "0+++0+++0+0+0+++")
```

D.

```
music = HIP_HOP_DRUMS4_2M
for measure in range(5, 8):
   makeBeat(music,1, measure, "0+++0+++0+0+0+++")
```

E. I don't know.

On day four, participants were asked to complete a survey measuring seven engagement constructs [27]. The engagement instrument is comprised of five scales from Williams et al. [28]:

- computing confidence (e.g "I am sure I can do advanced work in computing"),
- computing enjoyment (e.g. "I feel comfortable working with a computer"),
- perceived usefulness of computing (e.g. "I will be able to get a good job if I learn how to use a computer"),
- motivation to succeed in computing (e.g. "I like solving computing problems"), and
- computing identify and belongingness (e.g. "I feel like I 'belong' in computer science").

The instrument also draws on a scale [14] designed to measure the extent to which participants see computing as a creative outlet (e.g. "I am able to be very expressive and creative while doing computing"). Finally, the instrument measures students' intention to persist in computing as a career (e.g. "Someday, I would like to have a career in computing"). The student engagement survey was administered retrospectively, such that students' answered how they felt before the camp and at the end. This instrument was administered at the end of the fourth (of five) day of camp. The analysis consisted of a paired samples t-test whereby statistically significant changes from pre to post were assessed.

4.2 Results

Overall, the results suggest that students' attitudes positively and statistically significantly increased across 3 constructs at $p<.01$:

Computing Confidence, Motivation to Succeed in Computing, and Creativity. This suggests that the workshop is effective at enhancing students' perceptions that they can tackle advanced computing work and get good grades in computing (Computing Confidence). Likewise, the workshop increases students' motivations to persevere on complex computing problems (Motivation to Succeed in Computing). Originality and expressivity are also enhanced as a result (Creativity). Students' enjoyment and perceptions of the importance and usefulness of computers were, comparatively, high both before and after the workshop; this suggests that the workshop maintained students' positive perceptions of computing. Students indicate that they are statistically significantly more likely to see themselves in a computing field in the future as a result of the workshop.

Table 1. Change from before to after along the seven engagement constructs

CONSTRUCTS									
Constructs		n	Mean	Paired Samples *t-test*	SD	D	N	A	SA
Computing Confidence	Before	16	3.20	0.008**	14%	18%	24%	22%	21%
	Now	17	4.11		3%	3%	18%	33%	43%
Computing Enjoyment	Before	17	4.31	0.838	2%	5%	11%	25%	57%
	Now	17	4.34		1%	5%	10%	27%	57%
Perceived Usefulness of Computing	Before	17	4.39	0.945	2%	1%	9%	32%	56%
	Now	17	4.38		3%	6%	8%	17%	66%
Motivation to Succeed in Computing	Before	17	3.57	0.000**	3%	19%	21%	34%	24%
	Now	17	4.03		1%	7%	17%	39%	36%
Computing Identity and Belongingness	Before	17	3.59	0.277	2%	20%	27%	20%	31%
	Now	17	3.76		4%	14%	22%	24%	37%
Intention to Persist	Before	17	3.58	0.245	5%	12%	33%	22%	28%
	Now	17	3.70		5%	10%	28%	26%	32%
Creativity	Before	17	3.46	0.006**	9%	5%	38%	28%	21%
	Now	16	4.20		0%	0%	19%	42%	39%

**$p<.01$; *$p<.01$; negatively worded items were reverse coded prior to mean computation of the constructs. Only students with matched before and now scores were assessed for statistical significance. Note: We employed a 5pt. scale with the following response categories: Strongly Disagree (SD), Disagree (D), Neutral (N), Agree (A), and Strongly Agree (SA).

Table 2. Pearson correlation, n = 17

	Δ CKA overall	Δ Intent to Persist	Δ Confidence	Δ Enjoyment	Δ Importance & Perceived Usefulness	Δ Motivation	Δ Identity & Belongingness	Δ Creativity
Δ CKA (overall)	--							
Δ Intent to Persist	.083	--						
Δ Confidence	-.175	.583*	--					
Δ Enjoyment	.282	.093	.540*	--				
ΔImportance & Perceived Usefulness	.365	.366	.628**	.912**	--			
Δ Motivation	-.149	.431	.574*	.408	.364	--		
Δ Identity & Belongingness	.139	.740**	.815**	.646**	.839**	.507*	--	
Δ Creativity	-.242	.780**	.775**	.191	.333	.611**	.691**	--

**$p<.01$; *$p<.05$. Δ = Now-Before

To further investigate how the *EarSketch* program impacted students' intent to persist in computing, a correlation analysis was conducted whereby the change in responses (Δ) from Before to Now across the 7 survey constructs listed in Table 1 were entered into a Pearson's correlation. The results, presented in Table 2, indicate that to the extent that students gained in confidence, belongingness and creativity, their intent to persist in computing increased. Interestingly, growth in creativity was statistically significantly correlated with growth in confidence, motivation and belongingness. Further, the data indicate no significant correlation between a change in content knowledge and a change in the engagement constructs.

Figure 3 summarizes students' gains in content knowledge across all content knowledge assessment items, specifically examining content knowledge gains by item difficulty. The results clearly suggest that the workshop was statistically significantly effective in enhancing students' knowledge of programming concepts. Gains from pre to post were most evident for easy and moderate items. Though fewer students correctly answered the items that were rated as being hard, the results nonetheless show a statistically significant increase. The number of correctly answered content knowledge assessment items were also examined per individual student. On average, students made a 4 item gain from pre to post; that is, the average student answered 6 questions correctly at post and only 2 questions at pre. Perfect scores (10 out of 10) at post were found between two students. Further, female students made, on average, a 5-item gain from pre to post, and male students made a 4-item gain.

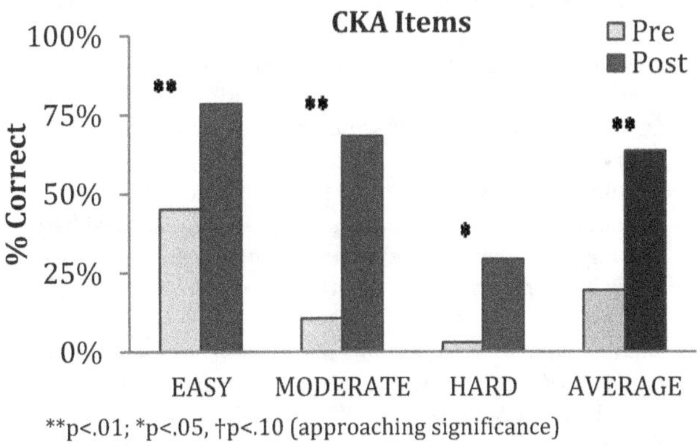

Figure 3. Pre/Post content knowledge assessment items by difficulty

When asked what aspects of the workshop students enjoyed the most, the vast majority indicated that they appreciated learning about programming and working on complex and interesting projects in computing and music. For example, one student noted "the best thing about this camp was the fact that we were introduced to programming, while also integrating it into musical concepts." Another student expresses her enthusiasm for the workshop projects by saying, "Learning how to create music using only code with minimal help from a DAW was very exciting and interesting. The code allows for a much easier and faster way to mix and remix music." Other aspects of the workshop that students valued were the supportive and positive environment created by the staff and the fellow campers.

5. RELATED WORK

5.1 Motivation

Learning how to program is a challenging task in itself, and there is a long history of research into building different types of programming environments intended to make computer science more accessible to a broader audience [13]. Much of this work has focused on targeting specific groups, such as women [23] and minorities [7,9,10,29] or leveraging interest in other areas, such as digital games [18,21,24], textiles [2], and music [16,17]. Particularly with respect to digital media, the hope is that a large and more diverse audience will be more interested in the creation of media-related content (as opposed to programming for its own merits). Because a novice audience will likely not have existing programming skills, these tools are intended to bridge the gap while maintaining students' attention.

5.2 Remixing Media

When remixing, musicians "weave samples from familiar songs into a new montage of sound," sampling melodic and harmonic riffs from existing recordings to create the rhythmic foundation for a new work [26]. This practice, which leverages creating, sharing, and listening to music as a potentially more ubiquitous cultural practice than seen in other computing educational domains, will serve as motivation for many students to program. Hip hop music, which we focus on as a means of engaging African-American students in particular (though hip hop is itself a widely popular domain), has already been successfully used as a culturally motivating domain in the recruitment of middle school students into computing in high school and beyond in coursework at North Carolina A&T State University (unpublished), for pre-computational education [7,9,10], as well as in other non computational domains, such as reading [19,20].

6. FUTURE WORK

We continue to iteratively review, refine, and evaluate all three components of *EarSketch* (curriculum, software toolset, and social network) as we prepare for a public release and broader deployment of the project. Near-term plans include a six-week pilot at an ethnically and socioeconomically diverse public high school in metro Atlanta in early 2013, to assess the success of our workshop curriculum in a more formal academic setting; and a two-week summer workshop in 2013 at Georgia Tech's Institute for Computing Education, to pilot additional curriculum modules focusing on more advanced computing and musical concepts. As the number of students participating in *EarSketch* pilots grows, we also hope to obtain statistically significant data about the learning outcomes and attitudes changes in students of different demographic backgrounds, so that we can better understand the impact of *EarSketch* on computing education for various under-represented populations.

We are also adding new functionality to the *EarSketch* software toolset and social media website. Some of our development is focused on improving usability and the seamless integration of multiple software components through changes such as new *EarSketch* menu items within *Reaper* and a cleaner project metadata entry page on the social media website. Other changes focus on new API functionality for the software toolset, in particular on functions to analyze sections of existing tracks or audio files and to design new effects to transform audio. This additional functionality will expand the creative possibilities of the environment, support the use of new computing concepts such as conditionals, and help make the toolset practical for use in more extended courses at the high school or college level. Finally, we are in the process of replacing the existing library of audio loops bundled with *EarSketch*, which were licensed to us only for use in pilot studies, with a more openly licensed library of audio content that has been created in collaboration with popular producers like Young Guru and Richard Devine. This library is a prerequisite to public dissemination and broad deployment of *EarSketch*.

7. ACKNOWLEDGEMENTS

This work heavily benefitted from our collaborations with Barbara Ericson, Christopher Michaud, Hera Kahn, and Mike Reilly. It has been funded by National Science Foundation grants CNS #1138469, #1234892, and #1237525.

8. REFERENCES

1. ArtisTech Media, LLC. ccMixter. *ccMixter: Download, Sample, Cut-up, Share.* http://ccmixter.org/.
2. Buechley, L., Eisenberg, M., Catchen, J., and Crockett, A. The LilyPad Arduino: using computational textiles to investigate engagement, aesthetics, and diversity in computer science education. *Proceeding of the twenty-sixth annual SIGCHI conference on Human factors in computing systems*, (2008), 423–432.
3. Burge, J.D. and Suarez, T.L. Preliminary analysis of factors affecting women and african americans in the computing sciences. *Proceedings of the 2005 conference on Diversity in computing*, ACM (2005), 53-56.
4. Chubin, D.E., May, G.S., and Babco, E.L. Diversifying the engineering workforce. *Journal of Engineering Education 94*, 1 (2005), 73–86.
5. Conway, M., Audia, S., Burnette, T., Cosgrove, D., and Christiansen, K. Alice: lessons learned from building a 3D system for novices. *Proceedings of the SIGCHI conference on Human factors in computing systems*, ACM (2000), 486-493.
6. Cuny, J. Address to the Computer Science Community. 2011.
7. Eglash, R., Bennett, A., O Donnell, C., Jennings, S., and Cintorino, M. Culturally situated design tools: Ethnocomputing from field site to classroom. *American anthropologist 108*, 2 (2006), 347.
8. Ericson, B., Guzdial, M., and Biggers, M. Improving secondary CS education: progress and problems. *ACM SIGCSE Bulletin*, (2007), 298–301.
9. Eugene, W. and Gilbert, J.E. C-PAL: cultural-based programming for adult learners. *Proceedings of the 46th Annual ACM Southeast Regional Conference*, ACM (2008), 450-453.
10. Eugene, W. and Gilbert, J.E. Mining for culture: reaching out of range. *Conference, University of Illinois at Urbana-Champaign, Champaign*, (2010).
11. Guzdial, M. A media computation course for non-majors. *ACM SIGCSE Bulletin*, (2003), 104–108.
12. Kafai, Y.B., Peppler, K.A., Burke, Q., Moore, M., and Glosson, D. Fröbel's forgotten gift: textile construction kits as pathways into play, design and computation. *Proceedings of the 9th International Conference on Interaction Design and Children*, (2010), 214–217.
13. Kelleher, C. and Pausch, R. Lowering the barriers to programming: A taxonomy of programming environments and languages for novice programmers. *ACM Comput. Surv. 37*, 2 (2005), 83-137.
14. Knezek, G. and Christensen, R. Validating the Computer Attitude Questionnaire (CAQ). (1996).
15. Krathwohl, D.R., Bloom, B.S., and Masia, B. *Taxonomy of educational objectives: The classification of educational goals.* David McKay Company, Inc., New York, 1956.
16. Meyers, A.L., Cole, M.C., Korth, E., and Pluta, S. Musicomputation: teaching computer science to teenage musicians. *Proceeding of the seventh ACM conference on Creativity and cognition*, ACM (2009), 29-38.
17. Misra, A., Blank, D., and Kumar, D. A music context for teaching introductory computing. *Proceedings of the 14th annual ACM SIGCSE conference on Innovation and technology in computer science education*, ACM (2009), 248-252.
18. Monroy-Hernández, A. and Resnick, M. Empowering kids to create and share programmable media. *interactions 15*, 2 (2008), 50-53.
19. Pinkard, N. Rappin Reader and Say Say Oh Playmate: Using Children's Childhood Songs as Literacy Scaffolds in Computer-Based Learning Environments. *Journal of Educational Computing Research 25*, 1 (2001), 17–34.
20. Pinkard, N.D. Lyric Reader: An architecture for creating intrinsically motivating and culturally responsive reading environments. *Interactive Learning Environments 7*, 1 (1999), 1–30.
21. Preston, J. and Morrison, B. Entertaining Education–Using Games-Based and Service-Oriented Learning to Improve STEM Education. *Transactions on Edutainment III*, (2009), 70–81.
22. Resnick, M., Maloney, J., Monroy-Hernández, A., et al. Scratch: programming for all. *Communications of the ACM 52*, 11 (2009), 60–67.
23. Rich, L., Perry, H., and Guzdial, M. A CS1 course designed to address interests of women. *Proceedings of the 35th SIGCSE technical symposium on Computer science education*, ACM (2004), 190-194.
24. Schulte, C. and Knobelsdorf, M. Attitudes towards computer science-computing experiences as a starting point and barrier to computer science. *Proceedings of the third international workshop on Computing education research*, ACM (2007), 27-38.
25. Vaidhyanathan, S. *Copyrights and copywrongs□: the rise of intellectual property and how it threatens creativity.* New York University Press, New York, 2003.
26. Wang, G., Trueman, D., Smallwood, S., and Cook, P.R. The Laptop Orchestra as Classroom. *Computer Music Journal 32*, 1 (2008), 26-37.
27. Wiebe, E., Williams, L., Yang, K., and Miller, C. Computer Science Attitude Survey. *computer 14*, 25 (2003), 0–86.
28. Williams, L., Wiebe, E., Yang, K., Ferzli, M., and Miller, C. In support of pair programming in the introductory computer science course. *Computer Science Education 12*, 3 (2002), 197–212.
29. Williams, L. Debunking the Nerd Stereotype with Pair Programming. *Computer 39*, 5 (2006), 83-85.
30. Xenakis, I. *Formalized Music: Thought and mathematics in composition.* Pendragon Press, 1992.
31. Computer Science: Principles. www.csprinciples.org.

Computer Science "Big Ideas" Play Well in Digital Sound and Music[i]

Jennifer Burg
Dept. of Computer Science
Wake Forest University
Winston-Salem, NC
(336) 758-4465
burg@wfu.edu

Jason Romney
School of Design and Production
UNC School of the Arts
Winston-Salem, NC
romneyj@uncsa.edu

Eric Schwartz
Sound Designer and
Audio Engineering
Athens, GA
schwartzsound@gmail.com

ABSTRACT

This paper reports the results of a four-year National Science Foundation CCLI grant that supported development and assessment of curricular material linking computer science (CS), digital audio, music, and sound design. A book and online learning aids were created and used in courses and summer workshops. The material was refined based on feedback from students and instructors. Learning was measured by pre- and post-tests. In this paper, we map the curricular material to the Big Ideas for CS Principles as well as to core CS courses. Objective and subjective assessment of the material over the course of the grant leads us to recommendations for *purposeful*, *parallel*, and *convergent* learning, concepts that are explained in the paper.

Categories and Subject Descriptors

K.3.2 Computer and Information Science Education
H.5.5 Sound and Music Computing
H.5.1 Multimedia Information

Keywords

digital media, computer science education, digital sound and music

1. MOTIVATION AND BACKGROUND

The motivation of this grant was a desire to create interdisciplinary curricular material that makes computer science learning more relevant and interesting to students by using sound and music as an application domain. Students' natural interest in sound and music gives us an entrée through which to introduce STEM concepts. It also provides a context in which students can learn to work with others of a different discipline. The interdisciplinary collaboration was intended to make learning more engaging while staying true to the fundamental purpose, which is to present CS and mathematical concepts and skills. The authors are not alone in advancing sound and music applications in computer science education. They have joined others active in this area [1] [5] [6] in creating a SIGCSE Committee on Computing and Music, and Sound and Music Computing is a category in the ACM Computing Classification System.

2. CURRICULAR MATERIAL FOR TEACHING DIGITAL SOUND AND MUSIC

During the grant period, a book and online learning supplements were created and assessed. The book was developed for an interdisciplinary audience, appropriate for students of computer science, music technology, or sound design. Each chapter except the last has three sections: (1) introduction of concepts relevant to all students (2) explanation of where these concepts are applied in sound design and music engineering, with hands-on examples (3) more depth on the mathematics, science, and algorithms, the underpinnings of the applications. There are eight chapters:

1. Getting Started
2. Sound Waves
3. Musical Sound
4. Sound Perception and Acoustics
5. Digitization
6. Sound Synthesis and MIDI
7. Sound Processing
8. Getting to Work

There are six types of learning supplements:

- interactive Flash tutorials
- MAX demos (Pure Data is free equivalent)
- MATLAB exercises (Octave is free equivalent)
- C and Java programming assignments
- video demonstrations
- practical exercises

Solutions are provided for exercises and programs. The curricular material is freely available online at the authors' website, http://digitalsoundandmusic.com.

3. PILOT TESTING AND ASSESSMENT

The curricular material was vetted and pilot tested in three two-day faculty workshops, two summer-long student workshops, and five courses, as listed in

Table 1. Student groups were small due to typical class sizes at the host universities, especially for a specialized topic. Also, scheduling constraints precluded having control groups for comparison. Thus, it was not possible to get statistically-significant results. However, the results were useful in helping us to refine the curricular material and to reveal the concepts students appeared to be learning or not learning well.

Assessment results for the Spring 2008 CSC191 course, offered to non-computer science majors, are given in Table 2. Students were asked to rate their understanding of key concepts before and after the course on a scale of 1 to 4, 4 reflecting the greatest understanding. In these results, it was gratifying to see that topics most closely associated with computer science – sampling and quantization, sampling rate and bit depth, and the difference between digital audio and MIDI (exemplifying numerical vs. symbolic representations) – were relatively well-understood at the end of the course, with a relatively high increase between what was understood before and after the course.

Pre- and post-tests of the chapter readings in the Summer 2011 workshop and the CSC191 course in Fall 2011 gave even more detailed information about the concepts that students missed most often. In particular, we tracked the average increase in correct or incorrect responses for each item on each test and tried to determine from these results if a concept was particularly difficult or poorly presented or a test questions was poorly composed. The questions on the post-tests were parallel to those on the pre-tests in that they always covered the same concepts, item-for-item, but not identically. The average increase in scores on the tests for Chapters 2, 3, 4, 5, and 7 (the chapters used in the course) were 31%, 24%, 16%, 38%, 42%, and 31%, respectively. These results, together with the student feedback from the Spring 2012 audio programming course at UNCA, helped to guide our refinement of the chapters and learning supplements.

Students were given a self-assessment of skills and knowledge before and after the CSC191 course in the fall 2011 semester. They were asked to rate their aptitude or interest in areas related to CS and music on a scale of 1 to 5, 5 being the greatest. Notably, their perception of their own aptitude increased on average from the beginning to the end of the course. Their perceived knowledge of the science of sound had the greatest increase. These results are given in Table 3.

The student assessments of the chapters and learning supplements used in the Audio Programming course, Spring 2012, were mostly positive. Students found the Flash and MAX demos particularly helpful in clarifying concepts. A few students were put off by the amount of physics they were asked to learn, and they found the readings long and dense. This has reinforced our desire to divide the curricular material into separate learning units that are easy to recognize, choose from, and access (See Future Work.)

Table 1 Assessment of interdisciplinary curricular material developed for digital sound and music

Course or Workshop	Place and Date	Audience	Assessment Done
Two-day faculty workshops	Wake Forest University (WFU), Summers 2008, 2009, and 2010	Faculty of CS and sound design	Feedback on perceived effectiveness of curricular material
Course: CSC 191 Digital Sound for Music and Theatre	WFU, Spring 2008	10 students interested in computer science, theatre, and music	Self-Assessment of knowledge before and after course
Student Summer Workshop	WFU, 8 weeks in Summer 2008	3 computer science students, 3 music students full time; 2 CS students part-time working on a separate project	Blogs Video and audio recordings of collaborative sessions
Course: First-Year Seminar, Digital Sound and Music	WFU, Fall 2009	15 freshmen students	Feedback on perceived effectiveness of curricular material
Student Summer Workshop	WFU, 8 weeks in Summer 2011	2 full-time CS students, 2 full-time music students, 2 part-time music students	Blogs with feedback on perceived effectiveness of curricular material Pre- and post-tests for book chapters to assess student learning
Course: CSC 191 Digital Sound and Music	WFU, Fall 2011	9 students interested in computer science and music. An attempt was made to get an approx. equal number of each type of student.	Blogs with feedback on perceived effectiveness of curricular material Self-assessment of skills and knowledge before and after course Pre- and post-tests for book chapters to assess student learning
Course: Audio Programming	UNC Asheville, Spring 2012	21 students of new media, computer science, and music technology	Feedback from students and instructor on perceived effectiveness of curricular material
Course: CSC 101, Overview of Computer Science	WFU, Fall 2012 (in progress)	41 students taking course for divisional credit (not counted toward CS major)	Pre- and post-tests measuring student understanding of and familiarity with CS Big Ideas

Table 2 Results from student self-assessment of knowledge before and after 100-level course in Digital Sound and Music

Numbers on a scale of 1–4	**the sense in which sound is a wave**	**sinusoidal nature of sound**	**frequency**	**amplitude**	**sampling and quanti-zation**	**decibels**	**dynamic range**	**bit depth**	**sampling rate**
average knowledge level at end of course	3.6	3	3.3	3.2	3.2	2.6667	3	3.1	3.1
average improvement	0.8	1.2	0.7	0.8	2.4	0.9	1.5	2	2.2
	aliasing	**EQ**	**Q-factor**	**Fourier transform**	**frequency response graph**	**condenser vs. dynamic mics**	**digital audio vs. MIDI**	**MIDI messages**	**sound synthesis for MIDI**
knowledge level at end of course	2.3	3	1.9	1.8	2.1	3.5	3.8	2.8	3
average improvement	1.7	1.5	1.5	1.6	1.4	2.6	2.4	2.2	2.4

Table 3 Assessment of skills, knowledge, and interest given to students before and after the CSC191 course, Fall 2011

Numbers on a scale of 1–5	**experience working with digital sound applications**	**aptitude for working with digital sound appli-cations**	**experience with MIDI**	**knowledge of science of sound**	**aptitude in math**	**interest in math**	**aptitude in physics**	**interest in physics**
average increase	0.875	0.375	1.5	1.125	0.375	0.5	0.625	0.125
	aptitude in electronics	**interest in electronics**	**aptitude in music theory**	**interest in music theory**	**experience in performing music**	**ability to read music**	**aptitude in working collaboratively**	**enjoyment in working collaboratively**
average increase	0.625	0.75	0.875	−0.25	0.25	0.375	0.625	0.125

4. PARALLEL, PURPOSEFUL, CONVERGENT LEARNING

Part of the assessment done in the project entailed video- or audiotaping interdisciplinary pairs or teams of students as they collaborated. The purpose was to discover synergies as well as moments when understanding digital sound processing or music from a lower level of abstraction shed light on the hands-on and creative endeavors. We were looking for ah-ha moments.

We discovered in this process that it was very difficult to be present just at the right moments when the students made breakthroughs in their creativity or understanding. The very presence of the microphones or cameras changed their collaborative behavior. Our conclusions about effective collaborative learning situations emerged from the totality of observations of students working together in all the workshops and courses, most of which could not be "caught on tape."

Over the course of the project, watching students of music and computer science interact in eight-week long summer workshop or seven (half semester) to fourteen week courses, we concluded that in many cases collaboration succeeds best in a mode of *parallel learning* and creative endeavor. By this we mean that we saw great benefit from having students of different disciplines working in the same lab, but not always on a shared project. Given the latitude, students gravitated toward projects of their own for which they could occasionally seek help from the person of the other discipline. The music students' goals were more musical (creating an arrangement of an original or mashed-up song), while the computer science students' goals were more technical (e.g., implementing a vocoder or autotuner). However, each group clearly learned from the others' expertise, the music students becoming more adept with sound drivers, latency, file types, etc., while the CS students were absorbing an understanding of keys, scales, and harmonies.

A second observation was that the creative projects that had the greatest success were those that were *purposeful*. That is, the projects grew out of an actual need or were aimed at a real presentation or performance. For example, two students worked on a program for loudspeaker placement, the program inspired by one of the author's dissatisfaction with the interface and output of existing software. The students working on this project were interested in completing and succeeding because they thought their software could be used, and perhaps even sold. A second project that the students attacked enthusiastically grew out of a performance of the musical "Floyd Collins" and a scene where the character sings with his own echoes. The challenge was to create the echoes of the singer's voice live and in sync with the actor, using MAX. Students implemented the MAX application, and we tested it in a performance auditorium with one of the students as the singer. A third successful project entailed doing a studio recording of a workshop participant's original song, with other participants accompanying or working the sound booth.

We had less success with trumped-up projects, like asking the students to create their own sampled and synthesized instruments, write an original composition, and play it on the their computers with the instruments they made. The students were at a loss as to what to compose, and they couldn't see the point in using their own sample banks and synthesized sounds, which they recognized as inferior to ones the supplied by Reason and Sonar, They were stalled in the composing process until it was suggested that they identify and adapt the chord sequence in Debussy's *Arabesque 1*. Then two separate music students created two separate and totally different compositions (one *mixing I've Got You Under My Skin* with *Arabesque I*, the other mixing the Beatles' *Blackbird*.) The computer science students served as audio engineering for the recording sessions, learning how to record in multiple sessions on multiple tracks and synchronize these.

A third observation grew out of the dilemma we faced in mixing hands-on, practical learning with science, mathematics, and abstract concepts. Where do you begin? At the high level of abstraction (high-level tools for audio processing), or at the low level (digitization of sound)? Our experience indicates that it's necessary to move from both directions – start high and work down, and also start low and work up. The places where the levels of abstraction converge are the potential ah-ha moments, when the students see the relationships between science/math and practical skills. This is what we call *convergent learning*.

An example of this convergence of practice and science/math understanding is the students' experience with latency. One of the students' immediate frustrations in the lab was the latency between their hitting a key on the MIDI keyboard and hearing the sound. Latency is a pervasive problem in sound processing. At first this situation was perceived by the students as simply a defect in the hardware and software. But as they began to understand buffering, drivers, analog to digital conversion, processing time, and the conversions that take place along the digital audio stream, they began to see that some amount of latency is unavoidable. (We also were inspired to create a helpful Flash animation of the audio stream as a result of our observations.)

Another ubiquitous problem in audio work is comb filtering. Bringing this problem to life for the students begins with letting them hear the phenomenon, and then progresses through having them calculate room modes, look at comb-shaped frequency response graphs in MATLAB or Octave, and understand algorithms that comb out given frequencies with an appropriate delay. These characterizations of sound deal with comb filtering from high and low levels of abstraction simultaneously.

5. INTEGRATING SOUND AND MUSIC THROUGH THE CS CURRICULUM

5.1 CS Principles via Sound and Music

Sound and music applications can be integrated throughout the computer science education, not only at introductory levels, but also through core courses like CS1, CS2, data structures and algorithms, and computer systems and networks. In the following sections, we give an overview of assignments and approaches to make this happen.

We are currently offering a CSC101 course (essentially CS Principles) in which we're adopting the learning objectives (LOs) from the CS Principles Big Ideas [7] using sound and music as an application domain. The Big Ideas are **creativity**, **abstraction**, **data**, **algorithms**, **programming**, **Internet**, and **impact**. Each of these can be engagingly explained or realized through applications in digital sound and music. Below, we give examples of only some of the LOs associated with the Big Ideas, as space allows.

Opportunities for interdisciplinary **creativity** abound in sound and music computation. Creative sound processing environments range from high level applications like Audacity and Sonar to programming languages like Java, Processing C/C++, or MAX. These environments provide endless opportunities to explore the LOs under **creativity** (e.g., LO2: *collaborate in the creation of computational artifacts*, and LO5: *use programming as a creative tool*).

Abstraction can be nicely illustrated with examples from sound and music. Consider three of the learning objectives in particular and what can be done with them:

LO 7: *explain how binary sequences are used to represent digital data;* LO10: *use models and simulations to raise and answer questions.*

Realization in sound: Show how sound is digitized. Simulate aliasing.

LO 9: *Use multiple levels of abstraction in computation.*

Realization in sound: Show how sound can be processed at different levels of abstraction with Audacity, Max, Octave, and PD, and a Java or C program, using a simple process like normalization as an example.

These are just a few examples. More examples can be inferred from the exercises suggested in

Table **4**.

Digital sound is a realm in which large amounts of **data** have to be processed quickly in real-time. This addresses LO 11: *Use computers to process information to gain insight and knowledge.* The Fourier transform, used to determine the frequency components of sound, serves as a good example of mathematical/algorithmic analysis of large amounts of data when applied to a long piece of music. Making students aware of the amount of data and the need for an efficient algorithm able to do this processing in real time is a good illustration of LO16: *Analyze the considerations involved in the computational manipulation of information.*

Sound and music processing **algorithms** are of sufficient variety and at different levels of complexity such that they can be used in courses from the introductory to the more advanced level. These algorithms then lead to **programming** in the language and at the level of abstraction appropriate to the purposes. In Section 5.2, we give examples of algorithms (or programming assignments, if you will) for sound processing, mapped to their appropriate CS level, with indications of the skills or concepts involved.

Sound and music applications can easily be associated with the Internet. As students create their own web pages and attach their own media to them, they become aware of the difference between client and server, where files must reside, how they are referenced, what file types are permitted and how they are handled, and so forth.

Finally, there are many topics under the heading of Impact that relate to sound and music. Under LO34: *analyze the beneficial and harmful effects of computing*; and LO33: *connect computing with innovations in other fields* – students can discuss how musical creativity is either heightened or compromised by sampled and synthesized MIDI music, vocoders, autotuners, and algorithmic music composition.

These Big Ideas and associated LOs are being used as the basis for labs in the current CSC101 course, Fall 2012. Students have taken a pre-course self-assessment of their knowledge of the Big Ideas, and at the end of the course they'll complete the assessment again. Some of the introductory-level material from our book and learning supplements is being used in the course.

5.2 Sound and Music in CS1 and Beyond

We now give specific examples of programming assignments or exercises that deal with sound and music. These could be woven throughout the core computer science curriculum as a way of teaching fundamental CS concepts and skills.

Table 4 lists these examples. Many of these have been written up as assignments in our online learning supplements, along with solutions at a password protected site. In most cases, we offer implementations in both MATLAB and C, and sometimes also in Java.

Note that in the audio programming assignments in

Table 4, the audio data can be played or output as text, depending on the programming language. If the language has high-level functions for playing notes of given frequencies or given MIDI numbers, then the sounds can be played. This is the case with Java and Processing. With MATLAB or Octave, students can generate arrays of numbers with single-statement array operations and play the arrays as sound. MATLAB and Octave have the advantage of allowing you to view the data graphically. With C, the students have to learn how to send data to the sound card, which entails dealing with sound libraries, sound devices, and programming at a lower level of abstraction.

In addition to our suggestions, [1] is an excellent sound for audio programming examples. The applications developed in [1] show that audio programming assignments do not have to be an end in themselves, but can also be used to teach good programming design and implementation. For example, a program for applying an amplitude envelope to a sound is made more efficient in increasingly refined versions, leading the author to observe this:

> The evolution of these programs demonstrates a principle that is easily overlooked by programmers. In the majority of cases … the required approach is to implement the same program several times…. We are already conscious of the need to approach the current task thinking of future needs…. [1]

The benefits of encapsulation are introduced as the authors develop a function for waveform synthesis. The point is that there are plenty of examples within the realm of sound to illustrate fundamental concepts of good programming practice.

6. FUTURE WORK

Our future work entails modularizing the curricular material to a greater extent, making it more accessible to educators at the K-12, community college, and university level. Sound and music applications are excellent for introducing STEM subjects, given that they combine mathematics, physics, electronics/engineering, CS, and programming. Much of the mathematics involved in sound and music applications is within the grasp of high school students – trigonometric functions, logarithms, exponents, base 2, summations, and simple arithmetic calculations. Using this application domain to illustrate the mathematics can be motivational to the students. There also are sufficient simple algorithms to introduce programming via sound applications at the high school level. Fortunately, high-level sound processing environments exist in freeware – Audacity, Octave, Pure Data, and Processing, for example – so cost need not be an obstacle in the public schools. To make our material useful at the high school level, we need to make clearly identifiable learning units on particular topics, indicating the appropriate sections of the book and associated learning supplements. These learning materials need to be annotated with the level of math and CS necessary for or gained from the module. We would also like to create larger groupings of the material useful in courses commonly taught in community colleges, technical schools, and universities to maximize the material's usefulness in fostering STEM education.

7. REFERENCES

[1] Beck, Robert, and Jennifer Burg. 2011. Report on the LIKES Workshop on Computer and Music. Retrieved 9/4/2012 from http://csweb.cs.wfu.edu/~burg/papers/ComputingAndMusicWorkshopReport.pdf.

[2] Boulanger, Richard, and Victor Lazzarini, eds. 2011. *The Audio Programming Book.* Cambridge, MA: MIT Press.

[3] Burg, Jennifer, Jason Romney, and Eric Schwartz. 2012. *Digital Sound and Music: Concepts, Practice, and Science* (with online learning supplements). Retrieved 9/3/2012 from http://www.cs.wfu.edu/~burg/CCLI.

[4] The College Board. 2012. Computer Science Principles: Computation Thinking and Practice. Retrieved 9/3/2102 from http://www.csprinciples.org/home/about-the-project/docs/Practices%2BBigIdeas-08-21-12.pdf?attredirects=0

[5] Ruthmann, S.A., Greher, G.R., & Heines, J.M. 2012. Real World Projects for Developing Musical and Computational Thinking. *30th International Society for Music Education (ISME) World Conference on Music Education.* Thessaloniki, Greece, July 15-20, 2012.

[6] Manaris, B., P. Roos, D. Krehbiel, T. Zalonis, and J.R. Armstrong. 2012. "Zipf's Law, Power Laws and Music Aesthetics." In T. Li, M. Ogihara, G. Tzanetakis, eds. *Music Data Mining*, Boca Raton, FL: CRC Press, pp. 169-216.

[7] The College Board. 2012. Computer Science Principles: Computation Thinking and Practice. Retrieved 9/3/2012 from http://www.csprinciples.org/home/about-the-project/docs/Practices%2BBigIdeas-08-21-12.pdf?attredirects=0

Table 4 Examples of sound- and music-based programming assignments and exercises

Programming Assignment or Exercise	additional CS or mathematics skills or concepts applied
straight line programs for doing simple computations (with or without conditional statements)	
get frequencies of harmonizing notes a third and a fifth away from a note (triad chord)	
given an air pressure amplitude, compute the sound in decibels, or vice versa	
calculate the frequency of a given MIDI note number	
compute the frequency of an undersampled sound wave that aliases	
compute room modes	
convert from one type of decibel to another	
create a major or minor triad, depending on user input	
programs with loops and conditions	
create and play major or minor scales, possibly comparing equal vs. just-tempered scales	
create and play chords of the user's choice	
programs with loops, conditions, and arrays	
simulate sampling by evaluating a sine wave, play the sound	
quantize an array of real numbers to the values possible for a given bit depth	
apply an amplitude envelope	
more advanced algorithms	
mu-law encoding – encode at one end, decode at the other, and compute the resulting error	bit operations
dithering and noise shaping	
determining endian-ness of a sound file	byte-ordering
reading and writing WAV files	file types, file formats
convolution	nested loops, domains of computation (time vs. frequency) , increased efficiency of computation in frequency domain, computational complexity
discrete Fourier transform, short-time Fourier transform (on windows of time data), applying windowing functions, Fast Fourier transform	complex numbers, summations, importance of computational complexity, attempting to do real-time computation as sound plays
wavetable synthesis; AM, PM, and FM synthesis	linear or cubic interpolation
applying delays, comb filtering, flanging	application of Fourier transform
creating vocoders, autotuners, pitch glides	application of Fourier transform
algorithmic music composition	experience in a visual programming language like MAX; also can be done in C or Java
writing a plugin, e.g. for Audacity	experience interfacing with existing software using APIs
writing a driver	experience with systems programming

[i] This paper is based on work supported by the National Science Foundation under CCLI Grant DUE 0717743, Jennifer Burg PI, Jason Romney, Co-PI.

Form, Function and Performances in a Musical Instrument MAKErs Camp

Blake Sawyer, Jason Forsyth, Taylor O'Connor, Brennon Bortz, Teri Finn, Liesl Baum, Ivica Ico Bukvic, Benjamin Knapp, Dane Webster
Institute for Creativity, Arts and Technology
Virginia Tech
Blacksburg, VA USA
{basawyer, jforsyth, jto2e, brennon, tfinn, licombs, ico, benknapp, webster}@vt.edu

ABSTRACT

This experience report presents the planning, execution and results of an exploratory 5-day musical instrument MAKErs camp for K-12 students. Students used various hardware sensors, a graphical programming environment and different physical prototyping techniques to create musical instruments. The design of a musical instrument introduces students to the full spectrum of the design process including form factor and function. Throughout the camp, students shared and performed in front of their peers to gain feedback as they iterated through the design of a musical instrument.

Categories and Subject Descriptors

K.3.2 [**Computers and Education**]: Computer and Information Science Education—*computer science education, curriculum*

Keywords

computer science education; GUI programming; MAKEr camp; musical instrument design

1. INTRODUCTION

Our changing world is a topic of constant conversation and strife within many areas of research and education. Creativity and innovation are abundant in areas of professional design and development and it is understood that this frame of mind, which encourages flexibility, risk-taking, and open-mindedness, will encourage success within industry. Yet, the question remains as to why such creative behaviors are not being fostered among students in K-12 and university. As things continue to rapidly progress, it becomes more apparent that students must be prepared to meet and match competition for success.

The MAKEr mindset [7] is one of creative and curious people, which is typically reserved for product designers. With the movement of making, those characteristics are being used to shift the relationship between the manufacturer and the consumer. MAKErs are simply unsettled by the final product, as it is slated to be, and carry an unwillingness to accept products in a final form. MAKErs view products as partially complete and concern themselves with the hackability and seek to redesign products to meet very specific, personal needs. Some view this as a DIY culture in which MAKErs are creating their own products, often for trivial needs. A more thorough look, however, reveals that the simple process of making may lead us to a deeper understanding of personal identity. John Seely Brown states that through this culture of tinkering, our "identity is defined by what [we] have created, and [what] others have ... built on it as well" as opposed to what our parents or upbringing have simply given [2].

With this idea in mind, we wanted to introduce the MAKEr concept to a group of K-12 students in hope of inspiring creativity in computer programming, computer hardware and the arts. During an exploratory 5-day summer camp, we challenged students to design and build an electronic musical instrument. This experience report presents the planning, execution and informal results of the camp. The remainder of the paper is outlined as follows, Section 2 will provide an overview of the camp preparation and schedule and discuss our rationale for using musical instruments as a platform for teaching computer programming, sensors and circuitry design, and physical prototyping. In Section 3, we present five teaching modules that form the basis of the camp where we expected students to learn a process of design. We discuss our experiences with the camp in Section 4 and describe how to move our informal process towards more formal educational environments. Lastly in Section 5, we conclude our paper and look towards future work.

2. MUSICAL MAKERS CAMP

Music and computation go hand and hand. And, due to music's wide applicability and interest, it is a commonly used method for teaching computer science to students of all ages. Ruthmann et al. [13] and Heines et al.'s [8] explored the idea of "performamatics" by combining music creation and computer science to build an interdisciplinary environment for teaching computation. Meyers et al. [10] successfully introduced computer science to a group of teenagers through computer music creation. We wanted to expand on these same methods by letting K-12 students design a musical instrument which introduces not only computer science

SIGCSE'13, March 6–9, 2013, Denver, Colorado, USA.

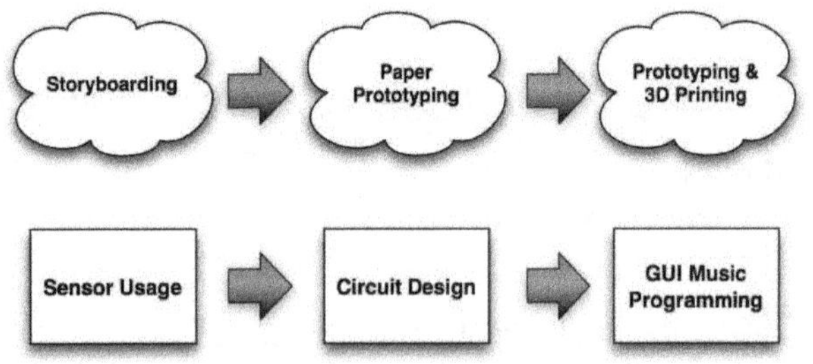

Figure 1: The design of an electronic musical instrument introduces students to the full spectrum of the design process including both form (above) and function (below).

and programming but other aspects of MAKE (e.g., creative design, physical prototyping, computer hardware, etc.)

The camp also introduced the students to the full spectrum of the design process in two ways: first, by designing the form of the instrument through storyboarding on whiteboards and constructing paper and 3D prototypes (top of Figure 1) and second, by designing the function of the instrument through sensor placement, circuitry design and using our GUI programming tool to program the music (bottom of Figure 1)

2.1 GUI Programming With PD-L2Ork

A critical component of the camp and the musical instrument design process is the conversion of sensor input into audio. Given that one of our core goals was to produce sound output, we sought a solution that provides minimal latency overhead (here we define latency as the amount of time between the sensor signal input to the computer and the resulting sound output from the speaker). In addition, in hope of fostering easy access to the platform of choice, we sought a free open-source solution. PD-L2Ork is a fork of Pure-Data [12], a real-time graphical programming environment for audio, video, and graphical processing actively developed as part of Virginia Tech's Linux Laptop Orchestra (L2Ork) project [5]. Its primary focus is to create a stable and usable environment designed specifically for music ensemble, and most recently on the development of a K12 education module. The current version is maintained exclusively on the Linux platform. For this reason, we chose to utilize the L2Ork hardware infrastructure, namely sixteen stations that include hemispherical speakers, external USB soundcard, MSI U-100 netbooks, and Wiimotes [4].

While the PD-L2Ork's K12 module was introduced as a pilot study in the spring 2012 and offered a flexible foundation, it was limited by its relatively small library of objects and its inability to store system-wide states (presets). Therefore, in preparation for the camp, the team set out to implement the global preset mechanism, and expand the system's library of coarsely-grained objects necessary for our K-12, target user population. Originally created for 4th and 5th grade students using WiiMote inputs to make music, PD-L2Ork was extended to accept inputs from an Arduino microprocessor [11] running the SARCduino firmware [9]. This firmware samples all inputs on the Arduino (12 digital and 6 analog) at 100 Hz. The new version includes over 40 new objects that allow students to seamlessly interact with each of these digital and analog signals coming from sensors on their instrument. No Arduino programming was necessary, only the GUI programming in PD-L2Ork.

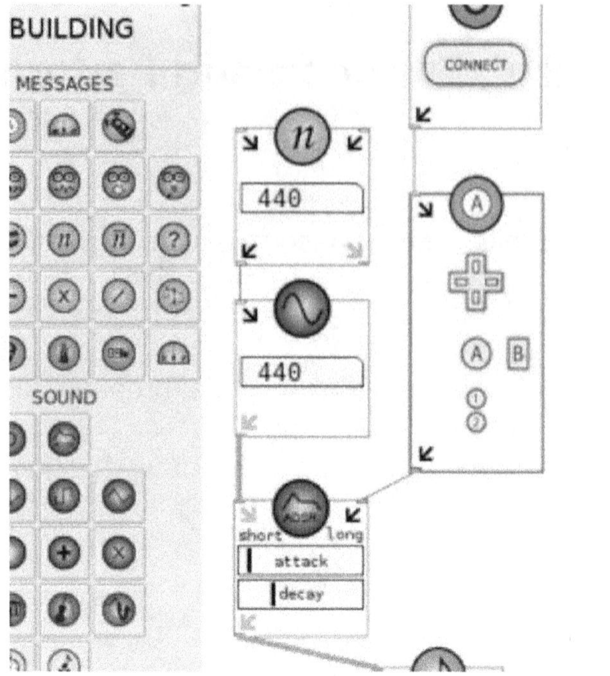

Figure 2: PD-L2Ork. The objects on the left can be dragged and connected within the workspace on the right.

A screenshot of PD-L2Ork's K12 programming environment is shown in Figure 2. In PD-L2Ork K12, objects can be connected via patch cords to allow their output to be sent to other objects. Patch cords as well as object inlets and outlets are colored differently to distinguish the difference between continuous audio streams (constant streams of 48,000 samples per second) and relatively sporadic sensor data streams (variable, up to 100 data points per second). This helps to reflect the objects' function and consequently legal/possible connections. For example, the K12 module features two sets of mathematical operator objects (one for manipulating sensor data streams, and one for manipulating audio streams) which are colored accordingly.

2.2 Team and Camp Preparation

The camp team consisted of four faculty, four graduate students and one undergraduate student. Together the camp team has expertise in creative design, education, engineering and music.

Preparation for the camp took 6 weeks. As a group, we discussed different types of electronic instruments that the students could build during the week. With 32 students attending the camp, we prepared four types of instruments the students would choose from. This allowed two groups of four students for each instrument. We also pre-built a fifth instrument that would be used as an early demonstration to the students at the camp.

Aside from preparing PD-L2Ork for use with an Arduino, each instrument had to be prototyped to determine required materials. We then prepared two "kits" for each of the four instruments. These kits included electronic sensors, Arduinos, wiring and some wooden enclosures and pieces they

Day	9:00-10:30	10:45-12:15	1:00-2:30	2:45-4:00
1	Introduction to MAKE using videos	Teaching creative process through group discussions	Introduce PD-L2Ork programming	Introduce different types of sensors; Build LED flashlight
2	Demonstrate laser harp instrument's circuitry and programming	Use LED flashlight to play 1-string light harp with light sensor and PD-L2Ork	Introduce 3D printing using paper prototyping and CAD software	Introduce 4 instruments students can choose from; Create instrument groups
3	First instrument group design time; white boarding and story boarding	Create 3D component using paper prototyping	Share and gain feedback on 3D component with other groups	Begin wiring and placing sensors on instrument
4	Finish wiring instrument	Create first music with instrument using PD-L2Ork	Share and gain feedback about instrument from other groups	Take field trip to 3D printing facilities to see their parts printing
5	Iterate their instrument both in form and function	Create and practice a performance with the instrument	Performance	Outro/Discussion about what students learned

Table 1: Daily Schedule for MAKEr Camp

could incorporate. We now describe each of these instruments, including what was put in each kit:

Percussion Instrument: The drum instrument provides up to four microphone sensors that can be configured by the students (e.g., putting them in cardboard boxes or inside a wooden enclosure). The microphone sensors detect vibrations which can be thresholded and play a sound or effect in PD-L2Ork.

Wind Instrument: The wind instrument has three types of sensors: a microphone detects when the player blows into the instrument, an accelerometer allows the player to move the instrument to create sounds, and four touch sensors for detecting when the player covers a hole on the wind instrument.

String Instrument: The string instrument resembles a stand-up bass with one string. It employs two types of sensors: a joystick that detects eight directions and a resistant stretch cord that can be pulled and plucked. The stretch cord can be attached to the joystick, so the player can pull and pluck in eight directions to create sounds and effects.

Room Instrument: This instrument uses an entire room separated into quadrants. Depending on the location of the player and the gestures they make, different sounds and effects can play. The player holds a device that includes an accelerometer to pickup gestures and IR sensors for determining their location in the room.

Laser Harp: We used a laser harp for demonstration purposes. This instrument consists of a harp-shaped device with four green lasers aimed at four photocell sensors. When the player's hand breaks the line of light, a sound or effect will play.

We also prepared materials for a simple LED "flashlight" that turned on through a force sensitive resistor.

The camp schedule was iterated throughout the preparation phase of the camp. In Table 1, the planned schedule consisting of four time blocks over the five days is summarized.

3. TEACHING A DESIGN PROCESS

To give students a plan for the week, as well as a design process, we wanted everyone to understand a common creative design framework of ideas, constraints, and prototypes. For any particular problem there are certain ideas that can be potential solutions, but the ideas have to be balanced against relevant constraints in the problem area. Often ideas have to be realized through prototyping and exploration to determine which ideas are best. The idea of iterating, building your own prototypes, and testing, are a core part of the MAKEr philosophy [7]. Having this framework gives the students a tool that can be used to resolve future open-ended problems, but also provides a rationale for the remainder of the week. In this way, students understand why we have them perform the activities during this week and they can appreciate the process, more than the final product.

From the outset we knew many students had their own projects and hobbies, and often followed this design process without knowing it. To help them understand the relationship between the intended design process and what they already do, we asked the students to share their own projects and discuss their own experiences making things. Many of the students shared their projects and reported that often they had to try several attempts before "getting things right."

To help reinforce the notion of iteration and prototypes, we showed several videos from animation studios where the designers are trying out new characters or studying how the characters move. Additionally, it was useful for the students to see that these grand characters did not begin fully formed, and had to be worked on several times to reach their final state.

After discussing iteration and prototypes, we conducted a few exercises to help identify ideas and constraints for a problem. In particular, we wanted to have the students consider constraints to a problem, as they are the main factors that shape a design. For this exercise we had the students consider a hypothetical trip to Mars. We felt this exercise was accessible to a majority of the students, and the constraints (such as time, distance, lack of oxygen, etc.) would be understandable to anyone.

Finally, we ran through a small design exercise where the students identified three musical instruments of interest, and then in groups, synthesized a new instrument from their ideas. Each group drew their ideas on white boards and presented them to the camp group. Figure 3 shows a student presenting their imaginary "slutar" instrument.

3.1 Exploring Functionality

3.1.1 Sensors and Circuitry

The electronic sensors and their circuitry provided a bridge between the physical world (i.e., form) and the music mak-

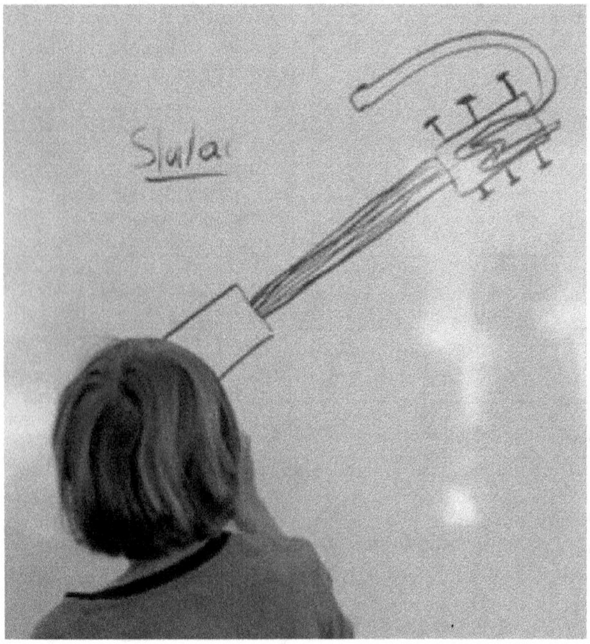

Figure 3: A student working on the whiteboard in front of the group as they discuss the design of an imaginary instrument called a "slutar".

ing software (i.e., function). Sensors and their different uses were introduced to the students early, during day one. After teaching the design process, time was committed to group discussions about everyday devices that use sensors (e.g., mouse and keyboard, phones, WiiMotes, etc.) This led to a more formal presentation of different types of sensors and their uses. The group went over accelerometers, touch and light sensors, and microphones.

At the end of day one, the laser harp was used as a target for discussion. The group discussed how to wire the four lasers and light sensors and then they spent time programming in PD-L2Ork together to make different sounds and effects for the laser harp.

Beginning on the second day, the group discussed more types of sensors including all the sensors available in the four prepared instruments. To apply this new knowledge and give them an idea of what they would be doing the rest of the week, the students built a 9V LED flash light that turned on through a pressure sensor attached to an enclosure. They then used this LED flash light to interact with a light sensor to play music (i.e., a 1-string light instrument). The LED flash light was given to the students to take home after the camp.

3.1.2 PD-L2Ork Programming

Throughout the camp students were exposed to a series of small workshops covering the basics of creating patches in PD-L2Ork as well as one-on-one tutoring. The latter proved to be critical in tackling project-specific challenges, particularly considering time constraints. Workshops tended to only cover the most basic, overarching concepts rather than specific needs of each student group. The ensuing projects exhibited a relatively high level of complexity so each group spent one-on-one time with a camp faculty member experienced in programming with PD-L2Ork. Figure 4 shows

Figure 4: Picture of a student working with the PD-L2Ork software to program a string instrument.

students working in PD-L2Ork to program the music for their string instrument.

PD-L2Ork's K12 module focused on visual approach to object-oriented programming environment. Akin to Labview, students placed various objects (abstractions) onto a canvas (a.k.a. patch). The coarse-grained nature of these objects shielded users from advanced, low-level tasks (e.g., dealing with the recognition of peripheral devices and the filtering of data streams), while still exposing them to core math and science challenges (e.g., through the use of basic math operations, such as addition, subtraction, multiplication, division, etc.) [3]. Each object contained GUI elements allowing its behavior to be easily customized. For example, the object which allows access to the analog Arduino data stream offers a channel selection, while a hit detection object allows for specifying thresholds, etc.

3.2 Exploring Form

3.2.1 3D Printing

3D printers are becoming less expensive, easier to operate and, therefore, more abundant to everyday people. It has been said that 3D printers might become as ubiquitous as our paper printers at home. And we may soon see dedicated "Kinko-esque" stores [1] and kiosks [6] for 3D printing services. During the third block of the second day of camp, we introduced the 3D printing process which included paper prototyping (discussed below) and 3D modeling. The group was shown 3D printed prototypes and given an overview of how to use the software to create different 3D models.

Later in the week as the students designed one of the four instrument, each group delivered one small, paper prototyped component of their instrument to be 3D printed. One of the camp workers took these designs, created 3D models and sent them off to be printed. The students had the opportunity later to see their designs being printed during a field trip to the 3D printer on the university's campus.

3.2.2 Paper Prototyping

Paper prototyping became a useful and concrete way for students to share their ideas throughout the camp. Students used cardboard, scissors and tape to construct paper prototypes at three points during the camp week: (1) when first introduced to 3D printing on day two, (2) when they first

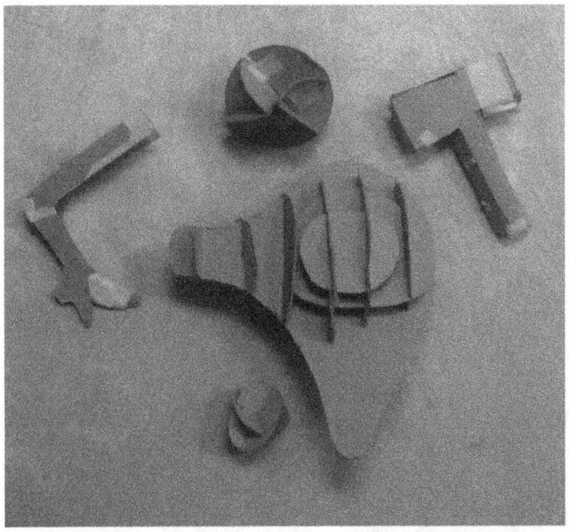

Figure 5: Examples of student paper prototypes

Figure 6: Students' performance of their "Nimbus" drum instrument.

began designing one of the four prepared instruments during days two and three and (3) when they designed a component to be 3D printed. Some examples of different paper prototypes can be seen in Figure 5. This paper prototyping technique became an important way for students to quickly transfer their imagination from a sketch to a physical artifact. This physical artifact could easily be shared with other people to gain feedback. For example, one group of students, when designing the enclosure of their wind instrument, decided to share two paper prototype designs with all the other groups. Paper prototyping enabled them to quickly build a design and then collect votes on the best enclosure to use for their wind instrument.

3.3 Sharing and Performances

Throughout the camp, and especially leading up to the performance at the end, we encouraged and set time aside for students and groups to share their ideas with their peers and camp workers. The act of presenting their ideas and receiving honest feedback from others motivated the students to do their best. We mentioned above how paper prototyping enabled sharing and critiquing. This was also accomplished using story boarding and white boarding to share ideas within and among groups. And, once groups began making music, students performed in front of others as a way of sharing their work. On several occasions during the camp, we took 10-15 minutes of time where the whole camp visited each group's work area having students present their current designs and receive feedback. Lastly, while we already planned a culminating performance at the end of the camp, we decided to invite all the parents to this performance, not only because parents were asking to come, but also to motivate the students to work even harder on their instruments and performances. Figure 6 shows a student group giving their final performance with drum instrument named "Nimbus".

4. DISCUSSION

In this Section we give an overview of the camp week, discuss how to move to more formal educational environments and how we were able to foster creativity throughout the camp week while still constrained by time.

4.1 Overview of the Week

Overall the camp was well attended with 28 students attending the full five days. Due to the many varied tasks of designing a musical instrument, most, if not all, students actively participated and collaborated in at least one or more tasks throughout the week. For example, some students spent the entire last half of the week prototyping different artifacts for the instruments while other students in their group spent the majority of their time programming in PD-L2Ork or wiring the hardware. Furthermore, during and after the camp, we received positive feedback, in the form of text messages and emails, from the students' parents, including requests to sign up for the camp next year.

When the camp week began, it became apparent that our planned schedule would need constant alteration and updating. Changes to the schedule occurred quickly as the day progressed and at the end of the day. Some major changes include: (1) spending extra time teaching and experimenting with the PD-L2Ork software, (2) using more paper prototyping to learn about 3D printing, create fantastical instrument and expand their instrument design, (3) including second field trip to a robotics lab to react to many students' interests in robotics, and (4) inviting parents to attend the final day performance.

4.2 Informal vs. Formal Education

The informal environment made the iterative nature of our camp schedule easy to manage. Since we had students for seven hours a day with no restrictions, we had the freedom to allow students a longer period of time if they seemed to require it. Similarly, if they finished a project more quickly than we anticipated, we could move on to the next portion of our day without the time constraint of a formal classroom environment.

The studio space in which we were located also lent itself well to flexibility. Student brainstorming sessions remained on the whiteboards for them to refer to all week, their projects could stay out on the work spaces without being in anyone's way, there was ample space to spread out and give each working group their own area in which to work. All of these factors led to an experience that felt effortless in many ways.

Implementing such an environment in a formal setting is not without its challenges, though. Teachers whose classroom time is confined by bell schedules or other constraints might consider teaming with other teachers who share a similar interest in encouraging a maker mindset. Such a tactic offers the potential to schedule larger blocks of time for project-based work yet still cover content from multiple disciplines. Once we, as teachers, demonstrate flexibility, openness, and willingness to invest in our own personal goals (i.e., implementing a maker project in the classroom), students will in turn be more willing to do the same.

4.3 Fostering Creativity With Time Constraints

One big challenge during the camp was allowing students to be creative with each of their designs, but also, when it came to actually building an instrument, we needed to constrain their designs so that they could finalize a design and be able to perform. This was accomplished in two ways. First we prepared partial "kits" for the four types of instruments before the camp began. These kits loosely defined each instrument by providing a set of sensors and a few physical artifacts. We were also careful in how we first presented the instruments to the students. The introduction was meant to be abstract, concentrating only on the sensors available (e.g., the stretch sensors for the string instrument or the location sensing for the room instrument). At this point, we did not want to constrain how the students would construct the instrument (i.e., form) or how it would sound musically (i.e., function).

Secondly, the paper prototyping module enabled students to stretch their creativity for designing their instruments. Most groups, when they first began, constructed very complicated instruments out of paper. As the week progressed, it was important that the students understood how they might actually build these complex instruments, but that they could only build and wire up a small part of this larger instrument.

5. CONCLUSION

As educators work to explore the potential of making within the classroom, it becomes increasingly clear that the benefits far outweigh the risks. The push for creativity, critical thinking, and innovative producers and seekers of knowledge creates a welcome environment for the MAKEr mindset and opens doors for students to play with knowledge. As students engage in making, they lead their curious minds through steps of design that are critical to creativity and innovation. Whether it is the design of a new product, or hacking of an existing product, the stages of curiosity, ideation, experimenting, and iterating encourage a mindset of risk-taking, openness, and ownership.

The current assessment of the camp's success is strictly anecdotal. We saw almost every student actively engaged in each of the design stages (i.e., ideation, iteration, sharing, ownership, etc.) as they explored both the form and function of their instrument. We plan to run this camp next summer in its same informal environment and we are currently coordinating with a local high school to move to more formal educational environments. In each setting we plan to set up mechanisms for more quantitative and qualitative assessment methods to measure the success of the camp.

Acknowledgments

We would like to thank all the students and parents for participating in the camp. The camp and this work is funded by the Institute for Creativity, Art & Technology at Virginia Tech with partial support by project grant NSF IIS-0954048.

6. REFERENCES

[1] R. Bilton. The future of 3d printing looks a lot like kinkos, http://venturebeat.com/2012/08/16/the-future-of-3d-printing-looks-a-lot-like-kinkos/, August 2012.

[2] J. S. Brown. Tinkering as a mode of knowledge production. Carnegie Foundation of the Advancement of Teaching, October 2008.

[3] I. I. Bukvic, L. Baum, B. Layman, and K. Woodard. Granular learning objects for instrument design and collaborative performance in k-12 education. In *Proceedings of the International Conference on New Interfaces for Musical Expression*, 2012.

[4] I. I. Bukvic, T. Martin, and M. Matthews. Moving beyond academia through open source solutions–introducing l2ork, virginia tech's linux laptop orchestra. *SEAMUS*, 2011.

[5] I. I. Bukvik, T. Martin, E. Standley, and M. Matthews. Introducing l2ork: Linux laptop orchestra. In *Proceedings of the International Conference on New Interfaces for Musical Expression*, 2010.

[6] V. T. Department of Mechanical Engineering. Dreamvendor, http://www.dreams.me.vt.edu/dreamvendor/index.html, 2012.

[7] D. Dougherty. Make magazine - http://makezine.com, 2012.

[8] J. M. Heines, G. R. Greher, and S. Kuhn. Music performamatics: interdisciplinary interaction. In *Proceedings of the 40th ACM technical symposium on Computer science education*, SIGCSE '09, pages 478–482, New York, NY, USA, 2009. ACM.

[9] J. Jaimovich. Sarcduino. *MuSE: Music Sensors And Emotion*, March 2010.

[10] A. L. Meyers, M. C. Cole, E. Korth, and S. Pluta. Musicomputation: teaching computer science to teenage musicians. In *Proceedings of the seventh ACM conference on Creativity and cognition*, C&C '09, pages 29–38, New York, NY, USA, 2009. ACM.

[11] E. Naone. Arduino uno. *Technology Review*, 114(2):78–79, April 2011.

[12] M. Puckette. Pure data: another integrated computer music environment. In *Proceedings of the International Computer Music Conference*, pages 37–41, 1996.

[13] A. Ruthmann, J. M. Heines, G. R. Greher, P. Laidler, and C. Saulters, II. Teaching computational thinking through musical live coding in scratch. In *Proceedings of the 41st ACM technical symposium on Computer science education*, SIGCSE '10, pages 351–355, New York, NY, USA, 2010. ACM.

Learning Mobile Security with Android Security Labware

Minzhe Guo
Prabir Bhattacharya
School of Computing Sciences and Informatics
University of Cincinnati
Cincinnati, OH 45221
guome@mail.uc.edu
bhattapr@ucmail.uc.edu

Ming Yang
Kai Qian
School of Computing and Software Engineering
Southern Polytechnic State University
Marietta, GA 30060
mingyang@spsu.edu
kqian@spsu.edu

Li Yang
Department of Computer Science and Engineering
University of Tennessee at Chattanooga
Chattanooga, TN 37403
Li-Yang@utc.edu

ABSTRACT
As smart mobile devices grow increasingly in popularity, so do the incentives for attackers. Recent surveys on mobile security describe the rapidly increasing number and sophistication of mobile attacks. Newer sources of risks are being introduced or explored in the mobile computing paradigm where traditional security threats are also evolving. The prevalence of mobile devices and the rapid growth of mobile threats have resulted in a shortage of mobile security personnel. Educational activities are needed to promote mobile security education and to meet the emerging industry and education needs. This paper presents our initial effort on exploring a learning approach to mobile security, which aims at taking advantages of the benefits of mobile devices and the best practices in learning information security, promoting students' interests, and improving students' self-efficacy. An Android security labware is designed to implement the environment and materials for the learning approach. We integrated the pilot modules of the labware into two security courses in two semesters. The majority of the students provided positive feedback and enjoyed the Android security practices.

Categories and Subject Descriptors: K.3.1 [**Computers and Education**]: Computer Uses in Education-*distance learning*; K.3.2 [**Computers and Education**]: Computer and Information Science Education-*computer science education*; D.4.6 [**Operating Systems**]: Security and Protection; K.6.5 [**Management of Computing and Information Systems**]: Security and Protection.

General Terms: Design, Experimentation, Security

Keywords: Android, Mobile Security, Labware

1. INTRODUCTION
Over the last decade, the use of mobile devices for both personal and business purposes has exploded. The arrival of smart mobile devices (smartphones and tablets) and the booming of mobile applications (apps) in recent years have only accelerated this trend. For the year 2011, the shipments of Apple-iOS-based and Google-Android-based smartphones and tablets were about 400 million units, compared to the 350 million units of netbooks, notebooks, and desktops in total [1]. More importantly, there have been more than 600,000 apps available for iOS and Android devices [2], turning these devices into powerful general-purpose computing platforms. More and more users and businesses use mobile devices for processing personal, financial, and commercial data, or use them to organize their work and private life. As mobile platforms grow increasingly in popularity, so do the incentives for attackers, especially when the value of mobile payment transactions is projected to reach almost $630 billion by 2014 [2]. Recent security surveys [2-5] describe the rapidly increasing number and sophistication of mobile attacks. According to the study, mobile infections will continue to rise significantly in these years [6]. The prevalence of mobile devices and the rapid growth of mobile threats have resulted in a shortage of personnel trained to handle mobile security [7].

Mobile security is an emerging security area of growing importance and increasing needs, but is a relatively weak area in the current computing curriculum at most schools. In this paper, we informally define mobile security as a subject at the intersection of wireless communication, mobile computing, and computer security, which covers the various security threats and protections involved in the use of smart mobile devices, especially the iOS-based and Android-based smartphones and tablets. The growing need for promoting mobile security education has been pointed out [8] and several security organizations have started to offer short-term training courses on mobile security, e.g., [9-11]. More and more academic institutions plan to integrate mobile security into their undergraduate computing curriculum. However, we find that there are at least two challenges in promoting the mobile security education. The first challenge is the unique characteristics of mobile security. Mobile security is new and evolving. Traditional security threats, e.g., malware or social engineering, are evolving in this new environment, such as using new attack vectors or adapting to the new platform. More importantly, new components (e.g., Global Positioning System (GPS)) and services (e.g., short message service (SMS) and mobile payment) in mobile platforms introduce new sources of risks. Few security courses cover the full spectrum of mobile security, especially those new and unique mobile security threats. The second challenge is the shortage of effective mobile security learning materials. Compared to the rich learning materials available for general computer security or other special security areas, e.g., web security or network security,

SIGCSE'13, March 6–9, 2013, Denver, Colorado, USA.

systematic materials designed specifically for mobile security remain sparse, not to mention the hands-on laboratory resources.

This paper presents our initial effort on dealing with the challenges through the exploration of a learning approach to mobile security, which takes advantage of the benefits of mobile devices and the best practices in learning information security, and the development of an Android security labware, which covers important mobile security knowledge and implements the environment and materials for the learning approach. We integrated the pilot modules of the labware in two security courses in two semesters. The majority of students surveyed provided positive feedback and enjoyed the Android security practices.

The reasons for our using Android as the platform for learning mobile security are as follows: (1) Android platform is open-sourced, while Apple iOS platform has license restrictions; (2) up to March 12, 2012, Android was ranked as the top mobile platform with 51 percent U. S. market share [12]; (3) the Android platform has become the chief target for malicious hackers [13]; (4) the Java-based app development on Android platform would impose a short learning curve for both students and faculties; and (5) many of the important mobile threats identified in the Android platform are common to all mobile platforms, though the detail implementations of the attacks and defenses can be different. The threat analysis and protection practice on Android platform can help students understand the mobile security in other platforms.

The rest of this paper is organized as follows. Section 2 presents the characteristics of the our learning approach to mobile security; Section 3 presents the Android security labware and demonstrates an example module in the labware; Section 4 discusses our experience in integrating the labware in security courses; Section 5 reviews the related work; and Section 6 concludes the paper and describe our future work.

2. A LEARNING APPROACH TO MOBILE SECURITY

For effective learning of mobile security, we desire a learning approach that takes advantages of the benefits of mobile devices (e.g., mobility and the closeness to students' daily lives) and the best practices in learning information security, promotes students' interests, and improves students' self-efficacy. This section presents the main characteristics of our learning approach that attempts to achieve these objectives.

(1) Experience-based Threat Analysis and Protection Practice

The first characteristic of our learning approach is its experience-based learning that couples mobile threat analysis with protection solution practices. The importance of experience-based learning or hands-on learning has long been recognized in the learning theory literature [14]. We develop hands-on materials specifically for mobile security. In addition, to make the learning more effective, for each specific mobile threat, our experience-based approach will first let students experience an actual attack instance, then instruct students on how to implement a protection solution using step-by-step tutorials. A protection solution practice can be a mobile app development (e.g., implement a filter to block malicious SMS), an open-sourced security tool practice (e.g., using reverse engineering tools *apktool* and *dex2jar*), or a configuration (e.g., configuration of Android app permission).

In traditional computer security classes, the protection principles and practices are the central topics. However, some academics have identified that, by experiencing actual attacks, the students will gain more insight, and that will enable them to design and implement better protections [15]. This attack/defend approach has been recognized as a highly effective approach to learning information security [16].

Our approach adopts the idea of understanding the protection task better from threat analysis, but ours differs from the attack/defend approach [15] in the following aspects: 1) we develop multimedia or mobile apps to demonstrate instances of attacks; 2) students will not design attacks and will not perform real attacks to harm servers or peers' mobile devices; 3) the developed attack apps are to facilitate students in analyzing mobile threats; they will be hard-coded and will not be effective in practice; and the complete source code is hidden from students and is not distributed.

(2) Real-world relevant learning

The second characteristic of our learning approach is its real-world relevant learning. A recent report pointed out that rather than teaching students only abstract concepts and assigning them abstract exercises, engaging students in real-world settings would benefit student effective learning in security education [17]. We approach real-world relevant learning in the following ways:

- Mobile app development with real devices. Unlike existing efforts on using mobile game development to improve engagement [18] or using mobile apps to help illustrate programming concepts [19], we directly use mobile app development as a means of protection solution practice. Students will be provided with step-by-step tutorials on developing mobile apps. Each app implements a certain protection solution. Students can debug and develop apps with emulators or real devices, and they can install their developed apps on real devices. This will help students obtain an instant gratification and confidence from the hands-on practice and encourage them to create their own apps. This also has the additional benefits of not only facilitating students to learn mobile programming skills but also heightening their awareness and understanding of secure programming principles.
- Up-to-date mobile threats and protections. We will provide students with the state-of-the-art mobile security knowledge. The materials are designed by collecting and analyzing a number of recent mobile security literatures from academics and industry [2-5, 20].
- Hands-on experiments with mobile devices directly. The mobile device itself is more relevant than other existing learning platforms to real world applications. It is close to the concepts and applications in students' daily lives. We design most of the security exercises in a way that they can be performed on mobile devices directly. This will help in creating a strong connection between the academic study and the reality of student's lives and engage student learning in mobile security.

(3) Mobile Learning

The last but not least characteristic of our learning approach is its mobile learning. The slides, tutorials, and demonstrations are designed to be friendly to mobile devices. Security exercises can be performed using mobile devices except those app development practices that use Eclipse IDE in personal computers. Materials are accessible from our dedicated repository using mobile devices.

3. THE ANDROID SECURITY LABWARE

To provide the environment and materials for our learning approach, we are developing an Android security labware, which is a collection of self-contained modules that provide both necessary concept introduction and hands-on laboratory exercises on mobile security. It consists of seven modules to introduce important mobile threats in three aspects of mobile security, including mobile device security & privacy, mobile app security, and mobile network & communication security. Each module includes pre-lab activities (concept introduction and lab preparation); hands-on lab activities (pairs of hands-on labs on analysis for the threats and their protection practice with smart devices); and post-lab activities (review questions, assignments, and case study). An open repository is developed to host the labware for wide access and collaboration. This section presents and demonstrates the design of the Android security labware.

3.1 Lab Modules

The modules in the labware are designed based on: (1) the ACM Computer Science Curricula 2013: Strawman Draft [21], (2) the authors' teaching experience on embedded systems and information security, and (3) recent mobile security reports [2-5, 20]. Table 1 presents the seven modules in the labware. They cover the important mobile threats in three aspects of mobile security, including: (1) mobile device security and privacy - mobile threats that are related to the security issues in a physical device and a mobile operating system; (2) mobile app security - mobile threats that are germane to the security issues in the development and distribution of mobile apps; and (3) mobile network and communication security - mobile threats that are relevant to security issues in mobile communication channels, network protocols, and mobile network/web activities. The Information Assurance and Security (IAS) topics, which are defined in ACM Computer Science Curricula 2013: Strawman Draft [21], are covered among the labs. All modules will follow the same pattern of design. We demonstrate an example module to illustrate the design in Section 3.2. In the following, we briefly present each module.

M 1: Threats of Lost or Stolen Mobile Devices. As a unique threat to mobile devices, lost or stolen mobile devices would result in leakage of the sensitive information stored in the device, such as fcontacts, passwords, bank information, or authorizations to business access. This module introduces to students the risks of lost or stolen mobile devices, and teach them protection methods to reduce their loss, including data encryption, data wiping for device lost, stolen phone locating, and device authentication.

M 2: Unauthorized Mobile Resource Access. This module introduces to students the threats of unauthorized access of users to mobile devices, the unauthorized access of apps to system resources, and the unauthorized inter-application resource access. For protection solutions, this module will provide students with the experience in the Android permission system. Students will learn the authentication protocols and practice the configuration of system permission and app permission.

M 3: Mobile Privacy Threats. This module introduces to students the privacy threats in mobile devices. Privacy threats may be caused by applications those are not necessarily malicious, but gather or use more sensitive information (e.g., location or user identity) than is necessary to perform their function or than a user is comfortable with [2]. Students will learn to know how firms or app developers can obtain their private data, and learn how to reduce the privacy leaks and how to use cryptography as a means to protect against theft of private information.

M 4: Mobile Malware. Mobile malware is mobile app designed to engage in malicious behavior on a mobile device [2]. This module will introduce to students the types of mobile malware, the attack vectors of mobile malware, the methodologies and tools to analyze mobile malware, the user education, and the tools for preventing damage from or detecting the mobile malware. It will demonstrate and analyze an app with a malicious payload. Students will also learn to use Android reverse engineering tools to analyze mobile malware.

M 5: Secure Mobile App Development. This module has two foci: secure mobile coding and tamper-resistant app development. On secure coding, this module will introduce the coding threats, e.g., buffer over-flow and injection. For preventing damage from coding threats, students will learn how to create a security-aware mobile app by enforcing the device management policies and practicing the mobile coding tips of Android *Activity*, *Intent*, *Broadcast*, and *ContentProvider*. On tamper resistance part, students will learn the threat of app tampering and learn how to anti-tamper using obfuscation.

Table 1. Lab Modules in the Android Security Labware

Category	Mobile Threat Analysis & Protection Modules	IAS Topics
Mobile Device Security & Privacy	M 1: Threats of Lost or Stolen Mobile Devices	• Fundamental Concepts • Security Architecture and Systems Administration • Cryptography
	M 2: Unauthorized Mobile Resource Access	
	M 3: Mobile Privacy Threat	
Mobile App Security	M 4: Mobile Malware	• Fundamental Concepts • Secure Software Design and Engineering • Security Architecture and Systems Administration
	M 5: Secure Mobile App Development	
Mobile Network & Communication Security	M 6: Mobile SMS Security	• Fundamental Concepts • Cryptography • Network Security • Security Policy and Governance
	M 7: Mobile Phishing Threats	

Mobile SMS Security

Description: Short Message Service (SMS) is one of the most popular functions in mobile devices. However, it also becomes a lucrative playground for various attacks and frauds. Mobile SMS threats are increasing, and will continue to do so over the coming years. This module introduces the SMS-based threats and protections. An instance of SMS attack will be demonstrated and students will develop strategies to protect against damage from this attack.

Learning Objectives:

- Students understand the SMS threats: what are the SMS-based threats, how the attacks happened, and their consequences;
- Students understand the principles of protection strategies; students know the best practices to ensure safe SMS messaging; students practice SMS filtering on Android devices.

Targeting Courses: Mobile Security, Mobile Computing, Mobile Programming

Activities:

- Pre-Lab Activities
  - Introduction to SMS (slides)
  - SMS Messaging in Android (slides)
  - Introduction to SMS-based Threats and Protections (slides)
  - User Education on Secure SMS Messaging Practices (slides)
- Lab Activities
  - Threat Analysis: Malicious SMS (slides, app-demo-on-emulator, video-demo-on-youtube)
  - Threat Protection: SMS Filtering (instructions, android-apk, eclipse project with code)
- Post-Lab Activities
  - Case Study: An instance of Smishing Attack (slides)
  - Review questions
  - Assignments

Figure 1. The Design of Mobile SMS Security Module

M 6: Mobile SMS Security. This module will introduce the mechanisms of SMS in mobile devices, the SMS-based attacks, and the protection solutions. An app-based SMS attack demonstration will be developed. Students will learn to develop filter-based protection solutions. The prototype of this module has been developed and integrated in class for evaluation.

M 7: Mobile Phishing Threats. Social engineering attacks, such as phishing, leverage social engineering to trick the user into disclosing sensitive information or installing malware [2]. So far, neither iOS nor Android devices have built-in security approaches to protect users from such attacks [5]. This module will introduce to students the mobile phishing threats and their protection solutions. The mobile phishing attack vectors will be discussed and an attack instance will be demonstrated. For protection, this module provides user education and detection tool practices. This module is under development.

M3 and M6 have been developed and evaluated in courses (Section 4 presents the evaluation results); M1 and M4 are developed and will be integrated into courses for evaluation soon; M2, M5, and M7 are under intensive development. In addition to the above seven modules, an *M0: Getting Started* module will be provided to introduce to students the setup of Android development environment and the fundamental concepts in information security and mobile computing. Students can learn basic programming skills with Android and know the ethics in information security. More modules will be designed in the future, such as the modules for mobile browser security.

3.2 Example Module

In this section, we briefly demonstrate an example module to illustrate the learning approach and labware. Figure 1 shows the design of the *Mobile SMS Security* Module, which aims at providing students with SMS threat analysis and protection experience. SMS is a distinctive function of mobile computing systems. Howevér, the convenience and popularity of SMS have also made the service a lucrative playground for various attacks and frauds such as spamming, phishing, and spoofing [22]. This module first provides the pre-lab activities that include the introduction to the SMS service in Android, threat types of SMS, the attacking surface of SMS, and the strategies for SMS threat protection solutions. The lab activities provide a pair of hands-on labs on threat analysis and protection practice. In the threat analysis part, the lab introduces important SMS attack principles with a mobile-app-based demonstration of an instance of SMS attacks. In the demo, an attacker installs a malicious SMS broadcast listener on the victim's mobile phone, which has four contacts, and then the attacker sends a malicious SMS message to the victim and steals the victim's contact. The victim has no idea of the attacker's messages. In the protection practice part, the lab instructs students on implementing a mobile app for protecting against this attack using SMS filtering. In the protection app, students practice using a filter to block suspicious SMS messages from unknown users. This app is workable in practice. Students can install the app in Android devices such that they can obtain an instant gratification from the hands-on practice and they can be encouraged to create their own apps. The post-lab activities include review questions, assignments, and case studies.

The intention of pairing up the threat analysis and protection practice is to help students to understand how the actual mobile attacks and protection solutions take effect and to help to foster students' knowledge of mobile security so that they can detect new types of attacks and develop corresponding protection solutions.

4. COURSE EXPRIENCE

The modules in the labware are designed to be self-contained so that they can both be used in a dedicated mobile security course and be integrated into existing courses. In this section, we present our experience in using pilot modules in a wireless security course in Spring 2012 (14 students) and in an information security course in Summer 2012 (26 students). In the wireless security course, labs in the *Mobile SMS Security* module were offered as part of the hands-on labs of the course; and in the information security course in Summer 2012, the RSA Encryption/Decryption labs in the *Mobile Privacy Threat* module and the labs in *Mobile SMS Security* Module were offered as part of the hands-on labs of the course. Students who participated were asked to complete a survey that consists of the following six questions to evaluate the idea and the effectiveness of the labware:

Q1. The labware helps me understand better about the mobile security concepts in the project.

Q2. The labware provides me with more hands-on experience on learning mobile security.

Q3. The labware is easy to follow and practice.

Q4. The labware promotes my interest and engagement in security.

Q5. The labware promotes my interest and engagement in mobile app development.

Q6. I gained real world security experience from the real world relevant hands-on mobile security labs.

Forty students participated in the lab activities and completed the survey. Figure 2 shows the students' feedback. On average, about 90% of students gave non-negative feedback on all evaluation questions, and about 70% students agreed with the design objectives of the labware. Since none of the forty students had prior mobile development experience, the result of Q3 is still satisfactory that over 60% students gave non-negative feedback.

Students also provided their comments. We list representative positive feedback in the following. Students found the labs fun, educational, and promoting their interests in both mobile security and Android app. They enjoyed the real hands-on experience with the Android security labs and gained self-efficacy from the practices.

- *This project gave me the interest of Android app and Mobile security. The topic of this project is one that we all could face on any daily basis. With the help of this lab, I am now more than ever interested in design an app.*
- *It was a real and more hands-on experience, which I really like and always wish to do with all courses.*
- *The project was very challenging which is something I like. It actually feels rewarding to see the project working and performing what you want it to do.*
- *I really liked the challenge of this lab. Much as the instructions was easy to follow. This lab has really raised my level of interest in android apps development.*

The representative negative comments provided by students are listed in the following. Their concerns were concentrated around the installation of the lab environment and the precision of lab instructions. This provides an explanation for the relatively high disagreement rate in the survey result of Q3 in Figure 2. In the future, we will work on reducing the complexity of the lab environment setup and improve the lab instructions. Some students suggested providing equivalent lab exercises on iPhone platform. While we explained our reasons for choosing Android in Section 1, we are also investigating the possibility of developing the security practices on iPhone platform.

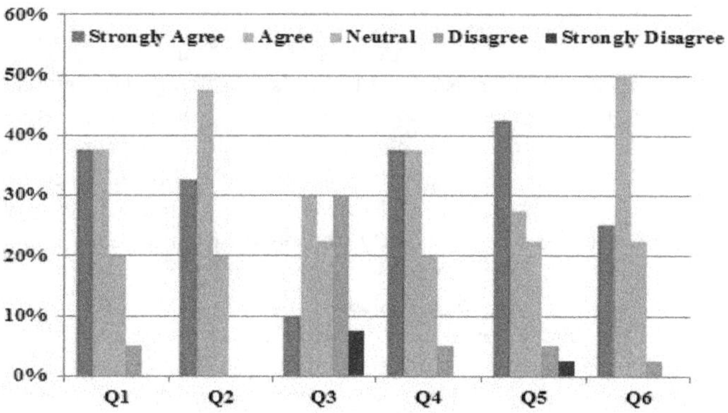

Figure 2. Survey Results

- *I liked the experience of building the project. The instructions could have been more precise.*
- *I really liked this project. Some of the problems I had with the software I had to Google for help and fortunately, it was there. The lab was not too hard, was not too easy. The only thing I found confusing was the links in the original word doc given us to us did not work.*
- *I would suggest having the lab environment set up before the assignment so that the emphasis can be on coding, programming, and applying cyber security concepts...*
- *Maybe because I am an iPhone fan, I wish we I had an option to choose (Apple or android), and I wish the lab was prepare and ready before we begin working on it.*

To sum up, our Android security labware and learning approach to mobile security received positive feedback from students and progress was made towards the objectives of promoting students' interests and improving their experience in mobile security and Android app development.

5. RELATED WORK

Courses focused on mobile security remain sparse in most computing curricula. Tague offered a mobile security course at the Carnegie Mellon University [23, 24]; however, it was a project-based course, which provided students with topics for discuss and exploration. In contrast, our work emphasizes learning mobile security through the hands-on experience, and we develop the lab environment and the materials for the learning.

The application of Android in the education of various computer science subjects is obtaining increasing interests. For example, Andrus and Nieh [25] developed a series of five Android kernel programming projects and an Android virtual laboratory to teach an introductory operating system course; Kurkovsky [18] used mobile game development as a motivational tool to engage students early in the curriculum; and Loveland [19] described the use of Google Android mobile platform and Google's Web Toolkit to provide students with experience in designing and implementing user interfaces for mobile and web applications. They all showed that the use of Android engaged students' interests in learning and improved effectiveness. Our work focuses on using Android to promote the study of mobile security and we directly use mobile apps for threat analysis and use mobile app development as a means of protection solution practice.

6. CONCLUSION

Mobile security is an emerging security area of growing importance and increasing needs, but is a relatively weak area in the current computing curriculum at most schools. This paper presents our initial effort on exploring the learning approach to mobile security and developing an Android-based security labware. We integrated the labware in two information security courses in two semesters. Forty students participated in the initial evaluation of our mobile security learning approaches and materials. The majority of students surveyed provided positive feedback and enjoyed the Android security practices. In the future, we plan to add more modules into the labware, such as the modules for mobile browser security, and Wi-Fi/Bluetooth communication security. We will improve the lab environment setup and the lab instructions. We will also work on offering a dedicated undergraduate mobile security course.

8. ACKNOWLEDGMENTS

The work is partially supported by the National Science Foundation under DUE award: SFS #1241651: Capacity Building in Mobile Security Through Curriculum and Faculty Development and CCLI #0942097, #0942140: Portable, Modular, and Modern Technology Infused labware for Broader Embedded Systems Education. Any opinions, findings, and conclusions or recommendations expressed in this material are those of the authors and do not necessarily reflect the views of the National Science Foundation

9. REFERENCES

[1] P. Alto, "Smart phones overtake client PCs in 2011," Canalys, Feb. 2012, accessed in Feb 2012, http://www.canalys.com/newsroom/smart-phones-overtake-client-pcs-2011.

[2] Lookout, Inc., "Lookout Mobile Security Report 2011," August 2011, accessed on Oct 12, 2011, https://www.mylookout.com/mobile-threat-report.

[3] Juniper Networks, Inc., "2011 Mobile Threats Report," Juniper Networks, Feb. 2012, accessed on Mar. 01, 2012, http://www.juniper.net/us/en/local/pdf/additional-resources/jnpr-2011-mobile-threats-report.pdf.

[4] McAfee® Labs™, "2012 Threats Predictions," McAfee, 2011, accessed on Mar. 1, 2012, http://www.mcafee.com/us/resources/reports/rp-threat-predictions-2012.pdf.

[5] C. Nachenberg, "A Window into Mobile Device Security," Symantec, 2011, http://www.symantec.com/content/en/us/about/media/pdfs/symc_mobile_device_security_june2011.pdf?om_ext_cid=biz_socmed_twitter_facebook_marketwire_linkedin_2011Jun_worldwide_mobilesecuritywp, accessed on Mar. 01, 2012.

[6] E. Geier, "2012 in Security: Rising Danger," PCWorld.com, Oct. 20, 2011, accessed on Mar. 10, 2012, http://www.pcworld.com/article/242174/2012_in_security_rising_danger.html.

[7] M.J. Schwartz, "Best Paying IT Security Jobs In 2012," InformationWeek.com, Nov. 25 2011, http://www.informationweek.com/news/security/management/232200152, accessed on Apr. 5, 2012.

[8] S. Diaz, "Mobile security needs more than just software, needs education," July 1, 2010, http://www.zdnet.com/blog/btl/mobile-security-needs-more-than-just-software-needs-education/36437, accessed on Jan 20, 2012.

[9] Stanford University, "XACS215 Mobile Security," accessed on May 1, 2012, http://scpd.stanford.edu/search/publicCourseSearchDetails.do?method=load&courseId=13070857.

[10] SANS.org, "Mobile Device Security," https://www.sans.org/security-training/mobile-device-security-5021-tid, accessed on Mar. 20, 2012.

[11] TONEX.com, "Course 90018: Mobile Applications Security Training - Mobile App Security Training course-Mobile Security Training," http://www.tonex.com/BootCamps/751, accessed on May 5, 2012.

[12] comSCORE, Inc., "comScore Reports March 2012 U.S. Mobile Subscriber Market Share," http://www.comscore.com/Press_Events/Press_Releases/2012/5/comScore_Reports_March_2012_U.S._Mobile_Subscriber_Market_Share, May 1, 2012, accessed on May 2, 2012.

[13] D. Reisigner, "Android Security Is a Major Threat: 10 Reasons Why," Apr. 04, 2012, http://mobile.eweek.com/c/a/Mobile-and-Wireless/Android-Security-Is-a-Major-Threat-10-Reasons-Why-148798, Apr. 06, 2012.

[14] W. Du, K. Jayaraman, and N. Gaubatz, "Enhancing Security Education with Hands-on Laboratory Exercises," In *Proceedings of the fifth Annual Symposium on Information Assurance (ASIA '10)*, June 16-17, 2010, Albany, New York.

[15] S. Caltagirone, P. Ortman, S. Melton, D. Manz, K. King, and P.W. Oman, "RADICL: A Reconfigurable Attack-Defend Instructional Computing Laboratory," *Security and Management*, Jun. 20-23, 2005, Las Vegas, Nevada, USA.

[16] W. Yurcik and D. Doss, "Different Approaches in the Teaching of Information Systems Security," in *Proceedings of the 2001 Information Systems Education Conference (ISECON'01)*, Nov. 2001, Cincinnati, OH, USA.

[17] EDUCAUSE, "The Future of Mobile Computing," 04/2011, accessed in Mar. 2012, http://net.educause.edu/ir/library/pdf/ESPNT1b.pdf.

[18] S. Kurkovsky, "Engaging Students through Mobile Game Development," *SIGCSE' 09*, Chattanooga, TN, Mar. 2009.

[19] S. Loveland, "Human computer interaction that reaches beyond desktop applications," In *Proceedings of SIGCSE 2011*, March 9-12, 2011, Dallas, Texas, USA.

[20] M. Ahamad, et al., "Emerging Cyber Threats Report 2012," Oct. 2011, accessed on Apr. 20, 2012, http://www.gtisc.gatech.edu/doc/emerging_cyber_threats_report2012.pdf.

[21] ACM/IEEE the Joint Task Force on Computing Curricula, Computer Science Curricula 2013: Strawman Draft, Feb. 2012, http://ai.stanford.edu/users/sahami/CS2013/strawman-draft/cs2013-strawman.pdf, accessed on Mar. 12, 2012.

[22] G. Yan, S. Eidenbenz, and E. Galli, "SMS-Watchdog: Profiling Social Behaviors of SMS Users for Anomaly Detection," in *Proceedings of the 12th International Symposium on Recent Advances in Intrusion Detection (RAID'09)*, Sept., 23-25, 2009, Saint-Malo, Brittany, France.

[23] P. Tague, "14-829: Mobile Security - Fall 2010," http://wnss.sv.cmu.edu/courses/14829-f10, 2010, accessed in Feb. 2012.

[24] P. Tague, "14-829: Mobile Security - Fall 2011," http://wnss.sv.cmu.edu/courses/14829-f11, 2011, accessed in Feb. 2012.

[25] J. Andrus and J. Nieh, "Teaching Operating Systems Using Android," *SIGCSE'12*, Feb. 29 – Mar. 3, Raleigh, NC, USA.

A Method for Incorporating Usable Security into Computer Security Courses

Binto George
School of Computer Sciences
Western Illinois University
Macomb, IL 61455
+1 309 298 1452
B-George@wiu.edu

Martha S Klems
School of Computer Sciences
Western Illinois University
Macomb, IL 61455
+1 309 298 1452
MS-Klems@wiu.edu

Anna Valeva
Economics and Decision Sciences
Western Illinois University
Macomb, IL 61455
+1 309 298 1403
AK-Valeva@wiu.edu

ABSTRACT

Since human factor security exploits are on the rise, ensuring Usable Security has become extremely important for the overall security of computer systems. However, traditional undergraduate computer security curriculum focuses heavily on technical aspects of security and generally ignores Usable Security. To address this problem, we developed a new 3P Learning Method that encourages students to view security problems from three different perspectives (i.e. 3P), namely: Defense, Offense, and Use. The 3P Method lets us incorporate Usable Security into the existing curriculum and helps students to consider Usable Security as an integral part of secure system design rather than an optional add-on.

Categories and Subject Descriptors

K.3.2 [**Computers and Education**]: Computer and Information Science Education –*curriculum.*

General Terms

Security, Human Factors.

Keywords

Usable Security, Security, 3P Learning Method, Computer Security Education.

1. INTRODUCTION

While the current computer security curriculum focuses on technological aspects, human factors are increasingly exploited to compromise security, as evidenced by the alarming increase in phishing, spoofing, pharming, and similar attacks. Although these attacks generally do not require very high technical skills, detection and prevention are usually complex. Hence, Usable Security - the study of the usability of security systems - is a much needed component of the undergraduate curriculum. However, we feel that the current computer science undergraduate curriculum does not adequately prepare students for tackling Usable Security issues. The practice has been to blame users for security problems whereas security professionals should have been focusing on making security functions usable for non-expert users.

Even in systems that have strong secure models or mathematical proof of security, effective security often depends on the users. Security measures that are easy and fun could be as effective as or even more effective than measures that are difficult to learn and use [1]. System designers should be aware of users' mental models and human factors that can potentially impact security.

While it is often understood that users must be trained and made aware of security risks, there is seldom any focus on preparing computer security professionals to design systems that can reduce or eliminate Usable Security problems. To address this lacuna, we revised our undergraduate computer security curriculum to include Usable Security.

Some computer security courses encourage students to view security from two perspectives: ***offense*** and ***defense***. Defense is the traditional role of the security professional – protect systems. Offense often assumes the vantage of an adversary exploiting the vulnerabilities of a system. By putting oneself in the shoes of an attacker, a student will learn to look for vulnerabilities. This was an effective strategy since most attacks used to exploit technical vulnerabilities. Now that attacks exploiting human factors are on the rise [2], the responsibility of protecting systems does not rest with users alone. Computer security professionals, therefore, should be able to build systems that are usably secure.

Only two out of the ten undergraduate computer security courses we surveyed had some Usable Security content. A few major universities offer elective courses on Usable Security. However, offering additional electives would entail additional resources. Besides, undergraduate programs are already packed with a large number of required courses. Since all security professionals should develop an understanding of Usable Security concepts, integration into existing courses appears a plausible option. Usable Security should be part of the system design process much like other aspects of security.

2. IMPORTANCE OF USABLE SECURITY

A recent report suggests that the top ten passwords of 32 million breached user accounts of a web-based enterprise were unacceptably weak **[4]**. The Anti-Phishing Working Group's latest report highlights more than 56,859 unique phishing sites detected in February 2012 **[2]**.

Because security is generally not a user's primary concern, effective security techniques require a different usability standard than the standards for user interfaces of other types of consumer software **[3]**. As evidenced in this study, the majority of users were unable to perform the simple task of signing and encrypting a message using PGP 5.0 in 90 minutes. The authors suggest that

SIGCSE'13, March 6–9, 2013, Denver, Colorado, USA.

"security usability alignment" is difficult to achieve when usability and security have not been integrated from the start. Other studies show that end-users of security systems find them difficult to use, resulting in potentially serious security problems **[5] [6]**.

3. SECURITY COURSES

A number of interesting approaches have been tried to teach computer security. Most computer security instructors use the methods of *defense assurance* and *attack understanding* [7]. The learning process can be improved by using a mixture of theory and concepts [8]. Louthan et. al. [9] brings offensive only exercises in a virtual enterprise network. Their experience shows that many students enjoy offensive exercises. Using honeynet for teaching computer security has also been proposed [10]. This work aims at providing real life experience to students in a distributed computing scenario. The approaches above focus mainly on technical aspects of security.

Visualization tools have been developed for teaching computer security [11]. The tools include a packet sniffer simulator, a Simulation of Kerberos Authentication Architecture, and a Visualization tool for Wireless Network Attacks. An undergraduate software security course described in [12] introduces a security development lifecycle model, and tools and techniques for designing trustworthy software.

In [13] a method to engage students in real-life relevant security exercises uses "second life". Students manage an online store and buy products from a number of websites set up for the purpose in second life environment. This activity can help students develop an understanding of how security works in real life beyond the narrow technical hands-on experiments in security labs. In the first phase, students review the security of stores before deciding to buy from there. Grades are assigned based on the security of websites from which they bought products. In the next phase, students set up their own storefronts and try to securely configure a router. Instructors launch an attack to see if the routers can be compromised or passwords can be cracked. Each time a password is cracked students pay $500.00 in "cyber money".

In general, computer security instructors tend to focus [15] on topics such as access control, encryption, security models, etc., while Certified Information Systems Security Professionals (CISSP) cite their top five priorities as: upper management support, user awareness and training, malware, patch management, vulnerability and risk assessment. These were consistently ranked lower by the computer science faculty. Consequently, many of the topics deemed important for the industry are not covered in a typical computer security course. In [15] it is argued that including risk assessment and modeling in traditional computer security courses can provide significant improvement and that students need background in HCI principles and Usable Security. We feel that CS faculty should consider broadening their topics list to include some of these areas. The teaching paradigm we propose is ideally suited to do just that within already existing computer security courses.

4. USABLE SECURITY IN COURSES

Epstein described an ethics and computer security course with a component that emphasizes the need for finding the right balance between usability and security [16] and introduced students to research projects in the area of Usable Authentication.

Some institutions, e.g., University of Pittsburgh, offer courses on computer security whose topical outline includes human factors in security. The reading list for Massachusetts Institute of Technology's open courseware includes papers on Usable Security. In a comprehensive undergraduate information assurance program described in [17], student teams from undergraduate institutions set up networks and try to secure them from attacks conducted by a team from the National Security Agency and the 1st Information Operations Command. While students learn about protecting national infrastructure from realistic attacks, the program could be augmented to include possible attacks against civilian systems by exploiting human factors.

In a Dartmouth college work [18] students are exposed to social engineering methods and explore how users' mental models diverge from technical reality in a "Hacker Curriculum" context. This may help students develop an insight into exploitation of users' (perceived as "naïve") mental models.

A number of elective courses in Usable Privacy and Security have been developed. Harvard University offers "Topics in User Interfaces: Security and Privacy Usability" with pre-requisite Introduction to Computer Science II. It includes current research in computer security and human-computer interaction. Harvard University Extension School offers a course on Security, Privacy, and Usability. Carnegie Mellon School of Computer Science has a graduate course on Usable Privacy and Security with weekly reading assignments, presentations, and a substantial group project commensurate with the students' degree program. Carleton University, Canada, offers an upper division course on Computer Security and Usability with computer security and operating systems as prerequisites.

5. OUR WORK: ADDING USABLE SECURITY

Instead of developing an elective course on Usable Security, we decided to synergistically embed Usable Security topics into existing computer security courses. We wanted to develop a learning method that will help students understand the importance of addressing Usable Security along with other security concerns during every stage of the system analysis, design, and development.

5.1 The 3 Perspectives (3P) Learning Method

Our 3P Learning Method encourages students to view computer security problems from ***Defense***, O***ffense***, and ***Use*** perspectives. Defense helps to protect computer systems by evaluating risks, identifying threats and mitigating them. Offense views the system from the adversaries' perspective to determine the vulnerabilities most likely to be exploited by an attacker. Use perspective tries to understand the system from the users' vantage in order to make security more usable and intuitive. The 3P Learning Method helps students achieve a unified vision of the security problem from three different perspectives.

5.2 Why Does the 3P Method Work?

In the 3P Learning Method students are trained to analyze security problems from perspectives of defense, use and offense. Our experience found this approach beneficial for our students. First, viewing each security problem from multiple perspectives makes the problem clearer which reinforces learning. Second, encouraging students to consider the users' viewpoint when designing systems emphasizes the importance of usability as part of computer security. Third, role playing the three perspectives improves classroom interaction and fosters an active learning process. Fourth, integrating usable security concepts along with traditional computer security topics enables us to cover more usable security topics than otherwise possible.

For example, consider the password based authentication explored by students:

Defense	**Problem**: How can I protect user information? **Solution**: Use passwords. **Learning Outcome**: Passwords can be used to protect user accounts.
Offense	**Problem**: How can I hack into the user account? **Solution**: Guess, break, or steal the password. **Learning Outcome**: Knowledge of available cracking tools. Password strength.
Use	**Problem**: How do I remember the password? It is embarrassing and a lot of trouble, if I forget. **Solution:** The system should help me choose good passwords and make it easier for me to securely reset the password if I forget. **Learning Outcome:** It is possible to devise passwords that are easy to remember but hard to guess.

Other examples: A student looking from the ***defense*** aspect of protecting a highly secure system may opt for partitioned design that isolates ***secret*** components of the system from ***public*** components. However, when students consider the ***use*** aspect, they would realize that it will lead to communication problems between ***secret*** level users and ***public*** level users. As a potential solution, students may (re)invent the Bell-LaPadula model [19]. When students view the system from ***offense*** perspective, they might think about setting up covert channels [20]. As students switch perspectives, their understanding becomes better.

When studying encryption, students quickly learn that the longer the key the stronger would be the cipher (***defense***). However, upon analyzing from the ***use*** perspective, they realize that people cannot remember long keys. So keys need to be stored. If those are stored in files, they may be stolen (***offense***). Thus the file should be password protected or the encryption key may be generated from a password (***Defense***). From ***use*** perspective, students understand that encryption is not a user's primary task and a suitable user interface that follows the user's mental model must be designed for ensuring security.

From the ***defense*** view, students learn that SSL uses encryption for data privacy. ***Offense*** point of view may detect a possibility of man-in-the-middle attack or the possibility that the private key be obtained by a hacker. However, when looking from the ***use*** side, students understand that security may be compromised despite strong encryption, e.g., if users give higher priority to their primary task of accessing the website at the expense of security by choosing to ignore SSL warnings.

The Receiver Operating Characteristics (ROC) curve of a biometric system visualizes two properties: False Match Rate (FMR) and False Non-Match Rate (FNMR). Students quickly realize that the FMR is very important from the ***defense*** perspective. Soon, they also see that the FNMR is important from the ***use*** viewpoint. Students understand the need for striking a balance between security and usability in civilian application domains.

The 3P Method enables us to systematically integrate Usable Security concepts into existing curriculum at all levels. For instance, introducing usable security as a security property along with confidentiality, integrity, availability and non-repudiation can help students view Usable Security as important as other security requirements.

We introduced the 3P Method into the computer security course for majors and systems security course for non-majors .

5.3 Usable Security in Course for Majors

The School of Computer Sciences has a Computer Security (SEC-M) course taken by undergraduate students from information science, computer science (traditional and business tracks), network technologies, and information systems. The pre-requisite for the course is CS1. We cannot assume any prior knowledge of security topics or advanced programming skills for the students taking this course.

In designing this course, in addition to the traditional security goals, we wanted students to understand that human factors are as important to system's security as technical factors.

5.3.1 Topics

We embedded Usable Security into the existing topics. We developed presentation materials and active learning tasks (available on our website) to encourage students to analyze security problems using our 3P Method. The topic list now includes [21]:

Week 1 Computer Security Principles, Scope and Dimensions of the Computer Security Problem (Security, Usability), Threats, Security Properties.
Week 2 Cryptography Basics. Classic Cryptography.
Week 3 Cryptographic Algorithms.
Week 4 Access Control, Authentication, Biometrics, Usable Access Control
Week 5 Application Security, Software Security: Secure Software Development, Secure Interface Design, Case Studies, Usability Testing.
Week 6 Threat Models, Vulnerability and Risk Assessment.
Week 7 Threat Modeling Case Study, Usable Security and Role of Human Factors in Security.
Week 8 Review/Practice/Midterm.
Week 9 Common Threats: Buffer Overflow, Denial of Service Attacks. Usable Security for Administrators.
Week 10 Phishing, Pharming, Human Factors Related Threats.
Week 11 Advanced Cryptography. Symmetric Key. Cryptography: AES, Encryption Modes, Public Key Systems: Knapsack, RSA, Diffie-Hellman, Elliptic Curve Cryptography, PGP, Usability of PGP.
Week 12 Public Key Infrastructure (PKI), Hash functions.
Week 13 SSL, Man-in-the-middle attacks, Digital Rights Management, Digital Watermarks.
Week 14 Operating Systems Security, Windows Usability Studies, Access Control (Discretionary, Mandatory, Rule Based, Role Based), Access Control Protocols.
Week 15 Firewalls, Usable Security of Firewalls, Project Presentations.
Week 16 Final Examination and Assessment.

5.3.2 Assignments and Projects

We redesigned the assignments and created a new course project utilizing 3P Method for reinforcing Usable Security.

5.3.2.1 *Using PGP for encryption*
PGP is a valuable tool for learning encryption. Students were asked to send and receive a message using PGP so that the confidentiality and integrity of the message can be ensured. This is also an opportunity to learn more about user interface design and users' mental models on encryption. Students interviewed everyday users to find out their understanding of different terms such as public key, private key, public key certificates and cryptography. Students also performed a cognitive walkthrough and heuristic evaluation of the PGP user interface.

5.3.2.2 *Threat Modeling*
Students were asked to identify threats arising from both technical and human factors. We augmented the traditional STRIDE threat model to specifically include human factor threats (STRIDE+H). Students analyzed a popular website (e.g., Facebook) to review the user interface and privacy policies. Alternatively, students may be asked to evaluate the user interface with the help of a non-expert user, who could be asked to "talk aloud" while performing a number of security functions using the interface.

5.3.2.3 *Usable Access Control Policy*
Students were asked to develop an access control policy for files to be created and shared by an imaginary enterprise team. Students were required to consider the usability security implications (analyze from ***use*** perspective) as a shift from assigning privileges following the principle of "least privilege" that shows how designing a system needing supervisor approval for too many common tasks may backfire since that may fatigue the supervisor into authorizing most requests without really paying attention, thereby resulting in less effective security.

5.3.2.4 *Secure Software Development Project*
Students were asked to implement a small secure software application. During each stage of the software development process, Usable Security was emphasized. In requirement analysis stage, students are asked to explore the Usable Security requirements along with confidentiality, integrity, availability and non-repudiation requirements (usability is considered as one of the fundamental security properties). During the preliminary design phase, students developed low fidelity prototypes (e.g., paper prototypes) of the interfaces for the major security functions. Later in the design phase, students performed a detailed threat analysis specifically looking for threats arising from human factors (using STRIDE+H threat model).

5.4 Usable Security in Course for Non-Majors
Our non-majors course is taken predominantly by law-enforcement majors, so topics such as phishing, pharming, and spoofing are of interest. We considered usable security in class discussions whenever possible, such as how setting certain security policies may actually work against security because of human factors. In our observation, non-majors often found it hard to use tools such as PGP (for encryption), making it easier for them to appreciate the need for usable security better than majors.

Students were asked how they would decide whether a website is legitimate and develop suggestions to improve security indicators on their browser. Can someone use the browser's interface to set the privacy settings he or she likes? Many students never realized that they could change security settings of a browser. Many did not know what security indicators meant or if there is any difference if they appear within the page or on the browser chrome.

The secure system design process was introduced with the simple example of adding two numbers. Requirement analysis would reveal if the numbers were real numbers or integers. What if the users entered other characters by accident? How would you develop a friendly interface that helps prevent user errors and provides feedback? How could they trust the results?

Non-majors were also asked to use the 3P Method to analyze different password systems such as text passwords, cognitive passwords and graphical passwords. Some students thought graphical password was "cool" and easier to remember, but realized someone could shoulder-surf unlike a text password.

Other possible exercises: choosing cognitive questions that are both secure and usable; designing a usable login interface that helps users set a secure password by giving realtime feedback on the strength of the password (design techniques such as parallel design, participatory design, etc. can be introduced); developing written policies for protecting employees from phishing.

5.5 Usable Security in Basic Courses
In [22] security is introduced in a CS1 course by adding two interesting assignments. We believe that it is important to embed Usable Security into CS1 and other courses whenever possible much like traditional security topics. The objective is to develop an understanding that users are often concerned about security but lack the tools or knowledge to protect the system. Therefore, the onus is on system designers to make system security functions intuitive and easier to use by closely following users' mental models.

Material does not have to be complex. A simple example is "redacting" secret information from a word document by placing a black rectangle over text. A non-expert user's mental model may assume that the text underneath will be unreadable. However, the text may be easily uncovered from the resulting PDF document. Examples such as above can illustrate how failure to follow users' mental models could result in inadequate security.

6. OUR CONTRIBUTIONS
The following is a list of our contributions:

1. Included usability as a security property at the level of confidentiality, integrity, availability, and non-repudiation. Thus, students consider the usability of security functions as important as other security properties.
2. Encouraged students to view security problems from three perspectives: ***Defense***, ***Offense***, and ***Use*** (the 3P Method) and developed course materials based on this method. Included security problems arising from usability in class discussions.
3. Modified a threat model (STRIDE [23]) to explicitly include human factors and encouraged students to explore threats arising from both technical and human factors. We call the modified threat model STRIDE+H.
4. Introduced usability design, inspection and user testing methods by adding a new module on Usable Security.
5. Developed assignments and lab materials to include Usable Security. Developed a secure software development project with emphasis on Usable Security.
6. Embedded Usable Security concepts into core courses such as Principles of Computer Science I and Data Structures I.

7. Added Usable Security into non-CS major course by developing course materials, examples and a lab exercise.

All course materials are available at:
http://www.wiu.edu/UsableSecurity/

7. ACTIVITIES, EXTERNAL REVIEWS AND LEARNING OUTCOMES

The Computer Security majors' course (SEC-M) may be taken by three undergraduate majors: Computer Science, Information Systems, and Network Technologies.

In Fall 2008 we offered a baseline SEC-M using the traditional approach for control purposes. Human factor security topics such as phishing, malware, user password security and biometrics were included.

In Spring 2009, we offered SEC-M with the 3P Learning Method. We also employed the discovery learning method [24] in conjunction with the 3P Learning Method since it seemed natural to combine the two to encourage critical thinking and foster student-centered learning.

Based on students' feedback, in Fall 2009, we combined the 3P Learning Method with a lecture based approach instead of discovery learning method. Over 350 slides and course materials were developed. The course project was clarified further by adding more Usable Security specific guidelines. The threat modeling procedure was modified to encourage looking for threats arising from human factors. We added case studies illustrating secure software design and Usable Security analysis and testing. We used the new materials in Spring and Fall 2010.

7.1 External Reviews

We conducted peer-review of the course materials in two rounds by CS faculty members not affiliated with our institution. After the first round, reviews were analyzed to improve the course materials further. Summative analysis was conducted with ten reviewers on a scale from 1 to 10 in terms of the following aspects (average scores and standard deviations of the scores are reported respectively):

Criteria	Average	SD
Teaching Methodology	9.00	0.82
Clarity of Materials	8.40	0.84
Coverage of Usable Security Topics	8.99	0.88
Coverage of Security Topics	8.3	1.16
Quality of Project/Assignments	8.8	1.03
Degree to which course materials meet the course objective	9.05	0.83

7.2 Student Final Assessment

In this Student Final Assessment (SFA) questionnaire, four questions were used to assess student awareness of usability issues in security systems and four other questions were used to assess students' Usable Security design knowledge. To evaluate the likelihood of students considering Usable Security as a factor in system design we requested they give a specific example to illustrate their concept of usability in the context of computer privacy and security.

After 4 semesters the Student Final Assessment showed a marked increase in at least some awareness of usability issues from 17% in the base class to 100% in the most recent class. It also showed an increase in usability design knowledge from 0% in the base class to 86% of students with some usability design knowledge.

In Spring 2012 the SEC-M course was taught by a different instructor under a format comparable to our baseline offering in Fall 2008. We administered the same SFA questionnaire and the results were consistent with those from Fall 2008: very little if any awareness or usability design knowledge.

7.3 Non-Major Computer Security Course

The non-major Computer Security (SEC-NM) course is taken primarily by law enforcement majors with a pre-requisite of Introduction to Computers.

The baseline SEC-NM class had an average of 25% on the SFA. In four short essay questions on aspects of computer security 55% failed to consider usability at all, 40% considered it in response to only one question, and only 5% considered it on two of the questions.

For Spring 2010 the SEC-NM was re-designed to emphasize Usable Security with the 3P Learning Method. The SFA average increased from the base mean of 25% to 48%. In Fall 2010, the emphasis on Usable Security and the 3P Learning Method continued. The course was enhanced with more examples and lab experience. The SFA average increased to 57%.

While SEC-M was taken by 5-10 students every semester, we had from 20 to 30 students taking SEC-NM each semester.

8. CONCLUSIONS

We introduced the 3P Learning Method to encourage students to view security problems from three perspectives: defense, offense and use. The 3P Method enabled us integrate Usable Security into existing courses. It also helped students to consider Usable Security as an integral part of secure system design rather than an optional add-on component.

Our learning assessment showed that our security courses using the 3P Method significantly improved Usable Security knowledge both for computer security major and non-major courses. Several improvements were made during the course offerings in multiple semesters, and while the improvement in SFA was not solely due to the 3P Learning Method, the 3P Learning Method was central to our course improvement process.

We felt that SEC-M students did not have secure system design knowledge for designing complex systems. An approach similar to "security across the curriculum" suggested in [25] to incorporate Usable Security into core courses may be beneficial. More research should focus on including Usable Security into the secure system design process, creating new threat models using the 3P paradigm and developing effective learning techniques.

We specifically designed a secure system design project to train students to incorporate security into all stages of the software development lifecycle. We introduced many system design examples, covering requirement analysis, design, and implementation by emphasizing security arising from both technical and human factors at each stage of the process. Our course materials were peer-reviewed and were made available on our website for download.

A few experts reviewing our course materials were of the opinion that security courses should focus on technical aspects and human factors can be easily learned. We also had experts stating usable security is very complex that it needed an elective on its own.

Developing specific Usable Security electives would be an approach that we did not consider for our students. This was due to resource constraints and because of our belief that all security courses should include Usable Security.

We feel that using the 3P Method improved the overall learning outcomes not only for usability, but for all aspects of computer security covered in the course. Our hypothesis is that the 3P Method is more interactive altogether, bringing the students' own experience as users and stirring up considerably more active attention to the learning process. However, this hypothesis must be verified by further learning assessments and research.

In closing, we hope that our fellow educators will find this paper useful when incorporating Usable Security into their curriculum as well as find novel applications of the 3P Learning Method.

9. ACKNOWLEDGEMENTS

Authors' contribution to this paper, in part, is based upon work supported by the National Science Foundation under Grant No. DUE-0736643.

10. REFERENCES

1 Talbot, Edward B, Frincke, Deborah, and Bishop, Matt. Demythifying Cyber Security. *IEEE Security and Privacy*, 8, 3 (May/June 2010), 56-59.

2 *Anti-Phishing Work Group (http://www.antiphishing.org/).*

3 Whitten, A. and Tygar, J. D. Why Johnny can't encrypt: a usablility evaluation of PGP 5.0. (Berkeley, CA 1999), Proceedings of the 8th Usenix Security Symposium.

4 Stinchcombe, N. *Imperva Releases Detailed Analysis of 32 Million Breached Consumer Passwords.* http://www.imperva.com/news/press/2010/01_21_Imperva_Releases_Detailed_Analysis_of_32_Million_Passwords.html, Retrieved 1st May, 2010.

5 Smetters, D. K. and Grinter, R. E. Moving from the Design of Usable Security Technologies to the Design of Useful Secure Applications. (2002), Proc. of the Workshop on New Security Paradigms.

6 Dourish, P. and Redmiles, D. An Approach to Usable Security Based on Event Monitorig and Visualization. (2002), Dourish, P., Redmiles, D., "An Approach to Usable Secu Proc. of the Workshop on New Security Paradigms.

7 Frincke, Deborah. Who Watches the Security Educators? *IEEE Security and Privacy*, 1, 3 (May 2003), 56-58.

8 Brynielsson, Joel. An Information Assurance Curriculum for Commanding Officers Using Hands-On Experiments. *SIGCSE Bull.*, 41, 1 (March 2009), 236-240.

9 Louthan, George, Roberts, Warren, Butler, Matthew, and Hale, John. An Offensive Exercise for Building Network, Systems and Web Security Awareness. In *Proc. of the 3rd Intl. Conf. on Cyber Security experimentation and test* (Washington, DC 2010), USENIX Association, 1-7.

10 Azadegan, Siva and McKenna, Vanessa. Use of Honeynets in Computer Security Education. (Jeju Island, S. Korea 2005), Proc. 4th Annual ACIS Intl. Conference on Computer and Information Science.

11 Yuan, Xiaohong, Vega, Percy, Qadah, Yaseen, Archer, Ricky, Yu, Huiming, and Xu, Jinsheng. Visualization Tools for Teaching Computer Security. *Trans. Comput. Educ.*, 9, 4 (January 2010), 20:1-20:28.

12 Lester, Cynthia Y and Jemerson, Frank. Designing an Undergraduate Software Security Course. (2008), The Second Intl. Conf. on Emerging Security Information, Systems and Technologies.

13 Ryoo, Jungwoo, Techatassanasoontorn, Angsana, and Lee, Dongwon. Security Education Using Second Life. *IEEE Security and Privacy*, 7, 2 (March 2009), 71-74.

14 Mullins, Barry E, Lacey, Timothy H, Mills, Robert F, Trechter, Joseph E, and Bass, Samuel D. How the Cyber Defense Exercise Shaped an Information-Assurance Curriculum. *IEEE Security and Privacy*, 5, 5 (September 2007), 40-49.

15 Swart, Richard S and Erbacher, Robert F. Educating Students to Create Trustworthy Systems. *IEEE Security and Privacy*, 5, 3 (May/June 2007).

16 Epstein, Richard G. An Ethics and Security Course for Students in Computer Science. (Houston, Texas, USA 2006), ACM SIGCSE.

17 Conti, Gregory, Hill, John, Lathrop, Scott, Alford, Kenneth, and Ragsdale, Daniel. A Comprehensive Undergrduate Information Assurance Program. In Irvine, Cynthia and Armstrong, Helen, eds., *Security Education and Critical Infrastructures*. Kluwer Academic Publishers, Norwell, MA, USA, 2003.

18 Bratus, Sergey and Masone, Christopher. Hacker Curriculum: How We Can Use It in Teaching. *IEEE Distributed Systems Online*, 8, 11 (November 2007).

19 Bell, E. D. and LaPadula, L. J. *Secure Computer Systems: Unified Exposition and MULTICS.* MITRE Corporation, 1976.

20 Lampson, B. W. A Note on the Confinement Problem. *CACM* (October 1973).

21 Stamp, Mark. *Information Security*. Wiley Inter-Science, 2006.

22 Kara, Nance. Teach Them When They Aren't Looking Introducing Computer Security in CS1. *IEEE Security and Privacy*, 7, 5 (September/October 2009), 53-55.

23 Swiderski, Frank and Snyder, Window. *Threat Modeling.* Microsoft Press, 2004.

24 Baldwin, Doug. Discovery learning in computer science. *ACM SIGCSE Bulletin* , 28, 1 (March 1996), 222-226.

25 Kaza, Siddharth, Taylor, Blair, Hochheiser, Harry, Azadegan, Shiva, and O□Leary, Mike. Injecting Security in the Curriculum – Experiences in Effective Dissemination and Assessment Design. (Baltimore, Maryland 2010), Proceedings of the 14th Colloquium for Information Systems Security Education.

Interactive Support for Secure Programming Education

Jun Zhu
Department of Software and Information Systems
University of North Carolina at Charlotte
Charlotte, NC 28223
jzhu16@uncc.edu

Heather Richter Lipford
Department of Software and Information Systems
University of North Carolina at Charlotte
Charlotte, NC 28223
Heather.Lipford@uncc.edu

Bill Chu
Department of Software and Information Systems
University of North Carolina at Charlotte
Charlotte, NC 28223
billchu@uncc.edu

ABSTRACT
Software flaws are a root cause of many of today's information security vulnerabilities. Current curricula emphasis on traditional information security issues does not address this root cause. We propose educating students on secure programming techniques through interactive tool support in the Integrated Development Environment (IDE). We believe this approach can complement other curricula efforts by teaching and providing continuous reinforcement of practices throughout programming tasks. In this paper, we evaluate our prototype tool, ASIDE, which provides instant security warnings, detailed explanations of vulnerabilities, and code generation. We report the results of an observational study on 20 students from an advanced Web programming course. The results provide early evidence that our tool could potentially help students learn about and practice secure programming in the context of their programming assignments.

Categories and Subject Descriptors
D.2.6 [**Software Engineering**]: Programming Environments – *integrated environments;* K3.2 [**Computers and Education**]: Computer and Information Science Education – *computer science education, information systems education.*

General Terms
Security, Human Factors, Experimentation

Keywords
Secure Programming, Security Education, IDE

1. INTRODUCTION
Many computer security problems are caused by software vulnerabilities, which often originate from the insecure code written by developers. While there are established sets of secure programming techniques and practices, such as CERT C Secure Coding Standards [14] and Secure Coding Guidelines for the Java Programming Language [10], only a very small fraction of developers are well trained in those practices. Computer Science, Software Engineering, and Information Technology educational programs train students in programming and application development. Yet, relatively few programs offer any education in secure software development – programming techniques that reduce the security bugs and vulnerabilities found in software. As a result, the programmers that we educate continue to inadvertently introduce security bugs, and attacks continue to cost organizations millions of dollars a year.

Despite the importance of secure software development, there is little research in how to effectively incorporate the training into existing degree programs and computing curricula. While some programs do offer secure programming training in a focused security course, security education researchers are recognizing that security education must be threaded throughout the entire computing curriculum [1, 6, 12]. Yet, this presents a number of challenges because most CS faculty have never been trained in secure programming. In addition, existing courses may not have the time or resources to cover additional secure programming topics on top of already extensive course content.

Our goal is to provide secure programming knowledge acquisition and practice development opportunities that are integrated into the student's curriculum alongside the programming constructs they are learning. Our approach is to provide training in, and support for, good secure programming practices as part of the tools that students use to program, namely the Integrated Development Environment (IDE). To that end, we are developing the Assured Software IDE (ASIDE) plug-in, a plug-in to the Eclipse Java development environment. The plug-in detects potential vulnerabilities in the code that students are working on, and interactively assists them in addressing those vulnerabilities, providing relevant and contextual explanations and training. This approach complements curricula-based approaches by serving as a continuous educational opportunity that adds to or reinforces the students' secure programming training while they are performing their coding activities. In this paper we present our current prototype of ASIDE and an initial evaluation of its use with students in an advanced Web programming course. Our results demonstrate that our approach is feasible, and that ASIDE can be used to provide awareness and knowledge while students work on assignments.

2. BACKGROUND
There is a large body of knowledge on techniques for designing, implementing, and testing software that is more secure and robust than existing software [3, 4]. Both government and industry efforts have been recently launched to codify and organize such knowledge. For example, the Department of Homeland Security (DHS) has developed a Common Body of Knowledge (CBK) for software assurance [18]. Several textbooks have also been written about secure software development [5, 8]. A number of universities have developed in-depth security courses teaching the analysis of software vulnerabilities and methods for preventing or repairing them [2]. However, there are disadvantages to only

SIGCSE'13, March 6–9, 2013, Denver, Colorado, USA.

providing concentrated courses: such dedicated security courses may be elective, and thus reach only a subset of computing students; there may not be room in the degree program for students to take the course; and students may not take the course until they are juniors or seniors. As students learn to program, the training and examples they learn from will heavily impact the practices they use in their own code [7]. Many programming textbooks have little mention of security, and may even contain vulnerabilities [13]. Thus, if students are not exposed to secure programming practices until later in their education, if at all, they may learn bad habits without being aware of the consequences.

Tayler et al proposed threading security touch points and risk analysis throughout computer science curricula by integrating secure programming modules into labs for programming-based courses, such CS0 and CS1, which they call security injections [15]. These injections consist of general vulnerability descriptions and problems, such as integer overflow, along with a security checklist for students to use to evaluate their code [16]. These lab modules have been shown to increase the students' awareness of security principles [17]. Nance also describes how to incorporate security concerns into the assignments in CS1 courses [9]. Our approach complements these efforts by examining whether providing interactive tool support in the IDE can aid students in writing secure code and learning secure programming practices.

3. ASIDE

The ASIDE prototype is a proof-of-concept Eclipse plugin for Java, which integrates secure programming support and education into the IDE. ASIDE works as a long running process in the background and scans a selected project for code patterns that match pre-defined heuristic rules of security vulnerabilities. Our first prototype is meant for an advanced Web application development class. Thus, ASIDE searches for vulnerabilities resulting from lack of input validation or output encoding, and the use of unsafe SQL statements. Whenever a match is found, ASIDE marks the corresponding source code line with a warning icon on the left margin of the code editor and also highlights the identified vulnerable code in red, shown in Figure 1.

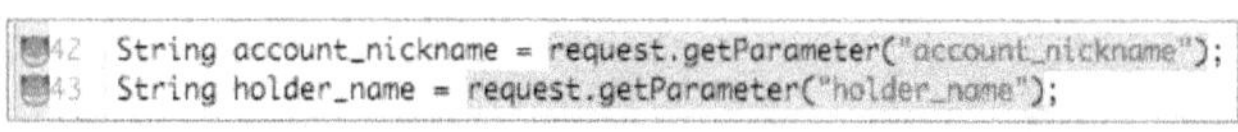

Figure 1. ASIDE vulnerable code warnings.

Users can click the warning icon or highlighted code to view several options, see Figure 2. Students can dismiss the warning with an Ignore This option. The Read More option opens a corresponding explanation page within Eclipse. While the warnings provide awareness as to where security vulnerabilities occur, the explanation pages provide the detailed knowledge as to what the vulnerability is, why it is important, how to fix the vulnerability, and how to use ASIDE to choose a quick fix if applicable. A portion of the explanation page for input validation is shown in Figure 3. Each explanation page consists of three or four small sections containing a concise summary of the most basic related secure programming knowledge, with buttons to expand for additional details and code examples. We structured the page in this way to provide an overview of the basic information at a glance, with additional details on demand. In addition, links to further or more comprehensive information on the Internet are provided for some of the sections.

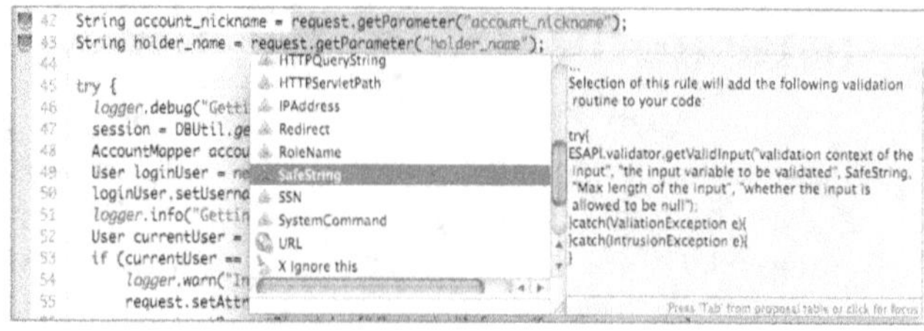

Figure 2. ASIDE provides a list of suggestions that can be applied to get explanations or address the selected warning.

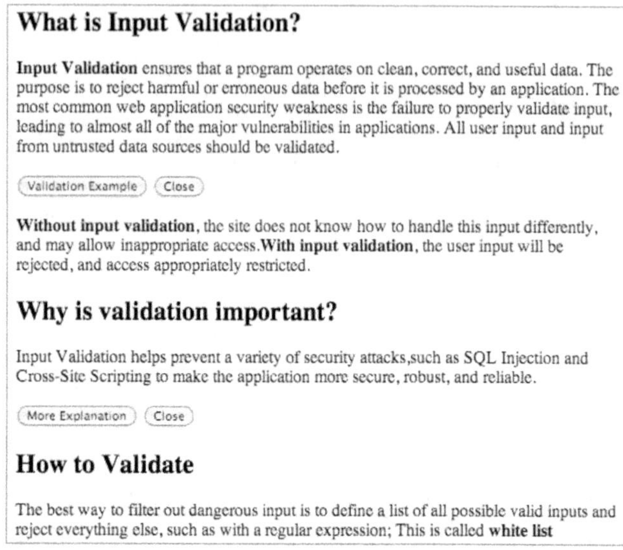

What is Input Validation?

Input Validation ensures that a program operates on clean, correct, and useful data. The purpose is to reject harmful or erroneous data before it is processed by an application. The most common web application security weakness is the failure to properly validate input, leading to almost all of the major vulnerabilities in applications. All user input and input from untrusted data sources should be validated.

(Validation Example) (Close)

Without input validation, the site does not know how to handle this input differently, and may allow inappropriate access. **With input validation**, the user input will be rejected, and access appropriately restricted.

Why is validation important?

Input Validation helps prevent a variety of security attacks,such as SQL Injection and Cross-Site Scripting to make the application more secure, robust, and reliable.

(More Explanation) (Close)

How to Validate

The best way to filter out dangerous input is to define a list of all possible valid inputs and reject everything else, such as with a regular expression; This is called **white list**

Figure 3. Portion of input validation explanation page.

Our goal with the tool is not only to provide knowledge on the security vulnerability, but also help students mitigate the vulnerability using standard best practice by reducing the effort in doing so. For warnings where this is possible, ASIDE performs automated code generation. Currently, this is done for input validation and output encoding vulnerabilities. Students must choose the type of input or output from the set of options displayed. The corresponding input validation or output encoding code segment is then inserted into the code, as illustrated in Figure 4. We use standard validation and encoding routines from ESAPI, an open source secure application development library [11]. ASIDE does not generate code for dynamic SQL statement warnings. Thus students would need to manually modify their code based upon the examples provided in the explanation.

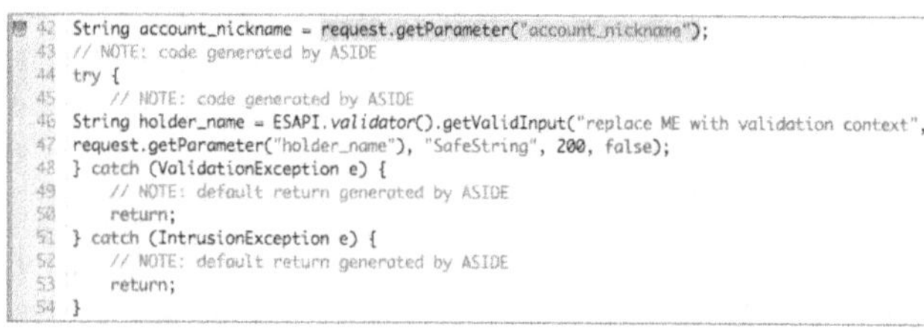

Figure 4. ASIDE generates a code segment based on the student's selection.

3.1 Previous ASIDE Research

ASIDE was originally conceived of and prototyped to provide professional developers with reminders, awareness, and assistance in creating more secure programs. We have previously performed both a security and usability analysis on ASIDE [19, 20]. In the usability study, we examined how developers would react to warnings, as well as two different methods for mitigation. One version of ASIDE provided only automated code generation functionality, similar to what is described above. The other version provided a brief explanation of the warning and its mitigation. We performed a comparison user study between the two versions of ASIDE with both IT professionals and students in the same Web application development course we used in this study (an earlier semester). The study results indicated that programmers appreciated the instant security warnings and did not find them annoying. The results also indicated that while some of the professionals were willing to attempt to write their own secure programming routines, the students were not. However, students did appreciate the code generation and wanted more explanations of the vulnerability and resulting code. While that study did not focus on the learning outcomes for these students, it did provide valuable lessons for our current educational prototype. We realized that even in an advanced programming course, students were even less aware of security than we realized, and needed simple yet detailed explanations of vulnerabilities and code. This also provided feedback that students would be likely to interact with ASIDE in order to utilize the automated code generation.

To focus on students and their training, we have extended our original prototype for educational use. We began with a focus on an advanced Web course to minimize changes to the developer version of ASIDE. Programs written for the Web are also the most commonly targeted applications, thus the secure programming practices taught alongside this course could have a big impact on students as they enter the workforce. We improved the comments ASIDE places in the code, made the prototype more robust, reduced the quick fix options provided, and developed the detailed explanation pages. The study we report here is our first study specifically focused on whether ASIDE would help students learn secure programming knowledge and practices.

4. USER STUDY METHODOLOGY

While our goal is to eventually release ASIDE for students to use throughout a course, our first evaluation utilized a laboratory study with short-term use to gather detailed observations and behaviors. Our goal was to obtain early feedback on whether this approach has potential to impact learning and practice, and to further improve the tool for broader use. The study goals include:

- How do students interact with the Read More option and the vulnerability explanations as they program?
- What are the students' impressions of the explanations? Are they easy to understand and helpful?
- Could students learn secure programming knowledge through using ASIDE?

4.1 Participants and Procedure

For this study, we recruited 20 students from a Java-based Web application development course that was offered to graduate and undergraduate students by our college in the Spring 2012. As part of the course, students were briefly introduced to basic secure programming techniques such as input validation and output encoding in a 30 minute lecture given by the course instructors prior to the study (the course instructors are not involved in this research). Project grades were based solely on the functional requirements rather than secure programming practices.

Part of the student's assignment was to incrementally build an online stock trading system over four projects throughout the semester using Java Servlet technology. Our study focused on the last increment of this project where the students were assigned to implement functionalities including add a banking account, display stock details, create a buy/sell stock transaction, and display transaction history. Students added these functions on top of their existing work artifacts, which included static Web pages, login, logout, and register functionalities.

4.2 Study Setup

We performed a controlled study where student participants were asked to our lab to work on their assignment for 3 hours. Each study session took ten minutes of pre-test and demographics survey, 3 hours of development, ten minutes of post-test, and fifteen minutes of interview. Participants were offered a gift card as compensation for completing the study session.

The students were first given a brief walkthrough of how the ASIDE plugin works while a technical assistant helped set up the development environment and screen recording software on the lab machines. The assistant also imported the participant's existing project into Eclipse and made sure it was compiled and could run on the local Web server. The student was then asked to launch the plugin before proceeding to development. Students were instructed to work as they wished on the assignment for 3 hours and respond to ASIDE warnings as they wanted to. The students worked on various parts of their own code, and upon completion of the session, none of them had completed the assignment (the assignment typically takes many more hours than provided in this session). Thus, students received different numbers and types of warnings, based upon the portions of the program they were working on during the study session.

4.3 Pre- and Post-test

Students were asked to take an online pre-test before the ASIDE walkthrough along with a demographic survey, and a post-test after the 3-hour development session. We designed two tests with similar questions and counterbalanced which test was given before or after the session. Both tests consisted of 18 true/false questions asking to identify which code statements required input validation or output encoding as well as more general questions about input validation, output encoding, and dynamic and prepared SQL statements. The following are three examples.

1. My application is only used by company employees; therefore I can trust the input from users and do not have to validate it.

2. Does the following statement contain variables that require encoding? log.info("failed to login user=" + request.getParameter("userid"));

3. Is the following statement subject to SQL Injection? statement.executeUpdate s("UPDATE customers SET addr = "+ customer.getAddress() + "'");

4.4 Semi-structured Interview

Each interview lasted 10 to 15 minutes. We began by asking students to describe their interactions with ASIDE, what they thought of the warnings and explanations pages, and the actions they took with ASIDE. We also asked participants what they thought they learned and took away from using ASIDE during the study session.

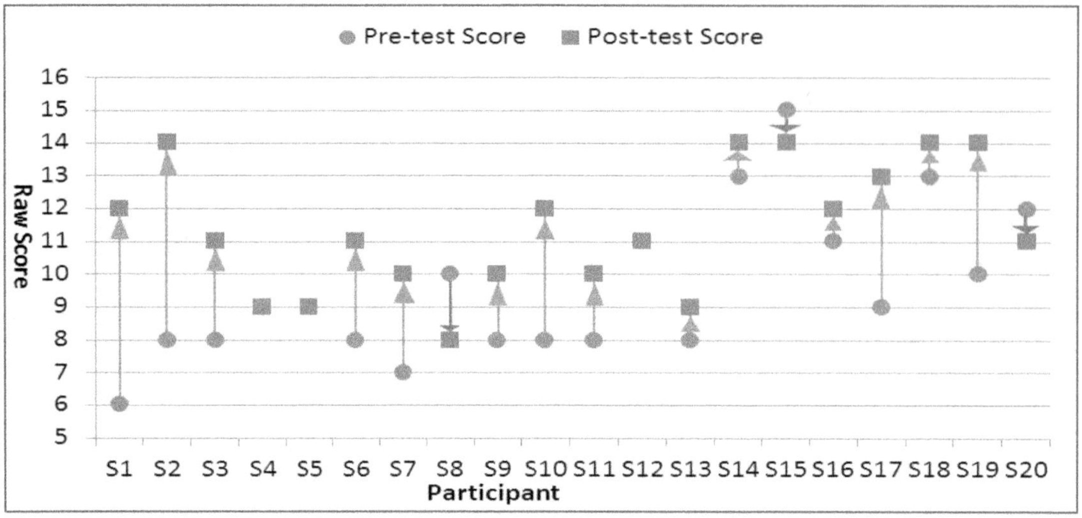

Figure 5. Comparison of pre- and post-test scores.

5. RESULTS

We had 20 student participants, including 12 male Master's students, 6 female Master's students and 2 male undergraduate students. Four of them reported that they knew a few but very limited security concepts prior to the study; none of them had secure programming experience before the study. For each student, we collected his/her answers to two tests, a 3-hour screen recording, and a recording of the interview. In addition, we collected the logs of ASIDE as a supplement to the screen recording. Due to an unexpected crash of the screen recording software during the study, we lost the screen recordings of 2 students, S19 and S20. Thus, all analysis of user behaviors was performed and reported for 18 participants.

5.1 Test Analysis

As we designed two tests, test A and test B, half of the students took test A as a pre-test and test B as a post-test (Group A), while half of the students took test B as a pre-test and test A as a post-test (Group B). Tests A and B were deemed equivalent by a chi square test. No significant differences were obtained for the number of correct responses obtained for Group A and Group B at pre-test.

Table 1. Test score summary

	Mean	Std. Deviation	Min	Max
Pre-score	9.55	2.30	6.00	15.00
Post-score	11.40	1.96	9.00	14.00
Pre-percentage	53.03%	12.81	33.33%	83.33%
Post-percentage	63.33%	10.86	44.44%	77.78%

The mean test scores are reported in Table 1. Scores increased from 9.55 (or 53.03% correct), a score close to what students would obtain by randomly choosing answers in the test, to 11.40 (or 63.33% correct), which constitutes a 1.45 increase after the 3-hour development session. We performed a Wilcoxon Signed Ranks Test, which showed that the difference between pre-test and post-test scores was statistically significant ($Z = -2.931$, $P = 0.003$), which indicates that using ASIDE did increased students' test scores. Figure 5 shows a comparison of the pre-test and post-test scores for each student. While most scores went up, three students had the same score, and 3 students had a lower score for the post-test. Thus 70% of students may have learned some secure programming knowledge from their experience using ASIDE.

5.2 Student Behavior

We used screen recordings to examine the ASIDE interaction behavior for 18 of our participants. Overall, 461 distinctive warnings were generated, which constitutes an average 25.6 warnings per participant. Out of all the 461 warnings, 321 were clicked (70%), and 217 were resolved (47%) mostly by choosing a quick fix and generating validation/encoding code (Figure 6). These results indicate that students interacted with ASIDE regularly, and did use it to resolve a number of security vulnerabilities.

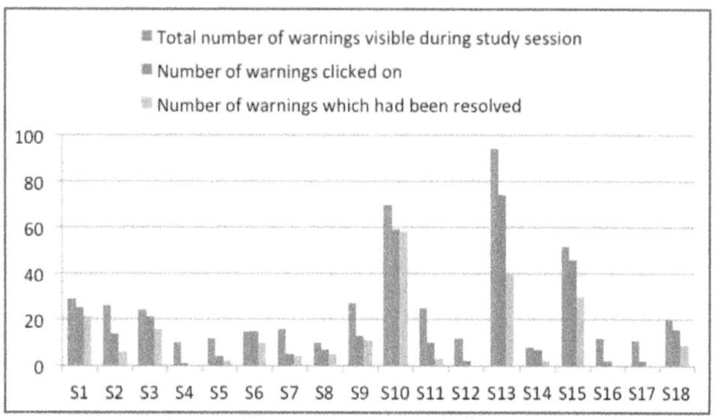

Figure 6. Metrics about warnings from students

We also examined their interaction with explanations. Among the 18 participants, 17 of them had input validation warnings and output encoding warnings. 76% of them clicked the ReadMore option and read the explanation page of input validation for an average of three minutes and 30 seconds, while 88% read the explanation page of output encoding for an average of two minutes and 43 seconds. 10 students had dynamic SQL statement warnings, and 80% of them clicked the ReadMore option to read the explanation for an average of three minutes and 47 seconds. Thus, not only did students click on the warnings, most students did spend several minutes reading explanations to learn more about the warnings.

For input validation and output encoding, ASIDE provides automatic code generation fixes, but for dynamic SQL statements, ASIDE only provides warnings and explanations. Students must then manually modify the dynamic SQL statement to a prepared SQL statement. 60% of the students who had this warning successfully wrote prepared statements after reading the explanation. This result is particularly notable because the course lectures, examples, and textbook only provided dynamic SQL statement examples. Thus, even a short exposure to ASIDE did result in a successful change in practice beyond merely automatically generating code.

One critical problem we discovered is that some students were confused about which "quick fix" rule option to apply for the input validation and output encoding warnings. The rule options were the type of input or type of output, which then impacted which validation or encoding routine was added to their code. Some of them hesitated for quite some time before they applied a rule option from the list, while several others blindly applied one single option for all warnings. This behavior indicates that the descriptions about these input validation and output encoding options are not sufficient, and need to be improved to reduce confusion. The labels of the options may also need to be modified to be more meaningful to students.

5.3 Student Perceptions

Almost all the students reported liking ASIDE as an interactive support tool. They appreciated the warnings as instant reminders for secure programming, and reported that they would neglect those vulnerabilities otherwise. For example, one student stated:

> [S6] *"So when I start coding, I am thinking of these security concepts, but as I progress through the code, I tend to forget it, or I tend to ignore it, or I tend to not understand why I should do that, but this tool actually told me where I can particularly look at, and change the code so that I can mitigate the security problem."*

Most of the students liked the ASIDE explanation Web pages; they thought they were easy to understand and very helpful. One student stated that:

> [S2] *"I think it was pretty good. I liked the explanations, and good examples to back them up. Actually, I got a decent understanding of what it was trying to do."*

More than half of the students responded that ASIDE indeed helped them write more secure code. For example:

> [S2] *"It helped me to look out for these things, because I really didn't know them before at all, so it definitely helped me to write more secure code."*

Students' responses during the interview also indicated that they learned at least a bit of secure programming knowledge. Several mentioned the specific secure programming concepts and terms covered in the warnings explanations. Students also reported that the tool helped them with the post-test, in which they could answer some questions confidently rather than guessing.

> [S3] *"When I did the survey after the session, I could answer what the encoding was doing, while before the session, I had very little knowledge about that, I just marked whatever I thought it was right, but at the end, I could choose the correct options."*

5.4 Limitations

Our study was an observational laboratory study, which has a number of limitations. First, we evaluated our tool with 20 student participants, which is a relatively small sample. The students were also advanced students, mostly graduate students, and ASIDE might be used differently by more novice programmers. The lab environment may have changed the students' behavior. Knowing the focus was on ASIDE, they may have been influenced to spend more time with the tool and be more positive about its use. On the other hand, the students already knew the assignment would not be graded based on the security of the application and there were no real-world security implications, reducing their interest. Despite these limitations, we believe our results provide an initial indication that ASIDE could be a successful learning tool, and provide us feedback as we move forward to evaluations of the longer term impacts.

6. DISCUSSION

Overall, the study results indicate that ASIDE has the potential to be an effective teaching tool. First, students were willing to spend multiple minutes reading the written material, 6:40 minutes on average per student. They did this in the middle of working on assignment functionality, as they encountered and dealt with their errors. None of the students reported that this was annoying or distracting from their primary goal. This is encouraging, and now needs to be investigated outside of a laboratory setting when students are not being directly observed.

Our results also indicate that students became more aware of secure programming implications after using ASIDE. Most of the students made strong statements about how they would not have thought about the security vulnerabilities otherwise during the interview. Students also did increase their test scores, indicating some learning of secure programming content. The increase in scores is not large, however. There are several reasons for this. First, the tests were relatively short. Because they were true/false questions, with guessing, expected scores would still be around 50%. A number of students also did not see the dynamic SQL statement errors, so those questions would not have been impacted by ASIDE. On the one hand, the post-test followed shortly after reading about secure programming, possibly helping the post-tests. On the other hand, the brief exposure may not have been significant enough to remember later. Finally, interview results indicated that some students felt more confident in the post-test. In retrospect, we could have also asked about their confidence in their answers to see where they felt like they were guessing and where they felt like they were not.

Another positive indication is that students did perform secure programming practices. They resolved about half the errors in their code. And 6 students manually changed their SQL statements to the secure prepared statements solely based on ASIDE. We did not follow up with these students to determine if they continued this practice after the session. This will be important as we begin to study longer-term behaviors and impacts of using ASIDE. Our goal is that ASIDE continues to reinforce secure practices even once students have learned them.

We can also draw some lessons for further improvements to ASIDE. First, we need to provide better explanations and examples on which rule options to apply for the warnings. The students also indicated that they would like the explanations to have more dynamic content, based on the context of the code that prompted the warning. The explanations we developed had annotated code examples. Unfortunately, we included these in the pages as images. Multiple students requested code examples that they could cut and paste directly into their code to further modify. We are actively working on these improvements in preparing for longer-term studies.

7. CONCLUSION AND FUTURE WORK

Educating current and future developers in secure programming techniques and practices is critical yet challenging. We believe our approach can help integrate security training across a computing curriculum, providing both knowledge and reinforcement of secure programming skills to students at all levels. Our initial evaluation provides positive evidence that such a programming tool can provide a learning opportunity and increase awareness and knowledge. Yet while this initial study is promising, many more questions need to be answered about the long-term effectiveness of a tool such as ASIDE. For example, do students improve and retain their awareness and knowledge over time? Do students become habituated to the warnings and eventually start to ignore them? When do they read the explanations, and do they return to read throughout a course? Will students be willing to perform secure programming practices if there is no impact on assignment grades?

Our long-term goal is to examine whether ASIDE can support students awareness and learning of secure programming throughout a curriculum. This will require adapting ASIDE to the needs of students from CS1 up to the advanced class our current prototype supports. We believe that in many cases the conceptual issues will be similar, such as to make sure that input is of the format and within the bounds of what is expected. However, the explanations and code examples provided and any code that is generated will need to be change based on the level of the student and course. We are currently adapting ASIDE for use in additional courses, and will be examining the educational impacts of its use across a number of courses and students.

8. ACKNOWLEDGEMENTS

We would like to thank all participants for their time. We thank Erik Northrop and Jing Xie for their assistance in conducting the user study, as well as Joel Kerr and Emmanuel Bello-Ogunu. This work is funded by NSF Grants #1044745 and #501562.

9. REFERENCES

[1] Azadegan, S. and O'Leary, M. 2006. Incorporating Security Concepts into First Course. *International Workshop on Informatics Education: Bridging the University/Industry Gap*, Santiago, Chile.

[2] Chu, B., Stranathan, W., Cody, J., Peterson, J., Wenner, A. and Yu, H. 2009. Teaching Secure Software Development. In *Proceedings of the 13th Colloquium for Information Systems Security Education,* Fairbanks, AK.

[3] Graff, M. and Wyk, K. R. 2003. *Secure Coding: Principles and Practices*, O'Reilly, Sebastopol, CA.

[4] Howard, M. and LeBlanc, D. 2003. *Writing Secure Code*. Microsoft Press, Redmond, WA.

[5] Howard, M. and Lipner, S. 2006. *The Security Development Lifecycle*. Microsoft Press, Redmond, WA.

[6] Irvine, C. E., Chin, S. and Frincke, D. 1998. Integrating Security into the Curriculum, *IEEE Computer* (Dec. 1998), 25-30.

[7] Lipford, H.R., Xie, J., Stranathan, W., Oakley, D., and Chu, B. 2010. The Impact of a Structured Application Framework on Web Application Security. In *Proceedings of the 14th Colloquium for Information Systems Security Education,* Baltimore, MD.

[8] McGraw Gary. 2006. *Software Security: Building Security In*. Addison-Wesley Professional, Boston, MA.

[9] Nance, K. 2009. Teach Them When They Aren't Looking: Introducing Security in CS1. *IEEE Security and Privacy*. 7, 5 (September 2009), 53-55.

[10] Oracle.com 2012. Secure Coding Guidelines for the Java Programming Language, Version 4.0. Retrieved September 5, 2012 from http://www.oracle.com/technetwork/java/seccodeguide-139067.html

[11] OWASP.org 2010. OWASP ESAPI. Retrieved September 5, 2012 from https://www.owasp.org/index.php/Category:OWASP_Enterprise_Security_API

[12] Perrone, L. F., Aburdene, M. and Meng, X. 2006. Approaches to undergraduate instruction in computer security. In *Proceedings of the 2006 American Society for Engineering Education Annual Conference and Exhibition,* Portland, OR.

[13] SANS Institute 2008. The SANS Awards for Finding Coding Books with Secure programming Flaws. Retrieved February 16, 2008 from http://www.sans-ssi.org/resources/Winners_of_insecure_coding_contest_20080721.pdf

[14] Seacord, R. C. 2008. *CERT C Secure Coding Standards*. Addison-Wesley Professional, Boston, MA.

[15] Taylor, B. and Azadegan, S. 2006. Threading Secure Coding Principles and Risk Analysis into the Undergraduate Computer Science and Information Systems Curriculum. In *Proceedings of Information Security Curriculum Development Conference,* Kennesaw, GA.

[16] Taylor, B. and Azadegan, S. 2007. Using Security Checklists and Scorecards in CS Curriculum. In *Proceedings of the National Colloquium for Information Systems Security Education,* Boston, MA.

[17] Taylor, B. and Azadegan, S. 2008. Moving beyond security tracks: integrating security in CS0 and CS1. In *Proceedings of the 39th SIGCSE technical symposium on Computer Science Education*, Vancouver, Canada.

[18] US Department of Homeland Security 2007. Software Assurance: A Curriculum Guide to the Common Body of Knowledge to Produce, Acquire, and Sustain Secure Software.

[19] Xie, J., Chu, B., and Lipford, H. R. 2011. ASIDE: IDE Support for Web Application Security. In *Proceedings of the 27th Annual Computer Security Applications Conference,* Orlando, FL.

[20] Xie, J., Lipford, H. R., and Chu, B. 2012. Evaluating interactive support for secure programming. In *Proceedings of the 2012 ACM Annual Conference on Human Factors in Computing Systems,* Austin, TX.

A Case for Course Capstone Projects in CS1

Saquib Razak
Carnegie Mellon University
Doha, Qatar
srazak@cmu.edu

ABSTRACT

Research shows that domain mastery requires three phases: acquiring core component skills, practicing integrating these skills, and then applying these skills to solve real-world problems. Although achieving domain mastery is the overall goal of the Computer Science (CS) curriculum, I will make the case that it is important to expose students to all three phases of learning in the first programming course. Having a mini-capstone project on a relevant problem gives the students the deep understanding of why these core components are needed and how they integrate as the students are learning them. In the process, working with a real application excites the students about computer science and can provide them with the confidence to engage in more challenging projects. This paper reports on an experiment where students implement a vehicle license plate number recognition project. Initial results from this experiment indicate that students who worked on the project perform better in the course learning objectives.

Categories and Subject Descriptors

K.3.2 [**Computers and Education**]: Computer and Information Science Education

General Terms

Algorithms, Experimentation

Keywords

Capstone project, CS1, License Plate Number Detection

1. INTRODUCTION

Most Computer Science programs have an Introduction to Programming course where students with little or no programming background learn the basic building blocks of a programming language. The goal of such a course is to have students master the basic programming constructs like variables, sequences, conditionals, loops, arrays, etc. and start students on the path towards logical thinking and problem-solving techniques.

Research shows that to master a skill, students require three levels of training: acquiring component skills, practicing integrating these skills, and then applying these skills to solve real-world problems [1]. In programming, these steps would include teaching students the individual structures and building blocks of a programming language (variables, loops, arrays, etc.), combining a few of these building blocks to demonstrate their integration to solve simple toy problems, and then using all the tools to solve a real world computational problem. Although, most introductory programming courses closely follow the first two steps, the third step where students apply their knowledge to solve real world problems is usually left for courses later in the curriculum.

In this paper, we present the results of a course capstone project that required students in our Introduction to Programming class, to solve a relevant but complex real-world problem. At first sight, the project seems too advanced for beginning students. However, we provided enough scaffolding to enable the students to focus on problem solving aspects of the project and learn to use the programming structures they have studied in class.

Most of the students who take this course have no previous programming experience. The course is taught in Java and is taken by students enrolled in the Computer Science, Information Systems, and Business Administration majors. The semester this experiment was conducted, this course had an enrollment of 84 students distributed among four sections. Two sections were taught by the author and two other faculty members taught each of the remaining two sections. Since the course is taught in Java, discussion on object-oriented programming is imperative, but not the focus of the course. The learning outcomes of the course focus on students being able to solve computational problems by programming a computer using Java. One of the goals of the course is to have the students master the basic building blocks and structures of a programming language. These concepts include: storing values using variables and arrays, sequential execution, operations and expressions, input and output, conditional executions, repetition using loops, reading files, and modular programming using functions.

The course capstone project, the focus of this paper, required the students to take an image of a license plate and write code that could determine the numbers on the license plates. The students worked through different phases of optical character recognition as discussed later in the paper.

We report on the results of an anonymous survey done in

SIGCSE'13, March 6–9, 2013, Denver, Colorado, USA.

class to evaluate student perception of the project. We also compare the performance of students on the final exam to evaluate the effectiveness of this project in helping students in course learning outcomes. Our results show that students with the project experience performed better on those final exam questions that required problem solving skills.

2. RELATED WORK

This project is not the first attempt at using a course capstone project to augment student learning. DeClue presents a project given to students in an introductory programming course [3]. His goal was to design a project that is relevant to real world software development, challenging and fun, and requires the students to synthesize concepts learned during the whole course. The author reports that overall students felt that they had a better understanding of course concepts after finishing the project.

Stevenson, et al. develop criteria for good real world project design for CS1 courses [9]. They argue that toy problems do not foster greater understanding of programming concepts in students, and that carefully designed problems that solve real-world issues are important aspect of student learning. They present two sample projects: a web crawler that reports on broken links and a spam evaluator.

Sturm, et al. experiment with introducing research based projects at CS1 level [10]. Their goal was to introduce students to research topics in computer science from the very beginning of their computer science program. Their experiment included giving a toy problem to one section of a course and a more sophisticated problem to the second section. The authors report that although most of the students were able to finish the more complex project given to the experimental group, there was no significant difference in students' perception of their experience with research in both sections.

Jimenez-Peris, et al. argue that programming projects should allow the students to practice programming concepts learned in class and at the same time, introduce students to computer science specific concepts that they will come across later in the curriculum [6]. They present projects like asteroids and tetris to introduce object oriented and concurrent programming concepts. Projects on card games developed familiarity with event driven programming and projects on edge enhancement and image compression introduced students to image processing.

Decker, et al. aim to introduce capstone assignments in the CS1 course [2]. They present a single-player game project where physics-related issues were encapsulated in classes and students were required to use the functionality of these classes using an API. The authors report that abstracting away the non-CS details of the project allowed the students to concentrate on the programming-specific part of the project.

Egbert, et al. introduce computer graphics research to the computer science curriculum. They emphasize the effectiveness of students "seeing" the result of applying CS theory to real-world problems [4]. In this process, they integrate computer vision-related modules in the core curriculum where the students work on an image transformation project. The authors report the results of a student survey that show that this project increased student understanding of course material, improved student programming skills, developed critical thinking among students, and changed their perception of computer vision.

In a paper similar to ours, Matzko and Davis present a computer graphics project for CS1 based on a research paper [7]. The project uses a well described and well understood color transformation algorithm presented in a published research paper. The students implement this algorithm as their final project and are able to visualize interesting color transformation on images. The authors, however, do not report on the effectiveness of this approach in increasing student interest in research or a better understanding of course learning outcomes. Similarly, Pattis argues the importance of using real-world problems. He reports on his approach of picking project ideas taken from newspapers, magazines, and advertisements. He presents one such idea where the students implement a cardioverter-defibrillator [8].

Several studies have looked at projects using interactive and visual components to increase student interest and understanding in introductory programming courses [5, 11].

Although the idea of using real-world projects to increase student understanding of basic building blocks of programming is not novel, our work makes the following contributions to this field of study:

- The project outlined in the study uses OCR(Optical Character Recognition) to determine numbers displayed in an image. This rather advanced topic takes normal image manipulation projects to a higher level.
- Delivering the information in the form of a pseudo research paper is a unique idea that encourages students to read scientific material. The accessibility of the paper allows the students to overcome barriers to reading and understanding research papers.
- Evaluating the effectiveness of this project-based approach, based on student performance, is not a well-studied area. Although there are several confounding variables in this study, the overall correlation of higher exam grades for students who worked on the project is striking.

3. THE PROJECT

Our University is located in Doha, Qatar and an image of a license plate with Arabic numerals is shown in Figure 1(a). The actual numbers on the plate are surrounded by extra text and colors. The goal of the project was to isolate each character of the license number and then identify each character. Normal assignments during the semester were one week long, while students were given two weeks to complete this project. The design of the project was governed by the following main principles:

- The project should solve a real world problem. The proposed project definitely meets this criteria since students are exposed to several applications like traffic cameras, automated parking garages, etc. where automated license plate algorithms are used.
- The second goal of the project was to provide something relevant to the students. Since the city where our university is located has extensive use of traffic cameras and most of our student commute to campus, the proposed project had a definite relevance for the students.
- We wanted a project that would be challenging and, hence, rewarding for the students.
- Our course is taught in Java and we have plans to migrate to Python next year. Since a lot of effort is made in designing this project, we wanted a project that would be language-independent in a way such that porting it to a different language would be trivial.

(a) Original Image.

(b) Normalization.

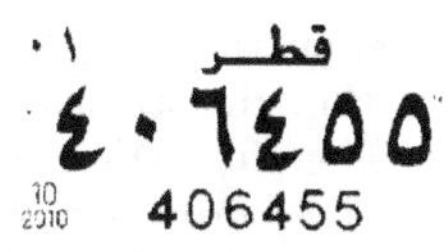

(c) Isolate Text.

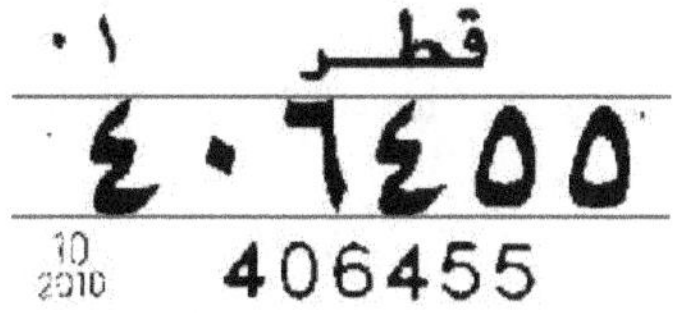

(d) Horizontal Segmentation.

(e) Vertical Segmentation.

Figure 1: Phases of Algorithm Applied to a License Plate.

- We have a large number of students with English as a second language. Students in general do not have an affinity or training in reading technical documents. One of our goals was to design a project that would require the students to read technical material.

Since the students who take this course are first time programmers, requiring them to perform optical image recognition algorithms is quite challenging. In fact, it would be unreasonable to expect all students to read the literature related to optical image recognition, understand the complicated algorithms outlined in these research papers, and then be able to implement these algorithms. In order to reduce this cognitive load on the students and to identify possible pitfalls students can fall into [9], I decided to design an algorithm that was, although not on par with current research, simple enough to produce reasonable results.

Since one of the goals of this project was to encourage students in reading technical material, I decided to write my algorithm in the form of a research paper and structure it as a regular conference paper with abstract, introduction, related work, background, and conclusions sections. The students were then asked to implement the algorithms outlined in the paper[1]. As section 3.1 will demonstrate, algorithms for different phases of the project were given in decreasing details in order to incite student creativity.

The students were also given a library that provided methods for image manipulation. More specifically, the library allowed the students to load an image from a bitmap file as an array of pixels, find height and width of the image, read and write individual pixels, and write the array of pixels to a file. The students used the library to read pixels from a bitmap file into an array. Students worked with this array of pixels for the implementation of the algorithms. The library code provided the students with means of displaying the current state of the image on the screen so they could check the progress of their algorithms. For example, once the students modified the array to change color of each pixel to black-and-white, they could update the image with this new data and view the updated image. When we transition to Python, we will only need to provide a new Python library for image manipulation and the same paper can then be used for a similar project in the new course. This provided the least amount of effort for project reuse with some sense of language independence.

[1]Interested readers can refer to the paper at `http://www.qatar.cmu.edu/~srazak/courses/15112-f12/hw/LicenseDetection.pdf`

3.1 Algorithms

Optical Character Recognition (OCR) is a mature field in computer science, where handwritten or printed text is translated into a string that is usable by a computer. Many existing algorithms isolate individual characters from within a document and then recognize each isolated character. Using OCR to detect the license plates of moving vehicles is also becoming widespread. The following four steps describe the process of automated license plate recognition:

3.1.1 Plate Localization and Orientation

This step involves: finding and isolating the license plate in the picture, compensating for the skew of the image and adjusting the dimensions to the required size. When the traffic cameras take a picture of a moving vehicle, often the license plate is embedded as part of the image. The license plate then needs to be extracted and isolated in order to avoid unnecessary noise in the image being processed. The project assumed that these steps of OCR have already been done and students already have an extracted image. The students were responsible for handling different sizes for license plates. This was explicitly spelled out in the research paper given as requirements for the project.

3.1.2 Normalization

The normalization phase involves adjusting the brightness and contrast of the image. This step required the students to convert the color image to black and white. This algorithm was given in the research paper as detailed text and required students to iterate through each row and each column of each row using nested loops. For each pixel, if the average of the RGB values was above a certain threshold, the pixel was changed to black; otherwise, the pixel was changed to white. This algorithm exercised loops, conditionals, arithmetic expressions, and methods. Figure 1(b) shows the license plate after the normalization phase. This part of the project accounted for 10% of the grade.

3.1.3 Character Segmentation

This phase finds the individual characters on the plates. Once the characters have been segmented, individual characters are processed to determine their value. This phase requires three main steps: the first requires the students to remove any extra information that might hinder the second and third steps. For this, the students had to remove the border around the license plate. Figure 1(c) shows the original license plate with the border removed. This algorithm was given in the paper as detailed text and exercised counting loops, conditional loops, conditional execution, and functional decomposition. This step accounted for 25 points on the project

The second step (Horizontal Segmentation) required horizontally localizing the group of characters that represent license number. At this stage, there are four horizontal blobs of black pixels that are still visible in the image as shown in Figure 1(d). A blob is defined as any consecutive rows where at least one pixel is black. Figure 1(d) shows that this particular plate has three horizontal blobs. The biggest blob happens to be the area where the license number is located. The algorithm, given in the paper as pseudo-code, required the students to identify all the blobs and isolate the biggest one. This required students to practice loops, finding maximum of a sequence of values, and storing multiple values using arrays. Horizontal segmentation was worth 25 points in the project.

The third step (Vertical Segmentation) isolated each character from the horizontally segmented section of the license plate. This algorithm was similar to horizontal segmentation but required students to iterate only those rows that were part of the maximum blob identified during horizontal segmentation. The algorithm stored the start and end of each character within this horizontal segment and required the students to use arrays since there could be a variable number of characters on each plate. Figure 1(e) shows the image of the license plate after vertical segmentation where all digits have been isolated. Students finishing this part successfully could receive a total of 85 points (25 points for this step). Completing the project up to this point gave the students a solid B.

3.1.4 Character Recognition

This phase takes a single character and determines its value. The algorithm for this part was briefly described in the paper but the students had to use their own creativity to find the exact solution. The algorithm used two stages: the first stage is called feature extraction, where the unique features of each digit are isolated and recorded. The second stage uses statistical analysis to compare these extracted features with all possible digits and predict the digit based on the best match.

The *Feature Extraction* stage requires that each digit be divided into four quadrants. Figure 2 shows the image of digit three segmented and then divided in four quadrants. The students then calculate the ratio of black and white pixels for each quadrant. In *Statistical Analysis* stage, the students then compare the differences between these calculated ratios with those provided in the paper for each possible digit or letter. The algorithm then determines the digit that has the least difference in each quadrant. This section accounted for 15 points.

4. EVALUATION

The goal of the Introduction to Programming course is to prepare students to analyze computation problems, design a solution, and be able to implement the solution by programming a computer. The project described in this paper

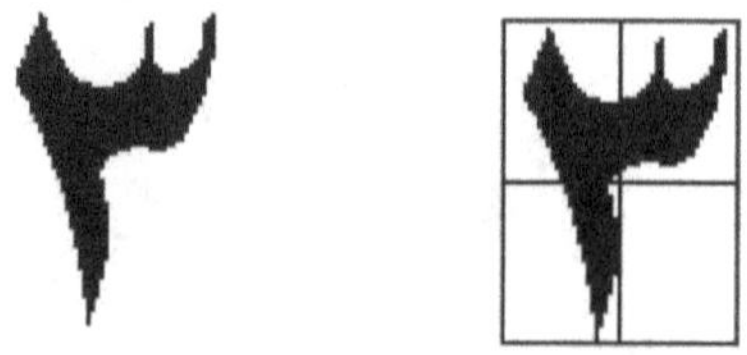

Figure 2: The digit "3" divided in four quadrants.

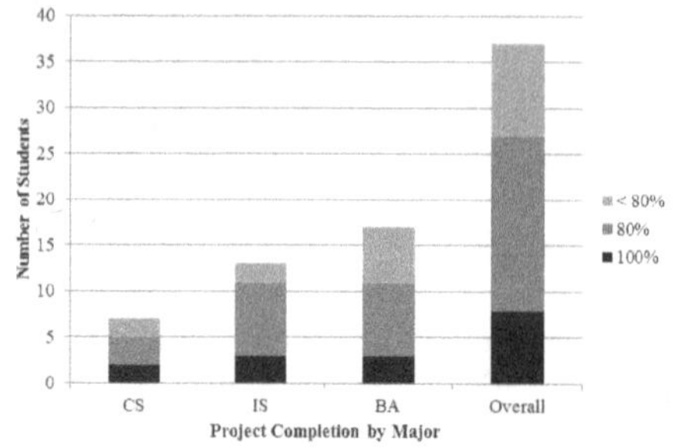

Figure 3: Students who completed the project.

was used as an experiment to improve student understanding of materials taught in the class. It is important for an evaluation of this experiment to measure the level of success (or failure) in achieving the overall goals of the course. This section presents the results of evaluating the level to which the design goals of the project were achieved, as well as the effect of the project on student performance in course learning outcomes.

4.1 Project Evaluation

This sections shows results of evaluating the success in achieving the design goals of the project. This evaluation is not the measure of student success in course goals (see section 4.2), but rather a measure of student perception of the project.

The data for this evaluation was obtained by an anonymous survey that was conducted during class. The survey asked multiple choice questions about how successful the students were in completing the project and their perception on the effect of the project in the learning goals of the course. The survey was conducted after the students submitted the project but before the project was graded.

This course had four sections, two of which were taught by the author and the other two which were taught by two other professors. There were 41 students in the two sections taught by the author. For the sake of simplicity, we will call this group the experimental group. There were 43 students in the other two sections combined which we will call the control group. The survey was only conducted by the students in experimental group . 37 out of 41 students (90%) completed the survey.

Figure 3 shows the number of students who were able to finish the project, segregated into majors. Eighty percent completion refers to those students who were able to complete vertical segmentation but could not finish the character recognition part. It is encouraging to see that a large number of students were able to finish 80 percent of the project. Figure 4 shows the number of students who felt that the project helped them better understand the concepts that were central to the course. It is interesting to note that most of the business students did not feel that the project helped

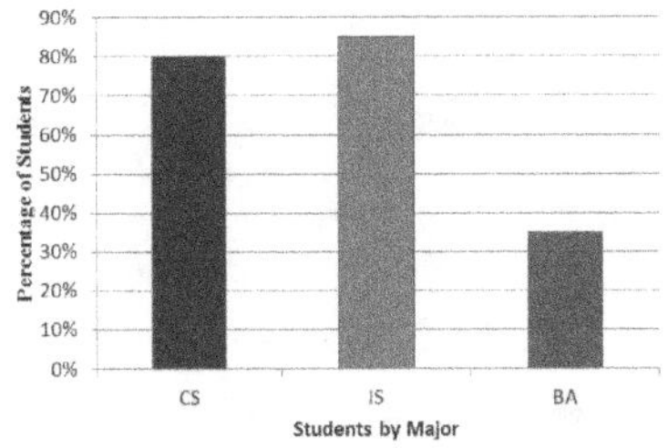

Figure 4: Students who felt project was useful.

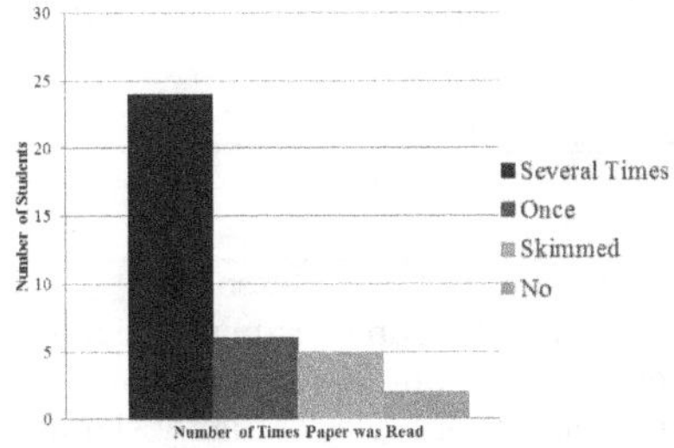

Figure 5: Students who read the paper.

them in understanding course material. A gut reaction for this data would be to conclude that Business students do not have the affinity for programming and hence do not take the project or course as seriously as Computer Science or Information Systems students. After working closely with these students, I feel that this conclusion would be faulty and a more accurate explanation could be that the theme of the project was more relevant to Computer Science, while the Business students failed to see its relevance to their program of study. If I had picked a project that had a more business background, I believe the Business students would have felt more comfortable with the project. I am planning on designing more business-oriented project at the same level of difficulty for future semesters to confirm this conclusion.

As I mentioned in section 3, one of the goals of the project was to train students in scientific reading. As can be seen in figure 5, a majority of students read the paper several times.

As the results of the survey show, the project was useful in helping students understand the course material and encouraged the students to read the research paper. There is still, however, a question mark on the participation of Business Administration students in the project.

4.2 Student Assessment

The second part of our assessment was to evaluate student learning. As mentioned earlier, this course was divided into four sections taught by three different faculty members. This project was only given to the students in author's sections while the other two sections were given more traditional assignments. This automatically created a control group and an experimental group. There was an equal distribution of students in each section, both in terms of number of students as well as their majors. There is no self-selection factor since these are freshmen students who do not get to choose their sections and are placed in the sections by the registrar alphabetically. This ensures that each section has the same number of students from each major.

To assess the effect of this project on student learning, I took the grades for the final exam of the course and studied

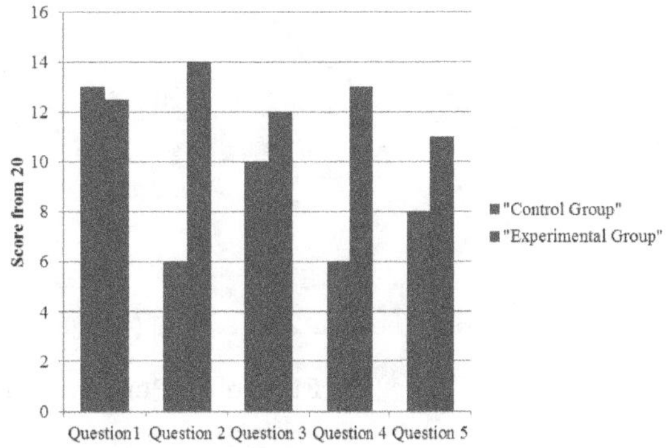

Figure 6: Median scores for two groups.

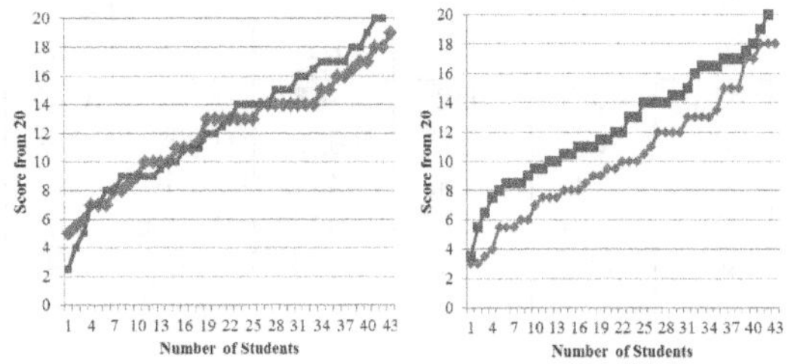

(a) Question 1. (b) Question 3.

Figure 7: Performance in Java Related Questions.

student performance on each question of the exam. This is a common exam taken by all students, and each faculty graded one or two questions for all students. Hence, there is no exam difficulty level or grading bias in the final exam scores. The final exam consisted of five questions and each question was worth 20 points. The author was not involved in setting any questions for the exam and only graded Question 3 from the final exam for all students in the course.

Question 1 and Question 3 were language-related questions, testing students grasp of the Java language and object-oriented paradigm. Question 2 was a problem solving question in Object Oriented Design, while questions 4 and 5 were purely problem-solving questions where the students were given a word problem and were asked to design and implement a solution in Java. The exam was a closed-book, paper based exam. Figure 6 shows the median scores for both groups for each question. The graph shows that the mean student performance for questions 1 and 3 was comparable for both groups but there was considerable difference in questions 2, 4, and 5. The experimental group performed better on questions that involved problem solving while performance in Java syntax related questions was comparable between the two groups.

Mean values of student scores may not properly represent the distribution of these scores. Figures 7(a), 7(b), 8(a), 8(b), and 8(c) show the cumulative distribution function (cdf) of student scores for both groups for each of the five questions. The x-axis shows the cumulative number of students while the y-axis shows the grade. Looking at a single point (x1,y1) on the graph for one group means that x1 number of students had a grade of y1 or lower.

Analyzing the grades for question 2 closely, we see that more than half the class (around 22 students) had a grade of 13 or better in the experimental group. Only 6 students in the control group had a grade of 13 or higher. On question 4, half the experimental group had a grade of at least 12

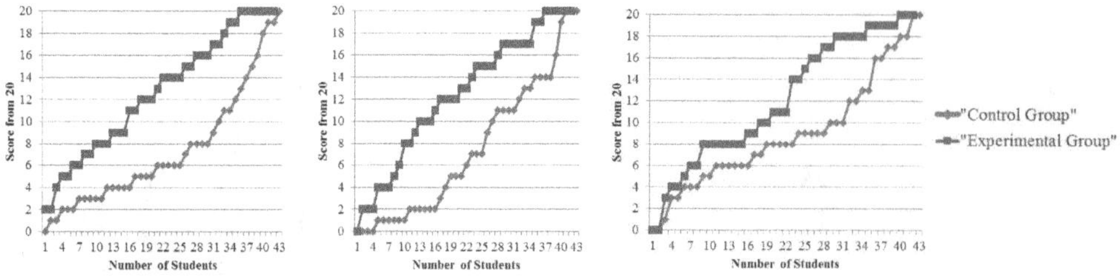

(a) Question 2. (b) Question 4. (c) Question 5.

Figure 8: Performance in Problem Solving Questions.

Table 1: Mann-Whitney Test Results for Grades ($n_{control} = 43, n_{experimental} = 41$)

	Mean Rank		U	P1	P2	z	Evaluation
	Ctrl.	Exp.					
Q1	41.3	43.7	932	0.65	0.32	0.45	The two samples are not significantly different.
Q2	32	543.5	1331	0.0001	0.0001	0.40	The difference between the two samples is highly significant.
Q3	36.3	49	1150	0.008	0.016	2.4	The difference between the two samples is marginally significant.
Q4	33.5	51.9	1267.5	0.0003	0.0006	3.45	The difference between the two samples is highly significant.
Q5	36.6	50.4	1146.5	.009	.02	2.37	The difference between the two samples is marginally significant.

while the control group had only 9 students at this level. Question 5 shows similar performance for both groups.

Table 1 shows the results of running a Mann-Whitney test on the exam score data where P1 stands for p-value one-tailed test and P2 stands for two-tailed test. For questions 1 and 3, the two groups of students have very similar grade distributions. The Mann-Whitney results show that the results for questions 2 and 4 are highly significant.

This evaluation shows that students who did the project performed well on questions that required problem-solving and coding skills. This experiment has several confounding variables. The two groups were taught by different instructors, and teaching style definitely affects student learning. Students did different assignments during the course of the semester. Although each homework exercised similar concepts, nonetheless their effects cannot be easily disregarded. In order to understand the effects of these confounding variables, we plan on doing a longitudinal study with this cohort at the end of their sophomore and junior years. We plan on conducting surveys and focus groups to study the effect of this project on their approach to learning.

5. CONCLUSIONS

This paper presents the results of an experiment conducted in an Introduction to Programming class where students were required to read a research paper and implement the algorithm presented in the paper. The algorithm presented the students with a solution to a real-world problem that is relevant to the students' every-day life. Besides being relevant and real world, the project's goal was to train students to read scientific material. Our evaluation results indicate that, with the correct level of scaffolding, the students were able to complete a project that initially seemed out of scope of their skill set. Although there is no definitive proof that the project did indeed improve student performance, there are clear indicators that point towards a strong correlation between student participation in the project and their increased skills in answering problem solving questions.

6. REFERENCES

[1] S. Ambrose, M. Bridges, M. DiPietro, M. Lovett, and M. Norman. How learning works: Seven research-based principles for smart teaching. 2010.

[2] A. Decker, S. Haydanek, and C. Egert. When objects collide: abstractions over common physics problems for capstone projects in cs1. *J. Comput. Small Coll.*, 21:12–18, December 2005.

[3] T. DeClue. A comprehensive capstone project in computer science i: getting the (instant) message. *J. Comput. Small Coll.*, 22:56–61, April 2007.

[4] D. Egbert, G. Bebis, M. McIntosh, N. LaTouttette, and A. Mitra. Computer vision research as a teaching tool in cs1. In *Frontiers in Education, 2002. FIE 2002. 32nd Annual*, volume 1, pages T4G–17 - T4G–22 vol.1, nov. 2002.

[5] K. Hunt. Using image processing to teach cs1 and cs2. *SIGCSE Bull.*, 35(4):86–89, Dec. 2003.

[6] R. Jiménez-Peris, S. Khuri, and M. Patiño Martínez. Adding breadth to cs1 and cs2 courses through visual and interactive programming projects. *SIGCSE Bull.*, 31:252–256, March 1999.

[7] S. Matzko and T. Davis. Using graphics research to teach freshman computer science. In *ACM SIGGRAPH 2006 Educators program*, SIGGRAPH '06, New York, NY, USA, 2006. ACM.

[8] R. E. Pattis. A philosophy and example of cs-1 programming projects. *SIGCSE Bull.*, 22(1):34–39, Feb. 1990.

[9] D. E. Stevenson and P. J. Wagner. Developing real-world programming assignments for cs1. *SIGCSE Bull.*, 38:158–162, June 2006.

[10] D. Sturm and S. Zelikovitz. Integrating research projects in cs1. *J. Comput. Small Coll.*, 25:55–59, 2010.

[11] R. Wicentowski and T. Newhall. Using image processing projects to teach cs1 topics. *SIGCSE Bull.*, 37(1):287–291, Feb. 2005.

Empirical Evaluation of Periodic Retrospective Assessment

Paul Gestwicki
Computer Science Department
Ball State University
Muncie, Indiana, USA
pvgestwicki@bsu.edu

Brian McNely
Writing, Rhetoric, and Digital Media
University of Kentucky
Lexington, Kentucky, USA
brian.mcnely@uky.edu

ABSTRACT

We propose the periodic retrospective assessment (PRA) technique for reflection-based evaluation of interdisciplinary, team-oriented learning experiences. PRA is characterized by two forms: an assessment at the end of each production iteration, followed by a summative assessment after production has ended. An empirical evaluation of PRA was conducted within a fifteen-week immersive studio—a student-driven, faculty-mentored learning experience in which all learner activity is directed toward a single project, undertaken in collaboration with a community partner. This evaluation reveals that students maintain primary focus on pragmatic production issues during the studio duration, although with secondary yet consistent focus on learning and development. PRA surfaces how the immersive studio produced positive learning outcomes with respect to interdisciplinary collaboration and lifetime learning.

Categories and Subject Descriptors

K.3.2 [**Computers and Education**]: Computer and Information Science Education—*Computer science education*; D.2.9 [**Software Engineering**]: Management—*Programming teams*

Keywords

assessment; evaluation; interdisciplinary; pedagogy; immersive; studio; qualitative; ethnography; Scrum

1. INTRODUCTION

Working in an interdisciplinary team with a community partner can be a high-impact learning experience for an undergraduate student [12], but it is challenging to design appropriate assessments that recognize the embodied, situated, social, and subjective natures of learning. We define *periodic retrospective assessments* (PRA) as a technique for assessing such learning experiences. This technique is designed to foster reflective practice [19], which helps a community of practice—comprising students, faculty, and external partners—to identify how and what it is learning. In this way, PRA is designed to improve metacognition and to provide affordances for intervention.

PRA is inspired by the Sprint Retrospectives of Scrum [20], and we have used this technique informally in several courses. An empirical evaluation of PRA was conducted as part of a major qualitative study in Spring 2012, in conjunction with an immersive learning seminar at the Virginia B. Ball Center for Creative Inquiry (VBC) at Ball State University. The overall goal of this study was to understand the impact of immersive learning on undergraduates, and so to understand the study, one must understand immersive learning.

The VBC defines and promotes "immersive learning" as a particular packaging of high-impact learning practices [15]. Specifically, an immersive learning experience is one that: carries academic credit; is student-driven and faculty mentored; generates a product; involves a team working on an interdisciplinary problem; involves community partners; focuses on student learning outcomes; and helps students define a career path or otherwise make connections to industry. We further define the *immersive studio* as an immersive learning experience in which the students are engaged solely in authentic inquiry-based learning experiences [6]. The immersive studio removes the accidental elements of education—such as tests, quizzes, and exams—in favor of authentic knowledge work within a community of practice [19, 23]. The word "studio" is carefully chosen to evoke a creative and collaborative work environment [cf. 9]. The model implementation of an immersive studio is a multidiscplinary team of students who collaborate to build communal knowledge while cooperating toward common goals, with a faculty mentor embedded as mediator and guide.

In a conventionally-designed learning experience, an instructor begins by identifying learning objectives and outcomes, and these drive the rest of the instructional design, including the assessment plan [1]. However, conventional assessment techniques are inadequate for assessing the immersive studio: the students themselves dynamically define the content and structure of the course, and so the syllabus cannot be separated from the community of learners [3]. General learning objectives related to interdisciplinary communication and collaboration can be identified ahead of time, but specific outcomes are too dependent upon the student-driven nature of the immersive studio. Because the syllabus is dynamic, the assessment strategy must be adaptive; because the syllabus is often implicit, the assessment strategy must also surface the values of the learning community.

SIGCSE'13, March 6–9, 2013, Denver, Colorado, USA.

2. RELATED WORK

The immersive studio can be described as a *rhizomatic learning*: the curriculum is communally designed in real time by the community of learners, and that knowledge is negotiated by this community [3]. Sharples et al. [21] identify rhizomatic learning as a pedagogic approach with potentially high impact. We note that such inquiry-based pedagogic approaches are powerful tools for learning how to learn (LHTL). Black et al. [2] identify the importance of LHTL as well as the challenges of designing authentic assessments for LHTL, or even distinguishing it from what we casually call *learning*.

The immersive studio provides a LHTL environment in which PRA provides assessment for learning [1]. This application of PRA is supported by the ecological approach to learning [8]. The ecological approach recognizes that learning is inseparable from the environment in which it takes place, and specifically that learning "is about becoming attuned to, perceiving, and being able to utilize specific sets of affordances that belong in specific practices" [13, p.2]. Indeed, one must learn to perceive affordances before one can act upon them, and the development of expertise "may involve learning to realize affordances unavailable to non-experts." [8, p.16] This is further supported by Engeström, whose study of expertise recognizes "the broader collaborative practice in which individuals are embedded" as part of a focus on the multivoiced, collectively embedded, and creative natures of expertise [4, p.199].

We make a distinction between *studio learning* [6] and *studio-based learning* (SBL), a successful pedagogic approach in Computer Science education [9]. As in studio-based learning, studio learning relies upon the creation of artifacts that represent learning and both formal and informal evaluation of these by experts and peers. Whereas most published implementations of SBL apply it within otherwise conventional higher educational idioms, studio learning is an SBL implementation in which *all* class activities directly support the team's communal objectives.

3. CONTEXT

PRA was formally evaluated within a fifteen-week immersive studio that took place in Spring 2012 and was mentored by Gestwicki. The subjects consisted of thirteen undergraduates who worked with the Children's Museum of Indianapolis to design and develop *Museum Assistant*, an educational video game about museums and collecting [7]. The students and faculty mentor met for eight hours a day, five days a week, in a dedicated space physically separate from the main university campus. The team consisted of eight Computer Science majors, one Music Technology major, one History major, one Visual Communication major, one student with majors in Electronic Art and Animation and Psychology, and one student with majors in Theater and Creative Writing. More than half the team—including all the non-CS majors—had no prior experience with game design and development. Students earned a full-semester's credit (15 credit hours) for their participation in the seminar: each student had a unique articulation of extant courses in which credit was earned, negotiated by the faculty mentor and dependent upon the student's grade level and major.

The first week of the semester was spent on orientation and training. The faculty mentor led the students through a series of scaffolded exercises designed to help the students understand fundamentals of design and interdisciplinary collaboration. The remainder of the semester was organized following principles of Scrum [20], particularly those encouraged by Keith [11] for agile game development. The team used two-week iterations—Scrum's "sprints"—with potentially shippable products created at the end of each of the seven sprints [16]. The final sprints coincided with two public exhibitions of the students' work.

The distinction between *client* and *community partner* is significant for this work. Museum staff provided feedback and guidance to the team, especially within their areas of expertise, but the team defined the essential characteristics of the game. To support this partnership, the faculty mentor took both the Scrum roles of Product Owner and Scrum Master: he articulated the team's designs as user stories while also assisting the team with the Scrum process and removing impediments to progress.

4. RESEARCH METHODS

Implementation of the immersive studio ran parallel to a major ethnographic study of immersive learning that sought empirical answers to a deceptively simple research question: how is immersive learning different than traditional post-secondary learning environments, and how do immersive experiences mediate learning? Ethnography is widely used in studies of human-computer interaction [17], interaction design [10], and computer-supported cooperative work [5], primarily because it is a methodology that facilitates rich understandings of participant experience across multiple forms of data and multiple instances of data collection. We designed a protocol, therefore, that provided our research team with wide-ranging access to the immersive studio—access that would lead to detailed understandings of participant experience. McNely led data collection, while Gestwicki had no access to the data, nor knowledge of participants, until after the semester had ended. Data collection was assisted by three additional field researchers who conducted over 135 collective hours of fieldwork in the immersive studio.

We collected seven forms of data over 83 site observations: fieldnotes and analytic memos (over 170,000 words); audio recordings (45 recordings of meetings, retrospectives, and collaboration sessions); three rounds of semi-structured interviews with each participant; documentary photographs (over 400 items); videos (three items); and most relevant to the present study, participant-produced artifacts (over 150 items, including written documents and images of whiteboard collaborations). Discussion of the full dataset is beyond the scope of this paper. Our analysis is primarily concerned with an important subset of this data: artifacts from each of seven Sprint Retrospective meetings and a final summative assessment meeting. Following Saldaña [18] and Stake [22], these artifacts were analyzed inductively, through a process of descriptive coding. As Saldaña [18] notes, the systematic description and categorization of data is foundational to qualitative inquiry. Through descriptive coding of our reduced dataset, we inductively derived patterns and themes of reflective practice among our participants, patterns which we were able to triangulate across other forms of data—primarily fieldnotes generated during retrospective sessions and the final round of semi-structured interviews that asked participants to reflect on their overall experience.

- Iteration retrospective at the end of each iteration
- Summative retrospective after the studio duration:
  1. Divergent identification of concepts
  2. Convergent selection of critical concepts
  3. Small-group reflection of critical concepts
  4. Studio discussion

Figure 1: PRA Overview

5. PERIODIC RETROSPECTIVE ASSESSMENT

PRA comprises two practices: iteration retrospectives and summative retrospectives. *Iteration retrospectives* occur periodically through the iterative and incremental production cycle, specifically at the end of each iteration. The *summative retrospective* is a single, structured meeting in four phases that occurs after production has completed. An overview is provided in Figure 1, and details of the two practices are provided below, illustrating their implementation with examples from the evaluation context.

5.1 Iteration retrospectives

Iteration retrospectives are formative assessments that occur at the end of each iteration. They highlight and foreground the knowledge generated during the iteration, recognizing that this knowledge is embodied and situated within the community of practice [23]. In Scrum, iteration retrospectives manifest as Sprint Retrospective meetings, the goal of which are for the team "to inspect itself and create a plan for improvements" [20, p.11].

We used two different formats for iteration retrospectives during the evaluation. The first, which we call *positive/negative format*, is a two-part meeting: during the first part, the team discusses what went well during the past sprint, and during the second part, the team discusses areas for improvement. In our study, this format was used for the first and last iteration retrospectives. The second format, used in sprints two through six, we call *start/stop/continue format*: in this format, team members recommend specific practices to start following, stop following, or continue following [11]. Regardless of format, general informal consensus is sought from the team for each articulated, except in cases where the instructor deems it necessary to exercise executive privilege to veto or mandate an item. Items are written publicly (such as on a whiteboard), digitally transcribed, and posted in prominent locations during the following sprint.

5.2 Summative Retrospective

The summative retrospective is a four-phase meeting held after the team's production obligations are completed, and hence after the final iteration retrospective. In the evaluation context, the summative retrospective was held during the final week of the semester—"finals week" for conventional courses. At this point, the project had been accepted by the community partner, the game was published to the Web, and all production activity had ceased.

The first phase of the summative retrospective is a time-boxed meeting during which students are asked to share what they learned. As a student mentions a concept—the articulations of which will vary in size, scope, and eloquence—it is publicly recorded, such as on a whiteboard. Unlike the iteration retrospectives, in which consensus is sought for action items, this phase is an exercise in divergent thinking: clarification may be sought, but discussion is prohibited. Elimination of redundancy may take place at the end of this first phase, although this proved unnecessary within the evaluation context.

The second phase permits convergence on common themes recognized by the team. Students are given a number of votes equal to ten percent of the total number of articulations, which each individual uses to mark the concepts he or she found most important. A student can only vote for an item once, and the definition of "important" is explicitly acknowledged to be subjective. This phase will result in a subset of concepts being highlighted as *critical concepts* for the community of practice. The number of concepts considered for this set depends upon the vote distribution, and our experience indicates ten percent as a reasonable heuristic

In the third phase, the team is divided into small discussion groups for a more intimate reflection on the critical concepts. A particular structure for the small-group reflection is not mandated, as long as each group generates an artifact—such as a list or short essay—that represents key points of their discussion. We note that for multidiscplinary teams, this is an opportunity to group students by discipline. Whereas iteration retrospectives foster articulation of knowledge held within the wider community, the third phase of the summative retrospective can foster disciplinary discourse and embrace the nuanced values of different academic traditions.

Finally, the fourth phase marks a return of the groups to the interdisciplinary whole. The entire studio is reconvened for each group to briefly share the highlights of their discussion. This practice recognizes the primacy of the community of practice to the studio experience, and it also provides the students a final opportunity to contrast personal, disciplinary, and community learning.

6. FINDINGS

The Spring 2012 immersive studio provided a context for formal evaluation of the PRA method of assessment. In this section, we describe the findings, first of the iteration retrospectives, then of the summative retrospectives, with a discussion of their relationship to follow.

6.1 Iteration Retrospectives

The students identified 258 items during the seven iteration retrospectives. Via the inductive coding process [22] described in Section 4, our participant data gave rise to four themes.

Collaboration Much of the students' discussion in iteration retrospectives centered around their own functioning as a team, including team management processes, use of space, communication patterns, information flows, and particular Scrum practices. Some of these items were mundane, such as "Clean and put away your own dishes," while others were deeply reflective, such as "Perseverance through prototyping." The team showed a consistent positive evaluation of using "downtime" for informal teambuilding (specifi-

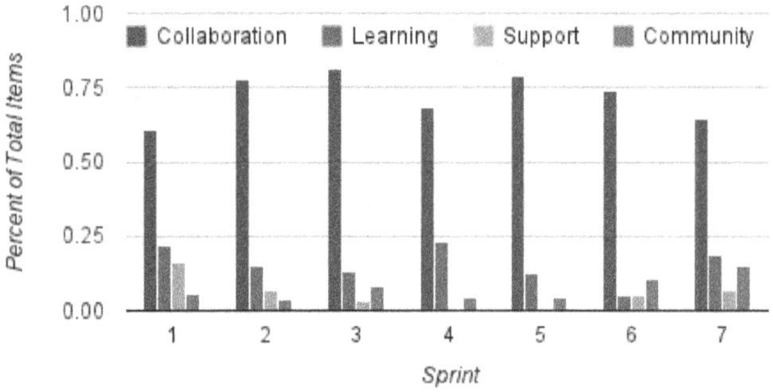

Figure 2: The team's relative focus on each theme during production

cally, Frisbee) and of sharing meals and treats together (specifically, cupcakes and root beer floats).

Learning The students demonstrated explicit awareness of the need to be learning. Early in the semester, there was a focus on game design, which is to be expected given that most of the team had little or no experience in this area. For example, in the first iteration retrospective, they recognized the value of reading the same game design references to build a "common-ground." Other items within this theme related to design process, such as "Learning that 'success' is not just a finished product" (that is, the project also needed to satisfy design constraints). Many of the comments about learning during the middle iterations related to the disciplinary reading groups that were established by the team. Toward the conclusion of the semester, the team articulated the positive value of learning about integration issues such as vertical slicing.

Support This theme dealt with the team's articulation of their external dependencies, including the project budget, faculty mentor, university staff, and the space in which the team worked.

Community This incorporates the team's considerations of the project's formal community sponsor as well as other community connections. External playtesters, for example, were mentioned in every retrospective except the first. In the final iteration retrospective, much of the discussion surrounded public display of the project, particularly the formal project showcase. The team also reflected positively upon how their work compared to similarly-themed projects created by industry professionals and the local game development community.

Figure 2 displays the occurrences of the themes over time, and these data can be used to approximate relative focus during the seven sprints. To be clear, this analysis of the iteration retrospectives is not meant to assess students' affective responses but rather to identify the themes on which their attention is focused. Practical issues of team operation appear to have dominated the students' focus during iteration reflections, which is to be expected of students who have never worked together in an immersive studio. Individual and communal learning was a continuous focus, though to a lesser extent than team operations. The focus on learning dropped in sprints four through six, correlating with the team's intensive focus on finishing the project to the exclusion of all else; it also corresponds with an increase in consideration of community issues, including the community partner, playtesting, and the project showcase. Concern for external team support follows an interesting path, starting high as the team was getting started, dropping to zero for the middle of production, and rising again as the team needed to ship its product and organize its public presentations.

We note that the iteration retrospectives drove discourse and activity during the subsequent sprints. This was evident in the recurrence of ideas and themes across sequential sprints, as the students struggled with difficult concepts and practices. Hence, we have qualitative evidence of the value of iteration retrospectives as formative assessments. In particular, this supports Sprint Retrospectives as a form of "assessment for learning" in Scrum teams [1, 2], confirming the claims of retrospective efficacy [11, 20].

Number of votes	6	5	4	3	2	1	0
Concepts	1	0	4	15	20	30	55

Figure 3: Summative retrospective vote distribution

Item	Votes
How to write clean code	6
Vertical slicing avoids wasted time	4
Learning through failure	4
Value of test-driven development	4
Value of just *doing* something	4

Figure 4: Summative retrospective critical concepts with four or more votes

6.2 Summative Retrospective

In the first phase of the summative retrospective, the team documented 125 critical concepts within the sixty-minute timebox. Each student was given twelve votes, corresponding to ten percent of the total number of concepts, and their distribution is shown in Figure 3. The team identified a convenient partitioning of items based on whether they earned three or fewer votes, or if they earned four or more. The latter were identified as the community's critical concepts, and they are listed in Figure 4.

The first item in Figure 4 is a reference to *Clean Code* [14], the team's development methodology. This is strongly related to the fourth critical concept, as test-driven development is a part of Clean Code. The second critical concept—*vertical slicing*—was introduced to the team by the faculty mentor early in production, although the concept proved elusive to the team. The third and sixth critical concepts in Figure 4 reflect the team's awareness of the danger of analysis paralysis. Building and testing prototypes are critical to the design process, and generally, the more iterations that are performed, the better the result. Through several rounds of paper and digital prototypes, the team developed an understanding and appreciation for the value of learning through prototyping. This phenomenon was described by one of the students during the studio duration as "just *make* something," reflecting the articulation in the critical concept list as "just *doing* something." We note that while iteration retrospectives reveal a community focus on production issues, the summative retrospective represents a transition of focus towards personal growth.

For the third phase of the summative retrospective, the team was divided into three groups. The "Arts and Humanities" group included all of the non-CS majors—none of whom were graduating—while the eight CS majors were divided into two groups of four based on whether they were graduating at the end of the semester. The highlights shared by each group in the fourth phase were transcribed by the faculty mentor, the notes then being shared with the team and collaboratively edited for clarity. In total, there were 446 words in 14 articulated points, and analysis of these reveals that each group had different interpretations of the learning experience, as explained below.

The Arts and Humanities group focused on the metacognitive nature of learning and the unexpected challenges of the semester. Their first point was that "just being able to say what we learned and being able to reflect on it was a fantastic part of the process," an implicit comparison being made to conventional higher educational practices. They pointed out that, although they knew that working on a team would be challenging, "it wasn't until [they] actually worked together for 15 weeks that [they] got to know how hard it really was." They also noted that the votes themselves "reveal how different people think and feel, and there are still some surprises after fifteen weeks together."

The non-graduating Computer Science students contrasted their immersive studio experience to conventional coursework; in fact, four of their five statements begin with the phrase, "In normal classes..." They highlighted how design thinking promotes a different approach than most conventional learning experiences, noting that "In a normal class, you're not meant to fail the first five assignments, but here you are." They were the only group that mentioned grades, acknowledging that grades were usually interpreted as "retribution or punishment for bad work."

The graduating Computer Science students showed more outward focus, potentially corresponding to the fact that all four had interviewed and accepted jobs during the semester. They recognized that despite the trappings of industrial practice, the value of the immersive studio was distinctly academic. They "appreciated this experience because of the 'real-world' situation... [They] could fail without risk of being fired and being homeless." This reflects an understanding of the university as a place for intellectual risks that may be impossible in industry. Where the Arts and Humanities group focused on the challenges of teamwork, the graduating Computer Science group reflected on self-awareness, noting that they "learned more about ourselves and our limitations and abilities and how to work within those."

7. DISCUSSION

PRA revealed that vertical slicing was a particularly difficult concept for the students to learn, and several factors triangulate towards this conclusion. Vertical slicing is absent from all iteration retrospectives despite it having been introduced and recommended by the project mentor throughout production. Both media asset production and source code demonstrate prominent horizontal slicing, which resulted in frustrations being articulated during retrospectives, interviews, and informal meetings.

We found that students in the immersive studio learned one of the most commonly-lauded but difficult to assess outcomes of higher education: preparation for lifetime learning. During iteration retrospectives, the students recognized the value of continuous improvement of personal practices as well as factual knowledge, while simultaneously demonstrating awareness of group learning within a community of practice—indications of learning how to learn [2]. In the summative retrospective, the graduating Computer Science group recognized that they had to take responsibility for personal failings, noting that they "recognize the danger of letting yourself off the hook when balancing quality of work vs. time left." They note that they became lax on elements of the agreed-upon methodology—specifically Clean Code and test-driven development—and that they "should hold [themselves] to higher standard" even in the face of this pressure; this echoes a prominent theme in Martin [14], which was studied by the CS majors' reading group.

A recognition of the challenges of open problems is woven through the periodic retrospective assessment. This is demonstrated in student comments about embracing failure as a learning opportunity and the value of iteration and vertical slicing, as shown in Figure 4. In the summative assessment, the non-graduating Computer Science group observed that "80% is good enough in many regular courses, but insufficient here: it had to be 100%." In the immersive studio, students learn how to approach open problems, and by matching affordances to those of an industrial setting, students are positioned to transfer this knowledge to the workplace. Validating the efficacy of this transfer is an area of future work.

We note that iteration retrospectives and summative retrospectives can be separated as distinct practices. As previously indicated, Scrum's Sprint Retrospectives are iteration retrospectives, and we have demonstrated how academic learning outcomes can be inferred by careful qualitative analysis of the retrospective. However, in our evaluation, the iteration retrospectives are strongly influenced by the pressures of production. Summative retrospectives, as a distinct practice, can be used to evaluate any learning experience in which divergent individual and convergent community perspectives are permitted. Indeed, we have used summative retrospectives informally in several project-oriented courses [6]. While the summative retrospective provides insight that may be aligned more closely with conventional learning objectives, our findings show that combining summative with iteration retrospectives can produce more detailed and nuanced understanding of a learning community.

PRA did not yield the fine-grained, disciplinary learning objectives one would expect to find in a syllabus. For example, students identified UML and C# as important concepts, but not specific parts of UML or features of C#; in the absence of these, one would have to look at additional artifacts such as diagrams and source code to determine whether specific concepts have been demonstrated. Individual interview data collected as part of the study does reveal more details about individual student accomplishment, but that is beyond the scope of the periodic retrospective assessments. Similarly, the iteration and summative retrospectives surfaced few non-CS concepts, despite their being raised in other parts of the study; one explanation for this is that a student who is the only representative of a discipline may not be inclined to speak up during the retrospective.

We introduced the context of the study as an immersive studio, where immersive learning is defined by seven criteria. Six of these seven criteria are represented throughout the PRA, the only absentee being that it was a credited learning experience. The lone mention of grades in the summative retrospective of the non-graduating CS group is the only indicator of this criterion. The implication is clear: one could expect that, outside of a credit-bearing university environment, PRA might function in a similar manner. Empirical software engineering researchers might consider instrumenting a Scrum team with end-of-project summative assessments and evaluating whether this leads to improved productivity as individuals develop better reflective practice.

Finally, we note that although the immersive studio framed our empirical study of PRA, this assessment technique is not bound to immersive learning. The anecdotal success of PRA outside of immersive learning experiences resonates with the specific findings of this study. Identifying the differences of these contexts is an area of future work.

8. ACKNOWLEDGMENTS

Museum Assistant was developed by Root Beer Float Studio [7]. The immersive studio was hosted by the Virginia B. Ball Center for Creative Inquiry, which is funded by the Edmund F. and Virginia B. Ball Foundation. Evaluation was supported through a Ball State University Provost's discretionary research grant. We are grateful to Anne Burke and Bridget Gelms for their assistance in data collection.

References

[1] P. Black and D. Wiliam. Inside the black box: Raising standards through classroom assessment. *Phi Delta Kappan*, 80(2):139–148, 1988.

[2] P. Black, R. McCormick, M. James, and D. Pedder. Learning how to learn and assessment for learning: a theoretical inquiry. *Research Papers in Education*, 12 (2):119–132, 2006.

[3] D. Cormier. Rhizomatic education: Community as curriculum. *Innovate: Journal of Online Education*, 4 (5), 2008.

[4] Y. Engeström. The tensions of judging: Handling cases of driving under the influence in Finland and California. In Y. Engeström and D. Middleton, editors, *Cognition and Communication at work*, pages 199–232. Cambridge University Press, Cambridge, 1996.

[5] Y. Engeström and D. Middleton. *Cognition and communication at work.* Cambridge University Press, Cambridge, 1996.

[6] P. Gestwicki. The entity system architecture and its application in an undergraduate game development studio. In *Proceedings of the International Conference on the Foundations of Digital Games*, FDG '12, pages 73–80, New York, NY, USA, 2012. ACM.

[7] P. Gestwicki and B. McNely. A case study of a five-step design thinking process in educational museum game design. In *Proceedings of Meaningful Play*, 2012. To be published.

[8] E. J. Gibson and A. D. Pick. *An Ecological Approach to Perceptual Learning and Development.* Oxford University Press, New York, 2003.

[9] C. D. Hundhausen, N. H. Narayanan, and M. E. Crosby. Exploring studio-based instructional models for computing education. In *Proceedings of the 39th SIGCSE technical symposium on Computer science education*, SIGCSE '08, pages 392–396, New York, NY, USA, 2008. ACM.

[10] V. Kaptelinin and B. A. Nardi. *Acting with technology: Activity theory and interaction design.* MIT Press, Cambridge, MA, 2006.

[11] C. Keith. *Agile Game Development with Scrum.* Addison–Wesley, Boston, MA, 2010.

[12] G. D. Kuh, J. Kinzie, J. H. Schuh, and E. J. Whitt. *Student Success in College: Creating Conditions that Matter.* Jossey–Bass, San Francisco, CA, 2010.

[13] J. Linderoth. Beyond the digital divide: An ecological approach to gameplay. In C. Marinka, K. Helen, and W. Annika, editors, *Think Design Play: The fifth international conference of the Digital Research Association (DIGRA)*, page 15, Hilversum, the Netherlands, September 2011. DiGRA/Utrecht School of the Arts.

[14] R. C. Martin. *Clean Code: A Handbook of Agile Software Craftsmanship.* Prentice Hall, Upper Saddle River, NJ, 2008.

[15] J. McKillip. Transformative undergraduate research: Students as the authors of and authorities on their own education. *CUR Quarterly*, 30(2):10–15, 2009.

[16] B. J. McNely, P. Gestwicki, A. Burke, and B. Gelms. Articulating everyday actions: an activity theoretical approach to scrum. In *Proceedings of the 30th ACM international conference on Design of communication*, SIGDOC '12, pages 95–104, New York, NY, USA, 2012. ACM.

[17] B. A. Nardi. *Context and Consciousness: Activity Theory and Human-Computer Interaction.* MIT Press, Cambridge, MA, 1996.

[18] J. Saldaña. *The Coding Manual for Qualitative Researchers.* Sage Publications Ltd, 2009.

[19] D. Schon. *The Reflective Practitioner: How Professionals Think in Action.* Basic Books, New York, 1983.

[20] K. Schwaber and J. Sutherland. *The Scrum Guide: The Definitive Guide to Scrum: The Rules of the Game.* 2011. Retrieved November 1, 2012, from http://scrum.org/Scrum-Guides.

[21] M. Sharples, P. McAndrew, M. Weller, R. Ferguson, E. FitzGerald, T. Hirst, Y. Mor, M. Gaved, and D. Whitelock. *Innovating Pedagogy 2012: Open University Innovation Report 1.* The Open University, Milton Keynes, 2012.

[22] R. E. Stake. *Qualitative Research: Studying How Things Work.* The Guilford Press, 2010.

[23] E. Wenger. *Communities of Practice: Learning, Meaning, and Identity.* Cambridge University Press, 1999.

Software Security Testing of an Online Banking System

A Unique Research Experience for Undergraduates and Computer Teachers

Dianxiang Xu
National Center for the Protection of the Financial Infrastructure
Dakota State University
Madison, SD 57042, USA
1-605-256-5694
dianxiang.xu@dsu.edu

ABSTRACT

This paper presents a unique summer project for a group of undergraduate students and high school computer teachers to gain research experiences in the area of cybersecurity. The students and teachers were selected from the participants in the NSF REU and RET programs at the host institution. Through the research on security testing of a real-world online banking system, the students and teachers have not only learned about the cutting-edge security testing techniques, but also made publishable contributions to the research base. The two collaborating graduate assistants served as an immediate role model for the undergraduates and an indirect role model for high school students through the teachers. With the help from the graduate assistants, the students and teachers were able to work effectively toward achieving their research objectives. The internal competition helped the participants get a better sense of achievement and satisfaction. The research experiences also prepared the teachers with the necessary knowledge for introducing cybersecurity topics (e.g., secure programming) into future classroom activity. As such, the project described in this paper provides a model summer program for undergraduate and/or K-12 teachers to gain research experiences.

Categories and Subject Descriptors

D.2.5 [**Testing and debugging**]: Testing tools (e.g., data generators, coverage testing). D.4.6 [**Security and protection**]: Access Controls. K.6.5 [**Security and protection**]: Authentication, Unauthorized access.

Keywords

Cybersecurity, security testing, software testing, access control, security attacks, mutation analysis.

1. INTRODUCTION

The widespread applications of Internet-based information systems have raised serious concerns about cybersecurity. Cybersecurity involves policies, procedures, methods, and techniques that protect and defend information and information systems by ensuring availability, integrity, authentication, confidentiality and non-repudiation. The cybersecurity workforce is key to assuring adequacy of security measures to protect and defend its information and information systems. According to the 2010 white paper of the CSIS commission on cybersecurity for the 44th Presidency [7], the United States is facing "a human capital crisis in cybersecurity." The U.S. Bureau of Labor statistics projects "there will be over 155,000 job openings for individuals with these important (cybersecurity) skills between now and 2018 - the 2nd fastest job growth rate in the United States" [1]. To strengthen the future cybersecurity environment, we need to motivate our young generations to develop a career interest in this important area. In particular, we need high quality educators to expand cybersecurity education at early age. Career planning and preparation during high school and postsecondary studies have an important impact on next generation workforce.

To meet the educational needs of cybersecurity, the author, in collaboration with his colleagues, has received grants from the US National Science Foundation (NSF) to establish the REU (Research Experiences for Undergraduates) and RET (Research Experiences for Teachers) Sites in Cybersecurity at Dakota State University. As South Dakota's information technology university, DSU is a national Center of Academic Excellence in Information Assurance Research and Education designated by the US National Security Agency and the US Department of Homeland Security. DSU offers undergraduate and graduate degrees in information assurance. In 2009, DSU established the National Center for the Protection of the Financial Infrastructure sponsored by the State of South Dakota, in partnership with Citibank, Wells Fargo, First Premier, the Federal Reserve, FDIC, and DHS. The goal of this center is to address the major security issues within the technical, business, legal and policy contexts of banking and finance through education and research.

In this paper, we present a project that is aligned with the center's mission as well as the objectives of the REU and RET sites. Specifically, the project involved two undergraduate students from the 2012 REU program and four high-school computer teachers from the 2012 RET program. Under the supervision of the faculty mentor (the author) and in collaboration with two graduate assistants, the students and teachers investigated the security testing of a real-world online banking system. They have not only learned about the cutting-edge security testing techniques, but also made contributions to the research base, which resulted in the publication of an international conference paper [13]. The collaborating graduate assistants served as an immediate role model for the undergraduates and an indirect role model for high school students through the teachers. An internal competition was held to help the participants get a better sense of achievement and satisfaction.

SIGCSE '13, March 6–9, 2013, Denver, Colorado, USA.

[1] http://mnc3.advanceitmn.org/

The remainder of this paper is organized as follows. Section 2 gives an introduction to the REU and RET Sites. Section 3 describes the technical background about the research project through which the students and teachers gained the research experiences. Section 4 introduces the project design. Section 5 presents the results of the project. Section 6 concludes this paper.

2. The REU and RET Sites in Cybersecurity

2.1 The REU Site

The REU Site in Cybersecurity is a three-year (2010, 2011, 2012) project that provides a diverse pool of motivated undergraduate students with a competitive research experience in cybersecurity. Each year, the REU site offers a nine-week summer program for nine undergraduate students to develop confidence as researchers and scientists. To assure the diversity of participants, 5-6 students (more than 50%) are selected from other institutions and 3-4 students are from DSU. Recruits are primarily junior or senior undergraduates majoring in computer science, computer and network security, software engineering, information systems, and related areas.

During the eight-week summer program, each student works with a faculty mentor on a carefully designed research project. In the first two weeks, students focus on developing projects. Tutorials and workshops are provided to help students establish necessary background knowledge and learn about how to conduct cybersecurity research. Students also work with their individual advisors, read literature, and design their projects. From week 3 through week 8, students carry out their projects under the supervision of their mentors. They also are required to attend the weekly seminars by faculty and invited industry speakers and report their weekly progress. During week 9, students prepare a written report in the format of an IEEE conference paper and an oral presentation modeled after a computer science conference.

Through the research experiences, the students are expected to improve their ability to formulate and solve a research problem, increase their communication proficiency, and establish a professional relationship with their faculty mentor. Some of them will be motivated to pursue graduate studies.

2.2 The RET Site

The RET Site in Cybersecurity is a three-year (2012, 2013, and 2014) project that provides in-service high school computer teachers across the State of South Dakota with an experience of conducting cutting-edge research in cybersecurity. It offers an eight-week summer program for ten teachers to conduct research with DSU faculty and continue to help them implement research-based activities in their classrooms throughout the subsequent academic year. During the summer program, the teachers are paired up to work with a DSU faculty mentor and his research team (graduate and undergraduate assistants) on a research project. Following the summer program, the teachers continue to develop learning materials for integrating their research experiences into their classroom activity.

Similar to the REU program, the schedule of the RET program consists of three phases: planning, execution, and presentation. In the first two weeks, teachers focus on developing project plans. They are paired up to work with their mentor and group members, read literature, and design their projects. From week 3 through week 7, they carry out their projects under the supervision of their mentor. During week 7, they prepare a written report in the format of an IEEE conference paper, an oral presentation modeled after a computer science conference, and a plan for curriculum development. The summer program also offers a three-credit course *Special Topics in Cybersecurity*. Through the integration of their research experiences and findings into classroom activity in the subsequent academic year, the high school teachers can expose their students to cybersecurity and motivate them to develop a career interest. A benefit for the faculty mentors is that they can disseminate the findings of their research programs to non-traditional audiences (high school teachers) and increase their understanding of high school computer technology education so as to improve their own teaching.

3. SOFTWARE SECURITY TESTING

In this section, we introduce the technical background of the research project. In addition to the basic concepts, we describe the advanced techniques that the students and teachers would learn from the research experience as well as the open research issues to which they could contribute.

Software security is a major source of cybersecurity risks. Many attacks against a company's network come at the application layer. They bypass the security mechanisms at the crypto, protocols and systems layers (e.g., firewall and intrusion detection). While secure coding is important, software security requires a lot more beyond coding [11]. For example, a large portion of the security flaws uncovered during Microsoft's "security push" in 2002 were closely related to design-level problems [4]. Principled use of assurance techniques needs to be considered throughout software development processes. Unfortunately, there is a lack of well-trained workforce for secure software development.

Software testing is a dominant practice for quality assurance of computer software. It aims at finding programming errors by executing a program with test cases, including test inputs and test oracles (i.e., expected results). A test fails if the actual result of its execution is different from its expected result. Software testing is an expensive and time-consuming activity, accounting for 50% or more of the total development costs. To create test cases, there are two basic strategies: black box and white box. The former views the system under test (SUT) as a block box and derives test cases from a requirements specification. The latter creates test cases based on the SUT's implementation (e.g., source or executable code). In this project, we focus on model-based security testing, a black box testing strategy that generates tests from security models (e.g., threat models and access control models).

Software security testing aims at finding vulnerabilities that may be exploited to violate security goals, such as confidentiality, integrity, and availability. Generally, it involves two perspectives: (a) testing whether or not a SUT has enforced its security policies, and (b) testing whether or not a SUT is subject to security attacks. Both are important for security assurance.

3.1 Testing Security Policy

Security policy plays an important role in security systems. For example, an access control policy regulates who can access what resources under what circumstances. It is a fundamental mechanism for preventing malicious or accidental violation of security requirements (e.g., confidentiality and integrity). While the specification of an access control policy can be supported by powerful verification techniques, a correctly specified policy may be implemented incorrectly for various reasons, such as programming errors, omissions, misunderstanding of the policy, and intricate interplay between business logic and access control policy [14]. The defects in an incorrect access control implementation may result in serious security problems, such as unauthorized accesses and escalation of privileges. Therefore, it is important to reveal the potential discrepancy between the policy specification and the actual system implementation.

On the other hand, traditional access control metrics are inadequate for assuring system accountability, which depends on "security procedures being faithfully carried out by computer systems and by human users" [5]. The actions in a security procedure range from administrative operations to business functions. They are often an obligatory part of the humans' job responsibilities. As such, specification and monitoring of obligation policy has recently gained increasing attention [10]. An obligation policy grants access "with strings attached" - access is granted with some obligations, i.e., behavioral constraints. Existing work on obligation policy has focused on policy languages for specifying and monitoring obligation requirements. In a computer software system, however, a correctly specified obligation policy may be implemented incorrectly. Existing work on testing obligation policies takes an implementation-based approach, targets those systems that specify obligation policy as rules in a database or input file, and derives test cases from the rules. In fact, few real-world applications have yet implemented obligations as part of security policy. In this project, we aim at a model-based approach to testing access control with obligatory constraints. It is independent of how the access control and obligation polices are implemented.

3.2 Testing Security Attacks

Security attacks typically result from unintended behaviors or invalid inputs. Testing for security is hard in that it is impossible to test a real-world program against all invalid inputs. Hence, it is highly desirable to develop automated (or partially automated), cost-effective testing techniques for detecting software vulnerabilities. Although existing work has provided useful recipes for specific types of vulnerabilities, more structured and automated approaches to systematic security testing are much needed. To address this issue, we have recently developed a tool-supported approach to automated security test generation with formal threat models [15]. Threat models are represented as Predicate/Transition (PrT) nets in MISTA [12], an automated model-based test generation tool developed by the author and adopted by industry. PrT nets are high-level Petri nets, a well-studied method for modeling and verifying distributed systems. When used for threat modeling, PrT nets are more expressive than attack trees (the most popular yet informal notation for threat modeling) because, for example, they can capture both control flows and data flows and complex attacks with partially ordered actions. Threat models can provide a basis for effective security testing because they describe security threats from the standpoint of how the adversary would attack or exploit a system. This meets the need of security testing to target the "presence of an intelligent adversary bent on breaking the system" [9].

There are a great variety of security attacks, depending on the given application. Testing security attacks in this project focused on SQL injection attacks and cross-site scripting (XSS) attacks. They have been the top security threats against web applications in recent years. Because many web applications make SQL queries to their database according to user-provided inputs, such as user name and password, a SQL injection attack tries to gain unauthorized access to a web application by injecting SQL query/command into user inputs. XSS attacks inject malicious client-site script into web pages viewed by other users so as to gain unauthorized access to the information (e.g., sensitive page content and session cookie) maintained by the browser on the user's behalf.

3.3 Security Mutation

Evaluating the effectiveness of a testing technique is a challenging issue in software testing. Because testing aims at finding bugs, a widely applied evaluation approach is mutation analysis, which creates mutants of a subject program by injecting faults [6]. The faults injected into the mutants mimic the bugs that likely occur in the development process. A mutant is said to be killed if at least one of the tests created by the given testing technique reports a failure. Usually, the percentage of mutants killed by the tests is a good indicator of the testing effectiveness. Key to mutation analysis is the fault model, which is a classification of bugs in the given programming language. Fault models used in traditional mutation testing research are often syntax-oriented and faults are injected by making syntactic changes to a target program or specification, such as modification of && (and) to || (or) in a condition. Obviously, syntactical mutants are unlikely security vulnerabilities because they have not taken the semantics into consideration. To evaluate our approach to automated security testing with formal threat models, we have created security mutants according to the common vulnerabilities of web applications (e.g., SQL injection and XSS) and C++ programs (buffer overflows and logic errors) [15].

Mutation analysis has been applied to the testing of access control and obligation policies. Le Traon et al., [8] created the mutants of role-based access control rules using five types of mutation operators: replacing permission rule with prohibition, replacing prohibition rule with permission, changing role, changing context, and adding a rule. Bertolino et al. [1] proposed a mutation-based approach to testing the PolPA authorization system that is based on the usage control and history-based access control model. The Policy Decision Point (PDP) is tested with the mutants of policy rules created by applying mutation operators to the policy rules. Elrakaiby et al. [2] also proposed a mutation-based approach to testing obligation policy enforcement, where obligation rules are independent of access control rules. In the above work, the access control or obligation policy is specified as rules in a database or input file and the test cases are derived from the rules. The mutants created from the syntax of access control and obligation rules in essence represent data or configuration errors, rather than programming bugs. From the mutation analysis perspective, this project considers both data error and programming bugs.

4. PROJECT DESIGN

In this section, we introduce the objective of the project, the organization of the project team, and the research tasks.

4.1 Objective

The main objective of the project was to provide an opportunity for the selected REU students and RET teachers to gain an experience of conducting cutting-edge research in cybersecurity. Through the experience, the students and teachers will not only learn about the advanced security techniques, but also contribute to the research base. To achieve this objective, the project was motivated by the author's newly developed techniques for threat-model-based security testing and model-based access control testing. These techniques had just been accepted for publication at prestigious venues when this project was first conceived [14] [15].

To make the project more interesting and engaging, a real-world application is critical. It can help researchers better formulate their research problems and evaluate their solutions. This consideration has lead to the adoption of Cyclos (http://project.cyclos.org/), an open source real-world online banking system being used by many organizations and communities all over the world. Using the online banking system is aligned with the goal of another funded project that aims at building a model online banking system as a research infrastructure for information assurance research and education. Banking security affects our daily life. Nowadays, more and more people rely on the Internet and mobile devices to manage financial activities. As the money is stored on and moved around the Internet, the intelligent criminal would migrate from the physical crime to the less dangerous options available online. Although the banks have made constant progress and innovation, the security threats to online banking are even greater. Falk et al. examined the web sites of 214 U.S. financial institutions and found that 76% of them suffered from at least one design flaw [3]. On the other hand, all participants of this project as a banking customer have some basic knowledge about banking and are familiar with Java, the programming language in which Cyclos is implemented. All RET teachers teach Java Programming I, Java Programming II, and AP Java Programming. Most of them also teach web design.

Cyclos is an open source online banking platform developed by STRO (Social Trade Organization). The main features include Internet banking, mobile banking, debit/credit cards and POS (Points Of Sale), e-commerce, and system administration and configuration. Cyclos is implemented based on MySQL, Tomcat, and several other Java frameworks, such as Spring (Application development framework for enterprise Java), Hibernate (for the storage and retrieval of Java domain objects via Object/Relational Mapping), and Struts (for creating web applications that utilize the Model-View-Controller architecture).

4.2 Project Team and Tasks

The project team consisted of a faculty member (the author), two REU students, four RET teachers, and two graduate assistants. The REU students were juniors from Pomona College and George State University, majoring in Computer Science. The RET teachers were from three public schools and one private school in South Dakota. The graduate assistants were third-year and first-year doctoral students with a research focus on information assurance. About two months before the REU program started, the author decided to use Cyclos as a real-world application for his research group and assigned the graduate assistants to begin learning about Cyclos. When the REU students and RET teachers joined the group, the graduate students had obtained a basic understanding about the Cyclos's functionality. For example, they were able to revise the source code as needed, re-compile and re-deploy Cyclos (this is critical to the mutation analysis) and present the basic features of Cyclos.

As Cyclos is a complex online banking platform, we chose to limit the scope of our study to the objects and activities related to loans, such as granting, viewing, repaying, and discarding a loan, creating a loan group, and adding a member of a loan group. This allowed us to focus on a manageable section of the system, which nevertheless remained broad enough to provide interesting results. Loan groups, a construct popular in the microfinance community in which a group of users are collectively responsible for a single loan, added an extra layer of complexity. In addition, we focused on the following four permission groups (i.e., roles): (a) *Full Member:* ordinary account holder; (b) *Full Broker:* broker who has read access to their clients' accounts; (c) *System Administrator*; (d) *Account Administrator:* admin with a subset of the System Administrator's permissions.

According to the research tasks, the project team was divided into the following four groups:

- Access control testing group. This group was responsible for validating Cyclos's access control policies by creating access control tests and performing the tests against the Cyclos implementation (Refer to Section 4.1 for technical background). It consisted of the third year doctoral student and one REU student;
- Obligation testing group. This group was responsible for defining obligation policies and designing and performing obligation tests (Refer to Section 4.1 for technical background). It consisted of two RET teachers;
- Attack testing group. This group was responsible for designing and performing SQL injection attacks and XSS attacks against Cyclos (Refer to Section 4.2 for technical background). It consisted of two RET teachers.
- Mutation analysis group. This group was responsible for creating security mutants of Cyclos (Refer to Section 4.3 for technical background). The mutants would be used by the testing groups for evaluating the effectiveness of their tests. The mutation analysis group consisted the first-year doctoral student and one REU student.

The 2012 REU and RET programs were held from May 28 through July 27 and from June 4 through July 27, respectively. The REU program started one week earlier than the RET program, but they ended in the same week. Before the summer programs started, the author contacted the REU students and the RET teachers and introduced reading materials for them to prepare for the summer program. The research groups were not formed until the first week of the RET program.

Beyond the research project, the REU students and RET teachers attended the following program-wide activities, which were helpful for them to perform the research project.

- A weekly three-hour class "Special Topics in Cybersecurity". This course was designed specifically for the REU and RET programs. It provides an overview of fundamental cybersecurity principles, including security goals, applied cryptography, network security, operating system security, software security, web security, malware, and digital forensics.
- Seminars such as "Conducting Publishable Research in Cybersecurity" and "Ethics in Research".
- Field trips to the Symantec (a well-known security company) site in Minneapolis and the Network and Security Department of USGS/EROS (Earth Resources Observation Systems) data center.
- Weekly REU or RET group meetings with the program director (i.e., the author).

The activities for this particular project included performing individual research tasks, holding group discussions, and attending weekly team meetings. During weekly team meetings, each member or group was required to update their progress, discuss the main research issues, and present a work plan for the next week. A common task for all project participants was to understand the related functional features and security goals of Cyclos. To this end, we built a model of the loan accounts according to the various access control activities and obligatory actions by the four roles. The model was represented by a PrT net in MISTA. Part of the model is included in the appendix.

To assure the objectivity of mutation testing, the mutation analysis group worked independently of the testing groups. In other words, they should not share with the testing groups any information about how they created the security mutants. The testing groups should not share with the mutation analysis group any information about how their tests were created. A few weeks later, we realized that the mutation analysis of Cyclos is too challenging. It requires a very good understanding about the complex Java source code of Cyclos as well as various plausible security vulnerabilities in several Java frameworks (Spring, Hibernate, Struts). Thus, we decided to limit the mutation analysis to access control policy and hold a competition between the access control testing group and the mutation analysis group. As an agreement negotiated by the two groups, the access control testing group would be the winner if their tests kill 60% or more of the mutants created by the mutation analysis group, otherwise the mutation analysis group would be the winner. Each member of the winning group will receive a 32GB USB drive as the prize.

5. RESULTS

In the first 3-4 weeks, all groups focused on understanding the related functionality and security requirements of Cyclos and learning about the principles of relevant security techniques (e.g., security testing with threat models and access control testing). Then they started creating their own artifacts.

The access control testing group created 47 access control tests according to the loan activities and access control metrics related to full member, full broker, account administrator, and system administrator. Each of these tests consists of a manually executable test script and an oracle value at one or more steps with the script. The test scripts are specified at the user interface level and thus performed from the user's perspective.

Due to the limited time and the complexity of Cyclos, the mutation analysis group focused on the mutation of access control rules. They created 10 security mutants by injecting access control faults into the relevant code or configuration. 5 of them have a programming error (e.g., missing access control check) and the rest involve incorrect privileges in the configuration database.

The access control testing group won the competition because their access control tests killed 90% of the security mutants created by the mutation analysis group. In fact, their tests would have killed the remaining mutant (mutant #5) if they had checked the oracle values carefully. In this mutant, the incorrect privilege for members has led to an unexpected change of the member's user interface. The access control testing group did not notice this change. In fact, this reflects one of the major reasons that software bugs go undetected – "looking, but not seeing".

The obligation testing group formulated five detailed obligation requirements and created scripts for testing these obligation requirements. Each of the scripts may yield multiple concrete tests with different parameters. A sample obligation is that, after an administrator has granted a loan to a member, the system should create a loan account for the member and the member should repay the loan within a period of time, otherwise a late fee will be charged (the duration and the amount of late fee are loan parameters, which are determined when the loan is granted).

The attack testing group identified numerous user input fields that are potentially subject to SQL injection and XSS attacks. For example, user name and password are two input fields, which lead to SQL queries to the database. We need to test whether SQL injection attacks can be launched through these inputs.

Based on the research activities, the REU students and RET teachers produced the following deliverables: (a) each REU student or RET pair made two presentations to the entire REU or RET group – one was about their project plan and the other was about their research result; (b) each REU student or RET pair wrote a paper on their project in the IEEE Proceedings format. (c) each RET teacher made a presentation on their teaching experience and a plan to integrate cybersecurity topics into their classroom activities. For example, most of them would introduce the concept of secure programming into their programming class.

In brief, the project has successfully achieved its goals. First, each REU student and RET teacher has learned about one of the specific security testing techniques. These techniques were newly developed and accepted for publication in prestigious venues. Second, most of them were able to make research contributions, which resulted in a paper accepted for publication and presentation by the 2013 *International Conference on Computing, Networking and Communications* [13]. To the best of our knowledge, the obligation testing was the first attempt to apply a model-based approach to the generation of obligation tests. The mutation analysis introduced access control bugs into the source code of Cyclos. This is different from the existing work on access control mutation that created mutants of access control rules according to their syntactic components.

There are several lessons that we have learned from this project. First, as the summer programs were short, preparation before the summer programs could be very helpful. The research project involved several subjects that were new to the participants. Getting some background knowledge related to the research project before the summer program would accelerate the warm-up process. Second, the graduate assistants played an important role in the project. They provided professional help to the REU students and RET teachers so that the students and teachers could work more effectively toward achieving their research goal. The graduate assistants also served an immediate role model for the undergraduates and an indirect role model for high school students through the teachers. Third, teamwork with both collaboration and competition made the research experience more effective and interesting. Through collaboration, the participants obtained a common understanding about the relevant functionality and security requirements of Cyclos. Through competition, they had a better sense of urgency, achievement, and satisfaction. Last, but not the least, Cyclos, as a real-world online banking system, intrigued the students' and teachers' interest and curiosity to investigate security issues.

6. CONCLUSIONS

We have presented a unique summer research project that involved undergraduate students from outside the host institution and high school computer teachers. Under the supervision of the faculty mentor and in collaboration with graduate assistants, they investigated several security testing issues of a real-world online banking system. Through the research activities, they have not only learned about advanced security testing techniques but also make publishable contributions to the research base. As the results were very encouraging, this project can be used as a model of summer programs for undergraduate students and/or K-12 teachers to gain research experiences.

7. ACKNOWLEDGMENTS

This work was supported in part by the US National Science Foundation (NSF) under grants CNS 1004843, CNS 1200648, and CNS 1123220.

8. REFERENCES

[1] Bertolino, A., Daoudagh, S., Lonetti, F., Marchetti, E., Martinelli, F., Mori, P. 2012. Testing of PolPA authorization systems. In *Proc. of 7th International Workshop on Automation of Software Test* (Zurich, Switzerland, June 2-3, 2012). AST'12. 8-14.

[2] Elrakaiby, Y., Mouelhi, T., Le Traon, Y. 2012. Testing obligation policy enforcement using mutation analysis. In *Proc. of the 7th International Workshop on Mutation Analysis* (Montréal, Canada, April 2012). 673-680.

[3] Falk, L., Prakash, A., Borders, K. 2008. Analyzing websites for user-visible security design flaws. In *Proc. of the Symposium on Usable Security and Privacy* (Pittsburg, USA, July 2008). SOUP'08. 117-126.

[4] Hoglund, G. and McGraw, G. 2004. *Exploiting Software: How to Break Code.* Addison-Wesley.

[5] Irwin, K., Yu, T., Winsborough, W.H. 2006. On the modeling and analysis of obligations. In *Proc. of the 13th ACM Conf. on Computer and Communications Security* (Chicago, USA, October 2006). CCS'06. 134-143.

[6] Jia, Y. and Harman, M. 2010. An analysis and survey of the development of mutation testing. *IEEE Trans. on Software Engineering*, 37, 5 (October 2010). 649-678.

[7] Langevin, J.R., McCaul, M.T., Charney, S. Raduege, H., Lewis, J.A. 2010. *A Human Capital Crisis in Cybersecurity: A White Paper of the CSIS commission on Cybersecurity for the 44th Presidency*, Center for Strategic & International Studies.

[8] Le Traon, Y., Mouelhi, T., Pretschner, A., and Baudry, B. 2008. Test-driven assessment of access control in legacy applications. In *Proc. of the First IEEE International Conference on Software, Testing, Verification and Validation* (Lillehammer, Norway, April 2008). ICST'08. 238-247.

[9] Potter, B., Allen, B., Mcgraw, G. 2004. Software security testing. *IEEE Security & Privacy*, (Sept. 2004). 32–36.

[10] Xu, C., Fong, P. W. L. 2012. The specification and compilation of obligation policies for program monitoring. In *Proc. of the 7th ACM Symposium on Information, Computer and Communications Security* (Seoul, South Korea, May 2012). ASIACCS'12.

[11] Xu, D. 2009. Software security, *Wiley Encyclopedia of Computer Science and Engineering*, B. W. Wah (Editor-In-Chief), Volume 5, John Wiley & Sons, Inc., Hoboken, NJ. 2703-2716.

[12] Xu, D. 2011. A tool for automated test code generation from high-level Petri nets. In *Proc. of Petri Nets'11* (Newcastle upon Tyne, UK, June 2011), LNCS 6709, 308-317.

[13] Xu, D., Sanford, M., Liu, Z., Emry, M., Brockmueller, B., Johnson, S., To, M. 2012. Testing access control and obligation policies. In *Proc. of the 2013 International Conference on Computing, Networking and Communications* (San Diego, January 2013). ICNC'13.

[14] Xu, D., Thomas, L., Kent, M., Mouelhi, T., and Le Traon, Y. 2012. A model-based approach to automated testing of access control policies. In *Proc. of the 17th ACM Symposium on Access Control Models and Technologies* (Newark, USA, June 2012), SACMAT'12. ACM. 209-218.

[15] Xu, D., Tu, M., Sanford, M., Thomas, L., Woodraska, D., and Xu, W. 2012. Automated security test generation with formal threat models. *IEEE Trans. on Dependable and Secure Computing*. 9, 4 (July/August 2012), 525-539.

Appendix. Partial test model of loan accounts in Cyclos [13]

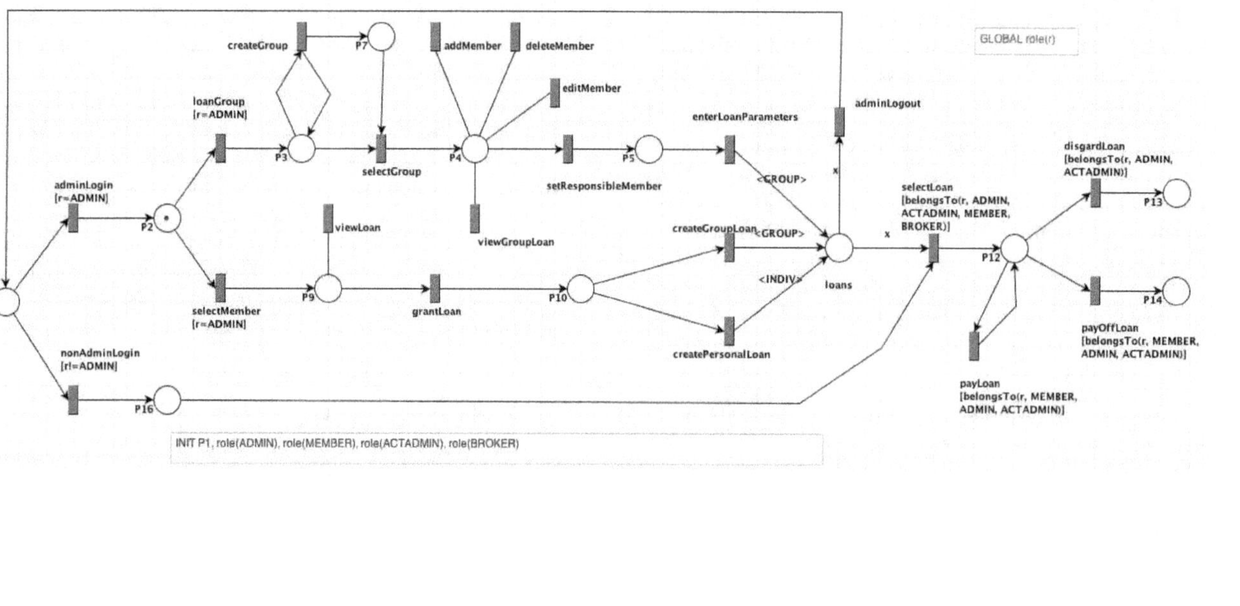

CE21–Maryland: The State of Computer Science Education in Maryland High Schools

Marie desJardins
Dept. of Computer Science and EE
University of Maryland, Baltimore County
Baltimore MD 21250
mariedj@cs.umbc.edu

Susan Martin
Center for Women in Technology
University of Maryland, Baltimore County
Baltimore MD 21250
susan@umbc.edu

ABSTRACT

The goals of UMBC's CE21-Maryland project are to build community and to increase the accessibility, diversity, and quality of high school CS education in Maryland. The ultimate objective is for all Maryland students to have access to high-quality, college preparatory CS courses. We present findings from a survey of high school computing teachers regarding the status of CS education in Maryland. Some findings of interest are that urban and rural students have less access to computing courses than suburban students; female teachers are more likely to attract female students and to have larger AP CS classes; and neither teacher race nor gender is correlated with the number of minority students enrolled in CS classes. We describe community building successes through two Google CS4HS workshops, a Maryland CSTA chapter, and statewide summit meetings for educators and administrators. We also discuss how our methodology can be used as a model for other states who are working towards CS education reform at the high school level.

Categories and Subject Descriptors

K.3.2 [**Computers and Education**]: Computer and Information Science Education—*Computer Science Education*

Keywords

High school teachers, professional development, community

1. INTRODUCTION

Despite the overall success of Maryland's K-12 education system, opportunities to study computer science vary tremendously among the 24 school systems and 247 high schools in the state. This disparity can be attributed to several factors previously identified by two Computer Science Teacher Association (CSTA) surveys: lack of a state-mandated CS high school graduation requirement, no state-required teacher certification in the discipline, and the absence of a standardized CS curriculum [5]. Many of these factors exacerbate gender, racial, and geographic disparities in access to computing education. Girls and underrepresented minorities (specifically African American and Hispanic students) are less likely to enroll in computer science classes in high school, including AP computer science. CS courses are less likely to be available in urban and rural schools than in suburban areas. However, when we began our project, little data existed about the actual situation in individual schools across the state, and teachers and administrators interested in CS education had not come together to discuss the challenges and possible strategies for change.

Computer science courses do not count towards high school graduation requirements in Maryland, are sometimes taught by teachers who are underprepared to teach the subject, and vary in content and quality among school systems and even among schools within a system. As a result, the vast majority of students leave high school without exposure to computational thinking skills, programming knowledge, or information about CS/IT career opportunities.

Maryland does theoretically have defined pathways to CS teacher certification, but few students are pursuing these options, and they are not well publicized or widely available. There is a severe shortage of qualified computer science high school teachers in the state. There are only two post-baccalaureate certificate programs in computer science in the state, but these programs have not been nationally certified, and no new teachers have been produced by either program in at least six years.

According the Running on Empty website, Maryland has adopted only 30% of ACM and CSTA's Level II curriculum standards and 10% of the Level III standards, placing it 23rd among all states [1]. High school computer science courses in Maryland are situated within what is referred to as Career and Technical Education (CTE), rather than being part of the overall academic requirements. Under Maryland high school graduation requirements, students are required to take one "tech-ed" course, but only a few counties offer a computer science foundational course as an option to satisfy this requirement. Moreover, these classes are typically not primarily focused on computational principles, since they must cover all of the engineering-focused technology education standards. Ultimately, the positioning of computer science courses within technology education, rather than as a stand-alone academic graduation requirement, contributes to the low number of students who study computing.

Changing state graduation requirements and increasing the availability of CS education to all students will require a complicated, long-term change process. Our focus in this

SIGCSE'13, March 6–9, 2013, Denver, Colorado, USA.

project is to gather data and evidence that can be used to provide support for systemic changes, and to build a community that can work together to create the conditions that will ultimately enable these changes. We describe the findings from an initial survey of computer science teachers across Maryland, then discuss our current and future community building efforts, including professional development workshops for teachers, the establishment of a Maryland chapter of the Computer Science Teachers Association, and two statewide summit meetings (one that was held in August 2012 and a larger summit to be held in May 2013).

2. RELATED WORK

Computing professionals are an essential ingredient of our nation's future economic success [8]. The availability of a diverse, highly skilled, and well educated technology workforce is critical for meeting workforce demands and for solving the myriad of complex social, environmental, health, and security challenges of the 21st century.

Unfortunately, the picture looks the bleakest for the computing disciplines just when these skills are most needed. Undergraduate enrollments in computer science have declined over the past decade: in 2010, only 2% of college-bound SAT takers reported that their intended major was computer science [9, 11]. There is a significant gender gap: in 2010-11, only 12.7% of computing degrees were awarded to women. Research indicates that differences in boys' and girls' attitudes, confidence, interest, and experience with computers affect their decision whether to study computer science in college [2]. Similarly, in 2010-11, only 4.6% of computing degrees were awarded to African Americans and 6.5% to Hispanics. Differences exist by race and ethnicity in the reasons for choosing computing majors and careers. Female, African American, and Hispanic students are all more likely to cite interest in "communal" careers: those that have the power to do good and make a difference to society. In addition, encouragement matters more than ability in terms of how likely women and underrepresented minorities are to complete a computing major and pursue a career in computing. The content and characteristics of the curriculum also have a substantial effect on the retention and progression of students in STEM majors, particularly for women and other underrepresented minorities [10, 12, 7, 6]. These results have implications for both the content and pedagogy of computer science education at the high school and college levels. If all high school students were exposed to computing content and careers as part of a required, introductory computer science class that emphasized collaboration, affiliation, and the societal good associated with computing, then more women and underrepresented minorities might be attracted to and retained in computing majors and careers.

It is a positive development that recently, undergraduate enrollments in CS have increased [13]. However, the gender and racial disparities persist. In order to ensure the success of *all* students in computer science, we must increase the quality and diversity of the pipeline by improving CS teaching standards, curriculum, teacher preparation, and availability of courses [1, 3, 4].

Efforts to increase the participation of diverse students in computing have been supported by the National Science Foundation's Broadening Participation Program in the past and now by the Computing and Computing Education for the 21st Century Program. Two states in particular, Georgia and Massachusetts, have made significant changes and improvements to computing education via Georgia Computes! and the Commonwealth Alliance for Information Technology Education (CAITE), respectively. Since 2006, the Georgia Computes! project has run K-12 summer camps, worked with faculty to offer and assess the impact of high-retention curricula, and used graduate students as mentors, material developers, and evaluators. CAITE, led by the University of Massachusetts, Amherst, has leveraged partnerships with community colleges in four regions of the state, as well as alliances with other STEM and information technology education initiatives, to offer programs and outreach activities for high school teachers, staff, and counselors. The dissemination of results and best practices from both of these projects is currently underway. As we begin our efforts in Maryland, we look to these projects as primary examples of the power of leveraging NSF research for long-term, statewide change. Our project is also anchored to the previous research conducted by CSTA to frame and quantify issues and challenges related to high school computer science education through the CSTA National Secondary Computer Science Survey and the Running on Empty data.

3. SURVEY OF TEACHERS

We conducted a baseline survey of computer science teachers to collect information about their backgrounds, their professional development needs, the computing courses they teach, the students in these classes, and the specific computer science offerings in their counties.[1] With respect to student demographics, we were particularly focused on gathering data that would help us to identify the nature and sources of possible gender, racial, and geographic disparities in the availability, depth, and quality of computing course offerings across the state. By sharing the data with our growing community of educators and administrators, we hope to build consensus for educational goals and objectives of which the broad community will be strongly supportive.

Maryland has 24 school systems: one in each of the 23 counties and one in Baltimore City. There are 222 traditional high schools, 16 Career Technology Education (CTE) Centers, and nine CTE high schools. Because CS is not a standardized subject and does not have its own department, teachers in different counties and schools are often located in different departments, teaching many different curricula, and holding varying credentials. As a result, no statewide database of CS teachers or courses exists. (The Maryland State Department of Education (MSDE) maintains a CTE mailing list, but not all of these teach computing courses, and not all computing teachers are on the list.)

We created an initial contact list of CS/IT teachers by reviewing the websites of the 247 Maryland high schools. This initial contact list included each school's mailing address, phone number, and guidance office staff contact. The task of identifying the computing teachers was challenging because of the variability of information available on individual school websites. Many schools had online staff directories while others did not, or the staff listing was not easily located on the website. For schools with staff listings,

[1]A summary of the survey questions and aggregated results, as well as crosstabulated results by gender, race, and school location, can be downloaded from `http://ce21maryland.umbc.edu/resources/` .

it was difficult to clearly identify computer science or IT teachers based on the job titles and departmental information. Contact information was gathered for teachers with job titles related to computing, information technology, career and technology, and business education. Follow-up phone calls were made to schools for which the information was not readily available, although little additional information was obtained by these phone calls, since administrative staff or guidance staff frequently referred our research assistants to the school website. Contact information was also added for CSTA-Maryland members who were not already in the database. This process resulted in 347 contact names and emails within Maryland public high schools. This initial contact list has been incorporated into a database to which contact names are continually added.

3.1 Survey Instrument

Our survey was based largely on the CSTA National Secondary Computer Science Survey (NSCSS),[2] which consists of 38 items regarding school and student characteristics, teacher characteristics, CS/IT offerings in the school, enrollment trends in CS classes, challenges faced by the teachers in teaching CS courses, and professional development opportunities. We added 15 other items about Maryland-specific topics such as certifications, school location, curriculum, and student demographics. In addition, we expanded the response list of possible challenges that teachers face.

In May 2012, we invited the 347 teachers in our contact database to take the survey. Survey recruitment was done through multiple channels: a postcard was sent in the mail; an initial invitation was sent by email; and three email reminders were also sent, as well as a reminder email from the MSDE CTE staff to their contact list. Of the 347 invitations, six explicitly opted out (requested no further emails) or were undeliverable (the email bounced). Of the 341 remaining invitees, 26% responded to the survey (88 teachers), as did nine additional respondents from the MSDE CTE mailing. A total of 97 respondents began the survey, although 12 of these did not answer all questions, so we have data for 85 completed surveys. (Answers for partially completed surveys are included in all response statistics.)

3.2 Results and Key Findings

The survey responses yielded insights about student demographics, course offerings, teacher preparation, professional development, and the challenges perceived by these teachers. Here we present a summary of the general findings in each area, as well as some of the potentially significant relationships that are present in the data. Note that this discussion represents only some of the key findings, since the survey is too extensive to present in full detail.

Student Demographics.

Table 1 summarizes the information provided by the survey respondents about the students who take their introductory and AP-level CS classes. Participants were asked to estimate the number of students in introductory and AP CS classes, the percentage of students in these classes who are female, and the percentage of students who are members of an ethnic minority.[3]

The dominant response for school size was 1001-2000 students (59.5% responding in this range). For a typical high school of 1500 students, therefore, the modal range of 11-25 students in introductory CS reflects only 1.2% of the student population in those classes. Even the next most frequent response of 26-50 students corresponds to only a 2.6% participation rate. Still, a significant number of schools (32.6%) do have over 50 students in introductory CS, whereas only 10.4% of schools have over 50 students in AP CS. That is, of the few students who take an introductory class, even fewer of them continue into advanced courses.

The numbers of students in introductory courses are comparable to national averages from NSCSS data, but with a stronger peak in the 11-50 range: fewer teachers in Maryland reported only 1-10 students taking introductory CS, but there were also fewer teachers who reported more than 50 students in these classes. A similar pattern holds for percentages of female students in introductory classes: the peak at 1-20% is stronger in Maryland than nationally, and there were fewer teachers in Maryland reporting high proportions (41-60%) of female students. However, this pattern is reversed for minority students: the peak at 1-20% has the same magnitude as nationally, but there are fewer teachers reporting no minority students and more teachers reporting higher percentages (21-80%) of minority students. This is likely because of the urban areas in Maryland which have high percentages of minority students overall.

At the AP level, teachers report more students taking these classes overall (with a peak at 11-25 students) than nationally (peak at 1-10 students). However, the pattern is somewhat different for female and minority populations. The peak at 1-20% is higher for both of these populations in Maryland than nationally, and fewer teachers report no minority or female students in AP classes—but fewer teachers also report higher proportions of female and minority students (21-80%) than nationally.

The respondents reported their school's geographic regions as 56.5% suburban, 24.7% rural, and 18.8% urban. While we do not have geographic labels for all of the schools, examining the county-by-county response rates shows a lower response rate in rural counties. The highest response rate (17 teachers, or 20% of the overall respondents) was in Montgomery County, an affluent suburban county. Only one response was provided from each of five counties, and no responses were received from four counties; all nine of these counties would be characterized as predominantly rural, most of them in the western (panhandle) part of the state and on the Eastern Shore of the Chesapeake Bay.

Course Offerings.

Nearly a tenth of the respondents (9.4%, or eight teachers) reported that their school offers no CS/IT courses. The most common reported reasons for a lack of CS/IT courses include insufficient student interest (five responses) and budget restrictions (five responses). All but one of these teachers felt that their school *should* offer CS courses.

Fewer than two-thirds of the schools offer an introductory computer science course (61.2%), and just over half offer AP courses (56.5%). A keyboarding class is offered in 37.6% of the schools; 24.7% offer an Oracle or Cisco Academy (four-

[2]http://csta.acm.org/Research/sub/Projects/ResearchFiles/CSTASurvey11CSResults.pdf

[3]The NSCSS questions regarding minority students do not specify which minority groups should be included, so these answers reflect not only underrepresented minorities but other ethnic minority groups as well.

Table 1: Demographics of students taking introductory and AP computer science

	Response	Intro CS		AP CS	
		Maryland	National	Maryland	National
Number of Students	1-10	4.3%	10%	25.0%	44%
	11-25	34.8%	24%	52.1%	36%
	26-50	28.3%	25%	12.5%	13%
	51-100	17.4%	20%	10.4%	6%
	101+	15.2%	21%	0%	2%
% Female	0%	8.7%	4%	10.4%	22%
	1-20%	60.9%	43%	77.1%	53%
	21-40%	26.1%	22%	10.4%	20%
	41-60%	4.3%	29%	2.1%	5%
	61-80%	0.0%	1.7%	0.0%	0.5%
% Minority	0%	2.2%	7%	6.3%	15%
	1-20%	52.5%	53%	66.7%	48%
	21-40%	26.1%	20%	12.5%	17%
	41-60%	10.9%	6%	8.3%	8%
	61-80%	6.3%	5%	0.0%	2%
	81-99%	0.0%	0%	6.3%	5%

course CTE "completer" sequences that lead to Oracle or Cisco certification); and 43.5% offer "other CS/IT courses" (see Figure 1 for response statistics on courses offered).

The geographic disparities are quite striking. Specifically, CS offerings are less available in rural and urban schools than in suburban ones, although the pattern of offerings is different in rural and urban schools. 28.6% of rural schools offered *no* CS/IT courses; this is the case for only 6.3% of urban schools and only 2.1% of suburban schools. Introductory CS courses are offered by 68.8% of suburban schools, but by only 50.0% and 52.4% of urban and rural schools, respectively. AP offerings are distributed similarly to introductory offerings: AP CS is offered by 62.5% of suburban schools, 43.8% of urban schools, and 52.4% of rural schools.

An interesting and very apparent finding is that female teachers are significantly more likely to attract more female students. 38.5% of female teachers reported having 21% or more female students in their classes, whereas only 16.7% of male teachers had this high a proportion of female students. (Male teachers are also more likely to have no female students (11.1%) than were female teachers (2%), although this difference represents only a few teachers, so no definitive conclusions can be drawn.) Female teachers also seemed to attract more students into AP CS in general, with 32% of female teachers having 26 or more students in AP classes, and only 9.5% of male teachers reporting this level of participation. As with introductory CS, female teachers were more likely to report 21% or more of their students being female (20%) than male teachers (4.8%), and male teachers were more likely to have no female students (14.3% vs. 8.0%). Teacher gender did not seem to affect minority participation. The race of the teacher did not appear to affect female or minority participation at the introductory or AP level; however, there is too little data to draw strong conclusions. (Of the 11 African American teachers, only three responded to the questions regarding introductory classes, and only three said their school offered an AP class.)

The numbers of students, particularly in AP courses, are also reflective of the offerings: in urban schools that do offer AP CS, most respondents indicate that only 1-10 students take the class each year. In suburban schools, the most

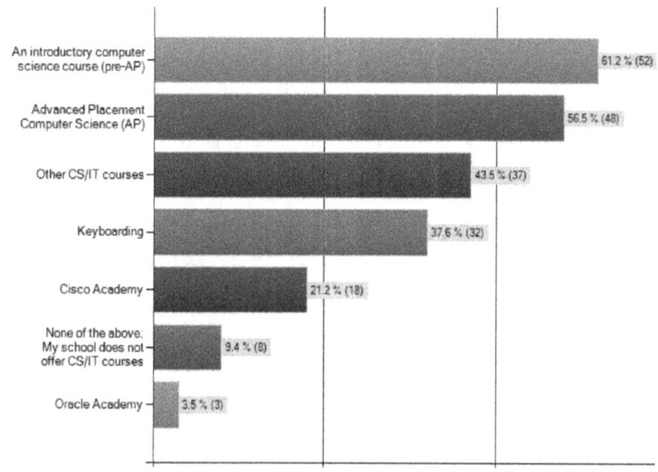

Figure 1: Survey responses about course offerings

common answer was 11-25 students, but some reported that there were 26-50 or even 51-100 students in AP CS.[4] In the rural schools with AP CS, most (70%) reported 11-25 students in the classes.

21.2% of schools overall offer the Cisco Academy, but almost none of these are in rural areas (only 4.8% of rural schools offer the Cisco academy, compared to 27.1% of suburban schools and 25.0% of urban schools). Similarly, 43.5% of schools overall offer other CS/IT courses, with these offerings being far more common in suburban schools (56.3%) than rural schools (only 14.3%).

Teacher Preparation and Professional Development.

The geographic disparities are again reflected in teacher certifications. Of the suburban teachers, 55.3% are certified to teach computer science, but only 25.0% of urban and 19.0% of urban teachers hold a CS certification. The most common certification in the latter schools is business education (43.8% of urban teachers and 38.1% of rural teach-

[4]These are likely to be teachers from magnet schools that have unusually large CS programs; to maintain anonymity, school names were not requested, but these responses are all from the two most affluent counties in Maryland, Howard and Montgomery.

ers). Technology education was also a common certification across all regions (43.8% of urban teachers, 46.8% of suburban teachers, and 33.3% of rural teachers). Mathematics was quite common in suburban schools (34.0%), but was seen less frequently in urban (18.8%) and rural (19.0%) schools.

Interestingly, teachers in both suburban and rural schools had more years of experience, with the dominant response for those regions being 15+ years (47.9% of suburban teachers and 52.4% of rural). Urban teachers were fairly evenly distributed across the experience ranges, but the slightly dominant response was 4-7 years (37.5%). Experience seems to matter for diversity: of the 13 teachers reporting more than 20% female students in introductory CS, for example, all but two had eight or more years of experience. Similarly, of the 20 teachers reporting more than 20% minority students in these classes, all but one had eight or more years of experience. This pattern continues to the AP level: all but one (i.e, 88%) of the eight teachers with fewer than eight years of experience had 1-20% female and 1-20% minority students in their AP classes; of the 38 more experienced teachers, 11 teachers (29%) had 21% or more minority students. (It is not possible from this data to tell whether there is causality in either direction: i.e., whether more experienced CS teachers attract more students, or whether schools with more CS students are able to hire more experienced teachers.)

Reflective of the urban demographics in Maryland, African American teachers were more common in those schools (25.0%) than in suburban (12.8%) or rural (4.8%) schools. Most teachers in all areas were Caucasian, with a few Asian American teachers and no Hispanic or Native American respondents. About half of the teachers were female, although suburban teachers were more likely to be male (61.7%) than were urban (43.8%) or rural (42.9%) teachers.

Challenges Perceived by Teachers.

Teachers reported experiencing a wide range of challenges in teaching CS classes. Again, in this area, there were some geographic differences. Rapidly changing technology was cited as a major challenge in 42.9% of urban schools and 52.9% of rural schools, but in only 23.9% of suburban schools. Similarly, lack of support by the staff was perceived as a major challenge by the plurality of urban (42.9%) and rural (50.0%) teachers but only as a moderate challenge by suburban teachers (41.3%). The same pattern was seen for "lack of curriculum resources," "lack of hardware/software resources," "lack of teacher subject knowledge," and "lack of professional development opportunities," among others.

"Difficult subject matter" was seen as less of an issue, but was still reported more often as a moderate challenge in urban (69.2%) and rural (52.9%) schools than in suburban (39.1%) schools. Interestingly, though, the related problem of "lack of student subject knowledge" was uniform across all school types, seen as a moderate challenge by urban (57.1%), rural (52.9%), and suburban (55.6%) teachers about equally.

The only challenge that was perceived as more of a concern by suburban teachers (with 43.5% reporting this as a major challenge) than urban (21.4%) or rural (31.3%) teachers was "being asked to teach multiple CS related courses in the same classroom at the same time." Presumably this is more of an issue at suburban schools because multiple CS classes are simply not offered at many of the rural and urban schools.

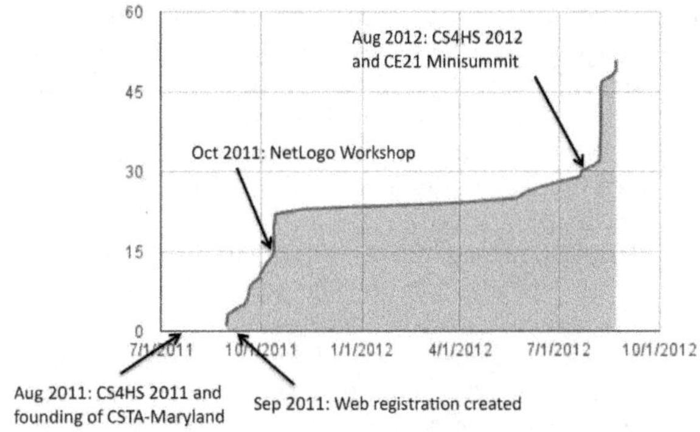

Figure 2: CSTA membership growth

4. COMMUNITY BUILDING

Our community building efforts are focused in three major areas: professional development opportunities for high school teachers, the establishment of a local chapter of CSTA, and statewide summit meetings for teachers, administrators, college faculty, and industry representatives.

4.1 Professional Development for Teachers

Our first outreach effort to high school teachers was a Google-sponsored CS4HS professional development workshop at UMBC in July 2011.[5] Twelve teachers attended; the event included sessions on Computing Education for the 21st Century, First Lego League robotics, Finch robots, NetLogo, Scratch programming, strategies for increasing diversity, and game programming. For several of the teachers, this workshop was the first opportunity they had had to meet and interact with other local CS teachers, and the event created a great deal of energy and zeal for improving CS education. The feedback that we received from the participants on our post-event survey was very positive: 88.9% rated the event overall as Excellent and 11.1% as Good. 90% of the teachers strongly agreed that they gained new ideas they can use in their CS classes, that they felt more connected to other high school CS teachers in the state, that their students would benefit from their experience, that they found the workshop to be worthwhile, and that attending CS4HS had enhanced their professional development.

Following the success of the first workshop, we offered a second CS4HS workshop in August 2012.[6] Twenty teachers attended this event, including two middle school teachers. The structure was similar to the first year, keeping some of the same sessions and adding sessions on the AP Computer Science Principles curriculum, cybersecurity, and AppInventor mobile app development. Our assessment data showed very similar outcomes to the 2012 workshop, with many teachers expressing a desire for additional professional development and networking activities.

4.2 CSTA–Maryland Local Chapter

At the end of the 2011 CS4HS workshop, we established a Maryland CSTA chapter,[7] with the officers elected from among the workshop attendees, and the initial members be-

[5]http://maple.cs.umbc.edu/cs4hs/schedule2011.html
[6]http://maple.cs.umbc.edu/cs4hs/schedule.html
[7]Chapter website: https://sites.google.com/site/cstamaryland/home.

ing the 12 teachers and several UMBC representatives. The 2011 CS4HS participants were very interested in further professional development, so we worked with the CSTA-Maryland leadership to organize a NetLogo workshop at UMBC in October 2011, which eight teachers attended.

The chapter has grown significantly since its creation. Figure 2 shows that each organized activity brought new members to the chapter: after the initial chapter members joined, ten teachers who attended or heard about the October 2011 workshop subsequently joined. The advertising for our August 2012 workshop brought a noticeable increase in membership in June and July 2012. The CSTA-Maryland chapter meeting that was held on the morning of the third day of the August CS4HS workshop was very lively: most of the 20 CS4HS participants attended, along with a number of teachers who had heard about the chapter or the minisummit that was being held that day (see Section 4.3). New board members were elected; several new positions (including industry liaison, middle school representative, and government liaison) were created; and a number of new initiatives (including another UMBC-hosted professional development workshop scheduled for October 2012) were proposed. Following the 2012 CS4HS workshop and minisummit, membership nearly doubled over a period of just a few weeks.

4.3 CE21–Maryland Summits

The final session of the 2012 CS4HS workshop overlapped with an all-day "minisummit" that brought high school teachers, college faculty, administrators, and industry representatives together to discuss the state of CS education in Maryland.[8] To take advantage of the overlap, we organized a panel of some of the teachers who had participated in CS4HS to share their experiences, and created an engaging video highlighting the teachers' thoughts and observations. (This video is currently in postproduction and will be available on our website in the near future.) The minisummit also included a keynote talk by Dr. Jan Cuny about NSF's diversity- and CS education-focused programs, a presentation of the national context of computing education, a presentation of our initial survey results, and an interactive session on future directions and how the community could work to improve CS education in the state. Feedback surveys were administered throughout the event, and we are currently analyzing responses to a followup survey.

In May 2015, we will host a larger summit meeting at UMBC. In addition to teachers, school administrators, and industry representatives, we also aim to have increased participation by higher education (four-year and community college) faculty county administrators, and state policymakers. The goal of the summit is to reach consensus on goals and initiatives that should be pursued at the state level to increase the consistency, availability, and quality of CS education in Maryland high schools.

5. CONCLUSIONS AND FUTURE WORK

Our teacher survey has provided the community with a broader and deeper understanding of the current situation and challenges surrounding CS education in Maryland. The community building activities that we have led over the past year have created a strong, active, and vocal community of educators and administrators who are committed to our shared mission of providing high-quality computing education to all students in the state of Maryland.

Our current focus areas are ensuring continued growth of CSTA–Maryland, creating a secondary CS teacher certification program at UMBC, performing further data analysis, and preparing for the summit to be held in Spring 2013.

We are also eager to collaborate and communicate with leaders of similar efforts in other regions of the country to share knowledge and resources for community building and for creating broad curricular change.

[8]Minisummit website: http://ce21maryland.umbc.edu/ce21-maryland-mini-summit/

Acknowledgements

This work was supported by the National Science Foundation (CE21-00007531 and CAREER-0545726). Thanks to our co-PI, Dr. Penny Rheingans, and to our research assistants: Rebecca Chhay, Shelby Clarke, James MacGlashan, Shawn Squire, and Abigail Williams.

6. REFERENCES

[1] ACM and CSTA. Running on empty: The failure to teach K-12 computer science in the digital age, 2010.

[2] L. Barker and W. Aspray. The state of research on girls and IT. In J. Cohoon and W. Aspray, editors, *Women and IT: Research on Underrepresentation*, pages 3–54. The MIT Press, 2006.

[3] CSTA. Ensuring exemplary teaching in an essential discipline: Addressing the crisis in computer science teacher education, 2008.

[4] J. Cuny. CS 10K project: Transforming high school computer science, 2011. CE21 community meeting handout.

[5] J. Gal-Ezer and C. Stephenson. The current state of computer science in US high schools: A report from two national surveys. *Journal for Computing Teachers*, Spring 2009.

[6] C. Hill, C. Corbett, and A. St. Rose. Why so few? women in science, technology, engineering and mathematics. Technical report, AAUW, 2010.

[7] National Academies of Science. Expanding underrepresented minority participation: America's science and technology talent at the crossroads, 2010.

[8] National Academy of Sciences. *Rising Above the Gathering Storm*. National Academies Press, 2007.

[9] National Science Board. Science and engineering indicators, 2010.

[10] C. Rypisi, L. Malcolm, and H. Kim. Environmental and developmental approaches to supporting women's success in stem fields. In S. Harper and S. J. Quay, editors, *Student Engagement in Higher Education*, pages 117–135. Routledge, 2009.

[11] The College Board. 2010 college-bound seniors, 2010.

[12] C. Zhao, R. Carini, and G. Kuh. Searching for the peach blossom Shangri-La: Student engagement of men and women STEM majors. *Review of Higher Education*, 28(4):503–25, 2006.

[13] S. Zweben. Computing degree and enrollment trends: From the 2010-2011 CRA Taulbee survey, 2012.

How Students Estimate the Effects of ICT and Programming Courses

Michail N. Giannakos*
Norwegian University of Science and Technology (NTNU)
Dep. of Computer & Information Science
Trondheim, NO-7491, Norway
michail.giannakos@idi.ntnu.no

Peter Hubwieser
Technische Universität München
Fakultät für Informatik
Boltzmannstr. 3. D-85478 Garching
peter.hubwieser@tum.de

Nikos Chrisochoides
Old Dominion University
Department of Computer Science
Norfolk, VA 23529, USA
nikos@cs.odu.edu

ABSTRACT

The curricula for Computer Science Education (CSE) of many countries comprise both Programming and Information and Communication Technology (ICT); however these two areas have substantial differences, inter alia the attitudes and beliefs of the students regarding the intended learning content. In this study, variables from the Unified Theory of Acceptance and Use of Technology and Social Cognitive Theory were chosen as important factors in students' behavior and attitude towards CSE. This hybrid framework aims to measure the level of the selected key variables on CSE and identify potential differences among ICT and Programming courses. Responses from the total of 126 Greek students, (71 attending ICT courses and 55 attending Programming Courses) were used to measure the variables and to identify the differences between ICT and Programming students. The results revealed several differences in the measured variables. The overall outcomes are expected to contribute to the understanding of students' likelihood to pursue computing related careers and promote the acceptance of CSE.

Categories and Subject Descriptors

K.3.2 [**Computer and Information Science Education**]: Computer Science Education, Curriculum.

General Terms

Measurement, Experimentation, Human Factors.

Keywords

ICT courses, Programming courses, Informatics, Secondary education, Students' Beliefs.

1. INTRODUCTION

The comparison of Computer Science Education (CSE) in different countries uncovers substantial disparities regarding the conception as well as the practice [14]. Some of these disparities are forced by the big differences in the Educational Systems, while others are caused by differences of traditions, national heritage or public opinion. In several CSE has been included in the curriculum as a distinct discipline in secondary education, while it was taught across curriculum in others [14]. Generally CSE focuses on basic concepts about the constructional principles of computers and networks (hardware) and the principles of programming, (formal languages, programming and software development), whereas Information and Communication Technology (ICT) is focused on how to use computers and how to apply software In many countries [14] CSE includes both ICT and programming courses, however, students' sometimes face these courses differently.

Several models and theories have been used to address students' perceptions and attitude towards learning media [8] and curricula [5]. The Unified Theory of Acceptance and Use of Technology (UTAUT) is one of the most widely and successfully used [13, 21]. Other researchers have empirically explained (using UTAUT or its initial form of TAM) several issues regarding students' attitude [8, 23]. As successful CS teaching largely depends on students' perception and beliefs, we aim to identify students' differences among programming and ICT courses. In this light, variables related to students' attitude were chosen and applied to programming and ICT courses respectively. Then a between group experiment was conducted among students participating ICT course and students participating programming course in the context of Greek educational system. Our empirical study aims to indentify the distinct differences among ICT and programming courses in order to provide a vehicle in the differentiation of educators' attitude in these courses which are mostly (in many countries) treated as a common course.

The purpose of this empirical investigation was to measure students' beliefs and to identify potential differences among ICT and Programming courses. As students' beliefs and attitude are highly correlated with their performance and students' perceptions have an impact on what they have already learned and what they choose to do next [18]. Our work is expected to contribute to the understanding of students' performance and intentions to pursue programming and ICT courses in their future studies.

2. RELATED WORK AND RESEARCH HYPOTHESES

All students' perceptions and intentions are considered as important determinants of the learning success. Reluctance towards adoption of CS content implies that research is needed to

* This work was carried out during the tenure of an ERCIM "Alain Bensoussan" Fellowship programme. The research leading to these results has received funding from the European Union Seventh Framework Programme (FP7/2007-2013) under grant agreement no 246016.

understand, more comprehensively, how students could be motivated. Although past research [1, 2] has empirically explained several issues regarding students perceptions and beliefs regards CSE, it is mostly focused on higher education and more specifically on CS departments. In addition, prior studies have studied CSE as a unified (both ICT and Programming) body. As a result, at present, there is lack of empirical studies on students CSE perceptions and the differences between ICT and Programming courses.

Several models and theories have been applied to address issues of students' attitude, perceptions and to identify the cause and the effect of different factors on the adoption of science education. For instance, UTAUT and SCT are some of the most widely applied theories in the context of students' behavior [5, 9]. In addition, Performance Expectancy (PE), Social Influence (SI), Satisfaction (STF), Self-Efficacy (SEF) and Perceive Behavioral Control (PBC) are some of the most commonly used factors [5, 9] affecting students' intention to attend a respective course. In the view of the above we aim to measure these factors for ICT and Programming courses and to identify potential difference in students' perceptions for these two courses. Thus, the study's set of hypotheses is formulated as follows:

H1. Students' Performance Expectancy is differentiated among ICT and Programming Courses.

H2. Students' Satisfaction is differentiated among ICT and Programming Courses.

H3. Students' Self-Efficacy is differentiated among ICT and Programming Courses.

H4. Students' Social Influence is differentiated among ICT and Programming Courses.

H5. Students' Perceived Behavioral Control is differentiated among ICT and Programming Courses.

H6. Students' Behavioral Intention is differentiated among ICT and Programming Courses.

3. ICT AND PROGRAMMING COURSES IN GREECE

The curricula of Secondary Education in Greece, since the school year 1998-1999, embody a single philosophy implemented by drafting up a Primary and Secondary Education Single Curriculum Framework. In the year 2003 the Interdisciplinary Unified Education Course Framework (DEPPS) and the new – detailed, Curricula (APS) were drawn up for compulsory education, which adopt the inter-disciplinary approach of knowledge. The new school books that were written based on the DEPPS and the new APS orientation have been introduced to the schools in 2006-2007.

In these compulsory education Curricula the importance of Information and Communication Technologies and the role these should play is widely recognized. ICT is not seen only as a separate subject of study, absolutely necessary today for students' technological literacy, but also as a multi-tool: cognitive teaching, information seeking, communicating knowledge etc. The theoretical model adopted, for introducing ICT in lower secondary education, is characterized by the teaching of an "informatics" course and the gradual use of computational and networking technologies as a means to support the cognitive process for all subjects of the programme of study.

The Cross-curricular Single Framework for Curricula for the lower secondary education, through the teaching of Informatics, foresees that the student is to:

- Be able to explain and analyze basic notions and terminology of Informatics (i.e. data, information, coding, data handling, file, save, programme, software, system software etc).
- Be aware of the operations of the main computer units and use with ease a computer system.
- Use generic software tools to record (write down) their ideas, to treat and present them in a variety of ways and means, to resolve simple problems, to use simple projection and control models in order to simulate and test simple problems or results from other cognitive domains.
- Be able to select, choose, analyse and evaluate information through different sources (electronic encyclopedias, electronic dictionaries, www etc) and utilize these for complex projects individual work or teamwork
- Utilize possibilities offered by Information and Communication Technologies (ICT) to communicate, exchange views, wonder, entertain, present their ideas and opinions (the way they choose) and apply simple knowledge of ICT in everyday life.
- Develop critical skills to be able to address problems using computer and to resolve simple problems in a programming environment.
- Cooperate to perform a given project, develop initiatives, design, set objectives, recognize the importance of teamwork in advancing the project, discuss and assess their work and the work of the others.
- Develop an ethics code in regards to their work in the lab, the respect of the work and differentiation of others.

In addition, Informatics has been introduced as a separate curriculum subject which is taught once a week by specialist IT teachers. In the course of Informatics ICT content dominates the curriculum throughout lower secondary education. By the end of the third year the students are introduced into fundamental algorithms and programming using Logo.

In the case of upper secondary education (Lyceum); the 1st grade operates as an orientation year with a general knowledge program. The 2nd grade offers three curricular directions or pathways: Theoretical, Scientific and Technological. In the 3rd grade Lyceum again has the same three directions/pathways. Students who follow the technological direction are taking a course which involves the development of algorithms and programming named Applications Development in a Programming Environment. This course has been taught for ten years. It focuses on the algorithmic approach and on the development of problem-solving skills in a programming environment. This subject is assigned to CS teachers.

The overall aim of 3rd Lyceum programming courses is to develop analytical and synthetic thinking, acquire methodological skills and be able to solve simple problems within a programming environment. This Programming course has not been designed to create programmers, and for this reason it is not designed to teach sophisticated programming techniques; it focuses on approaches and techniques of problem solving with emphasis on structured thinking. Many basic algorithmic and programming concepts, such as conditions, expressions and logical reasoning, are fundamentals of general knowledge and skills to be acquired in general education; these concepts are not presented in other disciplines.

The curriculum states that this subject must be taught (at least partially) in a computer lab. The Ministry of Education has certified specific Educational Software to support the lab work, especially for the Lyceum programming course. The Educational Software has been designed to support teaching, to complement the subject's needs and IT use and to help students consolidate the material. The certified software includes an activity space, a flow chart developer and a programming environment in accordance with the textbook. In addition to that, there are other educational software packages that have been developed by educators and are already in use in many schools.

4. METHODOLOGY

4.1 Context

The empirical study was conducted in the context of secondary education in Greece. As we previously mentioned, the relevant curriculum ICT courses (named Informatics) are mandatory during Gymnasium (middle school) years and aim to develop students' skills in the use of ICT (operating systems, word processing, spreadsheets, image processing etc). The first group in our experiment (ICT Group) consisted of students attending the 3rd class of Gymnasium. They have experience on ICT courses and they are asked for their perceptions regarding the ICT curriculum in the under investigation factors.

For the case of Lyceum (High School), ICT is taught as an elective or direction course since 1999. Thus, besides mandatory education (primary, lower secondary), students in all the classes of Lyceum can select certain ICT from a wide range of various subjects. In the last two classes of Lyceum, students select one of three directions, (technological, scientific or theoretical). If students in the last grade select the technological direction, they attend the programming course for which they are assessed through national exams. The second group in our experiment (Programming Group) consisted of students attending the 3rd class of Lyceum. They have experience on the programming course and they are asked for their perceptions regarding the programming curriculum in the under investigation factors.

In view of the above, our between group experiment was conducted among students' of 3rd of Gymnasium regarding ICT courses and students of 3rd of Lyceum regarding programming courses.

4.2 Sampling

The research methodology included a survey composed by questions on background information of the sample and on the six principal factors. The survey was open during the last three weeks of November 2011 at four public Gymnasiums (lower secondary education) and four public Lyceums (upper secondary education) in the northwestern Greece. The final sample of respondents comprised of 126 Students. From the total of students, 71 (56.35%) were 14 years and attended 3rd of Gymnasium (taught ICT course) and 55 (43.65%) were 17 years and attended the 3rd of Lyceum, in addition, 89 were males (70.6%) and 37 (29.4%) females.

Table 1. The Factors definitions and their Items

Factor	Operational Definition	Items*	Source Adopted
Performance Expectancy (PE)	The degree to which an individual believes that attending the respective course is useful for him/her.	Using programming improves my performance in a task. (PE1)	[21]
		Programming enhances my effectiveness in tasks progressing. (PE2)	
		Programming would make it easier to complete a task. (PE3)	
		Programming increases productivity in completing tasks. (PE4)	
Satisfaction (STF)	The degree to which a person positively feels with the respective course.	I am satisfied with the programming experience. (STF1)	[17]
		I am pleased with the programming experience. (STF2)	
		My decision to use programming was a wise one. (STF3)	
		My feeling to use programming was good. (STF4)	
Self-Efficacy (SEF)	The degree of conviction that one can successfully execute the operation required to produce the outcomes.	**I could complete a programming task …**	[23]
		if there was no one around to tell me what to do. (SEF1)	
		if I had never used it before. (SEF2)	
Social Influence (SI)	The degree to which an individual perceives that most people who are important to him think he should or should not attend the respective course.	People who are important to me think that I should learn programming. (SI1)	[13]
		People who influence my behavior encourage me to learn programming. (SI2)	
Perceived Behavioral Control (PBC)	The degree to which a person perceives how easy or difficult it would be to perform an operation in the respective course.	I would be able to complete programming tasks (PBC1)	[23]
		I have the knowledge and the ability to complete programming tasks. (PBC2)	
Behavioral Intention (BI)	The degree of students' willingness to attend the respective course	I intend to continue learning programming in the future. (BI1)	[16]
		I will continue learning programming in the future. (BI2)	
		I will regularly learn programming in the future. (BI3)	

* for the case of ICT courses the questions where the same with the only difference that the word programming has been replaced with ICT

4.3 Measures

The questionnaire handed out to the students was divided into two parts. The first included questions on the demographics of the sample (age and gender) and the second part included measures of the various factors identified in the literature from previous researches. Table 1 lists the questionnaire factors with their items, their operational definition, and the source from the literature review. In all cases, 7-point Likert scales were used to measure the variables.

4.4 Data Analysis

First, an analysis of reliability and dimensionality was carried out to check the validity of the scales used in the questionnaire. Regarding the reliability of the scales, Cronbach's α indicator was applied [6] and inter-item correlations statistics for the items of each variable were performed. According to Fornell & Larcker [7] and Hair et al. [12], Cronbach's α value greater than 0.60 for exploratory research indicates high reliability. In the next stage, the uni-dimensionality of the scales was evaluated, by carrying out a principal components analysis. The existence of uni-dimensionality is very important, since it allows calculating the average of the indicators that compose each construct. Consequently, it is possible to use a sole factor for representing each theoretical construct. Factorial analysis, with principal components and Varimax rotation, was carried out to test uni-dimensionality of our six scales. Afterwards, the differences of students' perceptions among ICT and Programming courses in each of the crucial factors it was examined using Mann–Whitney U-test.

5. RESEARCH FINDINGS

Fornell and Larcker [9] proposed three procedures to assess the convergent validity of any measure in a study: (1) composite reliability of each construct, (2) item reliability of the measure, and (3) the Average Variance Extracted (AVE).

First, we carried out an analysis of composite reliability and dimensionality to check the validity of the scale used in the questionnaire. Regarding the reliability of the scales, Cronbach's α indicators was applied [6] and inter-item correlations statistics for the items of the variable. As Table 2 demonstrates, the result of the test revealed acceptable indices of internal consistency in all the factors.

In the next stage, we proceeded to evaluate the reliability of the measure. The reliability of an item was assessed by measuring its factor loading onto the underlying construct. Hair et al. [12] recommended a factor loading of 0.5 to be good indicator of validity at the item level. The factor analysis identified six distinct factors; 1) Performance Expectancy (PE), 2) Satisfaction (STF), 3) Self-Efficacy (SEF), 4) Social Influence (SI), 5) Perceived Behavioral Control (PBC) and 6) Behavioral Intention (BI) (Table 2).

The third step for assessing the convergent validity is the average variance extracted (AVE); AVE measures the overall amount of variance that is attributed to the construct in relation to the amount of variance attributable to measurement error. Convergent validity is found to be adequate when the average variance extracted is equal or exceeds 0.50 [22].

Table 2. Summary of measurement scales

Factors	Items	Mean	S.D.	CR	Loadings	AVE
Performance Expectancy (PE)	PE1	4.61	1.81	0.89	0.75	0.65
	PE2	4.48	1.74		0.80	
	PE3	4.76	1.63		0.85	
	PE4	4.83	1.51		0.81	
Satisfaction (STF)	STF1	5.21	1.40	0.88	0.63	0.56
	STF2	5.20	1.39		0.66	
	STF3	5.63	1.35		0.85	
	STF4	5.41	1.36		0.83	
Self-Efficacy (SEF)	SEF1	3.56	1.90	0.71	0.86	0.71
	SEF2	4.04	1.77		0.82	
Social Influence (SI)	SN1	4.32	1.93	0.86	0.79	0.65
	SN2	4.09	1.92		0.82	
Perceived Behavioral Control (PBC)	PBC1	5.01	1.44	0.86	0.85	0.69
	PBC2	4.78	1.49		0.81	
Behavioral Intention (BI)	BI1	4.63	1.91	0.93	0.83	0.78
	BI2	4.56	1.93		0.90	
	BI3	4.00	1.91		0.91	

At the time of the survey, the respondents had enough exposure to CS courses (both ICT and Programming). Respondents expressed high STF (5.36/7) with CS courses. Additionally, they expressed slightly lower PE (4.67/7) and PBC (4.40/7). High levels of these factors indicate positive views concerning students' experience, usability, control and usefulness regarding CS courses. Also, respondents expressed their positive intentions to attend CS courses in the future BI (4.40/7). However, students' belief for social influence SI (4.21/7) from their friends and relatives in CS and especially their self-efficacy SEF (3.80/7) with computing are not in such a high level.

To examine the research questions regarding the differences in students' perceptions among ICT and programming courses, we used a Mann–Whitney *U*-test [19] including the six factors as dependent variables and the course taught (Programming or ICT) as independent variable. The Mann–Whitney U test does not require normality of distribution nor homogeneity of variance for the two groups in the study. The Mann–Whitney U test was therefore used instead of the t-test because of its usefulness with small samples test and his appropriateness for situations of unequal sample sizes and unequal variances [11]. All statistical analyses reported in this research were conducted with a significant level of 0.05.

As we can see from the outcome data in Table 3, course taught have an impact on students' performance expectancy, satisfaction, social influence and intention to attend. On the other hand courses taught do not exhibit a significant difference on students' self-efficacy and perceived behavioral control.

Table 3. Testing the differences among ICT and Programming

Factors	Mean (S.D.)		Differences	Z	U	p	Results
	ICT	Progr.					
PE	5.14 (1.16)	4.10 (1.58)	1,04	- 3.90	1160	**.000**	S.D
STF	5.63 (0.92)	5.03 (1.39)	0,6	- 2.28	1490	**.023**	S.D
SI	4.72 (1.55)	3.54 (1.90)	1,18	- 3.49	1246	**.000**	S.D
PBC	5.11 (1.22)	4.61 (1.48)	0,5	- 1.72	1601	.081	I.D.
SEF	3.57 (1.46)	4.10 (1.66)	-0,53	- 1.84	1580	.065	I.D.
BI	4.73 (1.59)	3.94 (1.97)	0,79	- 2.23	1501	**.026**	S.D

at level of significance $p<0.05$; S.D., Significant Difference; I.D. Insignificant Difference

6. CONCLUSION AND DISCUSSION

At the time of the survey, the students had enough exposure to each course, as the lessons starts at the middle of September. Both respondents' groups expressed high satisfaction in ICT and Programming course respectively. Additionally, they expressed slightly lower perceived behavioral control and performance expectancy. High levels of these factors indicate positive views concerning usability, control and usefulness regarding both courses. Also, respondents expressed their positive intentions to attend ICT courses in the future. However, students' belief in social influence from their friends and relatives in ICT is also ranges in high levels on the other hand their conviction to complete a task with ICT is not in such a high level.

Observing Figure 1, we notice that the scores of the ICT students are generally higher compared to the Programming students, except self-efficacy (SEF). This is the only factor indicating higher level at programming courses, although this difference is unfortunately not significant. Besides that we could summarize that ICT courses are more popular than programming courses. The most significant difference among the two courses is indicated in students' satisfaction (STF), this may be possibly based to the wide enrolment with ICT in the last few years. In addition PE, SI and BI, are also indicating significance difference among the two courses, this may be possible explained to the familiarity of ICT in students' daily life and the connection of ICT with entertaining processes. In addition, students have noted [3] that with informal learning, they were in control of what, how, and when they learned. When studying a difficult topic, they reported that the slower pace of informal learning was helpful. This possible explanation can shed a light into the high levels of ICT in many of our research factors. On the other hand, SEF and PBC does not indicate a significant difference. Hence, it seems that these factors ranged in the same levels in both courses.

Overall, figure 1 clearly exhibits several differences among students attitude regarding the two courses, so the common approach (of ICT and programming) in many countries may lead to ineffective teaching and confusing students perceive.

Overall, our study contributes to the literature in several ways. First, this study empirically measures students' perceptions and intentions for CSE. Additionally, this study identifies differences among ICT and Programming courses. The current study is one of the few so far, where a CSE empirical assessment is employed among students who attend ICT and Programming courses.

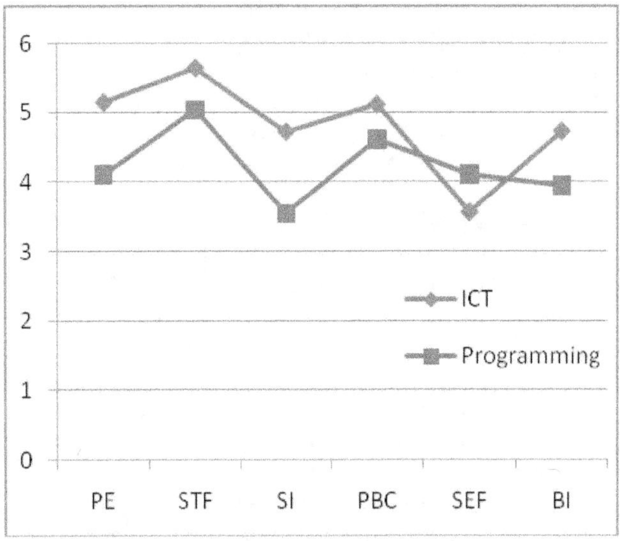

Figure 1. Average amount of each factor at each course, based on its items

Previous studies have shown that students' perceptions of what they have already learned affect their performance and what they choose to do next [18]. In view of the above students' performance and intentions to pursue programming and ICT courses is highly affected by their beliefs. As such, our findings have important implications for understanding how students perceive their learning and achievement in CSE. In addition, the results of the study allow us to argue that the enhancement of ICT in a Programming courses may benefit students' beliefs and change their attitude for programming.

As with any empirical study, there are some limitations. First, in this study the respondents are Greek students, who had attended the Greek educational system; this may limit the extend of the generalization of the findings. However, another study we have conducted among the secondary education students of Greece and Germany indicates that there is no significant difference on their perceptions regarding computer on these and many other factors [9]. Secondly, the data are based on self reported method, other methods such as depth interviews and observations could provide a complimentary picture of the findings through data triangulation. Thirdly, there are numerous factors affecting students' behavior, but this study focused on the specific factors raised from the literature as the most important ones. Last there is an age difference among the two groups (3years), this was made because we want each group to have the same exposure on the respective course, this age difference may have casual effect. However, we know from the literature that age do not impacts on students computers perceptions and anxiety [10]. In addition, Rosen and Maguire [20] reported that the results of 17 studies (8 of which were statistical) did not support the contention that age was a significant correlate of computer anxiety ([20], p. 181).

Future studies with larger sample from different countries (i.e., US, Norway) and educational systems' using wide variety of measures (i.e., observations, interviews) would valuable contribute on the understanding of students' attitude towards ICT and programming courses. In addition, we propose further work in examining the effect of these and probably additional factors on students' actual participation and performance in CS courses.

7. ACKNOWLEDGMENTS

The authors would like to thank all of the students and the schools' staff for their participation in the experiment. This work is also supported by NSF grants: CCF-1139864, CCF-1136538, and CSI-1136536 and by the Richard T. Cheng Endowment.

8. REFERENCES

[1] Barker, LJ, McDowell, C and Kalahar. K. 2009. Exploring factors that influence computer science introductory course students to persist in the major. *SIGCSE Bull.* 41, 153-157.

[2] Biggers, M, Brauer, A and Yilmaz. T. 2008. Student perceptions of computer science: a retention study comparing graduating seniors with cs leavers. In *Proceedings of the 39th SIGCSE technical symposium on Computer science education* (SIGCSE '08), 402-406.

[3] Boustedt, J., Eckerdal, A., McCartney, R., Sanders, K., Thomas, L. and Zander.C. (2011). Students' perceptions of the differences between formal and informal learning. In Proceedings of the seventh international workshop on Computing education research (ICER '11). ACM, New York, NY, USA, 61-68. DOI=10.1145/2016911.2016926

[4] Brinda, T., Puhlmann, H., Schulte, C. (2009). Bridging ICT and CS: educational standards for computer science in lower secondary education. SIGCSE Bull. 41, 3, 288-292.

[5] Chen, K., Razi, M. and Rienzo, T. (2011), Intrinsic Factors for Continued ERP Learning: A Precursor to Interdisciplinary ERP Curriculum Design. Decision Sciences Journal of Innovative Education, 9: 149–176.

[6] Cronbach, L.J. (1951). Coefficient alpha and the internal structure of tests. Psychometrika, 16(3), 297-334.

[7] Fornell, C., Larcker, D.F.: Evaluating structural equation models with unobservable variables and measurement error. Journal of Marketing Research, 48, 39--50 (1981).

[8] Giannakos MN, Vlamos P. 2012. Using Webcasts in Education: Evaluation of its Effectiveness. *British Journal of Educational Technology*. doi:10.1111/j.1467-8535.2012.01309.x

[9] Giannakos M, N., Hubwieser, P., and Ruf, A. (2012). Is Self-Efficacy in Programming Decreasing with the Level of Programming Skills?. In Proceedings of the 7th Workshop in Primary and Secondary Computing Education (WiPSCE '12).

[10] Gilroy, F. D., & Desai, H. B. (1986). Computer anxiety: Sex, race and age. International Journal of Man Machine Studies, 25, 711-719.

[11] Greasley, P. (2008). Quantitative data analysis using SPSS: an introduction for health and social studies. Maidenhead: Open University Press.

[12] Hair, J.F., Jr., Black, W.C., Babin, B.J., Anderson, R.E., & Tatham, R.L.: Multivariate data analysis, 6th edn. Upper saddle River, NJ: Prentice-Hall International (2006)

[13] Hsu, C.-L., and Lin, J.C.-C. (2008), Acceptance of Blog Usage: The Roles of Technology Acceptance, Social Influence and Knowledge Sharing Motivation. *Information and Management,* **45**, 1, 65-74.

[14] Hubwieser, P, Armoni, M, Brinda, T, Dagiene, V, Diethelm, I, Giannakos, MN, Knobelsdorf, M, Magenheim, J, Mittermeir, R, and Schubert, S. 2011. Computer science/informatics in secondary education. In *Proceedings of the 16th annual conference reports on Innovation and technology in computer science education - working group reports* (ITiCSE-WGR '11), ACM, New York, NY, USA, 19-38.

[15] Lang, C, Craig, A, Prey, J,. Egan, MA and Ayfer R. 2011. Outreach programs to promote computer science and ict to high school and middle school students. In *Proceedings of the 16th annual joint conference on Innovation and technology in computer science education* (ITiCSE '11). ACM, New York, NY, USA, 344-345.

[16] Lee, B.-C., Yoon J.-O,. & Lee, I. (2009). Learners' acceptance of e-learning in South Korea: theories and results. *Computers & Education,* **53**, 4, 1–44.

[17] Lin, C. S., Wu, S. & Tsai, R. J. (2005). Integrated perceived playfulness into expectation– confirmation model for web portal context. *Information & Management, 42*(5), 683-693.

[18] Metcalfe, J., & Finn, B. (2008). Evidence that judgments of learning are causally related to study choice. Psychonomic Bulletin & Review, 15,174 –179. DOI= 10.3758/PBR.15.1.174

[19] McKnight, P. E. and Najab, J. 2010. Mann-Whitney U Test. Corsini Encyclopedia of Psychology. 1. http://dx.doi.org/10.1002/9780470479216.corpsy0524

[20] Rosen, L. D., and Maguire, P. (1990). Myths and realities of computer phobia: A meta-analysis. Anxiety Research, 3 (3), 175-191. DOI:10.1080/08917779008248751

[21] Sanchez-Franco, M., J. (2010). WebCT – The Quasimoderating Effect of Perceived Affective Quality on An Extending Technology Acceptance Model. *Computers & Education, 54, 1*, 37-46.

[22] Segars, A.H. (1997). Assessing the unidimensionality of measurement: A paradigm and illustration within the context of information systems research. Omega International Journal of Management Science, 25(1), 107-121.

[23] Shih, H. (2008). Using a cognitive-motivation-control view to assess the adoption intention for Web-based learning. *Computer & Education, 50, (1),* 327-337. Spector, A. Z. 1989. Achieving application requirements. In *Distributed Systems*, S. Mullender, Ed. ACM Press Frontier Series. ACM, New York, NY, 19-33. http://doi.acm.org/10.1145/90417.90738

Using a Discourse-Intensive Pedagogy and Android's App Inventor for Introducing Computational Concepts to Middle School Students

Shuchi Grover
Stanford University
Graduate School of Education
Stanford, CA 94305
shuchig@stanford.edu

Roy Pea
Stanford University
Graduate School of Education/
H-STAR Institute
Stanford, CA 94305
roypea@stanford.edu

ABSTRACT
Past research on children and programming from the 1980s called for deepening the study of the pedagogy of programming in order to help children build better cognitive models of foundational concepts of CS. More recently, computing education researchers are beginning to recognize the need to apply the learning sciences to develop age- and grade-appropriate curricula and pedagogies for developing computational competencies among children. This paper presents the curriculum of an exploratory workshop that employed a discourse-intensive pedagogy to introduce middle school children to programming and foundational concepts of computer science through programming mobile apps in App Inventor for Android (AIA).

Categories and Subject Descriptors
K.3.2 [**Computers and Education**]: Computer and Information Science Education–*computer science education, curriculum, literacy*

General Terms
Design, Human Factors, Languages.

Keywords
App Inventor, Android, Computational Thinking, CS Ed Research, Experience Report, Introductory Programming, K-12 Instruction, Middle School.

1. INTRODUCTION
Wing's articles [22, 23] have been influential in arguing for adding computational thinking (CT) to every child's analytical ability as a vital ingredient of STEM learning in K-12. The tailwinds in the larger environment have further fanned this belief. The imperative for computing education in K-12 has gained momentum not only following alarming reports [21] but also due to the surging interest in STEM learning since the turn of the 21st century. There now appears to be growing consensus around the view that all children must learn CT and be offered a robust introductory exposure to computer science in K-12. Globally as well, countries around the world are beginning to act on the rationale for introducing computing education as early as middle school in order to train young minds in this discipline and way of thinking.

How do children best learn computational concepts? Seymour Papert's pioneering efforts in the 1980s around children, programming, and the development of procedural thinking skills through LOGO programming [16, 17] inspired a large body of research studies. This previous literature on children and programming (such as [7], among others) revealed the types of problems children experience on their way to understanding computing, and overwhelmingly called for a need to study the pedagogy of programming in order to help children build better cognitive models of foundational concepts of CS. However, most recent research in computing education and CT in K-12 that has used Wing's article as a springboard, has focused less on *pedagogy* and *process*, and more on *tools* for CT development, and learner-created programming *artifacts* to assess development of CT. Thus, despite the flurry of recent research activity on CT, many key questions still remain unanswered, and there is much that needs to be done to help develop a more lucid theoretical and practical understanding of how children come to understand computational concepts and thus how best to design the teaching and learning experience [5].

Pertinent to this context, it is a subsequent call from Jeannette Wing that deserves more attention than it has received thus far. At the "Workshop of Pedagogical Aspects of Computational Thinking," convened by the National Academy of Science, Wing argued for an application of research in the sciences of learning to design grade- and age-appropriate curricula for CT to maximize its impact on and significance for K-12 students [14]. In a view echoed by Alfred Aho at the same workshop, Wing acknowledged that the application of the learning sciences to fields like math had helped successfully develop learning progressions that have a solid foundation in research on the human brain and how it enables the learning of mathematical concepts. In contrast, computing has thus far been introduced to children in K-12 without much thought of how children will best learn CS concepts.

Key research findings in the learning sciences in the past couple of decades have been centered on learning as a *social endeavor*. These have included investigations of cognition and learning as it occurs in *socio-cultural contexts*, with all the attendant ideas of

SIGCSE'13, March 6–9, 2013, Denver, Colorado, USA.

situated learning, distributed intelligence, cognitive apprenticeship, embodied cognition, as well as activity, interaction and discourse analysis. Computing education curricula and pedagogy, as well as recent research in CT, have thus far not really leveraged these new developments on how children learn.

2. CLASSROOM DISCOURSE

The work presented in this paper draws on the well-known Vygotskian theoretical framework that emphasizes the importance of social interaction in the development of individual mental processes. Learning is a social activity, and speech unites the cognitive and the social [1]. Thus, in order to foster the development of any competency in a social context inside or outside the classroom, it is crucial that the pedagogy and curriculum pay attention to designing communication activities so that they foster better student learning. Learning scientists believe that in the process of guided knowledge construction, *tasks, representational tools, and talk are inextricably intertwined* [20] and that "sense-making and scaffolded discussion, calling for and elicited by particular forms of talk, are seen as primary mechanisms for promoting deep understanding of complex concepts and robust reasoning." Recent research on classroom discourse especially in math and science classrooms has revealed learning gains and better understanding through the use of discourse-intensive pedagogical practices where tasks are combined with interactions among learners, and productive teacher-led discussions.

3. PILOT AIA WORKSHOP FOR MIDDLE-SCHOOL STUDENTS

3.1 Designing for Discourse in a Computational Setting

Different domains and settings call for different types of tasks, discourse and activity [9]. The workshop pedagogy described here took the novel approach of bringing ideas of classroom discourse from the learning sciences to the teaching of introductory computational concepts. The curriculum of this pilot workshop was thus designed around what we would like to call out as ***"Computational Discourse," where learners would be introduced to ideas of computer science through building competencies in computational thinking by knowledge building discussions in concert with engaging in computationally rich activities.*** Based on past research on classroom discourse, the broader goal and belief was that through the process of "academically productive talk" [10], interactions, discussions and collaborations amongst learners and teacher, children would be supported in their "doing programming", making sense of computation concepts, thinking computationally, and developing a new vocabulary in practice. In doing so, learners would at the same time take on a new identity – that of computational thinker and computer scientist – which would build upon and transform their current understanding of computational concepts and ways of speaking about them and, ultimately, how these concepts and competencies relate to the goals that they have and what they imagine themselves doing in the future. Analogous arguments on the synergistic development in knowledge, skills, discourse and identity that learning environments should seek to support underlie the new K12 Science Education Framework and associated K12 Science Education Standards [15].

The following sections describe the pilot workshop, its curriculum, and the learning experience that evolved through teacher-learner discussions. The goals of the workshop (and the larger research on CT that it was a part of) were to understand and describe-

a) How computational discourse played a role in a computationally-rich learning setting that aimed to foster the development of CT, and

b) The appropriateness of App Inventor for Android (AIA) as a tool for fostering discourse and computational learning in such a setting.

3.2 Participants and Activities

Seven middle school students (3 girls, 4 boys; mean age: 13 years) with little to no prior programming experience were recruited to participate in a pilot workshop for middle school children titled 'Build Your Own Mobile Apps'. Since the workshop was part of a broader research to study the process of development of computational thinking in tweens and teens, the students were also informed that this entailed participation in a research study, and IRB-approved assent and consent was sought from the participants and their parents.

The study was conducted over a daylong workshop from 8:30 am to 5:30 pm in a university research lab. One of the authors was the lead researcher for this study as well as the sole facilitator of the workshop. A couple of volunteers provided minor assistance with video capture, and in helping one of the participant groups think through their final app project. Each participant was provided with a laptop and an Android mobile phone device that had been organized for the purpose of the workshop.

For the purposes of research, the following data was collected or captured:

1. The participants filled out brief pre- and post- workshop surveys. The pre survey aimed to gather basic information about the participant's age, grade and prior experience with programming and knowledge of mobile phone apps. The post survey aimed to get a sense for the participants' workshop experience, what they learned during the day, and how their views of what apps are and how they work had evolved.
2. Video capture of the whole room via 2 cameras.
3. Camtasia capture of each of the student laptop screens with picture-in-picture webcam capture of the participants as they worked on their apps.
4. Additional audio capture via recorders placed on the table around which the participants were seated.

3.2.1 AIA Workshop Curriculum

The workshop was divided into two distinct sessions separated by a lunch break. The morning session was spent introducing the participants to the basics of building mobile phone apps using AIA. Since the purpose of the research was to examine a discourse intensive pedagogy for introducing children to programming and foundational computational concepts, the curriculum was designed to be driven by discussion and questions emerging from three introductory collaborative programming exercises that were borrowed from the book, *App inventor: create your own android apps* [24], and performed as a whole group (See Table 1). The facilitator's laptop was connected to a large screen to facilitate discussion and activity involving the entire group, with each participant following along on his/her own laptop and mobile device as well.

Table 1: List of introductory examples

Activity	App and Features
App Example#1 –Hello Purr	Original "Hello Purr" App enhanced to include response to vibration sensor & clock timer events; picture taking and text-to-speech to greet when tapped; modified to have cat or tiger image appear randomly with 'meow' or 'roar' sound.
App Example #2 - Paint	Paint App enhanced to dynamically change radius of dots and width of line; subsequently modified to include features of Example#1 i.e. set canvas background to picture clicked and doodle on it
App Example #3 - Animation	Basic Animation- 2 sprites moving at random around the screen; timer events; coordinate system of phone screen; random number generation

At lunch, students worked in pairs to brainstorm ideas for the apps that they would build based on what they had learned in the course of the morning session. The afternoon was spent programming apps in pairs (except for 1 participant who preferred to work alone).

3.2.2 Final Projects

By the end of the day-long workshop, the participants had developed the following 4 apps that they demonstrated to the group—

- An app to help a child avatar gather all the candy on the screen by dragging him around to each candy. The app kept score of the candy gathered. The participants attempted to incorporate a countdown timer to gather all the candy within a specified time, but ran out of time before they could fully implement that feature.
- A whack-a-mole app that keeps score of the number of moles whacked; (note that the teacher had made passing reference to this game in the morning session, but the students developed it on their own. It was thus quite distinct from the *Mole Mash* example on the AIA website; it used images of moles that popped out of the ground (the background was carefully selected accordingly), and some moles appeared and then disappeared if they had not been whacked (this would impact the score). The students were in the process of developing a second level (after a certain score had been attained), which entailed having the moles appear at a faster rate.
- A bowling app where the goal is to have the ball hit a set of pins moving back and forth horizontally.
- A music jukebox app.

4. EVALUATION

4.1 How did Computational Discourse shape the learning experience?

Qualitative data analysis that involved coding for "discourse moves" in audio and video transcripts indicated the substantial and significant role that discourse--specifically learner questions and participant actions--played in the flow of the workshop curriculum. Group discussions significantly influenced the organic introduction and use of new vocabulary as well as important foundational computing concepts that the learners had been previously unaware of.

As an analytic strategy, we also looked for conditions in the context that precipitated learners' inquiry into, and use of, CT. In some instances it was the design invitation of an undesirable outcome or a critical omission that led to productive discourse and introduction of key CT ideas. In all these instances, the facilitator appropriately mediated these opportune "openings" to foster a discussion of key ideas of programming and computing.

Five illustrations of this phenomenon are provided in the subsections below. They describe the scenario that preceded a learner comment or action or question, and the ensuing discourse moves made by the facilitator. While these examples are merely illustrative, they provide clear evidence of how learner and facilitator responsiveness to *emergent issues* at the intersection of task, tools and talk in the course of a discourse-based introduction to simple programming concepts served to trigger opportunities for incorporating more advanced computing concepts, vocabulary, as well as features for learning and solving problems computationally in an organic and meaningful way.

Evidence from Camtasia screen and webcam captures of conversations during the app programming process, as well as pre-post surveys are still being analyzed, but preliminary results reveal a significant growth in CS vocabulary as well as use of important CT elements in the context of building mobile apps.

4.1.1 Illustrative Example #1

Scenario: In the original 'Hello Purr' app, the user taps the image of a cat and hears a 'meow' sound. The facilitator talked about the clock as another way of generating a 'timed' event at regular intervals and asked students to change the app to respond to a clock timer event (every one second) to play the "Meow" sound (instead of the initial design of responding to the user tapping the cat image). This led to the annoying (undesirable) result of 'meow' sounds every second.

Participant Question: "What if I, umm, just wanted the cat to meow five times?

Teacher-initiated Discourse Moves (that influence the curriculum trajectory): Design invitation of an undesirable outcome led to introduction of –

- Concept of keeping count using a 'counter'
- Variables (and explanation of what a 'variable' is)
- Conditional statements and if-then checks to make the program do one thing or another

Analysis: All these were new ideas and associated CT vocabulary terms that were organically introduced, arising from a learner need. These went far beyond the concepts introduced via the 'Hello Purr' app as described in the AIA tutorial.

4.1.2 Illustrative Example #2

Scenario: While the group was modifying the original 'Hello Purr' app as described above-

Participant Action: One participant discovered a way to program the app to take a picture using the phone camera.

Teacher-initiated Discourse Moves (that influence the curriculum trajectory): The facilitator's attention was drawn to this when she heard the click of the phone camera shutter. She decided that the next enhancement to the 'Hello Purr' app would be to have the students take a picture of themselves to replace the original image of the cat and say their name (using the "TextToSpeech" command) instead of playing the 'meow' sound.

Analysis: Two new features were introduced to a whole group as a result of a learner action – using an image clicked using the phone camera as well as the use of the TextToSpeech command.

4.1.3 *Illustrative Example #3*

Scenario: In the 'Paint' app, participants were taught how to draw a circle of a certain radius at the spot where the user taps the phone screen.

Participant Question: "Can we add a button or something to like change the radius?"

Teacher-initiated Discourse Moves (that influence the curriculum trajectory): The facilitator used this opportunity to explain the idea of *hard-coding* values versus being able to *dynamically* change a value based on *user input*. This led to a program enhancement where the idea of a "text box" for user input was introduced and the radius was set based on the value specified by the user.

Analysis: Crucial but oft-used mechanics of programming were introduced based on a perceived need in the app detected by a learner.

4.1.4 *Illustrative Example #4*

Scenario: The same 'Paint' app described above originally had only 4 buttons – one for each color red, blue, green, yellow. The participants were playing around with the app-

Participant Question: "Is there an Erase button to bring the screen back to a clean canvas?"

Teacher-initiated Discourse Moves (that influence the curriculum trajectory): This, again, was a design invitation of a critical omission of an essential feature that gave an opportunity to discuss how to "reset" a system state, and also how a user requirement dictates new functionality.

Analysis: Once again, a commonplace but crucial computational concept was introduced based on a perceived need in the app identified by a learner.

4.1.5 *Illustrative Example #5*

Scenario: After incorporating the 'Erase' button in the same 'Paint' app described in the subsections above, as students were playing around, making funny images like smiley faces, one participant made a rather pretty drawing of a flower and asked the following question.

Participant Question: "What if we wanted to save these drawings?"

Teacher-initiated Discourse Moves (that influence the curriculum trajectory): This, again, was a design invitation of an omission in the functionality. It prompted the facilitator to talk about persistence of data beyond the life of the program, working memory, RAM vs. hard disk storage, and a brief explanation of databases, too, even though it was not possible to incorporate these into the program just then.

Analysis: Once again, a perceived need in the app detected by a learner, prompted the organic introduction of fairly advanced CS concepts that would not normally be discussed so early in an introductory CS/programming session.

4.2 How did App Inventor for Android fare as a tool for fostering discourse and computational learning?

App Inventor for Android is a visual programming environment for developing mobile apps for the Android mobile platform that uses blocks like the popular Scratch programming platform. It was first developed at Google Labs by a team led by MIT's Hal Abelson and since early 2012 has transitioned to, and been freely available from MIT's Center for Mobile Learning. Like other visual graphical programming environments, it is relatively easy to use and allows early experiences to focus on designing and creating, while avoiding issues of programming syntax. By allowing novices to build programs by snapping together graphical blocks that control the actions of different dynamic actors on a screen, AIA, like Scratch, quite literally makes programming a snap. Recently published literature has described its efficacy in introducing computer science to high school students and teachers as well as introductory CS courses for undergraduates [4, 11, 19, 25], especially those with little prior background in computer programming. Also previously described are lists of what works and areas of improvement for AIA [19].

Little has been written about AIA for introducing programming and CS concepts to children in middle school. In our experience, AIA was an easy-to-use tool that was also excellent in motivating our 11 to 14 year old participants with little to no prior experience in programming to not only learn to program but also enjoy their first real programming experience. Mobile phone apps, and games in particular, are familiar territory for all tweens and teens today regardless of gender. In past literature, robotics and video game creation have been cited as suitable settings for children to learn computational thinking skills [18]. However, these as not very democratic in that they appeal more to male interests [6]. Recently introduced computational kits for creativity like e-Textiles seek to address this, but end up swinging almost all the way in the other direction, and appeal largely to girls. With the benefit of first-hand experience in introducing children to all these "tangible" computational tools in the past, we find AIA to be the most gender neutral and truly "democratic" among them all. Recent efforts to engage girls in computing, especially since stark enrollment numbers were published five years ago [13], as well as recommendations for engaging girls through "computing in context" [2, 8], provide a compelling rationale for the use of a tool such as this.

AIA helped us meet the primary goal of the workshop – that of providing a friendly platform that would allow novice middle school programmers to create exciting and fun apps. The thrill of hearing the first "meow" upon tapping the image on the screen was evident in the squeals, multiple utterances of "this is so cool" from around the table, as well as repetitive animal sounds as well as text-to-speech audio that filled the morning session as students repeatedly and excitedly tapped the screen or shook the phone. The complexity of the computational constructs that was demonstrated in the final projects by the end of the day was evidence of the completeness of the AIA feature set as a tool to expose novices to most all of the foundational elements of CS and CT that introductory computing curricula strive to cover.

Lastly, and perhaps most importantly (given the pedagogy employed in this curriculum), was the AIA's ability to foster natural engagement with the mechanics of programming and computational thinking through discussions and questions. Past studies on the language and structure that children and adults naturally use in solving problems before they have been exposed to programming show that "an event-based or rule-based structure" was often used, where actions were taken in response to events. "When PacMan loses all his lives, it's game over" would be an example of how people would generally describe their thinking process [12]. AIA's event-driven architecture for creating apps that responds to user or system-generated events was thus in keeping with the way novices approach problem-solving through programming; and was conducive for fostering organic discussions of how an app would be designed to achieve a desired result in response to user actions. Additionally, the complexity of event-driven programs the students were able to create with AIA in the course of a one day workshop went far beyond the limited "if-sensor-then-start/stop-motor (or LED)" type of programming that typically dominates the 'low floor', but not necessarily 'high ceiling' computational experiences in robotics and e-Textiles [3].

5. CONCLUSIONS

Despite the vast body of research on children and programming in the 1980s and the increased attention being given to computing education in K-12 today, educators are yet to establish the best pedagogies for introducing children to programming and computational concepts. It is thus worthwhile to bring research in the learning sciences to bear on the design of computing education curricula for younger children, and explore the value of the "social" aspect of the environment in the learning experience. This paper describes how talk, specifically, when used consciously and productively in an introductory CS curriculum for young learners can shape the ***process of development*** of CT. While data from other sources captured during this workshop needs to be analyzed to more closely investigate the impact of discourse on the development of specific elements of computational thinking, preliminary evidence from this exploratory study on the role of "computational discourse" for developing these competencies is very encouraging, and merits deeper inquiry as well as more widespread usage in curricula, especially for younger learners of CS and programming. Also, this opens the door to other possibilities in learning contexts as well. Through examining talk and interactions, targets of student difficulty could also be identified along with discursive strategies to deal with them.

Capturing teachable moments and facilitating additional learning for children is not a unique pedagogical practice; this approach is in fact fairly standard in good teaching for a variety of subjects. However, anecdotal evidence as well as a review of academic literature suggests that it is not usually employed in introductory programming or CS classrooms in K-12 (or even at the undergraduate level). Evidence from this workshop suggests that computationally rich environments may be consciously ***designed for computational discourse*** to help children develop a vocabulary that is faithful to CS as a discipline, as well as an understanding of the fundamentals of programming and computational thinking concepts and skills in a structured social setting inside or outside the traditional classroom.

As far as tools for computational thinking are concerned, App Inventor for Android appears to be emerging as a strong candidate-programming environment for use with early learners, especially those in the tween/teen age group. It stacks up well against current popular choices such as Scratch and Alice, and in some aspects appears to be an improvement on them by allowing for creative app building—something all teens, including girls, are eager and motivated to do—while still engaging with complex CT concepts including procedural and data abstraction, iterative and recursive thinking, structured task breakdown, conditional and logical thinking, and debugging.

To summarize, while this experience report is limited by a small sample size, and as such its findings are not generalizable, it is illustrative and provides a foundation—and direction—for much needed further work in the area of studying the development of computational competencies in school-age children including pedagogies and tools that support such efforts and appropriate curricula to achieve that goal.

6. ACKNOWLEDGMENTS

Our thanks to Prof. David Wolber at University of San Francisco for use of USF's HTC Android phones for this workshop, Prof. Paulo Blikstein for the use of the Transformative Learning Technologies Lab at the Stanford School of Education for conducting the workshop, audio/video recording equipment and laptops for the workshop participants. Thanks to the National Science Foundation (NSF) support of the LIFE Center (NSF-0835854) contributing to this work. Thanks also to the Stanford University School of Education for lending laptops for the workshop as well as providing funding for software, refreshments and honorariums for workshop volunteers.

7. REFERENCES

[1] Cazden, C.B. 2001. *Classroom discourse: The language of teaching and learning (2nd ed.).* Portsmouth, NH: Heinemann.

[2] Cooper, S., and Cunningham, S. 2010. Teaching computer science in context. *ACM Inroads.* 1,1, 5–8.

[3] Eisenberg, M., Elumeze, N., MacFerrin, M., and Buechley, L. 2009. Children's programming, reconsidered: settings, stuff, and surfaces. In *Proceedings of the 8th International Conference on Interaction Design and Children, Como, Italy.*

[4] Gray, J., Abelson, A., Wolber, D., and Friend, M. 2012. Teaching CS principles with app inventor. In *Proceedings of the 50th Annual Southeast Regional Conference* (ACM-SE '12). ACM, New York, NY, USA, 405-406

[5] Grover, S., and Pea, R. 2013. Computational Thinking in K–12: A Review of the State of the Field. *Educational Researcher.* To be published.

[6] Kafai, Y.B., Peppler, K.A., Burke, Q., Moore, M., and Glosson, D. 2010. Fröbel□s Forgotten Gift: Textile Construction Kits as Pathways into Play, Design and Computation. In *Proceedings of the 9th International Conference on Interaction Design and Children. Barcelona, Spain: ACM,* 214-217.

[7] Kurland, D.M, Pea, R.D., Clement, C., and Mawby, R. 1986. A study of the development of programming ability and thinking skills in high school students. *Journal of Educational Computing Research.* 2, 429-458.

[8] Margolis, J., & Fisher, A. 2002. *Unlocking the clubhouse: Women in computing.* Cambridge, MA: MIT Press.

[9] Michaels, S., Sohmer, R. E., and O'Connor, M. C. 2004. Classroom discourse. In H. Ammon, N. Dittmar, K. Mattheier, & P. Trudgill (Eds.), *Sociolinguistics: An international handbook of the science of language and society* (2nd ed., pp. 2351–2366). New York: Walter de Gruyter.

[10] Michaels, S., O'Connor, C., and Resnick, L. B. 2008. Deliberative discourse idealized and realized: Accountable

talk in the classroom and in civic life. *Studies in Philosophy and Education*. 27,4, 283–297.

[11] Morelli, R., de Lanerolle, T., Lake, P., Limardo, N., Tamotsu, E., and Uche, C. 2011. Can Android App Inventor Bring Computational Thinking to K-12? *Proc. 42nd ACM technical symposium on Computer science education (SIGCSE'11).*

[12] Myers, B. A., Pane, J. F. and Ko, A. 2004. Natural Programming Languages and Environments. *Comm. Of the ACM*, (Sept. 2004), 47-52.

[13] NCWIT. National Center for Women & Information Technology. (2007). NCWIT Scorecard 2007: A report on the status of women in information technology. Boulder, CO: National Center for Women & Information Technology. Retrieved September 15, 2008, from http://www.ncwit.org/pdf/2007_Scorecard_Web.pdf.

[14] National Research Council. 2011. Committee for the Workshops on Computational Thinking: *Report of a Workshop of Pedagogical Aspects of Computational Thinking*. Washington, DC: National Academies Press.

[15] National Research Council. 2012. *A framework for K-12 science education: Practices, cross-cutting concepts, and core ideas*. Washington DC: National Academy Press.

[16] Papert, S. 1980. *Mindstorms: children, computers, and powerful ideas*. New York: Basic Books.

[17] Papert, S. 1991. Situating Constructionism. In S. Papert & I. Harel (Eds.), *Constructionism*. Cambridge, MA: MIT Press.

[18] Repenning, A., Webb, D., and Ioannidou, A. 2010. Scalable game design and the development of a checklist for getting computational thinking into public schools. In *Proceedings of the 41st ACM technical symposium on Computer science education (SIGCSE '10)*, 265–269.

[19] Roy, K. 2012. App inventor for android: report from a summer camp. In *Proceedings of the 43rd ACM technical symposium on Computer Science Education* (SIGCSE '12). ACM, New York, NY, USA, 283-288.

[20] Sohmer, R., Michaels, S., O'Connor, M.C., and Resnick, L.B. 2009. Guided construction of knowledge in the classroom: The troika of talk, tasks and tools. In B. Schwarz, T. Dreyfus & R. Hershkowitz (Eds.), *Transformation of knowledge through classroom interaction* (pp. 105-129). Abingdon, UK: Routledge.

[21] Wilson, C., Sudol, L.A., Stephenson, C., and Stehlik, M. 2010. *Running on Empty: The Failure to Teach K-12 Computer Science in the Digital Age*. New York, NY: The Association for Computing Machinery and the Computer Science Teachers Association.

[22] Wing, J. 2006. Computational Thinking. *Communications of the ACM*. 49(3), 33-36.

[23] Wing, J. 2011. Research Notebook: Computational Thinking—What and Why? *The Link Magazine, Spring 2011*. Carnegie Mellon University, Pittsburgh. Retrieved September 7, 2012 from http://link.cs.cmu.edu/article.php?a=600

[24] Wolber, D., Abelson, H., Spertus, E. and Looney, L. 2011. *App inventor: create your own android apps. Sebastopol, CA: O'Reilly Media.*

[25] Wolber, D. 2011. App inventor and real-world motivation. In *Proceedings of the 42nd ACM technical symposium on Computer science education* (SIGCSE '11). ACM, New York, NY, USA, 601-606.

Poster Session 1

A Combat Robotics Course: Programming Meets Computer-Aided Design and Fabrication

Lewis Baumstark, *University of West Georgia*
Contact: lewisb@westga.edu

I report on experiences teaching a Senior-level Special Topics course in Combat Robotics during the Fall 2012 semester. The surface goal of the course was for student teams to design and build a three-pound remote-control combat robot conforming to the Robot Battles rules (http://robotbattles.com/rules) and then to compete against their peer teams at semester's end. The higher-level goal was to expose students to physical design and fabrication techniques – topics well outside our regular Computer Science curriculum – and integrate those techniques with software development. Students were required to:

- Design their robot using 3D Computer-Aided Design (CAD) software. The CAD model allowed students to experiment with design trade-offs, ensure proper fit and placement of parts, and to estimate the weight of the robot prior to build to ensure their design was under the limit.
- Fabricate parts for their robot using a Computer Numerical Control (CNC) milling machine (similar to that used by machinists and product designers in industry).
- Understand tool, machine, and workshop safety.
- Build and program a custom remote-control system using Arduino microcontrollers and Xbee wireless modules. This included soldering, obeying voltage and current limitations, serial communication, servo and motor control, and interfacing with other hardware (such as a Wii Nunchuck video game controller).

ACM Categories & Descriptors: J.2 Physical Sciences and Engineering; K.3.2 Computers and Education

Keywords: Robotics; Computer Numerical Control; Computer-Aided Design; Arduino; Xbee

Communication Patterns: A Tool for Analyzing Communication in Emerging Computer Science Educational Practices

Charles Wallace, *Michigan Technological University*
Shreya Kumar, *Michigan Technological University*
Contact: shreyak@mtu.edu

We introduce Communication Patterns (CPs) as a tool for rigorous qualitative analysis of project communication. Using our library of student capstone project case studies as a test bed, we describe our approach to communication analysis. We identify, analyze and compare the communication, at various granularities, that takes place in student projects. The patterns allow us to objectively describe the structure (what, how, who, where, when, why) of the different forms of communication that occur in a software project. Patterns range from strategic (choice of genre) to tactical (wording or tone). We use CPs to sensitize students to their communication choices as developers and users. The CP framework is familiar to students (akin to design patterns) and generative (readily extendible to new scenarios). In addition, we as researchers and instructors plan to use CPs to assess how new pedagogical practices, moving from traditional classroom communication towards more blended learning, are changing the student experience and assess the effectiveness of current software project communication practices. We use CPs to analyze the communication that occurs in teaching computer use to novice senior citizens. The examples illustrate how CPs can be used to study communication practices in many different contexts of software development or use.

ACM Categories & Descriptors: K.3 Computers and Education

Keywords: Communication; Education; Analytical Tool; Qualitative; Case Studies

Control-Alt-Hack™: A Card Game for Computer Security Outreach and Education

Tamara Denning, *University of Washington*
Tadayoshi Kohno, *University of Washington*
Adam Shostack, *Independent*
Contact: tdenning@cs.washington.edu

In this poster, we present Control-Alt-HackTM: White Hat Hacking for Fun and Profit—a card game for computer security outreach and education. A general lack of awareness about computer security contributes to the insecurity of new consumer technologies. We seek to increase people's prioritization of computer security and their understanding of the variety of attacks and technologies that can be vulnerable to compromise. We work towards this goal via a recreational tabletop card game where people play as white hat hackers, using their characters' skills to perform a variety of hacking Missions. We licensed a game mechanic from a hobbyist game company, worked with graphic designers and illustrators, and rewrote card text to make the game about working as a computer security professional. Visit www.controlalthack.com for supplementary educational materials and to request free educator copies.

ACM Categories & Descriptors: K.4.0 General; K.3.2 Computer and Information Science Education

Keywords: Awareness; Card Game; Computer Security; Education; Outreach; Security.

SIGCSE'13, March 6–9, 2013, Denver, Colorado, USA.
ACM 978-1-4503-1868-6/13/03..

K12 Outreach: Motivating K12 School Counselors to Embrace the Changing Face of Computing

Sarah Hug, *University of Colorado, Boulder*
Jane Krauss, *NCWIT*
Contact: hug@colorado.edu

K12 students have limited access to computer science curricula in United States' public schools. Individuals' perceptions of the field as a masculine, elite, and individualistic profession can restrict which K12 students are encouraged to pursue careers in computer science. The Counselors for Computing (C4C) campaign is designed to expand the profile of the "future computer scientist" by educating school counselors about the need for qualified professionals in this engaging, creative, collaborative, and rich field of study. This project is a collaboration with the American School Counselor Association (ASCA), the Computer Science Teachers' Association (CSTA) and more than thirty other members of NCWIT K-12 Alliance are partners in this campaign, developed to educate and equip academic school counselors to best advise students regarding computing careers. Advocates of computing who serve as academic school counselors can support student interest and aspirations towards computing through broadening course scheduling practices, linking students' current interest to computing (e.g., bioinformatics, media development), and considering multiple post-secondary paths in computer science. The C4C training program equips counselors to better inform youth about computing career paths, encourages counselors to focus on computing careers across pathways (e.g., for military, community college, and four year college/university bound students). In this poster presentation, the authors: a) describe the collaborative professional development approach taken in C4C, b) direct K12 computer science educators and stakeholders to free resources developed for C4C, and c) provide initial evidence of the program's effectiveness.

ACM Categories & Descriptors: K.3 Computers and Educaton, K.3.2 Computer and Information Science Education

Keywords: K12 computer science education, Computational thinking, computing careers

Sustainability Improves Student Learning (SISL) in Computing

Robert E Beck, *Villanova University*
Daniel Joyce, *Villanova University*
Contact: robert.beck@villanova.edu

Sustainability has been defined variously as the perpetual maintenance of diverse and productive environments upon which all life depends (Renewable Natural Resources Foundation); the responsible use of resources over an indefinite period of time (National Association of Biology Teachers); or "meet[ing] the needs of the present without compromising the ability of future generations to meet their own needs. (World Commission on Environment and Development)" A sustainable future depends on a workforce of professionals knowledgeable about creating practices, processes, and infrastructure to optimize resource management, and on a community informed about the ethics and influence of human activity on the integrated environmental, economic and social aspects of sustainability. For these reasons we believe that STEM education, which includes computing, is key to developing the knowledge, the technology, the skills, the motivation and the policies needed for a sustainable future. SIGCSE is one of eleven professional societies involved in the Sustainability Improves Student Learning (SISL) project, which seeks to engage those who teach computing in an effort to include sustainability ideas throughout the computing curriculum. This poster presents the current status and future plans of the SISL project, highlighting where and how computing plays a significant role (with special thanks to the ITiCSE sustainability-related working groups for the where and how information).

ACM Categories & Descriptors: K.3.2 Computer and Information Science Education; K.4.1 Public Policy Issues

Keywords: Sustainability

Creation of Interdisciplinary Programs in Computational Science

Steven I. Gordon, *Ohio Supercomputer Center*
Contact: sgordon@osc.edu

We present the components of model undergraduate and graduate programs in computational science that have been developed as part of the XSEDE Education Program. The models serve as a template to assist institutions in creating formal programs in computational science that span multiple disciplines including the sciences and engineering, mathematics, computer science, and, more recently, social sciences. The aim of the services is to encourage more institutions to consider computational science as a part of their core curriculum and to reduce the time it takes to integrate new materials and programs. The services provided include campus visits to explore program creation in the context of the interests of the current faculty conducting research and instruction that includes computational modeling. XSEDE also sponsors professional development workshops for faculty and students. These include one day to full week workshops focusing on computational science education in various disciplinary areas as well as technical training that focusing on a variety of computational tools and methods. XSEDE has also created an index to sharable instructional materials focused on building a virtual community interested in computational science education. The index will allow faculty and students to find reviewed examples of models, exercises, and instructions that can be incorporated into current and future courses.

ACM Categories & Descriptors: I.6 Simulation and Modeling; G.1 Numerical Analysis; G.3 Probability and Statistics; K.3.2 Computer and Information Science Education

Keywords: Computational science education, modeling, simulation

SIGCSE'13, March 6–9, 2013, Denver, Colorado, USA.
ACM 978-1-4503-1868-6/13/03.

Curriculum Collaboration, Customization, and Reuse: Creating Communities in Digital Repositories

Scott Britell, *Portland State University*
Lois Delcambre, *Portland State University*
Edward Fox, *Virginia Tech*
Randy Steele, *Olympia School District*
Contact: britell@cs.pdx.edu

With the proliferation of digital educational resources comes the requirement to provide educators with tools for collaboration, customization, and reuse of these resources. We describe our repository software built upon the Drupal content management system that allows educators to form curriculum-based online communities to create, share, and adapt educational resources and curricula. Teachers can create curricula from scratch, add to existing curricula, or clone and customize curricula to fit their teaching environment. We also show how our system can help educators see the usage contexts of their materials. The software is demonstrated in the STEMRobotics middle and high school robotics curricula repository and the MSScience middle school standards-based curriculum collaboration site.

ACM Categories & Descriptors: K.3.0 General

Keywords: Instructional Technologies, Curriculum Issues

Evaluation of the Emerging Scholars Program at Columbia University

Rita Powell, *University of Pennsylvania*
Christian Murphy, *University of Pennsylvania*
Adam Cannon, *Columbia University*
Joshua Gordon, *Columbia University*
Arthi Ramachandran, *Columbia University*
Contact: rpowell@cis.upenn.edu

The Columbia Emerging Scholars Program (CESP) in Computer Science is a Peer Led Team Learning (PLTL) approach to bringing undergraduates new to the discipline together with peer mentors to work on computational problems, and to expose them to the broad array of disciplines within computer science. CESP demonstrates that computer science is necessarily a collaborative activity that focuses more on problem solving and algorithmic thinking than on programming. In spring 2012 the computer science department at Columbia University completed the 9th iteration of CESP, with 104 women and 36 men having completed the program to date. Female enrollment at Columbia during the past four years has increased from 9% to 23%, but did CESP play a part in this increase? This poster presents our evaluation data, which indicates that CESP increased enrollment in the computer science major, especially for women. Students who took CESP along with the introduction to computer programming course in 2009-10 were three times more likely to major in computer science the following year than the students who took introduction to programming without CESP. 47% of CESP students subsequently chose the computer science major. In addition, survey results indicated that a large majority of students intended to take another computer science course, were enthusiastic about the program, and found the workshop topics exciting and engaging. Participants reported that they learned more about computer science in CESP, and would recommend CESP to others.

ACM Categories & Descriptors: K.3 Computers and Education; K.3.2 Computer and Information Science Education

Keywords: Computer Science Education, Recruiting, Emerging Scholars Program, Peer Led Team Learning, Women in Computer Science

Classroom Interventions to Reduce Failure & Course Withdrawal in CS1

Brian K. Hare, *University of Missouri – Kansas City*
Contact: hareb@umkc.edu

This poster reports on a set of classroom interventions at a public urban university to reduce the failure and withdrawal rate in CS1. Though unsuccessful in their original goal of reducing the number of students withdrawing from the course or receiving poor grades, the interventions provided valuable information suggesting contributors to poor course outcomes. These included concurrent full-time enrollment and full-time employment and lack of foundational skills. We also found that at-risk students could be identified with a one-page quiz the third week of the semester. We have made several course revisions going forward, including restructuring programming assignments and adding online practice problems, and revised our academic advising procedures.

ACM Categories & Descriptors: K.3.2 Computer and Information Science Educations

Keywords: CS1; retention; introductory programming

Using an Alternate Reality Game as a Course Backdrop

Matthew Lang, *Moravian College*
Contact: lang@moravian.edu

Education research has long borne that students who are the most successful are those that are intrinsically motivated. In the computer science education community there have been attempts to create intrinsic motivation in our students through the use of puzzles and games. At the same time, members of the community have advocated the use of storytelling to increase intrinsic motivation and student learning.

In an undergraduate computer science curriculum, large software projects and challenging lab assignments are necessary elements. While successful students thirst for these experiences, many students dread courses driven by large and challenging assignments.

In order to increase the intrinsic motivation of students in such a course, the assignments can be structured as elements of an alternate reality game (ARG) where successful participation in and completion of assignments advances a narrative set in the real world. The advantage of using a ARG in an educational context is many-fold: its storytelling and puzzle elements increase student engagement, it generates a sense of excitement in the class, and it increase student motivation to complete assignments.

SIGCSE'13, March 6–9, 2013, Denver, Colorado, USA.
ACM 978-1-4503-1868-6/13/03.

In an implementation of this course backdrop, student surveys indicate that students find the narrative element of the course fun, that they are more excited to do the lab assignments because of it, and that it makes them more excited about studying computer science. Furthermore, the excitement around the game helped to build community: interested students who completed the course helped in the preparation of the ARG for the next offering of the course.

ACM Categories & Descriptors: K.3.2 Computer and Information Science Education
Keywords: Active learning; Alternate reality games; Storytelling

Using Sequential Pattern Mining to Increase Graph Comprehension in Intelligent Tutoring System Student Data

Aaron Springer, *Eastern Mennonite University*
Matthew Johnson, *University of North Carolina Charlotte*
Michael Eagle, *University of North Carolina Charlotte*
Dr. Tiffany Barnes, *University of North Carolina Charlotte*
Contact: aaron.springer@emu.edu

Examining student interactions in multi-step problems from Intelligent Tutoring Systems currently involves examining thousands of interactions from hundreds of students. We designed and implemented a sequential pattern mining algorithm and a sequence rating algorithm that together recognize interesting student action sequences and display them to the user in the context of the larger graph system. With the added feature of our algorithms in the InVis system, we hope to allow teachers and tutoring system designers to better understand student action patterns and thus cater better to their learning.

ACM Categories & Descriptors: K.3.0 Computers and Education

Keywords: action mining, pattern mining, intelligent tutoringsystems, graph comprehension

MyCS: Middle-years Computer Science

Zachary Dodds, *Harvey Mudd College*
Michael Erlinger, *Harvey Mudd College*
Contact: dodds@cs.hmc.edu

MyCS (Middle-years Computer Science) is a one-semester CS curriculum that engages middle schoolers in computational skill-building. Scratch programming serves as a touchstone throughout the eighteen-week syllabus. Students punctuate that foundation with hands-on activities leveraged from excellent resources such as Exploring Computer Science, CS Principles, webdev tools, and CS unplugged. Over twenty classrooms and 700 students participated in MyCS's pilot years within the Pomona, CA and Lihue, HI school districts; 2013-15 will see an NSF-supported expansion of its summer workshops, academic-year classes, and program evaluation. This poster highlights our experiences developing MyCS, deploying it widely, and soliciting feedback on students' evolving computational identities.

SIGCSE'13, March 6–9, 2013, Denver, Colorado, USA.
ACM 978-1-4503-1868-6/13/03.

ACM Categories & Descriptors: K.3.2 [Computers and Education]: Computer Science Education

Keywords: Middle-school computer science

Cyberbulling and Game Models

Lila Ghemri, *Texas Southern University*
Rattikorn Hewett, *Texas Tech University*
Colleen Livingston, *Bemidji State University*
Contact: ghemri_lx@tsu.edu

The incidence of cyberbullying has been on the increase as more young people are spending time socializing online. Cyberbullying manifests itself through the sending of embarrassing pictures, mean-spirited text messages, emails and/or postings on social media. Technology has exacerbated the problem by allowing bullying to be accomplished easily and anonymously. The problem of cyberbulling has been brought at the forefront of many colleges and high schools because it is spreading. Indeed, studies show that 39% of social network users have been victims of cyberbulling, compared with 22% of online teens who do not use social networks. Additionally, 88% of teens using social media say they have witness an instance of cyberbulling. Victims of cyberbullying experience negative emotional, physical and social consequences, sometimes leading to the victim's suicide.
This module aims at increasing students' awareness of cyberbulling while introducing game theory. Game theory is used to model the bully and the victim and exposes the student to various 2-player models (zero-sum, predator-prey, Nash equilibrium) and strategies that produce the best outcome. This module will be 6 to 9 hours long and will present a definition of cyberbullying, statistics about its prevalence, and research done to prevent and deter cyberbullying. Next, concepts of game theory relevant to modeling a cyberbully and their victim, as 2x2 games, actions, payoffs will be introduced. As regards to learning objectives, it is anticipated that students, who complete this module, will be able to use simulation software to model various game strategies to represent a cyberbullying situation.

ACM Categories & Descriptors: K.4.1 Abuse and crime involving computers, K.4.2 Social Issues.

Keywords: cyberbullying; social media; game theory; 2x2 games

Enhance Computer Networks Learning with Hands-on Mobile Device Based Labware

Ming Yang, *Southern Polytechnic State University*
Gillermo Francia, *Jacksonville State University*
Li Yang, *University of Tennessee at Chattanooga*
Kai Qian, *Southern Polytechnic State University*
Minzhe Guo, *University of Cincinnati*
Prabir Bhattacharya, *University of Cincinnati*
Contact: mingyang@spsu.edu

Digital mobile devices, such as smart phones, have become an essential part of daily lives for the young generation, especially college students. The rapid growth of wireless and mobile technologies results in a huge demand on qualified professionals in this area. More and more schools started teaching wireless and mobile networking, but how to provide students with hands-on practice experience is still a challenge. The networking capabilities of smart mobile devices make it a perfect instructional tool for networking related course teaching. In this study, we have designed and developed a labware with Android smart phones that focuses on teaching and learning of fundamental data communications and networking concepts by making use of the mobile nature of smart phones and mobile devices. The goal of this labware is to provide students with hands-on experience with mobile devices to better understand networking concepts such as different layers of TCP/IP protocol, Bluetooth, Wi-Fi, and a wide range of networking methodologies/implementations in a easy-adoptable, affordable, and effective way.

ACM Categories & Descriptors: J. Computer Applications: J.7 Computers in Other Systems

Keywords: Mobile, Android, mobile device, networking, labware.

Women in Technology: An International Collaborative Celebration

Alison Clear, *Christchurch Polytechnic Institute of Technology*
Annemieke Craig, *Deakin University*
Catherine Lang, *Swinburne University of Technology*
Contact: alison.clear@cpit.ac.nz

The low numbers of female students in computing and computer science courses is still of concern. Initiatives to bring together women in technology to share their experiences, is an important aspect of increasing the numbers of female students entering the computing profession. A very successful celebration of Women in Technology was recently held in Australasia based on a tried and true US model. This model was adapted for the region and added to, other countries will be able to take the model and use it in their own environments and cultures. This poster will describe the recent event and give suggestions and models for other regions and countries to be able to replicate it.

ACM Categories & Descriptors: K.4.2 Social Issues, K.7.2 organizations

Keywords: Women in Technology, Collaboration, International

Creating an Educational Robot by Embedding a Learning Agent in the Physical World

Nan Li, *Carnegie Mellon University*
Apoorv Khandelwal, *Carnegie Mellon University*
Tung Phan, *Carleton College*
Dave S. Touretzky, *Carnegie Mellon University*
William W. Cohen, *Carnegie Mellon University*
Kenneth R. Koedinger, *Carnegie Mellon University*
Contact: nli1@cs.cmu.edu

SIGCSE'13, March 6–9, 2013, Denver, Colorado, USA.
ACM 978-1-4503-1868-6/13/03.

In the 21st century, educators want students not only to learn the content, but also to become better learners. To achieve this, it is crucial to improve understanding of how humans acquire knowledge and how students vary in their abilities to learn. Building an intelligent agent that models student learning would be a significant achievement in the learning sciences. Therefore, there have been considerable efforts towards this direction. SimStudent is a state-of-the-art intelligent agent that simulates a human's learning process. However, SimStudent has only been living in the world of graphical user interfaces. To construct a more human-like learning agent, we integrate SimStudent with a cognitive robot, Calliope5KP, to create a physical agent that is able to learn skill knowledge by interacting with users in the physical world. The robot version of SimStudent could provide a more engaging learning experience for students and help them acquire knowledge more effectively. We demonstrate the integration in a tic-tac-toe game, and show that the SimStudent robot is able to learn reasonably well with 12 games given two different curricula. The learning curves of the two different curricula are consistent with existing theories of human learning, where problems of interleaved order yield more effective learning than problems of blocked order.

ACM Categories & Descriptors: I.2.1 Applications and Expert Systems; I.2.6 Learning; I.2.9 Robotics

Keywords: Learning Agent, Educational Robot

Teaching Software Engineering with an Open-Source Humanitarian Software Project

Cameron Macdonell, *Grant MacEwan University*
Contact: macdonellc4@macewan.ca

A common criticism of undergraduate computer science is a disconnect from software development in the real world. To remedy this shortcoming, we introduced an actively developed open-source software project into a third-year software engineering course. We selected a humanitarian software project, Ushahidi, a crisis-mapping web application that is deployed worldwide to track events as diverse as election violence in developing countries, natural disasters and recently, Hurricane Sandy.

The primary learning outcome of working with open-source software is that communication skills are as important as programming skills when developing software on a large scale. Working with an active open-source project exposed students to interesting issues related to real-world software development and facilitated direct interaction with expert, professional developers. Positive experiences included successfully understanding, modifying and debugging software written by someone else – a rare activity in most curricula. The students also had to work with Ushahidi's distributed development model, common to many open-source projects, which reinforced the importance of communication skills and associated tools. Students also experienced some negative realities such as non-existent or outdated documentation and inconsistent software interfaces.

Aside from the technical learning outcomes, an intangible benefit of our approach was the motivation students experienced from having someone other than their instructor interested in their progress. As well, the use of a humanitarian software project exposed students to the changing face of computing from its business and scientific roots into new application areas.

ACM Categories & Descriptors: K.3.2 Computer and Information Science Education

Keywords: Software Engineering; Open Source; Computer Science Education

Computing in Context

Robert E. Beck, *Villanova University*
Edward Carr, *North Carolina A&T University*
Wingyan Chung, *Fayetteville State University*
Edward Fox, *Virginia Tech*
Christine Nass, *Villanova University*
Contact: robert.beck@villanova.edu

As computing moves into its sixth decade as a formal field of study, a great deal of attention is focused on the breadth of relationships between computing and other disciplines. Descriptors of this relationship include computing in context, computing with a purpose, computing + X, computational X, interdisciplinary computing, multi-disciplinary computing, and trans-disciplinary computing. Regardless of the descriptor, the goals for exploring the relationship remain the same: students need to understand how the power of computing informs and shapes ideas throughout the academy and society. They need to learn appropriate concepts in computing and to see these applied to other areas of study. This learning will be most effective when approached through active participation of students, as they tackle questions and problems coming from society's ever-growing and ever-changing reliance on computing devices and modes of interaction. Our NSF-funded project, titled Computing in Context, fosters interdisciplinary computing education by creating exemplars of curricular materials, testing these materials in undergraduate computing courses, and disseminating the materials through computingportal.org. We focus our effort on four areas of applied computing: computational linguistics, computing and music intelligence and security informatics, and web science. Our materials will be designed for inquiry-based learning, whether this occurs in lecture as a brief conversation between pairs of students or in lab as loosely formulated problem or scenario or as a multi-week, team-based project.

ACM Categories & Descriptors: K.3.2 Computer and Information Systems Education

Keywords: Computational linguistics; computing and music; intelligence and security informatics; web science

SIGCSE'13, March 6–9, 2013, Denver, Colorado, USA.
ACM 978-1-4503-1868-6/13/03.

Integrating Computer Science into Middle School Mathematics

Susan H. Rodger, *Duke University*
Dwayne C. Brown, Jr., *Duke University*
Michael Hoyle, *Duke University*
Michael Marion, *Duke University*
Contact: rodger@cs.duke.edu

Our project is part of the Adventures in Alice Programming project at Duke University. In particular, our project is integrating computer science into middle school math using Alice. We show several ways for students to improve their math skills while engaging their interest in programming. First, we have created Alice worlds for students to interact with to practice math concepts. Second, we have created tutorials to guide students on building such worlds. Third, we have created short challenge problems for students to focus on the math and the programming statements to complete a mostly built world. To encourage the use of Alice with projects we have developed many sample math projects. To encourage teachers to use Alice with math and computer science, we have been mapping our free curriculum materials to both the Common Core Math standards and the CSTA CS standards. Our curriculum materials are available at www.cs.duke.edu/csed/alice/aliceInSchools.

ACM Categories & Descriptors: K.3.2 Computer and Information Science Education

Keywords: Alice, virtual worlds, K-12 education, middle school, introductory computer science, mathematics

OpenDSA: Using an Active eTextbook to Teach Data Structures and Algorithms

Eric Fouh, *Virginia Tech*
Daniel Breakiron, *Virginia Tech*
Mai Elshehaly, *Virginia Tech*
T. Simin Hall, *Virginia Tech*
Ville Karavirta, *Aalto University*
Clifford A. Shaffer, *Virginia Tech*
Contact: shaffer@vt.edu

We present a study to evaluate OpenDSA, an open source, online system combining textbook-quality content with algorithm visualizations and interactive exercises for data structures and algorithms courses. We hypothesize that answering many questions and exercises with immediate feedback allows students to know whether they are on track with their learning. In a quasi-experimental study, a control group received lecture and textbook for three weeks. The treatment section spent class time working through equivalent content and exercises in OpenDSA. A post-test compared the two. An opinion survey examined students' perception and opinions about the experience. Detailed interaction logs were used to analyze student use of the tutorials and exercises to understand how they used the system.

ACM Categories & Descriptors: E.1 Data Structures; E.2 Data Storage Repreentations; K.3.2 Computers and Education: Computer and Information Science Education

Keywords: Algorithm visualization; automated assessment; eTextbooks

Making Images by Hand and by Code Motivating Students with Multi-Language Interactive Media Application Scripting

Chukwunweike T. Abuah, *Grinnell College*
Rogelio Calderon, *Grinnell College*
Martin Estrada, *Grinnell College*
Zarni Htet, *Central College*
Adriana M. Hurley, *Grinnell College*
Katherine Ingersoll, *Grinnell College*
Hart Russell, *Grinnell College*
Sydney Ryan, *Grinnell College*
Kimberly Spasaro, *Grinnell College*
Prashanna Tiwaree, *Grinnell College*
Samuel A. Rebelsky, *Grinnell College*
Contact: rebelsky@grinnell.edu

Calls are growing for computer science faculty to build a citizenry who are fluent with information technology and able to think computationally. While one might hope that our students would naturally understand the importance of such knowledge, many do not. CS faculty must therefore find ways to motivate such students.

In this project, we explore *interactive* scripting, scripting done while working in an application. Scripting applications allows non-programmers to explore creative spaces and more efficiently accomplish many tasks. The interactive scripting model allows students to mix work they do normally ("by hand") with scripts that they write to better interact with the system ("by code"). Rather than focusing on one language or programming environment, we explore a *multilingual* approach that supports scripting in the environment the student (or their professor) considers appropriate. The success of the Media Computation approach leads us to focus on *media* applications, primarily image making and manipulation.

We describe our experience (1) developing and using libraries to support interactive scripting in a functional language and an object-oriented language; (2) extending two open-source graphics applications, the GNU Image Manipulation Program and Inkscape, to support interactive multilingual scripting and (3) building novice-friendly examples and procedures.

ACM Categories & Descriptors: K.3.2 [**Computers and Education**]: Computer and Information Science Education-*computer science education.*

Keywords: FITness, Computational Thinking, Media Computation, Open-Source Software, Scripting Languages, Functional Programming

Selecting and Using a Parallel Programming Language

Michael Graf, *Knox College*
David Bunde, *Knox College*
David Ely, *The Ohio State University*
David Lucas, *Knox College*
Jens Mache, *Lewis & Clark College*
Chris Mitchell, *CloudBolt Software*
Andrei Papancea, *Knox College*
Miriam Robinson, *Lewis & Clark College*
Ben White, *Lewis & Clark College*
Contact: dbunde@knox.edu

One promising approach to teaching parallel programming is to use high-level parallel programming languages, which handle some of the more mundane details of parallel programming and allow both instructors and students to focus on the main ideas. How does one go about selecting the language to use? We present short descriptions of a variety of languages (Chapel, Cilk, CUDA, Habanero Java, Hadoop, OpenACC, OpenMP and Scala), including our assessment of their strengths and weaknesses, plus some general considerations to keep in mind when teaching parallel programming.

ACM Categories & Descriptors: D.3.2 Language classifications

Keywords: Parallel programming languages, High-level languages, Teaching parallel programming

A Comprehensive Software Engineering Education Program for Grades 6 to 12 in NYC Public Schools

Cameron L. Fadjo, *New York City Department of Education*
Contact: cfadjo@schools.nyc.gov

How do we best prepare middle and high school students for college and career pathways in software engineering? Current industry and academic trends suggest that students are best prepared for postsecondary success in new and emerging interdisciplinary fields through extensive training in higher-order thinking skills, such as creative thinking, problem solving, critical thinking, and computational thinking, as well as the development of advanced technical skills, such as applied computing and engineering. To address the urgent need to prepare students for postsecondary industry and educational pathways that utilize software engineering principles, the Office of Postsecondary Readiness (OPSR) within the NYC Department of Education has created a comprehensive curricular program in software engineering for students in grades 6 to 12 called the Software Engineering Pilot (SEP) program. OPSR seeks to improve college and career readiness for all students by placing the SEP program in twenty (20) NYC public schools --ten (10) middle schools and ten (10) high schools-- by the fall of 2013. In this poster session I will outline the various aspects of our comprehensive curriculum, including innovative approaches to teaching abstract concepts, and present the recommended overall curricular scope and sequence for introducing software engineering to students in grades 6 to 12.

SIGCSE'13, March 6–9, 2013, Denver, Colorado, USA.
ACM 978-1-4503-1868-6/13/03.

ACM Categories & Descriptors: K.3.2 [**Computers and Education**]: Computer and Information Science Education – *Computer science education.*

Keywords: Software Engineering Education, Computing Education, Curriculum Design, College and Career Readiness, Gender, Constructionism, Grounded Embodied Pedagogy, Instructional Embodiment

Teaching Data Structures with BeSocratic

Sam Bryfczynski, *Clemson University*
Brian C. Dean, *Clemson University*
Roy P. Pargas, *Clemson University*
Melanie M. Cooper, *Clemson University*
Michael Klymkowsky, *University of Colorado Boulder*
Contact: sbryfcz@gmail.com

Data structures are one of the fundamental concepts that all computer scientist students must learn if they are to succeed in their careers. Therefore, it is important to develop and assess questions targeted at improving the teaching of data structures. Unfortunately, research suggests that multiple choice or matching questions cannot be used to properly assess deep knowledge on a subject [1,2,3,4]. Students can often guess their way to the correct answer. We believe that students must construct these structures instead of simply identifying them. However, analyzing many hand-drawn data structures is time-consuming for large class sizes. This poster describes a web-based software tool, *BeSocratic,* designed to facilitate interactivity in a data structures course. *BeSocratic* allows students to build data structures intuitively using a combination of handwriting recognition and gestures. Using *BeSocratic*, instructors can create intelligent tutors that teach students to construct various data structures. These tutors are able to identify problems and provide multi-tiered feedback to students. Furthermore, *BeSocratic* records each action a student makes, so it may be replayed and visualized to gain deeper insights into how students construct data structures and complete algorithms. We have created and pilot-tested a *BeSocratic* activity, which teaches students how to construct splay trees.

ACM Categories & Descriptors: K.3.1 Computer Uses in Education

Keywords: Intelligent Tutors, Data Structors, Splay Trees, Feedback

RoboBuilder: A Computational Thinking Game

David Weintrop, *Northwestern University*
Uri Wilensky, *Northwestern University*
Contact: dweintrop@u.northwestern.edu

RoboBuilder is a blocks-based, program-to-play game designed to introduce students to core aspects of computational thinking in a fun and engaging environment. The game employs a constructionist design to challenge players to invent and implement strategies to control an on-screen robot using a specially designed visual programming language. During the game, players' robots compete against a series of progressively more challenging opponents in one-on-one battles. Through playing the game, players construct working programs, providing learners with the experience of reifying their own ideas using a computational medium, a practice central to our notion of computational thinking. This poster presents the design rationale for RoboBuilder and discusses key aspects of the game that contribute to giving learners a positive, hands-on introduction to core computational thinking skills including computationally expressing ideas, algorithmic thinking, and debugging.

ACM Categories & Descriptors: K.3.2 Computer and Information Science Education; D.1.7 Visual Programming

Keywords: Computational Thinking; Game-based Learning; Novice Programming Environments; Design

Modeling Student Programming with Multimodal Learning Analytics

Joseph F. Grafsgaard, *NC State University*
Joseph B. Wiggins, *NC State University*
Kristy Elizabeth Boyer, *NC State University*
Eric N. Wiebe, *NC State University*
James C. Lester, *NC State University*
Contact: jfgrafsg@ncsu.edu

Understanding how students solve computational problems is central to computer science education research. This goal is facilitated by recent advances in the availability and analysis of detailed multimodal data collected during student learning. Drawing on research into student problem-solving processes and findings on human posture and gesture, this poster utilizes a multimodal learning analytics framework that links automatically identified posture and gesture features with student problem-solving and dialogue events during one-on-one human tutoring of introductory computer science. The findings provide new insight into how bodily movements occur during computer science tutoring, and lay the foundation for programming feedback tools and deep analyses of student learning processes.

ACM Categories & Descriptors: K.3.2 [**Computer and Information Science Education**]: Computer science education; H.1.2 [**User/Machine Systems**]: Human factors, human information processing

Keywords: Computer science education research; multimodal learning analytics; computer programming; posture; gesture; nonverbal behavior; tutoring

SIGCSE'13, March 6–9, 2013, Denver, Colorado, USA.
ACM 978-1-4503-1868-6/13/03.

Poster Session 2

Embracing the Digital Humanities: A Course on Computing in the Humanities for Undergraduate Computer Science Minor Students

Deena Engel, *New York University*
Contact: deena@cs.nyu.edu

A review of literature in the Digital Humanities field reveals ongoing research on curriculum development. Case studies highlight projects as a means of teaching humanities computing. From a computing perspective, a literature review reveals studies on building successful programming curricula across disciplines; implementing project-based learning ; the role of Computer Science departments in inter-disciplinary studies and the role of teaching web programming to non-majors. Students must fulfill two pre-requisites in order to attend our class: at least one semester each in web design and programming in a high-level language (e.g. Python or Java). CS majors are welcome to take this as an elective. This course was given for the fourth time in the fall, 2012 semester. Topics in this course focus on the following subjects and projects: textual analysis by writing programs in Python; a text encoding project using XML with adherence to current Text Encoding Initiative standards (see TEI - http://www.tei-c.org/index.xml); building an on-line archive from primary source materials using xHTML/CSS, XML, XSLT and JavaScript; and creating works of software art using Processing /Java (http://processing.org/). Students are exposed to current research throughout the Digital Humanities by a series of guest lectures given by NYU faculty from the departments of English, History, Museum Studies, and Classics.

ACM Categories & Descriptors: **K.3.2** Computer and Information Science Education

Keywords: Multimedia; Curriculum Development; Web-based Techniques; Non-Majors

A Cloud Computing Curriculum for Undergraduate CS Majors

Edward Walker, *Whitworth University*
Contact: ewalker@whitworth.edu

We describe our approach in developing a Cloud Computing course for undergraduate CS majors. Teaching Cloud Computing can be a challenge, as there are many concepts that need to be covered within the limited time-frame of a three-credit hour semester course. Our approach focused on teaching the concepts and techniques for writing distributed client software using Cloud services, while covering other aspects of Cloud Computing at a higher-level using a story-telling approach. The core concepts were taught through a series of hands-on, scenario-driven, lectures and labs using Cloud services provided by Amazon.com. We share our experience in evaluating other Cloud Computing platforms for use in the class, and the challenges and false assumptions we encountered while teaching it.

ACM Categories & Descriptors: C.2.4 Distributed Systems; K.3.2 Computer and Information Science Education

Keywords: Cloud Computing; Curriculum Development; Distributed Computing; Undergraduate Computer Science Education

Using the Atmel AVR (Arduino Microcontroller) as the Foundation of Beginning Computer Organization Course

Susan M. Haynes, *Eastern Michigan University*
Contact: shaynes@emich.edu

This poster describes our experiences, materials and plans using the Atmel AVR, a RISC microprocessor, for teaching beginning computer organization at the college level. In particular, we use this microprocessor, typically packaged into the Arduino, to give hands-on experience with: (1) Assembly language programming, including ISA (16 bit instructions), multiple types of branches, multiple addressing modes, (2) C language programming, (3) interrupt programming, (4) I/O programming, and (5) programming on-board components, e.g., timers/counters. Because I/O pins are exposed, it is easy to use logic analyzer or oscilloscope to observe actual signals. Students are charmed and motivated by the physicality of the platform. It is an easy to use platform with a large and enthusiastic user community.

ACM Categories & Descriptors: C.5.3 Microcomputers

Keywords: interfacing; device driver

Technovation Challenge: Teaching Girls Computer Science & Entrepreneurship

AnnaLise Hoopes, *Iridescent*
Tara Chklovski, *Iridescent*
Dara Olmsted, *Iridescent*
Contact: tdenning@cs.washington.edu

Technovation Challenge introduces computer science to high school girls in a dynamic learning environment that offers exciting, real-world challenges to conquer; fresh new ways of thinking and problem solving; and the support of hands-on mentors drawn from academia and the tech industry. Over the course of 12 intensive weeks, students identify a problem drawn from their own real-life experiences and program a mobile phone application to solve it. They research their competition and identify ways in which they can win users and earn revenue. They practice their pitch with experienced investors who give them feedback on their app and business plan. The girls then pitch their ideas to a panel of venture capitalists. The winning team receives funding to take their app to market. Evaluations are conducted by an external evaluator. This past year, 67% of girls said they would like to go on to learn another

SIGCSE'13, March 6–9, 2013, Denver, Colorado, USA.
ACM 978-1-4503-1868-6/13/03.

programming language and we saw a 40% increase in girls' interest in studying computer science after completing the program. The number of girls who understand what a computer scientist does doubled, and the number of girls who said they knew how to write a computer program increased by 67%. Over the past three years over 800 high-school girls have programmed 163 mobile phone apps and learned how to launch their startups.

ACM Categories & Descriptors: A.0 General

Keywords: Girls, Programming, Apps

Making Programming Contest Practice Worthy of Academic Credit

Julie Johnson, *Vanderbilt University*
Contact: julie.l.johnson@vanderbilt.edu

The ACM Intercollegiate Programming Contest is probably the most prestigious competition of its kind. Decomposing problems into familiar algorithms; making tradeoffs between efficiency and complexity; working on a team under pressure; not only are these skills needed to compete successfully in such a contest, but are also highly valued in industry. The focus of this poster is to describe a course recently added to the curriculum at Vanderbilt University that centers on programming contest skills and yet, somewhat surprisingly, encompasses several significant learning objectives.

Because we already had a general idea of what the learning activities of a course like this would be, we were careful not to simply cobble together performance metrics and learning objectives to suit them. This common mistake leads to assessments that devolve into skills tests measuring basic knowledge instead of instruments that gauge a deeper understanding of the target learning objectives. To combat these pitfalls I broke down the learning activity by identifying the skills needed for success in such an exercise. I then classified each skill in two ways. (i) How could this ability play a part in the achievement of some broader, overarching concept and (ii) in what way might the learning and practice of this skill contribute to the deeper understanding of these larger concepts. Our goal is to inform faculty on how they might include a course like this in their programs and to demonstrate its value to the curriculum.

ACM Categories & Descriptors: K.3 Computers and Education

Keywords: Programming Contest, Course Design

Interdisciplinary Computing, Successes and Challenges

Lillian N. Cassel, *Villanova University*
Ursula Wolz, *Montclair State University*
Contact: cassel@acm.org

We summarize the results of our NSF funded exploration of interdisciplinary computing, including the following points:

- Interdisciplinary computing spans fields as diverse as visual art, music, the humanities and social sciences, health sciences, pure science, engineering, and mathematics. No field of inquiry in the 21st century extends its knowledge without the influence of computing.
- A bifurcation is occurring: at some institutions this climate of interdisciplinary work is nurtured, while at others it is thwarted by lack of motivation, resource limitations or simple inaccessibility.
- Interdisciplinary computing is inherently collaborative between computing specialists and specialists in other fields. It is not merely pair-wise: computational-X or Y-informatics, but often the collaboration draws from a number of fields.
- An important question is what is the breadth and depth of knowledge and skill required to engage in this work. Who needs to know what? What is the language of discourse? How is a methodology established and accepted, and how is subsequent work evaluated?
- The mundane concerns of intellectual ownership, boundaries on the discipline (e.g. silos), professional advancement, financial support, and institutional buy-in can diminish the pure intellectual joy that is evident in existing interdisciplinary work.
- Impediments are encountered in making the effective collaborations that are essential for the advancement of all the disciplines. The computing disciplines are essential to and also dependent on nearly all other branches of intellectual discovery.

ACM Categories & Descriptors: K.3.0 General

Keywords: Interdisciplinary computing, computational thinking

How Students Learn: Ripples in the Computer Science/Software Engineering Classroom

Alison Clear, *Christchurch Polytechnic Institute of Technology, New Zealand*
Michael Lance, *Christchurch Polytechnic Institute of Technology, New Zealand*
Amit Sarkar, *Christchurch Polytechnic Institute of Technology, New Zealand*
Contact: alison.clear@cpit.ac.nz

Learning cycle models have long offered structure and ideas for how to teach using a range of activities. Unfortunately recent studies have shown the models of learning styles and learning cycles are poorly supported by scientific evidence. In order to explore the answer to the question, how people learn, Race (2010) has put forward a model to simplify the terminology used in other learning models. The first two ripples are the Want ripple where the student has some want to learn, and the Need ripple where the learner has established that there is a need to learn the subject. These two ripples are considered the motivation aspects of the course. This poster describes the ripple model and then analyses the first two ripples in the context of Computer Science/Software Engineering students.

ACM Categories & Descriptors: D.1.5 Object-oriented Programming, K.3.2 Computer and Information Science Education

Keywords: Programming, Learning Styles, Education

SIGCSE'13, March 6–9, 2013, Denver, Colorado, USA.
ACM 978-1-4503-1868-6/13/03.

Kodu, Alice and Lego Robotics: A Three-step Model of Effective Introducing Middle School Students to Computer Programming and Robotics

Daniela Marghitu, *Auburn University*
Taha Ben Brahim, *Auburn University*
John Weaver, *Auburn University*
Yasmeen Rawajfih, *Auburn University*
Contact: marghda@auburn.edu

This poster describes a three-step ladder model of K 12 computing and robotics instruction beginning with a simpler programming environment (Kodu) and progressing to more challenging frameworks (Alice and Lego NXT). While moving between the three steps, students explore the similarities and differences in how concepts such as variables, conditionals, and looping are realized. Computer Science Unplugged activities are integrated and then implemented using Kodu, Alice and robots. This innovative model helps maintaining high levels of motivation, concentration, and fun during the entire six weeks of the camp. Feedback obtained from instructors, participants and participants' parents, reinforced by the results of the pre and post program evaluations, clearly indicated the program as a success.

ACM Categories & Descriptors: K.3.2 Computer and Information Science Education; K.3.1 Computer Uses in Education

Keywords: K12 Inclusive Outreach; Computational Thinking; Computer Science Unplugged

A Multi-Level Video Game for Teaching Security

Mario A.M. Guimaraes, *Zayed University*
Huwida Said, *Zayed University*
Contact: mario.guimaraes@zu.ac.ae

Video games can provide a secure and motivating active learning environment with practical scenarios. This video game project simulates a security competition where the player has to protect the system and keep the services running by reacting to injections that occur at random. The game has several modules (content areas) and levels. Modules have at least two levels. The first level requires installing and configuring hardware/software. For the second level players needs to respond to random events.

In the Network module, players install and configure network components such as a firewall/router, a WPA2 WIFI, a web filter/proxy, a spam filter and antivirus software. In the Database Module, players install Apache Web Server, the Data Management System (DBMS) and Database Applications. Players need to install the database and the web-server in a port different than their default port, disable default passwords and test for SQL injection before installing the database. In the Encryption Module, players will be given several scenarios and need to choose the best encrypting method perform the actions to ensure that the data is encrypted. The last module integrates content areas from all other modules.

ACM Categories & Descriptors: K.3.2 [Computer and Information Science Education]: *Games*

Keywords: Video games, prototypes, SDLC, IDE, Game Engine, Game Maker, Flash, Unity

Computing Foundations for the Scientist

Catherine Bareiss, *Olivet Nazarene University*
Larry Vail, *Olivet Nazarene University*
Contact: cbareiss@olivet.edu

There is a need for a new style of supporting a computer course. Although it is widely recognized that computer technology provides essential tools for all current scientific work, few university curricula adequately ground science majors in the fundamentals that underlie this technology. Introducing science students to computational thinking in the areas of algorithms and data structures, data representation and accuracy, abstraction, performance issues, and database concepts can enable future scientists to become intelligent, creative and effective users of this technology. The intent is not to turn scientists into computer scientists, but rather to enhance their ability to exploit computing tools to greatest scientific advantage. This poster demonstrates one course doing this.

ACM Categories & Descriptors: J.2. Phsyical Sciences and Engineering; J3. Life and Medical Sciences

Keywords: natural sciences, supporting course

On the Countably Many Misconceptions about #Hashtables

Elizabeth Patitsas, *University of Toronto*
Michelle Craig, *University of Toronto*
Steve Easterbrook, *University of Toronto*
Contact: patitsas@cs.toronto.edu

From an ongoing research project on teaching hash tables using worked examples, we present four preliminary observations. First, that rather than there being a small set of common misconceptions, student misconceptions are diverse and often unique to the student. Second, that students' naive language about hash tables when given a pretest is influenced by words from the Internet (e.g. "hashtag"). Third, we observed that students' language on concept questions evolves with repeated testing, becoming moreconceptually accurate but technically less precise. And finally, that students' code code correctness is not correlated to code style, but is correlated to how students performed on the concept questions.

ACM Categories & Descriptors: .K.3.2 Computer and Information Science Education

Keywords: data structures, CS2, code style

SIGCSE'13, March 6–9, 2013, Denver, Colorado, USA.
ACM 978-1-4503-1868-6/13/03.

Girls in IT: The Facts – A Comprehensive Look at the Latest Research on Gender and Technology in K-12 Contexts

Catherie Ashcraft, National Center for Women & IT, University of Colorado
Contact: catherine.ashcraft@colorado.edu

We introduce Communication Patterns (CPs) as a tool for rigorous qualitative analysis of project communication. Using our library of student capstone project case studies as a test bed, we describe our approach to communication analysis. We identify, analyze and compare the communication, at various

ACM Categories & Descriptors: K.3 Computers and Education

Keywords: Communication; Education; Analytical Tool; Qualitative; Case Studies

Introducing Privacy in a Data Mining Course

Lila Ghemri, *Texas Southern University*
Ping Chen, *University of Houston-Downtown*
Contact: ghemri_lx@tsu.edu

There has been a staggering increase in the volume of information exchanged over the Internet and the amount of personally identifiable information present online. Additionally, legislative mandates, such as the Sarbanes-Oxley Act of 2002, aim at monitoring organizational behavior and communication, and require organizations to safe keep all written corporate communication thus creating huge repositories of information, most of which must be access-restricted. IT carries the primary responsibility for ensuring that private digital information does not become public, through the implementation of access-security measures, together with constant monitoring to ensure that even authorized users behave responsibly and ethically. This situation requires CS educators to introduce students to data privacy and the ways to protect users' privacy.

We designed a privacy module, consisting of three lessons incorporated into a data mining course. The module aims at introducing students to privacy issues and legislations and the methods and technologies currently in use to protect privacy. The intended audience for this module is senior CS majors, with a working knowledge of database systems and basic data mining techniques. The module first presents students with an overview of privacy concepts and laws and regulations to protect it. Students are then introduced to data privacy-enhancing data manipulation methods as well as secure privacy preserving computation. Upon completion of this module, it is anticipated that students will acquire a good understanding of the concept of privacy, privacy laws and regulations and will become knowledgeable of the computational techniques used for preserving privacy in data mining.

ACM Categories & Descriptors: H.2.8 Data Mining; K.4.1 Public Policy Issues, Privacy

Keywords: Privacy; Data Mining; Privacy Laws

SIGCSE'13, March 6–9, 2013, Denver, Colorado, USA.
ACM 978-1-4503-1868-6/13/03.

"Dictionary Wars": An Inverted, Leaderboard-Driven Project for Learning Dictionary Data Structures

Kuba Karpierz, *University of British Columbia*
Joel Kitching, *University of British Columbia*
Brendan Shillingford, *University of British Columbia*
Elizabeth Patitsas, *University of Toronto*
Steven A. Wolfman, *University of British Columbia*
Contact: wolf@cs.ubc.ca

We present a highly reusable "inverted" project in which students learn asymptotic and practical behaviour of dictionary data structures--linked-lists, arrays, balanced trees, and hash tables--in an atmosphere of mild competition. Much like David Levine's Nifty Assignment "Sort Detective" [2], rather than implementing the dictionaries, students' programs generate input to our (unlabeled) implementations, and students use timing data to label the implementations. Much like Bryant and O'Halloran's computer architecture labs [1], students also compete to "convince" a web-based, automated system that their input generators distinguish the dictionaries based on trend-line behaviour. Initial assessment results suggest the project makes substantially improves students' understanding of practical performance of various dictionary data structures, particularly hash tables. UBC has used the project in three terms, and we plan to use it at UBC and U Toronto in coming terms.

ACM Categories & Descriptors: K.3.2 [Computers and Education]: Computer and Information Science Education---computer science education

Keywords: inverted assignment, leaderboard, dictionary abstract data type, map abstract data type

Computer Science-Education Outreach: An Interdisciplinary

Jennifer Rosato, *College of St. Scholastica*
Chery Takkunen, *College of St. Scholastica*
Contact: jrosato@css.edu

A recent focus in CS education has been at the K-12 level, developing CS and computational thinking skills. Oftentimes CS programs find it difficult to get into schools. At St. Scholastica a unique partnership exists between CS and Education. Together they sponsor workshops, write grants, conduct research and support a CSTA chapter. Activities have credibility with K-12 educators and involve subject matter experts. CS programs are able to reach their target audience, encouraging more teachers to include CS in their curriculum and to support their students in pursuing technical careers. Education programs have another way to partner with teachers and provide continuing education. The poster will share benefits for each program, collaborative activities, logistics and results.

ACM Categories & Descriptors: **K.3.2** Computer and Information Science Education

Keywords: K-12 outreach, computational thinking

Improving Hispanic High School Student Perceptions of Computing

Marvin Andujar, *Kean University*
Lauren Aguilera, *Kean University*
Yerika Jimenez, *Kean University*
Farah Zabe, *Kean University*
Patricia Morreale, *Kean University*
Contact: marvinandujar@gmail.com

A research study measuring perceptions of computing held by Hispanic high school students has been conducted using two visual programming interfaces. Undergraduates conducted regular weekend classes using both Alice and App Inventor lessons to provide computing instruction to the students enrolled in an enrichment program. The goal of this research was to identify and measure high school student perceptions of computing after being introduced computing using drag-drop programming interfaces. The results of this work demonstrates how student interest in computing increases once exposed to computing, but the interest increment is not enough for them to major in a computing area, highlighting the importance of ongoing engagement in computing throughout the high school years.

ACM Categories & Descriptors: K.3 Computers and Education

Keywords: Alice, App Inventor, Computer Perception, High School Minority Students, Hispanic Students

Developing Game-Like Instructional Modules to Enhance Student Learning in Lower Level Core Computer Science Courses

Jinghua Zhang, *Winston-Salem State University*
Mustafa Atay, *Winston-Salem State University*
Rebecca Caldwell, *Winston-Salem State University*
Elva J. Jones, *Winston-Salem State University*
Contact: zhangji@wssu.edu

Statistics have shown that fewer African Americans are pursuing Computer Science (CS) degrees relative to their proportion of the overall population and among those who do major in CS very few are employed as programmers. Struggling with the lower level core CS courses is the main barrier preventing students from declaring CS major and retaining students in the program. In this poster, we present our project of developing game-like instructional modules to enhance student learning in those gatekeeper courses namely Computer Programming I, Computer Programming II and Data Structures. The project involves implementing three components: Education, Assessment and Dissemination. The education component includes developing game-like instructional modules for those three courses, which will allow students to learn the difficult concepts in a gaming context. The assessment component includes establishing an advisory board for the project and implementing the evaluation plan. The advisory board, which consists of experienced CS faculty, education faculty and professionals from the game industry, assists in project development and the evaluation process. The dissemination component includes disseminating results through national conferences, outreach programs, computer science HBCU consortiums, publications and an HBCU faculty workshop. Several modules have been developed and evaluated in the computer programming classes at Winston-Salem State University. Initial assessment results show that game-like instructional modules had a positive impact on student learning.

ACM Categories & Descriptors: **K.3.2** Computer and Information Science Education

Keywords: Game-Like Modules; CS Education; Programming; Data Structures

Geospatial Intelligence as a Context for Computing Education

Sambit Bhattacharya, *Fayetteville State University*
Bogdan Czejdo, *Fayetteville State University*
Rakesh Malhotra, *Fayetteville State University*
Contact: sbhattac@uncfsu.edu

We present Geospatial Intelligence (GEOINT) as a context for computing education. GEOINT is a rich source of ideas for programming projects, algorithm design and use of databases. Students are interested in GEOINT due to its inherently visual subject matter and its strong ties with crime, espionage and social changes and upheavals. In short we are motivating computation as a subject that can provide solutions and insights into crime mysteries and complex events that unfold over time and space. In addition to keeping Computer Science majors interested, we also seek to attract students of other disciplines into computing. GEOINT and computing knowledge can provide initial preparation for certain jobs that are in demand and also for graduate school. Our assignments and programming projects that are inspired by GEOINT can be used in an introductory programming course or a more advanced course. These materials derive from well-known case studies and also fundamentals concepts in computing. Some programming projects are based on exploration of chronologies and timelines as tools that enable the geographical display of information as an order sequence of events. In general these geospatial displays can correlate information to help correct for possible gaps and inconsistencies in knowledge. These materials use multiple layered techniques of presenting information that use time, geographical location, weather conditions and static features of the earth's surface.

ACM Categories & Descriptors: H.2.8 Database Applications; K.3.2 Computer and Information Science Education

Keywords: geospatial intelligence; programming projects; algorithm design; databases; timelines

SIGCSE'13, March 6–9, 2013, Denver, Colorado, USA.
ACM 978-1-4503-1868-6/13/03.

CloudCoder: Building a Community for Creating, Assigning, Evaluating and Sharing Programming Exercises

David Hovemeyer, *York College*
Matthew Hertz, *Canisius College*
Jaime Spacco, *Knox College*
Andrei Papancea, *Knox College*
Paul Denny, *University of Auckland*
John Stamper, *Carnegie Mellon University*
Kelly Rivers, *Carnegie Mellon University*
Contact: jspacco@knox.edu

Automatically-tested online programming exercises can be useful in introductory programming courses as self-tests to accompany readings, for in-class assessment, for skills development, and to provide additional practice for students who need it. CloudCoder (http://cloudcoder.org) is an effort to build a community based on an open-source programming exercise system (currently supporting C, Java, and Python) tightly integrated with a repository of freely-redistributable programming exercises written and used by members of the community. The goal of the project is to make programming exercises easy and free to incorporate into any programming course.

ACM Categories & Descriptors: K.2.3.b Computer Science Education

Keywords: cs1, automated testing, cloudcoder

DISSECT: Integrating Computational Thinking in the Traditional K-12 Curricula Through Collaborative Teaching

Sarah Hug, *University of Colorado, Boulder*
Josh Sandry, *New Mexico State University*
Ryan Vordermann, *New Mexico State University*
Enrico Pontelli, *New Mexico State University*
Ben Wright, *New Mexico State University*
Contact: hug@colorado.edu

The goal of the DISSECT program is to integrate computational thinking lessons into general education K-12 classrooms via graduate student/teacher partnerships. The idea of combining the teaching of CT with other disciplines is not new and it has taken shape in a variety of recent efforts in the formal education of youth. What is promising and innovative is the approach as it is implemented in K12 DISSECT classrooms. Through a collaborative teaching partnership, teachers gain a new perspective regarding computer science, and in cooperation with graduate students well-versed in computer science concepts, develop lessons and course modules that serve two purposes: 1.) Address K-12 content standards in core disciplines (e.g., language arts, life science) and 2.) Introduce CT concepts, such as abstraction, algorithms, data analysis and modeling. This poster describes ways computational thinking (CT) is taught in general K-12 classrooms in New Mexico through cooperative teaching. Along with their potential to stimulate interest in computing, these pilot modules were viewed by K12 teachers as enhancing disciplinary course content that teachers are charged with teaching (e.g., middle school science, language arts), deemed vital for sustainability in K12 schools by participating teachers. Preliminary data indicate graduate student and teacher satisfaction with cooperative teaching of CT. Next steps for research will involve student level data collection and analysis.

ACM Categories & Descriptors: K.3 Computers and Educaton, K.3.2 Computer and Information Science Education

Keywords: K12 Outreach, Computational thinking

Ant Colony Simulation as an Engaging, Extendable, and Easily Gradable Programming Project

Roger West, *University of Illinois at Springfield*
Contact: rwest2@uis.edu

Simulations offer an engaging way to learn about decomposition of complex systems. Here I describe a project where the goal is to build a simulation of an ant colony consisting of five different ant behaviors in a 2D environment. Students design and build their simulations with no code provided except for the required GUI. Design issues include choice of appropriate data structures; traversal issues; and using inheritance to model ant behaviors. Students also learn about *emergence*, as characterized by the development of organized foraging trails by ants that respond only to their immediate surroundings. The visualization requirement enables students to quickly determine whether or not requirements have been met, and provides a way to rapidly grade a moderately large and complex assignment.

ACM Categories & Descriptors: D.1.5 Object-oriented Programming; E.1 Data Structures; F.2.2 Nonnumerical Algorithms and Problems; I.6.8 Types of Simulation

Keywords: Simulation, Data Structures, Algorithms, Grading, Ant Colony, Object-Oriented Programming, GUI, emergence

An Experiment to Test Bug Density in Students' Code

Zalia Shams, *Virginia Tech*
Stephen H. Edwards, *Virginia Tech*
Contact: zalia18@cs.vt.edu

A normal industry standard measure, bug density (bugs per thousand non-commented source line of code), is a through mechanism to assess code quality. If it is used for evaluating students' code, students will realize their ability to write bug free code from professional context. The main issues of using bug density for object oriented languages are creating a comprehensive test suit, and running them against all solutions as the test cases are written as part of solutions may fail to compile against other codes. We provide a novel four phase Java specific solution: 1) developing a comprehensive master test suit by collecting all the students written valid test cases; 2) transforming the test cases to use late binding so that they can run against any solution; 3) running the entire tests against all the programs and removing redundant test suits; and 4) estimating bugs/KSLOC by determining the relationship between test case failures in the master suite and latent bugs hidden in student programs. The first two phases of this ongoing research are applied to two programming assignments in two different courses encompassing 147 student programs and 240,158 individual test cases. Experimental results show that we have indeed removed compile-time dependencies from test cases using late binding and thus, have resolved the main technical challenge of using bug density for accessing students□ code. Our experimental results will help students to realize the quality of their code in terms of industry standard.

ACM Categories & Descriptors: D.1.5 Object-oriented Programming ; D.2.5 Testing and Debugging

Keywords: Test-driven development, automated assessment, software testing, programming assignments, test coverage, reflection, bytecode transformation

A Project Spine Framework for Software Engineering Education

Kevin A. Gary, *Arizona State University*
Srividya K. Bansal, *Arizona State University*
Arbi Ghazarian, *Arizona State University*
Contact: kgary@asu.edu

Software engineering (and by extension software engineering education) is a fast-paced and still emerging discipline (by historical comparison to traditional engineering), yet still immature. We argue this immaturity shows in software engineering education in two ways. First, significant efforts in the software engineering and computer science communities focus on content taxonomies or bodies of knowledge (BOKs), whereas BOKs are more established in traditional engineering disciplines. Second, project experiences are not viewed as a central integrating feature of a degree program's curricular implementation. Project experiences tend to be disjoint; there may be a "freshman project" or a "capstone" or an "undergraduate research experience" or merely a semester project undertaken by the individual initiative of an instructor. The Software Enterprise at Arizona State University uses project experiences as the contextual teaching and learning vehicle throughout the Bachelor of Science in Software Engineering degree program. Students engage in classroom learning, group-oriented lab exercises, implementation on scalable projects, and reflective assessment co-located in time for each concept. The result is a student who not only acquires a new skill, but also immediately understands how to put that skill in practice. The Software Enterprise, now in its 9th year, has evolved from an upperclassmen experience to the full-fledged *project spine* in the Software Engineering program. In a project spine, content is de-emphasized; foundational concepts are tied to project work throughout the undergraduate program. The Enterprise provides over 40 curricular modules (with labs), assessment tools, and pedagogical guidance on project-centered learning to computing educators.

ACM Categories & Descriptors: K.3.2 Computer Science Education; D.2.0 Software Engineering

Keywords: New Curriculum/Program/Degree Initiatives; CS Ed Research; Student Capstones

Student Development of Board Game Strategies in a Web-Based Graphical Infrastructure

Adam Oest, Rochester Institute of Technology
Ivona Bezáková, Rochester Institute of Technology
James Heliotis, Rochester Institute of Technology
Sean Strout, Rochester Institute of Technology
Contact: jeh@cs.rit.edu

We describe the design for a distributed game-playing environment suitable for student software development of player strategies. The framework has three main components: the game server, which runs as a RESTful web service on the Internet, the game client, which runs on the student's computer, and the graphical interface, which runs inside a web browser on the student's computer. Our earlier framework ran all components locally, and in a single programming language. The new framework supports single-user sessions, in which the student-implemented player plays against another, possibly faculty-supplied, software player, or against a human player. It also supports multi-user sessions, in which student players on two or more separate computers can play against each other in a single game. Supported by the NSF, award ID 1044721.

ACM Categories & Descriptors: K.3.2 Computer and Information Science Education, D.2.11 Software Architectures

Keywords: distributed, multi-player, strategy

Green Computing in the Introductory Curriculum

Susan Eileen Fox, *Macalester College*
Contact: fox@macalester.edu

Green computing is a catchall phrase that includes efforts to improve sustainability both within the IT industry and outside of it. The green IT movement seeks to reduce energy use, waste, and toxic substances by the IT industry. In many other industries, mobile and computing devices connected to the network enable sustainability through automation, virtualization, and reduced travel. Green computing is a topic of increasing importance within the IT industry. There are few green computing courses for undergraduates, and most are for advanced students. I present a "CS1 Lite" course centered on the theme of green computing. The course integrates programming activities with readings, discussion and online research. The first course module examined how the Internet and mobile networks enable sustainable practices, such as: the virtualization of goods and services, telecommuting and virtual meetings, and cloud computing. The second module examined the "Green IT" movement, including sustainability across the computer life cycle, and increasing energy efficiency, from individual computers up to data centers. The third module focused on "Smart Technology," where network-connected computing devices drive improvements. Topics included the smart energy grid, smart buildings, and applications in health care and agriculture. Throughout the course, programming assignments were tailored to problems relevant to the green computing topics. Students implemented simulations of green computing systems. Students exhibited increased interest and motivation for these projects, and learned naturally about data abstraction and computer networks.

ACM Categories & Descriptors: K.3.2 Computer and Information Science Education; K.4.0 Computers and Society, General; K.6.0 Management of Computing and Information Systems, General

Keywords: Computer Science 1; green computing; sustainable computing; theme-based introductory course

Interactive Exploration of Huffman Coding

Nicholas Brown, *Saint Louis University*
Michael H. Goldwasser, *Saint Louis University*
Contact: goldwamh@slu.edu

We present interactive software designed to support students' exploration of concepts involving Huffman coding. This software illustrates the association between binary code words and paths in a Huffman tree, the greedy algorithm that is used to construct an optimal tree, and the use of the tree in the decoding process. It allows the user to control the input upon which the code is built, to step forward and backward through an animation of the algorithm process for constructing a tree, and to choose data to encode or decode. We have used this software with students in an introductory computing principles course, a first-year data structures course, and an upper-level algorithms course. The software is publicly available as a Java applet at http://cs.slu.edu/~goldwasser/demos/huffman.

ACM Categories & Descriptors: E.4 Coding and Information Theory (data compaction and compression); K.3.2 Computer and Information Science Education

Keywords: Active Learning; Algorithm Animation; Huffman Coding

SIGCSE'13, March 6–9, 2013, Denver, Colorado, USA.
ACM 978-1-4503-1868-6/13/03.

Birds of a Feather: Flock 1

Teaching Computer Science Principles with Digital Sound and Music

Jennifer Burg, *Wake Forest University*
Susan Reiser, *UNC Asheville*
Contact: burg@wfu.edu

High school and CS0 computer science students often begin class having no computing education beyond studying office suite programs. Teaching digital audio, a ubiquitous application, allows an authentic and engaging context for the teaching of computer science principles as outlined at http://www.csprinciples.org. In particular, it demonstrates the interconnection of computer science with physics, mathematics, and audio engineering.

Students already use digital audio files and many have created digital audio. But we believe few CS0 students understand digital audio's underlying computer science. BOF attendees will be able to learn about our experiences in the classroom and test-drive the online curriculum materials. They can network with others interested in teaching digital media, so they can share teaching resources and techniques.

Do you teach digital audio or music technology? Are you interested in teaching these subjects? In this BOF we will discuss digital audio in computer science CS0 classes.

ACM Categories & Descriptors: K.3.2 **[Computers and education]:** Computer and Information Science Education – *computer science education; literacy*; J.5 **[Computer applications]**: Arts and Humanities – *music.*

Keywords: CS0; Digital Audio; Audio Programming

Test-First Java for Beginners

Viera K. Proulx, *Northeastern University*
Contact: vkp@ccs.neu.edu

Test-First Design is well-regarded process among software developers. Practitioner report that it encourages better program design, improves the testability and reliability, and reduces the stress.

We have used the test-first design approach in introductory Java-based programming courses for the past ten years. With the support of our *tester* library, students learn to design tests without any additional syntactic or structural overhead. A number of colleagues at other universities sued the *tester* library in a variety of courses.

Join us for a discussion on how you can help your students learn to design programs in the test-first style.

This work is sponsored by two NSF DUE CCLI grants: Redesigning Introductory Computing: The Design Discipline, Grant #00618543, and Integrating Test Design into Computing Curriculum from the Beginning, Grant #0920182.

ACM Categories & Descriptors: D.1.0 General Programming

Keywords: CS1/2, Curriculum Issues, K-12 Instruction, Object-Oriented Issues

Where Is Computing in General Education?

Catherine Bareiss, *Olivet Nazarene University*
Larry Vail, *Olivet Nazarene University*
Contact: cbareiss@olivet.edu

Have you been through a general education review, taught a general education computing course, or provided a service course in computing? Are computing skills and knowledge a college entrance requirement, upper level discipline specific tool, graduation goal, or knowledge for citizens in a free society? Sample computing courses include: Computer Applications in Business, Writing Process using Microsoft Word, Quantitative Social Science using SPSS, Computing equals Programming, AP CS Principles, Computer Ethics, Computers and Society, Computational Thinking, or Introduction to Computer Science. What has and hasn't worked? What should computing offer to the university? Come hear what others are doing and share your insights.

ACM Categories & Descriptors: K.0Computing Milieux: General

Keywords: general education

Automated Generation and Grading of Programming Assignments

Steven Shaffer, *Penn State University Park*
Cliff Shaffer, *Virginia Tech*
Contact: scs12@psu.edu

A problem with teaching large classes of introductory programming students is that students need copious practice but instructors do not have time to grade thousands of student programs. Large classes might require the instructor to restrict the graded programs to a handful. However, students need much more practice than this, and experience shows that if an assignment is not being graded then many students will not do it. Also, if the same problem is assigned to all students, copying of answers will occur. Programs that generate unique assignments and automatically grade submissions have been developed. Beginning with a brief example, this session will focus on experiences attendees have had with such approaches, and what an idealized system might look like, including exemplar use cases.

ACM Categories & Descriptors: K.3.2 Computer and Information Science Education

Keywords: computer science education; assignments; grading; assessment

SIGCSE'13, March 6–9, 2013, Denver, Colorado, USA.
ACM 978-1-4503-1868-6/13/03.

CSTA CS K-12 Instructional Standards and CS Curriculum

Deborah Seehorn, *NC Department of Public Instruction*
Chris Stephenson, *Computer Science Teachers Association*
Tammy Randall Pirmann, *School District of Springfield Township, Warrington, PA*
Kelly Powers, *Advanced Math & Science Academy Charter School, Marlborough, MA*
Contact: deborah.seehorn@dpi.nc.gov

In December 2011, CSTA published their new student learning standards for K–12 Computer Science. The current climate in K–12 schools is one of high stakes accountability with a strong focus on instructional standards. As a result, teachers, computer science education researchers, and K-12 outreach providers are increasingly being pressed to tie their content to national standards. The CSTA K–12 Computer Science Standards provide de facto national standards for all of these purposes. In addition, they help promote K–12 computer science as an essential academic discipline and allow educators and researchers alike to share a common understanding of what students should be learning throughout their K-12 experience.

ACM Categories & Descriptors: K.3.2 Computer and Information Science Education—computer science education, curriculum

Keywords: CS Curriculum; CS Standards; CS Instructional Standards; CSTA Standards; National Standards; Accountability

Birds of a Feather: Teaching with Alice

Donald J. Slater, *Carnegie Mellon University*
Wanda Dann, *Carnegie Mellon University*
Steve Cooper, *Stanford University*
Contact: dslater@cmu.edu

This session is for anyone currently using Alice 3.x and / or Alice 2.x, or exploring the possibility of using Alice in his or her curriculum. The discussion leaders and experienced Alice instructors will share teaching strategies, tips, and tricks with each other and those new to Alice. The session provides an arena for sharing Alice instructional materials and ideas for courses at all educational levels. This is an opportunity to share assignments and pointers to web sites where collections of instructional materials, such as syllabi, student projects, exams, and other resources are available.

ACM Categories & Descriptors: K.3.2 Computer and Information Science Education --- Computer Science Education, Curriculum, Literacy

Keywords: Your own keywords, Alice, Java, Mediated Transfer of Learning, 3D Graphics, Animation

SIGCSE'13, March 6–9, 2013, Denver, Colorado, USA.
ACM 978-1-4503-1868-6/13/03.

Nifty Computing In Society Case Studies

Jim Huggins, *Kettering University*
Alfreda Dudley, *Towson University*
Karla Carter, *Bellevue University*
Netiva Caftori, *Northeastern Illinois University*
Dee Weikle, *Eastern Mennonite University in Harrisonburg*
Contact: netivac@gmail.com

This session is being organized by ACM SIGCAS (Computers and Society) for those with an interest in addressing the social and ethical consequences of computing in our society within their curricula. This year we will share case studies as a means to teaching a variety of issues resulting from the impact of computing in our society. Our discussion leaders will introduce briefly favorite case studies in their fields of interest and will encourage all participants to share examples of their own. Ways for dealing and solving current problems will be tackled. We will provide a plan of how to incorporate the case studies presented into our classes along with a handout of how to do so. Topics of interest include legal issues, social media, privacy, and sustainability.

ACM Categories & Descriptors: K.4.2 Social Issues

Keywords: Computer ethics; society; case studies; social media; privacy; sustainability; legal issues

Integrating Communication Skills into the Computer Science Curriculum

Mark E. Hoffman, *Quinnipiac University*
Janet Burge, *Miami University*
Jerry Gannod, *Miami University*
Mladen Vouk, *North Carolina State University*
Contact: mark.hoffman@quinnipiac.edu

The fact that employers regularly list communication skills among their top requirements for graduates of Computer Science programs and that communication skills are specifically included in ABET program outcomes attests to their significance for Computer Science educators. To prepare students, Computer Science programs typically require students to take a course in technical communications or writing intensive courses. A recent trend emerging from the communication specialist suggests that integrating communication skills with content across the Computer Science curriculum is more effective strategy. The three-year NSF-funded CPATH II project (CCF-0939122 and CCF-0939081) "Incorporating Communication Skills into the Computer Science Curriculum" brought together 40 Computer Science educators and communications specialists to develop assignments and communications supports that implement content and communication skills integration. The results are available on the project website (http://cs-comm.lib.muohio.edu/). Computer Science educators who seek to provide graduates of Computer Science programs with excellent communication skills will find this approach relevant and valuable. Those who have developed integrated materials will be encouraged to contribute to the project repository. Those who are interested in increasing the amount of communication taught in their curriculum will be encouraged to adapt assignments from the repository to their needs.

ACM Categories & Descriptors: K.3.2 Computer Science Education; K.3.2 Curriculum

Keywords: Communication Skills; Computer Science Curriculum; Integrate Communication Skills

The Future of the ABET Computer Science Program Criteria

Allen Parrish, *The University of Alabama*
Cary Laxer, *Rose-Hulman Institute of Technology*
Contact: parrish@cs.ua.edu

The ABET Computing Accreditation Commission and CSAB (made up of representatives from ACM and IEEE-CS) are currently considering the next generation of changes to the computing accreditation criteria, with emphasis on the program criteria for the various disciplinary areas, including computer science. This Birds-of-A-Feather session will provide a platform for discussion of the types of changes that are currently under consideration, with a view toward obtaining feedback on those changes, as well as obtaining new ideas for revisions from the audience.

ACM Categories & Descriptors: D.3.2 Computer and Information Science Education

Keywords: Accreditation

Bringing Security into Traditional Computer Science Courses: Challenges and Support

Ambareen Siraj, *Tennessee Tech University*
Blair Taylor, *Towson University*
Steve Cooper, *Stanford University*
Contact: asiraj@tntech.edu

In today's world, it is critical that our students get exposure to security education as part of their Computer Science (CS) curriculum. The lack of security consciousness in digital workforce is costing businesses, government, and citizens severely every year. A significant reason behind this problem stems from the fact that the majority of higher education institutions do not have adequate resources to educate CS students in information assurance (IA) and security. While security is not required in the current CS curriculum, IA has been designated as a knowledge area in the proposed ACM/IEEE-CS CS Curricula 2013. Also, the absence of security topics in core CS subject matters not only leaves students security oblivious, but also prevents higher education institutions from applying for National Centers of Academic Excellence in Information Assurance Education Programs (CAE/IAE) accreditation, which provides access to government scholarships and grants. In this session, we will discuss challenges CS faculty face in integrating security topics in traditional CS courses and call attention to existing government funded supports that faculty can leverage in doing so. To share ideas and resources, we hope to bring together security educators who are active in this field with a community of CS educators who may not have any background in teaching security but recognize the need for it and are interested in teaching security topics as part of their regular course curriculum.

ACM Categories & Descriptors: K.3.2 Computer and Information Science Education; K.6.5 Security and Protection

Keywords: Security education, security integration, information asusrance knowledge area, ACM/IEEE-CS CS Curricula 2013

Technovation Challenge: Teaching Girls Computer Science & Entrepreneurship

Tara Chklovski, *Iridescent*
AnnaLise Hoopes, *Iridescent*
Dara Olmsted, *Iridescent*
Contact: annalise@iridescentlearning.org

Technovation Challenge introduces computer science to high school girls in a dynamic learning environment that offers exciting, real-world challenges to conquer; fresh new ways of thinking and problem solving; and the support of hands-on female mentors drawn from academia and the tech industry. Over the course of 12 intensive weeks, students identify a problem drawn from their own real-life experiences and program a mobile phone application to solve it. They practice their pitch with experienced investors who give them feedback on their app and business plan. After some more polishing and practice, the girls then pitch their ideas to a panel of venture capitalists. The winning team receives funding to take their app to market. A laptop is optional, but recommended.

ACM Categories & Descriptors: A.1 General Literature

Keywords: Girls

Replicating "Exploring Computer Science" (ECS)

Dale Reed, *University of Illinois Chicago*
Dan Yanek, *Northside College Prep*
Gail Chapman, *University of California Los Angeles*
Contact: dalereed@gmail.com

Exploring Computer Science (ECS) is engaging, hands-on high school curriculum and associated professional development that is being implemented at a systemic level in the Los Angeles Unified School District and is now being replicated in Chicago Public Schools and elsewhere. Unlike many introductory CS courses that are mostly programming, the ECS curriculum paired with the required professional development (PD) equips teachers and school districts for successful guided inquiry experiences across the breadth of CS for every student. Over 85 teachers across the country experienced this PD during the summer of 2012.

The key to success in Chicago has been establishing an active partnership. Connections to area public and private high school teachers were initiated through the 120-member Chicago CSTA. This active partnership connects Chicago and Los Angeles (UCLA), multiple Chicago universities (DePaul, UIC, Loyola) and Chicago Public Schools administrators. This model for replication is being explored in other states.

SIGCSE'13, March 6–9, 2013, Denver, Colorado, USA.
ACM 978-1-4503-1868-6/13/03.

This session is designed for high school teachers and university faculty currently partnering in implementing ECS, as well as those wanting to replicate ECS in their own cities. We'll begin with a brief activity coupled with small group discussion to give a very brief taste of ECS. This will be followed by discussion of what is special about this guided-inquiry curriculum as well as strategies for replication.

The ECS course is a natural precursor to the proposed new AP CS Principles course.

ACM Categories & Descriptors: K.3.2 Computer and Information Science Education

Keywords: CS Principles; Curriculum; Guided Inquiry; Professional Development

Teaching Track Faculty in CS

Mark Sherriff, *University of Virginia*
Daniel Garcia, *UC Berkeley*
Jody Paul, *Metropolitan State University at Denver*
Contact: sherriff@virginia.edu

Many computer science departments have chosen to hire faculty to teach in a teaching-track position that parallels the standard tenure-track position. These teaching-track positions include the possibility for promotion, longer-term contracts and greater pay as demonstrated by excellence in teaching, educational material development, and service. Since this type of position is relatively new in CS departments, the expectations and responsibilities for such faculty varies from one university to another, but they certainly differ from the traditional tenure-track positions. This birds-of-a-feather is designed to gather educators who are currently in such a position to share their experiences as members of the faculty of their departments and schools, and to provide opportunities for schools considering such positions to gather information. In past sessions, we have laid the groundwork for keeping this community together through online discussions and consolidating information about teaching-track positions at various universities together into an online database.

ACM Categories & Descriptors: K.3.2 Computer and Information Science Education: Computer Science Education

Keywords: Non-tenure track faculty, teaching faculty

Starting and Sustaining an Undergraduate Research Program in Computer Science

Adam Anthony, *Baldwin Wallace University*
Marie desJardins, *University of Maryland Baltimore County*
Contact: apanthon@bw.edu

The number of REU programs funded in Computer & Information Science and Engineering has increased from 6--12 per year prior to 2007 to a current level of 12--20 per year [www.nsf.gov]. Participation in research broadens students' experience base, increases their readiness for graduate school and the workforce, and develops their critical problem solving and communication skills. Research experiences are particularly effective at increasing the retention and success of women and minorities in computing fields [Cuny & Aspray, SIGCSE Bulletin 2002; Russell et al., Science 2007]. Despite the importance and prevalence of undergraduate research, many faculty are expected to involve undergraduates in research without having any direct experience or mentoring. Meanwhile, a growing interest in experiential learning at many institutions has led to a recent development of institutional environments in which undergraduate research is strongly supported. In many disciplines, such an environment naturally supports basic research programs that are inclusive of both under- and upperclassmen. However, computer science research at the undergraduate level presents a major challenge: most students who have the requisite knowledge to complete a novel research project are already close to graduation, which can make it difficult to involve undergraduates in longer-term research projects. In this bof, we hope to gather both experienced and novice research advisers to discuss strategies for running a continuous research effort across several graduating classes.

ACM Categories & Descriptors: K.3.0 General Computer Science Eduation

Keywords: Undergraduate Research

Multi-course Approaches to Curriculum 2013's Parallel and Distributed Computing

Richard Brown, *St. Olaf College*
Joel Adams, *Calvin College*
David Bunde, *Knox College*
Jens Mache, *Lewis & Clark College*
Elizabeth Shoop, *Macalester College*
Michael Smith, *Intel Corporation*
Paul Steinberg, *Intel Corporation*
Matthew Wolf, *Georgia Tech*
Contact: rab@stolaf.edu

The emerging CS2013 Curriculum recommendations call for greatly expanded emphasis on parallel and distributed computing (PDC), in response to recent industry changes. CS2013's PDC knowledge units relate to many undergraduate courses. Participants in this BOF will consider responses to CS2013 PDC recommendations that involve multiple undergraduate CS courses at an institution, as opposed to approaches that concentrate PDC topics primarily within a single course. This sharing and brainstorming session will bring together:

- people having experience with a multi-course or multi-level approach to teaching PDC;
- people contemplating a multi-course approach to introducing PDC material; and
- people wishing to provide and/or hear rationale for a multi-course strategy for teaching PDC

ACM Categories & Descriptors: K.3.2 Computer and Information Science Education – *Curriculum*; D.1.3 Concurrent programming – *Distributed programming, parallel programming*

Keywords: Parallel computing, parallelism, distributed computing, education, curricular recommendations, curriculum

SIGCSE'13, March 6–9, 2013, Denver, Colorado, USA.
ACM 978-1-4503-1868-6/13/03.

Brainstorming CS Principles Big Idea III: Data and Information

Suzanne W. Dietrich, *Arizona State University*
Don Goelman, *Villanova University*
Contact: dietrich@asu.edu

"Data and information facilitate the creation of knowledge" is Big Idea III in the Computer Science Principles effort. The June issue of ACM Inroads spotlighted some of the pilot offerings of CS Principles, which included spreadsheets, database structure, and XML as coverage of this big idea. The implementation of the CS Principles framework is quite flexible, as illustrated by these pilots. An article in the subsequent September ACM Inroads specifically mentioned the importance of big data and "Data Science." What concepts do you think should be included as part of data and information? The goal of this Birds-of-a-Feather session is to bring database educators together with those interested in teaching CS Principles to brainstorm this big idea.

ACM Categories & Descriptors: K.3.2 Computer and Information Science Education; H.2.m Database Management - Miscellaneous

Keywords: Data, Information, CS Principles

A Town Meeting: SIGCSE Committee on Expanding the Women-in-Computing Community

Gloria Childress Townsend, DePauw University
Contact: gct@depauw.edu

In January 2004, we organized the second SIGCSE Committee ("Expanding the Women-in-Computing Community"). Our annual Town Meeting provides dissemination of information concerning successful gender issues projects, along with group discussion and brainstorming, in order to create committee goals for the coming year. We select projects to highlight through listserv communication and through our connections with NCWIT, ABI, ACM-W, CRA-W, etc. This year we will highlight ACM-W Chapters and ACM-W Regional Celebrations.

ACM Categories & Descriptors: K.4.2 Social Issues; K.4 Computers and Society; K. Computing Milieu

Keywords: Gender Issues, Underrepresentation

SIGCSE'13, March 6–9, 2013, Denver, Colorado, USA.
ACM 978-1-4503-1868-6/13/03.

Birds of a Feather 2

Trends in CS Enrollments at Small, Liberal Arts Institutions

Barbara Anthony, *Southwestern University*
Lisa Bender, *Concordia College*
Christine Chung, *Connecticut College*
Mark Lewis, *Trinity University*
Contact: anthonyb@southwestern.edu

Enrollments in CS have been climbing dramatically in recent years at large schools, especially those in the top-tier for CS. This type of growth is part of the normal cycle for CS and is expected anytime that the public perceives that the job market for computing related fields is strong. It is unclear how much of this growth is currently seen on other campuses. The purpose of this BoF session is to discuss what educators at smaller campuses, and particularly liberal arts schools, are currently seeing in regards to enrollment in CS. This information could be of particular interest for those at schools considering cutting programs for economic reasons or those adjusting the number of faculty lines.

ACM Categories & Descriptors: K.3.2 Computer and Information Science Education

Keywords: Liberal Arts, Education

Logistics of Moving from Computer Fluency to Computational Thinking

Monika Sobolewska, *Michigan State University*
Contact: monika@msu.edu

As the theme of the conference indicates, computing is changing and so is its pedagogy. In the meantime, many computer science departments teach computer fluency service courses required by their universities, colleges, or other departments, in which the content of the course becomes highly challenged by institutional constraints (e.g. class size, university computer literacy requirement, etc.). This birds-of-a-feather is designed to gather educators who have been teaching fluency courses or may be teaching such courses in the future, so that they can share their experiences, learn from one another, and discuss the most effective ways of affecting change and delivering the content they deem most appropriate.

ACM Categories & Descriptors: K.3.2 Computer and Information Science Education

Keywords: Non-majors; Curriculum Issues; Computer Fluency; Computational Thinking; Computer Literacy

SIGCSE'13, March 6–9, 2013, Denver, Colorado, USA.
ACM 978-1-4503-1868-6/13/03.

Computer Scientists Put the Informatics into Bio, Health, and Medical Informatics Education

Bonnie MacKellar, *St John's University*
Margaret Menzin, *Simmons College*
Marc L. Smith, *Vassar College*
Tammy VanDeGrift, *University of Portland*
Contact: mackellb@stjohns.edu

There has been an explosion of interest in bioinformatics, medical informatics, and healthcare informatics in the past decade. As a result, many computer science departments are developing courses or degree programs in bioinformatics and/or health informatics. This session is aimed at faculty who are teaching, or developing courses that tie together computer science and biology, medicine, or healthcare. The discussion leaders all have experience teaching courses in healthcare informatics and/or bioinformatics within computer science departments. We will share our expertise and experience on such issues as effectively team teaching interdisciplinary courses, developing case studies and projects, and developing links with biologists and clinicians. Some of the questions we might tackle: What types of courses should be included in degree programs? What role do curricular standards, especially in healthcare, play? What topics belong in interdisciplinary bioinformatics courses? How do we cope with students who may have differing backgrounds and prerequisites? The hope is that we can create an informal network for sharing ideas which will persist after the session. To this end, we will also discuss ways for maintaining a community, perhaps as a mailing list, blog, or website.

ACM Categories & Descriptors: K..3.2 Computer and Information Science Education

Keywords: Bioinformatics education; Healthcare informatics education

Encouraging Faculty & Student Involvement in Humanitarian Free and Open Source Software (HFOSS)

Gregory W. Hislop, *Drexel University*
Heidi J. C. Ellis, *Western New England University*
Darci Burdge, *Nassau Community College*
Sean Goggins, *Drexel University*
Lori Postner, *Nassau Community College*
Stoney Jackson, *Western New England University*
Contact: ellis@wne.edu

Humanitarian Free and Open Source Software (HFOSS) projects provide a real-world application with an approachable and welcoming community for both faculty and students. Many faculty members are excited by the prospect of their students contributing to HFOSS. They perceive it as an opportunity to engage students, regardless of race or gender, in projects that have societal impact. However trying something new in the classroom though can be daunting, and many barriers to entry exist. Locating an appropriate project, trying to figure out how to incorporate a dynamic, real-world project into the curriculum and learning how to interact with the project's community each present their own set of challenges. This BOF provides a gathering place for faculty who are interested in student participation in FOSS or HFOSS. The discussion will include an overview of an NSF-funded project, OpenFE. The goal of OpenFE is to develop faculty expertise in working with HFOSS projects and to develop curriculum materials that support faculty members in bringing this approach into their classrooms. The members of the OpenFE team will discuss plans for this grant and welcome both novices and experienced contributors to join us and provide feedback.

ACM Categories & Descriptors: K.3.2 Computers and Education

Keywords: Open Source Software, Faculty Development, Computing Education Research

CSTA Chapters: Supporting Your Local Computer Science Educators

Frances P. Trees, *Rutgers University*
David Reed, *Creighton University*
Tammy Pirmann, *Springfield High School*
Contact: fran.trees@cs.rutgers.edu

As part of its commitment to developing a strong community of computer science educators, the Computer Science Teachers Association (CSTA) supports the development of regional CSTA chapters. A CSTA chapter is a local branch of CSTA designed to facilitate discussion of local issues, provision of member services at the local level, and to promote CSTA membership on the national level[1]. This BOF will provide a platform for the discussion of CSTA chapter formation and for the sharing of new resources to help chapters create dynamic and meaningful chapter activities.

ACM Categories & Descriptors: K.3.2 Compputer and Information Science Education

Keywords: K-12 Computer Science Education, Outreach

How PhD Students at Research Universities Can Prepare for a Career at a Liberal Arts College

Ann Irvine, *Johns Hopkins University*
Darakhshan Mir, *Rutgers University*
Michael Hay, *Colgate University*
Contact: annirvine@gmail.com

We will discuss how to better organize as graduate students and postdoctoral researchers seeking a career in liberal arts colleges (LACs). The BoF will bring together those who are interested in a career path to a LAC but do not have reliable advice and mentorship in their home departments and often turn out to be the only person in their department with such a career choice. Additionally, several people who have recently made a successful transition from graduate school to new faculty positions will attend the BoF.

ACM Categories & Descriptors: K.3.0 Computers and Education; K.3.2 Computer Science Education

Keywords: Graduate Students; Liberal Arts Colleges; Professional Development

Computer Science Principles: Necessary for ALL Students' Success?

Diane Baxter, *University of California San Diego*
Elizabeth Simon, *University of California San Diego*
Contact: dbaxter@ucsd.edu

Computing pervades students' academic and personal lives. Increasingly the core concepts of computational thinking are required for success in other fields. Should CS Principles become a general education requirement for all freshmen? This BOF will provide a platform for the discussion of whether or not the various courses taught as CS-0, Introduction to CS, or CS Principles have clearly defined a set of core competencies that should be required of all undergraduates. Do the national initiatives around computational thinking and CS 10K herald consensus or controversy around those core competencies? Discussion will include a look at one course that has been adopted as a general education requirement; its core concepts, textbooks and documented learning outcomes; and the institutional rationale for its acceptance as a general education requirement-filling course.

Related to this question is a proposed new CS Principles AP exam that is currently in development. The BoF will describe how the course above relates to the CS Principles AP Exam and the core competencies described through the CS Principles project. Discussion leaders will describe the value of the CS Principles AP initiative in gaining political and administrative support for introducing the course into high schools. They will share some initial data illustrating the wide variety of challenges encountered while introducing the same course as a pre-AP course into regional high schools.

ACM Categories & Descriptors: K.3.2 Computer and Information Science Education; K.4.0 Computers and Society

Keywords: Education, Principles; CS10K; Requirements; Advanced Placement; Computational Thinking Skills; Workforce

Broadening Mathematical Reasoning in Computing

Douglas Baldwin, *SUNY Geneseo*
Contact: baldwin@geneseo.edu

The pending revision of the ACM/IEEE CS curriculum guidelines for computer science, and the continuing broadening of the computing disciplines, among other considerations, make now a good time to review the role of mathematical reasoning in computing education. This birds-of-a-feather session provides an opportunity for people interested in mathematics and its role in computing education to reflect on and discuss the future of mathematical reasoning in our curricula, guided by the question of whether it should be broader than it has been, narrower, or if it is just right as it is.

SIGCSE'13, March 6–9, 2013, Denver, Colorado, USA.
ACM 978-1-4503-1868-6/13/03.

ACM Categories & Descriptors: K.3.2 Computer and Information Science Education; G.2.0 General

Keywords: Mathematical Thinking; Computing Education

Using Version Control in the Classroom

John Britton, *Education Liaison at GitHub*
Tim Berglund, *Trainer at GitHub*
Contact: jdb@github.com

Professional software developers depend on version control every day and that dependency will continue to grow as advances in version control technology continue. Students with experience using version control are more prepared and qualified to work in industry. We should expose students to version control early in their training not only as an additional skill but also as a tool to improve the learning experience. Version control can be leveraged to greatly improve assignment submission, grading, and feedback systems. In this session we will discuss strategies for incorporating the use of version control in the classroom as well as best practices for individual and group work submission, grading and feedback.

ACM Categories & Descriptors: D.1.0 Software Programming Techniques; D.2.3 Software Engineering Coding Tools and Techniques

Keywords: Version Control; Git; Collaboration; Industry Tools; Software Development

Including HCI and User Experience (UX) Methodologies in Computing Curriculum

Debra Lee Davis, *Florida International University*
Kip Irvine, *Florida International University*
Dave Berque, *DePauw University*
Janet Davis, *Grinnell College*
Brian Dorn, *University of Hartford*
Matt Jadud, *Berea College*
Contact: dledavis@cs.fiu.edu

With a growing awareness of the importance of Human Computer Interaction (HCI) and User Experience (UX) Design and Research in industry, many departments are examining ways to integrate this topic into their curriculum. What are the best ways to do this? Should HCI and UX be integrated into existing courses such as event-driven programming or mobile computing? Or should it be a separate course that integrates visual design, psychology and ergonomics? How important is this topic to students looking for internships and entry-level jobs? At what levels should these topics be taught in the curriculum? This is important as there is a growing demand in industry for User Experience specialists due to an increased focus on software quality and product success. A major complaint of employers is that this skill is lacking in many college graduates. Teaching computing students how to incorporate UX into the design and development process helps to address this critical need. This BOF will let participants share their ideas and learn from their peers. This is particularly relevant as the HCI Knowledge Area of the IEEE/ACM CS Curriculum 2013 is currently being developed. In fact, the chair of the HCI Knowledge Area (Sally Fincher) is seeking real examples of how HCI is taught in curricula across a variety of institutions and settings. After the BOF, we will share a summary of our BOF discussion with the chair.

SIGCSE'13, March 6–9, 2013, Denver, Colorado, USA.
ACM 978-1-4503-1868-6/13/03.

ACM Categories & Descriptors: K.3.2 Computer and Information Science Education; H.1.2 User/Machine Systems; H.5.2 User Interfaces; D.2.2 Design Tools and Techniques; D.2.10 Design

Keywords: Computing Curriculum; Human-Computer Interaction; User Experience; HCI; UX; Computing Instruction; Curriculum Issues

Taking Studio-based Learning Online

Yolanda Jacobs Reimer, *University of Montana*
Christopher Hundhausen, *Washington State University*
Phillip Conrad, *University of California, Santa Barbara*
Contact: reimer@cs.umt.edu

Studio-based learning (SBL), the centerpiece of architecture and fine arts education for over a century, has become increasingly attractive to computing educators. SBL can be conceptualized as an iterative process of solution refinement that relies heavily on shared physical space and design critiques. This session will explore ways in which CS educators can transition aspects of traditional or face-to-face SBL to an online learning environment. We will discuss the potential for online studios, how they might look and function, and how their effectiveness in promoting student learning might be gauged. As more and more CS courses assume an online presence, we seek to understand both the opportunities and the limitations associated with conducting critical studio work in a digital medium.

ACM Categories & Descriptors: K.3.1 Computer Uses in Education; K.3.2 Computer and Information Science Education

Keywords: Studio-based learning; online studio; design crits

Using POGIL Activities in Computer Science Classes

Helen H. Hu, *Westminster College*
Clifton Kussmaul, *Muhlenberg College*
Matthew Lang, *Moravian College*
Contact: hhu@westminstercollege.edu

POGIL activities are carefully designed to guide students to discover and explore concepts while encouraging students to practice process skills (*e.g.,* team work, leadership and problem solving). Many college instructors have written POGIL activities for CS 1, CS 2, Software Engineering and other upper division CS classes (http://www.cspogil.org). High school teachers are also writing POGIL activities for the AP Principles course. This BOF is an opportunity for educators to share POGIL activities and ideas for improving group dynamics and encouraging reflection. We welcome everyone interested in learning more about POGIL and will provide information on regional POGIL workshops.

ACM Categories & Descriptors: K.3.2 [Computer Milieux]: Computers and Education- Computer and Information Science Education[Computer science education]

Keywords: POGIL, active learning, process oriented guided inquiry learning, inquiry based learning, process skills

Technology that Educators of Computing Hail (TECH): Come, Share Your Favorites!

Daniel D. Garcia, *UC Berkeley*
Dan Armendariz, *UC Berkeley*
Contact: ddgarcia@cs.berkeley.edu

The pace of technology for use in computing education is staggering. In the last five years, the following tools / websites have completely transformed our teaching: Piazza, Google Docs, YouTube, Doodle and whenisgood.net, Skype and Google Hangout, and Khan Academy among others. Hardware has also played a part – we love our Zoom H2 digital voice recorder (for recording CD-quality lecture audio), Blue Yeti USB mike (for audio/videoconferences), and iClickers (for engaging students in class).

Do you wish you could easily share your favorites? Want to find out what the others know that you don't? Have a tool you've built and want to get some users? Come to this BOF! We'll also show the TECH website (part of the **ensemble** computing portal) we've built that attempts to collect all of these tools in one place. A laptop is recommended if the tool you wish to share is more involved than simply visiting a website.

ACM Categories & Descriptors: K.3.2 [Computer and Information Science Education]: Computer science education

Keywords: Technologies, Tools, ensemble, TECH

Teaching Security using Hands-On Exercises

Richard Weiss, *The Evergreen State College*
Michael E. Locasto, *The University of Calgary*
Jens Mache, *Lewis & Clark College*
Blair Taylor, *Towson University*
Elizabeth Hawthorne, *Union County College*
Contact: weissr@evergreen.edu

We see teaching cybersecurity through hands-on, interactive exercises as a way to engage students. Some of the exercises that we have seen require significant preparation on the part of the instructor. Having a community makes it easier to share exercises, knowing what works and what problems students and instructors have encountered. The purpose of this BOF is to bring together instructors who have used hands-on exercises and those who would like to. We recognize that few CS programs can afford new required courses, so we would be discussing ways to integrate security-related exercises into existing ones. This could include networking, OS, computer architecture, programming languages, software engineering and algorithms.

Recent hiring forecasts indicate that there is a tremendous need for skilled information security experts. This was evident at the last National Initiative for Cybersecurity Education (NICE) conference at NIST, and from sponsors of the Collegiate Cybersecurity CCDC. Security will be one of the core areas in the ACM/IEEE COMPUTER SCIENCE 2013 Curricula.

We think that it is particularly important to share stories from the classroom (what worked and what didn't), discuss ethical hacking, and discuss how to teach analytical skills. We also plan to discuss our own experiences, practices and ongoing efforts (e.g., our teaching experiences, the SISMAT program, Security Injections, EDURange and the dissemination of infosec interactive exercises). SISMAT includes a two-week summer intensive program based on the "Hacker Curriculum" and a combination of research and internship in cyberbersecurity for undergraduates.

ACM Categories & Descriptors: C.2.0 Network Security and Protection

Keywords: security; cybersecurity; information assurance; network security; laboratory exercises; teaching

Computational Literacy for Everyone: Opening a Dialogue Between STEM and the Digital Arts and Humanities

Nick Senske, *University of North Carolina at Charlotte*
Contact: nsenske@uncc.edu

Much has been said about the need to teach computer programming and the fundamental ideas of computer science in STEM education. Initiatives aimed at this audience propose new requirements, curricula, tools, and teaching methodologies to encourage widespread computational literacy. But what is being done in non-STEM disciplines to promote literacy? The goal of this panel is to open a discussion about advancing computer science education within the digital arts and humanities and how this might relate or combine with similar efforts in STEM. What can members of the digital arts and humanities community learn from each other about starting new curricula and teaching these subjects, and what can be learned and borrowed from STEM education? To begin the discussion, we will present a report on a computational methods course we developed for beginning architecture students and how this has led to an ongoing collaboration with our computer science department.

ACM Categories & Descriptors: J.5 Arts and Humanities, Architecture; K.3.2 Computer and Information Science Education

Keywords: Digital Arts, Digital Humanities, Computational Literacy, CS Fundamentals

Dual Degree Tracks for Computer Science Majors

Joanne F. Selinski, Johns Hopkins University
Kathie A. Yerion, Gonzaga University
Contact: joanne@cs.jhu.edu

Many institutions offer either a Bachelor of Science or a Bachelor of Arts degree program to computer science majors, often depending on what type of college or department houses the major. However, an increasing number of institutions have created dual degree tracks wherein students may choose to pursue either a BS or a BA, with a different set of requirements for each and possibly different credentialing as well. This BOF provides a forum for educators and administrators who currently

SIGCSE'13, March 6–9, 2013, Denver, Colorado, USA.
ACM 978-1-4503-1868-6/13/03.

offer dual degree options to share their experiences with those who are considering adding a second track. Issues of interest such as requirements within and outside the major, enrollment, accreditation, student outcomes, and possibly different career options may be discussed.

ACM Categories & Descriptors: K.3.2 Computer and Information Science Education

Keywords: Degree Tracks

Universal Access to Computing Education

Richard E. Ladner, *University of Washington*
Contact: ladner@cs.washington.edu

Approximately 10% of computer science and engineering majors have a disability of some kind. Those with disabilities are more likely to drop out of the major than those without disabilities. This BOF will bring together those who are interested in improving the success of these students. Strategies will be shared among the participants of the BOF to help each other do a better job of including these students in our classes and research projects.

ACM Categories & Descriptors: K.3.2 Computer Science Education .

Keywords: Universal Access, Disability

Multi-course Approaches to Curriculum 2013's Parallel and Distributed Computing

Richard Brown, *St. Olaf College*
Joel Adams, *Calvin College*
David Bunde, *Knox College*
Jens Mache, *Lewis & Clark College*
Elizabeth Shoop, *Macalester College*
Michael Smith, *Intel Corporation*
Paul Steinberg, *Intel Corporation*
Matthew Wolf, *Georgia Tech*
Contact: rab@stolaf.edu

The emerging CS2013 Curriculum recommendations call for greatly expanded emphasis on parallel and distributed computing (PDC), in response to recent industry changes. CS2013's PDC knowledge units relate to many undergraduate courses. Participants in this BOF will consider responses to CS2013 PDC recommendations that involve multiple undergraduate CS courses at an institution, as opposed to approaches that concentrate PDC topics primarily within a single course. This sharing and brainstorming session will bring together:

- people having experience with a multi-course or multi-level approach to teaching PDC;
- people contemplating a multi-course approach to introducing PDC material; and
- people wishing to provide and/or hear rationale for a multi-course strategy for teaching PDC

ACM Categories & Descriptors: K.3.2 Computer and Information Science Education – *Curriculum*; D.1.3 Concurrent programming – *Distributed programming, parallel programming*

Keywords: Parallel computing, parallelism, distributed computing, education, curricular recommendations, curriculum

The Joy of Word Games: Or, Putting the "Text" Back into Context

Michael P. Rogers, *Northwest Missouri State University*
Contact: mprogers@mac.com

We have heard much discussion, in recent years, about various contexts for teaching Computer Science. One that does not get a lot of attention, but frankly deserves more, is the notion of using word games — in which language plays a predominant role — to teach Computer Science. There is a plethora of clever and simply fun games that can be used to illustrate almost any concept that arises in CS1 and CS2. We would like to start a conversation with other SIGCSE attendees who are interested in these very entertaining, algorithmically stimulating games, and see what techniques they use, and what successes they have had, in incorporating them into the classroom.

ACM Categories & Descriptors: K.8.0 Games;

Keywords: Word Games; Linguistics; Programming Contexts; Introductory Programming; CS1; CS2

SIGCSE'13, March 6–9, 2013, Denver, Colorado, USA.
ACM 978-1-4503-1868-6/13/03.

Wednesday Workshop

ROS at Every Level: Using the Robot Operating System in CS 0, 1, 2, and Beyond

Julian Mason, *Duke University*
Zachary Dodds, *Harvey Mudd College*
William D. Smart, *Oregon State University*
Contact: mac@cs.duke.edu

After many years, the robotics research community has settled on standard middleware: the Robot Operating System (ROS). This standard presents a great opportunity for educational robotics. This hands-on workshop will engage participants in ROS-based curricula for CS 0–2 and advanced undergraduates. The workshop will highlight how ROS has simplified, enabled, and expanded "flipped" robotics curricula in CS 0–2. Our advanced materials show how ROS enables easy access to the robotics research community, permitting larger and more research-representative projects. This workshop is two long hands-on sessions punctuated with short reports from the presenters' experience. Participants will implement the first two assignments of our CS 2 curriculum. http://www.cs.hmc.edu/~dodds/ROSatSIGCSE2013. *Laptops optional.*

ACM Categories & Descriptors: I.2.9 Robotics, K.3.2 Curriculum

Keywords: Robotics, CS0, CS1, CS2, ROS, Robotics Curricula

Making Mathematical Reasoning Fun: Web-Integrated, Collaborative, and "Hands-On" Techniques

Jason O. Hallstrom, *Clemson University*
Joe Hollingsworth, *Indiana University Southeast*
Joan Krone, *Denison University*
Murali Sitaraman, *Clemson University*
Contact: jasonoh@cs.clemson.edu

Is it possible to excite students about learning the mathematical principles that underlie high-quality software? Can they use a development environment for "hands-on" experimentation with reasoning? Is this possible without displacing existing content? The answer is a resounding yes –from the experiences of professors at several institutions– but it takes the right set of pedagogical principles, reasoning tools, and "hands-on" exercises. This laboratory will help educators transfer the excitement of learning how to apply mathematical reasoning in building high quality software, by adopting one reasoning concept at a time.

The workshop will introduce a series of independent content modules that can be introduced in any course where mathematical reasoning might be taught – from introductory programming and software engineering to data structures and algorithms. They are designed to supplement, rather than replace, existing course materials.

Fees for this workshop will be covered for a limited number of attendees through an NSF award; limited travel support is also available. All participants are required to bring a laptop to participate in the computer-assisted exercises.

ACM Categories & Descriptors: K.3.2 Computer and Information Science Education

Keywords: Mathematical Reasoning, Software Development, Hands-on Exercises, Web-based Tools, Specification, Verification

Alice 3.1

Wanda Dann, *Carnegie Mellon University*
Steve Cooper, *Stanford University*
Don Slater, *Carnegie Mellon University*
Contact: wpdann@andrew.cmu.edu

This workshop is designed to offer a hands-on introduction to Alice 3.1 (now out of beta), as used in introductory courses in high school and early college levels. The focus of this workshop is on using program visualization for introducing fundamental concepts of programming. The introductory features of Alice 3.1 will be presented in an active-learning style. Although some comparisons between Alice 2.x and 3.1 will be included, the content of the workshop does not assume familiarity with Alice 2.x. Participants will receive latest 3.1 update and sneak peek at early textbook chapters. Attendees are expected to bring their own standard (no netbooks or tablets, please) laptop with a mouse (2-button).

ACM Categories & Descriptors: K.3 Computer & Information Science Education

Keywords: Alice; Introductory Programming; Visualization

Creative Computing: Introductory Programming Concepts with Processing.js

Semmy Purewal, *University of North Carolina at Asheville*
Contact: spurewal@unca.edu

Khan Academy recently announced that they will soon be teaching introductory Computer Science topics with the Processing.js language and an interactive, web-based code editor. At UNC Asheville, we have been using a similar pedagogical approach for over a year. Specifically, we have integrated Processing.js into our introductory course for non-majors by building an open-source, web-based editor which makes it easy for students to edit, save and share their Processing.js sketches. This workshop offers a hands-on introduction to Processing.js and our editor. Participants will also be given an overview of the programming module in Creative Computing, our recently re-imagined CS0 course. Curious individuals with a laptop, a modern web-browser and some basic programming experience are welcome.

ACM Categories & Descriptors: K.3.2 Computer and Information Science Education

Keywords: CS0, Computer Science Education, Processing, Processing.js

Computer Science Unplugged, Robotics, and Outreach Activities

Tim Bell, *University of Canterbury*
Daniela Marghitu, *Auburn University*
Lynn Lambert, *Christopher Newport University*
Paul Curzon, *Queen Mary University of London*
Contact: tim.bell@canterbury.ac.nz

You've been asked to talk to an elementary or high school class about Computer Science, but how can you ensure that the talk is engaging? Or perhaps you're trying to introduce a concept from Computer Science to a school group, but you want a fun way to get the class engaged. This workshop is a hands-on introduction to Computer Science Unplugged (www.csunplugged.org), a widely used set of kinesthetic, fun activities that cover many core areas of computer science without using high technology. We will explore how to use the activities in a variety of situations, including using them with robotics activities, school outreach, and computer clubs. Attendees will receive a CD with a copy of a handbook for teachers and a collection of videos demonstrating the activities. ***Laptops are optional.***

ACM Categories & Descriptors: K.3.2 Computer and Information Science Education

Keywords: K-12 outreach, Computational Thinking

Making the Most of Undergraduate Research

Andrea Danyluk, *Williams College*
Nancy Amato, *Texas A&M University*
Ran Libeskind-Hadas, *Harvey Mudd College*
Lori Pollock, *University of Delaware*
Susan Rodger, *Duke University*
Contact: andrea@cs.williams.edu

Involving undergraduates in Computer Science research has many benefits. It's an exciting way for students to gain independent problem solving skills. It exposes them to interesting projects and the research process, thereby keeping them in computer science, even encouraging them to go to graduate school. And especially in primarily teaching institutions, it's a rewarding way for faculty to remain engaged in their own research. In this workshop we will (1) present best practices for mentoring undergraduate research, (2) equip participants with resources for mentoring their own students, and (3) further develop (1) and (2) through breakout sessions on concerns of interest to attendees. For more, please see www.cs.williams.edu/~andrea/SIGCSE2013. This workshop is intended for all college level computer science educators. Laptop Optional.

ACM Categories & Descriptors: K.m Miscellaneous

Keywords: Undergraduate Research

Learn about Effective Proposal Writing via the Review Process

Guy-Alain Amoussou, *National Science Foundation*
Suzanne Westbrook, *National Science Foundation*
Contact: gamousso@nsf.gov

This interactive workshop focuses on the National Science Foundation grant proposal review process. By a close examination of the review process, participants gain an understanding of how to write good reviews and how to improve their own proposal writing. The topics for the workshop include: the proposal review process from submission to award or decline; elements of a good review; NSF merit criteria (intellectual merit and broader impacts); elements of good proposals; the format of the typical review panel process; how to volunteer to review.

The workshop uses a structured guided-interactive approach to lead participants through each topic by introducing related issues, engaging participants in group exercises designed to explore and share their understanding of the issues, and then providing some expert opinion on these issues.

Faculty members who wish to better understand the NSF review process or seek funding in support of undergraduate computing education are encouraged to attend. Participants will include novice proposal writers and those with more experience who seek to improve their proposal writing or reviewing skills.

ACM Categories & Descriptors: K.3.2 Computer and Information Science Education n

Keywords: National Science Foundation; outreach; funding; writing proposals; reviewing grant proposals; computing education

CSinParallel: Using MapReduce to Teach Parallel Programming Concepts Across the CS Curriculum

Richard Brown, *St. Olaf College*
Elizabeth Shoop, *Macalester College*
Joel Adams, *Calvin College*
Contact: rab@stolaf.edu

Map-reduce, the cornerstone computational framework for cloud computing applications, has star appeal to draw students to the study of parallelism. Participants will carry out hands-on exercises designed for students at CS1/intermediate/advanced levels that introduce data-intensive scalable computing concepts, using WebMapReduce (WMR), a simplified open-source interface to the widely used Hadoop map-reduce programming environment. These hands-on exercises enable students to perform data-intensive scalable computations carried out on the most widely deployed map-reduce framework, used by Facebook, Microsoft, Yahoo, and other companies. WMR supports programming in a choice of languages (including Java, Python, C++, C#, Scheme); participants will be able to try exercises with languages of their choice. Workshop includes brief introduction to direct Hadoop programming, and information about access to cluster resources supporting WMR. Workshop materials will reside on csinparallel.org, along with WMR software. Intended audience: CS instructors. Laptop required (Windows, Mac, or Linux).

ACM Categories & Descriptors: D.1.3 Concurrent programming; K.3.2 Computer and Information Science Education

Keywords: map-reduce computing, distributed computing, Hadoop, education, curriculum, CS1, introductory course, data-intensive scalable computing, WMR, WebMapReduce, CSinParallel

Hands-on CyberSecurity Exercises and the RAVE Virtual Environment

Richard Weiss, *The Evergreen State College*
Vincent Nestler, *California State University at San Bernadino*
Michael Locasto, *The University of Calgary*
Jens Mache, *Lewis & Clark College*
Brian Hay, *The University of Alaska, Fairbanks*
Contact: weissr@evergreen.edu

This workshop is intended for anyone who would like to use hands-on exercises in cybersecurity for a variety of classes including Networking, OS, Computer Security and Software Engineering. It has received increased attention nationally in the proposed ACM/IEEE CS2013 Curricula Guidelines. The goal of this workshop is to provide faculty with varied backgrounds (including none) in this area with some tools and interactive exercises to facilitate incorporating this knowledge area into their curriculum. We believe that it is important that students develop analytical skills, thus we include an introduction to EDURange and the Hacker Curriculum principles: (1) **understanding failure modes** and (2) **seeing across or through layers of abstraction according to a particular scenario**. We will guide attendees through exercises tailored to their level and interests. The exercises will include port scanning and setting up a firewall. These can be done at a range of levels from beginner to advanced. We will include an introduction to tools for packet inspection, which is an important part of analysis. Attendees will receive accounts on the RAVE with exercises that they can take back and use immediately with their classes. RAVE provides a number of VMs pre-configured for the exercises. RAVE is also a general purpose technology for other hands-on exercises. Laptop required.

ACM Categories & Descriptors: C.2.0 Network Security and Protection, C.2.2 Network Protocols,

Keywords: security; cybersecurity; information assurance; laboratory exercises; firewalls

Re-Imagining CS1/CS2 with Android Using the Sofia Framework

Stephen H. Edwards, *Virginia Tech*
Contact: edwards@cs.vt.edu

Android has seen increased use in introductory CS courses to motivate and excite students about their programming assignments, but using the standard Android libraries as a GUI platform in CS2 presents numerous challenges and using it in CS1 is nearly impossible. This workshop introduces participants to *Sofia,* the Simplified Open Framework for Innovative Android Applications, developed by the Web-CAT team at Virginia Tech. Sofia abstracts out many of the advanced concepts normally required to develop interesting applications, using a unique approach to event handling, binding GUI elements to Java code, and user interaction. The goal is to allow students to focus entirely on using Java programming skills to solve problems in the application domain, instead of writing monotonous glue code typically required to construct an Android application. *Laptop optional.*

ACM Categories & Descriptors: D.2.2 Software Engineering; D.1.5 Programming Techniques; K.3.2 Computers and Education

Keywords: android, Sofia, mobile, app, game, graphical user interface, GUI, Java, Greenfoot, CS1, CS2, library, framework

SNAP! (Build Your Own Blocks)

Brian Harvey, *University of California, Berkeley*
Daniel D. Garcia, *University of California, Berkeley*
Tiffany Barnes, *North Carolina State University*
Nathaniel Titterton, *University of California, Berkeley*
Dan Armendariz, *University of California, Berkeley*
Luke Segars, *Google, Inc.*
Eugene Lemon, *Ralph J Bunche High School*
Sean Morris, *Albany High School*
Josh Paley, *Henry M. Gunn High School*
Contact: bh@cs.berkeley.edu

This workshop is for high school and college teachers of general-interest ("CS 0") CS courses. It presents the programming environment used in two of the five initial AP CS Principles pilot courses.

SNAP! (Build Your Own Blocks) is a free, graphical, drag-and-drop extension to the Scratch programming language. Scratch, designed for 8-14 year olds, models programs as "scripts" without names, arguments, or return values. SNAP! adds support for older learners (14-20) by adding named procedures (thus recursion), procedures as data (thus higher order functions) structured lists, and sprites as first class objects with inheritance.

Participants will learn SNAP! through discussion, programming exercises, and exploration. See http://snap.berkeley.edu for details. Laptop required.

ACM Categories & Descriptors: D.1.7 Visual Programming; K.3.2 Computer and Information Science Education

Keywords: Programming language, visual programming, CS 0, AP CS Principles

Incorporating Version Control into Programming Courses

Tommy MacWilliam, *Harvard University*
Contact: tmacwilliam@cs.harvard.edu

This workshop, aimed at instructors of introductory or intermediate courses, introduces participants to version control via two popular source code management (SCM) tools: SVN and Git. Not only is proficiency with SCM tools an invaluable skill for aspiring software developers, but version control also allows students to collaborate effectively on projects. Participants will complete hands-on activities using distributed and centralized SCM tools, learn how to integrate version control into curricula, and discuss the pros and cons of various hosting solutions. Participants will also be introduced to version50, an open-source abstraction layer that provides a common, simplified interface for SCM tools aimed at making version control accessible to novice programmers. Laptop required.

ACM Categories & Descriptors: **D.2.3** Coding Tools and Techniques

Keywords: DVCS

SIGCSE'13, March 6–9, 2013, Denver, Colorado, USA.
ACM 978-1-4503-1868-6/13/03.

Friday Workshop

Computational Art and Creative Coding: Teaching CS1 with Processing

Ira Greenberg, *Southern Methodist University*
Deepak Kumar, *Bryn Mawr College*
Dianna Xu, *Bryn Mawr College*
Contact: igreenberg@smu.edu

This workshop showcases a new approach to teaching CS1 using computational art as a context. Participants will be introduced to the Processing programming language and environment, designed for the construction of 2D and 3D visual forms. Its IDE is light-weight, but well-suited for the rapid proto-typing needed for dynamic visual work. We hope to bring the excitement, creativity, and innovation fostered by Processing into the computer science education community. Instructors of all experience levels are welcome. Hands-on portion of the workshop will enable participants to explore Processing and create visual effects on the fly. Course materials and handouts detailing the software, curriculum, and teaching resources will be given out. All participants will need to bring their own laptops.
Supported by NSF Awards DUE-0942626 and CCF-0939370.

ACM Categories & Descriptors: K.3.2 Computer and Information Science Education

Keywords: CS1, Processing, Creative Computation, Generative Art

AP CS Principles & The Beauty and Joy of Computing Curriculum

Daniel D. Garcia, *UC Berkeley*
Brian Harvey, *UC Berkeley*
Tiffany Barnes, *NC State*
Nathaniel Titterton, *UC Berkeley*
Dan Armendariz, *UC Berkeley*
Luke Segars, *Google, Inc.*
Eugene Lemon, *Ralph J. Bunche High School*
Sean Morris, *Albany High School*
Josh Paley, *Henry M. Gunn High School*
Contact: ddgarcia@cs.berkeley.edu

The Beauty and Joy of Computing (BJC) is an introductory computer science curriculum developed at UC Berkeley (and adapted at the University of North Carolina, Charlotte), intended for high school juniors through university non-majors. It was used in two of the five initial pilot programs for the *AP CS Principles* course being developed by the College Board and the National Science Foundation. Our overall goal is to support the CS10K project by preparing instructors to teach the AP CS Principles course through the BJC curriculum. In this workshop, we will share our experiences as instructors of the course at the university and high school level, provide a glimpse into a typical week of the course, and share details of NSF-funded summer professional development opportunities. A laptop is strongly recommended.

ACM Categories & Descriptors: K.3.2 [Computer and Information Science Education]: Computer science education

Keywords: BJC, AP CS Principles, Non-Majors Intro CS, CS0

Introducing Secure Coding in CS0 and CS1

Matt Bishop, *University of California at Davis*
Blair Taylor, *Towson University*
Elizabeth Hawthorne, *Union County College*
Diana Burley, *George Washington University*
Siddharth Kaza, *Towson University*
Contact: skaza@towson.edu

The CS 2013 curriculum draft includes Information Assurance and Security as a pervasive knowledge area. However, introducing security in CS0 and CS1 is challenging because of lack of appropriate teaching resources and training. This workshop will provide a well-tested strategy for introducing secure coding concepts in CS0 and CS1. We will introduce attendees to secure coding through hands-on exercises, and provide self-contained, lab-based modules designed to be injected into CS0/CS1 with minimal impact on the course (www.towson.edu/securityinjections). Participants will be encouraged to bring in their own syllabus and labs to modify to include secure coding concepts. The first 15 participants will be reimbursed for the workshop cost on attendance. ***Laptop recommended.***

ACM Categories & Descriptors: K.3.2 Computers and Education

Keywords: CS0; CS1; Secure Coding; Security Injections

Experimenting with and Integrating Alice 2.3 into Many Disciplines

Susan H. Rodger, *Duke University*
Steve Cooper, *Stanford University*
Wanda Dann, *Carnegie Mellon University*
Dwayne C. Brown, Jr., *Duke University*
Jacobo Carrasquel, *Carnegie Mellon University*
Contact: rodger@cs.duke.edu

This interactive workshop will present the new features of Alice 2.3, and show how to integrate Alice 2.3 into multiple disciplines in middle school and high school. Participants will get hands-on experience with working with new Alice models and creating Alice projects. The workshop will also review curriculum materials and discuss mapping Alice to CSTA computer science standards. The curriculum materials presented could be used in middle school or high school in a variety of disciplines, or in college in a pre-CS 1 course. The target audience is middle school and high school teachers, and college faculty providing outreach to K-12 or teaching a pre-CS 1 course. Alice is available for free at www.alice.org. Curriculum materials are available at www.cs.duke.edu/csed/alice/aliceInSchools and at www.alice.org. ***A laptop is required, and a two-button mouse is recommended.***

SIGCSE'13, March 6–9, 2013, Denver, Colorado, USA.
ACM 978-1-4503-1868-6/13/03.

ACM Categories & Descriptors: K.3.2 Computer and Information Science Education

Keywords: Alice, virtual worlds, K-12 education, middle school, high school, introductory computer science

How to Plan and Run Computing Summer Camps for 4th-12th Grade Students

Barbara Ericson, *Georgia Institute of Technology*
Christopher Michaud, *Marist School*
Nannette Napier, *Georgia Gwinnett College*
Krishnendu Roy, *Valdosta State University*
Contact: ericson@cc.gatech.edu

This workshop will provide details on how to plan and run non-residential computing summer camps for 4th – 12th grade students. Georgia Tech has been offering computing summer camps since 2004. These camps are financially self-sustaining and effective. Items used in the camps include: CS Unplugged, LightBot, Scratch, Alice, LEGO robots (WeDo, NXT, and Tetrix), EarSketch, and App Inventor. Georgia Tech has also helped start other computing camps at eleven other colleges and universities in Georgia.
The workshop will include forms, a timeline, sample agendas, sample flyers, budget plans, a planning checklist, suggested projects, surveys, pre and post-tests, evaluation results, lessons learned, and more. **Laptop Recommended.**

ACM Categories & Descriptors: K.3.2 Computer and Information Science Education; Economics, Experimentation, Measurement

Keywords: Summer Camps, Alice, App Inventor, Scratch, LEGO, Outreach, Music, EarSketch

Pedagogy for Engaging Diverse Students in Computing

J. McGrath Cohoon, *University of Virginia*
James Cohoon, *University of Virginia*
Seth Reichelson, *Lake Brantley High School*
Susan Horwitz, *University of Wisconsin-Madison*
Laura Reasoner Jones, *Fairfax County Public School*
Contact: joanne.cohoon@gmail.com

Four research-supported teaching methods can make your computing courses more effective through improved student learning, comprehension, and motivation.
This workshop introduces and provides experience with those four methods

1. Collaborative learning, e.g., pair programming or peer led team learning
2. Examples and exercises in contexts that appeal to a broad range of students
3. Computing skills developed through practice
4. Developing spatial rotation abilities.

The presenters are among leading researchers and award-winning practitioners.

J. McGrath Cohoon: Senior Research Scientist at the National Center for Women & IT (NCWIT); Associate Professor of Science, Technology, and Society at the University of Virginia; conducts nationwide empirical studies of gender and computing.

Jim Cohoon: Computer Science professor at the University of Virginia; IEEE Computer Science highest education award recipient, and author of award-winning introductory textbooks.
Susan Horwitz: Professor of Computer Sciences at the University of Wisconsin - Madison; lead PI on an NSF grant that pioneered and evaluated use of Peer-Led Team Learning in introductory Computer-Science courses; recipient of University teaching awards.
Seth Reichelson: award-winning high school Computer Science teacher; nationally recognized for his approach to high school computing courses in general and AP Computer Science in particular.
Laura Jones: teaches in a public elementary school, writes frequently about girls and STEM careers, founded and directed the GEMS clubs (Girls Excelling in Math and Science) in 1995
Workshop participants will learn from these presenters how to employ the pedagogical methods for engaging and retaining diverse students in computer science courses. A ***laptop is optional.***

ACM Categories & Descriptors: K.3.2 Computer and Information Science Education

Keywords: Pedagogy, teaching methods, collaborative learning, PLTL, exercises and examples, spatial rotation

Teaching the CS Principles Curriculum with App Inventor

Ralph Morelli, *Trinity College*
David Wolber, *University of San Francisco*
Shaileen Pokress, *MIT Media Lab*
Franklyn Turbak, Wellesley College
Fred Martin, *University of Massachusetts Lowell*
Contact: ralph.morelli@trincoll.edu

The CS Principles Project is an NSF-funded initiative to develop a breadth-first advanced placement (AP) course in computer science. App Inventor is a visual, blocks-based programming language that makes sophisticated computing concepts accessible to a broad range of students. This hands-on workshop, aimed at high school and undergraduate teachers, will introduce participants to lessons, homework exercises, project assignments, and assessment materials (quizzes, grading rubrics) that can be used in an App Inventor-based CS0 course. Participants will develop simple Android apps, using devices provided by the workshop, and will use them in the context of lessons and assignments that fit within the CS Principles framework. A laptop is required. For additional details please visit : http://is.gd/sigcse2013appinv.

ACM Categories & Descriptors: K.3.1 Computer Uses in Education; K.3.2 Computer and Information Science Education

Keywords: Active learning, instructional technologies, non-majors, AP/IB courses and curricula

SIGCSE'13, March 6–9, 2013, Denver, Colorado, USA.
ACM 978-1-4503-1868-6/13/03.

Using Scala Strategically Across the Undergraduate Curriculum

Mark Lewis, *Trinity University*
Konstantin Läufer, *Loyola University Chicago*
George K. Thiruvathukal, *Loyola University Chicago*
Contact: mlewis@trinity.edu

Various hybrid-paradigm languages, designed to balance compile-time error detection, conciseness, and performance, have emerged. Scala, e.g., is interoperable with Java and has become an early leader in adoption, especially in the start-up and open-source spaces.

Workshop participants experience Scala's value as a teaching language in the CS curriculum through four lecture-lab modules: In CS1, the read-eval-print loop and simple, uniform syntax aid programming in the small. In CS2, higher-order methods allow concise, efficient manipulation of collections. Advanced topics include domain-specific languages, concurrency, web apps/services, and mobile apps.

Laptop recommended with Scala installed.

ACM Categories & Descriptors: D.1.0 General, D.1.1 Applicative (Functional) Programming, D.1.3 Concurrent Programming, D.1.4 Sequential Programming, D.1.5 Object-oriented Programming, D.3.3 Language Constructs and Features

Keywords: Scala, CS1, CS2, Advanced Programming Courses

NetLogo: Teaching with Turtles and Crossing Curricular Boundaries

Forrest Stonedahl, *Centre College*
David Weintrop, *Northwestern University*
Paulo Blikstein, *Stanford University*
Christine Shannon, *Centre College*
Contact: forrest.stonedahl@centre.edu

This workshop, intended for CS educators from middle school through undergrad, will introduce participants to NetLogo. NetLogo is an easy-to-learn multi-agent language and integrated modeling environment in widespread use in classrooms (and research labs) globally. This hands-on tutorial will highlight computational modeling in the natural and social sciences, tie in core computer science concepts, and discuss how to promote student thinking about decentralized systems. The workshop will draw on the presenters' own experiences teaching courses on computational science, computational art, theory of computation, and educational outreach events. Participants will learn first-hand how NetLogo can enrich a variety of computing courses. NetLogo runs on Mac/Linux/Windows. **Laptop required.**

ACM Categories & Descriptors: K.3.2 Computer Science Education; I.6.2 Simulation Languages

Keywords: NetLogo, agent-based modeling, computational science, programming languages, computer science education

Implementing the Inverted Classroom

Kate Lockwood, *Cal State Monterey Bay*
Jeff McCall, *Cal State Monterey Bay*
Barbara Beckmeyer, *Cal State Monterey Bay*
Marc Oehlman, *Cal State Monterey Bay*
Contact: klockwood@csumb.edu

The Inverted Classroom is an exciting pedagogical technique where more passive information assimilation activities (e.g. lectures) are assigned as homework and class time is reserved for active applied problem solving and group activities. With current technology, instructors wishing to implement inverted classroom have a variety of options to create engaging and accessible learning modules. In this workshop, we will provide an overview of inverted classroom philosophy and some initial data from successful pilots of the inverted classroom. Participants will work in small groups to develop small inverted classroom activities using software and technology provided by the presenters. We will wrap up with presentations from the groups and a discussion about assessment. ***Laptop Recommended.***

ACM Categories & Descriptors: K.3.1 Computer Uses in Education

Keywords: Inverted Classroom, Flipped Classroom, Pedagogy, Instructional Technology

LittleFe Buildout Workshop (Parts 1 & 2)

Charlie Peck, *Earlham College*
Tom Murphy, *Contra Costa College*
Skylar Thompson, *University of Washington*
Aaron Weeden, *Shodor Education Foundation*
Contact: charliep@cs.earlham.edu

LittleFe buildout events are training and infrastructure opportunities for teams of accepted faculty and students from educational institutions across the United States to assemble LittleFe educational appliances (http://littlefe.net) and learn to use them in the classroom to teach parallel programming, cluster computing, and computational/data enabled science & engineering (CDESE). The buildout consists of participants assembling their LittleFe unit from a kit; installing the Bootable Cluster CD (BCCD, http://bccd.net) software on it; learning about the curriculum modules available for teaching parallel programming, High Performance Computing (HPC) and CDESE; and learning how to develop new curriculum modules for the LittleFe/BCCD platform. ***At least one participant per team should bring a WiFi enabled laptop.***

ACM Categories & Descriptors: K.3.2 Computer and Information Science Education

Keywords: parallel computing; distributed computing; education

SIGCSE'13, March 6–9, 2013, Denver, Colorado, USA.
ACM 978-1-4503-1868-6/13/03.

Peer Instruction in CS: Introduction and Recent Developments

Daniel Zingaro, University of Toronto
Cynthia Bailey Lee, University of California, San Diego
John Glick, University of San Diego
Leo Porter, Skidmore College
Beth Simon, University of California, San Diego
Contact: daniel.zingaro@gmail.com

We introduce participants to Peer Instruction (PI): an active learning technique shown to be effective across the CS curriculum. In PI, Students work together to exchange perspectives and answer challenging conceptual questions and are supported by short teaching segments. We will introduce and motivate PI, demonstrate its use in combination with a clicker system, and describe ways to encourage student preparation for PI classes. Pre-lecture preparation may include reading quizzes or exploratory homeworks, two topics of recent interest in the computing research literature. We will explore this literature as part of our tour of a complete PI course: from pre-lecture, to lecture, to the course at large.
Participants will work in groups to develop new PI questions addressing challenges to their students' learning, and discuss numerous pedagogical benefits conferred through PI.

Instructors interested in increasing engagement in any CS course may attend. Participants are encouraged to bring current lecture materials. Laptop optional.

ACM Categories & Descriptors: K.3.2 [Computer Science Education]: Computer and Information Science Education

Keywords: CS1; peer instruction; classroom response; active learning

SIGCSE'13, March 6–9, 2013, Denver, Colorado, USA.
ACM 978-1-4503-1868-6/13/03.

Saturday Workshop

Android+Sphero: Teaching Mobile Computing and Robotics in a Single Course

Stan Kurkovsky, *Central Connecticut State University*
Contact: kurkovsky@ccsu.edu

Implications of using robotics and mobile computing in the curriculum extend far beyond motivation and engagement because skills in these areas can help students be more successful at the workplace. Our approach to teaching both subjects in one course focuses on using Sphero, a small ball-shaped wireless robot that can be controlled and programmed using an Android or iOS device via a Bluetooth link. Workshop participants will experience several hands-on projects that are offered to student in an Android+Sphero course, which culminates in a robot racing competition. This workshop is intended for high school and college faculty interested in mobile computing and/or robotics courses, projects, or activities. More information is available at http://www.cs.ccsu.edu/~stan/sigcse13/. Laptop recommended.

ACM Categories & Descriptors: K.3.2 Computer and Information Science Education

Keywords: Mobile Computing, Android, Robotics, Sphero

Computer Science via Digital Sound and Music: A Hands-on Introduction to Open Source Tools and New Curriculum Material to Introduce Computer Science Concepts

Jennifer Burg, *Wake Forest University*
Susan Reiser, *UNC Asheville*
Contact: burg@wfu.edu

In this workshop, participants will create and manipulate digital audio using open source software (Audacity, PureData, Processing's Minim Beta, Octave, and C/C++). The cross-disciplinary digital audio content links music, engineering, physics, mathematics, and computer science and was developed for and test-taught in computer science courses. Additionally, participants will access and use the freely available online videos, tutorials, and textbook that can be incorporated into their classrooms. The online content's development was funded by the National Science Foundation CCLI Grant, "Linking Science, Art, and Practice Through Digital Sound." Exercises that engage students in creative computational problem solving for sound and music applications will also be discussed. Laptops equipped with the open source applications mentioned above are strongly recommended but not required.

ACM Categories & Descriptors: I.3.2 Computer and Information Science Education; H.5.5 Sound and Music Computing

Keywords: digital sound and music, computer science education, creative computational problem solving

SIGCSE'13, March 6–9, 2013, Denver, Colorado, USA.
ACM 978-1-4503-1868-6/13/03.

Test-First Design in Introductory Java Programming

Viera K. Proulx, *Northeastern University*
Contact: vkp@ccs.neu.edu

While professional programmers report on the advantages of test-first design discipline, typical introductory programming courses do not require that students design comprehensive test suites for their programs. For the past ten years we (and a number of our adopters in a variety of settings) have used our *tester* library to support novice programmers in adopting test-first design.

This workshop illustrates hands-on the benefits of test-first pedagogy on a series of typical introductory programming assignments and shows how the focus on testing fosters a deeper understanding of fundamental concepts of object-oriented program design. The workshop prepares the participants to adopt test-first design approach in their introductory (and advanced) Java-based courses.

The *tester* library with tutorials, samples, and all downloads is available at: http://www.ccs.neu.edu/javalib/Tester and https://github.com/TesterViera/JavaLibTester/

A laptop is mandatory!

ACM Categories & Descriptors: AP/IB Courses and Curricula; CS1/2; Data Stuctures; Object-Oriented Issues

Keywords: Object-oriented programming, Test-first design, Java programming

Experiments with Network Security Threats in a Safe, Easy Sandbox

Michael J Jipping, *Hope College*
Acshi Haggenmiller, *Yale University*
Matthew Koster, *Calvin College*
Eric Ostrowski, *Grand Valley State University*
Contact: jipping@hope.edu

Computer and network security are important topics discussed in many places in the Computer Science curriculum. Security issues are difficult to experiment on in experiential based courses. Attacks on system security cannot be demonstrated on live campus networks. This workshop will demonstrate and experiment with several security attacks in a safe, sandbox-based virtual environment. We will begin two easy demonstrations and allow each participant to choose from six laboratory experiments. We will wrap up with an ethics discussion. Each experiment includes discussion of the area involved and tips on how to protect against the particular exploit under scrutiny. Each participant will be given a DVD with all exercise materials on it as a takeaway. This workshop is designed for instructors from all levels who want to add security experiments to classes. A laptop is mandatory. Each participant will receive copies of all experiments in the series. These experiments include discussion materials – introduction to the subject area, exploitation methods, and ways to avoid exploitation – as well as the procedures used to experience each activity.

ACM Categories & Descriptors: D.4.6 Security and Protection; K.4.2 Social Issues; K.6.5 Security and Protection

Keywords: Computer security, Network security, Experimentation, Sandboxing

Developing a Hands-on Undergraduate Parallel Programming Course with Pattern Programming

Barry Wilkinson, *University of North Carolina, Charlotte*
Clayton Ferner, *University of North Carolina, Wilmington*
Contact: abw@uncc.edu

Parallel programming has been taught for many years but has recently taken on greater significance with introduction of multicore and many-core processors. Still, most teaching has followed a traditional path of focusing on learning low-level tools such as MPI. This workshop introduces a new educational approach based upon first selecting a computational pattern and then using higher-level tools to create parallel executable code. A pattern programming framework has been developed to create a distributed application that avoids the need to use low-level routines. The framework self-deploys on distributed computers, clusters, and individual multicore computers. Several patterns have been implemented including workpool, pipeline, synchronous and iterative all-to-all, and stencil. The first pattern covered is the widely applicable workpool pattern and other patterns will be introduced. The workshop will describe how the approach can be used in the undergraduate curriculum and will provide hands-on experiences to participants. In our approach, students focus upon computational strategies. Programming is much easier and less likely to be flawed. Each workshop participant will receive a flash drive with all software and documentation pre-loaded for use in the workshop and afterwards in their classes. Laptop required.

ACM Categories & Descriptors: D.1.3 Concurrent Programming – *distributed programming, parallel programming.*

Keywords: Pattern Programming, Undergraduate Education

LINQ from a Database Perspective: Querying Relations and XML

Suzanne W. Dietrich, *Arizona State University*
Contact: dietrich@asu.edu

LINQ is a declarative language that provides a uniform paradigm for querying relations, objects, and XML. LINQ has from-where-select clauses, similar to SQL, but the clause order is based on its underlying formalism of functional programming. This workshop introduces LINQ from a database perspective with hands-on exercises over relational and XML data using a lightweight IDE for formative feedback. Participants will learn LINQ by experiencing sample exercises for incorporating LINQ into the database curriculum. The intended audience includes anyone with the knowledge of SQL who wants to learn LINQ. After learning LINQ to query relational data, participants will be introduced to XML and how LINQ can also be used to return, query, and transform XML data. Laptop recommended.

ACM Categories & Descriptors: H.2.3 Languages – *Query languages.*

Keywords: Database, Query Languages, LINQ, Relations, XML

Catalyzing & Sustaining Change in Computing Education

Lynn Andrea Stein, *Franklin W. Olin College of Engineering*
Contact: las@olin.edu

Why is change in academia so difficult? What risks and pitfalls await? How can we approach change so that it does not depend solely on our efforts or end when we are no longer there to maintain it? In this collaborative, interactive workshop, we will explore these questions and craft strategies to create sustainable change in computing curricula. This workshop is for those who want to create curricular change in their home departments, catalyze interdisciplinary curricula, or otherwise inspire innovation in teaching and learning at a scale that goes beyond a single classroom. Prereading (available online) will be expected. The workshop will end with the creation of concrete action plans. ***Laptop optional.***

ACM Categories & Descriptors: K.3.2 Computer and Information Science Education; A.m Miscellaneous

Keywords: Organizational Change; Curriculum; Academia

Drawing Machines: Exploring Embedded System Programming and Harware with an Artistic Flair

Erik Brunvand, *University of Utah*
Paul Stout, *University of Utah*
Jennifer (Ginger) Alford, *Trinity Valley School*
Contact: gralford@acm.org

This workshop introduces embedded programming and hardware using Arduino in a creative context to make machines that make drawings. This is a powerful way to introduce programming and physical computing concepts to students from high school to undergraduate, and to students who might not normally be intrigued by a computing course. Participants in this workshop will experience this curriculum first hand by using breadboards and electronic components to create circuits that they will control programmatically. Using the Arduino C-based software, participants will modify sample code, and develop their own code that will interact with the environment using light sensors, range finders, pressure sensors, and servos. In an engaging twist to a basic embedded hardware course, a supply of art materials will be used to turn the electronic circuits into mesmerizing contraptions that create interesting art pieces. A laptop is required but the Arduino and all electronic components will be provided for use during the workshop. Additional information and materials at www.buildingsteam.org.

SIGCSE'13, March 6–9, 2013, Denver, Colorado, USA.
ACM 978-1-4503-1868-6/13/03.

ACM Categories & Descriptors: K.3.2 Computer and Information Science Education; B.0.1 Hardware General

Keywords: kinetic art; education; engineering and art collaboration; drawing machine; hardware; microcontroller; Arduino

Using POGIL to Help Students Discover CS Concepts and Develop Process Skills

Clifton Kussmaul, *Muhlenberg College*
Helen Hu, *Westminster College*
Matthew Lang, *Moravian College*
Contact: kussmaul@muhlenberg.edu

This workshop is for anyone who teaches CS, and introduces process-oriented guided inquiry learning (POGIL) in computer science. POGIL is based on learning science, and shares characteristics with other forms of active, discovery, and inquiry learning. In a POGIL classroom, teams of 3-5 learners work on instructor-facilitated activities. Through scripted inquiry and investigation, learners discover concepts and construct their own knowledge. Using assigned team roles and meta-cognition, learners develop process skills and individual responsibility. Studies show that POGIL can significantly improve student performance. POGIL has particular potential for CS education. Software development is largely a team-based problem-solving activity, and POGIL helps students to learn from each other and develop problem-solving abilities as well as important team process skills. POGIL has been developed and validated over the last 15 years in a range of STEM disciplines.

The workshop consists primarily of hands-on team activities. Participants will work through CS activities and a set of meta-activities to explore POGIL practices and activity structures. Participants will also begin to draft parts of their own activities. More information and materials are available at http://cspogil.org and http://pogil.org, including sample activities for topics in a variety of CS courses. Laptops optional. This material is based upon work supported by the National Science Foundation under grant DUE-1044679.

ACM Categories & Descriptors: K.3.1 Computer Uses in Education; K.3.2 Computer and Information Science Education

Keywords: Active Learning; Communication; Guided Inquiry; POGIL; Process Skills; Teams

Augmenting Introductory Computer Science Classes with GameMaker and Mobile Apps

Tiffany Barnes, *NC State University*
Acey Boyce, *NC State University*
Veronica Catete, *NC State University*
Katelyn Doran, *Microsoft*
Drew Hicks, *NC State University*
Leslie Keller, *NC Virtual Public School*
Contact: tiffany.barnes@gmail.com

Students often take computing classes because they are eager to create games, to learn to create meaningful and useful software, or both. Connecting computing to real, cutting-edge applications has been shown to increase engagement of women and minorities. The new CS Principles curriculum, a pilot Advanced Placement course, seeks to broaden the participation in computing to a larger and more diverse audience. This curriculum emphasizes that computing is a creative activity where people work together to solve relevant problems. In this workshop, we introduce free software and curricula to enable novice high school and college students in a first computing course to learn basic game and mobile phone development. We discuss how these activities facilitate teaching high school and non-major (CS0) course topics, but they can also be used to illustrate more advanced topics. Participants will learn GameMaker and mobile phone programming using AppInventor, and/or Touch Develop. These tools allow students to create and have fun with computing while teaching object-oriented and event-driven programming and game architectures. If possible, Windows 7 phones will be provided for use during the workshop. We will provide links to curricular modules for the CS Principles: Beauty and Joy of Computing course, as well as links to the GameMaker, AppInventor, and Touch Develop platforms and tutorials. Participants must bring a network-connected laptop with a modern browser, and the latest version of Java (ideally with AppInventor installed), and may optionally bring an Android or Windows 7 phone.

ACM Categories & Descriptors: K.3.2 Computer and Information Science Education; Computer Science Education

Keywords: introductory course, game development, mobile applications, broadening participation

SIGCSE'13, March 6–9, 2013, Denver, Colorado, USA.
ACM 978-1-4503-1868-6/13/03.

SIGCSE 2013 SRC Undergraduate Student Research Abstracts

TreeHouse: Tools for Visualizing and Analyzing Datasets from Large-Scale Phylogenetic Inference

Mark Adamo, *Vassar College*

Large-scale phylogenetic inference may return sets of thousands of trees, each possibly containing hundreds of taxa. TreeHouse is a p hylogenetic tree-querying program that operates on large, highly-compressed sets of trees. I have extended TreeHouse to support multiple modes of visualization and have incorporated support for biological classification data, enabling entirely new hypothesis-testing analyses. New filtering operations allow for trees as well as tree sets to be edited, allowing tree data to be tailored to specialized areas of biological inquiry. Memory optimizations make TreeHouse's memory performance scale much better as the size of trees and trees sets increases.

A Cryptography Module for a Security Video Game

Abdulrahman Almarzooqi, *Zayed University*

This project is to create a cryptography model for video game that will help teach information security. Similar to a security competition, this game is being designed and implemented to provide students with real world scenarios where they have to make relevant security decisions involving how to apply cryptography. Interviewing Faculty and system administrators as well as downloading and testing related video game softwares provided great insight for the delopment of these prototypes. Tests with students and teachers will provide valuable insight to move from a prototype to a final product.

Teaching Network Security with a Video Game Simulating Security Competitions

Fatma Y. Beshwari, *Zayed University*

This project is to create a network module of a video game that will help teach information security. This game being designed is similar to a security competition, where students need to take quick actions to defend their resources. The target audience is university students preparing for a security competition or taking a class on penetration testing. Faculty and system administrators were interviewed to design the scenarios. The first prototype is being implemented in Game maker and after classroom testing we will implement it in Unity.

Metagenomic Data Analysis using Clustering

Sulochana Bramhacharya, *Hiram College*

Recombinant DNA technology and the decrease in sequencing costs have revolutionized the area of genetics. One of the biggest challenges right now is the analysis of gene sequences, gene clusters, and differences in composition of these clusters. Our program is a simple tool designed to cluster the gene sequences from samples and identify the outliers in two similar clusters from different samples. We took 16S gene sequences from two similar samples of different environmental conditions and clustered them using a g reedy incremental approach based on percent identity. We compared each cluster obtained from the first sample with each cluster in the second sample and determined two corresponding cluster pairs from both samples. If any of the clusters correspond, two different sets of data are obtained, i.e. one set of similar sequences in both clusters and another set of dissimilar sequences. The set of dissimilar sequences, also known as outliers, is useful to study about the factors causing the change in cluster composition in response to environmental changes. This program is aimed to be used by the students in their classroom and researchers.

An Improved User Interface for the Corona Project

Coty Collins, *Saint Bonaventure University*

Corona is a system that automates the process of creating JUnit tests for beginning programmers. In previous versions, users needed to know an arcane syntax to create a test. To address this, an improved user interface was developed. Syntactic overhead is reduced via a tree-like structure that allows users to specify objects. Parameters in a collection are also represented in the tree as children for the nodes in their containing class. Along with other improvements, the new user interface for Corona frees users of syntactic concerns and allows them to focus on input/output pairs; early studies suggest users are likely to generate more tests.

Debugging Using a Verifier

Carrie Eisengrein, *Clemson University*

Today, people normally find errors in programs by running tests. This can cause problems because there are occasions when tests cannot fully check every part of the system. Testing is not foolproof. The main goal in my area of study is to explore how to diagnose and fix errors in a program using verification conditions generated by the system, RESOLVE.

Automation of the Pre-Registration Process at Baldwin Wallace University

Aric F. Gady, *Baldwin Wallace University*

In an effort to aid student retention, Baldwin Wallace University implemented a pre-registration service for incoming first-year students that provides them with a pre-determined schedule as a starting point for planning their first semester. This program requires significant man-hours to create more than 600 schedules each year. The aim of this project is to automate the summer chairs' registration process for those incoming first-year students using simulated annealing. We have found that not only can the schedules be completed in less time, but also that the schedules may be of higher quality by some measures.

Porting Xinu to Raspberry Pi

Farzeen Harunani, *Marquette University*

As the field of computer science expands and becomes increasingly more complicated, two things happen. First, hardware and software get outdated regularly, and staying "up to date" can be expensive. Second, in terms of teaching computer science, it can be difficult for newcomers to the field (mainly students) to grasp the underlying concepts due to modern computing's ever-increasing system complexity. By merging an inexpensive piece of hardware with a simple Unix-like operating system, we can create a teaching tool that is accessible to anyone in terms of usability as well as monetary cost. This project proposes to utilize the XINU operating system in conjunction with the Raspberry Pi development board to achieve this goal.

The Robustness of Medical Decisions with Noisy Data - An analysis of the robustness of eGFR calculations using unreliable inputs

Nathan Lapinski, *University of Colorado*

Errors in medical data are one of the leading causes of fatalities in hospitals worldwide, leading to thousands of preventable deaths each year. In an effort to reduce this problem, many healthcare institutions have implemented clinical decision support software to aid practitioners in the patient care process. However, studies have shown that such software systems can actually lead to an increase in data errors, due in part to a lack of internal data validation mechanisms. We studied the role of a clinical decision support system in the diagnosis of renal disease and established that up to 27% of decisions made using such measures may be inaccurate. We propose a software solution to this problem that assesses the robustness of patient data inputs before they are used in clinical decision support software.

Digital Systems Test Bench
Amir Sabet, *AASTMT*

The purpose of this system is to test the digital circuits implemented by the students. The user either the student or the instructor supplies the design of the digital circuit in the form of HDL like text, for the simulation purpose. The main inputs and outputs of the circuit are connected to the computer for testing and error prediction. The proposed system software runs all the test inputs and compares the output from the circuit to the output from the simulation. Using the mismatching cases a prediction of the faulty connections is provided to assist the debugging of the circuit.

Enabling a Resource Limited Robot to Formulate Complex Plans
Demetrius Taylor, *Lamar University*

This study investigates the use of an existing planning system in conjunction with the INTERRAP architecture for autonomous agents to formulate plans for a resource limited task-oriented autonomous robot. The study creates a system that interfaces Dana Nau's hierarchical task network (HTN) planner with the local planning layer (LPL) of Jorg Muller's INTERRAP architecture. Since SHOP2 cannot run on the resource limited robot, a PC running SHOP2 formulates plans, and those plans are communicated to the LPL and executed by the robot. This enables the robot to achieve goals that require complex plans and permits reuse of a high-quality award-winning planner. The study presents the design, implementation highlights and a demonstration of an application of the INTERRAP-SHOP2 system.

Matching XML Checkpointing MCMCTree
Dimitri Wijesinghe, *Vassar College*

MCMCTree is a popular program for calculating the branch lengths of phylogenetic trees. It operates by taking an evolutionary tree and uses fossil data to estimate the origin times of each species, via the Markov Chain Monte Carlo probabilistic model. These calculations are computationally intensive and large datasets invite system failure. We have implemented a system of checkpointing for MCMCTree. With this system, MCMCTree can begin a calculation and save data as it goes along. If the system fails, calculations can be restored from the last checkpoint instead of starting from scratch. This infinitely increases the range of data the system can process. With checkpointing, MCMCTree can process trees of greater scope, and view evolution on a much broader scale than before.

Wireless Sensor Network Solution for Monitoring Earth Dams
Vladimir Yaremenko, *Colorado School of Mines*

For this project, I have written the firmware for a custom wireless device (mote) developed by our research group to monitor earth dams. A network of these motes is intended to replace current monitoring technology which is very limited in its data acquisition rate. With these motes placed in key points around the dam they will be able to provide a constant stream of data to a central location. Geophysicists will then be able to monitor the data and quickly detect any abnormalities. After implementing some form of time synchronization on these motes, they will be ready for full scale tests versus the current measuring equipment used for earth dams.

SIGCSE 2013 SRC Graduate Student Research Abstracts

Preserving Data Privacy Through Data Partitioning in Mobile Application

Mohammad Al-Mutawa, *University of Colorado*

To extend the capabilities of mobile devices, one can off-load computing tasks to more powerful remote nodes, which in many cases can improve performance and/or reduce power consumption. However, one of the problems associated with off-loading is the lose of data privacy. Our work use the concept of Data Partitioning to minimize, and in some case eliminate, the lose of personal data privacy. The overall execution consists of identifying sensitive data, shipping code and non-private data for remote execution and getting the results back, and then combining the results from local and remote executions on the mobile device.

Green Dolphin: A question and answer site for novice programmers

Chulakorn Aritajati, *Auburn University*

The Green Dolphin (GD) is a question and answer website. GD is designed to fulfill students' need for collaborative learning by allowing them to interact with and ask questions of the professional community consisting of their professors, TAs and classmates. GD gives students automatic feedbacks of their code quality. GD provides an expert system to suggest students who are experts. Therefore, users get fast and high quality answers, and professors spend less time to communicate with students. Students can gain new knowledge from the flow of questions and answers in the system. Students have opportunities to learn communication skills as well as programming and debugging skills.

Computing Computational Thinking Wacky Writing: Enhancing the XO Laptop Platform to Motivate Creative Writing by Children

Austin C. Bart, *Virginia Tech*

Creative Writing is an important expression of creativity, and there currently exists no satisfactory Learning Software for the widely-distributed XO Laptop Platform to fill this niche. This study created two new Creative Writing Learning Activities for the XO Laptop and intervened in a classroom to test their effect on the Intrinsic Motivation of children to write creatively using the XO laptop. The quantitative and qualitative results indicate that children were motivated to write using the software, leading the way to further improvements to the software for future benefit.

SLASH: Scratch-based visual programming in Second Life for introductory computer science education

Kara A. Behnke, *ATLAS Institute*

This research describes the application of SLASH, a modification of Scratch that generates syntax in Linden Scripting Language (LSL) through block-based programming. SLASH was recently deployed as the main programming tool in an introductory, undergraduate computer science course for non-majors. Students design objects in the virtual world Second Life and program object behaviors through the code generated by the SLASH environment. By using Second Life as the "laboratory" for the course, students were required to master programmatic constructs through block-generated code and apply the syntax-generated code into Second Life.

An Analysis of Optimizing Impact of Page Design Factor on Cyber Security

Ali Darwish, *University of Sharjah*

This study investigates the impact of Web page contents design on the effectiveness of browser security indicators. The natural and spontaneous behavior of users' eyes attention was studied during a security threat to understand what impact the page contents has on noticing security indicators. Sixty participants undertook a usability study that incorporated a controlled phishing attacks and an eye-tracker. The experiment was designed to enable the participants to respond to three phishing and two legitimate Websites. It revealed that there is a strong correlation between current web design and the security cues. This association might be responsible for the increasing number of phishing victims. The study aims to link the results of the experiment to the design recommendations for Web security indicators. These recommendations are based on the elements of design known as composition and the user experience with current designs.

Navigation in a Virtual Environment by Dichotic Listening: Initial Exploration of Audio Cues for BCI Classification

Ashish Dhital, *University of Wyoming*

Our research is focused on the initial exploration of the possibility of training a Brain Computer Interface (BCI) by using audio cues, instead of motor imagery. We have designed our BCI training and navigation to use audio cues that adhere to the dichotic listening (DL) mechanism so that users have an active choice for interaction or giving commands.

Preparing High School Teachers to Teach Computer Science

David P. Ely, *The Ohio State University*

Preliminary results of a computer science education study indicate that a successful teacher training project for high school mathematics teachers to teach computer science needs (1) to be in the form of a hands-on workshop with minimal syntax and even less lecture, (2) to use curriculum activities that involve mathematical problem solving. Both programming content knowledge and pedagogical content knowledge of the teachers is being tested. The study is examining a promising Computer Science teacher preparation model and curriculum that is heeding the call of the Transforming High School Computer Science: CS / 10K Project to attain the national goal of training 10,000 well-qualified, K-12 computer science teachers by 2015.

Real-time Visualization of Sentiment Tracking in Twitter

Kathleen Ericson, *Colorado State University*

Mining Twitter data for sentiment analysis can reveal underlying thought patterns within the Twitter user base. This information can be used to easily poll public sentiment and consumer trends. Previous work has focused on developing algorithms for analyzing tweets, as well as the feasibility of performing this processing in real time. Our work expands on this by moving analysis from file-based Hadoop to stream-based Granules. This should allow us to process streaming tweets more efficiently, allowing us to provide real-time results for visualization. One focus of this work is to allow users to easily visualize analyses on streaming data in real-time, allowing for a deeper understanding of results.

Real-time Visualization A Comprehensive Machine Learning Approach to Predicting and Maximizing Penetration Rates in Earth Pressure Balance (EPB) Tunnel Boring Machines

James Maher, *Colorado School of Mines*

Tunnel Boring Machines (TBMs) are massive circular drill bits that can be used to excavate small tunnels for utilities or large tunnels for subway systems. TBMs are preferred over traditional blasting and drilling methods because they have the capability to reduce surface deformations and provide a smooth, finished tunnel wall. Predicting the TBM's penetration rate based on these sensor readings can lead to increased accuracy in project cost estimation. Supervised machine learning models complex systems, based on prior data, to predict future performance. This project implements and evaluates linear regression, polynomial regression, multilinear regression, and support vector regression, to find the best penetration rate prediction model of an EPB TBM.

On-Mote Compressive Sampling in Wireless Seismic Sensor Networks

Mark J. Rubin, *Colorado School of Mines*

In this extended abstract, we summarize results from simulating compressive sampling as a data reduction technique in a wireless seismic sensor network. We simulated six combinations of sparsity domains and recovery algorithms on real-world passive seismic containing 78 avalanche events. After estimating the original seismic signal, we tested a machine learning workflow to automatically identify avalanche events. The results are promising; with only 30% of the original seismic data, we were able to estimate the original signal well enough to detect nearly 87% of the avalanche events (compared to 90% with full sampling). Lastly, we implemented a novel, lightweight, on-mote compressive sampling algorithm on an Arduino Fio wireless platform and successfully recorded a 220 Hz audio signal.

Author Index

www.ingramcontent.com/pod-product-compliance
Lightning Source LLC
LaVergne TN
LVHW080103011026
849160LV00013B/1020